CONSTITUTIONAL LAW AND AMERICAN DEMOCRACY

ASPEN COLLEGE SERIES

CONSTITUTIONAL LAW AND AMERICAN DEMOCRACY

Cases and Readings

COREY BRETTSCHNEIDER

Wolters Kluwer
Law & Business

Published by Wolters Kluwer Law & Business in New York.

Wolters Kluwer Law & Business serves customers worldwide with CCH, Aspen Publishers, and Kluwer Law International products. (www.wolterskluwerlb.com)

To contact Customer Service, e-mail customer.service@wolterskluwer.com, call 1-800-234-1660, fax 1-800-901-9075, or mail correspondence to:

Wolters Kluwer Law & Business
Attn: Order Department
PO Box 990
Frederick, MD 21705

Printed in the United States of America.

1 2 3 4 5 6 7 8 9 0

ISBN 978-0-7355-7982-8

Library of Congress Cataloging-in-Publication Data

Brettschneider, Corey Lang.
    Constitutional law and American democracy : cases and readings / Corey L. Brettschneider.
    p. cm. — (Aspen College Series)
    Includes index.
    ISBN 978-0-7355-7982-8
1. Constitutional law — United States. 2. Casebooks I. Title.
    KF4550.B725 2011
    342.73 — dc23

                                                    2011046345

About Wolters Kluwer Law & Business

Wolters Kluwer Law & Business is a leading global provider of intelligent information and digital solutions for legal and business professionals in key specialty areas, and respected educational resources for professors and law students. Wolters Kluwer Law & Business connects legal and business professionals as well as those in the education market with timely, specialized authoritative content and information-enabled solutions to support success through productivity, accuracy and mobility.

Serving customers worldwide, Wolters Kluwer Law & Business products include those under the Aspen Publishers, CCH, Kluwer Law International, Loislaw, Best Case, ftwilliam.com and MediRegs family of products.

CCH products have been a trusted resource since 1913, and are highly regarded resources for legal, securities, antitrust and trade regulation, government contracting, banking, pension, payroll, employment and labor, and healthcare reimbursement and compliance professionals.

Aspen Publishers products provide essential information to attorneys, business professionals and law students. Written by preeminent authorities, the product line offers analytical and practical information in a range of specialty practice areas from securities law and intellectual property to mergers and acquisitions and pension/benefits. Aspen's trusted legal education resources provide professors and students with high-quality, up-to-date and effective resources for successful instruction and study in all areas of the law.

Kluwer Law International products provide the global business community with reliable international legal information in English. Legal practitioners, corporate counsel and business executives around the world rely on Kluwer Law journals, looseleafs, books, and electronic products for comprehensive information in many areas of international legal practice.

Loislaw is a comprehensive online legal research product providing legal content to law firm practitioners of various specializations. Loislaw provides attorneys with the ability to quickly and efficiently find the necessary legal information they need, when and where they need it, by facilitating access to primary law as well as state-specific law, records, forms and treatises.

Best Case Solutions is the leading bankruptcy software product to the bankruptcy industry. It provides software and workflow tools to flawlessly streamline petition preparation and the electronic filing process, while timely incorporating ever-changing court requirements.

ftwilliam.com offers employee benefits professionals the highest quality plan documents (retirement, welfare and non-qualified) and government forms (5500/PBGC, 1099 and IRS) software at highly competitive prices.

MediRegs products provide integrated health care compliance content and software solutions for professionals in healthcare, higher education and life sciences, including professionals in accounting, law and consulting.

Wolters Kluwer Law & Business, a division of Wolters Kluwer, is headquartered in New York. Wolters Kluwer is a market-leading global information services company focused on professionals.

For my father, Eric Brettschneider,
who brought me to my first law class at age 6.

ABOUT THE AUTHOR

COREY BRETTSCHNEIDER is Associate Professor of Political Science at Brown University, where he teaches courses in political theory and public law. He is also Associate Professor, by courtesy, of Philosophy. Brettschneider has been a Rockefeller Faculty Fellow at the Princeton University Center for Human Values, a Visiting Associate Professor at Harvard Law School, and a Faculty Fellow at the Harvard Safra Center for Ethics.

Brettschneider received a Ph.D. in Politics from Princeton University and a J.D. from Stanford University. He is the author of *Value Democracy: Promoting Equality and Protecting Rights* (Princeton University Press, 2012) and *Democratic Rights: The Substance of Self-Government* (Princeton University Press, 2007). His articles have appeared in top journals. They include "The Politics of the Personal: A Liberal Approach," in *American Political Science Review* (2007), "A Transformative Theory of Religious Freedom," in *Political Theory* (2010), and "When the State Speaks, What Should It Say? Democratic Persuasion and the Freedom of Expression," in *Perspectives on Politics* (2011).

SUMMARY OF CONTENTS

CONTENTS

PART I: FOUNDATIONS

CHAPTER 1   JUDICIAL AUTHORITY   3

CHAPTER 2:   THEORIES OF INTERPRETATION   135

PART II: POWERS

CHAPTER 3: CONGRESSIONAL AUTHORITY AND ITS LIMITS 241

PART III: LIBERTY

CHAPTER 5:   FREE SPEECH   563

CHAPTER 6:   RELIGIOUS FREEDOM: THE FREE EXERCISE AND ESTABLISHMENT CLAUSES OF THE FIRST AMENDMENT   749

CHAPTER 7: SUBSTANTIVE DUE PROCESS AND FUNDAMENTAL RIGHTS 951

PART IV: EQUALITY

CHAPTER 8: RACE AND EQUALITY   1093

CHAPTER 9:　GENDER, SEXUAL ORIENTATION, AND EQUALITY　1247

PREFACE

Perhaps no other area of study brings together as many exciting and controversial issues as the study of constitutional law. The most hotly contested topics in our polity—from abortion rights to affirmative action to war—are found in the various areas that make up this field. But in addition to being contemporary, the topic is also by its nature historical. These contemporary topics are viewed through the lens of a document written in the eighteenth century. Thus, the study of constitutional law presents a major challenge: How can a document written so early in American history govern questions that those who wrote it could never have fathomed?

As we will see throughout this text, the question of how to interpret the Constitution, and how to apply it to today's issues, is itself contested. Debates rage among "originalists" devoted to the original meaning of the Constitution, "pragmatists" committed to future-oriented policy decisions, "proceduralists" concerned to see the document as reinforcing democracy, and those who advocate a "moral reading" of the Constitution, who emphasize the need to decide constitutional questions based on the document's underlying moral principles. Rather than shying away from the controversies at the heart of constitutional law, and the related debates among citizens and academics about these issues, this book is compiled with the aim of introducing you to the terrain of these debates. Through landmark and contemporary cases as well as through other seminal readings, historical writings, and commentary by leading scholars, you will learn how to think about the most complex and important legal challenges in our nation.

In addition to presenting some of the most important cases in American history, this book emphasizes readings that place these cases in the context of wider normative and historical debates, with the hope that it can be taught both in constitutional law classes and in those that seek to combine political theory and philosophy with a study of American political development and of the Supreme Court. The approach is designed to teach you the contours of the legal debates in the area of constitutional law. But as I see it, the role of teaching constitutional law is not primarily to train future litigators—although some of you might choose that path. It is rather to give you an understanding of the Constitution itself, the primary ways in which it has been interpreted by our political institutions, and the ways you can connect your own views on these subjects with distinctly legal questions. You will thus not only come away from this book with an understanding of the positions of the Supreme Court and of major scholars on a host of issues, but you will also have become constitutional interpreters yourselves.

Corey Brettschneider
Brown University
November 2011

ACKNOWLEDGMENTS

I began this project several years ago to create a casebook that teaches constitutional doctrine by tying it to fundamental themes from constitutional theory, political theory, political science, and the study of democracy. My aim was to write a book informed by the way many scholars teach constitutional law, and one that reflects the wide research interests of those who work in the subject.

I am grateful to the many students who have taken my courses at Brown University. The book grows out of what was originally my civil liberties course, later expanded to include a discussion of governmental powers. When I first came to Brown I worked with students to create a course that had the right balance between cases and readings on larger themes related to the U.S. Constitution. As I developed drafts of the book, I began teaching it. My students' feedback over the last three years has been fundamental in shaping the final product.

I am most indebted to the outstanding and inspiring team of Brown undergraduates who worked as research assistants on the project and who made its completion possible. They made working on the book a pleasure, and they were often the ones teaching me. Tobin Marcus provided invaluable support at the proposal stage. David McNamee and Manuel Possolo worked closely with me on all aspects of the book's first draft. Together we finalized the outline, selecting the readings and cases. David and Manuel helped to find the right tone and approach in the commentaries. They also created the charts and figures in Chapters 1 and 2 that give the theoretical frame of the entire project. Tobin, David, and Manuel have already achieved terrific success at top law and PhD programs, working in positions of responsibility for the federal government. Brittany Harwood also provided invaluable support on the first draft.

The second and final drafts saw another impressive team of Research Assistants: Jasleen Salwan, Andrea Matthews, and Anthony Badami helped add readings, rewrite much of the commentary, and respond to excellent suggestions from reviewers. This team was essential to finishing the book, and it was a pleasure to work with them. Jasleen in particular provided a heroic and efficient effort as the manuscript reached the final stages. Her work on the accompanying products, especially the instructor's manual, shows that she is already a brilliant teacher.

I thank not only my students, but also my teachers who introduced me to the subject of constitutional law. At Princeton, Amy Gutmann, George Kateb, Stephen Macedo, and Robert George taught me early on that political theorists have an obligation to engage with constitutional issues and have a valuable contribution to make in understanding the most important document of our government. I will always be grateful to these teachers, and I deeply appreciate their continued friendship and mentorship. At Stanford Law, Lawrence Lessig was an ideal mentor who showed me how to be rigorous yet creative in thinking about doctrine. I thank him too for his continued support of my research and career. Kathleen Sullivan taught what might be the most perfect first-year constitutional law course in existence. Tom Grey supervised my independent work and provided a model of how to integrate legal theory and constitutional law.

It is also a pleasure to thank my terrific colleagues who enthusiastically supported this project from the start. James Morone, John Tomasi, Sharon Krause, David Estlund, and Charles Larmore are an extraordinarily collegial group working across the boundaries of philosophy and political science. I have been happy to build the political theory program at Brown with them. Estlund and I taught a Harvard Law course in 2009 on "Democratic Theory and the Law," related to the materials in this book. I learned an immense amount from him and from our students in the course. Their insights are reflected in Chapters 5 and 6.

As I completed the final draft of this book I was fortunate to have two friends and colleagues who are also world-class constitutional law scholars help me to hone my presentation. Steve Calabresi has been an amazing colleague while visiting here at Brown. He provided invaluable assistance on Chapter 4. Gordon Silverstein, who was a fellow during our year at Princeton, worked with me to improve Chapter 3. He encouraged me to add more cases and provided assistance in creating better commentary. Together these two scholars made Part II on constitutional powers much better than it would have been.

I am indebted to the people at Aspen who made this book possible. In particular I would like to thank Carol McGeehan at Aspen for encouraging me to pursue this project, and Susan Boulanger for terrific editing work.

I thank the members of my family who talked with me about and supported this project, Allison Brettschneider, Sophie Helen Brettschneider, Susan Brettschneider, Kim Brettschneider, Jeanne Rostaing, Robert Klopfer, Patrick Heppell, John Weisz, and Jenny Weisz. Jenny provided helpful commentary on Chapter 7, drawing from her own legal background. I dedicate this book to my father, Eric Brettschneider, who began talking to me about the issues here when I first learned to speak in sentences. He was attending law school at the time, and was a terrific enough father to convince me at age six that I too was a student in his class.

Finally, I am grateful to the copyright holders for permission to reprint the following materials:

Bruce Ackerman, reprinted by permission of the publisher from We the People: Volume 1, Foundations by Bruce Ackerman, pp. 8-10, 40-44, 47-52, 105, Cambridge, Mass.: The Belknap Press of Harvard University Press, Copyright © 1991 by the President and Fellows of Harvard College.

Bruce Ackerman, reprinted by permission of the publisher from We the People, Volume 2, Transformations by Bruce Ackerman, pp. 268-271, 309-311, 314, Cambridge, Mass.: The Belknap Press of Harvard University Press, Copyright © 1998 by the President and Fellows of Harvard College.

Akhil Amar, "Of Sovereignty and Federalism," 96 Yale L.J. 1425-1450. The Yale Law Journal by Yale Law School. Copyright 1987 Reproduced with permission of Yale Law Journal Company, Inc. in the format Textbook and Other book via Copyright Clearance Center.

Raoul Berger, Government by Judiciary (1997). Reprinted by permission of Liberty Fund Press.

Justice Hugo Black, "The Bill of Rights," 35 N.Y.U. L. Rev. 865. Reprinted by permission of the publisher.

William Brennan, "The Constitution of the United States: Contemporary Ratification," Speech to the Text and Teaching Symposium, Georgetown University, 1985. Reprinted by permission of National Lawyers Guild.

Corey Brettschneider, "A Transformative Theory of Religious Freedom," 38 Pol. Theory 187. Used by permission of publisher.

Stephen Breyer, "Judicial Review: A Practicing Judge's Perspective," Oxford Journal of Legal Studies, Vol. 19, Summer 1999, by permission of Oxford University Press.

G. Calabresi & James Lindgren, "The President: Lightning Rod or King?" Yale Law Journal, Vol. 115, p. 2611, 2006. The Yale law journal by Yale Law School. Copyright 2006 Reproduced with permission of Yale Law Journal Company, Inc. in the format Textbook and Other book via Copyright Clearance Center.

Erwin Chemerinsky, "The Foulston Siefkin Lecture: Civil Liberties and the War on Terrorism," 45 Washburn L.J. 1, Fall 2005. Reprinted by permission of the publisher.

Ronald Dworkin, "The Moral Reading and the Majoritarian Premise" and "Roe in Danger" reprinted by permission of the publisher from Freedom's Law: The Moral Reading of the American Constitution by Ronald Dworkin, pp. 15-33, 44-59, Cambridge, Mass.: Harvard University Press, Copyright © 1996 by Ronald Dworkin.

Ronald Dworkin, "Women and Pornography," New York Review of Books. Reprinted with permission from The New York Review of Books. Copyright © 1993 NYREV, Inc.

Ronald Dworkin et al., "The Philosopher's Brief," New York Review of Books, March 27, 1997. Reprinted with permission from The New York Review of Books. Copyright © 1997 NYREV, Inc.

Chris Eisgruber & Lawrence Sager, "The Vulnerability of Conscience," 61 U. Chi. L. Rev. 1245 (1994), pp. 1248, 1254, 1256-1259, 1260-1265, 1282-1284, 1297-1298, 1315. The University of Chicago Law Review by University of Chicago. Copyright 1994. Reproduced with permission of University of Chicago Law School in the format Textbook and Other book via Copyright Clearance Center.

John Hart Ely, reprinted by permission of the publisher from Democracy and Distrust: A Theory of Judicial Review by John Hart Ely, pp. 11-14, 18-19, 39-40, 43-48, 69-81, 87-93, 98-103, Cambridge, Mass.: Harvard University Press, Copyright © 1980 by the President and Fellows of Harvard College.

John Hart Ely, "Wages of Crying Wolf: A Comment on Roe v. Wade," 82 Yale L.J. 920 (1973). The Yale law journal by Yale Law School. Copyright © 1973. Reproduced with permission of Yale Law Journal Company, Inc. in the format Textbook and Other Book via Copyright Clearance Center.

John Hart Ely, War and Responsibility. Copyright © 1993 Princeton University Press. Reprinted by permission of Princeton University Press.

Richard A. Epstein, How Progressives Rewrote the Constitution. Copyright © 2006. Reproduced with permission of Cato Institute in the format Textbook and Other Book via Copyright Clearance Center.

John Finnis, "The Good of Marriage and the Morality of Sexual Relations: Some Philosophical and Historical Observations," Am. J. Juris., 1997 42: 97. Reprinted by permission of the author and the publisher.

William A. Galston, "Parents, Government and Children" in Child, Family, and State, (nomos xliv) (Macedo Eds.: NYU Press, 2003).

Douglas Ginsburg, "On Constitutionalism," Cato Supreme Court Review 7, Washington, DC: Cato Institute, 2002-2003. Cato Supreme Court review 2003-2004 by Cato Institute. Center for Constitutional Studies Copyright © 2003. Reproduced with permission of Cato Institute in the format Textbook and Other Book via Copyright Clearance Center.

Mark Graber, "Desperately Ducking Slavery: Dred Scott and Contemporary Constitutional Theory," Constitutional Commentary 1997. Reprinted by permission of the publisher and the author.

Amy Gutmann, "Children, Paternalism, and Education: A Liberal Argument," Philosophy and Public Affairs, Vol. 9, No. 4 (Summer, 1980), pp. 338-358. Copyright © 1980 Blackwell Publishing Ltd. Reproduced with permission of Blackwell Publishing Ltd.

Amy Gutmann, "Responding to Racial Injustice" (pg 118). Appiah K. Anthony, Color Conscious. Copyright © 1996 by Princeton University Press. 1998 paperback edition reprinted by permission of Princeton University Press.

Sam Issacharoff, "Gerrymandering and Political Cartels," 116 Harv. L. Rev. 593 (2002). Harvard Law Review by Harvard Law Review Association. Copyright © 2002. Reproduced with permission of Harvard Law Review Association in the format Textbook via Copyright Clearance Center.

Leon Kass, "The Right to Life and Human Dignity," in The New Atlantis. Reprinted by permission of the publisher.

Andrew Koppelman, "Why Discrimination Against Lesbians and Gay Men Is Sex Discrimination," 69 N.Y.U. L. Rev. 197 (1994). Reproduced by permission of the publisher.

Larry Kramer, "We the Court," 115 Harv. L. Rev. 4 (2001), pp. 4-169. Harvard Law Review by Harvard Law Review Association. Copyright © 2001. Reproduced with permission of Harvard Law Review Association in the format Textbook and Other Book via Copyright Clearance Center.

Irving Kristol, "Pornography, Obscenity and the Case for Censorship," The New York Times Magazine, March 28, 1971, pp. 112-113. Reprinted by permission of the author's Estate.

Lawrence Lessig & Cass Sunstein, "The President and the Administration," Columbia Law Review, Vol. 94, No. 1, Jan. 1994. Copyright © 1994. Reproduced with permission of the authors and Columbia Law Review Association, Inc. in the format Textbook and Other Book via Copyright Clearance Center.

Catherine MacKinnon, "Pornography, Civil Rights, and Speech," Harv. CR-CLL Rev., 1985 20: 1. Harvard Civil Rights–Civil Liberties Law Review by Harvard Civil

Cass R. Sunstein & Randy E. Barnett, "Constitutive Commitments and Roosevelt's Second Bill of Rights: A Dialogue," 53 Drake L. Rev. 205, Winter, 2005. Sections I, II, VII. Reprinted by permission of Drake Law Review Copyright © 2005 in the format Textbook and Other Book via Copyright Clearance Center.

Gordon S. Wood, "The Origins of Judicial Review Revisited, or How the Marshall Court Made More Out of Less," 56 Wash. & Lee L. Rev. 787 (1999).

John Yoo, "The Continuation of Politics by Other Means: The Original Understanding of War Powers," Cal. L. Rev., Vol. 84, No. 2, Mar. 1996. Reprinted by permission of the author.

INTRODUCTION TO *CONSTITUTIONAL LAW AND AMERICAN DEMOCRACY*

In the United States, it is no longer contested that the Supreme Court has the power to strike down laws passed by Congress, the states, or municipalities that violate the Constitution. And while the Court operates under strict majoritarian rule—it takes only five of the nine justices to make these momentous decisions—the Court itself uses this power of judicial review to block and reverse the preferences of a national majority expressed through their elected representatives. This raises obvious questions: Why? Should the Supreme Court have this power? If so, how should it be exercised? These questions seem particularly puzzling in a democracy. Many Americans believe that they live in a system of self-government, in which majorities have a say in making law. Why, then, should such a small number of people be entitled to pass judgment on the preferences and will of hundreds of millions?

One answer to these questions appeals to the text of the Constitution itself. The justices, we might think, have the power to strike down legislation not in order to impose their own beliefs about policy, but rather as a means to enforce the document's requirements. The power of "judicial review," then, might be thought to stem from the Constitution's inherent supremacy over other governmental actions. Indeed, Article VI of the Constitution tells us that "this Constitution, and the Laws of the United States which shall be made in Pursuance thereof . . . shall be the supreme Law of the Land."

The claim that the Constitution is supreme, however, only raises a deeper question that will be at the heart of our inquiry into constitutional law in this book. Namely, although the Constitution is at times clear in its meaning, it is often ambiguous. In some places, it is hard to imagine much disagreement about its terms. For example, no one could argue that someone 22 years of age is eligible to be elected President of the United States. Article II, Section 1 of the Constitution explicitly states that the office excludes any "person . . . who shall not have attained to the Age of thirty five." Similarly, the Constitution is clear that "The Senate of the United States shall be composed of two Senators from each State." In contrast, consider whether the Eighth Amendment's prohibition of "cruel and unusual punishment" forbids the use of the electric chair in executions. What is "cruel"? What is "unusual"? According to whom? The Eighth Amendment does not set up a clear rule; rather, it creates a standard that must be subject to interpretation. Indeed, at points in American history, some have claimed that the death penalty constitutes "cruel and unusual" punishment. Others have disagreed, suggesting that because capital punishment is explicitly referenced in the Constitution, it cannot be prohibited by the document.

A course that merely focused on the least ambiguous provisions of the Constitution would not be very interesting. You would merely be asked obvious questions, such as the one I asked about the 22-year-old candidate for president, and would reach obvious conclusions. But fortunately, the bulk of constitutional inquiry that makes up the body of constitutional law, and that we will pursue here, is fraught with disagreement and contains some of the most interesting debates in American history. Indeed, in the United States, many of the issues discussed at our dinner tables and in our newspapers are "constitutionalized." The issues of abortion, the right to die, and the freedom of speech are among those that gain the most attention in our society. The Supreme Court, by limiting laws within these domains, has entered into the fray. Far from shying from controversy in this book, we will dive right into it.

Specifically, we will concern ourselves with two purposes. First, we will examine what the Supreme Court has said about a host of controversies. Second, rather than merely learn what the Court has said and done, we will challenge its conclusions and reasoning, taking on the task of constitutional interpretation ourselves.

Structure of the Book

Part I: Foundations

We begin the book with an inquiry into the foundations of judicial review. We ask first, in Chapter 1, why the Court should have the authority to strike down legislation passed by majoritarian institutions. Specifically, the chapter asks whether the reasoning in favor of this practice is sound through an examination of case law and commentary. We also examine the origin of the Court's power of judicial review, which is never explicitly granted by the Constitution. We proceed in Chapter 2 to tackle a variety of accounts that explain how the Court ought to interpret the Constitution if it does have the power of judicial review. As we will see in this chapter, just as some of the provisions of the document are ambiguous, so too there is great controversy over the way to read those provisions.

Part II: Powers

In the next part of the book, we move on to the question of which powers the particular branches of the government are afforded by the Constitution. Here, we will pivot from the question of judicial authority to questions about the powers and limits of the legislative and executive branches. To what extent can these branches make law, and enforce it? What should be done when conflicts emerge between the branches? In addition to these questions of "separation of powers," or more precisely, "conflicts of powers," we will examine the relationship between the federal government and the states. Where does the power of the states end and the power of the federal government begin?

Part III: Liberty

In the third part of the book, we move from questions of powers to questions of rights. In addition to establishing the various powers of government in its three branches, the Constitution guarantees individual rights. This part of the book will examine what these rights are and also will enable you to think for yourselves about what guarantees are provided by the Constitution. We begin with the Free Speech Clause of the First Amendment. Is the protection of free speech only a protection of political speech? Or does it extend to obscene materials as well? We move on in this section to consider religious protections afforded by two clauses in the First Amendment—the right to "free exercise of religion" and the prohibition against any "establishment of religion" by the government. Finally, we consider whether the Fourteenth Amendment of the Constitution establishes fundamental rights not explicitly enumerated by the Constitution, such as the right to privacy. The Court has protected some of these rights under the doctrine of "substantive due process." As we will see in this final section, such an inquiry takes us broadly into the areas of procreation, abortion, and the right to die.

Part IV: Equality

Whereas the first three parts of this book draw on a variety of provisions of the Constitution in carving out particular themes, the final section looks only at the Fourteenth Amendment, which guarantees citizens "equal protection of the laws." Here we will inquire into what kind of equality is protected by the Constitution. We will ask under what circumstances, if any, it is fair for laws to treat people differently on the basis of race, gender, or sexual orientation. We will also investigate the extent to which ideas of fairness bear upon our understanding of equal protection in these same areas.

Our inquiry, then, begins with two foundational problems in constitutional law—that concerning judicial authority, and that concerning constitutional interpretation. As is the case throughout this book, we are guided here both by the opinions of the Supreme Court and by the most important writers thinking about these issues.

How to Read and Brief a Case

It is important for you to note that there is a specific way to read, or to decode, the cases to follow. Namely, it will be helpful, especially in the first few cases that you read, to create a "case outline" or "brief." It is essential that this be done in a particular way to ensure that you have understood the case. I will include here some essential elements that must be included in a case brief, although your instructor might point you to others. First, it is essential to understand the basic facts of the case. In some instances, this will involve one party suing another; in others, an individual who has been arrested and accused of a crime; in still others, a contract dispute between two parties. In issues about a dispute between two parties, be sure to note who the original *plaintiff* and *defendant* were at the trial level. In criminal cases, the dispute is between the *government* and the *defendant*; there is no *plaintiff* in such cases. It is important, however, not to confuse plaintiff and defendant with the *petitioner* and *respondent*, terms that refer to the party who lost at the previous level, and the party who won, respectively. Usually, though not always, the petitioner's name will be first in the name of the case.

Second, it is essential to identify what is known as the legal issue in the case. The legal issue can be summarized in one sentence. Try to see in each case if you can identify one question that summarizes the legal issue, and then see how the Court answers it. Third, we want to identify the holding of the case. The holding is sometimes as short as "yes" or "no" respecting the legal issue. For instance, when you read *District of Columbia v. Heller*, the legal issue is: Does the District of Columbia's gun ban violate the Second Amendment? The holding here answers the question in the affirmative.

Fourth, you should be able to identify the legal reasoning that explains why the holding is reached. Here, you will have to reconstruct the legal argument in order to figure out its structure. Finally, be sure to understand the outcome of the case. In whose favor did the Court rule? What are the implications of the ruling? This will not always be as obvious as you might think. In some cases, the reasoning of the Court may appear to support one side, but the judgment may nevertheless fall in favor of another side for various reasons.

Legal Citations

As you read and brief cases, you may find it useful to understand the specialized legal citation format used by judges in the writing of opinions. Each case can be cited using a relatively concise citation consisting of the name of the case, the reporter, the volume number, and page number. The year of the decision is also often included. Supreme Court opinions, which comprise the bulk of the cases in this book, are published in the official *United States Reports*, available in any law library and on the Internet. These reports are referenced with the simple abbreviation "U.S." Thus, a complete citation might look like this:

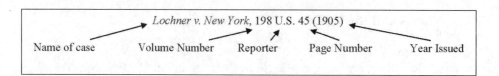

Lochner v. New York, 198 U.S. 45 (1905)

Name of case   Volume Number   Reporter   Page Number   Year Issued

Notice that the name of the case is always italicized. On second reference, judges or commentators may refer to a case by a shorter name and will omit the full citation—here, just *Lochner*. When judges wish to cite a particular location in a case, and not merely the case itself, they may cite two page numbers. Thus, a quotation on the third page of *Lochner* would be cited as *Lochner v. New York*, 198 U.S. 45, 47 (1905).

You will also come across citations of lower courts, such as those of federal circuit courts of appeals. These decisions are typically published in the *Federal Reporter* and are cited with the abbreviations F. or F.2d (for older cases) and F.3d (for more recent ones). Select opinions from district-level courts are published in the *Federal Supplement*, abbreviated as F. Supp. or F. Supp. 2d. Cases heard in state courts have varying citation formats, which you will not need to worry about for this book. It is usually possible, however, to decipher what they refer to.

The case law you will read in this book has been edited and abridged—indeed, many of the cases you will read run to 100 pages or more in the original. If you are curious to read the original versions of any of these cases, you can find them easily in any law library or online at Web sites such as FindLaw, Westlaw, or the Cornell Law Legal Information Institute. We have also listed these cases at the Web site that accompanies this book.

INTRODUCTION TO THE CONSTITUTION AND THE SUPREME COURT

Overview of the Constitution

Before we tackle the important and controversial issues that make up the bulk of this book, it is important to clarify some basic features of the Constitution, which form the basis for most constitutional issues. You should read the entire text of the document itself, included below, starting on page xlix, before reading what follows.

The first thing you should note about the document is that its first three articles establish the three branches of government. Article I creates Congress, the legislative branch; Article II the office of the President of the United States, the executive; and Article III the judiciary, including the Supreme Court. In establishing each of the branches, the Constitution grants certain powers as well as limits them. The federal government is thus known to be one of "enumerated" or "granted" powers. In contrast, the state governments have more general powers. For instance, among the powers often thought to be "reserved" to the states is the "police power" within their own jurisdictions to regulate the "welfare, health, safety, and morals" of citizens. The Tenth Amendment lays out the difference between the limited federal government and the states, declaring that "powers not delegated to the United States by the Constitution, or prohibited by it to the States, are reserved to the States respectively, or to the people."

The Three Branches of Government (Articles I, II, and III)

Article I of the Constitution creates and lays out the powers of Congress. As you look through Article I, many of the powers will seem to be straightforward. However, even several of those that seem simple at first glance turn out to be at the heart of the most difficult disputes over constitutional interpretation. Take, for instance, the Commerce Clause found in Section 8, which gives Congress the power to "regulate Commerce with foreign Nations, and among the several States." A fundamental question here is where this power of the Congress begins and where the power of states to regulate their own "intrastate" commerce ends. What kinds of activity are of an interstate nature, and what kinds belong only to the jurisdiction of one state?

As we will see in Chapter 3, this provision also became the basis for congressional legislation in the area of civil rights, ending segregation in places of "public accommodation." The debate over whether public accommodations, such as hotels and restaurants, were involved in interstate commerce served as a battleground for achieving equality for African Americans. Indeed, from the beginning, the provisions of Article I, Section 8 have been controversial. For example, early in Chapter 3, we will examine whether the so-called Necessary and Proper Clause authorized the creation of a national bank. We will soon wade into controversial territory, but for now it is worth familiarizing yourself with the various powers of the legislative branch by reading Article I. Pay particular attention to the powers to spend, to declare war, and to raise and support armies.

Article II of the Constitution establishes and delineates the powers of the executive branch. Among the powers granted to the president are the powers to make treaties, appoint judges, and choose subordinate officers. This article also states that the president shall be "Commander in Chief of the Army and Navy of the United States," a declaration that we will see used as a justification for broad executive authority in times of war. In addition, we will examine the debate over the potentially broad powers that come from the Constitution's declaration that executive power is "vested" in the presidency. Sometimes the division between the powers of Article I for Congress and those of Article II for the president is thought to outline a "separation of powers," but as will become evident in Chapter 4, many real controversies in constitutional law concern blurred lines between presidential and congressional power. For instance, consider the tension between Congress's power to declare war and the president's status as commander-in-chief. As we will see, one controversy concerns when the first power limits the second. Another question we will examine concerns the president's domestic powers in times of war. Does the president's role as commander-in-chief enhance his or her domestic powers when the country is in the midst of a major international conflict?

Article III of the Constitution establishes the Supreme Court and grants to Congress the power to establish "inferior" courts as needed. Perhaps most notable in this article, however, is the absence of any explicit authorization of judicial review. We will examine early in Chapter 1 the controversy this has caused in regard to the Supreme Court's authority to strike down laws passed by Congress and signed by the president. Despite not being explicitly grounded in the text of the Constitution, this power was famously declared early in the Court's history in the case of *Marbury v. Madison*. Also note the distinction between the Supreme Court's "original" and "appellate" jurisdiction. The Court's "original" jurisdiction, encompassing instances in which a case can be brought directly to the Supreme Court is quite limited. In such cases, the Court acts as a trial-level court. But in most instances, the Court does not conduct a trial, but rather acts as an appellate court. Appellate courts, in contrast to trial-level courts, only hear appeals from, or, in other words, review the decisions of, other courts. This review power, in the cases we will examine, allows the Supreme Court to correct lower-level courts when it determines that they have committed some error in constitutional interpretation. They are about controversies of law, not about disputes over the facts of a particular case. Notice too that justices are appointed for life-long terms, "during good Behavior."

The Amendment Process (Article V)

As this book will make clear, the Constitution—in addition to setting up a government—establishes a body of law. Thus, we will study not only the structure of government, but also certain legal controversies, such as those concerning freedom of speech, freedom of religion, and equal protection of the laws. Many of these provisions, however, were not contained in the original Constitution. Rather, they had to be created through a process of amendment. Article V sets the balance between "entrenching" the Constitution as a body of law that is more permanent than statutory law passed by Congress and the recognition that the people will sometimes wish to change it. It does this by creating a "supermajority" rule for amending the Constitution.

While statutes can be passed, or repealed, by simple majorities in both houses of Congress (assuming the president does not veto them), amending the Constitution requires the approval of two-thirds supermajorities of both houses of Congress and the consent of three-fourths of the states, either through their legislatures or through state ratifying conventions. In the more than 200 years since the Constitution was ratified, only 27 amendments have been passed, with the most recent taking effect in 1992. The first ten amendments, passed just a few years after the original Constitution, are collectively known as the Bill of Rights and contain many critical elements of the modern Constitution. Another major series of revisions to the Constitution, known as the Civil War Amendments, includes the abolishment of slavery and the guarantee of equal protection of the laws. Note too that Article V permits two-thirds of state legislatures to call a constitutional convention for the purpose of proposing new amendments to the Constitution, a power that has never been used.

The Supremacy Clause (Article VI)

Article VI of the Constitution, like Article V, references the status of the document itself. Critically, it declares that the "Constitution, and the Laws of the United States which shall be made in Pursuance thereof . . . shall be the supreme Law of the Land." As we will see in Chapter 1, this provision raises questions about judicial authority. Who has the right to interpret this supreme law? Some have argued that this is the exclusive role of the Supreme Court, while others have defended a shared role among the three branches of government.

Freedom of Expression and Religion (The First Amendment)

The First Amendment to the Constitution establishes several key areas of rights that we will examine in Part III of this book. For instance, the "free speech" provision has been interpreted as protecting a variety of kinds of expression, not merely verbal "speech." The amendment also contains the right to "free exercise of religion" and the prohibition on any "establishment of religion" by the government. Among the important topics we will work through are whether "speech" includes obscenity, whether the constitutional guarantee of the "free exercise" of religion requires the government to grant exemptions from generally applicable laws to religious individuals who believe such laws offend, and to what extent the prohibition of "establishment" requires a divide between religion and the state.

Notice that the First Amendment and other elements of the Bill of Rights limit certain powers of Congress but do not explicitly say anything about the powers of the states. But with the passage of the Fourteenth Amendment after the Civil War this changed. The Fourteenth Amendment, unlike the Bill of Rights, imposes explicit limits on state governments. Today, it is commonly thought by scholars and jurists that most of the important protections of the Bill of Rights also apply to the states by virtue of the Fourteenth Amendment.

In addition, the First Amendment's reference to what Congress can or cannot do highlights that the focus here is on the actions of the government, and the text suggests a broad doctrine of constitutional law known as the "state action" doctrine. According to this doctrine, constitutional cases are only triggered when some governmental entity has acted. Thus, it is widely thought that constitutional law does not prohibit private actors from engaging in certain activities that the "state," or government, is barred from. For example, a private high school that instituted speech codes would not implicate constitutional concerns in the way that a state-run public school likely would were it to implement the same policy.

Due Process (The Fourteenth Amendment)

As you read the Fourteenth Amendment, you should notice its resemblance to the Fifth Amendment of the Bill of Rights. While the latter refers to the federal government and the former to states, both protect individuals against deprivation of "life, liberty, or property, without due process of law." This right to "due process" is certainly among the Constitution's more ambiguous provisions. As we will see, "due process," while it seems to refer only to the procedural rights of citizens, has been thought to guarantee substantive rights as well. The potential confusion in this area of law is found in the very phrase "substantive due process." Sometimes a guarantee only of "due process" is thought of as the idea that any outcome of a process that is legitimate and fair is itself legitimate. In contrast, substantive guarantees are limits on particular kinds of policy outcomes. Thus, "substantive due process" is thought by some to be a contradiction in terms. But despite this criticism, the Court has developed a doctrine of substantive due process that holds that some liberties are so fundamental that they cannot be stripped from citizens by any "process" whatsoever. Thus, among the substantive rights associated with due process are a general right to privacy and specific rights to abortion and to contraception. Most recently, this doctrine has been used to protect gay individuals from criminal prosecution for consensual sexual relations.

We will also read about the doctrine of "economic substantive due process," now abandoned, which was once used by a conservative court to strike down many workers' rights laws passed during the New Deal. As you read this section, you should ask whether this Court was right to think that economic liberties such as the right to work were so fundamental as to require "due process" protections.

Equal Protection of the Laws (The Fourteenth Amendment)

In addition to guaranteeing "due process of law," the Fourteenth Amendment also guarantees citizens "the equal protection of the laws." The provision applies particularly in cases of discrimination based on race or ethnic background. As we will see in Chapter 9, the Court affords its highest level of protection, or what it calls "strict scrutiny," to legal distinction based on these characteristics, presuming laws that use such distinctions to be invalid absent a strong justification for their enactment. At the same time, however, the Equal Protection Clause does not explicitly mention either racial or ethnic discrimination. As you will see in Chapter 10, it has thus been expanded to encompass questions about the legality of distinctions based on gender and sexual orientation.

Unenumerated Powers and Rights (The Ninth and Tenth Amendments)

As we will see in depth in Chapter 2, there is great controversy over the role of the constitutional text in Supreme Court jurisprudence. In this debate, one of the more difficult and controversial provisions of the Constitution suggests an ambiguity on this issue. The Ninth Amendment to the Constitution reads: "The enumeration in the Constitution, of certain rights, shall not be construed to deny or disparage others retained by the people." The Ninth Amendment thus suggests that just because a right does not explicitly appear in the Constitution does not necessarily mean that it lacks constitutional protection. Some have gone so far as to suggest that the Ninth Amendment references a so-called "unwritten Constitution," which protects basic rights not enumerated in the document itself.

In addition, some have suggested that the Tenth Amendment clarifies the overall balance between federal and state power. This amendment declares: "The powers not delegated to the United States by the Constitution, nor prohibited by it to the States, are reserved to the States respectively, or to the people." As you read this amendment, consider whether it limits the powers of the federal government, and enhances the powers of the state, beyond what is said in Articles I and II.

History of the Constitution

As you can tell from our brief tour of the Constitution, the document is not just a piece of history. Rather, it forms the textual basis for an extremely important body of contemporary law. It serves as both a way of authorizing the powers of our government and also of limiting those powers. Although our focus in this book is on the relevance of this document to the ongoing practice of constitutional law, it is important to understand some historical context about the writing of the Constitution itself.

Before the modern Constitution was written, the country was governed by the Congress of the Confederation, which adhered to the Articles of Confederation.

In part due to the urging of those discontented with the Articles, famously including James Madison and Alexander Hamilton, a convention was called in Philadelphia during the summer of 1787 to consider amending this document. Among the common complaints about the Articles of Confederation was that it provided too weak a central government.

As you have seen from our examination so far, the new Constitution established both a Congress and an executive with a series of national powers. Structurally, the new Constitution retained some sovereignty for the states, but it also placed sovereignty in the hands of the federal government. The document thus dispensed with the idea that the United States was a mere alliance between fully sovereign states. As we will see in Chapters 3 and 4, this notion of "dual sovereignty" continues to pose challenges in constitutional interpretation. The convention in Philadelphia itself was not without controversy. Indeed, the final document we have today is widely regarded as the result of a series of compromises. In particular, the structure of Congress, which combines equal representation for all states in the Senate with proportional representation in the House of Representatives, is the result of a synthesis between the Virginia plan proposed by Madison, favored by large states, and the New Jersey plan, favored by small states.

Famously, too, the original document compromised on the issue of slavery. Questioning the legality of slavery was formally postponed until 1808. Notice too that Southern concerns that slaves be counted in the apportionment of representatives in the House despite not being able to vote were acknowledged by the so-called "Three-Fifths Clause," which counted slaves as just that fraction of a free person for apportionment purposes. Needless to say, this document grossly ignored the interests of African Americans, who in many states were relegated to bondage and in all were denied equal status. As we will see in the cases of African Americans and of women (Chapters 9 and 10), original defects in the Constitution would not be rectified for some time.

Because the document was to supersede the Articles of Confederation and incorporate the states into a new union of dual sovereignty, the Philadelphia convention agreed that three-quarters of the states would have to ratify it for it to take effect. During the debates in individual states about ratification, a group of leading "anti-Federalists" penned newspaper articles in opposition to the new Constitution and urged people to vote against it. Among their reasons, the anti-Federalists predicted that the new Constitution would consolidate too much power in the hands of a large government, which would fail to respect either the individual sovereignty of states or the rights of citizens. The debate between Federalists and anti-Federalists was particularly contentious in New York. In a series of periodicals, James Madison, John Jay, and Alexander Hamilton wrote articles—today known as *The Federalist Papers*—defending the Constitution and urging ratification. In this book, we have included several selections from these papers. Ultimately, the Federalists were victorious, and in mid-1788, the Constitution went into effect.

The legacy of the anti-Federalists, however, was not entirely lost. Despite the assurances of many Federalists that that the Constitution as enacted needed no explicit protections of individual rights, it was ultimately agreed to take up a Bill of Rights soon after the passage of the original document. Hamilton, for one, opposed the idea in *The Federalist* No. 84:

> I . . . affirm that bills of rights, in the sense and to the extent in which they are contended for, are not only unnecessary in the proposed Constitution, but would even be dangerous. They would contain various exceptions to powers not granted; and, on this very account, would afford a colorable pretext to claim more than were granted. For why declare that things shall not be done which there is no power to do? Why, for instance, should it be said that the liberty of the press shall not be restrained, when no power is given by which restrictions may be imposed? I will not contend that such a provision would confer a regulating power; but it is evident that it would furnish, to men disposed to usurp, a plausible pretense for claiming that power.

Despite this objection, a bill of rights was proposed by Congress in 1789 and ratified in 1791 in accordance with the Article V amendment process. Thus, of the 27 constitutional amendments that have been passed since the adoption of the original document, ten were accomplished in one fell swoop just a few years after the first version was ratified.

The Founding period is of course of significant interest to constitutional scholars. As we will see, the "originalist" school of constitutional interpretation in particular places great importance on understanding the meaning of the original document in the context in which it was written. But as will soon be evident, the constitutional convention by no means resolved the controversies that would come to dominate American political life. To the contrary, these issues could only be worked out through future argument and discussion.

The Path to the Supreme Court

The Supreme Court, as the highest court in the United States, hears only a very small fraction of the total cases filed throughout the country. Needless to say, the path to the Supreme Court is fraught with obstacles, and only seldom do litigants get the chance to present their cases before this body. While it is difficult to say exactly what makes a case reviewable by the Supreme Court, it is often a necessary condition that the question of law at issue be somewhat ambiguous and require clarification. The Supreme Court does not take just any case, but rather focuses on those in which it can clarify previous rulings, overturn precedent, or correct a conflict that exists among lower court rulings. In this section, we will begin by outlining the structure of the court system and the procedures by which a case might make it to the Supreme Court. We will then go on to outline various procedural hurdles that a case must overcome for the Court to reach a decision on the merits of a particular case.

The Structure of the Courts

As we noted earlier, Article III of the Constitution grants the Supreme Court a few select areas in which it has "original jurisdiction." In such cases, the Supreme Court acts as a trial-level court, meaning that it hears evidence and makes decisions about facts. In most instances, however, such "original jurisdiction" or "trial-level" cases begin at much lower levels of either the federal or the state system. Pursuant to Article III, Congress has established a series of "inferior" federal courts. The trial-level courts are called "district courts," and are found throughout the country. There are currently 94 federal district courts. The losing party in any one of these cases can make an appeal to "circuit" courts. There are thirteen of these "courts of appeals," twelve of which hear appeals from district courts based on geographic location, while a thirteenth court of appeals in Washington, D.C., the Federal Circuit, hears appeals nationwide from district court decisions on several technical subjects like patents and trademarks.

In addition to the federal court system, a parallel judicial system exists in each state, with trial-level and top-level courts. Most, but not all, states have appellate-level courts similar to those in the federal system. Although they go by different names, each state has established its own structure for handling legal claims. Often the highest appellate court is called the "Supreme Court" of the state. This is not a reliable way of determining the level of any given court, however. New York, for example, calls the trial-level courts "Supreme Court" and the highest court the "Court of Appeals." Although the rules by which it is decided whether a claim is rightly adjudicated in state or federal court are complicated, there are a few guiding principles. For instance, parties have a right to have their case heard by federal as opposed to state courts in matters of so-called "diversity jurisdiction," in which the parties are from different states. In addition, if the case implicates matters of federal law, parties can claim that there is a "federal question" at stake and seek to be heard by a federal court. Regardless, however, of whether a case originates in state or federal court, if a party claims its federal constitutional rights have been violated, it can apply for a "writ of certiorari" and seek to be heard by the Supreme Court of the United States once it has exhausted its appeals in the lower courts. Thus, the Supreme Court hears federal cases that arise both from the federal system and from the states.

Unlike at the district and circuit court level, parties do not have a right to have their case heard automatically at this level. Rather, they must petition the justices for certiorari. By custom, according to the so-called "rule of four," if at least four justices vote to hear a case, the Court will schedule it for briefing and argument and issue a ruling. The process of "granting cert" is itself the subject of much speculation. Certain features of a case might make it "cert-worthy," although no one feature is sufficient to ensure that it will be accepted. Many of the justices participate in a "cert pool" in which they share the process of review. Their clerks in particular, who are typically recent law school graduates, are particularly important at this stage of decision making, reading the petitions for certiorari and helping the justices decide which cases to take. The court receives thousands of certiorari petitions each year, but will typically hear no more than about 100 cases. Thus, only the most challenging and legally pressing matters will merit the attention of the nation's top judges.

When Does the Supreme Court Hear a Case?

In contrast to courts in many other countries, the Supreme Court of the United States cannot exercise its power of judicial review at will. Although it has the power to strike down laws—federal, state, and municipal—that are in conflict with the Constitution, it must do so only in the context of a particular case brought before it. This is because Article III of the Constitution contains what is called the Case or Controversy Clause. Specifically, before the Supreme Court (or any federal court) can make a decision about the constitutionality of a law or policy, it must be presented with a relevant conflict between two parties, one of which claims a harm or potential harm from the law at issue. The Court, for example, will not hear cases in which the legal question at issue has become moot because the facts have changed. Similarly, it will not hear cases that are not "ripe" for adjudication—if, for example, it is not certain that a potential harm will be realized as an actual harm, or if critical facts remain to be resolved. Additionally, the Supreme Court does not issue "advisory opinions" on the likely outcome of hypothetical cases. Some state courts, however, do engage in this practice, as does the International Court of Justice.

Related to the "case or controversy" requirement is the issue of standing. In order to have "standing" to bring a case to federal court or an appeal before the Supreme Court, a party must be directly involved in the matter being argued. In a variety of cases, the Supreme Court has asked whether individuals can have "third-party standing," meaning that they can claim that, because of a general harm posed by a law, they can sue on behalf of citizens at large. Granting third-party standing would entail that an individual before the Court would not have been directly harmed but rather would seek to litigate on behalf of some broader interest. Repeatedly, the Supreme Court has denied such standing, thus limiting its own review power.

Deciding a Case

In addition to the readings that frame many of the issues of these chapters, a good portion of our work in this book will involve analyzing Supreme Court opinions. Unlike the legislative and executive branches, the Supreme Court issues formal written arguments revealing not only its decisions, but the reasons for those decisions. These reasoned documents are known as "opinions."

The Process of Opinion Writing

After the Court has agreed to hear a case, a number of steps will occur. First, the parties to the case will submit written briefs outlining their arguments and the legal arguments they suggest the justices rely upon. The petitioners (those who are asking the Court to reverse the lower court, or those who "petitioned" for certiorari) are then invited to have a lawyer make an oral argument before the Court and respond to questions from the bench. In practice, lawyers prepare an oral presentation but are often interrupted by the justices' questions. These questions will respond either to the oral arguments or to the written briefs. At times, justices will ask for clarification of the facts, but then will engage in legal argument with the lawyers. For instance, justices might ask the lawyers about how their suggested rules would apply in hypothetical scenarios, and what the implications of their case might be for future cases if their reasoning were adopted. After oral argument, the Court convenes a conference in which all the justices will discuss the cases in which they recently heard argument and attempt to reach a consensus. Ultimately, however, each case is subject to a vote, with the majority determining the outcome. Depending on how the vote goes, a variety of opinions can potentially be issued by the Court.

If at least five of the nine justices agree, both about the judgment and the reasoning, the senior justice in the majority will assign one of the justices to write a "majority opinion," which the other members of the majority will sign to indicate their support. Sometimes, justices will agree on the outcome of the case but not on the reasoning. In such cases, justices will often write a "concurring opinion" to distinguish their reasoning from that of the "majority opinion," although they support the ultimate judgment of the case. In cases in which fewer than five justices agree on the legal reasoning of a decision, the controlling opinion is properly called a "plurality" opinion. In some cases, the Court will issue *per curiam* ("for the court") or unsigned opinions.

Lastly, justices who disagree with the outcome of the case and with the legal reasoning will file "dissenting" opinions, outlining the legal arguments they would have adopted instead. The role of dissenting opinions in constitutional law is multi-faceted. They provide alternative kinds of reasoning that is useful in formulating possible criticisms of the majority's reasoning. In addition, however, dissenting opinions are often cited in future opinions, and indeed can become the basis for new law. For instance, Justice Oliver Wendell Holmes penned a famous dissent in *Abrams v. United States* that was later used in the founding of modern free-speech law. We include many dissents in this book, sometimes because they ultimately turned out to be controlling after a subsequent case, and sometimes because they provide interesting legal arguments.

Legal Reasoning

Now that we have discussed the process of opinion writing, we can explore some of the content of these opinions. First, it is important to learn to identify the *holding* of Supreme Court opinions. The holding explains how, in a particular case, the law applies to the facts at hand. Usually the holding can be expressed in one sentence that ties together the legal issue discussed in the case with the decision about how this legal issue bears upon the facts. For instance, as you will see, the holding in *Lawrence v. Texas* is that state laws banning consensual sodomy violate couples' entitlement to substantive due process. Sometimes lawyers distinguish between the holding of the case and so-called *dicta*. Dicta is the area outside the specific legal adjudication, in which a particular justice will engage in reasoning that is either not strictly legal or is not necessary to decide the question before the court in the case at issue. Unlike the holding, it is not binding on future courts. The line between the holding and dicta, however, is sometimes blurry. Sometimes what is thought to be dicta becomes part of the holding, and ultimately part of the rule of law.

We will also see that much legal reasoning concerns the making and refuting of analogies to previous cases. The reason for this is that courts have an obligation to be consistent in their rulings over time, and to "treat like cases alike." In other words, the Supreme Court attempts to show respect for its prior precedent by continuing to apply similar rules to similar circumstances. The Court thus tends to follow a principle of *stare decisis*, roughly translated as "let the decision stand." Sometimes, however, the Court overturns a previous ruling. Famously, for example, the Court in *Brown v. Board of Education* overturned a previous case, *Plessy v. Ferguson*, which had enshrined the doctrine of "separate but equal." Sometimes, as in *Brown*, the Court will overrule a previous case explicitly. In other cases, such a reversal is never made explicit, though the Court may move away from or seek to marginalize a previous ruling. Thus, there is sometimes disagreement about whether a previous case has in fact been overruled.

THE CONSTITUTION OF THE UNITED STATES

We the People of the United States, in Order to form a more perfect Union, establish justice, insure domestic Tranquility, provide for the common defence, promote the general Welfare, and secure the Blessings of Liberty to ourselves and our Posterity, do ordain and establish this Constitution for the United States of America.

ARTICLE 1.

Section 1

All legislative Powers herein granted shall be vested in a Congress of the United States, which shall consist of a Senate and House of Representatives.

Section 2

The House of Representatives shall be composed of Members chosen every second Year by the People of the several States, and the Electors in each State shall have the Qualifications requisite for Electors of the most numerous Branch of the State Legislature.

No Person shall be a Representative who shall not have attained to the Age of twenty five Years, and been seven Years a Citizen of the United States, and who shall not, when elected, be an Inhabitant of that State in which he shall be chosen.

Representatives and direct Taxes shall be apportioned among the several States which may be included within this Union, according to their respective Numbers, which shall be determined by adding to the whole Number of free Persons, including those bound to Service for a Term of Years, and excluding Indians not taxed, three fifths of all other Persons.

The actual Enumeration shall be made within three Years after the first Meeting of the Congress of the United States, and within every subsequent Term of ten Years, in such Manner as they shall by Law direct. The Number of Representatives shall not exceed one for every thirty Thousand, but each State shall have at

Least one Representative; and until such enumeration shall be made, the State of New Hampshire shall be entitled to choose three, Massachusetts eight, Rhode Island and Providence Plantations one, Connecticut five, New York six, New Jersey four, Pennsylvania eight, Delaware one, Maryland six, Virginia ten, North Carolina five, South Carolina five and Georgia three.

When vacancies happen in the Representation from any State, the Executive Authority thereof shall issue Writs of Election to fill such Vacancies.

The House of Representatives shall choose their Speaker and other Officers; and shall have the sole Power of Impeachment.

Section 3

The Senate of the United States shall be composed of two Senators from each State, chosen by the Legislature thereof, for six Years; and each Senator shall have one Vote.

Immediately after they shall be assembled in Consequence of the first Election, they shall be divided as equally as may be into three Classes. The Seats of the Senators of the first Class shall be vacated at the Expiration of the second Year, of the second Class at the Expiration of the fourth Year, and of the third Class at the Expiration of the sixth Year, so that one third may be chosen every second Year; and if Vacancies happen by Resignation, or otherwise, during the Recess of the Legislature of any State, the Executive thereof may make temporary Appointments until the next Meeting of the Legislature, which shall then fill such Vacancies.

No person shall be a Senator who shall not have attained to the Age of thirty Years, and been nine Years a Citizen of the United States, and who shall not, when elected, be an Inhabitant of that State for which he shall be chosen.

The Vice President of the United States shall be President of the Senate, but shall have no Vote, unless they be equally divided.

The Senate shall choose their other Officers, and also a President pro tempore, in the absence of the Vice President, or when he shall exercise the Office of President of the United States.

The Senate shall have the sole Power to try all Impeachments. When sitting for that Purpose, they shall be on Oath or Affirmation. When the President of the United States is tried, the Chief Justice shall preside: And no Person shall be convicted without the Concurrence of two thirds of the Members present.

Judgment in Cases of Impeachment shall not extend further than to removal from Office, and disqualification to hold and enjoy any Office of honor, Trust or Profit under the United States: but the Party convicted shall nevertheless be liable and subject to Indictment, Trial, Judgment and Punishment, according to Law.

Section 4

The Times, Places and Manner of holding Elections for Senators and Representatives, shall be prescribed in each State by the Legislature thereof; but the Congress may at any time by Law make or alter such Regulations, except as to the Place of Choosing Senators.

The Congress shall assemble at least once in every Year, and such Meeting shall be on the first Monday in December, unless they shall by Law appoint a different Day.

Section 5

Each House shall be the Judge of the Elections, Returns and Qualifications of its own Members, and a Majority of each shall constitute a Quorum to do Business; but a smaller number may adjourn from day to day, and may be authorized to compel the Attendance of absent Members, in such Manner, and under such Penalties as each House may provide.

Each House may determine the Rules of its Proceedings, punish its Members for disorderly Behavior, and, with the Concurrence of two-thirds, expel a Member.

Each House shall keep a Journal of its Proceedings, and from time to time publish the same, excepting such Parts as may in their Judgment require Secrecy; and the Yeas and Nays of the Members of either House on any question shall, at the Desire of one fifth of those Present, be entered on the Journal.

Neither House, during the Session of Congress, shall, without the Consent of the other, adjourn for more than three days, nor to any other Place than that in which the two Houses shall be sitting.

Section 6

The Senators and Representatives shall receive a Compensation for their Services, to be ascertained by Law, and paid out of the Treasury of the United States. They shall in all Cases, except Treason, Felony and Breach of the Peace, be privileged from Arrest during their Attendance at the Session of their respective Houses, and in going to and returning from the same; and for any Speech or Debate in either House, they shall not be questioned in any other Place.

No Senator or Representative shall, during the Time for which he was elected, be appointed to any civil Office under the Authority of the United States which shall have been created, or the Emoluments whereof shall have been increased during such time; and no Person holding any Office under the United States, shall be a Member of either House during his Continuance in Office.

Section 7

All bills for raising Revenue shall originate in the House of Representatives; but the Senate may propose or concur with Amendments as on other Bills.

Every Bill which shall have passed the House of Representatives and the Senate, shall, before it become a Law, be presented to the President of the United States; If he approve he shall sign it, but if not he shall return it, with his Objections to that House in which it shall have originated, who shall enter the Objections at large on their Journal, and proceed to reconsider it. If after such Reconsideration two thirds of that House shall agree to pass the Bill, it shall be sent, together with the Objections, to the other House, by which it shall likewise be reconsidered, and if approved by two thirds of that House, it shall become a Law. But in all such Cases the Votes of both Houses shall be determined by Yeas and Nays, and the Names of the Persons voting for and against the Bill shall be entered on the Journal of each House respectively. If any Bill shall not be returned by the President within ten Days (Sundays excepted) after it shall have been presented to him, the Same shall be a Law, in like Manner as if he had signed it, unless the Congress by their Adjournment prevent its Return, in which Case it shall not be a Law.

Every Order, Resolution, or Vote to which the Concurrence of the Senate and House of Representatives may be necessary (except on a question of Adjournment) shall be presented to the President of the United States; and before the Same shall take Effect, shall be approved by him, or being disapproved by him, shall be repassed by two thirds of the Senate and House of Representatives, according to the Rules and Limitations prescribed in the Case of a Bill.

Section 8

The Congress shall have Power To lay and collect Taxes, Duties, Imposts and Excises, to pay the Debts and provide for the common Defence and general Welfare of the United States; but all Duties, Imposts and Excises shall be uniform throughout the United States;

To borrow money on the credit of the United States;

To regulate Commerce with foreign Nations, and among the several States, and with the Indian Tribes;

To establish an uniform Rule of Naturalization, and uniform Laws on the subject of Bankruptcies throughout the United States;

To coin Money, regulate the Value thereof, and of foreign Coin, and fix the Standard of Weights and Measures;

To provide for the Punishment of counterfeiting the Securities and current Coin of the United States;

To establish Post Offices and Post Roads;

To promote the Progress of Science and useful Arts, by securing for limited Times to Authors and Inventors the exclusive Right to their respective Writings and Discoveries;

To constitute Tribunals inferior to the supreme Court;

To define and punish Piracies and Felonies committed on the high Seas, and Offenses against the Law of Nations;

To declare War, grant Letters of Marque and Reprisal, and make Rules concerning Captures on Land and Water;

To raise and support Armies, but no Appropriation of Money to that Use shall be for a longer Term than two Years;

To provide and maintain a Navy;

To make Rules for the Government and Regulation of the land and naval Forces;

To provide for calling forth the Militia to execute the Laws of the Union, suppress Insurrections and repel Invasions;

To provide for organizing, arming, and disciplining the Militia, and for governing such Part of them as may be employed in the Service of the United States, reserving to the States respectively, the Appointment of the Officers, and the Authority of training the Militia according to the discipline prescribed by Congress;

To exercise exclusive Legislation in all Cases whatsoever, over such District (not exceeding ten Miles square) as may, by Cession of particular States, and the acceptance of Congress, become the Seat of the Government of the United States, and to exercise like Authority over all Places purchased by the Consent of the Legislature of the State in which the Same shall be, for the Erection of Forts, Magazines, Arsenals, dock-Yards, and other needful Buildings; And

To make all Laws which shall be necessary and proper for carrying into Execution the foregoing Powers, and all other Powers vested by this Constitution in the Government of the United States, or in any Department or Officer thereof.

Section 9

The Migration or Importation of such Persons as any of the States now existing shall think proper to admit, shall not be prohibited by the Congress prior to the Year one thousand eight hundred and eight, but a tax or duty may be imposed on such Importation, not exceeding ten dollars for each Person.

The privilege of the Writ of Habeas Corpus shall not be suspended, unless when in Cases of Rebellion or Invasion the public Safety may require it.

No Bill of Attainder or ex post facto Law shall be passed.

No capitation, or other direct, Tax shall be laid, unless in Proportion to the Census or Enumeration herein before directed to be taken.

No Tax or Duty shall be laid on Articles exported from any State.

No Preference shall be given by any Regulation of Commerce or Revenue to the Ports of one State over those of another: nor shall Vessels bound to, or from, one State, be obliged to enter, clear, or pay Duties in another.

No Money shall be drawn from the Treasury, but in Consequence of Appropriations made by Law; and a regular Statement and Account of the Receipts and Expenditures of all public Money shall be published from time to time.

No Title of Nobility shall be granted by the United States: And no Person holding any Office of Profit or Trust under them, shall, without the Consent of the Congress, accept of any present, Emolument, Office, or Title, of any kind whatever, from any King, Prince or foreign State.

Section 10

No State shall enter into any Treaty, Alliance, or Confederation; grant Letters of Marque and Reprisal; coin Money; emit Bills of Credit; make any Thing but gold and silver Coin a Tender in Payment of Debts; pass any Bill of Attainder, ex post facto Law, or Law impairing the Obligation of Contracts, or grant any Title of Nobility.

No State shall, without the Consent of the Congress, lay any Imposts or Duties on Imports or Exports, except what may be absolutely necessary for executing its inspection Laws: and the net Produce of all Duties and Imposts, laid by any State on Imports or Exports, shall be for the Use of the Treasury of the United States; and all such Laws shall be subject to the Revision and Control of the Congress.

No State shall, without the Consent of Congress, lay any duty of Tonnage, keep Troops, or Ships of War in time of Peace, enter into any Agreement or Compact with another State, or with a foreign Power, or engage in War, unless actually invaded, or in such imminent Danger as will not admit of delay.

ARTICLE 2.

Section 1

The executive Power shall be vested in a President of the United States of America. He shall hold his Office during the Term of four Years, and, together with the Vice-President chosen for the same Term, be elected, as follows:

Each State shall appoint, in such Manner as the Legislature thereof may direct, a Number of Electors, equal to the whole Number of Senators and Representatives to which the State may be entitled in the Congress: but no Senator or Representative, or Person holding an Office of Trust or Profit under the United States, shall be appointed an Elector.

The Electors shall meet in their respective States, and vote by Ballot for two persons, of whom one at least shall not lie an Inhabitant of the same State with themselves. And they shall make a List of all the Persons voted for, and of the Number of Votes for each; which List they shall sign and certify, and transmit sealed to the Seat of the Government of the United States, directed to the President of the Senate. The President of the Senate shall, in the Presence of the Senate and House of Representatives, open all the Certificates, and the Votes shall then be counted. The Person having the greatest Number of Votes shall be the President, if such Number be a Majority of the whole Number of Electors appointed; and if there be more than one who have such Majority, and have an equal Number of Votes, then the House of Representatives shall immediately choose by Ballot one of them for President; and if no Person have a Majority, then from the five highest on the List the said House shall in like Manner choose the President. But in choosing the President, the Votes shall be taken by States, the Representation from each State having one Vote; a quorum for this Purpose shall consist of a Member or Members from two-thirds of the States, and a Majority of all the States shall be necessary to a Choice. In every Case, after the Choice of the President, the Person having the greatest Number of Votes of the Electors shall be the Vice President. But if there should remain two or more who have equal Votes, the Senate shall choose from them by Ballot the Vice-President.

The Congress may determine the Time of choosing the Electors, and the Day on which they shall give their Votes; which Day shall be the same throughout the United States.

No person except a natural born Citizen, or a Citizen of the United States, at the time of the Adoption of this Constitution, shall be eligible to the Office of President; neither shall any Person be eligible to that Office who shall not have attained to the Age of thirty-five Years, and been fourteen Years a Resident within the United States.

In Case of the Removal of the President from Office, or of his Death, Resignation, or Inability to discharge the Powers and Duties of the said Office, the same shall devolve on the Vice President, and the Congress may by Law provide for the Case of Removal, Death, Resignation or Inability, both of the President and Vice President, declaring what Officer shall then act as President, and such Officer shall act accordingly, until the Disability be removed, or a President shall be elected.

The President shall, at stated Times, receive for his Services, a Compensation, which shall neither be increased nor diminished during the Period for which he shall have been elected, and he shall not receive within that Period any other Emolument from the United States, or any of them.

Before he enter on the Execution of his Office, he shall take the following Oath or Affirmation:

"I do solemnly swear (or affirm) that I will faithfully execute the Office of President of the United States, and will to the best of my Ability, preserve, protect and defend the Constitution of the United States."

Section 2

The President shall be Commander in Chief of the Army and Navy of the United States, and of the Militia of the several States, when called into the actual Service of the United States; he may require the Opinion, in writing, of the principal Officer in each of the executive Departments, upon any subject relating to the Duties of their respective Offices, and he shall have Power to Grant Reprieves and Pardons for Offenses against the United States, except in Cases of Impeachment.

He shall have Power, by and with the Advice and Consent of the Senate, to make Treaties, provided two thirds of the Senators present concur; and he shall nominate, and by and with the Advice and Consent of the Senate, shall appoint Ambassadors, other public Ministers and Consuls, Judges of the supreme Court, and all other Officers of the United States, whose Appointments are not herein otherwise provided for, and which shall be established by Law: but the Congress may by Law vest the Appointment of such inferior Officers, as they think proper, in the President alone, in the Courts of Law, or in the Heads of Departments.

The President shall have Power to fill up all Vacancies that may happen during the Recess of the Senate, by granting Commissions which shall expire at the End of their next Session.

Section 3

He shall from time to time give to the Congress Information of the State of the Union, and recommend to their Consideration such Measures as he shall judge necessary and expedient; he may, on extraordinary Occasions, convene both Houses, or either of them, and in Case of Disagreement between them, with Respect to the Time of Adjournment, he may adjourn them to such Time as he shall think proper; he shall receive Ambassadors and other public Ministers; he shall take Care that the Laws be faithfully executed, and shall Commission all the Officers of the United States.

Section 4

The President, Vice President and all civil Officers of the United States, shall be removed from Office on Impeachment for, and Conviction of, Treason, Bribery, or other high Crimes and Misdemeanors.

ARTICLE 3.

Section 1

The judicial Power of the United States, shall be vested in one supreme Court, and in such inferior Courts as the Congress may from time to time ordain and establish. The Judges, both of the supreme and inferior Courts, shall hold their Offices during good Behavior, and shall, at stated Times, receive for their Services a Compensation which shall not be diminished during their Continuance in Office.

Section 2

The judicial Power shall extend to all Cases, in Law and Equity, arising under this Constitution, the Laws of the United States, and Treaties made, or which shall be made, under their Authority; to all Cases affecting Ambassadors, other public Ministers and Consuls; to all Cases of admiralty and maritime Jurisdiction; to Controversies to which the United States shall be a Party; to Controversies between two or more States; between a State and Citizens of another State; between Citizens of different States; between Citizens of the same State claiming Lands under Grants of different States, and between a State, or the Citizens thereof, and foreign States, Citizens or Subjects.

In all Cases affecting Ambassadors, other public Ministers and Consuls, and those in which a State shall be Party, the supreme Court shall have original Jurisdiction. In all the other Cases before mentioned, the supreme Court shall have appellate Jurisdiction, both as to Law and Fact, with such Exceptions, and under such Regulations as the Congress shall make.

The Trial of all Crimes, except in Cases of Impeachment, shall be by Jury; and such Trial shall be held in the State where the said Crimes shall have been committed; but when not committed within any State, the Trial shall be at such Place or Places as the Congress may by Law have directed.

Section 3

Treason against the United States, shall consist only in levying War against them, or in adhering to their Enemies, giving them Aid and Comfort. No Person shall be convicted of Treason unless on the Testimony of two Witnesses to the same overt Act, or on Confession in open Court.

The Congress shall have power to declare the Punishment of Treason, but no Attainder of Treason shall work Corruption of Blood, or Forfeiture except during the Life of the Person attainted.

ARTICLE 4.

Section 1

Full Faith and Credit shall be given in each State to the public Acts, Records, and judicial proceedings of every other State. And the Congress may by general Laws prescribe the Manner in which such Acts, Records and Proceedings shall be proved, and the Effect thereof.

Section 2

The Citizens of each State shall be entitled to all Privileges and Immunities of Citizens in the several States.

A Person charged in any State with Treason, Felony, or other Crime, who shall flee from justice, and be found in another State, shall on demand of the executive Authority of the State from which he fled, be delivered up, to be removed to the State having Jurisdiction of the Crime.

No Person held to Service or Labour in one State, under the Laws thereof, escaping into another, shall, in Consequence of any Law or Regulation therein, be discharged from such Service or Labour, But shall be delivered up on Claim of the Party to whom such Service or Labour may be due.

Section 3

New States may be admitted by the Congress into this Union; but no new States shall be formed or erected within the Jurisdiction of any other State; nor any State be formed by the Junction of two or more States, or parts of States, without the Consent of the Legislatures of the States concerned as well as of the Congress.

The Congress shall have Power to dispose of and make all needful Rules and Regulations respecting the Territory or other Property belonging to the United States; and nothing in this Constitution shall be so construed as to Prejudice any Claims of the United States, or of any particular State.

Section 4

The United States shall guarantee to every State in this Union a Republican Form of Government, and shall protect each of them against Invasion; and on Application of the Legislature, or of the Executive (when the Legislature cannot be convened) against domestic Violence.

ARTICLE 5.

The Congress, whenever two thirds of both Houses shall deem it necessary, shall propose Amendments to this Constitution, or, on the Application of the

Legislatures of two thirds of the several States, shall call a Convention for proposing Amendments, which, in either Case, shall be valid to all Intents and Purposes, as part of this Constitution, when ratified by the Legislatures of three fourths of the several States, or by Conventions in three fourths thereof, as the one or the other Mode of Ratification may be proposed by the Congress; Provided that no Amendment which may be made prior to the Year One thousand eight hundred and eight shall in any Manner affect the first and fourth Clauses in the Ninth Section of the first Article; and that no State, without its Consent, shall be deprived of its equal Suffrage in the Senate.

ARTICLE 6.

All Debts contracted and Engagements entered into, before the Adoption of this Constitution, shall be as valid against the United States under this Constitution, as under the Confederation.

This Constitution, and the Laws of the United States which shall be made in Pursuance thereof; and all Treaties made, or which shall be made, under the Authority of the United States, shall be the supreme Law of the Land; and the Judges in every State shall be bound thereby, any Thing in the Constitution or Laws of any State to the Contrary notwithstanding.

The Senators and Representatives before mentioned, and the Members of the several State Legislatures, and all executive and judicial Officers, both of the United States and of the several States, shall be bound by Oath or Affirmation, to support this Constitution; but no religious Test shall ever be required as a Qualification to any Office or public Trust under the United States.

ARTICLE 7.

The Ratification of the Conventions of nine States, shall be sufficient for the Establishment of this Constitution between the States so ratifying the Same.

Done in Convention by the Unanimous Consent of the States present the Seventeenth Day of September in the Year of our Lord one thousand seven hundred and Eighty seven and of the Independence of the United States of America the Twelfth. In Witness whereof We have hereunto subscribed our Names.

Amendment 1

Congress shall make no law respecting an establishment of religion, or prohibiting the free exercise thereof; or abridging the freedom of speech, or of the press; or the right of the people peaceably to assemble, and to petition the Government for a redress of grievances.

Amendment 2

A well regulated Militia, being necessary to the security of a free State, the right of the people to keep and bear Arms, shall not be infringed.

Amendment 3

No Soldier shall, in time of peace be quartered in any house, without the consent of the Owner, nor in time of war, but in a manner to be prescribed by law.

Amendment 4

The right of the people to be secure in their persons, houses, papers, and effects, against unreasonable searches and seizures, shall not be violated, and no Warrants shall issue, but upon probable cause, supported by Oath or affirmation, and particularly describing the place to be searched, and the persons or things to be seized.

Amendment 5

No person shall be held to answer for a capital, or otherwise infamous crime, unless on a presentment or indictment of a Grand Jury, except in cases arising in the land or naval forces, or in the Militia, when in actual service in time of War or public danger; nor shall any person be subject for the same offense to be twice put in jeopardy of life or limb; nor shall be compelled in any criminal case to be a witness against himself, nor be deprived of life, liberty, or property, without due process of law; nor shall private property be taken for public use, without just compensation.

Amendment 6

In all criminal prosecutions, the accused shall enjoy the right to a speedy and public trial, by an impartial jury of the State and district wherein the crime shall have been committed, which district shall have been previously ascertained by law, and to be informed of the nature and cause of the accusation; to be confronted with the witnesses against him; to have compulsory process for obtaining witnesses in his favor, and to have the Assistance of Counsel for his defence.

Amendment 7

In Suits at common law, where the value in controversy shall exceed twenty dollars, the right of trial by jury shall be preserved, and no fact tried by a jury, shall be otherwise re-examined in any Court of the United States, than according to the rules of the common law.

Amendment 8

Excessive bail shall not be required, nor excessive fines imposed, nor cruel and unusual punishments inflicted.

Amendment 9

The enumeration in the Constitution, of certain rights, shall not be construed to deny or disparage others retained by the people.

Amendment 10

The powers not delegated to the United States by the Constitution, nor prohibited by it to the States, are reserved to the States respectively, or to the people.

Amendment 11

The Judicial power of the United States shall not be construed to extend to any suit in law or equity, commenced or prosecuted against one of the United States by Citizens of another State, or by Citizens or Subjects of any Foreign State.

Amendment 12

The Electors shall meet in their respective states, and vote by ballot for President and Vice-President, one of whom, at least, shall not be an inhabitant of the same state with themselves; they shall name in their ballots the person voted for as President, and in distinct ballots the person voted for as Vice-President, and they shall make distinct lists of all persons voted for as President, and of all persons voted for as Vice-President and of the number of votes for each, which lists they shall sign and certify, and transmit sealed to the seat of the government of the United States, directed to the President of the Senate;

The President of the Senate shall, in the presence of the Senate and House of Representatives, open all the certificates and the votes shall then be counted;

The person having the greatest Number of votes for President, shall be the President, if such number be a majority of the whole number of Electors appointed; and if no person have such majority, then from the persons having the highest numbers not exceeding three on the list of those voted for as President, the House of Representatives shall choose immediately, by ballot, the President. But in choosing the President, the votes shall be taken by states, the representation from each state having one vote; a quorum for this purpose shall consist of a member or members from two-thirds of the states, and a majority of all the states shall be necessary to a choice. And if the House of Representatives shall not choose a President whenever the right of choice shall devolve upon them, before the fourth day of March next following, then the Vice-President shall act as President, as in the case of the death or other constitutional disability of the President.

The person having the greatest number of votes as Vice-President, shall be the Vice-President, if such number be a majority of the whole number of Electors appointed, and if no person have a majority, then from the two highest numbers on the list, the Senate shall choose the Vice-President; a quorum for the purpose shall consist of two-thirds of the whole number of Senators, and a majority of the whole number shall be necessary to a choice. But no person constitutionally ineligible to the office of President shall be eligible to that of Vice-President of the United States.

Amendment 13

1. Neither slavery nor involuntary servitude, except as a punishment for crime whereof the party shall have been duly convicted, shall exist within the United States, or any place subject to their jurisdiction.

2. Congress shall have power to enforce this article by appropriate legislation.

Amendment 14

1. All persons born or naturalized in the United States, and subject to the jurisdiction thereof, are citizens of the United States and of the State wherein they reside. No State shall make or enforce any law which shall abridge the privileges or immunities of citizens of the United States; nor shall any State deprive any person of life, liberty, or property, without due process of law; nor deny to any person within its jurisdiction the equal protection of the laws.

2. Representatives shall be apportioned among the several States according to their respective numbers, counting the whole number of persons in each State, excluding Indians not taxed. But when the right to vote at any election for the choice of electors for President and Vice-President of the United States, Representatives in Congress, the Executive and Judicial officers of a State, or the members of the Legislature thereof, is denied to any of the male inhabitants of such State, being twenty-one years of age, and citizens of the United States, or in any way abridged, except for participation in rebellion, or other crime, the basis of representation therein shall be reduced in the proportion which the number of such male citizens shall bear to the whole number of male citizens twenty-one years of age in such State.

3. No person shall be a Senator or Representative in Congress, or elector of President and Vice-President, or hold any office, civil or military, under the United States, or under any State, who, having previously taken an oath, as a member of Congress, or as an officer of the United States, or as a member of any State legislature, or as an executive or judicial officer of any State, to support the Constitution of the United States, shall have engaged in insurrection or rebellion against the same, or given aid or comfort to the enemies thereof. But Congress may by a vote of two-thirds of each House, remove such disability.

4. The validity of the public debt of the United States, authorized by law, including debts incurred for payment of pensions and bounties for services in suppressing insurrection or rebellion, shall not be questioned. But neither the United States nor any State shall assume or pay any debt or obligation incurred in aid of insurrection or rebellion against the United States, or any claim for the loss

or emancipation of any slave; but all such debts, obligations and claims shall be held illegal and void.

5. The Congress shall have power to enforce, by appropriate legislation, the provisions of this article.

Amendment 15

1. The right of citizens of the United States to vote shall not be denied or abridged by the United States or by any State on account of race, color, or previous condition of servitude.

2. The Congress shall have power to enforce this article by appropriate legislation.

Amendment 16

The Congress shall have power to lay and collect taxes on incomes, from whatever source derived, without apportionment among the several States, and without regard to any census or enumeration.

Amendment 17

The Senate of the United States shall be composed of two Senators from each State, elected by the people thereof, for six years; and each Senator shall have one vote. The electors in each State shall have the qualifications requisite for electors of the most numerous branch of the State legislatures.

When vacancies happen in the representation of any State in the Senate, the executive authority of such State shall issue writs of election to fill such vacancies: Provided, That the legislature of any State may empower the executive thereof to make temporary appointments until the people fill the vacancies by election as the legislature may direct.

This amendment shall not be so construed as to affect the election or term of any Senator chosen before it becomes valid as part of the Constitution.

Amendment 18

1. After one year from the ratification of this article the manufacture, sale, or transportation of intoxicating liquors within, the importation thereof into, or the exportation thereof from the United States and all territory subject to the jurisdiction thereof for beverage purposes is hereby prohibited.

2. The Congress and the several States shall have concurrent power to enforce this article by appropriate legislation.

3. This article shall be inoperative unless it shall have been ratified as an amendment to the Constitution by the legislatures of the several States, as provided in the Constitution, within seven years from the date of the submission hereof to the States by the Congress.

Amendment 19

The right of citizens of the United States to vote shall not be denied or abridged by the United States or by any State on account of sex.

Congress shall have power to enforce this article by appropriate legislation.

Amendment 20

1. The terms of the President and Vice President shall end at noon on the 20th day of January, and the terms of Senators and Representatives at noon on the 3d day of January, of the years in which such terms would have ended if this article had not been ratified; and the terms of their successors shall then begin.

2. The Congress shall assemble at least once in every year, and such meeting shall begin at noon on the 3d day of January, unless they shall by law appoint a different day.

3. If, at the time fixed for the beginning of the term of the President, the President elect shall have died, the Vice President elect shall become President. If a President shall not have been chosen before the time fixed for the beginning of his term, or if the President elect shall have failed to qualify, then the Vice President elect shall act as President until a President shall have qualified; and the Congress may by law provide for the case herein neither a President elect nor a Vice President elect shall have qualified, declaring who shall then act as President, or the manner in which one who is to act shall be selected, and such person shall act accordingly until a President or Vice President shall have qualified.

4. The Congress may by law provide for the case of the death of any of the persons from whom the House of Representatives may choose a President whenever the right of choice shall have devolved upon them, and for the case of the death of any of the persons from whom the Senate may choose a Vice President whenever the right of choice shall have devolved upon them.

5. Sections 1 and 2 shall take effect on the 15th day of October following the ratification of this article.

6. This article shall be inoperative unless it shall have been ratified as an amendment to the Constitution by the legislatures of three-fourths of the several States within seven years from the date of its submission.

Amendment 21

1. The eighteenth article of amendment to the Constitution of the United States is hereby repealed.

2. The transportation or importation into any State, Territory, or possession of the United States for delivery or use therein of intoxicating liquors, in violation of the laws thereof, is hereby prohibited.

3. The article shall be inoperative unless it shall have been ratified as an amendment to the Constitution by conventions in the several States, as provided in the Constitution, within seven years from the date of the submission hereof to the States by the Congress.

Amendment 22

1. No person shall be elected to the office of the President more than twice, and no person who has held the office of President, or acted as President, for more than two years of a term to which some other person was elected President shall be elected to the office of the President more than once. But this Article shall not apply to any person holding the office of President, when this Article was proposed by the Congress, and shall not prevent any person who may be holding the office of President, or acting as President, during the term within which this Article becomes operative from holding the office of President or acting as President during the remainder of such term.

2. This article shall be inoperative unless it shall have been ratified as an amendment to the Constitution by the legislatures of three-fourths of the several States within seven years from the date of its submission to the States by the Congress.

Amendment 23

1. The District constituting the seat of Government of the United States shall appoint in such manner as the Congress may direct: A number of electors of President and Vice President equal to the whole number of Senators and Representatives in Congress to which the District would be entitled if it were a State, but in no event more than the least populous State; they shall be in addition to those appointed by the States, but they shall be considered, for the purposes of the election of President and Vice President, to be electors appointed by a State; and they shall meet in the District and perform such duties as provided by the twelfth article of amendment.

2. The Congress shall have power to enforce this article by appropriate legislation.

Amendment 24

1. The right of citizens of the United States to vote in any primary or other election for President or Vice President, for electors for President or Vice President, or for Senator or Representative in Congress, shall not be denied or abridged by the United States or any State by reason of failure to pay any poll tax or other tax.

2. The Congress shall have power to enforce this article by appropriate legislation.

Amendment 25

1. In case of the removal of the President from office or of his death or resignation, the Vice President shall become President.

2. Whenever there is a vacancy in the office of the Vice President, the President shall nominate a Vice President who shall take office upon confirmation by a majority vote of both Houses of Congress.

3. Whenever the President transmits to the President pro tempore of the Senate and the Speaker of the House of Representatives his written declaration that he is unable to discharge the powers and duties of his office, and until he transmits to them a written declaration to the contrary, such powers and duties shall be discharged by the Vice President as Acting President.

4. Whenever the Vice President and a majority of either the principal officers of the executive departments or of such other body as Congress may by law provide, transmit to the President pro tempore of the Senate and the Speaker of the House of Representatives their written declaration that the President is unable to discharge the powers and duties of his office, the Vice President shall immediately assume the powers and duties of the office as Acting President.

Thereafter, when the President transmits to the President pro tempore of the Senate and the Speaker of the House of Representatives his written declaration that no inability exists, he shall resume the powers and duties of his office unless the Vice President and a majority of either the principal officers of the executive department or of such other body as Congress may by law provide, transmit within four days to the President pro tempore of the Senate and the Speaker of the House of Representatives their written declaration that the President is unable to discharge the powers and duties of his office. Thereupon Congress shall decide the issue, assembling within forty eight hours for that purpose if not in session. If the Congress, within twenty one days after receipt of the latter written declaration, or, if Congress is not in session, within twenty one days after Congress is required to assemble, determines by two thirds vote of both Houses that the President is unable to discharge the powers and duties of his office, the Vice President shall continue to discharge the same as Acting President; otherwise, the President shall resume the powers and duties of his office.

Amendment 26

1. The right of citizens of the United States, who are eighteen years of age or older, to vote shall not be denied or abridged by the United States or by any State on account of age.

2. The Congress shall have power to enforce this article by appropriate legislation.

Amendment 27

No law, varying the compensation for the services of the Senators and Representatives, shall take effect, until an election of Representatives shall have intervened.

CONSTITUTIONAL LAW AND AMERICAN DEMOCRACY

PART I

FOUNDATIONS

JUDICIAL AUTHORITY

Is judicial review or judicial supremacy justified?
Is either constitutional? Is either democratic?

In the study of constitutional law, nothing is more problematic than the power of the Supreme Court itself. Many scholars of political science and constitutional law accept that the Court holds legitimate power to strike down both federal and state laws when those laws conflict with the U.S. Constitution. The potential problem with this power, however, lies in the fact that, at all levels of government, a large number of citizens are involved in the process of lawmaking. They do the hard work of crafting legislation, debating it in both formal and informal arenas, and participating either directly through plebiscites or indirectly through their elected representatives. In addition, at both the national and state levels of government, legislation must not only make it through the legislative branch, but must also win the approval of the executive branch, except in cases where an overwhelming supermajority in the legislature supports the legislation. Yet, in the U.S. system of government, the final decision as to whether laws are valid lies in the power of the Court to decide if legislation, despite all this effort, is consistent with the Constitution. If the Court finds that an act violates the Constitution, it has the power to strike down such legislation through the power of "judicial review." But what gives five out of nine justices of the Supreme Court the authority to make a decision about legislation approved by a majority of the people's representatives and that may affect millions of individuals?

All that is needed to spark the Court's review power is one person who contests the constitutionality of legislation by bringing a lawsuit. Although the Court does not have the power to initiate the review of laws on its own, each person subject to the law of and present in the United States has the right to bring suit challenging the constitutionality of laws that affect him or her. Article III of the Constitution in essence gives any one person the ability to challenge the constitutionality of legislative acts.

The readings and cases in this chapter attempt to address the question of why, in a democracy, the Supreme Court, prompted by suits brought by individuals or groups of individuals, should have the power of judicial review. The problem is described perhaps most famously by Alexander Bickel. Bickel addresses what he calls the "counter-majoritarian difficulty." For him, the fundamental question of the Constitution is whether we can regard the Court's power of judicial review as democratic given the minuscule number of people that are involved in the process of judicial review as compared to the number of people involved in the legislative process. He also challenges the idea that the Court is democratic given the fact that its members are not elected, but rather appointed by the president.

As you read through this chapter, it is important that you reflect on the possible answers to this challenge. The responses to this problem will help us to reflect on the question of judicial authority and the Court's review power. Indeed, the numerous questions that arise about the Constitution and its meaning throughout this book depend on our idea of judicial authority. When should the Court intercede in possible conflicts between Congress and the Constitution, or between the president and the Constitution, or even between Congress and the president? The question of intervention is no light matter, as throughout American history the courts have been involved through the power of judicial review in considering questions as fundamental as slavery, war, segregation, and abortion. Before we can discuss these specific issues, it is important to develop an understanding of when, if ever, the Court has the power and authority to intervene.

One possible line of argument that you should consider is that the rule of law itself provides an answer to the question of judicial authority. The courts, after all, are tasked with the job of interpreting the law. If the Constitution is a document of law, then it might follow that the courts should interpret the Constitution. In fact, this logic might go so far as to suggest that the Court should have the final say in various areas of law. In a contract suit, for example, the courts often are considered to have the final say. Should this finality also apply to matters of constitutional law? Something akin to this argument, as you will see, is prominent in the Court's decision in *Marbury v. Madison*, a case central to this chapter.

Those dissatisfied with grounding the Court's judicial review power in a claim about the nature of the rule of law find themselves in the company of a long line of critics of the Court's review power. While courts certainly can interpret law, it does not necessarily follow that they should be the exclusive interpreter of law. Thomas Jefferson, for instance, thought the other branches also capable of constitutional interpretation. Some advocates of "departmentalism" have advocated for a role for the other branches, aside from the Court, in constitutional interpretation. Moreover, Larry Kramer, whose article we excerpt in Section B, has argued that "the people themselves" have a role in constitutional interpretation.

Another line of argumentation in defense of the Court's review power draws from its potential democratic authority. Perhaps the will of the people itself demands ceding control to the Supreme Court in particular controversies. If the people endorse the idea of representative democracy, perhaps they also endorse the idea that particular decisions about matters of constitutional law should be left to the courts. A similar approach suggests that democracy itself must be protected by the courts. Perhaps the authority of the Supreme Court to enforce judicial review lies in its ability to bolster the democratic process. Similarly, those who believe rights to be fundamental to the American system might find appealing the idea that the Court's authority lies in its special ability to protect individual liberties.

What all the possible theories of the Court's authority and its review power make clear is that, to answer the counter-majoritarian difficulty, it might be necessary for you to ponder what you think democracy means. As the readings make clear, the definition of democracy is by no means obvious. Although simple majority rule is a common understanding of democratic rule, as you think about the role of the Court in a self-governing polity, also think about the meaning of democracy. Perhaps, as Ronald Dworkin believes, the protection of rights is fundamental to the meaning of democracy. Courts therefore might serve a democratic function when they protect rights, even if it means acting contrary to the will of the majority.

Some will be skeptical of both of these responses, and they will find themselves in the company of the strongest critics of judicial authority. According to some such thinkers, the Court's authority cannot be understood as anything other than antidemocratic. Some might conclude from this that there is no defense of the Court's judicial review power. But others might think that merely because it is an antidemocratic power does not mean that judicial review is not important or justified.

Indeed, even if judicial review should be a part of a system of democratic governance, as you will see, some legal scholars have debated the doctrine of "judicial supremacy." This debate concerns the question of whether the Court should be regarded as the final arbiter of the meaning of the Constitution or if that power should instead lie with another body of government.

In sum, in order to think about whether the Court should have the power of judicial review, it is essential that you grapple with the problem of judicial authority. As you read through this chapter you should seek to develop your own views about whether the Court should have *a* say, the *final* say, or *no* say in constitutional matters. This will enable you to develop informed views in other areas of constitutional controversy. The second chapter asks you to consider the content of the Constitution and what theories should motivate its interpretation. If you conclude that the Supreme Court should have the power of judicial review, it will also be incumbent on you to think about how the Court should exercise this review power. Having thought about the nature of the Supreme Court and its review power will prove invaluable in this task. Indeed, your view of the reason for judicial authority will inevitably be linked to the way you think this power should be exercised. For example, in Part II of this book, you will identify and evaluate the powers held by Congress and the president. These powers are derived from the Constitution, and interpretation of the Constitution is fundamental to the question of the nature of these powers. In Parts III and IV, you will be asked to think about the basic rights of liberty and equality to which those subject to the Constitution are entitled. But the Court's function in protecting these rights can only be answered if you have a general understanding of the role of the Court in the first place.

A.   THE ORIGINS OF JUDICIAL REVIEW

Although not labeled as such, the counter-majoritarian difficulty and the question of judicial authority in constitutional matters is a problem that has clearly been on the minds of scholars and jurists at least since the drafting of the Constitution. In *The Federalist* No. 78, Alexander Hamilton outlines two principal answers to this challenge that continue to be contested today. First, in the line of argument that would be repeated by Chief Justice John Marshall in the classic case of *Marbury v. Madison*, Hamilton argues that the Court's review power stems from the nature of the rule of law itself. If it is the role of courts to interpret law, and the Constitution is the law, then it follows that the courts should interpret the Constitution. This line of reasoning, often referred to as the "*Marbury* syllogism," is an often-repeated justification of the Court's authority. But this justification risks obscuring the difficult problems that underlie the counter-majoritarian difficulty not answered by this syllogism. In particular, why should the law itself command obedience? Why should courts be the exclusive interpreters of this law? The question of why the courts should have the power to interpret the law cannot be answered by reference to the law alone. Such an argument would be circular. Such questions cannot be answered without reference to a broader political theory about the justification for law. As we will see, Hamilton was aware of this problem and tried to outline a wider political theory of the power of judicial review that appealed to its importance in a democratic society. He claims in *The Federalist* that the very limits imposed by the Constitution have their source in the people themselves, as distinct from their elected representatives.

Throughout this chapter we examine various arguments that challenge Hamilton's understanding of the role of the Supreme Court within Article III of the Constitution. Many of these readings, however, share an assumption that the proper role of the Court should be read within the confines of Article III. These disagreements therefore are about how to interpret the Constitution. But before we examine these debates it is important to examine a fundamental challenge to Article III itself, and the very idea of a Supreme Court with review power. The excerpt included from Brutus, the pseudonym of a noted "anti-federalist" thinker, active in resisting the ratification of the Constitution by the states, suggests that the structure of Article III will lead to judicial tyranny. Inevitably, he suggests, the Court will need to answer questions left open by the Constitution, especially when it comes to applying broad provisions to specific facts. In such cases, the Court will have no guide. In this way, the potential arises for the Court to reach judgments that disregard the interests of the citizenry.

A more moderate critique does not seek to abolish the Supreme Court's power altogether, but would seek to limit it. The excerpt by Jefferson offers an interpretation of Article III distinct from the ones presented by both Hamilton and Brutus. Jefferson thought that a good account of democracy could not allow the Court the final word in interpreting the Constitution. In the included passage, he presents what became known later as the theory of departmentalism, or the idea that no one branch of government should have the final say in determining the meaning of the Constitution. In particular, notice his powerful metaphor about the Court's ability to mold law as though it were wax. If the Court is the final arbiter of the meaning of the Constitution, what is to prevent it from saying that the Constitution means merely what its justices wish it to say? The debate between Hamilton and Jefferson, therefore, raises a crucial issue of interpretation. Need the Constitution place its meaning in the hands of a final interpreter, or does that meaning stand apart from what any one institution claims it to mean? Does identifying the meaning of the Constitution require an institution to function as a final interpreter, or does that meaning stand on its own directly out of the document?

In his famous commentary on *Marbury v. Madison*, in which he coins the term, "counter-majoritarian difficulty," Bickel poses a fundamental challenge to both Hamilton's and Jefferson's views. He is deeply skeptical of the idea that the limits on majority rule imposed by the Constitution can be called democratic. For Bickel, it is the acts of participants in democratic rule that are the source of democratic authority, and he dismisses as chimerical the maneuvers of Hamilton and Chief Justice Marshall in suggesting otherwise. Yet Bickel is also concerned with protecting the guarantees of the Constitution, and arguably he still sees a role for the Court in doing so.

Before turning to our case selection for this chapter, you will explore Gordon Wood's attempt to provide a historical context for *Marbury v. Madison*. Wood raises interesting questions about the role of the decision in the Court's current practice of judicial review. Although *Marbury v. Madison* is often considered the basis of the Court's basic review power, Wood asks whether this is a modern invention rather than an obvious historical fact. Indeed, Wood's skepticism should give deep pause to anyone who wants to find the basis of judicial review in history alone.

The case selection in this chapter begins with *Calder v. Bull*. In that case the Court examined whether a state law violated the Constitution's ban on ex post facto laws. You will notice, too, that there is some commentary about the Court's possible power of judicial review. Although the review power is not clearly established in *Calder v. Bull*, you will see the issue examined in much greater depth when we turn next to the classic *Marbury v. Madison*, in which the Court is commonly regarded to have established the power of judicial review. You should notice how Chief Justice Marshall's argumentation appeals to the idea of law itself in establishing the Court's authority. You should note that, although the case does not grant the petitioner his claim, Chief Justice Marshall nevertheless uses the controversy as a means by which to assert greater power for the Court. Following *Marbury v. Madison*, which was predicated on a conflict at the federal level, you will find four cases in which the Court examined whether the actions of state governments violated the federal Constitution. The clauses of the Constitution here vary from issues regarding whether the prohibition on ex post facto laws has been violated to an examination of the meaning of the Contracts Clause. In addition to addressing issues of the Court's review power, these cases also inevitably raise the issue of the federal government's relationship to the states. As you will see, the Court in these cases breaks with its earlier reluctance to review and at times overturn state laws that violate the Constitution.

Alexander Bickel

THE LEAST DANGEROUS BRANCH

Chapter 1: Establishment and General Justification of Judicial Review

New Haven, CT: Yale University Press (1986)

The least dangerous branch of the American government is the most extraordinarily powerful court of law the world has ever known. The power which distinguishes the Supreme Court of the United States is that of constitutional review of actions of the other branches of government, federal and state. Curiously enough, this power of judicial review, as it is called, does not derive from any explicit constitutional command. The authority to determine the meaning and application of a written constitution is nowhere defined or even mentioned in the document itself. This is not to say that the power of judicial review cannot be placed in the Constitution; merely that it cannot be found there.

MARBURY v. MADISON

Congress was created very nearly full blown by the Constitution itself. The vast possibilities of the presidency were relatively easy to perceive and soon, inevitably, materialized. But the institution of the judiciary needed to be summoned up out of the constitutional vapors, shaped, and maintained; and the Great Chief Justice, John Marshall—not singlehanded, but first and foremost—was there to do it and did. If any social process can be said to have been "done" at a given time and by a given act, it is Marshall's achievement. The time was 1803; the act was the decision in the case of *Marbury v. Madison.*

William Marbury and some others sued Secretary Madison for delivery of their commissions as justices of the peace for the County of Washington in the District of Columbia, an office to which they had been appointed in the last moments of the administration of President John Adams. Marshall held that Marbury and the others were entitled to their commissions, but that the Supreme Court was without power to order Madison to deliver, because the section of the Judiciary Act of 1789 that purported to authorize the Court to act in such a case as this was itself unconstitutional. Thus did Marshall assume for his Court what is nowhere made explicit in the Constitution—the ultimate power to apply the Constitution, acts of Congress to the contrary notwithstanding.

"The question," Marshall's opinion begins, "whether an act repugnant to the Constitution, can become the law of the land, is a question deeply interesting to the United States; but, happily, not of an intricacy proportioned to its interest." Marshall's confidence that he could traverse the path ahead with ease is understandable, since he had already begged the question-in-chief, which was not whether an act repugnant to the Constitution could stand, but who should be empowered to decide that the act is repugnant. Marshall then posited the limited nature of the government established by the Constitution. It follows—and one may grant to Marshall that it follows as "a proposition too plain to be contested"—that the Constitution is a paramount law, and that ordinary legislative acts must conform to it. For Marshall it follows, further, that a legislative act contrary to the Constitution is not law and need not be given effect in court; else "written constitutions are absurd attempts, on the part of the people, to limit a power in its own nature illimitable." If two laws conflict, a court must obey the superior one. But Marshall knew (and, indeed, it was true in this very case) that a statute's repugnancy to the Constitution is in most instances not self-evident; it is, rather, an issue of policy that someone must decide. The problem is who: the courts, the legislature itself, the President, perhaps juries for purposes of criminal trials, or ultimately and finally the people through the electoral process?

This is the real question. Marshall addressed himself to it only partially and slightly. To leave the decision with the legislature, he said, is to allow those whose power is supposed to be limited themselves to set the limits—an absurd invitation to consistent abuse. Perhaps so, but the Constitution does not limit the power of the legislature alone. It limits that of the courts as well, and it may be equally absurd, therefore, to allow courts to set the limits. It is, indeed, more absurd, because courts are not subject to electoral control. (It may be argued that to leave the matter to the legislature is to leave it ultimately to the people at the polls. In this view the people as the principal would set the limits of the power that they have delegated to their agent.)

The case can be constructed where the conflict between a statute and the Constitution is self-evident in accordance with Marshall's general assumption. Even so, Marshall offers no real reason that the Court should have the power to nullify the statute. But Marshall did go on to some more specific textual references. His first was to Article III of the Constitution, which establishes the judiciary and reads in relevant part as follows:

SECTION 1. The judicial Power of the United States, shall be vested in one supreme Court, and in such inferior Courts as the Congress may from time to time ordain and establish. The Judges, both of the supreme and inferior Courts, shall hold their Offices during good Behavior, and shall, at stated Times, receive for their Services a Compensation which shall not be diminished during their Continuance in Office.

SECTION 2. The judicial Power shall extend to all Cases, in Law and Equity, arising under this Constitution, the Laws of the United States, and Treaties made, or which shall be made, under their Authority; — to all Cases affecting Ambassadors, or other public Ministers and Consuls; — to all Cases of admiralty and maritime Jurisdiction; — to Controversies to which the United States shall be a Party; — to Controversies between two or more States;—between a State and Citizens of another State; — between Citizens of different States; — between Citizens of the same State claiming Lands under Grants of different States, and between a State, or the Citizens thereof, and foreign States, Citizens or Subjects.

In all Cases affecting Ambassadors, other public Ministers and Consuls, and those in which a State shall be a Party, the supreme Court shall have original Jurisdiction. In all the other Cases before mentioned, the supreme Court shall have appellate Jurisdiction, both as to Law and Fact, with such Exceptions, and under such Regulations as the Congress shall make.

Could it be, Marshall asked, that those who granted the judicial power and extended it to all cases arising under the Constitution, laws, and treaties meant that cases arising under the Constitution should be decided without examination and application of the document itself? This was for Marshall "too extravagant to be maintained." Note well, however, that what the Constitution extends to cases arising under it is "the judicial

Power." Whether this power reaches as far as Marshall wanted it to go—namely, to reviewing acts of the legislature—is the question to be decided. What are the nature and extent of the function of the Court—the judicial power? Is the Court empowered, when it decides a case, to declare that a duly enacted statute violates the Constitution, and to invalidate the statute? Article III does not purport to describe the function of the Court; it subsumes whatever questions may exist as to that in the phrase "the judicial Power." It does not purport to tell the Court how to decide cases; it only specifies which kinds of cases the Court shall have jurisdiction to deal with at all. Thus, in giving jurisdiction in cases "arising under … the Laws" or "under … Treaties," the clause is not read as prescribing the process of decision to be followed. The process varies. In cases "under … the Laws" courts often leave determination of issues of fact and even issues that may be thought to be "of law" to administrative agencies. And under both "the Laws … and Treaties," much of the decision concerning meaning and applicability may be received ready-made from the Congress and the President. In some cases of all three descriptions, judicial decision may he withheld altogether—and it is for this reason that it will not do to place reliance on the word "all" in the phrase "all cases … arising …." To the extent that the Constitution speaks to such matters, it does so in the tightly packed phrase "judicial Power."

Only in the end, and then very lightly, does Marshall come to rest on the Supremacy Clause of Article VI, which in later times has seemed to many the most persuasive textual support. The Supremacy Clause is as follows:

> This Constitution and the Laws of the United States which shall be made in Pursuance thereof; and all Treaties made, or which shall be made, under the Authority of the United States, shall be the supreme Law of the Land; and the Judges in every State shall be bound thereby, any Thing in the Constitution or Laws of any State to the Contrary notwithstanding.

"It is also not entirely unworthy of observation," Marshall wrote—and this was all he had to say on the point—that in declaring what is to be the supreme law of the land, this clause mentions the Constitution first and then not the laws of the United States generally but only those which shall be made in pursuance of the Constitution. Marshall left it at that, and what is to be concluded from this remark? First, it must be noted that nothing here is addressed to federal courts. Any command to them will have to be inferred, if there is to be one at all. Only as a forensic amusement can the phrase "Judges in every State" be taken to include federal judges, on the ground that some of them sit in the states. After all, the Supreme Court does not. The clause speaks to the constituent states of the federation and tells them that federal law will supersede any contrary state law. Further, it goes over the heads of the state governments and speaks to state judges directly, telling them that it will be their duty to enforce the supreme federal law above any contrary state law. State judges need enforce, however, only such federal law as is made in pursuance of the Constitution. Conceivably the reference here might be to more than just the mechanical provisions that describe how a federal law is to be enacted—by the concurrence of both Houses and with the signature of the President. Conceivably state judges were to be authorized to measure federal law against the federal Constitution and uphold it or strike it down in accordance with their understanding of the relevant constitutional provision. But such an arrangement, standing alone, would have been extraordinary, and it would have been self-destructive.

Judiciary acts have, from the beginning, also given the Supreme Court jurisdiction to review state court cases in which is drawn in question the validity of a treaty or statute of the United States, presumably under the federal Constitution. If that was a grant to the Supreme Court of final authority to construe the Constitution as against acts of Congress, why, then, well and good. Nothing in the text prevents such a gesture of congressional abnegation, although in that event, what Congress can give away, Congress can, at least in theory, take back. But it is question-begging so to understand this provision of the first Judiciary Act. Reading no presuppositions into it, one may as easily conclude that the Supreme Court was meant only to enforce against state courts a rule that duly enacted federal statutes are constitutional by virtue of their due enactment. There is no similar ambiguity, however, in the first Judiciary Act's grant to the Supreme Court of jurisdiction to review cases which draw in question the validity of a statute of, or an authority exercised under, any state, on the ground of its being repugnant to the Constitution, treaties, or laws of the United States. This provision would be senseless unless it was intended to authorize the Court, in these circumstances, to construe and apply the federal Constitution as well as federal statute and treaty law. Only thus could this provision serve the interest of uniformity and of the superiority of federal power— and what other purpose could it have? As we have seen, the Supremacy Clause itself does not compel, although it permits and no doubt invites, this arrangement. This being so, Congress could change it all tomorrow. And perhaps it could, if textual

considerations were all that governed the matter, just as it could change the course of the Mississippi River, if all we had to indicate the location of its bed were some general description by a traveler of a body of water traversing the middle of the country from north to south.

THE COUNTER-MAJORITARIAN DIFFICULTY

The root difficulty is that judicial review is a counter-majoritarian force in our system. There are various ways of sliding over this ineluctable reality. Marshall did so when he spoke of enforcing, in behalf of "the people," the limits that they have ordained for the institutions of a limited government. But the word "people" so used is an abstraction. Not necessarily a meaningless or a pernicious one by any means; always charged with emotion, but nonrepresentational—an abstraction obscuring the reality that when the Supreme Court declares unconstitutional a legislative act or the action of an elected executive, it thwarts the will of representatives of the actual people of the here and now; it exercises control, not in behalf of the prevailing majority, but against it. That, without mystic overtones, is what actually happens. It is an altogether different kettle of fish, and it is the reason the charge can be made that judicial review is undemocratic.

Most assuredly, no democracy operates by taking continuous nose counts on the broad range of daily governmental activities. Representative democracies—that is to say, all working democracies—function by electing certain men for certain periods of time, then passing judgment periodically on their conduct of public office. . . . What we mean by democracy, therefore, is much more sophisticated and complex than the making of decisions in town meeting by a show of hands. It is true also that even decisions that have been submitted to the electoral process in some fashion are not continually resubmitted, and they are certainly not continually unmade. Once run through the process, once rendered by "the people" (using the term now in its mystic sense, because the reference is to the people in the past), myriad decisions remain to govern the present and the future despite what may well be fluctuating majorities against them at any given time. A high value is put on stability, and that is also a counter-majoritarian factor. Nevertheless, although democracy does not mean constant reconsideration of decisions once made, it does mean that a representative majority has the power to accomplish a reversal. This power is of the essence, and no less so because it is often merely held in reserve.

. . . The insights of Professor Truman and other writers into the role that groups play in our society and our politics have a bearing on judicial review. They indicate that there are other means than the electoral process, though subordinate and subsidiary ones, of making institutions of government responsive to the needs and wishes of the governed. Hence one may infer that judicial review, although not responsible, may have ways of being responsive. But nothing can finally depreciate the central function that is assigned in democratic theory and practice to the electoral process; nor can it be denied that the policy-making power of representative institutions, born of the electoral process, is the distinguishing characteristic of the system. Judicial review works counter to this characteristic.

It therefore does not follow from the complex nature of a democratic system that, because admirals and generals and the members, say, of the Federal Reserve Board or of this or that administrative

agency are not electorally responsible, judges who exercise the power of judicial review need not be responsible either, and in neither case is there a serious conflict with democratic theory. For admirals and generals and the like are most often responsible to officials who are themselves elected and through whom the line runs directly to a majority. What is more significant, the policies they make are or should be interstitial or technical only and are reversible by legislative majorities.

"For myself," said the late Judge Learned Hand,

it would be most irksome to be ruled by a bevy of Platonic Guardians, even if I knew how to choose them, which I assuredly do not. If they were in charge, I should miss the stimulus of living in a society where I have, at least theoretically, some part in the direction of public affairs. Of course I know how illusory would be the belief that my vote determined anything; but nevertheless when I go to the polls I have a satisfaction in the sense that we are all engaged in a common venture. If you retort that a sheep in the flock may feel something like it; I reply, following Saint Francis, "My brother, the Sheep."

. . . A further, crucial difficulty must also be faced. Besides being a counter-majoritarian check on the legislature and the executive, judicial review may, in a larger sense, have a tendency over time seriously to weaken the democratic process. Judicial review expresses, of course, a form of distrust of the legislature. "The legislatures," wrote James Bradley Thayer at the turn of the century,

are growing accustomed to this distrust and more and more readily inclined to justify it, and to shed the considerations of constitutional restraints, — certainly as concerning the exact extent of these restrictions, — turning that subject over to the courts; and what is worse, they insensibly fall into a habit of assuming that whatever they could constitutionally do they may do, — as if honor and fair dealing and common honesty were not relevant to their inquiries. The people, all this while, become careless as to whom they send to the legislature; too often they cheerfully vote for men whom they would not trust with an important private affair, and when these unfit persons are found to pass foolish and bad laws, and the courts step in and disregard them, the people are glad that these few wiser gentlemen on the bench are so ready to protect them against their more immediate representatives . . . . [I]t should be remembered that the exercise of it [the power of judicial review], even when unavoidable, is always attended with a serious evil, namely, that the correction of legislative mistakes comes from the outside, and the people thus lose the political experience, and the moral education and stimulus that comes from fighting the question out in the ordinary way, and correcting their own errors. The tendency of a common and easy resort to this great function, now lamentably too common, is to dwarf the political capacity of the people, and to deaden its sense of moral responsibility. It is no light thing to do that.

To this day, in how many hundreds of occasions does Congress enact a measure that it deems expedient, having essayed consideration of its constitutionality (that is to say, of its acceptability on principle), only to abandon the attempt in the declared confidence that the Court will correct errors of principle, if any? It may well be, as has been suggested, that any lowering of the level of legislative performance is attributable to many factors other than judicial review. Yet there is no doubt that what Thayer observed remains observable.

Finally, another, though related, contention has been put forward. It is that judicial review runs so fundamentally counter to democratic theory that in a society which in all other respects rests on that theory, judicial review cannot

ultimately be effective. We pay the price of a grave inner contradiction in the basic principle of our government, which is an inconvenience and a dangerous one; and in the end to no good purpose, for when the great test comes, judicial review will be unequal to it. The most arresting expression of this thought is in a famous passage from a speech of Judge Learned Hand. . . . Absent the institution of judicial review, Judge Hand said:

> I do not think that anyone can say what will be left of those [fundamental principles of equity and fair play which our constitutions enshrine]; I do not know whether they will serve only as counsels; but this much I think I do know—that a society so riven that the spirit of moderation is gone, no court can save; that a society where that spirit flourishes, no court need save; that in a society which evades its responsibility by thrusting upon the courts the nurture of that spirit, that spirit in the end will perish.

THE MORAL APPROVAL OF THE LINES: PRINCIPLE

The point of departure is a truism, perhaps it even rises to the unassailability of a platitude. It is that many actions of government have two aspects: their immediate, necessarily intended, practical effects, and their perhaps unintended or unappreciated bearing on values we hold to have more general and permanent interest. It is a premise we deduce not merely from the fact of a written constitution but from the history of the race, and ultimately as a moral judgment of the good society, that government should serve not only what we conceive from time to time to be our immediate material needs but also certain enduring values. This in part is what is meant by government under law. But such values do not present themselves ready-made. They have a past always, to be sure, but they must be continually derived, enunciated, and seen in relevant application. And it remains to ask which institution of our government—if any single one in particular—should be the pronouncer and guardian of such values.

Men in all walks or public life are able occasionally to perceive this second aspect of public questions. Sometimes they are also able to base their decisions on it; that is one of the things we like to call acting on principle. Often they do not do so, however, particularly when they sit in legislative assemblies. There, when the pressure for immediate results is strong enough and emotions ride high enough, men will ordinarily prefer to act on expediency rather than take the long view. Possibly legislators—everything else being equal—are as capable as other men of following the path of principle, where the path is clear or at any rate discernible. Our system, however, like all secular systems, calls for the evolution of principle in novel circumstances, rather than only for its mechanical application. Not merely respect for the rule of established principles but the creative establishment and renewal of a coherent body of principled rules—that is what our legislatures have proven themselves ill-equipped to give us.

Initially, great reliance for principled decision was placed in the Senators and the President, who have more extended terms of office and were meant to be elected only indirectly. Yet the Senate and the President were conceived of as less closely tied to, not as divorced from, electoral responsibility and the political marketplace. And so even then the need might have been felt for an institution which stands altogether aside from the current clash of interests, and which, insofar as is humanly possible, is concerned only with principle. We cannot know whether, as Thayer believed, our legislatures are what they are because we have judicial review, or whether we have judicial review and consider it necessary because legislatures are what they are. Yet it is arguable also that the partial separation of the legislative and judicial functions—and it is not meant to be absolute—is beneficial in any event, because it makes it possible for the desires of various groups and interests concerning immediate results to be heard clearly and unrestrainedly in one place. It may be thought fitting that somewhere in government, at some stage in the process of law-making, such felt needs should find unambiguous expression. Moreover, and more importantly, courts have certain capacities for dealing with matters of principle that legislatures and executives do not possess. Judges have, or should have, the leisure, the training, and the insulation to follow the ways of the scholar in pursuing the ends of government. This is crucial in sorting out the enduring values of a society, and it is not something that institutions can do well occasionally, while operating for the most part with a different set of gears. It calls for a habit of mind, and for undeviating institutional customs. Another advantage that courts have is that questions of principle never carry the same aspect for them as they did for the legislature or the executive. Statutes, after all, deal typically with abstract or dimly foreseen problems. The courts are concerned with the flesh and blood of an actual case. This tends to modify, perhaps to lengthen, everyone's view. It also provides an extremely salutary proving ground for all abstractions; it is conducive, in a phrase of Holmes, to thinking things, not words, and thus to the evolution of principle by a process that tests as it creates.

Their insulation and the marvelous mystery of time give courts the capacity to appeal to men's better natures, to call forth their aspirations, which may have been forgotten in the moment's hue and cry. This is what Justice Stone called the opportunity for "the sober second thought." Hence it is that the courts, although they may somewhat dampen the people's and the legislatures' efforts to educate themselves, are also a great and highly effective educational institution. Judge Gibson, in the very opinion mentioned earlier, highly critical as he was, took account of this. "In the business of government," he wrote, "a recurrence to first principles answers the end of an observation at sea with a view to correct the dead reckoning; and, for this purpose, a written constitution is an instrument of inestimable value. It is of inestimable value also, in rendering its principles familiar to the mass of the people. . . ." The educational institution that both takes the observation to correct the dead reckoning and makes it known is the voice of the Constitution: the Supreme Court exercising judicial review. The Justices, in Dean Rostow's phrase, "are inevitably teachers in a vital national seminar." No other branch of the American government is nearly so well equipped to conduct one. And such a seminar can do a great deal to keep our society from becoming so riven that no court will be able to save it. Of course, we have never quite been that society in which the spirit of moderation is so richly in flower that no court need save it.

Thus, as Professor Henry M. Hart, Jr., has written, and as surely most of the profession and of informed laity believe; for if not this, what and why? — thus the Court appears "predestined in the long run, not only by the thrilling tradition of Anglo-American law but also by the hard facts of its position in the structure of American institutions, to be a voice of reason, charged with the creative function of discerning afresh and of articulating and developing impersonal and durable principles. . . ." This line of thought may perhaps blunt, if it does not meet, the force of all the arguments on the other side. No doubt full consistency with democratic theory has not been established. The heart of the democratic faith is government by the consent of the governed. The further premise is not incompatible that the good society not only will want to satisfy the immediate needs of the greatest number but also will strive to support and maintain enduring general values. I have followed the view that the elected institutions are ill fitted, or not so well-fitted as the courts, to perform the latter task. This rests on the assumption that the people themselves, by direct action at the ballot box, are surely incapable of sustaining a working system of general values specifically applied. But that much we assume throughout, being a representative, deliberative democracy. Matters of expediency are not generally submitted to direct referendum. Nor should matters of principle, which require even more intensive deliberation, be so submitted. Reference of specific policies to the people for initial decision is, with few exceptions, the fallacy of the misplaced mystics, or the way of those who would use the forms of democracy to undemocratic ends. It is not the way in which working democracies live. But democracies do live by the idea, central to the process of gaining the consent of the governed, that the majority has the ultimate power to displace the decision-makers and to reject any part of their policy. With that idea, judicial review must achieve some measure of consonance.

Gordon Wood

THE ORIGINS OF JUDICIAL REVIEW REVISITED, OR HOW THE MARSHALL COURT MADE MORE OUT OF LESS

56 Wash. & Lee L. Rev. 787 (1999)

Alexander Hamilton called the judiciary the "weakest branch" of the three branches of government, but today we know better. To us not only does the unelected, life-tenured federal judiciary seem remarkably strong, but at times it actually seems bolder and more capable than the two elective branches in setting social policy. Certainly the federal judges, and especially the Justices of the Supreme Court, precisely because they do not have periodically to face an electorate, exercise an extraordinary degree of authority over our society and culture. The Supreme Court not only sets aside laws that popularly elected legislatures pass, but also interprets and construes the law with a freedom that sometimes is virtually legislative in scope. But it is not just the Supreme Court and other federal courts that are so powerful. Even the state courts, many of which are elected periodically, are extremely influential. . . .

We have usually given the name "judicial review" to this sweeping judicial authority. But if by judicial review we mean only the power of the Supreme Court and of other courts to set aside legislative acts in violation of the Constitution, then the term is too narrow, for voiding legislation is only the most prominent part of a broader manipulative power that courts exercise over wide areas of American life.

Commentators often have given the major responsibility for creating this power of judicial review to John Marshall, the great Chief Justice of the United States who served from 1801 to 1835. Marshall, nearly everyone acknowledges, was the greatest Chief Justice in American history. During his long career as Chief Justice of the Supreme Court, which spanned the administrations of five presidents, he helped to lay the foundations for both the Supreme Court's eventual independence and the constitutional supremacy of the national government over the states. But more important, at a stroke, his decision in *Marbury v. Madison* was supposed to have created the practice of judicial review. Even a constitutional scholar as sophisticated as Alexander M. Bickel thought that Marshall had done it all. "If any social process can be said to have been 'done' at a given time and by a given act," Bickel wrote in 1962, "it is Marshall's achievement. The time was 1803; the act was the decision in the case of *Marbury v. Madison.*"

Perhaps this is the way that many lawyers and jurists prefer to explain things. Perhaps they like to ransack the past in order to discover specific moments or concrete precedents, usually court decisions, which created important subsequent judicial practices and processes. The problem with this jurisprudential and unhistorical way of thinking is that it leaves its practitioners vulnerable to critics who can find other, more important precedents and moments in accounting for a practice or process. This has been the case recently with Marshall and judicial review. A number of revisionist legal scholars have argued that Marshall, in

Marbury v. Madison or elsewhere, did not create the modern practice of judicial review.

[W]e know that judicial review of some form did develop in these early decades of the new Republic. What was it? And how did it arise? No doubt the founders were confused over judicial review: some said it was improper and dangerous, while others seem to justify it. The sources of something as significant and forbidding as judicial review never could lie in the accumulation of a few sporadic judicial precedents, or even in the decision of *Marbury v. Madison*, but had to flow from fundamental changes taking place in the Americans' ideas of government and law.

Perhaps the most crucial of these changes involved reducing the representative character of the people's agents in the legislatures and enhancing the representative character of judges. Hamilton's argument in *Federalist* No. 78 was only the most prominent of efforts to do just this. The judges, Hamilton argued, had a right to oversee the acts of the presumably sovereign legislatures and to construe statutes and even set some of them aside if they thought they conflicted with either the federal or state constitutions. And the judges could do all this because the legislators were not really sovereign; they did not fully embody the people the way Parliament embodied the people of Britain. In America real and ultimate sovereignty rested with the people themselves, not with their representatives in the legislatures. Thus the legislators were not the people, but only one kind of servant of the people with a limited delegated authority to act on their behalf. Americans, said Hamilton, had no intention of enabling "the representatives of the people to substitute their will to that of their constituents." It was in fact "far more rational to suppose, that the courts

were designed to be an intermediate body between the people and the legislature, in order, among other things, to keep the latter within the limits assigned to their authority." Hamilton implied, and others drew out the implication much more fully in subsequent years, that the judges, though not elected, resembled the legislators and executives in being agents or servants of the people with a responsibility equal to that of the other two branches of government to carry out the people's will, even to the point of sharing in the making of law. Indeed, just such logic eventually would lead to the election of judges in many states. If the judges were agents of the people, not all that different from their other agents in the government, then by rights the people ought to elect them.

Redefining judges as agents of the sovereign people somehow equal in authority with the legislators and executives fundamentally altered the character of the judiciary in America and deeply affected its role in interpreting the law. But by itself it was not enough to create judicial review. Some historians and constitutional theorists have assumed that the idea of fundamental law and its embodiment in a written constitution were crucial as well.

Almost all eighteenth-century Englishmen on both sides of the Atlantic had recognized something called fundamental law as a guide to the moral rightness and constitutionality of ordinary law and politics. Nearly everyone repeatedly invoked Magna Carta and other fundamental laws of the English constitution. Theorists as different as Locke and Bolingbroke referred equally to the basic principles of the constitution as fundamental law. Even the rise of legislative sovereignty in eighteenth-century England—that is, the idea that law was the command of the legislature—did not displace this prevalent notion of fundamental law. Blackstone himself, despite his commitment to legislative sovereignty, believed that what he called an overriding natural law limited Parliament. Yet all these theoretical references to the principles of the constitution and fundamental law could not have much day-to-day practical importance. For most, this fundamental or natural law of the English constitution was seen as a kind of moral inhibition or conscience existing in the minds of legislators and others. It was so basic and primal, so imposing and political, that it really was enforceable only by the popular elective process or ultimately by the people's right of revolution. Eighteenth-century Englishmen talked about fundamental or natural law, invoked it constantly in their rhetoric, but despite the efforts of some jurists, they had difficulty calling upon this fundamental law in their everyday political and legal business.

The written constitutions of 1776 and 1777, however, gave revolutionary Americans a handle with which to grasp this otherwise insubstantial fundamental law. Suddenly the fundamental law and the first principles that Englishmen had referred to for generations had a degree of explicitness and reality that they never before quite had. The Constitution in America, said James Iredell of North Carolina in 1787, was not therefore "a mere imaginary thing, about which ten thousand different opinions may be formed, but a written document to which all may have recourse, and to which, therefore, the judges cannot willfully blind themselves."

But were the judges to have an exclusive authority to examine these fundamental laws and to determine what was constitutional and what was not? By the 1780s it seemed clear to many that legislatures in America were bound by explicitly written constitutions in ways that the English Parliament was not. But it was not yet clear that the courts by themselves were able to enforce those boundaries upon the legislatures. Said Iredell in 1786, summarizing the position of those opposed to judicial review,

> The great argument is that the Assembly have not a right to violate the constitution, yet if they in fact do so, the only remedy is, either by a humble petition that the law may be repealed, or a universal resistance of the people. But that in the mean time, their act, whatever it is, is to be obeyed as a law; for the judicial power is not to presume to question the power of an act of Assembly.

Both Jefferson and Madison thought that judges might act as the guardians of popular rights and might resist encroachments on these rights, but they never believed that judges had any special or unique power to interpret the Constitution. Madison admitted that "in the ordinary course of Government" the judiciary might interpret the laws and the Constitution, but surely, he said, it had no more right to determine the limits of the Constitution than did the executive or legislature. Both Jefferson and Madison remained convinced to the end of their lives that all parts of America's governments had equal authority to interpret the fundamental law of the Constitution—all departments had what Madison called "a concurrent right to expound the constitution." And when the several departments disagreed in their understanding of the fundamental law, wrote Madison in *Federalist* No. 49, only "an appeal to the people themselves, can alone declare its true meaning, and enforce its observance." Written constitutions, including the Bill of Rights, remained for Jefferson and Madison a set of great first principles that the several governmental departments, including the judiciary, could appeal to in those extraordinary occasions of violation. But because none of these departments could "pretend to an exclusive or superior right of settling the boundaries between their respective powers," the ultimate appeal in these quasi-revolutionary situations had to be to the people.

In other words, many revolutionaries or founders still thought that fundamental law, even when expressed in a written constitution, was so fundamental, so different in kind from ordinary law, that its invocation had to be essentially an exceptional and awesomely delicate political exercise. The courts might on occasion set aside legislation that violated fundamental law, but such an act could not be a part of routine judicial business. It necessarily had to be an extraordinary, even revolutionary, expression of public authority, the kind of extreme and remarkable action the people themselves would take if they could. This kind of judicial review, as Sylvia Snowiss has aptly described it, was "a substitute for revolution."

Everyone knew that setting aside legislative acts could be no ordinary matter. In *Calder v. Bull*, Justice Iredell admitted that the Supreme Court possessed the authority to declare a legislative act void, but he believed that doing so was of such "a delicate and awful nature, the Court will never resort to that authority, but in a clear and urgent case." Some congressmen actually debated establishing a regular procedure for federal judges to notify Congress officially when a court declared a law unconstitutional—so nervous were they over the gravity of such an action.

Judges realized that the burden of proving a legislative act unconstitutional beyond any doubt lay entirely with them. As Justice Samuel Chase said in *Hylton*

v. United States, if the constitutionality of Congress's tax on carriages had been "doubtful," he would have been bound "to receive the construction of the legislature." As late as 1800 in *Cooper v. Telfair*, Justices Bushrod Washington and William Paterson agreed that judicial review was an exceptional act, to be exercised only infrequently. "The presumption . . . must always be in favour of the validity of laws, if the contrary is not clearly demonstrated," declared Washington. For the Supreme Court "to pronounce any law void," said Paterson, there "must be a clear and unequivocal breach of the constitution, not a doubtful and argumentative implication."

Thus for many Americans in the 1790s judicial review of some sort did exist. But it remained an extraordinary and solemn political action, akin perhaps to the interposition of the states that Jefferson and Madison suggested in the Kentucky and Virginia Resolutions of 1798—something to be invoked only on the rare occasions of flagrant and unequivocal violations of the Constitution. It was not to be exercised in doubtful cases of unconstitutionality and was not yet accepted as an aspect of ordinary judicial activity.

This is where we begin to appreciate the achievement of the Marshall Court and other courts in the years following the Jeffersonian Republican revolution of 1800. The idea of fundamental law embodied in a written constitution by itself could never have accounted for the development of judicial review; indeed, emphasis on the fundamental character of the Constitution tended to inhibit the use of judicial review. Judicial review needed to be made less threatening, needed to become a normal and regular part of judicial business: This is, in fact, what the Marshall Court and other courts accomplished in the years after 1800.

In order for this to happen several things had to take place. First, America's written fundamental constitutions, its public laws, had to be transformed into laws that courts could interpret and construe as if they were routine statutes in the ordinary court system. What gives significance to our peculiar notion of a constitution is not that it is written or that it is fundamental, but rather that it runs in the ordinary court system. America's constitutions may be higher laws, special acts of the people in their sovereign capacity, but they are just like all the other lowly laws in that they are implemented through the normal practice of adversarial justice in the regular courts.

. . . American judges now treated the constitutions as commands of the sovereign people, super-statutes, if you will, that needed to be interpreted and integrated into the body of the law. In the process of reconciling constitutions and statutes, often in the name of reason and equity, courts tended to collapse the traditional distinction between fundamental and ordinary law. American judges now could construe the all-too brief words of the state and federal constitutions in relation to subject-matter, intention, context, and reasonableness as if they were the words of an ordinary statute. It was one of Marshall's great achievements, says Hobson, to apply "the familiar tools and methods of statutory construction . . . [t]o the novel task of expounding the Constitution of the United States." The result was the beginning of the creation of a special body of textual exegeses and legal expositions and precedents that we have come to call constitutional law. This accumulative body of constitutional law in America is now over two hundred years old; there is nothing quite like it anywhere else in the world.

This "legalization" of fundamental law, as Sylvia Snowiss has called it, domesticated the Constitution; it tamed what had hitherto been an object of fearful significance and wonder to the point where it could routinely run in the ordinary court system. Considering the Constitution as a kind of law that was cognizable in the regular courts permitted judges not only to expound and construe the Constitution as if it were an ordinary statute, but also to expect regular enforcement of the Constitution as if it were a simple statute. It was a momentous transformation. Because, in John Marshall's words, it was "emphatically the province and duty of the judicial department to say what the law is," treating the Constitution as mere law that judges had to expound and interpret and apply to particular cases gave special constitutional authority to American judges that judges elsewhere in the world did not share.

It was not enough, however, that constitutions run in the regular court system and be interpreted like ordinary statutes for judicial review to become acceptable. Something else was needed. If expounding constitutional law were to be simply part of the routine business of legal interpretation and not an earth-shaking political exercise, then it followed that the entire process of adjudication had to be removed from politics and from legislative tampering. Somehow or other judges had to carve out for themselves an exclusive sphere of professional legal activity.

After 1800 this is precisely what happened. Judges shed what had been a traditional political and magisterial role and adopted one that was much more exclusively legal. . . .

More and more, law grew separate from politics, all part of a larger separation between the private and public spheres that took place in these years.

This separation meant that the courts now tended to concentrate on individual cases and to avoid the most explosive and partisan political issues. Certainly the Marshall Court succeeded as well as it did because it retreated from the advanced and exposed political positions that the Federalists had tried to stake out for the national judiciary in the 1790s. . . .

The strategy behind the Marshall Court's judgments was always that less is more. The Court denied the belief of many Federalists that the common law of crimes ran in the federal court system, which was a major retreat, and it went out of its way to avoid any direct confrontation with the Republicans. In a series of conciliatory decisions, Marshall's Court recognized the authority of the Republican president and the Republican Congress over foreign affairs and matters of war. As Kent Newmyer has suggested, Marshall was so often able to get consensus out of what soon became a Republican-dominated Court because he used many of the Court's decisions to curtail governmental power—something that many Republicans eager to expand the areas of individual freedom could accept. In other words, the Marshall Court did not attempt to build up the power of the federal government, which immediately would have aroused Republican hostility everywhere. Instead, it moved to reduce governmental power, not at the federal but at the state level. By declaring a large number of state judicial interpretations and state laws invalid because they violated the national Constitution, the Court indirectly enhanced the supremacy of the nation and its own authority as well.

Even in the famous case of *Marbury v. Madison* in 1803, Marshall retreated rather than attacked. Many of the Federalists wanted Marshall to declare the Republicans' repeal of the judiciary act of 1801 unconstitutional for having abrogated the tenure of federal judges. But Marshall wisely realized that such a direct challenge to the Republicans could only harm the Court. Instead, he asserted the Court's authority to interpret the Constitution subtly and obliquely by declaring a portion of the earlier 1789 judiciary act unconstitutional for having granted the Supreme Court some original jurisdiction to which the Constitution had not entitled it.

The decision was so subtle and so oblique that most people did not see its implications. The Republicans actually liked the decision better than the Federalists. They thought that if Marshall wanted to circumscribe the original jurisdiction of his Court, then he had every right to do so. Even Jefferson conceded the right of the Court to interpret the Constitution in matters pertaining to the judiciary, but he continued to believe that the executive and the Congress retained equal authority to interpret the Constitution. In his *Marbury* decision Marshall did not explicitly disagree with Jefferson's position. Marshall in 1803 was not embarking on a crusade for judicial supremacy. His aim was to isolate the judiciary from partisan politics as much as possible.

The *Marbury* decision was all about separating legal issues from politics. As Marshall said, some questions were political; "they respect the nation, not individual rights," and thus were "only politically examinable." But questions involving the vested rights of individuals were different; vested rights were in their "nature, judicial, and must be tried by the judicial authority." By turning all questions of individual rights into exclusively judicial issues, Marshall appropriated an enormous amount of authority for the courts. After all, even Jefferson in 1789 had conceded that judges, "kept strictly to their own department," had the authority to protect the rights of individuals. Of course, Jefferson had not anticipated Marshall's expansive notion of rights.

As far as most Federalists were concerned, the laws of the land concerning individual rights now belonged exclusively to the courts. Getting the American people to believe this was a remarkable achievement, and the Marshall Court contributed greatly to this effort. But it would not have been possible without large numbers of influential people becoming increasingly disillusioned with the kind of democratic legislative politics that was emerging in the early Republic. As St. George Tucker pointed out in 1803, since the men of greatest talents, education, and virtue were not able to compete as well as others in the new scrambling, pushy, and interest-mongering world of popular electoral politics, they could best promote the science of the law in the judiciary. Marshall himself, like all "honest men who have honorable feelings," was increasingly "disgusted with . . . the political world" he saw around him, and was "much more gloomy" about the future. Everywhere the growth of democracy encouraged the insulating of legal issues from politics; "for," as Marshall put it, "nothing is more to be deprecated than the transfer of party politics to the seat of Justice." Only separating law from popular politics could protect the rights of individuals.

Many had come to believe that a society as enterprising, unruly, and democratic as America's not only required institutions and legal processes that could adapt readily to fast-moving economic circumstances, but needed as well the moderating influence of an aristocracy. Outside of the South, however, an American aristocracy was hard to come by; but necessity invented one. As Tocqueville later pointed out, lawyers in the early nineteenth century had come to constitute whatever aristocracy America possessed, at least in the North. Through their influence on the judiciary they tempered America's turbulent majoritarian governments and protected the rights of individuals and minorities from legislative abuse. "The courts of justice," Tocqueville said, "are the visible organs by which the legal profession is enabled to control the democracy."

Alexander Hamilton

THE FEDERALIST NO. 78

The Judiciary Department

Independent Journal, Saturday, June 14, 1788

After the Constitutional Convention, the Constitution was presented to the states to ratify. Specifically, Article Seven required ratification by 9 of the 13 states before it could be enacted. Writing under the pseudonym "Publius," James Madison, John Jay, and Alexander Hamilton argued in a series of New York newspapers for ratification.

The significance of the papers goes beyond this initial argument. They provided some of the most influential framing of debates about how to interpret the Constitution. In this excerpt, Hamilton addresses the role of the Supreme Court in the new Constitution and argues for its role in judicial review of legislation.

Whoever attentively considers the different departments of power must perceive, that, in a government in which they are separated from each other, the judiciary, from the nature of its functions, will always be the least dangerous to the political rights of the Constitution; because it will be least in a capacity to annoy or injure them. The Executive not only dispenses the honors, but holds the sword of the community. The legislature not only commands the purse, but prescribes the rules by which the duties and rights of every citizen are to be regulated. The judiciary, on the contrary, has no influence over either the sword or the purse; no direction either of the strength or of the wealth of the society; and can take no active resolution whatever. It may truly be said to have neither FORCE nor WILL, but merely judgment; and must ultimately depend upon the aid of the executive arm even for the efficacy of its judgments.

This simple view of the matter suggests several important consequences. It proves incontestably, that the judiciary is beyond comparison the weakest of the three departments of power; that it can never attack with success either of the other two; and that all possible care is requisite to enable it to defend itself against their attacks. It equally proves, that though individual oppression may now and then proceed from the courts of justice, the general liberty of the people can never be endangered from that quarter; I mean so long as the judiciary remains truly distinct from both the legislature and the Executive. For I agree, that "there is no liberty, if the power of judging be not separated from the legislative and executive powers." And it proves, in the last place, that as liberty can have nothing to fear from the judiciary alone, but would have everything to fear from its union with either of the other departments; that as

all the effects of such a union must ensue from a dependence of the former on the latter, notwithstanding a nominal and apparent separation; that as, from the natural feebleness of the judiciary, it is in continual jeopardy of being overpowered, awed, or influenced by its co-ordinate branches; and that as nothing can contribute so much to its firmness and independence as permanency in office, this quality may therefore be justly regarded as an indispensable ingredient in its constitution, and, in a great measure, as the citadel of the public justice and the public security.

The complete independence of the courts of justice is peculiarly essential in a limited Constitution. By a limited Constitution, I understand one which contains certain specified exceptions to the legislative authority; such, for instance, as that it shall pass no bills of attainder, no ex post facto laws, and the like. Limitations of this kind can be preserved in practice no other way than through the medium of courts of justice, whose duty it must be to declare all acts contrary to the manifest tenor of the Constitution void. Without this, all the reservations of particular rights or privileges would amount to nothing.

Some perplexity respecting the rights of the courts to pronounce legislative acts void, because contrary to the Constitution, has arisen from an imagination that the doctrine would imply a superiority of the judiciary to the legislative power. It is urged that the authority which can declare the acts of another void, must necessarily be superior to the one whose acts may be declared void. As this doctrine is of great importance in all the American constitutions, a brief discussion of the ground on which it rests cannot be unacceptable.

There is no position which depends on clearer principles, than that every act of a delegated authority, contrary to the tenor of the commission under which it is exercised, is void. No legislative act, therefore, contrary to the Constitution, can be valid. To deny this, would be to affirm, that the deputy is greater than his principal; that the servant is above his master; that the representatives of the people are superior to the people themselves; that men acting by virtue of powers, may do not only what their powers do not authorize, but what they forbid.

If it be said that the legislative body are themselves the constitutional judges of their own powers, and that the construction they put upon them is conclusive upon the other departments, it may be answered, that this cannot be the natural presumption, where it is not to be collected from any particular provisions in the Constitution. It is not otherwise to be supposed, that the Constitution could intend to enable the representatives of the people to substitute their will to that of their constituents. It is far more rational to suppose, that the courts were designed to be an intermediate body between the people and the legislature, in order, among other things, to keep the latter within the limits assigned to their authority. The interpretation of the laws is the proper and peculiar province of the courts. A constitution is, in fact, and must be regarded by the judges, as a fundamental law. It therefore belongs to them to ascertain its meaning, as well as the meaning of any particular act proceeding from the legislative body. If there should happen to be an irreconcilable variance between the two, that which has the superior obligation and validity ought, of course, to be preferred; or, in other words, the Constitution ought to be preferred to the statute, the intention of the people to the intention of their agents.

Nor does this conclusion by any means suppose a superiority of the judicial to the legislative power. It only supposes that the power of the people is superior to both; and that where the will of the legislature, declared in its statutes, stands in opposition to that of the people, declared in the Constitution, the judges ought to be governed by the latter rather than the former. They ought to regulate their decisions by the fundamental laws, rather than by those which are not fundamental.

This exercise of judicial discretion, in determining between two contradictory laws, is exemplified in a familiar instance. It not uncommonly happens, that there are two statutes existing at one time, clashing in whole or in part with each other, and neither of them containing any repealing clause or expression. In such a case, it is the province of the courts to liquidate and fix their meaning and operation. So far as they can, by any fair construction, be reconciled to each other, reason and law conspire to dictate that this should be done; where this is impracticable, it becomes a matter of necessity to give effect to one, in exclusion of the other. The rule which has obtained in the courts for determining their relative validity is, that the last in order of time shall be preferred to the first. But this is a mere rule of construction, not derived from any positive law, but from the nature and reason of the thing. It is a rule not enjoined upon the courts by legislative provision, but adopted by themselves, as consonant to truth and propriety, for the direction of their conduct as interpreters of the law. They thought it reasonable, that between the interfering acts of an EQUAL authority, that which was the last indication of its will should have the preference.

But in regard to the interfering acts of a superior and subordinate authority, of an original and derivative power, the nature and reason of the thing indicate the converse of that rule as proper to be followed. They teach us that the prior act of a superior ought to be preferred to the subsequent act of an inferior and subordinate authority; and that accordingly, whenever a particular statute contravenes the Constitution, it will be the duty of the judicial tribunals to adhere to the latter and disregard the former.

It can be of no weight to say that the courts, on the pretense of a repugnancy, may substitute their own pleasure to the constitutional intentions of the legislature. This might as well happen in the case of two contradictory statutes; or it might as well happen in every adjudication upon any single statute. The courts must declare the sense of the law; and if they should be disposed to exercise WILL instead of JUDGMENT, the consequence would equally be the substitution of their pleasure to that of the legislative body. The observation, if it prove any thing, would prove that there ought to be no judges distinct from that body.

If, then, the courts of justice are to be considered as the bulwarks of a limited Constitution against legislative encroachments, this consideration will afford a strong argument for the permanent tenure of judicial offices, since nothing will contribute so much as this to that independent spirit in the judges which must be essential to the faithful performance of so arduous a duty.

This independence of the judges is equally requisite to guard the Constitution and the rights of individuals from the effects of those ill humors, which the arts of designing men, or the influence of particular conjunctures, sometimes disseminate among the people themselves, and which, though they speedily give place to better information, and more deliberate reflection, have a tendency, in

the mean time, to occasion dangerous innovations in the government, and serious oppressions of the minor party in the community. Though I trust the friends of the proposed Constitution will never concur with its enemies, in questioning that fundamental principle of republican government, which admits the right of the people to alter or abolish the established Constitution, whenever they find it inconsistent with their happiness, yet it is not to be inferred from this principle, that the representatives of the people, whenever a momentary inclination happens to lay hold of a majority of their constituents, incompatible with the provisions in the existing Constitution, would, on that account, be justifiable in a violation of those provisions; or that the courts would be under a greater obligation to connive at infractions in this shape, than when they had proceeded wholly from the cabals of the representative body. Until the people have, by some solemn and authoritative act, annulled or changed the established form, it is binding upon themselves collectively, as well as individually; and no presumption, or even knowledge, of their sentiments, can warrant their representatives in a departure from it, prior to such an act. But it is easy to see, that it would require an uncommon portion of fortitude in the judges to do their duty as faithful guardians of the Constitution, where legislative invasions of it had been instigated by the major voice of the community.

But it is not with a view to infractions of the Constitution only, that the independence of the judges may be an essential safeguard against the effects of occasional ill humors in the society. These sometimes extend no farther than to the injury of the private rights of particular classes of citizens, by unjust and partial laws. Here also the firmness of the judicial magistracy is of vast importance in mitigating the severity and confining the operation of such laws. It not only serves to moderate the immediate mischiefs of those which may have been passed, but it operates as a check upon the legislative body in passing them; who, perceiving that obstacles to the success of iniquitous intention are to be expected from the scruples of the courts, are in a manner compelled, by the very motives of the injustice they meditate, to qualify their attempts. This is a circumstance calculated to have more influence upon the character of our governments, than but few may be aware of. The benefits of the integrity and moderation of the judiciary have already been felt in more States than one; and though they may have displeased those whose sinister expectations they may have disappointed, they must have commanded the esteem and applause of all the virtuous and disinterested. Considerate men, of every description, ought to prize whatever will tend to beget or fortify that temper in the courts: as no man can be sure that he may not be to-morrow the victim of a spirit of injustice, by which he may be a gainer to-day. And every man must now feel, that the inevitable tendency of such a spirit is to sap the foundations of public and private confidence, and to introduce in its stead universal distrust and distress.

That inflexible and uniform adherence to the rights of the Constitution, and of individuals, which we perceive to be indispensable in the courts of justice, can certainly not be expected from judges who hold their offices by a temporary commission. Periodical appointments, however regulated, or by whomsoever made, would, in some way or other, be fatal to their necessary independence. If the power of making them was committed either to the Executive or legislature, there would be danger of an improper complaisance to the branch which possessed it; if to both, there would be an unwillingness to hazard the displeasure of either; if to the people, or to persons chosen by them for the special purpose, there would be too great a disposition to consult popularity, to justify a reliance that nothing would be consulted but the Constitution and the laws.

Brutus

UNTITLED ESSAYS AGAINST RATIFICATION OF THE UNITED STATES CONSTITUTION

The New York Journal, 1787-1788

As the states decided whether they would or would not ratify the new Constitution, a series of essays by opponents of ratification were published in New York newspapers. These essays served as a counterbalance to The Federalist Papers, *which were meant to defend the proposed Constitution. In response to the arguments in favor of the judicial branch crafted by Article III of the Constitution, an author who called himself* "Brutus" *suggested why the new Supreme Court had powers that could become tyrannical and incompatible with the ideal of "free and equal government." Indeed, the name Brutus was meant to suggest a parallel between anti-federalists and the opponents of Julius Caesar.*

The essays, in addition to presaging future criticisms of the Court's judicial review power, help us to focus on some of the structural details of Article III. Notice in particular Brutus's worry that judicial power is left unchecked under the new Constitution. Article III requires that Supreme Court justices be appointed by the president and confirmed by the Senate. But, Brutus argues, this check does not suitably guard against the guarantee of life tenure and congressional inability to lower the salaries of the justices.

It is also worth noting as you read the argument against the review power of the Court that Brutus predicts that some justices will not stick to a literal, or what some call a "strict textual," reading of the Constitution. Instead, they will interpret the clauses broadly to claim a vast review power. This argument is reflected in the discussion of theories of interpretation in the next chapter. For now, however, consider whether this purported judicial role follows from the way the constitutional text is written. Does it authorize a broad review power in the way Brutus suggests? If so, is this a potential problem for democratic governance? Is Brutus correct that the British system of legislative supremacy is superior to the American system? Why?

BRUTUS 1 (OCTOBER 18, 1787)

This government is to possess absolute and uncontroulable power, legislative, executive and judicial, with respect to every object to which it extends, for by the last clause of section 8th, article 1st, it is declared "that the Congress shall have power to make all laws which shall be necessary and proper for carrying into execution the foregoing powers, and all other powers vested by this constitution, in the government of the United States; or in any department or office thereof. . . ."

The judicial power of the United States is to be vested in a supreme court, and in such inferior courts as Congress may from time to time ordain and establish. The powers of these courts are very extensive; their jurisdiction comprehends all civil causes, except such as arise between citizens of the same state; and it extends to all cases in law and equity arising under the constitution. . . . These courts will be, in themselves, totally independent of the states, deriving their authority from the United States, and receiving from them fixed salaries; and in the course of human events it is to be expected, that they will swallow up all the powers of the courts in the respective states.

Brutus.

BRUTUS 11 (JANUARY 31, 1788)

The nature and extent of the judicial power of the United States, proposed to be granted by this constitution, claims our particular attention.

. . . [B]ecause those who are to be vested with it, are to be placed in a situation altogether unprecedented in a free country. They are to be rendered totally independent, both of the people and the legislature, both with respect to their offices and salaries. No errors they may commit can be corrected by any power above them, if any such power there be, nor can they be removed from office for making ever so many erroneous adjudications.

The only causes for which they can be displaced, is, conviction of treason, bribery, and high crimes and misdemeanors.

This part of the plan is so modelled, as to authorise the courts, not only to carry into execution the powers expressly given, but where these are wanting or ambiguously expressed, to supply what is wanting by their own decisions.

That we may be enabled to form a just opinion on this subject, I shall, in considering it,

1st. Examine the nature and extent of the judicial powers — and

2d. Enquire, whether the courts who are to exercise them, are so constituted as to afford reasonable ground of confidence, that they will exercise them for the general good.

In article 3d, sect. 2d, it is said, "The judicial power shall extend to all cases in law and equity arising under this constitution, the laws of the United States, and treaties made, or which shall be made, under their authority, &c."

What latitude of construction this clause should receive, it is not easy to say. At first view, one would suppose, that it meant no more than this, that the courts under the general government should exercise, not only the powers of courts of law, but also that of courts of equity, in the manner in which those powers are usually exercised in the different states. But this cannot be the meaning, because the next clause authorises the courts to take cognizance of all cases in law and equity arising under the laws of the United States; this last article, I conceive, conveys as much power to the general judicial as any of the state courts possess.

This article, therefore, vests the judicial with a power to resolve all questions that may arise on any case on the construction of the constitution, either in law or in equity.

1st. According to this mode of construction, the courts are to give such meaning to the constitution as comports best with the common, and generally received acceptation of the words in which it is expressed, regarding their ordinary and popular use, rather than their grammatical propriety. Where words are dubious, they will be explained by the context.

The end of the clause will be attended to, and the words will be understood, as having a view to it; and the words will not be so understood as to bear no meaning or a very absurd one.

2d. The judicial are not only to decide questions arising upon the meaning of the constitution in law, but also in equity.

By this they are empowered, to explain the constitution according to the reasoning spirit of it, without being confined to the words or letter.

They will give the sense of every article of the constitution, that may from time to time come before them. And in their decisions they will not confine themselves to any fixed or established rules, but will determine, according to what appears to them, the reason and spirit of the constitution. The opinions of the supreme court, whatever they may be, will have the force of law; because there is no power provided in the constitution, that can correct their errors, or controul their adjudications. From this court there is no appeal. And I conceive the legislature themselves, cannot set aside a judgment of this court, because they are authorised by the constitution to decide in the last resort. The legislature must be controuled by the constitution, and not the constitution by them. They have therefore no more right to set aside any judgment pronounced upon the construction of the constitution, than they have to take from the president, the chief command of the army and navy, and commit it to some other person. The reason is plain; the judicial and executive derive their authority from the same source, that the legislature do theirs; and therefore in all cases, where the constitution does not make the one responsible to, or controulable by the other, they are altogether independent of each other.

The judicial power will operate to effect, in the most certain, but yet silent and imperceptible manner, what is evidently the tendency of the constitution: — I mean, an entire subversion of the legislative, executive and judicial powers of the individual states. Every adjudication of the supreme court, on any question that may arise upon the nature and extent of the general government, will affect the limits of the state jurisdiction. In proportion as the former enlarge the exercise of their powers, will that of the latter be restricted.

That the judicial power of the United States, will lean strongly in favour of the general government, and will give such an explanation to the constitution, as will favour an extension of its jurisdiction, is very evident from a variety of considerations.

1st. The constitution itself strongly countenances such a mode of construction. Most of the articles in this system, which convey powers of any considerable importance, are conceived in general and indefinite terms, which are either equivocal, ambiguous, or which require long definitions to unfold the extent of their meaning. The two most important powers committed to any government, those of raising money, and of raising and keeping up troops, have already been considered, and shewn to be unlimitted by any thing but the discretion of the legislature. The clause which vests the power to pass all laws which are proper and necessary, to carry the powers given into execution, it has been shewn, leaves the legislature at liberty, to do every thing, which in their judgment is best. It is said, I know, that this clause confers no power on the legislature, which they would not have had without it — though I believe this is not the fact, yet, admitting it to be, it implies that the constitution is not to receive an explanation strictly, according to its letter; but more power is implied than is expressed. And this clause, if it is to be considered, as explanatory of the extent of the powers given, rather than giving a new power, is to be understood as declaring, that in construing any of the articles conveying power, the spirit, intent and design of the clause, should be attended to, as well as the words in their common acceptation.

This constitution gives sufficient colour for adopting an equitable construction, if we consider the great end and design it professedly has in view — these appear from its preamble to be, "to form a more perfect union, establish justice, insure domestic tranquility, provide for the common defence, promote the general welfare, and secure the blessings of liberty to ourselves and posterity." The design of this system is here expressed, and it is proper to give such a meaning to the various parts, as will best promote the accomplishment of the end; this idea suggests itself naturally upon reading the preamble, and will countenance the court in giving the several articles such a sense, as will the most effectually promote the ends the constitution had in view — how this manner of explaining the constitution will operate in practice, shall be the subject of future enquiry.

2d. Not only will the constitution justify the courts in inclining to this mode of explaining it, but they will be interested in using this latitude of interpretation. Every body of men invested with office are tenacious of power; they feel interested, and hence it has become a kind of maxim, to hand down their offices, with all its rights and privileges, unimpaired to their successors; the same principle will influence them to extend their power, and increase their rights; this of itself will operate strongly upon the courts to give such a meaning to the constitution in all cases where it can possibly be done, as will enlarge the sphere of their own authority. Every extension of the power of the general legislature, as well as of the judicial powers, will increase the powers of the courts; and the dignity and importance of the judges, will be in proportion to the extent and magnitude of the powers they exercise. I add, it is highly probable the emolument of the judges will be increased, with the increase of the business they will have to transact and its importance. From these considerations the judges will be interested to extend the powers of the courts, and to construe the constitution as much as possible, in such a way as to favour it; and that they will do it, appears probable.

This power in the judicial, will enable them to mould the government, into almost any shape they please. — The manner in which this may be effected we will hereafter examine.

Brutus.

BRUTUS 15 (MARCH 20, 1788)

(Continued.)

I said in my last number, that the supreme court under this constitution would be exalted above all other power in the government, and subject to no controul. The business of this paper will be to illustrate this, and to shew the danger that will result from it. I question whether the world ever saw, in any period of it, a court of justice invested with such immense powers, and yet placed in a situation so little responsible. Certain it is, that in England, and in the several states, where we have been taught to believe, the courts of law are put upon the most prudent establishment, they are on a very different footing.

The judges in England are under the controul of the legislature, for they are bound to determine according to the laws passed by them. But the judges under this constitution will controul the legislature, for the supreme court are authorised in the last resort, to determine what is the extent of the powers of the Congress; they are to give the constitution an explanation, and there is no power above them to set aside their judgment. The framers of this constitution appear to have followed that of the British, in rendering the judges independent, by granting them their offices during good behavior, without following the constitution of England, in instituting a tribunal in which their errors may be corrected; and without adverting to this, that the judicial under this system have a power which is above the legislative, and which indeed transcends any power before given to a judicial by any free government under heaven.

Though in my opinion the judges ought to hold their offices during good behavior, yet I think it is clear, that the reasons in favour of this establishment of the judges in England, do by no means apply to this country.

The great reason assigned, why the judges in Britain ought to be commissioned during good behavior, is this, that they may be placed in a situation, not to be influenced by the crown, to give such decisions, as would tend to increase its powers and prerogatives. While the judges held their places at the will and pleasure of the king, on whom they depended not only for their offices, but also for their salaries, they were subject to every undue influence. If the crown wished to carry a favorite point, to accomplish which the aid of the courts of law was necessary, the pleasure of the king would be signified to the judges. And it required the spirit of a martyr, for the judges to determine contrary to the king's will. — They were absolutely dependent upon him both for their offices and livings. The king, holding his office during life, and transmitting it to his posterity as an inheritance, has much stronger inducements to increase the prerogatives of his office than those who hold their offices for stated periods, or even for life. Hence the English nation gained a great point, in favour of liberty. When they obtained the appointment of the judges, during good behavior, they got from the crown a concession, which deprived it of one of the most powerful engines with which it might enlarge the boundaries of the royal prerogative and encroach on the liberties of the people. But these reasons do not apply to this country, we have no hereditary monarch; those who appoint the judges do not hold their offices for life, nor do they descend to their children. The same arguments, therefore, which will conclude in favor of the tenor of the judge's offices for good behavior, lose a considerable part of their weight when applied to the state and condition of America. But much less can it be shewn, that the nature of our government requires that the courts should be placed beyond all account more independent, so much so as to be above controul.

I have said that the judges under this system will be independent in the strict sense of the word: To prove this I will shew — That there is no power above them that can controul their decisions, or correct their errors. There is no authority that can remove them from office for any errors or want of capacity, or lower their salaries, and in many cases their power is superior to that of the legislature.

1st. There is no power above them that can correct their errors or controul their decisions — The adjudications of this court are final and irreversible, for there is no court above them to which appeals can lie, either in error or on the merits. — In this respect it differs from the courts in England, for there the house of lords is

the highest court, to whom appeals, in error, are carried from the highest of the courts of law.

2d. They cannot be removed from office or suffer a diminution of their salaries, for any error in judgement or want of capacity.

It is expressly declared by the constitution, — "That they shall at stated times receive a compensation for their services which shall not be diminished during their continuance in office."

The only clause in the constitution which provides for the removal of the judges from office, is that which declares, that "the president, vice-president, and all civil officers of the United States, shall be removed from office, on impeachment for, and conviction of treason, bribery, or other high crimes and misdemeanors...." By this paragraph, civil officers, in which the judges are included, are removable only for crimes. Treason and bribery are named, and the rest are included under the general terms of high crimes and misdemeanors. — Errors in judgement, or want of capacity to discharge the duties of the office, can never be supposed to be included in these words, high crimes and misdemeanors. A man may mistake a case in giving judgment, or manifest that he is incompetent to the discharge of the duties of a judge, and yet give no evidence of corruption or want of integrity. To support the charge, it will be necessary to give in evidence some facts that will shew, that the judges committed the error from wicked and corrupt motives.

3d. The power of this court is in many cases superior to that of the legislature. I have shewed, in a former paper, that this court will be authorised to decide upon the meaning of the constitution, and that, not only according to the natural and ob[vious] meaning of the words, but also according to the spirit and intention of it.

In the exercise of this power they will not be subordinate to, but above the legislature. For all the departments of this government will receive their powers, so far as they are expressed in the constitution, from the people immediately, who are the source of power. The legislature can only exercise such powers as are given them by the constitution, they cannot assume any of the rights annexed to the judicial, for this plain reason, that the same authority which vested the legislature with their powers, vested the judicial with theirs — both are derived from the same source, both therefore are equally valid, and the judicial hold their powers independently of the legislature, as the legislature do of the judicial. — The supreme court then have a right, independent of the legislature, to give a construction to the constitution and every part of it, and there is no power provided in this system to correct their construction or do it away. . . . If, therefore, the legislature pass any laws, inconsistent with the sense the judges put upon the constitution, they will declare it void; and therefore in this respect their power is superior to that of the legislature.

Perhaps nothing could have been better conceived to facilitate the abolition of the state governments than the constitution of the judicial. They will be able to extend the limits of the general government gradually, and by insensible degrees, and to accommodate themselves to the temper of the people. Their decisions on the meaning of the constitution will commonly take place in cases which arise between individuals, with which the public will not be generally acquainted; one adjudication will form a precedent to the next, and this to a following one. These cases will immediately affect individuals only; so that a series of determinations will probably take place before

even the people will be informed of them. In the mean time all the art and address of those who wish for the change will be employed to make converts to their opinion. The people will be told, that their state officers, and state legislatures are a burden and expense without affording any solid advantage, for that all the laws passed by them, might be equally well made by the general legislature. If to those who will be interested in the change, be added, those who will be under their influence, and such who will submit to almost any change of government, which they can be persuaded to believe will ease them of taxes, it is easy to see, the party who will favor the abolition of the state governments would be far from being inconsiderable. — In this situation, the general legislature, might pass one law after another, extending the general and abridging the state jurisdictions, and to sanction their proceedings would have a course of decisions of the judicial to whom the constitution has committed the power of explaining the constitution. — If the states remonstrated, the constitutional mode of deciding upon the validity of the law, is with the supreme court, and neither people, nor state legislatures, nor the general legislature can remove them or reverse their decrees.

Had the construction of the constitution been left with the legislature, they would have explained it at their peril; if they exceed their powers, or sought to find, in the spirit of the constitution, more than was expressed in the letter, the people from whom they derived their power could remove them, and do themselves right; and indeed I can see no other remedy that the people can have against their rulers for encroachments of this nature. A constitution is a compact of a people with their rulers; if the rulers break the compact, the people have a right and ought to remove them and do themselves justice; but in order to enable them to do this with the greater facility, those whom the people chuse at stated periods, should have the power in the last resort to determine the sense of the compact; if they determine contrary to the understanding of the people, an appeal will lie to the people at the period when the rulers are to be elected, and they will have it in their power to remedy the evil; but when this power is lodged in the hands of men independent of the people, and of their representatives, and who are not, constitutionally, accountable for their opinions, no way is left to controul them but with a high hand and an outstretched arm.

Thomas Jefferson

LETTER TO JUDGE SPENCER ROANE

September 6, 1819

In contrast to the strong view of judicial authority defended by Alexander Hamilton, this selection from Thomas Jefferson advocates a role for each branch of government in interpreting the Constitution. Does the power of judicial review transform the Constitution into "a mere thing of wax in the hands of the judiciary," as Jefferson argues? As will become apparent in Section B of this chapter, the Court's role in interpreting the Constitution remains highly controversial.

I had read in the Enquirer, and with great approbation, the pieces signed Hampden, and have read them again with redoubled approbation, in the copies you have been so kind as to send me. I subscribe to every title of them. They contain the true principles of the revolution of 1800, for that was as real a revolution in the principles of our government as that of 1776 was in its form; not effected indeed by the sword, as that, but by the rational and peaceable instrument of reform, the suffrage of the people. The nation declared its will by dismissing functionaries of one principle, and electing those of another, in the two branches, executive and legislative, submitted to their election. Over the judiciary department, the constitution had deprived them of their control. That, therefore, has continued the reprobated system, and although new matter has been occasionally incorporated into the old, yet the leaven of the old mass seems to assimilate to itself the new, and after twenty years' confirmation of the federal system by the voice of the nation, declared through the medium of elections, we find the judiciary on every occasion, still driving us into consolidation.

In denying the right they usurp of exclusively explaining the constitution, I go further than you do, if I understand rightly your quotation from the Federalist, of an opinion that "the judiciary is the last resort in relation to the other departments of the government, but not in relation to the rights of the parties to the compact under which the judiciary is derived." If this opinion be sound, then indeed is our constitution a complete felo de se. For intending to establish three departments, co-ordinate and independent, that they might check and balance one another, it has given, according to this opinion, to one of them alone, the right to prescribe rules for the government of the others, and to that one too, which is unelected by, and independent of the nation. . . . The constitution, on this hypothesis, is a mere thing of wax in the hands of the judiciary, which they may twist, and shape into any form they please. It should be remembered, as an axiom of eternal truth in politics, that whatever power in any government is independent, is absolute also; in theory only, at first, while the spirit of the people is up, but in practice, as fast as that

relaxes. Independence can be trusted nowhere but with the people in mass. They are inherently independent of all but moral law. My construction of the constitution is very different from that you quote. It is that each department is truly independent of the others, and has an equal right to decide for itself what is the meaning of the constitution in the cases submitted to its action; and especially, where it is to act ultimately and without appeal. . . .

CALDER v. BULL
3 U.S. 386 (1798)

Majority: Chase, joined by Ellsworth, Wilson, Cushing, Paterson
Concurrence: Paterson
Concurrence: Iredell
Concurrence: Cushing

The following case considers whether the actions of the Connecticut legislature in retroactively canceling the will of a deceased citizen violated the Constitution's prohibition of ex post facto laws. An ex post facto law is legislation that retroactively alters the legal status of past acts, in contrast to legislation regulating future acts. In reading this case, consider why the Constitution might prohibit such laws. In addition to illuminating this substantive matter, this case serves as an early example of the Court's examination of the question as to whether the Supreme Court has the power of judicial review over legislative acts. How is this issue handled? Are any of Brutus's concerns about judicial tyranny present in this case? Pay particular attention as you read to the concurrence by Justice Iredell. What is his argument in favor of judicial review? Notice that the Court explicitly refuses to address

the question of judicial review of acts of Congress. We examine that question in our next case selection.

CHASE, J., *opinion.*

The Legislature of Connecticut, on the 2d Thursday of May, 1795, passed a resolution or law, which for the reasons assigned, set aside a decree of the court of Probate for Hartford, on the 21st of March, 1793, which decree disapproved of the will of Normand Morrison (the grandson) made the 21st of August, 1779, and refused to record the said will; and granted a new hearing by the said Court of Probate, with liberty of appeal therefrom, in six months. A new hearing was had, in virtue of this resolution, or law, before the said Court of Probate, who, on the 27th of July, 1795, approved the said will, and ordered it to be recorded. At August, 1795, appeal was then had to the superior court at Hartford, who at February term, 1796, affirmed the decree of the Court of Probate. Appeal was had to the Supreme Court of errors of Connecticut, who in June, 1796, adjudged, that there were no errors.

More than 18 months elapsed from the decree of the Court of Probate (on the 1st of March, 1793) and thereby Caleb Bull and wife were barred of all right of appeal, by a statute of Connecticut. There was no law of that State whereby a new hearing, or trial, before the said court of Probate might be obtained. Calder and wife claim the premises in question, in right of his wife, as heiress of N. Morrison, a physician; Bull and wife claim under the will of N. Morrison, the grandson.

The Counsel for the Plaintiffs in error, contend, that the said resolution or law of the Legislature of Connecticut, granting a new hearing, in the above case, is an ex post facto law, prohibited by the Constitution of the United States; that any law of the Federal government, or of the State governments, contrary to the constitution of the United States, is void; and that this court possesses the power to declare such law void.

It appears to me a self-evident proposition, that the several State Legislatures retain all the powers of legislation, delegated to them by the State Constitutions; which are not expressly taken away by the Constitution of the United States. . . .

The effect of the resolution or law of Connecticut, above stated, is to review a decision of one of its Inferior Courts, called the Court of Probate for Hartford, and to direct a new hearing of the case by the same Court of Probate, that passed the decree against the will of Normand Morrison. By the existing law of Connecticut a right to recover certain property had vested in Calder and his wife (the appellants) in consequence, this right to recover certain property declared to be in Bull and wife, the appellees. The sole enquiry is, whether this resolution or law of Connecticut, having such operation, is an ex post facto law, within the prohibition of the Federal Constitution?

Whether the Legislature of any of the States can revise and correct by law, a decision of any of its Courts of Justice, although not prohibited by the Constitution of the State, is a question of very great importance, and not necessary now to be determined; because the resolution or law in question does not go so far. I cannot subscribe to the omnipotence of a State Legislature, or that it is absolute and without controul; although its authority should not be expressly restrained by the Constitution, or fundamental law, of the State. There are acts which the Federal, or State, Legislature cannot do, without exceeding their authority. There are certain vital principles in our free Republican governments, which will determine and over-rule an apparent and flagrant abuse of legislative power; as to authorize manifest injustice by positive law; or to take away that security for personal liberty, or private property, for the protection whereof the government was established. An act of the Legislature (for I cannot call it a law) contrary to the great first principles of the social compact, cannot be considered a rightful exercise of legislative authority. . . . A law that punished a citizen for an innocent action, or, in other words, for an act, which when done, was in violation of no existing law; a law that destroys, or impairs, the lawful private contracts of citizens; a law that makes a man a Judge in his own cause; or a law that takes property from A and gives it to B. It is against all reason and justice, for a people to entrust a Legislature with such powers; and, therefore, it cannot be presumed that they have done it. The genius, the nature, and the spirit, of our State Governments, amount to a prohibition of such acts of legislation; and the general principles of law and reason forbid them. The Legislature may enjoin, permit, forbid, and punish; they may declare new crimes; and establish rules of conduct for all its citizens in future cases; they may command what is right, and prohibit what is wrong; but they cannot change innocence into guilt; or punish innocence as a crime; or violate the right of an antecedent lawful private contract; or the right of private property. To maintain that our Federal, or State, Legislature possesses such powers, if they had not been expressly restrained, would, in my opinion, be a political heresy, altogether inadmissible in our free republican governments.

The prohibition, in the letter, is not to pass any law concerning and after the fact; but the plain and obvious meaning and intention of the prohibition is this; that the Legislatures of the several states shall not pass laws, after a fact done by a subject, or citizen, which shall have relation to such fact, and shall punish him for having done it. The prohibition considered in this light, is an additional bulwark in favour of the personal security of the subject, to protect his person from punishment by legislative acts, having a retrospective operation. I do not think it was inserted to secure the citizen in his private rights, of either property, or contracts. The prohibition not to make any thing but gold and silver coin a tender in payment of debts, and not to pass any law impairing the obligation of contracts, were inserted to secure private rights; but the restriction not to pass any ex post facto law, was to secure the person of the subject from injury, or punishment, in consequence of such law. If the prohibition against making ex post facto laws was intended to secure personal rights from being affected, or injured, by such laws, and the prohibition is sufficiently extensive for that object, the other restraints, I have enumerated, were unnecessary, and therefore improper; for both of them are retrospective.

. . . In the present case, there is no fact done by Bull and wife, Plaintiff's in Error, that is in any manner affected by the law or resolution of Connecticut: It does not concern, or relate to, any act done by them. The decree of the Court of Probate of Hartford (on the 21st, March) in consequence of which Calder and wife claim a right to the property in question, was given before the said law or resolution, and in that sense, was affected and set aside by it; and in consequence of the law allowing a hearing and the decision in favor of the will, they have lost, what they would have been entitled to, if the Law or resolution, and the decision in consequence thereof, had not been made. The decree of the Court of probate is the only fact, on which the law or resolution operates. In my judgment the case of the Plaintiffs in Error, is not within the letter of the prohibition; and, for the reasons assigned, I am clearly of opinion, that it is not within the intention of the prohibition; and if within the intention, but out of the letter, I should not, therefore, consider myself justified to continue it within the prohibition, and therefore that the whole was void.

It was argued by the counsel for the plaintiffs in error, that the Legislature of Connecticut had no constitutional power to make the resolution (or law) in question, granting a new hearing, &c.

Without giving an opinion, at this time, whether this Court has jurisdiction to decide that any law made by Congress, contrary to the Constitution of the United States, is void; I am fully satisfied that this court has no jurisdiction to determine that any law of any state Legislature, contrary to the Constitution of such state is void. Further, if this court had such jurisdiction, yet it does not appear to me, that the resolution (or law) in question, is contrary to the charter of Connecticut, or its constitution, which is said by counsel to be composed of its charter, acts of assembly, and usages, and customs. I should think, that the courts of Connecticut are the proper tribunals to decide, whether laws, contrary to the constitution thereof, are void. In the present case they have, both in the inferior and superior courts, determined that the resolution (or law) in question was not contrary to either their state, or the federal, constitution.

I admit, an act unlawful in the beginning may, in some cases, become lawful by matter of after fact.

I also agree, that the words "ex post facto" have the meaning contended for, and no other, in the cases cited, and in all similar cases; where they are used unconnected with, and without relation to, Legislative acts, or laws.

There appears to me a manifest distinction between the case where one fact relates to, and affects another fact, as where an after fact, by operation of law, makes a former fact, either lawful or unlawful; and the case where a law made after a fact done, is to operate on, and to affect, such fact. In the first case both the acts are done by private persons. In the second case the first act is done by a private person, and the second act is done by the legislature to affect the first act.

If the term ex post facto law is to be construed to include and to prohibit the enacting any law after a fact, it will greatly restrict the power of the federal and state legislatures; and the consequences of such a construction may not be foreseen.

If the prohibition to make no ex post facto law extends to all laws made after the fact, the two prohibitions, not to make anything but old and silver coin a tender in payment of debts; and not to pass any law impairing the obligation of contracts, were improper and unnecessary.

It was further urged, that if the provision does not extend to prohibit the making any law after a fact, then all choses in action; all lands by Devise, all personal property by bequest, or distribution; by Elegit; by execution; by judgments, particularly on torts; will be unprotected from the legislative power of the states; rights vested may be divested at the will and pleasure of the state legislatures; and, therefore, that the true construction and meaning of the prohibition is, that the states pass no law to deprive a citizen of any right vested in him by existing laws.

It is not to be presumed, that the federal or state legislatures will pass laws to deprive citizens of rights vested in them by existing laws; unless for the benefit of the whole community; and on making full satisfaction. The restraint against making any ex post facto laws was not considered, by the framers of the constitution, as extending to prohibit the depriving a citizen even of a vested right to property; or the provision, "that private property should not be taken for public use, without just compensation," was unnecessary.

It seems to me, that the right of property, in its origin, could only arise from compact express, or implied, and I think it the better opinion, that the right as well as the mode, or manner, of acquiring property, and of alienating or transferring, inheriting, or transmitting it, is conferred by society; it is regulated by civil institution, and is always subject to the rules prescribed by positive law. When I say that a right is vested in a citizen, I mean, that he has the power to do certain actions; or to possess certain things, according to the law of the land.

I cannot agree, that a right to property vested in Calder and wife, in consequence of the decree (of the 21st of March, 1783) disapproving of the will of Morrison, the Grandson. If the will was valid, Mrs. Calder could have no right, as heiress of Morrison, the physician; but if the will was set aside, she had an undoubted title.

The resolution (or law) alone had no manner of effect on any right whatever vested in Calder and wife. The resolution (or law) combined with the new hearing, and the decision, in virtue of it, took away their right to recover the property in question. But when combined they took away no right of property vested in Calder and wife; because the decree against the will (21st. March, 1783) did not vest in or transfer any property to them.

I am under a necessity to give a construction, or explanation of the words "ex post facto laws," because they have not any certain meaning attached to them. But I will not go farther than I feel myself bound to do; and if I ever exercise the jurisdiction I will not decide any law to be void, but in a very clear case.

I am of opinion, that the decree of the Supreme Court of Errors of Connecticut be affirmed, with costs.

IREDELL, J. *[concurring in the judgment.]*

Though I concur in the general result of the opinions, which have been delivered, I cannot entirely adopt the reasons that are assigned upon the occasion.

From the best information to be collected, relative to the Constitution of Connecticut, it appears, that the Legislature of that State has been in the uniform, uninterrupted, habit of exercising a general superintending power over its courts of law, by granting new trials. It may, indeed, appear strange to some of us, that in any form, there should exist a power to grant, with respect to suits depending or adjudged, new rights of trial, new privileges of proceeding, not previously recognized and regulated by positive institutions; but such is the established usage of Connecticut, and it is obviously consistent with the general superintending authority of her Legislature. Nor is it altogether without some sanction for a Legislature to act as a court of justice. In England, we know, that one branch of the Parliament, the house of Lords, not only exercises a judicial power in cases of impeachment, and for the trial of its own members, but as the court of dernier resort,

takes cognizance of many suits at law, and in equity: And that in construction of law, the jurisdiction there exercised is by the King in full Parliament; which shews that, in its origin, the causes were probably heard before the whole Parliament. When Connecticut was settled, the right of empowering her Legislature to superintend the Courts of Justice, was, I presume, early assumed; and its expediency, as applied to the local circumstances and municipal policy of the State, is sanctioned by a long and uniform practice. The power, however, is judicial in its nature; and whenever it is exercised, as in the present instance, it is an exercise of judicial, not of legislative, authority.

But, let us, for a moment, suppose, that the resolution, granting a new trial, was a legislative act, it will by no means follow, that it is an act affected by the constitutional prohibition, that "no State shall pass any ex post facto law." I will endeavour to state the general principles, which influence me, on this point, succinctly and clearly, though I have not had an opportunity to reduce my opinion to writing.

If, then, a government, composed of Legislative, Executive and Judicial departments, were established, by a Constitution, which imposed no limits on the legislative power, the consequence would inevitably be, that whatever the legislative power chose to enact, would be lawfully enacted, and the judicial power could never interpose to pronounce it void. It is true, that some speculative jurists have held, that a legislative act against natural justice must, in itself, be void; but I cannot think that, under such a government, any Court of Justice would possess a power to declare it so. Sir William Blackstone, having put the strong case of an act of Parliament, which authorise a man to try his own cause, explicitly adds, that even in that case, "there is no court that has power to defeat the intent of the Legislature, when couched in such evident and express words, as leave no doubt whether it was the intent of the Legislature, or no." 1 Bl. Com. 91.

In order, therefore, to guard against so great an evil, it has been the policy of all the American states, which have, individually, framed their state constitutions since the revolution, and of the people of the United States, when they framed the Federal Constitution, to define with precision the objects of the legislative power, and to restrain its exercise within marked and settled boundaries. If any act of Congress, or of the Legislature of a state, violates those constitutional provisions, it is unquestionably void; though, I admit, that as the authority to declare it void is of a delicate and awful nature, the Court will never resort to that authority, but in a clear and urgent case. If, on the other hand, the Legislature of the Union, or the Legislature of any member of the Union, shall pass a law, within the general scope of their constitutional power, the Court cannot pronounce it to be void, merely because it is, in their judgment, contrary to the principles of natural justice. The ideas of natural justice are regulated by no fixed standard: the ablest and the purest men have differed upon the subject; and all that the Court could properly say, in such an event, would be, that the Legislature (possessed of an equal right of opinion) had passed an act which, in the opinion of the judges, was inconsistent with the abstract principles of natural justice. There are then but two lights, in which the subject can be viewed: 1st. If the Legislature pursue the authority delegated to them, their acts are valid. 2d. If they transgress the boundaries of that authority, their acts are invalid. In the former case, they exercise the discretion vested in them by the people, to whom alone they are responsible for the faithful discharge of their trust: but in the latter case, they violate a fundamental law, which must be our guide, whenever we are called

upon as judges to determine the validity of a legislative act.

Still, however, in the present instance, the act or resolution of the Legislature of Connecticut, cannot be regarded as an ex post facto law; for, the true construction of the prohibition extends to criminal, not to civil, cases. It is only in criminal cases, indeed, in which the danger to be guarded against, is greatly to be apprehended. The history of every country in Europe will furnish flagrant instances of tyranny exercised under the pretext of penal dispensations. Rival factions, in their efforts to crush each other, have superseded all the forms, and suppressed all the sentiments, of justice; while attainders, on the principle of retaliation and proscription, have marked all the vicissitudes of party triumph. The temptation to such abuses of power is unfortunately too alluring for human virtue; and, therefore, the framers of the American Constitutions have wisely denied to the respective Legislatures, Federal as well as State, the possession of the power itself: They shall not pass any ex post facto law; or, in other words, they shall not inflict a punishment for any act, which was innocent at the time it was committed; nor increase the degree of punishment previously denounced for any specific offence.

The policy, the reason and humanity, of the prohibition, do not, I repeat, extend to civil cases, to cases that merely affect the private property of citizens. Some of the most necessary and important acts of Legislation are, on the contrary, founded upon the principle, that private rights must yield to public exigencies. Highways are run through private grounds. Fortifications, Lighthouses, and other public edifices, are necessarily sometimes built upon the soil owned by individuals. In such, and similar cases, if the owners should refuse voluntarily to accommodate the public, they must be constrained, as far as the public necessities require; and justice is done, by allowing them a reasonable equivalent. Without the possession of this power the operations of Government would often be obstructed, and society itself would be endangered. It is not sufficient to urge, that the power may be abused, for, such is the nature of all power, — such is the tendency of every human institution: and, it might as fairly be said, that the power of taxation, which is only circumscribed by the discretion of the Body, in which it is vested, ought not to be granted, because the Legislature, disregarding its true objects, might, for visionary and useless projects, impose a tax to the amount of nineteen shillings in the pound. We must be content to limit power where we can, and where we cannot, consistently with its use, we must be content to repose a salutary confidence. It is our consolation that there never existed a Government, in ancient or modern times, more free from danger in this respect, than the Governments of America.

Upon the whole, though there cannot be a case, in which an ex post facto law in criminal matters is requisite, or justifiable (for Providence never can intend to promote the prosperity of any country by bad means) yet, in the present instance the objection doesnot [sic] arise: Because, 1st. if the act of the Legislature of Connecticut was a judicial act, it is not within the words of the Constitution; and 2d. even if it was a legislative act, it is not within the meaning of the prohibition.

MARBURY v. MADISON

5 U.S. 137 (1803)

Opinion: Marshall, joined by Paterson, Chase, Washington

After the controversial election of 1800, outgoing President John Adams made a series of "midnight appointments," filling intermediate-level civil service positions with loyal Federalists before the inauguration of Democratic-Republican President-elect Thomas Jefferson. Through these appointments, the Federalist Party attempted to retain influence over the judiciary even though it no longer controlled the presidency. Adams appointed William Marbury to serve as justice of the peace in the District of Columbia, but his commission was never delivered by the new administration. In this case, Marbury sought a writ of mandamus—a mandatory court order—requiring Jefferson's Secretary of State, James Madison, to deliver this commission.

Clearly, Chief Justice John Marshall must have realized that any attempt to take sides in this dispute by the Court would be seen as a partisan intervention. If Chief Justice Marshall were to issue the writ of mandamus, he risked the perception that the Supreme Court was not independent from partisan politics. In reading the case, consider whether this political and historical context influenced either the decision of the case or the kind of arguments presented in it. Does Chief Justice Marshall succeed in making an argument that both asserts the Court's power and that keeps it from seeming like it is merely acting in a partisan manner?

In addition to thinking about the political context of the case, it is also essential to understand the legal issues involved. Fundamental among them is the question of whether the Supreme Court has the power of judicial review in the first place. If you reread Article III of the Constitution, you will not find any explicit mention of the Court's review power. The Court therefore needed another argument for the establishment of this power aside from a clear grant from Article III. The case addresses a number of questions, including (a) whether Marbury has a legal right to his commission, (b) whether it is constitutional for the Judiciary Act of 1789 to allow Marbury to bring his case directly before the Supreme Court rather than beginning his litigation in a lower court, and (c) whether the Supreme Court can strike down an unconstitutional law. Bearing in mind the readings from Gordon Wood and Alexander Bickel, as well as Alexander Hamilton's claim in The Federalist No. 78 that, "The interpretation of the laws is the proper and peculiar province of the courts," it is important to consider how Chief Justice Marshall weaves these issues together. Is his case for judicial review persuasive?

As you prepare to read this case, it would be helpful to familiarize yourself with the processes by which the Supreme Court can hear a case by looking both to Box 1 below and to Article III itself. As you will see, the Court often acts as an "appellate court," reviewing the decision of lower courts for mistakes about the law. In these cases an "inferior" court will have heard a case before it comes to the Supreme Court on appeal. But in some cases it acts as a Court of "original jurisdiction" in which a litigant brings his or her original suit to the Supreme Court.

MR. CHIEF JUSTICE MARSHALL *delivered the opinion of the Court.*

In the order in which the court has viewed this subject, the following questions have been considered and decided.

1st. Has the applicant a right to the commission he demands?

2dly. If he has a right, and that right has been violated, do the laws of his country afford him a remedy?

3dly. If they do afford him a remedy, is it a mandamus issuing from this court?

The first object of enquiry is,

1st. Has the applicant a right to the commission he demands?

His right originates in an act of congress passed in February, 1801, concerning the district of Columbia.

After dividing the district into two counties, the 11th section of this law, enacts, "that there shall be appointed in and for each of the said counties, such number of discreet persons to be justices of the peace as the president of the United States shall, from time to time, think expedient, to continue in office for five years."

It appears, from the affidavits, that in compliance with this law, a commission for William Marbury as a justice of peace for the county of Washington, was signed by John Adams, then president of the United States; after which the seal of the United States was affixed to it; but the commission has never reached the person for whom it was made out.

In order to determine whether he is entitled to this commission, it becomes necessary to enquire whether he has been appointed to the office. For if he has been appointed, the law continues him in office for five years, and he is entitled to the possession of those evidences of office, which, being completed, became his property.

The 2d section of the 2d article of the constitution, declares, that "the president shall nominate, and, by and with the advice and consent of the senate, shall appoint ambassadors, other public ministers and consuls, and all other officers of the United States, whose appointments are not otherwise provided for."

The third section declares, that "he shall commission all the officers of the United States."

An act of congress directs the secretary of state to keep the seal of the United States, "to make out and record, and affix the said seal to all civil commissions to officers of the United States, to be appointed by the President, by and with the consent of the senate, or by the President alone; provided that the said seal shall not be affixed to any commission before the same shall have been signed by the President of the United States."

These are the clauses of the constitution and laws of the United States, which affect this part of the case. They seem to contemplate three distinct operations:

1st. The nomination. This is the sole act of the President, and is completely voluntary.

2d. The appointment. This is also the act of the President, and is also a voluntary act, though it can only be performed by and with the advice and consent of the senate.

3d. The commission. To grant a commission to a person appointed, might perhaps be deemed a duty enjoined by the constitution. "He shall," says that instrument, "commission all the officers of the United States."

This is an appointment by the President, by and with the advice and consent of the senate, and is evidenced by no act but the commission itself. In such a case therefore the commission and the appointment seem inseparable. . . . [T]he commission is not necessarily the appointment; though conclusive evidence of it.

It is . . . decidedly the opinion of the court, that when a commission has been signed by the President, the appointment is made; and that the commission is complete, when the seal of the United States has been affixed to it by the secretary of state.

Where an officer is removable at the will of the executive, the circumstance which completes his appointment is of no concern; because the act is at any time revocable; and the commission may be arrested, if still in the office. But when the officer is not removable at the will of the executive, the appointment is not revocable, and cannot be annulled. It has conferred legal rights which cannot be resumed.

The discretion of the executive is to be exercised until the appointment has been

made. But having once made the appointment, his power over the office is terminated in all cases, where, by law, the officer is not removable by him. The right to the office is then in the person appointed, and he has the absolute, unconditional, power of accepting or rejecting it.

Mr. Marbury, . . . since his commission was signed by the President, and sealed by the secretary of state, was appointed; and as the law creating the office, gave the officer a right to hold for five years, independent of the executive, the appointment was not revocable; but vested in the officer legal rights, which are protected by the laws of his country.

To withhold his commission, therefore, is an act deemed by the court not warranted by law, but violative of a vested legal right.

This brings us to the second enquiry; which is,

2dly. If he has a right, and that right has been violated, do the laws of his country afford him a remedy?

The very essence of civil liberty certainly consists in the right of every individual to claim the protection of the laws, whenever he receives an injury. One of the first duties of government is to afford that protection. In Great Britain the king himself is sued in the respectful form of a petition, and he never fails to comply with the judgment of his court.

The government of the United States has been emphatically termed a government of laws, and not of men. It will certainly cease to deserve this high appellation, if the laws furnish no remedy for the violation of a vested legal right.

By the constitution of the United States, the President is invested with certain important political powers, in the exercise of which he is to use his own discretion, and is accountable only to his country in his political character, and to his own conscience. To aid him in the performance of these duties, he is authorized to appoint certain officers, who act by his authority and in conformity with his orders.

In such cases, their acts are his acts; and whatever opinion may be entertained of the manner in which executive discretion may be used, still there exists, and can exist, no power to control that discretion. The subjects are political. They respect the nation, not individual rights, and being entrusted to the executive, the decision of the executive is conclusive. The application of this remark will be perceived by adverting to the act of congress for establishing the department of foreign affairs. This office, as his duties were prescribed by that act, is to conform precisely to the will of the President. He is the mere organ by whom that will is communicated. The acts of such an officer, as an officer, can never be examinable by the courts.

But when the legislature proceeds to impose on that officer other duties; when he is directed peremptorily to perform certain acts; when the rights of individuals are dependent on the performance of those acts; he is so far the officer of the law; is amenable to the laws for his conduct; and cannot at his discretion sport away the vested rights of others.

The conclusion from this reasoning is, that where the heads of departments are the political or confidential agents of the executive, merely to execute the will of the President, or rather to act in cases in which the executive possesses a constitutional or legal discretion, nothing can be more perfectly clear than that their acts are only politically examinable. But where a specific duty is assigned by law, and individual rights depend upon the performance of that duty, it seems equally clear that the individual who considers himself injured, has a right to resort to the laws of his country for a remedy.

If this be the rule, let us enquire how it applies to the case under the consideration of the court.

The power of nominating to the senate, and the power of appointing the person nominated, are political powers, to be exercised by the President according to his own discretion. When he has made an appointment, he has exercised his whole power, and his discretion has been completely applied to the case. If, by law, the officer be removable at the will of the President, then a new appointment may be immediately made, and the rights of the officer are terminated. But as a fact which has existed cannot be made never to have existed, the appointment cannot be annihilated; and consequently if the officer is by law not removable at the will of the President; the rights he has acquired are protected by the law, and are not resumable by the President. They cannot be extinguished by executive authority, and he has the privilege of asserting them in like manner as if they had been derived from any other source.

The question whether a right has vested or not, is, in its nature, judicial, and must be tried by the judicial authority. If, for example, Mr. Marbury had taken the oaths of a magistrate, and proceeded to act as one; in consequence of which a suit had been instituted against him, in which his defence had depended on his being a magistrate; the validity of his appointment must have been determined by judicial authority.

So, if he conceives that, by virtue of his appointment, he has a legal right, either to the commission which has been made out for him, or to a copy of that commission, it is equally a question examinable in a court, and the decision of the court upon it must depend on the opinion entertained of his appointment.

That question has been discussed, and the opinion is, that the latest point of time which can be taken as that at which the appointment was complete, and evidenced, was when, after the signature of the president, the seal of the United States was affixed to the commission.

It is then the opinion of the court,

1st. That by signing the commission of Mr. Marbury, the president of the United States appointed him a justice of peace, for the county of Washington in the district of Columbia; and that the seal of the United States, affixed thereto by the secretary of state, is conclusive testimony of the verity of the signature, and of the completion of the appointment; and that the appointment conferred on him a legal right to the office for the space of five years.

2dly. That, having this legal title to the office, he has a consequent right to the commission; a refusal to deliver which, is a plain violation of that right, for which the laws of his country afford him a remedy.

It remains to be enquired whether,

3dly. He is entitled to the remedy for which he applies. This depends on,

1st. The nature of the writ applied for, and,

2dly. The power of this court.

1st. The nature of the writ.

Blackstone, in the 3d volume of his commentaries, page 110, defines a mandamus to be, "a command issued in the King's name from the court of King's Bench, and directed to any person, corporation, or inferior court of judicature within the King's dominions, requiring them to do some particular thing therein specified, which appertains to their office and duty, and which the court of King's Bench has previously determined, or at least supposed, to be consonant to right and justice."

The province of the court is, solely, to decide on the rights of individuals, not to enquire how the executive, or executive officers, perform duties in which they have a discretion. Questions, in their nature political, or which are, by the constitution and laws, submitted to the executive, can never be made in this court.

It is not by the office of the person to whom the writ is directed, but the nature of the thing to be done that the propriety or impropriety of issuing a mandamus, is to be determined. Where the head of a department acts in a case, in which executive discretion is to be exercised; in which he is the mere organ of executive will; it is again repeated, that any application to a court to control, in any respect, his conduct, would be rejected without hesitation.

But where he is directed by law to do a certain act affecting the absolute rights of individuals, in the performance of which he is not placed under the particular direction of the President, and the performance of which, the President cannot lawfully forbid, and therefore is never presumed to have forbidden; as for example, to record a commission, or a patent for land, which has received all the legal solemnities; or to give a copy of such record; in such cases, it is not perceived on what ground the courts of the country are further excused from the duty of giving judgment, that right be done to an injured individual, than if the same services were to be performed by a person not the head of a department.

It was at first doubted whether the action of detinue was not a specified legal remedy for the commission which has been withheld from Mr. Marbury; in which case a mandamus would be improper. But this doubt has yielded to the consideration that the judgment in detinue is for the thing itself, or its value. The value of a public office not to be sold, is incapable of being ascertained; and the applicant has a right to the office itself, or to nothing. He will obtain the office by obtaining the commission, or a copy of it from the record.

This, then, is a plain case for a mandamus, either to deliver the commission, or a copy of it from the record; and it only remains to be enquired,

Whether it can issue from this court.

The act to establish the judicial courts of the United States authorizes the supreme court "to issue writs of mandamus, in cases warranted by the principles and usages of law, to any courts appointed, or persons holding office, under the authority of the United States."

The secretary of state, being a person holding an office under the authority of the United States, is precisely within the letter of the description; and if this court is not authorized to issue a writ of mandamus to such an officer, it must be because the law is unconstitutional, and therefore absolutely incapable of conferring the authority, and assigning the duties which its words purport to confer and assign.

The constitution vests the whole judicial power of the United States in one supreme court, and such inferior courts as congress shall, from time to time, ordain and establish. This power is expressly extended to all cases arising under the laws of the United States; and consequently, in some form, may be exercised over the present case; because the right claimed is given by a law of the United States.

In the distribution of this power it is declared that "the supreme court shall have original jurisdiction in all cases affecting ambassadors, other public ministers and consuls, and those in which a state shall be a party. In all other cases, the supreme court shall have appellate jurisdiction."

It has been insisted, at the bar, that as the original grant of jurisdiction, to the supreme and inferior courts, is general, and the clause, assigning original jurisdiction to the supreme court, contains no negative or restrictive words; the power remains to the legislature, to assign original jurisdiction to that court in other cases than those specified in the article which has been recited; provided those cases belong to the judicial power of the United States.

If it had been intended to leave it to the discretion of the legislature to apportion the judicial power between the supreme and inferior courts according to the will

of that body, it would certainly have been useless to have proceeded further than to have defined the judicial powers, and the tribunals in which it should be vested. The subsequent part of the section is mere surplusage, is entirely without meaning, if such is to be the construction. If congress remains at liberty to give this court appellate jurisdiction, where the constitution has declared their jurisdiction shall be original; and original jurisdiction where the constitution has declared it shall be appellate; the distribution of jurisdiction, made in the constitution, is form without substance.

Affirmative words are often, in their operation, negative of other objects than those affirmed; and in this case, a negative or exclusive sense must be given to them or they have no operation at all.

It cannot be presumed that any clause in the constitution is intended to be without effect; and therefore such a construction is inadmissible, unless the words require it.

That they should have appellate jurisdiction in all other cases, with such exceptions as congress might make, is no restriction; unless the words be deemed exclusive of original jurisdiction.

When an instrument organizing fundamentally a judicial system, divides it into one supreme, and so many inferior courts as the legislature may ordain and establish; then enumerates its powers, and proceeds so far to distribute them, as to define the jurisdiction of the supreme court by declaring the cases in which it shall take original jurisdiction, and that in others it shall take appellate jurisdiction; the plain import of the words seems to be, that in one class of cases its jurisdiction is original, and not appellate; in the other it is appellate, and not original. If any other construction would render the clause inoperative, that is an additional reason for rejecting such other construction, and for adhering to their obvious meaning.

To enable this court then to issue a mandamus, it must be shown to be an exercise of appellate jurisdiction, or to be necessary to enable them to exercise appellate jurisdiction.

It is the essential criterion of appellate jurisdiction, that it revises and corrects the proceedings in a cause already instituted, and does not create that cause. Although, therefore, a mandamus may be directed to courts, yet to issue such a writ to an officer for the delivery of a paper, is in effect the same as to sustain an original action for that paper, and therefore seems not to belong to appellate, but to original jurisdiction. Neither is it necessary in such a case as this, to enable the court to exercise its appellate jurisdiction.

The authority, therefore, given to the supreme court, by the act establishing the judicial courts of the United States, to issue writs of mandamus to public officers, appears not to be warranted by the constitution; and it becomes necessary to enquire whether a jurisdiction, so conferred, can be exercised.

The question, whether an act, repugnant to the constitution, can become the law of the land, is a question deeply interesting to the United States; but, happily, not of an intricacy proportioned to its interest. It seems only necessary to recognize certain principles, supposed to have been long and well established, to decide it.

That the people have an original right to establish, for their future government, such principles as, in their opinion, shall most conduce to their own happiness, is the basis, on which the whole American fabric has been erected. The exercise of this original right is a very great exertion; nor can it, nor ought it to be frequently repeated. The principles, therefore, so established, are deemed fundamental. And as the authority, from which they proceed, is supreme, and can seldom act, they are designed to be permanent.

This original and supreme will organizes the government, and assigns, to different departments, their respective powers. It may either stop here; or establish certain limits not to be transcended by those departments.

The government of the United States is of the latter description. The powers of the legislature are defined, and limited; and that those limits may not be mistaken, or forgotten, the constitution is written. To what purpose are powers limited, and to what purpose is that limitation committed to writing, if these limits may, at any time, be passed by those intended to be restrained? The distinction, between a government with limited and unlimited powers, is abolished, if those limits do not confine the persons on whom they are imposed, and if acts prohibited and acts allowed, are of equal obligation. It is a proposition too plain to be contested, that the constitution controls any legislative act repugnant to it; or, that the legislature may alter the constitution by an ordinary act.

Between these alternatives there is no middle ground. The constitution is either a superior, paramount law, unchangeable by ordinary means, or it is on a level with ordinary legislative acts, and like other acts, is alterable when the legislature shall please to alter it.

If the former part of the alternative be true, then a legislative act contrary to the constitution is not law: if the latter part be true, then written constitutions are absurd attempts, on the part of the people, to limit a power, in its own nature illimitable.

Certainly all those who have framed written constitutions contemplate them as forming the fundamental and paramount law of the nation, and consequently the theory of every such government must be, that an act of the legislature, repugnant to the constitution, is void.

This theory is essentially attached to a written constitution, and is consequently to be considered, by this court, as one of the fundamental principles of our society. It is not therefore to be lost sight of in the further consideration of this subject.

It is emphatically the province and duty of the judicial department to say what the law is. Those who apply the rule to particular cases, must of necessity expound and interpret that rule. If two laws conflict with each other, the courts must decide on the operation of each.

So if a law be in opposition to the constitution; if both the law and the constitution apply to a particular case, so that the court must either decide that case conformably to the law, disregarding the constitution; or conformably to the constitution, disregarding the law; the court must determine which of these conflicting rules governs the case. This is of the very essence of judicial duty.

If then the courts are to regard the constitution; and the constitution is superior to any ordinary act of the legislature; the constitution, and not such ordinary act, must govern the case to which they both apply.

Those then who controvert the principle that the constitution is to be considered, in court, as a paramount law, are reduced to the necessity of maintaining that courts must close their eyes on the constitution, and see only the law.

This doctrine would subvert the very foundation of all written constitutions. It would declare that an act, which, according to the principles and theory of our government, is entirely void; is yet, in practice, completely obligatory. It would declare, that if the legislature shall do what is expressly forbidden, such act, notwithstanding the express prohibition, is in reality effectual. It would be giving to the legislature a practical and real omnipotence, with the same breath which professes to restrict their powers within narrow limits. It is prescribing limits, and declaring that those limits may be passed at pleasure.

That it thus reduces to nothing what we have deemed the greatest improvement on political institutions a written constitution would of itself be sufficient, in America, where written constitutions have been viewed with so much reverence, for rejecting the construction. But the peculiar expressions of the constitution of the United States furnish additional arguments in favor of its rejection.

The judicial power of the United States is extended to all cases arising under the constitution.

Could it be the intention of those who gave this power, to say that, in using it, the constitution should not be looked into? That a case arising under the constitution should be decided without examining the instrument under which it arises?

This is too extravagant to be maintained.

In some cases then, the constitution must be looked into by the judges. And if they can open it at all, what part of it are they forbidden to read, or to obey?

There are many other parts of the constitution which serve to illustrate this subject.

It is declared that "no tax or duty shall be laid on articles exported from any state." Suppose a duty on the export of cotton, of tobacco, or of flour; and a suit instituted to recover it. Ought judgment to be rendered in such a case? Ought the judges to close their eyes on the constitution, and only see the law.

The constitution declares that "no bill of attainder or ex post facto law shall be passed."

If, however, such a bill should be passed and a person should be prosecuted under it; must the court condemn to death those victims whom the constitution endeavors to preserve?

"No person," says the constitution, "shall be convicted of treason unless on the testimony of two witnesses to the fame overt act, or on confession in open court."

Here the language of the constitution is addressed especially to the courts. It prescribes, directly for them, a rule of evidence not to be departed from. If the legislature should change that rule, and declare one witness, or a confession out of court, sufficient for conviction, must the constitutional principle yield to the legislative act?

From these, and many other selections which might be made, it is apparent, that the framers of the constitution contemplated that instrument, as a rule for the government of courts, as well as of the legislature.

It is also not entirely unworthy of observation, that in declaring what shall be the supreme law of the land, the constitution itself is first mentioned; and not the laws of the United States generally, but those only which shall be made in pursuance of the constitution, have that rank.

Thus, the particular phraseology of the constitution of the United States confirms and strengthens the principle, supposed to be essential to all written constitutions, that a law repugnant to the constitution is void; and that courts, as well as other departments, are bound by that instrument.

The rule must be discharged.

CASE QUESTIONS

1. Some commentators have argued that this opinion, which found against William Marbury, was an ingenious political move that succeeded in securing the power of judicial review for the Court without seeming like a partisan power grab. In claiming that the Supreme Court had the power of judicial review and by striking down the Judiciary Act of 1787, Chief Justice John Marshall gave legal precedence to the arguments of Alexander Hamilton and to his own Federalist Party. He also scored a moral victory for the Federalists by claiming, even while finding in James Madison's favor, that Marbury's rights had been denied.

   At the same time, Chief Justice Marshall was able to keep the Court above the partisan fray. Although he asserts the broader power of the Court to strike down unconstitutional laws, Chief Justice Marshall agrees with Thomas Jefferson's administration that the Court is powerless to enforce Marbury's particular claim. Even though Marbury has a "right" to have his appointment certified, Chief Justice Marshall rules that the procedures Marbury followed were unconstitutional. Does Chief Justice Marshall succeed in securing the power of the Court while retaining a sense of the Court's political independence? Consider here Gordon Wood's remarks about the challenges of a Supreme Court dominated by the Federalist Party retaining its power in a Democratic-Republican administration.

2. One crucial aspect of the case concerns the question of whether Congress can alter the kind of "original jurisdiction" held by the Supreme Court. While the Judiciary Act of 1789 provides that Marbury could bring his argument directly before the Supreme Court, Article III of the Constitution only allows this kind of "original jurisdiction" in a limited range of cases. Should Congress have been allowed to enhance the Supreme Court's powers of original jurisdiction? What does Chief Justice Marshall say about this issue?

3. This case is prominent because of Chief Justice Marshall's argument for the Court's judicial review power. What is his argument? Is it successful? Does it overcome concerns about the counter-majoritarian difficulty?

Box 1-1   The Pathways to the Supreme Court

In most cases (except for cases under original jurisdiction and limited instances of mandatory appeals), the Supreme Court has *discretionary* jurisdiction, which means that it can choose whether or not to hear an appeal. Often, the Court chooses to hear cases that might clear up areas of the law where lower courts have contradicted each other, or cases that bear on weighty legal issues. The Court agrees to hear an appeal by granting a petition for the writ of *certiorari*, also known as "granting cert."

Under Article III of the Constitution, the Supreme Court has the power to interpret the law in "all cases . . . arising under this Constitution, the laws of the United States, and treaties." Sometimes the Supreme Court, like lower federal courts, hears cases that concern matters of state law. Typically, these cases land in federal court under "diversity jurisdiction," when two parties in a civil matter hail from different states. The idea is that a federal court-room provides an impartial forum to decide such cases, but federal judges are required to apply relevant state law in these instances. The Court can also review the decisions of state courts, but only when state cases touch on matters of federal law as well, such as when a state law is alleged to violate the U.S. Constitution. In certain circumstances, a case in state court can jump to a federal court lower than the Supreme Court, as when a prisoner challenges her conviction in state court as unconstitutional.

In thinking about the issues raised in *Marbury v. Madison*, the following chart might be helpful. It outlines various routes by which a case might reach the Supreme Court:

Figure 1.1. Various Paths to the Supreme Court

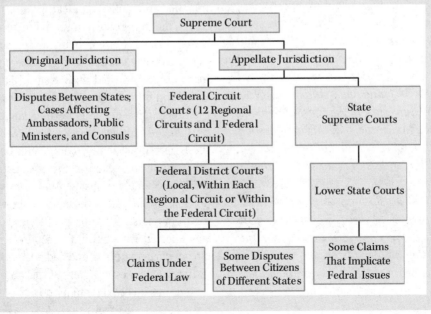

FLETCHER v. PECK

10 U.S. 87 (1810)

Opinion: Marshall, joined by Washington, Livingston, Todd
Dissent: Johnson

Under the "Yazoo Land Act," the State of Georgia sold very large tracts of land to private citizens. Believing that the Act and the process of selling the land had become deeply corrupted, a later legislature invalidated the sale. Of course, those who had bought land under this scheme were aggrieved by this result. Robert Fletcher had bought land from John Peck, one of the original purchasers of the land. When the sale was voided by the State of Georgia, Fletcher sued for damages, claiming the contract falsely represented Peck as the legal owner of the land. In order to decide whether Peck really was the legal owner, and thus entitled to sell the land to Fletcher, the Court focused on whether the law invalidating the purchases of the land was unconstitutional. Specifically, pay close attention to the discussion about whether the legislature is bound in this case from revoking the sale by the Contracts Clause of the U.S. Constitution, located in Article I, Section 10. You will notice that the Court pits the rights of individuals under this clause against the right of the legislature to make policy. Notice, too, that this is a question of the federal constitutionality of a state law, and thus raises questions about the relative power of the U.S. Constitution and that of state legislatures. Notice also that, in addition to the discussion of the Contracts Clause, this case raises an ex post facto question similar to the one we have just examined: Can a legislature invalidate a sale of land after the sale has occurred?

MR. CHIEF JUSTICE MARSHALL *delivered the opinion of the Court.*

The suit was instituted on several covenants contained in a deed made by John Peck, the defendant in error, conveying to Robert Fletcher, the plaintiff in error, certain lands which were part of a large purchase made by James Gunn and others, in the year 1795, from the State of Georgia, the contract for which was made in the form of a bill passed by the Legislature of that State.

. . . The . . . count . . . alleges that, in consequence of these practices and of other causes, a subsequent Legislature passed an act annulling and rescinding the law under which the conveyance to the original grantees was made, declaring that conveyance void, and asserting the title of the State to the lands it contained. The count proceeds to recite at large, this rescinding act, and concludes with averring that, by reason of this act, the title of the said Peck in the premises was constitutionally and legally impaired and rendered null and void.

. . . The importance and the difficulty of the questions, presented by these pleadings are deeply felt by the Court. The lands in controversy vested absolutely in James Gunn and others, the original grantees, by the conveyance of the Governor, made in pursuance of an act of assembly to which the Legislature was fully competent. Being thus in full possession of the legal estate, they, for a valuable consideration, conveyed portions of the land to those who were willing to purchase. If the original transaction was infected with fraud, these purchasers did not participate in it, and had no notice of it. They were innocent. Yet the Legislature of Georgia has involved them in the fate of the first parties to the transaction, and, if the act be valid, has annihilated their rights also.

The Legislature of Georgia was a party to this transaction, and for a party to pronounce its own deed invalid, whatever cause may be assigned for its invalidity, must be considered as a mere act of power which must find its vindication in a train of reasoning not often heard in courts of justice.

But the real party, it is said, are the people, and when their agents are unfaithful, the acts of those agents cease to be obligatory.

It is, however, to be recollected that the people can act only by these agents, and that, while within the powers conferred on them, their acts must be considered as the acts of the people. If the agents be corrupt, others may be chosen, and, if their contracts be examinable, the common sentiment, as well as common usage of mankind, points out a mode by which this examination may be made, and their validity determined.

. . . If the Legislature felt itself absolved from those rules of property which are common to all the citizens of the United States, and from those principles of equity which are acknowledged in all our courts, its act is to be supported by its power alone, and the same power may devest any other individual of his lands if it shall be the will of the Legislature so to exert it.

The principle is this: that a legislature may, by its own act, devest the vested estate of any man whatever, for reasons which shall, by itself, be deemed sufficient.

. . . Is the power of the Legislature competent to the annihilation of such title, and to a resumption of the property thus held?

The principle asserted is that one Legislature is competent to repeal any act which a former legislature was competent to pass, and that one legislature cannot abridge the powers of a succeeding legislature.

The correctness of this principle, so far as respects general legislation, can never be controverted. But if an act be done under a law, a succeeding legislature cannot undo it.

When, then, a law is in its nature a contract, when absolute rights have vested under that contract, a repeal of the law cannot devest those rights; and the act of annulling them, if legitimate, is rendered so by a power applicable to the case of every individual in the community.

It may well be doubted whether the nature of society and of government does not prescribe some limits to the legislative power; and, if any be prescribed, where are they to be found if the property of an individual, fairly and honestly acquired, may be seized without compensation?

To the Legislature all legislative power is granted, but the question whether the act of transferring the property of an individual to the public be in the nature of the legislative power is well worthy of serious reflection.

It is the peculiar province of the legislature to prescribe general rules for the government of society; the application of those rules to individuals in society would seem to be the duty of other departments. How far the power of giving the law may involve every other power, in cases where the Constitution is silent, never has been, and perhaps never can be, definitely stated.

The validity of this rescinding act, then, might well be doubted, were Georgia a single sovereign power. But Georgia cannot be viewed as a single, unconnected, sovereign power, on whose legislature no other restrictions are imposed than may be found in its own Constitution. She is a part of a large empire; she is a member of the American Union; and that Union has a Constitution the supremacy of which all acknowledge, and which imposes limits to the legislatures of the several States which none claim a right to pass. The Constitution of the United States declares that no State shall pass any bill of attainder, ex post facto law, or law impairing the obligation of contracts.

Does the case now under consideration come within this prohibitory section of the Constitution?

In considering this very interesting question, we immediately ask ourselves what is a contract? Is a grant a contract?

A contract is a compact between two or more parties, and is either executory or executed. An executory contract is one in which a party binds himself to do, or not to do, a particular thing; such was the law under which the conveyance was made by the Governor. A contract executed is one in which the object of contract is performed, and this, says Blackstone, differs in nothing from a grant. The contract between Georgia and the purchasers was executed by the grant. A contract executed, as well as one which is executory, contains obligations binding on the parties. A grant, in its own nature, amounts to an extinguishment of the right of the grantor, and implies a contract not to reassert that right. A party is therefore always estopped by his own grant.

Since, then, in fact, a grant is a contract executed, the obligation of which still continues, and since the Constitution uses the general term "contract" without distinguishing between those which are executory and those which are executed, it must be construed to comprehend the latter as well as the former. A law annulling conveyances between individuals, and declaring that the grantors should stand seised of their former estates, notwithstanding those grants, would be as repugnant to the Constitution as a law discharging the vendors of property from the obligation of executing their contracts by conveyances. It would be strange if a contract to convey was secured by the Constitution, while an absolute conveyance remained unprotected.

If, under a fair construction the Constitution, grants are comprehended under the term "contracts," is a grant from the State excluded from the operation of the provision? Is the clause to be considered as inhibiting the State from impairing the obligation of contracts between two individuals, but as excluding from that inhibition contracts made with itself?

The words themselves contain no such distinction. They are general, and are applicable to contracts of every description. If contracts made with the State are to be exempted from their operation, the exception must arise from the character of the contracting party, not from the words which are employed.

The State legislatures can pass no ex post facto law. An ex post facto law is one which renders an act punishable in a manner in which it was not punishable when it was committed. Such a law may inflict penalties on the person, or may inflict pecuniary penalties which swell the public treasury. The legislature is then prohibited from passing a law by which a man's estate, or any part of it, shall be seized for a crime which was not declared by some previous law to render him liable to that punishment. Why, then, should violence be done to the natural meaning of words for the purpose of leaving to the legislature the power of seizing for public use the estate of an individual in the form of a law annulling the title by which he holds that estate? The Court can perceive no sufficient grounds for making this distinction. This rescinding act would have the effect of an ex post facto law.

The argument in favour of presuming an intention to except a case not excepted by the words of the Constitution is susceptible of some illustration from a principle originally ingrafted in that instrument, though no longer a part of it. The Constitution, as passed, gave the courts of the United States jurisdiction in suits brought against individual States. A State, then, which violated its own contract was suable in the courts of the United States for that violation. Would it have been a defence in such a suit to say that the State had passed a law absolving itself from the contract? It is scarcely to be conceived that such a defence could be set up. And yet, if a State is neither restrained by the general principles of our political institutions nor by the words of the Constitution from impairing the obligation of its own contracts, such a defence would be a valid one. This feature is no longer found in the Constitution, but it aids in the construction of those clauses with which it was originally associated.

It is, then, the unanimous opinion of the Court that, in this case, the estate having passed into the hands of a purchaser for a valuable consideration, without notice, the State of Georgia was restrained, either by general principles which are common to our free institutions or by the particular provisions of the Constitution of the United States, from passing a law whereby the estate of the plaintiff in the premises so purchased could be constitutionally and legally impaired and rendered null and void. Judgement affirmed with costs.

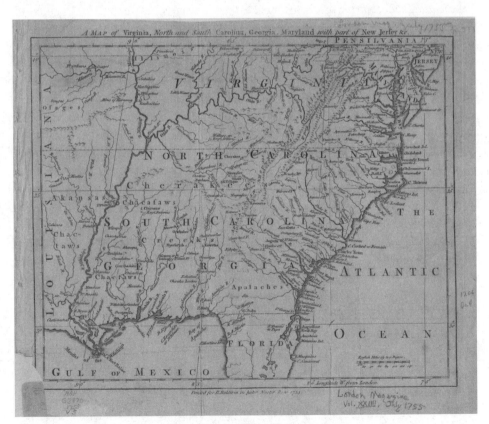

Courtesy of Hargrett Rare Book and Manuscript Library/University of Georgia Library

In Martin v. Hunter's Lessee, *the Supreme Court put an end to a dispute over land in Virginia, but also asserted the superiority of its rulings to those of state courts.*

MARTIN v. HUNTER'S LESSEE

14 U.S. 304 (1816)

Opinion: Story, joined by Duvall, Johnson, Livingston, Todd
Concurrence: Washington

Marbury v. Madison *declared the authority of the Supreme Court to review the constitutionality of federal laws. The Marshall Court extended its reasoning in* Marbury v. Madison *to establish judicial review of state laws as well in the landmark cases of* Martin v. Hunter's Lessee *and* Cohens v. Virginia.

Martin v. Hunter's Lessee *concerned a land dispute between the Commonwealth of Virginia and Denny Martin. Martin claimed the land as part of his inheritance from the British Lord Fairfax, and he argued that this inheritance was protected by a treaty between Britain and the United States. While the highest court of Virginia acknowledged that the U.S. treaty was superior to state law, it interpreted the treaty narrowly so that it did not prohibit the confiscation of Martin's property. On appeal, the U.S. Supreme Court held in Martin's favor that the confiscation was a violation of U.S. treaty obligations, and that, as the highest court in the land, its reading of the treaty trumped the Virginia court's interpretation. A central element of the Martin decision is its assertion that the Supreme Court can review state court rulings and has the final say on how to interpret federal law. In particular, at issue was the constitutionality of the 25th section of the Judiciary Act of 1789, which authorized the Supreme Court's jurisdiction in the case.*

As you read, consider whether the fact that these cases involve appeals from state—not federal—courts affects the Court's willingness to assert the power of judicial review. Should the Court's judicial review power be more deferential when reviewing state courts' interpretations of federal law within their territory?

MR. JUSTICE STORY *delivered the opinion of the Court.*

. . . The Constitution of the United States was ordained and established not by the States in their sovereign capacities, but emphatically, as the preamble of the Constitution declares, by "the people of the United States." There can be no doubt that it was competent to the people to invest the general government with all the powers which they might deem proper and necessary, to extend or restrain these powers according to their own good pleasure, and to give them a paramount and supreme authority. As little doubt can there be that the people had a right to prohibit to the States the exercise of any powers which were, in their judgment, incompatible with the objects of the general compact, to make the powers of the State governments, in given cases, subordinate to those of the nation, or to reserve to themselves those sovereign authorities which they might not choose to delegate to either. The Constitution was not, therefore, necessarily carved out of existing State sovereignties, nor a surrender of powers already existing in State institutions, for the powers of the States depend upon their own Constitutions, and the people of every State had the right to modify and restrain them according to their own views of the policy or principle. On the other hand, it is perfectly clear that the sovereign powers vested in the State governments by their respective Constitutions remained unaltered and unimpaired except so far as they were granted to the Government of the United States.

These deductions do not rest upon general reasoning, plain and obvious as they seem to be. They have been positively recognized by one of the articles in amendment of the Constitution, which declares that "The powers not delegated to the United States by the Constitution, nor prohibited by it to the States, are reserved to the States respectively, or to the people. . . ."

It was foreseen that, in the exercise of their ordinary jurisdiction, State courts would incidentally take cognizance of cases arising under the Constitution, the laws, and treaties of the United States. Yet to all these cases the judicial power, by the very terms of the Constitution, is to extend. It cannot extend by original jurisdiction if that was already rightfully and exclusively attached in the State courts, which (as has been already shown) may occur; it must therefore extend by appellate jurisdiction, or not at all. It would seem to follow that the appellate power of the United States must, in such cases, extend to State tribunals; and if in such cases, there is no reason why it should not equally attach upon all others within the purview of the Constitution.

It has been argued that such an appellate jurisdiction over State courts is inconsistent with the genius of our Governments, and the spirit of the Constitution. That the latter was never designed to act upon State sovereignties, but only upon the people, and that, if the power exists, it will materially impair the sovereignty of the States, and the independence of their courts. We cannot yield to the force of this reasoning; it assumes principles which we cannot admit, and draws conclusions to which we do not yield our assent. . . .

[The Constitution] is crowded with provisions which restrain or annul the sovereignty of the States in some of the highest branches of their prerogatives. The tenth section of the first article contains a long list of disabilities and prohibitions imposed upon the States. Surely, when such essential portions of State sovereignty are taken away or prohibited to be exercised, it cannot be correctly asserted that the Constitution does not act upon the States. The language of the Constitution is also imperative upon the States as to the performance of many duties. It is imperative upon the State legislatures to make laws prescribing the time, places, and manner of holding elections for senators and representatives, and for electors of President and Vice-President. And in these as well as some other cases, Congress have a right to revise, amend, or supersede the laws which may be passed by State legislatures. When therefore the States are stripped of some of the highest attributes of sovereignty, and the same are given to the United States; when the legislatures of the States are, in some respects, under the control of Congress, and in every case are, under the Constitution, bound by the paramount authority of the United States, it is certainly difficult to support the argument that the appellate power over the decisions of State courts is contrary to the genius of our institutions. The courts of the United States can, without question, revise the proceedings of the executive and legislative authorities of the States, and if they are found to be contrary to the Constitution, may declare them to be of no legal validity. Surely the exercise of the same right over judicial tribunals is not a higher or more dangerous act of sovereign power. . . .

On the whole, the Court are of opinion that the appellate power of the United States does extend to cases pending in the State courts, and that the 25th section of the judiciary act, which authorizes the exercise of this jurisdiction in the specified cases by a writ of error, is supported by the letter and spirit of the Constitution. We find no clause in that instrument which limits this power, and we dare not interpose a limitation where the people have not been disposed to create one. . . .

It is the opinion of the whole Court that the judgment of the Court of Appeals of Virginia, rendered on the mandate in this cause, be reversed, and the judgment of the District Court, held at Winchester, be, and the same is hereby, affirmed.

TRUSTEES OF DARTMOUTH COLLEGE v. WOODWARD
17 U.S. (4 Wheat.) 518 (1819)

Opinion: Marshall, joined by Johnson, Livingston
Concurrence: Washington, joined by Livingston
Concurrence: Story, joined by Livingston
Dissent: Duvall

Like Fletcher v. Peck, *this early act of judicial review concerned the Contracts Clause of the Constitution, which prohibits states from passing laws "impairing the obligation of contracts." When the trustees of Dartmouth College removed that college's president, the state legislature tried to make the college public in the hopes of reinstating him. The Court asked whether such an act violated the Contracts Clause. The case serves as an early example of the competition between judicial authority and the authority of state legislatures. As in* Fletcher v. Peck, *the narrower constitutional question concerns the degree to which the Constitution protects interests in private property from the control of state legislatures. Specifically, the Court investigates the entitlements of a private corporation to be protected from the state. In reading this case, you should focus on the distinct question of whether the Supreme Court has a role in enforcing the relationship between private ownership and the authority of state legislatures. Even if the Court is correct about the meaning of*

the Contracts Clause, should it attempt to enforce its interpretation over the objection of a state's legislature?

MR. CHIEF JUSTICE MARSHALL *delivered the opinion of the Court.*

This is an action of trover, brought by the Trustees of Dartmouth College against William H. Woodward, in the State court of New Hampshire, for the book of records, corporate seal, and other corporate property, to which the plaintiffs allege themselves to be entitled.

A special verdict, after setting out the rights of the parties, finds for the defendant, if certain acts of the Legislature of New Hampshire, passed on the 27th of June, and on the 18th of December 1816, be valid, and binding on the Trustees, without their assent, and not repugnant to the Constitution of the United States; otherwise, it finds for the plaintiffs.

The Superior Court of judicature of New Hampshire rendered a judgment upon this verdict for the defendant, which judgment has been brought before this court by writ of error. The single question now to be considered is do the acts to which the verdict refers violate the Constitution of the United States?

This court can be insensible neither to the magnitude nor delicacy of this question. The validity of a legislative act is to be examined; and the opinion of the highest law tribunal of a State is to be revised—an opinion which carries with it intrinsic evidence of the diligence, of the ability, and the integrity, with which it was formed. On more than one occasion, this Court has expressed the cautious circumspection with which it approaches the consideration of such questions, and has declared that in no doubtful case would it pronounce a legislative act to be contrary to the Constitution. But the American people have said in the Constitution of the United States that "no State shall pass any bill of attainder, ex post facto law, or law impairing the obligation of contracts." In the same instrument, they have also said, "that the judicial power shall extend to all cases in law and equity arising under the Constitution." On the judges of this Court, then, is imposed the high and solemn duty of protecting, from even legislative violation, those contracts which the Constitution of our country has placed beyond legislative control; and however irksome the task may be, this is a duty from which we dare not shrink.

. . . The defendant claims under three acts of the Legislature of New Hampshire, the most material of which was passed on the 27th of June, 1816, and is entitled "An act to amend the charter, and enlarge and improve the corporation of Dartmouth College." . . . The majority of the Trustees of the college have refused to accept this amended charter, and have brought this suit for the corporate property, which is in possession of a person holding by virtue of the acts which have been stated.

It can require no argument to prove that the circumstances of this case constitute a contract. . . . The points for consideration are, 1. Is this contract protected by the Constitution of the United States? 2. Is it impaired by the acts under which the defendant holds?

. . . This is plainly a contract to which the donors, the Trustees, and the Crown (to whose rights and obligations New Hampshire succeeds) were the original parties. . . . It is, then, a contract within the letter of the Constitution, and within its spirit also, unless the fact that the property is invested by the donors in Trustees for the promotion of religion and education, for the benefit of persons who are perpetually changing, though the objects remain the same, shall create a particular exception taking this case out of the prohibition contained in the Constitution.

It is more than possible that the preservation of rights of this description was not particularly in the view of the framers of the Constitution when the clause under consideration was introduced into that instrument. It is probable that interferences of more frequent occurrence, to which the temptation was stronger, and of which the mischief was more extensive, constituted the great motive for imposing this restriction on the State legislatures. But although a particular and a rare case may not, in itself, be of sufficient magnitude to induce a rule, yet it must be governed by the rule, when established, unless some plain and strong reason for excluding it can be given. It is not enough to say that this particular case was not in the mind of the convention when the article was framed, nor of the American people when it was adopted. It is necessary to go further and to say that, had this particular case been suggested, the language would have been so varied as to exclude it, or it would have been made a special exception. The case, being within the words of the rule, must be within its operation likewise, unless there be something in the literal construction so obviously absurd or mischievous or repugnant to the general spirit of the instrument as to justify those who expound the Constitution in making it an exception.

On what safe and intelligible ground can this exception stand? There is no expression in the Constitution, no sentiment delivered by its contemporaneous expounders, which would justify us in making it. In the absence of all authority of this kind, is there in the nature and reason of the case itself that which would sustain a construction of the Constitution not warranted by its words? Are contracts of this description of a character to excite so little interest that we must exclude them from the provisions of the Constitution as being unworthy of the attention of those who framed the instrument? Or does public policy so imperiously demand their remaining exposed to legislative alteration as to compel us, or rather permit us, to say that these words, which were introduced to give stability to contracts and which in their plain import comprehend this contract, must yet be so construed as to exclude it?

Almost all eleemosynary corporations, those which are created for the promotion of religion, of charity, or of education, are of the same character. The law of this case is the law of all. In every literary or charitable institution, unless the objects of the bounty be themselves incorporated, the whole legal interest is in Trustees, and can be asserted only by them. The donors, or claimants of the bounty, if they can appear in Court at all, can appear only to complain of the Trustees. In all other situations, they are identified with, and personated by, the Trustees, and their rights are to be defended and maintained by them. . . . Are they of so little estimation in the United States that contracts for their benefit must be excluded from the protection of words which in their natural import include them? Or do such contracts so necessarily require new modeling by the authority of the legislature that the ordinary rules of construction must be disregarded in order to leave them exposed to legislative alteration?

All feel that these objects are not deemed unimportant in the United States. The interest which this case has excited proves that they are not. The framers of the Constitution did not deem them unworthy of its care and protection. They have, though in a different mode, manifested their respect for science by reserving to the government of the Union the power "to promote the progress of science and useful arts by securing for limited times, to authors and inventors, the exclusive right to their respective writings and discoveries."

They have so far withdrawn science and the useful arts from the action of the State governments. Why then should they be supposed so regardless of contracts made for the advancement of literature as to intend to exclude them from provisions, made for the security of ordinary contracts between man and man? No reason for making this supposition is perceived.

The motives suggested at the bar grow out of the original appointment of the Trustees, which is supposed to have been in a spirit hostile to the genius of our government, and the presumption that, if allowed to continue themselves, they now are, and must remain forever, what they originally were. Hence is inferred the necessity of applying to this corporation, and to other similar corporations, the correcting and improving hand of the legislature.

The opinion of the Court, after mature deliberation, is that this is a contract the obligation of which cannot be impaired without violating the Constitution of the United States. This opinion appears to us to be equally supported by reason and by the former decisions of this Court.

2. We next proceed to the inquiry whether its obligation has been impaired

by those acts of the Legislature of New Hampshire to which the special verdict refers.

. . . It has been already stated that the act "to amend the charter, and enlarge and improve the corporation of Dartmouth College" increases the number of Trustees to twenty-one, gives the appointment of the additional members to the executive of the State, and creates a Board of Overseers, to consist of twenty-five persons, of whom twenty-one are also appointed by the Executive of New Hampshire, who have power to inspect and control the most important acts of the Trustees.

According to the tenor of the charter, then, the Trustees might, without impropriety, appoint a President and other professors from their own body. This is a power not entirely unconnected with an interest. Even if the proposition of the counsel for the defendant were sustained, if it were admitted that those contracts only are protected by the Constitution,

a beneficial interest in which is vested in the party, who appears in Court to assert that interest, yet it is by no means clear that the Trustees of Dartmouth College have no beneficial interest in themselves. But the Court has deemed it unnecessary to investigate this particular point, being of opinion on general principles that, in these private eleemosynary institutions, the body corporate, as possessing the whole legal and equitable interest and completely representing the donors for the purpose of executing the trust, has rights which are protected by the Constitution.

It results from this opinion that the acts of the Legislature of New Hampshire which are stated in the special verdict found in this cause are repugnant to the Constitution of the United States, and that the judgment on this special verdict ought to have been for the plaintiffs. The judgment of the State Court must, therefore, be reversed.

COHENS v. VIRGINIA

19 U.S. 264 (1821)

Opinion: Marshall, joined by Duvall, Johnson, Livingston, Story, Todd

In this case, two brothers violated state law by selling District of Columbia lottery tickets in Virginia. The brothers argued that, because Congress had authorized the sale of those tickets, their arrest was an unconstitutional violation of the Supremacy Clause found in Article VI, which reads, "This Constitution, and the Laws of the United States which shall be made in Pursuance thereof; and all Treaties made, or which shall be made, under the Authority of the United States, shall be the supreme Law of the Land; and the Judges in every State shall be bound thereby, any Thing in the Constitution or Laws of any State to the Contrary notwithstanding." Again, the Supreme Court articulated its power to review state court decisions. Although the Court upheld the defendants' convictions, it rejected the Virginia court's claim that it could not review the constitutionality of state criminal proceedings.

MR. CHIEF JUSTICE MARSHALL *delivered the opinion of the Court.*

The American States, as well as the American people, have believed a close and firm Union to be essential to their liberty and to their happiness. They have been taught by experience that this Union cannot exist without a government for the whole, and they have been taught by the same experience that this government would be a mere shadow, that must disappoint all their hopes, unless invested with large portions of that sovereignty which belongs to independent States. Under the influence of this opinion, and thus instructed by experience, the American people, in the conventions of their respective States, adopted the present Constitution.

If it could be doubted whether, from its nature, it were not supreme in all cases where it is empowered to act, that doubt would be removed by the declaration that "this Constitution, and the laws of the United States, which shall be made in pursuance thereof, and all treaties made, or which shall be made, under the authority of the United States, shall be the supreme law of the land; and the judges in every State shall be bound thereby; any thing in the Constitution or laws of any State to the contrary notwithstanding."

This is the authoritative language of the American people, and, if gentlemen please, of the American States. It marks, with lines too strong to be mistaken the characteristic distinction between the government of the Union and those of the States. The general government, though limited as to its objects, is supreme with respect to those objects. This principle is a part of the Constitution, and if there be any who deny its necessity, none can deny its authority.

The powers of the Union, on the great subjects of war, peace, and commerce, and on many others, are in themselves limitations of the sovereignty of the States; but, in addition to these, the sovereignty of the States is surrendered in many instances where the surrender can only operate to the benefit of the people, and where, perhaps, no other power is conferred on Congress than a conservative power to maintain the principles established in the Constitution. The maintenance of these principles in their purity is certainly among the great duties of the government. One of the instruments by which this duty may be peaceably performed is the judicial department. It is authorized to decide all cases of every description arising under the Constitution or laws of the United States. From this general grant of jurisdiction, no exception is made of those cases in which a State may be a party. When we consider the situation of the government of the Union and of a State in relation to each other; the nature of our Constitution; the subordination of the State governments to that Constitution; the great purpose for which jurisdiction over all cases arising under the Constitution and laws of the United States is confided to the judicial department; are we at liberty to insert in this general grant an exception of those cases in which a State may be a party? Will the spirit of the Constitution justify this attempt to control its words? We think it will not. We think a case arising under the Constitution or laws of the United States is cognizable in the Courts of the Union whoever may be the parties to that case.

Box 1-2   **Frequency of the Judicial Review Power**

In future chapters we will see that many of the significant instances of judicial review in the twentieth century concerned matters of individual rights, but as the cases in this chapter suggest, judicial review was originally invoked primarily in an attempt to define the proper scope of governmental powers. Another significant difference between judicial review in its early history and its later incarnations is the frequency of its use. In the twentieth century, the power was invoked much more frequently than in the nineteenth century. Does this suggest the impact of the decision in *Marbury v. Madison* was felt more strongly in the twentieth century than at the time it was decided? Figure 1.2 illustrates the number of laws struck down in the nineteenth and twentieth centuries, both state and federal, as well as the total number of laws (including local ordinances) invalidated by the Court. As shown in the graph, in the nineteenth century, judicial review was primarily directed against state governments. In the twentieth century, as the Court grew increasingly confident in striking down federal legislation, the number of invalidated state laws skyrocketed as well.

Figure 1.2. Cases Ruling Laws Unconstitutional

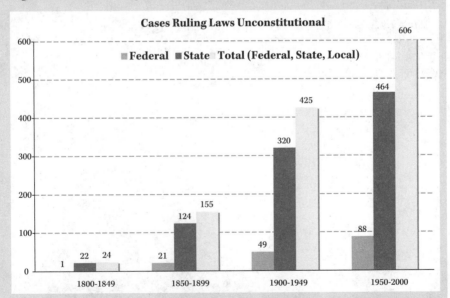

Data from *Analysis and Interpretation of the Constitution, Annotations of Cases Decided by the Supreme Court of the United States*, Senate Document No. 108-17, 2002 Edition. Available at *http://www. gpoaccess.gov/constitution/*.

Figure 1.3 paints a more fine-grained picture of the history of judicial review. Prior to the Civil War, the Supreme Court would occasionally strike down state laws, and it only invalidated two federal statutes: the Judiciary Act of 1789 in *Marbury v. Madison*, and the Missouri Compromise in the notorious case of *Dred Scott v. Sandford* (see Chapter 9). During the Reconstruction Era, the Court increasingly asserted its power, reacting against legislation ushered in by the overwhelmingly Republican Congress and enforcing the rights in the new Fourteenth Amendment against the states (although we will learn in Chapter 9 that the courts were little help to African Americans during this time). By the turn of the century, the Court was leaning heavily on the Fourteenth Amendment to protect economic liberty, striking down a bevy of progressive labor regulations at the state level. The Court also sought to obstruct President Franklin D. Roosevelt's first New Deal program, but eventually it backed down, ushering in a period of deference to democratically enacted law. Chief Justice Earl Warren's tenure during the 1960s witnessed new heights in the exercise of judicial review, expanding constitutional protections of individual rights. At the close of the twentieth century, a turn towards federalism led to a decline in the number of state statutes overturned, even as the amount of federal legislation invalidated increased.

Figure 1.3. Cases Ruling Laws Unconstitutional by 12-Year Period

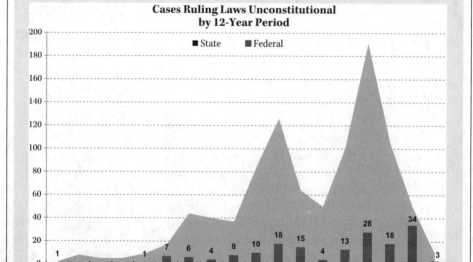

Data from *Analysis and Interpretation of the Constitution, Annotations of Cases Decided by the Supreme Court of the United States*, Senate Document No. 108-17, 2002 Edition, and 2008 Supplement. Available at *http://www.gpoaccess.gov/constitution/*.

SYNTHESIS QUESTIONS FOR FURTHER DISCUSSION: CHAPTER 1 SECTION A

1. The power of the Supreme Court to strike down federal laws as unconstitutional does not appear in the text of the Constitution itself. Does this fact give weight to Alexander Bickel's concern about whether the Court, an unelected body, should have the power to strike down laws passed by elected officials in a nation that considers itself democratic? Both Chief Justice John Marshall, in his opinion in *Marbury v. Madison*, and Alexander Hamilton, in *The Federalist*, attempt to answer this challenge by appeal to the idea of the rule of law itself. The Court's authority, they argue, derives from its role in interpreting law. Given that the Constitution is law, they claim, the Court should interpret it. Is this a persuasive argument for the Court's judicial review power?

    In evaluating the arguments of Chief Justice Marshall and Hamilton in favor of the Court's review power, it might be helpful to consider the following questions:

    a. Does the lack of constitutional text authorizing judicial review delegitimize this practice? Does the fact that *The Federalist*, including our reading from Hamilton, played a part in convincing citizens to ratify the Constitution mean that these papers themselves have a particular kind of constitutional weight? Note that this question also raises larger issues about the role of constitutional text in constitutional interpretation, issues pursued in depth in Chapter 2.

    b. Is there anything about the training of justices of the Supreme Court that gives them inherent authority over constitutional interpretation? For instance, although legal training is not required by the Constitution for appointment to the Court, does it matter that judges have been trained in law? Given that the ranks of top lawyers do not usually accurately reflect the population as a whole, is there an elitist element in the Court's decisions? Does legal training equip lawyers who are appointed to the Court with a set of skills that make the justices uniquely positioned to interpret the Constitution?

    c. The Court is appointed by the president in consultation with the Senate. Do the democratic credentials of these two bodies give the Court a further claim to authority?

2. Bickel challenges the Court's power of judicial review, and others have argued further that this power inheres also in the other branches of government. Thomas Jefferson's challenge to Hamilton is commonly seen as the original view of the theory of constitutional interpretation now known as departmentalism. In his letter, Jefferson stresses that the rights enshrined in the Constitution have a meaning independent of any particular institutional actor's interpretation. Why then, Jefferson asks, should

any one body, even the Supreme Court, have a monopoly on constitutional interpretation? In particular, Jefferson is concerned with the potential fallibility of the Court. If we assume that the Court is the final arbiter of the Constitution, might that inhibit citizens from recognizing its mistakes? It might be interesting to consider how Hamilton and Chief Justice Marshall would have responded to this claim. Are there any reasons to suggest that the Supreme Court might make fewer mistakes in matters of constitutional interpretation than elected bodies?

3. While the letter from Jefferson to Judge Spencer Roane emphasizes the role of other branches of the federal government in constitutional interpretation, Jefferson also held the view that states should have a role in this process. In particular, when the Federalist President John Adams and Congress crafted the Alien and Sedition Acts, which limited the free speech rights of political dissidents, Jefferson and James Madison drafted the Kentucky and Virginia resolutions declaring these acts unconstitutional. The Supreme Court was notably silent on the constitutionality of the Alien and Sedition Acts, and after its failure to speak, Jefferson and Madison turned to state legislatures in an attempt to declare them unconstitutional. Is there reason to believe, given the example of the Alien and Sedition Acts, that it is beneficial to give the states, in addition to the Court, a role in constitutional interpretation? What problems might accompany a departmentalist theory that allows for constitutional interpretation among the various branches of government? What problems might accompany a theory that provides a role for the states in interpreting the ultimate meaning of the Constitution? In answering these questions, consider the Court opinions you read in which the Supreme Court reviewed the constitutionality of state as opposed to federal law.

4. Brutus's arguments against ratification tend to stress why the Court will inevitably become an unchecked power that will fail to respect the interests of citizens. In contrast to Hamilton's defense of the Court and its review power, does Jefferson's notion of departmentalism offer a different retort to Brutus? What might Jefferson say about Brutus's contentions about the power of the Court under Article III, including his contention that the Court will be unchecked because justices are appointed for life?

5. In *Dartmouth College v. Woodward*, you saw the Supreme Court invalidate an act by a state legislature attempting to turn the institution from a private to a public entity. Are there any particular problems for democratic self-government that are raised when the Court strikes down state as opposed to federal law? Consider whether this case challenges the Court's democratic credentials with respect to our readings from Bickel and Brutus.

B. FROM JUDICIAL REVIEW TO JUDICIAL SUPREMACY

In the previous section, we examined historical justifications for the Court's review power. At this point in American history, this power of the Supreme Court is well established and widely accepted. Yet, when it comes to the question of whether the Court *should* have this power, there is controversy among scholars. Not all contemporary polities, after all, have judicial review of legislation. In contrast to our system, some systems retain "legislative supremacy" in which the legislature, not the court, has the final word about review of legislation. In this section, we will see that the Supreme Court itself has now declared in *Boerne v. Flores* that it not only has the power of judicial review but that its word is the final, decisive interpretation of the Constitution. This view is widely known as "judicial supremacy." Our readings begin with a look at the Court's contemporary judicial review power and examine its legitimacy, or lack thereof.

Whereas the previous section grounded the question of judicial authority in debates that took place during the Founding, this section examines the contemporary extension of this controversy.

We begin with a reading by U.S. Supreme Court Justice Stephen Breyer, in which he tackles the problem of the Court's democratic nature. For Justice Breyer, the counter-majoritarian difficulty should be answered not by looking beyond democracy but rather by rethinking the meaning of democracy. Justice Breyer rejects the idea that democracy is brute majoritarianism. Instead, he focuses on the ways in which the Supreme Court can bring about results that themselves enhance democracy. Whereas Alexander Bickel had seen the Court as posing a threat to democracy, Breyer argues that there is in fact a role for the Supreme Court in promoting what he refers to as the "active liberty" of self-government.

Ronald Dworkin extends Justice Breyer's argument that the Court has a fundamentally democratic purpose. He argues that when the Court serves the goals of democracy by protecting rights, self-government suffers no loss. For instance, he argues that the decision by the Court to strike down an anti-flag burning law in Texas was not undemocratic because the right of free speech was protected even though the Court was forced to strike down a decision in which many had participated through the democratic process. You might also think about Dworkin's framework when reading *Cooper v. Aaron*, a case in which there was massive resistance to the Supreme Court's desegregation order by the people of Arkansas. It is clear that both Justice Breyer and Dworkin think that there is a strong role for judicial review in a democracy. But does either or both of them defend judicial supremacy, the notion that the Court's role is final? Does either of these thinkers leave any role for constitutional interpretation by the other branches, the "departmentalism" urged by Thomas Jefferson in the previous section? In examining the possible contemporary relevance of departmentalism, it is also helpful to consider instances where the Court refuses to even hear a dispute that concerns the other branches. In *Nixon v. United States*, the Court employed its "political question" doctrine, according to which it does not hear some disputes on the grounds that they are better resolved by the political, elected branches of government. We will consider whether this doctrine, which is clearly an instance of judicial restraint, is a form of departmentalism. (We introduce the political question doctrine here, but we also explore it further in Chapter 4.)

Whereas Justice Breyer and Dworkin are among the most prominent contemporary defenders of judicial review, Larry Kramer and Jeremy Waldron are among its greatest critics. Kramer in particular modernizes Jefferson's classic worry that judicial review by the Supreme Court could turn into judicial supremacy. Kramer argues that many of the Court's decisions in recent years have been a power grab in which the democratic process has been usurped by a few powerful individuals. In its *Boerne v. Flores* decision, which we excerpt here, the Supreme Court declared itself the sole authority in determining the meaning of the Constitution and rejected Congress's own attempt to correct the Court's interpretive framework. Indeed, Kramer goes so far as to claim that the Court's intervention in the 2000 election dispute between candidates George Bush and Al Gore is emblematic of its power grab. The Court is no mere interpreter of the Constitution, according to Kramer; rather, it has usurped the power of the democratic process in a way that verges upon tyranny.

Kramer does not dispute the Court's judicial review power, long established as part of the American tradition. Rather, he questions whether the Court has an exclusive right to interpret the Constitution, as it seems to suggest in several of its decisions. On a view of judicial supremacy, perhaps best exemplified by the *Boerne v. Flores* case, the Court's interpretation of the meaning of the Constitution cannot be corrected by any of the other branches, including direct attempts by Congress to reverse Supreme Court decisions by statute as opposed to constitutional amendment. One problem with an understanding of the Court as a supreme interpreter is that it seems to suggest that even when the Court interprets the Constitution in a way that is flawed (think, for instance, of *Plessy v. Ferguson*, establishing the principle that segregation is consistent with the Equal Protection Clause of the Fourteenth Amendment), its decisions still must be respected as final and authoritative interpretations. Such a view leaves no room for constitutional interpretation by either democratically elected branches or citizens. As you read through this chapter, consider whether Kramer's criticisms of judicial supremacy are correct.

Waldron, in contrast to any of the other thinkers we examine in this chapter, presents a comprehensive critique of judicial review in its entirety. Going further than Kramer, Waldron is with Bickel in thinking that the power of judicial review in the hands of the Court should be understood as fundamentally undemocratic. Rejecting the theories of democracy posited by Justice Breyer and Dworkin, as well as that of Alexander Hamilton, Waldron claims that democracy is best understood as majority rule. Moreover, unlike Bickel, he believes that there is no justification for overturning the people's power to decide. Like many other scholars that we have examined in this section, Waldron is concerned with the protection of rights. Because citizens disagree about the content of rights, Waldron claims, the power to determine such rights is best left to the legislature.

Our case selection includes two of the most central controversies in the modern practice of judicial review, *Boerne v. Flores* and *Bush v. Gore*. The cases are notable because in both the Court asserts power over other branches of government, thus clearly raising the specter of judicial supremacy. In reading *Boerne v. Flores* you will enter into one of the clearest conflicts between Congress and the Supreme Court over the meaning of the Constitution. As you will see, in this case Congress attempted to correct what it regarded as a mistaken Supreme Court interpretation of the First Amendment's Free Exercise Clause. While we will study this clause, as well as other nuances of the case, in greater depth in Chapter 6, here we ask whether Congress can correct the Court's interpretation of a fundamental right.

Bush v. Gore will likely be remembered as one of the Court's most controversial cases of all time. As was the case in *Marbury v. Madison*, *Bush v. Gore* raised potential issues of partisanship. Ultimately, the question the Court faced was whether it would, in effect, end the controversy over the 2000 election. As you will see, the legal issues in the case concern the Equal Protection Clause of the Fourteenth Amendment and the issue about the requirements of the Court's Article III powers. But as you read it, think (with *Marbury v. Madison* in mind) about whether the Court should have taken the case or issued a ruling with such a drastic consequence. Did the Court here rest its argument on an assumption of judicial supremacy?

Although this chapter contains many examples of what might be considered judicial supremacy as well as readings charging the Court with usurping the authority of the other branches, we also include here two cases that illustrate limits on the power of the contemporary Court. In *United States v. Nixon*, we examine the political question doctrine, which limits the power of the Court to overturn decisions that the Constitution leaves to other branches. We also examine, in *Lujan v. Defenders of Wildlife*, the "standing doctrine" and the "case or controversy" requirement as examples of procedural limits on the Court. As we will see, the Court has limitations on its ability to initiate policy that the executive and the legislative branches do not.

Justice Stephen Breyer

JUDICIAL REVIEW: A PRACTICING JUDGE'S PERSPECTIVE

19 Oxford J. Legal Stud. 153 (1999)

My description will try to help you evaluate one important criticism of "independent judicial review" by which I mean the grant of legal authority to judges to set aside statutes upon the ground that they violate provisions of a written constitution. Such a system, says the criticism, substitutes for the views of legislators the views of judges. The judges are unelected, they interpret highly abstract constitutional language, e.g. the word "liberty," and they work in an ivory tower. The results are undemocratic, subjective, and impractical.

At the outset let me remind you of several features of our Supreme Court and our Constitution, with which many of you are already familiar. I do so because of their relevance to the later discussion. First, the Court's membership reflects a diversity of backgrounds and points of view. Vacancies arise infrequently because a President must appoint, and the Senate confirm, each of its nine members (currently seven men, two women) "for life." American judges enter their judicial career typically in mid-life after experience elsewhere. Eight of the present justices have had previous judicial experience in lower courts; and, before that, six had experience as lawyers in government; four in private practice; four as law professors. Republican Presidents appointed seven of us; a Democratic President, two. Length of term and the appointment process tend to guarantee diversity of constitutional views.

Second, the Court's role in judicial decision-making is limited. Much of our work involves the resolution of lower court conflicts about the interpretation of federal law. That law—the federal Constitution, congressional statutes, federal agency action—is itself limited, because the 50 states, not the federal government, are responsible for much of American law, including family law, property law, contract law, tort law, most criminal law, and most other commercial law. Perhaps 95 per cent or more of all judicial proceedings take place in state courts. Moreover, within the area of federal law, we hear only a handful of cases. We receive about 7600 requests for hearings each year; we grant and decide fewer than 100. (Overall, there may be more than 10 million court cases brought annually in the USA.)

Third, our decisions, like those of Supreme, or Constitutional, Courts in other nations have considerable legal and practical significance. In part that is because, like the House of Lords, the cases we take, by definition, are those that present open legal issues, with strong arguments on both sides. In part it is because most of our decisions, as a practical matter, are final. In part it is because our history includes certain decisions, such as those involving desegregation or electoral reapportionment, that have changed the life of our nation. I shall return to the way in which the finality of our decisions can affect what we do. For the moment, simply keep in mind the fact that our Court is comprised of a small number of men and women of diverse views and backgrounds, appointed for life, who decide a small number of cases involving federal law, and whose decisions are usually final and frequently have considerable practical significance.

Let me also remind you of several relevant features of our Constitution. The document, adopted in 1789 and importantly amended after our 19th century Civil War, established the federal government and, in doing so, sets forth a framework for democratic government. It initially included: an explicit delegation of powers to the federal government (reserving all others to the states); an allocation of governmental powers (among three branches of federal government); protections of certain liberties (such as free speech, press, and religion, and against unreasonable searches and seizures) from federal interference; and guarantees of fair procedures for those threatened with criminal prosecution. The Civil War amendments extended the scope of these protections by guaranteeing them against infringement by state governments; and it added guarantees to individual citizens of fair, and equal, treatment by all government.

For present purposes it is important also to remember that: the document is brief—seven Articles, 27 Amendments. Often its language is open ended, e.g. "no state shall . . . deprive any person of life, liberty, or property, without due process of law; nor deny to any person . . . the equal protection of the laws." It is difficult to amend—amendment ordinarily requiring the affirmative vote of two-thirds of each house of Congress plus approval by three-quarters of the states (or a special "convention"). And it is not simply a set of aspirations, but a legal document setting forth rules with legal force.

Judicial interpretations of the Constitution have binding legal force, not subject to legislative override (except through constitutional amendment). The judicial power to set aside laws, including congressional statutes, as unconstitutional rests upon a judicial interpretation of the Constitution, which the Court made nearly 200 years ago, in *Marbury v. Madison*. The Court's authority to set aside unconstitutional laws is now accepted. The public defers to nearly all judicial interpretations of the document, even when those interpretations are unpopular, controversial, and of debatable merit.

To summarize: the framework-creating document is brief, general, permanent, and effective.

Let me now describe the "democratic anomaly," a matter central to how citizens, constitutional scholars, and judges think about constitutional decision-making, and which appears frequently as the subject of public and academic constitutional debate. The question at the heart of the anomaly is why a democracy—a political system based on representation and accountability—should entrust the final, or near final, making of such highly significant decisions to judges—unelected, independent, and insulated from the direct impact of public opinion.

I can narrow the anomaly by pointing out that all government, to achieve flexibility, must involve the exercise of delegated authority. Given delegation, enacted law will not necessarily reflect the views of a particular electorate; nor will law that takes the form of treaties, regulations, and administrative rulings necessarily reflect the views of a particular legislature. Democracies also delegate authority to judges—and properly so. Who would want to convict a person accused of murder on the basis of a popular vote? Nor could one reasonably advocate a system of civil law that instantly changed to reflect the views of a popular majority, for such law would lack the stability that any form of government under law requires. For that matter, any actual democracy contains many non-majoritarian institutions (e.g. a Senate) and procedures (e.g. seniority).

I can narrow the anomaly further by pointing out that many non-constitutional judicial decisions are already, in a sense, immune from later legislative revision. As a practical matter, lack of legislative time or interest or the popularity of a judicial decision, means that the legislature usually will not overturn a judge's statutory decision despite its legal power to do so. . . .

I may have narrowed the anomaly, but it still exists. In fact, one could claim that the very systems just described still embody that anomaly to the extent that they offer special protection from the popular will. In any event, our own system does not permit a legislative override (except through amendment). Can we "resolve" the remaining "democratic" anomaly by admitting it and then trying to justify it? Let me remind you of several classic efforts to do so.

Some have pointed out, for example, that many, though not all, of the basic rights that our Constitution protects are themselves important preconditions of a well-functioning democratic system of government. The guarantee of free speech, for example, by helping to secure citizens' access to even the most bizarre points of view assures voters the opportunity to exercise an informed democratic choice. Many "equal protection" guarantees mean that government will not improperly weigh the voice of one citizen more heavily than that of another.

Others have argued that the American Constitution, with its allocation of powers among many different governmental units, requires a "referee" (i.e. the courts) to prevent overreaching. Still others say that "democracy" simply is, not only majority rule, but also the protection of minority rights—a method, for example, of preventing the "people drunk" from undoing the will of the "people sober." Given the 20th century's history of governments unable to withstand popular demands for mistreatment of minorities and the abandonment of democracy, one might see judicial review as a kind of institutional ballast, helping to stabilize the kind of democracy that so many nations today enjoy.

Still, there remains much to reconcile with "majoritarian" democracy, for example, certain constitutional protections such as the Eighth Amendment's prohibition of "cruel and unusual punishments," or the Fourteenth Amendment's protection of certain aspects of family life that fall within the scope of the word "liberty." Nor can one easily justify, as necessary to the preservation of that democracy, the independent determination by judges of related claims, based either upon constitutional words such as "liberty" (e.g. the claim of a constitutionally protected "right to die") or upon the words in a Court opinion interpreting those words (such as a claim about the constitutionally required implementation of a court decree forbidding certain kinds of racial discrimination). And, of course, in a sense, once one feels it necessary to justify the "anomaly," one has thereby admitted the problem.

Thus, I should like to return to narrowing: our judiciary, aware of the anomaly, tries to minimize its impact through the use of rules, standards or canons that recognize the problem. For example, the standard of constitutionality applicable to statutes focuses, not on the statute's wisdom, but on its constitutionality, which often concerns the statute's "rationality"; the rule (stare decisis) for determining when to overrule a previous case is less strict in constitutional than in statutory matters; a canon of interpretation requires courts to try to save a statute by interpreting it in a way that will avoid a serious constitutional problem. There are others. I also believe it important to note that judges, aware of the anomaly, often seek through their interpretive attitude to reflect the constitutionally vested primacy of legislative decision-making, even in cases that do not fall squarely within an interpretive canon.

But however much I may narrow, ultimately there remains an important set of cases, for example, cases involving privacy or religious freedom, that can require us, when interpreting or applying the Constitution, directly to frustrate the legislature's express objective. I turn to that set of cases—those in which there is an inevitable tension between the will of the elected legislature and the work of the unelected judge. Does judicial decision-making there mean subjective, impractical decision-making—or, to return to Lord Copper, up to what point?

You are aware that language, history, and precedent will answer many constitutional questions. Moreover, some fine constitutional judges have believed that, even in more difficult cases, a single factor, such as the Constitution's language, or its history, can itself significantly constrain subjective decision-making. For myself, however, I cannot find a touchstone in any such single factor. Instead, I believe that a realistic appraisal of subjectivity must take account of certain constraints, related to each other, which I shall describe in five parts and follow with an example.

First, judges of a constitutional court, like all judges, find constraints in the "rules," canons, principles, and institutional understandings of the judicial enterprise itself. Judge Learned Hand answered the charge of "subjectivity" by pointing to "those books." I assume he meant metaphorically to include (in common law matters) the common law tradition, and (in statutory matters) language, structure, history, precedent, purpose, and consequences—all of which permit a judge to find a "better" and a "worse" answer even to the most difficult of statutory questions, even where language (for example, antitrust law's "contract, combination or conspiracy in restraint of trade") is open-ended.

Second, as is true of any craft, experience both teaches and constrains its practitioners. And constitutional court judges do develop a kind of special experience. Our work differs in kind from most trial court work, for unlike trial courts we do not determine facts or apply previously elaborated law to those facts. It also differs in kind from some of the work of the courts of appeals, in that we do not review for error the trial court's application of previously elaborated law to the facts of a particular case. As Chief Justice Taft pointed out in 1921, "Litigants . . . have [already] had two chances." Rather we most frequently hear and decide cases that involve conflicts of interpretation

among the lower courts, thereby producing uniform national law. That "law interpreting" work resembles that of the courts of appeals when it involves statutes. Our work does not resemble theirs when we interpret the Constitution. Since all federal and state courts have the power to interpret the Constitution, the difference is one of degree, not kind. But it is one of considerable degree, for open questions of constitutional law in our Court become a steady diet. And the difference in degree is important in that the experience, the steadiness, and diversity of a constitutional diet, naturally lead a judge to try to see, and to understand, the Constitution as a coherent whole.

Third, that effort, in my view, leads one to see the Constitution as a "framework"— a concept that I believe plays as central a role in our Constitutional decision-making as does the notion of "legislative purpose" in statutory interpretation, or "comparative institutional expertise" in administrative law. The concept acts as a functional limitation, for it reminds us that we almost always must determine, not whether a statute or other legal rule is wise (e.g. whether handguns should be regulated or whether doctors should be free to assist a patient's suicide), but rather who has the legal power to make such a decision: individual or government? state or federal government? executive, legislative, or judicial branch? And it reminds us (as does our small size and limited docket capacity) that a constitutional power-allocating answer must last, irrespective of today's politics, for many years to come.

The concept acts as a substantive limitation in that the Constitution's provisions (read together) create a framework for a certain kind of workable government: that government is characterized by the rule of law; democratic responsibility for decision-making; the protection of basic human liberties; fair procedures; equal treatment of citizens; and widespread dispersal of governmental powers (among different levels and branches of government) to assure that no small group of individuals becomes too powerful. . . .

Fourth, I find constraint in the need for each decision to fit within what one might call the legal "fabric," a fabric that is itself tied, through purpose and through consequence, to actual human behavior. To say this is, in a sense, to repeat my first point, for every legal decision interacts (one might say "horizontally") with other decisions, principles, standards, practices, and institutional understandings, always modifying the "web" of the law; and every decision affects (one might say "vertically") the way in which that web, in turn, affects the world. Judges must often take account of "vertical" effects both because individual laws have particular individual purposes that guide legal interpretation and because legal institutions themselves are designed to help us solve the human problems that called them into being.

I suggest, however, that, in respect to constitutional matters, estimates of "vertical" effects, i.e. the real world consequences of "horizontal" interactions, have a particularly important role to play. In order to write an opinion, one might for example, ask not only the obvious "horizontal" questions, about say language, history, and precedent, but also such "vertical" questions as: (a) How will lower courts, lawyers, government officials, and other institutions (e.g. businesses, trade unions), who must rely upon the Court's cases for authoritative guidance, implement the opinion's holding? For example, should a constitutional rule that excludes illegally seized evidence from criminal trials be applied to court officials who negligently fail to check a computer-generated suspect list, in light of the need for a uniform, easily administered basic rule, or should it except them from the rule on the ground that their inclusion is administratively unnecessary? (b) What theme or "music" does the opinion's rhetorical language generate? Consider the powerful practical effects, above and beyond an opinion's holding, that use of a word like "sovereignty," or a metaphor such as "public forum," can have in cases involving, say, Indian tribes or free speech. Think, too, of the disastrous practical impact of the phrase "separate but equal" on American life and the Court's consequent difficulties in extricating the law from the phrase's implication in the segregated society that it helped to bring about. (c) What effect will the opinion have upon the working relations between courts and other major governmental institutions? How will it affect the way in which the Court itself works as an institution? (d) Should the opinion focus only on the facts characterized narrowly—say, to avoid commitment to a "theme," where consequences are not known, or where such commitment might mislead the public, or will so narrow a focus prevent the opinion from generating any clear and important principle?

Ultimately, what is the opinion's real-world impact (its effect, not its popularity), considered in light of basic constitutional objectives?

The answers to these practical questions constrain. Where a serious discrepancy develops between the world as described in terms of the Constitution's ultimate objectives and the world a particular decision helped to create, the constitutional rule will change. The Supreme Court realized by 1954, for example, that the Constitution's Equal Protection Clause could not tolerate the racially segregated society that the Court's earlier "separate but equal" cases had helped to establish. It properly overruled those cases, thereby indicating that constitutional interpretation itself is an ongoing, iterative, and self-correcting process.

Fifth, constraints arise out of the judge's own need for personal consistency over time. Justice O'Connor has described a judge's initial decisions as creating footprints that later decisions will follow. Moreover, the appointment process likely assures that judges have awareness, through prior experience of the nation's history and cultural heritage. Those facts, combined with diversity of membership and longevity of service, help to dampen radical swings in the Court's approach to constitutional problems.

I have tried to put the classical criticisms—"undemocratic," "subjective," "impractical"—in perspective. Since the interpretive system I describe is not mechanical but depends upon human judgment, since the constraints I mention only bind to a degree, and since the Court at certain times in its history has gone seriously awry, I cannot deny that the criticisms retain validity—"up to a point." Why then, why, one might ask, as democratic forms of government have become increasingly prevalent, in for example, Latin America and the former Eastern Bloc, have democratic societies increasingly tried to create independent judiciaries with final, or near final, authority to interpret basic legal documents that guarantee basic rights?

The obvious answer is that these nations increasingly have measured the criticisms against what they see as a need, a need for the protection of democratically structured government and of basic liberties that an independent judiciary can help to provide. That independent judiciary may protect them by helping gradually to develop among citizens and legislators liberty-protecting habits based in part upon their expectation that liberty-infringing laws will turn out not to be laws. And such protection might seem particularly necessary in a new democracy or one with a highly diverse citizenry or sizeable minority groups. That independent judiciary may also protect through the kind of force—ultimately based upon habit and expectations—that a court can bring to bear when, faced with a law that clearly violates a constitutional provision, that court says "no."

Several months ago I heard Justice Kennedy at New York University Law School welcome members of Russia's constitutional court into a profession that he said was both lonely and demanding of "courage." He was not then referring to the need to resolve difficult line-drawing problems correctly; but rather to the courage required at some times and in some places, to provide the proper answer to a clear violation.

These countervailing benefits, considered in light of the size of the USA, the diversity of its population, its history, its reliance upon law, may help to explain why, in my country, there is general public support for the institution of judicial review, whether or not that public praises or deplores the result in any particular case. You may understand both need and benefits if, of the many cases I might mention, I remind you of only one, the desegregation case *Brown v. Board of Education.*

Ronald Dworkin

FREEDOM'S LAW: THE MORAL READING OF THE AMERICAN CONSTITUTION

Introduction

Cambridge, MA: Harvard University Press (1996)

THE MAJORITARIAN PREMISE

Democracy means government by the people. But what does that mean? No explicit definition of democracy is settled among political theorists or in the dictionary. On the contrary, it is a matter of deep controversy what democracy really is. People disagree about which techniques of representation, which allocation of power among local, state, and national governments, which schedule and pattern of elections, and which other institutional arrangements provide the best available version of democracy. But beneath these familiar arguments over the structures of democracy there lies, I believe, a profound philosophical dispute about democracy's fundamental value or point, and one abstract issue is crucial to that dispute, though this is not always recognized. Should we accept or reject what I shall call the majoritarian premise?

This is a thesis about the fair outcomes of a political process: it insists that political procedures should be designed so that, at least on important matters, the decision that is reached is the decision that a majority or plurality of citizens favors, or would favor if it had adequate information and enough time for reflection. That goal sounds very reasonable, and many people, perhaps without much reflection, have taken it to provide the very essence of democracy. They believe that the complex political arrangements that constitute the democratic process should be aimed at and tested by this goal: that the laws that

the complex democratic process enacts and the policies that it pursues should be those, in the end, that the majority of citizens would approve.

The majoritarian premise does not deny that individuals have important moral rights the majority should respect. It is not necessarily tied to some collectivist or utilitarian theory according to which such rights are nonsense. In some political communities, however—in Great Britain, for example—the majoritarian premise has been thought to entail that the community should defer to the majority's view about what these individual rights are, and how they are best respected and enforced. It is sometimes said that Britain has no constitution, but that is a mistake. Britain has an unwritten as well as a written constitution, and part of the former consists in understandings about what laws Parliament should not enact. It is part of the British constitution, for example, that freedom of speech is to be protected.

In the United States, however, most people who assume that the majoritarian premise states the ultimate definition of and justification for democracy nevertheless accept that on some occasions the will of the majority should not govern. They agree that the majority should not always be the final judge of when its own power should be limited to protect individual rights, and they accept that at least some of the Supreme Court's decisions that overturned popular legislation, as the *Brown* decision did, were right. The majoritarian premise does not rule out exceptions of that kind, but it does insist that in such cases, even if some derogation from majoritarian government is overall justified, something morally regrettable has happened, a moral cost has been paid. The premise supposes, in other words, that it is *always* unfair when a political majority is not allowed to have its way, so that even when there are strong enough countervailing reasons to justify this, the unfairness remains.

If we reject the majoritarian premise, we need a different, better account of the value and point of democracy. I will defend an account—which I call the constitutional conception of democracy—that does reject the majoritarian premise. It denies that it is a defining goal of democracy that collective decisions always or normally be those that a majority or plurality of citizens would favor if fully informed and rational. It takes the defining aim of democracy to be a different one that collective decisions be made by political institutions whose structure, composition, and practices treat all members of the community, as individuals, with equal concern and respect. This alternate account of the aim of democracy, it is true, demands much the same structure of government as the majoritarian premise does. It requires that day-to-day political decisions be made by officials who have been chosen in popular elections. But the constitutional conception requires these majoritarian procedures out of a concern for the equal status of citizens, and not out of any commitment to the goals of majority rule. So it offers no reason why some nonmajoritarian procedure should not be employed on special occasions when this would better protect or enhance the equal status that it declares to be the essence of democracy, and it does not accept that these exceptions are a cause of moral regret.

The constitutional conception of democracy, in short, takes the following attitude to majoritarian government. Democracy means government subject to conditions—we might call these the "democratic" conditions—of equal status for all citizens. When majoritarian institutions provide and respect the democratic conditions, then the verdicts of these institutions should be accepted by everyone for that reason. But when they do not, or when their provision or respect is defective, there can be no objection, in the name of democracy, to other procedures that protect and respect them better. The democratic conditions plainly include, for example, a requirement that public offices must in principle be open to members of all races and groups on equal terms. If some law provided that only members of one race were eligible for public office, then there would be no moral cost—no matter for moral regret at all—if a court that enjoyed the power to do so under a valid constitution struck down that law as unconstitutional. That would presumably be an occasion on which the majoritarian premise was flouted, but though this is a matter of regret according to the majoritarian conception of democracy, it is not according to the constitutional conception. Of course, it may be controversial what the democratic conditions, in detail, really are, and whether a particular law does offend them, But, according to the constitutional conception, it would be the question to object to a practice assigning those controversial questions for final decision to a court, on the ground that that practice is undemocratic, because that objection assumes that the laws in question respect the democratic conditions, and that is the very issue in controversy.

I hope it is now clear that the majoritarian premise has had a potent—if often unnoticed—grip on the imagination of

American constitutional scholars and lawyers. Only that diagnosis explains the near unanimous view I described: that judicial review compromises democracy, so that the central question of constitutional theory must be whether and when that compromise is justified. That opinion is the child of a majoritarian conception of democracy, and therefore the grandchild of the majoritarian premise. It provokes the pointless search I described, for an interpretive strategy "intermediate" between the moral reading and originalism, and it tempts distinguished theorists into constructing Ptolemaic epicycles trying to reconcile constitutional practice with majoritarian principles.

So a complex issue of political morality—the validity of the majoritarian premise—is in fact at the heart of the long constitutional argument. The argument will remain confused until that issue is identified and addressed.

WE THE PEOPLE

We say that in a democracy government is by the people; we mean that the people collectively do things—elect leaders, for example—that no individual does or can do alone. There are two kinds of collective action, however—statistical and communal—and our view of the majoritarian premise may well turn on which kind of collective action we take democratic government to require.

Collective action is statistical when what the group does is only a matter of some function, rough or specific, of what the individual members of the group do on their own, that is, with no sense of doing something as a group.

Collective action is communal, however, when it cannot be reduced just to some statistical function of individual action, when it presupposes a special,

distinct, collective *agency*. It is a matter of individuals acting together in a way that merges their separate actions into a further, unified, act that is together *theirs*.

I have already distinguished two conceptions of democracy: majoritarian and constitutional. The first accepts and the second rejects the majoritarian premise. The difference between statistical and communal collective action allows us to draw a second distinction, this time between two readings of the idea that democracy is government by "the people." The first reading is a statistical one: that in a democracy political decisions are made in accordance with the votes or wishes of some function—a majority or plurality—of individual citizens. The second is a communal reading: that in a democracy political decisions are taken by a distinct entity—the people as *such*—rather than by any set of individuals one by one.

DOES CONSTITUTIONALISM UNDERMINE LIBERTY?

The majoritarian premise insists that something of moral importance is lost or compromised whenever a political decision contradicts what the majority of citizens would prefer or judge right if they reflected on the basis of adequate information. We must try to identify that moral cost. What is lost or compromised? Many people think the answer is: equality. I shall consider that apparently natural answer shortly, but I begin with a different suggestion, which is that when constitutional disabling provisions, like those found in the Bill of Rights, limit what a majority can enact, the result is to compromise the community's freedom.

That suggestion plainly appeals to what Isaiah Berlin and others have called positive as distinct from negative liberty, and what Benjamin Constant described as the liberty of the ancients as distinct from that of the moderns. It is the kind of freedom that statesmen and revolutionaries and terrorists and humanitarians have in mind when they insist that freedom must include the right of "self-determination" or the right of the "people" to govern themselves. Since the suggestion that constitutional rights compromise freedom appeals to positive rather than negative liberty, it might be said to pit the two kinds of liberty against each other. Constitutionalism, on this view, protects "negative" liberties, like free speech and "privacy," at the cost of the "positive" freedoms of self-determination.

This means, however, that this argument from liberty we are considering must be based on a communal rather than a statistical reading of government by the "people." On the statistical reading, an individual's control over the collective decisions that affect his life is measured by his power, on his own, to influence the result, and in a large democracy the power of any individual over national decisions is so tiny that constitutional restraints cannot be thought to diminish it enough to count as objectionable for that reason. On the contrary, constraints on majority will might well expand any particular individual's control of his own fate. On the communal reading, however, liberty is a matter not of any relation between government and citizens one by one, but rather of the relation between government and the whole citizenry understood collectively. Positive liberty, so understood, is the state of affairs when "the people" rule their officials, at least in the final analysis, rather than vice versa, and that is the liberty said to be compromised when the majority is prevented from securing its will.

Self-determination is the most potent—and dangerous—political ideal of our time. People fervently want to be governed by a group not just to which they belong, but with which they identify in some particular way. They want to be governed by members of the same religion or race or nation or linguistic community or historical nation-state rather than by any other group, and they regard a political community that does not satisfy this demand as a tyranny, no matter how otherwise fair and satisfactory it is.

This is partly a matter of narrow self-interest. People think that decisions made by a group most of whose members share their values will be better decisions for them. The great power of the ideal lies deeper, however. It lies in half-articulate convictions about when people are free, because they govern themselves, in spite of the fact that in a statistical sense, as individuals, they are not free, because they must often bend to the will of others. For us moderns, the key to this liberty of the ancients lies in democracy. As John Kenneth Galbraith has said, "When people put their ballots in the boxes, they are, by that act, inoculated against the feeling that the government is not theirs. They then accept, in some measure, that its errors are their errors, its aberrations their aberrations, that any revolt will be against them." We think we are free when we accept a majority's will in place of our own, but not when we bow before the doom of a monarch or the ukase of any aristocracy of blood or faith or skill. It is not difficult to see the judiciary as an aristocracy claiming dominion. Learned Hand described judges who appeal to the moral reading of the Constitution as "a bevy of Platonic guardians," and said he could not bear to be ruled by such a body of elites even if he knew how to select those fit for the task.

But powerful as the idea of democratic self-governance is, it is also deeply mysterious. Why am I *free*—how could I be thought to be governing *myself*—when I must obey what other people decide even if I think it wrong or unwise or unfair to me and my family? What difference can it make how many people must think the decision right and wise and fair if it is not necessary that *I* do? What kind of freedom is that? The answer to these enormously difficult questions begins in the communal conception of collective action. If I am a genuine member of a political community, its act is in some pertinent sense my act, even when I argued and voted against it, just as the victory or defeat of a team of which I am a member is my victory or defeat even if my own individual contribution made no difference either way. On no other assumption can we intelligibly think that as members of a flourishing democracy we are governing ourselves.

What could *genuine* membership in a political community mean? And in what sense *can* a collective act of a group also be the act of each member? We must describe some connection between an individual and a group that makes it *fair* to treat him—and *sensible* that he treat himself—as responsible for what it does. Let us bring those ideas together in the concept of moral membership, by which we mean the kind of membership in a political community that engages self-government. If true democracy is government by the people, in the communal sense that provides self-government, then true democracy is based on moral membership.

In this section we are considering the argument that the moral cost incurred when the majoritarian premise is flouted is a cost in liberty. We have now clarified that argument: we must understand it to mean that the people govern themselves when the majoritarian premise is satisfied, and that any compromise of that

premise compromises that self-government. But that majoritarianism does not guarantee self-government unless all the members of the community in question are moral members, and the majoritarian premise acknowledges no such qualification. I do not mean that people who deny moral membership in their political community are always right. The test, as I said, is moral not psychological. But they are not wrong just because they have an equal vote with others in some standing majoritarian structure.

When I described the constitutional conception of democracy earlier, as a rival to the majoritarian conception that reflects the majoritarian premise, I said that the constitutional conception presupposes democratic conditions. These are the conditions that must be met before majoritarian decision-making can claim any automatic moral advantage over other procedures for collective decision. We have now identified the same idea through another route. The democratic conditions are the conditions of moral membership in a political community. So we can now state a strong conclusion: not just that positive liberty is not sacrificed whenever and just because the majoritarian premise is ignored, but that positive liberty is enhanced when that premise is rejected outright in favor of the constitutional conception of democracy. If it is true that self-government is possible only within a community that meets the conditions of moral membership, because only then are we entitled to refer to government by "the people" in a powerful communal rather than a barren statistical sense, we need a conception of democracy that insists that no democracy exists unless those conditions are met.

These are *relational* conditions: they describe how an individual must be treated by a genuine political community in order that he or she be a moral member of that community. A political community cannot count anyone as a moral member unless it gives that person a *part* in any collective decision, a *stake* in it, and *independence* from it. First, each person must have an opportunity to make a difference in the collective decisions, and the force of his role—the magnitude of the difference he can make—must not be structurally fixed or limited in ways that reflect assumptions about his worth or talent or ability, or the soundness of his convictions or tastes. It is that condition that insists on universal suffrage and effective elections and representation, even though it does not demand that these be the only avenues of collective decision. It also insists on free speech and expression for all opinion, not just on formal political occasions, but in the informal life of the community as well.

Second, the political process of a genuine community must express some bona fide conception of equal concern for the interests of all members, which means that political decisions that affect the distribution of wealth, benefits, and burdens must be consistent with equal concern for all. Moral membership involves reciprocity: a person is not a member unless he is treated as a member by others, which means that they treat the consequences of any collective decision for his life as equally significant a reason for or against that decision as are comparable consequences for the life of anyone else. So the communal conception of democracy explains an intuition many of us share: that a society in which the majority shows contempt for the needs and prospects of some minority is illegitimate as well as unjust.

The third condition—of moral independence—is likely to be more controversial than these first two. I believe it essential, however, in order to capture an aspect of moral membership that the first two conditions may be interpreted to omit. The root idea we are now exploring—that individual freedom is furthered by collective self-government—assumes that the members of a political community can appropriately regard themselves as partners in a joint venture, like members or a football team or orchestra in whose work and fate all share, even when that venture is conducted in ways they do not endorse. That idea is nonsense unless it can be accepted by people with self-respect, and whether it can be depends on which kinds of decisions the collective venture is thought competent to make. An orchestra's conductor can decide, for example, how the orchestra will interpret a particular piece: there must be a decision of that issue binding on all, and the conductor is the only one placed to make it. No musician sacrifices anything essential to his control over his own life, and hence to his self-respect, in accepting that someone else has that responsibility, but it would plainly be otherwise if the conductor tried to dictate not only how a violinist should play under his direction, but what standards of taste the violinist should try to cultivate. No one who accepted responsibility to decide questions of musical judgment for himself could regard himself as a partner in a joint venture that proposed to decide them for him.

People who take personal responsibility for deciding what kind of life is valuable for them can nevertheless accept that issues of justice—about how the different and sometimes competing interests of all citizens should be accommodated—must be decided collectively, so that one decision is taken as authoritative for all. There is nothing in that proposition that

challenges an individual's own responsibility to decide for himself what life to
live given the resources and opportunities
that such collective decisions leave to him.
So he can treat himself as bound together
with others in a joint effort to resolve such
questions, even when his views lose. But
it would be otherwise if the majority purported to decide what he should think or
say about its decisions, or what values or
ideals should guide how he votes or the
choices he makes with the resources it
assigns him. Someone who believes in his
own responsibility for the central values
of his life cannot yield that responsibility
to a group even if he has an equal vote in
its deliberations. A genuine political community must therefore be a community
of independent moral agents. It must not
dictate what its citizens think about matters of political or moral or ethical judgment, but must, on the contrary, provide
circumstances that encourage them to
arrive at beliefs on these matters through
their own reflective and finally individual
conviction.

EQUALITY?

Although the argument from liberty is
emotionally the most powerful of the
arguments that might be made for the
majoritarian premise, an argument from
equality is more familiar. The dimension
of equality in question is presumably
political equality, because there is nothing
in majoritarianism that could be thought
automatic to promote any other form
of equality, particularly not economic
equality. True, if a society's economic
structure is pyramidal, with progressively
more people at progressively lower economic levels, then universal suffrage and
majoritarian decisions might well push
toward greater economic equality. But in
the United States, and in other advanced

capitalist countries where the profile of
distribution is now very different, people
in the majority often vote to protect their
own wealth against the demands of those
worse off than they are.

So the argument that equality is compromised when the majoritarian premise
is ignored must appeal to some concept of
political equality. But which concept this
is depends on which of the two readings
of collective action we have in mind. If
we take government by "the people" to be
only a statistical matter, then the equality
in question is the political equality of citizens taken one by one. Such equality was
certainly denied before women were permitted to vote, and it was compromised by
the electoral system in Victorian Britain,
which in effect gave university graduates
extra votes. But what metric do we use in
making most judgments? What is political equality according to the statistical
concept of collective political action?

Perhaps surprisingly, we cannot capture political equality if we define it as
equality of political *power*, because we
have no interpretation of "power" that
would make equality of power even an
attractive, let alone an attainable, ideal.
Suppose we take political power to be a
matter of impact, understood in the following way: my political impact, as a citizen of the United States, is a matter of how
far my favoring a particular decision, just
on its own, increases the antecedent likelihood of that being the collective decision, making no assumptions about what
opinion any other citizen has or forms.
Impact cannot be equal in a representative democracy: it must inevitably make a
greater difference to the antecedent probability of a trade measure being approved
that any particular senator favors it than
that I do. In any case, impact does not
capture any intuitively appealing concept of political power, because impact is

insensitive to what is the most important source of unequal political power in modern democracies, which is the inequality of wealth that allows some people vast opportunity to influence public opinion. Ross Perot and I have only one vote each, but he can buy massive television time to persuade others to his opinion, and I cannot buy any.

This might suggest an improved account: that political power is a matter not of impact but of influence, understood as my overall power to affect political decisions, taking into account my power to affect the opinions of others. But equality of influence is plainly an unattractive—as well as unrealizable—goal. We do not want wealth to affect political decisions, but that is because wealth is unequally and unfairly distributed. We certainly do want influence to be unequal in politics for other reasons: we want those with better views, or who can argue more cogently, to have more influence. We could not eliminate differential influence from such sources without savage transformations of our whole society, and these would mean the end, not the triumph, of deliberation in our politics.

We must begin again. Political equality, on the statistical model of collective action, must be defined as a matter not of power but of the kind of *status* I discussed in connection with the conditions of democratic self-government. Male-only suffrage and university votes were inegalitarian because they presupposed that some people were worthier or better fit to participate in collective decisions than others. But mere political authority—the power attached to political office for which all are in principle eligible—carries no such presupposition. That is why the special power of political officials does not destroy true political equality, and it

does not matter, for that point, whether or not the officials are directly elected. Many officials who are appointed rather than elected wield great power. An acting ambassador to Iraq can create a Gulf War and the chairman of the Federal Reserve Board can bring the economy to its knees. There is no inegalitarian premise of status—no supposition of first- and second-class citizenship—in the arrangements that produce this power. Nor is there any inegalitarian premise in the parallel arrangements that give certain American judges, appointed and approved by elected officials, authority over constitutional adjudication.

So the statistical reading of collective political action makes little sense of the idea that political equality is compromised whenever majority will is thwarted. And this idea is silly anyway, if we have the statistical reading in mind. In a large, continental democracy, any ordinary citizen's political power is minuscule, on any understanding of what political power is, and the diminution of that individual power traceable to constitutional constraints on majority will is more minuscule still. The egalitarian argument for the majoritarian premise seems initially more promising, however, if we detach it from the statistical reading of collective action and recast it from the perspective of the communal reading. From that perspective, equality is not a matter of any relation among citizens one by one, but rather a relation between the citizenry, understood collectively as "the people," and their governors. Political equality is the state of affairs in which the people rule their officials, in the final analysis, rather than vice versa. This provides a less silly argument for the proposition that judicial review or other compromises of the majoritarian premise damage political equality. It might be said that when judges apply constitutional provisions to strike down legislation that the people, through their representatives, have enacted, the people are no longer in charge.

But this argument is exactly the same as the argument considered in the last section: it appeals, once again, to the ideals of political self-determination. Positive liberty and the sense of equality that we extracted from the communal understanding of "we the people" are the very same virtues. (That is hardly surprising, since liberty and equality are, in general, aspects of the same ideal, not, as is often supposed, rivals.) The objections described in the last section, which are fatal to any attempt to ground a majoritarian premise in positive liberty, are also decisive against the same argument when it cries equality instead.

WHAT FOLLOWS?

In a decent working democracy, like the United States, the democratic conditions set out in the Constitution are sufficiently met in practice so that there is no unfairness in allowing national and local legislatures the powers they have under standing arrangements. On the contrary, democracy would be extinguished by any general constitutional change that gave an oligarchy of unelected experts power to overrule and replace any legislative decision they thought unwise or unjust. It is different, however, when the question is plausibly raised whether some rule or regulation or policy itself undercuts or weakens the democratic character of the community, and the constitutional arrangement assigns *that* question to a court. Suppose the legislature enacts a law making it a crime for someone to burn his own American flag

as an act of protest. Suppose this law is challenged on the ground that it impairs democratic self-government, by wrongly constricting the liberty of speech, and a court accepts this charge and strikes down the law. If the court's decision is correct—if laws against flag-burning do in fact violate the democratic conditions set out in the Constitution as these have been interpreted and formed by American history—the decision is not antidemocratic, but, on the contrary, improves democracy. No moral cost has been paid, because no one, individually or collectively, is worse off in any of the dimensions we have now canvassed. No one's power to participate in a self-governing community has been worsened, because everyone's power in that respect has been improved. No one's equality has been compromised, because equality, in the only pertinent sense, has been strengthened. No one has been cheated of the ethical advantages of a role in principled deliberation if he or she had a chance to participate in the public discussion about whether the decision was right. If the court had not intervened— if the legislature's decision had been left standing—everyone would have been worse off, in all the dimensions of democracy, and it would be perverse to regard that as in any way or sense a democratic victory. Of course, if we assume that the court's decision was wrong, then none of this is true. Certainly it impairs democracy when an authoritative court makes the wrong decision about what the democratic conditions require—but no more than it does when a majoritarian legislature makes a wrong constitutional decision that is allowed to stand. The possibility of error is symmetrical. So the majoritarian premise is confused, and it must be abandoned.

Larry Kramer

WE THE COURT

115 Harv. L. Rev. 4 (2001)

In recent years, scholars have drawn on Thomas Jefferson's notion of departmentalism to argue against judicial supremacy. Even if the Supreme Court rightly has a power of judicial review, this should not mean, they argue, that the Supreme Court is the supreme arbiter of the Constitution. The idea that aside from the Court, the "people themselves," to use Larry Kramer's phrase, should have the power of judicial review might strike some people as problematic. After all, most people are not lawyers, so why should they be able to interpret the Constitution? But as you have seen, the question of what the Constitution means is itself deeply contested. Moreover, in the following excerpt, Kramer argues that there has historically been a tradition of the people interpreting the Constitution. The move to judicial supremacy, he suggests, is a recent one, found mostly in the doctrines of the Rehnquist Court. But this move from judicial review to judicial supremacy is a mistake, he argues. We should return at least some of the power of judicial interpretation to the people themselves.

In this selection, Kramer attempts to revive Jefferson's theory of departmentalism. Clearly, the debate over judicial authority did not die with Jefferson and Alexander Hamilton. It is very much alive today. As you read this selection, consider the ways in which Jefferson and Kramer agree. You might also ask what judicial review without judicial supremacy might look like in light of Kramer's suggestion that the two need not go together.

For all his genius, John Marshall is seldom included among American's great political or legal rhetoricians. He penned some decent enough lines, but nothing with the power routinely displayed by a Holmes or a Lincoln, or, even among his contemporaries, by a Jefferson or a Paine. There is one line, though, that every lawyer and law student knows by heart, almost by instinct: "It is, emphatically, the province and duty of the judicial department, to say what the law is." There supposedly, in one pithy sentence, is the Supreme Court's own Declaration of Independence.

But what does Marshall's statement mean—on the ground, in operation? In 1958, the Court insisted in the almost-as-famous case of *Cooper v. Aaron* that *Marbury* "declared the basic principle that the federal judiciary is supreme in the exposition of the law of the Constitution," adding that this idea "has ever since been respected by this Court and the Country as a permanent and indispensable feature of our constitutional system." Well, hardly. As we shall see below (though it is by now conventional wisdom), *Marbury* staked out a considerably more modest position, venturing only that it was proper for the Court to interpret the Constitution without in any way suggesting that its interpretations were superior to those of the other branches. And certainly, as we shall also see below (though this, too, is conventional wisdom), the idea of judicial supremacy was not cheerfully embraced in the years after *Marbury*. The Court's periodic tugs of war with the likes of Jefferson, Jackson, Lincoln, the Reconstruction Congress, and FDR, to name only a few, are familiar terrain even to non-historians.

But here is the striking thing: in the years since *Cooper v. Aaron*, the idea of judicial supremacy—the notion that judges have the last word when it comes to constitutional interpretation and that their decisions determine the meaning of the Constitution for everyone—has finally found widespread approbation. The Court's decisions are often still controversial. State legislatures sometimes enact laws they know the Justices will strike down, and compliance with the Court's most contentious rulings, like those on abortion and school prayer, is willfully slack in many places. But these incidents of non-compliance have become forms of protest more than claims of interpretive superiority. Outright defiance in the shape of denying that Supreme Court decisions define constitutional law has, quite simply, disappeared....

There is, I believe, a simple explanation both for the general acceptance of judicial supremacy and for the defensiveness of its critics. Put simply, everyone—friend or foe of supremacy—begins with a shared understanding of the Constitution as ordinary law. It is "supreme," meaning it is superior to other forms of positive law and so trumps them when conflicts arise. But in every other respect, the Constitution is just "law" in the conventional sense in which lawyers use the word. It follows, naturally and ineluctably, that judges should be the ones to interpret it. Law is, after all, the stuff of judges; it is what they do. If the law is unclear, interpreting it to clarify its meaning is among the judiciary's central missions. It follows, almost as ineluctably, that judicial interpretations should be treated as conclusive by the other branches. Insofar as questions arise about what a legal text means, courts are where we go to get answers. And once a court has spoken, or at least once the Supreme Court has done so, its interpretations are supposed to trump those of other political actors unless and until the law is formally changed. This is universally acknowledged when it comes to statutes, and insofar as the Constitution shares the same status as these of positive law, there is no reason suddenly to abandon the practice.

. . . If the Constitution is law, after all, it is not (supposed to be) politics. It is, of course, political, in the sense that all law is political: it has political consequences, those who interpret and apply it cannot help but bring their politics with them into the interpretive process, and so forth. But modern recognition of the inherently political nature and structure of law still accepts the fundamental premise that law can and should be separated from politics. Law is, if you will, the part of politics that is supposed to be left to courts and judges. Placing something in a "law" box thus shifts our expectations and assumptions about authority to interpret. If the Constitution is law, then it is those who would argue that courts should not be its authoritative expositor who bear the burden of justifying what amounts to an exception to our normal practice.

The Founding generation did not see the Constitution this way and, as a result, had very different views about the role of the judiciary. Their Constitution was not ordinary law, not peculiarly the stuff of courts and judges. It was, as Part II will show, a special form of popular law, law made by the people to bind their governors, and so subject to rules and considerations that made it qualitatively different from (and not just superior to) statutory or common law.

Americans of the Founding era felt the wonder of popular government in a way that we, who take so much for granted, do not. The United States was then the only country in the world with a government founded explicitly on the consent of its people, and the people who gave that consent were intensely, profoundly conscious of the fact. And proud. This pride, this awareness of the fragility and importance of their venture in popular government, informed everything the Founders did. It was, as Gordon Wood said, "the deeply felt meaning of the Revolution." Modern commentators, especially legal commentators, read the Founders' letters and speeches anachronistically, giving too much weight, or the wrong kind of weight, to complaints about "the excess of democracy." We depict the men who framed the Constitution as striving to create a self-correcting system of checks and balances whose fundamental operations would all take place from within the government itself, with minimal involvement or interference from the people. Our political grammar is saturated with this reading of the Founding, which sees the movement to write a new Constitution almost exclusively in anti-democratic terms.

. . . The Founding generation's ideas about constitutional reform remained thoroughly embedded in a political ideology that celebrated the central role of "the people" in supplying the government with its energy and direction. Preserving liberty demanded a constitution whose internal architecture was carefully arranged to check power, just as it demanded leaders of sufficient "character" and "virtue." But structural innovations and virtuous leadership were devices to channel and control popular politics, not to isolate or eliminate it. The people remained responsible for making things work.

When Tucker and his contemporaries invoked "the people," they were not conjuring an empty abstraction or describing a mythic philosophical justification for government. "The people" they knew could speak, and had done so. "The people" they knew had fought a revolution, expressed dissatisfaction with the first fruits of independence, and debated and adopted a new charter to govern itself. Certainly the Founders were concerned about the perils of popular government, some of them obsessively so. But they were also captivated by its possibilities and in awe of its importance. Their Constitution remained, fundamentally, an act of popular will: the people's charter, made by the people. And, as we shall see, it was the people themselves—working through or responding to their agents in the government—who were responsible for seeing that the Constitution was properly interpreted and implemented. The idea of turning this responsibility over to judges was unthinkable.

. . . The American people learned a great deal during the early years of their Republic[.] . . . Among the lessons they learned . . . were first, that it was difficult to keep courts out of the business of interpreting a written constitution, and second, that popular constitutionalism of the eighteenth-century variety was not well suited for American's new circumstances. That courts might play a role enforcing the Constitution had been understood by some even before Ratification; by the time *Marbury* was decided in 1803, this role had expanded to permit courts routinely to act on their own best understanding of the Constitution's meaning. That it might extend further, that judges might be assigned the final word in disputes over how to interpret the Constitution, was already being debated by the early decades of the nineteenth century. It may have taken until some time after *Cooper v. Aaron* for this proposition to achieve acceptance, but the idea of judicial supremacy had entered America's political lexicon by the 1830s.

There is, nevertheless, a world of difference between having the last word and having the only word: between judicial supremacy and judicial sovereignty. We may choose to accept judicial supremacy, because we need someone to settle certain constitutional questions and, for a variety of historical and jurisprudential reasons, the Supreme Court seems like our best option. But it does not follow either that the Court must wield its authority over every question or that, when it does, the Court can dismiss or too quickly supplant the views of other, more democratic institutions. Nothing in the doctrine of judicial supremacy, in other words, requires denying either that the Constitution has qualities that set it apart from ordinary law, or that these qualities confer legitimate interpretive authority on political actors as a means of ensuring continued popular input in shaping constitutional meaning.

The trick, of course, is to find the proper balance, a problem courts have struggled with throughout American history. The various tussles between prior Supreme Courts and prior Presidents and Congresses should be seen in this light, for they reflect both the historical persistence of popular constitutionalism and the country's efforts to reconcile it with the practice of judicial supremacy. For much of the nineteenth century, an expansive notion of "political questions" and a sharp law/politics distinction among issues of constitutional law served to reconcile these conflicting principles. This doctrinal framework broke down during the *Lochner* era, triggering a prolonged struggle that culminated in the New Deal settlement most famously reflected in *Carolene Products*' footnote four. The accommodation thus reached—roughly a division between questions of defining grants of power and questions of protecting individual rights—proved stable for more than half a century. The Warren Court was activist, for example, but it remained strictly within the terms of the New Deal accommodation.

Which brings us to the Rehnquist Court. [S]omething significant has happened on Chief Justice Rehnquist's watch: a subtle, unacknowledged shift in the Court's understanding of judicial review that has troubling consequences for constitutional doctrine and for constitutionalism generally. As opposition to judicial supremacy has receded, the seeming naturalness of the Court's power to interpret has grown, and with it the Court's own apparent sense that interpretation by non-judicial actors is somehow unnatural. The Court has reacted by abandoning the *Carolene Products* accommodation—not because it has a better or more sensible one in mind, but because this Court sees no need to accommodate the political branches at all. The Rehnquist Court no longer views itself as first among equals, but has instead staked its claim to being the only institution empowered to speak with authority when it comes to the meaning of the Constitution. The other branches get to have their say, of course, for they must interpret the Constitution when deciding whether and how to act—just as you or I must do with respect to whatever law governs us. But executive or legislative understandings of the Constitution are, in the eyes of the Rehnquist Court, hardly more authoritative than yours or mine. Only the Court's own interpretations matter; only these have the force of constitutional law. If deference is still given to the President or Congress (and this is becoming rarer by the term), it is because the Court views deferring as pragmatic or sees the Constitution as indifferent to a problem, not because it thinks these branches have equal standing to interpret the text. The last, faint traces of popular constitutionalism are fading, threatened by a Court that truly sees the Constitution as nothing more than ordinary law. Judicial supremacy is becoming judicial sovereignty.

We see this development reflected in the Court's thinking in a number of ways. It appears in the Justices' rhetoric, which increasingly ignores or affirmatively denies legitimacy to the views of other actors. It appears as well in their willingness to cast aside long-established doctrines created specifically to preserve the interpretive authority of other branches, especially that of Congress. These include rational basis scrutiny under the Commerce Clause and, more ominously, deferential review of congressional fact finding. But the effects of judicial sovereignty extend beyond the abandonment of deference, for the Court's felt need to protect its control over constitutional meaning has itself become a doctrine-shaping imperative. Where prior Courts put restrictions on judicial review to accommodate the views of other branches, this Court has revamped the doctrine to eliminate the other branches' interpretive space and protect its own exclusive custody of the Constitution. This, as we shall see, is a central thrust of the Court's recent federalism decisions, especially those limiting Congress's power under Section 5 of the Fourteenth Amendment. And, of course, this shift in the Court's attitude toward the competence of other branches to address constitutional questions goes far toward explaining its extraordinarily aggressive actions in last Term's most notorious decision, *Bush v. Gore*.

From one perspective, the historical development of judicial review stands as hugely ironic. We have moved from a world in which the interpretive authority of the political branches was clear and

that of the Supreme Court questionable and uncertain, to one in which the Court's authority stands unchallenged while that of everyone else is under siege. The point is not originalist, and I will make no claim that we should reserve space for popular constitutionalism just because the Founders did. The historical experience that led to the emergence of judicial review and judicial supremacy suggests reasons for preserving bounded versions of both practices. But nothing similar justifies the drift to judicial sovereignty. . . .

. . . [D]eliberations in Congress . . . attested to the widening acceptance of the possibility and rightness of judicial review as an element of the constitutional system. A lengthy debate in the House of Representatives over the President's removal power in June 1789 generated considerable discussion of the courts' role, and while there was a great deal of ambiguity about the theory and scope of judicial review, most of the speakers accepted or assumed its existence. . . .

Courts exercising judicial review made no claim to treat fundamental law as ordinary law. They justified their refusal to enforce laws as a "political-legal" act on behalf of the people, a responsibility required by their position as the people's faithful agents. Judicial review was a substitute for popular action, a device to maintain constitutional limits without the need for civil unrest. It was, moreover, a power to be employed cautiously, only where the unconstitutionality of a law was clear beyond doubt—though in making this determination judges were not confined strictly to the text but could draw on well-established principles of the customary constitution as well.

The emergence of judicial review, even in this limited and restrained form, still needed to be fit into a theory of the Constitution. The argument for review was ultimately straightforward—to wit, that judges, no less than any other citizen or government official, were bound to take notice of the Constitution if and when it became relevant in the ordinary course of business. Yet however innocuous the proposition might sound stated abstractly, its application in practice raised an embarrassing theoretical problem. James Madison pointed to the difficulty in his 1788 observations on Jefferson's draft constitution for Virginia: "As the Courts are generally the last in making their decisions," he explained, "it results to them by refusing or not refusing to execute a law, to stamp it with its final character. This makes the Judiciary Department paramount in fact to the Legislature, which was never intended and can never be proper."

The solution to this dilemma is known today as the "departmental" or "concurrent" or "coordinate" theory of review. Madison himself was one of its earliest and strongest proponents. During the 1789 debate over the President's removal power, and notwithstanding the misgivings he had communicated to Jefferson the previous year, Madison conceded the basic argument for judicial review. "I acknowledge, in the ordinary course of government, that the exposition of the laws and constitution devolves upon the judicial," he said. It did not follow, however, that judicial decisions should therefore acquire any special stature or status.

Thomas Jefferson, who embraced this theory throughout his political life, expressed the idea succinctly: "Each of the three departments has equally the right to decide for itself what is its duty under the constitution, without any regard to what the others may have decided for themselves under a similar question."

Modern commentators find this theory puzzling, seeing in it a formula for anarchy and chaos. Some openly concede to being "confused" by the argument. Others assume that proponents of the departmental theory must have recognized that it was incomplete and continued to search for an alternative "effective method of resolving differences over constitutional interpretation." One historian pejoratively labels the theory "arbitrary review" (because, he says, it provides no "principled functional limits" for resolving constitutional conflicts) and insists that Madison, at least, meant something other than what he quite plainly said. As noted in the introduction, even modern scholars who purport to endorse departmentalism seem to find Madison's and Jefferson's version of it unintelligible. Instead, they typically propose some sort of functional division in which different branches are assigned final authority for different questions.

This generic confusion is revealing of the extent to which we have come to see our Constitution as ordinary law. For what underlies it is the assumption not just that someone must have final authority to resolve routine constitutional conflicts, but that this someone must be a governmental entity. Such an assumption belongs to the culture of ordinary law, not the culture of popular constitutionalism. In a regime of popular constitutionalism, government officials are the regulated, not the regulators, and final interpretive authority rests with the people themselves. Thus, Madison and Jefferson had no difficulty whatsoever explaining how constitutional conflicts would finally be resolved: they would be decided by the people. Ideally, of course, the disputing branches would reach an accommodation on their own, though Jefferson once observed that "we have . . . in more than one instance, seen the opinions of different departments in opposition to each other, & no ill ensue." Accommodation among the branches, after all, was what all that checking and balancing in separation of powers theory was supposed to be about. But if no compromise was forthcoming and a final resolution was needed, it was obvious who would decide. The issue would be answered, in Madison's words, by "the will of the community, to be collected in some mode to be provided by the constitution, or one dictated by the necessity of the case." Jefferson, too, urged that "when the legislative or executive functionaries act unconstitutionally, they are responsible to the people in their elective capacity."

. . . However understood, the practice of popular constitutionalism seems, at first, difficult to harmonize with the principle of judicial supremacy. After all, there can be only one last word on the meaning of the Constitution. It may rest with the people (whether speaking independently, through parties, or through elected officials) or it may rest with the Supreme Court, but how can it rest with both? Yet this is much too simplistic a view. There is, in fact, a world of difference between having the final word and having the only word. We may come to accept judicial supremacy, because we need someone trustworthy to settle certain constitutional disputes once and for all, and for a variety of historical, jurisprudential, and political reasons, the Supreme Court seems like our best option. Given this sort of pragmatic justification, it simply does not follow that the Court must wield its authority over every question of constitutional law; nor does it follow that, when the Court does exercise review, it should dismiss or too easily supplant the views of other, more democratic institutions. Nothing in the doctrine of judicial supremacy, in other words, requires divesting either the people or the political branches

of legitimate interpretive authority. Some matters may call for close judicial scrutiny while others are best left for resolution in the political domain. It is all a matter of finding the most appropriate or workable accommodation. . . .

The fragility of any accommodation based on a law/politics distinction was revealed when the Justices finally struck down an important federal law in *Dred Scott v. Sandford*. The Court was savaged in the press and suffered wounds to its reputation that took nearly a generation to heal. Recoiling from Chief Justice Taney's hamfisted assertion of judicial supremacy, Abraham Lincoln declared his support for a version of the old departmental theory and invoked Andrew Jackson's defiance of the Court as precedent. Lincoln returned to the problem of *Dred Scott* in his First Inaugural Address, where he conceded that the Court's judgment should be enforced as to the parties immediately involved. "At the same time," he continued:

> The candid citizen must confess that if the policy of the government upon vital questions, affecting the whole people, is to be irrevocably fixed by decisions of the Supreme Court, the instant they are made, in ordinary litigation between parties, in personal actions, the people will have ceased to be their own rulers, having to that extent practically resigned their government into the hands of that eminent tribunal.

. . . [T]he Rehnquist Court has simply repudiated cardinal principles of twentieth-century jurisprudence (including rational basis scrutiny of ends-means relationships and deferential review of facts), casting aside a century and a half of hard-earned experience in a spasm of "law is law" formalism. Worse, the Court's felt need to maintain its interpretive supremacy—to ensure that it alone controls the meaning of the Constitution—has itself become a doctrine-shaping imperative. The Rehnquist Court has thus devised rules that artificially limit the authority of lawmakers because it finds such rules necessary to ensure its ability to dominate constitutional interpretation. The result is a Constitution that is less and does less, and for no better reasons than the Court's low opinion of Congress and desire to protect its position as king of the hill. . . .

[A]nxiety to squelch any appearance that other branches can render authoritative interpretations of the Constitution or that their views might affect the Court's interpretations is a recurring motif in the rhetoric of the Rehnquist Court. Apprehension along these lines played an important role in its opinion in *Casey*, for example, in which the Court emphasized its aversion to showing weakness by yielding to strongly held views from outside the Court, even if the Justices believe those views might be correct. "Whatever the premises of opposition may be," Justices O'Connor, Kennedy, and Souter wrote, "to overrule under fire in the absence of the most compelling reason to reexamine a watershed decision would subvert the Court's legitimacy beyond any serious question."

Concern for securing the Court's power to interpret was still more evident in *City of Boerne v. Flores*. In 1990, the Court had overturned three decades of precedent by ruling 5-4 that laws of general applicability do not violate the Free Exercise Clause simply because they prohibit or burden religious practices. Congress responded in 1993 with the Religious Freedom Restoration Act (RFRA), in which it sought to restore the old law by protecting such practices subject to a compelling interest test. That a unanimous House of Representatives and ninety-seven of the one hundred Senators (not to mention

prior Courts, four members of the current Court, and most nonjudicial commentators) thought this was the better interpretation affected the majority's thinking not at all. Quite the contrary, it provoked a lecture on how it is Congress's job to enforce the Constitution, not to say what it is:

> When the Court has interpreted the Constitution, it has acted within the province of the Judicial Branch, which embraces the duty to say what the law is. Marbury v. Madison, 1 Cranch, at 177. When the political branches of the Government act against the background of a judicial interpretation of the Constitution already issued, it must be understood that in later cases and controversies the Court will treat its precedents with the respect due them under settled principles, including stare decisis, and contrary expectations must be disappointed.

Running through these decisions, and others that could be cited, is the Rehnquist Court's skittishness about losing control over the Constitution to other branches. The Justices seemed annoyed when lawyers for Vice President Gore argued in the election litigation that a statutory scheme (not to mention the Constitution itself) required Congress to resolve the dispute. "Are you suggesting there could be any judicial review of a decision by the Congress to count one set of electoral votes?" asked a disbelieving Chief Justice, followed by Justice Kennedy's stern warning that "we must be very careful to preserve the role of the Court." In the end, the majority chose to ignore Gore's argument, and instead concluded its opinion with the jaw-droppingly disingenuous claim that it had been "forced to confront" an "unsought responsibility." . . .

Among the more striking aspects of the Court's opinion was the argument it offered to justify this heightened scrutiny; or, rather, the absence of argument, for there was none. Chief Justice Rehnquist merely laid out a "first principle"— that the Constitution "creates a Federal Government of enumerated powers"— from which he apparently thought heightened judicial scrutiny followed automatically and without question. This unreflective conflating of constitutional limits with judicial enforcement was apparent at the end of the opinion, where the Chief Justice responded to claims that the Court's newest test was vague. Uncertainty there may be, he conceded:

> But, so long as Congress' authority is limited to those powers enumerated in the Constitution, and so long as those enumerated powers are interpreted as having judicially enforceable outer limits, congressional legislation under the Commerce Clause always will engender "legal uncertainty." . . . The Constitution mandates this uncertainty by withholding from Congress a plenary police power that would authorize enactment of every type of legislation. . . . Any possible benefit from eliminating this "legal uncertainty" would be at the expense of the Constitution's system of enumerated powers.

What is astonishing about this statement . . . is the Court's unawareness that its analysis is question-begging. The issue, after all, was whether the Constitution mandated that the enumerated powers be interpreted as having "judicially enforceable" outer limits. Not outer limits, mind you, but judicially enforceable ones. Everyone, including everyone in Congress, agrees that the Constitution's delegations have limits. The question has always been deciding who should say what these limits are.

. . . One has to guess at the Rehnquist Court's reasons for launching this wide-ranging assault on Congress, since the Justices themselves have nowhere explained or justified it. Apart from political motivations, . . . what emerges is a Court driven by a formal understanding of the nature of the Constitution and of the roles of Court and Congress under it. This understanding is never clearly stated, but rather consists of implicit assumptions that must be teased out of the opinions. But what comes across is a vision of the Constitution as ordinary law, that is, as something that generates conventional legal problems of a kind that can properly be resolved only by a court. Further animating the Justices who have led this revolution is a palpable edginess about the Supreme Court's ability to resolve these problems in a way that sticks, and a sense that past Courts have already let too much of the Constitution slip into legislative hands. Rules that do not enable the Supreme Court sufficiently to control the substantive meaning of the Constitution—rules that enable Congress to enact laws that "may become substantive in operation and effect"—are rules that need to be changed. This is true whether they are rules of process (such as standards of review) or rules of substance (such as the scope of equal protection or the reach of the Commerce Clause). What matters, above all, is keeping the Constitution safely in the Court's sole custody. . . .

Bush v. Gore, it should by now be clear, is not such an exceptional case after all. Quite the opposite, it is from a certain perspective emblematic of the Rehnquist Court and its jurisprudence. The defining characteristic of that Court is not its commitment to political conservatism nor a love of states' rights. Such labels may accurately describe the Court's politics and outcomes, but at the base of its jurisprudence, facilitating if not driving decisions, lies the Justices' conviction that they and they alone are responsible for the Constitution. Apart from the narrow political question doctrine and a theoretic possibility of amendment, any notion that what the Constitution does or permits might best be left for the people to resolve using the ordinary devices available to express their will seems beyond the Rehnquist Court's compass. Politics begins where the Constitution leaves off, and what the Constitution allows the political branches to do is in all events to be decided by the Court. This is judicial sovereignty. . . .

It is important in this regard to understand how the Court reached the position it has, and why the Justices seem so confident that what they are doing is right. It is too easy, in my view, to ascribe the course of the Rehnquist Court to politics alone, at least to politics in the narrow sense. That the Justices do or do not like certain laws obviously plays a role, and the political conservatism of the five who have controlled the Court's major decisions in recent years is surely part of the story, maybe even a big part. But such an account is one-dimensional. It leaves out the fact that the Justices are also lawyers who have spent the better part of their lives working in and with law. Their ideology is more than an array of preferences for one or another outcome in particular cases. It includes an ideology of constitutional law itself, a set of beliefs or ideas about the nature and meaning of the Constitution that makes them think they are right to intercede in politics as aggressively as they have. That the Justices have not been fans of some of the laws in question may have had something to do with their willingness, indeed eagerness, to take this step, just as their preference for a Republican president presumably made them more open to calling a halt to the election. But their sense that the Constitution called for them to act is surely more important still. The conservative ideology of the Rehnquist Court is,

above all, a conservative jurisprudence, and it consists of certain mutually reinforcing ideas about the Constitution and the Court as well as of conservative politics in the narrow sense. These ideas constitute the intellectual matrix of the Rehnquist Court's conservative majority.

The first of these ideas—now shared, I think, by many liberals as well as by conservatives—is that the Constitution is nothing more than a species of ordinary law, hence something whose content and meaning are properly resolved by judges. Politics is where you go to amend the Constitution; courts are where you go to interpret it. The idea of constitutional politics outside the amendment process is, to the Rehnquist Court, a threatening and possibly oxymoronic prospect. A second idea seems to follow from this first one, inasmuch as conceiving the Constitution in ordinary-law terms could lead one to conclude that any limitations it imposes must be of a kind enforceable by courts. Indeed, "constitutional limitations" and "judicially enforceable" have become virtual synonyms for the Rehnquist Court, inseparable if not indistinguishable. The final piece of the puzzle is not so much an idea as an understanding of constitutional history, one that reaffirms the need for court-imposed limits by demonizing popular politics and celebrating the role of the judiciary in controlling the people. The conservative majority on the Rehnquist Court do not see themselves as usurpers. They do not see themselves as activists (because it is not activism to restore the "true" Constitution). Indeed, I have little doubt but that they see themselves as heroic, as close kin of the courageous judges who stood up against segregation in the South. *Bush v. Gore* was not a travesty from their perspective. It was their finest moment, a case of taking the political heat to do the right thing.

. . . The Founding generation did not solve the problem of constitutional interpretation and enforcement by delegating it to judges. Their thinking was more complex and, frankly, more imaginative than that. They were too steeped in republicanism to think that the solution to the problem of republican politics was to chop it off at the knees. Their structural solutions were meant to operate in politics: elections, bicameralism, an executive veto, political connections between state and national governments, and, above all, the capacity of politicians with competing interests to appeal for support to the people who made the Constitution. An idea of judicial review did eventually emerge, but it was fenced in by concern for preserving the essence of this popular constitutionalism. The precise terms on which these competing principles were accommodated have varied over time, but both have been with us all along. And no matter how often the Court repeats that it has been the ultimate expositor of the Constitution since *Marbury*, it still will not have been so. Popular constitutionalism—understood as a domain in which the people are free to settle questions of constitutional law by and for themselves in politics—has been a prominent feature of American constitutional practice from the beginning. We have never had the purely legal Constitution of the Rehnquist Court, a stripped-down fundamental law whose democratic essence has been abstracted to a distant horizon. Nor has stewardship of our Constitution ever been turned over exclusively to lawyers and judges.

I said at the outset that I would not make an originalist claim, and I do not mean to do so now. The point is not that the Rehnquist Court's vision of the Constitution is wrong because the Founding generation would have rejected it or because popular constitutionalism has been a vital part of our practice all along, though both things are true. I am not interested (here) in getting into a complex debate about how much normative weight history should carry in law. My present objective is more modest: to denaturalize a set of assumptions that are taken as natural by many, including especially the conservative majority on the Rehnquist Court and its supporters off the Court. Insofar as the Justices have chosen their path in the belief that, in doing so, they are vindicating the Constitution, either as it was originally understood or as it was viewed until recently, they are mistaken. It does not automatically follow that they are wrong to enlarge the scope of their authority. But it does follow that they need an explanation and a justification they have yet to provide. Certainly more needs to be done than quoting *Marbury* out of context or offering really bad renditions of the Founding.

Perhaps the argument should be stated more strongly. History may not compel us to embrace the Founders' exact understanding of popular constitutionalism, but it does suggest that one position at least is not plausible: the one embraced by the Rehnquist Court, which denies that popular constitutionalism is even a valid concept. In fact, both our theory and our practice have always reserved substantial space for the people to have a say in interpreting their Constitution, albeit in complex ways that have changed over time. Popular constitutionalism is not some quaint curiosity from the Founders' world. It is a vital principle that has been part of our constitutional tradition all along. To deny that there are spaces outside the Court where constitutional decisions are made, decisions to which judges are subservient, is a radical and unprecedented idea. There is a place for judicial supremacy, but it has bounds. There is no place for the totalizing claims of judicial sovereignty.

We are left, then, with a normative problem: What is the proper relationship between popular constitutionalism and judicial supremacy? How should we divide the world of constitutional law between the Court and politics? These are not easy questions, and answering them properly would require another article at least this long. We would, among other things, need to agree upon a theory of constitutional interpretation and to investigate a wide range of related philosophical and empirical matters. Anything less would not do justice to this important and daunting problem. It is enough for present purposes, I hope, to uncover the problem, and in doing so to highlight the radical nature of the Rehnquist Court's recent decisions. Beyond that, I want merely to offer some preliminary observations meant to help structure thinking about the larger normative questions that remain.

. . . [T]he Constitution is not and never has been ordinary law, that while it has many features we associate with ordinary law, it retains a substantial ingredient of popular constitutionalism. Why hold to a view of the Constitution that fails so miserably to explain our actual practice? It would be one thing if popular constitutionalism were normatively undesirable or inconsistent with the basic objectives or purposes of the Constitution. But exactly the opposite is true. The central objective of the Constitution is to facilitate democratic politics, to call into being a regime of republican self-government. Popular constitutionalism is, if anything, more consistent than judicial review with the basic concept of the Constitution—which is why it provided our historical starting point and why constitutional theorists in earlier generations thought they needed

to spend all their time struggling to justify judicial review at all.

I am not suggesting that we abolish judicial review, or even judicial supremacy. Surely we need not rehearse here the familiar arguments about the many ways courts exercising review can reinforce democratic politics and enhance constitutional values, arguments our historical experience offers plenty of reasons to accept. These benefits are, however, functional and instrumental, for the history makes equally clear that judicial review is not required by the structure of our Constitution, much less implicit in the very notion of a written constitution. Judicial review emerged in response to specific conditions and for specific reasons, and it has served identifiable purposes over time. Yet if anything is implicit in the Constitution, it is a general preference for democratic solutions: that, after all, was the whole point. And the more important the problem, the stronger that preference becomes. We may still conclude that we need or want courts to settle certain problems or to counter certain endemic pathologies of party politics and representative assemblies. But less is more when it comes to limiting self-government, and we should be thinking about a minimal model of judicial review that calls upon judges to intercede only where necessary. It goes without saying that such an approach is consistent with historical experience. Yet it is virtually the opposite of the approach taken by the present Supreme Court, which presumes that questions respecting the Constitution are, by virtue of that alone, questions to be resolved by them and not us.

History may not tell us what to do. But it can tell us who we were and in this way help us understand who we have become. Legend has it that, as he left the

Constitutional Convention, Benjamin Franklin was approached by a woman who asked him, "What have you given us, Dr. Franklin?" "A republic," he replied, "if you can keep it." Have we? For all the disagreement about what we mean by "republic," no one has ever doubted that self-government is its essence and a constitution the purest distillate. What kind of republic removes its constitution from the process of self-governing? Certainly not the one our Founders gave us. Is it one we prefer? The choice, after all, is ours. The Supreme Court has made its grab for power. The question is: will we let them get away with it?

Jeremy Waldron

THE CORE OF THE CASE AGAINST JUDICIAL REVIEW

115 Yale L.J. 1346 (2006)

INTRODUCTION

Should judges have the authority to strike down legislation when they are convinced that it violates individual rights? In many countries they do. The best known example is the United States. In November 2003, the Supreme Judicial Court of Massachusetts ruled that the state's marriage licensing laws violated state constitutional rights to due process and equal protection by implicitly limiting marriage to a union between a man and a woman.... A good decision and a process in which claims of rights are steadily and seriously considered—for many people these are reasons for cherishing the institution of judicial review.... We can, they argue, put up with an occasional bad outcome as the price of a practice that has given us decisions like *Lawrence, Roe,* and *Brown,* which upheld our society's commitment to individual rights in the face of prejudiced majorities.

. . . This Essay will argue that judicial review of legislation is inappropriate as a mode of final decisionmaking in a free and democratic society.

. . . In liberal political theory, legislative supremacy is often associated with popular self-government, and democratic ideals are bound to stand in an uneasy relation to any practice that says elected legislatures are to operate only on the sufferance of unelected judges. Alexander Bickel summed up the issue in the well-known phrase, "the counter-majoritarian difficulty." . . .

In countries that do not allow legislation to be invalidated in this way, the people themselves can decide finally, by ordinary legislative procedures, whether they want to permit abortion, affirmative action, school vouchers, or gay marriage. . . .

What I want to do is identify a core argument against judicial review that is independent of both its historical manifestations and questions about its particular effects—the decisions (good and bad) that it has yielded, the heartbreaks and affirmations it has handed down. . . .

The members of the community are committed to rights, but they disagree about rights. Most issues of rights are in need of settlement. We need settlement not so much to dispose of the issue— nothing can do that—but to provide a basis for common action when action is necessary. Now, there are all sorts of issues on which we do not need society-wide settlement—transubstantiation, the meaning of *Hamlet*, the value of a purely contemplative life—and that is fortunate, because there is little prospect of agreement in these areas. Unfortunately, on issues of rights, for which we do need settlement, there is little prospect of agreement either. The need for settlement does not make the fact of disagreement evaporate; rather, it means that a common basis for action has to be forged in the heat of our disagreements.

In the real world, the need for settlement confronts us in the legislative arena. We legislate in certain areas, and the legislation we enact raises issues of rights. Those issues may not be facially prominent in the legislation. The legislation may be on marriage formalities, minimum working hours, campaign finance reform, or the historic preservation of city centers, but what happens is that somebody notices that its application happens to raise an issue of rights and it is in connection with that issue—is the legislation to be applied according to its terms or not?—that the need for settlement arises.

Let us assume, for now, that the legislature is broadly aware of the issues of rights that a given bill gives rise to and that, having deliberated on the matter, it resolves—through debate and voting—to settle those issues in a particular way. The legislature takes sides on one or more of the disagreements we imagined in assumption four. The question we face is whether that resolution of the legislature should be dispositive or whether there is reason to have it second-guessed and perhaps overruled by the judiciary.

How should we answer this question? I have heard people say that the decision-rule should be this: The legislature's decision stands, except when it violates rights. But clearly this will not do. We are assuming that the members of the society disagree about whether a given legislative proposal violates rights. We need a way of resolving that disagreement. The point is as old as Hobbes: We must set up a decision-procedure whose operation will settle, not reignite, the controversies whose existence called for a decision-procedure in the first place. This means that even though the members of the society we are imagining disagree about rights, they need to share a theory of legitimacy for the decision-procedure that is to settle their disagreements. So, in thinking about the reasons for setting up such a procedure, we should think about reasons that can be subscribed to by people on both sides of any one of these disagreements.

No decision-procedure will be perfect. Whether it is a process of legislation that cannot be reviewed or whether it is a process of judicial review, it will sometimes come to the wrong decision, betraying rights rather than upholding them. This is a fact of life in politics. Everyone must concede that there will sometimes be a dissonance between what they take to be the right choice and what they take to be the choice yielded by the decision-procedure they regard as legitimate. Richard Wollheim called this "a paradox in the theory of democracy," because it allows one and the same citizen to assert that A ought not to be enacted, where A is the policy he voted against, and A ought to be enacted, because A is the policy chosen by the majority. But Wollheim was wrong to ascribe this paradox to democracy. It is a general paradox in the theory of politics affecting any political theory that complements its account of what ought to be done with an account of how decisions ought to be made when there is disagreement about what ought to be done.

With that caution in mind, what are the reasons that need to be taken into account in designing or evaluating a decision-procedure for settling disagreements about rights? Two sorts of reasons may be considered. I shall call them "outcome-related" and "process-related" reasons, though they are both relevant to the issue of decision-procedure.

Process-related reasons are reasons for insisting that some person make, or participate in making, a given decision that stand independently of considerations about the appropriate outcome. In personal life, we sometimes say that a parent has the right to make the decision as to whether her child should be disciplined for a given infraction: It is not for a passer-by on the street or another passenger on the bus to make that decision. We may say that while reserving judgment on whether the child should be disciplined. Indeed, we may say that even though we think the passer-by is likely to make a better decision on this than the parent. In politics, the most familiar process-related reasons are those based on political equality and the democratic right to vote, the right to have one's voice counted even when others disagree with what one says.

Outcome-related reasons, by contrast, are reasons for designing the decision-procedure in a way that will ensure the appropriate outcome (i.e., a good, just, or right decision). Our subject matter is disagreements about rights. Because rights are important, it is likewise important that we get them right and so we must take outcome-related reasons very seriously indeed. Wrong answers may be tolerable in matters of policy; but on matters of principle, if the wrong answer is given, then rights will be violated. The members of the society we are imagining understand how important it is to avoid such outcomes or minimize them to the extent they can.

Of course, it may not be easy to identify outcome-related reasons that people on opposing sides of rights-disagreements can agree upon. As I said earlier, the design of a decision-procedure must be independent of the particular disagreement it is supposed to settle; it is no good if it simply reignites it. So we must avoid outcome-related reasons that aim specifically at particular controversial outcomes—e.g., favoring a decision-procedure because it is more likely to generate a pro-choice than a pro-life outcome. A decision-procedure chosen on this basis will hardly command the allegiance of the pro-life advocates. Given the disagreement, the whole point here is to set up a procedure for generating settlements in a way that can be recognized as legitimate on both sides.

So, how do we weigh these process-related and outcome-related considerations? We face the familiar problem of trying to maximize the value of two variables, like asking someone to buy the fastest car at the lowest price. There are various ways we can set up the question. We could ask: "What method is most likely to get at the truth about rights, while at the same time adequately respecting the equal claim to be heard of the voices of those affected?" Or we could ask: "What method best respects the equal claim to be heard of the voices of those affected, while at the same time being reasonably likely to get at the truth about rights?" I think I can cut through this Gordian knot. What I will argue . . . is that the outcome-related reasons are at best inconclusive. They are important, but they do not (as is commonly thought) establish anything like a clear case for judicial review. The process-related reasons, however, are quite one-sided. They operate mainly to discredit judicial review while leaving legislative decisionmaking unscathed. Thus, it seems to me the legislative side wins on either formulation of the question. And that will be the core of the case against judicial review.

It is tempting to associate outcome-related reasons with the case for judicial review (and process-related reasons with the case against it). This is a mistake. It is true that many of the more important process-related reasons are participatory and therefore favor elective or representative institutions. But it does not follow that all or most outcome-related reasons argue the other way. Outcome-related reasons, as we shall see, cut in both directions. There are things about legislatures that sometimes make them vulnerable to the sorts of pressures that rights are supposed to guard against; but there are also things about courts that make it difficult for them to grapple directly with the moral issues that rights-disagreements present.

In general, what I notice when I read outcome-related arguments in favor of judicial review is that people assume that an outcome-related case must be able to be made in favor of courts, if only because the most familiar arguments against judicial review are non-outcome-related. People strain to associate outcome-related reasons with the judiciary, and in so doing they often peddle a quite unrealistic picture of what judicial decisionmaking is like. Opponents of judicial review are often accused of adopting a naively optimistic view of legislatures. But sometimes we do this deliberately, matching one optimistic picture with another in the face of the refusal of the defenders of courts to give a realistic account of what happens there.

People sometimes argue that the wonderful thing about judicial reasoning on rights (as opposed to legislative reasoning on rights) is that issues of rights present themselves to judges in the form of flesh-and-blood individual situations. . . .

But this is mostly a myth. By the time cases reach the high appellate levels we are mostly talking about in our disputes about judicial review, almost all trace of the original flesh-and-blood right-holders has vanished, and argument such as it is revolves around the abstract issue of the right in dispute. Plaintiffs or petitioners are selected by advocacy groups precisely in order to embody the abstract characteristics that the groups want to emphasize as part of a general public policy argument. . . .

The process of legislation is open to consideration of individual cases, through lobbying, in hearings, and in debate. Indeed, there is a tendency these days to initiate legislation on the basis of notorious individual cases—Megan's Law, for example. Hard cases make bad law, it is sometimes said. To the extent that this is true, it seems to me that legislatures are much better positioned to mount an assessment of the significance of an individual case in relation to a general issue of rights that affects millions and affects them in many different ways.

We are imagining a society with a Bill of Rights, and if there is to be judicial review of legislation, it will presumably center on the Bill of Rights. The Bill of Rights, we have assumed, has been adopted in the society pursuant to members' shared commitment to the idea of individual and minority rights notwithstanding the fact that they disagree about what these rights are and what they entail. Now, when rights-disagreements erupt in regard to legislation, there is a question about the role that the established Bill of Rights should play in the decision-process in which the issue is posed. From an outcome-related point of view, is it a good idea or a bad idea that rights-disagreements be fought out in relation to the terms of a Bill of Rights?

One reason for thinking it is a good idea is that the written formulations of the Bill of Rights can help disputants focus on the abstract rights-issues at stake. But there are powerful reasons on the other side. The forms of words used in the Bill of Rights will not have been chosen with rights-disagreements in mind. Or, if they were, they will have been chosen in order to finesse the disagreements about rights that existed at the time the Bill of Rights was set up. Their platitudes may be exactly the wrong formulations to focus clear-headed, responsible, and good faith explorations of rights-disagreements.

The written formulations of a Bill of Rights also tend to encourage a certain rigid textual formalism. A legal right that finds protection in a Bill of Rights finds it under the auspices of some canonical form of words in which the provisions of the Bill are enunciated. One lesson of American constitutional experience is that the words of each provision tend to take on a life of their own, becoming the obsessive catchphrase for expressing everything one might want to say about the right in question. . . .

. . . [C]ourts will tend to be distracted in their arguments about rights by side arguments about how a text like the Bill of Rights is best approached by judges. American experience bears this out: The proportion of argument about theories of interpretation to direct argument about the moral issues is skewed in most judicial opinions in a way that no one who thinks the issues themselves are important can possibly regard as satisfactory. This is partly because the legitimacy of judicial review is itself so problematic. Because judges (like the rest of us) are concerned about the legitimacy of a process that

permits them to decide these issues, they cling to their authorizing texts and debate their interpretation rather than venturing out to discuss moral reasons directly.

It is often thought that the great advantage of judicial decisionmaking on issues of individual rights is the explicit reasoning and reason-giving associated with it. Courts give reasons for their decisions, we are told, and this is a token of taking seriously what is at stake, whereas legislatures do not. In fact, this is a false contrast. Legislators give reasons for their votes just as judges do. The reasons are given in what we call debate and they are published in Hansard or the Congressional Record. . . .

Perhaps this argument is not really about the presence or absence of reason-giving, but rather about its quality. In my view, however, the reasons that courts tend to give when they are exercising powers of judicial review of legislation are seldom the reasons that would be canvassed in a full deliberative discussion. . . . Partly this is the point mentioned earlier—that the reasons will be oriented toward the terminology of the Bill of Rights. . . .

Courts' reason-giving also involves attempts to construct desperate analogies or disanalogies between the present decision they face and other decisions that happen to have come before them (and in which they were engaged in similar contortions). There is laborious discussion of precedent, even though it is acknowledged at the highest levels of adjudication that precedent does not settle the matter. (So there is also laborious discussion of the circumstances in which precedent should or shouldn't be overridden.) And all the time, the real issues at stake in the good faith disagreement about rights get pushed to the margins. . . .

. . . Courts are concerned about the legitimacy of their decisionmaking and so they focus their "reason-giving" on facts that tend to show that they are legally authorized—by constitution, statute, or precedent—to make the decision they are proposing to make. This is an understandable thing to do. But it counts heavily against the courts in the outcome-related argument about the preferability of judicial review over legislation. Distracted by these issues of legitimacy, courts focus on what other courts have done, or what the language of the Bill of Rights is, whereas legislators—for all their vices—tend at least to go directly to the heart of the matter.

I am sure there is more to be said on the outcome-related question. It is certainly the case that just as courts address questions of rights in ways that distort what is really at stake, so too can legislative reasoning be a disgrace, as legislative majorities act out of panic, recklessly, or simply parrot popular or sectarian slogans in their pseudo-debates. The question is this: Which defects in deliberation should be regarded as normal and which as aberrations in the way that the respective institutions—courts and legislatures—are supposed to behave? Despite Dworkin's rhetoric about "forums of principle," I think courts are expected to behave in the ways that I have criticized, focusing on precedent, text, doctrine, and other legalisms. Our assumption about courts—assumption two—is about institutions that behave in that way, indeed behave well by those (legalistic) standards. In the case of legislatures, however, hasty or sectarian legislating is not part of the normal theory of what legislatures are set up to do. It is not what we should assume for the core case of legislative decisionmaking in a society most of whose members respect rights. There may be some countries—perhaps the United States—in which peculiar legislative pathologies have developed. If that is so, then Americans should confine their non-core argument for judicial review to their own exceptional circumstances. . . .

COOPER v. AARON

358 U.S. 1 (1958)

Opinion: Warren, Black, Frankfurter, Douglas, Burton, Clark, Harlan, Brennan, Whittaker
Concurrence: Frankfurter

Following the Supreme Court's 1954 decision in Brown v. Board of Education, *which held that racial discrimination in public schools is an unconstitutional violation of the Equal Protection Clause of the Fourteenth Amendment, Little Rock, Arkansas, adopted a plan to integrate its schools beginning in 1957. Massive resistance in the form of popular discontent, mob violence, and obstructive measures by the state legislature and Governor Orval Faubus disrupted these efforts. Only the intervention of federal troops allowed the integrated schools to continue operating safely. In response to these difficulties, local officials sought to suspend implementation of the desegregation proposal. In a unanimous decision, the Supreme Court reaffirmed its holding in* Brown v. Board of Education *and maintained that state officials were bound to enforce and abide by that decision. In a separate concurrence, Justice Felix Frankfurter argued that the rule of law requires that the Court have the final say in the face of open resistance.*

Opinion of the Court by **THE CHIEF JUSTICE, MR. JUSTICE BLACK, MR. JUSTICE FRANKFURTER, MR. JUSTICE DOUGLAS, MR. JUSTICE BURTON, MR. JUSTICE CLARK, MR. JUSTICE HARLAN, MR. JUSTICE BRENNAN,** *and* **MR. JUSTICE WHITTAKER.**

The constitutional rights of respondents are not to be sacrificed or yielded to the violence and disorder which have followed upon the actions of the Governor and Legislature. As this Court said some 41 years ago in a unanimous opinion in a case involving another aspect of racial segregation: "It is urged that this proposed segregation will promote the public peace by preventing race conflicts. Desirable as this is, and important as is the preservation of the public peace, this aim cannot be accomplished by laws or ordinances which deny rights created or protected by the Federal Constitution." Thus law and order are not here to be preserved by depriving the Negro children of their constitutional rights. The record before us clearly establishes that the growth of the Board's difficulties to a magnitude beyond its unaided power to control is the product of state action. Those difficulties, as counsel for the Board forthrightly conceded on the oral argument in this Court, can also be brought under control by state action. The controlling legal principles are plain. The command of the Fourteenth Amendment is that no "State" shall deny to any person within its jurisdiction the equal protection of the laws. "A State acts by its legislative, its executive, or its judicial authorities. It can act in no other way. The constitutional provision, therefore, must mean that no agency of the State, or of the officers or agents by whom its powers are exerted, shall deny to any person within its jurisdiction the equal protection of the laws. Whoever, by virtue of public position under a State government, . . . denies or takes away the equal protection of the laws, violates the constitutional inhibition; and as he acts in the name and for the State, and is clothed with the State's power, his act is that of the State. This must be so, or the constitutional prohibition has no meaning." *Ex parte Virginia.* Thus the prohibitions of the Fourteenth Amendment extend to all action of the State denying equal protection of the laws; whatever the agency of the State taking the action, or whatever the guise in which it is taken. In short, the constitutional rights of children not to be discriminated against in school admission on grounds of race or color declared by this Court in the *Brown* case can neither be nullified openly and directly by state legislators or state executive or judicial officers, nor nullified indirectly by them through evasive schemes for segregation whether attempted "ingeniously or ingenuously."

. . . [W]e should answer the premise of the actions of the Governor and Legislature that they are not bound by our holding in the *Brown* case. It is necessary only to recall some basic constitutional propositions which are settled doctrine.

Article VI of the Constitution makes the Constitution the "supreme Law of the Land." In 1803, Chief Justice Marshall, speaking for a unanimous Court, referring to the Constitution as "the fundamental and paramount law of the nation," declared in the notable case of *Marbury v. Madison*, that "It is emphatically the province and duty of the judicial department to say what the law is." This decision declared the basic principle that the federal judiciary is supreme in the exposition of the law of the Constitution, and that principle has ever since been respected by this Court and the Country as a permanent and indispensable feature of our constitutional system. It follows that the interpretation of the Fourteenth

Amendment enunciated by this Court in the *Brown* case is the supreme law of the land, and Art. VI of the Constitution makes it of binding effect on the States "any Thing in the Constitution or Laws of any State to the Contrary notwithstanding." Every state legislator and executive and judicial officer is solemnly committed by oath taken pursuant to Art. VI, cl. 3, "to support this Constitution." Chief Justice Taney, speaking for a unanimous Court in 1859, said that this requirement reflected the framers' "anxiety to preserve it [the Constitution] in full force, in all its powers, and to guard against resistance to or evasion of its authority, on the part of a State. . . . "

No state legislator or executive or judicial officer can war against the Constitution without violating his undertaking to support it. Chief Justice Marshall spoke for a unanimous Court in saying that: "If the legislatures of the several states may, at will, annul the judgments of the courts of the United States, and destroy the rights acquired under those judgments, the constitution itself becomes a solemn mockery. . . . " A Governor who asserts a power to nullify a federal court order is similarly restrained. If he had such power, said Chief Justice Hughes, in 1932, also for a unanimous Court, "it is manifest that the fiat of a state Governor, and not the Constitution of the United States, would be the supreme law of the land; that the restrictions of the Federal Constitution upon the exercise of state power would be but impotent phrases. . . ."

It is, of course, quite true that the responsibility for public education is primarily the concern of the States, but it is equally true that such responsibilities, like all other state activity, must be exercised consistently with federal constitutional requirements as they apply to state action. The Constitution created a government dedicated to equal justice under law. The Fourteenth Amendment embodied and emphasized that ideal. State support of segregated schools through any arrangement, management, funds, or property cannot be squared with the Amendment's command that no State shall deny to any person within its jurisdiction the equal protection of the laws. The right of a student not to be segregated on racial grounds in schools so maintained is indeed so fundamental and pervasive that it is embraced in the concept of due process of law. *Bolling v. Sharpe.* The basic decision in *Brown* was unanimously reached by this Court only after the case had been briefed and twice argued and the issues had been given the most serious consideration. Since the first *Brown* opinion three new Justices have come to the Court. They are at one with the Justices still on the Court who participated in that basic decision as to its correctness, and that decision is now unanimously reaffirmed. The principles announced in that decision and the obedience of the States to them, according to the command of the Constitution, are indispensable for the protection of the freedoms guaranteed by our fundamental charter for all of us. Our constitutional ideal of equal justice under law is thus made a living truth.

JUSTICE FRANKFURTER, *concurring.*

By working together, by sharing in a common effort, men of different minds and tempers, even if they do not reach agreement, acquire understanding and thereby tolerance of their differences. This process was under way in Little Rock. The detailed plan formulated by the Little Rock School Board, in the light of local circumstances, had been approved by the United States District Court in Arkansas as satisfying the requirements of this Court's decree in *Brown v. Board of Education.* The Little Rock School Board had embarked on an educational effort "to obtain public acceptance" of its plan. Thus the process of the community's accommodation to new demands of law upon it, the development of habits of acceptance of the right of colored children to the equal protection of the laws guaranteed by the Constitution, had peacefully and promisingly begun. The condition in Little Rock before this process was forcibly impeded by those in control of the government of Arkansas was thus described by the District Court, and these findings of fact have not been controverted:

> "Up to this time, no crowds had gathered about Central High School and no acts of violence or threats of violence in connection with the carrying out of the plan had occurred. Nevertheless, out of an abundance of caution, the school authorities had frequently conferred with the Mayor and Chief of Police of Little Rock about taking appropriate steps by the Little Rock police to prevent any possible disturbances or acts of violence in connection with the attendance of the 9 colored students at Central High School. The Mayor considered that the Little Rock police force could adequately cope with any incidents which might arise at the opening of school. The Mayor, the Chief of Police, and the school authorities made no request to the Governor or any representative of his for State assistance in maintaining peace and order at Central High School. Neither the Governor nor any other official of the State government consulted with the Little Rock authorities about whether the Little Rock police were prepared to cope with any incidents which might arise at the school, about any need for State assistance in maintaining peace and order, or about stationing the Arkansas National Guard at Central High School."

All this was disrupted by the introduction of the state militia and by other obstructive measures taken by the State. The illegality of these interferences with the constitutional right of Negro children qualified to enter the Central High School is unaffected by whatever action or non-action the Federal Government had seen fit to take. Nor is it neutralized by the undoubted good faith of the Little Rock School Board in endeavoring to discharge its constitutional duty.

The use of force to further obedience to law is in any event a last resort and one not congenial to the spirit of our Nation. But the tragic aspect of this disruptive tactic was that the power of the State was used not to sustain law but as an instrument for thwarting law. The State of Arkansas is thus responsible for disabling one of its subordinate agencies, the Little Rock School Board, from peacefully carrying out the Board's and the State's constitutional duty. Accordingly, while Arkansas is not a formal party in these proceedings and a decree cannot go against the State, it is legally and morally before the Court.

We are now asked to hold that the illegal, forcible interference by the State of Arkansas with the continuance of what the Constitution commands, and the consequences in disorder that it entrained, should be recognized as justification for undoing what the School Board had formulated, what the District Court in 1955 had directed to be carried out, and what was in process of obedience. No explanation that may be offered in support of such a request can obscure the inescapable meaning that law should bow to force. To yield to such a claim would be to enthrone official lawlessness, and lawlessness if not checked is the precursor of anarchy. On the few tragic occasions in the history of the Nation, North and South, when law was forcibly resisted or systematically evaded, it has signaled the breakdown of constitutional processes of government on which ultimately rest the liberties of all. Violent resistance to law cannot be made a legal reason for its suspension without loosening the fabric of our society. What could this mean but to acknowledge that disorder under the aegis of a State has moral superiority over the law of the Constitution? For those in authority thus to defy the law of the land is profoundly subversive not only of our constitutional system but of the presuppositions of a democratic society. The State "must . . . yield to an authority that is paramount to the State." . . .

When defiance of law judicially pronounced was last sought to be justified before this Court, views were expressed which are now especially relevant:

"The historic phrase 'a government of laws and not of men' epitomizes the distinguishing character of our political society. When John Adams put that phrase into the Massachusetts Declaration of Rights he was not indulging in a rhetorical flourish. He was expressing the aim of those who, with him, framed the Declaration of Independence and founded the Republic. 'A government of laws and not of men' was the rejection in positive terms of rule by fiat, whether by the fiat of governmental or private power. Every act of government may be challenged by an appeal to law, as finally pronounced by this Court. Even this Court has the last say only for a time. Being composed of fallible men, it may err. But revision of its errors must be by orderly process of law. The Court may be asked to reconsider its decisions, and this has been done successfully again and again throughout our history. Or, what this Court has deemed its duty to decide may be changed by legislation, as it often has been, and, on occasion, by constitutional amendment.

"But from their own experience and their deep reading in history, the Founders knew that Law alone saves a society from being rent by internecine strife or ruled by mere brute power however disguised. 'Civilization involves subjection of force to reason, and the agency of this subjection is law.' The conception of a government by laws dominated the thoughts of those who founded this Nation and designed its Constitution, although they knew as well as the belittlers of the conception that laws have to be made, interpreted and enforced by men. To that end, they set apart a body of men, who were to be the depositories of law, who by their disciplined training and character and by withdrawal from the usual temptations of private interest may reasonably be expected to be 'as free, impartial, and independent as the lot of humanity will admit.' So strongly were the framers of the Constitution bent on securing a reign of law that they endowed the judicial office with extraordinary safeguards and prestige. No one, no matter how exalted his public office or how righteous his private motive, can be judge in his own case. That is what courts are for."

The duty to abstain from resistance to "the supreme Law of the Land," U.S. Const., Art. VI, para. 2, as declared by the organ of our Government for ascertaining it, does not require immediate approval of it nor does it deny the right of dissent. Criticism need not be stilled. Active obstruction or defiance is barred. Our kind of society cannot endure if the controlling authority of the Law as derived from the Constitution is not to be the tribunal specially charged with the duty of ascertaining and declaring what is "the supreme Law of the Land." Particularly is this so where the declaration of what "the supreme Law" commands on an underlying moral issue is not the dubious pronouncement of a gravely divided Court but is the unanimous conclusion of a long-matured deliberative process. The Constitution is not the formulation of the merely personal views of the members of this Court, nor can its authority be reduced to the claim that state officials are its controlling interpreters. Local customs, however hardened by time, are not decreed in heaven. Habits and feelings they engender may be counteracted and moderated. Experience attests that such local habits and feelings will yield, gradually though this be, to law and education. And educational influences are exerted not only by explicit teaching. They vigorously flow from the fruitful exercise of the responsibility of those charged with political official power and from the almost unconsciously transforming actualities of living under law.

The process of ending unconstitutional exclusion of pupils from the common school system—"common" meaning shared alike—solely because of color is no doubt not an easy, overnight task in a few States where a drastic alteration in the ways of communities is involved. Deep emotions have, no doubt, been stirred. They will not be calmed by letting violence loose—violence and defiance employed and encouraged by those upon whom the duty of law observance should have the strongest claim—nor by submitting to it under whatever guise employed. Only the constructive use of time will achieve what an advanced civilization demands and the Constitution confirms.

That the responsibility of those who exercise power in a democratic government is not to reflect inflamed public feeling but to help form its understanding, is especially true when they are confronted with a problem like a racially discriminating public school system. This is the lesson to be drawn from the heartening experience in ending enforced racial segregation in the public schools in cities with Negro populations of large proportions. Compliance with decisions of this Court, as the constitutional organ of the supreme Law of the Land, has often, throughout our history, depended on active support by state and local authorities. It presupposes such support. To withhold it, and indeed to use political power to try to paralyze the supreme Law, precludes the maintenance of our federal system as we have known and cherished it for one hundred and seventy years.

Lincoln's appeal to "the better angels of our nature" failed to avert a fratricidal war. But the compassionate wisdom of Lincoln's First and Second Inaugurals bequeathed to the Union, cemented with blood, a moral heritage which, when drawn upon in times of stress and strife, is sure to find specific ways and means to surmount difficulties that may appear to be insurmountable.

NIXON v. UNITED STATES

506 U.S. 224 (1993)

Opinion: Rehnquist, joined by O'Connor, Blackmun, Scalia, Kennedy, Thomas
Concurrence: White, joined by Blackmun
Concurrence: Stevens
Concurrence: Souter

Although, as we will see in the next case, the Supreme Court has suggested that it not only has a role in interpreting the Constitution but that its interpretive power is supreme, this has not meant that the modern Court has failed to show restraint in decisions involving the other branches of government. The following selection is an example of the Court's political question doctrine, under which it refuses to review a case because it deems it a matter under the authority of the other branches. In reading this case, consider whether the political question doctrine is compatible with the notion of judicial supremacy. Is deferring to the legislative branch of government on this issue equivalent to deferring to its interpretation of the Constitution?

The political question doctrine recognizes that the Constitution explicitly grants some powers of decision making to either the Congress or the executive branch and suggests that they might be the appropriate forum for judging the meaning of the Constitution in those arenas. The more expansive the political question doctrine, arguably, the more the Court exercises restraint in matters of constitutional interpretation. But, does the fact that the Court itself determines when the political question doctrine is appropriately invoked provide evidence that it is compatible with an idea of judicial supremacy? Consider this question as you read this case. Although we introduce the political question doctrine in this chapter, we revisit the concept throughout this book. For example, it will be relevant to whether the Supreme Court has a role in ensuring equal voting power in Chapter 8 as well as the question of whether the president has an authority to end treaties in Chapter 4.

CHIEF JUSTICE REHNQUIST *delivered the opinion of the Court.*

Petitioner Walter L. Nixon, Jr., asks this court to decide whether Senate Rule XI, which allows a committee of Senators to hear evidence against an individual who has been impeached and to report that evidence to the full Senate, violates the Impeachment Trial Clause, Art. I, §3, cl. 6. That Clause provides that the "Senate shall have the sole Power to try all Impeachments." But before we reach the merits of such a claim, we must decide whether it is "justiciable," that is, whether it is a claim that may be resolved by the courts. We conclude that it is not.

Nixon, a former Chief Judge of the United States District Court for the Southern District of Mississippi, was convicted by a jury of two counts of making false statements before a federal grand jury and sentenced to prison. The grand

jury investigation stemmed from reports that Nixon had accepted a gratuity from a Mississippi businessman in exchange for asking a local district attorney to halt the prosecution of the businessman's son. Because Nixon refused to resign from his office as a United States District Judge, he continued to collect his judicial salary while serving out his prison sentence.

On May 10, 1989, the House of Representatives adopted three articles of impeachment for high crimes and misdemeanors. The first two articles charged Nixon with giving false testimony before the grand jury and the third article charged him with bringing disrepute on the Federal Judiciary.

After the House presented the articles to the Senate, the Senate voted to invoke its own Impeachment Rule XI, under which the presiding officer appoints a committee of Senators to "receive evidence and take testimony." The Senate committee held four days of hearings, during which 10 witnesses, including Nixon, testified. Pursuant to Rule XI, the committee presented the full Senate with a complete transcript of the proceeding and a report stating the uncontested facts and summarizing the evidence on the contested facts. Nixon and the House impeachment managers submitted extensive final briefs to the full Senate and delivered arguments from the Senate floor during the three hours set aside for oral argument in front of that body. Nixon himself gave a personal appeal, and several Senators posed questions directly to both parties. The Senate voted by more than the constitutionally required two thirds majority to convict Nixon on the first two articles. The presiding officer then entered judgment removing Nixon from his office as United States District Judge.

Nixon thereafter commenced the present suit, arguing that Senate Rule XI violates the constitutional grant of authority to the Senate to "try" all impeachments because it prohibits the whole Senate from taking part in the evidentiary hearings. Nixon sought a declaratory judgment that his impeachment conviction was void and that his judicial salary and privileges should be reinstated. The District Court held that his claim was nonjusticiable, and the Court of Appeals for the District of Columbia Circuit agreed.

A controversy is nonjusticiable—*i.e.*, involves a political question—where there is "a textually demonstrable constitutional commitment of the issue to a coordinate political department; or a lack of judicially discoverable and manageable standards for resolving it. . . ." *Baker v. Carr*. But the courts must, in the first instance, interpret the text in question and determine whether and to what extent the issue is textually committed. *Powell v. McCormack*. As the discussion that follows makes clear, the concept of a textual commitment to coordinate political department is not completely separate from the concept of a lack of judicially discoverable and manageable standards for resolving it; the lack of judicially manageable standards may strengthen the conclusion that there is a textually demonstrable commitment to a coordinate branch.

In this case, we must examine Art. I, §3, cl. 6, to determine the scope of authority conferred upon the Senate by the Framers regarding impeachment. It provides:

> "The Senate shall have the sole Power to try all Impeachments. When sitting for that Purpose, they shall be on Oath or Affirmation. When the President of the United States is tried, the Chief Justice shall preside: And no Person shall be convicted without the Concurrence of two thirds of the Members present."

The language and structure of this Clause are revealing. The first sentence is a grant of authority to the Senate, and the word "sole" indicates that this authority is reposed in the Senate and nowhere else. The next two sentences specify requirements to which the Senate proceedings shall conform: the Senate shall be on oath or affirmation, a two thirds vote is required to convict, and when the President is tried the Chief Justice shall preside.

Petitioner argues that the word "try" in the first sentence imposes by implication an additional requirement on the Senate in that the proceedings must be in the nature of a judicial trial. From there petitioner goes on to argue that this limitation precludes the Senate from delegating to a select committee the task of hearing the testimony of witnesses, as was done pursuant to Senate Rule XI. "'[T]ry' means more than simply 'vote on' or 'review' or 'judge.' In 1787 and today, trying a case means hearing the evidence, not scanning a cold record." Petitioner concludes from this that courts may review whether or not the Senate "tried" him before convicting him.

There are several difficulties with this position which lead us ultimately to reject it. The word "try," both in 1787 and later, has considerably broader meanings than those to which petitioner would limit it. Older dictionaries define try as "[t]o examine" or "[t]o examine as a judge." In more modern usage the term has various meanings. For example, try can mean "to examine or investigate judicially," "to conduct the trial of," or "to put to the test by experiment, investigation, or trial." Petitioner submits that "try," as contained in T. Sheridan, *Dictionary of the English Language* (1796), means "to examine as a judge; to bring before a judicial tribunal." Based on the variety of definitions, however, we cannot say that the Framers used the word "try" as an implied limitation on the method by which the Senate might proceed in trying impeachments. "As a rule the Constitution speaks in general terms, leaving Congress to deal with subsidiary matters of detail as the public interests and changing conditions may require...." *Dillon v. Gloss.*

The conclusion that the use of the word "try" in the first sentence of the Impeachment Trial Clause lacks sufficient precision to afford any judicially manageable standard of review of the Senate's actions is fortified by the existence of the three very specific requirements that the Constitution does impose on the Senate when trying impeachments: the members must be under oath, a two thirds vote is required to convict, and the Chief Justice presides when the President is tried. These limitations are quite precise, and their nature suggests that the Framers did not intend to impose additional limitations on the form of the Senate proceedings by the use of the word "try" in the first sentence.

Petitioner devotes only two pages in his brief to negating the significance of the word "sole" in the first sentence of Clause 6. As noted above, that sentence provides that "[t]he Senate shall have the sole Power to try all Impeachments." We think that the word "sole" is of considerable significance. Indeed, the word "sole" appears only one other time in the Constitution—with respect to the House of Representatives' "*sole* Power of Impeachment." The common sense meaning of the word "sole" is that the Senate alone shall have authority to determine whether an individual should be acquitted or convicted. The dictionary definition bears this out. "Sole" is defined as "having no companion," "solitary," "being the only one," and "functioning...independently and without assistance or interference." If the courts may review the actions of the Senate in order to determine whether that body "tried" an impeached official, it is difficult to see how the Senate would be "functioning...independently and without assistance or interference."

The history and contemporary understanding of the impeachment provisions support our reading of the constitutional language. The parties do not offer evidence of a single word in the history of the Constitutional Convention or in contemporary commentary that even alludes to the possibility of judicial review in the context of the impeachment powers. This silence is quite meaningful in light of the several explicit references to the availability of judicial review as a check on the Legislature's power with respect to bills of attainder, *ex post-facto* laws, and statutes.

The Framers labored over the question of where the impeachment power should lie. Significantly, in at least two considered scenarios the power was placed with the Federal Judiciary. Indeed, Madison and the Committee of Detail proposed that the Supreme Court should have the power to determine impeachments. Despite these proposals, the Convention ultimately decided that the Senate would have "the sole Power to Try all Impeachments." According to Alexander Hamilton, the Senate was the "most fit depositary of this important trust" because its members are representatives of the people. The Supreme Court was not the proper body because the Framers "doubted whether the members of that tribunal would, at all times, be endowed with so eminent a portion of fortitude as would be called for in the execution of so difficult a task" or whether the Court "would possess the degree of credit and authority" to carry out its judgment if it conflicted with the accusation brought by the Legislature—the people's representative. In addition, the Framers believed the Court was too small in number: "The awful discretion, which a court of impeachments must necessarily have, to doom to honor or to infamy the most confidential and the most distinguished characters of the community, forbids the commitment of the trust to a small number of persons."

... We agree with the Court of Appeals that opening the door of judicial review to the procedures used by the Senate in trying impeachments would "expose the political life of the country to months, or perhaps years, of chaos." This lack of finality would manifest itself most dramatically if the President were impeached. The legitimacy of any successor, and hence his effectiveness, would be impaired severely, not merely while the judicial process was running its course, but during any retrial that a differently constituted Senate might conduct if its first judgment of conviction were invalidated. Equally uncertain is the question of what relief a court may give other than simply setting aside the judgment of conviction. Could it order the reinstatement of a convicted federal judge, or order Congress to create an additional judgeship if the seat had been filled in the interim?

... In the case before us, there is no separate provision of the Constitution which could be defeated by allowing the Senate final authority to determine the meaning of the word "try" in the Impeachment Trial Clause. We agree with Nixon that courts possess power to review either legislative or executive action that transgresses identifiable textual limits. As we have made clear, "whether the action of [either the Legislative or Executive Branch] exceeds whatever authority has been committed, is itself a delicate exercise in constitutional interpretation, and is a responsibility of this Court as ultimate interpreter of the Constitution." *Baker v. Carr.* But we conclude, after exercising that delicate responsibility, that the word "try" in the Impeachment Clause does not provide an identifiable textual limit on the authority which is committed to the Senate.

For the foregoing reasons, the judgment of the Court of Appeals is
Affirmed.

LUJAN v. DEFENDERS OF WILDLIFE

504 U.S. 555 (1992)

Opinion: With respect to Parts I, II, III-A, and IV: Scalia, joined by Rehnquist, White, Kennedy, Souter, Thomas
    With respect to Part III-B: Scalia, joined by Rehnquist, White, Thomas
Concurrence: Kennedy, joined by Souter
Concurrence: Stevens
Dissent: Blackmun, joined by O'Connor

Although there is a very real question about whether the Supreme Court now exercises judicial supremacy rather than just judicial review, it is important to keep in mind that there are procedural constraints on the Court's power that keep it from completely usurping the other two branches. In addition to the constraints suggested by the political question doctrine, which we examined the previous case, the Constitution's requirement that the Supreme Court only hear matters in which there is a "case or controversy" (Article III, Section 2) also poses a major limit on its power. In the following case, the Supreme Court denies standing to an individual who has not suffered a concrete enough injury that the Court can actually redress. In short, the Supreme Court, as this case makes clear, does not have the power to simply decide upon the constitutionality of a law or policy without an injured party bringing a suit. As you read this case, you might consider the degree to which the Court's decision not to grant unaffected parties "standing" limits the reach of the Court and perhaps pushes against any worries that it has become too powerful.

JUSTICE SCALIA *delivered the opinion of the Court.*

The ESA seeks to protect species of animals against threats to their continuing existence caused by man. The ESA instructs the Secretary of the Interior to promulgate by regulation a list of those species which are either endangered or threatened under enumerated criteria, and to define the critical habitat of these species. Section 7(a)(2) of the Act then provides, in pertinent part:

> "Each Federal agency shall, in consultation with and with the assistance of the Secretary [of the Interior], insure that any action authorized, funded, or carried out by such agency . . . is not likely to jeopardize the continued existence of any endangered species or threatened species or result in the destruction or adverse modification of habitat of such species which is determined by the Secretary, after consultation as appropriate with affected States, to be critical."

In 1978, the Fish and Wildlife Service (FWS) and the National Marine Fisheries Service (NMFS), on behalf of the Secretary of the Interior and the Secretary of Commerce respectively, promulgated a joint regulation stating that the obligations imposed by §7(a)(2) extend to actions taken in foreign nations. The next year, however, the Interior Department began to reexamine its position. A revised joint regulation, reinterpreting §7(a)(2) to require consultation only for actions taken in the United States or on the high seas, was proposed in 1983, and promulgated in 1986.

Shortly thereafter, respondents, organizations dedicated to wildlife conservation and other environmental causes, filed this action against the Secretary of the Interior, seeking a declaratory judgment that the new regulation is in error as to the geographic scope of §7(a)(2), and an injunction requiring the Secretary to promulgate a new regulation restoring the initial interpretation. The District Court granted the Secretary's motion to dismiss for lack of standing. The Court of Appeals for the Eighth Circuit reversed by a divided vote. On remand, the Secretary moved for summary judgment on the standing issue, and respondents moved for summary judgment on the merits. The District Court denied the Secretary's motion, on the ground that the Eighth Circuit had already determined the standing question in this case; it granted respondents' merits motion, and ordered the Secretary to publish a revised regulation. The Eighth Circuit affirmed. We granted certiorari.

While the Constitution of the United States divides all power conferred upon the Federal Government into "legislative Powers," "[t]he executive Power," and "[t]he judicial Power," it does not attempt to define those terms. To be sure, it limits the jurisdiction of federal courts to "Cases" and "Controversies," but an executive inquiry can bear the name "case" (the Hoffa case) and a legislative dispute can bear the name "controversy" (the Smoot Hawley controversy). Obviously, then, the Constitution's central mechanism of separation of powers depends largely upon common understanding of what activities are appropriate to legislatures, to executives, and to courts. In *The Federalist* No. 48, Madison expressed the view that "[i]t is not infrequently a question of real nicety in legislative bodies whether the operation of a particular measure will, or will not, extend beyond the legislative sphere," whereas "the executive power [is] restrained within a narrower compass and . . . more simple in its nature," and "the judiciary [is] described by landmarks still less uncertain." One of those landmarks, setting apart the "Cases" and "Controversies" that are of the justiciable sort referred to in Article III — "serv[ing] to identify those disputes which are appropriately resolved through the judicial process," *Whitmore v. Arkansas*—is the doctrine of standing. Though some of its elements express merely prudential considerations that are part of judicial self government, the core component of standing is an essential and unchanging part of the case or controversy requirement of Article III.

Over the years, our cases have established that the irreducible constitutional minimum of standing contains three elements: First, the plaintiff must have suffered an "injury in fact" — an invasion of a legally protected interest which is (a) concrete and particularized, and (b) "actual or imminent, not 'conjectural' or 'hypothetical.'" Second, there must be a causal connection between the injury and the conduct complained of — the injury has to be "fairly . . . trace[able] to the challenged action of the defendant, and not . . . th[e] result [of] the independent action of some third party not before the court." *Simon v. Eastern Kentucky Welfare Rights Org.* Third, it must be "likely," as opposed to merely "speculative," that the injury will be "redressed by a favorable decision."

The party invoking federal jurisdiction bears the burden of establishing these elements. See *FW/PBS, Inc. v. Dallas*. Since they are not mere pleading requirements but rather an indispensable part of the plaintiff's case, each element must be supported in the same way as any other matter on which the plaintiff bears the burden of proof, i.e., with the manner and degree of evidence required at the successive stages of the litigation. At the pleading stage, general

factual allegations of injury resulting from the defendant's conduct may suffice, for on a motion to dismiss we "presum[e] that general allegations embrace those specific facts that are necessary to support the claim," *National Wildlife Federation*. In response to a summary judgment motion, however, the plaintiff can no longer rest on such "mere allegations," but must "set forth" by affidavit or other evidence "specific facts," which for purposes of the summary judgment motion will be taken to be true. And at the final stage, those facts (if controverted) must be "supported adequately by the evidence adduced at trial," *Gladstone*.

When the suit is one challenging the legality of government action or inaction, the nature and extent of facts that must be averred (at the summary judgment stage) or proved (at the trial stage) in order to establish standing depends considerably upon whether the plaintiff is himself an object of the action (or forgone action) at issue. If he is, there is ordinarily little question that the action or inaction has caused him injury, and that a judgment preventing or requiring the action will redress it. When, however, as in this case, a plaintiff's asserted injury arises from the government's allegedly unlawful regulation (or lack of regulation) of *someone else*, much more is needed. In that circumstance, causation and redressability ordinarily hinge on the response of the regulated third party to the government action or inaction — and perhaps on the response of others as well. The existence of one or more of the essential elements of standing "depends on the unfettered choices made by independent actors not before the courts and whose exercise of broad and legitimate discretion the courts cannot presume either to control or to predict," *ASARCO Inc. v. Kadish* (opinion of Kennedy, J.); and it becomes the burden of the plaintiff to adduce facts showing that those choices have been or will be made in such manner as to produce causation and permit redressability of injury. Thus, when the plaintiff is not himself the object of the government action or inaction he challenges, standing is not precluded, but it is ordinarily "substantially more difficult" to establish. *Allen.*

. . . Ms. Kelly stated that she traveled to Egypt in 1986 and "observed the traditional habitat of the endangered nile crocodile there and intend[s] to do so again, and hope[s] to observe the crocodile directly," and that she "will suffer harm in fact as a result of [the] American . . . role . . . in overseeing the rehabilitation of the Aswan High Dam on the Nile . . . and [in] develop[ing] . . . Egypt's . . . Master Water Plan." Ms. Skilbred averred that she traveled to Sri Lanka in 1981 and "observed th[e] habitat" of "endangered species such as the Asian elephant and the leopard" at what is now the site of the Mahaweli Project funded by the Agency for International Development (AID), although she "was unable to see any of the endangered species"; "this development project," she continued, "will seriously reduce endangered, threatened, and endemic species habitat including areas that I visited . . . [, which] may severely shorten the future of these species"; that threat, she concluded, harmed her because she "intend[s] to return to Sri Lanka in the future and hope[s] to be more fortunate in spotting at least the endangered elephant and leopard." When Ms. Skilbred was asked at a subsequent deposition if and when she had any plans to return to Sri Lanka, she reiterated that "I intend to go back to Sri Lanka," but confessed that she had no current plans: "I don't know [when]. There is a civil war going on right now. I don't know. Not next year, I will say. In the future."

We shall assume for the sake of argument that these affidavits contain facts showing that certain agency funded projects threaten listed species — though that

is questionable. They plainly contain no facts, however, showing how damage to the species will produce "imminent" injury to . . . Kelly and Skilbred. That the women "had visited" the areas of the projects before the projects commenced proves nothing. As we have said in a related context, "'[p]ast exposure to illegal conduct does not in itself show a present case or controversy regarding injunctive relief . . . if unaccompanied by any continuing, present adverse effects.'" *Lyons.* And the affiant's profession of an "inten[t]" to return to the places they had visited before — where they will presumably, this time, be deprived of the opportunity to observe animals of the endangered species — is simply not enough. Such "some day" intentions — without any description of concrete plans, or indeed even any specification of *when* the some day will be — do not support a finding of the "actual or imminent" injury that our cases require.

Besides relying upon the Kelly and Skilbred affidavits, respondents propose a series of novel standing theories. The first, inelegantly styled "ecosystem nexus," proposes that any person who uses *any part* of a "contiguous ecosystem" adversely affected by a funded activity has standing even if the activity is located a great distance away. This approach, as the Court of Appeals correctly observed, is inconsistent with our opinion in *National Wildlife Federation*, which held that a plaintiff claiming injury from environmental damage must use the area affected by the challenged activity and not an area roughly "in the vicinity" of it. It makes no difference that the general purpose section of the ESA states that the Act was intended in part "to provide a means whereby the ecosystems upon which endangered species and threatened species depend may be conserved." To say that the Act protects ecosystems is not to say that the Act creates (if it were possible) rights of action in persons who have not been injured in fact, that is, persons who use portions of an ecosystem not perceptibly affected by the unlawful action in question.

Respondents' other theories are called, alas, the "animal nexus" approach, whereby anyone who has an interest in studying or seeing the endangered animals anywhere on the globe has standing; and the "vocational nexus" approach, under which anyone with a professional interest in such animals can sue. Under these theories, anyone who goes to see Asian elephants in the Bronx Zoo, and anyone who is a keeper of Asian elephants in the Bronx Zoo, has standing to sue because the Director of AID did not consult with the Secretary regarding the AID funded project in Sri Lanka. This is beyond all reason. Standing is not "an ingenious academic exercise in the conceivable," *United States v. Students Challenging Regulatory Agency Procedures (SCRAP)*, but as we have said requires, at the summary judgment stage, a factual showing of perceptible harm. It is clear that the person who observes or works with a particular animal threatened by a federal decision is facing perceptible harm, since the very subject of his interest will no longer exist. It is even plausible — though it goes to the outermost limit of plausibility — to think that a person who observes or works with animals of a particular species in the very area of the world where that species is threatened by a federal decision is facing such harm, since some animals that might have been the subject of his interest will no longer exist, see *Japan Whaling Assn. v. American Cetacean Soc.* It goes beyond the limit, however, and into pure speculation and fantasy, to say that anyone who observes or works with an endangered species, anywhere in the world, is appreciably harmed by a single project affecting some portion

of that species with which he has no more specific connection.

Besides failing to show injury, respondents failed to demonstrate redressability. Instead of attacking the separate decisions to fund particular projects allegedly causing them harm, the respondents chose to challenge a more generalized level of government action (rules regarding consultation), the invalidation of which would affect all overseas projects. This programmatic approach has obvious practical advantages, but also obvious difficulties insofar as proof of causation or redressability is concerned. As we have said in another context, "suits challenging, not specifically identifiable Government violations of law, but the particular programs agencies establish to carry out their legal obligations ... [are], even when premised on allegations of several instances of violations of law, ... rarely if ever appropriate for federal court adjudication." *Allen.*

The most obvious problem in the present case is redressability. Since the agencies funding the projects were not parties to the case, the District Court could accord relief only against the Secretary: He could be ordered to revise his regulation to require consultation for foreign projects. But this would not remedy respondents' alleged injury unless the funding agencies were bound by the Secretary's regulation, which is very much an open question. Whereas in other contexts the ESA is quite explicit as to the Secretary's controlling authority, with respect to consultation the initiative, and hence arguably the initial responsibility for determining statutory necessity, lies with the agencies. When the Secretary promulgated the regulation at issue here, he thought it was binding on the agencies. The Solicitor General, however, has repudiated that position here, and the agencies themselves apparently deny the Secretary's authority. (During the period when the

Secretary took the view that §7(a)(2) did apply abroad, AID and FWS engaged in a running controversy over whether consultation was required with respect to the Mahaweli project, AID insisting that consultation applied only to domestic actions.)

. . . The Court of Appeals found that respondents had standing for an additional reason: because they had suffered a "procedural injury." The so called "citizen suit" provision of the ESA provides, in pertinent part, that "any person may commence a civil suit on his own behalf (A) to enjoin any person, including the United States and any other governmental instrumentality or agency . . . who is alleged to be in violation of any provision of this chapter." The court held that, because §7(a)(2) requires interagency consultation, the citizen suit provision creates a "procedural righ[t]" to consultation in all "persons" — so that *anyone* can file suit in federal court to challenge the Secretary's (or presumably any other official's) failure to follow the assertedly correct consultative procedure, notwithstanding their inability to allege any discrete injury flowing from that failure. To understand the remarkable nature of this holding one must be clear about what it does *not* rest upon: This is not a case where plaintiffs are seeking to enforce a procedural requirement the disregard of which could impair a separate concrete interest of theirs (*e. g.*, the procedural requirement for a hearing prior to denial of their license application, or the procedural requirement for an environmental impact statement before a federal facility is constructed next door to them). Nor is it simply a case where concrete injury has been suffered by many persons, as in mass fraud or mass tort situations. Nor, finally, is it the unusual case in which Congress has created a concrete private interest in the outcome of a suit against a private party for the government's benefit,

by providing a cash bounty for the victorious plaintiff. Rather, the court held that the injury in fact requirement had been satisfied by congressional conferral upon *all* persons of an abstract, self contained, noninstrumental "right" to have the Executive observe the procedures required by law. We reject this view.

We have consistently held that a plaintiff raising only a generally available grievance about government — claiming only harm to his and every citizen's interest in proper application of the Constitution and laws, and seeking relief that no more directly and tangibly benefits him than it does the public at large — does not state an Article III case or controversy. For example, in *Fairchild v. Hughes*, we dismissed a suit challenging the propriety of the process by which the Nineteenth Amendment was ratified. Justice Brandeis wrote for the Court:

> "[This is] not a case within the meaning of . . . Article III. . . . Plaintiff has [asserted] only the right, possessed by every citizen, to require that the Government be administered according to law and that the public moneys be not wasted. Obviously this general right does not entitle a private citizen to institute in the federal courts a suit. . . ."

. . . To be sure, our generalized grievance cases have typically involved Government violation of procedures assertedly ordained by the Constitution rather than the Congress. But there is absolutely no basis for making the Article III inquiry turn on the source of the asserted right. Whether the courts were to act on their own, or at the invitation of Congress, in ignoring the concrete injury requirement described in our cases, they would be discarding a principle fundamental to the separate and distinct constitutional role of the Third Branch — one of the essential elements that identifies those "Cases" and "Controversies" that are the business of the courts rather than of the political branches. "The province of the court," as Chief Justice Marshall said in *Marbury v. Madison*, "is, solely, to decide on the rights of individuals." Vindicating the *public* interest (including the public interest in government observance of the Constitution and laws) is the function of Congress and the Chief Executive. The question presented here is whether the public interest in proper administration of the laws (specifically, in agencies' observance of a particular, statutorily prescribed procedure) can be converted into an individual right by a statute that denominates it as such, and that permits all citizens (or, for that matter, a subclass of citizens who suffer no distinctive concrete harm) to sue. If the concrete injury requirement has the separation of powers significance we have always said, the answer must be obvious: To permit Congress to convert the undifferentiated public interest in executive officers' compliance with the law into an "individual right" vindicable in the courts is to permit Congress to transfer from the President to the courts the Chief Executive's most important constitutional duty, to "take Care that the Laws be faithfully executed." It would enable the courts, with the permission of Congress, "to assume a position of authority over the governmental acts of another and co equal department," *Frothingham v. Mellon*, and to become "'virtually continuing monitors of the wisdom and soundness of Executive action.'"

JUSTICE BLACKMUN, *with whom* **JUSTICE O'CONNOR** *joins*.

. . . To survive petitioner's motion for summary judgment on standing, respondents need not prove that they are actually or imminently harmed. They need show only a "genuine issue" of material fact as to standing. Fed. Rule Civ. Proc. 56(c). This is not a heavy burden. A "genuine issue" exists so long as "the evidence is such that a reasonable jury could return a verdict for the nonmoving party [respondents]." *Anderson v. Liberty Lobby, Inc.* This Court's "function is not [it]self to weigh the evidence and determine the truth of the matter but to determine whether there is a genuine issue for trial." *Id.*, at 249.

The Court never mentions the "genuine issue" standard. Rather, the Court refers to the type of evidence it feels respondents failed to produce, namely, "affidavits or other evidence showing, through specific facts" the existence of injury. . . . The Court thereby confuses respondents' evidentiary burden (*i.e.*, affidavits asserting "specific facts") in withstanding a summary judgment motion under Rule 56(e) with the standard of proof (*i.e.*, the existence of a "genuine issue" of "material fact") under Rule 56(c).

Were the Court to apply the proper standard for summary judgment, I believe it would conclude that the sworn affidavits and deposition testimony of Joyce Kelly and Amy Skilbred advance sufficient facts to create a genuine issue for trial concerning whether one or both would be imminently harmed by the Aswan and Mahaweli projects. In the first instance, as the Court itself concedes, the affidavits contained facts making it at least "questionable" (and therefore within the province of the factfinder) that certain agency funded projects threaten listed species. . . . The only remaining issue, then, is whether Kelly and Skilbred have shown that they personally would suffer imminent harm.

I think a reasonable finder of fact could conclude from the information in the affidavits and deposition testimony that either Kelly or Skilbred will soon return to the project sites, thereby satisfying the "actual or imminent" injury standard. The Court dismisses Kelly's and Skilbred's general statements that they intended to revisit the project sites as "simply not enough." . . . But those statements did not stand alone. A reasonable finder of fact could conclude, based not only upon their statements of intent to return, but upon their past visits to the project sites, as well as their professional backgrounds, that it was likely that Kelly and Skilbred would make a return trip to the project areas. Contrary to the Court's contention that Kelly's and Skilbred's past visits "proves nothing," . . . the fact of their past visits could demonstrate to a reasonable factfinder that Kelly and Skilbred have the requisite resources and personal interest in the preservation of the species endangered by the Aswan and Mahaweli projects to make good on their intention to return again. Cf. *Los Angeles v. Lyons* ("Past wrongs were evidence bearing on whether there is a real and immediate threat of repeated injury") (internal quotations omitted). Similarly, Kelly's and Skilbred's professional backgrounds in wildlife preservation, see App. 100, 144, 309-310, also make it likely — at least far more likely than for the average citizen — that they would choose to visit these areas of the world where species are vanishing.

CITY OF BOERNE v. FLORES

521 U.S. 507 (1997)

> **Opinion:** Kennedy, joined by Rehnquist, Stevens, Thomas, Ginsburg
> Joined by Scalia in all but Part III-A-1
> **Concurrence:** Stevens
> **Concurrence:** Scalia, joined by Stevens
> **Dissent:** O'Connor joined by Breyer in all but a portion of Part I
> **Dissent:** Souter
> **Dissent:** Breyer

In Employment Division v. Smith, *the Supreme Court reversed an earlier line of cases and lessened the scrutiny it applied to laws allegedly infringing religious freedoms, establishing what it regarded as a more workable and sound approach to this issue. Many citizens throughout the country, however, were angered by the Court's shift to this position, believing that it had abandoned the Constitution's strong protection of religious freedom. Concerned that the Court was not doing enough to protect religious citizens, Congress enacted the Religious Freedom Restoration Act (RFRA). The RFRA required the Court to return to its previous jurisprudence in this area and to reject the standard of religious freedom that the Court sought to adopt in its* Employment Division v. Smith *decision, discussed in Chapter 6. Although the case raises questions of religious freedom, which we explore later in Chapter 6, we focus here on the case's discussion of the proper role of Congress and the Supreme Court in constitutional interpretation. Arguably, by attempting to change the kind of interpretation of religious freedom adopted by the Court in* Employment Division v. Smith, *Congress assumed that the Court's decision on this matter was not final or supreme. In this case, the Court examines the constitutionality of the RFRA. Its decision in this case is often considered the Court's definitive modern statement on the question of judicial review. As you will see, the Court considers whether Congress, in passing the RFRA, overreached its proper role by attempting to correct the Court's own understanding of religious freedom. Although the Court recognizes that Congress has some role in enforcing constitutional rights, it regards itself as the ultimate source of constitutional interpretation. But how far does the Supreme Court go in making this case? Is the Court's interpretation the right one, solely because it says so? Is constitutional interpretation best left to the judiciary alone in certain cases? What role should Congress play in discerning the meaning of the Constitution?*

As you consider these questions, keep in mind Larry Kramer's and Jeremy Waldron's critiques of judicial supremacy. You might also consider whether Ronald Dworkin, in his excerpt, provides any theoretical support for this case.

JUSTICE KENNEDY *delivered the opinion of the Court.*

Situated on a hill in the city of Boerne, Texas, some 28 miles northwest of San Antonio, is St. Peter Catholic Church. Built in 1923, the church's structure replicates the mission style of the region's earlier history. The church seats about 230 worshippers, a number too small for its growing parish. Some 40 to 60 parishioners cannot be accommodated at some Sunday masses. In order to meet the needs of the congregation the Archbishop of San Antonio gave permission to the parish to plan alterations to enlarge the building.

A few months later, the Boerne City Council passed an ordinance authorizing the city's Historic Landmark Commission to prepare a preservation plan with proposed historic landmarks and districts. Under the ordinance, the Commission must preapprove construction affecting historic landmarks or buildings in a historic district.

Soon afterwards, the Archbishop applied for a building permit so construction to enlarge the church could proceed. City authorities, relying on the ordinance and the designation of a historic district (which, they argued, included the church),

denied the application. The Archbishop brought this suit challenging the permit denial in the United States District Court for the Western District of Texas.

The complaint contained various claims, but to this point the litigation has centered on RFRA and the question of its constitutionality. The Archbishop relied upon RFRA as one basis for relief from the refusal to issue the permit. The District Court concluded that by enacting RFRA Congress exceeded the scope of its enforcement power under §5 of the Fourteenth Amendment. The court certified its order for interlocutory appeal and the Fifth Circuit reversed, finding RFRA to be constitutional. We granted certiorari and now reverse.

Congress enacted RFRA in direct response to the Court's decision in *Employment Div., Dept. of Human Resources of Ore. v. Smith.* There we considered a Free Exercise Clause claim brought by members of the Native American Church who were denied unemployment benefits when they lost their jobs because they had used peyote. Their practice was to ingest peyote for sacramental purposes, and they challenged an Oregon statute of general applicability which made use of the drug criminal. In evaluating the claim, we declined to apply the balancing test set forth in *Sherbert v. Verner,* under which we would have asked whether Oregon's prohibition substantially burdened a religious practice and, if it did, whether the burden was justified by a compelling government interest. We stated:

> "Government's ability to enforce generally applicable prohibitions of socially harmful conduct . . . cannot depend on measuring the effects of a governmental action on a religious objector's spiritual development. To make an individual's obligation to obey such a law contingent upon the law's coincidence with his religious beliefs, except where the State's interest is 'compelling' . . . contradicts both constitutional tradition and common sense."

The application of the *Sherbert* test, the *Smith* decision explained, would have produced an anomaly in the law, a constitutional right to ignore neutral laws of general applicability. The anomaly would have been accentuated, the Court reasoned, by the difficulty of determining whether a particular practice was central to an individual's religion. We explained, moreover, that it "is not within the judicial ken to question the centrality of particular beliefs or practices to a faith, or the validity of particular litigants' interpretations of those creeds."

Four Members of the Court disagreed. They argued the law placed a substantial burden on the Native American Church members so that it could be upheld only if the law served a compelling state interest and was narrowly tailored to achieve that end. . . .

These points of constitutional interpretation were debated by Members of Congress in hearings and floor debates. Many criticized the Court's reasoning, and this disagreement resulted in the passage of RFRA. . . .

RFRA prohibits "government" from "substantially burdening" a person's exercise of religion even if the burden results from a rule of general applicability unless the government can demonstrate the burden "(1) is in furtherance of a compelling governmental interest; and (2) is the least restrictive means of furthering that compelling governmental interest." . . .

Under our Constitution, the Federal Government is one of enumerated powers. The judicial authority to determine the constitutionality of laws, in cases and controversies, is based on the premise that the "powers of the legislature are defined and limited; and that those limits may not be mistaken, or forgotten, the constitution is written." *Marbury v. Madison.* Congress relied on its Fourteenth Amendment enforcement power in enacting the most far reaching and substantial of RFRA's provisions, those which impose its requirements on the States. The Fourteenth Amendment provides, in relevant part:

> "Section 1. . . . No State shall make or enforce any law which shall abridge the privileges or immunities of citizens of the United States; nor shall any State deprive any person of life, liberty, or property, without due process of law; nor deny to any person within its jurisdiction the equal protection of the laws. . . .
>
> "Section 5. The Congress shall have power to enforce, by appropriate legislation, the provisions of this article."

In defense of the Act respondent contends, with support from the United States as amicus, that RFRA is permissible enforcement legislation. Congress, it is said, is only protecting by legislation one of the liberties guaranteed by the Fourteenth Amendment's Due Process Clause, the free exercise of religion, beyond what is necessary under *Smith.* It is said the congressional decision to dispense with proof of deliberate or overt discrimination and instead concentrate on a law's effects accords with the settled understanding that §5 includes the power to enact legislation designed to prevent as well as remedy constitutional violations. It is further contended that Congress' §5 power is not limited to remedial or preventive legislation

All must acknowledge that §5 is "a positive grant of legislative power" to Congress. . . .

Legislation which deters or remedies constitutional violations can fall within the sweep of Congress' enforcement power even if in the process it prohibits conduct which is not itself unconstitutional and intrudes into "legislative spheres of autonomy previously reserved to the States." For example, the Court upheld a suspension of literacy tests and similar voting requirements under Congress' parallel power to enforce the provisions of the Fifteenth

Amendment, as a measure to combat racial discrimination in voting, despite the facial constitutionality of the tests under *Lassiter v. Northampton County Bd. of Elections.* We have also concluded that other measures protecting voting rights are within Congress' power to enforce the Fourteenth and Fifteenth Amendments, despite the burdens those measures placed on the States.

It is also true, however, that "as broad as the congressional enforcement power is, it is not unlimited." *Oregon* v. *Mitchell.* In assessing the breadth of §5's enforcement power, we begin with its text. Congress has been given the power "to enforce" the "provisions of this article." We agree with respondent, of course, that Congress can enact legislation under §5 enforcing the constitutional right to the free exercise of religion. The "provisions of this article," to which §5 refers, include the Due Process Clause of the Fourteenth Amendment. Congress' power to enforce the Free Exercise Clause follows from our holding in *Cantwell v. Connecticut* that the "fundamental concept of liberty embodied in [the Fourteenth Amendment's Due Process Clause] embraces the liberties guaranteed by the First Amendment."

Congress' power under §5, however, extends only to "enforcing" the provisions of the Fourteenth Amendment. The Court has described this power as "remedial." The design of the Amendment and the text of §5 are inconsistent with the suggestion that Congress has the power to decree the substance of the Fourteenth Amendment's restrictions on the States. Legislation which alters the meaning of the Free Exercise Clause cannot be said to be enforcing the Clause. Congress does not enforce a constitutional right by changing what the right is. It has been given the power "to enforce," not the power to determine what constitutes a constitutional violation. Were it

not so, what Congress would be enforcing would no longer be, in any meaningful sense, the "provisions of [the Fourteenth Amendment]."

While the line between measures that remedy or prevent unconstitutional actions and measures that make a substantive change in the governing law is not easy to discern, and Congress must have wide latitude in determining where it lies, the distinction exists and must be observed. There must be a congruence and proportionality between the injury to be prevented or remedied and the means adopted to that end. Lacking such a connection, legislation may become substantive in operation and effect. History and our case law support drawing the distinction, one apparent from the text of the Amendment.

The Fourteenth Amendment's history confirms the remedial, rather than substantive, nature of the Enforcement Clause. The Joint Committee on Reconstruction of the 39th Congress began drafting what would become the Fourteenth Amendment in January 1866. The objections to the Committee's first draft of the Amendment, and the rejection of the draft, have a direct bearing on the central issue of defining Congress' enforcement power. In February, Republican Representative John Bingham of Ohio reported the following draft amendment to the House of Representatives on behalf of the Joint Committee:

> "The Congress shall have power to make all laws which shall be necessary and proper to secure to the citizens of each State all privileges and immunities of citizens in the several States, and to all persons in the several States equal protection in the rights of life, liberty, and property."

The proposal encountered immediate opposition, which continued through three days of debate. Members of Congress from across the political spectrum criticized the

Amendment, and the criticisms had a common theme: The proposed Amendment gave Congress too much legislative power at the expense of the existing constitutional structure....

. . . Under the revised Amendment, Congress' power was no longer plenary but remedial. Congress was granted the power to make the substantive constitutional prohibitions against the States effective. Representative Bingham said the new draft would give Congress "the power . . . to protect by national law the privileges and immunities of all the citizens of the Republic . . . whenever the same shall be abridged or denied by the unconstitutional acts of any State." Representative Stevens described the new draft Amendment as "allowing Congress to correct the unjust legislation of the States." . . . The revised Amendment proposal did not raise the concerns expressed earlier regarding broad congressional power to prescribe uniform national laws with respect to life, liberty, and property....

The design of the Fourteenth Amendment has proved significant also in maintaining the traditional separation of powers between Congress and the Judiciary. The first eight Amendments to the Constitution set forth self-executing prohibitions on governmental action, and this Court has had primary authority to interpret those prohibitions. The Bingham draft, some thought, departed from that tradition by vesting in Congress primary power to interpret and elaborate on the meaning of the new Amendment through legislation. Under it, "Congress, and not the courts, was to judge whether or not any of the privileges or immunities were not secured to citizens in the several States." While this separation of powers aspect did not occasion the widespread resistance which was caused by the proposal's threat to the federal balance, it nonetheless attracted the attention of various Members. As enacted, the Fourteenth Amendment confers substantive rights against the States which, like the provisions of the Bill of Rights, are self-executing. The power to interpret the Constitution in a case or controversy remains in the Judiciary.

The remedial and preventive nature of Congress' enforcement power, and the limitation inherent in the power, were confirmed in our earliest cases on the Fourteenth Amendment. In the *Civil Rights Cases* [excerpted in Chapter 8], the Court invalidated sections of the Civil Rights Act of 1875 which prescribed criminal penalties for denying to any person "the full enjoyment of" public accommodations and conveyances, on the grounds that it exceeded Congress' power by seeking to regulate private conduct. The Enforcement Clause, the Court said, did not authorize Congress to pass "general legislation upon the rights of the citizen, but corrective legislation; that is, such as may be necessary and proper for counteracting such laws as the States may adopt or enforce, and which, by the amendment, they are prohibited from making or enforcing. . . . " The power to "legislate generally upon" life, liberty, and property, as opposed to the "power to provide modes of redress" against offensive state action, was "repugnant" to the Constitution. Although the specific holdings of these early cases might have been superseded or modified, see, e.g., *Heart of Atlanta Motel, Inc. v. United States*, their treatment of Congress' §5 power as corrective or preventive, not definitional, has not been questioned.

Recent cases have continued to revolve around the question of whether §5 legislation can be considered remedial. In *South Carolina v. Katzenbach*, we emphasized that "the constitutional propriety of [legislation adopted under the Enforcement Clause] must be judged with reference to the historical experience . . . it reflects."

There we upheld various provisions of the Voting Rights Act of 1965, finding them to be "remedies aimed at areas where voting discrimination has been most flagrant," and necessary to "banish the blight of racial discrimination in voting, which has infected the electoral process in parts of our country for nearly a century." We noted evidence in the record reflecting the subsisting and pervasive discriminatory—and therefore unconstitutional—use of literacy tests. The Act's new remedies, which used the administrative resources of the Federal Government, included the suspension of both literacy tests and, pending federal review, all new voting regulations in covered jurisdictions, as well as the assignment of federal examiners to list qualified applicants enabling those listed to vote. The new, unprecedented remedies were deemed necessary given the ineffectiveness of the existing voting rights laws, and the slow costly character of case-by-case litigation.

After *South Carolina v. Katzenbach*, the Court continued to acknowledge the necessity of using strong remedial and preventive measures to respond to the widespread and persisting deprivation of constitutional rights resulting from this country's history of racial discrimination. . . .

Any suggestion that Congress has a substantive, non-remedial power under the Fourteenth Amendment is not supported by our case law. In *Oregon v. Mitchell*, a majority of the Court concluded Congress had exceeded its enforcement powers by enacting legislation lowering the minimum age of voters from 21 to 18 in state and local elections. The five Members of the Court who reached this conclusion explained that the legislation intruded into an area reserved by the Constitution to the States. . . .

If Congress could define its own powers by altering the Fourteenth Amendment's meaning, no longer would the Constitution be "superior paramount law, unchangeable by ordinary means." It would be "on a level with ordinary legislative acts, and, like other acts, . . . alterable when the legislature shall please to alter it." *Marbury v. Madison*. Under this approach, it is difficult to conceive of a principle that would limit congressional power. Shifting legislative majorities could change the Constitution and effectively circumvent the difficult and detailed amendment process contained in Article V.

We now turn to consider whether RFRA can be considered enforcement legislation under §5 of the Fourteenth Amendment.

Respondent contends that RFRA is a proper exercise of Congress' remedial or preventive power. The Act, it is said, is a reasonable means of protecting the free exercise of religion as defined by *Smith*. It prevents and remedies laws which are enacted with the unconstitutional object of targeting religious beliefs and practices. To avoid the difficulty of proving such violations, it is said, Congress can simply invalidate any law which imposes a substantial burden on a religious practice unless it is justified by a compelling interest and is the least restrictive means of accomplishing that interest. If Congress can prohibit laws with discriminatory effects in order to prevent racial discrimination in violation of the Equal Protection Clause, then it can do the same, respondent argues, to promote religious liberty.

While preventive rules are sometimes appropriate remedial measures, there must be a congruence between the means used and the ends to be achieved. The appropriateness of remedial measures must be considered in light of the evil presented. Strong measures appropriate to address one harm may be an unwarranted response to another, lesser one. Id., at 334

A comparison between RFRA and the Voting Rights Act is instructive. In contrast to the record which confronted Congress and the judiciary in the voting rights cases, RFRA's legislative record lacks examples of modern instances of generally applicable laws passed because of religious bigotry. The history of persecution in this country detailed in the hearings mentions no episodes occurring in the past 40 years. . . . It is difficult to maintain that they are examples of legislation enacted or enforced due to animus or hostility to the burdened religious practices or that they indicate some widespread pattern of religious discrimination in this country. Congress' concern was with the incidental burdens imposed, not the object or purpose of the legislation. . . .

Regardless of the state of the legislative record, RFRA cannot be considered remedial, preventive legislation, if those terms are to have any meaning. RFRA is so out of proportion to a supposed remedial or preventive object that it cannot be understood as responsive to, or designed to prevent, unconstitutional behavior. It appears, instead, to attempt a substantive change in constitutional protections. Preventive measures prohibiting certain types of laws may be appropriate when there is reason to believe that many of the laws affected by the congressional enactment have a significant likelihood of being unconstitutional. Remedial legislation under §5 "should be adapted to the mischief and wrong which the [Fourteenth] Amendment was intended to provide against."

RFRA is not so confined. Sweeping coverage ensures its intrusion at every level of government, displacing laws and prohibiting official actions of almost every description and regardless of subject matter. RFRA's restrictions apply to every agency and official of the Federal, State, and local Governments. RFRA applies to all federal and state law, statutory or otherwise, whether adopted before or after its enactment. RFRA has no termination date or termination mechanism. Any law is subject to challenge at any time by any individual who alleges a substantial burden on his or her free exercise of religion.

The stringent test RFRA demands of state laws reflects a lack of proportionality or congruence between the means adopted and the legitimate end to be achieved. If an objector can show a substantial burden on his free exercise, the State must demonstrate a compelling governmental interest and show that the law is the least restrictive means of furthering its interest. Claims that a law substantially burdens someone's exercise of religion will often be difficult to contest. Requiring a State to demonstrate a compelling interest and show that it has adopted the least restrictive means of achieving that interest is the most demanding test known to constitutional law. If "'compelling interest' really means what it says . . . many laws will not meet the test. . . . [The test] would open the prospect of constitutionally required religious exemptions from civic obligations of almost every conceivable kind." Laws valid under *Smith* would fall under RFRA without regard to whether they had the object of stifling or punishing free exercise. We make these observations not to reargue the position of the majority in *Smith* but to illustrate the substantive alteration of its holding attempted by RFRA. Even assuming RFRA would be interpreted in effect to mandate some lesser test, say one equivalent to intermediate scrutiny, the statute nevertheless would require searching judicial scrutiny of state law with the attendant likelihood of invalidation. This is a considerable congressional intrusion into the States' traditional prerogatives and general authority to regulate for the health and welfare of their citizens.

Our national experience teaches that the Constitution is preserved best when each part of the government respects both the Constitution and the proper actions and determinations of the other branches. When the Court has interpreted the Constitution, it has acted within the province of the Judicial Branch, which embraces the duty to say what the law is. When the political branches of the Government act against the background of a judicial interpretation of the Constitution already issued, it must be understood that in later cases and controversies the Court will treat its precedents with the respect due them under settled principles, including stare decisis, and contrary expectations must be disappointed. RFRA was designed to control cases and controversies, such as the one before us; but as the provisions of the federal statute here invoked are beyond congressional authority, it is this Court's precedent, not RFRA, which must control.

It is for Congress in the first instance to "determine whether and what legislation is needed to secure the guarantees of the Fourteenth Amendment," and its conclusions are entitled to much deference. Congress' discretion is not unlimited, however, and the courts retain the power, as they have since *Marbury v. Madison*, to determine if Congress has exceeded its authority under the Constitution. Broad as the power of Congress is under the Enforcement Clause of the Fourteenth Amendment, RFRA contradicts vital principles necessary to maintain separation of powers and the federal balance. The judgment of the Court of Appeals sustaining the Act's constitutionality is reversed.

CASE QUESTIONS

1. Why is the Supreme Court asserting that the RFRA is unconstitutional? Is it because the RFRA interprets the Constitution in an incorrect way or because Congress should not be allowed to correct the Supreme Court on any matter of constitutional interpretation? Does the opinion leave any room for the departmentalist understanding of constitutional interpretation? Could the Court have decided *Boerne v. Flores* in a way that stopped short of judicial supremacy?

2. Read Section 5 of the Fourteenth Amendment. Does this provision grant Congress some power in constitutional interpretation? What does the Court say about the congressional power asserted in this section of the Fourteenth Amendment?

3. This case clearly raises questions about the Court's role in a democracy. In *Boerne v. Flores*, the Court overturned the RFRA. The RFRA's popularity was evidenced by its overwhelming support in the Senate, where it was passed by a vote of 97 to 3. The case is significant not only because it pitted the Court against popular will, but because it raised the question of whether Congress could offer its own judgments about constitutional interpretation. The Court's negative answer makes *Boerne v. Flores* the strongest and clearest rejection of departmentalism and the Court's most ardent statement in defense of judicial supremacy. The Constitution tasks Congress with the power to enforce the provisions of the Fourteenth Amendment, including protections of individual liberty and equal protection under the law. When Congress and the Court disagree about how far those rights extend, as with the controversy over the RFRA, must Congress let the Court have the last word?

BUSH v. GORE

531 U.S. 98 (2000)

Opinion: Per Curiam
Concurrence: Rehnquist, joined by
Scalia, Thomas
Dissent: Stevens joined by Ginsburg,
Breyer
Dissent: Souter, joined by Breyer and
by Stevens and Ginsburg in all but
Part C
Dissent: Ginsburg, joined by Stevens
and by Souter and Breyer in Part I
Dissent: Breyer, joined by Stevens and
Ginsburg in all but Part I-A-1 and by
Souter in Part I

*In the 2000 presidential election between
George Bush and Albert Gore, the electoral vote
was close, so close that a victory in Florida for
either candidate would have ensured a victory in the presidential election. On Sunday,
November 26, 2000, Florida Secretary of State
Katherine Harris certified Bush as the winner
of the election in the state. Subsequent litigation on behalf of Gore resulted in the Florida
Supreme Court ordering a recount. The following decision focuses on two legal issues, one
concerning equal protection and the second
concerning Article II of the Constitution. In
addition to thinking about the U.S. Supreme
Court's arguments with regard to these two
matters, you should think about whether the
Court is the proper body to resolve this dispute in the context of the larger questions of
judicial authority examined in this chapter. Is
this a proper use of the Court's review power?
Or is it an instance of the Court improperly
adjudicating a political question?*

PER CURIAM.

On December 8, 2000, the Supreme Court
of Florida ordered that the Circuit Court
of Leon County tabulate by hand 9,000
ballots in Miami-Dade County. It also
ordered the inclusion in the certified vote
totals of 215 votes identified in Palm Beach
County and 168 votes identified in Miami-
Dade County for Vice President Albert
Gore, Jr., and Senator Joseph Lieberman,
Democratic Candidates for President
and Vice President. The Supreme Court
noted that petitioner, Governor George W.
Bush asserted that the net gain for Vice
President Gore in Palm Beach County was
176 votes, and directed the Circuit Court
to resolve that dispute on remand. The
court further held that relief would require
manual recounts in all Florida counties
where so-called "undervotes" had not been
subject to manual tabulation. The court
ordered all manual recounts to begin at
once. Governor Bush and Richard Cheney,
Republican Candidates for the Presidency
and Vice Presidency, filed an emergency
application for a stay of this mandate. On
December 9, we granted the application,
treated the application as a petition for a
writ of certiorari, and granted certiorari.

The petition presents the following questions: whether the Florida Supreme Court
established new standards for resolving
Presidential election contests, thereby violating Art. II, §1, cl. 2, of the United States
Constitution and failing to comply with 3
U.S.C. §5, and whether the use of standardless manual recounts violates the Equal
Protection and Due Process Clauses. With
respect to the equal protection question,
we find a violation of the Equal Protection
Clause.

An early case in our one person, one vote
jurisprudence arose when a State accorded
arbitrary and disparate treatment to voters
in its different counties. The Court found a
constitutional violation. We relied on these

principles in the context of the Presidential selection process in *Moore v. Ogilvie*, where we invalidated a county-based procedure that diluted the influence of citizens in larger counties in the nominating process. There we observed that "the idea that one group can be granted greater voting strength than another is hostile to the one man, one vote basis of our representative government."

The State Supreme Court ratified this uneven treatment. It mandated that the recount totals from two counties, Miami-Dade and Palm Beach, be included in the certified total. The court also appeared to hold sub silentio that the recount totals from Broward County, which were not completed until after the original November 14 certification by the Secretary of State, were to be considered part of the new certified vote totals even though the county certification was not contested by Vice President Gore. Yet each of the counties used varying standards to determine what was a legal vote. Broward County used a more forgiving standard than Palm Beach County, and uncovered almost three times as many new votes, a result markedly disproportionate to the difference in population between the counties.

In addition, the recounts in these three counties were not limited to so-called undervotes but extended to all of the ballots. The distinction has real consequences. A manual recount of all ballots identifies not only those ballots which show no vote but also those which contain more than one, the so-called overvotes. Neither category will be counted by the machine. This is not a trivial concern. At oral argument, respondents estimated there are as many as 110,000 overvotes statewide. As a result, the citizen whose ballot was not read by a machine because he failed to vote for a candidate in a way readable by a machine may still have his vote counted

in a manual recount; on the other hand, the citizen who marks two candidates in a way discernible by the machine will not have the same opportunity to have his vote count, even if a manual examination of the ballot would reveal the requisite indicia of intent. Furthermore, the citizen who marks two candidates, only one of which is discernible by the machine, will have his vote counted even though it should have been read as an invalid ballot. The State Supreme Court's inclusion of vote counts based on these variant standards exemplifies concerns with the remedial processes that were under way.

That brings the analysis to yet a further equal protection problem. The votes certified by the court included a partial total from one county, Miami-Dade. The Florida Supreme Court's decision thus gives no assurance that the recounts included in a final certification must be complete. Indeed, it is respondent's submission that it would be consistent with the rules of the recount procedures to include whatever partial counts are done by the time of final certification, and we interpret the Florida Supreme Court's decision to permit this. This accommodation no doubt results from the truncated contest period established by the Florida Supreme Court in *Bush I*, at respondents' own urging. The press of time does not diminish the constitutional concern. A desire for speed is not a general excuse for ignoring equal protection guarantees.

In addition to these difficulties the actual process by which the votes were to be counted under the Florida Supreme Court's decision raises further concerns. That order did not specify who would recount the ballots. The county canvassing boards were forced to pull together ad hoc teams comprised of judges from various Circuits who had no previous training in handling and interpreting ballots.

Furthermore, while others were permitted to observe, they were prohibited from objecting during the recount.

The recount process, in its features here described, is inconsistent with the minimum procedures necessary to protect the fundamental right of each voter in the special instance of a statewide recount under the authority of a single state judicial officer. Our consideration is limited to the present circumstances, for the problem of equal protection in election processes generally presents many complexities.

The question before the Court is not whether local entities, in the exercise of their expertise, may develop different systems for implementing elections. Instead, we are presented with a situation where a state court with the power to assure uniformity has ordered a statewide recount with minimal procedural safeguards. When a court orders a statewide remedy, there must be at least some assurance that the rudimentary requirements of equal treatment and fundamental fairness are satisfied.

Given the Court's assessment that the recount process underway was probably being conducted in an unconstitutional manner, the Court stayed the order directing the recount so it could hear this case and render an expedited decision. The contest provision, as it was mandated by the State Supreme Court, is not well calculated to sustain the confidence that all citizens must have in the outcome of elections. The State has not shown that its procedures include the necessary safeguards. The problem, for instance, of the estimated 110,000 overvotes has not been addressed, although Chief Justice Wells called attention to the concern in his dissenting opinion.

Upon due consideration of the difficulties identified to this point, it is obvious that the recount cannot be conducted in compliance with the requirements of equal protection and due process without substantial additional work. It would require not only the adoption (after opportunity for argument) of adequate statewide standards for determining what is a legal vote, and practicable procedures to implement them, but also orderly judicial review of any disputed matters that might arise. In addition, the Secretary of State has advised that the recount of only a portion of the ballots requires that the vote tabulation equipment be used to screen out undervotes, a function for which the machines were not designed. If a recount of overvotes were also required, perhaps even a second screening would be necessary. Use of the equipment for this purpose, and any new software developed for it, would have to be evaluated for accuracy by the Secretary of State, as required by Fla. Stat. §101.015 (2000).

The Supreme Court of Florida has said that the legislature intended the State's electors to "participate fully in the federal electoral process," as provided in 3 U.S.C. §5. That statute, in turn, requires that any controversy or contest that is designed to lead to a conclusive selection of electors be completed by December 12. That date is upon us, and there is no recount procedure in place under the State Supreme Court's order that comports with minimal constitutional standards. Because it is evident that any recount seeking to meet the December 12 date will be unconstitutional for the reasons we have discussed, we reverse the judgment of the Supreme Court of Florida ordering a recount to proceed.

None are more conscious of the vital limits on judicial authority than are the members of this Court, and none stand more in admiration of the Constitution's design to leave the selection of the President to the people, through their legislatures, and to the political sphere. When contending parties invoke the process of the courts, however, it becomes our unsought responsibility to resolve the federal and constitutional issues the judicial system has been forced to confront.

The judgment of the Supreme Court of Florida is reversed, and the case is remanded for further proceedings not inconsistent with this opinion.

CHIEF JUSTICE REHNQUIST, *with whom* **JUSTICE SCALIA** *and* **JUSTICE THOMAS** *join, concurring.*

We join the per curiam opinion. We write separately because we believe there are additional grounds that require us to reverse the Florida Supreme Court's decision.

We deal here not with an ordinary election, but with an election for the President of the United States. . . .

In most cases, comity and respect for federalism compel us to defer to the decisions of state courts on issues of state law. That practice reflects our understanding that the decisions of state courts are definitive pronouncements of the will of the States as sovereigns. Of course, in ordinary cases, the distribution of powers among the branches of a State's government raises no questions of federal constitutional law, subject to the requirement that the government be republican in character. But there are a few exceptional cases in which the Constitution imposes a duty or confers a power on a particular branch of a State's government. This is one of them. Article II, §1, cl. 2, provides that "each State shall appoint, in such Manner as the *Legislature* thereof may direct," electors for President and Vice President. (Emphasis added.) Thus, the text of the election law itself, and not just its interpretation by the courts of the States, takes on independent significance.

3 U.S.C. §5 informs our application of Art. II, §1, cl. 2, to the Florida statutory scheme, which, as the Florida Supreme Court acknowledged, took that statute into account. Section 5 provides that the State's selection of electors "shall be conclusive, and shall govern in the counting of the electoral votes" if the electors are chosen under laws enacted prior to election day, and if the selection process is completed six days prior to the meeting of the electoral college. . . .

If we are to respect the legislature's Article II powers, therefore, we must ensure that post-election state-court actions do not frustrate the legislative desire to attain the "safe harbor" provided by §5.

. . . Though we generally defer to state courts on the interpretation of state law, there are of course areas in which the Constitution requires this Court to undertake an independent, if still deferential, analysis of state law.

The scope and nature of the remedy ordered by the Florida Supreme Court jeopardizes the "legislative wish" to take advantage of the safe harbor provided by 3 U.S.C. §5. December 12, 2000, is the last date for a final determination of the Florida electors that will satisfy §5. Yet in the late afternoon of December 8th—four days before this deadline—the Supreme Court of Florida ordered recounts of tens of thousands of so-called "undervotes" spread through 64 of the State's 67 counties. This was done in a search for elusive—perhaps delusive—certainty as to the exact count of 6 million votes. But no one claims that these ballots have not previously been tabulated; they were initially read by voting machines at the time of the election, and thereafter reread by virtue of Florida's automatic recount provision. No one claims there was any fraud in the election. The Supreme Court of Florida ordered this additional recount under the provision of the election code giving the circuit judge the authority to provide relief that is "appropriate under such circumstances."

Surely when the Florida Legislature empowered the courts of the State to grant "appropriate" relief, it must have meant relief that would have become final by the cut-off date of 3 U.S.C. §5. In light of the inevitable legal challenges and ensuing appeals to the Supreme Court of Florida and petitions for certiorari to this Court, the entire recounting process could not possibly be completed by that date. Whereas the majority in the Supreme Court of Florida stated its confidence that "the remaining undervotes in these counties can be [counted] within the required time frame," it made no assertion that the seemingly inevitable appeals could be disposed of in that time. Although the Florida Supreme Court has on occasion taken over a year to resolve disputes over local elections, it has heard and decided the appeals in the present case with great promptness. But the federal deadlines for the Presidential election simply do not permit even such a shortened process.

JUSTICE GINSBURG, *with whom* **JUSTICE STEVENS** *joins, and with whom* **JUSTICE SOUTER** *and* **JUSTICE BREYER** *join as to Part I, dissenting.*

Rarely has this Court rejected outright an interpretation of state law by a state high court. *Fairfax's Devisee v. Hunter's Lessee, NAACP v. Alabama ex rel. Patterson,* and *Bouie v. City of Columbia*, cited by the Chief Justice, are three such rare instances. But those cases are embedded in historical contexts hardly comparable to the situation here. . . .

The Chief Justice's casual citation of these cases might lead one to believe they are part of a larger collection of cases in which we said that the Constitution impelled us to train a skeptical eye on a state court's portrayal of state law. But one would be hard pressed, I think, to find additional cases that fit the mold. As Justice Breyer convincingly explains, this case involves nothing close to the kind of recalcitrance by a state high court that warrants extraordinary action by this Court. The Florida Supreme Court concluded that counting every legal vote was the overriding concern of the Florida Legislature when it enacted the State's Election Code. The court surely should not be bracketed with state high courts of the Jim Crow South.

The Chief Justice says that Article II, by providing that state legislatures shall direct the manner of appointing electors, authorizes federal superintendence over the relationship between state courts and state legislatures, and licenses a departure from the usual deference we give to state court interpretations of state law. The Framers of our Constitution, however, understood that in a republican government, the judiciary would construe the legislature's enactments. In light of the constitutional guarantee to States of a "Republican Form of Government," Article II can hardly be read to invite this Court to disrupt a State's republican regime. Yet the Chief Justice today would reach out to do just that. By holding that Article II requires our revision of a state court's construction of state laws in order to protect one organ of the State from another, the Chief Justice contradicts the basic principle that a State may organize itself as it sees fit. Article II does not call for the scrutiny undertaken by this Court.

The extraordinary setting of this case has obscured the ordinary principle that dictates its proper resolution: Federal courts defer to state high courts' interpretations of their state's own law. This principle reflects the core of federalism, on which all agree. "The Framers split the atom of sovereignty. It was the genius of their idea that our citizens would have two political capacities, one state and one federal, each protected from incursion by the other." Were the other members of this Court as mindful as they generally are of our system of dual sovereignty, they would affirm the judgment of the Florida Supreme Court.

The Court assumes that time will not permit "orderly judicial review of any disputed matters that might arise." But no one has doubted the good faith and diligence with which Florida election officials, attorneys for all sides of this controversy, and the courts of law have performed their duties. Notably, the Florida Supreme Court has produced two substantial opinions within 29 hours of oral argument. In sum, the Court's conclusion that a constitutionally adequate recount is impractical is a prophecy the Court's own judgment will not allow to be tested. Such an untested prophecy should not decide the Presidency of the United States.

I dissent.

JUSTICE BREYER, *with whom* **JUSTICE STEVENS** *and* **JUSTICE GINSBURG** *join except as to Part I-A-1, and with whom* **JUSTICE SOUTER** *joins as to Part I, dissenting.*

The Court was wrong to take this case. It was wrong to grant a stay. It should now vacate that stay and permit the Florida Supreme Court to decide whether the recount should resume.

I

The political implications of this case for the country are momentous. But the federal legal questions presented, with one exception, are insubstantial.

A

1

The majority raises three Equal Protection problems with the Florida Supreme Court's recount order: first, the failure to include overvotes in the manual recount; second, the fact that all ballots, rather than simply the undervotes, were recounted in some, but not all, counties; and third, the absence of a uniform, specific standard to guide the recounts. As far as the first issue is concerned, petitioners presented no evidence, to this Court or to any Florida court, that a manual recount of overvotes would identify additional legal votes. The same is true of the second, and, in addition, the majority's reasoning would seem to invalidate any state provision for a manual recount of individual counties in a statewide election.

The majority's third concern does implicate principles of fundamental fairness. The majority concludes that the Equal Protection Clause requires that a manual recount be governed not only by the uniform general standard of the "clear intent of the voter," but also by uniform subsidiary standards (for example, a uniform determination whether indented, but not perforated, "undervotes" should count). The opinion points out that the Florida Supreme Court ordered the inclusion of Broward County's undercounted "legal votes" even though those votes included ballots that were not perforated but simply "dimpled," while newly recounted ballots from other counties will likely include only votes determined to be "legal" on the basis of a stricter standard. In light of our previous remand, the Florida Supreme Court may have been reluctant to adopt a more specific standard than that provided for by the legislature for fear of exceeding its authority under Article II. However, since the use of different standards could favor one or the other of the candidates, since time was, and is, too short to permit the lower courts to iron out significant differences through ordinary judicial review, and since the relevant distinction was embodied in the order of the State's highest court,

I agree that, in these very special circumstances, basic principles of fairness may well have counseled the adoption of a uniform standard to address the problem. In light of the majority's disposition, I need not decide whether, or the extent to which, as a remedial matter, the Constitution would place limits upon the content of the uniform standard.

2

Nonetheless, there is no justification for the majority's remedy, which is simply to reverse the lower court and halt the recount entirely. An appropriate remedy would be, instead, to remand this case with instructions that, even at this late date, would permit the Florida Supreme Court to require recounting all undercounted votes in Florida, including those from Broward, Volusia, Palm Beach, and Miami-Dade Counties, whether or not previously recounted prior to the end of the protest period, and to do so in accordance with a single-uniform substandard.

By halting the manual recount, and thus ensuring that the uncounted legal votes will not be counted under any standard, this Court crafts a remedy out of proportion to the asserted harm. And that remedy harms the very fairness interests the Court is attempting to protect. The manual recount would itself redress a problem of unequal treatment of ballots. . . .

II

Despite the reminder that this case involves "an election for the President of the United States," no preeminent legal concern, or practical concern related to legal questions, required this Court to hear this case, let alone to issue a stay that stopped Florida's recount process in its tracks. With one exception, petitioners' claims do not ask us to vindicate a constitutional provision designed to protect a basic human right. See, e.g., *Brown v. Board of Education*. Petitioners invoke fundamental fairness, namely, the need for procedural fairness, including finality. But with the one "equal protection" exception, they rely upon law that focuses, not upon that basic need, but upon the constitutional allocation of power. Respondents invoke a competing fundamental consideration—the need to determine the voter's true intent. But they look to state law, not to federal constitutional law, to protect that interest. Neither side claims electoral fraud, dishonesty, or the like. And the more fundamental equal protection claim might have been left to the state court to resolve if and when it was discovered to have mattered. It could still be resolved through a remand conditioned upon issuance of a uniform standard; it does not require reversing the Florida Supreme Court.

Of course, the selection of the President is of fundamental national importance. But that importance is political, not legal. And this Court should resist the temptation unnecessarily to resolve tangential legal disputes, where doing so threatens to determine the outcome of the election.

The Constitution and federal statutes themselves make clear that restraint is appropriate. They set forth a road map of how to resolve disputes about electors, even after an election as close as this one. That road map foresees resolution of electoral disputes by state courts. But it nowhere provides for involvement by the United States Supreme Court.

To the contrary, the Twelfth Amendment commits to Congress the authority and responsibility to count electoral votes. A federal statute, the Electoral Count Act, enacted after the close 1876 Hayes-Tilden Presidential election, specifies that, after States have tried to resolve disputes (through "judicial" or other means), Congress is the body primarily authorized to resolve remaining disputes.

The legislative history of the Act makes clear its intent to commit the power to resolve such disputes to Congress, rather than the courts:

> "The two Houses are, by the Constitution, authorized to make the count of electoral votes. They can only count legal votes, and in doing so must determine, from the best evidence to be had, what are legal votes .... The power to determine rests with the two Houses, and there is no other constitutional tribunal."

... The decision by both the Constitution's Framers and the 1886 Congress to minimize this Court's role in resolving close federal presidential elections is as wise as it is clear. However awkward or difficult it may be for Congress to resolve difficult electoral disputes, Congress, being a political body, expresses the people's will far more accurately than does an unelected Court. And the people's will is what elections are about.

... I think it not only legally wrong, but also most unfortunate, for the Court simply to have terminated the Florida recount. Those who caution judicial restraint in resolving political disputes have described the quintessential case for that restraint as a case marked, among other things, by the "strangeness of the issue," its "intractability to principled resolution," its "sheer momentousness, . . . which tends to unbalance judicial judgment," and "the inner vulnerability, the self-doubt of an institution which is electorally irresponsible and has no earth to draw strength from." Those characteristics mark this case.

At the same time, as I have said, the Court is not acting to vindicate a fundamental constitutional principle, such as the need to protect a basic human liberty. No other strong reason to act is present.

Congressional statutes tend to obviate the need. And, above all, in this highly politicized matter, the appearance of a split decision runs the risk of undermining the public's confidence in the Court itself. That confidence is a public treasure. It has been built slowly over many years, some of which were marked by a Civil War and the tragedy of segregation. It is a vitally necessary ingredient of any successful effort to protect basic liberty and, indeed, the rule of law itself. We run no risk of returning to the days when a President (responding to this Court's efforts to protect the Cherokee Indians) might have said, "John Marshall has made his decision; now let him enforce it!" But we do risk a self-inflicted wound—a wound that may harm not just the Court, but the Nation.

I fear that in order to bring this agonizingly long election process to a definitive conclusion, we have not adequately attended to that necessary "check upon our own exercise of power," "our own sense of self-restraint." Justice Brandeis once said of the Court, "The most important thing we do is not doing." What it does today, the Court should have left undone. I would repair the damage done as best we now can, by permitting the Florida recount to continue under uniform standards.

I respectfully dissent.

CASE QUESTION

This case raises fundamental questions about the role of the Supreme Court in a democracy. The Court effectively determined the outcome of the 2000 presidential election. One argument in favor of the Court's intervention, proposed by federal judge and legal theorist Richard Posner, is that the decision ended what could have been a highly divisive and overly drawn out public battle over the election. In this sense, *Bush v. Gore* was pragmatic because it settled a critical matter that could have become destabilizing to the American polity. The included reading from Justice Stephen Breyer also lauds the importance of pragmatic decision making by the Court, but Justice Breyer opposed the Court's decision in *Bush v. Gore*. Is Justice Breyer's dissenting stance consistent with his pragmatist approach to judicial interpretation? Is there a way to give a pragmatist defense of his position?

SYNTHESIS QUESTIONS FOR FURTHER DISCUSSION: CHAPTER 1 SECTION B

1. The Court's claim to judicial supremacy has become closely associated with its attempt to desegregate the Southern states in the face of fierce opposition. Many Southern politicians invoked a version of departmentalism, arguing that the Court was mistaken in reading the Equal Protection Clause as forbidding segregation. Although this substantive question will be dealt with in depth in Chapter 9, for now it is important to note that some of these arguments also suggested that, because the Court was wrong, it could not impose its decision on Southern politicians who read the Constitution in a different way. The Court's decision in *Cooper v. Aaron,* enforcing a desegregation order in the face of a defiant governor and other local politicians, sought to deflate this debate by asserting judicial supremacy. Clearly the arguments of Larry Kramer and Jeremy Waldron are not caught up in the racism that motivated much of the resistance to the Court in the era of desegregation, but could there have been a way to decide *Cooper v. Aaron* without invoking judicial supremacy? Are arguments for desegregation potentially consistent with departmentalism?

2. The theory of departmentalism has been revived recently by thinkers, such as Kramer, who focus on issues in which the Court's substantive decisions are at odds with the views of most contemporary Americans. Kramer's version of departmentalism is known as "popular constitutionalism." It therefore makes sense that he would focus his readers' attention on matters where the Court's decisions seem at odds with popular will. In the late nineteenth and early twentieth centuries, the Court struck down a number of statutes including wage, hour, and safety regulations for workers, as well as child labor protections. In cases such as *Lochner v. New York* and *Hammer v. Dagenhart,* the Supreme Court invalidated these laws for being incompatible with economic liberty. Since that time, workers' rights legislation has come to be seen by a vast majority as essential to the American system of government. But at times the Court has challenged legislatures and Congress on issues of personal liberties, such as gay rights and civil rights. Ronald Dworkin argues that rights protections by the Court are sometimes important despite popular opposition. How might Kramer

reply to the challenge that some freedoms should be upheld even if they are violated by legislatures or Congress?

3.   Is there any way to reconcile the Court's act of restraint in *Nixon v. United States* with Kramer's charge that the Rehnquist Court fully embraced judicial supremacy? Is judicial supremacy compatible with the political question doctrine?

KEY TERMS

bill of attainder: Legislation that declares an individual guilty of a crime without the benefit of a trial.

Democratic-Republican Party: The party of Thomas Jefferson, the President of the United States when *Marbury v. Madison* was decided.

departmentalism: The view that the various branches of government ought to have a say in constitutional interpretation.

ex post facto law: A law retroactively imposed on parties, in contrast to laws that govern future action.

Federalist Party: The party of President John Adams, Chief Justice John Marshall, and William Marbury.

judicial review: The power to strike down legislative or executive acts on grounds that they are incompatible with a provision or provisions of the Constitution.

judicial supremacy: The view that the Court is the final and supreme interpreter of constitutional meaning.

original jurisdiction: The power of the Court to be the first court to hear a case. This is in contrast to appellate jurisdiction, where the Court reviews a lower court decision.

per curiam opinion: An unsigned opinion.

standing doctrine: The doctrine the Court uses to determine whether an individual has suffered a constitutionally cognizable harm sufficient to permit his or her claim to be heard in federal court.

THEORIES OF INTERPRETATION

Does the Constitution have a theory at its core, or does its text speak for itself? How should we determine what its provisions mean?

In the previous chapter, we examined possible sources of the Court's power to strike down legislation through judicial review. But a separate question remains: If the justices do have such a power, when should they exercise it? As Alexander Hamilton and other defenders of judicial review have made clear, if the Court has such a power, it is derived from its claim to protect the guarantees of the Constitution. But in order to know what the Constitution guarantees, we must first know what it says and how to understand its meaning.

This task might at first glance seem easier than it is. On some issues, the Constitution's meaning is extremely clear, and indeed, this would be a rather short course if all constitutional interpretation were so straightforward. As examples of matters requiring little or no constitutional interpretation, consider the requirement in Article I that members of the House of Representatives be at least 25 years of age, the statement in Article II that the president will serve four-year terms in office, and the mandate that the president give an oath of office. But in addition to these straightforward matters of interpretation, other matters prove to be much more complex. Look, for example, at the Eighth Amendment's prohibition of "cruel and unusual punishment." As we will see in Chapter 8, this country has engaged in a long debate about whether this provision is compatible with capital punishment. Similarly, consider the Fourteenth Amendment's guarantee of "equal protection of the laws." What exactly does this broad phrase mean? Does it require equality between men and women, or between members of different economic classes? The Constitution provides little indication of the correct method of interpretation because no mention of these matters is found in the text itself.

While some phrases in the document are clear, at other times a phrase that might seem straightforward, such as the "power to regulate commerce . . . among the states," has turned out to raise more complicated issues of interpretation. Need goods be transported over state lines in order to be part of "commerce among the states," or are some goods made and sold within one state part of interstate commerce? Is, for instance, the decision to grow marijuana in one's own home subject to regulation under this clause?

The meaning of "due process" in the Fifth and Fourteenth Amendments is yet another source of debate, and it constitutes one of the most controversial areas of contemporary constitutional law. In addition to its relevance to the rights of criminal defendants, the entitlement to due process has also been applied to matters as diverse as workers' rights legislation and abortion. In particular, this clause has been thought to guarantee an entitlement to "substantive due process" rights in matters such as contraception and abortion. Yet the phrase "substantive due process" is nowhere to be found in the Constitution. The phrase "nor shall any state deprive any person of life, liberty, or property, without due process of law" does appear in the Fourteenth Amendment of the Constitution, but it does not refer explicitly to any of the specific rights controversies now thought relevant to this provision. Indeed, the question of whether the Constitution protects the ability of individuals to purchase latex condoms, or to perform abortions, would not have occurred to the Founders, even though it is now a central issue. The question then of how to interpret the constitutional text, especially in the instances of these open-ended provisions, is controversial to say the least.

Thankfully, you do not need to grapple alone with the difficult question of how to interpret the Constitution. In this chapter, we present four of the most prominent theories used to evaluate problems of constitutional interpretation. While the list of theories we examine here is certainly not exhaustive, the authors in this chapter present a variety of general accounts of how to read and think about the Constitution. It will become clear, moreover, that just as there are complexities in the text of the Constitution, there is also great debate amongst jurists and legal thinkers about the best method of interpretation. It would, of course, be easier for you if this book presented only one of these methods, but that would not do justice to the fundamental question of how to determine what the Constitution means. We will instead work through these various theories in an attempt to make sense of the ways in which they conflict and also how they might be combined with one another. By the end of this chapter, you should begin to think for yourself about how best to approach constitutional interpretation generally, as this will then help you in the specific controversies that are examined in subsequent chapters. Some of the cases that you will examine through the different lenses of each theory of constitutional interpretation were actually brought before the Court before the development of the theories. Indeed, a good test of the theories of interpretation is whether they can be applied to issues that preceded them.

The readings of this chapter begin with perhaps the most well known of constitutional theories: originalism. This view has been defended by many scholars of the Constitution including Robert Bork, former Attorney General Edwin Meese, and perhaps most notably current U.S. Supreme Court Justice Antonin Scalia. For originalists such as Justice Scalia, the text of the Constitution as it would have been understood at the time of the Founding is the root of all constitutional interpretation. Justice Scalia, therefore, gives great importance to the historical context in which the document—and any amendment—was written. In this interpretation, Justice Scalia appeals directly to the ideal of democracy. If judges are to avoid imposing their own personal moral and political views on a democratic polity, he claims, then they must defer instead to the Founders' document, which was itself an expression of democratic will. Sometimes "originalism" is used as an umbrella term that can refer, for example, to the original public meaning of constitutional phrases or to the original intentions of the Founders who authored them. Although originalism is often used as a synonym for the idea of original intent, Justice Scalia is careful to distinguish between the two. He rejects the idea that the collective intentions of the Founders could ever be known and instead seeks to determine the common meaning of the words as they would have been understood in the time at which they were written.

Justice Scalia informs this chapter not only as a constitutional theorist but also as a practicing justice. His opinion in *District of Columbia v. Heller*, and its particular attention to the text of the Second Amendment, illustrates Justice Scalia's view of original public meaning in action. In that case, the Court struck down a D.C. law that placed stringent limits on the ownership and possession of personal firearms. One of the many items of interest in this opinion is Justice Scalia's approach to precedent. As you will see, in his view it is the original meaning of the Constitution, not precedent, that has the greatest weight in judicial adjudication. Additionally, his dissent in *Planned Parenthood v. Casey*, which reasserted a fundamental constitutional right to abortion under the doctrine of substantive due process, is a paradigm of originalist reasoning. The Due Process Clause of the Fourteenth Amendment would not have been understood at the time it was written as protecting abortion rights, and it is therefore illegitimate, he claims, to use it to enforce such a right today.

We turn next to the theory of John Hart Ely, which offers an alternative to Justice Scalia's views of both democracy and constitutional interpretation. For Ely, it is not enough to look to the text of the Constitution to understand its meaning. Rather, we must understand the general idea that underpins the document. For Ely, it is the entitlement to equal participation in democratic lawmaking that constitutes the central guarantee at the heart of the Constitution. The idea of equal participation therefore should inform a variety of areas of constitutional interpretation. For Ely, the role of judges is to reinforce the commitment that all citizens have an equal role to play in the political process. Indeed, for Ely, the Equal Protection Clause is clearly central to understanding the Constitution as a whole. As our reading from him makes clear, Ely's theory is deeply informed by the famous Footnote Four of U.S. Supreme Court Justice Harlan Stone's decision in *United States v. Carolene Products*. In that footnote, Justice Stone suggests a special role for the Court in protecting "discrete and insular minorities" and the functioning of the political process. In its seminal decision in *Reynolds v. Sims*, which you will also read in this chapter, the Court determined that judges have a role in intervening in the election process, and it constituted a clear victory for the judicial role advocated by Ely in defending the democratic process.

While Ely suggests that a concern to ensure fair democratic procedures is central to constitutional meaning and interpretation, another school of thought emphasizes the role of constitutional rights that constrain democratic procedures. The "moral reading" of the Constitution proposed by Ronald Dworkin, as well as a similar account of interpretation offered by U.S. Supreme Court Justice William Brennan, emphasizes the idea that there are substantive, not merely procedural, moral ideals embedded in the Constitution. For both of these thinkers, provisions like the Eighth Amendment's prohibition of cruel and unusual punishment are examples of how the Constitution's text invites us to think about the ways in which a democratic regime should protect the general dignity and rights of all individuals. On Dworkin's account, democratic interpretation entails the protection of the very rights that are the core of self-government. Moreover, he suggests, these rights go beyond concerns about democratic participation.

One puzzle for the moral reading is to ask what specific values the Constitution enacts. For Dworkin, opinions like *Griswold v. Connecticut*, in which the Court established a fundamental right to privacy, epitomize the moral reading of the Constitution. But critics of this view ask whether the Constitution might be consistent with other moral views, such as the economic libertarian theory of property rights exemplified in *Lochner v. New York*. We include both of these cases in our selection to further examine what kind of moral reading the Constitution might require. Critics of Dworkin's position accuse adherents of the moral reading of substituting their own moral and political philosophies for the meaning of the Constitution. In reading this section, you might consider whether it is important for proponents of the moral reading to distinguish these cases and how it might be possible to locate fundamental values espoused by the Constitution without simply inserting one's own.

Finally, we turn to a view of constitutional interpretation known as pragmatism. Pragmatists reject the emphasis on grand theories of judicial review that Justice Scalia, Ely, and Dworkin share, favoring instead a case-by-case analysis of particular outcomes. For pragmatists, general debate about the meaning of the Constitution is less helpful than thinking about how to bring about the best consequences in particular cases. In direct contrast to Justice Scalia's emphasis on looking to history to interpret the Constitution, thinkers such as U.S. Supreme Court Justice Oliver Wendell Holmes and Judge Richard Posner argue that the Constitution requires us to bring about the best consequences in particular cases or, in other words, to think exclusively about how the document can improve the future. Other pragmatists, such as Cass Sunstein, reject the notion that the Constitution has a comprehensive theory at all and instead suggest ways in which judges of all theoretical persuasions can reach a democratic consensus. You will then read U.S. Supreme Court Justice Stephen Breyer's dissent in *District of Columbia v. Heller* and evaluate how his view of pragmatism responds to Justice Scalia's originalist methodology.

While the majority opinion in *Lochner v. New York* springs from one version of the moral reading, the dissent by Justice Holmes is a primary example of legal pragmatism. In that opinion, Justice Holmes chastised the majority for relying on its own moral and economic theory, famously proclaiming that the Constitution does not "enact Mr. Herbert Spencer's social statics." Though Justice Holmes's dissent is as brilliant as it is concise, you should reflect on whether it is desirable or even possible to avoid constitutional theorizing.

You might wonder why it is worth studying possible theories of constitutional interpretation. For instance, some contend that Supreme Court justices are partisan in their opinions and that they simply endorse the views of the party that appointed them to the Court. Partisanship may or may not play a role, but it alone cannot explain the decisions many justices have reached over time. For instance, Justice Scalia is often thought to be a conservative, largely in line with the Republican Party. However, he has broken with his party on many occasions to argue in defense of the rights of criminal defendants and freedom of expression. For instance, in interpreting the Confrontation Clause, he argued that individuals suspected of sexual abuse have the right to confront witnesses, including the children claiming to have been abused by them, in person rather than via closed circuit television, and he surprised many by joining the liberal firebrand Justice Brennan in overturning laws prohibiting flag burning. On Justice Scalia's view, as you will see, it is the text that guides, rather than partisan politics. Those following in the tradition of Ely contend that they have no partisan agenda, but rather an overriding concern to ensure the proper functioning of the democratic process. As you read these various theories, you should consider for yourself whether or not they are compelling.

A. ORIGINALISM

We begin our readings by examining the originalist theory of Justice Antonin Scalia. Justice Scalia's originalism is sometimes confused with the idea that modern constitutional interpreters should defer to the intentions of the Founders. Justice Scalia points out, however, that this would be impossible to discern, given the multiplicity of Framers and their various intentions. Instead, Justice Scalia directs us to try to find the meaning of the Constitution as it would have been "originally understood" by the wider population at the time the document or the amendments were ratified. Justice Scalia therefore is an advocate of "textualism" in constitutional interpretation. In his view, constitutional interpreters should pay close attention to the text of the Constitution because it alone—and not the various intents or understandings of the Founders or any other group—is the fundamental law that was ratified by the people. This raises a question, however, as to what is to be said about terms that are not widely understood among the general population. For instance, many citizens may not know what an ex post facto law or a bill of attainder is, although both phrases are used in the Constitution. Justice Scalia has suggested that in such instances we should look at the generally understood meaning of the Constitution's clauses as they were understood by the educated legal community at the time they were written and ratified. It is therefore not the Founders' intent that matters, but the meaning of the text that they wrote.

In contrast to Justice Scalia's view of original meaning, the theory of original intent is another kind of originalism, which has been defended most prominently by former Attorney General Edwin Meese III. In a speech before the American Bar Association in 1985, Meese called for "a jurisprudence of original intention," or in other words, constitutional interpretation in accordance with the original intent of the Founders. For example, he criticized the Court for interpreting the Establishment Clause, which we examine in Chapter 6, in such a way that it "prevent[s] religious activity." In reality, Meese asserts, the Framers intended for the clause to protect against federal government interference in state policy, and the Court should therefore apply it accordingly. Keep in mind the similarities and differences between Meese's notion of original intent and Justice Scalia's originalism throughout this section.

Justice Scalia contends that the alternatives to originalism, with their emphasis outside the constitutional text, are approaches that would inevitably result in judges imposing their own values on the document. He argues that this imposition would be an insult to democracy that would be made worse by the fact that the Supreme Court is an elite institution not elected by the people. In contrast, an originalist concern to stay true to the original meaning of the text shows fidelity to democracy by respecting the words of those with the legislative authority to make fundamental law and to the actual document that was ratified by the people. Justice Scalia holds that the voters who ratified the Constitution and its amendments have fundamental democratic credentials that can be respected only by adhering to the text they enacted. He argues that a failure to respect the textual meaning of these amendments would be a failure to respect the democratic process.

Justice Scalia contrasts his view of constitutional interpretation with that of a "living" understanding of constitutional meaning. It is important to Justice Scalia that we think of our Constitution as a "dead" document in order to ensure faithfulness to democratic enactments. In contrast, any idea of the Constitution as an evolving document will necessarily serve as a way for judges to impose their own values on constitutional meaning. Justice Scalia's approach can be elucidated with reference to the guarantee against "cruel and unusual punishment" found in the Eighth Amendment. He contends that a living interpretation might extend this broad phrase to invalidate a number of punishments, including the death penalty. But Justice Scalia believes the "cruel and unusual" clause should invalidate only those punishments considered cruel and unusual at the time the amendment was passed. He points to the explicit recognition of capital punishment in multiple provisions of the Constitution as evidence that this form of punishment could not have been considered cruel and unusual.

Notice as you read that Justice Scalia recognizes that original meaning might at times lead to results that are unpalatable in the contemporary world. For instance, there is a real question as to whether the *Brown v. Board of Education* decision, which struck down segregation in public schools, could be justified on originalist grounds. In the face of such decisions, Justice Scalia declares that he is "faint-hearted" in the sense that he would not necessarily follow an originalist interpretation when the results would be unacceptable. Do you believe that these limits suggest a flaw with originalist interpretation?

As you read Justice Scalia's explanation of his originalist philosophy, as well as his Supreme Court opinions, consider what implications originalism might have for the traditional legal idea of *stare decisis*. Stare decisis literally means, "let the decision stand," and refers to the importance in law of deferring to precedent. What role, if any, does precedent have in Justice Scalia's view of constitutional interpretation, especially when precedent conflicts with the original understanding of the Constitution? Some have suggested that one of the main virtues of the rule of law is consistency and that prior cases should therefore be overturned only very infrequently. Does Justice Scalia break with this view? You will notice that in his dissent in *Planned Parenthood v. Casey*, a case in which he challenges the right to an abortion, and in his majority opinion in *District of Columbia v. Heller*, in which the Court announces a previously unrecognized individual right to own guns, Justice Scalia is not afraid to place the original meaning over and above precedent. Why?

Justice Antonin Scalia

ORIGINALISM: THE LESSER EVIL

57 U. Cin. L. Rev. 849 (1989)

It may surprise the layman, but it will surely not surprise the lawyers here, to learn that originalism is not, and had perhaps never been, the sole method of constitutional exegesis. It would be hard to count on the fingers of both hands and the toes of both feet, yea, even on the hairs of one's youthful head, the opinions that have in fact been rendered not on the basis of what the Constitution originally meant, but on the basis of what the judges currently thought it desirable for it to mean. That is, I suppose, the sort of behavior Chief Justice Hughes was referring to when he said the Constitution is what the judges say it is. But in the past, non-originalist opinions have almost always had the decency to lie, or at least to dissemble, about what they were doing—either ignoring strong evidence of original intent that contradicted the minimal recited evidence of an original intent congenial to the court's desires, or else not discussing original intent at all, speaking in terms of broad constitutional generalities with no pretense of historical support. It is only in relatively recent years, however, that non-originalist exegesis has, so to speak, come out of the closet, and put itself forward overtly as an intellectually legitimate device. To be sure, in support of its venerability as a legitimate interpretive theory there is often trotted out John Marshall's statement in *McCulloch v. Maryland* that "we must never forget it is a constitution we are expounding"—as though the implication of that statement was that our interpretation must change from age to age. But that is a canard. The real implication was quite the opposite: Marshall was saying that the Constitution had to be interpreted generously because the powers conferred upon Congress under it had to be broad enough to serve not only the needs of the federal government originally discerned but also the needs that might arise in the future. If constitutional interpretation could be adjusted as changing circumstances required, a broad initial interpretation would have been unnecessary.

The principal theoretical defect of non-originalism, in my view, is its incompatibility with the very principle that legitimizes judicial review of constitutionality. Nothing in the text of the Constitution confers upon the courts the power to inquire into, rather than passively assume, the constitutionality of federal statutes. That power is, however, reasonably implicit because, as Marshall said in *Marbury v. Madison*, (1) "[i]t is emphatically the province and duty of the judicial department to say what the law is," (2) "[i]f two laws conflict with each other, the courts must decide on the operation of each," and (3) "the constitution is to be considered, in court, as a paramount law." Central to that analysis, it seems to me, is the perception that the Constitution, though it has an effect superior to other laws, is in its nature the sort of "law" that is the business of the courts—an enactment that has a fixed meaning ascertainable through the usual devices familiar to those learned in the law. If the Constitution were not that sort of a "law," but a novel invitation to apply current societal values, what reason would there be to believe that the invitation was addressed to the courts rather than to the legislature? One simply cannot say, regarding that sort of novel enactment, that "[i]t is emphatically the province and

duty of the judicial department" to determine its content. Quite to the contrary, the legislature would seem a much more appropriate expositor of social values, and its determination that a statute is compatible with the Constitution should, as in England, prevail.

Apart from the frailty of its theoretical underpinning, non-originalism confronts a practical difficulty reminiscent of the truism of elective politics that "You can't beat somebody with nobody." It is not enough to demonstrate that the other fellow's candidate (originalism) is no good; one must also agree upon another candidate to replace him. Just as it is not very meaningful for a voter to vote "non-Reagan," it is not very helpful to tell a judge to be a "non-originalist." If the law is to make any attempt at consistency and predictability, surely there must be general agreement not only that judges reject one exegetical approach (originalism), but that they adopt another. And it is hard to discern any emerging consensus among the non-originalists as to what this might be. Are the "fundamental values" that replace original meaning to be derived from the philosophy of Plato, or of Locke, or Mills, or Rawls, or perhaps from the latest Gallup poll? This is not to say that originalists are in entire agreement as to what the nature of their methodology is; as I shall mention shortly, there are some significant differences. But as its name suggests, it by and large represents a coherent approach, or at least an agreed-upon point of departure. As the name "non-originalism" suggests (and I know no other, more precise term by which this school of exegesis can be described), it represents agreement on nothing except what is the wrong approach.

Finally, I want to mention what is not a defect of non-originalism, but one of its supposed benefits that seems to me illusory. A bit earlier I quoted one of the most prominent non-originalists, Professor Tribe, to the effect that the Constitution "invites us, and our judges, to expand on the . . . freedoms that are uniquely our heritage." I think it fair to say that that is a common theme of non-originalists in general. But why, one may reasonably ask—once the original import of the Constitution is cast aside to be replaced by the "fundamental values" of the current society—why are we invited only to "expand on" freedoms, and not to contract them as well? Last Term we decided a case, *Coy v. Iowa*, in which, at the trial of a man accused of taking indecent liberties with two young girls, the girls were permitted to testify separated from the defendant by a screen which prevented them from seeing him. We held that, at least absent a specific finding that these particular witnesses needed such protection, this procedure violated that provision of the Sixth Amendment that assures a criminal defendant the right "to be confronted with the witnesses against him." Let us hypothesize, however (a hypothesis that may well be true), that modern American society is much more conscious of, and averse to, the effects of "emotional trauma" than was the society of 1791, and that it is, in addition, much more concerned about the emotional frailty of children and the sensitivity of young women regarding sexual abuse. If that is so, and if the non-originalists are right, would it not have been possible for the Court to hold that, even though in 1791 the confrontation clause clearly would not have permitted a blanket exception for such testimony, it does so today? Such a holding, of course, could hardly be characterized as an "expansion upon" preexisting freedoms. Or let me give another example that is already

history: I think it highly probable that over the past two hundred years the Supreme Court, though not avowedly under the banner of "non-originalist" interpretation, has in fact narrowed the contract clause of the Constitution well short of its original meaning. Perhaps we are all content with that development— but can it possibly be asserted that it represented an expansion, rather than a contraction, of individual liberties? Our modern society is undoubtedly not as enthusiastic about economic liberties as were the men and women of 1789; but we should not fool ourselves into believing that because we like the result the result does not represent a contraction of liberty. Non-originalism, in other words, is a two-way street that handles traffic both to and from individual rights.

Let me turn next to originalism, which is also not without its warts. Its greatest defect, in my view, is the difficulty of applying it correctly. Not that I agree with, or even take very seriously, the intricately elaborated scholarly criticisms to the effect that (believe it or not) words have no meaning. They have meaning enough, as the scholarly critics themselves must surely believe when they choose to express their views in text rather than music. But what is true is that it is often exceedingly difficult to plumb the original understanding of an ancient text. Properly done, the task requires the consideration of an enormous mass of material—in the case of the Constitution and its Amendments, for example, to mention only one element, the records of the ratifying debates in all the states. Even beyond that, it requires an evaluation of the reliability of that material—many of the reports of the ratifying debates, for example, are thought to be quite unreliable. And further still, it requires immersing oneself in the political and intellectual atmosphere of the time—somehow placing out of mind knowledge that we have which an earlier age did not, and putting on beliefs, attitudes, philosophies, prejudices and loyalties that are not those of our day. It is, in short, a task sometimes better suited to the historian than the lawyer.

I can be much more brief in describing what seems to me the second most serious objection to originalism: In its undiluted form, at least, it is medicine that seems too strong to swallow. Thus, almost every originalist would adulterate it with the doctrine of stare decisis—so that *Marbury v. Madison* would stand even if Professor Raoul Berger should demonstrate unassailably that it got the meaning of the Constitution wrong. (Of course recognizing stare decisis is seemingly even more incompatible with non-originalist theory: If the most solemnly and democratically adopted text of the Constitution and its Amendments can be ignored on the basis of current values, what possible basis could there be for enforced adherence to a legal decision of the Supreme Court?) But stare decisis alone is not enough to prevent originalism from being what many would consider too bitter a pill. What if some state should enact a new law providing public lashing, or branding of the right hand, as punishment for certain criminal offenses? Even if it could be demonstrated unequivocally that these were not cruel and unusual measures in 1791, and even though no prior Supreme Court decision has specifically disapproved them, I doubt whether any federal judge—even among the many who consider themselves originalists— would sustain them against an Eighth Amendment challenge. It may well be, as Professor Henry Monaghan persuasively argues, that this cannot legitimately be reconciled with originalist philosophy— that it represents the unrealistic view of the Constitution as a document intended to create a perfect society for all ages to come, whereas in fact it was a political compromise that did not pretend to create a perfect society even for its own age (as its toleration of slavery, which a majority of the founding generation recognized as an evil, well enough demonstrates). Even so, I am confident that public flogging and handbranding would not be sustained by our courts, and any espousal of originalism as a practical theory of exegesis must somehow come to terms with that reality.

One way of doing so, of course, would be to say that it was originally intended that the cruel and unusual punishment clause would have an evolving content— that "cruel and unusual" originally meant "cruel and unusual for the age in question" and not "cruel and unusual in 1791." But to be faithful to originalist philosophy, one must not only say this but demonstrate it to be so on the basis of some textual or historical evidence. Perhaps the mere words "cruel and unusual" suggest an evolutionary intent more than other provisions of the Constitution, but that is far from clear; and I know of no historical evidence for that meaning. And if the faint-hearted originalist is willing simply to posit such an intent for the "cruel and unusual punishment" clause, why not for the due process clause, the equal protection clause, the privileges and immunity clause, etc.? When one goes down that road, there is really no difference between the faint-hearted originalist and the moderate non-originalist, except that the former finds it comforting to make up (out of whole cloth) an original evolutionary intent, and the latter thinks that superfluous. It is, I think, the fact that most originalists are faint-hearted and most non-originalists are moderate (that is, would not ascribe evolving content to such clear provisions as the requirement that the President be no less than thirty-five years of age) which accounts for the fact that the sharp divergence between the two philosophies does not produce an equivalently sharp divergence in judicial opinions.

Having described what I consider the principal difficulties with the originalist and non-originalist approaches, I suppose I owe it to the listener to say which of the two evils I prefer. It is originalism. I take the need for theoretical legitimacy seriously, and even if one assumes (as many non-originalists do not even bother to do) that the Constitution was originally meant to expound evolving rather than permanent values, . . . I see no basis for believing that supervision of the evolution would have been committed to the courts. At an even more general theoretical level, originalism seems to me more compatible with the nature and purpose of a Constitution in a democratic system. A democratic society does not, by and large, need constitutional guarantees to insure that its laws will reflect "current values." Elections take care of that quite well. The purpose of constitutional guarantees—and in particular those constitutional guarantees of individual rights that are at the center of this controversy—is precisely to prevent the law from reflecting certain changes in original values that the society adopting the Constitution thinks fundamentally undesirable. Or, more precisely, to require the society to devote to the subject the long and hard consideration required for a constitutional amendment before those particular values can be cast aside.

I also think that the central practical defect of non-originalism is fundamental and irreparable: the impossibility of achieving any consensus on what, precisely, is to replace original meaning, once that is abandoned. The practical defects of originalism, on the other hand, while genuine enough, seem to me less severe. While it may indeed be unrealistic to have substantial confidence that judges and lawyers will find the correct historical answer to such refined questions of original intent as the precise content of "the executive Power," for the vast majority of questions the answer is clear. The death penalty, for example, was not cruel and unusual punishment because it is referred to in the Constitution itself; and the right of confrontation by its plain language meant, at least, being face-to-face with the person testifying against one at trial. For the non-originalist, even these are open questions. As for the fact that originalism is strong medicine, and that one cannot realistically expect judges (probably myself included) to apply it without a trace of constitutional perfectionism: I suppose I must respond that this is a world in which nothing is flawless, and fall back upon G.K. Chesterton's observation that a thing worth doing is worth doing badly.

It seems to me, moreover, that the practical defects of originalism are defects more appropriate for the task at hand—that is, less likely to aggravate the most significant weakness of the system of judicial review and more likely to produce results acceptable to all. If one is hiring a reference-room librarian, and has two applicants, between whom the only substantial difference is that the one's normal conversational tone tends to be too loud and the other's too soft, it is pretty clear which of the imperfections should be preferred. Now the main danger in judicial interpretation of the Constitution—or, for that matter, in judicial interpretation of any law—is that the judges will mistake their own predilections for the law. Avoiding this error is the hardest part of being a conscientious judge; perhaps no conscientious judge ever succeeds entirely. Non-originalism, which under one or another formulation invokes "fundamental values" as the touchstone of constitutionality, plays precisely to this weakness. It is very difficult for a person to discern a difference between those political values that he personally thinks most important, and those political values that are "fundamental to our society." Thus, by the adoption of such a criterion judicial personalization of the law is enormously facilitated. (One might reduce this danger by insisting that the new "fundamental values" invoked to replace original meaning be clearly and objectively manifested in the laws of the society. But among all the varying tests suggested by non-originalist theoreticians, I am unaware that that one ever appears. Most if not all non-originalists, for example, would strike down the death penalty, though it continues to be widely adopted in both state and federal legislation.)

Originalism does not aggravate the principal weakness of the system, for it establishes a historical criterion that is conceptually quite separate from the preferences of the judge himself. And the principal defect of that approach—that historical research is always difficult and sometimes inconclusive—will, unlike non-originalism, lead to a more moderate rather than a more extreme result. The inevitable tendency of judges to think that the law is what they would like it to be will, I have no doubt, cause most errors in judicial historiography to be made in the direction of projecting upon the age of 1789 current, modern values—so that as applied, even as applied in the best of faith, originalism will (as

the historical record shows) end up as something of a compromise. Perhaps not a bad characteristic for a constitutional theory. Thus, non-originalists can say, concerning the principal defect of originalism, "Oh happy fault." Originalism is, it seems to me, the librarian who talks too softly.

Having made that endorsement, I hasten to confess that in a crunch I may prove a faint-hearted originalist. I cannot imagine myself, any more than any other federal judge, upholding a statute that imposes the punishment of flogging. But then I cannot imagine such a case's arising either. In any event, in deciding the cases before me I expect I will rarely be confronted with making the stark choice between giving evolutionary content (not yet required by stare decisis) and not giving evolutionary content to particular constitutional provisions. The vast majority of my dissents from non-originalist thinking (and I hope at least some of those dissents will be majorities) will, I am sure, be able to be framed in the terms that, even if the provision in question has an evolutionary content, there is inadequate indication that any evolution in social attitudes has occurred. That—to conclude this largely theoretical talk on a note of reality—is the real dispute that appears in the case: not between non-originalists on the one hand and pure originalists on the other, concerning the validity of looking at all to current values; but rather between, on the one hand, non-originalists, fainthearted originalists and pure-originalists-accepting-for-the-sake-of-argument-evolutionary-content, and, on the other hand, other adherents of the same three approaches, concerning the nature and degree of evidence necessary to demonstrate that constitutional evolution has occurred.

PLANNED PARENTHOOD v. CASEY

505 U.S. 833 (1992)

Opinion: O'Connor, Kennedy, Souter, joined by Stevens in Part V E and by Blackmun in Parts I, II, III, V A, V C, and VI
Partial Concurrence, Partial Dissent: Stevens
Partial Concurrence, Partial Dissent: Blackmun
Partial Concurrence, Partial Dissent: Rehnquist, joined by White, Scalia, Thomas
Partial Concurrence, Partial Dissent: Scalia, joined by Rehnquist, White, Thomas

In this case, the Court upheld its previous decision in Roe v. Wade, *which recognizes the fundamental right for a woman to procure an abortion, while at the same time validating a number of restrictions on that right. This case raises serious questions about sexual privacy and reproductive autonomy, which are discussed in detail in Chapter 7. The focus here and in all of the other cases in this chapter, however, is on the theories of interpretation adopted by various members of the Court. For this reason, in this chapter we excerpt only Justice Antonin Scalia's dissent in the case. He offers an originalist argument against a woman's right to choose an abortion. Specifically, Justice Scalia claims that this right cannot be found anywhere in the Constitution. Certainly, in his opinion, such a right would not have been understood as part of the original meaning of the Constitution. Is Justice Scalia's argument convincing?*

JUSTICE SCALIA, *with whom* **THE CHIEF JUSTICE, JUSTICE WHITE,** *and* **JUSTICE THOMAS** *join, concurring in part and dissenting in part.*

The States may, if they wish, permit abortion on demand, but the Constitution does not require them to do so. The permissibility of abortion, and the limitations upon it, are to be resolved like most important questions in our democracy: by citizens trying to persuade one another and then voting. As the Court acknowledges, "where reasonable people disagree the government can adopt one position or the other." The Court is correct in adding the qualification that this "assumes a state of affairs in which the choice does not intrude upon a protected liberty," ibid.—but the crucial part of that qualification is the penultimate word. A State's choice between two positions on which reasonable people can disagree is constitutional even when (as is often the case) it intrudes upon a "liberty" in the absolute sense. Laws against bigamy, for example—with which entire societies of reasonable people disagree—intrude upon men and women's liberty to marry and live with one another. But bigamy happens not to be a liberty specially "protected" by the Constitution.

That is, quite simply, the issue in these cases: not whether the power of a woman to abort her unborn child is a "liberty" in the absolute sense; or even whether it is a liberty of great importance to many women. Of course it is both. The issue is whether it is a liberty protected by the Constitution of the United States. I am sure it is not. I reach that conclusion not because of anything so exalted as my views concerning the "concept of existence, of meaning, of the universe, and of the mystery of human life."

Rather, I reach it for the same reason I reach the conclusion that bigamy is not constitutionally protected—because of two simple facts: (1) the Constitution says absolutely nothing about it, and (2) the longstanding traditions of American society have permitted it to be legally proscribed.

The authors of the joint opinion, of course, do not squarely contend that *Roe v. Wade* was a correct application of "reasoned judgment"; merely that it must be followed, because of stare decisis. But in their exhaustive discussion of all the factors that go into the determination of when stare decisis should be observed and when disregarded, they never mention "how wrong was the decision on its face?" Surely, if "the Court's power lies . . . in its legitimacy, a product of substance and perception," the "substance" part of the equation demands that plain error be acknowledged and eliminated. *Roe* was plainly wrong—even on the Court's methodology of "reasoned judgment," and even more so (of course) if the proper criteria of text and tradition are applied.

The emptiness of the "reasoned judgment" that produced *Roe* is displayed in plain view by the fact that, after more than 19 years of effort by some of the brightest (and most determined) legal minds in the country, after more than 10 cases upholding abortion rights in this Court, and after dozens upon dozens of amicus briefs submitted in these and other cases, the best the Court can do to explain how it is that the word "liberty" must be thought to include the right to destroy human fetuses is to rattle off a collection of adjectives that simply decorate a value judgment and conceal a political choice. The right to abort, we are told, inheres in "liberty" because it is among "a person's most basic decisions"; it involves a "most intimate and personal choice"; it is "central to personal dignity and autonomy"; it "originates within the zone of conscience and belief";

it is "too intimate and personal" for state interference; it reflects "intimate views" of a "deep, personal character"; it involves "intimate relationships" and notions of "personal autonomy and bodily integrity"; and it concerns a particularly "'important decision.'" But it is obvious to anyone applying "reasoned judgment" that the same adjectives can be applied to many forms of conduct that this Court (including one of the Justices in today's majority, see *Bowers v. Hardwick*) has held are not entitled to constitutional protection—because, like abortion, they are forms of conduct that have long been criminalized in American society. Those adjectives might be applied, for example, to homosexual sodomy, polygamy, adult incest, and suicide, all of which are equally "intimate" and "deeply personal" decisions involving "personal autonomy and bodily integrity," and all of which can constitutionally be proscribed because it is our unquestionable constitutional tradition that they are proscribable. It is not reasoned judgment that supports the Court's decision; only personal predilection.

I cannot agree with, indeed I am appalled by, the Court's suggestion that the decision whether to stand by an erroneous constitutional decision must be strongly influenced—against overruling, no less—by the substantial and continuing public opposition the decision has generated. The Court's judgment that any other course would "subvert the Court's legitimacy" must be another consequence of reading the error-filled history book that described the deeply divided country brought together by *Roe*. In my history book, the Court was covered with dishonor and deprived of legitimacy by *Dred Scott v. Sandford*, an erroneous (and widely opposed) opinion that it did not abandon, rather than by *West Coast Hotel Co. v. Parrish*, which produced the famous "switch in time" from the Court's erroneous (and widely opposed) constitutional opposition to the social measures of the New Deal. (Both *Dred Scott* and one line of the cases resisting the New Deal rested upon the concept of "substantive due process" that the Court praises and employs today. Indeed, *Dred Scott* was "very possibly the first application of substantive due process in the Supreme Court, the original precedent for *Lochner v. New York* and *Roe v. Wade*."

But whether it would "subvert the Court's legitimacy" or not, the notion that we would decide a case differently from the way we otherwise would have in order to show that we can stand firm against public disapproval is frightening. It is a bad enough idea, even in the head of someone like me, who believes that the text of the Constitution, and our traditions, say what they say and there is no fiddling with them. But when it is in the mind of a Court that believes the Constitution has an evolving meaning; that the Ninth Amendment's reference to "other" rights is not a disclaimer, but a charter for action; and that the function of this Court is to "speak before all others for [the people's] constitutional ideals" unrestrained by meaningful text or tradition—then the notion that the Court must adhere to a decision for as long as the decision faces "great opposition" and the Court is "under fire" acquires a character of almost czarist arrogance. . . .

There is a poignant aspect to today's opinion. Its length, and what might be called its epic tone, suggest that its authors believe they are bringing to an end a troublesome era in the history of our Nation and of our Court. "It is the dimension" of authority, they say, to "call the contending sides of national controversy to end their national division by accepting a common mandate rooted in the Constitution."

There comes vividly to mind a portrait by Emanuel Leutze that hangs in the Harvard Law School: Roger Brooke Taney, painted in 1859, the 82d year of his life, the 24th of his Chief Justiceship, the second after his opinion in *Dred Scott*. He is all in black, sitting in a shadowed red armchair, left hand resting upon a pad of paper in his lap, right hand hanging limply, almost lifelessly, beside the inner arm of the chair. He sits facing the viewer and staring straight out. There seems to be on his face, and in his deep-set eyes, an expression of profound sadness and disillusionment. Perhaps he always looked that way, even when dwelling upon the happiest of thoughts. But those of us who know how the luster of his great Chief Justiceship came to be eclipsed by *Dred Scott* cannot help believing that he had that case—its already apparent consequences for the Court and its soon-to-be-played-out consequences for the Nation—burning on his mind. I expect that two years earlier he, too, had thought himself "calling the contending sides of national controversy to end their national division by accepting a common mandate rooted in the Constitution."

It is no more realistic for us in this litigation, than it was for him in that, to think that an issue of the sort they both involved—an issue involving life and death, freedom and subjugation—can be "speedily and finally settled" by the Supreme Court, as President James Buchanan in his inaugural address said the issue of slavery in the territories would be. Quite to the contrary, by foreclosing all democratic outlet for the deep passions this issue arouses, by banishing the issue from the political forum that gives all participants, even the losers, the satisfaction of a fair hearing and an honest fight, by continuing the imposition of a rigid national rule instead of allowing for regional differences, the Court merely prolongs and intensifies the anguish.

We should get out of this area, where we have no right to be, and where we do neither ourselves nor the country any good by remaining.

DISTRICT OF COLUMBIA v. HELLER

554 U.S. 570 (2008)

Opinion: Scalia, joined by Roberts, Kennedy, Thomas, Alito
Dissent: Stevens, joined by Souter, Ginsburg, Breyer
Dissent: Breyer, joined by Stevens, Souter, Ginsburg

Prior to this case, the Second Amendment had never been interpreted by the Supreme Court as recognizing an individual right to possess guns. In this opinion, more than 200 years after its passage as part of the Bill of Rights, Justice Antonin Scalia led the Court in interpreting the original meaning of the Second Amendment in order to discern the constitutionality of a firearms ban in Washington, D.C. Notice that this case does not address whether the Second Amendment applies to the states because this case concerns the District of Columbia, which is a federal entity.

As you read the case, consider whether Justice Scalia's willingness to avoid reliance on precedent rests on his originalist understanding of the Constitution. What role, if any, should precedent play in originalism? Moreover, consider Justice Scalia's close analysis of the text of the Second Amendment. How does this textual focus relate to his notion of original meaning?

MR. JUSTICE SCALIA *delivered the opinion of the Court.*

The District of Columbia generally prohibits the possession of handguns. It is a crime to carry an unregistered firearm, and the registration of handguns is prohibited. Wholly apart from that prohibition, no person may carry a handgun without a license, but the chief of police may issue licenses for 1-year periods. District of Columbia law also requires residents to keep their lawfully owned firearms, such as registered long guns, "unloaded and dissembled or bound by a trigger lock or similar device" unless they are located in a place of business or are being used for lawful recreational activities.

Respondent Dick Heller is a D.C. special police officer authorized to carry a handgun while on duty at the Federal Judicial Center. He applied for a registration certificate for a handgun that he wished to keep at home, but the District refused. He thereafter filed a lawsuit in the Federal District Court for the District of Columbia seeking, on Second Amendment grounds, to enjoin the city from enforcing the bar on the registration of handguns, the licensing requirement insofar as it prohibits the carrying of a firearm in the home without a license, and the trigger-lock requirement insofar as it prohibits the use of "functional firearms within the home." . . . It held that the Second Amendment protects an individual right to possess firearms and that the city's total ban on handguns, as well as its requirement that firearms in the home be kept nonfunctional even when necessary for self-defense, violated that right. The Court of Appeals directed the District Court to enter summary judgment for respondent.

The Second Amendment provides: "A well regulated Militia, being necessary to the security of a free State, the right of the people to keep and bear Arms, shall not be infringed." In interpreting this text, we are guided by the principle that "[t]he Constitution was written to be understood by the voters; its words and phrases were used in their normal and ordinary as distinguished from technical meaning."

Normal meaning may of course include an idiomatic meaning, but it excludes secret or technical meanings that would not have been known to ordinary citizens in the founding generation.

The two sides in this case have set out very different interpretations of the Amendment. Petitioners and today's dissenting Justices believe that it protects only the right to possess and carry a firearm in connection with militia service. Respondent argues that it protects an individual right to possess a firearm unconnected with service in a militia, and to use that arm for traditionally lawful purposes, such as self-defense within the home.

The Second Amendment is naturally divided into two parts: its prefatory clause and its operative clause. The former does not limit the latter grammatically, but rather announces a purpose. The Amendment could be rephrased, "Because a well regulated Militia is necessary to the security of a free State, the right of the people to keep and bear Arms shall not be infringed." Although this structure of the Second Amendment is unique in our Constitution, other legal documents of the founding era, particularly individual-rights provisions of state constitutions, commonly included a prefatory statement of purpose.

Logic demands that there be a link between the stated purpose and the command. The Second Amendment would be nonsensical if it read, "A well regulated Militia, being necessary to the security of a free State, the right of the people to petition for redress of grievances shall not be infringed." That requirement of logical connection may cause a prefatory clause to resolve an ambiguity in the operative clause ("The separation of church and state being an important objective, the teachings of canons shall have no place in our jurisprudence." The preface makes clear that the operative clause refers not to canons of

interpretation but to clergymen.) But apart from that clarifying function, a prefatory clause does not limit or expand the scope of the operative clause. Therefore, while we will begin our textual analysis with the operative clause, we will return to the prefatory clause to ensure that our reading of the operative clause is consistent with the announced purpose.

The first salient feature of the operative clause is that it codifies a "right of the people." The unamended Constitution and the Bill of Rights use the phrase "right of the people" two other times, in the First Amendment's Assembly-and-Petition Clause and in the Fourth Amendment's Search-and-Seizure Clause. The Ninth Amendment uses very similar terminology ("The enumeration in the Constitution, of certain rights, shall not be construed to deny or disparage others retained by the people"). All three of these instances unambiguously refer to individual rights, not "collective" rights, or rights that may be exercised only through participation in some corporate body.

Three provisions of the Constitution refer to "the people" in a context other than "rights"—the famous preamble ("We the people"), §2 of Article I (providing that "the people" will choose members of the House), and the Tenth Amendment (providing that those powers not given the Federal Government remain with "the States" or "the people"). Those provisions arguably refer to "the people" acting collectively—but they deal with the exercise or reservation of powers, not rights. Nowhere else in the Constitution does a "right" attributed to "the people" refer to anything other than an individual right.

What is more, in all six other provisions of the Constitution that mention "the people," the term unambiguously refers to all members of the political community, not an unspecified subset. As we said in

United States v. Verdugo-Urquidez, 494 U.S. 259, 265 (1990):

> "'[T]he people' seems to have been a term of art employed in select parts of the Constitution. . . . [Its uses] sugges[t] that 'the people' protected by the Fourth Amendment, and by the First and Second Amendments, and to whom rights and powers are reserved in the Ninth and Tenth Amendments, refers to a class of persons who are part of a national community or who have otherwise developed sufficient connection with this country to be considered part of that community."

This contrasts markedly with the phrase "the militia" in the prefatory clause. As we will describe below, the "militia" in colonial America consisted of a subset of "the people"—those who were male, able bodied, and within a certain age range. Reading the Second Amendment as protecting only the right to "keep and bear Arms" in an organized militia therefore fits poorly with the operative clause's description of the holder of that right as "the people."

We start therefore with a strong presumption that the Second Amendment right is exercised individually and belongs to all Americans.

We move now from the holder of the right—"the people"—to the substance of the right: "to keep and bear Arms."

Before addressing the verbs "keep" and "bear," we interpret their object: "Arms." The 18th-century meaning is no different from the meaning today. The 1773 edition of Samuel Johnson's dictionary defined "arms" as "weapons of offence, or armour of defence." Timothy Cunningham's important 1771 legal dictionary defined "arms" as "any thing that a man wears for his defence, or takes into his hands, or useth in wrath to cast at or strike another."

The term was applied, then as now, to weapons that were not specifically designed for military use and were not employed in a military capacity. For instance, Cunning-

ham's legal dictionary gave as an example of usage: "Servants and labourers shall use bows and arrows on Sundays, &c. and not bear other arms." Although one founding-era thesaurus limited "arms" (as opposed to "weapons") to "instruments of offence generally made use of in war," even that source stated that all firearms constituted "arms."

Some have made the argument, bordering on the frivolous, that only those arms in existence in the 18th century are protected by the Second Amendment. We do not interpret constitutional rights that way. Just as the First Amendment protects modern forms of communications, and the Fourth Amendment applies to modern forms of search the Second Amendment extends, prima facie, to all instruments that constitute bearable arms, even those that were not in existence at the time of the founding.

We turn to the phrases "keep arms" and "bear arms." Johnson defined "keep" as, most relevantly, "[t]o retain; not to lose," and "[t]o have in custody." Webster defined it as "[t]o hold; to retain in one's power or possession." No party has apprised us of an idiomatic meaning of "keep Arms." Thus, the most natural reading of "keep Arms" in the Second Amendment is to "have weapons."

The phrase "keep arms" was not prevalent in the written documents of the founding period that we have found, but there are a few examples, all of which favor viewing the right to "keep Arms" as an individual right unconnected with militia service. William Blackstone, for example, wrote that Catholics convicted of not attending service in the Church of England suffered certain penalties, one of which was that they were not permitted to "keep arms in their houses." Petitioners point to militia laws of the founding period that required militia members to "keep" arms in connection with militia service, and they conclude from this that the phrase "keep Arms" has a militia-related connotation. This is rather like saying that, since there are many statutes that authorize aggrieved employees to "file complaints" with federal agencies, the phrase "file complaints" has an employment-related connotation. "Keep arms" was simply a common way of referring to possessing arms, for militiamen and everyone else.

At the time of the founding, as now, to "bear" meant to "carry." When used with "arms," however, the term has a meaning that refers to carrying for a particular purpose—confrontation. In *Muscarello v. United States*, in the course of analyzing the meaning of "carries a firearm" in a federal criminal statute, Justice Ginsburg wrote that "[s]urely a most familiar meaning is, as the Constitution's Second Amendment . . . indicate[s]: 'wear, bear, or carry . . . upon the person or in the clothing or in a pocket, for the purpose . . . of being armed and ready for offensive or defensive action in a case of conflict with another person.'" We think that Justice Ginsburg accurately captured the natural meaning of "bear arms." Although the phrase implies that the carrying of the weapon is for the purpose of "offensive or defensive action," it in no way connotes participation in a structured military organization.

From our review of founding-era sources, we conclude that this natural meaning was also the meaning that "bear arms" had in the 18th century. In numerous instances, "bear arms" was unambiguously used to refer to the carrying of weapons outside of an organized militia. The most prominent examples are those most relevant to the Second Amendment: Nine state constitutional provisions written in the 18th century or the first two decades of the 19th, which enshrined a right of citizens to "bear arms in defense of themselves and the state" or "bear arms in defense of himself and the state." It is clear from those

formulations that "bear arms" did not refer only to carrying a weapon in an organized military unit. Justice James Wilson interpreted the Pennsylvania Constitution's arms-bearing right, for example, as a recognition of the natural right of defense "of one's person or house"—what he called the law of "self preservation." That was also the interpretation of those state constitutional provisions adopted by pre-Civil War state courts. These provisions demonstrate—again, in the most analogous linguistic context—that "bear arms" was not limited to the carrying of arms in a militia.

Putting all of these textual elements together, we find that they guarantee the individual right to possess and carry weapons in case of confrontation. This meaning is strongly confirmed by the historical background of the Second Amendment. We look to this because it has always been widely understood that the Second Amendment, like the First and Fourth Amendments, codified a pre-existing right. The very text of the Second Amendment implicitly recognizes the pre-existence of the right and declares only that it "shall not be infringed." As we said in *United States v. Cruikshank*, "[t]his is not a right granted by the Constitution. Neither is it in any manner dependent upon that instrument for its existence. The Second Amendment declares that it shall not be infringed. . . ."

By the time of the founding, the right to have arms had become fundamental for English subjects. Blackstone, whose works, we have said, "constituted the preeminent authority on English law for the founding generation," cited the arms provision of the Bill of Rights as one of the fundamental rights of Englishmen. His description of it cannot possibly be thought to tie it to militia or military service. It was, he said, "the natural right of resistance and self-preservation." Other contemporary authorities concurred. Thus, the right secured in 1689 as a result of the Stuarts' abuses was by the time of the founding understood to be an individual right protecting against both public and private violence.

And, of course, what the Stuarts had tried to do to their political enemies, George III had tried to do to the colonists. In the tumultuous decades of the 1760's and 1770's, the Crown began to disarm the inhabitants of the most rebellious areas. That provoked polemical reactions by Americans invoking their rights as Englishmen to keep arms. A New York article of April 1769 said that "[i]t is a natural right which the people have reserved to themselves, confirmed by the Bill of Rights, to keep arms for their own defence." They understood the right to enable individuals to defend themselves. As the most important early American edition of Blackstone's Commentaries (by the law professor and former Antifederalist St. George Tucker) made clear in the notes to the description of the arms right, Americans understood the "right of self-preservation" as permitting a citizen to "repe[l] force by force" when "the intervention of society in his behalf, may be too late to prevent an injury."

There seems to us no doubt, on the basis of both text and history, that the Second Amendment conferred an individual right to keep and bear arms. Of course the right was not unlimited, just as the First Amendment's right of free speech was not. Thus, we do not read the Second Amendment to protect the right of citizens to carry arms for any sort of confrontation, just as we do not read the First Amendment to protect the right of citizens to speak for any purpose. Before turning to limitations upon the individual right, however, we must determine whether the prefatory clause of the Second Amendment comports with our interpretation of the operative clause.

Does the preface fit with an operative clause that creates an individual right to keep and bear arms? It fits perfectly, once one knows the history that the founding generation knew and that we have described above. That history showed that the way tyrants had eliminated a militia consisting of all the able-bodied men was not by banning the militia but simply by taking away the people's arms, enabling a select militia or standing army to suppress political opponents. This is what had occurred in England that prompted codification of the right to have arms in the English Bill of Rights.

The debate with respect to the right to keep and bear arms, as with other guarantees in the Bill of Rights, was not over whether it was desirable (all agreed that it was) but over whether it needed to be codified in the Constitution. During the 1788 ratification debates, the fear that the federal government would disarm the people in order to impose rule through a standing army or select militia was pervasive in Antifederalist rhetoric. John Smilie, for example, worried not only that Congress's "command of the militia" could be used to create a "select militia," or to have "no militia at all," but also, as a separate concern, that "[w]hen a select militia is formed; the people in general may be disarmed." Federalists responded that because Congress was given no power to abridge the ancient right of individuals to keep and bear arms, such a force could never oppress the people. It was understood across the political spectrum that the right helped to secure the ideal of a citizen militia, which might be necessary to oppose an oppressive military force if the constitutional order broke down.

It is therefore entirely sensible that the Second Amendment's prefatory clause announces the purpose for which the right was codified: to prevent elimination of the militia. The prefatory clause does not suggest that preserving the militia was the only reason Americans valued the ancient right; most undoubtedly thought it even more important for self-defense and hunting. But the threat that the new Federal Government would destroy the citizens' militia by taking away their arms was the reason that right—unlike some other English rights—was codified in a written Constitution. Justice Breyer's assertion that individual self-defense is merely a "subsidiary interest" of the right to keep and bear arms is profoundly mistaken. He bases that assertion solely upon the prologue—but that can only show that self-defense had little to do with the right's codification; it was the central component of the right itself.

Besides ignoring the historical reality that the Second Amendment was not intended to lay down a "novel principl[e]" but rather codified a right "inherited from our English ancestors," petitioners' interpretation does not even achieve the narrower purpose that prompted codification of the right. If, as they believe, the Second Amendment right is no more than the right to keep and use weapons as a member of an organized militia—if, that is, the organized militia is the sole institutional beneficiary of the Second Amendment's guarantee—it does not assure the existence of a "citizens' militia" as a safeguard against tyranny. For Congress retains plenary authority to organize the militia, which must include the authority to say who will belong to the organized force. That is why the first Militia Act's requirement that only whites enroll caused States to amend their militia laws to exclude free blacks. Thus, if petitioners are correct, the Second Amendment protects citizens' right to use a gun in an organization from which Congress has plenary authority to exclude them. It guarantees a select militia of the sort the Stuart kings found useful, but not the people's militia that was the concern of the founding generation.

Justice Stevens relies on the drafting history of the Second Amendment—the various proposals in the state conventions and the debates in Congress. It is dubious to rely on such history to interpret a text that was widely understood to codify a preexisting right, rather than to fashion a new one. But even assuming that this legislative history is relevant, Justice Stevens flatly misreads the historical record.

Justice Stevens thinks it significant that the Virginia, New York, and North Carolina Second Amendment proposals were "embedded . . . within a group of principles that are distinctly military in meaning," such as statements about the danger of standing armies. But so was the highly influential minority proposal in Pennsylvania, yet that proposal, with its reference to hunting, plainly referred to an individual right. Other than that erroneous point, Justice Stevens has brought forward absolutely no evidence that those proposals conferred only a right to carry arms in a militia. By contrast, New Hampshire's proposal, the Pennsylvania minority's proposal, and Samuel Adams' proposal in Massachusetts unequivocally referred to individual rights, as did two state constitutional provisions at the time. Justice Stevens' view thus relies on the proposition, unsupported by any evidence, that different people of the founding period had vastly different conceptions of the right to keep and bear arms. That simply does not comport with our longstanding view that the Bill of Rights codified venerable, widely understood liberties.

. . . [W]e take issue with Justice Stevens' equating of these sources with postenactment legislative history, a comparison that betrays a fundamental misunderstanding of a court's interpretive task. "Legislative history," of course, refers to the pre-enactment statements of those who drafted or voted for a law; it is considered persuasive by some, not because they reflect the general understanding of the disputed terms, but because the legislators who heard or read those statements presumably voted with that understanding. "Postenactment legislative history," a deprecatory contradiction in terms, refers to statements of those who drafted or voted for the law that are made after its enactment and hence could have had no effect on the congressional vote. It most certainly does not refer to the examination of a variety of legal and other sources to determine the public understanding of a legal text in the period after its enactment or ratification. That sort of inquiry is a critical tool of constitutional interpretation. . . .

[N]othing in our precedents forecloses our adoption of the original understanding of the Second Amendment. It should be unsurprising that such a significant matter has been for so long judicially unresolved. For most of our history, the Bill of Rights was not thought applicable to the States, and the Federal Government did not significantly regulate the possession of firearms by law-abiding citizens. Other provisions of the Bill of Rights have similarly remained un-illuminated for lengthy periods. This Court first held a law to violate the First Amendment's guarantee of freedom of speech in 1931, almost 150 years after the Amendment was ratified, and it was not until after World War II that we held a law invalid under the Establishment Clause. Even a question as basic as the scope of proscribable libel was not addressed by this Court until 1964, nearly two centuries after the founding. It is demonstrably not true that, as Justice Stevens claims, "for most of our history, the invalidity of Second-Amendment-based objections to firearms regulations has been well settled and uncontroversial." For most of our history the question did not present itself.

Like most rights, the right secured by the Second Amendment is not unlimited. From Blackstone through the 19th-century cases, commentators and courts routinely explained that the right was not a right to keep and carry any weapon whatsoever in any manner whatsoever and for whatever purpose. For example, the majority of the 19th-century courts to consider the question held that prohibitions on carrying concealed weapons were lawful under the Second Amendment or state analogues. Although we do not undertake an exhaustive historical analysis today of the full scope of the Second Amendment, nothing in our opinion should be taken to cast doubt on longstanding prohibitions on the possession of firearms by felons and the mentally ill, or laws forbidding the carrying of firearms in sensitive places such as schools and government buildings, or laws imposing conditions and qualifications on the commercial sale of arms.

We also recognize another important limitation on the right to keep and carry arms. Miller said, as we have explained, that the sorts of weapons protected were those "in common use at the time." We think that limitation is fairly supported by the historical tradition of prohibiting the carrying of "dangerous and unusual weapons."

It may be objected that if weapons that are most useful in military service—M-16 rifles and the like—may be banned, then the Second Amendment right is completely detached from the prefatory clause. But as we have said, the conception of the militia at the time of the Second Amendment's ratification was the body of all citizens capable of military service, who would bring the sorts of lawful weapons that they possessed at home to militia duty. It may well be true today that a militia, to be as effective as militias in the 18th century, would require sophisticated arms that are highly unusual in society at large. Indeed, it may be true that no amount of small arms could be useful against modern-day bombers and tanks. But the fact that modern developments have limited the degree of fit between the prefatory clause and the protected right cannot change our interpretation of the right.

We turn finally to the law at issue here. As we have said, the law totally bans handgun possession in the home. It also requires that any lawful firearm in the home be disassembled or bound by a trigger lock at all times, rendering it inoperable.

As the quotations earlier in this opinion demonstrate, the inherent right of self-defense has been central to the Second Amendment right. The handgun ban amounts to a prohibition of an entire class of "arms" that is overwhelmingly chosen by American society for that lawful purpose. The prohibition extends, moreover, to the home, where the need for defense of self, family, and property is most acute. Under any of the standards of scrutiny that we have applied to enumerated constitutional rights, banning from the home "the most preferred firearm in the nation to 'keep' and use for protection of one's home and family," would fail constitutional muster.

Justice Breyer moves on to make a broad jurisprudential point: He criticizes us for declining to establish a level of scrutiny for evaluating Second Amendment restrictions. He proposes, explicitly at least, none of the traditionally expressed levels (strict scrutiny, intermediate scrutiny, rational basis), but rather a judge-empowering "interest-balancing inquiry" that "asks whether the statute burdens a protected interest in a way or to an extent that is out of proportion to the statute's salutary effects upon other important governmental interests." After an exhaustive discussion of the arguments for and against gun control, Justice Breyer arrives at his interest-balanced answer: because handgun violence is a problem, because the law is limited to an urban area, and because there were somewhat similar restrictions

in the founding period (a false proposition that we have already discussed), the interest-balancing inquiry results in the constitutionality of the handgun ban. QED.

We know of no other enumerated constitutional right whose core protection has been subjected to a freestanding "interest-balancing" approach. The very enumeration of the right takes out of the hands of government—even the Third Branch of Government—the power to decide on a case-by-case basis whether the right is really worth insisting upon. A constitutional guarantee subject to future judges' assessments of its usefulness is no constitutional guarantee at all. Constitutional rights are enshrined with the scope they were understood to have when the people adopted them, whether or not future legislatures or (yes) even future judges think that scope too broad. We would not apply an "interest-balancing" approach to the prohibition of a peaceful neo-Nazi march through Skokie. The First Amendment contains the freedom-of-speech guarantee that the people ratified, which included exceptions for obscenity, libel, and disclosure of state secrets, but not for the expression of extremely unpopular and wrong-headed views. The Second Amendment is no different. Like the First, it is the very product of an interest-balancing by the people—which Justice Breyer would now conduct for them anew. And whatever else it leaves to future evaluation, it surely elevates above all other interests the right of law-abiding, responsible citizens to use arms in defense of hearth and home.

We are aware of the problem of handgun violence in this country, and we take seriously the concerns raised by the many amici who believe that prohibition of handgun ownership is a solution. The Constitution leaves the District of Columbia a variety of tools for combating that problem, including some measures regulating handguns. But the enshrinement of constitutional rights necessarily takes certain policy choices off the table. These include the absolute prohibition of handguns held and used for self-defense in the home. Undoubtedly some think that the Second Amendment is outmoded in a society where our standing army is the pride of our Nation, where well-trained police forces provide personal security, and where gun violence is a serious problem. That is perhaps debatable, but what is not debatable is that it is not the role of this Court to pronounce the Second Amendment extinct.

SYNTHESIS QUESTIONS FOR FURTHER DISCUSSION: CHAPTER 2 SECTION A

1. The reading by Justice Antonin Scalia emphasizes the importance of the "original meaning" or "original understanding" of the Constitution. But there are different versions of this school of thought. According to former Attorney General Edwin Meese, who served under President Ronald Reagan, original *intent* (rather than original *meaning*) should serve to guide interpretation. The difference between meaning and intent has important consequences for how to interpret the constitutional text. For Meese, it is the intentions of the Framers, who drafted the constitutional text, that ought to ground constitutional interpretation. But according to original meaning theorists such as Justice Scalia, intent is too vague and indiscernible a concept to guide interpretation. Famously, focusing on the case of legislative intent, Justice Scalia suggests that intentions might not only differ but that there might be no discernible intent in the first place (*A Matter of Interpretation*, Princeton University Press, 1997, pp. 18-23). Intent theories therefore, Justice Scalia argues, risk that judges might turn to their own views in lieu of the Founders' intent. This would undermine the democratic ideal of original fidelity to a legitimately enacted text and would make judges into legislators. It is well known that the writers of the Constitution disagreed about many issues. Does this fact of disagreement create problems for original intent views of the Constitution? Does it create problems for the original meaning view?

2. In contrast to an "original intent" theory, Justice Scalia argues that judges should seek constitutional meaning in the text as it was understood by the educated public at the time it was written. This argument stems from the idea that the constitutional text, as ratified by the sovereign people, enjoys the highest possible democratic pedigree (compared to the decisions of judges or even elected legislators). Does this focus on the meaning of the text rather than the intent of those who drafted the Constitution imply that the views of the Framers of the Constitution have no more importance than the views of those alive at the time who were not involved

in the writing of the document? Should dictionaries and *The Federalist Papers* be regarded as equally important in discerning the meaning of the Constitution's text? In interpreting the Constitution's meaning, should the writers of the Constitution be paid the same regard as educated citizens at the time the Constitution was written?

3. One big puzzle in constitutional interpretation concerns how meaning fixed in the eighteenth century can be used to think about technological advances. In reading *District of Columbia v. Heller*, it is important to consider how Justice Scalia might account for the fact that modern weaponry is quite different from that which existed in previous centuries. Does Justice Scalia stick to his originalist approach of constitutional interpretation in this case?

4. Justice Scalia often criticizes accounts of a "living" or evolving Constitution. Indeed, he has at times claimed that the Constitution should be regarded as a "dead" document because in a democracy constitutional meaning should be traced in its origin to some legislative process. In what ways is the Constitution similar to or different from legislation passed by Congress? What do these similarities or differences say about Justice Scalia's claim that the Constitution is democratic when its meaning is fixed at the date in which its provisions were enacted? Is Justice Scalia correct that any account of a living Constitution would violate a commitment to democracy?

B. PROCEDURALISM

Originalist thinkers often claim that fidelity to democracy requires fidelity to the original meaning of the Constitution. But are there any rights that are fundamental to democracy apart from the details of the constitutional text? In this section we examine a distinct theory of interpretation that focuses on the Constitution as a document that protects democratic rights. On John Hart Ely's view, the Constitution centrally protects a right of equal participation in democracy, and it is the role of the Court to "police" and guarantee this entitlement. His theory places fundamental importance on the Fourteenth Amendment's Equal Protection Clause, but he also attempts to read into other clauses a guarantee of fair democratic procedures.

Ely grounds his theory of proceduralism, sometimes referred to as process theory, in the famous "Footnote Four" of *U.S. v. Carolene Products* (see page 178). Although the case itself concerns the regulation of interstate commerce in regard to milk products, it is famous for a footnote that outlines a set of circumstances in which the Court might conduct "exacting" scrutiny of governmental actions. According to the footnote, the Court should readily use its power of judicial review to protect rights explicitly outlined in the first ten amendments to the Constitution, those associated with the political process, or those necessary for the protection of "discrete and insular" minorities. Ely claims that this footnote expresses his view that the central role of the Supreme Court's judicial review power is to reinforce democracy.

Our case selection focuses on whether the Court should be involved in the process of determining the contours of legislative districts. As you read through this selection you should ask whether Ely's theory requires that the Court have a role in policing the democratic process by intervening in the drawing of election districts and other matters fundamental in an electoral democracy. What rights are at issue in these cases that are central to the democratic process as Ely defines it? In addition to thinking about these specific cases, you should also ask more generally about the kinds of rights a theory like Ely's would have the Court protect. For instance, would it be possible to interpret the prohibition on cruel and unusual punishment or the right to free speech as a requirement of democracy? How might one do so?

John Hart Ely

DEMOCRACY AND DISTRUST: A THEORY OF JUDICIAL REVIEW

Cambridge, MA: Harvard University Press (1980)

CHAPTER 2: THE IMPOSSIBILITY OF A CLAUSE-BOUND INTERPRETIVISM

Given what it takes to amend the Constitution, it is likely that a recent amendment will represent, if not necessarily a consensus, at least the sentiment of a contemporary majority. The amendments most frequently in issue in court, however—to the extent that they ever represent the "voice of the people"—represent the voice of people who have been dead for a century or two. There were those who worried about this even at the beginning. Noah Webster opined that "the very attempt to make perpetual constitutions is the assumption of a right to control the opinions of future generations; and to legislate for those over whom we have as little authority as we have over a nation in Asia." And Jefferson wrote to Madison "'that the earth belongs in usufruct to the living'; that the dead have neither powers nor rights over it." His suggestion was that the Constitution expire naturally every nineteen years. Madison and others objected that this would be unworkable and undesirable. (Apparently Jefferson was convinced, since he was President nineteen years into the Republic and didn't suggest the convening of a convention under Article V.) In fact we chose quite the opposite course, ordinarily requiring the concurrence of two-thirds of both Houses of Congress and ratification by the legislatures of three-quarters of the states to get rid of a constitutional provision or to add a new one. I am certainly not saying this is a bad thing, but it does fatally undercut the idea that in applying the Constitution—even the written Constitution of the interpretivist—judges are simply applying the people's will.

Incompatibility with democratic theory is a problem that seems to confront interpretivist and non-interpretivist alike.

Interpretivism does seem to retain the substantial virtue of fitting better our ordinary notion of how law works: if your job is to enforce the Constitution then the Constitution is what you should be enforcing, not whatever may happen to strike you as a good idea at the time. Thus stated, the conclusion possesses the unassailability of a truism, and if acceptance of *that* were all it took to make someone an interpretivist, no sane person could be anything else. But the debate over interpretivism is not an argument about the truth of a tautology, for interpretivism involves a further claim, that "enforcing the Constitution" necessarily means proceeding from premises that are explicit or clearly implicit in the document itself.

At this point it is helpful to clarify the concept in a way the literature to date has not, in particular to distinguish two possible versions of interpretivism. One might admit that a number of constitutional phrases cannot intelligibly be given content solely on the basis of their language and surrounding legislative history, indeed that certain of them seem on their face to call for an injection of content from some source beyond the provision, but hold nonetheless that the theory one employs to supply that content should be derived from the general themes of the entire constitutional document and not from some source entirely beyond its four corners. It might even be hoped that this broad form of interpretivism is capable of avoiding the pitfalls of a narrower (or "clause-bound") interpretivism and at the same time preserving those comparative advantages of an interpretivist approach. . . . In fact, two chapters hence I shall be arriving at much that position and making much

that claim. . . . That position, however, will take some time to develop, and it is not what is generally recommended under the interpretivist flag. The suggestion instead is usually that the various provisions of the Constitution be approached essentially as self-contained units and interpreted on the basis of their language, with whatever interpretive help the legislative history can provide, without significant injection of content from outside the provision. We shall see, however, that this standard form of interpretivism runs into trouble—trouble precisely on its own terms, and so serious as to be dispositive. For the constitutional document itself, the interpretivist's Bible, contains several provisions whose invitation to look beyond their four corners—whose invitation, if you will, to become at least to that extent a non-interpretivist—cannot be construed away.

Constitutional provisions exist on a spectrum ranging from the relatively specific to the extremely open-textured. At one extreme—for example the requirement that the President "have attained to the Age of thirty five years"—the language is so clear that a conscious reference to purpose seems unnecessary. Other provisions, such as the one requiring that the President be a "natural born Citizen," may need a reference to historical usage so as to exclude certain alternative constructions—conceivably if improbably here, a requirement of legitimacy (or illegitimacy!) or non-Caesarian birth—but once that "dictionary function" is served, the provision becomes relatively easy to apply. Others, such as the First Amendment's prohibition of congressional laws "abridging the freedom of speech," seem to need more. For one thing, a phrase as terse as the others I have mentioned is here expected to govern a broader and more important range of problems. For another, and this may have something to do with the first, we somehow sense that a line of growth was intended, that the language was not intended to be restricted to its 1791 meaning. This realization would not faze Justice Black or most other interpretivists: the job of the person interpreting the provision, they would respond, is to identify the *sorts of evils* against which the provision was directed and to move against their contemporary counterparts. Obviously this will be difficult, but it will remain interpretivism—a determination of "the present scope and meaning of a decision that the nation, at an earlier time, articulated and enacted into the constitutional text."

Still other provisions, such as the Eighth Amendment's prohibition of "cruel and unusual punishments," seem even more insistently to call for a reference to sources beyond the document itself and a "framers' dictionary." It is possible to construe this prohibition as covering only those punishments that would have been regarded as "cruel and unusual" in 1791, but that construction seems untrue to the open-ended quality of the language. The interpretivist can respond as he did to the First Amendment, that even though it is true that the clause shouldn't be restricted to its 1791 meaning, it should be restricted to the general categories of evils at which the provision was aimed. If you pursue this mode of "interpretation" with regard to the Eighth Amendment, however—and the First Amendment case will come down to much the same thing—you'll soon find yourself, at worst, begging a lot of questions or, at best, attributing to the framers a theory that may be *consistent* with what they said but is hardly discoverable in their discussions or their dictionaries. But even admitting this, the disaster for the interpretivist remains less than complete. The Cruel and Unusual Punishment Clause does invite the person interpreting it to freelance to a degree, but the freelancing is bounded. The subject is punishments, not the entire range of government action, and even in that limited area the delegation to the interpreter is not entirely unguided: only those punishments that are in some way serious ("cruel") and susceptible to sporadic imposition ("unusual") are to be disallowed.

The Eighth Amendment does not mark the end of the spectrum, however. The Fourteenth Amendment—and I shall argue later that the Ninth Amendment is similar—contains provisions that are difficult to read responsibly as anything other than quite broad invitations to import into the constitutional decision process considerations that will not be found in the language of the amendment or the debates that led up to it.

Due Process

Let us then turn, surely we are long overdue, to the language of the Due Process Clause. It is a bit embarrassing to suggest that a text is informative "when so many, for so long, have found it to be only evocative," but there is simply no avoiding the fact that the word that follows "due" is "process." No evidence exists that "process" meant something different a century ago from what it does now—in fact as I've indicated the historical record runs somewhat the other way—and it should take more than occasional aberrational use to establish that those who rarified the Fourteenth Amendment had an eccentric definition in mind. Familiarity breeds inattention, and we apparently need periodic reminding that "substantive due process" is a contradiction in terms sort of like "green pastel redness."

It is interesting to speculate on how it got started, though. As I indicated, the law of procedural due process was not in serious disarray, and the proposition that the government should be able seriously to hurt you without due process of law is hardly one that cries out for affirmation. Part of the explanation may lie in the recent resurrection of substantive due process. So long as *Lochner* lay in disrepute, and substantive due process was therefore as good as dead—that is, nonexistent or reduced to an essentially meaningless requirement that the government behave "rationally"—there was little risk in the premise that any serious governmental hurt should proceed by due process of law. That just meant people were typically entitled to fair procedures. But once "due process" is reinvested with serious *substantive* content, things get pretty scary and judges will naturally begin to look for ways to narrow the scope of their authority. The reaction is one that might have suggested that the error was in resurrecting substantive due process, but instead it seems to have meant that due process, properly so called, has been constricted.

Suppose there were in the Constitution one or more provisions providing for the protection of ghosts. Can there be any doubt, now that we no longer believe there is any such thing, that we would be behaving properly in ignoring the provisions? The "ghost" here is natural law, and the argument would be that because natural law is the source from which the open-ended clauses of the Ninth and Fourteenth Amendments were expected to derive their content, we are justified, now that our society no longer believes in natural law, in ignoring the clauses altogether.

. . . [E]ven granting that clauses like those under consideration established constitutional rights, they do not readily lend themselves to principled *judicial*

enforcement and should therefore be treated as if they were directed exclusively to the political branches. (This suggestion I *have* seen—from the pen, surprisingly, of Felix Frankfurter, who indicated in correspondence in the late 1950s that he wished the Due Process Clause, his idea of an open-ended provision, had been so treated.) It would be a cheap shot to note that there is no legislative history specifically indicating an intention that the Ninth Amendment was to receive judicial enforcement. There was at the time of the original Constitution little legislative history indicating that *any* particular provision was to receive judicial enforcement: the Ninth Amendment was not singled out one way or the other. What is mildly instructive, and it cuts the other way, is that the precursor decisions typically cited as "proof" that judicial review was intended—though they are too few and unclear really to amount to that—were often "noninterpretivist" decisions, drawing their mandates not from any documentary prohibition but rather from some principle derived externally. As far as the Fourteenth Amendment is concerned, it is true that the (misplaced) anticipation seems to have been that it would receive its most meaningful enforcement by Congress, acting under Section 5, rather than by the courts. It is also true that at the time of its ratification only three Acts of Congress had been declared unconstitutional by the Supreme Court. That doesn't mean the authority went unnoticed, however. *Dred Scott* drew heavy fire, and even prior to that time,

> [W]e may draw two conclusions concerning the criticism of the Supreme Court: first, the court was criticized quite as much for not declaring congressional acts unconstitutional as for doing so; second, it seems clear that both Federalist and Republican

criticism during these years was directed not so much at the possession of the power of the court to pass on the validity of acts of Congress as at the effect of its exercise in supporting or invalidating some particular party measure.

It is also relevant that a number of *state* statutes had been struck down in the first half of the nineteenth century. The Reconstruction Amendments were, after all, primarily directed at the states. The Republican criticism of *Dred Scott*, and of *Barron v. Baltimore* as well, continued throughout the drafting and ratification processes. Naturally this sometimes spilled over into a general distrust of the institution of judicial review, but in general the institution was assumed and the attack was limited to the specific offending instances. Surely there was nothing remotely resembling a consensus that judicial authority to review was generally to be curtailed: if anything, the consensus ran the other way. More important for present purposes, there was no indication that the Fourteenth Amendment was to be treated any differently in this respect from other provisions.

This, however, is a question on which history cannot have the last word, at least not the last affirmative word. If a principled approach to judicial enforcement of the Constitution's open-ended provisions cannot be developed, one that is not hopelessly inconsistent with our nation's commitment to representative democracy, responsible commentators must consider seriously the possibility that courts simply should stay away from them. Given the transparent failure of the dominant mode of "noninterpretivist" review, Justice Black's instinct to decline the delegation was healthy. But the dominant mode can be improved upon, or at least that is the burden of the rest of this book.

CHAPTER 3: DISCOVERING FUNDAMENTAL VALUES

Since interpretivism—at least a clause-bound version of interpretivism—is hoist by its own petard, we should look again, and more closely, at its traditional competitor. The prevailing academic line has held for some time that the Supreme Court should give content to the Constitution's open-ended provisions by identifying and enforcing upon the political branches those values that are, by one formula or another, truly important or fundamental. Indeed we are told this is inevitable: "there is simply no way for courts to review legislation in terms of the Constitution without repeatedly making difficult substantive choices among competing values, and indeed among inevitably controverted political, social, and moral conceptions." "[C]onstitutional law must now be understood as the means by which effect is given to those ideas that from time to time are held to be fundamental, ... " The Court is "an institution charged with the evolution and application of society's fundamental principles," and its "constitutional function," accordingly, is "to define values and proclaim principles."

The Judge's Own Values

The view that the judge, in enforcing the Constitution, should use his or her *own values* to measure the judgment of the political branches is a methodology that is seldom endorsed in so many words. As we proceed through the various methodologies that are, however, I think we shall sense in many cases that although the judge or commentator in question may be talking in terms of some "objective," nonpersonal method of identification, what he is really likely to be "discovering," whether or not he is fully aware of it, are his own values. It is thus important at the outset to understand just why a "judge's own values" approach is unacceptable: that understanding will illumine the unacceptability of the entire enterprise.

How might one arrive at such a view? Much of the explanation seems to involve what might be called the fallacy of transformed realism. About forty years ago people "discovered" that judges were human and therefore were likely in a variety of legal contexts consciously or unconsciously to slip their personal values into their legal reasonings. From that earth-shattering insight it has seemed to some an easy inference that that is what judges *ought* to be doing. Two observations are in order, both obvious. The first is that such a "realist" theory of adjudication is not a theory of adjudication at all, in that it does not tell us *which* values should be imposed. The second is that the theory's "inference" does not even remotely follow: that people have always been tempted to steal does not mean that stealing is what they should be doing. This is all plain as a pikestaff, which means something else has to be going on. People who tend to this extreme realist view must consciously or unconsciously be envisioning a Court staffed by justices who think as they do. That assumption takes care of both the problems I've mentioned. It tells you what values are to be imposed (the commentator's own) and also explains (at least to the satisfaction of the commentator) why such a Court would be desirable. But it's a heroic assumption, and the argument that seems to score most heavily against such a "realist" outlook is one that is genuinely realistic—that there is absolutely no assurance that the Supreme Court's life-tenured members (or the other federal judges) will be persons who share your values.

But let that pass and grant the realists their strange assumption. There remains the immense and obvious problem of reconciling the attitude under discussion with the basic democratic theory of our government.

The Court may be purseless and swordless, but its ability importantly to influence the way the nation functions has proved great and seems to be growing all the time. It may be true that the Court cannot *permanently* thwart the will of a solid majority, but it can certainly delay its implementation for decades—workmen's compensation, child labor, and unionization are among the more obvious examples—and to the people affected, that's likely to be forever.

The formal checks on the Court have surely not proved to be of much consequence. Congress's control over the budget of the federal courts—note, though, that it cannot constitutionally reduce judicial salaries—has proved an instrument too blunt to be of any real control potential. The country needs functioning and competent federal courts, and everybody knows it does. Despite the two-thirds requirement, impeachment *might* have developed into an effective mode of controlling decision. However, in part precisely because of our allegiance to the idea of an independent judiciary, it didn't, and today it is understood to be a weapon reserved for the grossest of cases. (It is no easier to impeach a justice than a President, as Richard Nixon learned from both sides.) Congress's theoretical power to withdraw the Court's jurisdiction over certain classes of cases is so fraught with constitutional doubt that although talked about from time to time, it has not been invoked for over one hundred years. Altering the size of, or "packing," the Court was quite popular in the nineteenth century, but only once, during the Grant

Administration, is it even arguable that it had its desired effect. And that is the last time it's been done. Franklin Roosevelt tried it, and although he failed, the prevailing mythology for a time was that his effort had pressured the Court into mending its ways. More recently discovered Court records have indicated, however, that the Court's "switch" was independent of (in fact prior to) the announcement of his plan. The message is mixed, but what now seems important about the episode is that an immensely popular President riding an immensely popular cause had his lance badly blunted by his assault on judicial independence.

There is also the possibility of constitutional amendment, but even when this course works it takes time—during which the Court's roadblock stays in place—and in any event seldom works. Our recent experience with the Equal Rights Amendment, endorsed by both major parties and hardly advancing a radical proposition, corroborates the difficulty of amending the Constitution. In all our history only four decisions of the Supreme Court have been reversed by constitutional amendment. It is also true that often, though by no means always, the cooperation of political officials is required to enforce Supreme Court decisions. But they generally go along, however grudgingly: it is, after all, their perceived legal duty to do so. (One inclined to regard failure to obey as a viable means of controlling the Court would do well to reflect on the fact that the President of the United States—one hardly renowned for his reverence to the rule of law—did surrender those fatal tapes.) What's left is the fact that the President appoints and the Senate confirms the new members of the Court, and certainly there is something there. But it generally takes several successive presidential terms, and the concurrence of several successive Senates, to replace a majority of the justices.

It's because everybody down deep knows this that few come right out and argue for the judge's own value as a source of constitutional judgment. Instead the search purports to be objective and value neutral; the reference is to something "out there" waiting to be discovered, whether it be natural law or some supposed value consensus of historical America, today's America, or the America that is yet to be.

Predicting Progress

In his 1969 Holmes Lectures, subsequently published as *The Supreme Court and the Idea of Progress*, the thinking of Alexander Bickel apparently took a new tack. The Warren Court, he claimed, had tried to prefigure the future, to shape its constitutional principles in accord with its best estimate of what tomorrow's observers would be prepared to credit as progress. In this, he argued, it had failed: already the Warren Court's "bets on the future" were coming up political losers. Bickel was somewhat elusive about whether he himself was prepared to accredit "tomorrow's values" as a source of constitutional judgment; his formal claim was that that had been the criterion of the Warren Court and that by its own criterion that Court had to be judged a failure. Though the point is arguable, I believe there was a good deal of prescription folded into Bickel's description. In any event others, before and after, have endorsed the method, even if Bickel did not mean to.

The problems with this approach are the familiar ones, in more aggravated form. First—assuming for the moment that we really are talking about a predictive task—there is no reason to suppose that judges are well qualified to foresee the future development of popular opinion. Professor Bickel, whose historical sensitivity surely exceeded that of most lawyers and judges, fell on his face—or so at least it seems as of 1980—explaining a decade ago how the Warren Court's great desegregation and reapportionment decisions had (already) become irrelevant. That only proves he was human—we've all mistaken ripples for waves. But that's exactly the point: prediction is a risky enterprise for anyone, and there is no warrant for an appointed judge's supposing he is so much better at it than the legislature that he is going to declare their efforts unconstitutional on the basis of his predictions.

In addition, the reference is antidemocratic on its face. Controlling today's generation by the values of its grandchildren is no more acceptable than controlling it by the values of its grandparents: a "liberal accelerator" is neither less nor more consistent with democratic theory than a "conservative brake." Superimposed on this problem is one I noted in connection with a contemporary consensus approach; the imposition of allegedly majoritarian values is a mindless way of going about protecting minorities, and stipulating that the majority is to be a future majority does not suddenly make sense of it. But even assuming that by some miracle of logic we could convince ourselves that the sensible way to protect today's minorities from today's majority is to impose on today's majority the values of tomorrow's majority, it would remain a myth that "the values of tomorrow's majority" are data that prescient courts can discover in a value-neutral way. For today's judicial decision (no matter what its source of judgment) will inevitably have an important influence on the values of tomorrow's majority. The "prophecies" of people in power have an inevitably self-fulfilling character, even when what is being "prophesied" is popular opinion. This

may or may not be a bad thing, but it does mean that the Court cannot be heard to plead value-neutrality on the theory that it is "taking its values from the future" rather than imposing its values *on* it; the fact that things turned out as the Supreme Court predicted may prove only that the Supreme Court is the Supreme Court. Thus by predicting the future the justices will unavoidably help shape it, and by shaping the future they will unavoidably, indeed this is the point of the methodology, shape the present. Assuming it works, that amounts to the imposition of the justices' own values. That's just what the fundamental value theorists promised they wouldn't do to us; the fact that it's done with mirrors shouldn't count as a defense.

CHAPTER 4: POLICING THE PROCESS OF REPRESENTATION: THE COURT AS REFEREE

All this seems to leave us in a quandary. An interpretivist approach—at least one that approaches constitutional provisions as self-contained units—proves on analysis incapable of keeping faith with the evident spirit of certain of the provisions. When we search for an external source of values with which to fill in the Constitution's open texture, however— one that will not simply end up constituting the Court a council of legislative revision—we search in vain. Despite the usual assumption that these are the only options, however, they are not, for value imposition is not the only possible response to the realization that we have a Constitution that needs filling in. A quite different approach is available, and to discern its outlines we need look no further than to the Warren Court.

That Court's reputation as "activist" or interventionist is deserved. A good deal of carping to the contrary notwithstanding, however, that is where its similarity to earlier interventionist courts, in particular to the early twentieth-century Court that decided *Lochner v. New York* and its progeny, ends. For all the while the commentators of the Warren era were talking about ways of discovering fundamental values, the Court itself was marching to a different drummer. The divergence wasn't entirely self-conscious, and the Court did lapse occasionally into the language of fundamental values: it would be surprising if the thinking of earlier Courts and the writings of the day's preeminent commentators hadn't taken some toll. The toll, however, was almost entirely rhetorical: the constitutional decisions of the Warren Court evidence a deep structure significantly different from the value-oriented approach favored by the academy.

Many of the Warren Court's most controversial decisions concerned criminal procedure or other questions of what judicial or administrative process is due before serious consequences may be visited upon individuals—process-oriented decisions in the most ordinary sense. But a concern with process in a broader sense—with the process by which the laws that govern society are made—animate its other decisions as well. Its unprecedented activism in the fields of political expression and association obviously fits this broader pattern. Other Courts had recognized the connection between such political activity and the proper functioning of the democratic process; the Warren Court was the first seriously to act upon it. That Court was also the first to move into, and once there seriously to occupy, the voter qualification and malapportionment areas. These were certainly interventionist decisions,

but the interventionism was fueled not by a desire on the part of the Court to vindicate particular substantive values it had determined were important or fundamental, but rather by a desire to ensure that the political process—which is where such values are properly identified, weighed, and accommodated—was open to those of all viewpoints on something approaching an equal basis.

Finally there were the important decisions insisting on equal treatment for society's habitual unequals, notably racial minorities, but also aliens, "illegitimates," and poor people. But rather than announcing that good or value X was so important or fundamental it simply had to be provided or protected, the Court's message here was that insofar as political officials had chosen to provide or protect X for some people (generally people like themselves), they had better make sure that everyone was being similarly accommodated or be prepared to explain pretty convincingly why not. Whether these two broad concerns of the Warren Court—with clearing the channels of political change on the one hand, and with correcting certain kinds of discrimination against minorities on the other—fit together to form a coherent theory of representative government, or whether, as is sometimes suggested, they are actually inconsistent impulses, is a question I shall take up presently. But however that may be, it seems to be coming into focus that the pursuit of these "participational" goals of broadened access to the processes and bounty of representative government, as opposed to the more traditional and academically popular insistence upon the provision of a series of particular substantive goods or values deemed fundamental, was what marked the work of the Warren Court. Some condemn and others praise, but at least we're beginning to understand that something different from old-fashioned value imposition was for a time the order of the day.

The *Carolene Products* Footnote

The Warren Court's approach was foreshadowed in a famous footnote in *United States v. Carolene Products Co.*, decided in 1938. Justice Stone's opinion for the Court upheld a federal statute prohibiting the interstate shipment of filled milk, on the ground that all it had to be was "rational" and it assuredly was that. Footnote four suggested, however, that mere rationality might not always be enough:

> There may be narrower scope for operation of the presumption of constitutionality when legislation appears on its face to be within a specific prohibition of the Constitution, such as those of the first ten amendments, which are deemed equally specific when held to be embraced within the Fourteenth. . . .

> It is unnecessary to consider now whether legislation which restricts those political processes which can ordinarily be expected to bring about repeal of undesirable legislation, is to be subjected to more exacting judicial scrutiny under the general prohibitions of the Fourteenth Amendment than are most other types of legislation. . . .

> Nor need we enquire whether similar considerations enter into the review of statutes directed at particular religious . . . or national . . . or racial minorities . . . ; whether prejudice against discrete and insular minorities may be a special condition, which tends seriously to curtail the operation of those political processes ordinarily to be relied upon to protect minorities, and which may call for a correspondingly more searching judicial inquiry.

The first paragraph is pure interpretivism; it says the Court should enforce the "specific" provisions of the Constitution. We've seen, though, that interpretivism is incomplete; there are provisions in the Constitution that call for more. The second and third paragraphs give us a version of what that more might be. Paragraph two suggests that it is an appropriate function of the Court to keep the machinery of democratic government running as it should, to make sure the channels of political participation and communication are kept open. Paragraph three suggests that the Court should also concern itself with what majorities do to minorities, particularly mentioning laws "directed at" religious, national, and racial minorities and those infected by prejudice against them.

For all its notoriety and influence, the *Carolene Products* footnote has not been adequately elaborated. Paragraph one has always seemed to some commentators not quite to go with the other two. Professor Lusky, who as Stone's law clerk was substantially responsible for the footnote, has recently revealed that the first paragraph was added at the request of Chief Justice Hughes. Any implied substantive criticism seems misplaced: positive law has its claims, even when it doesn't fit some grander theory. It's true, though, that paragraphs two and three are more interesting, and it is the relationship between those two paragraphs that has not been adequately elaborated. Popular control and egalitarianism are surely both ancient American ideals; indeed, dictionary definitions of "democracy" tend to incorporate both. Frequent conjunction is not the same thing as consistency, however, and at least on the surface a principle of popular control suggests an ability on the part of a majority simply to outvote a minority and thus deprive its members of goods they desire. Borrowing Paul Freund's word, I have suggested that both *Carolene Products* themes are concerned with participation: they ask us to focus not on whether this or that substantive value is unusually important or fundamental, but rather on whether the opportunity to participate either in the political processes by which values are appropriately identified and accommodated, or in the accommodation those processes have reached, has been unduly constricted. But the fact that two concepts can fit under the same verbal umbrella isn't enough to render them consistent either, and a system of equal participation in the processes of government is by no means self-evidently linked to a system of preemptively equal participation in the benefits and costs that process generates; in many ways it seems calculated to produce just the opposite effect. To understand the ways these two sorts of participation join together in a coherent political theory, it is necessary to focus . . . on the American system of representative democracy.

Representative Government

Representative democracy is perhaps most obviously a system of government suited to situations in which it is for one reason or another impractical for the citizenry actually to show up and personally participate in the legislative process. But the concept of representation, as understood by our forebears, was richer than this. Prerevolutionary rhetoric posited a continuing conflict between the interests of "the rulers" on the one hand, and those of "the ruled" (or "the people") on the other. A solution was sought by building into the concept of representation the idea of an association of the interests of the two groups. The principal force envisioned was the ballot: the people in their self-interest would choose representatives whose interests intertwined with

theirs and by the critical reelection decision ensure that they stayed that way, in particular that the representatives did not shield themselves from the rigors of the laws they passed.

What the system, at least as described thus far, does *not* ensure is the effective protection of minorities whose interests differ from the interests of most of the rest of us. For if it is not the "many" who are being treated unreasonably but rather only some minority, the situation will not be so comfortably amenable to political correction. Indeed there may be political pressures to encourage our representatives to pass laws that treat the majority coalition on whose continued support they depend in one way, and one or more minorities whose backing they don't need less favorably.

. . . [E]very citizen was said to be entitled to equivalent respect, and equality was a frequently mentioned republican concern. Its place in the Declaration of Independence, for example, could hardly be more prominent. When it came to describing the actual mechanics of republican government in the Constitution, however, this concern for equality got comparatively little explicit attention. This seems to have been largely because of an assumption of "pure" republican political and social theory that we have brushed but not yet stressed: that "the people" were an essentially homogeneous group whose interests did not vary significantly.

The key assumption here, that everyone's interests are essentially identical, is obviously a hard one for our generation to swallow, and in fact we know perfectly well that many of our forebears were ambivalent about it too. Thus the document of 1789 and 1791, though at no point explicitly invoking the concept of equality, did strive by at least two strategies to protect the interests of minorities from the potentially destructive will of some majority coalition. The more obvious one may be the "list" strategy employed by the Bill of Rights, itemizing things that cannot be done to anyone, at least by the federal government (though even here the safeguards turn out to be mainly procedural). The original Constitution's more pervasive strategy, however, can be loosely styled a strategy of pluralism, one of structuring the government, and to a limited extent society generally, so that a variety of voices would be guaranteed their say and no majority coalition could dominate.

The crucial move from a confederation to a system with a stronger central government was so conceived. Madison has been conspicuously attacked for not understanding pluralist political theory, but in fact there is reason to suppose he understood it rather well. His theory, derived from David Hume and spelled out at length in *The Federalist*, was that although at a local level one "faction" might well have sufficient clout to be able to tyrannize others, in the national government no faction or interest group would constitute a majority capable of exercising control. The Constitution's various moves to break up and counterpoise governmental decision and enforcement authority, not only between the national government and the states but among the three departments of the national government as well, were of similar design.

It is a rightly renowned system, but it didn't take long to learn that from the standpoint of protecting minorities it was not enough. . . . Also relevant was the persistence of the institution of slavery. So long as blacks could conveniently be regarded as subhuman, they provided no proof that some people were tyrannizing others. Once that assumption began to blur, there came into focus another reason for doubting that the protection of the many was necessarily the protection of all.

Simultaneously we came to recognize that the existing constitutional devices for protecting minorities were simply not sufficient. No finite list of entitlements can possibly cover all the ways majorities can tyrannize minorities, and the informal and more formal mechanism of pluralism cannot always be counted on either. . . . The existing theory of representation had to be extended so as to ensure not simply that the representative would not sever his increases from those of a majority of his constituency but also that he would not serve a majority coalition's interests from those of various minorities. Naturally that cannot mean that groups that constitute minorities of the population can never be treated less favorably than the rest, but it does preclude a refusal to *represent* them, the denial to minorities of what Professor Dworkin has called "equal concern and respect in the design and administration of the political institutions that govern them." The Fourteenth Amendment's Equal Protection Clause is obviously our Constitution's most dramatic embodiment of this ideal. Before that amendment was ratified, however, its theory was understood, and functioned as a component—even on occasion as a judicially enforceable component—of the concept of representation that had been at the core of our Constitution from the beginning.

The remainder of this chapter will comprise three arguments in favor of a participation-oriented, representation-reinforcing approach to judicial review. The first will take longer than the others since it will necessitate a tour, albeit brisk, of the Constitution itself. What this tour will reveal, contrary to the standard characterization of the Constitution as "an enduring but evolving statement of general values," is that in fact the selection and accommodation of substantive values is left almost entirely to the political process and instead the document is overwhelmingly concerned, on the one hand, with procedural fairness in the resolution of individual disputes (process writ small), and on the other, with what might capaciously be designated process writ large—with ensuring broad participation in the processes and distributions of government. An argument by way of *ejusdem generis* seems particularly justified in this case, since the constitutional provisions for which we are attempting to identify modes of supplying content such as the Ninth Amendment and the Privileges or Immunities Clause, seem to have been included in a "we must have missed something here, so let's trust our successors to add what we missed" spirit. On my more expansive days, therefore, I am tempted to claim that the mode of review developed here represents the ultimate interpretivism. Our review will tell us something else that may be even more relevant to the issue before us—that the few attempts the various framers *have* made to freeze substantive values by designating them for special protection in the document have been ill-fated, normally resulting in repeal, either officially or by interpretative pretense. This suggests a conclusion with important implications for the task of giving content to the document's more open-ended provisions, that preserving fundamental values is not an appropriate constitutional task.

The other two arguments are susceptible to briefer statement but are not less important. The first is that a representation-reinforcing approach to judicial review, unlike its rival value-protecting approach, is not inconsistent with, but on the contrary (and quite by design) entirely supportive of, the underlying premises of the American system of representative democracy. The second is that such an approach, again in contradiction to its rival, involves tasks that courts, as experts on process and (more important) as political outsiders, can sensibly claim to be better qualified and situated to perform than political officials.

The Nature of the United States Constitution

Many of our colonial forebears' complaints against British rule were phrased in "constitutional" terms. Seldom, however, was the claim one of deprivation of some treasured good or substantive right: the American colonists, at least the white males, were among the freest and best-off people in the history of the world, and by and large they knew it. "Constitutional" claims thus were often jurisdictional—that Parliament lacked authority, say, to regulate the colonies' "internal commerce"—the foundation for the claim being generally that we were not represented in Parliament. (Obviously the colonists weren't any crazier about being taxed than anyone else is, but what they damned as tyrannical was taxation without representation.) Or they were arguments of inequality: claims of entitlement to "the rights of Englishmen" had an occasional natural law flavor, but the more common meaning was that suggested by the words, a claim for equality of treatment with those living in England. Thus the colonists' "constitutional" arguments drew on the two participational themes we have been considering: that (1) their input into the process by which they were governed was insufficient, and that (partly as a consequence) (2) they were being denied what others were receiving.

I don't suppose it will surprise anyone to learn that the body of the original Constitution is devoted almost entirely to structure, explaining who among the various actors—federal government, state government, Congress, executive, judiciary—has authority to do what, and going on to fill in a good bit of detail about how these persons are to be selected and to conduct their business. Even provisions that at first glance might seem primarily designed to assure or preclude certain substantive results seem on reflection to be principally concerned with process. Thus, for example, the provision that treason "shall consist only in levying War against [the United States], or in adhering to their Enemies, giving them Aid and Comfort," appears at least in substantial measure to have been a precursor of the First Amendment, reacting to the recognition that persons in power can disable their detractors by charging disagreement as treason. The prohibitions against granting titles of nobility seem rather plainly to have been designed to buttress the democratic ideal that all are equals in government. The Ex Post Facto and Bill of Attainder Clauses prove on analysis to be separation of powers provisions, enjoining the legislature to act prospectively and by general rule (just as the judiciary is implicitly enjoined by Article III to act retrospectively and by specific decree). And we have seen that the Privileges and Immunities Clause of Article IV, and at least in one aspect—the other being a grant of congressional power—the Commerce Clause as well, function as equality provisions, guaranteeing virtual representation to the politically powerless.

This needn't throw us into a tailspin: my claim is only that the original Constitution was principally, indeed I would say overwhelmingly, dedicated to concerns of process and structure and not to the identification and preservation of specific substantive values. Any claim that it was exclusively so conceived would be ridiculous (as would any comparable claim about any comparably complicated human undertaking). And indeed there are other provisions in the original document that seem almost entirely value-oriented, though my point, of course, is that they are few and far between. Thus "corruption of blood" is forbidden as a punishment for treason. Punishing people for their parents' transgressions is outlawed as a substantively unfair outcome: it just can't be done, irrespective of procedures and also irrespective of whether it is done to the children of all offenders. The federal government, along with the states, is precluded from taxing articles exported from any state. Here too an outcome is simply precluded; what might be styled a value, the economic value of free trade among the states, is protected. This short list, however, covers just about all the values protected in the original Constitution—save one. And a big one it was. Although an understandable squeamishness kept the word out of the document, slavery must be counted a substantive value to which the original Constitution meant to extend unusual protection from the ordinary legislative process, at least temporarily. Prior to 1808, Congress was forbidden to prohibit the slave trade into any state that wanted it, and the states were obliged to return escaping slaves to their "homes."

Of course a number of the state ratifying conventions remained apprehensive, and a bill of rights did emerge. Here too, however, the data are unruly. The expression-related provisions of the First Amendment—"Congress shall make no law . . . abridging the freedom of speech, or of the press; or the right of the people peaceably to assemble, and to petition the Government for a redress of grievances"— were centrally intended to help make our governmental processes work, to ensure the open and informed discussion of political issues, and to check our government when it gets out of bounds. We can attribute other functions to freedom of expression, and some of them must have played a role, but the exercise has the smell of the lamp about it: the view that free expression per se, without regard to what it means to the process of government, is our preeminent right has a highly elitist cast. Positive law has its claims, and I am not suggesting that such other purposes as are plausibly attributable to the language should not be attributed; the amendment's language is not limited to political speech and it should not be so limited by construction (even assuming someone could come up with a determinate definition of "political"), But we are at present engaged in an exploration of what sort of document our forebears thought they were putting together, and in that regard the linking of the politically oriented protections of speech, press, assembly, and petition is highly informative.

With one important exception, the Reconstruction Amendments do not designate substantive values for protection from the political process. The Fourteenth Amendment's Due Process Clause, we have seen, is concerned with process writ small, the processes by which regulations are enforced against individuals. Its Privileges or Immunities Clause is quite inscrutable, indicating only that there should exist some set of constitutional entitlements not explicitly enumerated in the document: it is one of the provisions for which we are seeking guides to construction. The Equal Protection Clause is also unforthcoming with details, though it at least gives us a clue: by its explicit concern with equality among the persons within a state's jurisdiction it constitutes the document's clearest, though not sole, recognition that technical access to the process may not always be sufficient to guarantee good-faith representation of all those putatively represented. The Fifteenth Amendment, forbidding abridgment of the right to vote on account of race, opens the process to persons who had previously been excluded and thus by another strategy seeks to enforce the representative's duty of equal concern and respect. The exception, of course, involves a value I have mentioned before, slavery. The Thirteenth Amendment can be forced into a "process" mold—slaves don't participate effectively in the political process—and it surely significantly reflects a concern with equality as well. Just as surely, however, it embodies a substantive judgment that human slavery is simply not morally tolerable. Thus at no point has the Constitution been neutral on this subject. Slavery was one of the few values the original document singled out for protection from the political branches; *non-slavery* is one of the few values it singles out for protection now.

What has happened to the Constitution in the second century of our nationhood, though ground less frequently plowed, is most instructive on the subject of what jobs we have learned our basic document is suited to. There were no amendments between 1870 and 1913, but there have been eleven since. Five of them have extended the franchise: the Seventeenth extends to all of us the right to vote for our Senators directly, the Twenty-Fourth abolishes the poll tax as a condition of voting in federal elections, the Nineteenth extends the vote to women, the Twenty-Third to residents of the District of Columbia, and the Twenty-Sixth to eighteen-year-olds. Extension of the franchise to groups previously excluded has therefore been the dominant theme of our constitutional development since the Fourteenth Amendment, and it pursues both of the broad constitutional themes we have observed from the beginning: the achievement of a political process open to all on an equal basis and a consequent enforcement of the representative's duty of equal concern and respect to minorities and majorities alike. Three other amendments—the Twentieth, Twenty-Second, and Twenty-Fifth—involve Presidential eligibility and succession. The Sixteenth, permitting a federal income tax, adds another power to the list of those that had previously been assigned to the central government. That's it, save two, and indeed one of those two did place a substantive value beyond the reach of the political process. The amendment was the Eighteenth, and the value shielded was temperance. It was, of course, repealed fourteen years later by the Twenty-First Amendment, precisely, I suggest, because such attempts to freeze substantive values do not belong in a constitution. In 1919 temperance obviously seemed like a fundamental value; in 1933 it obviously did not.

What has happened to the Constitution's other value-enshrining provisions is similar, and similarly instructive. Some surely have survived, but typically because they are so obscure that they don't become issues (corruption of blood, quartering of troops) or so interlaced with procedural concerns they seem appropriate in a constitution (self-incrimination, double jeopardy). Those sufficiently conspicuous and precise to be controvertible have not survived. The most dramatic examples, of course, were slavery and prohibition. Both were removed by repeal, in one case a repeal requiring unprecedented carnage. Two other substantive values that at least arguably were placed beyond the reach of the political process by the Constitution have been "repealed" by judicial construction—the right of individuals to bear arms, and freedom to set contract terms without significant state regulation. Maybe in fact our forebears did not intend very seriously to protect those values, but the fact that the Court, in the face of what must be counted at least plausible contrary arguments, so readily read these values out of the Constitution is itself instructive of American expectations of a constitution. Finally, there is the value of religion, still protected by the Free Exercise Clause. Something different has happened here. In recent years that clause has functioned primarily to protect what must be counted as discrete and insular minorities, such as the Amish, Seventh Day Adventists, and Jehovah's Witnesses. Whatever the original conception of the Free Exercise Clause, its function during essentially all of its effective life has been one akin to the Equal Protection Clause and thus entirely appropriate to a constitution.

Don't get me wrong: our Constitution has always been substantially concerned with preserving liberty. If it weren't, it would hardly be worth fighting for. The question that is relevant to our inquiry here, however, is how that concern has been pursued. The principal answers to that, we have seen, are by a quite extensive set of procedural protections, and by a still more elaborate scheme designed to ensure that in the making of substantive choices the decision process will be open to all on something approaching an equal basis, with the decision-makers held to a duty to take into account the interests of all those their decisions affect. (Most often the document has proceeded on the assumption that assuring access is the best way of assuring that someone's interests will be considered, and so in fact it usually is. Other provisions, however—centrally but not exclusively the Equal Protection Clause—reflect a realization that access will not always be sufficient.) The general strategy has therefore not been to root in the document a set of substantive rights entitled to permanent protection. The Constitution has instead proceeded from the quite sensible assumption that an effective majority will not inordinately threaten its own rights, and has sought to assure that such a majority not systematically treat others less well than it treats itself—by structuring decision processes at all levels to try to ensure, first, that everyone's interests will be actually or virtually represented (usually both) at the point of substantive decision, and second, that the processes of individual application will not be manipulated so as to reintroduce in practice the sort of discrimination that is impermissible in theory. We have noted a few provisions that do not comfortably conform to this pattern. But they're an odd assortment, the understandable products of particular historical circumstances—guns, religion, contract, and so on—and in any event they are few and far between. To represent them as a dominant theme of our constitutional document one would have to concentrate quite single-mindedly on hopping from stone to stone and averting one's eyes from the mainstream.

The American Constitution has thus by and large remained a constitution properly so called, concerned with constitutive questions. What has distinguished it, and indeed the United States itself, has been a process of government, not a governing ideology. Justice Linde has written: "As a charter of government a constitution must prescribe legitimate processes, not legitimate outcomes, if like ours (and unlike more ideological documents elsewhere) it is to serve many generations through changing times."

Democracy and Distrust

As I have tried to be scrupulous about indicating, the argument from the general contours of the Constitution is necessarily a qualified one. In fact the documentary dictation of particular substantive outcomes has been rare (and generally unsuccessful), but our Constitution is too complex a document to lie still for any pat characterization. Beyond that, the premise of the argument, that aids to construing the more open-ended provisions are appropriately found in the nature of the surrounding document, though it is a premise that seems to find acceptance on all sides, is not one with which it is impossible to disagree. Thus the two arguments that follow, each overtly normative, are if anything more important than the one I have just reviewed. The first is entirely obvious by now, that unlike an approach geared to the judicial imposition of "fundamental values," the representation-reinforcing orientation whose contours I have sketched and will develop further is not inconsistent with, but on the contrary is entirely supportive of, the American system of representative democracy. It recognizes the unacceptability of the claim that appointed and life-tenured judges are better reflectors of conventional values than elected representatives, devoting itself instead to policing the mechanisms by which the system seeks to ensure that our elected representatives will actually represent. There may be an illusion of circularity here; my approach is more consistent with representative democracy because that's the way it was planned. But of course it isn't any more circular than setting out to build an airplane and ending up with something that flies.

The final point worth serious mention is that (again unlike a fundamental values approach) a representation-reinforcing approach assigns judges a role they are conspicuously well situated to fill. My reference here is not principally to expertise. Lawyers are experts on process writ small, the processes by which facts are found and contending parties are allowed to present their claims. And to a degree they are experts on process writ larger, the processes by which issues of public policy are fairly determined: lawyers do seem genuinely to have a feel, indeed it is hard to see what other special value they have, for ways of insuring that everyone gets his or her fair say. But too much shouldn't be made of this. Others, particularly the full-time participants, can also claim expertise on how the political process allocates voice and power. And of course many legislators are lawyers themselves. So the point isn't so much one of expertise as it is one of perspective.

The approach to constitutional adjudication recommended here is akin to what might be called an "antitrust" as opposed to a "regulatory" orientation to economic affairs—rather than dictate substantive results it intervenes only when the "market," in our case the political market, is systemically malfunctioning, (A referee analogy is also not far off: the referee is to intervene only when one team is gaining unfair advantage, not because the "wrong" team has scored.) Our government cannot fairly be said to be "malfunctioning" simply because it sometimes generates outcomes with which we disagree, however strongly (and claims that it is reaching results with which "the people" really disagree or would "if they understood"—are likely to be little more than self-deluding projections). In a representative democracy value determinations are to be made by our elected representatives, and if in fact most of us disapprove we can vote them out of office. Malfunction occurs when the *process* is undeserving of trust, when (1) the ins are choking off the channels of political change to ensure that they will stay in and the outs will stay out, or (2) though no one is actually denied a voice or a vote, representatives beholden to an effective majority are systematically disadvantaging some minority out of simple hostility or a prejudiced refusal to recognize commonalities of interest, and thereby denying that minority the protection afforded other groups by a representative system.

Obviously our elected representatives are the last persons we should trust with identification of either of these situations. Appointed judges, however, are comparative outsiders in our governmental system, and need worry about continuance in office only very obliquely. This does not give them some special pipeline to the genuine values of the American people: in fact it goes far to ensure that they won't have one. It does, however, put them in a position objectively to assess claims—though no one could suppose the evaluation won't be full of judgment calls—that either by clogging the channels of change or by acting as accessories to majority tyranny, our elected representatives in fact are not representing the interests of those whom the system presupposes they are.

UNITED STATES v. CAROLENE PRODUCTS

304 U.S. 144 (1938)

Opinion: Stone, joined by Hughes, Brandeis, Roberts, and by Black in all but the part marked "Third"
Concurrence: Butler
Dissent (not filed): McReynolds

Although the issue in United States v. Carolene Products *concerns the regulation of shipments of milk, it has tremendous significance because of its famous Footnote Four, also excerpted here. Pay particular attention to the footnote's treatment of the political process. As you read it, consider its link to John Hart Ely's procedural theory of constitutional interpretation.*

MR. JUSTICE STONE *delivered the opinion of the Court.*

The question for decision is whether the "Filled Milk Act" of Congress, which prohibits the shipment in interstate commerce of skimmed milk compounded with any fat or oil other than milk fat, so as to resemble milk or cream, transcends the power of Congress to regulate interstate commerce or infringes the Fifth Amendment.

We may assume for present purposes that no pronouncement of a legislature can forestall attack upon the constitutionality of the prohibition which it enacts by applying opprobrious epithets to the prohibited act, and that a statute would deny due process which precluded the disproof in judicial proceedings of all facts which would show or tend to show that a statute depriving the suitor of life, liberty or property had a rational basis.

But such we think is not the purpose or construction of the statutory characterization of filled milk as injurious to health and as a fraud upon the public. There is no need to consider it here as more than a declaration of the legislative findings deemed to support and justify the action taken as a constitutional exertion of the legislative power, aiding informed judicial review, as do the reports of legislative committees, by revealing the rationale of the legislation. Even in the absence of such aids the existence of facts supporting the legislative judgment is to be presumed, for regulatory legislation affecting ordinary commercial transactions is not to be pronounced unconstitutional unless in the light of the facts made known or generally assumed it is of such a character as to preclude the assumption that it rests upon some rational basis within the knowledge and experience of the legislators.[4] The present statutory findings affect appellee no more than the reports of the Congressional committees; and since in the absence of the statutory findings they would be presumed, their incorporation in the statute is no more prejudicial than surplusage.

---

4. There may be narrower scope for operation of the presumption of constitutionality when legislation appears on its face to be within a specific prohibition of the Constitution, such as those of the first ten amendments, which are deemed equally specific when held to be embraced within the Fourteenth. . . .

It is unnecessary to consider now whether legislation which restricts those political processes which can ordinarily be expected to bring about repeal of undesirable legislation, is to be subjected to more exacting judicial scrutiny under the general prohibitions of the Fourteenth Amendment than are most other types of legislation. . . .

Nor need we enquire whether similar considerations enter into the review of statutes directed at particular religious . . . or national . . . or racial minorities . . . ; whether prejudice against discrete and insular minorities may be a special condition, which tends seriously to curtail the operation of those political processes ordinarily to be relied upon to protect minorities, and which may call for a correspondingly more searching judicial inquiry.

REYNOLDS v. SIMS

377 U.S. 533 (1964)

Opinion: Warren, joined by Black, Douglas, Brennan, White, Goldberg
Concurrence: Clark
Concurrence: Stewart
Dissent: Harlan

As you have seen, John Hart Ely's notion of proceduralism stresses the role of the Court in "policing" the representational system. In this case, the Court intervenes to correct a system of state legislative districts in Alabama, where there were concerns about whether these districts violated the constitutional principle of "one person, one vote." The Alabama legislature failed to update its system of districting, with the result that state legislators represented constituencies of vastly differing size, and therefore some voters had much more influence in the legislature than others. Does Ely's theory support judicial intervention into the political process in this way? Consider the ways in which this case and Ely's theory differ from the way an originalist might approach the problem of representation. As we saw in Chapter 1, any time the Court intervenes to overturn popular legislation, there is a concern about the "counter-majoritarian difficulty." Does the fact that the Court in this case is attempting to ensure equal representation sufficiently respond to this difficulty? Would it make a difference if Alabama were accused of actively "gerrymandering" districts, the process whereby a particular political party attempts to draw districts in a way that serves its own political interests and pursuit of power?

MR. CHIEF JUSTICE WARREN *delivered the opinion of the Court.*

On August 26, 1961, the original plaintiffs (appellees in No. 23), residents, taxpayers and voters of Jefferson County, Alabama, filed a complaint in the United States District Court for the Middle District of Alabama, in their own behalf and on behalf of all similarly situated Alabama voters, challenging the apportionment of the Alabama Legislature. Defendants below (appellants in No. 23), sued in their representative capacities, were various state and political party officials charged with the performance of certain duties in connection with state elections. The complaint alleged a deprivation of rights under the Alabama Constitution and under the Equal Protection Clause of the Fourteenth Amendment, and asserted that the District Court had jurisdiction under provisions of the Civil Rights Act. . . .

Plaintiffs below alleged that the last apportionment of the Alabama Legislature was based on the 1900 federal census, despite the requirement of the State Constitution that the legislature be reapportioned decennially. They asserted that, since the population growth in the State from 1900 to 1960 had been uneven, Jefferson and other counties were now victims of serious discrimination with respect to the allocation of legislative representation. As a result of the failure of the legislature to reapportion itself, plaintiffs asserted, they were denied "equal suffrage in free and equal elections . . . and the equal protection of the laws" in violation of the Alabama Constitution and the Fourteenth Amendment to the Federal Constitution. The complaint asserted that plaintiffs had no other adequate remedy, and that they had exhausted all forms of relief other than that available through the federal courts. They alleged that the Alabama Legislature had established a pattern of prolonged inaction from 1911 to the present which "clearly demonstrates that no reapportionment . . . shall be effected"; that representation at any future constitutional convention would be established by the legislature, making it unlikely that the membership of any such convention would be fairly representative; and that, while the Alabama Supreme Court had found that the legislature had not complied with the State Constitution in failing to reapportion according to population decennially, that court had nevertheless indicated that it would not interfere with matters of legislative reapportionment.

. . . [T]he District Court held that the inequality of the existing representation in the Alabama Legislature violated the Equal Protection Clause of the Fourteenth Amendment, a finding which the Court noted had been "generally conceded" by the parties to the litigation, since population growth and shifts had converted the 1901 scheme, as perpetuated some 60 years later, into an invidiously discriminatory plan completely lacking in rationality. Under the existing provisions, applying 1960 census figures, only 25.1% of the State's total population resided in districts represented by a majority of the members of the Senate, and only 25.7% lived in counties which could elect a majority of the members of the House of Representatives. Population-variance ratios of up to about 41-to-1 existed in the Senate, and up to about 16-to-1 in the House. . . .

After the District Court's decision, new primary elections were held pursuant to legislation enacted in 1962 at the same special session as the proposed constitutional amendment and the Crawford-Webb Act, to be effective in the event the Court itself ordered a particular reapportionment plan into immediate effect. The November 1962 general election was likewise conducted on the basis of the District Court's ordered apportionment of legislative seats, as Mr. Justice Black refused to stay the District Court's order. Consequently, the present Alabama Legislature is apportioned in accordance with the temporary plan prescribed by the District Court's decree. All members of both houses of the Alabama Legislature serve four-year terms, so that the next regularly scheduled election of legislators will not be held until 1966. The 1963 regular session of the Alabama Legislature produced no legislation relating to legislative apportionment, and the legislature, which meets biennially, will not hold another regular session until 1965.

No effective political remedy to obtain relief against the alleged malapportionment of the Alabama Legislature appears to have been available. No initiative procedure exists under Alabama law. Amendment of the State Constitution can be achieved only after a proposal is adopted by three-fifths of the members of both houses of the legislature and is approved by a majority of the people, or as a result of a constitutional convention convened after approval by the people of a convention call initiated by a majority of both houses of the Alabama Legislature.

Undeniably the Constitution of the United States protects the right of all qualified citizens to vote, in state as well as in federal elections. A consistent line of decisions by this Court in cases involving attempts to deny or restrict the right of suffrage has made this indelibly clear. It has been repeatedly recognized that all qualified voters have a constitutionally protected right to vote. . . . In *Mosley* the Court stated that it is "as equally unquestionable that the right to have one's vote counted is as open to protection . . . as the right to put a ballot in a box." The right to vote can neither be denied outright, nor destroyed by alteration of ballots, nor diluted by ballot-box stuffing. . . .

Racially based gerrymandering, *Gomillion v. Lightfoot*, and the conducting of white primaries, both of which result in denying to some citizens their right to vote, have been held to be constitutionally impermissible. And history has seen a continuing expansion of the scope of the right of suffrage in this country. The right to vote freely for the candidate of one's choice is of the essence of a democratic society, and any restrictions on that right strike at the heart of representative government. And the right of suffrage can be denied by a debasement or dilution of the weight of a citizen's vote just as effectively as by wholly prohibiting the free exercise of the franchise.

> "How . . . can one person be given twice or ten times the voting power of another person in a statewide election merely because he lives in a rural area or because he lives in the smallest rural county? Once the geographical unit for which a representative is to be chosen is designated, all who participate in the election are to have an equal vote— whatever their race, whatever their sex, whatever their occupation, whatever their income, and wherever their home may be in that geographical unit. This is required by the Equal Protection Clause of the Fourteenth Amendment. The concept of 'we the people' under the Constitution visualizes no preferred class of voters but equality among those who meet the basic qualifications. The idea that every voter is equal to every other voter in his State, when he casts his ballot in favor of one of several competing candidates, underlies many of our decisions."

"[T]here is no indication in the Constitution that home site or occupation affords a permissible basis for distinguishing between qualified voters within the State." And, finally, we concluded: "The conception of political equality from the Declaration of Independence, to Lincoln's Gettysburg Address, to the Fifteenth, Seventeenth, and Nineteenth Amendments can only mean one thing—one person, one vote."

A predominant consideration in determining whether a State's legislative apportionment scheme constitutes an invidious discrimination violative of rights asserted under the Equal Protection Clause is that the rights allegedly impaired are individual and personal in nature. As stated by the Court in *United States v. Bathgate*, "[t]he right to vote is personal. . . ." While the result of a court decision in a state legislative apportionment controversy may be to require the restructuring of the geographical distribution of seats in a state legislature, the judicial focus must be concentrated upon ascertaining whether there has been any discrimination against certain of the State's citizens which constitutes an impermissible impairment of their constitutionally protected right to vote. Like *Skinner v. Oklahoma*, such a case "touches a sensitive and important area of human rights," and "involves one of the basic civil rights of man," presenting questions of alleged "invidious discriminations . . . against groups or types of individuals in violation of the constitutional guaranty of just and equal laws." Undoubtedly, the right of suffrage is a fundamental matter in a free and democratic society. Especially since the right to exercise the franchise in a free and unimpaired manner is preservative of other basic civil and political rights, any alleged infringement of the right of citizens to vote must be carefully and meticulously scrutinized. Almost a century ago, in *Yick Wo v. Hopkins*, the Court referred to "the political franchise of voting" as "a fundamental political right, because preservative of all rights."

Legislators represent people, not trees or acres. Legislators are elected by voters, not farms or cities or economic interests. As long as ours is a representative form of government, and our legislatures are those instruments of government elected directly by and directly representative of the people, the right to elect legislators in a free and unimpaired fashion is a bedrock of our political system. It could hardly be gainsaid that a constitutional claim had been asserted by an allegation that certain otherwise qualified voters had been entirely prohibited from voting for members of their state legislature. And, if a State should provide that the votes of citizens in one part of the State should be given two times, or five times, or 10 times the weight of votes of citizens in another part of the State, it could hardly be contended that the right to vote of those residing in the disfavored areas had not been effectively diluted. It would appear extraordinary to suggest that a State could be constitutionally permitted to enact a law providing that certain of the State's voters could vote two, five, or 10 times for their legislative representatives, while voters living elsewhere could vote only once. And it is inconceivable that a state law to the effect that, in counting votes for legislators, the votes of citizens in one part of the State would be multiplied by two, five, or 10, while the votes of persons in another area would be counted only at face value, could be constitutionally sustainable. Of course, the effect of state legislative districting schemes which give the same number of representatives to unequal numbers of constituents is identical. Overweighting and overvaluation of the votes of those living here has the certain effect of dilution and undervaluation of the votes of those living there. The resulting discrimination against those individual voters living in disfavored areas is easily demonstrable mathematically. Their right to vote is simply not the same right to vote as that of those living in a favored part of the State. Two, five, or 10 of them must vote before

the effect of their voting is equivalent to that of their favored neighbor. Weighting the votes of citizens differently, by any method or means, merely because of where they happen to reside, hardly seems justifiable. . . .

To the extent that a citizen's right to vote is debased, he is that much less a citizen. The fact that an individual lives here or there is not a legitimate reason for overweighting or diluting the efficacy of his vote. The complexions of societies and civilizations change, often with amazing rapidity. A nation once primarily rural in character becomes predominantly urban. Representation schemes once fair and equitable become archaic and outdated. But the basic principle of representative government remains, and must remain, unchanged—the weight of a citizen's vote cannot be made to depend on where he lives. Population is, of necessity, the starting point for consideration and the controlling criterion for judgment in legislative apportionment controversies. A citizen, a qualified voter, is no more nor no less so because he lives in the city or on the farm. This is the clear and strong command of our Constitution's Equal Protection Clause. This is an essential part of the concept of a government of laws and not men. This is at the heart of Lincoln's vision of "government of the people, by the people, [and] for the people." The Equal Protection Clause demands no less than substantially equal state legislative representation for all citizens, of all places as well as of all races.

We hold that, as a basic constitutional standard, the Equal Protection Clause requires that the seats in both houses of a bicameral state legislature must be apportioned on a population basis. Simply stated, an individual's right to vote for state legislators is unconstitutionally impaired when its weight is in a substantial fashion diluted when compared with votes of citizens living in other parts of the State. Since, under neither the existing apportionment provisions nor either of the proposed plans was either of the houses of the Alabama Legislature apportioned on a population basis, the District Court correctly held that all three of these schemes were constitutionally invalid.

SYNTHESIS QUESTIONS FOR FURTHER DISCUSSION: CHAPTER 2 SECTION B

1. John Hart Ely and Justice Antonin Scalia both agree that the Constitution should be interpreted in the context of a wider theory of democracy. For Justice Scalia, this entails fidelity to the original democratic process of the constitutional convention and the democratic amendment process. This fidelity is realized through interpretation consistent with original meaning. Ely clearly has a different underlying theory of democracy. For Ely, a democratic constitution should be interpreted through the lens of "process" theory. In particular, Ely argues that the Court has a role in striking down legislation that undermines the democratic process. Given the questions raised in the cases in this section, such as *Reynolds v. Sims,* does Ely's approach seem more persuasive as an account of the requirements of democracy than is originalism? Imagine that the original understanding of the Fourteenth Amendment did not include the principle of "one person, one vote." Does this mean that the Court should not enforce it?

2. In the wider work from which the Ely excerpt is taken, he attempts to situate his theory between those that disregard the text of the Constitution entirely (non-textualism) and those that express fidelity to the text as written. On his view, process theory's placement of participatory rights at the center of the Constitution's meaning offers the most coherent way to understand the constitutional text as a whole. Which clauses most support Ely's understanding of the Constitution? Which clauses are hardest to reconcile with it?

C. MORAL READING OF THE CONSTITUTION

One challenge to John Hart Ely's theory of interpretation is that the Constitution protects rights distinct from those related to democratic procedure. For instance, the Cruel and Unusual Punishment Clause of the Eighth Amendment does not seem to be related to the political process; rather, it seems to aim to protect some other fundamental interest. Drawing on this insight, Ronald Dworkin proposes a theory of constitutional interpretation that he calls "the moral reading." On his view, many of the abstract phrases in the Constitution invite us to think about broader issues in political morality and moral philosophy. For instance, to understand what is cruel, we need to engage in a general inquiry about the moral meaning of the term. On Dworkin's view, understanding the meaning of the term cruel requires an inquiry into moral philosophy because cruelty cannot be understood solely in terms of a dictionary definition. Instead, the prohibition on cruelty is a moral ideal and must be treated as such. Interestingly, Dworkin can also claim to appeal to the original intent of the Founders. Dworkin claims that if the Founders had meant for their provisions to be read as strict rules rather than as general principles, they would have eschewed such broad language as "cruel or unusual punishment," or "equal protection of the laws," as they did, for instance, when they specified exact age thresholds for members of the House and the Senate.

Dworkin's view is a "substantive" theory of constitutional interpretation. This means that apart from considerations of democratic procedure, there should be limits on the kind of laws that any democracy can enact. Dworkin claims that this outcome-based view is still democratic. He argues that self-government is not just about procedure, but is also about the kind of treatment to which democratic citizens are entitled. This means that our constitutional democracy must not simply guarantee citizens the right to participate but must also guarantee certain rights to be protected from the state. In addition to the readings from Dworkin, we also include an excerpt from Justice William Brennan. Like Dworkin, Justice Brennan advocated a substantive approach to the Constitution that sees certain moral values as central. For Justice Brennan, the Constitution fundamentally protects "human dignity." As you read this piece, consider how it affirms or differs from Dworkin's account of the moral reading.

Our case selection includes two cases where the Court protected rights in a manner that might be thought justified on the moral reading. Under its doctrine of substantive due process, the Court in *Lochner v. New York* struck down a law limiting the hours of bakers on the grounds that it violated the Fourteenth Amendment's Due Process Clause. Dworkin himself believes this case was wrongly decided. But it arguably invokes a moral reading of the Constitution. According to *Lochner v. New York*, the morality of the Constitution is fundamentally concerned with the protection of the right to contract, and private property more generally. Some have called the *Lochner v. New York* Court's morality a libertarian morality. What grounds might Dworkin or another proponent of the moral reading have to reject the holding of this decision? Answering this question will help you to see how the same theory might yield different conclusions about specific cases.

In contrast to *Lochner v. New York*, Dworkin does endorse the moral reading found in our second case selection, *Griswold v. Connecticut*. As you will see, according to this case, the broad provisions found in the Bill of Rights establish a right to privacy that protects a specific right to contraception. As you read this case, consider how its moral reading draws from the specific textual provisions of the Constitution. Do you agree that a right to privacy is implied by the broad provisions cited by U.S. Supreme Court Justice William O. Douglas in this case?

Ronald Dworkin

FREEDOM'S LAW: THE MORAL READING OF THE AMERICAN CONSTITUTION

Introduction

Cambridge, MA: Harvard University Press (1996)

Most contemporary constitutions declare individual rights against the government in very broad and abstract language, like the First Amendment of the United States Constitution, which provides that Congress shall make no law abridging "the freedom of speech." The moral reading proposes that we all—judges, lawyers, citizens—interpret and apply these abstract clauses on the understanding that they invoke moral principles about political decency and justice. The First Amendment, for example, recognizes a moral principle—that it is wrong for government to censor or control what individual citizens say or publish—and incorporates it into American law. So when some novel or controversial constitutional issue arises—about whether, for instance, the First Amendment permits laws against pornography—people who form an opinion must decide how an abstract moral principle is best understood. They must decide whether the true ground of the moral principle that condemns censorship, in the form in which this principle has been incorporated into American law, extends to the case of pornography.

The moral reading therefore brings political morality into the heart of constitutional law. But political morality is inherently uncertain and controversial, so any system of government that makes such principles part of its law must decide whose interpretation and understanding will be authoritative. In the American

system judges—ultimately the justices of the Supreme Court—now have that authority, and the moral reading of the Constitution is therefore said by its critics to give judges absolute power to impose their own moral convictions on the public. I shall shortly try to explain why that crude charge is mistaken. I should make plain first, however, that there is nothing revolutionary about the moral reading in practice. So far as American lawyers and judges follow any coherent strategy of interpreting the Constitution at all, they already use the moral reading, as I hope this book will make plain.

That explains why both scholars and journalists find it reasonably easy to classify judges as "liberal" or "conservative": the best explanation of the differing patterns of their decisions lies in their different understandings of central moral values embedded in the Constitution's text. Judges whose political convictions are conservative will naturally interpret abstract constitutional principles in a conservative way, as they did in the early years of this century, when they wrongly supposed that certain rights over property and contract are fundamental to freedom. Judges whose convictions are more liberal will naturally interpret those principles in a liberal way, as they did in the halcyon days of the Warren Court. The moral reading is not, in itself, either a liberal or a conservative charter or strategy. It is true that in recent decades liberal judges have ruled more statutes or executive orders unconstitutional than conservative judges have. But that is because conservative political principles for the most part either favored or did not strongly condemn the measures that could reasonably be challenged on constitutional grounds in those decades. There have been exceptions to that generalization. Conservatives strongly disapprove, on moral grounds, . . . affirmative action programs . . . , which give certain advantages to minority applicants for universities or jobs, and conservative justices have not hesitated to follow their understanding of what the moral reading required in such cases.

THE MORAL READING

The clauses of the American Constitution that protect individuals and minorities from government are found mainly in the so-called Bill of Rights—the first several amendments to the document— and the further amendments added after the Civil War. Many of these clauses are drafted in exceedingly abstract moral language. The First Amendment refers to the "right" of free speech, for example, the Fifth Amendment to the process that is "due" to citizens, and the Fourteenth to protection that is "equal." According to the moral reading, these clauses must be understood in the way their language most naturally suggests: they refer to abstract moral principles and incorporate these by reference, as limits on government's power.

There is of course room for disagreement about the right way to restate these abstract moral principles, so as to make their force clearer for us, and to help us to apply them to more concrete political controversies. I favor a particular way of stating the constitutional principles at the most general possible level. I believe that the principles set out in the Bill of Rights, taken together, commit the United States to the following political and legal ideals: government must treat all those subject to its dominion as having equal moral and political status; it must attempt, in good faith, to treat them all with equal concern; and it must respect whatever individual freedoms are indispensable to those ends, including but not limited to the freedoms more specifically designated in the document, such as the freedoms of speech and religion.

Of course the moral reading is not appropriate to everything a constitution contains. The American Constitution includes a great many clauses that are neither particularly abstract nor drafted in the language of moral principle. Article II specifies, for example, that the President must be at least thirty-five years old, and the Third Amendment insists that government may not quarter soldiers in citizens' houses in peacetime. The latter may have been inspired by a moral principle; those who wrote and enacted it might have been anxious to give effect to some principle protecting citizens' rights to privacy, for example. But the Third Amendment is not itself a moral principle: its *content* is not a general principle of privacy. So the first challenge to my own interpretation of the abstract clauses might be put this way. What argument or evidence do I have that the equal protection clause of the Fourteenth Amendment (for example), which declares that no state may deny any person equal protection of the laws, has a moral principle as its content though the Third Amendment does not?

This is a question of interpretation or, if you prefer, translation. We must try to find language of our own that best captures, in terms we find clear, the content of what the "framers" intended it to say. (Constitutional scholars use the word "framers" to describe, somewhat ambiguously, the various people who drafted and enacted a constitutional provision.) History is crucial to that project, because we must know something about the circumstances in which a person spoke to have any good idea of what he meant to say in speaking as he did. We find nothing in history, however, to cause us any doubt about what the framers of the Third Amendment meant to say. Given the words they used, we cannot sensibly interpret them as laying down any moral principle at all, even if we believe they were inspired by one. They said what the words they used would normally be used to say: not that privacy must be protected, but that soldiers must not be quartered in houses in peacetime. The same process of reasoning—about what the framers presumably intended to say when they used the words they did—yields an opposite conclusion about the framers of the equal protection clause, however. Most of them no doubt had fairly clear expectations about what legal consequences the Fourteenth Amendment would have. They expected it to end certain of the most egregious Jim Crow practices of the Reconstruction period. They plainly did not expect it to outlaw official racial segregation in school—on the contrary, the Congress that adopted the equal protection clause itself maintained segregation in the District of Columbia school system. But they did not *say* anything about Jim Crow laws or school segregation or homosexuality or gender equality, one way or the other. They said that "equal protection of the laws" is required, which plainly describes a very general principle, not any concrete application of it.

The framers meant, then, to enact a general principle. But which general principle? That further question must be answered by constructing different elaborations of the phrase "equal protection of the laws," each of which we can recognize as a principle of political morality that might have won their respect, and then by asking which of these it makes most sense to attribute to them given everything else we know. The qualification that each of these possibilities must be recognizable as a political *principle* is absolutely crucial. We cannot capture a statesman's efforts to lay down a general constitutional principle by attributing to him something neither he nor we could recognize as a candidate for that role. But the qualification will typically leave many possibilities open. It was once debated, for example, whether the framers intended to stipulate, in the equal protection clause, only the relatively weak political principle that laws must be enforced in accordance with their terms, so that legal benefits conferred on everyone, including blacks, must not be denied, in practice, to anyone.

History seems decisive that the framers of the Fourteenth Amendment did not mean to lay down only so weak a principle as that one, however, which would have left states free to discriminate against blacks in any way they wished so long as they did so openly. Congressmen of the victorious nation, trying to capture the achievements and lessons of a terrible war, would be very unlikely to settle for anything so limited and insipid, and we should not take them to have done so unless the language leaves no other interpretation plausible. In any case, constitutional interpretation must take into account past legal and political practice as well as what the framers themselves intended to say, and it has now been settled by unchallengeable precedent that the political principle incorporated in the Fourteenth Amendment is not that very weak one, but something more robust.

Once that is conceded, however, then the principle must be something *much* more robust, because the only alternative, as a translation of what the framers actually *said* in the equal protection clause, is that they declared a principle of quite breathtaking scope and power: the principle that government must treat everyone as of equal status and with equal concern.

This brief discussion has mentioned two important restraints that sharply limit the latitude the moral reading gives to individual judges. First, under that reading constitutional interpretation must begin in what the framers said, and, just as our judgment about what friends and strangers say relies on specific information about them and the context in which they speak, so does our understanding of what the framers said. History is therefore plainly relevant. But only in a particular way. We turn to history to answer the question of what they intended to *say*, not the different question of what *other* intentions they had. We have no need to decide what they expected to happen, or hoped would happen, in consequence of their having said what they did, for example; their purpose, in that sense, is not part of our study. We are governed by what our lawmakers said—by the principles they laid down— not by any information we might have about how they themselves would have interpreted those principles or applied them in concrete cases.

Second, and equally important, constitutional interpretation is disciplined, under the moral reading, by the requirement of constitutional *integrity*. Judges may not read their own convictions into the Constitution. They may not read the abstract moral clauses as expressing any particular moral judgment, no matter how much that judgment appeals to them, unless they find it consistent in

principle with the structural design of the Constitution as a whole, and also with the dominant lines of past constitutional interpretation by other judges. They must regard themselves as partners with other officials, past and future, who together elaborate a coherent constitutional morality, and they must take care to see that what they contribute fits with the rest. (I have elsewhere said that judges are like authors jointly creating a chain novel in which each writes a chapter that makes sense as part of the story as a whole.) Even a judge who believes that abstract justice requires economic equality cannot interpret the equal protection clause as making equality of wealth, or collective ownership of productive resources, a constitutional requirement, because that interpretation simply does not fit American history or practice, or the rest of the Constitution.

Nor could a judge plausibly think that the constitutional structure commits any but basic, structural political rights to his care. He might think that a society truly committed to equal concern would award people with handicaps special resources, or would secure convenient access to recreational parks for everyone, or would provide heroic and experimental medical treatment, no matter how expensive or speculative, for anyone whose life might possibly be saved. But it would violate constitutional integrity for a judge to treat these mandates as part of constitutional law. Judges must defer to general, settled understandings about the character of the power the Constitution assigns them. The moral reading asks them to find the best conception of constitutional moral principles—the best understanding of what equal moral status for men and women really requires, for example—that fits the broad story of America's historical record. It does not ask them to follow the whisperings of their own consciences or the traditions of their own class or sect if these cannot be seen as embedded in that record. Of course judges can abuse their power—they can pretend to observe the important restraint of integrity while really ignoring it. But generals and presidents and priests can abuse their powers, too. The moral reading is a strategy for lawyers and judges acting in good faith, which is all any interpretive strategy can be.

I emphasize these constraints of history and integrity, because they show how exaggerated is the common complaint that the moral reading gives judges absolute power to impose their own moral convictions on the rest of us. Macauley was wrong when he said that the American Constitution is all sail and no anchor, and so are the other critics who say that the moral reading turns judges into philosopher-kings. Our constitution is law, and like all law it is anchored in history, practice, and integrity. Most cases at law—even most constitutional cases—are not hard cases. The ordinary craft of a judge dictates an answer and leaves no room for the play of personal moral conviction. Still, we must not exaggerate the drag of that anchor. Very different, even contrary, conceptions of a constitutional principle—of what treating men and women as equals really means, for example—will often fit language, precedent, and practice well enough to pass these tests, and thoughtful judges must then decide on their own which conception does most credit to the nation. So though the familiar complaint that the moral reading gives judges unlimited power is hyperbolic, it contains enough truth to alarm those who believe that such judicial power is inconsistent with a republican form of government. The constitutional sail is a broad one, and

many people do fear that it is too big for a democratic boat.

WHAT IS THE ALTERNATIVE?

Constitutional lawyers and scholars have therefore been anxious to find other strategies for constitutional interpretation, strategies that give judges less power. They have explored two different possibilities. The first, and most forthright, concedes that the moral reading is right—that the Bill of Rights can only be understood as a set of moral principles. But it denies that judges should have the final authority themselves to conduct the moral reading—that they should have the last word about, for example, whether women have a constitutional right to choose abortion or whether affirmative action treats all races with equal concern. It reserves that interpretive authority to the people. That is by no means a contradictory combination of views. The moral reading, as I said, is a theory about what the Constitution means, not a theory about whose view of what it means must be accepted by the rest of us.

This first alternate offers a way of understanding the arguments of a great American judge, Learned Hand. Hand thought that the courts should take final authority to interpret the Constitution only when this is absolutely necessary to the survival of government—only when the courts must be referees between the other departments of government because the alternative would be a chaos of competing claims to jurisdiction. No such necessity compels courts to test legislative acts against the Constitution's moral principles, and Hand therefore thought it wrong for judges to claim that authority. Though his view was once an open possibility, history has long excluded it; practice has now settled that courts do have a responsibility to declare and act on their best understanding of what the Constitution forbids. If Hand's view had been accepted, the Supreme Court could not have decided, as it did in its famous *Brown* decision in 1954, that the equal protection clause outlaws racial segregation in public schools. In 1958 Hand said, with evident regret, that he had to regard the *Brown* decision as wrong, and he would have had to take the same view about later Supreme Court decisions that expanded racial equality, religious independence, and personal freedoms such as the freedom to buy and use contraceptives. These decisions are now almost universally thought not only sound but shining examples of our constitutional structure working at its best.

The first alternative strategy, as I said, accepts the moral reading. The second alternative, which is called the "originalist" or "original intention" strategy, does not. The moral reading insists that the Constitution means what the framers intended to say. Originalism insists that it means what they expected their language to do, which as I said is a very different matter. (Though some originalists, including one of the most conservative justices now on the Supreme Court, Antonin Scalia, are unclear about the distinction.) According to originalism, the great clauses of the Bill of Rights should be interpreted not as laying down the abstract moral principles they actually describe, but instead as referring, in a kind of code or disguise, to the framers' own assumptions and expectations about the correct application of those principles. So the equal protection clause is to be understood as commanding not equal status but what the framers themselves thought was equal status in spite of the fact that, as I said, the framers clearly meant to lay down the former standard

not the latter one. The *Brown* decision I just mentioned crisply illustrates the distinction. The Court's decision was plainly required by the moral reading, because it is obvious now that official school segregation is not consistent with equal status and equal concern for all races. But the originalist strategy, consistently applied, would have demanded the opposite conclusion, because, as I said, the authors of the equal protection clause did not believe that school segregation, which they practiced themselves, was a denial of equal status, and did not expect that it would one day be deemed to be so. The moral reading insists that they misunderstood the moral principle that they themselves enacted into law. The originalist strategy would translate that mistake into enduring constitutional law.

That strategy, like the first alternative, would condemn not only the *Brown* decision but many other Supreme Court decisions that are now widely regarded as paradigms of good constitutional interpretation. For that reason, almost no one now embraces originalist strategy in anything like a pure form. Even Robert Bork, who remains one of its strongest defenders, qualified his support in the Senate hearings following his nomination to the Supreme Court—he conceded that the *Brown* decision was right, and said that even the Court's 1965 decision guaranteeing a right to use contraceptives, which we have no reason to think the authors of any pertinent constitutional clause either expected or would have approved, was right in its result. The originalist strategy is as indefensible in principle as it is unpalatable in result, moreover. It is as illegitimate to substitute a concrete, detailed provision for the abstract language of the equal protection clause as it would be to substitute some abstract principle of privacy for the concrete terms of the

Third Amendment, or to treat the clause imposing a minimum age for a President as enacting some general principle of disability for persons under that age.

So though many conservative politicians and judges have endorsed originalism, and some, like Hand, have been tempted to reconsider whether judges should have the last word about what the Constitution requires, there is in fact very little practical support for either of these strategies. Yet the moral reading is almost never explicitly endorsed, and is often explicitly condemned. If neither of the two alternatives I described is actually embraced by those who disparage the moral reading, what alternative do they have in mind? The surprising answer is none. Constitutional scholars often say that we must avoid the mistakes of both the moral reading, which gives too much power to judges, and of originalism, which makes the contemporary Constitution too much the dead hand of the past. The right method, they say, is something in between which strikes the right balance between protecting essential individual rights and deferring to popular will. But they do not indicate what the right balance is, or even what kind of scale we should use to find it. They say that constitutional interpretation must take both history and the general structure of the Constitution into account as well as moral or political philosophy. But they do not say why history or structure, both of which, as I said, figure in the moral reading, should figure in some further or different way, or what that different way is, or what general goal or standard of constitutional interpretation should guide us, in seeking a different interpretive strategy.

So though the call for an intermediate constitutional strategy is often heard, it has not been answered, except in unhelpful metaphors about balance and structure. That is extraordinary, particularly given the enormous and growing literature of American constitutional theory. If it is so hard to produce an alternative to the moral reading, why struggle to do so? One distinguished constitutional lawyer who insists that there must be an interpretive strategy somewhere between originalism and the moral reading recently announced, at a conference, that although he had not discovered it, he would spend the rest of his life looking. Why?

So of course the moral reading encourages lawyers and judges to read an abstract constitution in the light of what they take to be justice. How else could they answer the moral questions that abstract constitution asks them? It is no surprise, or occasion for ridicule or suspicion, that a constitutional theory reflects a moral stance. Text and integrity do act as important constraints, as I have been emphasizing throughout this discussion. But though these constraints shape and limit the impact of convictions of justice, they cannot eliminate that impact. The moral reading insists, however, that this influence is not disreputable, so long as it is openly recognized, and so long as the convictions are identified and defended honestly, by which I mean through proper arguments of principle not just thin slogans or tired metaphors.

This book does indeed offer a liberal view of the American Constitution. It provides arguments of liberal principle and claims that these provide the best interpretations of constitutional tradition we have inherited and whose trustees we now are. I believe, and try to show, that liberal opinion best fits our constitutional structure, which was, after all, first constructed in the bright morning of liberal thought. My arguments can certainly be resisted. But I hope they will be resisted in the right way: by pointing out their fallacies or by deploying different principles—more conservative or more radical ones—and showing why these different principles are better because they are grounded in a superior morality, or are more practicable, or are in some other way wiser or fairer. It is too late for the old, cowardly, story about judges not being responsible for making arguments like these, or competent to do so, or that it is undemocratic for them to try, or that their job is to enforce the law, not speculate about morality. That old story is philosophy too, but it is bad philosophy. It appeals to concepts—of law and democracy—that it does not begin to understand.

It is in the nature of legal interpretation—not just but particularly constitutional interpretation—to aim at happy endings. There is no alternative, except aiming at unhappy ones, because once the pure form of originalism is rejected there is no such thing as neutral accuracy. Telling it how it is means, up to a point, telling it how it should be. What is that point? The American constitutional novel includes, after all, the Supreme Court's *Dred Scott* decision, which treated slaves as a kind of property, and the Court's twentieth-century "rights of property" decisions, which nearly swamped Roosevelt's New Deal. How happy an overall view of that story is actually on offer? Many chapters raise that question, and it cannot be answered except through detailed interpretive arguments like those they provide. But political and intellectual responsibility, as well as cheerfulness, argue for optimism. The Constitution is America's moral sail, and we must hold to the courage of the conviction that fills it, the conviction that we can all be equal citizens of a moral republic. That is a noble faith, and only optimism can redeem it.

Justice William Brennan

THE CONSTITUTION OF THE UNITED STATES: CONTEMPORARY RATIFICATION

Address to the Text and Teaching Symposium at Georgetown University

October 12, 1985

Justice William Brennan was one of the most prominent advocates of a living Constitution. As you read this excerpt from one of his addresses, consider whether this interpretive lens simply results in Justice Brennan substituting his own moral and political opinions for the text of the Constitution. Is it difficult to make such distinctions? If this is impossible, does it discredit this interpretive theory?

[T]he Constitution embodies the aspiration to social justice, brotherhood, and human dignity that brought this nation into being. The Declaration of Independence, the Constitution and the Bill of Rights solemnly committed the United States to be a country where the dignity and rights of all persons were equal before all authority. In all candor we must concede that part of this egalitarianism in America has been more pretension than realized fact. But we are an aspiring people, a people with faith in progress. Our amended Constitution is the lodestar for our aspirations. Like every text worth reading, it is not crystalline. The phrasing is broad and the limitations of its provisions are not clearly marked. Its majestic generalities and ennobling pronouncements are both luminous and obscure. This ambiguity of course calls forth interpretation, the interaction of reader and text. . . .

When Justices interpret the Constitution they speak for their community, not for themselves alone. The act of interpretation must be undertaken with full consciousness that it is, in a very real sense, the community's interpretation that is sought. Justices are not platonic guardians appointed to wield authority according to their personal moral predilections. Precisely because coercive force must attend any judicial decision to countermand the will of a contemporary majority, the Justices must render constitutional interpretations that are received as legitimate. The source of legitimacy is, of course, a wellspring of controversy in legal and political circles. At the core of the debate is what the late Yale Law School professor Alexander Bickel labeled "the counter-majoritarian difficulty." Our commitment to self-governance in a representative democracy must be reconciled with vesting in electorally unaccountable Justices the power to invalidate the expressed desires of representative bodies on the ground of inconsistency with higher law. Because judicial power resides in the authority to give meaning to the Constitution, the debate is really a debate about how to read the text, about constraints on what is legitimate interpretation.

There are those who find legitimacy in fidelity to what they call "the intentions of the Framers." In its most doctrinaire incarnation, this view demands that Justices discern exactly what the Framers thought about the question under consideration and simply follow that intention in resolving the case before them. It is a view that feigns self-effacing deference to the specific judgments of those who forged our original social compact. But in truth it is little more than arrogance cloaked as humility. It is arrogant to pretend that from our vantage we can gauge accurately the intent of the Framers on application of principle to specific, contemporary questions. All too often, sources of potential enlightenment such as records of the ratification debates provide sparse or ambiguous evidence of the original intention. Typically, all that can be gleaned is that the Framers themselves did not agree about the application or meaning of particular constitutional provisions, and hid their differences in cloaks of generality. Indeed, it is far from clear whose intention is relevant—that of the drafters, the congressional disputants, or the ratifiers in the states?—or even whether the idea of an original intention is a coherent way of thinking about a jointly drafted document drawing its authority from a general assent of the states. And apart from the problematic nature of the sources, our distance of two centuries cannot but work as a prism refracting all we perceive. One cannot help but speculate that the chorus of lamentations calling for interpretation faithful to "original intention"—and proposing nullification of interpretations that fail this quick litmus test—must inevitably come from persons who have no familiarity with the historical record.

Perhaps most importantly, while proponents of this facile historicism justify it as a depoliticization of the judiciary, the political underpinnings of such a choice should not escape notice. A position that upholds constitutional claims only if they were within the specific contemplation of the Framers in effect establishes a presumption of resolving textual ambiguities against the claim of constitutional right. It is far from clear what justifies such a presumption against claims of right. Nothing intrinsic in the nature of interpretation—if there is such a thing as the "nature" of interpretation—commands such a passive approach to ambiguity. This is a choice no less political than any other; it expresses antipathy to claims of the minority rights against the majority. Those who would restrict claims of right to the values of 1789 specifically articulated in the Constitution turn a blind eye to social progress and eschew adaptation of overarching principles to changes of social circumstance.

Another, perhaps more sophisticated, response to the potential power of judicial interpretation stresses democratic theory: because ours is a government of the people's elected representatives, substantive value choices should by and large be left to them. This view emphasizes not the transcendent historical authority of the Framers but the predominant contemporary authority of the elected branches of government. Yet it has similar consequences for the nature of proper judicial interpretation. Faith in the majoritarian process counsels restraint. Even under more expansive formulations of this approach, judicial review is appropriate only to the extent of ensuring that our democratic process functions smoothly. Thus, for example, we would protect freedom of speech merely to ensure that the people are heard by their representatives, rather than as a separate, substantive value. When, by contrast, society tosses up to the Supreme Court a dispute that would require invalidation of a legislature's substantive policy choice, the Court generally would stay its hand because the Constitution was meant as a plan of government and not as an embodiment of fundamental substantive values.

The view that all matters of substantive policy should be resolved through the majoritarian process has appeal under some circumstances, but I think it ultimately will not do. Unabashed enshrinement of majority would permit the imposition of a social caste system or wholesale confiscation of property so long as a majority of the authorized legislative body, fairly elected, approved. Our Constitution could not abide such a situation. . . .

One cannot read the text without admitting that it embodies substantive value choices; it places certain values beyond the power of any legislature. Obvious are the separation of powers; the privilege of the Writ of Habeas Corpus; prohibition of Bills of Attainder and ex post facto laws; prohibition of cruel and unusual punishments; the requirement of just compensation for official taking of property; the prohibition of laws tending to establish religion or enjoining the free exercise of religion; and, since the Civil War, the banishment of slavery and official race discrimination. . . .

To remain faithful to the content of the Constitution, therefore, an approach to interpreting the text must account for the existence of these substantive value choices, and must accept the ambiguity inherent in the effort to apply them to modern circumstances. . . .

We current Justices read the Constitution in the only way that we can: as Twentieth Century Americans. We look to the history of the time of framing and to the intervening history of interpretation. But the ultimate question must be, what do the words of the text mean in our time. For the genius of the Constitution rests not in any static meaning it might have had in a world that is dead and gone, but in the adaptability of its great principles to cope with current problems and current needs. What the constitutional fundamentals meant to the wisdom of other times cannot be their measure to the vision of our time. Similarly, what those fundamentals mean for us, our descendants will learn, cannot be the measure to the vision of their time. . . .

Interpretation must account for the transformative purpose of the text. Our Constitution was not intended to preserve a preexisting society but to make a new one, to put in place new principles that the prior political community had not sufficiently recognized. Thus, for example, when we interpret the Civil War Amendments to the charter—abolishing slavery, guaranteeing blacks equality under law, and guaranteeing blacks the right to vote—we must remember that those who put them in place had no desire to enshrine the status quo. Their goal was to make over their world, to eliminate all vestige of slave caste.

The Constitution on its face is, in large measure, a structuring text, a blueprint for government. And when the text is not prescribing the form of government it is limiting the powers of that government. The original document, before addition of any of the amendments, does not speak primarily of the rights of man, but of the abilities and disabilities of government. When one reflects upon the text's preoccupation with the scope of government as well as its shape, however, one comes to understand that what this text is about is the relationship of the individual and the state. The text marks the metes and bounds of official authority and individual autonomy. When one studies the boundary that the text marks out, one gets a sense of the vision of the individual embodied in the Constitution.

As augmented by the Bill of Rights and the Civil War Amendments, this text is a sparkling vision of the supremacy of the human dignity of every individual. This vision is reflected in the very choice of democratic self-governance: the supreme value of a democracy is the presumed worth of each individual. And this vision manifests itself most dramatically in the specific prohibitions of the Bill of Rights, a term which I henceforth will apply to describe not only the original first eight amendments, but the Civil War amendments as well. It is a vision that has guided us as a people throughout our history, although the precise rules by which we have protected fundamental human dignity have been transformed over time in response to both transformations of social condition and evolution of our concepts of human dignity.

As government acts ever more deeply upon those areas of our lives once marked "private," there is an even greater need to see that individual rights are not curtailed or cheapened in the interest of what may temporarily appear to be the "public good." . . . Solutions of constitutional questions from that perspective have become the great challenge of the modern era. All the talk in the last half-decade about shrinking the government does not alter this reality or the challenge it imposes. The modern activist state is a concomitant of the complexity of modern society; it is inevitably with us. We must meet the challenge rather than wish it were not before us.

. . . [I]t is because we recognize that incarceration strips a man of his dignity that we demand strict adherence to fair procedure and proof of guilt beyond a reasonable doubt before taking such a drastic step. These requirements are, as Justice Harlan once said, "bottomed on a fundamental value determination of our society that it is far worse to convict an innocent man than to let a guilty man go free." In re Winship [397 U.S. 358, 372 (1970)] (concurring opinion). There is no worse injustice than wrongly to strip a man of his dignity. And our adherence to the constitutional vision of human dignity is so strict that even after convicting a person according to these stringent standards, we demand that his dignity be infringed only to the extent appropriate to the crime and never by means of wanton infliction of pain or deprivation. I interpret the Constitution plainly to embody these fundamental values.

Of course the constitutional vision of human dignity has, in this past quarter century, infused far more than our decisions about the criminal process. Recognition of the principle of "one person, one vote" as a constitutional one redeems the promise of self-governance by affirming the essential dignity of every citizen in the right to equal participation in the democratic process. Recognition of so-called "new property" rights in those receiving government entitlements affirms the essential dignity of the least fortunate among us by demanding that government treat with decency, integrity and consistency those dependent on its benefits for their very survival. . . . Likewise, recognition of full equality for women—equal protection of the laws—ensures that gender has no bearing on claims to human dignity.

Recognition of broad and deep rights of expression and of conscience reaffirm the vision of human dignity in many ways. They too redeem the promise of self-governance by facilitating—indeed demanding—robust, uninhibited and wide-open debate on issues of public importance. Such public debate is of course vital to the development and dissemination of political ideas. As importantly, robust public discussion is the crucible in which personal political convictions are forged. In our democracy, such discussion is a political duty, it is the essence of self government. The constitutional vision of human dignity rejects the possibility of political orthodoxy imposed from above; it respects the right of each individual to form and to express political judgments, however far they may deviate from the mainstream and however unsettling they might be to the powerful or the elite. Recognition of these rights of expression and conscience also frees up the private space for both intellectual and spiritual development free of government dominance, either blatant or subtle.

. . . [W]hen a Justice perceives an interpretation of the text to have departed so far from its essential meaning, that Justice is bound, by a larger constitutional duty to the community, to expose the departure and point toward a different path. On this issue, the death penalty, I hope to embody a community striving for human dignity for all, although perhaps not yet arrived.

If we are to be as a shining city upon a hill, it will be because of our ceaseless pursuit of the constitutional ideal of human dignity. For the political and legal ideals that form the foundation of much that is best in American institutions—ideals jealously preserved and guarded throughout our history—still form the vital force in creative political thought and activity within the nation today. As we adapt our institutions to the ever-changing conditions of national and international life, those ideals of human dignity—liberty and justice for all individuals—will continue to inspire and guide us because they are entrenched in our Constitution. The Constitution with its Bill of Rights thus has a bright future, as well as a glorious past, for its spirit is inherent in the aspirations of our people.

LOCHNER v. NEW YORK

198 U.S. 45 (1905)

Opinion: Peckham, joined by Fuller, Brewer, Brown, McKenna
Dissent: Harlan, joined by White, Day
Dissent: Holmes

Much of the discussion in this case centers on whether the state's "police powers" extended far enough to permit it to regulate bakers' working hours. Police powers are the right of a state to regulate the "welfare, health, safety, and morals" of its population. But as crucial, if not more so, is the claim that the New York law violates the Fourteenth Amendment. As you look through the case, you will see that there is no claim about a procedural, or process, violation, but rather a suggestion that the State of New York violated the right to contract. Do you agree that there is such a "substantive" right in the Constitution?

Ronald Dworkin has suggested that he thinks that the economic theory of the Constitution at the heart of the decision in Lochner v. New York is mistaken. But defenders of this theory might argue that economic rights are an essential part of a moral reading. Indeed, the right to property and the related right to contract might be thought essential natural rights of individuals. If we conceive of U.S. Supreme Court Justice Rufus Peckham's theory of economic freedom as elaborated here as a moral theory, why would a moral reading of the Constitution reject it? In short, what if anything makes one moral reading better than another? As you will see, the contrast between Lochner v. New York and the case that follows, Griswold v. Connecticut, will be essential in understanding the dispute between various moral readings of the Constitution.

MR. JUSTICE PECKHAM, *after making [a] statement of the facts, delivered the opinion of the Court.*

The indictment, it will be seen, charges that the plaintiff in error violated the one hundred and tenth section of article 8, chapter 415, of the Laws of 1897, known as the labor law of the State of New York, in that he wrongfully and unlawfully required and permitted an employee working for him to work more than sixty hours in one week. There is nothing in any of the opinions delivered in this case, either in the Supreme Court or the Court of Appeals of the State, which construes the section, in using the word "required," as referring to any physical force being used to obtain the labor of an employee. It is assumed that the word means nothing more than the requirement arising from voluntary contract for such labor in excess of the number of hours specified in the statute. There is no pretense in any of the opinions that the statute was intended to meet a case of involuntary labor in any form. All the opinions assume that there is no real distinction, so far as this question is concerned, between the words "required" and "permitted." The mandate of the statute that "no employee shall be required or permitted to work," is the substantial equivalent of an enactment that "no employee shall contract or agree to work," more than ten hours per day, and as there is no provision for special emergencies the statute is mandatory in all cases. It is not an act merely fixing the number of hours which shall constitute a legal day's work, but an absolute prohibition upon the employer, permitting, under any circumstances, more than ten hours work to be done in his establishment. The employee may desire to earn the extra money, which would arise from his working more than the prescribed time, but this statute forbids the employer from permitting the employee to earn it.

The statute necessarily interferes with the right of contract between the employer and employees, concerning the number of hours in which the latter may labor in the bakery of the employer. The general right to make a contract in relation to his business is part of the liberty of the individual protected by the Fourteenth Amendment of the Federal Constitution. Under that provision no State can deprive any person of life, liberty or property without due process of law. The right to purchase or to sell labor is part of the liberty protected by this amendment, unless there are circumstances which exclude the right. There are, however, certain powers, existing in the sovereignty of each State in the Union, somewhat vaguely termed police powers, the exact description and limitation of which have not been attempted by the courts. Those powers, broadly stated and without, at present, any attempt at a more specific limitation, relate to the safety, health, morals and general welfare of the public. Both property and liberty are held on such reasonable conditions as may be imposed by the governing power of the State in the exercise of those powers, and with such conditions the Fourteenth Amendment was not designed to interfere.

The State, therefore, has power to prevent the individual from making certain kinds of contracts, and in regard to them the Federal Constitution offers no protection. If the contract be one which the State, in the legitimate exercise of its police power, has the right to prohibit, it is not prevented from prohibiting it by the Fourteenth Amendment. Contracts in violation of a statute, either of the Federal or state government, or a contract to let one's property for immoral purposes, or to do any other unlawful act, could obtain no protection from the Federal Constitution, as coming under the liberty of person or of free contract. Therefore, when the State, by its legislature, in the assumed exercise of its police powers, has passed an act which seriously limits the right to labor or the right of contract in regard to their means of livelihood between persons who are sui juris (both employer and employee), it becomes of great importance to determine which shall prevail—the right of the individual to labor for such time as he may choose, or the right of the State to prevent the individual from laboring or from entering into any contract to labor, beyond a certain time prescribed by the State.

It must, of course, be conceded that there is a limit to the valid exercise of the police power by the State. There is no dispute concerning this general proposition. Otherwise the Fourteenth Amendment would have no efficacy and the legislatures of the States would have unbounded power, and it would be enough to say that any piece of legislation was enacted to conserve the morals, the health or the safety of the people; such legislation would be valid, no matter how absolutely without foundation the claim might be. The claim of the police power would be a mere pretext—become another and delusive name for the supreme sovereignty of the State to be exercised free from constitutional restraint. This is not contended for. In every case that comes before this court, therefore, where legislation of this character is concerned and where the protection of the Federal Constitution is sought, the question necessarily arises: Is this a fair, reasonable and appropriate exercise of the police power of the State, or is it an unreasonable, unnecessary and arbitrary interference with the right of the individual to his personal liberty or to enter into those contracts in relation to labor which may seem to him appropriate or necessary for the support of himself and his family? Of course the liberty of contract relating to labor includes both parties to it. The one has as much right to purchase as the other to sell labor.

This is not a question of substituting the judgment of the court for that of the legislature. If the act be within the power of the State it is valid, although the judgment of the court might be totally opposed to the enactment of such a law. But the question would still remain: Is it within the police power of the State? That question must be answered by the court.

The question whether this act is valid as a labor law, pure and simple, may be dismissed in a few words. There is no reasonable ground for interfering with the liberty of person or the right of free contract, by determining the hours of labor, in the occupation of a baker. There is no contention that bakers as a class are not equal in intelligence and capacity to men in other trades or manual occupations, or that they are not able to assert their rights and care for themselves without the protecting arm of the State, interfering with their independence of judgment and of action. They are in no sense wards of the State. Viewed in the light of a purely labor law, with no reference whatever to the question of health, we think that a law like the one before us involves neither the safety, the morals nor the welfare of the public, and that the interest of the public is not in the slightest degree affected by such an act. The law must be upheld, if at all, as a law pertaining to the health of the individual engaged in the occupation of a baker. It does not affect any other portion of the public than those who are engaged in that occupation. Clean and wholesome bread does not depend upon whether the baker works but ten hours per day or only sixty hours a week. The limitation of the hours of labor does not come within the police power on that ground.

It is a question of which of two powers or rights shall prevail—the power of the State to legislate or the right of the individual to liberty of person and freedom of contract. The mere assertion that the subject relates though but in a remote degree to the public health does not necessarily render the enactment valid. The act must have a more direct relation, as a means to an end, and the end itself must be appropriate and legitimate, before an act can be held to be valid which interferes with the general right of an individual to be free in his person and in his power to contract in relation to his own labor.

We think that there can be no fair doubt that the trade of a baker, in and of itself, is not an unhealthy one to that degree which would authorize the legislature to interfere with the right to labor, and with the right of free contract on the part of the individual, either as employer or employee. In looking through statistics regarding all trades and occupations, it may be true that the trade of a baker does not appear to be as healthy as some other trades, and is also vastly more healthy than still others. To the common understanding the trade of a baker has never been regarded as an unhealthy one. Very likely physicians would not recommend the exercise of that or of any other trade as a remedy for ill health. Some occupations are more healthy than others, but we think there are none which might not come under the power of the legislature to supervise and control the hours of working therein, if the mere fact that the occupation is not absolutely and perfectly healthy is to confer that right upon the legislative department of the Government. It might be safely affirmed that almost all occupations more or less affect the health. There must be more than the mere fact of the possible existence of some small amount of unhealthiness to warrant legislative interference with liberty. It is unfortunately true that labor, even in any department, may possibly carry with it the seeds of unhealthiness. But are we all, on that account, at the mercy of legislative majorities? A printer, a tinsmith, a locksmith, a carpenter, a cabinetmaker, a dry goods clerk, a bank's, a lawyer's or a physician's clerk, or a clerk in almost any kind of business, would all come under the power of the legislature, on this assumption. No trade, no occupation, no mode of earning one's living, could escape this all-pervading power, and the acts of the legislature in limiting the hours of labor in all employments would be valid, although such limitation might seriously cripple the ability of the laborer to support himself and his family. . . .

. . . The act is not, within any fair meaning of the term, a health law, but is an illegal interference with the rights of individuals, both employers and employees, to make contracts regarding labor upon such terms as they may think best, or which they may agree upon with the other parties to such contracts. Statutes of the nature of that under review, limiting the hours in which grown and intelligent men may labor to earn their living, are mere meddlesome interferences with the rights of the individual, and they are not saved from condemnation by the claim that they are passed in the exercise of the police power and upon the subject of the health of the individual whose rights are interfered with, unless there be some fair ground, reasonable in and of itself, to say that there is material danger to the public health or to the health of the employees, if the hours of labor are not curtailed. If this be not clearly the case the individuals, whose rights are thus made the subject of legislative interference, are under the protection of the Federal Constitution regarding their liberty of contract as well as of person; and the legislature of the State has no power to limit their right as proposed in this statute.

It was further urged on the argument that restricting the hours of labor in the case of bakers was valid because it tended to cleanliness on the part of the workers, as a man was more apt to be cleanly when not overworked, and if cleanly then his "output" was also more likely to be so. What has already been said applies with equal force to this contention. We do not admit the reasoning to be sufficient to justify the claimed right of such interference. The State in that case would assume the position of a supervisor, or pater familias, over every act of the individual, and its right of governmental interference with his hours of labor, his hours of exercise, the character thereof, and the extent to which it shall be carried would be recognized and upheld. In our judgment it is not possible in fact to discover the connection between the number of hours a baker may work in the bakery and the healthful quality of the bread made by the workman. The connection, if any exists, is too shadowy and thin to build any argument for the interference of the legislature. If the man works ten hours a day it is all right, but if ten and a half or eleven his health is in danger and his bread may be unhealthful, and, therefore, he shall not be permitted to do it. This, we think, is unreasonable and entirely arbitrary. When assertions such as we have adverted to become necessary in order to give, if possible, a plausible foundation for the contention that the law is a "health law," it gives rise to at least a suspicion that there was some other motive dominating the legislature than the purpose to subserve the public health or welfare.

CASE QUESTIONS

1. Central to this case is the claim that New York law violates the Fourteenth Amendment. But as you look through the case, you will see that there is no claim about a procedural, or process, violation, but rather a suggestion that the State of New York violated the right to contract. Do you find such a "substantive" right in the Constitution? Do you agree with John Hart Ely that substantive due process is a contradiction of terms akin to "green pastel redness"?

2. Given that Ronald Dworkin offers a substantive account of constitutional rights, does his theory commit him to endorsing the holding in this case? What might a proponent of the moral reading say in opposition to the holding in *Lochner v. New York*?

GRISWOLD v. CONNECTICUT

381 U.S. 479 (1965)

Opinion: Douglas, joined by Warren, Clark, Brennan, Goldberg
Concurrence: Goldberg, joined by Warren, Brennan
Concurrence: Harlan
Concurrence: White
Dissent: Black, joined by Stewart
Dissent: Stewart, joined by Black

As you will see in Chapter 7, the substantive due process era defined by Lochner v. New York *ended during President Franklin Roosevelt's administration in the case* West Coast Hotel Co. v. Parrish. *The doctrine lay dormant until it was revived in two concurrences in this case about the constitutionality of laws banning contraception. In what way does the opinion of Justice William O. Douglas reflect the moral reading suggested by Ronald Dworkin? In what ways does the opinion of U.S. Supreme Court Justice John Marshall Harlan II differ from the two concurring opinions, which we also include here? In what ways does the kind of reasoning illustrated by all three opinions differ from that in* Lochner v. New York? *We delve further into the legal issues of this case later in this book. For now, focus on its significance as a possible example of the moral reading of the Constitution.*

MR. JUSTICE DOUGLAS *delivered the opinion of the Court.*

Appellant Griswold is Executive Director of the Planned Parenthood League of Connecticut. Appellant Buxton is a licensed physician and a professor at the Yale Medical School who served as Medical Director for the League at its Center in New Haven—a center open and operating from November 1 to November 10, 1961, when appellants were arrested.

They gave information, instruction, and medical advice to married persons as to the means of preventing conception. They examined the wife and prescribed the best contraceptive device or material for her use. Fees were usually charged, although some couples were serviced free.

The statutes whose constitutionality is involved in this appeal are §§53-32 and 54-196 of the General Statutes of Connecticut. The former provides:

> "Any person who uses any drug, medicinal article or instrument for the purpose of preventing conception shall be fined not less than fifty dollars or imprisoned not less than sixty days nor more than one year or be both fined and imprisoned."

Section 54-196 provides:

> "Any person who assists, abets, counsels, causes, hires or commands another to commit any offense may be prosecuted and punished as if he were the principal offender."

The appellants were found guilty as accessories and fined $100 each, against the claim that the accessory statute as so applied violated the Fourteenth Amendment. The Appellate Division of the Circuit Court affirmed. The Supreme Court of Errors affirmed that judgment.

Coming to the merits, we are met with a wide range of questions that implicate the Due Process Clause of the Fourteenth Amendment. Overtones of some arguments suggest that *Lochner v. New York*, should be our guide. But we decline that invitation as we did in *West Coast Hotel Co. v. Parrish*. We do not sit as a super-legislature to determine the wisdom, need, and propriety of laws that touch economic problems, business affairs, or social conditions. This law, however, operates directly on an intimate relation of husband and wife and their physician's role in one aspect of that relation.

The association of people is not mentioned in the Constitution nor in the Bill of Rights. The right to educate a child in a school of the parents' choice—whether public or private or parochial—is also not mentioned. Nor is the right to study any particular subject or any foreign language.

Yet the First Amendment has been construed to include certain of those rights.

By *Pierce v. Society of Sisters*, supra, the right to educate one's children as one chooses is made applicable to the States by the force of the First and Fourteenth Amendments. By *Meyer v. Nebraska*, supra, the same dignity is given the right to study the German language in a private school. In other words, the State may not, consistently with the spirit of the First Amendment, contract the spectrum of available knowledge. The right of freedom of speech and press includes not only the right to utter or to print, but the right to distribute, the right to receive, the right to read and freedom of inquiry, freedom of thought, and freedom to teach indeed the freedom of the entire university community. Without those peripheral rights the specific rights would be less secure. And so we reaffirm the principle of the *Pierce* and the *Meyer* cases.

In *NAACP v. Alabama*, we protected the "freedom to associate and privacy in one's associations," noting that freedom of association was a peripheral First Amendment right. Disclosure of membership lists of a constitutionally valid association, we held, was invalid "as entailing the likelihood of a substantial restraint upon the exercise by petitioner's members of their right to freedom of association." Ibid. In other words, the First Amendment has a penumbra where privacy is protected from governmental intrusion. In like context, we have protected forms of "association" that are not political in the customary sense but pertain to the social, legal, and economic benefit of the members. The right of "association," like the right of belief, is more than the right to attend a meeting; it includes the right to express one's attitudes or philosophies by membership in a group or by affiliation with it or by other lawful means.

Association in that context is a form of expression of opinion; and while it is not expressly included in the First Amendment its existence is necessary in making the express guarantees fully meaningful.

The foregoing cases suggest that specific guarantees in the Bill of Rights have penumbras, formed by emanations from those guarantees that help give them life and substance. Various guarantees create zones of privacy. The right of association contained in the penumbra of the First Amendment is one, as we have seen. The Third Amendment in its prohibition against the quartering of soldiers "in any house" in time of peace without the consent of the owner is another facet of that privacy. The Fourth Amendment explicitly affirms the "right of the people to be secure in their persons, houses, papers, and effects, against unreasonable searches and seizures." The Fifth Amendment in its Self-Incrimination Clause enables the citizen to create a zone of privacy which government may not force him to surrender to his detriment. The Ninth Amendment provides: "The enumeration in the Constitution, of certain rights, shall not be construed to deny or disparage others retained by the people."

The present case, then, concerns a relationship lying within the zone of privacy created by several fundamental constitutional guarantees. And it concerns a law which, in forbidding the use of contraceptives rather than regulating their manufacture or sale, seeks to achieve its goals by means having a maximum destructive impact upon that relationship. Such a law cannot stand in light of the familiar principle, so often applied by this Court, that a "governmental purpose to control or prevent activities constitutionally subject to state regulation may not be achieved by means which sweep unnecessarily broadly and thereby invade the area of protected freedoms." Would we allow the police to search the sacred precincts of marital bedrooms for telltale signs of the use of contraceptives? The very idea is repulsive to the notions of privacy surrounding the marriage relationship.

We deal with a right of privacy older than the Bill of Rights—older than our political parties, older than our school system. Marriage is a coming together for better or for worse, hopefully enduring, and intimate to the degree of being sacred. It is an association that promotes a way of life, not causes; a harmony in living, not political faiths; a bilateral loyalty, not commercial or social projects. Yet it is an association for as noble a purpose as any involved in our prior decisions.

MR. JUSTICE GOLDBERG, *whom* **THE CHIEF JUSTICE** *and* **MR. JUSTICE BRENNAN** *join, concurring.*

I agree with the Court that Connecticut's birth-control law unconstitutionally intrudes upon the right of marital privacy, and I join in its opinion and judgment. Although I have not accepted the view that "due process" as used in the Fourteenth Amendment incorporates all of the first eight amendments, I do agree that the concept of liberty protects those personal rights that are fundamental, and is not confined to the specific terms of the Bill of Rights. My conclusion that the concept of liberty is not so restricted and that it embraces the right of marital privacy though that right is not mentioned explicitly in the Constitution is supported both by numerous decisions of this Court, referred to in the Court's opinion, and by the language and history of the Ninth Amendment. In reaching the conclusion that the right of marital privacy is protected, as being within the protected penumbra of specific guarantees of the Bill of Rights, the Court refers to the Ninth Amendment. I add these words to emphasize the relevance of that amendment to the Court's holding.

... The language and history of the Ninth Amendment reveal that the Framers of the Constitution believed that there are additional fundamental rights, protected from governmental infringement, which exist alongside those fundamental rights specifically mentioned in the first eight constitutional amendments.

... To hold that a right so basic and fundamental and so deep-rooted in our society as the right of privacy in marriage may be infringed because that right is not guaranteed in so many words by the first eight amendments to the Constitution is to ignore the Ninth Amendment and to give it no effect whatsoever. Moreover, a judicial construction that this fundamental right is not protected by the Constitution because it is not mentioned in explicit terms by one of the first eight amendments or elsewhere in the Constitution would violate the Ninth Amendment, which specifically states that "the enumeration in the Constitution, of certain rights, shall not be construed to deny or disparage others retained by the people."

A dissenting opinion suggests that my interpretation of the Ninth Amendment somehow "broaden[s] the powers of this Court." With all due respect, I believe that it misses the import of what I am saying. ... [T]his Court has held, often unanimously, that the Fifth and Fourteenth Amendments protect certain fundamental personal liberties from abridgment by the Federal Government or the States. The Ninth Amendment simply shows the intent of the Constitution's authors that other fundamental personal rights should not be denied such protection or disparaged in any other way simply because they are not specifically listed in the first eight constitutional amendments. I do not see how this broadens the authority of the Court; rather it serves to support what this Court has been doing in protecting fundamental rights.

In determining which rights are fundamental, judges are not left at large to decide cases in light of their personal and private notions. Rather, they must look to the "traditions and [collective] conscience of our people" to determine whether a principle is "so rooted [there] ... as to be ranked as fundamental." The inquiry is whether a right involved "is of such a character that it cannot be denied without violating those 'fundamental principles of liberty and justice which lie at the base of all our civil and political institutions'. ... ." "Liberty" also "gains content from the emanations of ... specific [constitutional] guarantees" and "from experience with the requirements of a free society."

I agree fully with the Court that, applying these tests, the right of privacy is a fundamental personal right, emanating "from the totality of the constitutional scheme under which we live."

The entire fabric of the Constitution and the purposes that clearly underlie its specific guarantees demonstrate that the rights to marital privacy and to marry and raise a family are of similar order and magnitude as the fundamental rights specifically protected.

Although the Constitution does not speak in so many words of the right of privacy in marriage, I cannot believe that it offers these fundamental rights no protection. The fact that no particular provision of the Constitution explicitly forbids the State from disrupting the traditional relation of the family—a relation as old and as fundamental as our entire civilization—surely does not show that the Government was meant to have the power to do so. Rather, as the Ninth Amendment expressly recognizes, there are fundamental personal rights such as this one, which are protected from abridgment by the Government though not specifically mentioned in the Constitution.

The logic of the dissents would sanction federal or state legislation that seems to me even more plainly unconstitutional than the statute before us. Surely the Government, absent a showing of a compelling subordinating state interest, could not decree that all husbands and wives must be sterilized after two children have been born to them. Yet by their reasoning such an invasion of marital privacy would not be subject to constitutional challenge because, while it might be "silly," no provision of the Constitution specifically prevents the Government from curtailing the marital right to bear children and raise a family. While it may shock some of my Brethren that the Court today holds that the Constitution protects the right of marital privacy, in my view it is far more shocking to believe that the personal liberty guaranteed by the Constitution does not include protection against such totalitarian limitation of family size, which is at complete variance with our constitutional concepts. Yet, if upon a showing of a slender basis of rationality, a law outlawing voluntary birth control by married persons is valid, then, by the same reasoning, a law requiring compulsory birth control also would seem to be valid. In my view, however, both types of law would unjustifiably intrude upon rights of marital privacy which are constitutionally protected.

Although the Connecticut birth-control law obviously encroaches upon a fundamental personal liberty, the State does not show that the law serves any "subordinating [state] interest which is compelling" or that it is "necessary . . . to the accomplishment of a permissible state policy." The State, at most, argues that there is some rational relation between this statute and what is admittedly a legitimate subject of state concern—the discouraging of extra-marital relations. It says that preventing the use of birth-control devices by married persons helps prevent the indulgence by some in such extra-marital relations. The rationality of this justification is dubious, particularly in light of the admitted widespread availability to all persons in the State of Connecticut, unmarried as well as married, of birth-control devices for the prevention of disease, as distinguished from the prevention of conception. But, in any event, it is clear that the state interest in safeguarding marital fidelity can be served by a more discriminately tailored statute, which does not, like the present one, sweep unnecessarily broadly, reaching far beyond the evil sought to be dealt with and intruding upon the privacy of all married couples. Here, as elsewhere, "precision of regulation must be the touchstone in an area so closely touching our most precious freedoms."

MR. JUSTICE HARLAN, *concurring in the judgment.*

I fully agree with the judgment of reversal, but find myself unable to join the Court's opinion. The reason is that it seems to me to evince an approach to this case very much like that taken by my Brothers Black and Stewart in dissent, namely: the Due Process Clause of the Fourteenth Amendment does not touch this Connecticut statute unless the enactment is found to violate some right assured by the letter or penumbra of the Bill of Rights.

In other words, what I find implicit in the Court's opinion is that the "incorporation" doctrine may be used to restrict the reach of Fourteenth Amendment Due Process. For me, this is just as unacceptable constitutional doctrine as is the use of the "incorporation" approach to impose upon the States all the requirements of the Bill of Rights as found in the provisions of the first eight amendments and in the decisions of this Court interpreting them. . . .

In my view, the proper constitutional inquiry in this case is whether this Connecticut statute infringes the Due Process Clause of the Fourteenth Amendment because the enactment violates basic values "implicit in the concept of ordered liberty." *Palko v. Connecticut*. For reasons stated at length in my dissenting opinion in *Poe v. Ullman*, supra, I believe that it does. While the relevant inquiry may be aided by resort to one or more of the provisions of the Bill of Rights, it is not dependent on them or any of their radiations. The Due Process Clause of the Fourteenth Amendment stands, in my opinion, on its own bottom.

A further observation seems in order respecting the justification of my Brothers Black and Stewart for their "incorporation" approach to this case. Their approach does not rest on historical reasons, which are, of course, wholly lacking, but on the thesis that, by limiting the content of the Due Process Clause of the Fourteenth Amendment to the protection of rights which can be found elsewhere in the Constitution, in this instance, in the Bill of Rights, judges will thus be confined to "interpretation" of specific constitutional provisions, and will thereby be restrained from introducing their own notions of constitutional right and wrong into the "vague contours of the Due Process Clause." *Rochin v. California*. While I could not more

heartily agree that judicial "self-restraint" is an indispensable ingredient of sound constitutional adjudication, I do submit that the formula suggested for achieving it is more hollow than real. "Specific" provisions of the Constitution, no less than "due process," lend themselves as readily to "personal" interpretations by judges whose constitutional outlook is simply to keep the Constitution in supposed "tune with the times."

Judicial self-restraint will not, I suggest, be brought about in the "due process" area by the historically unfounded incorporation formula long advanced by my Brother Black, and now in part espoused by my Brother Stewart. It will be achieved in this area, as in other constitutional areas, only by continual insistence upon respect for the teachings of history, solid recognition of the basic values that underlie our society, and wise appreciation of the great roles that the doctrines of federalism and separation of powers have played in establishing and preserving American freedoms. Adherence to these principles will not, of course, obviate all constitutional differences of opinion among judges, nor should it. Their continued recognition will, however, go farther toward keeping most judges from roaming at large in the constitutional field than will the interpolation into the Constitution of an artificial and largely illusory restriction on the content of the Due Process Clause.

CASE QUESTIONS

1. U.S. Supreme Court Justice Arthur Goldberg cites the Ninth Amendment in what might be referred to as a "non-textualist" interpretation of the Constitution. Is Justice Goldberg's

appeal to the Ninth Amendment as a defense of the right to contraception sound?

2. Though this case and *Lochner v. New York* are similar, the Constitution's text explicitly prevents the states from "impairing the obligation of contracts." Nowhere does it mention

contraception, privacy, or reproductive rights. Does this put *Lochner v. New York* on stronger footing when it comes to claiming the existence of a moral principle in the Constitution? Is it irrelevant? If not, does Justice William O. Douglas convincingly overcome this difficulty?

SYNTHESIS QUESTIONS FOR FURTHER DISCUSSION: CHAPTER 2 SECTION C

1. In a debate with Justice Antonin Scalia, Ronald Dworkin once claimed that he too was an originalist because the original intent of the Framers was for the broad and expansive language of these clauses to be interpreted broadly and based on a moral argument. Can Dworkin be considered as originalist as Justice Scalia? More originalist? What does this suggest about the way we should understand the penumbra argument in *Griswold v. Connecticut*? Would Dworkin's version of originalism rely on intent or public meaning of the text?

2. Like John Hart Ely, Dworkin also claims to offer a democratic reading of the Constitution. In his view, however, democracy should be understood as entailing substantive, not just procedural, commitments. In particular, democratic societies protect basic rights, such as privacy, not simply equal participation in the democratic process. According to Dworkin, when the Court protects basic rights, such as the right to contraception, it has a claim to be acting democratically even though such rights are not obviously part of the democratic process. Is it correct to claim that democracy is not just about process but about basic rights as well? Does this argument answer the "counter-majoritarian difficulty" raised by Alexander Bickel in the previous chapter?

3. One complaint that proceduralists such as Ely, as well as originalists such as Justice Scalia, have leveled against theories that would combine substantive morality and judicial interpretation is that they open the door for the judge to impose his or her own moral view in a case. Ely once famously quipped that such theories would lead to judges merely appealing to their favorite political philosopher, following this kind of confrontation: "*We* like Rawls, *you* like Nozick. We win, 6-3. Statute invalidated" (John Hart Ely, Democracy and Distrust, 1980, p. 58). This caricature taps into

concerns about "judicial activism" common in the public dialogue about the role of the Court. Dworkin himself holds the view that the Constitution has a distinct morality to which judges should appeal regardless of whether they personally share that morality. Sometimes the worry about judges imposing their own morality is described as a threat of an overly "activist" judiciary. But would a moral reading be more activist than originalism or process theory in the sense that it would result in the striking down of more laws?

D. PRAGMATISM AND CONSEQUENTIALISM

We turn now to consider a theory of constitutional interpretation that emphasizes the importance of concrete facts over abstract principles. Justice Oliver Wendell Holmes, whose dissent in *Lochner v. New York* is often thought to define this tradition, is in many ways the founder of this theory of constitutional interpretation. This constitutional approach has many modern defenders as well, including Judge Richard Posner and Cass Sunstein.

According to Justice Holmes's dissent in *Lochner v. New York*, the majority was incorrect because it attempted to impose a political and moral theory on the Court. While Justice Holmes himself was sympathetic to the philosopher Herbert Spencer, he especially admonished the majority for using Spencer's theory in interpreting the Constitution. The problem with *Lochner v. New York*'s majority opinion, Justice Holmes argued, was that it failed to recognize that law should begin by considering concrete matters of policy grounded in the actual empirical facts before it. The question before the Court should not be what a particular theory of morality, or what a particular political theory, demands, but rather what the right response to a particular policy dilemma should be. Justice Holmes's pragmatism lies in his rejection of all-encompassing moral or legal theories and his embrace of practical problems.

Following in Justice Holmes's tradition, Judge Posner attempts in the following piece to define pragmatism. Like Justice Holmes, Judge Posner thinks it is important to consider empirical evidence about the impact of any particular decision concerning public policy. To take empirical considerations into account, Judge Posner argues, we must look closely at the facts before the Court. One useful contrast here might be between Judge Posner's view and originalism. While originalism focuses on fidelity to *past* decisions, Judge Posner's view emphasizes the importance of efficient decision-making for the *future*. Moreover, unlike Ronald Dworkin, Judge Posner does not believe that his concern for good future consequences requires a moral reading of the Constitution.

Like Judge Posner, Sunstein also considers himself a pragmatist. He offers a distinct understanding of this view in the passage we include. Drawing on the insights of both Justice Holmes and Judge Posner, he argues that Supreme

Court justices should not presuppose one theory of interpretation. He defends an idea of "incompletely theorized" agreements. According to Sunstein, it is important to recognize that judicial decision-making is a group process; therefore, the pragmatics of compromise are essential in achieving goals as a member of the Court. He argues that rather than trying to impose a particular judicial philosophy on one another, the justices should bracket their particular theories and come together to decide policy in a way that is beneficial to the polity and litigants.

Although we group Judge Posner and Sunstein together, it is also interesting to pay attention to their differences. For instance, you might ask whether Judge Posner need adopt Sunstein's emphasis on decision-making as a group process that requires pragmatism. In addition to the dissent of Justice Holmes in *Lochner v. New York*, we also include Justice Stephen Breyer's dissent in the case of *District of Columbia v. Heller*. You have already seen why *District of Columbia v. Heller*, in its announcement of a Second Amendment right to gun ownership by individuals, is an example of originalist jurisprudence. In resisting this decision, the dissent included here draws on matters of policy in a way recommended by pragmatists. Do you agree with the dissent that the majority opinion is over-theorized and should instead be decided more along the lines recommended by pragmatist theory?

Judge   Richard   Posner

AGAINST CONSTITUTIONAL THEORY

73 N.Y.U. L. Rev. 1 (1998)

Constitutional theory, as I shall use the term, is the effort to develop a generally accepted theory to guide the interpretation of the Constitution of the United States. It is distinct on the one hand from inquiries of a social scientific character into the nature, provenance, and consequences of constitutionalism—the sort of thing one associates mainly with historians and political scientists . . . and on the other hand from commentary on specific cases and doctrines, the sort of thing one associates with legal doctrinalists. . . . Constitutional theorists are normativists; their theories are meant to influence the way judges decide difficult constitutional cases; when the theorists are law-trained, as most of them are, they cannot resist telling their readers which cases they think were decided consistently with or contrary to their theory. Most constitutional theorists, indeed, believe in social reform through judicial action.

Constitutional theory in the sense in which I am using the term is at least as old as the Federalist papers. And yet after more than two centuries no signs of closure or even, it seems to me, of progress, are visible. The reason is that constitutional theory has no power to command agreement from people not already predisposed to accept the theorist's policy prescriptions. It has no power partly because it is normative, partly because interpretation, the subject of constitutional theory, is not susceptible of theoretical resolution, and partly because normativists . . . do not like to be backed into a corner by committing themselves to a theory that might be falsified by data. . . . [C]onstitutional theory, while often rhetorically powerful, lacks the agreement-coercing power of the best natural and social science.

An even more serious problem is that constitutional theory is not responsive to, and indeed tends to occlude, the greatest need of constitutional adjudicators, which is the need for empirical knowledge. . . . I know that just getting the facts right can't decide a case. There has to be an analytic framework to fit the facts into; without it they can have no normative significance. Only I don't think that constitutional theory can supply that framework. Nor that the design of the framework, as distinct from fitting the facts into it, is the big problem in constitutional law today. The big problem is not lack of theory, but lack of knowledge—lack of the very knowledge that academic research, rather than the litigation process, is best designed to produce. But it is a different kind of research from what constitutional theorists conduct.

The problem in political theory to which constitutional theory is offered as a solution is that our judicially enforceable Constitution gives the judges an unusual amount of power. This was seen as problematic long before the democratic principle became as central to our concept of government as it is now. Hamilton's solution to the problem, drawing on what was already an age-old formalist tradition stretching back to Cicero and

shortly to be echoed by John Marshall, was to assert that it was the law that was supreme, not the judges, since judges are (in Blackstone's phrase, but it is also Hamilton's sense) just the oracles, the mouthpieces, of the law.

After a century of judicial willfulness, this position was difficult to maintain with a straight face. The Constitution had obviously made the judges a competing power center. James Bradley Thayer argued in the 1890s that this was bad because it sapped the other branches of government of initiative and responsibility. He urged courts to enforce a constitutional right only when the existence of the right, as a matter of constitutional interpretation, was clear beyond a reasonable doubt. He thought, in other words, that the erroneous grant of a constitutional right was a more serious error than the erroneous denial of such a right, in just the same way that the criminal justice system assumes that the erroneous conviction of an innocent person is a more serious error than the erroneous acquittal of a guilty person. But Thayer didn't explain where he had gotten his weighting of constitutional errors or why it was the correct weighting.

Thayer is the father of the "outrage" school of constitutional interpretation, whose most notable practitioner was Holmes. Holmes's position was not identical to Thayer's; nor were Cardozo's and Frankfurter's positions identical to Holmes's, though there are broad affinities among all four. This school teaches that to be justified in trying to stymie the elected branches of government it shouldn't be enough that the litigant claiming a constitutional right has the better of the argument; it has to be a lot better; the alleged violation of the Constitution has to be certain (Thayer's position), or stomach-turning (Holmes's "puke" test), or shocking to the conscience (Frankfurter's test), or, a synthesis of the positions (one supported by Holmes's dissent in *Lochner*), the sort of thing no reasonable person could defend. The school of outrage is almost interchangeable with the doctrine of judicial self-restraint when that doctrine is understood as seeking to minimize the occasions on which the courts annul the actions of other branches of government. The judge who is self-restrained in this sense wishes to take a back seat to the other branches of government, but is stirred to action if his sense of justice is sufficiently outraged.

I own to considerable sympathy with this way of approaching constitutional issues. And when the outrage approach is tied, as I have just suggested it can be, to the doctrine of judicial self-restraint—a doctrine that is founded on reasons—the approach is no longer so purely visceral as my initial description may have suggested. But I cannot pretend that outrage or even self-restraint furnishes much in the way of guidance to courts grappling with difficult issues. And I could defend the approach convincingly only by showing, what may be impossible as a practical matter to do, that decisions invalidating statutes or other official actions as unconstitutional, when the decision could not have been justified under Thayer's or Holmes's or Cardozo's or Frankfurter's approach, have done more harm than good.

Hamilton-style formalism now has a defender in Justice Scalia. But he lacks the courage of his convictions. For he takes extreme libertarian positions with respect to such matters as affirmative action and freedom of speech on the ground that these positions are dictated not by the Constitution but by the cases interpreting the Constitution. Take away the adventitious operation of stare decisis and Scalia is left with a body of constitutional law of remarkable meagerness—which is not an objection but which requires a greater effort at justification than he has been able to offer. Indeed he has offered little by way of justification other than bromides about democracy. Complaining that the Supreme Court is undemocratic begs the question. The Court is part of the Constitution, which in its inception was rich in undemocratic features, such as the indirect election of the President and of the Senate, and a highly restricted franchise. The Constitution still has major undemocratic features. They include the method of apportionment of the Senate, which results in weighting the votes of people in sparsely populated states much more heavily than the votes of people in densely populated states; the election of the President on the basis of electoral rather than popular votes, which could result in the election of a candidate who had lost the popular vote; the expansion of constitutional rights brought about by the Bill of Rights and the Fourteenth Amendment, which curtails the powers of the elected branches of government; and, of course, lifetime appointment of federal judges who exercise considerable political power by virtue of the expansion of rights to which I just referred. The Supreme Court is certainly undemocratic in a sense, but not in a sense that makes it anomalous in the political system created by the Constitution, given the other "undemocratic" features that I have mentioned. A further drawback to Scalia's approach is that it requires judges to be political theorists, so that they know what "democracy" is, and also to be historians, because it takes a historian to reconstruct the original meaning of centuries-old documents.

Most constitutional theorizing in this century has taken a nonformalistic direction, unlike that of a Hamilton or a Scalia. . . . Leading candidates include John Hart Ely's principle of "representation reinforcement" and Ronald Dworkin's principle of egalitarian natural justice. These are substantive political principles, and they founder on the authors' lack of steady interest in and firm grasp of the details of public policy. . . . People who devote most of their lives to the study of political theory and constitutional doctrine do not thereby equip themselves to formulate substantive principles designed to guide decision-making across the vast range of difficult issues that spans affirmative action and exclusionary zoning, legislative apportionment and prison administration, telecommunications and euthanasia, the education of alien children and the administration of capital punishment, to name just a few current and recent issues in constitutional law.

I would like to see an entirely different kind of constitutional theorizing. It would set itself the difficult—although, from the perspective of today's theorists, the intellectually modest—task of exploring the operation and consequences of constitutionalism. It would ask such questions as, what difference has it made for press freedom and police practices in the United States compared to England that we have a judicially enforceable Bill of Rights and England does not? How influenced are judges in constitutional cases by public opinion? How influenced is public opinion by constitutional decisions? Are constitutional issues becoming more complex,

and if so, what are the courts doing to keep abreast of the complexities? Does intrusive judicial review breed constitutionally dubious statutes by enabling legislators to shift political hot potatoes to the courts? What is the effect of judicial activism on judicial workloads and is there a feedback loop here, activism producing heavy workloads that in turn cause the judges to become restrained in order to reduce the number of cases and thus alleviate the workload pressures? Does the Court try to prevent the formation of interest groups that might obtain constitutional amendments that would curtail the Court's power or abrogate some of its doctrines, or to encourage the formation of interest groups that will defend the Court's prerogatives? And what role do interest groups play in constitution-making and -amending? In the appointment of Supreme Court Justices? In the reception of Supreme Court decisions by the media and through the media the public? Above all, what are the actual and likely effects of particular decisions and doctrines? Did *Brown v. Board of Education* improve the education of blacks? Did *Roe v. Wade* retard abortion law reform at the state level? What effect have the apportionment cases had on public policy? Did the Warren Court's decisions expanding the constitutional rights of criminal defendants contribute to the increase in the crime rate in the 1960s and 1970s and provoke a legislative backlash, increasing the severity of sentences? These questions have not been entirely ignored, but the literature on them is meager, and law professors have contributed very little to it. Exploring these questions would be a more fruitful use of academic time and brains than continuing the 200-hundred-year-old game of political rhetoricizing that we call constitutional theory. Some of these questions might actually be answerable, and the answers would alter constitutional practice more than theorizing has done or can do. Thus I am in radical disagreement with Dworkin, who insists that cases in which facts or consequences matter to sound constitutional decisionmaking are "rare."

I am not advocating the transformation of litigation into a setting for generating or marshaling social scientific data and for testing social scientific hypotheses. The capability of the courts to conduct scientific or social scientific research is extremely limited, and perhaps nil. But their assimilative powers are greater. I would like to see the legal professoriate redirect its research and teaching efforts toward fuller participation in the enterprise of social science, and by doing this make social science a better aid to judges' understanding of the social problems that get thrust at them in the form of constitutional issues. What the judges should do until the professoriate accepts this challenge and makes real progress in the study of race relations, sexual activity, euthanasia, education theory, and the other areas of social life that are generating constitutional issues these days is an issue that I shall defer until I have explained what seem to me to be the unfortunate consequences of judicial ignorance of the social realities behind the issues with which they grapple.

It is the lack of an empirical footing that is and always has been the Achilles heel of constitutional law, not the lack of a good constitutional theory. But this raises the question of what the courts are to do in difficult constitutional cases when their ignorance is irremediable, though one hopes only temporarily so. Judges don't yet know enough about the role of women in the military, or about the causes of homosexual orientation, to base decisions in cases such as *Romer* and *VMI* on the answers to these empirical questions. Inevitably, the judge's vote in such a case will turn on his values and temperament. Those judges who believe (a belief likely to reflect a judge's values and temperament rather than a theory of judicial review) in judicial self-restraint, in the sense of wanting to minimize the occasions on which the courts annul the actions of other branches of government, will consider ignorance of the consequences of a challenged governmental policy that is not completely outrageous a compelling reason for staying the judicial hand in the absence of sure guidance from constitutional text, history, or precedent. (An important qualification: many constitutional issues can be resolved on the basis of these conventional legal materials.) Activists will plow ahead. These poles will not meet until much more is known about the consequences of judicial activism and judicial self-restraint. So one thing that we may hope for through the application of the methods of scientific theory and empirical inquiry to constitutional law is the eventual accumulation of enough knowledge to enable judges at least to deal sensibly with their uncertainty about the consequences of their decisions. Ultimately many of the uncertainties may be dispelled. Until that happy day arrives, the most we can realistically ask of the judges is that they be mindful of the limitations of their knowledge. And I do not mean knowledge of constitutional theory.

Cass Sunstein

INCOMPLETELY THEORIZED AGREEMENTS

108 Harv. L. Rev. 1733 (1995)

The problem of social pluralism pervades the legal system. Some of the relevant disagreements are explicitly religious in character. Others might be described as quasi-religious in the sense that they involve people's deepest and most defining commitments. What is the appropriate conception of liberty and equality? How should people educate their children? Should government punish people on the basis of deterrence only or should it consider retribution as well? Is the free speech principle about democracy or instead individual autonomy?

There is much dispute about whether well-functioning democracies should try to resolve such disagreements, and about how they should do so if they do try. Perhaps government should seek an "overlapping consensus" among reasonable people, thus allowing agreements to be made among Kantians, utilitarians, Aristotelians, and others. Perhaps participants in a liberal democracy can agree on the right even if they disagree on the good. Thus a sympathetic observer describes the liberal "hope that we can achieve social unity in a democracy through shared commitment to abstract principles."

This is a promising approach, and in some settings, it may work. But an investigation of actual democracy, and of law in actual democracies, raises questions about this view. Democracies—and law in democracies—must deal with people who very much disagree on the right as well as the good. Democracies—and law in democracies—must deal with people who tend to distrust abstractions altogether. Participants in law are

no exception. Judges are certainly not ordinary citizens. But neither are they philosophers. Indeed, participants in law may be unwilling to commit themselves to large-scale theories of any kind, and they will likely disagree with one another if they seek to agree on such theories.

Judges also have to decide many cases, and they have to decide them quickly. Decisions must be made rapidly in the face of apparently intractable social disagreements on a wide range of first principles. These disagreements will be reflected within the judiciary and other adjudicative institutions as well as within the citizenry at large. At least this is so if adjudicative institutions include, as they should, some of the range of views that are included in society generally.

In addition to facing the pressures of time, these diverse people must find a way to continue to live with one another. They should also show each other a high degree of mutual respect and reciprocity. Mutual respect may well entail a reluctance to attack one another's most basic or defining commitments, at least if it is not necessary to do so in order to decide particular controversies. Participants in law, even more than in democratic debate generally, do well to follow this counsel.

My suggestion in this Commentary is that well-functioning legal systems often tend to adopt a special strategy for producing agreement amidst pluralism. Participants in legal controversies try to produce incompletely theorized agreements on particular outcomes. They agree on the result and on relatively narrow or low-level explanations for it. They need not agree on fundamental principle. They do not offer larger or more abstract explanations than are necessary to decide the case. When they disagree on an abstraction, they move to a level of greater particularity. The distinctive feature of this account is that it emphasizes agreement on (relative) particulars rather than on (relative) abstractions. This is an important source of social stability and an important way for diverse people to demonstrate mutual respect, in law especially but also in liberal democracy as a whole.

. . . People may believe that it is important to protect endangered species, while having quite diverse theories of why this is so. . . . So too, people may favor a rule of strict liability for certain torts from diverse starting points, with some people rooting their judgments in economic efficiency, others in distributive goals, and still others in conceptions of basic rights. . . . Complete agreement is unlikely in matters of this sort. Disagreement on foundations may produce disagreement on particulars. . . .

When the convergence on particular outcomes is incompletely theorized, it is because the relevant actors are clear on the result without being clear, either in their own minds or on paper, on the most general theory that accounts for it.

Often judges can agree on an opinion or rationale offering low-level or mid-level principles and taking a relatively narrow line. They may agree that a particular rule is binding and makes sense—a sixty-five mile-per-hour speed limit, a requirement that people be provided a hearing before losing their homes—without agreeing on or entirely understanding any set of purported foundations for their belief. They may accept an outcome—reaffirming *Roe v. Wade*, protecting sexually explicit art—without knowing or converging on an ultimate ground for that acceptance.

Reasons are almost always offered, and in this sense something in the way of abstraction accompanies the outcome; reasons are by definition more abstract than the outcome for which they account. But the relevant actors seek to stay at the lowest level of abstraction necessary for the decision of the case. They hope that the reasons that have been offered are compatible with an array of deeper possible reasons, and they refuse to make a choice among those deeper reasons if it is not necessary to do so. . . .

It is customary to lament an outcome that has not been completely theorized, on the ground that any such outcome has been inadequately justified; but there are special advantages to incompletely theorized agreements in law (and elsewhere). Such agreements are especially well suited to the institutional limits of the judiciary, which is composed in significant part of multimember bodies, consisting in turn of highly diverse people who must render many decisions, live together, avoid error to the extent possible, and show each other mutual respect.

Incompletely theorized agreements play a pervasive role in law and society. It is rare for a person, and especially for a group, to theorize any subject completely—that is, to accept both a highly abstract theory and a series of steps that relate the theory to a concrete conclusion. In fact, people often reach incompletely theorized agreements on a general principle. Such agreements are incompletely theorized in the sense that people who accept the principle need not agree on what it entails in particular cases. People know that murder is wrong, but they disagree about abortion. They favor racial equality, but they are divided on affirmative action. Hence there is a familiar phenomenon of a comfortable and even emphatic agreement on a general principle, accompanied by sharp disagreement about particular cases.

This sort of agreement is incompletely theorized in the sense that it is incompletely specified—a familiar phenomenon with constitutional provisions and regulatory standards in administrative law. Incompletely specified agreements have distinctive social uses. They may permit acceptance of a general aspiration when people are unclear about what the aspiration means, and in this sense, they can maintain a measure of both stability and flexibility over time. At the same time, they can conceal the fact of large-scale social disagreement about particular cases.

There is a second and quite different kind of incompletely theorized agreement. People may agree on a mid-level principle but disagree both about the more general theory that accounts for it and about outcomes in particular cases. They may believe that government cannot discriminate on the basis of race, without settling on a large-scale theory of equality, and without agreeing whether government may enact affirmative action programs or segregate prisons when racial tensions are severe. The connections are left unclear, either in people's minds or in authoritative public documents, between the mid-level principle and general theory; the connection is equally unclear between the mid-level principle and concrete cases. So too, people may think that government may not regulate speech unless it can show a clear and present danger, but fail to settle whether this principle is founded in utilitarian or Kantian considerations, and disagree about whether the principle allows government to regulate a particular speech by members of the Ku Klux Klan.

My special interest here is in a third kind of phenomenon—incompletely theorized agreements on particular outcomes, accompanied by agreements on the low-level principles that account for them. These terms contain some ambiguities. There is no algorithm by which to distinguish between a high-level theory and one that operates at an intermediate or low level. We might consider Kantianism and utilitarianism as conspicuous examples of high-level theories and see legal illustrations in the many (academic) efforts to understand such areas as tort law, contract law, free speech, and the law of equality to be undergirded by highly abstract theories of the right or the good. By contrast, we might think of low-level principles as including most of the ordinary material of legal doctrine—the general class of principles and justifications that are not said to derive from any particular large theories of the right or the good, that have ambiguous relations to large theories, and that are compatible with more than one such theory.

By the term "particular outcome," I mean the judgment about who wins and who loses a case. By the term "low-level principles," I refer to something relative, not absolute; a principle is low-level only when compared to more abstract alternatives. I also mean the terms "theories" and "abstractions" (which I use interchangeably) in a relative sense: the notions "low-level," "high-level," and "abstract" are best understood as comparative, like the terms "big" and "unusual." The "clear and present danger" test is abstract when compared with the judgment that members of the Nazi Party may march in Skokie, Illinois, but the test is relatively particular when compared with the constitutional abstraction "freedom of speech." The idea of "freedom of speech" is relatively abstract when measured against the notion that campaign finance laws are acceptable, but the same idea is less abstract than the grounds that justify free speech, such as the principle of autonomy. The notion of a completely theorized judgment can be understood in the abstract: it refers to a judgment on a particular set of facts combined with all relevant vertical and horizontal judgments, as in a judgment in a free speech case accompanied by an understanding of all other free speech cases, or perhaps of all cases, and of all principles, at all levels of generality, that explain or justify that judgment.

What I am emphasizing here is that when people diverge on some (relatively) high-level proposition, they might be able to agree if they lower the level of abstraction. People are sometimes able to converge on a point of less generality than the point at which agreement is difficult or impossible. In law, the point of agreement is often highly particularized—absolutely as well as relatively—in the sense that it involves a specific outcome and a set of reasons that typically do not venture far from the case at hand.

As I have said, reasons are, by their very nature, more abstract than the outcome for which they account. In analogical thinking, a judge cannot go from one particular to another; it is necessary to identify a principle or a reason to unify or separate the particulars. To the extent that law prizes reason-giving, it contains an impulse toward abstraction. Full particularity is rare. What I am emphasizing is the lawyer's impulse to offer reasons on which people can unite from widely diverse foundations.

Perhaps the participants in law endorse no high-level theory, or perhaps they believe that no such theory is yet available. Perhaps they find theoretical disputes irrelevant, confusing, or annoying. Perhaps they think that it is unnecessary to select a theory, because a certain outcome follows whatever theory they choose. Perhaps they disagree with one another as they enter into high-level debates. What is critical is that they agree on how a case must come out and on a low-level justification.

The argument emphatically applies to legal rules, whether set down by judges, legislators, or administrators. Legal rules are typically incompletely theorized in the sense that they can be accepted by people who disagree on many general issues. People may agree that a sixty-five mile-per-hour speed limit makes sense, and that it applies to defendant Jones, without having much of a theory about criminal punishment, and without making judgments about the domain of utilitarianism and the scope of paternalism. A key social function of rules is to allow people to agree on the meaning, authority, and even the soundness of a governing legal provision in the face of disagreements about much else. Much the same can be said about other devices found in the legal culture, including standards, factors, and emphatically analogical reasoning. Indeed, all of the lawyer's conventional tools can allow the achievement of incompletely theorized agreements on particular outcomes, though in interestingly different ways.

It should now be clear that I am especially concerned with the use of ambitious thinking to produce "depth"—full accounts of the foundations of a decision, in the form of attempts to find ever deeper reasons behind the outcome. Incompletely theorized agreements do not offer such accounts. But such agreements also fail along the dimension of "width"—that is, they do not try to rationalize the law by showing how an outcome in one case fits coherently with particular outcomes in the full range of other cases. Judges, of course, attempt to produce local coherence, especially through reasoning by analogy. But they do not try for global coherence.

It seems clear that people may converge on a correct outcome even though they do not have a full account for their judgments. Jones may know that dropped objects fall, that bee stings hurt, and that snow melts, without knowing exactly why these facts are true. Much the same is true for law and morality. Johnson may know that slavery is wrong, that government may not stop political protests, and that every person should have just one vote, without knowing exactly why these things are so. Judge Wilson may know that under the Constitution, discrimination against the handicapped is generally permitted, and that discrimination against women is generally banned, without having an account of why the Constitution is so understood. We may thus offer an epistemological point: people can know that X is true without entirely knowing why X is true. This is very often so for particular conclusions about law.

There is a political point as well. People can agree on individual judgments even if they disagree on general theory. Diverse judges may agree that *Roe v. Wade* should not be overruled, though the reasons that lead each of them to that conclusion sharply diverge. Perhaps the judges have different large-scale theories and can agree only on a low-level principle. Perhaps some of the judges have not developed ambitious accounts of the relevant area of the law at all. Thus some people emphasize that the Court should respect its own precedents; others think that *Roe* was rightly decided as a way of protecting women's equality; others think that the case was rightly decided as a way of protecting privacy; others think that the case has everything to do with state neutrality toward religion; others think that restrictions on abortion are unlikely

to protect fetuses, and so the case rightly reflects the fact that any regulation of abortion would be ineffective in promoting its own purposes. We can find incompletely theorized political agreements on particular outcomes in many areas of law and politics—on both sides of the affirmative action controversy, both sides of the dispute over the death penalty, and in all facets of the debate over health care reform.

There are two especially important methods by which law might resolve disputes without obtaining agreement on first principles: rules and analogies. Both of these methods attempt to promote a major goal of a heterogeneous society: to make it possible to obtain agreement where agreement is necessary, and to make it unnecessary to obtain agreement where agreement is impossible.

For purposes of law, reliance on rules might be incompletely theorized in three different ways. People might agree that rules are binding without having a full or agreed-upon account of why this is so. They can often agree on what rules mean even when they agree on very little else. They can even agree that certain rules are good without agreeing on exactly why they are good. And in the face of persistent disagreement or uncertainty about what morality generally requires, people can sometimes reason about particular cases by reference to analogies. They point to cases in which their judgments are firm, and proceed from those firm judgments to the more difficult ones. From different foundations, they may be able to agree on the plausibility of an analogical claim because they share a judgment about a governing low-level principle in the face of disagreement about the abstractions underlying that principle.

The fact that we can obtain an agreement of this sort—about the usefulness and meaning of a rule or the existence of a sound analogy—is no guarantee of a good outcome, whatever may be our criteria for deciding whether an outcome is good. The fact that there is agreement about a rule does not mean that the rule is desirable. Perhaps the rule is bad, or perhaps the judgments that go into its interpretation are bad. The resolution of the Sentencing Commission deserves approval only if average practices were not pervasively unjust. Perhaps the Sentencing Commission incorporated judgments that were based on ignorance, confusion, or prejudice. Perhaps a more deeply theorized approach would have produced better guidelines.

Some of the same things may be said about analogies. People in positions of authority may agree that a ban on same-sex marriages is analogous to a ban on marriages between uncles and nieces. But the analogy may be misconceived because there are relevant differences, because the similarities are far from decisive, or because the principle that accounts for the judgment of similarity cannot be sustained. The fact that people agree that case A is analogous to case B does not mean that case A or case B is rightly decided. Problems with analogies and low-level principles might lead us to be more ambitious. Participants in law may well be pushed in the direction of general theory—and toward broader and more ambitious claims—precisely because low-level reasoning offers an inadequate and incompletely theorized account of relevant similarities or relevant differences.

All this should be sufficient to show that the virtues of incompletely theorized outcomes—and the virtues of decisions by rule and by analogy—are partial. Those virtues should not be exaggerated, and sometimes participants will have to raise the theoretical stakes. But no system of law is likely to be either just or efficient if it dispenses with incompletely theorized agreements. In fact, it is not likely even to be feasible.

THE CASE FOR INCOMPLETE THEORIZATION

1. Multimember Institutions.—I begin with the special problem of public justification faced by a multimember body. The first and most obvious point is that incompletely theorized agreements are well suited to a world—especially a legal world—containing social disagreement on large-scale issues. By definition, such agreements have the large advantage of allowing a convergence on particular outcomes by people unable to reach anything like an accord on general principles. This advantage is associated not only with the simple need to decide cases but also with social stability, which could not exist if fundamental disagreements broke out in every case of public or private dispute.

Second, incompletely theorized agreements can promote two goals of a liberal democracy and a liberal legal system: to enable people to live together, and to permit them to show each other a measure of reciprocity and mutual respect. The use of rules or low-level principles allows judges on multimember bodies and hence citizens generally to find commonality—and a common way of life—without producing unnecessary antagonism. Perhaps more important, incompletely theorized agreements allow people to show each other a high degree of mutual respect, civility, or reciprocity. Ordinary people frequently disagree in some deep way on an issue—the Middle East, pornography, gay marriages—and sometimes they agree not to discuss that issue much, as a way of deferring to each other's strong convictions (even if they do not at all respect the particular conviction that is at stake). If reciprocity and mutual respect are desirable, it follows that judges, perhaps even more than ordinary people, should not challenge a litigant's or one another's deepest and most defining commitments, at least if those commitments are reasonable and if there is no need for them to do so. Thus, it would be better if judges intending to reaffirm *Roe v. Wade* could do so without challenging the belief that the fetus is a human being, or if judges seeking to invalidate the death penalty could do so without saying that the punishment of death is invalid because of its sheer brutality.

Institutional arguments in law, especially those involving judicial restraint, are typically designed to bracket fundamental questions and remove them from the realm of the judiciary. The allocation of certain roles has the important function of allowing outcomes to be reached without forcing courts to make decisions on fundamental issues. Those issues are resolved by reference to institutional competence, not on their merits.

To be sure, some fundamental commitments might appropriately be challenged in the legal system or within other multimember bodies. Some such commitments are ruled off-limits by the authoritative legal materials. Many provisions involving basic rights have this function. Of course, it is not always disrespectful to disagree with someone in a fundamental way; on the contrary, such disagreements may reflect profound respect. For example, objections to judgments based on prejudice may reflect respect for the person at the same time that they attempt to overcome the judgments at issue. When defining commitments are based on demonstrable errors of fact or logic, it is appropriate to contest them. The same is true when those commitments are rooted in a rejection of the basic dignity of all human beings, or when it is necessary to undertake the contest to resolve a genuine problem. But many cases can be resolved in an incompletely theorized way, and that is all I am suggesting here.

2. Multimember Institutions and Individual Judges.—I turn now to reasons that call for incompletely theorized agreements whether or not we are dealing with a multimember body. The first consideration here is that any simple general theory of a large area of the law—free speech, contracts, property—is likely to be too crude to fit with the best understandings of the multiple values that are at stake in that area. Monistic theories of free speech or property rights, for example, fail to accommodate the range of values that speech and property implicate. Human goods are plural and diverse, and they cannot be ranked along any unitary scale without doing violence to our understanding of the qualitative differences among those very goods. People value things not just in terms of weight but also in qualitatively different ways. In the area of free speech, a simple top-down theory—stressing, for example, autonomy or democracy—is likely to run afoul of powerful judgments about particular cases. For this reason, monistic theories are usually inadequate.

Of course, a "top-down" approach might reject monism and point to plural values. But any such approach is likely to owe its genesis and its proof—its point or points—to a range of particular cases, and considered judgments about particular cases, on which it can build. Top-down approaches based on plural values may seem convincing, but incompletely theorized judgments are well suited to a moral universe that is diverse and pluralistic, not only in the sense that people disagree, but also in the sense that each of us is attuned to pluralism when we are thinking well about any area of law.

Second, incompletely theorized agreements serve the crucial function of reducing the political cost of enduring disagreements. If judges disavow large-scale theories, then losers in particular cases lose much less. They lose a decision but not the world. They may win on another occasion. Their own theory has not been rejected or ruled inadmissible. When the authoritative rationale for the result is disconnected from abstract theories of the good or the right, the losers can submit to legal obligations, even if reluctantly, without being forced to renounce their deepest ideals. To be sure, some theories should be rejected or ruled inadmissible; this is sometimes the point of authoritative legal materials. But it is an advantage, from the stand point of freedom and stability, for a legal system to be able to tell most losers—many of whom are operating from foundations that have something to offer, or that cannot be ruled out a priori—that their own deepest convictions may play a role elsewhere in the law.

The third point is that incompletely theorized agreements may be valuable when what is sought is moral evolution over time. Consider the area of constitutional equality, where considerable change has occurred in the past and is likely to occur in the future. A completely theorized judgment—at least if it takes rule-like form—would be unable to accommodate changes in facts or values. Incompletely theorized agreements are a key to debates over constitutional equality, which raise issues about whether gender, sexual orientation, age, disability, and other characteristics are analogous to race. Incompletely theorized agreements have the important advantage of allowing a large degree of openness to new facts and perspectives. At one point, we might think that homosexual relations are akin to incest; at another point, we might find the analogy bizarre. A completely theorized judgment would, of course, have many virtues if it were correct. But at any particular moment in time, this is an unlikely prospect for human beings, including judges, in constitutional law or elsewhere.

Fourth, incompletely theorized agreements may be the best approach available for people with limited time and capacities. The search for full theorization may be simply too difficult for participants in law to complete, and so too for others attempting to reason through difficult problems. A single judge faces this problem as much as a member of a multimember panel. In this respect, the principle of stare decisis is crucial: attention to precedent is liberating, not merely confining, since it is far easier for judges to decide cases if they can take much law as settled. The rule of precedent thus assists in the process of obtaining agreements among people who disagree on first principles. Indeed, precedents can lower the level of theorization by making more foundational views irrelevant or even inappropriate and by binding judges to outcomes that they would like to reject. In any event, incompletely theorized agreements have the advantage, for ordinary lawyers and judges, of humility and modesty: they allow past judgments to be treated as given and make it unnecessary to create the law anew in each case.

Fifth, and finally, incompletely theorized agreements are well adapted to a system that should or must take precedents as fixed points. This is a large advantage over more ambitious methods, since ambitious thinkers, in order to reach horizontal and vertical coherence, will probably be forced to disregard many decided cases. In light of the sheer number of adjudicative officials, law cannot speak with one voice; full coherence in principle is unlikely in the extreme. The area of contract law is unlikely to cohere with the field of tort law, or property law; contract law is itself likely to contain multiple and sometimes inconsistent strands. Multiple and sometimes inconsistent strands are a natural outgrowth of incompletely theorized agreements, which are themselves a way of minimizing the extent and depth of conflict. To be sure, the existence of such agreements may increase conflict by virtue of inconsistency.

It is important, then, that analogical thinkers and rule-followers usually take precedents as given even if they disagree with those precedents as a matter of first principle. The fact that precedents are fixed points helps to bring about incompletely theorized agreements as well, by constraining the areas of reasonable disagreement. The result is a degree of stability and predictability that are important virtues for law.

. . . [W]e might begin to make distinctions between the role of high theory in the courtroom and the role of high theory in the political branches; these distinctions are central to the claims I am making here. In democratic arenas, there is no taboo, presumptive or otherwise, against invoking high-level theories of the good or the right. Such theories have played a role in many social movements with defining effects on American constitutionalism, including the Civil War, the New Deal, the women's movement, the civil rights movement, and the environmental movement. Many of the most abstract arguments of high principle have come from participants in deliberative democracy—James Madison, Thomas Jefferson, Abraham Lincoln, Franklin Delano Roosevelt, Martin Luther King, Jr., and Rachel Carson.

To be sure, incompletely theorized agreements play a key role in democratic arenas too; consider laws that are supportable by reference to diverse foundations, such as those protecting endangered species or granting unions a right to organize. But high-level theories are an indispensable part of democratic politics.

By contrast, use of large-scale theories by courts is usually problematic and understood as such, within the judiciary (as exemplified by judicial practice) if not within law schools. The skepticism is partly a result of the simple fact that judges who invoke large-scale theories may have to require large-scale social reforms, and courts are usually ineffective at implementing such reforms on their own. An important part of the problem lies in the fact that courts, in common law or constitutional cases, must decide on the legitimacy of rules that are aspects of complex systems. In invalidating or changing a single rule, courts may produce unfortunate systemic effects that are not visible to them at the time of decision and that may be impossible for them to correct thereafter. Legislatures are in a much better position on this score.

For those who believe that the Warren Court provides an enduring model for American constitutionalism, this cautionary note may be inadequate; perhaps courts can take important steps in producing justice where there is now injustice, and perhaps a degree of theoretical abstraction is necessary for them to perform this role. Even if this is so, constitutional law is only a small part of adjudication, not the whole picture, and in any case, a degree of social reform in the name of the Constitution might be produced through judgments that are not completely theorized. Moreover, constitutional courts are unlikely to want to produce large-scale social change; the mode of selecting judges, and American history itself, suggest that courts will rarely attempt to replicate the Warren Court's role. And judges who use such theories may well blunder. Judges are not trained as political philosophers, and in many cases, use of abstractions not developed by close reference to particular problems has led to major mistakes.

Even more fundamentally, judges lack a democratic pedigree, and it is in the absence of such a pedigree that the system of precedent, analogy, and incompletely theorized agreement has such an important place. The right to a democratic system is one of the rights to which people are entitled, and in such a system, judicial invocation of large theories to support large decisions against democratic processes should be a rare event. To be sure, judges have a duty to interpret the Constitution, and that duty authorizes them to invoke relatively large-scale principles, seen as part and parcel of the Constitution as democratically ratified. Many people think that judicial activity is best characterized by reference to use of such principles, and it would be wrong to deny that there are occasions on which this practice occurs and is legitimate.

To identify those occasions, it would be necessary to develop a full theory of legal interpretation. For present purposes, I urge something more modest. Most judicial activity does not involve constitutional interpretation, and the ordinary work of common law decision and statutory interpretation calls for low-level principles. Indeed, constitutional argument is itself based largely on low-level principles, not on high theory, except on those rare occasions when more ambitious thinking becomes necessary to resolve a case, or when the case for the ambitious theory is so insistent that a range of judges do and should converge on it.

All well-functioning legal systems value the enterprise of reason-giving. But there is a good reason to be wary of reason-giving: reasons may be both over- and under-inclusive. In this way, reasons are like rules, which are also over- and under-inclusive if measured by reference to their justifications. Whenever a court offers reasons, there is a risk of future regret—not simply because the court may be confined in a subsequent case and thus have to avoid inconsistency, but because the reasons offered in case A may turn out, on reflection, to generate a standard, a principle, or a rule that collides with the court's considered judgment about case B. The constraint produced by the reason may limit discretion and promote predictability, but it may also produce a bad result.

The distinction between holding and dictum helps reduce this problem. Indeed, the distinction squarely addresses the problem of excessively theorized judgments, and it helps to ensure that legal decisions are incompletely theorized. If we understand the holding to be the narrowest possible basis for the decision, a subsequent court is able to offer sufficiently narrow reasons for the outcome in the previous case—that is, reasons that ensure that the outcome in the previous case does not apply to a case that is genuinely different. In initially giving a reason, court one may be unaware of possible applications that will falsify that reason because of its imprecision and excessive generality. But court two, able to offer some narrower and better-fitting explanation for the outcome, can eliminate the difficulty. It can label the excessive generality "dicta."

There is another difficulty with reason-giving. One might sometimes know something without knowing the reasons for it. For example, one may know that this is

Martin's face, and no other face, without knowing, exactly, why one knows that fact. Or one might know that a certain act would be wrong, without knowing, exactly, why it would be wrong. It is certainly possible to know that something is true without knowing why it is true.

. . . [I]t is possible that experienced judges, like experienced lawyers, develop a faculty—best described as wisdom, perception, or judgment—that allows them to reach decisions very well and very quickly. This is a distinctive faculty. It seems to be associated with the ready and sympathetic apprehension of a wide range of diverse particulars and with an appreciation of the appropriate weight to be given to each. Certainly, we can imagine a class of people who have a wonderful capacity to tell whether one case is relevantly like another, or to decide who should win cases, but who lack much of a capacity to explain what underlies their ultimate judgments, or their convictions about relevant similarity and difference. They are not theorists at all. But they have a "good ear," unlike some others who have a "tin ear" for law.

Perhaps it would ultimately be possible for such people (or at least outside observers) to explain what underlies these good apprehensions, but this may not be so. It is important not to mystify these issues. What is asserted to be a capacity for perception may in fact be a product of bias or confusion, and reason-giving helps diminish this risk. The faculty of wisdom, perception, or judgment probably amounts to a capacity to think very quickly of a resolution that takes account of everything that matters, including a wide array of competing considerations, and that coheres well with the rest of our particular and general judgments.

Enthusiasm for incompletely theorized agreements meets with many adversaries.

An especially distinguished example is Ronald Dworkin, who urges, at least as an ideal, a high degree of theoretical self-consciousness in adjudication. Dworkin argues that when lawyers disagree about what the law is, they are disagreeing about "the best constructive interpretation of the community's legal practice." Dworkin claims that interpretation in law consists of different efforts to make a governing text "the best it can be." This is Dworkin's conception of law as integrity.

Dworkin's account appears to require judges to develop high-level theories, and it does not (to say the least) favor theoretical modesty. There is no presumption against abstraction. In his hands, the relevant theories are large and abstract; they sound like political philosophy or moral theory. These theories are derived from or brought to bear on particular problems. But this is not how real lawyers and real judges proceed. If they can, they avoid broad and abstract questions.

Because of his enthusiasm for abstractions, Hercules—Dworkin's patient and resourceful judge—could not really participate in ordinary judicial deliberations. He would probably be seen as a usurper, even an oddball. On a single judge court, he would suffer from the vice of hubris. On a multimember panel, he would lack some of the crucial virtues of a participant in legal deliberation. These virtues include collegiality and civility, which incline judges toward the lowest level of abstraction necessary to decide a case.

Dworkin's conception of law as integrity offers a theory of what it means for law to be legitimate. Hercules can produce vertical and horizontal consistency among judgments of principle in law. Do incompletely theorized agreements comport with any plausible conception of legitimacy? . . . In fact, the idea of integrity, insofar as it is a judicial product, is unlikely to provide a convincing theory of legitimacy. Indeed, it seems plausible to say that integrity, as Dworkin describes it, is neither necessary nor sufficient for legitimacy, judicial or otherwise. Legitimacy stems not simply from principled consistency on the part of adjudicators (or someone else) but from a justifiable exercise of public force. That theory should be founded in a theory of authority and hence (if we are democrats) in suitably constrained democratic considerations. In this light, Dworkin's conception of integrity offers an excessively court-centered conception of legitimacy. It sees legitimacy not as an exercise of legitimate authority, or as an outcome of well-functioning democratic procedures, but instead as a process of distinction-making undertaken by judges. . . . For reasons of both policy and principle, the development of large-scale theories of the right and the good is most fundamentally a democratic task, not a judicial one. . . .

Incompletely theorized agreements have virtues, but as I have noted, their virtues are partial. Stability, for example, is brought about by such agreements, and stability is usually desirable, but a system that is stable and unjust should probably be made less stable. Agreement is important, but disagreement is important too, for it can be a creative force in revealing error and injustice. In this final section, I offer some qualifications to what has been said thus far. In brief: some cases cannot be decided at all without introducing a fair amount in the way of theoretical ambition. Moreover, some cases cannot be decided well without increasing the level of theoretical ambition. If a good abstraction is available, and if diverse judges can be persuaded that the abstraction is good, there should be no taboo against its judicial acceptance. The claims on behalf of

incompletely theorized agreements are presumptive rather than conclusive.

I have urged that there are reasons for judges to offer the least ambitious argument necessary to resolve cases, in the hope that different people from their diverse standpoints can converge on that argument, and with the belief that abstractions may prove troublesome for later cases. But if judges can agree on an abstraction, and if the abstraction can be shown to be a good one, judicial acceptance of that abstraction may hardly be troubling but, on the contrary, an occasion for celebration. Who could object to judicial adoption of what is by hypothesis a good theory? If agreement is possible on a good abstraction, a legal system will have done its job especially well; consider, as possibilities, antitrust or equal protection law. But any abstractions will likely have been developed through the generalization and clarification of incompletely theorized outcomes, accomplished by constant reference to concrete cases against which the theory is measured. At least part of the test of the theory—if it is a theory of law meant for judicial adoption—is how well it accounts for the cases and for considered judgments about the cases, though of course judicial mistakes are possible, and these may be corrected by the theory, subject to the constraints of stare decisis.

I am thus declining to endorse what might be called a strong version of the argument offered here: a claim that incompletely theorized agreements are always the appropriate approach to law and that more ambitious theory is always illegitimate in law. What I am urging is a more modest point, keyed to the institutional characteristics of judges in any legal system we are likely to have. Judges should adopt a presumption rather than a taboo against high-level theorization. Usually, they should invoke the lowest levels of theoretical ambition necessary to decide the case. In many contexts, they will not be able to think of a good theory. In many cases, they will not be able to agree on any theory. The effort to reach agreement on relative abstractions may make it hard for judges or other people to live and work together, and unnecessary contests over theory can suggest an absence of respect for the deepest and most defining commitments of other people.

LOCHNER v. NEW YORK

198 U.S. 45 (1905)

You have already read Justice Rufus Peckham's opinion in Lochner v. New York *as a potential example of the moral reading of the Constitution. We now turn to a famous dissent in that case by Justice Oliver Wendell Holmes, often considered the founder of the school of pragmatist constitutional interpretation. In the case, notice Justice Holmes's attention to Herbert Spencer's philosophy. Specifically, Justice Holmes worried that Justice Peckham was reading into the Constitution the view associated with Spencer that governmental intervention hindered freedom to succeed or fail in a free market. Justice Holmes believes, as you will see, that such a theory has no place in constitutional interpretation, and that one should instead focus on future consequences. As you read this decision, consider how Justice Holmes presages both Cass Sunstein's worry about excessive theorizing in constitutional interpretation and Judge Richard Posner's embrace of consequentialism. To what extent does Justice Holmes synthesize these two views, and to what extent is his account different?*

MR. JUSTICE HOLMES *dissenting.*

I regret sincerely that I am unable to agree with the judgment in this case, and that I think it my duty to express my dissent.

This case is decided upon an economic theory which a large part of the country does not entertain. If it were a question whether I agreed with that theory I should desire to study it further and long before making up my mind. But I do not conceive that to be my duty, because I strongly believe that my agreement or disagreement has nothing to do with the right of a majority to embody their opinions in law. It is settled by various decisions of this court that state constitutions and state laws may regulate life in many ways which we as legislators might think as injudicious or if you like as tyrannical as this, and which equally with this interfere with the liberty to contract. Sunday laws and usury laws are ancient examples. A more modern one is the prohibition of lotteries. The liberty of the citizen to do as he likes so long as he does not interfere with the liberty of others to do the same, which has been a shibboleth for some well-known writers, is interfered with by school laws, by the Post Office, by every state or municipal institution which takes his money for purposes thought desirable, whether he likes it or not. The Fourteenth Amendment does not enact Mr. Herbert Spencer's Social Statics. The other day we sustained the Massachusetts vaccination law. *Jacobson v. Massachusetts.* United States and state statutes and decisions cutting down the liberty to contract by way of combination are familiar to this court. *Northern Securities Co. v. United States.* Two years ago we upheld the prohibition of sales of stock on margins or for future delivery in the constitution of California. *Otis v. Parker.* The decision sustaining an eight hour law for miners is still recent. *Holden v. Hardy.* Some of these laws embody convictions or prejudices which judges are likely to share. Some may not. But a constitution is not intended to embody a particular economic theory, whether of paternalism and the organic relation of the citizen to the State or of laissez faire. It is made for people of fundamentally differing views, and the accident of our finding certain opinions natural and familiar or novel and even shocking ought not to conclude our judgment upon the question whether statutes embodying them conflict with the Constitution of the United States.

General propositions do not decide concrete cases. The decision will depend on a judgment or intuition more subtle than any articulate major premise. But I think that the proposition just stated, if it is accepted, will carry us far toward the end. Every opinion tends to become a law. I think that the word liberty in the Fourteenth Amendment is perverted when it is held to prevent the natural outcome of a dominant opinion, unless it can be said that a rational and fair man necessarily would admit that the statute proposed would infringe fundamental principles as they have been understood by the traditions of our people and our law. It does not need research to show that no such sweeping condemnation can be passed upon the statute before us. A reasonable man might think it a proper measure on the score of health. Men whom I certainly could not pronounce unreasonable would uphold it as a first installment of a general regulation of the hours of work. Whether in the latter aspect it would be open to the charge of inequality I think it unnecessary to discuss.

DISTRICT OF COLUMBIA v. HELLER

554 U.S. 570 (2008)

We turn now to another dissent that illustrates the philosophy of pragmatism. As we have seen, the majority opinion by Justice Antonin Scalia in District of Columbia v. Heller *is an example of originalist jurisprudence. Consider how Justice Stephen Breyer offers an alternative way of thinking about the issue in the case. To what extent does he, like Cass Sunstein, eschew theory in constitutional interpretation? To what extent does he rely on policy arguments about future consequences as recommended by Judge Richard Posner?*

JUSTICE BREYER, *with whom* **JUSTICE STEVENS, JUSTICE SOUTER**, *and* **JUSTICE GINSBURG** *join, dissenting.*

We must decide whether a District of Columbia law that prohibits the possession of handguns in the home violates the Second Amendment. The majority, relying upon its view that the Second Amendment seeks to protect a right of personal self-defense, holds that this law violates that Amendment. In my view, it does not.

. . . [T]he protection the Amendment provides is not absolute. The Amendment permits government to regulate the interests that it serves. Thus, irrespective of what those interests are—whether they do or do not include an independent interest in self-defense—the majority's view cannot be correct unless it can show that the District's regulation is unreasonable or inappropriate in Second Amendment terms. This the majority cannot do.

. . . I shall show that the District's law is consistent with the Second Amendment even if that Amendment is interpreted as protecting a wholly separate interest in individual self-defense. That is so because the District's regulation, which focuses upon the presence of handguns in high-crime urban areas, represents a permissible legislative response to a serious, indeed life-threatening, problem.

Thus I here assume that one objective (but, as the majority concedes, not the primary objective) of those who wrote the Second Amendment was to help assure citizens that they would have arms available for purposes of self-defense. Even so, a legislature could reasonably conclude that the law will advance goals of great public importance, namely, saving lives, preventing injury, and reducing crime. The law is tailored to the urban crime problem in that it is local in scope and thus affects only a geographic area both limited in size and entirely urban; the law concerns handguns, which are specially linked to urban gun deaths and injuries, and which are the overwhelmingly favorite weapon of armed criminals; and at the same time, the law imposes a burden upon gun owners that seems proportionately no greater than restrictions in existence at the time the Second Amendment was adopted. In these circumstances, the District's law falls within the zone that the Second Amendment leaves open to regulation by legislatures.

Although I adopt for present purposes the majority's position that the Second Amendment embodies a general concern about self-defense, I shall not assume that the Amendment contains a specific untouchable right to keep guns in the house to shoot burglars. The majority, which presents evidence in favor of the former proposition, does not, because it cannot, convincingly show that the Second Amendment seeks to maintain the latter in pristine, unregulated form.

To the contrary, colonial history itself offers important examples of the kinds of gun regulation that citizens would then have thought compatible with the "right to keep and bear arms," whether embodied in Federal or State Constitutions, or the background common law. And those examples include substantial regulation of firearms in urban areas, including regulations that imposed obstacles to the use of firearms for the protection of the home.

This historical evidence demonstrates that a self-defense assumption is the beginning, rather than the end, of any constitutional inquiry. That the District law impacts self-defense merely raises questions about the law's constitutionality. But to answer the questions that are raised (that is, to see whether the statute is unconstitutional) requires us to focus on practicalities, the statute's rationale, the problems that called it into being, its relation to those objectives—in a word, the details. There are no purely logical or conceptual answers to such questions. All of which is to say that to raise a self-defense question is not to answer it.

. . . [A]ny attempt in theory to apply strict scrutiny to gun regulations will in practice turn into an interest-balancing inquiry, with the interests protected by the Second Amendment on one side and the governmental public-safety concerns on the other, the only question being whether the regulation at issue impermissibly burdens the former in the course of advancing the latter.

I would simply adopt such an interest-balancing inquiry explicitly. The fact that important interests lie on both sides of the constitutional equation suggests that review of gun-control regulation is not a context in which a court should effectively presume either constitutionality (as in rational-basis review) or unconstitutionality (as in strict scrutiny). Rather, "where a law significantly implicates competing constitutionally protected interests in complex ways," the Court generally asks whether the statute burdens a protected interest in a way or to an extent that is out of proportion to the statute's salutary effects upon other important governmental interests. Any answer would take account both of the statute's effects upon the competing interests and the existence of any clearly superior less restrictive alternative. Contrary to the majority's unsupported suggestion that this sort of "proportionality" approach is unprecedented, . . . the Court has applied it in various constitutional contexts, including election-law cases, speech cases, and due process cases.

In applying this kind of standard the Court normally defers to a legislature's empirical judgment in matters where a legislature is likely to have greater expertise and greater institutional fact finding capacity. Nonetheless, a court, not a legislature, must make the ultimate constitutional conclusion, exercising its "independent judicial judgment" in light of the whole record to determine whether a law exceeds constitutional boundaries.

The above-described approach seems preferable to a more rigid approach here for a further reason. Experience as much as logic has led the Court to decide that in one area of constitutional law or another the interests are likely to prove stronger on one side of a typical constitutional case than on the other. Here, we have little prior experience. Courts that do have experience in these matters have uniformly taken an approach that treats empirically-based legislative judgment with a degree of deference. . . .

The second District restriction requires that the lawful owner of a firearm keep his weapon "unloaded and disassembled or bound by a trigger lock or similar device" unless it is kept at his place of business or being used for lawful recreational purposes. The only dispute regarding this provision appears to be whether the Constitution requires an exception that would allow someone to render a firearm operational when necessary for self-defense (i.e., that the firearm may be operated under circumstances where the common law would normally permit a self-defense justification in defense against a criminal charge). The District concedes that such an exception exists. This Court has final authority (albeit not often used) to definitively interpret District law, which is, after all, simply a species of federal law. And because I see nothing in the District law that would preclude the existence of a background common-law self-defense exception, I would avoid the constitutional question by interpreting the statute to include it.

The third District restriction prohibits (in most cases) the registration of a handgun within the District. Because registration is a prerequisite to firearm possession, the effect of this provision is generally to prevent people in the District from possessing handguns. In determining whether this regulation violates the Second Amendment, I shall ask how the statute seeks to further the governmental interests that it serves, how the statute burdens the interests that the Second Amendment seeks to protect, and whether there are practical less burdensome ways of furthering those interests. The ultimate question is whether the statute imposes burdens that, when viewed in light of the statute's legitimate objectives, are disproportionate.

. . . [C]onsider the facts as the legislature saw them when it adopted the District statute. As stated by the local council committee that recommended its adoption, the major substantive goal of the

District's handgun restriction is "to reduce the potentiality for gun-related crimes and gun-related deaths from occurring within the District of Columbia." The committee concluded, on the basis of "extensive public hearings" and "lengthy research," that "[t]he easy availability of firearms in the United States has been a major factor contributing to the drastic increase in gun-related violence and crime over the past 40 years." It reported to the Council "startling statistics," regarding gun-related crime, accidents, and deaths, focusing particularly on the relation between handguns and crime and the proliferation of handguns within the District.

In the committee's view, the current District firearms laws were unable "to reduce the potentiality for gun-related violence," or to "cope with the problems of gun control in the District" more generally. In the absence of adequate federal gun legislation, the committee concluded, it "becomes necessary for local governments to act to protect their citizens, and certainly the District of Columbia as the only totally urban statelike jurisdiction should be strong in its approach." It recommended that the Council adopt a restriction on handgun registration to reflect "a legislative decision that, at this point in time and due to the gun-control tragedies and horrors enumerated previously" in the committee report, "pistols . . . are no longer justified in this jurisdiction."

Next, consider the facts as a court must consider them looking at the matter as of today. Petitioners, and their amici, have presented us with more recent statistics that tell much the same story that the committee report told 30 years ago. At the least, they present nothing that would permit us to second-guess the Council in respect to the numbers of gun crimes, injuries, and deaths, or the role of handguns.

Respondent and his many amici for the most part do not disagree about the figures set forth in the preceding subsection, but they do disagree strongly with the District's predictive judgment that a ban on handguns will help solve the crime and accident problems that those figures disclose. In particular, they disagree with the District Council's assessment that "freezing the pistol . . . population within the District" will reduce crime, accidents, and deaths related to guns. And they provide facts and figures designed to show that it has not done so in the past, and hence will not do so in the future.

The upshot is a set of studies and counterstudies that, at most, could leave a judge uncertain about the proper policy conclusion. But from respondent's perspective any such uncertainty is not good enough. That is because legislators, not judges, have primary responsibility for drawing policy conclusions from empirical fact. And, given that constitutional allocation of decision-making responsibility, the empirical evidence presented here is sufficient to allow a judge to reach a firm legal conclusion.

In particular this Court, in First Amendment cases applying intermediate scrutiny, has said that our "sole obligation" in reviewing a legislature's "predictive judgments" is "to assure that, in formulating its judgments," the legislature "has drawn reasonable inferences based on substantial evidence." And judges, looking at the evidence before us, should agree that the District legislature's predictive judgments satisfy that legal standard. That is to say, the District's judgment, while open to question, is nevertheless supported by "substantial evidence."

There is no cause here to depart from the standard set forth in *Turner*, for the District's decision represents the kind of empirically based judgment that legislatures, not courts, are best suited to make. In fact, deference to legislative judgment seems particularly appropriate here, where the judgment has been made by a local legislature, with particular knowledge of local problems and insight into appropriate local solutions. Different localities may seek to solve similar problems in different ways, and a "city must be allowed a reasonable opportunity to experiment with solutions to admittedly serious problems." "The Framers recognized that the most effective democracy occurs at local levels of government, where people with firsthand knowledge of local problems have more ready access to public officials responsible for dealing with them." We owe that democratic process some substantial weight in the constitutional calculus.

For these reasons, I conclude that the District's statute properly seeks to further the sort of life-preserving and public-safety interests that the Court has called "compelling."

... [T]he District's objectives are compelling; its predictive judgments as to its law's tendency to achieve those objectives are adequately supported; the law does impose a burden upon any self-defense interest that the amendment seeks to secure; and there is no clear less restrictive alternative. I turn now to the final portion of the "permissible regulation" question: Does the District's law disproportionately burden amendment-protected interests? Several considerations, taken together, convince me that it does not.

First, the District law is tailored to the life-threatening problems it attempts to address. The law concerns one class of weapons, handguns, leaving residents free to possess shotguns and rifles, along with ammunition. The area that falls within its scope is totally urban. That urban area suffers from a serious handgun-fatality problem. The District's law directly aims at that compelling problem. And there is no less restrictive way to achieve the problem-related benefits that it seeks.

Second, the self-defense interest in maintaining loaded handguns in the home to shoot intruders is not the primary interest, but at most a subsidiary interest, that the Second Amendment seeks to serve. The Second Amendment's language, while speaking of a "Militia," says nothing of "self-defense." As Justice Stevens points out, the Second amendment's drafting history shows that the language reflects the Framers' primary, if not exclusive, objective. And the majority itself says that "the threat that the new Federal Government would destroy the citizens' militia by taking away their arms was the reason that right ... was codified in a written Constitution." The way in which the Amendment's operative clause seeks to promote that interest—by protecting a right "to keep and bear Arms"—may in fact help further an interest in self-defense. But a factual connection falls far short of a primary objective. The amendment itself tells us that militia preservation was first and foremost in the Framers' minds.

Further, any self-defense interest at the time of the Framing could not have focused exclusively upon urban-crime related dangers. Two hundred years ago, most Americans, many living on the frontier, would likely have thought of self-defense primarily in terms of outbreaks of fighting with Indian tribes, rebellions such as Shays' Rebellion, marauders, and crime-related dangers to travelers on the roads, on footpaths, or along waterways. ... Insofar as the Framers focused at all on the tiny fraction of the population living in large cities, they would have been aware that these city dwellers were subject to firearm restrictions that their rural counterparts were not. They are unlikely then to have thought of a right to keep loaded handguns in homes to confront intruders in urban settings as central. And the subsequent development of modern urban police departments, by diminishing the need to keep loaded guns nearby in case of intruders, would have moved any such right even further away from the heart of the amendment's more basic protective ends....

Nor, for that matter, am I aware of any evidence that handguns in particular were central to the Framers' conception of the Second Amendment. The lists of militia-related weapons in the late 18th-century state statutes appear primarily to refer to other sorts of weapons, muskets in particular....

Third, irrespective of what the Framers could have thought, we know what they did think. Samuel Adams, who lived in Boston, advocated a constitutional amendment that would have precluded the Constitution from ever being "construed" to "prevent the people of the United States, who are peaceable citizens, from keeping their own arms." Samuel Adams doubtless knew that the Massachusetts Constitution contained somewhat similar protection. And he doubtless knew that Massachusetts law prohibited Bostonians from keeping loaded guns in the house. So how could Samuel Adams have advocated such protection unless he thought that the protection was consistent with local regulation that seriously impeded urban residents from using their arms against intruders? It seems unlikely that he meant to deprive the Federal Government of power (to enact Boston-type weapons regulation) that he knew Boston had and (as far as we know) he would have thought constitutional under the Massachusetts Constitution. Indeed, since the District of Columbia (the subject of the Seat of Government Clause, U.S. Const., Art. I, §8, cl. 17) was the only urban area under direct federal control, it seems unlikely that the Framers thought about urban gun control at all....

Regardless, why would the majority require a precise colonial regulatory analogue in order to save a modern gun regulation from constitutional challenge? After all, insofar as we look to history to discover how we can constitutionally regulate a right to self-defense, we must look, not to what 18th-century legislatures actually did enact, but to what they would have thought they could enact. There are innumerable policy-related reasons why a legislature might not act on a particular matter, despite having the power to do so. This Court has "frequently cautioned that it is at best treacherous to find in congressional silence alone the adoption of a controlling rule of law." *United States v. Wells.* It is similarly "treacherous" to reason from the fact that colonial legislatures did not enact certain kinds of legislation an unalterable constitutional limitation on the power of a modern legislature cannot do so. The question should not be whether a modern restriction on a right to self-defense duplicates a past one, but whether that restriction, when compared with restrictions originally thought possible, enjoys a similarly strong justification. At a minimum that similarly strong justification is what the District's modern law, compared with Boston's colonial law, reveals.

Fourth, a contrary view, as embodied in today's decision, will have unfortunate consequences. The decision will encourage legal challenges to gun regulation throughout the Nation. Because it says little about the standards used to evaluate regulatory decisions, it will leave the Nation without clear standards for resolving those challenges.... And litigation over the course of many years, or the mere specter of such litigation, threatens to leave cities without effective protection against gun violence and accidents during that time.

As important, the majority's decision threatens severely to limit the ability of more knowledgeable, democratically elected officials to deal with gun-related problems. The majority says that it leaves the District "a variety of tools for combating" such problems. It fails to list even one seemingly adequate replacement for the law it strikes down. I can understand how reasonable individuals can disagree about the merits of strict gun control as a crime-control measure, even in a totally urbanized area. But I cannot understand how one can take from the elected branches of government the right to decide whether to insist upon a handgun-free urban populace in a city now facing a serious crime problem and which, in the future, could well face environmental or other emergencies that threaten the breakdown of law and order.

The majority derides my approach as "judge-empowering." I take this criticism seriously, but I do not think it accurate. As I have previously explained, this is an approach that the Court has taken in other areas of constitutional law. Application of such an approach, of course, requires judgment, but the very nature of the approach—requiring careful identification of the relevant interests and evaluating the law's effect upon them— limits the judge's choices; and the method's necessary transparency lays bare the judge's reasoning for all to see and to criticize.

The majority's methodology is, in my view, substantially less transparent than mine. At a minimum, I find it difficult to understand the reasoning that seems to underlie certain conclusions that it reaches.

Given the purposes for which the Framers enacted the Second Amendment, how should it be applied to modern-day circumstances that they could not have anticipated? Assume, for argument's sake, that the Framers did intend the Amendment to offer a degree of self-defense protection. Does that mean that the Framers also intended to guarantee a right to possess a loaded gun near swimming pools, parks, and playgrounds? That they would not have cared about the children who might pick up a loaded gun on their parents' bedside table? That they (who certainly showed concern for the risk of fire) would have lacked concern for the risk of accidental deaths or suicides that readily accessible loaded handguns in urban areas might bring? Unless we believe that they intended future generations to ignore such matters, answering questions such as the questions in this case requires judgment—judicial judgment exercised within a framework for constitutional analysis that guides that judgment and which makes its exercise transparent. One cannot answer those questions by combining inconclusive historical research with judicial ipse dixit.

The argument about method, however, is by far the less important argument surrounding today's decision. Far more important are the unfortunate consequences that today's decision is likely to spawn. Not least of these, as I have said, is the fact that the decision threatens to throw into doubt the constitutionality of gun laws throughout the United States. I can find no sound legal basis for launching the courts on so formidable and potentially dangerous a mission. In my view, there simply is no untouchable constitutional right guaranteed by the Second Amendment to keep loaded handguns in the house in crime-ridden urban areas.

SYNTHESIS QUESTIONS FOR FURTHER DISCUSSION: CHAPTER 2 SECTION D

1. Pragmatism is sometimes described as an "anti-theory," meaning that it does not rely on any one perspective for deciding cases. But it can be linked

to a broad tradition of "consequentialism" in political and legal theory. Given pragmatism's place in the consequentialist tradition, does it reject the role of moral and political theorizing in constitutional law? Or does it instead merely apply a consequentialist morality to legal cases? You might think about whether there is a difference on this issue between Cass Sunstein, who emphasizes the need for group decision making in legal cases, and Judge Richard Posner, who some describe as a straightforward consequentialist. For instance, could we consider one case at a time without relying on consequentialism?

2. Justice Oliver Wendell Holmes's dissent in *Lochner v. New York* is one of the most famous instances of pragmatism. Justice Holmes suggests that the Constitution is not guided by a political theory. Although Justice Holmes himself was, according to some scholars, sympathetic to the philosophy of Social Darwinism as defended by Herbert Spencer, he explicitly claims that this philosophy is not embedded in the Constitution. Does this ability to bracket one's personal political philosophy make pragmatism unique among the theories examined in this chapter? Or is pragmatism just another theory itself?

3. In contemplating the differences between pragmatism and originalism, it is helpful to consider the dispute between Justices Antonin Scalia and Stephen Breyer in *District of Columbia v. Heller*. While Justice Scalia's majority opinion is a paradigmatic example of originalist jurisprudence, Justice Breyer's is a classic statement of pragmatism. How would Justice Scalia's argument change, if at all, if one million gun deaths could be tied to the decision to strike down the Washington, D.C., ordinance? How might Justice Breyer's argument change if it turned out that striking down the ordinance did not result in a single gun death?

4. One possible problem for pragmatism might be the traditional legal concept of precedent. The principle of stare decisis, or "let the decision stand," suggests that when courts—including the Supreme Court—make decisions, they should attempt to be consistent over time. Law, in this view, is inevitably tied to the past. Given pragmatism's emphasis on future policy consequences, does it permit any role for stare decisis? Are past precedents good guides to good future policy consequences?

   What role does precedent have in each of the other theories we have looked at in this chapter? For instance, should originalism disregard precedent when it violates the original understanding of the Constitution? Should process theorists overturn precedents or disregard them when they do not protect the democratic process? Does the moral reading suggest that it is unimportant to follow precedent when it impedes, or fails to protect, basic rights? Finally, can consequentialists account for any role for precedent even in the face of bad policy consequences?

5. In this chapter, several different approaches to constitutional interpretation have been examined, including originalism, process theory, the moral reading, and pragmatism. Most theories share a commitment, however, to interpreting the text of the Constitution. You might assume, therefore, that the text itself matters to constitutional meaning as a matter of common sense. In the last chapter, however, it came to light that *Marbury v. Madison* arguably established judicial review without a textual basis. It is also important to consider the Ninth Amendment, for example. Does its reference to rights that are not enumerated invite us to look beyond the text of the Constitution in determining what is guaranteed by it? In considering these questions, it may be wise to reflect on Justice Arthur Goldberg's concurrence in *Griswold v. Connecticut*. Although the focus in this chapter has been limited to theories that assume the centrality of constitutional text, some constitutional theorists, notably Thomas Grey, have gone so far as to urge a "non-interpretivist" approach to the Constitution ("Do We Have an Unwritten Constitution?," Stanford Law Review, 1975). Do some of the readings from this chapter make any gestures towards non-interpretivism or non-textualism?

Box 2-1   Moving from the Theoretical to the Concrete

It is sometimes helpful to consider hypothetical situations in order to elucidate an abstract theory. To get a better understanding of each of the four theories we have investigated, examine the following four fact situations. As you read each of them, consider what each of the theories would say about the fact situations presented. As you will see, multiple conclusions can be drawn depending on the theory utilized.

For the purposes of these questions, it might be helpful to take the amendments out of their historical context and to focus just on their content.

A. A state passes a law banning the use of contraception. A couple appeals the law, citing the Fourteenth Amendment's Due Process Clause.

B. A public high school devoted to African-American history and culture denies admission to a white student. The student appeals the denial of admission, citing the Fourteenth Amendment's Equal Protection Clause.

C. Districts for members of the U.S. House of Representatives are drawn unevenly. A voter in a district that has twice as many people as a neighboring district appeals, citing the Fourteenth Amendment's Equal Protection Clause.

D. Congress passes a law authorizing the sentence of death for first-degree murder. A convicted criminal appeals, claiming the sentence violates the Eighth Amendment's ban on cruel and unusual punishment.

Box 2-2 **Four Theories of Constitutional Interpretation**

	How Is Judicial Review Democratic?	How Should Constitutional Text Be Interpreted?	What Is the Role of Precedent?
Originalism	The Constitution has supreme democratic force: Judges can strike down unconstitutional laws, but constitutional meaning is determined by the circumstances of its enactment.	Interpretation must discover the original understanding of a text, so judges should look to the Framers' intentions or the original public meaning of the text. Where there is no discoverable constitutional meaning, democratically accountable legislators should make law.	With few exceptions, precedent matters only when it correctly interprets the Constitution's original meaning.
Proceduralism	Judicial review can reinforce the integrity of the democratic process and protect minorities, but judges should avoid controversial judgments about substantive values.	Judges should interpret constitutional text with an eye to protecting the political process. Although the Constitution empowers judges to ensure that all are adequately represented, value judgments should be left to legislatures.	Precedent should be generally binding, but not when it undermines the democratic process.
Moral Reading	Democracy requires more than majority rule: Judicial review can protect the fundamental substantive rights belonging to citizens in a democracy.	Interpreting the Constitution's abstract clauses requires making judgments of political morality. Being faithful to the Constitution's deep moral commitments means protecting individual rights.	Precedent is important in that it illuminates how the law has been morally justified, but the best moral reading of the Constitution will sometimes require abandoning precedent.
Pragmatism	Judges should defer to legislative decisions about cost and benefit; they should avoid imposing their own sweeping personal moral theories.	Judges should temper their interpretations about what the Constitution means with considerations about the practical effects of their decisions. The text is important, but consequences matter as well.	Judges should look to precedent for guidance on how the law achieves the best results, but it is not binding.

KEY TERMS

gerrymandering: The attempt by a state legislature to draw districts in a way that will benefit or disadvantage a particular political party or racial group.

interpretivism: As defined by John Hart Ely, the middle ground between strict textualism and open-ended non-textualism.

non-textualism: The view, most clearly articulated by Justice Arthur Goldberg in *Griswold v. Connecticut*, that there are rights not explicitly mentioned in the constitutional text. In making his case, Justice Goldberg cites the Ninth Amendment.

penumbra: A concept used to defend the idea that the Constitution guarantees rights based on implicit meanings of the text. Most famously used in Justice William O. Douglas's concurrence in *Griswold v. Connecticut* to articulate a right to privacy in the shadow of various provisions of the Bill of Rights.

police powers: The state's entitlement to regulate the welfare, health, safety, and morals of its population.

stare decisis: Literally, "let the decision stand." The idea that the Supreme Court should defer to legal precedents in the hope of treating "like cases like."

substantive due process: The theory famously articulated in *Lochner v. New York* and in *Griswold v. Connecticut* suggesting that the Due Process Clause protects some fundamental rights, even if they are unrelated to due process of law.

textualism: The view articulated by originalists and other thinkers that we should read the text of the Constitution in as literal a way as possible, and that constitutional interpretation should not look beyond the explicit text of the document.

PART II

POWERS

CHAPTER 3

CONGRESSIONAL AUTHORITY AND ITS LIMITS

In Part 1, we saw why and how thinking about the meaning of democracy can help us understand whether and when the Supreme Court should exercise its power of judicial review. While in Chapter 1 we asked whether the Court has the authority to strike down laws, in Chapter 2 we explored when it might justifiably exercise that authority. In both chapters we saw that the question of when the Court can rightly exercise its power of judicial review is complicated by the U.S. Constitution's silence about this power. In Part 2, we turn to the question of Congress's authority and power to make law. In contrast to the Court's judicial review power, Congress's specific powers are explicitly articulated in Article I of the Constitution. But despite this specific articulation, controversy remains about how far these powers extend and when they should be limited.

Specifically, in this chapter we explore the question of how far congressional power extends relative to state governments. In the next chapter, we go on to examine Congress's power in relation to the executive branch and the judiciary. Traditionally, questions about Congress's power relative to the states are referred to as the problems of "federalism," while the question of inter-branch authority is referred to as "separation of powers." Importantly, the question of federalism in regard to the relationship between the state governments and the federal government should not be confused with the specific positions of the "Federalist" party or of *The Federalist Papers*.

The first thing that should stand out about the question of Congress's power relative to that of state legislatures is that both are democratic branches of government. The Congress of the United States is made up of two houses, the Senate and the House of Representatives. Although the members of the Senate were originally appointed by state legislatures, this was changed by the Seventeenth Amendment, adopted in 1913. Since then, both Houses of Congress have been directly elected by the people. Just as the U.S. Congress has democratic credentials, so too do state legislatures, which are also made up of members directly elected by the people. Since both the state and the national legislatures can pass laws that govern the lives of individual citizens, we have to consider how to sort out the constitutional limits of the powers of each of these levels of government and what should happen if there is a conflict between them.

Drawing on the concern to ensure democratic governance that guided the theories of constitutional interpretation in the last chapter, we might think about how to resolve conflicts over powers by asking what would be the most democratic relationship between the federal and state governments. Some have argued that state governments are closer to the people—both geographically and in terms of the more intimate connection between the voters and their representatives, since state legislators usually represent vastly smaller constituencies. This suggests that state government might be inherently more democratic. The national and state governments also differ in the range of their powers. Article I spells out a specific list of powers allocated to the national legislature, and while the "Necessary and Proper Clause," sometimes referred to as the "Elastic Clause," certainly expands those powers, the Tenth Amendment suggests that there are limits to the powers of the national government: Specifically, the Tenth Amendment declares that "[t]he powers not delegated to the United States by the Constitution, nor prohibited by it to the States, are reserved to the States respectively, or to the people." This suggests that while there are some specific limits on what the states are allowed to do (Article I, Section 10), the national government may do only those things assigned to it—while the states are left free to do as they choose (unless their own state constitution blocks them). Among the key powers left to the states are what are known as the "police powers," which are defined as the right to regulate the health, safety, welfare, and morals of the population. In contrast to the states, the federal government enjoys no such general police power.

The national government's powers may be limited, but they are strong powers with wide reach—just how wide, of course, is a matter of much debate. Any such debate would include a close consideration of the so-called Elastic Clause: Article I gives Congress a long list of powers, and then adds that Congress has the authority to make laws "necessary and proper for carrying into execution the foregoing Powers and all other Powers vested by this Constitution in the Government of the United States, or in any Department or Officer thereof." As our readings from Thomas Jefferson and Alexander Hamilton make clear, controversy over the meaning of this clause was evident from the Founding. In addition to this clause, the Constitution grants federal legislation supremacy over state legislation. Article VI, paragraph 2 asserts that "the laws of the United States [are the] supreme Law of the Land; and the Judges in every State shall be bound thereby, any Thing in the Constitution or Laws of any State to the Contrary notwithstanding." This "Supremacy Clause" has been invoked to make federal legislation supreme in relation to state laws that conflict with it. According to the doctrine of "preemption," states are prohibited from enacting laws that invade the realm of congressional powers. Congress has exercised power under each of the allocations provided in Article I, Section 8—but it has made particularly extensive use of the power "to regulate Commerce with foreign Nations, and among the several States, and with the Indian Tribes." While the "Commerce Clause" would ultimately come to be interpreted in a broad way, the Court struggled for decades in an attempt to draw a clear line between commerce that was exclusively within one state and that was "among the states"— that is to say, interstate commerce.

As you read this chapter, you will see that there is now—and long has been—a debate over the meaning of the clauses that give Congress its various powers, as well as the scope, range, and reach of these powers, particularly as they clash with the powers thought to be reserved to the states. You will be asked to think about the proper constitutional balance between congressional and state power. As you will see, the Commerce Clause has been a frequent site of contestation between those who wish to expand federal power and those who wish to limit it. Part of our inquiry will be guided by the text of the Constitution, but we will also continue to examine approaches to constitutional interpretation that do not emphasize a strict textualism. As you saw in the previous chapters, there is a robust debate about how to interpret the Constitution in general, and the debate about how to interpret clauses related to congressional and state power is part of that discussion.

In order to understand the debate about how to interpret Congress's power, it is important for you to be familiar with some of the background debates that often framed these issues. Among the most profound struggles you will consider is one that emerged in the twentieth century. On one side of this debate were those who saw the Constitution as a document of strict limits on national government power; they argued for strict constitutional limits on governmental authority to interfere with individual property and economic rights. Notably, these supporters of limited governmental power asserted that a fundamental right to contract was enshrined in the Fourteenth Amendment. On the other side were those who saw the Constitution quite differently, asserting that the Constitution provided the government with the authority (and even the obligation) to ensure the economic welfare of all citizens, including protections against what was seen as a great inequality of power between employers and employees. Those who insisted on a strictly limited role for government might today be referred to as "libertarians"; many modern conservatives share many of these concerns and commitments. Those on the other side initially identified themselves as "progressives," and coalesced around Presidents Theodore Roosevelt and Woodrow Wilson, but they eventually galvanized under the leadership of President Franklin D. Roosevelt, seeking a vastly increased role for the federal government in regulating the economy and securing workers' rights.

The debate between progressives and libertarians came to a head in *Lochner v. New York*, which we excerpted in the previous chapter and which we will examine again in Chapter 7. In *Lochner v. New York*, the Court struck down an attempt by a state government to regulate the hours and working conditions of bread bakers. Supporters of this legislation argued that at its root, it was a legitimate exercise of governmental power designed to protect the health and safety of these workers and the public, which would consume the product of their labor. The Supreme Court saw the legislation in a very different light, arguing that the law infringed upon the economic rights of both the workers and their employers—the right of each to agree to contracts that would define hours and working conditions. This right to contract, they insisted, was a vital and fundamental right embedded in the Constitution.

Importantly, *Lochner v. New York* concerned legislation that originated in the State of New York. If the regulation at issue in *Lochner v. New York*, however, had originated in the U.S. Congress, its opponents might have questioned its authority on the grounds that the Congress had no constitutional power to regulate the economy. Indeed, this issue defined a face-off between progressives and libertarians in the 1930s, some years after *Lochner v. New York*, over a range of national efforts to regulate the economy and the relations between employers and employees. These debates in the 1930s concerned the limits of what the national government could regulate or forbid, including particularly contentious struggles over the power to delegate broad discretionary power to the president as well as the power to create executive and even independent governmental agencies that could protect workers' rights. Specifically, the debate at this time focused on the constitutionality of the "New Deal," a staggering array of legislation passed by Congress and signed into law during President Franklin Roosevelt's first term of office between 1933 and 1936. President Roosevelt's New Deal had sought a larger role for the federal government in regulating the economy (including banks, stock exchanges, and agriculture), in promoting employment, and in protecting workers' rights. This new role for the federal government raised the important question, however, of whether Congress, in passing the New Deal, was exceeding its authority under the Constitution. Opponents of the New Deal argued that Congress had no constitutional power to enact it. As our case selection will make clear, President Roosevelt faced a Supreme Court that challenged his contention that the federal government had the constitutional power and authority to carry out the New Deal.

With these political and historical considerations in mind, we can better appreciate the debate over constitutional interpretation in regards to federal power. Originalist interpretations of the clauses that grant federal power have tended to stress the limited nature of congressional authority. According to these readings, we should take a narrow rather than an expansive view of the clauses that grant federal power, including the Commerce Clause, the Necessary and Proper Clause, and the Supremacy Clause. But in contrast to originalist understandings, a pragmatist might stress the need for an increase of federal power. Indeed, many of the arguments faced by President Roosevelt and his administration in their quest to seek an expanded role for federal power in regulating the economy were born out of the Great Depression, and the belief that the Constitution must be read in a way that would allow the government to combat this great emergency. A pragmatic approach to constitutional interpretation might justify an expanded federal government's role on grounds that it would better ensure economic stability. Of course, such pragmatic arguments are also vulnerable to the worry that such a federal role might backfire. The role of the moral reading in interpreting these clauses would depend on the kind of morality one thinks is central to the Constitution. Those who favor the kind of philosophy exemplified by *Lochner v. New York* might suggest that the moral reading requires limiting federal power, while those who believe that the morality of the Constitution is consistent with protecting the rights of workers might defend a more expansive understanding of the powers of Congress to intervene in the economy. As you read through the chapter, you should ask yourself what kind of interpretation each of these theories might support.

Now that we have examined the ideological and interpretative debate surrounding congressional authority, it is important to provide a broad overview of the history of the Supreme Court's jurisprudence about the boundaries between congressional and state powers, especially in the twentieth century. This will give you the background necessary to understand the in-depth debates raised in the readings and case law we examine in this chapter. It will also give you a sense of how the historical cases you will read from previous centuries continue to shape and influence the major struggles in the twentieth century and on to the present. In the nineteenth century, congressional power remained somewhat limited. Although the Court had clearly recognized that Congress had the power to regulate some interstate economic interaction in *Gibbons v. Ogden*, which we examine in Section A, it also limited that right. In the late nineteenth century, the Court struck down attempts by Congress to regulate monopolies in *United States v. E.C. Knight Co.*, when it struck down portions of the Sherman Anti-Trust Act. But this case did not entirely gut Congress of its ability to regulate monopolies. In *Swift & Co. v. United States*, the Court upheld Congress's authority to regulate products in the "stream of commerce." But despite the Court's affirmation of Congress's Commerce Clause power in *Swift*, it would remain a limited power. In fact, the Court would soon begin to strike down major pieces of Progressive legislation.

After *Swift*, a conservative Supreme Court, seeking to protect property rights and fearful of increased federal power in economic regulation, sought to establish limits on congressional authority. In 1918, well before the New Deal, the Supreme Court in *Hammer v. Dagenhart* struck down workers' rights legislation aimed at protecting children. The notion that Congress had expansive authority under the Constitution, however, would find a champion in President Roosevelt, who sought to build upon the progressives' commitment to workers' rights and to establish a federal role in regulating the economy. In the face of the nation's deepest economic crisis, and under intense political pressure from President Roosevelt, the critical swing vote on a deeply divided Supreme Court (Justice Owen Roberts) shifted his vote away from the implacable conservative bloc of four justices (Justices Willis Van Devanter, James Clark McReynolds, George Sutherland, and Pierce Butler) and upheld a key New Deal provision. This change famously became known as the "switch in time that saved nine." Realizing that they were now consigned to be a permanent minority, the four conservatives soon left the Court (three retired; Justice Butler died), and they were all replaced by justices nominated by President Roosevelt. The Court would soon develop a very different jurisprudence, shifting from a narrow vision of national power to a very broad reading in which they would give Congress wide leeway in regulating the economy. The Court's announcement in *Wickard v. Filburn*, that Congress was free to regulate just about any activity that might have even an indirect and seemingly trivial impact on the national economy, opened the possibility of nearly limitless congressional power.

During the Civil Rights movement, it would be the Commerce Clause that would serve as the constitutional foundation for congressional power to end segregation not only in government institutions but in all sorts of areas that had traditionally been thought to be private businesses, including transportation, restaurants, hotels, amusement parks, recreation facilities, and other public accommodations. You might have thought that the constitutional basis for this legislation would have been found in the Fourteenth Amendment's guarantee of equal protection. But, as you will see in our in-depth discussion of equal protection in Chapter 9, this clause was interpreted narrowly by the Court in the years immediately following its addition to the Constitution, and would only be applied where the government itself was involved—it would be triggered only where there was "state action." But when a privately owned hotel or restaurant or bar decided to exclude African Americans from their property, there appeared to be no state action involved. This led President Lyndon Johnson's administration to rest its landmark Civil Rights Act of 1964—which banned such discrimination—on the Commerce Clause. This choice was ratified by the Supreme Court in two 1964 cases—*Heart of Atlanta Motel v. United States* and *Katzenbach v. McClung*. These cases, many would argue, marked the final and perhaps most dramatic expansion of the Commerce Clause as the critical and unassailable foundation for national power.

Or at least it seemed that way. By the late 1960s, it was widely assumed that there was virtually nothing that Congress might like to do that could not be grounded in the Commerce Clause. But that assumption was shaken in the mid-1970s as the liberal Warren Court was slowly replaced through retirement by far more conservative justices named to the Court by President Richard Nixon, including Chief Justice Warren Burger and then–Associate Justice William Rehnquist, who joined the Court in 1971. Echoing both Thomas Jefferson and the pre-New Deal Court, Justice Rehnquist sought to restore a textual limit to the reach of the Commerce Clause. In key cases concerning the power of the national government to regulate hand guns, domestic violence, and municipal workers' wages and hours, Justice Rehnquist led the Court in striking down legislation that the majority deemed to have exceeded congressional authority under the Commerce Clause, insisting that some commerce is truly local and thus not subject to the regulation of the national government.

The so-called "New Federalism" championed by Justice Rehnquist has appeared to many to be a conservative idea. Indeed, perhaps because of the Civil Rights Era in which the defenders of states' rights were regarded as defenders of segregation and racism, limits on the federal government were seen to suggest an anti-progressive agenda. But as the reading by Kathleen Sullivan at the end of this chapter suggests, it is arguable whether this debate should be understood along a left-right divide. As the federal government grew increasingly conservative in the early twenty-first century, with a Republican president and Congress, some liberals began to think that limits on federalism might be consistent with a progressive agenda. In particular, the federal government's restriction of medical marijuana, its foray into regulating the kinds of abortions that medical doctors can perform, and its resistance to same-sex marriage have all led progressives to question whether there is virtue in leaving these choices to the states rather than the national government. In other words, perhaps there is nothing inherently conservative or liberal about federal power over the states. Ask yourself whether you favor a limited or expansive federal government in the various policy areas presented in the cases and readings included in this chapter. Keep in mind how your position about the role of Congress's power relate to your views on the policies at hand.

A. THE IDEA OF ENUMERATED POWERS

What are the sources of congressional power? How does enumerating powers protect liberty? Does it lead to effective governance?

In this section, we turn to the origins of the Supreme Court's rulings on congressional power. As you will see, although the Constitution sets out a number of areas in which Congress is authorized to act, from the beginning of our nation's history there has been a question as to how far these powers extend. Part of the question here is interpretive. Should we interpret these powers in a broad or narrow way? But behind this interpretive question lies a puzzle about what powers are granted to Congress by the Constitution and what kind of balance between state and federal power it requires. Fundamental to any discussion of American federalism is the case of *McCulloch v. Maryland*, which concerned the constitutionality of the Second Bank of the United States and the related question as to whether the bank could be taxed by state governments. Nowhere in the Constitution is there a mention of a power for Congress to create a bank, but do other provisions allow for its creation?

In addition to this specific question about the bank lies the more general issue of the way to strike the balance between state and federal power in the American constitutional order. Those who argue against the bank's constitutionality stress the notion of state sovereignty. Pointing out, for instance, that the Constitution was ratified by the states, they argue that the heart of American democracy lies in state government. Therefore, if federal congressional power were extended beyond the narrow provisions in Article I, it might impede the power of the states, and thus the sovereign authority of the states as realized in the people. This defense of states' rights as the basis for American democracy is most closely associated with Thomas Jefferson, whose views we examine in this chapter. It was Jefferson's political party, the Democratic-Republicans, who most prominently promoted the view in the early Republic that state governments were closer to the people than the federal government and therefore could better represent their interests.

In contrast to Jefferson's emphasis on the power of the states, Alexander Hamilton emphasizes the power of a strong national government. You will see that Hamilton makes both pragmatic and textual arguments about the constitutionality of the bank. But more importantly, he is arguing that the structure of American democracy has a large role for the federal government and Congress. Although the debate between Hamilton and Jefferson concerned the constitutionality of the First Bank of the United States, it would not be until the establishment of a second bank that the Supreme Court would rule on this important issue. As you will see in his opinion, U.S. Supreme Court Chief Justice John Marshall rejects the arguments of Jefferson and of those who claim that the people's sovereignty is only realized through state governments. But Chief Justice Marshall does not entirely reject a role for the state governments or deny that they are one location of the people's sovereignty. Instead, he announces what has come to be known as a theory of "dual-sovereignty" in both the federal government and in the states. The challenge for a theory of dual-sovereignty, however, is how to balance state and federal power given that both are sovereign entities.

The cases in this section will guide you as you attempt to understand what it might mean for both the states and the federal government to be sovereign under the U.S. Constitution. As you read through *McCulloch v. Maryland* and the two other cases, you will focus on three clauses that grant congressional power: (1) the Necessary and Proper Clause (in *McCulloch v. Maryland*); (2) the Interstate Commerce Clause (in *Gibbons v. Ogden*); and (3) the Spending Clause (in *South Dakota v. Dole*). Some of our inquiry, therefore, will be about the meaning of these three provisions. But as you know from Chapter 2, questions of textual interpretation are also controversial. Through what lens should we read each of these three clauses? Some of you will be tempted to turn immediately to originalism. Originalists would ask what these clauses meant to the relevant legal community at the time they were written and would also interpret them based on a narrow reading, or "to the letter of the law." But one complication with the originalist approach, as will be made clear in our first two readings, is that Hamilton and Jefferson, two prominent members of the Founding generation, disagreed about how these clauses should be understood. While Jefferson argued for an understanding that was narrow and limited, Hamilton suggested the importance of reading the Necessary and Proper Clause and the other clauses enumerating congressional authority in a broad way so as to heighten congressional power. For instance, in addition to the Necessary and Proper Clause, Congress is given the power to spend money raised through taxation. Together these clauses might be thought to suggest a more general power to intervene in national economic matters. As you will see, the controversy over how broadly or narrowly to read these clauses has not disappeared. Indeed, the Spending Clause itself has in the past 100 years become a central way that Congress has expanded its power. In *South Dakota v. Dole*, for instance, you will see that federal power to spend money on highways becomes linked to Congress's policy goal to create a national drinking age of 21. As you read the case, consider the kinds of arguments that Hamilton and Jefferson might have brought to this more recent controversy.

In contrast to originalists, pragmatists might place less emphasis on specific clauses and more on the general question of whether increased federal power would be beneficial to the country. In particular, the question of the Second Bank of the United States could be framed as one about the need to create a national economy. Some pragmatists might argue that increased federal power was necessary if the young United States was to develop a thriving national economy. But this empirical claim might be contested by others who have suggested that federal intervention into the economy at this time depressed rather than stimulated it. Should these considerations be taken into account in deciding the extent to which congressional power is authorized?

The lens of proceduralism stresses interpretations that reinforce democratic procedures. But these cases make clear that the proceduralist faces a puzzle: Which procedures should be enforced, those of federal or state government? As with pragmatism and originalism, it is not clear what kind of constitutional interpretation proceduralism recommends in these cases, but you might find it a helpful lens through which to examine textual authorizations of Congress's powers.

The moral reading might seem irrelevant to the clauses authorizing Congress's powers, which do not have obviously moral content. For instance, in *Gibbons v. Ogden*, we examine the extent to which the Commerce Clause authorizes federal power and limits trade between two states. This is not obviously a moral question, but it will become clearer in the next two sections that beneath questions of federalism lie fundamental moral issues. In particular, in Section B, the debate over the Commerce Clause moves from one solely concerned with commerce to one that is focused on race. The Civil Rights Act of 1964 outlawed segregation between the races in areas of so-called "public accommodations," such as restaurants and hotels. Where did Congress get this authority? As you will see, for reasons elaborated in Chapter 8, the Fourteenth Amendment was thought not to serve as a textual home for the power to enact this legislation because it had been narrowly interpreted by the Court in the *Civil Rights Cases* (see Chapter 8) shortly after it was ratified, and was thought to concern only discrimination that involved the government itself. By contrast, the Commerce Clause, which by 1964 had been broadly interpreted and applied, seemed a far more promising foundation for congressional authority. Opponents of this legislation argued that because many of these accommodations were not part of interstate commerce, Congress had no power to outlaw segregation as it did in this Act. Indeed, originalist interpreters of the Commerce Clause would have difficulty defending Congress's use of its Commerce Clause power in this way. But those who do defend congressional authority under the Commerce Clause to outlaw segregation in areas of public accommodations might do well to turn to the moral reading. Perhaps the legitimacy of the purpose of the legislation is as important as the textual meanings of the clauses. Similarly, proponents of the moral reading might defend President Franklin Roosevelt's push to use the

Commerce Clause power during the New Deal on such grounds. In other words, while the moral reading might not be obviously relevant to this section, as we study the development of the Commerce Clause in the next section, it will be central to our inquiry. In general, throughout this chapter, you should continue to ask how a variety of methods of interpretation might help us to analyze issues of congressional power and the problem of federalism.

Alexander Hamilton

OPINION AS TO THE CONSTITUTIONALITY OF THE BANK OF THE UNITED STATES*

1791

The creation of a national bank was one of the most heated controversies of the early Republic, both as a matter of public policy and as a question of constitutional interpretation. Congress's power to authorize a central bank is now well-settled, as reflected in Federal Reserve Chairman Ben Bernanke's broad control of America's money supply during the recent financial crisis. But from the time of the Founding through President Andrew Jackson's dramatic veto of the renewal of the charter of the Second Bank of the United States in 1832, the issue was never far from the heart of public partisan debate— not unlike contemporary disagreements over abortion rights and affirmative action.

In 1791, President Washington requested written opinions on the constitutionality of the bank charter before signing it into law. Alexander Hamilton, as Secretary of the Treasury, believed that a national bank was essential to creating financial stability and establishing the nation's credit. Thomas Jefferson, writing as Secretary of State, adamantly opposed the bank, as well as the excise taxes that would finance its incorporation. Their arguments as to the

constitutionality of incorporating the bank are reproduced below.

. . . [T]his general principle is inherent in the very definition of government, and essential to every step of progress to be made by that of the United States, namely: That every power vested in a government is in its nature sovereign, and includes, by force of the term, a right to employ all the means requisite and fairly applicable to the attainment of the ends of such power, and which are not precluded by restrictions and exceptions specified in the Constitution, or not immoral, or not contrary to the essential ends of political society.

This principle, in its application to government in general, would be admitted as an axiom; and it will be incumbent upon those who may incline to deny it, to prove a distinction, and to show that a rule which, in the general system of things, is essential to the preservation of the social order, is inapplicable to the United States.

The circumstance that the powers of sovereignty are in this country divided between the National and State governments, does not afford the distinction required. It does not follow from this, that each of the portion of powers delegated

*Available at *http://avalon.law.yale.edu/18th_century/
bank-ah.asp.

to the one or to the other, is not sovereign with regard to its proper objects. It will only follow from it, that each has sovereign power as to certain things, and not as to other things. To deny that the Government of the United States has sovereign power, as to its declared purposes and trusts, because its power does not extend to all cases would be equally to deny that the State governments have sovereign power in any case, because their power does not extend to every case. The tenth section of the first article of the Constitution exhibits a long list of very important things which they may not do. And thus the United States would furnish the singular spectacle of a political society without sovereignty, or of a people governed, without government.

If it would be necessary to bring proof to a proposition so clear, as that which affirms that the powers of the Federal Government, as to its objects, were sovereign, there is a clause of its Constitution which would be decisive. It is that which declares that the Constitution, and the laws of the United States made in pursuance of it, and all treaties made, or which shall be made, under their authority, shall be the supreme law of the land.

. . . [W]here the authority of the government is general, it can create corporations in all cases; where it is confined to certain branches of legislation, it can create corporations only in those cases.

. . . [A]ll government is a delegation of power. But how much is delegated in each case, is a question of fact, to be made out by fair reasoning and construction, upon the particular provisions of the Constitution, taking as guides the general principles and general ends of governments.

It is not denied that there are implied, as well as express powers, and that the former are as effectually delegated as the latter. . . . It will not be doubted, that if the United States should make a conquest of any of the territories of its neighbors, they would possess sovereign jurisdiction over the conquered territory. This would be rather a result, from the whole mass of the powers of the government, and from the nature of political society, than a consequence of either of the powers specially enumerated.

. . . [A]s a power of erecting a corporation may as well be implied as any other thing, it may as well be employed as an instrument or mean of carrying into execution any of the specified powers, as any other instrument or mean whatever. The only question must be in this, as in every other case, whether the mean to be employed or in this instance, the corporation to be erected, has a natural relation to any of the acknowledged objects or lawful ends of the government. Thus a corporation may not be erected by Congress for superintending the police of the city of Philadelphia, because they are not authorized to regulate the police of that city. But one may be erected in relation to the collection of taxes, or to the trade with foreign countries, or to the trade between the States, or with the Indian tribes; because it is the province of the Federal Government to regulate those objects, and because it is incident to a general sovereign or legislative power to regulate a thing, to employ all the means which relate to its regulation to the best and greatest advantage.

. . . To this mode of reasoning respecting the right of employing all the means requisite to the execution of the specified powers of the government, it is to be objected, that none but necessary and proper means are to be employed; and the Secretary of State maintains, that no means are to be considered necessary but those without which the grant of the power would be nugatory. Nay, so far does he go in his restrictive interpretation of the word, as even to make the case of necessity which shall warrant the constitutional exercise of the power to depend on casual and temporary circumstances; an idea which alone refutes the construction. The expediency of exercising a particular power, at a particular time, must, indeed, depend on circumstances; but the constitutional; right of exercising it must be uniform and invariable, the same to-day as to-morrow.

. . . It is certain that neither the grammatical nor popular sense of the term requires that construction. According to both, necessary often means no more than needful, requisite, incidental, useful, or conducive to. It is a common mode of expression to say, that it is necessary for a government or a person to do this or that thing, when nothing more is intended or understood, than that the interests of the government or person require, or will be promoted by, the doing of this or that thing. The imagination can be at no loss for exemplifications of the use of the word in this sense. And it is the true one in which it is to be understood as used in the Constitution. The whole turn of the clause containing it indicates, that it was the intent of the Convention, by that clause, to give a liberal latitude to the exercise of the specified powers. The expressions have peculiar comprehensiveness. They are, "to make all laws necessary and proper for carrying into execution the foregoing powers, and all other powers vested by the Constitution in the Government of the United States, or in any department or officer thereof."

To understand the word as the Secretary of State does, would be to depart from its obvious and popular sense, and to give it a restrictive operation, an idea never before entertained. It would be to give it the same force as if the word absolutely or indispensably had been prefixed to it.

Such a construction would beget endless uncertainty and embarrassment. The cases must be palpable and extreme, in which it could be pronounced, with certainty, that a measure was absolutely necessary, or one, without which the exercise of a given power would be nugatory. There are few measures of any government which would stand so severe a test. . . .

The practice of the government is against the rule of construction advocated by the Secretary of State. Of this, the act concerning lighthouses, beacons, buoys, and public piers, is a decisive example. This, doubtless, must be referred to the powers of regulating trade, and is fairly relative to it. But it cannot be affirmed that the exercise of that power in this instance was strictly necessary or that the power itself would be nugatory, without that of regulating establishments of this nature.

This restrictive interpretation of the word necessary is also contrary to this sound maxim of construction; namely, that the powers contained in a constitution of government, especially those which concern the general administration of the affairs of a country, its finances, trade, defence, etc., ought to be construed liberally in advancement of the public good. This rule does not depend on the particular form of a government, or on the particular demarcation of the boundaries of its powers, but on the nature and objects of government itself. The means by which national exigencies are to be provided for, national inconveniences obviated, national prosperity promoted, are of such infinite variety, extent, and complexity, that there must of necessity be great latitude of discretion in the selection and application of those means. Hence, consequently, the necessity and propriety of exercising the authorities intrusted to a government on principles of liberal construction.

. . . It is no valid objection to the doctrine to say, that it is calculated to extend the power of the General Government throughout the entire sphere of State legislation. The same thing has been said, and may be said, with regard to every exercise of power by implication or construction.

. . . But the doctrine which is contended for is not chargeable with the consequences imputed to it. It does not affirm that the National Government is sovereign in all respects, but that it is sovereign to a certain extent—that is, to the extent of the objects of its specified powers.

It leaves, therefore, a criterion of what is constitutional, and of what is not so. This criterion is the end, to which the measure relates as a means. If the end be clearly comprehended within any of the specified powers, and if the measure have an obvious relation to that end, and is not forbidden by any particular provision of the Constitution, it may safely be deemed to come within the compass of the national authority. There is also this further criterion, which may materially assist the decision: Does the proposed measure abridge a pre-existing right of any State or of any individual? If it does not, there is a strong presumption in favor of its constitutionality, and slighter relations to any declared object of the Constitution may be permitted to turn the scale.

. . . The proposed bank is to consist of an association of persons, for the purpose of creating a joint capital, to be employed chiefly and essentially in loans. So far the object is not only lawful, but it is the mere exercise of a right which the law allows to every individual. The Bank of New York, which is not incorporated, is an example of such an association. The bill proposes, in addition, that the government shall become a joint proprietor in this undertaking, and that it shall permit the bills of the company, payable on demand, to be receivable in its revenues; and stipulates that it shall not grant privileges, similar to those which are to be allowed to this company, to any others. All this is incontrovertibly within the compass of the discretion of the government. The only question is, whether it has a right to incorporate this company, in order to enable it the more effectually to accomplish ends which are in themselves lawful.

To establish such a right, it remains to show the relation of such an institution to one or more of the specified powers of the government. Accordingly it is affirmed that it has a relation, more or less direct, to the power of collecting taxes, to that of borrowing money, to that of regulating trade between the States, and to those of raising and maintaining fleets and armies. . . .

A bank relates to the collection of taxes in two ways—indirectly, by increasing the quantity of circulating medium and quickening circulation, which facilitates the means of paying directly, by creating a convenient species of medium in which they are to be paid.

To designate or appoint the money or thing in which taxes are to be paid, is not only a proper, but a necessary exercise of the power of collecting them. . . .

And among the expedients which may be adopted, is that of bills issued under the authority of the United States.

Now the manner of issuing these bills is again matter of discretion. The government might doubtless proceed in the following manner:

It might provide that they should be issued under the direction of certain officers, payable on demand; and, in order to support their credit, and give them a ready circulation, it might, besides giving them a currency in its taxes, set apart, out of any moneys in its treasury, a given sum, and appropriate it, under the direction of those officers, as a fund for answering the bills, as presented for payment.

The constitutionality of all this would not admit of a question, and yet it would amount to the institution of a bank, with a view to the more convenient collection of taxes. . . . [I]f the place where the fund to be set apart was kept should be made a receptacle of the moneys of all other persons who should incline to deposit them there for safe-keeping; and would become still more so, if the officers charged with the direction of the fund were authorized to make discounts at the usual rate of interest, upon good security. To deny the power of the government to add these ingredients to the plan, would be to refine away all government.

. . . Suppose, when the species of bank which has been described was about to be instituted, it was to be urged that, in order to secure to it a due degree of confidence, the fund ought not only to be set apart and appropriated generally, but ought to be specifically vested in the officers who were to have the direction of it, and in their successors in office, to the end that it might acquire the character of private property. . . . [S]uch a disposition of the thing would amount to the erection of a corporation; for the true definition of a corporation seems to be this: It is a legal person, or a person created by act of law, consisting of one or more natural persons authorized to hold property . . . .

. . . Suppose, also, that, by some of those adverse conjunctures which occasionally attend nations, there had been a very great drain of the specie of the country, so as not only to cause general distress for want of an adequate medium of circulation, but to produce, in consequence of that circumstance, considerable defalcations in the public revenues. Suppose, also, that there was no bank instituted in any State; in such a posture of things, would it not be most manifest, that the incorporation of a bank like that proposed by the bill would be a measure immediately relative to the effectual collection of the taxes, and completely within the province of the sovereign power of providing, by all laws necessary and proper, for that collection? . . .

A bank has a direct relation to the power of borrowing money, because it is a[n] usual, and in sudden emergencies an essential, instrument in the obtaining of loans to government.

A nation is threatened with a war; large sums are wanted on a sudden to make the necessary preparations. Taxes are laid for the purpose, but it requires time to obtain the benefit of them. Anticipation is indispensable. If there be a bank the supply can at once be had. If there be none, loans from individuals must be sought. The progress of these is often too slow for the exigency; in some situations they are not practicable at all. Frequently when they are, it is of great consequence to be able to anticipate the product of them by advance from a bank.

. . . Let it then be supposed that the necessity existed, (as but for a casualty would be the case), that proposals were made for obtaining a loan; that a number of individuals came forward and said, we are willing to accommodate the government with the money; . . . but in order to do this, it is indispensable that we should be incorporated as a bank. . . .

Can it be believed that a compliance with this proposition would be unconstitutional? . . .

The institution of a bank has also a natural relation to the regulation of trade between the States, in so far as it is conducive to the creation of a convenient medium of exchange between them, and to the keeping up a full circulation, by preventing the frequent displacement of the metals in reciprocal remittances. Money is the very hinge on which commerce turns. And this does not merely mean gold and silver; many other things have served the purpose, with different degrees of utility. Paper has been extensively employed.

The Secretary of State further argues, that if this was a regulation of commerce, it would be void, as extending as much to the internal commerce of every State as to its external. But what regulation of commerce does not extend to the internal commerce of every State? . . . [W]hat regulation of trade between the States but must affect the internal trade of each State? What can operate upon the whole, but must extend to every part?

The relation of a bank to the execution of the powers that concern the common defence has been anticipated. It has been noted, that, at this very moment, the aid of such an institution is essential to the measures to be pursued for the protection of our frontiers.

It now remains to show that the incorporation of a bank is within the operation of the provision which authorizes Congress to make all needful rules and regulations concerning the property of the United States. . . .

The support of government—the support of troops for the common defence—the payment of the public debt, are the true final causes for raising money. The disposition and regulation of it, when raised, are the steps by which it is applied to the ends

for which it was raised, not the ends themselves. Hence, therefore, the money to be raised by taxes, as well as any other personal property, must be supposed to come within the meaning, as they certainly do within the letter, of authority to make all needful rules and regulations concerning the property of the United States.

A power to make all needful rules and regulations concerning territory, has been construed to mean a power to erect a government. A power to regulate trade, is a power to make all needful rules and regulations concerning trade. Why may it not, then, include that of erecting a trading company, as well as, in other cases, to erect a government?

. . . [T]he very general power of laying and collecting taxes, and appropriating their proceeds—that of borrowing money indefinitely—that of coining money, and regulating foreign coins—that of making all needful rules and regulations respecting the property of the United States. These powers combined, as well as the reason and nature of the thing, speak strongly this language: that it is the manifest design and scope of the Constitution to vest in Congress all the powers requisite to the effectual administration of the finances of the United States. As far as concerns this object, there appears to be no parsimony of power. . . .

Thomas Jefferson

OPINION ON THE CONSTITUTIONALITY OF A NATIONAL BANK*

1791

. . . I consider the foundation of the Constitution as laid on this ground: That

*Available at *http://avalon.law.yale.edu/18th_century/ bank-tj.asp.*

"all powers not delegated to the United States, by the Constitution, nor prohibited by it to the States, are reserved to the States or to the people." To take a single step beyond the boundaries thus specially drawn around the powers of Congress, is to take possession of a boundless field of power, no longer susceptible of any definition.

The incorporation of a bank, and the powers assumed by this bill, have not, in my opinion, been delegated to the United States, by the Constitution.

I.

They are not among the powers specially enumerated: for these are:

1. A power to lay taxes for the purpose of paying the debts of the United States; but no debt is paid by this bill, nor any tax laid. Were it a bill to raise money, its origination in the Senate would condemn it by the Constitution.

2. "To borrow money." But this bill neither borrows money nor ensures the borrowing of it. The proprietors of the bank will be just as free as any other money holders, to lend or not to lend their money to the public. The operation proposed in the bill first, to lend them two millions, and then to borrow them back again, cannot change the nature of the latter act, which will still be a payment, and not a loan, call it by what name you please.

3. To "regulate commerce with foreign nations, and among the States, and with the Indian tribes." To erect a bank, and to regulate commerce, are very different acts. He who erects a bank, creates a subject of commerce in its bills, so does he who makes a bushel of wheat, or digs a dollar out of the mines; yet neither of these persons regulates commerce thereby. To make a thing which may be bought and sold, is not to prescribe regulations for buying and selling. Besides, if this was an exercise of the power of regulating commerce, it would be void, as

extending as much to the internal commerce of every State, as to its external. For the power given to Congress by the Constitution does not extend to the internal regulation of the commerce of a State (that is to say of the commerce between citizen and citizen) which remain exclusively with its own legislature; but to its external commerce only, that is to say, its commerce with another State, or with foreign nations, or with the Indian tribes. Accordingly the bill does not propose the measure as a regulation of trade, but as "productive of considerable advantages to trade." Still less are these powers covered by any other of the special enumerations.

II.

Nor are they within either of the general phrases, which are the two following:

1. To lay taxes to provide for the general welfare of the United States, that is to say, "to lay taxes for the purpose of providing for the general welfare." For the laying of taxes is the power, and the general welfare the purpose for which the power is to be exercised. They are not to lay taxes ad libitum for any purpose they please; but only to pay the debts or provide for the welfare of the Union. In like manner, they are not to do anything they please to provide for the general welfare, but only to lay taxes for that purpose. To consider the latter phrase, not as describing the purpose of the first, but as giving a distinct and independent power to do any act they please, which might be for the good of the Union, would render all the preceding and subsequent enumerations of power completely useless.

It would reduce the whole instrument to a single phrase, that of instituting a Congress with power to do whatever would be for the good of the United States; and, as they would be the sole judges of the good or evil, it would be also a power to do whatever evil they please.

It is an established rule of construction where a phrase will bear either of two meanings, to give it that which will allow some meaning to the other parts of the instrument, and not that which would render all the others useless. Certainly no such universal power was meant to be given them. It was intended to lace them up straitly within the enumerated powers, and those without which, as means, these powers could not be carried into effect. It is known that the very power now proposed as a means was rejected as an end by the Convention which formed the Constitution. A proposition was made to them to authorize Congress to open canals, and an amendatory one to empower them to incorporate. But the whole was rejected, and one of the reasons for rejection urged in debate was, that then they would have a power to erect a bank, which would render the great cities, where there were prejudices and jealousies on the subject, adverse to the reception of the Constitution.

2. The second general phrase is, "to make all laws necessary and proper for carrying into execution the enumerated powers." But they can all be carried into execution without a bank. A bank therefore is not necessary, and consequently not authorized by this phrase.

It has been urged that a bank will give great facility or convenience in the collection of taxes. Suppose this were true: yet the Constitution allows only the means which are "necessary," not those which are merely "convenient" for effecting the enumerated powers. If such a latitude of construction be allowed to this phrase as to give any non-enumerated power, it will go to everyone, for there is not one which ingenuity may not torture into a convenience in some instance or other, to

some one of so long a list of enumerated powers. It would swallow up all the delegated powers, and reduce the whole to one power, as before observed. Therefore it was that the Constitution restrained them to the necessary means, that is to say, to those means without which the grant of power would be nugatory.

But let us examine this convenience and see what it is. The report on this subject, page 3, states the only general convenience to be, the preventing the transportation and re-transportation of money between the States and the treasury (for I pass over the increase of circulating medium, ascribed to it as a want, and which, according to my ideas of paper money, is clearly a demerit). Every State will have to pay a sum of tax money into the treasury; and the treasury will have to pay, in every State, a part of the interest on the public debt, and salaries to the officers of government resident in that State. In most of the States there will still be a surplus of tax money to come up to the seat of government for the officers residing there. The payments of interest and salary in each State may be made by treasury orders on the State collector. This will take up the greater part of the money he has collected in his State, and consequently prevent the great mass of it from being drawn out of the State. If there be a balance of commerce in favor of that State against the one in which the government resides, the surplus of taxes will be remitted by the bills of exchange drawn for that commercial balance. And so it must be if there was a bank. But if there be no balance of commerce, either direct or circuitous, all the banks in the world could not bring up the surplus of taxes, but in the form of money. Treasury orders then, and bills of exchange may prevent the displacement of the main mass of the money collected, without the aid of any bank; and where these fail, it cannot be prevented even with that aid.

Perhaps, indeed, bank bills may be a more convenient vehicle than treasury orders. But a little difference in the degree of convenience cannot constitute the necessity which the Constitution makes the ground for assuming any non-enumerated power.

Besides, the existing banks will, without a doubt, enter into arrangements for lending their agency, and the more favorable, as there will be a competition among them for it; whereas the bill delivers us up bound to the national bank, who are free to refuse all arrangement, but on their own terms, and the public not free, on such refusal, to employ any other bank. That of Philadelphia I believe, now does this business, by their post-notes, which, by an arrangement with the treasury, are paid by any State collector to whom they are presented. This expedient alone suffices to prevent the existence of that necessity which may justify the assumption of a non-enumerated power as a means for carrying into effect an enumerated one. The thing may be done, and has been done, and well done, without this assumption, therefore it does not stand on that degree of necessity which can honestly justify it.

It may be said that a bank whose bills would have a currency all over the States, would be more convenient than one whose currency is limited to a single State.

So it would be still more convenient that there should be a bank, whose bills should have a currency all over the world. But it does not follow from this superior conveniency, that there exists anywhere a power to establish such a bank; or that the world may not go on very well without it.

Can it be thought that the Constitution intended that for a shade or two of convenience, more or less, Congress should be authorized to break down the most ancient and fundamental laws of the several States; such as those against Mortmain, the laws of Alienage, the rules of descent, the acts of distribution, the laws of escheat and forfeiture, the laws of monopoly? Nothing but a necessity invincible by any other means, can justify such a prostitution of laws, which constitute the pillars of our whole system of jurisprudence. Will Congress be too strait-laced to carry the Constitution into honest effect, unless they may pass over the foundation-laws of the State government for the slightest convenience of theirs?

The negative of the President is the shield provided by the Constitution to protect against the invasions of the legislature: 1. The right of the Executive. 2. Of the Judiciary. 3. Of the States and State legislatures. The present is the case of a right remaining exclusively with the States, and consequently one of those intended by the Constitution to be placed under its protection.

McCULLOCH v. MARYLAND

17 U.S. 316 (1819)

Opinion: Marshall, joined by Washington, Johnson, Livingston, Todd, Duvall, Story

While the charter for the First Bank of the United States expired in 1811, Congress passed a charter for a second bank in 1816. Maryland levied a tax against all banks not

chartered within the state, and the president of the Baltimore branch of the national bank, James McCulloch, refused to pay the tax. He claimed that the tax was unconstitutional because it interfered with a valid exercise of congressional power. In reading the case, pay particular attention to the kind of boundaries the holding establishes between federal and state power. According to Chief Justice Marshall, what is the source of congressional power to create the bank? In what ways does he think this power limits the various powers of the states? It is worth noting that by examining whether Congress had the power to authorize the bank, the Court was engaging in an early act of judicial review over federal legislation not long after Marbury v. Madison.

MR. CHIEF JUSTICE MARSHALL
delivered the opinion of the Court.

In the case now to be determined, the defendant, a sovereign State, denies the obligation of a law enacted by the legislature of the Union, and the plaintiff, on his part, contests the validity of an act which has been passed by the legislature of that State. . . .

The first question made in the cause is, has Congress power to incorporate a bank?

It has been truly said, that this can scarcely be considered as an open question, entirely unprejudiced by the former proceedings of the nation respecting it. The principle now contested was introduced at a very early period of our history, has been recognised by many successive legislatures, and has been acted upon by the judicial department, in cases of peculiar delicacy, as a law of undoubted obligation.

. . . [A] doubtful question, one on which human reason may pause, and the human judgment be suspended, in the decision of which the great principles of liberty are not

concerned, but the respective powers of those who are equally the representatives of the people, are to be adjusted; if not put at rest by the practice of the government, ought to receive a considerable impression from that practice. An exposition of the constitution, deliberately established by legislative acts, on the faith of which an immense property has been advanced, ought not to be lightly disregarded.

The power now contested was exercised by the first Congress elected under the present constitution. The bill for incorporating the bank of the United States did not steal upon an unsuspecting legislature, and pass unobserved. Its principle was completely understood, and was opposed with equal zeal and ability. After being resisted, first in the fair and open field of debate, and afterwards in the executive cabinet, with as much persevering talent as any measure has ever experienced, and being supported by arguments which convinced minds as pure and as intelligent as this country can boast, it became a law. The original act was permitted to expire; but a short experience of the embarrassments to which the refusal to revive it exposed the government, convinced those who were most prejudiced against the measure of its necessity, and induced the passage of the present law. . . .

. . . [T]he counsel for the State of Maryland have deemed it of some importance, in the construction of the constitution, to consider that instrument not as emanating from the people, but as the act of sovereign and independent States. The powers of the general government, it has been said, are delegated by the States, who alone are truly sovereign; and must be exercised in subordination to the States, who alone possess supreme dominion.

It would be difficult to sustain this proposition. . . . The government proceeds directly from the people; is "ordained and established" in the name of the people; and is declared to be ordained, "in order to form a more perfect union, establish justice, ensure domestic tranquillity, and secure the blessings of liberty to themselves and to their posterity." The assent of the States, in their sovereign capacity, is implied in calling a Convention, and thus submitting that instrument to the people. But the people were at perfect liberty to accept or reject it; and their act was final. It required not the affirmance, and could not be negatived, by the State governments. The constitution, when thus adopted, was of complete obligation, and bound the State sovereignties.

It has been said, that the people had already surrendered all their powers to the State sovereignties, and had nothing more to give. But, surely, the question whether they may resume and modify the powers granted to government does not remain to be settled in this country. Much more might the legitimacy of the general government be doubted, had it been created by the States. The powers delegated to the State sovereignties were to be exercised by themselves, not by a distinct and independent sovereignty, created by themselves. To the formation of a league, such as was the confederation, the State sovereignties were certainly competent. But when, "in order to form a more perfect union," it was deemed necessary to change this alliance into an effective government, possessing great and sovereign powers, and acting directly on the people, the necessity of referring it to the people, and of deriving its powers directly from them, was felt and acknowledged by all.

If any one proposition could command the universal assent of mankind, we might expect it would be this—that the government of the Union, though limited in its powers, is supreme within its sphere of action. This would seem to result necessarily from its nature. It is the government of all; its powers are delegated by all; it represents all, and acts for all. Though any one State may be willing to control its operations, no State is willing to allow others to control them. The nation, on those subjects on which it can act, must necessarily bind its component parts. But this question is not left to mere reason: the people have, in express terms, decided it, by saying, "this constitution, and the laws of the United States, which shall be made in pursuance thereof," "shall be the supreme law of the land," and by requiring that the members of the State legislatures, and the officers of the executive and judicial departments of the States, shall take the oath of fidelity to it.

The government of the United States, then, though limited in its powers, is supreme; and its laws, when made in pursuance of the constitution, form the supreme law of the land, "any thing in the constitution or laws of any State to the contrary notwithstanding."

Among the enumerated powers, we do not find that of establishing a bank or creating a corporation. But there is no phrase in the instrument which, like the articles of confederation, excludes incidental or implied powers; and which requires that every thing granted shall be expressly and minutely described. Even the 10th amendment, which was framed for the purpose of quieting the excessive jealousies which had been excited, omits the word "expressly," and declares only that the powers "not delegated to the United States, nor prohibited to the States, are reserved to the States or to the people;" thus leaving the question, whether the particular power which may become the subject of contest has been delegated to the one government, or prohibited to the other, to depend on a fair construction of the whole instrument. The men who drew and adopted this amendment had experienced the embarrassments resulting from the insertion of this word in the articles of confederation, and probably omitted it to avoid those embarrassments. A constitution, to contain an accurate detail of all the subdivisions of which its great powers will admit, and of all the means by which they may be carried into execution, would partake of the prolixity of a legal code, and could scarcely be embraced by the human mind. It would probably never be understood by the public. Its nature, therefore, requires, that only its great outlines should be marked, its important objects designated, and the minor ingredients which compose those objects be deduced from the nature of the objects themselves. . . . [W]e must never forget that it is a constitution we are expounding.

Although, among the enumerated powers of government, we do not find the word "bank" or "incorporation," we find the great powers to lay and collect taxes; to borrow money; to regulate commerce; to declare and conduct a war; and to raise and support armies and navies. . . . [A] government, entrusted with such ample powers, on the due execution of which the happiness and prosperity of the nation so vitally depends, must also be entrusted with ample means for their execution. The power being given, it is the interest of the nation to facilitate its execution. It can never be their interest, and cannot be presumed to have been their intention, to clog and embarrass its execution by withholding the most appropriate means. . . . Can we adopt that construction (unless the words imperiously require it) which would impute to the framers of that instrument, when granting these powers for the public good, the intention of impeding their exercise by withholding a choice of means? If, indeed, such be the mandate of the constitution, we have only to obey; but that instrument does not profess to enumerate the means by which the powers it confers may be executed; nor does

it prohibit the creation of a corporation, if the existence of such a being be essential to the beneficial exercise of those powers. It is, then, the subject of fair inquiry, how far such means may be employed.

The creation of a corporation, it is said, appertains to sovereignty. This is admitted. But to what portion of sovereignty does it appertain? Does it belong to one more than to another? In America, the powers of sovereignty are divided between the government of the Union, and those of the States. They are each sovereign, with respect to the objects committed to it, and neither sovereign with respect to the objects committed to the other. . . . The power of creating a corporation, though appertaining to sovereignty, is not, like the power of making war, or levying taxes, or of regulating commerce, a great substantive and independent power, which cannot be implied as incidental to other powers, or used as a means of executing them. It is never the end for which other powers are exercised, but a means by which other objects are accomplished. . . . The power of creating a corporation is never used for its own sake, but for the purpose of effecting something else. No sufficient reason is, therefore, perceived, why it may not pass as incidental to those powers which are expressly given, if it be a direct mode of executing them.

But the constitution of the United States has not left the right of Congress to employ the necessary means, for the execution of the powers conferred on the government, to general reasoning. To its enumeration of powers is added that of making "all laws which shall be necessary and proper, for carrying into execution the foregoing powers, and all other powers vested by this constitution, in the government of the United States, or in any department thereof."

The counsel for the State of Maryland have urged various arguments, to prove that this clause, though in terms a grant of power, is not so in effect; but is really restrictive of the general right, which might otherwise be implied, of selecting means for executing the enumerated powers. . . . Congress is not empowered by it to make all laws, which may have relation to the powers conferred on the government, but such only as may be "necessary and proper" for carrying them into execution. The word "necessary," is considered as controlling the whole sentence, and as limiting the right to pass laws for the execution of the granted powers, to such as are indispensable, and without which the power would be nugatory. That it excludes the choice of means, and leaves to Congress, in each case, that only which is most direct and simple.

Is it true, that this is the sense in which the word "necessary" is always used? . . . [W]e find that it frequently imports no more than that one thing is convenient, or useful, or essential to another. To employ the means necessary to an end, is generally understood as employing any means calculated to produce the end, and not as being confined to those single means, without which the end would be entirely unattainable. . . . The word "necessary" . . . admits of all degrees of comparison; and is often connected with other words, which increase or diminish the impression the mind receives of the urgency it imports. A thing may be necessary, very necessary, absolutely or indispensably necessary. To no mind would the same idea be conveyed, by these several phrases. This comment on the word is well illustrated, by the passage cited at the bar, from the 10th section of the 1st article of the constitution. It is, we think, impossible to compare the sentence which prohibits a State from laying "imposts, or duties on imports or exports, except what may be absolutely necessary for executing its inspection laws," with that which authorizes Congress "to make all laws which shall be necessary and

proper for carrying into execution" the powers of the general government, without feeling a conviction that the convention understood itself to change materially the meaning of the word "necessary," by prefixing the word "absolutely." This word, then, like others, is used in various senses; and, in its construction, the subject, the context, the intention of the person using them, are all to be taken into view.

. . . The subject is the execution of those great powers on which the welfare of a nation essentially depends. It must have been the intention of those who gave these powers, to insure, as far as human prudence could insure, their beneficial execution. This could not be done by confiding the choice of means to such narrow limits as not to leave it in the power of Congress to adopt any which might be appropriate, and which were conducive to the end. This provision is made in a constitution intended to endure for ages to come, and, consequently, to be adapted to the various crises of human affairs. To have prescribed the means by which government should, in all future time, execute its powers, would have been to change, entirely, the character of the instrument, and give it the properties of a legal code. It would have been an unwise attempt to provide, by immutable rules, for exigencies which, if foreseen at all, must have been seen dimly, and which can be best provided for as they occur. To have declared that the best means shall not be used, but those alone without which the power given would be nugatory, would have been to deprive the legislature of the capacity to avail itself of experience, to exercise its reason, and to accommodate its legislation to circumstances. If we apply this principle of construction to any of the powers of the government, we shall find it so pernicious in its operation that we shall be compelled to discard it. . . .

So, with respect to the whole penal code of the United States: whence arises the power to punish in cases not prescribed by the constitution? All admit that the government may, legitimately, punish any violation of its laws; and yet, this is not among the enumerated powers of Congress.

Take, for example, the power "to establish post offices and post roads." This power is executed by the single act of making the establishment. But, from this has been inferred the power and duty of carrying the mail along the post road, from one post office to another. And, from this implied power, has again been inferred the right to punish those who steal letters from the post office, or rob the mail. It may be said, with some plausibility, that the right to carry the mail, and to punish those who rob it, is not indispensably necessary to the establishment of a post office and post road. This right is indeed essential to the beneficial exercise of the power, but not indispensably necessary to its existence. So, of the punishment of the crimes of stealing or falsifying a record or process of a Court of the United States, or of perjury in such Court. To punish these offences is certainly conducive to the due administration of justice. But courts may exist, and may decide the causes brought before them, though such crimes escape punishment.

... This clause, as construed by the State of Maryland, would abridge, and almost annihilate this useful and necessary right of the legislature to select its means. That this could not be intended, is, we should think, had it not been already controverted, too apparent for controversy. We think so for the following reasons:

1st. The clause is placed among the powers of Congress, not among the limitations on those powers.

2nd. Its terms purport to enlarge, not to diminish the powers vested in the government. It purports to be an additional power, not a restriction on those already granted. No reason has been, or can be assigned for thus concealing an intention to narrow the discretion of the national legislature under words which purport to enlarge it. ...

The result of the most careful and attentive consideration bestowed upon this clause is, that if it does not enlarge, it cannot be construed to restrain the powers of Congress, or to impair the right of the legislature to exercise its best judgment in the selection of measures to carry into execution the constitutional powers of the government. If no other motive for its insertion can be suggested, a sufficient one is found in the desire to remove all doubts respecting the right to legislate on that vast mass of incidental powers which must be involved in the constitution, if that instrument be not a splendid bauble.

We admit, as all must admit, that the powers of the government are limited, and that its limits are not to be transcended. But we think the sound construction of the constitution must allow to the national legislature that discretion, with respect to the means by which the powers it confers are to be carried into execution, which will enable that body to perform the high duties assigned to it, in the manner most beneficial to the people. Let the end be legitimate, let it be within the scope of the constitution, and all means which are appropriate, which are plainly adapted to that end, which are not prohibited, but consist with the letter and spirit of the constitution, are constitutional.

That a corporation must be considered as a means not less usual, not of higher dignity, not more requiring a particular specification than other means, has been sufficiently proved. ... The power to "make all needful rules and regulations respecting the territory or other property belonging to the United States," is not more comprehensive, than the power "to make all laws which shall be necessary and proper for carrying into execution" the powers of the government. Yet all admit the constitutionality of a territorial government, which is a corporate body.

. . . Should Congress, in the execution of its powers, adopt measures which are prohibited by the constitution; or should Congress, under the pretext of executing its powers, pass laws for the accomplishment of objects not entrusted to the government; it would become the painful duty of this tribunal, should a case requiring such a decision come before it, to say that such an act was not the law of the land. But where the law is not prohibited, and is really calculated to effect any of the objects entrusted to the government, to undertake here to inquire into the degree of its necessity, would be to pass the line which circumscribes the judicial department, and to tread on legislative ground. This court disclaims all pretensions to such a power.

After this declaration, it can scarcely be necessary to say, that the existence of State banks can have no possible influence on the question. . . . [T]he choice of means implies a right to choose a national bank in preference to State banks, and Congress alone can make the election.

2. Whether the State of Maryland may, without violating the constitution, tax that branch?

That the power of taxation is one of vital importance; that it is retained by the States; that it is not abridged by the grant of a similar power to the government of the Union; that it is to be concurrently exercised by the two governments: are truths which have never been denied. But, such is the paramount character of the constitution, that its capacity to withdraw any subject from the action of even this power, is admitted. . . . [I]f it may restrain a State from the exercise of its taxing power on imports and exports; the same paramount

character would seem to restrain, as it certainly may restrain, a State from such other exercise of this power, as is in its nature incompatible with, and repugnant to, the constitutional laws of the Union. . . .

On this ground the counsel for the bank place its claim to be exempted from the power of a State to tax its operations. There is no express provision for the case, but the claim has been sustained on a principle which so entirely pervades the constitution, is so intermixed with the materials which compose it, so interwoven with its web, so blended with its texture, as to be incapable of being separated from it, without rending it into shreds.

This great principle is, that the constitution and the laws made in pursuance thereof are supreme; that they control the constitution and laws of the respective States, and cannot be controlled by them. From this, which may be almost termed an axiom, other propositions are deduced as corollaries, on the truth or error of which, and on their application to this case, the cause has been supposed to depend. These are, 1st. that a power to create implies a power to preserve. 2nd. That a power to destroy, if wielded by a different hand, is hostile to, and incompatible with these powers to create and to preserve. 3d. That where this repugnancy exists, that authority which is supreme must control, not yield to that over which it is supreme.

The power of Congress to create, and of course to continue, the bank, was the subject of the preceding part of this opinion; and is no longer to be considered as questionable.

That the power of taxing it by the States may be exercised so as to destroy it, is too obvious to be denied. But taxation is said to be an absolute power, which acknowledges no other limits than those expressly prescribed in the constitution, and like sovereign power of every other description, is trusted to the discretion of those who use it. But the very terms of this argument admit that the sovereignty of the State, in the article of taxation itself, is subordinate to, and may be controlled by the constitution of the United States. . . .

The argument on the part of the State of Maryland, is, not that the States may directly resist a law of Congress, but that they may exercise their acknowledged powers upon it, and that the constitution leaves them this right in the confidence that they will not abuse it.

[T]he power of taxing the people and their property is essential to the very existence of government, and may be legitimately exercised on the objects to which it is applicable, to the utmost extent to which the government may chuse to carry it. The only security against the abuse of this power, is found in the structure of the government itself. In imposing a tax the legislature acts upon its constituents. This is in general a sufficient security against erroneous and oppressive taxation.

The people of a State, therefore, give to their government a right of taxing themselves and their property, and as the exigencies of government cannot be limited, they prescribe no limits to the exercise of this right, resting confidently on the interest of the legislator, and on the influence of the constituents over their representative, to guard them against its abuse. But the means employed by the government of the Union have no such security, nor is the right of a State to tax them sustained by the same theory. Those means are not given by the people of a particular State, not given by the constituents of the legislature, which claim the right to tax them, but by the people of all the States. They are given by all, for the benefit of all—and upon theory, should be subjected to that government only which belongs to all.

If we apply the principle for which the State of Maryland contends, to the constitution generally, we shall find it capable of changing totally the character of that instrument. We shall find it capable of arresting all the measures of the government, and of prostrating it at the foot of the States. The American people have declared their constitution, and the laws made in pursuance thereof, to be supreme; but this principle would transfer the supremacy, in fact, to the States.

If the States may tax one instrument, employed by the government in the execution of its powers, they may tax any and every other instrument. They may tax the mail; they may tax the mint; they may tax patent rights; they may tax the papers of the custom-house; they may tax judicial process; they may tax all the means employed by the government, to an excess which would defeat all the ends of government. This was not intended by the American people. They did not design to make their government dependent on the States.

The question is, in truth, a question of supremacy; and if the right of the States to tax the means employed by the general government be conceded, the declaration that the constitution, and the laws made in pursuance thereof, shall be the supreme law of the land, is empty and unmeaning declamation.

[T]he States have no power, by taxation or otherwise, to retard, impede, burden, or in any manner control, the operations of the constitutional laws enacted by Congress to carry into execution the powers vested in the general government. This is, we think, the unavoidable consequence of that supremacy which the constitution has declared.

We are unanimously of opinion, that the law passed by the legislature of Maryland, imposing a tax on the Bank of the United States, is unconstitutional and void.

GIBBONS v. OGDEN
22 U.S. 1 (1824)

Opinion: Marshall, joined by
Washington, Todd, Duvall, Story
Concurrence: Johnson

While McCulloch v. Maryland established the framework for how we think about congressional power, perhaps the most significant source of Congress's authority is the Commerce Clause. Partly in response to economic inefficiencies and trade barriers under the Articles of Confederation, the founders gave Congress the power "to regulate commerce . . . among the several states." But the text alone leaves many questions open, and as we will see in the next section, the answers have evolved over time. Does all economic activity count as "commerce"? How extensive must this activity be in order to qualify as commerce among the states? An expansive answer to these questions would significantly enlarge the scope of congressional power, giving the federal government purview over broad swaths of economic life—just as a narrow answer would significantly weaken it.

The Supreme Court addressed these questions in Gibbons v. Ogden. After the State of New York granted his employer the exclusive navigation rights between New York and New Jersey, Thomas Gibbons sued to enjoin Aaron Ogden from operating a competing ferry service. Ogden countered that the New York monopoly violated federal law and was void. Notice once again that this case is about both an authorization for congressional action and also the limits that authorization presents for the powers of the states. It is important to note that in addition to being about Congress's commerce power, the case is significant in that it is often thought to be the origin of limits on state power currently referred to as the "dormant commerce clause."

According to this doctrine, it is implied in the grant of congressional power to regulate interstate commerce that the states cannot interfere with the regulation of interstate commerce. As you read, concentrate on the Court's perspective on whether Congress is authorized to regulate this area of economic activity and whether an individual state is prohibited from regulating it.

MR. CHIEF JUSTICE MARSHALL
delivered the opinion of the Court, and, after stating the case, proceeded as follows:

The appellant contends that this decree is erroneous, because the laws which purport to give the exclusive privilege it sustains, are repugnant to the constitution and laws of the United States.

The State of New-York maintains the constitutionality of these laws; and their Legislature, their Council of Revision, and their Judges, have repeatedly concurred in this opinion. . . .

. . . [W]hen these allied sovereigns [the states] converted their league into a government, when they converted their Congress of Ambassadors, deputed to deliberate on their common concerns, and to recommend measures of general utility, into a Legislature, empowered to enact laws on the most interesting subjects, the whole character in which the States appear, underwent a change, the extent of which must be determined by a fair consideration of the instrument by which that change was effected.

This instrument contains an enumeration of powers expressly granted by the people to their government. It has been said, that these powers ought to be construed strictly. . . . What do gentlemen mean, by a strict construction? . . . If they contend for that narrow construction which, in support of some theory not to be found in the constitution, would deny to the government those powers which the words of the grant, as usually understood, import, and which are consistent with the general views and objects of the instrument; for that narrow construction, which would cripple the government, and render it unequal to the object, for which it is declared to be instituted, and to which the powers given, as fairly understood, render it competent; then we cannot perceive the propriety of this strict construction, nor adopt it as the rule by which the constitution is to be expounded. . . . If, from the imperfection of human language, there should be serious doubts respecting the extent of any given power, it is a well settled rule, that the objects for which it was given, especially when those objects are expressed in the instrument itself, should have great influence in the construction. We know of no reason for excluding this rule from the present case. The grant does not convey power which might be beneficial to the grantor, if retained by himself, or which can enure solely to the benefit of the grantee; but is an investment of power for the general advantage, in the hands of agents selected for that purpose; which power can never be exercised by the people themselves, but must be placed in the hands of agents, or lie dormant. We know of no rule for construing the extent of such powers, other than is given by the language of the instrument which confers them, taken in connexion with the purposes for which they were conferred.

The words are, "Congress shall have power to regulate commerce with foreign nations, and among the several States, and with the Indian tribes."

The subject to be regulated is commerce; and our constitution being, as was aptly said at the bar, one of enumeration, and not of definition, to ascertain the extent of the power, it becomes necessary to settle the meaning of the word. The counsel for the appellee would limit it to traffic, to buying and selling, or the interchange of commodities, and do not admit that it comprehends navigation. This would restrict a general term, applicable to many objects, to one of its significations. Commerce, undoubtedly, is traffic, but it is something more: it is intercourse. It describes the commercial intercourse between nations, and parts of nations, in all its branches, and is regulated by prescribing rules for carrying on that intercourse. The mind can scarcely conceive a system for regulating commerce between nations, which shall exclude all laws concerning navigation, which shall be silent on the admission of the vessels of the one nation into the ports of the other, and be confined to prescribing rules for the conduct of individuals, in the actual employment of buying and selling, or of barter.

If commerce does not include navigation, the government of the Union has no direct power over that subject, and can make no law prescribing what shall constitute American vessels, or requiring that they shall be navigated by American seamen. Yet this power has been exercised from the commencement of the government, has been exercised with the consent of all, and has been understood by all to be a commercial regulation. All America understands, and has uniformly understood, the word "commerce," to comprehend navigation. . . .

It is a rule of construction, acknowledged by all, that the exceptions from a power mark its extent; for it would be absurd, as well as useless, to except from a granted power, that which was not granted—that which the words of the grant could not comprehend. If, then, there are in the constitution plain exceptions from the power over navigation, plain inhibitions to the exercise of that power in a particular way, it is a proof that those who made these exceptions, and prescribed these inhibitions, understood the power to which they applied as being granted.

The 9th section of the 1st article declares, that "no preference shall be given, by any regulation of commerce or revenue, to the ports of one State over those of another." This clause cannot be understood as applicable to those laws only which are passed for the purposes of revenue, because it is expressly applied to commercial regulations; and the most obvious preference which can be given to one port over another, in regulating commerce, relates to navigation. But the subsequent part of the sentence is still more explicit. It is, "nor shall vessels bound to or from one State, be obliged to enter, clear, or pay duties, in another." These words have a direct reference to navigation.

The universally acknowledged power of the government to impose embargoes, must also be considered as showing, that all America is united in that construction which comprehends navigation in the word commerce. . . .

The word used in the constitution, then, comprehends, and has been always understood to comprehend, navigation within its meaning; and a power to regulate navigation, is as expressly granted, as if that term had been added to the word "commerce."

To what commerce does this power extend? The constitution informs us, to commerce "with foreign nations, and among the several States, and with the Indian tribes."

It has, we believe, been universally admitted, that these words comprehend every species of commercial intercourse between the United States and foreign nations. . . .

If this be the admitted meaning of the word, in its application to foreign nations, it must carry the same meaning throughout the sentence, and remain a unit, unless there be some plain intelligible cause which alters it.

The subject to which the power is next applied, is to commerce "among the several States." The word "among" means intermingled with. A thing which is among others, is intermingled with them. Commerce among the States, cannot stop at the external boundary line of each State, but may be introduced into the interior.

Comprehensive as the word "among" is, it may very properly be restricted to that commerce which concerns more States than one. The phrase is not one which would probably have been selected to indicate the completely interior traffic of a State, because it is not an apt phrase for that purpose; and the enumeration of the particular classes of commerce, to which the power was to be extended, would not have been made, had the intention been to extend the power to every description. The enumeration presupposes something not enumerated; and that something, if we regard the language or the subject of the sentence, must be the exclusively internal commerce of a State. The genius and character of the whole government seem to be, that its action is to be applied to all the external concerns of the nation, and to those internal concerns which affect the States generally; but not to those which are completely within a particular State, which do not affect other States, and with which it is not necessary to interfere, for the purpose of executing some of the general powers of the government. The completely internal commerce of a State, then, may be considered as reserved for the State itself.

Can a trading expedition between two adjoining States, commence and terminate outside of each? And if the trading intercourse be between two States remote from each other, must it not commence in one, terminate in the other, and probably pass through a third? Commerce among the States must, of necessity, be commerce with the States. In the regulation of trade with the Indian tribes, the action of the law, especially when the constitution was made, was chiefly within a State. The power of Congress, then, whatever it may be, must be exercised within the territorial jurisdiction of the several States. . . .

It is the power to regulate; that is, to prescribe the rule by which commerce is to be governed. This power, like all others vested in Congress, is complete in itself, may be exercised to its utmost extent, and acknowledges no limitations, other than are prescribed in the constitution. These are expressed in plain terms, and do not affect the questions which arise in this case, or which have been discussed at the bar. If, as has always been understood, the sovereignty of Congress, though limited to specified objects, is plenary as to those objects, the power over commerce with foreign nations, and among the several States, is vested in Congress as absolutely as it would be in a single government, having in its constitution the same restrictions on the exercise of the power as are found in the constitution of the United States. The wisdom and the discretion of Congress, their identity with the people, and the influence which their constituents possess at elections, are, in this, as in many other instances, as that, for example, of declaring war, the sole restraints on which they have relied, to secure them from its abuse. They are the restraints on which the people must often rely solely, in all representative governments.

The power of Congress, then, comprehends navigation, within the limits of every State in the Union; so far as that navigation may be, in any manner, connected with "commerce with foreign nations, or among the several States, or with the Indian tribes." It may, of consequence, pass the jurisdictional line of New-York, and act upon the very waters to which the prohibition now under consideration applies.

But it has been urged with great earnestness, that, although the power of Congress to regulate commerce with foreign nations, and among the several States, be co-extensive with the subject itself, and have no other limits than are prescribed in the constitution, yet the States may severally exercise the same power, within their respective jurisdictions. In support of this argument, it is said, that they possessed it as an inseparable attribute of sovereignty, before the formation of the constitution, and still retain it, except so far as they have surrendered it by that instrument; that this principle results from the nature of the government, and is secured by the tenth amendment; that an affirmative grant of power is not exclusive, unless in its own nature it be such that the continued exercise of it by the former possessor is inconsistent with the grant, and that this is not of that description.

It has been contended by the counsel for the appellant, that, as the word "to regulate" implies in its nature, full power over the thing to be regulated, it excludes, necessarily, the action of all others that would perform the same operation on the same thing. That regulation is designed for the entire result, applying to those parts which remain as they were, as well as to those which are altered. It produces a uniform whole, which is as much disturbed and deranged by changing what the regulating power designs to leave untouched, as that on which it has operated.

There is great force in this argument, and the Court is not satisfied that it has been refuted.

Since, however, in exercising the power of regulating their own purely internal affairs, whether of trading or police, the States may sometimes enact laws, the validity of which depends on their interfering with, and being contrary to, an act of Congress passed in pursuance of the constitution, the Court will enter upon the inquiry, whether the laws of New-York, as expounded by the highest tribunal of that State, have, in their application to this case, come into collision with an act of Congress, and deprived a citizen of a right to which that act entitles him. Should this collision exist, it will be immaterial whether those laws were passed in virtue of a concurrent power "to regulate commerce with foreign nations and among the several States," or, in virtue of a power to regulate their domestic trade and police. In one case and the other, the acts of New-York must yield to the law of Congress; and the decision sustaining the privilege they confer, against a right given by a law of the Union, must be erroneous.

The nullity of any act, inconsistent with the constitution, is produced by the declaration, that the constitution is the supreme law. The appropriate application of that part of the clause which confers the same supremacy on laws and treaties, is to such acts of the State Legislatures as do not transcend their powers, but, though enacted in the execution of acknowledged State powers, interfere with, or are contrary to the laws of Congress, made in pursuance of the constitution, or some treaty made under the authority of the United States. In every such case, the act of Congress, or the treaty, is supreme; and the law of the State, though enacted in the exercise of powers not controverted, must yield to it.

. . . Congress has passed "an act for enrolling or licensing ships or vessels to be employed in the coasting trade and fisheries, and for regulating the same." The counsel for the respondent contend, that this act does not give the right to sail from port to port, but confines itself to regulating a pre-existing right, so far only as to confer certain privileges on enrolled and licensed vessels in its exercise.

It will at once occur, that, when a Legislature attaches certain privileges and exemptions to the exercise of a right over which its control is absolute, the law must imply a power to exercise the right. The privileges are gone, if the right itself be annihilated. It would be contrary to all reason, and to the course of human affairs, to say that a State is unable to strip a vessel of the particular privileges attendant on the exercise of a right, and yet may annul the right itself; that the State of New-York cannot prevent an enrolled and licensed vessel, proceeding from Elizabethtown, in New-Jersey, to New-York, from enjoying, in her course, and on her entrance into port, all the privileges conferred by the act of Congress; but can shut her up in her own port, and prohibit altogether her entering the waters and ports of another State. To the Court it seems very clear, that the whole act on the subject of the coasting trade, according to those principles which govern the construction of statutes, implies, unequivocally, an authority to licensed vessels to carry on the coasting trade.

If the power reside in Congress, as a portion of the general grant to regulate commerce, then acts applying that power to vessels generally, must be construed as comprehending all vessels. If none appear to be excluded by the language of the act, none can be excluded by construction. Vessels have always been employed to a greater or less extent in the transportation of passengers, and have never been supposed to be, on that account, withdrawn from the control or protection of Congress. Packets which ply along the coast, as well as those which make voyages between Europe and America, consider the transportation of passengers as an important part of their business. Yet it has never been suspected that the general laws of navigation did not apply to them. . . .

But all inquiry into this subject seems to the Court to be put completely at rest by the act already mentioned, entitled, "An act for the enrolling and licensing of steamboats."

This act authorizes a steamboat employed, or intended to be employed, only in a river or bay of the United States, owned wholly or in part by an alien, resident within the United States, to be enrolled and licensed as if the same belonged to a citizen of the United States.

This act demonstrates the opinion of Congress that steamboats may be enrolled and licensed, in common with vessels using sails. They are, of course, entitled to the same privileges, and can no more be restrained from navigating waters and entering ports which are free to such vessels than if they were wafted on their voyage by the winds, instead of being propelled by the agency of fire. The one element may be as legitimately used as the other for every commercial purpose authorized by the laws of the Union, and the act of a State inhibiting the use of either to any vessel having a license under the act of Congress comes, we think, in direct collision with that act.

As this decides the cause, it is unnecessary to enter in an examination of that part of the constitution which empowers Congress to promote the progress of science and the useful arts.

The Court is aware that, in stating the train of reasoning by which we have been conducted to this result, much time has been consumed in the attempt to demonstrate propositions which may have been thought axioms. It is felt that the tediousness inseparable from the endeavour to prove that which is already clear is imputable to a considerable part of this opinion. But it was unavoidable. The conclusion to which we have come depends on a chain of principles which it was necessary to preserve unbroken, and although some of them were thought nearly self-evident, the magnitude of the question, the weight of character belonging to those from whose judgment we dissent, and the argument at the bar demanded that we should assume nothing.

Powerful and ingenious minds, taking, as postulates, that the powers expressly granted to the government of the Union, are to be contracted by construction, into the narrowest possible compass, and that the original powers of the States are retained, if any possible construction will retain them, may, by a course of well digested, but refined and metaphysical reasoning, founded on these premises, explain away the constitution of our country, and leave it, a magnificent structure, indeed, to look at, but totally unfit for use. They may so entangle and perplex the understanding, as to obscure principles, which were before thought quite plain, and induce doubts where, if the mind were to pursue its own course, none would be perceived. In such a case, it is peculiarly necessary to recur to safe and fundamental principles to sustain those principles, and, when sustained, to make them the tests of the arguments to be examined.

MR. JUSTICE JOHNSON, *concurring.*

The judgment entered by the Court in this cause, has my entire approbation, but, having adopted my conclusions on views of the subject materially different from those of my brethren, I feel it incumbent on me to exhibit those views. . . .

The power of a sovereign state over commerce . . . amounts to nothing more than a power to limit and restrain it at pleasure. And since the power to prescribe the limits to its freedom necessarily implies the power to determine what shall remain unrestrained, it follows that the power must be exclusive; it can reside but in one potentate, and hence the grant of this power carries with it the whole subject, leaving nothing for the State to act upon. . . .

Commerce, in its simplest signification, means an exchange of goods, but in the advancement of society, labour, transportation, intelligence, care, and various mediums of exchange become commodities, and enter into commerce, the subject, the vehicle, the agent, and their various operations become the objects of commercial regulation. Shipbuilding, the carrying trade, and propagation of seamen are such vital agents of commercial prosperity that the nation which could not legislate over these subjects would not possess power to regulate commerce.

That such was the understanding of the framers of the Constitution is conspicuous from provisions contained in that instrument.

Box 3-1   Other Sources of Congressional Power

In addition to the Commerce power, the Constitution also enumerates a number of congressional powers, including the power to declare war, the power to regulate patents, and the power to pass laws governing bankruptcies. You should turn to Article I, Section 8, to review this list of powers and reflect on which modern-day laws these powers correspond to. The principle in *Gibbons v. Ogden* states that each of these enumerated powers is "plenary," which means that Congress has complete control over regulating these areas. The principle in *McCulloch v. Maryland* tells us that the Necessary and Proper Clause also generates certain implied powers—such as the power to incorporate a national bank—so long as they are sufficiently related to the other powers enumerated in the list. Together, these twin constitutional principles secure a broad foundation of congressional power.

Outside of Article I, several amendments after the Civil War also expressly grant congressional powers. These amendments sought to prohibit slavery (the Thirteenth Amendment), secure due process and equal protection rights for all citizens (the Fourteenth Amendment), and prevent discrimination in the right to vote based on race or sex (the Fifteenth and Nineteenth Amendments, respectively). In addition to articulating these substantive commitments, these amendments also empower Congress to enforce their provisions through legislation. *City of Boerne v. Flores*, which we read in Chapter 1, limited these textual provisions. According to the majority in *Boerne v. Flores*, only the Court has the power to interpret what these provisions mean or require, and Congress must enforce these requirements with remedies that are congruent and proportional to the constitutional harm.

SOUTH DAKOTA v. DOLE

483 U.S. 203 (1987)

Opinion: Rehnquist, joined by White, Marshall, Blackmun, Powell, Stevens, Scalia
Dissent: Brennan
Dissent: O'Connor

There are two key questions that tie together the cases and readings in this chapter. First, do the enumerated provisions of the Constitution grant Congress a significant amount of power, extending even beyond what the text itself prescribes? The second question concerns whether the ultimate extent of this power is limited and where the boundaries that constrain Congress's actions lie. One such limit might be thought to lie in the set of individual rights protected by the Constitution, which we discuss in the latter half of the book. The other chief limit might be thought to be the principle of federalism, embodied in the Tenth Amendment and considered to protect a certain sphere of activity that only states may regulate. Some of these areas have traditionally included family law, criminal law, and education.

But even if Congress cannot directly legislate in these areas, it can influence the decisions that states make through its power to tax and spend. Take, for example, education policy. While Congress may lack the power to impose standards on state governments, the federal government contributes to a significant portion of education spending each year. Should Congress have the authority to condition this funding on the state governments' meeting certain requirements? Or would such a policy merely be a guise for imposing unconstitutional demands on the states?

The Supreme Court evaluated the constitutionality of conditioning funds in South Dakota v. Dole. In exchange for a portion of federal highway funds, Congress demanded that all states raise the drinking age to at least 21. Chief Justice William Rehnquist's opinion discusses the line where "pressure turns into compulsion." Where does he draw that constitutional line? In Chief Justice Rehnquist's view, how closely related should the conditions be to the purpose of the funds in question?

CHIEF JUSTICE REHNQUIST delivered the opinion of the Court.

Petitioner South Dakota permits persons 19 years of age or older to purchase beer containing up to 3.2% alcohol. In 1984 Congress enacted 23 U.S.C. §158, which directs the Secretary of Transportation to withhold a percentage of federal highway funds otherwise allocable from States "in which the purchase or public possession . . . of any alcoholic beverage by a person who is less than twenty-one years of age is lawful." The State sued in United States District Court seeking a declaratory judgment that §158 violates the constitutional limitations on congressional exercise of the spending power and violates the Twenty-first Amendment to the United States Constitution. . . .

Here, Congress has acted indirectly under its spending power to encourage uniformity in the States' drinking ages. As we explain below, we find this legislative effort within constitutional bounds even if Congress may not regulate drinking ages directly.

The Constitution empowers Congress to "lay and collect Taxes, Duties, Imposts, and

Excises, to pay the Debts and provide for the common Defence and general Welfare of the United States." Incident to this power, Congress may attach conditions on the receipt of federal funds, and has repeatedly employed the power "to further broad policy objectives by conditioning receipt of federal moneys upon compliance by the recipient with federal statutory and administrative directives." The breadth of this power was made clear in United States v. Butler, 297 U.S. 1, 66 (1936), where the Court, resolving a longstanding debate over the scope of the Spending Clause, determined that "the power of Congress to authorize expenditure of public moneys for public purposes is not limited by the direct grants of legislative power found in the Constitution." Thus, objectives not thought to be within Article I's "enumerated legislative fields," id., at 65, may nevertheless be attained through the use of the spending power and the conditional grant of federal funds.

The spending power is of course not unlimited, but is instead subject to several general restrictions articulated in our cases. The first of these limitations is derived from the language of the Constitution itself: the exercise of the spending power must be in pursuit of "the general welfare." In considering whether a particular expenditure is intended to serve general public purposes, courts should defer substantially to the judgment of Congress. Second, we have required that if Congress desires to condition the States' receipt of federal funds, it "must do so unambiguously . . . , enabl[ing] the States to exercise their choice knowingly, cognizant of the consequences of their participation." Third, our cases have suggested (without significant elaboration) that conditions on federal grants might be illegitimate if they are unrelated "to the federal interest in particular national projects or programs." Finally, we have noted that other constitutional provisions may provide an independent bar to the conditional grant of federal funds.

South Dakota does not seriously claim that §158 is inconsistent with any of the first three restrictions mentioned above. We can readily conclude that the provision is designed to serve the general welfare, especially in light of the fact that "the concept of welfare or the opposite is shaped by Congress. . . ." Congress found that the differing drinking ages in the States created particular incentives for young persons to combine their desire to drink with their ability to drive, and that this interstate problem required a national solution. The means it chose to address this dangerous situation were reasonably calculated to advance the general welfare. The conditions upon which States receive the funds, moreover, could not be more clearly stated by Congress. And the State itself, rather than challenging the germaneness of the condition to federal purposes, admits that it "has never contended that the congressional action was . . . unrelated to a national concern in the absence of the Twenty-first Amendment." Indeed, the condition imposed by Congress is directly related to one of the main purposes for which highway funds are expended—safe interstate travel. This goal of the interstate highway system had been frustrated by varying drinking ages among the States. A Presidential commission appointed to study alcohol-related accidents and fatalities on the Nation's highways concluded that the lack of uniformity in the States' drinking ages created "an incentive to drink and drive" because "young persons commut[e] to border States where the drinking age is lower." By enacting §158, Congress conditioned the receipt of federal funds in a way reasonably calculated to address this particular impediment to a purpose for which the funds are expended.

The remaining question about the validity of §158—and the basic point of disagreement between the parties—is whether the Twenty-first Amendment constitutes an "independent constitutional bar" to the conditional grant of federal funds. . . . But our cases show that this "independent constitutional bar" limitation on the spending power is not of the kind petitioner suggests. *United States v. Butler*, for example, established that the constitutional limitations on Congress when exercising its spending power are less exacting than those on its authority to regulate directly.

We have also held that a perceived Tenth Amendment limitation on congressional regulation of state affairs did not concomitantly limit the range of conditions legitimately placed on federal grants. In Oklahoma v. Civil Service Comm'n, 330 U.S. 127 (1947), the Court considered the validity of the Hatch Act insofar as it was applied to political activities of state officials whose employment was financed in whole or in part with federal funds. The State contended that an order under this provision to withhold certain federal funds unless a state official was removed invaded its sovereignty in violation of the Tenth Amendment. Though finding that "the United States is not concerned with, and has no power to regulate, local political activities as such of state officials," the Court nevertheless held that the Federal Government "does have power to fix the terms upon which its money allotments to states shall be disbursed." The Court found no violation of the State's sovereignty because the State could, and did, adopt "the 'simple expedient' of not yielding to what she urges is federal coercion. The offer of benefits to a state by the United States dependent upon cooperation by the state with federal plans, assumedly for the general welfare, is not unusual."

These cases establish the "independent constitutional bar" limitation on the spending power is not, as petitioner suggests, a prohibition on the indirect achievement of objectives which Congress is not empowered to achieve directly. Instead, we think that the language in our earlier opinions stands for the unexceptionable proposition that the power may not be used to induce the States to engage in activities that would themselves be unconstitutional. Thus, for example, a grant of federal funds conditioned on invidiously discriminatory state action or the infliction of cruel and unusual punishment would be an illegitimate exercise of the Congress' broad spending power. But no such claim can be or is made here. Were South Dakota to succumb to the blandishments offered by Congress and raise its drinking age to 21, the State's action in so doing would not violate the constitutional rights of anyone.

Our decisions have recognized that in some circumstances the financial inducement offered by Congress might be so coercive as to pass the point at which "pressure turns into compulsion." Here, however, Congress has directed only that a State desiring to establish a minimum drinking age lower than 21 lose a relatively small percentage of certain federal highway funds. Petitioner contends that the coercive nature of this program is evident from the degree of success it has achieved. We cannot conclude, however, that a conditional grant of federal money of this sort is unconstitutional simply by reason of its success in achieving the congressional objective.

When we consider, for a moment, that all South Dakota would lose if she adheres to her chosen course as to a suitable minimum drinking age is 5% of the funds otherwise obtainable under specified highway grant programs, the argument as to coercion is shown to be more rhetoric than fact.

Here Congress has offered relatively mild encouragement to the States to enact higher minimum drinking ages than they would otherwise choose. But the enactment of such laws remains the prerogative of the States not merely in theory but in fact. Even if Congress might lack the power to impose a national minimum drinking age directly, we conclude that encouragement to state action found in §158 is a valid use of the spending power. Accordingly, the judgment of the Court of Appeals is Affirmed.

JUSTICE BRENNAN, *dissenting.*

I agree with Justice O'Connor that regulation of the minimum age of purchasers of liquor falls squarely within the ambit of those powers reserved to the States by the Twenty-first Amendment. . . . Since States possess this constitutional power, Congress cannot condition a federal grant in a manner that abridges this right. The Amendment, itself, strikes the proper balance between federal and state authority. I therefore dissent.

JUSTICE O'CONNOR, *dissenting.*

The Court today upholds the National Minimum Drinking Age Amendment, 23 U.S.C. §158 (1982 ed., Supp. III), as a valid exercise of the spending power conferred by Article I, §8. But §158 is not a condition on spending reasonably related to the expenditure of federal funds, and cannot be justified on that ground. Rather, it is an attempt to regulate the sale of liquor, an attempt that lies outside Congress' power to regulate commerce because it falls within the ambit of §2 of the Twenty-first Amendment.

My disagreement with the Court is relatively narrow on the spending power issue: it is a disagreement about the application of a principle, rather than a disagreement on the principle itself. I agree with the Court that Congress may attach conditions on the receipt of federal funds to further "the federal interest in particular national projects or programs. . . . "

But the Court's application of the requirement that the condition imposed be reasonably related to the purpose for which the funds are expended is cursory and unconvincing. We have repeatedly said that Congress may condition grants under the spending power only in ways reasonably related to the purpose of the federal program. . . . In my view, establishment of a minimum drinking age of 21 is not sufficiently related to interstate highway construction to justify so conditioning funds appropriated for that purpose. . . .

When Congress appropriates money to build a highway, it is entitled to insist that the highway be a safe one. But it is not entitled to insist as a condition of the use of highway funds that the State impose or change regulations in other areas of the State's social and economic life because of an attenuated or tangential relationship to highway use or safety. Indeed, if the rule were otherwise, the Congress could effectively regulate almost any area of a State's social, political, or economic life on the theory that use of the interstate transportation system is somehow enhanced. If, for example, the United States were to condition highway moneys upon moving the state capital, I suppose it might argue that interstate transportation is facilitated by locating local governments in places easily accessible to interstate highways—or, conversely, that highways might become overburdened if they had to carry traffic to and from the state capital. In my mind, such a relationship is hardly more attenuated than the one which the Court finds supports §158. *Cf.* Tr. of Oral Arg. 39 (counsel for the United States conceding that to condition a grant upon adoption of a unicameral legislature would violate the "germaneness" requirement).

There is a clear place at which the Court can draw the line between permissible and impermissible conditions on federal grants. It is the line identified in the Brief for the National Conference of State Legislatures *et al.* as *Amici Curiae*:

"Congress has the power to *spend* for the general welfare, it has the power to *legislate* only for delegated purposes...."

"The appropriate inquiry, then, is whether the spending requirement or prohibition is a condition on a grant or whether it is regulation. The difference turns on whether the requirement specifies in some way how the money should be spent, so that Congress' intent in making the grant will be effectuated. Congress has no power under the Spending Clause to impose requirements on a grant that go beyond specifying how the money should be spent. A requirement that is not such a specification is not a condition, but a regulation, which is valid only if it falls within one of Congress' delegated regulatory powers." *Id.* at 19-20....

The immense size and power of the Government of the United States ought not obscure its fundamental character. It remains a Government of enumerated powers.... Because 23 U.S.C. §158 (1982 ed., Supp. III) cannot be justified as an exercise of any power delegated to the Congress, it is not authorized by the Constitution. The Court errs in holding it to be the law of the land, and I respectfully dissent.

SYNTHESIS QUESTIONS FOR FURTHER DISCUSSION: CHAPTER 3 SECTION A

1. Alexander Hamilton contends that Congress possesses the "implied" power to incorporate a national bank, because this authority flows from other provisions enumerated in Article I. How persuasive is this claim? Is this argument compatible with the notion that the Constitution empowers Congress to legislate in only certain limited areas? What theories of interpretation might align with this political philosophy of implied power?

    By contrast, Thomas Jefferson places emphasis on strict boundaries for Article I's enumerated powers. Which interpretive theories might support this approach? For instance, is either Jefferson or Hamilton aided by originalist interpretations of the Constitution? Much of the debate between Hamilton and Jefferson boils down to what the phrase "necessary and proper" means—whether it limits or adds to what Congress can constitutionally regulate. Is Jefferson right to distinguish between incidental powers that are necessary and those that are merely convenient? In making his argument for a strict interpretation, Jefferson predicted that a broader reading would erode any meaningful limits on congressional power in the future. Was he right?

2. In *McCulloch v. Maryland*, how does Chief Justice John Marshall's opinion draw from Hamilton's and Jefferson's earlier arguments? Chief Justice Marshall proposes the following standard for determining whether the use

of congressional power is constitutional: First, is the purpose of the law constitutionally legitimate? Second, are the law's means plainly adapted to that end? Does this announced legal standard more closely reflect Jefferson's or Hamilton's approach?

What does Chief Justice Marshall mean when he states that "we must never forget that it is a constitution we are expounding," in contrast to "the prolixity of a legal code"? What kind of an interpretive approach does this reminder recommend? Is his standard for evaluating the limits of constitutional power found in the Constitution, as he claims, or does it rely on an interpretative approach that would go beyond the text of the Constitution?

3. In *Gibbons v. Ogden*, Chief Justice Marshall broadly construes "Commerce . . . among the several States" to cover all navigation, and he suggests that it encompasses a number of other related activities. On this theory, when the Constitution grants Congress an enumerated power, that power is "plenary," or complete, and state laws may not interfere with it. But at the same time, Chief Justice Marshall states that the federal government cannot regulate commerce that is "completely internal" to the state itself. Are these positions consistent? How limited or expansive does this decision leave Congress's commerce power? Finally, consider how this opinion reflects the power granted to Congress in *McCulloch v. Maryland*. In general, what do *Gibbons v. Ogden* and *McCulloch v. Maryland* suggest about where congressional power ends and state power begins?

4. The debate over implied powers continues in the modern era. Consider, for instance, the spending power discussed at the end of this section. Does such a power include a right to condition funds on certain public policy goals? Is this power implied by a power to spend? Does the spending power require that there be a connection between the public policy goal and the kind of spending that is authorized by Congress? What powers, if any, are not implied by the spending power?

B. THE BATTLE OVER ECONOMIC REGULATION

Do federal efforts to promote the general welfare and regulate the economy usurp states' powers? Are they consistent with liberty?

So far, we have seen that congressional authority depends on powers enumerated in Article I of the U.S. Constitution. In contrast to the general powers of the states, congressional powers to enact legislation must be granted through specific clauses in Article I. The twentieth century saw two major shifts in the scope of these powers. As you read through this section, you will be asked to evaluate whether these two shifts were consistent with the powers granted to Congress in Article I. In particular, we examine shifting understandings of the Commerce Clause, which grants Congress the power to regulate interstate commerce and implicitly limits the states from passing laws that impede this ability.

We begin this section with a discussion in *Swift & Co. v. United States* about the degree to which Congress has the authority to regulate economic activity and monopolistic practices. As you will see, this discussion highlights the notion of a stream of commerce, and provides some leeway for congressional legislation on matters of economic regulation. But despite the fact that *Swift & Co. v. United States* authorized congressional action, the early twentieth century is also marked by distinct limits on Congress's Commerce Clause power, especially as concerned much progressive legislation. You will note that in *Hammer v. Dagenhart* the Court limited Congress's power to regulate child labor. In many ways, *Hammer v. Dagenhart* marks the limits on congressional power, prominent in the Court's jurisprudence before the first shift we examine.

This first shift concerns President Franklin Roosevelt's decision during the New Deal era to expand the role of the federal government as a means of both regulating the national economy and stimulating economic growth. President Roosevelt believed that the Great Depression presented a major challenge to the nation's stability. On his view, the crisis of the Depression could be solved by an increased federal role in the economy, including providing jobs directly to citizens, creating new federal agencies, and seeking greater regulation of various economic sectors. As you will see in his famous "four freedoms" speech, President Roosevelt believed that government's role should not be limited to protecting private property, but should also include securing individual welfare for all. He thus rejected the "laissez-faire" approach to government, exemplified by the *Lochner v. New York* Court and libertarian thinkers such as Herbert Spencer, which suggested that financial markets and labor markets should be left free from government intervention. But President Roosevelt's attempt to expand the federal government raised a constitutional puzzle. What enumerated power granted Congress the ability to pass New Deal legislation? President Roosevelt's administration argued that the Commerce Clause provided the textual basis for much of the New Deal, as the nation had developed into one national economy in which interstate commerce was connected to a variety of aspects of life traditionally regulated by the states. President Roosevelt argued, moreover, that there was a need for a national effort to coordinate areas of economic life that the states, on their own, would be unable to do. The Supreme Court, however, struck down some New Deal legislation on grounds that it exceeded Congress's power under the Interstate Commerce Clause. For instance, in *Schechter Poultry Corp. v. United States*, the Court struck down President Roosevelt's National Industrial Recovery Act. In addition, in *Carter v. Carter Coal Company*, the Court struck down Congress's attempt at regulation of the coal industry.

President Roosevelt, however, was determined to push through his legislation over the Court's objections. He threatened to continue to add new justices to the Supreme Court, or "pack the Court," until the existing justices' votes were diluted. But President Roosevelt never had to follow through with this threat since, in 1937, Justice Owen Roberts changed his position from deeming the New Deal program and its economic regulations unconstitutional to upholding them. Justice Roberts's change in judicial philosophy (and his switch to join those upholding the President's position) became known as the "switch in time that saved nine." In other words, he saved the power of the nine Supreme Court justices from being diluted by a packed Court. Specifically, it was in a case about the State of Washington's minimum wage law, *West Coast Hotel v. Parrish* (excerpted in Chapter 7), that is generally considered the case in which the switch first occurred. Even though *West Coast Hotel v. Parrish* was about the constitutionality of state law and the end of the Court's use of its "substantive due process" doctrine to oppose economic regulations by the government, it signaled the end of opposition to the Court's willingness to strike down New Deal legislation at the federal level because of a perceived lack of congressional power. We examine *West Coast Hotel v. Parrish* and the Court's substantive due process doctrine in depth in Chapter 7, but here we focus on the impact of the "switch in time" on congressional power. Specifically, the Court's switch from striking down New Deal legislation to upholding it under the Commerce Clause raises a fundamental matter of constitutional interpretation. Should the Commerce Clause be understood to authorize a vast array of congressional powers to regulate and stimulate the economy? As you read this section, you should ask whether President Roosevelt's philosophy of the four freedoms should play a role in interpreting the Commerce Clause. What might a pragmatist say, for instance, about the extension of this power in order to provide for the general welfare? As you know, originalist theories of constitutional interpretation stress the importance of close textual readings. Could an originalist understand commerce to include such regulation? For example, if in a modern economy a vast amount of trade throughout the country means that all economic regulation is about interstate commerce, would an originalist be able to defend an expansive understanding of the Commerce Clause? What might other theories suggest about how to read this clause?

The second major shift in the scope of congressional power during the twentieth century came during the Civil Rights era. The Commerce Clause also played a critical role in this shift. In 1964, in the wake of President John F. Kennedy's assassination, Congress passed the Civil Rights Act. Among other things, the Act outlawed racial segregation in areas of so-called public accommodations, such as hotels and restaurants. Clearly the Civil Rights movement centered on the value of equality and was not, like the New Deal, primarily focused on economic regulation. But for reasons we examine in the *Civil Rights Cases* (Chapter 8), which addressed the constitutionality of a nineteenth-century civil rights act, the "Equal Protection Clause" was held to apply only to state action. Specifically, the Court's jurisprudence, starting in the nineteenth century and continuing into the twentieth, held that the Equal Protection Clause prohibited segregation in government institutions but not in public accommodations. Given this long-standing constraint, the Court instead chose to once again employ the Commerce Clause as the textual basis for congressional power to outlaw segregation in public accommodations. As you read the cases of *Heart of Atlanta Motel v. United States* and *Katzenbach v. McClung*, you should ask whether this was indeed the most compelling source of constitutional authorization for congressional power in the area of civil rights. One possible defense of the Court's action comes from the moral reading, given the inherent injustice of segregation. But is the moral reading an appropriate interpretive lens for a clause that seems to have no obvious concern for equality? Could a different lens of constitutional interpretation justify this use of the Commerce Clause?

Our readings in this section help to frame the controversy over the Commerce Clause during the New Deal era. For Bruce Ackerman, President Roosevelt's four freedoms are not part of the original understanding of the Constitution, but rather represent a new constitutional moment brought about by the New Deal. This moment of transformation, embodied in the Court's "switch in time," effectively amended the Constitution outside of Article V.

In Cass Sunstein's view, the four freedoms are fundamental aspects of the constitutional guarantee of welfare that should be understood alongside the more specific guarantees laid out in the Bill of Rights. The protections found in the National Labor Relations Act, the Fair Labor Standards Act, and the Social Security Act create what he refers to as "constitutive commitments" on a par with other constitutional guarantees. He therefore sees President Roosevelt not as declaring war on the meaning of the Constitution, but rather as using congressional power to pursue a fundamental mandate of the Constitution.

While Ackerman and Sunstein applaud President Roosevelt's expansion of congressional authority to bring about what they regard as economic freedom, Judge Douglas Ginsburg, a former Supreme Court nominee, and Richard Epstein argue for a different conception of economic freedom and offer an argument against President Roosevelt's expansion of congressional power. For Judge Ginsburg and Epstein, economic liberty entails protecting property rights and limiting the federal government's power to intrude upon a free market. Epstein in particular offers a defense of the pre–New Deal Court's framework for understanding Congress's authority under the Constitution on the grounds that it allowed for diverse policies among the states. Free citizens in a federal republic, he argues, should be able to choose among the several states when deciding where to live, work, or do business; these states should therefore have diverse social and economic circumstances. He thus applauds the earlier Court's restriction of congressional authority.

Although the focus of our readings is largely on the shift from a Commerce Clause that limited federal power to enact the New Deal to one that authorized it, these thinkers also offer insights that will be helpful in analyzing *Heart of Atlanta Motel v. United States* and *Katzenbach v. McClung* and the general power of Congress to enact the Civil Rights Act of 1964 under the Commerce Clause. Even if we grant that the Court shifts its understanding of the Commerce Clause in these cases, you should try to decide whether you think this shift is justified by the gravity of the Civil Rights movement and the need to eliminate segregation. Could Sunstein's suggestion that the general welfare provision of the Constitution serves as a textual basis for the New Deal also justify Congress's authority to enact civil rights legislation? Finally, do Judge Ginsburg's and Epstein's critiques of the New Deal also commit them to argue against Congress's power to enact civil rights legislation? Of course, the cases related to the New Deal and the Civil Rights Act dealt with very different subjects, but both concerned the Court's decision to expand congressional power through the Commerce Clause. Throughout this section, you should continue to ask whether these shifts in the Court's stance on congressional authority were or were not justified.

Bruce Ackerman

WE THE PEOPLE

Volume I: Foundations; and Volume II: Transformations

Cambridge, MA: Harvard University Press (1991)

Bruce Ackerman argues that the "switch in time"—Justice Owen Roberts's sudden shift in judicial philosophy to support New Deal policies—marked a "constitutional moment." According to Ackerman, a constitutional moment consists of a historical shift in the understanding of the Constitution that occurs outside of the normal amendment process. Although the Constitution requires an amendment to be formally changed, Ackerman believes that some shifts in judicial interpretation, backed by popular support, are so extreme that they also profoundly shift the meaning of the document. For example, in the following excerpt, he contends that the Court's subsequent decisions effectively ratified the New Deal as an amendment to the Constitution outside of Article V, which creates a formal process for amending the document. This is quite a striking claim, but it does command a certain degree of explanatory power. The New Deal indeed marks a discontinuity in our constitutional development, after which the federal government assumed responsibility for regulating the national economy. The rest of this section traces the history of that struggle.

You should consider the feasibility of Ackerman's theory of constitutional moments and how it figures into his understanding of the ways in which the Supreme Court responds to democratic will. How does it answer the counter-majoritarian difficulty outlined in Chapter 1, or compare to the theories of interpretation sketched in Chapter 2? Does Ackerman succeed in laying out clear criteria for when a constitutional moment occurs?

Above all else, a dualist Constitution seeks to distinguish between two different decisions that may be made in a democracy. The first is a decision by the American people; the second, by their government.

Decisions by the People occur rarely, and under special constitutional conditions. Before gaining the authority to make supreme law in the name of the People, a movement's political partisans must, first, convince an extraordinary number of their fellow citizens to take their proposed initiative with a seriousness that they do not normally accord to politics; second, they must allow their opponents a fair opportunity to organize their own forces; third, they must convince a majority of their fellow Americans to support their initiative as its merits are discussed, time and again, in the deliberative fora provided for "higher lawmaking." It is only then that a political movement earns the enhanced legitimacy the dualist Constitution accords to decisions made by the People.

Decisions made by the government occur daily, and also under special conditions. Most importantly, key officials must be held accountable regularly at the ballot box. In addition, they must be given incentives to take a broad view of the public interest without the undue influence of narrow interest groups. Even when this system of "normal lawmaking" is operating well, however, the dualist Constitution prevents elected politicians from exaggerating their authority.

They are not to assert that a normal electoral victory has given them a mandate to enact an ordinary statute that overturns the considered judgments previously reached by the People. If they wish to claim this higher form of democratic legitimacy, they must take to the specially onerous obstacle course provided by a dualist Constitution for purposes of higher lawmaking. Only if they succeed in mobilizing their fellow citizens and gaining their repeated support in response to their opponents' counterattacks may they finally earn the authority to proclaim that *the People* have changed their mind and have given their government new marching orders.

... [A]t its root, monism is very simple: Democracy requires the grant of plenary lawmaking authority to the winners of the last general election—so long, at least, as the election was conducted under free and fair ground rules and the winners don't try to prevent the next scheduled round of electoral challenges.

This idea motivates, in turn, a critical institutional conclusion: during the period between elections, all institutional checks upon the electoral victors are presumptively antidemocratic. For sophisticated monists, this is only a presumption. Perhaps certain constitutional checks may prevent the victors from abrogating the next scheduled election; perhaps others might be justified once one considers the deeper ways normal elections fail to satisfy our ideals of electoral fairness. While these exceptions may have great practical importance, monists refuse to let them obscure the main point: when the Supreme Court, or anybody else, invalidates a statute, it suffers from a "countermajoritarian difficulty" which must be overcome before a good democrat can profess satisfaction with this extraordinary action.

...The monist begs a big question when he asserts that the winner of a fair and open election is entitled to rule with the full authority of We the People. It is much better, of course, for electoral winners to take office rather than suffer an authoritarian putsch by the losers.

But it does not follow that all statutes gaining the support of a legislative majority in Washington, D.C., represent the considered judgment of a mobilized majority of American citizens. Instead, the dualist sees a profoundly democratic point to many of the distinctive practices that baffle the monist. For her, they express our Constitution's effort to require elected politicians to operate within a two-track system. If politicians hope to win normal democratic legitimacy for an initiative, they are directed down the normal lawmaking path and told to gain the assent of the House, Senate, and President in the usual ways. If they hope for higher lawmaking authority, they are directed down a specially onerous lawmaking path.... Only if a political movement successfully negotiates the special challenges of the higher lawmaking system can it rightfully claim that its initiative represents the constitutional judgment of We the People.

Once the two-track character of the system is recognized, the Supreme Court appears in a different light. Consider that all the time and effort required to push an initiative down the higher lawmaking track would be wasted unless the Constitution prevented future normal politicians from enacting statutes that ignored the movement's higher law achievement. If future politicians could so easily ignore established higher law, why would any mass movement take the trouble to overcome the special hurdles placed on the higher lawmaking track?

To maintain the integrity of higher lawmaking, all dualist constitutions must provide for one or more institutions to discharge a preservationist function. These institutions must effectively block efforts to repeal established constitutional principles by the simple expedient of passing a normal statute and force the reigning group of elected politicians to move onto the higher lawmaking track if they wish to question the judgments previously made by We the People. Only after negotiating this more arduous obstacle course can a political elite earn the authority to say that We the People have changed our mind.

It follows, then, that the dualist will view the Supreme Court from a very different perspective than the monist. The monist treats every act of judicial review as presumptively antidemocratic and strains to save the Supreme Court from the "counter-majoritarian difficulty" by one or another ingenious argument. In contrast, the dualist sees the discharge of the preservationist function by the courts as an essential part of a well-ordered democratic regime. Rather than threatening democracy by frustrating the statutory demands of the political elite in Washington, the courts serve democracy by protecting the hard-won principles of a mobilized citizenry against erosion by political elites who have failed to gain broad and deep popular support for their innovations....

... When modern lawyers and judges look to the deep past, they tell themselves a story that has a distinctive structure. Though special problems may lead them to appreciate the relevance of one or another aspect of America's constitutional history, three historical periods stand out from the rest. These eras have a pervasive significance: the lessons a judge draws from them organizes her entire approach to concrete cases. The first of these jurisgenerative eras is the Founding itself—the framing of the original Constitution and the Bill of Rights, the Supreme Court's initial assertion of judicial review in *Marbury v. Madison*. A second great period occurs two generations later, with the bloody struggles that ultimately yield the Reconstruction amendments. Then there is another pause of two generations before a third great turning point. This one centers on the 1930's and the dramatic confrontation between the New Deal and the Old Court that ends in the constitutional triumph of the activist welfare state.

... While all lawyers recognize that the 1930's mark the definitive constitutional triumph of activist national government, they tell themselves a story which denies that anything deeply creative was going on. This view of the 1930's is obtained by imagining a Golden Age in which Chief Justice Marshall got things right for all time by propounding a broad construction of the national government's lawmaking authority. The period between

Reconstruction and the New Deal can then be viewed as a (complex) story about the fall from grace—wherein most of the Justices strayed from the path of righteousness and imposed their laissez-faire philosophy on the nation through the pretext of constitutional interpretation. Predictably, these acts of judicial usurpation increasingly set the judges at odds with more democratic institutions, which acutely perceived the failure of laissez-faire to do justice to an increasingly interdependent world.

The confrontation between the New Deal and the Old Court climaxes this traditional morality play of decline, fall, and resurrection. Only Justice Roberts' "switch in time," and the departure of the worst judicial offenders, permitted the Court to expiate its counter-majoritarian sins without permanent institutional damage. If only the Justices had not strayed from Marshall's original path, perhaps all this unpleasantness could have been avoided!

... [I]n contrast to the first two turning points, modern lawyers do not describe either the substantive or the procedural aspects of the New Deal by telling themselves a tale of constitutional creation. The triumph of activist national government is mediated by a myth of rediscovery—as if the Founding Federalists had foreseen the works of Franklin Delano Roosevelt and would have been surprised to learn that the great struggles of the 1930's were necessary to gain the welfare state's constitutional legitimation.

... I mean to question the prevailing interpretive schema. Despite its familiarity, it is built on sand. If we return to our sources, they tell a very different story. They reveal both Reconstruction Republicans and New Deal Democrats engaging in self-conscious acts of constitutional creation that rivaled the Founding Federalists' in their scope and

depth. In each case, the new spokesmen for the people refused to follow the path of constitutional revision set out by their successors; like the Federalists before them, they transformed existing systems of higher lawmaking in the process of changing the fundamental direction of political development....

THE NEW DEAL

According to the modern myth of rediscovery: the New Dealers did not even contribute new substantive principles to our higher law, let alone rework the very process of higher lawmaking. Instead, their redefinition of American government involved little more than the recollection of some forgotten bits of Founding Wisdom.

My counterthesis: Like the Reconstruction Republicans, the New Deal Democrats relied on the national separation of powers between Congress, President, and Court to create a new institutional framework through which the American People might define, debate, and finally decide their constitutional future. The key institutional difference between the two periods involves the Presidency. Franklin Roosevelt remained at the helm of the reformist coalition throughout the Democrats' period of constitutional transformation, whereas Lincoln's assassination deprived Republican reformers of Presidential support during the critical struggle over the Fourteenth Amendment. Roosevelt's long tenure had fundamental, if unsurprising, implications for the Presidency's role in the process of higher lawmaking. While the Republicans successfully experimented with Presidential leadership in the process of legitimating the Thirteenth Amendment, they could not build on this experience once Andrew Johnson declared war on the Fourteenth Amendment. In contrast, the Democrats were in a position to develop the power of the Presidency in a far more incisive fashion.

When due allowances are made for the defection of President Johnson from the Republican coalition, however, it will be possible to identify remarkable similarities in the way in which the separation of powers tested, and finally legitimated, the constitutional revisions proposed by nineteenth-century Republicans and twentieth-century Democrats. Each higher lawmaking exercise began with the reformers in control of only part of the national government—in the case of the Republicans, it was Congress that took on the mantle of reform leadership with Johnson's defection; in the case of the Democrats, the Presidency was the leading reform branch. In both cases, the constitutional reformers' proposals were exposed to an initial period of incisive critique by conservative branches, which publicly appealed to the People to decisively reject the dangerous innovations proposed by the reformers. In the case of the Republicans, the leading conservative branch was the Presidency; for the Democrats, it was the Supreme Court.

These institutional differences were important, of course, in explaining the different dynamics of constitutional debate and decision. But it is even more important to see the deeper similarities. In both cases, the institutional deadlock in Washington forced both sides to mobilize their supporters in the country at large. These remarkable efforts at popular mobilization, in turn, gave extraordinary constitutional meaning to the next regularly scheduled election. If one or another side could win a decisive victory at the polls, it would try to use its popular support to break the institutional impasse.

This process of interbranch struggle and popular mobilization made the elections of 1866 and 1936 decisive events in constitutional history. On both occasions, the reformers returned to Washington with a clear victory at the polls. They proceeded to proclaim that the election results gave them a "mandate from the People," and that the time had come for the conservative branches to end their constitutional resistance.

This demand by the electorally victorious reformers inaugurated the period of ratification—in which the conservative branches considered whether to continue their resistance or to recognize that the People had indeed given their fixed support to the reformist movement. In both cases, this decision was not made in silent contemplation but in response to a challenge by the reformist branches to the conservatives' continued legitimacy. During Reconstruction, the reformist Congress finally threatened President Johnson with impeachment if he continued to use his office to sabotage ratification of the Fourteenth Amendment. During the New Deal, it was the reformist President's threat of packing the Court that provoked the conservative Justices to consider the wisdom of continued resistance. In both cases, however, the question was very much the same: Should the conservatives in the dissenting branches finally recognize that *the People had spoken*?

In both cases, the conservatives' answer was the same. Rather than escalating the constitutional crisis further, they decided, with evident reluctance, that further resistance would endanger too many of the very values they held fundamental. They made the "switch in time": Johnson called off his effort to prevent the formal ratification of the Fourteenth Amendment; the Supreme Court repudiated its doctrinal defense of laissez-faire capitalism and began to build new constitutional foundations for activist national government.

In turn, the victorious reformers responded in the same way. The Republicans refused to convict the President, allowing Johnson to remain in office to proclaim the validity of the Fourteenth Amendment; the Democrats called off the threat of court-packing, allowing the Old Court to proclaim that activist New Deal government was constitutionally legitimate.

As a consequence of these "switches in time," all three branches emerge from the period of democratic testing once again united, and the separation of powers remains intact for use by the next constitutional regime. But it is now in the service of the new constitutional solution that had previously been so controversial. . . .

Time and again, the New Dealers invoked Reconstruction precedents in their efforts to build a modern model of Presidential leadership in the higher lawmaking process. The challenge is to *listen* to these voices, not insist upon viewing the New Deal reformers as if they were exhausted epigones, capable only of returning to the forgotten wisdom of the Founders. Only after we define what is really new about the New Deal can we begin to confront the deep problems they left for us. Should the New Deal model of Presidential leadership once again be revised to better confront the higher lawmaking challenges of the next century?

FROM PAST TO PRESENT

. . . While the Reconstruction Republicans broke new ground in their use of the separation of powers as the principal engine of constitutional revision, they nonetheless managed to codify their reforms in legal instruments that bore the surface appearance of "constitutional amendments." These Reconstruction texts are only amendment-simulacra, since they were not generated in accordance with the principles laid down by the Federalist Constitution. Nonetheless, at least the Republicans managed to pour their new constitutional wine into old legal bottles.

In contrast, the New Dealers rejected the traditional form of an amendment; instead they relied on the New Deal Court to elaborate their new activist vision through a series of transformative opinions. It is worth emphasizing that this decision was entirely self-conscious and public. We will hear President Roosevelt and leading spokesmen of his Administration explaining why it was wrong to codify the New Deal transformation through forms sanctioned by Article Five; why we should rely instead on the appointment of new judges to give new meaning to the Constitution. After 1937, moreover, Roosevelt and Congress used this technique of transformative judicial appointment with unprecedented success. By the early 1940's, a reconstituted Court had not contented itself with rejecting a few offending decisions of a bygone era. It revolutionized reigning constitutional doctrine in a thoroughgoing way—to the point where the Court was now unanimously rejecting fundamental doctrines that shaped the entire body of constitutional law only a decade before. . . .

RETHINKING THE NEW DEAL

New Deal Democracy marked another great leap along the arc of nationalistic self-definition initiated by the American Revolution. Although the Founders broke with the state-centered Articles of Confederation, they did not clearly establish the priority of national over state citizenship; although the Reconstructers resolved this fundamental question in favor of the Union, they did not frontally challenge the Founding notion that the national government had limited powers over economic and social development; with the New Deal, this Founding principle was decisively repudiated. Henceforth, the federal government would operate as a truly national government, speaking for the People on all matters that sufficiently attracted the interest of lawmakers in Washington, D.C.

Not that the states were deprived of their general lawmaking jurisdiction. They too could legislate on any subject they found in the public interest—subject to preemption by national lawmakers and judicial scrutiny for prejudicial impact upon out-of-staters. A commitment to federalism, however, was no longer thought to require a constitutional strategy that restrained the national government to a limited number of enumerated powers over economic and social life.

... When the New Deal generation won positions of authority in the courts and the law schools, they took full advantage of their opportunity to warn their successors against repeating the Old Court's mistakes. These doctrinal teachings were greatly enhanced by the penetration of New Deal premises into American government. The millions of Social Security checks mailed each month attest to the government's ongoing concern with fair income distribution. The thousands of pages published annually in the *Federal Register* (founded in 1936) contain countless reminders by a host of alphabet agencies—SEC, NLRB, EPA, OSHA . . . —that unregulated capitalism endangers a series of fundamental values, ranging from environmental purity to worker dignity. Each day's headlines report on the ongoing

effort by the national government to sustain general prosperity through the flexible tools of macroeconomic policy made possible by the New Deal's repudiation of the Gold Standard. Until the Reagan Presidency, no victorious political movement had questioned the propriety of this complex governmental effort to improve upon the invisible hand. To one or another extent, each Administration had built upon the efforts of its predecessors in the three basic areas of activist concern marked out in the Roosevelt years: the pursuit of distributive justice, the correction of market failure, and the assurance of general prosperity.

Little wonder that modern lawyers have little trouble recalling the broad outlines of the great constitutional crisis of the 1930's. It is only their recollection of the Supreme Court's retreat before the New Deal that provides the vast statutory superstructure of the activist state with a firm constitutional foundation. It was different before 1932. Each new activist initiative then provoked anxious foreboding: How to evade the entrenched constitutional principles that cast intervention into the "free market" under a dark cloud? The answer, in particular cases, depended upon the complexities of constitutional doctrine and the vagaries of judicial personnel. But there was no mistaking the constitutionally problematic character of the activist enterprise. So far as the judges were concerned, We the People had *not* authorized state regulation of the marketplace whenever political majorities concluded that this would serve the nation's general welfare; the Constitution emerging after the Civil War contained fundamental limitations on such dubious enterprises.

These boundaries disintegrated during the New Deal revolution. A complex web of doctrine, woven by two generations of judges in the long period between 1873 and 1932, was swept away in the space of a decade. If the partisans of laissez-faire lost their battle in the legislature, they could no longer hope that the courts might reverse their opponents' victory. After the New Deal revolution, it became clear to judges that We the People had stripped free market solutions to social problems of their previously privileged position.

Lochner v. New York serves as the paradigm. In 1905, the Court struck down the effort by New York to limit the work week to sixty hours as a violation of freedom of contract. By the end of the Roosevelt era, *Lochner* became the symbol of a repudiated era of laissez-faire jurisprudence. Henceforward, courts would uphold the authority of American government to act against all forms of social or economic exploitation that were condemned by a democratically elected majority.

This turnaround was all the more wrenching in connection with the national government. The Supreme Court had never denied the states a broad (though not unlimited) power to police the economy, but it had taken a different view of Congressional authority. *Hammer v. Dagenhart* can serve as paradigm. In 1916, Congress had acted against child labor by excluding its products from interstate commerce. But the Court struck down this effort: "[t]he Commerce Clause was not intended to give to Congress a general authority to equalize ... conditions." If Congress could not take steps to express the nation's condemnation of a shocking abuse like child labor, its powers were limited indeed. If the New Deal was to prevail, this vision of limited government could not survive.

And it did not. By the early 1940's, the New Deal Court was ringing the death knell in unanimous decisions that would have astounded lawyers a decade before. But the bar proved very adaptable. Under the Court's emphatic tutelage, lawyers learned to look upon the case law of the preceding Republican regime with the peculiar mix of ignorance and contempt reserved for abandoned precedent. Whatever their personal political convictions, they quickly mastered the New Deal language for courtroom use. A half-century later, the New Deal Constitution— far less respectful of the rights of property and contract, far more respectful of national power—had been woven into the very fabric of the modern polity, shaping the expectations of ordinary citizens as well as the daily interactions of the President, Congress, and the Supreme Court. . . .

THE VIEW FROM ARTICLE FIVE

We can now begin to triangulate our problem by considering the New Deal's relationship to the Founding. Speaking broadly, the higher lawmaking efforts of the 1930's broke with the premises of Article Five in two ways.

The first involved a break from the Founding system of authorizing institutions. Article Five rests upon a federalist premise: in order to speak in the name of the People, a movement must gain the assent of *both* national and state institutions. The New Dealers took a more nation-centered course—using a series of national electoral victories as mandates that ultimately induced all three branches of the national government to recognize that the People had endorsed activist national government. So long, then, as modern lawyers suppose that all successful popular movements must take a federalist path to higher lawmaking authority, they will never surmount this first hurdle to a mature recognition of the New Deal's constitutional creativity.

But it shouldn't be too hard to jump over this hurdle. As we have seen, it was the Reconstruction Republicans, not the New Deal Democrats, who first established that We the People could speak through national institutions and demand that the states accept the primacy of American citizenship. If Reconstruction Republicans could use national institutions to legitimate their claims, why not New Deal Democrats, especially when they had gained the sustained consent of majorities in *all* regions of the country, while the Republicans had a lot more support in the North than in the South?

Which brings us to a second aspect of the New Deal break with Article Five. While the Reconstruction Republicans repudiated the federalist premises of the Founding, they memorialized their revolutionary reforms by placing them in legal packages that resemble Article Five amendments—bearing the numbers XIII and XIV and placing themselves in sober sequence with other amendments of less uncertain pedigree. In contrast, when modern lawyers seek to recall the New Deal's contribution, they do not turn to writings that pose as Article Five amendments but to *transformative judicial opinions* written in the aftermath of the Court-packing crisis. These great cases mark the decisive institutional moment at which the Supreme Court joined the other branches in rejecting the Republican vision of limited government, symbolized by *Hammer v. Dagenhart* and *Lochner v. New York*. Indeed, modern judges are more disturbed by the charge of *Lochner*ing than the charge of ignoring the intentions of the Federalists and Republicans who wrote the formal text. To mark this point, I shall say that the transformative opinions handed down by the New Deal Court

function as *amendment-analogues* that anchor constitutional meanings in the same symbolically potent way achieved by Article Five amendments.

Undoubtedly, this New Deal use of amendment-analogues requires thoughtful reappraisal of some pious platitudes—including the sense in which Americans live under a *written* constitution. Two centuries after the Founding, this platitude remains valid only on an expanded understanding of the constitutional canon. The corpus of authoritative texts includes not only those formal amendments generated by the procedures of Article Five but also: (a) the *amendment-simulacra* generated by the Republicans under the nationalistic procedures developed during Reconstruction and (b) the transformative opinions that serve as *amendment-analogues* under the nationalistic procedures developed by the Democrats during the Great Depression. So long as lawyers continue to accept the text-simulacra generated by the Reconstruction Republicans, they should not lightly reject the amendment-analogues generated by the New Deal Democrats.

Especially when this use of transformative opinions is hardly unprecedented in American constitutional history. As we already saw, the Republican Court's opinions in the *Legal Tender* and *Slaughterhouse Cases* discharged analogous constitutional functions toward the end of Reconstruction; and even before the Civil War, the opinions of the Taney Court had served to codify the constitutional meaning of Jacksonian Democracy.

Looking beyond the confines of constitutional law, there are countless other cases in which judicial opinions substitute for formal legislative texts. Consider the problem that arises when judges are obliged to coordinate statutory commands and the common law tradition.

In this familiar situation, common law courts regularly appeal to common law cases whenever they find a hole in a statutory scheme. Indeed, this use of judicial precedents in the absence of statutes is the single most important feature distinguishing Anglo-American legal systems from those dominant in Europe. From this vantage, the New Deal innovation is best seen as another case in which American lawyers, at moments of great crisis, creatively adapt traditional ideas (here, the common law use of cases in the absence of statutes) for new constitutional purposes (here, the use of cases in the absence of formal amendments). While this unconventional adaptation does challenge constitutional theory, this is the kind of challenge that has allowed the American people to sustain a continuous constitutional identity for the past two centuries. . . .

. . . The New Deal's substitution of transformative opinions for formal amendments was not the result of some inexplicable failure to attend to the terms of Article Five. It was a creative elaboration of higher lawmaking changes initiated much earlier in American history. The struggle over Reconstruction, not the Great Depression, first led Americans to break with the federalist premises of Article Five. The struggle over Reconstruction, not the Great Depression, first led the President, Congress, and Court to develop new higher lawmaking procedures more in keeping with the constitutive will of We the People of the United States. The basic New Deal innovation followed from the Democrats' greater success in sustaining their control over the Presidency throughout the period of constitutional creativity. . . .

. . . It is no small thing for a political system to focus on fundamentals in this incisive way. Most of the credit goes to the American people—who rejected the demagogues around them eager to drag them toward the moral abyss.

But the Constitution also deserves its share—for the way it structured the evolving struggle so as to allow the antagonists to join issue, rather than talk past one another. Despite Roosevelt's assertion to the contrary, the election of 1932 had little relationship to "the people's mandate" as he was now defining it. At that time, Americans had simply repudiated Hoover's style of progressive Republicanism as utterly inadequate; Roosevelt's mandate, as he well understood, was to experiment with more activist approaches—without any certainty that Americans would approve. Only with the 1934 elections could the President begin to claim genuine popular support for his more affirmative program. Even then his vision was very different from the one he was presenting to the Philadelphia convention. The NIRA was no assault on "economic royalism." If anything, it consolidated the hold of the business elite on their industrial fiefdoms—suspending the antitrust laws and giving dominant firms a central role in the emerging industrial order. This was, of course, why men like Brandeis enthusiastically joined in striking it down.

Only in response to the Supreme Court did Roosevelt and his New Dealers rethink their course—leading to the statutory initiatives of the Second New Deal and the Philadelphia effort to frame the meaning of their initiatives in self-consciously constitutional terms. Roosevelt's watchword was now the rebirth of freedom, not the imperative of central planning. But it was a new freedom, defined in the light of modern realities that would otherwise defeat the claims of equal opportunity. It was a freedom that could not be achieved in opposition to the state, but only through democratic control of the marketplace: "If the average citizen is guaranteed equal opportunity in the polling place, he must have equal opportunity in the market place."

This is the point where the Republicans jumped off the train. While [1936 Republican presidential nominee Governor Alfred] Landon was willing to endorse a more activist version of progressive Republicanism, he was unwilling to revise the old constitutional definition of freedom—tightly linked to principles of limited national government, freedom of contract, and private property. At most, he could endorse a constitutional amendment that authorized state (not federal) regulation of hours and wages. But he was entirely unwilling to accept the New Deal claim that modern freedom could only be achieved through the state and not against it; or endorse Roosevelt's assertion that the old constitutional regime had degenerated into a legalistic smokescreen for a world in which "life was no longer free; liberty no longer real; men could no longer follow the pursuit of happiness." To the contrary, the New Deal promise of freedom raised alarming prospects: "[Will] he attempt to get around the Constitution by tampering with the Supreme Court?"

With such questions ringing in their ears, Americans went to the polls— and gave Roosevelt and the New Deal Congress the greatest victory in American history. Landon gained the electoral votes of only Maine and New Hampshire; he managed to win only 36.5 percent of the popular vote, his share rising as high as 45 percent in no more than four states. The Republicans were left with eighty-nine seats in the House; sixteen in the Senate. No less important, the election of 1936 cemented the hold of the Democratic

Party on American life for the next generation. Indeed, we have yet to see another example of such a massive and enduring political realignment.

The same is true if we look backwards. Despite breakthroughs in the theory of popular sovereignty, the majoritarian achievements of the Federalists and the Republicans were actually quite modest. On both occasions, the revolutionary reformers won the consent of paper-thin majorities for their unconventional movements toward a "more perfect Union." In contrast, New Deal Democracy achieved in practice what Federalists and Republicans had sought in theory—the escalating support of a decisive majority of Americans throughout the nation in the face of an eloquent effort by conservatives to draw the line short of revolutionary reform.

Of course, all Americans had not been magically transformed into enthusiastic New Dealers. Alf Landon did attract 17 million voters into the Republican column in 1936, and the Supreme Court's resistance played an especially important role in reconciling these dissenters to the larger transformation. However bitterly the remaining Republicans might condemn "that man in the White House," there was something that none of them could reasonably deny. In gaining reelection, Roosevelt had been obliged to seek popular support in the face of a withering constitutional critique led by the Court. But when Landon energetically called the People to rise up in defense of their traditional Constitution, Americans were more impressed with the urgent need for revolutionary reform. While Republicans might conscientiously believe that their fellow citizens had made a tragic mistake, they could hardly deny that the People had given decisive support to the

Democrats with their eyes open. By raising the question of constitutional principle so eloquently during Roosevelt's first term of experimentation, the Supreme Court had played a key role in establishing, *even to New Deal opponents*, that the People were indeed supporting a change in their governing philosophy. . . .

. . . Roosevelt made the first big move with his plan for judicial reorganization—which would have allowed him to make six new appointments to the Supreme Court. This provoked a remarkably sophisticated constitutional debate. The President's leading opponents did not present themselves as staunch defenders of the traditional jurisprudence. No less than Roosevelt, they recognized that the People were demanding a fundamental change in constitutional direction.

They denied, however, that the President had hit upon the right way to implement the shift. On their view, there was only one way the President and his party could credibly speak for the People in a higher lawmaking voice—and that was by using the forms provided by Article Five of the original Constitution. To establish their good faith, opponents came forward with constitutional amendments and pleaded with the Administration to put its weight behind one or another proposal. In response, the President was obliged to explain why Article Five was inadequate, presenting an increasingly self-conscious defense of Presidential leadership in higher lawmaking.

The President's initiative, in short, catapulted the country into a great debate of central importance to my main thesis: Was the President right in claiming that the Democrats' electoral victories had given the New Dealers a mandate from the People to take unconventional action to constitutionalize their revolutionary reforms? Or were his opponents right in insisting on a monopolistic interpretation of Article Five?

Just then, the Court chose to make its switch in time. While particular decisions became landmarks, the Justices' new-found consistency was even more important. Never again would the Court find a New Deal reform beyond the power of government. As a consequence, the political protagonists relaxed their own creative efforts to work out the terms of a new constitutional solution and allowed the Court to codify the terms of the New Deal revolution . . . .

President   Franklin   Roosevelt

ADDRESS TO CONGRESS—"FOUR FREEDOMS"*

January 6, 1941

The following two speeches by President Franklin Roosevelt during 1941 and 1944 seek to anchor his New Deal programs in the context of World War II, painting the same joint purpose for them both: to secure and fulfill the great American promise of freedom. But President Roosevelt's vision is a significant break from the traditional idea that freedom requires only

*Available at *http://www.americanrhetoric.com/speeches/fdrthefourfreedoms.htm*.

protections against interference by the state. In contrast, President Roosevelt's conception of freedom includes an active role for government to help citizens navigate the dynamic economy and weather the storms of economic insecurity. How does this political theory help to justify expansive federal programs, such as wage and hour regulations, social security, and government works projects? Is this understanding of federal power consistent with Alexander Hamilton's or Thomas Jefferson's arguments, or does it go beyond either of them?

I address you, the members of this new Congress, at a moment unprecedented in the history of the union. I use the word "unprecedented" because at no previous time has American security been as seriously threatened from without as it is today.

I suppose that every realist knows that the democratic way of life is at this moment being directly assailed in every part of the world—assailed either by arms or by secret spreading of poisonous propaganda by those who seek to destroy unity and promote discord in nations that are still at peace. During 16 long months this assault has blotted out the whole pattern of democratic life in an appalling number of independent nations, great and small. And the assailants are still on the march, threatening other nations, great and small.

Therefore, as your President, performing my constitutional duty to "give to the Congress information of the state of the union," I find it unhappily necessary to report that the future and the safety of our country and of our democracy are overwhelmingly involved in events far beyond our borders.

As men do not live by bread alone, they do not fight by armaments alone. Those who man our defenses and those behind them who build our defenses must have the stamina and the courage which come from unshakable belief in the manner of life which they are defending. The mighty action that we are calling for cannot be based on a disregard of all the things worth fighting for.

The nation takes great satisfaction and much strength from the things which have been done to make its people conscious of their individual stake in the preservation of democratic life in America. Those things have toughened the fiber of our people, have renewed their faith and strengthened their devotion to the institutions we make ready to protect.

Certainly this is no time for any of us to stop thinking about the social and economic problems which are the root cause of the social revolution which is today a supreme factor in the world. For there is nothing mysterious about the foundations of a healthy and strong democracy.

The basic things expected by our people of their political and economic systems are simple. They are:

Equality of opportunity for youth and for others.

Jobs for those who can work.

Security for those who need it.

The ending of special privilege for the few.

The preservation of civil liberties for all.

The enjoyment—The enjoyment of the fruits of scientific progress in a wider and constantly rising standard of living.

These are the simple, the basic things that must never be lost sight of in the turmoil and unbelievable complexity of our modern world. The inner and abiding strength of our economic and political systems is dependent upon the degree to which they fulfill these expectations.

Many subjects connected with our social economy call for immediate improvement. As examples:

We should bring more citizens under the coverage of old-age pensions and unemployment insurance.

We should widen the opportunities for adequate medical care.

We should plan a better system by which persons deserving or needing gainful employment may obtain it.

I have called for personal sacrifice, and I am assured of the willingness of almost all Americans to respond to that call. A part of the sacrifice means the payment of more money in taxes. In my budget message I will recommend that a greater portion of this great defense program be paid for from taxation than we are paying for today. No person should try, or be allowed to get rich out of the program, and the principle of tax payments in accordance with ability to pay should be constantly before our eyes to guide our legislation.

If the Congress maintains these principles the voters, putting patriotism ahead pocketbooks, will give you their applause.

In the future days, which we seek to make secure, we look forward to a world founded upon four essential human freedoms.

The first is freedom of speech and expression—everywhere in the world.

The second is freedom of every person to worship God in his own way—everywhere in the world.

The third is freedom from want, which, translated into world terms, means economic understandings which will secure to every nation a healthy peacetime life for its inhabitants—everywhere in the world.

The fourth is freedom from fear, which, translated into world terms, means a world-wide reduction of armaments to such a point and in such a thorough fashion that no nation will be in a position to commit an act of physical aggression against any neighbor—anywhere in the world.

That is no vision of a distant millennium. It is a definite basis for a kind of world attainable in our own time and generation. That kind of world is the very antithesis of the so-called "new order" of tyranny which the dictators seek to create with the crash of a bomb.

To that new order we oppose the greater conception—the moral order. A good society is able to face schemes of world domination and foreign revolutions alike without fear.

Since the beginning of our American history we have been engaged in change, in a perpetual, peaceful revolution, a revolution which goes on steadily, quietly, adjusting itself to changing conditions without the concentration camp or the quicklime in the ditch. The world order which we seek is the cooperation of free countries, working together in a friendly, civilized society.

This nation has placed its destiny in the hands and heads and hearts of its millions of free men and women, and its faith in freedom under the guidance of God. Freedom means the supremacy of human rights everywhere. Our support goes to those who struggle to gain those rights and keep them. Our strength is our unity of purpose.

To that high concept there can be no end save victory.

President Franklin Roosevelt

STATE OF THE UNION MESSAGE TO CONGRESS— "SECOND BILL OF RIGHTS"*

January 11, 1944

To the Congress:

This Nation in the past two years has become an active partner in the world's greatest war against human slavery.

The one supreme objective for the future, which we discussed for each Nation individually, and for all the United Nations, can be summed up in one word: Security.

And that means not only physical security which provides safety from attacks by aggressors. It means also economic security, social security, moral security—in a family of Nations.

The best interests of each Nation, large and small, demand that all freedom-loving Nations shall join together in a just and durable system of peace. In the present world situation, evidenced by the actions of Germany, Italy, and Japan, unquestioned military control over disturbers of the peace is as necessary among Nations as it is among citizens in a community. And an equally basic essential to peace is a decent standard of living for all individual men and women and children in all Nations. Freedom from fear is eternally linked with freedom from want.

It is our duty now to begin to lay the plans and determine the strategy for the winning of a lasting peace and the establishment of an American standard of living higher than ever before known. We cannot be content, no matter how high that general standard of living may be, if some fraction of our people—whether it be one-third or one-fifth or one-tenth— is ill-fed, ill-clothed, ill-housed, and insecure.

This Republic had its beginning, and grew to its present strength, under the protection of certain inalienable political rights—among them the right of free speech, free press, free worship, trial by jury, freedom from unreasonable searches and seizures. They were our rights to life and liberty.

As our Nation has grown in size and stature, however—as our industrial economy expanded—these political rights proved inadequate to assure us equality in the pursuit of happiness.

We have come to a clear realization of the fact that true individual freedom cannot exist without economic security and independence. "Necessitous men are not free men." People who are hungry and out of a job are the stuff of which dictatorships are made.

In our day these economic truths have become accepted as self-evident. We have accepted, so to speak, a second Bill of Rights under which a new basis of security and prosperity can be established for all—regardless of station, race, or creed.

Among these are:

The right to a useful and remunerative job in the industries or shops or farms or mines of the Nation;

* Available at *http://www.fdrlibrary.marist.edu/archives/ address_text.html.*

The right to earn enough to provide adequate food and clothing and recreation;

The right of every farmer to raise and sell his products at a return which will give him and his family a decent living;

The right of every businessman, large and small, to trade in an atmosphere of freedom from unfair competition and domination by monopolies at home or abroad;

The right of every family to a decent home;

The right to adequate medical care and the opportunity to achieve and enjoy good health;

The right to adequate protection from the economic fears of old age, sickness, accident, and unemployment;

The right to a good education.

All of these rights spell security. And after this war is won we must be prepared to move forward, in the implementation of these rights, to new goals of human happiness and well-being.

America's own rightful place in the world depends in large part upon how fully these and similar rights have been carried into practice for our citizens. For unless there is security here at home there cannot be lasting peace in the world.

One of the great American industrialists of our day—a man who has rendered yeoman service to his country in this crisis—recently emphasized the grave dangers of "rightist reaction" in this Nation. All clear-thinking businessmen share his concern. Indeed, if such reaction should develop—if history were to repeat itself and we were to return to the so-called "normalcy" of the 1920's—then it is certain that even though we shall have conquered our enemies on the battlefields abroad, we shall have yielded to the spirit of Fascism here at home.

I ask the Congress to explore the means for implementing this economic bill of rights—for it is definitely the responsibility of the Congress so to do. Many of these problems are already before committees of the Congress in the form of proposed legislation. I shall from time to time communicate with the Congress with respect to these and further proposals. In the event that no adequate program of progress is evolved, I am certain that the Nation will be conscious of the fact.

Our fighting men abroad—and their families at home—expect such a program and have the right to insist upon it. It is to their demands that this Government should pay heed rather than to the whining demands of selfish pressure groups who seek to feather their nests while young Americans are dying.

The foreign policy that we have been following—the policy that guided us at Moscow, Cairo, and Teheran—is based on the common sense principle which was best expressed by Benjamin Franklin on July 4, 1776: "We must all hang together, or assuredly we shall all hang separately."

I have often said that there are no two fronts for America in this war. There is only one front. There is one line of unity which extends from the hearts of the people at home to the men of our attacking forces in our farthest outposts. When we speak of our total effort, we speak of the factory and the field, and the mine as well as of the battleground—we speak of the soldier and the civilian, the citizen and his Government.

Each and every one of us has a solemn obligation under God to serve this Nation in its most critical hour—to keep this Nation great—to make this Nation greater in a better world.

Cass R. Sunstein & Randy E. Barnett

CONSTITUTIVE COMMITMENTS AND ROOSEVELT'S SECOND BILL OF RIGHTS: A DIALOGUE

53 Drake L. Rev. 205 (Winter 2005)

We include here Cass Sunstein's defense of President Franklin Roosevelt's vision of freedom as well as a response to that defense by Randy Barnett. Notice that Barnett challenges Sunstein's constitutional argument and also President Roosevelt's conception of freedom. Does Sunstein succeed in providing a constitutional basis for President Roosevelt's vision?

I. ROOSEVELT'S SECOND BILL OF RIGHTS

Cass R. Sunstein

On January 11, 1944, the United States was involved in its longest conflict since the Civil War. The war effort was going well. In a remarkably short period, the tide had turned sharply in favor of the Allies. Ultimate victory was no longer in serious doubt. The real question was the nature of the peace.

At noon, America's optimistic, aging, self-assured, wheelchair-bound president, Franklin Delano Roosevelt, delivered his State of the Union Address to Congress. His speech was not elegant. It was messy, sprawling, unruly, a bit of a pastiche, and not at all literary. It was the opposite of Lincoln's tight, poetic Gettysburg Address. But because of what it said, this forgotten address, proposing a "Second Bill of Rights," has a strong claim to being the greatest speech of the twentieth century.

What made the Second Bill of Rights possible? Part of the answer lies in a simple idea, one pervasive in the American legal culture during Roosevelt's time: No one really opposes government intervention. Markets and wealth depend on government. Without government creating and protecting property rights, property itself cannot exist. Even the people who most loudly denounce government interference depend on it every day. Their own rights do not come from minimizing government but are a product of government.... Think, for example, of the owner of a radio station, a house in the suburbs, an expensive automobile, or a large bank account. Every such owner depends, every day of every year, on the protection given by a coercive and well-funded state, equipped with a police force, judges, prosecutors, and an extensive body of criminal and civil law.

From the beginning, Roosevelt's White House understood all this quite well. In accepting the Democratic nomination in 1932, Roosevelt insisted that "we must lay hold of the fact that economic laws are not made by nature. They are made by human beings." ...

In this light it was implausible to contend that government should simply "stay out of the way" or "let people fend for themselves." Against the backdrop of the Great Depression, and the threat from fascism, Roosevelt was entirely prepared to insist that government should "protect individualism" not only by protecting property rights but also by ensuring decent opportunities and minimal security for all. The ultimate result was his proposal for the Second Bill of Rights.

By virtue of its effect on the Universal Declaration, the Second Bill has influenced dozens of constitutions throughout the world. In one form or another, it can be found in countless political and legal documents. . . .

In fact the United States itself continues to live, at least some of the time, under Roosevelt's constitutional vision. A consensus underlies several of the rights he listed, including the right to education, the right to social security, and the right to be free from monopoly. In the 1950s and 1960s, the Supreme Court started to go much further, embarking on a process of giving constitutional recognition to some of the rights that Roosevelt listed.

In a short period from 1957 through 1969, the Court explored several of these issues, and it reacted sympathetically to people's complaints. In some of them, the Court went so far as to hold that the government must subsidize poor people in certain domains. In several, the Court ruled that indigent criminal defendants have a right to a lawyer at taxpayer expense. Building on "the right to protect your rights," the Court struck down poll taxes. In other cases, the Court went further still. In *Shapiro v. Thompson*, the Court seemed to come close to saying that the Constitution conferred a right to welfare benefits. . . .

In *Goldberg*, the Court abandoned the right-privilege distinction and ruled that welfare was indeed a form of constitutional "property." Under the Due Process Clause, the government must provide a hearing before it removes people from the rolls. In *Goldberg*, the Court emphasized the "brutal need" of those who depended on welfare benefits. In its most extraordinary passage, it noted that "from its founding the Nation's basic commitment has been to foster the dignity and well-being of all persons within its borders. We have come to recognize that forces not within the control of the poor contribute to their poverty." Here is a clear reminder of a central lesson of the Great Depression . . . .

. . . By the late 1960s, respected constitutional thinkers could conclude that the Court was on the verge of recognizing a right to be free from desperate conditions—a right that captures many of the rights that Roosevelt attempted to catalogue. But all this was undone as a result of the election of President Richard Nixon in 1968. President Nixon promptly appointed four justices—Warren Burger, William Rehnquist, Lewis Powell, and Harry Blackmun—who showed no interest in the Second Bill. In a series of decisions, the new justices, joined by one or two others, rejected the claim that the existing Constitution protects the rights that Roosevelt catalogued.

Roosevelt himself did not argue for constitutional change (and on this I believe that he was right). He wanted the Second Bill to be part of the nation's deepest commitments, to be recognized and vindicated by the public, not by federal judges. He thought that the Second Bill should be seen in the same way as the Declaration of Independence—as a statement of the fundamental aspirations of the United States, which we might see as the nation's constitutive commitments. . . .

II. CONSTITUTIVE COMMITMENTS

Cass R. Sunstein

It is standard to distinguish between constitutional requirements and mere policies. An appropriation for Head Start is a policy, which can be changed however Congress wishes; by contrast, the principle of free speech overrides whatever Congress seeks to do. But there is something important, rarely unnoticed, and in between—much firmer than mere policies, but falling short of constitutional requirements. These are constitutive commitments. . . .

Constitutive commitments have a special place in the sense that they are widely accepted and cannot be eliminated without a fundamental change in national understandings. These rights are "constitutive" in the sense that they help to create, or to constitute, a society's basic values. They are also commitments, in the sense that they have a degree of stability over time. A violation would amount to a kind of breach—a violation of a trust.

Current examples include the right to some kind of social security program; the right not to be fired by a private employer because of your skin color or your sex; the right to protection through some kind of antitrust law. As with constitutional provisions, we disagree about what, specifically, these rights entail; but there is not much national disagreement about the rights themselves. (At least not at the moment.)

We could learn a lot about a nation's history if we explored what falls in the category of constitutional rights, constitutive commitments, and mere policies—and even more if we identified migrations over time. Maybe some of the commitments just mentioned will turn into mere policies. Sometimes policies are rapidly converted into constitutive commitments (consider the 1964 Civil Rights Act). Sometimes constitutive commitments end up getting constitutional status (the right to sexual privacy is, to some extent, an example, with the line of cases from *Griswold v. Connecticut* to *Lawrence v. Texas*).

Back to FDR's Second Bill of Rights: He was not proposing a formal constitutional change; he did not want to alter a word of the founding document. He was proposing to identify a set of constitutive commitments. One possible advantage of that strategy is that it avoids a role for federal judges; another possible advantage is that it allows a lot of democratic debate, over time, about what the constitutive commitments specifically entail.

VII. Constitutive Commitments Do Not Matter, But If They Do . . .

Randy E. Barnett

Suppose I deny that there is a natural right to a decent home, by which I mean that one person has no enforceable moral claim on another person, or group of persons, to provide him with a house. Classical natural rights thinkers distinguished between "perfect rights" which ought to be enforceable and "imperfect rights" which entail unenforceable moral duties. By denying that there is a perfect right to a house, I would not be denying that some persons could decide to give a portion of their property to others so that they may afford a house. Likewise, a government program could be created to provide housing by means of tax dollars (unless taxation itself is theft, in which case such a program would be unjust for that reason). The denial of the alleged "right" to a home would be denying only that, in the absence of government, one person can demand that another person be compelled to labor for him to build him a house. What policies government chooses to adopt, even in the absence of an enforceable moral claim, is another matter.

Supposing that it is possible to identify the constitutive commitments of an entire society of 280 million diverse persons and that it matters what these commitments may be, the particular constitutive commitments emphasized by Cass are highly contestable. First, the exact content of the alleged commitment is contestable—for example, is a commitment to an enforceable or "perfect right" of the poor to the assistance of others, or a commitment to voluntarily honor an unenforceable duty or "imperfect right" to provide assistance to those in need by means of a voluntary public program? As a purely descriptive matter, it seems that it is the latter, not the former, that has "real foundations in our history," but who can be sure? And how could this interpretive dispute about unwritten constitutive commitments ever be settled? That is the point of my doubts about the uncertain conditions of what makes a commitment constitutive and how we would know one if it existed.

Second, assuming there are such things as constitutive commitments, it is not at all clear that ours today are the same as those in Roosevelt's day. In the 1940s, the idea of a national welfare state had great appeal among intellectuals. It promised a more effective means to achieve the liberal ends of individual well-being. Then it was tried. Remember "The Great Society" with its "War on Poverty" and "Urban Renewal," which was initiated during the Johnson Administration and greatly expanded by Richard Nixon (who also added the "War on Drugs" to the program)? Did poverty end? Were cities restored to their previous greatness? Was illicit drug use eradicated? Well, no. The underclass expanded as more people came to rely on government benefits as "entitlements." The inner cities grew more impoverished and dangerous. Government housing projects were erected and fell into the control of gangs and thugs, and are now being demolished. Government schools declined precipitously. Stagflation hit the national economy. The War on Drugs has fueled inner city street gangs and international terrorist organizations, and undermined democracy in Third World countries.

All these pernicious effects of implementing something like Roosevelt's Second Bill of Rights are the reasons why "welfare state" is now an epithet rather than a noble goal. Why courts in the 1980s backed away from imposing these policies as constitutional rights. Why Ronald Reagan was elected in 1980. Why Republicans took control of the House of Representatives in 1994, ending 50 years of Democratic dominance. Why all three branches of government are now controlled by Republicans. Why European social welfare states, all built on Rooseveltian foundations, are in grave economic crisis, with intractably high unemployment and obligations to pay for social programs outstripping the ability to tax those who work.

In short, our real world experience since the 1940s undermined any "constitutive commitment" that may have existed to a Second Bill of Rights in a manner that no academic argument ever could. But academic arguments explaining theoretically why Roosevelt's approach leads to disastrous consequences have also boomed since his speech, beginning with the explosive popularity of F.A. Hayek's *The Road to Serfdom* in 1949. If forced to choose whether the vision of Roosevelt or of Hayek is ascendant, I think clearly it is the latter. . . .

Nor were classical liberals somehow confused, as Cass seems to think, about the need for government to "positively" enforce properly defined natural rights of property and contract, when they opposed governmental interference with these rights. Indeed, the purpose for making claims of perfect rights is as much to justify government protection of these rights as it is to deny government the power to interfere with their proper exercise. That the first duty of government is the equal protection of properly defined rights was always at the heart of the Lockean justification of government itself. That government is thought to be needed to enforce properly defined rights, therefore, provides no support whatsoever for extending governmental enforcement to rights claims that themselves interfere with properly defined rights.

So what then are our "constitutive commitments" today? Today more than any time since the nineteenth century, American culture is committed to rights of private property and freedom of contract. It is against this intellectual tide that Cass Sunstein makes his plea, asserting Rooseveltian constitutive commitments as a sort of rear guard action. But this American commitment to property and contract is tempered by the age-old classical liberal concern with the welfare of those who slip between the cracks—the group that used to be called the "deserving poor."

True, today most still accept the Progressive proposition that government rather than private institutions should assist these people. Nevertheless, most also complain that the nondeserving poor are assisted as well as those who deserve aid, a complaint that led to historic welfare reforms in the 1990s. I believe both the deserving poor and the greater society would be better served if more of this well-motivated assistance were channeled through private competitive institutions, as it once was. Time will tell whether we will move farther in this direction or be frozen in place.

But the proof of the pudding is in the eating. To the extent it matters, Roosevelt's Second Bill of Rights was abandoned as a constitutive commitment—if it was ever truly adopted—by the bitter taste of the Great Society. If increased reliance on the voluntary duty of beneficence is allowed by the political establishment to be tried and it proves to work better in practice than government welfare programs, as theory says that it should, then such an approach is likely to expand. The principal obstacle to discovering who is correct as a practical matter is the effective obstruction of these reforms by reactionaries in academia, the media and public sector unions who call themselves, ironically, "Progressives." In the end, individual liberty is the one continuous constitutive commitment of the American polity. Only time will tell whether the best means to that end is Roosevelt's or Hayek's. I know on whom my bet would be placed.

Judge Douglas Ginsburg

ON CONSTITUTIONALISM*

Kenneth Simon Lecture in Constitutional Thought

September 17, 2002

Bruce Ackerman and Cass Sunstein contend that, at least in some sense, the New Deal effectively amended the Constitution outside of the formal Article V process.

*Available at *www.cato.org/pubs/scr/2003/constitutional.pdf*.

But does this kind of claim concede that President Franklin Roosevelt's efforts to regulate the national economy were in fact unconstitutional at the time they were proposed? Judge Douglas Ginsburg and libertarian scholar Richard Epstein express skepticism about whether the New Deal's expansion of the Commerce power was constitutional—or even desirable.

Does fidelity to the written nature of constitutional text require that its meaning remain fixed, insulated from changing conditions? From what interpretive theories—originalism, proceduralism, the moral reading, or pragmatism—do Judge Ginsburg and Epstein draw? Are political and policy judgments about the New Deal really separable from judgments about its constitutionality? If the critics are right and the New Deal was unconstitutional, what difference does 70 years of reliance on these mistaken precedents make? Would constitutional fidelity require uprooting these precedents, or simply "cutting our losses" and refusing to allow federal power to continue its growth?

I begin with an observation so fundamental, so straightforward and obvious, that it could be controversial only in the most elite law schools. That observation, to which I will devote considerable attention, is that ours is a written Constitution. When I say ours is a written constitution, I refer, of course, to the actual Constitution, the Constitution of the United States, the document reprinted in this little pamphlet in my hand. I do not refer to the legion of Supreme Court decisions interpreting the Constitution, applying it to particular factual situations, and in many cases providing us with an extended exegesis on its meaning. Those decisions are not the Constitution; as a practical matter, they are reasonably reliable guides to its application in future cases, but they are not the Constitution itself. To maintain otherwise is to ascribe to the Supreme Court a doctrine of infallibility it has never claimed for itself. . . .

To be faithful to our written Constitution, a jurist must recognize and respect the limiting nature of its terms. Granted, what a term such as "due process" requires in a particular circumstance is not always clear. Nevertheless, there should be no question at all about whether a 34-year-old or a naturalized citizen may become President of the United States. That the terms giving rise to most questions of constitutional meaning lie somewhere between inherent ambiguity and mathematical certainty is no excuse from the duty of fidelity to the text. Rather, to be faithful to the written Constitution a jurist must make it his goal to illuminate the meaning of the text as the Framers understood it. To be sure, there will be disagreements even among principled jurists whose only goal is fidelity to the text, but with the aid of historical sources such disagreements will be confined to the ordinarily narrow and determinate zone within which competing constructions of a word or phrase are reasonable.

Despite sporadic departures like *Dred Scott*, respect for the text of the Constitution was the norm from *Marbury* through the first third of the twentieth century. But the Great Depression and the determination of the Roosevelt Administration placed the Supreme Court's commitment to the Constitution as written under severe stress in the 1930s, and it was then that the wheels began to come off.

Among the powers granted to the Congress in the Constitution is the power "[t]o regulate commerce . . . among the several states." From early in the history of the Republic, this authority was recognized to extend to articles in commerce among the states, while jurisdiction over health, safety, or other exercises of the police power was reserved exclusively to the states. The Clause was deemed broad enough, therefore, to allow regulation not only of ferries and railroads that transported goods in interstate commerce, but also of ancillary facilities, such as stockyards, described as "a throat through which the current [of commerce] flows." The power did not encompass regulation of child labor, however, because "the use of interstate transportation was [not] necessary to the accomplishment of harmful results." Desirable though a prohibition upon child labor may have been, therefore, the Congress was without power to enact it. A contrary result would have allowed the Congress to regulate almost anything pursuant to its power over interstate commerce, regardless whether the subject regulated was within the police power of the states.

During the 1930s, President Roosevelt proposed and the Congress enacted New Deal legislation in the teeth of the Court's prior decisions explicating the limits of the written Constitution. In effect, the President and the Congress dared the Court to strike down laws with strong popular support. Then President Roosevelt announced, after his landslide victory in 1936, his plan to "pack" the Supreme Court—that is, in the name of efficiency, to add another seat to the Court for each active justice over the age of 70, which would have given him six additional appointments. The Court-packing plan was voted down overwhelmingly by the Senate, but until then the threat of some change in the composition of the Court must have added to the strain placed upon the Justices' adherence to their announced understanding of the Constitution. After all, the power of the sword of Damocles is not that it falls, but that it hangs.

It was under the threat of the Court-packing plan that the Justices decided *NLRB v. Jones & Laughlin Steel Corp.*, upholding the power of the Congress

to require employers to recognize and bargain with unions representing their employees. The Court's loose reasoning appears entirely too familiar from our contemporary perspective: strikes and other labor strife burden interstate commerce; therefore, employer-employee relations are subject to the power of the Congress to regulate interstate commerce.

In context, however, it is clear that the decision was a stark break from the Court's precedent. Whereas the Court had previously determined that the national government could not intrude upon the police power of the states by proscribing child labor, it now threw open the door to national regulation of employment relations—and much more. Not only interstate commerce but anything that affects interstate commerce came within the reach of the Congress. Indeed, not until *United States v. Lopez* in 1995 did the Court find another federally regulated subject beyond the reach of the Commerce Clause, and that was the possession near a school of a gun that was not shown to have moved in interstate commerce.

I have singled out the Court's interpretation of the Commerce Clause not because it is extreme but because it is illustrative. To take another example, the Constitution carefully separates legislative and executive powers. "All legislative powers herein granted shall be vested in a Congress of the United States," whereas "[t]he Executive Power shall be vested in a President of the United States of America." From that clear demarcation the Court had once inferred there must be a limit upon the ability of the Congress to delegate lawmaking functions to the executive branch. By delegating its legislative function the Congress avoids political accountability—therein lies the appeal of delegation—and frustrates the Framers' purpose in separating governmental powers. Accordingly, in the years before *Jones & Laughlin* the Supreme Court invalidated delegations of legislative power that contained no "intelligible principle to which the person or body authorized to take action is directed to conform." After the watershed New Deal cases expanding the reach of the Congress through the commerce power, however, the Court never again found an Act of Congress, however open-ended, to violate the Non-Delegation Doctrine.

If renewed fidelity to the Constitution as written is possible—and I think it is—then it will come only through a change in the legal culture. The ranks of scholars and judges advocating greater fidelity to constitutional text is still small but it is growing. Scholars are attending more to the original meaning of at least some of the clauses of the Constitution instead of focusing exclusively upon the Court's prior decisions. I daresay there has been more study of the Commerce Power and the Non-Delegation Doctrine in the last 10 years than in the prior half-century. Like archaeologists, legal and historical researchers have been rediscovering neglected clauses, dusting them off, and in some instances even imagining how they might be returned to active service. As the new legal scholarship gains acceptance, and students are exposed to the competing vision it represents, they will as lawyers begin to present more textual arguments, some of which may eventually win acceptance in the courts.

Richard Epstein

HOW PROGRESSIVES REWROTE THE CONSTITUTION

Washington, D.C.: Cato Institute (2006)

. . . The traditional classical liberal ideas of constitutional government—private property and freedom of contract, coupled with limited government and low levels of taxation and regulation, and, in the American context, federalism—may be traced to ancient times. They had a profound influence during the fertile founding period of our own Constitution. As historical landmarks, they stand as a constant reminder that it is possible to think of constitutional law without embracing the ideals of the modern social welfare state.

These debates swirl around many modern controversies, but they often come to a head whenever a new Supreme Court nomination is in the wings. However great my affection for the classical ideals that animated some, but not all, of the pre–New Deal jurisprudence, the opposition to that position is every bit as intense. Proponents of the modern position often make their lives far easier than they ought to be by their own extravagant misdescriptions of key doctrines of the now-reviled "Old Court." They are quite happy to place anyone opposed to their ideals in an imaginary "Constitution-in-Exile" movement, as though employing that term (Judge Douglas Ginsburg coined it) makes their opponents as legitimate as, say, deposed Bourbon royalists yearning for a return to some bygone age.

Overblown rhetoric to one side, just what might such a supposed movement support? We are often told that defenders of the pre–New Deal world order believe in an "unregulated America," when what they typically support is a legal order that does not regulate the prices, terms, and conditions on which goods and services are sold in a competitive market. It is often said that defenders of the pre–New Deal world believe that all property rights are inviolable. In fact, the classical liberal tradition in which I write accepts proportionate taxation. It also insists that government at all levels can use the power of eminent domain but only for public uses and upon payment of just compensation. That position also accepts the use of a police power that allows for regulation without compensation, which historically embraced law that addressed the public health, safety, morals, and general welfare, to use the formulation followed in the controversial case of *Lochner v. New York.* In some cases, that theory (like much of the modern law of privacy and sexual association) rejects some pre–New Deal legislation, such as that which is intended to promote the "morals" of the public at large. The classical liberal position is not "frozen" in the past; nor does it line up with modern left/right or Red/Blue divisions. The constant theme that drives the analysis is that of small government, which offers as little comfort to the new generation of religious and social conservatives as it does to the traditional American left.

Of course, I endorse some propositions that many other critics of modern American constitutional law most emphatically do not accept. Years ago, in my 1985 book *Takings,* I took the position that the standard interferences with employment contracts, such as minimum wage laws, antidiscrimination laws (in competitive markets only), collective bargaining laws, and Social Security

requirements, were unconstitutional, all on the ground that the state has no better knowledge of what individuals need than individuals themselves do. I stand unapologetically by those positions today and think that the invalidation of those programs rests not on some narrowly egoistical view of private property but on the correct *social* ground that this view does us more good in the long run than the endless creation of various "unfair" practices, such as those under modern labor law, that introduce various forms of state monopolies, each of which further saps the productive juices from American society. At the same time, I fully recognize that the mistakes of the past, such as the creation of Social Security, cannot be undone today in light of the extensive reliance interests that have been created. Many institutions that are not defensible as a matter of first principle become so embedded in our social life that they cannot be undone without grievous harm. But that acceptance of change should never be confused with the mistaken belief that long usage of accepted doctrine renders it necessarily immune from rational criticism and constitutional change; for if that were the case, then the doctrine of "separate-but-equal," announced in1896 in *Plessy v. Ferguson,* would have been affirmed, not overturned *58* years later in *Brown v. Board of Education.* There is no easy metric to solve the "second-best" of what, if anything, should be done to correct past constitutional errors. . . .

. . . [T]he same intellectuals who attacked the members of the Old Court because of their narrow and prescientific point of view were guilty of a massive disregard of the basic established principles of economics that were well known to Adam Smith and David Ricardo. Those principles were trampled by the mercantilist impulses of the day. No judgment about social welfare can be made simply by celebrating the gains to one preferred group. A complete social analysis must look at all the effects, negative and positive. Any program that works like a cartel makes sure that one group gets a larger share of a smaller pie from which it may profit in the long run (although long-term profitability could easily be impaired as others seek to evade legal restrictions). But the situation is always a double disaster for those individuals whom regulation leaves with a smaller share of a smaller pie.

The decisive criticism of the Progressive program, then, does not depend on any exaggerated sense of individualism—of the 18th century or of more modern vintage. It depends on an overall programmatic critique that examines the effect that policy initiatives have on the full range of relevant parties. The only programs that should survive are those that produce some *net* social improvement. Accordingly, there is no good sense in saying that one bad program justifies a second, any more than there is in insisting on making a second hole in the bottom of a boat instead of patching the first. Yet that is what happened under the Progressive regime where one bad turn justified a second. The workers whom the Progressives reflexively supported on matters of employment suffered under the agricultural regimes imposed to benefit dairy and wheat farmers, just as those farmers suffered from the legal regime that the Progressives adopted for labor unions. Neither error cancels out the other. Rather, the two errors compound each other. The intellectuals who scoffed at Adam Smith and his archaic conceptions of liberty fell into the timeless traps about which he so eloquently warned.

The Court's Commerce Clause jurisprudence thus represents a dubious textual reading for an antisocial political end.

The language of the clause is contorted so "commerce" now includes the home consumption that everyone took to be its verbal opposite. Politically, this tour-de-force of constitutional interpretation was justified by an ostensible social need to inject the federal government into problems too big to be left to the states. But so long as market liberalization is the path toward a rational agricultural and labor policy, the Progressive vision of American constitutionalism continues to prop up the most dubious of federal institutions. . . .

. . . [T]he Progressive tradition was . . . bankrupt on Commerce Clause and economic issues . . . in two distinct but related senses.

The first of these is that it failed as a matter of constitutional interpretation. Although inconsistent on several points, the Framers of the original Constitution, the Bill of Rights, and the Civil War Amendments did start with some strong preference in favor of protecting liberty, property, and the social institutions they foster—competition and free trade in all areas of human endeavor. A good theory of constitutional interpretation is not one that starts and stops with some rote meaning of text, but this charge could not be lodged against the Old Court whose understanding of the need to introduce the nontextual element of the police power shows a sensitivity to structure and function as well as text. Nor can it be said that the interpretation that the justices of the Old Court gave to liberty or property is at variance with ordinary usage or with the larger mission of strong individual protections under a regime of limited government. They made mistakes along the way, and they were forced to make peace with a doctrine that had more protectionist elements than is ideal. But it is hard to charge them with any wholesale betrayal of the original design.

The same cannot be said of the Progressives. They saw in constitutional interpretation the opportunity to rewrite a Constitution that showed at every turn the influence of John Locke and James Madison into a different Constitution, which reflected the wisdom of the leading intellectual reformers of their own time. That effort to switch the terms of discourse fails because it violates the first tenet of interpretation. If you disagree with the original text, then you cannot mend your disagreements by adding to its basic rule some exceptions that change the tenor and purpose of the document. That standard is not meant to privilege the Old Court against modern rivals. The same principle applies to modern constitutions that often are overendowed with positive rights: a right to decent housing does not become a right to purchase decent housing if you can afford it. A grant of positive rights, whether wise or foolish, should not disappear in a blaze of interpretation. The same applies to modern statutes. The National Labor Relations Act should not become the charter of free markets in labor, and the civil rights acts should not be interpreted to allow racial discrimination against any person in the name of ending discrimination. The point here is that anyone on any side of the political spectrum can play fast and loose with authoritative text, and those evasions are no more palatable when done by one side than by the other. The Progressives were wrong on matters of constitutional interpretation because they consciously used their intellectual powers to rewrite, not understand, key provisions of the constitutional text.

Worse perhaps, the Progressives were wrong as a matter of political theory. Assume that they could write their own constitution on a blank slate. What principles of political economy would so captivate their imaginations that they would want to preserve cartels and monopolies in all areas of social life? There are, of course, special cases—patents, telecommunications—where some guarded use of monopoly power may be needed to spur invention or to assemble network industries. But the Progressives were not interested in working through those special cases. Rather, they were determined that their vision of the managed economy should take precedence in all areas of life. Although they purported to have great sophistication on economic and social matters, their understanding of those matters was primitive, and their disdain for the evident signs of social improvement colored their vision of the success of the older order. In the end, they cannot hide behind any notion of judicial restraint or high-minded social virtue. The Progressives and their modern defenders have to live with the stark truth that the noblest innovations of the Progressive Era were its greatest failures.

SWIFT AND COMPANY v. UNITED STATES

196 U.S. 375 (1905)

Opinion: Holmes, joined by Harlan, Brewer, Brown, White, Peckham, McKenna, Day

Towards the end of the nineteenth century, members of the Progressive movement sought to apply the federal government's power to address social and economic problems such

as labor conditions, food safety, and monopolies. In response to this movement, the Court insisted on a narrow reading of Gibbons v. Ogden, distinguishing interstate commerce from purely local economic activity like production and consumption. Although the Court interpreted these latter spheres of activity to be within the purview of state governments alone, the justices struck down Progressive regulations at the state level—albeit on different grounds.

In United States v. E.C. Knight Co., the Supreme Court severely weakened the Sherman Anti-Trust Act. Because of its narrow reading of the commerce power, the Court construed the Act not to cover monopoly activity that occurred strictly within a state, such as in manufacturing. Although the justices did not invalidate this landmark legislation, their limited understanding of the Commerce power rendered it difficult to enforce.

However, despite denying Progressives the Commerce Clause power as a means of enacting legislation to regulate working conditions and wages within the states, the Court did allow the use of the commerce power to regulate what it labeled the "stream" of commerce. In Swift & Co. v. United States, the Court upheld the federal government's attempts to regulate cattle and prevent local monopolistic practices under the Sherman Anti-Trust Act. Even if each individual transaction involved in the cattle trade did not involve the crossing of state lines, the industry as a whole was involved, U.S. Supreme Court Justice Oliver Wendell Holmes argued, in a "stream of commerce." To some degree Swift & Co. v. United States might have marked a more lenient Commerce Clause jurisprudence. But as you will see in the following case, the Court was very concerned not to allow too much federal power to be authorized under this clause. As you read this case, you should pay attention to how broadly the Court reads the Commerce Clause.

MR. JUSTICE HOLMES *delivered the opinion of the Court.*

Although the combination alleged embraces restraint and monopoly of trade within a single state, its effect upon commerce among the states is not accidental, secondary, remote, or merely probable. On the allegations of the bill the latter commerce no less, perhaps even more, than commerce within a single state, is an object of attack. Moreover, it is a direct object; it is that for the sake of which the several specific acts and courses of conduct are done and adopted. Therefore the case is not like *United States v. E.C. Knight Co.*, where the subject-matter of the combination was manufacture, and the direct object monopoly of manufacture within a state. However likely monopoly of commerce among the states in the article manufactured was to follow from the agreement, it was not a necessary consequence nor a primary end. Here the subject-matter is sales, and the very point of the combination is to restrain and monopolize commerce among the states in respect to such sales. The two cases are near to each other, as sooner or later always must happen where lines are to be drawn, but the line between them is distinct.

So, again, the line is distinct between this case and *Hopkins v. United States*. All that was decided there was that the local business of commission merchants was not commerce among the states, even if what the brokers were employed to sell was an object of such commerce. The brokers were not like the defendants before us, themselves the buyers and sellers. They only furnished certain facilities for the sales. Therefore, there again the effects of the combination of brokers upon the commerce was only indirect, and not within the act.

For the foregoing reasons we are of opinion that the carrying out of the scheme alleged, by the means set forth, properly may be enjoined, and that the bill cannot be dismissed.

So far it has not been necessary to consider whether the facts charges in any single paragraph constitute commerce among the states or show an interference with it. There can be no doubt, we apprehend, as to the collective effect of all the facts, if true, and if the defendants entertain the intent alleged. We pass now to the particulars, and will consider the corresponding parts of the injunction at the same time. The first question arises on the 6th section. That charges a combination of independent dealers to restrict the competition of their agents when purchasing stock for them in the stock yards. The purchasers and their slaughtering establishments are largely in different States from those of the stockyards, and the sellers of the cattle, perhaps it is not too much to assume, largely in different States from either. The intent of the combination is not merely to restrict competition among the parties, but, as we have said, by force of the general allegation at the end of the bill, to aid in an attempt to monopolize commerce among the States.

It is said that this charge is too vague, and that it does not set forth a case of commerce among the States. Taking up the latter objection first, commerce among the States is not a technical legal conception, but a practical one, drawn from the course of business. When cattle are sent for sale from a place in one State, with the expectation that they will end their transit, after purchase, in another, and when, in effect, they do so, with only the interruption necessary to find a purchaser at the stockyards, and when this is a typical, constantly recurring course, the current thus existing is a current of commerce among the States, and the purchase of the cattle is a part and incident of such commerce. What we say is true at least of such a purchase by residents

in another State from that of the seller and of the cattle. And we need not trouble ourselves at this time as to whether the statute could be escaped by any arrangement as to the place where the sale, in point of law, is consummated. *See Norfolk & Western Ry. v. Sims*. But the sixth section of the bill charges an interference with such sales, a restraint of the parties by mutual contract and a combination not to compete in order to monopolize. It is immaterial if the section also embraces domestic transactions.

It should be added that the cattle in the stockyard are not at rest even to the extent that was held sufficient to warrant taxation in *American Steel & Wire Co. v. Speed*. But it may be that the question of taxation does not depend upon whether the article taxed may or may not be said to be in the course of commerce between the States, but depends upon whether the tax so far affects that commerce as to amount to a regulation of it. The injunction against taking part in a combination, the effect of which will be a restraint of trade among the States by directing the defendants' agents to refrain from bidding against one another at the sales of livestock, is justified so far as the subject matter is concerned.

The injunction, however, refers not to trade among the States in cattle, concerning which there can be no question of original packages, but to trade in fresh meats, as the trade forbidden to be restrained, and it is objected that the trade in fresh meats described in the second and third sections of the bill is not commerce among the States, because the meat is sold at the slaughtering places, or, when sold elsewhere, may be sold in less than the original packages. But the allegations of the second section, even if they import a technical passing of title at the slaughtering places, also import that the sales are to persons in other States, and that the shipments to other States are part of the transaction—"pursuant to such sales"—and the third section imports that the same things which are sent to agents are sold by them, and sufficiently indicates that some, at least, of the sales are of the original packages. Moreover, the sales are by persons in one State to persons in another. But we do not mean to imply that the rule which marks the point at which state taxation or regulation becomes permissible necessarily is beyond the scope of interference by Congress in cases where such interference is deemed necessary for the protection of commerce among the States. Nor do we mean to intimate that the statute under consideration is limited to that point. Beyond what we have said above, we leave those questions as we find them. They were touched upon in the *Northern Securities Company*'s case.

We are of opinion, further, that the charge in the sixth section is not too vague. The charge is not of a single agreement, but of a course of conduct intended to be continued. Under the act, it is the duty of the court, when applied to, to stop the conduct. The thing done and intended to be done is perfectly definite: with the purpose mentioned, directing the defendants' agents and inducing each other to refrain from competition in bids. The defendants cannot be ordered to compete, but they properly can be forbidden to give directions or to make agreements not to compete. *See Addyston Pipe & Steel Co. v. United States*. The injunction follows the charge. No objection was made on the ground that it is not confined to the places specified in the bill. It seems to us, however, that it ought to set forth more exactly the transactions in which such directions and agreements are forbidden. The trade in fresh meat referred to should be defined somewhat as it is in the bill, and the sales of stock should be confined to sales of stock at the stockyards named, which stock is sent from other States to the stockyards for sale or is bought at those yards for transport to another State.

HAMMER v. DAGENHART

247 U.S. 251 (1918)

Opinion: Day, joined by White, Pitney, Van Devanter, McReynolds
Dissent: Holmes, joined by McKenna, Brandeis, Clarke

Perhaps the most striking example of the Court's limits on the commerce power is Hammer v. Dagenhart. *The Child Labor Act of 1916 sought to ban the exchange of goods produced by child labor across state lines. This measure might seem to fit under even the narrowest understanding of "commerce . . . among the several states," because it did not directly ban child labor but instead concentrated on the products that were produced by that labor. But the Court argued that there was nothing dangerous or illicit about these products and thus this legislation was a poorly disguised effort to regulate wages and working conditions within the states themselves—which, they insisted, was beyond the reach of the Commerce Clause.*

As you read Hammer v. Dagenhart, *pay attention to the reasons why the legislation at issue is deemed not to be part of the stream of commerce. Why does the Court take this stance? Do you agree that this law is not authorized by the Commerce Clause? Pay particular attention to the dissent by Justice Oliver Wendell Holmes, the author of the majority decision in* Swift & Co. v. United States. *What arguments does he make against the Court's holding that this law is not authorized under the Commerce Clause?*

MR. JUSTICE DAY *delivered the opinion of the Court.*

A bill was filed in the United States District Court for the Western District of North Carolina by a father in his own behalf and as next friend of his two minor sons, one under the age of fourteen years and the other between the ages of fourteen and sixteen years, employees in a cotton mill at Charlotte, North Carolina, to enjoin the enforcement of the act of Congress intended to prevent interstate commerce in the products of child labor. Act of Sept. 1, 1916, c. 432, 39 Stat. 675:

> That no producer, manufacturer, or dealer shall ship or deliver for shipment in Interstate or foreign commerce any article or commodity the product of any mine or quarry, situated in the United States, in which within thirty days prior to the time of the removal of such product therefrom children under the age of sixteen years have been employed or permitted to work, or any article or commodity the product of any mill, cannery, workshop, factory, or manufacturing establishment, situated in the United States, in which within thirty days prior to the removal of such product there from children under the age of fourteen years have been employed or permitted to work, or children between the ages of fourteen years and sixteen years have been employed or permitted to work more than eight hours in any day, or more than six days in any week, or after the hour of seven o'clock postmeridian, or before the hour of six o'clock antemeridian.

Other sections of the act contain provisions for its enforcement and prescribe penalties for its violation.

The attack upon the act rests upon three propositions: First: It is not a regulation of interstate and foreign commerce; Second: It contravenes the Tenth Amendment to the Constitution; Third: It conflicts with the Fifth Amendment to the Constitution.

The controlling question for decision is: Is it within the authority of Congress in regulating commerce among the States to prohibit the transportation in interstate commerce of manufactured goods, the product of a factory in which, within thirty days prior to their removal there from, children under the age of fourteen have been employed or permitted to work, or children between the ages of fourteen and sixteen years have been employed or permitted to work more than eight hours in any day, or more than six days in any week, or after the hour of seven o'clock P.M. or before the hour of 6 o'clock A.M.?

The power essential to the passage of this act, the Government contends, is found in the Commerce Clause of the Constitution which authorizes Congress to regulate commerce with foreign nations and among the States.

. . . [T]he power is one to control the means by which commerce is carried on, which is directly the contrary of the assumed right to forbid commerce from moving and thus destroy it as to particular commodities. But it is insisted that adjudged cases in this court establish the doctrine that the power to regulate given to Congress incidentally includes the authority to prohibit the movement of ordinary commodities and therefore that the subject is not open for discussion. The cases demonstrate the contrary. They rest upon the character of the particular subjects dealt with and the fact that the scope of governmental authority, state or national, possessed over them is such that the authority to prohibit is as to them but the exertion of the power to regulate.

In each of these instances the use of interstate transportation was necessary to the accomplishment of harmful results. In other words, although the power over interstate transportation was to regulate, that could only be accomplished by prohibiting the use of the facilities of interstate commerce to effect the evil intended.

This element is wanting in the present case. The thing intended to be accomplished by this statute is the denial of the facilities of interstate commerce to those manufacturers in the States who employ children within the prohibited ages. The act in its effect does not regulate transportation among the States, but aims to standardize the ages at which children may be employed in mining and manufacturing within the States. The goods shipped are of themselves harmless. The act permits them to be freely shipped after thirty days from the time of their removal from the factory. When offered for shipment, and before transportation begins, the labor of their production is over, and the mere fact that they were intended for interstate commerce transportation does not make their production subject to federal control under the commerce power.

Commerce "consists of intercourse and traffic . . . and includes the transportation of persons and property, as well as the purchase, sale and exchange of commodities." The making of goods and the mining of coal are not commerce, nor does the fact that these things are to be afterwards shipped or used in interstate commerce, make their production a part thereof.

Over interstate transportation, or its incidents, the regulatory power of Congress is ample, but the production of articles, intended for interstate commerce, is a matter of local regulation.

When the commerce begins is determined, not by the character of the commodity, nor by the intention of the owner to transfer it to another state for sale, nor by his preparation of it for transportation, but by its actual delivery to a common carrier for transportation, or the actual commencement of its transfer to another state. . . . If it were otherwise, all manufacture intended for interstate shipment would be brought under federal control to the practical exclusion of the authority of the States, a result certainly not contemplated by the framers of the Constitution when they vested in Congress the authority to regulate commerce among the States.

It is further contended that the authority of Congress may be exerted to control interstate commerce in the shipment of child-made goods because of the effect of the circulation of such goods in other States where the evil of this class of labor has been recognized by local legislation, and the right to thus employ child labor has been more rigorously restrained than in the State of production. In other words, that the unfair competition, thus engendered, may be controlled by closing the channels of interstate commerce to manufacturers in those States where the local laws do not meet what Congress deems to be the more just standard of other States.

There is no power vested in Congress to require the States to exercise their police power so as to prevent possible unfair competition. Many causes may cooperate to give one State, by reason of local laws or conditions, an economic advantage over others. The Commerce Clause was not intended to give to Congress a general authority to equalize such conditions. In some of the States laws have been passed fixing minimum wages for women, in others the local law regulates the hours of labor of women in various employments. Business done in such States may be at an economic disadvantage when compared with States which have no such regulations; surely, this fact does not give Congress the power to deny transportation in interstate commerce to those who carry on business where the hours of labor and the rate of compensation for women have not been fixed by a standard in use in other States and approved by Congress.

The grant of power to Congress over the subject of interstate commerce was to enable it to regulate such commerce, and not to give it authority to control the States in their exercise of the police power over local trade and manufacture.

The grant of authority over a purely federal matter was not intended to destroy the local power always existing and carefully reserved to the States in the Tenth Amendment to the Constitution.

That there should be limitations upon the right to employ children in mines and factories in the interest of their own and the public welfare, all will admit. That such employment is generally deemed to require regulation is shown by the fact that the brief of counsel states that every State in the Union has a law upon the subject, limiting the right to thus employ children. In North Carolina, the State wherein is located the factory in which the employment was had in the present case, no child under twelve years of age is permitted to work.

It may be desirable that such laws be uniform, but our Federal Government is one of enumerated powers; "this principle," declared Chief Justice Marshall in *McCulloch v. Maryland,* 4 Wheat. 316, "is universally admitted."

The maintenance of the authority of the States over matters purely local is as essential to the preservation of our institutions as is the conservation of the supremacy of the federal power in all matters entrusted to the Nation by the Federal Constitution.

Thus the act in a twofold sense is repugnant to the Constitution. It not only transcends the authority delegated to Congress over commerce but also exerts a power as to a purely local matter to which the federal authority does not extend. The far reaching result of upholding the act cannot be more plainly indicated than by pointing out that if Congress can thus regulate matters entrusted to local authority by prohibition of the movement of commodities in interstate commerce, all freedom of commerce will be at an end, and the power of the States over local matters may be eliminated, and thus our system of government be practically destroyed.

MR. JUSTICE HOLMES, *dissenting.*

[I]f an act is within the powers specifically conferred upon Congress, it seems to me that it is not made any less constitutional because of the indirect effects that it may have, however obvious it may be that it will have those effects, and that we are not at liberty upon such grounds to hold it void.

The first step in my argument is to make plain what no one is likely to dispute—that the statute in question is within the power expressly given to Congress if considered only as to its immediate effects and that if invalid it is so only upon some collateral ground. The statute confines itself to prohibiting the carriage of certain goods in interstate or foreign commerce. Congress is given power to regulate such commerce in unqualified terms. It would not be argued today that the power to regulate does not include the power to prohibit. Regulation means the prohibition of something, and when interstate commerce is the matter to be regulated I cannot doubt that the regulation may prohibit any part of such commerce that Congress sees fit to forbid.

The question then is narrowed to whether the exercise of its otherwise constitutional power by Congress can be pronounced unconstitutional because of its possible reaction upon the conduct of the States in a matter upon which I have admitted that they are free from direct control. I should have thought that that matter had been disposed of so fully as to leave no room for doubt. I should have thought that most conspicuous decisions of this Court had made it clear that the power to regulate commerce and other constitutional powers could not be cut down or qualified by the fact that it might interfere with the carrying out of the domestic policy of any State.

The manufacture of oleomargarine is as much a matter of state regulation as the manufacture of cotton cloth. Congress levied a tax upon the compound when colored so as to resemble butter that was so great as obviously to prohibit the manufacture and sale. . . . Fifty years ago a tax on state banks, the obvious purpose and actual effect of which was to drive them, or at least their circulation, out of existence, was sustained, although the result was one that Congress had no constitutional power to require. . . . [T]he Sherman Act has been made an instrument for the breaking up on combinations in restraint of trade and monopolies, using the power to regulate commerce as a foothold, but not proceeding because that commerce was the end actually in mind. The objection that the control of the States over production was interfered with was urged again and again but always in vain.

The Pure Food and Drug Act which was sustained in *Hipolite Egg Co. v. United States*, with the intimation that "no trade can be carried on between the States to which it [the power of Congress to regulate commerce] does not extend," applies not merely to articles that the changing opinions of the time condemn as intrinsically harmful but to others innocent in themselves, simply on the ground that the order for them was induced by a preliminary fraud. It does not matter whether the supposed evil precedes or follows the transportation. It is enough that in the opinion of Congress the transportation encourages the evil.

The notion that prohibition is any less prohibition when applied to things now thought evil I do not understand. But if there is any matter upon which civilized countries have agreed—far more unanimously than they have with regard to intoxicants and some other matters over which this country is now emotionally aroused—it is the evil of premature and excessive child labor. I should have thought that if we were to introduce our own moral conceptions where in my opinion they do not belong, this was preeminently a case for upholding the exercise of all its powers by the United States.

But I had thought that the propriety of the exercise of a power admitted to exist in some cases was for the consideration of Congress alone and that this Court always had disavowed the right to intrude its judgment upon questions of policy or morals. It is not for this Court to pronounce when prohibition is necessary to regulation if it ever may be necessary—to say that it is permissible as against strong drink but not as against the product of ruined lives.

The act does not meddle with anything belonging to the States. They may regulate their internal affairs and their domestic commerce as they like. But when they seek to send their products across the state line they are no longer within their rights. If there were no Constitution and no Congress their power to cross the line would depend upon their neighbors. Under the Constitution such commerce belongs not to the States but to Congress to regulate. It may carry out its views of public policy whatever indirect effect they may have upon the activities of the States. Instead of being encountered by a prohibitive tariff at her boundaries the State encounters the public policy of the United States which it is for Congress to express.

The public policy of the United States is shaped with a view to the benefit of the nation as a whole. . . . The national welfare as understood by Congress may require a different attitude within its sphere from that of some self-seeking State. It seems to me entirely constitutional for Congress to enforce its understanding by all the means at its command.

A.L.A. SCHECHTER POULTRY CORP. v. UNITED STATES

295 U.S. 495 (1935)

Opinion: Hughes, joined by Van Devanter, McReynolds, Brandeis, Sutherland, Butler, Roberts
Concurrence: Cardozo, joined by Stone

During the initial attempts of President Franklin Roosevelt to implement his New Deal, the Court repeatedly struck down congressional legislation as lacking any federal power in the Constitution. Although Congress had tried to assert its Commerce Clause power in passing much of this legislation, the Court often held that Congress had exceeded its authority. For example, in Schechter Poultry Co. v. United States, *the Court struck down national labor and safety regulations as they applied to a New York slaughterhouse and poultry market. "Commerce . . . among the several states" did not extend to local production—and that meant that many of President Roosevelt's New Deal policies were unconstitutional. The following year, in* Carter v. Carter Coal Company, *the Court struck down an attempt by the federal government to regulate the coal industry on the grounds that it lacked the Commerce Clause power to do so.*

MR. CHIEF JUSTICE HUGHES *delivered the opinion of the Court.*

The question of the application of the provisions of the Live Poultry Code to intrastate transactions. Although the validity of the codes (apart from the question of delegation) rests upon the commerce clause of the Constitution, §3(a) is not, in terms, limited to interstate and foreign commerce. From the generality of its terms, and from the argument of the Government at the bar, it would appear that §3(a) was designed to authorize codes without that limitation. But, under §3(f), penalties are confined to violations of a code provision "in any transaction in or affecting interstate or foreign commerce." This aspect of the case presents the question whether the particular provisions of the Live Poultry Code, which the defendants were convicted for violating and for having conspired to violate, were within the regulating power of Congress.

These provisions relate to the hours and wages of those employed by defendants in their slaughterhouses in Brooklyn, and to the sales there made to retail dealers and butchers.

(1) Were these transactions "*in*" interstate commerce? Much is made of the fact that almost all the poultry coming to New York is sent there from other States. But the code provisions, as here applied, do not concern the transportation of the poultry from other States to New York, or the transactions of the commission men or others to whom it is consigned, or the sales made by such consignees to defendants. When defendants had made their purchases, whether at the West Washington

Market in New York City or at the railroad terminals serving the City, or elsewhere, the poultry was trucked to their slaughterhouses in Brooklyn for local disposition. The interstate transactions in relation to that poultry then ended. Defendants held the poultry at their slaughterhouse markets for slaughter and local sale to retail dealers and butchers who, in turn, sold directly to consumers. Neither the slaughtering nor the sales by defendants were transactions in interstate commerce. *Brown v. Houston; Public Utilities Comm'n v. Landon; Industrial Association v. States; Atlantic Coast Line v. Standard Oil Co.*

The undisputed facts thus afford no warrant for the argument that the poultry handled by defendants at their slaughterhouse markets was in a *"current"* or *"flow"* of interstate commerce, and was thus subject to congressional regulation. The mere fact that there may be a constant flow of commodities into a State does not mean that the flow continues after the property has arrived, and has become commingled with the mass of property within the State, and is there held solely for local disposition and use. So far as the poultry here in question is concerned, the flow in interstate commerce had ceased. The poultry had come to a permanent rest within the State. It was not held, used, or sold by defendants in relation to any further transactions in interstate commerce, and was not destined for transportation to other States. Hence, decisions which deal with a stream of interstate commerce—where goods come to rest within a State temporarily and are later to go forward in interstate commerce—and with the regulations of transactions involved in that practical continuity of movement, are not applicable here. *See Swift & Co. v. United States; Lemke v. Farmers Grain Co.; Stafford v. Wallace; Chicago Board of Trade v. Olsen; Tagg Bros. & Moorhead v. United States.*

(2) Did the defendants' transactions directly *"affect"* interstate commerce, so as to be subject to federal regulation? The power of Congress extends not only to the regulation of transactions which are part of interstate commerce, but to the protection of that commerce from injury. It matters not that the injury may be due to the conduct of those engaged in intrastate operations. Thus, Congress may protect the safety of those employed in interstate transportation "no matter what may be the source of the dangers which threaten it." *Southern Ry. Co. v. United States.* We said in *Second Employers' Liability Cases*, that it is the "effect upon interstate commerce," not "the source of the injury," which is "the criterion of congressional power." We have held that, in dealing with common carriers engaged in both interstate and intrastate commerce, the dominant authority of Congress necessarily embraces the right to control their intrastate operations in all matters having such a close and substantial relation to interstate traffic that the control is essential or appropriate to secure the freedom of that traffic from interference or unjust discrimination and to promote the efficiency of the interstate service. *The Shreveport Case; Wisconsin Railroad Comm'n v. Chicago, B. & Q. R. Co..* And combinations and conspiracies to restrain interstate commerce, or to monopolize any part of it, are nonetheless within the reach of the Anti-Trust Act because the conspirators seek to attain their end by means of intrastate activities. *Coronado Coal Co. v. United Mine Workers; Bedford Cut Stone Co. v. Stone Cutters Assn.*

We recently had occasion, in *Local 677 v. United States*, to apply this principle in connection with the live poultry industry. That was a suit to enjoin a conspiracy to restrain and monopolize interstate commerce in violation of the Anti-Trust Act. It was shown that marketmen, teamsters and slaughterers (*shochtim*) had conspired to burden the free movement of live poultry into the metropolitan area in and about New York City. Marketmen had organized an association, had allocated retailers among themselves, and had agreed to increase prices. To accomplish their objects, large amounts of money were raised by levies upon poultry sold, men were hired to obstruct the business dealers who resisted, wholesalers and retailers were spied upon, and, by violence and other forms of intimidation, were prevented from freely purchasing live poultry. Teamsters refused to handle poultry for recalcitrant marketmen, and members of the *shochtim* union refused to slaughter. In view of the proof of that conspiracy, we said that it was unnecessary to decide when interstate commerce ended and when intrastate commerce began. We found that the proved interference by the conspirators "with the unloading, the transportation, the sales by marketmen to retailers, the prices charged, and the amount of profits exacted" operated "substantially and directly to restrain and burden the untrammeled shipment and movement of the poultry" while unquestionably it was in interstate commerce. The intrastate acts of the conspirators were included in the injunction because that was found to be necessary for the protection of interstate commerce against the attempted and illegal restraint. *Id.* pp. 297, 299, 300.

The instant case is not of that sort. This is not a prosecution for a conspiracy to restrain or monopolize interstate commerce in violation of the Anti-Trust Act. Defendants have been convicted not upon direct charges of injury to interstate commerce or of interference with persons engaged in that commerce, but of violations of certain provisions of the Live Poultry Code and of conspiracy to commit these violations. Interstate commerce is brought in only upon the charge that violations of

these provisions—as to hours and wages of employees and local sales—"*affected*" interstate commerce.

In determining how far the federal government may go in controlling intrastate transactions upon the ground that they "affect" interstate commerce, there is a necessary and well established distinction between direct and indirect effects. The precise line can be drawn only as individual cases arise, but the distinction is clear in principle. Direct effects are illustrated by the railroad cases we have cited, as, *e.g.,* the effect of failure to use prescribed safety appliances on railroads which are the highways of both interstate and intrastate commerce, injury to an employee engaged in interstate transportation by the negligence of an employee engaged in an intrastate movement, the fixing of rates for intrastate transportation which unjustly discriminate against interstate commerce. But where the effect of intrastate transactions upon interstate commerce is merely indirect, such transactions remain within the domain of state power. If the commerce clause were construed to reach all enterprise and transactions which could be said to have an indirect effect upon interstate commerce, the federal authority would embrace practically all the activities of the people, and the authority of the State over its domestic concerns would exist only by sufferance of the federal government. Indeed, on such a theory, even the development of the State's commercial facilities would be subject to federal control.

The distinction between direct and indirect effects has been clearly recognized in the application of the Anti-Trust Act. Where a combination or conspiracy is formed, with the intent to restrain interstate commerce or to monopolize any part of it, the violation of the statute is clear. *Coronado Coal Co. v. United Mine Workers.* But where that intent is absent, and the objectives are limited to intrastate activities, the fact that there may be an indirect effect upon interstate commerce does not subject the parties to the federal statute, notwithstanding its broad provisions. This principle has frequently been applied in litigation growing out of labor disputes.

While these decisions related to the application of the federal statute, and not to its constitutional validity, the distinction between direct and indirect effects of intrastate transactions upon interstate commerce must be recognized as a fundamental one, essential to the maintenance of our constitutional system. Otherwise, as we have said, there would be virtually no limit to the federal power, and, for all practical purposes, we should have a completely centralized government. We must consider the provisions here in question in the light of this distinction.

The question of chief importance relates to the provisions of the Code as to the hours and wages of those employed in defendants' slaughterhouse markets. It is plain that these requirements are imposed in order to govern the details of defendants' management of their local business. The persons employed in slaughtering and selling in local trade are not employed in interstate commerce. Their hours and wages have no direct relation to interstate commerce. The question of how many hours these employees should work and what they should be paid differs in no essential respect from similar questions in other local businesses which handle commodities brought into a State and there dealt in as a part of its internal commerce. This appears from an examination of the considerations urged by the Government with respect to conditions in the poultry trade. Thus, the Government argues that hours and wages affect prices; that slaughterhouse men sell at a small margin above operating costs; that labor represents 50 to 60 percent of these costs; that a slaughterhouse operator paying lower wages or reducing his cost by exacting long hours of work translates his saving into lower prices; that this results in demands for a cheaper grade of goods, and that the cutting of prices brings about a demoralization of the price structure. Similar conditions may be adduced in relation to other businesses. The argument of the Government proves too much. If the federal government may determine the wages and hours of employees in the internal commerce of a State, because of their relation to cost and prices and their indirect effect upon interstate commerce, it would seem that a similar control might be exerted over other elements of cost also affecting prices, such as the number of employees, rents, advertising, methods of doing business, etc. All the processes of production and distribution that enter into cost could likewise be controlled. If the cost of doing an intrastate business is, in itself, the permitted object of federal control, the extent of the regulation of cost would be a question of discretion, and not of power.

The Government also makes the point that efforts to enact state legislation establishing high labor standards have been impeded by the belief that, unless similar action is taken generally, commerce will be diverted from the States adopting such standards, and that this fear of diversion has led to demands for federal legislation on the subject of wages and hours. The apparent implication is that the federal authority under the commerce clause should be deemed to extend to the establishment of rules to govern wages and hours in intrastate trade and industry generally throughout the country, thus overriding the authority of the States to deal with domestic problems arising from labor conditions in their internal commerce.

It is not the province of the Court to consider the economic advantages or disadvantage of such a centralized system.

It is sufficient to say that the Federal Constitution does not provide for it. Our growth and development have called for wide use of the commerce power of the federal government in its control over the expanded activities of interstate commerce, and in protecting that commerce from burdens, interferences, and conspiracies to restrain and monopolize it. But the authority of the federal government may not be pushed to such an extreme as to destroy the distinction, which the commerce clause itself establishes, between commerce "among the several States" and the internal concerns of a State. The same answer must be made to the contention that is based upon the serious economic situation which led to the passage of the Recovery Act—the fall in prices, the decline in wages and employment, and the curtailment of the market for commodities. Stress is laid upon the great importance of maintaining wage distributions which would provide the necessary stimulus in starting "the cumulative forces making for expanding commercial activity." Without in any way disparaging this motive, it is enough to say that the recuperative efforts of the federal government must be made in a manner consistent with the authority granted by the Constitution.

We are of the opinion that the attempt, through the provisions of the Code, to fix the hours and wages of employees of defendants in their intrastate business was not a valid exercise of federal power.

CARTER v. CARTER COAL COMPANY

298 U.S. 238 (1936)

Opinion: Sutherland, joined by Van Devanter, McReynolds, Butler, Roberts
Concurrence: Hughes
Dissent: Cardozo, joined by Brandeis, Stone

MR. JUSTICE SUTHERLAND *delivered the opinion of the Court.*

Another group of cases, of which *Swift & Co. v. United States*, is an example, rest upon the circumstance that the acts in question constituted direct interferences with the "flow" of commerce among the states. In the *Swift* case, livestock was consigned and delivered to stockyards—not as a place of final destination, but, as the court said in *Stafford v. Wallace*, "a throat through which the current flows." The sales which ensued merely changed the private interest in the subject of the current, without interfering with its continuity. *Industrial Assn. v. United States*. It was nowhere suggested in these cases that the interstate commerce power extended to the growth or production of the things which, after production, entered the flow. If the court had held that the raising of the cattle, which were involved in the *Swift* case, including the wages paid to and working conditions of the herders and others employed in the business, could be regulated by Congress, that decision and decisions holding similarly would be in point, for it is that situation, and not the one with which the court actually dealt, which here concerns us.

The distinction suggested is illustrated by the decision in *Arkadelphia Milling Co.*

v. St. Lois S.W. Ry. Co. That case dealt with orders of a state commission fixing railroad rates. One of the questions considered was whether certain shipments of rough material from the forest to mills in the same state for manufacture, followed by the forwarding of the finished product to points outside the state, was a continuous movement in interstate commerce. It appeared that, when the rough material reached the mills, it was manufactured into various articles which were stacked or placed in kilns to dry, the processes occupying several months. Markets for the manufactured articles were almost entirely in other states or in foreign countries. About 95% of the finished articles was made for outbound shipment. When the rough material was shipped to the mills, it was expected by the mills that this percentage of the finished articles would be so sold and shipped outside the state. And all of them knew and intended that this 95% of the finished product would be so sold and shipped. This court held that the state order did not interfere with interstate commerce, and that the *Swift* case was not in point, as it is not in point here.

The restricted field covered by the *Swift* and kindred cases is illustrated by the *Schechter* case, *supra*, p. 543. There, the commodity in question, although shipped from another state, had come to rest in the state of its destination, and, as the court pointed out, was no longer in a current or flow of interstate commerce. The *Swift* doctrine was rejected as inapposite. In the *Schechter* case, the flow had ceased. Here it had not begun. The difference is not one of substance. The applicable principle is the same.

But §1 (the preamble) of the act now under review declares that all production and distribution of bituminous coal "bear upon and directly affect its interstate commerce," and that regulation thereof is imperative for the protection of such commerce. The contention of the government is that the labor provisions of the act may be sustained in that view.

That the production of every commodity intended for interstate sale and transportation has some effect upon interstate commerce may be, if it has not already been, freely granted, and we are brought to the final and decisive inquiry, whether here that effect is direct, as the "preamble" recites, or indirect. The distinction is not formal, but substantial in the highest degree, as we pointed out in the *Schechter* case, *supra*, p. 546, *et seq.* "If the commerce clause were construed," we there said,

> to reach all enterprises and transactions which could be said to have an indirect effect upon interstate commerce, the federal authority would embrace practically all the activities of the people, and the authority of the State over its domestic concerns would exist only by sufferance of the federal government. Indeed, on such a theory, even the development of the State's commercial facilities would be subject to federal control.

It was also pointed out, p. 548, that

> the distinction between direct and indirect effects of intrastate transactions upon interstate commerce must be recognized as a fundamental one, essential to the maintenance of our constitutional system.

Whether the effect of a given activity or condition is direct or indirect is not always easy to determine. The word "direct" implies that the activity or condition invoked or blamed shall operate proximately—not mediately, remotely, or collaterally—to produce the effect. It connotes the absence of an efficient intervening agency or condition. And the extent of the effect bears no logical relation to its character. The distinction between a direct and an indirect effect turns not upon the magnitude of either the cause or the effect, but entirely upon the manner in which the effect has been brought about. If the production by one man of a single ton of coal intended for interstate sale and shipment, and actually so sold and shipped, affects interstate commerce indirectly, the effect does not become direct by multiplying the tonnage, or increasing the number of men employed, or adding to the expense or complexities of the business, or by all combined. It is quite true that rules of law are sometimes qualified by considerations of degree, as the government argues. But the matter of degree has no bearing upon the question here, since that question is not what is the extent of the local activity or condition, or the extent of the effect produced upon interstate commerce, but what is the relation between the activity or condition and the effect?

Much stress is put upon the evils which come from the struggle between employers and employees over the matter of wages, working conditions, the right of collective bargaining, etc., and the resulting strikes, curtailment and irregularity of production and effect on prices, and it is insisted that interstate commerce is greatly affected thereby. But, in addition to what has just been said, the conclusive answer is that the evils are all local evils over which the federal government has no legislative control. The relation of employer and employee is a local relation. At common law, it is one of the domestic relations. The wages are paid for the doing of local work. Working conditions are obviously local conditions. The employees are not engaged in or about commerce, but exclusively in producing a commodity. And the controversies and evils which it is the object of the act to regulate and minimize are local controversies and evils affecting local work undertaken to accomplish that local result. Such effect as they may have upon commerce, however extensive it may be, is secondary and indirect. An increase in the greatness of the effect adds to its importance. It does not alter its character.

NATIONAL LABOR RELATIONS BOARD v. JONES & LAUGHLIN STEEL CORP.

301 U.S. 1 (1937)

Opinion: Hughes, joined by Brandeis, Stone, Roberts, Cardozo
Dissent: McReynolds, joined by Van Devanter, Sutherland, Butler

Although the Supreme Court obstructed federal efforts to regulate the national economy for decades, culminating in the rejection of Congress's power to enact the early New Deal, the year 1937 saw the Court reverse course. In the following case, the Court began to embrace a far broader view of the Commerce power, and with it, much of President Franklin Roosevelt's New Deal.

This case was decided soon after West Coast Hotel v. Parrish, *often thought to be the case in which the Court's "switch in time" occurred. As some see it,* West Coast Hotel v. Parrish, *which concerns substantive due process (explored in Chapter 7), marked a change from the Court striking down New Deal legislation, as it did in* A.L.A. Schechter Poultry Corp. v. United States *and* Carter v. Carter Coal Co., *to upholding it. Some attribute the Court's change to President Roosevelt's threat to pack the Court with new justices. Regardless of the reasons, however, the change from the limits on Congress's Commerce Clause power before 1937, and the more expansive view of this power after 1937, is stark.*

The following three cases consider the National Labor Relations Act, the Fair Labor Standards Act, and the Agricultural Adjustment Act—each a cornerstone of President Roosevelt's economic recovery plan. It is important to read these cases as a group with the following questions in mind: How broadly do these cases define the stream of commerce? Does it only include production and other economic activity that cross state lines?

MR. CHIEF JUSTICE HUGHES *delivered the opinion of the Court.*

In a proceeding under the National Labor Relations Act of 1935, the National Labor Relations Board found that the respondent, Jones & Laughlin Steel Corporation, had violated the Act by engaging in unfair labor practices affecting commerce. . . . The unfair labor practices charged were that the corporation was discriminating against members of the union with regard to hire and tenure of employment, and was coercing and intimidating its employees in order to interfere with their self-organization. The discriminatory and coercive action alleged was the discharge of certain employees.

The National Labor Relations Board, sustaining the charge, ordered the corporation to cease and desist from such discrimination and coercion, to offer reinstatement to ten of the employees named, to make good their losses in pay, and to post for thirty days notices that the corporation would not discharge or discriminate against members, or those desiring to become members, of the labor union. As the corporation failed to comply, the Board petitioned the Circuit Court of Appeals to enforce the order. The court denied the petition, holding that the order lay beyond the range of federal power. We granted certiorari.

Contesting the ruling of the Board, the respondent argues (1) that the Act is in reality a regulation of labor relations and not of interstate commerce; (2) that the Act can have no application to the respondent's relations with its production employees because they are not subject to regulation by the federal government; and (3) that the provisions of the Act violate §2 of Article III and the Fifth and Seventh Amendments of the Constitution of the United States.

First. The scope of the Act.—The Act is challenged in its entirety as an attempt to regulate all industry, thus invading the reserved powers of the States over their local concerns. It is asserted that the references in the Act to interstate and foreign commerce are colorable at best; that the Act is not a true regulation of such commerce or of matters which directly affect it but on the contrary has the fundamental object of placing under the compulsory supervision of the federal government all industrial labor relations within the nation. . . .

If this conception of terms, intent and consequent inseparability were sound, the Act would necessarily fall by reason of the limitation upon the federal power which inheres in the constitutional grain, as well as because of the explicit reservation of the Tenth Amendment. But we are not at liberty to deny effect to specific provisions, which Congress has constitutional power to enact, by superimposing upon them inferences from general legislative declarations of an ambiguous character.

We think it clear that the National Labor Relations Act may be construed so as to operate within the sphere of constitutional authority. The jurisdiction conferred upon the Board, and invoked in this instance, is found in §10 (a), which provides:

"SEC. 10 (a). The Board is empowered, as hereinafter provided, to prevent any person from engaging in any unfair labor practice (listed in section 8) affecting commerce."

The critical words of this provision, prescribing the limits of the Board's authority in dealing with the labor practices, are "affecting commerce." The Act specifically defines the "commerce" to which it refers (§2(6)):

> "The term 'commerce' means trade, traffic, commerce, transportation, or communication among the several States ... or between points in the same State but through any other State or any Territory or the District of Columbia or any foreign country."

The Act also defines the term "affecting commerce" (§2 (7)):

> "The term 'affecting commerce' means in commerce, or burdening or obstructing commerce or the free flow of commerce, or having led or tending to lead to a labor dispute burdening or obstructing commerce or the free flow of commerce."

This definition is one of exclusion as well as inclusion. The grant of authority to the Board does not purport to extend to the relationship between all industrial employees and employers. Its terms do not impose collective bargaining upon all industry regardless of effects upon interstate or foreign commerce. It purports to reach only what may be deemed to burden or obstruct that commerce and, thus, qualified, it must be construed as contemplating the exercise of control within constitutional bounds. It is a familiar principle that acts which directly burden or obstruct interstate or foreign commerce, or its free flow, are within the reach of the congressional power. Acts having that effect are not rendered immune because they grow out of labor disputes. It is the effect upon commerce, not the source of the injury, which is the criterion. Whether or not particular action does affect commerce in such a close and intimate fashion as to be subject to federal control, and hence to lie within the authority conferred upon the Board, is left by the statute to be determined as individual cases arise. We are thus to inquire whether in the instant case the constitutional boundary has been passed.

Second. The unfair labor practices in question.—The unfair labor practices found by the Board are those defined in § 8, subdivisions (1) and (3). These provide:

> Sec. 8. It shall be an unfair labor practice for an employer—
> "(1) To interfere with, restrain, or coerce employees in the exercise of the rights guaranteed in section 7."
> "(3) By discrimination in regard to hire or tenure of employment or any term or condition of employment to encourage or discourage membership in any labor organization: ..."

Section 8, subdivision (1), refers to §7, which is as follows:

> "Sec. 7. Employees shall have the right to self-organization, to form, join, or assist labor organizations, to bargain collectively through representatives of their own choosing, and to engage in concerted activities, for the purpose of collective bargaining or other mutual aid or protection."

Thus, in its present application, the statute goes no further than to safeguard the right of employees to self-organization and to select representatives of their own choosing for collective bargaining or other mutual protection without restraint or coercion by their employer.

That is a fundamental right. Employees have as clear a right to organize and select their representatives for lawful purposes as the respondent has to organize its business and select its own officers and agents. Discrimination and coercion to prevent the free exercise of the right of employees to self-organization and representation is a proper subject for condemnation by competent legislative authority. Long ago we stated the reason for labor organizations. We said that they were organized out of the necessities of the situation; that a single employee was helpless in dealing with an employer; that he was dependent ordinarily on his daily wage for the maintenance of himself and family; that if the employer refused to pay him the wages that he thought fair, he was nevertheless unable to leave the employ and resist arbitrary and unfair treatment; that union was essential to give laborers opportunity to deal on an equality with their employer. . . .

Third. The application of the Act to employees engaged in production.—The principle involved.—Respondent says that whatever may be said of employees engaged in interstate commerce, the industrial relations and activities in the manufacturing department of respondent's enterprise are not subject to federal regulation. The argument rests upon the proposition that manufacturing in itself is not commerce.

The various parts of respondent's enterprise are described as interdependent and as thus involving "a great movement of iron ore, coal and limestone along well-defined paths to the steel mills, thence through them, and thence in the form of steel products into the consuming centers of the country—a definite and well-understood course of business." It is urged that these activities constitute a "stream" or "flow" of commerce, of which the Aliquippa manufacturing plant is the focal point, and that industrial strife at that point would cripple the entire movement.

. . . [But] we do not find it necessary to determine whether these features of defendant's business dispose of the asserted analogy to the "stream of commerce" cases. The instances in which that metaphor has been used are but particular, and not exclusive, illustrations of the protective power which the Government invokes

in support of the present Act. The congressional authority to protect interstate commerce from burdens and obstructions is not limited to transactions which can be deemed to be an essential part of a "flow" of interstate or foreign commerce. Burdens and obstructions may be due to injurious action springing from other sources. The fundamental principle is that the power to regulate commerce is the power to enact "all appropriate legislation" for "its protection and advancement"; to adopt measures "to promote its growth and insure its safety"; "to foster, protect, control and restrain." That power is plenary and may be exerted to protect interstate commerce "no matter what the source of the dangers which threaten it." Although activities may be intrastate in character when separately considered, if they have such a close and substantial relation to interstate commerce that their control is essential or appropriate to protect that commerce from burdens and obstructions, Congress cannot be denied the power to exercise that control. Undoubtedly the scope of this power must be considered in the light of our dual system of government and may not be extended so as to embrace effects upon interstate commerce so indirect and remote that to embrace them, in view of our complex society, would effectually obliterate the distinction between what is national and what is local and create a completely centralized government. The question is necessarily one of degree. . . .

The close and intimate effect which brings the subject within the reach of federal power may be due to activities in relation to productive industry although the industry when separately viewed is local. This has been abundantly illustrated in the application of the federal Anti-Trust Act. . . .

Upon the same principle, the Anti-Trust Act has been applied to the conduct of employees engaged in production. . . . The Court ruled that while the mere reduction in the supply of an article to be shipped in interstate commerce by the illegal or tortious prevention of its manufacture or production is ordinarily an indirect and remote obstruction to that commerce, nevertheless when the "intent of those unlawfully preventing the manufacture or production is shown to be to restrain or control the supply entering and moving in interstate commerce, or the price of it in interstate markets, their action is a direct violation of the Anti-Trust Act." And the existence of that intent may be a necessary inference from proof of the direct and substantial effect produced by the employees' conduct.

It is thus apparent that the fact that the employees here concerned were engaged in production is not determinative. The question remains as to the effect upon interstate commerce of the labor practice involved.

Fourth. Effects of the unfair labor practice in respondent's enterprise.—Giving full weight to respondent's contention with respect to a break in the complete continuity of the "stream of commerce" by reason of respondent's manufacturing operations, the fact remains that the stoppage of those operations by industrial strife would have a most serious effect upon interstate commerce. In view of respondent's far-flung activities, it is idle to say that the effect would be indirect or remote. It is obvious that it would be immediate and might be catastrophic. We are asked to shut our eyes to the plainest facts of our national life and to deal with the question of direct and indirect effects in an intellectual vacuum. . . . When industries organize themselves on a national scale, making their relation to interstate commerce the dominant factor in their activities, how can it be maintained that their industrial labor relations constitute a forbidden field into which Congress may not enter when it is necessary to protect interstate commerce from the paralyzing consequences of industrial war? We have often said that interstate commerce itself is a practical conception. It is equally true that interferences with that commerce must be appraised by a judgment that does not ignore actual experience.

Experience has abundantly demonstrated that the recognition of the right of employees to self-organization and to have representatives of their own choosing for the purpose of collective bargaining is often an essential condition of industrial peace. Refusal to confer and negotiate has been one of the most prolific causes of strife.

The steel industry is one of the great basic industries of the United States, with ramifying activities affecting interstate commerce at every point. The Government aptly refers to the steel strike of 1919–1920 with its far-reaching consequences. The fact that there appears to have been no major disturbance in that industry in the more recent period did not dispose of the possibilities of future and like dangers to interstate commerce which Congress was entitled to foresee and to exercise its protective power to forestall. It is not necessary again to detail the facts as to respondent's enterprise. Instead of being beyond the pale, we think that it presents in a most striking way the close and intimate relation which a manufacturing industry may have to interstate commerce and we have no doubt that Congress had constitutional authority to safeguard the right of respondent's employees to self-organization and freedom in the choice of representatives for collective bargaining.

UNITED STATES v. DARBY

312 U.S. 100 (1940)

Opinion: Stone, joined by Hughes, Roberts, Black, Reed, Frankfurter, Douglas, Murphy

MR. JUSTICE STONE *delivered the opinion of the Court.*

The two principal questions raised by the record in this case are, first, whether Congress has constitutional power to prohibit the shipment in interstate commerce of lumber manufactured by employees whose wages are less than a prescribed minimum or whose weekly hours of labor at that wage are greater than a prescribed maximum, and, second, whether it has power to prohibit the employment of workmen in the production of goods "for interstate commerce" at other than prescribed wages and hours. . . .

The Fair Labor Standards Act set up a comprehensive legislative scheme for preventing the shipment in interstate commerce of certain products and commodities produced in the United States under labor conditions as respects wages and hours which fail to conform to standards set up by the Act.

Section 15 of the statute prohibits certain specified acts and §16 (a) punishes willful violation of it by a fine of not more than $10,000 and punishes each conviction after the first by imprisonment of not more than six months or by the specified fine or both. Section 15 (1) makes unlawful the shipment in interstate commerce of any goods "in the production of which any employee was employed in violation of section 6 or section 7," which provide, among other things, that during the first year of

operation of the Act a minimum wage of 25 cents per hour shall be paid to employees "engaged in [interstate] commerce or the production of goods for [interstate] commerce," and that the maximum hours of employment for employees "engaged in commerce or the production of goods for commerce" without increased compensation for overtime, shall be forty-four hours a week.

There are numerous counts charging appellee with the shipment in interstate commerce from Georgia to points outside the state of lumber in the production of which, for interstate commerce, appellee has employed workmen at less than the prescribed minimum wage or more than the prescribed maximum hours without payment to them of any wage for overtime. . . .

The demurrer, so far as now relevant to the appeal, challenged the validity of the Fair Labor Standards Act under the Commerce Clause and the Fifth and Tenth Amendments. The district court quashed the indictment in its entirety upon the broad grounds that the Act, which it interpreted as a regulation of manufacture within the states, is unconstitutional. It declared that manufacture is not interstate commerce and that the regulation by the Fair Labor Standards Act of wages and hours of employment of those engaged in the manufacture of goods which it is intended at the time of production "may or will be" after production "sold in interstate commerce in part or in whole" is not within the congressional power to regulate interstate commerce.

While manufacture is not of itself interstate commerce, the shipment of manufactured goods interstate is such commerce and the prohibition of such shipment by Congress is indubitably a regulation of the commerce. The power to regulate commerce is the power "to prescribe the rule by which commerce is governed." It extends not only to those regulations which aid, foster and protect the commerce, but embraces those which prohibit it. It is conceded that the power of Congress to prohibit transportation in interstate commerce includes noxious articles, stolen articles, kidnapped persons, and articles such as intoxicating liquor or convict made goods, traffic in which is forbidden or restricted by the laws of the state of destination.

But it is said that the present prohibition falls within the scope of none of these categories; that . . . under the guise of a regulation of interstate commerce, it undertakes to regulate wages and hours within the state contrary to the policy of the state which has elected to leave them unregulated.

The power of Congress over interstate commerce "is complete in itself, may be exercised to its utmost extent, and acknowledges no limitations other than are prescribed in the Constitution." That power can neither be enlarged nor diminished by the exercise or non-exercise of state power. Congress, following its own conception of public policy concerning the restrictions which may appropriately be imposed on interstate commerce, is free to exclude from the commerce articles whose use in the states for which they are destined it may conceive to be injurious to the public health, morals or welfare, even though the state has not sought to regulate their use.

Such regulation is not a forbidden invasion of state power merely because either its motive or its consequence is to restrict the use of articles of commerce within the states of destination; and is not prohibited unless by other Constitutional provisions. It is no objection to the assertion of the power to regulate interstate commerce that its exercise is attended by the same incidents which attend the exercise of the police power of the states.

In the more than a century which has elapsed since the decision of *Gibbons v. Ogden*, these principles of constitutional interpretation have been so long and repeatedly recognized by this Court as applicable to the Commerce Clause, that there would be little occasion for repeating them now were it not for the decision of this Court twenty-two years ago in *Hammer v. Dagenhart*. In that case it was held by a bare majority of the Court over the powerful and now classic dissent of Mr. Justice Holmes setting forth the fundamental issues involved, that Congress was without power to exclude the products of child labor from interstate commerce. The reasoning and conclusion of the Court's opinion there cannot be reconciled with the conclusion which we have reached, that the power of Congress under the Commerce Clause is plenary to exclude any article from interstate commerce subject only to the specific prohibitions of the Constitution.

Hammer v. Dagenhart has not been followed. The distinction on which the decision was rested that Congressional power to prohibit interstate commerce is limited to articles which in themselves have some harmful or deleterious property—a distinction which was novel when made and unsupported by any provision of the Constitution—has long since been abandoned. . . . The conclusion is inescapable that *Hammer v. Dagenhart* was a departure from the principles which have prevailed in the interpretation of the Commerce Clause both before and since the decision and that such vitality, as a precedent, as it then had has long since been exhausted. It should be and now is overruled.

The power of Congress over interstate commerce is not confined to the regulation of commerce among the states. It extends to those activities intrastate which so affect interstate commerce or the exercise of the power of Congress over it as to make regulation of them appropriate means to the attainment of a legitimate end, the exercise of the granted power of Congress to regulate interstate commerce.

In the absence of Congressional legislation on the subject state laws which are not regulations of the commerce itself or its instrumentalities are not forbidden even though they affect interstate commerce.

But it does not follow that Congress may not by appropriate legislation regulate intrastate activities where they have a substantial effect on interstate commerce. A recent example is the National Labor Relations Act for the regulation of employer and employee relations in industries in which strikes, induced by unfair labor practices named in the Act, tend to disturb or obstruct interstate commerce. But long before the adoption of the National Labor Relations Act this Court had many times held that the power of Congress to regulate interstate commerce extends to the regulation through legislative action of activities intrastate which have a substantial effect on the commerce or the exercise of the Congressional power over it.

Congress, having by the present Act adopted the policy of excluding from interstate commerce all goods produced for the commerce which do not conform to the specified labor standards, it may choose the means reasonably adapted to the attainment of the permitted end, even though they involve control of intrastate activities. Such legislation has often been sustained with respect to powers, other than the commerce power granted to the national government, when the means chosen, although not themselves within the granted power, were nevertheless deemed appropriate aids to the accomplishment of some purpose within an admitted power of the national government. A familiar like exercise of power is the regulation of intrastate transactions which are so commingled with or related to interstate commerce that all must be regulated if the interstate commerce is to be effectively controlled. Similarly Congress may require inspection and preventive treatment of all cattle in a disease infected area in order to prevent shipment in interstate commerce of some of the cattle without the treatment. It may prohibit the removal, at destination, of labels required by the Pure Food & Drugs Act to be affixed to articles transported in interstate commerce. And we have recently held that Congress in the exercise of its power to require inspection and grading of tobacco shipped in interstate commerce may compel such inspection and grading of all tobacco sold at local auction rooms from which a substantial part but not all of the tobacco sold is shipped in interstate commerce.

The Sherman Act and the National Labor Relations Act are familiar examples of the exertion of the commerce power to prohibit or control activities wholly intrastate because of their effect on interstate commerce.

The means adopted by §15(a)(2) for the protection of interstate commerce by the suppression of the production of the condemned goods for interstate commerce is so related to the commerce and so affects it as to be within the reach of the commerce power. Congress, to attain its objective in the suppression of nationwide competition in interstate commerce by goods produced under substandard labor conditions, has made no distinction as to the volume or amount of shipments in the commerce or of production for commerce by any particular shipper or producer. It recognized that in present day industry, competition by a small part may affect the whole and that the total effect of the competition of many small producers may be great....

Our conclusion is unaffected by the Tenth Amendment which provides "The powers not delegated to the United States by the Constitution, nor prohibited by it to the States, are reserved to the States respectively, or to the people." The amendment states but a truism that all is retained which has not been surrendered. There is nothing in the history of its adoption to suggest that it was more than declaratory of the relationship between the national and state governments as it had been

established by the Constitution before the amendment or that its purpose was other than to allay fears that the new national government might seek to exercise powers not granted, and that the states might not be able to exercise fully their reserved powers.

From the beginning and for many years the amendment has been construed as not depriving the national government of authority to resort to all means for the exercise of a granted power which are appropriate and plainly adapted to the permitted end. Whatever doubts may have arisen of the soundness of that conclusion, they have been put at rest by the decisions under the Sherman Act and the National Labor Relations Act which we have cited.

WICKARD v. FILBURN

317 U.S. 111 (1942)

Opinion: Jackson, joined by Stone, Roberts, Black, Reed, Frankfurter, Douglas, Murphy

As you will see, Wickard v. Filburn *explains that Congress may regulate any economic activity that, in the aggregate, would "substantially affect" interstate commerce. If this proposition stretches so far as to cover a farmer who grows wheat for his own use, then is there any real limit on the commerce power?*

One puzzle that arises from the expanded commerce power concerns the meaning and relevance of the Tenth Amendment to the Constitution. That amendment claims that the "powers not delegated to the United States by the Constitution, nor prohibited by it to the

States, are reserved to the States respectively, or to the people." But are there any powers left to the states if the Commerce Clause grants such expansive powers to Congress? What should we make of U.S. Supreme Court Chief Justice Harlan F. Stone's claim in United States v. Darby *that the Tenth Amendment "states but a truism"? Even if the Court is right to overturn* Hammer v. Dagenhart, *does the Constitution nonetheless articulate some positive principle of state sovereignty?*

MR. JUSTICE JACKSON *delivered the opinion of the Court.*

The appellee for many years past has owned and operated a small farm in Montgomery County, Ohio, maintaining a herd of dairy cattle, selling milk, raising poultry, and selling poultry and eggs. It has been his practice to raise a small acreage of winter wheat, sown in the Fall and harvested in the following July; to sell a portion of the crop; to feed part to poultry and livestock on the farm, some of which is sold; to use some in making flour for home consumption; and to keep the rest for the following seeding. The intended disposition of the crop here involved has not been expressly stated.

In July of 1940, pursuant to the Agricultural Adjustment Act of 1938, as then amended, there were established for the appellee's 1941 crop a wheat acreage allotment of 11.1 acres and a normal yield of 20.1 bushels of wheat an acre. He was given notice of such allotment in July of 1940, before the Fall planting of his 1941 crop of wheat, and again in July of 1941, before it was harvested. He sowed, however, 23 acres, and harvested from his 11.9 acres of excess acreage 239 bushels, which under the terms of the Act as amended on May 26, 1941, constituted farm marketing excess, subject to a penalty of 49 cents a bushel, or $117.11 in all. . . .

The general scheme of the Agricultural Adjustment Act of 1938 as related to wheat is to control the volume moving in interstate and foreign commerce in order to avoid surpluses and shortages and the consequent abnormally low or high wheat prices and obstructions to commerce. Within prescribed limits and by prescribed standards the Secretary of Agriculture is directed to ascertain and proclaim each year a national acreage allotment for the next crop of wheat, which is then apportioned to the states and their counties, and is eventually broken up into allotments for individual farms. Loans and payments to wheat farmers are authorized in stated circumstances.

It is urged that under the Commerce Clause of the Constitution, Article I, §8, clause 3, Congress does not possess the power it has in this instance sought to exercise. The question would merit little consideration since our decision in *United States v. Darby*, sustaining the federal power to regulate production of goods for commerce, except for the fact that this Act extends federal regulation to production not intended in any part for commerce but wholly for consumption on the farm. The Act includes a definition of "market" and its derivatives, so that as related to wheat, in addition to its conventional meaning, it also means to dispose of "by feeding (in any form) to poultry or livestock which, or the products of which, are sold, bartered, or exchanged, or to be so disposed of." Hence, marketing quotas not only embrace all that may be sold without penalty but also what may be consumed on the premises. Wheat produced on excess acreage is designated as "available for marketing" as so defined, and the penalty is imposed thereon. Penalties do not depend upon whether any part of the wheat, either within or without the quota, is sold or intended to be sold. The sum of this is that the Federal Government fixes a quota including all that the farmer may harvest for sale or for his own farm needs, and declares that wheat produced on excess acreage may neither be disposed of nor used except upon payment of the penalty, or except it is stored as required by the Act or delivered to the Secretary of Agriculture.

Appellee says that this is a regulation of production and consumption of wheat. Such activities are, he urges, beyond the reach of Congressional power under the Commerce Clause, since they are local in character, and their effects upon interstate commerce are at most "indirect." In answer the Government argues that the statute regulates neither production nor consumption, but only marketing; and, in the alternative, that if the Act does go beyond the regulation of marketing it is sustainable as a "necessary and proper" implementation of the power of Congress over interstate commerce.

The Government's concern lest the Act be held to be a regulation of production or consumption, rather than of marketing, is attributable to a few dicta and decisions of this Court which might be understood to lay it down that activities such as "production," "manufacturing," and "mining" are strictly "local" and, except in special circumstances which are not present here, cannot be regulated under the commerce power because their effects upon interstate commerce are, as matter of law, only "indirect." Even today, when this power has been held to have great latitude, there is no decision of this Court that such activities may be regulated where no part of the product is intended for interstate commerce or intermingled with the subjects thereof. We believe that a review of the course of decision under the Commerce Clause will make plain, however, that questions of the power of Congress are not to be decided by reference to any formula which would give controlling force to nomenclature such as "production" and "indirect" and foreclose consideration of the actual effects of the activity in question upon interstate commerce.

The Court's recognition of the relevance of the economic effects in the application of the Commerce Clause . . . has made the mechanical application of legal formulas no longer feasible. Once an economic measure of the reach of the power granted to Congress in the Commerce Clause is accepted, questions of federal power cannot be decided simply by finding the activity in question to be "production," nor can consideration of its economic effects be foreclosed by calling them "indirect." The present Chief Justice has said in summary

of the present state of the law: "The commerce power is not confined in its exercise to the regulation of commerce among the states. It extends to those activities intrastate which so affect interstate commerce, or the exertion of the power of Congress over it, as to make regulation of them appropriate means to the attainment of a legitimate end, the effective execution of the granted power to regulate interstate commerce. . . . The power of Congress over interstate commerce is plenary and complete in itself, may be exercised to its utmost extent, and acknowledges no limitations other than are prescribed in the Constitution. . . . It follows that no form of state activity can constitutionally thwart the regulatory power granted by the Commerce Clause to Congress. Hence the reach of that power extends to those intrastate activities which in a substantial way interfere with or obstruct the exercise of the granted power."

Whether the subject of the regulation in question was "production," "consumption," or "marketing" is, therefore, not material for purposes of deciding the question of federal power before us. . . . [E]ven if appellee's activity be local and though it may not be regarded as commerce, it may still, whatever its nature, be reached by Congress if it exerts a substantial economic effect on interstate commerce, and this irrespective of whether such effect is what might at some earlier time have been defined as "direct" or "indirect."

The wheat industry has been a problem industry for some years. Largely as a result of increased foreign production and import restrictions, annual exports of wheat and flour from the United States during the ten-year period ending in 1940 averaged less than 10 per cent of total production, while during the 1920's they averaged more than 25 per cent. The decline in the export trade has left a large surplus in production which, in connection with an abnormally large supply of wheat and other grains in recent years, caused congestion in a number of markets; tied up railroad cars; and caused elevators in some instances to turn away grains, and railroads to institute embargoes to prevent further congestion.

In the absence of regulation, the price of wheat in the United States would be much affected by world conditions. During 1941, producers who cooperated with the Agricultural Adjustment program received an average price on the farm of about $1.16 a bushel, as compared with the world market price of 40 cents a bushel.

Differences in farming conditions, however, make these benefits mean different things to different wheat growers. . . . Except in regions of large-scale production, wheat is usually grown in rotation with other crops; for a nurse crop for grass seeding; and as a cover crop to prevent soil erosion and leaching. Some is sold, some kept for seed, and a percentage of the total production much larger than in areas of specialization is consumed on the farm and grown for such purpose. Such farmers, while growing some wheat, may even find the balance of their interest on the consumer's side.

The effect of consumption of home-grown wheat on interstate commerce is due to the fact that it constitutes the most variable factor in the disappearance of the wheat crop. Consumption on the farm where grown appears to vary in an amount greater than 20 per cent of average production. The total amount of wheat consumed as food varies but relatively little, and use as seed is relatively constant.

The maintenance by government regulation of a price for wheat undoubtedly can be accomplished as effectively by sustaining or increasing the demand as by limiting the supply. The effect of the statute before us is to restrict the amount which may be produced for market and the extent as well to which one may forestall resort to the market by producing to meet his own needs. That appellee's own contribution to the demand for wheat may be trivial by itself is not enough to remove him from the scope of federal regulation where, as here, his contribution, taken together with that of many others similarly situated, is far from trivial.

It is well established by decisions of this Court that the power to regulate commerce includes the power to regulate the prices at which commodities in that commerce are dealt in and practices affecting such prices. One of the primary purposes of the Act in question was to increase the market price of wheat, and to that end to limit the volume thereof that could affect the market. It can hardly be denied that a factor of such volume and variability as home-consumed wheat would have a substantial influence on price and market conditions. This may arise because being in marketable condition such wheat overhangs the market and, if induced by rising prices, tends to flow into the market and check price increases. But if we assume that it is never marketed, it supplies a need of the man who grew it which would otherwise be reflected by purchases in the open market. Home-grown wheat in this sense competes with wheat in commerce. The stimulation of commerce is a use of the regulatory function quite as definitely as prohibitions or restrictions thereon. This record leaves us in no doubt that Congress may properly have considered that wheat consumed on the farm where grown, if wholly outside the scheme of regulation, would have a substantial effect in defeating and obstructing its purpose to stimulate trade therein at increased prices.

The Heart of Atlanta Motel, whose practice of turning away African-American customers was held to violate the Civil Rights Act of 1964. The Supreme Court ruled that the Commerce Clause of the Constitution permitted the 1964 law.

HEART OF ATLANTA MOTEL, INC. v. UNITED STATES

379 U.S. 241 (1964)

Opinion: Clark, joined by Warren, Douglas, Harlan, Brennan, Stewart, White, Goldberg
Concurrence: Black
Concurrence: Douglas
Concurrence: Goldberg

The Civil Rights movement of the 1950s and '60s culminated in one of the nation's most important legislative legacies, the Civil Rights Act of 1964. This law far surpassed earlier legislation in its efforts to root out discrimination by federally funded entities, its allocation of meaningful enforcement power to the

Justice Department, and its nationwide prohibition against segregating public accommodations such as restaurants, hotels, and movie theaters.

After reviewing the various sources of congressional power laid out in the previous section, you might guess that this legislation finds its roots in the power to enforce the equal protection provision of the Fourteenth Amendment. But in the Civil Rights Cases *(1883), the Court ruled that the guarantee of equal protection applies only to state action, not to private conduct by business owners. Not wanting to disturb this 80-year-old precedent, the Court instead upheld the 1964 law on Commerce Clause grounds. In* Heart of Atlanta Motel v. United States *and* Katzenbach v. McClung, *the Supreme Court ruled that racial segregation imposes "a substantial and harmful effect" on interstate commerce, and thus Congress has the power to prohibit it. Does this ruling go farther than* United States v. Darby *and* Wickard v. Filburn? *Does it leave any activity to be regulated by the states? Are Commerce Clause grounds the best way to decide the case, or should the Court have instead overturned the* Civil Rights Cases *and found a textual home for this legislation in the Equal Protection Clause? What might pragmatists say about this issue? What might adherents of the moral reading say?*

MR. JUSTICE CLARK *delivered the opinion of the Court.*

The case comes here on admissions and stipulated facts. Appellant owns and operates the Heart of Atlanta Motel which has 216 rooms available to transient guests. The motel is . . . readily accessible to interstate highways 75 and 85 and state highways 23 and 41. Appellant solicits patronage from outside the State of Georgia through various national advertising media, including magazines of national circulation; it maintains over 50 billboards and highway signs within the State, soliciting patronage for the motel; it accepts convention trade from outside Georgia and approximately 75% of its registered guests are from out of State. Prior to passage of the [Civil Rights Act of 1964,] the motel had followed a practice of refusing to rent rooms to Negroes, and it alleged that it intended to continue to do so. In an effort to perpetuate that policy this suit was filed.

Title II of the Act . . . provides that:

"All persons shall be entitled to the full and equal enjoyment of the goods, services, facilities, privileges, advantages, and accommodations of any place of public accommodation, as defined in this section, without discrimination or segregation on the ground of race, color, religion, or national origin."

There are listed in §201 (b) four classes of business establishments, each of which "serves the public" and "is a place of public accommodation" within the meaning of §201 (a) "if its operations affect commerce, or if discrimination or segregation by it is supported by State action." The covered establishments are:

"(1) any inn, hotel, motel, or other establishment which provides lodging to transient guests, other than an establishment located within a building which contains not more than five rooms for rent or hire and which is actually occupied by the proprietor of such establishment as his residence;

"(2) any restaurant, cafeteria . . . [not here involved];

"(3) any motion picture house . . . [not here involved];

"(4) any establishment . . . which is physically located within the premises of any establishment otherwise covered by this subsection, or . . . within the premises of which is physically located any such covered establishment . . . [not here involved]. "

Section 201 (c) defines the phrase "affect commerce" as applied to the above establishments. It first declares that "any inn, hotel, motel, or other establishment which provides lodging to transient guests" affects commerce per se. Restaurants, cafeterias, etc., in class two affect commerce only if they serve or offer to serve interstate travelers or if a substantial portion of the food which they serve or products which they sell have "moved in commerce." Motion picture houses and other places listed in class three affect commerce if they customarily present films, performances, etc., "which move in commerce." And the establishments listed in class four affect commerce if they are within, or include within their own premises, an establishment "the operations of which affect commerce." Private clubs are excepted under certain conditions. See §201 (e).

Section 201 (d) declares that "discrimination or segregation" is supported by state action when carried on under color of any law, statute, ordinance, regulation or any custom or usage required or enforced by officials of the State or any of its subdivisions.

In addition, §202 affirmatively declares that all persons "shall be entitled to be free, at any establishment or place, from discrimination or segregation of any kind on the ground of race, color, religion, or national origin, if such discrimination or segregation is or purports to be required by any law, statute, ordinance, regulation, rule, or order of a State or any agency or political subdivision thereof."

Finally, §203 prohibits the withholding or denial, etc., of any right or privilege secured by §201 and §202 or the intimidation, threatening or coercion of any person with the purpose of interfering with any such right or the punishing, etc., of any person for exercising or attempting to exercise any such right.

The remaining sections of the Title are remedial ones for violations of any of the previous sections. . . .

It is admitted that the operation of the motel brings it within the provisions of §201 (a) of the Act and that appellant refused to provide lodging for transient Negroes because of their race or color and that it intends to continue that policy unless restrained.

The sole question posed is, therefore, the constitutionality of the Civil Rights Act of 1964 as applied to these facts. The legislative history of the Act indicates that Congress based the Act on §5 and the Equal Protection Clause of the Fourteenth Amendment as well as its power to regulate interstate commerce under Art. I, §8, cl. 3, of the Constitution.

The Senate Commerce Committee made it quite clear that the fundamental object of Title II was to vindicate "the deprivation of personal dignity that surely accompanies denials of equal access to public establishments." At the same time, however, it noted that such an objective has been and could be readily achieved "by congressional action based on the commerce power of the Constitution." Our study of the legislative record, made in the light of prior cases, has brought us to the conclusion that Congress possessed ample power in this regard, and we have therefore not considered the other grounds relied upon. This is not to say that the remaining authority upon which it acted was not adequate, a question upon which we do not pass, but merely that since the commerce power is sufficient for our decision here we have considered it alone. Nor is §201 (d) or §202, having to do with state action, involved here and we do not pass upon either of those sections.

In light of our ground for decision, it might be well at the outset to discuss the *Civil Rights Cases*, supra, which declared provisions of the Civil Rights Act of 1875 unconstitutional. We think that decision inapposite, and without precedential value in determining the constitutionality of the present Act. Unlike Title II of the present legislation, the 1875 Act broadly proscribed discrimination in "inns, public conveyances on land or water, theaters, and other places of public amusement," without limiting the categories of affected businesses to those impinging upon interstate commerce. In contrast, the applicability of Title II is carefully limited to enterprises having a direct and substantial relation to the interstate flow of goods and people, except where state action is involved. Further, the fact that certain kinds of businesses may not in 1875 have been sufficiently involved in interstate commerce to warrant bringing them within the ambit of the commerce power is not necessarily dispositive of the same question today. Our populace had not reached its present mobility, nor were facilities, goods and services circulating as readily in interstate commerce as they are today. . . . Finally, there is language in the *Civil Rights Cases* which indicates that the Court did not fully consider whether the 1875 Act could be sustained as an exercise of the commerce power.

While the Act as adopted carried no congressional findings the record of its passage through each house is replete with evidence of the burdens that discrimination by race or color places upon interstate commerce. This testimony included the fact that our people have become increasingly mobile with millions of people of all races traveling from State to State; that Negroes in particular have been the subject of discrimination in transient accommodations, having to travel great distances to secure the same; that often they have been unable to obtain accommodations and have had to call upon friends to put them up overnight, and that these conditions had become so acute as to require the listing of available lodging for Negroes in a special guidebook which was itself "dramatic testimony to the difficulties" Negroes encounter in travel.

. . . This testimony indicated a qualitative as well as quantitative effect on interstate travel by Negroes. The former was the obvious impairment of the Negro traveler's pleasure and convenience that resulted when he continually was uncertain of finding lodging. As for the latter, there was evidence that this uncertainty stemming from racial discrimination had the effect of discouraging travel on the part of a substantial portion of the Negro community. . . . We shall not burden this opinion with further details since the voluminous testimony presents overwhelming evidence that discrimination by hotels and motels impedes interstate travel.

The power of Congress to deal with these obstructions depends on the meaning of the Commerce Clause. . . . [T]he determinative test of the exercise of power by the Congress under the Commerce Clause is simply whether the activity sought to be regulated is "commerce which concerns more States than one" and has a real and substantial relation to the national interest. Let us now turn to this facet of the problem.

[I]n 1917 in *Caminetti v. United States*, Mr. Justice Day held for the Court:

> "The transportation of passengers in interstate commerce, it has long been settled, is within the regulatory power of Congress, under the Commerce Clause of the Constitution, and the authority of Congress to keep the channels of interstate commerce free from immoral and injurious uses has been frequently sustained, and is no longer open to question."

The same interest in protecting interstate commerce which led Congress to deal with segregation in interstate carriers and the white-slave traffic has prompted it to extend the exercise of its power to gambling, to criminal enterprises, to deceptive practices in the sale of products, to fraudulent security transactions, to misbranding of drugs, to wages and hours, *United States v. Darby*, to members of labor unions, to crop control, to discrimination against shippers, to the protection of small business from injurious price cutting, to resale price maintenance, to professional football, and to racial discrimination by owners and managers of terminal restaurants.

That Congress was legislating against moral wrongs in many of these areas rendered its enactments no less valid. In framing Title II of this Act Congress was also dealing with what it considered a moral problem. But that fact does not detract from the overwhelming evidence of the disruptive effect that racial discrimination has had on commercial intercourse. It was this burden which empowered Congress to enact appropriate legislation, and, given this basis for the exercise of its power, Congress was not restricted by the fact that the particular obstruction to interstate commerce with which it was dealing was also deemed a moral and social wrong.

It is said that the operation of the motel here is of a purely local character. But, assuming this to be true, "if it is interstate commerce that feels the pinch, it does not matter how local the operation which applies the squeeze." As Chief Justice Stone put it in *United States v. Darby*:

> "The power of Congress over interstate commerce is not confined to the regulation of commerce among the states. It extends to those activities intrastate which so affect interstate commerce or the exercise of the power of Congress over it as to make regulation of them appropriate means to the attainment of a legitimate end, the exercise of the granted power of Congress to regulate interstate commerce."

Thus the power of Congress to promote interstate commerce also includes the power to regulate the local incidents thereof, including local activities in both the States of origin and destination, which might have a substantial and harmful effect upon that commerce. One need only examine the evidence which we have discussed above to see Congress may—as it has—prohibit racial discrimination by motels serving travelers, however "local" their operations may appear.

We, therefore, conclude that the action of the Congress in the adoption of the Act as applied here to a motel which concededly serves interstate travelers is within the power granted it by the Commerce Clause of the Constitution, as interpreted by this Court for 140 years. It may be argued that Congress could have pursued other methods to eliminate the obstructions it found in interstate commerce caused by racial discrimination. But this is a matter of policy that rests entirely with the Congress not with the courts. How obstructions in commerce may be removed—what means are to be employed—is within the sound and exclusive discretion of the Congress. It is subject only to one caveat—that the means chosen by it must be reasonably adapted to the end permitted by the Constitution. We cannot say that its choice here was not so adapted. The Constitution requires no more.

APPENDIX TO OPINION OF THE COURT

Title II—Injunctive Relief Against Discrimination in Places of Public Accommodation

"SEC. 201. (a) All persons shall be entitled to the full and equal enjoyment of the goods, services, facilities, privileges, advantages, and accommodations of any place of public accommodation, as defined in this section, without discrimination or segregation on the ground of race, color, religion, or national origin.

"(b) Each of the following establishments which serves the public is a place of public accommodation within the meaning of this title if its operations affect commerce, or if discrimination or segregation by it is supported by State action:

"(1) any inn, hotel, motel, or other establishment which provides lodging to transient guests, other than an establishment located within a building which contains not more than five rooms for rent or hire and which is actually occupied by the proprietor of such establishment as his residence;

"(2) any restaurant, cafeteria, lunchroom, lunch counter, soda fountain, or other facility principally engaged in selling food for consumption on the premises, including, but not limited to, any such facility located on the premises of any retail establishment; or any gasoline station;

"(3) any motion picture house, theater, concert hall, sports arena, stadium or other place of exhibition or entertainment; and

"(4) any establishment (A)(i) which is physically located within the premises of any establishment otherwise covered by this subsection, or (ii) within the premises of which is physically located any such covered establishment, and (B) which holds itself out as serving patrons of such covered establishment.

"(c) The operations of an establishment affect commerce within the meaning of this title if (1) it is one of the establishments described in paragraph (1) of subsection (b); (2) in the case of an establishment described in

paragraph (2) of subsection (b), it serves or offers to serve interstate travelers or a substantial portion of the food which it serves, or gasoline or other products which it sells, has moved in commerce; (3) in the case of an establishment described in paragraph (3) of subsection (b), it customarily presents films, performances, athletic teams, exhibitions, or other sources of entertainment which move in commerce; and (4) in the case of an establishment described in paragraph (4) of subsection (b), it is physically located within the premises of, or there is physically located within its premises, an establishment the operations of which affect commerce within the meaning of this subsection. For purposes of this section, 'commerce' means travel, trade, traffic, commerce, transportation, or communication among the several States, or between the District of Columbia and any State, or between any foreign country or any territory or possession and any State or the District of Columbia, or between points in the same State but through any other State or the District of Columbia or a foreign country.

"(d) Discrimination or segregation by an establishment is supported by State action within the meaning of this title if such discrimination or segregation (1) is carried on under color of any law, statute, ordinance, or regulation; or (2) is carried on under color of any custom or usage required or enforced by officials of the State or political subdivision thereof; or (3) is required by action of the State or political subdivision thereof.

"(e) The provisions of this title shall not apply to a private club or other establishment not in fact open to the public, except to the extent that the facilities of such establishment are made available to the customers or patrons of an establishment within the scope of subsection (b).

"SEC. 202. All persons shall be entitled to be free, at any establishment or place, from discrimination or segregation of any kind on the ground of race, color, religion, or national origin, if such discrimination or segregation is or purports to be required by any law, statute, ordinance, regulation, rule, or order of a State or any agency or political subdivision thereof.

"SEC. 203. No person shall (a) withhold, deny, or attempt to withhold or deny, or deprive or attempt to deprive, any person of any right or privilege secured by section 201 or 202, or (b) intimidate, threaten, or coerce, or attempt to intimidate, threaten, or coerce any person with the purpose of interfering with any right or privilege secured by section 201 or 202, or (c) punish or attempt to punish any person for exercising or attempting to exercise any right or privilege secured by section 201 or 202.

"SEC. 204. (a) Whenever any person has engaged or there are reasonable grounds to believe that any person is about to engage in any act or practice prohibited by section 203, a civil action for preventive relief, including an application for a permanent or temporary injunction, restraining order, or other order, may be instituted by the person aggrieved and, upon timely application, the court may, in its discretion, permit the Attorney General to intervene in such civil action if he certifies that the case is of general public importance. Upon application by the complainant and in such circumstances as the court may deem just, the court may appoint an attorney for such complainant and may authorize the commencement of the civil action without the payment of fees, costs, or security.

"(b) In any action commenced pursuant to this title, the court, in its discretion, may allow the prevailing party, other than the United States, a reasonable attorney's fee as part of the costs, and the United States shall be liable for costs the same as a private person.

"(c) In the case of an alleged act or practice prohibited by this title which occurs in a State, or political subdivision of a State, which has a State or local law prohibiting such act or practice and establishing or authorizing a State or local authority to grant or seek relief from such practice or to institute criminal proceedings with respect thereto upon receiving notice thereof, no civil action may be brought under subsection (a) before the expiration of thirty days after written notice of such alleged act or practice has been given to the appropriate State or local authority by registered mail or in person, provided that the court may stay proceedings in such civil action pending the termination of State or local enforcement proceedings.

"(d) In the case of an alleged act or practice prohibited by this title which occurs in a State, or political subdivision of a State, which has no State or local law prohibiting such act or practice, a civil action may be brought under subsection (a): Provided, That the court may refer the matter to the Community Relations Service established by title X of this Act for as long as the court believes there is a reasonable possibility of obtaining voluntary compliance, but for not more than sixty days: Provided further, That upon expiration of such sixty-day period, the court may extend such period for an additional period, not to exceed a cumulative total of one hundred and twenty days, if it believes there then exists a reasonable possibility of securing voluntary compliance.

"SEC. 205. The Service is authorized to make a full investigation of any complaint referred to it by the court under section 204(d) and may hold such hearings with respect thereto as may be necessary. The Service shall conduct any hearings with respect to any such complaint in executive session, and shall not release any testimony given therein except by agreement of all parties involved in the complaint with the permission of the court, and the Service shall endeavor to bring about a voluntary settlement between the parties.

"SEC. 206. (a) Whenever the Attorney General has reasonable cause to believe that any person or group of persons is engaged in a pattern or practice of resistance to the full enjoyment of any of the rights secured by this title, and that the pattern or practice is of such a nature and is intended to deny the full exercise of the rights herein described, the Attorney General may bring a civil action in the appropriate district court of the United States by filing with it a complaint (1) signed by him (or in his absence the Acting Attorney General), (2) setting forth facts pertaining to such pattern or practice, and (3) requesting such preventive relief, including an application for a permanent or temporary injunction, restraining order or other order against the person or persons responsible for such pattern or practice, as he deems necessary to insure the full enjoyment of the rights herein described.

"(b) In any such proceeding the Attorney General may file with the clerk of such court a request that a court of three judges be convened to hear and determine the case. Such request by the Attorney General shall be accompanied by a certificate that, in his opinion, the case is of general public importance. A copy of the certificate and request for a three-judge court shall be immediately furnished by such clerk to the chief judge of the circuit (or in his absence, the presiding circuit judge of the circuit) in which the case is pending. Upon receipt of the copy of such request it shall be the duty of the chief judge of the circuit or the presiding circuit judge, as the case may be, to designate immediately three judges in such circuit, of whom at least one shall be a circuit judge and another of whom shall be a district judge of the court in which the proceeding was instituted, to hear and determine such case, and it shall be the duty of the judges so designated to assign the case for hearing at the earliest practicable date, to participate in the hearing and determination thereof, and to cause the case to be in every way expedited. An appeal from the final judgment of such court will lie to the Supreme Court.

"In the event the Attorney General fails to file such a request in any such proceeding, it shall be the duty of the chief judge of the district (or in his absence, the acting chief judge) in which the case is pending immediately to designate a judge in such district to hear and determine the case. In the event that no judge in the district is available to hear and determine the case, the chief judge of the district, or the acting chief judge, as the case may be, shall certify this fact to the chief judge of the circuit (or in his absence, the acting chief judge) who shall then designate a district or circuit judge of the circuit to hear and determine the case.

"It shall be the duty of the judge designated pursuant to this section to assign the case for hearing at the earliest practicable date and to cause the case to be in every way expedited.

"SEC. 207. (a) The district courts of the United States shall have jurisdiction of proceedings instituted pursuant to this title and shall exercise the same without regard to whether the aggrieved party shall have exhausted any administrative or other remedies that may be provided by law.

"(b) The remedies provided in this title shall be the exclusive means of enforcing the rights based on this title, but nothing in this title shall preclude any individual or any State or local agency from asserting any right based on any other Federal or State law not inconsistent with this title, including any statute or ordinance requiring nondiscrimination in public establishments or accommodations, or from pursuing any remedy, civil or criminal, which may be available for the vindication or enforcement of such right."

MR. JUSTICE DOUGLAS, *concurring.*

Though I join the Court's opinions, I am somewhat reluctant here . . . to rest solely on the Commerce Clause. My reluctance is not due to any conviction that Congress lacks power to regulate commerce in the interests of human rights. It is rather my belief that the right of people to be free of state action that discriminates against them because of race, like the "right of persons to move freely from State to State" (*Edwards v. California*) "occupies a more protected position in our constitutional system than does the movement of cattle, fruit, steel and coal across state lines." Moreover . . . the result reached by the Court is for me much more obvious as a protective measure under the Fourteenth Amendment than under the Commerce Clause. For the former deals with the constitutional status of the individual not with the impact on commerce of local activities or vice versa.

Hence I would prefer to rest on the assertion of legislative power contained in §5 of the Fourteenth Amendment which states: "The Congress shall have power to enforce, by appropriate legislation, the provisions of this article"—a power which the Court concedes was exercised at least in part in this Act.

A decision based on the Fourteenth Amendment would have a more settling effect, making unnecessary litigation over whether a particular restaurant or inn is within the commerce definitions of the Act or whether a particular customer is an interstate traveler. Under my construction, the Act would apply to all customers in all the enumerated places of public accommodation. And that construction would put an end to all obstructionist strategies and finally close one door on a bitter chapter in American history.

I think the Court is correct in concluding that the Act is not founded on the Commerce Clause to the exclusion of the Enforcement Clause of the Fourteenth Amendment.

In determining the reach of an exertion of legislative power, it is customary to read various granted powers together. As stated in *McCulloch v. Maryland*:

"We admit, as all must admit, that the powers of the government are limited, and that its limits are not to be transcended. But we think the sound construction of the constitution must allow to the national legislature that discretion, with respect to the means by which the powers it confers are to be carried into execution, which will enable that body to perform the high duties assigned to it, in the manner most beneficial to the people. Let the end be legitimate, let it be within the scope of the constitution, and all means which are appropriate, which are plainly adapted to that end, which are not prohibited, but consist with the letter and spirit of the constitution, are constitutional."

The "means" used in the present Act are in my view "appropriate" and "plainly adapted" to the end of enforcing Fourteenth Amendment rights as well as protecting interstate commerce.

Section 201(a) declares in Fourteenth Amendment language the right of equal access:

"All persons shall be entitled to the full and equal enjoyment of the goods, services, facilities, privileges, advantages, and accommodations of any place of public accommodation, as defined in this section, without discrimination or segregation on the ground of race, color, religion, or national origin."

The rights protected are clearly within the purview of our decisions under the Equal Protection Clause of the Fourteenth Amendment.

"State action"—the key to Fourteenth Amendment guarantees—is defined by §201(d) as follows:

"Discrimination or segregation by an establishment is supported by State action within the meaning of this title if such discrimination or segregation (1) is carried on under color of any law, statute, ordinance, or regulation; or (2) is carried on under color of any custom or usage required or enforced by officials of the State or political subdivision thereof; or (3) is required by action of the State or political subdivision thereof."

That definition is within our decision of *Shelley v. Kraemer*, for the "discrimination" in the present cases is "enforced by officials of the State," i.e., by the state judiciary under the trespass laws.

Section 202 declares the right of all persons to be free from certain kinds of state action at any public establishment—not just at the previously enumerated places of public accommodation:

"All persons shall be entitled to be free, at any establishment or place, from discrimination or segregation of any kind on the ground of race, color, religion, or national origin, if such discrimination or segregation is or purports to be required by any law, statute, ordinance, regulation, rule, or order of a State or any agency or political subdivision thereof."

Thus the essence of many of the guarantees embodied in the Act are those contained in the Fourteenth Amendment.

The Commerce Clause, to be sure, enters into some of the definitions of "place of public accommodation" in §§201(b) and (c). Thus a "restaurant" is included, §201(b)(2), "if . . . it serves or offers to serve interstate travelers or a substantial portion of the food which it serves . . . has moved in commerce." §201(c)(2). But any "motel" is included "which provides lodging to transient guests, other than an establishment located within a building which contains not more than five rooms for rent or hire and which is actually occupied by the proprietor of such establishment as his residence." §§201(b)(1) and (c)(1). Providing lodging "to transient guests" is not strictly Commerce Clause talk, for the phrase aptly describes any guest—local or interstate.

Thus some of the definitions of "place of public accommodation" in §201(b) are in Commerce Clause language and some are not. Indeed §201(b) is explicitly bifurcated. An establishment "which serves the public is a place of public accommodation," says §201(b), under either of two conditions: first, "if its operations affect commerce," or second, "if discrimination or segregation by it is supported by State action."

The House Report emphasizes these dual bases on which the Act rests—a situation which a minority recognized was being attempted and which it opposed.

Thus while I agree with the Court that Congress in fashioning the present Act used the Commerce Clause to regulate

racial segregation, it also used (and properly so) some of its power under §5 of the Fourteenth Amendment.

I repeat what I said earlier, that our decision should be based on the Fourteenth Amendment, thereby putting an end to all obstructionist strategies and allowing every person—whatever his race, creed, or color—to patronize all places of public accommodation without discrimination whether he travels interstate or intrastate.

KATZENBACH v. McCLUNG

379 U.S. 294 (1964)

Opinion: Clark, joined by Warren, Harlan, Brennan, Stewart, White
Concurrence: Douglas
Concurrence: Goldberg
Concurrence: Black

MR. JUSTICE CLARK *delivered the opinion of the Court.*

This case was argued with No. 515, *Heart of Atlanta Motel v. United States*, decided this date, . . . in which we upheld the constitutional validity of Title II of the Civil Rights Act of 1964 against an attack by hotels, motels, and like establishments.

Ollie's Barbecue is a family-owned restaurant in Birmingham, Alabama, specializing in barbecued meats and homemade pies, with a seating capacity of 220 customers. It is located on a state highway 11 blocks from an interstate one and a somewhat greater distance from railroad and bus stations. The restaurant caters to a family and white-collar trade with a take-

out service for Negroes. It employs 36 persons, two-thirds of whom are Negroes.

In the 12 months preceding the passage of the Act, the restaurant purchased locally approximately $150,000 worth of food, $69,683 or 46% of which was meat that it bought from a local supplier who had procured it from outside the State. The District Court expressly found that a substantial portion of the food served in the restaurant had moved in interstate commerce. The restaurant has refused to serve Negroes in its dining accommodations since its original opening in 1927, and since July 2, 1964, it has been operating in violation of the Act. . . .

The basic holding in *Heart of Atlanta Motel*, answers many of the contentions made by the appellees. There we outlined the overall purpose and operational plan of Title II and found it a valid exercise of the power to regulate interstate commerce insofar as it requires hotels and motels to serve transients without regard to their race or color. In this case we consider its application to restaurants which serve food a substantial portion of which has moved in commerce.

Section 201(a) of Title II commands that all persons shall be entitled to the full and equal enjoyment of the goods and services of any place of public accommodation without discrimination or segregation on the ground of race, color, religion, or national origin; and §201(b) defines establishments as places of public accommodation if their operations affect commerce or segregation by them is supported by state action. Sections 201(b)(2) and (c) place any "restaurant . . . principally engaged in selling food for consumption on the premises" under the Act "if . . . it serves or offers to serve interstate travelers or a substantial portion of the food which it serves . . . has moved in commerce."

Ollie's Barbecue admits that it is covered by these provisions of the Act. The Government makes no contention that the discrimination at the restaurant was supported by the State of Alabama. There is no claim that interstate travelers frequented the restaurant. The sole question, therefore, narrows down to whether Title II, as applied to a restaurant annually receiving about $70,000 worth of food which has moved in commerce, is a valid exercise of the power of Congress. The Government has contended that Congress had ample basis upon which to find that racial discrimination at restaurants which receive from out of state a substantial portion of the food served does, in fact, impose commercial burdens of national magnitude upon interstate commerce.

As we noted in *Heart of Atlanta Motel* both Houses of Congress conducted prolonged hearings on the Act. And, as we said there, while no formal findings were made, which of course are not necessary, it is well that we make mention of the testimony at these hearings. . . . The record is replete with testimony of the burdens placed on interstate commerce by racial discrimination in restaurants. A comparison of per capita spending by Negroes in restaurants, theaters, and like establishments indicated less spending, after discounting income differences, in areas where discrimination is widely practiced. . . . This diminutive spending springing from a refusal to serve Negroes and their total loss as customers has, regardless of the absence of direct evidence, a close connection to interstate commerce. The fewer customers a restaurant enjoys the less food it sells and consequently the less it buys. In addition, the Attorney General testified that this type of discrimination imposed "an artificial restriction on the market" and interfered with the flow of merchandise. In addition, there were many references to discriminatory situations causing wide unrest and having a depressant effect on general business conditions in the respective communities.

Moreover there was an impressive array of testimony that discrimination in restaurants had a direct and highly restrictive effect upon interstate travel by Negroes. This resulted, it was said, because discriminatory practices prevent Negroes from buying prepared food served on the premises while on a trip, except in isolated and unkempt restaurants and under most unsatisfactory and often unpleasant conditions. This obviously discourages travel and obstructs interstate commerce for one can hardly travel without eating. Likewise, it was said, that discrimination deterred professional, as well as skilled, people from moving into areas where such practices occurred and thereby caused industry to be reluctant to establish there.

We believe that this testimony afforded ample basis for the conclusion that established restaurants in such areas sold less interstate goods because of the discrimination, that interstate travel was obstructed directly by it, that business in general suffered and that many new businesses refrained from establishing there as a result of it.

It goes without saying that, viewed in isolation, the volume of food purchased by Ollie's Barbecue from sources supplied from out of state was insignificant when compared with the total foodstuffs moving in commerce. But, as our late Brother Jackson said for the Court in *Wickard v. Filburn*:

> "That appellee's own contribution to the demand for wheat may be trivial by itself is not enough to remove him from the scope of federal regulation where, as here, his contribution, taken together with that of many others similarly situated, is far from trivial."

Article I, §8, cl. 3, confers upon Congress the power "to regulate Commerce . . . among the several States" and Clause 18 of the same Article grants it the power "to make all Laws which shall be necessary and proper for carrying into Execution the foregoing Powers. . . . " This grant, as we have pointed out in *Heart of Atlanta Motel* "extends to those activities intrastate which so affect interstate commerce, or the exertion of the power of Congress over it, as to make regulation of them appropriate means to the attainment of a legitimate end, the effective execution of the granted power to regulate interstate commerce." Much is said about a restaurant business being local but "even if appellee's activity be local and though it may not be regarded as commerce, it may still, whatever its nature, be reached by Congress if it exerts a substantial economic effect on interstate commerce. . . ."

This Court has held time and again that this power extends to activities of retail establishments, including restaurants, which directly or indirectly burden or obstruct interstate commerce. We have detailed the cases in *Heart of Atlanta Motel*, and will not repeat them here.

Congress has determined for itself that refusals of service to Negroes have imposed burdens both upon the interstate flow of food and upon the movement of products generally. Of course, the mere fact that Congress has said when particular activity shall be deemed to affect commerce does not preclude further examination by this Court. But where we find that the legislators, in light of the facts and testimony before them, have a rational basis for finding a chosen regulatory scheme necessary to the protection of commerce, our investigation is at an end. The only remaining question—one answered in the affirmative by the court below—is whether the particular restaurant either serves or offers to serve interstate travelers or serves food a substantial portion of which has moved in interstate commerce.

Confronted as we are with the facts laid before Congress, we must conclude that it had a rational basis for finding that racial discrimination in restaurants had a direct and adverse effect on the free flow of interstate commerce. Insofar as the sections of the Act here relevant are concerned, §§201(b)(2) and (c), Congress prohibited discrimination only in those establishments having a close tie to interstate commerce, i.e., those, like the McClungs', serving food that has come from out of the State. We think in so doing that Congress acted well within its power to protect and foster commerce in extending the coverage of Title II only to those restaurants offering to serve interstate travelers or serving food, a substantial portion of which has moved in interstate commerce.

The absence of direct evidence connecting discriminatory restaurant service with the flow of interstate food, a factor on which the appellees place much reliance, is not, given the evidence as to the effect of such practices on other aspects of commerce, a crucial matter.

The power of Congress in this field is broad and sweeping; where it keeps within its sphere and violates no express constitutional limitation it has been the rule of this Court, going back almost to the founding days of the Republic, not to interfere. The Civil Rights Act of 1964, as here applied, we find to be plainly appropriate in the resolution of what the Congress found to be a national commercial problem of the first magnitude. We find it in no violation of any express limitations of the Constitution and we therefore declare it valid.

SYNTHESIS QUESTIONS FOR FURTHER DISCUSSION: CHAPTER 3 SECTION B

1. When President Franklin Roosevelt calls for a "Second Bill of Rights," does he actually advocate amending the text of the Constitution? What branch of government would be best suited to enforce these positive, socio-economic rights? Cass Sunstein believes that the New Deal successfully entrenched many of President Roosevelt's proposed rights as "constitutive commitments." Like Bruce Ackerman, Sunstein argues that these commitments, including landmark legislation such as the Social Security Act, register the same constitutional status as the text itself. Do you agree that these entitlements have similar constitutional status as some of the rights established by the Constitution? Does it matter that many of the rights are "negative" restrictions on state power as opposed to "positive" entitlements that grant citizens rights to receive certain benefits?

2. Issues regarding congressional power are sometimes couched in solely procedural terms, apart from any of the substantive or moral issues involved in these cases. Does it matter that child labor was a particularly controversial issue at the time? For instance, do you think Justice Oliver Wendell Holmes is justified in appealing to the "evil of premature and excessive child labor" in his dissent in *Hammer v. Dagenhart*, or is the morality of the legislation at issue in the "powers" cases in this chapter irrelevant to constitutional analysis?

3. In learning that the debate about civil rights legislation passed in the 1960s hinged on questions regarding the Commerce power, many students express surprise. The debate about civil rights, we often assume, is about equality, a value more closely enshrined in the Fourteenth Amendment's guarantee of "equal protection." Another route in discussing the constitutionality of this legislation would have been through the power granted to Congress under the fifth section of the Fourteenth Amendment, to enforce

laws related to equal protection. Should this have been the constitutional hook for Congress's civil rights legislation, instead of the Commerce Clause?

C. THE NEW FEDERALISM

Do states have a role in protecting liberty? How far does economic activity extend?

If some claim the New Deal illustrates an important lesson about the need for Congress to regulate the national economy, others believe it raises questions about whether this broad reach is compatible with a Constitution of limited federal powers. Under the sweeping reach of the Court's post-1937 decisions, Congress could regulate virtually any activity, so long as it produced some kind of "substantial effect" on interstate commerce. Furthermore, as we saw in *United States v. Carolene Products* in Chapter 2, courts have largely deferred to the legislature in economic judgments, such as how substantial an effect on commerce might be. The only constitutional requirement that an economic regulation would have to meet is that it possesses some rational basis.

But if "commerce . . . among the several states" can cover virtually any activity, then is Congress still limited to the specific powers enumerated in the Constitution? Or did the New Deal give rise to a single, unitary government? In determining whether questions of federalism—which for a time were forgotten as the public came to accept broader congressional powers without question— are important contemporary constitutional controversies, we examine a question of doctrine and a question of theory. First, where can we draw a clear line beyond which federal power cannot extend? Second, why do the principles of federalism matter in the first place?

In relation to the first question, the issue of balance between state authority and congressional authority might have been a moot point had it not been for a relatively recent development in constitutional law. As you saw in *Wickard v. Filburn* and in *Heart of Atlanta v. United States*, the Supreme Court after the switch in time adopted a broad understanding of interstate commerce. In *Wickard v. Filburn*, for instance, it upheld the regulation on the cultivation of wheat for private use on grounds that while the grower might use this wheat strictly for personal consumption, that would mean he was not buying that same wheat in the open market—thus depressing demand and therefore the price of wheat other farmers could command. While this one farmer might not be significant, if every wheat farmer in America did the same thing, the aggregation of these small effects would be substantial, and significantly affect the larger national market in wheat. After *Wickard v. Filburn*, it might appear that the question of congressional authority was largely settled and accepted as not only expansive but potentially limitless.

However, as you will see, decades later, in *National League of Cities v. Usery*, then–Associate Justice William Rehnquist, writing for the Court, revived the issue of federalism. Although Justice Rehnquist would face some setbacks, he played a crucial role in asserting the power of the states in relation to the federal government in contemporary constitutional jurisprudence. Indeed, some have suggested that his role in constitutional debates about federalism was central to what some have called the "Rehnquist Revolution" in the Supreme Court's recent history. Specifically, *National League of Cities v. Usery* concerned the federal government's regulation of state employees. Justice Rehnquist argued that the Tenth Amendment, which states that "powers not delegated to the United States by the Constitution . . . are reserved to the States," still presented significant limits on federal power, including limits on its power to regulate interstate commerce. In striking down the regulation, Justice Rehnquist hoped to signal the reemergence of boundaries on congressional authority and to reassert the power of the states. However, his plan faced a setback in *Garcia v. San Antonio Metropolitan Transit Authority* (1985), where the Court reversed *National League of Cities v. Usery*. It might appear that *Garcia v. San Antonio* would once and for all establish virtually unlimited congressional power in relation to the states. However, although the ruling in *Garcia v. San Antonio* seemed to signal continued expansive federal power, it contained a dissent from Justice Rehnquist, excerpted here, which presaged a pushback against the Court's expansive jurisprudence in regard to the Commerce Clause. Indeed, ten years later, in *United States v. Lopez*, the Supreme Court would strike down legislation establishing gun-free school zones on grounds that it exceeded Congress's power under the Commerce Clause. Again in *United States v. Morrison*, the Court would strike down the Violence Against Women Act on grounds that Congress lacked the authority to enact this legislation, which it deemed not a matter of interstate commerce. In both of these cases, the Court rejects the idea that commerce should be interpreted broadly to include matters that are not clearly economic. These cases, therefore, once again raise a puzzle about the meaning of this clause and the importance of federalism altogether.

The Court's revival of limits on Congress's commerce power came on the heels of another development in American politics. The development of constitutional interpretation is not merely an abstract exercise—it turns alongside the gears of history, evolving in step with the influence of political movements. Just as President Franklin Roosevelt eventually replaced the entire body of the Supreme Court, conservative presidents like Richard Nixon and Ronald Reagan have also left their mark on the Court. Specifically, during his terms in office, President Reagan announced a "New Federalism" that would restore power to the states. The idea of New Federalism was meant to serve as a direct rejection of President Roosevelt's New Deal. After President Reagan left office, the Court's decisions in *United States v. Lopez* and *United States v. Morrison* seemed to echo this call, ushering in a New Federalism jurisprudence under the leadership of appointees of Presidents Nixon and Reagan, including Justice Rehnquist, who was elevated to Chief Justice by President Reagan in 1986, after serving on the Court since 1972. The cases in this last section detail this development in constitutional law.

Although arguments for the New Federalism have traditionally been associated with the more conservative end of the political spectrum, in recent years progressives have begun to argue for the importance of constraints on congressional power. In the reading from Kathleen Sullivan, we see the suggestion that during periods of conservative dominance in Congress, federalist arguments in favor of states' rights might be an important tool for liberals to use in pushing back against encroachments on liberty. Although federalism is often associated with conservative resistance to the New Deal and civil rights in the name of states' rights, Sullivan's piece raises a question about whether those who defend more leftist understandings of economics and civil liberties might also appeal to this doctrine. In particular, defenders of a freedom to use medical marijuana might be tempted to agree with U.S. Supreme Court Justice Clarence Thomas's dissent in *Gonzales v. Raich*, which argued that the federal government does not have the power to outlaw and regulate medical marijuana. Is there room for those on the left of the political spectrum to embrace federalism? Should state governments have the leeway, free from congressional intervention, to pursue progressive ideas for promoting individual freedom and equality, including stem cell research, same-sex marriage, medical marijuana, and physician-assisted suicide?

We also read in this section a piece by Michael McConnell, who attempts to defend federalism by appealing to the history and political theory of the Constitution itself. These selections demonstrate that federalism is no longer a mere abstract question of philosophy, but rather fundamental to the Supreme Court's decisions and its jurisprudence. McConnell raises the relationship between federalism and democracy, and thus ties the topic of this chapter to a theme that has been prominent in this book. Specifically, notice McConnell's contention that state governments are closer to the people and more democratic, as opposed to the cumbersome, monopoly-like qualities of a centralized form of national government. Do you agree with McConnell that federalism is an inherently democratic idea and that it would be a mistake to move towards centralized control? Or, on the contrary, are you sympathetic to President Roosevelt's use of federal power and the Supreme Court's decision to grant that power under the Commerce Clause?

Michael W. McConnell

FEDERALISM: EVALUATING THE FOUNDERS' DESIGN

54 U. Chi. L. Rev. 1484 (1987)

During the debates over the drafting and ratification of the Constitution, supporters and opponents alike came to articulate complex and sophisticated theories of federalism (which, it should be stressed, was a uniquely American blend of national systems—like the French—and confederate systems—like the ancient Greek and early modern Dutch). The "natural attachment" of the people in 1787 to their states was augmented by practical arguments about how the new system of dual sovereignty would promote three complementary objectives: (1) "[t]o secure the public good," (2) to protect "private rights," and (3) "to preserve the spirit and form of popular government." Achievement of these ends, according to Madison, was the "great object" of the Constitution. To understand the "founders' design" we must look again at those arguments. As the people of 1987, we must look at them in light of modern experience and knowledge about political decision making. The arguments of 1787 stand up remarkably well.

A. TO "SECURE THE PUBLIC GOOD"

Rejecting both pure confederation and consolidation, the "Federal Farmer" (the ablest and most influential of the antifederalist pamphleteers) argued that a "partial consolidation" is the only system "that can secure the freedom and happiness of this people." He reasoned that "one government and general legislation alone, never can extend equal benefits to all parts of the United States: Different laws, customs, and opinions exist in the different states, which by a uniform system of laws would be unreasonably invaded." The framers sought, the Federal Farmer concluded, to preserve decentralized decision making because smaller units of government are better able to further the interests and general welfare of the people.

Three important advantages of decentralized decision making emerge from an examination of the founders' arguments and the modern literature. First, decentralized decision making is better able to reflect the diversity of interests

and preferences of individuals in different parts of the nation. Second, allocation of decision making authority to a level of government no larger than necessary will prevent mutually disadvantageous attempts by communities to take advantage of their neighbors. And third, decentralization allows for innovation and competition in government.

1. Responsiveness to diverse interests and preferences. The first, and most axiomatic, advantage of decentralized government is that local laws can be adapted to local conditions and local tastes, while a national government must take a uniform—and hence less desirable—approach. So long as preferences for government policies are unevenly distributed among the various localities, more people can be satisfied by decentralized decision making than by a single national authority. . . .

For example, assume that there are only two states, with equal populations of 100 each. Assume further that 70 percent of State A, and only 40 percent of State B, wish to outlaw smoking in public buildings. The others are opposed. If the decision is made on a national basis by a majority rule, 110 people will be pleased, and 90 displeased. If a separate decision is made by majorities in each state, 130 will be pleased, and only 70 displeased. The level of satisfaction will be still greater if some smokers in State A decide to move to State B, and some anti-smokers in State B decide to move to State A. In the absence of economies of scale in government services, significant externalities, or compelling arguments from justice, this is a powerful reason to prefer decentralized government. States are preferably governing units to the federal government, and local government to states. Modern public choice theory provides strong support for the framers' insight on this point.

2. Destructive competition for the benefits of government. A second consideration in designing a federal structure is more equivocal. The unit of decision making must be large enough so that decisions reflect the full costs and benefits, but small enough that destructive competition for the benefits of central government action is minimized. In economic language, this is the problem of "externalities."

Externalities present the principal countervailing consideration in favor of centralized government: if the costs of government action are borne by the citizens of State C, but the benefits are shared by the citizens of States D, E, and F, State C will be unwilling to expend the level of resources commensurate with the full social benefit of the action. This was the argument in Federalist 25 for national control of defense. Since an MX missile in Pennsylvania will deter a Soviet attack on Connecticut and North Carolina as well as Pennsylvania, optimal levels of investment in MX's require national decisions and national taxes. Or, similarly, since expenditures on water pollution reduction in Kentucky will benefit riparians all the way to New Orleans, it makes sense to nationalize decisions about water pollution regulation and treatment. Thus, as James Wilson explained to the Pennsylvania ratifying convention, "[w]hatever the object of government extends, in its operation, beyond the bounds of a particular state, should be considered as belonging to the government of the United States" (quoted at pp. 169-70).

That significant external effects of this sort provide justification for national decisions is well understood—hence federal funding of defense, interstate highways, national parks, and medical research, and federal regulation of interstate commerce, pollution, and national labor markets. It is less well understood that nationalizing

decisions where the impact is predominantly local has an equal and opposite effect. The framers' awareness that ill consequences flow as much from excessive as from insufficient centralization is fundamental to their insistence on enumerating and thus limiting the powers of the federal government. Hence the other half of Wilson's explanation: "Whatever object of government is confined in its operation and effect, within the bounds of a particular State, should be considered as belonging to the government of that State" (p. 169). This stands in marked contrast to the modern tendency to resolve all doubts in favor of federal control.

The point is quite general. It applies to lawmaking and regulation no less than to taxing and spending. A major effect of regulation is to shift burdens from one region or locality to another. Familiar examples are environmental laws that protect eastern "dirty" coal from competition from western "clean" coal and railroad regulation that enables low density areas to maintain service at the expense of other traffic. But the effect is especially obvious in the case of federal spending. If the national treasury is seen as a common pool resource for financing schemes of predominantly local benefit, it will be oversubscribed. Current budgetary woes are largely attributable to this fiscal "tragedy of the commons."

3. Innovation and competition in government. A final reason why federalism has been thought to advance the public good is that state and local governmental units will have greater opportunity and incentive to pioneer useful changes. A consolidated national government has all the drawbacks of a monopoly: it stifles choice and lacks the goad of competition.

Lower levels of government are more likely to depart from established consensus simply because they are smaller and more numerous. Elementary statistical theory holds that a greater number of independent observations will produce more instances of deviation from the mean. If innovation is desirable, it follows that decentralization is desirable. This statistical proposition is strengthened, moreover, by the political reality that a smaller unit of government is more likely to have a population with preferences that depart from the majority's. It is, therefore, more likely to try an approach that could not command a national majority.

Perhaps more important is that smaller units of government have an incentive, beyond the mere political process, to adopt popular policies. If a community can attract additional taxpayers, each citizen's share of the overhead costs of government is proportionately reduced. Since people are better able to move among states or communities than to emigrate from the United States, competition among governments for taxpayers will be far stronger at the state and local than at the federal level. Since most people are taxpayers, this means that there is a powerful incentive for decentralized governments to make things better for most people. In particular, the desire to attract taxpayers and jobs will promote policies of economic growth and expansion.

It is well known, for example, that families often choose a community on the basis of the school system; a better school system encourages development and raises property values. Competition among communities is therefore likely to result in superior education (as well as more cost-effective ways of providing it). This is especially likely given the strong business support for education. Because of the need for a well-educated work force, businesses often choose to locate in communities with a superior educational system and push for improved education in communities where they already have facilities. The chairman of Xerox Corporation has been quoted as saying, "Education is a bigger factor in productivity growth [rates] than increased capital, economies of scale or better allocation of resources."

To be sure, the results of competition among states and localities will not always be salutary. State-by-state determination of the laws of incorporation likely results in the most efficient forms of corporate organization, but state-by-state determination of the law of products liability seems to have created a liability monster. This is because each state can benefit in-state plaintiffs by more generous liability rules, the costs being exported to largely out-of-state defendants; while no state can do much to protect its in-state manufacturers from suits by plaintiffs in the other states. Thus, competition among the states in this arena leads to one-sidedly pro-plaintiff rules of law.

The most important example of this phenomenon is the effect of state-by-state competition on welfare and other redistributive policies. In most cases, immigration of investment and of middle- to upper-income persons is perceived as desirable, while immigration of persons dependent on public assistance is viewed as a drain on a community's finances. Yet generous welfare benefits paid by higher taxes will lead the rich to leave and the poor to come. This creates an incentive, other things being equal, against redistributive policies. Indeed, it can be shown that the level of redistribution in a decentralized system is likely to be lower even if there is virtually unanimous agreement among the citizens that higher levels would be desirable. Where redistribution is the objective, therefore, advocates should and do press for federal programs, or at least for minimum federal standards.

Thus, the competition among states has an uncertain effect: often salutary but sometimes destructive. There are races to the bottom as well as races to the top. Often one's view of the allocation of authority for specific issues will depend on a prediction as to substantive outcomes rather than a general theory of federalism.

B. TO PROTECT "PRIVATE RIGHTS"

The most important reason offered by the defenders of state sovereignty was that state and local governments are better protectors of liberty. Patrick Henry went to the heart of the matter when he told the Virginia ratifying convention:

> You are not to inquire how your trade may be increased, nor how you are to become a great and powerful people, but how your liberties can be secured; for liberty ought to be the direct end of your Government.

The most eloquent of the opponents of the Constitution, Henry stated flatly that in the "alarming transition, from a Confederacy to a consolidated Government," the "rights and privileges" of Americans were "endangered." He was far from alone in this fear.

At a distance of 200 years, it is this aspect of the Founders' thought that is most difficult for us to understand. After *Brown v. Board of Education* and the various civil rights acts, after the revolution in criminal procedure fostered by federal law and federal courts, after the imposition of uniform federal standards for basic liberties under the Bill of Rights, and after the proliferation of novel statutory "rights" arising from the interventions of the welfare-regulatory state, it is the federal government, not the states, that appears to be our system's primary protector of individual liberties. This seems to be the premise of the Fourteenth Amendment and of much of New Deal legislation. The view at the founding, however, was much more divided and ambivalent.

Madison's most important contribution to the debate over ratification is his challenging argument that individual liberties, such as property rights and freedom of religion, are better protected at the national than the state level. Madison's argument, greatly simplified, is that the most serious threat to individual liberty is the tyranny of a majority faction. Since any given faction is more likely to be concentrated in a particular locality, and to be no more than a small minority in the nation as a whole, it follows that factional tyranny is more likely in the state legislatures than in the Congress of the United States. This argument is supplemented by others, based on the "proper structure of the Union"—deliberative representation, separation of powers, and checks and balances—that also suggest that the federal government is a superior protector of rights. Here I shall concentrate on the argument from the "extent . . . of the Union." Madison's argument blunted the anti-federalists' appeal to state sovereignty as the guarantor of liberty. It was, however, only partially successful. Why?

Modern public choice theory has cast some doubt on elements of Madison's theory. In particular, Madison's assumption that the possibility of minority tyranny is neutralized by majority vote requirements and that minority factions are inherently vulnerable to majority tyranny is undermined by studies showing that a small, cohesive faction intensely interested in a particular outcome can exercise disproportionate influence in the political arena. Madison underestimated both the dangers of minority rule and the defensive resources of minority groups. Moreover, some observers have suggested that the conditions of modern federal politics—especially the balkanized, issue-oriented conjunction of bureaucratic agencies and committee staffs—is especially susceptible to factional politics. Professor Richard Stewart has dubbed the result "Madison's Nightmare." Proponents of greater state sovereignty in 1787-89 may have been rightly skeptical of Madison's claims that there would be less danger of factional oppression at the federal level.

But even taking Madison's fundamental insight as correct—and surely it has much to commend it—the argument on its own terms cautions against total centralization of authority in Washington. It points instead to a hybrid system in which states retain a major role in the protection of individual liberties. There are three basic reasons.

1. Liberty through mobility. Madison's argument demonstrates that factional oppression is more likely to occur in the smaller, more homogenous jurisdictions of individual states. But it does not deny that oppression at the federal level, when it occurs, is more dangerous. The lesser likelihood must be balanced against the greater magnitude of the danger. The main reason oppression at the federal level is more dangerous is that it is more difficult to escape. If a single state chose, for example, to prohibit divorce, couples seeking a divorce could move (or perhaps merely travel) to other states where their desires can be fulfilled. Oppressive measures at the state level are easier to avoid. Important recent examples of this phenomenon are the migration of homosexuals to cities like San Francisco, where they received official toleration, and the migration of individuals from Massachusetts to New Hampshire to escape high rates of taxation. A more contentious example is the regulation of abortion. If the power to regulate abortion is returned to the states, there is little likelihood of effective enforcement of anti-abortion laws, since permissive jurisdictions would attract business from more restrictive states. On the other hand, a nationwide rule—either voted by Congress or adopted by the courts as a construction of the due process clause—would have far more dramatic consequences.

2. Self-interested government. Madison held that there are two different and distinct dangers inherent in republican government: the "oppression of [the] . . . rulers" and the "injustice" of "one part of the society against . . . the other part." The first concern is that government officials will rule in their own interest instead of the interest of the people. The second is that some persons, organized in factions, will use the governmental powers to oppress others. Significantly, while Madison argued that the danger of faction is best met at the federal level (for the reasons summarized above), he conceded that the danger of self-interested representation is best tackled at the state level. "As in too small a sphere oppressive combinations may be too easily formed ag[ainst] the weaker party; so in too extensive a one, a defensive concert may be rendered too difficult against the oppression of those entrusted with the administration." Consequently, while powers most likely to be abused for factional advantage ought to be vested in the federal government, powers that are most likely to be abused by self-aggrandizing officials should be left in the states, where direct popular control is stronger.

3. Diffusion of power. Madison himself did not view his argument as establishing the superiority of a consolidated national government; rather, he presented his famous argument about the tyranny of factions in favor of the intermediate,

federalist solution of dual sovereignty. In Federalist 51, he underscored that "the rights of the people" are best protected in a system in which "two distinct governments," federal and state, "will control each other." The diffusion of power, in and of itself, is protective of liberty. In Tocqueville's evocative words, "Municipal bodies and county administrations are like so many hidden reefs retarding or dividing the flood of the popular will."

. . . [T]he framers of the Constitution and Bill of Rights believed that state governments were, in some vital respects, safer repositories of power over individual liberties than the federal government. It is thus no accident that the "police power"—the protection of public health, safety, and morals—was left to the states, with the federal government entrusted with less sensitive powers like those over interstate and foreign commerce. As Berger comments, "Moral issues . . . are best left to the States, precisely as the Founders intended" (p.146). Given the diversity of views about issues of morality, and the potential for oppression, it is natural that lovers of liberty would be inclined toward decentralized decision making.

At this point, an important qualification is in order. The arguments from the "public good" and from "private rights" make sense only if one presupposes that the decision in question is appropriate to democratic decision making at some level, be it state or federal. Some issues are so fundamental to basic justice that they must be taken out of majoritarian control altogether. This is why both state and federal governments are prohibited, for example, from passing ex post facto laws and bills of attainder. These issues are thus subject to a single national rule; the reason, however, has nothing to do with federalism. Federalism is a system for allocation of democratic decision making

power. For those few but important matters on which democracy itself cannot be trusted, neither the "public good" nor the "private rights" argument for state autonomy can hold sway.

C. TO PRESERVE "THE SPIRIT AND FORM OF POPULAR GOVERNMENT"

It was an article of faith among advocates of state autonomy that republicanism could survive only in a small jurisdiction. As stated by the prominent anti-federalist essayist, "Brutus," "a free republic cannot succeed over a country of such immense extent, containing such a number of inhabitants, and these increasing in such rapid progression as that of the whole United States." They believed consolidated national government would lead to aristocratic or despotic rule. Their reasons may be reduced to three major themes: (1) enforcement of laws, (2) nature of representation, and (3) cultivation of public spiritedness.

1. *Enforcement of laws.* Obedience to the law can arise from two different sources: fear of punishment and voluntary compliance. A republican government, which has a minimal coercive apparatus, must rely predominantly upon the latter. As Brutus explained, in a free republic "the government must rest for its support upon the confidence and respect which the people have for their government and laws." To the advocates of decentralized government, this necessarily implied that the units of government must be small and close to the people. . . .

2. *Nature of representation.* One of the principal arguments for substantial state autonomy was that representatives in a smaller unit of government will be closer to the people. Patrick Henry, for example, warned in the Virginia ratifying

convention that "throwing the country into large districts . . . will destroy that connection that ought to subsist between the electors and the elected." Assuming representative bodies of roughly the same number, any given representative will have fewer constituents and a smaller district at the state or local level. Each citizen's influence on his representative, therefore, will be proportionately greater, and geographically concentrated minorities are more likely to achieve representation.

Because federal electoral districts must of necessity be larger and more populous, representation is likely to be skewed in favor of the well-known few—what were known at the time as the "aristocratic" element. The Federal Farmer argued that increasing the number of representatives would make the nation "more democratical and secure, strengthen the confidence of the people in it, and thereby render it more nervous and energetic." However, the sheer size of the United States makes it impossible to increase the number of representatives sufficiently, without turning the Congress into what Madison called "the confusion of a multitude." . . .

3. Public spiritedness. Critics of governmental centralization warned that public spiritedness—then called "public virtue"—could be cultivated only in a republic of small dimensions. Republicanism, it was thought, depended to an extraordinary degree on the willingness of each citizen to submerge his own passions and interests for the common good. The only substitute for public virtue was an unacceptable degree of coercion, compatible only with nonrepublican forms of government.

There were two reasons to believe that a centralized government would undermine republican virtue. First, public spiritedness is a product of participation in deliberation over the public good. If the citizens are actively engaged in the public debate they will have more of a stake in the community. The federal government is too distant and its compass too vast to permit extensive participation by ordinary citizens in its policy formulations. By necessity, decision making will be delegated to agents. But as they are cut off from active participation in the commonwealth, the citizens will become less attached to it and more inclined to attend to their private affairs.

Second, the natural sentiment of benevolence, which lies at the heart of public spiritedness, is weaker as the distance grows between the individual and the objects of benevolence. An individual is most likely to sacrifice his private interests for the good of his family, and then for his neighbors and, by extension, his community. He is unlikely to place great weight upon the well-being of strangers hundreds of miles away. It is unlikely, therefore, that citizens of a nation as large as the United States will assume an attitude of republican virtue toward national affairs . . . .

K a t h l e e n   M .   S u l l i v a n

FROM STATES' RIGHTS BLUES TO BLUE STATES' RIGHTS: FEDERALISM AFTER THE REHNQUIST COURT

75 Fordham L. Rev. 799 (2006)

The Rehnquist Court dramatically revived the structural principles of federalism as grounds for judicial invalidation of statutes. For most of the twentieth century, the federal and state governments had been left to bargain or fight over their relationship in the realm of politics. The Rehnquist Court, by contrast, increasingly held that this relationship was a matter to be refereed in the courts. The Court grounded this approach in the history of the Founding: "Dual sovereignty is a defining feature of our Nation's constitutional blueprint. States, upon ratification of the Constitution, did not consent to become mere appendages of the Federal Government. Rather, they entered the Union with their sovereignty intact." In addition, the Court suggested that this relationship required judicial protection, not mere political self-help: "Federalism was our Nation's own discovery. The Framers split the atom of sovereignty. It was the genius of their idea that our citizens would have two political capacities, one state and one federal, each protected from incursion by the other."

For the most part, the Rehnquist Court's federalist revival restrained the federal government from incursion upon the states. In some lines of decision, the Court held that Congress had exceeded the scope of its powers. In others, it held that a federal law had wrongly intruded upon the sovereign autonomy of the states. Whether enforcing such internal or external limits on federal power, the Rehnquist Court took significant steps to rebalance power between the state and federal governments. The Court revived normative arguments for self-rule at more local levels of government and found textual and structural bases for vindicating such arguments against assertions of federal power that had gone unchallenged for decades.

Did these decisions establish a new constitutional order for federalism? . . . Any such extreme picture . . . is overstated. The Rehnquist Court surely revived the structural principles of federalism. But it maintained certain striking limits that kept these principles from bringing about a greater sea change in constitutional law. The Court did more to change the constitutional jurisprudence of federalism than it did to realign actual constitutional power. The question for the future is how much generative power this jurisprudence will have, for blue states and red states alike.

Even if the Rehnquist Court's federalism decisions did not shift power from the federal government to the states as dramatically as some have suggested, those decisions articulated a powerful set of constitutional ideals and principles supporting checks on federal incursions into state self-rule. . . . [T]his new jurisprudence . . . has the capacity to transcend traditional political alignments. States' rights have been associated historically with conservative causes, while federal power has been associated with increasing egalitarianism and protection of minorities from Reconstruction through the New Deal and the Civil Rights Acts of the 1960s. But now that federal power in all three branches has been consolidated in Republican hands to the greatest extent since 1954, champions of liberal causes might need to rethink any reflexive recoil from federalism. Gay weddings in San Francisco and Massachusetts, like popular initiatives authorizing physician-assisted suicide in Oregon and medicinal use of marijuana in California, exemplify recent progressive experimentation at the local level through policies that could not command a national majority. Under such political circumstances, liberals should hesitate before rejecting the Rehnquist Court's New Federalism. It might well contain seeds of a constitutional concept of social fluidity that can help to realize progressive as well as conservative ideals.

The first line of cases reintroduced, for the first time since the New Deal, judicial enforcement of the limits of power granted to Congress by the Commerce Clause. In *United States v. Lopez*, the Court invalidated a federal criminal prohibition on gun possession within the vicinity of a school, reasoning that gun possession, standing alone, does not have a substantial effect on interstate commerce. In *United States v. Morrison*, the Court invalidated the civil damages provisions of the federal Violence Against Women Act, reasoning that acts such as date rape or domestic battery are not economic activities with a substantial effect on interstate commerce. Both decisions declined to defer to congressional conclusions—in *Morrison*, conclusions based on quite extensive congressional factual findings—that a regulated activity has a substantial effect on interstate commerce.

These decisions signaled the end to an anything-goes approach to congressional commerce power, reviving the theory that enumeration of powers in Article I is a structural principle warranting judicial intervention to constrain federal overreaching. These striking new constraints on the federal commerce power, however, reached their outer limit in *Gonzalez v. Raich*, which upheld the application of federal controlled substance laws to the consumption of home-grown marijuana, despite California's efforts by popular initiative to allow such consumption for medicinal purposes. The majority reasoned that the principles of federalism did not compel an exemption from federal law, even for wholly intrastate activities expressly sanctioned by a state's government, so long as a product grown and consumed locally is fungible with products sold on interstate markets and the overall congressional scheme aims at activity that might be thought to have

a substantial effect on interstate commerce. Only three Justices from the *Lopez* and *Morrison* majorities stuck to their federalist guns, arguing in dissent that the Court's capacious conception of federal power over economic activities might well swallow up such wholly local activities as quilting bees.

. . . [Another] line of Rehnquist Court cases advanced federalism by limiting the federal government's ability to commandeer state officers and legislatures to serve federal ends. In *Printz v. United States*, the Court extended this holding to limit federal intrusion into state enforcement as well as enactment of law, invalidating portions of the Brady Handgun Violence Prevention Act that had required sheriffs and other local law enforcement officials to carry out federally mandated background checks on handgun purchasers.

But the Rehnquist Court's federalist revival was not as sweeping as it might appear. As described above, the Court set forth limiting principles to each of these lines. Even more important, the Court declined to go down four roads that would have pushed its New Federalism much further—despite having the apparent capacity to round up five votes to do so.

First, the Rehnquist Court never brought back the short-lived principle, set forth in 1976 in *National League of Cities v. Usery*, that there are some areas of reserved state autonomy over traditional and integral governmental functions that are absolutely immunized from federal control. *National League* was explicitly overruled a decade later by *Garcia v. San Antonio Metropolitan Transit Authority*. The bitter dissents in *Garcia* suggested that time and actuarial tables were on the side of the federalists. But Chief Justice William Rehnquist never cobbled a majority to bring back the federalist jurisprudence of *National League*, even though Presidents Ronald Reagan and George W. Bush added five new Justices to the Court, replacing most of the *Garcia* majority.

The failure to revive *National League* arguably renders the *Lopez* line of cases somewhat trivial. The majority opinion in *Lopez* spoke of criminal law, education, and family law as areas traditionally regulated by the states, suggesting a faint echo of *National League*'s notion of state islands in the stream of commerce. But if a traditional state activity does not enjoy affirmative immunity from congressional regulation, then the Rehnquist Court's internal limits on Congress's commerce power will provide thin constraint; it is a relatively small trick for Congress to make adequate findings that such an activity has a substantial effect on interstate commerce. If there is any doubt, Congress may simply employ an express jurisdictional nexus.

Second, the Rehnquist Court did not overrule *South Dakota v. Dole*, which held that Congress could condition federal highway funding for the states on their raising their minimum drinking age to twenty-one. The *Dole* decision takes a broad view of Congress's ability to use its spending power as leverage to obtain state commitments to regulation that Congress could not impose directly. The Court assumed that the Twenty-First Amendment, which preserves some measure of state autonomy over alcohol traffic, precluded Congress from directly imposing such a federal regulation in this area. It also assumed that if the drinking-age requirement were not germane to the purpose of highway funding, the federal law would impose an unconstitutional condition. But the Court found teenage alcohol sales germane enough to highway funding to surmount the unconstitutional

conditions problem, finding a sufficient nexus because, after all, teenage alcohol sales can cause drunk driving and drunk driving can cause damage to and require emergency services on the roads. Thus, spending conditions need only meet the most lenient test of rationality.

The failure to overrule *Dole* arguably renders trivial the . . . line of [commandeering] cases. Given the massive scale of federal spending and the large percentage of state budgets that depend upon federal subsidies, Congress has considerable leverage over the states through spending conditions. If, with little judicial oversight, Congress may bribe the states into enacting the very regulatory programs that Congress may not commandeer the states into enacting or enforcing, then the anti-commandeering cases can do little as a practical matter to shift power from the federal government to the states.

The Rehnquist Court's federalism revival was theoretically deep even if practically limited. The Rehnquist Court's federalism decisions suggested two principal theoretical bases for devolving greater power to local levels of government, one deontological and the other utilitarian. The first, deontological justification for federalism emphasizes self-rule: the notion of giving government to oneself. On this view, it is immoral to cede self-government to a distant bureaucrat in a remote capital rather than engaging in self-government alongside nearby neighbors. This position implies a default rule in favor of local power and requires very strong justifications for federal intervention.

The second justification, based on utilitarianism, takes the view that different levels of government have different expertise and competence in serving the general welfare. States are better at solving some and the nation better at solving other local and national problems. For example, the federal government can correct market failures that defy state control, such as regulating externalities like pollution that cross over state borders, providing public goods like national defense that would have free-rider problems if provided by the states, preventing races to the bottom that would occur if the states were left to compete among themselves on labor or welfare legislation, or providing a larger insurance pool for disasters such as earthquakes and hurricanes that would swamp local resources. On this view, state governments will be better at just about everything else because they are more efficient, more flexible given their smaller scale, and more responsive to problems that differ across localities. This justification applies a view of federalism that entrusts neutral technocratic expertise to make utilitarian judgments about which level of government has greater comparative advantage at solving different problems.

There is a third theoretical justification for federalism that is not well developed in the Rehnquist Court cases, but that might well be desirable to elaborate going forward, especially by those favoring liberal causes. This theory sees federalism as one among many guarantees in the Constitution facilitating social fluidity, and preventing the entrenchment of individual identity. On this theory, liberals should stop singing the states' rights blues and begin embracing blue states' rights.

This is so because the traditional federalism paradigm has been inverted by the entrenchment of Republican dominance of all three branches of government over the last six years. Under the traditional structural paradigm, liberals favor federal government while conservatives favor government by the states. On this view, liberals view the federal government as

an efficient means to correct market failures (as in the New Deal) and a just means to correct local tyranny (as in the Civil Rights Acts). At the same time, liberals traditionally view the states as backwaters of tyranny and discrimination epitomized by Jim Crow laws and continued resistance to desegregation in the South. On this traditional view, liberals endorse expansive views of federal governmental power and close checks on local options for the states. Conversely, under the traditional paradigm, conservatives view "big government" as the enemy, and the federal government as presumptively inefficient and unjust, stifling libertarian initiative and small business under a massive code of environmental, consumer protection, labor, and safety regulations. State governments, by contrast, traditionally appear to conservatives both more efficient and more responsive to the people, justifying, for example, the switch to block grants rather than formula grants to states during the Nixon and Reagan Administrations.

But once the Republican Party obtained simultaneous control of the White House, House, and Senate for the first time since 1954, local and state initiatives began to do more than federal programs to advance progressive social ends. Gay weddings took place through the executive action of Mayor Gavin Newsom of San Francisco and the state constitutional interpretation of Chief Justice Margaret Marshall writing for the Massachusetts Supreme Judicial Court. Oregon pioneered physician-assisted suicide while California experimented with allowing severely ill patients to use marijuana medicinally. Suddenly states' rights were no longer just for segregationist southerners. Conversely, conservatives have sought to transform entrenched control of the federal government into nationwide social restrictions—from regulating late-term abortion to limiting stem-cell research—that were once unthinkable at the federal level.

Against this backdrop, it is promising to articulate a third possible normative premise for federalism—one rooted in a larger constitutional norm of social fluidity. Social fluidity assumes that each individual has the freedom to shape and change identity without entrenchment into any fixed class, caste, nationality, religion, race, or locality. Our nation's lack of such entrenched national, tribal, or sectarian identity separates us from such balkanized societies as Belfast, Belgrade, and Beirut, in which national or religious identity determines all of one's social, economic, familial, and residential relationships.

The original Constitution contains a number of provisions that support this notion of social fluidity and that resist entrenchment of identity into fixed silos that go all the way down, constraining citizens within one group. The Establishment Clause forbids any national union of church and state. The Titles of Nobility Clause forbids the establishment of any aristocratic caste. In addition, the modern First Amendment has been held to imply a freedom of association that helps formalize Alexis de Tocqueville's observation that early nineteenth-century America had substituted ever-changing voluntary associations for fixed medieval hierarchies of guild and caste. If the Boy Scouts exclude someone for reason of sexual orientation, then there remains the option to start an alternative Boy Scouts instead. Another aspect of social fluidity is physical mobility. The right to migrate among the states, which itself migrated around the Constitution before the Court found a home for it in the Citizenship Clause, guarantees free movement across state boundaries without penalty for relocation or recency of state citizenship.

Federalism, by providing exit options from local repression, provides similar support to this crosscutting constitutional commitment to social fluidity. On this view, the answer to local prejudice is exit; a gay person inhibited by pre-*Lawrence v. Texas* Wyoming laws and social norms in a rural locale has the freedom to move to more welcoming urban environments. Federalism provides an opportunity for socially fluid self-definition according to each locality's different legislative and cultural environment. Such local norms provide an opportunity for self-definition and redefinition until a national consensus forms to extend any one local norm more universally.

This view of federalism as worthy of judicial protection to facilitate social fluidity is subject to several criticisms. First, it requires a presumption of strong judicial enforcement to maintain state and local autonomy from federal prohibitions on such activities as gay marriage and stem-cell research that fall outside the main purview of regulating the national market. This cannot please those who favor leaving issues of structure to the political safeguards of federalism. Second, by allowing economic decisions to be made at the national level while social decisions are made at the state level, such a view of federalism might seem to thwart decentralized economic policies that might allow for progressive local environmental, labor, antitakeover, and other laws. While such concepts of local economic rule might well be intuitively appealing, they also seem quixotic given the interconnectedness of a globalized economy. Third, some people will have more mobility than others to migrate across the lines that divide red and blue states—consider the gay cowboy who cannot leave Wyoming because ranching is the only job he knows and he has child support obligations, or the teenager in Montana for whom there is no in-state abortion provider. Where such constraints are present, federalism might appear to maroon some unlucky individuals in distinctly un-fluid backwaters. The only correction in such situations can be the national protection of individual rights through federal judicial decision or congressional exercise of Fourteenth Amendment enforcement powers. But there is reason to believe that federalist experimentation at the local level will help promote the ultimate spread of such norms. Massachusetts, for example, having launched an experiment in allowing gay marriage, declined the first legislative opportunity to roll back that experiment, apparently finding the effects of the experiment more salutary than pernicious.

The Rehnquist Court's revival of the structural principles of federalism has been unfairly maligned as an opportunistic vehicle for freeing gun-toters, wife-beaters, and other bigots from desirable federal laws. Under entrenched conservative dominance of all three branches of the federal government, however, federalism is better seen as protecting blue states and red states alike—that is, as a potential device for protecting progressive state and local experiments that advance the ends of liberty and equality. The Rehnquist Court did less than is often supposed to redistribute political power from the federal government to the states; its federalism decisions were qualified on their own terms and never reached as far as they might have. The Rehnquist Court did more than is often supposed, however, to redevelop the political theory of federalism, and to remind us of our more overarching constitutional commitments to social fluidity.

NATIONAL LEAGUE OF CITIES v. USERY
426 U.S. 833 (1976)

Opinion: Rehnquist, joined by Burger, Stewart, Powell
Concurrence: Blackmun
Dissent: Brennan, joined by White, Marshall
Dissent: Stevens

One clear lesson from the above readings is that the principle of federalism is an important structural feature of American constitutional government. The key question we must ask is whether this principle is compatible with Congress's power to regulate the national economy. Is there an upper boundary to the commerce power? If so, where might we draw the line? One possibility is

to say that the federal government lacks the power to regulate how sovereign states conduct their internal and administrative affairs in their capacity as employers. If the Tenth Amendment secures some kind of special autonomy for states, perhaps they are immune from the same kinds of regulations that bind ordinary employers in the national economy.

In National League of Cities v. Usery, the Court considered whether state employees were not subject to regulation because of the constitutional relationship between states and the national government. In particular, you should ask whether the Tenth Amendment requires the national government to defer to the states in matters concerning their own employees. Moreover, you should ask whether this decision begins to limit some of the federal power that we saw expanded during and after the New Deal in the previous section. In particular, how does this decision relate to the Court's decision in United States v. Darby *that the Fair Labor Standards Act (FLSA) was constitutional? In then-Associate Justice William Rehnquist's opinion for the Court he wrote, "FLSA . . . would interfere with traditional aspects of state sovereignty." Do you agree?*

MR. JUSTICE REHNQUIST *delivered the opinion of the Court.*

Appellee Secretary argues that the cases in which this Court has upheld sweeping exercises of authority by Congress, even though those exercises preempted state regulation of the private sector, have already curtailed the sovereignty of the States quite as much as the 1974 amendments to the Fair Labor Standards Act. We do not agree. It is one thing to recognize the authority of Congress to enact laws regulating individual businesses necessarily subject to the dual sovereignty of the government of the Nation and of the State in which they reside. It is quite another to uphold a similar exercise of congressional authority directed not to private citizens, but to the States as States. We have repeatedly recognized that there are attributes of sovereignty attaching to every state government which may not be impaired by Congress, not because Congress may lack an affirmative grant of legislative authority to reach the matter, but because the Constitution prohibits it from exercising the authority in that manner. In *Coyle v Oklahoma*, the Court gave this example of such an attribute:

> The power to locate its own seat of government and to determine when and how it shall be changed from one place to another,

and to appropriate its own public funds for that purpose, are essentially and peculiarly state powers. That one of the original thirteen States could now be shorn of such powers by an act of Congress would not be for a moment entertained.

Id. at 565.

One undoubted attribute of state sovereignty is the States' power to determine the wages which shall be paid to those whom they employ in order to carry out their governmental functions, what hours those persons will work, and what compensation will be provided where these employees may be called upon to work overtime. The question we must resolve here, then, is whether these determinations are "functions essential to separate and independent existence," *id.* at 580, quoting from *Lane County v. Oregon, supra*, at 76, so that Congress may not abrogate the States' otherwise plenary authority to make them.

In their complaint, appellants advanced estimates of substantial costs which will be imposed upon them by the 1974 amendments. Since the District Court dismissed their complaint, we take its well pleaded allegations as true, although it appears from appellee's submissions in the District Court and in this Court that resolution of the factual disputes as to the effect of the amendments is not critical to our disposition of the case.

Judged solely in terms of increased costs in dollars, these allegation show a significant impact on the functioning of the governmental bodies involved. The Metropolitan Government of Nashville and Davidson County, Tenn., for example, asserted that the Act will increase its costs of providing essential police and fire protection, without any increase in service or in current salary levels, by $938,000 per year. Cape Girardeau, Mo., estimated that its annual budget for fire protection may have to be increased by anywhere from

$250,000 to $400,000 over the current figure of $350,000. The State of Arizona alleged that the annual additional expenditures which will be required if it is to continue to provide essential state services may total $2.5 million. The State of California, which must devote significant portions of its budget to fire suppression endeavors, estimated that application of the Act to its employment practices will necessitate an increase in its budget of between $8 million and $16 million.

Increased costs are not, of course, the only adverse effects which compliance with the Act will visit upon state and local governments, and, in turn, upon the citizens who depend upon those governments. In its complaint in intervention, for example, California asserted that it could not comply with the overtime costs (approximately $750,000 per year) which the Act required to be paid to California Highway Patrol cadets during their academy training program. California reported that it had thus been forced to reduce its academy training program from 2,080 hours to only 960 hours, a compromise undoubtedly of substantial importance to those whose safety and welfare may depend upon the preparedness of the California Highway Patrol.

This type of forced relinquishment of important governmental activities is further reflected in the complaint's allegation that the city of Inglewood, Cal., has been forced to curtail its affirmative action program for providing employment opportunities for men and women interested in a career in law enforcement. The Inglewood police department has abolished a program for police trainees who split their week between on-the-job training and the classroom. The city could not abrogate its contractual obligations to these trainees, and it concluded that compliance with the Act in these circumstances was too financially burdensome to permit continuance of the classroom program. The city of Clovis, Cal., has been put to a similar choice regarding an internship program it was running in cooperation with a California State university. According to the complaint, because the interns' compensation brings them within the purview of the Act, the city must decide whether to eliminate the program entirely or to substantially reduce its beneficial aspects by doing away with any pay for the interns.

Quite apart from the substantial costs imposed upon the States and their political subdivisions, the Act displaces state policies regarding the manner in which they will structure delivery of those governmental services which their citizens require. The Act, speaking directly to the States *qua* States, requires that they shall pay all but an extremely limited minority of their employee the minimum wage rate currently chosen by Congress. It may well be that, as a matter of economic policy, it would be desirable that States, just as private employers, comply with these minimum wage requirement. But it cannot be gainsaid that the federal requirement directly supplant the considered policy choice of the States' elected officials and administrator as to how they wish to structure pay scale in state employment. The State might wish to employ persons with little or no training, or those who wish to work on a casual basis, or those who, for some other reason, do not possess minimum employment requirements, and pay them less than the federally prescribed minimum wage. It may wish to offer part-time or summer employment to teenagers at a figure less than the minimum wage, and, if unable to do so, may decline to offer such employment at all. But the Act would forbid such choice by the States. The only "discretion" left to them under the Act is either to attempt to increase their revenue to meet the additional financial burden imposed upon them by paying congressionally prescribed wages to their existing complement of employees or to reduce that complement to a number which can be paid the federal minimum wage without increasing revenue.

This dilemma presented by the minimum wage restriction may seem not immediately different from that faced by private employers, who have long been covered by the Act and who must find ways to increase their gross income if they are to pay higher wages while maintaining current earnings. The difference, however, is that a State is not merely a factor in the "shifting economic arrangements" of the private sector of the economy, *Kovacs v. Cooper* (Frankfurter, J., concurring), but is itself a coordinate element in the system established by the Framers for governing our Federal Union.

The degree to which the FLSA amendments would interfere with traditional aspects of state sovereignty can be seen even more clearly upon examining the overtime requirements of the Act. The general effect of these provisions is to require the States to pay their employees at premium rates whenever their work exceeds a specified number of hours in a given period. The asserted reason for these provisions is to provide a financial disincentive upon using employees beyond the work period deemed appropriate by Congress. According to appellee:

> This premium rate can be avoided if the [State] uses other employees to do the overtime work. This, in effect, tends to discourage overtime work and to spread employment, which is the result Congress intended.

Brief for Appellee 43. We do not doubt that this may be a salutary result, and that it has a sufficiently rational relationship to commerce to validate the application of the overtime provisions to private employers. But, like the minimum wage provisions, the vice of the Act as sought to be applied here is that it directly penalizes the States

for choosing to hire governmental employees on terms different from those which Congress has sought to impose.

This congressionally imposed displacement of state decisions may substantially restructure traditional ways in which the local governments have arranged their affairs. Although, at this point, many of the actual effects under the proposed amendments remain a matter of some dispute among the parties, enough can be satisfactorily anticipated for an outline discussion of their general import. The requirement imposing premium rates upon any employment in excess of what Congress has decided is appropriate for a governmental employee's workweek, for example, appears likely to have the effect of coercing the States to structure work periods in some employment areas, such as police and fire protection, in a manner substantially different from practices which have long been commonly accepted among local governments of this Nation. In addition, appellee represents that the Act will require that the premium compensation for overtime worked must be paid in cash, rather than with compensatory time off, unless such compensatory time is taken in the same pay period. Supplemental Brief for Appellee 9-10; *see Dunlop v. New Jersey, cert. pending sub nom. New Jersey v. Usery,* No. 75-532. This, too, appears likely to be highly disruptive of accepted employment practices in many governmental areas where the demand for a number of employees to perform important jobs for extended periods on short notice can be both unpredictable and critical. Another example of congressional choices displacing those of the States in the area of what are, without doubt, essential governmental decisions may be found in the practice of using volunteer firemen, a source of manpower crucial to many of our smaller towns' existence. Under the regulations proposed by appellee, whether individuals are indeed "volunteers" rather than "employees" subject to the minimum wage provisions of the Act are questions to be decided in the courts. *See* Brief for Appellee 49, and n. 41. It goes without saying that provisions such as these contemplate a significant reduction of traditional volunteer assistance which has been, in the past, drawn on to complement the operation of many local governmental functions.

Our examination of the effect of the 1974 amendments, as sought to be extended to the States and their political subdivisions, satisfies us that both the minimum wage and the maximum hour provisions will impermissibly interfere with the integral governmental functions of these bodies. We earlier noted some disagreement between the parties regarding the precise effect the amendments will have in application. We do not believe particularized assessments of actual impact are crucial to resolution of the issue presented, however. For even if we accept appellee's assessments concerning the impact of the amendments, their application will nonetheless significantly alter or displace the States' abilities to structure employer employee relationships in such areas as fire prevention, police protection, sanitation, public health, and parks and recreation. These activities are typical of those performed by state and local governments in discharging their dual functions of administering the public law and furnishing public services. Indeed, it is functions such as these which governments are created to provide, services such as these which the States have traditionally afforded their citizens. If Congress may withdraw from the States the authority to make those fundamental employment decisions upon which their systems for performance of these functions must rest, we think there would be little left of the States' "separate and independent existence." *Coyle.* Thus, even if appellants may have overestimated the effect which the Act will have upon their current levels and patterns of governmental activity, the dispositive factor is that Congress has attempted to exercise its Commerce Clause authority to prescribe minimum wages and maximum hours to be paid by the States in their capacities as sovereign governments. In so doing, Congress has sought to wield its power in a fashion that would impair the States' "ability to function effectively in a federal system." *Fry.* This exercise of congressional authority does not comport with the federal system of government embodied in the Constitution. We hold that, insofar as the challenged amendments operate to directly displace the States' freedom to structure integral operations in areas of traditional governmental functions, they are not within the authority granted Congress by Art. I, §8, cl. 3.

GARCIA v. SAN ANTONIO METROPOLITAN TRANSIT AUTHORITY

469 U.S. 528 (1985)

Opinion: Blackmun, joined by Brennan, White, Marshall, Stevens
Dissent: Powell, joined by Burger, Rehnquist, O'Connor
Dissent: Rehnquist
Dissent: O'Connor, joined by Rehnquist, Powell

Nine years after National League of Cities v. Usery, *U.S. Supreme Court Justice Harry Blackmun changed his vote to overturn that precedent in* Garcia v. San Antonio Metropolitan Transit Authority. *Is Justice Blackmun right that it is unworkable to distinguish between ordinary economic activity by states' governments and whatever activity reflects their special status as sovereigns?*

JUSTICE BLACKMUN *delivered the opinion of the Court.*

We revisit in these cases an issue raised in *National League of Cities v. Usery*. In that litigation, this Court, by a sharply divided vote, ruled that the Commerce Clause does not empower Congress to enforce the minimum-wage and overtime provisions of the Fair Labor Standards Act (FLSA) against the States "in areas of traditional governmental functions." Id., at 852. Although *National League of Cities* supplied some examples of "traditional governmental functions," it did not offer a general explanation of how a "traditional" function is to be distinguished from a "nontraditional" one. Since then, federal and state courts have struggled with the task, thus imposed, of identifying a traditional function for purposes of state immunity under the Commerce Clause.

In the present cases, a Federal District Court concluded that municipal ownership and operation of a mass-transit system is a traditional governmental function and thus, under *National League of Cities*, is exempt from the obligations imposed by the FLSA. Faced with the identical question, three Federal Courts of Appeals and one state appellate court have reached the opposite conclusion.

Our examination of this "function" standard applied in these and other cases over the last eight years now persuades us that the attempt to draw the boundaries of state regulatory immunity in terms of "traditional governmental function" is not only unworkable but is also inconsistent with established principles of federalism and, indeed, with those very federalism principles on which *National League of Cities* purported to rest. That case, accordingly, is overruled.

Appellees have not argued that SAMTA is immune from regulation under the FLSA on the ground that it is a local transit system engaged in intrastate commercial activity. In a practical sense, SAMTA's operations might well be characterized as "local." Nonetheless, it long has been settled that Congress' authority under the Commerce Clause extends to intrastate economic activities that affect interstate commerce. Were SAMTA a privately owned and operated enterprise, it could not credibly argue that Congress exceeded the bounds of its Commerce Clause powers in prescribing minimum wages and overtime rates for SAMTA's employees. Any constitutional exemption from the requirements of the FLSA therefore must rest on SAMTA's status as a governmental entity rather than on the "local" nature of its operations.

The prerequisites for governmental immunity under *National League of Cities* were summarized by this Court in *Hodel*. Under that summary, four conditions must be satisfied before a state activity may be deemed immune from a particular federal regulation under the Commerce Clause. First, it is said that the federal statute at issue must regulate "the 'States as States.'" Second, the statute must "address matters that are indisputably '[attributes] of state sovereignty.'" Third, state compliance with the federal obligation must "directly impair [the States'] ability 'to structure integral operations in areas of traditional governmental functions.'" Finally, the relation of state and federal interests must not be such that "the nature of the federal interest . . . justifies state submission."

Thus far, this Court itself has made little headway in defining the scope of the governmental functions deemed protected under *National League of Cities*. In that case the Court set forth examples of protected and unprotected functions, but provided no explanation of how those examples were identified. . . .

Many constitutional standards involve "[undoubted] . . . gray areas," and, despite the difficulties that this Court and other courts have encountered so far, it normally might be fair to venture the assumption that case-by-case development would lead to a workable standard for determining whether a particular governmental function should be immune from federal regulation under the Commerce Clause. A further cautionary note is sounded, however, by the Court's experience in the related field of state immunity from federal taxation. . . . If these tax-immunity cases had any common thread, it was in the attempt to distinguish between "governmental" and "proprietary" functions. . . .

The distinction the Court discarded as unworkable in the field of tax immunity has proved no more fruitful in the field of regulatory immunity under the Commerce Clause. Neither do any of the alternative standards that might be employed to distinguish between protected and unprotected governmental functions appear manageable. We rejected the possibility of making immunity turn on a purely historical standard of "tradition" in Long Island, and properly so. The most obvious defect of a historical approach to state immunity is that it prevents a court from accommodating changes in the historical functions of States, changes that have resulted in a number of once-private functions like education being assumed by the States and their subdivisions. At the same time, the only apparent virtue of a rigorous historical standard, namely, its promise of a reasonably objective measure for state immunity, is illusory. Reliance on history as an organizing principle results in line-drawing of the most arbitrary sort; the genesis of state governmental functions stretches over a historical continuum from before

the Revolution to the present, and courts would have to decide by fiat precisely how longstanding a pattern of state involvement had to be for federal regulatory authority to be defeated.

A nonhistorical standard for selecting immune governmental functions is likely to be just as unworkable as is a historical standard. The goal of identifying "uniquely" governmental functions, for example, has been rejected by the Court in the field of government tort liability in part because the notion of a "uniquely" governmental function is unmanageable. Another possibility would be to confine immunity to "necessary" governmental services, that is, services that would be provided inadequately or not at all unless the government provided them. The set of services that fits into this category, however, may well be negligible. The fact that an unregulated market produces less of some service than a State deems desirable does not mean that the State itself must provide the service; in most if not all cases, the State can "contract out" by hiring private firms to provide the service or simply by providing subsidies to existing suppliers. It also is open to question how well equipped courts are to make this kind of determination about the workings of economic markets.

We believe, however, that there is a more fundamental problem at work here, a problem that explains why the Court was never able to provide a basis for the governmental/proprietary distinction in the intergovernmental tax-immunity cases and why an attempt to draw similar distinctions with respect to federal regulatory authority under *National League of Cities* is unlikely to succeed regardless of how the distinctions are phrased. The problem is that neither the governmental/proprietary distinction nor any other that purports to separate out important governmental functions can be faithful to the role of federalism in a democratic society. The essence of our federal system is that within the realm of authority left open to them under the Constitution, the States must be equally free to engage in any activity that their citizens choose for the common weal, no matter how unorthodox or unnecessary anyone else—including the judiciary—deems state involvement to be. Any rule of state immunity that looks to the "traditional," "integral," or "necessary" nature of governmental functions inevitably invites an unelected federal judiciary to make decisions about which state policies it favors and which ones it dislikes. "The science of government . . . is the science of experiment," and the States cannot serve as laboratories for social and economic experiment if they must pay an added price when they meet the changing needs of their citizenry by taking up functions that an earlier day and a different society left in private hands. In the words of Justice Black:

> "There is not, and there cannot be, any unchanging line of demarcation between essential and non-essential governmental functions. Many governmental functions of today have at some time in the past been non-governmental. The genius of our government provides that, within the sphere of constitutional action, the people—acting not through the courts but through their elected legislative representatives—have the power to determine as conditions demand, what services and functions the public welfare requires."

We therefore now reject, as unsound in principle and unworkable in practice, a rule of state immunity from federal regulation that turns on a judicial appraisal of whether a particular governmental function is "integral" or "traditional." Any such rule leads to inconsistent results at the same time that it disserves principles of democratic self-governance, and it breeds inconsistency precisely because it is divorced from those principles. If there are to be limits on the Federal Government's power to interfere with state functions—as undoubtedly there are—we must look elsewhere to find them. We accordingly return to the underlying issue that confronted this Court in *National League of Cities*—the manner in which the Constitution insulates States from the reach of Congress' power under the Commerce Clause.

The central theme of *National League of Cities* was that the States occupy a special position in our constitutional system and that the scope of Congress' authority under the Commerce Clause must reflect that position. Of course, the Commerce Clause by its specific language does not provide any special limitation on Congress' actions with respect to the States. . . .

What has proved problematic is not the perception that the Constitution's federal structure imposes limitations on the Commerce Clause, but rather the nature and content of those limitations. One approach to defining the limits on Congress' authority to regulate the States under the Commerce Clause is to identify certain underlying elements of political sovereignty that are deemed essential to the States' "separate and independent existence." [T]he Court concluded that decisions by a State concerning the wages and hours of its employees are an "undoubted attribute of state sovereignty." . . .

We doubt that courts ultimately can identify principled constitutional limitations on the scope of Congress' Commerce Clause powers over the States merely by relying on a priori definitions of state sovereignty. In part, this is because of the elusiveness of objective criteria for "fundamental" elements of state sovereignty, a problem we have witnessed in the search for "traditional governmental functions." There is, however, a more fundamental reason: the sovereignty of the States is limited by the Constitution itself. A variety of sovereign powers, for example, are withdrawn from the States by Article I, §10. Section 8 of the same Article works an equally sharp contraction of state sovereignty by authorizing Congress to exercise a wide range of legislative powers and (in conjunction with the Supremacy Clause of Article VI) to displace contrary state legislation. By providing for final review of questions of federal law in this Court, Article III curtails the sovereign power of the States' judiciaries to make authoritative determinations of law. Finally, the developed application, through the Fourteenth Amendment, of the greater part of the Bill of Rights to the States limits the sovereign authority that States otherwise would possess to legislate with respect to their citizens and to conduct their own affairs.

The States unquestionably do "[retain] a significant measure of sovereign authority." They do so, however, only to the extent that the Constitution has not divested them of their original powers and transferred those powers to the Federal Government....

[T]he fact that the States remain sovereign as to all powers not vested in Congress or denied them by the Constitution offers no guidance about where the frontier between state and federal power lies. In short, we have no license to employ freestanding conceptions of state sovereignty when measuring congressional authority under the Commerce Clause.

Apart from the limitation on federal authority inherent in the delegated nature of Congress' Article I powers, the principal means chosen by the Framers to ensure the role of the States in the federal system lies in the structure of the Federal Government itself. It is no novelty to observe that the composition of the Federal Government was designed in large part to protect the States from overreaching by Congress. The Framers thus gave the States a role

in the selection both of the Executive and the Legislative Branches of the Federal Government. The States were vested with indirect influence over the House of Representatives and the Presidency by their control of electoral qualifications and their role in Presidential elections. They were given more direct influence in the Senate, where each State received equal representation and each Senator was to be selected by the legislature of his State. The significance attached to the States' equal representation in the Senate is underscored by the prohibition of any constitutional amendment divesting a State of equal representation without the State's consent.

[T]he Framers chose to rely on a federal system in which special restraints on federal power over the States inhered principally in the workings of the National Government itself, rather than in discrete limitations on the objects of federal authority. State sovereign interests, then, are more properly protected by procedural safeguards inherent in the structure of the federal system than by judicially created limitations on federal power.

We realize that changes in the structure of the Federal Government have taken place since 1789, not the least of which has been the substitution of popular election of Senators by the adoption of the Seventeenth Amendment in 1913, and that these changes may work to alter the influence of the States in the federal political process. Nonetheless, against this background, we are convinced that the fundamental limitation that the constitutional scheme imposes on the Commerce Clause to protect the "States as States" is one of process rather than one of result. Any substantive restraint on the exercise of Commerce Clause powers must find its justification in the procedural nature of this basic limitation, and it must be tailored to compensate for possible failings in the national political process rather than to dictate a "sacred province of state autonomy."

Insofar as the present cases are concerned, then, we need go no further than to state that we perceive nothing in the overtime and minimum-wage requirements of the FLSA, as applied to SAMTA, that is destructive of state sovereignty or violative of any constitutional provision. SAMTA faces nothing more than the same minimum-wage and overtime obligations that hundreds of thousands of other employers, public as well as private, have to meet.

JUSTICE POWELL, *with whom* **THE CHIEF JUSTICE**, **JUSTICE REHNQUIST**, *and* **JUSTICE O'CONNOR** *join, dissenting.*

The Court today, in its 5-4 decision, overrules *National League of Cities v. Usery*, a case in which we held that Congress lacked authority to impose the requirements of the Fair Labor Standards Act on state and local governments. Because I believe this decision substantially alters the federal system embodied in the Constitution, I dissent.

There are, of course, numerous examples over the history of this Court in which prior decisions have been reconsidered and overruled. There have been few cases, however, in which the principle of stare decisis and the rationale of recent decisions were ignored as abruptly as we now witness. The reasoning of the Court in *National League of Cities*, and the principle applied there, have been reiterated consistently over the past eight years. . . .

Whatever effect the Court's decision may have in weakening the application of stare decisis, it is likely to be less important than what the Court has done to the Constitution itself. A unique feature of the United States is the federal system of government guaranteed by the Constitution and implicit in the very name of our country. Despite

some genuflecting in the Court's opinion to the concept of federalism, today's decision effectively reduces the Tenth Amendment to meaningless rhetoric when Congress acts pursuant to the Commerce Clause. The Court holds that the Fair Labor Standards Act (FLSA) "contravened no affirmative limit on Congress' power under the Commerce Clause" to determine the wage rates and hours of employment of all state and local employees. . . .

To leave no doubt about its intention, the Court renounces its decision in *National League of Cities* because it "inevitably invites an unelected federal judiciary to make decisions about which state policies its favors and which ones it dislikes." In other words, the extent to which the States may exercise their authority, when Congress purports to act under the Commerce Clause, henceforth is to be determined from time to time by political decisions made by members of the Federal Government, decisions the Court says will not be subject to judicial review. I note that it does not seem to have occurred to the Court that it—an unelected majority of five Justices—today rejects almost 200 years of the understanding of the constitutional status of federalism. In doing so, there is only a single passing reference to the Tenth Amendment. Nor is so much as a dictum of any court cited in support of the view that the role of the States in the federal system may depend upon the grace of elected federal officials, rather than on the Constitution as interpreted by this Court.

The Court finds that the test of state immunity approved in *National League of Cities* and its progeny is unworkable and unsound in principle. In finding the test to be unworkable, the Court begins by mischaracterizing *National League of Cities* and subsequent cases. In concluding that efforts to define state immunity are unsound in principle, the Court radically departs from long-settled constitutional values and ignores the role of judicial review in our system of government.

Today's opinion does not explain how the States' role in the electoral process guarantees that particular exercises of the Commerce Clause power will not infringe on residual state sovereignty. Members of Congress are elected from the various States, but once in office they are Members of the Federal Government. Although the States participate in the Electoral College, this is hardly a reason to view the President as a representative of the States' interest against federal encroachment. We noted recently "[the] hydraulic pressure inherent within each of the separate Branches to exceed the outer limits of its power. . . ." *INS v. Chadha*. The Court offers no reason to think that this pressure will not operate when Congress seeks to invoke its powers under the Commerce Clause, notwithstanding the electoral role of the States.

The fact that Congress generally does not transgress constitutional limits on its power to reach state activities does not make judicial review any less necessary to rectify the cases in which it does do so. The States' role in our system of government is a matter of constitutional law, not of legislative grace. "The powers not delegated to the United States by the Constitution, nor prohibited by it to the States, are reserved to the States, respectively, or to the people."

More troubling than the logical infirmities in the Court's reasoning is the result of its holding, i.e., that federal political officials, invoking the Commerce Clause, are the sole judges of the limits of their own power. This result is inconsistent with the fundamental principles of our constitutional system. At least since *Marbury v. Madison* it has been the settled province of the federal judiciary "to say what the law is" with respect to the constitutionality of Acts of Congress. In rejecting the role of the judiciary in protecting the States from federal overreaching, the Court's opinion offers no explanation for ignoring the teaching of the most famous case in our history.

In our federal system, the States have a major role that cannot be pre-empted by the National Government. As contemporaneous writings and the debates at the ratifying conventions make clear, the States' ratification of the Constitution was predicated on this understanding of federalism. Indeed, the Tenth Amendment was adopted specifically to ensure that the important role promised the States by the proponents of the Constitution was realized.

Much of the initial opposition to the Constitution was rooted in the fear that the National Government would be too powerful and eventually would eliminate the States as viable political entities. This concern was voiced repeatedly until proponents of the Constitution made assurances that a Bill of Rights, including a provision explicitly reserving powers in the States, would be among the first business of the new Congress. . . . Antifederalists raised these concerns in almost every state ratifying convention. As a result, eight States voted for the Constitution only after proposing amendments to be adopted after ratification. All eight of these included among their recommendations some version of what later became the Tenth Amendment. So strong was the concern that the proposed Constitution was seriously defective without a specific bill of rights, including a provision reserving powers to the States, that in order to secure the votes for ratification, the Federalists eventually conceded that such provisions were necessary.

. . . Far from being "unsound in principle," . . . judicial enforcement of the Tenth Amendment is essential to maintaining the federal system so carefully designed by the Framers and adopted in the Constitution.

The Framers believed that the separate sphere of sovereignty reserved to the States would ensure that the States would serve as an effective "counterpoise" to the power of the Federal Government. The States would serve this essential role because they would attract and retain the loyalty of their citizens. The roots of such loyalty, the Founders thought, were found in the objects peculiar to state government. . . . [B]y usurping functions traditionally performed by the States, federal overreaching under the Commerce Clause undermines the constitutionally mandated balance of power between the States and the Federal Government, a balance designed to protect our fundamental liberties.

. . . [T]he Court today propounds a view of federalism that pays only lip service to the role of the States. [I]t fails to recognize the broad, yet specific areas of sovereignty that the Framers intended the States to retain. Indeed, the Court barely acknowledges that the Tenth Amendment exists. That Amendment states explicitly that "[the] powers not delegated to the United States . . . are reserved to the States." The Court recasts this language to say that the States retain their sovereign powers "only to the extent that the Constitution has not divested them of their original powers and transferred those powers to the Federal Government." This rephrasing is not a distinction without a difference; rather, it reflects the Court's unprecedented view that Congress is free under the Commerce Clause to assume a State's traditional sovereign power, and to do so without judicial review of its action. Indeed, the Court's view of federalism appears to relegate the States to precisely the trivial role that opponents of the Constitution feared they would occupy.

JUSTICE REHNQUIST, *dissenting.*

I join both Justice Powell's and Justice O'Connor's thoughtful dissents. Justice Powell's reference to the "balancing test" approved in National League of Cities is not identical with the language in that case, which recognized that Congress could not act under its commerce power to infringe on certain fundamental aspects of state sovereignty that are essential to "the States' separate and independent existence." Nor is either test, or Justice O'Connor's suggested approach, precisely congruent with Justice Blackmun's views in 1976, when he spoke of a balancing approach which did not outlaw federal power in areas "where the federal interest is demonstrably greater." But under any one of these approaches, the judgment in these cases should be affirmed, and I do not think it incumbent on those of us in dissent to spell out further the fine points of a principle that will, I am confident, in time again command the support of a majority of this Court.

JUSTICE O'CONNOR, *dissenting.*

The Court today surveys the battle scene of federalism and sounds a retreat. Like Justice Powell, I would prefer to hold the field and, at the very least, render a little aid to the wounded. I join Justice Powell's opinion. I also write separately to note my fundamental disagreement with the majority's views of federalism and the duty of this Court.

The Court overrules *National League of Cities v. Usery*, on the grounds that it is not "faithful to the role of federalism in a democratic society." . . . "The essence of our federal system," the Court concludes, "is that, within the realm of authority left open to them under the Constitution, the States must be equally free to engage in any activity that their citizens choose for the common weal. . . ." *Ibid. National League of Cities* is held to be inconsistent with this narrow view of federalism because it attempts to protect only those fundamental aspects of state sovereignty that are essential to the

States' separate and independent existence, rather than protecting all state activities "equally."

In my view, federalism cannot be reduced to the weak "essence" distilled by the majority today. There is more to federalism than the nature of the constraints that can be imposed on the States in "the realm of authority left open to them by the Constitution." The central issue of federalism, of course, is whether any realm is left open to the States by the Constitution— whether any area remains in which a State may act free of federal interference. "The issue . . . is whether the federal system has any *legal* substance, any core of constitutional right that courts will enforce." C. Black, *Perspectives in Constitutional Law* 30 (1963). The true "essence" of federalism is that the States, as States, have legitimate interests which the National Government is bound to respect even though its laws are supreme. If federalism so conceived and so carefully cultivated by the Framers of our Constitution is to remain meaningful, this Court cannot abdicate its constitutional responsibility to oversee the Federal Government's compliance with its duty to respect the legitimate interests of the States.

Due to the emergence of an integrated and industrialized national economy, this Court has been required to examine and review a breathtaking expansion of the powers of Congress. In doing so, the Court correctly perceived that the Framers of our Constitution intended Congress to have sufficient power to address national problems. But the Framers were not single-minded. The Constitution is animated by an array of intentions. *EEOC v. Wyoming* (Powell, J., dissenting). Just as surely as the Framers envisioned a National Government capable of solving national problems, they also envisioned a republic whose vitality was assured by the diffusion of power not only among the branches of the Federal Government, but also between the Federal Government and the States. *FERC v. Mississippi*, (O'Connor, J., dissenting). In the 18th century, these intentions did not conflict, because technology had not yet converted every local problem into a national one. A conflict has now emerged, and the Court today retreats rather than reconcile the Constitution's dual concerns for federalism and an effective commerce power.

We would do well to recall the constitutional basis for federalism and the development of the commerce power which has come to displace it. The text of the Constitution does not define the precise scope of state authority other than to specify, in the Tenth Amendment, that the powers not delegated to the United States by the Constitution are reserved to the States. In the view of the Framers, however, this did not leave state authority weak or defenseless; the powers delegated to the United States, after all, were "few and defined." *The Federalist* No. 45. The Framers' comments indicate that the sphere of state activity was to be a significant one, as Justice Powell's opinion clearly demonstrates. The States were to retain authority over those local concerns of greatest relevance and importance to the people. *The Federalist* No. 17. This division of authority, according to Madison, would produce efficient government and protect the rights of the people:

> "In a single republic, all the power surrendered by the people is submitted to the administration of a single government, and usurpations are guarded against by a division of the government into distinct and separate departments. In the compound republic of America, the power surrendered by the people is first divided between two distinct governments, and then the portion allotted to each subdivided among distinct and separate departments. Hence, a double security arises to the

rights of the people. The different governments will controul each other at the same time that each will be controuled by itself." *The Federalist* No. 51.

Of course, one of the "few and defined" powers delegated to the National Congress was the power "To regulate Commerce with foreign Nations, and among the several States, and with the Indian Tribes." U.S. Const., Art. I, §8, cl. 3. The Framers perceived the interstate commerce power to be important but limited, and expected that it would be used primarily, if not exclusively, to remove interstate tariffs and to regulate maritime affairs and large-scale mercantile enterprise. This perception of a narrow commerce power is important not because it suggests that the commerce power should be as narrowly construed today. Rather, it explains why the Framers could believe the Constitution assured significant state authority even as it bestowed a range of powers, including the commerce power, on the Congress. In an era when interstate commerce represented a tiny fraction of economic activity and most goods and services were produced and consumed close to home, the interstate commerce power left a broad range of activities beyond the reach of Congress.

In the decades since ratification of the Constitution, interstate economic activity has steadily expanded. Industrialization, coupled with advances in transportation and communications, has created a national economy in which virtually every activity occurring within the borders of a State plays a part. The expansion and integration of the national economy brought with it a coordinate expansion in the scope of national problems. This Court has been increasingly generous in its interpretation of the commerce power of Congress, primarily to assure that the National Government would be able to deal with national economic problems. Most significantly, the Court in *NLRB v. Jones & Laughlin Steel Corp.* and *United States v. Darby* rejected its previous interpretations of the commerce power which had stymied New Deal legislation. *Jones & Laughlin* and *Darby* embraced the notion that Congress can regulate intrastate activities that affect interstate commerce as surely as it can regulate interstate commerce directly. Subsequent decisions indicate that Congress, in order to regulate an activity, needs only a rational basis for a finding that the activity affects interstate commerce. *See Heart of Atlanta Motel, Inc. v. United States.* Even if a particular individual's activity has no perceptible interstate effect, it can be reached by Congress through regulation of that class of activity in general as long as that class, considered as a whole, affects interstate commerce. *Fry v. United States*; *Perez v. United States.*

Incidental to this expansion of the commerce power, Congress has been given an ability it lacked prior to the emergence of an integrated national economy. Because virtually every state activity, like virtually every activity of a private individual, arguably "affects" interstate commerce, Congress can now supplant the States from the significant sphere of activities envisioned for them by the Framers. It is in this context that recent changes in the workings of Congress, such as the direct election of Senators and the expanded influence of national interest groups . . . become relevant. These changes may well have lessened the weight Congress gives to the legitimate interests of States as States. As a result, there is now a real risk that Congress will gradually erase the diffusion of power between State and Nation on which the Framers based their faith in the efficiency and vitality of our Republic.

It would be erroneous, however, to conclude that the Supreme Court was blind to the threat to federalism when it expanded the commerce power. The Court based the expansion on the authority of Congress, through the Necessary and Proper Clause, "to resort to all means for the exercise of a granted power which are appropriate and plainly adapted to the permitted end." *United States v. Darby, supra,* at 124. It is through this reasoning that an intrastate activity "affecting" interstate commerce can be reached through the commerce power. Thus, in *United States v. Wrightwood Dairy Co.,* the Court stated:

> "The commerce power is not confined in its exercise to the regulation of commerce among the states. It extends to those activities intrastate which so affect interstate commerce, or the exertion of the power of Congress over it, as to make regulation of them appropriate means to the attainment of a legitimate end, the effective execution of the granted power to regulate interstate commerce . . . ."

United States v. Wrightwood Dairy Co. was heavily relied upon by *Wickard v. Filburn,* and the reasoning of these cases underlies every recent decision concerning the reach of Congress to activities affecting interstate commerce. *See, e.g., Fry v. United States, supra,* at 547; *Perez v. United States, supra,* at 151-152; *Heart of Atlanta Motel, Inc. v. United States, supra,* at 258-259.

It is worth recalling the cited passage in *McCulloch v. Maryland* that lies at the source of the recent expansion of the commerce power. "Let the end be legitimate, let it be within the scope of the constitution," Chief Justice Marshall said, "and all means which are appropriate, which are plainly adapted to that end, which are not prohibited, but consist with the letter and spirit of the constitution, are constitutional." The spirit of the Tenth Amendment, of course, is that the States will retain their integrity in a system in which the laws of the United States are nevertheless supreme. *Fry v. United States, supra,* at 547, n.7.

It is not enough that the "end be legitimate"; the means to that end chosen by Congress must not contravene the spirit of the Constitution. Thus, many of this Court's decisions acknowledge that the means by which national power is exercised must take into account concerns for state autonomy. ("Undoubtedly, the scope of this [commerce] power must be considered in the light of our dual system of government, and may not be extended so as to embrace effects upon interstate commerce so indirect and remote that to embrace them, in view of our complex society, would effectually obliterate the distinction between what is national and what is local and create a completely centralized government"); for example, Congress might rationally conclude that the location a State chooses for its capital may affect interstate commerce, but the Court has suggested that Congress would nevertheless be barred from dictating that location because such an exercise of a delegated power would undermine the state sovereignty inherent in the Tenth Amendment. Similarly, Congress, in the exercise of its taxing and spending powers, can protect federal savings and loan associations, but if it chooses to do so by the means of converting quasi-public state savings and loan associations into federal associations, the Court has held that it contravenes the reserved powers of the States because the conversion is not a reasonably necessary exercise of power to reach the desired end. The operative language of these cases varies, but the underlying principle is consistent: state autonomy is a relevant factor in assessing the means by which Congress exercises its powers.

UNITED STATES v. LOPEZ

514 U.S. 549 (1995)

Opinion: Rehnquist, joined by
  O'Connor, Scalia, Kennedy, Thomas
Concurrence: Kennedy, joined by
  O'Connor
Concurrence: Thomas
Dissent: Breyer, joined by Stevens,
  Souter, Ginsburg
Dissent: Stevens
Dissent: Souter

Although it looked like National League of
Cities v. Usery *might spark a resurgence of
the concern for the powers of the state as
opposed to the federal government, Justice
Harry Blackmun's opinion in* Garcia v. San
Antonio Metropolitan Transit Authority
*reversed that potential trajectory. Thus,
in some ways,* National League of Cities
v. Usery *was a false start for asserting the
sovereignty of states. Importantly, however, Justice William Rehnquist's dissent
in* Garcia v. San Antonio Metropolitan
Transit Authority *emphatically asserts
the importance of state sovereignty. It took
ten years for Justice Rehnquist's prediction
that the Court would rediscover the principles of federalism to be realized. By the
time the "New Federalism" finally emerged,
Justice Rehnquist had been promoted to
Chief Justice and liberal Justice Thurgood
Marshall had been replaced by conservative Justice Clarence Thomas.*

In United v. Lopez, *the Court struck down
a provision of the Gun-Free School Zones Act
prohibiting individuals from carrying a firearm within a certain distance of the a school.
In his opinion, Chief Justice Rehnquist argues
that the possession of a handgun does not
constitute "economic activity," nor does it
substantially affect interstate commerce,
and that therefore the law extends beyond*

*Congress's limited powers. Is the distinction
between economic activity and noneconomic
activity tenable? Is it consistent with all of
the landmark New Deal precedents? Recall
that the* McCulloch v. Maryland *framework
for congressional power is to ask whether the
law in question is an appropriate means to a
legitimate end. Is U.S. Supreme Court Justice
Stephen Breyer correct to say that the decision grants Congress considerably less deference than precedent requires?*

CHIEF JUSTICE REHNQUIST
delivered the opinion of the Court.

In the Gun-Free School Zones Act of 1990,
Congress made it a federal offense "for any
individual knowingly to possess a firearm
at a place that the individual knows, or
has reasonable cause to believe, is a school
zone." 18 U.S.C. §922(q)(1)(A). The Act
neither regulates a commercial activity
nor contains a requirement that the possession be connected in any way to interstate commerce. We hold that the Act
exceeds the authority of Congress "to
regulate Commerce . . . among the several
States. . . . "

On March 10, 1992, respondent, who
was then a 12th-grade student, arrived at
Edison High School in San Antonio, Texas,
carrying a concealed .38 caliber handgun
and five bullets. Acting upon an anonymous tip, school authorities confronted
respondent, who admitted that he was
carrying the weapon. He was arrested and
charged under Texas law with firearm possession on school premises. The next day,
the state charges were dismissed after federal agents charged respondent by complaint with violating the Gun-Free School
Zones Act of 1990.

We start with first principles. The Constitution creates a Federal Government of enumerated powers. As James Madison wrote, "the powers delegated by the proposed Constitution to the federal government are few and defined. Those which are to remain in the State governments are numerous and indefinite." This constitutionally mandated division of authority "was adopted by the Framers to ensure protection of our fundamental liberties . . . a healthy balance of power between the States and the Federal Government will reduce the risk of tyranny and abuse from either front."

The Court, through Chief Justice Marshall, first defined the nature of Congress' commerce power in *Gibbons v. Ogden*:

> "Commerce, undoubtedly, is traffic, but it is something more: it is intercourse. It describes the commercial intercourse between nations, and parts of nations, in all its branches, and is regulated by prescribing rules for carrying on that intercourse."

The commerce power "is the power to regulate; that is, to prescribe the rule by which commerce is to be governed. This power, like all others vested in congress, is complete in itself, may be exercised to its utmost extent, and acknowledges no limitations, other than are prescribed in the constitution." The *Gibbons* Court, however, acknowledged that limitations on the commerce power are inherent in the very language of the Commerce Clause.

. . . *Jones & Laughlin Steel*, *Darby*, and *Wickard* ushered in an era of Commerce Clause jurisprudence that greatly expanded the previously defined authority of Congress under that Clause. In part, this was a recognition of the great changes that had occurred in the way business was carried on in this country. Enterprises that had once been local or at most regional in nature had become national in scope. But the doctrinal change also reflected a view that earlier Commerce Clause cases artificially had constrained the authority of Congress to regulate interstate commerce.

But even these modern-era precedents which have expanded congressional power under the Commerce Clause confirm that this power is subject to outer limits. In *Jones & Laughlin Steel*, the Court warned that the scope of the interstate commerce power "must be considered in the light of our dual system of government and may not be extended so as to embrace effects upon interstate commerce so indirect and remote that to embrace them, in view of our complex society, would effectually obliterate the distinction between what is national and what is local and create a completely centralized government." Since that time, the Court has heeded that warning and undertaken to decide whether a rational basis existed for concluding that a regulated activity sufficiently affected interstate commerce.

. . . [W]e have identified three broad categories of activity that Congress may regulate under its commerce power. First, Congress may regulate the use of the channels of interstate commerce. Second, Congress is empowered to regulate and protect the instrumentalities of interstate commerce, or persons or things in interstate commerce, even though the threat may come only from intrastate activities. Finally, Congress' commerce authority includes the power to regulate those activities having a substantial relation to interstate commerce, i.e., those activities that substantially affect interstate commerce.

We now turn to consider the power of Congress, in the light of this framework, to enact §922(q). The first two categories of authority may be quickly disposed of: §922(q) is not a regulation of the use of the channels of interstate commerce, nor is it an attempt to prohibit the interstate transportation of a commodity through the channels of commerce; nor can §922(q) be justified as a regulation by which Congress has sought to protect an instrumentality of interstate commerce or a thing in interstate commerce. Thus, if §922(q) is to be sustained, it must be under the third category as a regulation of an activity that substantially affects interstate commerce.

First, we have upheld a wide variety of congressional Acts regulating intrastate economic activity where we have concluded that the activity substantially affected interstate commerce. Examples include the regulation of intrastate coal mining; intrastate extortionate credit transactions, restaurants utilizing substantial interstate supplies, inns and hotels catering to interstate guests, and production and consumption of homegrown wheat. These examples are by no means exhaustive, but the pattern is clear. Where economic activity substantially affects interstate commerce, legislation regulating that activity will be sustained.

Even *Wickard*, which is perhaps the most far reaching example of Commerce Clause authority over intrastate activity, involved economic activity in a way that the possession of a gun in a school zone does not.

. . . Section 922(q) is a criminal statute that by its terms has nothing to do with "commerce" or any sort of economic enterprise, however broadly one might define those terms. Section 922(q) is not an essential part of a larger regulation of economic activity, in which the regulatory scheme could be undercut unless the intrastate activity were regulated. It cannot, therefore, be sustained under our cases upholding regulations of activities that arise out of or are connected with a commercial transaction, which viewed in the aggregate, substantially affects interstate commerce.

Second, §922(q) contains no jurisdictional element which would ensure, through case-by-case inquiry, that the firearm possession in question affects interstate commerce. . . .

Although as part of our independent evaluation of constitutionality under the Commerce Clause we of course consider legislative findings, and indeed even congressional committee findings, regarding effect on interstate commerce, the Government concedes that "neither the statute nor its legislative history contain[s] express congressional findings regarding the effects upon interstate commerce of gun possession in a school zone." We agree with the Government that Congress normally is not required to make formal findings as to the substantial burdens that an activity has on interstate commerce. But to the extent that congressional findings would enable us to evaluate the legislative judgment that the activity in question substantially affected interstate commerce, even though no such substantial effect was visible to the naked eye, they are lacking here.

The Government's essential contention, in fine, is that we may determine here that §922(q) is valid because possession of a firearm in a local school zone does indeed substantially affect interstate commerce. The Government argues that possession of a firearm in a school zone may result in violent crime and that violent crime can be expected to affect the functioning of the national economy in two ways. First, the costs of violent crime are substantial, and, through the mechanism of insurance, those costs are spread throughout the population. Second, violent crime reduces the willingness of individuals to travel to areas within the country that are perceived to be unsafe. The Government also argues that the presence of guns in schools poses a substantial threat to the educational process by threatening the learning environment.

A handicapped educational process, in turn, will result in a less productive citizenry. That, in turn, would have an adverse effect on the Nation's economic well-being. As a result, the Government argues that Congress could rationally have concluded that §922(q) substantially affects interstate commerce.

We pause to consider the implications of the Government's arguments. The Government admits, under its "costs of crime" reasoning, that Congress could regulate not only all violent crime, but all activities that might lead to violent crime, regardless of how tenuously they relate to interstate commerce. Similarly, under the Government's "national productivity" reasoning, Congress could regulate any activity that it found was related to the economic productivity of individual citizens: family law (including marriage, divorce, and child custody), for example. Under the theories that the Government presents in support of §922(q), it is difficult to perceive any limitation on federal power, even in areas such as criminal law enforcement or education where States historically have been sovereign. Thus, if we were to accept the Government's arguments, we are hard pressed to posit any activity by an individual that Congress is without power to regulate.

Justice Breyer rejects our reading of precedent and argues that "Congress . . . could rationally conclude that schools fall on the commercial side of the line." Justice Breyer's rationale lacks any real limits because, depending on the level of generality, any activity can be looked upon as commercial. Under the dissent's rationale, Congress could just as easily look at child rearing as "falling on the commercial side of the line" because it provides a "valuable service—namely, to equip [children] with the skills they need to survive in life and, more specifically, in the workplace." We do not doubt that Congress has authority under the Commerce Clause to regulate numerous commercial activities that substantially affect interstate commerce and also affect the educational process. That authority, though broad, does not include the authority to regulate each and every aspect of local schools.

The possession of a gun in a local school zone is in no sense an economic activity that might, through repetition elsewhere, substantially affect any sort of interstate commerce. Respondent was a local student at a local school; there is no indication that he had recently moved in interstate commerce, and there is no requirement that his possession of the firearm have any concrete tie to interstate commerce.

To uphold the Government's contentions here, we would have to pile inference upon inference in a manner that would bid fair to convert congressional authority under the Commerce Clause to a general police power of the sort retained by the States. Admittedly, some of our prior cases have taken long steps down that road, giving great deference to congressional action. The broad language in these opinions has suggested the possibility of additional expansion, but we decline here to proceed any further. To do so would require us to conclude that the Constitution's enumeration of powers does not presuppose something not enumerated, and that there never will be a distinction between what is truly national and what is truly local. This we are unwilling to do.

JUSTICE BREYER, *with whom* **JUSTICE STEVENS, JUSTICE SOUTER**, *and* **JUSTICE GINSBURG** *join, dissenting.*

The issue in this case is whether the Commerce Clause authorizes Congress to enact a statute that makes it a crime to possess a gun in, or near, a school. In my view, the statute falls well within the scope of the commerce power as this Court has understood that power over the last half century.

In reaching this conclusion, I apply three basic principles of Commerce Clause interpretation. First, the power to "regulate Commerce . . . among the several States," encompasses the power to regulate local activities insofar as they significantly affect interstate commerce. As the majority points out, the Court, in describing how much of an effect the Clause requires, sometimes has used the word "substantial" and sometimes has not. . . . I use the word "significant" because the word "substantial" implies a somewhat narrower power than recent precedent suggests. . . .

Second, in determining whether a local activity will likely have a significant effect upon interstate commerce, a court must consider, not the effect of an individual act (a single instance of gun possession), but rather the cumulative effect of all similar instances (i.e., the effect of all guns possessed in or near schools).

Third, the Constitution requires us to judge the connection between a regulated activity and interstate commerce, not directly, but at one remove. Courts must give Congress a degree of leeway in determining the existence of a significant factual connection between the regulated activity and interstate commerce—both because the Constitution delegates the commerce power directly to Congress and because the determination requires an empirical judgment of a kind that a legislature is more likely than a court to make with accuracy. The traditional words "rational basis" capture this leeway. Thus, the specific question before us, as the Court recognizes, is not whether the "regulated activity sufficiently affected interstate commerce," but, rather, whether Congress could have had "a rational basis" for so concluding.

I recognize that we must judge this matter independently. . . . And, I also recognize that Congress did not write specific "interstate commerce" findings into the law under which Lopez was convicted. Nonetheless, as I have already noted, the matter that we review independently (i.e., whether there is a "rational basis") already has considerable leeway built into it. And, the absence of findings, at most, deprives a statute of the benefit of some extra leeway. This extra deference, in principle, might change the result in a close case, though, in practice, it has not made a critical legal difference. It would seem particularly unfortunate to make the validity of the statute at hand turn on the presence or absence of findings. . . . [T]here is no special need here for a clear indication of Congress' rationale. The statute does not interfere with the exercise of state or local authority. . . .

Applying these principles to the case at hand, we must ask whether Congress could have had a rational basis for finding a significant (or substantial) connection between gun-related school violence and interstate commerce. Or, to put the question in the language of the explicit finding that Congress made when it amended this law in 1994: Could Congress rationally have found that "violent crime in school zones," through its effect on the "quality of education," significantly (or substantially) affects "interstate" or "foreign commerce"? As long as one views the commerce connection, not as a "technical legal conception," but as "a practical one," the answer to this question must be yes. Numerous reports and studies—generated both inside and outside government—make clear that Congress could reasonably have found the empirical connection that its law, implicitly or explicitly, asserts.

For one thing, reports, hearings, and other readily available literature make clear that the problem of guns in and around schools is widespread and extremely serious. These materials report, for example, that four percent of American high school students (and six percent of inner-city high school students) carry a gun to school at least occasionally, that 12 percent of urban high school students have had guns fired at them, that 20 percent of those students have been threatened with guns, and that, in any 6-month period, several hundred thousand schoolchildren are victims of violent crimes in or near their schools. And, they report that this widespread violence in schools throughout the Nation significantly interferes with the quality of education in those schools. Based on reports such as these, Congress obviously could have thought that guns and learning are mutually exclusive. Congress could therefore have found a substantial educational problem—teachers unable to teach, students unable to learn—and concluded that guns near schools contribute substantially to the size and scope of that problem.

Having found that guns in schools significantly undermine the quality of education in our Nation's classrooms, Congress could also have found, given the effect of education upon interstate and foreign commerce, that gun-related violence in and around schools is a commercial, as well as a human, problem. Education, although far more than a matter of economics, has long been inextricably intertwined with the Nation's economy. Scholars estimate that nearly a quarter of America's economic growth in the early years of this century is traceable directly to increased schooling, that investment in "human capital" (through spending on education) exceeded investment in "physical capital" by a ratio of almost two to one, and that the economic returns to this investment in education exceeded the returns to conventional capital investment.

In recent years the link between secondary education and business has

strengthened, becoming both more direct and more important. Scholars on the subject report that technological changes and innovations in management techniques have altered the nature of the workplace so that more jobs now demand greater educational skills. . . .

Increasing global competition also has made primary and secondary education economically more important. The portion of the American economy attributable to international trade nearly tripled between 1950 and 1980, and more than 70 percent of American-made goods now compete with imports. Yet, lagging worker productivity has contributed to negative trade balances and to real hourly compensation that has fallen below wages in 10 other industrialized nations. At least some significant part of this serious productivity problem is attributable to students who emerge from classrooms without the reading or mathematical skills necessary to compete with their European or Asian counterparts, and, presumably, to high school dropout rates of 20 to 25 percent (up to 50 percent in inner cities). . . .

Finally, there is evidence that, today more than ever, many firms base their location decisions upon the presence, or absence, of a work force with a basic education. . . . In light of this increased importance of education to individual firms, it is no surprise that half of the Nation's manufacturers have become involved with setting standards and shaping curricula for local schools, that 88 percent think this kind of involvement is important, that more than 20 States have recently passed educational reforms to attract new business, and that business magazines have begun to rank cities according to the quality of their schools.

The economic links I have just sketched seem fairly obvious. Why then is it not equally obvious, in light of those links, that a widespread, serious, and substantial physical threat to teaching and learning also substantially threatens the commerce to which that teaching and learning is inextricably tied? That is to say, guns in the hands of six percent of inner-city high school students and gun-related violence throughout a city's schools must threaten the trade and commerce that those schools support. The only question, then, is whether the latter threat is (to use the majority's terminology) "substantial." The evidence of (1) the extent of the gun-related violence problem, see supra, at 619, (2) the extent of the resulting negative effect on classroom learning, see ibid., and (3) the extent of the consequent negative commercial effects, see supra, at 620-622, when taken together, indicate a threat to trade and commerce that is "substantial." At the very least, Congress could rationally have concluded that the links are "substantial."

Specifically, Congress could have found that gun-related violence near the classroom poses a serious economic threat (1) to consequently inadequately educated workers who must endure low paying jobs, and (2) to communities and businesses that might (in today's "information society") otherwise gain, from a well-educated work force, an important commercial advantage, of a kind that location near a railhead or harbor provided in the past. Congress might also have found these threats to be no different in kind from other threats that this Court has found within the commerce power, such as the threat that loan sharking poses to the "funds" of "numerous localities," and that unfair labor practices pose to instrumentalities of commerce. As I have pointed out, Congress has written that "the occurrence of violent crime in school zones" has brought about a "decline in the quality of education" that "has an adverse impact on interstate commerce and the foreign commerce of the United States."

The violence-related facts, the educational facts, and the economic facts, taken together, make this conclusion rational. And, because under our case law, the sufficiency of the constitutionally necessary Commerce Clause link between a crime of violence and interstate commerce turns simply upon size or degree, those same facts make the statute constitutional.

To hold this statute constitutional is not to "obliterate" the "distinction between what is national and what is local," nor is it to hold that the Commerce Clause permits the Federal Government to "regulate any activity that it found was related to the economic productivity of individual citizens," to regulate "marriage, divorce, and child custody," or to regulate any and all aspects of education. First, this statute is aimed at curbing a particularly acute threat to the educational process—the possession (and use) of life-threatening firearms in, or near, the classroom. The empirical evidence that I have discussed above unmistakably documents the special way in which guns and education are incompatible. This Court has previously recognized the singularly disruptive potential on interstate commerce that acts of violence may have. Second, the immediacy of the connection between education and the national economic well-being is documented by scholars and accepted by society at large in a way and to a degree that may not hold true for other social institutions. It must surely be the rare case, then, that a statute strikes at conduct that (when considered in the abstract) seems so removed from commerce, but which (practically speaking) has so significant an impact upon commerce.

The majority's holding—that §922 falls outside the scope of the Commerce Clause—creates three serious legal problems. First, the majority's holding runs contrary to modern Supreme Court cases that have upheld congressional actions despite connections to interstate or foreign commerce that are less significant than the effect of school violence. . . .

The second legal problem the Court creates comes from its apparent belief that it can reconcile its holding with earlier cases by making a critical distinction between "commercial" and noncommercial "transaction[s]." That is to say, the Court believes the Constitution would distinguish between two local activities, each of which has an identical effect upon interstate commerce, if one, but not the other, is "commercial" in nature. As a general matter, this approach fails to heed this Court's earlier warning not to turn "questions of the power of Congress" upon "formula[s]" that would give "controlling force to nomenclature such as 'production' and 'indirect' and foreclose consideration of the actual effects of the activity in question upon interstate commerce."
. . . Although the majority today attempts to categorize *Perez*, *McClung*, and *Wickard* as involving intrastate "economic activity," the Courts that decided each of those cases did not focus upon the economic nature of the activity regulated. Rather, they focused upon whether that activity affected interstate or foreign commerce.
. . . [I]f there is a principled distinction that could work both here and in future cases, Congress (even in the absence of vocational classes, industry involvement, and private management) could rationally conclude that schools fall on the commercial side of the line. In 1990, the year Congress enacted the statute before us, primary and secondary schools spent $230 billion—that is, nearly a quarter of a trillion dollars—which accounts for a significant portion of our $5.5 trillion gross domestic product for that year. . . . Why could Congress, for Commerce Clause purposes, not consider schools as roughly analogous to commercial investments from which the Nation derives the benefit of an educated work force?

The third legal problem created by the Court's holding is that it threatens legal uncertainty in an area of law that, until this case, seemed reasonably well settled. Congress has enacted many statutes (more than 100 sections of the United States Code), including criminal statutes (at least 25 sections), that use the words "affecting commerce" to define their scope. More importantly, in the absence of a jurisdictional element, are the courts nevertheless to take *Wickard* as inapplicable, and to judge the effect of a single noncommercial activity on interstate commerce without considering similar instances of the forbidden conduct? However these questions are eventually resolved, the legal uncertainty now created will restrict Congress' ability to enact criminal laws aimed at criminal behavior that, considered problem by problem rather than instance by instance, seriously threatens the economic, as well as social, well-being of Americans.

CASE QUESTION

After the decision, Congress responded by adding a jurisdictional requirement, requiring prosecutors to prove in each case that the gun in question moved in or otherwise affected interstate commerce. With this minor change, the Gun-Free School Zones Act of 1995 never again received a serious constitutional challenge. Given this fact, should we understand the *Lopez* decision to undermine the precedents found in the previous section, or instead as a warning requiring Congress to legislate with greater care?

UNITED STATES v. MORRISON

529 U.S. 598 (2000)

Opinion: Rehnquist, joined by
O'Connor, Scalia, Kennedy, Thomas
Concurrence: Thomas
Dissent: Souter, joined by Stevens,
Ginsburg, Breyer
Dissent: Breyer, joined by Stevens, and
by Souter and Ginsburg in Part I-A

United States v. Morrison *extends the ruling in* United States v. Lopez, *which cites education, criminal law, and family law as core examples of "noneconomic activity" beyond the purview of the Commerce Clause.* United States v. Morrison *strikes down parts of the Violence Against Women Act, limiting the use of the Commerce Clause to protect the rights of women through the use of criminal law. Does the logic of* Untied States v. Lopez *lead necessarily to this result? Is U.S. Supreme Court Justice David Souter correct to say that the holding here is incompatible with the Court's earlier rulings in* Heart of Atlanta Motel v. United States *and* Katzenbach v. McClung? *Does the holding in this case suggest that it is unwise to defend legislation protecting liberty and equality on Commerce Clause grounds?*

CHIEF JUSTICE REHNQUIST

delivered the opinion of the Court.

Petitioner Christy Brzonkala enrolled at Virginia Polytechnic Institute (Virginia Tech) in the fall of 1994. In September of that year, Brzonkala met respondents Antonio Morrison and James Crawford, who were both students at Virginia Tech and members of its varsity football team. Brzonkala alleges that, within 30 minutes of meeting Morrison and Crawford,

they assaulted and repeatedly raped her. After the attack, Morrison allegedly told Brzonkala, "You better not have any . . . diseases." In the months following the rape, Morrison also allegedly announced in the dormitory's dining room that he "like[d] to get girls drunk and. . . ." The omitted portions, quoted verbatim in the briefs on file with this Court, consist of boasting, debased remarks about what Morrison would do to women, vulgar remarks that cannot fail to shock and offend.

Brzonkala alleges that this attack caused her to become severely emotionally disturbed and depressed. She sought assistance from a university psychiatrist, who prescribed antidepressant medication. Shortly after the rape Brzonkala stopped attending classes and withdrew from the university.

In early 1995, Brzonkala filed a complaint against respondents under Virginia Tech's Sexual Assault Policy. During the school-conducted hearing on her complaint, Morrison admitted having sexual contact with her despite the fact that she had twice told him "no." After the hearing, Virginia Tech's Judicial Committee found insufficient evidence to punish Crawford, but found Morrison guilty of sexual assault and sentenced him to immediate suspension for two semesters.

Morrison appealed his second conviction through the university's administrative system. On August 21, 1995, Virginia Tech's senior vice president and provost set aside Morrison's punishment. She concluded that it was "excessive when compared with other cases where there has been a finding of violation of the Abusive Conduct Policy," 132 F.3d 949, 955 (CA4 1997). Virginia Tech did not inform Brzonkala of this decision.

After learning from a newspaper that Morrison would be returning to Virginia Tech for the fall 1995 semester, she dropped out of the university.

In December 1995, Brzonkala sued Morrison, Crawford, and Virginia Tech in the United States District Court for the Western District of Virginia. Her complaint alleged that Morrison's and Crawford's attack violated . . . the Violence Against Women Act of 1994. It states that "persons within the United States shall have the right to be free from crimes of violence motivated by gender." To enforce that right, subsection (c) declares:

> "A person (including a person who acts under color of any statute, ordinance, regulation, custom, or usage of any State) who commits a crime of violence motivated by gender and thus deprives another of the right declared in subsection (b) of this section shall be liable to the party injured, in an action for the recovery of compensatory and punitive damages, injunctive and declaratory relief, and such other relief as a court may deem appropriate."

Section 13981 defines a "crime" of violence motivated by "gender" as "a crime of violence committed because of gender or on the basis of gender, and due, at least in part, to an animus based on the victim's gender." . . .

Further clarifying the broad scope of §13981's civil remedy, subsection (e)(2) states that "nothing" in this section requires a prior criminal complaint, prosecution, or conviction to establish the elements of a cause of action under subsection (c) of this section." And subsection (e)(3) provides a §13981 litigant with a choice of forums: Federal and state courts "shall have concurrent jurisdiction" over complaints brought under the section.

Every law enacted by Congress must be based on one or more of its powers enumerated in the Constitution. "The powers of the legislature are defined and limited; and that those limits may not be mistaken or forgotten, the constitution is written." *Marbury v. Madison.* Congress explicitly identified the sources of federal authority on which it relied in enacting §13981. It said that a "federal civil rights cause of action" is established "pursuant" to the affirmative power of Congress . . . under section 5 of the Fourteenth Amendment to the Constitution, as well as under section 8 of Article I of the Constitution." 42 U.S.C. §13981(a). We address Congress' authority to enact this remedy under each of these constitutional provisions in turn.

Due respect for the decisions of a coordinate branch of Government demands that we invalidate a congressional enactment only upon a plain showing that Congress has exceeded its constitutional bounds. With this presumption of constitutionality in mind, we turn to the question whether §13981 falls within Congress' power under Article I, §8, of the Constitution. Brzonkala and the United States rely upon the third clause of the Article, which gives Congress power "to regulate Commerce with foreign Nations, and among the several States, and with the Indian Tribes." As we discussed at length in *Lopez*, our interpretation of the Commerce Clause has changed as our Nation has developed. We need not repeat that detailed review of the Commerce Clause's history here; it suffices to say that, in the years since *NLRB v. Jones & Laughlin Steel Corp.*, Congress has had considerably greater latitude in regulating conduct and transactions under the Commerce Clause than our previous case law permitted.

Lopez emphasized, however, that even under our modern, expansive interpretation of the Commerce Clause, Congress' regulatory authority is not without effective bounds.

"[E]ven [our] modern-era precedents which have expanded congressional power under the Commerce Clause confirm that this power is subject to outer limits. In *Jones & Laughlin Steel*, the Court warned that the scope of the interstate commerce power 'must be considered in the light of our dual system of government and may not be extended so as to embrace effects upon interstate commerce so indirect and remote that to embrace them, in view of our complex society, would effectually obliterate the distinction between what is national and what is local and create a completely centralized government.'" Id., at 556-557 (quoting *Jones & Laughlin Steel*, supra, at 37)

As we observed in *Lopez*, modern Commerce Clause jurisprudence has "identified three broad categories of activity that Congress may regulate under its commerce power. First, Congress may regulate the use of the channels of interstate commerce. Second, Congress is empowered to regulate and protect the instrumentalities of interstate commerce, or persons or things in interstate commerce, even though the threat may come only from intrastate activities. Finally, Congress' commerce authority includes the power to regulate those activities having a substantial relation to interstate commerce, . . . i.e., those activities that substantially affect interstate commerce."

Petitioners do not contend that these cases fall within either of the first two of these categories of Commerce Clause regulation. They seek to sustain §13981 as a regulation of activity that substantially affects interstate commerce. Given §13981's focus on gender-motivated violence wherever it occurs (rather than violence directed at the instrumentalities of interstate commerce, interstate markets, or things or persons in interstate commerce), we agree that this is the proper inquiry. . . . In *Lopez*, we held that the Gun-Free School Zones Act of 1990, which made it a federal crime to knowingly possess a firearm in a school zone, exceeded Congress' authority under the Commerce Clause. . . . *Lopez*'s review of Commerce Clause case law demonstrates that in those cases where we have sustained federal regulation of intrastate activity based upon the activity's substantial effects on interstate commerce, the activity in question has been some sort of economic endeavor.

The second consideration that we found important in analyzing §922(q) was that the statute contained "no express jurisdictional element which might limit its reach to a discrete set of firearm possessions that additionally have an explicit connection with or effect on interstate commerce." Such a jurisdictional element may establish that the enactment is in pursuance of Congress' regulation of interstate commerce. Third, we noted that neither §922(q) "nor its legislative history contains express congressional findings regarding the effects upon interstate commerce of gun possession in a school zone." While "Congress normally is not required to make formal findings as to the substantial burdens that an activity has on interstate commerce," the existence of such findings may "enable us to evaluate the legislative judgment that the activity in question substantially affects interstate commerce, even though no such substantial effect [is] visible to the naked eye." Finally, our decision in *Lopez* rested in part on the fact that the link between gun possession and a substantial effect on interstate commerce was attenuated.

With these principles underlying our Commerce Clause jurisprudence as reference points, the proper resolution of the present cases is clear. Gender-motivated crimes of violence are not, in any sense of the phrase, economic activity. While we need not adopt a categorical rule against aggregating the effects of any noneconomic activity in order to decide these cases, thus far in our Nation's history our cases have upheld Commerce Clause regulation of intrastate activity only where that activity is economic in nature. Like the Gun-Free School Zones Act at issue in *Lopez*, §13981 contains no jurisdictional element establishing that the federal cause of action is in pursuance of Congress' power to regulate interstate commerce. Although *Lopez* makes clear that such a jurisdictional element would lend support to the argument that §13981 is sufficiently tied to interstate commerce, Congress elected to cast §13981's remedy over a wider, and more purely intrastate, body of violent crime.

In contrast with the lack of congressional findings that we faced in Lopez, §13981 is supported by numerous findings regarding the serious impact that gender-motivated violence has on victims and their families. But the existence of congressional findings is not sufficient, by itself, to sustain the constitutionality of Commerce Clause legislation. As we stated in *Lopez*, "[S]imply because Congress may conclude that a particular activity substantially affects interstate commerce does not necessarily make it so." Rather, "[w]hether particular operations affect interstate commerce sufficiently to come under the constitutional power of Congress to regulate them is ultimately a judicial rather than a legislative question, and can be settled finally only by this Court."

In these cases, Congress' findings are substantially weakened by the fact that they rely so heavily on a method of reasoning that we have already rejected as unworkable if we are to maintain the Constitution's enumeration of powers. Congress found that gender-motivated violence affects interstate commerce

"by deterring potential victims from traveling interstate, from engaging in employment in interstate business, and from transacting with business, and in places involved in interstate commerce; . . . by diminishing national

productivity, increasing medical and other costs, and decreasing the supply of and the demand for interstate products."

Given these findings and petitioners' arguments, the concern that we expressed in *Lopez* that Congress might use the Commerce Clause to completely obliterate the Constitution's distinction between national and local authority seems well founded. The reasoning that petitioners advance seeks to follow the but-for causal chain from the initial occurrence of violent crime (the suppression of which has always been the prime object of the States' police power) to every attenuated effect upon interstate commerce. If accepted, petitioners' reasoning would allow Congress to regulate any crime as long as the nationwide, aggregated impact of that crime has substantial effects on employment, production, transit, or consumption. Indeed, if Congress may regulate gender-motivated violence, it would be able to regulate murder or any other type of violence since gender-motivated violence, as a subset of all violent crime, is certain to have lesser economic impacts than the larger class of which it is a part.

Petitioners' reasoning, moreover, will not limit Congress to regulating violence but may, as we suggested in *Lopez*, be applied equally as well to family law and other areas of traditional state regulation since the aggregate effect of marriage, divorce, and child rearing on the national economy is undoubtedly significant. Congress may have recognized this specter when it expressly precluded §13981 from being used in the family law context. Under our written Constitution, however, the limitation of congressional authority is not solely a matter of legislative grace.

We accordingly reject the argument that Congress may regulate noneconomic, violent criminal conduct based solely on that conduct's aggregate effect on interstate commerce. The Constitution requires a distinction between what is truly national and what is truly local. In recognizing this fact we preserve one of the few principles that has been consistent since the Clause was adopted. The regulation and punishment of intrastate violence that is not directed at the instrumentalities, channels, or goods involved in interstate commerce has always been the province of the States. Indeed, we can think of no better example of the police power, which the Founders denied the National Government and reposed in the States, than the suppression of violent crime and vindication of its victims....

Because we conclude that the Commerce Clause does not provide Congress with authority to enact §13981, we address petitioners' alternative argument that the section's civil remedy should be upheld as an exercise of Congress' remedial power under §5 of the Fourteenth Amendment. As noted above, Congress expressly invoked the Fourteenth Amendment as a source of authority to enact §13981.

The principles governing an analysis of congressional legislation under §5 are well settled. Section 5 states that Congress may "'enforce,' by 'appropriate legislation'" the constitutional guarantee that no State shall deprive any person of 'life, liberty or property, without due process of law,' nor deny any person 'equal protection of the laws.'" *City of Boerne v. Flores*. Section 5 is "a positive grant of legislative power" that includes authority to "prohibit conduct which is not itself unconstitutional and [to] intrude into 'legislative spheres of autonomy previously reserved to the States.'" However, "[a]s broad as the congressional enforcement power is, it is not unlimited." In fact, as we discuss in detail below, several limitations inherent in §5's text and constitutional context have been recognized since the Fourteenth Amendment was adopted.

Petitioners' §5 argument is founded on an assertion that there is pervasive bias in various state justice systems against victims of gender-motivated violence. This assertion is supported by a voluminous congressional record. Specifically, Congress received evidence that many participants in state justice systems are perpetuating an array of erroneous stereotypes and assumptions. Congress concluded that these discriminatory stereotypes often result in insufficient investigation and prosecution of gender-motivated crime, inappropriate focus on the behavior and credibility of the victims of that crime, and unacceptably lenient punishments for those who are actually convicted of gender-motivated violence. Petitioners contend that this bias denies victims of gender-motivated violence the equal protection of the laws and that Congress therefore acted appropriately in enacting a private civil remedy against the perpetrators of gender-motivated violence to both remedy the States' bias and deter future instances of discrimination in the state courts.

As our cases have established, state-sponsored gender discrimination violates equal protection unless it "serves 'important governmental objectives and . . . the discriminatory means employed' are 'substantially related to the achievement of those objectives.'" However, the language and purpose of the Fourteenth Amendment place certain limitations on the manner in which Congress may attack discriminatory conduct. These limitations are necessary to prevent the Fourteenth Amendment from obliterating the Framers' carefully crafted balance of power between the States and the National Government. Foremost among these limitations is the time-honored principle that the Fourteenth Amendment, by its very terms, prohibits only state action. "The principle has become firmly embedded in our constitutional law that the action inhibited by the first section of the Fourteenth Amendment is only such action as may fairly be said to be that of the States. That Amendment erects no shield against merely private conduct, however discriminatory or wrongful."

Shortly after the Fourteenth Amendment was adopted, we decided . . . the *Civil Rights Cases*. In those consolidated cases, we held that the public accommodation provisions of the Civil Rights Act of 1875, which applied to purely private conduct, were beyond the scope of the §5 enforcement power.

The force of the doctrine of stare decisis behind these decisions stems not only from the length of time they have been on the books, but also from the insight attributable to the Members of the Court at that time. Every Member had been appointed by President Lincoln, Grant, Hayes, Garfield, or Arthur—and each of their judicial appointees obviously had intimate knowledge and familiarity with the events surrounding the adoption of the Fourteenth Amendment. . . .

Petitioners alternatively argue that, unlike the situation in the *Civil Rights Cases*, here there has been gender-based disparate treatment by state authorities, whereas in those cases there was no indication of such state action. There is abundant evidence, however, to show that the Congresses that enacted the Civil Rights Acts of 1871 and 1875 had a purpose similar to that of Congress in enacting §13981: There were state laws on the books bespeaking equality of treatment, but in the administration of these laws there was discrimination against newly freed slaves. . . . Section 13981 is not aimed at proscribing discrimination by officials which the Fourteenth Amendment might not itself proscribe; it is directed not at any State or state actor, but at individuals who have committed criminal acts motivated by gender bias. . . .

Petitioner Brzonkala's complaint alleges that she was the victim of a brutal assault. But Congress' effort in §13981 to provide a federal civil remedy can be sustained neither under the Commerce Clause nor under §5 of the Fourteenth Amendment. If the allegations here are true, no civilized system of justice could fail to provide her a remedy for the conduct of respondent Morrison. But under our federal system that remedy must be provided by the Commonwealth of Virginia, and not by the United States. The judgment of the Court of Appeals is Affirmed.

JUSTICE THOMAS, *concurring.*

The majority opinion correctly applies our decision in *United States v. Lopez*, and I join it in full. I write separately only to express my view that the very notion of a "substantial effects" test under the Commerce Clause is inconsistent with the original understanding of Congress' powers and with this Court's early Commerce Clause cases. By continuing to apply this rootless and malleable standard, however circumscribed, the Court has encouraged the Federal Government to persist in its view that the Commerce Clause has virtually no limits. Until this Court replaces its existing Commerce Clause jurisprudence with a standard more consistent with the original understanding, we will continue to see Congress appropriating state police powers under the guise of regulating commerce.

JUSTICE SOUTER, *with whom* **JUSTICE STEVENS**, **JUSTICE GINSBURG**, *and* **JUSTICE BREYER** *join, dissenting.*

The Court says both that it leaves Commerce Clause precedent undisturbed and that the Civil Rights Remedy of the Violence Against Women Act of 1994 exceeds Congress's power under that Clause. I find the claims irreconcilable and respectfully dissent.

Our cases, which remain at least nominally undisturbed, stand for the following propositions. Congress has the power to legislate with regard to activity that, in the aggregate, has a substantial effect on interstate commerce. The fact of such a substantial effect is not an issue for the courts in the first instance, ibid., but for the Congress, whose institutional capacity for gathering evidence and taking testimony far exceeds ours. By passing legislation, Congress indicates its conclusion, whether explicitly or not, that facts support its exercise of the commerce power. The business of the courts is to review the congressional assessment, not for soundness but simply for the rationality of concluding that a jurisdictional basis exists in fact. Any explicit findings that Congress chooses to make, though not dispositive of the question of rationality, may advance judicial review by identifying factual authority on which Congress relied. Applying those propositions in these cases can lead to only one conclusion.

One obvious difference from *United States v. Lopez*, is the mountain of data assembled by Congress, here showing the effects of violence against women on interstate commerce. Passage of the Act in 1994 was preceded by four years of hearings, which included testimony from physicians and law professors; from survivors of rape and domestic violence; and from representatives of state law enforcement and private business. The record includes reports on gender bias from task forces in 21 States, and we have the benefit of specific factual findings in the eight separate Reports issued by Congress and its committees over the long course leading to enactment.

Based on the data ... Congress found that

"crimes of violence motivated by gender have a substantial adverse effect on interstate commerce, by deterring potential victims from traveling interstate, from engaging in employment in interstate business, and from transacting with business, and in places involved, in interstate commerce ... [,] by diminishing national productivity, increasing medical and other costs, and decreasing the supply of and the demand for interstate products...."

Congress thereby explicitly stated the predicate for the exercise of its Commerce Clause power. Is its conclusion irrational in view of the data amassed? True, the methodology of particular studies may be challenged, and some of the figures arrived at may be disputed. But the sufficiency of the evidence before Congress to provide a rational basis for the finding cannot seriously be questioned.

Indeed, the legislative record here is far more voluminous than the record compiled by Congress and found sufficient in two prior cases upholding Title II of the Civil Rights Act of 1964 against Commerce Clause challenges. In *Heart of Atlanta Motel, Inc. v. United States*, and *Katzenbach v. McClung*, the Court referred to evidence showing the consequences of racial discrimination by motels and restaurants on interstate commerce. Congress had relied on compelling anecdotal reports that individual instances of segregation cost thousands to millions of dollars.

While Congress did not, to my knowledge, calculate aggregate dollar values for the nationwide effects of racial discrimination in 1964, in 1994 it did rely on evidence of the harms caused by domestic violence and sexual assault, citing annual costs of $3 billion in 1990 and $5 to $10 billion in 1993. Equally important, though, gender-based violence in the 1990's was shown to operate in a manner similar to racial discrimination in the 1960's in reducing the mobility of employees and their production and consumption of goods shipped in interstate commerce. Like racial discrimination, gender-based violence bars its most likely targets—women—from full participation in the national economy.

If the analogy to the Civil Rights Act of 1964 is not plain enough, one can always look back a bit further. In *Wickard*, we upheld the application of the Agricultural Adjustment Act to the planting and consumption of homegrown wheat. The effect on interstate commerce in that case followed from the possibility that wheat grown at home for personal consumption could either be drawn into the market by rising prices, or relieve its grower of any need to purchase wheat in the market. The Commerce Clause predicate was simply the effect of the production of wheat for home consumption on supply and demand in interstate commerce. Supply and demand for goods in interstate commerce will also be affected by the deaths of 2,000 to 4,000 women annually at the hands of domestic abusers, and by the reduction in the work force by the 100,000 or more rape victims who lose their jobs each year or are forced to quit. Violence against women may be found to affect interstate commerce and affect it substantially.

… [T]he elusive heart of the majority's analysis in these cases is its statement that Congress's findings of fact are "weakened" by the presence of a disfavored "method of reasoning." This seems to suggest that the "substantial effects" analysis is not a factual enquiry, for Congress in the first instance with subsequent judicial review looking only to the rationality of the congressional conclusion, but one of a rather different sort, dependent upon a uniquely judicial competence.

The premise that the enumeration of powers implies that other powers are withheld is sound; the conclusion that some particular categories of subject matter are therefore presumptively beyond the reach of the commerce power is, however, a non sequitur. From the fact that Art. I, §8, cl. 3 grants an authority limited to regulating commerce, it follows only that Congress may claim no authority under that section to address any subject that does not affect commerce. It does not at all follow that an activity affecting commerce nonetheless falls outside the commerce power, depending on the specific character of the activity, or the authority of a State to regulate it along with Congress. My disagreement with the majority is not, however, confined to logic, for history has shown that categorical exclusions have proven as unworkable in practice as they are unsupportable in theory.

Why is the majority tempted to reject the lesson so painfully learned in 1937? An answer emerges from contrasting *Wickard* with one of the predecessor cases it superseded. It was obvious in *Wickard* that growing wheat for consumption right on the farm was not "commerce" in the common vocabulary, but that did not matter constitutionally so long as the aggregated activity of domestic wheat growing affected commerce substantially. Just a few years before *Wickard*, however, it had certainly been no less obvious that "mining" practices could substantially affect commerce, even though *Carter Coal Co.*, supra, had held mining regulation beyond the national commerce power. When we try to fathom the difference between the two cases, it is clear that they did not go in different directions because the *Carter Coal* Court could not understand a causal connection that the *Wickard* Court could grasp; the difference, rather, turned on the fact that the Court in *Carter Coal* had a reason for trying to maintain its categorical, formalistic distinction, while that reason had been abandoned by the time *Wickard* was decided. The reason was laissez-faire economics, the point of which was to keep government interference to a minimum. The Court in *Carter Coal* was still trying to create a laissez-faire world out of the 20th-century economy, and formalistic commercial distinctions were thought to be useful instruments in achieving that object. The Court in *Wickard* knew it could not do any such thing and in the aftermath of the New Deal had long since stopped attempting the impossible.

If we now ask why the formalistic economic/noneconomic distinction might matter today, after its rejection in *Wickard*, the answer is not that the majority fails to see causal connections in an integrated economic world. The answer is that in the minds of the majority there is a new animating theory that makes categorical formalism seem useful again. Just as the old formalism had value in the service of an economic conception, the new one is useful in serving a conception of federalism. It is the instrument by which assertions of national power are to be limited in favor of preserving a supposedly discernible, proper sphere of state autonomy to legislate or refrain from legislating as the individual States see fit. The legitimacy of the Court's current emphasis on the noncommercial nature of regulated activity, then, does not turn on any logic serving the text of the Commerce Clause or on the realism of the majority's view of the national economy. The essential issue is rather the

strength of the majority's claim to have a constitutional warrant for its current conception of a federal relationship enforceable by this Court through limits on otherwise plenary commerce power. This conception is the subject of the majority's second categorical discount applied today to the facts bearing on the substantial effects test.

All of this convinces me that today's ebb of the commerce power rests on error, and at the same time leads me to doubt that the majority's view will prove to be enduring law. There is yet one more reason for doubt. Although we sense the presence of *Carter Coal*, *Schechter*, and *Usery* once again, the majority embraces them only at arm's-length. Where such decisions once stood for rules, today's opinion points to considerations by which substantial effects are discounted. . . . As our predecessors learned then, the practice of such ad hoc review cannot preserve the distinction between the judicial and the legislative, and this Court, in any event, lacks the institutional capacity to maintain such a regime for very long. This one will end when the majority realizes that the conception of the commerce power for which it entertains hopes would inevitably fail the test expressed in Justice Holmes's statement that "the first call of a theory of law is that it should fit the facts." The facts that cannot be ignored today are the facts of integrated national commerce and a political relationship between States and Nation much affected by their respective treasuries and constitutional modifications adopted by the people. The federalism of some earlier time is no more adequate to account for those facts today than the theory of laissez-faire was able to govern the national economy 70 years ago.

GONZALES v. RAICH

545 U.S. 1 (2005)

Opinion: Stevens, joined by Kennedy, Souter, Ginsburg, Breyer
Concurrence: Scalia
Dissent: O'Connor, joined by Rehnquist and Thomas in all but Part III
Dissent: Thomas

Although California state law expressly allows certain individuals to grow their own marijuana as a treatment for various medical conditions, the federal Controlled Substances Act classifies marijuana as an illegal drug and bans its possession. Does Congress have the power to regulate marijuana even though California legalizes growing it and using it for some purposes? In Gonzales v. Raich, *the Court upheld Congress's power to authorize Drug Enforcement Administration officials to seize and destroy Angel Raich's supply of medical marijuana. Although Ms. Raich did not intend to sell or distribute her crop, the Court relied on* Wickard v. Filburn *to uphold her conviction. Do you agree with the Court that the Commerce Clause authorizes federal action in this case? Consider also U.S. Supreme Court Justice Antonin Scalia's concurrence. Do you think it is consistent with the majority positions in* United States v. Lopez *and* United States v. Morrison, *which he joined?*

JUSTICE STEVENS *delivered the opinion of the Court.*

The question presented in this case is whether the power vested in Congress by Article I, §8, of the Constitution "[t]o make all Laws which shall be necessary and proper for carrying into Execution" its authority to "regulate Commerce with foreign Nations, and among the several States" includes the power to prohibit the local cultivation and use of marijuana in compliance with California law.

Respondents Angel Raich and Diane Monson are California residents who suffer from a variety of serious medical conditions and have sought to avail themselves of medical marijuana pursuant to the terms of the Compassionate Use Act. They are being treated by licensed, board-certified family practitioners, who have concluded, after prescribing a host of conventional medicines to treat respondents' conditions and to alleviate their associated symptoms, that marijuana is the only drug available that provides effective treatment. Both women have been using marijuana as a medication for several years pursuant to their doctors' recommendation, and both rely heavily on cannabis to function on a daily basis. Indeed, Raich's physician believes that forgoing cannabis treatments would certainly cause Raich excruciating pain and could very well prove fatal.

On August 15, 2002, county deputy sheriffs and agents from the federal Drug Enforcement Administration (DEA) came to Monson's home. After a thorough investigation, the county officials concluded that her use of marijuana was entirely lawful as a matter of California law. Nevertheless, after a 3-hour standoff, the federal agents seized and destroyed all six of her cannabis plants.

Respondents thereafter brought this action against the Attorney General of the United States and the head of the DEA seeking injunctive and declaratory relief prohibiting the enforcement of the federal Controlled Substances Act to the extent it prevents them from possessing, obtaining, or manufacturing cannabis for their personal medical use. In their complaint and supporting affidavits, Raich and Monson described the severity of their afflictions, their repeatedly futile attempts to obtain relief with conventional medications, and the opinions of their doctors concerning their need to use marijuana....

The question before us, however, is not whether it is wise to enforce the statute in these circumstances; rather, it is whether Congress' power to regulate interstate markets for medicinal substances encompasses the portions of those markets that are supplied with drugs produced and consumed locally. Well-settled law controls our answer. The CSA is a valid exercise of federal power, even as applied to the troubling facts of this case.

Title II of that Act, the CSA, repealed most of the earlier antidrug laws in favor of a comprehensive regime to combat the international and interstate traffic in illicit drugs. The main objectives of the CSA were to conquer drug abuse and to control the legitimate and illegitimate traffic in controlled substances. Congress was particularly concerned with the need to prevent the diversion of drugs from legitimate to illicit channels.

To effectuate these goals, Congress devised a closed regulatory system making it unlawful to manufacture, distribute, dispense, or possess any controlled substance except in a manner authorized by the CSA. . . . In enacting the CSA, Congress classified marijuana as a Schedule I drug . . . because of [its] high potential for abuse, lack of any accepted medical use, and absence of any accepted safety for use in medically supervised treatment.

Respondents in this case do not dispute that passage of the CSA, as part of the Comprehensive Drug Abuse Prevention and Control Act, was well within Congress' commerce power. Nor do they contend that any provision or section of the CSA amounts to an unconstitutional exercise of congressional authority. Rather, respondents' challenge is actually quite limited; they argue that the CSA's categorical prohibition of the manufacture and possession of marijuana as applied to the intrastate manufacture and possession of marijuana for medical purposes pursuant to California law exceeds Congress' authority under the Commerce Clause.

Our case law firmly establishes Congress' power to regulate purely local activities that are part of an economic "class of activities" that have a substantial effect on interstate commerce. As we stated in *Wickard*, "even if appellee's activity be local and though it may not be regarded as commerce, it may still, whatever its nature, be reached by Congress if it exerts a substantial economic effect on interstate commerce." . . . When Congress decides that the "total incidence" of a practice poses a threat to a national market, it may regulate the entire class.

Our decision in *Wickard* is of particular relevance. In *Wickard*, we upheld the application of regulations promulgated under the Agricultural Adjustment Act of 1938, which were designed to control the volume of wheat moving in interstate and foreign commerce in order to avoid surpluses and consequent abnormally low prices. The regulations established an allotment of 11.1 acres for Filburn's 1941 wheat crop, but he sowed 23 acres, intending to use the excess by consuming it on his own farm. Filburn argued that even though we had sustained Congress' power to regulate the production of goods for commerce, that power did not authorize "federal regulation [of] production not intended in any part for commerce but wholly for consumption on the farm." Justice Jackson's opinion for a unanimous Court rejected this submission. He wrote:

"The effect of the statute before us is to restrict the amount which may be produced for market and the extent as well to which one may forestall resort to the market by producing to meet his own needs. That appellee's own contribution to the demand for wheat may be trivial by itself is not enough to remove him from the scope of federal regulation where, as here, his contribution, taken together with that of many others similarly situated, is far from trivial."

Wickard thus establishes that Congress can regulate purely intrastate activity that is not itself "commercial," in that it is not produced for sale, if it concludes that failure to regulate that class of activity would undercut the regulation of the interstate market in that commodity.

The similarities between this case and *Wickard* are striking. Like the farmer in *Wickard*, respondents are cultivating, for home consumption, a fungible commodity for which there is an established, albeit illegal, interstate market. Just as the Agricultural Adjustment Act was designed "to control the volume [of wheat] moving in interstate and foreign commerce in order to avoid surpluses . . ." and consequently control the market price, a primary purpose of the CSA is to control the supply and demand of controlled substances in both lawful and unlawful drug markets. In *Wickard*, we had no difficulty concluding that Congress had a rational basis for believing that, when viewed in the aggregate, leaving home-consumed wheat outside the regulatory scheme would have a substantial influence on price and market conditions. Here too, Congress had a rational basis for concluding that leaving home-consumed marijuana outside federal control would similarly affect price and market conditions.

More concretely, one concern prompting inclusion of wheat grown for home consumption in the 1938 Act was that rising market prices could draw such wheat into the interstate market, resulting in lower market prices. The parallel concern making it appropriate to include marijuana grown for home consumption in the CSA is the likelihood that the high demand in the interstate market will draw such marijuana into that market. While the diversion of homegrown wheat tended to frustrate the federal interest in stabilizing prices by regulating the volume of commercial transactions in the interstate market, the diversion of homegrown marijuana tends to frustrate the federal interest in eliminating commercial transactions in the interstate market in their entirety. In both cases, the regulation is squarely within Congress' commerce power because production of the commodity meant for home consumption, be it wheat or marijuana, has a substantial effect on supply and demand in the national market for that commodity.

Nonetheless, respondents suggest that *Wickard* differs from this case in three respects: (1) the Agricultural Adjustment Act, unlike the CSA, exempted small farming operations; (2) *Wickard* involved a "quintessential economic activity"—a commercial farm—whereas respondents do not sell marijuana; and (3) the *Wickard* record made it clear that the aggregate production of wheat for use on farms had a significant impact on market prices. Those differences, though factually accurate, do not diminish the precedential force of this Court's reasoning.

The fact that Wickard's own impact on the market was "trivial by itself" was not a sufficient reason for removing him from the scope of federal regulation. That the Secretary of Agriculture elected to exempt even smaller farms from regulation does not speak to his power to regulate all those whose aggregated production was significant, nor did that fact play any role in the Court's analysis. Moreover, even though Wickard was indeed a commercial farmer, the activity he was engaged in—the cultivation of wheat for home consumption—was not treated by the Court as part of his commercial farming operation. And while it is true that the record in the *Wickard* case itself established the causal connection between the production for local use and the national market, we have before us findings by Congress to the same effect.

... Respondents nonetheless insist that the CSA cannot be constitutionally applied to their activities because Congress did not make a specific finding that the intrastate cultivation and possession of marijuana for medical purposes based on the recommendation of a physician would substantially affect the larger interstate marijuana market. Be that as it may, we have never required Congress to make particularized findings in order to legislate, absent a special concern such as the protection of free speech. While congressional findings are certainly helpful in reviewing the substance of a congressional statutory scheme, particularly when the connection to commerce is not self-evident, and while we will consider congressional findings in our analysis when they are available, the absence of particularized findings does not call into question Congress' authority to legislate.

In assessing the scope of Congress' authority under the Commerce Clause, we stress that the task before us is a modest one. We need not determine whether respondents' activities, taken in the aggregate, substantially affect interstate commerce in fact, but only whether a "rational basis" exists for so concluding. Given the enforcement difficulties that attend distinguishing between marijuana cultivated locally and marijuana grown elsewhere and concerns about diversion into illicit channels, we have no difficulty concluding that Congress had a rational basis for believing that failure to regulate the

intrastate manufacture and possession of marijuana would leave a gaping hole in the CSA. Thus, as in *Wickard*, when it enacted comprehensive legislation to regulate the interstate market in a fungible commodity, Congress was acting well within its authority to "make all Laws which shall be necessary and proper" to "regulate Commerce . . . among the several States."

To support their contrary submission, respondents rely heavily on two of our more recent Commerce Clause cases. In their myopic focus, they overlook the larger context of modern-era Commerce Clause jurisprudence preserved by those cases. Moreover, even in the narrow prism of respondents' creation, they read those cases far too broadly.

Those two cases, of course, are *Lopez*, and *Morrison*. As an initial matter, the statutory challenges at issue in those cases were markedly different from the challenge respondents pursue in the case at hand. Here, respondents ask us to excise individual applications of a concededly valid statutory scheme. In contrast, in both *Lopez* and *Morrison*, the parties asserted that a particular statute or provision fell outside Congress' commerce power in its entirety. This distinction is pivotal for we have often reiterated that "[w]here the class of activities is regulated and that class is within the reach of federal power, the courts have no power 'to excise, as trivial, individual instances' of the class."

Unlike those at issue in *Lopez* and *Morrison*, the activities regulated by the CSA are quintessentially economic. "Economics" refers to "the production, distribution, and consumption of commodities." The CSA is a statute that regulates the production, distribution, and consumption of commodities for which there is an established, and lucrative, interstate market. Prohibiting the intrastate possession or manufacture of an article of commerce is a rational (and commonly utilized) means of regulating commerce in that product. Such prohibitions include specific decisions requiring that a drug be withdrawn from the market as a result of the failure to comply with regulatory requirements as well as decisions excluding Schedule I drugs entirely from the market. Because the CSA is a statute that directly regulates economic, commercial activity, our opinion in *Morrison* casts no doubt on its constitutionality.

. . . [T]he mere fact that marijuana—like virtually every other controlled substance regulated by the CSA—is used for medicinal purposes cannot possibly serve to distinguish it from the core activities regulated by the CSA.

Nor can it serve as an "objective marke[r]" or "objective facto[r]" to arbitrarily narrow the relevant class as the dissenters suggest. More fundamentally, if, as the principal dissent contends, the personal cultivation, possession, and use of marijuana for medicinal purposes is beyond the "'outer limits' of Congress' Commerce Clause authority," it must also be true that such personal use of marijuana (or any other homegrown drug) for recreational purposes is also beyond those "outer limits," whether or not a State elects to authorize or even regulate such use. Justice Thomas' separate dissent suffers from the same sweeping implications. That is, the dissenters' rationale logically extends to place any federal regulation (including quality, prescription, or quantity controls) of any locally cultivated and possessed controlled substance for any purpose beyond the "outer limits" of Congress' Commerce Clause authority. One need not have a degree in economics to understand why a nationwide exemption for the vast quantity of marijuana (or other drugs) locally cultivated for personal use (which presumably would include use by friends, neighbors, and family members) may have a substantial impact on the interstate

market for this extraordinarily popular substance. The congressional judgment that an exemption for such a significant segment of the total market would undermine the orderly enforcement of the entire regulatory scheme is entitled to a strong presumption of validity. . . .

Second, limiting the activity to marijuana possession and cultivation "in accordance with state law" cannot serve to place respondents' activities beyond congressional reach. The Supremacy Clause unambiguously provides that if there is any conflict between federal and state law, federal law shall prevail. . . .

Respondents . . . contend that their activities were not "an essential part of a larger regulatory scheme" because they had been "isolated by the State of California, and [are] policed by the State of California," and thus remain "entirely separated from the market." The dissenters fall prey to similar reasoning. The notion that California law has surgically excised a discrete activity that is hermetically sealed off from the larger interstate marijuana market is a dubious proposition, and, more importantly, one that Congress could have rationally rejected.

. . . Respondents also raise a substantive due process claim and seek to avail themselves of the medical necessity defense. These theories of relief were set forth in their complaint but were not reached by the Court of Appeals. We therefore do not address the question whether judicial relief is available to respondents on these alternative bases. We do note, however, the presence of another avenue of relief. As the Solicitor General confirmed during oral argument, the statute authorizes procedures for the reclassification of Schedule I drugs. But perhaps even more important than these legal avenues is the democratic process, in which the voices of voters allied with these respondents may one day be heard in the halls of Congress. Under the present state of the law, however, the judgment of the Court of Appeals must be vacated. The case is remanded for further proceedings consistent with this opinion.

JUSTICE SCALIA, *concurring in the judgment.*

I agree with the Court's holding that the Controlled Substances Act (CSA) may validly be applied to respondents' cultivation, distribution, and possession of marijuana for personal, medicinal use. I write separately because my understanding of the doctrinal foundation on which that holding rests is, if not inconsistent with that of the Court, at least more nuanced.

Since *Perez v. United States*, our cases have mechanically recited that the Commerce Clause permits congressional regulation of three categories: (1) the channels of interstate commerce; (2) the instrumentalities of interstate commerce, and persons or things in interstate commerce; and (3) activities that "substantially affect" interstate commerce. The first two categories are self-evident, since they are the ingredients of interstate commerce itself. The third category, however, is different in kind, and its recitation without explanation is misleading and incomplete.

It is misleading because, unlike the channels, instrumentalities, and agents of interstate commerce, activities that substantially affect interstate commerce are not themselves part of interstate commerce, and thus the power to regulate them cannot come from the Commerce Clause alone. Rather . . . Congress's regulatory authority over intrastate activities that are not themselves part of interstate commerce (including activities that have a substantial effect on interstate commerce) derives from the Necessary and Proper Clause. And the category of

"activities that substantially affect interstate commerce," is incomplete because the authority to enact laws necessary and proper for the regulation of interstate commerce is not limited to laws governing intrastate activities that substantially affect interstate commerce. Where necessary to make a regulation of interstate commerce effective, Congress may regulate even those intrastate activities that do not themselves substantially affect interstate commerce.

Our cases show that the regulation of intrastate activities may be necessary to and proper for the regulation of interstate commerce in two general circumstances. Most directly, the commerce power permits Congress not only to devise rules for the governance of commerce between States but also to facilitate interstate commerce by eliminating potential obstructions, and to restrict it by eliminating potential stimulants. That is why the Court has repeatedly sustained congressional legislation on the ground that the regulated activities had a substantial effect on interstate commerce. . . .

This principle is not without limitation. In *Lopez* and *Morrison*, the Court—conscious of the potential of the "substantially affects" test to "obliterate the distinction between what is national and what is local"—rejected the argument that Congress may regulate noneconomic activity based solely on the effect that it may have on interstate commerce through a remote chain of inferences . . . .

As we implicitly acknowledged in *Lopez*, however, Congress's authority to enact laws necessary and proper for the regulation of interstate commerce is not limited to laws directed against economic activities that have a substantial effect on interstate commerce. . . . As the Court put it in *Wrightwood Dairy*, where Congress has the authority to enact a regulation of interstate commerce, "it possesses every power needed to make that regulation effective."

Although this power "to make . . . regulation effective" commonly overlaps with the authority to regulate economic activities that substantially affect interstate commerce, and may in some cases have been confused with that authority, the two are distinct. The regulation of an intrastate activity may be essential to a comprehensive regulation of interstate commerce even though the intrastate activity does not itself "substantially affect" interstate commerce. Moreover . . . Congress may regulate even noneconomic local activity if that regulation is a necessary part of a more general regulation of interstate commerce. . . .

Today's principal dissent objects that, by permitting Congress to regulate activities necessary to effective interstate regulation, the Court reduces *Lopez* and *Morrison* to "little more than a drafting guide." (opinion of O'Connor, J.). I think that criticism unjustified. Unlike the power to regulate activities that have a substantial effect on interstate commerce, the power to enact laws enabling effective regulation of interstate commerce can only be exercised in conjunction with congressional regulation of an interstate market, and it extends only to those measures necessary to make the interstate regulation effective. As Lopez itself states, and the Court affirms today, Congress may regulate noneconomic intrastate activities only where the failure to do so "could . . . undercut" its regulation of interstate commerce.

Lopez and *Morrison* affirm that Congress may not regulate certain "purely local" activity within the States based solely on the attenuated effect that such activity may have in the interstate market. But those decisions do not declare noneconomic intrastate activities to be categorically beyond the reach of the Federal Government. . . . To dismiss this distinction as "superficial and formalistic" is to misunderstand the nature of the Necessary and Proper Clause, which empowers Congress to enact laws in effectuation of its enumerated powers that are not within its authority to enact in isolation. See *McCulloch v. Maryland*.

The application of these principles to the case before us is straightforward. In the CSA, Congress has undertaken to extinguish the interstate market in Schedule I controlled substances, including marijuana. The Commerce Clause unquestionably permits this. The power to regulate interstate commerce "extends not only to those regulations which aid, foster and protect the commerce, but embraces those which prohibit it." To effectuate its objective, Congress has prohibited almost all intrastate activities related to Schedule I substances—both economic activities (manufacture, distribution, possession with the intent to distribute) and noneconomic activities (simple possession). . . . Congress's authority to enact all of these prohibitions of intrastate controlled-substance activities depends only upon whether they are appropriate means of achieving the legitimate end of eradicating Schedule I substances from interstate commerce.

By this measure, I think the regulation must be sustained. Not only is it impossible to distinguish "controlled substances manufactured and distributed intrastate" from "controlled substances manufactured and distributed interstate," but it hardly makes sense to speak in such terms. Drugs like marijuana are fungible commodities. As the Court explains, marijuana that is grown at home and possessed for personal use is never more than an instant from the interstate market—and this is so whether or not the possession is for medicinal use or lawful use under the laws of a particular State. . . .

JUSTICE THOMAS, *dissenting.*

Respondents Diane Monson and Angel Raich use marijuana that has never been bought or sold, that has never crossed state lines, and that has had no demonstrable effect on the national market for marijuana. If Congress can regulate this under the Commerce Clause, then it can regulate virtually anything—and the Federal Government is no longer one of limited and enumerated powers.

I

Respondents' local cultivation and consumption of marijuana is not "Commerce . . . among the several States." By holding that Congress may regulate activity that is neither interstate nor commerce under the Interstate Commerce Clause, the Court abandons any attempt to enforce the Constitution's limits on federal power. The majority supports this conclusion by invoking, without explanation, the Necessary and Proper Clause. Regulating respondents' conduct, however, is not "necessary and proper for carrying into Execution" Congress' restrictions on the interstate drug trade. Thus, neither the Commerce Clause nor the Necessary and Proper Clause grants Congress the power to regulate respondents' conduct.

. . . [A]t the time of the founding, the term "'commerce' consisted of selling, buying, and bartering, as well as transporting for these purposes." Commerce, or trade, stood in contrast to productive activities like manufacturing and agriculture. Throughout founding-era dictionaries, Madison's notes from the Constitutional Convention, *The Federalist Papers*, and the ratification debates, the term "commerce" is consistently used to mean trade or exchange—not all economic or gainful activity that has some attenuated connection to trade

or exchange. . . . Certainly no evidence from the founding suggests that "commerce" included the mere possession of a good or some purely personal activity that did not involve trade or exchange for value. In the early days of the Republic, it would have been unthinkable that Congress could prohibit the local cultivation, possession, and consumption of marijuana.

On this traditional understanding of "commerce," the Controlled Substances Act regulates a great deal of marijuana trafficking that is interstate and commercial in character. The CSA does not, however, criminalize only the interstate buying and selling of marijuana. Instead, it bans the entire market—intrastate or interstate, noncommercial or commercial—for marijuana. Respondents are correct that the CSA exceeds Congress' commerce power as applied to their conduct, which is purely intrastate and noncommercial.

More difficult, however, is whether the CSA is a valid exercise of Congress' power to enact laws that are "necessary and proper for carrying into Execution" its power to regulate interstate commerce. The Necessary and Proper Clause is not a warrant to Congress to enact any law that bears some conceivable connection to the exercise of an enumerated power. Nor is it, however, a command to Congress to enact only laws that are absolutely indispensable to the exercise of an enumerated power.

To act under the Necessary and Proper Clause . . . Congress must select a means that is "appropriate" and "plainly adapted" to executing an enumerated power; the means cannot be otherwise "prohibited" by the Constitution; and the means cannot be inconsistent with "the letter and spirit of the [C]onstitution". . . . However, in order to be "necessary," the intrastate ban must be more than "a reasonable means [of] effectuat[ing] the regulation of interstate commerce." It must be "plainly adapted" to regulating interstate marijuana trafficking—in other words, there must be an "obvious, simple, and direct relation" between the intrastate ban and the regulation of interstate commerce. . . .

California's Compassionate Use Act sets respondents' conduct apart from other intrastate producers and users of marijuana. The Act channels marijuana use to "seriously ill Californians," and prohibits "the diversion of marijuana for nonmedical purposes." California strictly controls the cultivation and possession of marijuana for medical purposes. To be eligible for its program, California requires that a patient have an illness that cannabis can relieve, such as cancer, AIDS, or arthritis, and that he obtain a physician's recommendation or approval. Qualified patients must provide personal and medical information to obtain medical identification cards, and there is a statewide registry of cardholders. . . . This class of intrastate users is therefore distinguishable from others. . . .

But even assuming that States' controls allow some seepage of medical marijuana into the illicit drug market, there is a multibillion-dollar interstate market for marijuana. It is difficult to see how this vast market could be affected by diverted medical cannabis, let alone in a way that makes regulating intrastate medical marijuana obviously essential to controlling the interstate drug market.

In sum, neither in enacting the CSA nor in defending its application to respondents has the Government offered any obvious reason why banning medical marijuana use is necessary to stem the tide of interstate drug trafficking. Congress' goal of curtailing the interstate drug trade would not plainly be thwarted if it could not apply the CSA to patients like Monson and Raich.

Even assuming the CSA's ban on locally cultivated and consumed marijuana is "necessary," that does not mean it is also "proper." The means selected by Congress to regulate interstate commerce cannot be "prohibited" by, or inconsistent with the "letter and spirit" of, the Constitution.

Here, Congress has encroached on States' traditional police powers to define the criminal law and to protect the health, safety, and welfare of their citizens. Further, the Government's rationale—that it may regulate the production or possession of any commodity for which there is an interstate market—threatens to remove the remaining vestiges of States' traditional police powers. This would convert the Necessary and Proper Clause into precisely what Chief Justice Marshall did not envision, a "pretext . . . for the accomplishment of objects not intrusted to the government."

The majority holds that Congress may regulate intrastate cultivation and possession of medical marijuana under the Commerce Clause, because such conduct arguably has a substantial effect on interstate commerce. The majority's decision is further proof that the "substantial effects" test is a "rootless and malleable standard" at odds with the constitutional design.

The majority's treatment of the substantial effects test is rootless, because it is not tethered to either the Commerce Clause or the Necessary and Proper Clause. Under the Commerce Clause, Congress may regulate interstate commerce, not activities that substantially affect interstate commerce—any more than Congress may regulate activities that do not fall within, but that affect, the subjects of its other Article I powers. Whatever additional latitude the Necessary and Proper Clause affords, the question is whether Congress' legislation is essential to the regulation of interstate commerce itself—not whether the legislation extends only to economic activities that substantially affect interstate commerce.

The majority's treatment of the substantial effects test is malleable, because the majority expands the relevant conduct. By defining the class at a high level of generality (as the intrastate manufacture and possession of marijuana), the majority overlooks that individuals authorized by state law to manufacture and possess medical marijuana exert no demonstrable effect on the interstate drug market.

This Court has never held that Congress can regulate noneconomic activity that substantially affects interstate commerce. To evade even that modest restriction on federal power, the majority defines economic activity in the broadest possible terms as "the production, distribution, and consumption of commodities." This carves out a vast swath of activities that are subject to federal regulation. If the majority is to be taken seriously, the Federal Government may now regulate quilting bees, clothes drives, and potluck suppers throughout the 50 States. This makes a mockery of Madison's assurance to the people of New York that the "powers delegated" to the Federal Government are "few and defined," while those of the States are "numerous and indefinite."

If the majority is correct that *Lopez* and *Morrison* are distinct because they were facial challenges to "particular statute[s] or provision[s]," then congressional power turns on the manner in which Congress packages legislation. Under the majority's reasoning, Congress could not enact—either as a single-subject statute or as a separate provision in the CSA—a prohibition on the intrastate possession or cultivation of marijuana. Nor could it enact an intrastate ban simply to supplement existing drug regulations. However, that same prohibition is perfectly constitutional when integrated into a piece of legislation that reaches other regulable conduct.

Our federalist system, properly understood, allows California and a growing number of other States to decide for themselves how to safeguard the health and welfare of their citizens. I would affirm the judgment of the Court of Appeals. I respectfully dissent.

SYNTHESIS QUESTIONS FOR FURTHER DISCUSSION: CHAPTER 3 SECTION C

1. A significant argument in Justice Harry Blackmun's *Garcia v. San Antonio Metropolitan Transit Authority* opinion is that America's robust system of federalism does not require enforcement by the courts. Instead, the very structure of the federal government protects states' interests, with multiple veto points for policy changes, the Electoral College for presidential elections, and equal representation in the Senate. This was a popular argument among scholars who defended the New Deal, made most prominently by Herbert Wechsler. See Herbert Wechsler, "The Political Safeguards of Federalism: The Role of the States in the Composition and Selection of the National Government," *Columbia Law Review*, 54, no. 4 (Apr. 1954), pp. 543-560.

   Is Justice Blackmun's argument persuasive? Political safeguards also exist to protect individual rights, but many defenders of judicial review believe that courts should not simply defer to majority rule on these matters of constitutional principle. Is it possible to distinguish these two types of cases?

2.   Is U.S. Supreme Court Justice John Paul Stevens's result in *Gonzales v. Raich* required by *Wickard v. Filburn*? What theory might support national economic regulation but still find that Ms. Raich has the right—under the protection of state law—to grow medical marijuana? What role do *United States v. Lopez* and *United States v. Morrison* play in the reasoning in the decision? Consider Justice Antonin Scalia's concurrence, which draws from the broad *McCulloch* framework for congressional power. Are his arguments here consistent with his votes in *United States v. Lopez* and *United States v. Morrison*? How does this case differ from the way we might expect the "liberal" and "conservative" justices to vote?

3.   Previously we noted that Justice Oliver Wendell Holmes could not resist moral evaluation in regard to a case about child labor even though the constitutional arguments revolved around issues of congressional and state powers. In *Gonzales v. Raich*, one of the attorneys before the Supreme Courts, Randy Barnett, argued that in addition to the powers question, medical marijuana also raised issues of basic liberty. Specifically, Barnett argued that limits on medical marijuana violated constitutional rights under the doctrine of substantive due process. Should the issue of personal liberty help to frame the powers debate, or is it irrelevant to the kind of considerations we have explored in this chapter?

KEY TERMS

dual-sovereignty: The theory that suggests that both the states and the federal government are sovereign entities under the Constitution. On this theory, each retains certain exclusive powers. In particular, it holds that the Tenth Amendment and other provisions ensure a particular role for state power and limit federal power.

enumerated powers: Those powers specifically granted to Congress by the Constitution, in contrast to the states' more general police powers to regulate the "welfare, health, safety, and morals" of its population.

implied powers: Powers not explicitly stated in the Constitution, but thought granted by general phrases such as the Necessary and Proper Clause and the General Welfare Clause, often thought central to the decision in *McCulloch v. Maryland*.

New Federalism: The philosophy usually associated with the Reagan revolution, which sought to retrench the role of the federal government in the economic sphere; this also might refer to the Court's jurisprudence in pulling back congressional power under the Commerce Clause.

plenary powers: Exclusive powers explicitly granted to Congress, not shared with the states.

Progressive movement: A movement of the early twentieth century that sought increased roles for government in guaranteeing basic welfare for all and increased federal regulation of the economy and in stimulating economic growth.

PRESIDENTIAL AUTHORITY AND ITS LIMITS

In this chapter, we examine the power of the executive branch of government. Some of the Framers of the Constitution feared that the power endowed in this branch had significant potential for abuse, and they sought to ensure that the presidency was not vulnerable to the same abuses they thought defined monarchy. The danger of the presidency arguably inheres in the very idea of the execution of law. While lawmaking and adjudication are obviously important functions, it is in the act of carrying out the law that coercive power is most present. *The Federalist* No. 78 suggests, for instance, that the president "holds the sword of the community." In absolute monarchies and dictatorships, the power to execute the law is combined with the power to make law and to judge when it has been violated. But drawing on Montesquieu, an eighteenth-century French political theorist widely read by the drafters of the American Constitution, the Founders worried that such a consolidation of the powers of government would invariably lead to infringements upon individual liberty.

Montesquieu proposed the idea of the separation of powers as a way to avoid the dangers present in regimes, such as absolute monarchies, where powers to execute the laws were consolidated with the power to actually write the laws and interpret them. According to Montesquieu, liberty could best be protected by creating different institutions to carry out the three primary functions of government. Montesquieu suggests in one of our readings that "when the legislative and executive powers are united in the same person, or in the same body of magistrates, there can be no liberty." This same concern for liberty motivates the theories of federalism laid out in Chapter 3. In that chapter, you saw that the Founders created a structure of vertical separation of powers, dividing power between the national and the state governments; in this chapter, you will see how they also established a horizontal scheme at the federal level that sets the executive, legislative, and judicial powers against each other, creating a system of checks and balances. Dividing power among rival branches, they believed, would best preserve liberty and prevent tyranny.

The philosophy of the separation of powers is embodied not only in the writings of Montesquieu and the Founders, but also in the Constitution itself. Articles I, II, and III of the Constitution specify distinct functions for lawmaking, the execution of laws, and adjudication. Within each of these articles, specific powers are enumerated to delineate varying functions. It is tempting to see these specific enumerations as separating out the powers of the branches of government into distinct institutional entities. But as you will see in the cases and readings in this chapter, the manner in which such separation should occur is not obvious or uncontested. The greatest challenges for constitutional governance have occurred at the intersection of the functions outlined by Montesquieu. In particular, we examine various conflicts between the branches. Indeed, while the topic of this chapter is often referred to as "separation of powers," it might be more accurate to think of it as "conflicts of powers."

The source of conflicts between the branches is found partly in the fact that the powers of the executive, as outlined in Article II, are somewhat general and vague. It is important to note the contrast here with Article I. Whereas Article I grants to Congress only the powers that are "herein granted," such as the power to regulate commerce, Article II states simply that "the executive power shall be vested in the President." Note, though, that the Constitution never defines the meaning of the word "executive." Although Article II does enumerate specific powers for the president, such as the power to appoint cabinet officers, to veto legislation passed by Congress, and to serve as Commander-in-Chief of the military, there may also be functions inherent in "the executive power" besides these explicit grants of power. Additionally, Article II states that the president "shall take care that the laws be faithfully executed," an obligation that some scholars have argued implies a significant amount of latitude and discretion for executive authority.

Perhaps because the language vesting the executive power in the president is vague, questions remain as to what precisely executive power means. Most importantly, we are left with the question of whether the president has exclusive power in all matters of executive concern or whether his power must be shared with the legislature. For example, does the power of the president to appoint executive officers also imply that he has the exclusive power to remove such officers, or is he required to obtain the advice and consent of the Senate? What power does the president have to act without congressional authorization? Moreover, can power be delegated between the executive and legislative branches? For example, if executive power lies with the president, can Congress establish laws that allow this power to be shared either with independent agencies or with Congress itself?

As you will see in the cases throughout this chapter that deal with the above questions, although the powers of Congress and the executive branch at times appear to be clearly demarcated, in many other instances they come into conflict. This is particularly the case where powers are shared. Most obviously, while the president is the Commander-in-Chief, the Congress retains the power to declare war, the power to raise and support an army and a navy, and the power to pass the regulations that will govern those armed forces. We must ask in such instances where the Constitution draws the boundaries between these two branches.

The conflicts we examine here between the president and Congress open up larger issues about our constitutional democracy, which we first introduced in

Chapter 1. In that chapter we questioned why the Supreme Court, an unelected body, should have the power to strike down laws passed by democratic representatives. But what does democracy demand in instances of conflict between two representative branches? Although many have raised concerns about the Electoral College in the wake of *Bush v. Gore*, which we read in Chapter 1, the fact remains that the president and vice president are the only government officials elected by all of the nation's citizens. Some, such as Steven Calabresi, believe that this gives the presidency a particularly high level of democratic legitimacy, because he or she is accountable to the people as a whole. Others worry, however, that unchecked by Congress, the executive could become too powerful and thwart the will of the people. Indeed, a democratic election is no guarantee that principles such as the rule of law and respect for the interests of all citizens will be respected. We need only be reminded that dictators have often come to power through elections to see this point.

As you will see in *Youngstown Sheet & Tube Co. v. Sawyer*, which involved President Harry Truman's decision to seize private steel mills in a time of war, executive power is constitutionally limited by congressional authority. The executive power cannot encroach on areas in which Congress retains authority. Indeed, an effective way to ensure that the president has limited power is to grant another elected branch authority over some matters. The debate over war powers that we examine in Section B, for instance, also highlights how the potential danger of presidential control over the military is mitigated by Congress's authority.

In the final section of this chapter, we examine the relationship between the presidency and the rule of law. In addition to being tempered by Congress, presidential power is also limited by the Constitution itself. What role do the courts have in limiting executive power through enforcing the law? Famously, Richard Nixon declared in his post-Watergate interview with David Frost that "when the president does it, that means that it is not illegal." But, as you will see, our constitutional tradition has come to a different conclusion.

The most obvious difficulty with executive power is the worry that the president will become too powerful and either ignore the will of Congress or the rule of law altogether. But, as you will see, another modern issue at the heart of this chapter concerns the democratic accountability of administrative agencies. Part of President Franklin Roosevelt's New Deal included a vast expansion of what has become known as the "administrative state." Independent agencies such as the Federal Communications Commission, the Federal Election Commission, and the Federal Aviation Authority are appointed by the president but are not regarded as a part of the executive branch in the same way that cabinet departments are. The rationale is that some regulation should be carried out by parties that are insulated from political considerations. However, some have questioned the constitutionality of granting enormous power to these agencies of our government. The Constitution creates three branches of government, but it is unclear under which branch these agencies fall. In particular, *Humphrey's Executor v. United States* reveals that when it comes to the removal of the heads of these agencies, it is not straightforward which branch of government controls them. For originalists, there is a question as to what kind of constitutional status these agencies have since the administrative state was not anticipated by the Founding generation. Indeed, according to some thinkers, the existence of these agencies may very well violate the Constitution. Others have articulated a more limited critique, demanding that the lines of accountability be clear. Do these administrative agencies have too much independence from both the executive and congressional branches? Are there examples in which the president's power over executive agencies needs to be stronger in order to ensure democratic accountability?

In considering issues related to both the rule of the law, as well as those concerning the independence of administrative agencies, the theoretical debate, as well as the legal one, centers on the meaning of the "unitary executive." At the Founding, there was a lively debate about whether we should have more than one person serve as the chief executive. The Framers agreed, however, that there should be one president—in other words, a unitary executive. In contemporary politics, some have proposed that we rethink this decision. For instance, instead of having the president as the only nationally elected official who has power over the attorney general, some have proposed independent elections for some cabinet members. But in the realm of constitutional interpretation, the existence of only one executive is settled. The debate, rather, is about the meaning of this structure of government, in particular in its relation to the other branches regarding the separation of powers and foreign policy. Advocates of the unitary executive generally argue that the power of the president should not be shared with any other branch. Such thinkers conceptualize separation of powers as a commitment to complete and total separation between the various branches of government. In their article, law professors Lawrence Lessig and Cass Sunstein suggest that, although the Founders did not envision a unitary executive, it has become increasingly desirable over the course of history. However, some legal scholars oppose the idea of a unitary executive. They claim that, in fact, there should be some sharing or overlap in power between Congress and the president when it comes to the execution of the laws. As you read the cases included here, you should consider not only whether the Constitution endorses a unitary executive, but also whether such a scheme of power is in fact desirable in the context of the modern administrative state.

In discerning what exactly separation of powers entails, the readings of this chapter look to history and the text of the Constitution. But another way to think about this problem is to theorize about the executive function itself. According to many, the very idea of the executive includes a range of "inherent" powers that are necessary for the execution of the laws. Arguably, one such inherent power is control over foreign affairs. It might be thought that a nation needs to engage in foreign relations with one clear voice. But the notion that foreign relations are the exclusive power of the president is in conflict with Article I, Section 8, which grants Congress the power to declare war, regulate foreign trade, coin money, raise taxes, and raise and support an army and navy, as well as Article II, Section 2's requirement that treaties be made with the "advice and consent" of the Senate. In Section B, we consider the ways in which the debate over the unitary executive influences arguments about the president's powers when it comes to foreign affairs. Authors such as John Yoo argue that the president's power over foreign affairs is almost entirely exclusive and that the power to declare war is a narrow one. In contrast, John Hart Ely suggests that while the executive is responsible for carrying out the execution of war, the clear constitutional responsibility for its declaration, or commencement, mandates a large role for congressional deliberation in the formation of a national consensus.

The first two sections of the chapter examine the scope of presidential power in executing legislation in matters of domestic and foreign policy. The final section asks whether and how the rule of law limits the president when executive authority oversteps its bounds. The readings and cases of that section broaden our area of concern and force us to question the degree to which the president is subjected to the law. A number of cases probe the question of whether the president enjoys immunity from suit or evidentiary privileges. Together, these topics point to a larger controversy over presidential prerogative. Is the president ever above the law?

A. THE EXECUTIVE AND THE SEPARATION OF POWERS

What sources determine the power of the president, and how does the executive branch fit within the idea of the separation of powers? Are executive powers inherent, enumerated, or subject to congressional authorization?

This chapter begins with a selection from Montesquieu, whose writings directly influenced the thinking of the Founders. Although Montesquieu's writings about separation of powers are philosophical, they clearly provided a guide for those who were tasked with creating actual institutions of governance at the Constitutional Convention in 1787. His view is cited explicitly in *The Federalist Papers*. Despite the Founders' concern to show how the executive would be checked by both Congress and the judiciary, the Anti-Federalists worried that the executive power as it appeared in the Constitution would be tantamount to monarchy. We include from the Anti-Federalists a writing by "An Old Whig" that criticizes the presidency as the implementation of tyranny.

The modern debate about executive power revolves in large part around disputes over the interpretation of both Montesquieu and the Federalists. Defenders of a strong executive, what they label the unitary executive, argue that power should be held exclusively by the president and not shared with other branches or agencies. The unitary executive theory, defended by Lawrence Lessig, and Cass Sunstein resists such developments in American history as the independent prosecutor law and the development of shared responsibility for administrative agencies, such as the Federal Trade Commission, by the president and Congress.

Despite their many agreements, it also important to note the differences in the arguments about the unitary executive presented by Lessig and Sunstein, on the one hand, and Steven Calabresi and James Lindgren, on the other. For instance, Lessig and Sunstein pay close attention to the text of the Constitution and attempt to give an interpretation of executive power that is consistent with what they view as the original meaning of the document. With that said, their approach highlights the importance of adapting the original meaning of the Constitution to modern conditions and constraints that the Founders might not have foreseen. You might want to note the similarities between Lessig and Sunstein's arguments here and the earlier account of pragmatism that we excerpted in Chapter 2, including an earlier article by Sunstein. Although Calabresi previously has made use of originalist arguments in his work, his contribution here is noteworthy for its straightforward empirical arguments grounding his defense of an independent executive in arguments about democratic accountability. Calabresi addresses the worry that the presidency might be too strong, and in doing so makes way for arguments for a strong unitary executive. As you read through the case selection, keep in mind how each case raises questions about the original meaning of the Constitution, the text itself, and the more general question of the democratic accountability of the president, Congress, and the administrative agencies. To what extent do originalist arguments support limiting or expanding the power of the presidency? To what extent do concerns about democratic accountability shape the debate over the strength of the president's power?

Included in our case selection is *Youngstown Sheet & Tube Co. v. Sawyer*, the most influential modern legal formulation of how to understand conflicts between the branches. It is also notable because the opinion that has had the greatest influence was a concurrence, by U.S. Supreme Court Justice Robert H. Jackson, rather than the majority opinion. Justice Jackson's concurrence sets up a three-part structure for thinking about executive power. At one extreme are those cases where the president acts with the explicit approval of Congress. Here he acts with the maximum latitude. At the other extreme are those instances where the president acts despite congressional disapproval. Here he can do only those things explicitly assigned to the executive branch. In between is what Justice Jackson calls "the zone of twilight"—cases where Congress is silent and where the president lacks clear, explicit constitutional authority.

We also examine the question of the president's power to remove administrative appointees from office. The Constitution, you will recall, states that most administrative appointments must be made with the advice and consent of Congress—but says nothing about how these officials can be removed. This question was initially resolved in *Myers v. United States*, where the Court affirmed President Herbert Hoover's power to remove the postmaster general. But in *Humphrey's Executor v. United States*, the Court took a different view, ruling that the president's authority to remove officials could be constrained in those instances where Congress had established an explicit term of office for appointees in independent agencies. Those concerned with democratic accountability, including proponents of the unitary executive theory, worry that this undermines the ability of the public to hold these agencies accountable. This concern reached something of a zenith in a case challenging the constitutionality of the appointment of an independent prosecutor in *Morrison v. Olson*. This was a particularly fraught case, since leaving control over prosecutions of cases involving political corruption seemed to require independence from those who might actually be accused of these crimes—and the law being challenged here had been passed specifically in response to concerns about the abuse of prosecutorial discretion in the Watergate scandal.

Two cases in this section, *INS v. Chadha* and *Clinton v. New York*, address instances in which Congress attempted to alter the fundamental relationship between the legislative and executive branches by either increasing or weakening its own power in relation to the executive. In *INS v. Chadha*, the Court rejected an attempt by Congress to gain greater control over individual immigration cases through the so-called legislative veto. In *Clinton v. New York*, in contrast, the Court rejected an attempt by Congress to give away some of its constitutional power to write laws by granting the executive a line item veto, or the power to veto parts of congressional spending bills rather than to veto or accept in its entirety a bill passed by Congress.

As you examine both the readings and cases in this section, you should formulate your own ideas about the proper balance of power between Congress and the executive. Do you think that independent agencies of the type discussed in *Myers v. United States* and *Humphrey's Executor v. United States* should be under the complete control of the executive, or should there be shared power between Congress and the executive in the appointment and approval of the officers of these agencies? Moreover, you should pay particular attention to the framework outlined by Justice Jackson in the *Youngstown Sheet & Tube Co. v. Sawyer* case. Does this three-part framework accommodate the concerns about democracy that we struggled with in Chapter 1, as well as those raised in this chapter?

In many ways, the cases and readings in this section serve as a framework for the rest of this chapter. In particular, you should keep in mind how arguments about the unitary executive relate to more specific debates about the foreign policy powers of the presidency and whether the president should be immune to lawsuits.

Montesquieu

THE SPIRIT OF THE LAWS

Book XI, Section 6

New York, NY: Hafner Publishing Company (1949)

Political liberty is to be found only in moderate governments; and even in these it is not always found. It is there only when there is no abuse of power. But constant experience shows us that every man invested with power is apt to abuse it, and to carry his authority as far as it will go. Is it not strange, though true, to say that virtue itself has need of limits? To prevent this abuse, it is necessary from the very nature of things that power should be a check to power.

In every government there are three sorts of power: the legislative; the executive in respect to things dependent on the law of nations; and the executive in regard to matters that depend on the civil law.

By virtue of the first, the prince or magistrate enacts temporary or perpetual laws, and amends or abrogates those that have been already enacted. By the second, he makes peace or war, sends or receives embassies, establishes the public security, and provides against invasions. By the third, he punishes criminals, or determines the disputes that arise between individuals. The latter we shall call the judiciary power, and the other simply the executive power of the state.

The political liberty of the subject is a tranquillity of mind arising from the opinion each person has of his safety. In order to have this liberty, it is requisite the government be so constituted as one man need not be afraid of another.

When the legislative and executive powers are united in the same person, or in the same body of magistrates, there can be no liberty; because apprehensions may arise, lest the same monarch or senate should enact tyrannical laws, to execute them in a tyrannical manner.

Again, there is no liberty, if the judiciary power be not separated from the legislative and executive. Were it joined with the legislative, the life and liberty of the subject would be exposed to arbitrary control; for the judge would be then the legislator. Were it joined to the executive power, the judge might behave with violence and oppression.

There would be an end of everything, were the same man or the same body, whether of the nobles or of the people, to exercise those three powers, that of enacting laws, that of executing the public resolutions, and of trying the causes of individuals.

The judiciary power ought not to be given to a standing senate; it should be exercised by persons taken from the body of the people at certain times of the year, and consistently with a form and manner prescribed by law, in order to erect a tribunal that should last only so long as necessity requires.

By this method the judicial power, so terrible to mankind, not being annexed to any particular state or profession, becomes, as it were, invisible. People have not then the judges continually present to their view; they fear the office, but not the magistrate.

The other two powers may be given rather to magistrates or permanent bodies, because they are not exercised on any private subject; one being no more than the general will of the state, and the other the execution of that general will.

As in a country of liberty, every man who is supposed a free agent ought to be his own governor; the legislative power should reside in the whole body of the people. But since this is impossible in large states, and in small ones is subject to many inconveniences, it is fit the people should transact by their representatives what they cannot transact by themselves.

The executive power ought to be in the hands of a monarch, because this branch of government, having need of despatch, is better administered by one than by many: on the other hand, whatever depends on the legislative power is oftentimes better regulated by many than by a single person.

But if there were no monarch, and the executive power should be committed to a certain number of persons selected from the legislative body, there would be an end then of liberty; by reason the two powers would be united, as the same persons would sometimes possess, and would be always able to possess, a share in both.

THE

FEDERALIST:

A COLLECTION

O F

E   S   S   A   Y   S,

WRITTEN IN FAVOUR OF THE

NEW CONSTITUTION,

AS AGREED UPON BY THE FEDERAL CONVENTION,
SEPTEMBER 17, 1787.

IN TWO VOLUMES.

VOL. I.

NEW-YORK:

PRINTED AND SOLD BY J. AND A. M'LEAN,
No. 41, HANOVER-SQUARE.
M, DCC, LXXXVIII.

Title page of the first volume of The Federalist.

James Madison

THE FEDERALIST NO. 51

The Structure of the Government Must Furnish the Proper Checks and Balances Between the Different Departments

Independent Journal, Wednesday, February 6, 1788

To the People of the State of New York:

To what expedient, then, shall we finally resort, for maintaining in practice the necessary partition of power among the several departments, as laid down in the Constitution? The only answer that can be given is, that as all these exterior provisions are found to be inadequate, the defect must be supplied, by so contriving the interior structure of the government as that its several constituent parts may, by their mutual relations, be the means of keeping each other in their proper places. Without presuming to undertake a full development of this important idea, I will hazard a few general observations, which may perhaps place it in a clearer light, and enable us to form a more correct judgment of the principles and structure of the government planned by the convention.

In order to lay a due foundation for that separate and distinct exercise of the different powers of government, which to a certain extent is admitted on all hands to be essential to the preservation of liberty, it is evident that each department should have a will of its own; and consequently should be so constituted that the members of each should have as little agency as possible in the appointment of the members of the others. Were this principle rigorously adhered to, it would require that all the appointments for the supreme executive, legislative, and judiciary magistracies should be drawn from the same fountain of authority, the people, through channels having no communication whatever with one another. Perhaps such a plan of constructing the several departments would be less difficult in practice than it may in contemplation appear. Some difficulties, however, and some additional expense would attend the execution of it. Some deviations, therefore, from the principle must be admitted. In the constitution of the judiciary department in particular, it might be inexpedient to insist rigorously on the principle: first, because peculiar qualifications being essential in the members, the primary consideration ought to be to select that mode of choice which best secures these qualifications; secondly, because the permanent tenure by which the appointments are held in that department, must soon destroy all sense of dependence on the authority conferring them.

It is equally evident, that the members of each department should be as little dependent as possible on those of the others, for the emoluments annexed to their offices. Were the executive magistrate, or the judges, not independent of the legislature in this particular, their independence in every other would be merely nominal.

But the great security against a gradual concentration of the several powers in the same department, consists in giving to those who administer each department the necessary constitutional means and personal motives to resist encroachments of the others. The provision for defense must in this, as in all other cases, be made commensurate to the danger of attack. Ambition must be made to counteract ambition. The interest of the man must be connected with the constitutional rights of the place. It may be a reflection on human nature, that such devices should be necessary to control the abuses of government. But what is government itself, but the greatest of all reflections on human nature? If men were angels, no government would be necessary. If angels were to govern men, neither external nor internal controls on government would be necessary. In framing a government which is to be administered by men over men, the great difficulty lies in this: you must first enable the government to control the governed; and in the next place oblige it to control itself. A dependence on the people is, no doubt, the primary control on the government; but experience has taught mankind the necessity of auxiliary precautions.

This policy of supplying, by opposite and rival interests, the defect of better motives, might be traced through the whole system of human affairs, private as well as public. We see it particularly displayed in all the subordinate distributions of power, where the constant aim is to divide and arrange the several offices in such a manner as that each may be a check on the other—that the private interest of every individual may be a sentinel over the public rights. These inventions of prudence cannot be less requisite in the distribution of the supreme powers of the State.

AN OLD WHIG V

Philadelphia Independent Gazetteer, November 1, 1787

. . . [T]he office of President of the United States appears to me to be clothed with such powers as are dangerous. To be the fountain of all honors in the United States, commander in chief of the army, navy and militia, with the power of making treaties and of granting pardons, and to be vested with an authority to put a negative upon all laws, unless two thirds of both houses shall persist in enacting it, and put their names down upon calling the yeas and nays for that purpose, is in reality to be a KING as much *a King as the King of Great Britain*, and a King too of the worst kind;—an elective King.—If such powers as these are to be trusted in the hands of any man, they ought for the sake of preserving the peace of the community at once to be made hereditary.—Much as I abhor kingly government, yet I venture to pronounce where kings are admitted to rule they should most certainly be vested with hereditary power. The election of a King whether it be in America or Poland, will be a scene of horror and confusion; and I am perfectly serious when I declare that, as a friend to my country, I shall despair of any happiness in the United States until this office is either reduced to a lower pitch of power or made perpetual and hereditary.—When I say that our future President will be as much a king as the king of Great-Britain, I only ask of my readers to look into the constitution of that country, and then tell me what important prerogative the King of Great-Britain is entitled to, which does not also belong to the President during his continuance in office.—The King of Great-Britain it is true can create nobility which our President cannot; but our President will have the power of making all the *great men*, which comes to the same thing.—All the difference is that we shall be embroiled in contention about the choice of the man, whilst they are at peace under the security of an hereditary succession.—To be tumbled headlong from the pinnacle of greatness and be reduced to a shadow of departed royalty is a shock almost too great for human nature to endure. It will cost a man many struggles to resign such eminent powers, and ere long, we shall find, some one who will be very unwilling to part with them.—Let us suppose this man to be a favorite with his army, and that they are unwilling to part with their beloved commander in chief; or to make the thing familiar, let us suppose, a future President and commander in chief adored by his army and the militia to as great a degree as our late illustrious commander in chief; and we have only to suppose one thing more, that this man is without the virtue, the moderation and love of liberty which possessed the mind of our late general, and this country will be involved at once in war and tyranny. So far is it from its being improbable that the man who shall hereafter be in a situation to make the attempt to perpetuate his own power, should want the virtues of General Washington; that it is perhaps a chance of one hundred millions to one that the next age will not furnish an example of so disinterested a use of great power. We may also suppose, without trespassing upon the bounds of probability, that this man may not have the means of supporting in private life the dignity of his former station; that like Caesar, he may be at once ambitious and poor, and deeply involved in debt.—Such a man would die a thousand deaths rather than sink from the heights of splendor and power into obscurity and wretchedness. We are certainly about giving our president too much or too little; and in the course of less than twenty years we shall find that we have given him enough to enable him to take all. It would be infinitely more prudent to give him at once as much as would content him, so that we might be able to retain the rest in peace; for if once power is seized by violence not the least fragment of liberty will survive the shock. I would therefore advise my country-men seriously to ask themselves this question;—Whether they are prepared TO RECEIVE A KING? If they are to say at once, and make the kingly office hereditary; to frame a constitution that should set bounds to his power, and, as far as possible secure the liberty of the subject. If we are not prepared to *receive a king*, let us call another convention to revise the proposed constitution, and form it anew on the principles of a confederacy of free republics; but by no means, under pretence of a republic, to lay the foundation for a military government, which is the worst of all tyrannies.

Alexander Hamilton

THE FEDERALIST NO. 70

The Executive Department Further Considered

Independent Journal, Saturday, March 15, 1788

To the People of the State of New York:

Energy in the Executive is a leading character in the definition of good government. It is essential to the protection of the community against foreign attacks; it is not less essential to the steady administration of the laws; to the protection of property against those irregular and high-handed combinations which sometimes interrupt the ordinary course of justice; to the security of liberty against the enterprises and assaults of ambition, of faction, and of anarchy. Every man the least conversant in Roman history, knows how often that republic was obliged to take refuge in the absolute power of a single man, under the formidable title of Dictator, as well against the intrigues of ambitious individuals who aspired to the tyranny, and the seditions of whole classes of the community whose conduct threatened the existence of all government, as against the invasions of external enemies who menaced the conquest and destruction of Rome.

There can be no need, however, to multiply arguments or examples on this head. A feeble Executive implies a feeble execution of the government. A feeble execution is but another phrase for a bad execution; and a government ill executed, whatever it may be in theory, must be, in practice, a bad government.

Taking it for granted, therefore, that all men of sense will agree in the necessity of an energetic Executive, it will only remain to inquire, what are the ingredients which constitute this energy? How far can they be combined with those other ingredients which constitute safety in the republican sense? And how far does this combination characterize the plan which has been reported by the convention?

The ingredients which constitute energy in the Executive are, first, unity; secondly, duration; thirdly, an adequate provision for its support; fourthly, competent powers.

The ingredients which constitute safety in the republican sense are, first, a due dependence on the people, secondly, a due responsibility.

Those politicians and statesmen who have been the most celebrated for the soundness of their principles and for the justice of their views, have declared in favor of a single Executive and a numerous legislature. They have with great propriety, considered energy as the most necessary qualification of the former, and have regarded this as most applicable to power in a single hand, while they have, with equal propriety, considered the latter as best adapted to deliberation and wisdom, and best calculated to conciliate the confidence of the people and to secure their privileges and interests.

That unity is conducive to energy will not be disputed. Decision, activity, secrecy, and despatch will generally characterize the proceedings of one man in a much more eminent degree than the proceedings of any greater number; and in proportion as the number is increased, these qualities will be diminished.

This unity may be destroyed in two ways: either by vesting the power in two or more magistrates of equal dignity and authority; or by vesting it ostensibly in one man, subject, in whole or in part, to the control and co-operation of others, in the capacity of counsellors to him. Of the first, the two Consuls of Rome may serve as an example; of the last, we shall find examples in the constitutions of several of the States. New York and New Jersey, if I recollect right, are the only States which have intrusted the executive authority wholly to single men. Both these methods of destroying the unity of the Executive have their partisans; but the votaries of an executive council are the most numerous. They are both liable, if not to equal, to similar objections, and may in most lights be examined in conjunction.

The experience of other nations will afford little instruction on this head. As far, however, as it teaches any thing, it teaches us not to be enamoured of plurality in the Executive. We have seen that the Achaeans, on an experiment of two Praetors, were induced to abolish one. The Roman history records many instances of mischiefs to the republic from the dissensions between the Consuls, and between the military Tribunes, who were at times substituted for the Consuls. But it gives us no specimens of any peculiar advantages derived to the state from the circumstance of the plurality of those magistrates. That the dissensions between them were not more frequent or more fatal, is a matter of astonishment, until we advert to the singular position in which the republic was almost continually placed, and to the prudent policy pointed out by the circumstances of the state, and pursued by the Consuls, of making a division of the government between them. The patricians engaged in a perpetual struggle with the plebeians for the preservation of their ancient authorities and dignities; the Consuls, who were generally chosen out of the former body, were commonly united by the personal interest they had in the defense of the privileges of their order. In addition to this motive of union, after the arms of the republic had considerably expanded the bounds of its empire, it became an established custom with the Consuls to divide the administration between themselves by lot—one of them remaining at Rome to govern the city and its environs, the other taking the command in the more distant provinces. This expedient must, no doubt, have had great influence in preventing those collisions and rivalships which might otherwise have embroiled the peace of the republic.

But quitting the dim light of historical research, attaching ourselves purely to the dictates of reason and good sense, we shall discover much greater cause to reject than to approve the idea of plurality in the Executive, under any modification whatever.

Wherever two or more persons are engaged in any common enterprise or pursuit, there is always danger of difference of opinion. If it be a public trust or office, in which they are clothed with equal dignity and authority, there is peculiar danger of personal emulation and even animosity. From either, and especially from all these causes, the most bitter dissensions are apt to spring. Whenever these happen, they lessen the respectability, weaken the authority, and distract the plans and operation of those whom they divide. If they should unfortunately assail the supreme executive magistracy of a country, consisting of a plurality of persons, they might impede or frustrate the most important measures of the government, in the most critical emergencies of the state. And what is still worse, they might split the community into the most violent and irreconcilable factions, adhering differently to the different individuals who composed the magistracy.

Men often oppose a thing, merely because they have had no agency in planning it, or because it may have been planned by those whom they dislike. But if they have been consulted, and have happened to disapprove, opposition then becomes, in their estimation, an indispensable duty of self-love. They seem to think themselves bound in honor, and by all the motives of personal infallibility, to defeat the success of what has been resolved upon contrary to their sentiments. Men of upright, benevolent tempers have too many opportunities of remarking, with horror, to what desperate lengths this disposition is sometimes carried, and how often the great interests of society are sacrificed to the vanity, to the conceit, and to the obstinacy of individuals, who have credit enough to make their passions and their caprices interesting to mankind. Perhaps the question now before the public may, in its consequences, afford melancholy proofs of the effects of this despicable frailty, or rather detestable vice, in the human character.

Upon the principles of a free government, inconveniences from the source just mentioned must necessarily be submitted to in the formation of the legislature; but it is unnecessary, and therefore unwise, to introduce them into the constitution of the Executive. It is here too that they may be most pernicious. In the legislature, promptitude of decision is oftener an evil than a benefit. The differences of opinion, and the jarrings of parties in that department of the government, though they may sometimes obstruct salutary plans, yet often promote deliberation and circumspection, and serve to check excesses in the majority. When a resolution too is once taken, the opposition must be at an end. That resolution is a law, and resistance to it punishable. But no favorable circumstances palliate or atone for the disadvantages of dissension in the executive department. Here, they are pure and unmixed. There is no point at which they cease to operate. They serve to embarrass and weaken the execution of the plan or measure to which they relate, from the first step to the final conclusion of it. They constantly counteract those qualities in the Executive which are the most necessary ingredients in its composition—vigor and expedition, and this without any counterbalancing good. In the conduct of war, in which the energy of the Executive is the bulwark of the national security, every thing would be to be apprehended from its plurality.

But one of the weightiest objections to a plurality in the Executive, and which lies as much against the last as the first plan, is, that it tends to conceal faults and destroy responsibility.

Responsibility is of two kinds—to censure and to punishment. The first is the more important of the two, especially in an elective office. Man, in public trust, will much oftener act in such a manner as to render him unworthy of being any longer trusted, than in such a manner as to make him obnoxious to legal punishment. But the multiplication of the Executive adds to the difficulty of detection in either case. It often becomes impossible, amidst mutual accusations, to determine on whom the blame or the punishment of a pernicious measure, or series of pernicious measures, ought really to fall. It is shifted from one to another with so much dexterity, and under such plausible appearances, that the public opinion is left in suspense about the real author. The circumstances which may have led to any national miscarriage or misfortune are sometimes so complicated that, where there are a number of actors who may have had different degrees and kinds of agency, though we may clearly see upon the whole that there has been mismanagement, yet it may be impracticable to pronounce to whose account the evil which may have been incurred is truly chargeable.

It is evident from these considerations, that the plurality of the Executive tends to deprive the people of the two greatest securities they can have for the faithful exercise of any delegated power, *first*, the restraints of public opinion, which lose their efficacy, as well on account of the division of the censure attendant on bad measures among a number, as on account of the uncertainty on whom it ought to fall; and, *second*, the opportunity of discovering with facility and clearness the misconduct of the persons they trust, in order either to their removal from office or to their actual punishment in cases which admit of it.

The idea of a council to the Executive, which has so generally obtained in the State constitutions, has been derived from that maxim of republican jealousy which considers power as safer in the hands of a number of men than of a single man. If the maxim should be admitted to be applicable to the case, I should contend that the advantage on that side would not counterbalance the numerous disadvantages on the opposite side. But I do not think the rule at all applicable to the executive power. I clearly concur in opinion, in this particular, with a writer whom the celebrated Junius pronounces to be "deep, solid, and ingenious," that "the executive power is more easily confined when it is ONE"; that it is far more safe there should be a single object for the jealousy and watchfulness of the people; and, in a word, that all multiplication of the Executive is rather dangerous than friendly to liberty.

Lawrence Lessig & Cass R. Sunstein

THE PRESIDENT AND THE ADMINISTRATION

94 Colum L. Rev. 1 (Jan. 1994)

INTRODUCTION

Many think that under our constitutional system, the President must have the authority to control all government officials who implement the laws. The text, structure, and history of the Constitution, we are told, plainly require this result. Under this view, it is therefore something of an embarrassment that the Supreme Court has permitted conspicuous exceptions to this constitutional imperative. We now have independent special counsels, independent agencies, and other such exceptions, commonly thought to be inconsistent with the basic founding commitment to a unitary executive.

Some believe that this conception of unitariness derives from something that the framers decided—that the framers constitutionalized a strongly unitary executive, and that anyone following the original design must follow this structural pattern.

We think that the view that the framers constitutionalized anything like this vision of the executive is just plain myth. It is a creation of the twentieth century, not the eighteenth. It derives from twentieth century categories applied unreflectively to an eighteenth-century document. It ignores strong evidence that the framers imagined not a clear executive hierarchy with the President at the summit, but a large degree of congressional power to structure the administration as it thought proper.

We reach this conclusion with reluctance. A strongly unitary executive can promote important values of accountability, coordination, and uniformity in the execution of the laws, and to whatever extent these were the framers' values, they are certainly now ours. If these values are not advanced by the original design, we seemingly face an unpleasant dilemma—either we adhere to that design and sacrifice important institutional values, or we advance these institutional values and sacrifice fidelity to the original design. History apparently leads us to choose between the original design and a design many now view as indispensable.

At least this is so unless there is a compelling nonhistorical argument supporting a strong unitary design. We believe that there is indeed a plausible structural argument on behalf of the hierarchical conception of the unitary executive. This is an argument that emphasizes changed circumstances since the eighteenth century, and that accommodates the framers' design within this changed constitutional context—an argument, that is, that translates the framers' original design from the language and context of the eighteenth century into the world today. . . .

NEW CIRCUMSTANCES, OLD COMMITMENTS

We are concerned with the task of preserving initial constitutional commitments in light of changes in the constitutional context. In what follows, we first outline some relevant initial commitments, and then sketch two types of contextual change that make new applications necessary if these old commitments are to be maintained.

From our focus on what the framers said and did, we can identify a number of values that bear on whether we categorize a particular institution as executive (and hence requiring plenary presidential control) and that affect whether a particular limit on presidential control is proper. Unitariness was unquestionably one such value. As we have seen, the framers rejected a plural executive, and the Decision of 1789 shows that for some decisions, presidential control was indeed required. The framers believed that unitariness advanced the interests of coordination, accountability, and efficiency in the execution of the laws. All of these policies argued against a fragmented executive. In certain cases, it was critical that the executive be able to act with dispatch and without dissent. To account for those cases, the framers decided that the executive structure should be unitary.

The Vesting Clause of Article II—by placing the executive in one rather than many presidents—embodied this judgment. It is therefore clear that the constitutional text and structure reflect commitments to the unitary virtues of coordination, accountability, and efficiency in government. These commitments account for the unitariness of the presidency and of the executive power across a certain domain.

But it is equally certain that in some cases other values were relevant, and these values may at times constitutionally trump unitariness. On the founding view, efficiency not only justifies unitariness but also occasional legislative departures from that notion; it explains something of the relative independence of the district attorneys. So too does fear of executive and judicial aggrandizement. We have already noted the complexities in the Decision of 1789, but one lesson of that story was that sometimes the values of independence from the President could rightfully trump the interests of unitariness. The independence of adjudicative officers is one such interest. Maintaining congressional control over spending, to take another example, led the framers to reduce executive control over the Treasury, unitarian considerations notwithstanding.

From these distinct values we can draw together two that are for our purposes central. First is a value in accountability—where no special reason existed to separate responsibility from the President, the pattern of original executive structures strongly supports the conclusion that the President remains accountable for the actions of government officers. Of course, the general idea of accountability is embodied not only in the allocation of executive power, but also in the grant of legislative power to Congress, accompanied by a ban on open-ended delegations of legislative power. Second is a value of avoiding faction. This goal is, of course, at the center of the constitutional structure, and it helps explain the system of checks and balances in general.

Accountability and avoidance of factionalism, then, are two central values of the framers' original executive. Let us focus now on two sorts of changes in the current constitutional context that may require accommodation to continue to preserve these two original values.

The first, and least controversial, type of change is in the functions of what we are calling administrative agencies. What agencies do—the nature of their power and the way that power is exercised—is very different now from what it was at the framing period. Lawmaking and law-interpreting authority is now concentrated in an extraordinary array of regulatory agencies. This development has ensured that domestic policymaking is often done, not at the state level or even through Congress, but through large national bureaucracies.

This massive transformation in the institutional framework of American public law was entirely unanticipated by the framers, and it fundamentally altered the original constitutional design. We do not contend that administration was itself unanticipated, or that at the founding period it was trivial. On the contrary, the original period contained a precursor of the modern administrative state. But what we do now is not what was done then. General managerial functions were not within the domain of the national government, much less the President. Much of the organization of the national economy was left to state courts. By contrast, the national government restricted itself largely to national improvements, subsidies, tariffs, patents, tonnage, and the disposal of public lands. Whether or not Articles I and II were designed for congressional dominance, it seems clear that the early presidency involved little policymaking role in domestic affairs.

Things are of course different today. To take just one example, the Federal Communications Commission (FCC) sets national policy with respect to broadcasting. The FCC is not fully analogous to the administrative institutions at the founding, which never (or almost never) had such broad policymaking discretion. The problem is intensified when we recall that the FCC is merely one of a bewildering array of national administrative entities armed with similar power. Perhaps the immunization of such entities from presidential authority would now compromise constitutional commitments, indeed the very commitments that underlay the decision to create a (kind of) unitary presidency. Consider the original interest in coordination and the extent to which that interest would be compromised by allowing Congress to prevent the President from overseeing environmental or energy policy. For this reason, some institutions currently denominated administrative could arguably fall under presidential control as a matter of constitutional compulsion. This is because what administrative institutions do now is, in nature and scope, quite different from what administrative institutions did then—indeed, what such institutions do now is in terms of sheer importance more analogous to what unquestionably executive agencies did at the founding period. We will lay principal stress on this difference, suggesting that the framers' acquiescence in allowing some institutions to be independent of the President does not entail the conclusion that current, very different institutions can be similarly independent.

Second, and more controversially, some values may have become more or less important because we now have a better pragmatic understanding about how institutions actually function and a better understanding of the nature of the values at issue. This is the lesson from experience. Here the change consists not of new institutions raising unforeseen issues, but instead of new understandings of what certain governmental activities entail. At one time, for example, it may have been thought that an independent agency would best advance the policy interests of program X, but experience reveals that with independence, an independent agency is highly likely to fall victim to factional capture. Or it may have been thought that some sufficiently protected agencies could engage in apolitical, scientific, technocratic implementation of the laws; but now many believe that the notion of purely apolitical implementation is impossible, at least when discretionary judgments are involved. Of course assessments of this kind should be made principally by nonjudicial officials. But they may bear on constitutional interpretation as well. If either change occurred, then entities that Congress legitimately made independent when either view reigned must, perhaps, now be placed under the wing of the President as a matter of constitutional compulsion.

We begin, then, with the values of accountability and avoidance of faction, and we are confronted with changes in the types of function performed by modern regulatory agencies and in the lessons provided by experience with regulation. Consider how these two changes might work together to suggest that the modern executive must be strongly unitary, even if the framers' executive was not.

In the original understanding, officials who exercise the President's enumerated powers must operate under his control. But Congress was originally entitled to immunize some officials from presidential control when it thought proper—in particular, if those officials operated like judges, or if their duties were ministerial, or even if (as in the case of the Comptroller) their actions were discretionary but properly separated from the President's. All this of course operated in the context of a presidency that had an exceptionally narrow range of discretionary policymaking authorities in the domestic arena, at least compared to what we now find routine. Most of the functions performed by what we call the federal executive branch were originally the province of state legislatures and state courts, which had principal authority over regulation of the economy.

Now consider the character of the modern presidency. In the aftermath of the New Deal, administrative agencies carry out a wide range of highly discretionary policymaking tasks in the domestic arena. Because of delegations of discretionary authority to administrative agencies, the functions of those who execute the law have dramatically altered. Because of this discretionary authority, these agencies are now principal national policymakers—in practice, crucial lawmakers, both through regulation and interpretation. For example, control of the environment is in large measure a policy decision of the administrator of the Environmental Protection Agency. Parallel observations might be made for decisions relating to occupational safety and health, consumer products, and energy, including nuclear power. The same is true of implementation decisions. Rather than being ministerial, they involve highly discretionary choices about the content of domestic policy.

To say this is not to say that administrators at the founding had no policymaking power; of course they did. But it is hard to dispute the view that there has been a fundamental change in the legal context, involving the scope and nature of policymaking discretion that members of administrative agencies now possess. As the scope of the discretion of administrators has increased, their function has dramatically changed. At the founding, ministerial functions were freed from presidential control, and a wide range of administrative tasks plausibly could have been considered ministerial. Similarly, entities that performed judicial functions, or that engaged in tasks related to the purse, were also free of executive control. But now many administrators exercise what seem uncontroversially to be political functions, in the sense that their actions involve a great deal of discretion about policy and principle in implementing federal law. It remains true that many administrators also adjudicate; but the very process of adjudication frequently involves the creation of national policy under vague standards, as in, for example, the work of the National Labor Relations Board, the Federal Communications Commission, the Securities and Exchange Commission, and the Federal Trade Commission.

In short, in a period in which administrators exercise a wide range of discretionary authority, the very meaning of immunizing them from presidential control changes dramatically. When fundamental policy decisions are made by administrators, immunizing them from presidential control would have two significant consequences: first, it would segment fundamental policy decisions from direct political accountability and thus the capacity for coordination and democratic control; and second, it would subject these institutions to the perverse incentives of factions, by removing the insulating arm of the President, and increasing the opportunity for influence by powerful private groups. Neither of these consequences was favored by the framers. Indeed, both problems were specifically what the framers sought to avoid. For both these reasons—retaining accountability and avoiding factions—an interpreter could reasonably conclude either that it makes sense to understand the term executive to include more of the administrative power than the framers would have (specifically) included, or alternatively, that a legislative effort to insulate what is misleadingly labeled administration from the President is an improper exercise of legislative authority under the Necessary and Proper Clause.

All this describes how the function of administration has changed, and in ways that raise doubts about whether independence can be given to administrators, consistent with original constitutional commitments. Now consider a second change, one equally important.

In the last two centuries, there have been large-scale shifts in the nature of our understanding of what the administrators' power is. What was striking about the nineteenth-century view was the faith in the ability of administrative bodies to stand impartial in some scientific search for the true (rather than best) policy judgment. This was the progressive faith in administrative expertise. As Grundstein, a turn of the century theorist, wrote:

> Administration . . . was the realm of the professional, the scientist and the neutral technician, in the affairs of government, . . . set . . . apart from Politics in the sense that while the latter had to do with policies or expressions of the state will administration had to do with their execution.

But the post–New Deal view questions the very presupposition of this nineteenth-century model—the presupposition that the political can be so sharply separated from the administrative. To be sure, many insist on technocratic rationality—on the importance of expertise in helping people to make informed judgments about the relations between means and ends. This is an enduring theme in administrative law. We do not mean to disparage the importance of expertise in providing the foundation for sound public judgments. On the contrary, the absence of expertise, or the distortion of expert judgment through anecdote and interest-group power, is an important obstacle to a well-functioning system of regulatory law. But there has been an unmistakable and we believe fully warranted diminution in the progressive era's faith in the ability of expertise to solve regulatory problems on its own. This diminution has brought about a significant shift. As noted by (it is reported) Judge Scalia in the per curiam decision of a three-judge district court striking a portion of the Gramm-Rudman-Hollings Act,

> "These cases reflect considerable shifts over the course of time, not only in the Supreme Court's resolutions of particular issues relating to the removal power, but more importantly in the constitutional premises underlying those resolutions." It is not clear, moreover, that these shifts are at an end. Justice Sutherland's decision in *Humphrey's Executor* (1935) . . . is stamped with some of the political science preconceptions characteristic of its era and not of the present day. . . . It is not as obvious today as it seemed in the 1930s that there can be such things as genuinely 'independent' regulatory agencies, bodies of impartial experts whose independence from the President does not entail correspondingly greater dependence upon the committees of Congress to which they are then immediately accountable; or indeed, that the decisions of such agencies so clearly involve scientific judgment rather than political choice that it is even theoretically desirable to insulate them from the democratic process.

In a world where administration is conceived as apolitical, granting administrators relatively independent authority could be thought to raise few constitutional issues. If the administrators are simply executing a technical skill, there is little reason to make their judgment subject to the review of the President. In such a world, the grant of authority to independent commissions could build directly on two precedents provided in the framing period—ministerial duties, which by definition do not involve discretion, and the quasi-adjudicative Comptroller. The Supreme Court accepted this highly technocratic conception of administration in *Humphrey's Executor v. United States*, the heyday of the progressive model within the judiciary. On progressive assumptions, *Humphrey's Executor* builds quite directly on framing premises and precedents insofar as the Court emphasized quasi-legislative and quasi-adjudicative functions—an irony in view of the widespread view that the case was a bizarre and unfounded exercise in constitutional innovation.

But once this view of administration changes—once one sees the nature of administration as fundamentally political—new questions are raised about the extent to which courts may permit this power to be independent of the President. The presupposition behind independent administration—what made it capable of drawing on analogies like the Comptroller General and the Postmaster in the founding period—is no longer sustainable. The question for interpretation is how to accommodate this fundamental change in understanding.

If all this is true, an argument for the strongly unitary executive under modern conditions takes the following form. From the actual administrative entities that the framers established, we can infer that the framers did not intend to allow administrative officials exercising broad policymaking authority to operate independently of the President. With respect to such officials, they made no explicit judgment, for their existence was not foreseen. The framers anticipated a much smaller national government, in which states would have the fundamental role and in which Congress would engage in basic policymaking, and they believed that the President would exercise a good deal of discretionary authority only in international relations. The execution of federal domestic law would often be mechanical, and crucially, nonpolitical. For this reason, the founding commitment to a unitary executive could coexist with a range of federal officials not directly subject to presidential control.

To the framers, centralization of executive power in the President was indeed designed to promote accountability, expedition, and coordination in federal law, and nothing we have said questions their commitment to a unitary executive at this level of generality. Indeed, these were fundamental constitutional principles. Our point is only that the framers did not believe that those principles would be compromised by insulating particular administrators from presidential control.

It was in the nineteenth century that one of the features distinguishing the framers' world from ours changed. Here was the rise of a massive federal bureaucracy; but unlike the legal culture today, the culture of the nineteenth-century theorists was firm in its faith in the scientific model of administration, so that the theorists did not see constitutional problems with relatively independent agencies. The nineteenth-century culture could accommodate the growth in bureaucracy by approving relatively independent agencies while staying within the bounds of fidelity.

But for us, the central fact of the eighteenth-century executive (limited national government and limited delegations to federal administrators) has changed, and the central assumption of the nineteenth-century solution (neutral, scientific administration) has failed. For now, we not only have a large administrative bureaucracy, but we also have profound skepticism about whether it is possible and desirable for that bureaucracy to operate free from political judgment. Echoing Justice Brandeis (quoting Justice Holmes) in *Erie R.R. Co. v. Tompkins*, we could say that administration in the sense in which courts speak of it today can no longer be understood to be neutral, or scientific. Politics is at its core, in the sense that value judgments are pervasive and democratic controls on policymaking are indispensable. This raises a central problem for a modern bureaucratic state. The question the interpreter must answer is how best to accommodate this current skepticism—what structure makes most sense of the framers' design, given the change in the extent of the bureaucracy and the change in our understanding of what bureaucracy is.

The answer to this question is not simple. No doubt our understandings are complex and multiple, and no doubt the principal place for registering changes in understanding is the legislature, not the judiciary. Congress' diminished enthusiasm for the independent agency form attests to the possibility that new views about expertise and factionalism can influence legislative judgments, informed by constitutional considerations, about appropriate structures. It would be possible to say that courts should not take account of changed understandings in the process of constitutional interpretation. But it is also possible to think that changes of this kind are relevant to interpretation as well as to lawmaking.

A structural argument for a unitary executive, then, comes down to this: Where the framers allocated a power that they thought of as political, that power was allocated to people who were themselves politically accountable. This was part of the fundamental commitments to accountability and avoidance of factionalism. At the founding period, the existence of a degree of independence in administration could not realistically have been thought to compromise these commitments. Today, by contrast, a strong presumption of unitariness is necessary in order to promote the original constitutional commitments. The legislative creation of domestic officials operating independently of the President but exercising important discretionary policymaking power now stands inconsistent with founding commitments.

It follows that in order to be faithful to the founding vision in changed circumstances, courts must now bar Congress, at least as a presumption, from immunizing from presidential control the activities of officials who exercise discretionary policymaking authority—at least if those officials are not adjudicators. In order to be faithful to the original design, that is, the interpreter must see as part of the constitutional structure a constraint not explicitly stated in that design, requiring that certain kinds of policymaking remain within the control of the executive.

A contrary view, set out forcefully by Abner Greene, could also be suggested by this same history—one that argues against a strongly unitary executive. Perhaps the original design reflected a carefully calibrated set of judgments about institutional authority, with a division between lawmaking and law implementation; perhaps the most important changed circumstance was the disturbance of this calibration through the delegation of policymaking authority to the President. On this view, the key founding commitments call for diffusion of power and for checks and balances between the legislature and the executive. The principal threat of the post–New Deal period lies in the concentration of lawmaking and law-executing power within the presidency. To restore the original balance, courts must now allow a high degree of independence from presidential power, so as to prevent what the framers dreaded most: the concentration of governmental power in a single institution—here, the executive.

This argument also stresses the need to maintain fidelity with the original constitutional design. It too is an argument of translation. But it takes the post–New Deal developments as a reason for more rather than less caution about unitariness in administration. The new circumstances mean that unitariness is a far greater threat than it once was—not that unitariness is a constitutionally compelled solution.

More particularly, this view fears that the new delegations have threatened to confer excessive power on the executive branch—to create an imperial presidency. The changed circumstances argue in favor of a narrow reading of executive power and for broad congressional authority under the Necessary and Proper Clause, precisely in the interest of maintaining the original commitment to a system of checks and balances. On this view, congressional power to insulate administration from presidential control is a necessary quid pro quo for the exercise of discretionary lawmaking power by people other than legislators. The rise of lawmaking by nonlegislative bodies—most especially, the downfall of the nondelegation doctrine—makes it especially necessary to insist on congressional prerogatives under the Necessary and Proper Clause,

in order to prevent an aggregation of powers in the presidency. In short, Greene urges, the post–New Deal developments mean that modern interpreters should place less value on unitariness than did the framers, because of the need to maintain fidelity with the commitment to the diffusion of power.

This argument is hardly without force. It shows that there is no algorithm for deciding how to maintain fidelity with past instructions in the face of changed circumstances. But we do not believe that the argument is ultimately persuasive. The first and most fundamental problem is that the argument treats diffusion of power as an end in itself, rather than as an instrument for serving various purposes connected with the preservation of liberty. The second problem is that even if broad delegations of authority are the problem, independent agencies are not the solution.

Perhaps Congress can point to the need to limit presidential authority in order to support some isolated efforts to prevent concentration of power in the President. But it seems clear that the changed circumstances do not justify the immunization of all or most bureaucratic power from the President. This is because it is hard to identify how independent administration is a realistic solution to the constitutional problems caused by changed circumstances. Indeed, independent administration would sacrifice many values the founders saw as essential.

We conclude that if the framers thought that the realm of executive power was roughly coextensive with the realm of political choice, it makes sense to say that most of modern administration must fall under the power of the executive; and this is so even if the framers had a relatively capacious, but not specifically constitutionalized, conception of what counted as the administrative. Their conception of administrative (or permissibly nonexecutive) power certainly did not extend to the broad-scale selection of domestic policies for the country as a whole. If we are to translate their structural choices into current conditions, we may conclude that a largely hierarchical executive branch is the best way of keeping faith with the original plan. At least this is so if we are asking whether the President has a degree of removal and supervisory power over people who are authorized to make high-level discretionary decisions about the content of national policy.

Steven G. Calabresi & James Lindgren

THE PRESIDENT: LIGHTNING ROD OR KING?

115 Yale L.J. 2611 (2006)

I. THE POWERS OF A KING?

There is an idea current in the land today that presidential power has grown to the point where it is a threat to democracy. The *New York Times* editorial page writers and leading Democrats regularly accuse President George W. Bush of acting like a king or seeking kingly powers. In the academic community, Professor Bruce Ackerman has written powerfully about what he sees as the danger that presidential power poses to democracy itself. In this symposium issue, Professors Bill Marshall and Jennifer Martinez argue that the presidency has become too powerful. Marshall goes so far as to argue for reducing presidential power by separately electing the Attorney General.

In this Commentary, we suggest that when political power is examined more broadly, presidents and their parties generally have less power in the United States than commentators usually recognize. We believe the president today is less of a king than a lightning rod. Indeed, the constitutional and practical weakness of the presidency is, if not a threat to American democracy, at least a worrisome limitation on it. . . .

II. A WEAK OFFICE UNDER THE CONSTITUTION

Every four years Americans focus intently for ten months on the nation's presidential race. That race formally begins in late January with the Iowa caucuses and the New Hampshire primary, and it continues non-stop until November with a torrent of primaries, nominating conventions, presidential and vice presidential debates, and opinion polls. The unmistakable message sent to the voters is that this is it: the selection of a new president will determine which direction we go in as a society for the next four years. Electing the president is the democratic decision that really counts.

The problem with this idea is that it is not true. The president's formal powers under the Constitution are far too narrow to justify the hoopla that surrounds presidential elections. Under the Constitution, for example, presidents have very limited power over domestic policy. Anyone who doubts this should consider the fate of President Bush's proposals to reform social security and the tax code or President Clinton's attempt to introduce national health care.

The main levers that the Constitution gives the president over domestic policy are the veto power and the power to appoint principal officers in the executive and judicial branches subject to senatorial advice and consent. But the allegedly imperial George Bush has not yet vetoed even one piece of Congressional legislation. And it is easy to make too much of even the president's significant power over appointments. It is hard to induce most federal agencies to change directions (the NLRB is a notable exception), as is suggested by the successful thwarting of George Bush's recent attempts to reform the culture at the CIA. One must remember that federal departments and agencies are called *bureaucracies* for a reason. Even the significant effects of Bush's judicial appointments will be felt mainly in the period after he leaves office.

Ah, but a skeptic might say that the president has the dominant voice in foreign policy. Perhaps it is this formidable presidential power that justifies our quadrennial year-long presidential selection spectacle? Consider, however, just how little power a president really has even in this realm. Presidents can start military actions, but those military actions can be waged successfully only to the extent that Congress is willing to pay for them. Presidents can offer foreign aid, but again only to the extent Congress is willing to pay the bill. Presidents can propose free trade zones, but only if Congress is willing by a vote of both houses to go along. Presidents can negotiate treaties, but they become law only if two-thirds of the Senate approves. In short, while the president is the dominant player in foreign policy, there is almost nothing vital that the president can do even in this realm without some help from Congress. On its face, the power that voters grant to a

president every four years is less than is generally supposed.

III. OF COATTAILS, MIDTERM BACKLASHES, AND LIGHTNING RODS

A. Losses in Midterm Congressional Elections

In a broader political sense, elections convey even less power to presidents and their parties than we have just described. First, as the substantial political science literature on midterm elections documents, it is an iron law of politics that the president's party almost always loses seats in Congress during the biennial midterm elections and especially during the second midterm election of an eight-year presidency. The data are consistent with the anecdotal evidence that the party holding the presidency six years into an eight-year tenure becomes a lightning rod for voter discontent.

Recently it is not just the second midterm election that has been a disaster for most presidents: often it is the first midterm election as well. Midterm losses in a president's first term can lead to his party losing control of both houses of Congress, as happened to Bill Clinton in 1994, or simply to losing enough seats that the president can no longer push his agenda, as happened to Ronald Reagan in 1982....

B. Losses in State Elections

Strikingly, this midterm backlash is not confined just to federal elections. As James Campbell has nicely documented, there is a backlash against the president's party in the midterm elections for seats in state legislatures. Campbell shows that in state legislative races in presidential election years, the winning president's party benefits from his coattails, but in midterm elections the president's party suffers losses in state legislative races that approximately cancel out the gains from his coattails. Further, in an article published 35 years ago, Stephen Turrett analyzed incumbent governors' races in 1900–1969, noticing that incumbent governors were more likely to be re-elected in midterm elections if the president was of the opposing party. Turrett limited his analysis of this midterm effect to incumbent governors running for re-election and interpreted it as merely offsetting the coattail effect in presidential election years.

When one adds all gubernatorial races to the analysis, as we do in Charts 1 and 2, the backlash against the president's party in state races during a president's term is actually *stronger* overall than the coattail effect in the presidential election year. To be more specific, we find that four years after a party wins a presidential election it holds on average three *fewer* statehouses than it had *before it won* the presidential election! Perversely, winning the presidency seems to lead very shortly to losing power in the states. Since 1932 there have been eight changes of party control of the White House (1933, 1953, 1961, 1969, 1977, 1981, 1993, and 2001). In every instance but one, the party that seized the White House held more governorships in the year before they took office than in the year they lost the election leading to their leaving the White House. The only exception is that in 1980 Republicans held four fewer governorships than they held in 1992, immediately before the Republicans were voted out of the White House. Similarly, of the eleven presidents since 1933, every one except two (Kennedy and Reagan) left office with fewer governorships than his party had before he took office. Chart 1 shows this pattern.

The four-year pattern of a federal election cycle is shown in Chart 2. If one looks at the pattern since 1968, in his first year in office a president's party controls

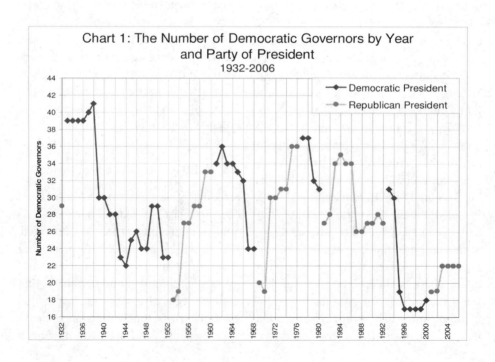

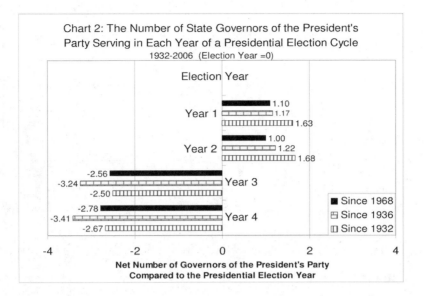

Chart 2: The Number of State Governors of the President's Party Serving in Each Year of a Presidential Election Cycle 1932-2006 (Election Year =0)

only 1.1 more governorships than the party had in the election year. Once in office, there is a backlash against the sitting president's party. On average since 1968, by the third and fourth years of a four-year presidential administration he has lost nearly four seats (3.7-3.9) from his first year, thus losing not only that one "coattail effect"

seat, but nearly three more governorships as well. One sees a similar, but slightly stronger pattern since 1936. If one looks at just two-term administrations since the 1950s, by the seventh year of the administration, the party winning the White House has 6 fewer governorships on average than it had before it won the White House.

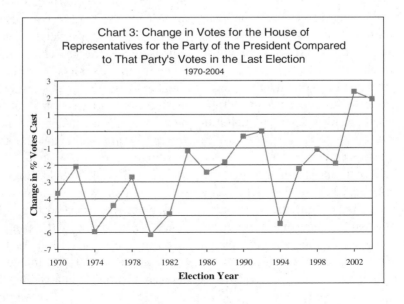

Chart 3: Change in Votes for the House of Representatives for the Party of the President Compared to That Party's Votes in the Last Election 1970-2004

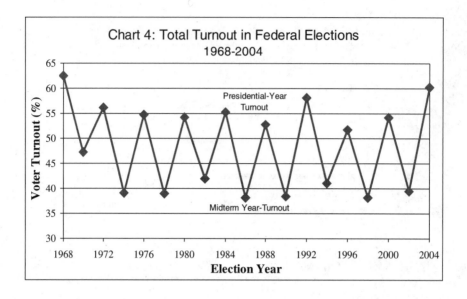

C. Why We See a Lightning
Rod Effect

What is driving the backlash we are documenting here? First, and most obviously, presidents become lightning rods for everything that goes wrong. Most presidents leave office less popular than when they entered, with Ronald Reagan and Bill Clinton being the only exceptions since at least Dwight Eisenhower. Even the exceptions (Reagan and Clinton) suffered major Congressional losses in their first midterm elections, at times when their job approval ratings were down substantially. Thus, the response of voters is to blame the president for whatever goes wrong, and probably as a result, to punish that president's party in midterm elections.

In Chart 3, we show that in the eighteen federal elections since 1970, in all but three of them (1992, 2002, and 2004), the party controlling the White House at the time of the election lost some of its proportion of the electorate for the House, compared with its proportion of the House vote two years before.

Second, as Chart 4 shows, not everyone votes in the midterm elections. Voter turnout is, in fact, significantly lower in midterm elections than it is during presidential years, and, as is well known, even American voter turnout in presidential years is low compared with the turnout in other Western democracies. Typically, turnout in a presidential year is about 55% of registered voters and turnout in midterm elections hovers around 40% of registered voters (Chart 4). The reasons for this are not hard to find. Americans are taught to think that the choice of a president is the key choice that gets made in their democracy, so that is the election everyone focuses on and votes in. The midterm election is of interest only to political junkies and to those voters who are mad about the direction in which the nation is going when the midterm election is held. Those angry voters in 1982 were disproportionately Democrats who were hostile to Ronald Reagan's dismantling of the safety net set up during the New Deal and Great Society years. Conversely, in 1994 the angry voters were disproportionately Republicans who were mad about everything from national health care, to gun control, to gay rights.

The effect therefore of successfully mobilizing to win the 1980 election for Ronald Reagan or the 1992 election for Bill Clinton was almost to guarantee the triumph of one's political opponents two years hence in an election where the turnout was around 40% of all registered voters, so that a mere 21% of registered voters constituted a majority. This midterm election allocated nearly as much federal power as did the presidential election and more power in the states. Yet this midterm election was one in which one's political opponents were much more likely to turn out and vote than one's allies—a very strange form of democracy indeed. Moreover, the losses suffered in the 1982 or 1994 midterm elections were of such a nature that they were unlikely to be undone until the other party again held the lightning rod office of the presidency.

The third reason for the strength of the perverse lightning rod effect is that in the mid-twentieth century, some states moved their governors' races to off-years in part to minimize the president's coattail effect and thus the effects of the presidential election cycle on state politics. Now only eleven states elect their governors on the same day as they vote for the president, while 36 states elect their governors during the year of a presidential midterm. Five other states, Kentucky, Mississippi, Louisiana, New Jersey, and Virginia, pick their governors during an odd numbered, non-presidential election year. All of the most populous (and thus politically powerful) states pick their governors during the midterm year, including California, Georgia, Florida, Illinois, Massachusetts, Michigan, New York, Pennsylvania, Ohio, and Texas. In a presidential year, the presidency, one third of the Senate, the entire House of Representatives, and eleven governorships are up for election. In the midterm year, one third of the Senate, the entire House of Representatives, and 36 governorships, including all the most important ones, are up for election with another five governorships up in odd numbered years. The huge number of governorships that are open in midterm and odd numbered years make the midterm elections of central importance to government in the United States.

In Reagan's second year, 1982, Republicans went from holding twenty-four governorships to holding sixteen—a reduction of 33%. In Clinton's second year, 1994, Republicans went from holding twenty governorships to holding thirty—an increase of 50%. The same pattern occurred in the 1960's and 1970's. In 1968, at the end of the Kennedy-Johnson years, Republicans held thirty-one governorships. In 1976, at the end of the Nixon-Ford years, Republicans held only twelve governorships.

IV. CONCLUSION

The American political landscape changes, not just every four years, but every two years as well. What has not been adequately recognized in the scholarly literature is that the changes in control in the states in the gubernatorial off-year elections are indeed larger than any coattail effect in the presidential election year, largely because only eleven small states elect their governors at the same time as they vote for president. The net effect is that by the time a president is up for re-election, his party controls fewer governorships than even before he won the election. Winning the presidency seems to lead very shortly to losing power, not only in Congress, but in state governorships as well. When one adds this perverse effect to the constitutional weakness of the presidency, the extraordinary emphasis on the presidential election every four years seems misplaced.

No American president has ever seriously threatened our democratic system of government, but democracy may be undermined when people regularly mobilize for and participate in a presidential election that is likely to produce on balance the opposite policy consequences from those that the people have voted for. Rather than worrying about imaginary threats of dictatorship, we ought to be worried today about an electoral system that may be regularly frustrating the popular will.

MYERS v. UNITED STATES

272 U.S. 52 (1926)

Opinion: Taft, joined by Van Devanter, Sutherland, Butler, Sanford, Stone
Dissent: Holmes
Dissent: McReynolds
Dissent: Brandeis

This is the first of three cases included in this section that concern the power of the president to remove executive officers. In this case, the Court decided that the president has full power to remove individuals exercising executive functions. This decision, however, was qualified over the course of time. The majority decision here and the dissent of U.S. Supreme Court Justice Louis Brandeis are part of a debate that has persisted from the time of the writing of the Constitution until the present. In your opinion, what, if any, are the appropriate limits on the power of the president to remove executive officers? As you begin to read these cases, you should consider what implications the power of the president to appoint executive officers has for his removal power. Is it essential to democratic accountability that the president have the authority to hire and fire? As you consider this, you might pick up on the possible tension noted by Justice Brandeis between the efficiency of the executive function and the risk that the president will retain arbitrary power.

MR. CHIEF JUSTICE TAFT *delivered the opinion of the Court.*

This case presents the question whether, under the Constitution, the President has the exclusive power of removing executive officers of the United States whom he has appointed by and with the advice and consent of the Senate.

Myers was, on July 21, 1917, appointed by the President, by and with the advice and consent of the Senate, to be a postmaster of the first class at Portland, Oregon, for a term of four years. On January 20, 1920, Myers' resignation was demanded. He refused the demand. On February 2, 1920, he was removed from office by order of the Postmaster General, acting by direction of the President. He protested to the Department against his removal, and continued to do so until the end of his term. He pursued no other occupation, and drew compensation for no other service during the interval. On April 21, 1921, he brought this suit in the Court of Claims for his salary from the date of his removal, which, as claimed by supplemental petition filed after July 21, 1921, the end of his term, amounted to $8,838.71.

By the 6th section of the Act of Congress of July 12, 1876, under which Myers was appointed with the advice and consent of the Senate as a first-class postmaster, it is provided that

> Postmasters of the first, second and third classes shall be appointed and may be removed by the President by and with the advice and consent of the Senate and shall hold their offices for four years unless sooner removed or suspended according to law.

The Senate did not consent to the President's removal of Myers during his term. If this statute, in its requirement that his term should be four years unless sooner removed by the President by and with the consent of the Senate, is valid, the appellant is entitled to recover his unpaid salary for his full term. The Government maintains that the requirement is invalid for the reason that, under Article II of the Constitution the President's power of removal of executive officers appointed by him with the advice and consent of the Senate is full and complete without consent of the Senate. If this view is sound, the removal of Myers by the President without the Senate's consent was legal. We are therefore confronted by the constitutional question, and cannot avoid it.

The question where the power of removal of executive officers appointed by the President by and with the advice and consent of the Senate was vested was presented early in the first session of the First Congress. There is no express provision respecting removals in the Constitution, except as Section 4 of Article II provides for removal from office by impeachment. The subject was not discussed in the Constitutional Convention. Under the Articles of Confederation, Congress was given the power of appointing certain executive officers of the Confederation, and, during the Revolution and while the Articles were given effect, Congress exercised the power of removal.

First. Mr. Madison insisted that Article II, by vesting the executive power in the President, was intended to grant to him the power of appointment and removal of executive officers except as thereafter expressly provided in that Article. He pointed out that one of the chief purposes of the Convention was to separate the legislative from the executive functions. He said:

> If there is a principle in our Constitution, indeed in any free Constitution, more sacred than another, it is that which separates the Legislative, Executive and Judicial powers. If there is any point in which the separation of the Legislative and Executive powers ought to be maintained with great caution, it is that which relates to officers and offices.

1 Annals of Congress, 581.

Their union under the Confederation had not worked well, as the members of the convention knew. Montesquieu's view that the maintenance of independence as between the legislative, the executive, and the judicial branches was a security for the people had their full approval. Accordingly, the Constitution was so framed as to vest in the Congress all legislative powers therein granted, to vest in the President the executive power, and to vest in one Supreme Court and such inferior courts as Congress might establish the judicial power. From this division on principle, the reasonable construction of the Constitution must be that the branches should be kept separate in all cases in which they were not expressly blended, and the Constitution should be expounded to blend them no more than it affirmatively requires.

The vesting of the executive power in the President was essentially a grant of the power to execute the laws. But the President, alone and unaided, could not execute the laws. He must execute them by the assistance of subordinates. As he is charged specifically to take care that they be faithfully executed, the reasonable implication, even in the absence of express words, was that, as part of his executive power, he should select those who were to act for him under his direction in the execution of the laws. The further implication must be, in the absence of any express limitation respecting removals, that, as his selection of administrative officers is essential to the execution of the laws by him, so must be his power of removing those for whom he cannot continue to be responsible.

The executive power was given in general terms, strengthened by specific terms where emphasis was regarded as appropriate, and was limited by direct expressions where limitation was needed, and the fact that no express limit was placed on the power of removal by the Executive was convincing indication that none was intended.

The reason for the principle is that those in charge of and responsible for administering functions of government who select their executive subordinates need, in meeting their responsibility, to have the power to remove those whom they appoint.

For the reasons given, we must therefore hold that the provision of the law of 1876, by which the unrestricted power of removal of first class postmasters is denied to the President, is in violation of the Constitution, and invalid.

MR. JUSTICE BRANDEIS, *dissenting*.

The Act of July 12, 1876, c. 17, §6, 19 Stat. 78, 80, reenacting earlier legislation, provided that "postmasters of the first, second, and third classes shall be appointed and may be removed by the President by and with the advice and consent of the Senate, and shall hold their offices for four years unless sooner removed or suspended according to law." That statute has been in force unmodified for half a century. Throughout the period, it has governed a large majority of all civil offices to which appointments are made by and with the advice and consent of the Senate. May the President, having acted under the statute insofar as it creates the office and authorizes the appointment, ignore, while the Senate is in session, the provision which prescribes the condition under which a removal may take place?

It is this narrow question, and this only, which we are required to decide.

In *Marbury v. Madison*, it was assumed, as the basis of decision, that the President, acting alone, is powerless to remove an inferior civil officer appointed for a fixed term with the consent of the Senate, and that case was long regarded as so deciding. In no case has this Court determined that the President's power of removal is beyond control, limitation, or regulation by Congress. Nor has any lower federal court ever so decided. This is true of the power as it affects officers in the Army or the Navy and the high political officer like heads of departments, as well as of the power in respect to inferior statutory offices in the executive branch. Continuously for the last fifty-eight years, laws comprehensive in character, enacted from time to time with the approval of the President, have made removal from the great majority of the inferior presidential offices dependent upon the consent of the Senate. Throughout that period these laws have been continuously applied. We are requested to disregard the authority of *Marbury v. Madison* and to overturn this long established constitutional practice.

The contention that Congress is powerless to make consent of the Senate a condition of removal by the President from an executive office rests mainly upon the clause in §1 of Article II which declares that

"The executive Power shall be vested in a President." The argument is that appointment and removal of officials are executive prerogatives; that the grant to the President of "the executive Power" confers upon him, as inherent in the office, the power to exercise these two functions without restriction by Congress, except insofar a the power to restrict his exercise of them is expressly conferred upon Congress by the Constitution; that, in respect to appointment, certain restrictions of the executive power are so provided for; but that, in respect to removal, there is no express grant to Congress of any power to limit the President's prerogative.

It is true that the exercise of the power of removal is said to be an executive act, and that, when the Senate grants or withholds consent to a removal by the President, it participates in an executive act. But the Constitution has confessedly granted to Congress the legislative power to create offices, and to prescribe the tenure thereof, and it has not in terms denied to Congress the power to control removals.

The separation of the powers of government did not make each branch completely autonomous. It left each in some measure dependent upon the others, as it left to each power to exercise, in some respects, functions in their nature executive, legislative and judicial. Obviously the President cannot secure full execution of the laws, if Congress denies to him adequate means of doing so. Full execution may be defeated because Congress declines to create offices indispensable for that purpose. Or because Congress, having created the office, declines to make the indispensable appropriation. Or because Congress, having both created the office and made the appropriation, prevents, by restrictions which it imposes, the appointment of officials who in quality and character are indispensable to the efficient execution of the law. If, in any such way, adequate means are denied to the President, the fault will lie with Congress. The President performs his full constitutional duty if, with the means and instruments provided by Congress and within the limitations prescribed by it, he uses his best endeavors to secure the faithful execution of the laws enacted. *Compare Kendall v. United States.* Checks and balances were established in order that this should be "a government of laws, and not of men."

The doctrine of the separation of powers was adopted by the convention of 1787 not to promote efficiency, but to preclude the exercise of arbitrary power. The purpose was not to avoid friction but, by means of the inevitable friction incident to the distribution of the governmental powers among three departments, to save the people from autocracy. In order to prevent arbitrary executive action, the Constitution provided in terms that presidential appointments be made with the consent of the Senate, unless Congress should otherwise provide, and this clause was construed by Alexander Hamilton in *The Federalist*, No. 77, as requiring like consent to removals.

Nothing in support of the claim of uncontrollable power can be inferred from the silence of the Convention of 1787 on the subject of removal. For the outstanding fact remains that every specific proposal to confer such uncontrollable power upon the President was rejected. In America, as in England, the conviction prevailed then that the people must look to representative assemblies for the protection of their liberties. And protection of the individual, even if he be an official, from the arbitrary or capricious exercise of power was then believed to be an essential of free government.

HUMPHREY'S EXECUTOR v. UNITED STATES

295 U.S. 602 (1935)

Opinion: Sutherland, joined by Hughes, Van Devanter, McReynolds, Brandeis, Butler, Stone, Roberts, Cardozo

In this case, the Supreme Court considered the constitutionality of a legislative act that limited the power of the president to remove from office individuals performing "quasi-legislative" or "quasi-judicial" functions. The Court decided that the president does not have limitless authority to remove such officers. To what extent does the reasoning in this case mark a departure from that in Myers v. United States, *in which the Court decided that the president has complete power to remove executive officers? Is it in fact possible to differentiate in a meaningful way between officers that perform quasi-legislative or quasi-judicial functions and those that perform purely executive duties? In other words, does this case provide a useful constitutional standard?*

MR. JUSTICE SUTHERLAND *delivered the opinion of the Court.*

Plaintiff brought suit in the Court of Claims against the United States to recover a sum of money alleged to be due the deceased for salary as a Federal Trade Commissioner from October 8, 1933, when the President undertook to remove him from office, to the time of his death on February 14, 1934.

William E. Humphrey, the decedent, on December 10, 1931, was nominated by President Hoover to succeed himself as a member of the Federal Trade Commission, and was confirmed by the United States Senate. He was duly commissioned for a term of seven years expiring September 25, 1938; and, after taking the required oath of office, entered upon his duties. On July 25, 1933, President Roosevelt addressed a letter to the commissioner asking for his resignation, on the ground "that the aims and purposes of the Administration with respect to the work of the Commission can be carried out most effectively with personnel of my own selection," but disclaiming any reflection upon the commissioner personally or upon his services. The commissioner replied, asking time to consult his friends.

The commissioner declined to resign, and on October 7, 1933, the President wrote him:

> Effective as of this date, you are hereby removed from the office of Commissioner of the Federal Trade Commission.

Humphrey never acquiesced in this action, but continued thereafter to insist that he was still a member of the commission, entitled to perform its duties and receive the compensation provided by law at the rate of $10,000 per annum. Upon these and other facts set forth in the certificate, which we deem it unnecessary to recite, the following questions are certified:

> 1. Do the provisions of section 1 of the Federal Trade Commission Act, stating that "any commissioner may be removed by the President for inefficiency, neglect of duty, or malfeasance in office," restrict or limit the power of the President to remove a commissioner except upon one or more of the causes named?
>
> If the foregoing question is answered in the affirmative, then—
>
> 2. If the power of the President to remove a commissioner is restricted or limited as shown by the foregoing interrogatory and the answer made thereto, is such a restriction or limitation valid under the Constitution of the United States?

The Federal Trade Commission Act creates a commission of five members to be appointed by the President by and with the advice and consent of the Senate, and §1 provides:

Not more than three of the commissioners shall be members of the same political party. The first commissioners appointed shall continue in office for terms of three, four, five, six, and seven years, respectively, from the date of the taking effect of this Act, the term of each to be designated by the President, but their successors shall be appointed for terms of seven years, except that any person chosen to fill a vacancy shall be appointed only for the unexpired term of the commissioner whom he shall succeed. The commission shall choose a chairman from its own membership. No commissioner shall engage in any other business, vocation, or employment. Any commissioner may be removed by the President for inefficiency, neglect of duty, or malfeasance in office.

The legislative reports in both houses of Congress clearly reflect the view that a fixed term was necessary to the effective and fair administration of the law.

The debates in both houses demonstrate that the prevailing view was that the commission was not to be "subject to anybody in the government, but . . . only to the people of the United States"; free from "political domination or control" or the "probability or possibility of such a thing"; to be "separate and apart from any existing department of the government—not subject to the orders of the President."

Thus, the language of the act, the legislative reports, and the general purposes of the legislation as reflected by the debates all combine to demonstrate the Congressional intent to create a body of experts who shall gain experience by length of service—a body which shall be independent of executive authority *except in its selection*, and free to exercise its judgment without the leave or hindrance of any other official or any department of the government. To the accomplishment of these purposes it is clear that Congress was of opinion that length and certainty of tenure would vitally contribute. And to hold that, nevertheless, the members of the commission continue in office at the mere will of the President might be to thwart, in large measure, the very ends which Congress sought to realize by definitely fixing the term of office.

We conclude that the intent of the act is to limit the executive power of removal to the causes enumerated, the existence of none of which is claimed here, and we pass to the second question.

To support its contention that the removal provision of §1, as we have just construed it, is an unconstitutional interference with the executive power of the President, the government's chief reliance is *Myers v. United States*. That case has been so recently decided, and the prevailing and dissenting opinions so fully review the general subject of the power of executive removal, that further discussion would add little of value to the wealth of material there collected. These opinions examine at length the historical, legislative and judicial data bearing upon the question, beginning with what is called "the decision of 1789" in the first Congress and coming down almost to the day when the opinions were delivered. Nevertheless, the narrow point actually decided was only that the President had power to remove a postmaster of the first class without the advice and consent of the Senate as required by act of Congress.

The office of a postmaster is so essentially unlike the office now involved that the decision in the *Myers* case cannot be accepted as controlling our decision here. A postmaster is an executive officer restricted to the performance of executive functions. He is charged with no duty at all related to either the legislative or judicial power. The actual decision in the *Myers* case finds support in the theory that such an officer is merely one of the units in the executive department, and, hence, inherently subject to the exclusive and illimitable power of removal by the Chief Executive, whose subordinate and aid he is. It goes no farther; much less does it include an officer who occupies no place in the executive department, and who exercises no part of the executive power vested by the Constitution in the President.

The Federal Trade Commission is an administrative body created by Congress to carry into effect legislative policies embodied in the statute in accordance with the legislative standard therein prescribed, and to perform other specified duties as a legislative or as a judicial aid. Such a body cannot in any proper sense be characterized as an arm or an eye of the executive. Its duties are performed without executive leave, and, in the contemplation of the statute, must be free from executive control. In administering the provisions of the statute in respect of "unfair methods of competition"—that is to say, in filling in and administering the details embodied by that general standard—the commission acts in part *quasi*-legislatively and in part *quasi*-judicially. In making investigations and reports thereon for the information of Congress under §6, in aid of the legislative power, it acts as a legislative agency. Under §7, which authorizes the commission to act as a master in chancery under rules prescribed by the court, it acts as an agency of the judiciary. To the extent that it exercises any executive function—as distinguished from executive power in the constitutional sense—it does so in the discharge and effectuation of its *quasi*-legislative or *quasi*-judicial powers, or as an agency of the legislative or judicial departments of the government.

If Congress is without authority to prescribe causes for removal of members of the trade commission and limit executive power of removal accordingly, that power at once becomes practically all-inclusive in respect of civil officers with the exception of the judiciary provided for by the Constitution. The Solicitor General, at the bar, apparently recognizing this to be true, with commendable candor, agreed that his view in respect of the removability of members of the Federal Trade Commission necessitated a like view in respect of the Interstate Commerce Commission and the Court of Claims. We are thus confronted with the serious question whether not only the members of these *quasi*-legislative and *quasi*-judicial bodies, but the judges of the legislative Court of Claims, exercising judicial power (*Williams v. United States*), continue in office only at the pleasure of the President.

We think it plain under the Constitution that illimitable power of removal is not possessed by the President in respect of officers of the character of those just named. The authority of Congress, in creating *quasi*-legislative or *quasi*-judicial agencies, to require them to act in discharge of their duties independently of executive control cannot well be doubted, and that authority includes, as an appropriate incident, power to fix the period during which they shall continue in office, and to forbid their removal except for cause in the meantime. For it is quite evident that one who holds his office only during the pleasure of another cannot be depended upon to maintain an attitude of independence against the latter's will.

The fundamental necessity of maintaining each of the three general departments of government entirely free from the control or coercive influence, direct or indirect, of either of the others has often been stressed, and is hardly open to serious question. So much is implied in the very fact of the separation of the powers of these departments by the Constitution, and in the rule which recognizes their essential coequality. The sound application of a principle that makes one master in his own house precludes him from imposing his control in the house of another who is master there.

The power of removal here claimed for the President falls within this principle, since its coercive influence threatens the independence of a commission which is not only wholly disconnected from the executive department, but which, as already fully appears, was created by Congress as a means of carrying into operation legislative and judicial powers, and as an agency of the legislative and judicial departments.

The result of what we now have said is this: whether the power of the President to remove an officer shall prevail over the authority of Congress to condition the power by fixing a definite term and precluding a removal except for cause will depend upon the character of the office; the *Myers* decision, affirming the power of the President alone to make the removal, is confined to purely executive officers, and,

as to officers of the kind here under consideration, we hold that no removal can be made during the prescribed term for which the officer is appointed except for one or more of the causes named in the applicable statute. To the extent that, between the decision in the *Myers* case, which sustains the unrestrictable power of the President to remove purely executive officers, and our present decision that such power does not extend to an office such as that here involved, there shall remain a field of doubt, we leave such cases as may fall within it for future consideration and determination as they may arise.

Table 4.1.   List of Administrative Agencies, Their Function, and Year Created

Agency Name	Function	Year Created
Agency for International Development	Supports economic growth, health, and democracy around the globe	1961
Bureau of Indian Affairs	Administers programs for American Indian tribes and Alaska natives, such as social services, natural resources management, and disaster relief	1824
Bureau of Labor Statistics	Measures working conditions, labor market activity, and price changes in the national economy	1884 as Bureau of Labor; transferred to Department of Labor in 1913 where it is located today
Centers for Medicare and Medicaid Services	Administers the federal insurance programs for the elderly and the poor	1977 as Health Care Financing Administration
Environmental Protection Agency	Enforces federal environmental legislation	1970
Government Accountability Office	Monitors federal government spending	1921
Immigration and Customs Enforcement	Enforces federal criminal and civil legislation related to immigration, trade, customs, and border control	2003
Securities and Exchange Commission	Regulates the securities industry	1934
Social Security Administration	Administers Social Security retirement, disability, and survivors' benefits programs	1935 as Social Security Board

YOUNGSTOWN SHEET & TUBE CO. v. SAWYER

343 U.S. 579 (1952)

Opinion: Black, joined by Frankfurter,
  Douglas, Jackson, Burton
Concurrence: Frankfurter
Concurrence: Douglas
Concurrence: Jackson
Concurrence: Burton
Concurrence: Clark
Dissent: Vinson, joined by Reed,
  Minton

Does the president's authority as Chief Executive and Commander-in-Chief enable him to take control of domestic private steel industries producing materials for the military during the Korean War? This case addresses that question in the context of a factory. During that war, steel workers were in a highly contentious negotiation with the mill owners, and the workers threatened to go on strike. But a strike in the steel mills might have cut off vital war supplies for troops fighting thousands of miles away in Korea. President Harry Truman ordered the secretary of commerce to seize most of the country's steel mills. The owners went to Court, arguing that President Truman had violated their property rights and usurped legislative power by acting beyond his constitutional authority.

In this case, the Court had to consider the limits of executive power and the relationship between the legislative and executive branches. Pay close attention not only to the majority opinion written by U.S. Supreme Court Justice Hugo Black, but also to Justice Robert H. Jackson's concurrence, in which he proposes a framework for determining the proper level of constitutional scrutiny that should be applied to executive action under different political circumstances—a framework that continues to shape constitutional rulings in this area to this day. Note particularly the difference between how the Court *might treat executive action in the absence of congressional authorization and the Court's view of executive actions that are opposed by Congress. But what should happen where Congress is silent, ambiguous, or unclear? What happens in Justice Jackson's "zone of twilight"? Is Justice Jackson's framework a compelling reading of the Constitution's provisions for the separation of powers?*

MR. JUSTICE BLACK *delivered the opinion of the Court.*

We are asked to decide whether the President was acting within his constitutional power when he issued an order directing the Secretary of Commerce to take possession of and operate most of the Nation's steel mills. The mill owners argue that the President's order amounts to lawmaking, a legislative function which the Constitution has expressly confided to the Congress, and not to the President. The Government's position is that the order was made on findings of the President that his action was necessary to avert a national catastrophe which would inevitably result from a stoppage of steel production, and that, in meeting this grave emergency, the President was acting within the aggregate of his constitutional powers as the Nation's Chief Executive and the Commander in Chief of the Armed Forces of the United States. The issue emerges here from the following series of events:

In the latter part of 1951, a dispute arose between the steel companies and their employees over terms and conditions that should be included in new collective bargaining agreements. Long-continued conferences failed to resolve the dispute. On December 18, 1951, the employees' representative, United Steelworkers of America, CIO, gave notice of an intention to strike when the existing bargaining agreements expired on December 31. The Federal Mediation and Conciliation Service then intervened in an effort to get labor and management to agree. This failing, the President on December 22, 1951, referred the dispute to the Federal Wage Stabilization Board to investigate and make recommendations for fair and equitable terms of settlement. This Board's report resulted in no settlement. On April 4, 1952, the Union gave notice of a nationwide strike called to begin at 12:01 A.M. April 9. The indispensability of steel as a component of substantially all weapons and other war materials led the President to believe that the proposed work stoppage would immediately jeopardize our national defense and that governmental seizure of the steel mills was necessary in order to assure the continued availability of steel. Reciting these considerations for his action, the President, a few hours before the strike was to begin, issued Executive Order 10340. . . . The order directed the Secretary of Commerce to take possession of most of the steel mills and keep them running. The Secretary immediately issued his own possessory orders, calling upon the presidents of the various seized companies to serve as operating managers for the United States. They were directed to carry on their activities in accordance with regulations and directions of the Secretary. The next morning the President sent a message to Congress reporting his action. Cong. Rec. April 9, 1952, p. 3962. Twelve days later, he sent a second message. Cong. Rec. April 21, 1952, p. 4192. Congress had taken no action.

Obeying the Secretary's orders under protest, the companies brought proceedings against him in the District Court. Their complaints charged that the seizure was not authorized by an act of Congress or by any constitutional provisions. The District Court was asked to declare the orders of the President and the Secretary invalid and to issue preliminary and permanent injunctions restraining their enforcement. Opposing the motion for preliminary injunction, the United States asserted that a strike disrupting steel production for even a brief period would so endanger the well being and safety of the Nation that the President had "inherent power" to do what he had done—power "supported by the Constitution, by historical precedent, and by court decisions."

The President's power, if any, to issue the order must stem either from an act of Congress or from the Constitution itself. There is no statute that expressly authorizes the President to take possession of property as he did here. Nor is there any act of Congress to which our attention has been directed from which such a power can fairly be implied. Indeed, we do not understand the Government to rely on statutory authorization for this seizure. There are two statutes which do authorize the President to take both personal and real property under certain conditions. However, the Government admits that these conditions were not met, and that the President's order was not rooted in either of the statutes. The Government refers to the seizure provisions of one of these statutes (§201(b) of the Defense Production Act) as "much too cumbersome, involved, and time-consuming for the crisis which was at hand."

Moreover, the use of the seizure technique to solve labor disputes in order to prevent work stoppages was not only unauthorized by any congressional enactment; prior to this controversy, Congress had refused to adopt that method of settling labor disputes. When the Taft-Hartley Act was under consideration in 1947, Congress rejected an amendment which would have authorized such governmental seizures in cases of emergency. Apparently it was thought that the technique of seizure, like that of compulsory arbitration, would interfere with the process of collective bargaining. Consequently, the plan Congress adopted in that Act did not provide for seizure under any circumstances. Instead, the plan sought to bring about settlements by use of the customary devices of mediation, conciliation, investigation by boards of inquiry, and public reports. In some instances, temporary injunctions were authorized to provide cooling-off periods. All this failing, unions were left free to strike after a secret vote by employees as to whether they wished to accept their employers' final settlement offer.

It is clear that, if the President had authority to issue the order he did, it must be found in some provision of the Constitution. And it is not claimed that express constitutional language grants this power to the President. The contention is that presidential power should be implied from the aggregate of his powers under the Constitution. Particular reliance is placed on provisions in Article II which say that "The executive Power shall be vested in a President . . . "; that "he shall take Care that the Laws be faithfully executed," and that he "shall be Commander in Chief of the Army and Navy of the United States."

The order cannot properly be sustained as an exercise of the President's military power as Commander in Chief of the Armed Forces. The Government attempts to do so by citing a number of cases upholding broad powers in military commanders engaged in day-to-day fighting in a theater of war. Such cases need not concern us here. Even though "theater of war" be an expanding concept, we cannot with faithfulness to our constitutional system hold that the Commander in Chief of the Armed Forces has the ultimate power as such to take possession of private property in order to keep labor disputes from stopping production.

This is a job for the Nation's lawmakers, not for its military authorities.

Nor can the seizure order be sustained because of the several constitutional provisions that grant executive power to the President. In the framework of our Constitution, the President's power to see that the laws are faithfully executed refutes the idea that he is to be a lawmaker. The Constitution limits his functions in the lawmaking process to the recommending of laws he thinks wise and the vetoing of laws he thinks bad. And the Constitution is neither silent nor equivocal about who shall make laws which the President is to execute. The first section of the first article says that "All legislative Powers herein granted shall be vested in a Congress of the United States. . . ."

The President's order does not direct that a congressional policy be executed in a manner prescribed by Congress—it directs that a presidential policy be executed in a manner prescribed by the President. The preamble of the order itself, like that of many statutes, sets out reasons why the President believes certain policies should be adopted, proclaims these policies as rules of conduct to be followed, and again, like a statute, authorizes a government official to promulgate additional rules and regulations consistent with the policy proclaimed and needed to carry that policy into execution. The power of Congress to adopt such public policies as those proclaimed by the order is beyond question. It can authorize the taking of private property for public use. It can make laws regulating the relationships between employers and employees, prescribing rules designed to settle labor disputes, and fixing wages and working conditions in certain fields of our economy. The Constitution does not subject this lawmaking power of Congress to presidential or military supervision or control.

The Founders of this Nation entrusted the lawmaking power to the Congress alone in both good and bad times. It would do no good to recall the historical events, the fears of power, and the hopes for freedom that lay behind their choice. Such a review would but confirm our holding that this seizure order cannot stand.

MR. JUSTICE JACKSON, *concurring in the judgment and opinion of the Court.*

That comprehensive and undefined presidential powers hold both practical advantages and grave dangers for the country will impress anyone who has served as legal adviser to a President in time of transition and public anxiety. While an interval of detached reflection may temper teachings of that experience, they probably are a more realistic influence on my views than the conventional materials of judicial decision which seem unduly to accentuate doctrine and legal fiction. But, as we approach the question of presidential power, we half overcome mental hazards by recognizing them. The opinions of judges, no less than executives and publicists, often suffer the infirmity of confusing the issue of a power's validity with the cause it is invoked to promote, of confounding the permanent executive office with its temporary occupant. The tendency is strong to emphasize transient results upon policies—such as wages or stabilization—and lose sight of enduring consequences upon the balanced power structure of our Republic.

A judge, like an executive adviser, may be surprised at the poverty of really useful and unambiguous authority applicable to concrete problems of executive power as they actually present themselves. Just what our forefathers did envision, or would have envisioned had they foreseen modern conditions, must be divined from materials almost as enigmatic as the dreams Joseph was called upon to interpret for Pharaoh. A century and a half of partisan debate and scholarly speculation yields no net result, but only supplies more or less apt quotations from respected sources on each side of any question. They largely cancel each other. And court decisions are indecisive because of the judicial practice of dealing with the largest questions in the most narrow way.

The actual art of governing under our Constitution does not, and cannot, conform to judicial definitions of the power of any of its branches based on isolated clauses, or even single Articles torn from context. While the Constitution diffuses power the better to secure liberty, it also contemplates that practice will integrate the dispersed powers into a workable government. It enjoins upon its branches separateness but interdependence, autonomy but reciprocity. Presidential powers are not fixed but fluctuate depending upon their disjunction or conjunction with those of Congress. We may well begin by a somewhat over-simplified grouping of practical situations in which a President may doubt, or others may challenge, his powers, and by distinguishing roughly the legal consequences of this factor of relativity.

1. When the President acts pursuant to an express or implied authorization of Congress, his authority is at its maximum, for it includes all that he possesses in his own right plus all that Congress can delegate. In these circumstances, and in these only, may he be said (for what it may be worth) to personify the federal sovereignty. If his act is held unconstitutional under these circumstances, it usually means that the Federal Government, as an undivided whole, lacks power. A seizure executed by the President pursuant to an Act of Congress would be supported by the strongest of presumptions and the widest

latitude of judicial interpretation, and the burden of persuasion would rest heavily upon any who might attack it.

2. When the President acts in absence of either a congressional grant or denial of authority, he can only rely upon his own independent powers, but there is a zone of twilight in which he and Congress may have concurrent authority, or in which its distribution is uncertain. Therefore, congressional inertia, indifference or quiescence may sometimes, at least, as a practical matter, enable, if not invite, measures on independent presidential responsibility. In this area, any actual test of power is likely to depend on the imperatives of events and contemporary imponderables, rather than on abstract theories of law.

3. When the President takes measures incompatible with the expressed or implied will of Congress, his power is at its lowest ebb, for then he can rely only upon his own constitutional powers minus any constitutional powers of Congress over the matter. Courts can sustain exclusive presidential control in such a case only by disabling the Congress from acting upon the subject. Presidential claim to a power at once so conclusive and preclusive must be scrutinized with caution, for what is at stake is the equilibrium established by our constitutional system.

Into which of these classifications does this executive seizure of the steel industry fit? It is eliminated from the first by admission, for it is conceded that no congressional authorization exists for this seizure. That takes away also the support of the many precedents and declarations which were made in relation, and must be confined, to this category.

Can it then be defended under flexible tests available to the second category? It seems clearly eliminated from that class, because Congress has not left seizure of private property an open field, but has covered it by three statutory policies inconsistent with this seizure.

None of these were invoked. In choosing a different and inconsistent way of his own, the President cannot claim that it is necessitated or invited by failure of Congress to legislate upon the occasions, grounds and methods for seizure of industrial properties.

This leaves the current seizure to be justified only by the severe tests under the third grouping, where it can be supported only by any remainder of executive power after subtraction of such powers as Congress may have over the subject. In short, we can sustain the President only by holding that seizure of such strike-bound industries is within his domain and beyond control by Congress. Thus, this Court's first review of such seizures occurs under circumstances which leave presidential power most vulnerable to attack and in the least favorable of possible constitutional postures.

The Solicitor General seeks the power of seizure in three clauses of the Executive Article, the first reading, "The executive Power shall be vested in a President of the United States of America." Lest I be thought to exaggerate, I quote the interpretation which his brief puts upon it: "In our view, this clause constitutes a grant of all the executive powers of which the Government is capable." If that be true, it is difficult to see why the forefathers bothered to add several specific items, including some trifling ones.

The example of such unlimited executive power that must have most impressed the forefathers was the prerogative exercised by George III, and the description of its evils in the Declaration of Independence leads me to doubt that they were creating their new Executive in his image.

The clause on which the Government next relies is that "The President shall be Commander in Chief of the Army and Navy of the United States...." These cryptic words have given rise to some of the most persistent controversies in our constitutional history. Of course, they imply something more than an empty title. But just what authority goes with the name has plagued presidential advisers who would not waive or narrow it by nonassertion, yet cannot say where it begins or ends. It undoubtedly puts the Nation's armed forces under presidential command. Hence, this loose appellation is sometimes advanced as support for any presidential action, internal or external, involving use of force, the idea being that it vests power to do anything, anywhere, that can be done with an army or navy.

Assuming that we are in a war *de facto*, whether it is or is not a war *de jure*, does that empower the Commander in Chief to seize industries he thinks necessary to supply our army? The Constitution expressly places in Congress power "to raise and support Armies" and "to provide and maintain a Navy." This certainly lays upon Congress primary responsibility for supplying the armed forces. Congress alone controls the raising of revenues and their appropriation, and may determine in what manner and by what means they shall be spent for military and naval procurement. I suppose no one would doubt that Congress can take over war supply as a Government enterprise. On the other hand, if Congress sees fit to rely on free private enterprise collectively bargaining with free labor for support and maintenance of our armed forces, can the Executive, because of lawful disagreements incidental to that process, seize the facility for operation upon Government-imposed terms?

There are indications that the Constitution did not contemplate that the title Commander in Chief *of the Army and Navy* will constitute him also Commander in Chief of the country, its industries and its inhabitants. He has no monopoly of "war powers," whatever they are. While Congress cannot deprive the President of the command of the army and navy, only Congress can provide him an army or navy to command.

That military powers of the Commander in Chief were not to supersede representative government of internal affairs seems obvious from the Constitution and from elementary American history.

We should not use this occasion to circumscribe, much less to contract, the lawful role of the President as Commander in Chief. I should indulge the widest latitude of interpretation to sustain his exclusive function to command the instruments of national force, at least when turned against the outside world for the security of our society. But, when it is turned inward not because of rebellion, but because of a lawful economic struggle between industry and labor, it should have no such indulgence.

The third clause in which the Solicitor General finds seizure powers is that "he shall take Care that the Laws be faithfully executed. . . . That authority must be matched against words of the Fifth Amendment that "No person shall be . . . deprived of life, liberty or property, without due process of law. . . ." One gives a governmental authority that reaches so far as there is law, the other gives a private right that authority shall go no farther. These signify about all there is of the principle that ours is a government of laws, not of men, and that we submit ourselves to rulers only if under rules.

In the practical working of our Government, we already have evolved a technique within the framework of the Constitution by which normal executive powers may be considerably expanded to meet an emergency. Congress may and has granted extraordinary authorities which lie dormant in normal times but may be called into play by the Executive in war or upon proclamation of a national emergency.

Under this procedure, we retain Government by law—special, temporary law, perhaps, but law nonetheless. The public may know the extent and limitations of the powers that can be asserted, and persons affected may be informed from the statute of their rights and duties.

The executive action we have here originates in the individual will of the President, and represents an exercise of authority without law. No one, perhaps not even the President, knows the limits of the power he may seek to exert in this instance, and the parties affected cannot learn the limit of their rights. We do not know today what powers over labor or property would be claimed to flow from Government possession if we should legalize it, what rights to compensation would be claimed or recognized, or on what contingency it would end. With all its defects, delays and inconveniences, men have discovered no technique for long preserving free government except that the Executive be under the law, and that the law be made by parliamentary deliberations. Such institutions may be destined to pass away. But it is the duty of the Court to be last, not first, to give them up.

MR. JUSTICE DOUGLAS, *concurring.*

There can be no doubt that the emergency which caused the President to seize these steel plants was one that bore heavily on the country. But the emergency did not create power; it merely marked an occasion when power should be exercised. And the fact that it was necessary that measures be taken to keep steel in production does not mean that the President, rather than the Congress, had the constitutional authority to act. The Congress, as well as the President, is trustee of the national welfare. The President can act more quickly than the Congress. The President, with the

armed services at his disposal, can move with force, as well as with speed. All executive power—from the reign of ancient kings to the rule of modern dictators—has the outward appearance of efficiency.

Legislative power, by contrast, is slower to exercise. There must be delay while the ponderous machinery of committees, hearings, and debates is put into motion. That takes time, and, while the Congress slowly moves into action, the emergency may take its toll in wages, consumer goods, war production, the standard of living of the people, and perhaps even lives. Legislative action may indeed often be cumbersome, time-consuming, and apparently inefficient. But, as Mr. Justice Brandeis stated in his dissent in *Myers v. United States*:

> The doctrine of the separation of powers was adopted by the Convention of 1787 not to promote efficiency, but to preclude the exercise of arbitrary power. The purpose was not to avoid friction, but, by means of the inevitable friction incident to the distribution of the governmental powers among three departments, to save the people from autocracy.

We therefore cannot decide this case by determining which branch of government can deal most expeditiously with the present crisis. The answer must depend on the allocation of powers under the Constitution. That, in turn, requires an analysis of the conditions giving rise to the seizure, and of the seizure itself.

The legislative nature of the action taken by the President seems to me to be clear. When the United States takes over an industrial plant to settle a labor controversy, it is condemning property. The seizure of the plant is a taking in the constitutional sense. *United States v. Pewee Coal Co.* A permanent taking would amount to the nationalization of the industry. A temporary taking falls short of that goal. But though the seizure is only for a week or a month, the condemnation is complete, and the United States must pay compensation for the temporary possession. *United States v. General Motors Corp.*; *United States v. Pewee Coal Co., supra.*

The power of the Federal Government to condemn property is well established. *Kohl v. United States.* It can condemn for any public purpose, and I have no doubt but that condemnation of a plant, factory, or industry in order to promote industrial peace would be constitutional. But there is a duty to pay for all property taken by the Government. The command of the Fifth Amendment is that no "private property be taken for public use, without just compensation." That constitutional requirement has an important bearing on the present case.

The President has no power to raise revenues. That power is in the Congress by Article I, Section 8 of the Constitution. The President might seize, and the Congress, by subsequent action, might ratify the seizure. But, until and unless Congress acted, no condemnation would be lawful. The branch of government that has the power to pay compensation for a seizure is the only one able to authorize a seizure or make lawful one that the President has effected. That seems to me to be the necessary result of the condemnation provision in the Fifth Amendment. It squares with the theory of checks and balances expounded by Mr. Justice Black in the opinion of the Court, in which I join.

We could not sanction the seizures and condemnations of the steel plants in this case without reading Article II as giving the President not only the power to execute the laws, but to make some. Such a step would most assuredly alter the pattern of the Constitution.

MR. JUSTICE FRANKFURTER,
concurring.

The question before the Court comes in this setting. Congress has frequently—at least 16 times since 1916—specifically provided for executive seizure of production, transportation, communications, or storage facilities. In every case, it has qualified this grant of power with limitations and safeguards. This body of enactments demonstrates that Congress deemed seizure so drastic a power as to require that it be carefully circumscribed whenever the President was vested with this extraordinary authority. The power to seize has uniformly been given only for a limited period or for a defined emergency, or has been repealed after a short period. Its exercise has been restricted to particular circumstances such as "time of war or when war is imminent," the needs of "public safety" or of "national security or defense," or "urgent and impending need." The period of governmental operation has been limited, as, for instance, to "sixty days after the restoration of productive efficiency." Seizure statutes usually make executive action dependent on detailed conditions: for example, (a) failure or refusal of the owner of a plant to meet governmental supply needs or (b) failure of voluntary negotiations with the owner for the use of a plant necessary for great public ends. Congress often has specified the particular executive agency which should seize or operate the plants or whose judgment would appropriately test the need for seizure. Congress also has not left to implication that just compensation be paid; it has usually legislated in detail regarding enforcement of this litigation-breeding general requirement.

Congress, in 1947, was again called upon to consider whether governmental seizure should be used to avoid serious industrial shutdowns. Congress decided against conferring such power generally and in advance, without special Congressional enactment to meet each particular need. Under the urgency of telephone and coal strikes in the winter of 1946, Congress addressed itself to the problems raised by "national emergency" strikes and lockouts. The termination of wartime seizure powers on December 31, 1946, brought these matters to the attention of Congress with vivid impact. A proposal that the President be given powers to seize plants to avert a shutdown where the "health or safety" of the Nation was endangered was thoroughly canvassed by Congress, and rejected. No room for doubt remains that the proponents as well as the opponents of the bill which became the Labor Management Relations Act of 1947 clearly understood that, as a result of that legislation, the only recourse for preventing a shutdown in any basic industry, after failure of mediation, was Congress. Authorization for seizure as an available remedy for potential dangers was unequivocally put aside. The Senate Labor Committee, through its Chairman, explicitly reported to the Senate that a general grant of seizure powers had been considered and rejected in favor of reliance on *ad hoc* legislation, as a particular emergency might call for it. An amendment presented in the House providing that, where necessary "to preserve and protect the public health and security," the President might seize any industry in which there is an impending curtailment of production, was voted down after debate, by a vote of more than three to one.

On a balance of considerations, Congress chose not to lodge this power in the President. It chose not to make available in advance a remedy to which both industry and labor were fiercely hostile. In deciding that authority to seize should be given to the President only after full consideration of the particular situation should show such legislation to be necessary, Congress presumably acted on experience with similar industrial conflicts in the past. It evidently assumed that industrial shutdowns in basic industries are not instances of spontaneous generation, and that danger warnings are sufficiently plain before the event to give ample opportunity to start the legislative process into action.

In any event, nothing can be plainer than that Congress made a conscious choice of policy in a field full of perplexity and peculiarly within legislative responsibility for choice. In formulating legislation for dealing with industrial conflicts, Congress could not more clearly and emphatically have withheld authority than it did in 1947. Perhaps as much so as is true of any piece of modern legislation, Congress acted with full consciousness of what it was doing, and in the light of much recent history. Previous seizure legislation had subjected the powers granted to the President to restrictions of varying degrees of stringency. Instead of giving him even limited powers, Congress, in 1947, deemed it wise to require the President, upon failure of attempts to reach a voluntary settlement, to report to Congress if he deemed the power of seizure a needed shot for his locker. The President could not ignore the specific limitations of prior seizure statutes. No more could he act in disregard of the limitation put upon seizure by the 1947 Act.

It cannot be contended that the President would have had power to issue this order had Congress explicitly negated such authority in formal legislation. Congress has expressed its will to withhold this power from the President as though it had said so in so many words. The authoritatively expressed purpose of Congress to disallow such power to the President and to require him, when in his mind the occasion arose for such a seizure, to put the matter to Congress and ask for specific authority from it, could not be more decisive if it had been written into the Labor Management Relations Act of 1947.

It is one thing to draw an intention of Congress from general language and to say that Congress would have explicitly written what is inferred, where Congress has not addressed itself to a specific situation. It is quite impossible, however, when Congress did specifically address itself to a problem, as Congress did to that of seizure, to find secreted in the interstices of legislation the very grant of power which Congress consciously withheld. To find authority so explicitly withheld is not merely to disregard in a particular instance the clear will of Congress. It is to disrespect the whole legislative process and the constitutional division of authority between President and Congress.

To be sure, the content of the three authorities of government is not to be derived from an abstract analysis. The areas are partly interacting, not wholly disjointed. The Constitution is a framework for government. Therefore, the way the framework has consistently operated fairly establishes that it has operated according to its true nature. Deeply embedded traditional ways of conducting government cannot supplant the Constitution or legislation, but they give meaning to the words of a text or supply them. It is an inadmissibly narrow conception of American constitutional law to confine it to the words of the Constitution and to disregard the gloss which life has written upon them. In short, a systematic, unbroken, executive practice, long pursued to the knowledge of the Congress and never before questioned, engaged in by Presidents who have also sworn to uphold the Constitution, making as it were such exercise of power part of the structure of our government, may be treated as a gloss on "executive Power" vested in the President by §1 of Art. II.

Down to the World War II period, the record is barren of instances comparable to the one before us.

A scheme of government like ours no doubt at times feels the lack of power to act with complete, all-embracing, swiftly moving authority. No doubt a government with distributed authority, subject to be challenged in the courts of law, at least long enough to consider and adjudicate the challenge, labors under restrictions from which other governments are free. It has not been our tradition to envy such governments. In any event, our government was designed to have such restrictions. The price was deemed not too high in view of the safeguards which these restrictions afford.

MR. CHIEF JUSTICE VINSON, *with whom* **MR. JUSTICE REED** *and* **MR. JUSTICE MINTON** *join, dissenting.*

The President of the United States directed the Secretary of Commerce to take temporary possession of the Nation's steel mills during the existing emergency because "a work stoppage would immediately jeopardize and imperil our national defense and the defense of those joined with us in resisting aggression, and would add to the continuing danger of our soldiers, sailors, and airmen engaged in combat in the field." In passing upon the question of Presidential powers in this case, we must first consider the context in which those powers were exercised.

Those who suggest that this is a case involving extraordinary powers should be mindful that these are extraordinary times. A world not yet recovered from the devastation of World War II has been forced to face the threat of another and more terrifying global conflict.

In 1950, when the United Nations called upon member nations "to render every assistance" to repel aggression in Korea, the United States furnished its vigorous support. For almost two full years, our armed forces have been fighting in Korea, suffering casualties of over 108,000 men. Hostilities have not abated. The "determination of the United Nations to continue its action in Korea to meet the aggression" has been reaffirmed. Congressional support of the action in Korea has been manifested by provisions for increased military manpower and equipment and for economic stabilization, as hereinafter described.

As an illustration of the magnitude of the over-all program, Congress has appropriated $130 billion for our own defense and for military assistance to our allies since the June, 1950, attack in Korea.

Over $5½ billion were appropriated for military assistance for fiscal year 1952, the bulk of that amount to be devoted to purchase of military equipment.

Congress, recognizing the "grim fact . . . that the United States is now engaged in a struggle for survival" and that "it is imperative that we now take those necessary steps to make our strength equal to the peril of the hour," granted authority to draft men into the armed forces. As a result, we now have over 3,500,000 men in our armed forces.

Appropriations for the Department of Defense, which had averaged less than $13 billion per year for the three years before attack in Korea, were increased by Congress to $48 billion for fiscal year 1951 and to $60 billion for fiscal year 1952.

The President has the duty to execute the foregoing legislative programs. Their successful execution depends upon continued production of steel and stabilized prices for steel. Accordingly, when the collective bargaining agreements between the Nation's steel producers and their employees, represented by the United Steel Workers, were due to expire on December 31, 1951, and a strike shutting down the entire basic steel industry was threatened, the President acted to avert a complete shutdown of steel production.

One is not here called upon even to consider the possibility of executive seizure of a farm, a corner grocery store or even a single industrial plant. Such considerations arise only when one ignores the central fact of this case—that the Nation's entire basic steel production would have shut down completely if there had been no Government seizure. Even ignoring for the moment whatever confidential information the President may possess as "the Nation's organ for foreign affairs," the uncontroverted affidavits in this record amply support the finding that "a work stoppage would immediately jeopardize and imperil our national defense."

Plaintiffs do not remotely suggest any basis for rejecting the President's finding that any stoppage of steel production would immediately place the Nation in peril.

Plaintiffs' counsel tells us that "sooner or later" the mills will operate again. That may satisfy the steel companies and, perhaps, the Union. But our soldiers and our allies will hardly be cheered with the assurance that the ammunition upon which their lives depend will be forthcoming—"sooner or later," or, in other words, "too little and too late."

Accordingly, if the President has any power under the Constitution to meet a critical situation in the absence of express statutory authorization, there is no basis whatever for criticizing the exercise of such power in this case.

A review of executive action demonstrates that our Presidents have on many occasions exhibited the leadership contemplated by the Framers when they made the President Commander in Chief, and imposed upon him the trust to "take Care that the Laws be faithfully executed." With or without explicit statutory authorization, Presidents have at such times dealt with national emergencies by acting promptly and resolutely to enforce legislative programs, at least to save those programs until Congress could act. Congress and the courts have responded to such executive initiative with consistent approval.

History bears out the genius of the Founding Fathers, who created a Government subject to law but not left subject to inertia when vigor and initiative are required.

Focusing now on the situation confronting the President on the night of April 8, 1952, we cannot but conclude that the President was performing his duty under the Constitution to "take Care that the Laws be faithfully executed"—a duty described by President Benjamin Harrison as "the central idea of the office."

The President reported to Congress the morning after the seizure that he acted because a work stoppage in steel production would immediately imperil the safety of the Nation by preventing execution of the legislative programs for procurement of military equipment. And, while a shutdown could be averted by granting the price concessions requested by plaintiffs, granting such concessions would disrupt the price stabilization program also enacted by Congress. Rather than fail to execute either legislative program, the President acted to execute both.

Much of the argument in this case has been directed at straw men. We do not now have before us the case of a President acting solely on the basis of his own notions of the public welfare. Nor is there any question of unlimited executive power in this case. The President himself closed the door to any such claim when he sent his Message to Congress stating his purpose to abide by any action of Congress, whether approving or disapproving his seizure action. Here, the President immediately made sure that Congress was fully informed of the temporary action he had taken only to preserve the legislative programs from destruction until Congress could act.

The absence of a specific statute authorizing seizure of the steel mills as a mode of executing the laws has not until today been thought to prevent the President from executing the laws. Unlike an administrative commission confined to the enforcement of the statute under which it was created, or the head of a department when administering a particular statute, the President is a constitutional officer charged with taking care that a "mass of legislation" be executed. Flexibility as to mode of execution to meet critical situations is a matter of practical necessity.

Whatever the extent of Presidential power on more tranquil occasions, and whatever the right of the President to execute legislative programs as he sees fit without reporting the mode of execution to Congress, the single Presidential purpose disclosed on this record is to faithfully execute the laws by acting in an emergency to maintain the *status quo*, thereby preventing collapse of the legislative programs until Congress could act. The President's action served the same purposes as a judicial stay entered to maintain the *status quo* in order to preserve the jurisdiction of a court. In his Message to Congress immediately following the seizure, the President explained the necessity of his action in executing the military procurement and anti-inflation legislative programs and expressed his desire to cooperate with any legislative proposals approving, regulating or rejecting the seizure of the steel mills. Consequently, there is no evidence whatever of any Presidential purpose to defy Congress or act in any way inconsistent with the legislative will.

In *United States v. Midwest Oil Co.,* *supra,* this Court approved executive action where, as here, the President acted to preserve an important matter until Congress could act—even though his action in that case was contrary to an express statute. In this case, there is no statute prohibiting the action taken by the President in a matter not merely important, but threatening the very safety of the Nation. Executive inaction in such a situation, courting national disaster, is foreign to the concept of energy and initiative in the Executive as created by the Founding Fathers. The Constitution was itself "adopted in a period of grave emergency. . . . While emergency does not create power, emergency may furnish the occasion for the exercise of power." The Framers knew, as we should know in these times of peril, that there is real danger in Executive weakness. There is no cause to fear Executive tyranny so long as the laws of Congress are being faithfully executed. Certainly there is no basis for fear of dictatorship when the Executive acts, as he did in this case, only to save the situation until Congress could act.

Faced with the duty of executing the defense programs which Congress had enacted and the disastrous effects that any stoppage in steel production would have on those programs, the President acted to preserve those programs by seizing the steel mills. There is no question that the possession was other than temporary in character, and subject to congressional direction—either approving, disapproving, or regulating the manner in which the mills were to be administered and returned to the owners. The President immediately informed Congress of his action, and clearly stated his intention to abide by the legislative will. No basis for claims of arbitrary action, unlimited powers, or dictatorial usurpation of congressional power appears from the facts of this case. On the contrary, judicial, legislative and executive precedents throughout our history demonstrate that, in this case, the President acted in full conformity with his duties under the Constitution.

IMMIGRATION AND NATURALIZATION SERVICE v. CHADHA

462 U.S. 919 (1983)

Opinion: Burger, joined by Brennan, Marshall, Blackmun, Stevens, O'Connor
Concurrence: Powell
Dissent: White
Dissent: Rehnquist, joined by White

In this case, the Supreme Court considered the constitutionality of a congressional act allowing for one House of Congress to invalidate by way of "legislative veto" a particular decision made by the executive branch. As you know, the veto power is usually thought of as a presidential prerogative, exercised in order to stop legislation passed by the House and the Senate. A central issue in this case is whether the procedure violates the Presentment Clause of Article I, Section 7 of the Constitution, which requires that every bill passed by Congress "shall . . . be presented to the President of the United States." Notice, too, the Court's discussion of the fact that the Constitution created Congress as a bicameral body, and its requirement that all legislation must pass through both the House and Senate. Can Congress ensure that the law is carried out in accordance with the will of the people if it cannot invalidate particular executive decisions? Is the Court *correct that congressional policy determinations that do not include both Houses are constitutionally problematic? How is the legislative veto different from other instances in which one House can act alone without the other, such as the Senate's entitlement to ratify treaties? Consider here the debate between U.S. Supreme Court Justice Byron White, who argues that the Court should ask if this innovative process is actually the best way to assure the functional integrity of the separation of powers, and the majority, who insist that the formal requirements of the Presentment and Bicameralism Clauses must be respected. As you read this case, consider whether you think there must be some flexibility in the structure of the U.S. government to allow it to meet modern challenges, including the growth of the government itself.*

CHIEF JUSTICE BURGER *delivered the opinion of the Court.*

[The case at hand] presents a challenge to the constitutionality of the provision in §244(c)(2) of the Immigration and Nationality Act, 66 Stat. 216, as amended, 8 U.S.C. §1254(c)(2), authorizing one House of Congress, by resolution, to invalidate the decision of the Executive Branch, pursuant to authority delegated by Congress to the Attorney General of the United States, to allow a particular deportable alien to remain in the United States.

Chadha is an East Indian who was born in Kenya and holds a British passport. He was lawfully admitted to the United States in 1966 on a nonimmigrant student visa. His visa expired on June 30, 1972. On October 11, 1973, the District Director of the Immigration and Naturalization Service ordered Chadha to show cause why he should not be deported for having "remained in the United States for a longer time than permitted." Pursuant to §242(b) of the Immigration and Nationality Act (Act), a deportation hearing was held before an Immigration Judge on January 11, 1974. Chadha conceded that he was deportable for overstaying his visa, and the hearing was adjourned to enable him to file an application for suspension of deportation under §244(a)(1) of the Act.

After Chadha submitted his application for suspension of deportation, the deportation hearing was resumed on February 7, 1974. On the basis of evidence adduced at the hearing, affidavits submitted with the application, and the results of a character investigation conducted by the INS, the Immigration Judge, on June 25, 1974, ordered that Chadha's deportation be suspended. The Immigration Judge found that Chadha met the requirements of §244(a)(1): he had resided continuously in the United States for over seven years, was of good moral character, and would suffer "extreme hardship" if deported.

Pursuant to §244(c)(1) of the Act, the Immigration Judge suspended Chadha's deportation and a report of the suspension was transmitted to Congress.

Once the Attorney General's recommendation for suspension of Chadha's deportation was conveyed to Congress, Congress had the power under §244(c)(2) of the Act, to veto the Attorney General's determination that Chadha should not be deported.

On December 12, 1975, Representative Eilberg, Chairman of the Judiciary Subcommittee on Immigration, Citizenship, and International Law, introduced a resolution opposing "the granting of permanent residence in the United States to [six] aliens," including Chadha. The resolution was referred to the House Committee on the Judiciary. On December 16, 1975, the resolution was discharged from further consideration by the House Committee on the Judiciary and submitted to the House of

Representatives for a vote. The resolution had not been printed and was not made available to other Members of the House prior to or at the time it was voted on. So far as the record before us shows, the House consideration of the resolution was based on Representative Eilberg's statement from the floor that

> [i]t was the feeling of the committee, after reviewing 340 cases, that the aliens contained in the resolution [Chadha and five others] did not meet these statutory requirements, particularly as it relates to hardship; and it is the opinion of the committee that their deportation should not be suspended.

Ibid. The resolution was passed without debate or recorded vote. Since the House action was pursuant to §244(c)(2), the resolution was not treated as an Art. I legislative act; it was not submitted to the Senate or presented to the President for his action.

We turn now to the question whether action of one House of Congress under §244(c)(2) violates strictures of the Constitution. We begin, of course, with the presumption that the challenged statute is valid. Its wisdom is not the concern of the courts; if a challenged action does not violate the Constitution, it must be sustained.

By the same token, the fact that a given law or procedure is efficient, convenient, and useful in facilitating functions of government, standing alone, will not save it if it is contrary to the Constitution....

Justice White undertakes to make a case for the proposition that the one-House veto is a useful "political invention," and we need not challenge that assertion. We can even concede this utilitarian argument, although the long-range political wisdom of this "invention" is arguable.

But policy arguments supporting even useful "political inventions" are subject to the demands of the Constitution, which defines powers and, with respect to this subject, sets out just how those powers are to be exercised.

Explicit and unambiguous provisions of the Constitution prescribe and define the respective functions of the Congress and of the Executive in the legislative process. Since the precise terms of those familiar provisions are critical to the resolution of these cases, we set them out verbatim. Article I provides:

> All legislative Powers herein granted shall be vested in a Congress of the United States, which shall consist of a Senate *and* House of Representatives.

Art. I, §1. (Emphasis added.)

> Every Bill which shall have passed the House of Representatives *and* the Senate, *shall*, before it becomes a law, be presented to the President of the United States....

Art. I, §7, cl. 2. (Emphasis added.)

> *Every* Order, Resolution, or Vote to which the Concurrence of the Senate and House of Representatives may be necessary (except on a question of Adjournment) *shall* be presented to the President of the United States; and before the Same shall take Effect, *shall* be approved by him, or being disapproved by him, *shall* be repassed by two thirds of the Senate and House of Representatives, according to the Rules and Limitations prescribed in the Case of a Bill.

Art. I, §7, cl. 3. (Emphasis added.)

These provisions of Art. I are integral parts of the constitutional design for the separation of powers. We have recently noted that "[t]he principle of separation of powers was not simply an abstract generalization in the minds of the Framers: it was woven into the document that they drafted in Philadelphia in the summer of 1787." *Buckley v. Valeo.* Just as we relied on the textual provision of Art. II, §2, cl. 2, to vindicate the principle of separation of powers in *Buckley*, we see that the purposes underlying the Presentment Clauses, Art. I, §7, cls. 2, 3, and the bicameral requirement of Art. I, §1, and §7, cl. 2, guide our resolution of the important question presented in these cases. The very structure of the Articles delegating and separating powers under Arts. I, II, and III exemplifies the concept of separation of powers, and we now turn to Art. I.

B. The Presentment Clauses

The records of the Constitutional Convention reveal that the requirement that all legislation be presented to the President before becoming law was uniformly accepted by the Framers. Presentment to the President and the Presidential veto were considered so imperative that the draftsmen took special pains to assure that these requirements could not be circumvented. During the final debate on Art. I, §7, cl. 2, James Madison expressed concern that it might easily be evaded by the simple expedient of calling a proposed law a "resolution" or "vote," rather than a "bill." As a consequence, Art. I, §7, cl. 3, was added.

The decision to provide the President with a limited and qualified power to nullify proposed legislation by veto was based on the profound conviction of the Framers that the powers conferred on Congress were the powers to be most carefully circumscribed. It is beyond doubt that lawmaking was a power to be shared by both Houses and the President.

The President's role in the lawmaking process also reflects the Framers' careful efforts to check whatever propensity a particular Congress might have to enact oppressive, improvident, or ill-considered measures. The President's veto role in the legislative process was described later during public debate on ratification:

> It establishes a salutary check upon the legislative body, calculated to guard the community against the effects of faction, precipitancy, or of any impulse unfriendly to the public good,

which may happen to influence a majority of that body.

> . . . The primary inducement to conferring the power in question upon the Executive is to enable him to defend himself; the secondary one is to increase the chances in favor of the community against the passing of bad laws, through haste, inadvertence, or design.

The Federalist No. 73 (A. Hamilton). The Court also has observed that the Presentment Clauses serve the important purpose of assuring that a "national" perspective is grafted on the legislative process:

> The President is a representative of the people just as the members of the Senate and of the House are, and it may be, at some times, on some subjects, that the President elected by all the people is rather more representative of them all than are the members of either body of the Legislature, whose constituencies are local and not countrywide. . . .

Myers v. United States, supra, at 123.

C. Bicameralism

The bicameral requirement of Art. I, §§1, 7, was of scarcely less concern to the Framers than was the Presidential veto, and indeed the two concepts are interdependent. By providing that no law could take effect without the concurrence of the prescribed majority of the Members of both Houses, the Framers reemphasized their belief, already remarked upon in connection with the Presentment Clauses, that legislation should not be enacted unless it has been carefully and fully considered by the Nation's elected officials. In the Constitutional Convention debates on the need for a bicameral legislature, James Wilson, later to become a Justice of this Court, commented:

> Despotism comes on mankind in different shapes, sometimes in an Executive, sometimes in a military, one. Is there danger of a Legislative despotism? Theory & practice both

proclaim it. If the Legislative authority be not restrained, there can be neither liberty nor stability; and it can only be restrained by dividing it within itself, into distinct and independent branches. In a single house there is no check but the inadequate one of the virtue & good sense of those who compose it.

However familiar, it is useful to recall that, apart from their fear that special interests could be favored at the expense of public needs, the Framers were also concerned, although not of one mind, over the apprehensions of the smaller states. Those states feared a commonality of interest among the larger states would work to their disadvantage; representatives of the larger states, on the other hand, were skeptical of a legislature that could pass laws favoring a minority of the people. It need hardly be repeated here that the Great Compromise, under which one House was viewed as representing the people and the other the states, allayed the fears of both the large and small states.

We see therefore that the Framers were acutely conscious that the bicameral requirement and the Presentment Clauses would serve essential constitutional functions. The President's participation in the legislative process was to protect the Executive Branch from Congress and to protect the whole people from improvident laws. The division of the Congress into two distinctive bodies assures that the legislative power would be exercised only after opportunity for full study and debate in separate settings. The President's unilateral veto power, in turn, was limited by the power of two-thirds of both Houses of Congress to overrule a veto, thereby precluding final arbitrary action of one person. It emerges clearly that the prescription for legislative action in Art. I, §§1, 7, represents the Framers' decision that the legislative power of the Federal Government be exercised in accord with a single, finely wrought and exhaustively considered, procedure.

Although not "hermetically" sealed from one another, *Buckley v. Valeo*, the powers delegated to the three Branches are functionally identifiable. When any Branch acts, it is presumptively exercising the power the Constitution has delegated to it. When the Executive acts, he presumptively acts in an executive or administrative capacity as defined in Art. II. And when, as here, one House of Congress purports to act, it is presumptively acting within its assigned sphere.

Beginning with this presumption, we must nevertheless establish that the challenged action under §244(c)(2) is of the kind to which the procedural requirements of Art. I, §7, apply. Not every action taken by either House is subject to the bicameralism and presentment requirements of Art. I. Whether actions taken by either House are, in law and fact, an exercise of legislative power depends not on their form, but upon "whether they contain matter which is properly to be regarded as legislative in its character and effect."

Examination of the action taken here by one House pursuant to §244(c)(2) reveals that it was essentially legislative in purpose and effect. In purporting to exercise power defined in Art. I, §8, cl. 4, to "establish an uniform Rule of Naturalization," the House took action that had the purpose and effect of altering the legal rights, duties, and relations of persons, including the Attorney General, Executive Branch officials and Chadha, all outside the Legislative Branch. Section 244(c)(2) purports to authorize one House of Congress to require the Attorney General to deport an individual alien whose deportation otherwise would be canceled under §244. The one-House veto operated in these cases to overrule the Attorney General and mandate Chadha's deportation; absent the House action, Chadha would remain in the United States. Congress has acted, and its action has altered Chadha's status.

The legislative character of the one-House veto in these cases is confirmed by the character of the congressional action it supplants. Neither the House of Representatives nor the Senate contends that, absent the veto provision in §244(c)(2), either of them, or both of them acting together, could effectively require the Attorney General to deport an alien once the Attorney General, in the exercise of legislatively delegated authority, had determined the alien should remain in the United States. Without the challenged provision in §244(c)(2), this could have been achieved, if at all, only by legislation requiring deportation. Similarly, a veto by one House of Congress under §244(c)(2) cannot be justified as an attempt at amending the standards set out in §244(a)(1), or as a repeal of §244 as applied to Chadha. Amendment and repeal of statutes, no less than enactment, must conform with Art. I.

The nature of the decision implemented by the one-House veto in these cases further manifests its legislative character. After long experience with the clumsy, time-consuming private bill procedure, Congress made a deliberate choice to delegate to the Executive Branch, and specifically to the Attorney General, the authority to allow deportable aliens to remain in this country in certain specified circumstances. It is not disputed that this choice to delegate authority is precisely the kind of decision that can be implemented only in accordance with the procedures set out in Art. I. Disagreement with the Attorney General's decision on Chadha's deportation—that is, Congress' decision to deport Chadha—no less than Congress' original choice to delegate to the Attorney General the authority to make that decision, involves determinations of policy that Congress can implement in only one way; bicameral passage followed by presentment to the President. Congress must abide by its delegation of authority

until that delegation is legislatively altered or revoked.

Finally, we see that, when the Framers intended to authorize either House of Congress to act alone and outside of its prescribed bicameral legislative role, they narrowly and precisely defined the procedure for such action. There are four provisions in the Constitution, explicit and unambiguous, by which one House may act alone with the unreviewable force of law, not subject to the President's veto:

(a) The House of Representatives alone was given the power to initiate impeachments. Art. I, §2, cl. 5;

(b) The Senate alone was given the power to conduct trials following impeachment on charges initiated by the House, and to convict following trial. Art. I, §3, cl. 6;

(c) The Senate alone was given final unreviewable power to approve or to disapprove Presidential appointments. Art. II, §2, cl. 2;

(d) The Senate alone was given unreviewable power to ratify treaties negotiated by the President. Art. II, §2, cl. 2.

Clearly, when the Draftsmen sought to confer special powers on one House, independent of the other House, or of the President, they did so in explicit, unambiguous terms. These carefully defined exceptions from presentment and bicameralism underscore the difference between the legislative functions of Congress and other unilateral but important and binding one-House acts provided for in the Constitution. These exceptions are narrow, explicit, and separately justified; none of them authorize the action challenged here. On the contrary, they provide further support for the conclusion that congressional authority is not to be implied, and for the conclusion that the veto provided for in §244(c)(2) is not authorized by the constitutional design of the powers of the Legislative Branch. . . .

We hold that the congressional veto provision in §244(c)(2) is severable from the Act, and that it is unconstitutional.

JUSTICE POWELL, *concurring in the judgment.*

The Court's decision, based on the Presentment Clauses, Art. I, §7, cls. 2 and 3, apparently will invalidate every use of the legislative veto. The breadth of this holding gives one pause. Congress has included the veto in literally hundreds of statutes, dating back to the 1930's. Congress clearly views this procedure as essential to controlling the delegation of power to administrative agencies. One reasonably may disagree with Congress' assessment of the veto's utility, but the respect due its judgment as a coordinate branch of Government cautions that our holding should be no more extensive than necessary to decide these cases. In my view, the cases may be decided on a narrower ground. When Congress finds that a particular person does not satisfy the statutory criteria for permanent residence in this country, it has assumed a judicial function in violation of the principle of separation of powers. Accordingly, I concur only in the judgment. . . .

II

On its face, the House's action appears clearly adjudicatory. The House did not enact a general rule; rather, it made its own determination that six specific persons did not comply with certain statutory criteria. It thus undertook the type of decision that traditionally has been left to other branches. Even if the House did not make a *de novo* determination, but simply reviewed the Immigration and Naturalization Service's findings, it still assumed a function ordinarily entrusted to the federal courts. *See*

5 U.S.C. §704 (providing generally for judicial review of final agency action); *cf. Foti v. INS* (holding that courts of appeals have jurisdiction to review INS decisions denying suspension of deportation). Where, as here, Congress has exercised a power "that cannot possibly be regarded as merely in aid of the legislative function of Congress," *Buckley v. Valeo*, the decisions of this Court have held that Congress impermissibly assumed a function that the Constitution entrusted to another branch.

The impropriety of the House's assumption of this function is confirmed by the fact that its action raises the very danger the Framers sought to avoid—the exercise of unchecked power. In deciding whether Chadha deserves to be deported, Congress is not subject to any internal constraints that prevent it from arbitrarily depriving him of the right to remain in this country. Unlike the judiciary or an administrative agency, Congress is not bound by established substantive rules. Nor is it subject to the procedural safeguards, such as the right to counsel and a hearing before an impartial tribunal, that are present when a court or an agency adjudicates individual rights. The only effective constraint on Congress' power is political, but Congress is most accountable politically when it prescribes rules of general applicability. When it decides rights of specific persons, those rights are subject to "the tyranny of a shifting majority."

Chief Justice Marshall observed:

> It is the peculiar province of the legislature to prescribe general rules for the government of society; the application of those rules to individuals in society would seem to be the duty of other departments.

Fletcher v. Peck. In my view, when Congress undertook to apply its rules to Chadha, it exceeded the scope of its constitutionally prescribed authority. I would not reach the broader question whether legislative vetoes are invalid under the Presentment Clauses.

JUSTICE WHITE, *dissenting.*

Today the Court not only invalidates §244(c)(2) of the Immigration and Nationality Act, but also sounds the death knell for nearly 200 other statutory provisions in which Congress has reserved a "legislative veto." For this reason, the Court's decision is of surpassing importance. And it is for this reason that the Court would have been well advised to decide the cases, if possible, on the narrower grounds of separation of powers, leaving for full consideration the constitutionality of other congressional review statutes operating on such varied matters as war powers and agency rule-making, some of which concern the independent regulatory agencies.

The prominence of the legislative veto mechanism in our contemporary political system and its importance to Congress can hardly be overstated. It has become a central means by which Congress secures the accountability of executive and independent agencies. Without the legislative veto, Congress is faced with a Hobson's choice: either to refrain from delegating the necessary authority, leaving itself with a hopeless task of writing laws with the requisite specificity to cover endless special circumstances across the entire policy landscape, or, in the alternative, to abdicate its lawmaking function to the Executive Branch and independent agencies. To choose the former leaves major national problems unresolved; to opt for the latter risks unaccountable policy-making by those not elected to fill that role. Accordingly, over the past five decades, the legislative veto has been placed in nearly 200 statutes. The device is known in every field of governmental concern: reorganization, budgets, foreign affairs, war powers, and regulation of trade, safety, energy, the environment, and the economy.

... [T]he legislative veto is more than "efficient, convenient, and useful." It is an important, if not indispensable, political invention that allows the President and Congress to resolve major constitutional and policy differences, assures the accountability of independent regulatory agencies, and preserves Congress' control over lawmaking. Perhaps there are other means of accommodation and accountability, but the increasing reliance of Congress upon the legislative veto suggests that the alternatives to which Congress must now turn are not entirely satisfactory.

II

If the legislative veto were as plainly unconstitutional as the Court strives to suggest, its broad ruling today would be more comprehensible. But the constitutionality of the legislative veto is anything but clear-cut. The issue divides scholars, courts, Attorneys General, and the two other branches of the National Government. If the veto devices so flagrantly disregarded the requirements of Art. I as the Court today suggests, I find it incomprehensible that Congress, whose Members are bound by oath to uphold the Constitution, would have placed these mechanisms in nearly 200 separate laws over a period of 50 years.

The reality of the situation is that the constitutional question posed today is one of immense difficulty over which the Executive and Legislative Branches—as well as scholars and judges—have understandably disagreed. That disagreement stems from the silence of the Constitution on the precise question: the Constitution does not directly authorize or prohibit the legislative veto. Thus, our task should be to determine whether the legislative veto is consistent with the purposes of Art. I and the principles of separation of powers which are reflected in that Article and throughout the Constitution. We should not find the lack of a specific constitutional authorization for the legislative veto surprising, and I would not infer disapproval of the mechanism from its absence. From the summer of 1787 to the present, the Government of the United States has become an endeavor far beyond the contemplation of the Framers. Only within the last half century has the complexity and size of the Federal Government's responsibilities grown so greatly that the Congress must rely on the legislative veto as the most effective, if not the only, means to insure its role as the Nation's lawmaker. But the wisdom of the Framers was to anticipate that the Nation would grow and new problems of governance would require different solutions. Accordingly, our Federal Government was intentionally chartered with the flexibility to respond to contemporary needs without losing sight of fundamental democratic principles. This was the spirit in which Justice Jackson penned his influential concurrence in the *Steel Seizure Case*:

> The actual art of governing under our Constitution does not and cannot conform to judicial definitions of the power of any of its branches based on isolated clauses or even single Articles torn from context. While the Constitution diffuses power the better to secure liberty, it also contemplates that practice will integrate the dispersed powers into a workable government.

Youngstown Sheet & Tube Co. v. Sawyer.

This is the perspective from which we should approach the novel constitutional questions presented by the legislative veto. In my view, neither Art. I of the Constitution nor the doctrine of separation of powers is violated by this mechanism by which our elected Representatives preserve their voice in the governance of the Nation.

III

B

. . . The Court's holding today that all legislative-type action must be enacted through the lawmaking process ignores that legislative authority is routinely delegated to the Executive Branch, to the independent regulatory agencies, and to private individuals and groups.

This Court's decisions sanctioning such delegations make clear that Art. I does not require all action with the effect of legislation to be passed as a law.

When agencies are authorized to prescribe law through substantive rulemaking, the administrator's regulation is not only due deference, but is accorded "legislative effect." These regulations bind courts and officers of the Federal Government, may preempt state law, and grant rights to and impose obligations on the public. In sum, they have the force of law.

If Congress may delegate lawmaking power to independent and Executive agencies, it is most difficult to understand Art. I as prohibiting Congress from also reserving a check on legislative power for itself. Absent the veto, the agencies receiving delegations of legislative or quasi-legislative power may issue regulations having the force of law without bicameral approval and without the President's signature. It is thus not apparent why the reservation of a veto over the exercise of that legislative power must be subject to a more exacting test. In both cases, it is enough that the initial statutory authorizations comply with the Art. I requirements.

Under the Court's analysis, the Executive Branch and the independent agencies may make rules with the effect of law while Congress, in whom the Framers confided the legislative power, Art. I, §1, may not exercise a veto which precludes such rules from having operative force. If the effective functioning of a complex modern government requires the delegation of vast authority which, by virtue of its breadth, is legislative or "quasi-legislative" in character, I cannot accept that Art. I—which is, after all, the source of the nondelegation doctrine—should forbid Congress to qualify that grant with a legislative veto.

C

The Court also takes no account of perhaps the most relevant consideration: however resolutions of disapproval under §244(c)(2) are formally characterized, in reality, a departure from the *status quo* occurs only upon the concurrence of opinion among the House, Senate, and President. Reservations of legislative authority to be exercised by Congress should be upheld if the exercise of such reserved authority is consistent with the distribution of and limits upon legislative power that Art. I provides.

1

The history of the Immigration and Nationality Act makes clear that §244(c)(2) did not alter the division of actual authority between Congress and the Executive. At all times, whether through private bills, or through affirmative concurrent resolutions, or through the present one-House veto, a permanent change in a deportable alien's status could be accomplished only with the agreement of the Attorney General, the House, and the Senate.

2

The central concern of the presentment and bicameralism requirements of Art. I is that, when a departure from the legal *status quo* is undertaken, it is done with the approval of the President and both Houses of Congress—or, in the event of a Presidential veto, a two-thirds majority in both Houses. This interest is fully satisfied by the operation of §244(c)(2). The President's approval is found in the Attorney General's action in recommending to Congress that the deportation order for a given alien be suspended. The House and the Senate indicate their approval of the Executive's action by not passing a resolution of disapproval within the statutory period. Thus, a change in the legal *status quo*—the deportability of the alien—is consummated only with the approval of each of the three relevant actors. The disagreement of any one of the three maintains the alien's preexisting status: the Executive may choose not to recommend suspension; the House and Senate may each veto the recommendation. The effect on the rights and obligations of the affected individuals and upon the legislative system is precisely the same as if a private bill were introduced but failed to receive the necessary approval.

Thus understood, §244(c)(2) fully effectuates the purposes of the bicameralism and presentment requirements.

Nor does §244 infringe on the judicial power, as Justice Powell would hold. Section 244 makes clear that Congress has reserved its own judgment as part of the statutory process. Congressional action does not substitute for judicial review of the Attorney General's decisions. The Act provides for judicial review of the refusal of the Attorney General to suspend a deportation and to transmit a recommendation to Congress. *INS v. Jong Ha Wang* (per curiam). But the courts have not been given the authority to review whether an alien should be given permanent status; review is limited to whether the Attorney General has properly applied the statutory standards for essentially denying the alien a recommendation that his deportable status be changed by the Congress.

V

I regret that I am in disagreement with my colleagues on the fundamental questions that these cases present. But even more I regret the destructive scope of the Court's holding. It reflects a profoundly different conception of the Constitution than that held by the courts which sanctioned the modern administrative state.

Today's decision strikes down in one fell swoop provisions in more laws enacted by Congress than the Court has cumulatively invalidated in its history. I fear it will now be more difficult to "insur[e] that the fundamental policy decisions in our society will be made not by an appointed official, but by the body immediately responsible to the people," *Arizona v. California* (Harlan, J., dissenting in part). I must dissent.

BOWSHER v. SYNAR

478 U.S. 714 (1986)

Opinion: Burger, joined by Brennan, Powell, Rehnquist, O'Connor
Concurrence: Stevens, joined by Marshall
Dissent: White
Dissent: Blackmun

In this case, the Court considers the constitutionality of an act in which Congress allocated power to play a critical role in the execution of its legislation to the comptroller general, an executive official who is subject to removal from office by congressional action. Would this unconstitutionally allow Congress to play a role not only in the creation of legislation but also in its execution? If so, is this a usurpation of executive power? Just how separate must the powers of the legislative and executive branches be? Is it possible to fully separate the two? How does the ability to fire an official relate to the broader issue of separation of powers?

CHIEF JUSTICE BURGER *delivered the opinion of the Court.*

The question presented by these appeals is whether the assignment by Congress to the Comptroller General of the United States of certain functions under the Balanced Budget and Emergency Deficit Control Act of 1985 violates the doctrine of separation of powers.

On December 12, 1985, the President signed into law the Balanced Budget and Emergency Deficit Control Act of 1985, popularly known as the "Gramm-Rudman-Hollings Act." The purpose of the Act is to eliminate the federal budget deficit. To that end, the Act sets a "maximum deficit amount" for federal spending for each of fiscal years 1986 through 1991. The size of that maximum deficit amount progressively reduces to zero in fiscal year 1991. If in any fiscal year the federal budget deficit exceeds the maximum deficit amount by more than a specified sum, the Act requires across-the-board cuts in federal spending to reach the targeted deficit level, with half of the cuts made to defense programs and the other half made to nondefense programs. The Act exempts certain priority programs from these cuts.

These "automatic" reductions are accomplished through a rather complicated procedure, spelled out in §251, the so-called "reporting provisions" of the Act. Each year, the Directors of the Office of Management and Budget (OMB) and the Congressional Budget Office (CBO) independently estimate the amount of the federal budget deficit for the upcoming fiscal year. If that deficit exceeds the maximum targeted deficit amount for that fiscal year by more than a specified amount, the Directors of OMB and CBO independently calculate, on a program-by-program basis, the budget reductions necessary to ensure that the deficit does not exceed the maximum deficit amount. The Act then requires the Directors to report jointly their deficit estimates and budget reduction calculations to the Comptroller General.

The Comptroller General, after reviewing the Directors' reports, then reports his conclusions to the President. §251(b). The President, in turn, must issue a "sequestration" order mandating the spending reductions specified by the Comptroller General. §252. There follows a period during which Congress may by legislation reduce spending to obviate, in whole or in part, the need for the sequestration order. If such reductions are not enacted, the sequestration order becomes effective and the spending reductions included in that order are made.

Anticipating constitutional challenge to these procedures, the Act also contains a "fallback" deficit reduction process to take effect "[i]n the event that any of the reporting procedures described in section 251 are invalidated." §274(f). Under these provisions, the report prepared by the Directors of OMB and the CBO is submitted directly to a specially created Temporary Joint Committee on Deficit Reduction, which must report in five days to both Houses a joint resolution setting forth the content of the Directors' report. Congress then must vote on the resolution under special rules, which render amendments out of order. If the resolution is passed and signed by the President, it then serves as the basis for a Presidential sequestration order.

Within hours of the President's signing of the Act, Congressman Synar, who had voted against the Act, filed a complaint seeking declaratory relief that the Act was unconstitutional. Eleven other Members later joined Congressman Synar's suit. A virtually identical lawsuit was also filed by the National Treasury Employees Union. The Union alleged that its members had been injured as a result of the Act's automatic spending reduction provisions, which have suspended certain cost-of-living benefit increases to the Union's members.

We noted recently that "[t]he Constitution sought to divide the delegated powers of the new Federal Government into three defined categories, Legislative, Executive, and Judicial." *INS v. Chadha.* The declared purpose of separating and dividing the powers of government, of course, was to "diffus[e] power the better to secure liberty." *Youngstown Sheet & Tube Co. v. Sawyer,* (Jackson, J., concurring). Justice Jackson's words echo the famous warning of Montesquieu, quoted by James Madison in *The Federalist* No. 47, that "'there can be no liberty where the legislative and executive powers are united in the same person, or body of magistrates'. . . ." *The Federalist* No. 47, p. 325 (J. Cooke ed. 1961).

Even a cursory examination of the Constitution reveals the influence of Montesquieu's thesis that checks and balances were the foundation of a structure of government that would protect liberty. The Framers provided a vigorous Legislative Branch and a separate and wholly independent Executive Branch, with each branch responsible ultimately to the people. The Framers also provided for a Judicial Branch equally independent, with "[t]he judicial Power . . . extend[ing] to all Cases, in Law and Equity, arising under this Constitution, and the Laws of the United States." Art. III, §2.

That this system of division and separation of powers produces conflicts, confusion, and discordance at times is inherent, but it was deliberately so structured to assure full, vigorous, and open debate on the great issues affecting the people, and to provide avenues for the operation of checks on the exercise of governmental power.

The Constitution does not contemplate an active role for Congress in the supervision of officers charged with the execution of the laws it enacts. The President appoints "Officers of the United States" with the "Advice and Consent of the Senate. . . ." Art. II, §2. Once the appointment has been made and confirmed, however, the Constitution explicitly provides for removal of Officers of the United States by Congress only upon impeachment by the House of Representatives and conviction by the Senate. An impeachment by the House and trial by the Senate can rest only on "Treason, Bribery or other high Crimes and Misdemeanors." Art. II, §4. A direct congressional role in the removal of officers charged with the execution of the laws beyond this limited one is inconsistent with separation of powers.

. . . [We] conclude that Congress cannot reserve for itself the power of removal of an officer charged with the execution of the laws except by impeachment. To permit the execution of the laws to be vested in an officer answerable only to Congress would, in practical terms, reserve in Congress control over the execution of the laws.

The structure of the Constitution does not permit Congress to execute the laws; it follows that Congress cannot grant to an officer under its control what it does not possess.

To permit an officer controlled by Congress to execute the laws would be, in essence, to permit a congressional veto. Congress could simply remove, or threaten to remove, an officer for executing the laws in any fashion found to be unsatisfactory to Congress. This kind of congressional control over the execution of the laws, *Chadha* makes clear, is constitutionally impermissible.

The dangers of congressional usurpation of Executive Branch functions have long been recognized. "[T]he debates of the Constitutional Convention, and the *Federalist Papers*, are replete with expressions of fear that the Legislative Branch of the National Government will aggrandize itself at the expense of the other two branches." *Buckley v. Valeo*. Indeed, we also have observed only recently that "[t]he hydraulic pressure inherent within each of the separate Branches to exceed the outer limits of its power, even to accomplish desirable objectives, must be resisted." *Chadha, supra*, at 951. With these principles in mind, we turn to consideration of whether the Comptroller General is controlled by Congress.

The critical factor lies in the provisions of the statute defining the Comptroller General's office relating to removability. Although the Comptroller General is nominated by the President from a list of three individuals recommended by the Speaker of the House of Representatives and the President *pro tempore* of the Senate, *see* 31 U.S.C. §703(a)(2), and confirmed by the Senate, he is removable only at the initiative of Congress. He may be removed not only by impeachment, but also by joint resolution of Congress "at any time" resting on any one of the following bases:

(i) permanent disability;
(ii) inefficiency;
(iii) neglect of duty;
(iv) malfeasance; or
(v) a felony or conduct involving moral turpitude.

31 U.S.C. §703(e)(1)B.

The statute permits removal for "inefficiency," "neglect of duty," or "malfeasance." These terms are very broad and, as interpreted by Congress, could sustain removal of a Comptroller General for any number of actual or perceived transgressions of the legislative will. The Constitutional Convention chose to permit impeachment of executive officers only for "Treason, Bribery, or other high Crimes and Misdemeanors." It rejected language that would have permitted impeachment for "maladministration," with Madison arguing that "[s]o vague a term will be equivalent to a tenure during pleasure of the Senate."

In constitutional terms, the removal powers over the Comptroller General's office dictate that he will be subservient to Congress.

It is clear that Congress has consistently viewed the Comptroller General as an officer of the Legislative Branch. The Reorganization Acts of 1945 and 1949, for example, both stated that the Comptroller General and the GAO are "a part of the legislative branch of the Government." 59 Stat. 616; 63 Stat. 205. Similarly, in the Accounting and Auditing Act of 1950, Congress required the Comptroller General to conduct audits "as an agent of the Congress." 64 Stat. 835.

Over the years, the Comptrollers General have also viewed themselves as part of the Legislative Branch. Against this background, we see no escape from the conclusion that, because Congress has retained removal authority over the Comptroller General, he may not be entrusted with executive powers. The remaining question is whether the Comptroller General has been assigned such powers in the Balanced Budget and Emergency Deficit Control Act of 1985.

Appellants suggest that the duties assigned to the Comptroller General in the Act are essentially ministerial and mechanical, so that their performance does not constitute "execution of the law" in a meaningful sense. On the contrary, we view these functions as plainly entailing execution of the law in constitutional terms. Interpreting a law enacted by Congress to implement the legislative mandate is the very essence of "execution" of the law. Under §251, the Comptroller General must exercise judgment concerning facts that affect the application of the Act. He must also interpret the provisions of the Act to determine precisely what budgetary calculations are required. Decisions of that kind are typically made by officers charged with executing a statute.

The executive nature of the Comptroller General's functions under the Act is revealed in §252(a)(3), which gives the Comptroller General the ultimate authority to determine the budget cuts to be made.

By placing the responsibility for execution of the Balanced Budget and Emergency Deficit Control Act in the hands of an officer who is subject to removal only by itself, Congress, in effect, has retained control over the execution of the Act, and has intruded into the executive function. The Constitution does not permit such intrusion.

JUSTICE WHITE, *dissenting.*

The Court, acting in the name of separation of powers, takes upon itself to strike down the Gramm-Rudman-Hollings Act, one of the most novel and far-reaching legislative responses to a national crisis since the New Deal. The basis of the Court's action is a solitary provision of another statute that was passed over 60 years ago and has lain dormant since that time. I cannot concur in the Court's action. Like the Court, I will not purport to speak to the wisdom of the policies incorporated in the legislation the Court invalidates; that is a matter for the Congress and the Executive, both of which expressed their assent to the statute barely half a year ago. I will, however, address the wisdom of the Court's willingness to interpose its distressingly formalistic view of separation of powers as a bar to the attainment of governmental objectives through the means chosen by the Congress and the President in the legislative process established by the Constitution....

II

If, as the Court seems to agree, the assignment of "executive" powers under Gramm-Rudman-Hollings to an officer not removable at will by the President would not, in itself, represent a violation of the constitutional scheme of separated powers, the question remains whether, as the Court concludes, the fact that the officer to whom Congress has delegated the authority to implement the Act is removable by a joint resolution of Congress should require invalidation of the Act. The Court's decision, as I have stated above, is based on a syllogism: the Act vests the Comptroller with "executive power"; such power may not be exercised by Congress or its agents; the Comptroller is an agent of Congress because he is removable by Congress; therefore the Act is invalid. I have no quarrel with the proposition that the powers exercised by the Comptroller under the Act may be characterized as "executive" in that they involve the interpretation and carrying out of the Act's mandate. I can also accept the general proposition that, although Congress has considerable authority in designating the officers who are to execute legislation, *see supra*, at

760-764, the constitutional scheme of separated powers does prevent Congress from reserving an executive role for itself or for its "agents." *Buckley v. Valeo* at 120-141; *id.* at 267-282 (White, J., concurring in part and dissenting in part). I cannot accept, however, that the exercise of authority by an officer removable for cause by a joint resolution of Congress is analogous to the impermissible execution of the law by Congress itself, nor would I hold that the congressional role in the removal process renders the Comptroller an "agent" of the Congress, incapable of receiving "executive" power....

The Act vesting budget-cutting authority in the Comptroller General represents Congress' judgment that the delegation of such authority to counteract ever-mounting deficits is "necessary and proper" to the exercise of the powers granted the Federal Government by the Constitution; and the President's approval of the statute signifies his unwillingness to reject the choice made by Congress. *Cf. Nixon v. Administrator of General Services.* Under such circumstances, the role of this Court should be limited to determining whether the Act so alters the balance of authority among the branches of government as to pose a genuine threat to the basic division between the lawmaking power and the power to execute the law. Because I see no such threat, I cannot join the Court in striking down the Act.

I dissent.

MORRISON v. OLSON

487 U.S. 654 (1988)

Opinion: Rehnquist, joined by Brennan, White, Marshall, Blackmun, Stevens, O'Connor
Dissent: Scalia

Calls for limits on executive power came with full force after the Watergate scandal of the Nixon administration. President Richard Nixon had been accused of hiring burglars to break into the headquarters of

the Democratic National Committee at the Watergate complex in Washington, D.C. The scandal eventually resulted in his resignation. During the scandal, President Nixon tried to exercise what many considered to be inappropriate control over the investigation of the break-in. Specifically, he ordered one Attorney General, Elliot Richardson, to fire an independent prosecutor, Archibald Cox, who had been appointed to investigate the Watergate break-in. Richardson resigned rather than fire Cox, but a subsequent acting Attorney General, Robert Bork, who was later nominated but not confirmed to serve on the Supreme Court, did fire Cox. These events raised traditional worries about the excessive power of the president, in particular when it came to investigations about his or her own wrongdoing. During the Carter administration, a series of reforms were passed by Congress that included a provision to ensure the independence of attorneys charged with investigating the executive branch.

This case concerns the constitutionality of a law allowing for the appointment of an independent counsel who may be removed from office not by the president but only by the attorney general, and even then only under extremely narrow and specific circumstances. It raises questions about the extent to which Congress may limit the power of the president to appoint and remove officials that perform executive functions. To what extent does the reasoning in this case build upon or depart from the reasoning in previous cases on the issue of the president's power to remove executive officers? Does this case repudiate Myers v. United States *and reaffirm* Humphrey's Executor v. United States? *To what extent should Congress be able to create executive offices that are independent from the control of the president? How, specifically, should the separation of powers be maintained? Also, if the president did have the* *power to fire any attorney charged with investigating him or her, would it be possible for that person to do his or her job effectively? Pay close attention to the arguments about democratic accountability in the dissent by U.S. Supreme Court Justice Antonin Scalia.*

CHIEF JUSTICE REHNQUIST *delivered the opinion of the Court.*

This case presents us with a challenge to the independent counsel provisions of the Ethics in Government Act of 1978, 28 U.S.C. §§49, 591 *et seq.* (1982 ed., Supp. V). We hold today that these provisions of the Act do not violate the Appointments Clause of the Constitution, Art. II, §2, cl. 2, or the limitations of Article III, nor do they impermissibly interfere with the President's authority under Article II in violation of the constitutional principle of separation of powers.

Briefly stated, Title VI of the Ethics in Government Act, 28 U.S.C. §§591-599 (1982 ed., Supp. V), allows for the appointment of an "independent counsel" to investigate and, if appropriate, prosecute certain high ranking Government officials for violations of federal criminal laws. The Act requires the Attorney General, upon receipt of information that he determines is "sufficient to constitute grounds to investigate whether any person [covered by the Act] may have violated any Federal criminal law," to conduct a preliminary investigation of the matter. When the Attorney General has completed this investigation, or 90 days has elapsed, he is required to report to a special court (the Special Division) created by the Act "for the purpose of appointing independent counsels." 28 U.S.C. §49 (1982 ed., Supp. V). If the Attorney General determines that "there are no reasonable grounds to believe that further investigation is warranted," then he must notify the Special Division of this result. In such a case, "the division of the court shall have no power to appoint an independent counsel." §592(b)(1). If, however, the Attorney General has determined that there are "reasonable grounds to believe that further investigation or prosecution is warranted," then he "shall apply to the division of the court for the appointment of an independent counsel."

Upon receiving this application, the Special Division "shall appoint an appropriate independent counsel and shall define that independent counsel's prosecutorial jurisdiction." §593(b).

With respect to all matters within the independent counsel's jurisdiction, the Act grants the counsel "full power and independent authority to exercise all investigative and prosecutorial functions and powers of the Department of Justice, the Attorney General, and any other officer or employee of the Department of Justice." §594(a). . . . In addition, whenever a matter has been referred to an independent counsel under the Act, the Attorney General and the Justice Department are required to suspend all investigations and proceedings regarding the matter. §597(a).

Two statutory provisions govern the length of an independent counsel's tenure in office. The first defines the procedure for removing an independent counsel. Section 596(a)(1) provides:

> An independent counsel appointed under this chapter may be removed from office, other than by impeachment and conviction, only by the personal action of the Attorney General and only for good cause, physical disability, mental incapacity, or any other condition that substantially impairs the performance of such independent counsel's duties.

If an independent counsel is removed pursuant to this section, the Attorney General is required to submit a report to both the Special Division and the Judiciary Committees of the Senate and the House "specifying the facts found and the ultimate grounds for such removal." §596(a)(2). Under the current version of the Act, an independent counsel can obtain judicial review of the Attorney General's action by filing a civil action in the United States District Court for the District of Columbia. The reviewing court is authorized to grant reinstatement or "other appropriate relief." §596(a)(3).

The other provision governing the tenure of the independent counsel defines the procedures for "terminating" the counsel's office. Under §596(b)(1), the office of an independent counsel terminates when he or she notifies the Attorney General that he or she has completed or substantially completed any investigations or prosecutions undertaken pursuant to the Act. In addition, the Special Division, acting either on its own or on the suggestion of the Attorney General, may terminate the office of an independent counsel at any time if it finds that "the investigation of all matters within the prosecutorial jurisdiction of such independent counsel . . . have been completed or so substantially completed that it would be appropriate for the Department of Justice to complete such investigations and prosecutions." §596(b)(2).

Finally, the Act provides for congressional oversight of the activities of independent counsel. An independent counsel may from time to time send Congress statements or reports on his or her activities. §595(a)(2). The "appropriate committees of the Congress" are given oversight jurisdiction in regard to the official conduct of an independent counsel, and the counsel is required by the Act to cooperate with Congress in the exercise of this jurisdiction. §595(a)(1). The counsel is required to inform the House of Representatives of "substantial and credible information which [the counsel] receives . . . that may constitute grounds for an impeachment." §595(c). In addition, the Act gives certain congressional committee members the power to "request in writing that the Attorney General apply for the appointment of an independent counsel." §592(g)(1). The Attorney General is required to respond to this request within a specified time, but is not required to accede to the request. §592(g)(2).

The proceedings in this case provide an example of how the Act works in practice. In 1982, two Subcommittees of the House of Representatives issued subpoenas directing the Environmental Protection Agency (EPA) to produce certain documents relating to the efforts of the EPA and the Land and Natural Resources Division of the Justice Department to enforce the "Superfund Law." At that time, appellee Olson was the Assistant Attorney General for the Office of Legal Counsel (OLC), appellee Schmults was Deputy Attorney General, and appellee Dinkins was the Assistant Attorney General for the Land and Natural Resources Division. Acting on the advice of the Justice Department, the President ordered the Administrator of EPA to invoke executive privilege to withhold certain of the documents on the ground that they contained "enforcement-sensitive information." The Administrator obeyed this order and withheld the documents. In response, the House voted to hold the Administrator in contempt, after which the Administrator and the United States together filed a lawsuit against the House. The conflict abated in March, 1983, when the administration agreed to give the House Committees limited access to the documents.

The following year, the House Judiciary Committee began an investigation into the Justice Department's role in the controversy over the EPA documents. During this investigation, appellee Olson testified before a House Subcommittee on March 10, 1983. Both before and after that testimony, the Department complied with several Committee requests to produce certain documents. Other documents were at first withheld, although these documents were eventually disclosed by the Department after the Committee learned of their existence. In 1985, the majority members of the Judiciary Committee published a lengthy report on the Committee's investigation. The report not only criticized various officials in the Department of Justice for their role in the EPA executive privilege dispute, but it also suggested that appellee Olson had given false and misleading testimony to the Subcommittee on March 10, 1983, and that appellees Schmults and Dinkins had wrongfully withheld certain documents from the Committee, thus obstructing the Committee's investigation. The Chairman of the Judiciary Committee forwarded a copy of the report to the Attorney General with a request, pursuant to 28 U.S.C. §592(c), that he seek the appointment of an independent counsel to investigate the allegations against Olson, Schmults, and Dinkins.

The Attorney General directed the Public Integrity Section of the Criminal Division to conduct a preliminary investigation. The Section's report concluded that the appointment of an independent counsel was warranted to investigate the Committee's allegations with respect to all three appellees. After consulting with other Department officials, however, the Attorney General chose to apply to the Special Division for the appointment of an independent counsel solely with respect to appellee Olson.

On April 23, 1986, the Special Division appointed James C. McKay as independent counsel to investigate "whether the testimony of . . . Olson and his revision of such testimony on March 10, 1983, violated either 18 U.S.C. §1505 or §1001, or any other provision of federal law." The court also ordered that the independent counsel shall have jurisdiction to investigate any other allegation of evidence of violation of any Federal criminal law by Theodore Olson developed during investigations, by the Independent Counsel, referred to above, and connected with or arising out of that investigation, and Independent Counsel shall have jurisdiction to prosecute for any such violation.

Order, Div. No. 86-1 (CADC Special Division, April 23, 1986). McKay later resigned as independent counsel, and on May 29, 1986, the Division appointed appellant Morrison as his replacement, with the same jurisdiction.

In January, 1987, appellant asked the Attorney General pursuant to §594(e) to refer to her as "related matters" the Committee's allegations against appellees Schmults and Dinkins. The Attorney General refused to refer the matters, concluding that his decision not to request the appointment of an independent counsel in regard to those matters was final under §592(b)(1). Appellant then asked the Special Division to order that the matters be referred to her under §594(e). On April 2, 1987, the Division ruled that the Attorney General's decision not to seek appointment of an independent counsel with respect to Schmults and Dinkins was final and unreviewable under §592(b)(1), and that therefore the court had no authority to make the requested referral. The court ruled, however, that its original grant of jurisdiction to appellant was broad enough to permit inquiry into whether Olson may have conspired with others, including Schmults and Dinkins, to obstruct the Committee's investigation.

Following this ruling, in May and June, 1987, appellant caused a grand jury to issue and serve subpoenas on appellees. All three appellees moved to quash the subpoenas, claiming, among other things, that the independent counsel provisions of the Act were unconstitutional, and that appellant accordingly had no authority to proceed.

The Appointments Clause of Article II reads as follows:

> [The President] shall nominate, and by and with the Advice and Consent of the Senate, shall appoint Ambassadors, other public Ministers and Consuls, Judges of the supreme Court, and all other Officers of the United States, whose Appointments are not herein otherwise provided for, and which shall be established by Law: but the Congress may by Law vest the Appointment of such inferior Officers, as they think proper, in the President alone, in the Courts of Law, or in the Heads of Departments.

U.S. Const., Art. II, §2, cl. 2. The parties do not dispute that "[t]he Constitution for purposes of appointment . . . divides all its officers into two classes." *United States v. Germaine.* As we stated in *Buckley v. Valeo*:

> Principal officers are selected by the President with the advice and consent of the Senate. Inferior officers Congress may allow to be appointed by the President alone, by the heads of departments, or by the Judiciary.

The initial question is, accordingly, whether appellant is an "inferior" or a "principal" officer. If she is the latter, as the Court of Appeals concluded, then the Act is in violation of the Appointments Clause.

The line between "inferior" and "principal" officers is one that is far from clear, and the Framers provided little guidance into where it should be drawn. We need not attempt here to decide exactly where the line falls between the two types of officers, because, in our view, appellant clearly falls on the "inferior officer" side of that line. Several factors lead to this conclusion.

First, appellant is subject to removal by a higher Executive Branch official. . . . Second, appellant is empowered by the Act to perform only certain, limited duties. An independent counsel's role is restricted primarily to investigation and, if appropriate, prosecution for certain federal crimes. . . .

Third, appellant's office is limited in jurisdiction. Not only is the Act itself restricted in applicability to certain federal officials suspected of certain serious federal crimes, but an independent counsel can only act within the scope of the jurisdiction that has been granted by the Special Division pursuant to a request by the Attorney General. Finally, appellant's office is limited in tenure. There is concededly no time limit on the appointment of a particular counsel. Nonetheless, the office of independent counsel is "temporary" in the sense that an independent counsel is appointed essentially to accomplish a single task, and when that task is over, the office is terminated, either by the counsel herself or by action of the Special Division. . . .

This does not, however, end our inquiry under the Appointments Clause. Appellees argue that, even if appellant is an "inferior" officer, the Clause does not empower Congress to place the power to appoint such an officer outside the Executive Branch. They contend that the Clause does not contemplate congressional authorization of "interbranch appointments," in which an officer of one branch is appointed by officers of another branch. The relevant language of the Appointments Clause is worth repeating. It reads:

> . . . but the Congress may by Law vest the Appointment of such inferior Officers, as they think proper, in the President alone, in the courts of Law, or in the Heads of Departments.

On its face, the language of this "excepting clause" admits of no limitation on interbranch appointments. Indeed, the inclusion of "as they think proper" seems clearly to give Congress significant discretion to determine whether it is "proper" to vest the appointment of, for example, executive officials in the "courts of Law."

We do not mean to say that Congress' power to provide for interbranch appointments of "inferior officers" is unlimited. In addition to separation of powers concerns, which would arise if such provisions for appointment had the potential to impair the constitutional functions assigned to one of the branches, *Siebold* itself suggested that Congress' decision to vest the appointment power in the courts would be improper if there was some "incongruity" between the functions normally performed by the courts and the performance of their duty to appoint. 100 U.S. at 398.

In this case, however, we do not think it impermissible for Congress to vest the power to appoint independent counsel in a specially created federal court. We thus disagree with the Court of Appeals' conclusion that there is an inherent incongruity about a court having the power to appoint prosecutorial officers. We have recognized that courts may appoint private attorneys to act as prosecutor for judicial contempt judgments. *See Young v. United States ex rel. Vuitton et Fils S.A.* In *Go-Bart Importing Co. v. United States*, we approved court appointment of United States commissioners, who exercised certain limited prosecutorial powers. *Id.* at 353, n. 2. In *Siebold*, as well, we indicated that judicial appointment of federal marshals, who are "executive officer[s]," would not be inappropriate.

Congress of course was concerned when it created the office of independent counsel with the conflicts of interest that could arise in situations when the Executive Branch is called upon to investigate its own high-ranking officers. If it were to remove the appointing authority from the Executive Branch, the most logical place to put it was in the Judicial Branch. In the light of the Act's provision making the judges of the Special Division ineligible to participate in any matters relating to an independent counsel they have appointed, 28 U.S.C. §49(f) (1982 ed., Supp. V), we do not think that appointment of the independent counsel by the court runs afoul of the constitutional limitation on "incongruous" interbranch appointments.

Appellees next contend that the powers vested in the Special Division by the Act conflict with Article III of the Constitution. We have long recognized that by the express provision of Article III, the judicial power of the United States is limited to "Cases" and "Controversies." See Muskrat v. United States. As a general rule, we have broadly stated that "executive or administrative duties of a nonjudicial nature may not be imposed on judges holding office under Art. III of the Constitution." Buckley, at 123 (citing United States v. Ferreira; Hayburn's Case). The purpose of this limitation is to help ensure the independence of the Judicial Branch and to prevent the judiciary from encroaching into areas reserved for the other branches. See United States Parole Comm'n v. Geraghty. With this in mind, we address in turn the various duties given to the Special Division by the Act.

Most importantly, the Act vests in the Special Division the power to choose who will serve as independent counsel and the power to define his or her jurisdiction. §593(b). Clearly, once it is accepted that the Appointments Clause gives Congress the power to vest the appointment of officials such as the independent counsel in the "courts of Law," there can be no Article III objection to the Special Division's exercise of that power, as the power itself derives from the Appointments Clause, a source of authority for judicial action that is independent of Article III. Appellees contend, however, that the Division's Appointments Clause powers do not encompass the power to define the independent counsel's jurisdiction. We disagree. In our view,

Congress' power under the Clause to vest the "Appointment" of inferior officers in the courts may, in certain circumstances, allow Congress to give the courts some discretion in defining the nature and scope of the appointed official's authority. Particularly when, as here, Congress creates a temporary "office" the nature and duties of which will by necessity vary with the factual circumstances giving rise to the need for an appointment in the first place, it may vest the power to define the scope of the office in the court as an incident to the appointment of the officer pursuant to the Appointments Clause. This said, we do not think that Congress may give the Division unlimited discretion to determine the independent counsel's jurisdiction. In order for the Division's definition of the counsel's jurisdiction to be truly "incidental" to its power to appoint, the jurisdiction that the court decides upon must be demonstrably related to the factual circumstances that gave rise to the Attorney General's investigation and request for the appointment of the independent counsel in the particular case.

We are more doubtful about the Special Division's power to terminate the office of the independent counsel pursuant to §596(b)(2). As appellees suggest, the power to terminate, especially when exercised by the Division on its own motion, is "administrative" to the extent that it requires the Special Division to monitor the progress of proceedings of the independent counsel and come to a decision as to whether the counsel's job is "completed." §596(b)(2). It also is not a power that could be considered typically "judicial," as it has few analogues among the court's more traditional powers. Nonetheless, we do not, as did the Court of Appeals, view this provision as a significant judicial encroachment upon executive power or upon the prosecutorial discretion of the independent counsel.

The termination provisions of the Act do not give the Special Division anything approaching the power to remove the counsel while an investigation or court proceeding is still underway—this power is vested solely in the Attorney General. As we see it, "termination" may occur only when the duties of the counsel are truly "completed" or "so substantially completed" that there remains no need for any continuing action by the independent counsel. It is basically a device for removing from the public payroll an independent counsel who has served his or her purpose, but is unwilling to acknowledge the fact. So construed, the Special Division's power to terminate does not pose a sufficient threat of judicial intrusion into matters that are more properly within the Executive's authority to require that the Act be invalidated as inconsistent with Article III.

We now turn to consider whether the Act is invalid under the constitutional principle of separation of powers. Two related issues must be addressed: the first is whether the provision of the Act restricting the Attorney General's power to remove the independent counsel to only those instances in which he can show "good cause," taken by itself, impermissibly interferes with the President's exercise of his constitutionally appointed functions. The second is whether, taken as a whole, the Act violates the separation of powers by reducing the President's ability to control the prosecutorial powers wielded by the independent counsel.

Unlike both *Bowsher* and *Myers*, this case does not involve an attempt by Congress itself to gain a role in the removal of executive officials other than its established powers of impeachment and conviction. The Act instead puts the removal power squarely in the hands of the Executive Branch; an independent counsel may be removed from office, "only by the personal action of the Attorney General, and only for good cause." §596(a)(1). There is no requirement of congressional approval of the Attorney General's removal decision, though the decision is subject to judicial review. §596(a)(3). In our view, the removal provisions of the Act make this case more analogous to *Humphrey's Executor v. United States*, and *Wiener v. United States*, than to *Myers* or *Bowsher*.

. . . Appellees contend that *Humphrey's Executor* and *Wiener* are distinguishable from this case because they did not involve officials who performed a "core executive function." They argue that our decision in *Humphrey's Executor* rests on a distinction between "purely executive" officials and officials who exercise "quasi-legislative" and "quasi-judicial" powers. In their view, when a "purely executive" official is involved, the governing precedent is *Myers*, not *Humphrey's Executor*. And, under *Myers*, the President must have absolute discretion to discharge "purely" executive officials at will.

We undoubtedly did rely on the terms "quasi-legislative" and "quasi-judicial" to distinguish the officials involved in *Humphrey's Executor* and *Wiener* from those in *Myers*, but our present considered view is that the determination of whether the Constitution allows Congress to impose a "good cause"–type restriction on the President's power to remove an official cannot be made to turn on whether or not that official is classified as "purely executive." The analysis contained in our removal cases is designed not to define rigid categories of those officials who may or may not be removed at will by the President, but to ensure that Congress does not interfere with the President's exercise of the "executive power" and his constitutionally appointed duty to "take care that the laws be faithfully executed" under Article II. . . .

Considering for the moment the "good cause" removal provision in isolation from the other parts of the Act at issue in this case, we cannot say that the imposition of a "good cause" standard for removal by itself unduly trammels on executive authority. There is no real dispute that the functions performed by the independent counsel are "executive" in the sense that they are law enforcement functions that typically have been undertaken by officials within the Executive Branch. As we noted above, however, the independent counsel is an inferior officer under the Appointments Clause, with limited jurisdiction and tenure and lacking policymaking or significant administrative authority. Although the counsel exercises no small amount of discretion and judgment in deciding how to carry out his or her duties under the Act, we simply do not see how the President's need to control the exercise of that discretion is so central to the functioning of the Executive Branch as to require as a matter of constitutional law that the counsel be terminable at will by the President.

Nor do we think that the "good cause" removal provision at issue here impermissibly burdens the President's power to control or supervise the independent counsel, as an executive official, in the execution of his or her duties under the Act. This is not a case in which the power to remove an executive official has been completely stripped from the President, thus providing no means for the President to ensure the "faithful execution" of the laws. Rather, because the independent counsel may be terminated for "good cause," the Executive, through the Attorney General, retains ample authority to assure that the counsel is competently performing his or her statutory responsibilities in a manner that comports with the provisions of the Act. Here, as with the provision of the Act conferring the appointment authority of the independent

counsel on the special court, the congressional determination to limit the removal power of the Attorney General was essential, in the view of Congress, to establish the necessary independence of the office. We do not think that this limitation as it presently stands sufficiently deprives the President of control over the independent counsel to interfere impermissibly with his constitutional obligation to ensure the faithful execution of the laws.

The final question to be addressed is whether the Act, taken as a whole, violates the principle of separation of powers by unduly interfering with the role of the Executive Branch. Time and again we have reaffirmed the importance in our constitutional scheme of the separation of governmental powers into the three coordinate branches. As we stated in *Buckley v. Valeo*, the system of separated powers and checks and balances established in the Constitution was regarded by the Framers as "a self-executing safeguard against the encroachment or aggrandizement of one branch at the expense of the other." *Id.* at 122. We have not hesitated to invalidate provisions of law which violate this principle. On the other hand, we have never held that the Constitution requires that the three Branches of Government "operate with absolute independence." *United States v. Nixon.* In the often-quoted words of Justice Jackson:

> While the Constitution diffuses power the better to secure liberty, it also contemplates that practice will integrate the dispersed powers into a workable government. It enjoins upon its branches separateness but interdependence, autonomy but reciprocity.

Youngstown Sheet & Tube Co. v. Sawyer (concurring opinion).

We observe first that this case does not involve an attempt by Congress to increase its own powers at the expense of the

Executive Branch. Unlike some of our previous cases, most recently *Bowsher v. Synar*, this case simply does not pose a "dange[r] of congressional usurpation of Executive Branch functions." at 727; *see also INS v. Chadha*. Indeed, with the exception of the power of impeachment—which applies to all officers of the United States—Congress retained for itself no powers of control or supervision over an independent counsel. The Act does empower certain Members of Congress to request the Attorney General to apply for the appointment of an independent counsel, but the Attorney General has no duty to comply with the request, although he must respond within a certain time limit. §592(g). Other than that, Congress' role under the Act is limited to receiving reports or other information and oversight of the independent counsel's activities, §595(a), functions that we have recognized generally as being incidental to the legislative function of Congress. *See McGrain v. Daugherty.*

Similarly, we do not think that the Act works any judicial usurpation of properly executive functions. As should be apparent from our discussion of the Appointments Clause above, the power to appoint inferior officers such as independent counsel is not, in itself, an "executive" function in the constitutional sense, at least when Congress has exercised its power to vest the appointment of an inferior office in the "courts of Law." We note nonetheless that, under the Act, the Special Division has no power to appoint an independent counsel *sua sponte*; it may only do so upon the specific request of the Attorney General, and the courts are specifically prevented from reviewing the Attorney General's decision not to seek appointment, §592(f). In addition, once the court has appointed a counsel and defined his or her jurisdiction, it has no power to supervise or control the activities of the counsel.

Finally, we do not think that the Act "impermissibly undermine[s]" the powers of the Executive Branch, *Schor supra*, at 856, or "disrupts the proper balance between the coordinate branches [by] prevent[ing] the Executive Branch from accomplishing its constitutionally assigned functions," *Nixon v. Administrator of General Services, supra*, at 443. It is undeniable that the Act reduces the amount of control or supervision that the Attorney General and, through him, the President exercises over the investigation and prosecution of a certain class of alleged criminal activity. The Attorney General is not allowed to appoint the individual of his choice; he does not determine the counsel's jurisdiction; and his power to remove a counsel is limited. Nonetheless, the Act does give the Attorney General several means of supervising or controlling the prosecutorial powers that may be wielded by an independent counsel. Most importantly, the Attorney General retains the power to remove the counsel for "good cause," a power that we have already concluded provides the Executive with substantial ability to ensure that the laws are "faithfully executed" by an independent counsel. No independent counsel may be appointed without a specific request by the Attorney General, and the Attorney General's decision not to request appointment if he finds "no reasonable grounds to believe that further investigation is warranted" is committed to his unreviewable discretion. The Act thus gives the Executive a degree of control over the power to initiate an investigation by the independent counsel. In addition, the jurisdiction of the independent counsel is defined with reference to the facts submitted by the Attorney General, and once a counsel is appointed, the Act requires that the counsel abide by Justice Department policy unless it is not "possible" to do so. Notwithstanding the fact that the counsel is to some degree "independent" and free from Executive supervision to a greater extent than other federal prosecutors, in our view, these features of the Act give the Executive Branch sufficient control over the independent counsel to ensure that the President is able to perform his constitutionally assigned duties.

In sum, we conclude today that it does not violate the Appointments Clause for Congress to vest the appointment of independent counsel in the Special Division; that the powers exercised by the Special Division under the Act do not violate Article III; and that the Act does not violate the separation of powers principle by impermissibly interfering with the functions of the Executive Branch.

JUSTICE SCALIA, *dissenting.*

. . . The notion that every violation of law should be prosecuted, including—indeed, *especially*—every violation by those in high places, is an attractive one, and it would be risky to argue in an election campaign that that is not an absolutely overriding value. *Fiat justitia, ruat coelum.* Let justice be done, though the heavens may fall. The reality is, however, that it is not an absolutely overriding value, and it was with the hope that we would be able to acknowledge and apply such realities that the Constitution spared us, by life tenure, the necessity of election campaigns. I cannot imagine that there are not many thoughtful men and women in Congress who realize that the benefits of this legislation are far outweighed by its harmful effect upon our system of government, and even upon the nature of justice received by those men and women who agree to serve in the Executive Branch. But it is difficult to vote not to enact, and even more difficult to vote to repeal, a statute called, appropriately enough, the Ethics in Government Act. If Congress is controlled by the party other than the one to which

the President belongs, it has little incentive to repeal it; if it is controlled by the same party, it dare not. By its shortsighted action today, I fear the Court has permanently encumbered the Republic with an institution that will do it great harm.

Worse than what it has done, however, is the manner in which it has done it. A government of laws means a government of rules. Today's decision on the basic issue of fragmentation of executive power is ungoverned by rule, and hence ungoverned by law. It extends into the very heart of our most significant constitutional function the "totality of the circumstances" mode of analysis that this Court has in recent years become fond of. Taking all things into account, we conclude that the power taken away from the President here is not really too much. The next time executive power is assigned to someone other than the President, we may conclude, taking all things into account, that it *is* too much. That opinion, like this one, will not be confined by any rule. We will describe, as we have today (though I hope more accurately) the effects of the provision in question, and will authoritatively announce: "The President's need to control the exercise of the [subject officer's] discretion is so central to the functioning of the Executive Branch as to require complete control." This is not analysis; it is *ad hoc* judgment. And it fails to explain why it is not true that—as the text of the Constitution seems to require, as the Founders seemed to expect, and as our past cases have uniformly assumed—all purely executive power must be under the control of the President.

The *ad hoc* approach to constitutional adjudication has real attraction, even apart from its work-saving potential. It is guaranteed to produce a result, in every case, that will make a majority of the Court happy with the law. The law is, by definition, precisely what the majority thinks, taking all things into account, it *ought* to be. I prefer to rely upon the judgment of the wise men who constructed our system, and of the people who approved it, and of

two centuries of history that have shown it to be sound. Like it or not, that judgment says, quite plainly, that "[t]he executive Power shall be vested in a President of the United States."

CLINTON v. CITY OF NEW YORK

524 U.S. 417 (1998)

Opinion: Stevens, joined by Rehnquist, Kennedy, Souter, Thomas, Ginsburg
Concurrence: Kennedy
Partial Concurrence, Partial Dissent: Scalia, joined by O'Connor and by Breyer in Part III
Dissent: Breyer, joined by O'Connor, Scalia in Part III

This case concerns the constitutionality of the Line Item Veto Act of 1996, which granted to the president the power to nullify particular provisions of congressional acts. The Court decided that the "line item veto" as granted in the Act violates the Presentment Clause of the Constitution. U.S. Supreme Court Justice Stephen Breyer, however, questions this conclusion in his dissent, which invokes a pragmatic theme. Could the line item veto in fact serve a legitimate and constitutional political purpose? For example, the line item veto would allow the president to eliminate the provisions unrelated to the topic of the bill that members of Congress often insert in major legislation. Even if the line item veto could be valuable in a democratic society, is it right to employ it? According to Justice Anthony Kennedy, "Failure of political will does not justify unconstitutional remedies." Do you agree, or do you think the ends justify the means? Does the majority's approach elevate form over substance?

JUSTICE STEVENS *delivered the opinion of the Court.*

The Line Item Veto Act (Act), 110 Stat. 1200, 2 U.S.C. §691 *et seq.* (1994 ed., Supp. II), was enacted in April 1996 and became effective on January 1, 1997. The following day, six Members of Congress who had voted against the Act brought suit in the District Court for the District of Columbia challenging its constitutionality. On April 10, 1997, the District Court entered an order holding that the Act is unconstitutional. *Byrd v. Raines.* In obedience to the statutory direction to allow a direct, expedited appeal to this Court, see §§692(b)-(c), we promptly noted probable jurisdiction and expedited review, 520 U.S. ___ (1997). We determined, however, that the Members of Congress did not have standing to sue because they had not "alleged a sufficiently concrete injury to have established Article III standing," *Raines v. Byrd*; thus, "in . . . light of [the] overriding and time-honored concern about keeping the Judiciary's power within its proper constitutional sphere," *id.*, we remanded the case to the District Court with instructions to dismiss the complaint for lack of jurisdiction.

Less than two months after our decision in that case, the President exercised his authority to cancel one provision in the Balanced Budget Act of 1997, and two provisions in the Taxpayer Relief Act of

1997. Appellees, claiming that they had been injured by two of those cancellations, filed these cases in the District Court. That Court again held the statute invalid, and we again expedited our review. We now hold that these appellees have standing to challenge the constitutionality of the Act and, reaching the merits, we agree that the cancellation procedures set forth in the Act violate the Presentment Clause, Art. I, §7, cl. 2, of the Constitution.

I

We begin by reviewing the canceled items that are at issue in these cases.

Section 4722(c) of the Balanced Budget Act

Title XIX of the Social Security Act, 79 Stat. 343, as amended, authorizes the Federal Government to transfer huge sums of money to the States to help finance medical care for the indigent. In 1991, Congress directed that those federal subsidies be reduced by the amount of certain taxes levied by the States on health care providers. In 1994, the Department of Health and Human Services (HHS) notified the State of New York that 15 of its taxes were covered by the 1991 Act, and that as of June 30, 1994, the statute therefore required New York to return $955 million to the United States. The notice advised the State that it could apply for a waiver on certain statutory grounds. New York did request a waiver for those tax programs, as well as for a number of others, but HHS has not formally acted on any of those waiver requests. New York has estimated that the amount at issue for the period from October 1992 through March 1997 is as high as $2.6 billion.

Because HHS had not taken any action on the waiver requests, New York turned to Congress for relief. On August 5, 1997,

Congress enacted a law that resolved the issue in New York's favor. Section 4722(c) of the Balanced Budget Act of 1997 identifies the disputed taxes and provides that they "are deemed to be permissible health care related taxes and in compliance with the requirements" of the relevant provisions of the 1991 statute.

On August 11, 1997, the President sent identical notices to the Senate and to the House of Representatives canceling "one item of new direct spending," specifying §4722(c) as that item, and stating that he had determined that "this cancellation will reduce the Federal budget deficit." He explained that §4722(c) would have permitted New York "to continue relying upon impermissible provider taxes to finance its Medicaid program" and that "[t]his preferential treatment would have increased Medicaid costs, would have treated New York differently from all other States, and would have established a costly precedent for other States to request comparable treatment."

Section 968 of the Taxpayer Relief Act

A person who realizes a profit from the sale of securities is generally subject to a capital gains tax. Under existing law, however, an ordinary business corporation can acquire a corporation, including a food processing or refining company, in a merger or stock-for-stock transaction in which no gain is recognized to the seller; the seller's tax payment, therefore, is deferred. If, however, the purchaser is a farmers' cooperative, the parties cannot structure such a transaction because the stock of the cooperative may be held only by its members; thus, a seller dealing with a farmers' cooperative cannot obtain the benefits of tax deferral.

In §968 of the Taxpayer Relief Act of 1997, Congress amended §1042 of the Internal Revenue Code to permit owners of certain food refiners and processors to defer the recognition of gain if they sell their stock to eligible farmers' cooperatives. The purpose of the amendment, as repeatedly explained by its sponsors, was "to facilitate the transfer of refiners and processors to farmers' cooperatives." The amendment to §1042 was one of the 79 "limited tax benefits" authorized by the Taxpayer Relief Act of 1997 and specifically identified in Title XVII of that Act as "subject to [the] line item veto."

On the same date that he canceled the "item of new direct spending" involving New York's health care programs, the President also canceled this limited tax benefit. In his explanation of that action, the President endorsed the objective of encouraging "value-added farming through the purchase by farmers' cooperatives of refiners or processors of agricultural goods," but concluded that the provision lacked safeguards and also "failed to target its benefits to small-and-medium-size cooperatives."

II

Appellees filed two separate actions against the President and other federal officials challenging these two cancellations. The plaintiffs in the first case are the City of New York, two hospital associations, one hospital, and two unions representing health care employees. The plaintiffs in the second are a farmers' cooperative consisting of about 30 potato growers in Idaho and an individual farmer who is a member and officer of the cooperative. The District Court consolidated the two cases and determined that at least one of the plaintiffs in each had standing under Article III of the Constitution.

IV

The Line Item Veto Act gives the President the power to "cancel in whole" three types of provisions that have been signed into law: "(1) any dollar amount of discretionary budget authority; (2) any item of new direct spending; or (3) any limited tax benefit." It is undisputed that the New York case involves an "item of new direct spending" and that the Snake River case involves a "limited tax benefit" as those terms are defined in the Act. It is also undisputed that each of those provisions had been signed into law pursuant to Article I, §7, of the Constitution before it was canceled.

The Act requires the President to adhere to precise procedures whenever he exercises his cancellation authority. In identifying items for cancellation he must consider the legislative history, the purposes, and other relevant information about the items. He must determine, with respect to each cancellation, that it will "(i) reduce the Federal budget deficit; (ii) not impair any essential Government functions; and (iii) not harm the national interest." Moreover, he must transmit a special message to Congress notifying it of each cancellation within five calendar days (excluding Sundays) after the enactment of the canceled provision. It is undisputed that the President meticulously followed these procedures in these cases.

A cancellation takes effect upon receipt by Congress of the special message from the President. If, however, a "disapproval bill" pertaining to a special message is enacted into law, the cancellations set forth in that message become "null and void." The Act sets forth a detailed expedited procedure for the consideration of a "disapproval bill," but no such bill was passed for either of the cancellations involved in these cases. A majority vote of both Houses is sufficient to enact a disapproval bill. The Act does not grant the President the authority to cancel a disapproval bill, but he does, of course, retain his constitutional authority to veto such a bill.

The effect of a cancellation is plainly stated in §691e, which defines the principal terms used in the Act. With respect to both an item of new direct spending and a limited tax benefit, the cancellation prevents the item "from having legal force or effect." Thus, under the plain text of the statute, the two actions of the President that are challenged in these cases prevented one section of the Balanced Budget Act of 1997 and one section of the Taxpayer Relief Act of 1997 "from having legal force or effect." The remaining provisions of those statutes, with the exception of the second canceled item in the latter, continue to have the same force and effect as they had when signed into law.

In both legal and practical effect, the President has amended two Acts of Congress by repealing a portion of each. "[R]epeal of statutes, no less than enactment, must conform with Art. I." *INS v. Chadha*. There is no provision in the Constitution that authorizes the President to enact, to amend, or to repeal statutes. Both Article I and Article II assign responsibilities to the President that directly relate to the lawmaking process, but neither addresses the issue presented by these cases. The President "shall from time to time give to the Congress Information on the State of the Union, and recommend to their Consideration such Measures as he shall judge necessary and expedient. . . . " Art. II, §3. Thus, he may initiate and influence legislative proposals. Moreover, after a bill has passed both Houses of Congress, but "before it become[s] a Law," it must be presented to the President. If he approves it, "he shall sign it, but if not he shall return it, with his Objections to that House in which it shall have originated, who shall enter the Objections at large on their Journal, and proceed to reconsider it." Art. I, §7, cl. 2. His "return" of a bill, which is usually described as a "veto," is subject to being overridden by a two-thirds vote in each House.

There are important differences between the President's "return" of a bill pursuant to Article I, §7, and the exercise of the President's cancellation authority pursuant to the Line Item Veto Act. The constitutional return takes place *before* the bill becomes law; the statutory cancellation occurs *after* the bill becomes law. The constitutional return is of the entire bill; the statutory cancellation is of only a part. Although the Constitution expressly authorizes the President to play a role in the process of enacting statutes, it is silent on the subject of unilateral Presidential action that either repeals or amends parts of duly enacted statutes.

There are powerful reasons for construing constitutional silence on this profoundly important issue as equivalent to an express prohibition. The procedures governing the enactment of statutes set forth in the text of Article I were the product of the great debates and compromises that produced the Constitution itself. Familiar historical materials provide abundant support for the conclusion that the power to enact statutes may only "be exercised in accord with a single, finely wrought and exhaustively considered, procedure." *Chadha.* Our first President understood the text of the Presentment Clause as requiring that he either "approve all the parts of a Bill, or reject it in toto." What has emerged in these cases from the President's exercise of his statutory cancellation powers, however, are truncated versions of two bills that passed both Houses of Congress. They are not the product of the "finely wrought" procedure that the Framers designed.

VI

Although they are implicit in what we have already written, the profound importance of these cases makes it appropriate to emphasize three points.

First, we express no opinion about the wisdom of the procedures authorized by the Line Item Veto Act. . . .

Second, although appellees challenge the validity of the Act on alternative grounds, the only issue we address concerns the "finely wrought" procedure commanded by the Constitution. *Chadha.*

Third, our decision rests on the narrow ground that the procedures authorized by the Line Item Veto Act are not authorized by the Constitution. The Balanced Budget Act of 1997 is a 500-page document that became "Public Law 105-33" after three procedural steps were taken: (1) a bill containing its exact text was approved by a majority of the Members of the House of Representatives; (2) the Senate approved precisely the same text; and (3) that text was signed into law by the President. The Constitution explicitly requires that each of those three steps be taken before a bill may "become a law." Art. I, §7. If one paragraph of that text had been omitted at any one of those three stages, Public Law 105-33 would not have been validly enacted. If the Line Item Veto Act were valid, it would authorize the President to create a different law—one whose text was not voted on by either House of Congress or presented to the President for signature. Something that might be known as "Public Law 105-33 as modified by the President" may or may not be desirable, but it is surely not a document that may "become a law" pursuant to the procedures designed by the Framers of Article I, §7, of the Constitution.

If there is to be a new procedure in which the President will play a different role in determining the final text of what may "become a law," such change must come not by legislation but through the amendment procedures set forth in Article V of the Constitution.

JUSTICE KENNEDY, *concurring.*

A nation cannot plunder its own treasury without putting its Constitution and its survival in peril. The statute before us, then, is of first importance, for it seems undeniable the Act will tend to restrain persistent excessive spending. Nevertheless, for the reasons given by Justice Stevens in the opinion for the Court, the statute must be found invalid. Failure of political will does not justify unconstitutional remedies.

I write to respond to my colleague Justice Breyer, who observes that the statute does not threaten the liberties of individual citizens, a point on which I disagree. The argument is related to his earlier suggestion that our role is lessened here because the two political branches are adjusting their own powers between themselves. To say the political branches have a somewhat free hand to reallocate their own authority would seem to require acceptance of two premises: first, that the public good demands it, and second, that liberty is not at risk. The former premise is inadmissible. The Constitution's structure requires a stability which transcends the convenience of the moment. The latter premise, too, is flawed. Liberty is always at stake when one or more of the branches seek to transgress the separation of powers.

Separation of powers was designed to implement a fundamental insight: concentration of power in the hands of a single branch is a threat to liberty. *The Federalist* states the axiom in these explicit terms: "The accumulation of all powers, legislative, executive, and judiciary, in the same hands . . . may justly be pronounced the very definition of tyranny." *The Federalist* No. 47.

In recent years, perhaps, we have come to think of liberty as defined by that word in the Fifth and Fourteenth Amendments and as illuminated by the other provisions of the Bill of Rights. The conception of liberty embraced by the Framers was not so confined. They used the principles of separation of powers and federalism to secure liberty in the fundamental political sense of the term, quite in addition to the idea of freedom from intrusive governmental acts. The idea and the promise were that when the people delegate some degree of control to a remote central authority, one branch of government ought not possess the power to shape their destiny without a sufficient check from the other two. In this vision, liberty demands limits on the ability of any one branch to influence basic political decisions.

It follows that if a citizen who is taxed has the measure of the tax or the decision to spend determined by the Executive alone, without adequate control by the citizen's Representatives in Congress, liberty is threatened. Money is the instrument of policy and policy affects the lives of citizens. The individual loses liberty in a real sense if that instrument is not subject to traditional constitutional constraints.

The principal object of the statute, it is true, was not to enhance the President's power to reward one group and punish another, to help one set of taxpayers and hurt another, to favor one State and ignore another. Yet these are its undeniable effects. The law establishes a new mechanism which gives the President the sole ability to hurt a group that is a visible target, in order to disfavor the group or to extract further concessions from Congress. The law is the functional equivalent of a line item veto and enhances the President's powers beyond what the Framers would have endorsed.

It is no answer, of course, to say that Congress surrendered its authority by its own hand; nor does it suffice to point out that a new statute, signed by the President or enacted over his veto, could restore to Congress the power it now seeks to relinquish. That a congressional cession of power is voluntary does not make it innocuous. The Constitution is a compact enduring for more than our time, and one Congress cannot yield up its own powers, much less those of other Congresses to follow.

JUSTICE BREYER, *with whom Justice O'Connor and Justice Scalia join as to Part III, dissenting.*

I

In my view the Line Item Veto Act does not violate any specific textual constitutional command, nor does it violate any implicit Separation of Powers principle. Consequently, I believe that the Act is constitutional.

II

I approach the constitutional question before us with three general considerations in mind. *First*, the Act represents a legislative effort to provide the President with the power to give effect to some, but not to all, of the expenditure and revenue-diminishing provisions contained in a single massive appropriations bill. And this objective is constitutionally proper.

When our Nation was founded, Congress could easily have provided the President with this kind of power. In that time period, our population was less than four million, federal employees numbered fewer than 5,000, annual federal budget outlays totaled approximately $4 million, and the entire operative text of Congress's first general appropriations law [contained only four provisions].

At that time, a Congress, wishing to give a President the power to select among appropriations, could simply have embodied each appropriation in a separate bill, each bill subject to a separate Presidential veto.

Today, however, our population is about 250 million, the Federal Government employs more than four million people, the annual federal budget is $1.5 trillion, and a typical budget appropriations bill may have a dozen titles, hundreds of sections, and spread across more than 500 pages of the Statutes at Large. Congress cannot divide such a bill into thousands, or tens of thousands, of separate appropriations bills, each one of which the President would have to sign, or to veto, separately. Thus, the question is whether the Constitution permits Congress to choose a particular novel *means* to achieve this same, constitutionally legitimate, end.

Second, the case in part requires us to focus upon the Constitution's generally phrased structural provisions, provisions that delegate all "legislative" power to Congress and vest all "executive" power in the President. The Court, when applying these provisions, has interpreted them generously in terms of the institutional arrangements that they permit.

Indeed, Chief Justice Marshall, in a well-known passage, explained,

> "To have prescribed the means by which government should, in all future time, execute its powers, would have been to change, entirely, the character of the instrument, and give it the properties of a legal code. It would have been an unwise attempt to provide, by immutable rules, for exigencies which, if foreseen at all, must have been seen dimly, and which can be best provided for as they occur."

McCulloch v. Maryland.

This passage calls attention to the genius of the Framers' pragmatic vision, which this Court has long recognized in cases that find constitutional room for necessary institutional innovation.

Third, we need not here referee a dispute among the other two branches. And, as the majority points out,

> "When this Court is asked to invalidate a statutory provision that has been approved by both Houses of the Congress and signed by the President, particularly an Act of Congress that confronts a deeply vexing national problem, it should only do so for the most compelling constitutional reasons."

These three background circumstances mean that, when one measures the *literal* words of the Act against the Constitution's *literal* commands, the fact that the Act may closely resemble a different, literally unconstitutional, arrangement is beside the point. To drive exactly 65 miles per hour on an interstate highway closely resembles an act that violates the speed limit. But it does not violate that limit, for small differences matter when the question is one of literal violation of law. No more does this Act literally violate the Constitution's words.

III

The Court believes that the Act violates the literal text of the Constitution. A simple syllogism captures its basic reasoning:

> Major Premise: The Constitution sets forth an exclusive method for enacting, repealing, or amending laws.
>
> Minor Premise: The Act authorizes the President to "repea[l] or amen[d]" laws in a different way, namely by announcing a cancellation of a portion of a previously enacted law.
>
> Conclusion: The Act is inconsistent with the Constitution.

I find this syllogism unconvincing, however, because its Minor Premise is faulty. When the President "canceled" the two appropriation measures now before us, he did not *repeal* any law nor did he *amend* any law. He simply *followed* the law, leaving the statutes, as they are literally written, intact.

To understand why one cannot say, *literally speaking*, that the President has repealed or amended any law, imagine how the provisions of law before us might have been, but were not, written. Imagine that the canceled New York health care tax provision at issue here, Pub. L. 105-33, §4722(c), 111 Stat. 515 . . . , had instead said the following:

> Section One. Taxes . . . that were collected by the State of New York from a health care provider before June 1, 1997 and for which a waiver of provisions [requiring payment] have been sought . . . are deemed to be permissible health care related taxes . . . *provided however that the President may prevent the just-mentioned provision from having legal force or effect if he determines x, y and z.* (Assume x, y and z to be the same determinations required by the Line Item Veto Act.)

Whatever a person might say, or think, about the constitutionality of this imaginary law, there is one thing the English language would prevent one from saying. One could not say that a President who "prevent[s]" the deeming language from "having legal force or effect" has either *repealed* or *amended* this particular hypothetical statute. Rather, the President has *followed* that law to the letter. He has exercised the power it explicitly delegates to him. He has executed the law, not repealed it.

Because one cannot say that the President's exercise of the power the Act grants is, literally speaking, a "repeal" or "amendment," the fact that the Act's procedures differ from the Constitution's exclusive procedures for enacting (or repealing) legislation is beside the point. The Act *itself* was enacted in accordance with these procedures, and its failure to require the President to satisfy those procedures does not make the Act unconstitutional.

IV

Because I disagree with the Court's holding of literal violation, I must consider whether the Act nonetheless violates Separation of Powers principles—principles that arise out of the Constitution's vesting of the "executive Power" in "a President," U.S. Const., Art. II, §1, and "[a]ll legislative Powers" in "a Congress," Art. I, §1. There are three relevant Separation of Powers questions here: (1) Has Congress given the President the wrong kind of power, *i.e.*, "non-Executive" power? (2) Has Congress given the President the power to "encroach" upon Congress' own constitutionally reserved territory? (3) Has Congress given the President too much power, violating the doctrine of "nondelegation?" These three limitations help assure "adequate control by the citizen's representatives in Congress," upon which Justice Kennedy properly insists. And with respect to *this* Act, the answer to all these questions is "no."

A

Viewed conceptually, the power the Act conveys is the right kind of power. It is "executive." As explained above, an exercise of that power "executes" the Act. Conceptually speaking, it closely resembles the kind of delegated authority—to spend or not to spend appropriations, to change or not to change tariff rates—that Congress has frequently granted the President, any differences being differences in degree, not kind.

B

The Act does not undermine what this Court has often described as the principal function of the Separation of Powers, which is to maintain the tripartite structure of the Federal Government—and thereby protect individual liberty—by providing a "safeguard against the encroachment or aggrandizement of one branch at the expense of the other." *Buckley v. Valeo* (per curiam); *Mistretta v. United States.*

[O]ne cannot say that the Act "encroaches" upon Congress' power, when Congress retained the power to insert, by simple majority, into any future appropriations bill, into any section of any such bill, or into any phrase of any section, a provision that says the Act will not apply.

Nor can one say the Act's grant of power "aggrandizes" the Presidential office. The grant is limited to the context of the budget. It is limited to the power to spend, or not to spend, particular appropriated items, and the power to permit, or not to permit, specific limited exemptions from generally applicable tax law from taking effect. These powers resemble those the President has exercised in the past on other occasions. The delegation of those powers to the President may strengthen the Presidency, but any such change in Executive Branch authority seems minute when compared with the changes worked by delegations of other kinds of authority that the Court in the past has upheld.

C

The "nondelegation" doctrine represents an added constitutional check upon Congress' authority to delegate power to the Executive Branch. And it raises a more serious constitutional obstacle here. The Constitution permits Congress to "see[k] assistance from another branch" of Government, the "extent and character" of that assistance to be fixed "according to common sense and the inherent necessities of the governmental co-ordination." *J. W. Hampton, Jr., & Co. v. United States*, 276 U.S., at 406. But there are limits on the way in which Congress can obtain such assistance; it "cannot delegate any part of its legislative power except under the limitation of a prescribed standard." *United States v. Chicago, M., St. P. & P. R. Co.* Or, in Chief Justice Taft's more familiar words, the

Constitution permits only those delegations where Congress "shall lay down by legislative act an *intelligible principle* to which the person or body authorized to [act] is directed to conform." *J.W. Hampton, supra,* at 409 (emphasis added).

The Act before us seeks to create such a principle in three ways. The first is procedural. The Act tells the President that, in "identifying dollar amounts [or] . . . items . . . for cancellation" (which I take to refer to his selection of the amounts or items he will "prevent from having legal force or effect"), he is to "consider," among other things,

> "the legislative history, construction, and purposes of the law which contains [those amounts or items, and] . . . any specific sources of information referenced in such law or . . . the best available information. . . ."

2 U.S.C. §691(b) (1994 ed., Supp. II).

The second is purposive. The clear purpose behind the Act, confirmed by its legislative history, is to promote "greater fiscal accountability" and to "eliminate wasteful federal spending and . . . special tax breaks." H.R. Conf. Rep. No. 104-491, p. 15 (1996).

The third is substantive. The President must determine that, to "prevent" the item or amount "from having legal force or effect" will "reduce the Federal budget deficit; . . . not impair any essential Government functions; and . . . not harm the national interest." 2 U.S.C. §691(a)(A) (1994 ed., Supp. II).

The resulting standards are broad. But this Court has upheld standards that are equally broad, or broader.

V

In sum, I recognize that the Act before us is novel. In a sense, it skirts a constitutional edge. But that edge has to do with means, not ends. The means chosen do not amount literally to the enactment, repeal, or amendment of a law. Nor, for that matter, do they amount literally to the "line item veto" that the Act's title announces. Those means do not violate any basic Separation of Powers principle. They do not improperly shift the constitutionally foreseen balance of power from Congress to the President. Nor, since they comply with Separation of Powers principles, do they threaten the liberties of individual citizens. They represent an experiment that may, or may not, help representative government work better. The Constitution, in my view, authorizes Congress and the President to try novel methods in this way. Consequently, with respect, I dissent.

SYNTHESIS QUESTIONS FOR FURTHER DISCUSSION: CHAPTER 4 SECTION A

1. Throughout this chapter, we investigate conflicts between the executive and the legislative branches. Justice Robert H. Jackson's concurrence in *Youngstown Sheet & Tube Co. v. Sawyer* lays out a three-part test for determining the extent of the president's power in a case of controversy:

    "1. When the President acts pursuant to an express or implied authorization of Congress, his authority is at its maximum, for it includes all that he possesses in his own right plus all that Congress can delegate. . . .

    2. When the President acts in absence of either a congressional grant or denial of authority, he can only rely upon his own independent powers, but there is a zone of twilight in which he and Congress may have concurrent authority, or in which its distribution is uncertain. . . .

    3. When the President takes measures incompatible with the expressed or implied will of Congress, his power is at its lowest ebb, for then he can rely only upon his own constitutional powers minus any constitutional powers of Congress over the matter. . . ."

    This three-part framework is suggested as a way that the Court might adjudicate between executive and congressional authority. But does the Court assume in *Youngstown Sheet & Tube Co. v. Sawyer* that it rightly has the power to adjudicate these disputes? Should it have this power? The lawyers representing the president suggested that *Youngstown Sheet & Tube Co. v. Sawyer* was rightly in the first category, while the Court found it to be in the third. Should the Court have the final word in this controversy, or is this a political question best settled between the executive and legislative branches?

    These questions are related to the issues of judicial authority and supremacy introduced in Chapter 1. Is it possible for the Court to be the primary or exclusive institution for discerning whether an issue concerns congressional or executive authority generally without usurping the legitimate power of the other branches?

2. President Harry Truman's decision to seize the steel mills, the issue at stake in *Youngstown Sheet & Tube Co. v. Sawyer*, took place during the Korean War. In defining the second category of presidential authority, Justice Jackson suggests that any "actual test of power is likely to depend on the imperatives of events and contemporary imponderables." Should the fact that the country was involved in a military conflict give the Court more reason to defer to congressional power? To executive power? Given that the president is the Commander-in-Chief, should his command over the military include the power to support the armed forces, even if doing so might infringe on domestic property rights? It is important to consider whether war time should automatically provide the president with greater domestic power, and if so, when, why, and how much? In the following section, the question will arise as to the president's power over foreign affairs at times of war. It will be important to keep in mind how his authority over foreign matters compares with that in the domestic realm, even in times of military crisis.

3. An "Old Whig" expressed the concern that the Constitution will empower the executive to such a degree that the president will become like a king. His argument focuses in part on the massive power a Commander-in-Chief is likely to wield among his or her own people. One aspect of executive power that the Founders likely did not anticipate derives from the vast network that makes up the administrative agencies in the federal government. Such agencies include the Federal Communications Commission (FCC), the Internal Revenue Service (IRS), and the Federal Election Commission (FEC). This is a different kind of power from that usually wielded by monarchs in that its power is dispersed throughout many different regulatory bodies rather than consolidated in one office. Do such agencies pose a threat to democratic self-governance and the rule of law? Defenders of congressional power might argue that the so-called "legislative veto" was simply a way to deflect a new threat to congressional authority posed by administrative agencies. Specifically, the ability of the INS or other executive agencies to carry out executive policy that does not reflect the legislative will could potentially undermine the power of the people to make laws. Given that these agencies are not elected and are not directly under the control of the president, what is the source of their legitimacy? Should Congress have the power to "veto" particular administrative choices that do not reflect congressional intent? If Congress lacks such power, does this jeopardize democratic self-government? Does it give the executive too much power? Consider the arguments against the "legislative veto" presented by the Court in *INS v. Chadha*.

4. While *INS v. Chadha* raises questions about whether administrative agencies might undermine the Congress's power to enact legislation according to the people's will, another modern development arguably presents a threat to the president's power. Bills passed by Congress are often joined

together into one large "omnibus" bill. In effect, they combine many different policy issues and controversies into one package. In order to combat this practice, the president asserted his power to carry out a line item veto. In other words, the president claimed to have the power to veto particular lines of legislative bills rather than having to veto the entire bill or nothing at all. Would this expand the veto power too far, or is it a way to ensure that the president, an elected official, has a sufficiently robust role in evaluating legislation passed by Congress by ensuring that the decision to veto can be based on the merits of a particular policy? Why did the Court rule against the line item veto in *Clinton v. City of New York*?

5. The excerpt from Alexander Hamilton's *The Federalist* No. 70 stresses why executive power should rest in one "unitary" government official— the president. Drawing on that thought, contemporary defenders of the unitary executive stress that there can be no "fourth" branch of government not under the total control of the executive or the legislature. Clearly, however, administrative agencies, whose officers must be confirmed by Congress, have some shared authority at the moment of appointment. But does this shared authority extend to the ability to remove an officer from one of those agencies? Defenders of the unitary executive theory suggest not. They argue at times on originalist grounds that the Founders through the Constitution granted the authority to the executive to fire. As you read the excerpts from James Madison and Hamilton, is there any evidence for this claim? In their article, Lawrence Lessig and Cass Sunstein argue that there is not, but still go on to consider efficiency and other non-originalist grounds for the claims of a unitary executive. Does the lack of an ability to fire the heads of administrative agencies constitute a threat to the executive power? Does the existence of these agencies themselves fit into one branch of government?

B. FOREIGN AFFAIRS AND THE POWER TO DECLARE WAR

Who has the power to declare war? Is it always necessary to declare war before engaging in military operations?

Whereas in the previous section we examined the general framework for evaluating conflicts between the president and Congress, we focus now on how these conflicts should be resolved in matters of foreign affairs. The question about the degree to which the president has exclusive power in foreign affairs has been controversial since first U.S. President George Washington's administration. The first reading in this section includes excerpts from the "Pacificus-Helvidius" debate between Alexander Hamilton and James Madison. In this debate, Hamilton and

Madison initiate what would become a central debate over whether and how power over foreign affairs is shared. In Hamilton's view, it is an inherent and exclusive power of the president to engage in foreign relations, except where that power has been explicitly limited by the Constitution, or assigned to another branch. Hamilton's arguments deeply worried Thomas Jefferson, but since he was a member of President Washington's cabinet, he turned to James Madison (then a Member of Congress) to challenge and refute Hamilton's arguments. Madison articulated a far more robust role for Congress in the making of foreign policy.

The question of the power to declare war, which the Constitution formally grants to Congress, has only been used five times in the nation's history: the War of 1812, the Mexican-American War, the Spanish-American War, World War I, and World War II. As a result, most of the conflicts to which the United States has been a party have occurred in what Justice Robert H. Jackson called the zone of twilight in his *Youngstown Sheet & Tube Co. v. Sawyer* decision. In the reading by John Hart Ely, the author criticizes Congress and president for failing to live up to their constitutional obligations in bringing the nation to war. He calls for greater deliberation and the establishment of a national consensus before entry to war. His arguments rebut the resolutions authorizing the use of force in the cases of the Vietnam and Iraq conflicts, excerpts of which are included as well. The article by John Yoo challenges Ely and defends a strong and autonomous role of the executive in determining when to engage in armed combat. Yoo extends the idea of the unitary executive and makes appeals to inherent presidential power in defending this robust role for the president.

We begin our case selection with the *Prize Cases*, which concerned whether President Abraham Lincoln could create a naval blockade of ports in the South during the Civil War without a formal declaration of war. The case reflected a trend towards presidential authority not only in war, but also more generally in cases of foreign affairs, which would continue into the twentieth century. In *United States v. Curtiss-Wright Export Corp.*, the Court considers whether Congress can delegate broad power to the executive in foreign affairs, as well as the source and scope of the president's independent power in foreign policy—themes that are developed in *Dames & Moore v. Regan*. These cases offer examples of the Court struggling to define just what might constitute congressional authorization and how to treat congressional silence in foreign affairs. In *Goldwater v. Carter*, the Court is asked to intervene and protect congressional prerogatives even where Congress itself has not directly confronted the president. While the Court declined to make a formal ruling in this case, *Goldwater v. Carter* does generate a set of important opinions about how and when the Court should—and should not—intervene in the separation of powers in foreign affairs, with some of the justices insisting that this constitutes a "political question" that should not be resolved by the Court.

When it invokes the political question doctrine, the Court refuses to decide the substance of the case because it considers the subject matter to be outside its jurisdiction. As you read *Goldwater v. Carter*, you might consider the differences and similarities between the issues in that case and those in the other cases we examine in this chapter.

As you read this section, you should continue to keep in mind the framework and debate from Section A. In particular, ask yourself whether Yoo correctly applies the idea of the unitary executive discussed in Section A to the president's power in foreign affairs. Specifically, you should ask whether Yoo's position is qualitatively different from those advanced in the previous section by Steven Calabresi as well as Lawrence Lessig and Cass Sunstein, or whether these views are continuous.

THE PROCLAMATION OF NEUTRALITY OF 1793 AND THE PACIFICUS-HELVIDIUS DEBATE

The following debate between Alexander Hamilton and James Madison arose over President George Washington's official proclamation of neutrality with regard to the conflict between European powers, specifically war between France and Great Britain, which the French revolutionary government declared in February 1793. As you will see in this excerpt, the proclamation, issued April 22, 1793, requires American citizens to remain neutral in these conflicts and declares that citizens who fail to obey this dictate will not be aided by the American government. What is constitutionally significant about this proclamation was that it was made unilaterally, without the consent of Congress. The proclamation was therefore an early example of what would come to be a fundamental debate over the president's power to make foreign policy outside of the formal grants he was given by the Constitution. In the following debate, Hamilton takes the position that the president's power is wide and that there is no constitutional limit on his power to make decisions concerning foreign policy. But as you will see, Madison challenges this position, arguing that the powers granted to the president do not include the power to make this proclamation. After the proclamation was issued and the debate ensued, Congress passed the Neutrality Act of 1794, bolstering President Washington's stated position of neutrality with congressional authorization.

PRESIDENT GEORGE WASHINGTON'S PROCLAMATION OF NEUTRALITY, 1793

Whereas it appears that a state of war exists between Austria, Prussia, Sardinia, Great Britain, and the United Netherlands, of the one part, and France on the other; and the duty and interest of the United States require, that they should with sincerity and good faith adopt and pursue a conduct friendly and impartial toward the belligerent Powers;

I have therefore thought fit by these presents to declare the disposition of the United States to observe the conduct aforesaid towards those Powers respectfully; and to exhort and warn the citizens of the United States carefully to avoid all acts and proceedings whatsoever, which may in any manner tend to contravene such disposition.

And I do hereby also make known, that whatsoever of the citizens of the United States shall render himself liable to punishment or forfeiture under the law of nations, by committing, aiding, or abetting hostilities against any of the said Powers, or by carrying to any of them those articles which are deemed contraband by the modern usage of nations, will not receive the protection of the United States, against such punishment or forfeiture; and further, that I have given instructions to those officers, to whom it belongs, to cause prosecutions to be instituted against all persons, who shall, within the cognizance of the courts of the United States, violate the law of nations, with respect to the Powers at war, or any of them.

In testimony whereof, I have caused the seal of the United States of America to be affixed to these presents, and signed the same with my hand. Done at the city of Philadelphia, the twenty-second day of April, one thousand seven hundred and ninety-three, and of the Independence of the United States of America the seventeenth.

ALEXANDER HAMILTON AND JAMES MADISON, PACIFICUS-HELVIDIUS DEBATE OF 1793

Pacificus (Alexander Hamilton)

No. 1

***

The objections [to President Washington's Proclamation of Neutrality] fall under four heads:

1. That the proclamation was without authority.

2. That it was contrary to our treaties with France.

3. That it was contrary to the gratitude which is due from this to that country, for the succors afforded to us in our own revolution.

4. That it was out of time and unnecessary. . . .

The inquiry then is, what department of our government is the proper one to make a declaration of neutrality, when the engagements of the nation permit, and its interests require that it should be done?

A correct mind will discern at once, that it can belong neither to the legislature nor judicial department, and of course must belong to the executive.

The legislative department is not the organ of intercourse between the United States and foreign nations. It is charged neither with making nor interpreting treaties. It is therefore not naturally that member of the government, which is to pronounce the existing condition of the nation, with regard to foreign powers, or to admonish the citizens of their obligations and duties in consequence; still less is it charged with enforcing the observance of those obligations and duties.

It is equally obvious, that the act in question is foreign to the judiciary department. The province of that department is to decide litigations in particular cases. It is indeed charged with the interpretation of treaties, but it exercises this function only where contending parties bring before it a specific controversy. It has no concern with pronouncing upon the external political relations of treaties between government and government. This position is too plain to need being insisted upon.

It must then of necessity belong to the executive department to exercise the function in question, when a proper case for it occurs.

It appears to be connected with that department in various capacities—As the organ of intercourse between the nation and foreign nations; as the interpreter of the national treaties, in those cases in which the judiciary is not competent, that is, between government and government; as the power which is charged with the execution of the laws, of which treaties form a part; as that which is charged with the command and disposition of the public force. . . .

The second article of the Constitution of the United States, section first, establishes this general proposition, that "the EXECUTIVE POWER shall be vested in a President of the United States of America." . . .

The general doctrine of our Constitution . . . is that the executive power of the nation is vested in the President; subject only to the exceptions and qualifications, which are expressed in the instrument.

Two of [the exceptions are] . . . the participation of the senate in the appointment of officers, and in the making of treaties. A third remains to be mentioned; the right of the legislature "to declare war, and grant letters of marque and reprisal." . . .

If on the one hand, the legislature have a right to declare war, it is on the other, the duty of the executive to preserve peace, till the declaration is made; and in fulfilling this duty, it must necessarily possess a right of judging what is the nature of the obligations which the treaties of the country impose on the government; and when it has concluded that there is nothing in them inconsistent with neutrality, it becomes both its province and its duty to enforce the laws incident to that state of the nation. The executive is charged with the execution of all laws, the law of nations, as well as the municipal law, by which the former are recognized and adopted. It is consequently bound, by executing faithfully the laws of neutrality, when the country is in a neutral position, to avoid giving cause of war to foreign powers. . . .

The right of the executive to receive ambassadors and other public ministers, may serve to illustrate the relative duties of the executive and legislative departments. This right includes that of judging, in the case of a revolution of government in a foreign country, whether the new rulers are competent organs of the national will, and ought to be recognized, or not; which, where a treaty antecedently exists between the United States and such nation, involves the power of continuing or suspending its operation. For until the new government is acknowledged, the treaties between the nations, so far at least as regards public rights, are of course suspended.

This power of determining virtually upon the operation of national treaties, as a consequence of the power to receive public ministers, is an important instance of the right of the executive, to decide upon the obligations of the country with regard to foreign nations. To apply it to the case of France, if there had been a treaty of alliance, offensive and defensive between the United States and that country, the unqualified acknowledgment of the new government would have put the United States in a condition to become an associate in the war with France, and would have laid the legislature under an obligation, if required, and there was otherwise no valid excuse, of exercising its power of declaring war.

This serves as an example of the right of the executive, in certain cases, to determine the condition of the nation, though it may, in its consequences, affect the exercise of the power of the legislature to declare war. Nevertheless, the executive cannot thereby control the exercise of that power. The legislature is still free to perform its duties, according to its own sense of them; though the executive, in the exercise of its constitutional powers, may establish an antecedent state of things, which ought to weigh in the legislative decision.

The division of the executive power in the Constitution, creates a concurrent authority in the cases to which it relates.

Hence, in the instance stated, treaties can only be made by the president and senate jointly; but their activity may be continued or suspended by the President alone. . . .

It deserves to be remarked, that as the participation of the senate in the making of treaties, and the power of the legislature to declare war, are exceptions out of the general "executive power" vested in the President, they are to be construed strictly, and ought to be extended no further than is essential to their execution.

While, therefore, the legislature can alone declare war, can alone actually transfer the nation from a state of peace to a state of hostility, it belongs to the "executive power" to do whatever else the law of nations, cooperating with the treaties of the country, enjoin in the intercourse of the United States with foreign powers.

In this distribution of authority, the wisdom of our Constitution is manifested. It is the province and duty of the executive to preserve to the nation the blessings of peace. The legislature alone can interrupt them by placing the nation in a state of war. . . .

Helvidius (James Madison)

No. 1

***

Let us examine [the doctrine being propounded by Pacificus]:

In the general distribution of powers, we find that of declaring war expressly vested in the congress, where every other legislative power is declared to be vested; and without any other qualifications than what is common to every other legislative act. The constitutional idea of this power would seem then clearly to be, that it is of a legislative and not an executive nature.

This conclusion becomes irresistible, when it is recollected, that the constitution cannot be supposed to have placed either any power legislative in its nature, entirely among executive powers, or any power executive in its nature, entirely among legislative powers, without charging the constitution, with that kind of intermixture and consolidation of different powers, which would violate a fundamental principle in the organization of free governments. If it were not unnecessary to enlarge on this topic here, it could be shown, that the constitution was originally vindicated, and has been constantly expounded, with a disavowal of any such intermixture.

The power of treaties is vested jointly in the president and in the senate, which is a branch of the legislature. From this arrangement merely, there can be no inference that would necessarily exclude the power from the executive class: since the senate is joined with the president in another power, that of appointing to offices, which, as far as relate to executive offices at least, is considered as of an executive nature. Yet on the other hand, there are sufficient indications that the power of treaties is regarded by the constitution as materially different from mere executive power, and as having more affinity to the legislative than to the executive character.

 . . . [T]hat treaties, when formed according to the constitutional mode, are confessedly to have force and operation of laws, and are to be a rule for the courts in controversies between man and man, as much as any other laws. They are even emphatically declared by the constitution to be "the supreme law of the land."

So far the argument from the constitution is precisely in opposition to the doctrine. As little will be gained in its favour from a comparison of the two powers, with those particularly vested in the president alone.

As there are but few, it will be most satisfactory to review them one by one.

"The president shall be commander in chief of the army and navy of the United States, and of the militia when called into the actual service of the United States."

There can be no relation worth examining between this power and the general power of making treaties. And instead of being analogous to the power of declaring war, it affords a striking illustration of the incompatibility of the two powers in the same hands. Those who are to conduct a war cannot in the nature of things, be proper or safe judges, whether a war ought to be commenced, continued, or concluded. They are barred from the latter functions by a great principle in free government, analogous to that which separates the sword from the purse, or the power of executing from the power of enacting laws. . . .

Thus it appears that by whatever standard we try this doctrine, it must be condemned as no less vicious in theory than it would be dangerous in practice. It is countenanced neither by the writers on law; nor by the nature of the powers themselves; nor by any general arrangements, or particular expressions, or plausible analogies, to be found in the constitution.

Whence then can the writer have borrowed it?

There is but one answer to this question.

The power of making treaties and the power of declaring war, are royal prerogatives in the British government, and are accordingly treated as executive prerogatives by British commentators. . . .

No. 2

***

Leaving however to the leisure of the reader deductions which the author,

having omitted, might not choose to own, I proceed to the examination of one, with which that liberty cannot be taken.

"However true it may be (says he) that the right of the legislature to declare war includes the right of judging, whether the legislature be under obligations to make war or not, it will follow that the executive is in any case excluded from a similar right of judging in the execution of its own functions." . . .

A concurrent authority in two independent departments, to perform the same function with respect to the same thing, would be as awkward in practice, as it is unnatural in theory.

If the legislature and executive have both a right to judge of the obligations to make war or not, it must sometimes happen, though not at present, that they will judge differently. The executive may proceed to consider the question today; may determine that the United States are not bound to take part in a war, and, in the execution of its functions, proclaim that declaration to all the world. Tomorrow the legislature may follow in the consideration of the same subject; may determine that the obligations impose war on the United States, and, in the execution of its functions, enter into a constitutional declaration, expressly contradicting the constitutional proclamation.

In what light does this present the constitution to the people who established it? In what light would it present to the world a nation, thus speaking, through two different organs, equally constitutional and authentic, two opposite languages, on the same subject, and under the same existing circumstances?

But it is not with the legislative rights alone that this doctrine interferes. The rights of the judiciary may be equally invaded. For it is clear that if a right declared by the constitution to be legislative, leaves, notwithstanding, a similar right in the executive, whenever a case for exercising it occurs, in the course of its functions; a right declared to be judiciary and vested in that department may, on the same principle, be assumed and exercised by the executive in the course of its functions; and it is evident that occasions and pretexts for the latter interference may be as frequent as for the former. So again the judiciary department may find equal occasions in the execution of its functions, for usurping the authorities of the executive; and the legislature for stepping into the jurisdiction of both. And thus all the power of government, of which a partition is so carefully made among the several branches, would be thrown into absolute hotchpot and exposed to a general scramble. . . .

John Hart Ely

WAR AND RESPONSIBILITY

Chapter 1: The Constitutional Framework

Princeton, NJ: Princeton University Press (1993)

This system will not hurry us into war; it is calculated to guard against it. It will not be in the power of a single man, or a single body of men, to involve us in such distress; for the important power of declaring war is vested in the legislature at large. . . .

—*James Wilson*

I didn't have to get permission from some old goat in the United States Congress to kick Saddam Hussein out of Kuwait.

—*George [H.W.] Bush*

One of the recurrent discoveries of academic writing about constitutional law—an all but certain ticket to tenure—is that from the standpoint of twentieth-century observers, the "original understanding" of the document's framers and ratifiers can be obscure to the point of inscrutability. Often this is true. In this case, however, it isn't. The power to declare war was constitutionally vested in Congress. The debates, and early practice, establish that this meant that all wars, big or small, "declared" in so many words or not—most weren't, even then—had to be legislatively authorized. Indeed, only one delegate to either the Philadelphia convention or any of the state ratifying conventions, Pierce Butler, is recorded as suggesting that authority to start a war be vested in the president. Elbridge Gerry, backed by others, responded that he "never expected to hear in a republic a motion to empower the Executive alone to declare war," and Butler subsequently disowned his earlier view.

There were several reasons for the founders' determination to vest the decision to go to war in the legislative process. The one they mentioned most often is the most obvious, a determination not to let such decisions be taken easily. The founders assumed that peace would (and should) be the customary state of the new republic—James Madison characterized war as "among the greatest of national calamities"—and sought to arrange the Constitution so as to assure that expectation. Their assumption was not that Congress was any more expert on the subject of war than the executive—if anything they assumed the contrary—but rather that requiring its assent would reduce the number of occasions on which we would become thus involved. There were various statements by influential framers to the effect that executives tended to be more warlike than legislative bodies.

Madison's is typical: "The constitution supposes, what the History of all Governments demonstrates, that the Executive is the branch of power most interested in war, and most prone to it. It has accordingly with studied care, vested the question of war in the Legislature." Patently the point was not to exclude the executive from the decision—if the president's not on board we're not going to have much of a war—but rather to "clog" the road to combat by requiring the concurrence of a number of people of various points of view. Justice Story wrote in 1833, "[T]he power of declaring war is not only the highest sovereign prerogative; but . . . it is in its own nature and effects so critical and calamitous, that it requires the utmost deliberation, and the successive review of all the councils of the nation." To invoke a more contemporary image, it takes more than one key to launch a missile: It should take quite a number to start a war.

Two other rationales that played a role can be highlighted by examining the (debated) decision to involve the House of Representatives in the decision to go to war. The House was certainly not included because of any perceived expertise: Indeed, because of its assumed lack thereof it was excluded from such foreign policy processes as the approval of treaties. Rather, authorization by the entire Congress was foreseeably calculated,

for one thing, to slow the process down, to insure that there would be a pause, a "sober second thought," before the nation was plunged into anything as momentous as war. Thus in defense of including the House, Story wrote that "[l]arge bodies necessarily move slowly; and where the co-operation of different bodies is required, the retardation of any measure must be proportionately increased." (Occasionally there won't be time for such deliberation, but we shall see that that is something the framers foresaw and accommodated.)

The House was included for another reason as well, that it was conceived as "the people's house." Given the way the burdens of war get distributed, it was felt that the people's representatives should have a say. (It was felt further that the involvement of "the people's representatives" would increase the participation of the people themselves in the debate.) The requirement of authorization by both houses of Congress was thus also calculated to increase the probability that the American people would support any war we entered into. The founders didn't need a Vietnam to teach them that wars unsupported by the people at large are unlikely to succeed. (Indeed, the difficulties of keeping the colonial troops in the field during the Revolution provided the beginnings of a similar lesson.)

This point applies a fortiori to the legislature. Unless Congress has unequivocally authorized a war at the outset, it is a good deal more likely later to undercut the effort, leaving it in a condition that satisfies neither the allies we induced to rely on us, our troops who fought and sometimes died, nor for that matter anyone else except, conceivably, the enemy. Admiral James Stockdale, who spent seven and a half years as a prisoner of war in Hanoi, put it well: "Our Constitution as written protected our fighting men from shedding blood in pointless exercises while a dissenting Congress strangled the effort. But what has evolved . . . affords them no such protection." Thus, he concludes, we cannot afford "to fight any more wars without a thoroughgoing national commitment in advance." In fact this is a position often taken, understandably, by military men. For example, General Alexander Haig testified at his confirmation hearing for the position of Secretary of State, "Heaven help us as a nation if we once again indulge in the expenditure of precious American blood without a clear demonstration of popular support for it. I think the legislature is the best manifestation of popular support."

It is true that an early draft of the Constitution vested the power "to make war" in Congress, and this language was changed during the editing process to the power "to declare war." This change was made for two reasons. The first was to make clear that once hostilities were congressionally authorized, the president, as "commander in chief," would assume tactical control (without constant congressional interference) of the way they were conducted. (Proponents of broad executive authority to involve the nation in military hostilities often rely on the constitutional designation of the president as "Commander in Chief of the Army and Navy of the United States," but the record is entirely clear that all this was meant to convey was command of the armed forces once Congress had authorized a war, that it did not carry authority to start one.) The second reason for the change in language was to reserve to the president the power, without advance congressional authorization, to "repel sudden attacks."

THE COUNTERARGUMENT FROM OBSOLESCENCE

The need for Presidents to have that power [to use force abroad without congressional approval], particularly in the modem age, should be obvious to almost everyone.

—Robert Bork

The clarity of the Constitution on this question leaves two strategies open to advocates of executive authority to start wars—though it can be demonstrated quite rapidly that neither will work. The first is simply to assert that the Constitution does not fit today's world—that it is, in a word, obsolete. In fact this is a line that is rarely taken in so many words, as the conventions of constitutional discourse do not recognize it as a legitimate move. For good reason: The most archaic-sounding provisions of our founding document, their purposes intelligently unpacked, generate commands of complete contemporary relevance. If there is a consensus that one of those commands has become unworkably burdensome—their point, of course, is to be at least somewhat burdensome—the appropriate response is repeal by the constitutionally prescribed method, not a unilateral declaration by the burdened official that the provision no longer applies, at least not to him.

In any event, the constitutional requirement that Congress express its formal approval before the president leads the nation into war is not remotely obsolete: The purposes that underlay it were rendered sufficiently transparent to permit their mapping onto contemporary conditions. Occasionally—though nowhere near as often as enthusiasts would have us believe—military emergencies can develop faster than Congress can convene and react. That was also true, however, in the late eighteenth century—in fact it was probably truer then than it is today, given that (a) Congress was out of session most of the time and it took weeks, not hours, to round its members up, and (b) its members and committees did not have significant staffs. The founders understood this, though, and consequently reserved to the president authority to respond on his own to "sudden attacks" until there was time for Congress to convene and confer: In such situations the president could respond militarily and seek authorization simultaneously.

It probably is the case, however, that enemy actions not actually amounting to attacks on the United States can more obviously threaten our national security now than they could when the Constitution was agreed to. This raises the question whether the reserved emergency presidential authority to "repel sudden attacks" should be (1) limited to actual attacks on United States territory or (2) "functionally" extended to other situations where a clear danger to our national security has developed so unexpectedly, and immediate military response is so imperative, that advance congressional authorization to respond militarily simply cannot be awaited (though such authorization must be requested, at the latest, simultaneously with the issuance of the order dispatching the troops, our military response discontinued if such authorization is not promptly forthcoming).

At first blush the language seems mildly helpful: "attack" might or might not mean "attack on the United States," but "sudden" does seem to suggest that time urgency is the point. This is building too much on too little, however, as the phrase appears not in the document but in Madison's notes on the debates. We therefore will make better progress by inquiring into the *purpose* of the reservation of authority to repel sudden attacks. One animating idea could have been that there would in the event of an attack on the United States inevitably be a consensus that a military response was in order, and thus a requirement of congressional approval would be a needless formality. If that was the idea, however, a limitation to actual attacks on U.S. territory seems highly questionable: The *preclusion* of such an attack by a preemptive strike seems likely to garner a similar consensus, as for that matter would an American military response to, say, a Soviet invasion of Mexico or Canada. But then how about Guatemala, Great Britain, or Japan? Thus if we construe the reservation in "likely consensus" terms we confront two choices, each unacceptable. Either we limit it to actual attacks on the United States, which seems to undershoot the posited rationale and thus constitute a questionable approach to constitutional language, or we expand it to all cases where the executive believes that "all sensible people" would agree with his response, in which case we can be quite certain it would be invoked whenever the executive himself thought a military response appropriate. (The tendency of virtually everyone to assume that all rational people, properly advised, would agree with him is one I assume I need not annotate.)

The most natural alternative construction of the reservation would focus on the word "sudden" and assume the point was to give the president authority to respond without advance authorization when there has not been time to secure it (so long as he seeks it simultaneously and subsides if it is not promptly forthcoming). This path appears more promising. In the first place, it fits a general theory of emergency power entertained by some of the founders, that under emergency conditions the executive can properly act in excess of legislative authorization, so long as he makes swift and full disclosure to the legislature and subsides if they do not approve. Second, it parallels a similar reservation of extraordinary military authority another section of Article I made in favor of the *states*: "No State shall, without the Consent of Congress . . . engage in War, unless actually invaded, *or* in such imminent Danger as will not admit of delay." Finally, unlike the "most sensible persons would agree" rationale, "there wasn't time to secure advance authorization so we had to seek it simultaneously" seems susceptible to principled limitation and thus may be given the sort of functional construction we are accustomed to according constitutional language. Thus although the point is arguable, I am inclined to construe the president's reserved authority to go ahead and respond militarily (and seek congressional authorization simultaneously) as extending to genuine and serious threats to our national security beyond actual attacks on United States territory.

Thus construed, the constitutional command is certainly not obsolete: In fact other changes have made it more urgent than ever. In the nineteenth century—indeed, up until World War II—the nation took quite seriously the founders' fear of a "standing army": Thus in order to lead the nation into combat the president needed not only a declaration of war or comparable statement of authorization, but also statutory authority to raise an army and a congressional appropriation of the funds needed to support it. Now, of course, we do effectively have a standing army, which means that today the requirement of congressional authorization is all that stands in the way of unfettered executive discretion to commit it to combat.

Another fact that might render the requirement of congressional authorization particularly important today is that at least for the present we have an all-volunteer army, thereby eliminating what might at certain periods in our history have been regarded as a further source of potential resistance to half-baked military schemes, namely draftees from all social classes (including politically influential ones) and their families and friends. I won't linger long on this one, however. This "check" was probably never terribly significant: I know I didn't emerge from basic training programmed for independent thinking. (For the moment at least it seems to be professional soldiers who provide the most reliable brake on the ill-conceived military schemes of amateurs, though obviously not so reliable that we should continue to tolerate the exclusion of Congress from the process.) Worth more attention is the fact that we have spent much of the late twentieth century in an era of "divided government" (president from one party, Congress from the other). Thank God it didn't happen, but as of, say, February 1992, the risk that the executive might start a war to demonstrate toughness and "leadership" in perilous political times (when, for example, the economy refuses to "jump-start" in time for an upcoming election) seemed anything but remote.

As far as the need to bring the American people on board is concerned, another change—actually in this case a return to the earlier traditions of the republic—seems relevant. We now have a citizenry more willing than those of prior decades to take on the administration on questions of foreign policy, particularly questions of war and peace. That this change too (at least assuming, as I do, that national unity behind authorized wars is generally a desirable goal) has increased the importance of the congressional authorization requirement was noted well in a student paper I received in the spring of 1991:

> [T]his writer must enter a personal note.... The congressional process that led to the authorization of January 12, 1991, had a significant bearing on my own attitude towards the war once it began. I was highly doubtful of the march to war, agreeing (as did congressional opponents of the war resolution) that the Iraqis ought to be ejected from Kuwait, but believing that sanctions and blockade were a wiser course, and that war was both hazardous and not necessary. Had President Bush gone to war by fiat, without authority from Congress . . . I believe I would have marched against it. But the war was in fact duly authorized, and I therefore believed it best to reserve my own doubts and not actively oppose a war which was entered into in a constitutional manner.

Another change of conditions repeatedly pressed by proponents of unencumbered presidential power is that the possible consequences of war are more serious now than they were in the eighteenth century. But this one too turns out on a moment's reflection to argue the other way—*in favor of* the original conclusion that "no one man should hold the power of bringing this oppression upon us." The fact that we can all be blown to kingdom come only reinforces the need, where there is time, for a "sober second thought" before war is entered into, and a collective judgment that it should be.

Of course, if he asked, the president probably would usually receive rather readily the support of both Congress and the American people when he decided to have a war. (Admittedly this is somewhat hard to judge, as of late congressional and popular opinion has generally not been permitted to register until the war is under way, at which point support notoriously increases.) From childhood we Americans are programmed to fall in when the bugle sounds, a fact that has caused no small percentage of my friends to ask me why, if approval is a foregone conclusion, I'm wasting my time worrying about increasing participation in such decisions. Is there any reason to suppose, given their respective performances, that Congress will prove wiser on issues of war and peace than the president? Actually I think our history does support, if slightly, the founders' judgment that Congress (if only because it is necessarily more deliberate) tends to be more responsible in this area than the executive. To answer the question on its own (comparative) terms, however, is to miss the point. The constitutional strategy was to require more than one set of keys to open the Pandora's box of war. As usual, Alexander Bickel said it well: "Singly, either the President or Congress can fall into bad errors.... So they can together too, but that is somewhat less likely, and in any event, together they are all we've got."

THE COUNTERARGUMENT FROM PRACTICE

The other argument that we can ignore the original demand of the Constitution here—this one is made more explicitly—is an argument from post-ratification practice, that the behavior of various presidents, and the acquiescence of various congresses, during the 200 years since the document was adopted have in essence amended it, effectively eliminating the requirement of congressional authorization. The most obvious answer here is one the Supreme Court has given many times, that past violations are only that—violations—and cannot change the meaning of the Constitution: "That an unconstitutional action has been taken before surely does not render that same action any less unconstitutional at a later date." Though that's got to be generally right, it may oversimplify somewhat, unduly assimilating constitutional provisions of relevantly different types. If, for example, the question before the Court were whether a certain action was appropriately classified as within the "legislative power" or the "executive power"—*and* there were no more precise provision suggesting an answer— one would rightly expect the judges to be interested in how various presidents and congresses, most particularly *early* presidents and congresses, had by action and acquiescence effectively classified it. Our question, however, does not present a case of one or more vague documentary vessels that must receive their meaning from subsequent experience. In language and recorded purpose the War Clause made an unmistakable point that needed no further gloss: Acts of war must be authorized by Congress. In cases like this the Court is quite right: Usurpation isn't precedent, it's usurpation.

Assume this were not so, however, and that on some oddly repotted "adverse possession" theory, post-ratification practice in violation of the Constitution could change it, still the argument could not work in this context. At the very least we would require "a systematic, unbroken, executive practice, long pursued to the knowledge of the Congress and never before questioned," a pattern that on every count is manifestly lacking here. Of course real life is never entirely neat and clean, but the original constitutional understanding was quite consistently honored from the framing until 1950. And when certain presidents did play a little fast and loose with congressional prerogatives—Polk at the start of the Mexican War; Wilson and Roosevelt, respectively, in the events leading up to the First and Second World Wars—they obscured or covered up the actual facts, pledging public fealty to the constitutional need for congressional authorization of military action. It is therefore impossible to build the occasional nonconforming presidential actions of this period into an argument that they had gradually altered the constitutional plan. Shifts of constitutional power, to the extent they are possible at all, must be accomplished in the open.

John Yoo

THE CONTINUATION OF POLITICS BY OTHER MEANS: THE ORIGINAL UNDERSTANDING OF WAR POWERS

84 Calif. L. Rev. 167 (Mar. 1996)

INTRODUCTION

Since the end of the Cold War, our nation has turned to the use of force in its foreign relations more frequently than some might have hoped. The increase in military interventions—in Lebanon, Grenada, the Persian Gulf, Panama, Kuwait, Somalia, Haiti, and now Bosnia—has been accompanied by increasing academic criticism of the way in which the federal government makes war. This criticism, which represents a diversity of political and intellectual positions, is striking both for its uniformity of opinion and its harshness of tone. Critics of the current war powers landscape accuse Presidents from Harry Truman to George Bush of waging "unconstitutional" wars, portray Congress as shirking its constitutional responsibilities, and point to the "powerful whiff of hypocrisy" found in the judiciary's hands-off attitude.

According to these scholars, the post–World War II era has witnessed nothing less than "the disappearance of the separation of powers, the system of checks and balances, as it applies to decisions to go to war." Arguing that the Framers intended Congress to have exclusive control over the decision to go to war, they interpret the Declare War Clause as a separation of powers provision that not only empowers Congress, but also limits executive abilities to make war. Under this approach, in order to wage war, the President must receive a declaration of war or its "functional equivalent" from Congress. Should the President overstep these constitutional boundaries, the federal courts must intervene to right the balance by declaring the war unconstitutional or even by enjoining the President's actions.

Historical practice, however, has contrasted starkly with these constitutional arguments. Congress has issued a declaration of war only five times in its history. The post-1945 era has borne witness to a litany of undeclared wars and an even longer list of less significant uses of the military. The President has initiated conflict, often without any formal signs of congressional approval, and certainly without a declaration of war. With few exceptions, the federal courts either have refused to hear constitutional challenges to these wars, or have upheld the propriety of the executive action.

This divergence of academic theory and political practice has led to an unusual arrangement of ideology and constitutional interpretation. "Liberals" who opposed unilateral executive authority have turned to the Framers' intent for support, arguing for a Constitution with a meaning fixed by the history of its drafting. "Conservatives" who favored enhanced presidential war powers have invoked the lessons of the recent past and the nation's post-ratification history to buttress a vision of a Constitution that has adapted to a dangerous world.

This Article argues, in a sense, that both sides are wrong. It agrees with the methodology employed by the critics of executive dominance over war powers but disagrees with their conclusions. When interpreting the text of the Constitution, we should seek to determine the meaning of its terms as understood by those who adopted its provisions. As the majority of scholars in the war powers area recognize, this is the best starting point to interpret the Constitution. As a written document, the Constitution's meaning does not change from the meaning it held for its drafters. Otherwise the Constitution's meaning would be as inconstant as, to paraphrase Horace, the times, or the mores.

Most works have focused on the short discussion of the Declare War Clause at the Constitutional Convention and a few selected comments from *The Federalist*. Others rely heavily on post-ratification evidence from the first quarter-century of the nation's youth to fill in the Constitution's perceived ambiguities. But these approaches fail to recognize that the Framers neither acted in a historical vacuum, nor wrote on a constitutional tabula rasa. Nor can we take as dispositive private comments that were not made known to the state ratifying conventions or to the people.

The historical evidence reveals a Constitution that does not prescribe one exclusive method for going to war. A war may be constitutional, even if no declaration of war has issued or if the President has acted unilaterally, so long as one branch has not usurped the textually enumerated power of another. The Constitution establishes a war-making process that can vary with the circumstances and with the relative political power of the President and Congress. It assumes that the political branches will exercise their constitutional powers sometimes cooperatively and sometimes antagonistically. Moreover, the Constitution did not inadvertently allocate all war powers to the two political branches; rather, the nature of the mutable process it created made judicial supervision unworkable and undesirable.

The Framers established a system which was designed to encourage presidential initiative in war, but which granted Congress an ultimate check on executive actions. Congress could express its opposition to executive war decisions only by exercising its powers over funding and impeachment. The Framers established this system because they were not excessively worried by the prospect of unilateral executive action. The President was seen as the protector and representative of the People. In contrast, the Framers expressed a deep concern regarding the damage that Congress, and the interest groups that could dominate it, might cause in the delicate areas of war and foreign policy.

Original understanding analysis illuminates the general framework that the Framers erected and what their expectations were. Because the Constitution fails to specify an exact relationship between the President and Congress in the area of war, examination of post-ratification practice confirms our understanding of the allocation of war powers between the branches. Ultimately, however, it is the constitutional framework that endures, while the exact processes of going to war within that framework may change over time.

I. WAR POWERS: ALLOCATION, PRACTICE, AND CRITICISM

A. The Constitutional Text

As with all constitutional questions, an analysis of war powers should begin with the constitutional text, which allocates war-making authority not to a single branch of government, but to both the executive and legislative departments. Article I gives Congress the power to "declare War, grant Letters of Marque and Reprisal, and make Rules concerning Captures on Land and Water." Congress also has the authority to "raise and support Armies," to "provide and maintain a Navy," to "make Rules for the Government and Regulation of the land and naval Forces," to "provide for calling forth the Militia to execute the Laws of the Union, suppress Insurrections and repel Invasions," and to "provide for organizing, arming, and disciplining, the Militia." Congress also possesses other powers related to foreign affairs, including the power to regulate international commerce, to establish immigration rules, to pass laws punishing piracy and felonies committed on the high seas, and to give its advice and consent to the appointment of ambassadors and the making of treaties.

Compared to this impressive list, the powers of the President at first glance appear somewhat paltry. Article II states that "the President shall be Commander in Chief of the Army and Navy of the United States, and of the Militia of the several States, when called into the actual Service of the United States." The President's other enumerated powers include the authority to receive ambassadors and, with the advice and consent of the Senate, to make treaties and appoint ambassadors. Finally, Article II vests "the executive Power" and the duty to execute the laws in the President.

The judiciary's powers are limited in the area of war powers, although the federal courts do have jurisdiction over cases that may relate to foreign affairs. Article III vests the judicial power of the United States in the federal courts, and gives them jurisdiction over cases arising under the Constitution, treaties, and other laws of the United States. No provision explicitly authorizes the federal courts to intervene directly in war powers questions.

1. Congress and President

The Constitution's division of authority establishes a framework that has evolved into the operational system of war powers we have today. The experiences of World Wars I and II might lead one to assume that because Congress declared war in those two wars, the Constitution requires a declaration to trigger the President's powers as Commander in Chief. However, formal declarations of war have constituted the exception rather than the rule in American history. . . . Although declarations of war have been rare, Congress has never been wholly absent from the war powers equation. For much of the nineteenth and early twentieth centuries, Congress assented to presidential uses of force abroad. Interventions undertaken without congressional approval were, for the most part, small-scale actions to protect American property, citizens, or honor abroad that had little risk of significant combat. Larger-scale actions required the President to seek congressional approval for expanded military forces. Given this relative inter-branch harmony, it is not surprising that the judiciary was not an active participant in war powers.

With the establishment of a large peacetime military force in the twentieth century, the prospect of unilateral presidential war-making appeared, concerns about congressional control emerged, and questions about the role of the judiciary arose. The Cold War period provoked almost continual struggles between the two branches over war powers. . . . A period of presidential weakness in the aftermath of the Vietnam War and Watergate prompted congressional efforts to assert control over the war-making process. In 1973, Congress passed the War Powers Resolution over President Nixon's veto to fulfill the intent of the framers . . . and insure that the collective judgment of both the Congress and the President will apply to the introduction of United States Armed Forces into hostilities, or into situations where imminent involvement in hostilities is clearly indicated by the circumstances, and to the continued use of such forces in hostilities or in such situations.

The Resolution further declares Congress' belief that the President can exercise his Commander-in-Chief powers "only pursuant to (1) a declaration of war, (2) specific statutory authorization, or (3) a national emergency created by attack upon the United States, its territories or possessions, or its armed forces." The Resolution attempts to prevent the President from sending the American military into combat without congressional approval, except in emergency situations.

Congress included three mechanisms in the Resolution designed to assure congressional participation in the war-making process. First, "the President in every possible instance shall consult with Congress" before introducing the armed forces into hostilities, whether imminent or actual. Second, the President must report to Congress within forty-eight hours of sending the military into (a) hostilities or imminent hostilities, (b) into the territory of another nation equipped for combat, or (c) in numbers which substantially increase the size of the American forces stationed in a foreign nation. This report must explain why the President sent the troops, describe the constitutional and legislative authority for the action, and estimate the scope and duration of the intervention.

The reporting requirement then triggers the third requirement: the controversial sixty-day clock. Once the President has reported military intervention to Congress, the Resolution requires the President to terminate the intervention within sixty days. Three events can forestall removal of American forces: (1) a declaration of war or specific congressional authorization; (2) congressional extension of the sixty-day period; or (3) congressional inability to meet due to armed attack on the United States. The President may also extend the sixty-day period once for thirty days if he certifies that the additional time is necessary to permit the safe withdrawal of American armed forces. Finally, the Resolution permits Congress to terminate an unauthorized presidential use of military force at any time by concurrent resolution.

Most commentators would agree that the Resolution has not proven to be a resounding success. No President has ever acknowledged its constitutionality, and no President has ever formally complied with its terms. The high watermark of presidential recognition of the Resolution was President Ford's messages to Congress in which he took "note" of the Resolution when he sent military forces to evacuate Americans from South Vietnam and Cambodia and to rescue American sailors in the S.S. *Mayaguez*

incident . . . of military action in messages that used similar language.

Despite presidential noncompliance, Congress has never sought to enforce the Resolution's terms either by using section 5's concurrent resolution mechanism or by removing funding for the military action. Congressional inaction has led challengers of the president's use of military force to seek judicial declarations that the President has violated the Constitution.

2. The Courts and the War Powers

Although individual members of Congress have criticized presidential actions in these various wars, Congress as a body has never sought to block executive war-making in the courts. But individuals who have been adversely affected by these military interventions have challenged presidential action by seeking redress in the courts. These actions have met with little success, because the Supreme Court has deferred to the conduct of international relations by the other branches, particularly the President. By relying on doctrines including political questions, ripeness, mootness, and standing, and by refusing to grant a writ of certiorari, the Court has studiously avoided becoming embroiled in war powers disputes.

From the earliest days of the Republic, the Court has recognized that the other branches must permit the President some amount of discretion in the conduct of foreign relations. When Chief Justice John Marshall was a Congressman, he declared that the President was "the sole organ of the nation in its external relations." Later, when he wrote *Marbury v. Madison*, Marshall made clear that there were "questions in their nature political" which were entrusted to the executive branch and removed from judicial review.

In discussing whether the Jefferson administration could withhold Marbury's commission, Marshall wrote:

> By the constitution of the United States, the president is invested with certain important political powers, in the exercise of which he is to use his own discretion, and is accountable only to his country in his political character, and to his own conscience. . . . The subjects are political . . . and being entrusted to the executive, the decision of the executive is conclusive.
>
> . . . Questions in their nature political, or which are, by the constitution and laws, submitted to the executive, can never be made in this court.

Even when faced with the modern wars of the twentieth century, the Court has continued to recognize that foreign affairs questions often are beyond judicial competence. In 1918, the Court in *Oetjen v. Central Leather Co.* declared, "The conduct of the foreign relations of our Government is committed by the Constitution to the Executive and Legislative—'the political'—Departments of the Government, and the propriety of what may be done in the exercise of this political power is not subject to judicial inquiry or decision." The twentieth-century Court also has held that the political question doctrine applies to the determination of when war has ended and whether the United States has recognized a foreign government.

The foremost statement of the convergence of judicial deference and executive discretion in foreign affairs came in Justice Sutherland's opinion in *United States v. Curtiss-Wright Export Corp.*:

> Not only . . . is the federal power over external affairs in origin and essential character different from that over internal affairs, but participation in the exercise of the power is significantly limited. In this vast external realm, with its important, complicated, delicate and manifold problems, the President alone has the power to speak or listen as a representative of the nation. It is important to bear in mind that we are here dealing . . . [with] the very delicate, plenary and exclusive power of the President as the sole organ of the federal government in the field of international relations. . . .

Baker v. Carr expresses the modern version of the political question doctrine. Although not a foreign affairs case, several of *Baker*'s justiciability factors apply with vigor to war powers and foreign affairs issues. Although "it is error to suppose that every case or controversy which touches foreign relations lies beyond judicial cognizance," Justice Brennan commented:

> Not only does resolution of such issues frequently turn on standards that defy judicial application, or involve the exercise of a discretion demonstrably committed to the executive or legislature; but many such questions uniquely demand single-voiced statement of the Government's views.

Baker's broad definition of the political question doctrine has permitted enhanced presidential powers in foreign affairs, primarily because the "single-voiced statement of the Government's views" has come almost exclusively from the executive branch. Over time, Chief Justice Marshall's original doctrine of presidential discretion in certain political areas involving the "nation, not individual rights," has neatly dovetailed with the President's growing control over foreign affairs.

Given these broad doctrines, it should come as no surprise that the Supreme Court has avoided challenges to the use of the war power. In the Korean and Vietnam Wars, for example, the Court regularly refused to grant a writ of certiorari for cases brought by draftees challenging the wars' constitutionality. Several times,

Justice Douglas dissented from the denial of certiorari on the ground "that the constitutional questions raised by conscription for a presidential war are both substantial and justiciable," but to no avail. Moreover, lower courts faced with Vietnam War suits regularly dismissed them as presenting political questions.

The judicial tradition of deference has continued during the post-Vietnam era, even in the context of the War Powers Resolution. When various plaintiffs challenged the Reagan administration's use of the American military in Central America in 1982 and the Persian Gulf in 1987, the D.C. Circuit dismissed the suits as presenting non-justiciable political questions. When twenty-nine Members of Congress sued President Reagan for allegedly sending illegal aid to El Salvador in violation of the War Powers Resolution, the same court held that whether the President had to comply with the Resolution's terms presented a non-justiciable political question.

Even though the modern Supreme Court has never ruled on the proper constitutional allocation of war powers among the three branches, what Professor Reisman calls an "operational code of competence" has formed among them. In other words, the President, Congress, and the federal courts have acted according to a set of norms and rules that they deem authoritative. In the war powers context, the President has taken the primary role in deciding when and how to wage war. Congress has fallen into the role of approving the interventions either through authorization before operations have begun or appropriations after the fact, while the judicial branch has abstained from inter-branch war powers disputes because they raise non-justiciable political questions. Put less charitably, we have a system which Professor Koh describes

as one of "executive initiative, congressional acquiescence, and judicial tolerance." Professor Koh's views are emblematic of a growing consensus among international and constitutional law scholars that the President's war powers grasp exceeds his constitutional reach.

C. The Academic Critique: The President Against the Professors

For the most part, legal academia has sharply criticized the current state of war powers. In a series of recent books, foreign relations and international law scholars such as John Hart Ely, Louis Henkin, Michael Glennon, Thomas Franck, Louis Fisher, and Harold Koh have taken the Presidents to task for waging unconstitutional war and have chastised the courts for abdicating their duty to adjudicate war power cases. These scholars rest their arguments on three bases: first, that the Framers intended Congress to exercise exclusive control over the decision to go to war; second, that modern separation of powers doctrine requires congressional approval of war; and third, that the courts have a constitutional duty to determine the proper allocation of warmaking power between the President and Congress.

In a curious reversal of roles, the war powers question displays critics of the legal theories of the Reagan and Bush administrations readily invoking the intent of the Framers. They claim that the Declare War Clause, in light of their reading of the thoughts of the Constitution's drafters, clearly indicates that the Framers intended that Congress play an equal, if not paramount, role in the decision to go to war. This original intent argument is an important part of the academic critique of presidential power that this Article intends to refute. . . .

IV. THE NEW CONSTITUTION

A. The Constitutional Text in Context

Our analysis begins with the constitutional text. In order to understand what the Constitution requires, we must place its text in the legal context of its day. Those who ratified the Constitution would not have understood its provisions in a vacuum, but instead would have compared and contrasted the document with both their legal understanding of the words and their understanding of how these provisions operated in the world of the eighteenth century.

The Framers included the declaration of war in the Constitution as a device to facilitate the federal government's representation of the nation in international affairs, and to make clear that the declaration of war was a power of the national government, not the state governments. As we have seen, a declaration of war performed a primarily juridical function under eighteenth-century international law, and it was this understanding that the Framers drew upon in giving Congress the authority to declare war. Critics, however, have misinterpreted it as primarily a separation of powers vehicle.

... [I]n the eighteenth-century mind, a declaration of war was not the same thing as a domestic authorization of war. In fact, a declaration of war was understood as what its name suggests: a declaration. Like a declaratory judgment, a declaration of war represented the judgment of Congress, acting in a judicial capacity (as it does in impeachments), that a state of war existed between the United States and another nation. Such a declaration could take place either before or after hostilities had commenced. While the power to "declare" war adds to Congress' store of powers, it does little to alter the relative domestic authorities of the executive and legislative branches. Its primary function was to trigger the international laws of war, which would clothe in legitimacy certain actions taken against one's own and enemy citizens. This was the meaning attributed to a declaration of war by seventeenth and eighteenth-century scholars on the laws of nations.

The Framers turned to international law to define phrases such as to "declare war" because it was international law (and international politics) which gave these powers meaning. Consistent with Chief Justice John Marshall's holding in *The Schooner Charming Betsy* that international law serves as a canon for statutory construction, it is appropriate to use international law as a canon of construction in the constitutional context.

American jurists in the decades following the ratification of the Constitution continued to interpret the declaration as a notification mechanism that defined the wartime rights of citizens and neutrals. Thus, Americans of the eighteenth century would have understood that the power to declare war dealt with setting the formal, legal relationship between two nations, and not with authorizing real hostilities. Once war was declared, a citizen of the United States could seize a ship flying French colors regardless of the state of relations between the two nations. However, if Congress has not declared a state of hostilities, the citizen must return the ship and pay damages; if a declaration has issued, he may sell the ship as a prize. But in neither case is a declaration of war necessary to "authorize," ex ante, the seizure of the ship.

Of course, in legitimating hostilities, this core function of a declaration of war could be thought to "authorize" war by justifying federal wartime policies. Because the declaration of war has a primary domestic effect of notifying the citizens of their new rights and obligations, it grants the government a different standard of conduct in relation to those rights and duties. Thus, a declaration of war would permit the government to treat its citizens in a way that restricted peacetime liberties in favor of a more effective war effort. The Fifth Amendment, for example, generally guarantees the right to an indictment or presentment by grand jury for capital crimes, "except in cases arising in the land or naval forces, or in the Militia, when in actual service in time of War or public danger." In time of war, Congress may authorize seizure of property belonging to foreigners without the need for compensations as required by the Takings Clause. During the Quasi-War, Federalists clamored for a declaration of war against France, because it would allow the passage at home of broad sedition laws, higher taxes, an expanded peacetime army, and other war measures. Thus, a declaration of war had a domestic function, which permitted new government actions in light of the changed legal status of its citizens. A declaration of war did not grant permission for executive action abroad, as we would expect of an "authorization" of war, but only set the stage for the exercise of domestic wartime powers, primarily by Congress.

Interpreting "declaration" to mean a judgment of a current status of relations, not an authorization of war, provides a new understanding of Congress' role in war, one which is not purely legislative. We should conceptualize the war clause as vesting the legislature with a judicial function, which involves a capacity for judgment in the manner of a court, rather than the enactment of positive law in the style of a legislature. Formally vesting one branch of government with powers that another branch inherently ought to

exercise did not trouble the Framers. They gave the President the right to veto legislation, which they thought of as a legislative power; they gave the President and the Senate the power to enter into treaties, which they also believed to be a legislative function. It is this formal mixing of powers that underlies Madison's famous argument in *The Federalist* No. 47 that the departments of government might have a "partial agency in, or . . . controul over the acts of each other."

Thinking of Congress as exercising judicial functions comes more easily when we consider that Article I already vests the legislature with the power of impeachment. Impeachment requires the Senate to act as nothing less than a court of first and last resort. As the Supreme Court implicitly recognized in *Nixon v. United States*, the Constitution vests Congress with a judicial function in impeachment, thereby precluding the federal courts from subsequent review. Although the Court in *Nixon* did not make the connection suggested here, and instead relied upon the political question doctrine, it reached the correct result because the Constitution already vests all judicial power over impeachments to Congress. In other words, the Court could not permit itself to review impeachment proceedings because to do so would vest Article III courts with appellate jurisdiction in derogation of the Senate's own judicial powers.

Analogizing to impeachment supports the legitimacy of the Article III courts' refusal to review war powers cases. Because the Constitution has vested Congress with the entire judicial power to decide whether the United States is in a state of war, no role for the courts is warranted. To be sure, the courts may still adjudicate cases that involve the ramifications of the nation's wartime or peacetime status, such as insurance cases that have wartime clauses. But the Constitution's allocation of the power "to declare war" in Congress divests the courts of any judicial power in war, just as the impeachment clause deprives the courts of any involvement in impeachments. The courts simply must accept the actions of the political branches in war matters as valid indications of whether a state of war exists.

Conclusions

This study has shown that the Framers intended Congress to participate in war-making by controlling appropriations. Although the Constitution gives the President the initiative in war by virtue of his powers over foreign relations and the military, it also forces the President to seek money and support from Congress at every turn. In making decisions whether to raise and support the requested forces, Congress can judge the benefits of a particular war as well as influence its means and ends. Such was the practice under the British Constitution and under the early American governments, elements of which provided models for the drafters of the new federal Constitution. Such was the explanation given by the supporters of the Constitution to its opponents.

Contrary to the arguments by today's scholars, the Declare War Clause does not add to Congress' store of war powers at the expense of the President. Rather, the Clause gives Congress a judicial role in declaring that a state of war exists between the United States and another nation, which bears significant legal ramifications concerning the rights and duties of American citizens. Congress' power to declare war also has the additional effect of ousting the courts from war powers disputes, because it deprives the courts

of the ability to second-guess Congress' determination of whether a formal state of war exists.

The Framers also may have believed judicial participation unwarranted because of the structure established in the war powers area. The potentially conflicting powers of the President and Congress establishes a system that demanded no constitutionally correct method of waging war, but instead permits flexible decision-making based on each branch's exercise of its powers. Aside perhaps from policing against the most extreme violations of those grants by another branch— such as if Congress attempted to "fire" the President as Commander in Chief—the courts have no constitutional standards to apply to a process the Framers left intentionally undefined. Instead, the Framers understood that the legislature and the executive would use their powers to defend the prerogatives of their departments, as well as to pursue their policy preferences against a recalcitrant coordinate branch. The Framers expected the branches to cooperate to wage a successful war, but also anticipated conflict should the two disagree.

A President sometimes must chart a risky course toward war because the Constitution places him squarely at the tiller. He is not alone; the Congress is at his side, either funding his decisions or frustrating them. This cooperative, and yet competitive, relationship has produced many different wars, and many different ways of going to war, in American history. It is perhaps ironic that as the United States today turns to its military more often in international affairs, the historical roots of war powers are so little understood by academia, or so ambiguously defined by the courts. The recent examples of presidential war-making and congressional inaction do not violate the

Constitution, nor should they cause the confusion they appear to. Instead, the elasticity of the war power process has resulted directly from the Framers' conscious design. They established an arena with wide markers to permit the executive and legislative branches to work in harmony, or to struggle for primacy, over issues of war.

As shown in Panama, Kuwait, Somalia, Haiti, and Bosnia, the end of the Cold War has not produced a relaxation in the need for American military force abroad. The approach of a new millennium does not seem to bring the prospects of a millennial peace any closer, either to the world or to the President and the Congress. Indeed the continuing struggle between the branches over the powers of war is only the fulfillment of the Framers' design and in the best interests of the People.

PRIZE CASES

67 U.S. 635 (1863)

Opinion: Grier, joined by Wayne, Swayne, Miller, Davis

Dissent: Nelson, joined by Clifford, Catron, Taney

On April 27, 1861, in the midst of the Civil War, President Abraham Lincoln ordered a naval blockade of southern ports in order to cut off supplies to insurrectionists. The central question in this case is whether President Lincoln had authority to order a blockade given that war had not been formally declared. The Court decided that the southern rebellion clearly instigated a state of war, warranting President Lincoln's actions. Notice that this case puts into tension the president's role as Commander-in-Chief and the role of Congress in declaring war.

In recent times, the question of what exactly constitutes a state of war has become increasingly complicated. Could a terrorist attack on the United States be considered an act of war warranting the president to engage in military conflict without congressional approval? The Civil War was not fought against an autonomous state, and terrorist networks generally transcend state boundaries. Does this case provide a relevant precedent for these kinds of issues?

MR. JUSTICE GRIER *delivered the opinion of the Court.*

Had the President a right to institute a blockade of ports in possession of persons in armed rebellion against the Government, on the principles of international law, as known and acknowledged among civilized States?

Neutrals have a right to challenge the existence of a blockade *de facto*, and also the authority of the party exercising the right to institute it. They have a right to enter the ports of a friendly nation for the purposes of trade and commerce, but are bound to recognize the rights of a belligerent engaged in actual war, to use this mode of coercion, for the purpose of subduing the enemy.

That a blockade *de facto* actually existed, and was formally declared and notified by the President on the 27th and 30th of April, 1861, is an admitted fact in these cases. That the President, as the Executive Chief of the Government and Commander-in-chief of the Army and Navy, was the proper person to make such notification has not been, and cannot be disputed.

The right of prize and capture has its origin in the "*jus belli*," and is governed and adjudged under the law of nations. To legitimate the capture of a neutral vessel or property on the high seas, a war must exist *de facto*, and the neutral must have knowledge or notice of the intention of one of the parties belligerent to use this mode of coercion against a port, city, or territory, in possession of the other.

Let us enquire whether, at the time this blockade was instituted, a state of war existed which would justify a resort to these means of subduing the hostile force. War has been well defined to be, "That state in which a nation prosecutes its right by force." The parties belligerent in a public war are independent nations. But it is not necessary, to constitute war, that both parties should be acknowledged as independent nations or sovereign States. A war may exist where one of the belligerents claims sovereign rights as against the other.

Insurrection against a government may or may not culminate in an organized rebellion, but a civil war always begins by insurrection against the lawful authority of the Government. A civil war is never solemnly declared; it becomes such by its accidents—the number, power, and organization of the persons who originate and carry it on. . . .

By the Constitution, Congress alone has the power to declare a national or foreign war. It cannot declare war against a State, or any number of States, by virtue of any clause in the Constitution. The Constitution confers on the President the whole Executive power. He is bound to take care that the laws be faithfully executed. He is Commander-in-chief of the Army and Navy of the United States, and of the militia of the several States when called into the actual service of the United States. He has no power to initiate or declare a war either against a foreign nation or a domestic State. But, by the Acts of Congress of February 28th, 1795, and 3d of March, 1807, he is authorized to call out the militia and use the military and naval forces of the United States in case of invasion by foreign nations and to suppress insurrection against the government of a State or of the United States.

If a war be made by invasion of a foreign nation, the President is not only authorized but bound to resist force by force. He does not initiate the war, but is bound to accept the challenge without waiting for any special legislative authority. And whether the hostile party be a foreign invader or States organized in rebellion, it is nonetheless a war although the declaration of it be "unilateral."

This greatest of civil wars was not gradually developed by popular commotion, tumultuous assemblies, or local unorganized insurrections. However long may have been its previous conception, it nevertheless sprung forth suddenly from the parent brain, a Minerva in the full panoply of war. The President was bound to meet it in the shape it presented itself, without waiting for Congress to baptize it with a name; and no name given to it by him or them could change the fact. It is not the less a civil war, with belligerent parties in hostile array, because it may be called an "insurrection" by one side, and the insurgents be considered as rebels or traitors. It is not necessary that the independence of the revolted province or State be acknowledged in order to constitute it a party belligerent in a war according to the law of nations.

Whether the President, in fulfilling his duties as Commander-in-chief in suppressing an insurrection, has met with such armed hostile resistance and a civil war of such alarming proportions as will compel him to accord to them the character of belligerents is a question to be decided by him, and this Court must be governed by the decisions and acts of the political department of the Government to which this power was entrusted. "He must determine what degree of force the crisis demands." The proclamation of blockade is itself official and conclusive evidence to the Court that a state of war existed which demanded and authorized a recourse to such a measure under the circumstances peculiar to the case.

. . . [T]herefore, we are of the opinion that the President had a right, *jure belli*, to institute a blockade of ports in possession of the States in rebellion which neutrals are bound to regard.

MR. JUSTICE NELSON, *dissenting.*

. . . The cases of the *United States v. Palmer*, *Divina Pastora*, and 4 *ibid.* 52, and that class of cases to be found in the reports are referred to as furnishing authority for the exercise of the war power claimed for the President in the present case. These cases hold that, when the Government of the United States recognizes a state of civil war to exist between a foreign nation and her colonies, but remaining itself neutral, the Courts are bound to consider as lawful all those acts which the new Government may direct against the enemy, and we admit the President who conducts the foreign relations of the Government may fitly recognize or refuse to do so, the existence of civil war in the foreign nation under the circumstances stated.

But this is a very different question from the one before us, which is whether the President can recognize or declare a civil war, under the Constitution, with all its belligerent rights, between his own Government and a portion of its citizens in a state of insurrection. That power, as we have seen, belongs to Congress. We agree when such a war is recognized or declared to exist by the warmaking power, but not otherwise, it is the duty of the Courts to follow the decision of the political power of the Government. . . .

Upon the whole, after the most careful consideration of this case which the pressure of other duties has admitted, I am compelled to the conclusion that no civil war existed between this Government and the States in insurrection till recognized by the Act of Congress 13th of July, 1861; that the President does not possess the power under the Constitution to declare war or recognize its existence within the meaning of the law of nations, which carries with it belligerent rights, and thus change the country and all its citizens from a state of peace to a state of war; that this power belongs exclusively to the Congress of the United States, and, consequently, that the President had no power to set on foot a blockade under the law of nations, and that the capture of the vessel and cargo in this case, and in all cases before us in which the capture occurred before the 13th of July, 1861, for breach of blockade, or as enemies' property, are illegal and void, and that the decrees of condemnation should be reversed, and the vessel and cargo restored.

MR. CHIEF JUSTICE TANEY,
MR. JUSTICE CATRON *and*
MR. JUSTICE CLIFFORD,
concurred in the dissenting opinion of
MR. JUSTICE NELSON.

UNITED STATES v. CURTISS-WRIGHT EXPORT CORP.

299 U.S. 304 (1936)

Opinion: Sutherland, joined by Hughes, Van Devanter, Brandeis, Butler, Roberts, Cardozo
Dissent (not filed): McReynolds

Defenders of a unitary executive in foreign policy with exclusive control over matters of foreign relations, such as John Yoo, often cite United States v. Curtiss-Wright *as supportive of their position. The case itself centers on two questions: Can the national government impose an arms embargo that will interfere with the rights of an American company to do business with foreign governments in a troubled region in South America? And if so, can the president decide whether and when to impose this embargo? Notice that U.S. Supreme Court Justice George Sutherland cites a joint resolution of Congress authorizing presidential action in this matter, which raises the question of delegation of powers. As you read this case, you should ask whether the president's power in this matter comes from his or her constitutional powers in foreign relations or from the statute in question. Does the case support the theory of a president with the discretion to act alone in matters of international relations? What is meant by the claim quoted by Justice Sutherland from former U.S. Supreme Court Chief Justice John Marshall, that the president is the "sole organ" in matters of international relations?*

Notice too that Justice Sutherland introduces a distinction between the national government's authority in internal domestic matters and external foreign policy matters. Is the president less constrained by the need to consult Congress in foreign as opposed to domestic matters?

MR. JUSTICE SUTHERLAND *delivered the opinion of the Court.*

On January 27, 1936, an indictment was returned in the court below, the first count of which charges that appellees, beginning with the 29th day of May, 1934, conspired to sell in the United States certain arms of war, namely fifteen machine guns, to Bolivia, a country then engaged in armed conflict in the Chaco, in violation of the Joint Resolution of Congress approved May 28, 1934, and the provisions of a proclamation issued on the same day by the President of the United States pursuant to authority conferred by §1 of the resolution.

It is contended that, by the Joint Resolution, the going into effect and continued operation of the resolution was conditioned (a) upon the President's judgment as to its beneficial effect upon the reestablishment of peace between the countries engaged in armed conflict in the Chaco; (b) upon the making of a proclamation, which was left to his unfettered discretion, thus constituting an attempted substitution of the President's will for that of Congress; (c) upon the making of a proclamation putting an end to the operation of the resolution, which again was left to the President's unfettered discretion, and (d) further, that the extent of its operation in particular cases was subject to limitation and exception by the President, controlled by no standard. In each of these particulars, appellees urge that Congress abdicated its essential functions and delegated them to the Executive.

Whether, if the Joint Resolution had related solely to internal affairs, it would be open to the challenge that it constituted an unlawful delegation of legislative power to the Executive we find it unnecessary to determine. The whole aim of the resolution is to affect a situation entirely external to the United States and falling within the category of foreign affairs. The determination which we are called to make, therefore, is whether the Joint Resolution, as applied to that situation, is vulnerable to attack under the rule that forbids a delegation of the lawmaking power. In other words, assuming (but not deciding) that the challenged delegation, if it were confined to internal affairs, would be invalid, may it nevertheless be sustained on the ground that its exclusive aim is to afford a remedy for a hurtful condition within foreign territory?

It will contribute to the elucidation of the question if we first consider the differences between the powers of the federal government in respect of foreign or external affairs and those in respect of domestic or internal affairs. That there are differences between them, and that these differences are fundamental, may not be doubted.

The two classes of powers are different both in respect of their origin and their nature. The broad statement that the federal government can exercise no powers except those specifically enumerated in the Constitution, and such implied powers as are necessary and proper to carry into effect the enumerated powers, is categorically true only in respect of our internal affairs. In that field, the primary purpose of the Constitution was to carve from the general mass of legislative powers then possessed by the states such portions as it was thought desirable to vest in the federal government, leaving those not included in the enumeration still in the states. *Carter v. Carter Coal Co.* That this doctrine applies only to powers which the states had is self-evident. And since the states severally never possessed international powers, such powers could not have been carved from the mass of state powers, but obviously were transmitted to the United States from some other source. During the colonial period, those powers were possessed exclusively by, and were entirely under the control of, the Crown. By the Declaration of Independence, "the Representatives of the United States of America" declared the United [not the several] Colonies to be free and independent states, and, as such, to have "full Power to levy War, conclude Peace, contract Alliances, establish Commerce, and to do all other Acts and Things which Independent States may of right do."

As a result of the separation from Great Britain by the colonies, acting as a unit, the powers of external sovereignty passed from the Crown not to the colonies severally,

but to the colonies in their collective and corporate capacity as the United States of America. Even before the Declaration, the colonies were a unit in foreign affairs, acting through a common agency—namely the Continental Congress, composed of delegates from the thirteen colonies. When, therefore, the external sovereignty of Great Britain in respect of the colonies ceased, it immediately passed to the Union. *See Penhallow v. Doane.* That fact was given practical application almost at once. The treaty of peace, made on September 23, 1783, was concluded between his Brittanic Majesty and the "United States of America." 8 Stat.—European Treaties—80.

The Union existed before the Constitution, which was ordained and established, among other things, to form "a more perfect Union." Prior to that event, it is clear that the Union, declared by the Articles of Confederation to be "perpetual," was the sole possessor of external sovereignty, and in the Union it remained without change save insofar as the Constitution, in express terms, qualified its exercise.

It results that the investment of the federal government with the powers of external sovereignty did not depend upon the affirmative grants of the Constitution. The powers to declare and wage war, to conclude peace, to make treaties, to maintain diplomatic relations with other sovereignties, if they had never been mentioned in the Constitution, would have vested in the federal government as necessary concomitants of nationality. Neither the Constitution nor the laws passed in pursuance of it have any force in foreign territory unless in respect of our own citizens (*see American Banana Co. v. United Fruit Co.*), and operations of the nation in such territory must be governed by treaties, international understandings and compacts, and the principles of international law. As a member of the family of nations, the right and power of the United States in that field are equal to the right and power of the other members of the international family. Otherwise, the United States is not completely sovereign. The power to acquire territory by discovery and occupation (*Jones v. United States*), the power to expel undesirable aliens (*Fong Yue Ting v. United States*), the power to make such international agreements as do not constitute treaties in the constitutional sense (*Altman & Co. v. United States*; Crandall, *Treaties, Their Making and Enforcement,* 2d ed., p. 102 and note 1), none of which is expressly affirmed by the Constitution, nevertheless exist as inherently inseparable from the conception of nationality. This the court recognized, and, in each of the cases cited, found the warrant for its conclusions not in the provisions of the Constitution, but in the law of nations.

Not only, as we have shown, is the federal power over external affairs in origin and essential character different from that over internal affairs, but participation in the exercise of the power is significantly limited. In this vast external realm, with its important, complicated, delicate and manifold problems, the President alone has the power to speak or listen as a representative of the nation. He makes treaties with the advice and consent of the Senate; but he alone negotiates. Into the field of negotiation the Senate cannot intrude, and Congress itself is powerless to invade it. As Marshall said in his great argument of March 7, 1800, in the House of Representatives, "The President is the sole organ of the nation in its external relations, and its sole representative with foreign nations."

It is important to bear in mind that we are here dealing not alone with an authority vested in the President by an exertion of legislative power, but with such an authority plus the very delicate, plenary and exclusive power of the President as the sole organ of the federal government in the field of international relations—a power which does not require as a basis for its exercise an act of Congress but which, of course, like every other governmental power, must be exercised in subordination to the applicable provisions of the Constitution. It is quite apparent that if, in the maintenance of our international relations, embarrassment—perhaps serious embarrassment—is to be avoided and success for our aims achieved, congressional legislation which is to be made effective through negotiation and inquiry within the international field must often accord to the President a degree of discretion and freedom from statutory restriction which would not be admissible were domestic affairs alone involved. Moreover, he, not Congress, has the better opportunity of knowing the conditions which prevail in foreign countries, and especially is this true in time of war. He has his confidential sources of information. He has his agents in the form of diplomatic, consular and other officials. Secrecy in respect of information gathered by them may be highly necessary, and the premature disclosure of it productive of harmful results.

When the President is to be authorized by legislation to act in respect of a matter intended to affect a situation in foreign territory, the legislator properly bears in mind the important consideration that the form of the President's action or, indeed, whether he shall act at all—may well depend, among other things, upon the nature of the confidential information which he has or may thereafter receive, or upon the effect which his action may have upon our foreign relations. This consideration, in connection with what we have already said on the subject, discloses the unwisdom of requiring Congress in this field of governmental power to lay down narrowly definite standards by which the President is to be governed.

In the light of the foregoing observations, it is evident that this court should not be in haste to apply a general rule which will have the effect of condemning legislation like that under review as constituting an unlawful delegation of legislative power. The principles which justify such legislation find overwhelming support in the unbroken legislative practice which has prevailed almost from the inception of the national government to the present day.

We deem it unnecessary to consider *seriatim* the several clauses which are said to evidence the unconstitutionality of the Joint Resolution as involving an unlawful delegation of legislative power. It is enough to summarize by saying that, both upon principle and in accordance with precedent, we conclude there is sufficient warrant for the broad discretion vested in the President to determine whether the enforcement of the statute will have a beneficial effect upon the reestablishment of peace in the affected countries; whether he shall make proclamation to bring the resolution into operation; whether and when the resolution shall cease to operate and to make proclamation accordingly, and to prescribe limitations and exceptions to which the enforcement of the resolution shall be subject.

GOLDWATER v. CARTER

444 U.S. 996 (1979)

Concurrence: Rehnquist, joined by Burger, Stewart, Stevens
Concurrence: Powell, Marshall
Concurrence: Blackmun, White
Dissent: Brennan

This case centers on President Jimmy Carter's decision to nullify unilaterally a treaty that had been signed with Taiwan limiting U.S. relations with China. President Carter had argued that while treaty ratification requires the advice and consent of the Senate, treaty nullification does not. As you will see, then-Associate U.S. Supreme Court Justice William Rehnquist in his opinion, joined by three other justices, argues that this issue is a political question and therefore it is an issue that the Court should not decide. In other words, four justices argued that this decision should be left to the other branches to resolve on their own. To what extent does this case differ from others concerning the authority of the president over foreign affairs in which the Court *did make a decision about what was required by the Constitution? Is the Court justified in removing itself from certain political disputes such as the one discussed here? Notice too the concurrence by U.S. Supreme Court Justice Lewis Powell, who provided the crucial fifth vote. Justice Powell suggests that the Court should not decide this case on the merits, but he provides a very different rationale from Justice Rehnquist for that decision. Does pragmatism play a role in this concurrence?*

MR. JUSTICE REHNQUIST, *with whom* **THE CHIEF JUSTICE, MR. JUSTICE STEWART,** *and* **MR. JUSTICE STEVENS** *join, concurring in the judgment.*

I am of the view that the basic question presented by the petitioners in this case is "political," and therefore nonjusticiable because it involves the authority of the President in the conduct of our country's foreign relations and the extent to which the Senate or the Congress is authorized to negate the action of the President. In *Coleman v. Miller*, a case in which members of the Kansas Legislature brought an action attacking a vote of the State Senate in favor of the ratification of the Child Labor Amendment, Mr. Chief Justice Hughes wrote in what is referred to as the "Opinion of the Court":

> "We think that . . . the question of the efficacy of ratifications by state legislatures, in the light of previous rejection or attempted withdrawal, should be regarded as a political question pertaining to the political departments, with the ultimate authority in the Congress in the exercise of its control over the promulgation of the adoption of the Amendment.
>
> "The precise question as now raised is whether, when the legislature of the State, as we have found, has actually ratified the proposed amendment, the Court should restrain the state officers from certifying the ratification to the Secretary of State, because of an earlier rejection, and thus prevent the question from coming before the political departments. We find no basis in either Constitution or statute for such judicial action. Article V, speaking solely of ratification, contains no provision as to rejection. . . ."

Id. at 307 U.S. 450.

Thus, Mr. Chief Justice Hughes' opinion concluded that "Congress, in controlling the promulgation of the adoption of a constitutional amendment, has the final determination of the question whether, by lapse of time, its proposal of the amendment had lost its vitality prior to the required ratifications." *Id.* at 307 U.S. 456.

I believe it follows *a fortiori* from *Coleman* that the controversy in the instant case is a nonjusticiable political dispute that should be left for resolution by the Executive and Legislative Branches of the Government. Here, while the Constitution is express as to the manner in which the Senate shall participate in the ratification of a treaty, it is silent as to that body's participation in the abrogation of a treaty. In this respect, the case is directly analogous to *Coleman, supra.* As stated in *Dyer v. Blair* (three-judge court):

> "A question that might be answered in different ways for different amendments must surely be controlled by political standards, rather than standards easily characterized as judicially manageable."

In light of the absence of any constitutional provision governing the termination of a treaty, and the fact that different termination procedures may be appropriate for different treaties (*see, e.g.,* 444 U.S. 1, *infra*), the instant case, in my view, also "must surely be controlled by political standards."

I think that the justifications for concluding that the question here is political in nature are even more compelling than in *Coleman,* because it involves foreign relations—specifically, a treaty commitment to use military force in the defense of a foreign government if attacked. . . .

The present case differs in several important respects from *Youngstown Sheet & Tube Co. v. Sawyer*, cited by petitioners as authority both for reaching the merits of this dispute and for reversing the Court of Appeals. In *Youngstown,* private litigants brought a suit contesting the President's authority under his war powers to seize the Nation's steel industry, an action of profound and demonstrable domestic impact. Here, by contrast, we are asked to settle a dispute between coequal branches of our Government, each of which has resources available to protect and assert its interests, resources not available to private litigants outside the judicial forum. Moreover, as in *Curtiss-Wright,* the effect of this action, as far as we can tell, is "entirely external to the United States, and [falls] within the category of foreign affairs." Finally, as already noted, the situation presented here is closely akin to that presented in *Coleman*, where the Constitution spoke only to the procedure for ratification of an amendment, not to its rejection.

Having decided that the question presented in this action is nonjusticiable, I believe that the appropriate disposition is for this Court to vacate the decision of the Court of Appeals and remand with instructions for the District Court to dismiss the complaint. . . .

MR. JUSTICE POWELL, *concurring.*

Although I agree with the result reached by the Court, I would dismiss the complaint as not ripe for judicial review.

I

This Court has recognized that an issue should not be decided if it is not ripe for judicial review. *Buckley v. Valeo* (per curiam). Prudential considerations persuade me that a dispute between Congress and the President is not ready for judicial review unless and until each branch has taken action asserting its constitutional authority. Differences between the President and the Congress are commonplace under our system. The differences should, and almost invariably do, turn on political, rather than legal, considerations. The Judicial Branch should not decide issues affecting the allocation of power between the President and Congress until the political branches reach a constitutional impasse. Otherwise, we would encourage small groups, or even individual Members, of Congress to seek judicial resolution of issues before the normal political process has the opportunity to resolve the conflict.

In the present posture of this case, we do not know whether there ever will be an actual confrontation between the Legislative and Executive Branches. . . . If the Congress chooses not to confront the President, it is not our task to do so. I therefore concur in the dismissal of this case.

II

Mr. Justice Rehnquist suggests, however, that the issue presented by this case is a nonjusticiable political question which can never be considered by this Court. I cannot agree. In my view, reliance upon the political question doctrine is inconsistent with our precedents. As set forth in the seminal case of *Baker v. Carr*, the doctrine incorporates three inquiries: (i) does the issue involve resolution of questions committed by the text of the Constitution to a coordinate branch of Government? (ii) would resolution of the question demand that a court move beyond areas of judicial expertise? (iii) do prudential considerations counsel against judicial intervention? In my opinion the answer to each of these inquiries would require us to decide this case if it were ready for review.

First, the existence of "a textually demonstrable constitutional commitment of the issue to a coordinate political department," *ibid.*, turns on an examination of the constitutional provisions governing the exercise of the power in question. *Powell v. McCormack*. No constitutional provision explicitly confers upon the President the power to terminate treaties. Further, Art. II, §2, of the Constitution authorizes the President to make treaties with the advice and consent of the Senate. Article VI provides that treaties shall be a part of the supreme law of the land. These provisions add support to the view that the text of the Constitution does not unquestionably commit the power to terminate treaties to the President alone. *Cf. Gilligan v. Morgan*; *Luther v. Borden*.

Second, there is no "lack of judicially discoverable and manageable standards for resolving" this case; nor is a decision impossible "without an initial policy determination of a kind clearly for nonjudicial discretion." *Baker v. Carr, supra,* at 369 U.S. 217. We are asked to decide whether the President may terminate a treaty under the Constitution without congressional approval. Resolution of the question may not be easy, but it only requires us to apply normal principles of interpretation to the constitutional provisions at issue. *See Powell v. McCormack, supra,* at 395 U.S. 548-549. The present case involves neither review of the President's activities as Commander in Chief nor impermissible interference in the field of foreign affairs. Such a case would arise if we were asked to decide, for example, whether a treaty required the President to order troops into a foreign country. But "it is error to suppose that every case or controversy which touches foreign relations lies beyond judicial cognizance." *Baker v. Carr, supra,* at 369 U.S. 211. This case "touches" foreign relations, but the question presented to us concerns only the constitutional division of power between Congress and the President.

A simple hypothetical demonstrates the confusion that I find inherent in Mr. Justice Rehnquist's opinion concurring in the judgment. Assume that the President signed a mutual defense treaty with a foreign country and announced that it would go into effect despite its rejection by the Senate. Under Mr. Justice Rehnquist's analysis, that situation would present a political question even though Art. II, §2, clearly would resolve the dispute. Although the answer to the hypothetical case seems self-evident because it demands textual, rather than interstitial, analysis, the nature of the legal issue presented is no different from the issue presented in the case before us. In both cases, the Court would interpret the Constitution to decide whether congressional approval

is necessary to give a Presidential decision on the validity of a treaty the force of law. Such an inquiry demands no special competence or information beyond the reach of the Judiciary. *Cf. Chicago & Southern Air Lines v. Waterman S.S. Corp.*

Finally, the political question doctrine rests in part on prudential concerns calling for mutual respect among the three branches of Government. Thus, the Judicial Branch should avoid "the potentiality of embarrassment [that would result] from multifarious pronouncements by various departments on one question." Similarly, the doctrine restrains judicial action where there is an "unusual need for unquestioning adherence to a political decision already made." *Baker v. Carr, supra,* at 369 U.S. 217.

If this case were ripe for judicial review, *see* Part I *supra,* none of these prudential considerations would be present. Interpretation of the Constitution does not imply lack of respect for a coordinate branch. *Powell v. McCormack, supra,* at 395 U.S. 548. If the President and the Congress had reached irreconcilable positions, final disposition of the question presented by this case would eliminate, rather than create, multiple constitutional interpretations. The specter of the Federal Government brought to a halt because of the mutual intransigence of the President and the Congress would require this Court to provide a resolution pursuant to our duty "'*to say what the law is.*'" *United States v. Nixon,* quoting *Marbury v. Madison.* . . .

MR. JUSTICE BLACKMUN, *with whom* **MR. JUSTICE WHITE** *joins, dissenting in part.*

In my view, the time factor and its importance are illusory; if the President does not have the power to terminate the treaty (a substantial issue that we should address only after briefing and oral argument), the notice of intention to terminate surely has no legal effect. It is also indefensible, without further study, to pass on the issue of justiciability or on the issues of standing or ripeness. While I therefore join in the grant of the petition for certiorari, I would set the case for oral argument and give it the plenary consideration it so obviously deserves.

MR. JUSTICE BRENNAN, *dissenting.*

I respectfully dissent from the order directing the District Court to dismiss this case, and would affirm the judgment of the Court of Appeals insofar as it rests upon the President's well established authority to recognize, and withdraw recognition from, foreign governments. App. to Pet. for Cert. 27A-29A.

In stating that this case presents a nonjusticiable "political question," Mr. Justice Rehnquist, in my view, profoundly misapprehends the political question principle as it applies to matters of foreign relations. Properly understood, the political question doctrine restrains courts from reviewing an exercise of foreign policy judgment by the coordinate political branch to which authority to make that judgment has been "constitutional[ly] commit[ted]." 369 U.S. 211-213 (1962). But the doctrine does not pertain when a court is faced with the antecedent question whether a particular branch has been constitutionally designated as the repository of political decisionmaking power. *Cf. Powell v. McCormack.* The issue of decisionmaking authority must be resolved as a matter of constitutional law, not political discretion; accordingly, it falls within the competence of the courts.

The constitutional question raised here is prudently answered in narrow terms. Abrogation of the defense treaty with Taiwan was a necessary incident to Executive recognition of the Peking Government, because the defense treaty was predicated upon the now-abandoned view that the Taiwan Government was the only legitimate political authority in China. Our cases firmly establish that the Constitution commits to the President alone the power to recognize, and withdraw recognition from, foreign regimes.

DAMES & MOORE v. REGAN

453 U.S. 654 (1981)

Opinion: Rehnquist, joined by Burger, Brennan, Stewart, White, Marshall, Blackmun, by Powell in all but n.6 and by Stevens in all but Part V
Concurrence: Stevens
Partial Concurrence, Partial Dissent: Powell

In negotiating for the release of American hostages captured in the Iranian hostage crisis in 1979, President Jimmy Carter ordered the transfer of Iranian assets and the settlement of legal claims brought against the state of Iran by companies in the United States to an international tribunal in Algeria. A central question in this case is whether President Carter had the authority to take such action. The Court decided that he did. But why? Here, the Dames & Moore Company argued that their right to have U.S. courts adjudicate their claims had been overridden by the President Carter without congressional authorization. Then–Associate Justice William Rehnquist, in his opinion for the Court, explained that a federal statute and subsequent amendments, while not explicitly authorizing what had been done here, did in fact suggest broad congressional approval. Justice Rehnquist revisits Justice Robert H. Jackson's categories from the Steel Seizure Case *and also engages in a discussion of the distinctions that can or should be made between "internal" and "external" affairs." To what degree does this case present a challenge to the distinction between internal and external affairs relied upon in* United States v. Curtiss-Wright? *Moreover, what role does the congressional action cited by Justice Rehnquist play in this case? Is it crucial to the president's power to act, or is it merely an additional piece of evidence that he has been granted this power by the Constitution?*

JUSTICE REHNQUIST *delivered the opinion of the Court.*

The questions presented by this case touch fundamentally upon the manner in which our Republic is to be governed. Throughout the nearly two centuries of our Nation's existence under the Constitution, this subject has generated considerable debate. We have had the benefit of commentators such a John Jay, Alexander Hamilton, and James Madison writing in *The Federalist Paper* at the Nation's very inception, the benefit of astute foreign observers of our system such as Alexis de Tocqueville and James Bryce writing during the first century of the Nation's existence, and the benefit of many other treatises, as well as more than 400 volumes of reports of decisions of this Court. As these writings reveal, it is doubtless both futile and perhaps dangerous to find any epigrammatical explanation of how this country has been governed. Indeed, as Justice Jackson noted, "[a] judge . . . may be surprised at the poverty of really useful and unambiguous

authority applicable to concrete problems of executive power as they actually present themselves." *Youngstown Sheet & Tube Co. v. Sawyer* (concurring opinion).

As we now turn to the factual and legal issues in this case, we freely confess that we are obviously deciding only one more episode in the never-ending tension between the President exercising the executive authority in a world that presents each day some new challenge with which he must deal, and the Constitution under which we all live and which no one disputes embodies some sort of system of checks and balances.

On November 4, 1979, the American Embassy in Tehran was seized and our diplomatic personnel were captured and held hostage. In response to that crisis, President Carter, acting pursuant to the International Emergency Economic Powers Act, 91 Stat. 1626, 50 U.S.C. §§1701-1706 (1976 ed., Supp. III) (hereinafter IEEPA), declared a national emergency on November 14, 1979, and blocked the removal or transfer of "all property and interests in property of the Government of Iran, its instrumentalities and controlled entities and the Central Bank of Iran which are or become subject to the jurisdiction of the United States. . . ." Exec. Order No. 12170, 3 CFR 457 (1980).

On December 19, 1979, petitioner Dames & Moore filed suit in the United States District Court for the Central District of California against the Government of Iran, the Atomic Energy Organization of Iran, and a number of Iranian banks. In its complaint, petitioner alleged that its wholly owned subsidiary, Dames & Moore International, S.R.L., was a party to a written contract with the Atomic Energy Organization, and that the subsidiary's entire interest in the contract had been assigned to petitioner. Under the contract, the subsidiary was to conduct site studies for a proposed nuclear power plant in Iran. As provided in the terms of the contract, the Atomic Energy Organization terminated the agreement for its own convenience on June 30, 1979. Petitioner contended, however, that it was owed $3,436,694.30 plus interest for services performed under the contract prior to the date of termination. The District Court issued orders of attachment directed against property of the defendants, and the property of certain Iranian banks was then attached to secure any judgment that might be entered against them.

On January 20, 1981, the Americans held hostage were released by Iran pursuant to an Agreement entered into the day before and embodied in two Declarations of the Democratic and Popular Republic of Algeria. The Agreement stated that "[i]t is the purpose of [the United States and Iran] ... to terminate all litigation as between the Government of each party and the nationals of the other, and to bring about the settlement and termination of all such claims through binding arbitration." In furtherance of this goal, the Agreement called for the establishment of an Iran–United States Claims Tribunal which would arbitrate any claims not settled within six months.

On January 19, 1981, President Carter issued a series of Executive Orders implementing the terms of the agreement.

On February 24, 1981, President Reagan issued an Executive Order in which he "ratified" the January 19th Executive Orders. Exec. Order No. 12294, 46 Fed. Reg. 14111. Moreover, he "suspended" all "claims which may be presented to the ... Tribunal," and provided that such claims "shall have no legal effect in any action now pending in any court of the United States."

On April 28, 1981, petitioner filed this action in the District Court for declaratory and injunctive relief against the United States and the Secretary of the Treasury, seeking to prevent enforcement of the Executive Orders and Treasury Department regulations implementing the Agreement with Iran. In its complaint, petitioner alleged that the actions of the President and the Secretary of the Treasury implementing the Agreement with Iran were beyond their statutory and constitutional powers, and, in any event, were unconstitutional to the extent they adversely affect petitioner's final judgment against the Government of Iran and the Atomic Energy Organization, its execution of that judgment in the State of Washington, its prejudgment attachments, and its ability to continue to litigate against the Iranian banks.

Not infrequently in affairs between nations, outstanding claims by nationals of one country against the government of another country are "sources of friction" between the two sovereigns. *United States v. Pink*. To resolve these difficulties, nations have often entered into agreements settling the claims of their respective nationals. Consistent with that principle, the United States has repeatedly exercised its sovereign authority to settle the claims of its nationals against foreign countries. Though those settlements have sometimes been made by treaty, there has also been a longstanding practice of settling such claims by executive agreement, without the advice and consent of the Senate. Under such agreements, the President has agreed to renounce or extinguish claims of United States nationals against foreign governments in return for lump-sum payments or the establishment of arbitration procedures.

It is clear that the practice of settling claims continues today. Since 1952, the President has entered into at least 10 binding settlements with foreign nations, including an $80 million settlement with the People's Republic of China.

Crucial to our decision today is the conclusion that Congress has implicitly approved the practice of claim settlement by executive agreement. This is best demonstrated by Congress' enactment of the International Claims Settlement Act of 1949, 64 Stat. 13, as amended, 22 U.S.C. §1621 *et seq.* (1976 ed. and Supp. IV). The Act had two purposes: (1) to allocate to United States nationals funds received in the course of an executive claims settlement with Yugoslavia, and (2) to provide a procedure whereby funds resulting from future settlements could be distributed. By creating a procedure to implement future settlement agreements, Congress placed its stamp of approval on such agreements.

Over the years, Congress has frequently amended the International Claims Settlement Act to provide for particular problems arising out of settlement agreements, thus demonstrating Congress' continuing acceptance of the President's claim settlement authority. With respect to the Executive Agreement with the People's Republic of China, for example, Congress established an allocation formula for distribution of the funds received pursuant to the Agreement. As with legislation involving other executive agreements, Congress did not question the fact of the settlement or the power of the President to have concluded it.

In addition to congressional acquiescence in the President's power to settle claims, prior cases of this Court have also recognized that the President does have some measure of power to enter into executive agreements without obtaining the advice and consent of the Senate. In *United States v. Pink*, for example, the Court upheld the validity of the Litvinov Assignment, which was part of an Executive Agreement whereby the Soviet Union assigned to the United States amounts owed to it by American nationals so that outstanding claims of other American nationals could be paid.

In light of all of the foregoing—the inferences to be drawn from the character of the legislation Congress has enacted in the area, such as the IEEPA and the Hostage Act, and from the history of acquiescence in executive claims settlement—we conclude that the President was authorized to suspend pending claims pursuant to Executive Order No. 12294. As Justice Frankfurter pointed out in *Youngstown*, "a systematic, unbroken, executive practice, long pursued to the knowledge of the Congress and never before questioned. . . may be treated as a gloss on 'Executive Power' vested in the President by §1 of Art. II." Past practice does not, by itself, create power, but "long-continued practice, known to and acquiesced in by Congress, would raise a presumption that the [action] had been [taken] in pursuance of its consent. . . ." *United States v. Midwest Oil Co.* Such practice is present here, and such a presumption is also appropriate. In light of the fact that Congress may be considered to have consented to the President's action in suspending claims, we cannot say that action exceeded the President's powers.

Finally, we reemphasize the narrowness of our decision. We do not decide that the President possesses plenary power to settle claims, even as against foreign governmental entities.

But where, as here, the settlement of claims has been determined to be a necessary incident to the resolution of a major foreign policy dispute between our country and another, and where, as here, we can conclude that Congress acquiesced in the President's action, we are not prepared to say that the President lacks the power to settle such claims.

CONGRESSIONAL RESOLUTIONS RELATING TO U.S. MILTARY ACTIONS

In order to clarify when the president has the power to engage the armed forces of the United States in military conflicts, Congress passed the 1973 War Powers Resolution. This resolution sets out specific guidelines for how the president may use the armed forces and under which circumstances he must ask for and obtain congressional approval for military action. Considered highly controversial and constitutionally suspect by many, the 1973 War Powers Resolution still provides the basic framework for obtaining authorization for U.S. military engagements. Does the resolution clarify the relationship between Congress and the president when it comes to the power to engage in armed conflict? Is it a positive development in our understanding of the constitutional doctrine of separation of powers?

We have included below the text of several congressional resolutions relating to the authorization of U.S. military actions: the Gulf of Tonkin Resolution, which authorized the military engagement in Vietnam and passed before the War Powers Resolution; the War Powers Resolution of 1973, which lays out the proper procedures for the authorization of U.S. military engagements; and the Authorization for Use of Military Force of 2001, which effectively authorized military intervention in Afghanistan and the "War on Terror."

Gulf of Tonkin Resolution (1964)

JOINT RESOLUTION of Congress H.J. Res. 1145

To promote the maintenance of international peace and security in southeast Asia.

Whereas naval units of the Communist regime in Vietnam, in violation of the principles of the Charter of the United Nations and of international law, have deliberately and repeatedly attacked United States naval vessels lawfully present in international waters, and have thereby created a serious threat to international peace; and

Whereas these attacks are part of a deliberate and systematic campaign of aggression that the Communist regime in North Vietnam has been waging against its neighbors and the nations joined with them in the collective defense of their freedom; and

Whereas the United States is assisting the peoples of southeast Asia to protect their freedom and has no territorial, military or political ambitions in the area, but desires only that these peoples should be left in peace to work out their own destinies in their own way: Now, therefore, be it

Resolved by the Senate and House of Representatives of the United States of America in Congress assembled, That the Congress approves and supports the determination of the President, as Commander in Chief, to take all necessary measures to repel any armed attack against the forces of the United States and to prevent further aggression.

Sec. 2. The United States regards as vital to its national interest and to world peace the maintenance of international peace and security in southeast Asia. Consonant with the Constitution of the United States and the Charter of the United Nations and in accordance with its obligations under the Southeast Asia Collective Defense Treaty, the United States is, therefore, prepared, as the President determines, to take all necessary steps, including the use of armed force, to assist any member or protocol state of the Southeast Asia Collective Defense Treaty requesting assistance in defense of its freedom.

Sec. 3. This resolution shall expire when the President shall determine that the peace and security of the area is reasonably assured by international conditions created by action of the United Nations or otherwise, except that it may be terminated earlier by concurrent resolution of the Congress.

War Powers Resolution (1973)

Public Law 93-148
93rd Congress
H.J. Res. 542
November 7, 1973

JOINT RESOLUTION
Concerning the war powers of Congress and the President. Resolved by the Senate and the House of Representatives of the United States of America in Congress assembled.

SEC. 1. SHORT TITLE. This joint resolution may be cited as the "War Powers Resolution."

SEC. 2. PURPOSE AND POLICY. (a) It is the purpose of this joint resolution to fulfill the intent of the framers of the Constitution of the United States and insure that the collective judgement of both the Congress and the President will apply to the introduction of United States Armed Forces into hostilities, or into situations where imminent involvement in hostilities is clearly indicated by the circumstances, and to the continued use of such forces in hostilities or in such situations.

(b) Under article I, section 8, of the Constitution, it is specifically provided that the Congress shall have the power to make all laws necessary and proper for carrying into execution, not only its own powers but also all other powers vested by the Constitution in the Government of the United States, or in any department or officer thereof.

(c) The constitutional powers of the President as Commander-in-Chief to introduce United States Armed Forces into hostilities, or into situations where imminent involvement in hostilities is clearly indicated by the circumstances, are exercised only pursuant to (1) a declaration of war, (2) specific statutory authorization, or (3) a national emergency created by attack upon the United States, its territories or possessions, or its armed forces.

SEC. 3. CONSULTATION. The President in every possible instance shall consult with Congress before introducing United States Armed Forces into hostilities or into situation where imminent involvement in hostilities is clearly indicated by the circumstances, and after every such introduction shall consult regularly with the Congress until United States Armed Forces are no longer engaged in hostilities or have been removed from such situations.

SEC. 4. REPORTING. (a) In the absence of a declaration of war, in any case in which United States Armed Forces are introduced—

(1) into hostilities or into situations where imminent involvement in hostilities is clearly indicated by the circumstances;

(2) into the territory, airspace or waters of a foreign nation, while equipped for combat, except for deployments which relate solely to supply, replacement, repair, or training of such forces; or

(3) in numbers which substantially enlarge United States Armed Forces equipped for combat already located in a foreign nation; the president shall submit within 48 hours to the Speaker of the House of Representatives and to the President pro tempore of the Senate a report, in writing, setting forth—

(A) the circumstances necessitating the introduction of United States Armed Forces;

(B) the constitutional and legislative authority under which such introduction took place; and

(C) the estimated scope and duration of the hostilities or involvement.

(b) The President shall provide such other information as the Congress may request in the fulfillment of its constitutional responsibilities with respect to committing the Nation to war and to the use of United States Armed Forces abroad.

(c) Whenever United States Armed Forces are introduced into hostilities or into any situation described in subsection (a) of this section, the President shall, so long as such armed forces continue to be engaged in such hostilities or situation, report to the Congress periodically on the status of such hostilities or situation as well as on the scope and duration of such hostilities or situation, but in no event shall he report to the Congress less often than once every six months.

SEC. 5. CONGRESSIONAL ACTION. (a) Each report submitted pursuant to section 4(a)(1) shall be transmitted to the Speaker of the House of Representatives and to the President pro tempore of the Senate on the same calendar day. Each report so transmitted shall be referred to the Committee on Foreign Affairs of the House of Representatives and to the Committee on Foreign Relations of the Senate for appropriate action. If, when the report is transmitted, the Congress has adjourned sine die or has adjourned for any period in excess of three calendar days, the Speaker of the House of Representatives and the President pro tempore of the Senate, if they deem it advisable (or if petitioned by at least 30 percent of the membership of their respective Houses) shall jointly request the President to convene Congress in order that it may consider the report and take appropriate action pursuant to this section.

(b) Within sixty calendar days after a report is submitted or is required to be submitted pursuant to section 4(a)(1), whichever is earlier, the President shall terminate any use of United States Armed Forces with respect to which such report was submitted (or required to be submitted), unless the Congress (1) has declared war or has enacted a specific authorization for such use of United States Armed Forces, (2) has extended by law such sixty-day period, or (3) is physically unable to meet as a result of an armed attack upon the United States. Such sixty-day period shall be extended for not more than an additional thirty days if the President determines and certifies to the Congress in writing that unavoidable military necessity respecting the safety of United States Armed Forces requires the continued use of such armed forces in the course of bringing about a prompt removal of such forces.

(c) Notwithstanding subsection (b), at any time that United States Armed Forces are engaged in hostilities outside the territory of the United States, its possessions and territories without a declaration of war or specific statutory authorization, such forces shall be removed by the President if the Congress so directs by concurrent resolution. . . .

SEC. 8. INTERPRETATION OF JOINT RESOLUTION. (a) Authority to introduce United States Armed Forces into hostilities or into situations wherein involvement in hostilities is clearly indicated by the circumstances shall not be inferred—

(1) from any provision of law (whether or not in effect before the date of the enactment of this joint resolution), including any provision contained in any appropriation Act, unless such provision specifically authorizes the introduction of United States Armed Forces into hostilities or into such situations and stating that it is intended to constitute specific statutory authorization within the meaning of this joint resolution; or

(2) from any treaty heretofore or hereafter ratified unless such treaty is implemented by legislation specifically authorizing the introduction of United States Armed Forces into hostilities or into such situations and stating that it is intended to constitute specific statutory authorization within the meaning of this joint resolution.

(b) Nothing in this joint resolution shall be construed to require any further specific statutory authorization to permit members of United States Armed Forces to participate jointly with members of the armed forces of one or more foreign countries in the headquarters operations of high-level military commands which were established prior to the date of enactment of this joint resolution and pursuant to the United Nations Charter or any treaty ratified by the United States prior to such date.

(c) For purposes of this joint resolution, the term "introduction of United States Armed Forces" includes the assignment of members of such armed forces to command, coordinate, participate in the movement of, or accompany the regular or irregular military forces of any foreign country or government when such military forces are engaged, or there exists an imminent threat that such forces will become engaged, in hostilities.

(d) Nothing in this joint resolution—

(1) is intended to alter the constitutional authority of the Congress or of the President, or the provision of existing treaties; or (2) shall be construed as granting any authority to the President with respect to the introduction of United States Armed Forces into hostilities or into situations wherein involvement in hostilities is clearly indicated by the circumstances which authority he would not have had in the absence of this joint resolution. . . .

Authorization for Use of Military Force (2001)

Public Law 107-40 [S.J. RES. 23]
107th CONGRESS
September 18, 2001

JOINT RESOLUTION
To authorize the use of United States Armed Forces against those responsible for the recent attacks launched against the United States.

Whereas, on September 11, 2001, acts of treacherous violence were committed against the United States and its citizens; and

Whereas, such acts render it both necessary and appropriate that the United States exercise its rights to self-defense and to protect United States citizens both at home and abroad; and

Whereas, in light of the threat to the national security and foreign policy of the United States posed by these grave acts of violence; and

Whereas, such acts continue to pose an unusual and extraordinary threat to the national security and foreign policy of the United States; and

Whereas, the President has authority under the Constitution to take action to deter and prevent acts of international terrorism against the United States: Now, therefore, be it

Resolved by the Senate and House of Representatives of the United States of America in Congress assembled,

Section 1. Short Title. This joint resolution may be cited as the 'Authorization for Use of Military Force.'

Section 2. Authorization for Use of United States Armed Forces. (a) IN GENERAL—That the President is authorized to use all necessary and appropriate force against those nations, organizations, or persons he determines planned, authorized, committed, or aided the terrorist attacks that occurred on September 11, 2001, or harbored such organizations or persons, in order to prevent any future acts of international terrorism against the United States by such nations, organizations or persons.

(b) War Powers Resolution Requirements—

(1) SPECIFIC STATUTORY AUTHORIZATION—Consistent with section 8(a)(1) of the War Powers Resolution, the Congress declares that this section is intended to constitute specific statutory authorization within the meaning of section 5(b) of the War Powers Resolution.

(2) APPLICABILITY OF OTHER REQUIREMENTS—Nothing in this resolution supercedes any requirement of the War Powers Resolution.

SYNTHESIS QUESTIONS FOR FURTHER DISCUSSION: CHAPTER 4 SECTION B

1. In many ways, the eighteenth-century dialogue between Alexander Hamilton and James Madison, known as the Pacificus-Helvidius debate, set the stage for the modern discussion of presidential power in foreign affairs. The Pacificus-Helvidius debate concerned the president's power to unilaterally declare neutrality in a foreign dispute. In what ways does Hamilton's defense of the president's unilateral power to declare neutrality parallel John Yoo's defense of modern presidential power in regard to the "Declare War" Clause? In what ways does it differ? In what ways does Madison's objection to President George Washington's unilateral action prefigure John Hart Ely's insistence that Congress be involved in foreign

affairs? One difference between the eighteenth-century debate between Madison and Hamilton and the twentieth-century debate between Yoo and Ely concerns topic area. While Madison and Hamilton are concerned with the power to declare neutrality, Ely and Yoo are concerned with war. Does this suggest a limit to drawing parallels between these two debates?

2. What would Hamilton and Madison have made of the controversies at issue in *United States v. Curtiss-Wright* and *Dames & Moore v. Regan*? Do these twentieth-century controversies raise issues they could not have imagined? What would Madison and Hamilton have made of the political question doctrine in *Goldwater v. Carter*? Think about these questions while keeping in mind the theory of originalism introduced in Chapter 2. Does this theory help us to think through these controversies given that even Hamilton and Madison disagreed about the nature of presidential power?

3. The Constitution gives Congress the power to declare war. But what exactly constitutes a war? Is a declaration of war necessary to "make" or "engage" in war? Are the semantic distinctions raised by Yoo about these distinctions instructive in thinking about presidential power and its limits? This problem seems especially pronounced in the case of the Civil War. Can the Court assert that the controversies in the *Prize Cases* occurred during a time of war?

4. Ely's argument in *War and Responsibility* was largely motivated by and concerned with events relating to the Vietnam War. Although war in Vietnam was never officially declared, the conflict was referred to as a war by most people. Was this an unconstitutional war given that Congress never passed a formal declaration of war? Advocates of the view that it was a constitutional armed action appeal to the Gulf of Tonkin resolution passed by Congress in 1964. Can such resolutions serve as the equivalent of a war declaration?

C. THE PRESIDENCY AND THE RULE OF LAW

Is the president ever above the law? How can the other branches provide effective checks and balances against the president? Should the president have any role in finding constitutional meaning?

We conclude this chapter with an examination of the relationship between the executive and the rule of law. While it is the role of the Court to interpret law and of Congress to make it, much of the executive's task is to execute the law. But some authors have suggested that the executive function goes beyond mere execution and also involves a role for the president in interpreting the Constitution itself. Others have even suggested a "prerogative power" that enables such a large degree of discretion that the president is in fact beyond the law, at least in some circumstances.

The arguments against the proposition that the president is above or beyond the law are to be found in the fundamental principles of constitutional democracy. Indeed, the notion that we are a "nation of laws, not men," is meant to contrast constitutional democracy with monarchy. In absolute monarchy, the sovereign has unlimited ability to act as he or she pleases. But in a constitutional democracy the people, and not their leader, are sovereign, and the constraints on governmental power apply to all political actors, including the executive. As we have seen, the structure of the Constitution subjects presidential authority, such as appointment and removal power, to limits imposed by Congress and the Constitution.

But the presidency also has a great deal of implied power that stems from the president's status as the Chief Executive. In order to carry out the execution of the law, discretion is involved. Not every action will be governed by principles and laws beyond the president's judgment. To what extent does the possibility of this inherent power require immunity from scrutiny of his or her actions? Is the president's workplace so sacred that it must be immunized from public scrutiny? As you read John Locke and Harvey Mansfield, who defend not only discretion for the presidency but arguably a degree of immunity from the law, consider whether some of the structures that bind the presidency need to be loosened when it comes to subjecting the president to judicial scrutiny. Is the president ever truly above the law? What are the ramifications of the various responses to this question? In considering the question and its implications, recall the following quote from *The Federalist* No. 70, excerpted in Section A: "Every man the least conversant in Roman history, knows how often that republic was obliged to take refuge in the absolute power of a single man, under the formidable title of Dictator."

The cases *United States v. Nixon, Nixon v. Fitzgerald,* and *Clinton v. Jones* ask whether sitting presidents can be subject to lawsuits. These cases generally suggest that the president can in fact be sued, though they make clear that the president is no ordinary citizen. While some of the readings in this section suggest that the president's extraordinary power might be reason for immunity, it is also important to consider the other side. Consider as you read these cases whether it is precisely because the president has so much power that he or she should be subject to lawsuits. Are personal lawsuits an appropriate way for citizens to check presidential power in addition to the structural checks that are inherent in our system of government?

As you read these cases, consider whether they refute the idea of "presidential prerogative," or the notion that the president is sometimes beyond the law. Do you agree with these decisions? Should the president be given more or less leeway than they allow?

John Locke

SECOND TREATISE OF GOVERNMENT

Chapter XIV: Of Prerogative

WHERE the legislative and executive power are in distinct hands, as they are in all moderated monarchies and well-framed governments, there the good of the society requires that several things should be left to the discretion of him that has the executive power. For the legislators not being able to foresee and provide by laws for all that may be useful to the community, the executor of the laws, having the power in his hands, has by the common law of Nature a right to make use of it for the good of the society, in many cases where the municipal law has given no direction, till the legislative can conveniently be assembled to provide for it; nay, many things there are which the law can by no means provide for, and those must necessarily be left to the discretion of him that has the executive power in his hands, to be ordered by him as the public good and advantage shall require; nay, it is fit that the laws themselves should in some cases give way to the executive power, or rather to this fundamental law of Nature and government—*viz.*, that as much as may be all the members of the society are to be preserved. For since many accidents may happen wherein a strict and rigid observation of the laws may do harm, as not to pull down an innocent man's house to stop the fire when the next to it is burning; and a man may come sometimes within the reach of the law, which makes no distinction of persons, by an action that may deserve reward and pardon; it is fit the ruler should have a power in many cases to mitigate the severity of the law, and pardon some offenders, since the end of government being the preservation of all as much as may be, even the guilty are to be spared where it can prove no prejudice to the innocent.

This power to act according to discretion for the public good, without the prescription of the law and sometimes even against it, is that which is called prerogative; for since in some governments the law-making power is not always in being and is usually too numerous, and so too slow for the dispatch requisite to execution, and because, also, it is impossible to foresee and so by laws to provide for all accidents and necessities that may concern the public, or make such laws as will do no harm, if they are executed with an inflexible rigor on all occasions and upon all persons that may come in their way; therefore there is a latitude left to the executive power to do many things of choice which the laws do not prescribe.

This power, whilst employed for the benefit of the community and suitably to the trust and ends of the government, is undoubted prerogative, and never is questioned. For the people are very seldom or never scrupulous or nice in the point or questioning of prerogative whilst it is in any tolerable degree employed for the use it was meant—that is, for the good of the people, and not manifestly against it. But if there comes to be a question between the executive power and the people about a thing claimed as a prerogative, the tendency of the exercise of such prerogative, to the good or hurt of the people, will easily decide that question.

It is easy to conceive that in the infancy of governments, when commonwealths differed little from families in number of people, they differed from them too but little in number of laws; and the governors, being as the fathers of them, watching over them for their good, the government was almost all prerogative. A few established laws served the turn, and the discretion and care of the ruler supplied the rest. But when mistake or flattery prevailed with weak princes, to make use of this power for private ends of their own and not for the public good, the people were fain, by express laws, to get prerogative determined in those points wherein they found disadvantage from it, and declared limitations of prerogative in those cases which they and their ancestors had left in the utmost latitude to the wisdom of those princes who made no other but a right use of it—that is, for the good of their people.

And therefore they have a very wrong notion of government who say that the people have encroached upon the prerogative when they have got any part of it to be defined by positive laws. For in so doing they have not pulled from the prince anything that of right belonged to him, but only declared that that power which they indefinitely left in his or his ancestors' hands, to be exercised for their good, was not a thing which they intended him, when he used it otherwise. For the end of government being the good of the community, whatsoever alterations are made in it tending to that end cannot be an encroachment upon anybody; since nobody in government can have a right tending to any other end; and those only are encroachments which prejudice or hinder the public good. Those who say otherwise speak as if the prince had a distinct and separate interest from the good of the community, and was not made for it; the root and source from which spring almost all those evils and disorders which happen in kingly governments. And

indeed, if that be so, the people under his government are not a society of rational creatures, entered into a community for their mutual good, such as have set rulers over themselves, to guard and promote that good; but are to be looked on as a herd of inferior creatures under the dominion of a master, who keeps them and works them for his own pleasure or profit. If men were so void of reason and brutish as to enter into society upon such terms, prerogative might indeed be, what some men would have it, an arbitrary power to do things hurtful to the people.

But since a rational creature cannot be supposed, when free, to put himself into subjection to another for his own harm (though where he finds a good and wise ruler he may not, perhaps, think it either necessary or useful to set precise bounds to his power in all things), prerogative can be nothing but the people's permitting their rulers to do several things of their own free choice where the law was silent, and sometimes too against the direct letter of the law, for the public good and their acquiescing in it when so done. For as a good prince, who is mindful of the trust put into his hands and careful of the good of his people, cannot have too much prerogative—that is, power to do good, so a weak and ill prince, who would claim that power his predecessors exercised, without the direction of the law, as a prerogative belonging to him by right of his office, which he may exercise at his pleasure to make or promote an interest distinct from that of the public, gives the people an occasion to claim their right and limit that power, which, whilst it was exercised for their good, they were content should be tacitly allowed.

And therefore he that will look into the history of England will find that prerogative was always largest in the hands of our wisest and best princes, because the people observing the whole tendency of their actions to be the public good, or if any human frailty or mistake (for princes are but men, made as others) appeared in some small declinations from that end, yet it was visible the main of their conduct tended to nothing but the care of the public. The people, therefore, finding reason to be satisfied with these princes, whenever they acted without, or contrary to the letter of the law, acquiesced in what they did, and without the least complaint, let them enlarge their prerogative as they pleased, judging rightly that they did nothing herein to the prejudice of their laws, since they acted conformably to the foundation and end of all laws—the public good.

Such God-like princes, indeed, had some title to arbitrary power by that argument that would prove absolute monarchy the best government, as that which God Himself governs the universe by, because such kings partake of His wisdom and goodness. Upon this is founded that saying, "That the reigns of good princes have been always most dangerous to the liberties of their people." For when their successors, managing the government with different thoughts, would draw the actions of those good rulers into precedent and make them the standard of their prerogative—as if what had been done only for the good of the people was a right in them to do for the harm of the people, if they so pleased—it has often occasioned contest, and sometimes public disorders, before the people could recover their original right and get that to be declared not to be prerogative which truly was never so; since it is impossible that anybody in the society should ever have a right to do the people harm, though it be very possible and reasonable that the people should not go about to set any bounds to the prerogative of those kings or rulers who

themselves transgressed not the bounds of the public good. For *"prerogative is nothing but the power of doing public good without a rule."*

The power of calling parliaments in England, as to precise time, place, and duration, is certainly a prerogative of the king, but still with this trust, that it shall be made use of for the good of the nation as the exigencies of the times and variety of occasion shall require. For it being impossible to foresee which should always be the fittest place for them to assemble in, and what the best season, the choice of these was left with the executive power, as might be best subservient to the public good and best suit the ends of parliament.

The old question will be asked in this matter of prerogative, *"But who shall be judge when this power is made a right use of?"* I answer: Between an executive power in being, with such a prerogative, and a legislative that depends upon his will for their convening, there can be no judge on earth. As there can be none between the legislative and the people, should either the executive or the legislative, when they have got the power in their hands, design, or go about to enslave or destroy them, the people have no other remedy in this, as in all other cases where they have no judge on earth, but to appeal to Heaven; for the rulers in such attempts, exercising a power the people never put into their hands, who can never be supposed to consent that anybody should rule over them for their harm, do that which they have not a right to do. And where the body of the people, or any single man, are deprived of their right, or are under the exercise of a power without right, having no appeal on earth they have a liberty to appeal to Heaven whenever they judge the cause of sufficient moment. And therefore, though the people cannot be judge, so as to have, by the constitution of that society, any superior power to determine and give effective sentence in the case, yet they have reserved that ultimate determination to themselves which belongs to all mankind, where there lies no appeal on earth, by a law antecedent and paramount to all positive laws of men, whether they have just cause to make their appeal to Heaven. And this judgment they cannot part with, it being out of a man's power so to submit himself to another as to give him a liberty to destroy him; God and Nature never allowing a man so to abandon himself as to neglect his own preservation. And since he cannot take away his own life, neither can he give another power to take it. Nor let any one think this lays a perpetual foundation for disorder; for this operates not till the inconvenience is so great that the majority feel it, and are weary of it, and find a necessity to have it amended. And this the executive power, or wise princes, never need come in the danger of; and it is the thing of all others they have most need to avoid, as, of all others, the most perilous.

Harvey Mansfield

THE CASE FOR THE STRONG EXECUTIVE: UNDER SOME CIRCUMSTANCES, THE RULE OF LAW MUST YIELD TO THE NEED FOR ENERGY

The Wall Street Journal, Wednesday, May 2, 2007

Complaints against the "imperial presidency" are back in vogue. With a view to President Bush, the late Arthur M. Schlesinger Jr. expanded and reissued the book of the same name he wrote against Richard Nixon, and Bush critics have taken up the phrase in a chorus. In response John Yoo and Richard Posner (and others) have defended the war powers of the president.

This is not the first time that a strong executive has been attacked and defended, and it will not be the last. Our Constitution, as long as it continues, will suffer this debate—I would say, give rise to it, preside over and encourage it. Though I want to defend the strong executive, I mainly intend to step back from that defense to show why the debate between the strong executive and its adversary, the rule of law, is necessary, good and—under the Constitution—never-ending.

In other circumstances I could see myself defending the rule of law. Americans are fortunate to have a Constitution that accommodates different circumstances. Its flexibility keeps it in its original form and spirit a "living constitution," ready for change, and open to new necessities and opportunities. The "living constitution" conceived by the Progressives actually makes it a prisoner of ongoing events and perceived trends. To explain the constitutional debate between the strong executive and the rule of law I will concentrate on its sources in political philosophy and, for greater clarity, ignore the constitutional law emerging from it.

The case for a strong executive should begin from a study, on this occasion a quick survey, of the American republic. The American republic was the first to have a strong executive that was intended to be republican as well as strong, and the success, or long life, of America's Constitution qualifies it as a possible model for other countries. Modern political science beginning from Machiavelli abandoned the best regime featured by classical political science because the best regime was utopian or imaginary. Modern political scientists wanted a practical solution, and by the time of Locke, followed by Montesquieu, they learned to substitute a model regime for the best regime; and this was the government of England. The model regime would not be applicable everywhere, no doubt, because it was not intended to be a lowest common denominator. But it would show what could be done in the best circumstances.

The American Founders had the ambition to make America the model regime, taking over from England. This is why they showed surprising respect for English government, the regime they had just rebelled against. America would not only make a republic for itself, but teach the world how to make a successful republic and thus improve republicanism and save the reputation of republics. For previous republics had suffered disastrous failure, alternating between anarchy and tyranny, seeming to force the conclusion that orderly government could come only from monarchy, the enemy of republics. Previous republics had put their faith in the rule of law as the best way to foil one-man rule. The rule of law would keep power in the hands of many, or at least a few, which was safer than in the hands of one. As the way to ensure the rule of law, Locke and Montesquieu fixed on the separation of powers. They were too realistic to put their faith in any sort of higher law; the rule of law would be maintained by a legislative process of institutions that both cooperated and competed.

Now the rule of law has two defects, each of which suggests the need for one-man rule. The first is that law is always imperfect by being universal, thus an average solution even in the best case, that is inferior to the living intelligence of a wise man on the spot, who can judge particular circumstances. This defect is discussed by Aristotle in the well-known passage in his "Politics" where he considers "whether it is more advantageous to be ruled by the best man or the best laws."

The other defect is that the law does not know how to make itself obeyed. Law assumes obedience, and as such seems oblivious to resistance to the law by the "governed," as if it were enough to require criminals to turn themselves in. No, the law must be "enforced," as we say. There must be police, and the rulers over the police must use energy (Alexander Hamilton's term) in addition to reason. It is a delusion to believe that governments can have energy without ever resorting to the use of force.

The best source of energy turns out to be the same as the best source of reason— one man. One man, or, to use Machiavelli's expression, *uno solo*, will be the greatest source of energy if he regards it as necessary to maintaining his own rule. Such a person will have the greatest incentive to be watchful, and to be both cruel and merciful in correct contrast and proportion. We are talking about Machiavelli's prince, the man whom in apparently unguarded moments he called a tyrant.

The American Founders heeded both criticisms of the rule of law when they created the presidency. The president would be the source of energy in government, that is, in the administration of government, energy being a neutral term that might include Aristotle's discretionary virtue and Machiavelli's tyranny—in which only partisans could discern the difference. The founders of course accepted the principle of the rule of law, as being required by the republican genius of the American people. Under this principle, the wise man or prince becomes and is called an "executive," one who carries out the will and instruction of others, of the legislature that makes the law, of the people who instruct or inspire the legislature. In this weak sense, the dictionary definition of "executive," the executive forbears to rule in his own name as one man. This means that neither one-man wisdom nor tyranny is admitted into the Constitution as such; if there is need for either, the need is subordinated to, or if you will, covered over by, the republican principle of the rule of law.

Yet the executive subordinated to the rule of law is in danger of being subordinate to the legislature. This was the fault in previous republics. When the separation of powers was invented in 17th-century England, the purpose was to keep the executive subordinate; but the trouble was the weakness of a subordinate executive. He could not do his job, or he could do his job only by overthrowing or cowing the legislature, as Oliver Cromwell had done. John Locke took the task in hand, and made a strong executive in a manner that was adopted by the American Founders.

Locke was a careful writer, so careful that he did not care if he appeared to be a confused writer. In his "Second Treatise of Government" he announces the supremacy of the legislature, which was the slogan of the parliamentary side in the English Civil War, as the principle that should govern a well-made constitution. But as the argument proceeds, Locke gradually "fortifies" (to use James Madison's term) the executive. Locke adds other related powers to the subordinate power of executing the laws: the federative power dealing with foreign affairs, which he presents as conceptually distinct from the power

of executing laws but naturally allied; the veto, a legislative function; the power to convoke the legislature and to correct its representation should it become corrupt; and above all, the prerogative, defined as "the power of doing public good without a rule." Without a rule! Even more: "sometimes too against the direct letter of the law." This is the very opposite of law and the rule of law—and "prerogative" was the slogan of the king's party in the same war.

Thus Locke combined the extraconstitutional with the constitutional in a contradiction; besides saying that the legislature is "the supreme power" of the commonwealth, he speaks of "the supreme executive power." Locke, one could say, was acting as a good citizen, bringing peace to his country by giving both sides in the Civil War a place in the constitution. In doing so he ensured that the war would continue, but it would be peaceful because he also ensured that, there being reason and force on both sides, neither side could win conclusively.

The American Constitution adopted this fine idea and improved it. The American Founders helped to settle Locke's deliberate confusion of supremacy by writing it into a document and ratifying it by the people rather than merely scattering it in the treatise of a philosopher. By being formalized the Constitution could become a law itself, but a law above ordinary law and thus a law above the rule of law in the ordinary sense of laws passed by the legislature. Thus some notion of prerogative—though the word "prerogative" was much too royal for American sensibilities—could be pronounced legal inasmuch as it was constitutional. This strong sense of executive power would be opposed, within the Constitution, to the rule of law in the usual, old-republican meaning, as represented by the two rule-of-law powers in the Constitution, the Congress which makes law and the judiciary which judges by the law.

The American Constitution signifies that it has fortified the executive by vesting the president with "the executive power," complete and undiluted in Article II, as opposed to the Congress in Article I, which receives only certain delegated and enumerated legislative powers. The president takes an oath "to execute the Office of President" of which only one function is to "take care that the laws be faithfully executed." In addition, he is commander-in-chief of the military, makes treaties (with the Senate), and receives ambassadors. He has the power of pardon, a power with more than a whiff of prerogative for the sake of a public good that cannot be achieved, indeed that is endangered, by executing the laws. In the *Federalist*, as already noted, the executive represents the need for energy in government, energy to complement the need for stability, satisfied mainly in the Senate and the judiciary.

Energy and stability are necessary in every form of government, but in their previous, sorry history, republics had failed to meet these necessities. Republican government cannot survive, as we would say, by ideology alone. The republican genius is dominant in America, where there has never been much support for anything like an *ancien régime,* but support for republicanism is not enough to make a viable republic. The republican spirit can actually cause trouble for republics if it makes people think that to be republican it is enough merely to oppose monarchy. Such an attitude tempts a republican people to republicanize everything so as to make government resemble a monarchy as little as possible.

Although the *Federalist* made a point of distinguishing a republic from a democracy (by which it meant a so-called pure, nonrepresentative democracy), the urge today to democratize everything has similar bad effects. To counter this reactionary republican (or democratic, in today's language) belief characteristic of shortsighted partisans, the *Federalist* made a point of holding the new, the novel, American republic to the test of good government as opposed merely to that of republican government.

The test of good government was what was necessary to all government. Necessity was put to the fore. In the first papers of the *Federalist*, necessity took the form of calling attention to the present crisis in America, caused by the incompetence of the republic established by the Articles of Confederation. The crisis was both foreign and domestic, and it was a crisis because it was urgent. The face of necessity, the manner in which it first appears and is most impressive, is urgency—in Machiavelli's words, *la necessità che non da tempo* (the necessity that allows no time). And what must be the character of a government's response to an urgent crisis? Energy. And where do we find energy in the government? In the executive. Actually, the *Federalist* introduces the need for energy in government considerably before it associates energy with the executive. To soothe republican partisans, the strong executive must be introduced by stages.

One should not believe that a strong executive is needed only for quick action in emergencies, though that is the function mentioned first. A strong executive is requisite to oppose majority faction produced by temporary delusions in the people. For the *Federalist*, a strong executive must exercise his strength especially against the people, not showing them "servile pliancy." Tocqueville shared this view. Today we think that a strong president is one who leads the people, that is, one who takes them where they want to go, like Andrew Jackson. But Tocqueville contemptuously regarded Jackson as weak for having been "the slave of the majority." Again according to the *Federalist*, the American president will likely have the virtue of responsibility, a new political virtue, now heard so often that it seems to be the only virtue, but first expounded in that work.

"Responsibility" is not mere responsiveness to the people; it means doing what the people would want done if they were apprised of the circumstances. Responsibility requires "personal firmness" in one's character, and it enables those who love fame—"the ruling passion of the noblest minds"—to undertake "extensive and arduous enterprises."

Only a strong president can be a great president. Americans are a republican people but they admire their great presidents. Those great presidents—I dare not give a complete list—are not only those who excelled in the emergency of war but those, like Washington, Lincoln and Franklin Roosevelt, who also deliberately planned and executed enterprises for shaping or reshaping the entire politics of their country.

This admiration for presidents extends beyond politics into society, in which Americans, as republicans, tolerate, and appreciate, an amazing amount of one-man rule. The CEO (chief executive officer) is found at the summit of every corporation including universities. I suspect that appreciation for private executives in democratic society was taught by the success of the Constitution's invention of a strong executive in republican politics.

The case for a strong executive begins from urgent necessity and extends to necessity in the sense of efficacy and even greatness. It is necessary not merely to respond to circumstances but also in a comprehensive way to seek to anticipate and form them. "Necessary to" the survival of a society expands to become "necessary for" the good life there, and indeed we look for signs in the way a government acts in emergencies for what it thinks to be good after the emergency has passed. A free government should show its respect for freedom even when it has to take it away. Yet despite the expansion inherent in necessity, the distinction between urgent crises and quiet times remains. Machiavelli called the latter *tempi pacifici*, and he thought that governments could not take them for granted. What works for quiet times is not appropriate in stormy times. John Locke and the American Founders showed a similar understanding to Machiavelli's when they argued for and fashioned a strong executive.

In our time, however, an opinion has sprung up in liberal circles particularly that civil liberties must always be kept intact regardless of circumstances. This opinion assumes that civil liberties have the status of natural liberties, and are inalienable. This means that the Constitution has the status of what was called in the 17th-century natural public law; it is an order as natural as the state of nature from which it emerges. In this view liberty has just one set of laws and institutions that must be kept inviolate, lest it be lost.

But Locke was a wiser liberal. His institutions were "constituted," less by creation than by modification of existing institutions in England, but not deduced as invariable consequences of disorder in the state of nature. He retained the difference, and so did the Americans, between natural liberties, inalienable but insecure, and civil liberties, more secure but changeable. Because civil liberties are subject to circumstances, a free constitution needs an institution responsive to circumstances, an executive able to be strong when necessary.

The lesson for us should be that circumstances are much more important for free government than we often believe. Civil liberties are for majorities as well as minorities, and no one should be considered to have rights against society whose exercise would bring society to ruin. The usual danger in a republic is tyranny of the majority, because the majority is the only legitimate dominant force. But in time of war the greater danger may be to the majority from a minority, and the government will be a greater friend than enemy to liberty. Vigilant citizens must be able to adjust their view of the source of danger, and change front if necessary. "Civil liberties" belong to all, not only to the less powerful or less esteemed, and the true balance of liberty and security cannot be taken as given without regard to the threat. Nor is it true that free societies should be judged solely by what they do in quiet times; they should also be judged by the efficacy, and the honorableness, of what they do in war in order to return to peace.

The American Constitution is a formal law that establishes an actual contention among its three separated powers. Its formality represents the rule of law, and the actuality arises from which branch better promotes the common good in the event, or in the opinion of the people. In quiet times the rule of law will come to the fore, and the executive can be weak. In stormy times, the rule of law may seem to require the prudence and force that law, or present law, cannot supply, and the executive must be strong. In judging the circumstances of a free society, two parties come to be formed around these two outlooks. These outlooks may not coincide with party principles because they often

depend on which branch a party holds and feels obliged to defend: Democrats today would be friendlier to executive power if they held the presidency—and Republicans would discover virtue in the rule of law if they held Congress.

The terms of the disagreement over a strong executive go back to the classic debate between Hamilton (as Pacificus) and Madison (as Helvidius) in 1793–94. Hamilton argued that the executive power, representing the whole country with the energy necessary to defend it, cannot be limited or exhausted. Madison replied that the executive power does not represent the whole country but is determined by its place in the structure of government, which is executing the laws. If carrying on war goes beyond executing the laws, that is all the more reason why the war power should be construed narrowly. Today Republicans and Democrats repeat these arguments when the former declare that we are at war with terrorists and the latter respond that the danger is essentially a matter of law enforcement.

As to the contention that a strong executive prompts a policy of imperialism, I would admit the possibility, and I promise to think carefully and prayerfully about returning Texas to Mexico. In its best moments, America wants to be a model for the world, but no more. In its less good moments, America becomes disgusted with the rest of the world for its failure to imitate our example and follow our advice. I believe that America is more likely to err with isolationism than with imperialism, and that if America is an empire, it is the first empire that always wants an exit strategy. I believe too that the difficulties of the war in Iraq arise from having wished to leave too much to the Iraqis, thus from a sense of inhibition rather than imperial ambition.

UNITED STATES v. NIXON

418 U.S. 683 (1974)

Opinion: Burger, joined by Douglas, Brennan, Stewart, White, Marshall, Blackmun, Powell

On June 17, 1972, five men were arrested for breaking into the Democratic National Committee headquarters at the Watergate building in Washington, D.C. Over time, it became apparent that these men broke into the office under orders from individuals in the administration of President Richard Nixon. As part of the investigation of this crime, a subpoena was issued requiring President Nixon to produce tapes, memoranda, and other documents relating to meetings that he held with certain individuals. President Nixon released some but not all of the requested materials and filed a motion to quash the subpoena. He claimed that the meetings in question were protected by executive privilege. In the case at hand, the Court considered the President's claim.

This case raises important questions about executive power, specifically in circumstances of suspected criminal activity in the executive branch. Is the president entitled to secrecy in his official meetings, or are his activities and words always a part of the public record? Here the Court explicitly endorses the idea that a president has a legitimate claim to privilege in certain matters. But how far does that claim extend? What is the best means to ensure that the president does not overstep his bounds? Do the courts have the authority to make such determinations?

MR. CHIEF JUSTICE BURGER *delivered the opinion of the Court.*

This litigation presents for review the denial of a motion, filed in the District Court on behalf of the President of the United States, in the case of *United States v. Mitchell*, to quash a third-party subpoena *duces tecum* issued by the United States District Court for the District of Columbia, pursuant to Fed. Rule Crim. Proc. 17(c). The subpoena directed the President to produce certain tape recordings and documents relating to his conversations with aides and advisers. The court rejected the President's claims of absolute executive privilege, of lack of jurisdiction, and of failure to satisfy the requirements of Rule 17(c).

On March 1, 1974, a grand jury of the United States District Court for the District of Columbia returned an indictment charging seven named individuals with various offenses, including conspiracy to defraud the United States and to obstruct justice. Although he was not designated as such in the indictment, the grand jury named the President, among others, as an unindicted coconspirator. On April 18, 1974, upon motion of the Special Prosecutor, a subpoena *duces tecum* was issued pursuant to Rule 17(c) to the President by the United States District Court and made returnable on May 2, 1974. This subpoena required the production, in advance of the September 9 trial date, of certain tapes, memoranda, papers, transcripts, or other writings relating to certain precisely identified meetings between the President and others. The Special Prosecutor was able to fix the time, place, and persons present at these discussions because the White House daily logs and appointment records had been delivered to him. On April 30, the President publicly released edited transcripts of 43 conversations; portions of 20 conversations subject to subpoena in the present case were included. On May 1, 1974, the President's counsel filed a "special appearance" and a motion to quash the subpoena under Rule 17(c). This motion was accompanied by a formal claim of privilege. At a subsequent hearing, further motions to expunge the grand jury's action naming the President as an unindicted coconspirator and for protective orders against the disclosure of that information were filed or raised orally by counsel for the President.

II. JUSTICIABILITY

In the District Court, the President's counsel argued that the court lacked jurisdiction to issue the subpoena because the matter was an intra-branch dispute between a subordinate and superior officer of the Executive Branch, and hence not subject to judicial resolution. That argument has been renewed in this Court with emphasis on the contention that the dispute does not present a "case" or "controversy" which can be adjudicated in the federal courts. The President's counsel argues that the federal courts should not intrude into areas committed to the other branches of Government. He views the present dispute as essentially a "jurisdictional" dispute within the Executive Branch which he analogizes to a dispute between two congressional committees. Since the Executive Branch has exclusive authority and absolute discretion to decide whether to prosecute a case, it is contended that a President's decision is final in determining what evidence is to be used in a given criminal case. Although his counsel concedes that the President has delegated certain specific powers to the Special Prosecutor, he has not "waived nor delegated to the Special Prosecutor the President's duty to claim privilege as to all materials . . . which fall within the President's inherent authority

to refuse to disclose to any executive officer." The Special Prosecutor's demand for the items therefore presents, in the view of the President's counsel, a political question under *Baker v. Carr*, 369 U.S. 186 (1962), since it involves a "textually demonstrable" grant of power under Art. II.

The mere assertion of a claim of an "intra-branch dispute," without more, has never operated to defeat federal jurisdiction; justiciability does not depend on such a surface inquiry. In *United States v. ICC*, the Court observed, "courts must look behind names that symbolize the parties to determine whether a justiciable case or controversy is presented."

Our starting point is the nature of the proceeding for which the evidence is sought—here, a pending criminal prosecution. It is a judicial proceeding in a federal court alleging violation of federal laws, and is brought in the name of the United States as sovereign. Under the authority of Art. II, §2, Congress has vested in the Attorney General the power to conduct the criminal litigation of the United States Government. It has also vested in him the power to appoint subordinate officers to assist him in the discharge of his duties. Acting pursuant to those statutes, the Attorney General has delegated the authority to represent the United States in these particular matters to a Special Prosecutor with unique authority and tenure. The regulation gives the Special Prosecutor explicit power to contest the invocation of executive privilege in the process of seeking evidence deemed relevant to the performance of these specially delegated duties.

So long as this regulation is extant, it has the force of law. In *United States ex rel. Accardi v. Shaughnessy*, regulations of the Attorney General delegated certain of his discretionary powers to the Board of Immigration Appeals and required that Board to exercise its own discretion on appeals in deportation cases. The Court held that, so long as the Attorney General's regulations remained operative, he denied himself the authority to exercise the discretion delegated to the Board even though the original authority was his and he could reassert it by amending the regulations.

Here, as in *Accardi*, it is theoretically possible for the Attorney General to amend or revoke the regulation defining the Special Prosecutor's authority. But he has not done so. So long as this regulation remains in force, the Executive Branch is bound by it, and indeed the United States, as the sovereign composed of the three branches, is bound to respect and to enforce it. Moreover, the delegation of authority to the Special Prosecutor in this case is not an ordinary delegation by the Attorney General to a subordinate officer: with the authorization of the President, the Acting Attorney General provided in the regulation that the Special Prosecutor was not to be removed without the "consensus" of eight designated leaders of Congress.

The demands of and the resistance to the subpoena present an obvious controversy in the ordinary sense, but that alone is not sufficient to meet constitutional standards. In the constitutional sense, controversy means more than disagreement and conflict; rather it means the kind of controversy courts traditionally resolve. Here at issue is the production or nonproduction of specified evidence deemed by the Special Prosecutor to be relevant and admissible in a pending criminal case. It is sought by one official of the Executive Branch within the scope of his express authority; it is resisted by the Chief Executive on the ground of his duty to preserve the confidentiality of the communications of the President. Whatever the correct answer on the merits, these issues are "of a type which are traditionally justiciable." *United States v. ICC.*

Moreover, since the matter is one arising in the regular course of a federal criminal prosecution, it is within the traditional scope of Art. III power. *Id.* at 198.

In light of the uniqueness of the setting in which the conflict arises, the fact that both parties are officers of the Executive Branch cannot be viewed as a barrier to justiciability. It would be inconsistent with the applicable law and regulation, and the unique facts of this case, to conclude other than that the Special Prosecutor has standing to bring this action, and that a justiciable controversy is presented for decision.

IV. THE CLAIM OF PRIVILEGE

A

. . . [W]e turn to the claim that the subpoena should be quashed because it demands "confidential conversations between a President and his close advisors that it would be inconsistent with the public interest to produce." The first contention is a broad claim that the separation of powers doctrine precludes judicial review of a President's claim of privilege. The second contention is that, if he does not prevail on the claim of absolute privilege, the court should hold as a matter of constitutional law that the privilege prevails over the subpoena *duces tecum.*

In the performance of assigned constitutional duties, each branch of the Government must initially interpret the Constitution, and the interpretation of its powers by any branch is due great respect from the others. The President's counsel, as we have noted, reads the Constitution as providing an absolute privilege of confidentiality for all Presidential communications. Many decisions of this Court, however, have unequivocally reaffirmed the holding of *Marbury v. Madison*, that "[i]t is emphatically the province and duty of the judicial department to say what the law is." No holding of the Court has defined the scope of judicial power specifically relating to the enforcement of a subpoena for confidential Presidential communications for use in a criminal prosecution, but other exercises of power by the Executive Branch and the Legislative Branch have been found invalid as in conflict with the Constitution. Since this Court has consistently exercised the power to construe and delineate claims arising under express powers, it must follow that the Court has authority to interpret claims with respect to powers alleged to derive from enumerated powers.

Our system of government "requires that federal courts on occasion interpret the Constitution in a manner at variance with the construction given the document by another branch." *Powell v. McCormack, supra*, at 549.

Notwithstanding the deference each branch must accord the others, the "judicial Power of the United States" vested in the federal courts by Art. III, §1, of the Constitution can no more be shared with the Executive Branch than the Chief Executive, for example, can share with the Judiciary the veto power, or the Congress share with the Judiciary the power to override a Presidential veto. Any other conclusion would be contrary to the basic concept of separation of powers and the checks and balances that flow from the scheme of a tripartite government. We therefore reaffirm that it is the province and duty of this Court "to say what the law is" with respect to the claim of privilege presented in this case.

B

In support of his claim of absolute privilege, the President's counsel urges two grounds, one of which is common to all governments and one of which is peculiar to our system of separation of powers. The first ground is the valid need for protection of communications between high Government officials and those who advise and assist them in the performance of their manifold duties; the importance of this confidentiality is too plain to require further discussion. Human experience teaches that those who expect public dissemination of their remarks may well temper candor with a concern for appearances and for their own interests to the detriment of the decisionmaking process. Whatever the nature of the privilege of confidentiality of Presidential communications in the exercise of Art. II powers, the privilege can be said to derive from the supremacy of each branch within its own assigned area of constitutional duties. Certain powers and privileges flow from the nature of enumerated powers; the protection of the confidentiality of Presidential communications has similar constitutional underpinnings.

The second ground asserted by the President's counsel in support of the claim of absolute privilege rests on the doctrine of separation of powers. Here it is argued that the independence of the Executive Branch within its own sphere insulates a President from a judicial subpoena in an ongoing criminal prosecution, and thereby protects confidential Presidential communications.

However, neither the doctrine of separation of powers nor the need for confidentiality of high-level communications, without more, can sustain an absolute, unqualified Presidential privilege of immunity from judicial process under all circumstances. The President's need for complete candor and objectivity from advisers calls for great deference from the courts. However, when the privilege depends solely on the broad, undifferentiated claim of public interest in the confidentiality of such conversations, a confrontation with other values arises. Absent a claim of need to protect military, diplomatic, or sensitive national security secrets, we find it difficult to accept the argument that even the very important interest in confidentiality of Presidential communications is significantly diminished by production of such material for *in camera* inspection with all the protection that a district court will be obliged to provide.

The impediment that an absolute, unqualified privilege would place in the way of the primary constitutional duty of the Judicial Branch to do justice in criminal prosecutions would plainly conflict with the function of the courts under Art. III. In designing the structure of our Government and dividing and allocating the sovereign power among three co-equal branches, the Framers of the Constitution sought to provide a comprehensive system, but the separate powers were not intended to operate with absolute independence.

To read the Art. II powers of the President as providing an absolute privilege as against a subpoena essential to enforcement of criminal statutes on no more than a generalized claim of the public interest in confidentiality of nonmilitary and non-diplomatic discussions would upset the constitutional balance of "a workable government" and gravely impair the role of the courts under Art. III.

C

Since we conclude that the legitimate needs of the judicial process may outweigh Presidential privilege, it is necessary to resolve those competing interests in a manner that preserves the essential functions of each branch. The right and indeed the duty to resolve that question does not free the Judiciary from according high respect to the representations made on behalf of the President.

The expectation of a President to the confidentiality of his conversations and correspondence, like the claim of confiden-

tiality of judicial deliberations, for example, has all the values to which we accord deference for the privacy of all citizens and, added to those values, is the necessity for protection of the public interest in candid, objective, and even blunt or harsh opinions in Presidential decisionmaking. A President and those who assist him must be free to explore alternatives in the process of shaping policies and making decisions, and to do so in a way many would be unwilling to express except privately. These are the considerations justifying a presumptive privilege for Presidential communications. The privilege is fundamental to the operation of Government, and inextricably rooted in the separation of powers under the Constitution.

But this presumptive privilege must be considered in light of our historic commitment to the rule of law. This is nowhere more profoundly manifest than, in our view, that "the twofold aim [of criminal justice] is that guilt shall not escape or innocence suffer." *Berger v. United States*. We have elected to employ an adversary system of criminal justice in which the parties contest all issues before a court of law. The need to develop all relevant facts in the adversary system is both fundamental and comprehensive. The ends of criminal justice would be defeated if judgments were to be founded on a partial or speculative presentation of the facts.

In this case, the President challenges a subpoena served on him as a third party requiring the production of materials for use in a criminal prosecution; he does so on the claim that he has a privilege against disclosure of confidential communications. He does not place his claim of privilege on the ground they are military or diplomatic secrets. As to these areas of Art. II duties, the courts have traditionally shown the utmost deference to Presidential responsibilities.

No case of the Court, however, has extended this high degree of deference to a President's generalized interest in confidentiality. Nowhere in the Constitution, as we have noted earlier, is there any explicit reference to a privilege of confidentiality, yet to the extent this interest relates to the effective discharge of a President's powers, it is constitutionally based.

The right to the production of all evidence at a criminal trial similarly has constitutional dimensions. The Sixth Amendment explicitly confers upon every defendant in a criminal trial the right "to be confronted with the witnesses against him" and "to have compulsory process for obtaining witnesses in his favor." Moreover, the Fifth Amendment also guarantees that no person shall be deprived of liberty without due process of law. It is the manifest duty of the courts to vindicate those guarantees, and to accomplish that it is essential that all relevant and admissible evidence be produced.

In this case, we must weigh the importance of the general privilege of confidentiality of Presidential communications in performance of the President's responsibilities against the inroads of such a privilege on the fair administration of criminal justice. The interest in preserving confidentiality is weighty indeed, and entitled to great respect. However, we cannot conclude that advisers will be moved to temper the candor of their remarks by the infrequent occasions of disclosure because of the possibility that such conversations will be called for in the context of a criminal prosecution.

On the other hand, the allowance of the privilege to withhold evidence that is demonstrably relevant in a criminal trial would cut deeply into the guarantee of due process of law and gravely impair the basic function of the court. A President's acknowledged need for confidentiality in the communications of his office is general in nature, whereas the constitutional need for production of relevant evidence in a criminal proceeding is specific and central to the fair adjudication of a particular criminal case in the administration of justice. Without access to specific facts, a criminal prosecution may be totally frustrated. The President's broad interest in confidentiality of communications will not be vitiated by disclosure of a limited number of conversations preliminarily shown to have some bearing on the pending criminal cases.

We conclude that, when the ground for asserting privilege as to subpoenaed materials sought for use in a criminal trial is based only on the generalized interest in confidentiality, it cannot prevail over the fundamental demands of due process of law in the fair administration of criminal justice. The generalized assertion of privilege must yield to the demonstrated, specific need for evidence in a pending criminal trial.

NIXON v. FITZGERALD

457 U.S. 731 (1982)

Opinion: Powell, joined by Burger, Rehnquist, Stevens, O'Connor
Concurrence: Burger
Dissent: White, joined by Brennan, Marshall, Blackmun
Dissent: Blackmun, joined by Brennan, Marshall

This case concerns the extent to which the president is immune from civil suit for actions made by him in his official capacity. It suggests a variety of questions. Is the president personally liable for the decisions he makes? Is it possible to distinguish adequately between the president as a person and the president as an officer of government? Do public needs, as the Court seems to suggest, justify the denial of civil claims brought against the president by private individuals?

JUSTICE POWELL *delivered the opinion of the Court.*

The plaintiff in this lawsuit seeks relief in civil damages from a former President of the United States. The claim rests on actions allegedly taken in the former President's official capacity during his tenure in office. The issue before us is the scope of the immunity possessed by the President of the United States.

I

In January, 1970 the respondent A. Ernest Fitzgerald lost his job as a management analyst with the Department of the Air Force. Fitzgerald's dismissal occurred in the context of a departmental reorganization and reduction in force, in which his job was eliminated. In announcing the reorganization, the Air Force characterized the action as taken to promote economy and efficiency in the Armed Forces.

Respondent's discharge attracted unusual attention in Congress and in the press. Fitzgerald had attained national prominence approximately one year earlier, during the waning months of the Presidency of Lyndon B. Johnson. On November 13, 1968, Fitzgerald appeared before the Subcommittee on Economy in Government of the Joint Economic Committee of the United States Congress. To the evident embarrassment of his superiors in the Department of Defense, Fitzgerald testified that cost-overruns on the CA transport plane could approximate $2 billion. He also revealed that unexpected technical difficulties had arisen during the development of the aircraft.

Concerned that Fitzgerald might have suffered retaliation for his congressional testimony, the Subcommittee on Economy in Government convened public hearings on Fitzgerald's dismissal. The press reported those hearings prominently, as it had the earlier announcement that his job was being eliminated by the Department of Defense. At a news conference on December 8, 1969, President Richard Nixon was queried about Fitzgerald's impending separation from Government service. The President responded by promising to look into the matter. Shortly after the news conference, the petitioner asked White House Chief of Staff H.R. Haldeman to arrange for Fitzgerald's assignment to another job within the administration. It also appears that the President suggested to Budget Director Robert Mayo that Fitzgerald might be offered a position in the Bureau of the Budget.

Fitzgerald's proposed reassignment encountered resistance within the administration. In an internal memorandum of January 20, 1970, White House aide Alexander Butterfield reported to Haldeman that "Fitzgerald is no doubt a top-notch cost expert, but he must be given very low marks in loyalty; and after all, loyalty is the name of the game." Butterfield therefore recommended that "[w]e should let him bleed, for a while at least." There is no evidence of White House efforts to reemploy Fitzgerald subsequent to the Butterfield memorandum.

Absent any offer of alternative federal employment, Fitzgerald complained to the Civil Service Commission. In a letter of January 20, 1970, he alleged that his separation represented unlawful retaliation for his truthful testimony before a congressional Committee. The Commission convened a closed hearing on Fitzgerald's allegations on May 4, 1971.

After hearing over 4,000 pages of testimony, the Chief Examiner for the Civil

Service Commission issued his decision in the Fitzgerald case on September 18, 1973. The Examiner held that Fitzgerald's dismissal had offended applicable civil service regulations. The Examiner based this conclusion on a finding that the departmental reorganization in which Fitzgerald lost his job, though purportedly implemented as an economy measure, was in fact motivated by "reasons purely personal to" respondent. As this was an impermissible basis for a reduction in force, the Examiner recommended Fitzgerald's reappointment to his old position or to a job of comparable authority.

Following the Commission's decision, Fitzgerald filed a suit for damages in the United States District Court. In it, he raised essentially the same claims presented to the Civil Service Commission. . . .

IV

Here a former President asserts his immunity from civil damages claims of two kinds. He stands named as a defendant in a direct action under the Constitution and in two statutory actions under federal laws of general applicability. In neither case has Congress taken express legislative action to subject the President to civil liability for his official acts.

Applying the principles of our cases to claims of this kind, we hold that petitioner, as a former President of the United States, is entitled to absolute immunity from damages liability predicated on his official acts. We consider this immunity a functionally mandated incident of the President's unique office, rooted in the constitutional tradition of the separation of powers and supported by our history.

A

The President occupies a unique position in the constitutional scheme. Article II, §1, of the Constitution provides that "[t]he executive Power shall be vested in a President of the United States. . . ." This grant of authority establishes the President as the chief constitutional officer of the Executive Branch, entrusted with supervisory and policy responsibilities of utmost discretion and sensitivity.

In arguing that the President is entitled only to qualified immunity, the respondent relies on cases in which we have recognized immunity of this scope for governors and cabinet officers. We find these cases to be inapposite. The President's unique status under the Constitution distinguishes him from other executive officials.

Because of the singular importance of the President's duties, diversion of his energies by concern with private lawsuits would raise unique risks to the effective functioning of government. As is the case with prosecutors and judges—for whom absolute immunity now is established— a President must concern himself with matters likely to "arouse the most intense feelings." Yet, as our decisions have recognized, it is in precisely such cases that there exists the greatest public interest in providing an official "the maximum ability to deal fearlessly and impartially with" the duties of his office. This concern is compelling where the officeholder must make the most sensitive and far-reaching decisions entrusted to any official under our constitutional system. Nor can the sheer prominence of the President's office be ignored. In view of the visibility of his office and the effect of his actions on countless people, the President would be an easily identifiable target for suits for civil damages. Cognizance of this personal vulnerability frequently could distract a President from his public duties, to the detriment of not only the President and his office but also the Nation that the Presidency was designed to serve.

B

Courts traditionally have recognized the President's constitutional responsibilities and status as factors counseling judicial deference and restraint. For example, while courts generally have looked to the common law to determine the scope of an official's evidentiary privilege, we have recognized that the Presidential privilege is "rooted in the separation of powers under the Constitution." *United States v. Nixon*. It is settled law that the separation of powers doctrine does not bar every exercise of jurisdiction over the President of the United States. But our cases also have established that a court, before exercising jurisdiction, must balance the constitutional weight of the interest to be served against the dangers of intrusion on the authority and functions of the Executive Branch. When judicial action is needed to serve broad public interests—as when the Court acts not in derogation of the separation of powers, but to maintain their proper balance, *cf. Youngstown Sheet & Tube Co. v. Sawyer*, *supra*, or to vindicate the public interest in an ongoing criminal prosecution, *see United States v. Nixon*, *supra*—the exercise of jurisdiction has been held warranted. In the case of this merely private suit for damages based on a President's official acts, we hold it is not.

C

In defining the scope of an official's absolute privilege, this Court has recognized that the sphere of protected action must be related closely to the immunity's justifying purposes. Frequently our decisions have held that an official's absolute immunity should extend only to acts in performance of particular functions of his office. But the Court also has refused to draw functional lines finer than history and reason would support. In view of the special nature of the President's constitutional office and functions, we think it appropriate to recognize absolute Presidential immunity from damages liability for acts within the "outer perimeter" of his official responsibility.

It clearly is within the President's constitutional and statutory authority to prescribe the manner in which the Secretary will conduct the business of the Air Force. Because this mandate of office must include the authority to prescribe reorganizations and reductions in force, we conclude that petitioner's alleged wrongful acts lay well within the outer perimeter of his authority.

V

A rule of absolute immunity for the President will not leave the Nation without sufficient protection against misconduct on the part of the Chief Executive. There remains the constitutional remedy of impeachment. In addition, there are formal and informal checks on Presidential action that do not apply with equal force to other executive officials. The President is subjected to constant scrutiny by the press. Vigilant oversight by Congress also may serve to deter Presidential abuses of office, as well as to make credible the threat of impeachment. Other incentives to avoid misconduct may include a desire to earn reelection, the need to maintain prestige as an element of Presidential influence, and a President's traditional concern for his historical stature.

The existence of alternative remedies and deterrents establishes that absolute immunity will not place the President "above the law." For the President, as for judges and prosecutors, absolute immunity merely precludes a particular private remedy for alleged misconduct in order to advance compelling public ends.

JUSTICE WHITE, *with whom* **JUSTICE BRENNAN**, **JUSTICE MARSHALL**, *and* **JUSTICE BLACKMUN** *join, dissenting.*

... The Court intimates that its decision is grounded in the Constitution. If that is the case, Congress cannot provide a remedy against Presidential misconduct, and the criminal laws of the United States are wholly inapplicable to the President. I find this approach completely unacceptable. I do not agree that, if the Office of President is to operate effectively, the holder of that Office must be permitted, without fear of liability and regardless of the function he is performing, deliberately to inflict injury on others by conduct that he knows violates the law....

Attaching absolute immunity to the Office of the President, rather than to particular activities that the President might perform, places the President above the law. It is a reversion to the old notion that the King can do no wrong....

IV

The majority may be correct in its conclusion that "[a] rule of absolute immunity ... will not leave the Nation without sufficient protection against misconduct on the part of the Chief Executive." ... Such a rule will, however, leave Mr. Fitzgerald without an adequate remedy for the harms that he may have suffered. More importantly, it will leave future plaintiffs without a remedy, regardless of the substantiality of their claims. The remedies in which the Court finds comfort were never designed to afford relief for individual harms. Rather, they were designed as political safety valves. Politics and history, however, are not the domain of the courts; the courts exist to assure each individual that he, as an individual, has enforceable rights that he may pursue to achieve a peaceful redress of his legitimate grievances.

I find it ironic, as well as tragic, that the Court would so casually discard its own role of assuring "the right of every individual to claim the protection of the laws," *Marbury v. Madison*, in the name of protecting the principle of separation of powers. Accordingly, I dissent.

CLINTON v. JONES

520 U.S. 681 (1997)

Opinion: Stevens, joined by Rehnquist, O'Connor, Scalia, Kennedy, Souter, Thomas, Ginsburg
Concurrence: Breyer

This case deals with the question of whether suits may be brought against the president for offenses allegedly committed before his entrance into office. The Court decided that the president was not immune from such suits. Is there a tension between the decision in this case and the Court's decision in Nixon v. Fitzgerald? *Lawsuits against the president inevitably require a great deal of attention from the administration. Would the nation be better served if civil suits against the president were delayed until after completion of his term of office, or is it best to ensure that he be held immediately accountable for prior actions?*

JUSTICE STEVENS *delivered the opinion of the Court.*

This case raises a constitutional and a prudential question concerning the Office of the President of the United States. Respondent, a private citizen, seeks to recover damages from the current occupant of that office based on actions allegedly taken before his term began. The President submits that in all but the most exceptional cases the Constitution requires federal courts to defer such litigation until his term ends and that, in any event, respect for the office warrants such a stay. Despite the force of the arguments supporting the President's submissions, we conclude that they must be rejected.

Petitioner, William Jefferson Clinton, was elected to the Presidency in 1992, and re-elected in 1996. His term of office expires on January 20, 2001. In 1991 he was the Governor of the State of Arkansas. Respondent, Paula Corbin Jones, is a resident of California. In 1991 she lived in Arkansas, and was an employee of the Arkansas Industrial Development Commission.

On May 6, 1994, she commenced this action in the United States District Court for the Eastern District of Arkansas by filing a complaint naming petitioner and Danny Ferguson, a former Arkansas State Police officer, as defendants. As the case comes to us, we are required to assume the truth of the detailed—but as yet untested—factual allegations in the complaint.

Those allegations principally describe events that are said to have occurred on the afternoon of May 8, 1991, during an official conference held at the Excelsior Hotel in Little Rock, Arkansas. The Governor delivered a speech at the conference; respondent—working as a state employee—staffed the registration desk. She alleges that Ferguson persuaded her to leave her desk and to visit the Governor in a business suite at the hotel, where he made "abhorrent" sexual advances that she vehemently rejected. She further claims that her superiors at work subsequently

dealt with her in a hostile and rude manner, and changed her duties to punish her for rejecting those advances. Finally, she alleges that after petitioner was elected President, Ferguson defamed her by making a statement to a reporter that implied she had accepted petitioner's alleged overtures, and that various persons authorized to speak for the President publicly branded her a liar by denying that the incident had occurred.

Respondent seeks actual damages of $75,000, and punitive damages of $100,000. With the exception of the last charge, which arguably may involve conduct within the outer perimeter of the President's official responsibilities, it is perfectly clear that the alleged misconduct of petitioner was unrelated to any of his official duties as President of the United States and, indeed, occurred before he was elected to that office.

In response to the complaint, petitioner promptly advised the District Court that he intended to file a motion to dismiss on grounds of Presidential immunity, and requested the court to defer all other pleadings and motions until after the immunity issue was resolved.

Petitioner's principal submission—that "in all but the most exceptional cases," the Constitution affords the President temporary immunity from civil damages litigation arising out of events that occurred before he took office—cannot be sustained on the basis of precedent.

Only three sitting Presidents have been defendants in civil litigation involving their actions prior to taking office. Complaints against Theodore Roosevelt and Harry Truman had been dismissed before they took office; the dismissals were affirmed after their respective inaugurations. Two companion cases arising out of an automobile accident were filed against John F.

Kennedy in 1960 during the Presidential campaign. After taking office, he unsuccessfully argued that his status as Commander in Chief gave him a right to a stay under the Soldiers' and Sailors' Civil Relief Act of 1940. The motion for a stay was denied by the District Court, and the matter was settled out of court. Thus, none of those cases sheds any light on the constitutional issue before us.

The principal rationale for affording certain public servants immunity from suits for money damages arising out of their official acts is inapplicable to unofficial conduct. In cases involving prosecutors, legislators, and judges we have repeatedly explained that the immunity serves the public interest in enabling such officials to perform their designated functions effectively without fear that a particular decision may give rise to personal liability.

That rationale provided the principal basis for our holding that a former President of the United States was "entitled to absolute immunity from damages liability predicated on his official acts," *Fitzgerald*, (citing *Ferri v. Ackerman*). Our central concern was to avoid rendering the President "unduly cautious in the discharge of his official duties."

This reasoning provides no support for an immunity for *unofficial* conduct. As we explained in *Fitzgerald*, "the sphere of protected action must be related closely to the immunity's justifying purposes." Because of the President's broad responsibilities, we recognized in that case an immunity from damages claims arising out of official acts extending to the "outer perimeter of his authority." But we have never suggested that the President, or any other official, has an immunity that extends beyond the scope of any action taken in an official capacity.

Moreover, when defining the scope of an immunity for acts clearly taken *within* an official capacity, we have applied a functional approach. "Frequently our decisions have held that an official's absolute immunity should extend only to acts in performance of particular functions of his office." Hence, for example, a judge's absolute immunity does not extend to actions performed in a purely administrative capacity. As our opinions have made clear, immunities are grounded in "the nature of the function performed, not the identity of the actor who performed it."

Petitioner's effort to construct an immunity from suit for unofficial acts grounded purely in the identity of his office is unsupported by precedent.

Petitioner's strongest argument supporting his immunity claim is based on the text and structure of the Constitution. He does not contend that the occupant of the Office of the President is "above the law," in the sense that his conduct is entirely immune from judicial scrutiny. The President argues merely for a postponement of the judicial proceedings that will determine whether he violated any law. His argument is grounded in the character of the office that was created by Article II of the Constitution, and relies on separation of powers principles that have structured our constitutional arrangement since the founding.

As a starting premise, petitioner contends that he occupies a unique office with powers and responsibilities so vast and important that the public interest demands that he devote his undivided time and attention to his public duties. He submits that— given the nature of the office—the doctrine of separation of powers places limits on the authority of the Federal Judiciary to interfere with the Executive Branch that would be transgressed by allowing this action to proceed.

We have no dispute with the initial premise of the argument. It does not follow, however, that separation of powers principles would be violated by allowing this action to proceed. The doctrine of separation of powers is concerned with the allocation of official power among the three co-equal branches of our Government.

Of course the lines between the powers of the three branches are not always neatly defined. But in this case there is no suggestion that the Federal Judiciary is being asked to perform any function that might in some way be described as "executive." Respondent is merely asking the courts to exercise their core Article III jurisdiction to decide cases and controversies. Whatever the outcome of this case, there is no possibility that the decision will curtail the scope of the official powers of the Executive Branch. The litigation of questions that relate entirely to the unofficial conduct of the individual who happens to be the President poses no perceptible risk of misallocation of either judicial power or executive power.

Rather than arguing that the decision of the case will produce either an aggrandizement of judicial power or a narrowing of executive power, petitioner contends that—as a by-product of an otherwise traditional exercise of judicial power—burdens will be placed on the President that will hamper the performance of his official duties. We have recognized that "[e]ven when a branch does not arrogate power to itself . . . the separation of powers doctrine requires that a branch not impair another in the performance of its constitutional duties." *Loving v. United States.* As a factual matter, petitioner contends that this particular case—as well as the potential additional litigation that an affirmance of the Court of Appeals judgment might spawn—may impose an unacceptable burden on the President's time and energy, and thereby impair the effective performance of his office.

Petitioner's predictive judgment finds little support in either history or the relatively narrow compass of the issues raised in this particular case. As we have already noted, in the more than 200-year history of the Republic, only three sitting Presidents have been subjected to suits for their private actions. If the past is any indicator, it seems unlikely that a deluge of such litigation will ever engulf the Presidency. As for the case at hand, if properly managed by the District Court, it appears to us highly unlikely to occupy any substantial amount of petitioner's time.

In sum, "[i]t is settled law that the separation of powers doctrine does not bar every exercise of jurisdiction over the President of the United States." *Fitzgerald.* If the Judiciary may severely burden the Executive Branch by reviewing the legality of the President's official conduct, and if it may direct appropriate process to the President himself, it must follow that the federal courts have power to determine the legality of his unofficial conduct. The burden on the President's time and energy that is a mere by-product of such review surely cannot be considered as onerous as the direct burden imposed by judicial review and the occasional invalidation of his official actions. We therefore hold that the doctrine of separation of powers does not require federal courts to stay all private actions against the President until he leaves office.

We add a final comment on two matters that are discussed at length in the briefs: the risk that our decision will generate a large volume of politically motivated harassing and frivolous litigation, and the danger that national security concerns might prevent the President from explaining a legitimate need for a continuance.

We are not persuaded that either of these risks is serious. Most frivolous and vexatious litigation is terminated at the pleading stage or on summary judgment, with little if any personal involvement by the defendant. Moreover, the availability of sanctions provides a significant deterrent to litigation directed at the President in his unofficial capacity for purposes of political gain or harassment. History indicates that the likelihood that a significant number of such cases will be filed is remote. Although scheduling problems may arise, there is no reason to assume that the District Courts will be either unable to accommodate the President's needs or unfaithful to the tradition—especially in matters involving national security—of giving "the utmost deference to Presidential responsibilities." Several Presidents, including petitioner, have given testimony without jeopardizing the Nation's security. In short, we have confidence in the ability of our federal judges to deal with both of these concerns.

If Congress deems it appropriate to afford the President stronger protection, it may respond with appropriate legislation. As petitioner notes in his brief, Congress has enacted more than one statute providing for the deferral of civil litigation to accommodate important public interests. If the Constitution embodied the rule that the President advocates, Congress, of course, could not repeal it. But our holding today raises no barrier to a statutory response to these concerns.

The Federal District Court has jurisdiction to decide this case. Like every other citizen who properly invokes that jurisdiction, respondent has a right to an orderly disposition of her claims.

JUSTICE BREYER, *concurring in the judgment.*

I agree with the majority that the Constitution does not automatically grant the President an immunity from civil lawsuits based upon his private conduct....

In my view, however, once the President sets forth and explains a conflict between judicial proceeding and public duties, the matter changes. At that point, the Constitution permits a judge to schedule a trial in an ordinary civil damages action (where postponement normally is possible without overwhelming damage to a plaintiff) only within the constraints of a constitutional principle—a principle that forbids a federal judge in such a case to interfere with the President's discharge of his public duties. I have no doubt that the Constitution contains such a principle applicable to civil suits, based upon Article II's vesting of the entire "executive Power" in a single individual, implemented through the Constitution's structural separation of powers, and revealed both by history and case precedent....

This case is a private action for civil damages in which, as the District Court here found, it is possible to preserve evidence and in which later payment of interest can compensate for delay. The District Court in this case determined that the Constitution required the postponement of trial during the sitting President's term. It may well be that the trial of this case cannot take place without significantly interfering with the President's ability to carry out his official duties. Yet, I agree with the majority that there is no automatic temporary immunity and that the President should have to provide the District Court with a reasoned explanation of why the immunity is needed; and I also agree that, in the absence of that explanation, the court's postponement of the trial date was premature. For those reasons, I concur in the result.

SYNTHESIS QUESTIONS FOR FURTHER DISCUSSION: CHAPTER 4 SECTION C

1.   "When the president does it that means it is not illegal." Former President Richard Nixon uttered these words in a famous interview with David Frost in 1977. Do John Locke and Harvey Mansfield agree with this statement? What arguments do they present for it?

2.   The idea of "sovereign immunity" suggests that government officials should not be subject to lawsuits. The idea goes back to a time of monarchy when the monarch was not thought to be bound by the law in a manner similar to the rest of the population. Did the Founders mean to extend the idea of prerogative to U.S. presidents? Is there a justification for such power that does not rest on the idea of monarchy? For instance, *United States v. Nixon* and *Clinton v. Jones* suggest limits on the power of the president to assert executive privilege to be immune from lawsuits. But are there cases in which such limits might in fact impair the president's ability to govern? The president's communications with other White House officials are generally considered part of the public record. Might this hinder the president from speaking as freely as he or she might otherwise?

KEY TERMS

bicameralism: The principle that the legislative branch should be composed of two chambers.

executive privilege: Areas in which the president might be immune or exempt from certain powers of Congress, including the subpoena power.

habeas corpus: The right of all citizens held by the government against their will to be provided with the legal justification for their incarceration; includes the right to be released if a court determines they are held without cause.

justiciable: Adjective describing a controversy that can be adjudicated by the courts.

legislative veto: A statutory mechanism formerly used by Congress to permit overriding an executive agency's action or determination.

line item veto: A proposed presidential power to veto specific sections of a bill, rather than the whole bill.

martial law: The declaration of military rule and the suspension of normal civil liberties in times of emergency.

unitary executive: The notion that the executive power must be held solely by one individual, not a committee. Its modern usage suggests that executive power should not be shared with the legislative branch or with independent agencies in matters such as the appointment and removal of officers. Also a theory associated with presidential control over federal agencies and with expanded presidential power during wartime.

prerogative: The discretionary power of the president not subject to control by legislation.

PART III

LIBERTY

CHAPTER 5

FREE SPEECH

The First Amendment declares that "Congress shall make no law . . . abridging the freedom of speech." Although the provision refers explicitly to Congress, modern-day First Amendment doctrine holds that the protection extends to state and local governments as well, under the doctrine of "incorporation." Given the prominence of free speech in American culture and jurisprudence, some might take it as self-evident that free speech is a right deserving of protection. But this is not obviously the case. The First Amendment has been held to defend ideologies that challenge the legitimacy of the Constitution itself, and of democratic governance. It has been used to protect racist speech and obscene content. Many other democracies, including Germany and the United Kingdom, impose limits upon kinds of speech that are protected by the First Amendment in the United States. Why, we might ask, should communication that offends the very basis of constitutional order be protected?

The controversies in this chapter help to establish the contours of the right to free speech and to test its limits. Before wading into these debates, carefully evaluate the theoretical readings, considering the different lenses they provide when examining the meaning of the Constitution's protection of free speech. What is it, exactly, that makes speech so important? Thinking about its purposes and core values may help you develop a working theory of what kinds of speech are deserving of protection and why.

Throughout this book, we have emphasized the centrality of the meaning of democracy in answering constitutional puzzles. We saw that the question of the Court's democratic credentials was central to discussions about its authority in Chapter 1, and to considerations of how the Constitution should be interpreted in Chapter 2. In Chapters 3 and 4, we evaluated the relative powers both among the branches and between national and state governments in terms of the degree to which their actions are authorized democratically. We move now from the question of powers to a fundamental right enshrined by the Constitution. Rights are sometimes thought of as constitutional constraints on democracy, but the right to free speech itself seems to have many democratic credentials. Without a right to say and hear political arguments, it might not be possible for the people to make fully informed decisions in voting for representatives and on other matters. Some have suggested that the First Amendment free speech provision is a core democratic right that prioritizes the importance of political speech as a means for citizens to be able to consent to law. Do you agree that all political speech must therefore be protected in a democracy? In Section A of this chapter, we will explore the theoretical arguments about the role of political speech under the First Amendment and case law.

In addition to considering the relationship between democracy, political speech, and the First Amendment, you will also consider whether speech that does not have obviously political content should be protected. Consider, for instance, whether artworks should be protected under the Free Speech Clause. Does art have a central place in democracy? Even if it does not, should it be protected? Even further removed from politics, it might be thought, are obscenity and pornography, speech that many believe lacks both artistic and political value. In Section B, you will be asked whether this constitutes "speech" and whether it is worthy of protection.

While pornography and obscenity might be thought to be valueless speech, other kinds of speech might actually be thought to threaten democracy. Consider, for instance, whether revolutionary propaganda that advocates the overthrow of the Constitution should be protected. One fundamental puzzle here is whether the First Amendment protects even those who would advocate its abolition. A different threat to democracy arguably comes from "hate speech." Although it is a fundamental tenet of American constitutionalism enshrined in the Fourteenth Amendment, that all persons are entitled to the equal protection of laws, hate groups often challenge this entitlement to equality under law. Perhaps no symbol in American history has been more hostile to this ideal of equality than the burning of crosses by the Ku Klux Klan. We also consider in Section B whether this expression, which arguably challenges the core of constitutional protections, is in fact protected by the First Amendment.

We begin our readings with the classic defense of free speech offered by John Stuart Mill in *On Liberty*. For Mill, it is not enough for an action to be offensive to justify banning it; rather, the action must cause "harm." Many forms of political speech might be offensive to others, but in Mill's view they should still enjoy protection. His argument is largely "consequentialist," meaning that he tries to show the benefits of the protection of free speech to society as a whole, rather than arguing for this freedom regardless of its effects in practice. In his view, freedom of speech creates what became widely known as a "marketplace of ideas," in which the eventual result is the discovery of truth. Allowing the state to ban speech, he fears, could result in the limitation of true statements, given the inevitable fallibility of the state. For Mill, merely expressing views that are partially true or entirely false, by forcing others to challenge and defend their own views, contributes to the discovery of truth and creates a public benefit. In short, according to Mill, the good consequence of speech is that true ideas will prevail.

Despite Mill's prominence, his views have been subjected to criticism. For instance, Irving Kristol argues that some contributions to debate seem not to have had a positive influence on society but rather to have led to a coarsening of public culture. Others have expressed skepticism toward the idea that there are such things as "true" political beliefs at all.

In addition to Mill's view, we also examine the work of Alexander Meiklejohn. Meiklejohn argues that it would be impossible for society to truly be self-governing if it lacked free speech. He asks us to imagine a town meeting in which participants are barred from speaking based on the content of their arguments. Such a town meeting, he argues, would be undemocratic on the grounds that citizens would be incapable of partaking in the essential processes of self-government. This example is meant to serve as a metaphor for the importance of free speech in the wider democratic process that the Constitution establishes and protects.

As you read through Section A, consider the degree to which the justifications offered for the protection of free speech by Mill and Meiklejohn extend to the particular controversies raised in the cases that follow. For instance, does a right to free speech entail a right to challenge the authority or validity of the Constitution itself? Should "subversive speech" that directly threatens the very foundation of constitutional order be allowed? Moreover, should our free speech arguments be informed by the particular historical context in which we find ourselves? For instance, the Court created a "clear and present danger" test during a period of political upheaval following World War I, when subversive speech seemed to many to threaten national security. Is it a mistake to take such historical factors into consideration when determining the constitutionality of specific speech?

Separate from the arguments of Mill and Meiklejohn, defenders of free speech have pointed to its importance as a mode of personal expression. For some, to allow people to become fully realized human beings, and to promote the value of tolerance in society, the state must respect the right of the individual not only to think freely but to speak freely as well. This justification of free speech goes beyond the realm of political debate and, as Ronald Dworkin suggests, extends to a wide variety of areas of speech. You might consider how Dworkin's arguments could be used to support protecting the kinds of speech that we examine in Section B.

The justification for protection of speech that you find most compelling will inevitably affect your views on how robust a protection the First Amendment should provide in political and other areas of expression that frequently come before the Court. You will be asked to consider not only the reasons you think speech should be protected, but also what kinds of speech should be protected. Your answers will likely differ depending on whether we are examining cases of political speech or issues of obscenity or hate speech. With regard to political speech, the Supreme Court has provided nearly absolute protection. However, it has not extended such a high degree of protection to obscenity. Legal thinkers such as Dworkin argue that we should extend greater protections of speech to obscenity. In contrast to those who defend absolute free speech protections, we also excerpt writings here from thinkers who would limit free speech. In particular, Catharine MacKinnon argues that the value of free speech should be balanced against a concern to ensure respect for equality, especially as it pertains to gender. For MacKinnon, freedom of speech is not absolute, even when it comes to political matters. For her, some limits on "hate speech" are justified in order to guarantee equality. As you develop your own positions on the issues raised in this chapter, you will be asked to consider whether you agree with MacKinnon that freedom of speech should sometimes be limited in the name of equality, or whether you believe instead that speech should be protected regardless of the viewpoint it expresses.

A.   POLITICAL SPEECH

Is protecting political speech fundamental to self-governance? Does it lead to good consequences? Should it ever be limited?

This section begins by exploring different theoretical frameworks for evaluating the freedom of speech. Why should speech be protected as a constitutional right? One way to think about the justifications for securing this liberty would appeal to good consequences, along the lines of the pragmatist view we examined in Chapter 2. However, one might worry that such a view could be vulnerable to failing to protect ideas not considered "good" or "true." But John Stuart Mill defends free speech on the grounds that even the protection of false opinions leads to the discovery of truth. In his view, a vigorous marketplace of ideas, unencumbered by censorship, will allow truth to prevail. In contrast to consequentialist defenses of free speech, Alexander Meiklejohn appeals to democratic justifications more along the lines of proceduralism or the moral reading. Meiklejohn argues that free speech is central to the democratic value of self-government. His metaphor of a town hall meeting assigns a crucial role for political speech in a democracy.

The theoretical readings from Mill and Meiklejohn help us to inquire into the justification for free speech, and they will also help us to evaluate the Supreme Court's doctrine on this subject. As you will see in this section, the Court has come to adopt a position known broadly as "viewpoint neutrality" in regard to free speech protection. A viewpoint, broadly speaking, is an opinion on a particular topic, including opinions about politics. If the Court deems a piece of legislation to be aimed at restricting a particular viewpoint, its modern tendency is to strike down the law. Both Meiklejohn and Mill could be understood to provide support for viewpoint neutrality in arguments against discrimination by the state based on particular opinions that individuals hold. You might also consider how U.S. Supreme Court Justice Hugo Black's absolutist defense of free speech, excerpted here, might serve as a defense of viewpoint neutrality.

In Section B, we examine the Court's more complicated approach to a broader category of restrictions, which it calls "content-based discrimination." Content often has to do with the subject or topic of speech rather than the specific opinion on that topic that is being expressed. Viewpoint-based discrimination is a subset of content-based discrimination in that any law that discriminates based on viewpoint also discriminates based on content, but the reverse is not necessarily true. As you will see, the Court allows in some instances for content discrimination in areas such as obscenity even though it does not tolerate limits on viewpoints.

But the current approach to free speech protection, in particular the doctrine of viewpoint neutrality, has evolved from a different jurisprudence that was less protective of unpopular viewpoints. As our first case selection makes clear, in the early 1900s the Court sought to balance the protection of the expression of viewpoints with the demands of security and the twin threats of fascism and socialism. In *Schenck v. United States*, *Abrams v. United States*, *Whitney v. California*, and *Dennis v. United States*, the Court established and eventually limited the clear and present danger test. According to this test, when deciding whether a limit on the expression of a political viewpoint is legitimate, the Court should take into consideration the actual danger to security posed by the speech in question. As some critics have pointed out, the test therefore tends to allow for the prohibition of dangerous speech only when it is potentially persuasive and successful in producing dangerous outcomes. Specifically, the threat of communism throughout the twentieth century was thought to challenge the basic idea of a Constitution that protects rights. Indeed, the danger of a communist revolution in the United States was thought to be a real possibility. Therefore, in some instances, such as in *Dennis v. United States*, the Court allowed for limits on subversive political speech that threatened revolution in this country. Eventually, the Court's balancing test gave way to a stronger protection of viewpoints and limitations on laws that limited speech based on its content.

Although the clear and present danger test has been abandoned in contemporary constitutional law, the question of balancing between security and free speech protections has reemerged in public debate. As you read this chapter, think about whether political ideologies that justify or advocate terrorism should receive protection under the First Amendment. On the one hand, following Meiklejohn, you might think that all political viewpoints should be protected, because a strong democracy can emerge only when citizens have the option of developing their own political opinions with full information about even subversive ideologies. But does the threat of terrorism in recent years limit the importance of protecting all political speech? For instance, imagine that a very powerful defense of Al-Qaeda's philosophy emerged on the Internet. Imagine further that the video contained only defenses of the ideology of extremist terrorist organizations. If such a video began to win converts, would there be an argument for limiting it? If you believe that the need to protect liberty should not be weighed against security considerations, it might be difficult to allow for such limitations. On the other hand, if you believe that such limits might be important, consider whether there might be some merit to the clear and present danger test. In the United Kingdom, for example, the Terrorism Act 2006 made it illegal to glorify acts of terrorism. In reading the selections in this chapter, consider whether U.K. Prime Minister Gordon Brown's defense of this law is persuasive.

Later, the chapter turns to *Brandenburg v. Ohio*, a case that clearly brought an end to the Court's reliance upon the clear and present danger test. According to the theory advanced in *Brandenburg v. Ohio*, only imminent threats to public order could be banned. Longer term threats, such as those posed by particular ideologies, are not seen as imminent on this standard. The case also raises a broader issue about whether an act of speech might constitute threatening conduct. Clearly, the First Amendment protection of free speech is not meant to extend to all instances of speech. For instance, the famous example of shouting fire in a crowded theater does create an imminent danger. Even though it is speech, it is not—and few would claim that it should be—protected. A related question concerns whether or not conduct could ever qualify as protected "speech." According to recent Supreme Court decisions, although an individual may not say or write anything, an act might still be expressive in nature and therefore protected under the First Amendment Free Speech Clause. The case of *Texas v. Johnson* explores the constitutionality of flag burning. Although flag burning is not speech, *per se*, there is a question as to whether it qualifies as expression of a viewpoint under the First Amendment.

We also consider two cases about the right to a free press, which is not only mentioned explicitly in the First Amendment but is intricately tied to the freedom of speech itself. In reading these cases, consider how Meiklejohn's argument about the necessity of freedom of speech for democracy extends to a right of citizens to know what the government is doing in their name. In *New York Times Co. v. United States*, often called the Pentagon Papers case, the Court considered how to balance this right with concerns about national security. As in *Brandenburg v. Ohio*, however, the Court decided that the fundamental right to know is more important than security concerns. In *New York Times Co. v. Sullivan*, the Court considered not whether the state had illegitimately limited speech but whether personal lawsuits based on the law of libel threaten free expression. Whereas all of the cases up to this point have dealt with the limits of government power, in examining this case consider the ways in which the First Amendment might affect relationships among citizens.

We also consider in this section the role of free speech in the political process. Is it a form of expression to give money as one wishes to a particular candidate? *Buckley v. Valeo* examines this issue. In *Citizens United v. Federal Elections Commission*, the question moved from the kind of speech that is protected to the question of to whom free speech extends, as the Court considered whether corporations have a right to run advertisements in support of or against particular candidates or policies. Ask yourself: Are corporations participants in the political process with rights equal or similar to those of citizens?

John Stuart Mill

ON LIBERTY AND OTHER ESSAYS

Chapter I: Introductory and Chapter II: Of the Liberty of Thought and Discussion

Oxford, England: Oxford University Press (2008)

CHAPTER I

Introductory

The object of this Essay is to assert one very simple principle, as entitled to govern absolutely the dealings of society with the individual in the way of compulsion and control, whether the means used be physical force in the form of legal penalties, or the moral coercion of public opinion. That principle is, that the sole end for which mankind are warranted, individually or collectively in interfering with the liberty of action of any of their number, is self-protection. That the only purpose for which power can be rightfully exercised over any member of a civilized community, against his will, is to prevent harm to others. His own good, either physical or moral, is not a sufficient warrant. He cannot rightfully be compelled to do or forbear because it will be better for him to do so, because it will make him happier, because, in the opinions of others, to do so would be wise, or even right. These are good reasons for remonstrating with him, or reasoning with him, or persuading him, or entreating him, but not for compelling him, or visiting him with any evil, in case he do otherwise. To justify that, the conduct from which it is desired to deter him must be calculated to produce evil to some one else. The only part of the conduct of any one, for which he is amenable to society, is that which concerns others. In the part which merely concerns himself, his independence is, of right, absolute. Over himself, over his own body and mind, the individual is sovereign.

It is, perhaps, hardly necessary to say that this doctrine is meant to apply only to human beings in the maturity of their faculties. We are not speaking of children, or of young persons below the age which the law may fix as that of manhood or womanhood. Those who are still in a state to require being taken care of by others, must be protected against their own actions as well as against external injury....

It is proper to state that I forego any advantage which could be derived to my argument from the idea of abstract right as a thing independent of utility. I regard utility as the ultimate appeal on all ethical questions; but it must be utility in the largest sense, grounded on the permanent interests of man as a progressive being. Those interests, I contend, authorize the subjection of individual spontaneity to external control, only in respect to those actions of each, which concern the interest of other people. If any one does an act hurtful to others, there is a prima facie case for punishing him, by law, or, where legal penalties are not safely applicable, by general disapprobation. There are also many positive acts for the benefit of others, which he may rightfully be compelled to perform; such as, to give evidence in a court of justice; to bear his fair share in the common defence, or in any other joint work necessary to the interest of the society of which he enjoys the protection; and to perform certain acts of individual beneficence, such as saving a fellow-creature's life, or interposing to protect the defenceless against ill-usage, things which whenever it is obviously a man's duty to do, he may rightfully be made responsible to society for not doing. A person may cause evil to others not only by his actions but by his inaction, and in neither case he is justly accountable to them for the injury. The latter case, it is true, requires a much more cautious exercise of compulsion than the former. To make any one answerable for doing evil to others, is the rule; to make him answerable for not preventing evil, is, comparatively speaking, the exception. Yet there are many cases clear enough and grave enough to justify that exception. In all things which regard the external relations of the individual, he is de jure amenable to those whose interests are concerned, and if need be, to society as their protector. There are often good reasons for not holding him to the responsibility; but these reasons must arise from the special expediencies of the case: either because it is a kind of case in which he is on the whole likely to act better, when left to his own discretion, than when controlled in any way in which society have it in their power to control him; or because the attempt to exercise control would produce other evils, greater than those which it would prevent. When such reasons as these preclude the enforcement of responsibility, the conscience of the agent himself should step into the vacant judgment-seat, and protect those interests of others which have no external protection; judging himself all the more rigidly, because the case does not admit of his being made accountable to the judgment of his fellow creatures.

But there is a sphere of action in which society, as distinguished from the individual, has, if any, only an indirect interest; comprehending all that portion of a person's life and conduct which affects only himself, or, if it also affects others, only with their free, voluntary, and undeceived consent and participation. When I say only himself, I mean directly, and in the first instance: for whatever affects himself, may affect others through himself; and the objection which may be grounded on this contingency, will receive consideration in the sequel. This, then, is the appropriate region of human liberty. It comprises, first, the inward domain of consciousness; demanding liberty of conscience, in the most comprehensive sense; liberty of thought and feeling; absolute freedom of opinion and sentiment on all subjects, practical or speculative, scientific, moral, or theological. The liberty of expressing and publishing opinions may seem to fall under a different principle, since it belongs to that part of the conduct of an individual which concerns other people; but, being almost of as much importance as the liberty of thought itself, and resting in great part on the same reasons, is practically inseparable from it. Secondly, the principle requires liberty of tastes and pursuits; of framing the plan of our life to suit our own character; of doing as we like, subject to such consequences as may follow; without impediment from our fellow-creatures, so long as what we do does not harm them even though they should think our conduct foolish, perverse, or wrong. Thirdly, from this liberty of each individual, follows the liberty, within the same limits, of combination among individuals; freedom to unite, for any purpose not involving harm to others: the persons combining being supposed to be of full age, and not forced or deceived.

No society in which these liberties are not, on the whole, respected, is free, whatever may be its form of government; and none is completely free in which they do not exist absolute and unqualified. The only freedom which deserves the name, is that of pursuing our own good in our own way, so long as we do not attempt to deprive others of theirs, or impede their efforts to obtain it. Each is the proper guardian of his own health, whether bodily, or mental or spiritual. Mankind are greater gainers by suffering each other to live as seems good to themselves, than by compelling each to live as seems good to the rest. . . .

CHAPTER II

Of the Liberty of Thought and Discussion

When we consider either the history of opinion, or the ordinary conduct of human life, to what is it to be ascribed that the one and the other are no worse than they are? Not certainly to the inherent force of the human understanding; for, on any matter not self-evident, there are ninety-nine persons totally incapable of judging of it, for one who is capable; and the capacity of the hundredth person is only comparative; for the majority of the eminent men of every past generation held many opinions now known to be erroneous, and did or approved numerous things which no one will now justify. Why is it, then, that there is on the whole a preponderance among mankind of rational opinions and rational conduct? If there really is this preponderance—which there must be, unless human affairs are, and have always been, in an almost desperate state—it is owing to a quality of the human mind, the source of everything respectable in man, either as an intellectual or as a moral being, namely, that his errors are corrigible. He is capable of rectifying his mistakes by discussion and experience. Not by experience alone. There must be discussion, to show how experience is to be interpreted. Wrong opinions and practices gradually yield to fact and argument: but facts and arguments, to produce any effect on the mind, must be brought before it. Very few facts are able to tell their own story, without comments to bring out their meaning. The whole strength and value, then, of human judgment, depending on the one property, that it can be set right when it is wrong, reliance can be placed on it only when the means of setting it right are kept constantly at hand. In the case of any person whose judgment is really deserving of confidence, how has it become so? Because he has kept his mind open to criticism of his opinions and conduct. Because it has been his practice to listen to all that could be said against him; to profit by as much of it as was just, and expound to himself, and upon occasion to others, the fallacy of what was fallacious. Because he has felt, that the only way in which a human being can make some approach to knowing the whole of a subject, is by hearing what can be said about it by persons of every variety of opinion, and studying all modes in which it can be looked at by every character of mind. No wise man ever acquired his wisdom in any mode but this; nor is it in the nature of human intellect to become wise in any other manner. The steady habit of correcting and completing his own opinion by collating it with those of others, so far from causing doubt and hesitation in carrying it into practice, is the only stable foundation for a just reliance on it: for, being cognizant of all that can, at least obviously, be said against him, and having taken up his position against all gainsayers knowing that he has sought for objections and difficulties, instead of avoiding them, and has shut out no light which can be thrown upon the subject from any quarter—he has a right to think his judgment better than that of any person, or any multitude, who have not gone through a similar process.

But, indeed, the dictum that truth always triumphs over persecution, is one of those pleasant falsehoods which men repeat after one another till they pass into commonplaces, but which all experience refutes. History teems with instances of truth put down by persecution. If not suppressed forever, it may be thrown back for centuries. To speak only of religious opinions: the Reformation broke out at least twenty times before Luther, and was put down. Arnold of Brescia was put down. Fra Dolcino was put down. Savonarola was put down. The Albigeois were put down. The Vaudois were put down. The Lollards were put down. The Hussites were put down. Even after the era of Luther, wherever persecution was persisted in, it was successful. In Spain, Italy, Flanders, the Austrian empire, Protestantism was rooted out; and, most likely, would have been so in England, had Queen Mary lived, or Queen Elizabeth died. Persecution has always succeeded, save where the heretics were too strong a party to be effectually persecuted. No reasonable person can doubt that Christianity might have been extirpated in the Roman empire. It spread, and became predominant, because the persecutions were only occasional, lasting but a short time, and separated by long intervals of almost undisturbed propagandism. It is a piece of idle sentimentality that truth, merely as truth, has any inherent power denied to error, of prevailing against the dungeon and the stake. Men are not more zealous for truth than they often are for error, and a sufficient application of legal or even of social penalties will generally succeed in stopping the propagation of either. The real advantage which truth has, consists in this, that when an opinion is true, it may be extinguished once, twice, or many times, but in the course of ages there will generally be found persons to rediscover it, until some one of its reappearances falls on a time when from favourable circumstances it escapes persecution until it has made such head as to withstand all subsequent attempts to suppress it. . . .

Let us now pass to the second division of the argument, and dismissing the supposition that any of the received opinions may be false, let us assume them to be true, and examine into the worth of the manner in which they are likely to be held, when their truth is not freely and openly canvassed. However unwillingly a person who has a strong opinion may admit the possibility that his opinion may be false, he ought to be moved by the consideration that however true it may be, if it is not fully, frequently, and fearlessly discussed, it will be held as a dead dogma, not a living truth.

There is a class of persons (happily not quite so numerous as formerly) who think it enough if a person assents undoubtingly to what they think true, though he has no knowledge whatever of the grounds of the opinion, and could not make a tenable defence of it against the most superficial objections. Such persons, if they can once get their creed taught from authority, naturally think that no good, and some harm, comes of its being allowed to be questioned. Where their influence prevails, they make it nearly impossible for the received opinion to be rejected wisely and considerately, though it may still be rejected rashly and ignorantly; for to shut out discussion entirely is seldom possible, and when it once gets in, beliefs not grounded on conviction are apt to give way before the slightest semblance of an argument. Waiving, however, this possibility—assuming that the true opinion abides in the mind, but abides as a prejudice, a belief independent of, and proof against, argument—this is not the way in which truth ought to be held by a rational being. This is not knowing the truth. Truth, thus held, is but one superstition the more, accidentally clinging to the words which enunciate a truth.

If the intellect and judgment of mankind ought to be cultivated, a thing which Protestants at least do not deny, on what can these faculties be more appropriately exercised by any one, than on the things which concern him so much that it is considered necessary for him to hold opinions on them? If the cultivation of the understanding consists in one thing more than in another, it is surely in learning the grounds of one's own opinions. Whatever people believe, on subjects on which it is of the first importance to believe rightly, they ought to be able to defend against at least the common objections. But, some one may say, "Let them be taught the grounds of their opinions. It does not follow that opinions must be merely parroted because they are never heard controverted. Persons who learn geometry do not simply commit the theorems to memory, but understand and learn likewise the demonstrations; and it would be absurd to say that they remain ignorant of the grounds of geometrical truths, because they never hear any one deny, and attempt to disprove them." Undoubtedly, and such teaching suffices on a subject like mathematics, where there is nothing at all to be said on the wrong side of the question. The peculiarity of the evidence of mathematical truths is, that all the argument is on one side. There are no objections, and no answers to objections. But on every subject on which difference of opinion is possible, the truth depends on a balance to be struck between two sets of conflicting reasons. Even in natural philosophy, there is always some other explanation possible of the same facts; some geocentric theory instead of heliocentric, some phlogiston instead of oxygen; and it has to be shown why that other theory cannot

be the true one: and until this is shown and until we know how it is shown, we do not understand the grounds of our opinion. But when we turn to subjects infinitely more complicated, to morals, religion, politics, social relations, and the business of life, three-fourths of the arguments for every disputed opinion consist in dispelling the appearances which favor some opinion different from it. The greatest orator, save one, of antiquity, has left it on record that he always studied his adversary's case with as great, if not with still greater, intensity than even his own. What Cicero practised as the means of forensic success, requires to be imitated by all who study any subject in order to arrive at the truth. He who knows only his own side of the case, knows little of that. His reasons may be good, and no one may have been able to refute them. But if he is equally unable to refute the reasons on the opposite side; if he does not so much as know what they are, he has no ground for preferring either opinion. The rational position for him would be suspension of judgment, and unless he contents himself with that, he is either led by authority, or adopts, like the generality of the world, the side to which he feels most inclination. Nor is it enough that he should hear the arguments of adversaries from his own teachers, presented as they state them, and accompanied by what they offer as refutations. This is not the way to do justice to the arguments, or bring them into real contact with his own mind. He must be able to hear them from persons who actually believe them; who defend them in earnest, and do their very utmost for them. He must know them in their most plausible and persuasive form; he must feel the whole force of the difficulty which the true view of the subject has to encounter and dispose of, else he will never really possess himself of the portion of truth which meets and removes that difficulty. Ninety-nine in a hundred of what are called educated men are in this condition, even of those who can argue fluently for their opinions. Their conclusion may be true, but it might be false for anything they know: they have never thrown themselves into the mental position of those who think differently from them, and considered what such persons may have to say; and consequently they do not, in any proper sense of the word, know the doctrine which they themselves profess. They do not know those parts of it which explain and justify the remainder; the considerations which show that a fact which seemingly conflicts with another is reconcilable with it, or that, of two apparently strong reasons, one and not the other ought to be preferred. All that part of the truth which turns the scale, and decides the judgment of a completely informed mind, they are strangers to; nor is it ever really known, but to those who have attended equally and impartially to both sides, and endeavored to see the reasons of both in the strongest light. So essential is this discipline to a real understanding of moral and human subjects, that if opponents of all important truths do not exist, it is indispensable to imagine them and supply them with the strongest arguments which the most skilful devil's advocate can conjure up.

If, however, the mischievous operation of the absence of free discussion, when the received opinions are true, were confined to leaving men ignorant of the grounds of those opinions, it might be thought that this, if an intellectual, is no moral evil, and does not affect the worth of the opinions, regarded in their influence on the character. The fact, however, is, that not only the grounds of the opinion are forgotten in the absence of discussion, but too often the meaning of the opinion itself. The words which convey it, cease to suggest ideas, or suggest only a small portion of those they were originally employed to communicate. Instead of a vivid conception and a living belief, there remain only a few phrases retained by rote; or, if any part, the shell and husk only of the meaning is retained, the finer essence being lost. The great chapter in human history which this fact occupies and fills, cannot be too earnestly studied and meditated on.

. . . We have now recognized the necessity to the mental wellbeing of mankind (on which all their other well-being depends) of freedom of opinion, and freedom of the expression of opinion, on four distinct grounds; which we will now briefly recapitulate.

First, if any opinion is compelled to silence, that opinion may, for aught we can certainly know, be true. To deny this is to assume our own infallibility.

Secondly, though the silenced opinion be an error, it may, and very commonly does, contain a portion of truth; and since the general or prevailing opinion on any object is rarely or never the whole truth, it is only by the collision of adverse opinions that the remainder of the truth has any chance of being supplied.

Thirdly, even if the received opinion be not only true, but the whole truth; unless it is suffered to be, and actually is, vigorously and earnestly contested, it will, by most of those who receive it, be held in the manner of a prejudice, with little comprehension or feeling of its rational grounds. And not only this, but, fourthly, the meaning of the doctrine itself will be in danger of being lost, or enfeebled, and deprived of its vital effect on the character and conduct: the dogma becoming a mere formal profession, inefficacious for good, but cumbering the ground, and preventing the growth of any real and heartfelt conviction, from reason or personal experience.

Before quitting the subject of freedom of opinion, it is fit to take notice of those who say, that the free expression of all opinions should be permitted, on condition that the manner be temperate, and do not pass the bounds of fair discussion. Much might be said on the impossibility of fixing where these supposed bounds are to be placed; for if the test be offence to those whose opinion is attacked, I think experience testifies that this offence is given whenever the attack is telling and powerful, and that every opponent who pushes them hard, and whom they find it difficult to answer, appears to them, if he shows any strong feeling on the subject, an intemperate opponent. But this, though an important consideration in a practical point of view, merges in a more fundamental objection. Undoubtedly the manner of asserting an opinion, even though it be a true one, may be very objectionable, and may justly incur severe censure. But the principal offences of the kind are such as it is mostly impossible, unless by accidental self-betrayal, to bring home to conviction. The gravest of them is, to argue sophistically, to suppress facts or arguments, to misstate the elements of the case, or misrepresent the opposite opinion. But all this, even to the most aggravated degree, is so continually done in perfect good faith, by persons who are not considered, and in many other respects may not deserve to be considered, ignorant or incompetent, that it is rarely possible on adequate grounds conscientiously to stamp the misrepresentation as morally culpable; and still less could law presume to interfere with this kind of controversial misconduct. With regard to what is commonly meant by intemperate discussion, namely, invective, sarcasm, personality, and the like, the denunciation of these weapons would deserve more sympathy if it were ever proposed to interdict them equally to both sides; but it is only desired to restrain the employment of them against the prevailing opinion: against the unprevailing they may not only be used without general disapproval, but will be likely to obtain for him who uses them the praise of honest zeal and righteous indignation. Yet whatever mischief arises from their use, is greatest when they are employed against the comparatively defenceless; and whatever unfair advantage can be derived by any opinion from this mode of asserting it, accrues almost exclusively to received opinions. The worst offence of this kind which can be committed by a polemic, is to stigmatize those who hold the contrary opinion as bad and immoral men. To calumny of this sort, those who hold any unpopular opinion are peculiarly exposed, because they are in general few and uninfluential, and nobody but themselves feels much interest in seeing justice done them; but this weapon is, from the nature of the case, denied to those who attack a prevailing opinion: they can neither use it with safety to themselves, nor if they could, would it do anything but recoil on their own cause. In general, opinions contrary to those commonly received can only obtain a hearing by studied moderation of language, and the most cautious avoidance of unnecessary offence, from which they hardly ever deviate even in a slight degree without losing ground: while unmeasured vituperation employed on the side of the prevailing opinion, really does deter people from professing contrary opinions, and from listening to those who profess them. For the interest, therefore, of truth and justice, it is far more important to restrain this employment of vituperative language than the other; and, for example, if it were necessary to choose, there would be much more need to discourage offensive attacks on infidelity, than on religion. It is, however, obvious that law and authority have no business with restraining either, while opinion ought, in every instance, to determine its verdict by the circumstances of the individual case; condemning every one, on whichever side of the argument he places himself, in whose mode of advocacy either want of candor, or malignity, bigotry or intolerance of feeling manifest themselves, but not inferring these vices from the side which a person takes, though it be the contrary side of the question to our own; and giving merited honor to every one, whatever opinion he may hold, who has calmness to see and honesty to state what his opponents and their opinions really are, exaggerating nothing to their discredit, keeping nothing back which tells, or can be supposed to tell, in their favor. This is the real morality of public discussion; and if often violated, I am happy to think that there are many controversialists who to a great extent observe it, and a still greater number who conscientiously strive towards it.

Alexander Meiklejohn

FREE SPEECH AND ITS RELATION TO SELF-GOVERNMENT

Chapter 1: The Rulers and the Ruled

Clark, NJ: The Law Book Exchange, Ltd. (2004)

The purpose of these lectures is to consider the freedom of speech which is guaranteed by the Constitution of the United States. The most general thesis of the argument is that, under the Constitution, there are two different freedoms of speech, and, hence, two different guarantees of freedom rather than only one.

More broadly, it may be asserted that our civil liberties, in general, are not all of one kind. They are of two kinds which, though radically different in constitutional status, are easily confused. And that confusion has been and is, disastrous in its effect upon our understanding of the relations between an individual citizen and the government of the United States. The argument of these lectures is an attempt to clear away that confusion.

As an instance of the first kind of civil liberty I would offer that of religious or irreligious belief. In this country of ours, so far as the Constitution is effective, men are free to believe and to advocate or to disbelieve and to argue against, any creed. And the government is unqualifiedly forbidden to restrict that freedom. As an instance of the second kind, we may take the liberty of an individual to own, and to use the income from, his labor or his property. It is agreed among us that every man has a right, a liberty, to such ownership and use. And yet it is also agreed that the government may take whatever part of a man's income it deems necessary for the promoting of the general welfare. The liberty of owning and using property is, then, as contrasted with that of religious belief, a limited one. It may be invaded by the government. And the Constitution authorizes such invasion. It requires only that the procedure shall be properly and impartially carried out and that it shall be justified by public need.

Our Constitution, then, recognizes and protects two different sets of freedoms. One of these is open to restriction the government. The other is not open to such restriction. It would be of great value to our argument and, in fact, to all attempts at political thinking in the United States, if there were available two sharply defined terms by which to identify these two fundamentally different kinds of civil liberty. But, alas, no such accurate use of words has been established among us. Men speak of freedom of belief and the freedom of property as if, in the Constitution, the word "freedom," as used these two cases, had the same meaning. Because of that confusion we are in constant danger of giving to a man's possessions the same dignity, the same status, as we give to the man himself. From that confusion our national life has suffered disastrous effects in all its phases. But for this disease of our minds there is, so far as I know, no specific semantic cure. All that we can do at present is to remember that such terms as liberty, freedom civil rights, etc., are ambiguous. We must, then, in each specific case, try to keep clear what meaning we are using.

I

We Americans think of ourselves as politically free. We believe in self-government. If men are to be governed, we say, then that governing must be done, not by others, but by themselves. So far, therefore, as our own affairs are concerned, we refuse to submit to alien control. That refusal, if need be, we will carry to the point of rebellion, of revolution. And if other men, within jurisdiction of our laws, are denied their right to political freedom, we will, in the same spirit, rise to their defense.

Governments, we insist, derive their just powers from the consent of the governed. If that consent be lacking governments have no just powers.

Now, this political program of ours, though passionately advocated by us, is not—as we all recognize—fully worked out in practice. Over one hundred and seventy years have gone by since the Declaration of Independence was written. But, to an unforgivable degree, citizens of the United States are still subjected to decisions in the making of which they have had no effective share. So far as that is true, we are not governed; we are not politically free. We are governed by others. And, perhaps worse, we are, without their consent, the governors of others.

But a more important point—which we Americans do not so readily recognize—is that of the intellectual difficulties which are inherent in the making and administering of this political program of ours. We do not see how baffling, even to the point of desperation, is the task of using our minds, to which we are summoned by our plan of government. That plan is not intellectually simple. Its victories are chiefly won, not by the carnage of battle, but by the sweat and agony of the mind. By contrast with it, the idea of alien government which we reject—whatever its other merits or defects—is easy to understand. It is suited to simple-minded people who are unwilling or unable to question their own convictions, who would defend their principles by suppressing that hostile criticism which is necessary for their clarification. The intellectual difficulty of which I am speaking is sharply indicated by Professor Edward Hallett Carr, in his recent book, *The Soviet Impact on the Western World*. Mr. Carr tells us that our American political program, as we formulate it, is not merely unclear. It is essentially self-contradictory and hence, nonsensical. "Confusion of thought," he says, "is often caused by the habit common among politicians and writers of the English-speaking world, of defining democracy in formal and conventional terms as 'self-government' or 'government by consent.'" What these terms define, he continues, "is not democracy, but anarchy. Government of some kind is necessary in the common interest precisely because men will not govern themselves. 'Government by consent' is a contradiction in terms; for the purpose of government is to compel people to do what they would not do of their own volition. In short, government is a process by which some people exercise compulsion on others."

Those words of Mr. Carr seem to me radically false. And, whatever else these lectures may do or fail to do, I hope that they may, in some measure, serve as a refutation of his contention. And yet the challenge of so able and well-balanced a mind cannot be ignored. If we believe in our principles we must make clear to others and to ourselves that self-government is not anarchy. We must show in what sense a free man, a free society, does practice self-direction. What, then, is the difference between a political system in which men do govern themselves and a political system in which men, without their consent, are governed by others? Unless we can make clear that distinction, discussion of freedom of speech or of any other freedom is meaningless and futile.

Alien government, we have said, is simple in idea. It is easy to understand. When one man or some self-chosen group holds control, without consent, over others, the relation between them is one of force and counterforce, of compulsion on the one hand and submission or resistance on the other. That relation is external and mechanical. It can be expressed in numbers—numbers of guns or planes or dollars or machines or policemen. The only basic fact is that one group "has the power" and the other group has not. In such a despotism, a ruler, by some excess of strength or guile or both, without the consent of his subjects, forces them into obedience. And in order to understand what he does, what they do, we need only measure the strength or weakness of the control and the strength or weakness of the resistance to it.

But government by consent—self-government—is not thus simple. It is, in fact, so complicated, so confusing, that, not only to the scholarly judgment of Mr. Carr, but also to the simple-mindedness which we call "shrewd, practical, calculating, common sense," it tends to seem silly, unrealistic, romantic, or—to use a favorite term of reproach—"idealistic." And the crux of the difficulty lies in the fact that, in such a society, the governors and the governed are not two distinct groups of persons. There is only one group—the self-governing people. Rulers and ruled are the same individuals. We, the People, are our own masters, our own subjects. But that inner relationship of men to themselves is utterly different in kind from the external relationship of one man to another. It cannot be expressed in terms of forces and compulsions. If we attempt to think about the political procedures of self-government by means of the ideas which are useful in describing the external control of a hammer over a nail or of a master over his slaves, the meaning slips through the fingers of our minds. For thinking which is done merely in terms of forces, political freedom does not exist.

At this point, a protest must be entered against the oversimplified advice which tells us that we should introduce into the realms of economics, politics, and morals the "methods" of the "sciences." Insofar as the advice suggests to us that we keep our beliefs within the limits of the evidence which warrants them, insofar as it tells us that our thinking about human relationships must be as exact and tentative, as orderly and inclusive, as is the work done by students of physical or biological fact, no one may challenge either its validity or its importance. To believe what one has no reason for believing is a crime of the first order. But, on the other hand, it must be urged that the chief source of our blundering ineptness in dealing with moral and political problems is that we do not know how to think about them except by quantitative methods which are borrowed from nonmoral, non-political, non-social sciences. In this sense we need to be, not more scientific, but less scientific, not more quantitative but other than quantitative. We must create and use methods of inquiry, methods of belief which are suitable to the study of men as self-governing persons but not suitable to the study of forces or of machines. In the understanding of a free society, scientific thinking has an essential part to play. But it is a secondary part. We shall not understand the Constitution of the United States if we think of men only as pushed around by forces. We must see them also as governing themselves.

But the statement just made must be guarded against two easy misinterpretations. First, when we say that self-government is hard to interpret, we are not saying that it is mysterious or magical or irrational. Quite the contrary is true. No idea which we have is more sane, more matter-of-fact, more immediately sensible, than that of self-government. Whether it be in the field of individual or of social activity, men are not recognizable as men unless, in any given situation, they are using their minds to give direction to their behavior. But the point which we are making is that

the externalized measuring of the play of forces which serves the purposes of business or of science is wholly unsuited to our dealing with problems of moral or political freedom. And we Americans seem characteristically blind to the distinction. We are at the top of the world in engineering. We are experts in the knowledge and manipulation of measurable forces, whether physical or psychological. We invent and run machines of ever new and amazing power and intricacy. And we are tempted by that achievement to see if we can manipulate men with the same skill and ingenuity. But the manipulation of men is the destruction of self-government. Our skill, therefore, threatens our wisdom. In this respect the United States with its "know-how" is, today, the most dangerous nation in the world.

And, second, what we have said must not be allowed to obscure the fact that a free government, established by common consent, may and often must use force in compelling citizens to obey the laws. Every government, as such, must have external power. It must, in fact, be more powerful than anyone of its citizens, than any group of them. Political freedom does not mean freedom from control. It means self-control. If, for example, a nation becomes involved in war, the government must decide who shall be drafted to leave his family and home, to risk his life, his health, his sanity, upon the battlefield. The government must also levy and collect and expend taxes. In general, it must determine how far and in what ways the customs and privileges of peace are to be swept aside. In all these cases it may be taken for granted that, in a self-governing society, minorities will disagree with the decisions which are made. May a minority man, then, by appeal to the principle of "consent," refuse to submit to military control? May he evade payment of taxes which he thinks unwise or unjust? May he say, "I did not approve of this measure; therefore, as a self-governing man, I claim the right to disobey it?"

Certainly not! At the bottom of every plan of self-government is a basic agreement, in which all the citizens have joined, that all matters of public policy shall be decided by corporate action, that such decisions shall be equally binding on all citizens, whether they agree with them or not, and that, if need be, they shall, by due legal procedure, be enforced upon anyone who refuses to conform to them. The man who rejects that agreement is not objecting to tyranny or despotism. He is objecting to political freedom. He is not a democrat. He is the anarchist of whom Mr. Carr speaks. Self-government is nonsense unless the "self" which governs is able and determined to make its will effective.

2

What, then, is this compact or agreement which underlies any plan for political freedom? It cannot be understood unless we distinguish sharply and persistently between the "submission" of a slave and the "consent" of a free citizen. In both cases it is agreed that obedience shall be required. Even when despotism is so extreme as to be practically indistinguishable from enslavement, a sort of pseudo consent is given by the subjects. When the ruling force is overwhelming, men are driven not only to submit, but also to agree to do so. For the time, at least, they decide to make the best of a bad situation rather than to struggle against hopeless odds. And, coordinate with this "submission" by the People, there are "concessions" by the ruler. For the avoiding of trouble, to establish his power, to manipulate one hostile force against another, he must take

account of the desires and interests of his subjects, must manage to keep them from becoming too rebellious. The granting of such "concessions" and the accepting of them are, perhaps, the clearest evidence that a government is not democratic but is essentially despotic and alien.

But the "consent" of free citizens is radically different in kind from this "submission" of slaves. Free men talk about their government, not in terms of its "favors" but in terms of their "rights." They do not bargain. They reason. Every one of them is, of course, subject to the laws which are made. But if the Declaration of Independence means what it says, if we mean what it says, then no man is called upon to obey a law unless he himself, equally with his fellows, has shared in making it. Under an agreement to which, in the closing words of the Declaration of Independence, "we mutually pledge to each other our Lives, our Fortunes, and our scared Honor," the consent which we give is not forced upon us. It expresses a voluntary compact among political equals. We, the People, acting together, either directly or through our representatives, make and administer law. We, the People, acting in groups or separately, are subject to the law. If we could make that double agreement effective, we would have accomplished the American Revolution. If we could understand that agreement we would understand the Revolution, which is still in the making. But the agreement can have meaning for us only as we clarify the tenuous and elusive distinction between a political "submission" which we abhor and a political "consent" in which we glory. Upon the effectiveness of that distinction rests the entire enormous and intricate structure of those free political institutions which we have pledged ourselves to build. If we can think that distinction clearly, we can be self-governing. If we lose our grip upon it, if, rightly or wrongly, we fall back into the prerevolutionary as alien and hostile to ourselves, nothing can save us from the slavery which, in 1776, we set out to destroy. . . .

3

Our own American constitutional procedure gives striking illustration of the double principle that no free government can submit to control other than its own and that, therefore, it must limit and control itself. For example, our agencies of government do their work under a scheme of mutual checks and balances. The Bill of Rights, also, sharply and explicitly defines boundaries beyond which acts of governing may not go. "Congress shall make no law . . ." it says. And again, "No person shall be held to answer for a capital or otherwise infamous crime unless. . . ." And again, "Excessive bail shall not be required, nor excessive fines imposed, nor cruel and unusual punishments inflicted." All these and many other limits are set to the powers of government. But in every case—let it be noted—these limits are set by government. These enactments were duly proposed, discussed, adopted, interpreted, and enforced by regular political procedure. And, as the years have gone by, We the People, who, by explicit compact, are the government, have maintained and interpreted and extended them. In some cases, we have reinterpreted them or have even abolished them. They are expressions of our own corporate self-control. They tell us that, by compact, explicit or implicit, we are self-governed. . . . That Constitution is based upon a twofold political agreement. It is ordained that all authority to exercise control, to determine common action, belongs to "We, the People." We, and we alone, are the rulers.

But it is ordained also that We, the People, are, all alike, subject to control. Every one of us may be told what he is allowed to do, what he is not allowed to do, what he is required to do. But this agreed-upon requirement of obedience does not transform a ruler into a slave. Citizens do not become puppets of the state when, having created it by common consent, they pledge allegiance to it and keep their pledge. Control by a self-governing nation is utterly different in kind from control by an irresponsible despotism. And to confuse these two is to lose all understanding of what political freedom is. Under actual conditions, there is no freedom for men except by the authority of government. Free men are not non-governed. They are governed—by themselves.

And now, after this long introduction, we are, I hope ready for the task of interpreting the First Amendment to the Constitution, of trying to clear away the confusions by which its meaning has been obscured and even lost.

4

"Congress shall make no law . . . abridging the freedom of speech . . ." says the First Amendment to the Constitution. As we turn now to the interpreting of those words, three preliminary remarks should be made.

First, let it be noted that, by those words, Congress is not debarred from all action upon freedom of speech. Legislation which abridges that freedom is forbidden, but not legislation to enlarge and enrich it. The freedom of mind which befits the members of a self-governing society is not a given and fixed part of human nature. It can be increased and established by learning, by teaching, by the unhindered flow of accurate information, by giving men health and vigor and security, by bringing them together in activities of communication and mutual understanding. And the federal legislature is not forbidden to engage in that positive enterprise of cultivating the general intelligence upon which the success of self-government so obviously depends. On the contrary, in that positive field the Congress of the United States has a heavy and basic responsibility to promote the freedom of speech.

And second, no one who reads with care the text of the First Amendment can fail to be startled by its absoluteness. The phrase, "Congress shall make no law . . . abridging the freedom of speech," is unqualified. It admits of no exceptions. To say that no laws of a given type shall be made means that no laws of that type shall, under any circumstances, be made. That prohibition holds good in war as in peace, in danger as in security. The men who adopted the Bill of Rights were not ignorant of the necessities of war or of national danger. It would, in fact, be nearer to the truth to say that it was exactly those necessities which they had in mind as they planned to defend freedom of discussion against them. Out of their own bitter experience they knew how terror and hatred, how war and strife, can drive men into acts of unreasoning suppression. They planned, therefore, both for the peace which they desired and for the wars which they feared. And in both cases they established an absolute, unqualified prohibition of the abridgment of the freedom of speech. That same requirement, for the same reasons, under the same Constitution, holds good today.

Against what has just been said it will be answered that twentieth-century America does not accept "absolutes" so readily as did the eighteenth century. But to this we must reply that the issue here involved cannot be dealt with by such twentieth-century a priori reasoning. It requires careful examination of the structure and

functioning of our political system as a whole to see what part the principle of the freedom of speech plays, here and now, in that system. And when that examination is made, it seems to me clear that for our day and generation, the words of the First Amendment mean literally what they say. And what they say is that under no circumstances shall the freedom of speech be abridged. Whether or not that opinion can be justified is the primary issue with which this argument tries to deal.

But, third, this dictum which we rightly take to express the most vital wisdom which men have won in their striving for political freedom is yet—it must be admitted—strangely paradoxical. No one can doubt that, in any well-governed society, the legislature has both the right and the duty to prohibit certain forms of speech. Libelous assertions may be, and must be, forbidden and punished. So too must slander. Words which incite men to crime are themselves criminal and must be dealt with as such. Sedition and treason may be expressed by speech or writing. And, in those cases, decisive repressive action by the government is imperative for the sake of the general welfare. All these necessities that speech be limited are recognized and provided for under the Constitution. They were not unknown to the writers of the First Amendment. That amendment, then, we may take it for granted, *does not forbid the abridging of speech*. But, at the same time, *it does forbid the abridging of the freedom of speech*. It is to the solving of that paradox, that apparent self-contradiction, that we are summoned if, as free men, we wish to know what the right of freedom of speech is.

5

As we proceed now to reflect upon the relations of a thinking and speaking individual to the government which guards his freedom, we may do well to turn back for a few moments to the analysis of those relations given by Plato. The Athenian philosopher of the fourth century B.C. was himself caught in our paradox. He saw the connection between self-government and intelligence with a clarity and wisdom and wit which have never been excelled. In his two short dialogues, the *Apology* and the *Crito*, he grapples with the problem which we are facing.

In both dialogues, Plato is considering the fight which a government has to demand obedience from its citizens. And in both dialogues, Socrates, a thinker and teacher who had aroused Plato from dogmatic slumber, is the citizen whose relations are discussed. The question is whether or not Socrates is in duty bound to obey the government. In the *Apology* the answer is "No." In the *Crito* the answer is "Yes." Plato is obviously using one of the favorite devices of the teacher. He is seeming to contradict himself. He is thereby demanding of his pupils that they save themselves and him from contradiction by making clear a basic and elusive distinction.

In the *Apology*, Socrates is on trial for his life. The charge against him is that in his teaching he has "corrupted the youth" and has "denied the Gods." On the evidence presented by a kind of un-Athenian Subversive Activities Committee he is found guilty. His judges do not wish to put him to death, but they warn him that, unless he will agree to stop his teaching or to change its tenor, they must order his execution. And to this demand for obedience to a decree abridging his freedom of speech, Socrates replies with a flat and unequivocal declaration of disobedient independence. My teaching, he says, is not, in that sense, under the abridging control of the government. Athens is a free

city. No official, no judge, he declares, may tell me what I shall, or shall not, teach or think. He recognizes that the government has the power and the legal right to put him to death. But so far as the content of his teaching is concerned, he claims unqualified independence. "Congress shall make no law abridging the freedom of speech," he seems to be saying. Present-day Americans who wish to understand the meaning, the human intention, expressed by the First Amendment, would do well to read and to ponder again Plato's *Apology*, written in Athens twenty-four centuries ago. It may well be argued that if the *Apology* had not been written—by Plato or by someone else—the First Amendment would not have been written. The relation here is one of trunk and branch.

But the argument of the *Crito* seems, at least, to contradict that of the *Apology*. Here Socrates, having been condemned to death, is in prison awaiting the carrying out of the sentence. His friend Crito urges him to escape, to evade the punishment. This he refuses to do. He has no right, he says, to disobey the decision of the government that he must drink the hemlock. That government has legal authority over the life and death of its citizens. Even though it is mistaken, and, therefore, unjust, they must, in this field, conform to its decisions. For Socrates, obedience to the laws which would abridge his life is here quite as imperative as was disobedience to laws which would abridge his belief and the expression of it. In passages of amazing beauty and insight, Socrates explains that duty to Crito. He represents himself as conversing with The Laws of Athens about the compact into which they and he have entered. The Laws, he says, remind him that for seventy years, he has "consented" to them, has accepted from them all the rights and privileges of an Athenian citizen. Will he now, they ask, because his own life is threatened, withdraw his consent, annul the compact? To do that would be a shameful thing, unworthy of a citizen of Athens.

Plato is too great a teacher to formulate for us, or for his more immediate pupils, the distinction which he is here drawing. He demands of us that we make it for ourselves. But that there is a distinction and that the understanding of it is essential for the practice of freedom, he asserts passionately and without equivocation. If the government attempts to limit the freedom of a man's opinions, he tells us, that man and his fellows with him, has both the right and the duty of disobedience. But if, on the other hand, by regular legal procedure, his life or his property are required of him, he must submit; he must let them go willingly. In one phase of a man's activities, the government may exercise control over him. In another phase, it may not. What then, are those two phases? Only as we see clearly the distinction between them, Plato is saying, do we know what government by consent of the governed means.

6

The difficulties of the paradox of freedom as applied to speech may perhaps be lessened if we now examine the procedure of the traditional American town meeting. That institution is commonly, and rightly, regarded as a model by which free political procedures may be measured. It is self-government in its simplest, most obvious form.

In the town meeting the people of a community assemble to discuss and to act upon matters of public interest—roads, schools, poorhouses, health, external defense, and the like. Every man is free to come. They meet as political equals. Each

has a right and a duty to think his own thoughts, to express them, and to listen to the arguments of others. The basic principle is that the freedom of speech shall be unabridged. And yet the meeting cannot even be opened unless, by common consent, speech is abridged. A chairman or moderator is, or has been, chosen. He "calls the meeting to order." And the hush which follows that call is a clear indication that restrictions upon speech have been set up. The moderator assumes, or arranges, that in the conduct of the business, certain rules of order will be observed. Except as he is overruled by the meeting as a whole, he will enforce those rules. His business on its negative side is to abridge speech. For example, it is usually agreed that no one shall speak unless "recognized by the chair." Also, debaters must confine their remarks to "the question before the house." If one man "has the floor," no one else may interrupt him except as provided by the rules. The meeting has assembled, not primarily to talk, but primarily by means of talking to get business done. And the talking must be regulated and abridged as the doing of the business under actual conditions may require. If a speaker wanders from the point at issue, if he is abusive or in other ways threatens to defeat the purpose of the meeting, he may be and should be declared "out of order." He must then stop speaking, at least in that way. And if he persists in breaking the rules, he may be "denied the floor" or, in the last resort, "thrown out" of the meeting. The town meeting, as it seeks for freedom of public discussion of public problems, would be wholly ineffectual unless speech were thus abridged. It is not a Hyde Park. It is a parliament or congress. It is a group of free and equal men, cooperating in a common enterprise, and using for that enterprise responsible and regulated discussion. It is not a dialectical free-for-all. It is self-government.

These speech-abridging activities of the town meeting indicate what the First Amendment to the Constitution does not forbid. When self-governing men demand freedom of speech they are not saying that every individual has an unalienable right to speak whenever, wherever, however he chooses. They do not declare that any man may talk as he pleases, when he pleases, about what he pleases, about whom he pleases, to whom he pleases. The common sense of any reasonable society would deny the existence of that unqualified right. No one, for example, may, without consent of nurse or doctor, rise up in a sickroom to argue for his principles or his candidate. In the sickroom, that question is not "before the house." The discussion is, therefore, "out of order." To you who now listen to my words, it is allowable to differ with me but it is not allowable for you to state that difference in words until I have finished my reading. Anyone who would thus irresponsibly interrupt the activities of a lecture, a hospital, a concert hall, a church, a machine shop, a classroom, a football field, or a home, does not thereby exhibit his freedom. Rather, he shows himself to be a boor, a public nuisance, who must be abated, by force if necessary.

What, then, does the First Amendment forbid? Here again the town meeting suggests an answer. That meeting is called to discuss and, on the basis of such discussion, to decide matters of public policy. For example, shall there be a school? Where shall it be located? Who shall teach? What shall be taught? The community has agreed that such questions as these shall be freely discussed and that, when the discussion is ended, decision upon them will be made by vote of the citizens. Now, in that method of political self-government, the point of ultimate interest is not the words of the speakers, but the minds of the hearers. The final aim of the meeting is the voting of wise decisions. The voters, therefore, must be made as wise as possible. The welfare of the community requires that those who decide issues shall understand them. They must know what they are voting about. And this, in turn, requires that so far as time allows, all facts and interests relevant to the problem shall be fully and fairly presented to the meeting. Both facts and interests must be given in such a way that all the alternative lines of action can be wisely measured in relation to one another. As the self-governing community seeks, by the method of voting, to gain wisdom in action, it can find it only in the minds of its individual citizens. If they fail, it fails. That is why freedom of discussion for those minds may not be abridged.

The First Amendment, then, is not the guardian of unregulated talkativeness. It does not require that, on every occasion, every citizen shall take part in public debate. Nor can it even give assurance that everyone shall have opportunity to do so. If, for example, at a town meeting, twenty like-minded citizens have become a "party," and if one of them has read to the meeting an argument which they have all approved, it would be ludicrously out of order for each of the others to insist on reading it again. No competent moderator would tolerate that wasting of the time available for free discussion. What is essential is not that everyone shall speak, but that everything worth saying shall be said. To this end, for example, it may be arranged that each of the known conflicting points of view shall have, and shall be limited to, an assigned share of the time available. But however it be arranged, the vital point, as stated negatively, is that no suggestion of policy shall be denied a hearing because it is on one side of the issue rather than another. And this means that though citizens may, on other grounds, be barred from speaking, they may not be barred because their views are thought to be false or dangerous. No plan of action shall be outlawed because someone in control thinks it unwise, unfair, un-American. No speaker may be declared "out of order" because we disagree with what he intends to say. And the reason for this equality of status in the field of ideas lies deep in the very foundations of the self-governing process. When men govern themselves, it is they—and no one else—who must pass judgment upon unwisdom and unfairness and danger. And that means that unwise ideas must have a hearing as well as wise ones, unfair as well as fair, dangerous as well as safe, un-American as well as American. Just so far as, at any point, the citizens who are to decide an issue are denied acquaintance with information or opinion or doubt or disbelief or criticism which is relevant to that issue, just so far the result must be ill-considered, ill-balanced planning for the general good. *It is that mutilation of the thinking process of the community against which the First Amendment to the Constitution is directed.* The principle of the freedom of speech springs from the necessities of the program of self-government. It is not a Law of Nature or of Reason in the abstract. It is a deduction from the basic American agreement that public issues shall be decided by universal suffrage.

If, then, on any occasion in the United States it is allowable to say that the Constitution is a good document it is equally allowable, in that situation, to say that the Constitution is a bad document. If a public building may be used in which to say, in time of war, that the war is justified, then the same building may be used in which to say that it is not justified. If it be publicly argued that conscription for armed service is moral and necessary, it may likewise be publicly argued that it is immoral and unnecessary. If it may be said that American political institutions are superior to those of England or Russia or Germany, it may, with equal freedom, be said that those of England or Russia or Germany are superior to ours. These conflicting views may be expressed, must be expressed, not because they are valid, but because they are relevant. If they are responsibly entertained by anyone, we, the voters, need to hear them. When a question of policy is "before the house," free men choose to meet it not with their eyes shut, but with their eyes open. To be afraid of ideas, any idea, is to be unfit for self-government. Any such suppression of ideas about the common good, the First Amendment condemns with its absolute disapproval. The freedom of ideas shall not be abridged.

Justice Hugo Black

THE BILL OF RIGHTS

35 N.Y.U. L. Rev. 865 (1960)

For much of the first half of the twentieth century, the Court employed a "balancing test" in thinking about free speech. The

"clear and present danger" test suggested in particular that a concern for government security should be balanced against

freedom of speech. Justice Hugo Black's argument in the following article suggests that such a balancing approach has no place in First Amendment jurisprudence. As an alternative to balancing, Justice Black defends an absolute interpretation of the First Amendment and the Bill of Rights. As you read this text, consider whether there are any instances in which the right to free speech should be balanced against the concern for some other value, such as security. Is Justice Black's argument that free speech should never be put aside for the protection of some other value convincing? Why does he believe that free speech in particular is so essential to protect?

What is a bill of rights? In the popular sense it is any document setting forth the liberties of the people. I prefer to think of our Bill of Rights as including all provisions of the original Constitution and Amendments that protect individual liberty by barring government from acting in a particular area or from acting except under certain prescribed procedures. I have in mind such clauses in the body of the Constitution itself as those which safeguard the right of habeas corpus, forbid bills of attainder and ex post facto laws, guarantee trial by jury, and strictly define treason and limit the way it can be tried and punished. I would certainly add to this list the last constitutional prohibition in Article Six that "no religious Test shall ever be required as a Qualification to any Office or public Trust under the United States."

I shall speak to you about the Bill of Rights only as it bears on powers of the Federal Government. Originally, the first ten amendments were not intended to apply to the states but, as the Supreme Court held in 1833 in *Barron v. Baltimore*, were adopted to quiet fears extensively entertained that the powers of the big new national government "might be exercised in a manner dangerous to liberty." I believe that by virtue of the Fourteenth Amendment, the first ten amendments are now applicable to the states, a view I stated in *Adamson v. California*. I adhere to that view. In this talk, however, I want to discuss only the extent to which the Bill of Rights limits the Federal Government.

In applying the Bill of Rights to the Federal Government there is today a sharp difference of views as to how far its provisions should be held to limit the lawmaking power of Congress. How this difference is finally resolved will, in my judgment, have far-reaching consequences upon our liberties. I shall first summarize what those different views are.

Some people regard the prohibitions of the Constitution, even its most unequivocal commands, as mere admonitions which Congress need not always observe. This viewpoint finds many different verbal expressions. For example, it is sometimes said that Congress may abridge a constitutional right if there is a clear and present danger that the free exercise of the right will bring about a substantive evil that Congress has authority to prevent. Or it is said that a right may be abridged where its exercise would cause so much injury to the public that this injury would outweigh the injury to the individual who is deprived of the right. Again, it is sometimes said that the Bill of Rights' guarantees must "compete" for survival against general powers expressly granted to Congress and that the individual's right must, if outweighed by the public interest, be subordinated to the Government's competing interest in denying the right. All of these formulations, and more with which you are doubtless familiar, rest, at least in part, on the premise that there are no, "absolute" prohibitions in the Constitution, and that all constitutional problems are questions of reasonableness, proximity, and degree. This view comes close to the English doctrine of legislative omnipotence, qualified only by the possibility of a judicial veto if the Supreme Court finds that a congressional choice between "competing" policies has no reasonable basis.

I cannot accept this approach to the Bill of Rights. It is my belief that there are "absolutes" in our Bill of Rights, and that they were put there on purpose by men who knew what words meant, and meant their prohibitions to be "absolutes." The whole history and background of the Constitution and Bill of Rights, as I understand it, belies the assumption or conclusion that our ultimate constitutional freedoms are no more than our English ancestors had when they came to this new land to get new freedoms. The historical and practical purposes of a Bill of Rights, the very use of a written constitution, indigenous to America, the language the Framers used, the kind of three-department government they took pains to set up, all point to the creation of a government which was denied all power to do some things under any and all circumstances, and all power to do other things except precisely in the manner prescribed. In this talk I will state some of the reasons why I hold this view. In doing so, however, I shall not attempt to discuss the wholly different and complex problem of the marginal scope of each individual amendment as applied to the particular facts of particular cases. For example, there is a question as to whether the First Amendment was intended to protect speech that courts find "obscene." I shall not stress this or similar differences of construction, nor shall I add anything to the views I expressed in the recent case of *Smith v. California*. I am primarily discussing here whether liberties admittedly covered by the Bill of Rights can nevertheless be abridged on the ground that a superior public interest justifies the abridgment. I think the Bill of Rights made its safeguards superior.

Today most Americans seem to have forgotten the ancient evils which forced their ancestors to flee to this new country and to form a government stripped of old powers used to oppress them. But the Americans who supported the Revolution and the adoption of our Constitution knew firsthand the dangers of tyrannical governments. They were familiar with the long existing practice of English persecutions of people wholly because of their religious or political beliefs. They knew that many accused of such offenses had stood, helpless to defend themselves, before biased legislators and judges.

To my way of thinking, at least, the history and language of the Constitution and the Bill of Rights, make it plain that one of the primary purposes of the Constitution with its amendments was to withdraw from the Government all power to act in certain areas—whatever the scope of those areas may be. If I am right in this then there is, at least in those areas, no justification whatever for "balancing" a particular right against some expressly granted power of Congress. If the Constitution withdraws from Government all power over subject matter in an area, such as religion, speech, press, assembly, and petition, there is nothing over which authority may be exerted.

The Framers were well aware that the individual rights they sought to protect might be easily nullified if subordinated to the general powers granted to Congress. One of the reasons for adoption of the Bill of Rights was to prevent just that. Specifically the people feared that the "necessary and proper" clause could be used to project the generally granted

Congressional powers into the protected areas of individual rights. One need only read the debates in the various states to find out that this is true. But if these debates leave any doubt, Mr. Madison's words to Congress should remove it. In speaking of the "necessary and proper" clause and its possible effect on freedom of religion he said, as reported in the Annals of Congress:

> Whether the words are necessary or not, he did not mean to say, but they had been required by some of the State Conventions, who seemed to entertain an opinion that under the clause of the Constitution, which gave power to Congress to make all laws necessary and proper to carry into execution the Constitution, and the laws made under it, enabled them to make laws of such a nature as might infringe the rights of conscience, and establish a national religion; to prevent these effects he presumed the amendment was intended, and he thought it as well expressed as the nature of the language would admit.

It seems obvious to me that Congress, in exercising its general powers, is expressly forbidden to use means prohibited by the Bill of Rights. Whatever else the phrase "necessary and proper" may mean, it must be that Congress may only adopt such means to carry out its powers as are "proper," that is, not specifically prohibited.

It has also been argued that since freedom of speech, press, and religion in England were narrow freedoms at best, and since there were many English laws infringing those freedoms, our First Amendment should not be thought to bar similar infringements by Congress. Again one needs only to look to the debates in Congress over the First Amendment to find that the First Amendment cannot be treated as a mere codification of English law. Mr. Madison made a clear explanation to Congress that it was the purpose of the First Amendment to grant greater protection than England afforded its citizens. He said:

> In the declaration of rights which that country has established, the truth is, they have gone no farther than to raise a barrier against the power of the Crown; the power of the Legislature is left altogether indefinite. Although I know whenever the great rights, the trial by jury, freedom of the press, or liberty of conscience, come in question in that body, the invasion of them is resisted by able advocates, yet their Magna Charta does not contain any one provision for the security of those rights, respecting which the people of America are most alarmed. The freedom of the press and rights of conscience, those choicest privileges of the people, are unguarded in the British Constitution.
>
> But although the case may be widely different, and it may not be thought necessary to provide limits for the legislative power in that country, yet a different opinion prevails in the United States.

It was the desire to give the people of America greater protection against the powerful Federal Government than the English had had against their government that caused the Framers to put these freedoms of expression, again in the words of Madison, "beyond the reach of this Government."

When closely analyzed the idea that there can be no "absolute" constitutional guarantees in the Bill of Rights is frightening to contemplate even as to individual safeguards in the original Constitution. Take, for instance, the last clause in Article Six that "no religious Test shall ever be required" for a person to hold office in the United States. Suppose Congress should find that some religious sect was dangerous because of its foreign affiliations. Such was the belief on which English test oaths rested for a long time and some of the states had test oaths on that assumption at the time, and after, our Constitution was adopted in 1789. Could Congress, or the Supreme Court, or both, put this precious privilege to be free from test oaths on scales, find it outweighed by some other public interest, and therefore make United States officials and employees swear they did not and never had belonged to or associated with a particular religious group suspected of disloyalty? Can Congress, in the name of overbalancing necessity, suspend habeas corpus in peacetime? Are there circumstances under which Congress could, after nothing more than a legislative bill of attainder, take away a man's life, liberty, or property? Hostility of the Framers toward bills of attainder was so great that they took the unusual step of barring such legislative punishments by the States as well as the Federal Government. They wanted to remove any possibility of such proceedings anywhere in this country. This is not strange in view of the fact that they were much closer than we are to the great Act of Attainder by the Irish Parliament, in 1688, which condemned between two and three thousand men, women, and children to exile or death without anything that even resembled a trial.

It seems to me that the "balancing" approach also disregards all of the unique features of our Constitution which I described earlier. In reality this approach returns us to the state of legislative supremacy which existed in England and which the Framers were so determined to change once and for all. On the one hand, it denies the judiciary its constitutional power to measure acts of Congress by the standards set down in the Bill of Rights. On the other hand, though apparently reducing judicial powers by saying that acts of Congress may be held unconstitutional only when they are found to have no rational legislative basis, this approach really gives the Court, along

with Congress, a greater power, that of overriding the plain commands of the Bill of Rights on a finding of weighty public interest. In effect, it changes the direction of our form of government from a government of limited powers to a government in which Congress may do anything that Courts believe to be "reasonable."

Of course the decision to provide a constitutional safeguard for a particular right, such as the fair trial requirements of the Fifth and Sixth Amendments and the right of free speech protection of the First, involves a balancing of conflicting interests. Strict procedures may release guilty men; protecting speech and press may involve dangers to a particular government. I believe, however, that the Framers themselves did this balancing when they wrote the Constitution and the Bill of Rights. They appreciated the risks involved and they decided that certain rights should be guaranteed regardless of these risks. Courts have neither the right nor the power to review this original decision of the Framers and to attempt to make a different evaluation of the importance of the rights granted in the Constitution. Where conflicting values exist in the field of individual liberties protected by the Constitution, that document settles the conflict, and its policy should not be changed without constitutional amendments by the people in the manner provided by the people.

Misuse of government power, particularly in times of stress, has brought suffering to humanity in all ages about which we have authentic history. Some of the world's noblest and finest men have suffered ignominy and death for no crime—unless unorthodoxy is a crime. Even enlightened Athens had its victims such as Socrates. Because of the same kind of bigotry, Jesus, the great Dissenter, was put to death on a wooden cross. The flames of inquisitions all over the world have warned that men endowed with unlimited government power, even earnest men, consecrated to a cause, are dangerous.

For my own part, I believe that our Constitution, with its absolute guarantees of individual rights, is the best hope for the aspirations of freedom which men share everywhere. I cannot agree with those who think of the Bill of Rights as an 18th Century straitjacket, unsuited for this age. It is old but not all old things are bad. The evils it guards against are not only old, they are with us now, they exist today. Almost any morning you open your daily paper you can see where some person somewhere in the world is on trial or has just been convicted of supposed disloyalty to a new group controlling the government which has set out to purge its suspected enemies and all those who had dared to be against its successful march to power. Nearly always you see that these political heretics are being tried by military tribunals or some other summary and sure method for disposition of the accused. Now and then we even see the convicted victims as they march to their execution.

Experience all over the world has demonstrated, I fear, that the distance between stable, orderly government and one that has been taken over by force is not so great as we have assumed. Our own free system to live and progress has to have intelligent citizens, citizens who cannot only think and speak and write to influence people, but citizens who are free to do that without fear of governmental censorship or reprisal.

The provisions of the Bill of Rights that safeguard fair legal procedures came about largely to protect the weak and the oppressed from punishment by the strong and the powerful who wanted to stifle the voices of discontent raised in protest against oppression and injustice in public affairs. Nothing that I have read in the Congressional debates on the Bill of Rights indicates that there was any belief that the First Amendment contained any qualifications. The only arguments that tended to look in this direction at all were those that said "that all paper barriers against the power of the community are too weak to be worthy of attention." Suggestions were also made in and out of Congress that a Bill of Rights would be a futile gesture since there would be no way to enforce the safeguards for freedom it provided. Mr. Madison answered this argument in these words:

> If they [the Bill of Rights amendments] are incorporated into the Constitution, independent tribunals of justice will consider themselves in a peculiar manner the guardians of those rights; they will be an impenetrable bulwark against any assumption of power in the Legislative or Executive; they will be naturally led to resist every encroachment upon rights expressly stipulated for in the Constitution by the declaration of rights.

I fail to see how courts can escape this sacred trust.

Since the earliest days philosophers have dreamed of a country where the mind and spirit of man would be free; where there would be no limits to inquiry; where men would be free to explore the unknown and to challenge the most deeply rooted beliefs and principles. Our First Amendment was a bold effort to adopt this principle—to establish a country with no legal restrictions of any kind upon the subjects people could investigate, discuss and deny. The Framers knew, better perhaps than we do today, the risks they were taking. They knew that free speech might be the friend of change and revolution. But they also knew that it is always the deadliest enemy of tyranny. With this knowledge they still believed that the ultimate happiness and security of a nation lies in its ability to explore, to change, to grow and ceaselessly to adapt itself to new knowledge born of inquiry free from any kind of governmental control over the mind and spirit of man. Loyalty comes from love of good government, not fear of a bad one.

The First Amendment is truly the heart of the Bill of Rights. The Framers balanced its freedoms of religion, speech, press, assembly and petition against the needs of a powerful central government, and decided that in those freedoms lies this nation's only true security. They were not afraid for men to be free. We should not be. We should be as confident as Jefferson was when he said in his First Inaugural Address:

> If there be any among us who would wish to dissolve this Union or to change its republican form, let them stand undisturbed as monuments of the safety with which error of opinion may be tolerated where reason is left free to combat it.

Gordon Brown

SPEECH ON TERRORISM

Address delivered to the Royal United Services Institute, London

February 13, 2006

Alexander Meiklejohn, John Stuart Mill, and Justice Hugo Black all provide a defense of a robust free-speech right. But in determining whether the right to free political speech is an absolute right or whether it should be balanced against other values, it is important to consider examples that highlight those values that might conflict with it. United Kingdom Prime Minister Gordon Brown's speech calls for the prohibition of certain kinds of political speech in the name of ensuring society's security. For instance, pay attention to what he says about the limits on "celebration of terrorism," and ask yourself whether this claim is at odds with the defenses of free speech delivered by our previous three authors. Moreover, keep in mind Prime Minister Brown's statements about the limits on dangerous speech as you consider the clear and present danger test that begins our case selection. In reading Prime Minister Brown's speech, also bear in mind the incident to which he is responding. On July 7, *2005, three London Underground trains as well as a double-decker bus were blown up in a coordinated series of bombings, resulting in the deaths of 52 people. Al-Qaeda claimed responsibility.*

Securing Our Future

As July 7 solemnly and starkly reminds us, the first responsibility of a government is to protect its citizens, keep people safe and ensure their security.

The reason is clear. Addressing the reality, causes and roots of international terrorism is one of the greatest new challenges of our times.

While we stood as one on and after July 7 there is a danger that in the aftermath of a terrorist incident as time passes, people's sense of the scale of the threat dims, that people's guard starts to drop, their vigilance lessens and their commitment to the tough and necessary security measures—all too clear on the morning after—weakens.

And there is also a danger that we fail to stand back and reflect and to make the long-term cool-headed assessment we need to have about the likely repetition of such events and to decide what, for the long term, needs to be done to strengthen our security.

The Changed Global Context

From 1945, the Cold War was fought with not only weapons that were military or intelligence based: it was fought through newspapers, journals, culture, the arts, literature. It was fought not just through governments but through foundations, trusts, civil society and civic organisations. Indeed we talked of a cultural Cold War—a Cold War of ideas and values—and one which the best ideas and values eventually triumphed.

And it is by power of argument, by debate and by dialogue that we will, in the long term, expose and defeat this extremist threat and we will have to argue not just against terrorism and terrorists but openly argue against the violent perversion of a peaceful religious faith.

Indeed, the very existence of the internet and the exchange of ideas across it means that instead of relying on old methods of censorship it is not only right now but necessary to take these ideas head on—a global battle for hearts and minds, and that will mean debate, discussion and dialogue through media, culture, arts, and literature. And not so much through governments, as through civil society and civic culture—in partnership with moderate Muslims and moderates everywhere—as globally we seek to isolate extremists from moderates.

We should also work with our allies and international organisations for reform and democracy; encourage interfaith cooperation such as the conferences we are involved in with Muslim thinkers; and in particular link young people here with young people in other countries.

Glorification

I think most people would agree that no one should be able to publicly celebrate and glorify what happened in London in July and walk away from the consequences, nor should they be able to form organisations to celebrate and glorify atrocities only to escape censure simply by adding a disclaimer that from the act of glorification it should not be assumed that anyone will emulate them. Indeed, if we withdraw glorification from the definition of indirect incitement or from the grounds for proscribing organisations this would send a signal that we could not reach a consensus on how serious this issue is.

None of this threatens our unshakeable commitment to freedom of speech; nor is it in any way whatever aimed at the decent law-abiding Muslim community of Britain—indeed I want to pay tribute to the way many organisations within the Muslim community condemned the protests.

Integration

We have had a great deal of success—especially since July—forging a common front against terrorism. And we should build on this—so we tackle together not just terrorism, but the roots of terrorism—the extremism which seeks to justify it, and the grievances that give it an audience.

In particular we must ensure that young Muslims have a voice in this debate and all the decisions that affect them. . . .

But the partnership we need is not only to tackle social and economic inequalities but also to expose the extremism which condones or encourages violence in place of dialogue and debate.

We should work to involve all parts of the British Muslim faith in ensuring that young Muslims have access to authoritative interpreters of Islam of their own generation and outlook. But the challenge of integration is one which if we are to succeed must draw in the whole of society.

Britishness

I have suggested that we do more to value the ideals of Britishness—our commitment to liberty, responsibility and fairness—and its symbols and institutions and in particular I suggest today we recognise and show we value the contribution of our police, emergency and security services, our military and our armed forces and the contribution of all those who fought in the great wars of the last century.

Conclusion

The global terrorist threat is such that we cannot afford not to be vigilant at all times.

I have suggested how this global terrorist problem must be fought globally —with all the means at our disposal: military, security, intelligence, economic and culture.

And around this I believe it is our responsibility to build a strong unified national consensus which reflects a modern patriotic purpose that—every day and without fail, we will do what is right to protect the security and liberties of our citizens and country, and in the face of global terrorism we will prevail.

SCHENCK v. UNITED STATES

249 U.S. 47 (1919)

Opinion: Holmes, joined by White, McKenna, Day, Van Devanter, Pitney, McReynolds, Brandeis, Clarke

In 1917, President Woodrow Wilson signed into law the Espionage Act, which aimed to curtail certain kinds of speech during World War I. Among other things, this law made it a crime to advocate for the cause of the enemy, to attempt to cause insubordination among the members of the armed forces, or to seek to interfere with recruiting or enlistment of military personnel in the United States. In two cases appearing before the Supreme Court in 1919, Schenck v. United States *and* Abrams v. United States, *individuals who were prosecuted under the Act for disseminating banned materials appealed their convictions, alleging that the Espionage Act was an unconstitutional violation of the First Amendment's guarantee of freedom of speech.*

In Schenck, *U.S. Supreme Court Justice Oliver Wendell Holmes, writing for the Court, argued that the Act did not violate free speech. Using the metaphor of an individual who cries fire in a crowded theater, he held that the circumstances surrounding an act of speech, in addition to its content, are of significance for a determination of constitutional claims arising under the right of free speech. In this case, Justice Holmes explained, the speech in question presented a "clear and present danger," meaning that it did not deserve protection.*

As you read this case, consider the possible implications of the clear and present danger test. One feature of the clear and present danger test is that it does not place an obvious time limit between expression of a dangerous idea and the acts of violence that might follow. Should timing matter? For instance, imagine that a dangerous idea took ten years to persuade the American people to take up arms against their government in revolution. In these circumstances, would the clear and present danger test still allow the government to ban the communication of that idea?

MR. JUSTICE HOLMES *delivered the opinion of the Court.*

This is an indictment in three counts. The first charges a conspiracy to violate the Espionage Act of June 15, 1917, by causing and attempting to cause insubordination, &c., in the military and naval forces of the United States, and to obstruct the recruiting and enlistment service of the United States, when the United States was at war with the German Empire, to-wit, that the defendants willfully conspired to have printed and circulated to men who had been called and accepted for military service under the Act of May 18, 1917, a document set forth and alleged to be calculated to cause such insubordination and obstruction. The count alleges overt acts in pursuance of the conspiracy, ending in the distribution of the document set forth. The second count alleges a conspiracy to commit an offence against the United States, to-wit, to use the mails for the transmission of matter declared to be non-mailable by Title XII, §2 of the Act of June 15, 1917, to-wit, the above mentioned document, with an averment of the same overt acts. The third count charges an unlawful use of the mails for the transmission of the same matter and otherwise as above. The defendants were found guilty on all the counts. They set up the First Amendment to the Constitution forbidding Congress to make any law abridging the freedom of speech, or of the press, and bringing the case here on that ground have argued some other points also of which we must dispose.

The document in question upon its first printed side recited the first section of the Thirteenth Amendment, said that the idea embodied in it was violated by the Conscription Act and that a conscript is little better than a convict. In impassioned language it intimated that conscription was despotism in its worst form and a monstrous wrong against humanity in the interest of Wall Street's chosen few. It said "Do not submit to intimidation," but in form at least confined itself to peaceful measures such as a petition for the repeal of the act. The other and later printed side of the sheet was headed "Assert Your Rights." It stated reasons for alleging that any one violated the Constitution when he refused to recognize "your right to assert your opposition to the draft," and went on "If you do not assert and support your rights, you are helping to deny or disparage rights which it is the solemn duty of all citizens and residents of the United States to retain." It described the arguments on the other side as coming from cunning politicians and a mercenary capitalist press, and even silent consent to the conscription law as helping to support an infamous conspiracy. It denied the power to send our citizens away to foreign shores to shoot up the people of other lands, and added that words could not express the condemnation such cold-blooded ruthlessness deserves, &c., winding up "You must do your share to maintain, support and uphold the rights of the people of this country." Of course the documents would not have been sent unless it had been intended to have some effect, and we do not see what effect it could be expected to have upon persons subject to the draft except to influence them to obstruct the carrying of it out. The defendants do not deny that the jury might find against them on this point.

But it is said, suppose that that was the tendency of this circular, it is protected by the First Amendment to the Constitution. Two of the strongest expressions are said to be quoted respectively from well-known public men. It well may be that the prohibition of laws abridging the freedom of speech is not confined to previous restraints, although to prevent them may have been the main purpose, as intimated in *Patterson v. Colorado*. We admit that in many places and in ordinary times the defendants in saying all that was said in the circular would have been within their constitutional rights. But the character of every act depends upon the circumstances in which it is done. The most stringent protection of free speech would not protect a man in falsely shouting fire in a theatre and causing a panic. It does not even protect a man from an injunction against uttering words that may have all the effect of force. The question in every case is whether the words used are used in such circumstances and are of such a nature as to create a clear and present danger that they will bring about the substantive evils that Congress has a right to prevent. It is a question of proximity and degree. When a nation is at war many things that might be said in time of peace are such a hindrance to its effort that their utterance will not be endured so long as men fight and that no Court could regard them as protected by any constitutional right. It seems to be admitted that if an actual obstruction of the recruiting service were proved, liability for words that produced that effect might be enforced. The statute of 1917 in §4 punishes conspiracies to obstruct as well as actual obstruction. If the act (speaking, or circulating a paper), its tendency and the intent with which it is done are the same, we perceive no ground for saying that success alone warrants making the act a crime.

Judgments affirmed.

ABRAMS v. UNITED STATES

250 U.S. 616 (1919)

Opinion: Clarke, joined by White, McKenna, Day, Van Devanter, Pitney, McReynolds
Dissent: Holmes, joined by Brandeis

In Abrams v. United States, *the Court once again considered whether the Espionage Act violated the right to free speech of defendants accused of spreading subversive ideas. Notice that despite his opinion in* Schenck v. United States, *Justice Oliver Wendell Holmes is in dissent in this case, arguing that the Espionage Act does violate the First Amendment rights of the defendants. In reading both cases, consider whether the circumstances were different enough to justify Justice Holmes's two positions under the clear and present danger test, or whether Justice Holmes abandoned the test.*

MR. JUSTICE CLARKE *delivered the opinion of the Court.*

On a single indictment, containing four counts, the five plaintiffs in error, hereinafter designated the defendants, were convicted of conspiring to violate provisions of the Espionage Act of Congress.

Each of the first three counts charged the defendants with conspiring, when the United States was at war with the Imperial Government of Germany, to unlawfully utter, print, write and publish: in the first count, "disloyal, scurrilous and abusive language about the form of Government of the United States;" in the second count, language "intended to bring the form of Government of the United States into contempt, scorn, contumely and disrepute;" and in the third count, language "intended to incite, provoke and encourage resistance to the United States in said war." The charge in the fourth count was that the defendants conspired "when the United States was at war with the Imperial German Government, unlawfully and willfully, by utterance, writing, printing and publication, to urge, incite and advocate curtailment of production of things and products, to wit, ordnance and ammunition, necessary and essential to the prosecution of the war." The offenses were charged in the language of the act of Congress.

It was charged in each count of the indictment that it was a part of the conspiracy that the defendants would attempt to accomplish their unlawful purpose by printing, writing and distributing in the City of New York many copies of a leaflet or circular, printed in the English language, and of another printed in the Yiddish language, copies of which, properly identified, were attached to the indictment.

All of the five defendants were born in Russia. They were intelligent, had considerable schooling, and at the time they were arrested they had lived in the United States terms varying from five to ten years, but none of them had applied for naturalization. Four of them testified as witnesses in their own behalf and of these, three frankly avowed that they were "rebels," "revolutionists," "anarchists," that they did not believe in government in any form, and they declared that they had no interest whatever in the Government of the United States. The fourth defendant testified that he was a "socialist" and believed in "a proper kind of government, not capitalistic," but in his classification the Government of the United States was "capitalistic."

It was admitted on the trial that the defendants had united to print and distribute the described circulars and that five thousand of them had been printed and distributed about the 22d day of August, 1918. The group had a meeting place in New York City, in rooms rented by defendant Abrams, under an assumed name, and there the subject of printing the circulars was discussed about two weeks before the defendants were arrested. The defendant Abrams, although not a printer, on July 27, 1918, purchased the printing outfit with which the circulars were printed and installed it in a basement room where the work was done at night. The circulars were distributed some by throwing them from a window of a building where one of the defendants was employed and others secretly, in New York City.

The defendants pleaded "not guilty," and the case of the Government consisted in showing the facts we have stated, and in introducing in evidence copies of the two printed circulars attached to the indictment, a sheet entitled "Revolutionists Unite for Action," written by the defendant Lipman, and found on him when he was arrested, and another paper, found at the headquarters of the group, and for which Abrams assumed responsibility.

Thus the conspiracy and the doing of the overt acts charged were largely admitted and were fully established.

On the record thus described it is argued, somewhat faintly, that the acts charged against the defendants were not unlawful because within the protection of that freedom of speech and of the press which is guaranteed by the First Amendment to the Constitution of the United States, and that the entire Espionage Act is unconstitutional because in conflict with that Amendment.

This contention is sufficiently discussed and is definitely negatived in *Schenck v. United States* and *Baer v. United States* and in *Frohwerk v. United States*.

The first of the two articles attached to the indictment is conspicuously headed, "The Hypocrisy of the United States and her Allies." After denouncing President Wilson as a hypocrite and a coward because troops were sent into Russia, it proceeds to assail our Government in general, saying:

> "His [the President's] shameful, cowardly silence about the intervention in Russia reveals the hypocrisy of the plutocratic gang in Washington and vicinity."

It continues:

> "He [the President] is too much of a coward to come out openly and say: 'We capitalistic nations cannot afford to have a proletarian republic in Russia.'"

Among the capitalistic nations Abrams testified the United States was included.

Growing more inflammatory as it proceeds, the circular culminates in:

> "The Russian Revolution cries: Workers of the World! Awake! Rise! Put down your enemy and mine!
>
> "Yes! friends, there is only one enemy of the workers of the world and that is CAPITALISM."

This is clearly an appeal to the "workers" of this country to arise and put down by force the Government of the United States which they characterize as their "hypocritical," "cowardly" and "capitalistic" enemy.

The second of the articles was printed in the Yiddish language and in the translation is headed, "Workers—Wake up." After referring to "his Majesty, Mr. Wilson, and

the rest of the gang; dogs of all colors!" it continues:

> "Workers, Russian emigrants, you who had the least belief in the honesty of our Government," which defendants admitted referred to the United States Government, "must now throw away all confidence, must spit in the face the false, hypocritic, military propaganda which has fooled you so relentlessly, calling forth your sympathy, your help, to the prosecution of the war."

The purpose of this obviously was to persuade the persons to whom it was addressed to turn a deaf ear to patriotic appeals in behalf of the Government of the United States, and to cease to render it assistance in the prosecution of the war.

It will not do to say, as is now argued, that the only intent of these defendants was to prevent injury to the Russian cause. Men must be held to have intended, and to be accountable for, the effects which their acts were likely to produce. Even if their primary purpose and intent was to aid the cause of the Russian Revolution, the plan of action which they adopted necessarily involved, before it could be realized, defeat of the war program of the United States, for the obvious effect of this appeal, if it should become effective, as they, hoped it might, would be to persuade persons of character such as those whom they regarded themselves as addressing, not to aid government loans and not to work in ammunition factories, where their work would produce "bullets, bayonets, cannon" and other munitions of war, the use of which would cause the "murder" of Germans and Russians.

Again, the spirit becomes more bitter as it proceeds to declare that—

> "America and her Allies have betrayed (the Workers). Their robberish aims are clear to all men. The destruction of the Russian Revolution, that is the politics of the march to Russia.

"Workers, our reply to the barbaric intervention has to be a general strike! An open challenge only will let the Government know that not only the Russian Worker fights for freedom, but also here in America lives the spirit of Revolution."

This is not an attempt to bring about a change of administration by candid discussion, for no matter what may have incited the outbreak on the part of the defendant anarchists, the manifest purpose of such a publication was to create an attempt to defeat the war plans of the Government of the United States, by bringing upon the country the paralysis of a general strike, thereby arresting the production of all munitions and other things essential to the conduct of the war.

That the interpretation we have put upon these articles, circulated in the greatest port of our land, from which great numbers of soldiers were at the time taking ship daily, and in which great quantities of war supplies of every kind were at the time being manufactured for transportation overseas, is not only the fair interpretation of them, but that it is the meaning which their authors consciously intended should be conveyed by them to others is further shown by the additional writings found in the meeting place of the defendant group and on the person of one of them. One of these circulars is headed: "Revolutionists! Unite for Action!"

After denouncing the President as "Our Kaiser" and the hypocrisy of the United States and her Allies, this article concludes:

"Socialists, Anarchists, Industrial Workers of the World, Socialists, Labor party men and other revolutionary organizations, Unite for action and let us save the Workers' Republic of Russia!

"Know you lovers of freedom that in order to save the Russian revolution, we must keep the armies of the allied countries busy at home."

Thus was again avowed the purpose to throw the country into a state of revolution if possible and to thereby frustrate the military program of the Government.

These excerpts sufficiently show, that while the immediate occasion for this particular outbreak of lawlessness, on the part of the defendant alien anarchists, may have been resentment caused by our Government sending troops into Russia as a strategic operation against the Germans on the eastern battle front, yet the plain purpose of their propaganda was to excite, at the supreme crisis of the war, disaffection, sedition, riots, and, as they hoped, revolution, in this country for the purpose of embarrassing and if possible defeating the military plans of the Government in Europe. A technical distinction may perhaps be taken between disloyal and abusive language applied to the form of our government or language intended to bring the form of our government into contempt and disrepute, and language of like character and intended to produce like results directed against the President and Congress, the agencies through which that form of government must function in time of war. But it is not necessary to a decision of this case to consider whether such distinction is vital or merely formal, for the language of these circulars was obviously intended to provoke and to encourage resistance to the United States in the war, as the third count runs, and, the defendants, in terms, plainly urged and advocated a resort to a general strike of workers in ammunition factories for the purpose of curtailing the production of ordnance and munitions necessary and essential to the prosecution of the war as is charged in the fourth count. Thus it is clear not only that some evidence but that much persuasive evidence was before the jury tending to prove that the defendants were guilty as charged in both the third and fourth counts of the indictment and under the long established rule of law hereinbe-fore stated the judgment of the District Court must be

Affirmed.

MR. JUSTICE HOLMES *dissenting.*

This indictment is founded wholly upon the publication of two leaflets which I shall describe in a moment. The first count charges a conspiracy pending the war with Germany to publish abusive language about the form of government of the United States, laying the preparation and publish-ing of the first leaflet as overt acts. The second count charges a conspiracy pend-ing the war to publish language intended to bring the form of government into con-tempt, laying the preparation and publish-ing of the two leaflets as overt acts. The third count alleges a conspiracy to encour-age resistance to the United States in the same war and to attempt to effectuate the purpose by publishing the same leaflets. The fourth count lays a conspiracy to incite curtailment of production of things neces-sary to the prosecution of the war and to attempt to accomplish it by publishing the second leaflet to which I have referred.

No argument seems to me necessary to show that these pronunciamentos in no way attack the form of government of the United States, or that they do not sup-port either of the first two counts. What little I have to say about the third count may be postponed until I have considered the fourth. With regard to that it seems too plain to be denied that the suggestion to workers in the ammunition factories that they are producing bullets to murder their dearest, and the further advocacy of a general strike, both in the second leaf-let, do urge curtailment of production of things necessary to the prosecution of the war within the meaning of the Act of May 16, 1918, c. 75, 40 Stat. 553, amending §3 of the earlier Act of 1917. But to make the conduct criminal that statute requires that it should be "with intent by such curtail-ment to cripple or hinder the United States in the prosecution of the war." It seems to me that no such intent is proved.

I never have seen any reason to doubt that the questions of law that alone were before this Court in the cases of *Schenck, Frohwerk* and *Debs*, were rightly decided. I do not doubt for a moment that by the same reasoning that would justify pun-ishing persuasion to murder, the United States constitutionally may punish speech that produces or is intended to produce a clear and imminent danger that it will bring about forthwith certain substantive evils that the United States constitutionally may seek to prevent. The power undoubt-edly is greater in time of war than in time of peace because war opens dangers that do not exist at other times.

But as against dangers peculiar to war, as against others, the principle of the right to free speech is always the same. It is only the present danger of immediate evil or an intent to bring it about that warrants Congress in setting a limit to the expres-sion of opinion where private rights are not concerned. Congress certainly cannot forbid all effort to change the mind of the country. Now nobody can suppose that the surreptitious publishing of a silly leaflet by an unknown man, without more, would present any immediate danger that its opinions would hinder the success of the government arms or have any appreciable tendency to do so. Publishing those opin-ions for the very purpose of obstructing however, might indicate a greater danger and at any rate would have the quality of an attempt. So I assume that the second leaf-let if published for the purposes alleged in the fourth count might be punishable. But it seems pretty clear to me that nothing less than that would bring these papers within the scope of this law. An actual intent in the sense that I have explained is necessary to constitute an attempt, where a further act of the same individual is required to complete the substantive crime, for reasons given in *Swift & Co. v. United States*. It is necessary where the success of the attempt depends upon others because if that intent is not present the actor's aim may be accomplished without bringing about the evils sought to be checked. An intent to prevent interference with the revolution in Russia might have been satisfied without any hindrance to carrying on the war in which we were engaged.

I do not see how anyone can find the intent required by the statute in any of the defendants' words. The second leaflet is the only one that affords even a foundation for the charge, and there, without invoking the hatred of German militarism expressed in the former one, it is evident from the beginning to the end that the only object of the paper is to help Russia and stop American intervention there against the popular government—not to impede the United States in the war that it was carrying on. To say that two phrases taken literally might import a suggestion of conduct that would have interference with the war as an indirect and probably undesired effect seems to me by no means enough to show an attempt to produce that effect.

I return for a moment to the third count. That charges an intent to provoke resistance to the United States in its war with Germany. Taking the clause in the statute that deals with that in connection with the other elaborate provisions of the act, I think that resistance to the United States means some forcible act of opposition to some proceeding of the United States in pursuance of the war. I think the intent must be the specific intent that I have described and for the reasons that I have given I think that no such intent was proved or existed in fact. I also think that there is no hint at resistance to the United States as I construe the phrase.

In this case sentences of twenty years imprisonment have been imposed for the publishing of two leaflets that I believe the defendants had as much right to publish as the Government has to publish the Constitution of the United States now vainly invoked by them. Even if I am technically wrong and enough can be squeezed from these poor and puny anonymities to turn the color of legal litmus paper; I will add, even if what I think the necessary intent were shown; the most nominal punishment seems to me all that possibly could be inflicted, unless the defendants are to be made to suffer not for what the indictment alleges but for the creed that they avow—a creed that I believe to be the creed of ignorance and immaturity when honestly held, as I see no reason to doubt that it was held here, but which, although made the subject of examination at the trial, no one has a right even to consider in dealing with the charges before the Court.

Persecution for the expression of opinions seems to me perfectly logical. If you have no doubt of your premises or your power and want a certain result with all your heart you naturally express your wishes in law and sweep away all opposition. To allow opposition by speech seems to indicate that you think the speech impotent, as when a man says that he has squared the circle, or that you do not care whole-heartedly for the result, or that you doubt either your power or your premises. But when men have realized that time has upset many fighting faiths, they may come to believe even more than they believe the very foundations of their own conduct that the ultimate good desired is better reached by free trade in ideas—that the best test of truth is the power of the thought to get itself accepted in the competition of the market, and that truth is the only ground upon which their wishes safely can be carried out. That at any rate is the theory of our Constitution. It is an experiment, as all life is an experiment. Every year if not every day we have to wager our salvation upon some prophecy based upon imperfect knowledge. While that experiment is part of our system I think that we should be eternally vigilant against attempts to check the expression of opinions that we loathe and believe to be fraught with death, unless they so imminently threaten immediate interference with the lawful and pressing purposes of the law that an immediate check is required to save the country. I wholly disagree with the argument of the Government that the First Amendment left the common law as to seditious libel in force. History seems to me against the notion. I had conceived that the United States through many years had shown its repentance for the Sedition Act of 1798, by repaying fines that it imposed. Only the emergency that makes it immediately dangerous to leave the correction of evil counsels to time warrants making any exception to the sweeping command, "Congress shall make no law . . . abridging the freedom of speech." Of course I am speaking only of expressions of opinion and exhortations,

which were all that were uttered here, but I regret that I cannot put into more impressive words my belief that in their conviction upon this indictment the defendants were deprived of their rights under the Constitution of the United States.

MR. JUSTICE BRANDEIS *concurs with the foregoing opinion.*

CASE QUESTION

Recall from Chapter 1 that Justice Oliver Wendell Holmes is often considered a founder of the pragmatist school of jurisprudence. Is his elaboration and defense of the clear and present danger test for free speech an example of pragmatism? It is widely noted that while Justice Holmes introduces the test in *Schenck v. United States* and employs it to uphold a restrictive law, he suggests in his *Abrams v. United States* dissent that a restriction on political speech should be struck down. Is he being inconsistent? Is there a way of reconciling these positions by appealing to pragmatism? Consider, too, how the facts of the two cases might be distinguished.

WHITNEY v. CALIFORNIA

274 U.S. 357 (1927)

Opinion: Sanford, joined by Taft, Van Devanter, McReynolds, Sutherland, Butler, Stone
Concurrence: Brandeis, joined by Holmes

In Whitney v. California, *the Court considered whether California's Criminal Syndicalism Act violated the free speech guarantee. The Act prohibited speech advocating the commission of a crime, sabotage, or unlawful acts of force and violence for the purpose of effecting political change. As you read the majority opinion, consider whether it invokes the clear and present danger test or some other standard. We include too a concurrence by U.S. Supreme Court Justice Louis Brandeis, who offers a robust defense of the right to free speech despite his upholding the law in question. What kind of defense does he offer? How does it resemble or differ from the arguments offered by John Stuart Mill and Alexander Meiklejohn?*

It is important to notice a distinctive feature about this case as compared to Schenck v. United States *and* Abrams v. United States. *Those cases concerned instances where federal legislation passed by Congress and signed by the president was alleged to violate the First Amendment. In this case, a state law is at issue. The legal distinction here should be evident upon a close reading of the First Amendment. Specifically, the First Amendment bans Congress from making laws that abridge the freedom of speech. But does this same provision apply to state legislatures as well? In a previous case,* Gitlow v. New York, *the Supreme Court did apply First Amendment analysis to a New York law, explaining, "For present purposes we may and do assume that freedom of speech and of the press—which are protected by the First Amendment from abridgment by Congress—are among the fundamental personal rights and 'liberties' protected by the due process clause of the Fourteenth Amendment from impairment by the States." This move by the Court in* Gitlow v. New York, *also followed by the Court in* Whitney v. California, *is commonly referred to as incorporation. The idea here is that by applying due process protections to the states, the Fourteenth Amendment also creates a protection of the rights enumerated in the Bill of Rights for individuals against state law. There is some controversy about which rights should be extended in this way under the doctrine of incorporation, but it is commonly accepted that the First Amendment right to free speech as well as the right to religious freedom, which we discuss in the next chapter, are incorporated against the states by the Fourteenth Amendment.*

MR. JUSTICE SANFORD *delivered the opinion of the Court.*

By a criminal information filed in the Superior Court of Alameda County, California, the plaintiff in error was charged, in five counts, with violations of the Criminal Syndicalism Act of that State. She was tried, convicted on the first count, and sentenced to imprisonment. The judgment was affirmed by the District Court of Appeal. Her petition to have the case heard by the Supreme Court was denied. And the case was brought here on a writ of error which was allowed by the Presiding Justice of the Court of Appeal, the highest court of the State in which a decision could be had.

On the first hearing in this Court, the writ of error was dismissed for want of jurisdiction. Thereafter, a petition for rehearing was granted, and the case was again heard and reargued both as to the jurisdiction and the merits.

The pertinent provisions of the Criminal Syndicalism Act are:

> "Section 1. The term 'criminal syndicalism' as used in this act is hereby defined as any doctrine or precept advocating, teaching or aiding and abetting the commission of crime, sabotage (which word is hereby defined as meaning willful and malicious physical damage or injury to physical property), or unlawful acts of force and violence or unlawful methods of terrorism as a means of accomplishing a change in industrial ownership or control, or effecting any political change.
>
> "Sec. 2. Any person who: . . . 4. Organizes or assists in organizing, or is or knowingly becomes a member of, any organization, society, group or assemblage of persons organized or assembled to advocate, teach or aid and abet criminal syndicalism. . . .
>
> "Is guilty of a felony and punishable by imprisonment."

The first count of the information, on which the conviction was had, charged that on or about November 28, 1919, in Alameda

County, the defendant, in violation of the Criminal Syndicalism Act, "did then and there unlawfully, willfully, wrongfully, deliberately and feloniously organize and assist in organizing, and was, is, and knowingly became a member of an organization, society, group and assemblage of persons organized and assembled to advocate, teach, aid and abet criminal syndicalism."

We proceed to the determination, upon the merits, of the constitutional question considered and passed upon by the Court of Appeal. Of course our review is to be confined to that question, since it does not appear, either from the order of the Court of Appeal or from the record otherwise, that any other federal question was presented in and either expressly or necessarily decided by that court. It is not enough that there may be somewhere hidden in the record a question which, if it had been raised, would have been of a federal nature. And this necessarily excludes from our consideration a question sought to be raised for the first time by the assignments of error here—not presented in or passed upon by the Court of Appeal—whether apart from the constitutionality of the Syndicalism Act, the judgment of the Superior Court, by reason of the rulings of that court on questions of pleading, evidence and the like, operated as a denial to the defendant of due process of law.

The following facts, among many others, were established on the trial by undisputed evidence: The defendant, a resident of Oakland, in Alameda County, California, had been a member of the Local Oakland branch of the Socialist Party. . . .

Shortly thereafter the Local Oakland withdrew from the Socialist Party, and sent accredited delegates, including the defendant, to a convention held in Oakland in November, 1919, for the purpose of organizing a California branch of the Communist Labor Party. The defendant, after taking out a temporary membership in the Communist Labor Party, attended this convention as a delegate and took an active part in its proceedings. She was elected a member of the Credentials Committee, and, as its chairman, made a report to the convention upon which the delegates were seated. She was also appointed a member of the Resolutions Committee, and as such signed the following resolution in reference to political action, among others proposed by the Committee: "The C.L.P. of California fully recognizes the value of political action as a means of spreading communist propaganda; it insists that in proportion to the development of the economic strength of the working class, it, the working class, must also develop its political power. The C.L.P. of California proclaims and insists that the capture of political power, locally or nationally by the revolutionary working class can be of tremendous assistance to the workers in their struggle of emancipation. Therefore, we again urge the workers who are possessed of the right of franchise to cast their votes for the party which represents their immediate and final interest—the C.L.P.—at all elections, being fully convinced of the utter futility of obtaining any real measure of justice or freedom under officials elected by parties owned and controlled by the capitalist class." The minutes show that this resolution, with the others proposed by the committee, was read by its chairman to the convention before the Committee on the Constitution had submitted its report. According to the recollection of the defendant, however, she herself read this resolution. . . .

In the light of this preliminary statement, we now take up, in so far as they require specific consideration, the various grounds upon which it is here contended that the Syndicalism Act and its application in this case is repugnant to the due process and equal protection clauses of the Fourteenth Amendment.

Nor is the Syndicalism Act as applied in this case repugnant to the due process clause as a restraint of the rights of free speech, assembly, and association.

That the freedom of speech which is secured by the Constitution does not confer an absolute right to speak, without responsibility, whatever one may choose, or an unrestricted and unbridled license giving immunity for every possible use of language and preventing the punishment of those who abuse this freedom; and that a State in the exercise of its police power may punish those who abuse this freedom by utterances inimical to the public welfare, tending to incite to crime, disturb the public peace, or endanger the foundations of organized government and threaten its overthrow by unlawful means, is not open to question.

By enacting the provisions of the Syndicalism Act the State has declared, through its legislative body, that to knowingly be or become a member of or assist in organizing an association to advocate, teach or aid and abet the commission of crimes or unlawful acts of force, violence or terrorism as a means of accomplishing industrial or political changes, involves such danger to the public peace and the security of the State, that these acts should be penalized in the exercise of its police power. That determination must be given great weight. Every presumption is to be indulged in favor of the validity of the statute; and it may not be declared unconstitutional unless it is an arbitrary or unreasonable attempt to exercise the authority vested in the State in the public interest.

The essence of the offense denounced by the Act is the combining with others in an association for the accomplishment of the desired ends through the advocacy and use of criminal and unlawful methods. It partakes of the nature of a criminal conspiracy. That such united and joint action involves even greater danger to the public peace and security than the isolated utterances and acts of individuals, is clear. We cannot hold that, as here applied, the Act is an unreasonable or arbitrary exercise of the police power of the State, unwarrantably infringing any right of free speech, assembly or association, or that those persons are protected from punishment by the due process clause who abuse such rights by joining and furthering an organization thus menacing the peace and welfare of the State.

We find no repugnancy in the Syndicalism Act as applied in this case to either the due process or equal protection clauses of the Fourteenth Amendment on any of the grounds upon which its validity has been here challenged.

The order dismissing the writ of error will be vacated and set aside, and the judgment of the Court of Appeal

Affirmed.

MR. JUSTICE BRANDEIS, *concurring.*

Miss Whitney was convicted of the felony of assisting in organizing, in the year 1919, the Communist Labor Party of California, of being a member of it, and of assembling with it. These acts are held to constitute a crime, because the party was formed to teach criminal syndicalism. The statute which made these acts a crime restricted the right of free speech and of assembly theretofore existing. The claim is that the statute, as applied, denied to Miss Whitney the liberty guaranteed by the Fourteenth Amendment.

The felony which the statute created is a crime very unlike the old felony of conspiracy or the old misdemeanor of unlawful assembly. The mere act of assisting in forming a society for teaching syndicalism, of becoming a member of it, or of assembling with others for that purpose is given the dynamic quality of crime. There is guilt although the society may not contemplate immediate promulgation of the doctrine. Thus the accused is to be punished, not for contempt, incitement or conspiracy, but for a step in preparation, which, if it threatens the public order at all, does so only remotely. The novelty in the prohibition introduced is that the statute aims, not at the practice of criminal syndicalism, nor even directly at the preaching of it, but at association with those who propose to preach it.

Despite arguments to the contrary which had seemed to me persuasive, it is settled that the due process clause of the Fourteenth Amendment applies to matters of substantive law as well as to matters of procedure. Thus all fundamental rights comprised within the term liberty are protected by the Federal Constitution from invasion by the States. The right of free speech, the right to teach and the right of assembly are, of course, fundamental rights. These may not be denied or abridged. But, although the rights of free speech and assembly are fundamental, they are not in their nature absolute. Their exercise is subject to restriction, if the particular restriction proposed is required in order to protect the State from destruction or from serious injury, political, economic or moral. That the necessity which is essential to a valid restriction does not exist unless speech would produce, or is intended to produce, a clear and imminent danger of some substantive evil which the State constitutionally may seek to prevent has been settled.

It is said to be the function of the legislature to determine whether at a particular time and under the particular circumstances the formation of, or assembly with, a society organized to advocate criminal syndicalism constitutes a clear and present danger of substantive evil; and that by enacting the law here in question the legislature of California determined that question in the affirmative. The legislature must obviously decide, in the first instance, whether a danger exists which calls for a particular protective measure. But where a statute is valid only in case certain conditions exist, the enactment of the statute cannot alone establish the facts which are essential to its validity. Prohibitory legislation has repeatedly been held invalid, because unnecessary, where the denial of liberty involved was that of engaging in a particular business. The power of the courts to strike down an offending law is no less when the interests involved are not property rights, but the fundamental personal rights of free speech and assembly.

This Court has not yet fixed the standard by which to determine when a danger shall be deemed clear; how remote the danger may be and yet be deemed present; and what degree of evil shall be deemed sufficiently substantial to justify resort to abridgment of free speech and assembly as the means of protection. To reach sound conclusions on these matters, we must bear in mind why a State is, ordinarily, denied the power to prohibit dissemination of social, economic and political doctrine which a vast majority of its citizens believes to be false and fraught with evil consequence.

Those who won our independence believed that the final end of the State was to make men free to develop their faculties; and that in its government the deliberative forces should prevail over the arbitrary. They valued liberty both as an end and as a means. . . . They believed liberty to be the secret of happiness and courage to be the secret of liberty. They believed that freedom to think as you will and to speak as you think are means indispensable to the discovery and spread of political truth; that without free speech and assembly discussion would be futile; that with them, discussion affords ordinarily adequate protection against the dissemination of noxious doctrine; that the greatest menace to freedom is an inert people; that public discussion is a political duty; and that this should be a fundamental principle of the American government. They recognized the risks to which all human institutions are subject. But they knew that order cannot be secured merely through fear of punishment for its infraction; that it is hazardous to discourage thought, hope and imagination; that fear breeds repression; that repression breeds hate; that hate menaces stable government; that the path of safety lies in the opportunity to discuss freely supposed grievances and proposed remedies; and that the fitting remedy for evil counsels is good ones. Believing in the power of reason as applied through public discussion, they eschewed silence coerced by law—the argument of force in its worst form. Recognizing the occasional tyrannies of governing majorities, they amended the Constitution so that free speech and assembly should be guaranteed.

Fear of serious injury cannot alone justify suppression of free speech and assembly. Men feared witches and burnt women. It is the function of speech to free men from the bondage of irrational fears. To justify suppression of free speech there must be reasonable ground to fear that serious evil will result if free speech is practiced. There must be reasonable ground to believe that the danger apprehended is imminent. There must be reasonable ground to believe that the evil to be prevented is a serious one. Every denunciation of existing law tends in some measure to increase the probability that there will be violation of it. Condonation of a breach enhances the probability. Expressions of approval add to the probability. Propagation of the criminal state of mind by teaching syndicalism increases it. Advocacy of law-breaking heightens it still further. But even advocacy of violation, however, reprehensible morally, is not a justification for denying free speech where the advocacy falls sort of incitement and there is nothing to indicate that the advocacy would be immediately acted on. The wide difference between advocacy and incitement, between preparation and attempt, between assembling and conspiracy, must be borne in mind. In order to support a finding of clear and present danger it must be shown either that immediate serious violence was to be expected or was advocated, or that the past conduct furnished reason to believe that such advocacy was then contemplated.

Those who won our independence by revolution were not cowards. They did not fear political change. They did not exalt order at the cost of liberty. To courageous, self-reliant men, with confidence in the power of free and fearless reasoning applied through the processes of popular government, no danger flowing from speech can be deemed clear and present, unless the incidence of the evil apprehended is so imminent that it may befall before there is opportunity for full discussion. If there be time to expose through discussion the falsehood and fallacies, to avert the evil by the processes of education, the remedy to be applied is more speech, not enforced silence. Only an emergency can justify repression. Such must be the rule if authority is to be reconciled with freedom. Such, in my opinion, is the command of the Constitution. It is therefore always open to Americans to challenge a law abridging free speech and assembly by showing that there was no emergency justifying it.

Moreover, even imminent danger cannot justify resort to prohibition of these functions essential to effective democracy, unless the evil apprehended is relatively serious. Prohibition of free speech and assembly is a measure so stringent that it would be inappropriate as the means for averting a relatively trivial harm to society. A police measure may be unconstitutional merely because the remedy, although effective as means of protection, is unduly harsh or oppressive. Thus, a State might, in the exercise of its police power, make any trespass upon the land of another a crime, regardless of the results or of the intent or purpose of the trespasser. It might, also, punish an attempt, a conspiracy, or an incitement to commit the trespass. But it is hardly conceivable that this Court would hold constitutional a statute which punished as a felony the mere voluntary assembly with a society formed to teach that pedestrians had the moral right to cross unenclosed, unposted, waste lands and to advocate their doing so, even if there was imminent danger that advocacy would lead to a trespass. The fact that speech is likely to result in some violence or in destruction of property is not enough to justify its suppression. There must be the probability of serious injury to the State. Among free men, the deterrents ordinarily to be applied to prevent crime are education and punishment for violations of the law, not abridgment of the rights of free speech and assembly.

The California Syndicalism Act recites in §4:

> "Inasmuch as this act concerns and is necessary to the immediate preservation of the public peace and safety, for the reason that at the present time large numbers of persons are going from place to place in this state advocating, teaching and practicing criminal syndicalism, this act shall take effect upon approval by the Governor."

This legislative declaration satisfies the requirement of the constitution of the State concerning emergency legislation. But it does not preclude enquiry into the question whether, at the time and under the circumstances, the conditions existed which are essential to validity under the Federal Constitution. As a statute, even if not void on its face, may be challenged because invalid as applied, the result of such an enquiry may depend upon the specific facts of the particular case. Whenever the fundamental rights of free speech and assembly are alleged to have been invaded, it must remain open to a defendant to present the issue whether there actually did exist at the time a clear danger; whether the danger, if any, was imminent; and whether the evil apprehended was one so substantial as to justify the stringent restriction interposed by the legislature. The legislative declaration, like the fact that the statute was passed and was sustained by the highest court of the State, creates merely a rebuttable presumption that these conditions have been satisfied.

Whether in 1919, when Miss Whitney did the things complained of, there was in California such clear and present danger of serious evil, might have been made the important issue in the case. She might have required that the issue be determined either by the court or the jury. She claimed below that the statute as applied to her violated the Federal Constitution; but she did not claim that it was void because there was no clear and present danger of serious evil, nor did she request that the existence of these conditions of a valid measure thus restricting the rights of free speech and assembly be passed upon by the court or a jury. On the other hand, there was evidence on which the court or jury might have found that such danger existed. I am unable to assent to the suggestion in the opinion of the Court that assembling with a political party, formed to advocate the desirability of a proletarian revolution by mass action at some date necessarily far in the future, is not a right within the protection of the Fourteenth Amendment. In the present case, however, there was other testimony which tended to establish the existence of a conspiracy, on the part of members of the International Workers of the World, to commit present serious crimes; and likewise to show that such a conspiracy would be furthered by the activity of the society of which Miss Whitney was a member. Under these circumstances the judgment of the state court cannot be disturbed.

Our power of review in this case is limited not only to the question whether a right guaranteed by the Federal Constitution was denied, but to the particular claims duly made below, and denied. We lack here the power occasionally exercised on review of judgments of lower federal courts to correct in criminal cases vital errors, although the objection was not taken in the trial court. This is a writ of error to a state court. Because we may not enquire into the errors now alleged, I concur in affirming the judgment of the state court.

DENNIS v. UNITED STATES

341 U.S. 494 (1951)

Opinion: Vinson, joined by Reed, Burton, Minton
Concurrence: Frankfurter
Concurrence: Jackson
Dissent: Black
Dissent: Douglas

In the following case, the Court considers the constitutionality of the Smith Act, which outlawed advocating the overthrow of the U.S. government. In particular, the case deals with an indictment against members of the Communist Party. The case is significant for its First Amendment analysis of government responses to the widely perceived threat of communism. As you read this case, consider whether you agree that the Communist Party itself constituted a clear and present danger to the United States, or whether this case mistakenly allowed for the suppression of political ideas. Consider further in what way, if at all, U.S. Supreme Court Chief Justice Fred M. Vinson alters the clear and present danger test compared to previous Court decisions. Pay particular attention to the dissent by Justice Hugo Black, which serves as an example of resistance to the clear and present danger test.

MR. CHIEF JUSTICE VINSON *announced the judgment of the Court and an opinion in which* **MR. JUSTICE REED,** **MR. JUSTICE BURTON** *and* **MR. JUSTICE MINTON** *join.*

Petitioners were indicted in July, 1948, for violation of the conspiracy provisions of the Smith Act, during the period of April, 1945, to July, 1948. The pretrial motion to quash the indictment on the grounds, *inter alia*, that the statute was unconstitutional was denied, *United States v. Foster*, and the case was set for trial on January 17, 1949. A verdict of guilty as to all the petitioners was returned by the jury on October 14, 1949. The Court of Appeals affirmed the convictions. We granted certiorari, limited to the following two questions: (1) Whether either §2 or §3 of the Smith Act, inherently or as construed and applied in the instant case, violates the First Amendment and other provisions of the Bill of Rights; (2) whether either §2 or §3 of the Act, inherently or as construed and applied in the instant case, violates the First and Fifth Amendments because of indefiniteness.

The trial of the case extended over nine months, six of which were devoted to the taking of evidence, resulting in a record of 16,000 pages. Our limited grant of the writ of certiorari has removed from our consideration any question as to the sufficiency of the evidence to support the jury's determination that petitioners are guilty of the offense charged. Whether, on this record, petitioners did, in fact, advocate the overthrow of the Government by force and violence is not before us, and we must base any discussion of this point upon the conclusions stated in the opinion of the Court of Appeals, which treated the issue in great detail. That court held that the record in this case amply supports the necessary finding of the jury that petitioners, the leaders of the Communist Party in this country, were unwilling to work within our framework of democracy, but intended to initiate a violent revolution whenever the propitious occasion appeared. Petitioners dispute the meaning to be drawn from the evidence, contending that the Marxist-Leninist doctrine they advocated taught that force and violence to achieve a Communist form of government in an existing democratic state would be necessary only because the ruling classes of that state would never permit the transformation to be accomplished peacefully, but would use force and violence to defeat any peaceful political and economic gain the Communists could achieve. But the Court of Appeals held that the record supports the following broad conclusions: by virtue of their control over the political apparatus of the Communist Political Association petitioners were able to transform that organization into the Communist Party; that the policies of the Association were changed from peaceful cooperation with the United States and its economic and political structure to a policy which had existed before the United States and the Soviet Union were fighting a common enemy, namely, a policy which worked for the overthrow of the Government by force and violence; that the Communist Party is a highly disciplined organization, adept at infiltration into strategic positions, use of aliases, and double meaning language; that the Party is rigidly controlled; that Communists, unlike other political parties, tolerate no dissension from the policy laid down by the guiding forces, but that the approved program is slavishly followed by the members of the Party; that the literature of the Party and the statements and activities of its leaders, petitioners here, advocate, and the general goal of the Party was, during the period in question, to achieve a successful overthrow of the existing order by force and violence.

II

The obvious purpose of the statute is to protect existing Government not from change by peaceable, lawful and constitutional means, but from change by violence, revolution and terrorism. That it is within the power of the Congress to protect the Government of the United States from armed rebellion is a proposition which requires little discussion. Whatever theoretical merit there may be to the argument that there is a "right" to rebellion against dictatorial governments is without force where the existing structure of the government provides for peaceful and orderly change. We reject any principle of governmental helplessness in the face of preparation for revolution, which principle, carried to its logical conclusion, must lead to anarchy. No one could conceive that it is not within the power of Congress to prohibit acts intended to overthrow the Government by force and violence. The question with which we are concerned here is not whether Congress has such power, but whether the means which it has employed conflict with the First and Fifth Amendments to the Constitution.

One of the bases for the contention that the means which Congress has employed are invalid takes the form of an attack on the face of the statute on the grounds that, by its terms, it prohibits academic discussion of the merits of Marxism-Leninism, that it stifles ideas and is contrary to all concepts of a free speech and a free press. Although we do not agree that the language itself has that significance, we must bear in mind that it is the duty of the federal courts to interpret federal legislation in a manner not inconsistent with the demands of the Constitution. *American Communications Assn. v. Douds.* We are not here confronted with cases similar to *Thornhill v. Alabama*; *Herndon v. Lowry*, and *De Jonge v. Oregon*, where a state court had given a meaning to a state statute which was inconsistent with the Federal Constitution. This is a federal statute which we must interpret as well as judge. Herein lies the fallacy of reliance upon the manner in which this Court has treated judgments of state courts. Where the statute as construed by the state court transgressed the First Amendment, we could not but invalidate the judgments of conviction.

III

Although no case subsequent to *Whitney* and *Gitlow* has expressly overruled the majority opinions in those cases, there is little doubt that subsequent opinions have inclined toward the Holmes-Brandeis rationale. And in *American Communications Ass'n v. Douds*, we were called upon to decide the validity of §9(h) of the Labor-Management Relations Act.

That section required officials of unions which desired to avail themselves of the facilities of the National Labor Relations Board to take oaths that they did not belong to the Communist Party and that they did not believe in the overthrow of the Government by force and violence. We pointed out that Congress did not intend to punish belief, but rather intended to regulate the conduct of union affairs. We therefore held that any indirect sanction on speech which might arise from the oath requirement did not present a proper case for the "clear and present danger" test, for the regulation was aimed at conduct rather than speech. In discussing the proper measure of evaluation of this kind of legislation, we suggested that the Holmes-Brandeis philosophy insisted that where there was a direct restriction upon speech, a "clear and present danger" that the substantive evil would be caused was necessary before the statute in question could be constitutionally applied. And we stated, "[The First] Amendment requires that one be permitted to believe what he will. It requires that one be permitted to advocate what he will unless there is a clear and present danger that a substantial public evil will result therefrom." But we further suggested that neither Justice Holmes nor Justice Brandeis ever envisioned that a shorthand phrase should be crystallized into a rigid rule to be applied inflexibly without regard to the circumstances of each case. Speech is not an absolute, above and beyond control by the legislature when its judgment, subject to review here, is that certain kinds of speech are so undesirable as to warrant criminal sanction. Nothing is more certain in modern society than the principle that there are no absolutes, that a name, a phrase, a standard has meaning only when associated with the considerations which gave birth to the nomenclature. To those who would paralyze our Government in the face of impending threat by encasing it in a semantic straitjacket we must reply that all concepts are relative.

In this case we are squarely presented with the application of the "clear and present danger" test, and must decide what that phrase imports. We first note that many of the cases in which this Court has reversed convictions by use of this or similar tests have been based on the fact that the interest which the State was attempting to protect was itself too insubstantial to warrant restriction of speech. Overthrow of the Government by force and violence is certainly a substantial enough interest for the Government to limit speech. Indeed, this is the ultimate value of any society, for if a society cannot protect its very structure from armed internal attack, it must follow that no subordinate value can be protected. If, then, this interest may be protected, the literal problem which is presented is what has been meant by the use of the phrase "clear and present danger" of the utterances bringing about the evil within the power of Congress to punish.

Obviously, the words cannot mean that before the Government may act, it must wait until the putsch is about to be executed, the plans have been laid and the signal is awaited. If Government is aware that a group aiming at its overthrow is attempting to indoctrinate its members and to commit them to a course whereby they will strike when the leaders feel the circumstances permit, action by the Government is required. The argument that there is no need for Government to concern itself, for Government is strong, it possesses ample powers to put down a rebellion, it may defeat the revolution with ease needs no answer. For that is not the question. Certainly an attempt to overthrow the Government by force, even though doomed from the outset because of inadequate numbers or power of the revolutionists, is

a sufficient evil for Congress to prevent. The damage which such attempts create both physically and politically to a nation makes it impossible to measure the validity in terms of the probability of success, or the immediacy of a successful attempt. In the instant case the trial judge charged the jury that they could not convict unless they found that petitioners intended to overthrow the Government "as speedily as circumstances would permit." This does not mean, and could not properly mean, that they would not strike until there was certainty of success. What was meant was that the revolutionists would strike when they thought the time was ripe. We must therefore reject the contention that success or probability of success is the criterion.

The situation with which Justices Holmes and Brandeis were concerned in *Gitlow* was a comparatively isolated event, bearing little relation in their minds to any substantial threat to the safety of the community. They were not confronted with any situation comparable to the instant one—the development of an apparatus designed and dedicated to the overthrow of the Government, in the context of world crisis after crisis.

Chief Judge Learned Hand, writing for the majority below, interpreted the phrase as follows: "In each case [courts] must ask whether the gravity of the 'evil,' discounted by its improbability, justifies such invasion of free speech as is necessary to avoid the danger." We adopt this statement of the rule. As articulated by Chief Judge Hand, it is as succinct and inclusive as any other we might devise at this time. It takes into consideration those factors which we deem relevant, and relates their significances. More we cannot expect from words.

IV

Although we have concluded that the finding that there was a sufficient danger to warrant the application of the statute was justified on the merits, there remains the problem of whether the trial judge's treatment of the issue was correct.

V

There remains to be discussed the question of vagueness—whether the statute as we have interpreted it is too vague, not sufficiently advising those who would speak of the limitations upon their activity. It is urged that such vagueness contravenes the First and Fifth Amendments. This argument is particularly nonpersuasive when presented by petitioners, who, the jury found, intended to overthrow the Government as speedily as circumstances would permit. A claim of guilelessness ill becomes those with evil intent. *Williams v. United States.*

We agree that the standard as defined is not a neat, mathematical formulary. Like all verbalizations it is subject to criticism on the score of indefiniteness. But petitioners themselves contend that the verbalization "clear and present danger" is the proper standard. We see no difference, from the standpoint of vagueness, whether the standard of "clear and present danger" is one contained *in haec verba* within the statute, or whether it is the judicial measure of constitutional applicability. We have shown the indeterminate standard the phrase necessarily connotes. We do not think we have rendered that standard any more indefinite by our attempt to sum up the factors which are included within its scope. We think it well serves to indicate to those who would advocate constitutionally prohibited conduct that there is a line beyond which they may not go—a line which they, in full knowledge of what they intend and the circumstances in which their activity takes place, will well appreciate and understand. Where there is doubt as to the intent of the defendants, the nature of their

activities, or their power to bring about the evil, this Court will review the convictions with the scrupulous care demanded by our Constitution. But we are not convinced that, because there may be borderline cases at some time in the future, these convictions should be reversed because of the argument that these petitioners could not know that their activities were constitutionally proscribed by the statute.

Affirmed.

MR. JUSTICE BLACK, *dissenting.*

Here again, as in *Breard v. Alexandria*, decided this day, my basic disagreement with the Court is not as to how we should explain or reconcile what was said in prior decisions, but springs from a fundamental difference in constitutional approach. Consequently, it would serve no useful purpose to state my position at length.

At the outset, I want to emphasize what the crime involved in this case is, and what it is not. These petitioners were not charged with an attempt to overthrow the Government. They were not charged with overt acts of any kind designed to overthrow the Government. They were not even charged with saying anything or writing anything designed to overthrow the Government. The charge was that they agreed to assemble and to talk and publish certain ideas at a later date: the indictment is that they conspired to organize the Communist Party and to use speech or newspapers and other publications in the future to teach and advocate the forcible overthrow of the Government. No matter how it is worded, this is a virulent form of prior censorship of speech and press, which I believe the First Amendment forbids. I would hold §3 of the Smith Act authorizing this prior restraint unconstitutional on its face and as applied.

The New York Times.

NEW YORK, TUESDAY, MARCH 29, 1960.

"The growing movement of peaceful mass demonstrations by Negroes is something new in the South, something understandable.... Let Congress heed their rising voices, for they will be heard."

—New York Times editorial
Saturday, March 19, 1960

Heed Their Rising Voices

As the whole world knows by now, thousands of Southern Negro students are engaged in widespread non-violent demonstrations in positive affirmation of the right to live in human dignity as guaranteed by the U. S. Constitution and the Bill of Rights. In their efforts to uphold these guarantees, they are being met by an unprecedented wave of terror by those who would deny and negate that document which the whole world looks upon as setting the pattern for modern freedom....

In Orangeburg, South Carolina, when 400 students peacefully sought to buy doughnuts and coffee at lunch counters in the business district, they were forcibly ejected, tear-gassed, soaked to the skin in freezing weather with fire hoses, arrested en masse and herded into an open barbed-wire stockade to stand for hours in the bitter cold.

In Montgomery, Alabama, after students sang "My Country, 'Tis of Thee" on the State Capitol steps, their leaders were expelled from school, and truckloads of police armed with shotguns and tear-gas ringed the Alabama State College Campus. When the entire student body protested to state authorities by refusing to re-register, their dining hall was padlocked in an attempt to starve them into submission.

In Tallahassee, Atlanta, Nashville, Savannah, Greensboro, Memphis, Richmond, Charlotte, and a host of other cities in the South, young American teenagers, in face of the entire weight of official state apparatus and police power, have boldly stepped forth as protagonists of democracy. Their courage and amazing restraint have inspired millions and given a new dignity to the cause of freedom.

Small wonder that the Southern violators of the Constitution fear this new, non-violent brand of freedom fighter . . . even as they fear the upswelling right-to-vote movement. Small wonder that they are determined to destroy the one man who, more than any other, symbolizes the new spirit now sweeping the South—the Rev. Dr. Martin Luther King, Jr., world-famous leader of the Montgomery Bus Protest. For it is his doctrine of non-violence which has inspired and guided the students in their widening wave of sit-ins; and it this same Dr. King who founded and is president of the Southern Christian Leadership Conference—the organization which is spearheading the surging right-to-vote movement. Under Dr. King's direction the Leadership Conference conducts Student Workshops and Seminars in the philosophy and technique of non-violent resistance.

Again and again the Southern violators have answered Dr. King's peaceful protests with intimidation and violence. They have bombed his home almost killing his wife and child. They have assaulted his person. They have arrested him seven times—for "speeding," "loitering" and similar "offenses." And now they have charged him with "perjury"—a felony under which they could imprison him for ten years. Obviously, their real purpose is to remove him physically as the leader to whom the students and millions

of others—look for guidance and support, and thereby to intimidate *all* leaders who may rise in the South. Their strategy is to behead this affirmative movement, and thus to demoralize Negro Americans and weaken their will to struggle. The defense of Martin Luther King, spiritual leader of the student sit-in movement, clearly, therefore, is an integral part of the total struggle for freedom in the South.

Decent-minded Americans cannot help but applaud the creative daring of the students and the quiet heroism of Dr. King. But this is one of those moments in the stormy history of Freedom when men and women of good will must do more than applaud the rising-to-glory of others. The America whose good name hangs in the balance before a watchful world, the America whose heritage of Liberty these Southern Upholders of the Constitution are defending, is *our* America as well as theirs . . .

We must heed their rising voices—yes—but we must add our own.

We must extend ourselves above and beyond moral support and render the material help so urgently needed by those who are taking the risks, facing jail, and even death in a glorious re-affirmation of our Constitution and its Bill of Rights.

We urge you to join hands with our fellow Americans in the South by supporting, with your dollars, this Combined Appeal for all three needs—the defense of Martin Luther King—the support of the embattled students—and the struggle for the right-to-vote.

Your Help Is Urgently Needed . . . NOW !!

Stella Adler
Raymond Pace Alexander
Shelly Appleton
Harry Van Arsdale
Harry Belafonte
Julie Belafonte
Dr. Algernon Black
Marc Blitzein
William Bowe
William Branch
Marlon Brando
Mrs. Ralph Bunche
Diahann Carroll
Dr. Alan Knight Chalmers

Joseph Cohen
Richard Coe
Nat King Cole
Cheryl Crawford
Dorothy Dandridge
Ossie Davis
Sammy Davis, Jr.
Ruby Dee
Harry Dolly
Scotty Eckford
Dr. Philip Elliott
Dr. Harry Emerson
Fosdick

Anthony Franciosa
Mathew Guinon
Lorraine Hansbury
Rev. Donald Harrington
Nat Hentoff
James Hicks
Mary Hinkson
Van Heflin
Langston Hughes
Morris Iushewitz
Mahalia Jackson
Paul Jennings
Mordecai Johnson
John Killens

Eartha Kitt
Rabbi Edward Klein
Hope Lange
John Lewis
Viveca Lindfors
David Livingston
William Michaelson
Carl Murphy
Don Murray
John Murray
A. J. Muste
Frederick O'Neal
Peter Ottley
L. Joseph Overton

Albert P. Palmer
Clarence Pickett
Shad Polier
Sidney Poitier
Michael Potoker
A. Philip Randolph
John Raitt
Elmer Rice
Cleveland Robinson
Jackie Robinson
Mrs. Eleanor Roosevelt
Bayard Rustin
Robert Ryan
Maureen Stapleton

Frank Silvera
Louis Simon
Hope Stevens
David Sullivan
Julius Sum
George Tabori
Rev. Gardner C. Taylor
Norman Thomas
Kenneth Tynan
Charles White
Shelley Winters
Max Youngstein

We in the south who are struggling daily for dignity and freedom warmly endorse this appeal

Rev. Ralph D. Abernathy
(Montgomery, Ala.)

Rev. Fred L. Shuttlesworth
(Birmingham, Ala.)

Rev. Kelley Miller Smith
(Nashville, Tenn.)

Rev. W. A. Dennis
(Chattanooga, Tenn.)

Rev. C. K. Steele
(Tallahassee, Fla.)

Rev. Matthew D. McCollom
(Orangeburg, S. C.)

Rev. William Holmes Borders
(Atlanta, Ga.)

Rev. Douglas Moore
(Durham, N. C.)

Rev. Wyatt Tee Walker
(Petersburg, Va.)

Rev. Walter L. Hamilton
(Norfolk, Va.)

I. S. Levy
(Columbia, S. C.)

Rev. Martin Luther King, Sr.
(Atlanta, Ga.)

Rev. Henry C. Bunton
(Memphis, Tenn.)

Rev. S. S. Seay, Sr.
(Montgomery, Ala.)

Rev. Samuel W. Williams
(Atlanta, Ga.)

Rev. A. L. Davis
(New Orleans, La.)

Mrs. Katie E. Whickham
(New Orleans, La.)

Rev. W. H. Hall
(Hattiesburg, Miss.)

Rev. J. E. Lowery
(Mobile, Ala.)

Rev. T. J. Jemison
(Baton Rouge, La.)

Please mail this coupon TODAY!

Committee To Defend Martin Luther King
and
The Struggle For Freedom In The South
312 West 125th Street, New York 27, N. Y.
UNiversity 6-1700

I am enclosing my contribution of $_____
for the work of the Committee.

(PLEASE PRINT)

Name _____

Address _____

City _____ Zone ____ State ____

☐ I want to help   ☐ Please send further information

Please make checks payable to:
Committee To Defend Martin Luther King

COMMITTEE TO DEFEND MARTIN LUTHER KING AND THE STRUGGLE FOR FREEDOM IN THE SOUTH
312 West 125th Street, New York 27, N. Y. UNiversity 6-1700

Chairmen: A. Philip Randolph, Dr. Gardner C. Taylor; *Chairmen of Cultural Division:* Harry Belafonte, Sidney Poitier; *Treasurer:* Nat King Cole; *Executive Director:* Bayard Rustin; *Chairmen of Church Division:* Father George B. Ford, Rev. Harry Emerson Fosdick, Rev. Thomas Kilgore, Jr., Rabbi Edward E. Klein; *Chairmen of Labor Division:* Morris Iushewitz, Cleveland Robinson

Advertisement in the New York Times challenged in New York Times Co. v. Sullivan.

But let us assume, contrary to all constitutional ideas of fair criminal procedure, that petitioners, although not indicted for the crime of actual advocacy, may be punished for it. Even on this radical assumption, the other opinions in this case show that the only way to affirm these convictions is to repudiate directly or indirectly the established "clear and present danger" rule. This the Court does in a way which greatly restricts the protections afforded by the First Amendment. The opinions for affirmance indicate that the chief reason for jettisoning the rule is the expressed fear that advocacy of Communist doctrine endangers the safety of the Republic. Undoubtedly a governmental policy of unfettered communication of ideas does entail dangers. To the Founders of this Nation, however, the benefits derived from free expression were worth the risk. They embodied this philosophy in the First Amendment's command that "Congress shall make no law . . . abridging the freedom of speech, or of the press. . . ." I have always believed that the First Amendment is the keystone of our Government, that the freedoms it guarantees provide the best insurance against destruction of all freedom. At least as to speech in the realm of public matters, I believe that the "clear and present danger" test does not "mark the furthermost constitutional boundaries of protected expression," but does "no more than recognize a minimum compulsion of the Bill of Rights." *Bridges v. California.*

So long as this Court exercises the power of judicial review of legislation, I cannot agree that the First Amendment permits us to sustain laws suppressing freedom of speech and press on the basis of Congress' or our own notions of mere "reasonableness." Such a doctrine waters down the First Amendment so that it amounts to little more than an admonition to Congress. The Amendment as so construed is not likely to protect any but those "safe" or orthodox views which rarely need its protection. I must also express my objection to the holding because, as Mr. Justice Douglas dissent shows, it sanctions the determination of a crucial issue of fact by the judge, rather than by the jury. Nor can I let this opportunity pass without expressing my objection to the severely limited grant of certiorari in this case which precluded consideration here of at least two other reasons for reversing these convictions: (1) the record shows a discriminatory selection of the jury panel which prevented trial before a representative cross-section of the community; (2) the record shows that one member of the trial jury was violently hostile to petitioners before and during the trial.

Public opinion being what it now is, few will protest the conviction of these Communist petitioners. There is hope, however, that, in calmer times, when present pressures, passions and fears subside, this or some later Court will restore the First Amendment liberties to the high preferred place where they belong in a free society.

NEW YORK TIMES CO. v. SULLIVAN

376 U.S. 254 (1964)

Opinion: Brennan, joined by Warren, Clark, Harlan, Stewart, White
Concurrence: Black, joined by Douglas
Concurrence: Goldberg, joined by Douglas

In New York Times Co. v. Sullivan, *the Supreme Court considered the extent to which the First Amendment protects libelous or untrue speech directed at public officials. Libelous speech must both harm or "defame" an individual and be published in some form. The Court found that the Constitution's protection of speech extends even to false speech, so long as it does not demonstrate actual malice toward the official or reckless disregard as to the truthfulness of the statement in question.*

In his opinion, U.S. Supreme Court Justice William J. Brennan emphasizes the importance of speech, even if it is untrue, for the process of political deliberation. You might recall John Stuart Mill's defense of the right to make flawed arguments here. To what extent, however, does false speech contribute to public discourse? Also, if politically motivated speech holds value, why not protect malicious speech? What is the appropriate standard for cases involving untrue or false speech, even if politically motivated? Individuals have a right to voice their opinions, but does the Constitution demand a basic level of integrity among participants in public discourse?

MR. JUSTICE BRENNAN *delivered the opinion of the Court.*

We are required in this case to determine for the first time the extent to which the constitutional protections for speech and press limit a State's power to award damages in a libel action brought by a public official against critics of his official conduct.

Respondent L.B. Sullivan is one of the three elected Commissioners of the City of Montgomery, Alabama. He testified that he was "Commissioner of Public Affairs, and the duties are supervision of the Police Department, Fire Department, Department of Cemetery and Department of Scales."

He brought this civil libel action against the four individual petitioners, who are Negroes and Alabama clergymen, and against petitioner the New York Times Company, a New York corporation which publishes the *New York Times*, a daily newspaper. A jury in the Circuit Court of Montgomery County awarded him damages of $500,000, the full amount claimed,

against all the petitioners, and the Supreme Court of Alabama affirmed.

Respondent's complaint alleged that he had been libeled by statements in a full-page advertisement that was carried in the *New York Times* on March 29, 1960. Entitled "Heed Their Rising Voices," the advertisement began by stating that, "As the whole world knows by now, thousands of Southern Negro students are engaged in widespread nonviolent demonstrations in positive affirmation of the right to live in human dignity as guaranteed by the U.S. Constitution and the Bill of Rights." It went on to charge that, "[I]n their efforts to uphold these guarantees, they are being met by an unprecedented wave of terror by those who would deny and negate that document which the whole world looks upon as setting the pattern for modern freedom. . . ."

Succeeding paragraphs purported to illustrate the "wave of terror" by describing certain alleged events. The text concluded with an appeal for funds for three purposes: support of the student movement, "the struggle for the right to vote," and the legal defense of Dr. Martin Luther King, Jr., leader of the movement, against a perjury indictment then pending in Montgomery.

The text appeared over the names of 64 persons, many widely known for their activities in public affairs, religion, trade unions, and the performing arts. Below these names, and under a line reading "We in the south who are struggling daily for dignity and freedom warmly endorse this appeal," appeared the names of the four individual petitioners and of 16 other persons, all but two of whom were identified as clergymen in various Southern cities. The advertisement was signed at the bottom of the page by the "Committee to Defend Martin Luther King and the Struggle for Freedom in the South," and the officers of the Committee were listed.

Of the 10 paragraphs of text in the advertisement, the third and a portion of the sixth were the basis of respondent's claim of libel.

They read as follows: Third paragraph: "In Montgomery, Alabama, after students sang 'My Country, 'Tis of Thee' on the State Capitol steps, their leaders were expelled from school, and truckloads of police armed with shotguns and tear-gas ringed the Alabama State College Campus. When the entire student body protested to state authorities by refusing to reregister, their dining hall was padlocked in an attempt to starve them into submission." Sixth paragraph: "Again and again, the Southern violators have answered Dr. King's peaceful protests with intimidation and violence. They have bombed his home, almost killing his wife and child. They have assaulted his person. They have arrested him seven times—for 'speeding,' 'loitering' and similar 'offenses.' And now they have charged him with 'perjury'—a *felony* under which they could imprison him for *ten years....*"

Although neither of these statements mentions respondent by name, he contended that the word "police" in the third paragraph referred to him as the Montgomery Commissioner who supervised the Police Department, so that he was being accused of "ringing" the campus with police. He further claimed that the paragraph would be read as imputing to the police, and hence to him, the padlocking of the dining hall in order to starve the students into submission. As to the sixth paragraph, he contended that, since arrests are ordinarily made by the police, the statement "They have arrested [Dr. King] seven times" would be read as referring to him; he further contended that the "They" who did the arresting would be equated with the "They" who committed the other described acts and with the "Southern violators." Thus, he argued, the paragraph would be read as accusing the Montgomery police, and hence him, of answering Dr. King's protests with "intimidation and violence," bombing his home, assaulting his person, and charging him with perjury. Respondent and six other Montgomery

residents testified that they read some or all of the statements as referring to him in his capacity as Commissioner.

It is uncontroverted that some of the statements contained in the two paragraphs were not accurate descriptions of events which occurred in Montgomery. Although Negro students staged a demonstration on the State Capitol steps, they sang the National Anthem and not "My Country, 'Tis of Thee." Although nine students were expelled by the State Board of Education, this was not for leading the demonstration at the Capitol, but for demanding service at a lunch counter in the Montgomery County Courthouse on another day. Not the entire student body, but most of it, had protested the expulsion, not by refusing to register, but by boycotting classes on a single day; virtually all the students did register for the ensuing semester. The campus dining hall was not padlocked on any occasion, and the only students who may have been barred from eating there were the few who had neither signed a preregistration application nor requested temporary meal tickets. Although the police were deployed near the campus in large numbers on three occasions, they did not at any time "ring" the campus, and they were not called to the campus in connection with the demonstration on the State Capitol steps, as the third paragraph implied. Dr. King had not been arrested seven times, but only four, and although he claimed to have been assaulted some years earlier in connection with his arrest for loitering outside a courtroom, one of the officers who made the arrest denied that there was such an assault.

On the premise that the charges in the sixth paragraph could be read as referring to him, respondent was allowed to prove that he had not participated in the events described. Although Dr. King's home had, in fact, been bombed twice when his wife and child were there, both of these occasions antedated respondent's tenure as Commissioner, and the police were not only not implicated in the bombings, but had made every effort to apprehend those who were. Three of Dr. King's four arrests took place before respondent became Commissioner. Although Dr. King had, in fact, been indicted (he was subsequently acquitted) on two counts of perjury, each of which carried a possible five-year sentence, respondent had nothing to do with procuring the indictment.

Respondent made no effort to prove that he suffered actual pecuniary loss as a result of the alleged libel. The cost of the advertisement was approximately $4800, and it was published by the *Times* upon an order from a New York advertising agency acting for the signatory Committee. The agency submitted the advertisement with a letter from A. Philip Randolph, Chairman of the Committee, certifying that the persons whose names appeared on the advertisement had given their permission. Mr. Randolph was known to the *Times'* Advertising Acceptability Department as a responsible person, and, in accepting the letter as sufficient proof of authorization, it followed its established practice. The manager of the Advertising Acceptability Department testified that he had approved the advertisement for publication because he knew nothing to cause him to believe that anything in it was false, and because it bore the endorsement of "a number of people who are well known and whose reputation" he "had no reason to question." Neither he nor anyone else at the *Times* made an effort to confirm the accuracy of the advertisement, either by checking it against recent *Times* news stories relating to some of the described events or by any other means.

The trial judge submitted the case to the jury under instructions that the statements in the advertisement were "libelous *per se*," and were not privileged, so that petitioners might be held liable if the jury found that they had published the advertisement and that the statements were made "of and concerning" respondent. The jury was instructed that, because the statements were libelous *per se*, "the law . . . implies legal injury from the bare fact of publication itself," "falsity and malice are presumed," "general damages need not be alleged or proved, but are presumed," and "punitive damages may be awarded by the jury even though the amount of actual damages is neither found nor shown." An award of punitive damages—as distinguished from "general" damages, which are compensatory in nature—apparently requires proof of actual malice under Alabama law, and the judge charged that "mere negligence or carelessness is not evidence of actual malice or malice in fact, and does not justify an award of exemplary or punitive damages." He refused to charge, however, that the jury must be "convinced" of malice, in the sense of "actual intent" to harm or "gross negligence and recklessness," to make such an award, and he also refused to require that a verdict for respondent differentiate between compensatory and punitive damages. The judge rejected petitioners' contention that his rulings abridged the freedoms of speech and of the press that are guaranteed by the First and Fourteenth Amendments. In affirming the judgment, the Supreme Court of Alabama sustained the trial judge's rulings and instructions in all respects.

Because of the importance of the constitutional issues involved, we granted the separate petitions for certiorari of the individual petitioners and of the Times. We reverse the judgment. We hold that the rule of law applied by the Alabama courts is constitutionally deficient for failure to provide the safeguards for freedom of speech and of the press that are required by the First and Fourteenth Amendments in a libel action brought by a public official against critics of his official conduct. We further hold that, under the proper safeguards, the evidence presented in this case is constitutionally insufficient to support the judgment for respondent.

Under Alabama law, as applied in this case, a publication is "libelous *per se*" if the words "tend to injure a person . . . in his reputation" or to "bring [him] into public contempt"; the trial court stated that the standard was met if the words are such as to "injure him in his public office, or impute misconduct to him in his office, or want of official integrity, or want of fidelity to a public trust. . . ." The jury must find that the words were published "of and concerning" the plaintiff, but, where the plaintiff is a public official, his place in the governmental hierarchy is sufficient evidence to support a finding that his reputation has been affected by statements that reflect upon the agency of which he is in charge. Once "libel *per se*" has been established, the defendant has no defense as to stated facts unless he can persuade the jury that they were true in all their particulars. His privilege of "fair comment" for expressions of opinion depends on the truth of the facts upon which the comment is based. Unless he can discharge the burden of proving truth, general damages are presumed, and may be awarded without proof of pecuniary injury. A showing of actual malice is apparently a prerequisite to recovery of punitive damages, and the defendant may, in any event, forestall a punitive award by a retraction meeting the statutory requirements. Good motives and belief in truth do not negate an inference of malice, but are relevant only in mitigation of punitive damages if the jury chooses to accord them weight.

The question before us is whether this rule of liability, as applied to an action brought by a public official against critics of his official conduct, abridges the freedom of speech and of the press that is guaranteed by the First and Fourteenth Amendments.

Respondent relies heavily, as did the Alabama courts, on statements of this Court to the effect that the Constitution does not protect libelous publications. Those statements do not foreclose our inquiry here. None of the cases sustained the use of libel laws to impose sanctions upon expression critical of the official conduct of public officials. Like insurrection, contempt, advocacy of unlawful acts, breach of the peace, obscenity, solicitation of legal business, and the various other formulae for the repression of expression that have been challenged in this Court, libel can claim no talismanic immunity from constitutional limitations. It must be measured by standards that satisfy the First Amendment.

The general proposition that freedom of expression upon public questions is secured by the First Amendment has long been settled by our decisions. The constitutional safeguard, we have said, "was fashioned to assure unfettered interchange of ideas for the bringing about of political and social changes desired by the people." *Roth v. United States.* "The maintenance of the opportunity for free political discussion to the end that government may be responsive to the will of the people and that changes may be obtained by lawful means, an opportunity essential to the security of the Republic, is a fundamental principle of our constitutional system." *Stromberg v. California.* "[I]t is a prized American privilege to speak one's mind, although not always with perfect good taste, on all public institutions," *Bridges v. California,* and this opportunity is to be afforded for "vigorous advocacy" no less than "abstract discussion." *NAACP v. Button.* The First Amendment, said Judge Learned Hand, "presupposes that right conclusions are more likely to be gathered out of a multitude of tongues than through any kind of authoritative selection. To many, this is, and always will be, folly, but we have staked upon it our all." *United States v. Associated Press.*

Thus, we consider this case against the background of a profound national commitment to the principle that debate on public issues should be uninhibited, robust, and wide-open, and that it may well include vehement, caustic, and sometimes unpleasantly sharp attacks on government and public officials. The present advertisement, as an expression of grievance and protest on one of the major public issues of our time, would seem clearly to qualify for the constitutional protection. The question is whether it forfeits that protection by the falsity of some of its factual statements and by its alleged defamation of respondent.

Authoritative interpretations of the First Amendment guarantees have consistently refused to recognize an exception for any test of truth—whether administered by judges, juries, or administrative officials—and especially one that puts the burden of proving truth on the speaker. The constitutional protection does not turn upon "the truth, popularity, or social utility of the ideas and beliefs which are offered." *NAACP v. Button*. As Madison said, "Some degree of abuse is inseparable from the proper use of every thing, and in no instance is this more true than in that of the press."

That erroneous statement is inevitable in free debate, and that it must be protected if the freedoms of expression are to have the "breathing space" that they "need . . . to survive," *NAACP v. Button*, was also recognized by the Court of Appeals for the District of Columbia Circuit in *Sweeney v. Patterson*. Judge Edgerton spoke for a unanimous court which affirmed the dismissal of a Congressman's libel suit based upon a newspaper article charging him with anti-Semitism in opposing a judicial appointment. Injury to official reputation affords no more warrant for repressing speech that would otherwise be free than does factual error.

If neither factual error nor defamatory content suffices to remove the constitutional shield from criticism of official conduct, the combination of the two elements is no less inadequate. This is the lesson to be drawn from the great controversy over the Sedition Act of 1798, which first crystallized a national awareness of the central meaning of the First Amendment. That statute made it a crime, punishable by a $5,000 fine

and five years in prison, "if any person shall write, print, utter or publish . . . any false, scandalous and malicious writing or writings against the government of the United States, or either house of the Congress . . . or the President . . . with intent to defame . . . or to bring them, or either of them, into contempt or disrepute; or to excite against them, or either or any of them, the hatred of the good people of the United States." The Act allowed the defendant the defense of truth, and provided that the jury were to be judges both of the law and the facts. Despite these qualifications, the Act was vigorously condemned as unconstitutional in an attack joined in by Jefferson and Madison.

Although the Sedition Act was never tested in this Court, the attack upon its validity has carried the day in the court of history. Fines levied in its prosecution were repaid by Act of Congress on the ground that it was unconstitutional. Calhoun, reporting to the Senate on February 4, 1836, assumed that its invalidity was a matter "which no one now doubts." Jefferson, as President, pardoned those who had been convicted and sentenced under the Act and remitted their fines.

There is no force in respondent's argument that the constitutional limitations implicit in the history of the Sedition Act apply only to Congress, and not to the States. It is true that the First Amendment was originally addressed only to action by the Federal Government, and that Jefferson, for one, while denying the power of Congress "to controul the freedom of the press," recognized such a power in the States. But this distinction was eliminated with the adoption of the Fourteenth Amendment and the application to the States of the First Amendment's restrictions.

The state rule of law is not saved by its allowance of the defense of truth. A rule compelling the critic of official conduct to guarantee the truth of all his factual assertions—and to do so on pain of libel judgments virtually unlimited in amount—leads to a comparable "self-censorship." Allowance of the defense of truth, with the burden of proving it on the defendant, does not mean that only false speech will be deterred. Even courts accepting this defense as an adequate safeguard have recognized the difficulties of adducing legal proofs that the alleged libel was true in all its factual particulars. Under such a rule, would-be critics of official conduct may be deterred from voicing their criticism, even though it is believed to be true and even though it is, in fact, true, because of doubt whether it can be proved in court or fear of the expense of having to do so. They tend to make only statements which "steer far wider of the unlawful zone." *Speiser v. Randall*. The rule thus dampens the vigor and limits the variety of public debate. It is inconsistent with the First and Fourteenth Amendments.

The constitutional guarantees require, we think, a federal rule that prohibits a public official from recovering damages for a defamatory falsehood relating to his official conduct unless he proves that the statement was made with "actual malice"—that is, with knowledge that it was false or with reckless disregard of whether it was false or not.

We hold today that the Constitution delimits a State's power to award damages for libel in actions brought by public officials against critics of their official conduct. Since this is such an action, the rule requiring proof of actual malice is applicable. While Alabama law apparently requires proof of actual malice for an award of punitive damages, where general damages are concerned malice is "presumed." Such a presumption is inconsistent with the federal rule.

Applying these standards, we consider that the proof presented to show actual malice lacks the convincing clarity which the constitutional standard demands, and hence that it would not constitutionally sustain the judgment for respondent under the proper rule of law. The case of the individual petitioners requires little discussion.

Even assuming that they could constitutionally be found to have authorized the use of their names on the advertisement, there was no evidence whatever that they were aware of any erroneous statements or were in any way reckless in that regard. The judgment against them is thus without constitutional support. As to the *Times*, we similarly conclude that the facts do not support a finding of actual malice.

Raising as it does the possibility that a good faith critic of government will be penalized for his criticism, the proposition relied on by the Alabama courts strikes at the very center of the constitutionally protected area of free expression. We hold that such a proposition may not constitutionally be utilized to establish that an otherwise impersonal attack on governmental operations was a libel of an official responsible for those operations. Since it was relied on exclusively here, and there was no other evidence to connect the statements with respondent, the evidence was constitutionally insufficient to support a finding that the statements referred to respondent.

The judgment of the Supreme Court of Alabama is reversed, and the case is remanded to that court for further proceedings not inconsistent with this opinion.

Reversed and remanded.

CASE QUESTION

One thing to notice about this case is that it departs in an important respect from the cases we have considered previously. In all of the cases you have read so far, there have been instances of clear "state action." For instance, in *Schenck v. United States*, an individual was arrested by the state. Police actions are perhaps the most obvious form of state action, which is usually thought to be required for First Amendment protection. Notice that the case arises from a lawsuit by a government official against a newspaper and private individuals. As you read, consider where the state action might be in this case. Is it simply that the state action is present because of the fact that the courts are involved in hearing libel suits? Or does a finding of state action hinge upon the involvement of a public official, in this case a "commissioner of public affairs," as the object of the speech in question? Or is there simply no state action in the case?

BRANDENBURG v. OHIO

395 U.S. 444 (1969)

Opinion: Per Curiam
Concurrence: Black
Concurrence: Douglas

The clear and present danger test, first outlined by Justice Oliver Wendell Holmes in Schenck v. United States, *came to a clear end in 1969, in* Brandenburg v. Ohio. *In its per curiam decision, the Court effectively did away with the clear and present danger test. According to* Brandenburg v. Ohio, *speech must not only advocate but also be likely to incite imminent lawless action in order for it to lose constitutional protection. This standard continues to guide jurisprudence in this area today. Another difference between the standard set up in this case and that of the clear and present danger test concerns the question of time. In* Brandenburg v. Ohio, *the Court indicates that speech must pose an imminent threat in order for it to be constitutionally prohibited. As you read this case, consider how you would characterize the difference between the clear and present danger test and the standard announced in* Brandenburg v. Ohio. *Is it a matter of degree, or are they different tests entirely? Accordingly, ask yourself whether it is constitutionally appropriate under the First Amendment that only threats inciting imminent lawless action lack constitutional protection*

PER CURIAM.

The appellant, a leader of a Ku Klux Klan group, was convicted under the Ohio Criminal Syndicalism statute for "advocat[ing] . . . the duty, necessity, or propriety of crime, sabotage, violence, or unlawful methods of terrorism as a means of accomplishing industrial or political reform" and for "voluntarily assembl[ing] with any society, group, or assemblage of persons formed to teach or advocate the doctrines of criminal syndicalism." He was fined $1,000 and sentenced to one to 10 years' imprisonment. The appellant challenged the constitutionality of the criminal syndicalism statute under the First and Fourteenth Amendments to the United States Constitution, but the intermediate appellate court of Ohio affirmed his conviction without opinion. The Supreme Court of Ohio dismissed his appeal, *sua sponte*, "for the reason that no substantial constitutional question exists herein." It did not file an opinion or explain its conclusions. Appeal was taken to this Court, and we noted probable jurisdiction. We reverse.

The record shows that a man, identified at trial as the appellant, telephoned an announcer-reporter on the staff of a Cincinnati television station and invited him to come to a Ku Klux Klan "rally" to be held at a farm in Hamilton County. With the cooperation of the organizers, the reporter and a cameraman attended the meeting and filmed the events. Portions of the films were later broadcast on the local station and on a national network.

The prosecution's case rested on the films and on testimony identifying the appellant as the person who communicated with the reporter and who spoke at the rally. The State also introduced into evidence several articles appearing in the film, including a pistol, a rifle, a shotgun, ammunition, a Bible, and a red hood worn by the speaker in the films.

One film showed 12 hooded figures, some of whom carried firearms. They were gathered around a large wooden cross, which they burned. No one was present other than the participants and the newsmen who made the film. Most of the words uttered during the scene were incomprehensible when the film was projected, but scattered phrases could be understood that were derogatory of Negroes and, in one instance, of Jews. Another scene on the same film showed the appellant, in Klan regalia, making a speech.

The second film showed six hooded figures one of whom, later identified as the appellant, repeated a speech very similar to that recorded on the first film. The reference to the possibility of "revengeance" was omitted, and one sentence was added: "Personally, I believe the nigger should be returned to Africa, the Jew returned to Israel." Though some of the figures in the films carried weapons, the speaker did not.

The Ohio Criminal Syndicalism Statute was enacted in 1919. From 1917 to 1920, identical or quite similar laws were adopted by 20 States and two territories. In 1927, this Court sustained the constitutionality of California's Criminal Syndicalism Act, the text of which is quite similar to that of the laws of Ohio. *Whitney v. California.* The Court upheld the statute on the ground that, without more, "advocating" violent means to effect political and economic change involves such danger to the security of the State that the State may outlaw it. But *Whitney* has been thoroughly discredited by later decisions. These later decisions have fashioned the principle that the constitutional guarantees of free speech and free press do not permit a State to forbid or proscribe advocacy of the use

of force or of law violation except where such advocacy is directed to inciting or producing imminent lawless action and is likely to incite or produce such action. As we said in *Noto v. United States*, "the mere abstract teaching . . . of the moral propriety or even moral necessity for a resort to force and violence, is not the same as preparing a group for violent action and steeling it to such action." A statute which fails to draw this distinction impermissibly intrudes upon the freedoms guaranteed by the First and Fourteenth Amendments. It sweeps within its condemnation speech which our Constitution has immunized from governmental control.

Measured by this test, Ohio's Criminal Syndicalism Act cannot be sustained. The Act punishes persons who "advocate or teach the duty, necessity, or propriety" of violence "as a means of accomplishing industrial or political reform"; or who publish or circulate or display any book or paper containing such advocacy; or who "justify" the commission of violent acts "with intent to exemplify, spread or advocate the propriety of the doctrines of criminal syndicalism"; or who "voluntarily assemble" with a group formed "to teach or advocate the doctrines of criminal syndicalism." Neither the indictment nor the trial judge's instructions to the jury in any way refined the statute's bald definition of the crime in terms of mere advocacy not distinguished from incitement to imminent lawless action.

Accordingly, we are here confronted with a statute which, by its own words and as applied, purports to punish mere advocacy and to forbid, on pain of criminal punishment, assembly with others merely to advocate the described type of action.[4] Such

---

4. Statutes affecting the right of assembly, like those touching on freedom of speech, must observe the established distinctions between mere advocacy and incitement to imminent lawless action, for as Chief Justice Hughes wrote in *De Jonge v. Oregon:* "The right of peaceable assembly is a right cognate to those of free speech and free press, and is equally fundamental." . . .

a statute falls within the condemnation of the First and Fourteenth Amendments. The contrary teaching of *Whitney v. California* cannot be supported, and that decision is therefore overruled.

Reversed.

MR. JUSTICE BLACK, *concurring.*

I agree with the views expressed by Mr. Justice Douglas in his concurring opinion in this case that the "clear and present danger" doctrine should have no place in the interpretation of the First Amendment. I join the Court's opinion, which, as I understand it, simply cites *Dennis v. United States,*

but does not indicate any agreement on the Court's part with the "clear and present danger" doctrine on which *Dennis* purported to rely.

CASE QUESTION

In what ways does *Brandenburg v. Ohio*'s criterion of imminence differ from the clear and present danger test? In order to answer this question, consider whether *Dennis v. United States* or *Schenck v. United States* would be decided differently under this standard.

NEW YORK TIMES CO. v. UNITED STATES

403 U.S. 713 (1971)

Opinion: Per Curiam
Concurrence: Black, joined by Douglas
Concurrence: Douglas, joined by Black
Concurrence: Brennan
Concurrence: Stewart, joined by White
Concurrence: White, joined by Stewart
Concurrence: Marshall
Dissent: Burger
Dissent: Harlan, joined by Blackmun, Burger
Dissent: Blackmun

In 1971, the New York Times *published a series of articles revealing information included in the Pentagon Papers, a classified government document detailing the history of the United States' involvement in the Vietnam War. The* Washington Post *subsequently followed suit. The government successfully sought an injunction, or a court order, against both newspapers preventing further publication of classified government documents. The cases*

quickly rose to the Supreme Court and were decided together in the per curiam opinion included here.

In reading this case, it is important to consider whether the First Amendment provides special protection against the "prior restraint" meaning official restriction prior to publication of expression by the press as opposed to punishment or damages after the fact of publication. Justice Hugo Black famously argued that the First Amendment protection of speech should generally be understood as providing absolute protection of speech. U.S. Supreme Court Chief Justice Warren E. Burger rejects this approach to the First Amendment in his dissent. Is there something special, however, about cases involving prior restraint, as Justice William J. Brennan seems to suggest?

In his dissent in this case, Chief Justice Burger also argues that the Court moved too hastily in reaching a decision without full consideration of the facts. Justice Black, in contrast, argues that the Court should have acted even more quickly. Who has the better argument? When matters of public concern are at stake, how should the Court balance the sometimes cumbersome judicial process with the right of news organizations to provide information to the people?

PER CURIAM

We granted certiorari in these cases in which the United States seeks to enjoin the *New York Times* and the *Washington Post* from publishing the contents of a classified study entitled "History of U.S. Decision-Making Process on Viet Nam Policy."

"Any system of prior restraints of expression comes to this Court bearing a heavy presumption against its constitutional validity." *Bantam Books, Inc. v. Sullivan.* The Government "thus carries a heavy burden of showing justification for the imposition of such a restraint." *Organization for a Better Austin v. Keefe.* The District Court for the Southern District of New York, in the *New York Times* case, and the District Court for the District of Columbia and the Court of Appeals for the District of Columbia Circuit, in the *Washington Post* case, held that the Government had not met that burden. We agree. . . .

MR. JUSTICE BLACK, *with whom* **MR. JUSTICE DOUGLAS** *joins, concurring.*

I adhere to the view that the Government's case against the *Washington Post* should have been dismissed, and that the injunction against the *New York Times* should have been vacated without oral argument when the cases were first presented to this Court. I believe that every moment's continuance of the injunctions against these newspapers amounts to a flagrant, indefensible, and continuing violation of the First Amendment. Furthermore, after oral argument, I agree completely that we must affirm

the judgment of the Court of Appeals for the District of Columbia Circuit and reverse the judgment of the Court of Appeals for the Second Circuit for the reasons stated by my Brothers Douglas and Brennan. In my view, it is unfortunate that some of my Brethren are apparently willing to hold that the publication of news may sometimes be enjoined. Such a holding would make a shambles of the First Amendment.

. . . Madison and the other Framers of the First Amendment, able men that they were, wrote in language they earnestly believed could never be misunderstood: "Congress shall make no law . . . abridging the freedom . . . of the press. . . ." Both the history and language of the First Amendment support the view that the press must be left free to publish news, whatever the source, without censorship, injunctions, or prior restraints.

In the First Amendment, the Founding Fathers gave the free press the protection it must have to fulfill its essential role in our democracy. The press was to serve the governed, not the governors. The Government's power to censor the press was abolished so that the press would remain forever free to censure the Government. The press was protected so that it could bare the secrets of government and inform the people. Only a free and unrestrained press can effectively expose deception in government. And paramount among the responsibilities of a free press is the duty to prevent any part of the government from deceiving the people and sending them off to distant lands to die of foreign fevers and foreign shot and shell. In my view, far from deserving condemnation for their courageous reporting, the *New York Times,* the *Washington Post,* and other newspapers should be commended for serving the purpose that the Founding Fathers saw so clearly. In revealing the workings of government that led to the

Vietnam war, the newspapers nobly did precisely that which the Founders hoped and trusted they would do.

The Government's case here is based on premises entirely different from those that guided the Framers of the First Amendment. The Solicitor General has carefully and emphatically stated:

> Now, Mr. Justice [Black], your construction of . . . [the First Amendment] is well known, and I certainly respect it. You say that no law means no law, and that should be obvious. I can only say, Mr. Justice, that to me it is equally obvious that "no law" does not mean "no law," and I would seek to persuade the Court that that is true. . . . [T]here are other parts of the Constitution that grant powers and responsibilities to the Executive, and . . . the First Amendment was not intended to make it impossible for the Executive to function or to protect the security of the United States.

And the Government argues in its brief that, in spite of the First Amendment,

> [t]he authority of the Executive Department to protect the nation against publication of information whose disclosure would endanger the national security stems from two interrelated sources: the constitutional power of the President over the conduct of foreign affairs and his authority as Commander-in-Chief.

In other words, we are asked to hold that, despite the First Amendment's emphatic command, the Executive Branch, the Congress, and the Judiciary can make laws enjoining publication of current news and abridging freedom of the press in the name of "national security." The Government does not even attempt to rely on any act of Congress. Instead, it makes the bold and dangerously far-reaching contention that the courts should take it upon themselves to "make" a law abridging freedom of the press in the name of equity, presidential power and national security, even when the representatives of the people in Congress have adhered to the command of the First Amendment and refused to make such a law. . . . To find that the President has "inherent power" to halt the publication of news by resort to the courts would wipe out the First Amendment and destroy the fundamental liberty and security of the very people the Government hopes to make "secure." No one can read the history of the adoption of the First Amendment without being convinced beyond any doubt that it was injunctions like those sought here that Madison and his collaborators intended to outlaw in this Nation for all time.

The word "security" is a broad, vague generality whose contours should not be invoked to abrogate the fundamental law embodied in the First Amendment. The guarding of military and diplomatic secrets at the expense of informed representative government provides no real security for our Republic. The Framers of the First Amendment, fully aware of both the need to defend a new nation and the abuses of the English and Colonial governments, sought to give this new society strength and security by providing that freedom of speech, press, religion, and assembly should not be abridged. . . .

MR. JUSTICE BRENNAN, *concurring.*

I

I write separately in these cases only to emphasize what should be apparent: that our judgments in the present cases may not be taken to indicate the propriety, in the future, of issuing temporary stays and restraining orders to block the publication of material sought to be suppressed by the Government. So far as I can determine, never before has the United States sought to enjoin a newspaper from publishing information in its possession. The relative novelty of the questions presented, the necessary haste with which decisions were reached, the magnitude of the interests asserted, and the fact that all the parties have concentrated their arguments upon the question whether permanent restraints were proper may have justified at least some of the restraints heretofore imposed in these cases. Certainly it is difficult to fault the several courts below for seeking to assure that the issues here involved were preserved for ultimate review by this Court. But even if it be assumed that some of the interim restraints were proper in the two cases before us, that assumption has no bearing upon the propriety of similar judicial action in the future. To begin with, there has now been ample time for reflection and judgment; whatever values there may be in the preservation of novel questions for appellate review may not support any restraints in the future. More important, the First Amendment stands as an absolute bar to the imposition of judicial restraints in circumstances of the kind presented by these cases.

II

The error that has pervaded these cases from the outset was the granting of any injunctive relief whatsoever, interim or otherwise. The entire thrust of the Government's claim throughout these cases has been that publication of the material sought to be enjoined "could," or "might," or "may" prejudice the national interest in various ways. But the First Amendment tolerates absolutely no prior judicial restraints of the press predicated upon surmise or conjecture that untoward consequences may result. Our cases, it is true, have indicated that there is a single, extremely narrow class of cases in which the First Amendment's ban on prior judicial restraint may be overridden. Our cases

have thus far indicated that such cases may arise only when the Nation "is at war," *Schenck v. United States*, during which times

> [n]o one would question but that a government might prevent actual obstruction to its recruiting service or the publication of the sailing dates of transports or the number and location of troops.

Near v. Minnesota. Even if the present world situation were assumed to be tantamount to a time of war, or if the power of presently available armaments would justify even in peacetime the suppression of information that would set in motion a nuclear holocaust, in neither of these actions has the Government presented or even alleged that publication of items from or based upon the material at issue would cause the happening of an event of that nature. "[T]he chief purpose of [the First Amendment's] guaranty [is] to prevent previous restraints upon publication." *Near v. Minnesota.* Thus, only governmental allegation and proof that publication must inevitably, directly, and immediately cause the occurrence of an event kindred to imperiling the safety of a transport already at sea can support even the issuance of an interim restraining order. In no event may mere conclusions be sufficient, for if the Executive Branch seeks judicial aid in preventing publication, it must inevitably submit the basis upon which that aid is sought to scrutiny by the judiciary. And, therefore, every restraint issued in this case, whatever its form, has violated the First Amendment—and not less so because that restraint was justified as necessary to afford the courts an opportunity to examine the claim more thoroughly. Unless and until the Government has clearly made out its case, the First Amendment commands that no injunction may issue.

MR. CHIEF JUSTICE BURGER, *dissenting.*

So clear are the constitutional limitations on prior restraint against expression that, from the time of *Near v. Minnesota,* until recently in *Organization for a Better Austin v. Keefe,* we have had little occasion to be concerned with cases involving prior restraints against news reporting on matters of public interest. There is, therefore, little variation among the members of the Court in terms of resistance to prior restraints against publication. Adherence to this basic constitutional principle, however, does not make these cases simple. In these cases, the imperative of a free and unfettered press comes into collision with another imperative, the effective functioning of a complex modern government, and, specifically, the effective exercise of certain constitutional powers of the Executive. Only those who view the First Amendment as an absolute in all circumstances—a view I respect, but reject—can find such cases as these to be simple or easy.

These cases are not simple for another and more immediate reason. We do not know the facts of the cases. No District Judge knew all the facts. No Court of Appeals judge knew all the facts. No member of this Court knows all the facts.

Why are we in this posture, in which only those judges to whom the First Amendment is absolute and permits of no restraint in any circumstances or for any reason, are really in a position to act?

I suggest we are in this posture because these cases have been conducted in unseemly haste. . . . The prompt setting of these cases reflects our universal abhorrence of prior restraint. But prompt judicial action does not mean unjudicial haste.

Here, moreover, the frenetic haste is due in large part to the manner in which

the *Times* proceeded from the date it obtained the purloined documents. It seems reasonably clear now that the haste precluded reasonable and deliberate judicial treatment of these cases, and was not warranted. The precipitate action of this Court aborting trials not yet completed is not the kind of judicial conduct that ought to attend the disposition of a great issue.

The newspapers make a derivative claim under the First Amendment; they denominate this right as the public "right to know"; by implication, the *Times* asserts a sole trusteeship of that right by virtue of its journalistic "scoop." The right is asserted as an absolute. Of course, the First Amendment right itself is not an absolute, as Justice Holmes so long ago pointed out in his aphorism concerning the right to shout "fire" in a crowded theater if there was no fire. There are other exceptions, some of which Chief Justice Hughes mentioned by way of example in *Near v. Minnesota.* There are no doubt other exceptions no one has had occasion to describe or discuss. Conceivably, such exceptions may be lurking in these cases and, would have been flushed had they been properly considered in the trial courts, free from unwarranted deadlines and frenetic pressures. An issue of this importance should be tried and heard in a judicial atmosphere conducive to thoughtful, reflective deliberation, especially when haste, in terms of hours, is unwarranted in light of the long period the *Times*, by its own choice, deferred publication.

It is not disputed that the *Times* has had unauthorized possession of the documents for three to four months, during which it has had its expert analysts studying them, presumably digesting them and preparing the material for publication. During all of this time, the *Times,* presumably in its capacity as trustee of the public's "right to know," has held up publication for purposes it considered proper, and thus public knowledge was delayed. No doubt this was for a good reason; the analysis of 7,000 pages of complex material drawn from a vastly greater volume of material would inevitably take time, and the writing of good news stories takes time. But why should the United States Government, from whom this information was illegally acquired by someone, along with all the counsel, trial judges, and appellate judges be placed under needless pressure? After these months of deferral, the alleged "right to know" has somehow and suddenly become a right that must be vindicated instanter.

Would it have been unreasonable, since the newspaper could anticipate the Government's objections to release of secret material, to give the Government an opportunity to review the entire collection and determine whether agreement could be reached on publication? Stolen or not, if security was not, in fact, jeopardized, much of the material could no doubt have been declassified, since it spans a period ending in 1968. With such an approach—one that great newspapers have in the past practiced and stated editorially to be the duty of an honorable press—the newspapers and Government might well have narrowed the area of disagreement as to what was and was not publishable, leaving the remainder to be resolved in orderly litigation, if necessary. To me, it is hardly believable that a newspaper long regarded as a great institution in American life would fail to perform one of the basic and simple duties of every citizen with respect to the discovery or possession of stolen property or secret government documents. That duty, I had thought—perhaps naively—was to report forthwith, to responsible public officers.

This duty rests on taxi drivers, Justices, and the *New York Times*. The course followed by the *Times*, whether so calculated or not, removed any possibility of orderly litigation of the issue. If the action of the judges up to now has been correct, that result is sheer happenstance.

Our grant of the writ of certiorari before final judgment in the *Times* case aborted the trial in the District Court before it had made a complete record pursuant to the mandate of the Court of Appeals for the Second Circuit.

The consequence of all this melancholy series of events is that we literally do not know what we are acting on. As I see it, we have been forced to deal with litigation concerning rights of great magnitude without an adequate record, and surely without time for adequate treatment either in the prior proceedings or in this Court. It is interesting to note that counsel on both sides, in oral argument before this Court, were frequently unable to respond to questions on factual points. Not surprisingly, they pointed out that they had been working literally "around the clock," and simply were unable to review the documents that give rise to these cases and were not familiar with them. This Court is in no better posture. . . .

I would affirm the Court of Appeals for the Second Circuit and allow the District Court to complete the trial aborted by our grant of certiorari, meanwhile preserving the *status quo* in the *Post* case. I would direct that the District Court, on remand, give priority to the *Times* case to the exclusion of all other business of that court, but I would not set arbitrary deadlines. . . .

We all crave speedier judicial processes, but, when judges are pressured, as in these cases, the result is a parody of the judicial function.

BUCKLEY v. VALEO

424 U.S. 1 (1976)

Opinion: Per Curiam
Partial Concurrence, Partial Dissent: Burger
Partial Concurrence, Partial Dissent: White
Partial Concurrence, Partial Dissent: Marshall
Partial Concurrence, Partial Dissent: Blackmun
Partial Concurrence, Partial Dissent: Rehnquist

So far we have considered the question of whether or not political speech is always protected by the First Amendment, or whether such protection has to be balanced against other concerns, such as the desire to maintain security or punish and deter libel. In this case, we move to a different aspect of speech expressing a political viewpoint. In particular, Buckley v. Valeo asks *to what degree the First Amendment protects the rights of citizens to fund political messages of their choice during campaigns for public office. Does the First Amendment grant to individuals the right to give unlimited funds to candidates of their choice? Consider these questions as you read the following First Amendment challenge to a campaign finance law.*

PER CURIAM

These appeals present constitutional challenges to the key provisions of the Federal Election Campaign Act of 1971 (Act), and related provisions of the Internal Revenue Code of 1954, all as amended in 1974.

The Court of Appeals, in sustaining the legislation in large part against various constitutional challenges, viewed it as "by far the most comprehensive reform legislation [ever] passed by Congress concerning the election of the President, Vice-President, and members of Congress." The statutes at issue, summarized in broad terms, contain the following provisions: (a) individual political contributions are limited to $1,000 to any single candidate per election, with an over-all annual limitation of $25,000 by any contributor; independent expenditures by individuals and groups "relative to a clearly identified candidate" are limited to $1,000 a year; campaign spending by candidates for various federal offices and spending for national conventions by political parties are subject to prescribed limits; (b) contributions and expenditures above certain threshold levels must be reported and publicly disclosed; (c) a system for public funding of Presidential campaign activities is established by Subtitle H of the Internal Revenue Code; and (d) a Federal Election Commission is established to administer and enforce the legislation.

I. CONTRIBUTION AND EXPENDITURE LIMITATIONS

The intricate statutory scheme adopted by Congress to regulate federal election campaigns includes restrictions on political contributions and expenditures that apply broadly to all phases of and all participants in the election process. The major contribution and expenditure limitations in the Act prohibit individuals from contributing more than $25,000 in a single year or more than $1,000 to any single candidate for an election campaign and from spending more than $1,000 a year "relative to a clearly identified candidate." Other provisions restrict a candidate's use of personal and family resources in his campaign and limit the over-all amount that can be spent by a candidate in campaigning for federal office.

The constitutional power of Congress to regulate federal elections is well established and is not questioned by any of the parties in this case. Thus, the critical constitutional questions presented here go not to the basic power of Congress to legislate in this area, but to whether the specific legislation that Congress has enacted interferes with First Amendment freedoms or invidiously discriminates against nonincumbent candidates and minor parties in contravention of the Fifth Amendment.

A. General Principles

The Act's contribution and expenditure limitations operate in an area of the most fundamental First Amendment activities. Discussion of public issues and debate on the qualifications of candidates are integral to the operation of the system of government established by our Constitution. The First Amendment affords the broadest protection to such political expression in order "to assure [the] unfettered interchange of ideas for the bringing about of political and social changes desired by the people." *Roth v. United States.* Although First Amendment protections are not confined to "the exposition of ideas," *Winters v. New York*, there is practically universal agreement that a major purpose of that Amendment was to protect the free discussion of governmental affairs, . . . of course includ[ing] discussions of candidates. . . . *Mills v. Alabama.* This no more than reflects our "profound national commitment to the principle that debate on public issues should be uninhibited, robust, and wide-open," *New York Times Co. v. Sullivan.* In a republic where the people are sovereign, the ability of the citizenry to make informed choices among candidates

for office is essential, for the identities of those who are elected will inevitably shape the course that we follow as a nation.

The expenditure limitations contained in the Act represent substantial, rather than merely theoretical, restraints on the quantity and diversity of political speech. The $1,000 ceiling on spending "relative to a clearly identified candidate," would appear to exclude all citizens and groups except candidates, political parties, and the institutional press from any significant use of the most effective modes of communication. Although the Act's limitations on expenditures by campaign organizations and political parties provide substantially greater room for discussion and debate, they would have required restrictions in the scope of a number of past congressional and Presidential campaigns and would operate to constrain campaigning by candidates who raise sums in excess of the spending ceiling.

By contrast with a limitation upon expenditures for political expression, a limitation upon the amount that any one person or group may contribute to a candidate or political committee entails only a marginal restriction upon the contributor's ability to engage in free communication. A contribution serves as a general expression of support for the candidate and his views, but does not communicate the underlying basis for the support. The quantity of communication by the contributor does not increase perceptibly with the size of his contribution, since the expression rests solely on the undifferentiated, symbolic act of contributing. At most, the size of the contribution provides a very rough index of the intensity of the contributor's support for the candidate. A limitation on the amount of money a person may give to a candidate or campaign organization thus involves little direct restraint on his political communication, for it permits the symbolic expression of support evidenced by a contribution but does not in any way infringe the contributor's freedom to discuss candidates and issues. While contributions may result in political expression if spent by a candidate or an association to present views to the voters, the transformation of contributions into political debate involves speech by someone other than the contributor. . . .

The Act's contribution and expenditure limitations also impinge on protected associational freedoms. Making a contribution, like joining a political party, serves to affiliate a person with a candidate. In addition, it enables like-minded persons to pool their resources in furtherance of common political goals. The Act's contribution ceilings thus limit one important means of associating with a candidate or committee, but leave the contributor free to become a member of any political association and to assist personally in the association's efforts on behalf of candidates.

In sum, although the Act's contribution and expenditure limitations both implicate fundamental First Amendment interests, its expenditure ceilings impose significantly more severe restrictions on protected freedoms of political expression and association than do its limitations on financial contributions.

B. Contribution Limitations

Section 608(b) provides, with certain limited exceptions, that no person shall make contributions to any candidate with respect to any election for Federal office which, in the aggregate, exceed $1,000.

Appellants contend that the $1,000 contribution ceiling unjustifiably burdens First Amendment freedoms, employs overbroad dollar limits, and discriminates against candidates opposing incumbent officeholders and against minor party candidates

in violation of the Fifth Amendment. We address each of these claims of invalidity in turn.

(A)

As the general discussion in Part I-A indicated, the primary First Amendment problem raised by the Act's contribution limitations is their restriction of one aspect of the contributor's freedom of political association. . . . It is unnecessary to look beyond the Act's primary purpose—to limit the actuality and appearance of corruption resulting from large individual financial contributions—in order to find a constitutionally sufficient justification for the $1,000 contribution limitation. . . . To the extent that large contributions are given to secure a political *quid pro quo* from current and potential office holders, the integrity of our system of representative democracy is undermined. Although the scope of such pernicious practices can never be reliably ascertained, the deeply disturbing examples surfacing after the 1972 election demonstrate that the problem is not an illusory one.

We find that, under the rigorous standard of review established by our prior decisions, the weighty interests served by restricting the size of financial contributions to political candidates are sufficient to justify the limited effect upon First Amendment freedoms caused by the $1,000 contribution ceiling.

(B)

Appellants' first overbreadth challenge to the contribution ceilings rests on the proposition that most large contributors do not seek improper influence over a candidate's position or an officeholder's action. Although the truth of that proposition may be assumed, it does not undercut the validity of the $1,000 contribution limitation.

Not only is it difficult to isolate suspect contributions but, more importantly, Congress was justified in concluding that the interest in safeguarding against the appearance of impropriety requires that the opportunity for abuse inherent in the process of raising large monetary contributions be eliminated.

(C)

Apart from these First Amendment concerns, appellants argue that the contribution limitations work such an invidious discrimination between incumbents and challengers that the statutory provisions must be declared unconstitutional on their face. . . . There is no such evidence to support the claim that the contribution limitations in themselves discriminate against major party challengers to incumbents. Challengers can and often do defeat incumbents in federal elections.

. . . In view of these considerations, we conclude that the impact of the Act's $1,000 contribution limitation on major party challengers and on minor party candidates does not render the provision unconstitutional on its face.

C. Expenditure Limitations

The Act's expenditure ceilings impose direct and substantial restraints on the quantity of political speech. The most drastic of the limitations restricts individuals and groups, including political parties that fail to place a candidate on the ballot to an expenditure of $1,000 "relative to a clearly identified candidate during a calendar year." Other expenditure ceilings limit spending by candidates, their campaigns, and political parties in connection with election campaigns. It is clear that a primary effect of these expenditure limitations is to restrict the quantity of campaign speech by individuals, groups,

and candidates. The restrictions, while neutral as to the ideas expressed, limit political expression "at the core of our electoral process and of the First Amendment freedoms." *Williams v. Rhodes.*

1. The $1,000 Limitation on Expenditures "Relative to a Clearly Identified Candidate"

Section 608(e)(1) provides that [n]o person may make any expenditure . . . relative to a clearly identified candidate during a calendar year which, when added to all other expenditures made by such person during the year advocating the election or defeat of such candidate, exceeds $1,000.

The plain effect of §608(e)(1) is to prohibit all individuals, who are neither candidates nor owners of institutional press facilities, and all groups, except political parties and campaign organizations, from voicing their views "relative to a clearly identified candidate" through means that entail aggregate expenditures of more than $1,000 during a calendar year. . . .

We agree that, in order to preserve the provision against invalidation on vagueness grounds, §608(e)(1) must be construed to apply only to expenditures for communications that, in express terms advocate the election or defeat of a clearly identified candidate for federal office.

We turn then to the basic First Amendment question—whether §608(e)(1), even as thus narrowly and explicitly construed, impermissibly burdens the constitutional right of free expression. The Court of Appeals summarily held the provision constitutionally valid on the ground that "section 608(e) is a loophole-closing provision only" that is necessary to prevent circumvention of the contribution limitations. We cannot agree.

We find that the governmental interest in preventing corruption and the appearance of corruption is inadequate to justify §608(e)(1)'s ceiling on independent expenditures. First, assuming, *arguendo*, that large independent expenditures pose the same dangers of actual or apparent *quid pro quo* arrangements as do large contributions, §608(e)(1) does not provide an answer that sufficiently relates to the elimination of those dangers. Unlike the contribution limitations' total ban on the giving of large amounts of money to candidates, §608(e)(1) prevents only some large expenditures. So long as persons and groups eschew expenditures that, in express terms advocate the election or defeat of a clearly identified candidate, they are free to spend as much as they want to promote the candidate and his views. The exacting interpretation of the statutory language necessary to avoid unconstitutional vagueness thus undermines the limitation's effectiveness as a loophole-closing provision by facilitating circumvention by those seeking to exert improper influence upon a candidate or officeholder. . . .

Second, quite apart from the shortcomings of §608(e)(1) in preventing any abuses generated by large independent expenditures, the independent advocacy restricted by the provision does not presently appear to pose dangers of real or apparent corruption comparable to those identified with large campaign contributions. The parties defending §608(e)(1) contend that it is necessary to prevent would-be contributors from avoiding the contribution limitations by the simple expedient of paying directly for media advertisements or for other portions of the candidate's campaign activities. They argue that expenditures controlled by or coordinated with the candidate and his campaign might well have virtually the same value to the candidate as a contribution and would pose similar dangers of abuse. Yet such controlled or coordinated expenditures are treated as contributions,

rather than expenditures under the Act. . . . By contrast, §608(e)(1) limits expenditures for express advocacy of candidates made totally independently of the candidate and his campaign. Unlike contributions, such independent expenditures may well provide little assistance to the candidate's campaign, and indeed may prove counterproductive. The absence of prearrangement and coordination of an expenditure with the candidate or his agent not only undermines the value of the expenditure to the candidate, but also alleviates the danger that expenditures will be given as a *quid pro quo* for improper commitments from the candidate. Rather than preventing circumvention of the contribution limitations, §608(e)(1) severely restricts all independent advocacy despite its substantially diminished potential for abuse.

While the independent expenditure ceiling thus fails to serve any substantial governmental interest in stemming the reality or appearance of corruption in the electoral process, it heavily burdens core First Amendment expression. For the First Amendment right to "speak one's mind . . . on all public institutions" includes the right to engage in "'vigorous advocacy' no less than 'abstract discussion.'" *New York Times Co. v. Sullivan* quoting *Bridges v. California* and *NAACP v. Button*. Advocacy of the election or defeat of candidates for federal office is no less entitled to protection under the First Amendment than the discussion of political policy generally or advocacy of the passage or defeat of legislation. It is argued, however, that the ancillary governmental interest in equalizing the relative ability of individuals and groups to influence the outcome of elections serves to justify the limitation on express advocacy of the election or defeat of candidates imposed by §608(e)(1)'s expenditure ceiling. But the concept that government may restrict the speech of some elements of our society in order to enhance the relative voice of others is wholly foreign to the First Amendment, which was designed "to secure 'the widest possible dissemination of information from diverse and antagonistic sources,'" and "to assure unfettered interchange of ideas for the bringing about of political and social changes desired by the people." *New York Times Co. v. Sullivan*, quoting *Associated Press v. United States* and *Roth v. United States*. The First Amendment's protection against governmental abridgment of free expression cannot properly be made to depend on a person's financial ability to engage in public discussion.

. . . For the reasons stated, we conclude that §608(e)(1)'s independent expenditure limitation is unconstitutional under the First Amendment.

2. Limitation on Expenditures by Candidates from Personal or Family Resources

The Act also sets limits on expenditures by a candidate "from his personal funds, or the personal funds of his immediate family, in connection with his campaigns during any calendar year." § 608(a)(1). These ceilings vary from $50,000 for Presidential or Vice Presidential candidates to $35,000 for senatorial candidates, and $25,000 for most candidates for the House of Representatives.

The ceiling on personal expenditures by candidates on their own behalf, like the limitations on independent expenditures contained in §608(e)(1), imposes a substantial restraint on the ability of persons to engage in protected First Amendment expression. The candidate, no less than any other person, has a First Amendment right to engage in the discussion of public issues and vigorously and tirelessly to advocate his own election and the election of other candidates. Indeed, it is of particular importance that candidates have the unfettered opportunity to make their views known so that the electorate may intelligently evaluate the candidates' personal qualities and their positions on vital public issues before choosing among them on election day. . . . Indeed, the use of personal funds reduces the candidate's dependence on outside contributions, and thereby counteracts the coercive pressures and attendant risks of abuse to which the Act's contribution limitations are directed.

The ancillary interest in equalizing the relative financial resources of candidates competing for elective office, therefore, provides the sole relevant rationale for §608(a)'s expenditure ceiling. That interest is clearly not sufficient to justify the provision's infringement of fundamental First Amendment rights. First, the limitation may fail to promote financial equality among candidates. A candidate who spends less of his personal resources on his campaign may nonetheless outspend his rival as a result of more successful fundraising efforts. Indeed, a candidate's personal wealth may impede his efforts to persuade others that he needs their financial contributions or volunteer efforts to conduct an effective campaign. Second, and more fundamentally, the First Amendment simply cannot tolerate §608(a)'s restriction upon the freedom of a candidate to speak without legislative limit on behalf of his own candidacy. We therefore hold that §608(a)'s restriction on a candidate's personal expenditures is unconstitutional.

3. Limitations on Campaign Expenditures

Section 608(c) places limitations on overall campaign expenditures by candidates seeking nomination for election and election to federal office.

No governmental interest that has been suggested is sufficient to justify the restriction on the quantity of political expression imposed by §608(c)'s campaign expenditure limitations. The major evil associated with rapidly increasing campaign expenditures is the danger of candidate dependence on large contributions. The interest in alleviating the corrupting influence of large contributions is served by the Act's contribution limitations and disclosure provisions, rather than by §608(c)'s campaign expenditure ceilings. . . .

The interest in equalizing the financial resources of candidates competing for federal office is no more convincing a justification for restricting the scope of federal election campaigns. Given the limitation on the size of outside contributions, the financial resources available to a candidate's campaign, like the number of volunteers recruited, will normally vary with the size and intensity of the candidate's support. There is nothing invidious, improper, or unhealthy in permitting such funds to be spent to carry the candidate's message to the electorate. Moreover, the equalization of permissible campaign expenditures might serve not to equalize the opportunities of all candidates, but to handicap a candidate who lacked substantial name recognition or exposure of his views before the start of the campaign.

. . . In any event, the mere growth in the cost of federal election campaigns, in and of itself, provides no basis for governmental restrictions on the quantity of campaign spending and the resulting limitation on the scope of federal campaigns. The First Amendment denies government the power to determine that spending to promote one's political views is wasteful, excessive, or unwise. In the free society ordained by our Constitution, it is not the government, but the people—individually, as citizens and candidates, and collectively,

as associations and political committees—who must retain control over the quantity and range of debate on public issues in a political campaign.

For these reasons, we hold that §608(c) is constitutionally invalid.

In sum, the provisions of the Act that impose a $1,000 limitation on contributions to a single candidate, a $5,000 limitation on contributions by a political committee to a single candidate, and a $25,000 limitation on total contributions by an individual during any calendar year, are constitutionally valid. These limitations, along with the disclosure provisions, constitute the Act's primary weapons against the reality or appearance of improper influence stemming from the dependence of candidates on large campaign contributions. The contribution ceilings thus serve the basic governmental interest in safeguarding the integrity of the electoral process without directly impinging upon the rights of individual citizens and candidates to engage in political debate and discussion. By contrast, the First Amendment requires the invalidation of the Act's independent expenditure ceiling, §608(e)(1), its limitation on a candidate's expenditures from his own personal funds, §608(a), and its ceilings on over-all campaign expenditures, §608(e). These provisions place substantial and direct restrictions on the ability of candidates, citizens, and associations to engage in protected political expression, restrictions that the First Amendment cannot tolerate. . . .

CONCLUSION

In summary, we sustain the individual contribution limits, the disclosure and reporting provisions, and the public financing scheme. We conclude, however, that the limitations on campaign expenditures, on independent expenditures by individuals and groups, and on expenditures by a candidate from his personal funds are constitutionally infirm. Finally, we hold that most of the powers conferred by the Act upon the Federal Election Commission can be exercised only by "Officers of the United States," appointed in conformity with Art. II, §2, cl. 2, of the Constitution, and therefore cannot be exercised by the Commission as presently constituted.

In No. 75-436, the judgment of the Court of Appeals is affirmed in part and reversed in part. The judgment of the District Court in No. 75-437 is affirmed. The mandate shall issue forthwith, except that our judgment is stayed, for a period not to exceed 30 days, insofar as it affects the authority of the Commission to exercise the duties and powers granted it under the Act.

TEXAS v. JOHNSON

491 U.S. 397 (1989)

> **Opinion:** Brennan, joined by Marshall, Blackmun, Scalia, Kennedy
> **Concurrence:** Kennedy
> **Dissent:** Rehnquist, joined by White and O'Connor
> **Dissent:** Stevens

When Texas v. Johnson *came before the Supreme Court in 1989, the laws of the federal government and 48 of the 50 states made the public burning of the flag of the United States a criminal offense. However, the Court decided in this case that a Texas law forbidding desecration of the flag violated the First Amendment guarantee of the freedom of speech.*

One puzzle raised by this case is whether conduct, namely the burning of a flag, should be considered "speech" according to the First Amendment. Of course the act of flag burning is not speech in the literal sense, but does the free-speech protection include some forms of expressive conduct?

Both dissents in this case also suggest that the flag, as a national symbol, deserves special protection. U.S. Supreme Court Justice John Paul Stevens argues that Johnson could very well have conveyed similar political ideas in a less offensive way. The dissents raise important questions. Does the First Amendment protect all acts of political expression, or does it exclude certain avenues of expressing a particular opinion? Should the fact of whether speech causes offense be a factor in considering what acts are protected by the First Amendment?

JUSTICE BRENNAN *delivered the opinion of the Court.*

After publicly burning an American flag as a means of political protest, Gregory Lee Johnson was convicted of desecrating a flag in violation of Texas law. This case presents the question whether his conviction is consistent with the First Amendment. We hold that it is not.

I

While the Republican National Convention was taking place in Dallas in 1984, respondent Johnson participated in a political demonstration dubbed the "Republican War Chest Tour." As explained in literature distributed by the demonstrators and in speeches made by them, the purpose of this event was to protest the policies of the Reagan administration and of certain Dallas-based corporations. The demonstrators marched through the Dallas streets, chanting political slogans and stopping at several corporate locations to stage "die-ins" intended to dramatize the consequences of nuclear war. On several occasions they spray-painted the walls of buildings and overturned potted plants, but Johnson himself took no part in such activities. He did, however, accept an American flag handed to him by a fellow protestor who had taken it from a flagpole outside one of the targeted buildings.

The demonstration ended in front of Dallas City Hall, where Johnson unfurled the American flag, doused it with kerosene, and set it on fire. While the flag burned, the protestors chanted: "America, the red, white, and blue, we spit on you." After the demonstrators dispersed, a witness to the flag burning collected the flag's remains and buried them in his backyard. No one was physically injured or threatened with injury, though several witnesses testified that they had been seriously offended by the flag burning.

Of the approximately 100 demonstrators, Johnson alone was charged with a crime. The only criminal offense with which he was charged was the desecration of a venerated object in violation of Tex. Penal Code Ann. §42.09(a)(3) (1989). After a trial, he was convicted, sentenced to one year in prison, and fined $2,000. The Court of Appeals for the Fifth District of Texas at Dallas affirmed Johnson's conviction, but the Texas Court of Criminal Appeals reversed, holding that the State could not, consistent with the First Amendment, punish Johnson for burning the flag in these circumstances.

II

Johnson was convicted of flag desecration for burning the flag rather than for uttering insulting words. This fact somewhat complicates our consideration of his conviction under the First Amendment. We must first determine whether Johnson's burning of the flag constituted expressive conduct, permitting him to invoke the First Amendment in challenging his conviction. If his conduct was expressive, we next decide whether the State's regulation is related to the suppression of free expression. If the State's regulation is not related to expression, then the less stringent standard we announced in *United States v. O'Brien* for regulations of noncommunicative conduct controls. If it is, then we are outside of *O'Brien*'s test, and we must ask whether this interest justifies Johnson's conviction under a more demanding standard. A third possibility is that the State's asserted interest is simply not implicated on these facts, and in that event the interest drops out of the picture.

The First Amendment literally forbids the abridgment only of "speech," but we have long recognized that its protection does not end at the spoken or written word. While we have rejected "the view that an apparently limitless variety of conduct can be labeled 'speech' whenever the person engaging in the conduct intends thereby to express an idea," *United States v. O'Brien*, we have acknowledged that conduct may be "sufficiently imbued with elements of communication to fall within the scope of the First and Fourteenth Amendments," *Spence*.

In deciding whether particular conduct possesses sufficient communicative elements to bring the First Amendment into play, we have asked whether "[a]n intent to convey a particularized message was present, and [whether] the likelihood was great that the message would be understood by those who viewed it." Hence, we have recognized the expressive nature of students' wearing of black armbands to protest American military involvement in Vietnam, *Tinker v. Des Moines Independent Community School Dist.*; of a sit-in by blacks in a "whites only" area to protest segregation, *Brown v. Louisiana*; of the wearing of American military uniforms in a dramatic presentation criticizing American involvement in Vietnam, *Schacht v. United States*; and of picketing about a wide variety of causes.

Especially pertinent to this case are our decisions recognizing the communicative nature of conduct relating to flags. Attaching a peace sign to the flag, *Spence*; refusing to salute the flag, *Barnette*; and displaying a red flag, *Stromberg v. California*, we have held, all may find shelter under the First Amendment. That we have had little difficulty identifying an expressive element in conduct relating to flags should not be surprising. The very purpose of a national flag is to serve as a symbol of our country; it is, one might say, "the one visible manifestation of two hundred years of nationhood."

Pregnant with expressive content, the flag as readily signifies this Nation as does the combination of letters found in "America."

We have not automatically concluded, however, that any action taken with respect to our flag is expressive. Instead, in characterizing such action for First Amendment purposes, we have considered the context in which it occurred. In *Spence*, for example, we emphasized that Spence's taping of a peace sign to his flag was "roughly simultaneous with and concededly triggered by the Cambodian incursion and the Kent State tragedy." The State of Washington had conceded, in fact, that Spence's conduct was a form of communication, and we stated that "the State's concession is inevitable on this record."

The State of Texas conceded for purposes of its oral argument in this case that Johnson's conduct was expressive conduct, and this concession seems to us as prudent as was Washington's in *Spence*. Johnson burned an American flag as part—indeed,

as the culmination—of a political demonstration that coincided with the convening of the Republican Party and its renomination of Ronald Reagan for President. The expressive, overtly political nature of this conduct was both intentional and overwhelmingly apparent. At his trial, Johnson explained his reasons for burning the flag as follows: "The American Flag was burned as Ronald Reagan was being renominated as President. And a more powerful statement of symbolic speech, whether you agree with it or not, couldn't have been made at that time. It's quite a just position [juxtaposition]. We had new patriotism and no patriotism." In these circumstances, Johnson's burning of the flag was conduct "sufficiently imbued with elements of communication," *Spence*, to implicate the First Amendment.

III

The government generally has a freer hand in restricting expressive conduct than it has in restricting the written or spoken word. It may not, however, proscribe particular conduct *because* it has expressive elements. "[W]hat might be termed the more generalized guarantee of freedom of expression makes the communicative nature of conduct an inadequate *basis* for singling out that conduct for proscription. A law *directed at* the communicative nature of conduct must, like a law directed at speech itself, be justified by the substantial showing of need that the First Amendment requires." *Community for Creative Non-Violence v. Watt* (Scalia, J., dissenting). It is, in short, not simply the verbal or nonverbal nature of the expression, but the governmental interest at stake, that helps to determine whether a restriction on that expression is valid.

Thus, although we have recognized that where "'speech' and 'nonspeech' elements are combined in the same course of conduct, a sufficiently important governmental interest in regulating the non-speech element can justify incidental limitations on First Amendment freedoms," *O'Brien*, we have limited the applicability of *O'Brien*'s relatively lenient standard to those cases in which "the governmental interest is unrelated to the suppression of free expression." In stating, moreover, that *O'Brien*'s test "in the last analysis is little, if any, different from the standard applied to time, place, or manner restrictions," *Clark*, we have highlighted the requirement that the governmental interest in question be unconnected to expression in order to come under *O'Brien*'s less demanding rule.

In order to decide whether *O'Brien*'s test applies here, therefore, we must decide whether Texas has asserted an interest in support of Johnson's conviction that is unrelated to the suppression of expression. If we find that an interest asserted by the State is simply not implicated on the facts before us, we need not ask whether *O'Brien*'s test applies. The State offers two separate interests to justify this conviction: preventing breaches of the peace and preserving the flag as a symbol of nationhood and national unity. We hold that the first interest is not implicated on this record and that the second is related to the suppression of expression.

A

Texas claims that its interest in preventing breaches of the peace justifies Johnson's conviction for flag desecration. However, no disturbance of the peace actually occurred or threatened to occur because of Johnson's burning of the flag. Although the State stresses the disruptive behavior of the protestors during their march toward City Hall, Brief for Petitioner 34-36, it admits that "no actual breach of the peace occurred at the time of the flag burning or in response

to the flag burning." The State's emphasis on the protestors' disorderly actions prior to arriving at City Hall is not only somewhat surprising given that no charges were brought on the basis of this conduct, but it also fails to show that a disturbance of the peace was a likely reaction to Johnson's conduct. The only evidence offered by the State at trial to show the reaction to Johnson's actions was the testimony of several persons who had been seriously offended by the flag burning.

The State's position, therefore, amounts to a claim that an audience that takes serious offense at particular expression is necessarily likely to disturb the peace and that the expression may be prohibited on this basis. Our precedents do not countenance such a presumption. On the contrary, they recognize that a principal "function of free speech under our system of government is to invite dispute. It may indeed best serve its high purpose when it induces a condition of unrest, creates dissatisfaction with conditions as they are, or even stirs people to anger." *Terminiello v. Chicago*. It would be odd indeed to conclude *both* that "if it is the speaker's opinion that gives offense, that consequence is a reason for according it constitutional protection," *FCC v. Pacifica Foundation* (opinion of Stevens, J.), *and* that the government may ban the expression of certain disagreeable ideas on the unsupported presumption that their very disagreeableness will provoke violence.

Thus, we have not permitted the government to assume that every expression of a provocative idea will incite a riot, but have instead required careful consideration of the actual circumstances surrounding such expression, asking whether the expression "is directed to inciting or producing imminent lawless action and is likely to incite or produce such action." *Brandenburg v. Ohio*. To accept Texas' arguments that it need only demonstrate "the potential for a breach of the peace," and that every flag burning necessarily possesses that potential, would be to eviscerate our holding in *Brandenburg*. This we decline to do.

Nor does Johnson's expressive conduct fall within that small class of "fighting words" that are "likely to provoke the average person to retaliation, and thereby cause a breach of the peace." *Chaplinsky v. New Hampshire*. No reasonable onlooker would have regarded Johnson's generalized expression of dissatisfaction with the policies of the Federal Government as a direct personal insult or an invitation to exchange fisticuffs.

We thus conclude that the State's interest in maintaining order is not implicated on these facts. The State need not worry that our holding will disable it from preserving the peace. We do not suggest that the First Amendment forbids a State to prevent "imminent lawless action." *Brandenburg*. And, in fact, Texas already has a statute specifically prohibiting breaches of the peace, which tends to confirm that Texas need not punish this flag desecration in order to keep the peace.

B

The State also asserts an interest in preserving the flag as a symbol of nationhood and national unity. In *Spence*, we acknowledged that the government's interest in preserving the flag's special symbolic value "is directly related to expression in the context of activity" such as affixing a peace symbol to a flag. We are equally persuaded that this interest is related to expression in the case of Johnson's burning of the flag. The State, apparently, is concerned that such conduct will lead people to believe either that the flag does not stand for nationhood and national unity, but instead reflects other, less positive concepts, or that the concepts reflected in the flag do not in fact exist, that

is, that we do not enjoy unity as a Nation. These concerns blossom only when a person's treatment of the flag communicates some message, and thus are related "to the suppression of free expression" within the meaning of *O'Brien*. We are thus outside of *O'Brien*'s test altogether.

It remains to consider whether the State's interest in preserving the flag as a symbol of nationhood and national unity justifies Johnson's conviction.

As in *Spence*, "[w]e are confronted with a case of prosecution for the expression of an idea through activity," and "[a]ccordingly, we must examine with particular care the interests advanced by [petitioner] to support its prosecution." Johnson was not, we add, prosecuted for the expression of just any idea; he was prosecuted for his expression of dissatisfaction with the policies of this country, expression situated at the core of our First Amendment values.

Moreover, Johnson was prosecuted because he knew that his politically charged expression would cause "serious offense." If he had burned the flag as a means of disposing of it because it was dirty or torn, he would not have been convicted of flag desecration under this Texas law: federal law designates burning as the preferred means of disposing of a flag "when it is in such condition that it is no longer a fitting emblem for display," and Texas has no quarrel with this means of disposal. The Texas law is thus not aimed at protecting the physical integrity of the flag in all circumstances, but is designed instead to protect it only against impairments that would cause serious offense to others. Texas concedes as much: "Section 42.09(b) reaches only those severe acts of physical abuse of the flag carried out in a way likely to be offensive. The statute mandates intentional or knowing abuse, that is, the kind of mistreatment that is not innocent, but rather is intentionally designed to seriously offend other individuals."

Whether Johnson's treatment of the flag violated Texas law thus depended on the likely communicative impact of his expressive conduct. Our decision in *Boos v. Barry*, tells us that this restriction on Johnson's expression is content based. In *Boos*, we considered the constitutionality of a law prohibiting "the display of any sign within 500 feet of a foreign embassy if that sign tends to bring that foreign government into 'public odium' or 'public disrepute.'" Rejecting the argument that the law was content neutral because it was justified by "our international law obligation to shield diplomats from speech that offends their dignity," we held that "[t]he emotive impact of speech on its audience is not a 'secondary effect'" unrelated to the content of the expression itself.

According to the principles announced in *Boos*, Johnson's political expression was restricted because of the content of the message he conveyed. We must therefore subject the State's asserted interest in preserving the special symbolic character of the flag to "the most exacting scrutiny." *Boos v. Barry*.

Texas argues that its interest in preserving the flag as a symbol of nationhood and national unity survives this close analysis. Quoting extensively from the writings of this Court chronicling the flag's historic and symbolic role in our society, the State emphasizes the "special place" reserved for the flag in our Nation. The State's argument is not that it has an interest simply in maintaining the flag as a symbol of *something*, no matter what it symbolizes; indeed, if that were the State's position, it would be difficult to see how that interest is endangered by highly symbolic conduct such as Johnson's. Rather, the State's claim is that it has an interest in preserving the flag as a symbol of *nationhood* and *national unity*, a symbol with a determinate range of meanings. According to Texas, if one physically treats the flag in a way that would tend to cast doubt on either the idea that nationhood and national unity are the flag's referents or that national unity actually exists, the message conveyed thereby is a harmful one and therefore may be prohibited.

If there is a bedrock principle underlying the First Amendment, it is that the government may not prohibit the expression of an idea simply because society finds the idea itself offensive or disagreeable.

We have not recognized an exception to this principle even where our flag has been involved. In *Street v. New York*, we held that a State may not criminally punish a person for uttering words critical of the flag. Rejecting the argument that the conviction could be sustained on the ground that Street had "failed to show the respect for our national symbol which may properly be demanded of every citizen," we concluded that "the constitutionally guaranteed 'freedom to be intellectually . . . diverse or even contrary,' and the 'right to differ as to things that touch the heart of the existing order,' encompass the freedom to express publicly one's opinions about our flag, including those opinions which are defiant or contemptuous." *Id*. Nor may the government, we have held, compel conduct that would evince respect for the flag. "To sustain the compulsory flag salute we are required to say that a Bill of Rights which guards the individual's right to speak his own mind, left it open to public authorities to compel him to utter what is not in his mind." *Id*.

In holding in *Barnette* that the Constitution did not leave this course open to the government, Justice Jackson described one of our society's defining principles in words deserving of their frequent repetition: "If there is any fixed star in our constitutional constellation, it is that no official, high or petty, can prescribe what shall be orthodox in politics, nationalism, religion, or other matters of opinion or force citizens to confess by word or act their faith therein." In *Spence*, we held that the same interest asserted by Texas here was insufficient to support a criminal conviction under a flag-misuse statute for the taping of a peace sign to an American flag. "Given the protected character of [Spence's] expression and in light of the fact that no interest the State may have in preserving the physical integrity of a privately owned flag was significantly impaired on these facts," we held, "the conviction must be invalidated."

In short, nothing in our precedents suggests that a State may foster its own view of the flag by prohibiting expressive conduct relating to it. To bring its argument outside our precedents, Texas attempts to convince us that even if its interest in preserving the flag's symbolic role does not allow it to prohibit words or some expressive conduct critical of the flag, it does permit it to forbid the outright destruction of the flag. The State's argument cannot depend here on the distinction between written or spoken words and nonverbal conduct. That distinction, we have shown, is of no moment where the nonverbal conduct is expressive, as it is here, and where the regulation of that conduct is related to expression, as it is here. In addition, both *Barnette* and *Spence* involved expressive conduct, not only verbal communication, and both found that conduct protected.

Texas' focus on the precise nature of Johnson's expression, moreover, misses the point of our prior decisions: their enduring lesson, that the government may not prohibit expression simply because it disagrees with its message, is not dependent on the particular mode in which one chooses to express an idea. If we were to hold that a State may forbid flag burning wherever it is likely to endanger the flag's symbolic role, but allow it wherever burning a flag promotes that role—as where, for example, a person ceremoniously burns a dirty flag—we would be saying that when it comes to impairing the flag's physical integrity, the flag itself may be used as a symbol—as a substitute for the written or spoken word or a "short cut from mind to mind"—only in one direction. We would be permitting a State to "prescribe what shall be orthodox" by saying that one may burn the flag to convey one's attitude toward it and its referents only if one does not endanger the flag's representation of nationhood and national unity.

We never before have held that the Government may ensure that a symbol be used to express only one view of that symbol or its referents. Indeed, in *Schacht v. United States*, we invalidated a federal statute permitting an actor portraying a member of one of our Armed Forces to "'wear the uniform of that armed force if the portrayal does not tend to discredit that armed force.'" This proviso, we held, "which leaves Americans free to praise the war in Vietnam but can send persons like Schacht to prison for opposing it, cannot survive in a country which has the First Amendment."

We perceive no basis on which to hold that the principle underlying our decision in *Schacht* does not apply to this case. To conclude that the government may permit designated symbols to be used to communicate only a limited set of messages would be to enter territory having no discernible or defensible boundaries. Could the government, on this theory, prohibit the burning of state flags? Of copies of the Presidential seal? Of the Constitution? In evaluating these choices under the First Amendment, how would we decide which symbols were sufficiently special to warrant this unique status? To do so, we would be forced to consult our own political preferences, and impose them on the citizenry, in the very way that the First Amendment forbids us to do.

There is, moreover, no indication—either in the text of the Constitution or in our cases interpreting it—that a separate juridical category exists for the American flag alone. Indeed, we would not be surprised to learn that the persons who framed our Constitution and wrote the Amendment that we now construe were not known for their reverence for the Union Jack. The First Amendment does not guarantee that other concepts virtually sacred to our Nation as a whole—such as the principle that discrimination on the basis of race is odious and destructive—will go unquestioned in the market-place of ideas. We decline, therefore, to create for the flag an exception to the joust of principles protected by the First Amendment.

It is not the State's ends, but its means, to which we object. It cannot be gainsaid that there is a special place reserved for the flag in this Nation, and thus we do not doubt that the government has a legitimate interest in making efforts to "preserv[e] the national flag as an unalloyed symbol of our country." *Spence.* We reject the suggestion, urged at oral argument by counsel for Johnson, that the government lacks "any state interest whatsoever" in regulating the manner in which the flag may be displayed. Congress has, for example, enacted precatory regulations describing the proper treatment of the flag, and we cast no doubt on the legitimacy of its interest in making such recommendations. To say that the government has an interest in encouraging proper treatment of the flag, however, is not to say that it may criminally punish a person for burning a flag as a means of political protest. "National unity as an end which officials may foster by persuasion and example is not in question. The problem is whether under our Constitution compulsion as here employed is a permissible means for its achievement." *Barnette.*

We are fortified in today's conclusion by our conviction that forbidding criminal punishment for conduct such as Johnson's will not endanger the special role played by our flag or the feelings it inspires. To paraphrase Justice Holmes, we submit that nobody can suppose that this one gesture of an unknown man will change our Nation's attitude towards its flag. Indeed, Texas' argument that the burning of an American flag "is an act having a high likelihood to cause a breach of the peace," and its statute's implicit assumption that physical mistreatment of the flag will lead to "serious offense," tend to confirm that the flag's special role is not in danger; if it were, no one would riot or take offense because a flag had been burned.

We are tempted to say, in fact, that the flag's deservedly cherished place in our community will be strengthened, not weakened, by our holding today. Our decision is a reaffirmation of the principles of freedom and inclusiveness that the flag best reflects, and of the conviction that our toleration of criticism such as Johnson's is a sign and source of our strength. Indeed, one of the proudest images of our flag, the one immortalized in our own national anthem, is of the bombardment it survived at Fort McHenry. It is the Nation's resilience, not its rigidity, that Texas sees reflected in the flag—and it is that resilience that we reassert today.

The way to preserve the flag's special role is not to punish those who feel differently about these matters. It is to persuade them that they are wrong. "To courageous, self-reliant men, with confidence in the power of free and fearless reasoning applied through the processes of popular government, no danger flowing from speech can be deemed clear and present, unless the incidence of the evil apprehended is so imminent that it may befall before there is opportunity for full discussion. If there be time to expose through discussion the falsehood and fallacies, to avert the evil by the processes of education, the remedy to be applied is more speech, not enforced silence." *Whitney v. California* (Brandeis, J., concurring). And, precisely because it is our flag that is involved, one's response to the flag burner may exploit the uniquely persuasive power of the flag itself. We can imagine no more appropriate response to burning a flag than waving one's own, no better way to counter a flag burner's message than by saluting the flag that burns, no surer means of preserving the dignity even of the flag that burned than by—as one witness here did—according its remains a respectful burial. We do not consecrate the flag by punishing its desecration, for in doing so we dilute the freedom that this cherished emblem represents.

V

Johnson was convicted for engaging in expressive conduct. The State's interest in preventing breaches of the peace does not support his conviction because Johnson's conduct did not threaten to disturb the peace. Nor does the State's interest in preserving the flag as a symbol of nationhood and national unity justify his criminal conviction for engaging in political expression. The judgment of the Texas Court of Criminal Appeals is therefore

Affirmed.

CHIEF JUSTICE REHNQUIST, *with whom* **JUSTICE WHITE** *and* **JUSTICE O'CONNOR** *join, dissenting.*

In holding this Texas statute unconstitutional, the Court ignores Justice Holmes' familiar aphorism that "a page of history is worth a volume of logic." *New York Trust Co. v. Eisner.* For more than 200 years, the American flag has occupied a unique position as the symbol of our Nation, a uniqueness that justifies a governmental prohibition against flag burning in the way respondent Johnson did here.

The American flag, throughout more than 200 years of our history, has come to be the visible symbol embodying our Nation. It does not represent the views of any particular political party, and it does not represent any particular political philosophy. The flag is not simply another "idea" or "point of view" competing for recognition in the marketplace of ideas. Millions and millions of Americans regard it with an almost mystical reverence regardless of what sort of social, political, or philosophical beliefs they may have. I cannot agree that the First Amendment invalidates the Act of Congress, and the laws of 48 of the 50 States, which make criminal the public burning of the flag.

More than 80 years ago in *Halter v. Nebraska*, this Court upheld the constitutionality of a Nebraska statute that forbade the use of representations of the American flag for advertising purposes upon articles of merchandise.

Only two Terms ago, in *San Francisco Arts & Athletics, Inc. v. United States Olympic Committee*, the Court held that Congress could grant exclusive use of the word "Olympic" to the United States Olympic Committee. The Court thought that this "restrictio[n] on expressive speech properly [was] characterized as incidental to the primary congressional purpose of encouraging and rewarding the USOC's activities." *Id.* As the Court stated, "when a word [or symbol] acquires value 'as the result of organization and the expenditure of labor, skill, and money' by an entity, that entity constitutionally may obtain a limited property right in the word [or symbol]." *Id*, Surely Congress or the States may recognize a similar interest in the flag.

But the Court insists that the Texas statute prohibiting the public burning of the American flag infringes on respondent Johnson's freedom of expression. Such freedom, of course, is not absolute. See *Schenck v. United States*. In *Chaplinsky v. New Hampshire*, a unanimous Court said: "Allowing the broadest scope to the language and purpose of the Fourteenth Amendment, it is well understood that the right of free speech is not absolute at all times and under all circumstances." The Court upheld Chaplinsky's conviction under a state statute that made it unlawful to "address any offensive, derisive or annoying word to any person who is lawfully in any street or other public place." Chaplinsky had told a local marshal, "'You are a God damned racketeer' and a 'damned Fascist and the whole government of Rochester are Fascists or agents of Fascists.'"

Here it may equally well be said that the public burning of the American flag by Johnson was no essential part of any exposition of ideas, and at the same time it had a tendency to incite a breach of the peace. Johnson was free to make any verbal denunciation of the flag that he wished; indeed, he was free to burn the flag in private. He could publicly burn other symbols of the Government or effigies of political leaders. He did lead a march through the streets of Dallas, and conducted a rally in front of the Dallas City Hall. He engaged in a "die-in" to protest nuclear weapons. He shouted out various slogans during the march, including: "Reagan, Mondale which will it be? Either one means World War III"; "Ronald Reagan, killer of the hour, Perfect example of U.S. power"; and "red, white and blue, we spit on you, you stand for plunder, you will go under." For none of these acts was he arrested or prosecuted; it was only when he proceeded to burn publicly an American flag stolen from its rightful owner that he violated the Texas statute.

The Court could not, and did not, say that Chaplinsky's utterances were not

expressive phrases—they clearly and succinctly conveyed an extremely low opinion of the addressee. The same may be said of Johnson's public burning of the flag in this case; it obviously did convey Johnson's bitter dislike of his country. But his act, like Chaplinsky's provocative words, conveyed nothing that could not have been conveyed and was not conveyed just as forcefully in a dozen different ways. As with "fighting words," so with flag burning, for purposes of the First Amendment: It is "no essential part of any exposition of ideas, and [is] of such slight social value as a step to truth that any benefit that may be derived from [it] is clearly outweighed" by the public interest in avoiding a probable breach of the peace. The highest courts of several States have upheld state statutes prohibiting the public burning of the flag on the grounds that it is so inherently inflammatory that it may cause a breach of public order.

The result of the Texas statute is obviously to deny one in Johnson's frame of mind one of many means of "symbolic speech." Far from being a case of "one picture being worth a thousand words," flag burning is the equivalent of an inarticulate grunt or roar that, it seems fair to say, is most likely to be indulged in not to express any particular idea, but to antagonize others. Only five years ago we said in *City Council of Los Angeles v. Taxpayers for Vincent*, that "the First Amendment does not guarantee the right to employ every conceivable method of communication at all times and in all places." The Texas statute deprived Johnson of only one rather inarticulate symbolic form of protest—a form of protest that was profoundly offensive to many—and left him with a full panoply of other symbols and every conceivable form of verbal expression to express his deep disapproval of national policy. Thus, in no way can it be said that Texas is punishing him because his hearers—or any other group of people—were profoundly opposed to the message that he sought to convey. Such opposition is no proper basis for restricting speech or expression under the First Amendment. It was Johnson's use of this particular symbol, and not the idea that he sought to convey by it or by his many other expressions, for which he was punished.

The uniquely deep awe and respect for our flag felt by virtually all of us are bundled off under the rubric of "designated symbols," that the First Amendment prohibits the government from "establishing." But the government has not "established" this feeling; 200 years of history have done that. The government is simply recognizing as a fact the profound regard for the American flag created by that history when it enacts statutes prohibiting the disrespectful public burning of the flag.

The Court concludes its opinion with a regrettably patronizing civics lecture, presumably addressed to the Members of both Houses of Congress, the members of the 48 state legislatures that enacted prohibitions against flag burning, and the troops fighting under that flag in Vietnam who objected to its being burned: "The way to preserve the flag's special role is not to punish those who feel differently about these matters. It is to persuade them that they are wrong." The Court's role as the final expositor of the Constitution is well established, but its role as a Platonic guardian admonishing those responsible to public opinion as if they were truant schoolchildren has no similar place in our system of government. The cry of "no taxation without representation" animated those who revolted against the English Crown to found our Nation—the idea that those who submitted to government should have some say as to what kind of laws would be passed. Surely one of the high purposes of a democratic society is to legislate against conduct that is regarded as evil and profoundly offensive to the

majority of people—whether it be murder, embezzlement, pollution, or flag burning.

Our Constitution wisely places limits on powers of legislative majorities to act, but the declaration of such limits by this Court "is, at all times, a question of much delicacy, which ought seldom, if ever, to be decided in the affirmative, in a doubtful case." *Fletcher v. Peck.* Uncritical extension of constitutional protection to the burning of the flag risks the frustration of the very purpose for which organized governments are instituted. The Court decides that the American flag is just another symbol, about which not only must opinions pro and con be tolerated, but for which the most minimal public respect may not be enjoined. The government may conscript men into the Armed Forces where they must fight and perhaps die for the flag, but the government may not prohibit the public burning of the banner under which they fight. I would uphold the Texas statute as applied in this case.

JUSTICE STEVENS, *dissenting.*

As the Court analyzes this case, it presents the question whether the State of Texas, or indeed the Federal Government, has the power to prohibit the public desecration of the American flag. The question is unique. In my judgment rules that apply to a host of other symbols, such as state flags, armbands, or various privately promoted emblems of political or commercial identity, are not necessarily controlling. Even if flag burning could be considered just another species of symbolic speech under the logical application of the rules that the Court has developed in its interpretation of the First Amendment in other contexts, this case has an intangible dimension that makes those rules inapplicable.

A country's flag is a symbol of more than "nationhood and national unity." It also signifies the ideas that characterize the society that has chosen that emblem as well as the special history that has animated the growth and power of those ideas. The fleurs-de-lis and the tricolor both symbolized "nationhood and national unity," but they had vastly different meanings. The message conveyed by some flags—the swastika, for example—may survive long after it has outlived its usefulness as a symbol of regimented unity in a particular nation.

So it is with the American flag. It is more than a proud symbol of the courage, the determination, and the gifts of nature that transformed 13 fledgling Colonies into a world power. It is a symbol of freedom, of equal opportunity, of religious tolerance, and of good will for other peoples who share our aspirations. The symbol carries its message to dissidents both at home and abroad who may have no interest at all in our national unity or survival.

The value of the flag as a symbol cannot be measured. Even so, I have no doubt that the interest in preserving that value for the future is both significant and legitimate. Conceivably that value will be enhanced by the Court's conclusion that our national commitment to free expression is so strong that even the United States as ultimate guarantor of that freedom is without power to prohibit the desecration of its unique symbol. But I am unpersuaded. The creation of a federal right to post bulletin boards and graffiti on the Washington Monument might enlarge the market for free expression, but at a cost I would not pay. Similarly, in my considered judgment, sanctioning the public desecration of the flag will tarnish its value—both for those who cherish the ideas for which it waves and for those who desire to don the robes of martyrdom by burning it. That tarnish is not justified by the trivial burden on free expression occasioned by requiring that an available, alternative mode of expression—including

uttering words critical of the flag, see *Street v. New York*—be employed.

It is appropriate to emphasize certain propositions that are not implicated by this case. The statutory prohibition of flag desecration does not "prescribe what shall be orthodox in politics, nationalism, religion, or other matters of opinion or force citizens to confess by word or act their faith therein." *West Virginia Board of Education v. Barnette*. The statute does not compel any conduct or any profession of respect for any idea or any symbol.

Nor does the statute violate "the government's paramount obligation of neutrality in its regulation of protected communication." *Young v. American Mini Theatres, Inc.* The content of respondent's message has no relevance whatsoever to the case. The concept of "desecration" does not turn on the substance of the message the actor intends to convey, but rather on whether those who view the *act* will take serious offense. Accordingly, one intending to convey a message of respect for the flag by burning it in a public square might nonetheless be guilty of desecration if he knows that others—perhaps simply because they misperceive the intended message—will be seriously offended. Indeed, even if the actor knows that all possible witnesses will understand that he intends to send a message of respect, he might still be guilty of desecration if he also knows that this understanding does not lessen the offense taken by some of those witnesses. Thus, this is not a case in which the fact that "it is the speaker's opinion that gives offense" provides a special "reason for according it constitutional protection," *FCC v. Pacifica Foundation*. The case has nothing to do with "disagreeable ideas." It involves disagreeable conduct that, in my opinion, diminishes the value of an important national asset.

The Court is therefore quite wrong in blandly asserting that respondent "was prosecuted for his expression of dissatisfaction with the policies of this country, expression situated at the core of our First Amendment values." Respondent was prosecuted because of the method he chose to express his dissatisfaction with those policies. Had he chosen to spray-paint—or perhaps convey with a motion picture projector—his message of dissatisfaction on the facade of the Lincoln Memorial, there would be no question about the power of the Government to prohibit his means of expression. The prohibition would be supported by the legitimate interest in preserving the quality of an important national asset. Though the asset at stake in this case is intangible, given its unique value, the same interest supports a prohibition on the desecration of the American flag.

The ideas of liberty and equality have been an irresistible force in motivating leaders like Patrick Henry, Susan B. Anthony, and Abraham Lincoln, schoolteachers like Nathan Hale and Booker T. Washington, the Philippine Scouts who fought at Bataan, and the soldiers who scaled the bluff at Omaha Beach. If those ideas are worth fighting for—and our history demonstrates that they are—it cannot be true that the flag that uniquely symbolizes their power is not itself worthy of protection from unnecessary desecration.

I respectfully dissent.

CASE QUESTION

The text of the First Amendment emphasizes protection for "speech." However, as you know from reading the *Texas v. Johnson* decision, the Court has extended this protection beyond mere written and spoken verbal expression. Flag burning, according to the Court, is symbolic expression protected by the Constitution. But to what extent does this protection of symbolic speech stray from the literal text? Could "textualist" theories of interpretation, such as originalism, or that advocated in this section by Justice Hugo Black, offer protection for symbolic expression? How should the Court distinguish between expressive conduct protected under the First Amendment and conduct that does not deserve such protection?

CITIZENS UNITED v. FEDERAL ELECTION COMMISSION

558 U.S. _____ (2010)

Opinion: Kennedy, joined by Roberts, Scalia, Alito, by Thomas in all but Part IV and by Stevens, Ginsburg, Breyer, Sotomayor in Part IV
Concurrence: Roberts, joined by Alito
Concurrence: Scalia, joined by Alito and by Thomas in part
Partial Concurrence, Partial Dissent: Stevens, joined by Ginsburg, Breyer, Sotomayor
Partial Concurrence, Partial Dissent: Thomas

In Buckley v. Valeo, *the Court established some First Amendment limits on campaign finance restrictions. In the following case, the Court considers whether restrictions on corporations' ability to fund political messages are valid under the First Amendment. As you read this case, consider whether the arguments of Alexander Meiklejohn or John Stuart Mill support the Court's reasoning about the rights of corporations under the First Amendment. Even if the speech in question clearly expresses a viewpoint, should it matter that the actor is a corporation rather than an individual?*

Should corporations' free speech rights be affected by the fact that they are not full participants in the political process (that is, they lack the right to vote)? Do citizens have the right to hear the views of corporations?

JUSTICE KENNEDY *delivered the opinion of the Court.*

Federal law prohibits corporations and unions from using their general treasury funds to make independent expenditures for speech defined as an "electioneering communication" or for speech expressly advocating the election or defeat of a candidate. Limits on electioneering communications were upheld in *McConnell v. Federal Election Comm'n.* The holding of *McConnell* rested to a large extent on an earlier case, *Austin v. Michigan Chamber of Commerce. Austin* had held that political speech may be banned based on the speaker's corporate identity.

In this case we are asked to reconsider *Austin* and, in effect, *McConnell.* It has been noted that "*Austin* was a significant departure from ancient First Amendment principles," *Federal Election Comm'n v. Wisconsin Right to Life, Inc. (WRTL)* (Scalia, J., concurring in part and concurring in judgment). We agree with that conclusion and hold that *stare decisis* does not compel the continued acceptance of *Austin.* The Government may regulate corporate political speech through disclaimer and disclosure requirements, but it may not suppress that speech altogether. We turn to the case now before us.

I

A

Citizens United is a nonprofit corporation. It brought this action in the United States District Court for the District of Columbia. A three-judge court later convened to hear the cause. The resulting judgment gives rise to this appeal.

Citizens United has an annual budget of about $12 million. Most of its funds are from donations by individuals; but, in addition, it accepts a small portion of its funds from for-profit corporations.

In January 2008, Citizens United released a film entitled *Hillary: The Movie.* We refer to the film as *Hillary.* It is a 90-minute documentary about then-Senator Hillary Clinton, who was a candidate in the Democratic Party's 2008 Presidential primary elections. *Hillary* mentions Senator Clinton by name and depicts interviews with political commentators and other persons, most of them quite critical of Senator Clinton. *Hillary* was released in theaters and on DVD, but Citizens United wanted to increase distribution by making it available through video-on-demand.

Video-on-demand allows digital cable subscribers to select programming from various menus, including movies, television shows, sports, news, and music. The viewer can watch the program at any time and can elect to rewind or pause the program. In December 2007, a cable company offered, for a payment of $1.2 million, to make *Hillary* available on a video-on-demand channel called "Elections '08." Some video-on-demand services require viewers to pay a small fee to view a selected program, but here the proposal was to make *Hillary* available to viewers free of charge.

To implement the proposal, Citizens United was prepared to pay for the video-on-demand; and to promote the film, it produced two 10-second ads and one 30-second ad for *Hillary.* Each ad includes a short (and, in our view, pejorative) statement about Senator Clinton, followed by the name of the movie and the movie's Website address. Citizens United desired to promote the video-on-demand offering by running advertisements on broadcast and cable television.

B

Before the Bipartisan Campaign Reform Act of 2002 (BCRA), federal law prohibited—and still does prohibit—corporations and unions from using general treasury funds to make direct contributions to candidates or independent expenditures that expressly advocate the election or defeat of a candidate, through any form of media, in connection with certain qualified federal elections. BCRA §203 amended §441b to prohibit any "electioneering communication" as well. An electioneering communication is defined as "any broadcast, cable, or satellite communication" that "refers to a clearly identified candidate for Federal office" and is made within 30 days of a primary or 60 days of a general election. The Federal Election Commission's (FEC) regulations further define an electioneering communication as a communication that is "publicly distributed." "In the case of a candidate for nomination for President . . . *publicly distributed* means" that the communication "[c]an be received by 50,000 or more persons in a State where a primary election . . . is being held within 30 days." Corporations and unions are barred from using their general treasury funds for express advocacy or electioneering communications. They may establish, however, a "separate segregated fund" (known as a political action committee, or PAC) for these purposes. The moneys received by the segregated fund are limited to donations from stockholders and employees of the corporation or, in the case of unions, members of the union.

C

Citizens United wanted to make *Hillary* available through video-on-demand within 30 days of the 2008 primary elections. It feared, however, that both the film and the ads would be covered by §441b's ban on corporate-funded independent expenditures, thus subjecting the corporation to civil and criminal penalties under §437g. In December 2007, Citizens United sought declaratory and injunctive relief against the FEC. It argued that (1) §441b is unconstitutional as applied to *Hillary*; and (2) BCRA's disclaimer and disclosure requirements, BCRA §§201 and 311, are unconstitutional as applied to *Hillary* and to the three ads for the movie.

The District Court denied Citizens United's motion for a preliminary injunction, and then granted the FEC's motion for summary judgment. The court held that §441b was facially constitutional under *McConnell*, and that §441b was constitutional as applied to *Hillary* because it was "susceptible of no other interpretation than to inform the electorate that Senator Clinton is unfit for office, that the United States would be a dangerous place in a President Hillary Clinton world, and that viewers should vote against her." The court also rejected Citizens United's challenge to BCRA's disclaimer and disclosure requirements. It noted that "the Supreme Court has written approvingly of disclosure provisions triggered by political speech even though the speech itself was constitutionally protected under the First Amendment."

We noted probable jurisdiction. The case was reargued in this Court after the Court asked the parties to file supplemental briefs addressing whether we should overrule either or both *Austin* and the part of *McConnell* which addresses the facial validity of 2 U.S.C. §441b.

III

The First Amendment provides that "Congress shall make no law . . . abridging the freedom of speech." Laws enacted to control or suppress speech may operate at different points in the speech process. The following are just a few examples of restrictions that have been attempted at different stages of the speech process—all laws found to be invalid: restrictions requiring a permit at the outset, *Watchtower Bible & Tract Soc. of N.Y., Inc. v. Village of Stratton*; imposing a burden by impounding proceeds on receipts or royalties, *Simon & Schuster, Inc. v. Members of N.Y. State Crime Victims Bd.*; seeking to exact a cost after the speech occurs, *New York Times Co. v. Sullivan*; and subjecting the speaker to criminal penalties, *Brandenburg v. Ohio*.

The law before us is an outright ban, backed by criminal sanctions. Section 441b makes it a felony for all corporations—including nonprofit advocacy corporations—either to expressly advocate the election or defeat of candidates or to broadcast electioneering communications within 30 days of a primary election and 60 days of a general election....

Section 441b is a ban on corporate speech notwithstanding the fact that a PAC created by a corporation can still speak. See *McConnell*. A PAC is a separate association from the corporation. So the PAC exemption from §441b's expenditure ban, does not allow corporations to speak. Even if a PAC could somehow allow a corporation to speak—and it does not—the option to form PACs does not alleviate the First Amendment problems with §441b....

Given the onerous restrictions, a corporation may not be able to establish a PAC in time to make its views known regarding candidates and issues in a current campaign.

Section 441b's prohibition on corporate independent expenditures is thus a ban on speech. As a "restriction on the amount of money a person or group can spend on political communication during a campaign," that statute "necessarily reduces the quantity of expression by restricting the number of issues discussed, the depth of their exploration, and the size of the audience reached." *Buckley v. Valeo*. Were the Court to uphold these restrictions, the Government could repress speech by silencing certain voices at any of the various points in the speech process....

Speech is an essential mechanism of democracy, for it is the means to hold officials accountable to the people. The right of citizens to inquire, to hear, to speak, and to use information to reach consensus is a precondition to enlightened self-government and a necessary means to protect it. The First Amendment "'has its fullest and most urgent application'" to speech uttered during a campaign for political office." *Eu v. San Francisco County Democratic Central Comm.*

For these reasons, political speech must prevail against laws that would suppress it, whether by design or inadvertence. Laws that burden political speech are "subject to strict scrutiny," which requires the Government to prove that the restriction "furthers a compelling interest and is narrowly tailored to achieve that interest." *WRTL*. While it might be maintained that political speech simply cannot be banned or restricted as a categorical matter, see *Simon & Schuster*, the quoted language from *WRTL* provides a sufficient framework for protecting the relevant First Amendment interests in this case. We shall employ it here.

Premised on mistrust of governmental power, the First Amendment stands against attempts to disfavor certain subjects or viewpoints. Prohibited, too, are restrictions distinguishing among different speakers, allowing speech by some but not others. See *First Nat. Bank of Boston v. Bellotti*. As instruments to censor, these categories are interrelated: Speech restrictions based on the identity of the speaker are all too often simply a means to control content.

Quite apart from the purpose or effect of regulating content, moreover, the Government may commit a constitutional wrong when by law it identifies certain preferred speakers. By taking the right to speak from some and giving it to others, the Government deprives the disadvantaged person or class of the right to use speech to strive to establish worth, standing, and respect for the speaker's voice. The Government may not by these means deprive the public of the right and privilege to determine for itself what speech and speakers are worthy of consideration. The First Amendment protects speech and speaker, and the ideas that flow from each.

The Court has upheld a narrow class of speech restrictions that operate to the disadvantage of certain persons, but these rulings were based on an interest in allowing governmental entities to perform their functions. . . . The corporate independent expenditures at issue in this case, however, would not interfere with governmental functions, so these cases are inapposite. These precedents stand only for the proposition that there are certain governmental functions that cannot operate without some restrictions on particular kinds of speech. By contrast, it is inherent in the nature of the political process that voters must be free to obtain information from diverse sources in order to determine how to cast their votes. At least before *Austin*, the Court had not allowed the exclusion of a class of speakers from the general public dialogue.

We find no basis for the proposition that, in the context of political speech, the Government may impose restrictions on certain disfavored speakers. Both history and logic lead us to this conclusion.

B

. . . The Court is thus confronted with conflicting lines of precedent: a pre-*Austin* line that forbids restrictions on political speech based on the speaker's corporate identity and a post-*Austin* line that permits them. . . .

2

. . . When Congress finds that a problem exists, we must give that finding due deference; but Congress may not choose an unconstitutional remedy. If elected officials succumb to improper influences from independent expenditures; if they surrender their best judgment; and if they put expediency before principle, then surely there is cause for concern. We must give weight to attempts by Congress to seek to dispel either the appearance or the reality of these influences. The remedies enacted by law, however, must comply with the First Amendment; and, it is our law and our tradition that more speech, not less, is the governing rule. An outright ban on corporate political speech during the critical preelection period is not a permissible remedy. Here Congress has created categorical bans on speech that are asymmetrical to preventing *quid pro quo* corruption. . . .

4

. . . We need not reach the question whether the Government has a compelling interest in preventing foreign individuals or associations from influencing our Nation's political process. Section 441b is not limited to corporations or associations that were created in foreign countries or funded predominately by foreign shareholders. Section 441b therefore would be overbroad even if we assumed, *arguendo*, that the Government has a compelling interest in limiting foreign influence over our political process. See *Broadrick*.

C

. . . Due consideration leads to this conclusion: *Austin* should be and now is overruled. We return to the principle established in *Buckley* and *Bellotti* that the Government may not suppress political speech on the basis of the speaker's corporate identity. No sufficient governmental interest justifies limits on the political speech of nonprofit or for-profit corporations.

D

Austin is overruled, so it provides no basis for allowing the Government to limit corporate independent expenditures. As the Government appears to concede, overruling *Austin* "effectively invalidate[s] not only BCRA Section 203, but also 2 U.S.C. 441b's prohibition on the use of corporate treasury funds for express advocacy." Brief for Appellee 33, n.12. Section 441b's restrictions on corporate independent expenditures are therefore invalid and cannot be applied to *Hillary*.

Given our conclusion we are further required to overrule the part of *McConnell* that upheld BCRA §203's extension of §441b's restrictions on corporate independent expenditures. The *McConnell* Court relied on the antidistortion interest recognized in *Austin* to uphold a greater restriction on speech than the restriction upheld in *Austin*, and we have found this interest unconvincing and insufficient. This part of *McConnell* is now overruled.

IV

A

Citizens United next challenges BCRA's disclaimer and disclosure provisions as applied to *Hillary* and the three advertisements for the movie.

. . . Although both provisions were facially upheld, the Court acknowledged that as-applied challenges would be available if a group could show a "reasonable probability" that disclosure of its contributors' names "will subject them to threats, harassment, or reprisals from either Government officials or private parties."

For the reasons stated below, we find the statute valid as applied to the ads for the movie and to the movie itself.

B

The Court has explained that disclosure is a less restrictive alternative to more comprehensive regulations of speech. In *Buckley*, the Court upheld a disclosure requirement for independent expenditures even though it invalidated a provision that imposed a ceiling on those expenditures. In *McConnell*, three Justices who would have found §441b to be unconstitutional nonetheless voted to uphold BCRA's disclosure and disclaimer requirements. And the Court has upheld registration and disclosure requirements on lobbyists, even though Congress has no power to ban lobbying itself. For these reasons, we reject Citizens United's contention that the disclosure requirements must be limited to speech that is the functional equivalent of express advocacy.

Shareholder objections raised through the procedures of corporate democracy can be more effective today because modern technology makes disclosures rapid and informative. A campaign finance system that pairs corporate independent expenditures with effective disclosure has not existed before today. It must be noted, furthermore, that many of Congress' findings in passing BCRA were premised on a system without adequate disclosure. With the advent of the Internet, prompt disclosure of expenditures can provide shareholders and citizens with the information needed to hold corporations and elected officials accountable for their positions and supporters. Shareholders can determine whether their corporation's political speech advances the corporation's interest in making profits, and citizens can see whether elected officials are " 'in the pocket' of so-called moneyed interests." The First Amendment protects political speech; and disclosure permits citizens and shareholders to react to the speech of corporate entities in a proper way. This transparency enables the electorate to make informed decisions and give proper weight to different speakers and messages.

V

... Modern day movies, television comedies, or skits on Youtube.com might portray public officials or public policies in unflattering ways. Yet if a covered transmission during the blackout period creates the background for candidate endorsement or opposition, a felony occurs solely because a corporation, other than an exempt media corporation, has made the "purchase, payment, distribution, loan, advance, deposit, or gift of money or anything of value" in order to engage in political speech. Speech would be suppressed in the realm where its necessity is most evident: in the public dialogue preceding a real election. Governments are often hostile to speech, but under our law and our tradition it seems stranger than fiction for our Government to make this political speech a crime. Yet this is the statute's purpose and design.

Some members of the public might consider *Hillary* to be insightful and instructive; some might find it to be neither high art nor a fair discussion on how to set the Nation's course; still others simply might suspend judgment on these points but decide to think more about issues and candidates. Those choices and assessments, however,

are not for the Government to make. "The First Amendment underwrites the freedom to experiment and to create in the realm of thought and speech. Citizens must be free to use new forms, and new forums, for the expression of ideas. The civic discourse belongs to the people, and the Government may not prescribe the means used to conduct it." *McConnell* (opinion of Kennedy, J.).

The judgment of the District Court is reversed with respect to the constitutionality of 2 U.S.C. §441b's restrictions on corporate independent expenditures. The judgment is affirmed with respect to BCRA's disclaimer and disclosure requirements. The case is remanded for further proceedings consistent with this opinion.

JUSTICE STEVENS, *with whom* **JUSTICE GINSBURG, JUSTICE BREYER,** *and* **JUSTICE SOTOMAYOR** *join, concurring in part and dissenting in part.*

The real issue in this case concerns how, not if, the appellant may finance its electioneering. Citizens United is a wealthy nonprofit corporation that runs a political action committee (PAC) with millions of dollars in assets. Under the Bipartisan Campaign Reform Act of 2002 (BCRA), it could have used those assets to televise and promote *Hillary: The Movie* wherever and whenever it wanted to. It also could have spent unrestricted sums to broadcast *Hillary* at any time other than the 30 days before the last primary election. Neither Citizens United's nor any other corporation's speech has been "banned". . . . All that the parties dispute is whether Citizens United had a right to use the funds in its general treasury to pay for broadcasts during the 30-day period. The notion that the First Amendment dictates an affirmative answer to that question is, in my judgment, profoundly misguided. Even more misguided is the notion that the Court must rewrite the law relating to campaign expenditures by *for-profit* corporations and unions to decide this case. . . .

V

Today's decision is backwards in many senses. It elevates the majority's agenda over the litigants' submissions, facial attacks over as-applied claims, broad constitutional theories over narrow statutory grounds, individual dissenting opinions over precedential holdings, assertion over tradition, absolutism over empiricism, rhetoric over reality. Our colleagues have arrived at the conclusion that *Austin* must be overruled and that §203 is facially unconstitutional only after mischaracterizing both the reach and rationale of those authorities, and after bypassing or ignoring rules of judicial restraint used to cabin the Court's lawmaking power. Their conclusion that the societal interest in avoiding corruption and the appearance of corruption does not provide an adequate justification for regulating corporate expenditures on candidate elections relies on an incorrect description of that interest, along with a failure to acknowledge the relevance of established facts and the considered judgments of state and federal legislatures over many decades.

In a democratic society, the longstanding consensus on the need to limit corporate campaign spending should outweigh the wooden application of judge-made rules. The majority's rejection of this principle "elevate[s] corporations to a level of deference which has not been seen at least since the days when substantive due process was regularly used to invalidate regulatory legislation thought to unfairly impinge upon established economic interests." *Bellotti*, at 817, n.13 (White, J., dissenting). At bottom, the Court's opinion is thus a rejection of the common sense of the American people, who have recognized a need to prevent corporations from undermining self-government since the founding, and who have fought against the distinctive corrupting potential of corporate electioneering since the days of Theodore Roosevelt. It is a strange time to repudiate that common sense. While American democracy is imperfect, few outside the majority of this Court would have thought its flaws included a dearth of corporate money in politics.

I would affirm the judgment of the District Court.

SYNTHESIS QUESTIONS FOR FURTHER DISCUSSION: CHAPTER 5 SECTION A

1. John Stuart Mill and Alexander Meiklejohn offer spirited defenses of free speech. While both theorists suggest the importance of protecting all political speech, they offer two different theories as to why speech should be protected. In the excerpt from Mill, notice his claim that free speech unfettered by coercion will lead to "truth." Mill suggests that partially or even completely false ideas will aid public discourse by clarifying the meaning and reasoning of true doctrines. This argument is a consequentialist one, emphasizing that free speech is instrumentally valuable

because it produces future public benefits. One question to consider, however, is whether even in the absence of such benefits speech still deserves protection. In particular, is a solely instrumentalist argument susceptible to the claim at the core of the clear and present danger test that certain rights must be suspended in times of great danger? In reading Meiklejohn's argument for free speech, consider whether his is an instrumental or an intrinsic argument. Is there any reason we should allow citizens to make and hear bad arguments even when this freedom might lead to bad policy results?

In reading the cases, think about whether either Mill's or Meiklejohn's argument is helpful in analyzing the cases that we have examined so far. For instance, does either of these authors help us to decide whether the clear and present danger test offers the right balance between protecting political speech and security? Meiklejohn himself was a critic of the clear and present danger test, but to what extent does his theory protect speech directed against democracy itself? Mill suggests that open-ended argument will lead to truth, but is speech celebrating terrorism part of open-ended argument, or is it rightly regarded as outside the boundaries of political discussion? Moreover, does burning a flag constitute the kind of speech that is important to the production of truth or to the guarantee of democracy?

2. The clear and present danger test was abandoned by the Supreme Court in its *Brandenburg v. Ohio* decision in favor of a much more robust protection of free political speech. Do Prime Minister Gordon Brown's statements about the danger of advocating for terrorism suggest a contemporary reason for returning to the clear and present danger test? Would the kind of "terrorist speech" Prime Minister Brown suggests might be banned in the United Kingdom be protected under the Court's standard in *Brandenburg v. Ohio*? If not, should a new standard be proposed? It was the premise of the clear and present danger test that when a nation is particularly susceptible to security threats it should offer less robust civil liberties protections. Is this vulnerability present in our own time? If so, how should we interpret the Constitution's protection of free speech?

As you consider this question of terrorism, you might think about whether this example actually vindicates the Court's clear and present danger standard in the early twentieth century. For instance, if we imagine that the documents distributed in *Schenck v. United States* or the circular that was distributed in *Abrams v. United States* in fact would lead to the overthrow of the U.S. government, would that justify the kind of balancing that the Court employed with the clear and present danger test? Is there any instance of danger to the U.S. government, whether terrorism or another threat, severe enough to justify the curtailment of free speech?

3. In his time, Meiklejohn was considered a strong advocate of free political speech and a forceful critic of the clear and present danger test. For

Meiklejohn, the right of democratic citizens to make and hear all political arguments is paramount if they are to have the capacity to consent to be governed. Does this argument risk ignoring forms of non-political expression? For instance, does his theory offer a defense of free expression in the domains of art and literature? To what extent, moreover, is Meiklejohn's defense aligned with a more general jurisprudence that makes the political process central to rights protections, along the lines of that articulated by John Hart Ely?

4. Meiklejohn argued that free political speech needed to be protected to ensure free deliberation among citizens. But is the participation of corporations in political deliberation essential to the democratic process? If so, are there any constitutional differences between corporations and individuals? What arguments does the Court present in *Citizens United v. Federal Elections Commission* for extending First Amendment protection to corporations? Do you agree? Moreover, is the ability to give money part of the democratic understanding of free speech, as concerning individuals or corporations?

Table 5.1.   Central Holdings of Key Supreme Court Cases on Free Speech

Supreme Court Case	Central Holding
Schenck v. United States	Speech that presents a clear and present danger does not receive First Amendment protection.
Whitney v. California	Speech that advocates, incites, or supports acts of violence or damage does not receive First Amendment protection. Expanded upon *Schenck v. United States*.
Brandenburg v. Ohio	Speech must not only advocate but actually be likely to incite imminent violent action in order for it to lose constitutional protection. Overturned *Whitney v. California* and rejected the clear and present danger test.
Texas v. Johnson	Expressive conduct is protected by the First Amendment.
New York Times Co. v. Sullivan	The First Amendment protects even untrue speech, so long as it does not demonstrate actual malice toward the official or reckless disregard for the truth or falsity of the statement in question.
Buckley v. Valeo	Although some aspects of campaign finance law are constitutionally valid, citizens have a First Amendment free speech interest in their ability to fund political candidates.
Citizens United v. FEC	The First Amendment protects the rights of corporations to directly fund advertisements in candidate elections.

B. OBSCENITY, PORNOGRAPHY, AND HATE SPEECH

Is obscene speech, pornography, or hate speech deserving of protection?

As we have seen, the Court today tends to eschew censorship of any political viewpoint under the doctrine known as viewpoint neutrality. Specifically, when the Court is evaluating laws that ban certain speech, it does not allow what it regards as "viewpoint discrimination." Generally, the Court goes beyond viewpoint neutrality to enforce a doctrine of "content neutrality," which includes the right to speak on all subjects free from restrictions based on the substance of one's speech. However, the Court does allow some exceptions to this broad prohibition on content-based discrimination. For example, when it comes to obscenity, the Court has allowed content-based limits on speech. Importantly, such content-based regulations prohibit all speech that falls under the category of obscenity rather than targeting obscene expression of a particular viewpoint.

In addition to analyzing the Supreme Court's approach to obscenity, we also examine a fervent critic of its approach to these issues. As we have seen, the Court's doctrine of viewpoint neutrality would not allow limits on pornography based on the particular message it expresses. However, Catharine MacKinnon argues that this is a mistake. On her view, pornography should be banned because it conveys the idea that women are subordinates. Rejecting viewpoint neutrality, she argues that such deeply inegalitarian viewpoints should be balanced and limited by a concern for the state to ensure women's equality.

We also examine a response to MacKinnon's view by Ronald Dworkin. According to Dworkin, if we were to abandon viewpoint neutrality, there would be no guarantee against laws that punished advocacy of inegalitarian ideas, a result that he takes as a problematic restriction on democratic rights.

Before we examine the Court's current jurisprudence on the issue of obscenity, we examine two cases that do not fall within the Court's obscenity doctrine. We begin with *Stanley v. Georgia*, which appears at first to be an obscenity case, but, as you will see, the Court declines to examine it through this lens, instead suggesting that it is appropriately analyzed in terms of the right to privacy that you saw in *Griswold v. Connecticut*. *Stanley v. Georgia* therefore helps to distinguish between questions of obscenity and questions of privacy. We turn next to the case of *Cohen v. California*, which raises questions about how to define obscenity. Like *Stanley v. Georgia*, *Cohen v. California* appears at first glance to be an obscenity case because it involves a curse word often associated with sex; however, as you will see, the Court claims that despite this seemingly obscene characteristic, Mr. Cohen deserves First Amendment protection.

The Court's current understanding of legitimate limits on expression in the area of obscenity was first articulated in *Miller v. California*. As you will see, although it allows for restrictions on obscenity, it limits such restrictions to the curtailment of speech that lacks serious expressive value of the kind found in politics, art, literature, or science. While *Miller v. California* concerns obscene mailings, *City of Erie v. Pap's A.M.* deals with the question of whether nude table-top dancing counts as an act of speech. *New York v. Ferber* examines a specific ban on child pornography. *United States v. Williams* raises the question of whether *New York v. Ferber's* protection extends to cases involving virtual pornography.

The Court has found that certain "indecent" speech, while it may not meet the technical standards of obscenity, might also be censored. *Federal Communications Commission v. Pacifica Foundation* considers whether comedian George Carlin's monologue on offensive language constitutes indecent speech and whether the Federal Communications Commission (FCC) has the power to limit the times at which it can be broadcast. Finally, in *American Booksellers v. Hudnut,* the U.S. Court of Appeals for the Seventh Circuit considers the constitutionality of a categorical ban on pornography.

There is a close connection between MacKinnon's reasons for limits on pornography and arguments about the limits of hate speech. Both hate speech and pornography are viewed by many as condoning or effectuating the subordination of women or minorities to such a degree that no interest in free speech can justify it. Hate speech thus "silences" the minorities at whom it is directed. Indeed, as MacKinnon sees it, the Fourteenth Amendment enshrines an entitlement to be treated as an equal, and these forms of speech undermine that entitlement. But the doctrine of viewpoint neutrality protects some forms of hate speech despite these arguments. Famously, in *National Socialist Party v. Skokie*, the Court ordered the Illinois Supreme Court to allow a group of neo-Nazis who had been prohibited from marching through a majority-Jewish suburb by the Circuit Court of Cook County, Illinois, to appeal the lower court's decision. Although the U.S. Supreme Court made its ruling in this case on procedural grounds rather than on the merits—that is, it sent the case back to the Illinois Supreme Court to decide whether the neo-Nazis had the right to march, rather than making that decision itself—the final ruling in the neo-Nazis' favor could be supported by the doctrine of viewpoint neutrality. One might reason that the judiciary could not limit a neo-Nazi march without abandoning viewpoint neutrality, which dictates that even viewpoints that advocate hate towards minorities are protected under the First Amendment.

The Court has taken a nuanced position on cases involving cross burning. In *R.A.V. v. City of St. Paul,* the Court protected an act of cross-burning as a form of expression. In *Virginia v. Black,* however, the Court held that cross-burning does not necessarily deserve protection when it constitutes a direct threat against specific individuals. How should we determine whether a given act of cross-burning constitutes such a threat?

It is also important as you consider these readings and cases to think about the more general justifications of free speech introduced in Section A, beyond the Court's specific jurisprudence in this area. For instance, the Court's jurisprudence on obscenity might be defended along the lines of Alexander Meiklejohn's protection of free political speech. If obscenity lacks political content, we might ask whether democracy requires its protection. Similarly, as you read, consider whether obscenity contributes to the marketplace of ideas that John Stuart Mill thought so important to the realization of truth. Consider, moreover, Irving

Kristol's argument that a society that allows the sale of obscenity cannot progress towards truth as Mill contended. What might Mill say in response to this contention? Should obscenity be considered an essential part of the marketplace of ideas? Does Kristol's argument justify the Court's approach to obscenity? Moreover, what might either Mill or Meiklejohn say about hate speech? Could either justify bans on political expression that demonized a particular group on the grounds that it undermined democracy or failed to contribute to beneficial political dialogue?

Catharine A. MacKinnon

PORNOGRAPHY, CIVIL RIGHTS, AND SPEECH

20 Harv. C.R.-C.L. L. Rev. 1 (1985)

In the philosophical terms of classical liberalism, an equality-freedom dilemma is produced: Freedom to make or consume pornography weighs against the equality of the sexes. Some people's freedom hurts other people's equality. There is something to this, but my formulation, as you might guess, comes out a little differently. If one asks whose freedom pornography represents, a tension emerges that is not a dilemma among abstractions so much as it is a conflict between groups. Substantive interests are at stake on *both* sides of the abstract issues, and women are allowed to matter in neither. If women's freedom is as incompatible with pornography's construction of our freedom as our equality is incompatible with pornography's construction of our equality, we get neither freedom nor equality under the liberal calculus. Equality for women is incompatible with a definition of men's freedom that is at our expense. What can freedom for women mean, so long as we remain unequal? Why should men's freedom to use us in this way be purchased with our second-class civil status?

I.

. . . In pornography, there it is, in one place, all of the abuses that women had to struggle so long even to begin to articulate, all the *unspeakable* abuse: the rape, the battery, the sexual harassment, the prostitution, and the sexual abuse of children. Only in the pornography it is called something else: sex, sex, sex, sex, and sex, respectively. Pornography sexualizes rape, battery, sexual harassment, prostitution, and child sexual abuse; it thereby celebrates, promotes, authorizes, and legitimizes them. More generally, it eroticizes the dominance and submission that is the dynamic common to them all. It makes hierarchy sexy and calls that "the truth about sex" or just a mirror of reality. Through this process, pornography constructs what a woman is as what men want from sex. This is what the pornography means. (I will talk about the way it works behaviorally, with the evidence on it, when I talk about the ordinance itself.)

Pornography constructs what a woman is in terms of its view of what men want sexually, such that acts of rape, battery, sexual harassment, prostitution, and sexual abuse of children become acts of sexual equality. Pornography's world of equality is a harmonious and balanced place. Men and women are perfectly complementary and perfectly bipolar. Women's desire to be fucked by men is equal to men's desire to fuck women. All the ways men love to take and violate women, women love to be taken and violated. The women who most love this are most men's equals, the most liberated; the most participatory child is the most grown-up, the most equal to an adult. Their consent merely expresses or ratifies these preexisting facts.

To give a set of rough epistemological translations, to defend pornography as consistent with the equality of the sexes is to defend the subordination of women to men as sexual equality. What in the pornographic view is love and romance looks a great deal like hatred and torture to the feminist. Pleasure and eroticism become violation. Desire appears as lust for dominance and submission. The vulnerability of women's projected sexual availability, that acting we are allowed (i.e. asking to be acted upon), is victimization. Play conforms to scripted roles. Fantasy expresses ideology, is not exempt from it. Admiration of natural physical beauty becomes objectification. Harmlessness becomes harm. Pornography is a harm of male supremacy made difficult to see because of its pervasiveness, potency, and, principally, because of its success in making the world a pornographic place. Specifically, its harm cannot be discerned, and will not be addressed, if viewed and approached neutrally, because it *is* so much of "what is." In other words, to the extent pornography succeeds in constructing social reality, it becomes invisible as harm. If we live in a world that pornography creates through the power of men in a male dominated situation the issue is not what the harm of pornography is, but how that harm is to become visible.

II.

Obscenity law provides a very different analysis and conception of the problem. In 1973, the legal definition of obscenity became that which the average person, applying contemporary community standards, would find that, taken as a whole, appeals to the prurient interest; that which depicts and describes in a patently offensive way—you feel like you're a cop reading someone's *Miranda* rights—sexual conduct as defined by the applicable state law; and that which, taken as a whole, lacks serious literary, artistic, political or scientific value. Feminism doubts whether the average gender-neutral person exists; has more questions about the content and process of defining what community standards are than it does about deviations from them; wonders why prurience counts but powerlessness does not, and why sensibilities are better protected from offense than women are from exploitation; defines sexuality, and thus its violation and expropriation, more broadly than does state law; and questions why a body of law which has not in practice been able to tell rape from intercourse should, without further guidance, be entrusted with telling pornography from anything less. Taking the work "as a whole" ignores that which the victims of pornography have long known: Legitimate settings diminish the injury perceived to be done to those whose trivialization and objectification it contextualizes. Besides, and this is a heavy one, if a woman is subjected, why should it matter that the work has other value? Maybe what redeems the work's value is what enhances its injury to women, not to mention that existing standards of literature, art, science, and politics, examined in a feminist light, are remarkably consonant with pornography's mode, meaning, and message. And finally—first and foremost, actually—although the subject of these materials is overwhelmingly women, their contents almost entirely comprised of women's bodies, our invisibility has been such, our equation as a sex *with* sex has been such, that the law of obscenity has never even considered pornography a woman's issue.

Obscenity, in this light, is a moral idea; an idea about judgments of good and bad. Pornography, by contrast, is a political practice, a practice of power and powerlessness. Obscenity is ideational and abstract; pornography is concrete and substantive. The two concepts represent two entirely different things. Nudity, excess of candor, arousal or excitement, prurient appeal, illegality of the acts depicted, and unnaturalness or perversion are all qualities that bother obscenity law when sex is depicted or portrayed. Sex forced on real women so that it can be sold at a profit to be forced on other real women; women's bodies trussed and maimed and raped and made into things to be hurt and obtained and accessed and this presented as the nature of women in a way that is acted on and acted out over and over; the coercion that is visible and the coercion that has become invisible—this and more bothers feminists about pornography. Obscenity as such probably does little harm. Pornography is integral to attitudes and behaviors of violence and discrimination which define the treatment and status of half the population.

III.

At the request of the city of Minneapolis, Andrea Dworkin and I conceived and designed a local human rights ordinance in accordance with our approach to the pornography issue. We define pornography as a practice of sex discrimination, a violation of women's civil rights, the opposite of sexual equality. Its point is to hold accountable, to those who are injured, those who profit from and benefit from that jury. It means that women's injury—our damage, our pain, our enforced inferiority—should outweigh their pleasure and their profits, or sex equality is meaningless.

... In order to focus upon what our law is, I will say what it is not. It is not a prior restraint. It does not go to possession. It does not turn on offensiveness. It is not a ban, unless relief for a proven injury is a "ban" on doing that injury again. Its principal enforcement mechanism is the civil rights commission, although it contains an option for direct access to court as well as de novo judicial review of administrative determinations, to ensure that no case will escape full judicial scrutiny and full due process. I will also not discuss various threshold issues, such as the sources of municipal authority, preemption, or abstention, or even issues of overbreadth or vagueness, nor will I defend the ordinance from views which never have been law, such as First Amendment absolutism. I will discuss the merits: how pornography by this definition is a harm, specifically how it is a harm of gender inequality, and how that harm outweighs any social interest in its protection by recognized First Amendment standards.

This law aspires to guarantee women's rights consistent with the First Amendment by making visible a conflict of rights between the equality guaranteed to all women and what, in some legal sense, is now the freedom of the pornographers to make and sell, and their consumers to have access to, the materials this ordinance defines. Judicial resolution of this conflict, if they do for women what they have done for others, is likely to entail a balancing of the rights of women arguing that our lives and opportunities, including our freedom of speech and action, are constrained by—and in many cases flatly precluded by, in, and through—pornography, against those who argue that the pornography is harmless, or harmful only in part but not in the whole of the definition; or that it is more important to preserve the pornography than it is to prevent or remedy whatever harm it does.

A.

The first victims of pornography are the ones in it.

Some of the same reasons children are granted some specific legal avenues for redress—relative lack of power, inability to command respect for their consent and self-determination, in some cases less physical strength or lowered legitimacy in using it, specific credibility problems, and lack of access to resources for meaningful self-expression—also hold true for women's comparative social position to men. It is therefore vicious to suggest, as many have, that women like Linda Marchiano should remedy their situations through the exercise of more speech. Pornography makes their speech impossible and where possible, worthless. Pornography makes women into objects. Objects do not speak. When they do, they are by then regarded as objects, not as humans, which is what it means to have no credibility. Besides, how Ms. Marchiano's speech is supposed to redress her injury, except by producing this legal remedy, is unclear since no amount of saying anything remedies what is being *done* to her in theatres and on home videos all over the world, where she is repeatedly raped for public entertainment and private profit.

What would justice look like for these women? Linda Marchiano said, "Virtually every time someone watches that film, they are watching me being raped."

As part of the relief for people who can prove this was done to them, our law provides an injunction to remove these materials from public view. The best authority we have for this is the *Ferber* case, which permits criminal prohibitions on child pornography. That case recognized that child pornography need not be obscene to be child abuse. The Court found such pornography harmful in part because it constituted "a permanent record of children's participation and the harm to the child is exacerbated by circulation." This was a film, by the way, largely of two boys masturbating. The sensitivities of obscenity law, the Court noted, were inapt because "a work which, taken on the whole, contains value may nevertheless embody the hardest core of child pornography." Whether a work appeals to the prurient interest is not the same as whether a child is physically or psychologically harmed to make it.

Both of these reasons apply to coerced women. Women are not children, but coerced women are effectively deprived of power over the expressive products of their coercion. Coerced pornography should meet the test that "the evil to be restricted . . . overwhelmingly outweighs the expressive interests, if any, at stake. . . ." Unless one wishes to retain the incentive structure that has introduced a profit motive into rape, pornography made this way should be able to be eliminated. . . .

C.

Specific pornography directly causes some assaults. Although police have known it for years, reported cases are increasingly noting the causal role of pornography in some sexual abuse. In a recent Minnesota case, a fourteen-year-old girl on a bicycle was stopped with a knife and forced into a car. Her hands were tied with a belt, she was pushed to the floor and covered with a blanket. The knife was then used to cut off her clothes, and fingers and a knife were inserted into her vagina. Then the man had her dress, drove her to a gravel pit, ordered her to stick a safety pin into the nipple of her left breast, and forced her to ask him to hit her. After hitting her, he forced her to commit fellatio and to submit to anal penetration, and made her use a cigarette to burn herself on her breast and near her pubic area. Then he defecated and urinated on her face, forced her to ingest some of the excrement and urine and made her urinate into a cup and drink it. He took a string from her blouse and choked her to the point of unconsciousness, leaving burn marks on her neck, and after cutting her with his knife in a couple of places, drove her back to where he had gotten her and let her go. The books that were found with this man were: *Violent Stories of Kinky Humiliation, Violent Stories of Dominance and Submission*—you think feminists made up these words?—*Bizarre Sex Crimes, Shamed Victims,* and *Water Sports Fetish, Enemas and Golden Showers.* The Minnesota Supreme Court said "It appears that in committing these various acts, the defendant was giving life to some stories he had read in various pornographic books."

D.

To reach the magnitude of this problem on the scale it exists, our law makes trafficking in pornography—production, sale, exhibition, or distribution—actionable. Under the obscenity rubric, much legal and psychological scholarship has centered on a search for the elusive link between pornography defined as obscenity and harm. They have looked high and low—in the mind of the male consumer, in society or in its "moral fabric," in correlations between variations in levels of anti-social acts and liberalization of obscenity laws. The only harm they have found has been one they have attributed to "the social interest in order and morality." Until recently, no one looked very persistently for harm to women, particularly harm to women through men. The rather obvious fact that the sexes *relate* has been overlooked in the inquiry into the male consumer and his mind. The pornography doesn't just drop out of the sky, go into his head and stop there. Specifically, men rape, batter, prostitute, molest, and sexually harass women. Under conditions of inequality, they also hire, fire, promote, and grade women, decide how much or whether or not we are worth paying and for what, define and approve and disapprove of women in ways that count, that determine our lives.

Recent experimental research on pornography shows that the materials covered by our definition cause measurable harm to women through increasing men's attitudes and behaviors of discrimination in both violent and nonviolent forms. Exposure to some of the pornography in our definition increases normal men's immediately subsequent willingness to aggress against women under laboratory conditions. It makes normal men more closely resemble convicted rapists attitudinally, although as a group they don't look all that different from them to start with. It also significantly increases attitudinal measures known to correlate with rape and self-reports of aggressive acts, measures such as hostility toward women, propensity to rape, condoning rape, and predicting that one would rape or force sex on a woman if one knew one would not get caught. This latter measure, by the way, begins with rape at about a third of all men and moves to half with "forced sex."

Pornography stimulates and reinforces, it does not cathect or mirror, the connection between one-sided freely available sexual access to women and masculine sexual excitement and sexual satisfaction. The catharsis hypothesis is fantasy. The fantasy theory is fantasy. Reality is: Pornography conditions male orgasm to female subordination. It tells men what sex means, what a real woman is, and codes them together in a way that is behaviorally reinforcing. This is a real five-dollar sentence but I'm going to say it anyway: Pornography is a set of hermeneutical equivalences that work on the epistemological level. Substantively, pornography defines the meaning of what a woman is by connecting access to her sexuality with masculinity through orgasm. The behavioral data show that what pornography means *is* what it does.

So far, opposition to our ordinance centers on the trafficking provision. This means not only that it is difficult to comprehend a group injury in a liberal culture—that what it *means* to be a woman is defined by this and that it is an injury for all women, even if not for all women equally. It is not only that the pornography has got to be accessible, which is the bottom line of virtually every objection to this law. It is also that power, as I said, is when you say something, it is taken for reality. If you talk about rape, it will be agreed that rape is awful. But rape is a conclusion. If a victim describes the facts of a rape, maybe she was asking for it, or enjoyed it, or at least consented to it, or the man might have thought she did, or maybe she had had sex before. It is now agreed that there is something wrong with sexual harassment. But describe what happened to you, and it may be trivial or personal

or paranoid, or maybe you should have worn a bra that day. People are against discrimination. But describe the situation of a real woman, and they are not so sure she wasn't just unqualified. In law, all these disjunctions between women's perspective on our injuries and the standards we have to meet go under dignified legal rubrics like burdens of proof, credibility, defenses, elements of the crime, and so on. These standards all contain a definition of what a woman is in terms of what sex is and the low value placed on us through it. They reduce injuries done to us to authentic expressions of who we are. Our silence is written all over them. So is the pornography.

By contrast, we have as yet encountered comparatively little objection to the coercion, force, or assault provisions of our ordinance. I think that's partly because the people who make and approve laws may not yet see what they do as that. They *know* they use the pornography as we have described it in this law, and our law defines that, the reality of pornography, as a harm to women. If they suspect that they might on occasion engage in or benefit from coercion or force or assault, they may think that the victims won't be able to prove it—and they're right. Women who charge men with sexual abuse are not believed. The pornographic view of them is: They want it; they all want it. When women bring charges of sexual assault, motives such as veniality or sexual repression must be invented, because we cannot really have been hurt. Under the trafficking provision, women's lack of credibility cannot be relied upon to negate the harm. There's no woman's story to destroy, no credibility-based decision on what happened. The hearings establish the harm. The definition sets the standard. The grounds of reality definition are authoritatively shifted. Pornography is bigotry, *period.* We are now—*in* the world pornography has decisively defined—having to meet the burden of proving, once and for all, for all of the rape and torture and battery, all of the sexual harassment, all of the child sexual abuse, all of the forced prostitution, *all* of it that the pornography is part of and that is part of the pornography, that the harm *does happen* and that when it happens it looks like this. Which may be why all this evidence never seems to be enough.

E.

It is worth considering what evidence has been enough when other harms involving other purported speech interests have been allowed to be legislated against. By comparison to our trafficking section, analytically similar restrictions have been allowed under the First Amendment, with a legislative basis far less massive, detailed, concrete, and conclusive. Our statutory language is more ordinary, objective, and precise, and covers a harm far narrower than its legislative record substantiates. Under *Miller*, obscenity was allowed to be made criminal in the name of the "danger of offending the sensibilities of unwilling recipients, or exposure to juveniles." Under our law, we have direct evidence of harm, not just a conjectural danger, that unwilling women in considerable numbers are not simply offended in their sensibilities, but are violated in their persons and restricted in their options. Obscenity law also suggests that the applicable standard for legal adequacy in measuring such connections may not be statistical certainty. The Supreme Court has said that it is not their job to resolve empirical uncertainties that underlie state obscenity legislation. Rather, it is for them to determine whether a legislature could reasonably have determined that a connection might exist between the prohibited material and harm of a kind in which the state has legitimate interest. Equality should be such an area. The Supreme Court recently recognized that prevention of sexual exploitation and abuse of children is, in their words, "a governmental objective of surpassing importance." This might also be the case for sexual exploitation and abuse of women, although I think a civil remedy is initially more appropriate to the goal of empowering adult women than a criminal prohibition would be.

Other rubrics provide further support for the argument that this law is narrowly tailored to further a legitimate governmental interest consistent with the interests underlying the First Amendment. Exceptions to the First Amendment—you may have gathered from this—exist. The reason they exist is that the harm done by some speech outweighs its expressive value, if any. In our law, a legislature recognizes that pornography, as defined and made actionable, undermines sex equality. One can say—and I have—that pornography is a causal factor in violations of women; one can also say that women will be violated so long as pornography exists; but one can also say simply that pornography violates women. Perhaps this is what the woman had in mind who testified at our hearings that whether or not pornography causes violent acts to be perpetrated against some women is not her only issue. "Porn is already a violent act against women. It is our mothers, our daughters, our sisters, and our wives that are for sale for pocket change at the newsstands in this country." *Chaplinsky v. New Hampshire* recognizes the ability to restrict as "fighting words" speech which, "by its very utterance inflicts injury. . . ." Perhaps the only reason that pornography has not been "fighting words"—in the sense of words which by their utterance tend to incite immediate breach of the peace—is that women have seldom fought back, yet.

Some concerns close to those of this ordinance underlie group libel laws, although the differences are equally important. In group libel law, as Justice Frankfurter's opinion in *Beauharnais* illustrates, it has been understood that individuals' treatment and alternatives in life may depend as much on the reputation of the group to which such a person belongs as on their own merit. Not even a partial analogy can be made to group libel doctrine without examining the point made by Justice Brandeis, and recently underlined by Larry Tribe: Would more speech, rather than less, remedy the harm? In the end, the answer may be yes, but not under the abstract system of free speech, which only enhances the power of the pornographers while doing nothing substantively to guarantee the free speech of women, for which we need civil equality. The situation in which women presently find ourselves with respect to the pornography is one in which more *pornography* is inconsistent with rectifying or even counterbalancing its damage through speech, because so long as the pornography exists in the way it does there *will not be more speech by women.* Pornography strips and devastates women of credibility, from our accounts of sexual assault to our everyday reality of sexual subordination. We are deauthorized and reduced and devalidated and silenced. Silenced here means that the purposes of the First Amendment, premised upon conditions presumed and promoted by protecting free speech, do not pertain to women because they are not our conditions. Consider then: How does pornography promote our individual self-fulfillment? How does sexual

inequality even permit it? Even if she can form words, who listens to a woman with a penis in her mouth? Facilitating consensus—to the extent pornography does so, it does so one-sidedly by silencing protest over the injustice of sexual subordination. Participation in civic life—central to Professor Meiklejohn's theory—how does pornography enhance women's participation in civic life? Anyone who cannot walk down the street or even lie down in her own bed without keeping her eyes cast down and her body clenched against assault is unlikely to have much to say about the issues of the day, still less will she become Tolstoy. Facilitating change *this law* facilitates the change the existing First Amendment theory has been used to throttle. Any system of freedom of expression that does not address a problem where the free speech of men silences the free speech of women, a real conflict between speech interests as well as between people, is not serious about securing freedom of expression in this country.

For those of you who still think pornography is only an idea, consider the possibility that obscenity law got one thing right. Pornography is more act-like than thought-like. The fact that pornography, in a feminist view, furthers the idea of the sexual inferiority of women, which is a political idea, doesn't make the pornography itself into a political idea. One can express the idea a practice embodies. That does not make that practice into an idea. Segregation expresses the idea of the inferiority of one group to another on the basis of race. That does not make segregation an idea. A sign that says "Whites Only" is only words. Is it therefore protected by the First Amendment? Is it not an act, a practice, of segregation because of the inseparability of what it means from what it does? *Law* is only words.

The issue here is whether the fact that the central link in the cycle of abuse that I have connected is words and pictures will immunize that entire cycle, about which we cannot do anything without doing something about the pornography. As Justice Stewart said in *Ginsburg*, "When expression occurs in a setting where the capacity to make a choice is absent, government regulation of that expression may coexist with and *even implement* First Amendment guarantees." I would even go so far as to say that the pattern of evidence we have closely approaches Justice Douglas' requirement that "freedom of expression can be suppressed if, and to the extent that, it is so closely brigaded with illegal action as to be an inseparable part of it." Those of you who have been trying to separate the acts from the speech—that's an act, that's an act, there's a law against that act, regulate that act, don't touch the speech—*notice here* that the fact that the acts involved are illegal doesn't mean that the speech that is "brigaded with" it, *cannot* be regulated. It is when it *can* be.

I take one of two penultimate points from Andrea Dworkin, who has often said that pornography is not speech for women, it is the silence of women. Remember the mouth taped, the woman gagged, "Smile, I can get a lot of money for that." The smile is not her expression. It is her silence, and it is not her expression not because it didn't happen, but because it *did* happen. The screams of the women in pornography are silence, like Kitty Genovese's screams, whose plight was misinterpreted by some onlookers as a lovers' quarrel. The flat expressionless voice of the woman in the New Bedford gang rape, testifying, is the silence of women. She was raped as men cheered and watched like they do in and with the pornography. When women resist and men say, "Like this, you stupid bitch, here

is how to do it" and shove their faces into the pornography, this "truth of sex" is the silence of women. When they say, "If you love me, you'll try," the enjoyment we fake, the enjoyment we learn, is silence. Women who submit because there is more dignity in it than in losing the fight over and over live in silence. Having to sleep with your publisher or director to get access to what men call speech is silence. Being humiliated on the basis of your appearance, whether by approval or disapproval, because you have to look a certain way for a certain job, whether you get the job or not, is silence. The absence of a woman's voice, everywhere that it cannot be heard, is silence. And anyone who thinks that what women say in pornography is women's speech—the "Fuck me, do it to me, harder," all of that—has never heard the sound of a woman's voice.

The most basic assumption underlying First Amendment adjudication is that, socially, speech is free. The first amendment says Congress shall not abridge the freedom of speech. Free speech, get it, *exists*. Those who wrote the First Amendment *had* speech—they wrote the Constitution. *Their* problem was to keep it free from the only power that realistically threatened it: the federal government. They designed the First Amendment to prevent government from constraining that which if unconstrained by government was free, meaning *accessible to them*. At the same time, we can't tell much about the intent of the Framers with regard to the question of women's speech, because I don't think we crossed their minds. It is consistent with this analysis that their posture to freedom of speech tends to presuppose that whole segments of the population are not systematically silenced, socially, prior to government action. If everyone's power were equal to theirs, if this were a non-hierarchical society, that might make sense. But the place of pornography in the inequality of the sexes makes the assumption of equal power untrue.

This is a hard question. It involves risks. Classically, opposition to censorship has involved keeping government off the backs of people. Our law is about getting some people off the backs of other people. The risks that it will be misused have to be measured against the risks of the status quo. Women will never have that dignity, security, compensation that is the promise of equality so long as the pornography exists as it does now. The situation of women suggests that the urgent issue of our freedom of speech is not primarily the avoidance of state intervention as such, but getting affirmative access to speech for those to whom it has been denied.

Ronald Dworkin

WOMEN IN PORNOGRAPHY

Review of Only Words, *by Catharine A. MacKinnon*

The New York Review of Books, October 21, 1993

1.

People once defended free speech to protect the rights of firebrands attacking government, or dissenters resisting an established church, or radicals campaigning for unpopular political causes. Free speech was plainly worth fighting for, and it still is in many parts of the world where these rights hardly exist. But in America now, free-speech partisans find themselves defending mainly racists shouting "nigger" or Nazis carrying swastikas or—most often—men looking at pictures of naked women with their legs spread open.

Pornography seems vulnerable on principle. The conventional explanation of why freedom of speech is important is Mill's theory that truth is most likely to emerge from a "marketplace" of ideas freely exchanged and debated. But most pornography makes no contribution at all to political or intellectual debate: it is preposterous to think that we are more likely to reach truth about anything at all because pornographic videos are available. So liberals defending a right to pornography find themselves triply on the defensive: their view is politically weak, deeply offensive to many women, and intellectually doubtful. Why, then, should we defend pornography? Why should we care if people can no longer watch films of people copulating for the camera, or of women being whipped and enjoying it? What would we lose, except a repellent industry?

Professor Catharine MacKinnon's new book of three short essays, *Only Words*, offers a sharp answer to the last of these questions: society would lose nothing if all pornography were banned, she says, except that women would lose their chains.

She argues that even if the publication of literature degrading to women is protected by the First Amendment, as the Seventh Circuit declared, such material offends another, competing constitutional value: the ideal of equality embedded in the equal protection clause of the Fourteenth Amendment, which declares that no state may deprive any person of the equal protection of the laws. If so, she says, then the courts must balance the two constitutional values, and since pornography contributes nothing of any importance to political debate, they should resolve the conflict in favor of equality and censorship.

Unlike MacKinnon's other arguments, this claim has application far beyond the issue of pornography. If her analysis is right, national and state governments have much broader constitutional powers than most lawyers think to prohibit or censor any "politically incorrect" expression that might reasonably be thought to sustain or exacerbate the unequal positions of women or of racial, ethnic, or other minorities. I shall therefore concentrate on this new argument, but I shall first comment briefly on MacKinnon's more conventional points.

. . . [One of MacKinnon's arguments is] that pornography should be banned because it "silences" women by making it more difficult for them to speak and less likely that others will understand what they say.

On this view, which has been argued more elaborately by others, it is women not pornographers who need First Amendment protection, because pornography humiliates or frightens them into silence and conditions men to misunderstand what they say. (It conditions them to think, for example—as some stupid judges have instructed juries in rape trials—that when a woman says no she sometimes means yes.) Because this argument cites the First Amendment as a reason for banning, not for protecting, pornography, it has the appeal of paradox. But it is premised on an unacceptable proposition: that the right to free speech includes a right to circumstances that encourage one to speak, and a right that others grasp and respect what one means to say.

These are obviously not rights that any society can recognize or enforce. Creationists, flat-earthers, and bigots, for example, are ridiculed in many parts of America now; that ridicule undoubtedly dampens the enthusiasm many of them have for speaking out and limits the attention others pay to what they say. Many political and constitutional theorists, it is true, insist that if freedom of speech is to have any value, it must include some right to the opportunity to speak: they say that a society in which only the rich enjoy access to newspapers, television, or other public media does not accord a genuine right to free speech. But it goes far beyond that to insist that freedom of speech includes not only opportunity to speak to the public but a guarantee of a sympathetic or even competent understanding of what one says.

I should mention [another] consideration that MacKinnon puts forward, though it is difficult to find an argument in it. She says that much pornography is not just speech—it is not "only words"—because it produces erections in men and provides them with masturbatory fantasies . . . she thinks that pornography's physiological power deprives it of First Amendment protection: "An orgasm is not an argument," she says, "and cannot be argued with. Compared with a thought, it raises far less difficult speech issues, if it raises any at all." But that seems a plain non sequitur: a piece of music or a work of art or poetry does not lose whatever protection the First Amendment affords it when some people find it sexually arousing, even if that effect does not depend on its argumentative or aesthetic merits, or whether it has any such merits at all. . . .

3.

In the most interesting parts of *Only Words*, MacKinnon offers a new argument that is also designed to transcend mere repulsion. She says that the way in which pornography is offensive—that it portrays women as submissive victims who enjoy torture and mutilation—contributes to the unequal opportunities of women in American society, and therefore contradicts the values meant to be protected by the equal protection clause. She concedes, for the sake of this argument, that in spite of its minimal contribution to intellectual or political debate, pornography is protected under the First Amendment. But that First Amendment protection must be balanced, she says, against the Fourteenth Amendment's requirement that people be treated equally. "The law of equality and the law of freedom of speech are on a collision course in this country," she says, and she argues that the balance, which has swung too far toward liberty, must now be redressed.

The censorship of pornography, she says, should be regarded as like other kinds of government action designed to create genuine equality of opportunity. It is now accepted by almost everyone that government may properly prohibit discrimination against blacks and women in employment and education, for example. But such discrimination may take the form, not merely of refusing them jobs or university places, but of subjecting those who do manage to find jobs or places to an environment of insult and prejudice that makes work or education less attractive or even impossible. Government prohibits racial or sexual harassment at work—it punishes employers who subject blacks to racial insult or women to sexual pressures, in spite of the fact that these objectionable practices are carried out through speech—and many universities have adopted "speech codes" that prohibit racial insults in classrooms or on campus.

Banning or punishing pornography, MacKinnon suggests, should be regarded as a more general remedy of the same kind. If pornography contributes to the general subordination of women by picturing them as sexual or servile objects, as she believes it does, then eliminating pornography can also be defended as serving equality of opportunity even though it restricts liberty. The "egalitarian" argument for censorship is in many ways like the "silencing" argument I described earlier: it supposes not that pornography significantly increases sexual crimes of violence, but that it works more insidiously to damage the standing and power of women within the community. But the "egalitarian" argument is in two ways different and apparently more cogent.

First, it claims not a new and paradoxical conflict within the idea of liberty, as the silencing argument does, but a conflict between liberty and equality, two ideals that many political philosophers think are often in conflict. Second, it is more limited in its scope. The "silencing" argument supposes that everyone—the bigot and the creationist as well the social reformer—has a right to whatever respectful attention on the part of others is necessary to encourage him to speak his mind and to guarantee that he will be correctly understood; and that is absurd. The "egalitarian" argument, on the contrary, supposes only that certain groups—those that are victims of persisting disadvantage in our society—should not be subjected to the kind of insult, harassment, or abuse that has contributed to that disadvantage.

But the "egalitarian" argument is nevertheless much broader and more dangerous in its scope than might first appear. The analogies MacKinnon proposes—to sexual harassment laws and university speech codes—are revealing, because though each of these forms of regulation might be said to serve a general egalitarian purpose, they are usually defended on much more limited and special grounds. Laws against sexual harassment are designed to protect women not from the diffuse effects of whatever derogatory opinions about them are part of the general culture, but from direct sexual taunts and other degrading language in the workplace. University speech codes are defended on a different ground: they are said to serve an educational purpose by preserving the calm and reflective atmosphere of mutual respect and of appreciation for a diversity of cultures and opinions that is essential for effective teaching and research.

I do not mean that such regulations raise no problems about free speech. They do. Even if university speech codes, for example, are enforced fairly and scrupulously (and in the charged atmosphere of university politics they often are not) they sometimes force teachers and students to compromise or suppress their opinions by erring on the side of safety, and some speech codes may actually be unconstitutional. I mean only that constraints on speech at work and on the campus can be defended without appealing to the frightening principle that considerations of equality require that some people not be free to express their tastes or convictions or preferences anywhere. MacKinnon's argument for banning pornography from the community as a whole does presuppose this principle, however, and accepting her argument would therefore have devastating consequences.

Government could then forbid the graphic or visceral or emotionally charged expression of any opinion or conviction that might reasonably offend a disadvantaged group. It could outlaw performances of *The Merchant of Venice*, or films about professional women who neglect their children, or caricatures or parodies of homosexuals in nightclub routines.

Courts would have to balance the value of such expression, as a contribution to public debate or learning, against the damage it might cause to the standing or sensibilities of its targets. MacKinnon thinks that pornography is different from other forms of discriminatory or hostile speech. But the argument she makes for banning it would apply to much else. She pointedly declares that freedom of speech is respected too much by Americans and that the Supreme Court was right in 1952 when it sustained a prosecution of anti-Semitic literature—a decision it has since abandoned—and wrong in 1978 when it struck down an ordinance banning a Nazi march in Illinois.

So if we must make the choice between liberty and equality that MacKinnon envisages—if the two constitutional values really are on a collision course—we should have to choose liberty because the alternative would be the despotism of thought-police.

But is she right that the two values do conflict in this way? Can we escape despotism only by cheating on the equality the Constitution also guarantees? The most fundamental egalitarian command of the Constitution is for equality throughout the political process. We can imagine some compromises of political equality that would plainly aid disadvantaged groups—it would undoubtedly aid blacks and women, for example, if citizens who have repeatedly expressed racist or sexist or bigoted views were denied the vote altogether. That would be unconstitutional, of course; the Constitution demands that everyone be permitted to play an equal part in the formal process of choosing a president, a Congress, and other officials, that no one be excluded on the ground that his opinions or tastes are too offensive or unreasonable or despicable to count.

Elections are not all there is to politics, however. Citizens play a continuing part in politics between elections, because informal public debate and argument influences what responsible officials—and officials anxious for re-election—will do. So the First Amendment contributes a great deal to political equality: it insists that just as no one may be excluded from the vote because his opinions are despicable, so no one may be denied the right to speak or write or broadcast because what he will say is too offensive to be heard.

That amendment serves other goals as well, of course: free speech helps to expose official stupidity and corruption, and it allows vigorous public debate that sometimes generates new ideas and refutes old ones. But the First Amendment's egalitarian role is independent of these other goals: it forbids censoring cranks or neo-Nazis not because anyone thinks that their contributions will prevent corruption or improve public debate, but just because equality demands that everyone, no matter how eccentric or despicable, have a chance to influence policies as well as elections. Of course it does not follow that government will in the end respect everyone's opinion equally, or that official decisions will be equally congenial to all groups. Equality demands that everyone's opinion be given a chance for influence, not that anyone's opinion will triumph or even be represented in what government eventually does.

The First Amendment's egalitarian role is not confined, however, to political speech. People's lives are affected not just by their political environment—not just by what their presidents and legislators and other public officials do—but even more comprehensively by what we might call their moral environment. How others treat me—and my own sense of identity and self-respect—are determined in part by the mix of social conventions,

opinions, tastes, convictions, prejudices, life styles, and cultures that flourish in the community in which I live. Liberals are sometimes accused of thinking that what people say or think in private has no impact on anyone except themselves, and that is plainly wrong. Someone to whom religion is of fundamental importance, for example, will obviously lead a very different and perhaps more satisfying life in a community in which most other people share his convictions than in a dominantly secular society of atheists for whom his beliefs are laughable superstitions. A woman who believes that explicit sexual material degrades her will likely lead a very different, and no doubt more satisfying, life among people who also despise pornography than in a community where others, including other women, think it liberating and fun.

Exactly because the moral environment in which we all live is in good part created by others, however, the question of who shall have the power to help shape that environment, and how, is of fundamental importance, though it is often neglected in political theory. Only one answer is consistent with the ideals of political equality: that no one may be prevented from influencing the shared moral environment, through his own private choices, tastes, opinions, and example, just because these tastes or opinions disgust those who have the power to shut him up or lock him up. Of course, the ways in which anyone may exercise that influence must be limited in order to protect the security and interests of others. People may not try to mold the moral climate by intimidating women with sexual demands or by burning a cross on a black family's lawn, or by refusing to hire women or blacks at all, or by making their working conditions so humiliating as to be intolerable.

But we cannot count, among the kinds of interests that may be protected in this way, a right not to be insulted or damaged just by the fact that others have hostile or uncongenial tastes, or that they are free to express or indulge them in private. Recognizing that right would mean denying that some people—those whose tastes these are—have any right to participate in forming the moral environment at all. Of course it should go without saying that no one has a right to *succeed* in influencing others through his own private choices and tastes. Sexists and bigots have no right to live in a community whose ideology or culture is even partially sexist or bigoted: they have no right to any proportional representation for their odious views. In a genuinely egalitarian society, however, those views cannot be locked out, in advance, by criminal or civil law: they must instead be discredited by the disgust, outrage, and ridicule of other people.

MacKinnon's "egalitarian" argument for censorship is important mainly because it reveals the most important reason for resisting her suggestions, and also because it allows us to answer her charge that liberals who oppose her are crypto-pornographers themselves. . . .

That charge is based on the inadequacy of the conventional explanation, deriving from John Stuart Mill, that pornography must be protected so that truth may emerge. What is actually at stake in the argument about pornography, however, is not society's chance to discover truth, but its commitment to the very ideal of equality that MacKinnon thinks underrated in the American community. Liberals defend pornography, though most of them despise it, in order to defend a conception of the First Amendment that includes, as at least one of its purposes, protecting equality in the processes through which the moral as well as the political environment is formed. First Amendment liberty is not equality's enemy, but the other side of equality's coin.

If we abandon our traditional understanding of equality for a different one that allows a majority to define some people as too corrupt or offensive or radical to join in the informal moral life of the nation, we will have begun a process that ends, as it has in so many other parts of the world, in making equality something to be feared rather than celebrated, a mocking, "correct" euphemism for tyranny.

Andrea Dworkin & Catharine MacKinnon

MODEL ANTIPORNOGRAPHY CIVIL RIGHTS ORDINANCE

in Pornography and Civil Rights: A New Day for Women's Equality

Minneapolis, MN: Organizing Against Pornography (1988)

We include here a model ordinance written by Andrea Dworkin and Catharine MacKinnon in 1983, which would have permitted women to initiate civil suits against purveyors of pornography. Although this ordinance does not provide for criminal charges against such purveyors, some have argued that it reaches *beyond obscenity and introduces a viewpoint-based category for limiting pornography. As you read the statute, consider whether the ordinance advances a specific political viewpoint in its approach. For instance, does the ordinance allow all rights of action against the purveyors of all depictions of sex, or only a kind of purveyor that promotes a particular political message? The contrast between this ordinance and the Court's approach in* Miller v. California *will become apparent as we begin our case selection. Moreover, this contrast will be highlighted even further when* *we examine an appellate court's scrutiny of this statute. As you read through the cases, consider whether you endorse MacKinnon's approach to the issue of pornography, the Court's approach to what it calls obscenity, or neither.*

Model Antipornography Civil Rights Ordinance

Section 1. STATEMENT OF POLICY

1. Pornography is a practice of sex discrimination. It exists in [place], threatening the health, safety, peace, welfare, and equality of citizens in our community. Existing laws are inadequate to solve these problems in [place].

2. Pornography is a systematic practice of exploitation and subordination based on sex that differentially harms and disadvantages women. The harm of pornography includes dehumanization, psychic assault, sexual exploitation, forced sex, forced prostitution, physical injury, and social and sexual terrorism and inferiority presented as entertainment. The bigotry and contempt pornography promotes, with the acts of aggression it fosters, diminish opportunities for equality of rights in employment, education, property, public accommodations, and public services; create public and private harassment, persecution, and denigration; promote injury and degradation such as rape, battery, sexual abuse of children, and prostitution, and inhibit just enforcement of laws against these acts; expose individuals who appear in pornography against their will to contempt, ridicule, hatred, humiliation, and embarrassment and target such women in particular for abuse and physical aggression; demean the reputations and diminish the occupational opportunities of individuals and groups on the basis of sex; contribute significantly to restricting women in particular from full exercise of citizenship and participation in the life of the community; lower the human dignity, worth, and civil status of women and damage mutual respect between the sexes; and undermine women's equal exercise of rights to speech and action guaranteed to all citizens under the [Constitutions] and [laws] of [place].

Section 2. DEFINITIONS

1. "Pornography" means the graphic sexually explicit subordination of women through pictures and/or words that also includes one or more of the following:

a. women are presented dehumanized as sexual objects, things or commodities; or

b. women are presented as sexual objects who enjoy humiliation or pain; or

c. women are presented as sexual objects experiencing sexual pleasure in rape, incest, or other sexual assault; or

d. women are presented as sexual objects tied up or cut up or mutilated or bruised or physically hurt; or

e. women are presented in postures or positions of sexual submission, servility, or display; or

f. women's body parts—including but not limited to vaginas, breasts, or buttocks—are exhibited such that women are reduced to those parts; or

g. women are presented being penetrated by objects or animals; or

h. women are presented in scenarios of degradation, humiliation, injury, torture, shown as filthy or inferior, bleeding, bruised or hurt in a context that makes these conditions sexual.

2. The use of men, children, or transsexuals in the place of women in (a) of this definition is also pornography for purposes of this law.

3. "Person" shall include child or transsexual.

Section 3. CAUSES OF ACTION

1. *Coercion into pornography.* It is sex discrimination to coerce, intimidate, or fraudulently induce (hereafter, "coerce") any person into performing for pornography, which injury may date from any appearance or sale of any product(s) of such performance(s). The maker(s), seller(s), exhibitor(s) and/or distributor(s) of said pornography may be sued for damages and for an injunction, including to eliminate the product(s) of the performance(s) from the public view.

Proof of one or more of the following facts or conditions shall not, without more, preclude a finding of coercion:

a. that the person is a woman; or

b. that the person is or has been a prostitute; or

c. that the person has attained the age of majority; or

d. that the person is connected by blood or marriage to anyone involved in or related to the making of the pornography; or

e. that the person has previously had, or been thought to have had, sexual relations with anyone, including anyone involved in or related to the making of the pornography; or

f. that the person has previously posed for sexually explicit pictures with or for anyone, including anyone involved in or related to the making of the pornography; or

g. that anyone else, including a spouse or other relative, has given permission on the person's behalf; or

h. that the person actually consented to a use of a performance that is then changed into pornography; or

i. that the person knew that the purpose of the acts or events in question was to make pornography; or

j. that the person showed no resistance or appeared to cooperate actively in the photographic sessions or events that produced the pornography; or

k. that the person signed a contract, or made statements affirming a willingness to cooperate in the production of the pornography; or

l. that no physical force, threats, or weapons were used in the making of the pornography; or

m. that the person was paid or otherwise compensated.

2. *Forcing pornography on a person.* It is sex discrimination to force pornography on a person in any place of employment, education, home, or any public place. Complaints may be brought only against the perpetrator of the force and/or the entity or institution responsible for the force.

3. *Assault or physical attack due to pornography.* It is sex discrimination to assault, physically attack, or injure any person in a way that is directly caused by specific pornography. Complaints may be brought against the perpetrator of the assault or attack, and/or against the maker(s), distributor(s), seller(s), and/or exhibitor(s) of the specific pornography.

4. *Defamation through pornography.* It is sex discrimination to defame any person through the unauthorized use in pornography of their proper name, image, and/or recognizable personal likeness. For purposes of this section, public figures shall be treated as private persons. Authorization once given can be revoked in writing any time prior to any publication.

5. *Trafficking in pornography.* It is sex discrimination to produce, sell, exhibit, or distribute pornography, including through private clubs.

a. Municipal, state, and federally funded public libraries or private and public university and college libraries in which pornography is available for study, including on open shelves but excluding special display presentations, shall not be construed to be trafficking in pornography.

b. Isolated passages or isolated parts shall not be the sole basis for complaints under this section.

c. Any woman may bring a complaint hereunder as a woman acting against the subordination of women. Any man, child, or transsexual who alleges injury by pornography in the way women are injured by it may also complain.

Section 4. DEFENSES

1. It shall not be a defense to a complaint under this law that the respondent did not know or intend that the materials at issue were pornography or sex discrimination.

2. No damages or compensation for losses shall be recoverable under Sec. 3(5) or other than against the perpetrator of the assault or attack in Sec. 3(3) unless the defendant knew or had reason to know that the materials were pornography.

3. In actions under Sec. 3(5) or other than against the perpetrator of the assault or attack in Sec. 3(3), no damages or compensation for losses shall be recoverable against maker(s) for pornography made, against distributor(s) for pornography distributed, against seller(s) for pornography sold, or against exhibitor(s) for pornography exhibited, prior to the effective date of this law.

Section 5. ENFORCEMENT

1. *Civil Action.* Any person who has a cause of action under this law may complain directly to a court of competent jurisdiction for relief.

2. *Damages.*

a. Any person who has a cause of action under this law, or their estate, may seek nominal, compensatory, and/or punitive damages without limitation, including for loss, pain, suffering, reduced enjoyment of life, and special damages, as well as for reasonable costs, including attorneys' fees and costs of investigation.

b. In claims under Sec. 3(5), or other than against the perpetrator of the assault or attack under Sec. 3(3), no damages or compensation for losses shall be recoverable against maker(s) for pornography made, against distributor(s) for pornography distributed, against seller(s) for pornography sold, or against exhibitor(s) for pornography exhibited, prior to the effective date of this law.

3. *Injunctions.* Any person who violates this law may be enjoined except that:

a. In actions under Sec. 3(5), and other than against the perpetrator of the assault or attack under Sec. 3(3), no temporary or permanent injunction shall issue prior to a final judicial determination that the challenged activities constitute a violation of this law.

b. No temporary or permanent injunction shall extend beyond such pornography that, having been described with reasonable specificity by said order(s), is determined to be validly proscribed under this law.

5. *Other Remedies.* The availability of relief under this law is not intended to be exclusive and shall not preclude, or be precluded by, the seeking of any other relief, whether civil or criminal.

6. *Limitation of Action.* Complaints under this law shall be brought within six years of the accrual of the cause of action or from when the complainant reaches the age of majority, whichever is later.

7. *Severability.* Should any part(s) of this law be found legally invalid, the remaining part(s) remain valid. A judicial declaration that any part(s) of this law cannot be applied validly in a particular manner or to a particular case or category of cases shall not affect the validity of that part or parts as otherwise applied, unless such other application would clearly frustrate the [legislative body's] intent in adopting this law.

Irving Kristol

PORNOGRAPHY, OBSCENITY, AND THE CASE FOR CENSORSHIP

in Conservatism: An Anthology of Social and Political Thought from David Hume to the Present *(Jerry Z. Muller ed.)*

Princeton, NJ: Princeton University Press (1997)

Recall from the previous section that John Stuart Mill argued that an unfettered marketplace of ideas protected by free speech would lead to truth. As you read Irving Kristol's argument, consider whether he offers a refutation of a Millian defense of a right to free speech as it might apply to obscenity.

If you believe that no one was ever corrupted by a book, you have also to believe that no one was ever improved by a book. You have to believe, in other words, that art is morally trivial and that education is morally irrelevant.

To be sure, it is extremely difficult to trace the effects of any single book (or play or movie) on any reader. But we all know that the ways in which we use our minds and imaginations do shape our characters and help define us as persons. That those

who certainly know this are moved to deny it merely indicates how a dogmatic resistance to the idea of censorship can result in a mindless insistence on the absurd.

For the plain fact is that we all believe that there is a point at which the public authorities ought to step in to limit the "self-expression" of an individual or a group. A theatrical director might find someone willing to commit suicide on the stage. We would not allow that. And I know of no one who argues that we ought to permit public gladiatorial contests, even between consenting adults.

No society can be utterly indifferent to the ways its citizens publicly entertain themselves. Bearbaiting and cockfighting are prohibited only in part out of compassion for the animals; the main reason is that such spectacles were felt to debase and brutalize the citizenry who flocked to witness them. The question with regard to pornography and obscenity is whether they will brutalize and debase our citizenry. We are, after all, not dealing with one book or one movie. We are dealing with a general tendency that is suffusing our entire culture.

Pornography's whole purpose, it seems to me, is to treat human beings obscenely, to deprive them of their specifically human dimension. Imagine a well-known man in a hospital ward, dying an agonizing death. His bladder and bowels empty themselves of their own accord. His consciousness is overwhelmed by pain, so that he cannot communicate with us, nor we with him. Now, it would be technically easy to put a television camera in his room and let the whole world witness this spectacle. We don't do it—at least not yet—because we regard this as an obscene invasion of privacy. And what would make the spectacle obscene is that we would be witnessing the extinguishing of humanity in a human animal.

Sex, like death, is an activity that is both animal and human. There are human sentiments and human ideals involved in this animal activity. But when sex is public, I do not believe the viewer can see the sentiments and the ideals, but sees only the animal coupling. And that is why when most men and women make love, they prefer to be alone because it is only when you are alone that you can make love, as distinct from merely copulating. When sex is a public spectacle, a human relationship has been debased into a mere animal connection.

But even if all this is granted, it doubtless will be said that we ought not to be unduly concerned. Free competition in the cultural marketplace, it is argued by those who have never otherwise had a kind word to say for laissez-faire, will dispose of the problem; in the course of time, people will get bored with pornography and obscenity.

I would like to be able to go along with this reasoning, but I think it is false, and for two reasons. The first reason is psychological, the second, political.

In my opinion, pornography and obscenity appeal to and provoke a kind of sexual regression. The pleasure one gets from pornography and obscenity is infantile and autoerotic; put bluntly, it is a masturbatory exercise of the imagination. Now, people who masturbate do not get bored with masturbation, just as sadists don't get bored with sadism, and voyeurs don't get bored with voyeurism. In other words, like all infantile sexuality, it can quite easily become a permanent self-reinforcing neurosis. And such a neurosis, on a mass scale, is a threat to our civilization and humanity, nothing less.

I am already touching upon a political aspect of pornography when I suggest that it is inherently subversive of civilization. But there is another political aspect, which has to do with the relationship of pornography and obscenity to democracy, and especially to the quality of public life on which democratic government ultimately rests.

Today a "managerial" conception of democracy prevails wherein democracy is seen as a set of rules and procedures, and nothing but a set of rules and procedures, by which majority rule and minority rights are reconciled into a state of equilibrium. Thus, the political system can be fully reduced to its mechanical arrangements.

There is, however, an older idea of democracy fairly common until about the beginning of this century for which the conception of the quality of public life is absolutely crucial. This idea starts from the proposition that democracy is a form of self-government, and that you are entitled to it only if that "self" is worthy of governing. Because the desirability of self-government depends on the character of the people who govern, the older idea of democracy was very solicitous of the condition of this character. This older democracy had no problem in principle with pornography and obscenity; it censored them; it was not about to permit people to corrupt themselves. But can a liberal—today—be for censorship? Yes, but he ought to favor liberal form of censorship.

I don't think this is a contradiction terms. We have no problem contrasting repressive laws governing alcohol, drugs and tobacco with laws regulating (that is, discouraging the sale of) alcohol, drugs and tobacco. We have not made smoking a criminal offense. We have, however, and with good liberal conscience, prohibited cigarette advertising on television. The idea of restricting individual freedom, in a liberal way, is not at all unfamiliar to us.

I therefore see no reason why we should not be able to distinguish repressive censorship from liberal censorship of the written and spoken word. In Britain, until a few years ago, you could perform almost any play you wished but certain plays, judged to be obscene, had to be performed in private theatrical clubs. In the United States, all of us who grew up using public libraries are familiar with the circumstances under which certain books could be circulated only to adults, while still other books had to be read in the library. In both cases, a small minority that was willing to make a serious effort to see an obscene play or book could do so. But the impact of obscenity was circumscribed, and the quality of public life was only marginally affected.

It is a distressing fact that any system of censorship is bound, upon occasion, to treat unjustly a particular work of art to find pornography where there is only gentle eroticism, to find obscenity where none really exists, or to find both where the work's existence ought to be tolerated because it serves a larger moral purpose. That is the price one has to be prepared to pay for censorship, even liberal censorship.

But if you look at the history of American or English literature, there is precious little damage you can point to as a consequence of the censorship that prevailed throughout most of that history. I doubt that many works of real literary merit ever were suppressed. Nor did I notice that hitherto suppressed masterpieces flooded the market when censorship was eased. I should say, to the contrary, that literature has lost quite a bit now that so much is permitted. It seems to me that the cultural market in the United States today is awash in dirty books, dirty movies, dirty theater. Our cultural condition has not improved as a result of the new freedom.

I'll put it bluntly: if you care for the quality of life in our American democracy, then you have to be for censorship.

STANLEY v. GEORGIA

394 U.S. 557 (1969)

Opinion: Marshall, joined by Fortas, Harlan, Douglas, Warren
Concurrence: Black
Concurrence: Stewart, joined by Brennan, White

As you read this case, consider why the Court declines to review it on grounds of obscenity and instead invokes the right of privacy. In what way does the Court preserve the obscenity doctrine when refusing to apply it in this case?

MR. JUSTICE MARSHALL *delivered the opinion of the Court.*

An investigation of appellant's alleged bookmaking activities led to the issuance of a search warrant for appellant's home. Under authority of this warrant, federal and state agents secured entrance. They found very little evidence of bookmaking activity, but, while looking through a desk drawer in an upstairs bedroom, one of the federal agents, accompanied by a state officer, found three reels of eight-millimeter film. Using a projector and screen found in an upstairs living room, they viewed the films. The state officer concluded that they were obscene and seized them. Since a further examination of the bedroom indicated that appellant occupied it, he was charged with possession of obscene matter and placed under arrest. He was later indicted for "knowingly hav[ing] possession of . . . obscene matter" in violation of Georgia law. Appellant was tried before a jury and convicted. The Supreme Court of Georgia affirmed. . . .

Appellant raises several challenges to the validity of his conviction. We find it necessary to consider only one. Appellant argues here, and argued below, that the Georgia obscenity statute, insofar as it punishes mere private possession of obscene matter, violates the First Amendment, as made applicable to the States by the Fourteenth Amendment. For reasons set forth below, we agree that the mere private possession of obscene matter cannot constitutionally be made a crime.

. . . The State and appellant both agree that the question here before us is whether "a statute imposing criminal sanctions upon the mere [knowing] possession of obscene matter" is constitutional. In this context, Georgia concedes that the present case appears to be one of "first impression

. . . on this exact point," but contends that, since "obscenity is not within the area of constitutionally protected speech or press," *Roth v. United States*, the States are free, subject to the limits of other provisions of the Constitution, *see, e.g., Ginsberg v. New York*, to deal with it any way deemed necessary, just as they may deal with possession of other things thought to be detrimental to the welfare of their citizens. If the State can protect the body of a citizen, may it not, argues Georgia, protect his mind?

It is true that *Roth* does declare, seemingly without qualification, that obscenity is not protected by the First Amendment. . . . However, neither *Roth* nor any subsequent decision of this Court dealt with the precise problem involved in the present case. . . . None of the statements cited by the Court in *Roth* for the proposition that "this Court has always assumed that obscenity is not protected by the freedoms of speech and press" were made in the context of a statute punishing mere private possession of obscene material. . . . Moreover, none of this Court's decisions subsequent to *Roth* involved prosecution for private possession of obscene materials. . . .

In this context, we do not believe that this case can be decided simply by citing *Roth. Roth* and its progeny certainly do mean that the First and Fourteenth Amendments recognize a valid governmental interest in dealing with the problem of obscenity. But the assertion of that interest cannot, in every context, be insulated from all constitutional protections. Neither *Roth* nor any other decision of this Court reaches that far. . . .

It is now well established that the Constitution protects the right to receive information and ideas. . . . This right to receive information and ideas, regardless of their social worth, *see Winters v. New York*, is fundamental to our free society....

These are the rights that appellant is asserting in the case before us. He is asserting the right to read or observe what he pleases—the right to satisfy his intellectual and emotional needs in the privacy of his own home. He is asserting the right to be free from state inquiry into the contents of his library. Georgia contends that appellant does not have these rights, that there are certain types of materials that the individual may not read or even possess. Georgia justifies this assertion by arguing that the films in the present case are obscene. But we think that mere categorization of these films as "obscene" is insufficient justification for such a drastic invasion of personal liberties guaranteed by the First and Fourteenth Amendments. Whatever may be the justifications for other statutes regulating obscenity, we do not think they reach into the privacy of one's own home. If the First Amendment means anything, it means that a State has no business telling a man, sitting alone in his own house, what books he may read or what films he may watch. Our whole constitutional heritage rebels at the thought of giving government the power to control men's minds.

And yet, in the face of these traditional notions of individual liberty, Georgia asserts the right to protect the individual's mind from the effects of obscenity. We are not certain that this argument amounts to anything more than the assertion that the State has the right to control the moral content of a person's thoughts. To some, this may be a noble purpose, but it is wholly inconsistent with the philosophy of the First Amendment. . . . Its guarantee is not confined to the expression of ideas that are conventional or shared by a majority. . . . And, in the realm of ideas, it protects expression which is eloquent no less than that which is unconvincing. Nor is it relevant that obscene materials in general, or the particular films before the Court, are arguably devoid of any ideological content. The line between the transmission of ideas and mere entertainment is much too elusive for this Court to draw, if indeed such a line can be drawn at all. See *Winters v. New York*. Whatever the power of the state to control public dissemination of ideas inimical to the public morality, it cannot constitutionally premise legislation on the desirability of controlling a person's private thoughts....

We hold that the First and Fourteenth Amendments prohibit making mere private possession of obscene material a crime. *Roth* and the cases following that decision are not impaired by today's holding. As we have said, the States retain broad power to regulate obscenity; that power simply does not extend to mere possession by the individual in the privacy of his own home. Accordingly, the judgment of the court below is reversed and the case is remanded for proceedings not inconsistent with this opinion.

COHEN v. CALIFORNIA

403 U.S. 15 (1971)

Opinion: Harlan, joined by Douglas, Brennan, Stewart, Marshall
Dissent: Blackmun, joined by Burger, Black and by White in part

On April 26, 1968, Paul Robert Cohen was arrested at the Los Angeles County Courthouse for wearing a jacket marked with the words "F**k the Draft." In this case, the Supreme Court considered whether this *act was entitled to constitutional protection. U.S. Supreme Court Justice John Marshall Harlan II, writing for the Court, held that it was protected under the First Amendment guarantee of the freedom of speech.*

This case raises fundamental questions about the value of free speech in a democratic society. How should the Court weigh the right of the individual to express himself against the interest of society to restrain speech that is offensive, shocking, or even aggressive? Does vulgar speech deserve the heightened level of constitutional protection accorded to political speech? The Court has decided that obscene speech does not. Is vulgar speech any different? To what extent does it matter whether the speech in question has meaningful or political content?

MR. JUSTICE HARLAN *delivered the opinion of the Court.*

This case may seem at first blush too inconsequential to find its way into our books, but the issue it presents is of no small constitutional significance.

Appellant Paul Robert Cohen was convicted in the Los Angeles Municipal Court of violating that part of California Penal Code §415 which prohibits "maliciously and willfully disturb[ing] the peace or quiet of any neighborhood or person . . . by . . . offensive conduct. . . ." He was given 30 days' imprisonment. The facts upon which his conviction rests are detailed in the opinion of the Court of Appeal of California, Second Appellate District, as follows:

> "On April 26, 1968, the defendant was observed in the Los Angeles County Courthouse in the corridor outside of division 20 of the municipal court wearing a jacket bearing the words 'Fuck the Draft' which were plainly visible. There were women and children present in the corridor. The defendant was arrested. The defendant testified that he wore the jacket knowing that the words were on the jacket as

a means of informing the public of the depth of his feelings against the Vietnam War and the Draft.

> "The defendant did not engage in, nor threaten to engage in, nor did anyone as the result of his conduct in fact commit or threaten to commit any act of violence. The defendant did not make any loud or unusual noise, nor was there any evidence that he uttered any sound prior to his arrest."

In affirming the conviction the Court of Appeal held that "offensive conduct" means "behavior which has a tendency to provoke *others* to acts of violence or to in turn disturb the peace," and that the State had proved this element because, on the facts of this case, "it was certainly reasonably foreseeable that such conduct might cause others to rise up to commit a violent act against the person of the defendant or attempt to forceably remove his jacket." The California Supreme Court declined review by a divided vote. We brought the case here, postponing the consideration of the question of our jurisdiction over this appeal to a hearing of the case on the merits. We now reverse.

The question of our jurisdiction need not detain us long. Throughout the proceedings below, Cohen consistently claimed that, as construed to apply to the facts of this case, the statute infringed his rights to freedom of expression guaranteed by the First and Fourteenth Amendments of the Federal Constitution. That contention has been rejected by the highest California state court in which review could be had. Accordingly, we are fully satisfied that Cohen has properly invoked our jurisdiction by this appeal.

I

In order to lay hands on the precise issue which this case involves, it is useful first to canvass various matters which this record does *not* present.

The conviction quite clearly rests upon the asserted offensiveness of the *words* Cohen used to convey his message to the public. The only "conduct" which the State sought to punish is the fact of communication. Thus, we deal here with a conviction resting solely upon "speech," not upon any separately identifiable conduct which allegedly was intended by Cohen to be perceived by others as expressive of particular views but which, on its face, does not necessarily convey any message and hence arguably could be regulated without effectively repressing Cohen's ability to express himself. Further, the State certainly lacks power to punish Cohen for the underlying content of the message the inscription conveyed. At least so long as there is no showing of an intent to incite disobedience to or disruption of the draft, Cohen could not, consistently with the First and Fourteenth Amendments, be punished for asserting the evident position on the inutility or immorality of the draft his jacket reflected. *Yates v. United States.*

Appellant's conviction, then, rests squarely upon his exercise of the "freedom of speech" protected from arbitrary governmental interference by the Constitution and can be justified, if at all, only as a valid regulation of the manner in which he exercised that freedom, not as a permissible prohibition on the substantive message it conveys. This does not end the inquiry, of course, for the First and Fourteenth Amendments have never been thought to give absolute protection to every individual to speak whenever or wherever he pleases, or to use any form of address in any circumstances that he chooses. In this vein, too, however, we think it important to note that several issues typically associated with such problems are not presented here.

In the first place, Cohen was tried under a statute applicable throughout the entire State. Any attempt to support this conviction on the ground that the statute seeks to preserve an appropriately decorous atmosphere in the courthouse where Cohen was arrested must fail in the absence of any language in the statute that would have put appellant on notice that certain kinds of otherwise permissible speech or conduct would nevertheless, under California law, not be tolerated in certain places. No fair reading of the phrase "offensive conduct" can be said sufficiently to inform the ordinary person that distinctions between certain locations are thereby created.

In the second place, as it comes to us, this case cannot be said to fall within those relatively few categories of instances where prior decisions have established the power of government to deal more comprehensively with certain forms of individual expression simply upon a showing that such a form was employed. This is not, for example, an obscenity case. Whatever else may be necessary to give rise to the States' broader power to prohibit obscene expression, such expression must be, in some significant way, erotic. It cannot plausibly be maintained that this vulgar allusion to the Selective Service System would conjure up such psychic stimulation in anyone likely to be confronted with Cohen's crudely defaced jacket.

This Court has also held that the States are free to ban the simple use, without a demonstration of additional justifying circumstances, of so-called "fighting words," those personally abusive epithets which, when addressed to the ordinary citizen, are, as a matter of common knowledge, inherently likely to provoke violent reaction. *Chaplinsky v. New Hampshire.* While the four-letter word displayed by Cohen in relation to the draft is not uncommonly employed in a personally provocative fashion, in this instance it was clearly not "directed to the person of the hearer." *Cantwell v. Connecticut.* No individual actually or likely to be present could reasonably have regarded the words on appellant's jacket as a direct personal insult. Nor do we have here an instance of the exercise of the State's police power to prevent a speaker from intentionally provoking a given group to hostile reaction. There is, as noted above, no showing that anyone who saw Cohen was in fact violently aroused or that appellant intended such a result.

Finally, in arguments before this Court much has been made of the claim that Cohen's distasteful mode of expression was thrust upon unwilling or unsuspecting viewers, and that the State might therefore legitimately act as it did in order to protect the sensitive from otherwise unavoidable exposure to appellant's crude form of protest. Of course, the mere presumed presence of unwitting listeners or viewers does not serve automatically to justify curtailing all speech capable of giving offense. While this Court has recognized that government may properly act in many situations to prohibit intrusion into the privacy of the home of unwelcome views and ideas which cannot be totally banned from the public dialogue, *e.g., Rowan v. Post Office Dept.,* we have at the same time consistently stressed that "we are often 'captives' outside the sanctuary of the home and subject to objectionable speech." The ability of government, consonant with the Constitution, to shut off discourse solely to protect others from hearing it is, in other words, dependent upon a showing that substantial privacy interests are being invaded in an essentially intolerable manner. Any broader view of this authority would effectively empower a majority to silence dissidents simply as a matter of personal predilections.

In this regard, persons confronted with Cohen's jacket were in a quite different posture than, say, those subjected to the raucous emissions of sound trucks blaring outside their residences. Those in the Los Angeles courthouse could effectively avoid further bombardment of their sensibilities simply by averting their eyes. And, while it may be that one has a more substantial claim to a recognizable privacy interest when walking through a courthouse corridor than, for example, strolling through Central Park, surely it is nothing like the interest in being free from unwanted expression in the confines of one's own home. Given the subtlety and complexity of the factors involved, if Cohen's "speech" was otherwise entitled to constitutional protection, we do not think the fact that some unwilling "listeners" in a public building may have been briefly exposed to it can serve to justify this breach of the peace conviction where, as here, there was no evidence that persons powerless to avoid appellant's conduct did in fact object to it, and where that portion of the statute upon which Cohen's conviction rests evinces no concern, either on its face or as construed by the California courts, with the special plight of the captive auditor, but, instead, indiscriminately sweeps within its prohibitions all "offensive conduct" that disturbs "any neighborhood or person."

II

Against this background, the issue flushed by this case stands out in bold relief. It is whether California can excise, as "offensive conduct," one particular scurrilous epithet from the public discourse, either upon the theory of the court below that its use is inherently likely to cause violent reaction or upon a more general assertion that the States, acting as guardians of public morality, may properly remove this offensive word from the public vocabulary.

The rationale of the California court is plainly untenable. At most it reflects an "undifferentiated fear or apprehension of disturbance [which] is not enough to overcome the right to freedom of expression." *Tinker v. Des Moines Indep. Community School Dist.* We have been shown no evidence that substantial numbers of citizens are standing ready to strike out physically at whoever may assault their sensibilities with execrations like that uttered by Cohen. There may be some persons about with such lawless and violent proclivities, but that is an insufficient base upon which to erect, consistently with constitutional values, a governmental power to force persons who wish to ventilate their dissident views into avoiding particular forms of expression. The argument amounts to little more than the self-defeating proposition that to avoid physical censorship of one who has not sought to provoke such a response by a hypothetical coterie of the violent and lawless, the States may more appropriately effectuate that censorship themselves.

Admittedly, it is not so obvious that the First and Fourteenth Amendments must be taken to disable the States from punishing public utterance of this unseemly expletive in order to maintain what they regard as a suitable level of discourse within the body politic. We think, however, that examination and reflection will reveal the shortcomings of a contrary viewpoint.

At the outset, we cannot overemphasize that, in our judgment, most situations where the State has a justifiable interest in regulating speech will fall within one or more of the various established exceptions, discussed above but not applicable here, to the usual rule that governmental bodies may not prescribe the form or content of individual expression. Equally important to our conclusion is the constitutional backdrop against which our decision must be made. The constitutional right of free expression is powerful medicine in a society as diverse and populous as ours. It is designed and intended to remove governmental restraints from the arena of public discussion, putting the decision as to what views shall be voiced largely into the hands of each of us, in the hope that use of such freedom will ultimately produce a more capable citizenry and more perfect polity and in the belief that no other approach would comport with the premise of individual dignity and choice upon which our political system rests.

To many, the immediate consequence of this freedom may often appear to be only verbal tumult, discord, and even offensive utterance. These are, however, within established limits, in truth necessary side effects of the broader enduring values which the process of open debate permits us to achieve. That the air may at times seem filled with verbal cacophony is, in this sense not a sign of weakness but of strength. We cannot lose sight of the fact that, in what otherwise might seem a trifling and annoying instance of individual distasteful abuse of a privilege, these fundamental societal values are truly implicated. That is why "wholly neutral futilities . . . come under the protection of free speech as fully as do Keats' poems or Donne's sermons," *Winters v. New York* (Frankfurter, J., dissenting), and why "so long as the means are peaceful, the communication need not meet standards of acceptability," *Organization for a Better Austin v. Keefe.*

Against this perception of the constitutional policies involved, we discern certain more particularized considerations that peculiarly call for reversal of this conviction. First, the principle contended for by the State seems inherently boundless. How is one to distinguish this from any other offensive word? Surely the State has no right to cleanse public debate to the point where it is grammatically palatable to the most squeamish among us. Yet no readily ascertainable general principle exists for stopping short of that result were we to affirm the judgment below. For, while the particular four-letter word being litigated here is perhaps more distasteful than most others of its genre, it is nevertheless often true that one man's vulgarity is another's lyric. Indeed, we think it is largely because governmental officials cannot make principled distinctions in this area that the Constitution leaves matters of taste and style so largely to the individual.

Additionally, we cannot overlook the fact, because it is well illustrated by the episode involved here, that much linguistic expression serves a dual communicative function: it conveys not only ideas capable of relatively precise, detached explication, but otherwise inexpressible emotions as well. In fact, words are often chosen as much for their emotive as their cognitive force. We cannot sanction the view that the Constitution, while solicitous of the cognitive content of individual speech, has little or no regard for that emotive function which, practically speaking, may often be the more important element of the overall message sought to be communicated. Indeed, as Mr. Justice Frankfurter has said, "one of the prerogatives of American citizenship is the right to criticize public men and measures— and that means not only informed and responsible criticism but the freedom to speak foolishly and without moderation." *Baumgartner v. United States.*

Finally, and in the same vein, we cannot indulge the facile assumption that one can forbid particular words without also running a substantial risk of suppressing ideas in the process. Indeed, governments might soon seize upon the censorship of particular words as a convenient guise for banning the expression of unpopular views. We have been able, as noted above, to discern little social benefit that might result from running the risk of opening the door to such grave results.

It is, in sum, our judgment that, absent a more particularized and compelling reason for its actions, the State may not, consistently with the First and Fourteenth Amendments, make the simple public display here involved of this single four-letter expletive a criminal offense. Because that is the only arguably sustainable rationale for the conviction here at issue, the judgment below must be

Reversed.

MR. JUSTICE BLACKMUN, *with whom* **THE CHIEF JUSTICE** *and* **MR. JUSTICE BLACK** *join, dissenting.*

Cohen's absurd and immature antic, in my view, was mainly conduct and little speech. The California Court of Appeal appears so to have described it, and I cannot characterize it otherwise. Further, the case appears to me to be well within the sphere of *Chaplinsky v. New Hampshire,* where Mr. Justice Murphy, a known champion of First Amendment freedoms, wrote for a unanimous bench. As a consequence, this Court's agonizing over First Amendment values seems misplaced and unnecessary.

MILLER v. CALIFORNIA

413 U.S. 15 (1973)

Opinion: Burger, joined by White,
  Blackmun, Powell, Rehnquist
Dissent: Douglas
Dissent: Brennan, joined by Stewart,
  Marshall

The Supreme Court struggled for a long time over how—and whether—obscene or pornographic materials fit within the First Amendment's protection of the freedom of speech. In Miller v. California, *the Court established a general standard for cases involving obscenity. One of the prongs of the "*Miller *test" established here exempts obscenity from First Amendment protection so long as the work in question lacks serious literary, artistic, political, and scientific value. To what extent does this qualification protect the freedom of speech? Is it a necessary qualification? Does it go far enough in protecting the right of individuals to express their views?*

Another prong of the Miller *test addresses the relevant standards for determining what is obscene. In a previous case,* Roth v. United States, *the Court had attempted to articulate a national standard for determining what is obscene. In* Miller v. California, *the Court abandoned the notion of a national standard, instead favoring more local standards for determining what is offensive and therefore obscene. Does such an approach resolve the ambiguities associated with defining what is offensive? Do you think a standard that focuses on local, as opposed to national, sensibilities is desirable? Finally, note another prong of the* Miller *test, requiring that the work appeal to the "prurient interest in sex." Do you agree that speech that is obscene under* Miller v. California *should have less First Amendment protection than*

other forms of speech? Should it have no protection?

MR. CHIEF JUSTICE BURGER *delivered the opinion of the Court.*

This is one of a group of "obscenity-pornography" cases being reviewed by the Court in a re-examination of standards enunciated in earlier cases involving what Mr. Justice Harlan called "the intractable obscenity problem." *Interstate Circuit, Inc. v. Dallas.*

Appellant conducted a mass mailing campaign to advertise the sale of illustrated books, euphemistically called "adult" material. After a jury trial, he was convicted of violating California Penal Code §311.2(a), a misdemeanor, by knowingly distributing obscene matter, and the Appellate Department, Superior Court of California, County of Orange, summarily affirmed the judgment without opinion. Appellant's conviction was specifically based on his conduct in causing five unsolicited advertising brochures to be sent through the mail in an envelope addressed to a restaurant in Newport Beach, California. The envelope was opened by the manager of the restaurant and his mother. They had not requested the brochures; they complained to the police.

The brochures advertise four books entitled "Intercourse," "Man-Woman," "Sex Orgies Illustrated," and "An Illustrated History of Pornography," and a film entitled "Marital Intercourse." While the brochures contain some descriptive printed material, primarily they consist of pictures and drawings very explicitly depicting men and women in groups of two or more engaging in a variety of sexual activities, with genitals often prominently displayed.

I

This case involves the application of a State's criminal obscenity statute to a situation in which sexually explicit materials have been thrust by aggressive sales action upon unwilling recipients who had in no way indicated any desire to receive such materials. This Court has recognized that the States have a legitimate interest in prohibiting dissemination or exhibition of obscene material when the mode of dissemination carries with it a significant danger of offending the sensibilities of unwilling recipients or of exposure to juveniles. It is in this context that we are called on to define the standards which must be used to identify obscene material that a State may regulate without infringing on the First Amendment as applicable to the States through the Fourteenth Amendment.

The dissent of Mr. Justice Brennan reviews the background of the obscenity problem, but since the Court now undertakes to formulate standards more concrete than those in the past, it is useful for us to focus on two of the landmark cases in the somewhat tortured history of the Court's obscenity decisions. In *Roth v. United States*, the Court sustained a conviction under a federal statute punishing the mailing of "obscene, lewd, lascivious or filthy . . ." materials. The key to that holding was the Court's rejection of the claim that obscene materials were protected by the First Amendment. Five Justices joined in the opinion stating:

"All ideas having even the slightest redeeming social importance—unorthodox ideas, controversial ideas, even ideas hateful to the prevailing climate of opinion—have the full protection of the [First Amendment] guaranties, unless excludable because they encroach upon the limited area of more important interests. But implicit in the history of the First Amendment is the rejection of obscenity as utterly without redeeming social importance. This is the same judgment expressed by this Court in *Chaplinsky v. New Hampshire*.

Nine years later, in *Memoirs v. Massachusetts*, the Court veered sharply away from the *Roth* concept and, with only three Justices in the plurality opinion, articulated a new test of obscenity. The plurality held that under the *Roth* definition

"as elaborated in subsequent cases, three elements must coalesce: it must be established that (a) the dominant theme of the material taken as a whole appeals to a prurient interest in sex; (b) the material is patently offensive because it affronts contemporary community standards relating to the description or representation of sexual matters; and (c) the material is utterly without redeeming social value." *Id.*

The sharpness of the break with *Roth*, represented by the third element of the *Memoirs* test and emphasized by Mr. Justice White's dissent, was further underscored when the *Memoirs* plurality went on to state:

"The Supreme Judicial Court erred in holding that a book need not be 'unqualifiedly worthless before it can be deemed obscene.' A book cannot be proscribed unless it is found to be *utterly* without redeeming social value."

While *Roth* presumed "obscenity" to be "utterly without redeeming social importance," *Memoirs* required that to prove obscenity it must be affirmatively established that the material is "*utterly* without redeeming social value." Thus, even as they repeated the words of *Roth*, the *Memoirs* plurality produced a drastically altered test that called on the prosecution to prove a negative, *i.e.*, that the material was "*utterly* without redeeming social value"—a burden virtually impossible to discharge under our criminal standards of proof. Such considerations caused Mr. Justice Harlan to wonder if the "*utterly* without redeeming social value" test had any meaning at all. See *Memoirs v. Massachusetts* (Harlan, J., dissenting).

Apart from the initial formulation in the *Roth* case, no majority of the Court has at any given time been able to agree on a standard to determine what constitutes obscene, pornographic material subject to regulation under the States' police power. We have seen "a variety of views among the members of the Court unmatched in any other course of constitutional adjudication." *Interstate Circuit, Inc. v. Dallas* (Harlan, J., concurring and dissenting). This is not remarkable, for in the area of freedom of speech and press the courts must always remain sensitive to any infringement on genuinely serious literary, artistic, political, or scientific expression. This is an area in which there are few eternal verities.

The case we now review was tried on the theory that the California Penal Code §311 approximately incorporates the three-stage *Memoirs* test. But now the *Memoirs* test has been abandoned as unworkable by its author, and no Member of the Court today supports the *Memoirs* formulation.

II

This much has been categorically settled by the Court, that obscene material is unprotected by the First Amendment. "The First and Fourteenth Amendments have never been treated as absolutes [footnote omitted]." *Breard v. Alexandria*, and cases cited. We acknowledge, however, the inherent dangers of undertaking to regulate any form of expression. State statutes designed to regulate obscene materials must be carefully limited. As a result, we now confine the permissible scope of such regulation to works which depict or describe sexual conduct.

That conduct must be specifically defined by the applicable state law, as written or authoritatively construed. A state offense must also be limited to works which, taken as a whole, appeal to the prurient interest in sex, which portray sexual conduct in a patently offensive way, and which, taken as a whole, do not have serious literary, artistic, political, or scientific value.

The basic guidelines for the trier of fact must be: (a) whether "the average person, applying contemporary community standards" would find that the work, taken as a whole, appeals to the prurient interest, *Kois v. Wisconsin*; (b) whether the work depicts or describes, in a patently offensive way, sexual conduct specifically defined by the applicable state law; and (c) whether the work, taken as a whole, lacks serious literary, artistic, political, or scientific value. We do not adopt as a constitutional standard the "*utterly* without redeeming social value" test of *Memoirs v. Massachusetts*; that concept has never commanded the adherence of more than three Justices at one time. If a state law that regulates obscene material is thus limited, as written or construed, the First Amendment values applicable to the States through the Fourteenth Amendment are adequately protected by the ultimate power of appellate courts to conduct an independent review of constitutional claims when necessary.

We emphasize that it is not our function to propose regulatory schemes for the States. That must await their concrete legislative efforts. It is possible, however, to give a few plain examples of what a state statute could define for regulation under part (b) of the standard announced in this opinion, *supra*:

(a) Patently offensive representations or descriptions of ultimate sexual acts, normal or perverted, actual or simulated.

(b) Patently offensive representations or descriptions of masturbation, excretory functions, and lewd exhibition of the genitals.

Sex and nudity may not be exploited without limit by films or pictures exhibited or sold in places of public accommodation any more than live sex and nudity can be exhibited or sold without limit in such public places. At a minimum, prurient, patently offensive depiction or description of sexual conduct must have serious literary, artistic, political, or scientific value to merit First Amendment protection. For example, medical books for the education of physicians and related personnel necessarily use graphic illustrations and descriptions of human anatomy. In resolving the inevitably sensitive questions of fact and law, we must continue to rely on the jury system, accompanied by the safeguards that judges, rules of evidence, presumption of innocence, and other protective features provide, as we do with rape, murder, and a host of other offenses against society and its individual members.

Mr. Justice Brennan, author of the opinions of the Court, or the plurality opinions, in *Roth v. United States; Jacobellis v. Ohio; Ginzburg v. United States; Mishkin v. New York*; and *Memoirs v. Massachusetts*, has abandoned his former position and now maintains that no formulation of this Court, the Congress, or the States can adequately distinguish obscene material unprotected by the First Amendment from protected expression, *Paris Adult Theatre I v. Slaton* (Brennan, J., dissenting). Paradoxically, Mr. Justice Brennan indicates that suppression of unprotected obscene material is permissible to avoid exposure to unconsenting adults, as in this case, and to juveniles, although he gives no indication of how the division between protected and non-protected materials may be drawn with greater precision for these purposes than

for regulation of commercial exposure to consenting adults only. Nor does he indicate where in the Constitution he finds the authority to distinguish between a willing "adult" one month past the state law age of majority and a willing "juvenile" one month younger.

Under the holdings announced today, no one will be subject to prosecution for the sale or exposure of obscene materials unless these materials depict or describe patently offensive "hard core" sexual conduct specifically defined by the regulating state law, as written or construed. We are satisfied that these specific prerequisites will provide fair notice to a dealer in such materials that his public and commercial activities may bring prosecution. If the inability to define regulated materials with ultimate, god-like precision altogether removes the power of the States or the Congress to regulate, then "hard core" pornography may be exposed without limit to the juvenile, the passerby, and the consenting adult alike, as, indeed, Mr. Justice Douglas contends. In this belief, however, Mr. Justice Douglas now stands alone.

Mr. Justice Brennan also emphasizes "institutional stress" in justification of his change of view. Noting that "the number of obscenity cases on our docket gives ample testimony to the burden that has been placed upon this Court," he quite rightly remarks that the examination of contested materials "is hardly a source of edification to the members of this Court." *Paris Adult Theatre I v. Slaton*. He also notes, and we agree, that "uncertainty of the standards creates a continuing source of tension between state and federal courts. . . ." "The problem is . . . that one cannot say with certainty that material is obscene until at least five members of this Court, applying inevitably obscure standards, have pronounced it so."

It is certainly true that the absence, since *Roth*, of a single majority view of this Court as to proper standards for testing obscenity has placed a strain on both state and federal courts. But today, for the first time since *Roth* was decided in 1957, a majority of this Court has agreed on concrete guidelines to isolate "hard core" pornography from expression protected by the First Amendment. Now we may abandon the casual practice of *Redrup v. New York*, and attempt to provide positive guidance to federal and state courts alike.

This may not be an easy road, free from difficulty. But no amount of "fatigue" should lead us to adopt a convenient "institutional" rationale—an absolutist, "anything goes" view of the First Amendment—because it will lighten our burdens. "Such an abnegation of judicial supervision in this field would be inconsistent with our duty to uphold the constitutional guarantees." *Jacobellis v. Ohio* (opinion of Brennan, J.). Nor should we remedy "tension between state and federal courts" by arbitrarily depriving the States of a power reserved to them under the Constitution, a power which they have enjoyed and exercised continuously from before the adoption of the First Amendment to this day. "Our duty admits of no 'substitute for facing up to the tough individual problems of constitutional judgment involved in every obscenity case.'"

III

Under a National Constitution, fundamental First Amendment limitations on the powers of the States do not vary from community to community, but this does not mean that there are, or should or can be, fixed, uniform national standards of precisely what appeals to the "prurient interest" or is "patently offensive." These are essentially questions of fact, and our Nation is simply too big and too diverse for this Court to reasonably expect that such standards could be articulated for all 50 States in a single formulation, even assuming the prerequisite consensus exists. When triers of fact are asked to decide whether "the average person, applying contemporary community standards" would consider certain materials "prurient," it would be unrealistic to require that the answer be based on some abstract formulation. The adversary system, with lay jurors as the usual ultimate factfinders in criminal prosecutions, has historically permitted triers of fact to draw on the standards of their community, guided always by limiting instructions on the law. To require a State to structure obscenity proceedings around evidence of a *national* "community standard" would be an exercise in futility.

As noted before, this case was tried on the theory that the California obscenity statute sought to incorporate the tripartite test of *Memoirs*. This, a "national" standard of First Amendment protection enumerated by a plurality of this Court, was correctly regarded at the time of trial as limiting state prosecution under the controlling case law. The jury, however, was explicitly instructed that, in determining whether the "dominant theme of the material as a whole . . . appeals to the prurient interest" and in determining whether the material "goes substantially beyond customary limits of candor and affronts contemporary community standards of decency," it was to apply "contemporary community standards of the State of California."

During the trial, both the prosecution and the defense assumed that the relevant "community standards" in making the factual determination of obscenity were those of the State of California, not some hypothetical standard of the entire United States of America. Defense counsel at trial never objected to the testimony of the State's expert on community standards or to the instructions of the trial judge on "statewide" standards. On appeal to the Appellate Department, Superior Court of California, County of Orange, appellant for the first time contended that application of state, rather than national, standards violated the First and Fourteenth Amendments.

We conclude that neither the State's alleged failure to offer evidence of "national standards," nor the trial court's charge that the jury consider state community standards, were constitutional errors. Nothing in the First Amendment requires that a jury must consider hypothetical and unascertainable "national standards" when attempting to determine whether certain materials are obscene as a matter of fact. . . .

People in different States vary in their tastes and attitudes, and this diversity is not to be strangled by the absolutism of imposed uniformity. As the Court made clear in *Mishkin v. New York*, the primary concern with requiring a jury to apply the standard of "the average person, applying contemporary community standards" is to be certain that, so far as material is not aimed at a deviant group, it will be judged by its impact on an average person, rather than a particularly susceptible or sensitive person—or indeed a totally insensitive one. We hold that the requirement that the jury evaluate the materials with reference to "contemporary standards of the State of California" serves this protective purpose and is constitutionally adequate.

The dissenting Justices sound the alarm of repression. But, in our view, to equate the free and robust exchange of ideas and political debate with commercial exploitation of obscene material demeans the grand conception of the First Amendment and its high purposes in the historic struggle for freedom. It is a "misuse of the great guarantees of free speech and free press. . . ." *Breard v. Alexandria*. The First Amendment protects works which, taken as a whole, have serious literary, artistic, political, or scientific value, regardless of whether the government or a majority of the people approve of the ideas these works represent. "The protection given speech and press was fashioned to assure unfettered interchange of *ideas* for the bringing about of political and social changes desired by the people," *Roth v. United States*. But the public portrayal of hard-core sexual conduct for its own sake, and for the ensuing commercial gain, is a different matter.

There is no evidence, empirical or historical, that the stern 19th century American censorship of public distribution and display of material relating to sex, see *Roth v. United States*, in any way limited or affected expression of serious literary, artistic, political, or scientific ideas. On the contrary, it is beyond any question that the era following Thomas Jefferson to Theodore Roosevelt was an "extraordinarily vigorous period," not just in economics and politics, but in *belles lettres* and in "the outlying fields of social and political philosophies." We do not see the harsh hand of censorship of ideas—good or bad, sound or unsound—and "repression" of political liberty lurking in every state regulation of commercial exploitation of human interest in sex.

Mr. Justice Brennan finds "it is hard to see how state-ordered regimentation of our minds can ever be forestalled." *Paris Adult Theatre I v. Slaton* (Brennan, J., dissenting). These doleful anticipations assume that courts cannot distinguish commerce in ideas, protected by the First Amendment, from commercial exploitation of obscene material. Moreover, state regulation of hard-core pornography so as to make it unavailable to nonadults, a regulation which Mr. Justice Brennan finds constitutionally permissible, has all the elements of "censorship" for adults; indeed even more rigid enforcement techniques may be called for with such dichotomy of regulation. See *Interstate Circuit, Inc. v. Dallas.* One can concede that the "sexual revolution" of recent years may have had useful byproducts in striking layers of prudery from a subject long irrationally kept from needed ventilation. But it does not follow that no regulation of patently offensive "hard core" materials is needed or permissible; civilized people do not allow unregulated access to heroin because it is a derivative of medicinal morphine.

In sum, we (a) reaffirm the *Roth* holding that obscene material is not protected by the First Amendment; (b) hold that such material can be regulated by the States, subject to the specific safeguards enunciated above, without a showing that the material is "*utterly* without redeeming social value"; and (c) hold that obscenity is to be determined by applying "contemporary community standards," see *Kois v. Wisconsin,* not "national standards." The judgment of the Appellate Department of the Superior Court, Orange County, California, is vacated and the case remanded to that court for further proceedings not inconsistent with the First Amendment standards established by this opinion.

Vacated and remanded.

MR. JUSTICE DOUGLAS, *dissenting.*

I

Today we leave open the way for California to send a man to prison for distributing brochures that advertise books and a movie under freshly written standards defining obscenity which until today's decision were never the part of any law.

Today we would add a new three-pronged test: "(a) whether 'the average person, applying contemporary community standards' would find that the work, taken as a whole, appeals to the prurient interest, . . . (b) whether the work depicts or describes, in a patently offensive way, sexual conduct specifically defined by the applicable state law, and (c) whether the work, taken as a whole, lacks serious literary, artistic, political, or scientific value."

Those are the standards we ourselves have written into the Constitution. Yet how under these vague tests can we sustain convictions for the sale of an article prior to the time when some court has declared it to be obscene?

Today the Court retreats from the earlier formulations of the constitutional test and undertakes to make new definitions. This effort, like the earlier ones, is earnest and well intentioned. The difficulty is that we do not deal with constitutional terms, since "obscenity" is not mentioned in the Constitution or Bill of Rights. And the First Amendment makes no such exception from "the press" which it undertakes to protect nor, as I have said on other occasions, is an exception necessarily implied, for there was no recognized exception to the free press at the time the Bill of Rights was adopted which treated "obscene" publications differently from other types of papers, magazines, and books. So there are no constitutional guidelines for deciding what is and what is not "obscene." The Court is at large because we deal with tastes and standards of literature. What shocks me may be sustenance for my neighbor. What causes one person to boil up in rage over one pamphlet or movie may reflect only his neurosis, not shared by others. We deal here with a regime of censorship which, if adopted, should be done by constitutional amendment after full debate by the people.

Obscenity cases usually generate tremendous emotional outbursts. They have no business being in the courts. If a constitutional amendment authorized censorship, the censor would probably be an administrative agency. Then criminal prosecutions could follow as, if, and when publishers defied the censor and sold their literature. Under that regime a publisher would know when he was on dangerous ground. Under the present regime—whether the old standards or the new ones are used—the criminal law becomes a trap. A brand new test would put a publisher behind bars under a new law improvised by the courts after the publication. That was done in *Ginzburg* and has all the evils of an *ex post facto* law.

My contention is that until a civil proceeding has placed a tract beyond the pale, no criminal prosecution should be sustained. For no more vivid illustration of vague and uncertain laws could be designed than those we have fashioned. As Mr. Justice Harlan has said:

> "The upshot of all this divergence in viewpoint is that anyone who undertakes to examine the Court's decisions since *Roth* which have held particular material obscene or not obscene would find himself in utter bewilderment." *Interstate Circuit, Inc. v. Dallas.*

. . . In any case—certainly when constitutional rights are concerned—we should not allow men to go to prison or be fined when they had no "fair warning" that what they did was criminal conduct.

II

If a specific book, play, paper, or motion picture has in a civil proceeding been condemned as obscene and review of that finding has been completed, and thereafter a person publishes, shows, or displays that particular book or film, then a vague law has been made specific. There would remain the underlying question whether the First Amendment allows an implied exception in the case of obscenity. I do not think it does and my views on the issue have been stated over and over again. But

at least a criminal prosecution brought at that juncture would not violate the time-honored void-for-vagueness test.

No such protective procedure has been designed by California in this case. Obscenity—which even we cannot define with precision—is a hodge-podge. To send men to jail for violating standards they cannot understand, construe, and apply is a monstrous thing to do in a Nation dedicated to fair trials and due process.

III

While the right to know is the corollary of the right to speak or publish, no one can be forced by government to listen to disclosure that he finds offensive. That was the basis of my dissent in *Public Utilities Comm'n v. Pollak*, where I protested against making streetcar passengers a "captive" audience. There is no "captive audience" problem in these obscenity cases. No one is being compelled to look or to listen. Those who enter newsstands or bookstalls may be offended by what they see. But they are not compelled by the State to frequent those places; and it is only state or governmental action against which the First Amendment, applicable to the States by virtue of the Fourteenth, raises a ban.

The idea that the First Amendment permits government to ban publications that are "offensive" to some people puts an ominous gloss on freedom of the press. That test would make it possible to ban any paper or any journal or magazine in some benighted place. The First Amendment was designed "to invite dispute," to induce "a condition of unrest," to "create dissatisfaction with conditions as they are," and even to stir "people to anger." *Terminiello v. Chicago.* The idea that the First Amendment permits punishment for ideas that are "offensive" to the particular judge or jury sitting in judgment is astounding. No greater leveler of speech or literature has ever been designed. To give the power to the censor, as we do today, is to make a sharp and radical break with the traditions of a free society. The First Amendment was not fashioned as a vehicle for dispensing tranquilizers to the people. Its prime function was to keep debate open to "offensive" as well as to "staid" people. The tendency throughout history has been to subdue the individual and to exalt the power of government. The use of the standard "offensive" gives authority to government that cuts the very vitals out of the First Amendment. As is intimated by the Court's opinion, the materials before us may be garbage. But so is much of what is said in political campaigns, in the daily press, on TV, or over the radio. By reason of the First Amendment—and solely because of it—speakers and publishers have not been threatened or subdued because their thoughts and ideas may be "offensive" to some.

The standard "offensive" is unconstitutional in yet another way. In *Coates v. City of Cincinnati*, we had before us a municipal ordinance that made it a crime for three or more persons to assemble on a street and conduct themselves "in a manner annoying to persons passing by." We struck it down, saying:

> "If three or more people meet together on a sidewalk or street corner, they must conduct themselves so as not to annoy any police officer or other person who should happen to pass by. In our opinion this ordinance is unconstitutionally vague because it subjects the exercise of the right of assembly to an unascertainable standard, and unconstitutionally broad because it authorizes the punishment of constitutionally protected conduct.
>
> "Conduct that annoys some people does not annoy others. Thus, the ordinance is vague, not in the sense that it requires a person to conform his conduct to an imprecise but comprehensive normative standard, but rather in the sense that no standard of conduct is specified at all." *Id.*

How we can deny Ohio the convenience of punishing people who "annoy" others and allow California power to punish people who publish materials "offensive" to some people is difficult to square with constitutional requirements.

If there are to be restraints on what is obscene, then a constitutional amendment should be the way of achieving the end. There are societies where religion and mathematics are the only free segments. It would be a dark day for America if that were our destiny. But the people can make it such if they choose to write obscenity into the Constitution and define it.

We deal with highly emotional, not rational, questions. To many the Song of Solomon is obscene. I do not think we, the judges, were ever given the constitutional power to make definitions of obscenity. If it is to be defined, let the people debate and decide by a constitutional amendment what they want to ban as obscene and what standards they want the legislatures and the courts to apply. Perhaps the people will decide that the path towards a mature, integrated society requires that all ideas competing for acceptance must have no censor. Perhaps they will decide otherwise. Whatever the choice, the courts will have some guidelines. Now we have none except our own predilections.

CASE QUESTION

In the first prong of the so-called *Miller* test, the Court acknowledges that the question of obscenity is in some ways dependent on local taste. But notice it makes no such provision or claim about its third prong. Is there an "objective test," not dependent on local standards, for determining whether a work has literary, social, artistic, or political value? For

instance, imagine a film that depicts sex in the manner common in pornographic films, but that also has a political theme. What would the Court say about such a film, and its third prong announced in *Miller v. California*? Is the mere mention of politics in such a film enough to guarantee it protection?

NATIONAL SOCIALIST PARTY v. SKOKIE

432 U.S. 43 (1977)

Opinion: Per Curiam
Dissent: Rehnquist, joined by Burger, Stewart
Dissent (not filed): White

PER CURIAM

On April 29, 1977, the Circuit Court of Cook County entered an injunction against petitioners. The injunction prohibited them from performing any of the following actions within the village of Skokie, Ill.: "[m]arching, walking or parading in the uniform of the National Socialist Party of America; [m]arching, walking or parading or otherwise displaying the swastika on or off their person; [d]istributing pamphlets or displaying any materials which incite or promote hatred against persons of Jewish faith or ancestry or hatred against persons of any faith or ancestry, race or religion." The Illinois Appellate Court denied an application for stay pending appeal. Applicants then filed a petition for a stay in the Illinois Supreme Court, together with a request for a direct expedited appeal to that court. The Illinois Supreme Court denied both the stay and leave for an expedited appeal. Applicants then filed an application for a stay with Mr. Justice Stevens, as Circuit Justice, who referred the matter to the Court.

Treating the application as a petition for certiorari from the order of the Illinois

Supreme Court, we grant certiorari and reverse the Illinois Supreme Court's denial of a stay. That order is a final judgment for purposes of our jurisdiction, since it involved a right "separable from, and collateral to" the merits, *Cohen v. Beneficial Loan Corp.* It finally determined the merits of petitioners' claim that the outstanding injunction will deprive them of rights protected by the First Amendment during the period of appellate review which, in the normal course, may take a year or more to complete. If a State seeks to impose a restraint of this kind, it must provide strict procedural safeguards, *Freedman v. Maryland*, including immediate appellate review. Absent such review, the State must instead allow a stay. The order of the Illinois Supreme Court constituted a denial of that right.

Reversed and remanded for further proceedings not inconsistent with this opinion.

MR. JUSTICE WHITE *would deny the stay.*

MR. JUSTICE REHNQUIST, *with whom* THE CHIEF JUSTICE *and* MR. JUSTICE STEWART *join, dissenting.*

The Court treats an application filed here to stay a judgment of the Circuit Court of Cook County as a petition for certiorari to review the refusal of the Supreme Court of Illinois to stay the injunction. It summarily reverses this refusal of a stay. I simply do not see how the refusal of the Supreme

Court of Illinois to stay an injunction granted by an inferior court within the state system can be described as a "[f]inal judgmen[t] or decre[e] rendered by the highest court of a State in which a decision could be had," which is the limitation that Congress has imposed on our jurisdiction to review state-court judgments under 28 U.S.C. 1257. *Cox Broadcasting Corp. v. Cohn*, relied upon by the Court, which surely took as liberal a view of this jurisdictional grant as can reasonably be taken, does not support the result reached by the Court here. In *Cox* there had been a final decision on the federal claim by the Supreme Court of Georgia, which was the highest court of that State in which such a decision could be had. Here all the Supreme Court of Illinois has done is, in the exercise of the discretion possessed by every appellate

court, to deny a stay of a lower court ruling pending appeal. No Illinois appellate court has heard or decided the merits of applicants' federal claim.

I do not disagree with the Court that the provisions of the injunction issued by the Circuit Court of Cook County are extremely broad, and I would expect that if the Illinois appellate courts follow cases such as *Freedman v. Maryland*, and *Nebraska Press Assn. v. Stuart*, relied upon by the Court, the injunction will be at least substantially modified by them. But I do not believe that in the long run respect for the Constitution or for the law is encouraged by actions of this Court which disregard the limitations placed on us by Congress in order to assure that an erroneous injunction issued by a state trial court does not wrongly interfere with the constitutional rights of those enjoined.

FEDERAL COMMUNICATIONS COMMISSION v. PACIFICA FOUNDATION

438 U.S. 726 (1978)

Opinion: Stevens, joined by Burger and Rehnquist in Parts I-III and IV-C, by Blackmun and Powell in all but parts IV-A and IV-B, and by Burger and Rehnquist in Parts IV-A and IV-B
Concurrence: Powell, joined by Blackmun
Dissent: Brennan, joined by Marshall
Dissent: Stewart, joined by Brennan, White, Marshall

This case deals with indecent speech transmitted via radio broadcast. In reading this case, it is important to consider the Court's distinction between indecent and obscene speech. To what extent is it possible to differentiate between the two? Are they entitled to different degrees of constitutional scrutiny?

MR. JUSTICE STEVENS *delivered the opinion of the Court (Parts I, II, III, and IV-C) and an opinion in which* **THE CHIEF JUSTICE** *and* **MR. JUSTICE REHNQUIST** *joined (Parts IV-A and IV-B).*

This case requires that we decide whether the Federal Communications Commission has any power to regulate a radio broadcast that is indecent but not obscene.

A satiric humorist named George Carlin recorded a 12-minute monologue entitled "Filthy Words" before a live audience in a California theater. He began by referring to his thoughts about "the words you couldn't say on the public, ah, airwaves, um, the ones you definitely wouldn't say, ever." He proceeded to list those words and repeat them over and over again in a variety of colloquialisms.

At about 2 o'clock in the afternoon on Tuesday, October 30, 1973, a New York radio station, owned by respondent Pacifica Foundation, broadcast the "Filthy Words" monologue. A few weeks later a man, who stated that he had heard the broadcast while driving with his young son, wrote a letter complaining to the Commission.

The complaint was forwarded to the station for comment. In its response, Pacifica explained that the monologue had been played during a program about contemporary society's attitude toward language and that, immediately before its broadcast, listeners had been advised that it included "sensitive language which might be regarded as offensive to some." Pacifica characterized George Carlin as "a significant social satirist" who "like Twain and Sahl before him, examines the language of ordinary people. . . . Carlin is not mouthing obscenities, he is merely using words to satirize as harmless and essentially silly our attitudes towards those words." Pacifica stated that it was not aware of any other complaints about the broadcast.

On February 21, 1975, the Commission issued a declaratory order granting the complaint and holding that Pacifica "could have been the subject of administrative sanctions."

In its memorandum opinion the Commission stated that it intended to "clarify the standards which will be utilized in considering" the growing number of complaints about indecent speech on the airwaves. *Id.*, at 94. Advancing several reasons for treating broadcast speech differently from other forms of expression, the Commission found a power to regulate indecent broadcasting in two statutes: 18 U.S.C. §1464, which forbids the use of "any obscene, indecent, or profane language by means of radio communications," and 47 U.S.C. §303 (g), which

requires the Commission to "encourage the larger and more effective use of radio in the public interest."

The Commission characterized the language used in the Carlin monologue as "patently offensive," though not necessarily obscene, and expressed the opinion that it should be regulated by principles analogous to those found in the law of nuisance where the "law generally speaks to *channeling* behavior more than actually prohibiting it. . . . [The] concept of 'indecent' is intimately connected with the exposure of children to language that describes, in terms patently offensive as measured by contemporary community standards for the broadcast medium, sexual or excretory activities and organs, at times of the day when there is a reasonable risk that children may be in the audience."

Applying these considerations to the language used in the monologue as broadcast by respondent, the Commission concluded that certain words depicted sexual and excretory activities in a patently offensive manner, noted that they "were broadcast at a time when children were undoubtedly in the audience (i.e., in the early afternoon)," and that the prerecorded language, with these offensive words "repeated over and over," was "deliberately broadcast." In summary, the Commission stated: "We therefore hold that the language as broadcast was indecent and prohibited by 18 U.S.C. [§]1464."

After the order issued, the Commission was asked to clarify its opinion by ruling that the broadcast of indecent words as part of a live newscast would not be prohibited. The Commission issued another opinion in which it pointed out that it "never intended to place an absolute prohibition on the broadcast of this type of language, but rather sought to channel it to times of day when children most likely would not be exposed to it."

The United States Court of Appeals for the District of Columbia Circuit reversed, with each of the three judges on the panel writing separately.

Having granted the Commission's petition for certiorari, we must decide: (1) whether the scope of judicial review encompasses more than the Commission's determination that the monologue was indecent "as broadcast"; (2) whether the Commission's order was a form of censorship forbidden by §326; (3) whether the broadcast was indecent within the meaning of §1464; and (4) whether the order violates the First Amendment of the United States Constitution.

B

When the issue is narrowed to the facts of this case, the question is whether the First Amendment denies government any power to restrict the public broadcast of indecent language in any circumstances. For if the government has any such power, this was an appropriate occasion for its exercise.

The words of the Carlin monologue are unquestionably "speech" within the meaning of the First Amendment. . . .

The question in this case is whether a broadcast of patently offensive words dealing with sex and excretion may be regulated because of its content. Obscene materials have been denied the protection of the First Amendment because their content is so offensive to contemporary moral standards. *Roth v. United States*. But the fact that society may find speech offensive is not a sufficient reason for suppressing it. Indeed, if it is the speaker's opinion that gives offense, that consequence is a reason for according it constitutional protection. For it is a central tenet of the First Amendment that the government must remain neutral in the marketplace of ideas. If there were any reason to believe that the Commission's characterization of the Carlin monologue as offensive could be traced to its political content—or even to the fact that it satirized contemporary attitudes about four-letter words—First Amendment protection might be required. But that is simply not this case. These words offend for the same reasons that obscenity offends. Their place in the hierarchy of First Amendment values was aptly sketched by Mr. Justice Murphy when he said: "[Such] utterances are no essential part of any exposition of ideas, and are of such slight social value as a step to truth that any benefit that may be derived from them is clearly outweighed by the social interest in order and morality." *Chaplinsky v. New Hampshire.*

Although these words ordinarily lack literary, political, or scientific value, they are not entirely outside the protection of the First Amendment. Some uses of even the most offensive words are unquestionably protected. Indeed, we may assume, *arguendo*, that this monologue would be protected in other contexts. Nonetheless, the constitutional protection accorded to a communication containing such patently offensive sexual and excretory language need not be the same in every context. It is a characteristic of speech such as this that both its capacity to offend and its "social value," to use Mr. Justice Murphy's term, vary with the circumstances. Words that are commonplace in one setting are shocking in another. To paraphrase Mr. Justice Harlan, one occasion's lyric is another's vulgarity.

In this case it is undisputed that the content of Pacifica's broadcast was "vulgar," "offensive," and "shocking." Because content of that character is not entitled to absolute constitutional protection under all circumstances, we must consider its context in order to determine whether the

Commission's action was constitutionally permissible.

C

We have long recognized that each medium of expression presents special First Amendment problems. *Joseph Burstyn, Inc. v. Wilson*. And of all forms of communication, it is broadcasting that has received the most limited First Amendment protection. Thus, although other speakers cannot be licensed except under laws that carefully define and narrow official discretion, a broadcaster may be deprived of his license and his forum if the Commission decides that such an action would serve "the public interest, convenience, and necessity." Similarly, although the First Amendment protects newspaper publishers from being required to print the replies of those whom they criticize, *Miami Herald Publishing Co. v. Tornillo*, it affords no such protection to broadcasters; on the contrary, they must give free time to the victims of their criticism. *Red Lion Broadcasting Co. v. FCC*.

The reasons for these distinctions are complex, but two have relevance to the present case. First, the broadcast media have established a uniquely pervasive presence in the lives of all Americans. Patently offensive, indecent material presented over the airwaves confronts the citizen, not only in public, but also in the privacy of the home, where the individual's right to be left alone plainly outweighs the First Amendment rights of an intruder. *Rowan v. Post Office Dept*. Because the broadcast audience is constantly tuning in and out, prior warnings cannot completely protect the listener or viewer from unexpected program content. To say that one may avoid further offense by turning off the radio when he hears indecent language is like saying that the remedy for an assault is to run away after the first blow. One may

hang up on an indecent phone call, but that option does not give the caller a constitutional immunity or avoid a harm that has already taken place.

Second, broadcasting is uniquely accessible to children, even those too young to read. Although Cohen's written message might have been incomprehensible to a first grader, Pacifica's broadcast could have enlarged a child's vocabulary in an instant. Other forms of offensive expression may be withheld from the young without restricting the expression at its source. Bookstores and motion picture theaters, for example, may be prohibited from making indecent material available to children. . . .

It is appropriate, in conclusion, to emphasize the narrowness of our holding. This case does not involve a two-way radio conversation between a cab driver and a dispatcher, or a telecast of an Elizabethan comedy. We have not decided that an occasional expletive in either setting would justify any sanction or, indeed, that this broadcast would justify a criminal prosecution. The Commission's decision rested entirely on a nuisance rationale under which context is all-important. The concept requires consideration of a host of variables. The time of day was emphasized by the Commission. The content of the program in which the language is used will also affect the composition of the audience, and differences between radio, television, and perhaps closed-circuit transmissions, may also be relevant. As Mr. Justice Sutherland wrote, a "nuisance may be merely a right thing in the wrong place,—like a pig in the parlor instead of the barnyard." *Euclid v. Ambler Realty Co*. We simply hold that when the Commission finds that a pig has entered the parlor, the exercise of its regulatory power does not depend on proof that the pig is obscene.

The judgment of the Court of Appeals is reversed.

MR. JUSTICE POWELL, *with whom*
MR. JUSTICE BLACKMUN *joins,*
concurring in part and concurring in
the judgment.

I join Parts I, II, III, and IV-C of Mr. Justice Stevens' opinion. Because I do not subscribe to all that is said in Part IV, however, I state my views separately.

I

... In essence, the Commission sought to "channel" the monologue to hours when the fewest unsupervised children would be exposed to it. In my view, this consideration provides strong support for the Commission's holding.

The Court has recognized society's right to "adopt more stringent controls on communicative materials available to youths than on those available to adults ..."

In most instances, the dissemination of this kind of speech to children may be limited without also limiting willing adults' access to it. Sellers of printed and recorded matter and exhibitors of motion pictures and live performances may be required to shut their doors to children, but such a requirement has no effect on adults' access. The difficulty is that such a physical separation of the audience cannot be accomplished in the broadcast media. During most of the broadcast hours, both adults and unsupervised children are likely to be in the broadcast audience, and the broadcaster cannot reach willing adults without also reaching children. This, as the Court emphasizes, is one of the distinctions between the broadcast and other media to which we often have adverted as justifying a different treatment of the broadcast media for First Amendment purposes. In my view, the Commission was entitled to give substantial weight to this difference in reaching its decision in this case.

A second difference, not without relevance, is that broadcasting—unlike most other forms of communication—comes directly into the home, the one place where people ordinarily have the right not to be assaulted by uninvited and offensive sights and sounds. Although the First Amendment may require unwilling adults to absorb the first blow of offensive but protected speech when they are in public before they turn away, a different order of values obtains in the home. "That we are often 'captives' outside the sanctuary of the home and subject to objectionable speech and other sound does not mean we must be captives everywhere." *Rowan v. Post Office Dept.* The Commission also was entitled to give this factor appropriate weight in the circumstances of the instant case. This is not to say, however, that the Commission has an unrestricted license to decide what speech, protected in other media, may be banned from the airwaves in order to protect unwilling adults from momentary exposure to it in their homes. Making the sensitive judgments required in these cases is not easy. But this responsibility has been reposed initially in the Commission, and its judgment is entitled to respect.

The Commission's holding does not prevent willing adults from purchasing Carlin's record, from attending his performances, or, indeed, from reading the transcript reprinted as an appendix to the Court's opinion. On its face, it does not prevent respondent Pacifica Foundation from broadcasting the monologue during late evening hours when fewer children are likely to be in the audience, nor from broadcasting discussions of the contemporary use of language at any time during the day. ...

II

As the foregoing demonstrates, my views are generally in accord with what is said in Part IV-C of Mr. Justice Stevens' opinion. I therefore join that portion of his opinion. I do not join Part IV-B, however, because I do not subscribe to the theory that the Justices of this Court are free generally to decide on the basis of its content which speech protected by the First Amendment is most "valuable" and hence deserving of the most protection, and which is less "valuable" and hence deserving of less protection. In my view, the result in this case does not turn on whether Carlin's monologue, viewed as a whole, or the words that constitute it, have more or less "value" than a candidate's campaign speech. This is a judgment for each person to make, not one for the judges to impose upon him.

MR. JUSTICE BRENNAN, *with whom* **MR. JUSTICE MARSHALL** *joins, dissenting.*

I find the Court's misapplication of fundamental First Amendment principles so patent, and its attempt to impose *its* notions of propriety on the whole of the American people so misguided, that I am unable to remain silent.

I

A

Without question, the privacy interests of an individual in his home are substantial and deserving of significant protection. In finding these interests sufficient to justify the content regulation of protected speech, however, the Court commits two errors. First, it misconceives the nature of the privacy interests involved where an individual voluntarily chooses to admit radio communications into his home. Second, it ignores the constitutionally protected interests of both those who wish to transmit and those who desire to receive broadcasts that many—including the FCC and this Court— might find offensive.

"The ability of government, consonant with the Constitution, to shut off discourse solely to protect others from hearing it is . . . dependent upon a showing that substantial privacy interests are being invaded in an essentially intolerable manner. Any broader view of this authority would effectively empower a majority to silence dissidents simply as a matter of personal predilections." *Cohen v. California.* I am in wholehearted agreement with my Brethren that an individual's right "to be let alone" when engaged in private activity within the confines of his own home is encompassed within the "substantial privacy interests" to which Mr. Justice Harlan referred in *Cohen*, and is entitled to the greatest solicitude. *Stanley v. Georgia.* However, I believe that an individual's actions in switching on and listening to communications transmitted over the public airways and directed to the public at large do not implicate fundamental privacy interests, even when engaged in within the home. Instead, because the radio is undeniably a public medium, these actions are more properly viewed as a decision to take part, if only as a listener, in an ongoing public discourse. Although an individual's decision to allow public radio communications into his home undoubtedly does not abrogate all of his privacy interests, the residual privacy interests he retains vis-a-vis the communication he voluntarily admits into his home are surely no greater than those of the people present in the corridor of the Los Angeles courthouse in *Cohen* who bore witness to the words "Fuck the Draft" emblazoned across Cohen's jacket. Their privacy interests were held insufficient to justify punishing Cohen for his offensive communication.

The Court's balance, of necessity, fails to accord proper weight to the interests of listeners who wish to hear broadcasts the FCC deems offensive. It permits majoritarian tastes completely to preclude a protected message from entering the homes of a receptive, unoffended minority. No decision of this Court supports such a result. Where the individuals constituting the offended majority may freely choose to reject the material being offered, we have never found their privacy interests of such moment to warrant the suppression of speech on privacy grounds. *Rowan v. Post Office Dept.*, relied on by the FCC and by the opinions of my Brothers Powell and Stevens, confirms rather than belies this conclusion. In *Rowan*, the Court upheld a statute, 39 U.S.C. §4009, permitting householders to require that mail advertisers stop sending them lewd or offensive materials and remove their names from mailing lists. Unlike the situation here, householders who wished to receive the sender's communications were not prevented from doing so. Equally important, the determination of offensiveness *vel non* under the statute involved in *Rowan* was completely within the hands of the individual householder; no governmental evaluation of the worth of the mail's content stood between the mailer and the householder. In contrast, the visage of the censor is all too discernible here.

B

Most parents will undoubtedly find understandable as well as commendable the Court's sympathy with the FCC's desire to prevent offensive broadcasts from reaching the ears of unsupervised children. Unfortunately, the facial appeal of this justification for radio censorship masks its constitutional insufficiency. Although the government unquestionably has a special interest in the well-being of children and consequently "can adopt more stringent controls on communicative materials available to youths than on those available to adults," *Erznoznik v. Jacksonville*, the Court

has accounted for this societal interest by adopting a "variable obscenity" standard that permits the prurient appeal of material available to children to be assessed in terms of the sexual interests of minors....

Because the Carlin monologue is obviously not an erotic appeal to the prurient interests of children, the Court, for the first time, allows the government to prevent minors from gaining access to materials that are not obscene, and are therefore protected, as to them. It thus ignores our recent admonition that "[speech] that is neither obscene as to youths nor subject to some other legitimate proscription cannot be suppressed solely to protect the young from ideas or images that a legislative body thinks unsuitable for them." The Court's refusal to follow its own pronouncements is especially lamentable since it has the anomalous subsidiary effect, at least in the radio context at issue here, of making completely unavailable to adults material which may not constitutionally be kept even from children.

The opinion of my Brother Powell acknowledges that there lurks in today's decision a potential for "[reducing] the adult population . . . to [hearing] only what is fit for children," but expresses faith that the FCC will vigilantly prevent this potential from ever becoming a reality. I am far less certain than my Brother Powell that such faith in the Commission is warranted; and even if I shared it, I could not so easily shirk the responsibility assumed by each Member of this Court jealously to guard against encroachments on First Amendment freedoms.

In concluding that the presence of children in the listening audience provides an adequate basis for the FCC to impose sanctions for Pacifica's broadcast of the Carlin monologue, the opinions of my Brother Powell, and my Brother Stevens, both stress the time-honored right of a parent to raise his child as he sees fit—a right this Court has consistently been vigilant to protect. Yet this principle supports a result directly contrary to that reached by the Court. *Yoder* and *Pierce* hold that parents, *not* the government, have the right to make certain decisions regarding the upbringing of their children. As surprising as it may be to individual Members of this Court, some parents may actually find Mr. Carlin's unabashed attitude towards the seven "dirty words" healthy, and deem it desirable to expose their children to the manner in which Mr. Carlin defuses the taboo surrounding the words. Such parents may constitute a minority of the American public, but the absence of great numbers willing to exercise the right to raise their children in this fashion does not alter the right's nature or its existence. Only the Court's regrettable decision does that.

C

As demonstrated above, neither of the factors relied on by both the opinion of my Brother Powell and the opinion of my Brother Stevens—the intrusive nature of radio and the presence of children in the listening audience—can, when taken on its own terms, support the FCC's disapproval of the Carlin monologue. These two asserted justifications are further plagued by a common failing: the lack of principled limits on their use as a basis for FCC censorship. No such limits come readily to mind, and neither of the opinions constituting the Court serve to clarify the extent to which the FCC may assert the privacy and children-in-the-audience rationales as justification for expunging from the airways protected communications the Commission finds offensive. Taken to their logical extreme, these rationales would support the cleansing of public radio of any "four-letter words" whatsoever, regardless

of their context. The rationales could justify the banning from radio of a myriad of literary works, novels, poems, and plays by the likes of Shakespeare, Joyce, Hemingway, Ben Jonson, Henry Fielding, Robert Burns, and Chaucer; they could support the suppression of a good deal of political speech, such as the Nixon tapes; and they could even provide the basis for imposing sanctions for the broadcast of certain portions of the Bible.

In order to dispel the specter of the possibility of so unpalatable a degree of censorship, and to defuse Pacifica's overbreadth challenge, the FCC insists that it desires only the authority to reprimand a broadcaster on facts analogous to those present in this case, . . . The opinions of both my Brother Powell and my Brother Stevens take the FCC at its word, and consequently do no more than permit the Commission to censor the afternoon broadcast of the "sort of verbal shock treatment," opinion of Mr. Justice Powell, involved here. To insure that the FCC's regulation of protected speech does not exceed these bounds, my Brother Powell is content to rely upon the judgment of the Commission while my Brother Stevens deems it prudent to rely on this Court's ability accurately to assess the worth of various kinds of speech. For my own part, even accepting that this case is limited to its facts, I would place the responsibility and the right to weed worthless and offensive communications from the public airways where it belongs and where, until today, it resided: in a public free to choose those communications worthy of its attention from a marketplace unsullied by the censor's hand.

II

. . . My Brother Stevens, in reaching a result apologetically described as narrow, takes comfort in his observation that "[a] requirement that indecent language be avoided will have its primary effect on the form, rather than the content, of serious communication," and finds solace in his conviction that "[there] are few, if any, thoughts that cannot be expressed by the use of less offensive language." The idea that the content of a message and its potential impact on any who might receive it can be divorced from the words that are the vehicle for its expression is transparently fallacious. A given word may have a unique capacity to capsule an idea, evoke an emotion, or conjure up an image. Indeed, for those of us who place an appropriately high value on our cherished First Amendment rights, the word "censor" is such a word. Mr. Justice Harlan, speaking for the Court, recognized the truism that a speaker's choice of words cannot surgically be separated from the ideas he desires to express when he warned that "we cannot indulge the facile assumption that one can forbid particular words without also running a substantial risk of suppressing ideas in the process." *Cohen v. California*. Moreover, even if an alternative phrasing may communicate a speaker's abstract ideas as effectively as those words he is forbidden to use, it is doubtful that the sterilized message will convey the emotion that is an essential part of so many communications. This, too, was apparent to Mr. Justice Harlan and the Court in *Cohen*.

My Brother Stevens also finds relevant to his First Amendment analysis the fact that "[adults] who feel the need may purchase tapes and records or go to theaters and nightclubs to hear [the tabooed] words." My Brother Powell agrees: "The Commission's holding does not prevent willing adults from purchasing Carlin's record, from attending his performances, or, indeed, from reading the transcript reprinted as an appendix to the Court's opinion." The opinions of my Brethren display both a sad insensitivity to the fact that

these alternatives involve the expenditure of money, time, and effort that many of those wishing to hear Mr. Carlin's message may not be able to afford, and a naive innocence of the reality that in many cases, the medium may well be the message.

The Court apparently believes that the FCC's actions here can be analogized to the zoning ordinances upheld in *Young v. American Mini Theatres, Inc.* For two reasons, it is wrong. First, the zoning ordinances found to pass constitutional muster in *Young* had valid goals other than the channeling of protected speech. No such goals are present here. Second, and crucial to the opinions of my Brothers Powell and Stevens in *Young*—opinions, which, as they do in this case, supply the bare five-person majority of the Court—the ordinances did not restrict the access of distributors or exhibitors to the market or impair the viewing public's access to the regulated material. Again, this is not the situation here. Both those desiring to receive Carlin's message over the radio and those wishing to send it to them are prevented from doing so by the Commission's actions. Although, as my Brethren point out, Carlin's message may be disseminated or received by other means, this is of little consolation to those broadcasters and listeners who, for a host of reasons, not least among them financial, do not have access to, or cannot take advantage of, these other means.

Moreover, it is doubtful that even those frustrated listeners in a position to follow my Brother Powell's gratuitous advice and attend one of Carlin's performances or purchase one of his records would receive precisely the same message Pacifica's radio station sent its audience. The airways are capable not only of carrying a message, but also of transforming it. A satirist's monologue may be most potent when delivered to a live audience; yet the choice whether this will in fact be the manner in which the message is delivered and received is one the First Amendment prohibits the government from making.

III

It is quite evident that I find the Court's attempt to unstitch the warp and woof of First Amendment law in an effort to reshape its fabric to cover the patently wrong result the Court reaches in this case dangerous as well as lamentable. Yet there runs throughout the opinions of my Brothers Powell and Stevens another vein I find equally disturbing: a depressing inability to appreciate that in our land of cultural pluralism, there are many who think, act, and talk differently from the Members of this Court, and who do not share their fragile sensibilities. It is only an acute ethnocentric myopia that enables the Court to approve the censorship of communications solely because of the words they contain.

The words that the Court and the Commission find so unpalatable may be the stuff of everyday conversations in some, if not many, of the innumerable subcultures that compose this Nation.

Academic research indicates that this is indeed the case.

Today's decision will thus have its greatest impact on broadcasters desiring to reach, and listening audiences composed of, persons who do not share the Court's view as to which words or expressions are acceptable and who, for a variety of reasons, including a conscious desire to flout majoritarian conventions, express themselves using words that may be regarded as offensive by those from different socio-economic backgrounds. In this context, the Court's decision may be seen for what, in the broader perspective, it really is: another of the dominant culture's inevitable efforts to force those groups who do not share its mores to conform to its way of thinking, acting, and speaking. See *Moore v. East Cleveland* (Brennan, J., concurring).

In confirming Carlin's prescience as a social commentator by the result it reaches today, the Court evidences an attitude toward the "seven dirty words" that many others besides Mr. Carlin and Pacifica might describe as "silly." Whether today's decision will similarly prove "harmless" remains to be seen. One can only hope that it will.

NEW YORK v. FERBER

458 U.S. 747 (1982)

Opinion: White, joined by Burger, Powell, Rehnquist, O'Connor
Concurrence: O'Connor
Concurrence: Brennan, joined by Marshall
Concurrence: Stevens
Concurrence (not filed): Blackmun

The standard for cases involving obscenity was established by the Court in Miller v. California. *In this case, the Court considered* *whether greater leeway for state regulation of child pornography might be warranted. To what extent is the case of children distinctive or deserving of special constitutional treatment?*

JUSTICE WHITE *delivered the opinion of the Court.*

At issue in this case is the constitutionality of a New York criminal statute which prohibits persons from knowingly promoting sexual performances by children under the age of 16 by distributing material which depicts such performances.

I

In recent years, the exploitative use of children in the production of pornography has become a serious national problem. The Federal Government and 47 States have sought to combat the problem with statutes specifically directed at the production of child pornography. At least half of such statutes do not require that the materials produced be legally obscene. Thirty-five States and the United States Congress have also passed legislation prohibiting the distribution of such materials; 20 States prohibit the distribution of material depicting children engaged in sexual conduct without requiring that the material be legally obscene.

New York is one of the 20. In 1977, the New York Legislature enacted Article 263 of its Penal Law. Section 263.05 criminalizes as a class C felony the use of a child in a sexual performance:

At issue in this case is §263.15, defining a class D felony:

"A person is guilty of promoting a sexual performance by a child when, knowing the character and content thereof, he produces, directs or promotes any performance which includes sexual conduct by a child less than sixteen years of age."

This case arose when Paul Ferber, the proprietor of a Manhattan bookstore specializing in sexually oriented products, sold two films to an undercover police officer. The films are devoted almost exclusively to depicting young boys masturbating. Ferber was indicted on two counts of violating §263.10 and two counts of violating §263.15, the two New York laws controlling dissemination of child pornography. After a jury trial, Ferber was acquitted of the two counts of promoting an obscene sexual performance, but found guilty of the two counts under §263.15, which did not require proof that the films were obscene. Ferber's convictions were affirmed without opinion by the Appellate Division of the New York State Supreme Court.

The New York Court of Appeals reversed, holding that §263.15 violated the First Amendment. . . . We granted the State's petition for certiorari, presenting the single question:

"To prevent the abuse of children who are made to engage in sexual conduct for commercial purposes, could the New York State Legislature, consistent with the First Amendment, prohibit the dissemination of material which shows children engaged in sexual conduct, regardless of whether such material is obscene?"

We believe our inquiry should begin with the question of whether a State has somewhat more freedom in proscribing works which portray sexual acts or lewd exhibitions of genitalia by children.

In *Miller v. California,* a majority of the Court agreed that a "state offense must also be limited to works which, taken as a whole, appeal to the prurient interest in sex, which portray sexual conduct in a patently offensive way, and which, taken as a whole, do not have serious literary, artistic, political, or scientific value." Over the past decade, we have adhered to the guidelines expressed in *Miller,* which subsequently has been followed in the regulatory schemes of most States.

B

The *Miller* standard, like its predecessors, was an accommodation between the State's interests in protecting the "sensibilities of unwilling recipients" from exposure to pornographic material and the dangers of censorship inherent in unabashedly content-based laws. Like obscenity statutes, laws directed at the dissemination of child pornography run the risk of suppressing protected expression by allowing the hand of the censor to become unduly heavy. For the following reasons, however, we are persuaded that the States are entitled to greater leeway in the regulation of pornographic depictions of children.

First. It is evident beyond the need for elaboration that a State's interest in "safeguarding the physical and psychological well-being of a minor" is "compelling." *Globe Newspaper Co. v. Superior Court.* "A democratic society rests, for its continuance, upon the healthy, well-rounded growth of young people into full maturity as citizens." *Prince v. Massachusetts.* Accordingly, we have sustained legislation aimed at protecting the physical and emotional well-being of youth even when the laws have operated in the sensitive area of constitutionally protected rights. In *Prince v. Massachusetts,* the Court held that a statute prohibiting use of a child to distribute literature on the street was valid notwithstanding the statute's effect on a First Amendment activity. In *Ginsberg v. New York,* we sustained a New York law protecting children from exposure to nonobscene literature. Most recently, we held that the Government's interest in the "well-being of its youth" justified special treatment of indecent broadcasting received by adults as well as children. *FCC v. Pacifica Foundation.*

The prevention of sexual exploitation and abuse of children constitutes a government objective of surpassing importance. The legislative findings accompanying passage of the New York laws reflect this concern:

"[There] has been a proliferation of exploitation of children as subjects in sexual performances. The care of children is a sacred trust and should not be abused by those who seek to profit through a commercial network based upon the exploitation of children. The public policy of the state demands the protection of children from exploitation through sexual performances."

We shall not second-guess this legislative judgment. Respondent has not intimated that we do so. Suffice it to say that virtually all of the States and the United States have passed legislation proscribing the production of or otherwise combating "child pornography." The legislative judgment, as well as the judgment found in the relevant literature, is that the use of children as subjects of pornographic materials is harmful to the physiological, emotional, and mental health of the child. That judgment, we think, easily passes muster under the First Amendment.

Second. The distribution of photographs and films depicting sexual activity by juveniles is intrinsically related to the sexual abuse of children in at least two ways. First, the materials produced are a permanent record of the children's participation and the harm to the child is exacerbated by their circulation. Second, the distribution network for child pornography must be closed if the production of material which requires the sexual exploitation of children is to be effectively controlled. Indeed, there is no serious contention that the legislature was unjustified in believing that it is difficult, if not impossible, to halt the exploitation of children by pursuing only those who produce the photographs and movies. While the production of pornographic materials is a low-profile, clandestine industry, the need to market the resulting products requires a visible apparatus of distribution. The most expeditious if not the only practical method of law enforcement may be to dry up the market for this material by imposing severe criminal penalties on persons selling, advertising, or otherwise promoting the product.

Respondent does not contend that the State is unjustified in pursuing those who distribute child pornography. Rather, he argues that it is enough for the State to prohibit the distribution of materials that are legally obscene under the *Miller* test. While some States may find that this approach properly accommodates its interests, it does not follow that the First Amendment prohibits a State from going further. The *Miller* standard, like all general definitions of what may be banned as obscene, does not reflect the State's particular and more compelling interest in prosecuting those who promote the sexual exploitation of children. Thus, the question under the *Miller* test of whether a work, taken as a whole, appeals to the prurient interest of the average person bears no connection to the issue of whether a child has been physically or psychologically harmed in the production of the work. Similarly, a sexually explicit depiction need not be "patently offensive" in order to have required the sexual exploitation of a child for its production. In addition, a work which, taken on the whole, contains serious literary, artistic, political, or scientific value may nevertheless embody the hardest core of child pornography. "It is irrelevant to the child [who has been abused] whether or not the material . . . has a literary, artistic, political or social value." We therefore cannot conclude that the *Miller* standard is a satisfactory solution to the child pornography problem.

Third. The advertising and selling of child pornography provide an economic motive for and are thus an integral part of the production of such materials, an activity illegal throughout the Nation. "It rarely has been suggested that the constitutional freedom for speech and press extends its immunity to speech or writing used as an integral part of conduct in violation of a valid criminal statute." *Giboney v. Empire Storage*

& Ice Co. We note that were the statutes outlawing the employment of children in these films and photographs fully effective, and the constitutionality of these laws has not been questioned, the First Amendment implications would be no greater than that presented by laws against distribution: enforceable production laws would leave no child pornography to be marketed.

Fourth. The value of permitting live performances and photographic reproductions of children engaged in lewd sexual conduct is exceedingly modest, if not *de minimis*. We consider it unlikely that visual depictions of children performing sexual acts or lewdly exhibiting their genitals would often constitute an important and necessary part of a literary performance or scientific or educational work. As a state judge in this case observed, if it were necessary for literary or artistic value, a person over the statutory age who perhaps looked younger could be utilized. Simulation outside of the prohibition of the statute could provide another alternative. Nor is there any question here of censoring a particular literary theme or portrayal of sexual activity. The First Amendment interest is limited to that of rendering the portrayal somewhat more "realistic" by utilizing or photographing children.

Fifth. Recognizing and classifying child pornography as a category of material outside the protection of the First Amendment is not incompatible with our earlier decisions. "The question whether speech is, or is not, protected by the First Amendment often depends on the content of the speech." *Young v. American Mini Theatres, Inc.* Leaving aside the special considerations when public officials are the target, *New York Times Co. v. Sullivan*, a libelous publication is not protected by the Constitution. *Beauharnais v. Illinois.* Thus, it is not rare that a content-based classification of speech has been accepted because it may be appropriately generalized that within the confines of the given classification, the evil to be restricted so overwhelmingly outweighs the expressive interests, if any, at stake, that no process of case-by-case adjudication is required. When a definable class of material, such as that covered by §263.15, bears so heavily and pervasively on the welfare of children engaged in its production, we think the balance of competing interests is clearly struck and that it is permissible to consider these materials as without the protection of the First Amendment.

C

There are, of course, limits on the category of child pornography which, like obscenity, is unprotected by the First Amendment. As with all legislation in this sensitive area, the conduct to be prohibited must be adequately defined by the applicable state law, as written or authoritatively construed. Here the nature of the harm to be combated requires that the state offense be limited to works that *visually* depict sexual conduct by children below a specified age. The category of "sexual conduct" proscribed must also be suitably limited and described.

The test for child pornography is separate from the obscenity standard enunciated in *Miller*, but may be compared to it for the purpose of clarity. The *Miller* formulation is adjusted in the following respects: A trier of fact need not find that the material appeals to the prurient interest of the average person; it is not required that sexual conduct portrayed be done so in a patently offensive manner; and the material at issue need not be considered as a whole. We note that the distribution of descriptions or other depictions of sexual conduct, not otherwise obscene, which do not involve live performance or photographic or other visual reproduction of live performances,

retains First Amendment protection. As with obscenity laws, criminal responsibility may not be imposed without some element of scienter on the part of the defendant. *Smith v. California.*

D

Section 263.15's prohibition incorporates a definition of sexual conduct that comports with the above-stated principles. The forbidden acts to be depicted are listed with sufficient precision and represent the kind of conduct that, if it were the theme of a work, could render it legally obscene: "actual or simulated sexual intercourse, deviate sexual intercourse, sexual bestiality, masturbation, sado-masochistic abuse, or lewd exhibition of the genitals." The term "lewd exhibition of the genitals" is not unknown in this area and, indeed, was given in *Miller* as an example of a permissible regulation. A performance is defined only to include live or visual depictions: "any play, motion picture, photograph or dance . . . [or] other visual representation exhibited before an audience." Section 263.15 expressly includes a scienter requirement.

We hold that §263.15 sufficiently describes a category of material the production and distribution of which is not entitled to First Amendment protection. It is therefore clear that there is nothing unconstitutionally "underinclusive" about a statute that singles out this category of material for proscription. It also follows that the State is not barred by the First Amendment from prohibiting the distribution of unprotected materials produced outside the State.

III

It remains to address the claim that the New York statute is unconstitutionally overbroad because it would forbid the distribution of material with serious literary, scientific, or educational value or material which does not threaten the harms sought to be combated by the State. Respondent prevailed on that ground below, and it is to that issue that we now turn.

A

The traditional rule is that a person to whom a statute may constitutionally be applied may not challenge that statute on the ground that it may conceivably be applied unconstitutionally to others in situations not before the Court. By focusing on the factual situation before us, and similar cases necessary for development of a constitutional rule, we face "flesh-and-blood" legal problems with data "relevant and adequate to an informed judgment." This practice also fulfills a valuable institutional purpose: it allows state courts the opportunity to construe a law to avoid constitutional infirmities.

What has come to be known as the First Amendment overbreadth doctrine is one of the few exceptions to this principle and must be justified by "weighty countervailing policies." *United States v. Raines.* The doctrine is predicated on the sensitive nature of protected expression: "persons whose expression is constitutionally protected may well refrain from exercising their rights for fear of criminal sanctions by a statute susceptible of application to protected expression." *Village of Schaumburg v. Citizens for a Better Environment.* It is for this reason that we have allowed persons to attack overly broad statutes even though the conduct of the person making the attack is clearly unprotected and could be proscribed by a law drawn with the requisite specificity.

The scope of the First Amendment overbreadth doctrine, like most exceptions to established principles, must be carefully tied to the circumstances in which facial invalidation of a statute is truly warranted. Because of the wide-reaching effects of striking down a statute on its face at the request of one whose own conduct may be punished despite the First Amendment, we have recognized that the overbreadth doctrine is "strong medicine" and have employed it with hesitation, and then "only as a last resort." *Broadrick.* We have, in consequence, insisted that the overbreadth involved be "substantial" before the statute involved will be invalidated on its face.

We accordingly held that "particularly where conduct and not merely speech is involved, we believe that the overbreadth of a statute must not only be real, but substantial as well, judged in relation to the statute's plainly legitimate sweep."

The premise that a law should not be invalidated for overbreadth unless it reaches a substantial number of impermissible applications is hardly novel. On most occasions involving facial invalidation, the Court has stressed the embracing sweep of the statute over protected expression.

The requirement of substantial overbreadth is directly derived from the purpose and nature of the doctrine. While a sweeping statute, or one incapable of limitation, has the potential to repeatedly chill the exercise of expressive activity by many individuals, the extent of deterrence of protected speech can be expected to decrease with the declining reach of the regulation. This observation appears equally applicable to the publication of books and films as it is to activities, such as picketing or participation in election campaigns, which have previously been categorized as involving conduct plus speech. We see no appreciable difference between the position of a publisher or bookseller in doubt as to the reach of New York's child pornography law and the situation faced by the Oklahoma state employees with respect to that State's restriction on partisan political activity. Indeed, it could reasonably be argued that the bookseller, with an economic incentive to sell materials that may fall within the statute's scope, may be less likely to be deterred than the employee who wishes to engage in political campaign activity.

B

Applying these principles, we hold that §263.15 is not substantially overbroad. We consider this the paradigmatic case of a state statute whose legitimate reach dwarfs its arguably impermissible applications. New York, as we have held, may constitutionally prohibit dissemination of material specified in §263.15. While the reach of the statute is directed at the hard core of child pornography, the Court of Appeals was understandably concerned that some protected expression, ranging from medical textbooks to pictorials in the *National Geographic* would fall prey to the statute. How often, if ever, it may be necessary to employ children to engage in conduct clearly within the reach of §263.15 in order to produce educational, medical, or artistic works cannot be known with certainty. Yet we seriously doubt, and it has not been suggested, that these arguably impermissible applications of the statute amount to more than a tiny fraction of the materials within the statute's reach. Nor will we assume that the New York courts will widen the possibly invalid reach of the statute by giving an expansive construction to the proscription on "lewd [exhibitions] of the genitals." Under these circumstances, §263.15 is "not substantially overbroad and . . . whatever overbreadth may exist should be cured through case-by-case analysis of the fact situations to which its sanctions, assertedly, may not be applied." *Broadrick v. Oklahoma.*

IV

Because §263.15 is not substantially overbroad, it is unnecessary to consider its application to material that does not depict sexual conduct of a type that New York may restrict consistent with the First Amendment. As applied to Paul Ferber and to others who distribute similar material, the statute does not violate the First Amendment as applied to the States through the Fourteenth. The judgment of the New York Court of Appeals is reversed, and the case is remanded to that court for further proceedings not inconsistent with this opinion.

JUSTICE O'CONNOR, *concurring.*

Although I join the Court's opinion, I write separately to stress that the Court does not hold that New York must except "material with serious literary, scientific, or educational value," from its statute. The Court merely holds that, even if the First Amendment shelters such material, New York's current statute is not sufficiently overbroad to support respondent's facial attack. The compelling interests identified in today's opinion suggest that the Constitution might in fact permit New York to ban knowing distribution of works depicting minors engaged in explicit sexual conduct, regardless of the social value of the depictions. For example, a 12-year-old child photographed while masturbating surely suffers the same psychological harm whether the community labels the photograph "edifying" or "tasteless." The audience's appreciation of the depiction is simply irrelevant to New York's asserted interest in protecting children from psychological, emotional, and mental harm.

An exception for depictions of serious social value, moreover, would actually increase opportunities for the content-based censorship disfavored by the First

Amendment. As drafted, New York's statute does not attempt to suppress the communication of particular ideas. The statute permits discussion of child sexuality, forbidding only attempts to render the "[portrayals] somewhat more 'realistic' by utilizing or photographing children." Thus, the statute attempts to protect minors from abuse without attempting to restrict the expression of ideas by those who might use children as live models.

On the other hand, it is quite possible that New York's statute is overbroad because it bans depictions that do not actually threaten the harms identified by the Court. For example, clinical pictures of adolescent sexuality, such as those that might appear in medical textbooks, might not involve the type of sexual exploitation and abuse targeted by New York's statute. Nor might such depictions feed the poisonous "kiddie porn" market that New York and other States have attempted to regulate. Similarly, pictures of children engaged in rites widely approved by their cultures, such as those that might appear in issues of the *National Geographic*, might not trigger the compelling interests identified by the Court. It is not necessary to address these possibilities further today, however, because this potential overbreadth is not sufficiently substantial to warrant facial invalidation of New York's statute.

JUSTICE BRENNAN, *with whom* **JUSTICE MARSHALL** *joins, concurring in the judgment.*

I agree with much of what is said in the Court's opinion. As I made clear in the opinion I delivered for the Court in *Ginsburg v. New York*, the State has a special interest in protecting the well-being of its youth. See also *Globe Newspaper Co. v. Superior Court*. This special and compelling interest, and the particular vulnerability of children,

afford the State the leeway to regulate pornographic material, the promotion of which is harmful to children, even though the State does not have such leeway when it seeks only to protect consenting adults from exposure to such material. *Ginsburg v. New York*. I also agree with the Court that the "tiny fraction" of material of serious artistic, scientific, or educational value that could conceivably fall within the reach of the statute is insufficient to justify striking the statute on the grounds of overbreadth. See *Broadrick v. Oklahoma*.

But in my view application of §263.15 or any similar statute to depictions of children that in themselves do have serious literary, artistic, scientific, or medical value, would violate the First Amendment. In short, it is inconceivable how a depiction of a child that is itself a serious contribution to the world of art or literature or science can be deemed "material outside the protection of the First Amendment."

I, of course, adhere to my view that, in the absence of exposure, or particular harm, to juveniles or unconsenting adults, the State lacks power to suppress sexually oriented materials. With this understanding, I concur in the Court's judgment in this case.

JUSTICE STEVENS, *concurring in the judgment.*

Two propositions seem perfectly clear to me. First, the specific conduct that gave rise to this criminal prosecution is not protected by the Federal Constitution; second, the state statute that respondent violated prohibits some conduct that is protected by the First Amendment. The critical question, then, is whether this respondent, to whom the statute may be applied without violating the Constitution, may challenge the statute on the ground that it conceivably may be applied unconstitutionally to others in situations not before the Court. I agree with the Court's answer to this question but not with its method of analyzing the issue.

I would refuse to apply overbreadth analysis for reasons unrelated to any prediction concerning the relative number of protected communications that the statute may prohibit. Specifically, I would postpone decision of my hypothetical case until it actually arises. Advocates of a liberal use of overbreadth analysis could object to such postponement on the ground that it creates the risk that the exhibitor's uncertainty may produce self-censorship. But that risk obviously interferes less with the interest in free expression than does an abstract, advance ruling that the film is simply unprotected whenever it contains a lewd scene, no matter how brief.

My reasons for avoiding overbreadth analysis in this case are more qualitative than quantitative. When we follow our traditional practice of adjudicating difficult and novel constitutional questions only in concrete factual situations, the adjudications tend to be crafted with greater wisdom. Hypothetical rulings are inherently treacherous and prone to lead us into unforeseen errors; they are qualitatively less reliable than the products of case-by-case adjudication.

Moreover, it is probably safe to assume that the category of speech that is covered by the New York statute generally is of a lower quality than most other types of communication. On a number of occasions, I have expressed the view that the First Amendment affords some forms of speech more protection from governmental regulation than other forms of speech. Today the Court accepts this view, putting the category of speech described in the New York statute in its rightful place near the bottom of this hierarchy. Although I disagree with the Court's position that such speech is totally without First Amendment protection, I agree that generally marginal speech does not warrant the extraordinary protection afforded by the overbreadth doctrine.

AMERICAN BOOKSELLERS ASS'N v. HUDNUT

771 F. 2d 323 (7th Cir. 1985)

In this case, the U.S. Court of Appeals for the Seventh Circuit considered the constitutionality of a city ordinance defining "pornography" as an act of discrimination against women rather than as an act of obscenity. What is the difference between obscenity and pornography? Why did the Seventh Circuit find the definition of pornography in the ordinance at issue unconstitutional even though it recognizes that obscenity might be constitutionally subject to limits? As you read this case recall Catharine MacKinnon's arguments from the excerpt above. In what ways does her approach to the issue of pornography clash with the opinion here?

EASTERBROOK, Circuit Judge.

Indianapolis enacted an ordinance defining "pornography" as a practice that discriminates against women. "Pornography" is to be redressed through the administrative and judicial methods used for other discrimination. The City's definition of "pornography" is considerably different from "obscenity," which the Supreme Court has held is not protected by the First Amendment.

To be "obscene" under *Miller v. California,* "a publication must, taken as a whole, appeal to the prurient interest, must contain patently offensive depictions or descriptions of specified sexual conduct, and on the whole have no serious literary, artistic, political, or scientific value." *Brockett v. Spokane Arcades, Inc.* Offensiveness must be assessed under the standards of the community. Both offensiveness and an appeal to something other than "normal, healthy sexual desires" are essential elements of "obscenity."

"Pornography" under the ordinance is "the graphic sexually explicit subordination of women, whether in pictures or in words, that also includes one or more of the following:

(1) Women are presented as sexual objects who enjoy pain or humiliation; or

(2) Women are presented as sexual objects who experience sexual pleasure in being raped; or

(3) Women are presented as sexual objects tied up or cut up or mutilated or bruised or physically hurt, or as dismembered or truncated or fragmented or severed into body parts; or

(4) Women are presented as being penetrated by objects or animals; or

(5) Women are presented in scenarios of degradation, injury, abasement, torture, shown as filthy or inferior, bleeding, bruised, or hurt in a context that makes these conditions sexual; or

(6) Women are presented as sexual objects for domination, conquest, violation, exploitation, possession, or use, or through postures or positions of servility or submission or display."

The statute provides that the "use of men, children, or transsexuals in the place of women in paragraphs (1) through (6) above shall also constitute pornography under this section." The ordinance as passed in April 1984 defined "sexually explicit" to mean actual or simulated intercourse or the uncovered exhibition of the genitals, buttocks or anus. An amendment in June 1984 deleted this provision, leaving the term undefined.

The Indianapolis ordinance does not refer to the prurient interest, to offensiveness, or to the standards of the community. It demands attention to particular depictions, not to the work judged as a whole. It is irrelevant under the ordinance whether the work has literary, artistic, political, or scientific value. The City and many amici point to these omissions as virtues. They maintain that pornography influences attitudes, and the statute is a way to alter the socialization of men and women rather than to vindicate community standards of offensiveness. And as one of the principal drafters of the ordinance has asserted, "if a woman is subjected, why should it matter that the work has other value?" Catharine A. MacKinnon, *Pornography, Civil Rights, and Speech.*

Civil rights groups and feminists have entered this case as amici on both sides. Those supporting the ordinance say that it will play an important role in reducing the tendency of men to view women as sexual objects, a tendency that leads to both unacceptable attitudes and discrimination in the workplace and violence away from it. Those opposing the ordinance point out that much radical feminist literature is explicit and depicts women in ways forbidden by the ordinance and that the ordinance would reopen old battles. It is unclear how Indianapolis would treat works from James Joyce's *Ulysses* to Homer's *Iliad*; both depict women as submissive objects for conquest and domination.

We do not try to balance the arguments for and against an ordinance such as this. The ordinance discriminates on the ground of the content of the speech. Speech treating women in the approved way—in sexual encounters "premised on equality" (MacKinnon)—is lawful no matter how sexually explicit. Speech treating women in the disapproved way—as submissive in matters sexual or as enjoying humiliation—is unlawful no matter how significant the literary, artistic, or political qualities of the work taken as a whole. The state may not ordain preferred viewpoints in this way. The Constitution forbids the state to declare one perspective right and silence opponents.

I

The ordinance contains four prohibitions. People may not "traffic" in pornography, "coerce" others into performing in pornographic works, or "force" pornography on anyone. Anyone injured by someone who has seen or read pornography has a right of action against the maker or seller.

The district court held the ordinance unconstitutional. The court concluded that the ordinance regulates speech rather than the conduct involved in making pornography. The regulation of speech could be justified, the court thought, only by a compelling interest in reducing sex discrimination, an interest Indianapolis had not established. The ordinance is also vague and overbroad, the court believed, and establishes a prior restraint of speech.

II

The plaintiffs are a congeries of distributors and readers of books, magazines, and films. The American Booksellers Association comprises about 5,200 bookstores and chains. The Association for American Publishers includes most of the country's publishers. Video Shack, Inc., sells and rents video cassettes in Indianapolis. Kelly Bentley, a resident of Indianapolis, reads books and watches films. There are many more plaintiffs. Collectively the plaintiffs (or their members, whose interests they represent) make, sell, or read just about every kind of material that could be affected by the ordinance, from hard-core films to W.B. Yeats's poem "Leda and the Swan" (from the myth of Zeus in the form of a swan impregnating an apparently subordinate Leda), to the collected works of James Joyce, D.H. Lawrence, and John Cleland.

The interests of Bentley and many of the members of the organizational plaintiffs are directly affected by the ordinance, which gives them standing to attack it. . . . *Buckley v. Valeo.*

III

"If there is any fixed star in our constitutional constellation, it is that no official, high or petty, can prescribe what shall be orthodox in politics, nationalism, religion, or other matters of opinion or force citizens to confess by word or act their faith therein." *West Virginia State Board of Education v. Barnette.* Under the First Amendment the government must leave to the people the evaluation of ideas. Bald or subtle, an idea is as powerful as the audience allows it to be. A belief may be pernicious—the beliefs of Nazis led to the death of millions, those of the Klan to the repression of millions. A pernicious belief may prevail. Totalitarian governments today rule much of the planet, practicing suppression of billions and spreading dogma that may enslave others. One of the things that separates our society from theirs is our absolute right to propagate opinions that the government finds wrong or even hateful.

The ideas of the Klan may be propagated. *Brandenburg v. Ohio.* Communists may speak freely and run for office. *DeJonge v. Oregon.* The Nazi Party may march through a city with a large Jewish population. People may criticize the President by misrepresenting his positions, and they have a right to post their misrepresentations on public property. People may seek to repeal laws guaranteeing equal opportunity in employment or to revoke the constitutional amendments granting the vote to blacks and women. They may do this because "above all else, the First Amendment means that government has no power to restrict expression because of its message [or] its ideas. . . ." *Police Department v. Mosley.*

Under the ordinance graphic sexually explicit speech is "pornography" or not depending on the perspective the author adopts. Speech that "subordinates" women and also, for example, presents women as enjoying pain, humiliation, or rape, or even simply presents women in "positions of servility or submission or display" is forbidden, no matter how great the literary or political value of the work taken as a whole. Speech that portrays women in positions of equality is lawful, no matter how graphic the sexual content. This is thought control. It establishes an "approved" view of women, of how they may react to sexual encounters, of how the sexes may relate to each other. Those who espouse the approved view may use sexual images; those who do not, may not.

Indianapolis justifies the ordinance on the ground that pornography affects thoughts. Men who see women depicted as subordinate are more likely to treat them so. Pornography is an aspect of dominance. It does not persuade people so much as change them. It works by socializing, by establishing the expected and the permissible. In this view pornography is not an idea; pornography is the injury.

There is much to this perspective. Beliefs are also facts. People often act in accordance with the images and patterns they find around them. People raised in a religion tend to accept the tenets of that religion, often without independent examination. People taught from birth that black people are fit only for slavery rarely rebelled against that creed; beliefs coupled with the self-interest of the masters established a social structure that inflicted great harm while enduring for centuries. Words and images act at the level of the subconscious before they persuade at the level of the conscious. Even the truth has little chance unless a statement fits within the framework of beliefs that may never have been subjected to rational study.

Therefore we accept the premises of this legislation. Depictions of subordination tend to perpetuate subordination. The subordinate status of women in turn leads to affront and lower pay at work, insult and injury at home, battery and rape on the streets. In the language of the legislature, "pornography is central in creating and maintaining sex as a basis of discrimination. Pornography is a systematic practice of exploitation and subordination based on sex which differentially harms women. The bigotry and contempt it produces, with the acts of aggression it fosters, harm women's opportunities for equality and rights [of all kinds]."

Yet this simply demonstrates the power of pornography as speech. All of these unhappy effects depend on mental intermediation. Pornography affects how people see the world, their fellows, and social relations. If pornography is what pornography does, so is other speech. Hitler's orations affected how some Germans saw Jews. Communism is a world view, not simply a *Manifesto* by Marx and Engels or a set of speeches. Efforts to suppress communist speech in the United States were based on the belief that the public acceptability of such ideas would increase the likelihood of totalitarian government. Religions affect socialization in the most pervasive way. The opinion in *Wisconsin v. Yoder*, shows how a religion can dominate an entire approach to life, governing much more than the relation between the sexes. Many people believe that the existence of television, apart from the content of specific programs, leads to intellectual laziness, to a penchant for violence, to many other ills. The Alien and Sedition Acts passed during the administration of John Adams rested on a sincerely held belief that disrespect for the government leads to social collapse and revolution—a belief with support in the history of many nations. Most governments of the world act on this empirical regularity, suppressing critical speech. In the United States, however, the strength of the support for this belief is irrelevant. Seditious libel is protected speech unless the danger is not only grave but also imminent.

Racial bigotry, anti-semitism, violence on television, reporters' biases—these and many more influence the culture and shape our socialization. None is directly answerable by more speech, unless that speech too finds its place in the popular culture. Yet all is protected as speech, however insidious. Any other answer leaves the government in control of all of the institutions of culture, the great censor and director of which thoughts are good for us.

Sexual responses often are unthinking responses, and the association of sexual arousal with the subordination of women therefore may have a substantial effect. But almost all cultural stimuli provoke unconscious responses. Religious ceremonies condition their participants. Teachers convey messages by selecting what not to cover; the implicit message about what is off limits or unthinkable may be more powerful than the messages for which they present rational argument. Television scripts contain unarticulated assumptions. People may be conditioned in subtle ways. If the fact that speech plays a role in a process of conditioning were enough to permit

governmental regulation, that would be the end of freedom of speech.

It is possible to interpret the claim that the pornography is the harm in a different way. Indianapolis emphasizes the injury that models in pornographic films and pictures may suffer. The record contains materials depicting sexual torture, penetration of women by red-hot irons and the like. These concerns have nothing to do with written materials subject to the statute, and physical injury can occur with or without the "subordination" of women. As we discuss in Part IV, a state may make injury in the course of producing a film unlawful independent of the viewpoint expressed in the film.

The more immediate point, however, is that the image of pain is not necessarily pain. In *Body Double*, a suspense film directed by Brian DePalma, a woman who has disrobed and presented a sexually explicit display is murdered by an intruder with a drill. The drill runs through the woman's body. The film is sexually explicit and a murder occurs—yet no one believes that the actress suffered pain or died. In *Barbarella* a character played by Jane Fonda is at times displayed in sexually explicit ways and at times shown "bleeding, bruised, [and] hurt in a context that makes these conditions sexual"—and again no one believes that Fonda was actually tortured to make the film. In *Carnal Knowledge* a woman grovels to please the sexual whims of a character played by Jack Nicholson; no one believes that there was a real sexual submission, and the Supreme Court held the film protected by the First Amendment. *Jenkins v. Georgia*. And this works both ways. The description of women's sexual domination of men in *Lysistrata* was not real dominance. Depictions may affect slavery, war, or sexual roles, but a book about slavery is not itself slavery, or a book about death by poison a murder.

Much of Indianapolis's argument rests on the belief that when speech is "unanswerable," and the metaphor that there is a "marketplace of ideas" does not apply, the First Amendment does not apply either. The metaphor is honored; Milton's *Aeropagitica* and John Stewart Mill's *On Liberty* defend freedom of speech on the ground that the truth will prevail, and many of the most important cases under the First Amendment recite this position. The Framers undoubtedly believed it. As a general matter it is true. But the Constitution does not make the dominance of truth a necessary condition of freedom of speech. To say that it does would be to confuse an outcome of free speech with a necessary condition for the application of the amendment.

A power to limit speech on the ground that truth has not yet prevailed and is not likely to prevail implies the power to declare truth. At some point the government must be able to say (as Indianapolis has said): "We know what the truth is, yet a free exchange of speech has not driven out falsity, so that we must now prohibit falsity." If the government may declare the truth, why wait for the failure of speech? Under the First Amendment, however, there is no such thing as a false idea, *Gertz v. Robert Welch, Inc.*, so the government may not restrict speech on the ground that in a free exchange truth is not yet dominant.

At any time, some speech is ahead in the game; the more numerous speakers prevail. Supporters of minority candidates may be forever "excluded" from the political process because their candidates never win, because few people believe their positions. This does not mean that freedom of speech has failed.

The Supreme Court has rejected the position that speech must be "effectively answerable" to be protected by the Constitution. For example, in *Buckley v. Valeo*, the Court held unconstitutional limitations on expenditures that were neutral with regard to the speakers' opinions and designed to make it easier for one person to answer another's speech. In *Mills v. Alabama*, the Court held unconstitutional a statute prohibiting editorials on election day—a statute the state had designed to prevent speech that came too late for answer. In cases from *Eastern Railroad Presidents Conference v. Noerr Motor Freight, Inc.* through *NAACP v. Claiborne Hardware Co.*, the Court has held that the First Amendment protects political stratagems—obtaining legislation through underhanded ploys and outright fraud in *Noerr*, obtaining political and economic ends through boycotts in *Clairborne Hardware*—that may be beyond effective correction through more speech.

We come, finally, to the argument that pornography is "low value" speech, that it is enough like obscenity that Indianapolis may prohibit it. Some cases hold that speech far removed from politics and other subjects at the core of the Framers' concerns may be subjected to special regulation. These cases do not sustain statutes that select among viewpoints, however. In *Pacifica* the FCC sought to keep vile language off the air during certain times. The Court held that it may; but the Court would not have sustained a regulation prohibiting scatological descriptions of Republicans but not scatological descriptions of Democrats, or any other form of selection among viewpoints.

At all events, "pornography" is not low value speech within the meaning of these cases. Indianapolis seeks to prohibit certain speech because it believes this speech influences social relations and politics on a grand scale, that it controls attitudes at home and in the legislature. This precludes a characterization of the speech as low value. True, pornography and obscenity have sex in common. But Indianapolis left out of its definition any reference to literary, artistic, political, or scientific value. The ordinance applies to graphic sexually explicit subordination in works great and small. The Court sometimes balances the value of speech against the costs of its restriction, but it does this by category of speech and not by the content of particular works. Indianapolis has created an approved point of view and so loses the support of these cases.

Any rationale we could imagine in support of this ordinance could not be limited to sex discrimination. Free speech has been on balance an ally of those seeking change. Governments that want stasis start by restricting speech. Culture is a powerful force of continuity; Indianapolis paints pornography as part of the culture of power. Change in any complex system ultimately depends on the ability of outsiders to challenge accepted views and the reigning institutions. Without a strong guarantee of freedom of speech, there is no effective right to challenge what is.

IV

The definition of "pornography" is unconstitutional. No construction or excision of particular terms could save it. The offense of trafficking in pornography necessarily falls with the definition. We express no view on the district court's conclusions that the ordinance is vague and that it establishes a prior restraint. Neither is necessary to our judgment. We also express no view on the argument presented by several amici that the ordinance is itself a form of discrimination on account of sex.

Section 8 of the ordinance is a strong severability clause, and Indianapolis asks that we parse the ordinance to save what we can. If a court could do this by surgical excision, this might be possible. But a federal court may not completely reconstruct a local ordinance, and we conclude

that nothing short of rewriting could save anything.

The offense of coercion to engage in a pornographic performance, for example, has elements that might be constitutional. Without question a state may prohibit fraud, trickery, or the use of force to induce people to perform—in pornographic films or in any other films. Such a statute may be written without regard to the viewpoint depicted in the work. *New York v. Ferber*, suggests that when a state has a strong interest in forbidding the conduct that makes up a film (in *Ferber* sexual acts involving minors), it may restrict or forbid dissemination of the film in order to reinforce the prohibition of the conduct. A state may apply such a rule to non-sexual coercion (although it need not). We suppose that if someone forced a prominent political figure, at gunpoint, to endorse a candidate for office, a state could forbid the commercial sale of the film containing that coerced endorsement. The same principle allows a court to enjoin the publication of stolen trade secrets and award damages for the publication of copyrighted matter without permission.

But the Indianapolis ordinance, unlike our hypothetical statute, is not neutral with respect to viewpoint. The ban on distribution of works containing coerced performances is limited to pornography; coercion is irrelevant if the work is not "pornography," and we have held the definition of "pornography" to be defective root and branch. A legislature might replace "pornography" in §16-3(g)(4) with "any film containing explicit sex" or some similar expression, but even the broadest severability clause does not permit a federal court to rewrite as opposed to excise. Rewriting is work for the legislature of Indianapolis.

The offense of forcing pornography on unwilling recipients is harder to assess. Many kinds of forcing (such as giving texts to students for translation) may themselves be protected speech. *Rowan v. Post Office*, shows that a state may permit people to insulate themselves from categories of speech—in *Rowan* sexual mail—but that the government must leave the decision about what items are forbidden in the hands of the potentially offended recipients. Exposure to sex is not something the government may prevent, see *Erznoznik v. City of Jacksonville*. We therefore could not save the offense of "forcing" by redefining "pornography" as all sexually-offensive speech or some related category. The statute needs a definition of "forcing" that removes the government from the role of censor. See also *Planned Parenthood Ass'n*, holding that the "captive audience" problem does not permit a government to discriminate on account of the speaker's message.

The section creating remedies for injuries and assaults attributable to pornography also is salvageable in principle, although not by us. The First Amendment does not prohibit redress of all injuries caused by speech. Injury to reputation is redressed through the law of libel, which is constitutional subject to strict limitations. Cases such as *Brandenburg v. Ohio* and *NAACP v. Claiborne Hardware* hold that a state may not penalize speech that does not cause immediate injury. But we do not doubt that if, immediately after the Klan's rally in *Brandenburg*, a mob had burned to the ground the house of a nearby black person, that person could have recovered damages from the speaker who whipped the crowd into a frenzy. All of the Justices assumed in *Claiborne Hardware* that if the threats in Charles Evers's incendiary speech had been a little less veiled and had led directly to an assault against a person shopping in a store owned by a white merchant, the victim of the assault and even the merchant could have recovered damages from the speaker.

The law of libel has the potential to muzzle the press, which led to *New York Times v. Sullivan*. A law awarding damages for assaults caused by speech also has the power to muzzle the press, and again courts would place careful limits on the scope of the right. Certainly no damages could be awarded unless the harm flowed directly from the speech and there was an element of intent on the part of the speaker, as in *Sullivan* and *Brandenburg*.

Much speech is dangerous. Chemists whose work might help someone build a bomb, political theorists whose papers might start political movements that lead to riots, speakers whose ideas attract violent protesters, all these and more leave loss in their wake. Unless the remedy is very closely confined, it could be more dangerous to speech than all the libel judgments in history. The constitutional requirements for a valid recovery for assault caused by speech might turn out to be too rigorous for any plaintiff to meet. But the Indianapolis ordinance requires the complainant to show that the attack was "directly caused by specific pornography," and it is not beyond the realm of possibility that a state court could construe this limitation in a way that would make the statute constitutional. We are not authorized to prevent the state from trying.

Again, however, the assault statute is tied to "pornography," and we cannot find a sensible way to repair the defect without seizing power that belongs elsewhere. Indianapolis might choose to have no ordinance if it cannot be limited to viewpoint-specific harms, or it might choose to extend the scope to all speech, just as the law of libel applies to all speech. An attempt to repair this ordinance would be nothing but a blind guess.

No amount of struggle with particular words and phrases in this ordinance can leave anything in effect. The district court came to the same conclusion. Its judgment is therefore

Affirmed.

R.A.V. v. CITY OF ST. PAUL

505 U.S. 377 (1992)

Opinion: Scalia, joined by Rehnquist, Kennedy, Souter, Thomas
Concurrence: White, joined by Blackmun, O'Connor and by Stevens except in Part I-A
Concurrence: Blackmun
Concurrence: Stevens, joined by White and Blackmun in Part I

JUSTICE SCALIA *delivered the opinion of the Court.*

In the predawn hours of June 21, 1990, petitioner and several other teenagers allegedly assembled a crudely made cross by taping together broken chair legs. They then allegedly burned the cross inside the fenced yard of a black family that lived across the street from the house where petitioner was staying. Although this conduct could have been punished under any of a number of laws, one of the two provisions under which respondent city of St. Paul chose to charge petitioner (then a juvenile) was the St. Paul Bias Motivated Crime Ordinance, which provides:

> "Whoever places on public or private property a symbol, object, appellation, characterization or graffiti, including, but not limited to, a burning cross or Nazi swastika, which one knows or has reasonable grounds to know arouses anger, alarm or resentment in others on the basis of race, color, creed, religion or gender commits disorderly conduct and shall be guilty of a misdemeanor."

Petitioner moved to dismiss this count on the ground that the St. Paul ordinance was substantially overbroad and impermissibly content based and therefore facially invalid under the First Amendment. The trial court granted this motion, but the Minnesota Supreme Court reversed.... We granted certiorari.

. . . Accordingly, we accept the Minnesota Supreme Court's authoritative statement that the ordinance reaches only those expressions that constitute "fighting words" within the meaning of *Chaplinsky*. . . . Assuming, *arguendo*, that all of the expression reached by the ordinance is proscribable under the "fighting words" doctrine, we nonetheless conclude that the ordinance is facially unconstitutional in that it prohibits otherwise permitted speech solely on the basis of the subjects the speech addresses.

The First Amendment generally prevents government from proscribing speech, see, *e.g.*, *Cantwell v. Connecticut*, or even expressive conduct, see, *e.g.*, *Texas v. Johnson*, because of disapproval of the ideas expressed. Content based regulations are presumptively invalid. . . .

It is not true that "fighting words" have at most a "*de minimis*" expressive content, *ibid.*, or that their content is *in all respects* "worthless and undeserving of constitutional protection," . . . ; sometimes they are quite expressive indeed. We have not said that they constitute "*no* part of the expression of ideas," but only that they constitute "no *essential* part of any exposition of ideas." *Chaplinsky*, (emphasis added).

. . . In other words, the exclusion of "fighting words" from the scope of the First Amendment simply means that, for purposes of that Amendment, the unprotected features of the words are, despite their verbal character, essentially a "nonspeech" element of communication. Fighting words are thus analogous to a noisy sound truck: Each is, as Justice Frankfurter recognized, a "mode of speech," *Niemotko v. Maryland*, (Frankfurter, J., concurring in result); both can be used to convey an idea; but neither has, in and of itself, a claim upon the First Amendment. As with the sound truck, however, so also with fighting words: The government may not regulate use based on hostility—or favoritism—towards the underlying message expressed. . . .

Applying these principles to the St. Paul ordinance, we conclude that, even as narrowly construed by the Minnesota Supreme Court, the ordinance is facially unconstitutional. Although the phrase in the ordinance, "arouses anger, alarm or resentment in others," has been limited by the Minnesota Supreme Court's construction to reach only those symbols or displays that amount to "fighting words," the remaining, unmodified terms make clear that the ordinance applies only to "fighting words" that insult, or provoke violence, "on the basis of race, color, creed, religion or gender." . . .

In its practical operation, moreover, the ordinance goes even beyond mere content discrimination, to actual viewpoint discrimination. Displays containing some words—odious racial epithets, for example—would be prohibited to proponents of all views. But "fighting words" that do not themselves invoke race, color, creed, religion, or gender—aspersions upon a person's mother, for example—would seemingly be usable *ad libitum* in the placards of those arguing *in favor* of racial, color, etc. tolerance and equality, but could not be used by that speaker's opponents. . . .

What we have here, it must be emphasized, is not a prohibition of fighting words that are directed at certain persons or groups (which would be *facially* valid if it met the requirements of the Equal Protection Clause); but rather, a prohibition of fighting words that contain (as the Minnesota Supreme Court repeatedly emphasized) messages of "bias motivated" hatred and in particular, as applied to this case, messages "based on virulent notions of racial supremacy."

. . . Despite the fact that the Minnesota Supreme Court and St. Paul acknowledge that the ordinance is directed at expression of group hatred, Justice Stevens suggests that this "fundamentally misreads" the ordinance. It is directed, he claims, not to speech of a particular content, but to particular "injur[ies]" that are "qualitatively different" from other injuries. This is word play. What makes the anger, fear, sense of dishonor, etc. produced by violation of this ordinance distinct from the anger, fear, sense of dishonor, etc. produced by other fighting words is nothing other than the fact that it is caused by a distinctive idea, conveyed by a distinctive message. The First Amendment cannot be evaded that easily. . . .

The content based discrimination reflected in the St. Paul ordinance . . . assuredly does not fall within the exception for content discrimination based on the very reasons why the particular class of speech at issue (here, fighting words) is proscribable. As explained earlier, the reason why fighting words are categorically excluded from the protection of the First Amendment is not that their content communicates any particular idea, but that their content embodies a particularly intolerable (and socially unnecessary) *mode* of expressing *whatever* idea the speaker wishes to convey. St. Paul has not singled out an especially offensive mode of expression—it has not, for example, selected for prohibition only those fighting words that communicate ideas in a threatening (as opposed to a merely obnoxious) manner. Rather, it has proscribed fighting words of whatever manner that communicate messages of racial, gender, or religious intolerance. Selectivity of this sort creates the possibility that the city is seeking to handicap the expression of particular ideas. That possibility would alone be enough to render the ordinance presumptively invalid, but St. Paul's comments and concessions in this case elevate the possibility to a certainty. . . .

The dispositive question in this case, therefore, is whether content discrimination is reasonably necessary to achieve St. Paul's compelling interests; it plainly is not. An ordinance not limited to the favored topics, for example, would have precisely the same beneficial effect. In fact the only interest distinctively served by the content limitation is that of displaying the city council's special hostility towards the particular biases thus singled out. That is precisely what the First Amendment forbids. The politicians of St. Paul are entitled to express that hostility—but not through the means of imposing unique limitations upon speakers who (however benightedly) disagree.

Let there be no mistake about our belief that burning a cross in someone's front yard is reprehensible. But St. Paul has sufficient means at its disposal to prevent such behavior without adding the First Amendment to the fire. The judgment of the Minnesota Supreme Court is reversed, and the case is remanded for proceedings not inconsistent with this opinion.

CITY OF ERIE v. PAP'S A.M.

529 U.S. 277 (2000)

Opinion: O'Connor, joined by Rehnquist, Kennedy, Souter, Breyer in Parts I and II and by Rehnquist, Kennedy, Breyer in parts III and IV
Concurrence: Scalia, joined by Thomas
Partial Concurrence, Partial Dissent: Souter
Dissent: Stevens, joined by Ginsburg

In this case, the Supreme Court considered whether a city ordinance banning public nudity violates the First Amendment's protection of freedom of speech. In reading this case, it is important to consider the distinction between speech and conduct. Is it possible to distinguish between conduct that is expressive and conduct that is not? Even speech, at times, has been found by the Court to lack meaningful expressive content and therefore to be undeserving of constitutional protection. How should the Court determine an appropriate test for discriminating between those acts which deserve protection and those that do not?

JUSTICE O'CONNOR *announced the judgment of the Court and delivered the opinion of the Court with respect to Parts I and II, and an opinion with respect to Parts III and IV, in which* **THE CHIEF JUSTICE, JUSTICE KENNEDY,** *and* **JUSTICE BREYER** *join.*

The city of Erie, Pennsylvania, enacted an ordinance banning public nudity. Respondent Pap's A.M. (hereinafter Pap's), which operated a nude dancing establishment in Erie, challenged the constitutionality of the ordinance and sought a permanent injunction against its enforcement. The Pennsylvania Supreme Court, although noting that this Court in *Barnes v. Glen Theatre, Inc.*, had upheld an Indiana ordinance that was "strikingly similar" to Erie's, found that the public nudity sections of the ordinance violated respondent's right to freedom of expression under the United States Constitution. This case raises the question whether the Pennsylvania Supreme Court properly evaluated the ordinance's constitutionality under the First Amendment. We hold that Erie's ordinance is a content-neutral regulation that satisfies the four-part test of *United States v. O'Brien*. Accordingly, we reverse the decision of the Pennsylvania Supreme Court and remand for the consideration of any remaining issues.

I

On September 28, 1994, the city council for the city of Erie, Pennsylvania, enacted Ordinance 75-1994, a public indecency ordinance that makes it a summary offense to knowingly or intentionally appear in public in a "state of nudity." Respondent Pap's, a Pennsylvania corporation, operated an establishment in Erie known as "Kandyland" that featured totally nude erotic dancing performed by women. To comply with the ordinance, these dancers must wear, at a minimum, "pasties" and a "G-string."

III

Being "in a state of nudity" is not an inherently expressive condition. As we explained in *Barnes*, however, nude dancing of the type at issue here is expressive conduct, although we think that it falls only within the outer ambit of the First Amendment's protection. See *Barnes v. Glen Theatre, Inc.*; *Schad v. Mount Ephraim*.

To determine what level of scrutiny applies to the ordinance at issue here, we must decide "whether the State's regulation is related to the suppression of expression." *Texas v. Johnson*; see also *United States v. O'Brien*. If the governmental purpose in enacting the regulation is unrelated to the suppression of expression, then the regulation need only satisfy the "less stringent" standard from *O'Brien* for evaluating restrictions on symbolic speech. *Texas v.*

Johnson; *United States v. O'Brien*. If the government interest is related to the content of the expression, however, then the regulation falls outside the scope of the *O'Brien* test and must be justified under a more demanding standard. *Texas v. Johnson*.

In *Barnes*, we analyzed an almost identical statute, holding that Indiana's public nudity ban did not violate the First Amendment, although no five Members of the Court agreed on a single rationale for that conclusion. We now clarify that government restrictions on public nudity such as the ordinance at issue here should be evaluated under the framework set forth in *O'Brien* for content-neutral restrictions on symbolic speech.

The ordinance here, like the statute in *Barnes*, is on its face a general prohibition on public nudity. By its terms, the ordinance regulates conduct alone. It does not target nudity that contains an erotic message; rather, it bans all public nudity, regardless of whether that nudity is accompanied by expressive activity. And like the statute in *Barnes*, the Erie ordinance replaces and updates provisions of an "Indecency and Immorality" ordinance that has been on the books since 1866, predating the prevalence of nude dancing establishments such as Kandyland....

Justice Stevens argues that the ordinance enacts a complete ban on expression. We respectfully disagree with that characterization. The public nudity ban certainly has the effect of limiting one particular means of expressing the kind of erotic message being disseminated at Kandyland. But simply to define what is being banned as the "message" is to assume the conclusion. We did not analyze the regulation in *O'Brien* as having enacted a total ban on expression. Instead, the Court recognized that the regulation against destroying one's draft card was justified by the Government's interest in preventing the harmful "secondary effects" of that conduct (disruption to the Selective Service System), even though that regulation may have some incidental effect on the expressive element of the conduct. Because this justification was unrelated to the suppression of O'Brien's antiwar message, the regulation was content neutral. Although there may be cases in which banning the means of expression so interferes with the message that it essentially bans the message, that is not the case here.

Similarly, even if Erie's public nudity ban has some minimal effect on the erotic message by muting that portion of the expression that occurs when the last stitch is dropped, the dancers at Kandyland and other such establishments are free to perform wearing pasties and G-strings. Any effect on the overall expression is *de minimis*.

This case is, in fact, similar to *O'Brien*, *Community for Creative Non-Violence*, and *Ward*. The justification for the government regulation in each case prevents harmful "secondary" effects that are unrelated to the suppression of expression. While the doctrinal theories behind "incidental burdens" and "secondary effects" are, of course, not identical, there is nothing objectionable about a city passing a general ordinance to ban public nudity (even though such a ban may place incidental burdens on some protected speech) and at the same time recognizing that one specific occurrence of public nudity—nude erotic dancing—is particularly problematic because it produces harmful secondary effects.

We conclude that Erie's asserted interest in combating the negative secondary effects associated with adult entertainment establishments like Kandyland is unrelated to the suppression of the erotic message conveyed by nude dancing. The ordinance prohibiting public nudity is therefore valid if it satisfies the four-factor

test from *O'Brien* for evaluating restrictions on symbolic speech.

IV

Applying that standard here, we conclude that Erie's ordinance is justified under *O'Brien*. The first factor of the *O'Brien* test is whether the government regulation is within the constitutional power of the government to enact. Here, Erie's efforts to protect public health and safety are clearly within the city's police powers. The second factor is whether the regulation furthers an important or substantial government interest. The asserted interests of regulating conduct through a public nudity ban and of combating the harmful secondary effects associated with nude dancing are undeniably important. And in terms of demonstrating that such secondary effects pose a threat, the city need not "conduct new studies or produce evidence independent of that already generated by other cities" to demonstrate the problem of secondary effects, "so long as whatever evidence the city relies upon is reasonably believed to be relevant to the problem that the city addresses." *Renton v. Playtime Theatres, Inc.* Because the nude dancing at Kandyland is of the same character as the adult entertainment at issue in *Renton*, *Young v. American Mini Theatres, Inc.* and *California v. LaRue*, it was reasonable for Erie to conclude that such nude dancing was likely to produce the same secondary effects. . . .

In any event, Erie also relied on its own findings. The preamble to the ordinance states that "the Council of the City of Erie *has, at various times over more than a century, expressed its findings* that certain lewd, immoral activities carried on in public places for profit are highly detrimental to the public health, safety and welfare, and lead to the debasement of both women and men, promote violence, public intoxication, prostitution and other serious criminal activity." The city council members, familiar with commercial downtown Erie, are the individuals who would likely have had first-hand knowledge of what took place at and around nude dancing establishments in Erie, and can make particularized, expert judgments about the resulting harmful secondary effects. . . . Here, Kandyland has had ample opportunity to contest the council's findings about secondary effects—before the council itself, throughout the state proceedings, and before this Court. Yet to this day, Kandyland has never challenged the city council's findings or cast any specific doubt on the validity of those findings. Instead, it has simply asserted that the council's evidentiary proof was lacking. In the absence of any reason to doubt it, the city's expert judgment should be credited. And the study relied on by *amicus curiae* does not cast any legitimate doubt on the Erie city council's judgment about Erie.

Finally, it is worth repeating that Erie's ordinance is on its face a content neutral restriction that regulates conduct, not First Amendment expression. And the government should have sufficient leeway to justify such a law based on secondary effects. As we have said, so long as the regulation is unrelated to the suppression of expression, "the government generally has a freer hand in restricting expressive conduct than it has in restricting the written or spoken word." *Texas v. Johnson.*

The ordinance also satisfies *O'Brien's* third factor, that the government interest is unrelated to the suppression of free expression. The fourth and final *O'Brien* factor—that the restriction is no greater than is essential to the furtherance of the government interest—is satisfied as well. The ordinance regulates conduct, and any incidental impact on the expressive element of nude dancing is *de minimis*. The

requirement that dancers wear pasties and G-strings is a minimal restriction in furtherance of the asserted government interests, and the restriction leaves ample capacity to convey the dancer's erotic message. Justice Souter points out that zoning is an alternative means of addressing this problem. It is far from clear, however, that zoning imposes less of a burden on expression than the minimal requirement implemented here. In any event, since this is a content-neutral restriction, least restrictive means analysis is not required. See *Ward.*

We hold, therefore, that Erie's ordinance is a content-neutral regulation that is valid under *O'Brien*. Accordingly, the judgment of the Pennsylvania Supreme Court is reversed, and the case is remanded for further proceedings not inconsistent with this opinion.

JUSTICE SCALIA, *with whom* **JUSTICE THOMAS** *joins, concurring in the judgment.*

I would dismiss this case for want of jurisdiction. Because the Court resolves the threshold mootness question differently and proceeds to address the merits, I will do so briefly as well. I agree that the decision of the Pennsylvania Supreme Court must be reversed, but disagree with the mode of analysis the Court has applied.

The city of Erie self-consciously modeled its ordinance on the public nudity statute we upheld against constitutional challenge in *Barnes v. Glen Theatre, Inc.,* calculating (one would have supposed reasonably) that the courts of Pennsylvania would consider themselves bound by our judgment on a question of federal constitutional law. In *Barnes*, I voted to uphold the challenged Indiana statute "not because it survives some lower level of First Amendment scrutiny, but because, as a general law regulating conduct and not specifically directed at expression, it is not subject to First Amendment scrutiny at all." Erie's ordinance, too, by its terms prohibits not merely nude dancing, but the act—irrespective of whether it is engaged in for expressive purposes—of going nude in public. The facts that a preamble to the ordinance explains that its purpose, in part, is to "limit a recent increase in nude live entertainment," that city council members in supporting the ordinance commented to that effect, and that the ordinance includes in the definition of nudity the exposure of devices simulating that condition, neither make the law any less general in its reach nor demonstrate that what the municipal authorities *really* find objectionable is expression rather than public nakedness.

There is no basis for the contention that the ordinance does not apply to nudity in theatrical productions such as *Equus* or *Hair*. Its text contains no such limitation. It was stipulated in the trial court that no effort was made to enforce the ordinance against a production of *Equus* involving nudity that was being staged in Erie at the time the ordinance became effective. One instance of nonenforcement—against a play already in production that prosecutorial discretion might reasonably have "grandfathered"—does not render this ordinance discriminatory on its face.

Moreover, even were I to conclude that the city of Erie had specifically singled out the activity of nude dancing, I still would not find that this regulation violated the First Amendment unless I could be persuaded (as on this record I cannot) that it was the communicative character of nude dancing that prompted the ban. When conduct other than speech itself is regulated, it is my view that the First Amendment is violated only "where the government prohibits conduct precisely because of its communicative attributes." *Barnes*. Here, even if one hypothesizes that the city's object was

to suppress only nude dancing, that would not establish an intent to suppress what (if anything) nude dancing communicates. The traditional power of government to foster good morals (*bonos mores*), and the acceptability of the traditional judgment (if Erie wishes to endorse it) that nude public dancing *itself* is immoral, have not been repealed by the First Amendment.

JUSTICE STEVENS, *with whom* **JUSTICE GINSBURG** *joins, dissenting.*

Far more important than the question whether nude dancing is entitled to the protection of the First Amendment are the dramatic changes in legal doctrine that the Court endorses today. Until now, the "secondary effects" of commercial enterprises featuring indecent entertainment have justified only the regulation of their location. For the first time, the Court has now held that such effects may justify the total suppression of protected speech. Indeed, the plurality opinion concludes that admittedly trivial advancements of a State's interests may provide the basis for censorship. The Court's commendable attempt to replace the fractured decision in *Barnes v. Glen Theatre, Inc.*, with a single coherent rationale is strikingly unsuccessful; it is supported neither by precedent nor by persuasive reasoning.

I

As the preamble to Ordinance No. 75-1994 candidly acknowledges, the council of the city of Erie enacted the restriction at issue "for the purpose of limiting a recent increase in nude live entertainment within the City." Prior to the enactment of the ordinance, the dancers at Kandyland performed in the nude. As the Court recognizes, after its enactment they can perform precisely the same dances if they wear "pasties and G-strings." In both instances, the erotic messages conveyed by the dancers to a willing audience are a form of expression protected by the First Amendment. Despite the similarity between the messages conveyed by the two forms of dance, they are not identical.

If we accept Chief Judge Posner's evaluation of this art form, see *Miller v. South Bend*, the difference between the two messages is significant. The plurality assumes, however, that the difference in the content of the message resulting from the mandated costume change is "*de minimis*." Although I suspect that the patrons of Kandyland are more likely to share Chief Judge Posner's view than the plurality's, for present purposes I shall accept the assumption that the difference in the message is small. The crucial point to remember, however, is that whether one views the difference as large or small, nude dancing still receives First Amendment protection, even if that protection lies only in the "outer ambit" of that Amendment. Erie's ordinance, therefore, burdens a message protected by the First Amendment. If one assumes that the same erotic message is conveyed by nude dancers as by those wearing miniscule costumes, one means of expressing that message is banned; if one assumes that the messages are different, one of those messages is banned. In either event, the ordinance is a total ban.

The Court relies on the so-called "secondary effects" test to defend the ordinance. The present use of that rationale, however, finds no support whatsoever in our precedents. Never before have we approved the use of that doctrine to justify a total ban on protected First Amendment expression. On the contrary, we have been quite clear that the doctrine would not support that end.

The reason we have limited our secondary effects cases to zoning and declined to extend their reasoning to total bans is clear and straightforward: A dispersal that simply limits the places where speech may occur is a minimal imposition whereas a total ban is the most exacting of restrictions. The State's interest in fighting presumed secondary effects is sufficiently strong to justify the former, but far too weak to support the latter, more severe burden. Yet it is perfectly clear that in the present case—to use Justice Powell's metaphor in *American Mini Theatres*—the city of Erie has totally silenced a message the dancers at Kandyland want to convey. The fact that this censorship may have a laudable ulterior purpose cannot mean that censorship is not censorship.

The Court's use of the secondary effects rationale to permit a total ban has grave implications for basic free speech principles. Ordinarily, laws regulating the primary effects of speech, *i.e.,* the intended persuasive effects caused by the speech, are presumptively invalid. Under today's opinion, a State may totally ban speech based on its secondary effects—which are defined as those effects that "happen to be associated" with speech, *Boos v. Barry*—yet the regulation is not presumptively invalid. Because the category of effects that "happen to be associated" with speech includes the narrower subset of effects caused by speech, today's holding has the effect of swallowing whole a most fundamental principle of First Amendment jurisprudence.

II

The Court's mishandling of our secondary effects cases is not limited to its approval of a total ban. It compounds that error by dramatically reducing the degree to which the State's interest must be furthered by the restriction imposed on speech, and by ignoring the critical difference between secondary effects caused by speech and the incidental effects on speech that may be caused by a regulation of conduct.

In what can most delicately be characterized as an enormous understatement, the plurality concedes that "requiring dancers to wear pasties and G-strings may not greatly reduce these secondary effects." To believe that the mandatory addition of pasties and a G-string will have *any* kind of noticeable impact on secondary effects requires nothing short of a titanic surrender to the implausible. Nevertheless, the plurality concludes that the "less stringent" test announced in *United States v. O'Brien*, "requires only that the regulation further the interest in combating such effects." It is one thing to say, however, that *O'Brien* is more lenient than the "more demanding standard" we have imposed in cases such as *Texas v. Johnson*. It is quite another to say that the test can be satisfied by nothing more than the mere possibility of *de minimis* effects on the neighborhood.

The Court is also mistaken in equating our secondary effects cases with the "incidental burdens" doctrine applied in cases such as *O'Brien*; and it aggravates the error by invoking the latter line of cases to support its assertion that Erie's ordinance is unrelated to speech. The incidental burdens doctrine applies when "'speech' and 'nonspeech' elements are combined in the same course of conduct," and the government's interest in regulating the latter justifies incidental burdens on the former. *O'Brien*. Secondary effects, on the other hand, are indirect consequences of protected speech and may justify regulation of the places where that speech may occur. When a State enacts a regulation, it might focus on the secondary effects of speech as its aim, or it might concentrate on nonspeech related concerns, having no thoughts at all with respect to how its regulation will affect speech—and only later, when the regulation is found to burden speech, justify the imposition as an unintended incidental consequence. But those interests are not the same, and the Court cannot ignore their differences and insist that both aims are equally unrelated to speech simply because Erie might have "recognized" that it could possibly have had either aim in mind. One can think of an apple and an orange at the same time; that does not turn them into the same fruit.

Correct analysis of the issue in this case should begin with the proposition that nude dancing is a species of expressive conduct that is protected by the First Amendment. Indeed, both the text of the ordinance and the reasoning in the Court's opinion make it pellucidly clear that the city of Erie has prohibited nude dancing "*precisely because of its communicative attributes.*" *Barnes* (Scalia, J., concurring in judgment).

III

The censorial purpose of Erie's ordinance precludes reliance on the judgment in *Barnes* as sufficient support for the Court's holding today. Several differences between the Erie ordinance and the statute at issue in *Barnes* belie the Court's assertion that the two laws are "almost identical."

As its preamble forthrightly admits, the ordinance's "purpose" is to "limit" a protected form of speech; its invocation of *Barnes* cannot obliterate that professed aim.

Erie's ordinance differs from the statute in *Barnes* in another respect. In *Barnes*, the Court expressly observed that the Indiana statute had not been given a limiting construction by the Indiana Supreme Court. As presented to this Court, there was nothing about the law itself that would confine its application to nude dancing in adult entertainment establishments. Erie's ordinance, however, comes to us in a much different posture. Indeed, as *stipulated* in the record, the city permitted a production of *Equus* to proceed without prosecution, even after the ordinance was in effect, and despite its awareness of the nudity involved in the production. Even if, in light of its broad applicability, the statute in *Barnes* was not aimed at a particular form of speech, Erie's ordinance is quite different. As presented to us, the ordinance is deliberately targeted at Kandyland's type of nude dancing (to the exclusion of plays like *Equus*), in terms of both its applicable scope and the city's enforcement.

It is clear beyond a shadow of a doubt that the Erie ordinance was a response to a more specific concern than nudity in general, namely, nude dancing of the sort found in Kandyland. Given that the Court has not even tried to defend the ordinance's total ban on the ground that its censorship of protected speech might be justified by an overriding state interest, it should conclude that the ordinance is patently invalid. For these reasons, as well as the reasons set forth in Justice White's dissent in *Barnes,* I respectfully dissent.

JUSTICE SOUTER, *concurring in part and dissenting in part.*

I join Parts I and II of the Court's opinion and agree with the analytical approach that the plurality employs in deciding this case. Erie's stated interest in combating the secondary effects associated with nude dancing establishments is an interest unrelated to the suppression of expression under *United States v. O'Brien*, and the city's regulation is thus properly considered under the *O'Brien* standards. I do not believe, however, that the current record allows us to say that the city has made a sufficient evidentiary showing to sustain its regulation, and I would therefore vacate the decision of the Pennsylvania Supreme Court and remand the case for further proceedings.

I

In several recent cases, we have confronted the need for factual justifications to satisfy intermediate scrutiny under the First Amendment. Those cases do not identify with any specificity a particular quantum of evidence, nor do I seek to do so in this brief concurrence. What the cases do make plain, however, is that application of an intermediate scrutiny test to a government's asserted rationale for regulation of expressive activity demands some factual justification to connect that rationale with the regulation in issue.

By these standards, the record before us today is deficient in its failure to reveal any evidence on which Erie may have relied, either for the seriousness of the threatened harm or for the efficacy of its chosen remedy. The plurality does the best it can with the materials to hand, but the pickings are slim. The city council's closest approach to an evidentiary record on secondary effects and their causes was the statement of one councilor, during the debate over the ordinance, who spoke of increases in sex crimes in a way that might be construed as a reference to secondary effects. Nor does the invocation of *Barnes v. Glen Theatre, Inc.* in one paragraph of the preamble to Erie's ordinance suffice. The plurality opinion in *Barnes* made no mention of evidentiary showings at all, and though my separate opinion did make a pass at the issue, I did not demand reliance on germane evidentiary demonstrations, whether specific to the statute in question or developed elsewhere. To invoke *Barnes*, therefore, does not indicate that the issue of evidence has been addressed.

There is one point, however, on which an evidentiary record is not quite so hard to find, but it hurts, not helps, the city. The final *O'Brien* requirement is that the incidental speech restriction be shown to be no greater than essential to achieve the government's legitimate purpose. To deal with this issue, we have to ask what basis there is to think that the city would be unsuccessful in countering any secondary effects by the significantly lesser restriction of zoning to control the location of nude dancing, thus allowing for efficient law enforcement, restricting effects on property values, and limiting exposure of the public. The record shows that for 23 years there has been a zoning ordinance on the books to regulate the location of establishments like Kandyland, but the city has not enforced it. . . . Even on the plurality's view of the evidentiary burden, this hurdle to the application of *O'Brien* requires an evidentiary response.

II

The record before us now does not permit the conclusion that Erie's ordinance is reasonably designed to mitigate real harms. This does not mean that the required showing cannot be made, only that, on this record, Erie has not made it. I would remand to give it the opportunity to do so. Accordingly, although I join with the plurality in adopting the *O'Brien* test, I respectfully dissent from the Court's disposition of the case.

VIRGINIA v. BLACK

538 U.S. 343 (2003)

Opinion: O'Connor, joined by Rehnquist, Stevens, Scalia, Breyer in Parts I, II, and III and by Rehnquist, Stevens, Breyer in Parts IV and V
Concurrence: Stevens
Partial Concurrence, Partial Dissent: Scalia, joined by Thomas in Parts I and II
Partial Concurrence, Partial Dissent: Souter, joined by Kennedy, Ginsburg
Dissent: Thomas

So far in this section we have examined the question of whether or not obscenity is a category protected by the First Amendment. We now move from the question of obscenity to that of hateful expression. Cross burning has a long history in the United States of being associated with the Ku Klux Klan's violent hostility to equality for African Americans. Indeed, the Court points out in this case that a founding ambition of the Klan was to oppose the Fourteenth Amendment's guarantee of equal protection. One worry, however, about bans on cross burning is that they infringe on political viewpoints. Do concerns about the right to the expression of any viewpoint, even a hateful one, apply in this case? As you read, consider the distinction the Court draws between crosses burned at a rally of the Ku Klux Klan and a cross burned on a lawn directed at a particular individual.

JUSTICE O'CONNOR *delivered the opinion of the Court.*

In this case we consider whether the Commonwealth of Virginia's statute banning cross burning with "an intent to intimidate a person or group of persons" violates the First Amendment. Va. Code Ann. §18.2-423 (1996). We conclude that while a State, consistent with the First Amendment, may ban cross burning carried out with the intent to intimidate, the provision in the Virginia statute treating any cross burning as prima facie evidence of intent to intimidate renders the statute unconstitutional in its current form.

I

Respondents Barry Black, Richard Elliott, and Jonathan O'Mara were convicted separately of violating Virginia's cross-burning statute, §18.2-423. That statute provides:

> "It shall be unlawful for any person or persons, with the intent of intimidating any person or group of persons, to burn, or cause to be burned, a cross on the property of another, a highway or other public place. Any person who shall violate any provision of this section shall be guilty of a Class 6 felony.
>
> "Any such burning of a cross shall be prima facie evidence of an intent to intimidate a person or group of persons."

On August 22, 1998, Barry Black led a Ku Klux Klan rally in Carroll County, Virginia. Twenty-five to thirty people attended this gathering, which occurred on private property with the permission of the owner, who was in attendance. The property was located on an open field just off Brushy Fork Road (State Highway 690) in Cana, Virginia.

When the sheriff of Carroll County learned that a Klan rally was occurring in his county, he went to observe it from the side of the road. During the approximately one hour that the sheriff was present, about 40 to 50 cars passed the site, a "few" of which stopped to ask the sheriff what was happening on the property. App. 71. Eight to ten houses were located in the vicinity of the rally. Rebecca Sechrist, who was related to the owner of the property where the rally took place, "sat and watched to see wha[t] [was] going on" from the lawn of her in-laws' house. She looked on as the Klan prepared for the gathering and subsequently conducted the rally itself. *Id.*, at 103.

During the rally, Sechrist heard Klan members speak about "what they were" and "what they believed in." *Id.*, at 106. The speakers "talked real bad about the blacks and the Mexicans." *Id.*, at 109. One speaker told the assembled gathering that "he would love to take a .30/.30 and just random[ly] shoot the blacks." *Ibid.* The speakers also talked about "President Clinton and Hillary Clinton," and about how their tax money "goes to . . . the black people." *Ibid.* Sechrist testified that this language made her "very . . . scared." *Id.*, at 110.

At the conclusion of the rally, the crowd circled around a 25- to 30-foot cross. The cross was between 300 and 350 yards away from the road. According to the sheriff, the cross "then all of a sudden . . . went up in a flame." *Id.*, at 71. As the cross burned, the Klan played "Amazing Grace" over the loudspeakers. Sechrist stated that the cross burning made her feel "awful" and "terrible." *Id.*, at 110.

When the sheriff observed the cross burning, he informed his deputy that they needed to "find out who's responsible and explain to them that they cannot do this in the State of Virginia." *Id.*, at 72. The sheriff then went down the driveway, entered the rally, and asked "who was responsible for burning the cross." *Id.*, at 74. Black responded, "I guess I am because I'm the head of the rally." *Ibid.* The sheriff then told Black, "[T]here's a law in the State of Virginia that you cannot burn a cross and I'll have to place you under arrest for this." *Ibid.*

Black was charged with burning a cross with the intent of intimidating a person or group of persons, in violation of §18.2423. At his trial, the jury was instructed that "intent to intimidate means the motivation to intentionally put a person or a group of persons in fear of bodily harm. Such fear must arise from the willful conduct of the accused rather than from some mere temperamental timidity of the victim." *Id.*, at 146. The trial court also instructed the jury that "the burning of a cross by itself is sufficient evidence from which you may infer the required intent." *Ibid.* When Black objected to this last instruction on First Amendment grounds, the prosecutor responded that the instruction was "taken straight out of the [Virginia] Model Instructions." *Id.,* at 134. The jury found Black guilty, and fined him $2,500. The Court of Appeals of Virginia affirmed Black's conviction. Rec. No. 1581993 (Va. App., Dec. 19, 2000), App. 201.

On May 2, 1998, respondents Richard Elliott and Jonathan O'Mara, as well as a third individual, attempted to burn a cross on the yard of James Jubilee. Jubilee, an African American, was Elliott's next-door neighbor in Virginia Beach, Virginia. Four months prior to the incident, Jubilee and his family had moved from California to Virginia Beach. Before the cross burning, Jubilee spoke to Elliott's mother to inquire about shots being fired from behind the Elliott home. Elliott's mother explained to Jubilee that her son shot firearms as a hobby, and that he used the backyard as a firing range.

On the night of May 2, respondents drove a truck onto Jubilee's property, planted a cross, and set it on fire. Their apparent motive was to "get back" at Jubilee for complaining about the shooting in the backyard. *Id.,* at 241. Respondents were not affiliated with the Klan. The next morning, as Jubilee was pulling his car out of the driveway, he noticed the partially burned cross approximately 20 feet from his house. After seeing the cross, Jubilee was "very nervous" because he "didn't know what would be the next phase," and because "a cross burned in your yard . . . tells you that it's just the first round." *Id.,* at 231.

Elliott and O'Mara were charged with attempted cross burning and conspiracy to commit cross burning. O'Mara pleaded guilty to both counts, reserving the right to challenge the constitutionality of the cross-burning statute. The judge sentenced O'Mara to 90 days in jail and fined him $2,500. The judge also suspended 45 days of the sentence and $1,000 of the fine.

At Elliott's trial, the judge originally ruled that the jury would be instructed "that the burning of a cross by itself is sufficient evidence from which you may infer the required intent." *Id.,* at 221222. At trial, however, the court instructed the jury that the Commonwealth must prove that "the defendant intended to commit cross burning," that "the defendant did a direct act toward the commission of the cross burning," and that "the defendant had the intent of intimidating any person or group of persons." *Id.,* at 250. The court did not instruct the jury on the meaning of the word "intimidate," nor on the prima facie evidence provision of §18.2423. The jury found Elliott guilty of attempted cross burning and acquitted him of conspiracy to commit cross burning. It sentenced Elliott to 90 days in jail and a $2,500 fine. The Court of Appeals of Virginia affirmed the convictions of both Elliott and O'Mara. *O'Mara v. Commonwealth.*

Each respondent appealed to the Supreme Court of Virginia, arguing that §18.2-423 is facially unconstitutional. The Supreme Court of Virginia consolidated all three cases, and held that the statute is unconstitutional on its face. 262 Va. 764, 553 S.E.2d 738 (2001). It held that the Virginia cross-burning statute "is analytically indistinguishable from the ordinance found unconstitutional in *R.A.V.* [*v. St. Paul*]." *Id.,* at 772, 553 S.E.2d, at 742. The Virginia statute, the court held, discriminates on the basis of content since it "selectively chooses only cross burning because of its distinctive message." *Id.,* at 774, 553 S.E.2d, at 744. The court also held that the prima facie evidence provision renders the statute overbroad because "[t]he enhanced probability of prosecution under the statute chills the expression of protected speech." *Id.*, at 777, 553 S.E.2d, at 746.

Three justices dissented, concluding that the Virginia cross-burning statute passes constitutional muster because it proscribes only conduct that constitutes a true threat. The justices noted that unlike the ordinance found unconstitutional in *R.A.V. v. St. Paul*, the Virginia statute does not just target cross burning "on the basis of race, color, creed, religion or gender." 262 Va., at 791, 553 S.E.2d, at 791. Rather, "the Virginia statute applies to any individual who burns a cross for any reason provided the cross is burned with the intent to intimidate." *Ibid.* The dissenters also disagreed with the majority's analysis of the prima facie provision because the inference alone "is clearly insufficient to establish beyond a reasonable doubt that a defendant burned a cross with the intent to intimidate." *Id.*, at 795, 553 S.E.2d, at 756. The dissent noted that the burden of proof still remains on the Commonwealth to prove intent to intimidate. We granted certiorari. 535 U.S. 1094 (2002).

. . . The First Amendment, applicable to the States through the Fourteenth Amendment, provides that "Congress shall make no law . . . abridging the freedom of speech." The hallmark of the protection of free speech is to allow "free trade in ideas"—even ideas that the overwhelming majority of people might find distasteful or discomforting. *Abrams v. United States* (Holmes, J., dissenting); see also *Texas v. Johnson*. . . .

The protections afforded by the First Amendment, however, are not absolute, and we have long recognized that the government may regulate certain categories of expression consistent with the Constitution. . . .

Thus, for example, a State may punish those words "which by their very utterance inflict injury or tend to incite an immediate breach of the peace." *Chaplinsky v. New Hampshire*; see also *R.A.V. v. City of St. Paul*. We have consequently held that fighting words—"those personally abusive epithets which, when addressed to the ordinary citizen, are, as a matter of common knowledge, inherently likely to provoke violent reaction"—are generally proscribable under the First Amendment. . . .

"True threats" encompass those statements where the speaker means to communicate a serious expression of an intent to commit an act of unlawful violence to a particular individual or group of individuals. . . . As noted in Part II, supra, the history of cross burning in this country shows that cross burning is often intimidating, intended to create a pervasive fear in victims that they are a target of violence.

B

The Supreme Court of Virginia ruled that in light of *R.A.V. v. City of St. Paul*, even if it is constitutional to ban cross burning in a content-neutral manner, the Virginia cross-burning statute is unconstitutional because it discriminates on the basis of content and viewpoint. It is true, as the Supreme Court of Virginia held, that the burning of a cross is symbolic expression. The reason why the Klan burns a cross at its rallies, or individuals place a burning cross on someone else's lawn, is that the burning cross represents the message that the speaker wishes to communicate. Individuals burn crosses as opposed to other means of communication because cross burning carries a message in an effective and dramatic manner. . . .

We did not hold in *R.A.V.* that the First Amendment prohibits all forms of content-based discrimination within a proscribable area of speech. Rather, we specifically stated that some types of content discrimination did not violate the First Amendment:

"When the basis for the content discrimination consists entirely of the very reason the entire class of speech at issue is proscribable, no significant danger of idea or viewpoint discrimination exists. Such a reason, having been adjudged neutral enough to support exclusion of the entire class of speech from First Amendment protection, is also neutral enough to form the basis of distinction within the class." . . .

The First Amendment permits Virginia to outlaw cross burnings done with the intent to intimidate because burning a cross is a particularly virulent form of intimidation. Instead of prohibiting all intimidating messages, Virginia may choose to regulate this subset of intimidating messages in light of cross-burning's long and pernicious history as a signal of impending violence. Thus, just as a State may regulate only that obscenity which is the most obscene due to its prurient content, so too may a State choose to prohibit only those forms of intimidation that are most likely to inspire fear of bodily harm. A ban on cross burning carried out with the intent to intimidate is fully consistent with our holding in *R.A.V.* and is proscribable under the First Amendment.

IV

The Supreme Court of Virginia ruled in the alternative that Virginia's cross-burning statute was unconstitutionally overbroad due to its provision stating that "[a]ny such burning of a cross shall be prima facie evidence of an intent to intimidate a person or group of persons." The Commonwealth added the prima facie provision to the statute in 1968. The court below did not reach whether this provision is severable from the rest of the cross-burning statute under Virginia law. In this Court, as in the Supreme Court of Virginia, respondents do not argue that the prima facie evidence provision is unconstitutional as applied

to any one of them. Rather, they contend that the provision is unconstitutional on its face.

The Supreme Court of Virginia has not ruled on the meaning of the prima facie evidence provision. It has, however, stated that "the act of burning a cross alone, with no evidence of intent to intimidate, will nonetheless suffice for arrest and prosecution and will insulate the Commonwealth from a motion to strike the evidence at the end of its case-in-chief." The jury in the case of Richard Elliott did not receive any instruction on the prima facie evidence provision, and the provision was not an issue in the case of Jonathan O'Mara because he pleaded guilty. The court in Barry Black's case, however, instructed the jury that the provision means: "The burning of a cross, by itself, is sufficient evidence from which you may infer the required intent." This jury instruction is the same as the Model Jury Instruction in the Commonwealth of Virginia.

The prima facie evidence provision, as interpreted by the jury instruction, renders the statute unconstitutional. Because this jury instruction is the Model Jury Instruction, and because the Supreme Court of Virginia had the opportunity to expressly disavow the jury instruction, the jury instruction's construction of the prima facie provision "is a ruling on a question of state law that is as binding on us as though the precise words had been written into" the statute. As construed by the jury instruction, the prima facie provision strips away the very reason why a State may ban cross burning with the intent to intimidate. The prima facie evidence provision permits a jury to convict in every cross-burning case in which defendants exercise their constitutional right not to put on a defense. And even where a defendant like Black presents a defense, the prima facie evidence provision makes it more likely that the jury will find an intent to intimidate regardless of the particular facts of the case. The provision permits the Commonwealth to arrest, prosecute, and convict a person based solely on the fact of cross burning itself.

It is apparent that the provision as so interpreted "would create an unacceptable risk of the suppression of ideas." *Secretary of State of Md. v. Joseph H. Munson Co.* The act of burning a cross may mean that a person is engaging in constitutionally proscribable intimidation. But that same act may mean only that the person is engaged in core political speech. The prima facie evidence provision in this statute blurs the line between these two meanings of a burning cross. As interpreted by the jury instruction, the provision chills constitutionally protected political speech because of the possibility that a State will prosecute—and potentially convict—somebody engaging only in lawful political speech at the core of what the First Amendment is designed to protect.

As the history of cross burning indicates, a burning cross is not always intended to intimidate. Rather, sometimes the cross burning is a statement of ideology, a symbol of group solidarity. It is a ritual used at Klan gatherings, and it is used to represent the Klan itself. Thus, "[b]urning a cross at a political rally would almost certainly be protected expression." *R.A.V. v. St. Paul* (White, J., concurring in judgment). Indeed, occasionally a person who burns a cross does not intend to express either a statement of ideology or intimidation. Cross burnings have appeared in movies such as *Mississippi Burning,* and in plays such as the stage adaptation of Sir Walter Scott's *The Lady of the Lake.*

The prima facie provision makes no effort to distinguish among these different types of cross burnings. It does not distinguish between a cross burning done with the purpose of creating anger or resentment and a cross burning done with the purpose of threatening or intimidating a victim. It does not distinguish between a cross burning at a public rally or a cross burning on a neighbor's lawn. It does not treat the cross burning directed at an individual differently from the cross burning directed at a group of like-minded believers. It allows a jury to treat a cross burning on the property of another with the owner's acquiescence in the same manner as a cross burning on the property of another without the owner's permission. To this extent I agree with Justice Souter that the prima facie evidence provision can "skew jury deliberations toward conviction in cases where the evidence of intent to intimidate is relatively weak and arguably consistent with a solely ideological reason for burning."

It may be true that a cross burning, even at a political rally, arouses a sense of anger or hatred among the vast majority of citizens who see a burning cross. But this sense of anger or hatred is not sufficient to ban all cross burnings. As Gerald Gunther has stated, "The lesson I have drawn from my childhood in Nazi Germany and my happier adult life in this country is the need to walk the sometimes difficult path of denouncing the bigot's hateful ideas with all my power, yet at the same time challenging any community's attempt to suppress hateful ideas by force of law." The prima facie evidence provision in this case ignores all of the contextual factors that are necessary to decide whether a particular cross burning is intended to intimidate. The First Amendment does not permit such a shortcut.

For these reasons, the prima facie evidence provision, as interpreted through the jury instruction and as applied in Barry Black's case, is unconstitutional on its face. We recognize that the Supreme Court of Virginia has not authoritatively interpreted the meaning of the prima facie evidence provision. Unlike Justice Scalia, we refuse to speculate on whether any interpretation of the prima facie evidence provision would satisfy the First Amendment. Rather, all we hold is that because of the interpretation of the prima facie evidence provision given by the jury instruction, the provision makes the statute facially invalid at this point. We also recognize the theoretical possibility that the court, on remand, could interpret the provision in a manner different from that so far set forth in order to avoid the constitutional objections we have described. We leave open that possibility. We also leave open the possibility that the provision is severable, and if so, whether Elliott and O'Mara could be retried under §18.2-423.

V

With respect to Barry Black, we agree with the Supreme Court of Virginia that his conviction cannot stand, and we affirm the judgment of the Supreme Court of Virginia. With respect to Elliott and O'Mara, we vacate the judgment of the Supreme Court of Virginia, and remand the case for further proceedings.

JUSTICE THOMAS, *dissenting.*

In every culture, certain things acquire meaning well beyond what outsiders can comprehend. That goes for both the sacred, see *Texas v. Johnson* (Rehnquist, C.J., dissenting), and the profane. I believe that cross burning is the paradigmatic example of the latter.

I

Although I agree with the majority's conclusion that it is constitutionally permissible to "ban . . . cross burning carried out with intent to intimidate," I believe that the majority errs in imputing an expressive component to the activity in question. In my view, whatever expressive value cross burning has, the legislature simply wrote it out by banning only intimidating conduct undertaken by a particular means. A conclusion that the statute prohibiting cross burning with intent to intimidate sweeps beyond a prohibition on certain conduct into the zone of expression overlooks not only the words of the statute but also reality.

A

"In holding [the ban on cross burning with intent to intimidate] unconstitutional, the Court ignores Justice Holmes' familiar aphorism that 'a page of history is worth a volume of logic.' *Texas v. Johnson* (Rehnquist, C. J., dissenting).

> "The world's oldest, most persistent terrorist organization is not European or even Middle Eastern in origin. Fifty years before the Irish Republican Army was organized, a century before Al Fatah declared its holy war on Israel, the Ku Klux Klan was actively harassing, torturing and murdering in the United States. Today . . . its members remain fanatically committed to a course of violent opposition to social progress and racial equality in the United States."

To me, the majority's brief history of the Ku Klux Klan only reinforces this common understanding of the Klan as a terrorist organization, which, in its endeavor to intimidate, or even eliminate those its dislikes, uses the most brutal of methods. . . .

B

. . . Accordingly, this statute prohibits only conduct, not expression. And, just as one cannot burn down someone's house to make a political point and then seek refuge in the First Amendment, those who hate cannot terrorize and intimidate to make their point. In light of my conclusion that the statute here addresses only conduct, there is no need to analyze it under any of our First Amendment tests. . . .

UNITED STATES v. WILLIAMS

553 U.S. 285 (2008)

Opinion: Scalia, joined by Roberts,
   Stevens, Kennedy, Thomas, Breyer,
   Alito
Concurrence: Stevens, joined by Breyer
Dissent: Souter, joined by Ginsburg

This case concerns the extent to which offers to provide or requests to obtain child pornography are entitled to constitutional protection. The Court held that such acts are categorically excluded from the First Amendment protection for the freedom of speech.

JUSTICE SCALIA *delivered the opinion of the Court.*

Section 2252A(a)(3)(B) of Title 18, United States Code, criminalizes, in certain specified circumstances, the pandering or solicitation of child pornography. This case presents the question whether that statute is overbroad under the First Amendment or impermissibly vague under the Due Process Clause of the Fifth Amendment....

B

The following facts appear in the opinion of the Eleventh Circuit. On April 26, 2004, respondent Michael Williams, using a sexually explicit screen name, signed in to a public Internet chat room. A Secret Service agent had also signed in to the chat room under the moniker "Lisa n Miami." The agent noticed that Williams had posted a message that read: "Dad of toddler has 'good' pics of her an [sic] me for swap of your toddler pics, or live cam." The agent struck up a conversation with Williams, leading to an electronic exchange of nonpornographic pictures of children. (The agent's picture

was in fact a doctored photograph of an adult.) Soon thereafter, Williams messaged that he had photographs of men molesting his 4-year-old daughter. Suspicious that "Lisa n Miami" was a law-enforcement agent, before proceeding further Williams demanded that the agent produce additional pictures. When he did not, Williams posted the following public message in the chat room: "HERE ROOM; I CAN PUT UPLINK CUZ IM FOR REAL—SHE CANT." Appended to this declaration was a hyperlink that, when clicked, led to seven pictures of actual children, aged approximately 5 to 15, engaging in sexually explicit conduct and displaying their genitals. The Secret Service then obtained a search warrant for Williams's home, where agents seized two hard drives containing at least 22 images of real children engaged in sexually explicit conduct, some of it sadomasochistic.

Williams was charged with one count of pandering child pornography under §2252A(a)(3)(B) and one count of possessing child pornography under §2252A(a)(5)(B). He pleaded guilty to both counts but reserved the right to challenge the constitutionality of the pandering conviction. The District Court rejected his challenge, and sentenced him to concurrent 60-month sentences on the two counts. The United States Court of Appeals for the Eleventh Circuit reversed the pandering conviction, holding that the statute was both overbroad and impermissibly vague.

II

A

According to our First Amendment overbreadth doctrine, a statute is facially invalid if it prohibits a substantial amount of protected speech. The doctrine seeks to strike a balance between competing social costs. *Virginia v. Hicks*. On the one hand, the threat of enforcement of an overbroad law deters people from engaging in constitutionally protected speech, inhibiting the free exchange of ideas. On the other hand, invalidating a law that in some of its applications is perfectly constitutional—particularly a law directed at conduct so antisocial that it has been made criminal—has obvious harmful effects. In order to maintain an appropriate balance, we have vigorously enforced the requirement that a statute's overbreadth be *substantial*, not only in an absolute sense, but also relative to the statute's plainly legitimate sweep. . . .

. . . Rather than targeting the underlying material, this statute bans the collateral speech that introduces such material into the child-pornography distribution network. Thus, an Internet user who solicits child pornography from an undercover agent violates the statute, even if the officer possesses no child pornography.

The statute's definition of the material or purported material that may not be pandered or solicited precisely tracks the material held constitutionally proscribable in *Ferber* and *Miller*: obscene material depicting (actual or virtual) children engaged in sexually explicit conduct, and any other material depicting actual children engaged in sexually explicit conduct. . . .

B

. . . Offers to engage in illegal transactions are categorically excluded from First Amendment protection. One would think that this principle resolves the present case, since the statute criminalizes only offers to provide or requests to obtain contraband—child obscenity and child pornography involving actual children,

both of which are proscribed, and the proscription of which is constitutional. The Eleventh Circuit, however, believed that the exclusion of First Amendment protection extended only to *commercial* offers to provide or receive contraband:

This mistakes the rationale for the categorical exclusion. It is based not on the less privileged First Amendment status of commercial speech, but on the principle that offers to give or receive what it is unlawful to possess have no social value and thus, like obscenity, enjoy no First Amendment protection. . . . It would be an odd constitutional principle that permitted the government to prohibit offers to sell illegal drugs, but not offers to give them away for free.

To be sure, there remains an important distinction between a proposal to engage in illegal activity and the abstract advocacy of illegality. The Act before us does not prohibit advocacy of child pornography, but only offers to provide or requests to obtain it. There is no doubt that this prohibition falls well within constitutional bounds. . . .

The Eleventh Circuit believed it a constitutional difficulty that no child pornography need exist to trigger the statute. In its view, the fact that the statute could punish a "braggart, exaggerator, or outright liar" rendered it unconstitutional. That seems to us a strange constitutional calculus. Although we have held that the government can ban *both* fraudulent offers, *and* offers to provide illegal products, the Eleventh Circuit would forbid the government from punishing *fraudulent offers to provide illegal products.* We see no logic in that position; if anything, such statements are doubly excluded from the First Amendment. . . .

The Eleventh Circuit found "particularly objectionable" the fact that the "reflects the belief" prong of the statute could ensnare a person who mistakenly believes that material is child pornography. This objection has two conceptually distinct parts. First, the Eleventh Circuit thought that it would be unconstitutional to punish someone for mistakenly distributing virtual child pornography as real child pornography. We disagree. Offers to deal in illegal products or otherwise engage in illegal activity do not acquire First Amendment protection when the offeror is mistaken about the factual predicate of his offer. . . .

Under this heading the Eleventh Circuit also thought that the statute could apply to someone who subjectively believes that an innocuous picture of a child is "lascivious." (Clause (v) of the definition of "sexually explicit conduct" is "lascivious exhibition of the genitals or pubic area of any person.") That is not so. The defendant must believe that the picture contains certain material, and that material in fact (and not merely in his estimation) must meet the statutory definition. Where the material at issue is a harmless picture of a child in a bathtub and the defendant, knowing that material, erroneously believes that it constitutes a "lascivious display of the genitals," the statute has no application.

It was also suggested at oral argument that the statute might cover documentary footage of atrocities being committed in foreign countries, such as soldiers raping young children. Perhaps so, if the material rises to the high level of explicitness that we have held is required. That sort of documentary footage could of course be the subject of an as-applied challenge. The courts presumably would weigh the educational interest in the dissemination of information about the atrocities against the government's interest in preventing the distribution of materials that constitute "a permanent record" of the children's degradation whose dissemination increases "the harm to the child." *Ferber*. Assuming that the constitutional balance would have to be struck in favor of the documentary, the existence of that exception would not establish that the statute is *substantially overbroad*. . . .

Finally, the dissent accuses us of silently overruling our prior decisions in *Ferber* and *Free Speech Coalition*. According to the dissent, Congress has made an end-run around the First Amendment's protection of virtual child pornography by prohibiting proposals to transact in such images rather than prohibiting the images themselves. But an offer to provide or request to receive virtual child pornography is not prohibited by the statute. A crime is committed only when the speaker believes or intends the listener to believe that the subject of the proposed transaction depicts *real* children. It is simply not true that this means "a protected category of expression [will] inevitably be suppressed." Simulated child pornography will be as available as ever, so long as it is offered and sought *as such*, and not as real child pornography. . . .

III

As an alternative ground for facial invalidation, the Eleventh Circuit held that §2252A(a)(3)(B) is void for vagueness. Vagueness doctrine is an outgrowth not of the First Amendment, but of the Due Process Clause of the Fifth Amendment. A conviction fails to comport with due process if the statute under which it is obtained fails to provide a person of ordinary intelligence fair notice of what is prohibited, or is so standardless that it authorizes or encourages seriously discriminatory enforcement. . . .

. . . [T]he Eleventh Circuit's error lies in the belief that the mere fact that close cases can be envisioned renders a statute vague. That is not so. Close cases can be imagined under virtually any statute. . . .

What renders a statute vague is not the possibility that it will sometimes be difficult to determine whether the incriminating fact it establishes has been proved; but rather the indeterminacy of precisely what that fact is. Thus, we have struck down statutes that tied criminal culpability to whether the defendant's conduct was "annoying" or "indecent"—wholly subjective judgments without statutory definitions, narrowing context, or settled legal meanings.

There is no such indeterminacy here. The statute requires that the defendant hold, and make a statement that reflects, the belief that the material is child pornography; or that he communicate in a manner intended to cause another so to believe. Those are clear questions of fact. . . .

Child pornography harms and debases the most defenseless of our citizens. Both the State and Federal Governments have sought to suppress it for many years, only to find it proliferating through the new medium of the Internet. This Court held unconstitutional Congress's previous attempt to meet this new threat, and Congress responded with a carefully crafted attempt to eliminate the First Amendment problems we identified. As far as the provision at issue in this case is concerned, that effort was successful.

The judgment of the Eleventh Circuit is reversed.

JUSTICE STEVENS, *with whom* **JUSTICE BREYER** *joins, concurring.*

My conclusion that this statutory provision is not facially unconstitutional is buttressed by two interrelated considerations on which Justice Scalia finds it unnecessary to rely. First, I believe the result to be compelled by the principle that "every reasonable construction must be resorted to, in order to save a statute from unconstitutionality," *Hooper v. California*; see also *Edward J. DeBartolo Corp. v. Florida Gulf*

Coast Building & Constr. Trades Council (collecting cases).

Second, to the extent the statutory text alone is unclear, our duty to avoid constitutional objections makes it especially appropriate to look beyond the text in order to ascertain the intent of its drafters. It is abundantly clear from the provision's legislative history that Congress' aim was to target materials advertised, promoted, presented, distributed, or solicited with a lascivious purpose—that is, with the intention of inciting sexual arousal.

The dissent argues that the statute impermissibly undermines our First Amendment precedents insofar as it covers proposals to transact in constitutionally protected material. It is true that proof that a pornographic but not obscene representation did not depict real children would place that representation on the protected side of the line. But any constitutional concerns that might arise on that score are surely answered by the construction the Court gives the statute's operative provisions; that is, proposing a transaction in such material would not give rise to criminal liability under the statute unless the defendant actually believed, or intended to induce another to believe, that the material in question depicted real children.

Accordingly, when material which is protected—particularly if it possesses serious literary, artistic, political, or scientific value—is advertised, promoted, presented, distributed, or solicited for some lawful and nonlascivious purpose, such conduct is not captured by the statutory prohibition.

JUSTICE SOUTER, *with whom* **JUSTICE GINSBURG** *joins, dissenting.*

Dealing in obscenity is penalized without violating the First Amendment, but as a general matter pornography lacks the harm to justify prohibiting it. If, however, a photograph (to take the kind of image in this case) shows an actual minor child as a pornographic subject, its transfer and even its possession may be made criminal. *New York v. Ferber*; *Osborne v. Ohio*. The exception to the general rule rests not on the content of the picture but on the need to foil the exploitation of child subjects, *Ferber*, and the justification limits the exception: only pornographic photographs of actual children may be prohibited, see *id.*; *Ashcroft v. Free Speech Coalition*. Thus, just six years ago the Court struck down a statute outlawing particular material merely represented to be child pornography, but not necessarily depicting actual children. *Id.*

The Court holds it is constitutional to prohibit these proposals, and up to a point I do not disagree. In particular, I accept the Court's explanation that Congress may criminalize proposals unrelated to any extant image. I part ways from the Court, however, on the regulation of proposals made with regard to specific, existing representations. Under the new law, the elements of the pandering offense are the same, whether or not the images are of real children. As to those that do not show real children, of course, a transaction in the material could not be prosecuted consistently with the First Amendment, and I believe that maintaining the First Amendment protection of expression we have previously held to cover fake child pornography requires a limit to the law's criminalization of pandering proposals. In failing to confront the tension between ostensibly protecting the material pandered while approving prosecution of the pandering of that same material, and in allowing the new pandering prohibition to suppress otherwise protected speech, the Court undermines *Ferber* and *Free Speech Coalition* in both reasoning and result. This is the significant element of today's holding, and I respectfully dissent from it. . . .

IV

I said that I would not pay the price enacted by the Act without a substantial justification, which I am at a loss to find here. I have to assume that the Court sees some grounding for the Act that I do not, however, and I suppose the holding can only be explained as an uncritical acceptance of a claim made both to Congress and to this Court. In each forum the Government argued that a jury's appreciation of the mere possibility of simulated or virtual child pornography will prevent convictions for the real thing, by inevitably raising reasonable doubt about whether actual children are shown. The Government voices the fear that skeptical jurors will place traffic in child pornography beyond effective prosecution unless it can find some way to avoid the *Ferber* limitation, skirt *Free Speech Coalition*, and allow prosecution whether pornography shows actual children or not.

The claim needs to be taken with a grain of salt. There has never been a time when some such concern could not be raised. Long before the Act was passed, for example, pornographic photos could be taken of models one day into adulthood, and yet there is no indication that prosecution has ever been crippled by the need to prove young-looking models were underage.

Still, if I were convinced there was a real reason for the Government's fear stemming from computer simulation, I would be willing to reexamine *Ferber*. Conditions can change, and if today's technology left no other effective way to stop professional and amateur pornographers from exploiting children there would be a fair claim that some degree of expressive protection had to yield to protect the children.

But the Government does not get a free pass whenever it claims a worthy objective for curtailing speech, and I have further doubts about the need claimed here.

Although Congress found that child pornography defendants "almost universally rais[e]" the defense that the alleged child pornography could be simulated or virtual, neither Congress nor this Court has been given the citation to a single case in which a defendant's acquittal is reasonably attributable to that defense.

Perhaps I am wrong, but without some demonstration that juries have been rendering exploitation of children unpunishable, there is no excuse for cutting back on the First Amendment and no alternative to finding overbreadth in this Act. I would hold it unconstitutional on the authority of *Ferber* and *Free Speech Coalition*.

SYNTHESIS QUESTIONS FOR FURTHER DISCUSSION: CHAPTER 5 SECTION B

1. Catharine MacKinnon uses the term "pornography" in contrast to the term "obscenity," which is employed by the Court. What is the difference? Compare the Court's test for obscenity in *Miller v. California* with the test set forth in MacKinnon's model ordinance and in her article. In *American Booksellers Ass'n v. Hudnut*, the Seventh Circuit was concerned with the political nature of the Indianapolis ordinance and in particular its concern for material depicting subordination. The court suggests that a standard of obscenity is easier to uphold. What might MacKinnon argue in response?

2. Notice that MacKinnon's ordinance has no exception for materials that have literary or artistic value. Does that mean that some "high art," not traditionally considered pornographic, might be a violation under the ordinance? Might other materials—for instance, an advertisement that employs pictures of a sexual and subordinate nature—be classified as pornography under the statute? Do your answers to these questions suggest that the statute is too broad in its definition or not? In other respects, might MacKinnon's standard in fact be too narrow in its definition? For instance, is it possible that a film could depict sex of a nonsubordinate nature? Although such a film might qualify as obscenity under the *Miller* test, would it necessarily count as pornography under MacKinnon's?

3. John Stuart Mill famously argues that allowing even bad ideas into public discourse will lead to truth through deliberation and debate. To what extent does his argument for the "harm principle" extend to materials the Court would deem obscene under *Miller v. California*? Does the argument not work because obscene materials are not "ideas"? Are you convinced by Irving Kristol's argument that legalizing such materials undermines public discourse and the marketplace of ideas? Although Kristol's arguments seem to address instrumental defenses of protections of pornography, are

there any intrinsic defenses of protections for obscenity? For instance, could one reconstruct any of Alexander Meiklejohn's arguments to suggest why access to obscenity is necessary in a democracy?

4.   In what ways do the arguments for banning pornography apply to hate speech? Do both involve subordination of a kind that is unacceptable in a democratic society? To what extent does the Court's current jurisprudence take this into consideration? For instance, consider the difference in *Virginia v. Black* between the cross burned on the field and the one burned on the lawn. Does the protection of the Klan's political viewpoints unacceptably allow this group to challenge the equality of African Americans, or do you believe that even heinous viewpoints such as the Klan's deserve protection under the First Amendment? In your answer, consider Justice Clarence Thomas's dissent in *Virginia v. Black* about the meaning of cross burning in America.

KEY TERMS

clear and present danger: A test in free speech jurisprudence that balanced free speech with the need for security.

consequentialism: View in moral, political, and legal theory that good results justify a decision. Often contrasted with "deontological" views, which emphasize that decisions should be constrained for moral and other reasons even if they would lead to good consequences.

content neutrality: The First Amendment doctrine that suggests that the court should not discriminate based on the content of speech; broader than the idea of **viewpoint neutrality**. Exclusions include obscenity and threats.

facially invalid: The idea that a law as written, as opposed to how it is applied to a specific instance, is invalid.

fighting words doctrine: The Court's doctrine for limiting threatening speech. Established in *Chaplinsky v. New Hampshire*. Relevant in some hate speech cases.

***Miller* test:**   The current test for recognizing obscenity. Chief Warren E. Justice Burger wrote, "The basic guidelines for the trier of fact must be: (a) whether 'the average person, applying contemporary community standards' would find that the work, taken as a whole, appeals to the prurient interest . . . (b) whether the work depicts or describes, in a patently offensive way, sexual conduct specifically defined by the applicable state law; and (c) whether the work, taken as a whole, lacks serious literary, artistic, political, or scientific value."

overbreadth doctrine: The idea in First Amendment jurisprudence that a particular law that aims at banning unprotected speech might also impact protected speech, and therefore should be struck down. This concept is related to the idea of vagueness, which suggests that if it is not clear which kind of speech is being regulated, a law can be invalid under the First Amendment.

prior restraint: Attempts to censor speech before it occurs, for instance through an injunction, as opposed to attempts to punish speech, for instance through libel laws.

seditious libel: Libel that calls into question one's fidelity to the government, usually a statement thought to incite hatred towards the government. It is usually considered unconstitutional to punish someone for seditious libel under the First Amendment protection of free speech, given that it is usually a statement of political viewpoint. Criminalized by Congress during President John Adams's administration in the "Alien and Sedition Acts," which were allowed to expire according to a sunset provision during the presidency of Thomas Jefferson.

state action: The doctrine that suggests that free speech claims are only triggered when the government has acted.

viewpoint neutrality: The notion that the laws that discriminate based on the opinion expressed by a given act of speech are unconstitutional.

CHAPTER 6

RELIGIOUS FREEDOM: THE FREE EXERCISE AND ESTABLISHMENT CLAUSES OF THE FIRST AMENDMENT

The United States of America has always been home to large numbers of people with deeply held religious beliefs and commitments. Many of the original settlers in America fled religious persecution in European countries. Yet from at least the time of the Founding, the effort to balance a respect for the practice of religion with an assurance that no one religion would dominate others or infringe on individual liberty has been a major challenge in U.S. constitutional law.

You will notice that some of the cases that we examine in this chapter concern issues related to free speech. In some ways, the question of what constitutes free exercise of religion, a central theme here, is about what might be thought of as religious expression. Other issues are more akin to concerns about discrimination against religious believers. In some ways, those themes will resemble issues we consider in Chapters 8 and 9 on the Equal Protection Clause. These overlaps might lead you to ask why the Constitution singles out religious freedom in the First Amendment. Why do other clauses guaranteeing civil liberties not serve as sufficient protection for freedom of religion? One question we examine throughout this chapter concerns whether religion is "special" in needing distinct kinds of protection, beyond those afforded by the other rights provisions in the U.S. Constitution.

The two Religion Clauses of the Constitution are found in the First Amendment of the Bill of Rights. The first, known as the Establishment Clause, states that "Congress shall make no law respecting the establishment of religion." The second, known as the Free Exercise Clause, affords similar protections against laws "prohibiting the free exercise thereof." Taken together, these two clauses attempt to balance the guarantee of religious freedom for all against the possibility of an established church dominating the polity.

Our examination of the Free Exercise Clause largely centers on questions of "exemptions" to otherwise valid laws. This question differs from many others in this book. So far, we have often examined cases about whether a statute as a whole should be struck down. Instead, the debate over accommodation focuses on whether individuals should be allowed to opt out of or not be subject to laws that are otherwise constitutional. For instance, it is clear that a law banning the worship of Jesus Christ would fail constitutional muster. However, while a law mandating that all public buildings, including churches, be closed on Sunday might not be unconstitutional *per se*, the First Amendment might call for exemptions for religious groups that honor the Sabbath on Sunday. Such issues are especially salient when otherwise valid general laws adversely affect minority religions. As you will see in a case selection, employment practices that infringe on religions that celebrate the Sabbath on a Saturday is an example of this kind of question.

In considering whether the First Amendment's Free Exercise Clause creates a right of an individual or a group to be exempted from a general law, the Supreme Court balances competing interests. On the one hand, these cases involve some state policy that has allegedly infringed on the religious beliefs or practices of an individual or a group. On the other hand, the state often has valid reasons for passing such laws. As you read each of these cases, consider whether granting an exemption would adversely affect the state's ability to pursue a legitimate goal, and if so, whether it is still important to grant the exemption in question. In *Employment Division v. Smith*, U.S. Supreme Court Justice Antonin Scalia explains that the Court's willingness to grant exemptions in Free Exercise Clause cases could overwhelm the courts with a slew of lawsuits, thus undermining their ability to function effectively. Others would place more weight on the rights of individuals, protecting them even when they adversely impact state functions as a whole. Consider how you might balance such interests as you read.

In Section B, our Establishment Clause cases center on the question of whether governmental support for religious activities or organizations, whether symbolic or financial, constitutes legislation with "respect" to an establishment of religion, thus violating a freedom protected by the First Amendment. The most obvious violations of the Establishment Clause would occur if the state were to attempt to institute a national religion. For instance, if Congress were to pass a bill declaring that the United States is fundamentally a Methodist nation, this would certainly be a violation of the core meaning of the clause. But as you will see, the question of whether an action "respect[s] an establishment of religion" also bears on more difficult cases. For instance, do religious displays on government property violate the Establishment Clause? The cases you will read demonstrate that the Court has taken at least two positions on such matters, and we will ask you to decide whether these positions are consistent. Another fundamental issue in establishment cases concerns state funding. In the United States, there is a history of religious organizations providing education and charity work. Is any funding of such organizations a violation of the Establishment Clause?

Although we will study the two Religion Clauses separately, at the end of the chapter try to formulate ideas about how these two clauses relate to each other. You might notice potential tensions between them. For instance, the Free Exercise Clause is meant to guarantee freedom from intervention by the state in people's religious beliefs and practices. But what if one wishes to give voice to his or her religion by requiring the state to fund religious organizations or celebrate religious holidays? It seems that the Establishment Clause in some ways might risk limiting the kind of free exercise that is also guaranteed. At a minimum, there is a challenge in thinking about how these two clauses fit together. Are they in conflict, or can they be understood as working in tandem to protect religious freedom?

One theory of how these clauses fit together centers on Thomas Jefferson's metaphor of the "wall of separation" between church and state. The Free Exercise Clause, on this view, prevents the state from interfering with religious practice. At the same time, the Establishment Clause prohibits the government from being involved in any way with religious affairs. Recently, however, both liberal and conservative religious thinkers have criticized this metaphor of separation. According to critics, religious life is intricately tied to and affected by a variety of government functions. Regardless of whether a policy was intended to affect religious practice or not, it is in the nature of government and the rule of law that every policy has the potential to impact religious organizations or activities in some way. For instance, a fire code might inadvertently affect the size of a church's congregation, yet few would question the validity of such a requirement. Similarly, there is no impropriety if the state provides firefighting services to a church that catches fire. Therefore, a complete wall between church and state is difficult to achieve.

In the readings by Michael McConnell, Martha Nussbaum, Amy Gutmann, and Chris Eisgruber and Lawrence Sager, the authors suggest an alternative to the idea of a wall of separation. All agree that religion will, and even should, have a place in discussions about public policy. Yet they disagree about the extent to which religious believers should be "accommodated" in the face of adverse laws. For Nussbaum and McConnell, religious freedom occupies a position of special dignity in the scheme of constitutional liberties, and the state should go to great lengths to avoid burdening believers with laws that violate their consciences. On their view, the Free Exercise Clause demands robust protection for religious minorities in the face of laws that would limit their practice.

In contrast to the arguments made by Nussbaum and McConnell, the readings by Eisgruber and Sager and Gutmann argue that we should not grant exemptions to religious groups even when religion might be adversely affected. These authors are particularly concerned to promote public values such as equality and are willing to accept the costs that such a pursuit by the state might have for religious liberty. In the case of *Bob Jones University v. United States*, the Court considered whether an organization with racist policies on its campus was entitled to an exemption from non-profit regulations that prohibited discrimination. While thinkers such as McConnell defend such exemptions on the grounds of freedom of religious conscience, others seek to balance this freedom with a general concern for equal protection. Eisgruber and Sager extend this concern for equality to explain the purpose of the Free Exercise Clause. According to them, the First Amendment should protect minorities not by treating them differently but by affording them the same "equal regard" as all citizens. This tension between an approach emphasizing the importance of religious exemptions and one stressing a balance between such exemptions and the value of equality is evident throughout the cases in this chapter.

While questions about the free exercise of religion and exemption from general laws constitute one aspect of religious freedom, the other problem of the Religion Clauses concerns the power of one religion to impose itself upon others through the coercive apparatus of the state. At the Founding, those such as James Madison and Thomas Jefferson, who defended the Establishment Clause, argued against thinkers like Phillips Payson and Richard Lee, who claimed that civic virtue could only be maintained by state-sponsored religion. In the modern debate about the Establishment Clause, most thinkers oppose the establishment of religion. However, there is deep disagreement about the way in which the government should interact with religious organizations, especially in the provision of public funding. The question here is whether public support for religious organizations that provide secular services such as education constitutes an unconstitutional establishment of religion. For instance, when the government provides vouchers to students who choose to attend parochial rather than public schools, does it indirectly or perhaps even inadvertently "establish" a religion? This question is made more difficult by the Clause's ambiguous language, which prohibits not simply all establishments of religion, but all laws *respecting* such establishments.

Thinkers such as McConnell argue for a robust role for religious groups in providing public services such as education. They defend the right of religious groups to receive state funding, which some believe should extend only to secular organizations. Consider, as we turn to our case selection, to what degree McConnell's view is adopted by the Court. In the case of school funding, the Court's decision in *Lemon v. Kurtzman* created a test that requires that public aid to religious groups be put toward a secular purpose, exhibit neutrality between faiths, and avoid excessive "entanglement" between religious groups and the state. These requirements place significant restrictions on the state's funding of religion. However, the *Lemon* test clearly allows some funding for religious groups.

A related issue concerns the place of religious practice in public life. For instance, we consider in this chapter whether and when public nondenominational prayers constitute an establishment of religion. The question here is whether the Establishment Clause prohibits the specific advancement of a particular religion, or whether it limits religious ideals in public life as a whole. In particular, does the inclusion of any public religious symbol entail the establishment of religion? For example, is the presence of religious symbols in public squares during Christmas constitutionally permissible? The question is complicated by the large role that religious imagery has in common elements of public life, such as in the Pledge of Allegiance. Moreover, the Court's own practice raises questions about the metaphoric wall of separation: Before every Supreme Court proceeding, the bailiff intones, "May God save the United States and this honorable Court."

Throughout the chapter, we examine the controversies about each of the individual Religion Clauses as well as ask how they might function together to protect religious liberty.

A. FREE EXERCISE AND ACCOMMODATION

To what extent should religious believers be exempt from the law? How do we reconcile religious freedom with demands for equality?

This section on the Free Exercise Clause of the First Amendment begins with an early set of readings that prefigure the contemporary debate about the meaning of the Clause. Although John Locke and Roger Williams wrote before the U.S. Constitution was drafted, their debate in many ways sets the stage for the contemporary debate about how the law ought to accommodate religious believers. For Locke, religious freedom is essential to preserve the liberty of conscience, to protect individual property rights, and to prevent wars of religion. Yet he is skeptical of excessive concessions to religion in lawmaking. For Williams, on the other hand, the freedom to worship, even when that worship conflicts with general laws, should be a primary concern of government.

In a contemporary defense of religious liberty, Martha Nussbaum argues for the kind of freedom of conscience espoused by Williams, believing it should result in a robust doctrine of what is known as religious exemption, or the notion that individuals should be granted exceptions to the requirements of those laws that conflict with their religious beliefs. Our reading from Michael McConnell echoes Nussbaum's line of reasoning, arguing against the principle that the Constitution should be blind to religion. In contrast, Chris Eisgruber and Lawrence Sager draw on a concern for the equal freedom of citizens. On their view, religious liberty should not regard religious belief as having special weight; rather, it should be protected under a broader principle of toleration. Amy Gutmann emphasizes the unique role that children play in the debate over the balance between the value of equality and the freedom of religious expression. For her, the state has a profound interest in guaranteeing equality for children, even when the state finds itself at odds with the religious beliefs of their parents. In her discussion of *Wisconsin v. Yoder*, Gutmann stresses the importance of mandated schooling despite the religious concerns raised by the Amish.

Using these readings as a guide, we turn to case law about religious exemptions in the area of free exercise jurisprudence. In *Sherbert v. Verner*, the Court considered whether a Seventh-day Adventist was entitled to unemployment benefits despite her refusal to work on a Saturday, a holy day of worship for her religious group. According to the Court's test at the time, every time a religious belief is adversely affected, the Court should presume that the impacted party should be granted an exemption.

Under the standard established in *Sherbert v. Verner*, any governmental action that has an adverse impact on religion triggers "strict scrutiny." This is the first time we are encountering this idea, but it will become important in latter chapters. In understanding the idea of strict scrutiny, it is first important to note that the Court's approach to the protection of rights often involves balancing. We saw, for instance, in Chapter 5 that the "clear and present danger" test balanced concerns for liberty against concerns for security. In instances where the Court wants to employ a balancing test that favors the rights of individuals strongly but still avoid an absolute prohibition on certain laws, it often employs a strict scrutiny test. In the case of protecting free exercise, strict scrutiny offers a way of strongly presuming that the interests of individuals in the free exercise of religion should outweigh the importance of achieving the purpose of the law in question. In other contexts, strict scrutiny is often a presumption about the invalidity of a law as a whole. But in the context of free exercise, it is a presumption that an exemption should be granted to an otherwise valid general law. Specifically, under a strict scrutiny test for free exercise, if the state is to show that an exemption should not be granted, it faces a very heavy burden: It must demonstrate that the challenged law serves a "compelling interest" and is "narrowly tailored" to meet this interest. In other contexts you will see the Court require that the general purpose of a law as a whole constitute a compelling interest and that it be narrowly tailored, but here those requirements apply to the denial of the exemption.

What is meant by a compelling interest? On this standard, the law in question must further a fundamental goal that would be impeded by a grant of religious exemption. What is meant by narrowly tailored? This standard measures the "fit" between the means of denying the exemption and the goal served by the law. In other words, is it necessary to deny the exemption in order to further the compelling interest? To be narrowly tailored, that "means-ends" fit must be very tight.

In *Sherbert v. Verner*, the Court applied strict scrutiny to the question of religious exemption, which you will see is comparable to that found in equal protection law. The analysis in *Sherbert v. Verner* fits well with Nussbaum, McConnell, and Williams's understanding of the importance of religious conscience and the need for religious exemptions in order to protect that fundamental liberty. Examining the standard set in *Sherbert v. Verner*, we will continue to explore the ways in which the Court used the strict scrutiny standard in examining issues of religious freedom. To this end, we present seven additional cases in which the Court deployed this standard.

Despite the Court's long use of strict scrutiny in matters of free exercise and exemption, it abandoned this test in the realm of free exercise law in *Employment Division v. Smith*. We closely examine the reasons why the Court finally rejected this test as unworkable. Specifically, a worry had emerged among some members of the Court that it was not actually employing the strict scrutiny standard it claimed to apply. On this account, the Court was claiming to presume an individual entitlement to exemptions when it was in fact denying them regularly out of necessity. In six of the eight cases listed before *Employment Division v. Smith*, the Court found in favor of the state. As you read, consider the extent to which the Court is actually employing a strict scrutiny standard. Bear this contention in mind when you read Justice Antonin Scalia's majority opinion in *Employment Division v. Smith*, which was meant to correct the supposed flaws in the earlier line of cases. In addition to arguing that the Court was failing to employ its stated standard, Justice Scalia explained that strict scrutiny is too high a standard for instances in which the law does not intentionally discriminate against religion and is crafted in a generally applicable way.

In *Employment Division v. Smith*, Justice Scalia, writing for the majority, articulated a new standard for analyzing when laws limiting the free exercise of religion require exemptions. In contrast to strict scrutiny, which presumes the need for an exemption when generally applicable laws adversely impact religion, "rational review" presumes the validity of these laws. According to rational review, the state need only show that its laws have a rational basis and have a rationally related fit between the denial of the exemption and the purposes of a law in order to constitutionally deny exemption.

Although the majority of the Court supported Justice Scalia's opinion in *Employment Division v. Smith*, Congress reacted unfavorably to it. In addition to the cases and the readings, we include here the Religious Freedom Restoration Act (RFRA), which Congress passed in 1993. Concerned that the Court's ruling in *Employment Division v. Smith* had overly weakened the protection of religious liberty, Congress intervened by mandating the application of strict scrutiny to cases alleging the infringement of religious freedom. But in *Boerne v. Flores*, the Court struck down this law.

In many ways, the Court's recent free exercise jurisprudence has involved a dialogue between Congress and the Court. When, in the RFRA, it sought to "restore" the Court's pre-*Employment Division v. Smith* jurisprudence and the strict scrutiny test for facially neutral laws, Congress attempted to engage in its own constitutional interpretation. In *Boerne v. Flores*, the Court therefore faced two questions. The first concerned the kind of free exercise jurisprudence it should adopt, but the second question concerned whether Congress had a role in guiding that decision. As we noted in Chapter 1, the Court rejected a congressional role in determining such jurisprudence, and arguably announced a doctrine of judicial supremacy. As you read *Boerne v. Flores*, consider whether the Court is declaring that it should have the final word on the question of what level of scrutiny to adopt in examining facially neutral laws, or whether it is claiming a broader understanding of its role as the ultimate interpreter of the Constitution. Moreover, decide whether you agree with Congress that the strict scrutiny standard is appropriate for analyzing the question of religious exemptions, or whether you agree with the standard in *Employment Division v. Smith* and the contention made by Justice Scalia that strict scrutiny is untenable.

As we have seen, the controversy over how to interpret the Free Exercise Clause is largely one about balancing. Specifically, the Court switches between two views of how to set the balance between the state's various interests and individuals' interests based on exemptions. Although we have been framing this question of balancing in a general way, it is helpful to also examine the question of balancing in light of specific state interests. Throughout this section, we pay particular attention to the state's interests in guaranteeing equality. At times, this interest conflicts with demands for religious exemptions. Two cases in this section deal with the possible tension between the value of equality and religious freedom. The first is a pre–*Employment Division v. Smith* case, while the second comes after *Employment Division v. Smith*. In *Bob Jones University v. United States*, the Court is confronted with the question of whether the Free Exercise Clause protects Bob Jones University's racially discriminatory policies. In particular, the case asks whether Bob Jones University's religiously based discrimination, such as its refusal to allow interracial dating or the presence of single black men on campus at night, could be the basis for revoking its tax-exempt status. The University argued that it was entitled to an exemption because its policies were based on its interpretation of the Bible. While in *Bob Jones University v. United States* the Court addresses the question of whether the Free Exercise Clause requires the government to ignore religious institutions' discrimination in allocating benefits, the Court in *Church of Lukumi Babalu Aye v. City of Hialeah* confronts a case in which the state itself is accused of discriminating. In particular, this case asks whether a Florida municipality's law banning "animal sacrifice" violates the Free Exercise Clause if the law specifically targets practitioners of the Santeria religion. Both of these cases highlight the intersection between questions of equality and those of religious freedom, but each provides a different answer. Is equality a value that cuts against religious liberty, as in *Bob Jones University v. United States*, or is equality instead the principal source of religious freedom, as it is in *Church of Lukumi Babalu Aye v. City of Hialeah*?

You will notice, beginning with our first case, that several of the cases in this section concern a possible violation of the Free Exercise Clause by state or local governments. These cases rely on the holding in *Cantwell v. Connecticut* that the Free Exercise Clause is subject to the doctrine of incorporation, applying the protection of free exercise against state as well as federal governments.

John Locke

A LETTER CONCERNING TOLERATION

Translated by William Popple

1689

John Locke's "A Letter Concerning Toleration" was translated from Latin and published in 1689, well before the U.S. Constitution was written. Nevertheless, it offers an important starting point for discussion of the reasons why the authors of the Constitution chose to include the two Religion Clauses in the Bill of Rights. The letter makes a clear argument not only for the protection of the freedom of religious conscience, but also for the protection of religious practices. Such protections are

*at the core of the Free Exercise Clause.
Locke's notion of the separation of civil
and religious authority, moreover, offers
the grounds for a theoretical defense of the
Establishment Clause. It is important to
note that while Locke extends protection
to non-Christian religions, he does not
avoid religious reasoning himself in arguing for such protections. Does this contradict his commitment to religious freedom?
In addition, while Locke is concerned with
protecting religious conscience and practices, he makes clear that the state should
pursue the "civil" interest. Does this argument leave any room for exemptions to
general laws for religious believers who
find themselves at odds with laws that
are in the civil interest? This question is
crucial for thinking about how Locke's
approach fits into modern debates about
religion and the First Amendment.*

Honoured Sir,

Since you are pleased to inquire what are
my thoughts about the mutual toleration
of Christians in their different professions
of religion, I must needs answer you freely
that I esteem that toleration to be the chief
characteristic mark of the true Church.

The toleration of those that differ from
others in matters of religion is so agreeable to the Gospel of Jesus Christ, and to
the genuine reason of mankind, that it
seems monstrous for men to be so blind
as not to perceive the necessity and advantage of it in so clear a light. I will not here
tax the pride and ambition of some, the
passion and uncharitable zeal of others.
These are faults from which human affairs
can perhaps scarce ever be perfectly freed;
but yet such as nobody will bear the plain
imputation of, without covering them with
some specious colour; and so pretend to
commendation, whilst they are carried
away by their own irregular passions. But,
however, that some may not colour their

spirit of persecution and unchristian cruelty with a pretence of care of the public
weal and observation of the laws; and that
others, under pretence of religion, may
not seek impunity for their libertinism
and licentiousness; in a word, that none
may impose either upon himself or others, by the pretences of loyalty and obedience to the prince, or of tenderness and
sincerity in the worship of God; I esteem
it above all things necessary to distinguish
exactly the business of civil government
from that of religion and to settle the just
bounds that lie between the one and the
other. If this be not done, there can be no
end put to the controversies that will be
always arising between those that have, or
at least pretend to have, on the one side,
a concernment for the interest of men's
souls, and, on the other side, a care of the
commonwealth.

The commonwealth seems to me to
be a society of men constituted only for
the procuring, preserving, and advancing
their own civil interests.

Civil interests I call life, liberty, health,
and indolency of body; and the possession
of outward things, such as money, lands,
houses, furniture, and the like.

It is the duty of the civil magistrate, by
the impartial execution of equal laws, to
secure unto all the people in general and
to every one of his subjects in particular
the just possession of these things belonging to this life. If anyone presume to violate the laws of public justice and equity,
established for the preservation of those
things, his presumption is to be checked
by the fear of punishment, consisting of
the deprivation or diminution of those
civil interests, or goods, which otherwise
he might and ought to enjoy. But seeing
no man does willingly suffer himself to be
punished by the deprivation of any part
of his goods, and much less of his liberty
or life, therefore, is the magistrate armed
with the force and strength of all his

subjects, in order to the punishment of those that violate any other man's rights.

Now that the whole jurisdiction of the magistrate reaches only to these civil concernments, and that all civil power, right and dominion, is bounded and confined to the only care of promoting these things; and that it neither can nor ought in any manner to be extended to the salvation of souls, these following considerations seem unto me abundantly to demonstrate.

First, because the care of souls is not committed to the civil magistrate, any more than to other men. It is not committed unto him, I say, by God; because it appears not that God has ever given any such authority to one man over another as to compel anyone to his religion. Nor can any such power be vested in the magistrate by the consent of the people, because no man can so far abandon the care of his own salvation as blindly to leave to the choice of any other, whether prince or subject, to prescribe to him what faith or worship he shall embrace. For no man can, if he would, conform his faith to the dictates of another. All the life and power of true religion consist in the inward and full persuasion of the mind; and faith is not faith without believing. Whatever profession we make, to whatever outward worship we conform, if we are not fully satisfied in our own mind that the one is true and the other well pleasing unto God, such profession and such practice, far from being any furtherance, are indeed great obstacles to our salvation. For in this manner, instead of expiating other sins by the exercise of religion, I say, in offering thus unto God Almighty such a worship as we esteem to be displeasing unto Him, we add unto the number of our other sins those also of hypocrisy and contempt of His Divine Majesty.

In the second place, the care of souls cannot belong to the civil magistrate, because his power consists only in outward force; but true and saving religion consists in the inward persuasion of the mind, without which nothing can be acceptable to God. And such is the nature of the understanding, that it cannot be compelled to the belief of anything by outward force. Confiscation of estate, imprisonment, torments, nothing of that nature can have any such efficacy as to make men change the inward judgement that they have framed of things....

In the third place, the care of the salvation of men's souls cannot belong to the magistrate; because, though the rigour of laws and the force of penalties were capable to convince and change men's minds, yet would not that help at all to the salvation of their souls. For there being but one truth, one way to heaven, what hope is there that more men would be led into it if they had no rule but the religion of the court and were put under the necessity to quit the light of their own reason, and oppose the dictates of their own consciences, and blindly to resign themselves up to the will of their governors and to the religion which either ignorance, ambition, or superstition had chanced to establish in the countries where they were born? In the variety and contradiction of opinions in religion, wherein the princes of the world are as much divided as in their secular interests, the narrow way would be much straitened; one country alone would be in the right, and all the rest of the world put under an obligation of following their princes in the ways that lead to destruction; and that which heightens the absurdity, and very ill suits the notion of a Deity, men would owe their eternal happiness or misery to the places of their nativity.

These considerations, to omit many others that might have been urged to the same purpose, seem unto me sufficient to conclude that all the power of civil government relates only to men's civil interests, is confined to the care of the things of this world, and hath nothing to do with the world to come. . . .

It follows now that we consider what is the power of this church and unto what laws it is subject.

Forasmuch as no society, how free soever, or upon whatsoever slight occasion instituted, whether of philosophers for learning, of merchants for commerce, or of men of leisure for mutual conversation and discourse, no church or company, I say, can in the least subsist and hold together, but will presently dissolve and break in pieces, unless it be regulated by some laws, and the members all consent to observe some order. Place and time of meeting must be agreed on; rules for admitting and excluding members must be established; distinction of officers, and putting things into a regular course, and suchlike, cannot be omitted. But since the joining together of several members into this church-society, as has already been demonstrated, is absolutely free and spontaneous, it necessarily follows that the right of making its laws can belong to none but the society itself; or, at least (which is the same thing), to those whom the society by common consent has authorised thereunto.

. . . In the last place, let us now consider what is the magistrate's duty in the business of toleration, which certainly is very considerable.

We have already proved that the care of souls does not belong to the magistrate. . . . But what if he neglect the care of his soul? I answer: What if he neglect the care of his health or of his estate, which things are nearlier related to the government of the magistrate than the other? Will the magistrate provide by an express law that such a one shall not become poor or sick? Laws provide, as much as is possible, that the goods and health of subjects be not injured by the fraud and violence of others; they do

not guard them from the negligence or ill-husbandry of the possessors themselves. No man can be forced to be rich or healthful whether he will or no. Nay, God Himself will not save men against their wills. . . .

But, after all, the principal consideration, and which absolutely determines this controversy, is this: Although the magistrate's opinion in religion be sound, and the way that he appoints be truly Evangelical, yet, if I be not thoroughly persuaded thereof in my own mind, there will be no safety for me in following it. No way whatsoever that I shall walk in against the dictates of my conscience will ever bring me to the mansions of the blessed. In a word, whatsoever may be doubtful in religion, yet this at least is certain, that no religion which I believe not to be true can be either true or profitable unto me. In vain, therefore, do princes compel their subjects to come into their Church communion, under pretence of saving their souls? If they believe, they will come of their own accord, if they believe not, their coming will nothing avail them. How great soever, in fine, may be the pretence of good-will and charity, and concern for the salvation of men's souls, men cannot be forced to be saved whether they will or no. And therefore, when all is done, they must be left to their own consciences.

Having thus at length freed men from all dominion over one another in matters of religion, let us now consider what they are to do. All men know and acknowledge that God ought to be publicly worshipped; why otherwise do they compel one another unto the public assemblies? Men, therefore, constituted in this liberty are to enter into some religious society, that they meet together, not only for mutual edification, but to own to the world that they worship God and offer unto His Divine Majesty such service as they themselves are not ashamed of and such as they think not unworthy of Him, nor unacceptable to Him; and, finally, that by the purity of doctrine, holiness of life, and decent form of worship, they may draw others unto the love of the true religion, and perform such other things in religion as cannot be done by each private man apart. . . .

But as in every Church there are two things especially to be considered—the outward form and rites of worship, and the doctrines and articles of things must be handled each distinctly that so the whole matter of toleration may the more clearly be understood.

Concerning outward worship, I say, in the first place, that the magistrate has no power to enforce by law, either in his own Church, or much less in another, the use of any rites or ceremonies whatsoever in the worship of God. And this, not only because these Churches are free societies, but because whatsoever is practised in the worship of God is only so far justifiable as it is believed by those that practise it to be acceptable unto Him. To impose such things, therefore, upon any people, contrary to their own judgment, is in effect to command them to offend God, which, considering that the end of all religion is to please Him, and that liberty is essentially necessary to that end, appears to be absurd beyond expression. . . .

In the next place: As the magistrate has no power to impose by his laws the use of any rites and ceremonies in any Church, so neither has he any power to forbid the use of such rites and ceremonies as are already received, approved, and practised by any Church; because, if he did so, he would destroy the Church itself: the end of whose institution is only to worship God with freedom after its own manner.

You will say, by this rule, if some congregations should have a mind to sacrifice infants, or (as the primitive Christians were falsely accused) lustfully pollute themselves in promiscuous uncleanness, or practise any other such heinous enormities, is the magistrate obliged to tolerate them, because they are committed in a religious assembly? I answer: No. These things are not lawful in the ordinary course of life, nor in any private house; and therefore neither are they so in the worship of God, or in any religious meeting. But, indeed, if any people congregated upon account of religion should be desirous to sacrifice a calf, I deny that that ought to be prohibited by a law. . . . For no injury is thereby done to any one, no prejudice to another man's goods. . . . The part of the magistrate is only to take care that the commonwealth receive no prejudice, and that there be no injury done to any man, either in life or estate. . . . But if peradventure such were the state of things that the interest of the commonwealth required all slaughter of beasts should be forborne for some while, in order to the increasing of the stock of cattle that had been destroyed by some extraordinary murrain, who sees not that the magistrate, in such a case, may forbid all his subjects to kill any calves for any use whatsoever? Only it is to be observed that, in this case, the law is not made about a religious, but a political matter; nor is the sacrifice, but the slaughter of calves, thereby prohibited.

By this we see what difference there is between the Church and the Commonwealth. Whatsoever is lawful in the Commonwealth cannot be prohibited by the magistrate in the Church. Whatsoever is permitted unto any of his subjects for their ordinary use, neither can nor ought to be forbidden by him to any sect of people for their religious uses. . . . But those things that are prejudicial to the commonweal of a people in their ordinary use and are, therefore, forbidden by laws, those things ought not to be permitted to Churches in their sacred rites. Only the magistrate ought always to be very careful that he do not misuse his authority to the oppression of any Church, under pretence of public good. . . .

Thus far concerning outward worship. Let us now consider articles of faith.

The articles of religion are some of them practical and some speculative. Now, though both sorts consist in the knowledge of truth, yet these terminate simply in the understanding, those influence the will and manners. Speculative opinions, therefore, and articles of faith (as they are called) which are required only to be believed, cannot be imposed on any Church by the law of the land. For it is absurd that things should be enjoined by laws which are not in men's power to perform. And to believe this or that to be true does not depend upon our will. But of this enough has been said already. "But," will some say; "let men at least profess that they believe." A sweet religion, indeed, that obliges men to dissemble and tell lies, both to God and man, for the salvation of their souls! If the magistrate thinks to save men thus, he seems to understand little of the way of salvation. And if he does it not in order to save them, why is he so solicitous about the articles of faith as to enact them by a law?

Further, the magistrate ought not to forbid the preaching or professing of any speculative opinions in any Church because they have no manner of relation to the civil rights of the subjects. If a Roman Catholic believe that to be really the body of Christ which another man calls bread, he does no injury thereby to his neighbour. If a Jew do not believe the New Testament to be the Word of God, he does not thereby alter anything in men's civil rights. If a heathen doubt of both Testaments, he is not therefore to be punished as a pernicious citizen. The power of the magistrate and the estates of the people may be equally secure whether any man believe these things or no. I readily grant that these opinions are false and absurd. But the business of laws is not to provide for the truth of opinions, but for the safety and security of the commonwealth and of every particular man's

goods and person. And so it ought to be. For the truth certainly would do well enough if she were once left to shift for herself. She seldom has received and, I fear, never will receive much assistance from the power of great men, to whom she is but rarely known and more rarely welcome. She is not taught by laws, nor has she any need of force to procure her entrance into the minds of men. Errors, indeed, prevail by the assistance of foreign and borrowed succours. But if Truth makes not her way into the understanding by her own light, she will be but the weaker for any borrowed force violence can add to her. Thus much for speculative opinions. Let us now proceed to practical ones.

A good life, in which consist not the least part of religion and true piety, concerns also the civil government; and in it lies the safety both of men's souls and of the commonwealth. Moral actions belong, therefore, to the jurisdiction both of the outward and inward court; both of the civil and domestic governor; I mean both of the magistrate and conscience. Here, therefore, is great danger, lest one of these jurisdictions intrench upon the other, and discord arise between the keeper of the public peace and the overseers of souls. But if what has been already said concerning the limits of both these governments be rightly considered, it will easily remove all difficulty in this matter.

Every man has an immortal soul, capable of eternal happiness or misery; whose happiness depending upon his believing and doing those things in this life which are necessary to the obtaining of God's favour, and are prescribed by God to that end. It follows from thence, first, that the observance of these things is the highest obligation that lies upon mankind and that our utmost care, application, and diligence ought to be exercised in the search and performance of them; because there is nothing in this world that is of any consideration in comparison with eternity. Secondly, that seeing one man does not violate the right of another by his erroneous opinions and undue manner of worship, nor is his perdition any prejudice to another man's affairs, therefore, the care of each man's salvation belongs only to himself. But I would not have this understood as if I meant hereby to condemn all charitable admonitions and affectionate endeavours to reduce men from errors, which are indeed the greatest duty of a Christian. Any one may employ as many exhortations and arguments as he pleases, towards the promoting of another man's salvation. But all force and compulsion are to be forborne. Nothing is to be done imperiously. Nobody is obliged in that matter to yield obedience unto the admonitions or injunctions of another, further than he himself is persuaded. Every man in that has the supreme and absolute authority of judging for himself. And the reason is because nobody else is concerned in it, nor can receive any prejudice from his conduct therein.

But besides their souls, which are immortal, men have also their temporal lives here upon earth; the state whereof being frail and fleeting, and the duration uncertain, they have need of several outward conveniences to the support thereof, which are to be procured or preserved by pains and industry. For those things that are necessary to the comfortable support of our lives are not the spontaneous products of nature, nor do offer themselves fit and prepared for our use. This part, therefore, draws on another care and necessarily gives another employment. But the pravity of mankind being such that they had rather injuriously prey upon the fruits of other men's labours than take pains to provide for themselves, the necessity of preserving men in the possession of what honest industry has already acquired and also of preserving their liberty and strength, whereby they may acquire what

they farther want, obliges men to enter into society with one another, that by mutual assistance and joint force they may secure unto each other their properties, in the things that contribute to the comfort and happiness of this life, leaving in the meanwhile to every man the care of his own eternal happiness, the attainment whereof can neither be facilitated by another man's industry, nor can the loss of it turn to another man's prejudice, nor the hope of it be forced from him by any external violence. But, forasmuch as men thus entering into societies, grounded upon their mutual compacts of assistance for the defence of their temporal goods, may, nevertheless, be deprived of them, either by the rapine and fraud of their fellow citizens, or by the hostile violence of foreigners, the remedy of this evil consists in arms, riches, and multitude of citizens; the remedy of the other in laws; and the care of all things relating both to one and the other is committed by the society to the civil magistrate. This is the original, this is the use, and these are the bounds of the legislative (which is the supreme) power in every commonwealth. I mean that provision may be made for the security of each man's private possessions; for the peace, riches, and public commodities of the whole people; and, as much as possible, for the increase of their inward strength against foreign invasions.

These things being thus explained, it is easy to understand to what end the legislative power ought to be directed and by what measures regulated; and that is the temporal good and outward prosperity of the society; which is the sole reason of men's entering into society, and the only thing they seek and aim at in it. And it is also evident what liberty remains to men in reference to their eternal salvation, and that is that every one should do what he in his conscience is persuaded to be acceptable to the Almighty, on whose good pleasure and acceptance depends their eternal happiness. For obedience is due, in the first place, to God and, afterwards to the laws.

But some may ask: "What if the magistrate should enjoin anything by his authority that appears unlawful to the conscience of a private person?" I answer that, if government be faithfully administered and the counsels of the magistrates be indeed directed to the public good, this will seldom happen. But if, perhaps, it do so fall out, I say, that such a private person is to abstain from the action that he judges unlawful, and he is to undergo the punishment which it is not unlawful for him to bear. For the private judgement of any person concerning a law enacted in political matters, for the public good, does not take away the obligation of that law, nor deserve a dispensation. But if the law, indeed, be concerning things that lie not within the verge of the magistrate's authority (as, for example, that the people, or any party amongst them, should be compelled to embrace a strange religion, and join in the worship and ceremonies of another Church), men are not in these cases obliged by that law, against their consciences. For the political society is instituted for no other end, but only to secure every man's possession of the things of this life. The care of each man's soul and of the things of heaven, which neither does belong to the commonwealth nor can be subjected to it, is left entirely to every man's self. Thus the safeguard of men's lives and of the things that belong unto this life is the business of the commonwealth; and the preserving of those things unto their owners is the duty of the magistrate. And therefore the magistrate cannot take away these worldly things from this man or party and give them to that; nor change propriety amongst fellow subjects (no not even by a law), for a cause that has no relation to the end of civil government, I mean for their religion, which whether it be true or false does no prejudice to the worldly concerns of their fellow subjects, which are the things that only belong unto the care of the commonwealth.

But what if the magistrate believe such a law as this to be for the public good? I answer: As the private judgement of any particular person, if erroneous, does not exempt him from the obligation of law, so the private judgement (as I may call it) of the magistrate does not give him any new right of imposing laws upon his subjects, which neither was in the constitution of the government granted him, nor ever was in the power of the people to grant, much less if he make it his business to enrich and advance his followers and fellow-sectaries with the spoils of others. But what if the magistrate believe that he has a right to make such laws and that they are for the public good, and his subjects believe the contrary? Who shall be judge between them? I answer: God alone. For there is no judge upon earth between the supreme magistrate and the people. God, I say, is the only judge in this case, who will retribute unto every one at the last day according to his deserts; that is, according to his sincerity and uprightness in endeavouring to promote piety, and the public weal, and peace of mankind. But What shall be done in the meanwhile? I answer: The principal and chief care of every one ought to be of his own soul first, and, in the next place, of the public peace; though yet there are very few will think it is peace there, where they see all laid waste.

There are two sorts of contests amongst men, the one managed by law, the other by force; and these are of that nature that where the one ends, the other always begins. But it is not my business to inquire into the power of the magistrate in the different constitutions of nations. I only know what usually happens where controversies arise without a judge to determine them. You will say, then, the magistrate being the stronger will have his will and carry his point. Without doubt; but the question is not here concerning the doubtfulness of the event, but the rule of right....

Ecclesiastical assemblies and sermons are justified by daily experience and public allowance. These are allowed to people of some one persuasion; why not to all? If anything pass in a religious meeting seditiously and contrary to the public peace, it is to be punished in the same manner and no otherwise than as if it had happened in a fair or market. These meetings ought not to be sanctuaries for factious and flagitious fellows. Nor ought it to be less lawful for men to meet in churches than in halls; nor are one part of the subjects to be esteemed more blamable for their meeting together than others. Every one is to be accountable for his own actions, and no man is to be laid under a suspicion or odium for the fault of another. Those that are seditious, murderers, thieves, robbers, adulterers, slanderers, etc., of whatsoever Church, whether national or not, ought to be punished and suppressed. But those whose doctrine is peaceable and whose manners are pure and blameless ought to be upon equal terms with their fellow-subjects. Thus if solemn assemblies, observations of festivals, public worship be permitted to any one sort of professors, all these things ought to be permitted to the Presbyterians, Independents, Anabaptists, Arminians, Quakers, and others, with the same liberty. Nay, if we may openly speak the truth, and as becomes one man to another, neither Pagan nor Mahometan, nor Jew, ought to be excluded from the civil rights of the commonwealth because of his religion. The Gospel commands no such thing. The Church which "judgeth not those that are without" wants it not. And the commonwealth, which embraces indifferently all men that are honest, peaceable, and industrious, requires it not. Shall we suffer a Pagan to deal and trade with us, and shall we not suffer him to pray unto and worship God? If we allow the Jews to have private houses and dwellings amongst us, why should we not allow them to have synagogues? Is their doctrine more false, their worship more abominable, or is the civil peace more endangered by their meeting in public than in their private houses? But if these things may be granted to Jews and Pagans, surely the condition of any Christians ought not to be worse than theirs in a Christian commonwealth.

You will say, perhaps: "Yes, it ought to be; because they are more inclinable to factions, tumults, and civil wars." I answer: Is this the fault of the Christian religion? If it be so, truly the Christian religion is the worst of all religions and ought neither to be embraced by any particular person, nor tolerated by any commonwealth. For if this be the genius, this the nature of the Christian religion, to be turbulent and destructive to the civil peace, that Church itself which the magistrate indulges will not always be innocent.... Now as it is very difficult for men patiently to suffer themselves to be stripped of the goods which they have got by their honest industry, and, contrary to all the laws of equity, both human and divine, to be delivered up for a prey to other men's violence and rapine; especially when they are otherwise altogether blameless; and that the occasion for which they are thus treated does not at all belong to the jurisdiction of the magistrate, but entirely to the conscience of every particular man for the conduct of which he is accountable to God only; what else can be expected but that these men, growing weary of the evils under which they labour, should in the end think it lawful for them to resist force with force, and to defend their natural rights (which are not forfeitable upon account of religion) with arms as well as they can?

That this has been hitherto the ordinary course of things is abundantly evident in history, and that it will continue to be so hereafter is but too apparent in reason. It cannot indeed, be otherwise so long as the principle of persecution for religion shall prevail, as it has done hitherto, with magistrate and people, and so long as those that ought to be the preachers of peace and concord shall continue with all their art and strength to excite men to arms and sound the trumpet of war. But that magistrates should thus suffer these incendiaries and disturbers of the public peace might justly be wondered at if it did not appear that they have been invited by them unto a participation of the spoil, and have therefore thought fit to make use of their covetousness and pride as means whereby to increase their own power.

For who does not see that these good men are, indeed, more ministers of the government than ministers of the Gospel and that, by flattering the ambition and favouring the dominion of princes and men in authority, they endeavour with all their might to promote that tyranny in the commonwealth which otherwise they should not be able to establish in the Church? This is the unhappy agreement that we see between the Church and State. Whereas if each of them would contain itself within its own bounds—the one attending to the worldly welfare of the commonwealth, the other to the salvation of souls—it is impossible that any discord should ever have happened between them.... God Almighty grant, I beseech Him, that the gospel of peace may at length be preached, and that civil magistrates, growing more careful to conform their own consciences to the law of God and less solicitous about the binding of other men's consciences by human laws, may, like fathers of their country, direct all their counsels and endeavours to promote universally the civil welfare of all their children, except only of such as are arrogant, ungovernable, and injurious to their brethren; and that all ecclesiastical men, who boast themselves to be the successors of the Apostles, walking peaceably and modestly in the Apostles' steps, without intermeddling with State Affairs, may apply themselves wholly to promote the salvation of souls.

FAREWELL.

Thomas Jefferson

LETTER TO DANBURY BAPTISTS

Library of Congress, 1802

In his letter to the Danbury Baptists, Thomas Jefferson refers to a "wall of separation" between church and state, a requirement that he suggests is guaranteed by natural rights. According to some natural rights theorists, however, such rights are themselves granted by God. In reading this letter, it is important to consider how the idea of the wall of separation and the concept of natural rights might or might not be compatible. In particular, consider whether the phrase used by Jefferson is consistent with the development of the Court's Establishment Clause jurisprudence as you examine it throughout this chapter. As you read the Court's opinions on the Establishment Clause, consider the kind of interpretations that they bring to this concept.

To messers. Nehemiah Dodge, Ephraim Robbins, & Stephen S. Nelson, a committee of the Danbury Baptist association in the state of Connecticut.

Gentlemen

The affectionate sentiments of esteem and approbation which you are so good as to express towards me, on behalf of the Danbury Baptist association, give me the highest satisfaction. My duties dictate a faithful and zealous pursuit of the interests of my constituents, & in proportion as they are persuaded of my fidelity to those duties, the discharge of them becomes more and more pleasing.

Believing with you that religion is a matter which lies solely between Man & his God, that he owes account to none other for his faith or his worship, that the legitimate powers of government reach actions only, & not opinions, I contemplate with sovereign reverence that act of the whole American people which declared that their legislature should "make no law respecting an establishment of religion, or prohibiting the free exercise thereof," thus building a wall of separation between Church & State. Adhering to this expression of the supreme will of the nation in behalf of the rights of conscience, I shall see with sincere satisfaction the progress of those sentiments which tend to restore to man all his natural rights, convinced he has no natural right in opposition to his social duties.

I reciprocate your kind prayers for the protection & blessing of the common father and creator of man, and tender you for yourselves & your religious association, assurances of my high respect & esteem.

Th Jefferson Jan, 1, 1802.

Roger Williams

A PLEA FOR RELIGIOUS LIBERTY

an excerpt from **The Bloudy Tenent of Persecution, for Cause of Conscience**

1644

Roger Williams, one of the founders of Rhode Island, led an intellectual life pursuing questions of political and religious freedom. Martha Nussbaum, whose work you will read next, believes that Williams offers the best lens from which to view the Religion Clauses of the First Amendment. Like John Locke, Williams bases many of his arguments for religious freedom on religious reasoning. For instance, he thinks there are religious reasons to restrict forced conversion. Also, notice his claim that religious freedom will protect religion from corruption by secular authorities. Is his argument compatible with the wall of separation metaphor?

First, that the blood of so many hundred thousand souls of Protestants and Papists, spilt in the wars of present and former ages, for their respective consciences, is not required nor accepted by Jesus Christ the Prince of Peace. . . .

Fourthly, the doctrine of persecution for cause of conscience is proved guilty of all the blood of the souls crying for vengeance under the altar.

Fifthly, all civil states with their officers of justice in their respective constitutions and administrations are proved essentially civil, and therefore not judges, governors, or defenders of the spiritual or Christian state and worship.

Sixthly, it is the will and command of God that (since the coming of his Son the Lord Jesus) a permission of the most paganish, Jewish, Turkish, or antichristian consciences and worships, be granted to all men in all nations and countries; and they are only to be fought against with that sword which is only (in soul matters) able to conquer, to wit, the sword of God's Spirit, the Word of God.

Seventhly, the state of the Land of Israel, the kings and people thereof in peace and war, is proved figurative and ceremonial, and no pattern nor president for any kingdom or civil state in the world to follow.

Eighthly, God requireth not a uniformity of religion to be enacted and enforced in any civil state; which enforced uniformity (sooner or later) is the greatest occasion of civil war, ravishing of conscience, persecution of Christ Jesus in his servants, and of the hypocrisy and destruction of millions of souls. . . .

Eleventhly, the permission of other consciences and worships than a state professeth only can (according to God) procure a firm and lasting peace (good assurance being taken according to the wisdom of the civil state for uniformity of civil obedience from all forts).

TRUTH. I acknowledge that to molest any person, Jew or Gentile, for either professing doctrine, or practicing worship merely religious or spiritual, it is to persecute him, and such a person (whatever his doctrine or practice be, true or false) suffereth persecution for conscience.

But withal I desire it may be well observed that this distinction is not full and complete: for beside this that a man may be persecuted because he holds or practices what he believes in conscience to be a truth (as Daniel did, for which he was cast into the lions' den, Dan. 6), and many thousands of Christians, because

they durst not cease to preach and practice what they believed was by God commanded, as the Apostles answered (Acts 4 & 5), I say besides this a man may also be persecuted, because he dares not be constrained to yield obedience to such doctrines and worships as are by men invented and appointed. . . .

PEACE. I add that a civil sword (as woeful experience in all ages has proved) is so far from bringing or helping forward an opposite in religion to repentance that magistrates sin grievously against the work of God and blood of souls by such proceedings. Because as (commonly) the sufferings of false and antichristian teachers harden their followers, who being blind, by this means are occasioned to tumble into the ditch of hell after their blind leaders, with more inflamed zeal of lying confidence. So, secondly, violence and a sword of steel begets such an impression in the sufferers that certainly they conclude (as indeed that religion cannot be true which needs such instruments of violence to uphold it so) that persecutors are far from soft and gentle commiseration of the blindness of others. . . .

First, the proper means whereby the civil power may and should attain its end are only political. . . . Secondly, the means whereby the church may and should attain her ends are only ecclesiastical. . . .

So that magistrates, as magistrates, have no power of setting up the form of church government, electing church officers, punishing with church censures, but to see that the church does her duty herein. And on the other side, the churches as churches, have no power (though as members of the commonweal they may have power) of erecting or altering forms of civil government, electing of civil officers, inflicting civil punishments (no not on persons excommunicate) as by deposing magistrates from their civil authority, or withdrawing the hearts of the people against them, to their laws, no more than to discharge wives, or children, or servants, from due obedience to their husbands, parents, or masters; or by taking up arms against their magistrates, though he persecute them for conscience: for though members of churches who are public officers also of the civil state may suppress by force the violence of usurpers, as Iehoiada did Athaliah, yet this they do not as members of the church but as officers of the civil state.

TRUTH. Here are diverse considerable passages which I shall briefly examine, so far as concerns our controversy.

First, whereas they say that the civil power may erect and establish what form of civil government may seem in wisdom most meet, I acknowledge the proposition to be most true, both in itself and also considered with the end of it, that a civil government is an ordinance of God, to conserve the civil peace of people, so far as concerns their bodies and goods, as formerly hath been said.

But from this grant I infer (as before hath been touched) that the sovereign, original, and foundation of civil power lies in the people (whom they must needs mean by the civil power distinct from the government set up). And, if so, that a people may erect and establish what form of government seems to them most meet for their civil condition; it is evident that such governments as are by them erected and established have no more power, nor for no longer time, than the civil power or people consenting and agreeing shall betrust them with. This is clear not only in reason but in the experience of all commonweals, where the people are not deprived of their natural freedom by the power of tyrants.

And, if so, that the magistrates receive their power of governing the church from the people, undeniably it follows that a people, as a people, naturally consider (of what nature or nation soever in Europe, Asia, Africa, or America), have fundamentally and originally, as men, a power to govern the church, to see her do her duty, to correct her, to redress, reform, establish, etc. And if this be not to pull God and Christ and Spirit out of heaven, and subject them unto natural, sinful, inconstant men, and so consequently to Satan himself, by whom all peoples naturally are guided, let heaven and earth judge. . . .

The God of Peace, the God of Truth will shortly seal this truth, and confirm this witness, and make it evident to the whole world, that the doctrine of persecution for cause of conscience, is most evidently and lamentably contrary to the doctrine of Christ Jesus the Prince of Peace. Amen.

Martha Nussbaum

LIBERTY OF CONSCIENCE: THE ATTACK ON EQUAL RESPECT

8 J. Hum. Dev. 337 (2007)

This piece by the philosopher Martha Nussbaum serves as a bridge between the theories of Roger Williams and John Locke and modern case law on religious freedom. Nussbaum forcefully defends the idea that individuals should be granted "exemptions" from general laws that impinge on their religious freedom, even in cases where the laws have a noble purpose. This kind of argument appears quite prominently in various cases in this chapter. What problems might arise if such exemptions are allowed? Furthermore, assuming religious exemption is at times justifiable, how should the Court decide when to grant an exemption?

—*Your Selvs praetend libertie of Conscience, but alas, it is but selfe (the great God Selfe) only to Your Selves.*
(Roger Williams, letter to the Governors of Massachusetts and Connecticut 1670, in Williams, 1988, vol. II)

EQUAL LIBERTY OF CONSCIENCE

. . . All modern democracies are currently in a state of fear, and growing religious diversity is one of the things that most keenly inspires fear. Just as in the nineteenth century America saw a panic about Catholic immigration, and otherwise reasonable people hastened to demonize the entirety of the Roman Catholic faith, arguing that Catholicism and Catholics were incompatible with democracy, so too today we hear, in North America and especially in Europe, the same sweeping and unsubtle arguments about Islam and Muslims. . . .

In this paper I shall argue that the only decent antidote to that fear, and to the unjust behavior that it often inspires, lies in renewed commitment to a long tradition of equal respect for conscience that played a formative role in both European and American institutions, but that is frequently honored more in the breach than in the observance—renewed commitment

to that tradition and to the governmental and legal policies that it entails.

What are those policies? . . . In short, respecting liberty of conscience equally entails that the state may not create a two-tiered system of citizenship by establishing a religious orthodoxy that gives rights to others on unequal terms. As U.S. Supreme Court Justice Jackson put it in a famous opinion holding that Jehovah's Witnesses may not be compelled to recite the Pledge of Allegiance in school (which their religion forbids, as a form of idolatry): "If there is any fixed star in our constitutional constellation, it is that no official, high or petty, can prescribe what shall be orthodox in politics, nationalism, religion, or other matters of opinion or force citizens to confess by word or act their faith therein. If there are any circumstances which permit an exception, they do not now occur to us" (*Board of Education v. Barnette*, 1943).

Let us look at two cases that illustrate the issues vividly. . . . In a famous judgment in 1963, the U.S. Supreme Court (*Sherbert v. Verner*, 1963) . . . held that benefits could not be made conditional on a violation of a person's religious scruples: this was just like fining someone for Saturday worship. In other words, the denial of benefits was a violation of Mrs. Sherbert's equal freedom, as a citizen, to worship in her own way. Free exercise does not mean simply that nobody can come and put Mrs. Sherbert in jail for her non-standard religious practices. It means, as well, that the conditions of liberty must be the same for all. The Court held that no person may suffer a "substantial burden" to their religious liberty without a "compelling state interest"—which clearly did not exist in this case.

Workplace arrangements are always made for the benefit of the majority.

The holidays observed, the work-days chosen, all are tailored to suit the local majority; in this case Christian. There is nothing inherently wrong with this—so long as care is taken to prevent this convenient arrangement from turning into a fundamental inequality in freedom and respect. The Free Exercise Clause, the Court held, guarantees that equal freedom.

The Allegheny County Courthouse stands on public property in downtown Pittsburgh. In the late 1980s, the County set up two holiday season displays. The first, inside the Courthouse, consisted of a crèche (Nativity scene), donated by a local Roman Catholic organization, and labeled to that effect. Placed on the Grand Staircase of the Courthouse, with no other displays around it, the Nativity scene bore a sign—carried by an angel above the manger—saying "Gloria in Excelsis Deo" ("Glory to God in the highest").

The second display was outside, on the Courthouse lawn. It consisted of a Hanukkah menorah 18 feet tall, standing next to the city's 45-foot decorated Christmas tree. At the foot of the tree was a message from the mayor saying that the display was a "salute to liberty." (In fact, the menorah is a symbol of liberty, since the holiday of Hanukkah commemorates the Maccabees' courageous rebellion against political oppression. It is difficult to say whether a Christmas tree represents liberty, but it is such an all-purpose symbol that the mayor can probably declare this without implausibility.) Local residents took both displays to court, charging that they violated the Establishment Clause.

The Court obviously considered this a very difficult case. Ultimately a split Court judged that the first display violated the Establishment Clause and the second did

not (*County of Allegheny v. ACLU*, 1989). The crucial question they asked was whether each display communicated the message that the county was giving its endorsement to a particular set of religious beliefs and practices, thus threatening equality. The first display seemed to the majority to communicate such an endorsement: the religious Christian display stood alone, in a position of special prominence and honor. The second display was different: the fact that more than one religion was honored, and that the theme connecting the tree with the menorah was that of liberty, a theme that could include all citizens, whatever their religion or non-religion, meant to at least the Court's center that the people of Pittsburgh would not be likely "to perceive the combined display of the tree, the sign, and the menorah as an 'endorsement' or 'disapproval . . . of their individual religious choices.'"

We can grant that this is a difficult case to decide, and we can even differ about whether it was correctly decided, while yet agreeing about the immense importance of the principle involved. Some religious symbols, set up by government, threaten the equal standing of citizens in the public realm. They attach the imprimatur of orthodoxy to Christian observance, while demoting the beliefs and practices of others.

These cases show us that making law in a pluralistic democracy is a delicate matter, requiring great sensitivity to a variety of contextual and cultural factors. They also show us, however, that all is not well just because no overt violence occurs between members of one religion and those of another. The United States has had its share of outright violence, particularly against members of unpopular new religions—Catholics, Mormons,

Jehovah's Witnesses. What these recent cases show, however, is that there is also violence in the subtle assault on equal dignity that consists in being told that you are not a fully equal citizen because of your commitment to your religion. Europe and the United States plume themselves on their respect for pluralism and their civilized behavior toward religious minorities: and yet, problems like this occur all the time. Until we really counter these more subtle threats and commit ourselves to developing democracies that are really places of equal respect, especially equal respect for new immigrants whom we do not like and whom we fear, we do not have the right to pride ourselves just because there is not very much physical violence. Roger Williams, the great seventeenth-century thinker about religious pluralism, who founded the first colony in which genuine religious equality obtained, called this subtle violence to conscience "soul rape".... We need to think hard about how we can develop democracies that are not places of soul rape....

THE MODERN CONSTITUTIONAL CONSENSUS: FREE EXERCISE ACCOMMODATION

What does it take to defend religious liberty in a truly even-handed way? One philosophical tradition, beginning with Locke (who wrote 50 years after Williams), holds that it takes two things only: first, laws that do not penalize religious belief and practice; and, second, laws that are fair, setting up the same conditions for all citizens in matters that touch on their religion.... For example, says Locke, if it is legal to speak Latin in a school, it ought to be legal to speak Latin

in a church: a law that says otherwise is a covert form of unfairness to Roman Catholics....

Locke's position has modern defenders on the U.S. Supreme Court, in particular Justice Antonin Scalia, who is prepared to strike down laws that expressly discriminate against minorities, but who opposes any special accommodations of their practices....

For a long American tradition that begins in the seventeenth century, the Locke-Scalia position is insufficient, and even Alito's modest extension of it is not quite enough. This tradition reasons that laws, in a democracy, are always made by the majority. They express majority ideas of convenience, and they will incorporate the religious preferences of the majority.... Such laws, even if they do not involve any hostility to minorities, are apt to be heedless, not noticing the special burdens that minorities have to face. Already before the war of independence, the colonists had become used to such problems. Quakers refused to take off their hats in court, although the law required this. Jews refused to give testimony on a Saturday when served with a subpoena. Both Quakers and Mennonites refused required military service.

The position that emerged was one that favored special exemptions in such cases. In a famous letter to the Quakers written shortly after Independence, George Washington, the first U.S. President, said: "I assure you very explicitly, that in my opinion the conscientious scruples of all men should be treated with great delicacy and tenderness: and it is my wish and desire, that the laws may always be as extensively accommodated to them, as a due regard for the protection and essential interests of the nation may justify and permit". . . . He did not require them to perform military service, and he also did not ask them, as Locke would have, to pay the legal penalty. . . .

It was on account of this tradition that Adell Sherbert got her unemployment compensation. The Supreme Court reasoned that imposing such an unequal burden could be done only if the state could show what they called a "compelling interest" in the uniformity in question—for example, by showing that peace and safety were at stake. . . .

THE MODERN CONSTITUTIONAL CONSENSUS: NON-ESTABLISHMENT WITH EQUAL RESPECT

As I said, the liberty-of-conscience tradition quickly became skeptical of any sort of religious establishment, on the grounds that it is 'soul rape' to impose any sort of orthodoxy on the striving individual conscience. Establishments were worst when they threatened liberty, penalizing people for non-orthodox worship, or forcing them to affirm orthodox sentiments that they might not believe, or attaching conditions of religious orthodoxy to a person's civil rights or ability to hold office. It was quickly understood, however, that even an apparently benign establishment fostered inequality, by making a statement that the government of the nation endorses a particular brand of religion. This endorsement is at the same time, inevitably, a dis-endorsement, creating an in group and an out group. As James Madison said, "[A]ll men are to be considered as entering into Society on equal conditions," and even a non-coercive establishment violates that equality. . . . In 1984,

discussing the U.S. Constitution's ban on religious establishment, Justice Sandra Day O'Connor recapitulated the long Madisonian tradition:

> The Establishment Clause prohibits government from making adherence to a religion relevant in any way to a person's standing in the political community. . . . Endorsement sends a message to non-adherents that they are outsiders, not full members of the political community, and an accompanying message to adherents that they are insiders, favored members of the political community. Disapproval sends the opposite message.

(*Lynch v. Donnelly*, 1984)

According to Justice O'Connor's very helpful analysis, the right question to ask of any potentially problematic policy in the area of religious establishment is the following one: would an objective observer, acquainted with all the relevant historical and contextual facts, view the policy in question as one that makes a public statement of endorsement or disapproval, sending a message of inequality?

. . . Here, as before, what is important to see is the importance of the equality analysis. We must always ask whether a given form of aid expresses government favor for religion or a particular religion, or whether, by contrast, a given refusal of aid expresses actual disfavor for religion.

So far in this talk I have not used the words "separation of church and state," so often used, especially by the left, in this connection. My avoidance of these words is deliberate. This slogan was, in fact, not part of our original constitutional tradition. It is not to be found in our Constitution, and none of the framers used it; they preferred the language of liberty and equality. The slogan arose in the mid-nineteenth century during the panic over Catholic immigration, and it expressed people's fear that the Catholic church was going to take over American institutions. To some extent, the words can rise above their tawdry history, and in the mouths of some thoughtful liberals they do express admirable values of liberty and equality. But the idea of separation does not direct thought well. Total separation of church from state, if we think of it literally, is both impossible and undesirable. We do not want to deny the church the benefits of the fire department and the police. We also do not want to deny priests and ministers the right to run for office, although at some times in our history people have held that view. How much separation is a good thing, and how much is a bad thing? That is the question we must ask. And we can answer it well only with recourse to other more fundamental values, in particular those of equal standing in the political community and equal liberty....

THE ATTACK ON THE TRADITION OF EQUAL LIBERTY

The tradition I have praised has many enemies, but we can reduce them all to two, both rather common in decent modern liberal democracies, and it is with these assailants that I want to conclude. Neither is a double-dyed villain, but both, I believe, fail to understand something essential about what equal respect for persons requires. The first opponent I shall call the *establishmentarian*. This person thinks that good order and public safety require a public commitment to a religious orthodoxy, a dominant religious tradition. Life with so many different religions is too chaotic, too fraught, unless we can state quite clearly that this is who we are as a nation: this is our creed, our tradition, these are our religious values, and anyone who wants to live in peace among us has to acknowledge this and assimilate to it....

What is wrong with this view is that it does not treat people as equals. It asks some to subordinate their conscientious commitments to those of others. Even a benign establishmentarianism can have quite far-reaching effects disadvantageous to minorities. It can support policies that use taxpayer money to fund schools only of a particular religious sort, policies that allow religious tests for public office, and so on. But even when an establishment does not do this—as with the one in Virginia that James Madison criticized, which allowed people to opt out of the tax donation to the established church—as Madison said, such a policy nonetheless, just by announcing a preferred state religion, tells minorities that they do not enter the public square "on equal conditions." It asks them to live on terms of permanent second-class citizenship and a certain degree of humiliation, as public ceremonials announce again and again that the outsiders are not really equal.

It is easy to frown on this opponent—at least for American intellectuals, for whom these views are associated with the religious right, whom American intellectuals are accustomed to think of as very different from themselves, and not very bright. It is less easy to frown on my second opponent, who is found, mostly, on the left. This opponent I shall call the *anti-religionist*. This position, as you shall see, is the obverse of Rehnquist's. The anti-religionist thinks that all religion should be disfavored in the public square—not for reasons of equality, or liberty, but because he or she thinks religion somewhat embarrassing, a relic of a pre-scientific era, and a source of nothing but trouble. We can best build lasting democracies, thinks the anti-religionist, if we discourage religion and build on secular scientific rationality. Of course we should not repress religion or legally penalize religious people or religious observance. But we should certainly discourage it, and there is absolutely no reason to bend over backwards to give it space to unfold itself. . . .

What is wrong with anti-religionism? Well, the first thing that has been wrong with most actual versions of it is that it is likely to be especially harsh toward minority religions. The religion of the majority does not look particularly religious, because it is so much a part of dominant laws and customs that it does not stand out. . . .

The second problem with anti-religionism is that it is likely to be stingy with accommodations. Because it thinks that religion is fundamentally not very important, it is not likely to go out of its way to give people dispensations from laws of general applicability on grounds of conscience. Drug laws, laws about work days, all of these will be arranged to suit the convenience of the modern administrative state. If the anti-religionist thinks a particular war wrong, then he or she may uphold a limited right to conscientious objection in wartime. But not on grounds of conscience in the traditional sense. Anti-religionists simply do not have very much respect for the capability of conscience, not in so far as it exercises itself in a religious way.

Third and most basic: even a fair anti-religionism is not compatible with a thoroughgoing commitment to equal respect. Anti-religionism says, here we are, the enlightened ones—philosopher Daniel Dennett calls himself and his fellow anti-religionists the "brights." We "brights" see more clearly than you benighted people over there. This is not a very good stance to take toward one's fellow citizens, in a world full of mystery and complexity, where it is a very good bet that nobody, not the anti-religionist either, has the ultimate solution to questions about the meaning of life and death that have plagued humanity ever since humanity began to exist. If scientific anti-religionists think they do have the answer—in the form, for example, of a reductive physiological account of the life and death of organisms—we should protest that this is an answer so drained of mystery and genuine curiosity that it is this answer, not the traditions of the religions, which demeans humanity and compromises the project of building a rich multifaceted state based on respect for humanity. (The framers of the Universal Declaration of Human Rights agreed not to base the declaration on any specific religious or ethical comprehensive doctrine, but they did need to agree, they thought, on a moral view of human dignity that made human beings not mere bundles of matter, not mere objects to be used for the ends of efficiency.)

. . . The human internal capability of conscience is a delicate and vulnerable thing. It needs support from laws and institutions. Because it is worthy of equal respect, it is worthy of equal support. An approach to political principles based on the idea of human capability should learn from the tradition I have described, and reject both establishmentarianism and anti-religionism—in order to be fully respectful and fully fair to all human beings.

Amy Gutmann

CHILDREN, PATERNALISM, AND EDUCATION: A LIBERAL ARGUMENT

9 Phil. & Pub. Aff. 338 (1980)

This reading by Amy Gutmann suggests why granting exemptions might be problematic in some cases. Guttmann argues that significant constitutional tension can arise in cases where the child's interests might conflict with the parents' conscience, such as in the case of Wisconsin v. Yoder. *In discerning what is in the best interest of children, and what their basic rights are, to what extent should society defer to their parents' beliefs? How should conflicts between children's interests and rights and those of their parents be resolved?*

The liberal principle concerning *paternalism* does not comprehend all of parents' justified interference with their children's liberty. Parents also have rights of action that are not based upon evidence that parents will thereby serve the interests of their children better than any other available agents. Charles Fried argues that "the right to form one's child's values, one's child's life plan and the right to lavish attention on the child are extensions of the basic right not to be interfered with in doing these things for oneself." But why should a liberal society permit any *extensions* of a person's negative rights of action to include rights of action over *other people*?

. . . Let us begin with parents' rights to free exercise of their religion. Most of us assume that this right extends to a right to educate one's children into one's own religion. But why ought this extension of a personal right to a right over another (albeit immature) person be regarded as legitimate? After all, although we believe

that free exercise of religion is a primary good, many of us do not think that religion itself is a primary good or that religious education is in the *best* interests of children. Do parents' rights of religious education have a source other than our common understanding of what constitutes their children's best interests? Our answer, I think, must be a qualified yes. But Fried's argument supporting this conclusion is troubling, for he suggests that parents have rights to educate children in their own values because children are extensions of their parents' personalities and because these rights are therefore a measure of parents' own autonomy. To this extent parents' rights must operate regardless not only of democratic determination but also of their children's interests. Given the tenets of many religions, free exercise for parents necessarily entails raising their children according to the precepts of their own religion. This is certainly true of Orthodox Jews, the Amish, and members of many other religious groups whose religions constitute ways of *family* life for their followers. Freedom of belief for parents who lack traditional religious affiliations may similarly be inseparable from freedom to teach a preferred system of values to their children. In this sense, Fried is correct in suggesting that parents' rights to raise their children are extensions of other basic negative rights granted to adults by a liberal state. However, these negative rights of parents over their children are not, as Fried's basic argument implies, very broad or inviolable. Parents' rights are seriously constrained by the rights of their children, which are in turn dependent upon the nature of the society within which children are to be raised. Consider the free exercise rights of Amish parents. Their objection to formal education of their children beyond the eighth grade is grounded in the central tenets of their religion: the Amish "object to the high school . . . because the values they teach are in marked variance with Amish values and the Amish way of life; they view secondary school education as an impermissible exposure of their children to a 'worldly' influence in conflict with their beliefs." In *Wisconsin v. Yoder*, the Supreme Court ruled that Amish parents could not be forced to send their children to any school beyond the eighth grade, although Wisconsin law mandated formal schooling for all children until they reached the age of sixteen. The Court held that Amish parents' right to the free exercise of their religion was abrogated by Wisconsin's attempt to enforce the state's school attendance law upon Amish children. The Court's ruling appears consistent with the argument that parents' rights over their children are extensions of their own negative rights in this case, of their right to religious freedom.

Perhaps the stakes in the *Yoder* case were too small to impress the dilemma it posed upon us; only one or two years of compulsory schooling were in dispute. But imagine if another well-established religious group in the United States otherwise identical to the Amish were to forbid *all* formal education for their children for the same reasons that the Amish prohibit schooling beyond the eighth grade. What ought a court to rule concerning the claim by members of this religious group that educating their children in schools would expose them "to worldly influences in terms of attitudes, goals, and values contrary to beliefs," and would substantially interfere with their religious development and integration into their community's way of life? Here we have a free exercise claim of parents pitted against their own children's right to an education that will prepare them for choosing competently among a broad range of conceptions of the good life and for participating intelligently in the political life of their society. The choice the court must make is clear: it can uphold either the parents' or the children's rights. Competing rights claims are never easy to adjudicate. But this case is more difficult than usual. How does one balance the parents' right over their children (by extension of their own free exercise right) against the right to education made on behalf of those same children by the liberal state acting as *parens patriae*?

Before attempting an answer, we must briefly examine the meaning of a child's right to education within a liberal society. If children have rights in virtue of their basic needs and interests as future adult citizens, one of those rights will be a right to education, or what some theorists have called "a right to socialization." The content of children's right to education will depend upon what is adequate for living a full life within their society—for being capable of choosing among available conceptions of the good and of participating intelligently in democratic politics if they so choose. I have no doubt that this criterion imposes substantially greater obligations upon us than we fulfill by our current educational, and other related, practices. But beyond this point, education ceases to be a right, even if it remains an important human good. On this understanding, a child's right to compulsory education is a precondition to becoming a rational human being and a full citizen of a liberal democratic society. Without any formal schooling, children will be incapable of intelligently exercising their civil or political rights within our society. The assertion on the part of parents of an unconstrained right of free exercise therefore entails the assertion of a right to deprive their children of two fundamental goods for which a liberal democratic state exists: the making of an informed choice among conceptions of the good life, and participation in meaningful democratic self-government. Rawls' conclusion that liberty has priority over other primary goods is not appropriate to this case of ordering primary goods, however appropriate it may be to ordering entitlements among adult citizens. We rank children's rights to education above their rights to religious freedom since we believe that this restriction of their present liberty is necessary to create the conditions for future enjoyment of religious and other freedoms.

Without education, liberal freedoms lose a great deal, even if not all, of their value. We are left now with the problem of ordering the religious freedom of parents and the right of children to an adequate education. The appropriate rule is that a child's right to education be given priority over his or her parents' right to religious exercise. This is, I think, the correct priority for the following reasons:

(1) A child's right to education is a necessary precondition for the development of capacities to choose a conception of the good life and to employ the political freedoms of democratic citizenship.

(2) Even if one considers that the constraint of parents' free exercise is a denial to their child of his or her present freedom of religion, a concurrent denial of the child's educational right calls into question the grounds of his or her acceptance of those religious beliefs.

(3) Although this priority allows the liberal state to abridge parents' religious freedom, the state is justified in limiting only that portion of parents' freedom that extends to dominion over their child *and* restricts their child's basic rights.

(4) The value of a liberal democracy to its citizens is in large part contingent upon the ability of its citizens to exercise their political rights intelligently as well as to choose among alternative conceptions of the good life. Allowing parents to deprive their children of the right to education blocks realization of these basic future freedoms of personal and political choice.

One can concede that any practical standard of education will eliminate some options that might otherwise be open to children when they mature, but so long as we must choose among paternalistic standards we are required to choose those that are most neutral among competing conceptions of the good, standards that expand rather than contract a child's future ability to exercise meaningful choice. Since by placing the child's right to education above his or her parents' claims of free exercise we diminish, but do not negate the meaningfulness of their religious freedom, we ought to conclude that parental rights of free exercise cannot override a child's right to education. My argument so far constitutes a response to one common "liberal" defense of ceding parents full rights to educate their children as they see fit: that if liberalism is based upon respect for individual choice among differing conceptions of the good and upon granting individuals the freedom to practice their differing conceptions, we cannot justify restricting parents' rights to educate and socialize their children into what they consider the most worthy modes of life. On the contrary, we *can* justify limitations upon parents' rights because our valuation of liberal freedom to pursue differing conceptions of the good is dependent upon that freedom being exercised by beings who have been raised under conditions conducive to choice. Nor is it a valid objection to say that the democratic state (on my view) is simply imposing *its* values upon children. Some values must be imposed in any case. What is at issue here is not *whose* values but *what* values ought to be imposed upon children. I have defended a liberal concern for fostering conditions that facilitate the development of capacities for personal choice and democratic citizenship. If our present state is not more reliable at enforcing this paternalistic standard than individual parents are, then my argument certainly does not support its standards above those of parents. The priority of children's rights to education over parental rights of religion only justifies state regulation of private and public education to the extent that such regulation provides the best guarantee to all children of an education adequate to full and equal citizenship. Once a liberal state insures that every child is so educated, it has no further rights of paternalistic agency over children with regard to education.

Chris Eisgruber & Lawrence Sager

THE VULNERABILITY OF CONSCIENCE: THE CONSTITUTIONAL BASIS FOR PROTECTING RELIGIOUS CONDUCT

61 U. Chi. L. Rev. 1245 (1994)

Like Martha Nussbaum, Chris Eisgruber and Lawrence Sager appeal to a notion of equality as the basis of the Freedom of Religion Clauses. They suggest, however, that religious exemptions should be granted only in a certain set of circumstances, in part because they do not seem to share Nussbaum's conviction that there is anything special about religious belief per se. Instead, they offer a model of non-discrimination against religion as the basis for interpreting the Religion Clauses. To what extent, if at all, is this secular defense of religious freedom compatible with religious exemption? Does it give enough weight to the role of religion in American life? Most importantly, is religious belief distinct from or more important than deeply held non-religious beliefs?

What is needed is a fresh start. We need to abandon the idea that it is the unique value of religious practices that sometimes entitles them to constitutional attention. What properly motivates constitutional solicitude for religious practices is their distinct vulnerability to discrimination, not their distinct value; and what is called for, in turn, is protection against discrimination, not privilege against legitimate governmental concerns. When we have replaced value with vulnerability, and the paradigm of privilege with that of protection, then it will be possible both to make sense of our constitutional past in this area and to chart an appealing constitutional future. That is the project of this Article. We hope to demonstrate that the privilege view of religious exemptions is normatively unjustified and unattractive in its practical implications, while the protection view is both justified and attractive in its consequences. . . .

. . . Most modern commentary has proceeded on the assumption that the constitutional status of religious exemptions rises or falls on the degree to which religious practices are constitutionally privileged—privileged in the way, for example, that speech is privileged. If religiously motivated people are to be exempt from the application of laws that they would otherwise be required to obey, it is assumed, this must be because religion is esteemed by the Constitution in a way that most other human commitments, however intense or laudable, are not . . . the paradigm of privilege itself is deeply misdirecting as a guide to religious liberty in general, and to the problem of religious exemptions in particular. A closer look at the privileging view strongly confirms this initial assessment.

THE CASE AGAINST THE PRIVILEGING OF RELIGIOUS EXEMPTIONS

A. The Privileging of Religion Made More Precise: Unimpaired Flourishing

The underlying logic of the privileging view of religious exemptions is this: It is a matter of constitutional regret whenever government prevents or discourages persons from honoring their religious commitments; accordingly, government should act so as to avoid placing religious believers at a substantial disadvantage by virtue of their efforts to conform their conduct to their beliefs. This is the principle of unimpaired flourishing.

Unimpaired flourishing is sometimes offered as a principle of equity, as though it functions merely to make those who respond to the strong demands of their religious beliefs no worse off than others. But unimpaired flourishing is different than that: it privileges religious commitments over other deep commitments that persons have. Members of our political community are not generally entitled to governmental arrangements that enable them to honor their important commitments without being placed at a substantial disadvantage. . . .

Unimpaired Flourishing Applied

Welfare-driven measures of justice have an endemic normative burden: idiosyncracies in the welfare functions of some individuals will support extreme and intuitively discreditable demands on social resources on their behalf-demands that seem to contradict the underlying project of securing justice. . . . As a conception of religious freedom, unimpaired flourishing presents a striking variant on this normative difficulty. Religious belief need not be founded in reason, guided by reason, or governed in any way by the reasonable. Accordingly, the demands that religions place on the faithful, and the demands that the faithful can in turn place on society in the name of unimpaired flourishing, are potentially extravagant. The potential of religious beliefs to be arbitrarily demanding, to be greedy in their demands on both the individual and the society committed to the unimpaired flourishing of its religiously faithful, is compounded by the possible all-or-nothing quality of religious dictates. In other domains, well-being is generally incremental—having the requirements of well-being partially satisfied is a benefit. But religious demands can be absolute or categorical. They can assume the form: "A, B, and C must all be fully in place or you are condemned to eternal damnation." The principle of unimpaired flourishing, as a result, commends a vision of a world that is unrecognizable, unattractive, and ultimately incoherent. In this world, the faithful would be licensed to do as their faith requires, with little regard for the consequences as seen from the vantage of secular society. In this world, wealth would be distributed so as to support comfortably those whose religious commitments diverted them from remunerative pursuits, or otherwise required great investments of time and money. In this world, the faithful whose beliefs so required would receive disproportionate authority over decisions about the use of collective authority. The chaotic picture that emerges is ultimately incoherent in this sense: the demands of one faith would ultimately extend so far as to come into sharp conflict with the requirements of other religions, and some mechanism, presumably secular, would have to arbitrate. But, of course, no proponent of the constitutional privileging of religion actually means to take us into this ungainly world.

Significantly, almost all judges and commentators who urge something like the principle of unimpaired flourishing nevertheless want collective authority in the United States to remain pretty much as it is; they merely want to find a haven for religiously motivated conduct at the margins of state authority. This produces incoherence of a much more immediate and troubling sort: proponents of unimpaired flourishing are in the unhappy position of offering an unexplainably selective, comparatively modest, practical agenda for reform, on the basis of a sweeping and deeply radical principle of political justice. The result is an analytical scramble. Various limitations are offered, often in combination. Religiously motivated acts that harm others, it is sometimes suggested, may be curtailed by state law, but the state may not interfere with religious believers on paternalistic grounds. As to the support of religious believers who cannot earn or must spend as a consequence of their beliefs, a baseline grounded, in effect, on the existing distribution of wealth and opportunity is urged, and claims to improve on the status quo for needy religious believers are disavowed. Or, it is suggested, secular needs must be balanced against religious needs. These attempts to rescue unimpaired flourishing from its own logic are unsatisfying. If religious motivation signifies legal immunity only at the margins of state authority, there is good reason to suppose that in these cases we are actually responding to well-founded—if inarticulate—doubts about state authority in general rather than to the needs of religion in particular. On this account, if we valued liberty in general to the appropriate degree, there would be no need for the additional feature of religious motivation to enter the story.

Indeed, important constitutional benefits depend upon our willingness to recognize this connection between specifically religious interests and more general principles of privilege. Religious groups perform a valuable service in a freedom-loving society: they push at the margins of liberty. But that service is best realized when the regime of law refuses to privilege religion, so that the systematic but idiosyncratic impulses of organized religion act on behalf of us all when they help to maintain or expand the ambit of constitutionally secure choice....

The Normative Difficulties of Unimpaired Flourishing

1. The sectarian defect

In a liberal democracy, the claim that one particular set of practices or one particular set of commitments ought to be privileged (as we have used that term) bears a substantial burden of justification. As we shall see, the background circumstances—that religion is singled out for distinct and emphatic treatment in the text of the Constitution, that many of the colonists fled religious persecution under circumstances that would have made religious liberty vital, that there are various features of religious liberty in our working constitutional tradition that seem at once important and well settled—do not in themselves support the proposition that religion ought to be privileged. An attractive and full account of religion's place in our constitutional tradition can proceed from protection rather than privilege. Justification for the privileging of religion must proceed on normative grounds.

In a nation with many groups, many values, and many views of the commitments by which a good life is shaped, the shared understanding among some groups that they are each bound by the commandments of a (different) god they believe deserves/demands obeisance is unacceptably sectarian as a basis for the constitutional privileging of religion. Their claim, as a union of groups within a broader, pluralistic society is no different in principle than the sectarian claim of the religious believer we first considered, who reasoned, wholly from within his own religious tradition, that his God

was the true, supreme god, and thus the state must permit each believer in the true God to subordinate the state's commands to those of God. As against the artist for whom art is the highest command of life, the activist to whom the pursuit of racial justice is all, or any of us who happen not to be members of the union of the deeply religious, the members of the union have no reason to offer, from within their own beliefs, for the privileging of their commitments that the rest of us lack with regard to our deep commitments.

2. Two nonsectarian strategies

There are, however, two arguments for the constitutional privileging of religion that do not suffer from this sectarian defect. The first appeals to persons within our political community to recognize—from the outside, in effect—the anguished state of the religious believer who is under state fiat to behave in a way that flatly contradicts the demands of her religion. The second suggests that organized religion enables our society to maintain an important place for the moral, non-self-regarding aspects of life.

One version of the first argument asks us to consider the potential stakes for the religious believer of disobeying her God's commandments. They may be such that it is an understatement to speak of them as matters of life and death; they may be no less than eternal paradise or damnation. We cannot be expected to act as though those are the stakes, of course, but we can appreciate the unhappy state of someone who regards them as the stakes. This seems an unpromising way to put the case. It asks us to assume—in a way that seems especially inappropriate when it comes to matters spiritual—that self-interest rather than conscience is the stronger human drive. It expects us to treat the religious believer's very long-term (possibly abstract, metaphorical) self—interested reasons for obedience as motivationally more powerful than other persons' immediate self-interest and driving passions—the deeply devoted artist, the parent with a hungry child, or the lover overwrought with love, who are driven to disobey the law. Furthermore, it asks us either to treat all religions as having the structure of eternal reward/punishment because some do, or to parse among religions on this peculiar ground. Interestingly (and this may not be a criticism), it also asks us to accept as true for the believer that heaven and hell are at stake, while holding to the contrary as a matter of our own belief.

The better version of this first argument for privileging religion emphasizes mortal conscience rather than eternal consequences. It encourages us to see that the religious believer is in the grip of conscience—a motivation that is at once powerful and laudable—and to regard that circumstance as grounds for excusing her from obedience to laws that force her to choose between her conscience and her well-being at the hands of the state. But while conscience is the better motivational grounds for privileging religion, there remain persuasive objections to the claim.

Again, religious conscience is just one of many very strong motivations in human life, and there is no particular reason to suppose that it is likely to matter more in the run of religious lives generally than will other very powerful forces in the lives of both the nonreligious and the religious. This is not to trivialize religious interests. We have no trouble agreeing with Douglas Laycock when he argues that it would be

an error to maintain that "[a] soldier who believes he must cover his head before an omnipresent God is constitutionally indistinguishable from a soldier who wants to wear a Budweiser gimme cap." Likewise, we agree with Michael McConnell that a Saturday work schedule imposes qualitatively different burdens on those who "like to go sailing on Saturdays" and those who "observe the Sabbath" on that day. But these comparisons largely beg the question. Of course, burdens upon religious practice differ from burdens upon tastes in fashion and recreation. Do they also differ from the considerably more weighty burdens imposed by secular commitments to one's family, or by secular moral obligations, or by physical disabilities?

Consider two cases:

(1) Goldman is an army officer. His faith requires him to wear a yarmulke. The yarmulke is inconsistent with the Army uniform. The Army insists that Goldman must resign his commission or comply with the uniform regulation. The Army relies entirely on its interest in uniform appearance; it does not contend that Goldman's obligation to wear the yarmulke will in any other way impair his performance.

(2) Collar is an army officer. He has a rare skin disorder on his neck that prevents him from wearing a tie. Army uniform regulations require that all officers wear ties on certain occasions. The Army insists that Collar must resign his commission or comply with the regulation. The Army relies entirely on its interest in uniform appearance; it does not contend that Collar's disability will in any other way impair his performance.

Should we regard Goldman's interests as more weighty than Collar's? Does the

Army have a constitutional obligation to accommodate Goldman's religious burden if it accommodates Collar's disability, or vice-versa? To maintain that the Constitution privileges religion, we would have to uncover some ground for constitutionally favoring Goldman's interests over Collar's, a ground that is not impermissibly sectarian or partisan; and that is precisely what is lacking in the case for privileging religion.

The second nonsectarian argument for the constitutional privileging of religion appeals to our desire as a society to remain alive to the moral, non-self-regarding aspects of life, and sees organized religion as a taproot of this vital aspect of human flourishing. But while religion sponsors the highest forms of community, compassion, love, and sacrifice, one need only look around the world, or probe our own history, to recognize that it also sponsors discord, hate, intolerance, and violence. Religion is enormously varied in the demands it places on the faithful. As we observed earlier, religious faith or belief need not be founded in reason, guided by reason, or governed in any way by the reasonable. . . .

IV. THE PROTECTION OF MINORITY BELIEF AS A RATIONALE FOR RELIGIOUS EXEMPTIONS

A. A New Approach: Equal Regard

We advocate a new approach to religious exemptions, founded on protection rather than privilege. Protection can explain and justify the distinct status of religion in our constitutional tradition, offer a workable and attractive approach to religious exemptions, and—surprisingly—make some sense out of the patchwork of precedent regarding religious exemptions.

In place of the mistaken claim that religion is uniquely valued by the Constitution, an approach based on protection depends upon the special vulnerability of minority religious beliefs to hostility or indifference. Where privilege sponsored the principle of unimpaired flourishing, protection offers the principle of equal regard. Equal regard requires simply that government treat the deep, religiously inspired concerns of minority religious believers with the same regard as that enjoyed by the deep concerns of citizens generally. Equal regard needs to be on the active agenda of the judiciary because of the confluence of two circumstances. First, for many religious believers, being able to conform their conduct to the dictates of their beliefs is a matter of deep concern. Second, the religious provenance of these strong behavioral impulses makes them highly vulnerable to discrimination by official decision makers. Both of these propositions are widely acknowledged and do not require detailed support here. But the second bears elaboration. Religious commandments are not necessarily founded on or limited by reasons accessible to nonbelievers; often they are understood to depend on fiat or covenant and to implicate forces or beings beyond human challenge or comprehension. Religion is often the hub of tightly knit communities, whose habits, rituals, and values are deeply alien to outsiders. At best, this is likely to produce a chronic interfaith "tone deafness," in which the persons of one faith do not easily empathize with the concerns of persons in other faiths. At worst, it may produce hostility, even murderous hatred, among different religious groups.

The axis of antagonism—even with its broad range from indifference to hostility—does not fully capture the subtle pattern of religious vulnerability. From the perspective of some faiths, it is desirable to convert nonbelievers rather than to injure them. Such messianic faiths may have the welfare of the nonbelievers genuinely and fully in mind as they zealously seek converts to the true faith; they may even have the welfare of the nonbelievers fully in mind as they seek to shape the legal regime to discourage or prevent the nonbelievers from pursuing their own beliefs.

These nonantagonist variations may be "kinder, gentler" forms of discrimination, but they remain stark failures of equal regard. The possibility of nonantagonistic disregard of minority concerns makes religious discrimination particularly subtle and complex. This will be important to bear in mind as we turn to the task of sketching a jurisprudence of equal regard.

D. Equal Regard and Equal Protection

As we flesh out the idea of equal regard, it may seem to resemble a robust jurisprudence of equal protection. Robust in this sense: contemporary equal protection doctrine protects African Americans and women by barring both facial distinctions disfavoring those groups and facially neutral governmental action that is motivated by animus toward those groups; it does not bar facially neutral governmental action that has only a disparate impact on protected groups. Equal regard seems more demanding in this respect than equal protection, and our readers may wonder whether we mean to argue that religion should enjoy special protection, that the Supreme Court has erred in excluding disparate impact from close constitutional scrutiny in equal protection cases, or some third proposition not yet on the table. Certainly equal regard and equal protection have much in common—not only because both invoke the general norm of equality, but also because, as we observed earlier, the Supreme Court's jurisprudence of racial equality is the most prominent example of the paradigm of protection in constitutional law. Moreover, as we shall see in a moment, one of our specific recommendations may well have implications outside the context of religious liberty. Nevertheless, it would be a mistake to conflate equal regard with traditional equal protection doctrine in general or with a new sensitivity to disparate impact in particular. Extant equal protection jurisprudence assumes that governmental behavior operating to disadvantage a vulnerable group is either purposefully designed to accomplish that result or is innocent of any constitutionally cognizable harm. Equal regard, of course, condemns governmental behavior that purposefully harms a religious group; but it also identifies and condemns behavior that lies in a middle ground between purposeful discrimination and unintended disparate harm. Governmental action that betrays a failure to treat the serious concerns of minority religious believers with the same regard extended to the deep concerns of citizens generally is vulnerable to a distinct constitutional objection. . . .

CONCLUSION

Cast in the mold of constitutional privilege, the idea of religious liberty is self-contradictory. The problem is not simply that religious liberty at its margins may conflict with other constitutional precepts, or even that under the umbrella of religious liberty we may find subsidiary principles that are at times in conflict. The problem is deeper than either of these familiar observations. At its core, religious liberty is about the toleration—the celebration—of the divergent ways that members of our society come to understand the foundational coordinates of a well-formed life. To single out one of the ways that persons come to understand what is important in life, and grant those who choose that way a license to disregard legal norms that the rest of us are obliged to obey, is to defeat rather than fulfill our commitment to toleration. Yet that favoritism is precisely what the privileging view of religious liberty requires. Yet, if the defects of the privileging view are patent, so too are the conditions that make constitutional solicitude for religion essential. Religious persecution drove many of the settlers of the colonies from Europe to America and drove some from their newfound homes in America. Religious discrimination is not merely an artifact of constitutional history. Within the memory of many adults, it was a prominent feature of our national landscape, and it would be far too optimistic to think that we have outgrown the human impulse to respond badly to the basic differences of culture, habit, and belief that attach to diverse religious faiths. So while the root infirmity of conferring constitutional privilege on religious belief has been sufficiently well understood to curb the Court's enthusiasm for such a privilege, the impulse to preserve nonmainstream religious belief from hostile or indifferent governmental treatment has had a durable—and deserved—place in constitutional adjudication. The resulting tension has made a hash of the jurisprudence of religious accommodation. The problem lies not with religious liberty but with the paradigm of constitutional privilege and with the principle of unimpaired flourishing that paradigm sponsors. If we replace privilege with protection and replace unimpaired flourishing with equal regard, we can rebuild the jurisprudence of religious accommodation. We can make sense of what has seemed scattered precedent, and we can make religious liberty compatible with its own roots in toleration—and hence with the whole of our tradition of constitutional liberty.

Corey Brettschneider

A TRANSFORMATIVE THEORY OF RELIGIOUS FREEDOM

38 Pol. Theory 187 (2010)

Most of the readings so far have focused on the protections provided by the First Amendment for religious groups. In this article, I examine the ways in which the state might seek to promote equality, even in cases where religious groups reject this value. I suggest that efforts by the state to promote equality may in fact be compatible with rights against coercion.

My argument proceeds in three stages, each of which is designed to allay fears that a transformative account of religious freedom is antireligious and antiliberal. First, I argue that religious freedom is a principled commitment that requires the transformation of religious viewpoints at odds with it. Second, I place this transformative account in the context of a wider theory of political liberalism. I argue that this transformative account does not require an all-or-nothing choice between a commitment to liberalism or to religion. Finally, I emphasize the compatibility of my transformative account of religious freedom with basic rights such as freedom of association. Throughout this article, I draw on U.S. Supreme Court cases related to the free exercise clause of the First Amendment. But I do so to develop an argument in political theory about how religious freedom should be understood, not to affirm existing case law or develop a new free-exercise jurisprudence.

RELIGION v. RELIGIOUS FREEDOM: THE *LUKUMI* PRINCIPLE

On a static analysis of religious freedom, such as that suggested by accommodationist thinkers, the first concern should be whether laws intentionally or unintentionally burden religious practices. On this view, an account of religious freedom must be sensitive not only to the dangers of the state's directly attacking religious belief but also to unintended effects of policy on religious exercise. Accommodationists assume that religious freedom is endangered whenever existing religious beliefs are burdened or changed. Accommodationist thinking figured strongly in the Supreme Court's jurisprudence prior to *Employment Division v. Smith* in 1990. A fundamental flaw in static views that associate religious freedom with the preservation of existing religious beliefs is that they cannot account for the potential tensions between these beliefs and the desire to protect religious freedom.

Consider, for instance, the Court's decision to strike down municipal legislation prohibiting animal sacrifice in *Church of*

the Lukumi Babalu Aye v. City of Hialeah. In this case, the city of Hialeah, Florida, had deliberately targeted the practice of the Santeria religion, which involves the sacrifice of live animals. The legislation was designed to single out animal sacrifice in particular for criminal sanction, although similar forms of animal slaughter were permitted. A unanimous Court suggested that this legislation could not be explained on any basis other than animus toward the Santeria religion. I suggest that we study this example to understand the tensions present in thinking about the political morality of religious freedom. In particular, I wish to use this case because it is commonly thought to be a paradigmatic example of the judicial protection of religious freedom. I hope to push this common understanding of *Lukumi* to show that religious freedom at times requires attempts at transformation. My aim is not to oppose the accommodationists' claim that religious freedom requires some exemptions to general laws. Rather, I examine the philosophical inadequacy of such an approach when issues of equal citizenship are implicated.

Since the ordinance at issue in *Lukumi* hindered religious practices, a static analysis would likely suggest that it should be struck down. Not only did the Hialeah city councilmen who passed the law limit the religious practice of animal sacrifice, but they apparently did so with the intent of burdening the Santeria religion specifically. The flaws and limits of the static approach, however, can be found by looking at the transcript of the meeting in which the city as a whole discussed the ordinance. The transcript, quoted in Justice Kennedy's majority opinion, reveals that the ordinances were themselves religiously motivated. One councilman justified his opposition to the practice of animal sacrifice by stating, "I don't believe the Bible allows that." The chaplain of the Hialeah police department variously described Santeria practices as "an abomination to the Lord" and the worship of "demons." Thus, whatever the Court's decision in *Lukumi*, there would have been an adverse effect on some religion. The Santeria practitioners would have been adversely affected if the law had been allowed to stand. On the other hand, striking down the law would apparently burden the religious views of the councilmen and others, who hold that it is a Christian moral duty to ban animal sacrifice. In striking down the ordinance, the Court not only protected the Santeria religion from illiberal, coercive legislation. It also served to condemn the illiberal beliefs behind the legislation. The fact that these beliefs were motivated by religion does not immunize them from condemnation. As I see it, the Court's decision to strike down this law also expressed the message that those particular views of the councilmen that led them to pass the ordinance, regardless of whether they were religious or not, have no place in a free society's deliberations about coercion.

We are thus confronted by a seeming paradox of religious freedom. It is usually understood that religious freedom protects certain religious practices. In a related vein, religious freedom is thought to protect the religious beliefs that underlie such practices. But not all religious practices, and not all religious beliefs, should be protected. Some religious practices and religious beliefs are at odds with the principle that citizens should be allowed to practice their religion and to believe what they wish free of state sanction. These beliefs are rightly condemned and discouraged by the legitimate state. In particular, the religious "practice" of the councilmen to ban the Santeria religion—as well as the religious beliefs

behind this practice—are rightly subject to transformation. Specifically, the case of the Hialeah ordinance suggests that those who seek to use the power of the state to restrict a religious belief or practice, even when motivated by their own religious beliefs, should be stopped as well as criticized. Of course, when a law such as the Hialeah ordinance is struck down on First Amendment free exercise grounds, those who passed the law are not sanctioned through criminal law. But the Court's decision should be interpreted, on my view, to legally prohibit them from implementing policies at odds with the ideal of religious freedom while also sending a message that the beliefs and arguments that led to this statute, even if religious in nature, are incompatible with religious freedom....

Therefore, in rulings like *Lukumi*, the Supreme Court acts as an "exemplar" of public reason in two senses. First, it acts as an enforcer of public reason by striking down unconstitutional laws, such as those that constrain the practice of one religion because it is viewed as incompatible with another. Second, it acts as a model for the wider citizenry, including public officials who deliberate about and make law, when it explains why such laws are illegitimate and when it speaks in defense of the values of free and equal citizenship. Supreme Court opinions certainly are concerned with the immediate task of whether to strike down law. But their audience also rightly includes all those potentially involved in lawmaking, including citizens concerned to think and deliberate publicly about lawmaking. In *Lukumi* specifically, the primary purpose of the Court's decision was to strike down a law violating religious freedom. But it did more than this. The decision also expressed disapproval of the reasons its proponents gave for passing this law, and it issued a rebuke to them for violating their duty to respect religious freedom. That the reasons of the law's proponents, including the councilmen's, were themselves religious does not immunize them from this rebuke. Nor does the fact that their free-speech rights protect them from being punished merely for holding these views entail that they cannot be criticized by those who defend the core principle of religious freedom. The Court's decision expressed a principled disapproval of the kind of religious reasoning that would use the state to impose religious beliefs on others and therefore directly criticized the views expressed by the Hialeah proponents. The decision, moreover, is relevant for all those who would attempt to use similar reasoning to pass equivalent laws in other locales. . . .

In the promulgating of reasons for rights, and in seeking to transform beliefs at odds with these reasons, it is essential that the legitimate state respect two distinct limitations. The first concerns the method through which transformation should be attempted and the principle of equal citizenship promoted. The second concerns limits on the content of the beliefs targeted for transformation. The first, which I call the "means-based" limit, requires that the state not pursue transformation of citizens' views through any method that violates fundamental rights such as freedom of expression, conscience, and association. For example, it cannot prohibit meetings of the Anti-Santeria Society or threaten criminal sanctions against the Hialeah councilmen for holding and expressing beliefs in conflict with the *Lukumi* principle. However, a public articulation of why the councilmen's views are inconsistent with religious freedom would not violate their rights, even if this point were

articulated by state officials. The *Lukumi* principle ideally should be defended by those in power as well as by citizens participating in democratic debate. Ideally, citizens and their representatives will successfully defend the *Lukumi* principle such that laws that would violate will not come before the court. As I have argued elsewhere, it is better for public principles to be defended through majoritarian processes than through judicial review. It is only as a last resort, when lawmakers and citizens fail to heed this duty, that they are rightly rebuked by the courts.

On my view, which I develop throughout this essay, the state can avoid violating the "means-based" limit by confining its attempts at transformation or promotion to its expressive rather than its coercive capacities. For example, public officials and citizens may make arguments that defend the *Lukumi* principle when engaged in public discussion, even in the face of religious opposition. Moreover, as I suggest in the next section, there is a role for educators to teach the importance of religious toleration even if some parents hold religious objections. The right to hold and express a belief at odds with the ideal of equal citizenship which underlies the *Lukumi* principle does not entail a right to hold it unchallenged. I take the position that mere reasoning by the state addressed to citizens is not tantamount to coercion. It is a familiar Millian point that the fact that I have a right to free speech does not keep you from convincing me that some of my opinions are wrong. Moreover, if you are successful in persuading me through reason, and my views are transformed, this is certainly not evidence that I have been coerced. To the contrary, we tend to regard such "transformations" as freely chosen. One need not be a full-blown Kantian to accept as much. When we move from the question of individual persuasion to state persuasion, we should observe that the state has a particular interest in advancing principles, such as the ideal of religious freedom articulated in *Lukumi*, that are essential to its own legitimacy. It is also essential that the state use as much as possible the means of reasoning to defend its most fundamental principles. Like the Supreme Court, state officials should reason by means of an appeal to public principles. . . .

As such, it is not the belief in the superiority of one's religion per se that transformation should target but rather the belief that certain religious reasons should be imposed by law. Moreover, the substance-based limit suggests that it is only those beliefs most blatantly at odds with the principles of equal citizenship that are rightly subject to transformation. For instance, reasonable people might disagree about the implications of equal citizenship for issues such as affirmative action—and no position on this issue should rightly be subject to transformation. Rather, it is those beliefs, religious and otherwise, that are openly hostile to or implausibly consistent with the values of equal citizenship that the state should seek to transform. . . .

There is, in short, no way of getting around the fact that attempting to transform an illiberal belief is sometimes tantamount to attempting to intentionally transform a religious belief. Indeed, Rawls maintained, despite his claim of "neutrality of intent" toward religious doctrines, that he hoped unreasonable religions would become reasonable over time. But I have argued that the account of transformation should not, as Rawls suggests, be a mere "hope." It is rather a commitment that is fundamental to the idea of religious freedom itself.

THE RIGHT TO RESIST RELIGIOUS TRANSFORMATION AND THE FREEDOM OF ASSOCIATION

I have suggested an alternative to static conceptions of religious freedom; on my view, the state should promote principles of free and equal citizenship even in the face of religious doctrines that oppose them. Because of the substance-based limit on such transformation, some groups whose internal policies make them appear hostile to these principles might not rightly be subject to transformation as long as they do not seek to impose their religious beliefs on others with the force of law. However, if we also adhere to what I have called the means-based limit, even those groups that do seek to impose their religious beliefs on others by law—those who are actively hostile to the ideal of free and equal citizenship—retain certain rights to resist transformation.

Core liberal commitments to the freedoms of expression, association, and conscience require that the state not use force to change religious viewpoints. Of course, the state should not view religious belief as justification for violent crimes, and it rightly punishes even those who give religious reasons for such actions. But policies involving coercive sanction cannot serve as the means of transforming illiberal beliefs. To ensure this, an account of religious transformation must endorse a robust conception of freedom of association.

The right to freedom of association entails what might be called a series of rights to resist or "opt out" of the process of liberal dialectic, which I defended in the previous section. . . . Subject to the reasonable limitations that accompany any rights, the rights to exist and to congregate should be granted to even deeply illiberal groups. Moreover, absent public subsidy, private associations have a fundamental right to decide on their own membership and to keep their membership lists private. This right is particularly important when membership is connected to a group's expressive purpose. For instance, I take it to be a right of religious groups to exclude nonbelievers. Often, these rights protect matters of internal membership and organization, matters that do not necessarily violate the political ideals of free and equal citizenship. However, even for groups with views clearly opposed to these ideals, the rights of association must be protected. I therefore stress in this section why, alongside the state's role in promoting public values of equal citizenship through its expressive capacity and its role as an effective subsidizer of nonprofits, there exists a right for groups or individuals to resist transformation.

In sum, if religious groups that hold such illiberal discrete views wish to opt out of the dialectical process, they should be allowed to do so as a matter of law. These rights to opt out, however, do not imply an acceptance by the state of these views nor an acknowledgment that they are consistent with freestanding public principles fundamental to legitimacy.

CONCLUSION

In this essay, I suggested why static conceptions of religion neglect the fact that a commitment to religious freedom itself requires transformation of some religious beliefs. Religions, on my view, are not rightfully protected by a metaphorical "wall" or private space into which public values cannot interfere. On the contrary, the "*Lukumi* principle" I have proposed suggests that when conflicts emerge between existing religious views and the freestanding public values central to legitimacy, the state should work to transform religious belief. I argued, moreover, that such transformation must respect both a "means-based" and a "substance-based" limit. The state should seek transformation through persuasion, not coercion, and should attempt to change only those beliefs at odds with the shared values of free and equal citizenship. In recognizing these limits, the legitimate state can promote its own values while respecting the rights of all citizens.

My approach therefore grounds a transformative theory of religious freedom in the promulgation and promotion of the reasons that underlie rights, including rights of religious freedom.

Exemptions and Strict Scrutiny: Introduction to the Free Exercise Cases

As we discuss further in Chapter 9, the Court's protection of rights is often achieved through "balancing" rather than an absolute conception of rights. Specifically, the Court seeks to weigh the state's interest in pursuing some general goal against the interest of the individuals who have claimed that a right has been violated. It is important to note that the Court employs different kinds of balancing tests in different contexts.

As will become clear after reading the cases in this chapter, the debate over how to interpret the Free Exercise Clause of the First Amendment has largely been a debate over what kind of balancing test the Court should use in the area of free exercise. Historically, the Court has at different times used two kinds of balancing between the state's interest in promoting some aspect of the general welfare and claims of the individual to religious freedom of conscience. We begin our case selection with the cases that the Court considered under strict scrutiny.

In *Sherbert v. Verner*, the Court announced the strict scrutiny test for balancing between the interests of the state and the individual in cases concerning the free exercise of religion. The strict scrutiny standard requires that, any time a religious practice is adversely affected by legislation, the Court presume that the person who has been affected is entitled to an exemption. More specifically, the Court's decision in *Sherbert v. Verner* held that religious exemptions might be denied only in cases in which there exists a government goal that is so important it constitutes a compelling interest. In addition to imposing a high standard for the goals of legislation, the Court also uses the strict scrutiny test to ensure that the means of achieving that goal are narrowly tailored. In order to deny an exemption under the strict scrutiny standard test, therefore, the government faces a very high burden in explaining its reasons for legislation and its means for achieving it. It also faces a high burden in explaining why both the goal and the means for achieving it are incompatible with religious exemptions.

As you read the cases that follow, identify the compelling interests that the state uses to justify denying a religious exemption. Ask yourself whether you feel those goals are truly compelling, as well as whether the state's means are truly narrowly tailored.

WEST VIRGINIA STATE BOARD OF EDUCATION v. BARNETTE

319 U.S. 624 (1943)

Opinion: Jackson, joined by Byrnes and Stone
Concurrence: Black, joined by Douglas
Concurrence: Murphy
Dissent: Frankfurter, joined by Reed and Roberts

MR. JUSTICE JACKSON *delivered the opinion of the Court.*

Following the decision by this Court on June 3, 1940, in *Minersville School District v. Gobitis*, the West Virginia . . . Board of Education on January 9, 1942, adopted a resolution containing recitals taken largely from the Court's *Gobitis* opinion and ordering that the salute to the flag become "a regular part of the program of activities in the public schools," that all teachers and pupils "shall be required to participate in the salute honoring the Nation represented by the Flag; provided, however, that refusal to salute the Flag be regarded as an act of insubordination, and shall be dealt with accordingly."

The resolution originally required the "commonly accepted salute to the Flag," which it defined. Objections to the salute as "being too much like Hitler's" were raised by the Parent and Teachers Association, the Boy and Girl Scouts, the Red Cross, and the Federation of Women's Clubs. Some modification appears to have been made in deference to these objections, but no concession was made to Jehovah's Witnesses. What is now required is the "stiff-arm" salute, the saluter to keep the right hand raised with palm turned up while the following is repeated: "I pledge allegiance to the Flag of the United States of America and to the Republic for which it stands; one Nation, indivisible, with liberty and justice for all."

Failure to conform is "insubordination," dealt with by expulsion. Readmission is denied by statute until compliance. Meanwhile, the expelled child is "unlawfully absent," and may be proceeded against as a delinquent. His parents or guardians are liable to prosecution, and, if convicted, are subject to fine not exceeding $50 and jail term not exceeding thirty days.

Appellees, citizens of the United States and of West Virginia, brought suit in the United States District Court for themselves and others similarly situated asking its injunction to restrain enforcement of these laws and regulations against Jehovah's Witnesses. The Witnesses are an unincorporated body teaching that the obligation imposed by law of God is superior to that of laws enacted by temporal government. Their religious beliefs include a literal version of Exodus, Chapter 20, verses 4 and 5, which says: "Thou shalt not make unto thee any graven image, or any likeness of anything that is in heaven above, or that is in the earth beneath, or that is in the water under the earth; thou shalt not bow down thyself to them nor serve them." They consider that the flag is an "image" within this command. For this reason, they refuse to salute it.

Children of this faith have been expelled from school and are threatened with exclusion for no other cause. Officials threaten to send them to reformatories maintained for criminally inclined juveniles. Parents of such children have been prosecuted, and are threatened with prosecutions for causing delinquency.

The Board of Education moved to dismiss the complaint, setting forth these facts and alleging that the law and regulations are an unconstitutional denial of religious freedom, and of freedom of speech, and are invalid under the "due process" and "equal protection" clauses of the Fourteenth Amendment to the Federal Constitution. The cause was submitted on the pleadings to a District Court of three judges. It restrained enforcement as to the plaintiffs and those of that class. The Board of Education brought the case here by direct appeal. . . .

The freedom asserted by these appellees does not bring them into collision with rights asserted by any other individual. It is such conflicts which most frequently require intervention of the State to determine where the rights of one end and those of another begin. But the refusal of these persons to participate in the ceremony does not interfere with or deny rights of others to do so. Nor is there any question in this case that their behavior is peaceable and orderly. The sole conflict is between authority and rights of the individual. The State asserts power to condition access to public education on making a prescribed sign and profession and at the same time to coerce attendance by punishing both parent and child. The latter stand on a right of self-determination in matters that touch individual opinion and personal attitude.

As the present Chief Justice said in dissent in the *Gobitis* case, the State may "require teaching by instruction and study of all in our history and in the structure and organization of our government, including the guaranties of civil liberty, which tend to inspire patriotism and love of country." Here, however, we are dealing with a compulsion of students to declare a belief. They are not merely made acquainted with the flag salute so that they may be informed as to what it is or even what it means. The issue here is whether this slow and easily neglected route to aroused loyalties constitutionally may be short-cut by substituting a compulsory salute and slogan. This issue is not prejudiced by the Court's previous holding that, where a State, without compelling attendance, extends college facilities to pupils who voluntarily enroll, it may prescribe military training as part of the course without offense to the Constitution. It was held that those who take advantage of its opportunities may not, on ground of conscience, refuse compliance with such conditions. *Hamilton v. Regents.* In the present case, attendance is not optional. That case is also to be distinguished from the present one, because, independently of college privileges or requirements, the State has power to raise militia and impose the duties of service therein upon its citizens.

There is no doubt that, in connection with the pledges, the flag salute is a form of utterance. Symbolism is a primitive but effective way of communicating ideas. The use of an emblem or flag to symbolize some system, idea, institution, or personality is a short-cut from mind to mind. Causes and nations, political parties, lodges, and ecclesiastical groups seek to knit the loyalty of their followings to a flag or banner, a color or design. The State announces rank, function, and authority through crowns and maces, uniforms and black robes; the church speaks through the Cross, the Crucifix, the altar and shrine, and clerical raiment. Symbols of State often convey political ideas, just as religious symbols come to convey theological ones. Associated with many of these symbols are appropriate gestures of acceptance or respect: a salute, a bowed or bared head, a bended knee. A person gets from a symbol the meaning he puts into it, and what is one man's comfort and inspiration is another's jest and scorn. . . .

Whether the First Amendment to the Constitution will permit officials to order observance of ritual of this nature does not depend upon whether as a voluntary exercise we would think it to be good, bad or merely innocuous. Any credo of nationalism is likely to include what some disapprove or to omit what others think essential, and to give off different overtones as it takes on different accents or interpretations. If official power exists to coerce acceptance of any patriotic creed, what it shall contain cannot be decided by courts, but must be largely discretionary with the ordaining authority, whose power to prescribe would no doubt include power to amend. Hence, validity of the asserted power to force an American citizen publicly to profess any statement of belief, or to engage in any ceremony of assent to one, presents questions of power that must be considered independently of any idea we may have as to the utility of the ceremony in question.

Nor does the issue, as we see it, turn on one's possession of particular religious views or the sincerity with which they are held. While religion supplies appellees' motive for enduring the discomforts of making the issue in this case, many citizens who do not share these religious views hold such a compulsory rite to infringe constitutional liberty of the individual. It is not necessary to inquire whether nonconformist beliefs will exempt from the duty to salute unless we first find power to make the salute a legal duty.

. . . The question which underlies the flag salute controversy is whether such a ceremony so touching matters of opinion and political attitude may be imposed upon the individual by official authority under powers committed to any political organization under our Constitution. . . .

The case is made difficult not because the principles of its decision are obscure, but because the flag involved is our own. Nevertheless, we apply the limitations of the Constitution with no fear that freedom to be intellectually and spiritually diverse or even contrary will disintegrate the social organization. To believe that patriotism will not flourish if patriotic ceremonies are voluntary and spontaneous, instead of a compulsory routine, is to make an unflattering estimate of the appeal of our institutions to free minds. We can have intellectual individualism and the rich cultural diversities that we owe to exceptional minds only at the price of occasional eccentricity and abnormal attitudes. When they are so harmless to others or to the State as those we deal with here, the price is not too great. But freedom to differ is not limited to things that do not matter much. That would be a mere shadow of freedom. The test of its substance is the right to differ as to things that touch the heart of the existing order.

If there is any fixed star in our constitutional constellation, it is that no official, high or petty, can prescribe what shall be orthodox in politics, nationalism, religion, or other matters of opinion, or force citizens to confess by word or act their faith therein. If there are any circumstances which permit an exception, they do not now occur to us.

We think the action of the local authorities in compelling the flag salute and pledge transcends constitutional limitations on their power, and invades the sphere of intellect and spirit which it is the purpose of the First Amendment to our Constitution to reserve from all official control. . . .

MR. JUSTICE FRANKFURTER,
dissenting.

The essence of the religious freedom guaranteed by our Constitution is therefore this: no religion shall either receive the state's support or incur its hostility. Religion is outside the sphere of political government. This does not mean that all matters on which religious organizations or beliefs may pronounce are outside the sphere of government. Were this so, instead of the separation of church and state, there would be the subordination of the state on any matter deemed within the sovereignty of the religious conscience. Much that is the concern of temporal authority affects the spiritual interests of men. But it is not enough to strike down a nondiscriminatory law that it may hurt or offend some dissident view. It would be too easy to cite numerous prohibitions and injunctions to which laws run counter if the variant interpretations of the Bible were made the tests of obedience to law. The validity of secular laws cannot be measured by their conformity to religious doctrines. It is only in a theocratic state that ecclesiastical doctrines measure legal right or wrong.

An act compelling profession of allegiance to a religion, no matter how subtly or tenuously promoted, is bad. But an act promoting good citizenship and national allegiance is within the domain of governmental authority, and is therefore to be judged by the same considerations of power and of constitutionality as those involved in the many claims of immunity from civil obedience because of religious scruples.

That claims are pressed on behalf of sincere religious convictions does not, of itself, establish their constitutional validity. Nor does waving the banner of religious freedom relieve us from examining into the power we are asked to deny the states. Otherwise, the doctrine of separation of church and state, so cardinal in the history of this nation and for the liberty of our people, would mean not the disestablishment of a state church, but the establishment of all churches, and of all religious groups.

The subjection of dissidents to the general requirement of saluting the flag, as a measure conducive to the training of children in good citizenship, is very far from being the first instance of exacting obedience to general laws that have offended deep religious scruples. Compulsory vaccination, see *Jacobson v. Massachusetts*, food inspection regulations, see *Shapiro v. Lyle*, the obligation to bear arms, see *Hamilton v. Regents*, testimonial duties, see *Stansbury v. Marks*, compulsory medical treatment, see *People v. Vogelesang*—these are but illustrations of conduct that has often been compelled in the enforcement of legislation of general applicability even though the religious consciences of particular individuals rebelled at the exaction.

Law is concerned with external behavior, and not with the inner life of man. It rests in large measure upon compulsion. Socrates lives in history partly because he gave his life for the conviction that duty of obedience to secular law does not presuppose consent to its enactment or belief in its virtue. The consent upon which free government rests is the consent that comes from sharing in the process of making and unmaking laws. The state is not shut out from a domain because the individual conscience may deny the state's claim. The individual conscience may profess what faith it chooses. It may affirm and promote that faith—in the language of the Constitution, it may "exercise" it freely—but it cannot thereby restrict community action through political organs in matters of community concern, so long as the action is not asserted in a discriminatory way, either openly or by stealth. One may have the right to practice one's religion and at the same time owe the duty of formal obedience to laws that run counter to one's belief. Compelling belief implies denial of opportunity to combat it and to assert dissident views. Such compulsion is one thing.

Quite another matter is submission to conformity of action while denying its wisdom or virtue, and with ample opportunity for seeking its change or abrogation.

When dealing with religious scruples, we are dealing with an almost numberless variety of doctrines and beliefs entertained with equal sincerity by the particular groups for which they satisfy man's needs in his relation to the mysteries of the universe. There are, in the United States, more than 250 distinctive established religious denominations. In the State of Pennsylvania, there are 120 of these, and, in West Virginia, as many as 65. But if religious scruples afford immunity from civic obedience to laws, they may be invoked by the religious beliefs of any individual even though he holds no membership in any sect or organized denomination. Certainly this Court cannot be called upon to determine what claims of conscience should be recognized, and what should be rejected as satisfying the "religion" which the Constitution protects. That would, indeed, resurrect the very discriminatory treatment of religion which the Constitution sought forever to forbid.

Consider the controversial issue of compulsory Bible reading in public schools. The educational policies of the states are in great conflict over this, and the state courts are divided in their decisions on the issue whether the requirement of Bible reading offends constitutional provisions dealing with religious freedom. The requirement of Bible reading has been justified by various state courts as an appropriate means of inculcating ethical precepts and familiarizing pupils with the most lasting expression of great English literature. Is this Court to overthrow such variant state educational policies by denying states the right to entertain such convictions in regard to their school systems because of a belief that the King James version is, in fact, a sectarian text to which parents of the Catholic and

Jewish faiths and of some Protestant persuasions may rightly object to having their children exposed? On the other hand, the religious consciences of some parents may rebel at the absence of any Bible reading in the schools. Or is this Court to enter the old controversy between science and religion by unduly defining the limits within which a state may experiment with its school curricula? The religious consciences of some parents may be offended by subjecting their children to the Biblical account of creation, while another state may offend parents by prohibiting a teaching of biology that contradicts such Biblical account.

There are other issues in the offing which admonish us of the difficulties and complexities that confront states in the duty of administering their local school systems. All citizens are taxed for the support of public schools, although this Court has denied the right of a state to compel all children to go to such schools, and has recognized the right of parents to send children to privately maintained schools. Parents who are dissatisfied with the public schools thus carry a double educational burden. Children who go to public school enjoy in many states derivative advantages, such as free textbooks, free lunch, and free transportation in going to and from school. What of the claims for equality of treatment of those parents who, because of religious scruples, cannot send their children to public schools? What of the claim that, if the right to send children to privately maintained schools is partly an exercise of religious conviction, to render effective this right, it should be accompanied by equality of treatment by the state in supplying free textbooks, free lunch, and free transportation to children who go to private schools? What of the claim that such grants are offensive to the cardinal constitutional doctrine of separation of church and state?

These questions assume increasing importance in view of the steady growth of parochial schools, both in number and in population. I am not borrowing trouble by adumbrating these issues, nor am I parading horrible examples of the consequences of today's decision. I am aware that we must decide the case before us, and not some other case. But that does not mean that a case is dissociated from the past, and unrelated to the future. We must decide this case with due regard for what went before and no less regard for what may come after. Is it really a fair construction of such a fundamental concept as the right freely to exercise one's religion that a state cannot choose to require all children who attend public school to make the same gesture of allegiance to the symbol of our national life because it may offend the conscience of some children, but that it may compel all children to attend public school to listen to the King James version although it may offend the consciences of their parents? And what of the larger issue of claiming immunity from obedience to a general civil regulation that has a reasonable relation to a public purpose within the general competence of the state?

. . . We are told that a flag salute is a doubtful substitute for adequate understanding of our institutions. The states that require such a school exercise do not have to justify it as the only means for promoting good citizenship in children, but merely as one of diverse means for accomplishing a worthy end. We may deem it a foolish measure, but the point is that this Court is not the organ of government to resolve doubts as to whether it will fulfill its purpose. Only if there be no doubt that any reasonable mind could entertain can we deny to the states the right to resolve doubts their way, and not ours.

That which to the majority may seem essential for the welfare of the state may offend the consciences of a minority. But, so long as no inroads are made upon the actual exercise of religion by the minority, to deny the political power of the majority to enact laws concerned with civil matters, simply because they may offend the consciences of a minority, really means that the conscience of a minority are more sacred and more enshrined in the Constitution than the consciences of a majority.

SHERBERT v. VERNER

374 U.S. 398 (1963)

Opinion: Brennan, joined by Warren, Black, Clark, Goldberg
Concurrence: Douglas
Concurrence: Stewart
Dissent: Harlan, joined by White

MR. JUSTICE BRENNAN *delivered the opinion of the Court.*

Appellant, a member of the Seventh-day Adventist Church, was discharged by her South Carolina employer because she would not work on Saturday, the Sabbath Day of her faith. When she was unable to obtain other employment because, from conscientious scruples, she would not take Saturday work, she filed a claim for unemployment compensation benefits under the South Carolina Unemployment Compensation Act. That law provides that, to be eligible for benefits, a claimant must be "able to work and . . . available for work"; and, further, that a claimant is ineligible for benefits "[i]f . . . he has failed, without good cause . . . to accept available suitable work when offered him by the employment office or the employer. . . ." The appellee Employment Security Commission, in administrative proceedings under the statute, found that appellant's restriction upon her availability for Saturday work brought her within the provision disqualifying for benefits insured workers who fail, without good cause, to accept "suitable work when

offered . . . by the employment office or the employer. . . ." The Commission's finding was sustained by the Court of Common Pleas for Spartanburg County. That court's judgment was, in turn, affirmed by the South Carolina Supreme Court, which rejected appellant's contention that, as applied to her, the disqualifying provisions of the South Carolina statute abridged her right to the free exercise of her religion secured under the Free Exercise Clause of the First Amendment through the Fourteenth Amendment. The State Supreme Court held specifically that appellant's ineligibility infringed no constitutional liberties because such a construction of the statute "places no restriction upon the appellant's freedom of religion, nor does it in any way prevent her in the exercise of her right and freedom to observe her religious beliefs in accordance with the dictates of her conscience." We noted probable jurisdiction of appellant's appeal. We reverse the judgment of the South Carolina Supreme Court and remand for further proceedings not inconsistent with this opinion.

I

The door of the Free Exercise Clause stands tightly closed against any governmental regulation of religious beliefs as such, *Cantwell v. Connecticut.* Government may neither compel affirmation of a repugnant belief, *Torcaso v. Watkins,* nor penalize or discriminate against individuals or groups because they hold religious views abhorrent to the authorities, *Fowler v. Rhode Island*, nor employ the taxing power to inhibit the dissemination of particular religious views, *Murdock v. Pennsylvania*, *Follett v. McCormick*. On the other hand, the Court has rejected challenges under the Free Exercise Clause to governmental regulation of certain overt acts prompted by religious beliefs or principles, for "even when the action is in accord with one's religious convictions, [it] is not totally free from legislative restrictions." *Braunfeld v. Brown*. The conduct or actions so regulated have invariably posed some substantial threat to public safety, peace or order. . . .

Plainly enough, appellant's conscientious objection to Saturday work constitutes no conduct prompted by religious principles of a kind within the reach of state legislation. If, therefore, the decision of the South Carolina Supreme Court is to withstand appellant's constitutional challenge, it must be either because her disqualification as a beneficiary represents no infringement by the State of her constitutional rights of free exercise, or because any incidental burden on the free exercise of appellant's religion may be justified by a "compelling state interest in the regulation of a subject within the State's constitutional power to regulate. . . ." *NAACP v. Button*.

II

We turn first to the question whether the disqualification for benefits imposes any burden on the free exercise of appellant's religion. We think it is clear that it does. In a sense, the consequences of such a disqualification to religious principles and practices may be only an indirect result of welfare legislation within the State's general competence to enact; it is true that no criminal sanctions directly compel appellant to work a six-day week. But this is only the beginning, not the end, of our inquiry. For "[i]f the purpose or effect of a law is to impede the observance of one or all religions or is to discriminate invidiously between religions, that law is constitutionally invalid even though the burden may be characterized as being only indirect." *Braunfeld v. Brown*. Here, not only is it apparent that appellant's declared ineligibility for benefits derives solely from the practice of her religion, but the pressure upon her to forego that practice is unmistakable. The ruling forces her to choose between following the precepts of her religion and forfeiting benefits, on the one hand, and abandoning one of the precepts of her religion in order to accept work, on the other hand. Governmental imposition of such a choice puts the same kind of burden upon the free exercise of religion as would a fine imposed against appellant for her Saturday worship.

Nor may the South Carolina court's construction of the statute be saved from constitutional infirmity on the ground that unemployment compensation benefits are not appellant's "right," but merely a "privilege." It is too late in the day to doubt that the liberties of religion and expression may be infringed by the denial of or placing of conditions upon a benefit or privilege. (*American Communications Assn. v. Douds*; *Wieman v. Updegraff*; *Hannegan v. Esquire, Inc.*) For example, in *Flemming v. Nestor*, the Court recognized with respect to Federal Social Security benefits that "[t]he interest of a covered employee under the Act is of sufficient substance to fall within the protection from arbitrary governmental action afforded by the Due Process Clause." In *Speiser v. Randall*, we emphasized that conditions upon public benefits cannot be sustained if they so operate, whatever their purpose, as to inhibit or deter the exercise of First Amendment freedoms. We there struck down a condition which limited the availability of a tax exemption to those members of the exempted class who affirmed their loyalty to the state government granting the exemption. While the State was surely under no obligation to afford such an exemption, we held that the imposition of such a condition upon even a gratuitous benefit inevitably deterred or discouraged the exercise of First Amendment rights of expression, and thereby threatened to "produce a result which the State could not command directly." "To deny an exemption to claimants who engage in certain forms of speech is, in effect, to penalize them for such speech." Likewise, to condition the availability of benefits upon this appellant's willingness to violate a cardinal principle of her religious faith effectively penalizes the free exercise of her constitutional liberties.

Significantly, South Carolina expressly saves the Sunday worshipper from having to make the kind of choice which we here hold infringes the Sabbatarian's religious liberty. When, in times of "national emergency," the textile plants are authorized by the State Commissioner of Labor to operate on Sunday, "no employee shall be required to work on Sunday . . . who is conscientiously opposed to Sunday work, and if any employee should refuse to work on Sunday on account of conscientious . . . objections, he or she shall not jeopardize his or her seniority by such refusal or be discriminated against in any other manner." No question of the disqualification of a Sunday worshipper for benefits is likely to arise, since we cannot suppose that an employer will discharge him in violation of this statute. The unconstitutionality of the disqualification of the Sabbatarian is thus compounded by the religious discrimination which South Carolina's general statutory scheme necessarily effects.

III

We must next consider whether some compelling state interest enforced in the eligibility provisions of the South Carolina statute justifies the substantial infringement of appellant's First Amendment right. It is basic that no showing merely of a rational relationship to some colorable state interest would suffice; in this highly sensitive constitutional area, "[o]nly the gravest abuses, endangering paramount interests, give occasion for permissible limitation," *Thomas v. Collins*. No such abuse or danger has been advanced in the present case. The appellees suggest no more than a possibility that the filing of fraudulent claims by unscrupulous claimants feigning religious objections to Saturday work might not only dilute the unemployment compensation fund, but also hinder the scheduling by employers of necessary Saturday work. But that possibility is not apposite here, because no such objection appears to have been made before the South Carolina Supreme Court, and we are unwilling to assess the importance of an asserted state interest without the views of the state court. Nor, if the contention had been made below, would the record appear to sustain it; there is no proof whatever to warrant such fears of malingering or deceit as those which the respondents now advance. Even if consideration of such evidence is not foreclosed by the prohibition against judicial inquiry into the truth or falsity of religious beliefs, *United States v. Ballard*—a question as to which we intimate no view, since it is not before us—it is highly doubtful whether such evidence would be sufficient to warrant a substantial infringement of religious liberties. For even if the possibility of spurious claims did threaten to dilute the fund and disrupt the scheduling of work, it would plainly be incumbent upon the appellees to demonstrate that no alternative forms of regulation would combat such abuses without infringing First Amendment rights.

In these respects, then, the state interest asserted in the present case is wholly dissimilar to the interests which were found to justify the less direct burden upon religious practices in *Braunfeld v. Brown.* The Court recognized that the Sunday closing law which that decision sustained undoubtedly served "to make the practice of [the Orthodox Jewish merchants'] . . . religious beliefs more expensive." But the statute was nevertheless saved by a countervailing factor which finds no equivalent in the instant case—a strong state interest in providing one uniform day of rest for all workers. That secular objective could be achieved, the Court found, only by declaring Sunday to be that day of rest. Requiring exemptions for Sabbatarians, while theoretically possible, appeared to present an administrative problem of such magnitude, or to afford the exempted class so great a competitive advantage, that such a requirement would have rendered the entire statutory scheme unworkable. In the present case, no such justifications underlie the determination of the state court that appellant's religion makes her ineligible to receive benefits.

IV

In holding as we do, plainly we are not fostering the "establishment" of the Seventh-day Adventist religion in South Carolina, for the extension of unemployment benefits to Sabbatarians in common with Sunday worshippers reflects nothing more than the governmental obligation of neutrality in the face of religious differences, and does not represent that involvement of religious with secular institutions which it is the object of the Establishment Clause to forestall. *See School District of Abington Township v. Schempp.* Nor does the recognition of the appellant's right to unemployment benefits under the state statute serve to abridge any other person's religious liberties. Nor do we, by our decision today, declare the existence of a constitutional right to unemployment benefits on the part of all persons whose religious convictions are the cause of their unemployment. This is not a case in which an employee's religious convictions serve to make him a nonproductive member of society. Finally, nothing we say today constrains the States to adopt any particular form or scheme of unemployment compensation. Our holding today is only that South Carolina may not constitutionally apply the eligibility provisions so as to constrain a worker to abandon his religious convictions respecting the day of rest. This holding but reaffirms a principle that we announced a decade and a half ago, namely that no State may "exclude individual Catholics, Lutherans, Mohammedans, Baptists, Jews, Methodists, Non-believers, Presbyterians, or the members of any other faith, because of their faith, or lack of it, from receiving the benefits of public welfare legislation."

MR. JUSTICE HARLAN, *whom* **MR. JUSTICE WHITE** *joins, dissenting.*

Today's decision is disturbing both in its rejection of existing precedent and in its implications for the future. The significance of the decision can best be understood after an examination of the state law applied in this case.

South Carolina's Unemployment Compensation Law was enacted in 1936 in response to the grave social and economic problems that arose during the depression of that period. . . .

> . . . the purpose of the legislature was to tide people over, and to avoid social and economic chaos, during periods when *work was*

unavailable. But, at the same time, there was clearly no intent to provide relief for those who, for purely personal reasons, were or became *unavailable for work....*

The South Carolina Supreme Court has uniformly applied this law in conformity with its clearly expressed purpose. It has consistently held that one is not "available for work" if his unemployment has resulted not from the inability of industry to provide a job, but rather from personal circumstances, no matter how compelling....

In the present case, all that the state court has done is to apply these accepted principles. Since virtually all of the mills in the Spartanburg area were operating on a six-day week, the appellant was "unavailable for work," and thus ineligible for benefits, when personal considerations prevented her from accepting employment on a full-time basis in the industry and locality in which she had worked. The fact that these personal considerations sprang from her religious convictions was wholly without relevance to the state court's application of the law. Thus, in no proper sense can it be said that the State discriminated against the appellant on the basis of her religious beliefs or that she was denied benefits *because* she was a Seventh-day Adventist....

... [T]he implications of the present decision are far more troublesome than its apparently narrow dimensions would indicate at first glance. The meaning of today's holding, as already noted, is that the State must furnish unemployment benefits to one who is unavailable for work if the unavailability stems from the exercise of religious convictions. The State, in other words, must *single out* for financial assistance those whose behavior is religiously motivated, even though it denies such assistance to others whose identical behavior (in this case, inability to work on Saturdays) is not religiously motivated.... I cannot subscribe to the conclusion that the State is constitutionally compelled to carve out an exception to its general rule of eligibility in the present case. Those situations in which the Constitution may require special treatment on account of religion are, in my view, few and far between, and this view is amply supported by the course of constitutional litigation in this area.... Such compulsion in the present case is particularly inappropriate in light of the indirect, remote, and insubstantial effect of the decision below on the exercise of appellant's religion and in light of the direct financial assistance to religion that today's decision requires.

For these reasons I respectfully dissent from the opinion and judgment of the Court.

Box 6-1   **Strict in Theory but Fatal in Fact? The Court's Use of Strict Scrutiny in Free Exercise Jurisprudence**

In choosing to adopt the standard of strict scrutiny in any given case, the Court supposedly presumes that a constitutional right has been violated. In theory, the Court must then balance the interest of the individual against the interest of the state. In fact, however, the Court often finds that individual rights have been violated. This result raises the question as to whether strict scrutiny is really a balancing test at all. If the Court always finds that rights have been violated when it applies strict scrutiny, is it really employing a balancing test? Some commentators have suggested that strict scrutiny is actually not a balancing test but rather window dressing on an absolute bar to certain kinds of legislation. For this reason, some have argued that the strict scrutiny test is "strict in theory but fatal in fact."

For instance, in *Wisconsin v. Yoder*, which concerned the question of whether Amish children should be given an exemption from a law requiring attendance at school past eighth grade, the Court applied strict scrutiny. Arguably, because this test created a presumptive rights violation, the Amish were able to succeed in ultimately gaining this exemption. Such cases support the contention that strict scrutiny is strict in theory but fatal in fact.

However, in many of the other cases that you will study in this chapter, even though strict scrutiny is applied, the Court ruled in favor of the state. Some have argued that issues of free exercise are an exception to the adage "strict in theory but fatal in fact." For example, in *Bob Jones University v. United States*, the Court applied strict scrutiny and yet failed to grant an exemption to the adversely affected religious group. The Court decided in that case that the government met its burden of showing a compelling interest for denial of a tax exemption to Bob Jones University.

In *United States v. Lee*, the Court applied strict scrutiny but denied the Amish relief from a general law about taxes. In *Bowen v. Roy*, Native Americans were denied an exemption to a requirement to provide a social security number despite applying strict scrutiny. In *Goldman v. Weinberger*, the Court denied Goldman's right to an exemption to the military's requirements regarding soldier's uniforms. As you can see, although the Court repeatedly applied strict scrutiny, it still often found for the government. It is clear from this line of cases that at least in the free exercise area, strict scrutiny was not strict in theory and fatal in fact. Indeed, the Court so often found for the government in this line of cases that it raised the question of whether it was applying strict scrutiny at all in the area of free exercise. As you read through these cases, ask whether the Court is presuming the laws at issue invalid or whether it really was employing a less strict test.

WISCONSIN v. YODER

406 U.S. 205 (1972)

Opinion: Burger, joined by Brennan, Stewart, White, Marshall, Blackmun
Concurrence: Stewart, joined by Brennan
Concurrence: White, joined by Brennan, Stewart
Partial Dissent: Douglas

MR. CHIEF JUSTICE BURGER
delivered the opinion of the Court.

. . . Respondents Jonas Yoder and Wallace Miller are members of the Old Order Amish religion, and respondent Adin Yutzy is a member of the Conservative Amish Mennonite Church. They and their families are residents of Green County, Wisconsin. Wisconsin's compulsory school attendance law required them to cause their children to attend public or private school until reaching age 16, but the respondents declined to send their children, ages 14 and 15, to public school after they completed the eighth grade. The children were not enrolled in any private school, or within any recognized exception to the compulsory attendance law, and they are conceded to be subject to the Wisconsin statute.

On complaint of the school district administrator for the public schools, respondents were charged, tried, and convicted of violating the compulsory attendance law in Green County Court, and were fined the sum of $5 each. Respondents defended on the ground that the application of the compulsory attendance law violated their rights under the First and Fourteenth Amendments. The trial testimony showed that respondents believed, in accordance with the tenets of Old Order Amish communities generally, that their children's attendance at high school, public or private, was contrary to the Amish religion and way of life. They believed that, by sending their children to high school, they would not only expose themselves to the danger of the censure of the church community, but, as found by the county court, also endanger their own salvation and that of their children. The State stipulated that respondents' religious beliefs were sincere. . . .

The Amish do not object to elementary education through the first eight grades as a general proposition, because they agree that their children must have basic skills in the "three R's" in order to read the Bible, to be good farmers and citizens, and to be able to deal with non-Amish people when necessary in the course of daily affairs. They view such a basic education as acceptable because it does not significantly expose their children to worldly values or interfere with their development in the Amish community during the crucial adolescent period. While Amish accept compulsory elementary education generally, wherever possible they have established their own elementary schools, in many respects like the small local schools of the past. In the Amish belief, higher learning tends to develop values they reject as influences that alienate man from God.

I

There is no doubt as to the power of a State, having a high responsibility for education of its citizens, to impose reasonable regulations for the control and duration of basic education. . . . Providing public schools ranks at the very apex of the function of a State. Yet even this paramount responsibility was, in *Pierce*, made to yield to the right of parents to provide an equivalent education in a privately operated system. There, the Court held that Oregon's statute compelling attendance in a public school from age eight to age 16 unreasonably interfered with the interest of parents in directing the rearing of their offspring, including their education in church-operated schools. As that case suggests, the values of parental direction of the religious upbringing and education of their children in their early and formative years have a high place in our society. . . . Thus, a State's interest in universal education, however highly we rank it, is not totally free from a balancing process when it impinges on fundamental rights and interests, such as those specifically protected by the Free Exercise Clause of the First Amendment, and the traditional interest of parents with respect to the religious upbringing of their children so long as they, in the words of *Pierce*, "prepare [them] for additional obligations."

It follows that, in order for Wisconsin to compel school attendance beyond the eighth grade against a claim that such attendance interferes with the practice of a legitimate religious belief, it must appear either that the State does not deny the free exercise of religious belief by its requirement or that there is a state interest of sufficient magnitude to override the interest claiming protection under the Free Exercise Clause. Long before there was general acknowledgment of the need for universal formal education, the Religion Clauses had specifically and firmly fixed the right to free exercise of religious beliefs, and buttressing this fundamental right was an equally firm, even if less explicit, prohibition against the establishment of any religion by government. The values underlying these two provisions relating to religion have been zealously protected, sometimes even at the expense of other interests of admittedly high social importance. The invalidation of financial aid to parochial schools by government grants for a salary subsidy for teachers is but one example of the extent to which courts have gone in this regard, notwithstanding that such aid programs were legislatively determined to be in the public interest and the service of sound educational policy by States and by Congress. . . .

The essence of all that has been said and written on the subject is that only those interests of the highest order and those not otherwise served can overbalance legitimate claims to the free exercise of religion. We can accept it as settled, therefore, that, however strong the State's interest in universal compulsory education, it is by no means absolute to the exclusion or subordination of all other interests. . . .

II

. . . The impact of the compulsory attendance law on respondents' practice of the Amish religion is not only severe, but inescapable, for the Wisconsin law affirmatively compels them, under threat of criminal sanction, to perform acts undeniably at odds with fundamental tenets of their religious beliefs. . . . Nor is the impact of the compulsory attendance law confined to grave interference with important Amish religious tenets from a subjective point of view. It carries with it precisely the kind of objective danger to the free exercise of religion that the First Amendment was designed to prevent. As the record shows, compulsory school attendance to age 16 for Amish children carries with it a very real threat of undermining the Amish community and religious practice as they exist today; they must either abandon belief and be assimilated into society at large or be forced to migrate to some other and more tolerant region.

In sum, the unchallenged testimony of acknowledged experts in education and religious history, almost 300 years of consistent practice, and strong evidence of a sustained faith pervading and regulating respondents' entire mode of life support the claim that enforcement of the State's requirement of compulsory formal education after the eighth grade would gravely endanger, if not destroy, the free exercise of respondents' religious beliefs.

III

Neither the findings of the trial court nor the Amish claims as to the nature of their faith are challenged in this Court by the State of Wisconsin. Its position is that the State's interest in universal compulsory formal secondary education to age 16 is so great that it is paramount to the undisputed claims of respondents that their mode of preparing their youth for Amish life, after the traditional elementary education, is an essential part of their religious belief and practice. Nor does the State undertake to meet the claim that the Amish mode of life and education is inseparable from and a part of the basic tenets of their religion—indeed, as much a part of their religious belief and practices as baptism, the confessional, or a sabbath may be for others.

Wisconsin concedes that, under the Religion Clauses, religious beliefs are absolutely free from the State's control, but it argues that "actions," even though religiously grounded, are outside the protection of the First Amendment. But our decisions have rejected the idea that religiously grounded conduct is always outside the protection of the Free Exercise Clause. It is true that activities of individuals, even when religiously based, are often subject to regulation by the States in the exercise of their undoubted power to promote the health, safety, and general welfare, or the Federal Government in the exercise of its delegated powers. . . . But to agree that religiously grounded conduct must often be subject to the broad police power of the State is not to deny that there are areas of conduct protected by the Free Exercise Clause of the First Amendment, and thus beyond the power of the State to control, even under regulations of general applicability. . . . This case, therefore, does not become easier because respondents were convicted for their "actions" in refusing to send their children to the public high school; in this context, belief and action cannot be neatly confined in logic-tight compartments.

Nor can this case be disposed of on the grounds that Wisconsin's requirement for school attendance to age 16 applies uniformly to all citizens of the State and does not, on its face, discriminate against religions or a particular religion, or that it is motivated by legitimate secular concerns. A regulation neutral on its face may, in its application, nonetheless offend the constitutional requirement for governmental

neutrality if it unduly burdens the free exercise of religion. . . .

We turn, then, to the State's broader contention that its interest in its system of compulsory education is so compelling that even the established religious practices of the Amish must give way. Where fundamental claims of religious freedom are at stake, however, we cannot accept such a sweeping claim; despite its admitted validity in the generality of cases, we must searchingly examine the interests that the State seeks to promote by its requirement for compulsory education to age 16, and the impediment to those objectives that would flow from recognizing the claimed Amish exemption. . . .

The State advances two primary arguments in support of its system of compulsory education. It notes, as Thomas Jefferson pointed out early in our history, that some degree of education is necessary to prepare citizens to participate effectively and intelligently in our open political system if we are to preserve freedom and independence. Further, education prepares individuals to be self-reliant and self-sufficient participants in society. We accept these propositions.

However, the evidence adduced by the Amish in this case is persuasively to the effect that an additional one or two years of formal high school for Amish children in place of their long-established program of informal vocational education would do little to serve those interests. . . .

The State attacks respondents' position as one fostering "ignorance" from which the child must be protected by the State. No one can question the State's duty to protect children from ignorance, but this argument does not square with the facts disclosed in the record. Whatever their idiosyncrasies as seen by the majority, this record strongly shows that the Amish community has been a highly successful social unit within our society, even if apart from the conventional "mainstream." Its members are productive and very law-abiding members of society; they reject public welfare in any of its usual modern forms. The Congress itself recognized their self-sufficiency by authorizing exemption of such groups as the Amish from the obligation to pay social security taxes.

It is neither fair nor correct to suggest that the Amish are opposed to education beyond the eighth grade level. What this record shows is that they are opposed to conventional formal education of the type provided by a certified high school because it comes at the child's crucial adolescent period of religious development. . . .

. . . There can be no assumption that today's majority is "right," and the Amish and others like them are "wrong." A way of life that is odd or even erratic but interferes with no rights or interests of others is not to be condemned because it is different.

The State, however, supports its interest in providing an additional one or two years of compulsory high school education to Amish children because of the possibility that some such children will choose to leave the Amish community, and that, if this occurs, they will be ill-equipped for life. The State argues that, if Amish children leave their church, they should not be in the position of making their way in the world without the education available in the one or two additional years the State requires. However, on this record, that argument is highly speculative. There is no specific evidence of the loss of Amish adherents by attrition, nor is there any showing that, upon leaving the Amish community, Amish children, with their practical agricultural training and habits of industry and self-reliance, would become burdens on society because of educational shortcomings. Indeed, this argument of the State appears to rest primarily on the State's mistaken

assumption, already noted, that the Amish do not provide any education for their children beyond the eighth grade, but allow them to grow in "ignorance". To the contrary, not only do the Amish accept the necessity for formal schooling through the eighth grade level, but continue to provide what has been characterized by the undisputed testimony of expert educators as an "ideal" vocational education for their children in the adolescent years. . . .

IV

Finally, the State, on authority of *Prince v. Massachusetts*, argues that a decision exempting Amish children from the State's requirement fails to recognize the substantive right of the Amish child to a secondary education, and fails to give due regard to the power of the State as *parens patriae* to extend the benefit of secondary education to children regardless of the wishes of their parents. . . .

Our holding in no way determines the proper resolution of possible competing interests of parents, children, and the State in an appropriate state court proceeding in which the power of the State is asserted on the theory that Amish parents are preventing their minor children from attending high school despite their expressed desires to the contrary. Recognition of the claim of the State in such a proceeding would, of course, call into question traditional concepts of parental control over the religious upbringing and education of their minor children recognized in this Court's past decisions. It is clear that such an intrusion by a State into family decisions in the area of religious training would give rise to grave questions of religious freedom comparable to those raised here and those presented in *Pierce v. Society of Sisters*. On this record, we neither reach nor decide those issues. . . .

Indeed, it seems clear that, if the State is empowered, as *parens patriae*, to "save" a child from himself or his Amish parents by requiring an additional two years of compulsory formal high school education, the State will, in large measure, influence, if not determine, the religious future of the child. Even more markedly than in *Prince*, therefore, this case involves the fundamental interest of parents, as contrasted with that of the State, to guide the religious future and education of their children. The history and culture of Western civilization reflect a strong tradition of parental concern for the nurture and upbringing of their children. This primary role of the parents in the upbringing of their children is now established beyond debate as an enduring American tradition....

However read, the Court's holding in *Pierce* stands as a charter of the rights of parents to direct the religious upbringing of their children. And, when the interests of parenthood are combined with a free exercise claim of the nature revealed by this record, more than merely a "reasonable relation to some purpose within the competency of the State" is required to sustain the validity of the State's requirement under the First Amendment. To be sure, the power of the parent, even when linked to a free exercise claim, may be subject to limitation under *Prince* if it appears that parental decisions will jeopardize the health or safety of the child, or have a potential for significant social burdens. But, in this case, the Amish have introduced persuasive evidence undermining the arguments the State has advanced to support its claims in terms of the welfare of the child and society as a whole. The record strongly indicates that accommodating the religious objections of the Amish by forgoing one, or at most two, additional years of compulsory education will not impair the physical or mental health of the child or result in an inability to be self-supporting or to discharge the duties and responsibilities of citizenship, or in any other way materially detract from the welfare of society.

In the face of our consistent emphasis on the central values underlying the Religion Clauses in our constitutional scheme of government, we cannot accept a *parens patriae* claim of such all-encompassing scope and with such sweeping potential for broad and unforeseeable application as that urged by the State.

V

For the reasons stated we hold, with the Supreme Court of Wisconsin, that the First and Fourteenth Amendments prevent the State from compelling respondents to cause their children to attend formal high school to age 16. Our disposition of this case, however, in no way alters our recognition of the obvious fact that courts are not school boards or legislatures, and are ill-equipped to determine the "necessity" of discrete aspects of a State's program of compulsory education. This should suggest that courts must move with great circumspection in performing the sensitive and delicate task of weighing a State's legitimate social concern when faced with religious claims for exemption from generally applicable educational requirements. It cannot be overemphasized that we are not dealing with a way of life and mode of education by a group claiming to have recently discovered some "progressive" or more enlightened process for rearing children for modern life.

Aided by a history of three centuries as an identifiable religious sect and a long history as a successful and self-sufficient segment of American society, the Amish in this case have convincingly demonstrated the sincerity of their religious beliefs, the interrelationship of belief with their mode of life, the vital role that belief and daily conduct play in the continued survival of Old Order Amish communities and their religious organization, and the hazards presented by the State's enforcement of a statute generally valid as to others. Beyond this, they have carried the even more difficult burden of demonstrating the adequacy of their alternative mode of continuing informal vocational education in terms of precisely those overall interests that the State advances in support of its program of compulsory high school education. In light of this convincing showing, one that probably few other religious groups or sects could make, and weighing the minimal difference between what the State would require and what the Amish already accept, it was incumbent on the State to show with more particularity how its admittedly strong interest in compulsory education would be adversely affected by granting an exemption to the Amish....

Affirmed.

MR. JUSTICE DOUGLAS *dissenting in part.*

I agree with the Court that the religious scruples of the Amish are opposed to the education of their children beyond the grade schools, yet I disagree with the Court's conclusion that the matter is within the dispensation of parents alone. The Court's analysis assumes that the only interests at stake in the case are those of the Amish parents, on the one hand, and those of the State, on the other. The difficulty with this approach is that, despite the Court's claim, the parents are seeking to vindicate not only their own free exercise claims, but also those of their high-school-age children.

It is argued that the right of the Amish children to religious freedom is not presented by the facts of the case, as the issue before the Court involves only the Amish parents' religious freedom to defy a state criminal statute imposing upon them an affirmative duty to cause their children to attend high school.

First, respondents' motion to dismiss in the trial court expressly asserts not only the religious liberty of the adults, but also that of the children, as a defense to the prosecutions. It is, of course, beyond question that the parents have standing as defendants in a criminal prosecution to assert the religious interests of their children as a defense. Although the lower courts and a majority of this Court assume an identity of interest between parent and child, it is clear that they have treated the religious interest of the child as a factor in the analysis.

Second, it is essential to reach the question to decide the case not only because the question was squarely raised in the motion to dismiss, but also because no analysis of religious liberty claims can take place in a vacuum. If the parents in this case are allowed a religious exemption, the inevitable effect is to impose the parents' notions of religious duty upon their children. Where the child is mature enough to express potentially conflicting desires, it would be an invasion of the child's rights to permit such an imposition without canvassing his views. As in *Prince v. Massachusetts*, it is an imposition resulting from this very litigation. As the child has no other effective forum, it is in this litigation that his rights should be considered. And if an Amish child desires to attend high school, and is mature enough to have that desire respected, the State may well be able to override the parents' religiously motivated objections.

Religion is an individual experience. It is not necessary, nor even appropriate, for every Amish child to express his views on the subject in a prosecution of a single adult. Crucial, however, are the views of the child whose parent is the subject of the suit. Frieda Yoder has in fact, testified that her own religious views are opposed to high-school education. I therefore join the judgment of the Court as to respondent Jonas Yoder. But Frieda Yoder's views may not be those of Vernon Yutzy or Barbara Miller. I must dissent, therefore, as to respondents Adin Yutzy and Wallace Miller, as their motion to dismiss also raised the question of their children's religious liberty. . . .

The Court rightly rejects the notion that actions, even though religiously grounded, are always outside the protection of the Free Exercise Clause of the First Amendment. In so ruling, the Court departs from the teaching of *Reynolds v. United States*, where it was said, concerning the reach of the Free

Exercise Clause of the First Amendment, "Congress was deprived of all legislative power over mere opinion, but was left free to reach actions which were in violation of social duties or subversive of good order." In that case, it was conceded that polygamy was a part of the religion of the Mormons. Yet the Court said, "It matters not that his belief [in polygamy] was a part of his professed religion: it was still belief, and belief only."

Action which the Court deemed to be antisocial could be punished even though it was grounded on deeply held and sincere religious convictions. What we do today, at least in this respect, opens the way to give organized religion a broader base than it has ever enjoyed, and it even promises that in time *Reynolds* will be overruled.

UNITED STATES v. LEE

455 U.S. 252 (1982)

Opinion: Burger, joined by Brennan, White, Marshall, Blackmun, Powell, Rehnquist, O'Connor
Concurrence: Stevens

CHIEF JUSTICE BURGER *delivered the opinion of the Court.*

We noted probable jurisdiction to determine whether imposition of social security taxes is unconstitutional as applied to persons who object on religious grounds to receipt of public insurance benefits and to payment of taxes to support public insurance funds. The District Court concluded that the Free Exercise Clause prohibits forced payment of social security taxes when payment of taxes and receipt of benefits violate the taxpayer's religion. We reverse.

I

Appellee, a member of the Old Order Amish, is a farmer and carpenter. From 1970 to 1977, appellee employed several other Amish to work on his farm and in his carpentry shop. He failed to file the quarterly social security tax returns required of employers, withhold social security tax from his employees, or pay the employer's share of social security taxes.

In 1978, the Internal Revenue Service assessed appellee in excess of $27,000 for unpaid employment taxes; he paid $91— the amount owed for the first quarter of 1973—and then sued in the United States District Court for the Western District of Pennsylvania for a refund, claiming that imposition of the social security taxes violated his First Amendment free exercise rights and those of his Amish employees.

The District Court held the statutes requiring appellee to pay social security and unemployment insurance taxes unconstitutional as applied. The court noted that the Amish believe it sinful not to provide for their own elderly and needy, and therefore are religiously opposed to the national social security system. The court also accepted appellee's contention that the Amish religion not only prohibits the acceptance of social security benefits, but also bars all contributions by Amish to the social security system. . . . The court's holding was based on both the exemption statute for the self-employed and the First Amendment; appellee and others "who fall within the carefully circumscribed definition provided in §142(g) are relieved from paying the employer's share of [social security taxes], as it is an unconstitutional infringement upon the free exercise of their religion." Direct appeal from the judgment of the District Court was taken.

II

The exemption provided by §1402(g) is available only to self-employed individuals, and does not apply to employers or employees. Consequently, appellee and his employees are not within the express provisions of §1402(g). Thus, any exemption from payment of the employer's share of social security taxes must come from a constitutionally required exemption.

A

The preliminary inquiry in determining the existence of a constitutionally required exemption is whether the payment of social security taxes and the receipt of benefits interferes with the free exercise rights of the Amish. The Amish believe that there

is a religiously based obligation to provide for their fellow members the kind of assistance contemplated by the social security system. Although the Government does not challenge the sincerity of this belief, the Government does contend that payment of social security taxes will not threaten the integrity of the Amish religious belief or observance. It is not within "the judicial function and judicial competence," however, to determine whether appellee or the Government has the proper interpretation of the Amish faith; "[c]ourts are not arbiters of scriptural interpretation." *Thomas v. Review Bd. of Indian Employment Security Div.* We therefore accept appellee's contention that both payment and receipt of social security benefits is forbidden by the Amish faith. Because the payment of the taxes or receipt of benefits violates Amish religious beliefs, compulsory participation in the social security system interferes with their free exercise rights.

The conclusion that there is a conflict between the Amish faith and the obligations imposed by the social security system is only the beginning, however, and not the end, of the inquiry. Not all burdens on religion are unconstitutional. The state may justify a limitation on religious liberty by showing that it is essential to accomplish an overriding governmental interest.

B

Because the social security system is nationwide, the governmental interest is apparent. The social security system in the United States serves the public interest by providing a comprehensive insurance system with a variety of benefits available to all participants, with costs shared by employers and employees. The social security system is by far the largest domestic governmental program in the United States today, distributing approximately $11 billion monthly to 36 million Americans. The design of the system requires support by mandatory contributions from covered employers and employees. This mandatory participation is indispensable to the fiscal vitality of the social security system. . . . Thus, the Government's interest in assuring mandatory and continuous participation in, and contribution to, the social security system is very high.

C

The remaining inquiry is whether accommodating the Amish belief will unduly interfere with fulfillment of the governmental interest. In *Braunfeld v. Brown*, this Court noted that "to make accommodation between the religious action and an exercise of state authority is a particularly delicate task . . . because resolution in favor of the State results in the choice to the individual of either abandoning his religious principle or facing . . . prosecution." The difficulty in attempting to accommodate religious beliefs in the area of taxation is that "we are a cosmopolitan nation made up of people of almost every conceivable religious preference." *Braunfeld.* The Court has long recognized that balance must be struck between the values of the comprehensive social security system, which rests on a complex of actuarial factors, and the consequences of allowing religiously based exemptions. To maintain an organized society that guarantees religious freedom to a great variety of faiths requires that some religious practices yield to the common good. Religious beliefs can be accommodated, but there is a point at which accommodation would "radically restrict the operating latitude of the legislature." *Braunfeld.* Unlike the situation presented in *Wisconsin v. Yoder*, it would be difficult to accommodate the comprehensive social security system with myriad exceptions flowing from a wide variety of religious beliefs. The obligation to pay the social security tax initially is not fundamentally different from the obligation to pay income taxes; the difference—in theory at least—is that the social security tax revenues are segregated for use only in furtherance of the statutory program. There is no principled way, however, for purposes of this case, to distinguish between general taxes and those imposed under the Social Security Act. . . . The tax system could not function if denominations were allowed to challenge the tax system because tax payments were spent in a manner that violates their religious belief. Because the broad public interest in maintaining a sound tax system is of such a high order, religious belief in conflict with the payment of taxes affords no basis for resisting the tax.

III

Congress has accommodated, to the extent compatible with a comprehensive national program, the practices of those who believe it a violation of their faith to participate in the social security system. In §1402(g), Congress granted an exemption, on religious grounds, to self-employed Amish and others. Confining the §1402(g) exemption to the self-employed provided for a narrow category which was readily identifiable. Self-employed persons in a religious community having its own "welfare" system are distinguishable from the generality of wage earners employed by others.

Congress and the courts have been sensitive to the needs flowing from the Free Exercise Clause, but every person cannot be shielded from all the burdens incident to exercising every aspect of the right to practice religious beliefs. When followers of a particular sect enter into commercial activity as a matter of choice, the limits they accept on their own conduct as a matter of conscience and faith are not to be superimposed on the statutory schemes which are binding on others in that activity. Granting an exemption from social security taxes to an employer operates to impose the employer's religious faith on the employees. Congress drew a line in §1402(g), exempting the self-employed Amish but not all persons working for an Amish employer. The tax imposed on employers to support the social security system must be uniformly applicable to all, except as Congress provides explicitly otherwise.

Accordingly, the judgment of the District Court is reversed, and the case is remanded for proceedings consistent with this opinion.

BOB JONES UNIVERSITY v. UNITED STATES

461 U.S. 574 (1983)

Opinion: Burger, joined by Brennan, White, Marshall, Blackmun, Stevens, O'Connor, and by Powell in part III
Concurrence: Powell
Dissent: Rehnquist

CHIEF JUSTICE BURGER *delivered the opinion of the Court.*

We granted certiorari to decide whether petitioners, nonprofit private schools that prescribe and enforce racially discriminatory admissions standards on the basis of religious doctrine, qualify as tax-exempt organizations under §501(c)(3) of the Internal Revenue Code of 1954.

I

A

Until 1970, the Internal Revenue Service granted tax-exempt status to private schools, without regard to their racial admissions policies, under §501(c)(3) of the Internal Revenue Code and granted charitable deductions for contributions to such schools under §170 of the Code.

On January 12, 1970, a three-judge District Court for the District of Columbia issued a preliminary injunction prohibiting the IRS from according tax-exempt status to private schools in Mississippi that discriminated as to admissions on the basis of race. Thereafter, in July, 1970, the IRS concluded that it could "no longer legally justify allowing tax-exempt status [under §501(c)(3)] to private schools which practice racial discrimination." At the same time, the IRS announced that it could not "treat gifts to such schools as charitable deductions for income tax purposes [under §170]." By letter dated November 30, 1970, the IRS formally notified private schools, including those involved in this litigation, of this change in policy, "applicable to all private schools in the United States at all levels of education." . . .

The revised policy on discrimination was formalized in Revenue Ruling 71-447, 1971-2 Cum. Bull. 230:

Both the courts and the Internal Revenue Service have long recognized that the statutory requirement of being "organized and operated exclusively for religious, charitable, . . . or educational purposes" was intended to express the basic common law concept [of "charity"].... All charitable trusts, educational or otherwise, are subject to the requirement that the purpose of the trust may not be illegal or contrary to public policy.

Based on the "national policy to discourage racial discrimination in education," the IRS ruled that "a [private] school not having a racially nondiscriminatory policy as to students is not 'charitable' within the common law concepts reflected in sections 170 and 501(c)(3) of the Code."

B

Bob Jones University is a nonprofit corporation located in Greenville, S.C. Its purpose is "to conduct an institution of learning . . . giving special emphasis to the Christian religion and the ethics revealed in the Holy Scriptures." The corporation operates a school with an enrollment of approximately 5,000 students, from kindergarten through college and graduate school. Bob Jones University is not affiliated with any religious denomination, but is dedicated to the teaching and propagation of its fundamentalist Christian religious beliefs. It is both a religious and educational institution. Its teachers are required to be devout Christians, and all courses at the University are taught according to the Bible. Entering students are screened as to their religious beliefs, and their public and private conduct is strictly regulated by standards promulgated by University authorities.

The sponsors of the University genuinely believe that the Bible forbids interracial dating and marriage. To effectuate these views, Negroes were completely excluded until 1971. From 1971 to May, 1975, the University accepted no applications from unmarried Negroes, but did accept applications from Negroes married within their race.

Following the decision of the United States Court of Appeals for the Fourth Circuit in *McCrary v. Runyon*, prohibiting racial exclusion from private schools, the University revised its policy. Since May 29, 1975, the University has permitted unmarried Negroes to enroll; but a disciplinary rule prohibits interracial dating and marriage. That rule reads:

There is to be no interracial dating.

1. Students who are partners in an interracial marriage will be expelled.
2. Students who are members of or affiliated with any group or organization which holds as one of its goals or advocates interracial marriage will be expelled.
3. Students who date outside of their own race will be expelled.
4. Students who espouse, promote, or encourage others to violate the University's dating rules and regulations will be expelled.

The University continues to deny admission to applicants engaged in an interracial marriage or known to advocate interracial marriage or dating.

Until 1970, the IRS extended tax-exempt status to Bob Jones University under §501(c)(3). By the letter of November 30, 1970, that followed the injunction issued in *Green v. Kennedy*, the IRS formally notified the University of the change in IRS policy, and announced its intention to challenge the tax-exempt status of private schools practicing racial discrimination in their admissions policies....

. . . On January 19, 1976, the IRS officially revoked the University's tax-exempt status, effective as of December 1, 1970, the day after the University was formally notified of the change in IRS policy. The University subsequently filed returns under the Federal Unemployment Tax Act for the period from December 1, 1970, to

December 31, 1975, and paid a tax totaling $21 on one employee for the calendar year of 1975. After its request for a refund was denied, the University instituted the present action, seeking to recover the $21 it had paid to the IRS. The Government counterclaimed for unpaid federal unemployment taxes for the taxable years 1971 through 1975, in the amount of $489,675.59, plus interest....

II

A

In Revenue Ruling 71-447, the IRS formalized the policy, first announced in 1970, that §170 and §501(c)(3) embrace the common law "charity" concept. Under that view, to qualify for a tax exemption pursuant to §501(c)(3), an institution must show, first, that it falls within one of the eight categories expressly set forth in that section, and second, that its activity is not contrary to settled public policy.

Section 501(c)(3) provides that "[c]orporations . . . organized and operated exclusively for religious, charitable . . . or educational purposes" are entitled to tax exemption. Petitioners argue that the plain language of the statute guarantees them tax-exempt status. They emphasize the absence of any language in the statute expressly requiring all exempt organizations to be "charitable" in the common law sense, and they contend that the disjunctive "or" separating the categories in §501(c)(3) precludes such a reading. Instead, they argue that, if an institution falls within one or more of the specified categories it is automatically entitled to exemption, without regard to whether it also qualifies as "charitable." The Court of Appeals rejected that contention and concluded that petitioners' interpretation of the statute "tears section 501(c)(3) from its roots."

It is a well-established canon of statutory construction that a court should go beyond the literal language of a statute if reliance on that language would defeat the plain purpose of the statute....

Section 501(c)(3) therefore must be analyzed and construed within the framework of the Internal Revenue Code and against the background of the congressional purposes. Such an examination reveals unmistakable evidence that, underlying all relevant parts of the Code, is the intent that entitlement to tax exemption depends on meeting certain common law standards of charity—namely, that an institution seeking tax-exempt status must serve a public purpose and not be contrary to established public policy....

Tax exemptions for certain institutions thought beneficial to the social order of the country as a whole, or to a particular community, are deeply rooted in our history, as in that of England. The origins of such exemptions lie in the special privileges that have long been extended to charitable trusts.

More than a century ago, this Court announced the caveat that is critical in this case:

> [I]t has now become an established principle of American law that courts of chancery will sustain and protect . . . a gift . . . to public charitable uses, *provided the same is consistent with local laws and public policy. . . . Perin v. Carey. . . .*

When the Government grants exemptions or allows deductions all taxpayers are affected; the very fact of the exemption or deduction for the donor means that other taxpayers can be said to be indirect and vicarious "donors." Charitable exemptions are justified on the basis that the exempt entity confers a public benefit—a benefit which the society or the community may not itself choose or be able to provide, or which supplements and advances the work of public institutions already supported by tax revenues. History buttresses logic to make clear that, to warrant exemption under §501(c)(3), an institution must fall within a category specified in that section and must demonstrably serve and be in harmony with the public interest. The institution's purpose must not be so at odds with the common community conscience as to undermine any public benefit that might otherwise be conferred.

B

We are bound to approach these questions with full awareness that determinations of public benefit and public policy are sensitive matters with serious implications for the institutions affected; a declaration that a given institution is not "charitable" should be made only where there can be no doubt that the activity involved is contrary to a fundamental public policy. But there can no longer be any doubt that racial discrimination in education violates deeply and widely accepted views of elementary justice. Prior to 1954, public education in many places still was conducted under the pall of *Plessy v. Ferguson*; racial segregation in primary and secondary education prevailed in many parts of the country. This Court's decision in *Brown v. Board of Education* signalled an end to that era. Over the past quarter of a century, every pronouncement of this Court and myriad Acts of Congress and Executive Orders attest a firm national policy to prohibit racial segregation and discrimination in public education.

An unbroken line of cases following *Brown v. Board of Education* establishes beyond doubt this Court's view that racial discrimination in education violates a most fundamental national public policy, as well as rights of individuals. . . .

Few social or political issues in our history have been more vigorously debated and more extensively ventilated than the issue of racial discrimination, particularly in education. Given the stress and anguish of the history of efforts to escape from the shackles of the "separate but equal" doctrine of *Plessy v. Ferguson*, it cannot be said that educational institutions that, for whatever reasons, practice racial discrimination, are institutions exercising "beneficial and stabilizing influences in community life," *Walz v. Tax Comm'n*, or should be encouraged by having all taxpayers share in their support by way of special tax status.

There can thus be no question that the interpretation of §170 and §501(c)(3) announced by the IRS in 1970 was correct. That it may be seen as belated does not undermine its soundness. It would be wholly incompatible with the concepts underlying tax exemption to grant the benefit of tax-exempt status to racially discriminatory educational entities, which "exer[t] a pervasive influence on the entire educational process." *Norwood v. Harrison*. Whatever may be the rationale for such private schools' policies, and however sincere the rationale may be, racial discrimination in education is contrary to public policy. Racially discriminatory educational institutions cannot be viewed as conferring a public benefit within the "charitable" concept discussed earlier, or within the congressional intent underlying §170 and §501(c)(3). . . .

III

Petitioners contend that, even if the Commissioner's policy is valid as to non-religious private schools, that policy cannot constitutionally be applied to schools that engage in racial discrimination on the basis of sincerely held religious beliefs. As to such schools, it is argued that the IRS construction of §170 and §501(c)(3) violates their free exercise rights under the Religion Clauses of the First Amendment. This contention presents claims not heretofore considered by this Court in precisely this context.

This Court has long held the Free Exercise Clause of the First Amendment to be an absolute prohibition against governmental regulation of religious beliefs, *Wisconsin v. Yoder*, *Sherbert v. Verner*, *Cantwell v. Connecticut*. As interpreted by this Court, moreover, the Free Exercise Clause provides substantial protection for lawful conduct grounded in religious belief (*Wisconsin v. Yoder*; *Thomas v. Review Board of Indiana Employment Security Div.*; *Sherbert v. Verner*). However, "[n]ot all burdens on religion are unconstitutional. . . . The state may justify a limitation on religious liberty by showing that it is essential to accomplish an overriding governmental interest." *United States v. Lee.*

On occasion, this Court has found certain governmental interests so compelling as to allow even regulations prohibiting religiously based conduct. In *Prince v. Massachusetts*, for example, the Court held that neutrally cast child labor laws prohibiting sale of printed materials on public streets could be applied to prohibit children from dispensing religious literature. The Court found no constitutional infirmity in "excluding [Jehovah's Witness children] from doing there what no other children may do." *Id.* Denial of tax benefits will inevitably have a substantial impact on the operation of private religious schools, but will not prevent those schools from observing their religious tenets.

The governmental interest at stake here is compelling. As discussed in Part II-B, *supra*, the Government has a fundamental, overriding interest in eradicating racial discrimination in education—discrimination that prevailed, with official approval, for the first 165 years of this Nation's constitutional history. That governmental interest substantially outweighs whatever burden denial of tax benefits places on petitioners' exercise of their religious beliefs. The interests asserted by petitioners cannot be accommodated with that compelling governmental interest, *see United States v. Lee*, and no "less restrictive means," *see Thomas v. Review Board of Indiana Employment Security Div.*, are available to achieve the governmental interest.

IV

The remaining issue is whether the IRS properly applied its policy to these petitioners. . . . Petitioner Bob Jones University . . . contends that it is not racially discriminatory. It emphasizes that it now allows all races to enroll, subject only to its restrictions on the conduct of all students, including its prohibitions of association between men and women of different races, and of interracial marriage. Although a ban on intermarriage or interracial dating applies to all races, decisions of this Court firmly establish that discrimination on the basis of racial affiliation and association is a form of racial discrimination. (*Loving v. Virginia*; *McLaughlin v. Florida*; *Tillman v. Wheaton-Haven Recreation Assn.*). We therefore find that the IRS properly applied Revenue Ruling 71-447 to Bob Jones University.

JUSTICE REHNQUIST, *dissenting.*

The Court points out that there is a strong national policy in this country against racial discrimination. To the extent that the Court states that Congress, in furtherance of this policy, could deny tax-exempt status to educational institutions that promote racial discrimination, I readily agree. But, unlike the Court, I am convinced that Congress simply has failed to take this action and, as this Court has said over and over again, regardless of our view on the propriety of Congress' failure to legislate, we are not constitutionally empowered to act for it. . . .

Almost a century of statutory history proves that Congress itself intended to decide what §501(c)(3) requires. Congress has expressed its decision in the plainest of terms in §501(c)(3) by providing that tax-exempt status is to be given to any corporation, or community chest, fund, or foundation that is organized for one of the eight enumerated purposes, operated on a nonprofit basis, and uninvolved in lobbying activities or political campaigns. The IRS certainly is empowered to adopt regulations for the enforcement of these specified requirements, and the courts have authority to resolve challenges to the IRS's exercise of this power, but Congress has left it to neither the IRS nor the courts to select or add to the requirements of §501(c)(3). . . .

Therefore, it is my view that, unless and until Congress affirmatively amends §501(c)(3) to require more, the IRS is without authority to deny petitioners §501(c)(3) status. For this reason, I would reverse the Court of Appeals.

BOWEN v. ROY

476 U.S. 693 (1986)

Opinion: Burger, joined by Brennan, Marshall, Blackmun, Powell, Rehnquist, Stevens, O'Connor in Parts I and II and by Powell, Rehnquist in Part III
Concurrence: Blackmun
Concurrence: Stevens
Partial Concurrence, Partial Dissent: O'Connor
Dissent: White

CHIEF JUSTICE BURGER *announced the judgment of the Court and delivered the opinion of the Court with respect to Parts I and II, and an opinion with respect to Part III, in which* **JUSTICE POWELL** *and* **JUSTICE REHNQUIST** *join.*

The question presented is whether the Free Exercise Clause of the First Amendment compels the Government to accommodate a religiously based objection to the statutory requirements that a Social Security number be provided by an applicant seeking to receive certain welfare benefits, and that the States use these numbers in administering the benefit programs.

I

Appellees Stephen J. Roy and Karen Miller applied for and received benefits under the Aid to Families with Dependent Children program and the Food Stamp program. They refused to comply, however, with the requirement that participants in these programs furnish their state welfare agencies with the Social Security numbers of the members of their household as a condition of receiving benefits. Appellees contended that obtaining a Social Security number for their 2-year-old daughter, Little Bird of the Snow, would violate their Native American religious beliefs. The Pennsylvania Department of Public Welfare thereafter terminated AFDC and medical benefits payable to appellees on the child's behalf and instituted proceedings to reduce the level of food stamps that appellees' household was receiving. Appellees then filed this action against the Secretary of the Pennsylvania Department of Public Welfare, the Secretary of Health and Human Services, and the Secretary of Agriculture, arguing that the Free Exercise Clause entitled them to an exemption from the Social Security number requirement.... At trial, Roy testified that he had recently developed a religious objection to obtaining a Social Security number for Little Bird of the Snow. Roy is a Native American descended from the Abenaki Tribe, and he asserts a religious belief that control over one's life is essential to spiritual purity, and indispensable to "becoming a holy person." Based on recent conversations with an Abenaki chief, Roy believes that technology is "robbing the spirit of man." In order to prepare his daughter for greater spiritual power, therefore, Roy testified to his belief that he must keep her person and spirit unique, and that the uniqueness of the Social Security number as an identifier, coupled with the other uses of the number over which she has no control, will serve to "rob the spirit" of his daughter and prevent her from attaining greater spiritual power.

. . . Citing our decision in *United States v. Lee*, the court entered an injunction containing two basic components. *First*, the Secretary of Health and Human Services was permanently restrained from making any use of the social security number which was issued in the name of Little Bird of the Snow Roy and from disseminating the number to any agency, individual, business entity, or any other third party. *Second*, the federal and state defendants were enjoined until Little Bird of the Snow's 16th birthday from denying Roy cash assistance, medical assistance, and food stamps "because of the [appellees'] refusal to provide a social security number for her." We noted probable jurisdiction, and we vacate and remand.

II

Appellees raise a constitutional challenge to two features of the statutory scheme here. They object to Congress' requirement that a state AFDC plan *must . . .* provide (A) that, *as a condition of eligibility* under the plan, *each* applicant for or recipient of aid *shall* furnish to the State agency his social security account number. They also object to Congress' requirement that "such State agency *shall utilize* such account numbers . . . in the administration of such plan." *Ibid.* We analyze each of these contentions, turning to the latter contention first.

Our cases have long recognized a distinction between the freedom of individual belief, which is absolute, and the freedom of individual conduct, which is not absolute. This case implicates only the latter concern....

Never to our knowledge has the Court interpreted the First Amendment to require the Government *itself* to behave in ways that the individual believes will further his or her spiritual development or that of his or her family. The Free Exercise Clause simply cannot be understood to require the Government to conduct its own internal affairs in ways that comport with the religious beliefs of particular citizens. Just as the Government may not insist that appellees engage in any set form of religious observance, so appellees may not demand that the Government join in their chosen religious practices by refraining from using a number to identify their daughter. "[T]he Free Exercise Clause is written in terms of what the government cannot do to the individual, not in terms of what the individual can extract from the government." *Sherbert v. Verner.* . . .

. . . The Free Exercise Clause affords an individual protection from certain forms of governmental compulsion; it does not afford an individual a right to dictate the conduct of the Government's internal procedures.

... We conclude then that government regulation that indirectly and incidentally calls for a choice between securing a governmental benefit and adherence to religious beliefs is wholly different from governmental action or legislation that criminalizes religiously inspired activity or inescapably compels conduct that some find objectionable for religious reasons. Although the denial of government benefits over religious objection can raise serious Free Exercise problems, these two very different forms of government action are not governed by the same constitutional standard. A governmental burden on religious liberty is not insulated from review simply because it is indirect, *Thomas v. Review Board of Indiana Employment Security Div.*, but the nature of the burden is relevant to the standard the government must meet to justify the burden.

The test applied in cases like *Wisconsin v. Yoder*, is not appropriate in this setting. In the enforcement of a facially neutral and uniformly applicable requirement for the administration of welfare programs reaching many millions of people, the Government is entitled to wide latitude. ... Absent proof of an intent to discriminate against particular religious beliefs or against religion in general, the Government meets its burden when it demonstrates that a challenged requirement for governmental benefits, neutral and uniform in its application, is a reasonable means of promoting a legitimate public interest.

... Here there is nothing whatever suggesting antagonism by Congress towards religion generally, or towards any particular religious beliefs. The requirement that applicants provide a Social Security number is facially neutral, and applies to all applicants for the benefits involved.

Congress has made no provision for individual exemptions to the requirement in the two statutes in question.... The Social Security number requirement clearly promotes a legitimate and important public interest. No one can doubt that preventing fraud in these benefits programs is an important goal....

We also think it plain that the Social Security number requirement is a reasonable means of promoting that goal. . . . [T]he District Court found:

> Social security numbers are used in making the determination that benefits in the programs are properly paid and that there is no duplication of benefits or failure of payment. ... Utilization in the computer system of the name of a benefit recipient alone frequently is not sufficient to ensure the proper payment of benefits.

... [I]n any event, we know of no case obligating the Government to tolerate a slight risk of "one or perhaps a few individuals" fraudulently obtaining benefits in order to satisfy a religious objection to a requirement designed to combat that very risk. Appellees may not use the Free Exercise Clause to demand Government benefits, but only on their own terms, particularly where that insistence works a demonstrable disadvantage to the Government in the administration of the programs.

As the Court has recognized before, given the diversity of beliefs in our pluralistic society and the necessity of providing governments with sufficient operating latitude, some incidental neutral restraints on the free exercise of religion are inescapable. As a matter of legislative policy, a legislature might decide to make religious accommodations to a general and neutral system of awarding benefits, "[b]ut our concern is not with the wisdom of legislation, but with its constitutional limitation." *Braunfeld v. Brown.* We conclude that the

Congress' refusal to grant appellees a special exemption does not violate the Free Exercise Clause.

The judgment of the District Court is vacated and the case is remanded.

JUSTICE O'CONNOR, *with whom* **JUSTICE BRENNAN** *and* **JUSTICE MARSHALL** *join, concurring in part and dissenting in part.*

. . . Granting an exemption to Little Bird of the Snow, and to the handful of others who can be expected to make a similar religious objection to providing the Social Security number in conjunction with the receipt of welfare benefits, will not demonstrably diminish the Government's ability to combat welfare fraud. The District Court found that the governmental appellants had hardly shown that a significant number of other individuals were likely to make a claim similar to that at issue here. . . .

The danger that a religious exemption would invite or encourage fraudulent applications seeking to avoid cross-matching performed with the use of Social Security numbers is remote on the facts as found by the District Court: few would-be lawbreakers would risk arousing suspicion by requesting an exemption granted only to a very few. And the sincerity of appellees' religious beliefs is here undisputed. There is therefore no reason to believe that our previous standard for determining whether the Government must accommodate a free exercise claim does not apply.

. . . Here, although prevention of welfare fraud is concededly a compelling interest, the Government asserts only administrative efficiency as its reason for refusing to exempt appellees from furnishing the Social Security number. The District Court found that assertion sorely wanting, and our conclusion that part of the resulting injunction was overbroad only makes the Government's assertion less plausible. Surely the fact that the Court was willing in *Bob Jones University* to give overriding weight to the Government's interest in eradicating the scourge of racial discrimination does not mean that the Court must also give overriding weight to the unanchored anxieties of the welfare bureaucracy. . . .

I would merely vacate that portion of the injunction issued by the District Court that enjoins the Government from using or disseminating the Social Security number already in its possession.

GOLDMAN v. WEINBERGER

475 U.S. 503 (1986)

Opinion: Rehnquist, joined by Burger, White, Powell, Stevens
Concurrence: Stevens, joined by White, Powell
Dissent: Brennan, joined by Marshall
Dissent: Blackmun
Dissent: O'Connor, joined by Marshall

JUSTICE REHNQUIST *delivered the opinion of the Court.*

Petitioner S. Simcha Goldman contends that the Free Exercise Clause of the First Amendment to the United States Constitution permits him to wear a yarmulke while in uniform, notwithstanding an Air Force regulation mandating uniform dress for Air Force personnel. The District Court for the District of Columbia permanently enjoined the Air Force from enforcing its regulation against petitioner and from penalizing him for wearing his yarmulke.

The Court of Appeals for the District of Columbia Circuit reversed on the ground that the Air Force's strong interest in discipline justified the strict enforcement of its uniform dress requirements. We granted certiorari because of the importance of the question, and now affirm.

Petitioner Goldman is an Orthodox Jew and ordained rabbi. In 1973, he was accepted into the Armed Forces Health Professions Scholarship Program.... After completing his Ph.D. in psychology, petitioner entered active service in the United States Air Force as a commissioned officer, in accordance with a requirement that participants in the scholarship program serve one year of active duty for each year of subsidized education. Petitioner was stationed at March Air Force Base in Riverside, California, and served as a clinical psychologist at the mental health clinic on the base.

Until 1981, petitioner was not prevented from wearing his yarmulke on the base. He avoided controversy by remaining close to his duty station in the health clinic and by wearing his service cap over the yarmulke when out of doors. But in April, 1981, after he testified as a defense witness at a court-martial wearing his yarmulke but not his service cap, opposing counsel lodged a complaint with Colonel Joseph Gregory, the Hospital Commander, arguing that petitioner's practice of wearing his yarmulke was a violation of Air Force Regulation (AFR) 35-10. This regulation states in pertinent part that "[h]eadgear will not be worn ... [w]hile indoors except by armed security police in the performance of their duties."

. . . Petitioner then sued respondent Secretary of Defense and others, claiming that the application of AFR 35-10 to prevent him from wearing his yarmulke infringed upon his First Amendment freedom to exercise his religious beliefs....

Petitioner argues that AFR 35-10, as applied to him, prohibits religiously motivated conduct, and should therefore be analyzed under the standard enunciated in *Sherbert v. Verner.* But we have repeatedly held that "the military is, by necessity, a specialized society separate from civilian society." *Parker v. Levy.* "[T]he military must insist upon a respect for duty and a discipline without counterpart in civilian life," *Schlesinger v. Councilman,* in order to prepare for and perform its vital role.

Our review of military regulations challenged on First Amendment grounds is far more deferential than constitutional review of similar laws or regulations designed for civilian society. The military need not encourage debate or tolerate protest to the extent that such tolerance is required of the civilian state by the First Amendment; to accomplish its mission, the military must foster instinctive obedience, unity, commitment, and *esprit de corps.* The essence of military service "is the subordination of the desires and interests of the individual to the needs of the service." *Orloff v. Willoughby.*

These aspects of military life do not, of course, render entirely nugatory in the military context the guarantees of the First Amendment. But "within the military community, there is simply not the same [individual] autonomy as there is in the larger civilian community." *Parker v. Levy.* In the context of the present case, when evaluating whether military needs justify a particular restriction on religiously motivated conduct, courts must give great deference to the professional judgment of military authorities concerning the relative importance of a particular military interest....

The considered professional judgment of the Air Force is that the traditional outfitting of personnel in standardized uniforms encourages the subordination of personal preferences and identities in favor of the overall group mission. Uniforms encourage a sense of hierarchical unity by tending to eliminate outward individual distinctions except for those of rank. The Air Force considers them as vital during peacetime as during war, because its personnel must be ready to provide an effective defense on a moment's notice; the necessary habits of discipline and unity must be developed in advance of trouble. We have acknowledged that [t]he inescapable demands of military discipline and obedience to orders cannot be taught on battlefields; the habit of immediate compliance with military procedures and orders must be virtually reflex, with no time for debate or reflection. *Chappell v. Wallace.*

... But whether or not expert witnesses may feel that religious exceptions to AFR 35-10 are desirable is quite beside the point. The desirability of dress regulations in the military is decided by the appropriate military officials, and they are under no constitutional mandate to abandon their considered professional judgment. Quite obviously, to the extent the regulations do not permit the wearing of religious apparel such as a yarmulke, a practice described by petitioner as silent devotion akin to prayer, military life may be more objectionable for petitioner and probably others. But the First Amendment does not require the military to accommodate such practices in the face of its view that they would detract from the uniformity sought by the dress regulations. The Air Force has drawn the line essentially between religious apparel that is visible and that which is not, and we hold that those portions of the regulations challenged here reasonably and evenhandedly regulate dress in the interest of the military's perceived need for uniformity. The First Amendment therefore does not prohibit them from being applied to petitioner, even though their effect is to restrict the wearing of the headgear required by his religious beliefs. The judgment of the Court of Appeals is

Affirmed.

Free Exercise Cases: From Strict Scrutiny to Rational Review

We have already raised the possibility that the Court was not genuinely invoking a strict scrutiny standard in the line of cases that you have just read—those falling between *Sherbert v. Verner* and *Employment Division v. Smith*. In *Employment Division v. Smith*, as you will see, the Court decided that its previous free exercise jurisprudence was unworkable and should be changed. Specifically, the case changed the kind of scrutiny that is used in First Amendment case law concerning the Free Exercise Clause, from a strict scrutiny standard to one of rational review. Rather than presuming that laws adversely affecting religion should be subject to exemptions, the Court used its rational review standard to impose a much higher burden for those who wished to be granted an exemption. Namely, if a law was generally applicable, it was necessary to show that it was based on intentional discrimination toward a particular religion, not just that it had an adverse effect on that religion. According to this standard, religious exemptions could be denied as long as the law in question served a rational interest and did not intentionally target a religion.

In comparing the strict scrutiny and rational review standards, it is helpful to think about two questions. First, what are the government's goals for the legislation at issue, and how weighty are they? Second, what are the methods that the state uses to achieve these goals? Under the previous strict scrutiny test, in order to deny an exemption, the government's goals needed to be extremely weighty. In the Court's terms, the state needed to show a compelling interest. Moreover, strict scrutiny also demanded that Congress try to achieve these goals in the narrowest possible manner. Under this standard, it was very difficult for the government to show that it was justified in denying an exemption. In contrast, the standard of rational review announced in *Employment Division v. Smith* is much easier for the government to meet when it seeks to deny an exemption. It requires only that the government show that it has some good reason for denying the exemption, both in terms of having a legitimate goal to achieve and using reasonable means to attain that goal. For an in-depth discussion of these different tiers of scrutiny, see the chart in Chapter 9 on page 1263.

EMPLOYMENT DIVISION v. SMITH

494 U.S. 872 (1990)

Opinion: Scalia, joined by Rehnquist, White, Stevens, Kennedy
Concurrence: O'Connor, joined by Brennan, Marshall, Blackmun in Parts I and II without concurring in the judgment
Dissent: Blackmun, joined by Brennan, Marshall

In Employment Division v. Smith, *the Court considered whether a Native American group was entitled to an exemption to a general law prohibiting the use of peyote. The group claimed it was entitled to an exemption under the standards set in* Sherbert v. Verner *because the use of peyote was essential to its religious beliefs and practices. The Native American group did not challenge the legitimacy of a general prohibition on peyote, but rather sought to be exempted from the enforcement of this ban when it came to its own*

religious practices. Under the Sherbert v. Verner *standard, the Court would have had to show that a denial of the exemption supported a compelling interest and that there was no alternative to realizing this interest without denying the exemption. But, as you are about to see, Justice Antonin Scalia uses the occasion of this case to abandon the strict scrutiny standard for granting exemptions to neutral laws. Instead, he explains that because this case does not involve an intent to discriminate against the petitioners' religion, rational basis is the appropriate constitutional standard.*

As you read this case, consider why the Court decided to change its standard from strict scrutiny to rational review. Moreover, in thinking about the consequences of this change for actual litigants, it might be useful to consider whether Employment Division v. Smith *would have been decided differently under the old strict scrutiny test that is rejected here.*

JUSTICE SCALIA *delivered the opinion of the Court.*

This case requires us to decide whether the Free Exercise Clause of the First Amendment permits the State of Oregon to include religiously inspired peyote use within the reach of its general criminal prohibition on use of that drug, and thus permits the State to deny unemployment benefits to persons dismissed from their jobs because of such religiously inspired use.

I

Oregon law prohibits the knowing or intentional possession of a "controlled substance" unless the substance has been prescribed by a medical practitioner. The law defines "controlled substance" as a drug classified in Schedules I through V of the Federal Controlled Substances Act. Persons who violate this provision by possessing a controlled substance listed on Schedule I are "guilty of a Class B felony." As compiled by the State Board of Pharmacy under its statutory authority, Schedule I contains the drug peyote, a hallucinogen derived from the plant *Lophophora williamsii Lemaire.*

Respondents Alfred Smith and Galen Black were fired from their jobs with a private drug rehabilitation organization because they ingested peyote for sacramental purposes at a ceremony of the Native American Church, of which both are members. When respondents applied to petitioner Employment Division for unemployment compensation, they were determined to be ineligible for benefits because they had been discharged for work-related "misconduct." The Oregon Court of Appeals reversed that determination, holding that

the denial of benefits violated respondents' free exercise rights under the First Amendment. . . .

II

A

The Free Exercise Clause of the First Amendment, which has been made applicable to the States by incorporation into the Fourteenth Amendment, *see Cantwell v. Connecticut,* provides that "Congress shall make no law respecting an establishment of religion, or *prohibiting the free exercise thereof.* . . ." The free exercise of religion means, first and foremost, the right to believe and profess whatever religious doctrine one desires. Thus, the First Amendment obviously excludes all "governmental regulation of religious beliefs as such." *Sherbert v. Verner.* . . .

But the "exercise of religion" often involves not only belief and profession but the performance of (or abstention from) physical acts: assembling with others for a worship service, participating in sacramental use of bread and wine, proselytizing, abstaining from certain foods or certain modes of transportation. It would be true, we think (though no case of ours has involved the point), that a state would be "prohibiting the free exercise [of religion]" if it sought to ban such acts or abstentions only when they are engaged in for religious reasons, or only because of the religious belief that they display. It would doubtless be unconstitutional, for example, to ban the casting of "statues that are to be used for worship purposes," or to prohibit bowing down before a golden calf.

Respondents in the present case, however, seek to carry the meaning of "prohibiting the free exercise [of religion]" one large step further. They contend that their religious motivation for using peyote places them beyond the reach of a criminal law that is not specifically directed at their religious practice, and that is concededly constitutional as applied to those who use the drug for other reasons. They assert, in other words, that "prohibiting the free exercise [of religion]" includes requiring any individual to observe a generally applicable law that requires (or forbids) the performance of an act that his religious belief forbids (or requires). As a textual matter, we do not think the words must be given that meaning. It is no more necessary to regard the collection of a general tax, for example, as "prohibiting the free exercise [of religion]" by those citizens who believe support of organized government to be sinful than it is to regard the same tax as "abridging the freedom . . . of the press" of those publishing companies that must pay the tax as a condition of staying in business. It is a permissible reading of the text, in the one case as in the other, to say that, if prohibiting the exercise of religion (or burdening the activity of printing) is not the object of the tax, but merely the incidental effect of a generally applicable and otherwise valid provision, the First Amendment has not been offended. . . .

Our decisions reveal that the latter reading is the correct one. We have never held that an individual's religious beliefs excuse him from compliance with an otherwise valid law prohibiting conduct that the State is free to regulate. On the contrary, the record of more than a century of our free exercise jurisprudence contradicts that proposition. As described succinctly by Justice Frankfurter in *Minersville School Dist. Bd. of Educ. v. Gobitis*: "Conscientious scruples have not, in the course of the long struggle for religious toleration, relieved the individual from obedience to a general law not aimed at the promotion or restriction of religious beliefs. The mere possession of religious convictions which contradict the relevant concerns of a political society does not relieve the citizen from the discharge of political responsibilities." We first had occasion to assert that principle in *Reynolds v. United States*, where we rejected the claim that criminal laws against polygamy could not be constitutionally applied to those whose religion commanded the practice. "Laws," we said, "are made for the government of actions, and while they cannot interfere with mere religious belief and opinions, they may with practices. . . . Can a man excuse his practices to the contrary because of his religious belief? To permit this would be to make the professed doctrines of religious belief superior to the law of the land, and in effect to permit every citizen to become a law unto himself."

Subsequent decisions have consistently held that the right of free exercise does not relieve an individual of the obligation to comply with a "valid and neutral law of general applicability on the ground that the law proscribes (or prescribes) conduct that his religion prescribes (or proscribes)." *United States v. Lee* (Stevens, J., concurring in judgment). . . .

The only decisions in which we have held that the First Amendment bars application of a neutral, generally applicable law to religiously motivated action have involved not the Free Exercise Clause alone, but the Free Exercise Clause in conjunction with other constitutional protections, such as freedom of speech and of the press. . . . Some of our cases prohibiting compelled expression, decided exclusively upon free speech grounds, have also involved freedom of religion. . . . And it is easy to envision a case in which a challenge on freedom of association grounds would likewise be reinforced by Free Exercise Clause concerns. . . .

The present case does not present such a hybrid situation, but a free exercise claim unconnected with any communicative activity or parental right. Respondents urge us to hold, quite simply, that when otherwise prohibitable conduct is accompanied by religious convictions, not only the convictions but the conduct itself must be free from governmental regulation. We have never held that, and decline to do so now. There being no contention that Oregon's drug law represents an attempt to regulate religious beliefs, the communication of religious beliefs, or the raising of one's children in those beliefs, the rule to which we have adhered ever since *Reynolds* plainly controls. "Our cases do not at their farthest reach support the proposition that a stance of conscientious opposition relieves an objector from any colliding duty fixed by a democratic government." *Gillette v. United States.*

B

Respondents argue that, even though exemption from generally applicable criminal laws need not automatically be extended to religiously motivated actors, at least the claim for a religious exemption must be evaluated under the balancing test set forth in *Sherbert v. Verner.* Under the *Sherbert* test, governmental actions that substantially burden a religious practice must be justified by a compelling governmental interest. Applying that test, we have, on three occasions, invalidated state unemployment compensation rules that conditioned the availability of benefits upon an applicant's willingness to work under conditions forbidden by his religion. (*Sherbert v. Verner*; *Thomas v. Review Board, Indiana Employment Div.*; *Hobbie v. Unemployment Appeals Comm'n of Florida.*) We have never invalidated any governmental action on the basis of the *Sherbert* test except the denial of unemployment compensation. Although we have sometimes purported to apply the *Sherbert* test in contexts other than that,

we have always found the test satisfied. (*United States v. Lee*; *Gillette v. United States.*) In recent years we have abstained from applying the *Sherbert* test (outside the unemployment compensation field) at all. In *Bowen v. Roy*, we declined to apply *Sherbert* analysis to a federal statutory scheme that required benefit applicants and recipients to provide their Social Security numbers. The plaintiffs in that case asserted that it would violate their religious beliefs to obtain and provide a Social Security number for their daughter. We held the statute's application to the plaintiffs valid regardless of whether it was necessary to effectuate a compelling interest. In *Lyng v. Northwest Indian Cemetery Protective Assn.*, we declined to apply *Sherbert* analysis to the Government's logging and road construction activities on lands used for religious purposes by several Native American Tribes, even though it was undisputed that the activities "could have devastating effects on traditional Indian religious practices." In *Goldman v. Weinberger*, we rejected application of the *Sherbert* test to military dress regulations that forbade the wearing of yarmulkes. In *O'Lone v. Estate of Shabazz*, we sustained, without mentioning the *Sherbert* test, a prison's refusal to excuse inmates from work requirements to attend worship services.

. . . As the plurality pointed out in *Roy*, our decisions in the unemployment cases stand for the proposition that where the State has in place a system of individual exemptions, it may not refuse to extend that system to cases of "religious hardship" without compelling reason. *Bowen v. Roy.*

Whether or not the decisions are that limited, they at least have nothing to do with an across-the-board criminal prohibition on a particular form of conduct. Although, as noted earlier, we have sometimes used the *Sherbert* test to analyze free exercise challenges to such laws (*United States v. Lee*; *Gillette v. United States*), we have never applied the test to invalidate one. We conclude today that the sounder approach, and the approach in accord with the vast majority of our precedents, is to hold the test inapplicable to such challenges. The government's ability to enforce generally applicable prohibitions of socially harmful conduct, like its ability to carry out other aspects of public policy, "cannot depend on measuring the effects of a governmental action on a religious objector's spiritual development." *Lyng*. To make an individual's obligation to obey such a law contingent upon the law's coincidence with his religious beliefs, except where the State's interest is "compelling"— permitting him, by virtue of his beliefs, "to become a law unto himself," *Reynolds v. United States*—contradicts both constitutional tradition and common sense.

The "compelling government interest" requirement seems benign, because it is familiar from other fields. But using it as the standard that must be met before the government may accord different treatment on the basis of race, or before the government may regulate the content of speech, is not remotely comparable to using it for the purpose asserted here. What it produces in those other fields—equality of treatment, and an unrestricted flow of contending speech—are constitutional norms; what it would produce here—a private right to ignore generally applicable laws—is a constitutional anomaly.

Nor is it possible to limit the impact of respondents' proposal by requiring a "compelling state interest" only when the conduct prohibited is "central" to the individual's religion. It is no more appropriate for judges to determine the "centrality" of religious beliefs before applying a "compelling interest" test in the free

exercise field than it would be for them to determine the "importance" of ideas before applying the "compelling interest" test in the free speech field. What principle of law or logic can be brought to bear to contradict a believer's assertion that a particular act is "central" to his personal faith? Judging the centrality of different religious practices is akin to the unacceptable "business of evaluating the relative merits of differing religious claims." *United States v. Lee* (Stevens, J., concurring). As we reaffirmed only last Term, "[i]t is not within the judicial ken to question the centrality of particular beliefs or practices to a faith, or the validity of particular litigants' interpretation of those creeds." *Hernandez v. Commissioner*. Repeatedly and in many different contexts, we have warned that courts must not presume to determine the place of a particular belief in a religion or the plausibility of a religious claim. . . .

If the "compelling interest" test is to be applied at all, then, it must be applied across the board, to all actions thought to be religiously commanded. Moreover, if "compelling interest" really means what it says (and watering it down here would subvert its rigor in the other fields where it is applied), many laws will not meet the test. Any society adopting such a system would be courting anarchy, but that danger increases in direct proportion to the society's diversity of religious beliefs, and its determination to coerce or suppress none of them. Precisely because "we are a cosmopolitan nation made up of people of almost every conceivable religious preference," *Braunfeld v. Brown*, and precisely because we value and protect that religious divergence, we cannot afford the luxury of deeming *presumptively invalid*, as applied to the religious objector, every regulation of conduct that does not protect an interest of the highest order. . . .

Values that are protected against government interference through enshrinement in the Bill of Rights are not thereby banished from the political process. Just as a society that believes in the negative protection accorded to the press by the First Amendment is likely to enact laws that affirmatively foster the dissemination of the printed word, so also a society that believes in the negative protection accorded to religious belief can be expected to be solicitous of that value in its legislation as well. It is therefore not surprising that a number of States have made an exception to their drug laws for sacramental peyote use. . . . But to say that a nondiscriminatory religious practice exemption is permitted, or even that it is desirable, is not to say that it is constitutionally required, and that the appropriate occasions for its creation can be discerned by the courts. It may fairly be said that leaving accommodation to the political process will place at a relative disadvantage those religious practices that are not widely engaged in; but that unavoidable consequence of democratic government must be preferred to a system in which each conscience is a law unto itself or in which judges weigh the social importance of all laws against the centrality of all religious beliefs.

Because respondents' ingestion of peyote was prohibited under Oregon law, and because that prohibition is constitutional, Oregon may, consistent with the Free Exercise Clause, deny respondents unemployment compensation when their dismissal results from use of the drug. The decision of the Oregon Supreme Court is accordingly reversed.

It is so ordered.

JUSTICE O'CONNOR, *with whom* **JUSTICE BRENNAN, JUSTICE MARSHALL**, *and*

JUSTICE BLACKMUN *join as to Parts I and II, concurring in the judgment.*

Although I agree with the result the Court reaches in this case, I cannot join its opinion. In my view, today's holding dramatically departs from well settled First Amendment jurisprudence, appears unnecessary to resolve the question presented, and is incompatible with our Nation's fundamental commitment to individual religious liberty.

I

At the outset, I note that I agree with the Court's implicit determination that the constitutional question upon which we granted review—whether the Free Exercise Clause protects a person's religiously motivated use of peyote from the reach of a State's general criminal law prohibition—is properly presented in this case. As the Court recounts, respondents Alfred Smith and Galen Black were denied unemployment compensation benefits because their sacramental use of peyote constituted work-related "misconduct," not because they violated Oregon's general criminal prohibition against possession of peyote. We held, however, in *Employment Div., Dept. of Human Resources of Oregon v. Smith*, that whether a State may, consistent with federal law, deny unemployment compensation benefits to persons for their religious use of peyote depends on whether the State, as a matter of state law, has criminalized the underlying conduct. The Oregon Supreme Court, on remand from this Court, concluded that "the Oregon statute against possession of controlled substances, which include peyote, makes no exception for the sacramental use of peyote." . . .

II

The Court today extracts from our long history of free exercise precedents the single categorical rule that "if prohibiting the exercise of religion . . . is . . . merely the incidental effect of a generally applicable and otherwise valid provision, the First Amendment has not been offended." Indeed, the Court holds that, where the law is a generally applicable criminal prohibition, our usual free exercise jurisprudence does not even apply. To reach this sweeping result, however, the Court must not only give a strained reading of the First Amendment but must also disregard our consistent application of free exercise doctrine to cases involving generally applicable regulations that burden religious conduct.

A

The Free Exercise Clause of the First Amendment commands that "Congress shall make no law . . . prohibiting the free exercise [of religion]." In *Cantwell v. Connecticut*, we held that this prohibition applies to the States by incorporation into the Fourteenth Amendment and that it categorically forbids government regulation of religious beliefs. As the Court recognizes, however, the "free exercise" of religion often, if not invariably, requires the performance of (or abstention from) certain acts. . . . "[B]elief and action cannot be neatly confined in logic-tight compartments." *Wisconsin v. Yoder*. Because the First Amendment does not distinguish between religious belief and religious conduct, conduct motivated by sincere religious belief, like the belief itself, must therefore be at least presumptively protected by the Free Exercise Clause.

The Court today, however, interprets the Clause to permit the government to prohibit, without justification, conduct mandated by an individual's religious beliefs, so long as that prohibition is generally applicable. . . . But a law that prohibits certain conduct—conduct that happens to be an act of worship for someone—manifestly does prohibit that person's free exercise of his religion. A person who is barred from engaging in religiously motivated conduct is barred from freely exercising his religion. Moreover, that person is barred from freely exercising his religion regardless of whether the law prohibits the conduct only when engaged in for religious reasons, only by members of that religion, or by all persons. It is difficult to deny that a law that prohibits religiously motivated conduct, even if the law is generally applicable, does not at least implicate First Amendment concerns.

The Court responds that generally applicable laws are "one large step" removed from laws aimed at specific religious practices. The First Amendment, however, does not distinguish between laws that are generally applicable and laws that target particular religious practices. Indeed, few States would be so naive as to enact a law directly prohibiting or burdening a religious practice as such. Our free exercise cases have all concerned generally applicable laws that had the effect of significantly burdening a religious practice. If the First Amendment is to have any vitality, it ought not be construed to cover only the extreme and hypothetical situation in which a State directly targets a religious practice. As we have noted in a slightly different context, "[s]uch a test has no basis in precedent and relegates a serious First Amendment value to the barest level of minimum scrutiny that the Equal Protection Clause already provides." *Hobbie v. Unemployment Appeals Comm'n of Florida*.

To say that a person's right to free exercise has been burdened, of course, does not mean that he has an absolute right to engage in the conduct. Under our established First Amendment jurisprudence, we have recognized that the freedom to act, unlike the freedom to believe, cannot be absolute.... Instead, we have respected both the First Amendment's express textual mandate and the governmental interest in regulation of conduct by requiring the Government to justify any substantial burden on religiously motivated conduct by a compelling state interest and by means narrowly tailored to achieve that interest.... The compelling interest test effectuates the First Amendment's command that religious liberty is an independent liberty, that it occupies a preferred position, and that the Court will not permit encroachments upon this liberty, whether direct or indirect, unless required by clear and compelling governmental interests "of the highest order," *Yoder*. "Only an especially important governmental interest pursued by narrowly tailored means can justify exacting a sacrifice of First Amendment freedoms as the price for an equal share of the rights, benefits, and privileges enjoyed by other citizens." *Roy*.

The Court attempts to support its narrow reading of the Clause by claiming that "[w]e have never held that an individual's religious beliefs excuse him from compliance with an otherwise valid law prohibiting conduct that the State IS free to regulate." But as the Court later notes, as it must, in cases such as *Cantwell* and *Yoder*, we have in fact interpreted the Free Exercise Clause to forbid application of a generally applicable prohibition to religiously motivated conduct. Indeed, in *Yoder* we expressly rejected the interpretation the Court now adopts:

[O]ur decisions have rejected the idea that religiously grounded conduct is always outside the protection of the Free Exercise Clause. It is true that activities of individuals, even when religiously based, are often subject to regulation by the States in the exercise of their undoubted power to promote the health, safety, and general welfare, or the Federal Government in the exercise of its delegated powers. But to agree that religiously grounded conduct must often be subject to the broad police power of the State is not to deny that there are areas of conduct protected by the Free Exercise Clause of the First Amendment and thus beyond the power of the State to control, *even under regulations of general applicability*....

... A regulation neutral on its face may, in its application, nonetheless offend the constitutional requirement for government neutrality if it unduly burdens the free exercise of religion.

The Court endeavors to escape from our decisions in *Cantwell* and *Yoder* by labeling them "hybrid" decisions, but there is no denying that both cases expressly relied on the Free Exercise Clause, and that we have consistently regarded those cases as part of the mainstream of our free exercise jurisprudence. Moreover, in each of the other cases cited by the Court to support its categorical rule, we rejected the particular constitutional claims before us only after carefully weighing the competing interests.... That we rejected the free exercise claims in those cases hardly calls into question the applicability of First Amendment doctrine in the first place. Indeed, it is surely unusual to judge the vitality of a constitutional doctrine by looking to the win-loss record of the plaintiffs who happen to come before us.

B

Respondents, of course, do not contend that their conduct is automatically immune from all governmental regulation simply because it is motivated by their sincere religious beliefs. . . . Rather, respondents invoke our traditional compelling interest test to argue that the Free Exercise Clause requires the State to grant them a limited exemption from its general criminal prohibition against the possession of peyote. The Court today, however, denies them even the opportunity to make that argument, concluding that "the sounder approach, and the approach in accord with the vast majority of our precedents, is to hold the [compelling interest] test inapplicable to" challenges to general criminal prohibitions.

In my view, however, the essence of a free exercise claim is relief from a burden imposed by government on religious practices or beliefs, whether the burden is imposed directly through laws that prohibit or compel specific religious practices, or indirectly through laws that, in effect, make abandonment of one's own religion or conformity to the religious beliefs of others the price of an equal place in the civil community. As we explained in *Thomas*:

> Where the state conditions receipt of an important benefit upon conduct proscribed by a religious faith, or where it denies such a benefit because of conduct mandated by religious belief, thereby putting substantial pressure on an adherent to modify his behavior and to violate his beliefs, a burden upon religion exists. . . .

. . . Once it has been shown that a government regulation or criminal prohibition burdens the free exercise of religion, we have consistently asked the Government to demonstrate that unbending application of its regulation to the religious objector "is essential to accomplish an overriding governmental interest," *Lee*, or represents "the least restrictive means of achieving some compelling state interest." *Thomas*.

. . . To me, the sounder approach—the approach more consistent with our role as judges to decide each case on its individual merits—is to apply this test in each case to determine whether the burden on the specific plaintiffs before us is constitutionally significant, and whether the particular criminal interest asserted by the State before us is compelling. . . .

Moreover, we have not "rejected" or "declined to apply" the compelling interest test in our recent cases. Recent cases have instead affirmed that test as a fundamental part of our First Amendment doctrine. . . . The cases cited by the Court signal no retreat from our consistent adherence to the compelling interest test. . . .

Similarly, the other cases cited by the Court for the proposition that we have rejected application of the *Sherbert* test outside the unemployment compensation field, are distinguishable because they arose in the narrow, specialized contexts in which we have not traditionally required the government to justify a burden on religious conduct by articulating a compelling interest. . . . That we did not apply the compelling interest test in these cases says nothing about whether the test should continue to apply in paradigm free exercise cases such as the one presented here.

The Court today gives no convincing reason to depart from settled First Amendment jurisprudence. There is nothing talismanic about neutral laws of general applicability or general criminal prohibitions, for laws neutral toward religion can coerce a person to violate his religious conscience or intrude upon his religious duties just as effectively as laws aimed at religion. Although the Court suggests that the compelling interest test, as applied to generally applicable laws, would result in a "constitutional anomaly," the First Amendment unequivocally makes freedom of religion, like freedom from race discrimination and freedom of speech, a "constitutional nor[m]," not an "anomaly." Nor would application of our established free exercise doctrine to this case necessarily be incompatible with our equal protection cases. . . . We have, in any event, recognized that the Free Exercise Clause protects values distinct from those protected by the Equal Protection Clause. . . . As the language of the Clause itself makes clear, an individual's free exercise of religion is a preferred constitutional activity. . . . A law that makes criminal such an activity therefore triggers constitutional concern—and heightened judicial scrutiny—even if it does not target the particular religious conduct at issue. Our free speech cases similarly recognize that neutral regulations that affect free speech values are subject to a balancing, rather than categorical, approach. . . . The Court's parade of horribles not only fails as a reason for discarding the compelling interest test, it instead demonstrates just the opposite: that courts have been quite capable of applying our free exercise jurisprudence to strike sensible balances between religious liberty and competing state interests.

Finally, the Court today suggests that the disfavoring of minority religions is an "unavoidable consequence" under our system of government, and that accommodation of such religions must be left to the political process. In my view, however, the First Amendment was enacted precisely to protect the rights of those whose religious practices are not shared by the majority and may be viewed with hostility. The history of our free exercise doctrine amply demonstrates the harsh impact majoritarian rule has had on unpopular or emerging religious groups such as the Jehovah's Witnesses

and the Amish. Indeed, the words of Justice Jackson in *West Virginia Board of Education v. Barnette* are apt:

> The very purpose of a Bill of Rights was to withdraw certain subjects from the vicissitudes of political controversy, to place them beyond the reach of majorities and officials and to establish them as legal principles to be applied by the courts. One's right to life, liberty, and property, to free speech, a free press, freedom of worship and assembly, and other fundamental rights may not be submitted to vote; they depend on the outcome of no elections.

. . . The compelling interest test reflects the First Amendment's mandate of preserving religious liberty to the fullest extent possible in a pluralistic society. For the Court to deem this command a "luxury," is to denigrate "[t]he very purpose of a Bill of Rights." . . .

JUSTICE BLACKMUN, *with whom* **JUSTICE BRENNAN** *and* **JUSTICE MARSHALL** *join, dissenting.*

This Court over the years painstakingly has developed a consistent and exacting standard to test the constitutionality of a state statute that burdens the free exercise of religion. Such a statute may stand only if the law in general, and the State's refusal to allow a religious exemption in particular, are justified by a compelling interest that cannot be served by less restrictive means.

Until today, I thought this was a settled and inviolate principle of this Court's First Amendment jurisprudence. The majority, however, perfunctorily dismisses it as a "constitutional anomaly." As carefully detailed in Justice O'Connor's concurring opinion, the majority is able to arrive at this view only by mischaracterizing this Court's precedents. The Court discards leading free exercise cases such as *Cantwell v. Connecticut*, and *Wisconsin v. Yoder*, as "hybrid." The Court views traditional free exercise analysis as somehow inapplicable to criminal prohibitions (as opposed to conditions on the receipt of benefits), and to state laws of general applicability (as opposed, presumably, to laws that expressly single out religious practices). The Court cites cases in which, due to various exceptional circumstances, we found strict scrutiny inapposite, to hint that the Court has repudiated that standard altogether. In short, it effectuates a wholesale overturning of settled law concerning the Religion Clauses of our Constitution. One hopes that the Court is aware of the consequences, and that its result is not a product of overreaction to the serious problems the country's drug crisis has generated.

This distorted view of our precedents leads the majority to conclude that strict scrutiny of a state law burdening the free exercise of religion is a "luxury" that a well-ordered society cannot afford, and that the repression of minority religions is an "unavoidable consequence of democratic government." I do not believe the Founders thought their dearly bought freedom from religious persecution a "luxury," but an essential element of liberty—and they could not have thought religious intolerance "unavoidable," for they drafted the Religion Clauses precisely in order to avoid that intolerance.

For these reasons, I agree with Justice O'Connor's analysis of the applicable free exercise doctrine, and I join parts I and II of her opinion. As she points out, "the critical question in this case is whether exempting respondents from the State's general criminal prohibition 'will unduly interfere with fulfillment of the governmental interest.'" I do disagree, however, with her specific answer to that question.

I

In weighing respondents' clear interest in the free exercise of their religion against Oregon's asserted interest in enforcing its drug laws, it is important to articulate in precise terms the state interest involved. It is not the State's broad interest in fighting the critical "war on drugs" that must be weighed against respondents' claim, but the State's narrow interest in refusing to make an exception for the religious, ceremonial use of peyote....

The State's interest in enforcing its prohibition, in order to be sufficiently compelling to outweigh a free exercise claim, cannot be merely abstract or symbolic. The State cannot plausibly assert that unbending application of a criminal prohibition is essential to fulfill any compelling interest if it does not, in fact, attempt to enforce that prohibition. In this case, the State actually has not evinced any concrete interest in enforcing its drug laws against religious users of peyote. Oregon has never sought to prosecute respondents, and does not claim that it has made significant enforcement efforts against other religious users of peyote. The State's asserted interest thus amounts only to the symbolic preservation of an unenforced prohibition. But a government interest in "symbolism, even symbolism for so worthy a cause as the abolition of unlawful drugs," *Treasury Employees v. Von Raab*, (Scalia, J., dissenting), cannot suffice to abrogate the constitutional rights of individuals.

Similarly, this Court's prior decisions have not allowed a government to rely on mere speculation about potential harms, but have demanded evidentiary support for a refusal to allow a religious exception. (*Thomas*; *Yoder*; *Sherbert v. Verner*.) In this case, the State's justification for refusing to recognize an exception to its criminal laws for religious peyote use is entirely speculative.

The State proclaims an interest in protecting the health and safety of its citizens from the dangers of unlawful drugs. It offers, however, no evidence that the religious use of peyote has ever harmed anyone. The factual findings of other courts cast doubt on the State's assumption that religious use of peyote is harmful. . . .

The fact that peyote is classified as a Schedule I controlled substance does not, by itself, show that any and all uses of peyote, in any circumstance, are inherently harmful and dangerous. The Federal Government, which created the classifications of unlawful drugs from which Oregon's drug laws are derived, apparently does not find peyote so dangerous as to preclude an exemption for religious use. Moreover, other Schedule I drugs have lawful uses.

The State also seeks to support its refusal to make an exception for religious use of peyote by invoking its interest in abolishing drug trafficking. There is, however, practically no illegal traffic in peyote. Also, the availability of peyote for religious use, even if Oregon were to allow an exemption from its criminal laws, would still be strictly controlled by federal regulations, and by the State of Texas, the only State in which peyote grows in significant quantities. Peyote simply is not a popular drug; its distribution for use in religious rituals has nothing to do with the vast and violent traffic in illegal narcotics that plagues this country.

Finally, the State argues that granting an exception for religious peyote use would erode its interest in the uniform, fair, and certain enforcement of its drug laws. The State fears that, if it grants an exemption for religious peyote use, a flood of other claims to religious exemptions will follow. It would then be placed in a dilemma, it says, between allowing a patchwork of exemptions that would hinder its law enforcement efforts, and risking a violation of the Establishment Clause by arbitrarily limiting its religious exemptions. This argument, however, could be made in almost any free exercise case. See Lupu, "Where Rights Begin: The Problem of Burdens on the Free Exercise of Religion," 102 Harv. L. Rev. 933, 947 (1989) ("Behind every free exercise claim is a spectral march; grant this one, a voice whispers to each judge, and you will be confronted with an endless chain of exemption demands from religious deviants of every stripe"). This Court, however, consistently has rejected similar arguments in past free exercise cases, and it should do so here as well. See *Frazee v. Illinois Dept. of Employment Security*; *Thomas*; *Sherbert*.

CASE QUESTION

In this case, the Court changed its standard of scrutiny when considering whether or not an exemption should be granted for religious individuals or groups to laws that are general and neutral. It moved the standard from one that was extremely demanding on the government, that of strict scrutiny, to the famously lenient standard of rational review. But it is difficult to think about the implications of this test without also considering how it would actually affect specific cases. Would any of the cases you have just read have been decided differently under a rational basis test?

| Box 6-2 | Oscillating Levels of Scrutiny—From *Sherbert* to *Boerne* |

The figure in this box illustrates the various tests that have been applied to free exercise claims. In *Employment Division v. Smith*, the Court shifted the standard for considering religious exemptions under the Free Exercise Clause from strict scrutiny to rational review. Although the RFRA attempted to reverse that decision and restore the strict scrutiny standard, the Court in *Boerne v. Flores* retained its rational review standard. The following chart depicts both the original state of the law in *Sherbert v. Verner* and the three subsequent changes.

Figure 6.1. Oscillating Levels of Scrutiny

Standards	*Sherbert* (1963)	*Smith* (1990)	*RFRA* (1993)	*Boerne* (1997)
Strict Scrutiny	X		X	
Rational Review		X		X

CHURCH OF LUKUMI BABALU AYE, INC. v. CITY OF HIALEAH

508 U.S. 520 (1993)

Opinion: Kennedy, joined by Rehnquist, White, Stevens, Scalia, Souter, Thomas in Parts I, II, and IV, by Rehnquist, White, Stevens, Scalia, Thomas in Part II-B, by Rehnquist, Stevens, Scalia, Thomas in Parts II-A-1 and II-A-3, by Stevens in Part II-A-2
Concurrence: Scalia, joined by Rehnquist
Concurrence: Souter
Concurrence: Blackmun, joined by O'Connor

In Church of Lukumi Babalu Aye, Inc. v. City of Hialeah, *the Court makes it clear that after* Employment Division v. Smith *there should be a clear distinction between cases in which there is intentional targeting of religious freedom and those cases in which a neutral general law adversely affects religion. In the former, the Court is especially skeptical of challenged laws, whereas in the latter, the Court gives much more deference. As you read the case, try to discern how we might distinguish between adverse effects on religion and legislation that deliberately targets religion. Should the actual motives of legislators be relevant to the constitutionality of the policies they enact? Some of the councilmen who passed the law at issue in this case explicitly criticized members of the Santeria religion during a meeting about this law. Should that matter in deciding whether this group has been intentionally targeted? Consider whether this standard might permit lawmakers with discriminatory intentions to insulate their discrimination from constitutional attacks simply by failing to articulate the real motivation for their legislation. Notice too that unlike many of our previous cases, the current case concerns the question of whether to strike down a law altogether rather than whether to grant an exemption. Should the Court be more reluctant to strike down a law on grounds of religious freedom as opposed to merely granting an exemption?*

JUSTICE KENNEDY *delivered the opinion of the Court, except as to Part II-A-2.*

The principle that government may not enact laws that suppress religious belief or practice is so well understood that few violations are recorded in our opinions. Concerned that this fundamental nonpersecution principle of the First Amendment was implicated here, however, we granted certiorari.

Our review confirms that the laws in question were enacted by officials who did not understand, failed to perceive, or chose to ignore the fact that their official actions violated the Nation's essential commitment to religious freedom. The challenged laws had an impermissible object; and in all events, the principle of general applicability was violated because the secular ends asserted in defense of the laws were pursued only with respect to conduct motivated by religious beliefs. We invalidate the challenged enactments, and reverse the judgment of the Court of Appeals.

I

A

This case involves practices of the Santeria religion, which originated in the nineteenth century. When hundreds of thousands of members of the Yoruba people were brought as slaves from eastern Africa to Cuba, their traditional African religion absorbed significant elements of Roman Catholicism. The resulting syncretion, or fusion, is Santeria, "the way of the saints." The Cuban Yoruba express their devotion to spirits, called orishas, through the iconography of Catholic saints, Catholic symbols are often present at Santeria rites, and Santeria devotees attend the Catholic sacraments. . . .

The Santeria faith teaches that every individual has a destiny from God, a destiny fulfilled with the aid and energy of the orishas. The basis of the Santeria religion is the nurture of a personal relation with the orishas, and one of the principal forms of devotion is an animal sacrifice. . . .

According to Santeria teaching, the orishas are powerful, but not immortal. They depend for survival on the sacrifice. Sacrifices are performed at birth, marriage, and death rites, for the cure of the sick, for the initiation of new members and priests, and during an annual celebration. Animals sacrificed in Santeria rituals include chickens, pigeons, doves, ducks, guinea pigs, goats, sheep, and turtles. The animals are killed by the cutting of the carotid arteries in the neck. The sacrificed animal is cooked and eaten, except after healing and death rituals.

Santeria adherents faced widespread persecution in Cuba, so the religion and its rituals were practiced in secret. The open practice of Santeria and its rites remains infrequent. . . . The religion was brought to this Nation most often by exiles from the Cuban revolution. The District Court estimated that there are at least 50,000 practitioners in South Florida today. . . .

B

Petitioner Church of the Lukumi Babalu Aye, Inc. (Church), is a not-for-profit corporation organized under Florida law in 1973. The Church and its congregants practice the Santeria religion. . . . In April, 1987, the Church leased land in the city of Hialeah, Florida, and announced plans to establish a house of worship as well as a school, cultural center, and museum. . . . The Church began the process of obtaining utility service and receiving the necessary licensing, inspection, and zoning approvals. Although the Church's efforts at obtaining the necessary licenses and permits were far from smooth, it appears that it received all needed approvals by early August, 1987.

The prospect of a Santeria church in their midst was distressing to many members of the Hialeah community, and the announcement of the plans to open a Santeria church in Hialeah prompted the city council to hold an emergency public session on June 9, 1987. . . .

. . . First, the city council adopted Resolution 87-66, which noted the "concern" expressed by residents of the city "that certain religions may propose to engage in practices which are inconsistent with public morals, peace or safety," and declared that "[t]he City reiterates its commitment to a prohibition against any and all acts of any and all religious groups which are inconsistent with public morals, peace or safety." Next, the council approved an emergency ordinance, Ordinance 87-40, that incorporated in full, except as to penalty, Florida's animal cruelty laws. Among other things, the incorporated state law subjected to criminal punishment "[w]hoever . . . unnecessarily or cruelly . . . kills any animal." . . .

In September, 1987, the city council adopted three substantive ordinances addressing the issue of religious animal sacrifice. Ordinance 87-52 defined "sacrifice" as "to unnecessarily kill, torment, torture, or mutilate an animal in a public or private ritual or ceremony not for the primary purpose of food consumption,"

and prohibited owning or possessing an animal "intending to use such animal for food purposes." It restricted application of this prohibition, however, to any individual or group that "kills, slaughters or sacrifices animals for any type of ritual, regardless of whether or not the flesh or blood of the animal is to be consumed." The ordinance contained an exemption for slaughtering by "licensed establishment[s]" of animals "specifically raised for food purposes." Declaring, moreover, that the city council "has determined that the sacrificing of animals within the city limits is contrary to the public health, safety, welfare and morals of the community," the city council adopted Ordinance 87-71. That ordinance defined sacrifice as had Ordinance 87-52, and then provided that "[i]t shall be unlawful for any person, persons, corporations or associations to sacrifice any animal within the corporate limits of the City of Hialeah, Florida." The final Ordinance, 87-72, defined "slaughter" as "the killing of animals for food," and prohibited slaughter outside of areas zoned for slaughterhouse use. The ordinance provided an exemption, however, for the slaughter or processing for sale of "small numbers of hogs and/or cattle per week in accordance with an exemption provided by state law." All ordinances and resolutions passed the city council by unanimous vote. Violations of each of the four ordinances were punishable by fines not exceeding $500 or imprisonment not exceeding 60 days, or both.

Following enactment of these ordinances, the Church . . . filed this action pursuant to 42 U.S.C. §1983 in the United States District Court for the Southern District of Florida. . . .

After a 9-day bench trial on the remaining claims, the District Court ruled for the city, finding no violation of petitioners' rights under the Free Exercise Clause. . . .

II

The Free Exercise Clause of the First Amendment, which has been applied to the States through the Fourteenth Amendment, *see Cantwell v. Connecticut*, provides that "Congress shall make no law respecting an establishment of religion, or *prohibiting the free exercise thereof. . . .*" The city does not argue that Santeria is not a "religion" within the meaning of the First Amendment. Nor could it. Although the practice of animal sacrifice may seem abhorrent to some, "religious beliefs need not be acceptable, logical, consistent, or comprehensible to others in order to merit First Amendment protection." *Thomas v. Review Bd. of Indiana Employment Security Div.* Given the historical association between animal sacrifice and religious worship, petitioners' assertion that animal sacrifice is an integral part of their religion "cannot be deemed bizarre or incredible." *Frazee v. Illinois Dept. of Employment Security*. Neither the city nor the courts below, moreover, have questioned the sincerity of petitioners' professed desire to conduct animal sacrifices for religious reasons. We must consider petitioners' First Amendment claim.

In addressing the constitutional protection for free exercise of religion, our cases establish the general proposition that a law that is neutral and of general applicability need not be justified by a compelling governmental interest even if the law has the incidental effect of burdening a particular religious practice. *Employment Div., Dept. of Human Resources of Oregon v. Smith.* Neutrality and general applicability are interrelated, and, as becomes apparent in this case, failure to satisfy one requirement is a likely indication that the other has not been satisfied. A law failing to satisfy these requirements must be justified by a compelling governmental interest, and must be narrowly tailored to advance that interest.

These ordinances fail to satisfy the *Smith* requirements. We begin by discussing neutrality.

A

In our Establishment Clause cases, we have often stated the principle that the First Amendment forbids an official purpose to disapprove of a particular religion or of religion in general. . . . These cases, however, for the most part, have addressed governmental efforts to benefit religion or particular religions, and so have dealt with a question different, at least in its formulation and emphasis, from the issue here. Petitioners allege an attempt to disfavor their religion because of the religious ceremonies it commands, and the Free Exercise Clause is dispositive in our analysis.

At a minimum, the protections of the Free Exercise Clause pertain if the law at issue discriminates against some or all religious beliefs or regulates or prohibits conduct because it is undertaken for religious reasons. . . . Indeed, it was "historical instances of religious persecution and intolerance that gave concern to those who drafted the Free Exercise Clause." *Bowen v. Roy* (opinion of Burger, C.J.). . . . These principles, though not often at issue in our Free Exercise Clause cases, have played a role in some. In *McDaniel v. Paty*, for example, we invalidated a State law that disqualified members of the clergy from holding certain public offices, because it "impose[d] special disabilities on the basis of . . . religious status." *Employment Div., Dept. of Human Resources of Oregon v. Smith*. On the same principle, in *Fowler v. Rhode Island*, we found that a municipal ordinance was applied in an unconstitutional manner when interpreted to prohibit preaching in a public park by a Jehovah's Witness, but to permit preaching during the course of a Catholic mass or Protestant church service. . . .

1

Although a law targeting religious beliefs as such is never permissible, if the object of a law is to infringe upon or restrict practices because of their religious motivation, the law is not neutral, *see Employment Div., Dept. of Human Resources of Oregon v. Smith*, and it is invalid unless it is justified by a compelling interest and is narrowly tailored to advance that interest. There are, of course, many ways of demonstrating that the object or purpose of a law is the suppression of religion or religious conduct. To determine the object of a law, we must begin with its text, for the minimum requirement of neutrality is that a law not discriminate on its face. A law lacks facial neutrality if it refers to a religious practice without a secular meaning discernable from the language or context. Petitioners contend that three of the ordinances fail this test of facial neutrality because they use the words "sacrifice" and "ritual": words with strong religious connotations. We agree that these words are consistent with the claim of facial discrimination, but the argument is not conclusive. The words "sacrifice" and "ritual" have a religious origin, but current use admits also of secular meanings. The ordinances, furthermore, define "sacrifice" in secular terms, without referring to religious practices.

We reject the contention advanced by the city that our inquiry must end with the text of the laws at issue. Facial neutrality is not determinative. The Free Exercise Clause, like the Establishment Clause, extends beyond facial discrimination. The Clause "forbids subtle departures from neutrality," *Gillette v. United States*, and "covert suppression of particular religious

beliefs." *Bowen v. Roy* (opinion of Burger, C.J.). Official action that targets religious conduct for distinctive treatment cannot be shielded by mere compliance with the requirement of facial neutrality. The Free Exercise Clause protects against governmental hostility which is masked, as well as overt. . . .

The record in this case compels the conclusion that suppression of the central element of the Santeria worship service was the object of the ordinances. First, though use of the words "sacrifice" and "ritual" does not compel a finding of improper targeting of the Santeria religion, the choice of these words is support for our conclusion. There are further respects in which the text of the city council's enactments discloses the improper attempt to target Santeria. Resolution 87-66, adopted June 9, 1987, recited that "residents and citizens of the City of Hialeah have expressed their concern that certain religions may propose to engage in practices which are inconsistent with public morals, peace or safety," and "reiterate[d]" the city's commitment to prohibit "any and all [such] acts of any and all religious groups." No one suggests, and, on this record, it cannot be maintained, that city officials had in mind a religion other than Santeria.

It becomes evident that these ordinances target Santeria sacrifice when the ordinances' operation is considered. Apart from the text, the effect of a law in its real operation is strong evidence of its object. To be sure, adverse impact will not always lead to a finding of impermissible targeting. For example, a social harm may have been a legitimate concern of government for reasons quite apart from discrimination. . . . The subject at hand does implicate, of course, multiple concerns unrelated to religious animosity, for example, the suffering or mistreatment visited upon the sacrificed animals, and health hazards from improper disposal. But the ordinances, when considered together, disclose an object remote from these legitimate concerns. The design of these laws accomplishes, instead, a "religious gerrymander," *Walz v. Tax Comm'n of New York City* (Harlan, J., concurring), an impermissible attempt to target petitioners and their religious practices.

It is a necessary conclusion that almost the only conduct subject to Ordinances 8740, 87-52, and 87-71 is the religious exercise of Santeria church members. The texts show that they were drafted in tandem to achieve this result. We begin with Ordinance 87-71. It prohibits the sacrifice of animals, but defines sacrifice as "to unnecessarily kill . . . an animal in a public or private ritual or ceremony not for the primary purpose of food consumption." The definition excludes almost all killings of animals except for religious sacrifice, and the primary purpose requirement narrows the proscribed category even further, in particular by exempting Kosher slaughter. We need not discuss whether this differential treatment of two religions is, itself, an independent constitutional violation. It suffices to recite this feature of the law as support for our conclusion that Santeria alone was the exclusive legislative concern. The net result of the gerrymander is that few, if any, killings of animals are prohibited other than Santeria sacrifice, which is proscribed because it occurs during a ritual or ceremony and its primary purpose is to make an offering to the orishas, not food consumption. Indeed, careful drafting ensured that, although Santeria sacrifice is prohibited, killings that are no more necessary or humane in almost all other circumstances are unpunished. . . .

In sum, the neutrality inquiry leads to one conclusion: the ordinances had as their object the suppression of religion. The pattern we have recited discloses animosity to Santeria adherents and their

religious practices; the ordinances, by their own terms, target this religious exercise; the texts of the ordinances were gerrymandered with care to proscribe religious killings of animals but to exclude almost all secular killings; and the ordinances suppress much more religious conduct than is necessary in order to achieve the legitimate ends asserted in their defense. These ordinances are not neutral, and the court below committed clear error in failing to reach this conclusion.

B

We turn next to a second requirement of the Free Exercise Clause, the rule that laws burdening religious practice must be of general applicability. *Employment Div., Dept. of Human Resources of Oregon v. Smith.* All laws are selective to some extent, but categories of selection are of paramount concern when a law has the incidental effect of burdening religious practice. The Free Exercise Clause "protect[s] religious observers against unequal treatment," *id.* All laws are selective to some extent, but categories of selection are of paramount concern when a law has the incidental effect of burdening religious practice. The Free Exercise Clause "protect[s] religious observers against unequal treatment," *Hobbie v. Unemployment Appeals Comm'n of Florida* (Stevens, J., concurring in judgment), and inequality results when a legislature decides that the governmental interests it seeks to advance are worthy of being pursued only against conduct with a religious motivation.

The principle that government, in pursuit of legitimate interests, cannot in a selective manner impose burdens only on conduct motivated by religious belief is essential to the protection of the rights guaranteed by the Free Exercise Clause. The principle underlying the general applicability requirement has parallels in our First Amendment jurisprudence.... In this case, we need not define with precision the standard used to evaluate whether a prohibition is of general application, for these ordinances fall well below the minimum standard necessary to protect First Amendment rights.

Respondent claims that Ordinances 87-40, 87-52, and 87-71 advance two interests: protecting the public health and preventing cruelty to animals. The ordinances are underinclusive for those ends. They fail to prohibit nonreligious conduct that endangers these interests in a similar or greater degree than Santeria sacrifice does. The underinclusion is substantial, not inconsequential. Despite the city's proffered interest in preventing cruelty to animals, the ordinances are drafted with care to forbid few killings but those occasioned by religious sacrifice. Many types of animal deaths or kills for nonreligious reasons are either not prohibited or approved by express provision....

The city concedes that "neither the State of Florida nor the City has enacted a generally applicable ban on the killing of animals." It asserts, however, that animal sacrifice is "different" from the animal killings that are permitted by law. According to the city, it is "self-evident" that killing animals for food is "important"; the eradication of insects and pests is "obviously justified"; and the euthanasia of excess animals "makes sense." These *ipse dixits* do not explain why religion alone must bear the burden of the ordinances, when many of these secular killings fall within the city's interest in preventing the cruel treatment of animals....

Ordinance 87-72, which prohibits the slaughter of animals outside of areas zoned for slaughterhouses, is underinclusive on its face. The ordinance includes an exemption for "any person, group, or organization"

that "slaughters or processes for sale, small numbers of hogs and/or cattle per week in accordance with an exemption provided by state law." Respondent has not explained why commercial operations that slaughter "small numbers" of hogs and cattle do not implicate its professed desire to prevent cruelty to animals and preserve the public health. Although the city has classified Santeria sacrifice as slaughter, subjecting it to this ordinance, it does not regulate other killings for food in like manner.

We conclude, in sum, that each of Hialeah's ordinances pursues the city's governmental interests only against conduct motivated by religious belief. The ordinances "ha[ve] every appearance of a prohibition that society is prepared to impose upon [Santeria worshippers], but not upon itself." *The Florida Star v. B.J.F.* (Scalia, J., concurring in part and concurring in judgment). This precise evil is what the requirement of general applicability is designed to prevent.

III

A law burdening religious practice that is not neutral or not of general application must undergo the most rigorous of scrutiny. To satisfy the commands of the First Amendment, a law restrictive of religious practice must advance "'interests of the highest order,'" and must be narrowly tailored in pursuit of those interests. *McDaniel v. Paty*. The compelling interest standard that we apply once a law fails to meet the *Smith* requirements is not "water[ed] ... down" but "really means what it says." *Employment Div., Dept. of Human Resources of Oregon v. Smith*. A law that targets religious conduct for distinctive treatment or advances legitimate governmental interests only against conduct with a religious motivation will survive strict scrutiny only in rare cases. It follows from what we have already said that these ordinances cannot withstand this scrutiny.

First, even were the governmental interests compelling, the ordinances are not drawn in narrow terms to accomplish those interests. As we have discussed, all four ordinances are overbroad or underinclusive in substantial respects. The proffered objectives are not pursued with respect to analogous nonreligious conduct, and those interests could be achieved by narrower ordinances that burdened religion to a far lesser degree. The absence of narrow tailoring suffices to establish the invalidity of the ordinances. *See Arkansas Writers' Project, Inc. v. Ragland.*

Respondent has not demonstrated, moreover, that, in the context of these ordinances, its governmental interests are compelling. Where government restricts only conduct protected by the First Amendment and fails to enact feasible measures to restrict other conduct producing substantial harm or alleged harm of the same sort, the interest given in justification of the restriction is not compelling. . . . As we show above, the ordinances are underinclusive to a substantial extent with respect to each of the interests that respondent has asserted, and it is only conduct motivated by religious conviction that bears the weight of the governmental restrictions. There can be no serious claim that those interests justify the ordinances.

IV

The Free Exercise Clause commits government itself to religious tolerance, and upon even slight suspicion that proposals for state intervention stem from animosity to religion or distrust of its practices, all officials must pause to remember their own high duty to the Constitution and to the rights it secures. Those in office must be resolute in resisting importunate demands and must ensure that the sole reasons for imposing the burdens of law and regulation are secular. Legislators may not devise mechanisms, overt or disguised, designed to persecute or oppress a religion or its practices. The laws here in question were enacted contrary to these constitutional principles, and they are void.

Reversed.

Religious Freedom Restoration Act (1993)

In 1993, by a vast majority, Congress passed legislation to reverse the Court's decision in Employment Division v. Smith *by changing the standard of scrutiny in free exercise cases to rational review. This legislation, called the Religious Freedom and Restoration Act (RFRA), was signed into law by President Bill Clinton. Although the Court has occasionally reversed its own decisions, what is significant about this Act is that Congress is attempting to reverse a decision of the Supreme Court. In* Boerne v. Flores, *the Court found the law unconstitutional. In reading this legislation, think back to the discussion in Chapter 1 about judicial authority. Is the Court right to conclude that Congress lacks the authority to overturn its decision in* Employment Division v. Smith?

H.R.1308

TITLE: To protect the free exercise of religion. Be it enacted by the Senate and House of Representatives of the United States of America in Congress assembled,

SECTION 1. SHORT TITLE.

This Act may be cited as the "Religious Freedom Restoration Act of 1993."

SEC. 2. CONGRESSIONAL FINDINGS AND DECLARATION OF PURPOSES.

(a) Findings: The Congress finds that—

(1) the framers of the Constitution, recognizing free exercise of religion as an unalienable right, secured its protection in the First Amendment to the Constitution;

(2) laws "neutral" toward religion may burden religious exercise as surely as laws intended to interfere with religious exercise;

(3) governments should not substantially burden religious exercise without compelling justification;

(4) in *Employment Division v. Smith,* the Supreme Court virtually eliminated the requirement that the government justify burdens on religious exercise imposed by laws neutral toward religion; and

(5) the compelling interest test as set forth in prior Federal court rulings is a workable test for striking sensible balances between religious liberty and competing prior governmental interests.

(b) Purposes: The purposes of this Act are—

(1) to restore the compelling interest test as set forth in *Sherbert v. Verner and Wisconsin v. Yoder,* and to guarantee its application in all cases where free exercise of religion is substantially burdened; and

(2) to provide a claim or defense to persons whose religious exercise is substantially burdened by government.

SEC. 3. FREE EXERCISE OF RELIGION PROTECTED.

(a) In General: Government shall not substantially burden a person's exercise of religion even if the burden results from a rule of general applicability, except as provided in subsection (b).

(b) Exception: Government may substantially burden a person's exercise of religion only if it demonstrates that application of the burden to the person—

(1) is in furtherance of a compelling governmental interest; and

(2) is the least restrictive means of furthering that compelling governmental interest.

(c) Judicial Relief: A person whose religious exercise has been burdened in violation of this section may assert that violation as a claim or defense in a judicial proceeding and obtain appropriate relief against a government. Standing to assert a claim or defense under this section shall be governed by the general rules of standing under article III of the Constitution. . . .

SEC. 5. DEFINITIONS.

As used in this Act—

(1) the term "government" includes a branch, department, agency, instrumentality, and official (or other person acting under color of law) of the United States, a State, or a subdivision of a State;

(2) the term "State" includes the District of Columbia, the Commonwealth of Puerto Rico, and each territory and possession of the United States;

(3) the term "demonstrates" means meets the burdens of going forward with the evidence and of persuasion; and

(4) the term "exercise of religion" means the exercise of religion under the First Amendment to the Constitution.

SEC. 6. APPLICABILITY.

(a) In General.—This Act applies to all Federal and State law, and the implementation of that law, whether statutory or otherwise, and whether adopted before or after the enactment of this Act.

(b) Rule of Construction.—Federal statutory law adopted after the date of the enactment of this Act is subject to this Act unless such law explicitly excludes such application by reference to this Act.

(c) Religious Belief Unaffected.—Nothing in this Act shall be construed to authorize any government to burden any religious belief.

CITY OF BOERNE v. P.F. FLORES

521 U.S. 507 (1997)

Opinion: Kennedy, joined by Thomas, Ginsburg, Rehnquist
Concurrence: Scalia, joined by Stevens
Concurrence: Stevens
Dissent: Souter
Dissent: Breyer
Dissent: O'Connor, joined by Breyer

As you have just read, the RFRA sought to "restore" religious freedom in two senses: Most generally, the Act was an attempt to reclaim a deeper level of respect for religious freedom in this country that its proponents believed was lost in Employment Division v. Smith. *But more specifically, it sought to actually restore the old standard of review that the Court had abandoned in* Employment Division v. Smith, *that of strict scrutiny.*

As a result of the RFRA, the Court faced two questions that it answers in the following case. First, it re-examines the question of whether Employment Division v. Smith *was correct in changing the standard of scrutiny from strict to rational basis in this area of law. Second, it faces the question of whether in determining the standard of review in free exercise cases, it should take into consideration Congress's opinion and perhaps, by implication, that of*

the American people. The second issue combines the questions we have been examining about religious freedom with those regarding judicial supremacy introduced in Chapter 1. Does the Court have the final and exclusive word about the meaning of free exercise, and generally, about the U.S. Constitution? As you read this case, keep in mind our earlier discussion about issues of judicial authority, and consider how they relate to this controversy over the Free Exercise Clause and the RFRA.

JUSTICE KENNEDY *delivered the opinion of the Court.*

A decision by local zoning authorities to deny a church a building permit was challenged under the Religious Freedom Restoration Act of 1993 (RFRA). The case calls into question the authority of Congress to enact RFRA. We conclude the statute exceeds Congress' power. . . .

I

Congress enacted RFRA in direct response to the Court's decision in *Employment Div., Dept. of Human Resources of Ore. v. Smith.* There we considered a Free Exercise Clause claim brought by members of the Native American Church who were denied unemployment benefits when they lost their jobs because they had used peyote. Their practice was to ingest peyote for sacramental purposes, and they challenged an Oregon statute of general applicability which made use of the drug criminal. In evaluating the claim, we declined to apply the balancing test set forth in *Sherbert v. Verner*, under which we would have asked whether Oregon's prohibition substantially burdened a religious practice and, if it did, whether the burden was justified by a compelling government interest. . . .

The application of the *Sherbert* test, the *Smith* decision explained, would have produced an anomaly in the law, a constitutional right to ignore neutral laws of general applicability. The anomaly would have been accentuated, the Court reasoned, by the difficulty of determining whether a particular practice was central to an individual's religion. We explained, moreover, that it "is not within the judicial ken to question the centrality of particular beliefs or practices to a faith, or the validity of particular litigants' interpretations of those creeds." . . .

. . . *Smith* held that neutral, generally applicable laws may be applied to religious practices even when not supported by a compelling governmental interest.

Four Members of the Court disagreed. They argued the law placed a substantial burden on the Native American Church members so that it could be upheld only if the law served a compelling state interest and was narrowly tailored to achieve that end. Justice O'Connor concluded Oregon had satisfied the test, while Justice Blackmun, joined by Justice Brennan and Justice Marshall, could see no compelling interest justifying the law's application to the members.

These points of constitutional interpretation were debated by Members of Congress in hearings and floor debates.

Many criticized the Court's reasoning, and this disagreement resulted in the passage of RFRA. Congress announced:

"(1) [T]he framers of the Constitution, recognizing free exercise of religion as an unalienable right, secured its protection in the First Amendment to the Constitution;

"(2) laws 'neutral' toward religion may burden religious exercise as surely as laws intended to interfere with religious exercise;

"(3) governments should not substantially burden religious exercise without compelling justification;

"(4) in *Employment Division v. Smith*, the Supreme Court virtually eliminated the requirement that the government justify burdens on religious exercise imposed by laws neutral toward religion; and

"(5) the compelling interest test as set forth in prior Federal court rulings is a workable test for striking sensible balances between religious liberty and competing prior governmental interests."

The Act's stated purposes are:

"(1) to restore the compelling interest test as set forth in *Sherbert v. Verner and Wisconsin v. Yoder*, and to guarantee its application in all cases where free exercise of religion is substantially burdened; and

"(2) to provide a claim or defense to persons whose religious exercise is substantially burdened by government." . . .

II

A

Under our Constitution, the Federal Government is one of enumerated powers. *McCulloch v. Maryland*. The judicial authority to determine the constitutionality of laws, in cases and controversies, is based on the premise that the "powers of the legislature are defined and limited; and that those limits may not be mistaken, or forgotten, the Constitution is written." *Marbury v. Madison*.

Congress relied on its Fourteenth Amendment enforcement power in enacting the most far reaching and substantial of RFRA's provisions, those which impose its requirements on the States. . . . The Fourteenth Amendment provides, in relevant part:

> "Section 1. . . . No State shall make or enforce any law which shall abridge the privileges or immunities of citizens of the United States; nor shall any State deprive any person of life, liberty, or property, without due process of law; nor deny to any person within its jurisdiction the equal protection of the laws. . . .
>
> "Section 5. The Congress shall have power to enforce, by appropriate legislation, the provisions of this article."

The parties disagree over whether RFRA is a proper exercise of Congress' §5 power "to enforce" by "appropriate legislation" the constitutional guarantee that no State shall deprive any person of "life, liberty, or property, without due process of law" nor deny any person "equal protection of the laws."

In defense of the Act respondent contends, with support from the United States as *amicus*, that RFRA is permissible enforcement legislation. Congress, it is said, is only protecting by legislation one of the liberties guaranteed by the Fourteenth Amendment's Due Process Clause, the free exercise of religion, beyond what is necessary under *Smith*. It is said the congressional decision to dispense with proof of deliberate or overt discrimination and instead concentrate on a law's effects accords with the settled understanding that §5 includes the power to enact legislation designed to prevent as well as remedy constitutional violations. It is further contended that Congress' §5 power is not limited to remedial or preventive legislation.

All must acknowledge that §5 is "a positive grant of legislative power" to Congress, *Katzenbach v. Morgan*. . . .

Congress' power under §5, however, extends only to "enforc[ing]" the provisions of the Fourteenth Amendment. The Court has described this power as "remedial," *South Carolina v. Katzenbach*. The design of the Amendment and the text of §5 are inconsistent with the suggestion that Congress has the power to decree the substance of the Fourteenth Amendment's restrictions on the States. Legislation which alters the meaning of the Free Exercise Clause cannot be said to be enforcing the Clause. Congress does not enforce a constitutional right by changing what the right is. It has been given the power "to enforce," not the power to determine what constitutes a constitutional violation. Were it not so, what Congress would be enforcing would no longer be, in any meaningful sense, the "provisions of [the Fourteenth Amendment]." . . .

1

The remedial and preventive nature of Congress' enforcement power, and the limitation inherent in the power, were confirmed in our earliest cases on the Fourteenth Amendment. In the *Civil Rights Cases*, the Court invalidated sections of the Civil Rights Act of 1875 which prescribed criminal penalties for denying to any person "the full enjoyment of" public accommodations and conveyances, on the grounds that it exceeded Congress' power by seeking to regulate private conduct. The Enforcement Clause, the Court said, did not authorize Congress to pass "general legislation upon the rights of the citizen, but corrective legislation; that is, such as may be necessary and proper for counteracting such laws as the States may adopt or enforce, and which, by the amendment, they are prohibited from making or enforcing. . . ." *Id*. The power to "legislate generally upon" life, liberty, and property, as opposed to the "power to provide modes of redress" against offensive state action, was "repugnant" to the Constitution. *Id.* . . . Although the specific holdings of these early cases might have been superseded or modified, . . . their treatment of Congress' §5 power as corrective or preventive, not definitional, has not been questioned. . . .

2

Any suggestion that Congress has a substantive, non-remedial power under the Fourteenth Amendment is not supported by our case law. In *Oregon v. Mitchell*, a majority of the Court concluded Congress had exceeded its enforcement powers by enacting legislation lowering the minimum age of voters from 21 to 18 in state and local elections. The five Members of the Court who reached this conclusion explained that the legislation intruded into an area reserved by the Constitution to the States. . . . Four of these five were explicit in rejecting the position that §5 endowed Congress with the power to establish the meaning of constitutional provisions. . . . Justice Black's rejection of this position might be inferred from his disagreement with Congress' interpretation of the Equal Protection Clause. See *id.* . . .

If Congress could define its own powers by altering the Fourteenth Amendment's meaning, no longer would the Constitution be "superior paramount law, unchangeable by ordinary means." It would be "on a level with ordinary legislative acts, and, like other acts, . . . alterable when the legislature shall please to alter it." *Marbury v. Madison.* Under this approach, it is difficult to conceive of a principle that would limit congressional power. . . . Shifting legislative majorities could change the Constitution and effectively circumvent the difficult and detailed amendment process contained in Article V.

We now turn to consider whether RFRA can be considered enforcement legislation under §5 of the Fourteenth Amendment.

B

Respondent contends that RFRA is a proper exercise of Congress' remedial or preventive power. The Act, it is said, is a reasonable means of protecting the free exercise of religion as defined by *Smith*. It prevents and remedies laws which are enacted with the unconstitutional object of targeting religious beliefs and practices. . . . To avoid the difficulty of proving such violations, it is said, Congress can simply invalidate any law which imposes a substantial burden on a religious practice unless it is justified by a compelling interest and is the least restrictive means of accomplishing that interest. If Congress can prohibit laws with discriminatory effects in order to prevent racial discrimination in violation of the Equal Protection Clause, . . . then it can do the same, respondent argues, to promote religious liberty.

While preventive rules are sometimes appropriate remedial measures, there must be a congruence between the means used and the ends to be achieved. The appropriateness of remedial measures must be considered in light of the evil presented. See *South Carolina v. Katzenbach*. Strong measures appropriate to address one harm may be an unwarranted response to another, lesser one. *Id.* . . .

Regardless of the state of the legislative record, RFRA cannot be considered remedial, preventive legislation, if those terms are to have any meaning. RFRA is so out of proportion to a supposed remedial or preventive object that it cannot be understood as responsive to, or designed to prevent, unconstitutional behavior. It appears, instead, to attempt a substantive change in constitutional protections. Preventive measures prohibiting certain types of laws may be appropriate when there is reason to believe that many of the laws affected by the congressional enactment have a significant likelihood of being unconstitutional. . . . Remedial legislation under §5 "should be adapted to the mischief and wrong which the [Fourteenth] [A]mendment was intended to provide against." *Civil Rights Cases.*

RFRA is not so confined. Sweeping coverage ensures its intrusion at every level of government, displacing laws and prohibiting official actions of almost every description and regardless of subject matter. RFRA's restrictions apply to every agency and official of the Federal, State, and local Governments. RFRA applies to all federal and state law, statutory or otherwise, whether adopted before or after its enactment. RFRA has no termination date or termination mechanism. Any law is subject to challenge at any time by any individual who alleges a substantial burden on his or her free exercise of religion. . . .

The stringent test RFRA demands of state laws reflects a lack of proportionality or congruence between the means adopted and the legitimate end to be achieved. If an objector can show a substantial burden on his free exercise, the State must demonstrate a compelling governmental interest and show that the law is the least restrictive means of furthering its interest. Claims that a law substantially burdens someone's exercise of religion will often be difficult to contest. . . . Requiring a State to demonstrate a compelling interest and show that it has adopted the least restrictive means of achieving that interest is the most demanding test known to constitutional law. If "'compelling interest' really means what it says . . . many laws will not meet the test. . . . [The test] would open the prospect of constitutionally required religious exemptions from civic obligations of almost every conceivable kind." *Smith.* Laws valid under *Smith* would fall under RFRA without regard to whether they had the object of stifling or punishing free exercise. We make these observations not to reargue the position of the majority in *Smith* but to illustrate the substantive alteration of its holding attempted by RFRA. Even assuming RFRA would be interpreted in effect to mandate some lesser test, say one equivalent to intermediate scrutiny, the statute nevertheless would require searching judicial scrutiny of state law with the attendant likelihood of invalidation. This is a considerable congressional intrusion into the States' traditional prerogatives and general authority to regulate for the health and welfare of their citizens.

The substantial costs RFRA exacts, both in practical terms of imposing a heavy litigation burden on the States and in terms of curtailing their traditional general regulatory power, far exceed any pattern or practice of unconstitutional conduct under the Free Exercise Clause as interpreted in *Smith.* Simply put, RFRA is not designed to identify and counteract state laws likely to be unconstitutional because of their treatment of religion. In most cases, the state laws to which RFRA applies are not ones which will have been motivated by religious bigotry. If a state law disproportionately burdened a particular class of religious observers, this circumstance might be evidence of an impermissible legislative motive. RFRA's substantial burden test, however, is not even a discriminatory effects or disparate impact test. It is a reality of the modern regulatory state that numerous state laws, such as the zoning regulations at issue here, impose a substantial burden on a large class of individuals. When the exercise of religion has been burdened in an incidental way by a law of general application, it does not follow that the persons affected have been burdened any more than other citizens, let alone burdened because of their religious beliefs. In addition, the Act imposes in every case a least restrictive means requirement—a requirement that was not used in the pre-*Smith* jurisprudence RFRA purported to codify—which also indicates that the legislation is broader than is appropriate if the goal is to prevent and remedy constitutional violations....

Our national experience teaches that the Constitution is preserved best when each part of the government respects both the Constitution and the proper actions and determinations of the other branches. When the Court has interpreted the Constitution, it has acted within the province of the Judicial Branch, which embraces the duty to say what the law is. *Marbury v. Madison*. When the political branches of the Government act against the background of a judicial interpretation of the Constitution already issued, it must be understood that in later cases and controversies the Court will treat its precedents with the respect due them under settled principles, including *stare decisis*, and contrary expectations must be disappointed. RFRA was designed to control cases and controversies, such as the one before us; but as the provisions of the federal statute here invoked are beyond congressional authority, it is this Court's precedent, not RFRA, which must control.

It is for Congress in the first instance to "determin[e] whether and what legislation is needed to secure the guarantees of the Fourteenth Amendment," and its conclusions are entitled to much deference. *Katzenbach v. Morgan*. Congress' discretion is not unlimited, however, and the courts retain the power, as they have since *Marbury v. Madison*, to determine if Congress has exceeded its authority under the Constitution. Broad as the power of Congress is under the Enforcement Clause

of the Fourteenth Amendment, RFRA contradicts vital principles necessary to maintain separation of powers and the federal balance. The judgment of the Court of Appeals sustaining the Act's constitutionality is reversed.

JUSTICE O'CONNOR, *with whom* **JUSTICE BREYER** *joins except as to a portion of Part I, dissenting.*

I dissent from the Court's disposition of this case. I agree with the Court that the issue before us is whether the Religious Freedom Restoration Act (RFRA) is a proper exercise of Congress' power to enforce §5 of the Fourteenth Amendment. But as a yardstick for measuring the constitutionality of RFRA, the Court uses its holding in *Employment Div., Dept. of Human Resources of Ore. v. Smith*, the decision that prompted Congress to enact RFRA as a means of more rigorously enforcing the Free Exercise Clause. I remain of the view that *Smith* was wrongly decided, and I would use this case to reexamine the Court's holding there. Therefore, I would direct the parties to brief the question whether *Smith* represents the correct understanding of the Free Exercise Clause and set the case for reargument. If the Court were to correct the misinterpretation of the Free Exercise Clause set forth in *Smith*, it would simultaneously put our First Amendment jurisprudence back on course and allay the legitimate concerns of a majority in Congress who believed that *Smith* improperly restricted religious liberty. We would then be in a position to review RFRA in light of a proper interpretation of the Free Exercise Clause.

The Court's analysis of whether RFRA is a constitutional exercise of Congress' §5 power, set forth in Part III-B of its opinion, is premised on the assumption that *Smith* correctly interprets the Free Exercise Clause. This is an assumption that I do not accept. I continue to believe that *Smith* adopted an improper standard for deciding free exercise claims. In *Smith*, five Members of this Court—without briefing or argument on the issue—interpreted the Free Exercise Clause to permit the government to prohibit, without justification, conduct mandated by an individual's religious beliefs, so long as the prohibition is generally applicable. Contrary to the Court's holding in that case, however, the Free Exercise Clause is not simply an anti-discrimination principle that protects only against those laws that single out religious practice for unfavorable treatment. See *Smith* (O'Connor, J., concurring in judgment). Rather, the Clause is best understood as an affirmative guarantee of the right to participate in religious practices and conduct without impermissible governmental interference, even when such conduct conflicts with a neutral, generally applicable law. Before *Smith*, our free exercise cases were generally in keeping with this idea: where a law substantially burdened religiously motivated conduct—regardless whether it was specifically targeted at religion or applied generally—we required government to justify that law with a compelling state interest and to use means narrowly tailored to achieve that interest. (*Smith*; *Hobbie v. Unemployment Appeals Comm'n of Fla.*; *United States v. Lee*; *McDaniel v. Paty*; *Wisconsin v. Yoder*; *Gillette v. United States*; *Sherbert v. Verner*.)

The Court's rejection of this principle in *Smith* is supported neither by precedent nor, as discussed below, by history. The decision has harmed religious liberty. For example, a Federal District Court, in reliance on *Smith*, ruled that the Free Exercise Clause was not implicated where Hmong natives objected on religious grounds to their son's autopsy, conducted pursuant to a generally applicable state law. The Court of Appeals for the Eighth Circuit held that application of a city's zoning laws to prevent a church from conducting services in an area zoned for commercial uses raised no free exercise concerns, even though the city permitted secular not-for-profit organizations in that area. These cases demonstrate that lower courts applying *Smith* no longer find necessary a searching judicial inquiry into the possibility of reasonably accommodating religious practice.

Stare decisis concerns should not prevent us from revisiting our holding in *Smith*. "[S]tare decisis is a principle of policy and not a mechanical formula of adherence to the latest decision, however recent and questionable, when such adherence involves collision with a prior doctrine more embracing in its scope, intrinsically sounder, and verified by experience." *Adarand Constructors, Inc. v. Peña.* This principle is particularly true in constitutional cases, where—as this case so plainly illustrates—"correction through legislative action is practically impossible." *Seminole Tribe of Fla. v. Florida.* I believe that, in light of both our precedent and our Nation's tradition of religious liberty, *Smith* is demonstrably wrong. Moreover, it is a recent decision. As such, it has not engendered the kind of reliance on its continued application that would militate against overruling it.

Accordingly, I believe that we should reexamine our holding in *Smith*, and do so in this very case. In its place, I would return to a rule that requires government to justify any substantial burden on religiously motivated conduct by a compelling state interest and to impose that burden only by means narrowly tailored to achieve that interest.

CASE QUESTION

Now that you have read the Court's decision in *Boerne v. Flores*, you are in a position to evaluate whether it should have allowed Congress to reverse its decision in *Employment Division v. Smith*. Assuming *Employment Division v. Smith* was rightly decided, was the Court correct here to keep the standard in the face of a congressional attempt to reverse it?

SYNTHESIS QUESTIONS FOR FURTHER DISCUSSION: CHAPTER 6 SECTION A

1. It is common to view the Free Exercise and Establishment Clauses of the First Amendment as creating a wall of separation between church and state. This language is evoked explicitly in Thomas Jefferson's "Letter to the Danbury Baptists." Arguably, the idea is also found in John Locke's "A Letter Concerning Toleration" in the notion that there is a division of authority between divine and secular matters. The idea of a wall of separation between church and state, however, has come under criticism in recent years from a range of interpreters of the Religion Clauses. Thinkers ranging from Martha Nussbaum to Lawrence Sager and Chris Eisgruber disagree about the meaning of the clauses and how they should be interpreted, but they all agree that there can be no wall of separation. One reason for their rejection of the metaphor is their perception of an inevitable clash between religious interests and rights of individuals. Amy Guttmann argues, for instance, that *Wisconsin v. Yoder* pits the rights of children against the possibly conflicting right of parents to bring their children up in accordance with a particular set of religious beliefs. *Bob Jones University v. United States* measures a religious belief about race against a governmental interest in building a society free from racism. Given these clashes, is there any way to preserve a separation metaphor? Must religious and secular interests inevitably clash?

2. Most of the free exercise cases we have examined concern the question of whether a religious individual or group is entitled to an exemption from a general law. *Sherbert v. Verner*, for example, is not about whether South Carolina's official day of rest should be switched from Sunday to Saturday but about whether a particular individual should be excused from a general policy of setting Sunday as that day. In *Employment Division v. Smith*, the Native American group was not seeking to legalize peyote but only to receive an exemption from generally valid drug control laws. Does the fact that rights of religious freedom can often be protected by making an exemption make them easier to protect than assertions that require striking down general laws? Should we be eager to accommodate religious groups in this way? As you consider these questions, you might ask about

the validity of Justice Antonin Scalia's argument in *Employment Division v. Smith* that allowing exemptions in individual cases will result in endless litigation.

3.   One of the central questions at issue between "accommodationist" interpreters of the Religion Clauses, like Nussbaum, and non-accommodationist thinkers, such as Eisgruber and Sager, is whether there is anything about religious belief as such that requires special recognition. In defense of the idea that it does require special recognition, some theorists point to the fact that the First Amendment specifically requires protection of religion. Eisgruber and Sager suggest, however, that the Religion Clauses are meant only to recognize that discrimination has often been brought to bear on religious groups, thus meriting special attention but not special protection. One way to approach these issues is to ask whether a claim to free exercise of religion is distinctive from a free speech claim. For instance, in *Board of Education v. Barnette*, the Jehovah's Witnesses claim that being forced to salute the flag violates both their free speech and free exercise rights. Do the religious claims here add anything to the claims of free speech? Would protection have been granted even if their reason for refusing to salute the flag had been merely secular rather than religious?

4.   Some of the free exercise cases in this chapter concern exemptions to laws banning particular kinds of behavior. For instance, *Employment Division v. Smith* addresses the question of whether Native Americans should receive an exemption to a ban on using controlled substances. But should it make a difference if the issue is not whether a behavior or practice should be banned but whether a religious organization should receive a financial benefit or burden from partaking in a particular activity? *Bob Jones University v. United States* concerns the question of whether non-profit status can be denied to a religious organization due to its policy banning interracial dating. Does the fact that the case is about non-profit status make it different from other exemption cases that are about outright bans on certain behavior, such as drug use? The question of government funding for religious institutions will be examined in the next section, but it might be worth considering how the Court's holdings in the free exercise cases, especially in *Bob Jones University v. United States*, relate to its decisions in cases relating to the Establishment Clause. Another question raised by *Bob Jones University v. United States* is whether non-egalitarian religious beliefs deserve protection under the First Amendment given that they conflict with what many think of as the egalitarian values central to the Constitution. Should it matter in cases of the First Amendment protection of free exercise if one's religious beliefs endorse a view of racial inequality at odds with the spirit of the Fourteenth Amendment?

B. ESTABLISHMENT, PUBLIC FUNDING, AND PRAYER

Are religious groups entitled to public funding or public prayer? What is the balance of religion and liberalism in public life?

The question of whether the states or the federal government should "establish" an official religion led to a heated debate among the Founders. James Madison, in his "Memorial and Remonstrance," argues against a proposal in Virginia to establish Anglicanism as that state's official religion. His arguments prefigure those that would serve as the basis for the Establishment Clause of the U.S. Constitution. Like John Locke and Roger Williams, Madison is concerned with protecting individuals' freedom of conscience in choosing their own religion and preventing state coercion in matters of belief. The Establishment Clause serves as a complement to the liberty protected by the Free Exercise Clause, he suggests, because it prevents state coercion on behalf of an official religion. Inevitably, he suggests, an official church would exclude other faiths. The readings by Richard Henry Lee and Phillips Payson challenge Madison's argument by suggesting that a common official religion instills public virtue. Without an official religion, they argue, there would be no way to instill morality in the public as a whole, and this would risk the loss of social and democratic stability.

Given the fact of religious pluralism, the contemporary debate about the Establishment Clause has moved beyond the question of whether the United States should establish an official religion. Modern jurists instead consider the extent to which private organizations should be involved in public functions. In particular, the topic has garnered a great deal of attention as a result of former President George W. Bush's "compassionate conservatism," which attempted to employ religious groups in such public functions as welfare provision and education. Thinkers such as Michael McConnell argue that a wide role for religious groups in such functions is consistent not only with the principles of the Founding but also with the best reading of the Establishment Clause itself. For McConnell, the very idea of a wall of separation, proposed by Thomas Jefferson, overlooks the various ways in which a plurality of religious groups can and should be involved in public life. One source for secular limits on the role of religion in public life might be found in the work of John Rawls. Rawls argues for a kind of "public reason," the idea that government must base its actions on reasons shared among all citizens, both religious and non-religious. As you read Rawls's account, consider whether it offers the basis for an argument against substantial government funding for religion in public service roles.

As you read through the case selection, notice the major but ambiguous role of the wall of separation metaphor. In *Engel v. Vitale*, the Court employs the wall of separation metaphor in striking down mandated prayer in a New York public school. Such prayer, the Court argues, would constitute an unconstitutional establishment of religion. The Court extended this holding more recently in *Lee v. Weisman* and *Santa Fe Independent School District v. Doe*, in which it rejected variations on the kind of school prayer found in *Engel v. Vitale*. In reading these three cases, consider the degree to which state coercion or establishment was involved in each of them, and in particular whether clergy-led prayer or student-led prayer constitutes an establishment of religion.

In addition to the issue of school prayer, we focus on the controversy over the provision of public funding for religious schools. Here the wall of separation seems at times to be more porous. In *Lemon v. Kurtzman*, the Court announced its modern Establishment Clause test when it rejected funding for students of secular subjects in parochial schools. Though *Lemon v. Kurtzman* seems to set a clear standard for state entanglement in religious schools, the Court's more recent decisions on the matter have involved more ambivalence about state funding to religious schools. As you read, think about why the Court rejected funding for scholarships for religious study in *Locke v. Davey* but allowed the provision of vouchers to students attending religious schools in *Zelman v. Simmons-Harris*.

The wall of separation metaphor suggests a clean divide between public and private spaces, but in American life the town square, perhaps the most paradigmatic public space, has often been used for religious displays. Is the "wall" dividing religious and public life porous in this area, or is it rigid? Consider this as you examine the Court's struggle with determining what kinds of public religious imagery are consistent with the First Amendment ban on establishment. In *Lynch v. Donnelly* and *County of Allegheny v. ACLU*, the Court examines the question of whether the public display of religious symbols such as the Christian crèche, the Jewish menorah, and the Christmas tree are consistent with the constitutional prohibition of the establishment of religion. Similarly, in *Van Orden v. Perry* and *McCreary County v. ACLU of Kentucky*, the Court considers whether the public display of the Ten Commandments violates the prohibition of the establishment of religion. To what extent does context matter in determining whether a symbolic display represents an endorsement of a particular faith? Is there a clear principle to distinguish acceptable displays from those that are constitutionally problematic?

As you will see throughout this book, at times the Court's jurisprudence in a particular area is very clear. This, however, is not one of those areas. The Court's establishment jurisprudence is somewhat unsettled, and its doctrine varies a significant amount. In earlier cases like *Everson v. Board of Education* and *Schempp v. Abingdon School District*, the Court vigorously upheld the rigid separation of church and state, and in *Lemon v. Kurtzman* the Court formulated a three-pronged test for policing this separation. However, in more recent cases the Court has frequently, though never categorically, strayed from

Lemon v. Kurtzman, and formulated different tests: U.S. Supreme Court Justice Sandra Day O'Connor's endorsement test in *Lynch v. Donnelly*, U.S. Supreme Court Justice Anthony Kennedy's coercion test in *County of Allegheny v. ACLU*, and U.S. Supreme Court Justice Stephen Breyer's more nuanced test in *Van Orden v. Perry*. These three tests continue to compete with *Lemon v. Kurtzman*, and no one analysis has gained the unqualified approval of a stable majority of the Court. As you read the following cases, consider the many different tests the Court has articulated. Would the older cases like *Everson v. Board of Education* and *Engel v. Vitale* have been decided differently under one of the newer tests? Which test, if any, do you believe best expresses the meaning of the Establishment Clause?

Patrick Henry

A BILL ESTABLISHING A PROVISION FOR TEACHERS OF THE CHRISTIAN RELIGION

1784

At its most basic and literal level, the Establishment Clause of the First Amendment prohibits the establishment of a national religion. Less obvious, however, is the question of whether particular kinds of governmental action, short of outright establishment, also violate the prohibition on the establishment of religion. From the time of the Founding, one of the central questions in establishment jurisprudence has concerned public funding for religious groups. We begin our readings with Patrick Henry's attempt to introduce legislation in Virginia to provide funding for religious education. We continue with James Madison's seminal and highly influential argument for rejecting this bill, which would have funded teachers of Christianity out of Virginia's treasury. Although the debate between Henry and Madison took place before the ratification of the Bill of Rights and the passage of the Establishment Clause, Madison's argument against Henry's bill helps to shed light on

modern questions regarding public funding for religious groups. Madison was the primary drafter and congressional sponsor of the First Amendment, and in debating the Amendment, the Framers were heavily influenced by Madison's experience in Virginia. In reading that document, consider whether Madison argues against any and all funding for religious institutions with state money or merely against funding for religious education, a distinction that will prove important in modern Establishment Clause cases. Consider, too, how Madison might reply to the arguments of Richard Henry Lee and Phillips Payson, which follow that excerpt, suggesting that religion itself might serve a secular purpose in that it is necessary to develop the kind of social ethos that can serve the Republic. Is religious education necessary for that purpose?

Whereas the general diffusion of Christian knowledge hath a natural tendency to correct the morals of men, restrain their vices, and preserve the peace of society; which cannot be effected without a competent provision for learned teachers, who may be thereby enabled to devote their time and attention to the duty of instructing such citizens, as from their circumstances and want of education, cannot otherwise attain such knowledge; and it is judged that such provision may be made by the Legislature, without counteracting the liberal principle heretofore adopted and intended to be preserved by abolishing all distinctions of preeminence amongst the different societies or communities of Christians;

Be it therefore enacted by the General Assembly, that for the support of Christian teachers,—per centum on the amount, or—in the pound on the sum payable for tax on the property within this Commonwealth, is hereby assessed, and shall be paid by every person chargeable with the said tax at the time the same shall become due; and the Sheriffs of the several Counties shall have power to levy and collect the same in the same manner and under the like restrictions and limitations, as are or may be prescribed by the laws for raising the Revenues of this State.

And be it enacted, That for every sum so paid, the Sheriff or Collector shall give a receipt, expressing therein to what society of Christians the person from whom he may receive the same shall direct the money to be paid, keeping a distinct account thereof in his books. The Sheriff of every County, shall, on or before the __ day of __ in every year, return to the Court, upon oath, two alphabetical lists of the payments to him made, distinguishing in columns opposite to the names of the persons who shall have paid the same, the society to which the money so paid was by them appropriated; and one column for the names where no appropriation shall be made. One of which lists, after being recorded in a book to be kept for that purpose, shall be filed by the Clerk in his office; the other shall by the Sheriff be fixed up in the Courthouse, there to remain for the inspection of all concerned. And the Sheriff, after deducting five per centum for the collection, shall forthwith pay to such person or persons as shall be appointed to receive the same by the Vestry, Elders, or Directors, however, denominated of each such society, the sum so stated to be due to that society; or in default thereof, upon the motion of such person or persons to the next or any succeeding Court, execution shall be awarded for the same against the Sheriff and his security, his and their executors or administrators; provided that ten days previous notice be given of such motion. An upon every such execution, the Officer serving the same shall proceed to immediate sale of the estate taken, and shall not accept of security for payment at the end of three months, nor to have the goods forthcoming at the day of sale; for his better direction wherein, the Clerk shall endorse upon every such execution that no security of any kind shall be taken. And be it further enacted, That the money to be raised by virtue of this Act, shall be by the Vestries, Elders, or Directors of each religious society, appropriated to a provision for a Minister or Teacher of the Gospel of their denomination, or the providing place of divine worship, and to none other use whatsoever; except in the denominations of Quakers and Mennonites, who may receive what is collected from their members, and place it in their general fund, to be disposed of in a manner which they shall think best calculated to promote their particular mode of worship. . . .

James Madison

MEMORIAL AND REMONSTRANCE AGAINST RELIGIOUS ASSESSMENTS

1785

To the Honorable the General Assembly of the Commonwealth of Virginia

A MEMORIAL AND REMONSTRANCE

We the subscribers, citizens of the said Commonwealth, having taken into serious consideration, a Bill printed by order of the last Session of General Assembly, entitled "A Bill establishing a provision for Teachers of the Christian Religion," and conceiving that the same if finally armed with the sanctions of a law, will be a dangerous abuse of power, are bound as faithful members of a free State to remonstrate against it, and to declare the reasons by which we are determined. We remonstrate against the said Bill,

1. Because we hold it for a fundamental and undeniable truth, "that Religion or the duty which we owe to our Creator and the manner of discharging it, can be directed only by reason and conviction, not by force or violence." The Religion then of every man must be left to the conviction and conscience of every man; and it is the right of every man to exercise it as these may dictate. This right is in its nature an unalienable right. It is unalienable, because the opinions of men, depending only on the evidence contemplated by their own minds cannot follow the dictates of other men: It is unalienable also, because what is here a right towards men, is a duty towards the Creator. It is the duty of every man to render to the Creator such homage and

such only as he believes to be acceptable to him. This duty is precedent, both in order of time and in degree of obligation, to the claims of Civil Society. Before any man can be considered as a member of Civil Society, he must be considered as a subject of the Governor of the Universe: And if a member of Civil Society, do it with a saving of his allegiance to the Universal Sovereign. We maintain therefore that in matters of Religion, no man's right is abridged by the institution of Civil Society and that Religion is wholly exempt from its cognizance. True it is, that no other rule exists, by which any question which may divide a Society, can be ultimately determined, but the will of the majority; but it is also true that the majority may trespass on the rights of the minority.

2. Because Religion be exempt from the authority of the Society at large, still less can it be subject to that of the Legislative Body. The latter are but the creatures and vicegerents of the former. Their jurisdiction is both derivative and limited: it is limited with regard to the co-ordinate departments, more necessarily is it limited with regard to the constituents. The preservation of a free Government requires not merely, that the metes and bounds which separate each department of power be invariably maintained; but more especially that neither of them be suffered to overleap the great Barrier which defends the rights of the people. The Rulers who are guilty of such an encroachment, exceed the commission

from which they derive their authority, and are Tyrants. The People who submit to it are governed by laws made neither by themselves nor by an authority derived from them, and are slaves.

3. Because it is proper to take alarm at the first experiment on our liberties. We hold this prudent jealousy to be the first duty of Citizens, and one of the noblest characteristics of the late Revolution. The free men of America did not wait till usurped power had strengthened itself by exercise, and entangled the question in precedents. They saw all the consequences in the principle, and they avoided the consequences by denying the principle. We revere this lesson too much soon to forget it. Who does not see that the same authority which can establish Christianity, in exclusion of all other Religions, may establish with the same ease any particular sect of Christians, in exclusion of all other Sects? that the same authority which can force a citizen to contribute three pence only of his property for the support of any one establishment, may force him to conform to any other establishment in all cases whatsoever.

4. Because the Bill violates the equality which ought to be the basis of every law, and which is more indispensable, in proportion as the validity or expediency of any law is more liable to be impeached. If "all men are by nature equally free and independent," all men are to be considered as entering into Society on equal conditions; as relinquishing no more, and therefore retaining no less, one than another, of their natural rights. Above all are they to be considered as retaining an "*equal* title to the free exercise of Religion according to the dictates of Conscience." Whilst we assert for ourselves a freedom to embrace, to profess and to observe the Religion which we believe to be of

divine origin, we cannot deny an equal freedom to those whose minds have not yet yielded to the evidence which has convinced us. If this freedom be abused, it is an offence against God, not against man: To God, therefore, not to man, must an account of it be rendered. As the Bill violates equality by subjecting some to peculiar burdens, so it violates the same principle, by granting to others peculiar exemptions. Are the Quakers and Menonists the only sects who think a compulsive support of their Religions unnecessary and unwarrantable? Can their piety alone be entrusted with the care of public worship? Ought their Religions to be endowed above all others with extraordinary privileges by which proselytes may be enticed from all others? We think too favorably of the justice and good sense of these denominations to believe that they either covet preeminences over their fellow citizens or that they will be seduced by them from the common opposition to the measure.

5. Because the Bill implies either that the Civil Magistrate is a competent Judge of Religious Truth; or that he may employ Religion as an engine of Civil policy. The first is an arrogant pretension falsified by the contradictory opinions of Rulers in all ages, and throughout the world: the second an unhallowed perversion of the means of salvation.

6. Because the establishment proposed by the Bill is not requisite for the support of the Christian Religion. To say that it is, is a contradiction to the Christian Religion itself, for every page of it disavows a dependence on the powers of this world: it is a contradiction to fact; for it is known that this Religion both existed and flourished, not only without the support of human laws, but in spite of every opposition from them, and not only during the period

of miraculous aid, but long after it had been left to its own evidence and the ordinary care of Providence. Nay, it is a contradiction in terms; for a Religion not invented by human policy, must have pre-existed and been supported, before it was established by human policy. It is moreover to weaken in those who profess this Religion a pious confidence in its innate excellence and the patronage of its Author; and to foster in those who still reject it, a suspicion that its friends are too conscious of its fallacies to trust it to its own merits.

7. Because experience witnesseth that ecclesiastical establishments, instead of maintaining the purity and efficacy of Religion, have had a contrary operation. During almost fifteen centuries has the legal establishment of Christianity been on trial. What have been its fruits? More or less in all places, pride and indolence in the Clergy, ignorance and servility in the laity, in both, superstition, bigotry and persecution. Enquire of the Teachers of Christianity for the ages in which it appeared in its greatest luster; those of every sect, point to the ages prior to its incorporation with Civil policy. Propose a restoration of this primitive State in which its Teachers depended on the voluntary rewards of their flocks, many of them predict its downfall. On which Side ought their testimony to have greatest weight, when for or when against their interest?

8. Because the establishment in question is not necessary for the support of Civil Government. If it be urged as necessary for the support of Civil Government only as it is a means of supporting Religion, and it be not necessary for the latter purpose, it cannot be necessary for the former. If Religion be not within the cognizance of Civil Government how can its legal establishment be necessary to Civil Government? What influence in fact have ecclesiastical establishments had on Civil Society? In some instances they have been seen to erect a spiritual tyranny on the ruins of the Civil authority; in many instances they have been seen upholding the thrones of political tyranny: in no instance have they been seen the guardians of the liberties of the people. Rulers who wished to subvert the public liberty, may have found an established Clergy convenient auxiliaries. A just Government instituted to secure & perpetuate it needs them not. Such a Government will be best supported by protecting every Citizen in the enjoyment of his Religion with the same equal hand which protects his person and his property; by neither invading the equal rights of any Sect, nor suffering any Sect to invade those of another.

9. Because the proposed establishment is a departure from the generous policy, which, offering an Asylum to the persecuted and oppressed of every Nation and Religion, promised a luster to our country, and an accession to the number of its citizens. What a melancholy mark is the Bill of sudden degeneracy? Instead of holding forth an Asylum to the persecuted, it is itself a signal of persecution. It degrades from the equal rank of Citizens all those who see opinions in Religion do not bend to those of the Legislative authority. Distant as it may be in its present form from the Inquisition, it differs from it only in degree. The one is the first step, the other the last in the career of intolerance. The magnanimous sufferer under this cruel scourge in foreign Regions, must view the Bill as a Beacon on our Coast, warning him to seek some other haven, where liberty and philanthropy in their due extent, may offer a more certain repose from his Troubles.

10. Because it will have a like tendency to banish our Citizens. The allurements presented by other situations are every day thinning their number. To super add a fresh motive to emigration by revoking the liberty which they now enjoy, would be the same species of folly which has dishonored and depopulated flourishing kingdoms.

11. Because it will destroy that moderation and harmony which the forbearance of our laws to intermeddle with Religion has produced among its several sects. Torrents of blood have been spilt in the old world, by vain attempts of the secular arm, to extinguish Religious discord, by proscribing all difference in Religious opinion. Time has at length revealed the true remedy. Every relaxation of narrow and rigorous policy, wherever it has been tried, has been found to assuage the disease. The American Theater has exhibited proofs that equal and complete liberty, if it does not wholly eradicate it, sufficiently destroys its malignant influence on the health and prosperity of the State. If with the salutary effects of this system under our own eyes, we begin to contract the bounds of Religious freedom, we know no name that will too severely reproach our folly. At least let warning be taken at the first fruits of the threatened innovation. The very appearance of the Bill has transformed "that Christian forbearance, love and charity," which of late mutually prevailed, into animosities and jealousies, which may not soon be appeased. What mischiefs may not be dreaded, should this enemy to the public quiet be armed with the force of a law?

12. Because the policy of the Bill is adverse to the diffusion of the light of Christianity. The first wish of those who enjoy this precious gift ought to be that it may be imparted to the whole race of mankind. Compare the number of those who have as yet received it with the number still remaining under the dominion of false Religions; and how small is the former! Does the policy of the Bill tend to lessen the disproportion? No; it at once discourages those who are strangers to the light of revelation from coming into the Region of it; and countenances by example the nations who continue in darkness, in shutting out those who might convey it to them. Instead of Leveling as far as possible, every obstacle to the victorious progress of Truth, the Bill with an ignoble and unchristian timidity would circumscribe it with a wall of defense against the encroachments of error.

13. Because attempts to enforce by legal sanctions, acts obnoxious to so great a proportion of Citizens, tend to enervate the laws in general, and to slacken the bands of Society. If it be difficult to execute any law which is not generally deemed necessary or salutary, what must be the case, where it is deemed invalid and dangerous? And what may be the effect of so striking an example of impotency in the Government, on its general authority? . . .

15. Because finally, "the equal right of every citizen to the free exercise of his Religion according to the dictates of conscience" is held by the same tenure with all our other rights. If we recur to its origin, it is equally the gift of nature; if we weigh its importance, it cannot be less dear to us; if we consult the "Declaration of those rights which pertain to the good people of Virginia, as the basis and foundation of Government," it is enumerated with equal solemnity, or rather studied emphasis. Either then, we must say, that the Will of the Legislature is the only measure of their authority; and that in the plenitude of this authority, they may sweep away all our fundamental rights; or,

that they are bound to leave this particular right untouched and sacred: Either we must say, that they may control the freedom of the press, may abolish the Trial by Jury, may swallow up the Executive and Judiciary Powers of the State; nay that they may despoil us of our very right of suffrage, and erect themselves into an independent and hereditary Assembly or, we must say, that they have no authority to enact into the law the Bill under consideration.

We the Subscribers say, that the General Assembly of this Commonwealth have no such authority: And that no effort may be omitted on our part against so dangerous an usurpation, we oppose to it, this remonstrance; earnestly praying, as we are in duty bound, that the Supreme Lawgiver of the Universe, by illuminating those to whom it is addressed, may on the one hand, turn their Councils from every act which would affront his holy prerogative, or violate the trust committed to them: and on the other, guide them into every measure which may be worthy of his blessing, may redound to their own praise, and may establish more firmly the liberties, the prosperity and the happiness of the Commonwealth.

Richard Henry Lee

LETTER TO JAMES MADISON

November 26, 1784

Trenton November 26, 1784
Dear Sir,

I received your agreeable letter the day after mine of the 28th instant had been dispatched. I thank you Sir for the very particular and satisfactory information that you have favord me with. It is certainly comfortable to know that the Legislature of our country is engaged in beneficial pursuits—for I conceive that the Gen. Assessment, and a wise digest of our militia laws are very important concerns: the one to secure our peace, and the other our morals. Refiners may weave as fine a web of reason as they please, but the experience of all times shews Religion to be the guardian of morals—And he must be a very inattentive observer in our Country, who does not see that avarice is accomplishing the destruction of religion, for want of a legal obligation to contribute something to its support. The declaration of Rights, it seems to me, rather contends against forcing modes of faith and forms of worship, than against compelling contribution for the support of religion in general. I fully agree with the Presbyterians, that true freedom embraces the Mahomitan and the Gentoo as well as the Christian religion. And upon this liberal ground I hope our Assembly will conduct themselves. I believe there is no doubt but that the population of our country depends eminently upon our Revenue laws, they therefore, demand intense consideration. It is natural for men to fly from oppression to ease, and whilst our taxes are extremely heavy, and North Carolina & Georgia pay little or no tax, it is not to be wonderd that so many of our people flock to these States & unfortunately they are carrying to Georgia & South Carolina the cultivation of Tobacco. I do not mean by this, that we should suffer ill example to prevent us from honorably and punctually paying our debts. But I think that we may fairly practise here, as other Nations the most honest do—I mean, exactly to pay the interest, and slowly to sink the principal. An attempt to do the latter too suddenly, will ruin, by depopulating, the country. The only mode appears to be, a funding of the whole debt, so as certainly to pay the interest, and slowly the principal. Cannot a sinking fund be brought to bear upon the latter, by throwing all overflowings of taxes into a Reservoir for gathering interest upon interest? I suppose that at all events, the facilities offerd by Congress in their Act of the 28th of April last will be among the amendments to the Revenue law this Session. . . .

I am dear Sir, with great esteem and regard Your most obedient and very humble servant,

Richard Henry Lee

Phillips Payson

MASSACHUSETTS ELECTION SERMON OF 1778

Boston, 1778

But Jerusalem, Which Is Above, Is Free, Which Is the Mother of Us All. So Then, Brethren, We Are Not Children of the Bond Woman, But of the Free.—Gal. iv. 26, 31.

It is common for the inspired writers to speak of the gospel dispensation in terms applicable to the heavenly world, especially when they view it in comparison with the law of Moses. In this light they consider the church of God, and good men upon earth, as members of the church and family of God above, and liken the liberty of Christians to that of the citizens of the heavenly Zion. We doubt not but the Jerusalem above, the heavenly society, possesses the noblest liberty to a degree of perfection of which the human mind can have no adequate conception in the present state. The want of that knowledge and rectitude they are endowed with above renders liberty and government so imperfect here below. . . .

Much depends upon the mode and administration of civil government to complete the blessings of liberty; for although the best possible plan of government never can give an ignorant and vicious people the true enjoyment of liberty, yet a state may be enslaved though its inhabitants in general may be knowing, virtuous, and heroic. The voice of reason and the voice of God both teach us that the great object or end of government is the public good. Nor is there less certainty in determining that a free and righteous government originates from the people, and is under their direction and control; and therefore a free, popular model of government—of the republican kind—may be judged the most friendly to the rights and liberties of the people, and the most conducive to the public welfare. . . .

In this view, it is obvious to observe that a spirit of liberty should in general prevail among a people; their minds should be possessed with a sense of its worth and nature. Facts and observation abundantly teach us that the minds of a community, as well as of individuals, are subject to different and various casts and impressions. The inhabitants of large and opulent empires and kingdoms are often entirely lost to a sense of liberty, in which case they become an easy prey to usurpers and tyrants. Where the spirit of liberty is found in its genuine vigor it produces its genuine effects; urging to the greatest vigilance and exertions, it will surmount great difficulties; [so] that it is no easy matter to deceive or conquer a people determined to be free. The exertions and effects of this great spirit in our land have already been such as may well astonish the world; and so long as it generally prevails it will be quiet with no species of government but what befriends and protects it. Its jealousy for its safety may sometimes appear as if verging to faction; but it means well, and can never endanger a state unless its root and source is corrupted. . . .

I must not forget to mention religion, both in rulers and people, as of the highest importance to the public. This is the most sacred principle that can dwell in the human breast. It is of the highest importance to men—the most perfective of the human soul. The truths of the gospel are the most pure, its motives the most noble and animating, and its comforts the most supporting to the mind. The importance of religion to civil society and government is great indeed, as it keeps alive the best sense of moral obligation, a matter of such extensive utility, especially in respect to an oath, which is one of the principal instruments of government. The fear and reverence of God, and the terrors of eternity, are the most powerful restraints upon the minds of men; and hence it is of special importance in a free government, the spirit of which being always friendly to the sacred rights of conscience, it will hold up the gospel as the great rule of faith and practice. Established modes and usages in religion, more especially the stated public worship of God, so generally form the principles and manners of a people, that changes or alterations in these, especially when nearly conformed to the spirit and simplicity of the gospel, may well be esteemed very dangerous experiments in government. For this, and other reasons, the thoughtful and wise among us trust that our civil fathers, from a regard to gospel worship and the constitution of these churches, will carefully preserve them, and at all times guard against every innovation that might tend to overset the public worship of God, though such innovations may be urged from the most foaming zeal. Persons of a gloomy, ghostly, and mystic cast, absorbed in visionary scenes, deserve but little notice in matters either of religion or government. Let the restraints of religion once be broken down, as they infallibly would be by leaving the subject of public worship to the humors of the multitude, and we might well defy all human wisdom and power to support and preserve order and government in the state. Human conduct and character can never be better formed than upon the principles of our holy religion; they give the justest sense, the most adequate views, of the duties between rulers and people, and are the best principles in the world to carry the ruler through the duties of his station; and in case a series of faithful services should be followed with popular censure, as may be the case, yet the religious ruler will find the approbation of his conscience a noble reward.

Many other things might be mentioned as circumstances much in favor of a free government and public liberty, as where the inhabitants of a state can, in general, give their suffrages in person, and men of abilities are dispersed in the several parts of a state capable of public office and station; especially if there is a general distribution of property, and the landed interest not engrossed by a few, but possessed by the inhabitants in general through the state. Things of this nature wear a kind aspect. But, for the preservation and permanence of the state, it is of still higher importance that its internal strength be supported upon the great pillars of capacity, defence, and union. The full liberty of the press—that eminent instrument of promoting knowledge, and great palladium of the public liberty—being enjoyed, the learned professions directed to the public good, the great principles of legislation and government, the great examples and truths of history, the maxims of generous and upright policy, and the severer truths of philosophy investigated and apprehended by a general application to books, and by observation and experiment,—are means by which the capacity of a state will be strong and respectable, and the number of superior minds will be daily increasing. Strength, courage, and military discipline being, under God, the great defence of a state, as these are cultivated and improved the public defence will increase; and if there is added to these a general union, a spirit of harmony, the internal strength and beauty of the state will be great indeed. The variety and freedom of opinion is apt to check the union of a free state; and in case the union be interrupted merely from the freedom of opinion, contesting for real rights and privileges, the state and its government may still be strong and secure, as was, in fact, the case in ancient Rome, in the more disinterested periods of that republic. But if parties and factions, arising from false ambition, avarice, or revenge, run high, they endanger the state, which was the case in the latter periods of the republic of Rome. Hence the parties in a free state, if aimed at the public liberty and welfare, are salutary; but if selfish interest

and views are their source, they are both dangerous and destructive. . . .

A state and its inhabitants thus circumstanced in respect to government, principle, morals, capacity, union, and rulers, make up the most striking portrait, the liveliest emblem of the Jerusalem that is above, that this world can afford. That this may be the condition of these free, independent, and sovereign states of America, we have the wishes and prayers of all good men.

. . . In this stage of our struggle we are by no means to indulge to a supine and dilatory spirit, which might yet be fatal, nor have we to take our resolutions from despair. Far from this, we have the noblest motives, the highest encouragements. I know the ardor of the human mind is apt in time to abate, though the subject be ever so important; but surely the blood of our friends and countrymen, still crying in our ears, like the souls of the martyrs under the altar, must arouse and fire every nobler passion of the mind. Moreover, to anticipate the future glory of America from our present hopes and prospects is ravishing and transporting to the mind. In this light we behold our country, beyond the reach of all oppressors, under the great charter of independence, enjoying the purest liberty; beautiful and strong in its union; the envy of tyrants and devils, but the delight of God and all good men; a refuge to the oppressed; the joy of the earth; each state happy in a wise model of government, and abounding with wise men, patriots, and heroes; the strength and abilities of the whole continent, collected in a grave and venerable council, at the head of all, seeking and promoting the good of the present and future generations. Hail, my happy country, saved of the Lord! Happy land, emerged from the deluges of the Old World, drowned in luxury and lewd excess! Hail, happy posterity, that shall reap the peaceful fruits of our suffering, fatigues, and wars! With such prospects, such transporting views, it is difficult to keep the passions or the tongue within the bounds of Christian moderation. But far be it from us to indulge vain-glory, or return railing for railing, or to insult our foes; we cultivate better principles of humanity and bravery, and would much rather cherish the feelings of pity, especially to those of our enemies of better minds, whose names, with the baser, may appear in the pages of impartial history with indelible blemish. We wish, from the infatuation, and wickedness, and fate of our enemies, the world would learn lessons in wisdom and virtue; that princes would learn never to oppress their subjects; that the vaunting generals of Britain would learn never more to despise and contemn their enemy, nor prove blasphemers of God and religion. We wish the whole world may learn the worth of liberty. And may the inhabitants of these states, when their independence and freedom shall be completed, bless God for ever and ever; for thine, O Lord, is the power, and the glory, and the victory.

But, under our raised expectations of seeing the good of God's chosen, let us think soberly, let us act wisely. The public still calls aloud for the united efforts both of rulers and people; nor have we as yet put off the harness. We have many things amiss among ourselves that need to be reformed,—many internal diseases to cure, and secret internal enemies to watch against, who may aim a fatal blow while making the highest pretensions to our cause; for plausible pretences are common covers to the blackest designs. We wish we had more public virtue, and that people would not be so greedy of cheating themselves and their neighbors. We wish for much greater exertions to promote education, and knowledge, and virtue, and piety. But in all states there will be such as want no learning, no government, no religion at all.

For the cure of our internal political diseases, and to promote the health and vigor, the defence and safety, of the state, our eyes, under God, are directed to our rulers; and, from that wisdom and prudence with which they have conducted our public affairs in the most trying times, we have the highest encouragement to look to them.

As a token of unfeigned respect, the honorable gentlemen of both Houses of Assembly present will permit me, by way of address, to observe, that the freemen of this state, by delegating their powers to you, my civil fathers, have reposed the greatest trust and confidence in you, from whence, we doubt not but you are sensible, arises the most sacred obligation to fidelity. Preserving a constant sense of this, and keeping the public welfare as your great object in view, we trust you will never be wanting in your best endeavors and most vigorous exertions to defend and deliver your country. The matters of the war will undoubtedly, at present, claim your first and principal attention,—always esteeming its great object, the liberty of your country, of more inestimable value than all the treasure of the world; and therefore, to obtain and secure it, no necessary charges or costs are to be spared. The internal matters of the state that claim your attention, though they may pass a severe scrutiny, will be noticed with all justice and impartiality; and in the choice of a Council— that important branch of our Legislature from which we have experienced such eminent services—of which branch, or one nearly similar, we hope this state will never be destitute,—in this choice, persons of known ability, of public virtue and religion, and possessed of the spirit of liberty, will have the preference. . . .

My hearers, let us all harken to the calls of our country, to the calls of God, and learn those lessons in wisdom which are so forcibly inculcated upon us in these times, and by such wonderful measures in Providence. From a sacred regard both to the goodness and severity of God, let us follow the guidance of his providence, and in the way of duty leave ourselves and all events with God. Remembering that Jerusalem which is above is the mother of us all, that we are children "not of the bond woman, but of the free," let us stand fast in the liberty where-with Christ hath made us free, and be not entangled again with the yoke of bondage. Imitating the virtue, the piety, the love of liberty, so conspicuous in our pious ancestors, like them let us exert ourselves for the good of posterity. With diligence let us cultivate the spirit of liberty, of public virtue, of union and religion, and thus strengthen the hands of government and the great pillars of the state. Our own consciences will reproach us, and the world condemn us, if we do not properly respect, and obey, and reverence the government of our own choosing. The eyes of the whole world are upon us in these critical times, and, what is yet more, the eyes of Almighty God. Let us act worthy of our professed principles, of our glorious cause, that in some good measure we may answer the expectations of God and of men. Let us cultivate the heavenly temper, and sacredly regard the great motive of the world to come. And God of his mercy grant the blessings of peace may soon succeed to the horrors of war, and that from the enjoyment of the sweets of liberty here we may in our turn and order go to the full enjoyment of the nobler liberties above, in that New Jerusalem, that city of the living God, that is enlightened by the glory of God and of the Lamb. Amen.

Michael McConnell

RELIGIOUS PARTICIPATION IN PUBLIC PROGRAMS: RELIGIOUS FREEDOM AT A CROSSROADS

69 U. Chi. L. Rev. 115 (1992)

According to Michael McConnell, the Supreme Court has often been too restrictive in its understanding of the role religion should play in public life. Historically, McConnell argues, religious institutions have contributed significantly to social welfare, including education and the provision of social services. It would be a mistake, he claims, to read the Establishment Clause as limiting this role. Indeed, such a reading of the Establishment Clause would have the faulty effect of crowding out the legitimate role religion might play in serving many civil purposes. How does McConnell's interpretation of the Establishment Clause fit in the debate between James Madison and his critics? How does his view challenge the notion of separation of church and state? In what ways do his arguments draw on an originalist approach to constitutional interpretation?

A RELIGION CLAUSE JURISPRUDENCE FOR A PLURALISTIC NATION

A jurisprudence of the Religion Clauses must begin with a proper understanding of the ideals of the Clauses and the evils against which they are directed. We can then formulate legal doctrine.

The great mistake of the Warren and Burger Courts was to embrace the ideal of the secular state, with its corresponding tendencies toward indifference or hostility to religion. The mistake of the emerging jurisprudence of the Rehnquist Court is to defer to majoritarian decisionmaking. A better understanding of the ideal of the Religion Clauses, both normatively and historically, is that they guarantee a pluralistic republic in which citizens are free to exercise their religious differences without hindrance from the state (unless necessary to important purposes of civil government), whether that hindrance is for or against religion. . . . When scrutinizing a law or governmental practice under the Religion Clauses, the courts should ask the following question: is the purpose or probable effect to increase religious uniformity, either by inhibiting religious practice (a Free Exercise Clause violation) or by forcing or inducing a contrary religious practice (an Establishment Clause violation), without sufficient justification? The baseline for these judgments is the hypothetical world in which individuals make decisions about religion on the basis of their own religious conscience, without the influence of government. The underlying principle is that governmental action should have the minimum possible effect on religion, consistent with achievement of the government's legitimate purposes.

A. A Pluralist Approach to the Free Exercise Clause

. . . Apart from the question of generally applicable laws, at issue in Smith, there are two other currents of change in free exercise jurisprudence, one from the right and one from the left. From the right comes the movement to resuscitate the right-privilege distinction by limiting the Free Exercise Clause to outright "prohibitions" of religious practice. From the left comes the movement to transform the free exercise right into a right of personal autonomy or self-definition. Both should be confronted and resisted.

1. *"Prohibitions" of religious practice and conditions on government aid.*

In *Lyng*, the Court emphasized that the "the crucial word in the constitutional text is 'prohibit.'" From this, the Court concluded that the Free Exercise Clause does not limit how the government controls its property, even when, as in *Lyng*, the government owns holy sites indispensable for religious worship. Thus the Forest Service could build a road over an American Indian holy site and "virtually destroy" the religion. By the same reasoning, the Free Exercise Clause would not limit the government's exercise of other nonregulatory powers, even if the government's action or inaction made the exercise of religion difficult or impossible. The Free Exercise Clause would apply only when the government made religious practice unlawful (and even then, under *Smith*, the Clause would not apply if the prohibition were generally applicable and not directed at religion). . . .

2. Free exercise and the rights of conscience.

On the other hand, some would expand the scope of the Free Exercise Clause by treating the free exercise right as a right of personal autonomy or self-definition. . . . This treats religion as an individualistic choice rather than as the irresistible conviction of the authority of God. The most obvious manifestation of this shift is the move to extend free exercise protections to any and all claims arising from "conscience," understood as the reflective judgment of the individual. David A.J. Richards perhaps best exemplifies this move: he argues that constitutional protections for religious freedom are ultimately based on "respect for the person as an independent source of value." Relying on this premise, Richards argues that it is illegitimate to distinguish between the free exercise of religion and the free exercise of any other personal belief or value. Free exercise becomes an undifferentiated right of personal autonomy. The essence of "religion" is that it acknowledges a normative authority independent of the judgment of the individual or of the society as a whole. Thus, the Virginia Declaration of Rights defined religion as the "duty which we owe to our Creator, and the manner of discharging it." Madison said that the law protects religious freedom because the duties arising from spiritual authority are "precedent both in order of time and degree of obligation, to the claims of Civil Society." The Free Exercise Clause does not protect autonomy; it protects obligation.

B.   A Pluralist Approach to the Establishment Clause

A pluralist approach to the Establishment Clause requires more explication, since the Supreme Court has never had a satisfactory Establishment Clause doctrine. The Court's first Establishment Clause case in this century was in 1947, and thereafter the Court fell quickly into the secularist interpretations that I have already criticized, most notably the three-pronged *Lemon* test. Unlike the *Lemon* test, a pluralistic approach would not ask whether the purpose or effect of the challenged action is to "advance religion," but whether it is to foster religious uniformity or otherwise distort the process of reaching and practicing religious convictions. A governmental policy that gives free rein to individual decisions (secular and religious) does not offend the Establishment Clause, even if the effect is to increase the number of religious choices. The concern of the Establishment Clause is with governmental actions that constrain individual decisionmaking with respect to religion, by favoring one religion over others, or by favoring religion over nonreligion.

1.   The roots of the pluralist approach: McDaniel, Widmar, and Witters.

a) *McDaniel v. Paty.* In *McDaniel*, the Court struck down a provision of the Tennessee Constitution that disqualified clergymen from legislative office. The court below had upheld the provision because it would "prevent those most intensely involved in religion from injecting sectarian goals and policies into the lawmaking process, and thus [would] avoid fomenting religious strife or the fusing of church with state affairs." The plurality of the Supreme Court had no difficulty rejecting this theory on the ground that it lacked any "persuasive support."

Justice Brennan, however, voted to invalidate the exclusion on more interesting and wide-ranging grounds. First, as a doctrinal matter, Justice Brennan maintained that "government may not use religion as a basis of classification for the imposition of duties, penalties, privileges or benefits" except when it does so "for purposes of accommodating our traditions of religious liberty." He further explained his idea of "accommodation": [G]overnment may take religion into account . . . to exempt, when possible, from generally applicable governmental regulation individuals whose religious beliefs and practices would otherwise thereby be infringed, or to create without state involvement an atmosphere in which voluntary religious exercise may flourish. Under this conception, the government must be "religion-blind" except when it accommodates religion—i.e., removes burdens on independently adopted religious practice. Brennan's was the first clear statement of the accommodation principle in any Supreme Court opinion.

Second, the Brennan opinion was noteworthy for its treatment of the role of religion in public life. The Tennessee provision was based on the proposition that religion is an inherently sectarian and divisive influence, which must be radically privatized in order to protect the democratic process. This can be seen as a reflection of the Deweyite philosophy, discussed above, which molded Supreme Court thinking during the Warren and Burger periods and underlay the movement to secularize the public sphere. Its principal doctrinal incarnation was the "political divisiveness" element of the entanglement test. The Court explained in *Lemon*: Ordinarily political debate and division, however vigorous or even partisan, are normal and healthy manifestations of our democratic system of government, but political division along religious lines was one of the principal evils against which the First Amendment

was intended to protect. The potential divisiveness of such conflict is a threat to the normal political process.

. . . The history of many countries attests to the hazards of religion's intruding into the political arena. Without noting its roots in *Lemon*, Justice Brennan took sharp issue with this reasoning in McDaniel, stating that it "manifest[ed] patent hostility toward, not neutrality respecting, religion." He denied that the divisiveness of religious entry into political debate is a "threat" to the democratic process. Rather, he said that "religious ideas, no less than any other, may be the subject of debate which is 'uninhibited, robust, and wide-open,'" reminding his readers that "church and religious groups in the United States have long exerted powerful political pressures on state and national legislatures, on subjects as diverse as slavery, war, gambling, drinking, prostitution, marriage, and education." Brennan took the view that religions are among the many points of view held by people of the United States, and that all such points of view are entitled to equal respect and an equal place in the public councils. "Religionists no less than members of any other group enjoy the full measure of protection afforded speech, association, and political activity generally." He warned against using the Establishment Clause "as a sword to justify repression of religion or its adherents from any aspect of public life." Brennan thus saw religion not as a threat to pluralism, but as an essential and legitimate part of it.

b) *Widmar v. Vincent.* In *Widmar*, a public university banned religious student groups from meeting on campus—a privilege extended to all other student groups—on the theory that allowing them to meet would "advance religion" in violation of the Establishment Clause.

. . . But Justice Powell's opinion for the majority of the Court recognized that this understanding of "advancement" would commit the government to a policy of discriminating against religion. Since the "forum is available to a broad class of nonreligious as well as religious speakers," Powell noted, any benefit to religion is purely "incidental." Like Brennan's concurrence in *McDaniel*, the decision treated religion as an appropriate and legitimate element in the mix of ideas in American life.

c) *Witters v. Department of Services.* In *Witters*, a blind man challenged the refusal of the Washington Department of Services for the Blind to pay for his program of vocational education, to which he was otherwise statutorily entitled. The State contended that to pay for his religious education would violate the Establishment Clause, because his chosen profession was the ministry and his course of study consisted of a degree program at a Bible college. But the Supreme Court unanimously rejected the state's argument. Although the Bible college at which Witters matriculated was a pervasively sectarian institution and many of the courses for which he was registered contained specifically religious content, the Court held that it would not violate the Establishment Clause for the state to pay the bill. Employing reasoning similar to that in *Widmar*, the opinion for the Court stressed that "[a]ny aid provided under Washington's program that ultimately flows to religious institutions does so only as a result of the genuinely independent and private choices of aid recipients" and "is in no way skewed towards religion. . . ." Justice Powell, however—in an opinion apparently supported by four other Justices and hence commanding majority

support—argued that the decision should not turn on how many students choose religious or secular education. According to Powell, "state programs that are wholly neutral in offering educational assistance to a class defined without reference to religion do not violate" the effects prong of the *Lemon* test. The difference between the two opinions is narrow but important. The opinion for the Court in *Witters* was willing to accept religion as one element in the public culture, on nondiscriminatory terms, but only when religion was an insignificant minority. Justice Powell, by contrast, was concerned only that the terms of the program be "wholly neutral"; it did not matter what choices the recipients made.

This line of cases escapes the mistakes of both the emerging Rehnquist Court jurisprudence and that of the Warren and Burger Courts. The decisions did not defer to majoritarian decisionmaking. Indeed, in each of the three cases, the government lost. Justice White's plea in *Widmar* that the States should "be a good deal freer to formulate policies that affect religion in divergent ways" did not attract a single additional vote. Instead, the decisions uphold the principle—to use Madison's language—that religious citizens have "full and equal rights." The opinions also abjure the secularist orientation so common in the other opinions of the Warren and Burger Courts. Whether in the political sphere (Brennan in *McDaniel*), in the interchange of ideas exemplified by the university (*Widmar*), or in the area of government financial assistance (*Witters*), these opinions treat religious perspectives as welcome and legitimate parts of our pluralistic public culture. Although the opinion for the Court in *Witters* hinted that the government-supported sector must remain predominantly secular, the opinions were unanimous in rejecting the idea that it must be entirely secular. In these opinions, the Justices seem to be moving toward the salutary position that the degree of secularism and of religiosity must be left to the people, not dictated by the Constitution, and not subject to the influence or control of the legislature.

2.   *Coping with the regulatory state.*

As Justice Brennan recognized in *McDaniel*, it is sometimes necessary for the government to "take religion into account" in order to ensure that government regulation does not infringe religious freedom. While always true to some extent, this has become far more important as government regulation has penetrated so much more deeply into both private life and the operations of the non-profit sector. As discussed above, the Rehnquist Court's adoption of a formal neutrality approach to the Free Exercise Clause has eliminated constitutional protection for religious individuals and institutions whose practices run contrary to the secular rules of the modern state. But the Court's more deferential approach to the Establishment Clause has the opposite effect: it permits the political branches wide latitude to soften the effect of regulation on religious practice through appropriate accommodations. Fortunately, the value of religious liberty is well recognized in the political sphere, and accommodations are not uncommon, even for the benefit of relatively small religious groups. . . .

Under the Burger Court, legislative accommodations of religion were treated with suspicion, and not infrequently invalidated on flimsy pretexts. The Court never held that accommodation is unconstitutional in principle, but the *Lemon* test made accommodations difficult to defend. Accommodations of religion have no "secular purpose," if "secular purpose" means a purpose solely relating to nonreligious concerns. The effect of accommodations is to make the practice of religion easier, and therefore, in all probability, more widespread. And some accommodations require the government to make judgments regarding religious beliefs and needs. This is easily characterized as "entanglement."

3.   *Equal access to public resources.*

One of the most important eighteenth-century abuses against which the no-establishment principle was directed was mandatory support for churches and ministers. This system was support for religion qua religion; it singled out religion as such for financial benefit. Secular institutions, activities, and ideologies received no comparable form of assistance. Religious assessments were eliminated in Virginia, Maryland, and most of the southern states by 1789, and in New England by 1834. As the Supreme Court has noted, the struggle against religious assessments was a central event in the development of the philosophy of the Religion Clauses of the First Amendment.

In the ensuing 150 years, the government began to assist in a wide range of charitable and educational activities, formerly left to private (frequently religious) endeavor. Frequently, the government chose to enter these fields not by setting up its own agencies, but by making financial contributions to private institutions that supplied services to the public. Common examples included higher education, hospitals, and orphanages. An advantage of private administration over public was that it preserved diversity, since different institutions would bring a different perspective and approach to the activity. The ultimate beneficiaries thus had a degree of choice. A student interested in a Catholic education could go to a Catholic college; a patient needing to keep to a kosher diet could go to a Jewish hospital; a dying mother wanting her child to be raised as a Protestant could designate a Protestant orphanage. A citizen need not forfeit public benefits as a condition to exercising the religious option. . . .

The Court's analysis failed to recognize the effect of the change in governmental roles. When the government provides no financial support to the nonprofit sector except for churches, it aids religion. But when the government provides financial support to the entire nonprofit sector, religious and nonreligious institutions alike, on the basis of objective criteria, it does not aid religion. It aids higher education, health care, or child care; it is neutral to religion. Indeed, to deny equal support to a college, hospital, or orphanage on the ground that it conveys religious ideas is to penalize it for being religious. It is a penalty whether the government excludes the religious institution from the program altogether, as in *Lemon*, *Nyquist*, and *Grand Rapids*, or requires the institution to secularize a portion of its program, as in *Tilton v. Richardson*, *Roemer*, or *Hunt v. McNair*.

The underlying issue is precisely the same as that in *Sherbert v. Verner*. The question in *Sherbert* was whether the state could deny benefits to an individual otherwise eligible for unemployment compensation on the ground that she refused to make herself available for work on her sabbath day. The Court recognized that the denial of a benefit, under such circumstances, is equivalent

to a "fine" for adhering to her religious convictions. Justice Douglas, a ferocious opponent of nondiscriminatory "aid" to religious institutions, well understood the point in *Sherbert*: The fact that government cannot exact from me a surrender of one iota of my religious scruples does not, of course, mean that I can demand of government a sum of money, the better to exercise them. For the Free Exercise Clause is written in terms of what the government cannot do to the individual, not in terms of what the individual can exact from the government.

. . . This inconsistent application of the right-privilege distinction is the most fundamental cause of the contradiction between the *Lemon* test and the Free Exercise Clause. *Lemon* assumes an outmoded conception of government aid, which treats equal access as "aid." The Free Exercise Clause, at a minimum (that is, after *Smith*), prohibits discrimination against an institution solely on the ground that it is religious. The *Lemon* test outlaws nondiscriminatory treatment and the Free Exercise Clause requires it. We must therefore reject the central animating idea of modern Establishment Clause analysis: that taxpayers have a constitutional right to insist that none of their taxes be used for religious purposes. Properly conceived, the taxpayer has a right to insist that the government not give tax dollars to religion qua religion, or in a way that favors religion over nonreligion, or one religion over another. But the taxpayer has no right to insist that the government discriminate against religion in the distribution of public funds. In this pluralistic country, taxpayers come in all varieties of belief and unbelief. To tax everyone, but to dispense money only to secular organizations, is to use government's coercive power to disadvantage religion.

4.   *Government influence over education and culture.*

A final threat to religious autonomy arises from governmental control over many of the institutions of education and culture. In an earlier era, when these were under private control, the government's voice was far less prominent in the marketplace of ideas. The influence of government is likely to foster homogeneity with respect to religion, since it is likely to reflect a broadly acceptable, majoritarian view of religion—in short, to support a civil religion. If it were possible to insist that government be "neutral" in its speech about religion, this would be highly desirable. Unfortunately, in the context of government speech—unlike regulation and spending—"neutrality" is an unattainable ideal. Whenever the government communicates to the people, it will favor some ideas and oppose others. The only truly effective way to reduce government influence on our religious lives through its speech would be to reduce the governmental presence in our cultural and educational institutions. Requirements of accommodation and equal treatment can solve (or at least greatly mitigate) the problems created by the regulatory and spending powers, but there are no real solutions to the problems created by the government's vastly increased role in the culture.

There are three baselines from which the neutrality of government speech might theoretically be evaluated. The first is complete secularization of the public sphere. If the "neutral" position were one in which religion is completely relegated to the private sphere of family and the institutions of private choice, any reference to religion in the public sphere would be a departure from neutrality. This is the position advocated by Professor Sullivan, who says that the solution to the government speech problem is "simple" if we would only "[b]anish public sponsorship of religious symbols from the public square." Serious enforcement of this position would bring about a radical change in the cultural fabric of the nation. Initial litigation has focused on what have been called "distinctively religious elements," such as crèches, crosses, and menorahs. But multitudes of other symbols, deeply engrained in our public culture, are no less distinctively religious. Christmas trees are symbols of Christmas, too, and many non-Christians (not to mention some Christians) consider them inappropriate for secular institutions. Certainly the star on top of the tree is a religious symbol. And if the star is a religious symbol, so are the pretty lights along the sidewalks of Michigan Avenue in downtown Chicago. Although most of us do not recognize the symbolism, these lights signify the advent of what the gospel of John calls the "true light that enlightens every man." Thanksgiving conveys a religious message, as do the speeches of Abraham Lincoln and the Reverend Martin Luther King, Jr.—which would have to be censored before they could be made a part of public celebrations. Many of our cities have religious names; many of our historic sites reflect religious aspects of the culture. To strip public property of all religious elements (when public property is used to convey secular messages of every kind and description) would have a profoundly secularizing effect on the culture.

The problem with the secularization baseline is that it is not neutral in any realistic sense. A small government could be entirely secular, and would have little impact on culture. But when the government owns the street and parks, which are the principal sites for public communication and community celebrations, the schools, which are a principal means for transmitting ideas and values to future generations, and many of the principal institutions of culture, exclusion of religious ideas, symbols, and voices marginalizes religion in much the same way that the neglect of the contributions of African-American and other minority citizens, or of the viewpoints and contributions of women, once marginalized those segments of the society. Silence about a subject can convey a powerful message. When the public sphere is open to ideas and symbols representing nonreligious viewpoints, cultures, and ideological commitments, to exclude all those whose basis is "religious" would profoundly distort public culture. . . .

A . . . possible baseline is the degree of religious expression that an "objective observer" would deem appropriate in the public sphere—Justice O'Connor's endorsement test. But this actually states no baseline at all; it is merely a restatement of the question. These issues are passionately contested within our culture. For example, to some (heavily represented in legal academia), inclusion of a nativity scene in a Christmas display on government property is an act of blatant intolerance. With equal sincerity, others (less well represented in legal academia), maintain that deliberate exclusion of a nativity scene from a Christmas display places the prestige and influence of the government in favor of materialism and against religion. The "endorsement test" is justified on the ground that it will ensure that no class of citizens defined by religious perspective is made to feel like an "outsider" to the political community. If so, it is necessary to pay serious attention to both points of view. Both sides are sincere, and both consider themselves in danger of being marginalized. Unfortunately, it is not possible for both to prevail, and there

is no objective standpoint for choosing one over the other (that is, no standpoint that both could, in principle, accept). The "objective observer" does not, therefore, offer even a theoretically possible baseline for the evaluation of neutrality.

The third possible baseline is the state of public culture in the non-government-controlled sector. If the aspects of culture controlled by the government (public spaces, public institutions) exactly mirrored the culture as a whole, then the influence and effect of government involvement would be nil: the religious life of the people would be precisely the way it would be if the government were absent from the cultural sphere. In a pluralistic culture, this is the best of the possible understandings of "neutrality," since it will lead to a broadly inclusive public sphere, in which the public is presented a wide variety of perspectives, religious ones included. If a city displays many different cultural symbols during the course of the year, a nativity scene at Christmas or a menorah at Hannukah is likely to be perceived as an expression of pluralism rather than as an exercise in Christian or Jewish triumphalism. If the curriculum is genuinely diverse, exposing children to religious ideas will not have the effect of indoctrination. Individuals should be permitted to opt out of participating in those religious (or antireligious) aspects of the program that are objectionable to them on grounds of conscience, but there is no reason to extirpate all religious elements from the entire curriculum. The same is true of the public culture: opt-out rights should be freely accorded, but the general norm should be one of openness, diversity, and pluralism.

If members of minority religions (or other cultural groups) feel excluded by government symbols or speech, the best solution is to request fair treatment of alternative traditions, rather than censorship of more mainstream symbols. If a government refuses to cooperate with minority religious (and other cultural) groups within the community, there may be a basis for inferring that the choice of symbols was a deliberate attempt to use government influence to promote a particular religious position. Courts should not encourage the proliferation of litigation by offering the false hope that perfect neutrality can be achieved through judicial fine-tuning. Judicial scrutiny should be reserved for cases in which a particular religious position is given such public prominence that the overall message becomes one of conformity rather than pluralism. Certainly they should not allow official acts that declare one religion, or group of religions, superior to the rest, or give official sponsorship to symbols or ceremonies that are inherently exclusionary. Particular care should be taken where impressionable children are involved. But courts should be cautious about responding to particular contestable issues in isolation. It is impossible to tell whether a particular event, symbol, statement, or item is an indication of diversity or of favoritism if it is viewed without regard to wider context.

CONCLUSION

The religious freedom cases under the First Amendment have been distorted by the false choice between secularism and majoritarianism, neither of which faithfully reflects the pluralistic philosophy of the Religion Clauses. Instead, the Free Exercise and Establishment Clauses should protect against government-induced uniformity in matters of religion. In the modern welfare-regulatory state, this means that the state must not favor religion over nonreligion, nonreligion over religion, or one religion over another in distributing financial resources; that the state must create exceptions to laws of general applicability when these laws threaten the religious convictions or practices of religious institutions or individuals; and that the state should eschew both religious favoritism and secular bias in its own participation in the formation of public culture. This interpretation will tolerate a more prominent place for religion in the public sphere, but will simultaneously guarantee religious freedom for faiths both large and small.

John Rawls

THE IDEA OF PUBLIC REASON REVISITED

in The Law of Peoples

Cambridge, MA: Harvard University Press (1999)

While Michael McConnell stresses the importance of religion in public life, John Rawls provides a way of recognizing the limits of that role. In particular, Rawls's notion of public reason is meant to serve as a standard for evaluating when religious purposes or justifications rightly can serve as the basis for policy. In Rawls's view, such reasons can play a role in public life when they serve to reinforce reasons that could be given to citizens who lack any particular religious beliefs. Public reason is thus meant as a way of discerning which reasons are common to citizens. According to Rawls, religious motives should not be excluded from public life, but rather must be subject to a theoretical test that measures the degree to which they are also good objectives for non-religious people. Is this standard too restrictive of religious belief? Does it go beyond the requirement of the Establishment Clause in requiring a secular standard for law?

§3. RELIGION AND PUBLIC REASON IN DEMOCRACY

3.1. Before examining the idea of the wide view of public political culture, we ask: How is it possible for those holding religious doctrines, some based on religious authority, for example, the Church or the Bible, to hold at the same time a reasonable political conception that supports a reasonable constitutional democratic regime? Can these doctrines still be compatible for the right reasons with a liberal political conception? To attain this compatibility, it is not sufficient that these doctrines accept a democratic government merely as a *modus vivendi*. Referring to citizens holding religious doctrines as citizens of faith, we ask: How is it possible for citizens of faith to be wholehearted members of a democratic society who endorse society's intrinsic political ideals and values and do not simply acquiesce in the balance of political and social forces? Expressed more sharply: How is it possible—or is it—for those of faith, as well as the nonreligious (secular), to endorse a constitutional regime even when their comprehensive doctrines may not prosper under it, and indeed may decline? This last question brings out anew the significance of the idea of legitimacy and public reason's role in determining legitimate law. To clarify the question, consider two examples. The first is that of Catholics and Protestants in the sixteenth and seventeenth centuries when the principle of toleration was honored only as a *modus vivendi*.

This meant that should either party fully gain its way it would impose its own religious doctrine as the sole admissible faith. A society in which many faiths all share this attitude and assume that for the indefinite future their relative numbers will stay roughly the same might well have a constitution resembling that of the United States, fully protecting the religious liberties of sharply divided religions more or less equal in political power. The constitution is, as it were, honored as a pact to maintain civil peace. In this society political issues might be discussed in terms of political ideas and values so as not to open religious conflict and arouse sectarian hostility. The role of public reason here serves merely to quiet divisiveness and encourage social stability. However, in this case we do not have stability for the right reasons, that is, as secured by a firm allegiance to a democratic society's political (moral) ideals and values. Nor again do we have stability for the right reasons in the second example—a democratic society where citizens accept as political (moral) principles the substantive constitutional clauses that ensure religious, political, and civil liberties, when their allegiance to these constitutional principles is so limited that none is willing to see his or her religious or nonreligious doctrine losing ground in influence and numbers, and such citizens are prepared to resist or to disobey laws that they think undermine their positions. And they do this even though the full range of religious and other liberties is always maintained and the doctrine in question is completely secure. Here again democracy is accepted conditionally and not for the right reasons. What these examples have in common is that society is divided into separate groups, each of which has its own fundamental interest distinct from and opposed to the interests of the other groups and for which it is prepared to resist or to violate legitimate democratic law. In the first example, it is the interest of a religion in establishing its hegemony, while in the second, it is the doctrine's fundamental interest in maintaining a certain degree of success and influence for its own view, either religious or nonreligious. While a constitutional regime can fully ensure rights and liberties for all permissible doctrines, and therefore protect our freedom and security, a democracy necessarily requires that, as one equal citizen among others, each of us accept the obligations of legitimate law. While no one is expected to put his or her religious or nonreligious doctrine in danger, we must each give up forever the hope of changing the constitution so as to establish our religion's hegemony, or of qualifying our obligations so as to ensure its influence and success. To retain such hopes and aims would be inconsistent with the idea of equal basic liberties for all free and equal citizens.

3.2. To expand on what we asked earlier: How is it possible—or is it—for those of faith, as well as the nonreligious (secular), to endorse a constitutional regime even when their comprehensive doctrines may not prosper under it, and indeed may decline? Here the answer lies in the religious or nonreligious doctrine's understanding and accepting that, except by endorsing a reasonable constitutional democracy, there is no other way fairly to ensure the liberty of its adherents consistent with the equal liberties of other reasonable free and equal citizens. In endorsing a constitutional democratic regime, a religious doctrine may say that

such are the limits God sets to our liberty; a nonreligious doctrine will express itself otherwise. But in either case, these doctrines formulate in different ways how liberty of conscience and the principle of toleration can cohere with equal justice for all citizens in a reasonable democratic society. Thus, the principles of toleration and liberty of conscience must have an essential place in any constitutional democratic conception. They lay down the fundamental basis to be accepted by all citizens as fair and regulative of the rivalry between doctrines. Observe here that there are two ideas of toleration. One is purely political, being expressed in terms of the rights and duties protecting religious liberty in accordance with a reasonable political conception of justice. The other is not purely political but expressed from within a religious or a nonreligious doctrine, as when, for example, it was said above that such are the limits God sets on our liberty. Saying this offers an example of what I call reasoning from conjecture. In this case we reason from what we believe, or conjecture, may be other people's basic doctrines, religious or philosophical, and seek to show them that, despite what they might think, they can still endorse a reasonable political conception of justice. We are not ourselves asserting that ground of toleration but offering it as one they could assert consistent with their comprehensive doctrines.

§4. THE WIDE VIEW OF PUBLIC POLITICAL CULTURE

4.1. Now we consider what I call the wide view of public political culture and discuss two aspects of it. The first is that reasonable comprehensive doctrines, religious or nonreligious, may be introduced in public political discussion at any time, provided that in due course proper political reasons—and not reasons given solely by comprehensive doctrines—are presented that are sufficient to support whatever the comprehensive doctrines introduced are said to support. This injunction to present proper political reasons I refer to as *the proviso*, and it specifies public political culture as distinct from the background culture. The second aspect I consider is that there may be positive reasons for introducing comprehensive doctrines into public political discussion. I take up these two aspects in turn.

Obviously, many questions may be raised about how to satisfy the proviso. One is: when does it need to be satisfied? On the same day or some later day? Also, on whom does the obligation to honor it fall? It is important that it be clear and established that the proviso is to be appropriately satisfied in good faith. Yet the details about how to satisfy this proviso must be worked out in practice and cannot feasibly be governed by a clear family of rules given in advance. How they work out is determined by the nature of the public political culture and calls for good sense and understanding. It is important also to observe that the introduction into public political culture of religious and secular doctrines, provided the proviso is met, does not change the nature and content of justification in public reason itself. This justification is still given in terms of a family of reasonable political conceptions of justice.

However, there are no restrictions or requirements on how religious or secular doctrines are themselves to be expressed; these doctrines need not, for example, be by some standards logically correct, or open to rational appraisal, or evidentially supportable. Whether they are or not is a matter to be decided by those presenting them, and how they want what they say

to be taken. They will normally have practical reasons for wanting to make their views acceptable to a broader audience.

4.2. Citizens' mutual knowledge of one another's religious and nonreligious doctrines expressed in the wide view of public political culture recognizes that the roots of democratic citizens' allegiance to their political conceptions lie in their respective comprehensive doctrines, both religious and nonreligious. In this way citizens' allegiance to the democratic ideal of public reason is strengthened for the right reasons. We may think of the reasonable comprehensive doctrines that support society's reasonable political conceptions as those conceptions' vital social basis, giving them enduring strength and vigor. When these doctrines accept the proviso and only then come into political debate, the commitment to constitutional democracy is publicly manifested. Made aware of this commitment, government officials and citizens are more willing to honor the duty of civility, and their following the ideal of public reason helps foster the kind of society that ideal exemplifies. These benefits of the mutual knowledge of citizens' recognizing one another's reasonable comprehensive doctrines bring out a positive ground for introducing such doctrines, which is not merely a defensive ground, as if their intrusion into public discussion were inevitable in any case. . . .

4.3. Public reasoning aims for public justification. We appeal to political conceptions of justice, and to ascertainable evidence and facts open to public view, in order to reach conclusions about what we think are the most reasonable political institutions and policies. Public justification is not simply valid reasoning, but argument addressed to others; it proceeds correctly from premises we accept and think others could reasonably accept to conclusions we think they could also reasonably accept. This meets the duty of civility, since in due course the proviso is satisfied. There are two other forms of discourse that may also be mentioned, though neither expresses a form of public reasoning. One is declaration: here we each declare our own comprehensive doctrine, religious or nonreligious. This we do not expect others to share. Rather, each of us shows how, from our own doctrines, we can and do endorse a reasonable public political conception of justice with its principles and ideals. The aim of doing this is to declare to others who affirm different comprehensive doctrines that we also each endorse a reasonable political conception belonging to the family of reasonable such conceptions. On the wide view, citizens of faith who cite the Gospel parable of the Good Samaritan do not stop there, but go on to give a public justification for this parable's conclusions in terms of political values. In this way citizens who hold different doctrines are reassured, and this strengthens the ties of civic friendship. . . .

§6. QUESTIONS ABOUT PUBLIC REASON

I now turn to various questions and doubts about the idea of public reason and try to allay them.

6.1. First, it, may be objected that the idea of public reason would unreasonably limit the topics and considerations available for political argument and debate, and that we should adopt instead what we may call the open view with no constraints. I now discuss two examples to rebut this objection.

Of special interest in the example of school prayer is that it brings out that the idea of public reason is not a view about specific political institutions or policies.

Rather, it is a view about the kind of reasons on which citizens are to rest their political cases in making their political justifications to one another when they support laws and policies that invoke the coercive powers of government concerning fundamental political questions. Also of special interest in this example is that it serves to emphasize that the principles that support the separation of church and state should be such that they can be affirmed by all free and equal citizens, given the fact of reasonable pluralism. The reasons for the separation of church and state are these, among others: It protects religion from the state and the state from religion; it protects citizens from their churches and citizens from one another. It is a mistake to say that political liberalism is an individualist political conception, since its aim is the protection of the various interests in liberty, both associational and individual. And it is also a grave error to think that the separation of church and state is primarily for the protection of secular culture; of course it does protect that culture, but no more so than it protects all religions. The vitality and wide acceptance of religion in America is often commented upon, as if it were a sign of the peculiar virtue of the American people. Perhaps *so*, but it may also be connected with the fact that in this country the various religions have been protected by the First Amendment from the state, and none has been able to dominate and suppress the other religions by the capture and use of state power. . . . Some citizens of faith have felt that this separation is hostile to religion and have sought to change it. . . .

The relevant comparison is to those situations in which legislators enacting laws and judges deciding cases must make decisions. Here some political rule of action must be laid down and all must be able reasonably to endorse the process by which a decision is reached. Recall that public reason sees the office of citizen with its duty of civility as analogous to that of judge with its duty of deciding cases. Just as judges are to decide cases by legal grounds of precedent, recognized canons of statutory interpretation, and other relevant grounds, so citizens are to reason by public reason and to be guided by the criterion of reciprocity, whenever constitutional essentials and matters of basic justice are at stake.

In particular, when hotly disputed questions, such as that of abortion, arise which may lead to a stand-off between different political conceptions, citizens must vote on the question according to their complete ordering of political values. Indeed, this is a normal case: unanimity of views is not to be expected. Reasonable political conceptions of justice do not always lead to the same conclusion; nor do citizens holding the same conception always agree on particular issues. Yet the outcome of the vote, as I said before, is to be seen as legitimate provided all government officials, supported by other reasonable citizens, of a reasonably just constitutional regime sincerely vote in accordance with the idea of public reason. This doesn't mean the outcome is true or correct, but that it is reasonable and legitimate law, binding on citizens by the majority principle. Some may, of course, reject a legitimate decision, as Roman Catholics may reject a decision to grant a right to abortion. They may present an argument in public reason for denying it and fail to win a majority. But they need not themselves exercise the right to abortion. . . .

I emphasize that this idea of public reason is fully compatible with the many forms of nonpublic reason. These belong to the internal life of the many associations in civil society, and they are not of course all the same; different nonpublic reasons of different religious associations shared by their members are not those of scientific societies. Since we seek a shareable public basis of justification for all citizens in society, giving justifications to particular persons and groups here and there until all are covered fails to do this. To speak of all persons in society is still too broad, unless we suppose that they are in their nature basically the same. In political philosophy one role of ideas about our nature has been to think of people in a standard, or canonical, fashion so that they might all accept the same kind of reasons. In political liberalism, however, we try to avoid natural or psychological views of this kind, as well as theological or secular doctrines. Accounts of human nature we put aside and rely on a political conception of persons as citizens instead.

6.3. As I have stressed throughout, it is central to political liberalism that free and equal citizens affirm both a comprehensive doctrine and a political conception. However, the relation between a comprehensive doctrine and its accompanying political conception is easily misunderstood when political liberalism speaks of a reasonable overlapping consensus of comprehensive doctrines? It means that all of these doctrines, both religious and nonreligious, support a political conception of justice underwriting a constitutional democratic society whose principles, ideals, and standards satisfy the criterion of reciprocity. Thus, all reasonable doctrines affirm such a society with its corresponding political institutions: equal basic rights and liberties for all citizens, including liberty of conscience and the freedom of religion. On the other hand, comprehensive doctrines that cannot support such a democratic society are not reasonable. Their principles and ideals do not satisfy the criterion of reciprocity, and in various ways they fail to establish the equal basic liberties. As examples, consider the many fundamentalist religious doctrines, the doctrine of the divine right of monarchs and the various forms of aristocracy, and, not to be overlooked, the many instances of autocracy and dictatorship. . . .

In a reasonable comprehensive doctrine, in particular a religious one, the ranking of values may not be what we might expect. Thus, suppose we call *transcendent* such values as salvation and eternal life—the *Visio Dei*. This value, let's say, is higher, or superior to, the reasonable political values of a constitutional democratic society. These are worldly values and therefore on a different, and as it were lower, plane than those transcendent values. It doesn't follow, however, that these lower yet reasonable values are overridden by the transcendent values of the religious doctrine. In fact, a *reasonable* comprehensive doctrine is one in which they are not overridden; it is the unreasonable doctrines in which reasonable political values are overridden. This is a consequence of the idea of the politically reasonable as set out in political liberalism. Recall that it was said: In endorsing a constitutional democratic regime, a religious doctrine may say that such are the limits God sets to our liberty.

§7. CONCLUSION

7.1. Throughout, I have been concerned with a torturing question in the contemporary world, namely: Can democracy and comprehensive doctrines, religious or nonreligious, be compatible? And if *so*, how? At the moment a number of conflicts between religion and democracy

raise this question. To answer it political liberalism makes the distinction between a self-standing political conception of justice and a comprehensive doctrine. A religious doctrine resting on the authority of the Church or the Bible is not, of course, a liberal comprehensive doctrine: its leading religious and moral values are not those, say, of Kant or Mill. Nevertheless, it may endorse a constitutional democratic society and recognize its public reason. Here it is basic that public reason is a political idea and belongs to the category of the political. Its content is given by the family of (liberal) political conceptions of justice satisfying the criterion of reciprocity. It does not trespass upon religious beliefs and injunctions insofar as these are consistent with the essential constitutional liberties, including the freedom of religion and liberty of conscience. There is, or need be, no war between religion and democracy. In this respect political liberalism is sharply different from and rejects Enlightenment Liberalism, which historically attacked orthodox Christianity. . . .

Of course, citizens may think that the grounding reasons for toleration and for the other elements of a constitutional democratic society are not political but rather are to be found in their religious or nonreligious doctrines. And these reasons, they may well say, are the true or the right reasons; and they may see the political reasons as superficial, the grounding ones as deep. Yet there is no conflict here, but simply concordant judgments made within political conceptions of justice on the one hand, and within comprehensive doctrines on the other.

There are limits, however, to reconciliation by public reason. Three main kinds of conflicts set citizens at odds: those deriving from irreconcilable comprehensive doctrines, those deriving from differences in status, class position, or occupation, or from differences in ethnicity, gender, or race, and finally, those deriving from the burdens of judgment. Political liberalism concerns primarily the first kind of conflict. It holds that even though our comprehensive doctrines are irreconcilable and cannot be compromised, nevertheless citizens who affirm reasonable doctrines may share reasons of another kind, namely, public reasons given in terms of political conceptions of justice. I also believe that such a society can resolve the second kind of conflict, which deals with conflicts between citizens' fundamental interests, political, economic, and social. . . .

7.2. Reasonable comprehensive doctrines do not reject the essentials of a constitutional democratic polity. Moreover, reasonable persons are characterized in two ways: First, they stand ready to offer fair terms of social cooperation between equals, and they abide by these terms if others do also, even should it be to their advantage not to; second, reasonable persons recognize and accept the consequences of the burdens of judgment, which leads to the idea of reasonable toleration in a democratic society. Finally we come to the idea of legitimate law, which reasonable citizens understand to apply to the general structure political authority. They know that in political life unanimity can rarely if ever be expected, so a reasonable democratic constitution must include majority or other plurality voting procedures in order to reach decisions. The idea of the politically reasonable is sufficient unto itself for the purposes of public reason when basic political questions are at stake. Of course, fundamentalist religious doctrines and autocratic and dictatorial rulers will reject the ideas of public reason and deliberative democracy. They will say that democracy leads to a culture contrary to their religion, or denies the values that only autocratic or dictatorial rule can secure. They assert that the religiously true, or the philosophically true, overrides the politically reasonable. We simply say that such a doctrine is politically unreasonable. Within political liberalism nothing more need be said.

EVERSON v. BOARD OF EDUCATION

330 U.S. 1 (1947)

Opinion: Black, joined by Vinson, Reed, Douglas, Murphy
Dissent: Jackson, joined by Frankfurter
Dissent: Rutledge, joined by
    Frankfurter, Jackson, Burton

Despite embracing the metaphorical wall of separation between church and state, the Court has struggled with the constitutionality of state funding for religiously affiliated institutions. This case addresses the question of transportation of school children. In particular, the Court asks whether funding such transportation for some children who attend religious schools constitutes an establishment of religion. As you read this case, ask yourself whether the state is aiding the religious schools or the children and their parents. Does the answer to this question make a difference in your evaluation of the decision? Can the state fund students who attend religious schools without funding the schools themselves? These issues will become increasingly salient in future cases involving state funding, such as in Zelman v. Simmons-Harris *and* Locke v. Davey, *which we explore toward the end of this case selection. Notice that as in* Gitlow v. New York *and* Whitney v. California, *this case concerns the question of the establishment of religion by a state, namely, New Jersey. One significance of* Everson v. Board of Education *is the decision of the Court to incorporate the prohibition on religious establishment to apply to states, despite the Establishment Clause's explicit reference to the federal government.*

MR. JUSTICE BLACK *delivered the opinion of the Court.*

A New Jersey statute authorizes its local school districts to make rules and contracts for the transportation of children to and from schools. The appellee, a township board of education, acting pursuant to this statute, authorized reimbursement to parents of money expended by them for the bus transportation of their children on regular busses operated by the public transportation system. Part of this money was for the payment of transportation of some children in the community to Catholic parochial schools. These church schools give their students, in addition to secular education, regular religious instruction conforming to the religious tenets and modes of worship of the Catholic Faith. The superintendent of these schools is a Catholic priest.

The appellant, in his capacity as a district taxpayer, filed suit in a state court challenging the right of the Board to reimburse parents of parochial school students. . . . The New Jersey Court of Errors and Appeals reversed, holding that neither the statute nor the resolution passed pursuant to it was in conflict with the State constitution or the provisions of the Federal

Constitution in issue. The case is here on appeal.

. . . The only contention here is that the state statute and the resolution, insofar as they authorized reimbursement to parents of children attending parochial schools, violate the Federal Constitution . . . in these two respects, which to some extent overlap. *First.* They authorize the State to take by taxation the private property of some and bestow it upon others to be used for their own private purposes. This, it is alleged, violates the due process clause of the Fourteenth Amendment. *Second.* The statute and the resolution forced inhabitants to pay taxes to help support and maintain schools which are dedicated to, and which regularly teach, the Catholic Faith. This is alleged to be a use of state power to support church schools contrary to the prohibition of the First Amendment which the Fourteenth Amendment made applicable to the states. . . .

Second. The New Jersey statute is challenged as a "law respecting an establishment of religion." The First Amendment, as made applicable to the states by the Fourteenth, *Murdock v. Pennsylvania*, commands that a state "shall make no law respecting an establishment of religion, or prohibiting the free exercise thereof. . . ." Whether this New Jersey law is one respecting an "establishment of religion" requires an understanding of the meaning of that language, particularly with respect to the imposition of taxes. Once again, therefore, it is not inappropriate briefly to review the background and environment of the period in which that constitutional language was fashioned and adopted. . . .

The imposition of taxes to pay ministers' salaries and to build and maintain churches and church property aroused [Founding-era Americans'] indignation. It was these feelings which found expression in the First Amendment. No one locality and no one group throughout the Colonies can rightly be given entire credit for having aroused the sentiment that culminated in adoption of the Bill of Rights' provisions embracing religious liberty. But Virginia, where the established church had achieved a dominant influence in political affairs and where many excesses attracted wide public attention, provided a great stimulus and able leadership for the movement. The people there, as elsewhere, reached the conviction that individual religious liberty could be achieved best under a government which was stripped of all power to tax, to support, or otherwise to assist any or all religions, or to interfere with the beliefs of any religious individual or group.

The movement toward this end reached its dramatic climax in Virginia in 1785–86 when the Virginia legislative body was about to renew Virginia's tax levy for the support of the established church. Thomas Jefferson and James Madison led the fight against this tax. Madison wrote his great Memorial and Remonstrance against the law. In it, he eloquently argued that a true religion did not need the support of law; that no person, either believer or non-believer, should be taxed to support a religious institution of any kind; that the best interest of a society required that the minds of men always be wholly free; and that cruel persecutions were the inevitable result of government-established religions. Madison's Remonstrance received strong support throughout Virginia, and the Assembly postponed consideration of the proposed tax measure until its next session. When the proposal came up for consideration at that session, it not only died in committee, but the Assembly enacted the famous "Virginia Bill for Religious Liberty" originally written by Thomas Jefferson. The preamble to that Bill stated among other things that

"Almighty God hath created the mind free; that all attempts to influence it by temporal punishments, or burdens, or by civil incapacitations, tend only to beget habits of hypocrisy and meanness, and are a departure from the plan of the Holy author of our religion who being Lord both of body and mind, yet chose not to propagate it by coercions on either . . .; that to compel a man to furnish contributions of money for the propagation of opinions which he disbelieves, is sinful and tyrannical; that even the forcing him to support this or that teacher of his own religious persuasion, is depriving him of the comfortable liberty of giving his contributions to the particular pastor, whose morals he would make his pattern. . . ."

And the statute itself enacted:

"That no man shall be compelled to frequent or support any religious worship, place, or ministry whatsoever, nor shall be enforced, restrained, molested, or burdened in his body or goods, nor shall otherwise suffer on account of his religious opinions or belief. . . ."

This Court has previously recognized that the provisions of the First Amendment, in the drafting and adoption of which Madison and Jefferson played such leading roles, had the same objective, and were intended to provide the same protection against governmental intrusion on religious liberty as the Virginia statute. (*Reynolds v. United States*; *Watson v. Jones*; *Davis v. Beason*.) Prior to the adoption of the Fourteenth Amendment, the First Amendment did not apply as a restraint against the states. Most of them did soon provide similar constitutional protections for religious liberty. But some states persisted for about half a century in imposing restraints upon the free exercise of religion and in discriminating against particular religious groups. In recent years, so far as the provision against the establishment of a religion is concerned, the question has most frequently arisen in connection with proposed state aid to church schools and efforts to carry on religious teachings in the public schools in accordance with the tenets of a particular sect. Some churches have either sought or accepted state financial support for their schools. Here again, the efforts to obtain state aid or acceptance of it have not been limited to any one particular faith. The state courts, in the main, have remained faithful to the language of their own constitutional provisions designed to protect religious freedom and to separate religions and governments. Their decisions, however, show the difficulty in drawing the line between tax legislation which provides funds for the welfare of the general public and that which is designed to support institutions which teach religion.

. . . The "establishment of religion" clause of the First Amendment means at least this: neither a state nor the Federal Government can set up a church. Neither can pass laws which aid one religion, aid all religions, or prefer one religion over another. Neither can force nor influence a person to go to or to remain away from church against his will or force him to profess a belief or disbelief in any religion. No person can be punished for entertaining or professing religious beliefs or disbeliefs, for church attendance or non-attendance. No tax in any amount, large or small, can be levied to support any religious activities or institutions, whatever they may be called, or whatever form they may adopt to teach or practice religion. Neither a state nor the Federal Government can, openly or secretly, participate in the affairs of any religious organizations or groups, and vice versa. In the words of Jefferson, the clause against establishment of religion by law was intended to erect "a wall of separation between church and State." *Reynolds v. United States.*

We must consider the New Jersey statute in accordance with the foregoing limitations imposed by the First Amendment.

But we must not strike that state statute down if it is within the State's constitutional power, even though it approaches the verge of that power. *See Interstate Ry. v. Massachusetts*, Holmes, J. New Jersey cannot consistently with the "establishment of religion" clause of the First Amendment contribute tax-raised funds to the support of an institution which teaches the tenets and faith of any church. . . . While we do not mean to intimate that a state could not provide transportation only to children attending public schools, we must be careful, in protecting the citizens of New Jersey against state-established churches, to be sure that we do not inadvertently prohibit New Jersey from extending its general state law benefits to all its citizens without regard to their religious belief.

Measured by these standards, we cannot say that the First Amendment prohibits New Jersey from spending tax-raised funds to pay the bus fares of parochial school pupils as a part of a general program under which it pays the fares of pupils attending public and other schools. It is undoubtedly true that children are helped to get to church schools. There is even a possibility that some of the children might not be sent to the church schools if the parents were compelled to pay their children's bus fares out of their own pockets when transportation to a public school would have been paid for by the State. The same possibility exists where the state requires a local transit company to provide reduced fares to school children including those attending parochial schools, or where a municipally owned transportation system undertakes to carry all school children free of charge. Moreover, state-paid policemen, detailed to protect children going to and from church schools from the very real hazards of traffic, would serve much the same purpose and accomplish much the same result as state provisions intended to guarantee free transportation of a kind which the state deems to be best for the school children's welfare. And parents might refuse to risk their children to the serious danger of traffic accidents going to and from parochial schools, the approaches to which were not protected by policemen. Similarly, parents might be reluctant to permit their children to attend schools which the state had cut off from such general government services as ordinary police and fire protection, connections for sewage disposal, public highways and sidewalks. Of course, cutting off church schools from these services so separate and so indisputably marked off from the religious function would make it far more difficult for the schools to operate. But such is obviously not the purpose of the First Amendment. That Amendment requires the state to be a neutral in its relations with groups of religious believers and nonbelievers; it does not require the state to be their adversary. State power is no more to be used so as to handicap religions than it is to favor them.

This Court has said that parents may, in the discharge of their duty under state compulsory education laws, send their children to a religious, rather than a public, school if the school meets the secular educational requirements which the state has power to impose. *See Pierce v. Society of Sisters.* It appears that these parochial schools meet New Jersey's requirements. The State contributes no money to the schools. It does not support them. Its legislation, as applied, does no more than provide a general program to help parents get their children, regardless of their religion, safely and expeditiously to and from accredited schools.

The First Amendment has erected a wall between church and state. That wall must be kept high and impregnable. We could not approve the slightest breach. New Jersey has not breached it here.

Affirmed.

MR. JUSTICE RUTLEDGE, *with whom* **MR. JUSTICE FRANKFURTER, MR. JUSTICE JACKSON** *and* **MR. JUSTICE BURTON** *agree, dissenting.*

... This case forces us to determine squarely for the first time what was "an establishment of religion" in the First Amendment's conception; and by that measure to decide whether New Jersey's action violates its command....

I

Not simply an established church, but any law respecting an establishment of religion is forbidden. The Amendment was broadly but not loosely phrased. It is the compact and exact summation of its author's views formed during his long struggle for religious freedom. In Madison's own words characterizing Jefferson's Bill for Establishing Religious Freedom, the guaranty he put in our national charter, like the bill he piloted through the Virginia Assembly, was "a Model of technical precision, and perspicuous brevity." Madison could not have confused "church" and "religion," or "an established church" and "an establishment or religion."

The Amendment's purpose was not to strike merely at the official establishment of a single sect, creed or religion, outlawing only a formal relation such as had prevailed in England and some of the colonies. Necessarily it was to uproot all such relationships. But the object was broader than separating church and state in this narrow sense. It was to create a complete and permanent separation of the spheres of religious activity and civil authority by comprehensively forbidding every form of public aid or support for religion. In proof the Amendment's wording and history unite with this Court's consistent utterances whenever attention has been fixed directly upon the question.

"Religion" appears only once in the Amendment. But the word governs two prohibitions and governs them alike. It does not have two meanings, one narrow to forbid "an establishment" and another, much broader, for securing "the free exercise thereof." "Thereof" brings down "religion" with its entire and exact content, no more and no less, from the first into the second guaranty, so that Congress and now the states are as broadly restricted concerning the one as they are regarding the other.

No one would claim today that the Amendment is constricted, in "prohibiting the free exercise" of religion, to securing the free exercise of some formal or creedal observance, of one sect or of many. It secures all forms of religious expression, creedal, sectarian or nonsectarian wherever and however taking place, except conduct which trenches upon the like freedoms of others or clearly and presently endangers the community's good order and security. For the protective purposes of this phase of the basic freedom street preaching, oral or by distribution of literature, has been given "the same high estate under the First Amendment as . . . worship in the churches and preaching from the pulpits." And on this basis parents have been held entitled to send their children to private, religious schools. *Pierce v. Society of Sisters.* Accordingly, daily religious education commingled with secular is "religion" within the guaranty's comprehensive scope. So are religious training and teaching in whatever form. The word connotes the broadest content, determined not by the form or formality of the teaching or where it occurs, but by its essential nature regardless of those details.

"Religion" has the same broad significance in the twin prohibition concerning "an establishment." The Amendment was not duplicitous. "Religion" and "establishment" were not used in any formal or technical sense. The prohibition broadly forbids state support, financial or other, of religion in any guise, form or degree. It outlaws all use of public funds for religious purposes. . . .

New Jersey's action therefore exactly fits the type of exaction and the kind of evil at which Madison and Jefferson struck. Under the test they framed it cannot be said that the cost of transportation is no part of the cost of education or of the religious instruction given. That it is a substantial and a necessary element is shown most plainly by the continuing and increasing demand for the state to assume it. Nor is there pretense that it relates only to the secular instruction given in religious schools or that any attempt is or could be made toward allocating proportional shares as between the secular and the religious instruction. It is precisely because the instruction is religious and relates to a particular faith, whether one or another, that parents send their children to religious schools under the *Pierce* doctrine. And the very purpose of the state's contribution is to defray the cost of conveying the pupil to the place where he will receive not simply secular, but also and primarily religious, teaching and guidance. . . .

By no declaration that a gift of public money to religious uses will promote the general or individual welfare, or the cause of education generally, can legislative bodies overcome the Amendment's bar. Nor may the courts sustain their attempts to do so by finding such consequences for appropriations which in fact give aid to or promote religious uses. Legislatures are free to make, and courts to sustain, appropriations only when it can be found that in fact they do not aid, promote, encourage or sustain religious teaching or observances, be the amount large or small. No such finding has been or could be made in this case. The Amendment has removed this form of promoting the public welfare from legislative and judicial competence to make a public function. It is exclusively a private affair.

TORCASO v. WATKINS

367 U.S. 488 (1961)

Opinion: Black, joined by Warren, Douglas, Clark, Brennan, Whittaker, Stewart
Concurrence (not filed): Frankfurter
Concurrence (not filed): Harlan

The following case involved a challenge by an atheist to a law requiring public officials to profess belief in God. As you read it, consider whether the Establishment Clause requires law and other governmental actions to be neutral, not only between different religions but also between religion and irreligion.

MR. JUSTICE BLACK *delivered the opinion of the Court.*

Article 37 of the Declaration of Rights of the Maryland Constitution provides:

"[N]o religious test ought ever to be required as a qualification for any office of profit or trust in this State, other than a declaration of belief in the existence of God...."

The appellant Torcaso was appointed to the office of Notary Public by the Governor of Maryland but was refused a commission to serve because he would not declare his belief in God....

There is, and can be, no dispute about the purpose or effect of the Maryland Declaration of Rights requirement before us—it sets up a religious test which was designed to and, if valid, does bar every person who refuses to declare a belief in God from holding a public "office of profit or trust" in Maryland. The power and authority of the State of Maryland thus is put on the side of one particular sort of believers—those who are willing to say they believe in "the existence of God." It is true that there is much historical precedent for such laws. Indeed, it was largely to escape religious test oaths and declarations that a great many of the early colonists left Europe and came here hoping to worship in their own way. It soon developed, however, that many of those who had fled to escape religious test oaths turned out to be perfectly willing, when they had the power to do so, to force dissenters from their faith to take test oaths in conformity with that faith. This brought on a host of laws in the new Colonies imposing burdens and disabilities of various kinds upon varied beliefs depending largely upon what group happened to be politically strong enough to legislate in favor of its own beliefs. The effect of all this was the formal or practical "establishment" of particular religious faiths in most of the Colonies, with consequent burdens imposed on the free exercise of the faiths of nonfavored believers.

... When our Constitution was adopted, the desire to put the people "securely beyond the reach" of religious test oaths brought about the inclusion in Article VI of that document of a provision that "no religious Test shall ever be required as a Qualification to any Office or public Trust under the United States." Article VI supports the accuracy of our observation in *Girouard v. United States*, that "[t]he test oath is abhorrent to our tradition." Not satisfied, however, with Article VI and other guarantees in the original Constitution, the First Congress proposed and the States very shortly thereafter adopted our Bill of Rights, including the First Amendment. That Amendment broke new constitutional ground in the protection it sought to afford to freedom of religion, speech, press, petition and assembly....

We repeat and again reaffirm that neither a State nor the Federal Government can constitutionally force a person "to profess a belief or disbelief in any religion." Neither can constitutionally pass laws or impose requirements which aid all religions as against non-believers, and neither can aid those religions based on a belief in the existence of God as against those religions founded on different beliefs. . . .

This Maryland religious test for public office unconstitutionally invades the appellant's freedom of belief and religion and therefore cannot be enforced against him.

The judgment of the Court of Appeals of Maryland is accordingly reversed and the cause is remanded for further proceedings not inconsistent with this opinion.

ENGEL v. VITALE

370 U.S. 421 (1962)

Opinion: Black, joined by Warren, Clark, Harlan, Brennan
Concurrence: Douglas
Dissent: Stewart

In this case, the Supreme Court declared the practice of school prayer led by a public school principal unconstitutional. As you read the case, ask whether the fact that an official led the prayer converted it into involuntary activity on the part of students. Should this question itself resolve the matter of whether the prayer constituted an establishment of religion—in other words, should it matter whether participation in the prayer was "involuntary" or not?

MR. JUSTICE BLACK *delivered the opinion of the Court.*

The respondent Board of Education of Union Free School District No. 9, New Hyde Park, New York, acting in its official capacity under state law, directed the School District's principal to cause the following prayer to be said aloud by each class in the presence of a teacher at the beginning of each school day:

> "Almighty God, we acknowledge our dependence upon Thee, and we beg Thy blessings upon us, our parents, our teachers and our Country."

This daily procedure was adopted on the recommendation of the State Board of Regents, a governmental agency created by the State Constitution to which the New York Legislature has granted broad supervisory, executive, and legislative powers over the State's public school system. These state officials composed the prayer which they recommended and published as a part of their "Statement on Moral and Spiritual Training in the Schools," saying: "We believe that this Statement will be subscribed to by all men and women of good will, and we call upon all of them to aid in giving life to our program." . . .

We think that by using its public school system to encourage recitation of the Regents' prayer, the State of New York has adopted a practice wholly inconsistent with the Establishment Clause. There can, of course, be no doubt that New York's program of daily classroom invocation of God's blessings as prescribed in the Regents' prayer is a religious activity. It is a solemn avowal of divine faith and supplication for the blessings of the Almighty. The nature of such a prayer has always been religious, none of the respondents has denied this and the trial court expressly so found. . . .

The petitioners contend among other things that the state laws requiring or permitting use of the Regents' prayer must be struck down as a violation of the Establishment Clause because that prayer was composed by governmental officials as a part of a governmental program to further religious beliefs. For this reason, petitioners argue, the State's use of the Regents' prayer in its public school system breaches the constitutional wall of separation between Church and State. We agree with that contention since we think that the constitutional prohibition against laws respecting an establishment of religion must at least mean that in this country it is no part of the business of government to compose official prayers for any group of the American people to recite as a part of a religious program carried on by government.

It is a matter of history that this very practice of establishing governmentally composed prayers for religious services was one of the reasons which caused many of our early colonists to leave England and seek religious freedom in America. The Book of Common Prayer, which was created under governmental direction and which was approved by Acts of Parliament in 1548 and 1549, set out in minute detail the accepted form and content of prayer and other religious ceremonies to be used in the established, tax-supported Church of England. The controversies over the Book and what should be its content repeatedly threatened to disrupt the peace of that country as the accepted forms of prayer in the established church changed with the views of the particular ruler that happened to be in control at the time. Powerful groups representing some of the varying religious views of the people struggled among themselves to impress their particular views upon the Government and obtain amendments of the Book more suitable to their respective notions of how religious services should be conducted in order that the official religious establishment would advance their particular religious beliefs. Other groups, lacking the necessary political power to influence the Government on the matter, decided to leave England and its established church and seek freedom in America from England's governmentally ordained and supported religion. . . .

By the time of the adoption of the Constitution, our history shows that there was a widespread awareness among many Americans of the dangers of a union of Church and State. . . . The Constitution was intended to avert a part of this danger by leaving the government of this country in the hands of the people rather than in the hands of any monarch. But this safeguard was not enough. Our Founders were no more willing to let the content of their prayers and their privilege of praying whenever they pleased be influenced by the ballot box than they were to let these vital matters of personal conscience depend upon the succession of monarchs. The First Amendment was added to the Constitution to stand as a guarantee that neither the power nor the prestige of the Federal Government would be used to control, support or influence the kinds of prayer the American people can say that the people's religions must not be subjected to the pressures of government for change each time a new political administration is elected to office. Under that Amendment's prohibition against governmental establishment of religion, as reinforced by the provisions of the Fourteenth Amendment, government in this country, be it state or federal, is without power to prescribe by law any particular form of prayer which is to be used as an official prayer in carrying on any program of governmentally sponsored religious activity.

There can be no doubt that New York's state prayer program officially establishes the religious beliefs embodied in the Regents' prayer. The respondents' argument to the contrary, which is largely based upon the contention that the Regents' prayer is "non-denominational" and the fact that the program, as modified and approved by state courts, does not require all pupils to recite the prayer but permits those who wish to do so to remain silent or be excused from the room, ignores the essential nature of the program's constitutional defects. Neither the fact that the prayer may be denominationally neutral nor the fact that its observance on the part of the students is voluntary can serve to free it from the limitations of the Establishment Clause, as it might from the Free Exercise Clause, of the First Amendment, both of which are operative against the States by virtue of the Fourteenth Amendment. Although these two clauses may in certain instances overlap, they forbid two quite different kinds of governmental encroachment upon religious freedom. The Establishment Clause, unlike the Free Exercise Clause, does not depend upon any showing of direct governmental compulsion and is violated by the enactment of laws which establish an official religion whether those laws operate directly to coerce nonobserving individuals or not. This is not to say, of course, that laws officially prescribing a particular form of religious worship do not involve coercion of such individuals. When the power, prestige and financial support of government is placed behind a particular religious belief, the indirect coercive pressure upon religious minorities to conform to the prevailing officially approved religion is plain. But the purposes underlying the Establishment Clause go much further than that. Its first and most immediate purpose rested on the belief that a union of government and religion tends to destroy government and to degrade religion. Another purpose of the Establishment Clause rested upon an awareness of the historical fact that governmentally established religions and religious persecutions go hand in hand. . . . It was in large part to get completely away from this sort of systematic religious persecution that the Founders brought into being our Nation, our Constitution, and our Bill of Rights with its prohibition against any governmental establishment of religion. The New York laws officially prescribing the Regents' prayer are inconsistent both with the purposes of the Establishment Clause and with the Establishment Clause itself.

It has been argued that to apply the Constitution in such a way as to prohibit state laws respecting an establishment of religious services in public schools is to indicate a hostility toward religion or toward prayer. Nothing, of course, could be more wrong. The history of man is inseparable from the history of religion. And perhaps it is not too much to say that since the beginning of that history many people have devoutly believed that "More things are wrought by prayer than this world dreams of." . . . It is neither sacrilegious nor antireligious to say that each separate government in this country should stay out of the business of writing or sanctioning official prayers and leave that purely religious function to the people themselves and to those the people choose to look to for religious guidance.

MR. JUSTICE STEWART, *dissenting.*

A local school board in New York has provided that those pupils who wish to do so may join in a brief prayer at the beginning of each school day, acknowledging their dependence upon God and asking His blessing upon them and upon their parents, their teachers, and their country. The Court today decides that in permitting this brief nondenominational prayer the school board has violated the Constitution of the United States. I think this decision is wrong. . . .

With all respect, I think the Court has misapplied a great constitutional principle. I cannot see how an "official religion" is established by letting those who want to say a prayer say it. On the contrary, I think that to deny the wish of these school children to join in reciting this prayer is to deny them the opportunity of sharing in the spiritual heritage of our Nation. . . .

At the opening of each day's Session of this Court we stand, while one of our officials invokes the protection of God. Since the days of John Marshall our Crier has said, "God save the United States and this Honorable Court." Both the Senate and the House of Representatives open their daily Sessions with prayer. Each of our Presidents, from George Washington to John F. Kennedy, has upon assuming his Office asked the protection and help of God. . . . Countless similar examples could be listed, but there is no need to belabor the obvious. It was all summed up by this Court just ten years ago in a single sentence: "We are a religious people whose institutions presuppose a Supreme Being." I do not believe that this Court, or the Congress, or the President has by the actions and practices I have mentioned established an "official religion" in violation of the Constitution. And I do not believe the State of New York has done so in this case. What each has done has been to recognize and to follow the deeply entrenched and highly cherished spiritual traditions of our Nation—traditions which come down to us from those who almost two hundred years ago avowed their "firm Reliance on the Protection of divine Providence" when they proclaimed the freedom and independence of this brave new world.

I dissent.

LEMON v. KURTZMAN

403 U.S. 602 (1971)

Opinion: Burger, joined by Black, Douglas, Harlan, Stewart, Blackmun and by Marshall in Nos. 569 and 570
Concurrence: Douglas, joined by Black and by Marshall in Nos. 569 and 570, filing a separate statement
Concurrence: Brennan
Partial Concurrence, Partial Dissent: White

We turn now to Lemon v. Kurtzman, *which outlines what is often considered the modern standard for evaluating whether a law "establishes" a religion. In reading this case, it is important to think about the ways in which the principles outlined in James Madison's* Remonstrance *might apply here. Does it matter that the funding policy in question in* Lemon v. Kurtzman *provides monetary support only to teachers of secular subjects, even though they are based in religious schools? This case is significant because the Court created the so-called* Lemon *test. According to this test, a state action must have a secular legislative purpose, must not have the primary effect of advancing or inhibiting religion, and must not result in "excessive government entanglement" with religion, in order for it to be valid under the First Amendment.*

In Lemon v. Kurtzman, *the Court decided that public payment for teachers in private (mostly Catholic) schools to teach secular subjects using the same materials as in public schools involved excessive government entanglement in religion. But, as you will see, in* Zelman v. Simmons-Harris, *the Court found constitutional a voucher program for private education in part because funding went directly to students, who could choose between a number of secular or religious private schools, rather than to teachers based in religious schools. It is important to note, however, that in this case the public schools in question were failing to provide an adequate education, and for this reason the state had a particularly strong reason for providing alternate sources of education. How important is this failure of secular alternatives?*

MR. CHIEF JUSTICE BURGER
delivered the opinion of the Court.

These two appeals raise questions as to Pennsylvania and Rhode Island statutes providing state aid to church-related elementary and secondary schools. Both statutes are challenged as violative of the Establishment and Free Exercise Clauses of the First Amendment and the Due Process Clause of the Fourteenth Amendment.

Pennsylvania has adopted a statutory program that provides financial support to non-public elementary and secondary schools by way of reimbursement for the cost of teachers' salaries, textbooks, and instructional materials in specified secular subjects. Rhode Island has adopted a statute under which the State pays directly to teachers in nonpublic elementary schools a supplement of 15% of their annual salary. Under each statute state aid has been given to church-related educational institutions. We hold that both statutes are unconstitutional. . . .

II

. . . The language of the Religion Clauses of the First Amendment is at best opaque,

particularly when compared with other portions of the Amendment. Its authors did not simply prohibit the establishment of a state church or a state religion, an area history shows they regarded as very important and fraught with great dangers. Instead they commanded that there should be "no law respecting an establishment of religion." A law may be one "respecting" the forbidden objective while falling short of its total realization. A law "respecting" the proscribed result, that is, the establishment of religion, is not always easily identifiable as one violative of the Clause. A given law might not establish a state religion but nevertheless be one "respecting" that end in the sense of being a step that could lead to such establishment and hence offend the First Amendment.

In the absence of precisely stated constitutional prohibitions, we must draw lines with reference to the three main evils against which the Establishment Clause was intended to afford protection: "sponsorship, financial support, and active involvement of the sovereign in religious activity." *Walz v. Tax Commission.*

Every analysis in this area must begin with consideration of the cumulative criteria developed by the Court over many years. Three such tests may be gleaned from our cases. First, the statute must have a secular legislative purpose; second, its principal or primary effect must be one that neither advances nor inhibits religion, *Board of Education v. Allen;* finally, the statute must not foster "an excessive government entanglement with religion."

Inquiry into the legislative purposes of the Pennsylvania and Rhode Island statutes affords no basis for a conclusion that the legislative intent was to advance religion. On the contrary, the statutes themselves clearly state that they are intended to enhance the quality of the secular education in all schools covered by the compulsory attendance laws. There is no reason to believe the legislatures meant anything else. A State always has a legitimate concern for maintaining minimum standards in all schools it allows to operate. As in *Allen*, we find nothing here that undermines the stated legislative intent; it must therefore be accorded appropriate deference.

In *Allen* the Court acknowledged that secular and religious teachings were not necessarily so intertwined that secular textbooks furnished to students by the State were in fact instrumental in the teaching of religion. The legislatures of Rhode Island and Pennsylvania have concluded that secular and religious education are identifiable and separable. In the abstract we have no quarrel with this conclusion.

The two legislatures, however, have also recognized that church-related elementary and secondary schools have a significant religious mission and that a substantial portion of their activities is religiously oriented. They have therefore sought to create statutory restrictions designed to guarantee the separation between secular and religious educational functions and to ensure that State financial aid supports only the former. All these provisions are precautions taken in candid recognition that these programs approached, even if they did not intrude upon, the forbidden areas under the Religion Clauses. We need not decide whether these legislative precautions restrict the principal or primary effect of the programs to the point where they do not offend the Religion Clauses, for we conclude that the cumulative impact of the entire relationship arising under the statutes in each State involves excessive entanglement between government and religion.

III

In order to determine whether the government entanglement with religion is excessive, we must examine the character and purposes of the institutions that are benefited, the nature of the aid that the State provides, and the resulting relationship between the government and the religious authority. Mr. Justice Harlan, in a separate opinion in *Walz*, echoed the classic warning as to "programs, whose very nature is apt to entangle the state in details of administration. . . ." Here we find that both statutes foster an impermissible degree of entanglement. . . .

IV

A broader base of entanglement of yet a different character is presented by the divisive political potential of these state programs. In a community where such a large number of pupils are served by church-related schools, it can be assumed that state assistance will entail considerable political activity. Partisans of parochial schools, understandably concerned with rising costs and sincerely dedicated to both the religious and secular educational missions of their schools, will inevitably champion this cause and promote political action to achieve their goals. Those who oppose state aid, whether for constitutional, religious, or fiscal reasons, will inevitably respond and employ all of the usual political campaign techniques to prevail. Candidates will be forced to declare and voters to choose. It would be unrealistic to ignore the fact that many people confronted with issues of this kind will find their votes aligned with their faith.

Ordinarily political debate and division, however vigorous or even partisan, are normal and healthy manifestations of our democratic system of government, but political division along religious lines was one of the principal evils against which the First Amendment was intended to protect. The potential divisiveness of such conflict is a threat to the normal political process. To have States or communities divide on the issues presented by state aid to parochial schools would tend to confuse [and obscure] other issues of great urgency. We have an expanding array of vexing issues, local and national, domestic and international, to debate and divide on. It conflicts with our whole history and tradition to permit questions of the Religion Clauses to assume such importance in our legislatures and in our elections that they could divert attention from the myriad issues and problems that confront every level of government. The highways of church and state relationships are not likely to be one-way streets, and the Constitution's authors sought to protect religious worship from the pervasive power of government. The history of many countries attests to the hazards of religion's intruding into the political arena or of political power intruding into the legitimate and free exercise of religious belief. . . .

V

In *Walz* it was argued that a tax exemption for places of religious worship would prove to be the first step in an inevitable progression leading to the establishment of state churches and state religion. That claim could not stand up against more than 200 years of virtually universal practice imbedded in our colonial experience and continuing into the present.

The progression argument, however, is more persuasive here. We have no long history of state aid to church-related educational institutions comparable to 200 years of tax exemption for churches. Indeed, the state programs before us today represent something of an innovation. We have already noted that modern governmental programs have self-perpetuating and self-expanding propensities. These internal pressures are only enhanced when the schemes involve institutions whose legitimate needs are growing and whose interests have substantial political support. Nor can we fail to see that in constitutional adjudication some steps, which when taken were thought to approach "the verge," have become the platform for yet further steps. A certain momentum develops in constitutional theory and it can be a "downhill thrust" easily set in motion but difficult to retard or stop. Development by momentum is not invariably bad; indeed, it is the way the common law has grown, but it is a force to be recognized and reckoned with. The dangers are increased by the difficulty of perceiving in advance exactly where the "verge" of the precipice lies. As well as constituting an independent evil against which the Religion Clauses were intended to protect, involvement or entanglement between government and religion serves as a warning signal.

Finally, nothing we have said can be construed to disparage the role of church-related elementary and secondary schools in our national life. Their contribution has been and is enormous. Nor do we ignore their economic plight in a period of rising costs and expanding need. Taxpayers generally have been spared vast sums by the maintenance of these educational institutions by religious organizations, largely by the gifts of faithful adherents.

The merit and benefits of these schools, however, are not the issue before us in these cases. The sole question is whether state aid to these schools can be squared with the dictates of the Religion Clauses. Under our system the choice has been made that government is to be entirely excluded from the area of religious instruction and churches excluded from the affairs of government. The Constitution decrees that religion must be a private matter for the individual, the family, and the institutions of private choice, and that while some involvement and entanglement are inevitable, lines must be drawn.

The judgment of the Rhode Island District Court in No. 569 and No. 570 is affirmed. The judgment of the Pennsylvania District Court in No. 89 is reversed, and the case is remanded for further proceedings consistent with this opinion.

MARSH v. CHAMBERS

463 U.S. 783 (1983)

Opinion: Burger, joined by White, Blackmun, Powell, Rehnquist, O'Connor
Dissent: Brennan, joined by Marshall
Dissent: Stevens

For more than ten years, the Court applied the test articulated in Lemon v. Kurtzman *consistently. In declaring constitutional the longstanding practice in legislatures throughout the nation of opening their sessions with a prayer,* Marsh v. Chambers *did not clearly invoke the test. Does the Court depart from* Lemon v. Kurtzman *here? If so, how? Also, if it did depart from* Lemon v. Kurtzman, *should it have provided a rationale for doing so? As you read this case, consider whether legislative prayer could have been upheld under the* Lemon *test had the Court applied it. Additionally, as you will see,* Marsh v. Chambers *was the beginning of a long line of modern Establishment Clause cases that did not clearly rely on the* Lemon *test.*

CHIEF JUSTICE BURGER *delivered the opinion of the Court.*

The question presented is whether the Nebraska Legislature's practice of opening each legislative day with a prayer by a chaplain paid by the State violates the Establishment Clause of the First Amendment....

II

The opening of sessions of legislative and other deliberative public bodies with prayer is deeply embedded in the history and tradition of this country. From colonial times through the founding of the Republic and ever since, the practice of legislative prayer has coexisted with the principles of disestablishment and religious freedom. In the very courtrooms in which the United States District Judge and later three Circuit Judges heard and decided this case, the proceedings opened with an announcement that concluded, "God save the United States and this Honorable Court." The same invocation occurs at all sessions of this Court.

The tradition in many of the Colonies was, of course, linked to an established church, but the Continental Congress, beginning in 1774, adopted the traditional procedure of opening its sessions with a prayer offered by a paid chaplain. Although prayers were not offered during the Constitutional Convention, the First Congress, as one of its early items of business, adopted the policy of selecting a chaplain to open each session with prayer. Thus, on April 7, 1789, the Senate appointed a committee "to take under consideration the manner of electing Chaplains." On April 9, 1789, a similar committee was appointed by the House of Representatives. On April 25, 1789, the Senate elected its first chaplain; the House followed suit on May 1, 1789. A statute providing for the payment of these chaplains was enacted into law on September 22, 1789.

On September 25, 1789, three days after Congress authorized the appointment of paid chaplains, final agreement was reached on the language of the Bill of Rights. Clearly the men who wrote the First Amendment Religion Clauses did not view paid legislative chaplains and opening prayers as a violation of that Amendment, for the practice of opening sessions with prayer has continued without interruption ever since that early session of Congress. It has also been followed consistently in most of the states, including Nebraska, where the institution of opening legislative sessions with prayer was adopted even before the State attained statehood.

Standing alone, historical patterns cannot justify contemporary violations of constitutional guarantees, but there is far more here than simply historical patterns. In this context, historical evidence sheds light not only on what the draftsmen intended the Establishment Clause to mean, but also on how they thought that Clause applied to the practice authorized by the First Congress—their actions reveal their intent. An Act

> "passed by the first Congress assembled under the Constitution, many of whose members had taken part in framing that instrument, . . . is contemporaneous and weighty evidence of its true meaning." *Wisconsin v. Pelican Ins. Co.*

In *Walz v. Tax Comm'n*, we considered the weight to be accorded to history:

> "It is obviously correct that no one acquires a vested or protected right in violation of the Constitution by long use, even when that span of time covers our entire national existence and indeed predates it. Yet an unbroken practice . . . is not something to be lightly cast aside." . . .

This unique history leads us to accept the interpretation of the First Amendment draftsmen who saw no real threat to the Establishment Clause arising from a practice of prayer similar to that now challenged. We conclude that legislative prayer presents no more potential for establishment than the provision of school transportation, *Everson v. Board of Education*, beneficial grants for higher education, *Tilton v. Richardson*, or tax exemptions for religious organizations, *Walz*. . . .

In light of the unambiguous and unbroken history of more than 200 years, there can be no doubt that the practice of opening legislative sessions with prayer has become part of the fabric of our society. To invoke Divine guidance on a public body entrusted with making the laws is not, in these circumstances, an "establishment" of religion or a step toward establishment; it is simply a tolerable acknowledgment of beliefs widely held among the people of this country. As Justice Douglas observed, "[w]e are a religious people whose institutions presuppose a Supreme Being." *Zorach v. Clauson.*

III

. . . We do not doubt the sincerity of those, who like respondent, believe that to have prayer in this context risks the beginning of the establishment the Founding Fathers feared. But this concern is not well founded, for as Justice Goldberg aptly observed in his concurring opinion in *Abington* . . . :

> "It is of course true that great consequences can grow from small beginnings, but the measure of constitutional adjudication is the ability and willingness to distinguish between real threat and mere shadow."

The unbroken practice for two centuries in the National Congress and for more than a century in Nebraska and in many other states gives abundant assurance that there is no real threat "while this Court sits," *Panhandle Oil Co. v. Mississippi ex rel. Knox* (Holmes, J., dissenting).

The judgment of the Court of Appeals is Reversed.

JUSTICE BRENNAN, *with whom* **JUSTICE MARSHALL** *joins, dissenting.*

The Court today has written a narrow and, on the whole, careful opinion. In effect, the Court holds that officially sponsored legislative prayer, primarily on account of its "unique history," is generally exempted from the First Amendment's prohibition against "an establishment of religion." . . .

I

The Court makes no pretense of subjecting Nebraska's practice of legislative prayer to any of the formal "tests" that have traditionally structured our inquiry under the Establishment Clause. That it fails to do so is, in a sense, a good thing, for it simply confirms that the Court is carving out an exception to the Establishment Clause rather than reshaping Establishment Clause doctrine to accommodate legislative prayer. For my purposes, however, I must begin by demonstrating what should be obvious: that, if the Court were to judge legislative prayer through the unsentimental eye of our settled doctrine, it would have to strike it down as a clear violation of the Establishment Clause.

The most commonly cited formulation of prevailing Establishment Clause doctrine is found in *Lemon v. Kurtzman*:

> "Every analysis in this area must begin with consideration of the cumulative criteria developed by the Court over many years. Three such tests may be gleaned from our cases. First, the statute [at issue] must have a secular legislative purpose; second, its principal or primary effect must be one that neither advances nor inhibits religion; finally, the statute must not foster 'an excessive government entanglement with religion.'"

That the "purpose" of legislative prayer is pre-eminently religious rather than secular seems to me to be self-evident. "To invoke Divine guidance on a public body entrusted with making the laws," is nothing but a religious act. Moreover, whatever secular functions legislative prayer might play—formally opening the legislative session, getting the members of the body to quiet down, and imbuing them with a sense of seriousness and high purpose—could so plainly be performed in a purely nonreligious fashion that to claim a secular purpose for the prayer is an insult to the perfectly honorable individuals who instituted and continue the practice.

The "primary effect" of legislative prayer is also clearly religious. As we said in the context of officially sponsored prayers in the public schools, "prescribing a particular form of religious worship," even if the individuals involved have the choice not to participate, places "indirect coercive pressure upon religious minorities to conform to the prevailing officially approved religion. . . ." *Engel v. Vitale.* More importantly, invocations in Nebraska's legislative halls explicitly link religious belief and observance to the power and prestige of the State. "[T]he mere appearance of a joint exercise of legislative authority by Church and State provides a significant symbolic benefit to religion in the minds of some by reason of the power conferred." *Larkin v. Grendel's Den, Inc.*

Finally, there can be no doubt that the practice of legislative prayer leads to excessive "entanglement" between the State and religion. *Lemon* pointed out that "entanglement" can take two forms: First, a state statute or program might involve the state impermissibly in monitoring and overseeing religious affairs. In the case of legislative prayer, the process of choosing a "suitable" chaplain, whether on a permanent or rotating basis, and insuring that the chaplain limits himself or herself to "suitable" prayers, involves precisely the sort of supervision that agencies of government should if at all possible avoid.

Second, excessive "entanglement" might arise out of "the divisive political potential" of a state statute or program.

> "Ordinarily political debate and division, however vigorous or even partisan, are normal and healthy manifestations of our democratic system of government, but political division along religious lines was one of the principal evils against which the First Amendment was intended to protect. The potential divisiveness of such conflict is a threat to the normal political process." Ibid.

In this case, this second aspect of entanglement is also clear. The controversy between Senator Chambers and his colleagues, which had reached the stage of difficulty and rancor long before this lawsuit was brought, has split the Nebraska Legislature precisely on issues of religion and religious conformity. The record in this case also reports a series of instances, involving legislators other than Senator Chambers, in which invocations by Reverend Palmer and others led to controversy along religious lines. And in general, the history of legislative prayer has been far more eventful—and divisive—than a hasty reading of the Court's opinion might indicate.

In sum, I have no doubt that, if any group of law students were asked to apply the principles of *Lemon* to the question of legislative prayer, they would nearly unanimously find the practice to be unconstitutional.

LYNCH v. DONNELLY

465 U.S. 668 (1984)

Opinion: Burger, joined by White, Powell, Rehnquist, O'Connor
Concurrence: O'Connor
Dissent: Brennan, joined by Marshall, Blackmun, Stevens
Dissent: Blackmun, joined by Stevens

Many towns have historically celebrated the Christmas holiday by displaying a crèche, or a religious nativity scene, in a town square or other public space. In Lynch v. Donnelly, *the Court considers whether such a display in Pawtucket, Rhode Island, violates the Establishment Clause because it endorses Christianity. In reading this case, consider in what ways the crèche is different from or the same as a Christmas tree. How would the decision bear upon the public display of decorated trees during Christmas? Keep this question in mind when reading* Allegheny v. ACLU, *which concerns, on the one hand, the display of a crèche, and on the other, the display of a Christmas tree and a menorah, a symbol of the Jewish holiday of Chanukah. Is there a significant difference between these various displays in these two cases? Why are certain displays found unconstitutional and others not? Another question concerns the comparison between the two crèches in* Lynch v. Donnelly *and* Allegheny v. ACLU. *What does the Court think is different between these two crèches? Is the distinction between the two constitutionally significant?*

This case is also important because Justice Sandra Day O'Connor, for a long time the swing vote on the Court in Establishment Clause cases, articulates her "endorsement" test. In her concurrence, Justice O'Connor insists that the test is merely a "clarification" of the Lemon *test. Consider whether you agree, or whether you instead think it is a more sweeping change in jurisprudence.*

CHIEF JUSTICE BURGER *delivered the opinion of the Court.*

We granted certiorari to decide whether the Establishment Clause of the First Amendment prohibits a municipality from including a crèche, or Nativity scene, in its annual Christmas display.

I

Each year, in cooperation with the downtown retail merchants' association, the city of Pawtucket, R.I., erects a Christmas display as part of its observance of the Christmas holiday season. The display is situated in a park owned by a nonprofit organization and located in the heart of the shopping district. The display is essentially like those to be found in hundreds of towns or cities across the Nation—often on public grounds—during the Christmas season. The Pawtucket display comprises many of the figures and decorations traditionally associated with Christmas, including, among other things, a Santa Claus house, reindeer pulling Santa's sleigh, candy-striped poles, a Christmas tree, carolers, cutout figures representing such characters as a clown, an elephant, and a teddy bear, hundreds of colored lights, a large banner that reads "SEASONS GREETINGS," and the crèche at issue here. All components of this display are owned by the city.

The crèche, which has been included in the display for 40 or more years, consists of the traditional figures, including the Infant Jesus, Mary and Joseph, angels, shepherds, kings, and animals, all ranging in height from 5" to 5'. In 1973, when the present crèche was acquired, it cost the city $1,365; it now is valued at $200. The erection and dismantling of the crèche costs the city about $20 per year; nominal expenses are incurred in lighting the crèche. No money has been expended on its maintenance for the past 10 years.

Respondents, Pawtucket residents and individual members of the Rhode Island affiliate of the American Civil Liberties Union, and the affiliate itself, brought this action in the United States District Court for Rhode Island, challenging the city's inclusion of the crèche in the annual display. The District Court held that the city's inclusion of the crèche in the display violates the Establishment Clause, which is binding on the states through the Fourteenth Amendment. The District Court found that, by including the crèche in the Christmas display, the city has "tried to endorse and promulgate religious beliefs," and that "erection of the crèche has the real and substantial effect of affiliating the City with the Christian beliefs that the crèche represents." This "appearance of official sponsorship," it believed, "confers more than a remote and incidental benefit on Christianity." Last, although the court acknowledged the absence of administrative entanglement, it found that excessive entanglement has been fostered as a result of the political divisiveness of including the crèche in the celebration. The city was permanently enjoined from including the crèche in the display.

A divided panel of the Court of Appeals for the First Circuit affirmed. We granted certiorari, and we reverse.

II

A

This Court has explained that the purpose of the Establishment and Free Exercise Clauses of the First Amendment is "to prevent, as far as possible, the intrusion of either [the church or the state] into the precincts of the other." *Lemon v. Kurtzman*.

At the same time, however, the Court has recognized that

"total separation is not possible in an absolute sense. Some relationship between government and religious organizations is inevitable." Ibid.

In every Establishment Clause case, we must reconcile the inescapable tension between the objective of preventing unnecessary intrusion of either the church or the state upon the other, and the reality that, as the Court has so often noted, total separation of the two is not possible.

The Court has sometimes described the Religion Clauses as erecting a "wall" between church and state. The concept of a "wall" of separation is a useful figure of speech probably deriving from views of Thomas Jefferson. The metaphor has served as a reminder that the Establishment Clause forbids an established church or anything approaching it. But the metaphor itself is not a wholly accurate description of the practical aspects of the relationship that in fact exists between church and state.

No significant segment of our society and no institution within it can exist in a vacuum or in total or absolute isolation from all the other parts, much less from government. "It has never been thought either possible or desirable to enforce a regime of total separation. . . ." *Cmte. for Public Educ. & Relig. Liberty v. Nyquist*. Nor does the Constitution require complete separation of church and state; it affirmatively mandates accommodation, not merely tolerance, of all religions, and forbids hostility toward any. (*Zorach v. Clauson*; *Illinois ex rel. McCollum v. Bd. of Educ.*). Anything less would require the "callous indifference" we have said was never intended by the Establishment Clause. *Zorach*. Indeed, we have observed, such hostility would

bring us into "war with our national tradition as embodied in the First Amendment's guaranty of the free exercise of religion." *McCollum*.

B

The Court's interpretation of the Establishment Clause has comported with what history reveals was the contemporaneous understanding of its guarantees. A significant example of the contemporaneous understanding of that Clause is found in the events of the first week of the First Session of the First Congress in 1789. In the very week that Congress approved the Establishment Clause as part of the Bill of Rights for submission to the states, it enacted legislation providing for paid Chaplains for the House and Senate. In *Marsh v. Chambers*, we noted that 17 Members of that First Congress had been Delegates to the Constitutional Convention where freedom of speech, press, and religion and antagonism toward an established church were subjects of frequent discussion. We saw no conflict with the Establishment Clause when Nebraska employed members of the clergy as official legislative Chaplains to give opening prayers at sessions of the state legislature. The interpretation of the Establishment Clause by Congress in 1789 takes on special significance in light of the Court's emphasis that the First Congress

"was a Congress whose constitutional decisions have always been regarded, as they should be regarded, as of the greatest weight in the interpretation of that fundamental instrument," *Myers v. United States*.

It is clear that neither the 17 draftsmen of the Constitution who were Members of the First Congress, nor the Congress of 1789, saw any establishment problem in the employment of congressional Chaplains to offer daily prayers in the Congress, a practice that has continued for nearly two centuries. It would be difficult to identify a more striking example of the accommodation of religious belief intended by the Framers. . . .

III

. . . The Court consistently has declined to take a rigid, absolutist view of the Establishment Clause. We have refused "to construe the Religion Clauses with a literalness that would undermine the ultimate constitutional objective as illuminated by history." *Walz v. Tax Comm'n*. In our modern, complex society, whose traditions and constitutional underpinnings rest on and encourage diversity and pluralism in all areas, an absolutist approach in applying the Establishment Clause is simplistic and has been uniformly rejected by the Court.

Rather than mechanically invalidating all governmental conduct or statutes that confer benefits or give special recognition to religion in general or to one faith—as an absolutist approach would dictate—the Court has scrutinized challenged legislation or official conduct to determine whether, in reality, it establishes a religion or religious faith, or tends to do so. See *Walz*. Joseph Story wrote a century and a half ago:

> "The real object of the [First] Amendment was . . . to prevent any national ecclesiastical establishment, which should give to an hierarchy the exclusive patronage of the national government."

In each case, the inquiry calls for line-drawing; no fixed, per se rule can be framed. The Establishment Clause like the Due Process Clauses is not a precise, detailed provision in a legal code capable of ready application. The purpose of the Establishment Clause "was to state an objective, not to write a statute." *Walz*. The line between permissible relationships and those barred by the Clause can no more be straight and unwavering than due process can be defined in a single stroke or phrase or test. The Clause erects a "blurred, indistinct, and variable barrier depending on all the circumstances of a particular relationship." *Lemon*.

In the line-drawing process we have often found it useful to inquire whether the challenged law or conduct has a secular purpose, whether its principal or primary effect is to advance or inhibit religion, and whether it creates an excessive entanglement of government with religion. *Lemon*. But, we have repeatedly emphasized our unwillingness to be confined to any single test or criterion in this sensitive area. In two cases, the Court did not even apply the *Lemon* "test." We did not, for example, consider that analysis relevant in *Marsh v. Chambers*. Nor did we find *Lemon* useful in *Larson v. Valente*, where there was substantial evidence of overt discrimination against a particular church. . . .

The narrow question is whether there is a secular purpose for Pawtucket's display of the crèche. The display is sponsored by the city to celebrate the Holiday and to depict the origins of that Holiday. These are legitimate secular purposes. The District Court's inference, drawn from the religious nature of the crèche, that the city has no secular purpose was, on this record, clearly erroneous. . . .

We are unable to discern a greater aid to religion deriving from inclusion of the crèche than from these benefits and endorsements previously held not violative of the Establishment Clause. What was said about the legislative prayers in *Marsh*, and implied about the Sunday Closing Laws in *McGowan* is true of the city's inclusion of the crèche: its "reason or effect merely happens to coincide or harmonize with the tenets of some . . . religions." *McGowan*.

. . . The dissent asserts some observers may perceive that the city has aligned itself with the Christian faith by including a Christian symbol in its display and that this serves to advance religion. We can assume, *arguendo*, that the display advances religion in a sense; but our precedents plainly contemplate that on occasion some advancement of religion will result from governmental action. The Court has made it abundantly clear, however, that "not every law that confers an 'indirect,' 'remote,' or 'incidental' benefit upon [religion] is, for that reason alone, constitutionally invalid." *Nyquist*. Here, whatever benefit there is to one faith or religion or to all religions, is indirect, remote, and incidental; display of the crèche is no more an advancement or endorsement of religion than the Congressional and Executive recognition of the origins of the Holiday itself as "Christ's Mass," or the exhibition of literally hundreds of religious paintings in governmentally supported museums.

The District Court found that there had been no administrative entanglement between religion and state resulting from the city's ownership and use of the crèche. . . . Entanglement is a question of kind and degree. In this case, however, there is no reason to disturb the District Court's finding on the absence of administrative entanglement. . . .

The Court of Appeals correctly observed that this Court has not held that political divisiveness alone can serve to invalidate otherwise permissible conduct. And we decline to so hold today. This case does not involve a direct subsidy to church-sponsored schools or colleges, or other religious institutions, and hence no inquiry into potential political divisiveness is even called for. In any event, apart from this litigation there is no evidence of political friction or divisiveness over the crèche in the 40-year history of Pawtucket's Christmas celebration. The District Court stated that the inclusion of the crèche for the 40-years has been "marked by no apparent dissension" and that the display has had a "calm history." Curiously, it went on to hold that the political divisiveness engendered by this lawsuit was evidence of excessive entanglement. A litigant cannot, by the very act of commencing a lawsuit, however, create the appearance of divisiveness and then exploit it as evidence of entanglement.

We are satisfied that the city has a secular purpose for including the crèche, that the city has not impermissibly advanced religion, and that including the crèche does not create excessive entanglement between religion and government.

IV

Justice Brennan describes the crèche as a "re-creation of an event that lies at the heart of Christian faith." The crèche, like a painting, is passive; admittedly it is a reminder of the origins of Christmas. Even the traditional, purely secular displays extant at Christmas, with or without a crèche, would inevitably recall the religious nature of the Holiday. The display engenders a friendly community spirit of goodwill in keeping with the season. The crèche may well have special meaning to those whose faith includes the celebration of religious Masses, but none who sense the origins of the Christmas celebration would fail to be aware of its religious implications. That the display brings people into the central city, and serves commercial interests and benefits merchants and their employees, does not, as the dissent points out, determine the character of the display. That a prayer invoking Divine guidance in Congress is preceded and followed by debate and partisan conflict over taxes, budgets, national defense, and myriad mundane subjects, for example, has never been thought to demean or taint the sacredness of the invocation.

Of course the crèche is identified with one religious faith but no more so than the examples we have set out from prior cases in which we found no conflict with the Establishment Clause. It would be ironic, however, if the inclusion of a single symbol of a particular historic religious event, as part of a celebration acknowledged in the Western World for 20 centuries, and in this country by the people, by the Executive Branch, by the Congress, and the courts for 2 centuries, would so "taint" the city's exhibit as to render it violative of the Establishment Clause. To forbid the use of this one passive symbol—the crèche—at the very time people are taking note of the season with Christmas hymns and carols in public schools and other public places, and while the Congress and legislatures open sessions with prayers by paid chaplains, would be a stilted overreaction contrary to our history and to our holdings. If the presence of the crèche in this display violates the Establishment Clause, a host of other forms of taking official note of Christmas, and of our religious heritage, are equally offensive to the Constitution. . . .

VI

We hold that, notwithstanding the religious significance of the crèche, the city of Pawtucket has not violated the Establishment Clause of the First Amendment. Accordingly, the judgment of the Court of Appeals is reversed.

JUSTICE O'CONNOR, *concurring.*

I concur in the opinion of the Court. I write separately to suggest a clarification of our Establishment Clause doctrine. The suggested approach leads to the same result in this case as that taken by the Court, and the Court's opinion, as I read it, is consistent with my analysis.

I

The Establishment Clause prohibits government from making adherence to a religion relevant in any way to a person's standing in the political community. Government can run afoul of that prohibition in two principal ways. One is excessive entanglement with religious institutions, which may interfere with the independence of the institutions, give the institutions access to government or governmental powers not fully shared by nonadherents of the religion, and foster the creation of political constituencies defined along religious lines. The second and more direct infringement is government endorsement or disapproval of religion. Endorsement sends a message to nonadherents that they are outsiders, not full members of the political community, and an accompanying message to adherents that they are insiders, favored members of the political community. Disapproval sends the opposite message.

Our prior cases have used the three-part test articulated in *Lemon v. Kurtzman*, as a guide to detecting these two forms of unconstitutional government action. It has never been entirely clear, however, how the three parts of the test relate to the principles enshrined in the Establishment Clause. Focusing on institutional entanglement and on endorsement or disapproval of religion clarifies the *Lemon* test as an analytical device. . . .

III

The central issue in this case is whether Pawtucket has endorsed Christianity by its display of the crèche. To answer that question, we must examine both what Pawtucket intended to communicate in displaying the crèche and what message the city's display actually conveyed. The purpose and effect prongs of the *Lemon* test represent these two aspects of the meaning of the city's action.

The meaning of a statement to its audience depends both on the intention of the speaker and on the "objective" meaning of the statement in the community. Some listeners need not rely solely on the words themselves in discerning the speaker's intent: they can judge the intent by, for example, examining the context of the statement or asking questions of the speaker. Other listeners do not have or will not seek access to such evidence of intent. They will rely instead on the words themselves; for them the message actually conveyed may be something not actually intended. If the audience is large, as it always is when government "speaks" by word or deed, some portion of the audience will inevitably receive a message determined by the "objective" content of the statement, and some portion will inevitably receive the intended message. Examination of both the subjective and the objective components of the message communicated by a government action is therefore necessary to determine whether the action carries a forbidden meaning.

The purpose prong of the *Lemon* test asks whether government's actual purpose is to endorse or disapprove of religion. The effect prong asks whether, irrespective of government's actual purpose, the practice under review in fact conveys a message of endorsement or disapproval. An affirmative answer to either question should render the challenged practice invalid.

A

The purpose prong of the *Lemon* test requires that a government activity have a secular purpose. That requirement is not satisfied, however, by the mere existence of some secular purpose, however dominated by religious purposes. In *Stone v.*

Graham, for example, the Court held that posting copies of the Ten Commandments in schools violated the purpose prong of the *Lemon* test, yet the State plainly had some secular objectives, such as instilling most of the values of the Ten Commandments and illustrating their connection to our legal system. The proper inquiry under the purpose prong of *Lemon*, I submit, is whether the government intends to convey a message of endorsement or disapproval of religion.

Applying that formulation to this case, I would find that Pawtucket did not intend to convey any message of endorsement of Christianity or disapproval of non-Christian religions. The evident purpose of including the crèche in the larger display was not promotion of the religious content of the crèche but celebration of the public holiday through its traditional symbols. Celebration of public holidays, which have cultural significance even if they also have religious aspects, is a legitimate secular purpose.

The District Court's finding that the display of the crèche had no secular purpose was based on erroneous reasoning. The District Court believed that it should ascertain the city's purpose in displaying the crèche separate and apart from the general purpose in setting up the display. It also found that, because the tradition-celebrating purpose was suspect in the court's eyes, the city's use of an unarguably religious symbol "raises an inference" of intent to endorse. When viewed in light of correct legal principles, the District Court's finding of unlawful purpose was clearly erroneous.

B

Focusing on the evil of government endorsement or disapproval of religion makes clear that the effect prong of the *Lemon* test is properly interpreted not to require invalidation of a government practice merely because it in fact causes, even as a primary effect, advancement or inhibition of religion. The laws upheld in *Walz v. Tax Comm'n*, (tax exemption for religious, educational, and charitable organizations), in *McGowan v. Maryland*, (mandatory Sunday closing law), and in *Zorach v. Clauson* (released time from school for off-campus religious instruction), had such effects, but they did not violate the Establishment Clause. What is crucial is that a government practice not have the effect of communicating a message of government endorsement or disapproval of religion. It is only practices having that effect, whether intentionally or unintentionally, that make religion relevant, in reality or public perception, to status in the political community.

Pawtucket's display of its crèche, I believe, does not communicate a message that the government intends to endorse the Christian beliefs represented by the crèche. Although the religious and indeed sectarian significance of the crèche, as the District Court found, is not neutralized by the setting, the overall holiday setting changes what viewers may fairly understand to be the purpose of the display—as a typical museum setting, though not neutralizing the religious content of a religious painting, negates any message of endorsement of that content. The display celebrates a public holiday, and no one contends that declaration of that holiday is understood to be an endorsement of religion. The holiday itself has very strong secular components and traditions. Government celebration of the holiday, which is extremely common, generally is not understood to endorse the religious content of the holiday, just as government celebration of Thanksgiving is not so understood. The crèche is a traditional symbol of the holiday that is very commonly displayed along with purely secular symbols, as it was in Pawtucket.

These features combine to make the government's display of the crèche in this particular physical setting no more an endorsement of religion than such governmental "acknow-

ledgements" of religion as legislative prayers of the type approved in *Marsh v. Chambers*, government declaration of Thanksgiving as a public holiday, printing of "In God We Trust" on coins, and opening court sessions with "God save the United States and this honorable court." Those government acknowledgments of religion serve, in the only ways reasonably possible in our culture, the legitimate secular purposes of solemnizing public occasions, expressing confidence in the future, and encouraging the recognition of what is worthy of appreciation in society. For that reason, and because of their history and ubiquity, those practices are not understood as conveying government approval of particular religious beliefs. The display of the crèche likewise serves a secular purpose—celebration of a public holiday with traditional symbols. It cannot fairly be understood to convey a message of government endorsement of religion. It is significant in this regard that the crèche display apparently caused no political divisiveness prior to the filing of this lawsuit, although Pawtucket had incorporated the crèche in its annual Christmas display for some years. For these reasons, I conclude that Pawtucket's display of the crèche does not have the effect of communicating endorsement of Christianity.

JUSTICE BRENNAN, *with whom* **JUSTICE MARSHALL**, **JUSTICE BLACKMUN**, *and* **JUSTICE STEVENS** *join, dissenting.*

. . . After reviewing the Court's opinion, I am convinced that this case appears hard not because the principles of decision are obscure, but because the Christmas holiday seems so familiar and agreeable. Although the Court's reluctance to disturb a community's chosen method of celebrating such an agreeable holiday is understandable, that cannot justify the Court's departure from controlling precedent. In my view, Pawtucket's maintenance and display at public expense of a symbol as distinctively sectarian as a crèche simply cannot be squared with our prior cases. And it is plainly contrary to the purposes and values of the Establishment Clause to pretend, as the Court does, that the otherwise secular setting of Pawtucket's nativity scene dilutes in some fashion the crèche's singular religiosity, or that the city's annual display reflects nothing more than an "acknowledgment" of our shared national heritage. Neither the character of the Christmas holiday itself nor our heritage of religious expression supports this result. . . .

A

. . . The "primary effect" of including a nativity scene in the city's display is, as the District Court found, to place the government's imprimatur of approval on the particular religious beliefs exemplified by the crèche. Those who believe in the message of the nativity receive the unique and exclusive benefit of public recognition and approval of their views. For many, the city's decision to include the crèche as part of its extensive and costly efforts to celebrate Christmas can only mean that the prestige of the government has been conferred on the beliefs associated with the crèche, thereby providing "a significant symbolic benefit to religion. . . ." *Larkin v. Grendel's Den, Inc., supra*, at 125-126. The effect on minority religious groups, as well as on those who may reject all religion, is to convey the message that their views are not similarly worthy of public recognition nor entitled to public support. It was precisely this sort of religious chauvinism that the Establishment Clause was intended forever to prohibit. . . .

IV

. . . But the city's action should be recognized for what it is: a coercive, though perhaps small, step toward establishing the sectarian preferences of the majority at the expense of the minority, accomplished by placing public facilities and funds in support of the religious symbolism and theological tidings that the crèche conveys. . . .

I dissent.

COUNTY OF ALLEGHENY v. ACLU
492 U.S. 573 (1989)

Opinion: Blackmun, joined by Brennan, Marshall, Stevens, O'Connor in Parts III-A, IV, and V, by Stevens, O'Connor in Parts I and II, by Stevens in Part III-B, by O'Connor in Part VII

Concurrence: O'Connor, joined by Brennan, Stevens in Part II

Partial Concurrence, Partial Dissent: Brennan, joined by Marshall, Stevens

Partial Concurrence, Partial Dissent: Stevens, joined by Brennan, Marshall

Partial Concurrence, Partial Dissent: Kennedy, joined by Rehnquist, White, Scalia

In the following case, the justices split over whether two separate religious displays on public land were constitutional. In the first, the government of Allegheny County, Pennsylvania, had erected a nativity scene near the grand staircase of its main courthouse. In the second, the county had placed a Christmas tree and a menorah in front of the county's office building. As you will see, four justices considered both displays constitutional, three considered both unconstitutional, and U.S. Supreme Court Justices Harry Blackmun and Sandra Day O'Connor provided the final votes to declare the nativity scene unconstitutional and the menorah constitutional. As you read this case, consider whether any coherent rule of law can be gleaned from the numerous

The Supreme Court ruled that the display of this nativity scene inside the Allegheny County Courthouse violated the Establishment Clause.

This menorah, on the other hand, was held not to violate the Establishment Clause in the same case.

opinions. Pay attention to the dissent as well, in which Justice Anthony Kennedy first articulates his "coercion" test. Consider whether this effectively creates a competitor to the Lemon *test and Justice O'Connor's endorsement test.*

JUSTICE BLACKMUN *announced the judgment of the Court and delivered the opinion of the Court with respect to Parts III-A, IV, and V, an opinion with respect to Parts I and II, in which* **JUSTICE STEVENS** *and* **JUSTICE O'CONNOR** *join, an opinion with respect to Part III-B, in which* **JUSTICE STEVENS** *joins, an opinion with respect to Part VII, in which* **JUSTICE O'CONNOR** *joins, and an opinion with respect to Part VI.*

This litigation concerns the constitutionality of two recurring holiday displays located on public property in downtown Pittsburgh. The first is a crèche placed on the Grand Staircase of the Allegheny County Courthouse. The second is a Chanukah menorah placed just outside the City-County Building, next to a Christmas

tree and a sign saluting liberty. The Court of Appeals for the Third Circuit ruled that each display violates the Establishment Clause of the First Amendment because each has the impermissible effect of endorsing religion. We agree that the crèche display has that unconstitutional effect but reverse the Court of Appeals' judgment regarding the menorah display. . . .

In the course of adjudicating specific cases, this Court has come to understand the Establishment Clause to mean that government may not promote or affiliate itself with any religious doctrine or organization, may not discriminate among persons on the basis of their religious beliefs and practices, may not delegate a governmental power to a religious institution, and may not involve itself too deeply in such an institution's affairs. . . . Our subsequent decisions further have refined the definition of governmental action that unconstitutionally advances religion. In recent years, we have paid particularly close attention to whether the challenged governmental practice either has the purpose or effect of "endorsing" religion, a concern that has long had a place in our Establishment Clause jurisprudence. . . . Of course, the word "endorsement" is not self-defining. Rather, it derives its meaning from other words that this Court has found useful over the years in interpreting the Establishment Clause. Thus, it has been noted that the prohibition against governmental endorsement of religion "preclude[s] government from conveying or attempting to convey a message that religion or a particular religious belief is favored or preferred."

. . . Whether the key word is "endorsement," "favoritism," or "promotion," the essential principle remains the same. The Establishment Clause, at the very least, prohibits government from appearing to take a position on questions of religious belief or from "making adherence to a religion relevant in any way to a person's standing in the political community." *Lynch v. Donnelly*, (O'Connor, J., concurring).

B

. . . The rationale of the majority opinion in *Lynch* is none too clear: the opinion contains two strands, neither of which provides guidance for decision in subsequent cases. First, the opinion states that the inclusion of the crèche in the display was "no more an advancement or endorsement of religion" than other "endorsements" this Court has approved in the past, but the opinion offers no discernible measure for distinguishing between permissible and impermissible endorsements. Second, the opinion observes that any benefit the government's display of the crèche gave to religion was no more than "indirect, remote, and incidental," ibid.—without saying how or why.

Although Justice O'Connor joined the majority opinion in *Lynch*, she wrote a concurrence that differs in significant respects from the majority opinion. The main difference is that the concurrence provides a sound analytical framework for evaluating governmental use of religious symbols.

First and foremost, the concurrence squarely rejects any notion that this Court will tolerate some government endorsement of religion. Rather, the concurrence recognizes any endorsement of religion as "invalid," id., at 690, because it "sends a message to nonadherents that they are outsiders, not full members of the political community, and an accompanying message to adherents that they are insiders, favored members of the political community."

Second, the concurrence articulates a method for determining whether the government's use of an object with religious meaning has the effect of endorsing religion. The effect of the display depends upon the message that the government's practice communicates: the question is "what viewers may fairly understand to be the purpose of the display." That inquiry, of necessity, turns upon the context in which the contested object appears: "[A] typical museum setting, though not neutralizing the religious content of a religious painting, negates any message of endorsement of that content." Ibid. The concurrence thus emphasizes that the constitutionality of the crèche in that case depended upon its "particular physical setting," ibid., and further observes: "Every government practice must be judged in its unique circumstances to determine whether it [endorses] religion," id., at 694. The concurrence concluded that both because the crèche is "a traditional symbol" of Christmas, a holiday with strong secular elements, and because the crèche was "displayed along with purely secular symbols," the crèche's setting "changes what viewers may fairly understand to be the purpose of the display" and "negates any message of endorsement" of "the Christian beliefs represented by the crèche."

. . . [T]he five Justices in concurrence and dissent in *Lynch* agreed upon the relevant constitutional principles: the government's use of religious symbolism is unconstitutional if it has the effect of endorsing religious beliefs, and the effect of the government's use of religious symbolism depends upon its context. These general principles are sound, and have been adopted by the Court in subsequent cases. Since *Lynch*, the Court has made clear that, when evaluating the effect of government conduct under the Establishment Clause, we must ascertain whether "the challenged governmental action is sufficiently likely to be perceived by adherents of the controlling denominations as an endorsement, and by the nonadherents as a disapproval, of their individual religious choices." *Grand Rapids*. Accordingly, our present task is to determine whether the display of the crèche and the menorah, in their respective "particular physical settings," has the effect of endorsing or disapproving religious beliefs.

IV

We turn first to the county's crèche display. There is no doubt, of course, that the crèche itself is capable of communicating a religious message. . . . Under the Court's holding in *Lynch*, the effect of a crèche display turns on its setting. Here, unlike in *Lynch*, nothing in the context of the display detracts from the crèche's religious message. The *Lynch* display comprised a series of figures and objects, each group of which had its own focal point. Santa's house and his reindeer were objects of attention separate from the crèche, and had their specific visual story to tell. Similarly, whatever a "talking" wishing well may be, it obviously

was a center of attention separate from the crèche. Here, in contrast, the crèche stands alone: it is the single element of the display on the Grand Staircase. . . . No viewer could reasonably think that it occupies this location without the support and approval of the government. Thus, by permitting the "display of the crèche in this particular physical setting," *Lynch* (O'Connor, J., concurring), the county sends an unmistakable message that it supports and promotes the Christian praise to God that is the crèche's religious message.

The fact that the crèche bears a sign disclosing its ownership by a Roman Catholic organization does not alter this conclusion. On the contrary, the sign simply demonstrates that the government is endorsing the religious message of that organization, rather than communicating a message of its own. But the Establishment Clause does not limit only the religious content of the government's own communications. It also prohibits the government's support and promotion of religious communications by religious organizations. Indeed, the very concept of "endorsement" conveys the sense of promoting someone else's message. Thus, by prohibiting government endorsement of religion, the Establishment Clause prohibits precisely what occurred here: the government's lending its support to the communication of a religious organization's religious message. . . .

In sum, *Lynch* teaches that government may celebrate Christmas in some manner and form, but not in a way that endorses Christian doctrine. Here, Allegheny County has transgressed this line. It has chosen to celebrate Christmas in a way that has the effect of endorsing a patently Christian message: Glory to God for the birth of Jesus Christ. Under *Lynch*, and the rest of our cases, nothing more is required to demonstrate a violation of the Establishment Clause. The display of the crèche in this context, therefore, must be permanently enjoined. . . .

VI

The display of the Chanukah menorah in front of the City-County Building may well present a closer constitutional question. The menorah, one must recognize, is a religious symbol: it serves to commemorate the miracle of the oil as described in the Talmud. But the menorah's message is not exclusively religious. The menorah is the primary visual symbol for a holiday that, like Christmas, has both religious and secular dimensions.

Moreover, the menorah here stands next to a Christmas tree and a sign saluting liberty. While no challenge has been made here to the display of the tree and the sign, their presence is obviously relevant in determining the effect of the menorah's display. The necessary result of placing a menorah next to a Christmas tree is to create an "overall holiday setting" that represents both Christmas and Chanukah—two holidays, not one.

The mere fact that Pittsburgh displays symbols of both Christmas and Chanukah does not end the constitutional inquiry. If the city celebrates both Christmas and Chanukah as religious holidays, then it violates the Establishment Clause. The simultaneous endorsement of Judaism and Christianity is no less constitutionally infirm than the endorsement of Christianity alone. . . .

Accordingly, the relevant question for Establishment Clause purposes is whether the combined display of the tree, the sign, and the menorah has the effect of endorsing both Christian and Jewish faiths, or rather simply recognizes that both Christmas and Chanukah are part of the same winter-holiday season, which has attained a secular status in our society. Of the two

interpretations of this particular display, the latter seems far more plausible and is also in line with Lynch.

VII

Lynch v. Donnelly confirms, and in no way repudiates, the longstanding constitutional principle that government may not engage in a practice that has the effect of promoting or endorsing religious beliefs. The display of the crèche in the county courthouse has this unconstitutional effect. The display of the menorah in front of the City-County Building, however, does not have this effect, given its "particular physical setting."

The judgment of the Court of Appeals is affirmed in part and reversed in part, and the cases are remanded for further proceedings.

It is so ordered.

JUSTICE O'CONNOR, *with whom* **JUSTICE BRENNAN** *and* **JUSTICE STEVENS** *join as to Part II, concurring in part and concurring in the judgment.*

I

. . . I agree that the crèche displayed on the Grand Staircase of the Allegheny County Courthouse, the seat of county government, conveys a message to nonadherents of Christianity that they are not full members of the political community, and a corresponding message to Christians that they are favored members of the political community. In contrast to the crèche in *Lynch*, which was displayed in a private park in the city's commercial district as part of a broader display of traditional secular symbols of the holiday season, this crèche stands alone in the county courthouse. The display of religious symbols in public areas of core government buildings runs a special risk of "mak[ing] religion relevant, in reality or public perception, to status in the political community." The Court correctly concludes that placement of the central religious symbol of the Christmas holiday season at the Allegheny County Courthouse has the unconstitutional effect of conveying a government endorsement of Christianity.

III

For reasons which differ somewhat from those set forth in Part VI of Justice Blackmun's opinion, I also conclude that the city of Pittsburgh's combined holiday display of a Chanukah menorah, a Christmas tree, and a sign saluting liberty does not have the effect of conveying an endorsement of religion.... In my view, the relevant question for Establishment Clause purposes is whether the city of Pittsburgh's display of the menorah, the religious symbol of a religious holiday, next to a Christmas tree and a sign saluting liberty sends a message of government endorsement of Judaism or whether it sends a message of pluralism and freedom to choose one's own beliefs. The message of pluralism conveyed by the city's combined holiday display is not a message that endorses religion over nonreligion.

JUSTICE BRENNAN, *with whom* **JUSTICE MARSHALL** *and* **JUSTICE STEVENS** *join, concurring in part and dissenting in part.*

. . . I continue to believe that the display of an object that "retains a specifically Christian [or other] religious meaning," is incompatible with the separation of church and state demanded by our Constitution. I therefore agree with the Court that Allegheny County's display of a crèche at the county courthouse signals an endorsement of the Christian faith in violation of the Establishment Clause, and join Parts III-A, IV, and V of the Court's opinion. I cannot agree, however, that the city's display of a 45-foot Christmas tree and an 18-foot Chanukah menorah at the entrance to the building housing the mayor's office shows no favoritism towards Christianity, Judaism, or both. Indeed, I should have thought that the answer as to the first display supplied the answer to the second.

JUSTICE STEVENS, *with whom* **JUSTICE BRENNAN** *and* **JUSTICE MARSHALL** *join, concurring in part and dissenting in part.*

In my opinion the Establishment Clause should be construed to create a strong presumption against the display of religious symbols on public property. There is always a risk that such symbols will offend nonmembers of the faith being advertised as well as adherents who consider the particular advertisement disrespectful. Some devout Christians believe that the crèche should be placed only in reverential settings, such as a church or perhaps a private home; they do not countenance its use as an aid to commercialization of Christ's birthday. In this very suit, members of the Jewish faith firmly opposed the use to which the menorah was put by the particular sect that sponsored the display at Pittsburgh's City-County Building. Even though "[p]assersby who disagree with the message conveyed by these displays are free to ignore them, or even to turn their backs," displays of this kind inevitably have a greater tendency to emphasize sincere and deeply felt differences among individuals than to achieve an ecumenical goal. The Establishment Clause does not allow public bodies to foment such disagreement.

JUSTICE KENNEDY, *with whom* **THE CHIEF JUSTICE, JUSTICE WHITE,** *and* **JUSTICE SCALIA** *join, concurring in the judgment in part and dissenting in part.*

The majority holds that the County of Allegheny violated the Establishment Clause by displaying a crèche in the county court-house, because the "principal or primary effect" of the display is to advance religion within the meaning of *Lemon v. Kurtzman.* This view of the Establishment Clause reflects an unjustified hostility toward religion, a hostility inconsistent with our history and our precedents, and I dissent from this holding. The crèche display is constitutional, and, for the same reasons, the display of a menorah by the city of Pittsburgh is permissible as well. On this latter point, I concur in the result, but not the reasoning, of Part VI of Justice Blackmun's opinion.

I

. . . Rather than requiring government to avoid any action that acknowledges or aids religion, the Establishment Clause permits government some latitude in recognizing and accommodating the central role religion plays in our society. (*Lynch v. Donnelly*; *Walz v. Tax Comm'n of New York City.*) Any approach less sensitive to our heritage would border on latent hostility toward religion, as it would require government in all its multifaceted roles to acknowledge only the secular, to the exclusion and so to the detriment of the religious. A categorical approach would install federal courts as jealous guardians of an absolute "wall of separation," sending a clear message of disapproval. In this century, as the modern administrative state expands to touch the lives of its citizens in such diverse ways and redirects their financial choices through programs of its own, it is difficult to maintain the fiction that requiring government

to avoid all assistance to religion can in fairness be viewed as serving the goal of neutrality.

The ability of the organized community to recognize and accommodate religion in a society with a pervasive public sector requires diligent observance of the border between accommodation and establishment. Our cases disclose two limiting principles: government may not coerce anyone to support or participate in any religion or its exercise; and it may not, in the guise of avoiding hostility or callous indifference, give direct benefits to religion in such a degree that it in fact "establishes a [state] religion or religious faith, or tends to do so."

It is no surprise that without exception we have invalidated actions that further the interests of religion through the coercive power of government. Forbidden involvements include compelling or coercing participation or attendance at a religious activity, requiring religious oaths to obtain government office or benefits, *Torcaso v. Watkins*, or delegating government power to religious groups, *Larkin v. Grendel's Den, Inc.* The freedom to worship as one pleases without government interference or oppression is the great object of both the Establishment and the Free Exercise Clauses. Barring all attempts to aid religion through government coercion goes far toward attainment of this object. (*McGowan v. Maryland*; *Cantwell v. Connecticut.*)

As Justice Blackmun observes, some of our recent cases reject the view that coercion is the sole touchstone of an Establishment Clause violation. That may be true if by "coercion" is meant direct coercion in the classic sense of an establishment of religion that the Framers knew. But coercion need not be a direct tax in aid of religion or a test oath. Symbolic recognition or accommodation of religious faith may violate the Clause in an extreme case.

I doubt not, for example, that the Clause forbids a city to permit the permanent erection of a large Latin cross on the roof of city hall. This is not because government speech about religion is per se suspect, as the majority would have it, but because such an obtrusive year-round religious display would place the government's weight behind an obvious effort to proselytize on behalf of a particular religion. Speech may coerce in some circumstances, but this does not justify a ban on all government recognition of religion. As Chief Justice Burger wrote for the Court in *Walz*:

> "The general principle deducible from the First Amendment and all that has been said by the Court is this: that we will not tolerate either governmentally established religion or governmental interference with religion. Short of those expressly proscribed governmental acts there is room for play in the joints productive of a benevolent neutrality which will permit religious exercise to exist without sponsorship and without interference."

This is most evident where the government's act of recognition or accommodation is passive and symbolic, for in that instance any intangible benefit to religion is unlikely to present a realistic risk of establishment. Absent coercion, the risk of infringement of religious liberty by passive or symbolic accommodation is minimal. Our cases reflect this reality by requiring a showing that the symbolic recognition or accommodation advances religion to such a degree that it actually "establishes a religion or religious faith, or tends to do so." . . .

II

These principles are not difficult to apply to the facts of the cases before us. In permitting the displays on government property of the menorah and the crèche, the city and county sought to do no more than "celebrate the season," and to acknowledge, along with many of their citizens, the historical background and the religious, as well as secular, nature of the Chanukah and Christmas holidays. This interest falls well within the tradition of government accommodation and acknowledgment of religion that has marked our history from the beginning. It cannot be disputed that government, if it chooses, may participate in sharing with its citizens the joy of the holiday season, by declaring public holidays, installing or permitting festive displays, sponsoring celebrations and parades, and providing holiday vacations for its employees. All levels of our government do precisely that. As we said in *Lynch*, "Government has long recognized—indeed it has subsidized—holidays with religious significance."

If government is to participate in its citizens' celebration of a holiday that contains both a secular and a religious component, enforced recognition of only the secular aspect would signify the callous indifference toward religious faith that our cases and traditions do not require; for by commemorating the holiday only as it is celebrated by nonadherents, the government would be refusing to acknowledge the plain fact, and the historical reality, that many of its citizens celebrate its religious aspects as well. Judicial invalidation of government's attempts to recognize the religious underpinnings of the holiday would signal not neutrality but a pervasive intent to insulate government from all things religious. The Religion Clauses do not require government to acknowledge these holidays or their religious component; but our strong tradition of government accommodation and acknowledgment permits government to do so.

There is no suggestion here that the government's power to coerce has been used to further the interests of Christianity or Judaism in any way. No one was compelled to observe or participate in any religious ceremony or activity. Neither the city nor the county contributed significant amounts of tax money to serve the cause of one religious faith. The crèche and the menorah are purely passive symbols of religious holidays. Passersby who disagree with the message conveyed by these displays are free to ignore them, or even to turn their backs, just as they are free to do when they disagree with any other form of government speech.

LEE v. WEISMAN

505 U.S. 577 (1992)

Opinion: Kennedy, joined by Blackmun, Stevens, O'Connor, Souter
Concurrence: Blackmun, joined by Stevens, O'Connor
Concurrence: Souter, joined by Stevens, O'Connor
Dissent: Scalia, joined by Rehnquist, White, Thomas

Lee v. Weisman *and* Santa Fe Independent School District v. Doe *both concern the role of prayer in schools. In* Lee v. Weisman, *the principal of the school provided guidance to a rabbi who would lead a prayer at a graduation ceremony about what he should say. In his opinion in this case, Justice Anthony Kennedy finds this problematic because it entails excessive entanglement of government in religion. Notice as well that Justice Kennedy applies the coercion test he first articulated in* Allegheny v. ACLU. *Is his application of the test here consistent with the test he outlined in that case? Consider also whether the test Justice Kennedy employs here is consistent with the* Lemon *test.*

JUSTICE KENNEDY *delivered the opinion of the Court.*

Deborah Weisman graduated from Nathan Bishop Middle School, a public school in Providence, at a formal ceremony in June 1989. She was about 14 years old. For many years it has been the policy of the Providence School Committee and the Superintendent of Schools to permit principals to invite members of the clergy to give invocations and benedictions at middle school and high school graduations. Many, but not all, of the principals elected to include prayers as part of the graduation ceremonies. Acting for himself and his daughter, Deborah's father, Daniel Weisman, objected to any prayers at Deborah's middle school graduation, but to no avail. The school principal, petitioner Robert E. Lee, invited a rabbi to deliver prayers at the graduation exercises for Deborah's class. Rabbi Leslie Gutterman, of the Temple Beth El in Providence, accepted.

It has been the custom of Providence school officials to provide invited clergy with a pamphlet entitled "Guidelines for Civic Occasions," prepared by the National Conference of Christians and Jews. The Guidelines recommend that public prayers at nonsectarian civic ceremonies be composed with "inclusiveness and sensitivity," though they acknowledge that "[p]rayer of any kind may be inappropriate on some civic occasions." The principal gave Rabbi Gutterman the pamphlet before the graduation and advised him the invocation and benediction should be nonsectarian. . . .

These dominant facts mark and control the confines of our decision: State officials direct the performance of a formal religious exercise at promotional and graduation ceremonies for secondary schools. Even for those students who object to the religious exercise, their attendance and participation in the state sponsored religious activity are in a fair and real sense obligatory, though the school district does not require attendance as a condition for receipt of the diploma....

[The] controlling precedents as they relate to prayer and religious exercise in primary and secondary public schools compel the holding here that the policy of the city of Providence is an unconstitutional one. We can decide the case without reconsidering the general constitutional framework by which public schools' efforts to accommodate religion are measured. Thus we do not accept the invitation of petitioners and *amicus* the United States to reconsider our decision in *Lemon v. Kurtzman.* The government involvement with religious activity in this case is pervasive, to the point of creating a state-sponsored and state-directed religious exercise in a public school. Conducting this formal religious observance conflicts with settled rules pertaining to prayer exercises for students, and that suffices to determine the question before us.

The principle that government may accommodate the free exercise of religion does not supersede the fundamental limitations imposed by the Establishment Clause. It is beyond dispute that, at a minimum, the Constitution guarantees that government may not coerce anyone to support or participate in religion or its exercise, or otherwise act in a way which "establishes a [state] religion or religious faith, or tends to do so." *Lynch.* The State's involvement in the school prayers challenged today violates these central principles.

That involvement is as troubling as it is undenied. A school official, the principal, decided that an invocation and a benediction should be given; this is a choice attributable to the State, and from a constitutional perspective it is as if a state statute decreed that the prayers must occur. The principal chose the religious participant, here a rabbi, and that choice is also attributable to the State....

Divisiveness, of course, can attend any state decision respecting religions, and neither its existence nor its potential necessarily invalidates the State's attempts to accommodate religion in all cases. The potential for divisiveness is of particular relevance here, though, because it centers around an overt religious exercise in a secondary school environment where, as we discuss below, subtle coercive pressures exist, and where the student had no real alternative which would have allowed her to avoid the fact or appearance of participation.

The State's role did not end with the decision to include a prayer and with the choice of clergyman. Principal Lee provided Rabbi Gutterman with a copy of the "Guidelines for Civic Occasions," and advised him that his prayers should be nonsectarian. Through these means the principal directed and controlled the content of the prayer. Even if the only sanction for ignoring the instructions were that the rabbi would not be invited back, we think no religious representative who valued his or her continued reputation and effectiveness in the community would incur the State's displeasure in this regard. It is a cornerstone principle of our Establishment Clause jurisprudence that "it is no part of the business of government to compose official prayers for any group of the American people to recite as a part of a religious program carried on by government," *Engel v. Vitale,* and that is what the school officials attempted to do....

The First Amendment's Religion Clauses mean that religious beliefs and religious expression are too precious to be either proscribed or prescribed by the State. The design of the Constitution is that preservation and transmission of religious beliefs and worship is a responsibility and a choice committed to the private sphere, which itself is promised freedom to pursue that mission. . . .

We turn our attention now to consider the position of the students, both those who desired the prayer and she who did not. . . . To endure the speech of false ideas or offensive content and then to counter it is part of learning how to live in a pluralistic society, a society which insists upon open discourse towards the end of a tolerant citizenry. And tolerance presupposes some mutuality of obligation. It is argued that our constitutional vision of a free society requires confidence in our own ability to accept or reject ideas of which we do not approve, and that prayer at a high school graduation does nothing more than offer a choice. By the time they are seniors, high school students no doubt have been required to attend classes and assemblies and to complete assignments exposing them to ideas they find distasteful or immoral or absurd, or all of these. Against this background, students may consider it an odd measure of justice to be subjected during the course of their educations to ideas deemed offensive and irreligious, but to be denied a brief, formal prayer ceremony that the school offers in return. This argument cannot prevail, however. It overlooks a fundamental dynamic of the Constitution.

The First Amendment protects speech and religion by quite different mechanisms. Speech is protected by ensuring its full expression even when the government participates, for the very object of some of our most important speech is to persuade the government to adopt an idea as its own.

The method for protecting freedom of worship and freedom of conscience in religious matters is quite the reverse. In religious debate or expression, the government is not a prime participant, for the Framers deemed religious establishment antithetical to the freedom of all. The Free Exercise Clause embraces a freedom of conscience and worship that has close parallels in the speech provisions of the First Amendment, but the Establishment Clause is a specific prohibition on forms of state intervention in religious affairs, with no precise counterpart in the speech provisions. The explanation lies in the lesson of history that was and is the inspiration for the Establishment Clause, the lesson that, in the hands of government, what might begin as a tolerant expression of religious views may end in a policy to indoctrinate and coerce. A state-created orthodoxy puts at grave risk that freedom of belief and conscience which are the sole assurance that religious faith is real, not imposed. . . .

As we have observed before, there are heightened concerns with protecting freedom of conscience from subtle coercive pressure in the elementary and secondary public schools. . . . What to most believers may seem nothing more than a reasonable request that the nonbeliever respect their religious practices, in a school context may appear to the nonbeliever or dissenter to be an attempt to employ the machinery of the State to enforce a religious orthodoxy.

We need not look beyond the circumstances of this case to see the phenomenon at work. The undeniable fact is that the school district's supervision and control of a high school graduation ceremony places public pressure, as well as peer pressure, on attending students to stand as a group or, at least, maintain respectful silence during the Invocation and Benediction. This pressure, though subtle and indirect, can be as real as any overt compulsion. Of course, in our culture standing or remaining silent can signify adherence to a view or simple respect for the views of others. And no doubt some persons who have no desire to join a prayer have little objection to standing as a sign of respect for those who do. But for the dissenter of high school age, who has a reasonable perception that she is being forced by the State to pray in a manner her conscience will not allow, the injury is no less real. There can be no doubt that for many, if not most, of the students at the graduation, the act of standing or remaining silent was an expression of participation in the Rabbi's prayer. That was the very point of the religious exercise. It is of little comfort to a dissenter, then, to be told that for her the act of standing or remaining in silence signifies mere respect, rather than participation. What matters is that, given our social conventions, a reasonable dissenter in this milieu could believe that the group exercise signified her own participation or approval of it. . . .

The injury caused by the government's action, and the reason why Daniel and Deborah Weisman object to it, is that the State, in a school setting, in effect required participation in a religious exercise. It is, we concede, a brief exercise during which the individual can concentrate on joining its message, meditate on her own religion, or let her mind wander. But the embarrassment and the intrusion of the religious exercise cannot be refuted by arguing that these prayers, and similar ones to be said in the future, are of a *de minimis* character. To do so would be an affront to the Rabbi who offered them and to all those for whom the prayers were an essential and profound recognition of divine authority. And for the same reason, we think that the intrusion is greater than the two minutes or so of time consumed for prayers like these. Assuming, as we must, that the prayers were offensive

to the student and the parent who now object, the intrusion was both real and, in the context of a secondary school, a violation of the objectors' rights. That the intrusion was in the course of promulgating religion that sought to be civic or nonsectarian rather than pertaining to one sect does not lessen the offense or isolation to the objectors. At best it narrows their number, at worst increases their sense of isolation and affront. . . . The Government's argument gives insufficient recognition to the real conflict of conscience faced by the young student. The essence of the Government's position is that with regard to a civic, social occasion of this importance it is the objector, not the majority, who must take unilateral and private action to avoid compromising religious scruples, here by electing to miss the graduation exercise. This turns conventional First Amendment analysis on its head. It is a tenet of the First Amendment that the State cannot require one of its citizens to forfeit his or her rights and benefits as the price of resisting conformance to state sponsored religious practice. To say that a student must remain apart from the ceremony at the opening invocation and closing benediction is to risk compelling conformity in an environment analogous to the classroom setting, where we have said the risk of compulsion is especially high. . . .

We do not hold that every state action implicating religion is invalid if one or a few citizens find it offensive. People may take offense at all manner of religious as well as nonreligious messages, but offense alone does not in every case show a violation. We know too that sometimes to endure social isolation or even anger may be the price of conscience or nonconformity. But, by any reading of our cases, the conformity required of the student in this case was too high an exaction to withstand the test of the Establishment

Clause. The prayer exercises in this case are especially improper because the State has in every practical sense compelled attendance and participation in an explicit religious exercise at an event of singular importance to every student, one the objecting student had no real alternative to avoid.

Our jurisprudence in this area is of necessity one of line-drawing, of determining at what point a dissenter's rights of religious freedom are infringed by the State.

The sole question presented is whether a religious exercise may be conducted at a graduation ceremony in circumstances where, as we have found, young graduates who object are induced to conform. No holding by this Court suggests that a school can persuade or compel a student to participate in a religious exercise. That is being done here, and it is forbidden by the Establishment Clause of the First Amendment.

For the reasons we have stated, the judgment of the Court of Appeals is
Affirmed.

SANTA FE INDEPENDENT SCHOOL DISTRICT v. DOE

530 U.S. 290 (2000)

Opinion: Stevens, joined by O'Connor, Kennedy, Souter, Ginsburg, Breyer
Dissent: Rehnquist, joined by Scalia, Thomas

In Lee v. Weisman, *Justice Anthony Kennedy is concerned that allowing prayer in schools may have a significant potential to coerce students into a particular set of beliefs. But in the following case, the prayer at issue is student-led. Is the worry about coercion more or less salient in light of this difference?*

JUSTICE STEVENS *delivered the opinion of the Court.*

Prior to 1995, the Santa Fe High School student who occupied the school's elective office of student council chaplain delivered a prayer over the public address system before each varsity football game for the entire season. This practice, along with others, was challenged in District Court as a violation of the Establishment Clause of the First Amendment. While

these proceedings were pending in the District Court, the school district adopted a different policy that permits, but does not require, prayer initiated and led by a student at all home games. The District Court entered an order modifying that policy to permit only nonsectarian, nonproselytizing prayer. The Court of Appeals held that, even as modified by the District Court, the football prayer policy was invalid.

I

Respondents commenced this action in April 1995 and moved for a temporary restraining order to prevent the District from violating the Establishment Clause at the imminent graduation exercises. In their complaint the Does alleged that the District had engaged in several proselytizing practices, such as promoting attendance at a Baptist revival meeting, encouraging membership in religious clubs, chastising children who held minority religious beliefs, and distributing Gideon Bibles on school premises. They also alleged that the District allowed students to read Christian invocations and benedictions from the stage at graduation ceremonies, and to deliver overtly Christian prayers over the public address system at home football games.

. . . The policy authorized two student elections, the first to determine whether "invocations" should be delivered, and the second to select the spokesperson to deliver them. [I]t contained two parts, an initial statement that omitted any requirement that the content of the invocation be "nonsectarian and nonproselytising," and a fallback provision that automatically added that limitation if the preferred policy should be enjoined. On August 31, 1995, according to the parties' stipulation, "the district's high school students voted to determine whether a student would deliver prayer at varsity football games. . . . The students chose to allow a student to say a prayer at football games." A week later, in a separate election, they selected a student "to deliver the prayer at varsity football games."

The final policy . . . omits the word "prayer" from its title, and refers to "messages" and "statements" as well as "invocations." It is the validity of that policy that is before us.

. . . We granted the District's petition for certiorari, limited to the following question: "Whether petitioner's policy permitting student-led, student-initiated prayer at football games violates the Establishment Clause." We conclude, as did the Court of Appeals, that it does.

II

The first Clause in the First Amendment to the Federal Constitution provides that "Congress shall make no law respecting an establishment of religion, or prohibiting the free exercise thereof." The Fourteenth Amendment imposes those substantive limitations on the legislative power of the States and their political subdivisions. *Wallace v. Jaffree.* In *Lee v. Weisman,* we held that a prayer delivered by a rabbi at a middle school graduation ceremony violated that Clause. Although this case involves student prayer at a different type of school function, our analysis is properly guided by the principles that we endorsed in *Lee.*

. . . In this case the District first argues that this principle is inapplicable to its policy because the messages are private student speech, not public speech. It reminds us that "there is a crucial difference between *government* speech endorsing religion, which the Establishment Clause forbids, and *private* speech endorsing religion, which the Free Speech and Free Exercise Clauses protect." . . . We certainly agree with that distinction, but we are not persuaded that the pregame invocations should be regarded as "private speech."

These invocations are authorized by a government policy and take place on government property at government-sponsored school-related events. Of course, not every message delivered under such circumstances is the government's own. We have held, for example, that an individual's contribution to a government-created forum was not government speech. See *Rosenberger v. Rector and Visitors of Univ. of Va.* Although the District relies heavily on *Rosenberger* and similar cases involving such forums, it is clear that the pregame ceremony is not the type of forum discussed in those cases. The Santa Fe school officials simply do not "evince either 'by policy or by practice,' any intent to open the [pregame ceremony] to 'indiscriminate use,' . . . by the student body generally." *Hazelwood School Dist. v. Kuhlmeier.* Rather, the school allows only one student, the same student for the entire season, to give the invocation. The statement or invocation, moreover, is subject to particular regulations that confine the content and topic of the student's message.

Granting only one student access to the stage at a time does not, of course, necessarily preclude a finding that a school has created a limited public forum. Here, however, Santa Fe's student election system ensures that only those messages deemed "appropriate" under the District's policy may be delivered. That is, the majoritarian process implemented by the District guarantees, by definition, that minority candidates will never prevail and that their views will be effectively silenced.

Recently, in *Board of Regents of Univ. of Wis. System v. Southworth*, we explained why student elections that determine, by majority vote, which expressive activities shall receive or not receive school benefits are constitutionally problematic:

> "To the extent the referendum substitutes majority determinations for viewpoint neutrality it would undermine the constitutional protection the program requires. The whole theory of viewpoint neutrality is that minority views are treated with the same respect as are majority views. Access to a public forum, for instance, does not depend upon majoritarian consent. That principle is controlling here."

Like the student referendum for funding in *Southworth*, this student election does nothing to protect minority views but rather places the students who hold such views at the mercy of the majority. Because "fundamental rights may not be submitted to vote; they depend on the outcome of no elections," *West Virginia Bd. of Ed. v. Barnette*, the District's elections are insufficient safeguards of diverse student speech.

In *Lee*, the school district made the related argument that its policy of endorsing only "civic or nonsectarian" prayer was acceptable because it minimized the intrusion on the audience as a whole. We rejected that claim by explaining that such a majoritarian policy "does not lessen the offense or isolation to the objectors. At best it narrows their number, at worst increases their sense of isolation and affront." Similarly, while Santa Fe's majoritarian election might ensure that *most* of the students are represented, it does nothing to protect the minority; indeed, it likely serves to intensify their offense.

Moreover, the District has failed to divorce itself from the religious content in the invocations. It has not succeeded in doing so, either by claiming that its policy is "'one of neutrality rather than endorsement'" or by characterizing the individual student as the "circuit-breaker" in the process. Contrary to the District's repeated assertions that it has adopted a "hands-off" approach to the pregame invocation, the realities of the situation plainly reveal that its policy involves both perceived and actual endorsement of religion. In this case, as we found in *Lee*, the "degree of school involvement" makes it clear that the pregame prayers bear "the imprint of the State and thus put school-age children who objected in an untenable position."

The District has attempted to disentangle itself from the religious messages by developing the two-step student election process. The text of the October policy, however, exposes the extent of the school's entanglement. The elections take place at all only because the school "board *has chosen to permit* students to deliver a brief invocation and/or message." The elections thus "shall" be conducted "by the high school student council" and "[u]pon advice and direction of the high school principal." The decision whether to deliver a message is first made by majority vote of the entire student body, followed by a choice of the speaker in a separate, similar majority election. Even though the particular words used by the speaker are not determined by those votes, the policy mandates that the "statement or invocation" be "consistent with the goals and purposes of this policy," which are "to solemnize the event, to promote good sportsmanship and student safety, and to establish the appropriate environment for the competition."

In addition to involving the school in the selection of the speaker, the policy, by its terms, invites and encourages religious messages. The policy itself states that the purpose of the message is "to solemnize the event." A religious message is the most obvious method of solemnizing an event. Moreover, the requirements that the message "promote good citizenship" and "establish the appropriate environment for competition" further narrow the types of message deemed appropriate, suggesting that a solemn, yet nonreligious, message, such as commentary on United States foreign policy, would be prohibited. Indeed, the only type of message that is expressly endorsed in the text is an "invocation"—a term that primarily describes an appeal for divine assistance. In fact, as used in the past at Santa Fe High School, an "invocation" has always entailed a focused religious message. Thus, the expressed purposes of the policy encourage the selection of a religious message, and that is precisely how the students understand the policy. The results of the elections described in the parties' stipulation make it clear that the students understood that the central question before them was whether prayer should be a part of the pregame ceremony. We recognize the important role that public worship plays in many communities, as well as the sincere desire to include public prayer as a part of various occasions so as to mark those occasions' significance. But such religious activity in public schools, as elsewhere, must comport with the First Amendment.

The actual or perceived endorsement of the message, moreover, is established by factors beyond just the text of the policy. Once the student speaker is selected and the message composed, the invocation is then delivered to a large audience assembled as part of a regularly scheduled, school-sponsored function conducted on school property. The message is broadcast over the school's public address system, which remains subject to the control of school officials. It is fair to assume that the pregame ceremony is clothed in the traditional indicia of school sporting events, which generally include not just the team, but also cheerleaders and band members dressed in uniforms sporting the school name and mascot. The school's name is likely written in large print across the field and on banners and flags. The crowd will certainly include many who display the school colors and insignia on their school T-shirts, jackets, or hats and who may also be waving signs displaying the school name. It is in a setting such as this that "[t]he board has chosen to permit" the elected student to rise and give the "statement or invocation."

In this context the members of the listening audience must perceive the pregame message as a public expression of the views of the majority of the student body delivered with the approval of the school administration. In cases involving state participation in a religious activity, one of the relevant questions is "whether an objective observer, acquainted with the text, legislative history, and implementation of the statute, would perceive it as a state endorsement of prayer in public schools." Regardless of the listener's support for, or objection to, the message, an objective Santa Fe High School student will unquestionably perceive the inevitable pregame prayer as stamped with her school's seal of approval....

School sponsorship of a religious message is impermissible because it sends the ancillary message to members of the audience who are nonadherents "that they are outsiders, not full members of the political community, and an accompanying message to adherents that they are insiders, favored members of the political community." *Lynch v. Donnelly.* The delivery of such a message—over the school's public address system, by a speaker representing the student body, under the supervision of school faculty, and pursuant to a school policy that explicitly and implicitly encourages public prayer—is not properly characterized as "private" speech.

III

The District next argues that its football policy is distinguishable from the graduation prayer in *Lee* because it does not coerce students to participate in religious observances. . . . Attendance at a high school football game, unlike showing up for class, is certainly not required in order to receive a diploma. Moreover, we may assume that the District is correct in arguing that the informal pressure to attend an athletic event is not as strong as a senior's desire to attend her own graduation ceremony.

There are some students, however, such as cheerleaders, members of the band, and, of course, the team members themselves, for whom seasonal commitments mandate their attendance, sometimes for class credit. The District also minimizes the importance to many students of attending and participating in extracurricular activities as part of a complete educational experience. . . . High school home football games are traditional gatherings of a school community; they bring together students and faculty as well as friends and family from years present and past to root for a common cause. Undoubtedly, the games are not important to some students, and they voluntarily choose not to attend. For many others, however, the choice between whether to attend these games or to risk facing a personally offensive religious ritual is in no practical sense an easy one. The Constitution, moreover, demands that the school may not force this difficult choice upon these students for "[i]t is a tenet of the First Amendment that the State cannot require one of its citizens to forfeit his or her rights and benefits as the price of resisting conformance to state-sponsored religious practice."

Even if we regard every high school student's decision to attend a home football game as purely voluntary, we are nevertheless persuaded that the delivery of a pregame prayer has the improper effect of coercing those present to participate in an act of religious worship. For "the government may no more use social pressure to enforce orthodoxy than it may use more direct means." As in *Lee,* "[w]hat to most believers may seem nothing more than a reasonable request that the nonbeliever respect their religious practices, in a school context may appear to the nonbeliever or dissenter to be an attempt to employ the machinery of the State to enforce a religious orthodoxy." The constitutional command will not permit the District "to exact religious conformity from a student as the price" of joining her classmates at a varsity football game.

The Religion Clauses of the First Amendment prevent the government from making any law respecting the establishment of religion or prohibiting the free exercise thereof. By no means do these commands impose a prohibition on all religious activity in our public schools. Indeed, the common purpose of the Religion Clauses "is to secure religious liberty." *Engel v. Vitale.* Thus, nothing in the Constitution as interpreted by this Court prohibits any public school student from voluntarily praying at any time before, during, or after the school-day. But the religious liberty protected by the Constitution is abridged when the State affirmatively sponsors the particular religious practice of prayer.

IV

Our examination of those circumstances above leads to the conclusion that this policy does not provide the District with the constitutional safe harbor it sought. The policy is invalid on its face because it establishes an improper majoritarian election on religion, and unquestionably has the purpose and creates the perception of encouraging the delivery of prayer at a series of important school events.

The judgment of the Court of Appeals is, accordingly, affirmed.

ZELMAN v. SIMMONS-HARRIS

536 U.S. 639 (2002)

Opinion: Rehnquist, joined by O'Connor, Scalia, Kennedy, Thomas
Concurrence: O'Connor
Concurrence: Thomas
Dissent: Stevens
Dissent: Souter, joined by Stevens, Ginsburg, Breyer
Dissent: Breyer, joined by Stevens, Souter

CHIEF JUSTICE REHNQUIST *delivered the opinion of the Court.*

The State of Ohio has established a pilot program designed to provide educational choices to families with children who reside in the Cleveland City School District. The question presented is whether this program offends the Establishment Clause of the United States Constitution. We hold that it does not.

There are more than 75,000 children enrolled in the Cleveland City School District. The majority of these children are from low-income and minority families. Few of these families enjoy the means to send their children to any school other than an inner-city public school. For more than a generation, however, Cleveland's public schools have been among the worst performing public schools in the Nation. In 1995, a Federal District Court declared a "crisis of magnitude" and placed the entire Cleveland school district under state control. Shortly thereafter, the state auditor found that Cleveland's public schools were in the midst of a "crisis that is perhaps unprecedented in the history of American education." The district had failed to meet any of the 18 state standards for minimal acceptable performance. Only 1 in 10 ninth graders could pass a basic proficiency examination, and students at all levels performed at a dismal rate compared with students in other Ohio public schools. More than two-thirds of high school students either dropped or failed out before graduation. Of those students who managed to reach their senior year, one of every four still failed to graduate. Of those students who did graduate, few could read, write, or compute at levels comparable to their counterparts in other cities.

It is against this backdrop that Ohio enacted, among other initiatives, its Pilot Project Scholarship Program. The program provides financial assistance to families in any Ohio school district that is or has been "under federal court order requiring supervision and operational management of the district by the state superintendent." Cleveland is the only Ohio school district to fall within that category.

The program provides two basic kinds of assistance to parents of children in a covered district. First, the program provides tuition aid for students in kindergarten through third grade, expanding each year through eighth grade, to attend a participating public or private school of their parent's choosing. Second, the program provides tutorial aid for students who choose to remain enrolled in public school.

The tuition aid portion of the program is designed to provide educational choices to parents who reside in a covered district. Any private school, whether religious or nonreligious, may participate in the program and accept program students so long as the school is located within the boundaries of a covered district and meets statewide educational standards. Participating private schools must agree not to discriminate on the basis of race, religion, or ethnic background, or to "advocate or foster unlawful behavior or teach hatred of any person or group on the basis of race, ethnicity, national origin, or religion." . . . The program has been in operation within the Cleveland City School District since the 1996–1997 school year. In the 1999–2000 school year, 56 private schools participated in the program, 46 (or 82%) of which had a religious affiliation. None of the public schools in districts adjacent to Cleveland have elected to participate. More than 3,700 students participated in the scholarship program, most of whom (96%) enrolled in religiously affiliated schools. Sixty percent of these students were from families at or below the poverty line. In the 1998-1999 school year, approximately 1,400 Cleveland public school students received tutorial aid. This number was expected to double during the 1999–2000 school year.

In July 1999, respondents filed this action in United States District Court, seeking to enjoin the program on the ground that it violated the Establishment Clause of the United States Constitution. In August 1999, the District Court issued a preliminary injunction barring further implementation of the program, which we stayed pending review by the Court of Appeals. In December 1999, the District Court granted summary judgment for respondents. In December 2000, a divided panel of the Court of Appeals affirmed the judgment of the District Court, finding that the program had the "primary effect" of advancing religion in violation of the Establishment Clause. The Court of Appeals stayed its mandate pending disposition in this Court. We granted certiorari, and now reverse the Court of Appeals.

The Establishment Clause of the First Amendment, applied to the States through the Fourteenth Amendment, prevents a State from enacting laws that have the "purpose" or "effect" of advancing or inhibiting religion. *Agostini v. Felton.* There is no dispute that the program challenged here was enacted for the valid secular purpose of providing educational assistance to poor children in a demonstrably failing public school system. Thus, the question presented is whether the Ohio program nonetheless has the forbidden "effect" of advancing or inhibiting religion.

To answer that question, our decisions have drawn a consistent distinction between government programs that provide aid directly to religious schools, *Mitchell v. Helms*, and programs of true private choice, in which government aid reaches religious schools only as a result of the genuine and independent choices of private individuals. (*Mueller v. Allen*; *Witters v. Washington Dept. of Servs. for Blind*; *Zobrest v.*

Catalina Foothills School Dist.) While our jurisprudence with respect to the constitutionality of direct aid programs has "changed significantly" over the past two decades, our jurisprudence with respect to true private choice programs has remained consistent and unbroken. Three times we have confronted Establishment Clause challenges to neutral government programs that provide aid directly to a broad class of individuals, who, in turn, direct the aid to religious schools or institutions of their own choosing. Three times we have rejected such challenges.

In *Mueller*, we rejected an Establishment Clause challenge to a Minnesota program authorizing tax deductions for various educational expenses, including private school tuition costs, even though the great majority of the program's beneficiaries (96%) were parents of children in religious schools. We began by focusing on the class of beneficiaries, finding that because the class included "*all* parents," including parents with "children [who] attend nonsectarian private schools or sectarian private schools," the program was "not readily subject to challenge under the Establishment Clause." Then, viewing the program as a whole, we emphasized the principle of private choice, noting that public funds were made available to religious schools "only as a result of numerous, private choices of individual parents of school-age children." This, we said, ensured that "'no imprimatur of state approval' can be deemed to have been conferred on any particular religion, or on religion generally." We thus found it irrelevant to the constitutional inquiry that the vast majority of beneficiaries were parents of children in religious schools, saying:

> "We would be loath to adopt a rule grounding the constitutionality of a facially neutral law on annual reports reciting the extent to which various classes of private citizens claimed benefits under the law."

That the program was one of true private choice, with no evidence that the State deliberately skewed incentives toward religious schools, was sufficient for the program to survive scrutiny under the Establishment Clause.

In *Witters*, we used identical reasoning to reject an Establishment Clause challenge to a vocational scholarship program that provided tuition aid to a student studying at a religious institution to become a pastor. Looking at the program as a whole, we observed that "[a]ny aid . . . that ultimately flows to religious institutions does so only as a result of the genuinely independent and private choices of aid recipients." We further remarked that, as in *Mueller*, "[the] program is made available generally without regard to the sectarian-nonsectarian, or public-nonpublic nature of the institution benefited." In light of these factors, we held that the program was not inconsistent with the Establishment Clause.

Five Members of the Court, in separate opinions, emphasized the general rule from *Mueller* that the amount of government aid channeled to religious institutions by individual aid recipients was not relevant to the constitutional inquiry. Our holding thus rested not on whether few or many recipients chose to expend government aid at a religious school but, rather, on whether recipients generally were empowered to direct the aid to schools or institutions of their own choosing.

Finally, in *Zobrest*, we applied *Mueller* and *Witters* to reject an Establishment Clause challenge to a federal program that permitted sign-language interpreters to assist deaf children enrolled in religious schools. Reviewing our earlier decisions, we stated that "government programs that neutrally provide benefits to a broad class of citizens defined without reference to religion are not readily subject to an Establishment Clause challenge." Looking once again to the challenged program as a whole, we observed that the program "distributes benefits neutrally to any child qualifying as 'disabled.'" Its "primary beneficiaries," we said, were "disabled children, not sectarian schools."

We further observed that "[b]y according parents freedom to select a school of their choice, the statute ensures that a government-paid interpreter will be present in a sectarian school only as a result of the private decision of individual parents." Our focus again was on neutrality and the principle of private choice, not on the number of program beneficiaries attending religious schools. ("*Zobrest* did not turn on the fact that James Zobrest had, at the time of litigation, been the only child using a publicly funded sign-language interpreter to attend a parochial school.") Because the program ensured that parents were the ones to select a religious school as the best learning environment for their handicapped child, the circuit between government and religion was broken, and the Establishment Clause was not implicated.

Mueller, Witters, and *Zobrest* thus make clear that where a government aid program is neutral with respect to religion, and provides assistance directly to a broad class of citizens who, in turn, direct government aid to religious schools wholly as a result of their own genuine and independent private choice, the program is not readily subject to challenge under the Establishment Clause. A program that shares these features permits government aid to reach religious institutions only by way of the deliberate choices of numerous individual recipients. The incidental advancement of a religious mission, or the perceived endorsement of a religious message, is reasonably attributable to the individual recipient, not to the government, whose role ends with the disbursement of benefits. As a plurality of this Court recently observed:

"[I]f numerous private choices, rather than the single choice of a government, determine the distribution of aid, pursuant to neutral eligibility criteria, then a government cannot, or at least cannot easily, grant special favors that might lead to a religious establishment."

. . . It is precisely for these reasons that we have never found a program of true private choice to offend the Establishment Clause.

We believe that the program challenged here is a program of true private choice, consistent with *Mueller, Witters*, and *Zobrest*, and thus constitutional. As was true in those cases, the Ohio program is neutral in all respects toward religion. It is part of a general and multifaceted undertaking by the State of Ohio to provide educational opportunities to the children of a failed school district. It confers educational assistance directly to a broad class of individuals defined without reference to religion, *i.e.*, any parent of a school-age child who resides in the Cleveland City School District. The program permits the participation of *all* schools within the district, religious or nonreligious. Adjacent public schools also may participate and have a financial incentive to do so. Program benefits are available to participating families on neutral terms, with no reference to religion. The only preference stated anywhere in the program is a preference for low-income families, who receive greater assistance and are given priority for admission at participating schools.

There are no "financial incentive[s]" that "ske[w]" the program toward religious schools. Such incentives "[are] not present . . . where the aid is allocated on the basis of neutral, secular criteria that neither favor nor disfavor religion, and is made available to both religious and secular beneficiaries on a nondiscriminatory basis." The program here in fact creates financial *dis*incentives for religious schools, with private schools receiving only half the government assistance given to community schools and one-third the assistance given to magnet schools. Adjacent public schools, should any choose to accept program students, are also eligible to receive two to three times the state funding of a private religious school. Families too have a financial disincentive to choose a private religious school over other schools. Parents that choose to participate in the scholarship program and then to enroll their children in a private school (religious or nonreligious) must copay a portion of the school's tuition. Families that choose a community school, magnet school, or traditional public school pay nothing. Although such features of the program are not necessary to its constitutionality, they clearly dispel the claim that the program "creates . . . financial incentive[s] for parents to choose a sectarian school."

Respondents suggest that even without a financial incentive for parents to choose a religious school, the program creates a "public perception that the State is endorsing religious practices and beliefs." But we have repeatedly recognized that no reasonable observer would think a neutral program of private choice, where state aid reaches religious schools solely as a result of the numerous independent decisions of private individuals, carries with it the *imprimatur* of government endorsement. The argument is particularly misplaced here since "the reasonable observer in the endorsement inquiry must be deemed aware" of the "history and context" underlying a challenged program. Any objective observer familiar with the full history and context of the Ohio program would reasonably view it as one aspect of a broader undertaking to assist poor children in failed schools, not as an endorsement of religious schooling in general.

There also is no evidence that the program fails to provide genuine opportunities for Cleveland parents to select secular educational options for their school-age children. Cleveland schoolchildren enjoy a range of educational choices: They may remain in public school as before, remain in public school with publicly funded tutoring aid, obtain a scholarship and choose a religious school, obtain a scholarship and choose a nonreligious private school, enroll in a community school, or enroll in a magnet school. That 46 of the 56 private schools now participating in the program are religious schools does not condemn it as a violation of the Establishment Clause. The Establishment Clause question is whether Ohio is coercing parents into sending their children to religious schools, and that question must be answered by evaluating *all* options Ohio provides Cleveland schoolchildren, only one of which is to obtain a program scholarship and then choose a religious school. . . .

. . . Respondents finally claim that we should look to *Committee for Public Ed. & Religious Liberty v. Nyquist*, to decide these cases. We disagree for two reasons. First, the program in *Nyquist* was quite different from the program challenged here. *Nyquist* involved a New York program that gave a package of benefits exclusively to private schools and the parents of private school enrollees. Although the program was enacted for ostensibly secular purposes, we found that its "function" was "*unmistakably* to provide desired financial support for nonpublic, sectarian institutions." Its genesis, we said, was that private religious schools faced "increasingly grave fiscal problems." The program thus provided direct money grants to religious schools. It provided tax benefits "unrelated to the amount of money actually expended by any parent on tuition," ensuring a windfall to parents of children in religious schools. It similarly provided tuition reimbursements designed explicitly to "offe[r] . . . an incentive to parents to send their children to sectarian schools." Indeed, the program flatly prohibited. Ohio's program shares none of these features.

Second, were there any doubt that the program challenged in *Nyquist* is far removed from the program challenged here, we expressly reserved judgment with respect to "a case involving some form of public assistance (*e.g.*, scholarships) made available generally without regard to the sectarian-nonsectarian, or public-nonpublic nature of the institution benefited." That, of course, is the very question now before us, and it has since been answered, first in *Mueller*. To the extent the scope of *Nyquist* has remained an open question in light of these later decisions, we now hold that *Nyquist* does not govern neutral educational assistance programs that, like the program here, offer aid directly to a broad class of individual recipients defined without regard to religion. In sum, the Ohio program is entirely neutral with respect to religion. It provides benefits directly to a wide spectrum of individuals, defined only by financial need and residence in a particular school district. It permits such individuals to exercise genuine choice among options public and private, secular and religious. The program is therefore a program of true private choice. In keeping with an unbroken line of decisions rejecting challenges to similar programs, we hold that the program does not offend the Establishment Clause.

The judgment of the Court of Appeals is reversed.

JUSTICE SOUTER, *with whom* **JUSTICE STEVENS, JUSTICE GINSBURG**, *and* **JUSTICE BREYER** *join, dissenting.*

The Court's majority holds that the Establishment Clause is no bar to Ohio's payment of tuition at private religious elementary and middle schools under a scheme that systematically provides tax money to support the schools' religious missions. The occasion for the legislation thus upheld is the condition of public education in the city of Cleveland. The record indicates that the schools are failing to serve their objective, and the vouchers in issue here are said to be needed to provide adequate alternatives to them. If there were an excuse for giving short shrift to the Establishment Clause, it would probably apply here. But there is no excuse. Constitutional limitations are placed on government to preserve constitutional values in hard cases, like these. . . .

B

. . . If the divisiveness permitted by today's majority is to be avoided in the short term, it will be avoided only by action of the political branches at the state and national levels. Legislatures not driven to desperation by the problems of public education may be able to see the threat in vouchers negotiable in sectarian schools. Perhaps even cities with problems like Cleveland's will perceive the danger, now that they know a federal court will not save them from it.

My own course as a judge on the Court cannot, however, simply be to hope that the political branches will save us from the consequences of the majority's decision. *Everson*'s statement is still the touchstone of sound law, even though the reality is that in the matter of educational aid the Establishment Clause has largely been read away. True, the majority has not approved vouchers for religious schools alone, or aid earmarked for religious instruction. But no scheme so clumsy will ever get before us, and in the cases that we may see, like these, the Establishment Clause is largely silenced. I do not have the option to leave it silent, and I hope that a future Court will reconsider today's dramatic departure from basic Establishment Clause principle.

LOCKE v. DAVEY

540 U.S. 712 (2004)

Opinion: Rehnquist, joined by Stevens,
O'Connor, Kennedy, Souter,
Ginsburg, Breyer
Dissent: Scalia, joined by Thomas
Dissent: Thomas

We now turn to a case that raises issues of free exercise as well as establishment. At issue in the case is whether a publicly funded scholarship can constitutionally be withheld from students pursuing devotional theology. This is a good time to reflect on the relationship between the Free Exercise Clause and the Establishment Clause. Do strict restrictions on the establishment of religion, including funding that can be used for religious purposes, ultimately result in a curtailment in the free exercise of religion?

CHIEF JUSTICE REHNQUIST *delivered the opinion of the Court.*

The State of Washington established the Promise Scholarship Program to assist academically gifted students with postsecondary education expenses. In accordance with the State Constitution, students may not use the scholarship at an institution where they are pursuing a degree in devotional theology. We hold that such an exclusion from an otherwise inclusive aid program does not violate the Free Exercise Clause of the First Amendment.

The Washington State Legislature found that "[s]tudents who work hard . . . and successfully complete high school with high academic marks may not have the financial ability to attend college because they cannot obtain financial aid or the financial aid is insufficient." In 1999, to assist these high-achieving students, the legislature created

the Promise Scholarship Program, which provides a scholarship, renewable for one year, to eligible students for postsecondary education expenses. Students may spend their funds on any education-related expense, including room and board. The scholarships are funded through the State's general fund, and their amount varies each year depending on the annual appropriation, which is evenly prorated among the eligible students. The scholarship was worth $1,125 for academic year 1999–2000 and $1,542 for 2000–2001.

To be eligible for the scholarship, a student must meet academic, income, and enrollment requirements. A student must graduate from a Washington public or private high school and either graduate in the top 15% of his graduating class, or attain on the first attempt a cumulative score of 1,200 or better on the Scholastic Assessment Test I or a score of 27 or better on the American College Test. The student's family income must be less than 135% of the State's median. Finally, the student must enroll "at least half time in an eligible postsecondary institution in the state of Washington," and may not pursue a degree in theology at that institution while receiving the scholarship. Private institutions, including those religiously affiliated, qualify as "eligible postsecondary institution[s]" if they are accredited by a nationally recognized accrediting body. A "degree in theology" is not defined in the statute, but, as both parties concede, the statute simply codifies the State's constitutional prohibition on providing funds to students to pursue degrees that are "devotional in nature or designed to induce religious faith."

A student who applies for the scholarship and meets the academic and income requirements is notified that he is eligible for the scholarship if he meets the enrollment requirements. Once the student enrolls at an eligible institution, the institution must certify that the student is enrolled at least half time and that the student is not pursuing a degree in devotional theology. The institution, rather than the State, determines whether the student's major is devotional. If the student meets the enrollment requirements, the scholarship funds are sent to the institution for distribution to the student to pay for tuition or other educational expenses. Respondent, Joshua Davey, was awarded a Promise Scholarship, and chose to attend Northwest College. Northwest is a private, Christian college affiliated with the Assemblies of God denomination, and is an eligible institution under the Promise Scholarship Program. Davey had "planned for many years to attend a Bible college and to prepare [himself] through that college training for a lifetime of ministry, specifically as a church pastor." To that end, when he enrolled in Northwest College, he decided to pursue a double major in pastoral ministries and business management/administration. There is no dispute that the pastoral ministries degree is devotional and therefore excluded under the Promise Scholarship Program.

At the beginning of the 1999–2000 academic year, Davey met with Northwest's director of financial aid. He learned for the first time at this meeting that he could not use his scholarship to pursue a devotional theology degree. He was informed that to receive the funds appropriated for his use, he must certify in writing that he was not pursuing such a degree at Northwest. He refused to sign the form and did not receive any scholarship funds.

Davey then brought an action under against various state officials (hereinafter State) in the District Court for the Western District of Washington to enjoin the State from refusing to award the scholarship solely because a student is pursuing a devotional theology degree, and for damages. He argued the denial of his scholarship based on his decision to pursue a theology degree violated, *inter alia*, the Free Exercise, Establishment, and Free Speech Clauses of the First Amendment, as incorporated by the Fourteenth Amendment, and the Equal Protection Clause of the Fourteenth Amendment. After the District Court denied Davey's request for a preliminary injunction, the parties filed cross-motions for summary judgment. The District Court rejected Davey's constitutional claims and granted summary judgment in favor of the State.

A divided panel of the United States Court of Appeals for the Ninth Circuit reversed. The court concluded that the State had singled out religion for unfavorable treatment and thus under our decision in *Church of Lukumi Babalu Aye, Inc. v. Hialeah*, the State's exclusion of theology majors must be narrowly tailored to achieve a compelling state interest.

The Religion Clauses of the First Amendment provide: "Congress shall make no law respecting an establishment of religion, or prohibiting the free exercise thereof." These two Clauses, the Establishment Clause and the Free Exercise Clause, are frequently in tension. In other words, there are some state actions permitted by the Establishment Clause but not required by the Free Exercise Clause.

This case involves that "play in the joints" described above. Under our Establishment Clause precedent, the link between government funds and religious training is broken by the independent and private choice of recipients. As such, there is no doubt that the State could, consistent with the Federal Constitution, permit Promise Scholars to pursue a degree in devotional theology, and the State does not contend otherwise. The question before us, however, is whether Washington, pursuant to its own constitution, which has been authoritatively interpreted as prohibiting even indirectly funding religious instruction that will prepare students for the ministry . . . can deny them such funding without violating the Free Exercise Clause.

Davey urges us to answer that question in the negative. He contends that under the rule we enunciated in *Church of Lukumi Babalu Aye, Inc. v. Hialeah,* the program is presumptively unconstitutional because it is not facially neutral with respect to religion. We reject his claim of presumptive unconstitutionality, however; to do otherwise would extend the *Lukumi* line of cases well beyond not only their facts but their reasoning. In *Lukumi,* the city of Hialeah made it a crime to engage in certain kinds of animal slaughter. We found that the law sought to suppress ritualistic animal sacrifices of the Santeria religion. In the present case, the State's disfavor of religion (if it can be called that) is of a far milder kind. It imposes neither criminal nor civil sanctions on any type of religious service or rite. It does not deny to ministers the right to participate in the political affairs of the community. And it does not require students to choose between their religious beliefs and receiving a government benefit. The State has merely chosen not to fund a distinct category of instruction.

Justice Scalia argues, however, that generally available benefits are part of the "baseline against which burdens on religion are measured." Because the Promise Scholarship Program funds training for all secular professions, Justice Scalia contends the State must also fund training for religious professions. But training for religious professions and training for secular professions are not fungible. Training someone to lead a congregation is an essentially

religious endeavor. Indeed, majoring in devotional theology is akin to a religious calling as well as an academic pursuit. And the subject of religion is one in which both the United States and state constitutions embody distinct views—in favor of free exercise, but opposed to establishment—that find no counterpart with respect to other callings or professions. That a State would deal differently with religious education for the ministry than with education for other callings is a product of these views, not evidence of hostility toward religion.

Even though the differently worded Washington Constitution draws a more stringent line than that drawn by the United States Constitution, the interest it seeks to further is scarcely novel. In fact, we can think of few areas in which a State's antiestablishment interests come more into play. Since the founding of our country, there have been popular uprisings against procuring taxpayer funds to support church leaders, which was one of the hallmarks of an "established" religion.

Most States that sought to avoid an establishment of religion around the time of the founding placed in their constitutions formal prohibitions against using tax funds to support the ministry. The plain text of these constitutional provisions prohibited *any* tax dollars from supporting the clergy. We have found nothing to indicate, as Justice Scalia contends, that these provisions would not have applied so long as the State equally supported other professions or if the amount at stake was *de minimis.* That early state constitutions saw no problem in explicitly excluding *only* the ministry from receiving state dollars reinforces our conclusion that religious instruction is of a different ilk.

Far from evincing the hostility toward religion which was manifest in *Lukumi,* we believe that the entirety of the Promise

Scholarship Program goes a long way toward including religion in its benefits. The program permits students to attend pervasively religious schools, so long as they are accredited. As Northwest advertises, its "concept of education is distinctly Christian in the evangelical sense." Davey notes all students at Northwest are required to take at least four devotional courses, "Exploring the Bible," "Principles of Spiritual Development," "Evangelism in the Christian Life," and "Christian Doctrine," and some students may have additional religious requirements as part of their majors. In short, we find neither in the history or text of Article I, §11 of the Washington Constitution, nor in the operation of the Promise Scholarship Program, anything that suggests animus towards religion. Given the historic and substantial state interest at issue, we therefore cannot conclude that the denial of funding for vocational religious instruction alone is inherently constitutionally suspect.

Without a presumption of unconstitutionality, Davey's claim must fail. The State's interest in not funding the pursuit of devotional degrees is substantial and the exclusion of such funding places a relatively minor burden on Promise Scholars. If any room exists between the two Religion Clauses, it must be here. We need not venture further into this difficult area in order to uphold the Promise Scholarship Program as currently operated by the State of Washington.

The judgment of the Court of Appeals is therefore reversed.

JUSTICE SCALIA, *with whom* **JUSTICE THOMAS** *joins, dissenting.*

. . . When the State makes a public benefit generally available, that benefit becomes part of the baseline against which burdens on religion are measured; and when the State withholds that benefit from some individuals solely on the basis of religion, it violates the Free Exercise Clause no less than if it had imposed a special tax.

That is precisely what the State of Washington has done here. It has created a generally available public benefit, whose receipt is conditioned only on academic performance, income, and attendance at an accredited school. It has then carved out a solitary course of study for exclusion: theology. Wash. Rev. Code §28B.119.010(8) (Supp. 2004); Wash. Admin. Code §250-80-020(12)(g) (2003). No field of study but religion is singled out for disfavor in this fashion. Davey is not asking for a special benefit to which others are not entitled. Cf. *Lyng v. Northwest Indian Cemetery Protective Assn.* He seeks only *equal* treatment—the right to direct his scholarship to his chosen course of study, a right every other Promise Scholar enjoys. . . .

II

. . . Today's holding is limited to training the clergy, but its logic is readily extendible, and there are plenty of directions to go. What next? Will we deny priests and nuns their prescription-drug benefits on the ground that taxpayers' freedom of conscience forbids medicating the clergy at public expense? This may seem fanciful, but recall that France has proposed banning religious attire from schools, invoking interests in secularism no less benign than those the Court embraces today. . . . When the public's freedom of conscience is invoked to justify denial of equal treatment, benevolent motives shade into indifference and ultimately into repression. Having accepted the justification in this case, the Court is less well equipped to fend it off in the future. I respectfully dissent.

AP Photo/Harry Cabluck

The display of the Ten Commandments on the grounds of the Texas State Capitol, the constitutionality of which was challenged, but upheld, by the Court in Van Orden v. Perry.

VAN ORDEN v. PERRY

545 U.S. 677 (2005)

Opinion: Rehnquist, joined by Scalia, Kennedy, Thomas
Concurrence: Scalia
Concurrence: Thomas
Concurrence: Breyer
Dissent: Stevens, joined by Ginsburg
Dissent: O'Connor
Dissent: Souter, joined by Stevens, Ginsburg

As we have already seen, in some cases the Court upholds religious displays against Establishment Clause challenges because they have a secular purpose, while in other instances they are struck down as lacking such a purpose. For instance, we saw in Allegheny v. ACLU *and* Lynch v. Donnelly *that a crèche has to be examined in the context in which it is displayed to determine whether it violates the First Amendment. We turn now to the question of whether the public display of the Ten Commandments violates the Establishment Clause. Here, too, the Court eschews any formal test, including the* Lemon *test. Instead, the Court focuses on the specific display in determining whether it has a secular meaning. What, if anything, distinguishes the following two displays of the Ten Commandments, and do these distinctions justify the Court's differing decisions about their constitutionality? Pay particular attention to Justice Stephen Breyer's concurrence. Note that although he ultimately agrees with the Court that the Ten Commandments display does not violate the Establishment Clause, he does not concur in the Court's reasoning. Does Justice Breyer announce a new test, an exception to previous tests, or simply a clarification? Given the split ruling in this case, is there any concrete "holding" or "rule of law" that you can identify?*

CHIEF JUSTICE REHNQUIST *announced the judgment of the Court and delivered an opinion, in which* **JUSTICE SCALIA**, **JUSTICE KENNEDY**, *and* **JUSTICE THOMAS** *join.*

The question here is whether the Establishment Clause of the First Amendment allows the display of a monument inscribed with the Ten Commandments on the Texas State Capitol grounds. We hold that it does.

The 22 acres surrounding the Texas State Capitol contain 17 monuments and 21 historical markers commemorating the "people, ideals, and events that compose Texan identity." The monolith challenged here stands 6-feet high and 3-feet wide. It is located to the north of the Capitol building, between the Capitol and the Supreme Court building. Its primary content is the text of the Ten Commandments. An eagle grasping the American flag, an eye inside of a pyramid, and two small tablets with what appears to be an ancient script are carved above the text of the Ten Commandments. Below the text are two Stars of David and the superimposed Greek letters Chi and Rho, which represent Christ. The bottom of the monument bears the inscription "PRESENTED TO THE PEOPLE AND YOUTH OF TEXAS BY THE FRATERNAL ORDER OF EAGLES OF TEXAS 1961."

The legislative record surrounding the State's acceptance of the monument from the Eagles—a national social, civic, and patriotic organization—is limited to legislative journal entries. After the monument was accepted, the State selected a site for the monument based on the recommendation of the state organization responsible for maintaining the Capitol grounds. The Eagles paid the cost of erecting the monument, the dedication of which was presided over by two state legislators.

Petitioner Thomas Van Orden is a native Texan and a resident of Austin. At one time he was a licensed lawyer, having graduated from Southern Methodist Law School. Van Orden testified that, since 1995, he has encountered the Ten Commandments monument during his frequent visits to the Capitol grounds. His visits are typically for the purpose of using the law library in the Supreme Court building, which is located just northwest of the Capitol building.

Forty years after the monument's erection and six years after Van Orden began to encounter the monument frequently, he sued numerous state officials in their official capacities under 42 U.S.C. §1983 seeking both a declaration that the monument's placement violates the Establishment Clause and an injunction requiring its removal. After a bench trial, the District Court held that the monument did not contravene the Establishment Clause. It found that the State had a valid secular purpose in recognizing and commending the Eagles for their efforts to reduce juvenile delinquency. The District Court also determined that a reasonable observer, mindful of the history, purpose, and context, would not conclude that this passive monument conveyed the message that the State was seeking to endorse religion. The Court of Appeals affirmed the District Court's holdings with respect to the monument's purpose and effect. We granted certiorari, and now affirm.

This case, like all Establishment Clause challenges, presents us with the difficulty of respecting both faces. Our institutions presuppose a Supreme Being, yet these institutions must not press religious observances upon their citizens. One face looks to the past in acknowledgment of our Nation's heritage, while the other looks to the present in demanding a separation between church and state.

Whatever may be the fate of the *Lemon* test in the larger scheme of Establishment

Clause jurisprudence, we think it not useful in dealing with the sort of passive monument that Texas has erected on its Capitol grounds. Instead, our analysis is driven both by the nature of the monument and by our Nation's history.

As we explained in *Lynch v. Donnelly*: "There is an unbroken history of official acknowledgment by all three branches of government of the role of religion in American life from at least 1789." For example, both Houses passed resolutions in 1789 asking President George Washington to issue a Thanksgiving Day Proclamation to "recommend to the people of the United States a day of public thanksgiving and prayer, to be observed by acknowledging, with grateful hearts, the many and signal favors of Almighty God."

Recognition of the role of God in our Nation's heritage has also been reflected in our decisions. We have acknowledged, for example, that "religion has been closely identified with our history and government," *School Dist. of Abington Township v. Schempp*, and that "[t]he history of man is inseparable from the history of religion," *Engel v. Vitale*. This recognition has led us to hold that the Establishment Clause permits a state legislature to open its daily sessions with a prayer by a chaplain paid by the State. *Marsh v. Chambers*. Such a practice, we thought, was "deeply embedded in the history and tradition of this country." As we observed there, "it would be incongruous to interpret [the Establishment Clause] as imposing more stringent First Amendment limits on the states than the draftsmen imposed on the Federal Government." In this case we are faced with a display of the Ten Commandments on government property outside the Texas State Capitol. Such acknowledgments of the role played by the Ten Commandments in our Nation's heritage are common throughout America. We need only look within our own Courtroom. Since 1935, Moses has stood, holding two tablets that reveal portions of

the Ten Commandments written in Hebrew, among other lawgivers in the south frieze. Representations of the Ten Commandments adorn the metal gates lining the north and south sides of the Courtroom as well as the doors leading into the Courtroom. Moses also sits on the exterior east facade of the building holding the Ten Commandments tablets.

Of course, the Ten Commandments are religious—they were so viewed at their inception and so remain. The monument, therefore, has religious significance. According to Judeo-Christian belief, the Ten Commandments were given to Moses by God on Mt. Sinai. But Moses was a lawgiver as well as a religious leader. And the Ten Commandments have an undeniable historical meaning, as the foregoing examples demonstrate. Simply having religious content or promoting a message consistent with a religious doctrine does not run afoul of the Establishment Clause. (*Lynch v. Donnelly*; *Marsh v. Chambers*; *McGowan v. Maryland*; *Walz v. Tax Comm'n of City of New York*.)

There are, of course, limits to the display of religious messages or symbols. For example, we held unconstitutional a Kentucky statute requiring the posting of the Ten Commandments in every public schoolroom. *Stone v. Graham*.

The placement of the Ten Commandments monument on the Texas State Capitol grounds is a far more passive use of those texts than was the case in *Stone*, where the text confronted elementary school students every day. Indeed, Van Orden, the petitioner here, apparently walked by the monument for a number of years before bringing this lawsuit. The monument is therefore also quite different from the prayers involved in *Schempp* and *Lee v. Weisman*. Texas has treated her Capitol grounds monuments as representing the several strands in the State's political and legal history. The inclusion of the Ten Commandments monument in this group has a dual significance, partaking of both religion and government. We cannot say that Texas' display of this monument violates the Establishment Clause of the First Amendment.

The judgment of the Court of Appeals is affirmed.

JUSTICE BREYER, *concurring in the judgment.*

In *School Dist. of Abington Township v. Schempp,* Justice Goldberg, joined by Justice Harlan, wrote, in respect to the First Amendment's Religion Clauses, that there is "no simple and clear measure which by precise application can readily and invariably demark the permissible from the impermissible." One must refer instead to the basic purposes of those Clauses. They seek to "assure the fullest possible scope of religious liberty and tolerance for all." They seek to avoid that divisiveness based upon religion that promotes social conflict, sapping the strength of government and religion alike. *Zelman v. Simmons-Harris* (Breyer, J., dissenting). They seek to maintain that "separation of church and state" that has long been critical to the "peaceful dominion that religion exercises in [this] country," where the "spirit of religion" and the "spirit of freedom" are productively "united," "reign[ing] together" but in separate spheres "on the same soil." A. de Tocqueville, Democracy in America. They seek to further the basic principles set forth today by Justice O'Connor in her concurring opinion in *McCreary County v. American Civil Liberties Union of Ky.*

The Court has made clear, as Justices Goldberg and Harlan noted, that the realization of these goals means that government must "neither engage in nor compel religious practices," that it must "effect no favoritism among sects or between religion and nonreligion," and that it must "work deterrence of no religious belief." (*Schempp;*

Lee v. Weisman; Everson v. Board of Ed. of Ewing.) The government must avoid excessive interference with, or promotion of, religion. (*County of Allegheny v. American Civil Liberties Union; Zelman* (Breyer, J., dissenting).) But the Establishment Clause does not compel the government to purge from the public sphere all that in any way partakes of the religious. See, *e.g., Marsh v. Chambers.* Such absolutism is not only inconsistent with our national traditions, but would also tend to promote the kind of social conflict the Establishment Clause seeks to avoid.

Thus, as Justices Goldberg and Harlan pointed out, the Court has found no single mechanical formula that can accurately draw the constitutional line in every case. *Schempp.* Where the Establishment Clause is at issue, tests designed to measure "neutrality" alone are insufficient, both because it is sometimes difficult to determine when a legal rule is "neutral," and because "untutored devotion to the concept of neutrality can lead to invocation or approval of results which partake not simply of that noninterference and noninvolvement with the religious which the Constitution commands, but of a brooding and pervasive devotion to the secular and a passive, or even active, hostility to the religious." *Ibid.*

Neither can this Court's other tests readily explain the Establishment Clause's tolerance, for example, of the prayers that open legislative meetings; certain references to, and invocations of, the Deity in the public words of public officials; the public references to God on coins, decrees, and buildings; or the attention paid to the religious objectives of certain holidays, including Thanksgiving.

If the relation between government and religion is one of separation, but not of mutual hostility and suspicion, one will inevitably find difficult borderline cases. And in such cases, I see no test-related substitute for the exercise of legal judgment.

That judgment is not a personal judgment. Rather, as in all constitutional cases, it must reflect and remain faithful to the underlying purposes of the Clauses, and it must take account of context and consequences measured in light of those purposes. While the Court's prior tests provide useful guideposts—and might well lead to the same result the Court reaches today, no exact formula can dictate a resolution to such fact-intensive cases.

The case before us is a borderline case. It concerns a large granite monument bearing the text of the Ten Commandments located on the grounds of the Texas State Capitol. On the one hand, the Commandments' text undeniably has a religious message, invoking, indeed emphasizing, the Diety. On the other hand, focusing on the text of the Commandments alone cannot conclusively resolve this case. Rather, to determine the message that the text here conveys, we must examine how the text is *used*. And that inquiry requires us to consider the context of the display.

In certain contexts, a display of the tablets of the Ten Commandments can convey not simply a religious message but also a secular moral message (about proper standards of social conduct). And in certain contexts, a display of the tablets can also convey a historical message (about a historic relation between those standards and the law)—a fact that helps to explain the display of those tablets in dozens of courthouses throughout the Nation, including the Supreme Court of the United States.

Here the tablets have been used as part of a display that communicates not simply a religious message, but a secular message as well. The circumstances surrounding the display's placement on the capitol grounds and its physical setting suggest that the State itself intended the latter, nonreligious aspects of the tablets' message to predominate. And the monument's 40-year history

on the Texas state grounds indicates that that has been its effect.

The group that donated the monument, the Fraternal Order of Eagles, a private civic (and primarily secular) organization, while interested in the religious aspect of the Ten Commandments, sought to highlight the Commandments' role in shaping civic morality as part of that organization's efforts to combat juvenile delinquency. The Eagles' consultation with a committee composed of members of several faiths in order to find a nonsectarian text underscores the group's ethics-based motives. The tablets, as displayed on the monument, prominently acknowledge that the Eagles donated the display, a factor which, though not sufficient, thereby further distances the State itself from the religious aspect of the Commandments' message.

The physical setting of the monument, moreover, suggests little or nothing of the sacred. The monument sits in a large park containing 17 monuments and 21 historical markers, all designed to illustrate the "ideals" of those who settled in Texas and of those who have lived there since that time. The setting does not readily lend itself to meditation or any other religious activity. But it does provide a context of history and moral ideals. It (together with the display's inscription about its origin) communicates to visitors that the State sought to reflect moral principles, illustrating a relation between ethics and law that the State's citizens, historically speaking, have endorsed. That is to say, the context suggests that the State intended the display's moral message—an illustrative message reflecting the historical "ideals" of Texans—to predominate.

If these factors provide a strong, but not conclusive, indication that the Commandments' text on this monument conveys a predominantly secular message, a further factor is determinative here. As far as I can tell, 40 years passed in which the presence of this monument, legally speaking, went unchallenged (until the single legal objection raised by petitioner). And I am not aware of any evidence suggesting that this was due to a climate of intimidation. Hence, those 40 years suggest more strongly than can any set of formulaic tests that few individuals, whatever their system of beliefs, are likely to have understood the monument as amounting, in any significantly detrimental way, to a government effort to favor a particular religious sect, primarily to promote religion over nonreligion, to "engage in" any "religious practic[e]," to "compel" any "religious practic[e]," or to "work deterrence" of any "religious belief." *Schempp* (Goldberg, J., concurring). Those 40 years suggest that the public visiting the capitol grounds has considered the religious aspect of the tablets' message as part of what is a broader moral and historical message reflective of a cultural heritage.

This case, moreover, is distinguishable from instances where the Court has found Ten Commandments displays impermissible. The display is not on the grounds of a public school, where, given the impressionability of the young, government must exercise particular care in separating church and state. (*Weisman; Stone v. Graham.*) This case also differs from *McCreary County*, where the short (and stormy) history of the courthouse Commandments' displays demonstrates the substantially religious objectives of those who mounted them, and the effect of this readily apparent objective upon those who view them. That history there indicates a governmental effort substantially to promote religion, not simply an effort primarily to reflect, historically, the secular impact of a religiously inspired document. And, in today's world, in a Nation of so many different religious and comparable nonreligious fundamental beliefs, a more contemporary state effort to focus attention upon a religious text is certainly likely to prove divisive in a way that this longstanding, pre-existing monument has not.

For these reasons, I believe that the Texas display—serving a mixed but primarily nonreligious purpose, not primarily "advanc[ing]" or "inhibit[ing] religion," and not creating an "excessive government entanglement with religion,"—might satisfy this Court's more formal Establishment Clause tests. (*Lemon; Capitol Square* (O'Connor, J., concurring in part).) But, as I have said, in reaching the conclusion that the Texas display falls on the permissible side of the constitutional line, I rely less upon a literal application of any particular test than upon consideration of the basic purposes of the First Amendment's Religion Clauses themselves. This display has stood apparently uncontested for nearly two generations. That experience helps us understand that as a practical matter of *degree* this display is unlikely to prove divisive. And this matter of degree is, I believe, critical in a borderline case such as this one.

At the same time, to reach a contrary conclusion here, based primarily upon on the religious nature of the tablets' text would, I fear, lead the law to exhibit a hostility toward religion that has no place in our Establishment Clause traditions. Such a holding might well encourage disputes concerning the removal of longstanding depictions of the Ten Commandments from public buildings across the Nation. And it could thereby create the very kind of religiously based divisiveness that the Establishment Clause seeks to avoid. *Zelman* (Breyer, J., dissenting).

Justices Goldberg and Harlan concluded in *Schempp* that

"[t]he First Amendment does not prohibit practices which by any realistic measure create none of the dangers which it is designed to prevent and which do not so directly or substantially involve the state in religious exercise or in the favoring of religion as to have meaningful and practical impact."

That kind of practice is what we have here. I recognize the danger of the slippery slope. Still, where the Establishment Clause is at issue, we must "distinguish between real threat and mere shadow." *Ibid.* Here, we have only the shadow.

In light of these considerations, I cannot agree with today's plurality's analysis. Nor can I agree with Justice Scalia's dissent in *McCreary County.* I do agree with Justice O'Connor's statement of principles in *McCreary County,* . . . though I disagree with her evaluation of the evidence as it bears on the application of those principles to this case.

I concur in the judgment of the Court.

McCREARY COUNTY v. ACLU OF KENTUCKY

545 U.S. 844 (2005)

Opinion: Souter, joined by Stevens, O'Connor, Ginsburg, Breyer
Concurrence: O'Connor
Dissent: Scalia, joined by Rehnquist, Thomas, and by Kennedy in Parts II and III

JUSTICE SOUTER *delivered the opinion of the Court.*

Executives of two counties posted a version of the Ten Commandments on the walls of their courthouses. After suits were filed charging violations of the Establishment Clause, the legislative body of each county adopted a resolution calling for a more extensive exhibit meant to show that the Commandments are Kentucky's "precedent legal code." The result in each instance was a modified display of the Commandments surrounded by texts containing religious references as their sole common element. After changing counsel, the counties revised the exhibits again by eliminating some documents, expanding the text set out in another, and adding some new ones.

The issues are whether a determination of the counties' purpose is a sound basis for ruling on the Establishment Clause complaints, and whether evaluation of the counties' claim of secular purpose for the ultimate displays may take their evolution into account. We hold that the counties' manifest objective may be dispositive of the constitutional enquiry, and that the development of the presentation should be considered when determining its purpose.

In the summer of 1999, petitioners McCreary County and Pulaski County, Kentucky (hereinafter Counties), put up in their respective courthouses large, goldframed copies of an abridged text of the King James version of the Ten Commandments, including a citation to the Book of Exodus. In McCreary County, the placement of the Commandments responded to an order of the county legislative body requiring "the display [to] be posted in 'a very high traffic area' of the courthouse." In Pulaski County, amidst reported controversy over the propriety of the display, the Commandments were hung in a ceremony presided over by the county Judge-Executive, who called them "good rules to live by" and who recounted the story of an astronaut who became convinced "there must be a divine God" after viewing the Earth from the moon. The Judge-Executive was accompanied by the pastor of his church, who called the Commandments "a creed of ethics" and told the press after the ceremony that displaying the Commandments was "one of the greatest things the judge could have done to close out the millennium."

Assembled with the Commandments are framed copies of the Magna Carta, the Declaration of Independence, the Bill of Rights, the lyrics of the Star Spangled Banner, the Mayflower Compact, the National Motto, the Preamble to the Kentucky Constitution, and a picture of Lady Justice. The collection is entitled "The Foundations of American Law and Government Display" and each document comes with a statement about its historical and legal significance. . . .

A

. . . The touchstone for our analysis is the principle that the "First Amendment mandates governmental neutrality between religion and religion, and between religion and nonreligion." (*Epperson v. Arkansas*; *Everson v. Board of Ed. of Ewing*; *Wallace v. Jaffree*). When the government acts with the ostensible and predominant purpose of advancing religion, it violates that central Establishment Clause value of official religious neutrality, there being no neutrality when the government's ostensible object is to take sides. *Corporation of Presiding Bishop of Church of Jesus Christ of Latter-day Saints v. Amos.* Manifesting a purpose to favor one faith over another, or adherence to religion generally, clashes with the "understanding, reached . . . after decades of religious war, that liberty and social stability demand a religious tolerance that respects the religious views of all citizens. . . ."

Zelman v. Simmons-Harris (Breyer, J., dissenting). By showing a purpose to favor religion, the government "sends the . . . message to . . . nonadherents 'that they are outsiders, not full members of the political community, and an accompanying message to adherents that they are insiders, favored members. . . .'" *Santa Fe Independent School Dist. v. Doe.*

Indeed, the purpose apparent from government action can have an impact more significant than the result expressly decreed: when the government maintains Sunday closing laws, it advances religion only minimally because many working people would take the day as one of rest regardless, but if the government justified its decision with a stated desire for all Americans to honor Christ, the divisive thrust of the official action would be inescapable. This is the teaching of *McGowan v. Maryland*, which upheld Sunday closing statutes on practical, secular grounds after finding that the government had forsaken the religious purposes behind centuries-old predecessor laws.

Lemon said that government action must have "a secular . . . purpose," and after a host of cases it is fair to add that although a legislature's stated reasons will generally get deference, the secular purpose required has to be genuine, not a sham, and not merely secondary to a religious objective. See, *e.g.*, *Santa Fe Independent School Dist. v. Doe* ("When a governmental entity professes a secular purpose for an arguably religious policy, the government's characterization is, of course, entitled to some deference. But it is nonetheless the duty of the courts to 'distinguis[h] a sham secular purpose from a sincere one'"); *Edwards* [*v. Aguillard*]; *Stone*).

Even the Counties' own cited authority confirms that we have not made the purpose test a pushover for any secular claim. True, *Wallace* said government action is tainted by its object "if it is entirely motivated by a purpose to advance religion," a remark that suggests, in isolation, a fairly complaisant attitude. But in that very case the Court declined to credit Alabama's stated secular rationale of "accommodation" for legislation authorizing a period of silence in school for meditation or voluntary prayer, given the implausibility of that explanation in light of another statute already accommodating children wishing to pray. As we said, the Court often does accept governmental statements of purpose, in keeping with the respect owed in the first instance to such official claims. But in those unusual cases where the claim was an apparent sham, or the secular purpose secondary, the unsurprising results have been findings of no adequate secular object, as against a predominantly religious one. . . .

The Counties' second proffered limitation can be dispatched quickly. They argue that purpose in a case like this one should be inferred, if at all, only from the latest news about the last in a series of governmental actions, however close they may all be in time and subject. But the world is not made brand new every morning, and the Counties are simply asking us to ignore perfectly probative evidence; they want an absentminded objective observer, not one presumed to be familiar with the history of the government's actions and competent to learn what history has to show. (*Santa Fe Independent School Dist. v. Doe*; *Edwards*; *Capitol Square Review and Advisory Bd. v. Pinette* (O'Connor, J., concurring in part and concurring in judgment).) The Counties' position just bucks common sense: reasonable observers have reasonable memories, and our precedents sensibly forbid an observer "to turn a blind eye to the context in which [the] policy arose." *Santa Fe Independent School Dist. v. Doe*.

While the dissent fails to show a consistent original understanding from which to argue that the neutrality principle should be rejected, it does manage to deliver a surprise. As mentioned, the dissent says that the deity the Framers had in mind was the God of monotheism, with the consequence that government may espouse a tenet of traditional monotheism. This is truly a remarkable view. Other members of the Court have dissented on the ground that the Establishment Clause bars nothing more than governmental preference for one religion over another, *e.g.*, *Wallace v. Jaffree* (Rehnquist, J., dissenting), but at least religion has previously been treated inclusively. Today's dissent, however, apparently means that government should be free to approve the core beliefs of a favored religion over the tenets of others, a view that should trouble anyone who prizes religious liberty. Certainly history cannot justify it; on the contrary, history shows that the religion of concern to the Framers was not that of the monotheistic faiths generally, but Christianity in particular, a fact that no member of this Court takes as a premise for construing the Religion Clauses. Justice Story probably reflected the thinking of the framing generation when he wrote in his Commentaries that the purpose of the Clause was "not to countenance, much less to advance, Mahometanism, or Judaism, or infidelity, by prostrating Christianity; but to exclude all rivalry among Christian sects." The Framers would, therefore, almost certainly object to the dissent's unstated reasoning that because Christianity was a monotheistic "religion," monotheism with Mosaic antecedents should be a touchstone of establishment interpretation. Even on originalist critiques of existing precedent there is, it seems, no escape from interpretative consequences that would surprise the Framers. Thus, it appears to be common ground in the interpretation of a Constitution "intended to endure for ages to come," *McCulloch v. Maryland*, that applications unanticipated by the Framers are inevitable.

Historical evidence thus supports no solid argument for changing course (whatever force the argument might have when directed at the existing precedent), whereas public discourse at the present time certainly raises no doubt about the value of the interpretative approach invoked for 60 years now. We are centuries away from the St. Bartholomew's Day massacre and the treatment of heretics in early Massachusetts, but the divisiveness of religion in current public life is inescapable. This is no time to deny the prudence of understanding the Establishment Clause to require the Government to stay neutral on religious belief, which is reserved for the conscience of the individual.

V

Given the ample support for the District Court's finding of a predominantly religious purpose behind the Counties' third display, we affirm the Sixth Circuit in upholding the preliminary injunction.

JUSTICE O'CONNOR, *concurring*.

. . . Reasonable minds can disagree about how to apply the Religion Clauses in a given case. But the goal of the Clauses is clear: to carry out the Founders' plan of preserving religious liberty to the fullest extent possible in a pluralistic society. By enforcing the Clauses, we have kept religion a matter for the individual conscience, not for the prosecutor or bureaucrat. At a time when we see around the world the violent consequences of the assumption of religious authority by government, Americans may count themselves fortunate: Our regard for constitutional boundaries has protected us

from similar travails, while allowing private religious exercise to flourish. . . .

Our guiding principle has been James Madison's—that "[t]he Religion . . . of every man must be left to the conviction and conscience of every man." To that end, we have held that the guarantees of religious freedom protect citizens from religious incursions by the States as well as by the Federal Government. (*Everson v. Board of Ed. of Ewing*; *Cantwell v. Connecticut*.) Government may not coerce a person into worshiping against her will, nor prohibit her from worshiping according to it. It may not prefer one religion over another or promote religion over nonbelief. *Everson*. It may not entangle itself with religion. *Walz v. Tax Comm'n of City of New York*. And government may not, by "endorsing religion or a religious practice," "mak[e] adherence to religion relevant to a person's standing in the political community." *Wallace v. Jaffree* (O'Connor, J., concurring in judgment).

When we enforce these restrictions, we do so for the same reason that guided the Framers—respect for religion's special role in society. Our Founders conceived of a Republic receptive to voluntary religious expression, and provided for the possibility of judicial intervention when government action threatens or impedes such expression. Voluntary religious belief and expression may be as threatened when government takes the mantle of religion upon itself as when government directly interferes with private religious practices. When the government associates one set of religious beliefs with the state and identifies nonadherents as outsiders, it encroaches upon the individual's decision about whether and how to worship. In the marketplace of ideas, the government has vast resources and special status. Government religious expression therefore risks crowding out private observance and distorting the natural interplay between competing beliefs. Allowing government to be a potential mouthpiece for competing religious ideas risks the sort of division that might easily spill over into suppression of rival beliefs. Tying secular and religious authority together poses risks to both.

Given the history of this particular display of the Ten Commandments, the Court correctly finds an Establishment Clause violation. The purpose behind the counties' display is relevant because it conveys an unmistakable message of endorsement to the reasonable observer. *Lynch v. Donnelly* (O'Connor, J., concurring).

It is true that many Americans find the Commandments in accord with their personal beliefs. But we do not count heads before enforcing the First Amendment. *West Virginia Bd. of Ed. v. Barnette*. Nor can we accept the theory that Americans who do not accept the Commandments' validity are outside the First Amendment's protections. There is no list of approved and disapproved beliefs appended to the First Amendment—and the Amendment's broad terms ("free exercise," "establishment," "religion") do not admit of such a cramped reading. It is true that the Framers lived at a time when our national religious diversity was neither as robust nor as well recognized as it is now. They may not have foreseen the variety of religions for which this Nation would eventually provide a home. They surely could not have predicted new religions, some of them born in this country. But they did know that line-drawing between religions is an enterprise that, once begun, has no logical stopping point. They worried that "the same authority which can establish Christianity, in exclusion of all other Religions, may establish with the same ease any particular sect of Christians, in exclusion of all other Sects." The Religion Clauses, as a result, protect adherents of all religions, as well as those who believe in no religion at all.

JUSTICE SCALIA, *with whom* **THE CHIEF JUSTICE** *and* **JUSTICE THOMAS** *join, and with whom* **JUSTICE KENNEDY** *joins as to Parts II and III, dissenting.*

I would uphold McCreary County and Pulaski County, Kentucky's (hereinafter Counties) displays of the Ten Commandments. I shall discuss first, why the Court's oft repeated assertion that the government cannot favor religious practice is false; second, why today's opinion extends the scope of that falsehood even beyond prior cases; and third, why even on the basis of the Court's false assumptions the judgment here is wrong.

What distinguishes the rule of law from the dictatorship of a shifting Supreme Court majority is the absolutely indispensable requirement that judicial opinions be grounded in consistently applied principle. That is what prevents judges from ruling now this way, now that—thumbs up or thumbs down—as their personal preferences dictate. Today's opinion forthrightly (or actually, somewhat less than forthrightly) admits that it does not rest upon consistently applied principle. In a revealing footnote, the Court acknowledges that the "Establishment Clause doctrine" it purports to be applying "lacks the comfort of categorical absolutes." What the Court means by this lovely euphemism is that sometimes the Court chooses to decide cases on the principle that government cannot favor religion, and sometimes it does not. The footnote goes on to say that "[i]n special instances we have found good reason" to dispense with the principle, but "[n]o such reasons present themselves here." It does not identify all of those "special instances," much less identify the "good reason" for their existence.

I have cataloged elsewhere the variety of circumstances in which this Court— even *after* its embrace of *Lemon*'s stated prohibition of such behavior—has approved government action "undertaken with the specific intention of improving the position of religion," *Edwards v. Aguillard* (Scalia, J., dissenting). Suffice it to say here that when the government relieves churches from the obligation to pay property taxes, when it allows students to absent themselves from public school to take religious classes, and when it exempts religious organizations from generally applicable prohibitions of religious discrimination, it surely means to bestow a benefit on religious practice— but we have approved it. (*Amos*; *Walz v. Tax Comm'n of City of New York*; *Zorach.*) Indeed, we have even approved (post-*Lemon*) government-led prayer to God. In *Marsh v. Chambers*, the Court upheld the Nebraska State Legislature's practice of paying a chaplain to lead it in prayer at the opening of legislative sessions. The Court explained that "[t]o invoke Divine guidance on a public body entrusted with making the laws is not . . . an 'establishment' of religion or a step toward establishment; it is simply a tolerable acknowledgment of beliefs widely held among the people of this country." (Why, one wonders, is not respect for the Ten Commandments a tolerable acknowledgment of beliefs widely held among the people of this country?) Turning at last to the displays actually at issue in this case, the Court faults the Counties for not *repealing* the resolution expressing what the Court believes to be an impermissible intent. Under these circumstances, the Court says, "no reasonable observer could swallow the claim that the Counties had cast off the objective so unmistakable in the earlier displays." Even were I to accept all that the Court has said before, I would not agree with that assessment. To begin with, of course, it is unlikely that a reasonable observer *would even have been aware* of the resolutions, so there would be nothing to "cast off." The Court implies that the Counties may have

been able to remedy the "taint" from the old resolutions by enacting a new one. But that action would have been wholly unnecessary in light of the explanation that the Counties included *with the displays themselves*: A plaque next to the documents informed all who passed by that each display "contains documents that played a significant role in the foundation of our system of law and government." Additionally, there was no reason for the Counties to repeal or repudiate the resolutions adopted with the hanging of the second displays, since they related *only to the second displays*. After complying with the District Court's order to remove the second displays "immediately," and erecting new displays that in content and by express assertion reflected a *different* purpose from that identified in the resolutions, the Counties had no reason to believe that their previous resolutions would be deemed to be the basis for their actions. After the Counties discovered that the sentiments expressed in the resolutions could be attributed to their most recent displays (in oral argument before this Court), they repudiated them immediately. In sum: The first displays did not necessarily evidence an intent to further religious practice; nor did the second displays, or the resolutions authorizing them; and there is in any event no basis for attributing whatever intent motivated the first and second displays to the third. Given the presumption of regularity that always accompanies our review of official action, the Court has identified no evidence of a purpose to advance religion in a way that is inconsistent with our cases. The Court may well be correct in identifying the third displays as the fruit of a desire to display the Ten Commandments, but neither our cases nor our history support its assertion that such a desire renders the fruit poisonous.

For the foregoing reasons, I would reverse the judgment of the Court of Appeals.

SYNTHESIS QUESTIONS FOR FURTHER DISCUSSION: CHAPTER 6 SECTION B

1. In moving from questions of free exercise to those of establishment, it is worth thinking about how the two Religion Clauses relate to one another. Is it possible to defend religious freedom without in some way engaging in the "establishment of religion"? Paradigmatically, the Establishment Clause is understood to prohibit the creation of a national church or a national religion. In thinking about whether this prohibition is required for religious freedom, consider whether a nation that has an established church—such as the United Kingdom—might also sufficiently guarantee religious freedom. Thinking back to the "Memorial and Remonstrance," how might James Madison answer this question? Do you agree? A related question concerns whether actions short of the establishment of a national church should be considered an unconstitutional attempt at the establishment of religion. For instance, based on Madison's thought, do public subsidies or tax exemptions for churches constitute an unconstitutional establishment of religion? Does such funding threaten religious freedom? You will notice that all of these issues help us to think more clearly about the more general question raised in the introduction to this chapter of whether there is an inevitable clash between the Free Exercise and Establishment Clauses of the First Amendment.

2. While support for religious believers and practices is clearly part of the central mission of religious institutions, many churches, mosques, and synagogues also provide social services to the public. For example, many operate homeless shelters, soup kitchens, and schools. Does the government violate the Establishment Clause when it supports these activities? Can some of these endeavors be classified as secular? Consider in your answer Michael McConnell's argument that religious groups have a large part to play in providing social services. Indeed, historically they have played a large role in this area. Should they be allowed to continue to do so? In *Lemon v. Kurtzman*, the Court struck down subsidies to religious schools, while in *Zelman v. Simmons-Harris*, it upheld vouchers for students, many of whom chose to attend parochial schools. What is the difference between these cases? Is the Court distinguishing between two separate circumstances, or are the rulings inconsistent? In considering your answer to this question, you might revisit your reflections on whether the Religion Clauses erect a wall of separation between church and state.

3. In his article, John Rawls argues that the public sphere should be governed by public reason. Specifically, he claims that religious argument should play

a role in public life only if it can be translated into terms that reasonable non-believers can accept. How does this claim relate to the debate over religious symbols displayed in public by the state? For instance, in *Lynch v. Donnelly*, the Court finds acceptable a crèche in the city of Pawtucket, but in *Allegheny v. ACLU* it rules that a different crèche is unconstitutional. The Court suggests that the salient difference is that one display was primarily cultural and secular whereas the other was overtly religious. Does this standard constrain the role of religion in public life by requiring "translation" of religious symbols into secular ones? If this is the case, is the public expression of less widespread religions more likely to be denied simply because such religions involve practices not part of the current public culture?

We have included both displays here. What difference, if any, is there between them?

© Courtesy of Professor Thomas Metzloff, Duke University

This Pawtucket, Rhode Island, crèche was the subject of the Supreme Court case Lynch v. Donnelly.

Pittsburgh Post-Gazette, Zoll. Reprinted with Permission.

The Supreme Court decision in Allegheny v. ACLU *examined this crèche in the main staircase of the Allegheny County Courthouse.*

4. The question of the constitutionality of the display of the Ten Commandments in many ways parallels the question of the constitutionality of the crèche. Do you agree with the Court that the Ten Commandments might at times be displayed in a manner that furthers a secular purpose? How can we tell when this is the case? Just as we explored this question with the aid of two pictures in regard to the crèche, we also display here two different displays of the Ten Commandments. Is there a constitutionally significant difference between the two displays? Do you agree with the Court's distinction between these displays?

Do these displays of the Ten Commandments meet the standard of public reason as defined by Rawls? You should consider in particular the difference between the first four, which define the relationship between God and humans, and the next six, which deal with interpersonal relations.

AP Photo/Harry Cabluck

This slab containing the Ten Commandments, installed on the lawn outside the Texas State Capitol in Austin, was the focus of the Supreme Court case Van Orden v. Perry.

© Photo by Franz Jantzen, Collection of the U.S. Supreme Court

The central figure in the U.S. Supreme Court pediment sculpture showing great lawmakers of history depicts Moses holding the Ten Commandments.

5. Consider all of the Establishment Clause cases that you have read in this chapter. Which of the various approaches or tests employed by the Court—or by Justices in concurrences or dissents—strikes you as the most faithful to the original understanding of the Clause? Which is the best method of applying the Clause's meaning to our diverse, modern society? Are your answers to these two questions different? Would you propose a different analysis?

    Now that you have read the major cases concerning the establishment of religion, you might rethink whether some of the free exercise cases might be understood through this lens. For instance, in *Church of Lukumi Babalu Aye v. City of Hialeah*, a free exercise analysis might focus on the impact of the ban on animal sacrifice for members of the Santeria religion. But could an establishment argument be made in this case that focuses on the councilmen's invocation of religious language to pass this law? Would such an analysis be sufficient to describe the constitutional problems with this law?

KEY TERMS

animus: Term used by the Court to refer to rationales for legislation that fail the rational basis test because they exhibit an unconstitutional hostility to a particular group as the basis for law. Although these rationales might be stated as reasons, in the Court's current jurisprudence, they fail to meet a standard of "rationality."

comprehensive doctrine: John Rawls's term for a religious or secular view that encompasses an understanding not just of justice, but of all moral questions. Comprehensive doctrines are contrasted with doctrines that are solely about politics.

entanglement: The Court's term for programs or legislation that overly involve relations between government and religion, relevant in Establishment Clause jurisprudence.

exemption: When the Court grants an exception to otherwise generally valid laws to individuals or groups for religious reasons.

facially neutral: As the Court explains in *Church of Lukumi Babalu Aye v. City of Hialeah*, a law that does not by its express terms discriminate against one religion or another, though it may have the incidental effect of doing so.

incorporation doctrine: The constitutional doctrine that holds that the Fourteenth Amendment's Due Process Clause creates a protection of the basic liberties of the Bill of Rights against the states in addition to Congress. At this point, most of the Bill of Rights has been subject to this doctrine, including the Free Speech and Religion Clauses. Provisions that have not been formally subject to the doctrine include but are not limited to the right to a jury trial in certain civil trials, guaranteed by the Seventh Amendment, as well as the right to an indictment by a grand jury in a criminal trial, guaranteed by the Fifth Amendment.

public reason: Rawls's phrase for the appropriate kind of arguments that are appealed to in justifying coercion.

rational review: When the Court presumes that a law is valid so long as the state can demonstrate that the law is "rationally related" to pursuing a "legitimate interest."

strict scrutiny: When the Court presumes that a law is invalid unless it is a "narrowly tailored" means of pursuing a "compelling interest."

wall of separation: The metaphor employed by some theorists of the First Amendment that suggests that the prohibition on the establishment of religion creates a sharp divide between religious and governmental institutions.

CHAPTER 7

SUBSTANTIVE DUE PROCESS AND FUNDAMENTAL RIGHTS

What rights, if any, are so fundamental as to be immune from the political process? Must they be found in the text?

In this chapter, we move from controversies surrounding rights that are explicitly written into the Constitution to a debate about legal rights that are not explicitly enumerated. Chapters 5 and 6 examined controversial cases involving the freedom of speech and the free exercise of religion. These controversies centered on the meaning of "enumerated" rights made explicit in the First Amendment. In *West Virginia v. Barnette*, U.S. Supreme Court Justice Robert H. Jackson explains that these rights are inviolable and immune from interference by political majorities:

> The very purpose of a Bill of Rights was to withdraw certain subjects from the vicissitudes of political controversy, to place them beyond the reach of majorities and officials and to establish them as legal principles to be applied by the courts. One's right to life, liberty, and property, to free speech, a free press, freedom of worship and assembly, and other fundamental rights may not be submitted to vote; they depend on the outcome of no elections.

Justice Jackson here is talking about why rights written into the text of the Constitution cannot be infringed by state legislatures or Congress. But can the Constitution ever constrain democratic majorities absent a clear and specific textual mandate? Are there some rights that are implicit in the text of the Constitution?

Unlike the First Amendment protections of free speech and religious liberty, the topic of this chapter, the entitlement to a guarantee of substantive due process, is not clearly discernible in the text of the Constitution. But the fact that a right is not explicitly mentioned or defined by the Constitution is not a sufficient reason, according to many constitutional thinkers, to rule out the possibility that it is fundamental to our constitutional order. For instance, the Court recognizes that the First Amendment protects freedom of association, a right that is considered ancillary to that of free speech but is not mentioned in the Constitution. Moreover, parts of the Constitution seem in fact to refer us beyond the text itself. Consider, for example, the Ninth Amendment's declaration that "the enumeration . . . of certain rights shall not be construed to deny or disparage" other fundamental rights that deserve protection. Here the Ninth Amendment might be understood to suggest that just because a right is not made explicit in the text of the Constitution, this does not mean that it does not exist. But this understanding of the Ninth Amendment raises some further problems. If the rights are not explicit, how do we know what they are? Many have thought that this issue is so problematic that the Ninth Amendment should not serve as a ground for constitutionally protected rights.

In contrast to the Ninth Amendment, the Fourteenth Amendment might provide more of a guide to the kind of rights implicit in the constitutional text. Although the term "substantive due process" does not appear in the Constitution, it has a foundation in the Fourteenth Amendment's guarantee that "no state shall . . . deprive any person of life, liberty, or property, without due process of law." It might be thought that the clause authorizes the deprivation of life, liberty, or property with due process of law. But the doctrine of substantive due process suggests otherwise. It suggests that no amount of due process can justify the deprivation of these guarantees. The idea here is that some liberties are so fundamental that they should be protected even if the legal and democratic processes lead to their violation. Substantive due process thus aims to limit the risks posed by the "tyranny of the majority." Although many think substantive due process suspect, it grounds many important constitutional rights. The rights to contraception, to an abortion, to autonomy in deciding whether and with whom to have sex are all grounded in the modern doctrine of substantive due process. These rights are, of course, among the most controversial of those protected by the Court. For example, the statute at issue in *Lawrence v. Texas*, which banned gay sodomy, was enacted by a duly elected legislature through a democratically legitimate process, yet the Court ruled on substantive due process grounds that this statute violated individuals' fundamental right to sexual privacy and intimacy. We will see that in addition to these contemporary rights, the Court also protected a right to contract that invalidated many worker protections under the doctrine of substantive due process in the early part of the twentieth century. This right was controversial and eventually abandoned by the Court. Indeed, one of the tasks of those who have defended the modern doctrine of substantive due process is to distinguish it from the earlier abandoned doctrine of economic substantive due process.

So far we have given a sense of the doctrine of substantive due process and have mentioned why there might be general skepticism about substantive due process. Now we will briefly explore how this skepticism and a response to it can be grounded in the theories of constitutional interpretation we explored in Chapter 2. Originalists and proceduralists tend to be skeptical of expanding the doctrine of substantive due process and of its foundation in the Constitution. In contrast, the moral reading offers a robust defense of the doctrine. Pragmatic theories of constitutional interpretation also potentially defend the doctrine.

The first type of skepticism is found in theories that stress the importance of textualism. The term "substantive" is often defined as "not-procedural," leading textualists to suggest that the phrase "substantive due process" is a contradiction in terms. Indeed, the non-textual aspect of the substantive due process doctrine has made it a central point of contention for those concerned about what Alexander Bickel called the "counter-majoritarian difficulty." Given that the rights guaranteed by substantive due process are not explicitly enumerated in the Constitution, many constitutional commentators have questioned why such rights should be protected in cases where state legislatures do not recognize them.

Given the close relationship between textualism and originalism, it is not surprising that proponents of that theory are often hostile to substantive due process. But U.S. Supreme Court Justice Antonin Scalia, whose theory of originalism we examined in Chapter 2, has a somewhat more nuanced position than outright rejection of the doctrine. According to Justice Scalia, liberty protected under the Due Process Clause would not have been understood at the time of the ratification of the Fourteenth Amendment to guarantee reproductive freedoms or gay rights. Any unconditional liberty protected by the Fourteenth Amendment, in his view, must be "deeply rooted in history and tradition." This same logic leads to his rejection of rights of sexual intimacy in his dissent in *Lawrence v. Texas*. Because these rights depart from tradition, they cannot be a part of the original public meaning of the Fourteenth Amendment, and because they depart from the original meaning, they are foreign to the Constitution. Any judge who identifies these rights as fundamental smuggles her own values into the Constitution and flouts the will of elected majorities.

John Hart Ely's procedural theory of democracy is also potentially hostile to the doctrine of substantive due process. For Ely, the democratic process is not only enshrined in the text of the Fourteenth Amendment, but it also serves as a primary justification for and limit on judicial review of legislation. Although Ely believes that the Court should guarantee rights related to voting, for instance, he claims that substantive rights are not grounded in the Constitution and that judicial review over such matters short-circuits legitimate democratic procedures. A right to use contraception or to engage in sexual intimacy might be important, but in Ely's view they are not central to democratic functioning and therefore should be decided in legislatures and not by the courts. Consider how Ely's procedural theory functions as a critique of *Roe v. Wade* in his article, "The Wages of Crying Wolf."

In contrast to these critics, however, the moral reading of the Constitution advanced by Ronald Dworkin sees substantive due process as a key structural feature of the Constitution. The political morality of individual liberty, on his view, is the basis and guiding principle of the entire text of the Constitution. Dworkin therefore advocates an expansive understanding of substantive due process. In *Life's Dominion*, he defends a right to abortion on the grounds that liberty includes the freedom for individuals to make crucial life choices. For Dworkin, making these judgments of political morality is necessary to interpret the Constitution and to satisfy the substantive requirements of democracy.

In contrast to the other three theories, pragmatists such as U.S. Supreme Court Justice Stephen Breyer, Cass Sunstein, and Judge Richard Posner eschew such sweeping constitutional theories. For them, the doctrine of substantive due process is only a tool that can be used to achieve good consequences. Rather than interpreting substantive due process to include a fixed set of liberties, they would uphold the doctrine in those cases where doing so would benefit society, and reject it if it could lead to adverse outcomes.

The doctrine of substantive due process has its historical origin, as we noted in Chapter 5, in a certain theory of economic liberty centered on a right to con-tract. The modern doctrine of substantive due process, however, is about per-sonal rather than economic liberty. Specifically, it protects a variety of personal liberties, including the right to purchase and use contraceptives. In reading *Griswold v. Connecticut*, think about the ways in which the Court's protection of a right to privacy, including a right to use contraception, might raise some of the same problems that arose in considering *Lochner v. New York*. Are the justices in both these cases merely imposing their personal morality upon the people? Does substantive due process have a legitimate role in a democratic society? The theories that we have considered here suggest how *Griswold v. Connecticut* and *Lochner v. New York* might be grouped together (think of the originalist and proceduralist understandings), or how they might be distinguished from one another (think of Dworkin's moral reading). Use these two cases as guideposts in developing your own view about this controversial doctrine.

Note that in *Griswold v. Connecticut*, which established a "right to privacy" that includes a right to use contraception free from state intervention, the Court goes to great lengths to avoid relying on substantive due process as a consti-tutional grounding or "hook." Indeed, U.S. Supreme Court Justice William O. Douglas explains that a right to privacy is grounded in other provisions of the Bill of Rights besides the Fourteenth Amendment. Arguably, he is trying to avoid being accused of "*Lochner*izing" or, in other words, of using what many saw as the faulty logic behind the right to contract that characterized the era of sub-stantive due process in the economic realm. U.S. Supreme Court Justice Arthur Goldberg also attempts to avoid *Lochner*izing by grounding the right to privacy in the Ninth Amendment. But U.S Supreme Court Justice John Harlan's concur-rence does cite the doctrine of substantive due process, and ultimately, Justice Harlan's view came to ground the right to privacy in current constitutional doc-trine. As you read *Griswold v. Connecticut*, perhaps the most important case of this chapter, consider which justice offers the best defense of substantive due process. Take note too of the dissents in this case. Do you agree that the idea of a right to privacy lacks a solid constitutional basis?

Although substantive due process can be traced back at least to *Lochner v. New York*, the contemporary extensions of this doctrine have a more direct lin-eage in cases about the rights of the family. In *Meyer v. Nebraska*, for instance, the

Court announced certain fundamental rights that parents have over their children when it comes to child rearing and education. In *Griswold v. Connecticut*, the Court drew directly upon the rights of the family in announcing a fundamental right to decide whether or not to have a child. In particular, the Court relied on the inviolable privacy of the "marital bedroom." Despite basing the right to procreation in the rights of families, the Court moved in *Eisenstadt v. Baird* to establish substantive due process as an individual right. The Court's decisions about abortion rights and gay rights likewise have moved away from the family framework—although the Court did rely upon the fundamental right of marriage in striking down miscegenation laws in *Loving v. Virginia*.

The doctrine of substantive due process has had a wide range of applications and touched numerous areas of public policy interest. We begin this chapter with the origins of the doctrine as one of economic liberty to contract and consider the extent to which the rights of families and of parents to raise their children are fundamental. *Meyer v. Nebraska* and *Pierce v. Society of Sisters*, in particular, address a possible tension between certain public education goals and the rights of families. We then consider cases involving reproductive freedom, including rights to use contraception and to obtain abortions. We examine the deep controversy about legalizing abortion along with Ely's critique of the Court's intervention into this area. Few contemporary controversies approach the intensity of the abortion debate, except perhaps those about gay rights, which we consider in Section C of this chapter. In *Bowers v. Hardwick* and *Lawrence v. Texas*, the Court considers the extent to which intimate sexual conduct deserves protection under the doctrine of substantive due process. We consider in this section the Court's decision to recognize the right of gay and heterosexual couples to have consensual sex. Finally, we examine the implications of the doctrine of substantive due process for families making decisions about whether to continue medical care to seriously ill relatives as well as the related issue of whether the doctrine of substantive due process extends to protect assisted suicide.

A. ECONOMIC SUBSTANTIVE DUE PROCESS

This section introduces the doctrine of substantive due process, which, as we have seen, extends into a wide variety of areas in constitutional law. Its origin, however, is in an area of rights no longer covered by the doctrine—that of economic liberty. Thus, this section explores the question of what "economic substantive due process" *was* rather than what it *is*. As you read these cases, however, ask whether the demise of economic substantive due process also suggests a flaw in the modern doctrine of substantive due process.

As we noted in both Chapters 2 and 3, an important early articulation of substantive due process is found in the case of *Lochner v. New York*. Specifically, *Lochner v. New York* examined whether a New York law that limited the hours of bakers violated the economic rights both of owners and of workers to make contracts as they wished. The name of the doctrine is confusing, because the

Lochner v. New York case asserted no "procedural" violation. Instead, the idea of the case is that certain liberties, such as the right to contract, are so fundamental to our constitutional scheme that they can never be infringed upon by the state, regardless of the "process" observed.

Thus, critics of the doctrine have argued that the very term "substantive due process" is an oxymoron, because substance is often defined as non-procedural. In considering whether *Lochner v. New York* rightly places the doctrine of substantive due process in the context of the Fourteenth Amendment, think back to the differing theories of constitutional interpretation that we studied in Chapter 2.

Many criticisms of the decision in *Lochner v. New York*, including U.S. Supreme Court Justice Oliver Wendell Holmes's dissent, suggest that the case mistakenly reads into the Constitution a libertarian theory of liberty. According to certain libertarian thinkers, one of the primary justifications of the state is to protect private property. Some libertarians thus defend a "minimal state" that greatly limits the power of government over the economic sphere. In order to see various arguments connected to libertarian thought, we have included excerpts here from John Locke and Robert Nozick. Although Nozick's place in the libertarian tradition is not contested, scholars cannot agree whether Locke himself can properly be understood as a libertarian. Some point to Locke's embrace of certain rights of welfare as necessary complements to property to argue that there is parity between these two entitlements. Although most our readings in this section define and defend strong property rights and a weak role for the state in economic policy and intervention, it would be helpful to revisit the progressive philosophy of President Franklin Roosevelt, who took a different approach to these issues, excerpted in Chapter 3, Section B. You will recall that President Roosevelt announced the "four freedoms" that defended a strong role for government in economic policy, with the aim of protecting workers rights and securing a decent standard of living for all. Also, revisit the readings from Cass Sunstein and Bruce Ackerman, who defended a progressive approach to the economy and civil liberties. Sunstein, you will also recall from Chapter 2, introduced us to the constitutional theory of pragmatism, which was very much present in his defense of President Roosevelt's ideas about the government's role in regulating the national economy.

The *Lochner v. New York* case stands not just for the particular issue concerning maximum-hours laws, which we examine here, but also for a long line of cases in which the Supreme Court appealed to the doctrine of economic substantive due process to strike down labor laws during and before the New Deal. For instance, we also include here an excerpt from *Adkins v. Children's Hospital*, in which the Court struck down minimum wage laws in the District of Columbia. The era of economic substantive due process, however, came to an end with *West Coast Hotel v. Parrish*, another minimum wage law case from the State of Washington. In Chapter 3 we saw that although *West Coast Hotel v. Parrish* is about state law, it signaled an end to the Court's opposition to President Roosevelt's New Deal at the federal level of government. Here we examine it as the end of the era of the use of the doctrine of substantive due process to strike down economic regulations. In *West Coast Hotel v. Parrish*, the Court directly overturned *Adkins v. Children's Hospital*, making the textual argument that the word "contract" does not appear in the Due Process Clause of the Fourteenth Amendment. Liberty, the Court held, is not the same as the right to contract.

The transition between the *Lochner v. New York* era of substantive due process and its demise in *West Coast Hotel v. Parrish* is no mere philosophical change. It occurs in the context of one of the most controversial parts of the Court's history. In particular, President Roosevelt, frustrated with the Court's opposition to his New Deal programs, threatened the Court with his famous "court packing plan," as we explained in Chapter 3. Roosevelt proposed that Congress pass legislation to add justices to the Court until the existing justices' votes were diluted, arguably causing the "switch in time that saved nine," where U.S. Supreme Court Justice Owen Roberts provided the critical swing vote for abandoning economic substantive due process. *West Coast Hotel v. Parrish*, therefore, not only raises a question about the legitimacy of the Court's libertarian philosophy in the *Lochner v. New York* line of cases, but it also raises a fundamental question about democracy. Was President Roosevelt usurping judicial independence in threatening the Court? Or, was the doctrine of substantive due process so undemocratic that it legitimated the President's strong action in threatening the Court?

John Locke

SECOND TREATISE OF GOVERNMENT

Chapter II; Chapter V

1698

The philosophy of John Locke is often thought to have had a strong influence on the Constitution and its underlying philosophy. For Locke, the purpose of a constitution is to guarantee a set of natural rights that are owed to all people regardless of the time or place in which they live.

The question of whether the Constitution guarantees such rights is certainly controversial. You will remember from Chapter 2 that there is significant disagreement among scholars about the degree to which the Constitution enshrines moral ideals. Moreover, one of the most controversial questions among those who agree that the Constitution does ensure natural rights is which specific rights are guaranteed.

In this passage, Locke argues that the right to hold property free from state interference is among the most basic of all human rights. As you read through this passage, think about Locke's argument for why property is such a basic right. Locke is thought to be such an advocate of private property that many regard him as a "property libertarian." According to such thinkers, the right to private property is so fundamental that its protection should be considered the primary purpose of society. Certainly Locke agrees. Are his arguments convincing? Importantly, think about whether his arguments are so strong that they entail that property must be core to any legitimate constitution, including the U.S. Constitution. Such a claim might reinforce the arguments of the justices of the Lochner v. New York *era who did see the right to private property as core to the Constitution's meaning.*

CHAPTER II: OF THE STATE OF NATURE

Sec. 4. To understand political power right, and derive it from its original, we must consider, what state all men are naturally in, and that is, a state of perfect freedom to order their actions, and dispose of their possessions and persons, as they think fit, within the bounds of the law of nature, without asking leave, or depending upon the will of any other man.

A state also of equality, wherein all the power and jurisdiction is reciprocal, no one having more than another; there being nothing more evident, than that creatures of the same species and rank, promiscuously born to all the same advantages of nature, and the use of the same faculties, should also be equal one amongst another without subordination or subjection, unless the lord and master of them all should, by any manifest declaration of his will, set one above another, and confer on him, by an evident and clear appointment, an undoubted right to dominion and sovereignty.

Sec. 6. But though this be a state of liberty, yet it is not a state of license: though man in that state have an uncontroulable liberty to dispose of his person or possessions, yet he has not liberty to destroy himself, or so much as any creature in his possession, but where some nobler use than its bare preservation calls for it. The state of nature has a law of nature to govern it, which obliges every one: and reason, which is that law, teaches all mankind, who will but consult it, that being all equal and independent, no one ought to harm another in his life, health, liberty, or possessions: for men being all the workmanship of one omnipotent, and infinitely wise maker; all the servants of one sovereign master, sent into the world by his order, and about his business; they are his property, whose workmanship they are, made to last during his, not one another's pleasure: and being furnished with like faculties, sharing all in one community of nature, there cannot be supposed any such subordination among us, that may authorize us to destroy one another, as if we were made for one another's uses, as the inferior ranks of creatures are for our's. Every one, as he is bound to preserve himself, and not to quit his station wilfully, so by the like reason, when his own preservation comes not in competition, ought he, as much as he can, to preserve the rest of mankind, and may not, unless it be to do justice on an offender, take away, or impair the life, or what tends to the preservation of the life, the liberty, health, limb, or goods of another.

Sec. 7. And that all men may be restrained from invading others rights, and from doing hurt to one another, and the law of nature be observed, which willeth the peace and preservation of all mankind, the execution of the law of nature is, in that state, put into every man's hands, whereby every one has a right to punish the transgressors of that law to such a degree, as may hinder its violation: for the law of nature would, as all other laws that concern men in this world 'be in vain, if there were no body that in the state of nature had a power to execute that law, and thereby preserve the innocent and restrain offenders. And if any one in the state of nature may punish another for any evil he has done, every one may do so: for in that state of perfect equality, where naturally there is no superiority or jurisdiction of one over another, what any may do in prosecution of that law, every one must needs have a right to do.

Sec. 8. And thus, in the state of nature, one man comes by a power over another; but yet no absolute or arbitrary power, to use a criminal, when he has got him in his hands, according to the passionate heats, or boundless extravagancy of his own will; but only to retribute to him, so far as calm reason and conscience dictate, what is proportionate to his transgression, which is so much as may serve for reparation and restraint: for these two are the only reasons, why one man may lawfully do harm to another, which is that we call punishment. In transgressing the law of nature, the offender declares himself to live by another rule than that of reason and common equity, which is that measure God has set to the actions of men, for their mutual security; and so he becomes dangerous to mankind, the tye, which is to secure them from injury and violence, being slighted and broken by him. Which being a trespass against the whole species, and the peace and safety of it, provided for by the law of nature, every man upon this score, by the right he hath to preserve mankind in general, may restrain, or where it is necessary, destroy things noxious to them, and so may bring such evil on any one, who hath transgressed that law, as may make him repent the doing of it, and thereby deter him, and by his example others, from doing the like mischief. And in the case, and upon this ground, EVERY MAN HATH A RIGHT TO PUNISH THE OFFENDER, AND BE EXECUTIONER OF THE LAW OF NATURE.

Sec. 9. I doubt not but this will seem a very strange doctrine to some men: but before they condemn it, I desire them to resolve me, by what right any prince or state can put to death, or punish an alien, for any crime he commits in their country. It is certain their laws, by virtue of any sanction they receive from the promulgated will of the legislative, reach not a stranger: they speak not to him, nor, if they did, is he bound to hearken to them. The legislative authority, by which they are in force over the subjects of that commonwealth, hath no power over him. Those who have the supreme power of making laws in England, France or Holland, are to an Indian, but like the rest of the world, men without authority: and therefore, if by the law of nature every man hath not a power to punish offences against it, as he soberly judges the case to require, I see not how the magistrates of any community can punish an alien of another country; since, in reference to him, they can have no more power than what every man naturally may have over another.

Sec. 10. Besides the crime which consists in violating the law, and varying from the right rule of reason, whereby a man so far becomes degenerate, and declares himself to quit the principles of human nature, and to be a noxious creature, there is commonly injury done to some person or other, and some other man receives damage by his transgression: in which case he who hath received any damage, has, besides the right of punishment common to him with other men, a particular right to seek reparation from him that has done it: and any other person, who finds it just, may also join with him that is injured, and assist him in recovering from the offender so much as may make satisfaction for the harm he has suffered.

CHAPTER V: OF PROPERTY

Sec. 25. Whether we consider natural reason, which tells us, that men, being once born, have a right to their preservation, and consequently to meat and drink, and such other things as nature affords for their subsistence: or revelation, which gives us an account of those grants God made of the world to Adam, and to Noah, and his sons, it is very clear, that God, as king David says, Psal. cxv. 16. has given the earth to the children of men; given it to mankind in common. But this being supposed, it seems to some a very great difficulty, how any one should ever come to have a property in any thing: I will not content myself to answer, that if it be difficult to make out property, upon a supposition that God gave the world to Adam, and his posterity in common, it is impossible that any man, but one universal monarch, should have any property upon a supposition, that God gave the world to Adam, and his heirs in succession, exclusive of all the rest of his posterity. But I shall endeavour to shew, how men might come to have a property in several parts of that which God gave to mankind in common, and that without any express compact of all the commoners.

Sec. 26. God, who hath given the world to men in common, hath also given them reason to make use of it to the best advantage of life, and convenience. The earth, and all that is therein, is given to men for the support and comfort of their being. And tho' all the fruits it naturally produces, and beasts it feeds, belong to mankind in common, as they are produced by the spontaneous hand of nature; and no body has originally a private dominion, exclusive of the rest of mankind, in any of them, as they are thus in their natural state: yet being given for the use of men, there must of necessity be a means to appropriate them some way or other, before they can be of any use, or at all beneficial to any particular man. The fruit, or venison, which nourishes the wild Indian, who knows no enclosure, and is still a tenant in common, must be his, and so his, i.e. a part of him, that another can no longer

have any right to it, before it can do him any good for the support of his life.

Sec. 27. Though the earth, and all inferior creatures, be common to all men, yet every man has a property in his own person: this no body has any right to but himself. The labour of his body, and the work of his hands, we may say, are properly his. Whatsoever then he removes out of the state that nature hath provided, and left it in, he hath mixed his labour with, and joined to it something that is his own, and thereby makes it his property. It being by him removed from the common state nature hath placed it in, it hath by this labour something annexed to it, that excludes the common right of other men: for this labour being the unquestionable property of the labourer, no man but he can have a right to what that is once joined to, at least where there is enough, and as good, left in common for others.

Sec. 28. He that is nourished by the acorns he picked up under an oak, or the apples he gathered from the trees in the wood, has certainly appropriated them to himself. No body can deny but the nourishment is his. I ask then, when did they begin to be his? when he digested? or when he eat? or when he boiled? or when he brought them home? or when he picked them up? and it is plain, if the first gathering made them not his, nothing else could. That labour put a distinction between them and common: that added something to them more than nature, the common mother of all, had done; and so they became his private right. And will any one say, he had no right to those acorns or apples, he thus appropriated, because he had not the consent of all mankind to make them his? Was it a robbery thus to assume to himself what belonged to all in common? If such a consent as that was necessary, man had starved, notwithstanding the plenty God had given him.

We see in commons, which remain so by compact, that it is the taking any part of what is common, and removing it out of the state nature leaves it in, which begins the property; without which the common is of no use. And the taking of this or that part, does not depend on the express consent of all the commoners. Thus the grass my horse has bit; the turfs my servant has cut; and the ore I have digged in any place, where I have a right to them in common with others, become my property, without the assignation or consent of any body. The labour that was mine, removing them out of that common state they were in, hath fixed my property in them.

Sec. 29. By making an explicit consent of every commoner, necessary to any one's appropriating to himself any part of what is given in common, children or servants could not cut the meat, which their father or master had provided for them in common, without assigning to every one his peculiar part. Though the water running in the fountain be every one's, yet who can doubt, but that in the pitcher is his only who drew it out? His labour hath taken it out of the hands of nature, where it was common, and belonged equally to all her children, and hath thereby appropriated it to himself.

Sec. 30. Thus this law of reason makes the deer that Indian's who hath killed it; it is allowed to be his goods, who hath bestowed his labour upon it, though before it was the common right of every one. And amongst those who are counted the civilized part of mankind, who have made and multiplied positive laws to determine property, this original law of nature, for the beginning of property, in what was before common, still takes place; and by virtue thereof, what fish any one catches in the ocean, that great and still remaining common of mankind; or what ambergrise any one takes up here, is by the labour that removes it out of that common state nature left it in, made his property, who takes that pains about it. And even amongst us, the hare that any one is hunting, is thought his who pursues her during the chase: for being a beast that is still looked upon as common, and no man's private possession; whoever has employed so much labour about any of that kind, as to find and pursue her, has thereby removed her from the state of nature, wherein she was common, and hath begun a property.

Sec. 32. But the chief matter of property being now not the fruits of the earth, and the beasts that subsist on it, but the earth itself; as that which takes in and carries with it all the rest; I think it is plain, that property in that too is acquired as the former. As much land as a man tills, plants, improves, cultivates, and can use the product of, so much is his property. He by his labour does, as it were, inclose it from the common. Nor will it invalidate his right, to say every body else has an equal title to it; and therefore he cannot appropriate, he cannot inclose, without the consent of all his fellow-commoners, all mankind. God, when he gave the world in common to all mankind, commanded man also to labour, and the penury of his condition required it of him. God and his reason commanded him to subdue the earth, i.e. improve it for the benefit of life, and therein lay out something upon it that was his own, his labour. He that in obedience to this command of God, subdued, tilled and sowed any part of it, thereby annexed to it something that was his property, which another had no title to, nor could without injury take from him.

Sec. 40. Nor is it so strange, as perhaps before consideration it may appear, that the property of labour should be able to over-balance the community of land: for it is labour indeed that puts the difference of value on every thing; and let any one consider what the difference is between an acre of land planted with tobacco or sugar, sown with wheat or barley, and an acre of the same land lying in common, without any husbandry upon it, and he will find, that the improvement of labour makes the far greater part of the value. I think it will be but a very modest computation to say, that of the products of the earth useful to the life of man nine tenths are the effects of labour: nay, if we will rightly estimate things as they come to our use, and cast up the several expences about them, what in them is purely owing to nature, and what to labour, we shall find, that in most of them ninety-nine hundredths are wholly to be put on the account of labour.

Sec. 41. There cannot be a clearer demonstration of any thing, than several nations of the Americans are of this, who are rich in land, and poor in all the comforts of life; whom nature having furnished as liberally as any other people, with the materials of plenty, i.e. a fruitful soil, apt to produce in abundance, what might serve for food, raiment, and delight; yet for want of improving it by labour, have not one hundredth part of the conveniencies we enjoy: and a king of a large and fruitful territory there, feeds, lodges, and is clad worse than a day-labourer in England.

Sec. 42. To make this a little clearer, let us but trace some of the ordinary provisions of life, through their several progresses, before they come to our use, and see how much they receive of their value from human industry. Bread, wine and cloth, are things of daily use, and great plenty; yet notwithstanding, acorns, water and leaves, or skins, must be our bread, drink and cloathing, did not labour furnish us with these more useful commodities:

for whatever bread is more worth than acorns, wine than water, and cloth or silk, than leaves, skins or moss, that is wholly owing to labour and industry; the one of these being the food and raiment which unassisted nature furnishes us with; the other, provisions which our industry and pains prepare for us, which how much they exceed the other in value, when any one hath computed, he will then see how much labour makes the far greatest part of the value of things we enjoy in this world: and the ground which produces the materials, is scarce to be reckoned in, as any, or at most, but a very small part of it; so little, that even amongst us, land that is left wholly to nature, that hath no improvement of pasturage, tillage, or planting, is called, as indeed it is, waste; and we shall find the benefit of it amount to little more than nothing.

This shews how much numbers of men are to be preferred to largeness of dominions; and that the increase of lands, and the right employing of them, is the great art of government: and that prince, who shall be so wise and godlike, as by established laws of liberty to secure protection and encouragement to the honest industry of mankind, against the oppression of power and narrowness of party, will quickly be too hard for his neighbours: but this by the by. To return to the argument in hand,

Sec. 43. An acre of land, that bears here twenty bushels of wheat, and another in America, which, with the same husbandry, would do the like, are, without doubt, of the same natural intrinsic value: but yet the benefit mankind receives from the one in a year, is worth 5 pounds, and from the other possibly not worth a penny, if all the profit an Indian received from it were to be valued, and sold here; at least, I may truly say, not one thousandth. It is labour then which puts the greatest part of value upon land, without which it would scarcely be worth any thing: it is to that we owe the greatest part of all its useful products; for all that the straw, bran, bread, of that acre of wheat, is more worth than the product of an acre of as good land, which lies waste, is all the effect of labour: for it is not barely the ploughman's pains, the reaper's and thresher's toil, and the baker's sweat, is to be counted into the bread we eat; the labour of those who broke the oxen, who digged and wrought the iron and stones, who felled and framed the timber employed about the plough, mill, oven, or any other utensils, which are a vast number, requisite to this corn, from its being feed to be sown to its being made bread, must all be charged on the account of labour, and received as an effect of that: nature and the earth furnished only the almost worthless materials, as in themselves. It would be a strange catalogue of things, that industry provided and made use of, about every loaf of bread, before it came to our use, if we could trace them; iron, wood, leather, bark, timber, stone, bricks, coals, lime, cloth, dying drugs, pitch, tar, masts, ropes, and all the materials made use of in the ship, that brought any of the commodities made use of by any of the workmen, to any part of the work; all which it would be almost impossible, at least too long, to reckon up.

Sec. 44. From all which it is evident, that though the things of nature are given in common, yet man, by being master of himself, and proprietor of his own person, and the actions or labour of it, had still in himself the great foundation of property; and that, which made up the great part of what he applied to the support or comfort of his being, when invention and arts had improved the conveniencies of life, was perfectly his own, and did not belong in common to others.

H e r b e r t   S p e n c e r

SOCIAL STATICS

Chapter X: The Right of Property

1851

Herbert Spencer's defense of private property and his attack on redistributivist policies derives largely from John Locke's theory. We include it here because this work is mentioned by name by Justice Oliver Wendell Holmes in his famous dissent in Lochner v. New York. *As you read it, think about why Spencer sees property as fundamental, and keep his philosophy in mind as a possible justification for the Court's decision in* Lochner v. New York.

We have seen that, without any infraction of the law of equal freedom, an individual may lease from society a given surface of soil, by agreeing to pay in return a stated amount of the produce he obtains from that soil. We found that, in doing this, he does no more than what every other man is equally free with himself to do—that each has the same power with himself to become the tenant—and that the rent he pays accrues alike to all. Having thus hired a tract of land from his fellow-men, for a given period, for understood purposes, and on specified terms—having thus obtained, for a time, the exclusive use of that land by a definite agreement with its owners, it is manifest that an individual may, without any infringement of the rights of others, appropriate to himself that portion of produce which remains after he has paid to mankind the promised rent. He has now, to use Locke's expression—mixed his labour with—certain products of the earth; and his claim to them is in this case valid, because he obtained the *consent* of society before so expending his labour; and having fulfilled the condition which society, imposed in giving that consent—the payment of rent—society, to fulfil its part of the agreement, must acknowledge his title to that surplus which remains after the rent has been paid.—Provided you deliver to us a stated share of the produce which by cultivation you can obtain from this piece of land, we give you the exclusive use of the remainder of that produce:—these are the words of the contract; and in virtue of this contract, the tenant may equitably claim the supplementary share as his private property: may so claim it without any disobedience to the law of equal freedom; and has therefore a *right* so to claim it. . . .

An argument fatal to the communist theory, is suggested by the fact, that a desire for property is one of the elements of our nature. Repeated allusion has been made to the admitted truth, that acquisitiveness is an unreasoning impulse quite distinct from the desires whose gratifications property secures—an impulse that is often obeyed at the expense of those desires. And if a propensity to personal acquisition be really a component of man's constitution, then that cannot be a right form of society which affords it no scope. Socialists do indeed allege that private appropriation is an abuse of this propensity, whose normal function, they say, is to impel us to accumulate for the benefit of the public at large. But in thus attempting to escape from one difficulty, they do but entangle themselves in another. Such an explanation overlooks the fact that the

use and *abuse* of a faculty (whatever the etymology of the words may imply) differ only in *degree*; whereas their assumption is, that they differ in *kind*. Gluttony is an abuse of the desire for food; timidity, an abuse of the feeling which in moderation produces prudence; servility, an abuse of the sentiment that generates respect; obstinacy, of that from which firmness springs: in all of which cases we find that the legitimate manifestations differ from the illegitimate ones, merely in quantity, and not in quality. So also with the instinct of accumulation. It may be quite true that its dictates have been, and still are, followed to an absurd excess; but it is also true that no change in the state of society will alter its nature and its office. To whatever extent moderated, it must still be a desire for personal acquisition. Whence it follows that a system affording opportunity for its exercise must ever be retained; which means, that the system of private property must be retained; and this presupposes a *right* of private property, for by right we mean that which harmonizes with the human constitution as divinely ordained.

. . . Further argument appears to be unnecessary. We have seen that the right of property is deducible from the law of equal freedom—that it is presupposed by the human constitution—and that its denial involves absurdities.

Were it not that we shall frequently have to refer to the fact hereafter, it would be scarcely needful to show that the taking away another's property is an infringement of the law of equal freedom, and is therefore wrong. If A appropriate to himself something belonging to B, one of two things must take place: either B does the like to A, or he does not. If A has no property, or if his property is inaccessible to B, B has evidently no opportunity of exercising equal freedom with A, by claiming from him something of like value; and A has therefore assumed a greater share of freedom than he allows B, and has broken the law. If again, A's property is open to B, and A permits B to use like freedom with himself by taking an equivalent, there is no violation of the law; and the affair practically becomes one of barter. But such a transaction will never take place save in theory; for A has no motive to appropriate B's property with the intention of letting B take an equivalent: seeing that if he really means to let B have what B thinks an equivalent, he will prefer to make the exchange by consent in the ordinary way. The only case simulating this, is one in which A takes from B a thing that B does not wish to part with; that is, a thing for which A can give B nothing that B thinks an equivalent; and as the amount of gratification which B has in the possession of this thing, is the measure of its value to him, it follows that if A cannot give B a thing which affords B equal gratification, or in other words what he thinks an equivalent, then A has taken from B what affords A satisfaction, but does not return to B what affords B satisfaction; and has therefore broken the law by assuming the greater share of freedom. Wherefore we find it to be a logical deduction from the law of equal freedom, that no man can rightfully take property from another against his will.

Robert Nozick

ANARCHY, STATE, AND UTOPIA

New York, NY: Basic Books (1974)

In addition to the historical argument you have read from John Locke, we include here a modern variant on Locke's view by the contemporary libertarian Robert Nozick. Does his concept of voluntary exchanges support a doctrine of economic substantive due process?

VOLUNTARY EXCHANGE

Some readers will object to my speaking frequently of voluntary exchanges on the grounds that some actions (for example, workers accepting a wage position) are not really voluntary because one party faces severely limited options, with all the others being much worse than the one he chooses. Whether a person's actions are voluntary depends on what it is that limits his alternatives. If facts of nature do so, the actions are voluntary. (I may voluntarily walk to someplace I would prefer to fly to unaided.) Other people's actions place limits on one's available opportunities. Whether this makes one's resulting action non-voluntary depends upon whether these others had the right to act as they did.

Consider the following example. Suppose there are twenty-six women and twenty-six men each wanting to be married. For each sex, all of that sex agree on the same ranking of the twenty-six members of the opposite sex in terms of desirability as marriage partners: call them A to Z and A' to Z' respectively in decreasing preferential order. A and A' voluntarily choose to get married, each preferring the other to any other partner. B would most prefer to marry A', and B' would most prefer to marry *A*, but by their choices *A* and *A'* have removed these options. When *B* and *B'* marry, their choices are not made nonvoluntary merely by the fact that there is something else they each would rather do. This other most preferred option requires the cooperation of others who have chosen, as is their right, not to cooperate. *B* and *B'* chose among fewer options than did *A* and *A'*. This contraction of the range of options continues down the line until we come to *Z* and *Z'*, who each face a choice between marrying the other or remaining unmarried. Each prefers anyone of the twenty-five other partners who by their choices have removed themselves from consideration by *Z* and *Z'*. *Z* and *Z'* voluntarily choose to marry each other. The fact that their only other alternative is (in their view) much worse, and the fact that others chose to exercise their rights in certain ways, thereby shaping the external environment of options in which *Z* and *Z'* choose, does not mean they did not marry voluntarily.

Similar considerations apply to market exchanges between workers and owners of capital. *Z* is faced with working or starving; the choices and actions of all other persons do not add up to providing *Z* with some other option. (He may have various options about what job to take.) Does *Z* choose to work voluntarily? (Does someone on a desert island who must work to survive?) *Z* does choose voluntarily if the other individuals *A* through *Y* each acted voluntarily and within their rights. We then have to ask the question about the others. We ask it up the line until we reach *A*, or *A* and *B* who chose to act in certain ways thereby shaping the external choice environment in which *C* chooses. We move back down the line with *A* through *C*'s voluntary choice affecting *D*'s choice environment, and *A* through *D*'s choices affecting *E*'s choice environment, and

so on back down to *Z*. A person's choice among differing degrees of unpalatable alternatives is not rendered nonvoluntary by the fact that others voluntarily chose and acted within their rights in a way that did not provide him with a more palatable alternative.

We should note an interesting feature of the structure of rights to engage in relationships with others, including voluntary exchanges. The right to engage in a certain relationship is not a right to engage in it with anyone, or even with anyone who wants to or would choose to, but rather it is a right to do it with anyone who has the right to engage in it (with someone who has the right to engage in it . . .). Rights to engage in relationships or transactions have hooks on them, which must attach to the corresponding hook of another's right that comes out to meet theirs. My right of free speech is not violated by a prisoner's being kept in solitary confinement so that he cannot hear me, and my right to hear information is not violated if this prisoner is prevented from communicating with me. The rights of members of the press are not violated if Edward Everett Hale's "man without a country" is not permitted to read some of their writings, nor are the rights of readers violated if Josef Goebbels is executed and thereby prevented from providing them with additional reading material. In each case, the right is a right to a relationship with someone else who *also* has the right to be the other party in such a relationship. Adults normally will have the right to such a relationship with any other consenting adult who has this right, but the right *may* be forfeited in punishment for wrongful acts. This complication of hooks on rights will *not* be relevant to any cases we discuss. But it does have implications; for example it complicates an immediate condemnation of the disruption of speakers in a *public* place, solely on the grounds that this disruption violates the rights of other people to *hear* whatever opinions they choose to listen to. If rights to engage in relationships go out only half-way, these others do have a right to hear whatever opinions they please, but only from persons who have a right to communicate them. Hearers' rights are not violated *if* the speaker has no hook to reach out to join up with theirs. (The speaker can lack a hooked right only because of something he has done, not because of the *content* of what he is about to say.) My reflections here are not intended to justify disruption, merely to warn against the too simple grounds for condemnation which I myself have been prone to use.

LOCHNER v. NEW YORK

198 U.S. 45 (1905)

Opinion: Peckham, joined by Fuller, Brewer, Brown, McKenna
Dissent: Harlan, joined by White, Day
Dissent: Holmes

In Lochner v. New York, *the Supreme Court struck down, on grounds of substantive due process, a state law limiting the working hours of bakers. The "right to contract," the majority held, has a fundamental place in a constitutional regime designed to protect property rights. To what extent is this philosophy read into the Constitution through a version of the moral reading introduced by Ronald Dworkin in Chapter 2? Pay particular attention to Justice Oliver Wendell Holmes's dissent, which, as you will see, makes explicit reference to Herbert Spencer's views on property that we just examined. Does the opinion rest on the kind of philosophy you just saw defended by John Locke, Robert Nozick, or Herbert Spencer? Do you agree with Justice Holmes that these philosophers' ideas, in particular Spencer's views, have no place in constitutional interpretation?*

MR. JUSTICE PECKHAM, *after making [a] statement of the facts, delivered the opinion of the Court.*

The indictment, it will be seen, charges that the plaintiff in error violated the one hundred and tenth section of article 8, chapter 415, of the Laws of 1897, known as the labor law of the State of New York, in that he wrongfully and unlawfully required and permitted an employee working for him to work more than sixty hours in one week. There is nothing in any of the opinions delivered in this case, either in the Supreme Court or the Court of Appeals of the State, which construes the section, in using the word "required," as referring to any physical force being used to obtain the labor of an employee. It is assumed that the word means nothing more than the requirement arising from voluntary contract for such labor in excess of the number of hours specified in the statute. There is no pretense in any of the opinions that the statute was intended to meet a case of involuntary labor in any form. All the opinions assume that there is no real distinction, so far as this question is concerned, between the words "required" and "permitted." The mandate of the statute that "no employee shall be required or permitted to work," is the substantial equivalent of an enactment that "no employee shall contract or agree to work," more than ten hours per day, and as there is no provision for special emergencies the statute is mandatory in all cases. It is not an act merely fixing the number of hours which shall constitute a legal day's work, but an absolute prohibition upon the employer, permitting, under any circumstances, more than ten hours work to be done in his establishment. The employee may desire to earn the extra money, which would arise from his working more than the prescribed time, but this statute forbids the employer from permitting the employee to earn it.

The statute necessarily interferes with the right of contract between the employer and employees, concerning the number of hours in which the latter may labor in the bakery of the employer. The general right to make a contract in relation to his business is part of the liberty of the individual protected by the Fourteenth Amendment of the Federal Constitution. Under that provision no State can deprive any person of life, liberty or property without due process of law. The right to purchase or to sell labor is part of the liberty protected by this amendment, unless there are circumstances which exclude the right. There are, however, certain powers, existing in the sovereignty of each State in the Union, somewhat vaguely termed police powers, the exact description and limitation of which have not been attempted by the courts. Those powers, broadly stated and without, at present, any attempt at a more specific limitation, relate to the safety, health, morals and general welfare of the public. Both property and liberty are held on such reasonable conditions as may be imposed by the governing power of the State in the exercise of those powers, and with such conditions the Fourteenth Amendment was not designed to interfere.

The State, therefore, has power to prevent the individual from making certain kinds of contracts, and in regard to them the Federal Constitution offers no protection.

If the contract be one which the State, in the legitimate exercise of its police power, has the right to prohibit, it is not prevented from prohibiting it by the Fourteenth Amendment. Contracts in violation of a statute, either of the Federal or state government, or a contract to let one's property for immoral purposes, or to do any other unlawful act, could obtain no protection from the Federal Constitution, as coming under the liberty of person or of free contract. Therefore, when the State, by its legislature, in the assumed exercise of its police powers, has passed an act which seriously limits the right to labor or the right of contract in regard to their means of livelihood between persons who are sui juris (both employer and employee), it becomes of great importance to determine which shall prevail—the right of the individual to labor for such time as he may choose, or the right of the State to prevent the individual from laboring or from entering into any contract to labor, beyond a certain time prescribed by the State.

It must, of course, be conceded that there is a limit to the valid exercise of the police power by the State. There is no dispute concerning this general proposition. Otherwise the Fourteenth Amendment would have no efficacy and the legislatures of the States would have unbounded power, and it would be enough to say that any piece of legislation was enacted to conserve the morals, the health or the safety of the people; such legislation would be valid, no matter how absolutely without foundation the claim might be. The claim of the police power would be a mere pretext—become another and delusive name for the supreme sovereignty of the State to be exercised free from constitutional restraint. This is not contended for. In every case that comes before this court, therefore, where legislation of this character is concerned and where the protection of the Federal

Constitution is sought, the question necessarily arises: Is this a fair, reasonable and appropriate exercise of the police power of the State, or is it an unreasonable, unnecessary and arbitrary interference with the right of the individual to his personal liberty or to enter into those contracts in relation to labor which may seem to him appropriate or necessary for the support of himself and his family? Of course the liberty of contract relating to labor includes both parties to it. The one has as much right to purchase as the other to sell labor.

This is not a question of substituting the judgment of the court for that of the legislature. If the act be within the power of the State it is valid, although the judgment of the court might be totally opposed to the enactment of such a law. But the question would still remain: Is it within the police power of the State? That question must be answered by the court.

The question whether this act is valid as a labor law, pure and simple, may be dismissed in a few words. There is no reasonable ground for interfering with the liberty of person or the right of free contract, by determining the hours of labor, in the occupation of a baker. There is no contention that bakers as a class are not equal in intelligence and capacity to men in other trades or manual occupations, or that they are not able to assert their rights and care for themselves without the protecting arm of the State, interfering with their independence of judgment and of action. They are in no sense wards of the State. Viewed in the light of a purely labor law, with no reference whatever to the question of health, we think that a law like the one before us involves neither the safety, the morals nor the welfare of the public, and that the interest of the public is not in the slightest degree affected by such an act. The law must be upheld, if at all, as a law pertaining to the health of the individual engaged in the occupation of a baker. It does not affect any other portion of the public than those who are engaged in that occupation. Clean and wholesome bread does not depend upon whether the baker works but ten hours per day or only sixty hours a week. The limitation of the hours of labor does not come within the police power on that ground.

It is a question of which of two powers or rights shall prevail—the power of the State to legislate or the right of the individual to liberty of person and freedom of contract. The mere assertion that the subject relates though but in a remote degree to the public health does not necessarily render the enactment valid. The act must have a more direct relation, as a means to an end, and the end itself must be appropriate and legitimate, before an act can be held to be valid which interferes with the general right of an individual to be free in his person and in his power to contract in relation to his own labor.

We think that there can be no fair doubt that the trade of a baker, in and of itself, is not an unhealthy one to that degree which would authorize the legislature to interfere with the right to labor, and with the right of free contract on the part of the individual, either as employer or employee. In looking through statistics regarding all trades and occupations, it may be true that the trade of a baker does not appear to be as healthy as some other trades, and is also vastly more healthy than still others. To the common understanding the trade of a baker has never been regarded as an unhealthy one. Very likely physicians would not recommend the exercise of that or of any other trade as a remedy for ill health. Some occupations are more healthy than others, but we think there are none which might not come under the power of the legislature to supervise and control the hours of working therein, if the mere fact that the occupation is not absolutely and perfectly healthy is to confer that right upon the legislative department of the Government. It might be safely affirmed that almost all occupations more or less affect the health. There must be more than the mere fact of the possible existence of some small amount of unhealthiness to warrant legislative interference with liberty. It is unfortunately true that labor, even in any department, may possibly carry with it the seeds of unhealthiness. But are we all, on that account, at the mercy of legislative majorities? A printer, a tinsmith, a locksmith, a carpenter, a cabinetmaker, a dry goods clerk, a bank's, a lawyer's or a physician's clerk, or a clerk in almost any kind of business, would all come under the power of the legislature, on this assumption. No trade, no occupation, no mode of earning one's living, could escape this all-pervading power, and the acts of the legislature in limiting the hours of labor in all employments would be valid, although such limitation might seriously cripple the ability of the laborer to support himself and his family. . . .

. . . The act is not, within any fair meaning of the term, a health law, but is an illegal interference with the rights of individuals, both employers and employees, to make contracts regarding labor upon such terms as they may think best, or which they may agree upon with the other parties to such contracts. Statutes of the nature of that under review, limiting the hours in which grown and intelligent men may labor to earn their living, are mere meddlesome interferences with the rights of the individual, and they are not saved from condemnation by the claim that they are passed in the exercise of the police power and upon the subject of the health of the individual whose rights are interfered with, unless there be some fair ground, reasonable in and of itself, to say that there is material danger to the public health or to the health of the employees, if the hours of labor are not curtailed. If this be not clearly the case the individuals, whose rights are thus made the subject of legislative interference, are under the protection of the Federal Constitution regarding their liberty of contract as well as of person; and the legislature of the State has no power to limit their right as proposed in this statute.

It was further urged on the argument that restricting the hours of labor in the case of bakers was valid because it tended to cleanliness on the part of the workers, as a man was more apt to be cleanly when not overworked, and if cleanly then his "output" was also more likely to be so. What has already been said applies with equal force to this contention. We do not admit the reasoning to be sufficient to justify the claimed right of such interference. The State in that case would assume the position of a supervisor, or pater familias, over every act of the individual, and its right of governmental interference with his hours of labor, his hours of exercise, the character thereof, and the extent to which it shall be carried would be recognized and upheld. In our judgment it is not possible in fact to discover the connection between the number of hours a baker may work in the bakery and the healthful quality of the bread made by the workman. The connection, if any exists, is too shadowy and thin to build any argument for the interference of the legislature. If the man works ten hours a day it is all right, but if ten and a half or eleven his health is in danger and his bread may be unhealthful, and, therefore, he shall not be permitted to do it. This, we think, is unreasonable and entirely arbitrary. When assertions such as we have adverted to become necessary in order to give, if possible, a plausible foundation for the contention that the law is a "health law," it gives rise to at least a suspicion that there was some other motive dominating the legislature than the purpose to subserve the public health or welfare.

MR. JUSTICE HOLMES *dissenting.*

I regret sincerely that I am unable to agree with the judgment in this case, and that I think it my duty to express my dissent.

This case is decided upon an economic theory which a large part of the country does not entertain. If it were a question whether I agreed with that theory I should desire to study it further and long before making up my mind. But I do not conceive that to be my duty, because I strongly believe that my agreement or disagreement has nothing to do with the right of a majority to embody their opinions in law. It is settled by various decisions of this court that state constitutions and state laws may regulate life in many ways which we as legislators might think as injudicious or if you like as tyrannical as this, and which equally with this interfere with the liberty to contract. Sunday laws and usury laws are ancient examples. A more modern one is the prohibition of lotteries. The liberty of the citizen to do as he likes so long as he does not interfere with the liberty of others to do the same, which has been a shibboleth for some well-known writers, is interfered with by school laws, by the Post Office, by every state or municipal institution which takes his money for purposes thought desirable, whether he likes it or not. The Fourteenth Amendment does not enact Mr. Herbert Spencer's Social Statics. The other day we sustained the Massachusetts vaccination law. *Jacobson v. Massachusetts*. United States and state statutes and decisions cutting down the liberty to contract by way of combination are familiar to this court. *Northern Securities Co. v. United States*. Two years

ago we upheld the prohibition of sales of stock on margins or for future delivery in the constitution of California. *Otis v. Parker*. The decision sustaining an eight-hour law for miners is still recent. *Holden v. Hardy*. Some of these laws embody convictions or prejudices which judges are likely to share. Some may not. But a constitution is not intended to embody a particular economic theory, whether of paternalism and the organic relation of the citizen to the State or of laissez faire. It is made for people of fundamentally differing views, and the accident of our finding certain opinions natural and familiar or novel and even shocking ought not to conclude our judgment upon the question whether statutes embodying them conflict with the Constitution of the United States.

General propositions do not decide concrete cases. The decision will depend on a judgment or intuition more subtle than any articulate major premise. But I think that the proposition just stated, if it is accepted, will carry us far toward the end. Every opinion tends to become a law. I think that the word liberty in the Fourteenth Amendment is perverted when it is held to prevent the natural outcome of a dominant opinion, unless it can be said that a rational and fair man necessarily would admit that the statute proposed would infringe fundamental principles as they have been understood by the traditions of our people and our law. It does not need research to show that no such sweeping condemnation can be passed upon the statute before us. A reasonable man might think it a proper measure on the score of health. Men whom I certainly could not pronounce unreasonable would uphold it as a first installment of a general regulation of the hours of work. Whether in the latter aspect it would be open to the charge of inequality I think it unnecessary to discuss.

ADKINS v. CHILDREN'S HOSPITAL

261 U.S. 525 (1923)

Opinion: Sutherland, joined
by McKenna, Van Devanter,
McReynolds, Butler
Dissent: Taft, joined by Sanford
Dissent: Holmes

In the following case, the Court extends the logic of substantive due process, relied upon in Lochner v. New York *to protect the economic interest in private property, to strike down minimum wage laws. Before you read the case, you might consider the possible reasons for such laws. Are they necessary for social justice or to ensure that all can achieve a decent standard of living? It is important to recall from Chapter 3 President Franklin Roosevelt's arguments for such laws, including his notion of "four freedoms," before continuing in this section. Note that this case was decided before the New Deal. Do you agree with the Court that the Constitution is incompatible with minimum wage laws?*

MR. JUSTICE SUTHERLAND *delivered the opinion of the Court.*

The question presented for determination by these appeals is the constitutionality of the Act of September 19, 1918, providing for the fixing of minimum wages for women and children in the District of Columbia.

The appellee in the first case is a corporation maintaining a hospital for children in the District. It employs a large number of women in various capacities, with whom it had agreed upon rates of wages and compensation satisfactory to such employees, but which in some instances were less than the minimum wage fixed by an order of the board made in pursuance of the act.

The women with whom appellee had so contracted were all of full age and under no legal disability. The instant suit was brought by the appellee in the Supreme Court of the District to restrain the board from enforcing or attempting to enforce its order on the ground that the same was in contravention of the Constitution, and particularly the due process clause of the Fifth Amendment.

In the second case, the appellee, a woman twenty-one years of age, was employed by the Congress Hall Hotel Company as an elevator operator, at a salary of $35 per month and two meals a day. She alleges that the work was light and healthful, the hours short, with surroundings clean and moral, and that she was anxious to continue it for the compensation she was receiving, and that she did not earn more. Her services were satisfactory to the Hotel Company, and it would have been glad to retain her but was obliged to dispense with her services by reason of the order of the board and on account of the penalties prescribed by the act. The wages received by this appellee were the best she was able to obtain for any work she was capable of performing, and the enforcement of the order, she alleges, deprived her of such employment and wages. An injunction was prayed as in the other case. . . .

The statute now under consideration is attacked upon the ground that it authorizes an unconstitutional interference with the freedom of contract included within the guaranties of the due process clause of the Fifth Amendment. That the right to contract about one's affairs is a part of the liberty of the individual protected by this clause, is settled by the decisions of this Court and is no longer open to question. *Lochner v. New York*. Within this liberty are contracts of employment of labor. In making such contracts, generally speaking, the parties have an equal right to obtain from each other the best terms they can as the result of private bargaining.

An interference with this liberty so serious as that now under consideration, and so disturbing of equality of right, must be deemed to be arbitrary unless it be supportable as a reasonable exercise of the police power of the State.

There is, of course, no such thing as absolute freedom of contract. It is subject to a great variety of restraints. But freedom of contract is, nevertheless, the general rule, and restraint the exception, and the exercise of legislative authority to abridge it can be justified only by the existence of exceptional circumstances.

If now, in the light furnished by the . . . exceptions to the general rule forbidding legislative interference with freedom of contract, we examine and analyze the statute in question, we shall see that it differs from them in every material respect. . . . It is simply and exclusively a price-fixing law, confined to adult women (for we are not now considering the provisions relating to minors), who are legally as capable of contracting for themselves as men. It forbids two parties having lawful capacity—under penalties as to the employer—to freely contract with one another in respect of the price for which one shall render service to the other in a purely private employment where both are willing, perhaps anxious, to agree, even though the consequence may be to oblige one to surrender a desirable engagement and the other to dispense with the services of a desirable employee. The price fixed by the board need have no relation to the capacity or earning power of the employee, the number of hours which may happen to constitute the day's work,

the character of the place where the work is to be done, or the circumstances or surroundings of the employment; and, while it has no other basis to support its validity than the assumed necessities of the employee, it takes no account of any independent resources she may have. It is based wholly on the opinions of the members of the board and their advisers—perhaps an average of their opinions, if they do not precisely agree—as to what will be necessary to provide a living for a woman, keep her in health and preserve her morals. It applies to any and every occupation in the District, without regard to its nature or the character of the work.

The standard furnished by the statute for the guidance of the board is so vague as to be impossible of practical application with any reasonable degree of accuracy. What is sufficient to supply the necessary cost of living for a woman worker and maintain her in good health and protect her morals is obviously not a precise or unvarying sum—not even approximately so. The amount will depend upon a variety of circumstances: the individual temperament, habits of thrift, care, ability to buy necessaries intelligently, and whether the woman live alone or with her family. To those who practice economy, a given sum will afford comfort, while to those of contrary habit the same sum will be wholly inadequate. The cooperative economics of the family group are not taken into account though they constitute an important consideration in estimating the cost of living, for it is obvious that the individual expense will be less in the case of a member of a family than in the case of one living alone. The relation between earnings and morals is not capable of standardization. It cannot be shown that well-paid women safeguard their morals more carefully than those who are poorly paid. Morality rests upon other considerations than wages, and there is, certainly, no such prevalent connection between the two as to justify a broad attempt to adjust the latter with reference to the former. As a means of safeguarding morals the attempted classification in our opinion, is without reasonable basis. No distinction can be made between women who work for others and those who do not; nor is there ground for distinction between women and men, for, certainly, if women require a minimum wage to preserve their morals men require it to preserve their honesty. For these reasons, and others which might be stated, the inquiry in respect of the necessary cost of living and of the income necessary to preserve health and morals, presents an individual, and not a composite, question, and must be answered for each individual considered by herself, and not by a general formula prescribed by a statutory bureau.

The law takes account of the necessities of only one party to the contract. It ignores the necessities of the employer by compelling him to pay not less than a certain sum not only whether the employee is capable of earning it, but irrespective of the ability of his business to sustain the burden, generously leaving him, of course, the privilege of abandoning his business as an alternative for going on at a loss. Within the limits of the minimum sum, he is precluded, under penalty of fine and imprisonment, from adjusting compensation to the differing merits of his employees. It compels him to pay at least the sum fixed in any event, because the employee needs it, but requires no service of equivalent value from the employee. It therefore undertakes to solve but one-half of the problem. The other half is the establishment of a corresponding standard of efficiency, and this forms no part of the policy of the legislation, although in practice the former half without the latter must lead to ultimate failure, in accordance with the inexorable

law that no one can continue indefinitely to take out more than he puts in without ultimately exhausting the supply. The law is not confined to the great and powerful employers, but embraces those whose bargaining power may be as weak as that of the employee. It takes no account of periods of stress and business depression, of crippling losses, which may leave the employer himself without adequate means of livelihood. To the extent that the sum fixed exceeds the fair value of the services rendered, it amounts to a compulsory exaction from the employer for the support of a partially indigent person, for whose condition there rests upon him no peculiar responsibility, and therefore, in effect, arbitrarily shifts to his shoulders a burden which, if it belongs to anybody, belongs to society as a whole.

The feature of this statute which, perhaps more than any other, puts upon it the stamp of invalidity is that it exacts from the employer an arbitrary payment for a purpose and upon a basis having no causal connection with his business, or the contract or the work the employee engages to do. The declared basis, as already pointed out, is not the value of the service rendered, but the extraneous circumstance that the employee needs to get a prescribed sum of money to insure her subsistence, health and morals. The ethical right of every worker, man or woman, to a living wage may be conceded. One of the declared and important purposes of trade organizations is to secure it. And with that principle, and with every legitimate effort to realize it in fact, no one can quarrel; but the fallacy of the proposed method of attaining it is that it assumes that every employer is bound at all events to furnish it. The moral requirement implicit in every contract of employment, *viz.*, that the amount to be paid and the service to be rendered shall bear to each other some relation of just equivalence, is completely ignored. The necessities of the employee are alone considered, and these arise outside of the employment, are the same when there is no employment, and as great in one occupation as in another. Certainly the employer, by paying a fair equivalent for the service rendered, though not sufficient to support the employee, has neither caused nor contributed to her poverty. On the contrary, to the extent of what he pays, he has relieved it. In principle, there can be no difference between the case of selling labor and the case of selling goods. If one goes to the butcher, the baker or grocer to buy food, he is morally entitled to obtain the worth of his money, but he is not entitled to more. If what he gets is worth what he pays, he is not justified in demanding more simply because he needs more, and the shopkeeper, having dealt fairly and honestly in that transaction, is not concerned in any peculiar sense with the question of his customer's necessities. Should a statute undertake to vest in a commission power to determine the quantity of food necessary for individual support and require the shopkeeper, if he sell to the individual at all, to furnish that quantity at not more than a fixed maximum, it would undoubtedly fall before the constitutional test. The fallacy of any argument in support of the validity of such a statute would be quickly exposed. The argument in support of that now being considered is equally fallacious, though the weakness of it may not be so plain. A statute requiring an employer to pay in money, to pay at prescribed and regular intervals, to pay the value of the services rendered, even to pay with fair relation to the extent of the benefit obtained from the service, would be understandable. But a statute which prescribes payment without regard to any of these things and solely with relation to circumstances apart from the contract of employment, the business affected by it and the work done under it, is so clearly the product of a naked, arbitrary

exercise of power that it cannot be allowed to stand under the Constitution of the United States.

Finally, it may be said that if, in the interest of the public welfare, the police power may be invoked to justify the fixing of a minimum wage, it may, when the public welfare is thought to require it, be invoked to justify a maximum wage. The power to fix high wages connotes, by like course of reasoning, the power to fix low wages. If, in the face of the guaranties of the Fifth Amendment, this form of legislation shall be legally justified, the field for the operation of the police power will have been widened to a great and dangerous degree. If, for example, in the opinion of future lawmakers, wages in the building trades shall become so high as to preclude people of ordinary means from building and owning homes, an authority which sustains the minimum wage will be invoked to support a maximum wage for building laborers and artisans, and the same argument which has been here urged to strip the employer of his constitutional liberty of contract in one direction will be utilized to strip the employee of his constitutional liberty of contract in the opposite direction. A wrong decision does not end with itself: it is a precedent, and, with the swing of sentiment, its bad influence may run from one extremity of the arc to the other.

It has been said that legislation of the kind now under review is required in the interest of social justice, for whose ends freedom of contract may lawfully be subjected to restraint. The liberty of the individual to do as he pleases, even in innocent matters, is not absolute. It must frequently yield to the common good, and the line beyond which the power of interference may not be pressed is neither definite nor unalterable, but may be made to move, within limits not well defined, with changing need and circumstance. Any attempt to fix a rigid boundary would be unwise, as well as futile. But, nevertheless, there are limits to the power, and when these have been passed, it becomes the plain duty of the courts in the proper exercise of their authority to so declare. To sustain the individual freedom of action contemplated by the Constitution is not to strike down the common good, but to exalt it, for surely the good of society as a whole cannot be better served than by the preservation against arbitrary restraint of the liberties of its constituent members.

It follows from what has been said that the act in question passes the limit prescribed by the Constitution, and, accordingly, the decrees of the court below are

Affirmed.

MR. CHIEF JUSTICE TAFT, *dissenting.*

... Legislatures, in limiting freedom of contract between employee and employer by a minimum wage, proceed on the assumption that employees, in the class receiving least pay, are not upon a full level of equality of choice with their employer, and, in their necessitous circumstances, are prone to accept pretty much anything that is offered. They are peculiarly subject to the overreaching of the harsh and greedy employer. The evils of the sweating system and of the long hours and low wages which are characteristic of it are well known. Now I agree that it is a disputable question in the field of political economy how far a statutory requirement of maximum hours or minimum wages may be a useful remedy for these evils, and whether it may not make the case of the oppressed employee worse than it was before. But it is not the function of this Court to hold congressional acts invalid simply because they are passed to carry out economic views which the Court believes to be unwise or unsound.....

The right of the legislature under the Fifth and Fourteenth Amendments to limit the hours of employment on the score of the health of the employee, it seems to me, has been firmly established. As to that, one would think, the line had been pricked out so that it has become a well formulated rule. In *Holden v. Hardy*, it was applied to miners and rested on the unfavorable environment of employment in mining and smelting. In *Lochner v. New York*, it was held that restricting those employed in bakeries to ten hours a day was an arbitrary and invalid interference with the liberty of contract secured by the Fourteenth Amendment. Then followed a number of cases, beginning with *Muller v. Oregon*, sustaining the validity of a limit on maximum hours of labor for women, to which I shall hereafter allude, and, following these cases, came *Bunting v. Oregon*. In that case, this Court sustained a law limiting the hours of labor of any person, whether man or woman, working in any mill, factory or manufacturing establishment to ten hours a day with a proviso as to further hours to which I shall hereafter advert. The law covered the whole field of industrial employment, and certainly covered the case of persons employed in bakeries. Yet the opinion in the *Bunting* case does not mention the *Lochner* case. No one can suggest any constitutional distinction between employment in a bakery and one in any other kind of a manufacturing establishment which should make a limit of hours in the one invalid and the same limit in the other permissible. It is impossible for me to reconcile the *Bunting* case and the *Lochner* case, and I have always supposed that the *Lochner* case was thus overruled *sub silentio*. Yet the opinion of the Court herein in support of its conclusion quotes from the opinion in the *Lochner* case as one which has been sometimes distinguished but never overruled. Certainly there was no attempt to distinguish it in the *Bunting* case.....

I am authorized to say that **MR. JUSTICE SANFORD** concurs in this opinion.

MR. JUSTICE HOLMES, *dissenting.*

. . . The earlier decisions upon the same words in the Fourteenth Amendment began within our memory and went no farther than an unpretentious assertion of the liberty to follow the ordinary callings. Later, that innocuous generality was expanded into the dogma, Liberty of Contract. Contract is not specially mentioned in the text that we have to construe. It is merely an example of doing what you want to do, embodied in the word liberty. But pretty much all law consists in forbidding men to do some things that they want to do, and contract is no more exempt from law than other acts. . . .

I confess that I do not understand the principle on which the power to fix a minimum for the wages of women can be denied by those who admit the power to fix a maximum for their hours of work. I fully assent to the proposition that here, as elsewhere, the distinctions of the law are distinctions of degree, but I perceive no difference in the kind or degree of interference with liberty, the only matter with which we have any concern, between the one case and the other. . . .

This statute does not compel anybody to pay anything. It simply forbids employment at rates below those fixed as the minimum requirement of health and right living. It is safe to assume that women will not be employed at even the lowest wages allowed unless they earn them, or unless the employer's business can sustain the burden. In short, the law, in its character and operation, is like hundreds of so-called police laws that have been upheld. . . .

I am of opinion that the statute is valid, and that the decree should be reversed.

WEST COAST HOTEL CO. v. PARRISH

300 U.S. 379 (1937)

Opinion: Hughes, joined by Brandeis, Stone, Roberts, Cardozo
Dissent: Sutherland, joined by Van Devanter, McReynolds, Butler

In 1932, the property libertarian philosophy of the Supreme Court was at odds with that of many elected politicians, including the newly elected president of the United States. President Franklin Roosevelt's New Deal attempted to create a variety of protections for workers. Some of these measures were at odds with the idea that the Court's primary purpose was the protection of private property and the guarantee of libertarian property rights. In West Coast Hotel v. Parrish, *the Court reversed its position in* Adkins v. Children's Hospital, *and more generally, ended the era of substantive due process protections for the kind of property rights protections favored by libertarians. Many believe the Court backed down in response to pressure from President Roosevelt, in particular because of his threat to "pack the court" by adding more justices through Congress. This case is often regarded as the moment in which the switch in time that saved nine occurred. The idea is that by abandoning the doctrine of substantive due process, the Court averted President Roosevelt's plan to pack it with justices sympathetic to his position.*

You will notice that this case concerns state law, but it also coincided with President

Roosevelt's attempt to pass similar laws protecting workers' rights at the national level and expanding the role of the federal government in the economy. Had it not been abandoned here, the doctrine of substantive due process potentially would have limited the ability of President Roosevelt to pursue the goals of the New Deal. What reasoning do the justices provide for reversing Adkins v. Children's Hospital? *Are they convincing?*

MR. CHIEF JUSTICE HUGHES *delivered the opinion of the Court.*

This case presents the question of the constitutional validity of the minimum wage law of the State of Washington.

The appellant conducts a hotel. The appellee, Elsie Parrish, was employed as a chambermaid and (with her husband) brought this suit to recover the difference between the wages paid her and the minimum wage fixed pursuant to the state law. The minimum wage was $14.50 per week of 48 hours. The appellant challenged the act as repugnant to the due process clause of the Fourteenth Amendment of the Constitution of the United States.

The appellant relies upon the decision of this Court in *Adkins v. Children's Hospital*, which held invalid the District of Columbia Minimum Wage Act, which was attacked under the due process clause of the Fifth Amendment. On the argument at bar, counsel for the appellees attempted to distinguish the *Adkins* case upon the ground that the appellee was employed in a hotel, and that the business of an innkeeper was affected with a public interest. That effort at distinction is obviously futile, as it appears that, in one of the cases ruled by the *Adkins* opinion, the employee was a woman employed as an elevator operator in a hotel.

The Supreme Court of Washington has upheld the minimum wage statute of that State. It has decided that the statute is a reasonable exercise of the police power of the State. In reaching that conclusion, the state court has invoked principles long established by this Court in the application of the Fourteenth Amendment. The state court has refused to regard the decision in the *Adkins* case as determinative, and has pointed to our decisions both before and since that case as justifying its position. We are of the opinion that this ruling of the state court demands on our part a reexamination of the *Adkins* case. The importance of the question, in which many States having similar laws are concerned, the close division by which the decision in the *Adkins* case was reached, and the economic conditions which have supervened, and in the light of which the reasonableness of the exercise of the protective power of the State must be considered, make it not only appropriate, but we think imperative, that, in deciding the present case, the subject should receive fresh consideration.

The principle which must control our decision is not in doubt. The constitutional provision invoked is the due process clause of the Fourteenth Amendment, governing the States, as the due process clause invoked in the *Adkins* case governed Congress. In each case, the violation alleged by those attacking minimum wage regulation for women is deprivation of freedom of contract. What is this freedom? The Constitution does not speak of freedom of contract. It speaks of liberty and prohibits the deprivation of liberty without due process of law. In prohibiting that deprivation, the Constitution does not recognize an absolute and uncontrollable liberty. Liberty in each of its phases has its history and connotation. But the liberty safeguarded is liberty in a social organization which requires the protection of law against the evils which menace the health, safety, morals and welfare of the people. Liberty under the Constitution is thus necessarily subject to the restraints of due process, and regulation which is reasonable in relation to its subject and is adopted in the interests of the community is due process.

> ... There is no absolute freedom to do as one wills or to contract as one chooses. The guaranty of liberty does not withdraw from legislative supervision that wide department of activity which consists of the making of contracts, or deny to government the power to provide restrictive safeguards. Liberty implies the absence of arbitrary restraint, not immunity from reasonable regulations and prohibitions imposed in the interests of the community.

Chicago, B. & Q.R. Co. v. McGuire.

This power under the Constitution to restrict freedom of contract has had many illustrations. That it may be exercised in the public interest with respect to contracts between employer and employee is undeniable. Thus, statutes have been sustained limiting employment in underground mines and smelters to eight hours a day (*Holden v. Hardy*); in requiring redemption in cash of store orders or other evidences of indebtedness issued in the payment of wages (*Knoxville Iron Co. v. Harbison*); in forbidding the payment of seamen's wages in advance (*Patterson v. Bark Eudora*); in making it unlawful to contract to pay miners employed at quantity rates upon the basis of screened coal instead of the weight of the coal as originally produced in the mine (*McLean v. Arkansas*); in prohibiting contracts limiting liability for injuries to employees (*Chicago, B. & Q. R. Co. v. McGuire*); in limiting hours of work of employees in manufacturing establishments (*Bunting v. Oregon*), and in maintaining workmen's compensation laws (*New York Central R. Co. v. White; Mountain Timber Co. v. Washington*). In dealing with the relation of employer and employed, the legislature has necessarily a wide field of discretion in order that there may be

suitable protection of health and safety, and that peace and good order may be promoted through regulations designed to insure wholesome conditions of work and freedom from oppression.

The point that has been strongly stressed that adult employees should be deemed competent to make their own contracts was decisively met nearly forty years ago in *Holden v. Hardy*, where we pointed out the inequality in the footing of the parties. We said:

> The legislature has also recognized the fact, which the experience of legislators in many States has corroborated, that the proprietors of these establishments and their operatives do not stand upon an equality, and that their interests are, to a certain extent, conflicting. The former naturally desire to obtain as much labor as possible from their employees, while the latter are often induced by the fear of discharge to conform to regulations which their judgment, fairly exercised, would pronounce to be detrimental to their health or strength. In other words, the proprietors lay down the rules and the laborers are practically constrained to obey them. In such cases, self-interest is often an unsafe guide, and the legislature may properly interpose its authority.

And we added that the fact "that both parties are of full age and competent to contract does not necessarily deprive the State of the power to interfere where the parties do not stand upon an equality, or where the public health demands that one party to the contract shall be protected against himself." "The State still retains an interest in his welfare, however reckless he may be. The whole is no greater than the sum of all the parts, and when the individual health, safety and welfare are sacrificed or neglected, the State must suffer."

We think that the views thus expressed are sound and that the decision in the *Adkins* case was a departure from the true application of the principles governing the regulation by the State of the relation of employer and employed.

There is an additional and compelling consideration which recent economic experience has brought into a strong light. The exploitation of a class of workers who are in an unequal position with respect to bargaining power, and are thus relatively defenceless against the denial of a living wage, is not only detrimental to their health and wellbeing, but casts a direct burden for their support upon the community. What these workers lose in wages, the taxpayers are called upon to pay. The bare cost of living must be met. We may take judicial notice of the unparalleled demands for relief which arose during the recent period of depression and still continue to an alarming extent despite the degree of economic recovery which has been achieved. It is unnecessary to cite official statistics to establish what is of common knowledge through the length and breadth of the land. While, in the instant case, no factual brief has been presented, there is no reason to doubt that the State of Washington has encountered the same social problem that is present elsewhere. The community is not bound to provide what is, in effect, a subsidy for unconscionable employers.

Our conclusion is that the case of *Adkins v. Children's Hospital*, should be, and it is, overruled. The judgment of the Supreme Court of the State of Washington is

Affirmed.

MR. JUSTICE SUTHERLAND, *dissenting:*

Mr. Justice Van Devanter, Mr. Justice McReynolds, Mr. Justice Butler and I think the judgment of the court below should be reversed. The principles and authorities relied upon to sustain the judgment were considered in *Adkins v. Children's Hospital*, and *Morehead v. New York ex rel. Tipaldo*, and their lack of application to cases like the one in hand was pointed out.

A sufficient answer to all that is now said will be found in the opinions of the court in those cases. Nevertheless, in the circumstances, it seems well to restate our reasons and conclusions.

Under our form of government, where the written Constitution, by its own terms, is the supreme law, some agency, of necessity, must have the power to say the final word as to the validity of a statute assailed as unconstitutional. The Constitution makes it clear that the power has been intrusted to this court when the question arises in a controversy within its jurisdiction, and, so long as the power remains there, its exercise cannot be avoided without betrayal of the trust.

... The judicial function is that of interpretation; it does not include the power of amendment under the guise of interpretation. To miss the point of difference between the two is to miss all that the phrase "supreme law of the land" stands for, and to convert what was intended as inescapable and enduring mandates into mere moral reflections.

If the Constitution, intelligently and reasonably construed in the light of these principles, stands in the way of desirable legislation, the blame must rest upon that instrument, and not upon the court for enforcing it according to its terms. The remedy in that situation—and the only true remedy—is to amend the Constitution.

... The *Adkins* case dealt with an act of Congress which had passed the scrutiny both of the legislative and executive branches of the government. We recognized that thereby these departments had affirmed the validity of the statute, and properly declared that their determination must be given great weight, but we then concluded, after thorough consideration, that their view could not be sustained. ... Coming, then, to a consideration of the Washington statute, it first is to be observed that it is in every substantial respect identical with the statute involved in the *Adkins* case. Such vices as existed in the latter are present in the former. And if the *Adkins* case was properly decided, as we who join in this opinion think it was, it necessarily follows that the Washington statute is invalid.

In support of minimum wage legislation it has been urged, on the one hand, that great benefits will result in favor of underpaid labor, and, on the other hand, that the danger of such legislation is that the minimum will tend to become the maximum, and thus bring down the earnings of the more efficient toward the level of the less efficient employees. But with these speculations we have nothing to do. We are concerned only with the question of constitutionality.

That the clause of the Fourteenth Amendment which forbids a state to deprive any person of life, liberty or property without due process of law includes freedom of contract is so well settled as to be no longer open to question. Nor reasonably can it be disputed that contracts of employment of labor are included in the rule. *Adair v. United States*; *Coppage v. Kansas*. . . . We then pointed out that minimum wage legislation such as that here involved does not deal with any business charged with a public interest, or with public work, or with a temporary emergency, or with the character, methods or periods of wage payments, or with hours of labor, or with the protection of persons under legal disability, or with the prevention of fraud. It is, simply and exclusively, a law fixing wages for adult women who are legally as capable of contracting for themselves as men, and cannot be sustained unless upon principles apart from those involved in cases already decided by the court.

. . . The feature of this statute which, perhaps more than any other, puts upon it the stamp of invalidity is that it exacts from the employer an arbitrary payment for a purpose and upon a basis having no causal connection with his business, or the contract, or the work the employee engages to do. The declared basis, as already pointed out, is not the value of the service rendered, but the extraneous circumstance that the employee needs to get a prescribed sum of money to insure her subsistence, health and morals. The ethical right of every worker, man or woman, to a living wage may be conceded. One of the declared and important purposes of trade organizations is to secure it. And with that principle and with every legitimate effort to realize it, in fact, no one can quarrel; but the fallacy of the proposed method of attaining it is that it assumes that every employer is bound at all events to furnish it. The moral requirement implicit in every contract of employment, *viz.*, that the amount to be paid and the service to be rendered shall bear to each other some relation of just equivalence, is completely ignored. The necessities of the employee are alone considered, and these arise outside of the employment, are the same when there is no employment, and as great in one occupation as in another. Certainly the employer, by paying a fair equivalent for the service rendered, though not sufficient to support the employee, has neither caused nor contributed to her poverty. On the contrary, to the extent of what he pays, he has relieved it. In principle, there can be no difference between the case of selling labor and the case of selling goods. If one goes to the butcher, the baker or grocer to buy food, he is morally entitled to obtain the worth of his money, but he is not entitled to more. If what he gets is worth what he pays, he is not justified in demanding more simply because he needs more, and the shopkeeper, having dealt fairly and honestly in that transaction, is not concerned in any peculiar sense with the question of his customer's necessities. Should a statute undertake to vest in a commission power to determine the quantity of food necessary for individual support and require the shopkeeper, if he sell to the individual at all, to furnish that quantity at not more than a fixed maximum, it would undoubtedly fall before the constitutional test. The fallacy of any argument in support of the validity of such a statute would be quickly exposed. The argument in support of that now being considered is equally fallacious, though the weakness of it may not be so plain. A statute requiring an employer to pay in money, to pay at prescribed and regular intervals, to pay the value of the services rendered, even to pay with fair relation to the extent of the benefit obtained from the service, would be understandable. But a statute which prescribes payment without regard to any of these things, and solely with relation to circumstances apart from the contract of employment, the business affected by it and the work done under it, is so clearly the product of a naked, arbitrary exercise of power that it cannot be allowed to stand under the Constitution of the United States.

SYNTHESIS QUESTIONS FOR FURTHER DISCUSSION: CHAPTER 7 SECTION A

1. In his dissent in *Lochner v. New York*, Justice Oliver Wendell Holmes accuses the majority of trying to read into the Constitution a certain economic theory of liberty that its text does not enshrine. Is this the theory of libertarianism endorsed in the selection by Robert Nozick? Is it the theory of property endorsed by John Locke? Although the Due Process Clause itself does not reference the idea of a right to contract, this practice is referenced elsewhere. Article I, Section 10 of the Constitution reads: "No state shall . . . pass any . . . Law impairing the Obligation of Contracts." Does this suggest that there might be merit to the majority's argument in *Lochner v. New York*?

2. Read the Due Process Clause of the Fourteenth Amendment in isolation from the rest of the Constitution. Does a strictly textual reading seem to suggest that economic rights are liberties of which individuals can be deprived, given due process of law?

3. What might Locke or Nozick say in response to the Court's decision in *West Coast Hotel v. Parrish*? Are their defenses of private property compatible with the Court's ruling in this case?

4. Is there any account of a right to private property besides the Lockean account? Although *West Coast Hotel v. Parrish* is widely seen to have ended the era of substantive due process protections for a right to property, does it leave room for the protection of any property rights?

5. As we have noted, *West Coast Hotel v. Parrish* was decided in the context of President Franklin Roosevelt's threat to pack the Court. Was President Roosevelt's threat legitimate? Assume that President Roosevelt was correct that the *Lochner v. New York*–era justices were wrong to rely on a theory of property libertarianism. Would the rightness of his position justify his actions?

B.   RIGHTS OF THE FAMILY

In considering the doctrine of substantive due process, we begin this section with two cases that center upon the rights of families. Although, as we have noted, the Court expounded the doctrine of substantive due process to protect economic liberties in *Lochner v. New York*, it then applied the doctrine to non-economic liberties in *Meyer v. Nebraska* and in *Pierce v. Society of Sisters*. Both of these latter cases deal with the question of parents' rights over their children's education. *Meyer v. Nebraska* addresses the right of parents to be free from governmental prohibitions on their children learning a foreign language. In turn, *Pierce v. Society of Sisters* concerns whether parents have a right to enroll their children in private rather than public schools. Both cases elaborate a fundamental right of parents that is relatively uncontroversial today. But both cases also open up the question of how the Court should discern fundamental rights that are not enumerated in the Constitution.

In *Michael H. v. Gerald D.*, Justice Antonin Scalia suggests an exclusive method for determining fundamental rights. He states that "a rule of law that binds neither by text nor by any particular, identifiable tradition is no rule of law at all." On this view, absent an explicit textual protection, the Court must proceed carefully in establishing which liberties the Due Process Clause protects. First, judges must define the right in question with a very narrow level of specificity, i.e., the right to engage in gay sodomy rather than the right to intimate sexual conduct, or the right of an illegitimate father to custody rather than the right to depart from society's conventions. Second, the Court must locate the right in a clearly defined tradition spanning the nation's history. While this method seems to be compatible with protecting the rights of families, as in *Meyer v. Nebraska* and *Pierce v. Society of Sisters*, many critics of substantive due process use this logic to criticize the expansive use of the doctrine in cases such as *Lawrence v. Texas*, which we discuss in Section C.

In addition to discerning fundamental rights by looking to tradition, the Court has turned to approaches that stress the values of the Constitution. U.S. Supreme Court Justice Benjamin Cardozo explains in *Palko v. Connecticut* that some rights are so fundamental as to be "implicit in the concept of ordered liberty." Unlike with Justice Scalia's originalism, references to tradition or history alone might not satisfy this line of reasoning. Instead, it demands that judges evaluate whether the law strikes an appropriate balance between individual freedom and the legitimate goals of the state. A right is fundamental when its infringement calls this very balance into question. Although there will inevitably be disagreement about which rights, exactly, count as fundamental, the Court has long held that fundamental rights exist that cannot be violated by majoritarian institutions. In *Hebert v. Louisiana*, the Court appealed to something like the moral reading we studied in Chapter 2 when it suggested that these rights are grounded in the "principles of liberty and justice which lie at the base of all our civic and political institutions." These principles, the Court suggested in *Snyder v. Massachusetts*, are "so rooted in the . . . conscience of our people as to be ranked as fundamental."

The rights examined throughout this chapter, including the rights to contraception, abortion, and sexual intimacy for gay couples, are not explicitly granted in the Constitution. But while these specific rights are not linked to tradition, their defenders argue that they are linked to the fundamental liberties enshrined in the Constitution. In particular, the doctrine of substantive due process is thought according to the modern Court to establish a broad "right to privacy." As you will see, this right was established in *Griswold v. Connecticut*, a case about contraception, but it is significant for its claim that this specific right is part of a more general set of privacy rights. In *Griswold v. Connecticut*, Justice William O. Douglas specifically referenced the privacy rights of the "marital bedroom," drawing implicitly on the idea, explored here, that families were entitled to rights to make private decisions.

Our readings for this section emphasize a theoretical dilemma that will become apparent in the Court's later cases. William Galston defends the rights of families announced in *Meyer v. Nebraska* and *Pierce v. Society of Sisters*. Harder cases pit the rights of parents against individual rights and pressing concerns of equality. One might argue that the rights of families are a kind of group right, which is in tension with the individual rights of children. As Amy Gutmann argued in Chapter 6, sometimes the rights of individual children should outweigh the rights of parents. Thus, she rejected the extension of the protection guaranteed in *Meyer v. Nebraska* and *Pierce v. Society of Sisters* to exempting Amish children from laws requiring them to attend school altogether in *Wisconsin v. Yoder*. This dilemma will also prove relevant to Section C, where you must grapple with the question of whether privacy rights are protections of individuals or of the family unit as a whole.

William A. Galston

PARENTS, GOVERNMENT, AND CHILDREN: AUTHORITY OVER EDUCATION IN THE LIBERAL DEMOCRATIC STATE

in **Child, Family, and State** *(Stephen Macedo & Iris Marion Young eds.)*

New York, NY: New York University Press (2003)

In the following excerpt, William Galston suggests why the rights of families should be thought of as fundamental rights. Do his arguments provide support for the use of substantive due process to protect these liberties in matters of education? Keep them in mind when you read the case selection.

I. INTRODUCTION

Some years ago, my wife and I engaged in a series of discussions about where to send our son to school. His experience in a District of Columbia primary school had been perfectly satisfactory, and we could have easily let him continue there.

Ultimately, although neither my wife nor I am particularly religious, we decided to send him to a Jewish day school. The determining factors were, first, our desire that our son learn systematically about his heritage and second, that he learn in a recognizably moral community where shared premises—justice, care for others, moral responsibility, and self-discipline, among others—are applied to the concrete issues of school life.

Our decision occurred within a context of assumptions that we took for granted without much thought. The government has the right (and perhaps duty) to require the education of all children up through the mid-teens and to regulate some basic features of their education. Parents bear principal responsibility for seeing to it that their children meet this requirement, but they have the right to choose among a wide range of options for meeting it. While government has the right to tax all its citizens to finance and operate a system of public schools open to all, it cannot create a public school monopoly that prevents parents from sending their children to nonpublic schools.

Each of these assumptions was contested earlier in the history of the United States; all now enjoy near-universal support. In my judgment, this shift represents more than bare historical contingency or practical necessity. These widely accepted assumptions are consistent with a defensible version of liberal democratic theory as well as with the practical requirements of life in liberal democracies under modern circumstances.

The underlying theory goes something like this: In establishing the aims of—and control over—education, three sets of considerations must somehow be coordinated. First, the conditions for the normal development of children must be secured, their ability to become contributing members of the economy and society must be fostered, and the growth over time in their capacity for sound independent judgment must be recognized. Second, the liberal democratic state must act, not only to safeguard the developmental interests of children, but also to promote the effective functioning of its basic institutions. Third, the special relationship between parents and children must be reflected in the allocation of educational authority, and so must what I shall call the "expressive interest" of parents in raising their children in a manner consistent with their understanding of what gives meaning and value to life.

While each of the values must find appropriate expression in practical decisions, there is no guarantee that they will fit together into a harmonious whole. Pressed to the hilt, any one of them will entail costs to the others that may well be judged excessive. Sound education policy cannot be exclusively state centered, parent centered, or child centered. Among other implications, this schema means that civic concerns do not function as trumps in discussions of educational policy. A particular course of action designed to promote important civic objectives may nonetheless be the wrong thing to do for other reasons: for example, the government cannot rightly compel school children to join in a flag salute ceremony contrary to the dictates of their conscience. This remains the case even if the flag salute proves to be an effective means of fostering patriotism. It is equally true that parental concerns do not function as trumps; in some cases the damage to core civic concerns, or to the child's interests, will be too extensive.

While I shall not offer anything like a full exposition (let alone defense) of this thesis, I should underscore three of its features at the outset.

First, liberal democracies are not civic republics. The liberal democratic state does not have plenipotentiary power, and public-spirited aims need not govern the actions of its citizens in all spheres and circumstances. And while feminism has reinterpreted and relocated the boundary between public and private matters, it does not necessarily deny the appropriateness of the distinction as such or the value of privacy, rightly understood, in human life. If the liberal democratic state were to legislate a conception of child or governmental interests that in effect nullified parental educational choice, it would exceed the legitimate bounds of its authority.

Much the same can be said of liberal democratic justice. Whichever conception of liberal democratic justice one prefers, it cannot be so comprehensive and stringent as to expunge a substantial zone of diversity and choice. Justice establishes a framework of claims that individuals and (for some purposes) groups may ask the state to enforce. But potential claimants need not press their justified claims to the hilt. They may choose not to exercise some of their entitlements in return for other goods that seem preferable, all things considered. The proposition "It would be unjust for you to deprive me of A" does not imply the conclusion "It would be wrong for me not to exercise my claim to A against you." The nonexercise of a justified claim becomes questionable when the potential claimant is subject to intimidation or is deprived of the information and self-confidence required for independent judgment. The free exercise of independent and group choice within the framework of liberal democratic judgment generates a zone of diverse ways of life that are permissible and safeguarded from external intervention even when we could not imagine choosing them for ourselves....

Second, when I invoke parental authority over education, I presuppose a fair division of decision-making power between the parents (assuming that more than one is in the picture). I make no assumptions about who can be a parent, about how one becomes a parent, or about the parent's legal status in relation to another parent or to the child. I do not address the circumstances in which the presumption in favor of the parent may be rebutted by parental misconduct or incapacity. Nor do I intend to enter into, or to prejudge, the knotty questions that arise when marriages dissolve or when a child's relatives other than parents (grandparents, for example) make claims on a share of decision-making authority. My discussion, then, takes place within a simplified model of family life. I leave for another occasion the question of how my arguments and conclusions would change in response to various real-world alterations of the model.

Third, to insist, as I do, that control over education is a function of distinct and sometimes competing normative dimensions is to say almost nothing about how these variables should be weighted or rank-ordered in determining individual decisions. This gap can be filled only by thick descriptions of specific decision contexts and by deliberative arguments about the relative importance of different dimensions of value within these contexts. Even after careful description and deliberation, in many situations it will not prove possible to reach full closure, leaving wide latitude for appropriate processes of political decision making.

While the multivalued pluralist perspective I am urging is not enough to produce unique affirmative results, it does yield an important negative consequence. This approach makes it impossible to argue directly from the premise

"Option A yields important gains along dimension X" to the conclusion "We should choose A," for others may reasonably contend that the sacrifices of value along other dimensions are significant enough to outweigh the gains along X. From this perspective, then, it never suffices to claim that a particular course of action serves the interests of children, or parents, or civic life; all must somehow be taken into account.

II. EDUCATION IN U.S. HISTORY

John Stuart Mill regarded the right of the state to compel parents to educate their children as "almost a self-evident axiom." Yet writing in 1859, he observed that in practice few of his fellow citizens were willing to affirm its force. While most acknowledged the moral duty of parents to educate their children, they denied that the state had the right to enforce it. Much the same situation prevailed on the other side of the Atlantic. Despite the spread of the "common school" ideal in the early nineteenth century, as late as the eve of the Civil War, only two states (Massachusetts and New York) had enacted compulsory education statutes. Many citizens who conceded that the policy would promote the general welfare nonetheless denied that the state could properly—and constitutionally—go down this road.

Within decades, matters had changed radically. By 1900, thirty-two states had passed compulsory attendance laws. By 1918, such laws were universal throughout the United States. Despite its readiness to strike down a wide range of social legislation as infringements of individual liberty, not even the *Lochner*-era Supreme Court was willing to raise constitutional questions about the power of the states to enforce such laws. (Given the late development of the policy of universal compulsory education, this agreement is all the more noteworthy.)

III. FROM HISTORY TO THEORY

A resort to theory may not prove conclusive, but it is surely necessary.

As we have seen, John Stuart Mill regards it as virtually self-evident that the state "should require and compel the education, up to a certain standard, of every human being who is born its citizen." In his account, the state's authority derives from parental responsibility. The bare fact of causing the existence of another human being brings into play more responsibilities than does virtually any other human act. In particular, "[I]t is one of the most sacred duties of the parents (or, as law and usage now stand, the father), after summoning a human being into the world, to give to that being an education fitting him to perform his part well in life toward others and toward himself." The failure to do so is a "moral crime, both against the unfortunate offspring and against society; and . . . if the parent does not fulfill this obligation, the State ought to see it fulfilled."

Mill assumes that this educational duty flows directly from the fact of biological generation, coupled with broad features of the individual and social good. Parents do not have the right to neglect the education of their children in ways that impose avoidable burdens on their fellow citizens—for example, by raising children unable to contribute to the economy or unwilling to obey the law. Nor do they have the right to deprive their children of what Mill assumes to be the profound and pervasive benefits of education: the development of human faculties is at the core of what he terms the "permanent interests of man as a progressive being." Mill accepts a version of the thesis

I earlier termed limited perfectionism; the necessity of education reflects, not only the contextually specific requisites of advanced economies, but also noncontextual features of the human condition. The state has a legitimate interest in enforcing parental responsibility, both to enhance social utility and to create human beings in the "maturity of their faculties" who are "capable of being improved by free and equal discussion."

Mill suggests that this parental responsibility is material as well as moral: parents must finance their children's education to the extent they can. His insistence on individual responsibility is striking: the "moral crime" lies not only in willfully depriving a child of education but also in bringing a child into the world without a "fair prospect" of being able to afford a basic education. (He even endorses the legitimacy of Continental laws forbidding couples to marry unless they have the means to support a family.) But he also stresses the element of social responsibility: when the state makes education compulsory, it must provide sliding-scale subsidies for lower-income families and pay outright for the education of children whose parents cannot afford to contribute anything. So all members of the society must do their part to sustain a system of compulsory education that benefits society as a whole.

Mill distinguishes between state-enforced compulsory education and direct state provision of education. He opposes all policies that lead to state dominance over or monopoly of education. Diversity of character and opinion is the key to both individual flourishing and social progress. But a state-dominated system of education is a "mere contrivance for molding people to be exactly like one another" that "establishes a despotism over the mind." A state system of education "should only exist, if it exist at all, as one among many competing experiments, carried on for the purpose of example and stimulus to keep the others up to a certain standard of excellence." . . .

One may of course question Mill's point of departure. But there is much to be said in favor of the proposition that children are not uniform blank slates that others may inscribe as they please. Most parents I know have been led by their own experience to acknowledge the existence and importance of each child's natural bent. Good parenting—and by extension good education—finds ways of accomplishing its essential purposes with rather than against the grain.

The crucial issue is whether our upbringing will accommodate and encourage, or rather pinch and repress, the development of our distinctiveness. But there is no guarantee that a system of parental educational choice would promote individuality as Mill understands it. He is critical of patriarchy, but he does not draw the obvious connection that a father's choice may prove just as Procrustean for a child as would the state's. Instead of a single despotic power there might be a multiplicity of smaller ones. (Mill of all people should have been exquisitely sensitive to this possibility.) Mill's proposed system would promote educational diversity, to be sure, but not necessarily individuality.

There is more to be said in defense of Mill's position, however. Educational diversity is at least a necessary condition for the cultivation of individuality. Assuming, as Mill does, the diversity of human types, it is hard to see how any single unitary system of education could accommodate all of them equally well. The existence of a range of educational choices offers the possibility of a better fit between institutional settings and individual needs.

While children can be consulted, more-over, they cannot make these choices for themselves, especially in the early years. Either parents will make these choices, or the state will make them for them. While parents may often fail to choose wisely, there are reasons to believe that the state typically will do even worse. On average, parents understand their children's individual traits better than public authorities do, their concern for their children's well-being is deeper, and they are not subject to the homogenizing imperatives of even the best bureaucracies in the modem state. In practice, the legal system must create a presumption in one direction or the other, and the case for a presumption in favor of parents is strong.

But that presumption is rebuttable. While the range of parental discretion is wide, the state properly enforces numerous limits on parental authority. Laws against abuse and neglect mean that parents are not free to injure their children or to deprive them of the basic goods needed for normal physical, mental, and emotional development. Nor may parents invoke their deepest religious convictions to prevent their children's immunization or deprive them of essential medical care. By the same token, the state may act to prevent what amounts to educational abuse and neglect, through measures such as compulsory education statutes and basic standards of education attainment. But the state cannot legitimately define a concept of the child's best interests so extensive and detailed that its enforcement would in practice eviscerate the power of parents to make decisions concerning their children's education. . . .

IV. EXPRESSIVE LIBERTY AND PARENTAL INTERESTS

By *expressive liberty* I mean the absence of constraints imposed by some individuals or groups on others that make it impossible or significantly more difficult for the affected individuals or groups to live their lives in ways that express their deepest beliefs about what gives meaning and value to life. An example of such constraints is the Inquisition, which forced Iberian Jews either to endure persecution or to renounce their religious practices.

Expressive liberty offers us the opportunity to enjoy a fit between inner and outer, conviction and deed. Not all sets of practices will themselves rest on, or reflect a preference for, liberty as ordinarily understood. For example, being Jewish is not always (indeed, is not usually) understood as a matter of choice. But once that fact is established through birth and circumstance, it becomes a matter of great importance for Jews to live in a society that permits them to live in accordance with an identity that is given rather than chosen and that is structured by obligations whose binding power does not depend on individual acceptance. For Jews, and for many others as well, the ability to revise one's conception of the good is hardly a good thing. In short, because not all sets of beliefs and practices value (let alone give pride of place to) liberty, expressive liberty protects the ability of individuals and groups to live in ways that others would regard as unfree.

Expressive liberty is an important value because it is a precondition for leading a complete and satisfying life. The reason is straightforward: part of what it means to have deep beliefs about how one should live is the desire to live in accordance with them. Only in rare cases (perhaps certain kinds of Stoicism) do constraints imposed by other individuals and by social structures have negligible effects on the ability of believers to live in accordance with their convictions. Most of us experience impediments to acting on our deepest beliefs as sources of deprivation and unhappiness, resentment and anger. The absence of expressive liberty is a misfortune that few would willingly endure.

Although expressive liberty is a great good, it is not the only good, and it is certainly not without limits. No one would seriously argue that the expressive liberty of parents would legitimate the ritual sacrifice of their children or that expressive liberty could be invoked to blunt the force of responsibility to our fellow citizens and to legitimate public institutions. But because it is a core value, it cannot rightly be infringed without countervailing reasons of considerable weight. . . .

What I want to argue is that the ability of parents to raise their children in a manner consistent with their deepest commitments is an essential element of expressive liberty. As Eamonn Callan rightly suggests, parenting is typically undertaken as one of the central meaning-giving tasks of our lives. We cannot detach our aspirations for our children from our understanding of what is good and virtuous. As Stephen Gilles insists, loving and nurturing a child cannot in practice be divorced from shaping that child's values. In so doing as parents, we cannot but draw on the comprehensive understanding that gives our values whatever coherence and grounding they may possess. Moreover, we hope for relations of intimacy with our children, as they develop and when they are grown. But estrangement is the enemy of intimacy. It is understandable for parents to fear that their children may become embroiled in ways of life they regard as alien and distasteful and, within limits, act to reduce the risk that this fear will be realized. Callan links these parental expressive interests with core liberal freedoms:

The rights to freedom of conscience and association are widely accepted as among the necessary requirements of any recognizably liberal regime. But the freedom to rear our children according to the dictates of conscience is for most of us as important as any other expression of conscience, and the freedom to organize and sustain the life of the family in keeping with our own values is as significant as our liberty to associate outside the family for any purpose whatever.

Conversely, one of the most disturbing features of illiberal regimes is the wedge their governments typically seek to drive between parents and children and the effort they make to replace a multiplicity of family traditions with a unitary, state-administered culture.

The appropriate parental role is structured in part by the vulnerability, dependency, and developmental needs of children. The model of fiduciary responsibility developed by Locke and endorsed by contemporary thinkers such as Richard Arneson and Ian Shapiro well captures this dimension of the parent-child relationship. But the expressive interests of parents are not reducible to their fiduciary duty to promote their children's interests. A better model is more nearly reciprocal: parents and children serve, and are served by, one another in complex ways. To quote Callan once more:

[I]f a moral theory interprets the child's role so as to make individual children no more than instruments of their parents' good it would be open to damning moral objections. But parallel objections must be decisive against any theory that interprets the parent's role in ways that make individual parents no more than instruments of their children's good. We should want a conception of parents' rights in education that will not license the oppression of children. But we should also want a conception that will do justice to the hopes that parents have and the sacrifices they make in rearing their children.

... Like any other value, the expressive interests of parents can be pushed too far. To begin with, as children develop, their own expressive interests must be given increased weight. Consider the well-known case of *Wisconsin v. Yoder*. This case presented a clash between a Wisconsin state law, which required school attendance until age sixteen, and three Old Order Amish parents, who claimed that mandating their children's school attendance after age fourteen would undermine their community-based religious practices. While the Supreme Court decided in favor of the parents, a number of justices declared that the adolescent children had liberty claims independent of their parents. The record offered no evidence of religious disagreement between the Amish children and their parents. If the children had expressed the desire to continue their education, these justices would have voted to uphold the state's enforcement of its attendance laws against the wishes of the parents. At a minimum, the children's freestanding religious claims imply enforceable rights of exit from the boundaries of community defined by their parents. I would add that the exit rights must be more than formal. Communities cannot rightly act in ways that disempower individuals intellectually, emotionally, or practically from living successfully outside their bounds.

But should the expressed views of the children be taken as dispositive? Arneson and Shapiro say not: even if the children acquiesce, the parents may still be in violation of their fiduciary responsibility. A parent, they insist, "cannot pretend to speak for the child while really regarding the child as an empty vessel for the parent's own religious convictions. As a fiduciary, the parent is bound to preserve the child's own future religious freedom." Even if we accept this premise (and it may

be questioned from several perspectives), it is by no means clear what practical conclusions we are compelled to draw from it. Does respect for a child's religious freedom mean that the parent is required to treat all comprehensive views equally, taking the child on a tour of different faiths and secular philosophical outlooks and then saying in effect, you choose? Few parents, whatever their outlook, would accept this proposition; even fewer would endorse its enforcement by the state; and I do not see considerations weighty enough to warrant such a sharp break with established practices. At the very least, parents are entitled to introduce their children to what they regard as vital sources of meaning and value and to hope that their children will come to share this orientation. One might also argue that instructing children within a particular tradition, far from undermining intellectual or religious freedom, may in fact promote it. Knowing what it means to live within a coherent framework of value and belief may well contribute to an informed adult choice between one's tradition of origin and those encountered later in life. . . .

While these arguments clarify some moral intuitions, they also suggest that practical issues of educational authority cannot be resolved on the plane of moral abstractions. The acceptability of parental decisions must be evaluated within the full context of influences shaping children's awareness of alternatives and ability to weight them. And it is not enough to judge the intention of parents' educational decisions; we must also look at their concrete results. . . .

Even if *Yoder* does not violate the present or potential expressive liberty of Amish young people, it may be argued that the decision gives inadequate weight to the state's interest in fostering good citizens. According to this line of argument, good citizens participate actively in public affairs, using developed powers of critical reason to deliberate on and decide among competing policies and representatives. But Amish education discourages both active participation and critical reasoning and thus fails to meet legitimate basic state requirements.

There are three sorts of reply to this line of argument. First, as we have seen, the proposition that X is instrumental to (or even necessary for) the creation of good citizens does not, as a matter of constitutional law or liberal democratic theory, warrant the conclusion that X is right or legitimate, all things considered. There may be compelling moral and human considerations that prevent the state from enforcing otherwise acceptable policies on dissenting individuals or groups.

Second, even if we accept the premise that critical reasoning is a sine qua non of liberal democratic citizenship, there is no reason to believe that the Amish are incapable of exercising it in the relevant respect. I recently read a newspaper article (regrettably I cannot locate the reference) written by a Catholic theologian concerning U.S. tactics in the Kosovo conflict. Reasoning from and applying the principles of Catholic "justice in war" doctrine, he concluded that high-altitude bombing safeguarded pilots at a morally unacceptable cost in civilian lives. This is an example of critical reasoning *within* or *from* a tradition rather than *about* that tradition. But it would be unreasonable for a conception—especially an enforceable conception—of liberal democratic citizenship to demand that citizens somehow set aside, or adopt a stance of open-minded neutrality toward, the beliefs around which they organize they lives when reasoning about public affairs. The Amish have demonstrated their capacity

for critical reasoning in the ways that it is publicly reasonable to expect.

Finally, the active deliberative/participatory virtues are not the only virtues of citizenship we should care about. Law-abidingness, personal and family responsibility, and tolerance of social diversity are also important for the successful functioning of contemporary liberal democracies. In these respects, among others, the Amish score high. They may not be the best of citizens, but may we not say that they are good enough? At least they fulfill the political version of the Hippocratic oath—to do no harm. I might add that if nonvoting and civic withdrawal are taken as sufficient evidence of parental and pedagogical failure warranting state intervention, then our indictment extends far beyond the minute numbers of Amish to implicate more than half the families and graduates of public schools in the United States.

V. PARENTAL AUTHORITY, EXPRESSIVE LIBERTY, AND PUBLIC EDUCATION

Today, after two decades of hand-wringing about the quality of public education, roughly 90 percent of all school-age children still attend public schools. There is no compelling reason to believe that the emphasis I have placed on expressive liberty and the role of parents, if taken as the basis for actual policy, would significantly erode the dominant position the public schools now enjoy. Nor does my thesis undermine the legitimate role of the state in requiring all parents to educate their children and in establishing basic standards for all educational institutions. (In these important respects, all elementary and secondary education in the United States is "public.") Rather, my account merely makes explicit the moral and theoretical underpinnings of the long-standing U.S. constitutional commitment to the principle that parents may choose among a range of options—public and private, secular and religious, heterogeneous and homogeneous—for discharging their obligation to educate their children.

Nonetheless, my stance does reflect an underlying understanding that some may find objectionable. I believe that in a society characterized by a deep diversity of moral and religious views, and accordingly by diverse family and communal ways of life, both empirical consent and normative legitimacy require that, to the maximum extent consistent with the maintenance of civic unity and stability, all permissible ways of life be able to find expression in the key choices families and communities must make. Among these choices, the venue and conduct of education rank high. I would argue that genuine civic unity rests on unforced consent.

States that permit their citizens to live in ways that express their values are likely to enjoy widespread support, even gratitude. By contrast, state coercion is likely to produce dissent, resistance, and withdrawal.

Granted, sometimes the state has no choice. If families, schools, or local communities are acting in ways that violate the basic rights of citizens, then the state must step in. And if the result is resistance—even "massive resistance" in the face of compulsory school desegregation—that is the price that must be paid for defending the rightful claims of all citizens. My point is rather that the state must be parsimonious in defining the realm in which uniformity must be secured through coercion. An educational program based on an expansive and contestable definition of good citizenship or civic unity will not ordinarily justify the forcible suppression of expressive liberty.

MEYER v. NEBRASKA

262 U.S. 390 (1923)

Opinion: McReynolds, joined by Taft, McKenna, Van Devanter, Brandeis, Butler, Sanford
Dissent: Holmes, joined by Sutherland

MR. JUSTICE McREYNOLDS *delivered the opinion of the Court.*

Plaintiff in error was tried and convicted in the district court for Hamilton county, Nebraska, under an information which charged that on May 25, 1920, while an instructor in Zion Parochial School he unlawfully taught the subject of reading in the German language to Raymond Parpart, a child of 10 years, who had not attained and successfully passed the eighth

grade. The information is based upon "An act relating to the teaching of foreign languages in the state of Nebraska," approved April 9, 1919, which follows:

"Section 1. No person, individually or as a teacher, shall, in any private, denominational, parochial or public school, teach any subject to any person in any language than the English language.

"Sec. 2. Languages, other than the English language, may be taught as languages only after a pupil shall have attained and successfully passed the eighth grade as evidenced by a certificate of graduation issued by the county superintendent of the county in which the child resides.

"Sec. 3. Any person who violates any of the provisions of this act shall be deemed guilty of a misdemeanor and upon conviction, shall be subject to a fine of not less than twenty-five dollars ($25), nor more than one hundred dollars ($100), or be confined in the county jail for any period not exceeding thirty days for each offense.

"Sec. 4. Whereas, an emergency exists, this act shall be in force from and after its passage and approval."

. . . The problem for our determination is whether the statute as construed and applied unreasonably infringes the liberty guaranteed to the plaintiff in error by the Fourteenth Amendment.

While this court has not attempted to define with exactness the liberty thus guaranteed, the term has received much consideration and some of the included things have been definitely stated. Without doubt, it denotes not merely freedom from bodily restraint but also the right of the individual to contract, to engage in any of the common occupations of life, to acquire useful knowledge, to marry, establish a home and bring up children, to worship God according to the dictates of his own conscience, and generally to enjoy those privileges long recognized at common law as essential to the orderly pursuit of happiness by free men. The established doctrine is that this liberty may not be interfered with, under the guise of protecting the public interest, by legislative action which is arbitrary or without reasonable relation to some purpose within the competency of the state to effect. Determination by the Legislature of what constitutes proper exercise of police power is not final or conclusive but is subject to supervision by the courts. *Lawton v. Steele*.

The American people have always regarded education and acquisition of knowledge as matters of supreme importance which should be diligently promoted. The Ordinance of 1787 declares:

"Religion, morality and knowledge being necessary to good government and the happiness of mankind, schools and the means of education shall forever be encouraged."

Corresponding to the right of control, it is the natural duty of the parent to give his children education suitable to their station in life; and nearly all the states, including Nebraska, enforce this obligation by compulsory laws.

Practically, education of the young is only possible in schools conducted by especially qualified persons who devote themselves thereto. The calling always has been regarded as useful and honorable, essential, indeed, to the public welfare. Mere knowledge of the German language cannot reasonably be regarded as harmful. Heretofore it has been commonly looked upon as helpful and desirable. Plaintiff in error taught this language in school as part of his occupation. His right thus to teach and the right of parents to engage him so to instruct their children, we think, are within the liberty of the amendment.

The challenged statute forbids the teaching in school of any subject except in English; also the teaching of any other language until the pupil has attained and successfully passed the eighth grade, which is not usually accomplished before the age of twelve. The Supreme Court of the state has held that "the so-called ancient or dead languages" are not "within the spirit or the purpose of the act." Latin, Greek, Hebrew are not proscribed; but German, French, Spanish, Italian, and every other alien speech are within the ban. Evidently the Legislature has attempted materially to interfere with the calling of modern language teachers, with the opportunities of pupils to acquire knowledge, and with the power of parents to control the education of their own.

It is said the purpose of the legislation was to promote civic development by inhibiting training and education of the immature in foreign tongues and ideals before they could learn English and acquire American ideals, and "that the English language should be and become the mother tongue of all children reared in this state." It is also affirmed that the foreign-born population is very large, that certain communities commonly use foreign words, follow foreign leaders, move in a foreign atmosphere, and that the children are thereby hindered from becoming citizens of the most useful type and the public safety is imperiled.

That the state may do much, go very far, indeed, in order to improve the quality of its citizens, physically, mentally and morally, is clear; but the individual has certain fundamental rights which must be respected. The protection of the Constitution extends to all, to those who speak other languages as well as to those born with English on the tongue. Perhaps it would be highly advantageous if all had ready understanding of our ordinary speech, but this cannot be coerced by methods which conflict with the Constitution—a desirable end cannot be promoted by prohibited means. . . .

The desire of the Legislature to foster a homogeneous people with American ideals prepared readily to understand current discussions of civic matters is easy to appreciate. Unfortunate experiences during the late war and aversion toward every character of truculent adversaries were certainly enough to quicken that aspiration. But the means adopted, we think, exceed the limitations upon the power of the state and conflict with rights assured to plaintiff in error. The interference is plain enough and no adequate reason therefore in time of peace and domestic tranquility has been shown. . . .

As the statute undertakes to interfere only with teaching which involves a modern language, leaving complete freedom as to other matters, there seems no adequate foundation for the suggestion that the

purpose was to protect the child's health by limiting his mental activities. It is well known that proficiency in a foreign language seldom comes to one not instructed at an early age, and experience shows that this is not injurious to the health, morals or understanding of the ordinary child.

The judgment of the court below must be reversed and the cause remanded for further proceedings not inconsistent with this opinion.

Reversed.

MR. JUSTICE HOLMES, *dissenting.*

We all agree, I take it, that it is desirable that all the citizens of the United States should speak a common tongue, and therefore that the end aimed at by the statute is a lawful and proper one. The only question is whether the means adopted deprive teachers of the liberty secured to them by the Fourteenth Amendment. It is with hesitation and unwillingness that I differ from my brethren with regard to a law like this, but I cannot bring my mind to believe that, in some circumstances, and circumstances existing, it is said, in Nebraska, the statute might not be regarded as a reasonable or even necessary method of reaching the desired result. The part of the act with which we are concerned deals with the teaching of young children. Youth is the time when familiarity with a language is established and if there are sections in the state where a child would hear only Polish or French or German spoken at home, I am not prepared to say that it is unreasonable to provide that, in his early years, he shall hear and speak only English at school. But, if it is reasonable, it is not an undue restriction of the liberty either of teacher or scholar. No one would doubt that a teacher might be forbidden to teach many things, and the only criterion of his liberty under the Constitution that I can think of is "whether, considering the end in view, the statute passes the bounds of reason and assumes the character of a merely arbitrary fiat." *Purity Extract & Tonic Co. v. Lynch; Hebe Co. v. Shaw; Jacob Ruppert v. Caffey.* I think I appreciate the objection to the law, but it appears to me to present a question upon which men reasonably might differ, and therefore I am unable to say that the Constitution of the United States prevents the experiment's being tried.

I agree with the Court as to the special proviso against the German language contained in the statute dealt with in *Bohning v. Ohio.*

MR. JUSTICE SUTHERLAND *concurs in this opinion.*

PIERCE v. SOCIETY OF SISTERS

268 U.S. 510 (1925)

Opinion: McReynolds, joined by Taft, Holmes, Van Devanter, Brandeis, Sutherland, Butler, Sanford, Stone

MR. JUSTICE McREYNOLDS *delivered the opinion of the Court.*

The challenged Act, effective September 1, 1926, requires every parent, guardian or other person having control or charge or custody of a child between eight and sixteen years to send him "to a public school for the period of time a public school shall be held during the current year" in the district where the child resides, and failure so to do is declared a misdemeanor. . . . The manifest purpose is to compel general attendance at public schools by normal children, between eight and sixteen, who have not completed the eighth grade. And without doubt enforcement of the statute would seriously impair, perhaps destroy, the profitable features of appellees' business and greatly diminish the value of their property.

Appellee, the Society of Sisters, is an Oregon corporation, organized in 1880, with power to care for orphans, educate and instruct the youth, establish and maintain academies or schools, and acquire necessary real and personal property. It has long devoted its property and effort to the secular and religious education and care of children, and has acquired the valuable good will of many parents and guardians. It conducts interdependent primary and high schools and junior colleges, and maintains orphanages for the custody and control of children between eight and sixteen. In its primary schools, many children between those ages are taught the subjects usually pursued in Oregon public schools during the first eight years. Systematic religious instruction and moral training according to the tenets of the Roman Catholic Church are also regularly provided. All courses of study, both temporal and religious, contemplate continuity of training under appellee's charge; the primary schools are essential to the system and the most profitable.

After setting out the above facts, the Society's bill alleges that the enactment conflicts with the right of parents to choose schools where their children will receive appropriate mental and religious training, the right of the child to influence the parents' choice of a school, the right of schools and teachers therein to engage in a useful business or profession, and is accordingly repugnant to the Constitution and void.

And, further, that, unless enforcement of the measure is enjoined the corporation's business and property will suffer irreparable injury.

Appellee, Hill Military Academy, is a private corporation organized in 1908 under the laws of Oregon, engaged in owning, operating and conducting for profit an elementary, college preparatory and military training school for boys between the ages of five and twenty-one years. Appellants, law officers of the State and County, have publicly announced that the Act of November 7, 1922, is valid, and have declared their intention to enforce it. By reason of the statute and threat of enforcement, appellee's business is being destroyed and its property depreciated; parents and guardians are refusing to make contracts for the future instruction of their sons, and some are being withdrawn.

The Academy's bill states the foregoing facts and then alleges that the challenged Act contravenes the corporation's rights guaranteed by the Fourteenth Amendment and that, unless appellants are restrained from proclaiming its validity and threatening to enforce it, irreparable injury will result. The prayer is for an appropriate injunction. . . .

The inevitable practical result of enforcing the Act under consideration would be destruction of appellees' primary schools, and perhaps all other private primary schools for normal children within the State of Oregon. These parties are engaged in a kind of undertaking not inherently harmful, but long regarded as useful and meritorious. Certainly there is nothing in the present records to indicate that they have failed to discharge their obligations to patrons, students or the State. And there are no peculiar circumstances or present emergencies which demand extraordinary measures relative to primary education.

Under the doctrine of *Meyer v. Nebraska*, we think it entirely plain that the Act of 1922 unreasonably interferes with the liberty of parents and guardians to direct the upbringing and education of children under their control: as often heretofore pointed out, rights guaranteed by the Constitution may not be abridged by legislation which has no reasonable relation to some purpose within the competency of the State. The fundamental theory of liberty upon which all governments in this Union repose excludes any general power of the State to standardize its children by forcing them to accept instruction from public teachers only. The child is not the mere creature of the State; those who nurture him and direct his destiny have the right, coupled with the high duty, to recognize and prepare him for additional obligations.

Appellees are corporations, and therefore, it is said, they cannot claim for themselves the liberty which the Fourteenth Amendment guarantees. Accepted in the proper sense, this is true. (*Northwestern Life Ins. Co. v. Riggs*; *Western Turf Association v. Greenberg*.) But they have business and property for which they claim protection. These are threatened with destruction through the unwarranted compulsion which appellants are exercising over present and prospective patrons of their schools. And this court has gone very far to protect against loss threatened by such action. (*Truax v. Raich*; *Truax v. Corrigan*; *Terrace v. Thompson*.)

The courts of the State have not construed the Act, and we must determine its meaning for ourselves. Evidently it was expected to have general application, and cannot be construed as though merely intended to amend the charters of certain private corporations, as in *Berea College v. Kentucky*. No argument in favor of such view has been advanced.

Generally it is entirely true, as urged by counsel, that no person in any business has such an interest in possible customers as to enable him to restrain exercise of proper power of the State upon the ground that he will be deprived of patronage. But the injunctions here sought are not against the exercise of any proper power. Plaintiffs asked protection against arbitrary, unreasonable and unlawful interference with their patrons and the consequent destruction of their business and property. . . .

The suits were not premature. The injury to appellees was present and very real, not a mere possibility in the remote future. If no relief had been possible prior to the effective date of the Act, the injury would have become irreparable. Prevention of impending injury by unlawful action is a well recognized function of courts of equity.

SYNTHESIS QUESTIONS FOR FURTHER DISCUSSION: CHAPTER 7 SECTION B

1. In contrast to economic substantive due process, Section B traces another iteration of this doctrine. In addition to protecting economic liberties, some of these cases suggest, substantive due process protects the liberty of families. But is the liberty of families primarily about the interests of parents, or does it include a recognition that children sometimes have interests distinct from, and even opposed to, those of their parents? For instance, imagine that the question in *Pierce v. Society of Sisters* was not about the right of parents to send their children to a religious school, but about the right of parents to prevent their children from attending any school whatsoever. Does the Constitution guarantee such a right? Should it? In considering this question, read the case of *Wisconsin v. Yoder*, included in Chapter 6.

2. In the next section, you will see that the case of *Griswold v. Connecticut* ties the modern doctrine of substantive due process, usually referred to as the right to privacy, to the rights of married couples to pursue their own family planning. Does such a framework abandon the notion that the Constitution protects individual rights? Does the conceptualization of rights as attaching to families prioritize group rights over individual rights? What problems might such a conception represent?

3. *Pierce v. Society of Sisters* guarantees a right of families to send their children to private schools and struck down a requirement of public school funding. Does this ruling grant too much power to families over their children's education, or is it correct to think that parents should have such power? Would the case have come out any differently if evidence were introduced that the majority of students in the Society of Sisters's schools had wanted to attend the public school and were in private school only because of their parents' wishes? Does granting substantive due process rights to parents over their children infringe upon children's rights? What liberties should children be granted?

C.   THE RIGHT TO PRIVACY: SEXUAL RELATIONS, REPRODUCTIVE FREEDOM, ABORTION, AND ASSISTED SUICIDE

In this section, we consider whether the doctrine of substantive due process protects personal liberty in the areas of reproduction, abortion, and sexual relations. An early attempt was made by litigants in *Buck v. Bell* to establish a substantive due process right to bodily autonomy and control over one's own reproductive choices. As you will see, a litigant unsuccessfully challenged a forced sterilization program on the grounds that it violated the doctrine of substantive due process. If this case were argued today, it likely would have a different outcome. The contemporary Supreme Court has recognized that some rights in the area of reproductive freedom and sexuality are so fundamental that they can never be taken away, even by democratic majorities. Although we will cover a vast array of areas—from the right to contraception to abortion to rights to engage in consensual sex—the Court protects fundamental rights in these areas under one modern doctrine of substantive due process or, as the Court describes this cluster of rights, the right to privacy.

Griswold v. Connecticut marks perhaps the most important modern articulation of the doctrine of substantive due process, although the doctrine was only cited explicitly in one of the concurring opinions in the case. The case is about whether a Connecticut law banning the sale and use of contraception violates the Constitution. Justice William O. Douglas famously writes that "specific guarantees in the Bill of Rights have penumbras, formed by emanations from those guarantees that help give them life and substance." He draws upon the First, Third, Fourth, Fifth, and Ninth Amendments in declaring that the various entitlements of these amendments create "zones of privacy." Although specific provisions, such as the Third Amendment's prohibition on quartering troops in a person's home, might seem unrelated to the issue of contraception, Justice Douglas explains that it, alongside the other amendments, suggests a broad right to privacy. That right, he reasons, should extend beyond the kinds of parental rights discussed in the previous section to more general rights of married couples. The sacredness of the marital bedroom, he claims, ensures a right to purchase and use contraception.

You should also pay particular attention to Justice John Harlan's opinion, which relies explicitly on the Fourteenth Amendment's protection of liberty. It is Justice Harlan's opinion that most clearly gestures to the doctrine of substantive due process. Unlike Justice Harlan, it is likely that most of the justices who wrote opinions in *Griswold v. Connecticut*, including Justice Douglas writing for the majority, were taking pains to avoid the kind of substantive due process arguments found in *Lochner v. New York*. But ultimately it is the Fourteenth Amendment that has served as the textual basis for modern protections of liberty. Again, think about whether Justice Douglas's opinion in *Griswold v. Connecticut* serves to distinguish this kind of personal liberty from that found in *Lochner v. New York*.

One clear difference between *Lochner v. New York* and *Griswold v. Connecticut* concerns the topic areas of each case; the personal issue of contraception is a long way from the economic issue of the right to contract. But had *Griswold v. Connecticut* merely established a right to contraception, it would not have had such enduring significance in constitutional law. Rather, the case was ultimately viewed as protecting not only rights to contraception, but also a more general zone of privacy in which individuals can make their own autonomous decisions free from government coercion.

As you will see, a puzzle soon emerged about whether the Constitution guaranteed a broad right to privacy after the *Griswold v. Connecticut* decision. Did the right also pertain to non-married couples? Did it extend, literally, beyond the marital bedroom? Future cases, beginning with *Eisenstadt v. Baird*, would hold that it did. Indeed, while *Eisenstadt v. Baird* itself dealt with the question of contraception, the Court soon would move beyond this specific issue to consider the right to an abortion in *Roe v. Wade*. Later, in *Lawrence v. Texas*, the doctrine of privacy would be expanded to include same-sex couples as well. Although the original right to privacy, grounded in the married couple's relationship, arguably had some similarity to the rights of families we considered in Section B, after *Eisenstadt v. Baird* the right to privacy was generally considered an individual right. As you read through the specific cases, consider whether the idea of a general right to privacy successfully captures this broad variety of specific rights.

While *Roe v. Wade* establishes the right to an abortion in the first trimester, over the course of future cases the Court would secure certain aspects of this right while curtailing others. For example, *Planned Parenthood v. Casey* questions *Roe v. Wade*'s rigid trimester framework, which distinguished between acceptable forms of regulation depending on what three-month period of pregnancy a woman was in, but secures its core holding, ruling that "undue burdens" on the right to an abortion are unconstitutional. Consider to what extent the Court's refusal to require a right to have an abortion funded in *Maher v. Roe* or its acceptance of a ban on "partial-birth abortions" in *Gonzales v. Carhart* undercut *Roe v. Wade*.

It is perhaps the Court's decision in *Roe v. Wade*, as well as its subsequent clarification and curtailment in further cases, which has stirred the greatest amount of public controversy. The question of whether a fetus is a life is a matter of deep theological and moral dispute. As some commentators see it, the Court's decision cannot be divorced from morality. Some, such as John Hart Ely, see the Court's foray into this area as an encroachment on non-legal territory. Others, such as Ronald Dworkin, defend the Court's intervention in this area as necessary for elaborating the Constitution's morality.

As you read this section, consider how the Court's modern doctrine of substantive due process differs and draws from its earlier iterations, both during the *Lochner v. New York* era and in the cases that recognize family rights. You will notice, for instance, that although the Court begins in *Griswold v. Connecticut* by talking about a right of families, it moves very quickly to conceiving of substantive due process as an individual right in *Eisenstadt v. Baird*. Thus, while the Court rejects the *Lochner v. New York* era's focus on economic rights, it still conceives of substantive due process as a right of individuals, as was the case in the *Lochner v. New York* era. At the same time, consider whether the modern Court's focus on personal liberty shares anything with the kind of rights protected in the cases we considered in the previous section. Arguably, although the Court rejects the notion that substantive due process is a right of families, it is building upon its earlier jurisprudence in this area. You might consider too, as you read these cases, whether this modern doctrine of substantive due process is itself at odds with the ideal of democracy. In determining whether these cases were rightly decided, does it matter that many of them were extremely controversial? Should public opinion be relevant when it comes to issues of fundamental rights?

Although the doctrine of substantive due process originated with the protection of economic liberty, it has developed to encompass a wide variety of areas. Controversially, some have sought to extend this protection to the case of assisted suicide. On this view, the liberty provision of the Fourteenth Amendment protects not only fundamental life choices such as whether to have a child, but also the right to determine when one may end one's own life. The debate over the right to die and the right to contraception are bound together by their common implications for decisional autonomy. Both the decision of whether or not to bear a child and the decision of whether or not to terminate care at the end of life are among the most fundamental decisions an individual can make. If the privacy doctrine is understood as a broad protection of individuals' entitlements to make decisions as long they do not harm others, then we can see why it might extend to a right to die. Those who would defend such a link would broaden privacy beyond issues of sex and reproduction, a move that opponents of a right to die find dubious.

We conclude this section with two cases that touch on this topic. In *Cruzan v. Missouri*, the Court considers whether the Constitution protects a parent's right to refuse life-supporting medical treatment on behalf of his or her incapacitated child. Although the Court is sympathetic to Cruzan's parents' desire to terminate her treatment, it does not extend substantive due process protection in this case. Instead, Chief Justice William Rehnquist explains that in the absence of "clear and convincing evidence" that Cruzan, who was in a vegetative state, wished to refuse treatment, the right of her parents to do so on her behalf is outweighed by the state's interest in preserving life. In *Washington v. Glucksberg*, the Court considers more directly whether a patient has a right to physician-assisted suicide when suffering a terminal illness. Again in this case, the Court refuses to extend substantive due process protection in this area, stressing the traditional domain of the state in protecting the health of its citizens. As you read these cases, consider whether you believe the doctrine of substantive due process should extend to these areas.

Ronald Dworkin

FREEDOM'S LAW: THE MORAL READING OF THE AMERICAN CONSTITUTION

Chapter 1: Roe *in Danger*

Cambridge, MA: Harvard University Press (1996)

The following two readings by Ronald Dworkin and John Hart Ely, legal theorists that we studied in depth in Chapter 2, serve to introduce us to opposing perspectives on the doctrine of the right to privacy closely associated with the modern doctrine of substantive due process. Note not only what they say about whether the right to privacy includes a right to an abortion, but also what they say about privacy more generally. In particular, how do their positions on these issues reflect their more general constitutional theories? How does Dworkin apply the moral reading to these issues? How does Ely's focus on procedure impact his thinking about the right to privacy?

No judicial decision in our time has aroused as much sustained public outrage, emotion, and physical violence, or as much intemperate professional criticism, as the Supreme Court's 1973 decision in *Roe v. Wade*, which declared, by a seven to two majority, that women have a constitutionally protected right to abortion in the early stages of pregnancy. In the years since, anti-abortion groups and political conservatives have campaigned with single-minded conviction to reverse that decision. They proposed without success a series of constitutional amendments, sponsored unsuccessful bills asking Congress to declare that a fetus's life begins at conception, persuaded President Reagan to appoint anti-abortion judges to the federal courts, waged single-issue political campaigns against candidates

who support a right to abortion, and disrupted and bombed abortion clinics. The public at large is divided in different ways about different aspects of the abortion issue. A *Los Angeles Times* national survey reported that 61 percent of Americans think abortion morally wrong—57 percent think it murder—and yet 74 percent nevertheless believe that "abortion is a decision that has to be made by every woman for herself."

Courts cannot avoid deciding the legal question whether a fetus is a constitutional person because it makes no sense to consider what constitutional rights some people do or do not have, in any area of constitutional law, without first deciding who *else* has rights a state must or may also recognize. The Supreme Court has held, for example, that the citizens of each state have a constitutional right that state elections be conducted under districting arrangements that ensure one person one vote, and a state could not undermine that principle by counting as people whole classes of entities that the Constitution, properly interpreted, does not. A state could not declare corporations persons, for instance, by providing separate votes for them, and cut down the voting power of real people. The question of whether and in what sense corporations are constitutional persons, with rights of their own, has been much debated throughout constitutional history. But it has never been doubted that because that question affects the rights of everyone else, it must be decided judicially, at the national constitutional level. Of course a state may promote the interests of its corporations in a wide variety of ways. But it cannot endow them with rights whose force is to curtail the constitutional rights enjoyed by others. Only the Constitution can do that.

So the question of who is a constitutional person must be settled at the constitutional level, by the Supreme Court, as part of deciding what constitutional rights anyone has, and the question whether a fetus is a constitutional person is pivotal to the abortion debate. In *Roe v. Wade* the Court decided that a fetus is not a constitutional person before birth, and though its opinion has been criticized by several academic lawyers, it is largely persuasive once that premise is accepted. Earlier Supreme Court decisions had established that a person has a fundamental constitutional right to control his or her own role in procreation—the Court had decided, for example, that for this reason a state may not prohibit the sale of contraceptives. If a fetus is not a constitutional person, then a fetus's right to live cannot be cited as a justification for denying that right after pregnancy begins, though of course a state can nevertheless protect the fetus's interests in a great variety of other ways.

But if the fetus is a constitutional person, then *Roe v. Wade* is plainly wrong, as the Court's opinion in that case conceded. The Fourteenth Amendment declares that no state may deny any person "equal protection of the laws." If the fetus is protected by that clause, then of course a state is entitled to protect its life in the same way it protects the lives of other people under its care, and for that reason is entitled to say that a woman's right to control the use of her body for procreation ends, at least when her health is not at stake,

when pregnancy begins. Indeed, it would be difficult to resist a very much stronger conclusion: that a state is not only entitled but *required* to take that view, so that states like New York, which decided to permit abortion in early pregnancy even before *Roe v. Wade* was decided, would be constitutionally *prohibited* from doing so.

The equal protection clause requires states to extend the protection of their laws against murder and assault equally to all persons, and if fetuses were constitutional persons any state legislation that discriminated against them in that respect, by permitting abortion, would be "suspect," under equal protection principles, and the Supreme Court would have an obligation to review such legislation to determine whether the state's justification for that discrimination was "compelling." In some cases it would be: when a state permitted abortion to protect the health of a mother, for example, or perhaps in cases of rape or incest. But if a woman is well aware of the physical and emotional consequences of pregnancy and voluntarily has sexual intercourse knowing that she risks becoming pregnant, a state that permits her or her doctor to abort her fetus has no compelling justification for doing so if the fetus is entitled to equal protection of the laws. For a state fails to show equal concern for both mother and fetus when it allows the mother to regain the freedom of her body at the expense of the fetus's life.

It is true, as a number of legal scholars have pointed out, that the law does not generally require people to make any sacrifice at all to save the life of another person who needs their aid. A person ordinarily has no legal duty to save a stranger from drowning even if he can do so at no risk to himself and with minimal effort. But abortion normally requires a physical attack on a fetus, not just the failure to come to its aid. And in any case parents are invariably made an exception to the general doctrine under which people are not required to save others. Parents have a legal duty to care for their children, and if a fetus is a person from conception a state would not be justified in discriminating between fetuses and infants. If it did not permit killing infants or abandoning them in circumstances in which they would inevitably die, it could not permit abortion either. The physical and emotional and economic burdens of pregnancy are intense, of course, but so are the parallel burdens of parenthood.

I stress this point because it is important to notice that those who urge the Supreme Court to leave the question of abortion to the states, to decide as their politics dictate, have in effect conceded that a fetus is *not* a constitutional person. In oral argument, Justice Byron White asked Charles Fried whether in his view there is "some problem about the state permitting abortion." Fried replied, "Oh, no," and said very firmly that it would be a serious mistake for the Court to "constitutionalize" the issue at any "point in the spectrum" by requiring constitutional scrutiny of permissive abortion legislation by a state. That position is preposterous except on the assumption that the Constitution itself offers a fetus's life no protection at all.

But Fried could hardly have given White's question any other answer. It would be political madness for the Court to try to force unwilling states to outlaw abortion; and neither the government nor any other responsible group has asked it to do so. The damage to the community, to the Court's authority, and to the Constitution would be far greater if it did try to force the states to outlaw abortion than if it simply left the law where it stands. But the Court can avoid that

inconceivable decision, legitimately, only by confirming *Roe v. Wade*'s explicit decision that a fetus is not a constitutional person. So the most complex and difficult of the legal issues in the abortion dispute has been removed from the controversy by a kind of practical necessity. I do not mean to suggest, by emphasizing these practical arguments for that view, that it is not the correct view in law. On the contrary, I think that it is.

The question is one of legal interpretation. The principle that the fetus is not a constitutional person fits better with other parts of our law and also with our sense of how related issues would and should be decided if they arose than the rival principle that it is. Even if the fetus is a human being, it is in a unique situation politically as well as biologically for a reason that could properly be thought sufficient to deny it constitutional status. The state can take action that affects it, in order to protect or advance its interests, only through its mother, and only through means that would necessarily restrict her freedom in ways no man's or other woman's freedom could constitutionally be limited; by dictating her diet and other personal and intimate behavior, for example. Apart from anti-abortion statutes, there are few signs in our law of the kind of regulation of pregnancy that would be appropriate if the fetus were a constitutional person, and the Supreme Court has never suggested any constitutional requirement of such protection.

The best historical evidence shows, moreover, that even anti-abortion laws, which were not prevalent in the United States before the middle of the nineteenth century, were adopted to protect the health of the mother and the privileges of the medical profession, not out of any recognition of a fetus's rights. Even states that had the most stringent anti-abortion laws before *Roe v. Wade*, moreover, did not punish abortion as severely as murder, as they should have done if they thought a fetus a constitutional person. Nor did they try to outlaw or penalize a woman's procuring an abortion in another state or abroad.

So the better interpretation of our constitutional law and practice holds that a fetus is not a constitutional person. That conclusion could be accepted, as I suggested, even by someone who thinks abortion a heinous sin: not every sin is or could be punished by law. But it will of course be easier to accept for someone who believes that a human being has no moral right to life until it has developed self-consciousness as a being whose life extends over time. On the assumption that this condition is not reached until some time after birth, the interpretive conclusion, that a human being becomes a constitutional person no earlier than at that point, seems even sounder.

It is therefore not an acceptable argument, against the claim that women have a constitutional right to choose an abortion in early pregnancy, that the fetus is a constitutional person whose competing right to live would overcome any such right.

Abortion cannot be disentangled from contraception, even medically, however, because the IUD and the most popular and safest birth control pills act as abortifacients; that is, they destroy fertilized ova. So the Court could not hold that a woman's right to control her role in procreation ends with fertilization without permitting states to outlaw the contraceptives now in use. That would be in effect to overrule *Griswold*, which Fried said was a correct decision. Even if contraception and abortion did not overlap medically in that way, they could not be distinguished in principle, once it is assumed that a fetus is not a constitutional person.

The Court's previous privacy decisions can be justified only on the assumption that decisions affecting marriage and childbirth are so important, so intimate and personal, so crucial to the development of personality and sense of moral responsibility, and so closely tied to religious and ethical convictions protected by the First Amendment, that people must be allowed to make these decisions for themselves, consulting their own conscience, rather than allowing society to thrust its collective decision on them. The abortion decision is at least as much a private decision in that sense as any other the Court has protected. In many ways it is more private, because the decision involves a woman's control not just of her connections to others, but of the use of her own body, and the Constitution recognizes in a variety of ways the special intimacy of a person's connection to her own physical integrity.

If a fetus were a constitutional person, then abortion could of course be distinguished from at least contraception that did not involve abortifacients, because a state could properly cite a compelling interest in protecting the fetus's right to life and to be treated with equal concern. But given the assumption that a fetus is not a constitutional person, that reason for distinguishing abortion from contraception, and from other activities permitted by decisions protecting privacy, fails. Fried tried to distinguish the contraception cases on the ground that *Griswold v. Connecticut* was based not on any general right to control one's own procreation, but on the different basis that the police could enforce a prohibition on the use of contraceptives only by searching the marital bedroom, which would be offensive. It is true that one opinion in *Griswold v. Connecticut* mentioned that reason for invalidating a prohibition on married couples using contraceptives. But it is a silly reason, not only because prohibitions on the use of contraceptives could be enforced without breaking down bedroom doors, but because the Court has upheld other criminal statutes that might be thought just as difficult to enforce without offensive and impermissible searches.

In any case, the later contraception cases rejected that interpretation of *Griswold v. Connecticut*, and they are inconsistent with it. In *Eisenstadt v. Baird*, Justice Brennan, for the Court, stated the point of the past privacy cases this way: "If the right of privacy means anything, it is the right of the *individual*, married or not, to be free from government intrusion into matters so fundamentally affecting a person as the decision whether to bear or beget a child."

And one of the justices who dissented in the *Griswold* case, Potter Stewart, joined the majority in *Roe v. Wade*, on the ground that if one accepts the *Griswold* decision, as he then did on grounds of precedent, one has to accept *Roe v. Wade* as well. Fried's claim that the privacy decisions were really only about searching bedrooms proved too bizarre for him to defend with any confidence. When Justice Sandra Day O'Connor asked a direct question, "Do you say there is no fundamental right to decide whether to have a child or not?" he could only answer, "I would hesitate to formulate the right in such abstract terms."

So the argument from precedent in favor of *Roe v. Wade* seems a strong one: Supreme Court precedents established a constitutional right of control over one's own role in childbirth, and, if a fetus is not a constitutional person, that right naturally extends to abortion. But we must now consider the opposing arguments made by those lawyers, including the justices dissenting in that case, who insist it was wrong and should now be discarded. They say that the right to abortion is "judge-made" and has "little or no cognizable roots in the language or design of the Constitution." Or that the right has "no moorings in the text of our Constitution or in familiar constitutional doctrine, and cannot be sustained by 'the interpretive tradition of the legal community.'" Or that the right does not exist because the subject of abortion is "one upon which the Constitution is silent."

But these various complaints beg the question. Of course if the judges who decided *Roe v. Wade* made up the constitutional rights they announced, or if those rights have no roots in the language or design of the Constitution, or if they cannot be established as drawn from the Constitution by interpretive methods traditional to legal reasoning, then the decision was certainly wrong. But we cannot decide whether these complaints are justified without some theory of how judges *should* interpret the abstract provisions of the Constitution, such as the provision that requires due process of law. How should judges decide which rights do and which do not have "roots" in the abstract language?

The various government briefs in *Webster* sometimes suggest an answer to that question which our legal tradition has decisively rejected: that abstract language should never be interpreted to yield a right that the historical framers who enacted the abstract provision did not accept themselves. The briefs argue that the Fourteenth Amendment cannot be thought to include a right to abortion because abortion laws were being enacted by states throughout the country when that amendment was added to the Constitution. But the Congress that enacted the Fourteenth Amendment itself segregated the public schools of the

District of Columbia, and no one now argues that *Brown v. Board of Education*, which held that segregation violated the rights provided by that amendment, was wrong.

The briefs of the Bush administration and the state of Missouri also rely on a variety of other interpretive suggestions. They propose that the Constitution should be understood to contain only "enumerated" rights, that is, rights explicitly mentioned in the text. But that ignores the fact that the same legal situation can be described in different ways. The Supreme Court decided, in 1952, that the police may not pump out a suspect's stomach for evidence. Shall we say that the Court decided that the right to due process of law, which is mentioned in the text of the Constitution, applied to the particular facts of that case? Or that it decided that people have a right not to have their stomachs pumped, which is derived from the due process clause but which is not itself mentioned in the text? There is only a verbal difference between these two formulations and neither is more accurate than the other.

In any case, if we must reject the right to an abortion because abortion is not mentioned in the Constitution, then we must also reject a great number of other, unquestioned constitutional rights that lawyers frequently describe in language not to be found there either. These include the right to use contraceptives, which the government now argues is part of the Constitution in spite of the fact that contraception is not mentioned. They also include the right to vote, to marry, to travel between states, to live with one's extended family, to educate one's children privately in schools meeting educational standards, and to attend racially desegregated schools. If these are all "unenumerated" rights, and so "judge-

made" constitutional law, it hardly counts against *Roe v. Wade* that it falls into the same category.

One of the government briefs replies to that objection with a metaphor. It says that the supposed right of abortion "travels further from its point of departure in the text" than these other rights. But how do we measure the distance between a right and the constitutional language from which it is drawn? How can we tell whether the distance between abortion and the constitutional language of due process is greater than the distance between contraception or stomach pumping and that language? Or the distance between the other "unenumerated" rights I listed and the constitutional language in which these were rooted?

Our legal tradition gives a very different, less metaphorical and superficial, answer to the question how abstract constitutional provisions should be interpreted. Judges should seek to identify the principles latent in the Constitution as a whole, and in past judicial decisions applying the Constitution's abstract language, in order to enforce the same principles in new areas and so make the law steadily more coherent. In that way, the principles that have been relied on to justify rights for one group or in one situation are extended, so far as that is possible, to everyone else to whom they equally apply. That common law process was used in *Roe v. Wade* to argue that the principles latent in the earlier privacy decisions about sterilization and family and contraception must be applied to the abortion case as well. These earlier privacy decisions can themselves be defended in a similar way, as part of a broader project of the Court, begun earlier in the century, to identify and enforce the principles implicit in what the Court called "the concept of ordered liberty," which means the principle a society truly committed to individual liberty and dignity must recognize. A right to control one's part in procreation finds support in that general project, as well as in the more closely related decisions protecting privacy, because that right is crucially important to the moral, social, and economic freedom of women.

These are the arguments that the opponents of *Roe v. Wade* must meet, and they should try to meet them in the traditional way, by explaining why principles different from those mentioned, which do not yield a right to abortion, provide a more satisfactory interpretation of the Constitution as a whole and of the Court's past decisions under it. Of course different judges will come to very different conclusions about which principles provide the best interpretation of the Constitution, and since there is no neutral standpoint from which it can be proved which side is right, each justice must in the end rely on his or her convictions about which argument is best. But that is an inevitable feature of a political system, like ours, which conceives of its Constitution as a charter of principle rather than a particular collection of political settlements.

Certainly the present critics of *Roe v. Wade* offer no alternative. Since their question-begging rhetoric about "judge-made law" and "new rights" rests on no reasoned intellectual basis, it provides even less discipline than the traditional interpretive method, because the latter does demand coherent and extended argument, not just name-calling. The question-begging rhetoric, on the contrary, leaves lawyers free to accept constitutional rights now popular in the community, such as the right to legally integrated education and to the use of contraceptives, and to oppose rights politically more troublesome, such as the right to abortion, without having to explain what the difference between the constitutional standing of these rights actually is.

Though *Roe v. Wade* held that women have a right in principle to control their part in procreation, it added that states have a legitimate interest in protecting "potential life," and that any statement of a woman's constitutional right to an abortion must take that interest into account. It decided that the state's interest becomes compelling enough in late pregnancy, when the fetus has become viable, to permit the state to regulate or prohibit abortions after that point, except as necessary to protect the mother's health. Unfortunately, the Court did not satisfactorily explain what kind of interest a state is permitted to take in "potential life," or why its concern grows stronger or more legitimate after a fetus becomes viable.

The Court did not mean, of course, that a state has a legitimate interest in increasing the birth rate, because that interest would apply with equal strength at all times in pregnancy and, indeed, would justify a state's opposing contraception as vigorously as abortion. Nor did the Court mean that a state may legitimately decide that a being with potential life has rights of its own which the state may take an interest in protecting. As we saw, the Court rightly held that the question whether a fetus is a constitutional person, and thus a person whose rights can be competitive with the constitutional rights of others, must be settled at the constitutional level, not by state legislation, and it then held that the fetus is not such a person. What else could a state's interest in "potential life" mean?

The most persuasive answer which takes the Court's subsequent decisions into account, is, I believe, the following. Even though a fetus is not a constitutional person, it is nevertheless an entity of considerable moral and emotional significance in our culture, and a state may recognize and try to protect that significance in ways that fall short of any substantial abridgment of a woman's constitutional right over the use of her own body. A state might properly fear the impact of widespread abortion on its citizens' instinctive respect for the value of human life and their instinctive horror at human destruction or suffering, which are values essential for the maintenance of a just and decently civil society. A political community in which abortion became commonplace and a matter of ethical indifference, like appendectomy, would certainly be a more callous and insensitive community, and it might be a more dangerous one as well.

A state's concern for the moral significance of a fetus increases as pregnancy advances, and it is particularly intense after viability, when the fetus has assumed a post-natal baby's form. This is a matter of resemblance. People's instinctive respect for life is unlikely to be lessened significantly if they come to regard the abortion of a just-fertilized ovum as permissible, any more than it is lessened when they accept contraception. But the assault on instinctive values is likely to be almost as devastating when a nearly full-term baby is aborted as when a week-old child is killed.

So the state's concern is greatest after the point at which a fetus, under present technology, is viable, and a prohibition on elective abortion after that time will not significantly burden or compromise a woman's constitutional right. Her right is a right to make fundamental decisions for herself, and that right is satisfied when she has had ample time after discovering her pregnancy to consider whether she wishes to continue it and to arrange a safe and convenient abortion if she does not. *Roe v. Wade*, understood in that way, did not balance a woman's rights against the competing rights of a fetus or of anyone else. Rather it identified a scheme of

regulation that could meet a state's most powerful needs without substantially compromising a woman's rights at all.

The Court had to pick a particular event or period of pregnancy in constructing that scheme in order to make it clear enough to be administered by officials and judges. If the Court had said simply that a state must allow a woman "ample" or "reasonable" time after the discovery of pregnancy to decide about abortion, it would have faced a succession of test cases provoked by state legislatures defining the cut-off line earlier and earlier, so that it would eventually have been forced to draw a line in any case. The Court's decision to make the crucial event viability, which occurs at approximately twenty-three or twenty-four weeks, has much to recommend it. Viability marks a distinct stage of pregnancy after which the difference between a fetus and a premature infant is a matter not of development but only of environment. Since viability follows "quickening," or the point at which a pregnant woman feels movement in her womb, it is late enough to provide her a reasonable opportunity for an abortion after pregnancy is discovered. (Teenage women, particularly, may easily be unaware of pregnancy before quickening; their periods may have been erratic or missing before pregnancy and they may not "show," or look pregnant, before then.)

Some critics feared that advances in medical technology would make fetuses viable much earlier, requiring the Court to change its standard; in an earlier case Justice O'Connor said that *Roe v. Wade* was for that reason on "a collision course" with itself. But a consensus of medical opinion now declares that fear unfounded: there is, according to the brief filed in the *Webster* case by the American Medical Association and other medical groups, an "anatomical threshold for fetal survival of about twenty-three to twenty-four weeks of gestation . . . because the fetal lung does not mature sufficiently to permit normal or even mechanically-assisted respiration before [that time]."

An established Supreme Court decision, particularly one that recognizes that individual constitutional rights, should not be overruled unless it is clearly wrong or has proved thoroughly unworkable. *Roe v. Wade* is not wrong, and it certainly is not clearly wrong. Justice Blackmun's opinion might have been clearer in some respects, and the Court might have chosen an event in pregnancy other than viability but which occurs at roughly the same time, such as neocortical functioning, to mark the point at which abortion might be prohibited. But these are hardly reasons to tear apart constitutional law by overturning the decision now. The Court should refuse to nourish the cynical view, already popular among its critics, that constitutional law is only a matter of which President appointed the last few justices.

If the Court declines to overrule or substantially restrict *Roe v. Wade*, as it should, it must decide the more limited constitutional issues raised by the *Webster* case. As I said, the lower courts declared unconstitutional a variety of clauses in Missouri's statute. The state does not now contest some of these rulings, and urges implausible but benign interpretations of others in order to save them from unconstitutionality. The important remaining controversy concerns the state's ban on the use of public facilities in connection with abortion even when the abortion is performed by a private doctor and paid for by private funds.

The statute defines public facilities very broadly as "any public institution, public facility, public equipment, or any physical asset owned, leased, or controlled by this state or any agency or

political subdivision thereof." So it would forbid abortion in the Truman Medical Center in Kansas City—where 97 percent of all hospital abortions at sixteen weeks or later in Missouri were performed in 1985—in spite of the fact that the center is a private hospital staffed mainly by private doctors, and administered by private corporations, just because that hospital is located on ground leased from a political subdivision of the state.

Missouri defends the provision by appealing to earlier decisions of the Supreme Court. In *Maher v. Roe*, the Court sustained a state's right to provide medical assistance funds for childbirth but not for abortion, and in *Poelker v. Doe* it allowed a state to provide childbirth but not abortion facilities in a public city hospital. The Court said that although a state may not forbid abortions, it need not go into the abortion business itself. It might constitutionally adopt a preference for childbirth to abortion, and provide funds only for the former.

The decisions in the *Maher* and *Poelker* cases have been criticized because they permit states to take action to discourage people from exercising their constitutional rights. But even if we accept these decisions as sound they do not support Missouri's broad prohibition. Of course a state need not subsidize or support the exercise of every constitutional right, and it may pursue policies of its own choice in the benefits it awards. It may without violating anyone's rights to free speech publish literature encouraging conservation while refusing to distribute other political material.

But Missouri's argument overlooks a crucial distinction. It is one thing for a state to decline to participate in some act it disapproves in circumstances in which it would itself be the author of the act, or would plausibly be taken to be, if it did. A state, for example, may refuse to distribute political criticism of its own government without violating anyone's rights to free speech. It is quite another thing for a state to use its economic power or control of crucial resources to discourage citizens from exercising their constitutional rights when there is no question of the state being seen as the author of, or as in any way supporting, what they do. A city cannot force newsstands in shopping centers built on public land to sell only papers it approves. It cannot force theaters it supplies with water and power and police protection to perform only plays it likes.

Perhaps a state that itself pays for abortions, or provides them in free public hospitals, will in effect have declared itself neutral between abortion and childbirth, or will be understood to have done so. For the state is necessarily the author of its own public funding and public medical provision. But it is preposterous that a state should be understood as itself performing abortions carried out by private doctors on their own initiative and paid for with private funds, just because the hospital in which this is done is in other ways state-supported, or because it is on land the state, as it happens, owns.

The true explanation of why Missouri adopted its stringent prohibition is not, of course, that it wants to avoid declaring itself neutral about abortion, but that it wants to make abortion as difficult and as expensive as possible in order to discourage its residents from exercising their constitutional rights. It enacts whatever measures to that end its officials can devise and the federal courts have not yet condemned, including measures so obviously unconstitutional that its lawyers do not seriously defend them when they are challenged. That is impermissible: a state must not declare war on its own people because it is angry that the law is on their side.

Unhappily, if the Court in any way now signals itself more ready to accept constraints on abortion than it has been in the past, that dismal spectacle will continue. Other states will adopt more and more restrictive statutes to provoke more and more test cases to see how far the Court will actually go. Charles Fried anticipated exactly that at the close of his oral argument. He asked the justices, even if they did not overrule *Roe v. Wade*, at least not to say anything "that would further entrench this decision as a secure premise for reasoning in future cases." The Justices would do best for constitutional order and decorum, as well as principle, if they refused to take that bad advice.

J o h n   H a r t   E l y

WAGES OF CRYING WOLF: A COMMENT ON *ROE v. WADE*

82 Yale L.J. 920 (1973)

"The interests of the mother and the fetus are opposed. On which side should the State throw its weight? The issue is volatile; and it is resolved by the moral code which an individual has."

In *Roe v. Wade*, decided January 22, 1973, the Supreme Court—Justice Blackmun speaking for everyone but Justices White and Rehnquist—held unconstitutional Texas's (and virtually every other state's) criminal abortion statute. The broad outlines of its argument are not difficult to make out:

1. The right to privacy, though not explicitly mentioned in the Constitution, is protected by the Due Process Clause of the Fourteenth Amendment.

2. This right "is broad enough to encompass a woman's decision whether or not to terminate her pregnancy."

3. This right to an abortion is "fundamental" and can therefore be regulated only on the basis of a "compelling" state interest.

4. The state does have two "important and legitimate" interests here, the first in protecting maternal health, the second in protecting the life (or potential life) of the fetus. But neither can be counted "compelling" throughout the entire pregnancy: Each matures with the unborn child. These interests are separate and distinct. Each grows in substantiality as the woman approaches term and, at a point during pregnancy, each becomes "compelling."

5. During the first trimester of pregnancy, neither interest is sufficiently compelling to justify any interference with the decision of the woman and her physician. Appellants have referred the Court to medical data indicating that mortality rates for women undergoing early abortions, where abortion is legal, "appear to be as low as or lower than the rates for normal childbirth." Thus the state's interest in protecting maternal health is not compelling during the first trimester. Since the interest in protecting the fetus is not yet compelling either, during the first trimester the state can neither prohibit an abortion nor regulate the conditions under which one is performed.

6. As we move into the second trimester, the interest in protecting the fetus remains less than compelling, and the decision to have an abortion thus continues to control. However, at this point the health risks of abortion begin to exceed those of childbirth. "It follows that, from and after this point, a State may regulate the abortion procedure to the extent that the regulation reasonably relates to the preservation and protection of maternal health." Abortion may not be prohibited during the second trimester, however.

7. At the point at which the fetus becomes viable the interest in protecting it becomes compelling, and therefore from that point on the state can prohibit abortions except—and this limitation is also apparently a constitutional command, though it receives no justification in the opinion—when they are necessary to protect maternal life or health.

I

A number of fairly standard criticisms can be made of *Roe*. A plausible narrower basis of decision, that of vagueness, is brushed aside in the rush toward broader ground. The opinion strikes the reader initially as a sort of guidebook, addressing questions not before the Court and drawing lines with an apparent precision one generally associates with a commissioner's regulations. On closer examination, however, the precision proves largely illusory. Confusing signals are emitted, particularly with respect to the nature of the doctor's responsibilities and the permissible scope of health regulations after the first trimester. The Court seems, moreover, to get carried away on the subject of remedies: Even assuming the case can be made for an unusually protected constitutional right to an abortion, it hardly seems necessary to have banned during the first trimester all state regulation of the conditions under which abortions can be performed. By terming such criticisms "standard," I do not mean to suggest they are unimportant, for they are not. But if they were all that was wrong with *Roe*, it would not merit special comment.

II

Let us not underestimate what is at stake: Having an unwanted child can go a long way toward ruining a woman's life. And at bottom *Roe* signals the Court's judgment that this result cannot be justified by any good that anti-abortion legislation accomplishes. This surely is an understandable conclusion—indeed it is one with which I agree—but ordinarily the Court claims no mandate to second-guess legislative balances, at least not when the Constitution has designated neither of the values in conflict as entitled to special protection. But even assuming it would be a good idea for the Court to assume this function, *Roe* seems a curious place to have begun. Laws prohibiting the use of "soft" drugs or, even more obviously, homosexual acts between consenting adults can stunt "the preferred life styles" of those against whom enforcement is threatened in very serious ways. It is clear such acts harm no one besides the participants, and indeed the case that the participants are harmed is a rather shaky one. Yet such laws survive, on the theory that there exists a societal consensus that the behavior involved is revolting or at any rate immoral. Of course the consensus is not universal but it is sufficient, and this is what is counted crucial, to get the laws passed and keep them on the books. Whether anti-abortion legislation cramps the life style of an unwilling mother more significantly than anti-homosexuality legislation cramps the life style of a homosexual is a close question. But even granting that it does, the other side of the balance looks very different. For there is more than simple societal revulsion to support legislation restricting abortion: Abortion ends (or if it makes a difference, prevents) the life of a human being other than the one making the choice. The Court's response here is simply not adequate. It agrees, indeed it holds, that after the point of viability (a concept it fails to note will become even less clear than it is now as the technology of birth continues to develop) the interest in protecting the fetus is compelling. Exactly why that is the magic moment is not made clear: Viability, as the Court defines it, is achieved some six to twelve weeks after quickening. (Quickening is the point at which the fetus begins discernibly to move independently of the mother and the point that has historically been deemed crucial—to the extent any point between conception and birth has been focused on.) But no, it is viability that is constitutionally critical: the Court's defense seems to mistake a definition for a syllogism.

> With respect to the State's important and legitimate interest in potential life, the "compelling" point is at viability. This is so because the fetus then presumably has the capacity of meaningful life outside the mother's womb.

With regard to why the state cannot consider this "important and legitimate interest" prior to viability, the opinion is even less satisfactory. The discussion begins sensibly enough: The interest asserted is not necessarily tied to the question whether the fetus is "alive," for whether or not one calls it a living being, it is an entity with the potential for (and indeed the likelihood of) life. But all of arguable relevance that follows are arguments that fetuses (a) are not recognized as "persons in the whole sense" by legal doctrine generally and (b) are not "persons" protected by the Fourteenth Amendment.

The canons of construction employed here are perhaps most intriguing when they are contrasted with those invoked to derive the constitutional right to an abortion. But in any event, the argument that fetuses lack constitutional rights is simply irrelevant. For it has never been held or even asserted that the state interest needed to justify forcing a person to refrain from an activity, whether or not that activity is constitutionally protected, must implicate either the life or the constitutional rights of another person. Dogs are not "persons in the whole sense" nor have they constitutional rights, but that does not mean the state cannot prohibit killing them: It does not even mean the state cannot prohibit killing them in the exercise of the First Amendment right of political protest. Come to think of it, draft cards aren't persons either. Thus even assuming the Court ought generally to get into the business of second-guessing legislative balances, it has picked a strange case with which to begin. Its purported evaluation of the balance that produced anti-abortion legislation simply does not meet the issue: That the life plans of the mother must, not simply may, prevail over the state's desire to protect the fetus simply does not follow from the judgment that the fetus is not a person. Beyond all that, however, the Court has no business getting into that business.

III

Were I a legislator I would vote for a statute very much like the one the Court ends up drafting. I hope this reaction reflects more than the psychological phenomenon that keeps bombardiers sane—the fact that it is somehow easier to "terminate" those you cannot see—and am inclined to think it does: that the mother, unlike the unborn child, has begun to imagine a future for herself strikes me as morally quite significant. But God knows I'm not happy with that resolution. Abortion is too much like infanticide on the one hand, and too much like contraception on the other, to leave one comfortable with any answer; and the moral issue it poses is as fiendish as any philosopher's hypothetical.

Of course, the Court often resolves difficult moral questions, and difficult questions yield controversial answers. I doubt, for example, that most people would agree that letting a drug peddler go unapprehended is morally preferable to letting the police kick down his door without probable cause. The difference, of course, is that the Constitution, which legitimates and theoretically controls judicial intervention, has some rather pointed things to say about this choice. There will of course be difficult questions about the applicability of its language to specific facts, but at least the document's special concern with one of the values in conflict is manifest. It simply says nothing, clear or fuzzy, about abortion.

What the Court does assert is that there is a general right of privacy granted special protection—that is, protection above and beyond the baseline requirement of "rationality"—by the Fourteenth Amendment, and that that right "is broad enough to encompass" the right to an abortion. The general right of privacy is inferred, as it was in *Griswold v. Connecticut*, from various provisions of the Bill of Rights manifesting a concern with privacy, notably the Fourth Amendment's guarantee against unreasonable searches, the Fifth Amendment's privilege against self-incrimination, and the right, inferred from the First Amendment, to keep one's political associations secret.

Thus it seems to me entirely proper to infer a general right of privacy, so long as some care is taken in defining the sort of right the inference will support. Those aspects of the First, Fourth and Fifth Amendments to which the Court refers all limit the ways in which, and the circumstances under which, the government can go about gathering information about a person he would rather it did not have. *Katz v. United States* limiting governmental tapping of telephones, may not involve what the framers would have called a "search," but it plainly involves this general concern with privacy. *Griswold* is a long step, even a leap, beyond this, but at least the connection is discernible. Had it been a case that purported to discover in the Constitution a "right to contraception," it would have been *Roe*'s strongest precedent. But the Court in *Roe* gives no evidence of so regarding it, and rightly not. Commentators tend to forget, though the Court plainly has not, that the Court in *Griswold* stressed that it was invalidating only that portion of the Connecticut law that proscribed the use, as opposed to the manufacture, sale, or other distribution of contraceptives. That distinction (which would be silly were the right to contraception being constitutionally enshrined) makes sense if the case is rationalized on the ground that the section of the law whose constitutionality was in issue was such that its enforcement would have been virtually impossible without the most outrageous sort of governmental prying into the privacy of the home. And this, indeed, is the theory on which the Court appeared rather explicitly to settle:

The present case, then, concerns a relationship lying within the zone of privacy created by several fundamental constitutional guarantees. And it concerns a law which, in forbidding the use of contraceptives rather than regulating their manufacture or sale, seeks to achieve its goals by means having a maximum destructive impact upon that relationship. Such a law cannot stand in light of the familiar principle, so often applied by this Court, that "a governmental purpose to control or prevent activities constitutionally subject to state regulation may not be achieved by means which sweep unnecessarily broadly and thereby invade the area of protected freedoms." NAACP v. Alabama, 377 U.S. 288, 307. Would we allow the police to search the sacred precincts of marital bedrooms for telltale signs of the use of contraceptives? The very idea is repulsive to the notions of privacy surrounding the marriage relationship.

Thus even assuming (as the Court surely seemed to) that a state can constitutionally seek to minimize or eliminate the circulation and use of contraceptives, Connecticut had acted unconstitutionally by selecting a means, that is a direct ban on use, that would generate intolerably intrusive modes of data-gathering. No such rationalization is attempted by the Court in *Roe*—and understandably not, for whatever else may be involved, it is not a case about governmental snooping.

The Court reports that some amici curiae argued for an unlimited right to do as one wishes with one's body. This theory holds, for me at any rate, much appeal. However, there would have been serious problems with its invocation in this case. In the first place, more than the mother's own body is involved in a decision to have an abortion; a fetus may not be a "person in the whole sense," but it is certainly not nothing. Second, it is difficult to find a basis for thinking that the theory was meant to be given constitutional sanction:

Surely it is no part of the "privacy" interest the Bill of Rights suggests.

> [I]t is not clear to us that the claim . . . that one has an unlimited right to do with one's body as one pleases bears a close relationship to the right of privacy. . . .

Unfortunately, having thus rejected the amici's attempt to define the bounds of the general constitutional right of which the right to an abortion is a part, on the theory that the general right described has little to do with privacy, the Court provides neither an alternative definition nor an account of why it thinks privacy is involved. It simply announces that the right to privacy "is broad enough to encompass a woman's decision whether or not to terminate her pregnancy." Apparently this conclusion is thought to derive from the passage that immediately follows it:

> The detriment that the State would impose upon the pregnant woman by denying this choice altogether is apparent. Specific and direct harm medically diagnosable even in early pregnancy may be involved. Maternity, or additional offspring, may force upon the woman a distressful life and future. Psychological harm may be imminent. Mental and physical health may be taxed by child care. There is also the distress, for all concerned, associated with the unwanted child, and there is the problem of bringing a child into a family already unable, psychologically and otherwise, to care for it. In other cases, as in this one, the additional difficulties and continuing stigma of unwed motherhood may be involved.

All of this is true and ought to be taken very seriously. But it has nothing to do with privacy in the Bill of Rights sense or any other the Constitution suggests. I suppose there is nothing to prevent one from using the word "privacy" to mean the freedom to live one's life without governmental interference. But the Court obviously does not so use the term. Nor could it, for such a right is at stake in every case. Our life styles are constantly limited, often seriously, by governmental regulation; and while many of us would prefer less direction, granting that desire the status of a preferred constitutional right would yield a system of "government" virtually unrecognizable to us and only slightly more recognizable to our forefathers. The Court's observations concerning the serious, life-shaping costs of having a child prove what might to the thoughtless have seemed unprovable: That even though a human life, or a potential human life, hangs in the balance, the moral dilemma abortion poses is so difficult as to be heartbreaking. What they fail to do is even begin to resolve that dilemma so far as our governmental system is concerned by associating either side of the balance with a value inferable from the Constitution.

Of course a woman's freedom to choose an abortion is part of the "liberty" the Fourteenth Amendment says shall not be denied without due process of law, as indeed is anyone's freedom to do what he wants. But "due process" generally guarantees only that the inhibition be procedurally fair and that it have some "rational" connection—though plausible is probably a better word—with a permissible governmental goal. What is unusual about *Roe* is that the liberty involved is accorded a far more stringent protection, so stringent that a desire to preserve the fetus's existence is unable to overcome it—a protection more stringent, I think it fair to say, than that the present Court accords the freedom of the press explicitly guaranteed by the First Amendment. What is frightening about *Roe* is that this super-protected right is not inferable from the language of the Constitution, the framers' thinking respecting the specific problem in issue, any general value derivable from the provisions they included, or the nation's governmental structure. Nor is it explainable in terms of the unusual political impotence of the group judicially protected vis-à-vis the interest that legislatively prevailed over it. And that, I believe—the predictable early reaction to *Roe* notwithstanding ("more of the same Warren-type activism")—is a charge that can responsibly be leveled at no other decision of the past twenty years. At times the inferences the Court has drawn from the values the Constitution marks for special protection have been controversial, even shaky, but never before has its sense of an obligation to draw one been so obviously lacking.

IV

Not in the last thirty-five years at any rate. For, as the received learning has it, this sort of thing did happen before, repeatedly. From its 1905 decision in *Lochner v. New York* into the 1930's the Court, frequently though not always under the rubric of "liberty of contract," employed the Due Process Clauses of the Fourteenth and Fifth Amendments to invalidate a good deal of legislation. According to the dissenters at the time and virtually all the commentators since, the Court had simply manufactured a constitutional right out of whole cloth and used it to superimpose its own view of wise social policy on those of the legislatures. So indeed the Court itself came to see the matter, and its reaction was complete:

> There was a time when the Due Process Clause was used by this Court to strike down laws which were thought unreasonable, that is, unwise or incompatible with some particular economic or social philosophy. In this manner the Due Process Clause was used, for example, to nullify

laws prescribing maximum hours for work in bakeries, Lochner v. New York, 198 U.S. 45 (1905), outlawing "yellow dog" contracts, Coppage v. Kansas, 236 U.S. 1 (1915), setting minimum wages for women, Adkins v. Children's Hospital, 261 U.S. 525 (1923), and fixing the weight of loaves of bread, Jay Burns Baking Co. v. Bryan, 264 U.S. 504 (1924). This intrusion by the judiciary into the realm of legislative value judgments was strongly objected to at the time. . . . Mr. Justice Holmes said,

"I think the proper course is to recognize that a state legislature can do whatever it sees fit to do unless it is restrained by some express prohibition in the Constitution of the United States or of the State, and that Courts should be careful not to extend such prohibitions beyond their obvious meaning by reading into them conceptions of public policy that the particular Court may happen to entertain."

> . . . The doctrine that prevailed in *Lochner*, *Coppage*, *Adkins*, *Burns*, and like cases— that due process authorizes courts to hold laws unconstitutional when they believe the legislature has acted unwisely—has long since been discarded. We have returned to the original constitutional proposition that courts do not substitute their social and economic beliefs for the judgment of legislative bodies, who are elected to pass laws.

It may be, however—at least it is not the sort of claim one can disprove— that the "right to an abortion," or non-economic rights generally, accord more closely with "this generation's idealization of America" than the "rights" asserted in either *Lochner* or *Dandridge*. But that attitude, of course, is precisely the point of the *Lochner* philosophy, which would grant unusual protection to those "rights" that somehow seem most pressing, regardless of whether the Constitution suggests any special solicitude for them. The

Constitution has little to say about contract, less about abortion, and those who would speculate about which the framers would have been more likely to protect may not be pleased with the answer. The Court continues to disavow the philosophy of *Lochner*. Yet as Justice Stewart's concurrence admits, it is impossible candidly to regard *Roe* as the product of anything else. That alone should be enough to damn it. Criticism of the *Lochner* philosophy has been virtually universal and will not be rehearsed here. I would, however, like to suggest briefly that although *Lochner* and *Roe* are twins to be sure, they are not identical. While I would hesitate to argue that one is more defensible than the other in terms of judicial style, there are differences in that regard that suggest *Roe* may turn out to be the more dangerous precedent. All the "superimposition of the Court's own value choices" talk is, of course, the characterization of others and not the language of *Lochner* or its progeny. Indeed, those cases did not argue that "liberty of contract" was a preferred constitutional freedom, but rather represented it as merely one among the numerous aspects of "liberty" the Fourteenth Amendment protects, therefore requiring of its inhibitors a "rational" defense.

Thus the test *Lochner* and its progeny purported to apply is that which would theoretically control the same questions today: whether a plausible argument can be made that the legislative action furthers some permissible governmental goal. The trouble, of course, is they misapplied it. *Roe*, on the other hand, is quite explicit that the right to an abortion is a "fundamental" one, requiring not merely a "rational" defense for its inhibition but rather a "compelling" one.

A second difference between *Lochner* et al. and *Roe* has to do with the nature of the legislative judgments being second-guessed. In the main, the "refutations" tendered by the *Lochner* series were of two sorts. The first took the form of declarations that the goals in terms of which the legislatures' actions were defended were impermissible. Thus, for example, the equalization of unequal bargaining power and the strengthening of the labor movement are simply ends the legislature had no business pursuing, and consequently its actions cannot thereby be justified. The second form of "refutation" took the form not of denying the legitimacy of the goal relied on but rather of denying the plausibility of the legislature's empirical judgment that its action would promote that goal.

The *Roe* opinion's "refutation" of the legislative judgment that anti-abortion statutes can be justified in terms of the protection of the fetus takes neither of these forms. The Court grants that protecting the fetus is an "important and legitimate" governmental goal, and of course it does not deny that restricting abortion promotes it. What it does, instead, is simply announce that that goal is not important enough to sustain the restriction. There is little doubt that judgments of this sort were involved in *Lochner* et al., but what the Court said in those cases was not that the legislature had incorrectly balanced two legitimate but competing goals, but rather that the goal it had favored was impermissible or the legislation involved did not really promote it. Perhaps this is merely a rhetorical difference, but it could prove to be important. *Lochner* et al. were thoroughly disreputable decisions, but at least they did us the favor of sowing the seeds of their own destruction. To say that the equalization of bargaining power or the fostering of the labor movement is a goal outside the ambit of a "police power" broad enough to forbid all contracts the state legislature can reasonably regard "as inconsistent with the public interests or as hurtful to the public order or as detrimental to the common good" is to say something that is, in a word, wrong. And it is just as obviously wrong to declare, for example, that restrictions on long working hours cannot reasonably be said to promote health and safety. *Roe's* "refutation" of the legislative judgment, on the other, is not obviously wrong, for the substitution of one nonrational judgment for another concerning the relative importance of a mother's opportunity to live the life she has planned and a fetus's opportunity to live at all, can be labeled neither wrong nor right. The problem with *Roe* is not so much that it bungles the question it sets itself, but rather that it sets itself a question the Constitution has not made the Court's business. It looks different from *Lochner*—it has the shape if not the substance of a judgment that is very much the Court's business, one vindicating an interest the Constitution marks as special—and it is for that reason perhaps more dangerous. Of course in a sense it is more candid than *Lochner*. But the employment of a higher standard of judicial review, no matter how candid the recognition that it is indeed higher, loses some of its admirability when it is accompanied by neither a coherent account of why such a standard is appropriate nor any indication of why it has not been satisfied.

BUCK v. BELL

274 U.S. 200 (1927)

Opinion: Holmes, joined by Taft, Van Devanter, McReynolds, Brandeis, Sutherland, Sanford, Stone
Dissent (not filed): Butler

Mr. JUSTICE HOLMES *delivered the opinion of the Court.*

This is a writ of error to review a judgment of the Supreme Court of Appeals of the State of Virginia affirming a judgment of the Circuit Court of Amherst County by which the defendant in error, the superintendent of the State Colony for Epileptics and Feeble Minded, was ordered to perform the operation of salpingectomy upon Carrie Buck, the plaintiff in error, for the purpose of making her sterile. The case comes here upon the contention that the statute authorizing the judgment is void under the Fourteenth Amendment as denying to the plaintiff in error due process of law and the equal protection of the laws.

Carrie Buck is a feeble-minded white woman who was committed to the State Colony above mentioned in due form. She is the daughter of a feeble-minded mother in the same institution, and the mother of an illegitimate feeble-minded child. She was eighteen years old at the time of the trial of her case in the Circuit Court, in the latter part of 1924. An Act of Virginia, approved March 20, 1924, recites that the health of the patient and the welfare of society may be promoted in certain cases by the sterilization of mental defectives, under careful safeguard, etc.; that the sterilization may be effected in males by vasectomy and in females by salpingectomy, without serious pain or substantial danger to life; that the Commonwealth is supporting in various institutions many defective persons who, if now discharged, would become a menace, but, if incapable of procreating, might be discharged with safety and become self-supporting with benefit to themselves and to society, and that experience has shown that heredity plays an important part in the transmission of insanity, imbecility, etc. The statute then enacts that, whenever the superintendent of certain institutions, including the above-named State Colony, shall be of opinion that it is for the best interests of the patients and of society that an inmate under his care should be sexually sterilized, he may have the operation performed upon any patient afflicted with hereditary forms of insanity, imbecility, etc., on complying with the very careful provisions by which the act protects the patients from possible abuse.

The superintendent first presents a petition to the special board of directors of his hospital or colony, stating the facts and the grounds for his opinion, verified by affidavit. Notice of the petition and of the time and place of the hearing in the institution is to be served upon the inmate, and also upon his guardian, and if there is no guardian, the superintendent is to apply to the Circuit Court of the County to appoint one. If the inmate is a minor, notice also is to be given to his parents, if any, with a copy of the petition. The board is to see to it that the inmate may attend the hearings if desired by him or his guardian. The evidence is all to be reduced to writing, and, after the board has made its order for or against the operation, the superintendent, or the inmate, or his guardian, may appeal to the Circuit Court of the County. The Circuit Court may consider the record of the board and the evidence before it and such other admissible evidence as may be offered, and may affirm, revise, or reverse the order of the board and enter such order as it deems just. Finally any party may apply to the Supreme Court of Appeals, which, if it grants the appeal, is to hear the case upon the record of the trial in the Circuit Court, and may enter such order as it thinks the Circuit Court should have entered. There can be no doubt that, so far as procedure is concerned, the rights of the patient are most carefully considered, and, as every step in this case was taken in scrupulous compliance with the statute and after months of observation, there is no doubt that, in that respect, the plaintiff in error has had due process of law.

The attack is not upon the procedure, but upon the substantive law. It seems to be contended that in no circumstances could such an order be justified. It certainly is contended that the order cannot be justified upon the existing grounds. The judgment finds the facts that have been recited, and that Carrie Buck is the probable potential parent of socially inadequate offspring, likewise afflicted, that she may be sexually sterilized without detriment to her general health, and that her welfare and that of society will be promoted by her sterilization, and thereupon makes the order. In view of the general declarations of the legislature and the specific findings of the Court, obviously we cannot say as matter of law that the grounds do not exist, and, if they exist, they justify the result. We have seen more than once that the public welfare may call upon the best citizens for their lives. It would be strange if it could not call upon those who already sap the strength of the State for these lesser sacrifices, often not felt to be such by those concerned, in order to prevent our being swamped with incompetence. It is better for all the world if, instead of waiting to execute degenerate offspring for crime or to let them starve for their imbecility, society can prevent those who are manifestly unfit from continuing their kind. The principle that sustains compulsory vaccination is broad enough to cover cutting the Fallopian tubes. *Jacobson v. Massachusetts.* Three generations of imbeciles are enough.

But, it is said, however it might be if this reasoning were applied generally, it fails when it is confined to the small number who are in the institutions named and is not applied to the multitudes outside. It is the usual last resort of constitutional arguments to point out shortcomings of this sort. But the answer is that the law does all that is needed when it does all that it can, indicates a policy, applies it to all within the lines, and seeks to bring within the lines all similarly situated so far and so fast as its means allow. Of course, so far as the operations enable those who otherwise must be kept confined to be returned to the world, and thus open the asylum to others, the equality aimed at will be more nearly reached.

Judgment affirmed.

MR. JUSTICE BUTLER *dissents.*

GRISWOLD v. CONNECTICUT

381 U.S. 479 (1965)

Opinion: Douglas, joined by Warren, Clark, Brennan, Goldberg
Concurrence: Goldberg, joined by Warren, Brennan
Concurrence: Harlan
Concurrence: White
Dissent: Black, joined by Stewart
Dissent: Stewart, joined by Black

You will remember that we excerpted Griswold v. Connecticut *as an example of the moral reading in Chapter 2. We include a longer version here to stress the importance of the right to privacy, a right that will frame all of the cases in the rest of this chapter. This time, consider the ways in which the argument for this right differs from its previous iteration during the* Lochner v. New York *era. Moreover, in what ways does this right draw upon the rights of families discussed in Section B?*

Also as you read this case, notice how each opinion presents a different theory of the right to privacy. In particular, pay attention to Justice William O. Douglas's emphasis on freedom of association and Justice Arthur Goldberg's conception of fundamental personal liberties as distinct from due process rights. In cases such as these, is there a distinction between liberty and privacy? If there is, does it matter? What do these perspectives on privacy have in common? How do they differ? Compare and contrast each of them to the rejection of an abstract right to privacy delineated in the dissent. Which of the arguments do you find most persuasive?

MR. JUSTICE DOUGLAS *delivered the opinion of the Court.*

Appellant Griswold is Executive Director of the Planned Parenthood League of Connecticut. Appellant Buxton is a licensed physician and a professor at the Yale Medical School who served as Medical Director for the League at its Center in New Haven—a center open and operating from November 1 to November 10, 1961, when appellants were arrested.

They gave information, instruction, and medical advice to married persons as to the means of preventing conception. They examined the wife and prescribed the best contraceptive device or material for her use. Fees were usually charged, although some couples were serviced free.

The statutes whose constitutionality is involved in this appeal are §§53-32 and 54-196 of the General Statutes of Connecticut. The former provides:

"Any person who uses any drug, medicinal article or instrument for the purpose of preventing conception shall be fined not less than fifty dollars or imprisoned not less than sixty days nor more than one year or be both fined and imprisoned."

Section 54-196 provides:

"Any person who assists, abets, counsels, causes, hires or commands another to commit any offense may be prosecuted and punished as if he were the principal offender."

The appellants were found guilty as accessories and fined $100 each, against the claim that the accessory statute as so applied violated the Fourteenth Amendment. The Appellate Division of the Circuit Court affirmed. The Supreme Court of Errors affirmed that judgment.

Coming to the merits, we are met with a wide range of questions that implicate the Due Process Clause of the Fourteenth Amendment. Overtones of some arguments suggest that *Lochner v. New York* should be our guide. But we decline that invitation as we did in *West Coast Hotel Co. v. Parrish*. We do not sit as a super-legislature to determine the wisdom, need, and propriety of laws that touch economic problems, business affairs, or social conditions. This law, however, operates directly on an intimate relation of husband and wife and their physician's role in one aspect of that relation.

The association of people is not mentioned in the Constitution nor in the Bill of Rights. The right to educate a child in a school of the parents' choice—whether public or private or parochial—is also not mentioned. Nor is the right to study any particular subject or any foreign language. Yet the First Amendment has been construed to include certain of those rights.

By *Pierce v. Society of Sisters*, the right to educate one's children as one chooses is made applicable to the States by the force of the First and Fourteenth Amendments. By *Meyer v. Nebraska*, the same dignity is given the right to study the German language in a private school. In other words, the State may not, consistently with the spirit of the First Amendment, contract the spectrum of available knowledge. The right of freedom of speech and press includes not only the right to utter or to print, but the right to distribute, the right to receive, the right to read and freedom of inquiry, freedom of thought, and freedom to teach indeed the freedom of the entire university community. Without those peripheral rights the specific rights would be less secure. And so we reaffirm the principle of the *Pierce* and the *Meyer* cases.

In *NAACP v. Alabama*, we protected the "freedom to associate and privacy in one's associations," noting that freedom of association was a peripheral First Amendment right. Disclosure of membership lists of a constitutionally valid association, we held, was invalid "as entailing the likelihood of a substantial restraint upon the exercise by petitioner's members of their right to freedom of association." Ibid. In other words, the First Amendment has a penumbra where privacy is protected from governmental intrusion. In like context, we have protected forms of "association" that are not political in the customary sense but pertain to the social, legal, and economic benefit of the members. The right of "association," like the right of belief is more than the right to attend a meeting; it includes the right to express one's attitudes or philosophies by membership in a group or by affiliation with it or by other lawful means. Association in that context is a form of expression of opinion; and while it is not expressly included in the First Amendment its existence is necessary in making the express guarantees fully meaningful.

The foregoing cases suggest that specific guarantees in the Bill of Rights have penumbras, formed by emanations from those guarantees that help give them life and substance. Various guarantees create zones of privacy. The right of association contained in the penumbra of the First Amendment is one, as we have seen. The Third Amendment in its prohibition against the quartering of soldiers "in any house" in time of peace without the consent of the owner is another facet of that privacy. The Fourth Amendment explicitly affirms the "right of the people to be secure in their persons, houses, papers, and effects, against unreasonable searches and seizures." The Fifth Amendment in its Self-Incrimination Clause enables the citizen to create a zone of privacy which government may not force him to surrender to his detriment. The Ninth Amendment provides: "The enumeration in the Constitution, of certain rights, shall not be construed to deny or disparage others retained by the people."

The present case, then, concerns a relationship lying within the zone of privacy created by several fundamental constitutional guarantees. And it concerns a law which, in forbidding the use of contraceptives rather than regulating their manufacture or sale, seeks to achieve its goals by means having a maximum destructive impact upon that relationship. Such a law cannot stand in light of the familiar principle, so often applied by this Court, that a "governmental purpose to control or prevent activities constitutionally subject to state regulation may not be achieved by means which sweep unnecessarily broadly and thereby invade the area of protected freedoms." Would we allow the police to search the sacred precincts of marital bedrooms for telltale signs of the use of contraceptives? The very idea is repulsive to the notions of privacy surrounding the marriage relationship.

We deal with a right of privacy older than the Bill of Rights—older than our political parties, older than our school system.

Marriage is a coming together for better or for worse, hopefully enduring, and intimate to the degree of being sacred. It is an association that promotes a way of life, not causes; a harmony in living, not political faiths; a bilateral loyalty, not commercial or social projects. Yet it is an association for as noble a purpose as any involved in our prior decisions.

MR. JUSTICE GOLDBERG, *whom* **THE CHIEF JUSTICE** *and* **MR. JUSTICE BRENNAN** *join, concurring.*

I agree with the Court that Connecticut's birth-control law unconstitutionally intrudes upon the right of marital privacy, and I join in its opinion and judgment. Although I have not accepted the view that "due process" as used in the Fourteenth Amendment incorporates all of the first eight Amendments, I do agree that the concept of liberty protects those personal rights that are fundamental, and is not confined to the specific terms of the Bill of Rights. My conclusion that the concept of liberty is not so restricted and that it embraces the right of marital privacy though that right is not mentioned explicitly in the Constitution is supported both by numerous decisions of this Court, referred to in the Court's opinion, and by the language and history of the Ninth Amendment. In reaching the conclusion that the right of marital privacy is protected, as being within the protected penumbra of specific guarantees of the Bill of Rights, the Court refers to the Ninth Amendment. I add these words to emphasize the relevance of that Amendment to the Court's holding.

. . . The language and history of the Ninth Amendment reveal that the Framers of the Constitution believed that there are additional fundamental rights, protected from governmental infringement, which exist alongside those fundamental rights specifically mentioned in the first eight constitutional amendments.

. . . To hold that a right so basic and fundamental and so deep-rooted in our society as the right of privacy in marriage may be infringed because that right is not guaranteed in so many words by the first eight amendments to the Constitution is to ignore the Ninth Amendment and to give it no effect whatsoever. Moreover, a judicial construction that this fundamental right is not protected by the Constitution because it is not mentioned in explicit terms by one of the first eight amendments or elsewhere in the Constitution would violate the Ninth Amendment, which specifically states that "the enumeration in the Constitution, of certain rights, shall not be construed to deny or disparage others retained by the people."

A dissenting opinion suggests that my interpretation of the Ninth Amendment somehow "broaden[s] the powers of this Court." With all due respect, I believe that it misses the import of what I am saying. . . . [T]his Court has held, often unanimously, that the Fifth and Fourteenth Amendments protect certain fundamental personal liberties from abridgment by the Federal Government or the States. The Ninth Amendment simply shows the intent of the Constitution's authors that other fundamental personal rights should not be denied such protection or disparaged in any other way simply because they are not specifically listed in the first eight constitutional amendments. I do not see how this broadens the authority of the Court; rather it serves to support what this Court has been doing in protecting fundamental rights.

In determining which rights are fundamental, judges are not left at large to decide cases in light of their personal and private notions. Rather, they must look to the "traditions and [collective] conscience of our people" to determine whether a principle is "so rooted [there] . . . as to be ranked as fundamental." The inquiry is whether a right involved "is of such a character that it cannot be denied without violating those 'fundamental principles of liberty and justice which lie at the base of all our civil and political institutions'. . . ." "Liberty" also "gains content from the emanations of . . . specific [constitutional] guarantees" and "from experience with the requirements of a free society."

I agree fully with the Court that, applying these tests, the right of privacy is a fundamental personal right, emanating "from the totality of the constitutional scheme under which we live."

The entire fabric of the Constitution and the purposes that clearly underlie its specific guarantees demonstrate that the rights to marital privacy and to marry and raise a family are of similar order and magnitude as the fundamental rights specifically protected.

Although the Constitution does not speak in so many words of the right of privacy in marriage, I cannot believe that it offers these fundamental rights no protection. The fact that no particular provision of the Constitution explicitly forbids the State from disrupting the traditional relation of the family—a relation as old and as fundamental as our entire civilization—surely does not show that the Government was meant to have the power to do so. Rather, as the Ninth Amendment expressly recognizes, there are fundamental personal rights such as this one, which are protected from abridgment by the Government though not specifically mentioned in the Constitution.

The logic of the dissents would sanction federal or state legislation that seems to me even more plainly unconstitutional than the statute before us. Surely the Government, absent a showing of a compelling subordinating state interest, could not decree that all husbands and wives must be sterilized after two children have been born to them. Yet by their reasoning such an invasion of marital privacy would not be subject to constitutional challenge because, while it might be "silly," no provision of the Constitution specifically prevents the Government from curtailing the marital right to bear children and raise a family. While it may shock some of my Brethren that the Court today holds that the Constitution protects the right of marital privacy, in my view it is far more shocking to believe that the personal liberty guaranteed by the Constitution does not include protection against such totalitarian limitation of family size, which is at complete variance with our constitutional concepts. Yet, if upon a showing of a slender basis of rationality, a law outlawing voluntary birth control by married persons is valid, then, by the same reasoning, a law requiring compulsory birth control also would seem to be valid. In my view, however, both types of law would unjustifiably intrude upon rights of marital privacy which are constitutionally protected.

Although the Connecticut birth-control law obviously encroaches upon a fundamental personal liberty, the State does not show that the law serves any "subordinating [state] interest which is compelling" or that it is "necessary . . . to the accomplishment of a permissible state policy." The State, at most, argues that there is some rational relation between this statute and what is admittedly a legitimate subject of state concern—the discouraging of extra-marital relations. It says that preventing the use of birth-control devices by married persons helps prevent the indulgence by

some in such extra-marital relations. The rationality of this justification is dubious, particularly in light of the admitted widespread availability to all persons in the State of Connecticut, unmarried as well as married, of birth-control devices for the prevention of disease, as distinguished from the prevention of conception. But, in any event, it is clear that the state interest in safeguarding marital fidelity can be served by a more discriminately tailored statute, which does not, like the present one, sweep unnecessarily broadly, reaching far beyond the evil sought to be dealt with and intruding upon the privacy of all married couples. Here, as elsewhere, "precision of regulation must be the touchstone in an area so closely touching our most precious freedoms."

MR. JUSTICE HARLAN, *concurring in the judgment.*

I fully agree with the judgment of reversal, but find myself unable to join the Court's opinion. The reason is that it seems to me to evince an approach to this case very much like that taken by my Brothers Black and Stewart in dissent, namely: the Due Process Clause of the Fourteenth Amendment does not touch this Connecticut statute unless the enactment is found to violate some right assured by the letter or penumbra of the Bill of Rights.

In other words, what I find implicit in the Court's opinion is that the "incorporation" doctrine may be used to restrict the reach of Fourteenth Amendment Due Process. For me, this is just as unacceptable constitutional doctrine as is the use of the "incorporation" approach to impose upon the States all the requirements of the Bill of Rights as found in the provisions of the first eight amendments and in the decisions of this Court interpreting them. *See, e.g.,* my concurring opinions in *Pointer v. Texas*, and *Griffin v. California*, and my dissenting opinion in *Poe v. Ullman*. In my view, the proper constitutional inquiry in this case is whether this Connecticut statute infringes the Due Process Clause of the Fourteenth Amendment because the enactment violates basic values "implicit in the concept of ordered liberty," *Palko v. Connecticut*. For reasons stated at length in my dissenting opinion in *Poe v. Ullman, supra*, I believe that it does. While the relevant inquiry may be aided by resort to one or more of the provisions of the Bill of Rights, it is not dependent on them or any of their radiations. The Due Process Clause of the Fourteenth Amendment stands, in my opinion, on its own bottom.

A further observation seems in order respecting the justification of my Brothers Black and Stewart for their "incorporation" approach to this case. Their approach does not rest on historical reasons, which are, of course, wholly lacking but on the thesis that, by limiting the content of the Due Process Clause of the Fourteenth Amendment to the protection of rights which can be found elsewhere in the Constitution, in this instance, in the Bill of Rights, judges will thus be confined to "interpretation" of specific constitutional provisions, and will thereby be restrained from introducing their own notions of constitutional right and wrong into the "vague contours of the Due Process Clause." *Rochin v. California*. While I could not more heartily agree that judicial "self-restraint" is an indispensable ingredient of sound constitutional adjudication, I do submit that the formula suggested for achieving it is more hollow than real. "Specific" provisions of the Constitution, no less than "due process," lend themselves as readily to "personal" interpretations by judges

whose constitutional outlook is simply to keep the Constitution in supposed "tune with the times". . . . Need one go further than to recall last Term's reapportionment cases, where a majority of the Court "interpreted" "by the People" (Art. I, §2) and "equal protection" (Amdt. 14) to command "one person, one vote," an interpretation that was made in the face of irrefutable and still unanswered history to the contrary? *See* my dissenting opinions in those cases.

Judicial self-restraint will not, I suggest, be brought about in the "due process" area by the historically unfounded incorporation formula long advanced by my Brother Black, and now in part espoused by my Brother Stewart. It will be achieved in this area, as in other constitutional areas, only by continual insistence upon respect for the teachings of history, solid recognition of the basic values that underlie our society, and wise appreciation of the great roles that the doctrines of federalism and separation of powers have played in establishing and preserving American freedoms. Adherence to these principles will not, of course, obviate all constitutional differences of opinion among judges, nor should it. Their continued recognition will, however, go farther toward keeping most judges from roaming at large in the constitutional field than will the interpolation into the Constitution of an artificial and largely illusory restriction on the content of the Due Process Clause.*

---

*Indeed, my Brother Black, in arguing his thesis, is forced to lay aside a host of cases in which the Court has recognized fundamental rights in the Fourteenth Amendment without specific reliance upon the Bill of Rights. . . .

MR. JUSTICE BLACK, *with whom*
MR. JUSTICE STEWART *joins, dissenting.*

I agree with my Brother Stewart's dissenting opinion. And, like him, I do not to any extent whatever base my view that this Connecticut law is constitutional on a belief that the law is wise, or that its policy is a good one. In order that there may be no room at all to doubt why I vote as I do, I feel constrained to add that the law is every bit as offensive to me as it is to my Brethren of the majority and my Brothers Harlan, White and Goldberg, who, reciting reasons why it is offensive to them, hold it unconstitutional. There is no single one of the graphic and eloquent strictures and criticisms fired at the policy of this Connecticut law either by the Court's opinion or by those of my concurring Brethren to which I cannot subscribe—except their conclusion that the evil qualities they see in the law make it unconstitutional.

Had the doctor defendant here, or even the nondoctor defendant, been convicted for doing nothing more than expressing opinions to persons coming to the clinic that certain contraceptive devices, medicines or practices would do them good and would be desirable, or for telling people how devices could be used, I can think of no reasons at this time why their expressions of views would not be protected by the First and Fourteenth Amendments, which guarantee freedom of speech. But speech is one thing; conduct and physical activities are quite another. The two defendants here were active participants in an organization which gave physical examinations to women, advised them what kind of contraceptive devices or medicines would most likely be satisfactory for them, and then supplied the devices themselves, all for a graduated scale of fees, based on the family income. Thus, these defendants admittedly engaged with others in a planned course of conduct to help people violate the Connecticut law. . . . The Court talks about a constitutional "right of privacy" as though there is some constitutional provision or provisions forbidding any law ever to be passed which might abridge the "privacy" of individuals. But there is not. There are, of course, guarantees in certain specific constitutional provisions which are designed in part to protect privacy at certain times and places with respect to certain activities. Such, for example, is the Fourth Amendment's guarantee against "unreasonable searches and seizures." But I think it belittles that Amendment to talk about it as though it protects nothing but "privacy." To treat it that way is to give it a niggardly interpretation, not the kind of liberal reading I think any Bill of Rights provision should be given. The average man would very likely not have his feelings soothed any more by having his property seized openly than by having it seized privately and by stealth. He simply wants his property left alone. And a person can be just as much, if not more, irritated, annoyed and injured by an unceremonious public arrest by a policeman as he is by a seizure in the privacy of his office or home.

One of the most effective ways of diluting or expanding a constitutionally guaranteed right is to substitute for the crucial word or words of a constitutional guarantee another word or words, more or less flexible and more or less restricted in meaning. This fact is well illustrated by the use of the term "right of privacy" as a comprehensive substitute for the Fourth Amendment's guarantee against "unreasonable searches and seizures." "Privacy" is a broad, abstract and ambiguous concept which can easily be shrunken in meaning but which can also, on the other hand, easily be interpreted as a constitutional ban against many things other than searches and seizures. I have expressed the view many times that First Amendment freedoms, for example, have suffered from a failure of the courts to stick to the simple language of the First Amendment in construing it, instead of invoking multitudes of words substituted for those the Framers used. For these reasons, I get nowhere in this case by talk about a constitutional "right of privacy" as an emanation from one or more constitutional provisions. I like my privacy as well as the next one, but I am nevertheless compelled to admit that government has a right to invade it unless prohibited by some specific constitutional provision. For these reasons, I cannot agree with the Court's judgment and the reasons it gives for holding this Connecticut law unconstitutional.

I repeat, so as not to be misunderstood, that this Court does have power, which it should exercise, to hold laws unconstitutional where they are forbidden by the Federal Constitution. My point is that there is no provision of the Constitution which either expressly or impliedly vests power in this Court to sit as a supervisory agency over acts of duly constituted legislative bodies and set aside their laws because of the Court's belief that the legislative policies adopted are unreasonable, unwise, arbitrary, capricious or irrational. The adoption of such a loose flexible. uncontrolled standard for holding laws unconstitutional, if ever it is finally achieved, will amount to a great unconstitutional shift of power to the courts which I believe and am constrained to say will be bad for the courts, and worse for the country. Subjecting federal and state laws to such an unrestrained and unrestrainable judicial control as to the wisdom of legislative enactments would, I fear, jeopardize the separation of governmental powers that the Framers set up, and, at the same time, threaten to take away much of the power of States to govern themselves which the Constitution plainly intended them to have.

I realize that many good and able men have eloquently spoken and written, sometimes in rhapsodical strains, about the duty of this Court to keep the Constitution in tune with the times. The idea is that the Constitution must be changed from time to time, and that this Court is charged with a duty to make those changes. For myself, I must, with all deference, reject that philosophy. The Constitution makers knew the need for change, and provided for it. Amendments suggested by the people's elected representatives can be submitted to the people or their selected agents for ratification. That method of change was good for our Fathers, and, being somewhat old-fashioned, I must add it is good enough for me. And so I cannot rely on the Due Process Clause or the Ninth Amendment or any mysterious and uncertain natural law concept as a reason for striking down this state law. The Due Process Clause, with an "arbitrary and capricious" or "shocking to the conscience" formula, was liberally used by this Court to strike down economic legislation in the early decades of this century, threatening, many people thought, the tranquility and stability of the Nation. *See, e.g., Lochner v. New York.* That formula, based on subjective considerations of "natural justice," is no less dangerous when used to enforce this Court's views about personal rights than those about economic rights. I had thought that we had laid that formula, as a means for striking down state legislation, to rest once and for all in cases like *West Coast Hotel Co. v. Parrish, Olsen v. Nebraska ex rel. Western Reference & Bond Assn.,* and many other opinions.

ROE v. WADE

410 U.S. 113 (1973)

Opinion: Blackmun, joined by Burger, Douglas, Brennan, Stewart, Marshall, Powell
Concurrence: Burger
Concurrence: Douglas
Concurrence: Stewart
Dissent: White, joined by Rehnquist
Dissent: Rehnquist

Although Griswold v. Connecticut *established a specific right to use contraception free from government prohibition, it also referenced a broader right of privacy. In* Roe v. Wade, *the Court drew on the notion of a right to privacy to hold that women had the right to terminate their own pregnancies in some circumstances. What grounds does the Court use for extending privacy beyond contraception to this more controversial area? How much of the ground was laid in* Griswold v. Connecticut *for the extension of privacy to this new area of law? Is the argument in* Griswold v. Connecticut *sufficient to sustain not only a right of privacy in regard to contraception, but to bodily autonomy more generally?*

As was the case in Griswold v. Connecticut, *your particular theory of constitutional interpretation will guide your answers to these questions. Originalists, for instance, will likely resist the move towards reading into the Constitution broad principles that recognize a right to privacy that protects abortion, a right not conceived of by the Founders. On the contrary, those who support a moral reading might find in* Roe v. Wade *exactly the kind of constitutional interpretation central to their theory. Consider too what a pragmatist or proceduralist interpretation of the Constitution might say about* Roe v. Wade. *You have seen the excerpt from John Hart Ely about privacy rights. Is there any democratic*

defense for this decision? Similarly, what pragmatic arguments might be raised either for or against it?

In addition to considering these case-specific questions, also think about two approaches to the kinds of holdings that can be established in case law. Constitutional lawyers often distinguish between "rules" and "standards" in judicial opinions. Rules set clear boundaries between what is lawful and what is not, while standards establish more general principles. In reading the Constitution itself, for example, we noted that age requirements establish clear rules, while other phrases such as the prohibition on cruel and unusual punishment suggested standards. The distinction between rules and standards is particularly important in noting the differences between the kind of decisions the Court made in Griswold v. Connecticut *and in* Roe v. Wade. *Notice as you read this case that it establishes clear rules as to when states are permitted to regulate abortion. As you read the opinion, consider the pitfalls that might come with such a rule-oriented decision, and in particular with the trimester framework established. Should the opinion have been more like that in* Griswold v. Connecticut, *which avoided specific rule-like claims in favor of a more principled approach?*

MR. JUSTICE BLACKMUN *delivered the opinion of the Court.*

This Texas federal appeal and its Georgia companion, *Doe v. Bolton*, present constitutional challenges to state criminal abortion legislation. The Texas statutes under attack here are typical of those that have been in effect in many States for approximately a century. The Georgia statutes, in contrast, have a modern cast and are a legislative product that, to an extent at least, obviously reflects the influences of recent attitudinal change, of advancing medical knowledge and techniques, and of new thinking about an old issue.

We forthwith acknowledge our awareness of the sensitive and emotional nature of the abortion controversy, of the vigorous opposing views, even among physicians, and of the deep and seemingly absolute convictions that the subject inspires. One's philosophy, one's experiences, one's exposure to the raw edges of human existence, one's religious training, one's attitudes toward life and family and their values, and the moral standards one establishes and seeks to observe, are all likely to influence and to color one's thinking and conclusions about abortion.

In addition, population growth, pollution, poverty, and racial overtones tend to complicate and not to simplify the problem.

Our task, of course, is to resolve the issue by constitutional measurement, free of emotion and of predilection. We seek earnestly to do this, and, because we do, we have inquired into, and in this opinion place some emphasis upon, medical and medical-legal history and what that history reveals about man's attitudes toward the abortion procedure over the centuries. We bear in mind, too, Mr. Justice Holmes' admonition in his now-vindicated dissent in *Lochner v. New York*:

> "[The Constitution] is made for people of fundamentally differing views, and the accident of our finding certain opinions natural and familiar or novel and even shocking ought not to conclude our judgment upon the question whether statutes embodying them conflict with the Constitution of the United States."

The Texas statutes that concern us here . . . make it a crime to "procure an abortion," as therein defined, or to attempt one, except with respect to "an abortion procured or attempted by medical advice for the purpose of saving the life of the mother." Similar statutes are in existence in a majority of the States.

Jane Roe, a single woman who was residing in Dallas County, Texas, instituted this federal action in March 1970 against the District Attorney of the county. She sought a declaratory judgment that the Texas criminal abortion statutes were unconstitutional on their face, and an injunction restraining the defendant from enforcing the statutes.

Roe alleged that she was unmarried and pregnant; that she wished to terminate her pregnancy by an abortion "performed by a competent, licensed physician, under safe, clinical conditions"; that she was unable to get a "legal" abortion in Texas because her life did not appear to be threatened by the continuation of her pregnancy; and that she could not afford to travel to another jurisdiction in order to secure a legal abortion under safe conditions. She claimed that the Texas statutes were unconstitutionally vague and that they abridged her right of personal privacy, protected by the First, Fourth, Fifth, Ninth, and Fourteenth Amendments. By an amendment to her complaint Roe purported to sue "on behalf of herself and all other women" similarly situated. . . .

The principal thrust of appellant's attack on the Texas statutes is that they improperly invade a right, said to be possessed by the pregnant woman, to choose to terminate her pregnancy. Appellant would discover this right in the concept of personal "liberty" embodied in the Fourteenth Amendment's Due Process Clause; or in personal, marital, familial, and sexual privacy said to be protected by the Bill of Rights or its penumbras, (*Griswold v. Connecticut*; *Eisenstadt v. Baird*), or among those rights reserved to the people by the

Ninth Amendment, *Griswold v. Connecticut* (Goldberg, J., concurring). Before addressing this claim, we feel it desirable briefly to survey, in several aspects, the history of abortion, for such insight as that history may afford us, and then to examine the state purposes and interests behind the criminal abortion laws. . . .

This right of privacy, whether it be founded in the Fourteenth Amendment's concept of personal liberty and restrictions upon state action, as we feel it is, or, as the District Court determined, in the Ninth Amendment's reservation of rights to the people, is broad enough to encompass a woman's decision whether or not to terminate her pregnancy. The detriment that the State would impose upon the pregnant woman by denying this choice altogether is apparent. Specific and direct harm medically diagnosable even in early pregnancy may be involved. Maternity, or additional offspring, may force upon the woman a distressful life and future. Psychological harm may be imminent. Mental and physical health may be taxed by child care. There is also the distress, for all concerned, associated with the unwanted child, and there is the problem of bringing a child into a family already unable, psychologically and otherwise, to care for it. In other cases, as in this one, the additional difficulties and continuing stigma of unwed motherhood may be involved. All these are factors the woman and her responsible physician necessarily will consider in consultation.

On the basis of elements such as these, appellant and some amici argue that the woman's right is absolute and that she is entitled to terminate her pregnancy at whatever time, in whatever way, and for whatever reason she alone chooses. With this we do not agree. Appellant's arguments that Texas either has no valid interest at all in regulating the abortion decision, or no interest strong enough to support any limitation upon the

woman's sole determination, are unpersuasive. The Court's decisions recognizing a right of privacy also acknowledge that some state regulation in areas protected by that right is appropriate. As noted above, a State may properly assert important interests in safeguarding health, in maintaining medical standards, and in protecting potential life. At some point in pregnancy, these respective interests become sufficiently compelling to sustain regulation of the factors that govern the abortion decision. The privacy right involved, therefore, cannot be said to be absolute.

We, therefore, conclude that the right of personal privacy includes the abortion decision, but that this right is not unqualified and must be considered against important state interests in regulation.

Where certain "fundamental rights" are involved, the Court has held that regulation limiting these rights may be justified only by a "compelling state interest" (*Kramer v. Union Free School District*; *Shapiro v. Thompson*; *Sherbert v. Verner*), and that legislative enactments must be narrowly drawn to express only the legitimate state interests at stake. (*Griswold v. Connecticut*; *Aptheker v. Secretary of State*; *Cantwell v. Connecticut*.)

In the recent abortion cases, cited above, courts have recognized these principles. Those striking down state laws have generally scrutinized the State's interests in protecting health and potential life, and have concluded that neither interest justified broad limitations on the reasons for which a physician and his pregnant patient might decide that she should have an abortion in the early stages of pregnancy. Courts sustaining state laws have held that the State's determinations to protect health or prenatal life are dominant and constitutionally justifiable.

The District Court held that the appellee failed to meet his burden of demonstrating that the Texas statute's infringement upon Roe's rights was necessary to support a compelling state interest, and that, although the appellee presented "several compelling justifications for state presence in the area of abortions," the statutes outstripped these justifications and swept "far beyond any areas of compelling state interest." Appellant and appellee both contest that holding. Appellant, as has been indicated, claims an absolute right that bars any state imposition of criminal penalties in the area. Appellee argues that the State's determination to recognize and protect prenatal life from and after conception constitutes a compelling state interest. As noted above, we do not agree fully with either formulation.

The appellee and certain amici argue that the fetus is a "person" within the language and meaning of the Fourteenth Amendment. In support of this, they outline at length and in detail the well-known facts of fetal development. If this suggestion of personhood is established, the appellant's case, of course, collapses, for the fetus' right to life would then be guaranteed specifically by the Amendment.

The Constitution does not define "person" in so many words. Section 1 of the Fourteenth Amendment contains three references to "person." The first, in defining "citizens," speaks of "persons born or naturalized in the United States."

All this, together with our observation, supra, that throughout the major portion of the 19th century prevailing legal abortion practices were far freer than they are today, persuades us that the word "person," as used in the Fourteenth Amendment, does not include the unborn. This is in accord with the results reached in those few cases where the issue has been squarely presented. Indeed, our decision in *United States v. Vuitch* inferentially is to the same effect, for we there would not have indulged in

statutory interpretation favorable to abortion in specified circumstances if the necessary consequence was the termination of life entitled to Fourteenth Amendment protection.

This conclusion, however, does not of itself fully answer the contentions raised by Texas, and we pass on to other considerations.

The pregnant woman cannot be isolated in her privacy. She carries an embryo and, later, a fetus, if one accepts the medical definitions of the developing young in the human uterus. The situation therefore is inherently different from marital intimacy, or bedroom possession of obscene material, or marriage, or procreation, or education, with which *Eisenstadt* and *Griswold*, *Stanley*, *Loving*, *Skinner*, and *Pierce* and *Meyer* were respectively concerned. As we have intimated above, it is reasonable and appropriate for a State to decide that at some point in time another interest, that of health of the mother or that of potential human life, becomes significantly involved. The woman's privacy is no longer sole and any right of privacy she possesses must be measured accordingly.

Texas urges that, apart from the Fourteenth Amendment, life begins at conception and is present throughout pregnancy, and that, therefore, the State has a compelling interest in protecting that life from and after conception. We need not resolve the difficult question of when life begins. When those trained in the respective disciplines of medicine, philosophy, and theology are unable to arrive at any consensus, the judiciary, at this point in the development of man's knowledge, is not in a position to speculate as to the answer.

It should be sufficient to note briefly the wide divergence of thinking on this most sensitive and difficult question. There has always been strong support for the view that life does not begin until live birth. This was the belief of the Stoics. It appears to be the predominant, though not the unanimous, attitude of the Jewish faith. It may be taken to represent also the position of a large segment of the Protestant community, insofar as that can be ascertained; organized groups that have taken a formal position on the abortion issue have generally regarded abortion as a matter for the conscience of the individual and her family. As we have noted, the common law found greater significance in quickening. Physicians and their scientific colleagues have regarded that event with less interest and have tended to focus either upon conception, upon live birth, or upon the interim point at which the fetus becomes "viable," that is, potentially able to live outside the mother's womb, albeit with artificial aid. Viability is usually placed at about seven months (28 weeks) but may occur earlier, even at 24 weeks. The Aristotelian theory of "mediate animation," that held sway throughout the Middle Ages and the Renaissance in Europe, continued to be official Roman Catholic dogma until the 19th century, despite opposition to this "ensoulment" theory from those in the Church who would recognize the existence of life from the moment of conception. Substantial problems for precise definition of this view are posed, however, by new embryological data that purport to indicate that conception is a "process" over time, rather than an event, and by new medical techniques such as menstrual extraction, the "morning-after" pill, implantation of embryos, artificial insemination, and even artificial wombs.

In view of all this, we do not agree that, by adopting one theory of life, Texas may override the rights of the pregnant woman that are at stake. We repeat, however, that the State does have an important and legitimate interest in preserving and protecting the health of the pregnant woman, whether she be a resident of the State or a non-resident who seeks medical consultation and treatment there, and that it has still another important and legitimate interest in protecting the potentiality of human life. These interests are separate and distinct. Each grows in substantiality as the woman approaches term and, at a point during pregnancy, each becomes "compelling."

With respect to the State's important and legitimate interest in the health of the mother, the "compelling" point, in the light of present medical knowledge, is at approximately the end of the first trimester. This is so because of the now-established medical fact that until the end of the first trimester mortality in abortion may be less than mortality in normal childbirth. It follows that, from and after this point, a State may regulate the abortion procedure to the extent that the regulation reasonably relates to the preservation and protection of maternal health. Examples of permissible state regulation in this area are requirements as to the qualifications of the person who is to perform the abortion; as to the licensure of that person; as to the facility in which the procedure is to be performed, that is, whether it must be a hospital or may be a clinic or some other place of less-than-hospital status; as to the licensing of the facility; and the like.

This means, on the other hand, that, for the period of pregnancy prior to this "compelling" point, the attending physician, in consultation with his patient, is free to determine, without regulation by the State, that, in his medical judgment, the patient's pregnancy should be terminated. If that decision is reached, the judgment may be effectuated by an abortion free of interference by the State.

With respect to the State's important and legitimate interest in potential life, the "compelling" point is at viability. This is so because the fetus then presumably has the capability of meaningful life outside the mother's womb. State regulation protective of fetal life after viability thus has both logical and biological justifications. If the State is interested in protecting fetal life after viability, it may go so far as to proscribe abortion during that period, except when it is necessary to preserve the life or health of the mother.

Measured against these standards, Art. 1196 of the Texas Penal Code, in restricting legal abortions to those "procured or attempted by medical advice for the purpose of saving the life of the mother," sweeps too broadly. The statute makes no distinction between abortions performed early in pregnancy and those performed later, and it limits to a single reason, "saving" the mother's life, the legal justification for the procedure. The statute, therefore, cannot survive the constitutional attack made upon it here.

This conclusion makes it unnecessary for us to consider the additional challenge to the Texas statute asserted on grounds of vagueness. See *United States v. Vuitch*.

To summarize and to repeat:

> 1. A state criminal abortion statute of the current Texas type, that excepts from criminality only a lifesaving procedure on behalf of the mother, without regard to pregnancy stage and without recognition of the other interests involved, is violative of the Due Process Clause of the Fourteenth Amendment.
>
> (a) For the stage prior to approximately the end of the first trimester, the abortion decision and its effectuation must be left to the medical judgment of the pregnant woman's attending physician.
>
> (b) For the stage subsequent to approximately the end of the first trimester, the State, in promoting its interest in the health of the mother, may, if it chooses, regulate the abortion procedure in ways that are reasonably related to maternal health.
>
> (c) For the stage subsequent to viability, the State in promoting its interest in the

> potentiality of human life may, if it chooses, regulate, and even proscribe, abortion except where it is necessary, in appropriate medical judgment, for the preservation of the life or health of the mother.
>
> 2. The State may define the term "physician," as it has been employed in the preceding paragraphs of this Part XI of this opinion, to mean only a physician currently licensed by the State, and may proscribe any abortion by a person who is not a physician as so defined.

In *Doe v. Bolton*, procedural requirements contained in one of the modern abortion statutes are considered. That opinion and this one, of course, are to be read together.

This holding, we feel, is consistent with the relative weights of the respective interests involved, with the lessons and examples of medical and legal history, with the lenity of the common law, and with the demands of the profound problems of the present day. The decision leaves the State free to place increasing restrictions on abortion as the period of pregnancy lengthens, so long as those restrictions are tailored to the recognized state interests. The decision vindicates the right of the physician to administer medical treatment according to his professional judgment up to the points where important state interests provide compelling justifications for intervention. Up to those points, the abortion decision in all its aspects is inherently, and primarily, a medical decision, and basic responsibility for it must rest with the physician. If an individual practitioner abuses the privilege of exercising proper medical judgment, the usual remedies, judicial and intra-professional, are available.

The judgment of the District Court as to intervenor Hallford is reversed, and Dr. Hallford's complaint in intervention is dismissed. In all other respects, the judgment of the District Court is affirmed. Costs are allowed to the appellee.

MR. JUSTICE WHITE, *with whom* **MR. JUSTICE REHNQUIST** *joins, dissenting.*

At the heart of the controversy in these cases are those recurring pregnancies that pose no danger whatsoever to the life or health of the mother but are, nevertheless, unwanted for any one or more of a variety of reasons—convenience, family planning, economics, dislike of children, the embarrassment of illegitimacy, etc. The common claim before us is that, for any one of such reasons, or for no reason at all, and without asserting or claiming any threat to life or health, any woman is entitled to an abortion at her request if she is able to find a medical advisor willing to undertake the procedure.

The Court, for the most part, sustains this position: during the period prior to the time the fetus becomes viable, the Constitution of the United States values the convenience, whim, or caprice of the putative mother more than the life or potential life of the fetus; the Constitution, therefore, guarantees the right to an abortion as against any state law or policy seeking to protect the fetus from an abortion not prompted by more compelling reasons of the mother.

With all due respect, I dissent. I find nothing in the language or history of the Constitution to support the Court's judgment. The Court simply fashions and announces a new constitutional right for pregnant mothers and, with scarcely any reason or authority for its action, invests that right with sufficient substance to override most existing state abortion statutes. The upshot is that the people and the legislatures of the 50 States are constitutionally dissentitled to weigh the relative importance of the continued existence and development of the fetus, on the one hand, against a spectrum of possible impacts on the mother, on the other hand. As an exercise of raw judicial power, the Court perhaps has authority to do what it does today; but, in my view, its judgment is an improvident and extravagant exercise of the power of judicial review that the Constitution extends to this Court.

The Court apparently values the convenience of the pregnant mother more than the continued existence and development of the life or potential life that she carries. Whether or not I might agree with that marshaling of values, I can in no event join the Court's judgment because I find no constitutional warrant for imposing such an order of priorities on the people and legislatures of the States. In a sensitive area such as this, involving as it does issues over which reasonable men may easily and heatedly differ, I cannot accept the Court's exercise of its clear power of choice by interposing a constitutional barrier to state efforts to protect human life and by investing mothers and doctors with the constitutionally protected right to exterminate it. This issue, for the most part, should be left with the people and to the political processes the people have devised to govern their affairs.

It is my view, therefore, that the Texas statute is not constitutionally infirm because it denies abortions to those who seek to serve only their convenience, rather than to protect their life or health. Nor is this plaintiff, who claims no threat to her mental or physical health, entitled to assert the possible rights of those women whose pregnancy assertedly implicates their health. This, together with *United States v. Vuitch*, dictates reversal of the judgment of the District Court.

Likewise, because Georgia may constitutionally forbid abortions to putative mothers who, like the plaintiff in this case, do not fall within the reach of §26-1202(a) of its criminal code, I have no occasion, and the District Court had none, to consider the constitutionality of the procedural requirements of the Georgia statute as applied to those pregnancies posing substantial hazards to either life or health. I would reverse the judgment of the District Court in the Georgia case.

MR. JUSTICE REHNQUIST, *dissenting.*

The Court's opinion brings to the decision of this troubling question both extensive historical fact and a wealth of legal scholarship. While the opinion thus commands my respect, I find myself nonetheless in fundamental disagreement with those parts of it that invalidate the Texas statute in question, and therefore dissent.

I

The Court's opinion decides that a State may impose virtually no restriction on the performance of abortions during the first trimester of pregnancy. Our previous decisions indicate that a necessary predicate for such an opinion is a plaintiff who was in her first trimester of pregnancy at some time during the pendency of her lawsuit. While a party may vindicate his own constitutional rights, he may not seek vindication for the rights of others. (*Moose Lodge v. Irvis*; *Sierra Club v. Morton.*) The Court's statement of facts in this case makes clear, however, that the record in no way indicates the presence of such a plaintiff. We know only that plaintiff Roe at the time of filing her complaint was a pregnant woman; for aught that appears in this record, she may have been in her last trimester of pregnancy as of the date the complaint was filed.

Nothing in the Court's opinion indicates that Texas might not constitutionally apply its proscription of abortion as written to a woman in that stage of pregnancy. Nonetheless, the Court uses her complaint against the Texas statute as a fulcrum for deciding that States may impose virtually no restrictions on medical abortions performed during the first trimester of pregnancy. In deciding such a hypothetical lawsuit, the Court departs from the longstanding admonition that it should never "formulate a rule of constitutional law broader than is required by the precise facts to which it is to be applied." *Liverpool, New York & Philadelphia S.S. Co. v. Commissioners of Emigration.*

II

Even if there were a plaintiff in this case capable of litigating the issue which the Court decides, I would reach a conclusion opposite to that reached by the Court. I have difficulty in concluding, as the Court does, that the right of "privacy" is involved in this case. Texas, by the statute here challenged, bars the performance of a medical abortion by a licensed physician on a plaintiff such as Roe. A transaction resulting in an operation such as this is not "private" in the ordinary usage of that word. Nor is the "privacy" that the Court finds here even a distant relative of the freedom from searches and seizures protected by the Fourth Amendment to the Constitution, which the Court has referred to as embodying a right to privacy. *Katz v. United States.*

If the Court means by the term "privacy" no more than that the claim of a person to be free from unwanted state regulation of consensual transactions may be a form of "liberty" protected by the Fourteenth Amendment, there is no doubt that similar claims have been upheld in our earlier decisions on the basis of that liberty. I agree with the statement of Mr. Justice Stewart in his concurring opinion that the "liberty," against deprivation of which without due process the Fourteenth Amendment protects, embraces more than the rights found in the Bill of Rights. But that liberty is not guaranteed absolutely against deprivation, only against deprivation without due process of law. The test traditionally applied in the area of social and economic legislation is whether or not a law such as that challenged has a rational relation to a valid state objective. *Williamson v. Lee Optical Co.* The Due Process Clause of the Fourteenth Amendment undoubtedly does place a limit, albeit a broad one, on legislative power to enact laws such as this. If the Texas statute were to prohibit an abortion even where the mother's life is in jeopardy, I have little doubt that such a statute would lack a rational relation to a valid state objective under the test stated in Williamson. But the Court's sweeping invalidation of any restrictions on abortion during the first trimester is impossible to justify under that standard, and the conscious weighing of competing factors that the Court's opinion apparently substitutes for the established test is far more appropriate to a legislative judgment than to a judicial one.

The Court eschews the history of the Fourteenth Amendment in its reliance on the "compelling state interest" test. See *Weber v. Aetna Casualty & Surety Co.* (dissenting opinion). But the Court adds a new wrinkle to this test by transposing it from the legal considerations associated with the Equal Protection Clause of the Fourteenth Amendment to this case arising under the Due Process Clause of the Fourteenth Amendment. Unless I misapprehend the consequences of this transplanting of the "compelling state interest test," the Court's opinion will accomplish the seemingly impossible feat of leaving this area of the law more confused than it found it.

While the Court's opinion quotes from the dissent of Mr. Justice Holmes in *Lochner v. New York*, the result it reaches is more closely attuned to the majority opinion of Mr. Justice Peckham in that case. As in *Lochner* and similar cases applying substantive due process standards to

economic and social welfare legislation, the adoption of the compelling state interest standard will inevitably require this Court to examine the legislative policies and pass on the wisdom of these policies in the very process of deciding whether a particular state interest put forward may or may not be "compelling." The decision here to break pregnancy into three distinct terms and to outline the permissible restrictions the State may impose in each one, for example, partakes more of judicial legislation than it does of a determination of the intent of the drafters of the Fourteenth Amendment.

The fact that a majority of the States reflecting, after all, the majority sentiment in those States, have had restrictions on abortions for at least a century is a strong indication, it seems to me, that the asserted right to an abortion is not "so rooted in the traditions and conscience of our people as to be ranked as fundamental," *Snyder v. Massachusetts.* Even today, when society's views on abortion are changing, the very existence of the debate is evidence that the "right" to an abortion is not so universally accepted as the appellant would have us believe.

To reach its result, the Court necessarily has had to find within the scope of the Fourteenth Amendment a right that was apparently completely unknown to the drafters of the Amendment. As early as 1821, the first state law dealing directly with abortion was enacted by the Connecticut Legislature. By the time of the adoption of the Fourteenth Amendment in 1868, there were at least 36 laws enacted by state or territorial legislatures limiting abortion. While many States have amended or updated their laws, 21 of the laws on the books in 1868 remain in effect today. Indeed, the Texas statute struck down today was, as the majority notes, first enacted in 1857 and "has remained substantially unchanged to the present time."

There apparently was no question concerning the validity of this provision or of any of the other state statutes when the Fourteenth Amendment was adopted. The only conclusion possible from this history is that the drafters did not intend to have the Fourteenth Amendment withdraw from the States the power to legislate with respect to this matter.

III

Even if one were to agree that the case that the Court decides were here, and that the enunciation of the substantive constitutional law in the Court's opinion were proper, the actual disposition of the case by the Court is still difficult to justify. The Texas statute is struck down in toto, even though the Court apparently concedes that at later periods of pregnancy Texas might impose these selfsame statutory limitations on abortion. My understanding of past practice is that a statute found to be invalid as applied to a particular plaintiff, but not unconstitutional as a whole, is not simply "struck down" but is, instead, declared unconstitutional as applied to the fact situation before the Court. *Yick Wo v. Hopkins*; *Street v. New York*.

For all of the foregoing reasons, I respectfully dissent.

MAHER v. ROE

432 U.S. 464 (1977)

Opinion: Powell, joined by Burger, Stewart, White, Rehnquist, Stevens
Concurrence: Burger
Dissent: Brennan, joined by Marshall, Blackmun
Dissent: Marshall
Dissent: Blackmun, joined by Brennan, Marshall

In the following case, the Court considers whether or not citizens are entitled to funding for abortion as a matter of right. Sometimes, political theorists and lawyers distinguish between positive and negative rights. Negative rights are rights to be free from government coercion. In contrast, positive rights require the government to act affirmatively in some manner—by subsidizing an activity or providing a service, for example. As you read this opinion, consider whether the government has an obligation not only to protect negative rights, but also to provide positive rights. If there is a right to an abortion, should the government subsidize that right?

MR. JUSTICE POWELL *delivered the opinion of the Court.*

In *Beal v. Doe*, we hold today that Title XIX of the Social Security Act does not require the funding of nontherapeutic abortions as a condition of participation in the joint federal-state Medicaid program established by that statute. In this case, as a result of our decision in *Beal*, we must decide whether the Constitution requires a participating State to pay for nontherapeutic abortions when it pays for childbirth.

The Constitution imposes no obligation on the States to pay the pregnancy-related medical expenses of indigent women, or indeed to pay any of the medical expenses of indigents. But when a State decides to alleviate some of the hardships of poverty by providing medical care, the manner in which it dispenses benefits is subject to constitutional limitations. Appellees' claim is that Connecticut must accord equal treatment to both abortion and childbirth, and may not evidence a policy preference by funding only the medical expenses incident to childbirth. This challenge to the classifications established by the Connecticut regulation presents a question arising under the Equal Protection Clause of the Fourteenth Amendment. The basic framework of analysis of such a claim is well settled:

> We must decide, first, whether [state legislation] operates to the disadvantage of some suspect class or impinges upon a fundamental right explicitly or implicitly protected by the Constitution, thereby requiring strict judicial scrutiny. . . . If not, the [legislative] scheme must still be examined to determine whether it rationally furthers some legitimate, articulated state purpose and therefore does not constitute an invidious discrimination. . . .

San Antonio School Dist. v. Rodriguez. Applying this analysis here, we think the District Court erred in holding that the Connecticut regulation violated the Equal Protection Clause of the Fourteenth Amendment.

[II]

A

This case involves no discrimination against a suspect class. An indigent woman desiring an abortion does not come within the limited category of disadvantaged classes so recognized by our cases. Nor does the fact that the impact of the regulation falls upon those who cannot pay lead to a different conclusion. In a sense, every denial of welfare to an indigent creates a wealth classification as compared to nonindigents who are able to pay for the desired goods or services. But this Court has never held that

financial need alone identifies a suspect class for purposes of equal protection analysis. Accordingly, the central question in this case is whether the regulation "impinges upon a fundamental right explicitly or implicitly protected by the Constitution." The District Court read our decisions in *Roe v. Wade*, and the subsequent cases applying it, as establishing a fundamental right to abortion, and therefore concluded that nothing less than a compelling state interest would justify Connecticut's different treatment of abortion and childbirth. We think the District Court misconceived the nature and scope of the fundamental right recognized in *Roe*.

B

At issue in *Roe* was the constitutionality of a Texas law making it a crime to procure or attempt to procure an abortion, except on medical advice for the purpose of saving the life of the mother. Drawing on a group of disparate cases restricting governmental intrusion, physical coercion, and criminal prohibition of certain activities we concluded that the Fourteenth Amendment's concept of personal liberty affords constitutional protection against state interference with certain aspects of an individual's personal "privacy," including a woman's decision to terminate her pregnancy.

We held that only a compelling state interest would justify such a sweeping restriction on a constitutionally protected interest, and we found no such state interest during the first trimester. Even when judged against this demanding standard, however, the State's dual interest in the health of the pregnant woman and the potential life of the fetus were deemed sufficient to justify substantial regulation of abortions in the second and third trimesters.

The Texas law in *Roe* was a stark example of impermissible interference with the pregnant woman's decision to terminate her pregnancy. In subsequent cases, we have invalidated other types of restrictions, different in form but similar in effect, on the woman's freedom of choice. Thus, in *Planned Parenthood of Central Missouri v. Danforth*, we held that Missouri's requirement of spousal consent was unconstitutional because it granted [the husband] the right to prevent unilaterally, and for whatever reason, the effectuation of his wife's and her physician's decision to terminate her pregnancy.

Missouri had interposed an "*absolute obstacle* to a woman's decision that *Roe* held to be constitutionally protected from such interference." Although a state-created obstacle need not be absolute to be impermissible (*Doe v. Bolton*; *Carey v. Population Services International*), we have held that a requirement for a lawful abortion "is not unconstitutional unless it unduly burdens the right to seek an abortion." We therefore declined to rule on the constitutionality of a Massachusetts statute regulating a minor's access to an abortion until the state courts had had an opportunity to determine whether the statute authorized a parental veto over the minor's decision or the less burdensome requirement of parental consultation.

These cases recognize a constitutionally protected interest "in making certain kinds of important decisions" free from governmental compulsion. *Whalen v. Roe.*

The Connecticut regulation before us is different in kind from the laws invalidated in our previous abortion decisions. The Connecticut regulation places no obstacles—absolute or otherwise—in the pregnant woman's path to an abortion. An indigent woman who desires an abortion suffers no disadvantage as a consequence of Connecticut's decision to fund childbirth; she continues as before to be dependent on private sources for the service she desires. The State may have made

childbirth a more attractive alternative, thereby influencing the woman's decision, but it has imposed no restriction on access to abortions that was not already there. The indigency that may make it difficult—and in some cases, perhaps, impossible—for some women to have abortions is neither created nor in any way affected by the Connecticut regulation. We conclude that the Connecticut regulation does not impinge upon the fundamental right recognized in *Roe*.

C

Our conclusion signals no retreat from *Roe* or the cases applying it. There is a basic difference between direct state interference with a protected activity and state encouragement of an alternative activity consonant with legislative policy. Constitutional concerns are greatest when the State attempts to impose its will by force of law; the State's power to encourage actions deemed to be in the public interest is necessarily far broader.

This distinction is implicit in two cases cited in *Roe* in support of the pregnant woman's right under the Fourteenth Amendment. *Meyer v. Nebraska* involved a Nebraska law making it criminal to teach foreign languages to children who had not passed the eighth grade. Nebraska's imposition of a criminal sanction on the providers of desired services makes *Meyer* closely analogous to *Roe*. In sustaining the constitutional challenge brought by a teacher convicted under the law, the Court held that the teacher's "right thus to teach and the right of parents to engage him so to instruct their children" were "within the liberty of the Amendment." In *Pierce v. Society of Sisters*, the Court relied on *Meyer* to invalidate an Oregon criminal law requiring the parent or guardian of a child to send him to a public school, thus precluding the choice of a private school. Reasoning that the Fourteenth Amendment's concept of liberty "excludes any general power of the State to standardize its children by forcing them to accept instruction from public teachers only," the Court held that the law "unreasonably interfere[d] with the liberty of parents and guardians to direct the upbringing and education of children under their control."

Both cases invalidated substantial restrictions on constitutionally protected liberty interests: in *Meyer*, the parent's right to have his child taught a particular foreign language; in *Pierce*, the parent's right to choose private, rather than public school education. But neither case denied to a State the policy choice of encouraging the preferred course of action. Indeed, in *Meyer*, the Court was careful to state that the power of the State "to prescribe a curriculum" that included English and excluded German in its free public schools "is not questioned."

D

The question remains whether Connecticut's regulation can be sustained under the less demanding test of rationality that applies in the absence of a suspect classification or the impingement of a fundamental right. This test requires that the distinction drawn between childbirth and nontherapeutic abortion by the regulation be "rationally related" to a "constitutionally permissible" purpose. (*Lindsey v. Normet*; *Massachusetts Bd. of Retirement v. Murgia*.) We hold that the Connecticut funding scheme satisfies this standard.

The decision whether to expend state funds for nontherapeutic abortion is fraught with judgments of policy and value over which opinions are sharply divided. Our conclusion that the Connecticut regulation is constitutional is not based on

a weighing of its wisdom or social desirability, for this Court does not strike down state laws "because they may be unwise, improvident, or out of harmony with a particular school of thought." *Williamson v. Lee Optical Co.*, quoted in *Dandridge v. Williams*. Indeed, when an issue involves policy choices as sensitive as those implicated by public funding of nontherapeutic abortions, the appropriate forum for their resolution in a democracy is the legislature. We should not forget that "legislatures are ultimate guardians of the liberties and welfare of the people in quite as great a degree as the courts." *Missouri, K. & T.R. Co. v. May* (Holmes, J.).

In conclusion, we emphasize that our decision today does not proscribe government funding of nontherapeutic abortions. It is open to Congress to require provision of Medicaid benefits for such abortions as a condition of state participation in the Medicaid program. Also, under Title XIX as construed in *Beal v. Doe*, Connecticut is free—through normal democratic processes—to decide that such benefits should be provided. We hold only that the Constitution does not require a judicially imposed resolution of these difficult issues.

The judgment of the District Court is reversed, and the case is remanded for further proceedings consistent with this opinion.

It is so ordered.

MR. JUSTICE BRENNAN, *with whom* **MR. JUSTICE MARSHALL** *and* **MR. JUSTICE BLACKMUN** *join, dissenting.*

This Court reverses on the ground that "the District Court misconceived the nature and scope of the fundamental right recognized in *Roe* [*v. Wade*]," and therefore that Connecticut was not required to meet the "compelling interest" test to justify its discrimination against elective abortion, but only "the less demanding test of rationality that applies in the absence of . . . the impingement of a fundamental right." This holding, the Court insists, "places no obstacles—absolute or otherwise—in the pregnant woman's path to an abortion"; she is still at liberty to finance the abortion from "private sources." True, the State may [by funding childbirth] have made childbirth a more attractive alternative, thereby influencing the woman's decision, but it has imposed no restriction on access to abortions that was not already there. True, also, indigency "may make it difficult—and in some cases, perhaps impossible—for some women to have abortions," but that regrettable consequence "is neither created nor in any way affected by the Connecticut regulation."

But a distressing insensitivity to the plight of impoverished pregnant women is inherent in the Court's analysis. The stark reality for too many, not just "some," indigent pregnant women is that indigency makes access to competent licensed physicians not merely "difficult," but "impossible." As a practical matter, many indigent women will feel they have no choice but to carry their pregnancies to term because the State will pay for the associated medical services, even though they would have chosen to have abortions if the State had also provided funds for that procedure, or indeed if the State had provided funds for neither procedure. This disparity in funding by the State clearly operates to coerce indigent pregnant women to bear children they would not otherwise choose to have, and just as clearly, this coercion can only operate upon the poor, who are uniquely the victims of this form of financial pressure. Mr. Justice Frankfurter's words are apt:

> "To sanction such a ruthless consequence, inevitably resulting from a money hurdle erected by the State, would justify a latter-day Anatole France to add one more item to his ironic comments on the 'majestic equality' of the law. 'The law, in its majestic equality, forbids the rich as well as the poor to sleep under bridges, to beg in the streets, and to steal bread.'. . . ." *Griffin v. Illinois.*

The Court's premise is that only an equal protection claim is presented here. Claims of interference with enjoyment of fundamental rights have, however, occupied a rather protean position in our constitutional jurisprudence. Whether or not the Court's analysis may reasonably proceed under the Equal Protection Clause, the Court plainly errs in ignoring, as it does, the unanswerable argument of appellees, and the holding of the District Court, that the regulation unconstitutionally impinges upon their claim of privacy derived from the Due Process Clause.

Roe v. Wade and cases following it hold that an area of privacy invulnerable to the State's intrusion surrounds the decision of a pregnant woman whether or not to carry her pregnancy to term. The Connecticut scheme clearly impinges upon that, area of privacy by bringing financial pressures on indigent women that force them to bear children they would not otherwise have. . . . Yet the Court concludes that "the Connecticut regulation does not impinge upon [that] fundamental right." This conclusion is based on a perceived distinction, on the one hand, between the imposition of criminal penalties for the procurement of an abortion present in *Roe v. Wade* and *Doe v. Bolton* and the absolute prohibition present in *Planned Parenthood of Central Missouri v. Danforth*, and, on the other, the assertedly lesser inhibition imposed by the Connecticut scheme.

The last time our Brother Powell espoused the concept in an abortion case that . . . [t]here is a basic difference between direct state interference with a protected activity and state encouragement of an alternative activity consonant with legislative policy, the Court refused to adopt it. *Singleton v. Wulff*....

We have also rejected this approach in other abortion cases.... Most recently, also in a privacy case, the Court squarely reaffirmed that the right of privacy was fundamental, and that an infringement upon that right must be justified by a compelling state interest. *Carey v. Population Services International*.... In words that apply fully to Connecticut's statute, and that could hardly be more explicit, *Carey* stated: "'Compelling' is, of course, the key word; where a decision as fundamental as that whether to bear or beget a child is involved, regulations imposing a burden on it may be justified only by compelling state interests, and must be narrowly drawn to express only those interests." *Carey* relied specifically upon *Roe*, *Doe*, and *Planned Parenthood*, and interpreted them in a way flatly inconsistent with the Court's interpretation today: "The significance of these cases is that they establish that the same test must be applied to state regulations that burden an individual's right to decide to prevent conception or terminate pregnancy by substantially limiting access to the means of effectuating that decision as is applied to state statutes that prohibit the decision entirely."

Finally, cases involving other fundamental rights also make clear that the Court's concept of what constitutes an impermissible infringement upon the fundamental right of a pregnant woman to choose to have an abortion makes new law. We have repeatedly found that infringements of fundamental rights are not limited to outright denials of those rights.... Until today, I had not thought the nature of the fundamental right established in *Roe* was open to question, let alone susceptible of the interpretation advanced by the Court. The fact that the Connecticut scheme may not operate as an absolute bar preventing all indigent women from having abortions is not critical. What is critical is that the State has inhibited their fundamental right to make that choice free from state interference....

Bellotti v. Baird held, and the Court today agrees, that a state requirement is unconstitutional if it "unduly burdens the right to seek an abortion." Connecticut has "unduly" burdened the fundamental right of pregnant women to be free to choose to have an abortion because the State has advanced no compelling state interest to justify its interference in that choice.

BOWERS v. HARDWICK

478 U.S. 186 (1986)

Opinion: White, joined by Burger, Powell, Rehnquist, O Connor
Concurrence: Burger
Concurrence: Powell
Dissent: Blackmun, joined by Brennan, Marshall, Stevens
Dissent: Stevens, joined by Brennan, Marshall

So far, we have considered cases about women's reproductive autonomy, but now we turn to the question of whether the right to privacy protects the right of gay couples to have consensual sexual relations. You will notice that the challenged statute in this case, in banning sodomy, does not distinguish between heterosexual and homosexual couples. Nevertheless, both the majority and U.S. Supreme Court

Chief Justice Warren Burger concentrate exclusively on the law's prohibition on same-sex conduct. Notice also how in arguing for the constitutionality of this anti-sodomy law, both the majority and Chief Justice Burger attempt to narrow the right at issue to one specifically about consensual sodomy rather than about a more general right to privacy. We will revisit rights in matters of consensual sexual relations in the case of Lawrence v. Texas, *which, as you will see, overrules the decision in* Bowers v. Hardwick. *We will also revisit the case in Chapter 9, as it, like many of the cases in this book, raises both substantive due process and equal protection issues.*

JUSTICE WHITE *delivered the opinion of the Court.*

In August, 1982, respondent Hardwick (hereafter respondent) was charged with violating the Georgia statute criminalizing sodomy by committing that act with another adult male in the bedroom of respondent's home. . . .

This case does not require a judgment on whether laws against sodomy between consenting adults in general, or between homosexuals in particular, are wise or desirable. It raises no question about the right or propriety of state legislative decisions to repeal their laws that criminalize homosexual sodomy, or of state court decisions invalidating those laws on state constitutional grounds. The issue presented is whether the Federal Constitution confers a fundamental right upon homosexuals to engage in sodomy, and hence invalidates the laws of the many States that still make such conduct illegal, and have done so for a very long time. The case also calls for some judgment about the limits of the Court's role in carrying out its constitutional mandate.

We first register our disagreement with the Court of Appeals and with respondent that the Court's prior cases have construed the Constitution to confer a right of privacy that extends to homosexual sodomy and, for all intents and purposes, have decided this case. The reach of this line of cases was sketched in *Carey v. Population Services International. Pierce v. Society of Sisters* and *Meyer v. Nebraska* were described as dealing with childrearing and education; *Prince v. Massachusetts* with family relationships; *Skinner v. Oklahoma ex rel. Williamson* with procreation; *Loving v. Virginia* with marriage; *Griswold v. Connecticut* and *Eisenstadt v. Baird* with contraception; and *Roe v. Wade* with abortion. The latter three cases were interpreted as construing the Due Process Clause of the Fourteenth Amendment to confer a fundamental individual right to decide whether or not to beget or bear a child. *Carey v. Population Services International.*

Accepting the decisions in these cases and the above description of them, we think it evident that none of the rights announced in those cases bears any resemblance to the claimed constitutional right of homosexuals to engage in acts of sodomy that is asserted in this case. No connection between family, marriage, or procreation, on the one hand, and homosexual activity, on the other, has been demonstrated, either by the Court of Appeals or by respondent. Moreover, any claim that these cases nevertheless stand for the proposition that any kind of private sexual conduct between consenting adults is constitutionally insulated from state proscription is unsupportable. Indeed, the Court's opinion in *Carey* twice asserted that the privacy right, which the *Griswold* line of cases found to be one of the protections provided by the Due Process Clause, did not reach so far.

Precedent aside, however, respondent would have us announce, as the Court of Appeals did, a fundamental right to engage in homosexual sodomy. This we are quite unwilling to do. It is true that, despite the language of the Due Process Clauses of the

Fifth and Fourteenth Amendments, which appears to focus only on the processes by which life, liberty, or property is taken, the cases are legion in which those Clauses have been interpreted to have substantive content, subsuming rights that to a great extent are immune from federal or state regulation or proscription. Among such cases are those recognizing rights that have little or no textual support in the constitutional language.

Striving to assure itself and the public that announcing rights not readily identifiable in the Constitution's text involves much more than the imposition of the Justices' own choice of values on the States and the Federal Government, the Court has sought to identify the nature of the rights qualifying for heightened judicial protection. In *Palko v. Connecticut*, it was said that this category includes those fundamental liberties that are "implicit in the concept of ordered liberty," such that "neither liberty nor justice would exist if [they] were sacrificed."

It is obvious to us that neither of these formulations would extend a fundamental right to homosexuals to engage in acts of consensual sodomy. Proscriptions against that conduct have ancient roots. Sodomy was a criminal offense at common law, and was forbidden by the laws of the original 13 States when they ratified the Bill of Rights. Against this background, to claim that a right to engage in such conduct is "deeply rooted in this Nation's history and tradition" or "implicit in the concept of ordered liberty" is, at best, facetious.

Nor are we inclined to take a more expansive view of our authority to discover new fundamental rights imbedded in the Due Process Clause. The Court is most vulnerable and comes nearest to illegitimacy when it deals with judge-made constitutional law having little or no cognizable roots in the language or design of the Constitution.

That this is so was painfully demonstrated by the face-off between the Executive and the Court in the 1930's, which resulted in the repudiation of much of the substantive gloss that the Court had placed on the Due Process Clauses of the Fifth and Fourteenth Amendments. There should be, therefore, great resistance to expand the substantive reach of those Clauses, particularly if it requires redefining the category of rights deemed to be fundamental. Otherwise, the Judiciary necessarily takes to itself further authority to govern the country without express constitutional authority. The claimed right pressed on us today falls far short of overcoming this resistance.

Even if the conduct at issue here is not a fundamental right, respondent asserts that there must be a rational basis for the law, and that there is none in this case other than the presumed belief of a majority of the electorate in Georgia that homosexual sodomy is immoral and unacceptable. This is said to be an inadequate rationale to support the law. The law, however, is constantly based on notions of morality, and if all laws representing essentially moral choices are to be invalidated under the Due Process Clause, the courts will be very busy indeed. Even respondent makes no such claim, but insists that majority sentiments about the morality of homosexuality should be declared inadequate. We do not agree, and are unpersuaded that the sodomy laws of some 25 States should be invalidated on this basis.

Accordingly, the judgment of the Court of Appeals is

Reversed.

CHIEF JUSTICE BURGER, *concurring.*

I join the Court's opinion, but I write separately to underscore my view that, in constitutional terms, there is no such thing as a fundamental right to commit homosexual sodomy.

As the Court notes, the proscriptions against sodomy have very "ancient roots." Decisions of individuals relating to homosexual conduct have been subject to state intervention throughout the history of Western civilization. Condemnation of those practices is firmly rooted in Judeo-Christian moral and ethical standards. Homosexual sodomy was a capital crime under Roman law. During the English Reformation, when powers of the ecclesiastical courts were transferred to the King's Courts, the first English statute criminalizing sodomy was passed. Blackstone described "the infamous *crime against nature*" as an offense of "deeper malignity" than rape, a heinous act "the very mention of which is a disgrace to human nature," and "a crime not fit to be named." The common law of England, including its prohibition of sodomy, became the received law of Georgia and the other Colonies. In 1816, the Georgia Legislature passed the statute at issue here, and that statute has been continuously in force in one form or another since that time. To hold that the act of homosexual sodomy is somehow protected as a fundamental right would be to cast aside millennia of moral teaching.

This is essentially not a question of personal "preferences," but rather of the legislative authority of the State. I find nothing in the Constitution depriving a State of the power to enact the statute challenged here.

JUSTICE BLACKMUN, *with whom* **JUSTICE BRENNAN, JUSTICE MARSHALL,** *and* **JUSTICE STEVENS** *join, dissenting.*

This case is no more about "a fundamental right to engage in homosexual sodomy," as the Court purports to declare, than *Stanley v. Georgia* was about a fundamental right to watch obscene movies, or *Katz v. United States* was about a fundamental right to place interstate bets from a telephone booth. Rather, this case is about "the most comprehensive of rights and the right most valued by civilized men," namely, "the right to be let alone." *Olmstead v. United States* (Brandeis, J., dissenting).

I believe we must analyze respondent Hardwick's claim in the light of the values that underlie the constitutional right to privacy. If that right means anything, it means that, before Georgia can prosecute its citizens for making choices about the most intimate aspects of their lives, it must do more than assert that the choice they have made is an "abominable crime not fit to be named among Christians."

First, the Court's almost obsessive focus on homosexual activity is particularly hard to justify in light of the broad language Georgia has used. Unlike the Court, the Georgia Legislature has not proceeded on the assumption that homosexuals are so different from other citizens that their lives may be controlled in a way that would not be tolerated if it limited the choices of those other citizens. Rather, Georgia has provided that "[a] person commits the offense of sodomy when he performs or submits to any sexual act involving the sex organs of one person and the mouth or anus of another." The sex or status of the persons who engage in the act is irrelevant as a matter of state law. In fact, to the extent I can discern a legislative purpose for Georgia's 1968 enactment of §16-6-2, that purpose seems to have been to broaden the coverage of the law to reach heterosexual as well as homosexual activity. Michael Hardwick's standing may rest in significant part on Georgia's apparent willingness to enforce against homosexuals a law it seems not to have any desire to enforce against heterosexuals. But his claim that §16-6-2 involves an unconstitutional intrusion into his privacy and his right of intimate association does not depend in any way on his sexual orientation.

The Court concludes today that none of our prior cases dealing with various decisions that individuals are entitled to make free of governmental interference "bears any resemblance to the claimed constitutional right of homosexuals to engage in acts of sodomy that is asserted in this case." While it is true that these cases may be characterized by their connection to protection of the family, *see Roberts v. United States Jaycees*, the Court's conclusion that they extend no further than this boundary ignores the warning in *Moore v. East Cleveland* against "clos[ing] our eyes to the basic reasons why certain rights associated with the family have been accorded shelter under the Fourteenth Amendment's Due Process Clause." We protect those rights not because they contribute, in some direct and material way, to the general public welfare, but because they form so central a part of an individual's life. We protect the decision whether to have a child because parenthood alters so dramatically an individual's self-definition, not because of demographic considerations or the Bible's command to be fruitful and multiply. And we protect the family because it contributes so powerfully to the happiness of individuals, not because of a preference for stereotypical households.

The Court claims that its decision today merely refuses to recognize a fundamental right to engage in homosexual sodomy; what the Court really has refused to recognize is the fundamental interest all individuals have in controlling the nature of their intimate associations with others.

MICHAEL H. v. GERALD D.

491 U.S. 110 (1989)

Opinion: Scalia, joined by Rehnquist and by O'Connor, Kennedy in all but note 6
Concurrence: O'Connor, joined by Kennedy
Concurrence: Stevens
Dissent: Brennan, joined by Marshall, Blackmun
Dissent: White, joined by Brennan

In this case, we return to the question of whether a right to privacy is connected to a right of parenthood. In many ways the case directly relates to the cases from the previous section connecting substantive due process to the rights of families. As you read this case, consider how the Court's rulings in Maher v. Roe *and* Pierce v. Society of Sisters *relate to this modern understanding of substantive due process. Consider also what Justice Antonin Scalia says about "history and tradition" in footnote 6. How does this relate to a jurisprudence of constitutional rights?*

JUSTICE SCALIA *announced the judgment of the Court and delivered an opinion, in which* **THE CHIEF JUSTICE** *joins, and in all but note 6 of which* **JUSTICE O'CONNOR** *and* **JUSTICE KENNEDY** *join.*

Under California law, a child born to a married woman living with her husband is presumed to be a child of the marriage. The presumption of legitimacy may be rebutted only by the husband or wife, and then only in limited circumstances. The instant appeal presents the claim that this presumption infringes upon the due process rights of a man who wishes to establish his paternity of a child born to the wife of another man, and the claim that it infringes upon the constitutional right of the child to maintain a relationship with her natural father.

I

The facts of this case are, we must hope, extraordinary. On May 9, 1976, in Las Vegas, Nevada, Carole D., an international model, and Gerald D., a top executive in a French oil company, were married. The couple established a home in Playa del Rey, California, in which they resided as husband and wife when one or the other was not out of the country on business. In the summer of 1978, Carole became involved in an adulterous affair with a neighbor, Michael H. In September, 1980, she conceived a child, Victoria D., who was born on May 11, 1981. Gerald was listed as father on the birth certificate, and has always held Victoria out to the world as his daughter. Soon after delivery of the child, however, Carole informed Michael that she believed he might be the father.

In the first three years of her life, Victoria remained always with Carole, but found herself within a variety of quasi-family units. In October, 1981, Gerald moved to New York City to pursue his business interests, but Carole chose to remain in California. At the end of that month, Carole and Michael had blood tests of themselves and Victoria, which showed a 98.07% probability that Michael was Victoria's father. . . .

In November, 1982, rebuffed in his attempts to visit Victoria, Michael filed a filiation action in California Superior Court to establish his paternity and right to visitation. In March, 1983, the court appointed an attorney and guardian *ad litem* to represent Victoria's interests. Victoria then filed a cross-complaint asserting that, if she had more than one psychological or *de facto* father, she was entitled to maintain her filial relationship, with all of the attendant rights, duties, and obligations, with both.

In May, 1983, Carole filed a motion for summary judgment. . . . In April, 1984, Carole and Michael signed a stipulation that Michael was Victoria's natural father. . . .

In May, 1984, Michael and Victoria, through her guardian *ad litem*, sought visitation rights for Michael *pendente lite*. To assist in determining whether visitation would be in Victoria's best interests, the Superior Court appointed a psychologist to evaluate Victoria, Gerald, Michael, and Carole. The psychologist recommended that Carole retain sole custody, but that Michael be allowed continued contact with Victoria pursuant to a restricted visitation schedule. The court concurred, and ordered that Michael be provided with limited visitation privileges *pendente lite*.

On October 19, 1984, Gerald, who had intervened in the action, moved for summary judgment on the ground that . . . there were no triable issues of fact as to Victoria's paternity. This law provides that "the issue of a wife cohabiting with her husband, who is not impotent or sterile, is conclusively presumed to be a child of the marriage." . . . On January 28, 1985, having found that affidavits submitted by Carole and Gerald sufficed to demonstrate that the two were cohabiting at conception and birth, and that Gerald was neither sterile nor impotent, the Superior Court granted Gerald's motion for summary judgment, rejecting Michael's and Victoria's challenges to the constitutionality of §621. The court also denied their motions for continued visitation. . . .

III

. . . We address first the claims of Michael. At the outset, it is necessary to clarify what he sought and what he was denied. California law, like nature itself, makes no provision for dual fatherhood. Michael was seeking to be declared the father of Victoria. The immediate benefit he evidently sought to obtain from that status was visitation rights. But if Michael were successful in being declared the father, other rights would follow—most importantly, the right to be considered as the parent who should have custody....

... Michael contends as a matter of substantive due process that, because he has established a parental relationship with Victoria, protection of Gerald's and Carole's marital union is an insufficient state interest to support termination of that relationship. This argument is, of course, predicated on the assertion that Michael has a constitutionally protected liberty interest in his relationship with Victoria.

It is an established part of our constitutional jurisprudence that the term "liberty" in the Due Process Clause extends beyond freedom from physical restraint. (*Pierce v. Society of Sisters*; *Meyer v. Nebraska*.) Without that core textual meaning as a limitation, defining the scope of the Due Process Clause "has at times been a treacherous field for this Court," giving "reason for concern lest the only limits to . . . judicial intervention become the predilections of those who happen at the time to be Members of this Court." *Moore v. East Cleveland*.

In an attempt to limit and guide interpretation of the Clause, we have insisted not merely that the interest denominated as a "liberty" be "fundamental" (a concept that, in isolation, is hard to objectify), but also that it be an interest traditionally protected by our society. As we have put it, the Due Process Clause affords only those protections "so rooted in the traditions and conscience of our people as to be ranked as fundamental." *Snyder v. Massachusetts*. Our cases reflect "continual insistence upon respect for the teachings of history [and] solid recognition of the basic values

that underlie our society. . . ." *Griswold v. Connecticut*.

This insistence that the asserted liberty interest be rooted in history and tradition is evident, as elsewhere, in our cases according constitutional protection to certain parental rights. Michael reads the landmark case of *Stanley v. Illinois*, and the subsequent cases of *Quilloin v. Walcott*, *Caban v. Mohammed*, and *Lehr v. Robertson*, as establishing that a liberty interest is created by biological fatherhood plus an established parental relationship—factors that exist in the present case as well. We think that distorts the rationale of those cases. As we view them, they rest not upon such isolated factors but upon the historic respect—indeed, sanctity would not be too strong a term—traditionally accorded to the relationships that develop within the unitary family.

. . . Thus, the legal issue in the present case reduces to whether the relationship between persons in the situation of Michael and Victoria has been treated as a protected family unit under the historic practices of our society, or whether, on any other basis, it has been accorded special protection. We think it impossible to find that it has. In fact, quite to the contrary, our traditions have protected the marital family (Gerald, Carole, and the child they acknowledge to be theirs) against the sort of claim Michael asserts.

. . . What Michael asserts here is a right to have himself declared the natural father, and thereby to obtain parental prerogatives. What he must establish, therefore, is not that our society has traditionally allowed a natural father in his circumstances to establish paternity, but that it has traditionally accorded such a father parental rights, or at least has not traditionally denied them. Even if the law in all States had always been that the entire world could challenge the marital presumption and obtain a declaration as to who was the natural father, that would not advance Michael's claim. Thus, it is ultimately irrelevant, even for purposes of determining current social attitudes towards the alleged substantive right Michael asserts, that the present law in a number of States appears to allow the natural father—including the natural father who has not established a relationship with the child—the theoretical power to rebut the marital presumption. What counts is whether the States in fact award substantive parental rights to the natural father of a child conceived within, and born into, an extant marital union that wishes to embrace the child. We are not aware of a single case, old or new, that has done so. This is not the stuff of which fundamental rights qualifying as liberty interests are made.[6]

We do not understand why, having rejected our focus upon the societal tradition regarding the natural father's rights vis-à-vis a child whose mother is married to another man, Justice Brennan would choose to focus instead upon "parenthood." Why should the relevant category not be even more general—perhaps "family relationships"; or "personal relationships"; or even "emotional attachments in general"? Though the dissent has no basis for the level of generality it would select, we do: We refer to the most specific level at which a relevant tradition protecting, or denying protection to, the asserted right can be identified. If, for example, there were no societal tradition, either way, regarding the rights of the natural father of a child adulterously conceived, we would have to consult, and (if possible) reason from, the traditions regarding natural fathers in general. But there is such a more specific tradition, and it unqualifiedly denies protection to such a parent.

One would think that Justice Brennan would appreciate the value of consulting the most specific tradition available, since he acknowledges that "[e]ven if we can agree . . . that 'family' and 'parenthood' are part of the good life, it is absurd to assume that we can agree on the content of those terms and destructive to pretend that we do." Because such general traditions provide such imprecise guidance, they permit judges to dictate rather than discern the society's views. The need, if arbitrary decisionmaking is to be avoided, to adopt the most specific tradition as the point of reference—or at least to announce, as Justice Brennan declines to do, some other criterion for selecting among the innumerable relevant traditions that could be consulted—is well enough exemplified by the fact that in the present case Justice Brennan's opinion and Justice O'Connor's opinion, which disapproves this footnote, both appeal to the tradition, but on the basis of the tradition they select reach opposite results. Although assuredly having the virtue (if it be that) of leaving judges free to decide as they think best when the unanticipated occurs, a rule of law that binds neither by text nor by any particular, identifiable tradition is no rule of law at all.

Finally, we may note that this analysis is not inconsistent with the result in cases such as *Griswold v. Connecticut* or *Eisenstadt*

---

6. Justice Brennan criticized our methodology in using historical traditions specifically relating to the rights of an adulterous natural father, rather than inquiring more generally "whether parenthood is an interest that historically has received our attention and protection." There seems to us no basis for the contention that this methodology is "nove[l]." For example, in *Bowers v. Hardwick*, we noted that at the time the Fourteenth Amendment was ratified all but 5 of the 37 States had criminal sodomy laws, that all 50 of the States had such laws prior to 1961, and that 24 States and the District of Columbia continued to have them; and we concluded from that record, regarding that very specific aspect of sexual conduct, that "to claim that a right to engage in such conduct is 'deeply rooted in this Nation's history and tradition' or 'implicit in the concept of ordered liberty' is, at best, facetious." In *Roe v. Wade*, we spent about a fifth of our opinion negating the proposition that there was a longstanding tradition of laws proscribing abortion.

v. Baird. None of those cases acknowledged a longstanding and still extant societal tradition withholding the very right pronounced to be the subject of a liberty interest and then rejected it. Justice Brennan must do so here. In this case, the existence of such a tradition, continuing to the present day, refutes any possible contention that the alleged right is "so rooted in the traditions and conscience of our people as to be ranked as fundamental," *Snyder v. Massachusetts,* or "implicit in the concept of ordered liberty," *Palko v. Connecticut....*

IV

We have never had occasion to decide whether a child has a liberty interest, symmetrical with that of her parent, in maintaining her filial relationship. We need not do so here because, even assuming that such a right exists, Victoria's claim must fail. Victoria's due process challenge is, if anything, weaker than Michael's.

... Whatever the merits of the guardian *ad litem's* belief that such an arrangement can be of great psychological benefit to a child, the claim that a State must recognize multiple fatherhood has no support in the history or traditions of this country. Moreover, even if we were to construe Victoria's argument as forwarding the lesser proposition that, whatever her status *vis-à-vis* Gerald, she has a liberty interest in maintaining a filial relationship with her natural father, Michael, we find that, at best, her claim is the obverse of Michael's, and fails for the same reasons.

... We apply, therefore, the ordinary "rational relationship" test to Victoria's equal protection challenge. The primary rationale underlying §621's limitation on those who may rebut the presumption of legitimacy is a concern that allowing persons other than the husband or wife to do so may undermine the integrity of the marital union. When the husband or wife contests the legitimacy of their child, the stability of the marriage has already been shaken. In contrast, allowing a claim of illegitimacy to be pressed by the child—or, more accurately, by a court-appointed guardian *ad litem*—may well disrupt an otherwise peaceful union. Since it pursues a legitimate end by rational means, California's decision to treat Victoria differently from her parents is not a denial of equal protection.

The judgment of the California Court of Appeal is

Affirmed.

JUSTICE BRENNAN, *with whom* **JUSTICE MARSHALL** *and* **JUSTICE BLACKMUN** *join, dissenting.*

In a case that has yielded so many opinions as has this one, it is fruitful to begin by emphasizing the common ground shared by a majority of this Court. Five Members of the Court refuse to foreclose "the possibility that a natural father might ever have a constitutionally protected interest in his relationship with a child whose mother was married to, and cohabiting with, another man at the time of the child's conception and birth." Five Justices agree that the flaw inhering in a conclusive presumption that terminates a constitutionally protected interest without any hearing whatsoever is a procedural one. Four Members of the Court agree that Michael H. has a liberty interest in his relationship with Victoria, and one assumes for purposes of this case that he does.

In contrast, only one other Member of the Court fully endorses Justice Scalia's view of the proper method of analyzing questions arising under the Due Process Clause. Nevertheless, because the plurality opinion's exclusively historical analysis portends a significant and unfortunate departure from our prior cases and from sound constitutional decisionmaking, I devote a substantial portion of my discussion to it.

I

Once we recognized that the "liberty" protected by the Due Process Clause of the Fourteenth Amendment encompasses more than freedom from bodily restraint, today's plurality opinion emphasizes, the concept was cut loose from one natural limitation on its meaning. This innovation paved the way, so the plurality hints, for judges to substitute their own preferences for those of elected officials. Dissatisfied with this supposedly unbridled and uncertain state of affairs, the plurality casts about for another limitation on the concept of liberty.

It finds this limitation in "tradition." Apparently oblivious to the fact that this concept can be as malleable and as elusive as "liberty" itself, the plurality pretends that tradition places a discernible border around the Constitution. The pretense is seductive; it would be comforting to believe that a search for "tradition" involves nothing more idiosyncratic or complicated than poring through dusty volumes on American history. Yet, as Justice White observed in his dissent in *Moore v. East Cleveland*: "What the deeply rooted traditions of the country are is arguable." Indeed, wherever I would begin to look for an interest "deeply rooted in the country's traditions," one thing is certain: I would not stop (as does the plurality) at Bracton, or Blackstone, or Kent, or even the American Law Reports in conducting my search. Because reasonable people can disagree about the content of particular traditions, and because they can disagree even about which traditions are relevant to the definition of "liberty," the plurality has not found the objective boundary that it seeks.

Even if we could agree, moreover, on the content and significance of particular

traditions, we still would be forced to identify the point at which a tradition becomes firm enough to be relevant to our definition of liberty and the moment at which it becomes too obsolete to be relevant any longer. The plurality supplies no objective means by which we might make these determinations. Indeed, as soon as the plurality sees signs that the tradition upon which it bases its decision (the laws denying putative fathers like Michael standing to assert paternity) is crumbling, it shifts ground and says that the case has nothing to do with that tradition, after all. "[W]hat is at issue here," the plurality asserts after canvassing the law on paternity suits, "is not entitlement to a state pronouncement that Victoria was begotten by Michael." But that is precisely what is at issue here, and the plurality's last-minute denial of this fact dramatically illustrates the subjectivity of its own analysis.

It is ironic that an approach so utterly dependent on tradition is so indifferent to our precedents. Citing barely a handful of this Court's numerous decisions defining the scope of the liberty protected by the Due Process Clause to support its reliance on tradition, the plurality acts as though English legal treatises and the American Law Reports always have provided the sole source for our constitutional principles. They have not. Just as common-law notions no longer define the "property" that the Constitution protects, see *Goldberg v. Kelly*, neither do they circumscribe the "liberty" that it guarantees. On the contrary, "'[l]iberty' and 'property' are broad and majestic terms. They are among the '[g]reat [constitutional] concepts . . . purposely left to gather meaning from experience. . . . [T]hey relate to the whole domain of social and economic fact, and the statesmen who founded this Nation knew too well that only a stagnant society remains unchanged.'" *Board of Regents of State Colleges v. Roth.*

It is not that tradition has been irrelevant to our prior decisions. Throughout our decisionmaking in this important area runs the theme that certain interests and practices—freedom from physical restraint, marriage, childbearing, childrearing, and others—form the core of our definition of "liberty." Our solicitude for these interests is partly the result of the fact that the Due Process Clause would seem an empty promise if it did not protect them, and partly the result of the historical and traditional importance of these interests in our society. In deciding cases arising under the Due Process Clause, therefore, we have considered whether the concrete limitation under consideration impermissibly impinges upon one of these more generalized interests.

Today's plurality, however, does not ask whether parenthood is an interest that historically has received our attention and protection; the answer to that question is too clear for dispute. Instead, the plurality asks whether the specific variety of parenthood under consideration—a natural father's relationship with a child whose mother is married to another man—has enjoyed such protection.

If we had looked to tradition with such specificity in past cases, many a decision would have reached a different result. Surely the use of contraceptives by unmarried couples, *Eisenstadt v. Baird*, or even by married couples, *Griswold v. Connecticut*; the freedom from corporal punishment in schools, *Ingraham v. Wright*; the freedom from an arbitrary transfer from a prison to a psychiatric institution, *Vitek v. Jones*; and even the right to raise one's natural but illegitimate children, *Stanley v. Illinois*, were not "interest[s] traditionally protected by our society" at the time of their consideration by this Court. If we had asked, therefore, in *Eisenstadt*, *Griswold*, *Ingraham*, *Vitek*, or *Stanley* itself whether the specific

interest under consideration had been traditionally protected, the answer would have been a resounding "no." That we did not ask this question in those cases highlights the novelty of the interpretive method that the plurality opinion employs today.

The plurality's interpretive method is more than novel; it is misguided. It ignores the good reasons for limiting the role of "tradition" in interpreting the Constitution's deliberately capacious language. In the plurality's constitutional universe, we may not take notice of the fact that the original reasons for the conclusive presumption of paternity are out of place in a world in which blood tests can prove virtually beyond a shadow of a doubt who sired a particular child and in which the fact of illegitimacy no longer plays the burdensome and stigmatizing role it once did. Nor, in the plurality's world, may we deny "tradition" its full scope by pointing out that the rationale for the conventional rule has changed over the years . . . ; instead, our task is simply to identify a rule denying the asserted interest and not to ask whether the basis for that rule—which is the true reflection of the values undergirding it—has changed too often or too recently to call the rule embodying that rationale a "tradition." Moreover, by describing the decisive question as whether Michael's and Victoria's interest is one that has been "traditionally protected by our society," rather than one that society traditionally has thought important (with or without protecting it), and by suggesting that our sole function is to "discern the society's views," the plurality acts as if the only purpose of the Due Process Clause is to confirm the importance of interests already protected by a majority of the States. Transforming the protection afforded by the Due Process Clause into a redundancy mocks those who, with care and purpose, wrote the Fourteenth Amendment.

In construing the Fourteenth Amendment to offer shelter only to those interests specifically protected by historical practice, moreover, the plurality ignores the kind of society in which our Constitution exists. We are not an assimilative, homogeneous society, but a facilitative, pluralistic one, in which we must be willing to abide someone else's unfamiliar or even repellent practice because the same tolerant impulse protects our own idiosyncracies. Even if we can agree, therefore, that "family" and "parenthood" are part of the good life, it is absurd to assume that we can agree on the content of those terms and destructive to pretend that we do. In a community such as ours,

"liberty" must include the freedom not to conform. The plurality today squashes this freedom by requiring specific approval from history before protecting anything in the name of liberty.

The document that the plurality construes today is unfamiliar to me. It is not the living charter that I have taken to be our Constitution; it is instead a stagnant, archaic, hidebound document steeped in the prejudices and superstitions of a time long past. This Constitution does not recognize that times change, does not see that sometimes a practice or rule outlives its foundations. I cannot accept an interpretive method that does such violence to the charter that I am bound by oath to uphold.

PLANNED PARENTHOOD v. CASEY

505 U.S. 833 (1992)

Opinion: O'Connor, Kennedy and Souter, joined by Blackmun in Parts I, II, III, V-A, V-C, and VI and by Stevens in Part V-E

Partial Concurrence, Partial Dissent: Stevens

Partial Concurrence, Partial Dissent: Blackmun

Partial Concurrence, Partial Dissent: Rehnquist, joined by White, Scalia, Thomas

Partial Concurrence, Partial Dissent: Scalia, joined by Rehnquist, White, Thomas

As you will recall, in Roe v. Wade *the Court established a trimester framework for protecting a right to abortion. In this case, the Court considers several regulations on abortion, and suggests the inadequacy of the*

trimester framework in dealing with their potential constitutionality. The "undue burden" test proposed here replaces a clear rule, the trimester framework, with a standard. Consider how the less rule-based and more standard-based undue burden test stands in comparison to the trimester framework. Does this new standard weaken the right to an abortion? You might reflect here on the general differences between rules and standards in constitutional law and their implications for protecting rights.

Also as you read this case, pay attention to the opinion's concern about the legitimacy of the Court. U.S. Supreme Court Justice Sandra Day O'Connor writes, "A decision to overrule Roe's essential holding under the existing circumstances would address error, if error there was, at the cost of both profound and unnecessary damage to the Court's legitimacy, and to the Nation's commitment to the rule of law." Does the desire to preserve the Court's legitimacy provide strong support for the decision reached in this case? Should it influence the Court's decisions in general? Why or why not? As you consider this question, it might be helpful to think back to some of the issues raised in Chapter 1.

JUSTICE O'CONNOR, JUSTICE KENNEDY, *and* **JUSTICE SOUTER** *delivered the opinion of the Court.*

Liberty finds no refuge in a jurisprudence of doubt. Yet, 19 years after our holding that the Constitution protects a woman's right to terminate her pregnancy in its early stages [*Roe v. Wade*], that definition of liberty is still questioned. . . .

At issue in these cases are five provisions of the Pennsylvania Abortion Control Act. . . . The Act requires that a woman seeking an abortion give her informed consent prior to the abortion procedure, and specifies that she be provided with certain information at least 24 hours before the abortion is performed. For a minor to obtain an abortion, the Act requires the informed consent of one of her parents, but provides for a judicial bypass option if the minor does not wish to or cannot obtain a parent's consent. Another provision of the Act requires that, unless certain exceptions apply, a married woman seeking an abortion must sign a statement indicating that she has notified her husband of her intended abortion. The Act exempts compliance with these three requirements in the event of a "medical emergency". . . .

. . . [A]t oral argument in this Court, the attorney for the parties challenging the statute took the position that none of the enactments can be upheld without overruling *Roe v. Wade*. We disagree with that analysis; but we acknowledge that our decisions after *Roe* cast doubt upon the meaning and reach of its holding.

After considering the fundamental constitutional questions resolved by *Roe*, principles of institutional integrity, and the rule of stare decisis, we are led to conclude this: the essential holding of *Roe v. Wade* should be retained and once again reaffirmed.

It must be stated at the outset and with clarity that *Roe*'s essential holding, the holding we reaffirm, has three parts. First is a recognition of the right of the woman to choose to have an abortion before viability and to obtain it without undue interference from the State. Before viability, the State's interests are not strong enough to support a prohibition of abortion or the imposition of a substantial obstacle to the woman's effective right to elect the procedure. Second is a confirmation of the State's power to restrict abortions after fetal viability if the law contains exceptions for pregnancies which endanger the woman's life or health. And third is the principle that the State has legitimate interests from the outset of the pregnancy in protecting the health of the woman and the life of the fetus that may become a child. These principles do not contradict one another; and we adhere to each.

The inescapable fact is that adjudication of substantive due process claims may call upon the Court in interpreting the Constitution to exercise that same capacity which, by tradition, courts always have exercised: reasoned judgment. Its boundaries are not susceptible of expression as a simple rule. That does not mean we are free to invalidate state policy choices with which we disagree; yet neither does it permit us to shrink from the duties of our office. . . . Men and women of good conscience can disagree, and we suppose some always shall disagree, about the profound moral and spiritual implications of terminating a pregnancy, even in its earliest stage. Some of us as individuals find abortion offensive to our most basic principles of morality, but that cannot control our decision. Our obligation is to define the liberty of all, not to mandate our own moral code. The underlying constitutional issue is whether the State can resolve these philosophic questions in such a definitive way that a woman lacks all choice in the matter, except perhaps in those rare circumstances in which the pregnancy is itself a danger to her own life or health, or is the result of rape or incest.

Our law affords constitutional protection to personal decisions relating to marriage, procreation, contraception, family relationships, child rearing, and education. Our cases recognize the right of the individual, married or single, to be free from unwarranted governmental intrusion into matters so fundamentally affecting a person as the decision whether to bear or beget a child. Our precedents "have respected the private realm of family life which the state cannot enter." [*Prince v. Massachusetts.*] These matters, involving the most intimate and personal choices a person may make in a lifetime, choices central to personal dignity and autonomy, are central to the liberty protected by the Fourteenth Amendment. At the heart of liberty is the right to define one's own concept of existence, of meaning, of the universe, and of the mystery of human life. Beliefs about these matters could not define the attributes of personhood were they formed under compulsion of the State.

These considerations begin our analysis of the woman's interest in terminating her pregnancy, but cannot end it, for this reason: though the abortion decision may originate within the zone of conscience and belief, it is more than a philosophic exercise. Abortion is a unique act. It is an act fraught with consequences for others: for the woman who must live with the implications of her decision; for the persons who perform and assist in the procedure; for the spouse, family, and society which must confront the knowledge that these procedures exist, procedures some deem nothing short of an act of violence against innocent human life; and, depending on one's beliefs, for the life or potential life that is aborted. Though abortion is conduct, it does not follow that the State is entitled to proscribe it in all instances. That is because the liberty of the woman is at stake in a sense unique to the human condition, and so, unique to the law. Her suffering is too intimate and personal for the State to insist, without more, upon its own vision of the woman's role, however dominant that vision has been in the course of our history and our culture. The destiny of the woman must be shaped to a large extent on her own conception of her spiritual imperatives and her place in society. . . .

The obligation to follow precedent begins with necessity, and a contrary necessity marks its outer limit . . . we recognize that no judicial system could do society's work if it eyed each issue afresh in every case that raised it. Indeed, the very concept of the rule of law underlying our own Constitution requires such continuity over time that a respect for precedent is, by definition, indispensable.

We have seen how time has overtaken some of *Roe*'s factual assumptions: advances in maternal health care allow for abortions safe to the mother later in pregnancy than was true in 1973. . . . But these facts go only to the scheme of time limits on the realization of competing interests, and the divergences from the factual premises of 1973 have no bearing on the validity of *Roe*'s central holding, that viability marks the earliest point at which the State's interest in fetal life is constitutionally adequate to justify a legislative ban on nontherapeutic abortions. The soundness or unsoundness of that constitutional judgment in no sense turns on whether viability occurs at approximately 28 weeks, as was usual at the time of *Roe*, at 23 to 24 weeks, as it sometimes does today, or at some moment even slightly earlier in pregnancy, as it may if fetal respiratory capacity can somehow be enhanced in the future.

The Court's duty in the present case is clear. In 1973, it confronted the already-divisive issue of governmental power to limit personal choice to undergo abortion, for which it provided a new resolution based on the due process guaranteed by the Fourteenth Amendment. Whether or not a new social consensus is developing on that issue, its divisiveness is no less today than in 1973, and pressure to overrule the decision, like pressure to retain it, has grown only more intense. A decision to overrule *Roe*'s essential holding under the existing circumstances would address error, if error there was, at the cost of both profound and unnecessary damage to the Court's legitimacy, and to the Nation's commitment to the rule of law. It is therefore imperative to adhere to the essence of *Roe*'s original decision, and we do so today. . . .

From what we have said so far, it follows that it is a constitutional liberty of the woman to have some freedom to terminate her pregnancy. We conclude that the basic decision in *Roe* was based on a constitutional analysis which we cannot now repudiate. The woman's liberty is not so unlimited, however, that, from the outset, the State cannot show its concern for the life of the unborn and, at a later point in fetal development, the State's interest in life has sufficient force so that the right of the woman to terminate the pregnancy can be restricted.

. . . We conclude the line should be drawn at viability, so that, before that time, the woman has a right to choose to terminate her pregnancy. We adhere to

this principle for two reasons. First, as we have said, is the doctrine of stare decisis. Any judicial act of line-drawing may seem somewhat arbitrary, but *Roe* was a reasoned statement, elaborated with great care. We have twice reaffirmed it in the face of great opposition. . . . The second reason is that the concept of viability, as we noted in *Roe*, is the time at which there is a realistic possibility of maintaining and nourishing a life outside the womb, so that the independent existence of the second life can, in reason and all fairness, be the object of state protection that now overrides the rights of the woman. Consistent with other constitutional norms, legislatures may draw lines which appear arbitrary without the necessity of offering a justification. But courts may not. We must justify the lines we draw. And there is no line other than viability which is more workable. To be sure, as we have said, there may be some medical developments that affect the precise point of viability, but this is an imprecision within tolerable limits, given that the medical community and all those who must apply its discoveries will continue to explore the matter. The viability line also has, as a practical matter, an element of fairness. In some broad sense, it might be said that a woman who fails to act before viability has consented to the State's intervention on behalf of the developing child.

The woman's right to terminate her pregnancy before viability is the most central principle of *Roe v. Wade*. It is a rule of law and a component of liberty we cannot renounce.

On the other side of the equation is the interest of the State in the protection of potential life . . . it must be remembered that *Roe v. Wade* speaks with clarity in establishing not only the woman's liberty but also the State's "important and legitimate interest in potential life." That portion of the decision in *Roe* has been given too little acknowledgment and implementation by the Court in its subsequent cases. Those cases decided that any regulation touching upon the abortion decision must survive strict scrutiny, to be sustained only if drawn in narrow terms to further a compelling state interest. Not all of the cases decided under that formulation can be reconciled with the holding in *Roe* itself that the State has legitimate interests in the health of the woman and in protecting the potential life within her. In resolving this tension, we choose to rely upon *Roe*, as against the later cases. . . .

We reject the trimester framework, which we do not consider to be part of the essential holding of *Roe*. Measures aimed at ensuring that a woman's choice contemplates the consequences for the fetus do not necessarily interfere with the right recognized in *Roe*, although those measures have been found to be inconsistent with the rigid trimester framework announced in that case. A logical reading of the central holding in *Roe* itself, and a necessary reconciliation of the liberty of the woman and the interest of the State in promoting prenatal life, require, in our view, that we abandon the trimester framework as a rigid prohibition on all pre-viability regulation aimed at the protection of fetal life. The trimester framework suffers from these basic flaws: in its formulation, it misconceives the nature of the pregnant woman's interest; and in practice, it undervalues the State's interest in potential life, as recognized in *Roe*. . . .

Though the woman has a right to choose to terminate or continue her pregnancy before viability, it does not at all follow that the State is prohibited from taking steps to ensure that this choice is thoughtful and informed. Even in the earliest stages of pregnancy, the State may enact rules and regulations designed to encourage her to know that there are philosophic and social arguments of great weight that can be brought to bear in favor of continuing the pregnancy to full term, and that there are procedures and institutions to allow adoption of unwanted children as well as a certain degree of state assistance if the mother chooses to raise the child herself. . . . As our jurisprudence relating to all liberties save perhaps abortion has recognized, not every law which makes a right more difficult to exercise is, ipso facto, an infringement of that right. An example clarifies the point. We have held that not every ballot access limitation amounts to an infringement of the right to vote.

The abortion right is similar. Numerous forms of state regulation might have the incidental effect of increasing the cost or decreasing the availability of medical care, whether for abortion or any other medical procedure. The fact that a law which serves a valid purpose, one not designed to strike at the right itself, has the incidental effect of making it more difficult or more expensive to procure an abortion cannot be enough to invalidate it. Only where state regulation imposes an undue burden on a woman's ability to make this decision does the power of the State reach into the heart of the liberty protected by the Due Process Clause. . . .

A finding of an undue burden is a shorthand for the conclusion that a state regulation has the purpose or effect of placing a substantial obstacle in the path of a woman seeking an abortion of a nonviable fetus. A statute with this purpose is invalid because the means chosen by the State to further the interest in potential life must be calculated to inform the woman's free choice, not hinder it. . . . Understood another way, we answer the question, left open in previous opinions discussing the undue burden formulation, whether a law designed to further the State's interest in fetal life which imposes an undue burden on the woman's decision before fetal viability could be constitutional. The answer is no.

. . . [However], what is at stake is the woman's right to make the ultimate decision, not a right to be insulated from all others in doing so. Regulations which do no more than create a structural mechanism by which the State, or the parent or guardian of a minor, may express profound respect for the life of the unborn are permitted, if they are not a substantial obstacle to the woman's exercise of the right to choose. Unless it has that effect on her right of choice, a state measure designed to persuade her to choose childbirth over abortion will be upheld if reasonably related to that goal. Regulations designed to foster the health of a woman seeking an abortion are valid if they do not constitute an undue burden.

The Court of Appeals applied what it believed to be the undue burden standard, and upheld each of the provisions except for the husband notification requirement. We agree generally with this conclusion, but refine the undue burden analysis in accordance with the principles articulated above. . . . [The Court then turns to the specifics of the Pennsylvania statute.]

For each abortion performed, a report must be filed identifying: the physician (and the second physician where required); the facility; the referring physician or agency; the woman's age; the number of prior pregnancies and prior abortions she has had; gestational age; the type of abortion procedure; the date of the abortion; whether there were any preexisting medical conditions which would complicate pregnancy; medical complications with the abortion; where applicable, the basis for the determination that the abortion was medically necessary; the weight of the aborted fetus; and whether the woman was married, and if so, whether notice was provided or the basis for the failure to give notice. Every abortion facility must also file quarterly reports showing the number of abortions performed broken down by trimester. In all events, the identity of each woman who has had an abortion remains confidential. . . .

In *Danforth*, we held that recordkeeping and reporting provisions that are reasonably directed to the preservation of maternal health and that properly respect a patient's confidentiality and privacy are permissible. We think that, under this standard, all the provisions at issue here except that relating to spousal notice are constitutional. Although they do not relate to the State's interest in informing the woman's choice, they do relate to health. . . . Nor do we find that the requirements impose a substantial obstacle to a woman's choice. At most, they might increase the cost of some abortions by a slight amount. While at some point increased cost could become a substantial obstacle, there is no such showing on the record before us. . . .

Our Constitution is a covenant running from the first generation of Americans to us, and then to future generations. It is a coherent succession. Each generation must learn anew that the Constitution's written terms embody ideas and aspirations that must survive more ages than one. We accept our responsibility not to retreat from interpreting the full meaning of the covenant in light of all of our precedents. We invoke it once again to define the freedom guaranteed by the Constitution's own promise, the promise of liberty.

JUSTICE BLACKMUN, *concurring in part, concurring in the judgment in part, and dissenting in part.*

. . . I do not underestimate the significance of today's joint opinion. Yet I remain steadfast in my belief that the right to reproductive choice is entitled to the full protection afforded by this Court before *Webster*. And I fear for the darkness as four Justices anxiously await the single vote necessary to extinguish the light. . . .

Make no mistake, the joint opinion of Justices O'Connor, Kennedy, and Souter is an act of personal courage and constitutional principle. In contrast to previous decisions in which Justices O'Connor and Kennedy postponed reconsideration of *Roe v. Wade*, the authors of the joint opinion today join Justice Stevens and me in concluding that "the essential holding of *Roe* should be retained and once again reaffirmed." . . .

Today, no less than yesterday, the Constitution and decisions of this Court require that a State's abortion restrictions be subjected to the strictest of judicial scrutiny. Our precedents and the joint opinion's principles require us to subject all non *de minimis* abortion regulations to strict scrutiny. Under this standard, the Pennsylvania statute's provisions requiring content based counseling, a 24-hour delay, informed parental consent, and reporting of abortion related information must be invalidated. . . .

But, we are reassured, there is always the protection of the democratic process. While there is much to be praised about our democracy, our country since its founding has recognized that there are certain fundamental liberties that are not to be left to the whims of an election. A woman's right to reproductive choice is one of those fundamental liberties. Accordingly, that liberty need not seek refuge at the ballot box.

In one sense, the Court's approach is worlds apart from that of The Chief Justice and Justice Scalia. And yet, in another sense, the distance between the two approaches is short—the distance is but a single vote.

I am 83 years old. I cannot remain on this Court forever, and when I do step down, the confirmation process for my successor well may focus on the issue before us today. That, I regret, may be exactly where the choice between the two worlds will be made.

JUSTICE SCALIA, *with whom* **THE CHIEF JUSTICE**, **JUSTICE WHITE**, *and* **JUSTICE THOMAS JOIN**, *concurring in the judgment in part and dissenting in part.*

. . . A State's choice between two positions on which reasonable people can disagree is constitutional even when (as is often the case) it intrudes upon a "liberty" in the absolute sense. . . .

That is, quite simply, the issue in this case: not whether the power of a woman to abort her unborn child is a "liberty" in the absolute sense; or even whether it is a liberty of great importance to many women. Of course it is both. The issue is whether it is a liberty protected by the Constitution of the United States. I am sure it is not. I reach that conclusion not because of anything so exalted as my views concerning the "concept of existence, of meaning, of the universe, and of the mystery of human life." *Ibid.* Rather, I reach it for the same reason I reach the conclusion that bigamy is not constitutionally protected—because of two simple facts: (1) the Constitution says absolutely nothing about it, and (2) the longstanding traditions of American society have permitted it to be legally proscribed. . . .

We should get out of this area, where we have no right to be, and where we do neither ourselves nor the country any good by remaining.

LAWRENCE v. TEXAS

539 U.S. 558 (2003)

Opinion: Kennedy, joined by Stevens,
   Souter, Ginsburg, Breyer
Concurrence: O'Connor
Dissent: Scalia, joined by Rehnquist,
   Thomas
Dissent: Thomas

Despite the defense of stare decisis (the notion that the Court should let previous decisions "stand") you just read in Planned Parenthood v. Casey, *the Supreme Court has the ability to reverse its own prior opinions.* Lawrence v. Texas *is a clear example of the Court reversing a previous precedent. In this case, the Supreme Court overturns its decision in* Bowers v. Hardwick *and broadens the right to privacy to matters of consensual sex. Specifically, the Court strikes down an ordinance banning sodomy among gay couples. What reasons does the Court give for reversing itself in such a dramatic fashion? In particular, pay attention to the relation between the Court's opinion in* Lawrence v. Texas *and U.S. Supreme Court Justice Harry Blackmun's dissent in* Bowers v. Hardwick.

Note too that the Court had the option of striking this law down solely on equal protection grounds and not expanding the doctrine of substantive due process. Should it have done so?

When the Court reverses a decision, prior dissents often play a large role in governing the reasoning of the reversal. What similarities are there between this opinion and Justice Blackmun's rejection of the idea that sodomy laws are about a right to narrow sexual acts as opposed to broader issues of privacy? You might consider the distinction again between rules and standards in comparing Bowers v. Hardwick *and* Lawrence v. Texas.

JUSTICE KENNEDY *delivered the opinion of the Court.*

Liberty protects the person from unwarranted government intrusions into a dwelling or other private places. In our tradition the State is not omnipresent in the home. And there are other spheres of our lives and existence, outside the home, where the State should not be a dominant presence. Freedom extends beyond spatial bounds. Liberty presumes an autonomy of self that includes freedom of thought, belief, expression, and certain intimate conduct. The instant case involves liberty of the person both in its spatial and more transcendent dimensions.

The question before the Court is the validity of a Texas statute making it a crime for two persons of the same sex to engage in certain intimate sexual conduct.

In Houston, Texas, officers of the Harris County Police Department were dispatched to a private residence in response to a reported weapons disturbance. They entered an apartment where one of the petitioners, John Geddes Lawrence, resided. The right of the police to enter does not seem to have been questioned. The officers observed Lawrence and another man, Tyron Garner, engaging in a sexual act. The two petitioners were arrested, held in custody over night, and charged and convicted before a Justice of the Peace.

The complaints described their crime as "deviate sexual intercourse, namely anal sex, with a member of the same sex (man)." The applicable state law is Tex. Penal Code Ann. §21.06(a). It provides: "A person commits an offense if he engages in deviate sexual intercourse with another individual of the same sex." The statute defines "[d]eviate sexual intercourse" as follows:

"(A) any contact between any part of the genitals of one person and the mouth or anus of another person; or

"(B) the penetration of the genitals or the anus of another person with an object."

The Court of Appeals for the Texas Fourteenth District considered the petitioners' federal constitutional arguments under both the Equal Protection and Due Process Clauses of the Fourteenth Amendment. After hearing the case en banc the court, in a divided opinion, rejected the constitutional arguments and affirmed the convictions.

We granted certiorari to consider three questions:

1. Whether Petitioners' criminal convictions under the Texas "Homosexual Conduct" law—which criminalizes sexual intimacy by same-sex couples, but not identical behavior by different-sex couples—violate the Fourteenth Amendment guarantee of equal protection of laws?

2. Whether Petitioners' criminal convictions for adult consensual sexual intimacy in the home violate their vital interests in liberty and privacy protected by the Due Process Clause of the Fourteenth Amendment?

3. Whether *Bowers v. Hardwick* should be overruled? We conclude the case should be resolved by determining whether the petitioners were free as adults to engage in the private conduct in the exercise of their liberty under the Due Process Clause of the Fourteenth Amendment to the Constitution. For this inquiry we deem it necessary to reconsider the Court's holding in *Bowers*.

There are broad statements of the substantive reach of liberty under the Due Process Clause in earlier cases, including *Pierce v. Society of Sisters* and *Meyer v. Nebraska*; but the most pertinent beginning point is our decision in *Griswold v. Connecticut*.

In *Griswold* the Court invalidated a state law prohibiting the use of drugs or devices of contraception and counseling or aiding and abetting the use of contraceptives. The Court described the protected interest as a right to privacy and placed emphasis on the marriage relation and the protected space of the marital bedroom. After *Griswold* it was established that the right to make certain decisions regarding sexual conduct extends beyond the marital relationship. In *Eisenstadt v. Baird*, the Court invalidated a law prohibiting the distribution of contraceptives to unmarried persons. The case was decided under the Equal Protection Clause; but with respect to unmarried persons, the Court went on to state the fundamental proposition that the law impaired the exercise of their personal rights. It quoted from the statement of the Court of Appeals finding the law to be in conflict with fundamental human rights, and it followed with this statement of its own:

"It is true that in *Griswold* the right of privacy in question inhered in the marital relationship. . . . If the right of privacy means anything, it is the right of the *individual*, married or single, to be free from unwarranted governmental intrusion into matters so fundamentally affecting a person as the decision whether to bear or beget a child."

The opinions in *Griswold* and *Eisenstadt* were part of the background for the decision in *Roe v. Wade*. As is well known, the case involved a challenge to the Texas law prohibiting abortions, but the laws of other States were affected as well. Although the Court held the woman's rights were not absolute, her right to elect an abortion did have real and substantial protection as an exercise of her liberty under the Due Process Clause. The Court cited cases that protect spatial freedom and cases that go well beyond it. *Roe* recognized the right of a woman to make certain fundamental decisions affecting her destiny and confirmed once more that the protection of liberty under the Due Process Clause has a substantive dimension of fundamental significance in defining the rights of the person.

The facts in *Bowers* had some similarities to the instant case. A police officer, whose right to enter seems not to have been in question, observed Hardwick, in his own bedroom, engaging in intimate sexual conduct with another adult male. The conduct was in violation of a Georgia statute making it a criminal offense to engage in sodomy. One difference between the two cases is that the Georgia statute prohibited the conduct whether or not the participants were of the same sex, while the Texas statute, as we have seen, applies only to participants of the same sex. Hardwick was not prosecuted, but he brought an action in federal court to declare the state statute invalid. He alleged he was a practicing homosexual and that the criminal prohibition violated rights guaranteed to him by the Constitution. The Court, in an opinion by Justice White, sustained the Georgia law. Chief Justice Burger and Justice Powell joined the opinion of the Court and filed separate, concurring opinions. Four Justices dissented. The Court began its substantive discussion in *Bowers* as follows: "The issue presented is whether the Federal Constitution confers a fundamental right upon homosexuals to engage in sodomy and hence invalidates the laws of the many States that still make such conduct illegal and have done so for a very long time." That statement, we now conclude, discloses the Court's own failure to appreciate the extent of the liberty at stake. To say that the issue in *Bowers* was simply the right to engage in certain sexual conduct demeans the claim the individual put forward, just as it would demean a married couple were it to be said marriage is simply about the right to have sexual intercourse. The laws involved in *Bowers* and here are, to be sure, statutes that purport to do no more than prohibit a particular sexual act. Their penalties and purposes, though, have more far-reaching consequences, touching upon the most private human conduct, sexual behavior, and in the most private of places, the home. The statutes do seek to control a personal relationship that, whether or not entitled to formal recognition in the law, is within the liberty of persons to choose without being punished as criminals.

This, as a general rule, should counsel against attempts by the State, or a court, to define the meaning of the relationship or to set its boundaries absent injury to a person or abuse of an institution the law protects. It suffices for us to acknowledge that adults may choose to enter upon this relationship in the confines of their homes and their own private lives and still retain their dignity as free persons. When sexuality finds overt expression in intimate conduct with another person, the conduct can be but one element in a personal bond that is more enduring. The liberty protected by the Constitution allows homosexual persons the right to make this choice.

It must be acknowledged, of course, that the Court in *Bowers* was making the broader point that for centuries there have been powerful voices to condemn homosexual conduct as immoral. The condemnation has been shaped by religious beliefs, conceptions of right and acceptable behavior, and respect for the traditional family. For many persons these are not trivial concerns but profound and deep convictions accepted as ethical and moral principles to which they aspire and which thus determine the course of their lives. These considerations do not answer the question before us, however. The issue is whether the majority may use the power of the State to enforce these views on the whole society through operation of the criminal law. "Our obligation is to define the liberty of all, not to mandate our own moral code." *Planned*

Parenthood of Southeastern Pa. v. Casey. Two principal cases decided after *Bowers* cast its holding into even more doubt. In *Planned Parenthood of Southeastern Pa. v. Casey,* the Court reaffirmed the substantive force of the liberty protected by the Due Process Clause. The *Casey* decision again confirmed that our laws and tradition afford constitutional protection to personal decisions relating to marriage, procreation, contraception, family relationships, child rearing, and education. In explaining the respect the Constitution demands for the autonomy of the person in making these choices, we stated as follows:

> "These matters, involving the most intimate and personal choices a person may make in a lifetime, choices central to personal dignity and autonomy, are central to the liberty protected by the Fourteenth Amendment. At the heart of liberty is the right to define one's own concept of existence, of meaning, of the universe, and of the mystery of human life. Beliefs about these matters could not define the attributes of personhood were they formed under compulsion of the State."

Persons in a homosexual relationship may seek autonomy for these purposes, just as heterosexual persons do. The decision in *Bowers* would deny them this right.

The second post-*Bowers* case of principal relevance is *Romer v. Evans.* There the Court struck down class-based legislation directed at homosexuals as a violation of the Equal Protection Clause. *Romer* invalidated an amendment to Colorado's constitution which named as a solitary class persons who were homosexuals, lesbians, or bisexual either by "orientation, conduct, practices or relationships," and deprived them of protection under state antidiscrimination laws. We concluded that the provision was "born of animosity toward the class of persons affected" and further that it had no rational relation to a legitimate governmental purpose. As an alternative argument in this case, counsel for the petitioners and some *amici* contend that *Romer* provides the basis for declaring the Texas statute invalid under the Equal Protection Clause. That is a tenable argument, but we conclude the instant case requires us to address whether *Bowers* itself has continuing validity. Were we to hold the statute invalid under the Equal Protection Clause some might question whether a prohibition would be valid if drawn differently, say, to prohibit the conduct both between same-sex and different-sex participants.

Equality of treatment and the due process right to demand respect for conduct protected by the substantive guarantee of liberty are linked in important respects, and a decision on the latter point advances both interests. If protected conduct is made criminal and the law which does so remains unexamined for its substantive validity, its stigma might remain even if it were not enforceable as drawn for equal protection reasons. When homosexual conduct is made criminal by the law of the State, that declaration in and of itself is an invitation to subject homosexual persons to discrimination both in the public and in the private spheres. The central holding of *Bowers* has been brought in question by this case, and it should be addressed. Its continuance as precedent demeans the lives of homosexual persons.

The stigma this criminal statute imposes, moreover, is not trivial. The offense, to be sure, is but a class C misdemeanor, a minor offense in the Texas legal system. Still, it remains a criminal offense with all that imports for the dignity of the persons charged. The petitioners will bear on their record the history of their criminal convictions.

The foundations of *Bowers* have sustained serious erosion from our recent decisions in *Casey* and *Romer*. When our precedent has been thus weakened, criticism from other sources is of greater significance. In the United States criticism of *Bowers* has been substantial and continuing, disapproving of its reasoning in all respects, not just as to its historical assumptions.

The doctrine of *stare decisis* is essential to the respect accorded to the judgments of the Court and to the stability of the law. It is not, however, an inexorable command. *Payne v. Tennessee*. In *Casey* we noted that when a Court is asked to overrule a precedent recognizing a constitutional liberty interest, individual or societal reliance on the existence of that liberty cautions with particular strength against reversing course. The holding in *Bowers*, however, has not induced detrimental reliance comparable to some instances where recognized individual rights are involved. Indeed, there has been no individual or societal reliance on *Bowers* of the sort that could counsel against overturning its holding once there are compelling reasons to do so. *Bowers* itself causes uncertainty, for the precedents before and after its issuance contradict its central holding.

The rationale of *Bowers* does not withstand careful analysis. In his dissenting opinion in *Bowers*, Justice Stevens came to these conclusions:

> "Our prior cases make two propositions abundantly clear. First, the fact that the governing majority in a State has traditionally viewed a particular practice as immoral is not a sufficient reason for upholding a law prohibiting the practice; neither history nor tradition could save a law prohibiting miscegenation from constitutional attack. Second, individual decisions by married persons, concerning the intimacies of their physical relationship, even when not intended to produce offspring, are a form of 'liberty' protected by the Due Process Clause of the Fourteenth Amendment.

> Moreover, this protection extends to intimate choices by unmarried as well as married persons."

Justice Stevens' analysis, in our view, should have been controlling in *Bowers* and should control here. *Bowers* was not correct when it was decided, and it is not correct today. It ought not to remain binding precedent. *Bowers v. Hardwick* should be and now is overruled.

The present case does not involve minors. It does not involve persons who might be injured or coerced or who are situated in relationships where consent might not easily be refused. It does not involve public conduct or prostitution. It does not involve whether the government must give formal recognition to any relationship that homosexual persons seek to enter. The case does involve two adults who, with full and mutual consent from each other, engaged in sexual practices common to a homosexual lifestyle. The petitioners are entitled to respect for their private lives. The State cannot demean their existence or control their destiny by making their private sexual conduct a crime. Their right to liberty under the Due Process Clause gives them the full right to engage in their conduct without intervention of the government. "It is a promise of the Constitution that there is a realm of personal liberty which the government may not enter." *Casey*. The Texas statute furthers no legitimate state interest which can justify its intrusion into the personal and private life of the individual.

Had those who drew and ratified the Due Process Clauses of the Fifth Amendment or the Fourteenth Amendment known the components of liberty in its manifold possibilities, they might have been more specific. They did not presume to have this insight. They knew times can blind us to certain truths and later generations can see that laws once thought necessary and proper in fact serve only to oppress. As the Constitution endures, persons in every generation can invoke its principles in their own search for greater freedom.

The judgment of the Court of Appeals for the Texas Fourteenth District is reversed, and the case is remanded for further proceedings not inconsistent with this opinion.

JUSTICE SCALIA, *with whom* **THE CHIEF JUSTICE** *and* **JUSTICE THOMAS JOIN**, *dissenting.*

"Liberty finds no refuge in a jurisprudence of doubt." *Planned Parenthood of Southeastern Pa. v. Casey.* That was the Court's sententious response, barely more than a decade ago, to those seeking to overrule *Roe v. Wade.* The Court's response today, to those who have engaged in a 17-year crusade to overrule *Bowers v. Hardwick*, is very different. The need for stability and certainty presents no barrier.

Most of the rest of today's opinion has no relevance to its actual holding—that the Texas statute "furthers no legitimate state interest which can justify" its application to petitioners under rational-basis review . . . (overruling *Bowers* to the extent it sustained Georgia's anti-sodomy statute under the rational-basis test). Though there is discussion of "fundamental proposition[s]," . . . and "fundamental decisions," *ibid.* nowhere does the Court's opinion declare that homosexual sodomy is a "fundamental right" under the Due Process Clause; nor does it subject the Texas law to the standard of review that would be appropriate (strict scrutiny) if homosexual sodomy *were* a "fundamental right." Thus, while overruling the *outcome* of *Bowers*, the Court leaves strangely untouched its central legal conclusion: "[R]espondent would have us announce . . . a fundamental right to engage in homosexual sodomy. This we are quite unwilling

to do." 478 U.S., at 191. Instead the Court simply describes petitioners' conduct as "an exercise of their liberty"—which it undoubtedly is—and proceeds to apply an unheard-of form of rational-basis review that will have far-reaching implications beyond this case. . . .

I

I begin with the Court's surprising readiness to reconsider a decision rendered a mere 17 years ago in *Bowers v. Hardwick.* I do not myself believe in rigid adherence to *stare decisis* in constitutional cases; but I do believe that we should be consistent rather than manipulative in invoking the doctrine. Today's opinions in support of reversal do not bother to distinguish—or indeed, even bother to mention—the paean to *stare decisis* co-authored by three Members of today's majority in *Planned Parenthood v. Casey.* There, when *stare decisis* meant preservation of judicially invented abortion rights, the widespread criticism of *Roe* was strong reason to *reaffirm* it:

> "Where, in the performance of its judicial duties, the Court decides a case in such a way as to resolve the sort of intensely divisive controversy reflected in *Roe*[,] . . . its decision has a dimension that the resolution of the normal case does not carry. . . . [T]o overrule under fire in the absence of the most compelling reason . . . would subvert the Court's legitimacy beyond any serious question."

Today, however, the widespread opposition to *Bowers*, a decision resolving an issue as "intensely divisive" as the issue in *Roe*, is offered as a reason in favor of *overruling* it. Gone, too, is any "enquiry" (of the sort conducted in *Casey*) into whether the decision sought to be overruled has "proven 'unworkable.'"

Today's approach to *stare decisis* invites us to overrule an erroneously decided precedent (including an "intensely divisive" decision) *if:* (1) its foundations have been "eroded" by subsequent decisions . . . ; (2) it has been subject to "substantial and continuing" criticism, *ibid.*; and (3) it has not induced "individual or societal reliance" that counsels against overturning. . . . The problem is that *Roe* itself—which today's majority surely has no disposition to overrule—satisfies these conditions to at least the same degree as *Bowers.*

(1) A preliminary digressive observation with regard to the first factor: The Court's claim that *Planned Parenthood v. Casey, supra,* "casts some doubt" upon the holding in *Bowers* (or any other case, for that matter) does not withstand analysis. As far as its holding is concerned, *Casey* provided a *less* expansive right to abortion than did *Roe, which was already on the books when* Bowers *was decided.* And if the Court is referring not to the holding of *Casey,* but to the dictum of its famed sweet-mystery-of-life passage ("At the heart of liberty is the right to define one's own concept of existence, of meaning, of the universe, and of the mystery of human life"): That "casts some doubt" upon either the totality of our jurisprudence or else (presumably the right answer) nothing at all. I have never heard of a law that attempted to restrict one's "right to define" certain concepts; and if the passage calls into question the government's power to regulate *actions based on* one's self-defined "concept of existence, etc.," it is the passage that ate the rule of law.

I do not quarrel with the Court's claim that *Romer v. Evans* (1996) "eroded" the "foundations" of *Bowers'* rational-basis holding. But *Roe* and *Casey* have been equally "eroded" by *Washington v. Glucksberg,* which held that *only* fundamental rights which are "deeply rooted in

this Nation's history and tradition" qualify for anything other than rational basis scrutiny under the doctrine of "substantive due process." *Roe* and *Casey,* of course, subjected the restriction of abortion to heightened scrutiny without even attempting to establish that the freedom to abort *was* rooted in this Nation's tradition.

(2) *Bowers,* the Court says, has been subject to "substantial and continuing [criticism], disapproving of its reasoning in all respects, not just as to its historical assumptions." . . . Exactly what those nonhistorical criticisms are, and whether the Court even agrees with them, are left unsaid, although the Court does cite two books. Of course, *Roe* too (and by extension *Casey*) had been (and still is) subject to unrelenting criticism, including criticism from the two commentators cited by the Court today.

(3) That leaves, to distinguish the rock-solid, unamendable disposition of *Roe* from the readily overrulable *Bowers,* only the third factor. "[T]here has been," the Court says, "no individual or societal reliance on *Bowers* of the sort that could counsel against overturning its holding. . . ." . . . It seems to me that the "societal reliance" on the principles confirmed in *Bowers* and discarded today has been overwhelming. Countless judicial decisions and legislative enactments have relied on the ancient proposition that a governing majority's belief that certain sexual behavior is "immoral and unacceptable" constitutes a rational basis for regulation. We ourselves relied extensively on *Bowers* when we concluded, in *Barnes v. Glen Theatre, Inc.,* that Indiana's public indecency statute furthered "a substantial government interest in protecting order and morality," *ibid.* (plurality opinion); State laws against bigamy, same-sex marriage, adult incest, prostitution,

masturbation, adultery, fornication, bestiality, and obscenity are likewise sustainable only in light of *Bowers'* validation of laws based on moral choices. Every single one of these laws is called into question by today's decision; the Court makes no effort to cabin the scope of its decision to exclude them from its holding. The impossibility of distinguishing homosexuality from other traditional "morals" offenses is precisely why *Bowers* rejected the rational-basis challenge. "The law," it said, "is constantly based on notions of morality, and if all laws representing essentially moral choices are to be invalidated under the Due Process Clause, the courts will be very busy indeed."

What a massive disruption of the current social order, therefore, the overruling of *Bowers* entails. Not so the overruling of *Roe*, which would simply have restored the regime that existed for centuries before 1973, in which the permissibility of and restrictions upon abortion were determined legislatively State-by-State. *Casey*, however, chose to base its *stare decisis* determination on a different "sort" of reliance. "[P]eople," it said, "have organized intimate relationships and made choices that define their views of themselves and their places in society, in reliance on the availability of abortion in the event that contraception should fail." 505 U.S., at 856. This falsely assumes that the consequence of overruling *Roe* would have been to make abortion unlawful. It would not; it would merely have *permitted* the States to do so. Many States would unquestionably have declined to prohibit abortion, and others would not have prohibited it within six months (after which the most significant reliance interests would have expired). Even for persons in States other than these, the choice would not have been between abortion and childbirth, but between abortion nearby and abortion in a neighboring State.

To tell the truth, it does not surprise me, and should surprise no one, that the Court has chosen today to revise the standards of *stare decisis* set forth in *Casey*. It has thereby exposed *Casey's* extraordinary deference to precedent for the result-oriented expedient that it is.

AP photo / Joe Marquette

Decades after Roe v. Wade, *abortion remains a polarizing issue in American politics.*

GONZALES v. CARHART

550 U.S. 124 (2007)

Opinion: Kennedy, joined by Roberts, Scalia, Thomas, Alito
Concurrence: Thomas, joined by Scalia
Dissent: Ginsburg, joined by Stevens, Souter, Breyer

In Planned Parenthood v. Casey, *the Court established the undue burden standard for regulating abortion. As you read this case, consider whether the undue burden standard is distinct from what you believed it to be when you read* Planned Parenthood v. Casey. *How might this decision have been different had the Court applied the trimester framework established in* Roe v. Wade *rather than the undue burden standard? Finally, notice that this case concerns a law regulating the kinds of procedures doctors use with their patients. Should the special relationship between doctor and patient play any role in the Court's decision in this case?*

JUSTICE KENNEDY *delivered the opinion of the Court.*

These cases require us to consider the validity of the Partial-Birth Abortion Ban Act of 2003 (Act), a federal statute regulating abortion procedures. We conclude the Act should be sustained against the objections lodged by the broad, facial attack brought against it.

The Act proscribes a particular manner of ending fetal life, so it is necessary here to discuss abortion procedures in some detail.

Abortion methods vary depending to some extent on the preferences of the physician and, of course, on the term of the pregnancy and the resulting stage of the unborn child's development. Between 85 and 90 percent of the approximately 1.3 million abortions performed each year in the United States take place in the first three months of pregnancy, which is to say in the first trimester. The most common first-trimester abortion method is vacuum aspiration (otherwise known as suction curettage) in which the physician vacuums out the embryonic tissue. Early in this trimester an alternative is to use medication, such as mifepristone (commonly known as RU-486), to terminate the pregnancy. The Act does not regulate these procedures.

Of the remaining abortions that take place each year, most occur in the second trimester. The surgical procedure referred to as "dilation and evacuation" or "D&E" is the usual abortion method in this trimester. Although individual techniques for performing D&E differ, the general steps are the same.

A doctor must first dilate the cervix at least to the extent needed to insert surgical instruments into the uterus and to maneuver them to evacuate the fetus.

After sufficient dilation the surgical operation can commence. The doctor, often guided by ultrasound, inserts grasping forceps through the woman's cervix and into the uterus to grab the fetus. The doctor grips a fetal part with the forceps and pulls it back through the cervix and vagina, continuing to pull even after meeting resistance from the cervix. The friction causes the fetus to tear apart. For example, a leg might be ripped off the fetus as it is pulled through the cervix and out of the woman. The process of evacuating the fetus piece by piece continues until it has been completely removed. A doctor may make 10 to 15 passes with the forceps to evacuate the fetus in its entirety, though sometimes removal is completed with fewer passes. Once the fetus has been evacuated, the placenta and any remaining fetal material are suctioned or scraped out of the uterus.

Some doctors, especially later in the second trimester, may kill the fetus a day or two before performing the surgical evacuation. They inject digoxin or potassium chloride into the fetus, the umbilical cord, or the amniotic fluid. Fetal demise may cause contractions and make greater dilation possible. Once dead, moreover, the fetus' body will soften, and its removal will be easier.

The abortion procedure that was the impetus for the numerous bans on "partial-birth abortion," including the Act, is a variation of this standard D&E. For discussion purposes this D&E variation will be referred to as intact D&E. The main difference between the two procedures is that in intact D&E a doctor extracts the fetus intact or largely intact with only a few passes.

In an intact D&E procedure the doctor extracts the fetus in a way conducive to pulling out its entire body, instead of ripping it apart.

In 2003 . . . Congress passed the Act at issue here.

Congress found, among other things, that "[a] moral, medical, and ethical consensus exists that the practice of performing a partial-birth abortion . . . is a gruesome and inhumane procedure that is never medically necessary and should be prohibited."

The principles set forth in the joint opinion in *Planned Parenthood of Southeastern Pa. v. Casey*, did not find support from all those who join the instant opinion. Whatever one's views concerning the *Casey* joint opinion, it is evident a premise central to its conclusion—that the government has a legitimate and substantial interest in preserving and promoting fetal life—would

be repudiated were the Court now to affirm the judgments of the Courts of Appeals.

Casey involved a challenge to *Roe v. Wade*. The opinion contains this summary:

"It must be stated at the outset and with clarity that *Roe's* essential holding, the holding we reaffirm, has three parts. First is a recognition of the right of the woman to choose to have an abortion before viability and to obtain it without undue interference from the State. Before viability, the State's interests are not strong enough to support a prohibition of abortion or the imposition of a substantial obstacle to the woman's effective right to elect the procedure. Second is a confirmation of the State's power to restrict abortions after fetal viability, if the law contains exceptions for pregnancies which endanger the woman's life or health. And third is the principle that the State has legitimate interests from the outset of the pregnancy in protecting the health of the woman and the life of the fetus that may become a child. These principles do not contradict one another; and we adhere to each."

Though all three holdings are implicated in the instant cases, it is the third that requires the most extended discussion; for we must determine whether the Act furthers the legitimate interest of the Government in protecting the life of the fetus that may become a child.

We assume the following principles for the purposes of this opinion. Before viability, a State "may not prohibit any woman from making the ultimate decision to terminate her pregnancy." It also may not impose upon this right an undue burden, which exists if a regulation's "purpose or effect is to place a substantial obstacle in the path of a woman seeking an abortion before the fetus attains viability." On the other hand, "[r]egulations which do no more than create a structural mechanism by which the State, or the parent or guardian of a minor, may express profound respect for the life of the unborn are permitted, if they are not a substantial obstacle to the woman's exercise of the right to choose." *Casey*, in short, struck a balance. The balance was central to its holding. We now apply its standard to the cases at bar.

Because D&E is the most common second-trimester abortion method, respondents suggest the Act imposes an undue burden. In this litigation the Attorney General does not dispute that the Act would impose an undue burden if it covered standard D&E.

We determine . . . [t]he Act prohibits intact D&E; and, notwithstanding respondents' arguments, it does not prohibit the D&E procedure in which the fetus is removed in parts.

The Act prohibits a doctor from intentionally performing an intact D&E. The dual prohibitions of the Act, both of which are necessary for criminal liability, correspond with the steps generally undertaken during this type of procedure. First, a doctor delivers the fetus until its head lodges in the cervix, which is usually past the anatomical landmark for a breech presentation. Second, the doctor proceeds to pierce the fetal skull with scissors or crush it with forceps. This step satisfies the overt-act requirement because it kills the fetus and is distinct from delivery.

The Act excludes most D&Es in which the fetus is removed in pieces, not intact. If the doctor intends to remove the fetus in parts from the outset, the doctor will not have the requisite intent to incur criminal liability. Removing the fetus in this manner does not violate the Act because the doctor will not have delivered the living fetus to one of the anatomical landmarks or committed an additional overt act that kills the fetus after partial delivery.

Under the principles accepted as controlling here, the Act, as we have interpreted it, would be unconstitutional "if its purpose or effect is to place a substantial obstacle in the path of a woman seeking an abortion before the fetus attains viability." The abortions affected by the Act's regulations take place both previability and postviability; so the quoted language and the undue burden analysis it relies upon are applicable. The question is whether the Act, measured by its text in this facial attack, imposes a substantial obstacle to late-term, but previability, abortions.

The Act proscribes a method of abortion in which a fetus is killed just inches before completion of the birth process. Congress stated as follows: "Implicitly approving such a brutal and inhumane procedure by choosing not to prohibit it will further coarsen society to the humanity of not only newborns, but all vulnerable and innocent human life, making it increasingly difficult to protect such life." The Act expresses respect for the dignity of human life.

Congress was concerned, furthermore, with the effects on the medical community and on its reputation caused by the practice of partial-birth abortion. The findings in the Act explain:

> "Partial-birth abortion . . . confuses the medical, legal, and ethical duties of physicians to preserve and promote life, as the physician acts directly against the physical life of a child, whom he or she had just delivered, all but the head, out of the womb, in order to end that life."

There can be no doubt the government "has an interest in protecting the integrity and ethics of the medical profession." Under our precedents it is clear the State has a significant role to play in regulating the medical profession.

Casey reaffirmed these governmental objectives. The government may use its voice and its regulatory authority to show its profound respect for the life within the woman. A central premise of the opinion was that the Court's precedents after *Roe* had "undervalue[d] the State's interest in potential life." The plurality opinion indicated "[t]he fact that a law which serves a valid purpose, one not designed to strike at the right itself, has the incidental effect of making it more difficult or more expensive to procure an abortion cannot be enough to invalidate it." This was not an idle assertion. The three premises of *Casey* must coexist. The third premise, that the State, from the inception of the pregnancy, maintains its own regulatory interest in protecting the life of the fetus that may become a child, cannot be set at naught by interpreting *Casey's* requirement of a health exception so it becomes tantamount to allowing a doctor to choose the abortion method he or she might prefer. Where it has a rational basis to act, and it does not impose an undue burden, the State may use its regulatory power to bar certain procedures and substitute others, all in furtherance of its legitimate interests in regulating the medical profession in order to promote respect for life, including life of the unborn.

The Act's ban on abortions that involve partial delivery of a living fetus furthers the Government's objectives. No one would dispute that, for many, D&E is a procedure itself laden with the power to devalue human life.

It is a reasonable inference that a necessary effect of the regulation and the knowledge it conveys will be to encourage some women to carry the infant to full term, thus reducing the absolute number of late-term abortions. The medical profession, furthermore, may find different and less shocking methods to abort the fetus in the second trimester, thereby accommodating legislative demand. The State's interest in respect for life is advanced by the dialogue that better informs the political and legal systems, the medical profession, expectant mothers, and society as a whole of the consequences that follow from a decision to elect a late-term abortion.

It is objected that the standard D&E is in some respects as brutal, if not more, than the intact D&E, so that the legislation accomplishes little. What we have already said, however, shows ample justification for the regulation. Partial-birth abortion, as defined by the Act, differs from a standard D&E because the former occurs when the fetus is partially outside the mother to the point of one of the Act's anatomical landmarks. It was reasonable for Congress to think that partial-birth abortion, more than standard D&E, "undermines the public's perception of the appropriate role of a physician during the delivery process, and perverts a process during which life is brought into the world."

The Act's furtherance of legitimate government interests bears upon, but does not resolve, the next question: whether the Act has the effect of imposing an unconstitutional burden on the abortion right because it does not allow use of the barred procedure where "necessary, in appropriate medical judgment, for [the] preservation of the . . . health of the mother." The prohibition in the Act would be unconstitutional, under precedents we here assume to be controlling, if it "subject[ed] [women] to significant health risks." . . .[W]hether the Act creates significant health risks for women has been a contested factual question. The evidence presented in the trial courts and before Congress demonstrates both sides have medical support for their position.

The question becomes whether the Act can stand when this medical uncertainty persists. The Court's precedents instruct that the Act can survive this facial attack. The Court has given state and federal legislatures wide discretion to pass legislation in areas where there is medical and scientific uncertainty.

Physicians are not entitled to ignore regulations that direct them to use reasonable alternative procedures. The law need not give abortion doctors unfettered choice in the course of their medical practice, nor should it elevate their status above other physicians in the medical community.

Medical uncertainty does not foreclose the exercise of legislative power in the abortion context any more than it does in other contexts. The medical uncertainty over whether the Act's prohibition creates significant health risks provides a sufficient basis to conclude in this facial attack that the Act does not impose an undue burden.

As the previous sections of this opinion explain, respondents have not demonstrated that the Act would be unconstitutional in a large fraction of relevant cases. It is neither our obligation nor within our traditional institutional role to resolve questions of constitutionality with respect to each potential situation that might develop.

Respondents have not demonstrated that the Act, as a facial matter, is void for vagueness, or that it imposes an undue burden on a woman's right to abortion based on its overbreadth or lack of a health exception. For these reasons the judgments of the Courts of Appeals for the Eighth and Ninth Circuits are reversed.

It is so ordered.

JUSTICE THOMAS, *with whom* **JUSTICE SCALIA JOINS**, *concurring.*

I join the Court's opinion because it accurately applies current jurisprudence, including *Planned Parenthood v. Casey*. I write separately to reiterate my view that the Court's abortion jurisprudence, including *Casey* and *Roe v. Wade*, has no basis in the Constitution. I also note that whether the Act constitutes a permissible exercise of Congress' power under the Commerce Clause is not before the Court. The parties

did not raise or brief that issue; it is outside the question presented; and the lower courts did not address it.

JUSTICE GINSBURG, *with whom* **JUSTICE STEVENS, JUSTICE SOUTER,** *and* **JUSTICE BREYER** *join, dissenting.*

In *Planned Parenthood of Southeastern Pa. v. Casey*, the Court declared that "[l]iberty finds no refuge in a jurisprudence of doubt." There was, the Court said, an "imperative" need to dispel doubt as to "the meaning and reach" of the Court's 7-to-2 judgment, rendered nearly two decades earlier in *Roe v. Wade*. Responsive to that need, the Court endeavored to provide secure guidance to "[s]tate and federal courts as well as legislatures throughout the Union," by defining "the rights of the woman and the legitimate authority of the State respecting the termination of pregnancies by abortion procedures."

Taking care to speak plainly, the *Casey* Court restated and reaffirmed *Roe*'s essential holding. First, the Court addressed the type of abortion regulation permissible prior to fetal viability. It recognized "the right of the woman to choose to have an abortion before viability and to obtain it without undue interference from the State." Second, the Court acknowledged "the State's power to restrict abortions *after fetal viability*, if the law contains exceptions for pregnancies which endanger the woman's life *or health*." Third, the Court confirmed that "the State has legitimate interests from the outset of the pregnancy in protecting *the health of the woman* and the life of the fetus that may become a child."

In reaffirming *Roe*, the *Casey* Court described the centrality of "the decision whether to bear . . . a child," *Eisenstadt v. Baird*, to a woman's "dignity and autonomy," her "personhood" and "destiny," her "conception of . . . her place in society." Of signal importance here, the *Casey* Court stated with unmistakable clarity that state regulation of access to abortion procedures, even after viability, must protect "the health of the woman."

Seven years ago, in *Stenberg v. Carhart*, the Court invalidated a Nebraska statute criminalizing the performance of a medical procedure that, in the political arena, has been dubbed "partial-birth abortion." With fidelity to the *Roe-Casey* line of precedent, the Court held the Nebraska statute unconstitutional in part because it lacked the requisite protection for the preservation of a woman's health.

Today's decision is alarming. It refuses to take *Casey* and *Stenberg* seriously. It tolerates, indeed applauds, federal intervention to ban nationwide a procedure found necessary and proper in certain cases by the American College of Obstetricians and Gynecologists. It blurs the line, firmly drawn in *Casey*, between previability and postviability abortions. And, for the first time since *Roe*, the Court blesses a prohibition with no exception safeguarding a woman's health.

I dissent from the Court's disposition. Retreating from prior rulings that abortion restrictions cannot be imposed absent an exception safeguarding a woman's health, the Court upholds an Act that surely would not survive under the close scrutiny that previously attended state-decreed limitations on a woman's reproductive choices.

I

A

As *Casey* comprehended, at stake in cases challenging abortion restrictions is a woman's "control over her [own] destiny." "There was a time, not so long ago," when women were "regarded as the center of home and family life, with attendant special responsibilities that precluded full and independent legal status under the Constitution." Those views, this Court made clear in *Casey*, "are no longer consistent with our understanding of the family, the individual, or the Constitution." Women, it is now acknowledged, have the talent, capacity, and right "to participate equally in the economic and social life of the Nation." Their ability to realize their full potential, the Court recognized, is intimately connected to "their ability to control their reproductive lives." Thus, legal challenges to undue restrictions on abortion procedures do not seek to vindicate some generalized notion of privacy; rather, they center on a woman's autonomy to determine her life's course, and thus to enjoy equal citizenship stature.

In keeping with this comprehension of the right to reproductive choice, the Court has consistently required that laws regulating abortion, at any stage of pregnancy and in all cases, safeguard a woman's health.... We have thus ruled that a State must avoid subjecting women to health risks not only where the pregnancy itself creates danger, but also where state regulation forces women to resort to less safe methods of abortion.

In *Stenberg*, we expressly held that a statute banning intact D&E was unconstitutional in part because it lacked a health exception. We noted that there existed a "division of medical opinion" about the relative safety of intact D&E, but we made clear that as long as "substantial medical authority supports the proposition that banning a particular abortion procedure could endanger women's health," a health exception is required. ... Thus, we reasoned, division in medical opinion "at most means uncertainty, a factor that signals the presence of risk, not its absence." "[A] statute that altogether forbids [intact D&E] . . . consequently must contain a health exception."

II

A

The Court offers flimsy and transparent justifications for upholding a nationwide ban on intact D&E *sans* any exception to safeguard a women's health. Today's ruling, the Court declares, advances "a premise central to [*Casey's*] conclusion"—*i.e.*, the Government's "legitimate and substantial interest in preserving and promoting fetal life." . . . But the Act scarcely furthers that interest: The law saves not a single fetus from destruction, for it targets only a *method* of performing abortion. See *Stenberg*. And surely the statute was not designed to protect the lives or health of pregnant women. . . . In short, the Court upholds a law that, while doing nothing to "preserv[e] . . . fetal life," bars a woman from choosing intact D&E although her doctor "reasonably believes [that procedure] will best protect [her]." *Stenberg*.

As another reason for upholding the ban, the Court emphasizes that the Act does not proscribe the nonintact D&E procedure. But why not, one might ask. Nonintact D&E could equally be characterized as "brutal," involving as it does "tear[ing] [a fetus] apart" and "ripp[ing] off" its limbs. "[T]he notion that either of these two equally gruesome procedures . . . is more akin to infanticide than the other, or that the State furthers any legitimate interest by banning one but not the other, is simply irrational." *Stenberg*.

Delivery of an intact, albeit nonviable, fetus warrants special condemnation, the Court maintains, because a fetus that is not dismembered resembles an infant. But so, too, does a fetus delivered intact after it is terminated by injection a day or two before the surgical evacuation, or a fetus delivered through medical induction or cesarean. Yet, the availability of those procedures—along with D&E by dismemberment—the Court says, saves the ban on intact D&E from a declaration of unconstitutionality. Never mind that the procedures deemed acceptable might put a woman's health at greater risk.

Ultimately, the Court admits that "moral concerns" are at work, concerns that could yield prohibitions on any abortion. . . . Notably, the concerns expressed are untethered to any ground genuinely serving the Government's interest in preserving life. By allowing such concerns to carry the day and case, overriding fundamental rights, the Court dishonors our precedent. . . .

Revealing in this regard, the Court invokes an antiabortion shibboleth for which it concededly has no reliable evidence: Women who have abortions come to regret their choices, and consequently suffer from "[s]evere depression and loss of esteem." Because of women's fragile emotional state and because of the "bond of love the mother has for her child," the Court worries, doctors may withhold information about the nature of the intact D&E procedure. The solution the Court approves, then, is *not* to require doctors to inform women, accurately and adequately, of the different procedures and their attendant risks. *Casey*. Instead, the Court deprives women of the right to make an autonomous choice, even at the expense of their safety.

This way of thinking reflects ancient notions about women's place in the family and under the Constitution—ideas that have long since been discredited. . . . Though today's majority may regard women's feelings on the matter as "self-evident," this Court has repeatedly confirmed that "[t]he destiny of the woman must be shaped . . . on her own conception of her spiritual imperatives and her place in society." *Casey*.

B

In cases on a "woman's liberty to determine whether to [continue] her pregnancy," this

Court has identified viability as a critical consideration. See *Casey*. . . . Today, the Court blurs that line, maintaining that "[t]he Act [legitimately] appl[ies] both previability and postviability because . . . a fetus is a living organism while within the womb, whether or not it is viable outside the womb." Instead of drawing the line at viability, the Court refers to Congress' purpose to differentiate "abortion and infanticide" based not on whether a fetus can survive outside the womb, but on where a fetus is anatomically located when a particular medical procedure is performed.

One wonders how long a line that saves no fetus from destruction will hold in face of the Court's "moral concerns." . . . The Court's hostility to the right *Roe* and *Casey* secured is not concealed. . . . Instead of the heightened scrutiny we have previously applied, the Court determines that a "rational" ground is enough to uphold the Act. And, most troubling, *Casey*'s principles, confirming the continuing vitality of "the essential holding of *Roe*," are merely "assume[d]" for the moment, rather than "retained" or "reaffirmed," *Casey*.

III

A

The Court further confuses our jurisprudence when it declares that "facial attacks" are not permissible in "these circumstances," *i.e.*, where medical uncertainty exists. ("In an as-applied challenge the nature of the medical risk can be better quantified and balanced than in a facial attack.") This holding is perplexing given that, in materially identical circumstances we held that a statute lacking a health exception was unconstitutional on its face. *Stenberg*.

Without attempting to distinguish *Stenberg* and earlier decisions, the majority

asserts that the Act survives review because respondents have not shown that the ban on intact D&E would be unconstitutional "in a large fraction of relevant cases." But *Casey* makes clear that, in determining whether any restriction poses an undue burden on a "large fraction" of women, the relevant class is *not* "all women," nor "all pregnant women," nor even all women "seeking abortions." Rather, a provision restricting access to abortion, "must be judged by reference to those [women] for whom it is an actual rather than an irrelevant restriction." . . . It makes no sense to conclude that this facial challenge fails because respondents have not shown that a health exception is necessary for a large fraction of second-trimester abortions, including those for which a health exception is unnecessary: The very purpose of a health *exception* is to protect women in *exceptional* cases. . . .

IV

As the Court wrote in *Casey*, "overruling *Roe*'s central holding would not only reach an unjustifiable result under principles of *stare decisis*, but would seriously weaken the Court's capacity to exercise the judicial power and to function as the Supreme Court of a Nation dedicated to the rule of law." "[T]he very concept of the rule of law underlying our own Constitution requires such continuity over time that a respect for precedent is, by definition, indispensable."

Though today's opinion does not go so far as to discard *Roe* or *Casey*, the Court, differently composed than it was when we last considered a restrictive abortion regulation, is hardly faithful to our earlier invocations of "the rule of law" and the "principles of *stare decisis*." . . . A decision so at odds with our jurisprudence should not have staying power.

In sum, the notion that the Partial-Birth Abortion Ban Act furthers any legitimate governmental interest is, quite simply, irrational. The Court's defense of the statute provides no saving explanation. In candor, the Act, and the Court's defense of it, cannot be understood as anything other than an effort to chip away at a right declared again and again by this Court—and with increasing comprehension of its centrality to women's lives. When "a statute burdens constitutional rights and all that can be said on its behalf is that it is the vehicle that legislators have chosen for expressing their hostility to those rights, the burden is undue." *Stenberg.*

For the reasons stated, I dissent from the Court's disposition and would affirm the judgments before us for review.

CRUZAN v. DIRECTOR, MISSOURI DEPARTMENT OF HEALTH

497 U.S. 261 (1990)

Opinion: Rehnqust, joined by White, O'Connor, Scalia, Kennedy
Concurrence: O'Connor
Concurrence: Scalia
Dissent: Brennan, joined by Marshall, Blackmun
Dissent: Stevens

In this case, the Court considers the right of an individual to terminate life support to a permanently incapacitated family member. One issue to consider is whether, in the event that the patient had clearly and demonstrably expressed a will not to be kept on life support, that patient's family has the right to terminate its usage. Arguably, this case shares with many of the other cases we have considered a concern with a right of privacy, but it also shares a special affinity with issues about the rights of families that we explored in Section B. Could one make an argument on behalf of Cruzan's family based on any of the education cases explored in that section? Is the Court correct in limiting the rights of families in the ways that it does in this case?

CHIEF JUSTICE REHNQUIST *delivered the opinion of the Court.*

Petitioner Nancy Beth Cruzan was rendered incompetent as a result of severe injuries sustained during an automobile accident. Co-petitioners Lester and Joyce Cruzan, Nancy's parents and coguardians, sought a court order directing the withdrawal of their daughter's artificial feeding and hydration equipment after it became apparent that she had virtually no chance of recovering her cognitive faculties. The Supreme Court of Missouri held that, because there was no clear and convincing evidence of Nancy's desire to have life-sustaining treatment withdrawn under such circumstances, her parents lacked authority to effectuate such a request. We granted certiorari and now affirm.

We granted certiorari to consider the question of whether Cruzan has a right under the United States Constitution which would require the hospital to withdraw life-sustaining treatment from her under these circumstances.

At common law, even the touching of one person by another without consent and without legal justification was a battery. Before the turn of the century, this Court observed that "[n]o right is held more sacred, or is more carefully guarded by the common law, than the right of every individual to the possession and control of his own person, free from all restraint or interference of others, unless by clear and unquestionable authority of law." This notion of bodily integrity has been embodied in the requirement that informed consent is generally required for medical treatment. Justice Cardozo, while on the Court of Appeals of New York, aptly described this doctrine: "Every human being of adult years and sound mind has a right to determine what shall be done with his own body, and a surgeon who performs an operation without his patient's consent commits an assault, for which he is liable in damages."

Most of the earlier cases involved patients who refused medical treatment forbidden by their religious beliefs, thus implicating First Amendment rights as well as common law rights of self-determination. More recently, however, with the advance of medical technology capable of sustaining life well past the point where natural forces would have brought certain death in earlier times, cases involving the right to refuse life-sustaining treatment have burgeoned.

In the *Quinlan* case, young Karen Quinlan suffered severe brain damage as the result of anoxia, and entered a persistent vegetative state. Karen's father sought judicial approval to disconnect his daughter's respirator. Noting that the State's interest "weakens and the individual's right to privacy grows as the degree of bodily invasion increases and the prognosis dims," the court concluded that the state interests had to give way in that case. The court also concluded that the "only practical way" to prevent the loss of Karen's privacy right due to her incompetence was to allow her guardian and family to decide "whether she would exercise it in these circumstances." Ibid.

After *Quinlan*, however, most courts have based a right to refuse treatment either solely on the common law right to informed consent or on both the common law right and a constitutional privacy right. Reasoning that an incompetent person retains the same rights as a competent individual "because the value of human dignity extends to both," the court adopted a "substituted judgment" standard whereby courts were to determine what an incompetent individual's decision would have been under the circumstances.

While recognizing that a federal right of privacy might apply in the case, the court, contrary to its approach in *Quinlan*, decided to base its decision on the common law right to self-determination and informed consent. "On balance, the right to self-determination ordinarily outweighs any countervailing state interests, and competent persons generally are permitted to refuse medical treatment, even at the risk of death. Most of the cases that have held otherwise, unless they involved the interest in protecting innocent third parties, have concerned the patient's competency to make a rational and considered choice."

Reasoning that the right of self-determination should not be lost merely because an individual is unable to sense a violation of it, the court held that incompetent individuals retain a right to refuse treatment. It also held that such a right could be exercised by a surrogate decisionmaker using a "subjective" standard when there was clear evidence that the incompetent person would have exercised it. Where such evidence was lacking, the court held that an individual's right could still be invoked in certain circumstances under objective "best interest" standards. Thus, if some trustworthy evidence existed that the individual would have wanted to terminate treatment, but not enough to clearly establish a person's wishes for purposes of the subjective standard, and the burden of a prolonged life from the experience of pain and suffering markedly outweighed its satisfactions, treatment could be terminated under a "limited-objective" standard. Where no trustworthy evidence existed, and a person's suffering would make the administration of life-sustaining treatment inhumane, a "pure-objective" standard could be used to terminate treatment. If none of these conditions obtained, the court held it was best to err in favor of preserving life.

The court also rejected certain categorical distinctions that had been drawn in prior refusal-of-treatment cases as lacking substance for decision purposes: the distinction between actively hastening death by terminating treatment and passively allowing a person to die of a disease; between treating individuals as an initial matter versus withdrawing treatment afterwards; between ordinary versus extraordinary treatment; and between treatment by artificial feeding versus other forms of life-sustaining medical procedures. As to the last item, the court acknowledged the "emotional significance" of food, but noted that feeding by implanted tubes is a "medical procedur[e] with inherent risks and possible side effects, instituted by skilled healthcare providers to compensate for impaired physical functioning" which analytically was equivalent to artificial breathing using a respirator.

In contrast to *Conroy*, the Court of Appeals of New York recently refused to accept less than the clearly expressed wishes of a patient before permitting the exercise of her right to refuse treatment by a surrogate decisionmaker. There, the court, over the objection of the patient's family members, granted an order to insert a feeding tube into a 77-year-old woman rendered incompetent as a result of several strokes. While continuing to recognize a common law right to refuse treatment,

the court rejected the substituted judgment approach for asserting it "because it is inconsistent with our fundamental commitment to the notion that no person or court should substitute its judgment as to what would be an acceptable quality of life for another. Consequently, we adhere to the view that, despite its pitfalls and inevitable uncertainties, the inquiry must always be narrowed to the patient's expressed intent, with every effort made to minimize the opportunity for error." The court held that the record lacked the requisite clear and convincing evidence of the patient's expressed intent to withhold life-sustaining treatment.

. . . [T]he common law doctrine of informed consent is viewed as generally encompassing the right of a competent individual to refuse medical treatment. Beyond that, these decisions demonstrate both similarity and diversity in their approach to decision of what all agree is a perplexing question with unusually strong moral and ethical overtones. State courts have available to them for decision a number of sources—state constitutions, statutes, and common law—which are not available to us. In this Court, the question is simply and starkly whether the United States Constitution prohibits Missouri from choosing the rule of decision which it did. This is the first case in which we have been squarely presented with the issue of whether the United States Constitution grants what is in common parlance referred to as a "right to die." We follow the judicious counsel of our decision in *Twin City Bank v. Nebeker*, where we said that, in deciding "a question of such magnitude and importance . . . it is the [better] part of wisdom not to attempt, by any general statement, to cover every possible phase of the subject."

The Fourteenth Amendment provides that no State shall "deprive any person of life, liberty, or property, without due process of law." The principle that a competent person has a constitutionally protected liberty interest in refusing unwanted medical treatment may be inferred from our prior decisions. In *Jacobson v. Massachusetts*, for instance, the Court balanced an individual's liberty interest in declining an unwanted smallpox vaccine against the State's interest in preventing disease. Decisions prior to the incorporation of the Fourth Amendment into the Fourteenth Amendment analyzed searches and seizures involving the body under the Due Process Clause and were thought to implicate substantial liberty interests. *Breithaupt v. Abram*.

Just this Term, in the course of holding that a State's procedures for administering antipsychotic medication to prisoners were sufficient to satisfy due process concerns, we recognized that prisoners possess "a significant liberty interest in avoiding the unwanted administration of antipsychotic drugs under the Due Process Clause of the Fourteenth Amendment." *Washington v. Harper*. Still other cases support the recognition of a general liberty interest in refusing medical treatment. (*Vitek v. Jones*; *Parham v. J.R.*)

But determining that a person has a "liberty interest" under the Due Process Clause does not end the inquiry; "whether respondent's constitutional rights have been violated must be determined by balancing his liberty interests against the relevant state interests." *Youngberg v. Romeo*.

Petitioners insist that, under the general holdings of our cases, the forced administration of life-sustaining medical treatment, and even of artificially-delivered food and water essential to life, would implicate a competent person's liberty interest. Although we think the logic of the cases discussed above would embrace such a liberty interest, the dramatic consequences involved in refusal of such treatment would inform the inquiry as to whether the deprivation of that interest is constitutionally permissible. But for purposes of this case, we assume that the United States Constitution would grant a competent person a constitutionally protected right to refuse lifesaving hydration and nutrition.

Petitioners go on to assert that an incompetent person should possess the same right in this respect as is possessed by a competent person. They rely primarily on our decisions in *Parham v. J.R.* and *Youngberg v. Romeo*. In *Parham*, we held that a mentally disturbed minor child had a liberty interest in "not being confined unnecessarily for medical treatment," but we certainly did not intimate that such a minor child, after commitment, would have a liberty interest in refusing treatment. In *Youngberg*, we held that a seriously retarded adult had a liberty interest in safety and freedom from bodily restraint. *Youngberg*, however, did not deal with decisions to administer or withhold medical treatment.

The difficulty with petitioners' claim is that, in a sense, it begs the question: an incompetent person is not able to make an informed and voluntary choice to exercise a hypothetical right to refuse treatment or any other right. Such a "right" must be exercised for her, if at all, by some sort of surrogate. Here, Missouri has in effect recognized that, under certain circumstances, a surrogate may act for the patient in electing to have hydration and nutrition withdrawn in such a way as to cause death, but it has established a procedural safeguard to assure that the action of the surrogate conforms as best it may to the wishes expressed by the patient while competent. Missouri requires that evidence of the incompetent's wishes as to the withdrawal of treatment be proved by clear and convincing evidence. The question, then, is whether the United States Constitution forbids the establishment of this procedural requirement by the State. We hold that it does not.

Whether or not Missouri's clear and convincing evidence requirement comports with the United States Constitution depends in part on what interests the State may properly seek to protect in this situation. Missouri relies on its interest in the protection and preservation of human life, and there can be no gainsaying this interest. As a general matter, the States—indeed, all civilized nations—demonstrate their commitment to life by treating homicide as serious crime. Moreover, the majority of States in this country have laws imposing criminal penalties on one who assists another to commit suicide. We do not think a State is required to remain neutral in the face of an informed and voluntary decision by a physically able adult to starve to death.

But in the context presented here, a State has more particular interests at stake. The choice between life and death is a deeply personal decision of obvious and overwhelming finality. We believe Missouri may legitimately seek to safeguard the personal element of this choice through the imposition of heightened evidentiary requirements. It cannot be disputed that the Due Process Clause protects an interest in life as well as an interest in refusing life-sustaining medical treatment. Not all incompetent patients will have loved ones available to serve as surrogate decisionmakers. And even where family members are present, "[t]here will, of course, be some unfortunate situations in which family members will not act to protect a patient." A State is entitled to guard against potential abuses in such situations. Similarly, a State is entitled to consider that a judicial proceeding to make a determination regarding an incompetent's wishes may very well not be an adversarial one, with the added guarantee of accurate factfinding that the adversary

process brings with it. *Ohio v. Akron Center for Reproductive Health.* Finally, we think a State may properly decline to make judgments about the "quality" of life that a particular individual may enjoy, and simply assert an unqualified interest in the preservation of human life to be weighed against the constitutionally protected interests of the individual.

In our view, Missouri has permissibly sought to advance these interests through the adoption of a "clear and convincing" standard of proof to govern such proceedings. "The function of a standard of proof, as that concept is embodied in the Due Process Clause and in the realm of factfinding, is to 'instruct the factfinder concerning the degree of confidence our society thinks he should have in the correctness of factual conclusions for a particular type of adjudication.'" *Addington v. Texas.* "This Court has mandated an intermediate standard of proof—'clear and convincing evidence'—when the individual interests at stake in a state proceeding are both 'particularly important' and 'more substantial than mere loss of money.'" *Santosky v. Kramer.*

We think it self-evident that the interests at stake in the instant proceedings are more substantial, both on an individual and societal level, than those involved in a run-of-the-mine civil dispute. But not only does the standard of proof reflect the importance of a particular adjudication, it also serves as "a societal judgment about how the risk of error should be distributed between the litigants." (*Santosky*; *Addington.*) The more stringent the burden of proof a party must bear, the more that party bears the risk of an erroneous decision. We believe that Missouri may permissibly place an increased risk of an erroneous decision on those seeking to terminate an incompetent individual's life-sustaining treatment. An erroneous decision not to terminate results in a maintenance of the status quo;

the possibility of subsequent developments such as advancements in medical science, the discovery of new evidence regarding the patient's intent, changes in the law, or simply the unexpected death of the patient despite the administration of life-sustaining treatment, at least create the potential that a wrong decision will eventually be corrected or its impact mitigated. An erroneous decision to withdraw life-sustaining treatment, however, is not susceptible of correction. In *Santosky*, one of the factors which led the Court to require proof by clear and convincing evidence in a proceeding to terminate parental rights was that a decision in such a case was final and irrevocable. The same must surely be said of the decision to discontinue hydration and nutrition of a patient such as Nancy Cruzan, which all agree will result in her death.

It is also worth noting that most, if not all, States simply forbid oral testimony entirely in determining the wishes of parties in transactions which, while important, simply do not have the consequences that a decision to terminate a person's life does. At common law and by statute in most States, the parol evidence rule prevents the variations of the terms of a written contract by oral testimony. The statute of frauds makes unenforceable oral contracts to leave property by will, and statutes regulating the making of wills universally require that those instruments be in writing.

In sum, we conclude that a State may apply a clear and convincing evidence standard in proceedings where a guardian seeks to discontinue nutrition and hydration of a person diagnosed to be in a persistent vegetative state. We note that many courts which have adopted some sort of substituted judgment procedure in situations like this, whether they limit consideration of evidence to the prior expressed wishes of the incompetent individual, or whether they allow more general proof of what the individual's decision would have been, require a clear and convincing standard of proof for such evidence....

The Supreme Court of Missouri held that, in this case, the testimony adduced at trial did not amount to clear and convincing proof of the patient's desire to have hydration and nutrition withdrawn. In so doing, it reversed a decision of the Missouri trial court, which had found that the evidence "suggest[ed]" Nancy Cruzan would not have desired to continue such measures, but which had not adopted the standard of "clear and convincing evidence" enunciated by the Supreme Court. The testimony adduced at trial consisted primarily of Nancy Cruzan's statements, made to a housemate about a year before her accident, that she would not want to live should she face life as a "vegetable," and other observations to the same effect. The observations did not deal in terms with withdrawal of medical treatment or of hydration and nutrition. We cannot say that the Supreme Court of Missouri committed constitutional error in reaching the conclusion that it did.

Petitioners alternatively contend that Missouri must accept the "substituted judgment" of close family members even in the absence of substantial proof that their views reflect the views of the patient. They rely primarily upon our decisions in *Michael H. v. Gerald D.* and *Parham v. J.R.* But we do not think these cases support their claim. In *Michael H.*, we upheld the constitutionality of California's favored treatment of traditional family relationships; such a holding may not be turned around into a constitutional requirement that a State must recognize the primacy of those relationships in a situation like this. And in *Parham*, where the patient was a minor, we also upheld the constitutionality of a state scheme in which parents made certain decisions for mentally ill minors. Here again, petitioners would seek to turn a decision which allowed a State to rely on family decisionmaking into a constitutional requirement that the State recognize such decisionmaking. But constitutional law does not work that way.

No doubt is engendered by anything in this record but that Nancy Cruzan's mother and father are loving and caring parents. If the State were required by the United States Constitution to repose a right of "substituted judgment" with anyone, the Cruzans would surely qualify. But we do not think the Due Process Clause requires the State to repose judgment on these matters with anyone but the patient herself. Close family members may have a strong feeling—a feeling not at all ignoble or unworthy, but not entirely disinterested, either—that they do not wish to witness the continuation of the life of a loved one which they regard as hopeless, meaningless, and even degrading. But there is no automatic assurance that the view of close family members will necessarily be the same as the patient's would have been had she been confronted with the prospect of her situation while competent. All of the reasons previously discussed for allowing Missouri to require clear and convincing evidence of the patient's wishes lead us to conclude that the State may choose to defer only to those wishes, rather than confide the decision to close family members.

The judgment of the Supreme Court of Missouri is

Affirmed.

JUSTICE BRENNAN, *with whom* **JUSTICE MARSHALL** *and* **JUSTICE BLACKMUN** *join, dissenting.*

. . . A grown woman at the time of the accident, Nancy had previously expressed her wish to forgo continuing medical care under circumstances such as these. Her family and her friends are convinced that this is what she would want. . . . Yet the Missouri Supreme Court, alone among state courts deciding such a question, has determined that an irreversibly vegetative patient will remain a passive prisoner of medical technology—for Nancy, perhaps for the next 30 years. . . .

I

A

The question before this Court is a relatively narrow one: whether the Due Process Clause allows Missouri to require a now-incompetent patient in an irreversible persistent vegetative state to remain on life-support absent rigorously clear and convincing evidence that avoiding the treatment represents the patient's prior, express choice. . . . If a fundamental right is at issue, Missouri's rule of decision must be scrutinized under the standards this Court has always applied in such circumstances. As we said in *Zablocki v. Redhail,* if a requirement imposed by a State "significantly interferes with the exercise of a fundamental right, it cannot be upheld unless it is supported by sufficiently important state interests and is closely tailored to effectuate only those interests." The Constitution imposes on this Court the obligation to "examine carefully . . . the extent to which [the legitimate government interests advanced] are served by the challenged regulation." *Moore v. East Cleveland.* See also *Carey v. Population Services International* (invalidating a requirement that bore "no relation to the State's interest"). An evidentiary rule, just as a substantive prohibition, must meet these standards if it significantly burdens a fundamental liberty interest. . . .

B

... The right to be free from medical attention without consent, to determine what shall be done with one's own body, *is* deeply rooted in this Nation's traditions, as the majority acknowledges. ...

II

A

The right to be free from unwanted medical attention is a right to evaluate the potential benefit of treatment and its possible consequences according to one's own values and to make a personal decision whether to subject oneself to the intrusion. For a patient like Nancy Cruzan, the sole benefit of medical treatment is being kept metabolically alive. Neither artificial nutrition nor any other form of medical treatment available today can cure or in any way ameliorate her condition. Irreversibly vegetative patients are devoid of thought, emotion and sensation; they are permanently and completely unconscious. ...

There are also affirmative reasons why someone like Nancy might choose to forgo artificial nutrition and hydration under these circumstances. Dying is personal. And it is profound. For many, the thought of an ignoble end, steeped in decay, is abhorrent. A quiet, proud death, bodily integrity intact, is a matter of extreme consequence. ...

IV

... Yet Missouri and this Court have displaced Nancy's own assessment of the processes associated with dying. They have discarded evidence of her will, ignored her values, and deprived her of the right to a decision as closely approximating her own choice as humanly possible. They have done so disingenuously in her name, and openly in Missouri's own. That Missouri and this Court may truly be motivated only by concern for incompetent patients makes no matter. As one of our most prominent jurists warned us decades ago: "Experience should teach us to be most on our guard to protect liberty when the government's purposes are beneficent. ... The greatest dangers to liberty lurk in insidious encroachment by men of zeal, well meaning but without understanding." *Olmstead v. United States* (Brandeis, J., dissenting).

I respectfully dissent.

WASHINGTON v. GLUCKSBERG

521 U.S. 702 (1997)

Opinion: Rehnquist, joined by
  O'Connor, Scalia, Kennedy, Thomas
Concurrence: O'Connor, joined in part
  by Ginsburg, Breyer
Concurrence: Stevens
Concurrence: Souter
Concurrence: Ginsberg
Concurrence: Breyer

Sometimes the breadth of the Supreme Court's holding in a particular case actually does not become clear until a later case develops it. In Washington v. Glucksberg, *the Court considers whether* Cruzan v. Missouri *established a broad principle of a right to die that would extend to cases of assisted suicide. As you read* Washington v. Glucksberg, *consider the import of the Court's earlier claim in* Cruzan v. Missouri *that a clear will to terminate life support should be respected by the state. Did this specific claim, which, as we have seen, was tangential to the actual ruling in the case, establish a broad right to die?*

What arguments does Chief Justice William Rehnquist bring against such a broadening of the Cruzan v. Missouri *opinion? Notice that as in the previous section, the issue here is about how broad substantive due process protections are in areas of decisional autonomy and the end of life.*

CHIEF JUSTICE *Rehnquist delivered the opinion of the Court.*

The question presented in this case is whether Washington's prohibition against "caus[ing]" or "aid[ing]" a suicide offends the Fourteenth Amendment to the United States Constitution. We hold that it does not.

It has always been a crime to assist a suicide in the State of Washington. In 1854, Washington's first Territorial Legislature outlawed "assisting another in the commission of self murder." Today, Washington law provides: "A person is guilty of promoting a suicide attempt when he knowingly causes or aids another person to attempt suicide." "Promoting a suicide attempt" is a felony, punishable by up to five years' imprisonment and up to a $10,000 fine. At the same time, Washington's Natural Death Act, enacted in 1979, states that the "withholding or withdrawal of life sustaining treatment" at a patient's direction "shall not, for any purpose, constitute a suicide."

Petitioners in this case are the State of Washington and its Attorney General. Respondents Harold Glucksberg, M.D., Abigail Halperin, M.D., Thomas A. Preston, M.D., and Peter Shalit, M.D., are physicians who practice in Washington. These doctors occasionally treat terminally ill, suffering patients, and declare that they would assist these patients in ending their lives if not for Washington's assisted suicide ban. In January 1994, respondents, along with three gravely ill, pseudonymous plaintiffs who have since died and Compassion in Dying, a nonprofit organization that counsels people considering physician assisted suicide, sued in the United States District Court, seeking a declaration that Wash Rev. Code 9A.36.060(1) is, on its face, unconstitutional.

The plaintiffs asserted "the existence of a liberty interest protected by the Fourteenth Amendment which extends to a personal choice by a mentally competent, terminally ill adult to commit physician assisted suicide." Relying primarily on *Planned Parenthood v. Casey* and *Cruzan v. Director, Missouri Dept. of Health*, the District Court agreed, and concluded that Washington's assisted suicide ban is unconstitutional because it "places an undue burden on the exercise of [that] constitutionally protected liberty interest." The District Court also decided that the Washington statute violated the Equal Protection Clause's requirement that " 'all persons similarly situated . . . be treated alike.' "

The Due Process Clause guarantees more than fair process, and the "liberty" it protects includes more than the absence of physical restraint. *Collins v. Harker Heights.* The Clause also provides heightened protection against government interference with certain fundamental rights and liberty interests. (*Reno v. Flores*; *Casey*). In a long line of cases, we have held that, in addition to the specific freedoms protected by the Bill of Rights, the "liberty" specially protected by the Due Process Clause includes the rights to marry, *Loving v. Virginia*; to have children, *Skinner v. Oklahoma ex rel. Williamson*; to direct the education and upbringing of one's children, *Meyer v. Nebraska, Pierce v. Society of Sisters*; to marital privacy, *Griswold v. Connecticut*; to use contraception, *ibid., Eisenstadt v. Baird*; to bodily integrity, *Rochin v. California*; and to abortion, *Casey.* We have also assumed, and strongly suggested, that the Due Process Clause protects the traditional right to refuse unwanted lifesaving medical treatment. *Cruzan.*

But we "ha[ve] always been reluctant to expand the concept of substantive due process because guideposts for responsible decisionmaking in this unchartered area are scarce and open ended." By extending constitutional protection to an asserted right or liberty interest, we, to a great extent, place the matter outside the arena of public debate and legislative action. We must therefore "exercise the utmost care whenever we are asked to break new ground in this field," ibid., lest the liberty protected by the Due Process Clause be subtly transformed into the policy preferences of the members of this Court.

Our established method of substantive due process analysis has two primary features: First, we have regularly observed that the Due Process Clause specially protects those fundamental rights and liberties which are, objectively, "deeply rooted in this Nation's history and tradition," *Snyder v. Massachusetts*, and "implicit in the concept of ordered liberty," such that "neither liberty nor justice would exist if they were sacrificed," *Palko v. Connecticut*. Second, we have required in substantive due process cases a "careful description" of the asserted fundamental liberty interest. Our Nation's history, legal traditions, and practices thus provide the crucial "guideposts for responsible decisionmaking," *Collins*, that direct and restrain our exposition of the Due Process Clause. As we stated recently in *Flores*, the Fourteenth Amendment "forbids the government to infringe . . . 'fundamental' liberty interests at all, no matter what process is provided, unless the infringement is narrowly tailored to serve a compelling state interest."

Justice Souter, relying on Justice Harlan's dissenting opinion in *Poe v. Ullman*, would largely abandon this restrained methodology, and instead ask "whether

[Washington's] statute sets up one of those 'arbitrary impositions' or 'purposeless restraints' at odds with the Due Process Clause of the Fourteenth Amendment." In our view, however, the development of this Court's substantive due process jurisprudence, described briefly above, has been a process whereby the outlines of the "liberty" specially protected by the Fourteenth Amendment—never fully clarified, to be sure, and perhaps not capable of being fully clarified—have at least been carefully refined by concrete examples involving fundamental rights found to be deeply rooted in our legal tradition. This approach tends to rein in the subjective elements that are necessarily present in due process judicial review. In addition, by establishing a threshold requirement—that a challenged state action implicate a fundamental right—before requiring more than a reasonable relation to a legitimate state interest to justify the action, it avoids the need for complex balancing of competing interests in every case.

Turning to the claim at issue here, the Court of Appeals stated that "[p]roperly analyzed, the first issue to be resolved is whether there is a liberty interest in determining the time and manner of one's death," or, in other words, "[i]s there a right to die?" Similarly, respondents assert a "liberty to choose how to die" and a right to "control of one's final days," and describe the asserted liberty as "the right to choose a humane, dignified death," and "the liberty to shape death." As noted above, we have a tradition of carefully formulating the interest at stake in substantive due process cases. For example, although *Cruzan* is often described as a "right to die" case (*Cruzan* recognized "the more specific interest in making decisions about how to confront an imminent death"), we were, in fact, more precise: we assumed that the Constitution granted competent persons a "constitutionally protected right to refuse lifesaving hydration and nutrition." *Cruzan*.

The history of the law's treatment of assisted suicide in this country has been and continues to be one of the rejection of nearly all efforts to permit it. That being the case, our decisions lead us to conclude that the asserted "right" to assistance in committing suicide is not a fundamental liberty interest protected by the Due Process Clause. The Constitution also requires, however, that Washington's assisted suicide ban be rationally related to legitimate government interests.

First, Washington has an "unqualified interest in the preservation of human life." *Cruzan*. This interest is symbolic and aspirational as well as practical:

> "While suicide is no longer prohibited or penalized, the ban against assisted suicide and euthanasia shores up the notion of limits in human relationships. It reflects the gravity with which we view the decision to take one's own life or the life of another, and our reluctance to encourage or promote these decisions."

Respondents admit that "[t]he State has a real interest in preserving the lives of those who can still contribute to society and enjoy life." Washington, however, has rejected this sliding scale approach and, through its assisted suicide ban, insists that all persons' lives, from beginning to end, regardless of physical or mental condition, are under the full protection of the law.

Relatedly, all admit that suicide is a serious public health problem, especially among persons in otherwise vulnerable groups.

Those who attempt suicide—terminally ill or not—often suffer from depression or other mental disorders. The New York Task Force, however, expressed its concern that, because depression is difficult to diagnose, physicians and medical professionals often fail to respond adequately to seriously ill patients' needs. Thus, legal physician assisted suicide could make it more difficult for the State to protect depressed or mentally ill persons, or those who are suffering from untreated pain, from suicidal impulses.

The State also has an interest in protecting the integrity and ethics of the medical profession. In contrast to the Court of Appeals' conclusion that "the integrity of the medical profession would [not] be threatened in any way by [physician assisted suicide]," the American Medical Association, like many other medical and physicians' groups, has concluded that "[p]hysician assisted suicide is fundamentally incompatible with the physician's role as healer."

The State's interest here goes beyond protecting the vulnerable from coercion; it extends to protecting disabled and terminally ill people from prejudice, negative and inaccurate stereotypes, and "societal indifference." The State's assisted suicide ban reflects and reinforces its policy that the lives of terminally ill, disabled, and elderly people must be no less valued than the lives of the young and healthy, and that a seriously disabled person's suicidal impulses should be interpreted and treated the same way as anyone else's.

Finally, the State may fear that permitting assisted suicide will start it down the path to voluntary and perhaps even involuntary euthanasia. The Court of Appeals struck down Washington's assisted suicide ban only "as applied to competent, terminally ill adults who wish to hasten their deaths by obtaining medication prescribed by their doctors." Washington insists, however, that the impact of the court's decision will not and cannot be so limited. If suicide is protected as a matter of constitutional right, it is argued, "every man and woman in the United States must enjoy it." *Compassion in Dying*. The Court of Appeals' decision, and its expansive reasoning, provide ample support for the State's concerns.

The court noted, for example, that the "decision of a duly appointed surrogate decision maker is for all legal purposes the decision of the patient himself," that "in some instances, the patient may be unable to self administer the drugs and . . . administration by the physician . . . may be the only way the patient may be able to receive them"; and that not only physicians, but also family members and loved ones, will inevitably participate in assisting suicide. Thus, it turns out that what is couched as a limited right to "physician assisted suicide" is likely, in effect, a much broader license, which could prove extremely difficult to police and contain. Washington's ban on assisting suicide prevents such erosion.

This concern is further supported by evidence about the practice of euthanasia in the Netherlands. The Dutch government's own study revealed that in 1990, there were 2,300 cases of voluntary euthanasia (defined as "the deliberate termination of another's life at his request"), 400 cases of assisted suicide, and more than 1,000 cases of euthanasia without an explicit request. In addition to these latter 1,000 cases, the study found an additional 4,941 cases where physicians administered lethal morphine overdoses without the patients' explicit consent. This study suggests that, despite the existence of various reporting procedures, euthanasia in the Netherlands has not been limited to competent, terminally ill adults who are enduring physical suffering, and that

regulation of the practice may not have prevented abuses in cases involving vulnerable persons, including severely disabled neonates and elderly persons suffering from dementia. The New York Task Force, citing the Dutch experience, observed that "assisted suicide and euthanasia are closely linked," and concluded that the "risk of . . . abuse is neither speculative nor distant." Washington, like most other States, reasonably ensures against this risk by banning, rather than regulating, assisting suicide. See *United States v. 12 200-ft Reels of Super 8MM Film*.

We need not weigh exactingly the relative strengths of these various interests. They are unquestionably important and legitimate, and Washington's ban on assisted suicide is at least reasonably related to their promotion and protection. We therefore hold that Wash. Rev. Code 9A.36.060(1) (1994) does not violate the Fourteenth Amendment, either on its face or "as applied to competent, terminally ill adults who wish to hasten their deaths by obtaining medication prescribed by their doctors."

Throughout the Nation, Americans are engaged in an earnest and profound debate about the morality, legality, and practicality of physician assisted suicide. Our holding permits this debate to continue, as it should in a democratic society. The decision of the en banc Court of Appeals is reversed, and the case is remanded for further proceedings consistent with this opinion.

SYNTHESIS QUESTIONS FOR FURTHER DISCUSSION: CHAPTER 7 SECTION C

1. John Hart Ely's article in this section suggests that the modern doctrine of privacy does not have a sound constitutional basis. But is there any way that his theory, which we examined in depth in Chapter 2, could provide such a basis? Could the moral reading provide such a basis?

2. In *Eisenstadt v. Baird*, the Court extended the right of privacy beyond the domain of married relationships and the family. Does this case break in this respect with the kind of substantive due process rights that we examined in the previous section? Is this a good development in constitutional law?

3. Prior to *Roe v. Wade*, abortion was regulated on a state-by-state basis. However, Ronald Dworkin argues against what he calls a "checkerboard" approach to the Constitution. On his view, there is a problem with failing to reach a national decision about whether or not to protect abortion. He argues that either a right to abortion is protected by the privacy guarantee under *Griswold v. Connecticut* or the fetus has an independent right of life that is guaranteed under due process and equal protection law. Specifically, because each state has murder laws, there would be an equal protection violation in not punishing as murderers those who destroyed fetuses. Is there, however, an argument to be made for states to have a role in regulating abortion? In answering this question, you might reflect back to the arguments concerning democracy that we read in Chapter 1.

4. One of the newest areas in which substantive due process guarantees have been recognized is that of gay rights. Do you see a clear line from *Eisenstadt v. Baird* to *Lawrence v. Texas*? One thing to notice about the *Lawrence v. Texas* case is that it explicitly overturns *Bowers v. Hardwick*. What does U.S. Supreme Court Justice Anthony Kennedy write in *Lawrence v. Texas* to refute the argument in *Bowers v. Hardwick* that "there is no constitutional right to sodomy"?

5. *Maher v. Roe* concerned the question not of "negative" rights to be free from state intervention, but of "positive" entitlements to be provided a service, here the right to receive Medicaid reimbursement for an abortion. Does the Constitution in general protect only "negative" rights to be free from state intervention, or also "positive" rights to receive certain goods? Consider, for instance, the Preamble of the Constitution's statement about providing for the "general welfare."

6. Rights of privacy are sometimes thought linked to more general interests that persons have in "decisional autonomy." Perhaps the ultimate element of "decisional autonomy" is the capacity to choose whether to end one's own life. Does the Constitution extend privacy rights to this area? Do the restrictions upheld in *Washington v. Glucksberg* and *Cruzan v. Missouri* suggest that the Supreme Court has conclusively determined that there is no fundamental "right to die"?

7. As you have seen, the Court in *Cruzan v. Missouri* considered whether or not a family has the right to terminate life support for an adult child. Would it make a difference in the case of a minor? Consider this question in light of the cases in this section as well as the arguments examined in Section B.

KEY TERMS

euthanasia: In contrast to instances in which an individual is able to take his or her own life, euthanasia involves another person initiating such a course of action. It is distinguished into two categories, voluntary (the ending of life by another with consent) and involuntary (no consent). Sometimes it is colloquially referred to as mercy-killing. In the context of this chapter, euthanasia is discussed with reference to individuals who have an incurable, debilitating, or fatal disease.

libertarianism: The political philosophy that holds that the primary purpose of government is the protection of private property. This theory also rejects the notion of government provision for welfare.

negative rights: Rights to be free from government coercion.

New Deal: President Franklin Roosevelt's series of social programs to stimulate the economy, provide for employment, and enhance the general welfare.

positive rights: Rights to be given certain material goods by the state.

quickening: The moment during pregnancy in which a woman can feel her fetus, dismissed by the Court in *Roe v. Wade* as an inappropriate guideline for regulating abortion.

state of nature: A rhetorical device used by political theorists such as John Locke to describe situations in which there is no state. It is often used to consider what fundamental rights exist independently of government. In turn, the state of nature is used by Locke and his followers to constrain the actions of government.

trimester framework: The framework announced in *Roe v. Wade* regulating abortion, dividing pregnancy into three sections, each lasting three months.

undue burden: The standard announced by the Court in *Planned Parenthood v. Casey* for determining whether infringements on the right to have an abortion, such as spousal or parental notification laws, can be sustained. It provides a test for balancing the interests of the individual woman seeking an abortion with the interests of the state.

viability: The ability of the fetus to live outside the womb, cited as the key point at which the state could lawfully prohibit abortion in the trimester framework employed in *Roe v. Wade*.

PART IV

EQUALITY

CHAPTER 8

RACE AND EQUALITY

The Preamble to the U.S. Constitution begins by invoking "We the People" as the Constitution's ultimate source. Commonly, the phrase is associated with democratic self-rule and the notion that all persons subject to the law should be treated as free and equal. But any careful look at the text of the Constitution should raise a healthy skepticism about the original Constitution's commitment to equality. Although the term "slavery" is never used in the document, the original Constitution clearly does not explicitly outlaw its practice. Indeed, in the Three-Fifths Clause, under which three-fifths of the slave population was counted for tax distribution and the allocation of House representatives, and in Article I, Section 9, which postpones the potential abolition of the slave trade until 1808, the Constitution makes euphemistic references to the existence of slavery without explicitly acknowledging its existence. For instance, it uses the phrase "Importation of such Persons" to refer to the slave trade. Moreover, Article IV provides that slaves who manage to escape servitude are subject to the laws of their original, slave-owning jurisdictions. Finally, no African Americans participated in the Constitutional Convention, despite their substantial presence within the states. All of these facts reveal that despite the rhetoric of equality that often surrounds discussions of the original Constitution, it was far from an egalitarian document.

Over the course of two centuries, the Constitution has evolved from condoning to repudiating the institutions of slavery and later racial segregation. In this chapter, you will read U.S. Supreme Court Justice Thurgood Marshall's bicentennial speech, which seeks to dissuade people from overly glorifying the original Constitution. As Justice Marshall points out, it was not until the Constitution was amended after the Civil War that the ideal of equality was enshrined in the document. The Fourteenth Amendment in many ways serves as a demarcation between an earlier constitution that tolerated both racism and segregation and one that enshrined an explicit idea of equality before the law regardless of race.

However, as you will see in this chapter, despite the ideals of the Fourteenth Amendment's dedication to "equal protection of the laws" and the Fifteenth Amendment's guarantee of African Americans' right to vote, the puzzle of how to combat racism was just emerging. Indeed, it is perhaps because equality is such an elusive ideal that much of the Constitution's history has centered on debates about the meaning of the Fourteenth Amendment's guarantee of "equal protection." Although segregation has few defenders in contemporary American society, the Court's earlier struggle about the meaning of equal protection concerned whether it prohibited segregation by the state. Indeed, at one point the Court held that the practice of state segregation was consistent with the Equal Protection Clause of the Fourteenth Amendment. What were the arguments the Supreme Court used to justify its determination that racial segregation by the government did not violate "equal protection of the laws" in *Plessy v. Ferguson*? Moreover, why did a unanimous Court in *Brown v. Board of Education* reverse that earlier understanding of equal protection? These two cases and their differing views of segregation are central to our inquiry in this chapter.

In contemporary constitutional practice, *Brown v. Board of Education* is accepted as settled law and *Plessy v. Ferguson* is widely viewed as one of the Court's most flawed decisions. Indeed, it is sometimes said that no constitutional theory of interpretation is acceptable if it cannot explain why *Brown v. Board of Education* was decided correctly. It is more than a landmark; it is a super-precedent. But the consensus over the correctness of the *Brown v. Board of Education* decision has not ended the debate about the meaning of the Equal Protection Clause. Just as in an earlier era, in contemporary debates about the meaning of the Fourteenth Amendment there is widespread disagreement about what it means to secure equal protection. As our readings in Section B make clear, this divide has centered on two interpretations, both claiming to inherit the legacy of *Brown v. Board of Education*.

On one side, a color-conscious view, developed most explicitly by Amy Gutmann, suggests that policies that aim to combat discrimination and racism sometimes need to draw distinctions based on race in order to be effective. In particular, Gutmann argues for color-conscious affirmative action policies on the grounds that they are needed to resolve deep discrimination in American society. But in contrast to a color-conscious interpretation of the Equal Protection Clause, some have argued that the Constitution must be colorblind. On this view, the Constitution does not permit the government to take race into consideration, even in order to further worthy goals.

This controversy between colorblind and color-conscious approaches to the Constitution frames not only the debate over affirmative action, as you will see in Section B, but also our inquiry into voter discrimination in Section C. There we will ask whether the Constitution allows for or prohibits attempts to ensure African-American representation in Congress by taking race into account. As you will see, while proponents of a colorblind view believe that congressional districts must be drawn without reference to race, those with a color-conscious perspective advocate the creation of "majority-minority" districts that will elect minority representatives. As you read through Sections B and C, you will note the consensus that the earlier racism of the Constitution before the Fourteenth Amendment was a mistake, but you will also be confronted with the contemporary dispute over the meaning of equality. As you work your way through these cases, consider whether you believe the Constitution should be colorblind or color-conscious. Ask yourself, moreover, how your answer to this question impacts your specific views on affirmative action and voter discrimination.

Although much of this chapter focuses on the implications of equal protection for issues of discrimination against racial and ethnic minorities, we begin by confronting the Constitution's original deep association with slavery. The legacy of slavery has shaped American history and created a moral dilemma for constitutional interpretation that persists to this day. How can those who value the Constitution's structure and its protection of individual rights reconcile these virtues with the evil of slavery? Because of its accommodations of slavery, the abolitionist William Lloyd Garrison called the Constitution "a covenant with death and an agreement with Hell." It is clear that after the passage of the Thirteenth, Fourteenth, and Fifteenth Amendments that the Constitution prohibits slavery, but there is a debate among historians and constitutional theorists over whether, before the passage of these amendments, the Constitution allowed for or prohibited slavery. One way to explore this debate is to examine in depth the case of *Dred Scott v. Sandford*, which is the focus of the first section of this chapter.

Dred Scott, a slave, sued for his freedom on the grounds that he had been relocated into one of the new territories that prohibited slavery. In one of the most morally and legally contested decisions of American history, however, the Supreme Court denied Scott his freedom on the grounds that he did not have standing as a citizen, and that furthermore, the Missouri Compromise was unconstitutional because Congress did not have the power to enact it. For the time being, the Supreme Court legally sanctioned the evil of slavery, although it would continue to be a source of contentious debate that served as a catalyst for the Civil War.

The first section in this chapter uses *Dred Scott v. Sandford* as a window into the broader question of whether the antebellum Constitution had the resources, given that there was not yet a Fourteenth Amendment, to confront the morally suspect practices of racism, slavery, and segregation. Consider whether the Constitution's aspirations of freedom and equality or its textual concessions to slavery mean that *Dred Scott v. Sandford* was, legally speaking, rightly or wrongly decided at the time. Our selection from Mark Graber argues that the various theories of interpretation we have studied cannot avoid the kind of constitutional evil that *Dred Scott v. Sandford* presents. According to Graber, each theory has certain commitments that might plausibly point it toward the *Dred Scott v. Sandford* Court's majority decision. Originalists, like U.S. Supreme Court Justice Antonin Scalia, are bound by the Constitution's textual accommodations of slavery. Proceduralists, such as John Hart Ely, are reluctant to rest constitutional interpretation on a substantive account of equality and defer to the kind of public support that the *Dred Scott v. Sandford* decision enjoyed at the time. Adherents to the "moral reading" of the Constitution, such as Ronald Dworkin, must make room in their analysis for the pro-slavery aspirations found in the Constitution as well as the egalitarian ones. Elsewhere, Graber has argued that pragmatists might endorse *Dred Scott v. Sandford* because they prefer "constitutional peace" to "constitutional justice." Consider how each theoretical approach might respond to Graber's claims. How might each of these theories suggest that even without the Fourteenth Amendment, *Dred Scott v. Sandford* was wrongly decided? In answering this question, you can see that the evils of racism pose a serious challenge for constitutional interpretation.

It took the Civil War and a series of constitutional amendments in the Reconstruction Era that followed to resolve the problem of legally sanctioned slavery in the United States. The Thirteenth Amendment, ratified in December 1865, abolished the institution of slavery, and the Fourteenth Amendment, ratified in July 1868, guaranteed equal protection of laws and made clear that all persons born or naturalized in the United States are citizens under the Constitution. No longer was there any ambiguity about whether African Americans were entitled to legal standing under the Constitution. But the resolution of these debates gave rise to two new constitutional dilemmas. First, in the *Civil Rights Cases*, included here, the Court was asked to determine how far the reach of equal protection extended. In announcing the "state action" doctrine, the Court interpreted the phrase "equal protection of the laws" to mean freedom from discrimination by the state, but not by private organizations or individuals. Thus, much civil rights legislation passed in the mid-twentieth century—such as that preventing restaurants or hotels from discriminating against minorities—was sanctioned under the Commerce Clause and not the Equal Protection Clause. But another constitutional dilemma centers not on the role of segregation in restaurants or hotels, but on state-sponsored segregation, which includes public schools. Was the Fourteenth Amendment's guarantee of equal protection compatible with state-sponsored segregation? From an originalist point of view, the Fourteenth Amendment was passed when segregation was pervasive not only in Southern states but also in Washington, D.C., the very place where it was crafted and enacted. Is this fact significant in deciding the Equal Protection Clause's impact on state-sponsored segregation?

In 1896, *Plessy v. Ferguson* raised the question of whether segregation mandated by the state was compatible with the guarantee of equal protection. Opponents of segregation, who challenged the practice of legally required segregation on railway cars, argued that separation could not be reconciled with equal protection. In a clear rebuff to that argument, however, a nearly unanimous Court decided that segregation by the state was constitutionally acceptable. By legitimizing the doctrine of "separate but equal," it established that segregation and equal protection were constitutionally compatible. In reading *Plessy v. Ferguson*, take note of U.S. Supreme Court Justice John Marshall Harlan's dissent. Justice Harlan disagrees with the majority's stance on the constitutionality of segregation, arguing that "there is no caste here. Our Constitution is colorblind, and neither knows nor tolerates classes among citizens." These two ideas—that the state should disregard an individual's color and that the Constitution does not tolerate a system of racial castes—fit together in opposing segregation, but they form the intellectual foundation for future controversies about affirmative action. As you read the rest of this chapter, you will see that Justice Harlan's dissent and the notion of colorblind constitutionalism are invoked in a variety of areas from affirmative action to voting discrimination. As you read Justice Harlan's dissent in *Plessy v. Ferguson*, think about whether there are any obvious implications for those topics contained in his opinion. Moreover, is there a way to oppose the majority's opinion in *Plessy v. Ferguson* without invoking color-blind constitutionalism? Consider which argument better fits the requirements of the Equal Protection Clause.

In a dramatic reversal of its own precedent, the Court outlawed segregation in public schools in *Brown v. Board of Education* on the grounds that separate treatment is in fact unequal treatment. U.S. Supreme Court Chief Justice Earl Warren cited social science data showing that segregation produced a sense of inferiority in black schoolchildren, a result it deemed incompatible with equal protection under the law. Although the reasoning of *Brown v. Board of Education* continues to generate controversy, the ruling itself is seen as a bedrock of contemporary jurisprudence. *Brown v. Board of Education* is likely at the front of Justice Scalia's mind when, in the reading from Chapter 2, he claims that he is a "faint-hearted originalist" because he endorses *Brown v. Board of Education* despite its potential tensions with originalist theory.

This difficulty for originalism recalls Graber's challenge that constitutional theories cannot wholly banish the reasoning behind *Dred Scott v. Sandford*. In reading this chapter, consider the extent to which originalism, proceduralism, the moral reading, and pragmatism authorize judges to battle racism when endorsed by the state.

In addition to *Brown v. Board of Education*, we include here another landmark case to highlight the Court's role in combating state-sponsored segregation. Among the bulwarks of segregation in the United States, the prohibition of so-called "miscegenation" or interracial marriage was fundamental. In the wake of *Brown v. Board of Education* and the ensuing Civil Rights movement, the Supreme Court invalidated state laws banning interracial marriage as inconsistent with the Equal Protection Clause and substantive due process in *Loving v. Virginia*. The case highlights again that the Court was willing to employ the guarantee of equal protection in limiting segregation by the states.

Although *Brown v. Board of Education* is settled law, a modern controversy over the Equal Protection Clause concerns whether it prohibits affirmative action. During the Civil Rights movement, President Lyndon B. Johnson and other proponents of desegregation argued that, in order to achieve equality and remedy past injustices, African Americans should receive some form of preferential treatment in areas such as employment and college admissions. As President Johnson dramatically illustrated in his commencement speech at Howard University, included here, "you do not take a person who, for years, has been hobbled by chains and liberate him, bring him up to the starting line of a race and then say, 'you are free to compete with all the others.'" Opponents of affirmative action, however, scored a victory in *Regents v. Bakke*, which outlawed race-based quotas setting a fixed number of places for minorities at a state medical school. The Court in *Regents v. Bakke* seemed to invoke an ideal of colorblind constitutionalism in using the Equal Protection Clause to limit affirmative action. Amy Gutmann offers a retort to proponents of the "colorblind" Constitution. She argues that the basis of affirmative action should not be, as President Johnson suggested, righting the wrongs of slavery and Jim Crow, but rather the goal of building an inclusive and diverse society. To reach the goal of diversity, Gutmann argues, we must take into account the color of an individual's skin. In the Court's decision in *Grutter v. Bollinger*, the Court adopted a "goal-oriented" approach. In many ways, the decision vindicates the idea that affirmative action policy must be grounded in justifications that look to future ends, such as diversity, rather than in rectification-based rationales like that proposed by President Johnson.

As you will see, the debate between color-conscious and colorblind approaches to the Constitution is filtered by the Court through its doctrine of strict scrutiny. The Court has tended to view laws that make distinctions based on race with the utmost suspicion. Yet, as is usually the case, the Court has not issued a categorical legal ban upon all racial classifications, but rather has applied a balancing test between governmental interest and the rights of citizens to be free from discrimination. In legal terms, it applies its highest level of scrutiny, or "strict scrutiny," to these cases. Strict scrutiny mandates that the Court presume any distinction based on race to be invalid unless the government can show that a policy of discrimination serves a "compelling state interest" and that the policy is "narrowly tailored" to meet the goals of that interest. When the Court applies this standard, the challenged statute is usually struck down. But the Court, at times, does find that the state has a compelling interest that is narrowly tailored, and thus upholds a law. Consider what possible rationales advocated by color-conscious proponents might rise to a compelling interest. When you read Guttman's arguments defending affirmative action, decide whether they could survive the test of strict scrutiny.

This chapter concludes by examining the role that the Court has played in ensuring equal voting rights for African Americans. The Fifteenth Amendment, ratified in February 1870, explicitly grants African Americans the right to vote, but concerns have lingered throughout subsequent history regarding African Americans' equal access to the political process. Such concerns perhaps made themselves most apparent in the controversy over legislative redistricting. After staying clear of the issue of redistricting for some time on the grounds that it was a political question, the Court first entered fully into the debate with its decision in *Baker v. Carr*. As you will see, contemporary debate on this question concerns so-called majority-minority districts, in which there is an attempt to ensure minority representation by drawing districts that contain a majority of that particular racial minority. Again, the question of colorblindness and color-consciousness will serve to guide you as you consider this difficult issue. As you will see, throughout this chapter proponents of color-consciousness claim that the only way to fight discrimination is to be aware of race in public policy. In contrast, proponents of colorblindness argue that it is a mistake to try to fight discrimination with discrimination. Which of these approaches do you find most compelling in thinking about the Equal Protection Clause?

A.   SLAVERY, SEGREGATION, AND RACISM

In this section, we examine the constitutional legacy of race in historical debates over slavery and segregation. We include readings by William Lloyd Garrison and Frederick Douglass, as well as a famous 1858 speech by Abraham Lincoln, then a candidate for the Senate, to give you some background on the debates that shaped our modern constitutional understanding of these issues. Garrison regards the Constitution as a vile compromise tainted by its concessions to slavery, and argues that those who seek the abolition of slavery should also seek the abandonment of the Constitution. Douglass, a former slave, offers a more moderate view, claiming that the best reading of the antebellum Constitution had outgrown any accommodations to slavery. The speech by Lincoln—denouncing his opponent, Stephen Douglas—reflects these controversies and more, as he enters into the debate about the meaning of the Court's decision in *Dred Scott v. Sandford* and the role of popular sovereignty in settling the slavery dispute. Two additional readings provide a modern perspective on these disputes. Justice Thurgood Marshall's piece highlights the tensions between constitutional aspirations and the historical constitutional problems regarding the treatment of African Americans. Mark Graber, while acknowledging the moral evil of slavery, defends the *Dred Scott v. Sandford* decision as consistent with the constitutional and legal culture of the time, and moreover, suggests the compatibility of this argument with several constitutional theories.

As you read *Dred Scott v. Sandford* and the other materials in this section, consider whether the Constitution could be said to support or prohibit institutionalized racism before the passage of the Thirteenth, Fourteenth, and Fifteenth Amendments. Do you agree with Garrison that the document was so tainted that abolitionists should have opposed the Constitution itself, or do you believe that it had elements worthy of reform? In many ways, your view of U.S. Supreme Court Chief Justice Roger Taney's opinion in *Dred Scott v. Sandford* will help to inform your views on these broader matters. As you read Chief Justice Taney's opinion in *Dred Scott v. Sandford*, you will be prompted to consider the various issues of judicial authority along with the more general theories of constitutional interpretation that we have used to frame this entire book.

This section then moves from discussion of slavery to issues of segregation. We examine *Plessy v. Ferguson* and *Brown v. Board of Education*, two cases central to the nation's attempt to grapple with the legacy of slavery and Jim Crow. The Thirteenth and Fourteenth Amendments clearly reversed *Dred Scott v. Sandford*. No longer was there a question as to whether African Americans had standing under the law and under the Constitution to claim their basic rights. Moreover, the Equal Protection Clause of the Fourteenth Amendment clearly states that African Americans are entitled to "equal protection of the laws." The constitutional puzzle after the passage of the Fourteenth Amendment, then, concerned precisely what was meant by "equal protection." The scope of this protection was limited in a fundamental way. First, the clause applied only to equal protection under the law, which the Court ruled to mean that it applied only to instances of state action. We saw in Chapter 3 that when the Civil Rights Act of 1964 was passed, it was done under the guise of the Commerce Clause because of this limitation in the Equal Protection Clause. The limit posed by the state action doctrine on the applicability and scope of the Equal Protection Clause is defended on the grounds that it protects freedom of association in the private sphere, which includes private organizations. Is this distinction valid?

In addition to the limit posed by state action, however, there was also a limit suggested by the Court's understanding of equality. Specifically, in *Plessy v. Ferguson*, the Court asked whether the institution of Jim Crow or segregation, which separated African Americans and whites by law in such varied areas of life as transportation and education, was consistent with the guarantee of equal protection. In particular, *Plessy v. Ferguson* concerned a Louisiana law that mandated segregation in railroad cars. Although the prohibition constituted state action, the Court focused its decision on whether segregation itself violated the Equal Protection Clause. Under the doctrine of "separate but equal," it suggested that separation of the races did not inherently result in the inferior treatment of African Americans.

Many years later, in *Brown v. Board of Education*, the Court explicitly overturned the doctrine of separate but equal announced in *Plessy v. Ferguson*. However, as you will see in several subsequent cases, the precise meaning of *Brown v. Board of Education* was far from clear. The section concludes with several such cases dealing with aspects of judicially enforced desegregation in the aftermath of *Brown v. Board of Education*. One subsequent question about how to interpret *Brown v. Board of Education* to consider is whether it stands for the principle that the Constitution is colorblind, an idea announced in Justice John Marshall Harlan's dissent in *Plessy v. Ferguson*. The question of whether the Constitution is indeed colorblind or rather, according to Amy Gutmann, "color conscious," plays a major role in the contemporary debate about affirmative action. This section's debate about the meaning of equal protection, then, sets the stage for the contemporary controversies over affirmative action and voting discrimination that we will consider in the next two sections.

William Lloyd Garrison

ON THE CONSTITUTION AND THE UNION

The Liberator, December 1832

We begin our readings with a selection from William Lloyd Garrison, a noted abolitionist. This essay was published in his abolitionist newspaper, The Liberator, in December 1832. As you read, consider the extent to which Garrison acknowledges that the Constitution permits slavery. In contrast to many of the readings we have examined in previous chapters, Garrison seems to concede here that the correct interpretation of the Constitution will lead to an evil result. As you work your way through this passage, keep in mind that it was written before the passage of the Thirteenth, Fourteenth, and Fifteenth Amendments.

There is much declamation about the sacredness of the compact which was formed between the free and slave states, on the adoption of the Constitution. A sacred compact, forsooth! We pronounce it the most bloody and heaven-daring arrangement ever made by men for the continuance and protection of a system of the most atrocious villainy ever exhibited on earth.

Yes—we recognize the compact, but with feelings of shame and indignation; and it will be held in everlasting infamy by the friends of justice and humanity throughout the world. It was a compact formed at the sacrifice of the bodies and souls of millions of our race, for the sake of achieving a political object—an unblushing and monstrous coalition to do evil that good might come. Such a compact was, in the nature of things and according to the law of God, null and void from the beginning. No body of men ever had the right to guarantee the holding of human beings in bondage. Who or what were the framers of our government, that they should dare confirm and authorise such high-handed villainy—such a flagrant robbery of the inalienable rights of man—such a glaring violation of all the precepts and injunctions of the gospel—such a savage war upon a sixth part of our whole population? —They were men, like ourselves—as fallible, as sinful, as weak, as ourselves. By the infamous bargain which they made between themselves, they virtually dethroned the Most High God, and trampled beneath their feet their own solemn and heaven-attested Declaration, that all men are created equal, and endowed by their Creator with certain inalienable rights—among which are life, liberty, and the pursuit of happiness. They had no lawful power to bind themselves, or their posterity, for one hour—for one moment—by such an unholy alliance. It was not valid then—it is not valid now. Still they persisted in maintaining it—and still do their successors, the people of Massachusetts, of New-England, and of the twelve free States, persist in maintaining it. A sacred compact! A sacred compact! What, then, is wicked and ignominious?

This, then, is the relation in which we of New-England stand to the holders of slaves at the south, and this is virtually our language toward them—"Go on, most worthy associates, from day to day, from month to month, from year to year, from generation to generation, plundering two millions of human beings of their liberty and the fruits of their toil—driving them into the fields like cattle—starving and lacerating their bodies—selling the husband from his wife, the wife from her husband, and children from their parents—spilling their blood—withholding the bible from their hands and all knowledge from their minds—and kidnapping annually sixty thousand infants, the offspring of pollution and shame! Go on, in these practices—we do not wish nor mean to interfere, for the rescue of your victims, even by expostulation or warning—we like your company too well to offend you by denouncing your conduct—'although we know that by every principle of law which does not utterly disgrace us by assimilating us to pirates, that they have as good and as true a right to the equal protection of the law as we have; and although we ourselves stand prepared to die, rather than submit even to a fragment of the intolerable load of oppression to which we are subjecting them—yet, never mind—let that be—they have grown old in suffering and we iniquity—and we have nothing to do now but to speak *peace, peace,* to one another in our sins. We are too wicked ever to love them as God commands us to do—we are so resolute in our wickedness as not even to desire to do so—and we are so proud in our iniquity that we will hate and revile whoever disturbs us in it. We want, like the devils of old, to be let alone in our sin. We are unalterably determined, and neither God nor man shall move us from this resolution, that our colored fellow subjects never shall be free or happy in their native land.' Go on, from bad to worse—add link to link to the chains upon the bodies of your victims—add constantly to the intolerable burdens under which they groan—and if, goaded to desperation by your cruelties; they should rise to assert their rights and redress their wrongs, fear nothing—we are pledged, by a sacred compact, to shoot them like dogs and rescue you from their vengeance! Go on—we never will forsake you, for 'there is honor among thieves'— our swords are ready to leap from their scabbards, and our muskets to pour forth deadly vollies, as soon as you are in danger. We pledge you our physical strength, by the sacredness of the national compact—a compact by which we have enabled you already to plunder, persecute and destroy two millions of slaves, who now lie beneath the sod; and by which we now give you the same piratical license to prey upon a much larger number of victims and all their posterity. Go on—and by this sacred instrument, the Constitution of the United States, *dripping as it is with human blood,* we solemnly pledge you our lives, our fortunes, and our sacred honor, that we will stand by you to the last."

People of New-England, and of the free States! is it true that slavery is no concern of yours? Have you no right even to protest against it, or to seek its removal? Are you not the main pillars of its support? How long do you mean to be answerable to God and the world, for spilling the blood of the poor innocents? Be not afraid to look the monster SLAVERY boldly in the face. He is your implacable foe—the vampyre who is sucking your life-blood—the ravager of a large portion of your country, and the enemy of God and man. Never hope to be a united, or happy, or prosperous people while he exists. He has an appetite like the grave—a spirit as malignant as that of the bottomless pit—and an influence as dreadful as the corruption of death. Awake to your danger! the struggle is a mighty one—it cannot be avoided—it should not be, if it could.

It is said that if you agitate this question, you will divide the Union. Believe it not; but should disunion follow, the fault will not be yours. You must perform your duty, faithfully, fearlessly and promptly, and leave the consequences to God: that duty clearly is, to cease from giving countenance and protection to southern kidnappers. Let them separate, if they can muster courage enough—and the liberation of their slaves is certain. Be assured that slavery will very speedily destroy this Union, *if it be let alone*; but even if the Union can be preserved by treading upon the necks, spilling the blood, and destroying the souls of millions of your race, we say it is not worth a price like this, and that it is in the highest degree criminal for you to continue the present compact. Let the pillars thereof fall—let the superstructure crumble into dust—if it must be upheld by robbery and oppression.

Frederick Douglass

WHAT TO THE SLAVE IS THE FOURTH OF JULY?

Address given at Corinthian Hall, Rochester, New York

July 5, 1852

Frederick Douglass escaped slavery as a young man and became a celebrated orator and writer. He delivered the following address *on July 5, 1852, at Corinthian Hall in Rochester, New York. Although, like William Lloyd Garrison, Douglass was a well-known abolitionist, the following selection highlights their different views of the Constitution. Consider in particular Douglass's claim that the Constitution is a "glorious liberty document." In his view, the Constitution's general commitment to principles of liberty is at odds with more specific provisions that seem to condone slavery. As you read this passage, consider its parallel with modern debates about the tension between specific rule-like provisions of the Constitution and what Ronald Dworkin called its "majestic generalities." For instance, you might want to refer to the debate between originalists and thinkers such as Dworkin, outlined in Chapter 2.*

Mr. President, Friends and Fellow Citizens: He who could address this audience without a quailing sensation, has stronger nerves than I have. I do not remember ever to have appeared as a speaker before any assembly more shrinkingly, nor with greater distrust of my ability, than I do this day.

The papers and placards say, that I am to deliver a 4th [of] July oration. This certainly sounds large, and out of the common way, for it is true that I have often had the privilege to speak in this beautiful Hall, and to address many who now honor me with their presence. But neither their familiar faces, nor the perfect gage I think I have of Corinthian Hall, seems to free me from embarrassment.

The fact is, ladies and gentlemen, the distance between this platform and the slave plantation, from which I escaped, is considerable and the difficulties to be overcome in getting from the latter to the former, are by no means slight. That I am here to-day is, to me, a matter of astonishment as well as of gratitude. You will not, therefore, be surprised, if in what I have to say I evince no elaborate preparation, nor

grace my speech with any high sounding exordium.

Fellow-citizens, I shall not presume to dwell at length on the associations that cluster about this day. The simple story of it is that, 76 years ago, the people of this country were British subjects. The style and title of your "sovereign people" (in which you now glory) was not then born. You were under the British Crown.

But, your fathers, who had not adopted the fashionable idea of this day, of the infallibility of government, and the absolute character of its acts, presumed to differ from the home government in respect to the wisdom and the justice of some of those burdens and restraints. They went so far in their excitement as to pronounce the measures of government unjust, unreasonable, and oppressive, and altogether such as ought not to be quietly submitted to.

On the 2d of July, 1776, the old Continental Congress, to the dismay of the lovers of ease, and the worshipers of property, clothed that dreadful idea with all the authority of national sanction. They did so in the form of a resolution; and as we seldom hit upon resolutions, drawn up in our day whose transparency is at all equal to this, it may refresh your minds and help my story if I read it. "Resolved, That these united colonies are, and of right, ought to be free and Independent States; that they are absolved from all allegiance to the British Crown; and that all political connection between them and the State of Great Britain is, and ought to be, dissolved."

Citizens, your fathers made good that resolution. They succeeded; and to-day you reap the fruits of their success. The freedom gained is yours; and you, therefore, may properly celebrate this anniversary. The 4th of July is the first great fact in your nation's history—the very ringbolt in the chain of your yet undeveloped destiny.

We have to do with the past only as we can make it useful to the present and to the future. To all inspiring motives, to noble deeds which can be gained from the past, we are welcome. But now is the time, the important time. Your fathers have lived, died, and have done their work, and have done much of it well. You live and must die, and you must do your work. You have no right to enjoy a child's share in the labor of your fathers, unless your children are to be blest by your labors. You have no right to wear out and waste the hard-earned fame of your fathers to cover your indolence. Washington could not die till he had broken the chains of his slaves. Yet his monument is built up by the price of human blood, and the traders in the bodies and souls of men, shout—We have Washington to "*our father.*" Alas! that it should be so; yet so it is.

"The evil that men do, lives after them, The good is oft' interred with their bones."

What have I, or those I represent, to do with your national independence?

This Fourth of July is yours, not mine. You may rejoice, I must mourn. To drag a man in fetters into the grand illuminated temple of liberty, and call upon him to join you in joyous anthems, were inhuman mockery and sacrilegious irony.

I shall see, this day, and its popular characteristics, from the slave's point of view. Standing, there, identified with the American bondman, making his wrongs mine, I do not hesitate to declare, with all my soul, that the character and conduct of this nation never looked blacker to me than on this 4th of July! America is false to the past, false to the present, and solemnly binds herself to be false to the future.

On what branch of the subject do the people of this country need light? Must I undertake to prove that the slave is a man? That point is conceded already. There are seventy-two crimes in the State of Virginia, which, if committed by a black man, (no matter how ignorant he be), subject him to the punishment of death; while only two of the same crimes will subject a white man to the like punishment. What is this but the acknowledgement that the slave is a moral, intellectual and responsible being? It is admitted in the fact that Southern statute books are covered with enactments forbidding, under severe fines and penalties, the teaching of the slave to read or to write. When you can point to any such laws, in reference to the beasts of the field, then I may consent to argue the manhood of the slave.

Must I argue the wrongfulness of slavery? Is that a question for Republicans? Is it to be settled by the rules of logic and argumentation, as a matter beset with great difficulty, involving a doubtful application of the principle of justice, hard to be understood? There is not a man beneath the canopy of heaven, that does not know that slavery is wrong for him.

What, then, remains to be argued? Is it that slavery is not divine; that God did not establish it; that our doctors of divinity are mistaken? There is blasphemy in the thought.

What, to the American slave, is your 4th of July? I answer: a day that reveals to him, more than all other days in the year, the gross injustice and cruelty to which he is the constant victim.

But it is answered in reply to all this, that precisely what I have now denounced is, in fact, guaranteed and sanctioned by the Constitution of the United States; that the right to hold and to hunt slaves is a part of that Constitution framed by the illustrious Fathers of this Republic.

Fellow-citizens! there is no matter in respect to which, the people of the North have allowed themselves to be so ruinously imposed upon, as that of the pro-slavery character of the Constitution. In that instrument I hold there is neither warrant, license, nor sanction of the hateful thing; but, interpreted as it ought to be interpreted, the Constitution is a GLORIOUS LIBERTY DOCUMENT. Read its preamble, consider its purposes. Is slavery among them? Is it at the gateway? or is it in the temple? It is neither. While I do not intend to argue this question on the present occasion, let me ask, if it be not somewhat singular that, if the Constitution were intended to be, by its framers and adopters, a slave-holding instrument, why neither slavery, slave-holding, nor slave can anywhere be found in it. What would be thought of an instrument, drawn up, legally drawn up, for the purpose of entitling the city of Rochester to a track of land, in which no mention of land was made?

Now, take the constitution according to its plain reading, and I defy the presentation of a single pro-slavery clause in it. On the other hand it will be found to contain principles and purposes, entirely hostile to the existence of slavery.

Allow me to say, in conclusion, notwithstanding the dark picture I have this day presented of the state of the nation, I do not despair of this country. There are forces in operation, which must inevitably work the downfall of slavery. "The arm of the Lord is not shortened," and the doom of slavery is certain. I, therefore, leave off where I began, with hope. While drawing encouragement from the Declaration of Independence, the great principles it contains, and the genius of American Institutions, my spirit is also cheered by the obvious tendencies of the age. Walled cities and empires have become unfashionable. The arm of commerce has borne away the gates of the strong city. Intelligence is penetrating the darkest corners of the globe. It makes its pathway over and under the sea, as well as on the earth. Wind, steam, and lightning are its chartered agents. Oceans no longer divide, but link nations together. From Boston to London is now a holiday excursion. Space is comparatively annihilated. Thoughts expressed on one side of the Atlantic are, distinctly heard on the other. The far off and almost fabulous Pacific rolls in grandeur at our feet. The Celestial Empire, the mystery of ages, is being solved. The fiat of the Almighty, "Let there be Light," has not yet spent its force. No abuse, no outrage whether in taste, sport or avarice, can now hide itself from the all-pervading light.

Abraham Lincoln

A HOUSE DIVIDED

June 17, 1858

The series of debates in 1858 between Abraham Lincoln, the Republican nominee for senator from Illinois, and his opponent, Democratic Senator Stephen Douglas, offered perhaps the most famous encapsulation of *the national discussion over slavery. Many see in those famous debates the seeds of civil war and a reconstituting of the Constitution's position on race, created by the Thirteenth, Fourteenth, and Fifteenth Amendments.*

Pay particular attention to two things as you work your way through this speech, often called the "House Divided" speech. First, drawing upon our readings from Chapter 3, note the degree to which both pro-slavery and anti-slavery positions were couched in concerns about federalism. Second, note Lincoln's response to the Dred Scott v. Sandford *decision, which struck down the Missouri Compromise in declaring that Congress did not have the power to ban slavery.*

Mr. President and Gentlemen of the Convention: If we could first know where we are, and whither we are tending, we could better judge what to do, and how to do it. We are now far into the fifth year since a policy was initiated with the avowed object and confident promise of putting an end to slavery agitation. Under the operation of that policy, that agitation has not only not ceased, but has constantly augmented. In my opinion, it will not cease until a crisis shall have been reached and passed. "A house divided against itself cannot stand." I believe this government cannot endure permanently half slave and half free. I do not expect the Union to be dissolved; I do not expect the house to fall; but I do expect it will cease to be divided. It will become all one thing, or all the other. Either the opponents of slavery will arrest the further spread of it, and place it where the public mind shall rest in the belief that it is in the course of ultimate extinction, or its advocates will push it forward till it shall become alike lawful in all the States, old as well as new, North as well as South.

Have we no tendency to the latter condition?

Let any one who doubts, carefully contemplate that now almost complete legal combination—piece of machinery, so to speak—compounded of the Nebraska doctrine and the *Dred Scott* decision.

The new year of 1854 found slavery excluded from more than half the States by State Constitutions, and from most of the National territory by Congressional prohibition. Four days later, commenced the struggle which ended in repealing that Congressional prohibition. This opened all the National territory to slavery, and was the first point gained.

But, so far, Congress only had acted; and an indorsement by the people, real or apparent, was indispensable to save the point already gained, and give chance for more.

This necessity had not been overlooked; but had been provided for, as well as might be, in the notable argument of "squatter sovereignty," otherwise called "sacred right of self-government," which latter phrase, though expressive of the only rightful basis of any government, was so perverted in this attempted use of it as to amount to just this: That if any *one* man choose to enslave *another*, no *third* man shall be allowed to object. That argument was incorporated into the Nebraska bill itself, in the language which follows: "It being the true intent and meaning of this Act not to legislate slavery into any Territory or State, nor to exclude it therefrom; but to leave the people thereof perfectly free to form and regulate their domestic institutions in their own way, subject only to the Constitution of the United States." Then opened the roar of loose declamation in favor of "squatter sovereignty," and "sacred right of self-government." "But," said opposition members, "let us amend the bill so as to expressly declare that the people of the Territory may exclude slavery." "Not we," said the friends of the measure; and down they voted the amendment.

While the Nebraska bill was passing through Congress, a *law case* involving the question of a negro's freedom, by reason of his owner having voluntarily taken him first into a free State and then into a Territory covered by the Congressional prohibition, and held him as a slave for a long time in each, was passing through the United States Circuit Court for the District of Missouri; and both Nebraska bill and law suit were brought to a decision in the same month of May, 1854. The negro's name was "Dred Scott," which name now designates the decision finally made in the case.

The election came. Mr. Buchanan was elected, and the indorsement, such as it was, secured. That was the second point gained. The indorsement, however, fell short of a clear popular majority by nearly four hundred thousand votes, and so, perhaps, was not overwhelmingly reliable and satisfactory.

At length a squabble springs up between the President and the author of the Nebraska bill, on the mere question of *fact*, whether the Lecompton Constitution was or was not, in any just sense, made by the people of Kansas; and in that quarrel the latter declares that all he wants is a fair vote for the people, and that he cares not whether slavery be voted *down* or voted *up*. I do not understand his declaration that he cares not whether slavery be voted down or voted up, to be intended by him other than as an apt definition of the policy he would impress upon the public mind—the principle for which he declares he has suffered so much, and is ready to suffer to the end. His [Douglas's] late joint struggle with the Republicans, against the Lecompton Constitution [a proposed pro-slavery constitution for Kansas], involves nothing of the original Nebraska doctrine. That struggle was made on a point—the right of a people to make their own constitution—upon which he and the Republicans have never differed.

The several points of the *Dred Scott* decision, in connection with Senator Douglas's "care not" policy, constitute the piece of machinery, in its present state of advancement. This was the third point gained. The working points of that machinery are:—

Firstly, That no negro slave, imported as such from Africa, and no descendant of such slave, can ever be a citizen of any State, in the sense of that term as used in the Constitution of the United States. This point is made in order to deprive the negro, in every possible event, of the benefit of that provision of the United States Constitution which declares that "The citizens of each State shall be entitled to all privileges and immunities of citizens in the several States."

Secondly, That "subject to the Constitution of the United States," neither Congress nor a Territorial Legislature can exclude slavery from any United States territory. This point is made in order that individual men may fill up the Territories with slaves, without danger of losing them as property, and thus to enhance the chances of permanency to the institution through all the future.

Thirdly, That whether the holding a negro in actual slavery in a free State, makes him free, as against the holder, the United States courts will not decide, but will leave to be decided by the courts of any slave State the negro may be forced into by the master. This point is made, not to be pressed immediately; but, is acquiesced in for awhile, and apparently indorsed by the people at an election, then to sustain the logical conclusion that what Dred Scott's master might lawfully do with Dred Scott, in the free State of Illinois, every other master may lawfully do with any other one, or one thousand slaves, in Illinois, or in any other free State.

Auxiliary to all this, and working hand in hand with it, the Nebraska doctrine, or what is left of it, is to educate and mould public opinion, at least Northern public opinion, not to care whether slavery is voted down or voted up. This shows exactly where we now are; and partially, also, whither we are tending.

It will throw additional light on the latter, to go back and run the mind over the string of historical facts already stated. Several things will now appear less dark and mysterious than they did when they were transpiring. The people were to be left "perfectly free," "subject only to the Constitution." What the Constitution had to do with it, outsiders could not then see. Plainly enough now, it was an exactly fitted niche, for the *Dred Scott* decision to afterward come in, and declare the perfect freedom of the people to be just no freedom at all. Why was the amendment, expressly declaring the right of the people, voted down? Plainly enough now: the adoption of it would have spoiled the niche for the *Dred Scott* decision. Why was the court decision held up? Why even a Senator's individual opinion withheld, till after the Presidential election? Plainly enough now: the speaking out then would have damaged the perfectly free argument upon which the election was to be carried. Why the outgoing President's felicitation on the indorsement? Why the delay of a re-argument? Why the incoming President's advance exhortation in favor of the decision? These things look like the cautious patting and petting of a spirited horse preparatory to mounting him, when it is dreaded that he may give the rider a fall. And why the hasty after-indorsement of the decision by the President and others?

We cannot absolutely know that all these exact adaptations are the result of preconcert. But when we see a lot of framed timbers, different portions of which we know have been gotten out at different times and places and by different workmen,—Stephen, Franklin, Roger and James, for instance,—and when we see these timbers joined together, and see they exactly make the frame of a house or a mill, all the tenons and mortises exactly fitting, and all the lengths and proportions of the different pieces exactly adapted to their respective places, and not a piece too many or too few—not omitting even scaffolding—or, if a single piece be lacking, we see the place in the frame exactly fitted and prepared yet to bring such piece in—in such a case, we find it impossible not to believe that Stephen and Franklin and Roger and James all understood one another from the beginning, and all worked upon a common plan or draft drawn up before the first blow was struck.

It should not be overlooked that, by the Nebraska bill, the people of a *State* as well as Territory, were to be left "perfectly free," "subject only to the Constitution." Why mention a State? They were legislating for Territories, and not for or about States. Certainly the people of a State are and ought to be subject to the Constitution of the United States; but why is mention of this lugged into this merely Territorial law? Why are the people of a Territory and the people of a State therein lumped together, and their relation to the Constitution therein treated as being precisely the same? While the opinion of the court, by Chief Justice Taney, in the *Dred Scott* case, and the separate opinions of all the concurring Judges, expressly declare that the Constitution of the United States neither permits Congress nor a Territorial Legislature to exclude slavery from any United States Territory, they all omit to declare whether or not the same Constitution permits a State, or the people of a State, to exclude it. *Possibly*, this is a mere omission; but who can be quite sure, if McLean or Curtis had sought to get into the opinion a declaration of unlimited power in the people of a State to exclude slavery from their limits, just as Chase and Mace sought to get such declaration, in behalf of the people of a Territory, into the Nebraska bill,—I ask, who can be quite sure that it would not have been voted down in the one case as it had been in the other? The nearest approach to the point of declaring the power of a State over slavery, is made by Judge Nelson. He approaches it more than once, using the precise idea, and almost the language, too, of the Nebraska act. On one occasion, his exact language is, "Except in cases where the power is restrained by the Constitution of the United States, the law of the State is supreme over the subject of slavery within its jurisdiction." In what cases the power of the States is so restrained by the United States Constitution, is left an open question, precisely as the same question, as to the restraint on the power of the Territories, was left open in the Nebraska act. Put this and that together, and we have another nice little niche, which we may, ere long, see filled with another Supreme Court decision, declaring that the Constitution of the United States does not permit a *State* to exclude slavery from its limits. And this may especially be expected if the doctrine of "care not whether slavery be voted down or voted up" shall gain upon the public mind sufficiently to give promise that such a decision can be maintained when made.

Such a decision is all that slavery now lacks of being alike lawful in all the States. Welcome, or unwelcome, such a decision is probably coming, and will soon be upon us, unless the power of the present political dynasty shall be met and overthrown. We shall lie down pleasantly dreaming that the people of Missouri are on the verge of making their State free, and we shall awake to the reality instead that the Supreme Court has made Illinois a Slave State. To meet and overthrow the power of that dynasty, is the work now before all those who would prevent that consummation. That is what we have to do. How can we best do it?

There are those who denounce us openly to their own friends, and yet whisper us softly, that Senator Douglas is the aptest instrument there is with which to effect that object. How can he oppose the advances of slavery? He don't care anything about it. His avowed mission is impressing the "public heart" to *care nothing about it.* For years he has labored to prove it a sacred right of white men to take negro slaves into the new Territories. Can he possibly show that it is less a sacred right to buy them where they can be bought cheapest? And unquestionably they can be bought cheaper in Africa than in Virginia. He has done all in his power to reduce the whole question of slavery to one of a mere right of property; and as such, how can he oppose the foreign slave trade—how can he refuse that trade in that "property" shall be "perfectly free"—unless he does it as a protection to the home production?

Our cause, then, must be intrusted to, and conducted by, its own undoubted friends—those whose hands are free, whose hearts are in the work, who *do care* for the result. We shall not fail; if we stand firm, we *shall not fail.* Wise counsels may accelerate, or mistakes delay it, but sooner or later, the victory is sure to come.

Thurgood Marshall

THE BICENTENNIAL SPEECH

Address given at the San Francisco Patent and Trademark Law Association

May 6, 1987

Justice Thurgood Marshall was the first African American appointed to the Supreme Court. He famously argued before the Court in Brown v. Board of Education, _among other important desegregation cases. Although his speech at the bicentennial of the adoption of the U.S. Constitution comes more than 100 years after the writings of William Lloyd Garrison and Frederick Douglass, notice how it reflects some of the same concerns expressed in their remarks. Does Justice Marshall's approach to the issue of slavery at the Founding resonate more with Garrison's or Douglass's understanding of the original Constitution?_

1987 marks the 200th anniversary of the United States Constitution. A Commission has been established to coordinate the celebration. The official meetings, essay contests, and festivities have begun.

Patriotic feelings will surely swell, prompting proud proclamations of the wisdom, foresight, and sense of justice shared by the Framers and reflected in a written document now yellowed with age. This is unfortunate—not the patriotism itself, but the tendency for the celebration to oversimplify, and overlook the many other events that have been instrumental to our achievements as a nation. The focus of this celebration invites a complacent belief that the vision of those who debated and compromised in Philadelphia yielded the "more perfect Union" it is said we now enjoy.

I cannot accept this invitation, for I do not believe that the meaning of the Constitution was forever "fixed" at the Philadelphia Convention. Nor do I find

the wisdom, foresight, and sense of justice exhibited by the Framers particularly profound. To the contrary, the government they devised was defective from the start, requiring several amendments, a civil war, and momentous social transformation to attain the system of constitutional government, and its respect for the individual freedoms and human rights, we hold as fundamental today. When contemporary Americans cite "The Constitution," they invoke a concept that is vastly different from what the Framers barely began to construct two centuries ago.

No doubt it will be said, when the unpleasant truth of the history of slavery in America is mentioned during this bicentennial year, that the Constitution was a product of its times, and embodied a compromise which, under other circumstances, would not have been made. But the effects of the Framers' compromise have remained for generations. They arose from the contradiction between guaranteeing liberty and justice to all, and denying both to Negroes.

It took a bloody civil war before the 13th Amendment could be adopted to abolish slavery, though not the consequences slavery would have for future Americans.

While the Union survived the civil war, the Constitution did not. In its place arose a new, more promising basis for justice and equality, the 14th Amendment, ensuring protection of the life, liberty, and property of all persons against deprivations without due process, and guaranteeing equal protection of the laws. And yet almost another century would pass before any significant recognition was obtained of the rights of black Americans to share equally even in such basic opportunities as education, housing, and employment, and to have their votes counted, and counted equally. In the meantime, blacks joined America's military to fight its wars and invested untold hours working in its factories and on its farms, contributing to the development of this country's magnificent wealth and waiting to share in its prosperity.

What is striking is the role legal principles have played throughout America's history in determining the condition of Negroes. They were enslaved by law, emancipated by law, disenfranchised and segregated by law; and, finally, they have begun to win equality by law. Along the way, new constitutional principles have emerged to meet the challenges of a changing society. The progress has been dramatic, and it will continue.

The men who gathered in Philadelphia in 1787 could not have envisioned these changes. They could not have imagined, nor would they have accepted, that the document they were drafting would one day be construed by a Supreme Court to which had been appointed a woman and the descendant of an African slave. "We the People" no longer enslave, but the credit does not belong to the Framers. It belongs to those who refused to acquiesce in outdated notions of "liberty," "justice," and "equality," and who strived to better them.

And so we must be careful, when focusing on the events which took place in Philadelphia two centuries ago, that we not overlook the momentous events which followed, and thereby lose our proper sense of perspective. Otherwise, the odds are that for many Americans the bicentennial celebration will be little more than a blind pilgrimage to the shrine of the original document now stored in a vault in the National Archives. If we seek, instead, a sensitive understanding of the Constitution's inherent defects, and its promising evolution through 200 years of history, the celebration of the "Miracle at Philadelphia" will, in my view, be a far more meaningful and humbling experience. We will see that the true miracle was not the birth of the Constitution, but its life, a life nurtured through two turbulent centuries of our own making, and a life embodying much good fortune that was not.

Thus, in this bicentennial year, we may not all participate in the festivities with flagwaving fervor. Some may more quietly commemorate the suffering, struggle, and sacrifice that has triumphed over much of what was wrong with the original document, and observe the anniversary with hopes not realized and promises not fulfilled. I plan to celebrate the bicentennial of the Constitution as a living document, including the Bill of Rights and the other amendments protecting individual freedoms and human rights.

Mark Graber

DESPERATELY DUCKING SLAVERY: *DRED SCOTT* AND CONTEMPORARY CONSTITUTIONAL THEORY

14 Const. Comment. 271 (1997)

The following piece of legal commentary by Mark Graber serves as an introduction to the Court's decision in Dred Scott v. Sandford, *often thought of as one of the*

Court's most flawed decisions. As you read it, you should be attuned to the connections he draws between the constitutional theories outlined in Chapter 2 and this infamous case. Is he correct in positing that any or all of these theories could offer a plausible defense of the decision reached in Dred Scott v. Sandford?

Contemporary constitutional theory rests on three premises. *Brown v. Board of Education* was correct, *Lochner v. New York* was wrong, and *Dred Scott v. Sandford* was also wrong. A few intrepid souls question whether *Brown* was correctly decided (although they would not have the Supreme Court overrule that decision). Some proponents of law and economics favor reviving the freedom of contract and the *Lochner* decision. No one, however, wishes to rethink the universal condemnation of *Dred Scott*.

This agreement that *Dred Scott* was a "public calamity" masks a deeper disagreement over exactly what was wrong with the Supreme Court's decision. Each school of contemporary constitutional thought claims *Dred Scott* embarrasses rival theories. Proponents of judicial restraint maintain that Chief Justice Roger Taney's opinion demonstrates the evils that result when federal justices prevent the elected branches of government from resolving major social disputes. Originalists maintain that the Taney opinion demonstrates the evils that result when constitutional authorities fail to be tethered by precedent or the original meaning of the constitution. Aspirational theorists maintain that the Taney opinion demonstrates the evils that result when constitutional authorities are too tethered by precedent or the original meaning of the constitution. Virtually every commentator who condemns *Dred Scott* insists that Taney could not have reached

that decision's proslavery and racist conclusions had he understood or adhered to the correct theory of the judicial function in constitutional cases. Following Robert Cover's analysis of fugitive slave cases, leading members of all schools of contemporary constitutional thought suggest that many Supreme Court justices who protected slavery and declared free blacks to be non-citizens supported those evils because they "shared a jurisprudence that fostered imprecise thinking about the nature of the choices available."

These contemporary uses of the *Dred Scott* decision to discredit rival theories are fruitless. No prominent approach to the judicial function compels any result in that case. Both the denial of congressional power over slavery in the territories and the claim that former slaves could not be American citizens can be supported (and opposed) by jurists sincerely committed to institutional, historical and aspirational theories. The majority opinions in *Dred Scott* used many different constitutional arguments to reach their immoral conclusions and the dissents in that case similarly relied on various constitutional logics. For these reasons, the standard analogies between *Dred Scott* and controversial twentieth century judicial opinions fail.

The argument laid out below is that *Dred Scott* is constitutionally *plausible* in any contemporary constitutional rhetoric, not that the result in that case follows logically from institutional, historical, or aspirational understandings of the judicial function in constitutional cases. All theories of contemporary constitutional interpretation are vulnerable to unique pro-slavery outcomes, circumstances in which that theory might compel a more pro-slavery result than rival theories.

This revisionist account of *Dred Scott* is less designed to rehabilitate the Taney

Court than to expose the result orientation of all schools of contemporary constitutional thought. Constitutional theorists ritually proclaim adherence to the distinction between constitutionality and justice, but few academic lawyers highlight the constitutional evils that they believe would result should judges adopt the "correct" theory of the judicial function in constitutional cases. Controversial cases in leading studies consistently come out "right," as "right" is defined by the theorist's political commitments. Conservative constitutional commentators insist that principled justices would sustain bans on abortion and strike down affirmative action policies; their liberal peers insist that principled justices would strike down bans on abortion and sustain affirmative action policies.

This consensus that *Dred Scott* was wrong (and *Brown* was right) inhibits serious discussion of constitutional evils. By highlighting the plausible constitutional arguments in favor of the result in *Dred Scott*, I hope to begin a better discussion among constitutional commentators as to the original constitution's imperfections and the reasons for adhering even to a constitution that might sanction evil results.

Dred Scott is not an example of what is wrong with any conception of the judicial function in constitutional cases. Rather, *Dred Scott* demonstrates how in the wrong hands or in the wrong circumstances all constitutional theories may yield unjust conclusions. The justices in the *Dred Scott* majority relied on institutional, historical and aspirational arguments that, while often strained, were not substantially weaker from a pure craft perspective than the institutional, historical and aspirational arguments made by the dissenters in *Dred Scott*. Taney was able to use these constitutional modalities in his opinion

because all forms of constitutional logic are capable of yielding evil results. Institutional arguments yield evil results whenever elected officials and popular majorities support evil laws. Historical arguments yield evil results whenever constitutional framers and ratifiers constitutionalize evil practices. Aspirational arguments yield evil results whenever constitutional framers and ratifiers have evil constitutional values.

In specific cases, of course, some theories perform better than others. *Dred Scott* may be no exception. Perhaps the Taney Court would have reached the just result in that case had the majority relied exclusively on the "right" theory of the judicial role in constitutional cases. Still, contemporary commentators who use *Dred Scott* to highlight how the constitutional theories advanced by their rivals may lead to injustice routinely ignore other issues raised by the American law of slavery where their preferred theory fares worse. All constitutional theories, when applied to the various constitutional controversies of the 1850s, are vulnerable to uniquely evil outcomes, proslavery results that might have been avoided had the justices relied on some other approach to the judicial function.

Institutionalists who advocate judicial deference to elected officials would be inclined to sustain constitutionally dubious proslavery legislation. Consider the Fugitive Slave Acts that Congress passed in 1793 and 1850. Both historical and aspirational theories provide strong grounds for declaring these statutes unconstitutional. An historicist could point out that the language used by the fugitive slave clause and its placement in Article IV rather than Article I of the Constitution (which lists national powers) indicates that the framers vested Congress with no power over fugitive slaves. The fugitive slave clause, in this common view, merely established state obligations. An antislavery aspirationalist would regard the fugitive slave clause as a constitutional contradiction that courts should either ignore or interpret as narrowly as possible. Proponents of judicial restraint, on the other hand, would probably be compelled to sustain the Fugitive Slave Acts because those measures were not clearly unconstitutional. If popular majorities believed that the federal government should assist slave catchers in the rendition process or give slave catchers immunities from hostile state laws, then a judge committed to institutionalism would have to let the people have their way.

Judges committed to historical theories of judicial review might feel obliged to strike down any federal antislavery legislation not limited to the territories or the international slave trade. Consider a federal law that promoted freedom within a state, say a measure requiring states to keep manumission legal (or even a total ban on slavery). Both institutional and aspirational theories provide strong reasons for sustaining such statutes. A proponent of judicial restraint would argue that the court should not second guess whatever slavery policies the people's national representatives thought best. An antislavery aspirationalist would see such measures as fulfilling the antislavery aspirations of the constitution. An historicist, however, might be compelled to declare such antislavery measures unconstitutional. At least in 1857, a clear consensus existed that "Congress had no power to interfere with slavery as it exists in the States, or to regulate what is called the slave trade among them."

The vulnerability of aspirational theories to unique proslavery outcomes is more complicated. An antislavery aspirationalist would reach every antislavery result that an institutionalist or historicist would reach, and might sometimes reach antislavery results that could not be obtained by alternative approaches to the judicial function. A proslavery aspirationalist, however, would not only reach every proslavery result that an institutionalist or historicist would reach, but such a judge would sometimes reach proslavery results that could not be obtained by other means. Consider the result of *Dred Scott* had Scott sued for his freedom in Illinois. Both institutional and aspirational theories seem to compel a judicial decision in favor of freedom. An institutionalist would, absent national legislation, defer to Illinois' judgment that slaves became free when voluntarily taken to Illinois. An historicist would defer to the framers' judgment that Illinois have the authority to determine the status of slavery in Illinois. A proslavery aspirationalist, however, could by citing the comity clause or perhaps a more general constitutional right to travel, insist that slaveowners had a right to bring their slaves along when they journeyed or temporarily resided in free states.

Dred Scott and law of slavery confound contemporary constitutional theorists who proclaim that the Constitution is nearly perfect when properly interpreted. All prominent theories of the judicial function in constitutional cases yield proslavery results in the right circumstances. No prominent theory could have promised perfectly just outcomes during the 1850s because American popular majorities supported racist practices, because the framers in 1787 provided some degree of protection for a racist institution, and because many framers had racist aspirations. *Dred Scott* is an evil decision because slavery and white supremacy are evil practices, and not because some flaw existed in the interpretive modalities adopted by the Taney Court. Unfortunately, constitutional commentators who pretend that devotees of their theory would see, say and do no evil never address the central question *Dred Scott* raises. What does a judge or any other person obligated to interpret the Constitution do when their preferred theory of constitutional interpretation yields an evil result?

DRED SCOTT v. SANDFORD

60 U.S. 393 (1857)

Opinion: Taney
Concurrence: Wayne
Concurrence: Nelson
Concurrence: Grier
Concurrence: Catron
Concurrence: Daniel
Concurrence: Campbell
Dissent: McLean
Dissent: Curtis

Dred Scott was a slave who had lived in both the State of Illinois and the Wisconsin federal territory, both places in which slavery was illegal. Under the theory that he could no longer be held in bondage under the laws of Illinois or the laws governing the Wisconsin territory, Scott sued for his freedom. The Wisconsin territory, he argued, was governed by the Missouri Compromise, which prohibited slavery and which required that he be freed. One central issue in the case concerned whether as a slave Scott had standing to sue in the first place. The Court examined this issue in light of the broader question of whether slaves or their descendeants could be citizens in the sense specified by the Constitution. The Court also considered the constitutionality of the Missouri Compromise, which outlawed slavery in some of the federal territories. Here the central issue was whether a federal law outlawing slavery unconstitutionally denied the owners of slaves their "property."

Chief Justice Roger Taney's majority opinion in Dred Scott v. Sandford *is at odds with many values that are central to modern American society. However, as Mark Graber suggests, despite its unjust result, the opinion may have a stronger basis in the Constitution as it then existed than some might think. As you read, you should consider whether Chief Justice Taney's arguments are consistent with any of the theories of constitutional interpretation that we have examined, bearing in mind that the Court was interpreting a pre-Thirteenth Amendment Constitution. Looking at the Constitution and the facts of the case, ask yourself how each theory would counsel the Court to rule. Regardless of the constitutional text, is the case inherently wrongly decided because it denies equal citizenship to all? Is there any constitutional theory that could affirm Chief Justice Taney's decision in regard to the Missouri Compromise and its discussion of slaves as property?*

Consider also any deeper flaws that might be presented in examining the various theories you have seen. For example, some claim that proceduralism as a theory would have been inappropriate to consider in constitutional interpretation before the passage of the Thirteenth and Fourteenth Amendments. Additionally, a pragmatic interpretation of Dred Scott v. Sandford *might be quite challenging because it would likely involve assessing the historical conflict looming between the free and slave states. Specifically, some have argued that if the Court had not decided* Dred Scott v. Sandford *the way that it did, it might have triggered the Civil War earlier by threatening an already suspicious group of Southern states. Should a Supreme*

Court justice take into account the likelihood of public resistance to a ruling when considering how to decide cases? What about a decision that could result in war? The moral reading imports a set of political values to evaluate case law. Is there any theory of morality that could defend Chief Justice Taney's decision? More importantly, is there any way that a proponent of the moral reading could come to a different result, given the absence of the Thirteenth and Fourteenth Amendments and the presence of clauses acknowledging slavery in the Constitution?

MR. CHIEF JUSTICE TANEY *delivered the opinion of the Court.*

. . . There are two leading questions presented by the record: 1. Had the Circuit Court of the United States jurisdiction to hear and determine the case between these parties? And 2. If it had jurisdiction, is the judgment it has given erroneous or not? The plaintiff in error, who was also the plaintiff in the court below, was, with his wife and children, held as slaves by the defendant, in the State of Missouri; and he brought this action in the Circuit Court of the United States for that district, to assert the title of himself and his family to freedom. . . .

The question is simply this: Can a negro, whose ancestors were imported into this country, and sold as slaves, become a member of the political community formed and brought into existence by the Constitution of the United States, and as such become entitled to all the rights, and privileges, and immunities, guaranteed by that instrument to the citizen? One of which rights is the privilege of suing in a court of the United States in the cases specified in the Constitution.

It will be observed, that the plea applies to that class of persons only whose ancestors were negroes of the African race, and imported into this country, and sold and held as slaves. The only matter in issue before the court, therefore, is, whether the descendants of such slaves, when they shall be emancipated, or who are born of parents who had become free before their birth, are citizens of a State, in the sense in which the word citizen is used in the Constitution of the United States. . . .

The words "people of the United States" and "citizens" are synonymous terms, and mean the same thing. They both describe the political body who, according to our republican institutions, form the sovereignty, and who hold the power and conduct the Government through their representatives. They are what we familiarly call the "sovereign people," and every citizen is one of this people, and a constituent member of this sovereignty. The question before us is, whether the class of persons described in the plea in abatement compose a portion of this people, and are constituent members of this sovereignty? We think they are not, and that they are not included, and were not intended to be included, under the word "citizens" in the Constitution, and can therefore claim none of the rights and privileges which that instrument provides for and secures to citizens of the United States. On the contrary, they were at that time considered as a subordinate and inferior class of beings, who had been subjugated by the dominant race, and, whether emancipated or not, yet remained subject to their authority, and had no rights or privileges but such as those who held the power and the Government might choose to grant them.

It is not the province of the court to decide upon the justice or injustice, the policy or impolicy, of these laws. The decision of that question belonged to the political or law-making power; to those who formed the sovereignty and framed the

Constitution. The duty of the court is, to interpret the instrument they have framed, with the best lights we can obtain on the subject, and to administer it as we find it, according to its true intent and meaning when it was adopted.

In discussing this question, we must not confound the rights of citizenship which a State may confer within its own limits, and the rights of citizenship as a member of the Union. It does not by any means follow, because he has all the rights and privileges of a citizen of a State, that he must be a citizen of the United States. He may have all of the rights and privileges of the citizen of a State, and yet not be entitled to the rights and privileges of a citizen in any other State. . . .

It is very clear, therefore, that no State can, by any act or law of its own, passed since the adoption of the Constitution, introduce a new member into the political community created by the Constitution of the United States. It cannot make him a member of this community by making him a member of its own. And for the same reason it cannot introduce any person, or description of persons, who were not intended to be embraced in this new political family, which the Constitution brought into existence, but were intended to be excluded from it.

The question then arises, whether the provisions of the Constitution, in relation to the personal rights and privileges to which the citizen of a State should be entitled, embraced the negro African race, at that time in this country, or who might afterwards be imported, who had then or should afterwards be made free in any State; and to put it in the power of a single State to make him a citizen of the United States, and endue him with the full rights of citizenship in every other State without their consent? Does the Constitution of the United States act upon him whenever he shall be made free under the laws of a State, and raised there to the rank of a citizen, and immediately clothe him with all the privileges of a citizen in every other State, and in its own courts?

The court think the affirmative of these propositions cannot be maintained. And if it cannot, the plaintiff in error could not be a citizen of the State of Missouri, within the meaning of the Constitution of the United States, and, consequently, was not entitled to sue in its courts.

It is true, every person, and every class and description of persons, who were at the time of the adoption of the Constitution recognised as citizens in the several States, became also citizens of this new political body; but none other; it was formed by them, and for them and their posterity, but for no one else. And the personal rights and privileges guarantied to citizens of this new sovereignty were intended to embrace those only who were then members of the several State communities, or who should afterwards by birthright or otherwise become members, according to the provisions of the Constitution and the principles on which it was founded. . . .

It becomes necessary, therefore, to determine who were citizens of the several States when the Constitution was adopted. And in order to do this, we must recur to the Governments and institutions of the thirteen colonies, when they separated from Great Britain and formed new sovereignties, and took their places in the family of independent nations. We must inquire who, at that time, were recognised as the people or citizens of a State, whose rights and liberties had been outraged by the English Government; and who declared their independence, and assumed the powers of Government to defend their rights by force of arms.

In the opinion of the court, the legislation and histories of the times, and the language used in the Declaration of Independence, show, that neither the class of persons who had been imported as slaves, nor their descendants, whether they had become free or not, were then acknowledged as a part of the people, nor intended to be included in the general words used in that memorable instrument.

It is difficult at this day to realize the state of public opinion in relation to that unfortunate race, which prevailed in the civilized and enlightened portions of the world at the time of the Declaration of Independence, and when the Constitution of the United States was framed and adopted. But the public history of every European nation displays it in a manner too plain to be mistaken.

They had for more than a century before been regarded as beings of an inferior order, and altogether unfit to associate with the white race, either in social or political relations; and so far inferior, that they had no rights which the white man was bound to respect; and that the negro might justly and lawfully be reduced to slavery for his benefit. He was bought and sold, and treated as an ordinary article of merchandise and traffic, whenever a profit could be made by it. This opinion was at that time fixed and universal in the civilized portion of the white race. It was regarded as an axiom in morals as well as in politics, which no one thought of disputing, or supposed to be open to dispute; and men in every grade and position in society daily and habitually acted upon it in their private pursuits, as well as in matters of public concern, without doubting for a moment the correctness of this opinion.

And in no nation was this opinion more firmly fixed or more uniformly acted upon than by the English Government and English people. They not only seized them on the coast of Africa, and sold them or held them in slavery for their own use; but they took them as ordinary articles of merchandise to every country where they could make a profit on them, and were far more extensively engaged in this commerce than any other nation in the world.

The opinion thus entertained and acted upon in England was naturally impressed upon the colonies they founded on this side of the Atlantic. And, accordingly, a negro of the African race was regarded by them as an article of property, and held, and bought and sold as such, in every one of the thirteen colonies which united in the Declaration of Independence, and afterwards formed the Constitution of the United States. The slaves were more or less numerous in the different colonies, as slave labor was found more or less profitable. But no one seems to have doubted the correctness of the prevailing opinion of the time. . . .

The province of Maryland, in 1717, passed a law declaring "that if any free negro or mulatto intermarry with any white woman, or if any white man shall intermarry with any negro or mulatto woman, such negro or mulatto shall become a slave during life, excepting mulattoes born of white women, who, for such intermarriage, shall only become servants for seven years, to be disposed of as the justices of the county court, where such marriage so happens, shall think fit; to be applied by them towards the support of a public school within the said county. And any white man or white woman who shall intermarry as aforesaid, with any negro or mulatto, such white man or white woman shall become servants during the term of seven years, and shall be disposed of by the justices as aforesaid, and be applied to the uses aforesaid." . . .

We refer to these historical facts for the purpose of showing the fixed opinions concerning that race, upon which the statesmen of that day spoke and acted. It is necessary to do this, in order to determine whether the general terms used in the Constitution of the United States, as to the rights of man and the rights of the people, was intended to include them, or to give to them or their posterity the benefit of any of its provisions.

The language of the Declaration of Independence is equally conclusive:

It begins by declaring that, "when in the course of human events it becomes necessary for one people to dissolve the political bands which have connected them with another, and to assume among the powers of the earth the separate and equal station to which the laws of nature and nature's God entitle them, a decent respect for the opinions of mankind requires that they should declare the causes which impel them to the separation."

It then proceeds to say: "We hold these truths to be self-evident: that all men are created equal; that they are endowed by their Creator with certain unalienable rights; that among them is life, liberty, and the pursuit of happiness; that to secure these rights, Governments are instituted, deriving their just powers from the consent of the governed."

The general words above quoted would seem to embrace the whole human family, and if they were used in a similar instrument at this day would be so understood. But it is too clear for dispute, that the enslaved African race were not intended to be included, and formed no part of the people who framed and adopted this declaration; for if the language, as understood in that day, would embrace them, the conduct of the distinguished men who framed the Declaration of Independence would have been utterly and flagrantly inconsistent with the principles they asserted; and instead of the sympathy of mankind, to which they so confidently appealed, they would have deserved and received universal rebuke and reprobation.

Yet the men who framed this declaration were great men—high in literary acquirements—high in their sense of honor, and incapable of asserting principles inconsistent with those on which they were acting. They perfectly understood the meaning of the language they used, and how it would be understood by others; and they knew that it would not in any part of the civilized world be supposed to embrace the negro race, which, by common consent, had been excluded from civilized Governments and the family of nations, and doomed to slavery. They spoke and acted according to the then established doctrines and principles, and in the ordinary language of the day, and no one misunderstood them. The unhappy black race were separated from the white by indelible marks, and laws long before established, and were never thought of or spoken of except as property, and when the claims of the owner or the profit of the trader were supposed to need protection. . . .

But there are two clauses in the Constitution which point directly and specifically to the negro race as a separate class of persons, and show clearly that they were not regarded as a portion of the people or citizens of the Government then formed.

One of these clauses reserves to each of the thirteen States the right to import slaves until the year 1808, if it thinks proper. And the importation which it thus sanctions was unquestionably of persons of the race of which we are speaking, as the traffic in slaves in the United States had always been confined to them. And by the other provision the States pledge themselves to each other to maintain the right of property of the master, by delivering up to him any slave who may have escaped from his service, and be found within their respective territories. By the first above-mentioned clause, therefore, the right to purchase and hold this property is directly sanctioned and authorized for twenty years by the people who framed the Constitution. And by the second, they pledge themselves to maintain and uphold the right of the master in the manner specified, as long as the Government they then formed should endure. And these two provisions show, conclusively, that neither the description of persons therein referred to, nor their descendants, were embraced in any of the other provisions of the Constitution; for certainly these two clauses were not intended to confer on them or their posterity the blessings of liberty, or any of the personal rights so carefully provided for the citizen. . . .

And if persons of the African race are citizens of a State, and of the United States, they would be entitled to all of these privileges and immunities in every State, and the State could not restrict them; for they would hold these privileges and immunities under the paramount authority of the Federal Government, and its courts would be bound to maintain and enforce them, the Constitution and laws of the State to the contrary notwithstanding. And if the States could limit or restrict them, or place the party in an inferior grade, this clause of the Constitution would be unmeaning, and could have no operation; and would give no rights to the citizen when in another State. He would have none but what the State itself chose to allow him. This is evidently not the construction or meaning of the clause in question. It guaranties rights to the citizen, and the State cannot withhold them. And these rights are of a character and would lead to consequences which make it absolutely certain that the African race were not included under the name of citizens of a State, and were not in the contemplation of the framers of the Constitution when these privileges and immunities were provided for the protection of the citizen in other States. . . .

The question with which we are now dealing is, whether a person of the African race can be a citizen of the United States, and become thereby entitled to a special privilege, by virtue of his title to that character, and which, under the Constitution, no one but a citizen can claim. . . .

This case, however, strikingly illustrates the consequences that would follow the construction of the Constitution which would give the power contended for to a State. It would in effect give it also to an individual. For if the [owner] of [a slave] had manumitted him in his lifetime, and sent him to reside in a State which recognised him as a citizen, he might have visited and sojourned in [a slave State] when he pleased, and as long as he pleased, as a citizen of the United States; and the State officers and tribunals would be compelled, by the paramount authority of the Constitution, to receive him and treat him as one of its citizens, exempt from the laws and police of the State in relation to a person of that description, and allow him to enjoy all the rights and privileges of citizenship, without respect to the laws of [that State], although such laws were deemed by it absolutely essential to its own safety. . . .

No one, we presume, supposes that any change in public opinion or feeling, in relation to this unfortunate race, in the civilized nations of Europe or in this country, should induce the court to give to the words of the Constitution a more liberal construction in their favor than they were intended to bear when the instrument was framed and adopted. Such an argument would be altogether inadmissible in any tribunal called on to interpret it. If any of its provisions are deemed unjust, there is a mode prescribed in the instrument itself by which it may be amended; but while it remains unaltered, it must be construed now as it was understood at the time of its adoption. It is not only the same in words, but the same in meaning, and delegates the same powers to the Government, and reserves and secures the same rights and privileges to the citizen; and as long as it continues to exist in its present form, it speaks not only in the same words, but with the same meaning and intent with which it spoke when it came from the hands of its framers, and was voted on and adopted by the people of the United States. Any other rule of construction would abrogate the judicial character of this court, and make it the mere reflex of the popular opinion or passion of the day. This court was not created by the Constitution for such purposes. Higher and graver trusts have been confided to it, and it must not falter in the path of duty.

What the construction was at that time, we think can hardly admit of doubt. We have the language of the Declaration of Independence and of the Articles of Confederation, in addition to the plain words of the Constitution itself; we have the legislation of the different States, before, about the time, and since, the Constitution was adopted; we have the legislation of Congress, from the time of its adoption to a recent period; and we have the constant and uniform action of the Executive Department, all concurring together, and leading to the same result. And if anything in relation to the construction of the Constitution can be regarded as settled, it is that which we now give to the word "citizen" and the word "people."

And upon a full and careful consideration of the subject, the court is of opinion, that, upon the facts stated in the plea in abatement, Dred Scott was not a citizen of Missouri within the meaning of the Constitution of the United States, and not entitled as such to sue in its courts; and, consequently, that the Circuit Court had no jurisdiction of the case, and that the judgment on the plea in abatement is erroneous.

We proceed, therefore, to inquire whether the facts relied on by the plaintiff entitled him to his freedom. . . .

In considering this part of the controversy, two questions arise: 1. Was he, together with his family, free in Missouri by reason of the stay in [a free territory]? And 2. If they were not, is Scott himself free by reason of his removal to Rock Island, in the State of Illinois, as stated in the above admissions?

We proceed to examine the first question.

The act of Congress, upon which the plaintiff relies, declares that slavery and involuntary servitude, except as a punishment for crime, shall be forever prohibited in all that part of the territory ceded by France, under the name of Louisiana, which lies north of thirty-six degrees thirty minutes north latitude, and not included within the limits of Missouri. And the difficulty which meets us at the threshold of this part of the inquiry is, whether Congress was authorized to pass this law under any of the powers granted to it by the Constitution; for if the authority is not given by that instrument, it is the duty of this court to declare it void and inoperative, and incapable of conferring freedom upon any one who is held as a slave under the have of any one of the States.

The counsel for the plaintiff has laid much stress upon that article in the Constitution which confers on Congress the power "to dispose of and make all needful rules and regulations respecting the territory or other property belonging to the United States"; but, in the judgment of the court, that provision has no bearing on the present controversy, and the power there given, whatever it may be, is confined, and was intended to be confined, to the territory which at that time belonged to, or was claimed by, the United States, and was within their boundaries as settled by the treaty with Great Britain, and can have no influence upon a territory afterwards acquired from a foreign Government. It was a special provision for a known and particular territory, and to meet a present emergency, and nothing more. . . .

It was to transfer to the new Government the property then held in common by the States, and to give to that Government power to apply it to the objects for which it had been destined by mutual agreement among the States before their league was dissolved. It applied only to the property which the States held in common at that time, and has no reference whatever to any territory or other property which the new sovereignty might afterwards itself acquire. . . .

This brings us to examine by what provision of the Constitution the present Federal Government, under its delegated and restricted powers, is authorized to acquire territory outside of the original limits of the United States, and what powers it may exercise therein over the person or property of a citizen of the United States, while it remains a Territory, and until it shall be admitted as one of the States of the Union.

There is certainly no power given by the Constitution to the Federal Government to establish or maintain colonies bordering on the United States or at a distance, to be ruled and governed at its own pleasure; nor to enlarge its territorial limits in any way, except by the admission of new States. That power is plainly given; and if a new State is admitted, it needs no further legislation by Congress, because the Constitution itself defines the relative rights and powers, and duties of the State, and the citizens of the State, and the Federal Government. But no power is given to acquire a Territory to be held and governed permanently in that character. . . .

[I]t may be safely assumed that citizens of the United States who migrate to a Territory belonging to the people of the United States, cannot be ruled as mere colonists, dependent upon the will of the General Government, and to be governed by any laws it may think proper to impose. The principle upon which our Governments rest, and upon which alone they continue to exist, is the union of States, sovereign and independent within their own limits in their internal and domestic concerns, and bound together as one people by a General Government, possessing certain enumerated and restricted powers, delegated to it by the people of the several States, and exercising supreme authority within the scope of the powers granted to it, throughout the dominion of the United States. A power, therefore, in the General Government to obtain and hold colonies and dependent territories, over which they might legislate without restriction, would be inconsistent with its own existence in its present form. Whatever it acquires, it acquires for the benefit of the people of the several States who created it. It is their trustee acting for them, and charged with the duty of promoting the interests of the whole people of the Union in the exercise of the powers specifically granted. . . .

But the power of Congress over the person or property of a citizen can never be a mere discretionary power under our Constitution and form of Government. The powers of the Government and the rights and privileges of the citizen are regulated and plainly defined by the Constitution itself. And when the Territory becomes a part of the United States, the Federal Government enters into possession in the character impressed upon it by those who created it. It enters upon it with its powers over the citizen strictly defined, and limited by the Constitution, from which it derives its own existence, and by virtue of which alone it continues to exist and act as a Government and sovereignty. It has no power of any kind beyond it; and it cannot, when it enters a Territory of the United States, put off its character, and assume discretionary or despotic powers which the Constitution has denied to it. It cannot create for itself a new character separated from the citizens of the United States, and the duties it owes them under the provisions of the Constitution. The Territory being a part of the United States, the Government and the citizen both enter it under the authority of the Constitution, with their respective rights defined and marked out; and the Federal Government can exercise no power over his person or property, beyond what that instrument confers, nor lawfully deny any right which it has reserved.

A reference to a few of the provisions of the Constitution will illustrate this proposition.

For example, no one, we presume, will contend that Congress can make any law in a Territory respecting the establishment of religion, or the free exercise thereof, or abridging the freedom of speech or of the press, or the right of the people of the Territory peaceably to assemble, and to petition the Government for the redress of grievances.

Nor can Congress deny to the people the right to keep and bear arms, nor the right to trial by jury, nor compel any one to be a witness against himself in a criminal proceeding.

These powers, and others, in relation to rights of person, which it is not necessary here to enumerate, are, in express and positive terms, denied to the General Government; and the rights of private property have been guarded with equal care. Thus the rights of property are united with the rights of person, and placed on the same ground by the fifth amendment to the Constitution, which provides that no person shall be deprived of life, liberty, and property, without due process of law.

And an act of Congress which deprives a citizen of the United States of his liberty or property, merely because he came himself or brought his property into a particular Territory of the United States, and who had committed no offence against the laws, could hardly be dignified with the name of due process of law. . . .

It seems, however, to be supposed, that there is a difference between property in a slave and other property, and that different rules may be applied to it in expounding the Constitution of the United States. . . .

[I]f the Constitution recognises the right of property of the master in a slave, and makes no distinction between that description of property and other property owned by a citizen, no tribunal, acting under the authority of the United States, whether it be legislative, executive, or judicial, has a right to draw such a distinction, or deny to it the benefit of the provisions and guarantees which have been provided for the protection of private property against the encroachments of the Government.

Now, as we have already said in an earlier part of this opinion, upon a different point, the right of property in a slave is distinctly and expressly affirmed in the Constitution. The right to traffic in it, like an ordinary article of merchandise and property, was guarantied to the citizens of the United States, in every State that might desire it, for twenty years. And the Government in express terms is pledged to protect it in all future time, if the slave escapes from his owner. This is done in plain words—too plain to be misunderstood. And no word can be found in the Constitution which gives Congress a greater power over slave property, or which entitles property of that kind to less protection than property of any other description. The only power conferred is the power coupled with the duty of guarding and protecting the owner in his rights.

Upon these considerations, it is the opinion of the court that the act of Congress which prohibited a citizen from holding and owning property of this kind in the territory of the United States north of the line therein mentioned, is not warranted by the Constitution, and is therefore void; and that neither Dred Scott himself, nor any of his family, were made free by being carried into this territory; even if they had been carried there by the owner, with the intention of becoming a permanent resident.

We have so far examined the case, as it stands under the Constitution of the United States, and the powers thereby delegated to the Federal Government.

But there is another point in the case which depends on State power and State law. And it is contended, on the part of the plaintiff, that he is made free by being taken to Rock Island, in the State of Illinois, independently of his residence in the territory of the United States; and being so made free, he was not again reduced to a state of slavery by being brought back to Missouri. . . .

As Scott was a slave when taken into the State of Illinois by his owner, and was there held as such, and brought back in that character, his status, as free or slave, depended on the laws of Missouri, and not of Illinois. . . .

[W]hatever doubts or opinions may, at one time, have been entertained upon this subject, we are satisfied, upon a careful examination of all the cases decided in the State courts of Missouri referred to, that it is now firmly settled by the decisions of the highest court in the State, that Scott and his family upon their return were not free, but were, by the laws of Missouri, the property of the defendant; and that the Circuit Court of the United States had no jurisdiction, when, by the laws of the State, the plaintiff was a slave, and not a citizen. . . .

Upon the whole, therefore, it is the judgment of this court, that it appears by the record before us that the plaintiff in error is not a citizen of Missouri, in the sense in which that word is used in the Constitution; and that the Circuit Court of the United States, for that reason, had no jurisdiction in the case, and could give no judgment in it. Its judgment for the defendant must, consequently, be reversed, and a mandate issued, directing the suit to be dismissed for want of jurisdiction.

MR. JUSTICE McLEAN *dissenting.*

. . . There is no averment in this plea which shows or conduces to show an inability in the plaintiff to sue in the Circuit Court. It does not allege that the plaintiff had his domicile in any other State, nor that he is not a free man in Missouri. He is averred to have had a negro ancestry, but this does not show that he is not a citizen of Missouri, within the meaning of the act of Congress authorizing him to sue in the Circuit Court. It has never been held necessary, to constitute a citizen within the act, that he should have the qualifications of an elector. Females and minors may sue in the Federal courts, and so may any individual who has a permanent domicile in the State under whose laws his rights are protected, and to which he owes allegiance.

Being born under our Constitution and laws, no naturalization is required, as one of foreign birth, to make him a citizen. The most general and appropriate definition of the term citizen is "a freeman." Being a freeman, and having his domicile in a State different from that of the defendant, he is a citizen within the act of Congress, and the courts of the Union are open to him.

It has often been held, that the jurisdiction, as regards parties, can only be exercised between citizens of different States, and that a mere residence is not sufficient;

but this has been said to distinguish a temporary from a permanent residence....

In the argument, it was said that a colored citizen would not be an agreeable member of society. This is more a matter of taste than of law. Several of the States have admitted persons of color to the right of suffrage, and in this view have recognised them as citizens; and this has been done in the slave as well as the free States. On the question of citizenship, it must be admitted that we have not been very fastidious. Under the late treaty with Mexico, we have made citizens of all grades, combinations, and colors. The same was done in the admission of Louisiana and Florida. No one ever doubted, and no court ever held, that the people of these Territories did not become citizens under the treaty. They have exercised all the rights of citizens, without being naturalized under the acts of Congress....

I prefer the lights of Madison, Hamilton, and Jay, as a means of construing the Constitution in all its bearings, rather than to look behind that period, into a traffic which is now declared to be piracy, and punished with death by Christian nations. I do not like to draw the sources of our domestic relations from so dark a ground. Our independence was a great epoch in the history of freedom; and while I admit the Government was not made especially for the colored race, yet many of them were citizens of the New England States, and exercised, the rights of suffrage when the Constitution was adopted, and it was not doubted by any intelligent person that its tendencies would greatly ameliorate their condition.

Many of the States, on the adoption of the Constitution, or shortly afterward, took measures to abolish slavery within their respective jurisdictions; and it is a well-known fact that a belief was cherished by the leading men, South as well as North, that the institution of slavery would gradually decline, until it would become extinct. The increased value of slave labor, in the culture of cotton and sugar, prevented the realization of this expectation. Like all other communities and States, the South were influenced by what they considered to be their own interests.

But if we are to turn our attention to the dark ages of the world, why confine our view to colored slavery? On the same principles, white men were made slaves. All slavery has its origin in power, and is against right.

The power of Congress to establish Territorial Governments, and to prohibit the introduction of slavery therein, is the next point to be considered....

On the 13th of July, the Ordinance of 1787 was passed, "for the government of the United States territory northwest of the river Ohio," with but one dissenting vote. This instrument provided there should be organized in the territory not less than three nor more than five States, designating their boundaries. It passed while the Federal Convention was in session, about two months before the Constitution was adopted by the Convention. The members of the Convention must therefore have been well acquainted with the provisions of the Ordinance. It provided for a temporary Government, as initiatory to the formation of State Governments. Slavery was prohibited in the territory.

Can any one suppose that the eminent men of the Federal Convention could have overlooked or neglected a matter so vitally important to the country, in the organization of temporary Governments for the vast territory northwest of the river Ohio? In the 3d section of the 4th article of the Constitution, they did make provision for the admission of new States, the sale of the public lands, and the temporary Government of the territory. Without a temporary Government, new States could not have been formed, nor could the public lands have been sold.

If the third section were before us now for consideration for the first time, under the facts stated, I could not hesitate to say there was adequate legislative power given in it. The power to make all needful rules and regulations is a power to legislate. This no one will controvert, as Congress cannot make "rules and regulations," except by legislation. But it is argued that the word territory is used as synonymous with the word land; and that the rules and regulations of Congress are limited to the disposition of lands and other property belonging to the United States. That this is not the true construction of the section appears from the fact that in the first line of the section "the power to dispose of the public lands" is given expressly, and, in addition, to make all needful rules and regulations. The power to dispose of is complete in itself, and requires nothing more. It authorizes Congress to use the proper means within its discretion, and any further provision for this purpose would be a useless verbiage. As a composition, the Constitution is remarkably free from such a charge.

In the discussion of the power of Congress to govern a Territory, in the case of *Atlantic Insurance Company v. Canter*, Chief Justice Marshall, speaking for the court, said, in regard to the people of Florida, "they do not, however, participate in political power; they do not share in the Government till Florida shall become a State; in the mean time, Florida continues to be a Territory of the United States, governed by virtue of that clause in the Constitution which empowers Congress 'to make all needful rules and regulations respecting the territory or other property belonging to the United States.'"

. . . And in the close of the opinion, the court say, "in legislating for them [the Territories,] Congress exercises the combined powers of the General and State Governments."

The prohibition of slavery north of thirty-six degrees thirty minutes, and of the State of Missouri, contained in the act admitting that State into the Union, was passed by a vote of 134, in the House of Representatives, to 42. Before Mr. Monroe signed the act, it was submitted by him to his Cabinet, and they held the restriction of slavery in a Territory to be within the constitutional powers of Congress. . . .

I will now consider the fourth head, which is: "The effect of taking slaves into a State or Territory, and so holding them, where slavery is prohibited."

If the principle laid down in the case of *Prigg v. Pennsylvania* is to be maintained, and it is certainly to be maintained until overruled, as the law of this court, there can be no difficulty on this point. In that case, the court says: "The state of slavery is deemed to be a mere municipal regulation, founded upon and limited to the range of the territorial laws." If this be so, slavery can exist nowhere except under the authority of law, founded on usage having the force of law, or by statutory recognition. And the court further says: "It is manifest, from this consideration, that if the Constitution had not contained the clause requiring the rendition of fugitives from labor, every non-slaveholding State in the Union would have been at liberty to have declared free all runaway slaves coming within its limits, and to have given them entire immunity and protection against the claims of their masters."

Now, if a slave abscond, he may be reclaimed; but if he accompany his master into a State or Territory where slavery is prohibited, such slave cannot be said to have left the service of his master where his services were legalized. And if slavery be limited to the range of the territorial laws, how can the slave be coerced to serve in a State or Territory, not only without the authority of law, but against its express provisions? What gives the master the right to control the will of his slave? The local law, which exists in some form. But where there is no such law, can the master control the will of the slave by force? Where no slavery exists, the presumption, without regard to color, is in favor of freedom. Under such a jurisdiction, may the colored man be levied on as the property of his master by a creditor? On the decease of the master, does the slave descend to his heirs as property? Can the master sell him? Any one or all of these acts may be done to the slave, where he is legally held to service. But where the law does not confer this power, it cannot be exercised. . . .

But there is another ground which I deem conclusive, and which I will re-state.

The Supreme Court of Missouri refused to notice the act of Congress or the Constitution of Illinois, under which Dred Scott, his wife and children, claimed that they are entitled to freedom. . . .

If a State court may do this, on a question involving the liberty of a human being, what protection do the laws afford? So far from this being a Missouri question, it is a question, as it would seem, within the twenty-fifth section of the judiciary act, where a right to freedom being set up under the act of Congress, and the decision being against such right, it may be brought for revision before this court, from the Supreme Court of Missouri. I think the judgment of the court below should be reversed.

CASE QUESTION

Some legal thinkers in the tradition of "legal positivism" suggest that we must divide legal analysis from moral analysis. Unjust laws, in their view, can still be valid laws. For instance, one might argue that the judges in this case were merely applying the Constitution as it was written. In his article, Mark Graber suggests why a variety of theories of constitutional interpretation might lead to the conclusion that *Dred Scott v. Sandford* was the "right" legal result. In his words, "*Dred Scott* is constitutionally plausible in any contemporary constitutional rhetoric." But such a suggestion requires bracketing common understandings of contemporary morality. Should we bracket these conceptions in doing constitutional analysis, and in judging Chief Justice Roger Taney's decision? Or, should the Court always follow the exact wording of the Constitution, even if it leads to an undeniably evil result?

The Civil War Amendments

The Thirteenth Amendment (1865)

1. Neither slavery nor involuntary servitude, except as a punishment for crime whereof the party shall have been duly convicted, shall exist within the United States, or any place subject to their jurisdiction.

2. Congress shall have power to enforce this article by appropriate legislation.

The Fourteenth Amendment (1868)

1. All persons born or naturalized in the United States, and subject to the jurisdiction thereof, are citizens of the United States and of the State wherein they reside. No

State shall make or enforce any law which shall abridge the privileges or immunities of citizens of the United States; nor shall any State deprive any person of life, liberty, or property, without due process of law; nor deny to any person within its jurisdiction the equal protection of the laws.

2. Representatives shall be apportioned among the several States according to their respective numbers, counting the whole number of persons in each State, excluding Indians not taxed. But when the right to vote at any election for the choice of electors for President and Vice-President of the United States, Representatives in Congress, the Executive and Judicial officers of a State, or the members of the Legislature thereof, is denied to any of the male inhabitants of such State, being twenty-one years of age, and citizens of the United States, or in any way abridged, except for participation in rebellion, or other crime, the basis of representation therein shall be reduced in the proportion which the number of such male citizens shall bear to the whole number of male citizens twenty-one years of age in such State.

3. No person shall be a Senator or Representative in Congress, or elector of President and Vice-President, or hold any office, civil or military, under the United States, or under any State, who, having previously taken an oath, as a member of Congress, or as an officer of the United States, or as a member of any State legislature, or as an executive or judicial officer of any State, to support the Constitution of the United States, shall have engaged in insurrection or rebellion against the same, or given aid or comfort to the enemies thereof. But Congress may by a vote of two-thirds of each House, remove such disability.

4. The validity of the public debt of the United States, authorized by law, including debts incurred for payment of pensions and bounties for services in suppressing insurrection or rebellion, shall not be questioned. But neither the United States nor any State shall assume or pay any debt or obligation incurred in aid of insurrection or rebellion against the United States, or any claim for the loss or emancipation of any slave; but all such debts, obligations and claims shall be held illegal and void.

5. The Congress shall have power to enforce, by appropriate legislation, the provisions of this article.

The Fifteenth Amendment (1870)

1. The right of citizens of the United States to vote shall not be denied or abridged by the United States or by any State on account of race, color, or previous condition of servitude.

2. The Congress shall have power to enforce this article by appropriate legislation.

THE CIVIL RIGHTS CASES

109 U.S. 3 (1883)

Opinion: Bradley, joined by Waite, Miller, Field, Hunt, Woods, Matthews, Gray
Dissent: Harlan

In reviewing the Fourteenth Amendment, it is important to take note of the fifth section, which grants to Congress the power to enforce the amendment's provisions by enacting appropriate legislation. Congress passed the Civil Rights Act of 1875 in an attempt to enforce the ideal of equal protection of the laws. Section 1 of the Act guaranteed "the full and equal enjoyment of the accommodations, advantages, facilities, and privileges of inns, public conveyances on land or water, theatres, and other places of public amusement, subject only to the conditions and limitations established by law and applicable alike to citizens of every race and color, regardless of any previous condition of servitude." In the Civil Rights Cases, the Court consolidated five cases that resulted from prosecutions under this law. Specifically, the decision focuses on whether Section 5 of the Fourteenth Amendment gave Congress the power to ensure equal protection in relationships among people or whether it was only meant to deny the government the ability to discriminate. As you will remember from Chapter 3, the Court's decision here only permits Congress to end discrimination by governmental entities rather than private ones; in other words, the discrimination must be the result of state action. As a result, when the Court considered the Civil Rights Act of 1964, almost a century later, it would have had to reverse the Civil Rights Cases in order to rely on the Equal Protection Clause. As you saw, the Court chose not to overturn this precedent, instead relying on the Commerce Clause.

As you read this case, consider whether you agree that the Fourteenth Amendment should apply only to state action or whether it should also have been read to authorize the Civil Rights Act of 1875. Notice too the dissent by Justice John Marshall Harlan, criticizing the state action doctrine.

MR. JUSTICE BRADLEY *delivered the opinion of the Court.*

These cases are all founded on the first and second sections of the act of congress known as the "Civil Rights Act," passed March 1, 1875, entitled "An act to protect all citizens in their civil and legal rights."

It is obvious that the primary and important question in all the cases is the constitutionality of the law; for if the law is unconstitutional none of the prosecutions can stand.

The sections of the law referred to provide as follows:

Section 1. That all persons within the jurisdiction of the United States shall be entitled to the full and equal enjoyment of the accommodations, advantages, facilities, and privileges of inns, public conveyances on land or water, theaters, and other places of public amusement; subject only to the conditions and limitations established by law, and applicable alike to citizens of every race and color, regardless of any previous condition of servitude.

SEC. 2. That any person who shall violate the foregoing section by denying to any citizen, except for reasons by law applicable to citizens of every race and color, and regardless of any previous condition of servitude, the full enjoyment of any of the accommodations, advantages, facilities, or privileges in said section enumerated, or by aiding or inciting such denial, shall for every such offence, forfeit and pay the sum of five hundred dollars to the person aggrieved thereby, to be recovered in an action of debt, with full costs, and shall also, for every such offence, be deemed guilty of a misdemeanor, and, upon conviction thereof, shall be fined not less than five hundred nor more than one thousand dollars, or shall be imprisoned not less than thirty days nor more than one year, *Provided,* that all persons may elect to sue for the penalty aforesaid, or to proceed under their rights at common law and by State statutes, and having so elected to proceed in the one mode or the other, their right to proceed in the other jurisdiction shall be barred. But this provision shall not apply to criminal proceedings, either under this act or the criminal law of any State; *and provided further,* that a judgment for the penalty in favor of the party aggrieved, or a judgment upon an indictment, shall be a bar to either prosecution respectively.

Are these sections constitutional? The first section, which is the principal one, cannot be fairly understood without attending to the last clause, which qualifies the preceding part.

The essence of the law is not to declare broadly that all persons shall be entitled to the full and equal enjoyment of the accommodations, advantages, facilities, and privileges of inns, public conveyances, and theatres, but that such enjoyment shall not be subject to any conditions applicable only to citizens of a particular race or color, or who had been in a previous condition of servitude. In other words, it is the purpose of the law to declare that, in the enjoyment of the accommodations and privileges of inns, public conveyances, theatres, and other places of public amusement, no distinction shall be made between citizens of different race or color or between those who have, and those who have not, been slaves. Its effect is to declare that, in all inns, public conveyances, and places of amusement, colored citizens, whether formerly slaves or not, and citizens of other races, shall have the same accommodations and privileges in all inns, public conveyances, and places of amusement as are enjoyed by white citizens, and vice versa. The second section makes it a penal offence in any person to deny to any citizen of any race or color, regardless of previous servitude, any of the accommodations or privileges mentioned in the first section.

Has Congress constitutional power to make such a law? Of course, no one will contend that the power to pass it was contained in the Constitution before the adoption of the last three amendments. The power is sought, first, in the Fourteenth Amendment, and the views and arguments of distinguished Senators, advanced whilst the law was under consideration, claiming authority to pass it by virtue of that amendment, are the principal arguments adduced in favor of the power. We have carefully considered those arguments, as was due to the eminent ability of those who put them forward, and have felt, in all its force, the weight of authority which always invests a law that Congress deems itself competent to pass. But the responsibility of an independent judgment is now thrown upon this court, and we are bound to exercise it according to the best lights we have.

The first section of the Fourteenth Amendment (which is the one relied on), after declaring who shall be citizens of the United States, and of the several States, is prohibitory in its character, and prohibitory upon the States. It declares that:

> No State shall make or enforce any law which shall abridge the privileges or immunities of citizens of the United States; nor shall any State deprive any person of life, liberty, or property without due process of law; nor deny to any person within its jurisdiction the equal protection of the laws.

It is State action of a particular character that is prohibited. Individual invasion of individual rights is not the subject matter of the amendment. It has a deeper and broader scope. It nullifies and makes void all State legislation, and State action of every kind, which impairs the privileges and immunities of citizens of the United States or which injures them in life, liberty or property without due process of law, or which denies to any of them the equal protection of the laws. It not only does this, but, in order that the national will, thus declared, may not be a mere *brutum fulmen*, the last section of the amendment invests Congress with power to enforce it by appropriate legislation. To enforce what? To enforce the prohibition. To adopt appropriate legislation for correcting the effects of such prohibited State laws and State acts, and thus to render them effectually null, void, and innocuous. This is the legislative power conferred upon Congress, and this is the whole of it. It does not invest Congress with power to legislate upon subjects which are within the domain of State legislation, but to provide modes of relief against State legislation, or State action, of the kind referred to. It does not authorize Congress to create a code of municipal law for the regulation of private rights, but to provide modes of redress against the operation of State laws and the action of State officers executive or judicial when these are subversive of the fundamental rights specified in the amendment. Positive rights and privileges are undoubtedly secured by the Fourteenth Amendment, but they are secured by way of prohibition against State laws and State proceedings affecting those rights and privileges, and by power given to Congress to legislate for the purpose of carrying such prohibition into effect, and such legislation must necessarily be predicated upon such supposed State laws or State proceedings, and be directed to the correction of their operation and effect.

MR. JUSTICE HARLAN *dissenting*.

The opinion in these cases proceeds, it seems to me, upon grounds entirely too narrow and artificial. I cannot resist the conclusion that the substance and spirit of the recent amendments of the Constitution have been sacrificed by a subtle and ingenious verbal criticism. "It is not the words of the law, but the internal sense of it that makes the law; the letter of the law is the body; the sense and reason of the law is the soul." Constitutional provisions, adopted in the interest of liberty and for the purpose of securing, through national legislation, if need be, rights inhering in a state of freedom and belonging to American citizenship have been so construed as to defeat the ends the people desired to accomplish, which they attempted to accomplish, and which they supposed they had accomplished by changes in their fundamental law. By this I do not

mean that the determination of these cases should have been materially controlled by considerations of mere expediency or policy. I mean only, in this form, to express an earnest conviction that the court has departed from the familiar rule requiring, in the interpretation of constitutional provisions, that full effect be given to the intent with which they were adopted.

The purpose of the first section of the act of Congress of March 1, 1875, was to prevent race discrimination in respect of the accommodations and facilities of inns, public conveyances, and places of public amusement. It does not assume to define the general conditions and limitations under which inns, public conveyances, and places of public amusement may be conducted, but only declares that such conditions and limitations, whatever they may be, shall not be applied so as to work a discrimination solely because of race, color, or previous condition of servitude. The second section provides a penalty against anyone denying, or aiding or inciting the denial, of any citizen, of that equality of right given by the first section except for reasons by law applicable to citizens of every race or color and regardless of any previous condition of servitude.

There seems to be no substantial difference between my brethren and myself as to the purpose of Congress, for they say that the essence of the law is not to declare broadly that all persons shall be entitled to the full and equal enjoyment of the accommodations, advantages, facilities, and privileges of inns, public conveyances, and theatres, but that such enjoyment shall not be subject to conditions applicable only to citizens of a particular race or color, or who had been in a previous condition of servitude. The effect of the statute, the court says, is that colored citizens, whether formerly slaves or not, and citizens of other races shall have the same accommodations and privileges in all inns, public conveyances, and places of amusement as are enjoyed by white persons, and vice versa.

The court adjudges, I think erroneously, that Congress is without power, under either the Thirteenth or Fourteenth Amendment, to establish such regulations, and that the first and second sections of the statute are, in all their parts, unconstitutional and void.

. . . The opinion of the court, as I have said, proceeds upon the ground that the power of Congress to legislate for the protection of the rights and privileges secured by the Fourteenth Amendment cannot be brought into activity except with the view, and as it may become necessary, to correct and annul State laws and State proceedings in hostility to such rights and privileges. In the absence of State laws or State action adverse to such rights and privileges, the nation may not actively interfere for their protection and security, even against

corporations and individuals exercising public or *quasi*-public functions. Such I understand to be the position of my brethren. If the grant to colored citizens of the United States of citizenship in their respective States imports exemption from race discrimination in their States in respect of such civil rights as belong to citizenship, then to hold that the amendment remits that right to the States for their protection, primarily, and stays the hands of the nation until it is assailed by State laws or State proceedings is to adjudge that the amendment, so far from enlarging the powers of Congress—as we have heretofore said it did—not only curtails them, but reverses the policy which the general government has pursued from its very organization. Such an interpretation of the amendment is a denial to Congress of the power, by appropriate legislation, to enforce one of its provisions.

Box 8-1	A Route Not Taken: The Privileges and Immunities Clause and the *Slaughter-House Cases* (1873)

In addition to cutting off the possible use of the Fourteenth Amendment's Section 5 power to authorize civil rights legislation, the Court limited another provision of that amendment. Many scholars insist that the Privileges and Immunities Clause of the Fourteenth Amendment could have been a compelling source of authority for civil rights legislation. This clause guarantees that "No State shall make or enforce any law which shall abridge the privileges or immunities of citizens of the United States." Surely, they argue, civil rights, such as those provided for in both the 1875 and the 1964 Civil Rights Acts, are among the "privileges and immunities" of citizenship. This argument, however, was derailed almost immediately after the ratification of the Fourteenth Amendment in the *Slaughter-House Cases* (1873). The case involved a number of butchers in New Orleans who argued that a Louisiana plan to restrict butchering to a limited, government-sponsored monopoly denied them the right to practice their trade and was an infringement of their property rights. The Court ruled against them, but in the course of the decision the Court considered, and rejected, the idea that the Privileges and Immunities Clause was meant to incorporate a wide array of rights at the national level and apply them against state and local governments. The Fourteenth Amendment, the Court held, gives Congress the power to enforce *national* rights—*national* privileges and immunities. As U.S. Supreme Court Justice Samuel F. Miller wrote in his opinion for the Court:

> The language is, "No State shall make or enforce any law which shall abridge the privileges or immunities of citizens of *the United States*." It is a little remarkable, if this clause was intended as a protection to the citizen of a State against the legislative power of his own State, that the word citizen of the State should be left out when it is so carefully used, and used in contradistinction to the citizens of the United States in the very sentence which precedes it. . . .
>
> [W]hen, as in the case before us, these consequences are so serious, so far-reaching and pervading, so great a departure from the structure and spirit of our institutions; when the effect is to fetter and degrade the State governments by subjecting them to the control of Congress in the exercise of powers heretofore universally conceded to them of the most ordinary and fundamental character; when, in fact, it radically changes the whole theory of the relations of the State and Federal governments to each other and of both these governments to the people, the argument has a force that is irresistible in the absence of language which expresses such a purpose too clearly to admit of doubt.
>
> We are convinced that no such results were intended by the Congress which proposed these amendments, nor by the legislatures of the States which ratified them.

What are those national privileges and immunities that the Court viewed the Fourteenth Amendment as protecting? As it turned out, these national privileges and communities were quite limited. For instance, they included the power to seek the protection of the national government when traveling abroad, the right to have access to seaports and harbors, and a few others.

With the Privileges and Immunities Clause construed so narrowly, this decision left the Equal Protection Clause as the next most likely source of national power to enforce civil rights. But, as you just saw, that too was very quickly narrowed by the *Civil Rights Cases*, in which the Court insisted that equal protection would only apply to those rights that involved public rather than private affairs. This meant that discrimination in places of public accommodation (such as transportation, restaurants, inns and hotels, shops, and movie theaters) was beyond the reach of the national government for a long period of American history. Thus, when the Lyndon B. Johnson Administration joined Congress to write the Civil Rights Act of 1964, they were reluctant to rest the law on either the Privileges and Immunities Clause or the Equal Protection Clause—since doing so would require the Court to overturn its long-standing precedents from those earlier cases. Instead, they turned to the Commerce Clause, as you saw in Chapter 3.

The colored waiting room was an example of state-mandated segregation, an issue that raised the question of "separate but equal" examined in Plessy v. Ferguson *and reevaluated in* Brown v. Board of Education.

PLESSY v. FERGUSON

163 U.S. 537 (1896)

Opinion: Brown, Shiras, Jackson, White, Fuller, Field, Gray
Dissent: Harlan

The Fourteenth Amendment, ratified in 1868, explicitly and deliberately granted all Americans, regardless of color, "equal protection of the laws." Despite this guarantee, well into the second half of the twentieth century, many states legally maintained a segregated society in which African Americans were forced into separate and clearly inferior schools and accommodations.

With this background information in mind, examine the Court's reasoning in its infamous decision in Plessy v. Ferguson *about the constitutionality of the principle of segregation. Specifically, in this case, the Court endorsed the principle of "separate but equal" in ruling that a Louisiana law requiring racial segregation in train cars did not violate the Constitution. Notice that there is clear state action in this case because there is a law at issue mandating segregation. Thus the state action requirement suggested by the* Civil Rights Cases *is met. Thus the Court is forced here to decide the case based upon the meaning of the Fourteenth Amendment's Equal Protection Clause. The Court had ruled in the case of* Yick Wo v. Hopkins *that San Francisco had applied its law regulating laundry operations in a way that denied Chinese laundry operators equal protection of the laws. Although the law did not discriminate "on its face" or as the law was written, it was discriminatory in the way it was applied. In this case, Plessy argued, the Court should extend the holding in* Yick Wo v. Hopkins *to strike down state-mandated segregation in railway cars.*

What arguments does U.S. Supreme Court Justice Henry B. Brown make to support his conclusion that state-mandated segregation is consistent with the Equal Protection Clause? Consider also that when the Thirteenth and Fourteenth Amendments were approved by Congress, the District of Columbia, which was governed directly by Congress itself, practiced segregation. What arguments does Justice John Marshall Harlan present in his dissent against the Court's decision? What does he mean when he says that the Constitution is "colorblind"? Do you agree with Justice Harlan's analysis? Does his evident racism undermine his argumentation? Or, on the contrary, does it strengthen his argument that even someone who holds racist positions recognizes the unconstitutionality of separate-but-equal facilities? Be sure to note the similarities and differences between Justice Harlan's dissent here and his dissent in the *Civil Rights Cases.*

MR. JUSTICE BROWN, *after stating the case, delivered the opinion of the Court.*

This case turns upon the constitutionality of an act of the General Assembly of the State of Louisiana, passed in 1890, providing for separate railway carriages for the white and colored races. Acts 1890, No. 111, p. 152.

The first section of the statute enacts "that all railway companies carrying passengers in their coaches in this State shall provide equal but separate accommodations for the white and colored races by providing two or more passenger coaches for each passenger train, or by dividing the passenger coaches by a partition so as to secure separate accommodations."

By the second section, it was enacted "that the officers of such passenger trains shall have power and are hereby required to assign each passenger to the coach or compartment used for the race to which such passenger belongs; any passenger insisting on going into a coach or compartment to which by race he does not belong shall be liable to a fine of twenty-five dollars, or in lieu thereof to imprisonment for a period of not more than twenty days in the parish prison, and any officer of any railroad insisting on assigning a passenger to a coach or compartment other than the one set aside for the race to which said passenger belongs shall be liable to a fine of twenty-five dollars, or in lieu thereof to imprisonment for a period of not more than twenty days in the parish prison; and should any passenger refuse to occupy the coach or compartment to which he or she is assigned by the officer of such railway, said officer shall have power to refuse to carry such passenger on his train, and for such refusal neither he nor the railway company which he represents shall be liable for damages in any of the courts of this State."

The information filed in the criminal District Court charged in substance that Plessy, being a passenger between two stations within the State of Louisiana, was assigned by officers of the company to the coach used for the race to which he belonged, but he insisted upon going into a coach used by the race to which he did not belong. Neither in the information nor plea was his particular race or color averred. The petition for the writ of prohibition averred that petitioner was seven-eighths Caucasian and one-eighth African blood; that the mixture of colored blood was not discernible in him, and that he was entitled to every right, privilege and immunity secured to citizens of the United States of the white race; and that, upon such theory, he took possession of a vacant seat in a coach where passengers of the white race were accommodated, and was ordered by the conductor to vacate said coach and take a seat in another assigned to persons of the colored race, and, having refused to comply with such demand, he was forcibly ejected with the aid of a police officer, and imprisoned in the parish jail to answer a charge of having violated the above act.

The constitutionality of this act is attacked upon the ground that it conflicts both with the Thirteenth Amendment of the Constitution, abolishing slavery, and the Fourteenth Amendment, which prohibits certain restrictive legislation on the part of the States.

1. That it does not conflict with the Thirteenth Amendment, which abolished slavery and involuntary servitude, except

as a punishment for crime, is too clear for argument. Slavery implies involuntary servitude—a state of bondage; the ownership of mankind as a chattel, or at least the control of the labor and services of one man for the benefit of another, and the absence of a legal right to the disposal of his own person, property and services.

A statute which implies merely a legal distinction between the white and colored races—a distinction which is founded in the color of the two races and which must always exist so long as white men are distinguished from the other race by color—has no tendency to destroy the legal equality of the two races, or reestablish a state of involuntary servitude.

2. By the Fourteenth Amendment, all persons born or naturalized in the United States and subject to the jurisdiction thereof are made citizens of the United States and of the State wherein they reside, and the States are forbidden from making or enforcing any law which shall abridge the privileges or immunities of citizens of the United States, or shall deprive any person of life, liberty, or property without due process of law, or deny to any person within their jurisdiction the equal protection of the laws.

The object of the amendment was undoubtedly to enforce the absolute equality of the two races before the law, but, in the nature of things, it could not have been intended to abolish distinctions based upon color, or to enforce social, as distinguished from political, equality, or a commingling of the two races upon terms unsatisfactory to either. Laws permitting, and even requiring, their separation in places where they are liable to be brought into contact do not necessarily imply the inferiority of either race to the other, and have been generally, if not universally, recognized as within the competency of the state legislatures in the exercise of their police power. The most common instance of this is connected with the establishment of separate schools for white and colored children, which has been held to be a valid exercise of the legislative power even by courts of States where the political rights of the colored race have been longest and most earnestly enforced.

The distinction between laws interfering with the political equality of the negro and those requiring the separation of the two races in schools, theatres and railway carriages has been frequently drawn by this court. Thus, in *Strauder v. West Virginia*, it was held that a law of West Virginia limiting to white male persons, 21 years of age and citizens of the State, the right to sit upon juries was a discrimination which implied a legal inferiority in civil society, which lessened the security of the right of the colored race, and was a step toward reducing them to a condition of servility. Indeed, the right of a colored man that, in the selection of jurors to pass upon his life, liberty and property, there shall be no exclusion of his race and no discrimination against them because of color has been asserted in a number of cases. So, where the laws of a particular locality or the charter of a particular railway corporation has provided that no person shall be excluded from the cars on account of color, we have held that this meant that persons of color should travel in the same car as white ones, and that the enactment was not satisfied by the company's providing cars assigned exclusively to people of color, though they were as good as those which they assigned exclusively to white persons. *Railroad Company v. Brown.*

Upon the other hand, where a statute of Louisiana required those engaged in the transportation of passengers among the States to give to all persons traveling within that State, upon vessels employed in that business, equal rights and privileges in all parts of the vessel, without distinction on account of race or color, and subjected to an action for damages the owner of such a vessel, who excluded colored passengers on account of their color from the cabin set aside by him for the use of whites, it was held to be, so far as it applied to interstate commerce, unconstitutional and void. *Hall v. De Cuir.* The court in this case, however, expressly disclaimed that it had anything whatever to do with the statute as a regulation of internal commerce, or affecting anything else than commerce among the States.

In the present case, no question of interference with interstate commerce can possibly arise, since the East Louisiana Railway appears to have been purely a local line, with both its termini within the State of Louisiana.

It is claimed by the plaintiff in error that, in any mixed community, the reputation of belonging to the dominant race, in this instance the white race, is property in the same sense that a right of action or of inheritance is property. Conceding this to be so for the purposes of this case, we are unable to see how this statute deprives him of, or in any way affects his right to, such property. If he be a white man and assigned to a colored coach, he may have his action for damages against the company for being deprived of his so-called property. Upon the other hand, if he be a colored man and be so assigned, he has been deprived of no property, since he is not lawfully entitled to the reputation of being a white man.

In this connection, it is also suggested by the learned counsel for the plaintiff in error that the same argument that will justify the state legislature in requiring railways to provide separate accommodations for the two races will also authorize them to require separate cars to be provided for people whose hair is of a certain color, or who are aliens, or who belong to certain nationalities, or to enact laws requiring colored people to walk upon one side of the street and white people upon the other, or requiring white men's houses to be painted white and colored men's black, or their vehicles or business signs to be of different colors, upon the theory that one side of the street is as good as the other, or that a house or vehicle of one color is as good as one of another color. The reply to all this is that every exercise of the police power must be reasonable, and extend only to such laws as are enacted in good faith for the promotion for the public good, and not for the annoyance or oppression of a particular class. Thus, in *Yick Wo v. Hopkins*, it was held by this court that a municipal ordinance of the city of San Francisco to regulate the carrying on of public laundries within the limits of the municipality violated the provisions of the Constitution of the United States if it conferred upon the municipal authorities arbitrary power, at their own will and without regard to discretion, in the legal sense of the term, to give or withhold consent as to persons or places without regard to the competency of the persons applying or the propriety of the places selected for the carrying on of the business. It was held to be a covert attempt on the part of the municipality to make an arbitrary and unjust discrimination against the Chinese race.

So far, then, as a conflict with the Fourteenth Amendment is concerned, the case reduces itself to the question whether the statute of Louisiana is a reasonable regulation, and, with respect to this, there must necessarily be a large discretion on the part of the legislature. In determining the question of reasonableness, it is at liberty to act with reference to the established usages, customs, and traditions of the people, and with a view to the promotion of their comfort and the preservation of the public peace and good order. Gauged by this standard, we cannot say that a law which authorizes or even requires the separation of the two races in public conveyances is

unreasonable, or more obnoxious to the Fourteenth Amendment than the acts of Congress requiring separate schools for colored children in the District of Columbia, the constitutionality of which does not seem to have been questioned, or the corresponding acts of state legislatures.

We consider the underlying fallacy of the plaintiff's argument to consist in the assumption that the enforced separation of the two races stamps the colored race with a badge of inferiority. If this be so, it is not by reason of anything found in the act, but solely because the colored race chooses to put that construction upon it. The argument necessarily assumes that if, as has been more than once the case and is not unlikely to be so again, the colored race should become the dominant power in the state legislature, and should enact a law in precisely similar terms, it would thereby relegate the white race to an inferior position. We imagine that the white race, at least, would not acquiesce in this assumption. The argument also assumes that social prejudices may be overcome by legislation, and that equal rights cannot be secured to the negro except by an enforced commingling of the two races. We cannot accept this proposition. If the two races are to meet upon terms of social equality, it must be the result of natural affinities, a mutual appreciation of each other's merits, and a voluntary consent of individuals.

Legislation is powerless to eradicate racial instincts or to abolish distinctions based upon physical differences, and the attempt to do so can only result in accentuating the difficulties of the present situation. If the civil and political rights of both races be equal, one cannot be inferior to the other civilly or politically. If one race be inferior to the other socially, the Constitution of the United States cannot put them upon the same plane.

The judgment of the court below is, therefore,

Affirmed.

MR. JUSTICE HARLAN, *dissenting.*

While there may be in Louisiana persons of different races who are not citizens of the United States, the words in the act "white and colored races" necessarily include all citizens of the United States of both races residing in that State. So that we have before us a state enactment that compels, under penalties, the separation of the two races in railroad passenger coaches, and makes it a crime for a citizen of either race to enter a coach that has been assigned to citizens of the other race.

Thus, the State regulates the use of a public highway by citizens of the United States solely upon the basis of race.

However apparent the injustice of such legislation may be, we have only to consider whether it is consistent with the Constitution of the United States.

In respect of civil rights common to all citizens, the Constitution of the United States does not, I think, permit any public authority to know the race of those entitled to be protected in the enjoyment of such rights. Every true man has pride of race, and, under appropriate circumstances, when the rights of others, his equals before the law, are not to be affected, it is his privilege to express such pride and to take such action based upon it as to him seems proper. But I deny that any legislative body or judicial tribunal may have regard to the race of citizens when the civil rights of those citizens are involved. Indeed, such legislation as that here in question is inconsistent not only with that equality of rights which pertains to citizenship, National and State, but with the personal liberty enjoyed by everyone within the United States.

The Thirteenth Amendment does not permit the withholding or the deprivation of any right necessarily inhering in freedom. It not only struck down the institution of slavery as previously existing in the United States, but it prevents the imposition of any burdens or disabilities that constitute badges of slavery or servitude. It decreed universal civil freedom in this country. This court has so adjudged. But that amendment having been found inadequate to the protection of the rights of those who had been in slavery, it was followed by the Fourteenth Amendment.

These two amendments, if enforced according to their true intent and meaning, will protect all the civil rights that pertain to freedom and citizenship.

These notable additions to the fundamental law were welcomed by the friends of liberty throughout the world. They removed the race line from our governmental systems. They had, as this court has said, a common purpose, namely to secure "to a race recently emancipated, a race that through many generations have been held in slavery, all the civil rights that the superior race enjoy." We also said: "The words of the amendment, it is true, are prohibitory, but they contain a necessary implication of a positive immunity, or right, most valuable to the colored race—the right to exemption from unfriendly legislation against them distinctively as colored—exemption from legal discriminations, implying inferiority in civil society. Lessening the security of their enjoyment of the rights which others enjoy, and discriminations which are steps towards reducing them to the condition of a subject race."

It was said in argument that the statute of Louisiana does not discriminate against either race, but prescribes a rule applicable alike to white and colored citizens. But this argument does not meet the difficulty. Everyone knows that the statute in question had its origin in the purpose not so much to exclude white persons from railroad cars occupied by blacks as to exclude colored people from coaches occupied by or assigned to white persons. Railroad corporations of Louisiana did not make discrimination among whites in the matter of accommodation for travelers. The thing to accomplish was, under the guise of giving equal accommodation for whites and blacks, to compel the latter to keep to themselves while traveling in railroad passenger coaches. No one would be so wanting in candor as to assert the contrary. The fundamental objection, therefore, to the statute is that it interferes with the personal freedom of citizens.

It is one thing for railroad carriers to furnish, or to be required by law to furnish, equal accommodations for all whom they are under a legal duty to carry. It is quite another thing for government to forbid citizens of the white and black races from traveling in the same public conveyance, and to punish officers of railroad companies for permitting persons of the two races to occupy the same passenger coach. If a State can prescribe, as a rule of civil conduct, that whites and blacks shall not travel as passengers in the same railroad coach, why may it not so regulate the use of the streets of its cities and towns as to compel white citizens to keep on one side of a street and black citizens to keep on the other? Why may it not, upon like grounds, punish whites and blacks who ride together in streetcars or in open vehicles on a public road or street? Why may it not require sheriffs to assign whites to one side of a courtroom and blacks to the other? And why may it not also prohibit the commingling of the two races in the galleries of legislative halls or in public assemblages convened for the consideration of the political questions of the day? Further, if this statute of Louisiana is consistent with the personal liberty of citizens, why may not the State require the separation in railroad coaches of native and

naturalized citizens of the United States, or of Protestants and Roman Catholics?

The answer given at the argument to these questions was that regulations of the kind they suggest would be unreasonable, and could not, therefore, stand before the law. Is it meant that the determination of questions of legislative power depends upon the inquiry whether the statute whose validity is questioned is, in the judgment of the courts, a reasonable one, taking all the circumstances into consideration? A statute may be unreasonable merely because a sound public policy forbade its enactment. But I do not understand that the courts have anything to do with the policy or expediency of legislation. A statute may be valid and yet, upon grounds of public policy, may well be characterized as unreasonable.

There is a dangerous tendency in these latter days to enlarge the functions of the courts by means of judicial interference with the will of the people as expressed by the legislature. Our institutions have the distinguishing characteristic that the three departments of government are coordinate and separate. Each must keep within the limits defined by the Constitution. And the courts best discharge their duty by executing the will of the lawmaking power, constitutionally expressed, leaving the results of legislation to be dealt with by the people through their representatives. Statutes must always have a reasonable construction. Sometimes they are to be construed strictly; sometimes liberally, in order to carry out the legislative will. But however construed, the intent of the legislature is to be respected, if the particular statute in question is valid, although the courts, looking at the public interests, may conceive the statute to be both unreasonable and impolitic. If the power exists to enact a statute, that ends the matter so far as the courts are concerned. The adjudged cases in which statutes have been held to be void because unreasonable are those in which the means employed by the legislature were not at all germane to the end to which the legislature was competent.

The white race deems itself to be the dominant race in this country. And so it is in prestige, in achievements, in education, in wealth and in power. So, I doubt not, it will continue to be for all time if it remains true to its great heritage and holds fast to the principles of constitutional liberty. But in view of the Constitution, in the eye of the law, there is in this country no superior, dominant, ruling class of citizens. There is no caste here. Our Constitution is colorblind, and neither knows nor tolerates classes among citizens. In respect of civil rights, all citizens are equal before the law. The humblest is the peer of the most powerful. The law regards man as man, and takes no account of his surroundings or of his color when his civil rights as guaranteed by the supreme law of the land are involved. It is therefore to be regretted that this high tribunal, the final expositor of the fundamental law of the land, has reached the conclusion that it is competent for a State to regulate the enjoyment by citizens of their civil rights solely upon the basis of race.

In my opinion, the judgment this day rendered will, in time, prove to be quite as pernicious as the decision made by this tribunal in the *Dred Scott Case*. It was adjudged in that case that the descendants of Africans who were imported into this country and sold as slaves were not included nor intended to be included under the word "citizens" in the Constitution, and could not claim any of the rights and privileges which that instrument provided for and secured to citizens of the United States.

The recent amendments of the Constitution, it was supposed, had eradicated these principles from our institutions. But it seems that we have yet, in some of the States, a dominant race—a superior class of citizens, which assumes to regulate the enjoyment of civil rights, common to all citizens, upon the basis of race. The present decision, it may well be apprehended, will not only stimulate aggressions, more or less brutal and irritating, upon the admitted rights of colored citizens, but will encourage the belief that it is possible, by means of state enactments, to defeat the beneficent purposes which the people of the United States had in view when they adopted the recent amendments of the Constitution, by one of which the blacks of this country were made citizens of the United States and of the States in which they respectively reside, and whose privileges and immunities, as citizens, the States are forbidden to abridge. Sixty millions of whites are in no danger from the presence here of eight millions of blacks. The destinies of the two races in this country are indissolubly linked together, and the interests of both require that the common government of all shall not permit the seeds of race hate to be planted under the sanction of law. What can more certainly arouse race hate, what more certainly create and perpetuate a feeling of distrust between these races, than state enactments which, in fact, proceed on the ground that colored citizens are so inferior and degraded that they cannot be allowed to sit in public coaches occupied by white citizens. That, as all will admit, is the real meaning of such legislation as was enacted in Louisiana.

The sure guarantee of the peace and security of each race is the clear, distinct, unconditional recognition by our governments, National and State, of every right that inheres in civil freedom, and of the equality before the law of all citizens of the United States, without regard to race.

State enactments regulating the enjoyment of civil rights upon the basis of race, and cunningly devised to defeat legitimate results of the war under the pretence of recognizing equality of rights, can have no other result than to render permanent peace impossible and to keep alive a conflict of races the continuance of which must do harm to all concerned. This question is not met by the suggestion that social equality cannot exist between the white and black races in this country. That argument, if it can be properly regarded as one, is scarcely worthy of consideration, for social equality no more exists between two races when traveling in a passenger coach or a public highway than when members of the same races sit by each other in a street car or in the jury box, or stand or sit with each other in a political assembly, or when they use in common the street of a city or town, or when they are in the same room for the purpose of having their names placed on the registry of voters, or when they approach the ballot box in order to exercise the high privilege of voting.

There is a race so different from our own that we do not permit those belonging to it to become citizens of the United States. Persons belonging to it are, with few exceptions, absolutely excluded from our country. I allude to the Chinese race. But, by the statute in question, a Chinaman can ride in the same passenger coach with white citizens of the United States, while citizens of the black race in Louisiana, many of whom, perhaps, risked their lives for the preservation of the Union, who are entitled, by law, to participate in the political control of the State and nation, who are not excluded, by law or by reason of their race, from public stations of any kind, and who have all the legal rights that belong to white citizens, are yet declared to be criminals, liable to imprisonment, if they ride in a public coach occupied by citizens of the white race. It is scarcely just to say that a colored citizen should not object to occupying a public coach assigned to his own race. He does not object, nor, perhaps, would he object to separate coaches for his race if his rights under the law were recognized. But he objecting, and ought never to cease objecting, to the proposition that citizens of the white and black race can be adjudged criminals because they sit, or claim the right to sit, in the same public coach on a public highway.

The arbitrary separation of citizens on the basis of race while they are on a public highway is a badge of servitude wholly inconsistent with the civil freedom and the equality before the law established by the Constitution. It cannot be justified upon any legal grounds.

If evils will result from the commingling of the two races upon public highways established for the benefit of all, they will be infinitely less than those that will surely come from state legislation regulating the enjoyment of civil rights upon the basis of race. We boast of the freedom enjoyed by our people above all other peoples. But it is difficult to reconcile that boast with a state of the law which, practically, puts the brand of servitude and degradation upon a large class of our fellow citizens, our equals before the law. The thin disguise of "equal" accommodations for passengers in railroad coaches will not mislead anyone, nor atone for the wrong this day done.

I am of opinion that the statute of Louisiana is inconsistent with the personal liberty of citizens, white and black, in that State, and hostile to both the spirit and letter of the Constitution of the United States. If laws of like character should be enacted in the several States of the Union, the effect would be in the highest degree mischievous. Slavery, as an institution tolerated by law would, it is true, have disappeared from our country, but there would remain a power in the States, by sinister legislation, to interfere with the full enjoyment of the

© Bettmann/Corbis

A newspaper headline announcing the Supreme Court's ruling in Brown v. Board of Education.

blessings of freedom to regulate civil rights, common to all citizens, upon the basis of race, and to place in a condition of legal inferiority a large body of American citizens now constituting a part of the political community called the People of the United States, for whom and by whom, through representatives, our government is administered. Such a system is inconsistent with the guarantee given by the Constitution

to each State of a republican form of government, and may be stricken down by Congressional action, or by the courts in the discharge of their solemn duty to maintain the supreme law of the land, anything in the constitution or laws of any State to the contrary notwithstanding.

For the reasons stated, I am constrained to withhold my assent from the opinion and judgment of the majority.

BROWN v. BOARD OF EDUCATION

347 U.S. 483 (1954)

Opinion: Warren, joined by Black, Reed, Frankfurter, Douglas, Jackson, Burton, Clark, Minton

In the 1940s, the National Association for the Advancement of Colored People (NAACP) attempted to persuade the courts to dismantle segregation by arguing that the notion of "separate but equal" was empirically false. They brought a series of cases that showed that supposedly equal facilities for African Americans were clearly inferior to the facilities provided to whites. The NAACP won

an important victory in Sweatt v. Painter, *when the Supreme Court recognized that the rejection of a black applicant to the University of Texas Law School constituted a violation of the Equal Protection Clause of the Fourteenth Amendment. But the Court stopped short of reversing the separate but equal doctrine: "We cannot, therefore, agree with respondents that the doctrine of* Plessy v. Ferguson *requires affirmance of the judgment below. Nor need we reach petitioner's contention that* Plessy v. Ferguson *should be re-examined in the light of contemporary knowledge respecting the purposes of the*

Fourteenth Amendment and the effects of racial segregation."

But in Brown v. Board of Education *the Court was asked to recognize that the whole purpose of segregation in the South was to maintain the legal inferiority of non-white citizens. As you will see, the Court unanimously overrules* Plessy v. Ferguson's *holding that segregation was compatible with the Equal Protection Clause. As you read, consider the basis for the decision. For instance, part of the argument for reversing* Plessy v. Ferguson *was the empirical observation that black children who attended segregated schools saw themselves as inferior to white children, as evidenced by the results of the famous "doll test" employed by psychologists Kenneth and Mamie Clark. They found that black children tended to prefer to play with white dolls and attribute positive characteristics to them while attributing negative qualities to black dolls. Is such evidence necessary to establish the principle that separate cannot be equal? Absent this social science data, should the Court still have ruled this way? Should the Court have relied upon empirical data to make what some might consider a fundamentally moral judgment?*

This case is also an important place to recall the theories of constitutional interpretation that we explored in Chapter 2. It has been said that any good theory of constitutional interpretation must explain why Brown v. Board of Education *is correct. Does each theory meet this requirement? For instance, can an originalist interpretation account for* Brown v. Board of Education *given that the Equal Protection Clause was passed at a time when government-mandated segregation existed in the nation's capital?*

MR. CHIEF JUSTICE WARREN *delivered the opinion of the Court.*

These cases come to us from the States of Kansas, South Carolina, Virginia, and Delaware. They are premised on different facts and different local conditions, but a common legal question justifies their consideration together in this consolidated opinion.

In each of the cases, minors of the Negro race, through their legal representatives, seek the aid of the courts in obtaining admission to the public schools of their community on a nonsegregated basis. In each instance, they had been denied admission to schools attended by white children under laws requiring or permitting segregation according to race. This segregation was alleged to deprive the plaintiffs of the equal protection of the laws under the Fourteenth Amendment. In each of the cases other than the Delaware case, a three-judge federal district court denied relief to the plaintiffs on the so-called "separate but equal" doctrine announced by this Court in *Plessy v. Ferguson*. Under that doctrine, equality of treatment is accorded when the races are provided substantially equal facilities, even though these facilities be separate. In the Delaware case, the Supreme Court of Delaware adhered to that doctrine, but ordered that the plaintiffs be admitted to the white schools because of their superiority to the Negro schools.

The plaintiffs contend that segregated public schools are not "equal" and cannot be made "equal," and that hence they are deprived of the equal protection of the laws. Because of the obvious importance of the question presented, the Court took jurisdiction. Argument was heard in the 1952 Term, and reargument was heard this Term on certain questions propounded by the Court.

Reargument was largely devoted to the circumstances surrounding the adoption of the Fourteenth Amendment in 1868. It covered exhaustively consideration of the Amendment in Congress, ratification by the states, then-existing practices in racial segregation, and the views of proponents and opponents of the Amendment. This discussion and our own investigation convince us that, although these sources cast some light, it is not enough to resolve the problem with which we are faced. At best, they are inconclusive. The most avid proponents of the post-War Amendments undoubtedly intended them to remove all legal distinctions among "all persons born or naturalized in the United States." Their opponents, just as certainly, were antagonistic to both the letter and the spirit of the Amendments and wished them to have the most limited effect. What others in Congress and the state legislatures had in mind cannot be determined with any degree of certainty.

An additional reason for the inconclusive nature of the Amendment's history with respect to segregated schools is the status of public education at that time. In the South, the movement toward free common schools, supported by general taxation, had not yet taken hold. Education of white children was largely in the hands of private groups. Education of Negroes was almost nonexistent, and practically all of the race were illiterate. In fact, any education of Negroes was forbidden by law in some states. Today, in contrast, many Negroes have achieved outstanding success in the arts and sciences, as well as in the business and professional world. It is true that public school education at the time of the Amendment had advanced further in the North, but the effect of the Amendment on Northern States was generally ignored in the congressional debates. Even in the North, the conditions of public education did not approximate those existing today. The curriculum was usually rudimentary; ungraded schools were common in rural areas; the school term was but three months a year in many states, and compulsory school attendance was virtually unknown.

As a consequence, it is not surprising that there should be so little in the history of the Fourteenth Amendment relating to its intended effect on public education.

In the first cases in this Court construing the Fourteenth Amendment, decided shortly after its adoption, the Court interpreted it as proscribing all state-imposed discriminations against the Negro race. The doctrine of "separate but equal" did not make its appearance in this Court until 1896 in the case of *Plessy v. Ferguson, supra,* involving not education but transportation. American courts have since labored with the doctrine for over half a century. In this Court, there have been six cases involving the "separate but equal" doctrine in the field of public education. In more recent cases, all on the graduate school level, inequality was found in that specific benefits enjoyed by white students were denied to Negro students of the same educational qualifications. In none of these cases was it necessary to reexamine the doctrine to grant relief to the Negro plaintiff. And in *Sweatt v. Painter, supra,* the Court expressly reserved decision on the question whether *Plessy v. Ferguson* should be held inapplicable to public education.

In the instant cases, that question is directly presented. Here, unlike *Sweatt v. Painter,* there are findings below that the Negro and white schools involved have been equalized, or are being equalized, with respect to buildings, curricula, qualifications and salaries of teachers, and other "tangible" factors. Our decision, therefore, cannot turn on merely a comparison of these tangible factors in the Negro and white schools involved in each of the cases. We must look instead to the effect of segregation itself on public education.

In approaching this problem, we cannot turn the clock back to 1868, when the Amendment was adopted, or even to 1896, when *Plessy v. Ferguson* was written. We must consider public education in the light of its full development and its present place in American life throughout the Nation. Only in this way can it be determined if segregation in public schools deprives these plaintiffs of the equal protection of the laws.

Today, education is perhaps the most important function of state and local governments. Compulsory school attendance laws and the great expenditures for education both demonstrate our recognition of the importance of education to our democratic society. It is required in the performance of our most basic public responsibilities, even service in the armed forces. It is the very foundation of good citizenship. Today it is a principal instrument in awakening the child to cultural values, in preparing him for later professional training, and in helping him to adjust normally to his environment. In these days, it is doubtful that any child may reasonably be expected to succeed in life if he is denied the opportunity of an education. Such an opportunity, where the state has undertaken to provide it, is a right which must be made available to all on equal terms.

We come then to the question presented: Does segregation of children in public schools solely on the basis of race, even though the physical facilities and other "tangible" factors may be equal, deprive the children of the minority group of equal educational opportunities? We believe that it does.

In *Sweatt v. Painter*, in finding that a segregated law school for Negroes could not provide them equal educational opportunities, this Court relied in large part on "those qualities which are incapable of objective measurement but which make for greatness in a law school." In *McLaurin v. Oklahoma State Regents*, the Court, in requiring that a Negro admitted to a white graduate school be treated like all other students, again resorted to intangible considerations: ". . . his ability to study, to engage in discussions and exchange views with other students, and, in general, to learn his profession." Such considerations apply with added force to children in grade and high schools. To separate them from others of similar age and qualifications solely because of their race generates a feeling of inferiority as to their status in the community that may affect their hearts and minds in a way unlikely ever to be undone. The effect of this separation on their educational opportunities was well stated by a finding in the Kansas case by a court which nevertheless felt compelled to rule against the Negro plaintiffs:

> "Segregation of white and colored children in public schools has a detrimental effect upon the colored children. The impact is greater when it has the sanction of the law, for the policy of separating the races is usually interpreted as denoting the inferiority of the negro group. A sense of inferiority affects the motivation of a child to learn. Segregation with the sanction of law, therefore, has a tendency to [retard] the educational and mental development of negro children and to deprive them of some of the benefits they would receive in a racial[ly] integrated school system."

Whatever may have been the extent of psychological knowledge at the time of *Plessy v. Ferguson*, this finding is amply supported by modern authority. Any language in *Plessy v. Ferguson* contrary to this finding is rejected.

We conclude that, in the field of public education, the doctrine of "separate but equal" has no place. Separate educational facilities are inherently unequal. Therefore, we hold that the plaintiffs and others similarly situated for whom the actions have been brought are, by reason of the segregation complained of, deprived of the equal protection of the laws guaranteed by the Fourteenth Amendment. This disposition makes unnecessary any discussion whether such segregation also violates the Due Process Clause of the Fourteenth Amendment.

Because these are class actions, because of the wide applicability of this decision, and because of the great variety of local conditions, the formulation of decrees in these cases presents problems of considerable complexity. On reargument, the consideration of appropriate relief was necessarily subordinated to the primary question—the constitutionality of segregation in public education. We have now announced that such segregation is a denial of the equal protection of the laws. It is so ordered.

BROWN v. BOARD OF EDUCATION II

349 U.S. 294 (1955)

Opinion: Warren, Black, Reed, Frankfurter, Douglas, Burton, Clark, Minton, Harlan

Brown v. Board of Education *held that racially segregated schools violated the Equal Protection Clause. But the process of desegregation did not come about instantly. In 1955, the year after* Brown v. Board of Education *was handed down, the Court issued instructions about how the transition to integration in public schools was to be achieved. Importantly, Southern officials were to complete desegregation "with all deliberate speed." As you read this case, you should consider whether this guideline is appropriate. Does it have the potential to undermine the decision in* Brown v. Board of Education *and its historic reversal of* Plessy v. Ferguson? *Should the Court have instead insisted that its ruling in* Brown v. Board of Education *be followed immediately?*

Even after Brown v. Board of Education II, *the issue of integration was far from settled in the nation, especially in Southern states. In a famous incident in 1957 that came to memorialize the aftermath of* Brown v. Board of Education, *the Governor of Arkansas, accompanied by a mob of angry protestors, attempted to block nine African-American students from enrolling in Little Rock's previously whites-only* Central High School. *Ultimately the students were permitted to attend, but they needed the assistance of the U.S. Army, acting on the orders of President Dwight D. Eisenhower.*

Recall that the Court's landmark ruling about judicial supremacy in Cooper v. Aaron *held that the State of Arkansas could not ignore its ruling in* Brown v. Board of Education. *How should the Court approach situations where its rulings face massive resistance by a large section of the country?*

MR. CHIEF JUSTICE WARREN *delivered the opinion of the Court.*

These cases were decided on May 17, 1954. The opinions of that date, declaring the fundamental principle that racial discrimination in public education is unconstitutional, are incorporated herein by reference. All provisions of federal, state, or local law requiring or permitting such discrimination must yield to this principle. There remains for consideration the manner in which relief is to be accorded.

Because these cases arose under different local conditions and their disposition will involve a variety of local problems, we requested further argument on the question of relief. In view of the nationwide importance of the decision, we invited the Attorney General of the United States and the Attorneys General of all states requiring or permitting racial discrimination in public education to present their views on that question. The parties, the United States, and the States of Florida, North Carolina, Arkansas, Oklahoma, Maryland, and Texas filed briefs and participated in the oral argument.

These presentations were informative and helpful to the Court in its consideration of the complexities arising from the transition to a system of public education freed of racial discrimination. The presentations also demonstrated that substantial steps to eliminate racial discrimination in public schools have already been taken, not only in some of the communities in which these cases arose, but in some of the states appearing as amici curiae, and in other states as well. Substantial progress has been made in the District of Columbia and in the communities in Kansas and Delaware involved in this litigation. The defendants in the cases coming to us from South Carolina and Virginia are awaiting the decision of this Court concerning relief.

Full implementation of these constitutional principles may require solution of varied local school problems. School authorities have the primary responsibility for elucidating, assessing, and solving these problems; courts will have to consider whether the action of school authorities constitutes good faith implementation of the governing constitutional principles. Because of their proximity to local conditions and the possible need for further hearings, the courts which originally heard these cases can best perform this judicial appraisal. Accordingly, we believe it appropriate to remand the cases to those courts.

In fashioning and effectuating the decrees, the courts will be guided by equitable principles. Traditionally, equity has been characterized by a practical flexibility in shaping its remedies and by a facility for adjusting and reconciling public and private needs. These cases call for the exercise of these traditional attributes of equity power. At stake is the personal interest of the plaintiffs in admission to public schools as soon as practicable on a nondiscriminatory basis. To effectuate this interest may call for elimination of a variety of obstacles in making the transition to school systems operated in accordance with the constitutional principles set forth in our May 17, 1954, decision. Courts of equity may properly take into account the public interest in the elimination of such obstacles in a systematic and effective manner. But it should go without saying that the vitality of these constitutional principles cannot be allowed to yield simply because of disagreement with them.

While giving weight to these public and private considerations, the courts will require that the defendants make a prompt and reasonable start toward full compliance with our May 17, 1954, ruling. Once such a start has been made, the courts may find that additional time is necessary to carry out the ruling in an effective manner. The burden rests upon the defendants to establish that such time is necessary in the public interest and is consistent with good faith compliance at the earliest practicable date. To that end, the courts may consider problems related to administration, arising from the physical condition of the school plant, the school transportation system, personnel, revision of school districts and attendance areas into compact units to achieve a system of determining admission to the public schools on a nonracial basis, and revision of local laws and regulations which may be necessary in solving the foregoing problems. They will also consider the adequacy of any plans the defendants may propose to meet these problems and to effectuate a transition to a racially nondiscriminatory school system. During this period of transition, the courts will retain jurisdiction of these cases.

The judgments below, except that in the Delaware case, are accordingly reversed and the cases are remanded to the District Courts to take such proceedings and enter such orders and decrees consistent with this opinion as are necessary and proper to admit to public schools on a racially nondiscriminatory basis with all deliberate speed the parties to these cases. The judgment in the Delaware case—ordering the immediate admission of the plaintiffs to schools previously attended only by white children—is affirmed on the basis of the principles stated in our May 17, 1954, opinion, but the case is remanded to the Supreme Court of Delaware for such further proceedings as that Court may deem necessary in light of this opinion.

LOVING v. VIRGINIA

388 U.S. 1 (1967)

Opinion: Warren, Black, Douglas, Clark, Harlan, Brennan, White, Fortas
Concurrence: Stewart

Long before segregation took root in the United States, American colonies began forbidding interracial marriages. These so-called anti-miscegenation laws were a key component of the legal construction upholding the separation of the races and the façade of white supremacy. They were one of the last vestiges of Jim Crow to be dismantled by the federal government, surviving even the Civil Rights Act of 1964.

The Court has repeatedly recognized that the right to marry is one of the most fundamental rights protected by the Constitution. The plaintiffs in this case argued for a right to interracial marriage by appealing to both the Equal Protection Clause and substantive due process. As you read this excerpt, pay particular attention to the equal protection arguments. To what extent do they draw on the insights in Brown v. Board of Education?

MR. CHIEF JUSTICE WARREN
delivered the opinion of the Court.

This case presents a constitutional question never addressed by this Court: whether a statutory scheme adopted by the State of Virginia to prevent marriages between persons solely on the basis of racial classifications violates the Equal Protection and Due Process Clauses of the Fourteenth Amendment. For reasons which seem to us to reflect the central meaning of those constitutional commands, we conclude that these statutes cannot stand consistently with the Fourteenth Amendment.

In June, 1958, two residents of Virginia, Mildred Jeter, a Negro woman, and Richard Loving, a white man, were married in the District of Columbia pursuant to its laws. Shortly after their marriage, the Lovings returned to Virginia and established their marital abode in Caroline County. At the October Term, 1958, of the Circuit Court of Caroline County, a grand jury issued an indictment charging the Lovings with violating Virginia's ban on interracial marriages. . . . [T]he Lovings pleaded guilty to the charge, and were sentenced to one year in jail; however, the trial judge suspended the sentence for a period of 25 years on the condition that the Lovings leave the State and not return to Virginia together for 25 years. He stated in an opinion that:

Almighty God created the races white, black, yellow, malay and red, and he placed them on separate continents. And, but for the interference with his arrangement, there would be no cause for such marriage. The fact that he separated the races shows that he did not intend for the races to mix.

While the state court is no doubt correct in asserting that marriage is a social relation subject to the State's police power, *Maynard v. Hill*, the State does not contend in its argument before this Court that its powers to regulate marriage are unlimited notwithstanding the commands of the Fourteenth Amendment. Nor could it do so in light of *Meyer v. Nebraska* and *Skinner v. Oklahoma*. Instead, the State argues that the meaning of the Equal Protection Clause, as illuminated by the statements of the Framers, is only that state penal laws containing an interracial element as part of the definition of the offense must apply equally to whites and Negroes in the sense that members of each race are punished to the same degree. Thus, the State contends that, because its miscegenation statutes punish equally both the white and the Negro participants in an interracial marriage, these statutes, despite their reliance on racial classifications, do not constitute an invidious discrimination based upon race. The second argument advanced by the State assumes the validity of its equal application theory. The argument is that, if the Equal Protection Clause does not outlaw miscegenation statutes because of their reliance on racial classifications, the question of constitutionality would thus become whether there was any rational basis for a State to treat interracial marriages differently from other marriages. On this question, the State argues, the scientific evidence is substantially in doubt and, consequently, this Court should defer to the wisdom of the state legislature in adopting its policy of discouraging interracial marriages.

Because we reject the notion that the mere "equal application" of a statute containing racial classifications is enough to remove the classifications from the Fourteenth Amendment's proscription of all invidious racial discriminations, we do not accept the State's contention that these statutes should be upheld if there is any possible basis for concluding that they serve a rational purpose. The mere fact of equal application does not mean that our analysis of these statutes should follow the approach we have taken in cases involving no racial discrimination where the Equal Protection Clause has been arrayed against a statute discriminating between the kinds of advertising which may be displayed on trucks in New York City, *Railway Express Agency, Inc. v. New York*, or an exemption in Ohio's *ad valorem* tax for merchandise owned by a nonresident in a storage warehouse, *Allied Stores of Ohio, Inc. v. Bowers*. In these cases, involving distinctions not drawn according to race, the Court has merely asked whether there is any rational foundation for the discriminations, and has deferred to the wisdom of the state legislatures. In the case at bar, however, we deal with statutes containing racial classifications, and the fact of equal application does not immunize the statute from the very heavy burden of justification which the Fourteenth Amendment has traditionally required of state statutes drawn according to race.

These statutes also deprive the Lovings of liberty without due process of law in violation of the Due Process Clause of the Fourteenth Amendment. The freedom to marry has long been recognized as one of the vital personal rights essential to the orderly pursuit of happiness by free men.

Marriage is one of the "basic civil rights of man," fundamental to our very existence and survival. *Skinner v. Oklahoma*. To deny this fundamental freedom on so unsupportable a basis as the racial classifications embodied in these statutes, classifications so directly subversive of the principle of equality at the heart of the Fourteenth Amendment, is surely to deprive all the State's citizens of liberty without due process of law. The Fourteenth Amendment requires that the freedom of choice to marry not be restricted by invidious racial discriminations. Under our Constitution, the freedom to marry, or not marry, a person of another race resides with the individual, and cannot be infringed by the State.

These convictions must be reversed.

ALEXANDER v. HOLMES COUNTY BOARD OF EDUCATION

396 U.S. 1218 (1969)

Opinion: Black

Though Brown v. Board of Education *was a tremendous victory in the Civil Rights movement, the Southern states began a campaign of massive resistance to the opinion. As you read, the Court in* Brown v. Board of Education II *failed to require immediate desegregation, and the Court's ambiguous and uncertain timeline for implementation encouraged delay.*

By 1969, fifteen years after Brown v. Board of Education, *desegregation had yet to be fully carried out in many states. In* Alexander v. Holmes County Board of Education, *the Court announced that the guideline of* Brown v. Board of Education II, *calling for "all deliberate speed" in desegregation, was getting in the way of realizing* Brown v. Board of Education's *purpose. In the words of U.S. Supreme Court Justice Hugo Black, "all deliberate speed" should not be used as a "soft euphemism for delay."*

MR. JUSTICE BLACK, *Circuit Justice.*

For a great many years Mississippi has had in effect what is called a dual system of public schools, one system for white students only and one system for Negro students only. On July 3, 1969, the Fifth Circuit Court of Appeals entered an order requiring the submission of new plans to be put into effect this fall to accelerate desegregation in 33 Mississippi school districts. On August 28, upon the motion of the Department of Justice and the recommendation of the Secretary of Health, Education & Welfare, the Court of Appeals suspended the July 3 order and postponed the date for submission of the new plans until December 1, 1969. I have been asked by Negro plaintiffs in 14 of these school districts to vacate the suspension of the July 3 order. Largely for the reasons set forth below, I feel constrained to deny that relief.

In *Brown v. Board of Education [I]* and *Brown v. Board of Education [II]*, we held that state-imposed segregation of students according to race denied Negro students the equal protection of the law guaranteed by the Fourteenth Amendment. *Brown I* was decided 15 years ago, but in Mississippi as well as in some other States the decision has not been completely enforced, and there are many schools in those States that are still either "white" or "Negro" schools and many that are still all-white or all-Negro. This has resulted in large part from the fact that in *Brown II* the Court declared that this unconstitutional denial of equal protection should be remedied, not immediately, but only "with all deliberate speed." Federal courts have ever since struggled with the phrase "all deliberate speed." Unfortunately this struggle has not eliminated dual school systems, and I am of the opinion that so long as that phrase is a relevant factor they will never be eliminated. "All deliberate speed" has turned out to be only a soft euphemism for delay.

In my opinion the phrase "with all deliberate speed" should no longer have any relevancy whatsoever in enforcing the constitutional rights of Negro students. The Fifth Circuit found that the Negro students in these school districts are being denied equal protection of the law, and in my view they are entitled to have their constitutional rights vindicated now without postponement for any reason.

It has been 15 years since we declared in the two *Brown* cases that a law which prevents a child from going to a public school because of his color violates the Equal Protection Clause. As this record conclusively shows, there are many places still in this country where the schools are either "white" or "Negro" and not just schools for all children as the Constitution requires. In my opinion there is no reason why such a wholesale deprivation of constitutional rights should be tolerated another minute. I fear that this long denial of constitutional rights is due in large part to the phrase "with all deliberate speed." I would do away with that phrase completely.

MISSOURI v. JENKINS

515 U.S. 70 (1995)

Opinion: Rehnquist, joined by
    O'Connor, Scalia, Kennedy, Thomas
Concurrence: O'Connor
Concurrence: Thomas
Dissent: Souter, joined by Stevens,
    Ginsburg, Breyer
Dissent: Ginsburg

More than 40 years after Brown v. Board of Education, *the Court was still confronted with questions about the reach of judicially supervised efforts at achieving racial equality in public schools. In this case, a 5-4 majority led by U.S. Supreme Court Chief Justice William Rehnquist attempts to curb the scope of judicial remedies for past segregation to removing the effects only of de jure, and not de facto, segregation. As you read this case, you should ask whether the majority is right to limit remedies in this way. Moreover, how should the difference between de facto and de jure segregation be ascertained? Do Chief Justice Rehnquist's limits to possible remedies for segregation*

weaken the holding in Brown v. Board of Education?

CHIEF JUSTICE REHNQUIST *delivered the opinion of the Court.*

In this case, the State of Missouri has challenged the District Court's order of salary increases for virtually all instructional and noninstructional staff within the Kansas City, Missouri, School District (KCMSD) and the District Court's order requiring the State to continue to fund remedial "quality education" programs because student achievement levels were still "at or below national norms at many grade levels."

This case has been before the same United States District Judge since 1977. In that year, the KCMSD, the school board, and the children of two school board members brought suit against the State and other defendants. Plaintiffs alleged that the State, the surrounding suburban school districts (SSD's), and various federal agencies had caused and perpetuated a system of racial segregation in the schools of the Kansas City metropolitan area. The KCMSD brought a cross claim against the State for its failure to eliminate the vestiges of its prior dual school system.

In June 1985, the District Court issued its first remedial order and established as its goal the "elimination of all vestiges of state imposed segregation." The District Court determined that "[s]egregation ha[d] caused a system wide *reduction* in student achievement in the schools of the KCMSD." The District Court also identified 25 schools within the KCMSD that had enrollments of 90% or more black students.

The District Court, pursuant to plans submitted by the KCMSD and the State, ordered a wide range of quality education programs for all students attending the KCMSD. First, the District Court ordered that the KCMSD be restored to an AAA classification, the highest classification awarded by the State Board of Education. Second, it ordered that the number of students per class be reduced so that the student to teacher ratio was below the level required for AAA standing. The District Court justified its reduction in class size as

> "an essential part of any plan to remedy the vestiges of segregation in the KCMSD. Reducing class size will serve to remedy the vestiges of past segregation by increasing individual attention and instruction, as well as increasing the potential for desegregative educational experiences for KCMSD students by maintaining and attracting non minority enrollment."

The District Court also set out to desegregate the KCMSD but believed that "[t]o accomplish desegregation within the boundary lines of a school district whose enrollment remains 68.3% black is a difficult task." Because it had found no interdistrict violation, the District Court could not order mandatory interdistrict redistribution of students between the KCMSD and the surrounding SSDs.

As part of its desegregation plan, the District Court has ordered salary assistance to the KCMSD. In 1987, the District Court initially ordered salary assistance only for teachers within the KCMSD. Since that time, however, the District Court has ordered salary assistance to all but three of the approximately 5,000 KCMSD employees. The total cost of this component of the desegregation remedy since 1987 is over $200 million.

The District Court's desegregation plan has been described as the most ambitious and expensive remedial program in the history of school desegregation. The annual cost per pupil at the KCMSD far exceeds that of the neighboring SSDs or of any school district in Missouri. Nevertheless, the KCMSD, which has pursued a "friendly adversary" relationship with the plaintiffs, has continued to propose ever more expensive programs. As a result, the desegregation costs have escalated and now are approaching an annual cost of $200 million. These massive expenditures have financed

> "high schools in which every classroom will have air conditioning, an alarm system, and 15 microcomputers; a 2,000-square-foot planetarium; green houses and vivariums; a 25-acre farm with an air conditioned meeting room for 104 people; a Model United Nations wired for language translation; broadcast capable radio and television studios with an editing and animation lab; a temperature controlled art gallery; movie editing and screening rooms; a 3,500-square-foot dust-free diesel mechanics room; 1,875-square-foot elementary school animal rooms for use in a zoo project; swimming pools; and numerous other facilities."

The State, through the operation of joint and several liability, has borne the brunt of these costs.

With this background, we turn to the present controversy. First, the State has challenged the District Court's requirement that it fund salary increases for KCMSD instructional and noninstructional staff. The State claimed that funding for salaries was beyond the scope of the District Court's remedial authority. Second, the State has challenged the District Court's order requiring it to continue to fund the remedial quality education programs for the 1992–1993 school year.

Because of the importance of the issues, we granted certiorari to consider the following: (1) whether the District Court exceeded its constitutional authority when it granted salary increases to virtually all instructional and noninstructional employees of the KCMSD, and (2) whether the District Court properly relied upon the fact that student achievement test scores had failed to rise to some unspecified level when it declined to find that the State had achieved partial unitary status as to the quality education programs.

Almost 25 years ago, in *Swann v. Charlotte Mecklenburg Bd. of Ed.*, we dealt with the authority of a district court to fashion remedies for a school district that had been segregated in law in violation of the Equal Protection Clause of the Fourteenth Amendment. Although recognizing the discretion that must necessarily adhere in a district court in fashioning a remedy, we also recognized the limits on such remedial power:

> "[E]limination of racial discrimination in public schools is a large task and one that should not be retarded by efforts to achieve broader purposes lying beyond the jurisdiction of the school authorities. One vehicle can carry only a limited amount of baggage. It would not serve the important objective of *Brown I* to seek to use school desegregation cases for purposes beyond their scope, although desegregation of schools ultimately will have impact on other forms of discrimination."

Three years later, in *Milliken I*, we held that a District Court had exceeded its authority in fashioning interdistrict relief where the surrounding school districts had not themselves been guilty of any constitutional violation. We said that a desegregation remedy "is necessarily designed, as all remedies are, to restore the victims of discriminatory conduct to the position they would have occupied in the absence of such conduct." "[W]ithout an interdistrict violation and interdistrict effect, there is no constitutional wrong calling for an interdistrict remedy." We also rejected "[t]he suggestion . . . that schools which have a majority of Negro students are not 'desegregated,' whatever the makeup of the school district's population and however neutrally the district lines have been drawn and administered."

Three years later, in *Milliken v. Bradley*, (*Milliken II*), we articulated a three-part framework derived from our prior cases to guide district courts in the exercise of their remedial authority.

> "In the first place, like other equitable remedies, the nature of the desegregation remedy is to be determined by the nature and scope of the constitutional violation. *Swann v. Charlotte Mecklenburg Board of Education.* The remedy must therefore be related to 'the *condition* alleged to offend the Constitution. . . .' *Milliken I.* Second, the decree must indeed be *remedial* in nature, that is, it must be designed as nearly as possible 'to restore the victims of discriminatory conduct to the position they would have occupied in the absence of such conduct.' Third, the federal courts in devising a remedy must take into account the interests of state and local authorities in managing their own affairs, consistent with the Constitution."

We added that the "principle that the nature and scope of the remedy are to be determined by the violation means simply that federal court decrees must directly address and relate to the constitutional violation itself."

The ultimate inquiry is "whether the [constitutional violator] ha[s] complied in good faith with the desegregation decree since it was entered, and whether the vestiges of past discrimination ha[ve] been eliminated to the extent practicable."

Proper analysis of the District Court's orders challenged here, then, must rest upon their serving as proper means to the end of restoring the victims of discriminatory conduct to the position they would have occupied in the absence of that conduct and their eventual restoration of "state and local authorities to the control of a school system that is operating in compliance with the Constitution." We turn to that analysis.

Here, the District Court has found, and the Court of Appeals has affirmed, that this case involved no interdistrict constitutional violation that would support interdistrict relief. Thus, the proper response by the District Court should have been to eliminate to the extent practicable the vestiges of prior *de jure* segregation within the KCMSD: a system wide reduction in student achievement and the existence of 25 racially identifiable schools with a population of over 90% black students.

The District Court and Court of Appeals, however, have felt that because the KCMSD's enrollment remained 68.3% black, a purely *intra*district remedy would be insufficient.

Instead of seeking to remove the racial identity of the various schools within the KCMSD, the District Court has set out on a program to create a school district that was equal to or superior to the surrounding SSDs. Its remedy has focused on "desegregative attractiveness," coupled with "suburban comparability." Examination of the District Court's reliance on "desegregative attractiveness" and "suburban comparability" is instructive for our ultimate resolution of the salary order issue.

The purpose of desegregative attractiveness has been not only to remedy the system wide reduction in student achievement, but also to attract nonminority students not presently enrolled in the KCMSD. This remedy has included an elaborate program of capital improvements, course enrichment, and extracurricular enhancement not simply in the formerly identifiable black schools, but in schools throughout the district. The District Court's remedial orders have converted every senior high school, every middle school, and one half of the elementary schools in the KCMSD into "magnet" schools. The District Court's remedial order has all but made the KCMSD itself into a magnet district.

The District Court's remedial plan in this case, however, is not designed solely to redistribute the students within the KCMSD in order to eliminate racially identifiable schools within the KCMSD. Instead, its purpose is to attract nonminority students from outside the KCMSD schools. But this *inter*district goal is beyond the scope of the *intra*district violation identified by the District Court. In effect, the District Court has devised a remedy to accomplish indirectly what it admittedly lacks the remedial authority to mandate directly: the interdistrict transfer of students.

Respondents argue that the District Court's reliance upon desegregative attractiveness is justified in light of the District Court's statement that segregation has "led to white flight from the KCMSD to suburban districts." The lower courts' "findings" as to "white flight" are both inconsistent internally, and inconsistent with the typical supposition, bolstered here by the record evidence, that "white flight" may result from desegregation, not *de jure* segregation. The United States, as *amicus curiae*, argues that the District Court's finding that "*de jure* segregation in the KCMSD caused white students to leave the system . . . is not inconsistent with the district court's earlier conclusion that the suburban districts did nothing to cause this white flight and therefore could not be included in a mandatory interdistrict remedy."

The District Court's pursuit of "desegregative attractiveness" cannot be reconciled with our cases placing limitations on a district court's remedial authority. It is certainly theoretically possible that the greater the expenditure per pupil within the KCMSD, the more likely it is that some unknowable number of nonminority students not presently attending schools in the KCMSD will choose to enroll in those schools. Under this reasoning, however, every increased expenditure, whether it be for teachers, noninstructional employees, books, or buildings, will make the KCMSD in some way more attractive, and thereby perhaps induce nonminority students to enroll in its schools. But this rationale is not susceptible to any objective limitation.

The District Court's pursuit of the goal of "desegregative attractiveness" results in so many imponderables and is so far removed from the task of eliminating the racial identifiability of the schools within the KCMSD that we believe it is beyond the admittedly broad discretion of the District Court. In this posture, we conclude that the District Court's order of salary increases, which was "grounded in remedying the vestiges of segregation by improving the desegregative attractiveness of the KCMSD," is simply too far removed from an acceptable implementation of a permissible means to remedy previous legally mandated segregation.

Similar considerations lead us to conclude that the District Court's order requiring the State to continue to fund the quality education programs because student achievement levels were still "at or below national norms at many grade levels" cannot be sustained. The State does not seek from this Court a declaration of partial unitary status with respect to the quality education programs. It challenges

the requirement of indefinite funding of a quality education program until national norms are met, based on the assumption that while a mandate for significant educational improvement, both in teaching and in facilities, may have been justified originally, its indefinite extension is not.

It may be that in education, just as it may be in economics, a "rising tide lifts all boats," but the remedial quality education program should be tailored to remedy the injuries suffered by the victims of prior *de jure* segregation.

The judgment of the Court of Appeals is reversed.

JUSTICE THOMAS, *concurring.*

. . . Without a basis in any real finding of intentional government action, the District Court's imposition of liability upon the State of Missouri improperly rests upon a theory that racial imbalances are unconstitutional. . . . In effect, the court found that racial imbalances constituted an ongoing constitutional violation that continued to inflict harm on black students. This position appears to rest upon the idea that any school that is black is inferior, and that blacks cannot succeed without the benefit of the company of whites. . . .

Two clear restraints on the use of the equity power—federalism and the separation of powers—derive from the very form of our Government. Federal courts should pause before using their inherent equitable powers to intrude into the proper sphere of the States. We have long recognized that education is primarily a concern of local authorities. . . . A structural reform decree eviscerates a State's discretionary authority over its own program and budgets and forces state officials to reallocate state resources and funds to the desegregation plan at the expense of other citizens, other government programs, and other institutions not represented in court. . . . When District Courts seize complete control over the schools, they strip state and local governments of one of their most important governmental responsibilities, and thus deny their existence as independent governmental entities....

Even if segregation were present, we must remember that a deserving end does not justify all possible means. The desire to reform a school district, or any other institution, cannot so captivate the Judiciary that it forgets its constitutionally mandated role. Usurpation of the traditionally local control over education not only takes the judiciary beyond its proper sphere, it also deprives the States and their elected officials of their constitutional powers. At some point, we must recognize that the judiciary is not omniscient, and that all problems do not require a remedy of constitutional proportions.

JUSTICE SOUTER, *with whom* **JUSTICE STEVENS, JUSTICE GINSBURG**, *and* **JUSTICE BREYER** *join, dissenting.*

In 1984, 30 years after our decision in *Brown v. Board of Education*, the District Court found that the State of Missouri and the Kansas City, Missouri School District (KCMSD) had failed to reform the segregated scheme of public school education in the KCMSD, previously mandated by the State, which had required black and white children to be taught separately according to race. *Jenkins v. Missouri*. After *Brown*, neither the State nor the KCMSD moved to dismantle this system of separate education "root and branch," *id.*, at 1505, despite their affirmative obligation to do that under the Constitution. *Green* v. *School Bd. of New Kent County*.... Consequently, on the 20th anniversary of *Brown* in 1974, 39 of the 77 schools in the KCMSD had student bodies that were more than 90 percent black, and 80 percent of all black schoolchildren in the KCMSD attended those schools. *Id.*, at 1492–1493. Ten years later, in the 1983–1984

school year, 24 schools remained racially isolated with more than 90 percent black enrollment. *Id.*, at 1493. Because the State and the KCMSD intentionally created this segregated system of education, and subsequently failed to correct it, the District Court concluded that the State and the district had "defaulted in their obligation to uphold the Constitution." *Id.*, at 1505....

On its face, the Court's opinion projects an appealing pragmatism in seeming to cut through the details of many facts by applying a rule of law that can claim both precedential support and intuitive sense, that there is error in imposing an interdistrict remedy to cure a merely intradistrict violation. Since the District Court has consistently described the violation here as solely intradistrict, and since the object of the magnet schools under its plan includes attracting students into the district from other districts, the Court's result seems to follow with the necessity of logic, against which arguments about detail or calls for fair warning may not carry great weight.

... [T]he District Court did not mean by an "intradistrict violation" what the Court apparently means by it today. The District Court meant that the violation within the KCMSD had not led to segregation outside of it, and that no other school districts had played a part in the violation. It did not mean that the violation had not produced effects of any sort beyond the district. Indeed, the record that we have indicates that the District Court understood that the violation here did produce effects spanning district borders and leading to greater segregation within the KCMSD, the reversal of which the District Court sought to accomplish by establishing magnet schools. Insofar as the Court assumes that this was not so in fact, there is at least enough in the record to cast serious doubt on its assumption....

I respectfully dissent.

SYNTHESIS QUESTIONS FOR FURTHER DISCUSSION: CHAPTER 8 SECTION A

1. Did the Constitution bar slavery before the passage of the Thirteenth Amendment? What are William Lloyd Garrison's and Frederick Douglass's views on this subject? Garrison's argument raises the potential conclusion that because it protected slavery, the Constitution was illegitimate before abolition. In his words, "Such a compact was, in the nature of things and according to the law of God, null and void from the beginning." What is Douglass's response to this claim? Consider whether these arguments draw more from text or from more general understandings of the Constitution.

2. One might suggest that *Dred Scott v. Sandford* was rightly decided as a matter of law, but that the judges should have committed a kind of civil disobedience and refused to follow "the law." Usually we think of civil disobedience as an act of citizens committed against the state. But when faced with a potentially evil decision, perhaps state officials should refuse to enforce the law in order to prevent an evil result. Therefore, even if you think Chief Justice Roger Taney's decision was correct as a matter of law, is there any argument that he should have committed "civil disobedience" and decided that case differently?

3. Looking back on the Founding, Justice Thurgood Marshall stresses the difference between the Founders' Constitution and the modern Constitution. After the passage of the Thirteenth Amendment (ban on slavery), Fourteenth Amendment (guarantee of equal protection), and the Fifteenth Amendment (guarantee of a right to vote), does the Constitution become a fundamentally different document? The idea of an amendment often suggests a partial change, but did these amendments radically restructure the Constitution? In Justice Marshall's words, "While the Union survived the Civil War, the Constitution did not." What does this mean? Consider Justice Marshall's argument for tempering reverence towards the Framers of the Constitution. Do his remarks echo the arguments of either Garrison or Douglass?

4. As we have seen, *Brown v. Board of Education* overturns the separate but equal doctrine announced by the majority in *Plessy v. Ferguson*. Famously, Justice John Marshall Harlan dissented in *Plessy v. Ferguson*, citing the claim that the Fourteenth Amendment requires a "colorblind" Constitution. Did the ruling in *Brown v. Board of Education* merely assert that Justice Harlan was correct after all? Or did it suggest a third path of constitutional interpretation of the Equal Protection Clause in regard to racial classifications?

5. Some have argued—as Justice Hugo Black did in *Alexander v. Holmes County Board of Education*—that in using the term "all deliberate speed" in *Brown*

v. Board of Education II, the Supreme Court undercut its original decision. This criticism raises the issue of whether rights must be guaranteed immediately or speedily to really count as rights in the first place. Do you believe that *Brown v. Board of Education II* undercuts *Brown v. Board of Education*? For a radical view on the ineffectiveness of *Brown*, see Gerald Rosenberg, *The Hollow Hope: Can Courts Bring About Social Change?* (University of Chicago Press, 1991). According to Rosenberg, the courts are particularly ineffective in implementing and enforcing rights. His book challenges the notion that *Brown v. Board of Education* led to successful desegregation, and thus serves as one argument in support of those skeptics who worry that *Brown v. Board of Education*, regardless of its content, was undermined in implementation.

B.   AFFIRMATIVE ACTION

Can the Constitution be color-conscious, or must it be colorblind?

In an important way, the debate about affirmative action centers on the meaning of the precedent established in *Brown v. Board of Education*. Both opponents and defenders of programs that emphasize preferential treatment for minorities in hiring and admissions in education appeal to *Brown v. Board of Education* in defense of their position. Opponents of affirmative action and defenders of colorblind approaches to the Constitution suggest that *Brown v. Board of Education* prohibits the state from ever taking race into consideration, even for noble purposes. These opponents cite Justice John Marshall Harlan's dissent in *Plessy v. Ferguson* in defense of their position. On the other hand, proponents of affirmative action suggest that *Brown v. Board of Education* and the subsequent attempts by the Court to bring about desegregation demonstrate that the state must take an active role in eliminating the effects of slavery and segregation in our society. Simply approaching policy from a colorblind perspective, they argue, will only leave the effects of segregation in place, albeit without laws that mandate it. Does *Brown v. Board of Education* support the proposition that the Constitution is a colorblind document? Or does it lay the foundation for future policies aimed at advancing underrepresented minority groups in a way that is color-conscious?

Before we proceed to examine both the general debate about justifications of affirmative action and to apply them to the cases, it is important to understand why the constitutional doctrine established in *Brown v. Board of Education* opened the door to challenges to affirmative action. *Brown v. Board of Education* came to be understood to stand for the proposition that any time a law made a distinction based on race, strict scrutiny should be triggered. Any time strict scrutiny is invoked, the state must show that a distinction based on race is made in pursuit of a goal so important as to constitute a "compelling interest."

In addition to the Court's emphasis on the high burden for the goal of any program that distinguishes based on race, it must also show that the particular policy that is being examined is narrowly tailored in meeting that goal. In other words, it is not only a high burden to show that the state's goal is a compelling interest, but also that the means of pursuing this goal must be the narrowest possible relative to alternative means. As you will see, public institutions have put forward a variety of arguments for why their affirmative action plans meet the standard of strict scrutiny.

Throughout this section, note the differences between the affirmative action programs that we examine in the following section. As you will see, a variety of programs that differ greatly in their methods are often lumped together under the category of "affirmative action." But the amount of deference the Court affords these programs largely depends on their specific methods. As you will see in *Regents v. Bakke*, and, to some degree, in *Gratz v. Bollinger*, the Court is skeptical of "quota" programs, which require a minimum number of minority candidates to receive positions in schools or jobs. As you will see in *Grutter v. Bollinger*, it is more tolerant of those programs that use race as a "plus factor" in admissions and hiring decisions, especially when it does so in a way that is individualized with respect to the specific applicants.

Traditionally, two arguments have been made for giving African Americans applying for public jobs and public institutions such a plus factor. The first emphasizes the need to rectify past injustices, including the evils of slavery and segregation. The second is more forward-looking and emphasizes the need to promote diversity in society at large. Without institutions that are diverse, some argue, we cannot have a society that functions freely or fairly.

We begin this section by considering general arguments for color-conscious versus colorblind approaches to affirmative action. You will see in the readings to come that John McWhorter takes a colorblind position, while Amy Gutmann, who emphasizes the future-oriented justification of affirmative action, believes that non-discrimination is compatible with a policy of racial preferences for minority applicants. You will then be asked to consider how color-conscious and colorblind approaches frame the case law on this subject.

President Lyndon B. Johnson

TO FULFILL THESE RIGHTS

Address given at Howard University, Washington, D.C.

June 4, 1965

As will become evident in the cases that follow, recent equal protection law has examined whether affirmative action programs that give some preference to minority applicants are constitutional. Challenges to these programs have suggested that they violate the Equal Protection Clause of the Fourteenth Amendment. Affirmative action as a means of rectifying discrimination was championed by President Lyndon B. Johnson, who offered a defense of these programs in a commencement address at Howard University on June 4, 1965. As you read the excerpt, keep in mind the extent to which President Johnson defends affirmative action policies on the grounds that they rectify past injustices. This kind of justification will come into conflict with the Supreme Court's own analysis in Gratz v. Bollinger *and* Grutter v. Bollinger. *Is affirmative action in hiring or college admissions best justified by reference to the rectification of past injustices? Are you convinced by President Johnson's argument?*

I am delighted at the chance to speak at this important and this historic institution. Howard has long been an outstanding center for the education of Negro Americans. Its students are of every race and color and they come from many countries of the world. It is truly a working example of democratic excellence.

. . . [N]othing in any country touches us more profoundly, and nothing is more freighted with meaning for our own destiny than the revolution of the Negro American.

In far too many ways American Negroes have been another nation: deprived of freedom, crippled by hatred, the doors of opportunity closed to hope.

In our time change has come to this Nation, too. The American Negro, acting with impressive restraint, has peacefully protested and marched, entered the courtrooms and the seats of government, demanding a justice that has long been denied. The voice of the Negro was the call to action. But it is a tribute to America that, once aroused, the courts and the Congress, the President and most of the people, have been the allies of progress.

Thus we have seen the high court of the country declare that discrimination based on race was repugnant to the Constitution, and therefore void. We have seen in 1957, and 1960, and again in 1964, the first civil rights legislation in this Nation in almost an entire century.

As majority leader of the United States Senate, I helped to guide two of these bills through the Senate. And, as your President, I was proud to sign the third. And now very soon we will have the fourth—a new law guaranteeing every American the right to vote.

That beginning is freedom; and the barriers to that freedom are tumbling down. Freedom is the right to share, share fully and equally, in American society—to vote, to hold a job, to enter a public place, to go to school. It is the right to be treated in every part of our national life as a person equal in dignity and promise to all others.

But freedom is not enough. You do not wipe away the scars of centuries by saying: Now you are free to go where you want, and do as you desire, and choose the leaders you please.

You do not take a person who, for years, has been hobbled by chains and liberate him, bring him up to the starting line of a race and then say, "you are free to compete with all the others," and still justly believe that you have been completely fair.

Thus it is not enough just to open the gates of opportunity. All our citizens must have the ability to walk through those gates.

This is the next and the more profound stage of the battle for civil rights. We seek not just freedom but opportunity. We seek not just legal equity but human ability, not just equality as a right and a theory but equality as a fact and equality as a result.

For the task is to give 20 million Negroes the same chance as every other American to learn and grow, to work and share in society, to develop their abilities—physical, mental and spiritual, and to pursue their individual happiness.

To this end equal opportunity is essential, but not enough, not enough. Men and women of all races are born with the same range of abilities. But ability is not just the product of birth. Ability is stretched or stunted by the family that you live with, and the neighborhood you live in—by the school you go to and the poverty or the richness of your surroundings. It is the product of a hundred unseen forces playing upon the little infant, the child, and finally the man.

This graduating class at Howard University is witness to the indomitable determination of the Negro American to win his way in American life.

The number of Negroes in schools of higher learning has almost doubled in 15 years. The number of nonwhite professional workers has more than doubled in 10 years. The median income of Negro college women tonight exceeds that of white college women.

But for the great majority of Negro Americans—the poor, the unemployed, the uprooted, and the dispossessed—there is a much grimmer story. They still, as we meet here tonight, are another nation. Despite the court orders and the laws, despite the legislative victories and the speeches, for them the walls are rising and the gulf is widening.

We are not completely sure why this is. We know the causes are complex and subtle. But we do know the two broad basic reasons.

First, Negroes are trapped—as many whites are trapped—in inherited, gateless poverty. They lack training and skills. They are shut in, in slums, without decent medical care. Private and public poverty combine to cripple their capacities.

But there is a second cause—much more difficult to explain, more deeply grounded, more desperate in its force. It is the devastating heritage of long years of slavery; and a century of oppression, hatred, and injustice.

For Negro poverty is not white poverty. Many of its causes and many of its cures are the same. But there are differences—deep, corrosive, obstinate differences—radiating painful roots into the community, and into the family, and the nature of the individual.

These differences are not racial differences. They are solely and simply the consequence of ancient brutality, past injustice, and present prejudice. They are anguishing to observe. For the Negro they are a constant reminder of oppression. For the white they are a constant reminder of guilt. But they must be faced and they must be dealt with and they must be overcome, if we are ever to reach the time when the only difference between Negroes and whites is the color of their skin.

Nor can we find a complete answer in the experience of other American minorities. For they did not have the heritage of centuries to overcome, and they did not have a cultural tradition which had been twisted and battered by endless years of hatred and hopelessness, nor were they excluded—these others—because of race or color—a feeling whose dark intensity is matched by no other prejudice in our society.

Nor can these differences be understood as isolated infirmities. They are a seamless web. They cause each other. They result from each other. They reinforce each other.

Much of the Negro community is buried under a blanket of history and circumstance. It is not a lasting solution to lift just one corner of that blanket. We must stand on all sides and we must raise the entire cover if we are to liberate our fellow citizens.

One of the differences is the increased concentration of Negroes in our cities. More than 73 percent of all Negroes live in urban areas compared with less than 70 percent of the whites. Most of these Negroes live in slums. Most of these Negroes live together—a separated people.

Men are shaped by their world. When it is a world of decay, ringed by an invisible wall, when escape is arduous and uncertain, and the saving pressures of a more hopeful society are unknown, it can cripple the youth and it can desolate the men.

There is also the burden that a dark skin can add to the search for a productive place in our society. Unemployment strikes most swiftly and broadly at the Negro, and this burden erodes hope. Blighted hope breeds despair. Despair brings indifferences to the learning which offers a way out. And despair, coupled with indifferences, is often the source of destructive rebellion against the fabric of society.

Perhaps most important—its influence radiating to every part of life—is the breakdown of the Negro family structure. For this, most of all, white America must accept responsibility. It flows from centuries of oppression and persecution of the Negro man. It flows from the long years of degradation and discrimination, which have attacked his dignity and assaulted his ability to produce for his family.

Only a minority—less than half—of all Negro children reach the age of 18 having lived all their lives with both of their parents. At this moment, tonight, little less than two-thirds are at home with both of their parents. Probably a majority of all Negro children receive federally-aided public assistance sometime during their childhood.

The family is the cornerstone of our society. More than any other force it shapes the attitude, the hopes, the ambitions, and the values of the child. And when the family collapses it is the children that are usually damaged. When it happens on a massive scale the community itself is crippled.

So, unless we work to strengthen the family, to create conditions under which most parents will stay together—all the rest: schools, and playgrounds, and public assistance, and private concern, will never be enough to cut completely the circle of despair and deprivation.

For what is justice?

It is to fulfill the fair expectations of man.

Thus, American justice is a very special thing. For, from the first, this has been a land of towering expectations. It was to be a nation where each man could be ruled by the common consent of all—enshrined in law, given life by institutions, guided by men themselves subject to its rule. And all—all of every station and origin—would be touched equally in obligation and in liberty.

Beyond the law lay the land. It was a rich land, glowing with more abundant promise than man had ever seen. Here, unlike any place yet known, all were to share the harvest.

And beyond this was the dignity of man. Each could become whatever his qualities of mind and spirit would permit—to strive, to seek, and, if he could, to find his happiness.

This is American justice. We have pursued it faithfully to the edge of our imperfections, and we have failed to find it for the American Negro.

So, it is the glorious opportunity of this generation to end the one huge wrong of the American Nation and, in so doing, to find America for ourselves, with the same immense thrill of discovery which gripped those who first began to realize that here, at last, was a home for freedom.

All it will take is for all of us to understand what this country is and what this country must become.

John McWhorter

REAL DIVERSITY AFTER *BAKKE*

New York Sun, April 23, 2003

While many justifications for affirmative action emphasize remedying past injustices, others stress the future-oriented goal of promoting diversity in society. As you will see, much of the debate over affirmative action focuses on whether or not universities should take race into account in admissions decisions for this purpose. The diversity rationale is potentially important in two fundamental ways. First, it has been said to enhance the learning experience of those attending the university. Second, diversity serves as a way to ensure that a variety of racial and ethnic groups are represented in the workplace. Educational institutions are gateways to many professions, and if these institutions are not diverse, then it will be difficult to have diversified professions. In the following two passages, we consider arguments for and against this so-called "diversity rationale." Consider in particular how the passage from Amy Gutmann differs in its defense of affirmative action from that given by President Lyndon B. Johnson. To what extent does John McWhorter's piece respond to the "future diversity" and "past injustice" justifications for affirmative action?

With the Supreme Court about to decide a set of cases that could overturn its 1978 *Bakke* decision and require colorblind admissions at colleges and universities, it's a good time to describe what a post affirmative-action admissions policy at a top school should look like—and explain why it would be fully compatible with minority success and real diversity.

The raison d'être of the nation's selective universities is to forge a well-educated, national elite. Thus, our post-preferences approach to admissions must be meritocratic, though few people would want schools simply to choose students with the best SAT scores and grades and call it a day.

Back in the early 1980s, at Simon's Rock Early College in Massachusetts, a smattering of my classmates fell into the 1,600 category. But thankfully, the school's administrators grasped that that kind of achievement represents only one of the forms of excellence that smart young people can bring to campus life. The school worked hard to attract a lively mix of students, who vastly enriched my years on campus. My cello playing, for example, took on new depth, because I had the opportunity to play with a brilliant musician whose talents on piano and violin scaled near-professional heights.

At school, I also met my first Mennonite and my first white Southerner. There were other blacks among the school's 300 or so students, too. Most, like me, were middle class, but there was one guy who had grown up in crumbling Camden, N.J. This student gave a lesson in one form of cultural "blackness" to his white classmates —he had real "street" cred. But far more important, after a rocky start and some coaching, he also proved he could do the schoolwork on the high level the school demanded. This was real diversity.

Since my undergraduate days, however, elite universities have come to mean something much different when they speak of "diversity": having as many brown faces on campus as possible, regardless of standards. The origin of the current notion of diversity was Justice Lewis Powell's opinion for the court in *Bakke*. Though strict racial quotas were unconstitutional, Justice Powell argued, schools could still use race as an "important element" in admissions in order to create a "diverse" campus that would enhance the quality of all students' educational experiences by exposing them to minority "opinions."

Justice Powell's argument was dishonest, in that it wasn't at bottom about broadening white students' horizons but providing a rationale for admitting blacks and Hispanics much less qualified than other applicants. Even on its own terms, however, Justice Powell's "diversity" argument is demeaning and offensive to minorities. What would be a black "opinion" on French irregular verbs? Or systolic pressure? The "black" views that most interest diversity advocates, of course, are those that illumine social injustice.

Black students understandably can find this whole diversity regime repugnant and even racist. "Professor McWhorter," students have asked me, "what about when I am called on for my opinion as a black person in class? Is it fair that I have to deal with that burden?" A continent away, the undergraduate-written "Black Guide to Life at Harvard" insists: "We are not here to provide diversity training for Kate or Timmy before they go out to take over the world."

Even as we seek diversity in the worthy, Simon's Rock sense, we must recognize that students need to be able to excel at college-level studies. The problem, then, is to find some way to measure a student's potential that still leaves administrators enough leeway to ensure that campus life benefits from a rich variety of excellences and life experiences.

As it turns out, we have—and use—the measure: the Scholastic Aptitude Test.

Nowadays, a creeping fashion dismisses the SAT as culturally biased. But while it is true that the SAT is far from perfect, the exam really does tend to forecast students' future success, as even William Bowen and Derek Bok admit in their valentine to racial preferences, *The Shape of the River*.

A post-preferences admissions policy must accept that below a certain cut-off point in SAT scores, a student runs a serious risk of failing to graduate. As Thomas Sowell, among others, has shown, placing minorities in schools that expect a performance level beyond what they have been prepared to meet leads to disproportionate dropout rates—41% of the black students in Berkeley's class of 1988, to take one typical example, did not complete their education, compared with 16% of whites. Many of these students may have flourished at slightly less competitive schools.

To prevent this kind of damage, the SAT could supply us with the rough parameters within which our admissions search for different kinds of merit—diversity, rightly understood—will proceed. Within our SAT range, there will be plenty of room for judgment calls. Grades, extracurricular activities, and character will all be key. Our admissions policy will be colorblind, but it won't ignore the working class and the poor—many of whom, as a practical matter, will be blacks or Hispanics.

The University of California at Berkeley, where I teach, is already on the right track. Not so long ago, the admissions committee I sat on matter-of-factly chose middle-class brown students, essentially "white" culturally, over equally deserving white students. I felt tremendous discomfort over the practice. Since California voted in a 1997 referendum to ban the use of race in admissions, things have changed. Berkeley still assesses students on grades and scores, but instead of race, it now considers the "hardships" that young men and women may have overcome while excelling at school. We recently gave fellowships, for example, to two needy white students who had shown sterling promise. I felt fundamentally right about these fellowships. "This is a racially blind process," emphasizes the chair of Berkeley's faculty committee on admissions, Calvin Moore.

The idea of a "racially blind process" makes today's "diversity" fans shudder, since they believe that it will lead to a tragic re-segregation of the best American universities and thus of American society. I'm sorry, but this is manipulative melodrama. In an America several decades past the Civil Rights Act, where far more black families are middle class than are poor, many black students will be ready for the top schools without dragging down the bar of evaluation.

Since the banning of racial preferences in California, there has been a 350% rise in the number of black teens taking calculus in preparation for college. Challenge people, and they respond.

It's time to step up to the plate. My years on college campuses have taught me that even those willing to acknowledge the injustices of preferences in private uphold the "diversity" party line in public—something *Bakke* allows them to do. Indeed, 25 years of *Bakke* show that, in practice, even a hint that race can be "a" factor in admissions will give college administrators, ever eager to "do the right thing," the go-ahead to continue fostering a second-tier class-within-a-class of "spunky" minorities on their campuses.

Justice Powell's *Bakke* opinion cited an amicus brief for "diversity" submitted by Harvard, Stanford, Columbia, and the University of Pennsylvania. The brief described how these schools had traditionally aimed to compose their classes with a mixture of "students from California, New York and Massachusetts; city dwellers and farm boys; violinists, painters and football players; biologists, historians and classicists; potential stockbrokers, academics and politicians." It's a wonderful, noble goal, this diversity—and we don't need to treat any group of citizens as lesser beings to accomplish it.

Amy Gutmann

RESPONDING TO RACIAL INJUSTICE

in *Color Conscious: The Political Morality of Race*

Princeton, NJ: Princeton University Press (1996)

In 1989, the school board of Piscataway High School faced budget cuts that required it to fire one of two teachers of typing and secretarial studies, Sharon Taxman and Debra Williams. Taxman and Williams had equal seniority, having been hired on the same day in 1980. Instead of flipping a coin to decide which teacher

to fire, the school board decided to fire Taxman and retain Williams, the only black teacher in the school's department of business education.

This example of color conscious action is an easy target for a color-blind perspective. The school board violated Taxman's right not to be discriminated against on grounds of race, and the school board's action should therefore be prohibited. It is beside any moral point admitted by a color-blind perspective to say that the board may have acted consistently with the aim of overcoming racial injustice, and that this kind of action can be morally distinguished from race conscious policies that reflect "prejudice and contempt for a disadvantaged group" or increase the disadvantage of an already disadvantaged group. "Discrimination on the basis of race," Alexander Bickel wrote in a famous defense of color blindness, "is illegal, immoral, unconstitutional, inherently wrong, and destructive of democratic society. Now this is to be unlearned, and we are told that this is not a matter of fundamental principle but only a matter of whose ox is gored." A contemporary critic echoes Bickel when he associates the Piscataway school board's action with "the most extreme form of racialism."

Many radically different arguments have been offered for and against preferential treatment, and I cannot review them all here. Instead, I focus on the morally strongest case that can be made in the context of our society for preferential treatment of black Americans. That case rests on the ideal of fairness or fair equality of opportunity, which also informs the principle of nondiscrimination. The strongest argument for preferential treatment from the perspective of anyone committed to justice as fairness is that it paves the way for a society in which fair equality of opportunity is a reality rather than merely an abstract promise. By giving preference to basically qualified black candidates over better qualified nonblack candidates, employers—especially those who control large-scale institutions—may help create the background conditions for fair equality of opportunity. How can they do so? By breaking down the racial stereotyping of jobs that has resulted from our racist past. Many scarce and highly valued jobs in our society remain racially stereotyped because of this past. In this context, even institutions that faithfully apply the principle of nondiscrimination in hiring may fail to convey a message of fair opportunity to blacks. Absent this message, hiring practices are also bound to fail the test of fair opportunity.

If preferential hiring of basically qualified blacks can help break down the racial stereotyping of jobs, then employers may legitimately consider not only a candidate's qualifications, which are specific to the job's purpose, but also a candidate's capacity to move society forward to a time when the principle of nondiscrimination works more fairly than it does today. It is reasonable to think that by hiring qualified blacks for stereotypically white positions in greater numbers than blacks would be hired by color-blind employers, the United States will move farther and faster in the direction of providing fair opportunity to all its citizens. There are three ways in which preferential hiring may help move our society in this direction: by *breaking down racial stereotypes,* by *creating identity role models* for black children and, as important, by *creating diversity role models* for all citizens. Identity role models teach black children that they too can realistically aspire to social accomplishment, while diversity role models teach all children and adults alike that blacks are accomplished contributors to our society from whom we all may learn. All three of these considerations—breaking racial stereotypes and creating identity and diversity role models—are of course color conscious.

REGENTS OF THE UNIVERSITY OF CALIFORNIA v. BAKKE

438 U.S. 265 (1978)

Opinion: Powell, joined by White in Parts I, III-A, and V-C and by Brenan, Marshall, Blackmun in Parts I and V-C

Partial Concurrence, Partial Dissent: Brennan, White, Marshall, Blackmun

Concurrence: White

Concurrence: Marshall

Concurrence: Blackmun

Partial Concurrence, Partial Dissent: Stevens, joined by Burger, Stewart, Rehnquist

This case involves a challenge to the University of California at Davis's medical school's method of conducting affirmative action in admissions, which involved reserving a certain number of spots for students of certain racial groups. The Court is clear that U.C. Davis's admission policy is unconstitutional in its use of quotas, but is the holding here incompatible with affirmative action altogether? Notice in particular the heavy burden put on U.C. Davis to justify its policy by a strict scrutiny analysis. Think about the possible future of affirmative action under the Constitution by distinguishing possible compelling interests that the school could have appealed to, and alternative means that it could have used to realize these interests.

MR. JUSTICE POWELL *announced the judgment of the Court.*

This case presents a challenge to the special admissions program of the petitioner, the Medical School of the University of California at Davis, which is designed to assure the admission of a specified number of students from certain minority groups.

The Medical School of the University of California at Davis opened in 1968 with an entering class of 50 students. Over the next two years, the faculty devised a special admissions program to increase the representation of "disadvantaged" students in each Medical School class. The special program consisted of a separate admissions system operating in coordination with the regular admissions process.

Under the regular admissions procedure, a candidate could submit his application to the Medical School beginning in July of the year preceding the academic year for which admission was sought. Because of the large number of applications, the admissions committee screened each one to select candidates for further consideration. Candidates whose overall undergraduate grade point averages fell below 2.5 on a scale of 4.0 were summarily rejected. About one out of six applicants was invited for a personal interview. Following the interviews, each candidate was rated on a scale of 1 to 100 by his interviewers and four other members of the admissions committee. The rating embraced the interviewers' summaries, the candidate's overall grade point average, grade point average in science courses, scores on the Medical College Admissions Test (MCAT), letters of recommendation, extracurricular activities, and other biographical data. The ratings were added together to arrive at each candidate's "benchmark" score. The full committee then reviewed the file and scores of each applicant and made offers of admission on a "rolling" basis. The chairman was responsible for placing names on the waiting list. They were not placed in strict numerical order; instead, the chairman had discretion to include persons with "special skills."

The special admissions program operated with a separate committee, a majority of whom were members of minority groups. On the 1973 application form, candidates were asked to indicate whether they wished to be considered as "economically and/or educationally disadvantaged" applicants; on the 1974 form the question was whether they wished to be considered as members of a "minority group," which the Medical School apparently viewed as "Blacks," "Chicanos," "Asians," and "American Indians." If these questions were answered affirmatively, the application was forwarded to the special admissions committee. No formal definition of "disadvantaged" was ever produced, but the chairman of the special committee screened each application to see whether it reflected economic or educational deprivation. Having passed this initial hurdle, the applications then were rated by the special committee in a fashion similar to that used by the general admissions committee, except that special candidates did not have to meet the 2.5 grade point average cutoff applied to regular applicants. About one-fifth of the total number of special applicants were invited for interviews in 1973 and 1974. Following each interview, the special committee assigned each special applicant a benchmark score. The special committee then presented its top choices to the general admissions committee. The latter did not rate or compare the special candidates against the general applicants, but could reject recommended special candidates for failure to meet course requirements or other specific deficiencies. The special committee continued to recommend special applicants until a number prescribed by faculty vote were admitted. While the overall class size was still 50, the prescribed number was 8; in 1973 and 1974, when the class size had doubled to 100, the prescribed number of special admissions also doubled, to 16.

Although disadvantaged whites applied to the special program in large numbers, none received an offer of admission through that process. Indeed, in 1974, at least, the special committee explicitly considered only "disadvantaged" special applicants who were members of one of the designated minority groups.

Allan Bakke is a white male who applied to the Davis Medical School in both 1973 and 1974. In both years, Bakke's application was considered under the general admissions program, and he received an interview. Despite a strong benchmark score of 468 out of 500, Bakke was rejected. His application had come late in the year, and no applicants in the general admissions process with scores below 470 were accepted after Bakke's application was completed. There were four special admissions slots unfilled at that time, however, for which Bakke was not considered.

Bakke's 1974 application was completed early in the year. Again, Bakke's application was rejected. In both years, applicants were admitted under the special program with grade point averages, MCAT scores, and benchmark scores significantly lower than Bakke's.

After the second rejection, Bakke filed the instant suit in the Superior Court of California. He alleged that the Medical School's special admissions program operated to exclude him from the school on the basis of his race, in violation of his rights under the Equal Protection Clause of the Fourteenth Amendment, Art. I, §21, of the California Constitution, and §601 of Title VI of the Civil Rights Act of 1964.

The language of §601, like that of the Equal Protection Clause, is majestic in its sweep:

> No person in the United States shall, on the ground of race, color, or national origin, be excluded from participation in, be denied the benefits of, or be subjected to discrimination

under any program or activity receiving Federal financial assistance.

The concept of "discrimination," like the phrase "equal protection of the laws," is susceptible of varying interpretations, for, as Mr. Justice Holmes declared,

> [a] word is not a crystal, transparent and unchanged, it is the skin of a living thought, and may vary greatly in color and content according to the circumstances and the time in which it is used.

Although isolated statements of various legislators, taken out of context, can be marshaled in support of the proposition that §601 enacted a purely colorblind scheme, without regard to the reach of the Equal Protection Clause, these comments must be read against the background of both the problem that Congress was addressing and the broader view of the statute that emerges from a full examination of the legislative debates.

The problem confronting Congress was discrimination against Negro citizens at the hands of recipients of federal moneys. Indeed, the color blindness pronouncements . . . generally occur in the midst of extended remarks dealing with the evils of segregation in federally funded programs. Over and over again, proponents of the bill detailed the plight of Negroes seeking equal treatment in such programs. There simply was no reason for Congress to consider the validity of hypothetical preferences that might be accorded minority citizens; the legislators were dealing with the real and pressing problem of how to guarantee those citizens equal treatment.

In view of the clear legislative intent, Title VI must be held to proscribe only those racial classifications that would violate the Equal Protection Clause or the Fifth Amendment.

Petitioner does not deny that decisions based on race or ethnic origin by faculties and administrations of state universities are reviewable under the Fourteenth Amendment. The parties do disagree as to the level of judicial scrutiny to be applied to the special admissions program. Petitioner argues that the court below erred in applying strict scrutiny, as this inexact term has been applied in our cases. That level of review, petitioner asserts, should be reserved for classifications that disadvantage "discrete and insular minorities." *See United States v. Carolene Products Co.* Respondent, on the other hand, contends that the California court correctly rejected the notion that the degree of Judicial scrutiny accorded a particular racial or ethnic classification hinges upon membership in a discrete and insular minority and duly recognized that the "lights established [by the Fourteenth Amendment] are personal rights."

En route to this crucial battle over the scope of judicial review, the parties fight a sharp preliminary action over the proper characterization of the special admissions program. Petitioner prefers to view it as establishing a "goal" of minority representation in the Medical School. Respondent, echoing the courts below, labels it a racial quota.

This semantic distinction is beside the point: the special admissions program is undeniably a classification based on race and ethnic background. To the extent that there existed a pool of at least minimally qualified minority applicants to fill the 16 special admissions seats, white applicants could compete only for 84 seats in the entering class, rather than the 100 open to minority applicants. Whether this limitation is described as a quota or a goal, it is a line drawn on the basis of race and ethnic status.

The guarantees of the Fourteenth Amendment extend to all persons. Its language is explicit: "No State shall . . . deny to any person within its jurisdiction the equal protection of the laws."

The guarantee of equal protection cannot mean one thing when applied to one individual and something else when applied to a person of another color. If both are not accorded the same protection, then it is not equal.

Petitioner urges us to adopt for the first time a more restrictive view of the Equal Protection Clause, and hold that discrimination against members of the white "majority" cannot be suspect if its purpose can be characterized as "benign." The clock of our liberties, however, cannot be turned back to 1868. It is far too late to argue that the guarantee of equal protection to all persons permits the recognition of special wards entitled to a degree of protection greater than that accorded others.

Once the artificial line of a "two-class theory" of the Fourteenth Amendment is put aside, the difficulties entailed in varying the level of judicial review according to a perceived "preferred" status of a particular racial or ethnic minority are intractable. The concepts of "majority" and "minority" necessarily reflect temporary arrangements and political judgments. As observed above, the white "majority" itself is composed of various minority groups, most of which can lay claim to a history of prior discrimination at the hands of the State and private individuals. Not all of these groups can receive preferential treatment and corresponding judicial tolerance of distinctions drawn in terms of race and nationality, for then the only "majority" left would be a new minority of white Anglo-Saxon Protestants. There is no principled basis for deciding which groups would merit "heightened judicial solicitude" and which would not. Courts would be asked to evaluate the extent of the prejudice and consequent harm suffered by various minority groups. Those whose societal injury is thought to exceed some arbitrary level of tolerability then would be entitled to preferential classifications at the expense of individuals belonging to other groups. Those classifications would be free from exacting judicial scrutiny. As these preferences began to have their desired effect, and the consequences of past discrimination were undone, new judicial rankings would be necessary. The kind of variable sociological and political analysis necessary to produce such rankings simply does not lie within the judicial competence—even if they otherwise were politically feasible and socially desirable.

Moreover, there are serious problems of justice connected with the idea of preference itself. First, it may not always be clear that a so-called preference is, in fact, benign. Courts may be asked to validate burdens imposed upon individual members of a particular group in order to advance the group's general interest. Nothing in the Constitution supports the notion that individuals may be asked to suffer otherwise impermissible burdens in order to enhance the societal standing of their ethnic groups. Second, preferential programs may only reinforce common stereotypes holding that certain groups are unable to achieve success without special protection based on a factor having no relationship to individual worth. Third, there is a measure of inequity in forcing innocent persons in respondent's position to bear the burdens of redressing grievances not of their making.

We have held that, in

> order to justify the use of a suspect classification, a State must show that its purpose or interest is both constitutionally permissible and substantial, and that its use of the classification is "necessary . . . to the accomplishment" of its purpose or the safeguarding of its interest.

The special admissions program purports to serve the purposes of: (i) "reducing the historic deficit of traditionally disfavored minorities in medical schools and in the medical profession"; (ii) countering the effects of societal discrimination; (iii) increasing the number of physicians who will practice in communities currently underserved; and (iv) obtaining the educational benefits that flow from an ethnically diverse student body. It is necessary to decide which, if any, of these purposes is substantial enough to support the use of a suspect classification.

If petitioner's purpose is to assure within its student body some specified percentage of a particular group merely because of its race or ethnic origin, such a preferential purpose must be rejected not as insubstantial, but as facially invalid. Preferring members of any one group for no reason other than race or ethnic origin is discrimination for its own sake. This the Constitution forbids.

The State certainly has a legitimate and substantial interest in ameliorating, or eliminating where feasible, the disabling effects of identified discrimination.

We have never approved a classification that aids persons perceived as members of relatively victimized groups at the expense of other innocent individuals in the absence of judicial, legislative, or administrative findings of constitutional or statutory violations. Without such findings of constitutional or statutory violations, it cannot be said that the government has any greater interest in helping one individual than in refraining from harming another. Thus, the government has no compelling justification for inflicting such harm.

Petitioner identifies, as another purpose of its program, improving the delivery of health care services to communities currently underserved. It may be assumed that, in some situations, a State's interest in facilitating the health care of its citizens is sufficiently compelling to support the use of a suspect classification. But there is virtually no evidence in the record indicating that petitioner's special admissions program is either needed or geared to promote that goal.

Petitioner simply has not carried its burden of demonstrating that it must prefer members of particular ethnic groups over all other individuals in order to promote better health care delivery to deprived citizens. Indeed, petitioner has not shown that its preferential classification is likely to have any significant effect on the problem.

The fourth goal asserted by petitioner is the attainment of a diverse student body. This clearly is a constitutionally permissible goal for an institution of higher education. Academic freedom, though not a specifically enumerated constitutional right, long has been viewed as a special concern of the First Amendment.

Ethnic diversity, however, is only one element in a range of factors a university properly may consider in attaining the goal of a heterogeneous student body. Although a university must have wide discretion in making the sensitive judgments as to who should be admitted, constitutional limitations protecting individual rights may not be disregarded. Respondent urges—and the courts below have held—that petitioner's dual admissions program is a racial classification that impermissibly infringes his rights under the Fourteenth Amendment. As the interest of diversity is compelling in the context of a university's admissions program, the question remains whether the program's racial classification is necessary to promote this interest.

It may be assumed that the reservation of a specified number of seats in each class for individuals from the preferred ethnic groups would contribute to the attainment of considerable ethnic diversity in the student body. But petitioner's argument that this is the only effective means of serving the interest of diversity is seriously flawed. The diversity that furthers a compelling state interest encompasses a far broader array of qualifications and characteristics, of which racial or ethnic origin is but a single, though important, element. Petitioner's special admissions program, focused solely on ethnic diversity, would hinder, rather than further, attainment of genuine diversity.

Nor would the state interest in genuine diversity be served by expanding petitioner's two-track system into a multi-track program with a prescribed number of seats set aside for each identifiable category of applicants. Indeed, it is inconceivable that a university would thus pursue the logic of petitioner's two-track program to the illogical end of insulating each category of applicants with certain desired qualifications from competition with all other applicants.

The experience of other university admissions programs, which take race into account in achieving the educational diversity valued by the First Amendment, demonstrates that the assignment of a fixed number of places to a minority group is not a necessary means toward that end.

In such an admissions program, race or ethnic background may be deemed a "plus" in a particular applicant's file, yet it does not insulate the individual from comparison with all other candidates for the available seats. The file of a particular black applicant may be examined for his potential contribution to diversity without the factor of race being decisive when compared, for example, with that of an applicant identified as an Italian-American if the latter is thought to exhibit qualities more likely to promote beneficial educational pluralism.

This kind of program treats each applicant as an individual in the admissions process. The applicant who loses out on the last available seat to another candidate receiving a "plus" on the basis of ethnic background will not have been foreclosed from all consideration for that seat simply because he was not the right color or had the wrong surname. It would mean only that his combined qualifications, which may have included similar nonobjective factors, did not outweigh those of the other applicant. His qualifications would have been weighed fairly and competitively, and he would have no basis to complain of unequal treatment under the Fourteenth Amendment.

The fatal flaw in petitioner's preferential program is its disregard of individual rights as guaranteed by the Fourteenth Amendment. Such rights are not absolute. But when a State's distribution of benefits or imposition of burdens hinges on ancestry or the color of a person's skin, that individual is entitled to a demonstration that the challenged classification is necessary to promote a substantial state interest. Petitioner has failed to carry this burden.

In enjoining petitioner from ever considering the race of any applicant, however, the courts below failed to recognize that the State has a substantial interest that legitimately may be served by a properly devised admissions program involving the competitive consideration of race and ethnic origin. For this reason, so much of the California court's judgment as enjoins petitioner from any consideration of the race of any applicant must be reversed.

With respect to respondent's entitlement to an injunction directing his admission to the Medical School, petitioner has conceded that it could not carry its burden of proving that, but for the existence of its unlawful special admissions program, respondent still would not have been admitted. Hence, respondent is entitled to the injunction, and that portion of the judgment must be affirmed.

MR. JUSTICE BRENNAN, MR. JUSTICE WHITE, MR. JUSTICE MARSHALL, and MR. JUSTICE BLACKMUN, *concurring in the judgment in part and dissenting in part.*

The difficulty of the issue presented—whether government may use race-conscious programs to redress the continuing effects of past discrimination—and the mature consideration which each of our Brethren has brought to it have resulted in many opinions, no single one speaking for the Court. But this should not and must not mask the central meaning of today's opinions: Government may take race into account when it acts not to demean or insult any racial group, but to remedy disadvantages cast on minorities by past racial prejudice, at least when appropriate findings have been made by judicial, legislative, or administrative bodies with competence to act in this area.

MR. JUSTICE POWELL agrees that some uses of race in university admissions are permissible and, therefore, he joins with us to make five votes reversing the judgment below insofar as it prohibits the University from establishing race-conscious programs in the future.

MR. JUSTICE STEVENS, *with whom* THE CHIEF JUSTICE, MR. JUSTICE STEWART, *and* MR. JUSTICE REHNQUIST *join, concurring in the judgment in part and dissenting in part.*

The statutory prohibition against discrimination in federally funded projects contained in §601 is more than a simple paraphrasing of what the Fifth or Fourteenth Amendment would require.

However, we need not decide the congruence—or lack of congruence—of the controlling statute and the Constitution since the meaning of the Title VI ban on exclusion is crystal clear: race cannot be the basis of excluding anyone from participation in a federally funded program.

In short, nothing in the legislative history justifies the conclusion that the broad language of §601 should not be given its natural meaning. We are dealing with a distinct statutory prohibition, enacted at a particular time with particular concerns in mind; neither its language nor any prior interpretation suggests that its place in the Civil Rights Act, won after long debate, is simply that of a constitutional appendage. In unmistakable terms, the Act prohibits the exclusion of individuals from federally funded programs because of their race.

CITY OF RICHMOND v. J.A. CROSON CO.
488 U.S. 469 (1989)

Opinion: O'Connor, joined by
Rehnquist, White, Stevens, Kennedy
in Parts I, III-B, IV, by Rehnquist,
White in Part II, and by Rehnquist,
White, Kennedy in Parts III-A and V
Concurrence: Stevens
Concurrence: Kennedy
Concurrence: Scalia
Dissent: Marshall, joined by Brennan,
Blackmun
Dissent: Blackmun, joined by Brennan

We have just looked at the question of whether affirmative action in matters of public university education triggers strict scrutiny. We now turn to consider whether the awarding of government contracts can take race into account. Should race-conscious policies meant to increase the number of minority contractors also be subject to strict scrutiny analysis? Consider, for instance, whether there are different rationales for taking race into account in the awarding of government contracts than for doing so in university admissions. Pay particular attention to the level of review the Court employs here. As you will see, strict scrutiny is used in both City of Richmond v. J.A. Croson Co. *and* Adarand Constructors v. Pena, *which follows this case. What possible compelling interest does the Court consider in its discussion of government contracts and affirmative action?*

JUSTICE O'CONNOR *announced the judgment of the Court and delivered the opinion of the Court with respect to Parts I, III-B, and IV, an opinion with respect to Part II, in which* **THE CHIEF JUSTICE** *and* **JUSTICE WHITE** *join, and an opinion with respect to Parts III-A and V, in which* **THE CHIEF JUSTICE, JUSTICE WHITE**, *and* **JUSTICE KENNEDY** *join.*

In this case, we confront once again the tension between the Fourteenth Amendment's guarantee of equal treatment to all citizens, and the use of race-based measures to ameliorate the effects of past discrimination on the opportunities enjoyed by members of minority groups in our society. In *Fullilove v. Klutznick*, we held that a congressional program requiring that 10% of certain federal construction grants be awarded to minority contractors did not violate the equal protection principles embodied in the Due Process Clause of the Fifth Amendment. Relying largely on our decision in *Fullilove*, some lower federal courts have applied a similar standard of review in assessing the constitutionality of state and local minority set-aside provisions under the Equal Protection Clause of the Fourteenth Amendment. Since our decision two Terms ago in *Wygant v. Jackson Board of Education*, the lower federal courts have attempted to apply its standards in evaluating the constitutionality of state and local programs which allocate a portion of public contracting opportunities exclusively to minority-owned businesses. We noted probable

jurisdiction in this case to consider the applicability of our decision in *Wygant* to a minority set-aside program adopted by the city of Richmond, Virginia.

I

On April 11, 1983, the Richmond City Council adopted the Minority Business Utilization Plan (the Plan). The Plan required prime contractors to whom the city awarded construction contracts to subcontract at least 30% of the dollar amount of the contract to one or more Minority Business Enterprises (MBE's).

The Plan defined an MBE as "[a] business at least fifty-one (51) percent of which is owned and controlled . . . by minority group members." "Minority group members" were defined as "[c]itizens of the United States who are Blacks, Spanish-speaking, Orientals, Indians, Eskimos, or Aleuts." There was no geographic limit to the Plan; an otherwise qualified MBE from anywhere in the United States could avail itself of the 30% set-aside. The Plan declared that it was "remedial" in nature, and enacted "for the purpose of promoting wider participation by minority business enterprises in the construction of public projects." The Plan expired on June 30, 1988, and was in effect for approximately five years. . . .

The Plan was adopted by the Richmond City Council after a public hearing. Seven members of the public spoke to the merits of the ordinance: five were in opposition. two in favor. Proponents of the set-aside provision relied on a study which indicated that, while the general population of Richmond was 50% black, only 0.67% of the city's prime construction contracts had been awarded to minority businesses in the 5-year period from 1978 to 1983. It was also established that a variety of contractors' associations, whose representatives appeared in opposition to the ordinance, had virtually no minority businesses within their membership. . . .

There was no direct evidence of race discrimination on the part of the city in letting contracts or any evidence that the city's prime contractors had discriminated against minority-owned subcontractors. . . .

II

The parties and their supporting amici fight an initial battle over the scope of the city's power to adopt legislation designed to address the effects of past discrimination. Relying on our decision in *Wygant*, appellee argues that the city must limit any race-based remedial efforts to eradicating the effects of its own prior discrimination. This is essentially the position taken by the Court of Appeals below. Appellant argues that our decision in *Fullilove* is controlling, and that as a result the city of Richmond enjoys sweeping legislative power to define and attack the effects of prior discrimination in its local construction industry. We find that neither of these two rather stark alternatives can withstand analysis. . . .

As a matter of state law, the city of Richmond has legislative authority over its procurement policies, and can use its spending powers to remedy private discrimination, if it identifies that discrimination with the particularity required by the Fourteenth Amendment. . . .

Thus, if the city could show that it had essentially become a "passive participant" in a system of racial exclusion practiced by elements of the local construction industry, we think it clear that the city could take affirmative steps to dismantle such a system. It is beyond dispute that any public entity, state or federal, has a compelling interest in assuring that public dollars, drawn from the tax contributions of all citizens, do not serve to finance the evil of private prejudice.

III

A

The Equal Protection Clause of the Fourteenth Amendment provides that "[n]o State shall . . . deny to any person within its jurisdiction the equal protection of the laws." As this Court has noted in the past, the "rights created by the first section of the Fourteenth Amendment are, by its terms, guaranteed to the individual. The rights established are personal rights." *Shelley v. Kraemer.* The Richmond Plan denies certain citizens the opportunity to compete for a fixed percentage of public contracts based solely upon their race. To whatever racial group these citizens belong, their "personal rights" to be treated with equal dignity and respect are implicated by a rigid rule erecting race as the sole criterion in an aspect of public decisionmaking.

Absent searching judicial inquiry into the justification for such race-based measures, there is simply no way of determining what classifications are "benign" or "remedial" and what classifications are in fact motivated by illegitimate notions of racial inferiority or simple racial politics. Indeed, the purpose of strict scrutiny is to "smoke out" illegitimate uses of race by assuring that the legislative body is pursuing a goal important enough to warrant use of a highly suspect tool. The test also ensures that the means chosen "fit" this compelling goal so closely that there is little or no possibility that the motive for the classification was illegitimate racial prejudice or stereotype.

Classifications based on race carry a danger of stigmatic harm. Unless they are strictly reserved for remedial settings, they may in fact promote notions of racial inferiority and lead to a politics of racial hostility. See *University of California Regents v. Bakke* (opinion of Powell, J.). We thus reaffirm the view expressed by the plurality in *Wygant* that the standard of review under the Equal Protection Clause is not dependent on the race of those burdened or benefited by a particular classification. *Wygant* (O'Connor, J., concurring in part and concurring in judgment).

Our continued adherence to the standard of review employed in *Wygant* does not, as Justice Marshall's dissent suggests, indicate that we view "racial discrimination as largely a phenomenon of the past" or that "government bodies need no longer preoccupy themselves with rectifying racial injustice." As we indicate, States and their local subdivisions have many legislative weapons at their disposal both to punish and prevent present discrimination and to remove arbitrary barriers to minority advancement. Rather, our interpretation . . . stems from our agreement with the view expressed by Justice Powell in *Bakke* that "[t]he guarantee of equal protection cannot mean one thing when applied to one individual and something else when applied to a person of another color." *Bakke*. . . .

Even were we to accept a reading of the guarantee of equal protection under which the level of scrutiny varies according to the ability of different groups to defend their interests in the representative process, heightened scrutiny would still be appropriate in the circumstances of this case. One of the central arguments for applying a less exacting standard to "benign" racial classifications is that such measures essentially involve a choice made by dominant racial groups to disadvantage themselves. If one aspect of the judiciary's role under the Equal Protection Clause is to protect "discrete and insular minorities" from majoritarian prejudice or indifference, see *United States v. Carolene Products Co.*, some

maintain that these concerns are not implicated when the "white majority" places burdens upon itself. See J. Ely, Democracy and Distrust.

In this case, blacks constitute approximately 50% of the population of the city of Richmond. Five of the nine seats on the city council are held by blacks. The concern that a political majority will more easily act to the disadvantage of a minority on unwarranted assumptions or incomplete facts would seem to militate for, not against, the application of heightened judicial scrutiny in this case. . . .

B

We think it clear that the factual predicate offered in support of the Richmond Plan suffers from the same two defects identified as fatal in *Wygant*. The District Court found the city council's "findings sufficient to ensure that, in adopting the Plan, it was remedying the present effects of past discrimination in the construction industry." Like the "role model" theory employed in *Wygant*, a generalized assertion that there has been past discrimination in an entire industry provides no guidance for a legislative body to determine the precise scope of the injury it seeks to remedy. It "has no logical stopping point." *Wygant*. "Relief" for such an ill-defined wrong could extend until the percentage of public contracts awarded to MBE's in Richmond mirrored the percentage of minorities in the population as a whole.

Appellant argues that it is attempting to remedy various forms of past discrimination that are alleged to be responsible for the small number of minority businesses in the local contracting industry. Among these the city cites the exclusion of blacks from skilled construction trade unions and training programs. This past discrimination has prevented them "from following the traditional path from laborer to entrepreneur." The city also lists a host of non-racial factors which would seem to face a member of any racial group attempting to establish a new business enterprise, such as deficiencies in working capital, inability to meet bonding requirements, unfamiliarity with bidding procedures, and disability caused by an inadequate track record.

While there is no doubt that the sorry history of both private and public discrimination in this country has contributed to a lack of opportunities for black entrepreneurs, this observation, standing alone, cannot justify a rigid racial quota in the awarding of public contracts in Richmond, Virginia. Like the claim that discrimination in primary and secondary schooling justifies a rigid racial preference in medical school admissions, an amorphous claim that there has been past discrimination in a particular industry cannot justify the use of an unyielding racial quota.

It is sheer speculation how many minority firms there would be in Richmond absent past societal discrimination, just as it was sheer speculation how many minority medical students would have been admitted to the medical school at Davis absent past discrimination in educational opportunities. Defining these sorts of injuries as "identified discrimination" would give local governments license to create a patchwork of racial preferences based on statistical generalizations about any particular field of endeavor. . . .

Justice Marshall apparently views the requirement that Richmond identify the discrimination it seeks to remedy in its own jurisdiction as a mere administrative headache, an "onerous documentary obligatio[n]." We cannot agree. In this regard, we are in accord with Justice Stevens' observation in *Fullilove*, that "[b]ecause racial characteristics so seldom provide a relevant basis for disparate treatment,

and because classifications based on race are potentially so harmful to the entire body politic, it is especially important that the reasons for any such classification be clearly identified and unquestionably legitimate." *Fullilove*. The "evidence" relied upon by the dissent, the history of school desegregation in Richmond and numerous congressional reports, does little to define the scope of any injury to minority contractors in Richmond or the necessary remedy. The factors relied upon by the dissent could justify a preference of any size or duration. . . .

In sum, none of the evidence presented by the city points to any identified discrimination in the Richmond construction industry. We, therefore, hold that the city has failed to demonstrate a compelling interest in apportioning public contracting opportunities on the basis of race. To accept Richmond's claim that past societal discrimination alone can serve as the basis for rigid racial preferences would be to open the door to competing claims for "remedial relief" for every disadvantaged group. The dream of a Nation of equal citizens in a society where race is irrelevant to personal opportunity and achievement would be lost in a mosaic of shifting preferences based on inherently unmeasurable claims of past wrongs. "Courts would be asked to evaluate the extent of the prejudice and consequent harm suffered by various minority groups. Those whose societal injury is thought to exceed some arbitrary level of tolerability then would be entitled to preferential classifications. . . ." *Bakke* (Powell, J.). We think such a result would be contrary to both the letter and spirit of a constitutional provision whose central command is equality.

The foregoing analysis applies only to the inclusion of blacks within the Richmond set-aside program. There is absolutely no evidence of past discrimination against Spanish-speaking, Oriental, Indian,

Eskimo, or Aleut persons in any aspect of the Richmond construction industry. The District Court took judicial notice of the fact that the vast majority of "minority" persons in Richmond were black. Supp. App. 207. It may well be that Richmond has never had an Aleut or Eskimo citizen. The random inclusion of racial groups that, as a practical matter, may never have suffered from discrimination in the construction industry in Richmond suggests that perhaps the city's purpose was not in fact to remedy past discrimination.

If a 30% set-aside was "narrowly tailored" to compensate black contractors for past discrimination, one may legitimately ask why they are forced to share this "remedial relief" with an Aleut citizen who moves to Richmond tomorrow? The gross overinclusiveness of Richmond's racial preference strongly impugns the city's claim of remedial motivation.

IV

As noted by the court below, it is almost impossible to assess whether the Richmond Plan is narrowly tailored to remedy prior discrimination since it is not linked to identified discrimination in any way. We limit ourselves to two observations in this regard.

First, there does not appear to have been any consideration of the use of race-neutral means to increase minority business participation in city contracting. See *United States v. Paradise*. Many of the barriers to minority participation in the construction industry relied upon by the city to justify a racial classification appear to be race neutral. If MBEs disproportionately lack capital or cannot meet bonding requirements, a race-neutral program of city financing for small firms would, a fortiori, lead to greater minority participation. The principal opinion in *Fullilove* found that Congress

had carefully examined and rejected race-neutral alternatives before enacting the MBE set-aside. There is no evidence in this record that the Richmond City Council has considered any alternatives to a race-based quota.

Second, the 30% quota cannot be said to be narrowly tailored to any goal, except perhaps outright racial balancing. It rests upon the "completely unrealistic" assumption that minorities will choose a particular trade in lockstep proportion to their representation in the local population.

Since the city must already consider bids and waivers on a case-by-case basis, it is difficult to see the need for a rigid numerical quota. As noted above, the congressional scheme upheld in *Fullilove* allowed for a waiver of the set-aside provision where an MBE's higher price was not attributable to the effects of past discrimination. Based upon proper findings, such programs are less problematic from an equal protection standpoint because they treat all candidates individually, rather than making the color of an applicant's skin the sole relevant consideration. Unlike the program upheld in *Fullilove*, the Richmond Plan's waiver system focuses solely on the availability of MBEs; there is no inquiry into whether or not the particular MBE seeking a racial preference has suffered from the effects of past discrimination by the city or prime contractors.

Given the existence of an individualized procedure, the city's only interest in maintaining a quota system rather than investigating the need for remedial action in particular cases would seem to be simple administrative convenience. But the interest in avoiding the bureaucratic effort necessary to tailor remedial relief to those who truly have suffered the effects of prior discrimination cannot justify a rigid line drawn on the basis of a suspect classification. Under Richmond's scheme, a successful black, Hispanic, or Oriental entrepreneur from anywhere in the country enjoys an absolute preference over other citizens based solely on their race. We think it obvious that such a program is not narrowly tailored to remedy the effects of prior discrimination.

V

Nothing we say today precludes a state or local entity from taking action to rectify the effects of identified discrimination within its jurisdiction. If the city of Richmond had evidence before it that nonminority contractors were systematically excluding minority businesses from subcontracting opportunities, it could take action to end the discriminatory exclusion. Where there is a significant statistical disparity between the number of qualified minority contractors willing and able to perform a particular service and the number of such contractors actually engaged by the locality or the locality's prime contractors, an inference of discriminatory exclusion could arise. Under such circumstances, the city could act to dismantle the closed business system by taking appropriate measures against those who discriminate on the basis of race or other illegitimate criteria. In the extreme case, some form of narrowly tailored racial preference might be necessary to break down patterns of deliberate exclusion.

Nor is local government powerless to deal with individual instances of racially motivated refusals to employ minority contractors. Where such discrimination occurs, a city would be justified in penalizing the discriminator and providing appropriate relief to the victim of such discrimination. Moreover, evidence of a pattern of individual discriminatory acts can, if supported by appropriate statistical proof, lend support to a local government's

determination that broader remedial relief is justified.

Even in the absence of evidence of discrimination, the city has at its disposal a whole array of race-neutral devices to increase the accessibility of city contracting opportunities to small entrepreneurs of all races. Simplification of bidding procedures, relaxation of bonding requirements, and training and financial aid for disadvantaged entrepreneurs of all races would open the public contracting market to all those who have suffered the effects of past societal discrimination or neglect. Many of the formal barriers to new entrants may be the product of bureaucratic inertia more than actual necessity, and may have a disproportionate effect on the opportunities open to new minority firms. Their elimination or modification would have little detrimental effect on the city's interests and would serve to increase the opportunities available to minority business without classifying individuals on the basis of race. The city may also act to prohibit discrimination in the provision of credit or bonding by local suppliers and banks. Business as usual should not mean business pursuant to the unthinking exclusion of certain members of our society from its rewards.

In the case at hand, the city has not ascertained how many minority enterprises are present in the local construction market nor the level of their participation in city construction projects. The city points to no evidence that qualified minority contractors have been passed over for city contracts or subcontracts, either as a group or in any individual case. Under such circumstances, it is simply impossible to say that the city has demonstrated "a strong basis in evidence for its conclusion that remedial action was necessary." *Wygant.*

Proper findings in this regard are necessary to define both the scope of the injury and the extent of the remedy necessary to cure its effects. Such findings also serve to assure all citizens that the deviation from the norm of equal treatment of all racial and ethnic groups is a temporary matter, a measure taken in the service of the goal of equality itself. Absent such findings, there is a danger that a racial classification is merely the product of unthinking stereotypes or a form of racial politics. "[I]f there is no duty to attempt either to measure the recovery by the wrong or to distribute that recovery within the injured class in an evenhanded way, our history will adequately support a legislative preference for almost any ethnic, religious, or racial group with the political strength to negotiate 'a piece of the action' for its members." *Fullilove* (Stevens, J., dissenting). Because the city of Richmond has failed to identify the need for remedial action in the awarding of its public construction contracts, its treatment of its citizens on a racial basis violates the dictates of the Equal Protection Clause. Accordingly, the judgment of the Court of Appeals for the Fourth Circuit is

Affirmed.

JUSTICE MARSHALL, *with whom* **JUSTICE BRENNAN** *and* **JUSTICE BLACKMUN** *join, dissenting.*

It is a welcome symbol of racial progress when the former capital of the Confederacy acts forthrightly to confront the effects of racial discrimination in its midst. In my view, nothing in the Constitution can be construed to prevent Richmond, Virginia, from allocating a portion of its contracting dollars for businesses owned or controlled by members of minority groups. Indeed, Richmond's set-aside program is indistinguishable in all meaningful respects from—and in fact was patterned upon—the federal set-aside plan which this Court upheld in *Fullilove v. Klutznick*.

A majority of this Court holds today, however, that the Equal Protection Clause of the Fourteenth Amendment blocks Richmond's initiative. The essence of the majority's position is that Richmond has failed to catalog adequate findings to prove that past discrimination has impeded minorities from joining or participating fully in Richmond's construction contracting industry. I find deep irony in second-guessing Richmond's judgment on this point. As much as any municipality in the United States, Richmond knows what racial discrimination is; a century of decisions by this and other federal courts has richly documented the city's disgraceful history of public and private racial discrimination. In any event, the Richmond City Council has supported its determination that minorities have been wrongly excluded from local construction contracting. Its proof includes statistics showing that minority-owned businesses have received virtually no city contracting dollars, and rarely if ever belonged to area trade associations; testimony by municipal officials that discrimination has been widespread in the local construction industry; and the same exhaustive and widely publicized federal studies relied on in *Fullilove*, studies which showed that pervasive discrimination in the Nation's tight-knit construction industry had operated to exclude minorities from public contracting. These are precisely the types of statistical and testimonial evidence which, until today, this Court had credited in cases approving of race-conscious measures designed to remedy past discrimination.

More fundamentally, today's decision marks a deliberate and giant step backward in this Court's affirmative action jurisprudence. Cynical of one municipality's attempt to redress the effects of past racial discrimination in a particular industry, the majority launches a grapeshot attack on race-conscious remedies in general. The majority's unnecessary pronouncements will inevitably discourage or prevent governmental entities, particularly States and localities, from acting to rectify the scourge of past discrimination. This is the harsh reality of the majority's decision, but it is not the Constitution's command.

ADARAND CONSTRUCTORS v. PENA

515 U.S. 200 (1995)

Opinion: O'Connor, joined by Rehnquist, Kennedy, Thomas and to an extent by Scalia in Parts I, II, III-A, III-B, III-D, and IV and by Kennedy in Part III-C
Concurrence: Scalia
Concurrence: Thomas
Dissent: Stevens, joined by Ginsburg
Dissent: Souter, joined by Ginsburg, Breyer
Dissent: Ginsburg, joined by Breyer

JUSTICE O'CONNOR *announced the judgment of the Court.*

Petitioner Adarand Constructors, Inc., claims that the Federal Government's practice of giving general contractors on government projects a financial incentive to hire subcontractors controlled by "socially and economically disadvantaged individuals," and in particular, the Government's use of race-based presumptions in identifying such individuals, violates the equal protection component of the Fifth Amendment's Due Process Clause.

In 1989, the Central Federal Lands Highway Division, which is part of the United States Department of Transportation, awarded the prime contract for a highway construction project in Colorado to Mountain Gravel & Construction Company. Mountain Gravel then solicited bids from subcontractors for the guardrail portion of the contract. Adarand, a Colorado-based highway construction company specializing in guardrail work, submitted the low bid. Gonzales Construction Company also submitted a bid.

The prime contract's terms provide that Mountain Gravel would receive additional compensation if it hired subcontractors certified as small businesses controlled by "socially and economically disadvantaged individuals." Gonzales is certified as such a business; Adarand is not. Mountain Gravel awarded the subcontract to Gonzales, despite Adarand's low bid, and Mountain Gravel's Chief Estimator has submitted an affidavit stating that Mountain Gravel would have accepted Adarand's bid, had it not been for the additional payment it received by hiring Gonzales instead.

The Government urges that "[t]he Subcontracting Compensation Clause program is . . . a program based on *disadvantage*, not on race," and thus that it is subject only to "the most relaxed judicial scrutiny." The Government concedes, however, that "the race-based rebuttable presumption used in some certification determinations under the Subcontracting Compensation Clause" is subject to some heightened level of scrutiny.

Adarand's claim arises under the Fifth Amendment to the Constitution, which provides that "No person shall . . . be deprived of life, liberty, or property, without due process of law." Although this Court has always understood that Clause to provide some measure of protection against *arbitrary* treatment by the Federal Government, it is not as explicit a guarantee of *equal* treatment as the Fourteenth Amendment, which provides that "No *State* shall . . . deny to any person within its jurisdiction the equal protection of the laws" (emphasis added). Our cases have accorded varying degrees of significance to the difference in the language of those two Clauses. We think it necessary to revisit the issue here.

Through the 1940s, this Court had routinely taken the view in non-race-related cases that, "[u]nlike the Fourteenth Amendment, the Fifth contains no equal protection clause and it provides no guaranty against discriminatory legislation by Congress." *Detroit Bank v. United States*. When the Court first faced a Fifth Amendment equal protection challenge to a federal racial classification, it adopted a similar approach, with most unfortunate results. In *Hirabayashi v. United States*, the Court considered a curfew applicable only to persons of Japanese ancestry.

The Court observed—correctly—that "[d]istinctions between citizens solely because of their ancestry are by their very nature odious to a free people whose institutions are founded upon the doctrine of equality," and that "racial discriminations are in most circumstances irrelevant and therefore prohibited." But it also cited *Detroit Bank* for the proposition that the Fifth Amendment "restrains only such discriminatory legislation by Congress as amounts to a denial of due process," and upheld the curfew because "circumstances within the knowledge of those charged with the responsibility for maintaining the national defense afforded a rational basis for the decision which they made."

Metro Broadcasting, Inc. v. FCC involved a Fifth Amendment challenge to two race-based policies of the Federal Communications Commission. In *Metro Broadcasting*, the Court repudiated the long-held notion that "it would be unthinkable that the same Constitution would impose a lesser duty on the Federal Government" than it does on a State to afford equal protection of the laws. It did so by holding that "benign" federal racial classifications need only satisfy intermediate scrutiny. "[B]enign" federal racial classifications, the Court said, "—even if those measures are not 'remedial' in the sense of being designed to compensate victims of past governmental or societal discrimination—are constitutionally permissible to the extent that they serve *important* governmental objectives within the power of Congress and are *substantially related* to achievement of those objectives." The Court did not explain how to tell whether a racial classification should be deemed "benign," other than to express "confiden[ce] that an 'examination of the legislative scheme and its history' will separate benign measures from other types of racial classifications."

. . . [S]trict scrutiny of all governmental racial classifications is essential:

> "Absent searching judicial inquiry into the justification for such race-based measures, there is simply no way of determining what classifications are 'benign' or 'remedial' and what classifications are in fact motivated by illegitimate notions of racial inferiority or simple racial politics."

We adhere to that view today, despite the surface appeal of holding "benign" racial classifications to a lower standard.

Second, *Metro Broadcasting* squarely rejected one of the three propositions established by the Court's earlier equal protection cases, namely, congruence between the standards applicable to federal and state racial classifications.

The propositions undermined by *Metro Broadcasting* all derive from the basic principle that the Fifth and Fourteenth Amendments to the Constitution protect *persons*, not *groups*. It follows from that principle that all governmental action based on race—a *group* classification long recognized as "in most circumstances irrelevant and therefore prohibited"—should be subjected to detailed judicial inquiry to ensure that the *personal* right to equal protection of the laws has not been infringed. These ideas have long been central to this Court's understanding of equal protection, and holding "benign" state and federal racial classifications to different standards does not square with them. Accordingly, we hold today that all racial classifications, imposed by whatever federal, state, or local governmental actor, must be analyzed by a reviewing court under strict scrutiny. In other words, such classifications are constitutional only if they are narrowly tailored measures that further compelling governmental interests. To the extent that *Metro Broadcasting* is inconsistent with that holding, it is overruled.

JUSTICE STEVENS, *with whom* **JUSTICE GINSBURG** *joins, dissenting.*

. . . The Court's concept of "consistency" assumes that there is no significant difference between a decision by the majority to impose a special burden on the members of a minority race and a decision by the majority to provide a benefit to certain members of that minority notwithstanding its incidental burden on some members of the majority. In my opinion that assumption is untenable. There is no moral or constitutional equivalence between a policy that is designed to perpetuate a caste system and one that seeks to eradicate racial subordination. Invidious discrimination is an engine of oppression, subjugating a disfavored group to enhance or maintain the power of the majority. Remedial race based preferences reflect the opposite impulse: a desire to foster equality in society. . . .

The Court's concept of "congruence" assumes that there is no significant difference between a decision by the Congress of the United States to adopt an affirmative action program and such a decision by a State or a municipality. In my opinion that assumption is untenable. It ignores important practical and legal differences between federal and state or local decision makers. . . .

The majority in *Metro Broadcasting* and the plurality in *Fullilove* were not alone in relying upon a critical distinction between federal and state programs. In his separate opinion in *Richmond v. J.A. Croson Co.*, Justice Scalia discussed the basis for this distinction. He observed that "it is one thing to permit racially based conduct by the Federal Government—whose legislative powers concerning matters of race were explicitly enhanced by the Fourteenth Amendment, see U.S. Const., Amdt. 14, §5—and quite another to permit it by the precise entities against whose conduct in matters of race that Amendment was specifically directed, see Amdt. 14, §1." *Id.*, at 521-522. Continuing, Justice Scalia explained why a "sound distinction between federal and state (or local) action based on race rests not only upon the substance of the Civil War Amendments, but upon social reality and governmental theory." *Id.*, at 522.

My skeptical scrutiny of the Court's opinion leaves me in dissent. The majority's concept of "consistency" ignores a difference, fundamental to the idea of equal protection, between oppression and assistance. The majority's concept of "congruence" ignores a difference, fundamental to our constitutional system, between the Federal Government and the States. And the majority's concept of *stare decisis* ignores the force of binding precedent. I would affirm the judgment of the Court of Appeals.

JUSTICE SOUTER, *with whom* **JUSTICE GINSBURG** *and* **JUSTICE BREYER** *join, dissenting.*

. . . When the extirpation of lingering discriminatory effects is thought to require a catch up mechanism, like the racially preferential inducement under the statutes considered here, the result may be that some members of the historically favored race are hurt by that remedial mechanism, however innocent they may be of any personal responsibility for any discriminatory conduct. When this price is considered reasonable, it is in part because it is a price to be paid only temporarily; if the justification for the preference is eliminating the effects of a past practice, the assumption is that the effects will themselves recede into the past, becoming attenuated and finally disappearing.

Surely the transition from the *Fullilove* plurality view (in which Justice Powell joined) to today's strict scrutiny (which will presumably be applied as Justice Powell employed it) does not signal a change in the standard by which the burden of a remedial racial preference is to be judged as reasonable or not at any given time. If in the District Court Adarand had chosen to press a challenge to the reasonableness of the burden of these statutes, more than a decade after *Fullilove* had examined such a burden, I doubt that the claim would have fared any differently from the way it will now be treated on remand from this Court.

GRUTTER v. BOLLINGER

539 U.S. 306 (2003)

Opinion: O'Connor, joined by Stevens, Ginsburg, Breyer and in part by Scalia, Thomas
Concurrence: Ginsburg, joined by Breyer
Partial Concurrence, Partial Dissent: Scalia, joined by Thomas
Partial Concurrence, Partial Dissent: Thomas, joined by Scalia in Parts I-VII
Dissent: Rehnquist, joined by Scalia, Kennedy, Thomas
Dissent: Kennedy

The Supreme Court decided two companion cases about affirmative action in 2003. As you will remember, Regents v. Bakke made clear that the Equal Protection Clause was incompatible with racial quotas as a means to pursue affirmative action. Although U.S. Supreme Court Justice Lewis F. Powell made clear that universities could permissibly take race into account in order to further the compelling governmental interest of promoting diversity, the question remained open exactly how the government could take race into account in university admissions. In Grutter v. Bollinger, *the Court considered the use of race as one factor in a multifaceted and holistic evaluation in the admissions decisions of the University of Michigan Law School. In* Gratz v. Bollinger, *the Court considered the acceptability under the Equal Protection Clause of a different admissions program for undergraduate students in which racial minority status always afforded a candidate a certain fixed number of points toward a total that would guarantee admission. As you read, think about what kind of justification for affirmative action the Court regarded as a compelling interest. Given that this compelling interest was present in both cases, what distinguishes the two?*

In particular, why is one policy narrowly tailored while another is not? What kind of affirmative action do these cases suggest is constitutional in light of the Court's prior decision in Regents v. Bakke?

JUSTICE O'CONNOR *delivered the opinion of the Court.*

This case requires us to decide whether the use of race as a factor in student admissions by the University of Michigan Law School is unlawful.

Petitioner Barbara Grutter is a white Michigan resident who applied to the Law School in 1996 with a 3.8 grade point average and 161 Law School Admissions Test (LSAT) score. The Law School initially placed petitioner on a waiting list, but subsequently rejected her application. Petitioner alleged that respondents discriminated against her on the basis of race in violation of the Fourteenth Amendment.

Dennis Shields, Director of Admissions when petitioner applied to the Law School, testified that he did not direct his staff to admit a particular percentage or number of minority students, but rather to consider an applicant's race along with all other factors. Shields testified that at the height of the admissions season, he would frequently consult the so-called "daily reports" that kept track of the racial and ethnic composition of the class (along with other information such as residency status and gender). This was done, Shields testified, to ensure that a critical mass of underrepresented minority students would be reached so as to realize the educational benefits of a diverse student body. Shields stressed, however, that he did not seek to admit any particular number or percentage of underrepresented minority students.

Erica Munzel, who succeeded Shields as Director of Admissions, testified that

"critical mass" means "meaningful numbers" or "meaningful representation," which she understood to mean a number that encourages underrepresented minority students to participate in the classroom and not feel isolated. Munzel also asserted that she must consider the race of applicants because a critical mass of underrepresented minority students could not be enrolled if admissions decisions were based primarily on undergraduate GPAs and LSAT scores.

The District Court heard extensive testimony from Professor Richard Lempert, who chaired the faculty committee that drafted the policy. Lempert explained that this language did not purport to remedy past discrimination, but rather to include students who may bring to the Law School a perspective different from that of members of groups which have not been the victims of such discrimination.

In the end, the District Court concluded that the Law School's use of race as a factor in admissions decisions was unlawful. Applying strict scrutiny, the District Court determined that the Law School's asserted interest in assembling a diverse student body was not compelling because "the attainment of a racially diverse class . . . was not recognized as such by *Bakke* and is not a remedy for past discrimination."

Sitting en banc, the Court of Appeals reversed the District Court's judgment. The Court of Appeals first held that Justice Powell's opinion in *Bakke* was binding precedent establishing diversity as a compelling state interest. The Court of Appeals also held that the Law School's use of race was narrowly tailored because race was merely a "potential 'plus' factor."

We granted certiorari to resolve the disagreement among the Courts of Appeals on a question of national importance: Whether diversity is a compelling interest that can justify the narrowly tailored use of race in selecting applicants for admission to public universities.

Since this Court's splintered decision in *Bakke*, Justice Powell's opinion announcing the judgment of the Court has served as the touchstone for constitutional analysis of race-conscious admissions policies. Public and private universities across the Nation have modeled their own admissions programs on Justice Powell's views on permissible race-conscious policies.

Justice Powell approved the university's use of race to further only one interest: "the attainment of a diverse student body."

Justice Powell was, however, careful to emphasize that in his view race "is only one element in a range of factors a university properly may consider in attaining the goal of a heterogeneous student body."

Before this Court, as they have throughout this litigation, respondents assert only one justification for their use of race in the admissions process: obtaining "the educational benefits that flow from a diverse student body."

Today, we hold that the Law School has a compelling interest in attaining a diverse student body.

The Law School's educational judgment that such diversity is essential to its educational mission is one to which we defer. The Law School's assessment that diversity will, in fact, yield educational benefits is substantiated by respondents and their *amici*. Our scrutiny of the interest asserted by the Law School is no less strict for taking into account complex educational judgments in an area that lies primarily within the expertise of the university.

In announcing the principle of student body diversity as a compelling state interest, Justice Powell invoked our cases recognizing a constitutional dimension, grounded in the First Amendment, of educational autonomy: "The freedom of a university to make its own judgments as to education includes the selection of its student body." From this premise, Justice Powell reasoned that by claiming "the right to select those students who will contribute the most to the 'robust exchange of ideas,'" a university "seek[s] to achieve a goal that is of paramount importance in the fulfillment of its mission." Our conclusion that the Law School has a compelling interest in a diverse student body is informed by our view that attaining a diverse student body is at the heart of the Law School's proper institutional mission, and that "good faith" on the part of a university is "presumed" absent "a showing to the contrary."

Even in the limited circumstance when drawing racial distinctions is permissible to further a compelling state interest, government is still "constrained in how it may pursue that end."

Since *Bakke*, we have had no occasion to define the contours of the narrow-tailoring inquiry with respect to race-conscious university admissions programs.

We find that the Law School's admissions program bears the hallmarks of a narrowly tailored plan. As Justice Powell made clear in *Bakke*, truly individualized consideration demands that race be used in a flexible, nonmechanical way. It follows from this mandate that universities cannot establish quotas for members of certain racial groups or put members of those groups on separate admissions tracks. Nor can universities insulate applicants who belong to certain racial or ethnic groups from the competition for admission. Universities can, however, consider race or ethnicity more flexibly as a "plus" factor in the context of individualized consideration of each and every applicant.

That a race-conscious admissions program does not operate as a quota does not, by itself, satisfy the requirement of individualized consideration. When using race as a "plus" factor in university admissions, a university's admissions program must remain flexible enough to ensure that each applicant is evaluated as an individual and not in a way that makes an applicant's race or ethnicity the defining feature of his or her application.

Here, the Law School engages in a highly individualized, holistic review of each applicant's file, giving serious consideration to all the ways an applicant might contribute to a diverse educational environment. The Law School affords this individualized consideration to applicants of all races.

Petitioner and the United States argue that the Law School's plan is not narrowly tailored because race-neutral means exist to obtain the educational benefits of student body diversity that the Law School seeks. We disagree. Narrow tailoring does not require exhaustion of every conceivable race-neutral alternative. Nor does it require a university to choose between maintaining a reputation for excellence or fulfilling a commitment to provide educational opportunities to members of all racial groups.

We take the Law School at its word that it would "like nothing better than to find a race-neutral admissions formula" and will terminate its race-conscious admissions program as soon as practicable. It has been 25 years since Justice Powell first approved the use of race to further an interest in student body diversity in the context of public higher education. Since that time, the number of minority applicants with high grades and test scores has indeed increased. We expect that 25 years from now, the use of racial preferences will no longer be necessary to further the interest approved today.

JUSTICE SCALIA, *with whom* **JUSTICE THOMAS** *joins, concurring in part and dissenting in part.*

I join the opinion of The Chief Justice. As he demonstrates, the University of Michigan Law School's mystical "critical mass" justification for its discrimination by race challenges even the most gullible mind. The admissions statistics show it to be a sham to cover a scheme of racially proportionate admissions. . . .

I add the following: The "educational benefit" that the University of Michigan seeks to achieve by racial discrimination consists, according to the Court, of "cross-racial understanding," and "better prepar[ation of] students for an increasingly diverse workforce and society," all of which is necessary not only for work, but also for good "citizenship." This is not, of course, an "educational benefit" on which students will be graded on their Law School transcript (Works and Plays Well with Others: B+) or tested by the bar examiners (Q: Describe in 500 words or less your cross-racial understanding). For it is a lesson of life rather than law—essentially the same lesson taught to (or rather learned by, for it cannot be "taught" in the usual sense) people three feet shorter and twenty years younger than the full-grown adults at the University of Michigan Law School, in institutions ranging from Boy Scout troops to public-school kindergartens. If properly considered an "educational benefit" at all, it is surely not one that is either uniquely relevant to law school or uniquely "teachable" in a formal educational setting. *And therefore*: If it is appropriate for the University of Michigan Law School to use racial discrimination for the purpose of putting together a "critical mass" that will convey generic lessons in socialization and good citizenship, surely it is no less appropriate—indeed, *particularly* appropriate—for the civil service system of the State of Michigan to do so. There, also, those exposed to "critical masses" of certain races will presumably become better Americans, better Michiganders, better civil servants. And surely private employers cannot be criticized—indeed, should be praised—if they also "teach" good citizenship to their adult employees through a patriotic, all-American system of racial discrimination in hiring. The nonminority individuals who are deprived of a legal education, a civil service job, or any job at all by reason of their skin color will surely understand.

Unlike a clear constitutional holding that racial preferences in state educational institutions are impermissible, or even a clear anticonstitutional holding that racial preferences in state educational institutions are OK, today's *Grutter-Gratz* split double header seems perversely designed to prolong the controversy and the litigation. Some future lawsuits will presumably focus on whether the discriminatory scheme in question contains enough evaluation of the applicant "as an individual," and sufficiently avoids "separate admissions tracks," to fall under *Grutter* rather than *Gratz*. Some will focus on whether a university has gone beyond the bounds of a "good faith effort" and has so zealously pursued its "critical mass" as to make it an unconstitutional *de facto* quota system, rather than merely "a permissible goal." (quoting *Sheet Metal Workers v. EEOC* (O'Connor, J., concurring in part and dissenting in part)). Other lawsuits may focus on whether, in the particular setting at issue, any educational benefits flow from racial diversity. (That issue was not contested in *Grutter*; and while the opinion accords "a degree of deference to a university's academic decisions,". . . "deference does not imply abandonment or abdication of judicial review," *Miller-El v. Cockrell*) Still other suits may challenge the bona fides of the institution's expressed commitment to the educational benefits of diversity that immunize

the discriminatory scheme in *Grutter*. (Tempting targets, one would suppose, will be those universities that talk the talk of multiculturalism and racial diversity in the courts but walk the walk of tribalism and racial segregation on their campuses—through minority-only student organizations, separate minority housing opportunities, separate minority student centers, even separate minority-only graduation ceremonies.) And still other suits may claim that the institution's racial preferences have gone below or above the mystical *Grutter*-approved "critical mass." Finally, litigation can be expected on behalf of minority groups intentionally short-changed in the institution's composition of its generic minority "critical mass." I do not look forward to any of these cases. The Constitution proscribes government discrimination on the basis of race, and state-provided education is no exception.

JUSTICE THOMAS, *with whom* **JUSTICE SCALIA** *joins, concurring in part and dissenting in part.*

. . . The majority upholds the Law School's racial discrimination not by interpreting the people's Constitution, but by responding to a faddish slogan of the cognoscenti. First, I agree with the Court insofar as its decision, which approves of only one racial classification, confirms that further use of race in admissions remains unlawful. Second, I agree with the Court's holding that racial discrimination in higher education admissions will be illegal in 25 years. I respectfully dissent from the remainder of the Court's opinion and the judgment, however, because I believe that the Law School's current use of race violates the Equal Protection Clause and that the Constitution means the same thing today as it will in 300 months.

GRATZ v. BOLLINGER

539 U.S. 244 (2003)

Opinion: Rehnquist, joined by
O'Connor, Scalia, Kennedy, Thomas
Concurrence: O'Connor, joined in part
by Breyer
Concurrence: Thomas
Concurrence: Breyer
Dissent: Stevens, joined by Souter
Dissent: Souter, joined by Ginsburg in
Part II
Dissent: Ginsburg, joined by Souter
and by Breyer in Part I

CHIEF JUSTICE REHNQUIST
delivered the opinion of the Court.

Petitioners Jennifer Gratz and Patrick
Hamacher both applied for admission to
the University of Michigan's (University)
College of Literature, Science, and the Arts
(LSA) as residents of the State of Michigan.
Both petitioners are Caucasian.

The University has changed its admissions guidelines a number of times during the period relevant to this litigation,
and we summarize the most significant
of these changes briefly. The University's
Office of Undergraduate Admissions (OUA)
oversees the LSA admissions process.

OUA considers a number of factors in
making admissions decisions, including
high school grades, standardized test scores,
high school quality, curriculum strength,
geography, alumni relationships, and leadership. OUA also considers race. During all periods relevant to this litigation, the University
has considered African-Americans, Hispanics,
and Native Americans to be "underrepresented minorities," and it is undisputed that
the University admits "virtually every qualified . . . applicant" from these groups.

During 1995 and 1996, OUA counselors evaluated applications according to

grade-point average combined with what
were referred to as the "SCUGA" factors.
These factors included the quality of an
applicant's high school (S), the strength of
an applicant's high school curriculum (C),
an applicant's unusual circumstances (U),
an applicant's geographical residence (G),
and an applicant's alumni relationships
(A). After these scores were combined to
produce an applicant's "GPA 2" score, the
reviewing admissions counselors referenced a set of "Guidelines" tables, which
listed GPA 2 ranges on the vertical axis, and
American College Test/Scholastic Aptitude
Test (ACT/SAT) scores on the horizontal
axis. Each table was divided into cells that
included one or more courses of action to
be taken, including admit, reject, delay for
additional information, or postpone for
reconsideration.

In both years, applicants with the same
GPA 2 score and ACT/SAT score were
subject to different admissions outcomes
based upon their racial or ethnic status. For
example, as a Caucasian in-state applicant,
Gratz's GPA 2 score and ACT score placed
her within a cell calling for a postponed
decision on her application. An in-state or
out-of-state minority applicant with Gratz's
scores would have fallen within a cell calling for admission.

In 1997, the University modified its
admissions procedure. Specifically, the
formula for calculating an applicant's GPA
2 score was restructured to include additional point values under the "U" category
in the SCUGA factors. Under this new system, applicants could receive points for
underrepresented minority status, socio-
economic disadvantage, or attendance at
a high school with a predominantly underrepresented minority population, or under-
representation in the unit to which the

student was applying (for example, men who sought to pursue a career in nursing). Under the 1997 procedures, Hamacher's GPA 2 score and ACT score placed him in a cell on the in-state applicant table calling for postponement of a final admissions decision. An underrepresented minority applicant placed in the same cell would generally have been admitted.

Beginning with the 1998 academic year, the OUA dispensed with the Guidelines tables and the SCUGA point system in favor of a "selection index," on which an applicant could score a maximum of 150 points.

Each application received points based on high school grade point average, standardized test scores, academic quality of an applicant's high school, strength or weakness of high school curriculum, in-state residency, alumni relationship, personal essay, and personal achievement or leadership. Of particular significance here, under a "miscellaneous" category, an applicant was entitled to 20 points based upon his or her membership in an underrepresented racial or ethnic minority group. The University explained that the "development of the selection index for admissions in 1998 changed only the mechanics, not the substance of how race and ethnicity were considered in admissions."

Petitioners asserted that the LSA's use of race as a factor in admissions violates Title VI of the Civil Rights Act of 1964 and the Equal Protection Clause of the Fourteenth Amendment. Respondents relied on Justice Powell's opinion in *Regents of Univ. of Cal. v. Bakke* to respond to petitioners' arguments. Respondents contended that the LSA has just such an interest in the educational benefits that result from having a racially and ethnically diverse student body and that its program is narrowly tailored to serve that interest.

Petitioners argue, first and foremost, that the University's use of race in under-graduate admissions violates the Fourteenth Amendment. Specifically, they contend that this Court has only sanctioned the use of racial classifications to remedy identified discrimination, a justification on which respondents have never relied. Petitioners further argue that "diversity as a basis for employing racial preferences is simply too open-ended, ill-defined, and indefinite to constitute a compelling interest capable of supporting narrowly-tailored means." But for the reasons set forth today in *Grutter v. Bollinger*, the Court has rejected these arguments of petitioners.

Petitioners alternatively argue that even if the University's interest in diversity can constitute a compelling state interest, the District Court erroneously concluded that the University's use of race in its current freshman admissions policy is narrowly tailored to achieve such an interest. Petitioners argue that the guidelines the University began using in 1999 do not "remotely resemble the kind of consideration of race and ethnicity that Justice Powell endorsed in *Bakke*."

We find that the University's policy, which automatically distributes 20 points, or one-fifth of the points needed to guarantee admission, to every single "underrepresented minority" applicant solely because of race, is not narrowly tailored to achieve the interest in educational diversity that respondents claim justifies their program.

In *Bakke*, Justice Powell reiterated that "[p]referring members of any one group for no reason other than race or ethnic origin is discrimination for its own sake." He then explained, however, that in his view it would be permissible for a university to employ an admissions program in which "race or ethnic background may be deemed a 'plus' in a particular applicant's file." He explained that such a program might allow for "[t]he file of a particular black applicant [to] be examined for his potential contribution to diversity without the factor of race being decisive when compared, for example, with that of an applicant identified as an Italian-American if the latter is thought to exhibit qualities more likely to promote beneficial educational pluralism."

Justice Powell's opinion in *Bakke* emphasized the importance of considering each particular applicant as an individual, assessing all of the qualities that individual possesses, and in turn, evaluating that individual's ability to contribute to the unique setting of higher education. The admissions program Justice Powell described, however, did not contemplate that any single characteristic automatically ensured a specific and identifiable contribution to a university's diversity.

The current LSA policy does not provide such individualized consideration. The LSA's policy automatically distributes 20 points to every single applicant from an "underrepresented minority" group, as defined by the University. The only consideration that accompanies this distribution of points is a factual review of an application to determine whether an individual is a member of one of these minority groups. Moreover, unlike Justice Powell's example, where the race of a "particular black applicant" could be considered without being decisive, see *Bakke*, the LSA's automatic distribution of 20 points has the effect of making "the factor of race . . . decisive" for virtually every minimally qualified underrepresented minority applicant.

Respondents contend that "[t]he volume of applications and the presentation of applicant information make it impractical for [LSA] to use the . . . admissions system" upheld by the Court today in *Grutter*. But the fact that the implementation of a program capable of providing individualized consideration might present administrative challenges does not render constitutional an otherwise problematic system. Nothing in Justice Powell's opinion in *Bakke* signaled that a university may employ whatever means it desires to achieve the stated goal of diversity without regard to the limits imposed by our strict scrutiny analysis.

JUSTICE GINSBURG, *with whom* **JUSTICE SOUTER** *joins, dissenting.*

Educational institutions, the Court acknowledges, are not barred from any and all consideration of race when making admissions decisions. But the Court once again maintains that the same standard of review controls judicial inspection of all official race classifications. This insistence on "consistency," would be fitting were our Nation free of the vestiges of rank discrimination long reinforced by law. But we are not far distant from an overtly discriminatory past, and the effects of centuries of law-sanctioned inequality remain painfully evident in our communities and schools.

The Constitution instructs all who act for the government that they may not "deny to any person . . . the equal protection of the laws." In implementing this equality instruction, as I see it, government decision-makers may properly distinguish between policies of exclusion and inclusion. Actions designed to burden groups long denied full citizenship stature are not sensibly ranked with measures taken to hasten the day when entrenched discrimination and its after effects have been extirpated.

Our jurisprudence ranks race a "suspect" category, "not because [race] is inevitably an impermissible classification, but because it is one which usually, to our national shame, has been drawn for the purpose of maintaining racial inequality." But where race is considered "for the purpose of achieving equality," no automatic proscription is in order. For, as insightfully explained, "[t]he Constitution is both color blind and color conscious. To avoid conflict with the equal protection clause, a classification that denies a benefit, causes harm, or imposes a burden must not be based on race. In that sense, the Constitution is color blind.

But the Constitution is color conscious to prevent discrimination being perpetuated and to undo the effects of past discrimination." Contemporary human rights documents draw just this line; they distinguish between policies of oppression and measures designed to accelerate *de facto* equality.

Examining in this light the admissions policy employed by the University of Michigan's College of Literature, Science, and the Arts (College), . . . I see no constitutional infirmity. Like other top-ranking institutions, the College has many more applicants for admission than it can accommodate in an entering class. Every applicant admitted under the current plan, petitioners do not here dispute, is qualified to attend the College. The racial and ethnic groups to which the College accords special consideration (African-Americans, Hispanics, and Native-Americans) historically have been relegated to inferior status by law and social practice; their members continue to experience class-based discrimination to this day. There is no suggestion that the College adopted its current policy in order to limit or decrease enrollment by any particular racial or ethnic group, and no seats are reserved on the basis of race. Nor has there been any demonstration that the College's program unduly constricts admissions opportunities for students who do not receive special consideration based on race.

The stain of generations of racial oppression is still visible in our society, and the determination to hasten its removal remains vital. One can reasonably anticipate, therefore, that colleges and universities will seek to maintain their minority enrollment—and the networks and opportunities thereby opened to minority graduates—whether or not they can do so in full candor through adoption of affirmative action plans of the kind here at issue. Without recourse to such plans, institutions of higher education may resort to camouflage. For example, schools may encourage applicants to write of their cultural traditions in the essays they submit, or to indicate whether English is their second language. Seeking to improve their chances for admission, applicants may highlight the minority group associations to which they belong, or the Hispanic surnames of their mothers or grandparents. In turn, teachers' recommendations may emphasize who a student is as much as what he or she has accomplished. If honesty is the best policy, surely Michigan's accurately described, fully disclosed College affirmative action program is preferable to achieving similar numbers through winks, nods, and disguises.

PARENTS INVOLVED IN COMMUNITY SCHOOLS v. SEATTLE SCHOOL DISTRICT NO. 1

551 U.S. 701 (2007)

Opinion: Roberts, joined by Scalia, Kennedy, Thomas, Alito in Parts I, II, III-A, and III-C and by Scalia, Thomas, Alito in Parts III-B and IV
Concurrence: Thomas
Concurrence: Kennedy
Dissent: Stevens
Dissent: Breyer, joined by Stevens, Souter, Ginsburg

As you have seen, the Court was heavily divided in Gratz v. Bollinger *and* Grutter v. Bollinger. *U.S. Supreme Court Justice Sandra Day O'Connor retired after these cases were decided and was replaced in 2006 by Justice Samuel Alito. This opened the possibility that the Court would go beyond merely limiting the kinds of acceptable affirmative action programs allowable under the Equal Protection Clause to banning them altogether. In the following case, the Court examines whether attempts to create racially diverse public high schools violate the Equal Protection Clause. You might consider whether there is a difference in the importance of ensuring diversity in universities as opposed to in high schools.*

Moreover, you will note the connection between this case and Brown v. Board of Education, Brown v. Board of Education II, *and* Alexander v. Holmes County Board of Education, *which we examined in Section A. Those cases examined both the constitutionality of segregation and the requirements for desegregation. One question about the case that follows is the degree to which it limits the ability of public school districts to desegregate. Certainly, in contemporary America, there is not de jure segregation of the kind the Court examined in* Brown v. Board of Education, *but was the Seattle School District's attempt to diversify schools an attempt to desegregate de facto segregated schools? Consider too the question of colorblind constitutionalism seemingly embraced by U.S. Supreme Court Chief Justice John Roberts's opinion, and how it contrasts with Amy Gutmann's theory of color-consciousness. Is Chief Justice Roberts correct in bringing this understanding of equal protection to bear on this case, or is color-consciousness more appropriate?*

CHIEF JUSTICE ROBERTS *announced the judgment of the Court.*

The school districts in these cases voluntarily adopted student assignment plans that rely upon race to determine which public schools certain children may attend. The Seattle school district classifies children as white or nonwhite; the Jefferson County school district as black or "other." In Seattle, this racial classification is used to allocate slots in oversubscribed high schools. In Jefferson County, it is used to

make certain elementary school assignments and to rule on transfer requests. In each case, the school district relies upon an individual student's race in assigning that student to a particular school, so that the racial balance at the school falls within a predetermined range based on the racial composition of the school district as a whole. Parents of students denied assignment to particular schools under these plans solely because of their race brought suit, contending that allocating children to different public schools on the basis of race violated the Fourteenth Amendment guarantee of equal protection. The Courts of Appeals below upheld the plans. We granted certiorari, and now reverse.

Seattle School District No. 1 operates 10 regular public high schools. The plan allows incoming ninth graders to choose from among any of the district's high schools, ranking however many schools they wish in order of preference.

Some schools are more popular than others. If too many students list the same school as their first choice, the district employs a series of "tiebreakers" to determine who will fill the open slots at the oversubscribed school. The first tiebreaker selects for admission students who have a sibling currently enrolled in the chosen school. The next tiebreaker depends upon the racial composition of the particular school and the race of the individual student. If an oversubscribed school is not within 10 percentage points of the district's overall white/nonwhite racial balance, it is what the district calls "integration positive," and the district employs a tiebreaker that selects for assignment students whose race "will serve to bring the school into balance." If it is still necessary to select students for the school after using the racial tiebreaker, the next tiebreaker is the geographic proximity of the school to the student's residence.

Seattle has never operated segregated schools—legally separate schools for students of different races—nor has it ever been subject to court-ordered desegregation. It nonetheless employs the racial tiebreaker in an attempt to address the effects of racially identifiable housing patterns on school assignments.

Petitioner Parents Involved in Community Schools is a nonprofit corporation comprising the parents of children who have been or may be denied assignment to their chosen high school in the district because of their race.

Jefferson County Public Schools operates the public school system in metropolitan Louisville, Kentucky. In 1973 a federal court found that Jefferson County had maintained a segregated school system, and in 1975 the District Court entered a desegregation decree. Jefferson County operated under this decree until 2000, when the District Court dissolved the decree after finding that the district had achieved unitary status by eliminating "[t]o the greatest extent practicable" the vestiges of its prior policy of segregation.

In 2001, after the decree had been dissolved, Jefferson County adopted the voluntary student assignment plan at issue in this case. The plan requires all nonmagnet schools to maintain a minimum black enrollment of 15 percent, and a maximum black enrollment of 50 percent.

It is well established that when the government distributes burdens or benefits on the basis of individual racial classifications, that action is reviewed under strict scrutiny. In order to satisfy this searching standard of review, the school districts must demonstrate that the use of individual racial classifications in the assignment plans here under review is "narrowly tailored" to achieve a "compelling" government interest.

Without attempting in these cases to set forth all the interests a school district might assert, it suffices to note that our prior cases, in evaluating the use of racial classifications in the school context, have recognized two interests that qualify as compelling. The first is the compelling interest of remedying the effects of past intentional discrimination. Yet the Seattle public schools have not shown that they were ever segregated by law, and were not subject to court-ordered desegregation decrees. Jefferson County does not rely upon an interest in remedying the effects of past intentional discrimination in defending its present use of race in assigning students.

Nor could it. We have emphasized that the harm being remedied by mandatory desegregation plans is the harm that is traceable to segregation, and that "the Constitution is not violated by racial imbalance in the schools, without more." Once Jefferson County achieved unitary status, it had remedied the constitutional wrong that allowed race-based assignments. Any continued use of race must be justified on some other basis.

The second government interest we have recognized as compelling for purposes of strict scrutiny is the interest in diversity in higher education upheld in *Grutter*. The diversity interest was not focused on race alone but encompassed "all factors that may contribute to student body diversity."

The entire gist of the analysis in *Grutter* was that the admissions program at issue there focused on each applicant as an individual, and not simply as a member of a particular racial group. The classification of applicants by race upheld in *Grutter* was only as part of a "highly individualized, holistic review." The point of the narrow tailoring analysis in which the *Grutter* Court engaged was to ensure that the use of racial classifications was indeed part of a broader assessment of diversity, and not simply an effort to achieve racial balance, which the Court explained would be "patently unconstitutional."

In the present cases, by contrast, race is not considered as part of a broader effort to achieve "exposure to widely diverse people, cultures, ideas, and viewpoints." It is not simply one factor weighed with others in reaching a decision, as in *Grutter*; it is *the* factor.

Even when it comes to race, the plans here employ only a limited notion of diversity, viewing race exclusively in white/non-white terms in Seattle and black/"other" terms in Jefferson County. But under the Seattle plan, a school with 50 percent Asian-American students and 50 percent white students but no African-American, Native-American, or Latino students would qualify as balanced, while a school with 30 percent Asian-American, 25 percent African-American, 25 percent Latino, and 20 percent white students would not. It is hard to understand how a plan that could allow these results can be viewed as being concerned with achieving enrollment that is "broadly diverse."

The Court in *Grutter* expressly articulated key limitations on its holding—defining a specific type of broad-based diversity and noting the unique context of higher education—but these limitations were largely disregarded by the lower courts in extending *Grutter* to uphold race-based assignments in elementary and secondary schools. The present cases are not governed by *Grutter*.

In *Grutter*, the number of minority students the school sought to admit was an undefined "meaningful number" necessary to achieve a genuinely diverse student body. Although the matter was the subject of disagreement on the Court, the majority concluded that the law school did not count back from its applicant pool to arrive at the "meaningful number" it regarded as necessary to diversify its student body.

Here the racial balance the districts seek is a defined range set solely by reference to the demographics of the respective school districts.

This working backward to achieve a particular type of racial balance, rather than working forward from some demonstration of the level of diversity that provides the purported benefits, is a fatal flaw under our existing precedent. We have many times over reaffirmed that "[r]acial balance is not to be achieved for its own sake."

Accepting racial balancing as a compelling state interest would justify the imposition of racial proportionality throughout American society, contrary to our repeated recognition that "[a]t the heart of the Constitution's guarantee of equal protection lies the simple command that the Government must treat citizens as individuals, not as simply components of a racial, religious, sexual or national class." Allowing racial balancing as a compelling end in itself would "effectively assur[e] that race will always be relevant in American life, and that the 'ultimate goal' of 'eliminating entirely from governmental decision-making such irrelevant factors as a human being's race' will never be achieved."

The principle that racial balancing is not permitted is one of substance, not semantics. Racial balancing is not transformed from "patently unconstitutional" to a compelling state interest simply by relabeling it "racial diversity." While the school districts use various verbal formulations to describe the interest they seek to promote—racial diversity, avoidance of racial isolation, racial integration—they offer no definition of the interest that suggests it differs from racial balance.

The districts have also failed to show that they considered methods other than explicit racial classifications to achieve their stated goals. Narrow tailoring requires "serious, good-faith consideration of workable race-neutral alternatives," and yet in Seattle several alternative assignment plans—many of which would not have used express racial classifications—were rejected with little or no consideration.

If the need for the racial classifications embraced by the school districts is unclear, even on the districts' own terms, the costs are undeniable. Government action dividing us by race is inherently suspect because such classifications promote "notions of racial inferiority and lead to a politics of racial hostility," "reinforce the belief, held by too many for too much of our history, that individuals should be judged by the color of their skin," and "endorse race-based reasoning and the conception of a Nation divided into racial blocs, thus contributing to an escalation of racial hostility and conflict."

All this is true enough in the contexts in which these statements were made—government contracting, voting districts, allocation of broadcast licenses, and electing state officers—but when it comes to using race to assign children to schools, history will be heard. In *Brown v. Board of Education*, we held that segregation deprived black children of equal educational opportunities regardless of whether school facilities and other tangible factors were equal, because government classification and separation on grounds of race themselves denoted inferiority.

The parties and their *amici* debate which side is more faithful to the heritage of *Brown*, but the position of the plaintiffs in *Brown* was spelled out in their brief and could not have been clearer: "[T]he Fourteenth Amendment prevents states from according differential treatment to American children on the basis of their color or race." What do the racial classifications at issue here do, if not accord differential treatment on the basis of race? As counsel who appeared before this Court for the plaintiffs in *Brown* put it: "We have one

fundamental contention which we will seek to develop in the course of this argument, and that contention is that no State has any authority under the equal-protection clause of the Fourteenth Amendment to use race as a factor in affording educational opportunities among its citizens." There is no ambiguity in that statement. And it was that position that prevailed in this Court, which emphasized in its remedial opinion that what was "[a]t stake is the personal interest of the plaintiffs in admission to public schools as soon as practicable *on a nondiscriminatory basis*," and what was required was "determining admission to the public schools *on a nonracial basis*." What do the racial classifications do in these cases, if not determine admission to a public school on a racial basis? Before *Brown*, schoolchildren were told where they could and could not go to school based on the color of their skin. The school districts in these cases have not carried the heavy burden of demonstrating that we should allow this once again—even for very different reasons. For schools that never segregated on the basis of race, such as Seattle, or that have removed the vestiges of past segregation, such as Jefferson County, the way "to achieve a system of determining admission to the public schools on a nonracial basis," is to stop assigning students on a racial basis. The way to stop discrimination on the basis of race is to stop discriminating on the basis of race.

JUSTICE BREYER, *with whom* **JUSTICE STEVENS, JUSTICE SOUTER**, *and* **JUSTICE GINSBURG** *join, dissenting.*

These cases consider the longstanding efforts of two local school boards to integrate their public schools. The school board plans before us resemble many others adopted in the last 50 years by primary and secondary schools throughout the

Nation. All of those plans represent local efforts to bring about the kind of racially integrated education that *Brown v. Board of Education* long ago promised—efforts that this Court has repeatedly required, permitted, and encouraged local authorities to undertake. This Court has recognized that the public interests at stake in such cases are "compelling." We have approved of "narrowly tailored" plans that are no less race-conscious than the plans before us. And we have understood that the Constitution *permits* local communities to adopt desegregation plans even where it does not *require* them to do so.

The plurality pays inadequate attention to this law, to past opinions' rationales, their language, and the contexts in which they arise. As a result, it reverses course and reaches the wrong conclusion. In doing so, it distorts precedent, it misapplies the relevant constitutional principles, it announces legal rules that will obstruct efforts by state and local governments to deal effectively with the growing resegregation of public schools, it threatens to substitute for present calm a disruptive round of race-related litigation, and it undermines *Brown*'s promise of integrated primary and secondary education that local communities have sought to make a reality. This cannot be justified in the name of the Equal Protection Clause.

I

The historical and factual context in which these cases arise is critical. In *Brown*, this Court held that the government's segregation of schoolchildren by race violates the Constitution's promise of equal protection. The Court emphasized that "education is perhaps the most important function of state and local governments." And it thereby set the Nation on a path toward public school integration.

In dozens of subsequent cases, this Court told school districts previously segregated by law what they must do at a minimum to comply with *Brown*'s constitutional holding. The measures required by those cases often included race-conscious practices, such as mandatory busing and race-based restrictions on voluntary transfers.

Beyond those minimum requirements, the Court left much of the determination of how to achieve integration to the judgment of local communities. Thus, in respect to race-conscious desegregation measures that the Constitution *permitted*, but did not *require* (measures similar to those at issue here), this Court unanimously stated:

> "School authorities are traditionally charged with broad power to formulate and implement educational policy and might well conclude, for example, that in order to prepare students to live in a pluralistic society each school should have a prescribed ratio of Negro to white students reflecting the proportion for the district as a whole. To do this as an educational policy is within the broad discretionary powers of school authorities." Swann v. Charlotte-Mecklenburg Bd. of Ed.

As a result, different districts—some acting under court decree, some acting in order to avoid threatened lawsuits, some seeking to comply with federal administrative orders, some acting purely voluntarily, some acting after federal courts had dissolved earlier orders—adopted, modified, and experimented with hosts of different kinds of plans, including race-conscious plans, all with a similar objective: greater racial integration of public schools.

Overall these efforts brought about considerable racial integration. More recently, however, progress has stalled. Between 1968 and 1980, the number of black children attending a school where minority children constituted more than half of the school fell from 77% to 63% in the Nation (from 81% to 57% in the South) but then reversed direction by the year 2000, rising from 63% to 72% in the Nation (from 57% to 69% in the South). Today, more than one in six black children attend a school that is 99–100% minority. In light of the evident risk of a return to school systems that are in fact (though not in law) resegregated, many school districts have felt a need to maintain or to extend their integration efforts.

The upshot is that myriad school districts operating in myriad circumstances have devised myriad plans, often with race-conscious elements, all for the sake of eradicating earlier school segregation, bringing about integration, or preventing retrogression. Seattle and Louisville are two such districts, and the histories of their present plans set forth typical school integration stories.

First, the school districts' plans serve "compelling interests" and are "narrowly tailored" on any reasonable definition of those terms. Second, the distinction between *de jure* segregation (caused by school systems) and *de facto* segregation (caused, *e.g.*, by housing patterns or generalized societal discrimination) is meaningless in the present context, thereby dooming the plurality's endeavor to find support for its views in that distinction. Third, real-world efforts to substitute racially diverse for racially segregated schools (however caused) are complex, to the point where the Constitution cannot plausibly be interpreted to rule out categorically all local efforts to use means that are "conscious" of the race of individuals.

Both districts sought greater racial integration for educational and democratic, as well as for remedial, reasons. Both sought to achieve these objectives while preserving their commitment to other educational goals, *e.g.*, districtwide commitment to high quality public schools, increased pupil assignment to neighborhood schools, diminished use of busing, greater student choice, reduced risk of white flight, and so forth. Consequently, the present plans expand student choice; they limit the burdens (including busing) that earlier plans had imposed upon students and their families; and they use race-conscious criteria in limited and gradually diminishing ways. In particular, they use race-conscious criteria only to mark the outer bounds of broad population-related ranges.

With this factual background in mind, I turn to the legal question: Does the United States Constitution prohibit these school boards from using race-conscious criteria in the limited ways at issue here?

II

A longstanding and unbroken line of legal authority tells us that the Equal Protection Clause permits local school boards to use race-conscious criteria to achieve positive race-related goals, even when the Constitution does not compel it. . . . [T]he Court set forth in *Swann* a basic principle of constitutional law—a principle of law that has found "wide acceptance in the legal culture."

Courts are not alone in accepting as constitutionally valid the legal principle that *Swann* enunciated—*i.e.*, that the government may voluntarily adopt race-conscious measures to improve conditions of race even when it is not under a constitutional obligation to do so. That principle has been accepted by every branch of government and is rooted in the history of the Equal Protection Clause itself. In fact, without being exhaustive, I have counted 51 federal statutes that use racial classifications. I have counted well over 100 state statutes that similarly employ racial classifications. Presidential administrations for the past half-century have used and supported various race-conscious measures. And during the same time, hundreds of local school districts have adopted student assignment plans that use race-conscious criteria.

That *Swann's* legal statement should find such broad acceptance is not surprising. For *Swann* is predicated upon a well-established legal view of the Fourteenth Amendment. That view understands the basic objective of those who wrote the Equal Protection Clause as forbidding practices that lead to racial exclusion. The Amendment sought to bring into American society as full members those whom the Nation had previously held in slavery.

There is reason to believe that those who drafted an Amendment with this basic purpose in mind would have understood the legal and practical difference between the use of race-conscious criteria in defiance of that purpose, namely to keep the races apart, and the use of race-conscious criteria to further that purpose, namely to bring the races together.

Sometimes Members of this Court have disagreed about the degree of leniency that the Clause affords to programs designed to include. But I can find no case in which this Court has followed Justice Thomas' "colorblind" approach. And I have found no case that otherwise repudiated this constitutional asymmetry between that which seeks to *exclude* and that which seeks to *include* members of minority races.

What does the plurality say in response? First, it seeks to distinguish *Swann* and other similar cases on the ground that those cases involved remedial plans in response to *judicial findings* of *de jure* segregation.... [T]hat is historically untrue. Many school districts in the South adopted segregation remedies (to which *Swann* clearly applies) without any such federal order. And, in any event, the histories of Seattle and Louisville make clear that this distinction—between court-ordered and voluntary desegregation—seeks a line that sensibly cannot be drawn.

Second, the plurality downplays the importance of *Swann* and related cases by frequently describing their relevant statements as "dicta."* These criticisms, however, miss the main point. *Swann* did not hide its understanding of the law in a corner of an obscure opinion or in a footnote, unread but by experts. It set forth its view prominently in an important opinion joined by all nine Justices, knowing that it would be read and followed throughout the Nation. The basic problem with the plurality's technical "dicta"-based response lies in its overly theoretical approach to case law, an approach that emphasizes rigid distinctions between holdings and dicta in a way that serves to mask the radical nature of today's decision. Law is not an exercise in mathematical logic. And statements of a legal rule set forth in a judicial opinion do not always divide neatly into "holdings" and "dicta." (Consider the legal "status" of Justice Powell's separate opinion in *Regents of Univ. of Cal. v. Bakke*.) The constitutional principle enunciated in *Swann*, reiterated in subsequent cases, and relied upon over many years, provides, and has widely been thought to provide, authoritative legal guidance. And if the plurality now chooses to reject that principle, it cannot adequately justify its retreat simply by affixing the label "dicta" to reasoning with which it disagrees. Rather, it must explain to the courts and to the Nation *why* it would abandon guidance set forth many years before, guidance that countless others have built upon over time, and which the law has continuously embodied.

Third, a more important response is the plurality's claim that later cases—in particular *Johnson*, *Adarand*, and *Grutter*—supplanted *Swann*. The plurality says that cases such as *Swann* and the others I have

---

*[*Obiter dicta*, or simply *dicta*, refers to legal reasoning that is not part of the technical holding of the case.—EDS.]

described all "were decided before this Court definitively determined that 'all racial classifications . . . must be analyzed by a reviewing court under strict scrutiny.' " This Court in *Adarand* added that "such classifications are constitutional only if they are narrowly tailored measures that further compelling governmental interests." And the Court repeated this same statement in *Grutter*.

Several of these cases were significantly more restrictive than *Swann* in respect to the degree of leniency the Fourteenth Amendment grants to programs designed to *include* people of all races. But that legal circumstance cannot make a critical difference here for two separate reasons.

First, no case—not *Adarand*, *Gratz*, *Grutter*, or any other—has ever held that the test of "strict scrutiny" means that all racial classifications—no matter whether they seek to include or exclude—must in practice be treated the same. The Court did not say in *Adarand* or in *Johnson* or in *Grutter* that it was overturning *Swann* or its central constitutional principle.

Indeed, in its more recent opinions, the Court recognized that the "fundamental purpose" of strict scrutiny review is to "take relevant differences" between "fundamentally different situations . . . into account." And the Court, using the very phrase that Justice Marshall had used to describe strict scrutiny's application to any *exclusionary* use of racial criteria, sought to "*dispel the notion* that strict scrutiny" is as likely to condemn *inclusive* uses of "race-conscious" criteria as it is to invalidate *exclusionary* uses. That is, it is *not* in all circumstances "strict in theory, but fatal in fact."

The upshot is that the cases to which the plurality refers, though all applying strict scrutiny, do not treat exclusive and inclusive uses the same. Rather, they apply the strict scrutiny test in a manner that is "fatal in fact" only to racial classifications that harmfully *exclude*; they apply the test in a manner that is *not* fatal in fact to racial classifications that seek to *include*.

The plurality cannot avoid this simple fact. Today's opinion reveals that the plurality would rewrite this Court's prior jurisprudence, at least in practical application, transforming the "strict scrutiny" test into a rule that is fatal in fact across the board. In doing so, the plurality parts company from this Court's prior cases, and it takes from local government the longstanding legal right to use race-conscious criteria for inclusive purposes in limited ways.

III

The principal interest advanced in these cases to justify the use of race-based criteria goes by various names. Sometimes a court refers to it as an interest in achieving racial "diversity." Other times a court, like the plurality here, refers to it as an interest in racial "balancing."

Regardless of its name, however, the interest at stake possesses three essential elements. First, there is a historical and remedial element: an interest in setting right the consequences of prior conditions of segregation. This refers back to a time when public schools were highly segregated, often as a result of legal or administrative policies that facilitated racial segregation in public schools. It is an interest in continuing to combat the remnants of segregation caused in whole or in part by these school-related policies, which have often affected not only schools, but also housing patterns, employment practices, economic conditions, and social attitudes.

Second, there is an educational element: an interest in overcoming the adverse educational effects produced by and associated with highly segregated schools. Studies suggest that children taken from those schools and placed in integrated settings often show positive academic gains.

Research suggests, for example, that black children from segregated educational environments significantly increase their achievement levels once they are placed in a more integrated setting. Indeed in Louisville itself the achievement gap between black and white elementary school students grew substantially smaller (by seven percentage points) after the integration plan was implemented in 1975. Conversely, to take another example, evidence from a district in Norfolk, Virginia, shows that resegregated schools led to a decline in the achievement test scores of children of all races.

Third, there is a democratic element: an interest in producing an educational environment that reflects the "pluralistic society" in which our children will live. It is an interest in helping our children learn to work and play together with children of different racial backgrounds. It is an interest in teaching children to engage in the kind of cooperation among Americans of all races that is necessary to make a land of three hundred million people one Nation.

The majority acknowledges that in prior cases this Court has recognized at least two interests as compelling: an interest in "remedying the effects of past intentional discrimination," and an interest in "diversity in higher education." But the plurality does not convincingly explain why those interests do not constitute a "compelling interest" here. How do the educational and civic interests differ in kind from those that underlie and justify the racial "diversity" that the law school sought in *Grutter*, where this Court found a compelling interest?

I next ask whether the plans before us are "narrowly tailored" to achieve these "compelling" objectives.

First, the race-conscious criteria at issue only help set the outer bounds of *broad* ranges. They constitute but one part of plans that depend primarily upon other, nonracial elements. To use race in this way is not to set a forbidden "quota."

In fact, the defining feature of both plans is greater emphasis upon student choice. *Choice*, therefore, is the "predominant factor" in these plans. *Race* is not.

Second, broad-range limits on voluntary school choice plans are less burdensome, and hence more narrowly tailored, than other race-conscious restrictions this Court has previously approved. Indeed, the plans before us are *more narrowly tailored* than the race-conscious admission plans that this Court approved in *Grutter*. Here, race becomes a factor only in a fraction of students' non-merit-based assignments—not in large numbers of students' merit-based applications.

Third, the manner in which the school boards developed these plans itself reflects "narrow tailoring." Each plan was devised to overcome a history of segregated public schools. Each plan embodies the results of local experience and community consultation. Each plan is the product of a process that has sought to enhance student choice, while diminishing the need for mandatory busing. And each plan's use of race-conscious elements is *diminished* compared to the use of race in preceding integration plans. . . .

VI

To show that the school assignment plans here meet the requirements of the Constitution, I have written at exceptional length.

Thus, the opinion's reasoning is long. But its conclusion is short: The plans before us satisfy the requirements of the Equal Protection Clause.

Four basic considerations have led me to this view. *First*, the histories of Louisville and Seattle reveal complex circumstances and a long tradition of conscientious efforts by local school boards to resist racial segregation in public schools.

Second, since this Court's decision in *Brown*, the law has consistently and unequivocally approved of both voluntary and compulsory race-conscious measures to combat segregated schools. The Equal Protection Clause, ratified following the Civil War, has always distinguished in practice between state action that excludes and thereby subordinates racial minorities and state action that seeks to bring together people of all races.

Third, the plans before us, subjected to rigorous judicial review, are supported by compelling state interests and are narrowly tailored to accomplish those goals. Just as diversity in higher education was deemed compelling in *Grutter*, diversity in public primary and secondary schools—where there is even more to gain—must be, a fortiori, a compelling state interest.

Fourth, the plurality's approach risks serious harm to the law and for the Nation. Its view of the law rests either upon a denial of the distinction between exclusionary and inclusive use of race-conscious criteria in the context of the Equal Protection Clause, or upon such a rigid application of its "test" that the distinction loses practical significance.

The last half-century has witnessed great strides toward racial equality, but we have not yet realized the promise of *Brown*. To invalidate the plans under review is to threaten the promise of *Brown*. The plurality's position, I fear, would break that promise. This is a decision that the Court and the Nation will come to regret.

I must dissent.

RICCI v. DeSTEFANO

555 U.S. _____ (2009)

Opinion: Kennedy, joined by Roberts, Scalia, Thomas, Alito
Concurrence: Scalia
Concurrence: Alito, joined by Scalia, Thomas
Dissent: Ginsburg, joined by Stevens, Souter, Breyer

The most recent important affirmative-action case to come before the Court was Ricci v. DeStefano, *which concerned so-called "reverse discrimination" in employment. The case received national attention during the Senate confirmation hearings of U.S. Supreme Court Justice Sonia Sotomayor, whose affirmation of the lower court's ruling as an appellate judge was reversed by the Supreme Court. Although U.S. Supreme Court Justice Anthony Kennedy, writing for a 5-4 majority, does not reach the equal protection claim made by the petitioners, consider the implications of the puzzle presented by this case for civil rights laws that attempt to prohibit discrimination. Can a desire to avoid one kind of discrimination sometimes inevitably lead to another?*

JUSTICE KENNEDY *delivered the opinion of the Court.*

In 2003, 118 New Haven firefighters took examinations to qualify for promotion to the rank of lieutenant or captain.

When the examination results showed that white candidates had outperformed minority candidates, the mayor and other local politicians opened a public debate that turned rancorous. Some firefighters argued the tests should be discarded because the results showed the tests to be discriminatory. They threatened a discrimination lawsuit if the City made promotions based on the tests. Other firefighters said the exams were neutral and fair. And they, in turn, threatened a discrimination lawsuit if the City, relying on the statistical racial disparity, ignored the test results and denied promotions to the candidates who had performed well. In the end the City took the side of those who protested the test results. It threw out the examinations.

The suit alleges that, by discarding the test results, the City and the named officials discriminated against the plaintiffs based on their race, in violation of both Title VII of the Civil Rights Act of 1964 and the Equal Protection Clause of the Fourteenth Amendment.

We conclude that race-based action like the City's in this case is impermissible under Title VII unless the employer can demonstrate a strong basis in evidence that, had it not taken the action, it would have been liable under the disparate-impact statute. In light of our ruling under the statutes, we need not reach the question whether respondents' actions may have violated the Equal Protection Clause.

Title VII prohibits both intentional discrimination (known as "disparate treatment") as well as, in some cases, practices that are not intended to discriminate but in fact have a disproportionately adverse effect on minorities (known as "disparate impact").

The Civil Rights Act of 1964 did not include an express prohibition on policies or practices that produce a disparate impact. But in *Griggs v. Duke Power Co.*, the Court interpreted the Act to prohibit, in some cases, employers' facially neutral practices that, in fact, are "discriminatory in operation." The *Griggs* Court stated that the "touchstone" for disparate-impact liability is the lack of "business necessity": "If an employment practice which operates to exclude [minorities] cannot be shown to be related to job performance, the practice is prohibited." Under those precedents, if an employer met its burden by showing that its practice was job-related, the plaintiff was required to show a legitimate alternative that would have resulted in less discrimination.

Twenty years after *Griggs*, the Civil Rights Act of 1991 was enacted. The Act included a provision codifying the prohibition on disparate-impact discrimination.

We consider, therefore, whether the purpose to avoid disparate-impact liability excuses what otherwise would be prohibited disparate-treatment discrimination.

The Court has held that certain government actions to remedy past racial discrimination—actions that are themselves based on race—are constitutional only where there is a "strong basis in evidence" that the remedial actions were necessary.

Applying the strong-basis-in-evidence standard to Title VII gives effect to both the disparate-treatment and disparate-impact provisions, allowing violations of one in the name of compliance with the other only in certain, narrow circumstances. The standard leaves ample room for employers' voluntary compliance efforts, which are essential to the statutory scheme and to Congress's efforts to eradicate workplace discrimination. And the standard appropriately constrains employers' discretion in making race-based decisions: It limits that discretion to cases in which there is a strong basis in evidence of disparate-impact liability, but it is not so restrictive that it allows employers to act only when there is a provable, actual violation.

On the record before us, there is no genuine dispute that the City lacked a strong basis in evidence to believe it would face disparate-impact liability if it certified the examination results. In other words, there is no evidence—let alone the required strong basis in evidence—that the tests were flawed because they were not job-related or because other, equally valid and less discriminatory tests were available to the City. Fear of litigation alone cannot justify an employer's reliance on race to the detriment of individuals who passed the examinations and qualified for promotions.

JUSTICE GINSBURG, *with whom* **JUSTICE STEVENS**, **JUSTICE SOUTER**, *and* **JUSTICE BREYER** *join, dissenting.*

In assessing claims of race discrimination, "[c]ontext matters." *Grutter v. Bollinger*. In 1972, Congress extended Title VII of the Civil Rights Act of 1964 to cover public employment. At that time, municipal fire departments across the country, including New Haven's, pervasively discriminated against minorities. The extension of Title VII to cover jobs in firefighting effected no overnight change. It took decades of persistent effort, advanced by Title VII litigation, to open firefighting posts to members of racial minorities.

The white firefighters who scored high on New Haven's promotional exams understandably attract this Court's sympathy. But they had no vested right to promotion. Nor have other persons received promotions in preference to them. New Haven maintains that it refused to certify the test results because it believed, for good cause, that it would be vulnerable to a Title VII disparate-impact suit if it relied on those results. The Court today holds that New Haven has not demonstrated "a strong basis in evidence" for its plea. . . . In so holding, the Court pretends that "[t]he City rejected the test

results solely because the higher scoring candidates were white." . . . That pretension, essential to the Court's disposition, ignores substantial evidence of multiple flaws in the tests New Haven used. The Court similarly fails to acknowledge the better tests used in other cities, which have yielded less racially skewed outcomes. By order of this Court, New Haven, a city in which African-Americans and Hispanics account for nearly 60 percent of the population, must today be served—as it was in the days of undisguised discrimination—by a fire department in which members of racial and ethnic minorities are rarely seen in command positions. . . .

B

. . . It is indeed regrettable that the City's non-certification decision would have required all candidates to go through another selection process. But it would have been more regrettable to rely on flawed exams to shut out candidates who may well have the command presence and other qualities needed to excel as fire officers. Yet that is the choice the Court makes today. . . .

This case presents an unfortunate situation, one New Haven might well have avoided had it utilized a better selection process in the first place. But what this case does not present is race-based discrimination in violation of Title VII. I dissent from the Court's judgment, which rests on the false premise that respondents showed "a significant statistical disparity," but "nothing more." . . .

SYNTHESIS QUESTIONS FOR FURTHER DISCUSSION: CHAPTER 8 SECTION B

1. Does the constitutional guarantee of equal protection require colorblindness? Or is the guarantee color-conscious, meaning that race can be taken into consideration in order to assure a diverse society? Consider this question in the context of the readings by Amy Gutmann and John McWhorter, as well as the *Grutter v. Bollinger* and *Regents v. Bakke* cases. Is the Court right in *Regents v. Bakke* to suggest that affirmative action in state institutions of higher learning cannot employ quotas that establish minimum numbers of racial minorities in order to combat discrimination? Is there a difference between minimum quotas ("floors") for racial minorities and maximum quotas ("ceilings") for groups based on race? Was the Court wrong in *Gratz v. Bollinger* and *Grutter v. Bollinger* to leave the door open to individualized programs of affirmative action such as those at the University of Michigan Law School? Why did it draw the line against a "point system" of admission?

2. In *Grutter v. Bollinger*, Justice Sandra Day O'Connor rejects appeals to justifications of affirmative action based on rectification of past injustice. Instead, she endorses the "diversity rationale," which appeals to the goal of having minorities present at all levels of society. According to Justice O'Connor, however, this rationale might only be temporary. She writes, "We expect that 25 years from now, the use of racial preferences will no longer be necessary to further the interest approved today." U.S. Supreme Court Justice Clarence Thomas, in dissent, argues that "the Constitution means the same thing today as it will in 300 months." Might affirmative action be justified in 2003, but not—if circumstances change in the way Justice O'Connor predicts—in 2028? Or do you agree with Justice Thomas's objection? Is Justice O'Connor's argument incompatible with those philosophies of interpretation, such as originalism, which reject the idea of a "living Constitution"?

3. In the case selections for this section, the Court applies the balancing test known as strict scrutiny. Under this test, an admissions or hiring policy by the state that has a race-based classification must meet two standards to avoid being struck down on equal protection grounds. First, it must be based in a goal that qualifies as a compelling interest. Second, the means of achieving a compelling interest must be narrowly tailored—or, in other words, very closely related—to the ends. Because this test is so demanding in its presumed invalidity of distinctions based on race, commentators have often said that the test is "strict in theory, but fatal in fact." In other words, this is so tough a standard that it cannot be met.

   But clearly, in its examination of the affirmative action cases, the Court left open the possibility that an admissions policy that made distinctions based on race could potentially be justifiable. Although it struck down policies that were justified on the basis of past discrimination, such as the undergraduate admissions policy at the University of Michigan, it allowed the distinctions employed by the law school. Why does one set of admissions criteria pass the test of strict scrutiny while the other does not?

4. Opponents of the Court's recent equal protection jurisprudence have worried that it has cut off the possibility of remedying segregation in schools. They claim that while *Brown v. Board of Education* outlawed state segregation, many schools remain segregated *de facto*. If schools cannot take race into account, how is it possible for them to try to remedy segregation that results from the socio-economic forces that segregate neighborhoods? Although *Parents Involved in Community Schools v. Seattle School District* does not formally overturn *Brown v. Board of Education*, does it leave any way for school systems to fight segregation?

C. VOTING DISCRIMINATION

Throughout this book, beginning in Chapter 1, we have explored the degree to which the ideal of democracy should inform our practice of constitutional interpretation. One major challenge for American constitutional democracy concerns the disenfranchisement of and discrimination against African-American citizens in matters of political representation. Most obviously, African Americans were denied the franchise before the Fifteenth Amendment, not only in the Southern slave states, but also, with few exceptions, in the North as well. The Thirteenth, Fourteenth, and Fifteenth Amendments passed after the Civil War were an attempt to rectify this discrimination and disenfranchisement. The Fifteenth Amendment in particular guarantees the right to vote to former slaves. It reads:

> Section 1. The right of citizens of the United States to vote shall not be denied or abridged by the United States or by any State on account of race, color, or previous condition of servitude.
> Section 2. The Congress shall have the power to enforce this article by appropriate legislation.

Yet the passage of these three amendments certainly did not end the practice of racial discrimination, either in matters of segregation or in discrimination when it came to voting. Some states fought against extending the franchise to African Americans through a variety of measures including mandatory literacy tests and poll taxes. As we will see in *Guinn v. United States*, Oklahoma—as did other states—crafted such a law, which required prospective voters to pass a literacy test, thus disenfranchising many African Americans who had not attained a formal education. But this law included a "grandfather clause" that had the effect of exempting illiterate white citizens. In its ruling, the Supreme Court cited the Fourteenth Amendment in striking down this exemption, underscoring the possible use of this amendment in limiting the kinds of voting policies that localities could employ.

One of the discriminatory practices states used was the widespread creation of "gerrymandered" districts, which were designed to dilute the votes of African Americans. Even if African Americans were guaranteed the right to vote, the weight of their vote could be diluted by the way districts were drawn—for example, by dividing African Americans among all districts so that they could not wield decisive electoral influence in any one district. One way to challenge this practice was through the courts. But this strategy raised fundamental questions, both about federalism and about the respective role of federal courts and state legislatures. Specifically, should federal institutions dictate that legislative districts ensure local representation? Should the Court play a role in policing the representative process to ensure that it is not discriminatory?

In our first reading, Raoul Berger suggests it would be fundamentally undemocratic for a court to resolve what he sees as a political problem that is properly considered outside the boundaries of judicial authority. In *Baker v. Carr*, the Supreme Court directly asserted that it has a role in policing unrepresentative districts. The Court announced that under the Equal Protection Clause, it was obligated to enter the fray in disputes of gerrymandered districts. The Court's decision here has resonance with the constitutional theory espoused by John Hart Ely, whose work we also excerpt here. For Ely, the Court's role is in ensuring representative government, and it therefore must enter controversies in which one of the bases of democracy itself has been threatened. Although *Baker v. Carr* established a role for the courts in policing gerrymandering, it was in *Reynolds v. Sims* that the Court faced the question of whether to strike down a scheme of apportionment that allegedly violated the Equal Protection Clause.

Despite the Court's forays into the areas of literacy tests and gerrymandering, arguably the greatest change in combating discrimination against African Americans in voting was achieved through the Voting Rights Act of 1965. The Act prohibited many of the techniques that states had used to disempower African Americans in the political process. It paid particular attention to issues of racial gerrymandering and vote dilution. Specifically, it required oversight of a variety of areas in the country in which there had been discrimination. Section 5 of the Act provided a mechanism by which the federal government would oversee legislative schemes to safeguard against discrimination.

The modern debate over racial gerrymandering, as Samuel Issacharoff points out, concerns in part the controversial decision to create so-called majority-minority districts, in its own way a form of purposeful racial gerrymandering. The argument for creating such districts is that real representation for African Americans must consist of African-American representatives. Historically, however, African-American votes have been diluted, and thus there has been a dearth of African-American representatives in Congress. By requiring some states to draw such majority-minority districts, the Voting Rights Act sought to rectify this disparity. But this concern hearkens back to many of the controversies that accompanied the race-conscious politics of affirmative action that we examined in the previous section. Specifically, does taking race into account when creating legislative districts conflict with the non-discrimination requirement of the Equal Protection Clause? As we saw previously, some have argued that the Equal Protection Clause not only bans segregation, but that it also requires a colorblind approach to the Constitution that does not take into account race in regard to any matter, including the drawing of legislative district lines. As you will see in our case selection, the Supreme Court has not repudiated the requirements of the Voting Rights Act that provide for a federal role in overseeing the drawing of legislative districts. But the Court did find in *Shaw v. Reno* and *Miller v. Johnson* that there are limits to the extent to which majority-minority districts may be drawn. As you read these cases, try to think about how the Court's jurisprudence fits into the more general debate about colorblind and color-conscious understandings of the Constitution. In drawing legislative districts, is it possible to take race into account in order to further minority representation without running afoul of the Equal Protection Clause?

We conclude our case selection with *Northwest Austin Municipal v. Holder*, which includes a dissent from Justice Clarence Thomas challenging the constitutionality of Section 5 of the Voting Rights Act, which provides oversight limiting racial gerrymandering. On his view, it is impossible to walk the line between a colorblind interpretation of the Constitution and current federal oversight over racial gerrymandering. Do you agree with Justice Thomas that colorblind constitutionalism should inform our analysis in this area?

Raoul Berger

GOVERNMENT BY JUDICIARY

Indianapolis, IN: Liberty Fund (1997)

The process of drawing congressional districts, left to state legislatures, is notoriously political. Those in power will often attempt to draw district lines so as to give their party a strategic advantage in future elections. Should the Supreme Court interfere in this practice of "gerrymandering"? Raoul Berger argues in the following excerpt that the practice of gerrymandering, while problematic for democracy, should not be corrected by courts. In his view, a nondemocratic fix to this problem within the framework of democracy would be deeply problematic, regardless of the results. He therefore denounces the Court's role in striking down redistricting plans as "activism."

Baker v. Carr (1962), the unprecedented reapportionment decision, said Paul Kauper, opened a "new chapter of judicial adventurism." When the issue was once again presented in *Reynolds v. Sims*, Justice Harlan wrote a dissent that to my mind is irrefutable. The majority of the Court made no pretense of meeting his historical demonstration; it remained for William Van Alstyne to essay a rebuttal. Harlan's reliance on the legislative history to establish the "original understanding," Van Alstyne writes, pertains solely to "exclusive state power over suffrage qualifications" and has no bearing on "the separate issue of malapportionment"; "there was almost no mention of the subject." That fact alone gives one pause: how can a revolution in *Northern* apportionment be based on nonmention?

The dominant purpose of the 39th Congress was to maintain Republican hegemony by reducing Southern representation; and only secondarily did they think to secure the "person and property" of the *Negro* from oppression. There were repeated disclaimers of any intention to interfere with State sovereignty beyond those objectives. Moreover, while Negro suffrage was predominantly a Southern problem, reapportionment would invade long-established State practices with respect to *white* voters in the North. But Van Alstyne argues that to read malapportionment in the equal protection clause "is to say *only* that among the enfranchised [white] elite," qualified by the State to vote, "no invidious distinction shall be permitted. The States may be as capricious as they please in withholding the ballot but not in perpetuating elites within the elite." That is a tremendous "only." Republicans who shrank from interfering with State control of Negro suffrage in the South would scarcely have dared to impose on the North a radical reconstruction of white apportionment patterns. Certainly there was no disclosure that such intrusion was contemplated; there is in fact striking evidence that malapportionment was an accepted practice. Speaking with respect to reduced representation, Blaine of Maine said,

> if you cut off the blacks from being enumerated in the basis of representation in the southern States the white population of those States will immediately distribute Representatives within their own territory on the basis of white population. Therefore the most densely populated negro districts will not be allowed to offset the most densely populated white districts. . . . Do you suppose that the upland districts of Georgia and South Carolina, inhabited largely by whites, will, in the event of adoption of this amendment, allow the distribution of Representatives to be made on the basis of the whole population? By no means. They will at once insist on the white basis within the State.

Not a hint that this would be unlawful, but, rather, clear recognition that States were free to apportion representation to *suit* themselves. Although, as Van Alstyne

notices, this would leave "areas populated by non-voters without representation (and not merely without a vote in the choice of 'their' representatives)," Bingham replied, "no possible amendment . . . will answer the purpose unless it is followed by further legislation." Bingham thus confirms Blaine's recital of the plenary State power over apportionment and implies that the "representation" (§2) proposal was not designed to meet this situation. Van Alstyne's comment that "Blaine's remarks were directed only to the apportionment of congressional rather than state representation" implausibly suggests that the States would be readier to surrender control over their own internal patterns—a suggestion that is incompatible with the pervasive attachment to State sovereignty.

Blaine's remarks did not reflect a fleeting improvisation, but responded to established practice. Earlier he had stated: "As an abstract proposition no one will deny that population is the true basis of representation; for women, children and other nonvoting classes may have as vital an interest in the legislation . . . as those who actually cast the ballot." But, he noted, recognizing existing practice, as had *Federalist* No. 54 and James Wilson long before, "the ratio of voters to population differs very widely in different sections, from a minimum of *nineteen per cent* to a maximum of *fifty-eight percent.*" Even that uncompromising abolitionist Charles Sumner was reconciled to such practices because they reflected "custom and popular faith," and could not be changed "unless supported by the permanent feelings and conditions of the people." Then, too, in the congressional debate of June 1868 (that is, prior to ratification of the Fourteenth Amendment), on the readmission of the rebel States, Farnsworth pointed out that the Florida apportionment provision gave "to the sparsely populated portions of the State the control of the Legislature." But Ben Butler responded that the Senate Judiciary Committee "have found the [Florida] constitution republican and proper," as did the Senate, the House Committee on Reconstruction, and the House itself, thus reaffirming that such malapportionment did not violate the guarantee of a "republican form of government," nor the equal protection clause which was the work of Butler and his fellows. The Blaine, Sumner, and Butler statements constitute hard evidence which is not overcome by mere speculation. Since, moreover, most of the States were malapportioned, it is a strained assumption that by ratification they surrendered a right they had excercised from the outset, and of which surrender they were totally unapprised.

When Van Alstyne dismissed Harlan's reading of the §2 phrase "or in any way abridged" because "once the congressional history" of this phrase is "canvassed . . . it becomes clear that the phrase had nothing at all to do with malapportionment," he scuttled his whole case. For, by the same token, the history of the equal protection clause likewise "had nothing at all to do with malapportionment." "There is," he states, "no evidence that §2 was applicable to abridgment of the right to vote resulting from malapportionment of state legislatures." "It is even likely," he avers, "that had the subject been discussed there might have been a disavowal of an intention to apply the Equal Protection Clause to malapportionment." But "hypothetical answers to hypothetical questions . . . would be a most dubious basis for expounding the content of 'equal protection' one hundred years later." There is no need to speculate because Blaine and others plainly recognized malapportionment as an existing practice that was left

untouched. I, too, prefer to eschew speculation, particularly when it is unnecessary. One who would bring an unmentioned departure from settled practice within the perimeter of the Amendment has the burden of proof, made heavier here by (1) the fact that Negro suffrage, on which the Court rested its case for reapportionment, was unmistakably excluded; (2) the plainly expressed attachment of the framers to State sovereignty and their intention to intrude no further than the limits of the Civil Rights Act; and (3) the presumption that a diminution of powers reserved to the States by the Tenth Amendment will be clearly stated.

In one form or another, Van Alstyne would put asunder what the Warren Court hath joined; he would jettison the Court's "one man, one vote" postulate. Granting arguendo State power "with respect to outright denials of the right to vote," he asks, "is it equally so with respect to partial disfranchisement through malapportionment?" The simple answer is that the greater includes the less. If a State may altogether *deny* the vote, it may *dilute* it. It was in these terms that Chief Justice Warren rationalized reapportionment: the Constitution, he held, protects the right to "vote," the "right to have one's vote counted." And "the right of Suffrage can be denied by a debasement or dilution of the weight of a citizen's vote just as effectively as by wholly prohibiting the free exercise of the franchise." His premise—that the Constitution, that is, the Fourteenth Amendment, protects the right to vote—is contradicted by historical facts. But his logic is impeccable and may be stated inversely: given a right to deny suffrage, it follows that there is a right to dilute it.

In the Convention Elbridge Gerry refused to set up the judges "as the guardians of the Rights of the people," preferring to rely "on the Representatives of the people as the guardians of their rights and interests." That belief was later echoed by Justice Brandeis, who referred to the deep-seated conviction of the American people that they "must look to representative assemblies for the protection of their liberties." Platonic Guardians have enjoyed small favor in our polity. Judge Learned Hand, one of the wisest judges, disclaimed any knowledge of how to choose Platonic Guardians and had no desire to live under their guardianship. And wonder of wonders, Justice Brennan declared "Justices are not platonic guardians appointed to wield authority according to their personal moral predilections." To be sure, this was said during his confirmation hearings; during his incumbency he became a veritable paragon of Platonic Guardians.

Judges are not oracles who, indifferent to the passions of the time, divine the true meaning of the Constitution. What a judge is "really discovering" on his interpretive voyage, correctly observes John Hart Ely, "are his own values." Judging in terms of personal preferences has long been condemned; Blackstone disapproved of judges whose decisions would be regulated "only by their own opinions." Marshall declared that "the judicial power is never exercised for the purpose of giving effect to the will of the judge." "Under the guise of interpreting the Constitution," said Justice Moody, "we must take care that we do not import into the discussion our personal views of what would be wise, just, and fitting rules . . . and confound them with constitutional limitations."

Recently Judge Richard Posner commented that "a judge ought not to substitute personal values for those that are part of the text, structure and history of the Constitution." Even activists acknowledge the rule, perhaps perceiving that the

substitution "of the individual sense of justice . . . would put an end to the rule of law." Then too, as James Wilson emphasized in the Convention, laws "may be unjust" and yet be "constitutional."

Activists seek to reshape the Constitution on behalf of "human rights" and of greater protection of "minorities." We have seen that the Founders were more concerned with the rights of the community than with those of the individual, that they regarded the rights expressed in Blackstone's triad as "fundamental," that this triad, the 39th Congress was told, also represented the American view. A leading activist theoretician, Paul Brest, acknowledges that "Many of what we have come to regard as the irreducible minima of rights are actually supra-constitutional; almost none of the others are entailed by the text or original understanding." Activists would have the courts decide, Michael Perry observes, "what rights, beyond those specified by the framers, individuals should . . . have against government."

Activist efforts to enlarge judicial protection of minorities would jettison a central tenet of our democratic system—majority rule. Of course, if specific provision is made in the Constitution for such protection, it must be given effect. But, as Hamilton stated in *Federalist* No. 22, "To give a minority a negative upon the majority . . . [is] to subject the sense of the greater number to that of the lesser." Madison was of the same mind; criticizing a proposal that more than a majority ought to be required for a quorum, he said that it would reverse a "fundamental principle of free government," because "It would be no longer the majority that would rule; the power would be transferred to the minority." And Jefferson concurred that the "will of the Majority should always prevail." Activists would substitute the "tyranny" of the minority for the "bugaboo" of majority "tyranny"; they would have the tail wag the dog. Randall Bridwell properly asks, "what makes the tyranny of the minority . . . better than the tyranny of the majority?" Activists' insistence on enlarged judicial protection illustrates once more their preference for judicial governance, as is exemplified by Robert Cover. He unabashedly thrust aside "the self-evident meaning of the Constitution" because "we" have decided to "entrust" judges with framing an "ideology" whereby to test legislation and, it may be added, discard the Framers' choices.

John Hart Ely

DEMOCRACY AND DISTRUST

Cambridge, MA: Harvard University Press (1986)

This piece might be read as a response to the arguments we have just seen from Raoul Berger. John Hart Ely attempts to justify the role of courts in striking down gerrymandering by appealing to his procedural theory of democracy, which we examined at length in Chapter 2. As you read this piece, consider not only the specific issue of gerrymandering and judicial intervention, but more generally, the Court's role in "reinforcing" democratic rights.

Although the right to vote seems equally central to a right of participation in the democratic process, there is less consensus among commentators on the propriety of judicial activism in the voting area. It is tempting to suppose that this is because the right to vote is not mentioned explicitly in the Constitution—at least the right to vote in state elections isn't—but we know that won't wash. Freedom of association is not mentioned in the First Amendment or anywhere else, and neither speech nor association is mentioned in the Fourteenth, yet those have quite properly been protected. Also, those who object to active review in voting cases tend as often as not to be people who are untroubled by "substantive due process"

elsewhere: something like "contraception, yes—voting, no" is not that uncommon a constellation. It should be clear from what has gone before that I think that's exactly upside down: unblocking stoppages in the democratic process is what judicial review ought preeminently to be about, and denial of the vote seems the quintessential stoppage.

Why, then, the resistance in so many quarters to active judicial review in the voting area? In fact most of the fire has been directed at the malapportionment cases, which we shall get to presently. Justice Harlan had a more fundamental objection however—one that goes to voter qualification cases equally—and that was that the Equal Protection Clause, which is the provision under which the Court has decided both kinds of cases, simply had not been intended by its framers to apply to voting. In fact the legislative history is not as clear as Harlan claimed it was, but it does seem probable that most of the framers (and ratifiers) of the Fourteenth Amendment did not specifically anticipate that its first section would be applied to voting rights. The problem comes in what Harlan thought that observation proved. Why on this of all issues should we get hung up—why, in particular, should Justice Harlan get hung up—on the specific intentions of the framers? As we have seen, the over-riding intention of those who wrote and ratified the Equal Protection Clause was apparently to state a general ideal whose specific applications would be supplied by posterity. They surely entertained no spe-cific intention that the Equal Protection Clause would cover antimiscegenation laws, or for that matter segregated school-ing either. But as Chief Justice Warren so correctly put it in *Brown v. Board of Education*, the legislative history relating specifically to schooling, and he might have added the legislative history bearing on all specific applications, was "incon-clusive." Unjustified discriminations in the distribution of the franchise fit com-fortably within the language of—and just as obviously violate the ideal expressed by—the Equal Protection Clause (and for that matter the Republican Form of Government Clause as well). That is what should count as important.

The sort of review that is appropriate in cases involving voter qualifications is related to that which is appropriate in First Amendment contexts. We cannot trust the ins to decide who stays out, and it is therefore incumbent on the courts to ensure not only that no one is denied the vote for no reason, but also that where there is a reason (as there will be) it had better be a very convincing one. Thus in *Carrington v. Rash*, decided in 1965, the Court invalidated a Texas law denying the franchise to those who had moved into the state on military service, and in *Harper v. Virginia Board of Elections*, decided a year later, it struck down Virginia's poll tax. Each of these voter qualifications, the Court said, was irrational. But nei-ther really was that. Military personnel do tend to be more transient than others

and in addition might well, as the state argued, end up dominating the politics of a town in or near which a military base is located. It may also be true, or at least it is not irrational to think so, that persons of some wealth tend to be more "respon-sible" citizens or, more plausibly still, that the willingness to pay a fee for voting is some reflection of serious interest in the election. So the language of irrationality was hyperbole, and the real point in each case was that a group of persons—the military in one case, those so poor that a fee might be a deterrent in the other—was being frozen out of the decision process for an insufficiently compelling reason.

However, the usual demand of the Equal Protection Clause is simply that the discrimination in question be ratio-nally explainable. Chief Justice Warren's opinion for the Court in *Reynolds* tried to suggest that any deviation from a one person, one vote standard was irrational, but that is nonsense. Various states, and the federal government as well, often and permissibly give special breaks to cer-tain groups in our society. Farmers, for example, frequently receive special gov-ernmental favors—subsidies, tax breaks, even exemptions from antitrust and other criminal statutes—as a way of fostering a strong agricultural economy. Another entirely rational way of pursuing the same goal is to give rural areas more legislative representatives per unit of population.

There is indeed a problem with this sort of defense, but it's not that it isn't rational, or even that it is incapable of meeting the rightfully stronger demand the Court has imposed in the voting area. The problem instead, if you will, is that such defenses work too well, that they can readily be pushed to the point of justifying govern-mental systems that we all would recog-nize as inconsistent with the plan of our Constitution. If protecting the agricultural economy is truly important to a state, and it obviously is to some, it would not be illogical to give farmers 90 percent of the effective voting power even though they make up only 10 percent of the population. That is too much for everyone, however. It was obviously to cope with such extended inferences that Justice Stewart, dissenting in *Reynolds* and its companion cases, added to the baseline equal protection requirement, that distinctions in voting strength be rationally defensible, the additional demand that the plan at issue "must be such as not to permit the systematic frustration of the will of a majority of the electorate of the State." . . .

Some commentators have suggested that the Court's role in protecting minorities should consist only in removing barriers to their participation in the political process. We have seen, however—and the realization is one that threads our constitutional document—that the duty of representation that lies at the core of our system requires more than a voice and a vote. No matter how open the process, those with most of the votes are in a position to vote themselves advantages at the expense of the others, or otherwise to refuse to take their interests into account. "'One person, one vote,' under these circumstances, makes a travesty of the equality principle." Not long ago the assurances of pluralist political theory, that any group whose members were not denied the franchise could protect itself by entering into the give and take of the political marketplace, dominated academic political science. Recently, however, pluralism has come under powerful attack, as more stress has been placed on the undeniable concentrations of power, and inequalities among the various competing groups, in American politics. Of course the pluralist model does work sometimes, and minorities *can* protect themselves by striking deals and stressing the ties that bind the interests of other groups to their own. But sometimes it doesn't, as the single example of how our society has treated its black minority (even after that minority had gained every official attribute of access to the process) is more than sufficient to prove.

One thing we know the Constitution, the Equal Protection Clause in particular, cannot mean is that everyone is entitled to equal treatment by every law. In fact much of the point of most laws is to sort people out for differential treatment, often quite seriously differential treatment. Neither can the Constitution coherently be interpreted as outlining some "appropriate" distributional pattern against which actual allocations of hurts and benefits can be traced to see if they are constitutional. The constitutionality of most distributions thus cannot be determined simply by looking to see who ended up with what, but rather can be approached intelligibly only by attending to the process that brought about the distribution in question—by what Robert Nozick has called a "historical" (as opposed to an "end result") approach. This is not the way one should approach a law withholding something to which the Constitution gives us a presumptive constitutional entitlement, such as the right to vote. That right simply cannot be denied (unless the state's lawyer can come up with a compelling justification for doing so). The Court's job in such cases is to look at the world as it exists and ask whether such a right is in fact being abridged, and if it is, to consider what reasons might be adduced in support of the deprivation, without regard to what actually occasioned it. To the extent that there is a stoppage, the system is malfunctioning, and the Court should unblock it without caring how it got that way.

Samuel Issacharoff

GERRYMANDERING AND POLITICAL CARTELS

116 Harv. L. Rev. 593 (2002)

As will become clear when you read Guinn v. United States, *questions of voting rights have been intertwined with race throughout American history.* Guinn v. United States *considered, for instance, the legitimacy of literacy tests used to exclude African Americans from voting. A more recent issue, explored here by Samuel Issacharoff, ties together issues of gerrymandering with those of race. Specifically, advocates of sending more African Americans to Congress have sought to create so-called majority-minority districts with the hope of increasing the likelihood that African-American candidates will be elected. Is race-consciousness in gerrymandering an appropriate way to promote diversity in Congress? Consider arguments for the creation of majority-minority districts that appeal to the diversity and remedying injustice arguments introduced by Amy Gutmann and President Lyndon B. Johnson, respectively, in Section B. Why might some consider the creation of such districts problematic from the perspective of the Fourteenth Amendment's Equal Protection Clause?*

Nearly forty years ago, the U.S. Supreme Court ushered in the rights era in the law governing the political process. Beginning with its intuition that redistricting may impermissibly alter the outcomes of elections, the Court created a regime of justiciable rights that redrew the contours of politics, from eligibility for the franchise, to the effect of electoral schemes on minority electoral prospects, to the funding of candidates and the political process.

The passage of time, and the extensive case law that has developed, permits a revisitation of the core principles animating American jurisprudence on the political process.

Over the past decade, the focus of constitutional attention in the redistricting arena has been on the imprecise boundaries the courts have drawn against the use of racial considerations in apportioning representation. Following the pathbreaking opinion in *Shaw v. Reno* (*Shaw I*), the battle lines in the courts and in the scholarship have been drawn over the application of familiar equal protection categories in the struggles over race and representation. Often overlooked in the profusion of scholarship following *Shaw I*, however, has been whether the battles over racial representation reveal a more systemic institutional failure in the redistricting process. Indeed, as I develop in this article, it is possible to see in the *Shaw* line of cases a manifestation of a more deeply rooted problem in the redistricting context, one stemming from the acceptance to date of insider manipulation of the process for partisan gain.

Examined from this perspective, the *Shaw* line of cases reveals not only ongoing doctrinal battles over the application of the antidiscrimination norm to state action deemed beneficial to racial minorities, but also something deeper about the relation between constitutional law and politics. To date, the Court has not developed any theoretical foundation deeper than its early insight that redistricting may be subject to systematic manipulation. Instead, the Court has articulated only a rudimentary concern that the susceptibility of redistricting to ends-oriented manipulation might result in impermissible discrimination or some other form of unfair partisan advantage. This limitation emerges most clearly not in the area of racial representation, but in the less normatively explosive context of partisan gerrymandering. Just as one may best observe a solar eclipse by focusing away from its brightest point, so too it may be that insights into the failings of current jurisprudence may be gained by diverting attention from the searing question of race.

The place to start, therefore, is the breakthrough case of *Davis v. Bandemer*, in which the Court first recognized a claim of unconstitutional discrimination in the redistricting context based on partisanship rather than the familiar equal protection category of racial classifications. In *Davis*, the Court grounded its constitutional concerns in the ability of political insiders to manipulate electoral boundaries to magnify their political power and frustrate the legitimate aspirations of their political rival, defined for all practical purposes as one or another of the two major parties. The conceptual underpinning of the Court's analysis in *Davis* is undeveloped but appears to rest on an unelaborated intuition of unfairness to the political party not enjoying the bounties of incumbent power. *Davis* introduces the actionable claim of political vote dilution, an uncomfortable analogue of the concept of minority vote dilution, which in turn is an extension of antidiscrimination law. But the analogy breaks down across many dimensions, and the unfortunate result is a new equal protection doctrine with an impossibly high burden of proof for actually making out a claim.

The conceptual weakness in how the Court has treated the potential for mischievous manipulation of redistricting is evident in a less criticized earlier case,

Gaffney v. Cummings. There, the Court found unobjectionable a political compromise between the Democrats and Republicans of Connecticut to partition the state so as to lock in the political status quo ante. The Court reasoned that there could be no partisan harm, regardless of the geographic contortions of the district lines, when the two parties had negotiated a redistricting plan without either of them seeking to exploit the other for legislative gain. The Connecticut experiment in a negotiated division of power, which political scientist Bruce Cain terms a "bipartisan gerrymander," does not present the problem of discrimination against one of the parties and thereby avoids the equal protection framework the Court has employed thus far. Put another way, if a legislative plan were to provide the two major political parties with reasonable prospects of achieving what they believed to be their appropriate shares of representation, what could be objectionable in such a coalition effort? From the vantage point of equal protection law, neither party should be considered a victim of discrimination under such a sharing of electoral opportunity.

The label "bipartisan gerrymander" suggests that there may be grounds for concern but does not elucidate the exact source of that concern. The invocation of the gerrymandering label may express an aesthetic objection to the contours of the districting lines, or it may hint at the stench of backroom politics improperly shielded from public scrutiny, but it does not capture any substantive conception of what is wrong with the outcome when the two incumbent parties carve up the state into mutually acceptable bailiwicks.

A simple analogy might cast the putative benefits of a partisan nonaggression pact in a different light. Imagine that instead of two political parties agreeing to territorially defined zones of influence, we found that two dominant rival firms producing interchangeable products—as with Coke and Pepsi, to take but the most obvious example—had made such an agreement. To pose the question is virtually to answer it since such a pact would be a first-order violation of the antitrust laws. Cartelization would produce monopoly rents in the market, and consumers would end up with fewer choices at higher prices. A more complete story would add concerns about long-term stagnation, incentives for product development, and so forth.

As redistricting returns to its decennial full bloom, it is worth pondering why the two stories elicit such different legal reactions. Why is it that geographical divisions into clearly identified zones of influence trigger condemnation under the antitrust laws but approval under constitutional scrutiny? Pushed further, is there anything specific in the political arena that insulates a standstill agreement between the two dominant parties from being defined as anything less than a serious threat to consumer (defined here as voter) welfare?

. . . [T]his form of political market manipulation threatens a core tenet of democratic legitimacy: accountability to shifting voter preferences. The basic move here is to argue that the risk in gerrymandering is not so much that of discrimination or lack of a formal ability to participate individually, but that of constriction of the competitive processes by which voters can express choice.

So long as the process is left in the hands of incumbent political officials whose self-interest runs strongly to what they can get away with, and so long as judicial oversight remains cumbersome and unpredictable, the private interest will likely continue to subsume the public interest. A strategy of reinforcing political competition by taking the process of redistricting out of the hands of partisan officials offers the prospect of realizing our constitutional values. Not only does it provide an exit strategy from the Court's entanglement with the bruising world of race and politics, but it also returns the core constitutional value in judicial oversight of the political process to what, at least aspirationally, it has been for over a century: securing the selection of representatives that as fully as possible stand for the "free and uncorrupted choice of those who have the right to take part in that choice."

GUINN v. UNITED STATES

238 U.S. 347 (1915)

Opinion: White, joined by McKenna, Holmes, Day, Hughes, Van Devanter, Lamar, Pitney

MR. CHIEF JUSTICE WHITE *delivered the opinion of the Court.*

Suffrage in Oklahoma was regulated by §1, Article III of the Constitution under which the State was admitted into the Union. Shortly after the admission, there was submitted an amendment to the Constitution making a radical change in that article which was adopted prior to November 8, 1910. At an election for members of Congress which followed the adoption of this Amendment, certain election officers, in enforcing its provisions, refused to allow certain negro citizens to vote who were clearly entitled to vote under the provision of the Constitution under which the State was admitted, that is, before the amendment, and who, it is equally clear, were not entitled to vote under the provision of the suffrage amendment if that amendment governed. The persons so excluded based their claim of right to vote upon the original Constitution and upon the assertion that the suffrage amendment was void because in conflict with the prohibitions of the Fifteenth Amendment, and therefore afforded no basis for denying them the right guaranteed and protected by that Amendment.

The questions which the court below asks are these:

1. Was the amendment to the constitution of Oklahoma, heretofore set forth, valid?
2. Was that amendment void insofar as it attempted to debar from the right or privilege of voting for a qualified candidate for a Member of Congress in Oklahoma, unless they were able to read and write any section of the constitution of Oklahoma, negro citizens of the United States who were otherwise qualified to vote for a qualified candidate for a Member of Congress in that State, but who were not, and none of whose lineal ancestors was entitled to vote under any form of government on January 1, 1866, or at any time prior thereto, because they were then slaves?

As these questions obviously relate to the provisions concerning suffrage in the original constitution and the amendment to those provisions which forms the basis of the controversy, we state the text of both. The original clause, so far as material, was this:

> The qualified electors of the State shall be male citizens of the United States, male citizens of the State, and male persons of Indian descent native of the United States, who are over the age of twenty-one years, who have resided in the State one year, in the county six months, and in the election precinct thirty days, next preceding the election at which any such elector offers to vote.

And this is the amendment:

> No person shall be registered as an elector of this State or be allowed to vote in any election herein, unless he be able to read and write any section of the constitution of the State of Oklahoma; but no person who was, on January 1, 1866, or at any time prior thereto, entitled to vote under any form of government, or who at that time resided in some foreign nation, and no lineal descendant of such person, shall be denied the right to register and vote because of his inability to so read and write sections of such constitution.

To avoid that which is unnecessary, let us at once consider and sift the propositions of the United States, on the one hand, and of the plaintiffs in error, on the other, in order to reach with precision the real and final question to be considered. The United States insists that the provision of the amendment which fixes a standard based upon January 1, 1866, is repugnant to the prohibitions of the Fifteenth Amendment because, in substance and effect, that provision, if not an express, is certainly an open, repudiation of the Fifteenth Amendment, and hence the provision in question was stricken with nullity in its inception by the self-operative force of the Amendment, and, as the result of the same power, was at all subsequent times devoid of any vitality whatever.

For the plaintiffs in error, on the other hand, it is said the States have the power to fix standards for suffrage, and that power was not taken away by the Fifteenth Amendment, but only limited to the extent of the prohibitions which that Amendment established. This being true, as the standard fixed does not in terms make any discrimination on account of race, color, or previous condition of servitude, since all, whether negro or white, who come within its requirements enjoy the privilege of voting, there is no ground upon which to rest the contention that the provision violates the Fifteenth Amendment.

On the other hand, the United States denies the relevancy of these contentions. It says state power to provide for suffrage is not disputed, although, of course, the authority of the Fifteenth Amendment and the limit on that power which it imposes is insisted upon. Hence, no assertion denying the right of a State to exert judgment and discretion in fixing the qualification of suffrage is advanced, and no right to question the motive of the State in establishing a standard as to such subjects under such circumstances or to review or supervise the same is relied upon, and no power to destroy an otherwise valid exertion of authority upon the mere ultimate operation of the power exercised is asserted. And, applying these principles to the very case in hand, the argument of the Government, in substance, says: no question is raised by the Government concerning the validity of the literacy test provided for in the amendment under consideration as an independent standard, since the conclusion is plain that that test rests on the exercise of state judgment, and therefore cannot be here assailed either by disregarding the State's power to judge on the subject or by testing its motive in enacting the provision. The real question involved, so the argument of the Government insists, is the repugnancy of the standard which the amendment makes, based upon the conditions existing on January 1, 1866, because, on its face and inherently, considering the substance of things, that standard is a mere denial of the restrictions imposed by the prohibitions of the Fifteenth Amendment, and by necessary result, recreates and perpetuates the

very conditions which the Amendment was intended to destroy. From this, it is urged that no legitimate discretion could have entered into the fixing of such standard which involved only the determination to directly set at naught or by indirection avoid the commands of the Amendment.

The questions then are: (1) giving to the propositions of the Government the interpretation which the Government puts upon them and assuming that the suffrage provision has the significance which the Government assumes it to have, is that provision, as a matter of law, repugnant to the Fifteenth Amendment? which leads us, of course, to consider the operation and effect of the Fifteenth Amendment. (2) If yes, has the assailed amendment, insofar as it fixes a standard for voting as of January 1, 1866, the meaning which the Government attributes to it? which leads us to analyze and interpret that provision of the amendment. (3) If the investigation as to the two prior subjects establishes that the standard fixed as of January 1, 1866, is void, what, if any, effect does that conclusion have upon the literacy standard otherwise established by the amendment? which involves determining whether that standard, if legal, may survive the recognition of the fact that the other or 1866 standard has not, and never had, any legal existence.

Let us consider these subjects under separate headings.

1. *The operation and effect of the Fifteenth Amendment.* This is its text:

> Section 1. The right of citizens of the United States to vote shall not be denied or abridged by the United States or by any State on account of race, color, or previous condition of servitude.
>
> Section 2. The Congress shall have power to enforce this article by appropriate legislation.

(a) Beyond doubt, the Amendment does not take away from the state governments in a general sense the power over suffrage which has belonged to those governments from the beginning, and without the possession of which power the whole fabric upon which the division of state and national authority under the Constitution and the organization of both governments rest would be without support and both the authority of the nation and the State would fall to the ground. In fact, the very command of the Amendment recognizes the possession of the general power by the State, since the Amendment seeks to regulate its exercise as to the particular subject with which it deals.

(b) But it is equally beyond the possibility of question that the Amendment, in express terms, restricts the power of the United States or the States to abridge or deny the right of a citizen of the United States to vote on account of race, color or previous condition of servitude.

But, while this is true, it is true also that the Amendment does not change, modify or deprive the States of their full power as to suffrage except, of course, as to the subject with which the Amendment deals and to the extent that obedience to its command is necessary. Thus, the authority over suffrage which the States possess and the limitation which the Amendment imposes are coordinate, and one may not destroy the other without bringing about the destruction of both.

(c) While, in the true sense, therefore, the Amendment gives no right of suffrage, it was long ago recognized that, in operation, its prohibition might measurably have that effect; that is to say, that, as the command of the Amendment was self-executing and reached without legislative action the conditions of discrimination against which it was aimed, the result might arise that as a consequence of the striking down of a discriminating clause a right of suffrage would be enjoyed by reason of the generic character of the provision which would remain after the discrimination was stricken out. A familiar illustration of this doctrine resulted from the effect of the adoption of the Amendment on state constitutions in which, at the time of the adoption of the Amendment, the right of suffrage was conferred on all white male citizens, since, by the inherent power of the Amendment, the word white disappeared, and therefore all male citizens, without discrimination on account of race, color or previous condition of servitude, came under the generic grant of suffrage made by the State.

With these principles before us, how can there be room for any serious dispute concerning the repugnancy of the standard based upon January 1, 1866 (a date which preceded the adoption of the Fifteenth Amendment), if the suffrage provision fixing that standard is susceptible of the significance which the Government attributes to it? Indeed, there seems no escape from the conclusion that to hold that there was even possibility for dispute on the subject would be but to declare that the Fifteenth Amendment not only had not the self-executing power which it has been recognized to have from the beginning, but that its provisions were wholly inoperative, because susceptible of being rendered inapplicable by mere forms of expression embodying no exercise of judgment and resting upon no discernible reason other than the purpose to disregard the prohibitions of the Amendment by creating a standard of voting which on its face was, in substance, but a revitalization of conditions which, when they prevailed in the past, had been destroyed by the self-operative force of the Amendment.

2. *The standard of January 1, 1866, fixed in the suffrage amendment and its significance.*

The inquiry, of course, here is, does the amendment as to the particular standard which this heading embraces involve the mere refusal to comply with the commands of the Fifteenth Amendment as previously stated?

It is true it contains no express words of an exclusion from the standard which it establishes of any person on account of race, color, or previous condition of servitude prohibited by the Fifteenth Amendment, but the standard itself inherently brings that result into existence, since it is based purely upon a period of time before the enactment of the Fifteenth Amendment, and makes that period the controlling and dominant test of the right of suffrage. In other words, we seek in vain for any ground which would sustain any other interpretation but that the provision, recurring to the conditions existing before the Fifteenth Amendment was adopted and the continuance of which the Fifteenth Amendment prohibited, proposed by, in substance and effect, lifting those conditions over to a period of time after the Amendment to make them the basis of the right to suffrage conferred in direct and positive disregard of the Fifteenth Amendment. And the same result, we are of opinion, is demonstrated by considering whether it is possible to discover any basis of reason for the standard thus fixed other than the purpose above stated. We say this because we are unable to discover how, unless the prohibitions of the Fifteenth Amendment were considered, the slightest reason was afforded for basing the classification upon a period of time prior to the Fifteenth Amendment. Certainly it cannot be said that there was any peculiar necromancy in the time named which engendered attributes affecting the qualification to vote which would not exist at another and different period unless the Fifteenth Amendment was in view.

3. *The determination of the validity of the literacy test and the possibility of its surviving the disappearance of the 1866 standard with which it is associated in the suffrage amendment.*

No time need be spent on the question of the validity of the literacy test, considered alone, since, as we have seen, its establishment was but the exercise by the State of a lawful power vested in it not subject to our supervision, and, indeed, its validity is admitted. Whether this test is so connected with the other one relating to the situation on January 1, 1866, that the invalidity of the latter requires the rejection of the former, is really a question of state law, but, in the absence of any decision on the subject by the Supreme Court of the State, we must determine it for ourselves. We are of opinion that neither forms of classification nor methods of enumeration should be made the basis of striking down a provision which was independently legal, and therefore was lawfully enacted because of the removal of an illegal provision with which the legal provision or provisions may have been associated. We state what we hold to be the rule thus strongly because we are of opinion that, on a subject like the one under consideration, involving the establishment of a right whose exercise lies at the very basis of government, a much more exacting standard is required than would ordinarily obtain where the influence of the declared unconstitutionality of one provision of a statute upon another and constitutional provision is required to be fixed. Of course, rigorous as is this rule and imperative as is the duty not to violate it, it does not mean that it applies in a case where it expressly appears that a contrary conclusion must be reached if the plain letter and necessary intendment of the provision under consideration so compels, or where such a result is rendered necessary because to follow the contrary course would give rise to such an extreme and anomalous situation as would cause it to be impossible to conclude that it could have been upon any hypothesis whatever within the mind of the lawmaking power.

Does the general rule here govern, or is the case controlled by one or the other of the exceptional conditions which we have just stated, is then the remaining question to be decided. Coming to solve it, we are of opinion that, by a consideration of the text of the suffrage amendment insofar as it deals with the literacy test, and to the extent that it creates the standard based upon conditions existing on January 1, 1866, the case is taken out of the general rule and brought under the first of the exceptions stated. We say this because, in our opinion, the very language of the suffrage amendment expresses, not by implication nor by forms of classification nor by the order in which they are made, but by direct and positive language, the command that the persons embraced in the 1866 standard should not be under any conditions subjected to the literacy test, a command which would be virtually set at naught if on the obliteration of the one standard by the force of the Fifteenth Amendment the other standard should be held to continue in force.

We answer the first question, No, and the second question, Yes.

BAKER v. CARR

369 U.S. 186 (1962)

Opinion: Brennan, joined by Warren, Black
Concurrence: Douglas
Concurrence: Clark
Concurrence: Stewart
Dissent: Frankfurter, joined by Harlan
Dissent: Harlan, joined by Frankfurter

Americans often think that they are living in a representative democracy, but historically there have been some questions about the extent to which our system actually guarantees equal representation. The most obvious counterpoint is the Senate, which provides unequal representation to individuals in order to provide equal representation to the states. In contrast, the House of Representatives is apportioned based on the population of each state in an attempt to more accurately represent individual interests. But, do these legislative districts that make up the House of Representatives themselves have to be apportioned in a way that provides for equal representation? Most state legislatures also have two chambers, in many cases based upon the federal system, with one of the chambers, like the Senate, representing counties equally, instead of individuals. Should the Equal Protection Clause be interpreted so as to require that these districts be drawn in such a way as to ensure one person, one vote, or the principle that every person's vote should have the same weight as everyone else's?

Our next set of cases examines these issues. As you read the first case, Baker v. Carr, *consider whether the Court's judicial authority should extend to policing the manner in which legislative districts are drawn. Does the Equal Protection Clause guarantee a right to have one's vote counted equally in federal as well as state elections? As you read, think about the debate between John Hart Ely and Raoul Berger over the role of the Supreme Court in policing the democratic process. Is Berger correct that so-called government by judiciary is in its nature undemocratic? Or is Ely correct that democratic government requires the guarantee of "one person, one vote"?*

MR. JUSTICE BRENNAN *delivered the opinion of the Court.*

Tennessee's standard for allocating legislative representation among her counties is the total number of qualified voters resident in the respective counties, subject only to minor qualifications. Decennial reapportionment in compliance with the constitutional scheme was effected by the General Assembly each decade from 1871 to 1901. In 1901, the General Assembly abandoned separate enumeration in favor of reliance upon the Federal Census, and passed the Apportionment Act here in controversy.

Between 1901 and 1961, Tennessee has experienced substantial growth and redistribution of her population. In 1901, the population was 2,020,616, of whom 487,380 were eligible to vote. The 1960 Federal Census reports the State's population at 3,567,089, of whom 2,092,891 are eligible to vote. The relative standings of the counties in terms of qualified voters have changed significantly.

The complaint concludes that

these plaintiffs and others similarly situated, are denied the equal protection of the laws accorded them by the Fourteenth Amendment to the Constitution of the United States by virtue of the debasement of their votes.

Because we deal with this case on appeal from an order of dismissal granted on appellees' motions, precise identification of the issues presently confronting us demands clear exposition of the grounds upon which the District Court rested in dismissing the case.

The District Court was uncertain whether our cases withholding federal judicial relief rested upon a lack of federal jurisdiction or upon the inappropriateness of the subject matter for judicial consideration—what we have designated "nonjusticiability."

Article III, §2, of the Federal Constitution provides that

The judicial Power shall extend to all Cases, in Law and Equity, arising under this Constitution, the Laws of the United States, and Treaties made, or which shall be made, under their Authority.

It is clear that the cause of action is one which "arises under" the Federal Constitution. The complaint alleges that the 1901 statute effects an apportionment that deprives the appellants of the equal protection of the laws in violation of the Fourteenth Amendment.

In holding that the subject matter of this suit was not justiciable, the District Court stated:

From a review of these decisions, there can be no doubt that the federal rule . . . is that the federal courts . . . will not intervene in cases of this type to compel legislative reapportionment.

We understand the District Court to have read the cited cases as compelling the conclusion that, since the appellants sought to have a legislative apportionment held unconstitutional, their suit presented a "political question," and was therefore nonjusticiable. We hold that this challenge to an apportionment presents no nonjusticiable "political question."

Of course, the mere fact that the suit seeks protection of a political right does not mean it presents a political question. Such an objection "is little more than a play upon words."

The nonjusticiability of a political question is primarily a function of the separation of powers. Much confusion results from the capacity of the "political question" label to obscure the need for case-by-case inquiry. Deciding whether a matter has in any measure been committed by the Constitution to another branch of government, or whether the action of that branch exceeds whatever authority has been committed, is itself a delicate exercise in constitutional interpretation, and is a responsibility of this Court as ultimate interpreter of the Constitution.

It is apparent that several formulations which vary slightly according to the settings in which the questions arise may describe a political question, although each has one or more elements which identify it as essentially a function of the separation of powers. Prominent on the surface of any case held to involve a political question is found a textually demonstrable constitutional commitment of the issue to a coordinate political department; or a lack of judicially discoverable and manageable standards for resolving it; or the impossibility of deciding without an initial policy determination of a kind clearly for nonjudicial discretion; or the impossibility of a court's undertaking independent resolution without expressing lack of the respect due coordinate branches of government; or an unusual need for unquestioning adherence to a political decision already made; or the potentiality of embarrassment from multifarious pronouncements by various departments on one question.

Unless one of these formulations is inextricable from the case at bar, there should be no dismissal for nonjusticiability on the ground of a political question's presence. The doctrine of which we treat is one of "political questions," not one of "political cases." The courts cannot reject as "no law suit" a *bona fide* controversy as to whether some action denominated "political" exceeds constitutional authority.

We come, finally, to the ultimate inquiry whether our precedents as to what constitutes a nonjusticiable "political question" bring the case before us under the umbrella of that doctrine. A natural beginning is to note whether any of the common characteristics which we have been able to identify and label descriptively are present. We find none: the question here is the consistency of state action with the Federal Constitution. We have no question decided, or to be decided, by a political branch of government coequal with this Court. Nor do we risk embarrassment of our government abroad, or grave disturbance at home if we take issue with Tennessee as to the constitutionality of her action here challenged. Nor need the appellants, in order to succeed in this action, ask the Court to enter upon policy determinations for which judicially manageable standards are lacking. Judicial standards under the Equal Protection Clause are well developed and familiar, and it has been open to courts since the enactment of the Fourteenth Amendment to determine, if, on the particular facts, they must, that a discrimination reflects no policy, but simply arbitrary and capricious action.

We conclude that the complaint's allegations of a denial of equal protection present a justiciable constitutional cause of action upon which appellants are entitled to a trial and a decision. The right asserted is within the reach of judicial protection under the Fourteenth Amendment.

The judgment of the District Court is reversed, and the cause is remanded for further proceedings consistent with this opinion.

MR. JUSTICE FRANKFURTER, *whom* **MR. JUSTICE HARLAN** *joins, dissenting.*

Such a massive repudiation of the experience of our whole past in asserting destructively novel judicial power demands a detailed analysis of the role of this Court in our constitutional scheme. Disregard of inherent limits in the effective exercise of the Court's "judicial Power" not only presages the futility of judicial intervention in the essentially political conflict of forces by which the relation between population and representation has time out of mind been, and now is, determined. It may well impair the Court's position as the ultimate organ of "the supreme Law of the Land" in that vast range of legal problems, often strongly entangled in popular feeling, on which this Court must pronounce. The Court's authority—possessed of neither the purse nor the sword—ultimately rests on sustained public confidence in its moral sanction. Such feeling must be nourished by the Court's complete detachment, in fact and in appearance, from political entanglements and by abstention from injecting itself into the clash of political forces in political settlements.

To charge courts with the task of accommodating the incommensurable factors of policy that underlie these mathematical puzzles is to attribute, however flatteringly, omnicompetence to judges. The Framers of the Constitution persistently rejected a proposal that embodied this assumption, and Thomas Jefferson never entertained it.

In effect, today's decision empowers the courts of the country to devise what should constitute the proper composition of the legislatures of the fifty States. If state courts should for one reason or another find themselves unable to discharge this task, the duty of doing so is put on the federal courts or on this Court, if State views do not satisfy this Court's notion of what is proper districting.

The Framers, carefully and with deliberate forethought, refused so to enthrone the judiciary. In this situation, as in others of like nature, appeal for relief does not belong here. Appeal must be to an informed, civically militant electorate. In a democratic society like ours, relief must come through an aroused popular conscience that sears the conscience of the people's representatives. In any event, there is nothing judicially more unseemly nor more self-defeating than for this Court to make *in terrorem* pronouncements, to indulge in merely empty rhetoric, sounding a word of

promise to the ear sure to be disappointing to the hope.

In sustaining appellants' claim, based on the Fourteenth Amendment, that the District Court may entertain this suit, this Court's uniform course of decision over the years is overruled or disregarded. Explicitly it begins with *Colegrove v. Green*, decided in 1946, but its roots run deep in the Court's historic adjudicatory process.

Colegrove held that a federal court should not entertain an action for declaratory and injunctive relief to adjudicate the constitutionality, under the Equal Protection Clause and other federal constitutional and statutory provisions, of a state statute establishing the respective districts for the State's election of Representatives to the Congress.

The *Colegrove* doctrine, in the form in which repeated decisions have settled it, was not an innovation. It represents long judicial thought and experience. From its earliest opinions, this Court has consistently recognized a class of controversies which do not lend themselves to judicial standards and judicial remedies.

The cases concerning war or foreign affairs, for example, are usually explained by the necessity of the country's speaking with one voice in such matters. While this concern alone undoubtedly accounts for many of the decisions, others do not fit the pattern. It would hardly embarrass the conduct of war were this Court to determine, in connection with private transactions between litigants, the date upon which war is to be deemed terminated. But the Court has refused to do so.

A controlling factor in such cases is that, decision respecting these kinds of complex matters of policy being traditionally committed not to courts but to the political agencies of government for determination by criteria of political expediency, there exists no standard ascertainable by settled judicial experience or process by reference to which a political decision affecting the question at issue between the parties can be judged. Where the question arises in the course of a litigation involving primarily the adjudication of other issues between the litigants, the Court accepts as a basis for adjudication the political departments' decision of it. But where its determination is the sole function to be served by the exercise of the judicial power, the Court will not entertain the action.

A federal court enforcing the Federal Constitution is not, to be sure, bound by the remedial doctrines of the state courts. But it must consider as pertinent to the propriety or impropriety of exercising its jurisdiction those state law effects of its decree which it cannot itself control. A federal court cannot provide the authority requisite to make a legislature the proper governing body of the State of Tennessee. And it cannot be doubted that the striking down of the statute here challenged on equal protection grounds, no less than on grounds of failure to reapportion decennially, would deprive the State of all valid apportionment legislation and deprive the State of an effective law-based legislative branch.

Although the District Court had jurisdiction in the very restricted sense of power to determine whether it could adjudicate the claim, the case is of that class of political controversy which, by the nature of its subject, is unfit for federal judicial action.

REYNOLDS v. SIMS

377 U.S. 533 (1964)

Opinion: Warren, joined by Black, Douglas, Brennan, White, Goldberg
Concurrence: Clark
Concurrence: Stewart
Dissent: Harlan

Though the Court took a significant step towards ending disproportionate representation in state legislatures by declaring such representational inequities justiciable in Baker v. Carr, *it was not until* Reynolds v. Sims *that the Court considered whether to actually strike down an apportionment scheme.*

MR. CHIEF JUSTICE WARREN

delivered the opinion of the Court.

On August 26, 1961, the original plaintiffs, residents, taxpayers and voters of Jefferson County, Alabama, filed a complaint in the United States District Court for the Middle District of Alabama, in their own behalf and on behalf of all similarly situated Alabama voters, challenging the apportionment of the Alabama Legislature.

Plaintiffs below alleged that the last apportionment of the Alabama Legislature was based on the 1900 federal census, despite the requirement of the State Constitution that the legislature be reapportioned decennially. They asserted that, since the population growth in the State from 1900 to 1960 had been uneven, Jefferson and other counties were now victims of serious discrimination with respect to the allocation of legislative representation. As a result of the failure of the legislature to reapportion itself, plaintiffs asserted, they were denied "equal suffrage in free and equal elections . . . and the equal protection of the laws," in violation of the Alabama Constitution and the Fourteenth Amendment to the Federal Constitution.

On July 21, 1962, the District Court held that the inequality of the existing representation in the Alabama Legislature violated the Equal Protection Clause of the Fourteenth Amendment, a finding which the Court noted had been "generally conceded" by the parties to the litigation, since population growth and shifts had converted the 1901 scheme, as perpetuated some 60 years later, into an invidiously discriminatory plan completely lacking in rationality. Population variance ratios of up to about 41-to-1 existed in the Senate, and up to about 16-to-1 in the House. Jefferson County, with over 600,000 people, was given only one senator, as was Lowndes County, with a 1960 population of only 15,417, and Wilcox County, with only 18,739 people.

Undeniably, the Constitution of the United States protects the right of all qualified citizens to vote, in state as well as in federal, elections. A consistent line of decisions by this Court in cases involving attempts to deny or restrict the right of suffrage has made this indelibly clear. . . . "Obviously included within the right to choose, secured by the Constitution, is the right of qualified voters within a state to cast their ballots and have them counted. . . ." Racially based gerrymandering, and the conducting of white primaries, both of which result in denying to some citizens their right to vote, have been held to be constitutionally impermissible. And the right of suffrage can be denied by a debasement or dilution of the weight of a citizen's vote just as effectively as by wholly prohibiting the free exercise of the franchise.

In *Baker v. Carr*, we held that a claim asserted under the Equal Protection Clause challenging the constitutionality of a State's apportionment of seats in its legislature, on the ground that the right to vote of certain citizens was effectively impaired, since debased and diluted, in effect presented a justiciable controversy subject to adjudication by federal courts. The spate of similar cases filed and decided by lower courts since our decision in *Baker* amply shows that the problem of state legislative malapportionment is one that is perceived to exist in a large number of the States. In *Baker*, a suit involving an attack on the apportionment of seats in the Tennessee Legislature, we remanded to the District Court, which had dismissed the action, for consideration on the merits. We intimated no view as to the proper constitutional standards for evaluating the validity of a state legislative apportionment scheme. Nor did we give any consideration to the question of appropriate remedies.

We indicated in *Baker*, however, that the Equal Protection Clause provides discoverable and manageable standards for use by lower courts in determining the constitutionality of a state legislative apportionment scheme, and we stated:

> Nor need the appellants, in order to succeed in this action, ask the Court to enter upon policy determinations for which judicially manageable standards are lacking. Judicial standards under the Equal Protection Clause are well developed and familiar, and it has been open to courts since the enactment of the Fourteenth Amendment to determine, if, on the particular facts, they must, that a discrimination reflects no policy, but simply arbitrary and capricious action.

In *Gray v. Sanders*, we held that the Georgia county unit system, applicable in statewide primary elections, was unconstitutional, since it resulted in a dilution of the weight of the votes of certain Georgia voters merely because of where they resided.... "The conception of political equality from the Declaration of Independence, to Lincoln's Gettysburg Address, to the Fifteenth, Seventeenth, and Nineteenth Amendments can mean only one thing—one person, one vote."

A predominant consideration in determining whether a State's legislative apportionment scheme constitutes an invidious discrimination violative of rights asserted under the Equal Protection Clause is that the rights allegedly impaired are individual and personal in nature. While the result of a court decision in a state legislative apportionment controversy may be to require the restructuring of the geographical distribution of seats in a state legislature, the judicial focus must be concentrated upon ascertaining whether there has been any discrimination against certain of the State's citizens which constitutes an impermissible impairment of their constitutionally protected right to vote.

Legislators represent people, not trees or acres. Legislators are elected by voters, not farms or cities or economic interests. As long as ours is a representative form of government, and our legislatures are those instruments of government elected directly by and directly representative of the people, the right to elect legislators in a free and unimpaired fashion is a bedrock of our political system. It could hardly be gainsaid that a constitutional claim had been asserted by an allegation that certain otherwise qualified voters had been entirely prohibited from voting for members of their state legislature. And, if a State should provide that the votes of citizens in one part of the State should be given two times, or five times, or 10 times the weight of votes of citizens in another part of the State, it could hardly be contended that the right to vote of those residing in the disfavored areas had not been effectively diluted. It would appear extraordinary to suggest that a State could be constitutionally permitted to enact a law providing that certain of the State's voters could vote two, five, or 10 times for their legislative representatives, while voters living elsewhere could vote only once. And it is inconceivable that a state law to the effect that, in counting votes for legislators, the votes of citizens in one part of the State would be multiplied by two, five, or 10, while the votes of persons in another area would be counted only at face value, could be constitutionally sustainable. Of course, the effect of state legislative districting schemes which give the same number of representatives to unequal numbers of constituents is identical. Overweighting and overvaluation of the votes of those living here has the certain effect of dilution and undervaluation of the votes of those living there. The resulting discrimination against those individual voters living in disfavored areas is easily demonstrable mathematically. Their right to vote is simply not the same right to vote as that of those living in a favored part of the State. Two, five, or 10 of them must vote before the effect of their voting is equivalent to that of their favored neighbor. Weighting the votes of citizens differently, by any method or means, merely because of where they happen to reside, hardly seems justifiable. One must be ever aware that the Constitution forbids "sophisticated, as well as simple-minded, modes of discrimination."

We are told that the matter of apportioning representation in a state legislature is a complex and many-faceted one. We are advised that States can rationally consider factors other than population in apportioning legislative representation. We are admonished not to restrict the power of the States to impose differing views as to political philosophy on their citizens. We are cautioned about the dangers of entering into political thickets and mathematical quagmires. Our answer is this: a denial of constitutionally protected rights demands judicial protection; our oath and our office require no less of us.

We hold that, as a basic constitutional standard, the Equal Protection Clause requires that the seats in both houses of a bicameral state legislature must be apportioned on a population basis. Simply stated, an individual's right to vote for state legislators is unconstitutionally impaired when its weight is in a substantial fashion diluted when compared with votes of citizens living in other parts of the State.

Since neither of the houses of the Alabama Legislature, under any of the three plans considered by the District Court, was apportioned on a population basis, we would be justified in proceeding no further. However, one of the proposed plans, that contained in the so-called 67-Senator Amendment, at least superficially resembles the scheme of legislative representation followed in the Federal Congress. Under this plan, each of Alabama's 67 counties is allotted one senator, and no counties are given more than one Senate seat. Arguably, this is analogous to the allocation of two Senate seats, in the Federal Congress, to each of the 50 States, regardless of population.

Much has been written since our decision in *Baker v. Carr* about the applicability of the so-called federal analogy to state legislative apportionment arrangements. After considering the matter, the court below concluded that no conceivable analogy could be drawn between the federal scheme and the apportionment of seats in the Alabama Legislature under the proposed constitutional amendment. We agree with the District Court, and find the federal analogy inapposite and irrelevant to state legislative districting schemes.

The system of representation in the two Houses of the Federal Congress is one ingrained in our Constitution, as part of the law of the land. It is one conceived out of compromise and concession indispensable to the establishment of our federal republic. Arising from unique historical circumstances, it is based on the consideration that, in establishing our type of federalism a group of formerly independent States bound themselves together under one national government. Admittedly, the original 13 States surrendered some of their sovereignty in agreeing to join together "to form a more perfect Union." But at the heart of our constitutional system remains the concept of separate and distinct governmental entities which have delegated some, but not all, of their formerly held powers to the single national government. The fact that almost three-fourths of our present States were never, in fact, independently sovereign does not detract from our view that the so-called federal analogy is inapplicable as a sustaining precedent for state legislative apportionments.

Political subdivisions of States—counties, cities, or whatever—never were and never have been considered as sovereign entities. Rather, they have been traditionally regarded as subordinate governmental instrumentalities created by the State to assist in the carrying out of state governmental functions.

Thus, we conclude that the plan contained in the 67-Senator Amendment for apportioning seats in the Alabama Legislature cannot be sustained by recourse to the so-called federal analogy. Nor can any other inequitable state legislative apportionment scheme be justified on such an asserted basis. This does not necessarily mean that such a plan is irrational, or involves something other than a "republican form of government." We conclude simply that such a plan is impermissible for the States under the Equal Protection Clause, since perforce resulting, in virtually every case, in submergence of the equal population principle in at least one house of a state legislature.

A State may legitimately desire to maintain the integrity of various political subdivisions, insofar as possible, and provide for compact districts of contiguous territory in designing a legislative apportionment scheme. Valid considerations may underlie such aims. Indiscriminate districting, without any regard for political subdivision or natural or historical boundary lines, may be little more than an open invitation to partisan gerrymandering. Single-member districts may be the rule in one State, while another State might desire to achieve some flexibility by creating multi-member or floterial districts. Whatever the means of accomplishment, the overriding objective must be substantial equality of population among the various districts, so that the vote of any citizen is approximately equal in weight to that of any other citizen in the State.

MR. JUSTICE HARLAN, *dissenting.*

Today's holding is that the Equal Protection Clause of the Fourteenth Amendment requires every State to structure its legislature so that all the members of each house represent substantially the same number of people; other factors may be given play only to the extent that they do not significantly encroach on this basic "population" principle. Whatever may be thought of this holding as a piece of political ideology—and even on that score, the political history and practices of this country from its earliest beginnings leave wide room for debate—I think it demonstrable that the Fourteenth Amendment does not impose this political tenet on the States or authorize this Court to do so.

Had the Court paused to probe more deeply into the matter, it would have found that the Equal Protection Clause was never intended to inhibit the States in choosing any democratic method they pleased for the apportionment of their legislatures. This is shown by the language of the Fourteenth Amendment taken as a whole, by the

understanding of those who proposed and ratified it, and by the political practices of the States at the time the Amendment was adopted. It is confirmed by numerous state and congressional actions since the adoption of the Fourteenth Amendment, and by the common understanding of the Amendment as evidenced by subsequent constitutional amendments and decisions of this Court before *Baker v. Carr, supra,* made an abrupt break with the past in 1962.

The failure of the Court to consider any of these matters cannot be excused or explained by any concept of "developing" constitutionalism. It is meaningless to speak of constitutional "development" when both the language and history of the controlling provisions of the Constitution are wholly ignored. Since it can, I think, be shown beyond doubt that state legislative apportionments, as such, are wholly free of constitutional limitations, save such as may be imposed by the Republican Form of Government Clause (Const., Art. IV, §4), the Court's action now bringing them within the purview of the Fourteenth Amendment amounts to nothing less than an exercise of the amending power by this Court.

So far as the Federal Constitution is concerned, the complaints in these cases should all have been dismissed below for failure to state a cause of action, because what has been alleged or proved shows no violation of any constitutional right.

SHAW v. RENO

509 U.S. 630 (1993)

Opinion: O'Connor, joined by
   Rehnquist, Scalia, Kennedy, Thomas
Dissent: White, joined by Blackmun,
   Stevens
Dissent: Blackmun
Dissent: Stevens
Dissent: Souter

It is clear that racial gerrymandering was traditionally used as a device to dilute the votes of African Americans, and the Voting Rights Act of 1965 made such practices illegal. But one puzzle we have seen throughout this chapter is whether a remedy for discrimination that is conscious of race runs afoul of the Equal Protection Clause. The

Voting Rights Act provides a role for the federal attorney general in overseeing districts that had a history of discrimination and gerrymandering. Such "covered jurisdictions" under the Act are required to submit any proposed changes to their voting or apportionment schemes to a federal panel for approval. In this case and in Miller v. Johnson, *which follows, two Southern states drew majority African-American congressional districts with the cooperation of the attorney general. These districts were drawn in an attempt to comply with the Voting Rights Act of 1965 and to further minority representation in Congress. The plaintiffs in these cases objected on the grounds that these districts violated the allegedly colorblind nature of the Equal Protection Clause by creating a segregated system of electoral politics. The cases pit the authority of the attorney general acting under the Voting Rights Act against the limitations of the Equal Protection Clause with regard to race-conscious polices. More generally, the Court asks whether the rectification of discrimination by creating majority-minority districts conflicts with the Equal Protection Clause. As you read, consider the extent to which you favor a colorblind or color-conscious interpretation of the Equal Protection Clause. How does that perspective impact the way you view the legitimacy of majority-minority districts?*

JUSTICE O'CONNOR *delivered the opinion of the Court.*

Forty of North Carolina's one hundred counties are covered by §5 of the Voting Rights Act of 1965, which prohibits a jurisdiction subject to its provisions from implementing changes in a "standard, practice, or procedure with respect to voting" without federal authorization.

The Attorney General, acting through the Assistant Attorney General for the Civil Rights Division, interposed a formal objection to the General Assembly's plan. The Attorney General specifically objected to the configuration of boundary lines drawn in the south central to southeastern region of the State. In the Attorney General's view, the General Assembly could have created a second majority minority district "to give effect to black and Native American voting strength in this area" by using boundary lines "no more irregular than [those] found elsewhere in the proposed plan," but failed to do so for "pretextual reasons."

The General Assembly enacted a revised redistricting plan that included a second majority black district. The General Assembly located the second district not in the south central to southeastern part of the State, but in the north central region along Interstate 85.

The first of the two majority black districts contained in the revised plan, District 1, is somewhat hook shaped. Centered in the northeast portion of the State, it moves southward until it tapers to a narrow band; then, with finger like extensions, it reaches far into the southernmost part of the State near the South Carolina border. District 1 has been compared to a "Rorschach ink blot test," and a "bug splattered on a windshield."

The second majority black district, District 12, is even more unusually shaped. It is approximately 160 miles long and, for much of its length, no wider than the I-85 corridor. It winds in snake like fashion through tobacco country, financial centers, and manufacturing areas "until it gobbles in enough enclaves of black neighborhoods." Northbound and southbound drivers on I-85 sometimes find themselves in separate districts in one county, only to "trade" districts when they enter the next county. Of the 10 counties through which District 12 passes, five are cut into three different districts; even towns are divided.

At one point the district remains contiguous only because it intersects at a single point with two other districts before crossing over them.

Appellants instituted the present action in the United States District Court for the Eastern District of North Carolina. Appellants alleged not that the revised plan constituted a political gerrymander, nor that it violated the "one person, one vote" principle, see *Reynolds v. Sims*, but that the State had created an unconstitutional *racial* gerrymander.

Appellants contended that the General Assembly's revised reapportionment plan violated several provisions of the United States Constitution, including the Fourteenth Amendment. They alleged that the General Assembly deliberately "create[d] two Congressional Districts in which a majority of black voters was concentrated arbitrarily—without regard to any other considerations, such as compactness, contiguousness, geographical boundaries, or political subdivisions" with the purpose "to create Congressional Districts along racial lines" and to assure the election of two black representatives to Congress.

That argument strikes a powerful historical chord: It is unsettling how closely the North Carolina plan resembles the most egregious racial gerrymanders of the past.

An understanding of the nature of appellants' claim is critical to our resolution of the case. In their complaint, appellants did not claim that the General Assembly's reapportionment plan unconstitutionally "diluted" white voting strength. They did not even claim to be white. Rather, appellants' complaint alleged that the deliberate segregation of voters into separate districts on the basis of race violated their constitutional right to participate in a "color blind" electoral process.

This Court never has held that race conscious state decisionmaking is impermissible in *all* circumstances. What appellants object to is redistricting legislation that is so extremely irregular on its face that it rationally can be viewed only as an effort to segregate the races for purposes of voting, without regard for traditional districting principles and without sufficiently compelling justification. For the reasons that follow, we conclude that appellants have stated a claim upon which relief can be granted under the Equal Protection Clause.

Classifications of citizens solely on the basis of race "are by their very nature odious to a free people whose institutions are founded upon the doctrine of equality." They threaten to stigmatize individuals by reason of their membership in a racial group and to incite racial hostility. Accordingly, we have held that the Fourteenth Amendment requires state legislation that expressly distinguishes among citizens because of their race to be narrowly tailored to further a compelling governmental interest.

These principles apply not only to legislation that contains explicit racial distinctions, but also to those rare statutes that, although race neutral, are, on their face, "unexplainable on grounds other than race."

Appellants contend that redistricting legislation that is so bizarre on its face that it is "unexplainable on grounds other than race" demands the same close scrutiny that we give other state laws that classify citizens by race. Our voting rights precedents support that conclusion.

In *Guinn v. United States*, the Court invalidated under the Fifteenth Amendment a statute that imposed a literacy requirement on voters but contained a "grandfather clause" applicable to individuals and their lineal descendants entitled to vote "on [or prior to] January 1, 1866." The determinative consideration for the Court was that the law, though ostensibly race-neutral, on its face "embod[ied] no exercise of judgment and rest[ed] upon no discernible reason" other than to circumvent the prohibitions of the Fifteenth Amendment. In other words, the statute was invalid because, on its face, it could not be explained on grounds other than race.

A reapportionment statute typically does not classify persons at all; it classifies tracts of land, or addresses. Moreover, redistricting differs from other kinds of state decisionmaking in that the legislature always is *aware* of race when it draws district lines, just as it is aware of age, economic status, religious and political persuasion, and a variety of other demographic factors. That sort of race consciousness does not lead inevitably to impermissible race discrimination. The district lines may be drawn, for example, to provide for compact districts of contiguous territory, or to maintain the integrity of political subdivisions.

The difficulty of proof, of course, does not mean that a racial gerrymander, once established, should receive less scrutiny under the Equal Protection Clause than other state legislation classifying citizens by race. Moreover, it seems clear to us that proof sometimes will not be difficult at all. "One need not use Justice Stewart's classic definition of obscenity—'I know it when I see it'—as an ultimate standard for judging the constitutionality of a gerrymander to recognize that dramatically irregular shapes may have sufficient probative force to call for an explanation."

Put differently, we believe that reapportionment is one area in which appearances do matter. A reapportionment plan that includes in one district individuals who belong to the same race, but who are otherwise widely separated by geographical and political boundaries, and who may have little in common with one another but the color of their skin, bears an uncomfortable resemblance to political apartheid. It reinforces the perception that members of the same racial group—regardless of their age, education, economic status, or the community in which the live—think alike, share the same political interests, and will prefer the same candidates at the polls. By perpetuating such notions, a racial gerrymander may exacerbate the very patterns of racial bloc voting that majority minority districting is sometimes said to counteract.

The message that such districting sends to elected representatives is equally pernicious. When a district obviously is created solely to effectuate the perceived common interests of one racial group, elected officials are more likely to believe that their primary obligation is to represent only the members of that group, rather than their constituency as a whole. This is altogether antithetical to our system of representative democracy.

In this case, the Attorney General suggested that North Carolina could have created a reasonably compact second majority minority district in the south central to southeastern part of the State. We express no view as to whether appellants successfully could have challenged such a district under the Fourteenth Amendment. We also do not decide whether appellants' complaint stated a claim under constitutional provisions other than the Fourteenth Amendment. Today we hold only that appellants have stated a claim under the Equal Protection Clause by alleging that the North Carolina General Assembly adopted a reapportionment scheme so irrational on its face that it can be understood only as an effort to segregate voters into separate voting districts because of their race, and that the separation lacks sufficient justification. If the allegation of racial gerrymandering remains uncontradicted, the District Court further must determine whether the North Carolina plan is narrowly tailored to further a compelling governmental interest. Accordingly, we reverse the judgment of the District Court and remand the case for further proceedings consistent with this opinion.

JUSTICE WHITE, *with whom* **JUSTICE BLACKMUN** *and* **JUSTICE STEVENS** *join, dissenting.*

... The grounds for my disagreement with the majority are simply stated: appellants have not presented a cognizable claim, because they have not alleged a cognizable injury. To date, we have held that only two types of state voting practices could give rise to a constitutional claim. The first involves direct and outright deprivation of the right to vote, for example by means of a poll tax or literacy test. ... Plainly, this variety is not implicated by appellants' allegations, and need not detain us further. The second type of unconstitutional practice is that which "affects the political strength of various groups," *Mobile v. Bolden* (Stevens, J., concurring in judgment), in violation of the Equal Protection Clause. As for this latter category, we have insisted that members of the political or racial group demonstrate that the challenged action have the intent and effect of unduly diminishing their influence on the political process. Although this severe burden has limited the number of successful suits, it was adopted for sound reasons.

The central explanation has to do with the nature of the redistricting process.

As the majority recognizes, "redistricting differs from other kinds of state decision-making in that the legislature always is aware of race when it draws district lines, just as it is *aware* of age, economic status, religious and political persuasion, and a variety of other demographic factors" (emphasis in original). "Being aware," in this context, is shorthand for "taking into account," and it hardly can be doubted that legislators routinely engage in the business of making electoral predictions based on group characteristics—racial, ethnic, and the like. ...

To the extent that no other racial group is injured, remedying a Voting Rights Act violation does not involve preferential treatment. Cf. *Wygant*, supra, at 295 (White, J., concurring in judgment). It involves, instead, an attempt to equalize treatment, and to provide minority voters with an effective voice in the political process. The Equal Protection Clause of the Constitution, surely, does not stand in the way.

IV

Since I do not agree that petitioners alleged an equal protection violation, and because the Court of Appeals faithfully followed the Court's prior cases, I dissent, and would affirm the judgment below.

MILLER v. JOHNSON

515 U.S. 900 (1995)

Opinion: Kennedy, joined by Rehnquist, O'Connor, Scalia, Thomas
Concurrence: O'Connor
Dissent: Stevens
Dissent: Ginsberg, joined by Stevens, Breyer and by Souter except in Part III-B

JUSTICE KENNEDY *delivered the opinion of the Court.*

The constitutionality of Georgia's congressional redistricting plan is at issue here. In *Shaw v. Reno*, we held that a plaintiff states a claim under the Equal Protection Clause by alleging that a state redistricting plan, on its face, has no rational explanation save as an effort to separate voters on the basis of race. The question we now decide is whether Georgia's new Eleventh District gives rise to a valid equal protection claim under the principles announced in *Shaw*, and, if so, whether it can be sustained nonetheless as narrowly tailored to serve a compelling governmental interest.

In 1965, the Attorney General designated Georgia a covered jurisdiction under §4(b) of the Voting Rights Act. In consequence, §5 of the Act requires Georgia to obtain either administrative preclearance by the Attorney General or approval by the United States District Court for the District of Columbia of any change in a "standard, practice, or procedure with respect to voting" made after November 1, 1964.

Between 1980 and 1990, one of Georgia's 10 congressional districts was a majority black district, that is, a majority of the district's voters were black. The 1990 Decennial Census indicated that Georgia's population of 6,478,216 persons, 27% of whom are black, entitled it to an additional eleventh congressional seat, prompting Georgia's General Assembly to redraw the State's congressional districts. Both the House and the Senate adopted redistricting guidelines which, among other things, required single-member districts of equal population, contiguous geography, non-dilution of minority voting strength, fidelity to precinct lines where possible, and compliance with §§2 and 5 of the Act. Only after these requirements were met did the guidelines permit drafters to consider other ends, such as maintaining the integrity of political subdivisions, preserving the core of existing districts, and avoiding contests between incumbents.

The legislature's plan contained two majority minority districts, the Fifth and Eleventh, and an additional district, the Second, in which blacks comprised just over 35% of the voting age population. Despite the plan's increase in the number of majority black districts from one to two and the absence of any evidence of an intent to discriminate against minority voters, the Department of Justice refused preclearance on January 21, 1992.

The General Assembly returned to the drawing board. A new plan was enacted and submitted for preclearance. The Justice Department refused preclearance again, relying on alternative plans proposing three majority minority districts. One of the alternative schemes relied on by the Department was the so called "max black" plan, drafted by the American Civil Liberties Union (ACLU) for the General Assembly's black caucus. The key to the ACLU's plan was the "Macon/Savannah trade." The dense black population in the Macon region would be transferred from the Eleventh District to the Second, converting the Second into a majority black district, and the Eleventh District's loss in black population would be offset by extending the Eleventh to include the black populations in Savannah. Pointing to the General Assembly's refusal to enact the Macon/Savannah swap into law, the Justice Department concluded that Georgia had "failed to explain adequately" its failure to create a third majority minority district.

Twice spurned, the General Assembly set out to create three majority minority districts to gain preclearance. Using the ACLU's "max black" plan as its benchmark, the General Assembly enacted a plan that

"bore all the signs of [the Justice Department's] involvement: The black population of Meriwether County was gouged out of the Third District and attached to the Second District by the narrowest of land bridges; Effingham and Chatham Counties were split to make way for the Savannah extension, which itself split the City of Savannah; and the plan as a whole split 26 counties, 23 more than the existing congressional districts."

The *Almanac of American Politics* has this to say about the Eleventh District: "Geographically, it is a monstrosity, stretching from Atlanta to Savannah. Its core is the plantation country in the center of the state, lightly populated, but heavily black. It links by narrow corridors the black neighborhoods in Augusta, Savannah and southern DeKalb County." Georgia's plan included three majority black districts, though, and received Justice Department preclearance on April 2, 1992.

On January 13, 1994, appellees, five white voters from the Eleventh District, filed this action against various state officials (Miller Appellants) in the United States District Court for the Southern District of Georgia. Their suit alleged that Georgia's Eleventh District was a racial gerrymander and so a violation of the Equal Protection Clause as interpreted in *Shaw v. Reno*.

A majority of the District Court panel agreed that the Eleventh District was invalid under *Shaw*, with one judge dissenting. After sharp criticism of the Justice Department for its use of partisan advocates in its dealings with state officials and for its close cooperation with the ACLU's vigorous advocacy of minority district maximization, the majority turned to a careful interpretation of our opinion in *Shaw*. It read *Shaw* to require strict scrutiny whenever race is the "overriding, predominant force" in the redistricting process. Citing much evidence of the legislature's purpose and intent in creating the final plan, as well as the irregular shape of the District (in particular several appendages drawn for the obvious purpose of putting black populations into the District), the court found that race was the overriding and predominant force in the districting determination. The court proceeded to apply strict scrutiny. Though rejecting proportional representation as a compelling interest, it was willing to assume that compliance with the Voting

Rights Act would be a compelling interest. As to the latter, however, the court found that the Act did not require three majority black districts, and that Georgia's plan for that reason was not narrowly tailored to the goal of complying with the Act.

Finding that the "evidence of the General Assembly's intent to racially gerrymander the Eleventh District is overwhelming, and practically stipulated by the parties involved," the District Court held that race was the predominant, overriding factor in drawing the Eleventh District. Appellants do not take issue with the court's factual finding of this racial motivation. Rather, they contend that evidence of a legislature's deliberate classification of voters on the basis of race cannot alone suffice to state a claim under *Shaw*. They argue that, regardless of the legislature's purposes, a plaintiff must demonstrate that a district's shape is so bizarre that it is unexplainable other than on the basis of race, and that appellees failed to make that showing here. Appellants' conception of the constitutional violation misapprehends our holding in *Shaw* and the Equal Protection precedent upon which *Shaw* relied.

Our observation in *Shaw* of the consequences of racial stereotyping was not meant to suggest that a district must be bizarre on its face before there is a constitutional violation. Nor was our conclusion in *Shaw* that in certain instances a district's appearance (or, to be more precise, its appearance in combination with certain demographic evidence) can give rise to an equal protection claim, a holding that bizarreness was a threshold showing, as appellants believe it to be. Our circumspect approach and narrow holding in *Shaw* did not erect an artificial rule barring accepted equal protection analysis in other redistricting cases. Shape is relevant not because bizarreness is a necessary element of the constitutional wrong or a threshold requirement of proof, but because it may be persuasive circumstantial evidence that race for its own sake, and not other districting principles, was the legislature's dominant and controlling rationale in drawing its district lines. The logical implication, as courts applying *Shaw* have recognized, is that parties may rely on evidence other than bizarreness to establish race-based districting.

Appellants and some of their *amici* argue that the Equal Protection Clause's general proscription on race-based decisionmaking does not obtain in the districting context because redistricting by definition involves racial considerations. Underlying their argument are the very stereotypical assumptions the Equal Protection Clause forbids. It is true that redistricting in most cases will implicate a political calculus in which various interests compete for recognition, but it does not follow from this that individuals of the same race share a single political interest.

In sum, we make clear that parties alleging that a State has assigned voters on the basis of race are neither confined in their proof to evidence regarding the district's geometry and makeup nor required to make a threshold showing of bizarreness. Today's case requires us further to consider the requirements of the proof necessary to sustain this equal protection challenge.

Federal court review of districting legislation represents a serious intrusion on the most vital of local functions. It is well settled that "reapportionment is primarily the duty and responsibility of the State." Electoral districting is a most difficult subject for legislatures, and so the States must have discretion to exercise the political judgment necessary to balance competing interests.

Although race-based decisionmaking is inherently suspect, until a claimant makes a showing sufficient to support

that allegation the good faith of a state legislature must be presumed. The courts, in assessing the sufficiency of a challenge to a districting plan, must be sensitive to the complex interplay of forces that enter a legislature's redistricting calculus. Redistricting legislatures will, for example, almost always be aware of racial demographics; but it does not follow that race predominates in the redistricting process. The distinction between being aware of racial considerations and being motivated by them may be difficult to make. This evidentiary difficulty, together with the sensitive nature of redistricting and the presumption of good faith that must be accorded legislative enactments, requires courts to exercise extraordinary caution in adjudicating claims that a state has drawn district lines on the basis of race. The plaintiff's burden is to show, either through circumstantial evidence of a district's shape and demographics or more direct evidence going to legislative purpose, that race was the predominant factor motivating the legislature's decision to place a significant number of voters within or without a particular district. To make this showing, a plaintiff must prove that the legislature subordinated traditional race neutral districting principles, including but not limited to compactness, contiguity, respect for political subdivisions or communities defined by actual shared interests, to racial considerations. Where these or other race neutral considerations are the basis for redistricting legislation, and are not subordinated to race, a state can "defeat a claim that a district has been gerrymandered on racial lines."

In our view, the District Court applied the correct analysis, and its finding that race was the predominant factor motivating the drawing of the Eleventh District was not clearly erroneous. The court found it was "exceedingly obvious" from the shape of the Eleventh District, together with the relevant racial demographics, that the drawing of narrow land bridges to incorporate within the District outlying appendages containing nearly 80% of the district's total black population was a deliberate attempt to bring black populations into the district. Although this evidence is quite compelling, we need not determine whether it was, standing alone, sufficient to establish a *Shaw* claim that the Eleventh District is unexplainable other than by race. The District Court had before it considerable additional evidence showing that the General Assembly was motivated by a predominant, overriding desire to assign black populations to the Eleventh District and thereby permit the creation of a third majority black district in the Second.

The court found that "it became obvious," both from the Justice Department's objection letters and the three preclearance rounds in general, "that [the Justice Department] would accept nothing less than abject surrender to its maximization agenda." It further found that the General Assembly acquiesced and as a consequence was driven by its overriding desire to comply with the Department's maximization demands.

Race was, as the District Court found, the predominant, overriding factor explaining the General Assembly's decision to attach to the Eleventh District various appendages containing dense majority black populations. As a result, Georgia's congressional redistricting plan cannot be upheld unless it satisfies strict scrutiny, our most rigorous and exacting standard of constitutional review.

There is a "significant state interest in eradicating the effects of past racial discrimination." The State does not argue, however, that it created the Eleventh District to remedy past discrimination, and with good reason: there is little doubt that the State's true interest in designing the Eleventh District was creating a third majority black district to satisfy the Justice Department's preclearance demands. Whether or not in some cases compliance with the Voting Rights Act, standing alone, can provide a compelling interest independent of any interest in remedying past discrimination, it cannot do so here. As we suggested in *Shaw*, compliance with federal antidiscrimination laws cannot justify race-based districting where the challenged district was not reasonably necessary under a constitutional reading and application of those laws. The congressional plan challenged here was not required by the Voting Rights Act under a correct reading of the statute.

We do not accept the contention that the State has a compelling interest in complying with whatever preclearance mandates the Justice Department issues. When a state governmental entity seeks to justify race-based remedies to cure the effects of past discrimination, we do not accept the government's mere assertion that the remedial action is required. Rather, we insist on a strong basis in evidence of the harm being remedied.

The Voting Rights Act, and its grant of authority to the federal courts to uncover official efforts to abridge minorities' right to vote, has been of vital importance in eradicating invidious discrimination from the electoral process and enhancing the legitimacy of our political institutions. Only if our political system and our society cleanse themselves of that discrimination will all members of the polity share an equal opportunity to gain public office regardless of race. As a Nation we share both the obligation and the aspiration of working toward this end. It takes a shortsighted and unauthorized view of the Voting Rights Act to invoke that statute, which has played a decisive role in redressing some of our worst forms of discrimination, to demand the very racial stereotyping the Fourteenth Amendment forbids.

The judgment of the District Court is affirmed, and the case is remanded for further proceedings consistent with this decision.

JUSTICE GINSBURG, *with whom* **JUSTICES STEVENS** *and* **BREYER** *join, and with whom* **JUSTICE SOUTER** *joins except as to Part III-B, dissenting.*

Legislative districting is highly political business. This Court has generally respected the competence of state legislatures to attend to the task. When race is the issue, however, we have recognized the need for judicial intervention to prevent dilution of minority voting strength. Generations of rank discrimination against African-Americans, as citizens and voters, account for that surveillance....

C

... Only after litigation—under either the Voting Rights Act, the Court's new *Miller* standard, or both—will States now be assured that plans conscious of race are safe. Federal judges in large numbers may be drawn into the fray. This enlargement of the judicial role is unwarranted. The reapportionment plan that resulted from Georgia's political process merited this Court's approbation, not its condemnation. Accordingly, I dissent.

NORTHWEST AUSTIN MUNICIPAL UTILITY DISTRICT NO. 1 v. HOLDER

557 U.S. _____ (2009)

Opinion: Roberts, joined by Stevens, Scalia, Kennedy, Souter, Ginsburg, Breyer, Alito
Partial Concurrence, Partial Dissent: Thomas

As you previously read, the Voting Rights Act of 1965 requires many Southern states to submit any changes to their voting systems for approval by the federal government. In the following case, a small utility district that, like all other state- or municipality-run agencies that rely on elections in Texas, was subject to this requirement challenged the requirement's constitutionality. Notice as you read the distinction between the question of whether an exemption or "bailout" might be granted to Section 5 of the Voting Rights Act and the question of whether this provision is unconstitutional. As you read Chief Justice John Roberts's *opinion for the Court, consider whether the Voting Rights Act's continuing imposition of burdens on certain states' electoral systems are justified by the Fifteenth Amendment. Notice too Justice Clarence Thomas's separate opinion, which issues a broad attack on the constitutionality of a key provision of the Voting Rights Act of 1965. Is Justice Thomas's position required by the notion of colorblind constitutionalism? Is it correct?*

CHIEF JUSTICE ROBERTS *delivered the opinion of the Court.*

The plaintiff in this case is a small utility district raising a big question—the constitutionality of §5 of the Voting Rights Act. The district has an elected board, and is required by §5 to seek preclearance from federal authorities in Washington, D.C., before it can change anything about those elections. This is required even though there has never been any evidence of racial discrimination in voting in the district.

The district filed suit seeking relief from these preclearance obligations under the "bailout" provision of the Voting Rights Act. That provision allows the release of a "political subdivision" from the preclearance requirements if certain rigorous conditions are met. The court below denied relief, concluding that bailout was unavailable to a political subdivision like the utility district that did not register its own voters. The district appealed, arguing that the Act imposes no such limitation on bailout, and that if it does, the preclearance requirements are unconstitutional.

That constitutional question has attracted ardent briefs from dozens of interested parties, but the importance of the question does not justify our rushing to decide it. Quite the contrary: Our usual practice is to avoid the unnecessary resolution of constitutional questions. We agree that the district is eligible under the Act to seek bailout. We therefore reverse, and do not reach the constitutionality of §5. . . .

II

The historic accomplishments of the Voting Rights Act are undeniable. When it was first passed, unconstitutional discrimination was rampant and the "registration of voting-age whites ran roughly 50 percentage points or more ahead" of black registration in many covered States. *Katzenbach*. Today, the registration gap between white and black voters is in single digits in the covered States; in some of those States, blacks now register and vote at higher rates than whites. Similar dramatic improvements have occurred for other racial minorities. "[M]any of the first generation barriers to minority voter registration and voter turnout that were in

place prior to the [Voting Rights Act] have been eliminated." . . .

Section 5 goes beyond the prohibition of the Fifteenth Amendment by suspending *all* changes to state election law—however innocuous—until they have been precleared by federal authorities in Washington, D.C. The preclearance requirement applies broadly, *NAACP v. Hampton County Election Comm'n*, and in particular to every political subdivision in a covered State, no matter how small, *United States v. Sheffield Bd. of Comm'rs*.

Some of the conditions that we relied upon in upholding this statutory scheme in *Katzenbach* and *City of Rome* have unquestionably improved. Things have changed in the South. Voter turnout and registration rates now approach parity. Blatantly discriminatory evasions of federal decrees are rare. And minority candidates hold office at unprecedented levels.

These improvements are no doubt due in significant part to the Voting Rights Act itself, and stand as a monument to its success. Past success alone, however, is not adequate justification to retain the preclearance requirements. It may be that these improvements are insufficient and that conditions continue to warrant preclearance under the Act. But the Act imposes current burdens and must be justified by current needs.

The Act also differentiates between the States, despite our historic tradition that all the States enjoy "equal sovereignty." *United States v. Louisiana.* Distinctions can be justified in some cases. "The doctrine of the equality of States . . . does not bar . . . remedies for *local* evils which have subsequently appeared." *Katzenbach.* But a departure from the fundamental principle of equal sovereignty requires a showing that a statute's disparate geographic coverage is sufficiently related to the problem that it targets.

These federalism concerns are underscored by the argument that the preclearance requirements in one State would be unconstitutional in another. See *Georgia v. Ashcroft* (Kennedy, J., concurring) ("Race cannot be the predominant factor in redistricting under our decision in *Miller v. Johnson*. Yet considerations of race that would doom a redistricting plan under the Fourteenth Amendment or §2 seem to be what save it under §5"). Additional constitutional concerns are raised in saying that this tension between §§2 and 5 must persist in covered jurisdictions and not elsewhere.

The evil that §5 is meant to address may no longer be concentrated in the jurisdictions singled out for preclearance. The statute's coverage formula is based on data that is now more than 35 years old, and there is considerable evidence that it fails to account for current political conditions. For example, the racial gap in voter registration and turnout is lower in the States originally covered by §5 than it is nationwide. Congress heard warnings from supporters of extending §5 that the evidence in the record did not address "systematic differences between the covered and the non-covered areas of the United States[,] . . . and, in fact, the evidence that is in the record suggests that there is more similarity than difference."

The parties do not agree on the standard to apply in deciding whether, in light of the foregoing concerns, Congress exceeded its Fifteenth Amendment enforcement power in extending the preclearance requirements. The district argues that "[t]here must be a congruence and proportionality between the injury to be prevented or remedied and the means adopted to that end,"; the Federal Government asserts that it is enough that the legislation be a "rational means to effectuate the constitutional prohibition." That question has been extensively briefed in this case, but we need not resolve it. The Act's preclearance requirements and its coverage formula raise serious constitutional questions under either test.

In assessing those questions, we are keenly mindful of our institutional role. We fully appreciate that judging the constitutionality of an Act of Congress is "the gravest and most delicate duty that this Court is called on to perform." *Blodgett v. Holden* (Holmes, J., concurring). "The Congress is a coequal branch of government whose Members take the same oath we do to uphold the Constitution of the United States." *Rostker v. Goldberg*. The Fifteenth Amendment empowers "Congress," not the Court, to determine in the first instance what legislation is needed to enforce it. Congress amassed a sizable record in support of its decision to extend the preclearance requirements, a record the District Court determined "document[ed] contemporary racial discrimination in covered states." The District Court also found that the record "demonstrat[ed] that section 5 prevents discriminatory voting changes" by "quietly but effectively deterring discriminatory changes."

We will not shrink from our duty "as the bulwar[k] of a limited constitution against legislative encroachments," *The Federalist* No. 78, but "[i]t is a well-established principle governing the prudent exercise of this Court's jurisdiction that normally the Court will not decide a constitutional question if there is some other ground upon which to dispose of the case," *Escambia County v. McMillan*. Here, the district also raises a statutory claim that it is eligible to bail out under §§4 and 5. Justice Thomas argues that the principle of constitutional avoidance has no pertinence here. He contends that even if we resolve the district's statutory argument in its favor, we would still have to reach the constitutional question, because the district's statutory argument would not afford it all the relief it seeks.

We disagree. The district expressly describes its constitutional challenge to §5 as being "in the alternative" to its statutory argument. The district's counsel confirmed this at oral argument. We therefore turn to the district's statutory argument.

III

. . . More than 40 years ago, this Court concluded that "exceptional conditions" prevailing in certain parts of the country justified extraordinary legislation otherwise unfamiliar to our federal system. *Katzenbach*. In part due to the success of that legislation, we are now a very different Nation. Whether conditions continue to justify such legislation is a difficult constitutional question we do not answer today. We conclude instead that the Voting Rights Act permits all political subdivisions, including the district in this case, to seek relief from its preclearance requirements.

The judgment of the District Court is reversed, and the case is remanded for further proceedings consistent with this opinion.

JUSTICE THOMAS, *concurring in the judgment in part and dissenting in part.*

This appeal presents two questions: first, whether appellant is entitled to bail out from coverage under the Voting Rights Act of 1965 (VRA); and second, whether the preclearance requirement of §5 of the VRA is unconstitutional. Because the Court's statutory decision does not provide appellant with full relief, I conclude that it is inappropriate to apply the constitutional avoidance doctrine in this case. I would therefore decide the constitutional issue presented and hold that §5 exceeds Congress' power to enforce the Fifteenth Amendment.

B

Several important principles emerge from *Katzenbach* and the decisions that followed it. First, §5 prohibits more state voting practices than those necessarily encompassed by the explicit prohibition on intentional discrimination found in the text of the Fifteenth Amendment. The explicit command of the Fifteenth Amendment is a prohibition on state practices that in fact deny individuals the right to vote "on account of" race, color, or previous servitude. In contrast, §5 is the quintessential prophylaxis; it "goes beyond the prohibition of the Fifteenth Amendment by suspending *all* changes to state election law—however innocuous—until they have been precleared by federal authorities in Washington, D.C."

Indeed, §5's preclearance requirement is "one of the most extraordinary remedial provisions in an Act noted for its broad remedies. Even the Department of Justice has described it as a 'substantial departure . . . from ordinary concepts of our federal system'; its encroachment on state sovereignty is significant and undeniable." *United States v. Sheffield Bd. of Comm'rs* (Stevens, J., dissenting). This "encroachment is especially troubling because it destroys local control of the means of self-government, one of the central values of our polity." *City of Rome* (Powell, J., dissenting). More than 40 years after its enactment, this intrusion has become increasingly difficult to justify.

C

The extensive pattern of discrimination that led the Court to previously uphold §5 as enforcing the Fifteenth Amendment no longer exists. Covered jurisdictions are not now engaged in a systematic campaign to deny black citizens access to the ballot through intimidation and violence.

And the days of "grandfather clauses, property qualifications, 'good character' tests, and the requirement that registrants 'understand' or 'interpret' certain matter," *Katzenbach*, are gone. There is thus currently no concerted effort in these jurisdictions to engage in the "unremitting and ingenious defiance of the Constitution" that served as the constitutional basis for upholding the "uncommon exercise of congressional power" embodied in §5.

The lack of sufficient evidence that the covered jurisdictions currently engage in the type of discrimination that underlay the enactment of §5 undermines any basis for retaining it. Punishment for long past sins is not a legitimate basis for imposing a forward-looking preventative measure that has already served its purpose. Those supporting §5's reenactment argue that without it these jurisdictions would return to the racially discriminatory practices of 30 and 40 years ago. But there is no evidence that public officials stand ready, if given the chance, to again engage in concerted acts of violence, terror, and subterfuge in order to keep minorities from voting. Without such evidence, the charge can only be premised on outdated assumptions about racial attitudes in the covered jurisdictions. Admitting that a prophylactic law as broad as §5 is no longer constitutionally justified based on current evidence of discrimination is not a sign of defeat. It is an acknowledgment of victory.

SYNTHESIS QUESTIONS FOR FURTHER DISCUSSION: CHAPTER 8 SECTION C

1. Is the Supreme Court's intervention into questions of how to draw congressional districts illegitimate judicial activism? Does it violate the right of the elected branches to govern themselves and enact legislation? Raoul Berger is quite critical of the idea that courts, rather than legislators, should act as defenders of individual rights. He writes, "Platonic Guardians have enjoyed small favor in our polity." Is this view consistent with John Hart Ely's theory of judicial review, which we introduced in Chapter 2?

2. Many have argued that for American society to overcome the evils of racism it is essential not only that African Americans have a right to vote, but that they be adequately represented in Congress. This representation is essential to putting issues that affect the African-American community on the agenda of congressional legislation, and in getting legislation passed that serves that community. But is there a tension between this goal and the principle of one person, one vote? Consider this in the context of *Shaw v. Reno*, in which the Court considered whether a "racial gerrymander" intended to ensure African-American representation in the House of Representatives was unconstitutional. Arguably, this case pits two ideas of equality at odds, one focused on equality in racial representation and one idea focused on the idea of equal voting strength.

3. As you have seen, the Voting Rights Act of 1965 authorizes a federal role in overseeing the drawing of legislative districts, but do you agree with Justice Clarence Thomas's separate opinion in *Northwest Austin Municipal Utility District No. 1 v. Holder*, in which he argues that those provisions of the Voting Rights Act run afoul of the Constitution? How might the analysis in *Shaw v. Reno* and *Miller v. Johnson* be used to counter Justice Thomas's arguments?

4. Can you reconcile the Court's approach to questions of equal protection in *Gratz v. Bollinger* and *Grutter v. Bollinger* with the approach used in *Shaw v. Reno* and *Miller v. Johnson*? Is the Court more accepting of a color-conscious approach in one of these areas than it is in the others?

KEY TERMS

bipartisan gerrymander: A district drawn on a bipartisan basis in order to guarantee the reelection of incumbents of both parties.

colorblind: The view that the Constitution cannot take race into account in equal protection analysis, often used as a basis for opposing affirmative action and racial gerrymanders.

color-conscious: The view that we must take race into account to combat discrimination in matters of deep segregation and equal protection.

de facto: A practical reality that is not established in law.

de jure: Established in or concerned with law.

Jim Crow: A name for the system of segregation at one time prevailing in the southern United States.

legal positivism: The view that there is a separation between legal validity and morality.

majority-minority districts: Districts drawn in such a way as to make a traditionally disadvantaged population the majority. The result aims for the election of minority officials.

Missouri Compromise: An agreement passed by Congress in 1820 to ban slavery in parts of the former Louisiana Territory; struck down in *Dred Scott v. Sandford*.

political question doctrine: The idea that the Supreme Court should not intervene in matters concerning the other branches of government because the issue is fundamentally "political," not legal; the doctrine is sometimes applied to issues of foreign policy.

poll tax: A tax imposed on each citizen as a prerequisite to voting. Given the extreme poverty of many African Americans after the Civil War, the poll tax was often used as a strategy for disenfranchisement.

racial gerrymander: The shaping of legislative districts to account for race. In particular, in the modern context, this refers to an attempt to create by gerrymander majority-minority districts or some density of minority voters that falls short of a majority.

racial quota: A method of affirmative action whereby numerical floors are used to ensure the representation of racial minorities.

vote dilution: The drawing of districts in such a way so as to weaken the voting power of a particular voting bloc.

CHAPTER 9

GENDER, SEXUAL ORIENTATION, AND EQUALITY

In the previous chapter, we looked at the Equal Protection Clause of the Fourteenth Amendment as it related to questions of race. As we saw in those cases, the Court applied strict scrutiny, which presumes that suspect classifications based on race are constitutionally invalid. In this chapter, we ask whether the Equal Protection Clause requires similar protections against discrimination based on gender and sexual orientation. Like African Americans, women have experienced a prolonged history of unequal treatment in America. Many have argued that gender-based classifications are just as morally arbitrary as race-based discrimination and therefore gender-based distinctions should receive the same level of scrutiny as those based on race. Similarly, we explore the protections afforded to gay citizens under the Equal Protection Clause. Some proponents of gay rights have suggested that discrimination against gays is as invidious as gender- and race-based distinctions and therefore should also receive strict scrutiny. As we will see in this chapter, the Court has extended protection to women and gays, but it has done so in a way that is distinct from the standard it uses for race and ethnicity under the Equal Protection Clause.

It is helpful to think about discrimination based on gender by considering the degree to which gender- and race-based classifications are analogous to one another. The reading by Susan Okin should help you to think about this issue because it answers the contention that differences based on gender are biological in contrast to distinctions based on race. In distinguishing between gender and sex, Okin claims that many of the assumed differences between men and women are not biological in nature, but rather socially constructed. Although differences between men and women might sometimes seem to be based on innate characteristics, Okin suggests that these differences reflect discriminatory upbringing and prevailing social norms. On Okin's view, most issues related to discrimination between men and women rest on arbitrary distinctions. In contrast, the reading by Phyllis Schlafly emphasizes that real biological differences between men and women lie at the root of seemingly discriminatory practices. Moreover, Schlafly suggests that these distinctions and the differential treatment that follows from them actually improve the welfare of women in society. We include Schlafly's view in part because it is often seen as central to the defeat of the Equal Rights Amendment (ERA), which we also discuss in this chapter.

Motivated in large part by arguments about the arbitrariness of sex discrimination, the ERA was first proposed in 1923. It followed on the heels of the Nineteenth Amendment's guarantee of suffrage for women in 1920. Proponents of the ERA, during this "first wave of feminism," had hoped for a pair of amendments that would reflect the Fourteenth and Fifteenth Amendments' guarantees of equality and voting rights to African Americans. Advocates of the ERA finally secured its passage in Congress in 1972, with a proviso: If three-quarters of the states had not ratified it within seven years, it could not take effect. Ultimately, opponents of the Amendment, such as Schlafly, secured its defeat. If the Amendment had been passed, it likely would have triggered the kind of strict scrutiny that the Court applies in race-based cases. But for reasons detailed here by Jane Mansbridge, it was not ratified.

Despite the failure to ratify the ERA, however, the Supreme Court, beginning in a series of cases in the 1970s, has applied the Equal Protection Clause of the Fourteenth Amendment to invalidate some gender-based classifications. The Court has decided that gender-based distinctions should receive an intermediate level of scrutiny. In *Craig v. Boren*, the Court establishes this new level of intermediate scrutiny, stating that "classifications by gender must serve important governmental objectives and must be substantially related to achievement of those objectives." In strict scrutiny cases, such as those involving racial classifications, the state requires a "compelling interest" and a "narrowly tailored" governmental purpose. Similarly, in gender-based cases, the Court requires a high level of justification from the government in order to establish that such laws are consistent with the Equal Protection Clause. But rather than requiring a "compelling" state interest, the Court requires simply an "important" governmental objective. Moreover, the Court requires not narrowly tailored means, but merely that the policy being challenged be substantially related to the goals of the state.

This area of law, however, is not straightforward. At times, the Court seems to take into account the differences between gender and sex. It sometimes suggests that biological differences, such as those related to pregnancy, are not arbitrary, and in such cases the Court seems to apply not intermediate scrutiny but rather the more lax rational review test. As you read these cases, think about the way in which the distinction between sex and gender, crucial to the debate between Okin and Schlafly, also plays a role in the Court's jurisprudence.

As in the case of gender, there is a major constitutional debate about the kind of scrutiny discrimination against gay citizens should receive under the Equal Protection Clause. In considering the kind of scrutiny that the Supreme Court applies to cases of gay rights, it might also be helpful to recall its category of "discrete and insular" minorities proposed in the *United States v. Carolene Products* Footnote Four that we discussed in Chapter 2. While African Americans are arguably a discrete and insular minority, women are discrete (they are recognizable), but not insular (they are integrated into society, not segregated). Are gay citizens a discrete and insular minority? Should this category be central to determining the level of scrutiny gays receive under the Equal Protection Clause? As you read the cases in the chapter, ask whether the characteristics of these three groups really do justify differing levels of scrutiny.

In deciding how to balance the rights of gay citizens against the interest of the state, the Supreme Court has applied its lowest level of scrutiny. While race-based classifications require a compelling state interest and gender-based classifications an important interest, laws that make a distinction based on sexual orientation must merely have a "rational basis" in order to be constitutionally justified. In employing the rational review test, the Court has extended protections of rights to gay citizens. In *Romer v. Evans*, the Court invalidated a Colorado law that it deemed to be based in "animus" or hatred towards gay citizens. In the Court's view, any law based in animus lacks rational justification and cannot constitute a legitimate governmental interest under the Equal Protection Clause. It is important to note that the Court, while employing the rational review standard, has not ruled out the possibility of employing a higher level of scrutiny in Equal Protection analysis of gay rights. As you read through this chapter, consider whether it should apply a higher level of scrutiny.

The current debate over gay rights centers on the question of whether the Equal Protection Clause protects a right to same-sex marriage. As we saw in Chapter 8, in *Loving v. Virginia*, the Court invalidated so-called anti-miscegenation laws prohibiting interracial marriage on grounds of equal protection. Consider whether this precedent also requires the finding that laws prohibiting same-sex couples from marrying are unconstitutional. In *In Re Marriage Cases*, the California Supreme Court applied the California Constitution's equivalent of the Equal Protection Clause to reach precisely this finding. Given the U.S. Supreme Court's rational review standard in gay rights cases, is it likely to make a similar move? As we saw in Chapter 8, *Loving v. Virginia* asserts a fundamental right to freely choose one's marriage partner. Does this right to marry apply only to straight couples, or also to same-sex couples?

We also include in this chapter another excerpt from *Lawrence v. Texas*, which deals with the question of whether a law banning homosexual sodomy is unconstitutional. You will remember from Chapter 7 that the Court struck down this law under the doctrine of substantive due process. However, in a concurrence, U.S. Supreme Court Justice Sandra Day O'Connor suggests that the Equal Protection Clause would be a more appropriate constitutional hook for reaching the same result. As you read this case, consider whether equal protection should replace substantive due process protections in this area or supplement it.

A. SEX AND GENDER

What level of scrutiny should gender discrimination receive? Does the question of "innate difference" aid constitutional inquiry? How does gender equality relate to freedom?

In the last chapter, we saw that the Court employs strict scrutiny in examining explicit distinctions based on race. According to this standard, there is a strong presumption against laws that explicitly distinguish based on race, ethnicity, or national origin. The justification for this presumption against such laws is grounded in the claim that such distinctions are arbitrary and morally unacceptable, in large part because an individual has no effective control over his or her race. But what is to be said about distinctions between men and women that are made explicit in legislation or policy? Should the Court employ as strong a presumption against such laws as it does in the case of race? Or are there arguments for employing a distinct level of scrutiny? As you will see throughout this chapter, there have been a variety of proposals both by the courts and by Congress that attempt to answer this question. This specific argument about the appropriate level of scrutiny is grounded in a deeper philosophical debate regarding the proper analogy (or lack thereof) between issues of race and those of gender and sex.

Until the mid-1970s, the Supreme Court rejected the idea that there should be heightened scrutiny for cases involving distinctions based on gender. The Court assumed that the Equal Protection Clause was fundamentally concerned with issues of discrimination based on race, ethnicity, and national origin. But even though it did not employ a "heightened" level of scrutiny, it still struck down what it regarded as arbitrary laws that discriminated based on gender or sex. For instance, in *Reed v. Reed*, the Court struck down as unconstitutionally discriminatory a law that gave men preference over women in matters of inheritance. The Court here employed what is known as the "rational basis test." You will recall that in contrast to strict scrutiny, which presumes the invalidity of a law, rational basis review assumes that a law is valid unless it can be shown that there is no acceptable reason for the legislation. This standard imposes a very heavy burden on those who would seek to invalidate a law. Nonetheless, the Court has invalidated some laws because it could discern no rational reason for their existence. For instance, as you will see in *Romer v. Evans*, the Court struck down a plebiscite that discriminated against gay citizens on the grounds that it lacked a rational basis.

Needless to say, despite the Court's earlier jurisprudence on the matter, many thinkers and citizens disagreed with the claim that discrimination based on gender and sex should be treated differently than discrimination based on race. As early as the 1920s, an "Equal Rights Amendment" was introduced in Congress. We focus here on the ERA passed by Congress in 1972 and in particular the debate about the ratification of that Amendment. The Amendment's text mirrored the language of the Fourteenth Amendment and would have had the effect of raising the level of scrutiny in distinctions based on gender from rational-basis review to strict scrutiny. Jane Mansbridge argues for the ERA as an important contribution to constitutional interpretation by citizens and suggests some explanations for why it was not ratified.

At the same time as the Amendment was being considered for ratification by the states, the Supreme Court adopted a new jurisprudence on women's rights, which we examine here in depth. Although the Court did not adopt a standard of strict scrutiny, as the ERA would have demanded, it did begin employing a higher level of scrutiny than rational review. Adopting "intermediate" scrutiny in between both rational basis and strict scrutiny in *Craig v. Boren*, the Court announced a new standard for applying the Equal Protection Clause to discrimination based on sex and gender. As we have noted, with this level of scrutiny, the state must show that it has an "important interest" in justifying distinctions between men and women and that its means is "substantially related" to its goal. In short, though the ERA was never fully ratified, the Court did adopt some of its ambitions, but still stopped short of endorsing a standard of strict scrutiny. As you read this chapter, ask yourself whether you think the Court ought to have adopted strict scrutiny as the ERA would have required.

Susan Okin

ON THE DISTINCTION BETWEEN SEX AND GENDER

in Justice, Gender, and the Family

New York, NY: Basic Books (1991)

Susan Okin was one of the most prominent political theorists to seriously examine the role that gender and sex play both in political thinking and in law. In her view, central to any theory that takes the rights of women seriously is recognition of the difference between sex and gender. We pay particularly close attention to Okin's contributions to political theory because of her discussion of this distinction and its importance for thinking about women's rights. Consider what Okin says about "false gender neutrality" and its relationship to ensuring the rights of women.

A central source of injustice for women these days is that the law, most noticeably in the event of divorce, treats more or less as equals those whom custom, workplace discrimination, and the still conventional division of labor within the family have made very unequal. Central to this socially created inequality are two commonly made but inconsistent presumptions: that women are primarily responsible for the rearing of children; and that serious and committed members of the work force (regardless of class) do not have primary responsibility, or even shared responsibility, for the rearing of children. The old assumption of the workplace, still implicit, is that workers have wives at home. It is built not only into the structure and expectations of the workplace but into other crucial social institutions, such as schools, which make no attempt to take account, in their scheduled hours or vacations, of the fact that parents are likely to hold jobs.

Now, of course, many wage workers do not have wives at home. Often, they *are* wives and mothers, or single, separated, or divorced mothers of small children. But neither the family nor the workplace has taken much account of this fact. Employed wives still do by far the greatest proportion of unpaid family work, such as child care and housework. Women are far more likely to take time out of the workplace or to work part-time because of family responsibilities than are their husbands or male partners. And they are much more likely to move because of their husbands' employment needs or opportunities than their own. All these tendencies, which are due to a number of factors, including the sex segregation and discrimination of the workplace itself, tend to be cyclical in their effects: wives advance more slowly than their husbands at work and thus gain less seniority, and the discrepancy between their wages increases over time. Then, because both the power structure of the family and what is regarded as consensual "rational" family decision making reflect the fact that the husband usually earns more, it will become even less likely as time goes on that the unpaid work of the family will be shared between the spouses. Thus the cycle of inequality is perpetuated. Often hidden from view within a marriage, it is in the increasingly likely event of marital breakdown that the socially constructed inequality of married women is at its most visible.

This is what I mean when I say that gender-structured marriage makes women vulnerable. These are not matters of natural necessity, as some people would believe. Surely nothing in our natures dictates that men should not be equal participants in the rearing of their children. Nothing in the nature of work makes it impossible to adjust it to the fact that people are parents as well as workers. That these things have not happened is part of the historically, socially constructed differentiation between the sexes that feminists have come to call *gender*. We live in a society that has over the years regarded the innate characteristic of sex as one of the clearest legitimizers of different rights and restrictions, both formal and informal. While the legal sanctions that uphold male dominance have begun to be eroded in the past century, and more rapidly in the last twenty years, the heavy weight of tradition, combined with the effects of socialization, still works powerfully to reinforce sex roles that are commonly regarded as of unequal prestige and worth. The sexual division of labor has not only been a fundamental part of the marriage contract, but so deeply influences us in our formative years that feminists of both sexes who try to reject it can find themselves struggling against it with varying degrees of ambivalence. Based on this linchpin, "gender"—by which I mean *the deeply entrenched institutionalization of sexual difference*—still permeates our society. . . .

Many academics in recent years have become aware of the objectionable nature of using the supposedly generic male forms of nouns and pronouns. As feminist scholars have demonstrated, these words have most often *not* been used, throughout history and the history of philosophy in particular, with the intent to include women. *Man, mankind,* and *he* are going out of style as universal representations, though they have by no means disappeared. But the gender-neutral alternatives that most contemporary theorists employ are often even more misleading than the blatantly sexist use of male terms of reference. For they serve to disguise the real and continuing failure of theorists to confront the fact that the human race consists of persons of two sexes. They are by this means able to ignore the fact that there are *some* socially relevant physical differences between women and men, and the even more important fact that the sexes have had very different histories, very different assigned social roles and "natures," and very different degrees of access to power and opportunity in all human societies up to and including the present.

False gender neutrality is not a new phenomenon. Aristotle, for example, used *anthropos*—"human being"—in discussions of "the human good" that turn out not only to exclude women but to depend on their subordination. Kant even wrote of "all rational beings" as such in making arguments that he did not mean to apply to women. But it was more readily apparent that such arguments or conceptions of the good were not about all of us, but only about male heads of families. For their authors usually gave at some point an explanation, no matter how inadequate, of why what they were saying did not apply to women and of the different characteristics and virtues, rights, and responsibilities they thought women ought to have. Nevertheless, their theories have often been read as though they pertain (or can easily be applied) to all of us. Feminist interpretations of the last fifteen years or so have revealed the falsity of this "add women and stir" method of reading the history of political thought.

The falseness of the gender-neutral language of contemporary political theorists is less readily apparent. Most, though not all, contemporary moral and political philosophers use "men and women," "he or she," "persons," or the increasingly ubiquitous "self." Sometimes they even get their computers to distribute masculine and feminine terms of reference randomly. Since they do not explicitly exclude or differentiate women, as most theorists in the past did, we may be tempted to read their theories as inclusive of all of us. But we cannot. Their merely terminological responses to feminist challenges, in spite of giving a superficial impression of tolerance and inclusiveness, often strain credulity and sometimes result in nonsense. They do this in two ways: by ignoring the irreducible biological differences between the sexes, and/or by ignoring their different assigned social roles and consequent power differentials, and the ideologies that have supported them. Thus gender-neutral terms frequently obscure the fact that so much of the real experience of "persons," so long as they live in gender-structured societies, *does* in fact depend on what sex they are.

False gender neutrality is by no means confined to the realm of theory. Its harmful effects can be seen in public policies that have directly affected large numbers of women adversely. It was used, for example, in the Supreme Court's 1976 decision that the exclusion of pregnancy-related disabilities from employers' disability insurance plans was "not a gender-based discrimination at all." In a now infamous phrase of its majority opinion, the Court explained that such plans did not discriminate against women because the distinction drawn by such plans was between pregnant women and "non-pregnant *persons*."

Examples of false gender neutrality in contemporary political theory will appear throughout this book; I will illustrate the concept here by citing just two examples. Ackerman's *Social Justice in the Liberal State* is a book containing scrupulously gender-neutral language. He breaks with this neutrality only, it seems, to *defy* existing sex roles; he refers to the "Commander," who plays the lead role in the theory, as "she." However, the argument of the book does not address the existing inequality or role differentiation between the sexes, though it has the potential for doing so. The full impact of Ackerman's gender-neutral language without attention to gender is revealed in his section on abortion: a two-page discussion written, with the exception of a single "she," in the completely gender-neutral language of fetuses and their "parents." The impression given is that there is no relevant respect in which the relationship of the two parents to the fetus differs. Now it is, of course, possible to imagine (and in the view of many feminists, would be desirable to achieve) a society in which differences in the relation of women and men to fetuses would be so slight as to reasonably play only a minor role in the discussion of abortion. But this would have to be a society without gender—one in which sexual difference carried no social significance, the sexes were equal in power and interdependence, and "mothering" and "fathering" a child meant the same thing, so that parenting and earning responsibilities were equally shared. We certainly do not live in such a society. Neither is there any discussion of one in Ackerman's theory, in which the division of labor between the sexes is not considered a matter of social (in)justice. In such a context, a "gender-neutral" discussion of abortion is almost as misleading as the Supreme Court's "gender-neutral" discussion of pregnancy.

A second illustration of false gender neutrality comes from Derek Phillips's *Toward a Just Social Order*. Largely because of the extent of his concern—rare among theorists of justice—with how we are to *achieve and maintain* a just social order, Phillips pays an unusual amount of attention to the family. He writes about the family as the locus for the development of a sense of justice and self-esteem, of an appreciation of the meaning of reciprocity, of the ability to exercise unforced choice, and of an awareness of alternative *ways* of life. The problem with this otherwise admirable discussion is that, apart from a couple of brief exceptions, the family itself is presented in gender-neutral terms that bear little resemblance to actual, gender-structured life. It is because of "parental affection," "parental nurturance," and "child rearing" that children in Phillips's families become the autonomous moral agents that his just society requires its citizens to be. The child's development of a sense of identity is very much dependent upon being raised *by* "parental figures who themselves have coherent and well-integrated personal identities," and we are told that such a coherent identity is "ideally one built around commitments to work and love." This all sounds very plausible. But it does not take account of the multiple inequalities of gender. In gender-structured societies—in which the child rearers are women, "parental nurturance" is largely mothering, and those who do what society regards as "meaningful work" are assumed not to be primary parents—women in even

the best of circumstances face considerable conflicts between love (a fulfilling family life) and "meaningful work." Women in less fortunate circumstances face even greater conflicts between love (even basic love of their children) and any kind of paid work at all.

It follows from Phillips's own premises that these conflicts are very likely to affect the strength and coherence in women of that sense of identity and self-esteem coming from love and meaningful work, that he regards as essential for being an autonomous moral agent. In turn, if they are mothers, it is also likely to affect their daughters' and sons' developing senses of their identity. Gender is clearly a major obstacle to the attainment of a social order remotely comparable to the just one Phillips aspires to—but his false gender-neutral language allows him to ignore this fact. Although he is clearly aware of how distant in some other respects his vision of a just social order is from contemporary societies, his use of falsely gender-neutral language leaves him quite unaware of the distance between the type of family that might be able to socialize just citizens and typical families today.

The combined effect of the omission of the family and the falsely gender-neutral language in recent political thought is that most theorists are continuing to ignore the highly political issue of gender. The language they use makes little difference to what they actually do, which is to write about men and about only those women who manage, in spite of the gendered structures and practices of the society in which they live, to adopt patterns of life that have been developed to suit the needs of men. The fact that human beings are born as helpless infants—not as the purportedly autonomous actors who populate political theories—is obscured by the implicit assumption of gendered families, operating outside the range of the theories. To a large extent, contemporary theories of justice, like those of the past, are about men with wives at home.

Box 9-1	The Equal Rights Amendment

Section 1. **Equality of rights under the law shall not be denied or abridged by the United States or by any state on account of sex.**

Section 2. **The Congress shall have the power to enforce, by appropriate legislation, the provisions of this article.**

Section 3. **This amendment shall take effect two years after the date of ratification.**

Phyllis Schlafly

THE POWER OF THE POSITIVE WOMAN

New York, NY: Arlington House (1977)

Phyllis Schlafly was noted for her role in helping to defeat the ERA. As you read this excerpt from her work, pay careful attention to what she considers to be "real differences" between men and women. As you read, ask whether she blurs Susan Okin's distinction between sex and gender and, if so, whether she is right to do so.

THE FIVE PRINCIPLES

When the women's liberationists enter the political arena to promote legislation and litigation in pursuit of their goals, their specific demands are based on five principles.

(1) They demand that a "gender-free" rule be applied to every federal and state law, bureaucratic regulation, educational institution, and expenditure of public funds. Based on their dogma that there is no real difference between men and women (except in sex organs), they demand that males and females have identical treatment always. Thus, if fathers are not expected to stay home and care for their infant children, then neither should mothers be expected to do so; and, therefore, it becomes the duty of the government to provide kiddy-care centers to relieve mothers of that unfair and unequal burden.

The women's lib dogma demands that the courts treat sex as a "suspect" classification—just as race is now treated—so that no difference of treatment or separation between the sexes will ever be permitted, no matter how reasonable or how much it is desired by reasonable people.

The nonsense of these militant demands was illustrated by the Department of Health, Education and Welfare (HEW) ruling in July, 1976, that all public school "functions such as father-son or mother-daughter breakfasts" would be prohibited because this "would be subjecting you to separate treatment." It was announced that violations would lead to a cutoff of federal assistance or court action by the Justice Department.

When President Gerald Ford read this in the newspaper, he was described by his press secretary as being "quite irritated" and as saying that he could not believe that this was the intent of Congress in passing a law against sex discrimination in education. He telephoned HEW Secretary David Mathews and told him to suspend the ruling.

The National Organization for Women, however, immediately announced opposition to President Ford's action, claiming that such events (fashion shows, softball games, banquets, and breakfasts) are sex-discriminatory and must be eliminated. It is clear that a prohibition against your right to make any difference or separation between the sexes anytime anywhere is a primary goal of the women's liberation movement.

No sooner had the father-son, mother-daughter flap blown over than HEW embroiled itself in another controversy by a ruling that an after-school choir of fifth and sixth grade boys violates the HEW regulation that bars single-sex choruses. The choir in Wethersfield, Connecticut, that precipitated the ruling had been established for boys whose "voices haven't changed yet," and the purpose was "to get boys interested in singing" at an early age so they would be willing to join coed choruses later. Nevertheless, HEW found that such a boy's chorus is by definition sex discriminatory.

The Positive Woman rejects the "gender-free" approach. She knows that there are many differences between male and female and that we are entitled to have our laws, regulations, schools, and courts reflect these differences and allow for reasonable differences in treatment and separations of activities that reasonable men and women want.

The Positive Woman also rejects the argument that sex discrimination should be treated the same as race discrimination. There is vastly more difference between a man and a woman than there is between a black and a white, and it is nonsense to adopt a legal and bureaucratic attitude that

pretends that those differences do not exist. Even the United States Supreme Court has, in recent and relevant cases, upheld "reasonable" sex-based differences of treatment by legislatures and by the military.

(2) The women's lib legislative goals seek an irrational mandate of "equality" at the expense of justice. The fact is that equality cannot always be equated with justice, and may sometimes even be highly unjust. If we had absolutely equal treatment in regard to taxes, then everyone would pay the same income tax, or perhaps the same rate of income tax, regardless of the size of the income.

If we had absolutely equal treatment in regard to federal spending programs, we would have to eliminate welfare, low-income housing benefits, food stamps, government scholarships, and many other programs designed to benefit low-income citizens. If we had absolutely equal treatment in regard to age, then seventeen-year-olds, or even ten-year-olds, would be permitted to vote, and we would have to eliminate Social Security unless all persons received the same benefits that only those over sixty-two receive now.

Our legislatures, our administrative departments, and our courts have always had and still retain the discretion to make reasonable differences in treatment based on age, income, or economic situation. The Positive Woman believes that it makes no sense to deprive us of the ability to make reasonable distinctions based on sex that reasonable men and women want.

(3) The women's liberation movement demands that women be given the benefit of "reverse discrimination." The Positive Woman recognizes that this is mutually exclusive with the principle of equal opportunity for all. Reverse discrimination is based on the theory that "group rights" take precedence over individual

rights, and that "reverse discrimination" (variously called "preferential treatment," "remedial action," or "affirmative action") should be imposed in order to compensate some women today for alleged past discriminations against other women. The word "quotas" is usually avoided, but it amounts to the same thing.

The fallacy of reverse discrimination has been aptly exposed by Professor Sidney Hook. No one would argue, he wrote, that because many years ago blacks and women were denied the right to vote, we should now compensate by giving them an extra vote or two; or by barring white men from voting at all.

But that is substantially what the women's liberationists are demanding—and getting by federal court orders—in education, employment, and politics when they ask for "affirmative action" to remedy past discrimination.

The Positive Woman supports equal opportunity for individuals of both sexes, as well as of all faiths and races. She rejects the theories of reverse discrimination and "group rights." It does no good for the woman who may have been discriminated against twenty-five years ago to know that an unqualified woman today receives preferential treatment at the expense of a qualified man. Only the vindictive radical would support such a policy of revenge.

(4) The women's liberation movement is based on the unproven theory that uniformity should replace diversity—or, in simpler language, the federalization of all remaining aspects of our life. The militant women demand that *all* educational institutions conform to federally determined rules about sex discrimination.

There is absolutely no evidence that HEW bureaucrats can do a better or fairer job of regulating our schools and colleges than local officials. Nor is there any evidence that individuals, or women, or society as a whole, would be better off under a uniform system enforced by the full power of the federal government than they would be under a free and competitive system, under local control, using diverse methods and regulations. It is hard to see why anyone would want to put more power into the hands of federal bureaucrats who cannot cope with the problems they already have.

The militant women demand the HEW regulations enforce a strict gender-free uniformity on all schools and colleges. Everything from sports to glee clubs must be coed, regardless of local customs or wishes. The militants deplore the differences from state to state in the laws governing marriage and divorce. Yet does anyone think our nation would be improved if we were made subject to a national divorce law devised by HEW?

The Positive Woman rejects the theory that Washington, D.C., is the fountainhead of all wisdom and professional skill. She supports the principle of leaving all possible control and discretion in the hands of local school and college officials and their elected boards.

(5) The women's liberation movement pushes its proposals on the premise that everything must be neutral as between morality and immorality, and as between the institution of the family and alternate lifestyles: for example, that homosexuals and lesbians should have just as much right to teach in the schools and to adopt children as anyone else; and that illegitimate babies and abortions by married or single mothers should be accepted as normal behavior for teachers—and funded by public money.

A good example of the rabid determination of the militant radicals to push every law and regulation to the far-out limit of moral neutrality is the HEW regulation on sex discrimination that implements the Education Amendments of 1972. Although the federal statute simply prohibits sex discrimination, the HEW regulation (1) requires that any medical benefit program administered by a school or college pay for abortions for married and unmarried students, (2) prohibits any school or college from refusing to employ or from firing an unmarried pregnant teacher or a woman who has had, or plans to have, an abortion, and (3) prohibits any school or college from refusing admission to any student who has had, or plans to have, an abortion. Abortion is referred to by the code words "termination of pregnancy."

This HEW regulation is illogical, immoral, and unauthorized by any reasonable reading of the 1972 Education Act. But the HEW regulation became federal law on July 18, 1975, after being signed by the president and accepted by Congress.

The Positive Woman believes that our educational institutions have not only the right, but the obligation, to set minimum standards of moral conduct at the local level. She believes that schools and colleges have no right to use our public money to promote conduct that is offensive to the religious and moral values of parents and taxpayers.

Jane J. Mansbridge

WHY WE LOST THE ERA

Chicago, IL: University of Chicago Press (1986)

Central to the debate over the ERA was the contention that it would increase the level of scrutiny courts would apply to discrimination on the basis of sex. According to Phyllis Schlafly, the Amendment would have prevented distinctions based on sex that are important for public policy. In this essay, Jane Mansbridge challenges this assumption. As you read this, consider whether strict scrutiny is compatible with making any legal distinctions between the sexes.

In March 1972 the Equal Rights Amendment to the United States Constitution— the ERA—passed the Senate of the United States with a vote of 84 to 8, seventeen votes more than the two-thirds required for constitutional amendments. In the ensuing ten years—from 1972 to 1982—a majority of Americans consistently told interviewers that they favored this amendment to the Constitution. Yet on June 30, 1982, the deadline for ratifying the amendment passed with only thirty-five of the required thirty-eight states having ratified.

How did this happen?

This book will argue that if the ERA had been ratified, the Supreme Court would have been unlikely to use it to bring about major changes in the relations between American men and women, at least in the foreseeable future. Nor did the American public want any significant change in gender roles, whether at work, at home, or in society at large. The groups that fought for the ERA and the groups that fought against it, however, had a stake in believing that the ERA *would* produce these kinds of changes. With both the proponents and the opponents exaggerating the likely effects of the ERA, legislators in wavering states became convinced that the ERA might, in fact, produce important substantive changes—and the necessary votes were lost. Considering the large number of legislative votes required to amend the Constitution, the puzzle is not why the ERA died but why it came so close to passing.

Contrary to widespread belief, public support for the ERA did not increase in the course of the ten-year struggle. In key wavering states where the ERA was most debated, public support actually declined. Much of the support for the Amendment was superficial, because it was based on a support for abstract rights, not for real changes. Many nominal supporters took strong antifeminist positions on other issues, and their support evaporated when the ERA became linked in their minds to feminist positions they rejected.

The irony in all this is that the ERA would have had much less substantive effect than either proponents or opponents claimed. Because the ERA applied only to the government and not to private businesses and corporations, it would have had no noticeable effect, at least in the short run, on the gap between men's and women's wages. Furthermore, during the 1970s, the Supreme Court began to use the Fourteenth Amendment to the Constitution to declare unconstitutional almost all the laws and practices that Congress had intended to make unconstitutional when it passed the ERA in 1972. The exceptions were laws and practices that most Americans approved. Thus, by the late 1970s it was hard to show that the ERA would have made any of the substantive changes that most Americans favored.

While the ERA would have had few immediate, tangible effects, I nonetheless believe that its defeat was a major setback for equality between men and women. Its direct effects would have been slight, but its indirect effects on both judges and legislators would probably have led in the long run to interpretations of existing laws and enactment of new laws that would have benefited women. The lack of immediate benefits did, however, deeply influence the course of the public debate. Because ERA activists had little of an immediate, practical nature to lose if the ERA was defeated, they had little reason to describe it in a way that would make it acceptable to middle-of-the-road legislators. As a consequence, the most influential leaders in the pro-ERA organizations and many of the activists in those organizations chose to interpret the ERA as delivering radical results.

Most proponents contended, for example, that the ERA would require the military to send women draftees into combat on the same basis as men. ERA proponents adopted this position even though it reduced their chances of achieving the short-run goal of passing the ERA and despite the fact that the Court was not likely to interpret the ERA as having this effect. They did so in part because their ideology called for full equality with men, not for equality with exceptions. In a somewhat similar manner, certain feminist lawyers argued in state courts that state ERAs required states to fund medically necessary abortions if they were funding all medically necessary services for men. Such arguments also reduced the chances that legislators in the key unratified states would vote for the federal ERA.

The struggle reveals how impossible it is, even in the most favorable circumstances, to dispense with "ideology" in favor of practical political reasoning when the actors in the drama give their energies voluntarily, without pay or other material incentives. Volunteers always have mixed motives, but most are trying to do good and promote justice. As a result, most would rather lose fighting for a cause they believe in than win fighting for a cause they feel is morally compromised.

Because the ERA offered its supporters no tangible benefits, activists worked hard for it only if they believed strongly in equality for women. They had no reason to "betray" that principle by compromise for compromise offered no concrete benefits, either to them personally or to women generally. ERA opponents took relatively extreme positions for similar reasons. But their "radicalism" cost them less, because they had only to disrupt an emerging consensus, not to produce one.

Refusing to compromise is, of course, often better than winning. It is not the focus on principle rather than practice that should give the reader of this story pause. It is the difficulty both sides had assimilating information about the struggle in which they were engaged. This institutionalized deafness meant that neither the activists nor the general public could make even an informed guess about what passage of the ERA would accomplish. As a result, there was no serious national debate about whether the Amendment was the best way of accomplishing what the proponents sought or whether it really threatened the values that opponents sought to defend. Nor did the proponents, who ran the gamut from feminist lawyers to grassroots activists, ever engage one another in a wide-ranging discussion of strategy.

The only possible way to have persuaded three more state legislatures to ratify the ERA would have been to insist—correctly—it would do relatively little in the short run, and to insist equally strongly—and correctly—on the importance of placing the principle in the Constitution to guide the Supreme Court in its long-run evolution of constitutional law. In addition, the pro-ERA movement would have had to develop an ongoing, district-based political network capable of turning generalized public sympathy for reforms that benefit women into political pressure on specific legislators in the marginal unratified states. But even this strategy might not have worked. Comparatively few state legislators were open to persuasion on this issue, and the troops for district-based organizing were often hard to mobilize—or keep mobilized.

The movement away from principle and the increasing focus on substantive effects was probably an inevitable result of the ten-year struggle for the ERA. Inevitable or not, the shift did occur. In the near future, therefore, the only way to convince legislators that the ERA would not have undesirable substantive effects would be to add explicit amendments limiting its application to the military, abortion, and so on. No principled feminist, including myself, favors an ERA that includes such "crippling" amendments. In the present political climate, therefore, the future of the ERA looks even dimmer than its past.

The death of the ERA was, of course, also related to broader changes in American political attitudes. Two of these changes were especially relevant: growing legislative skepticism about the consequences of giving the U.S. Supreme Court authority to review legislation, and the growing organizational power of the new Right.

Suspicion of the Supreme Court, and of the role of lawyers and judges generally, certainly played a significant role in the ERA's demise. For its advocates, the ERA was a device for allowing the Supreme Court to impose the principle of equality between the sexes on recalcitrant state legislators. For legislators, that was precisely the problem. They did not want their actions reviewed, much less reversed, by federal judges whom they did not even appoint. There was a larger problem as well. The ERA embodied a principle, which was supposed to apply, without exception, to specific pieces of legislation. But most people—including most legislators—do not derive their preferences from principles. Instead, they derive their principles from their preferences, endorsing principles they associate with outcomes they like. Because the justices of the Supreme Court of the United States put somewhat more weight than ordinary citizens do on the principles they have evolved from the Constitution, they often find themselves taking controversial or even unpopular stands. As a result, much of the public has come to view the Court as "out of control." Although the Court's unpopular decisions have not yet reduced its power, they took their toll on the ERA. If the primary cause of the ERA's defeat was the fear that it would lead to major changes in the roles of men and women, a major subsidiary cause was legislative backlash against "progressive" Court decisions, starting with the 1954 school desegregation decision. Many state legislators were unwilling to give the Court "new words to play with," rightly fearing that this could eventually have all sorts of unforeseeable consequences they might not like and would not be able to reverse.

The same sense of impotence in the face of national changes that fueled the reaction against the Court also fed the conservative backlash against feminism and the growth of the "new" Right. For many conservative Americans, the personal became political for the first time when questions of family, children, sexual behavior, and women's roles became subjects of political debate. Leaders of the "old" Radical Right, who had traditionally focused on national defense and the Communist menace, became aware of the organizing potential of these "women's" issues only slowly. Once assimilated, however, the "new" issues turned out to have two great organizational virtues. First, they provided a link with fundamentalist churches. The evangelizing culture and the stable geographic base of the fundamentalist churches made them powerful actors in state legislatures once they ventured into the political process. Second, "women's issues" not only gave a focus to the reaction against the changes in child rearing, sexual behavior, divorce, and the use of drugs that had taken place in the 1960s and 1970s, they also mobilized a group, traditional homemakers, that had lost status over the two previous decades and was feeling the psychological effects of the loss. The new women's issues, combined with improvements in computer technology that reduced the cost of processing large numbers of names, made it feasible for the first time to contact by direct mail and thus bring into concerted political activities many who had previously been concerned only with a single issue or not been involved in politics at all.

State legislators were predisposed to oppose a constitutional amendment that gave the federal government power in one of the few areas that was still primarily in the province of the states, namely, family law. The entry of new conservative activists into the political process enhanced this "natural" resistance. As fundamentalist women became more prominent in the opposition, the ERA came to be seen as an issue that pitted women against women and, moreover, women of the Right against women of the Left. Once the ERA lost its aura of benefiting all women and became a partisan issue, it lost its chance of gaining the supermajority required for a constitutional amendment.

There are two lessons to be learned from the story told here. The first is a lesson about the politics of promoting "the common good." We have known for a long time of the extraordinary inequities built into the way different groups can influence legislators in a pluralist democratic system. We have also known that because it is harder to organize for the general interest than for particular interests, the general interest will—all other things being equal—count less in the political process than most people want it to. The story of the ERA struggle reveals a third, less widely recognized, obstacle to promoting the common good. Organizing on behalf of the general interest usually requires volunteers, and mobilizing volunteers often requires an exaggerated, black or white vision of events to justify spending time and money on the cause. Ironically, the greatest cost in organizing for the public interest may be the distortion, in the course of organizing, of that interest itself.

A second, practical lesson follows from the first. While organizations that depend on volunteers to promote the common good seem to have an inherent tendency toward ideological purity and polarized perceptions, they can develop institutions that help correct these tendencies, ranging from small-group techniques through formal systems of representation. Although ongoing organizations are susceptible to the temptations of speaking only to themselves, they are also our main repositories of past experience and our main mechanism for avoiding the endless repetition of past errors. Effectively promoting the common good thus requires that we keep such organizations strong and consistently funded, while at the same time trying to ensure internal dialogue on substantive issues.

Box 9-2   Tiers of Scrutiny for Evaluating Discrimination

In the previous chapter, we examined the Court's balancing test in instances where laws or policies introduce a racial classification or distinction. Such cases trigger strict scrutiny, which mandates that for a law to avoid being struck down, it had to pass two distinct tests. First, the goal or end of the law must be shown to constitute a "compelling state interest." Second, the law must be narrowly tailored in order to meet this goal. In other words, the state must have a powerful reason to make a classification based on race. Furthermore, it must use the least restrictive means to achieve its policy goal. Strict scrutiny thus creates a strong presumption against the validity of laws that create racial distinctions.

In this chapter, we examine two other kinds of distinctions that broadly mirror the structure of the equal protection balancing test introduced in the previous chapter. Namely, the Court examines both the legitimacy of the ends of a law and the means by which it is achieved. But in contrast to race, when it comes to gender and sexual orientation, the "weights" of this balancing test are different. In the case of gender, the Court first applies a standard of "intermediate" or "heightened" scrutiny. Rather than needing to show that a distinction based on gender is based on a

Figure 9.1. Supreme Court Tiers of Scrutiny for Evaluating Discrimination

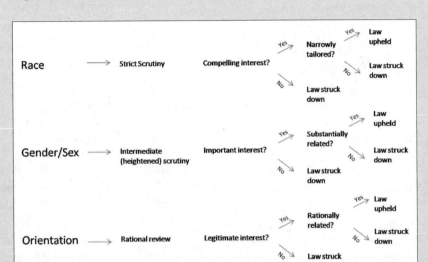

"compelling state interest," the state need only show that the distinction is based on an "important" interest. In evaluating the means by which an important state interest is achieved, the state need not show that the law is narrowly tailored, but merely that the law is "substantially related" to the goal.

In cases concerning distinctions based on sexual orientation, which we examine in Section B, the Court has so far applied an even more lenient standard than for distinctions based on race or gender. Rather than demonstrating a "compelling" or "important" interest, the state only need show that the end is a "legitimate" one. As for the means, the state must show that a law is "rationally related" to the goal, as opposed to being arbitrary or based in animus.

The above flow chart visually demonstrates these three different "tiers" of review. We place the "strict scrutiny" standard at the top to highlight the strongest presumption for the invalidity of laws that discriminate based on race, ethnicity, or national origin. We place the "intermediate scrutiny" test for gender in the middle to illustrate its status. Finally, the lowest level of scrutiny is placed at the bottom. Notice that in order for a law to survive any of these tests, it is first necessary to determine which level of scrutiny is appropriate, and then to determine whether a law passes an evaluation of both its ends and its means.

REED v. REED

404 U.S. 71 (1971)

Opinion: Burger, joined by Douglas, Brennan, Stewart, White, Marshall, Blackmun

For much of its history, the Supreme Court generally refused to invalidate gender discrimination under the Equal Protection Clause. Here the Court for the first time extends the Clause's protection to women, utilizing the permissive test of rational basis review. As you read the case, pay attention to the reasons the Court provides for invalidating the law despite the deference that laws normally receive under rational review. What characteristics does the law at issue in this case have that make it vulnerable to being overturned even under such a low level of scrutiny?

MR. CHIEF JUSTICE BURGER
delivered the opinion of the Court.

Richard Lynn Reed, a minor, died intestate in Ada County, Idaho, on March 29, 1967. His adoptive parents, who had separated sometime prior to his death, are the parties to this appeal. Approximately seven months after Richard's death, his mother, appellant Sally Reed, filed a petition in the Probate Court of Ada County, seeking appointment as administratrix of her son's estate. Prior to the date set for a hearing on the mother's petition, appellee Cecil Reed, the father of the decedent, filed a competing petition seeking to have himself appointed administrator of the son's estate. The court treated §§15–312 and 15–314 of the Idaho Code as the controlling statutes, and read those sections as compelling a preference for Cecil Reed because he was a male.

Section 15–312 designates the persons who are entitled to administer the estate of one who dies intestate. . . . Section 1314 provides, however, that

> [o]f several persons claiming and equally entitled [under §1312] to administer, males must be preferred to females, and relatives of the whole to those of the half blood.

. . . Having examined the record and considered the briefs and oral arguments of the parties, we have concluded that the arbitrary preference established in favor of males by §15–314 of the Idaho Code cannot stand in the face of the Fourteenth Amendment's command that no State deny the equal protection of the laws to any person within its jurisdiction.

Idaho does not, of course, deny letters of administration to women altogether. Indeed, under §15–312, a woman whose spouse dies intestate has a preference over a son, father, brother, or any other male relative of the decedent. Moreover, we can judicially notice that, in this country, presumably due to the greater longevity of women, a large proportion of estates, both intestate and under wills of decedents, are administered by surviving widows.

Section 15–314 is restricted in its operation to those situations where competing applications for letters of administration have been filed by both male and female members of the same entitlement class established by §15–312. In such situations, §15–314 provides that different treatment be accorded to the applicants on the basis of their sex; it thus establishes a classification subject to scrutiny under the Equal Protection Clause.

In applying that clause, this Court has consistently recognized that the Fourteenth Amendment does not deny to States the power to treat different classes of persons in different ways. The Equal Protection Clause of that amendment does, however, deny to States the power to legislate that different treatment be accorded to persons placed by a statute into different classes on the basis of criteria wholly unrelated to the objective of that statute. . . . The question presented by this case, then, is whether a difference in the sex of competing applicants for letters of administration bears a rational relationship to a state objective that is sought to be advanced by the operation of §§15–312 and 15–314.

Clearly the objective of reducing the workload on probate courts by eliminating one class of contests is not without some legitimacy. The crucial question, however, is whether §15–314 advances that objective in a manner consistent with the command of the Equal Protection Clause. We hold that it does not. To give a mandatory preference to members of either sex over members of the other, merely to accomplish the elimination of hearings on the merits, is to make the very kind of arbitrary legislative choice forbidden by the Equal Protection Clause of the Fourteenth Amendment; and whatever may be said as to the positive values of avoiding intrafamily controversy, the choice in this context may not lawfully be mandated solely on the basis of sex.

FRONTIERO v. RICHARDSON

411 U.S. 677 (1973)

Opinion: Brennan, joined by Douglas, White, Marshall
Concurrence: Stewart
Concurrence: Powell, joined by Burger, Blackmun
Dissent: Rehnquist

In this case, the Court is confronted with a military regulation that imposes a burden on married female service members but not on their male counterparts. This case is notable because a four-justice plurality determined that discrimination on the basis of gender should be evaluated under the strict scrutiny standard. Three justices concurred with the ruling but thought that they should not preempt the democratic process that was playing out as the country decided the very same issue in considering whether to ratify the ERA. Do you agree with the opinion? Do you think the dissenters were correct that the Court should have waited for the political resolution of the issue?

MR. JUSTICE BRENNAN *announced the judgment of the Court and an opinion in which* **MR. JUSTICE DOUGLAS**, **MR. JUSTICE WHITE**, *and* **MR. JUSTICE MARSHALL** *join.*

The question before us concerns the right of a female member of the uniformed services to claim her spouse as a "dependent" for the purposes of obtaining increased quarters allowances and medical and dental benefits . . . on an equal footing with male members. Under these statutes, a serviceman may claim his wife as a "dependent" without regard to whether she is in fact dependent upon him for any part of her support. A servicewoman, on the other hand, may not claim her husband as a "dependent" under these programs unless he is in fact dependent upon her for over one-half of his support. Thus, the question for decision is whether this difference in treatment constitutes an unconstitutional discrimination against servicewomen in violation of the Due Process Clause of the Fifth Amendment.

I

... Appellant Sharron Frontiero, a lieutenant in the United States Air Force, sought increased quarters allowances, and housing and medical benefits for her husband, appellant Joseph Frontiero, on the ground that he was her "dependent." Although such benefits would automatically have been granted with respect to the wife of a male member of the uniformed services, appellant's application was denied because she failed to demonstrate that her husband was dependent on her for more than one-half of his support. Appellants then commenced this suit, contending that, by making this distinction, the statutes unreasonably discriminate on the basis of sex in violation of the Due Process Clause of the Fifth Amendment. In essence, appellants asserted that the discriminatory impact of the statutes is twofold: first, as a procedural matter, a female member is required to demonstrate her spouse's dependency, while no such burden is imposed upon male members; and, second, as a substantive matter, a male member who does not provide more than one-half of his wife's support receives benefits, while a similarly situated female member is denied such benefits. Appellants therefore sought a permanent injunction against the continued enforcement of these statutes and an order directing the appellees to provide Lieutenant Frontiero with the same housing and medical benefits that a similarly situated male member would receive.

Although the legislative history of these statutes sheds virtually no light on the purposes underlying the differential treatment accorded male and female members, a majority of the three-judge District Court surmised that Congress might reasonably have concluded that, since the husband in our society is generally the "bread-winner" in the family—and the wife typically the "dependent" partner—"it would be more economical to require married female members claiming husbands to prove actual dependency than to extend the presumption of dependency to such members." Indeed, given the fact that approximately 99% of all members of the uniformed services are male, the District Court speculated that such differential treatment might conceivably lead to a "considerable saving of administrative expense and manpower."

II

At the outset, appellants contend that classifications based upon sex, like classifications based upon race, alienage, and national origin, are inherently suspect and must therefore be subjected to close judicial scrutiny. We agree and, indeed, find at least implicit support for such an approach in our unanimous decision only last Term in *Reed v. Reed.* . . .

There can be no doubt that our Nation has had a long and unfortunate history of sex discrimination. Traditionally, such discrimination was rationalized by an attitude of "romantic paternalism" which, in practical effect, put women, not on a pedestal, but in a cage. Indeed, this paternalistic attitude became so firmly rooted in our national consciousness that, 100 years ago, a distinguished Member of this Court was able to proclaim:

"Man is, or should be, woman's protector and defender. The natural and proper timidity and delicacy which belongs to the female sex evidently unfits it for many of the occupations of civil life. The constitution of the family organization, which is founded in the divine ordinance, as well as in the nature of things, indicates the domestic sphere as that which properly belongs to the domain and functions of womanhood. The harmony, not to say identity, of interests and views which belong, or should belong, to the family institution is repugnant to the idea of a woman adopting a distinct and independent career from that of her husband. . . .

". . . The paramount destiny and mission of woman are to fulfil the noble and benign offices of wife and mother. This is the law of the Creator." *Bradwell v. State* (Bradley, J., concurring).

As a result of notions such as these, our statute books gradually became laden with gross, stereotyped distinctions between the sexes and, indeed, throughout much of the 19th century the position of women in our society was, in many respects, comparable to that of blacks under the pre-Civil War slave codes. Neither slaves nor women could hold office, serve on juries, or bring suit in their own names, and married women traditionally were denied the legal capacity to hold or convey property or to serve as legal guardians of their own children. And although blacks were guaranteed the right to vote in 1870, women were denied even that right—which is itself "preservative of other basic civil and political rights" until adoption of the Nineteenth Amendment half a century later.

It is true, of course, that the position of women in America has improved markedly in recent decades. Nevertheless, it can hardly be doubted that, in part because of the high visibility of the sex characteristic, women still face pervasive, although at times more subtle, discrimination in our educational institutions, in the job market and, perhaps most conspicuously, in the political arena.

Moreover, since sex, like race and national origin, is an immutable characteristic determined solely by the accident of birth, the imposition of special disabilities upon the members of a particular sex because of their sex would seem to violate "the basic concept of our system that legal burdens should bear some relationship to individual responsibility. . . ." *Weber v. Aetna Casualty & Surety Co.* And what differentiates sex from such nonsuspect statuses as intelligence or physical disability, and aligns it with the recognized suspect criteria, is that the sex characteristic frequently bears no relation to ability to perform or contribute to society. As a result, statutory distinctions between the sexes often have the effect of invidiously relegating the entire class of females to inferior legal status without regard to the actual capabilities of its individual members. . . .

With these considerations in mind, we can only conclude that classifications based upon sex, like classifications based upon race, alienage, or national origin, are inherently suspect, and must therefore be subjected to strict judicial scrutiny. Applying the analysis mandated by that stricter standard of review, it is clear that the statutory scheme now before us is constitutionally invalid.

III

The sole basis of the classification established in the challenged statutes is the sex of the individuals involved. Thus, . . . a female member of the uniformed services seeking to obtain housing and medical benefits for her spouse must prove his dependency in fact, whereas no such burden is imposed upon male members. In addition, the statutes operate so as to deny benefits to a female member, such as appellant Sharron Frontiero, who provides less than one-half of her spouse's support, while at the same time granting such benefits to a male member who likewise provides less than one-half of his spouse's support. Thus, to this extent at least, it may fairly be said that these statutes command "dissimilar treatment for men and women who are . . . similarly situated." *Reed v. Reed.*

Moreover, the Government concedes that the differential treatment accorded men and women under these statutes serves no purpose other than mere "administrative convenience." In essence, the Government maintains that, as an empirical matter, wives in our society frequently are dependent upon their husbands, while husbands rarely are dependent upon their wives. Thus, the Government argues that Congress might reasonably have concluded that it would be both cheaper and easier simply conclusively to presume that wives of male members are financially dependent upon their husbands, while burdening female members with the task of establishing dependency in fact.

The Government offers no concrete evidence, however, tending to support its view that such differential treatment in fact saves the Government any money. In order to satisfy the demands of strict judicial scrutiny, the Government must demonstrate, for example, that it is actually cheaper to grant increased benefits with respect to all male members, than it is to determine which male members are in fact entitled to such benefits and to grant increased benefits only to those members whose wives actually meet the dependency requirement. Here, however, there is substantial evidence that, if put to the test, many of the wives of male members would fail to qualify for benefits. And in light of the fact that the dependency determination with respect to the husbands of female members is presently made solely on the basis of affidavits, rather than through the more costly hearing process, the Government's explanation of the statutory scheme is, to say the least, questionable.

In any case, our prior decisions make clear that, although efficacious administration of governmental programs is not without some importance, "the Constitution recognizes higher values than speed and efficiency." *Stanley v. Illinois.* And when we enter the realm of "strict judicial scrutiny," there can be no doubt that "administrative convenience" is not a shibboleth, the mere recitation of which dictates constitutionality. See *Shapiro v. Thompson*; *Carrington v. Rash*. On the contrary, any statutory scheme which draws a sharp line between the sexes, solely for the purpose of achieving administrative convenience, necessarily commands "dissimilar treatment for men and women who are . . . similarly situated," and therefore involves the "very kind of arbitrary legislative choice forbidden by the [Constitution]. . . ." *Reed v. Reed.* We therefore conclude that, by according differential treatment to male and female members of the uniformed services for the sole purpose of achieving administrative convenience, the challenged statutes violate the Due Process Clause of the Fifth Amendment insofar as they require a female member to prove the dependency of her husband.

Reversed.

MR. JUSTICE STEWART concurs in the judgment, agreeing that the statutes before us work an invidious discrimination in violation of the Constitution. . . .

MR. JUSTICE POWELL, *with whom* **THE CHIEF JUSTICE** *and* **MR. JUSTICE BLACKMUN** *join, concurring in the judgment.*

I agree that the challenged statutes constitute an unconstitutional discrimination against servicewomen in violation of the Due Process Clause of the Fifth Amendment, but I cannot join the opinion of Mr. Justice Brennan, which would hold that all classifications based upon sex, "like classifications based upon race, alienage, and national origin," are "inherently suspect and must therefore be subjected to close judicial scrutiny." It is unnecessary for the Court in this case to characterize sex as a suspect classification, with all of the far-reaching implications of such a holding. *Reed v. Reed*, which abundantly supports our decision today, did not add sex to the narrowly limited group of classifications which are inherently suspect. In my view, we can and should decide this case on the authority of *Reed* and reserve for the future any expansion of its rationale.

There is another, and I find compelling, reason for deferring a general categorizing of sex classifications as invoking the strictest test of judicial scrutiny. The Equal Rights Amendment, which if adopted will resolve the substance of this precise question, has been approved by the Congress and submitted for ratification by the States. If this Amendment is duly adopted, it will represent the will of the people accomplished in the manner prescribed by the Constitution. By acting prematurely and unnecessarily, as I view it, the Court has assumed a decisional responsibility at the very time when state legislatures, functioning within the traditional democratic process, are debating the proposed Amendment. It seems to me that this reaching out to pre-empt by judicial action a major political decision which is currently in process of resolution does not reflect appropriate respect for duly prescribed legislative processes.

There are times when this Court, under our system, cannot avoid a constitutional decision on issues which normally should be resolved by the elected representatives of the people. But democratic institutions are weakened, and confidence in the restraint of the Court is impaired, when we appear unnecessarily to decide sensitive issues of broad social and political importance at the very time they are under consideration within the prescribed constitutional processes.

GEDULDIG v. AIELLO

417 U.S. 484 (1974)

Opinion: Stewart, joined by Burger, White, Blackmun, Powell, Rehnquist
Dissent: Brennan, joined by Douglas, Marshall

Whatever you make of the disagreement between thinkers such as Susan Okin and Phyllis Schlafly, women's ability to become pregnant is clearly a biological difference between the sexes—perhaps the most salient such distinction. In this case, the Court examines how this biological difference should impact equal protection law as applied to issues of sex and gender. Do you agree with the Court's analysis about this real difference between men and women? Do you agree with

the Court's observation in footnote 20 that laws that burden pregnancies do not discriminate on the basis of sex, but rather between pregnant and non-pregnant persons?

MR. JUSTICE STEWART *delivered the opinion of the Court.*

For almost 30 years, California has administered a disability insurance system that pays benefits to persons in private employment who are temporarily unable to work because of disability not covered by workmen's compensation. The appellees brought this action to challenge the constitutionality of a provision of the California program that, in defining "disability," excludes from coverage certain disabilities resulting from pregnancy.

California's disability insurance system is funded entirely from contributions deducted from the wages of participating employees. Participation in the program is mandatory unless the employees are protected by a voluntary private plan approved by the State. Each employee is required to contribute one percent of his salary, up to an annual maximum of $85. These contributions are placed in the Unemployment Compensation Disability Fund, which is established and administered as a special trust fund within the state treasury. It is from this Disability Fund that benefits under the program are paid.

In return for his one-percent contribution to the Disability Fund, the individual employee is insured against the risk of disability stemming from a substantial number of "mental or physical illness[es] and mental or physical injur[ies]." It is not every disabling condition, however, that triggers the obligation to pay benefits under the program. As already noted, for example, any disability of less than eight days' duration is not compensable, except when the employee is hospitalized. Conversely, no benefits are payable for any single disability beyond 26 weeks. Further, disability is not compensable if it results from the individual's court commitment as a dipsomaniac, drug addict, or sexual psychopath. Finally, §2626 of the Unemployment Insurance Code excludes from coverage certain disabilities that are attributable to pregnancy.

Appellees are four women who have paid sufficient amounts into the Disability Fund to be eligible for benefits under the program. Each of the appellees became pregnant and suffered employment disability as a result of her pregnancy.

The District Court, finding

"that the exclusion of pregnancy-related disabilities is not based upon a classification having a rational and substantial relationship to a legitimate state purpose,"

held that the exclusion was unconstitutional under the Equal Protection Clause.

It is clear that California intended to establish this benefit system as an insurance program that was to function essentially in accordance with insurance concepts. Since the program was instituted in 1946, it has been totally self-supporting, never drawing on general state revenues to finance disability or hospital benefits.

Over the years, California has demonstrated a strong commitment not to increase the contribution rate above the one-percent level. The State has sought to provide the broadest possible disability protection that would be affordable by all employees, including those with very low incomes. Because any larger percentage or any flat dollar amount rate of contribution would impose an increasingly regressive levy bearing most heavily upon those with the lowest incomes, the State has resisted any attempt to change the required contribution from the one-percent level.

In ordering the State to pay benefits for disability accompanying normal pregnancy and delivery, the District Court acknowledged the State's contention

"that coverage of these disabilities is so extraordinarily expensive that it would be impossible to maintain a program supported by employee contributions if these disabilities are included."

There is considerable disagreement between the parties with respect to how great the increased costs would actually be, but they would clearly be substantial. For purposes of analysis, the District Court accepted the State's estimate, which was in excess of $100 million annually, and stated:

"[I]t is clear that including these disabilities would not destroy the program. The increased costs could be accommodated quite easily by making reasonable changes in the contribution rate, the maximum benefits allowable, and the other variables affecting the solvency of the program."

We cannot agree that the exclusion of this disability from coverage amounts to invidious discrimination under the Equal Protection Clause. California does not discriminate with respect to the persons or groups which are eligible for disability insurance protection under the program.

This Court has held that, consistently with the Equal Protection Clause, a State

"may take one step at a time, addressing itself to the phase of the problem which seems most acute to the legislative mind.... The legislature may select one phase of one field and apply a remedy there, neglecting the others...."

Particularly with respect to social welfare programs, so long as the line drawn by the State is rationally supportable, the courts will not interpose their judgment as to the appropriate stopping point.

The State has a legitimate interest in maintaining the self-supporting nature of its insurance program. Similarly, it has an interest in distributing the available resources in such a way as to keep benefit payments at an adequate level for disabilities that are covered, rather than to cover all disabilities inadequately. Finally, California has a legitimate concern in maintaining the contribution rate at a level that will not unduly burden participating employees, particularly low income employees who may be most in need of the disability insurance.

These policies provide an objective and wholly noninvidious basis for the State's decision not to create a more comprehensive insurance program than it has. There is no evidence in the record that the selection of the risks insured by the program worked to discriminate against any definable group or class in terms of the aggregate risk protection derived by that group or class from the program.[20] There is no risk from which men are protected and women are not. Likewise, there is no risk from which women are protected and men are not.

The appellee simply contends that, although she has received insurance protection equivalent to that provided all other participating employees, she has suffered discrimination because she encountered a risk that was outside the program's protection. For the reasons we have stated, we hold that this contention is not a valid one under the Equal Protection Clause of the Fourteenth Amendment.

MR. JUSTICE BRENNAN, *with whom* **MR. JUSTICE DOUGLAS** *and* **MR. JUSTICE MARSHALL** *join, dissenting.*

Relying upon *Dandridge v. Williams* and *Jefferson v. Hackney*, the Court today rejects appellees' equal protection claim and upholds the exclusion of normal-pregnancy-related disabilities from coverage under California's disability insurance program on the ground that the legislative classification rationally promotes the State's legitimate cost-saving interests in "maintaining

---

20. The dissenting opinion to the contrary, this case is thus a far cry from cases like *Reed v. Reed* and *Frontiero v. Richardson*, involving discrimination based upon gender as such. The California insurance program does not exclude anyone from benefit eligibility because of gender but merely removes one physical condition—pregnancy—from the list of compensable disabilities. While it is true that only women can become pregnant it does not follow that every legislative classification concerning pregnancy is a sex-based classification like those considered in *Reed* and *Frontiero*. Normal pregnancy is an objectively identifiable physical condition with unique characteristics. Absent a showing that distinctions involving pregnancy are mere pretexts designed to effect an invidious discrimination against the members of one sex or the other, lawmakers are constitutionally free to include or exclude pregnancy from the coverage of legislation such as this on any reasonable basis, just as with respect to any other physical condition. The lack of identity between the excluded disability and gender as such under this insurance program becomes clear upon the most cursory analysis. The program divides potential recipients into two groups—pregnant women and nonpregnant persons. While the first group is exclusively female, the second includes members of both sexes. The fiscal and actuarial benefits of the program thus accrue to members of both sexes.

the self-supporting nature of its insurance program[,] . . . distributing the available resources in such a way as to keep benefit payments at an adequate level for disabilities that are covered, . . . [and] maintaining the contribution rate at a level that will not unduly burden participating employees. . .." Because I believe that *Reed v. Reed* and *Frontiero v. Richardson* mandate a stricter standard of scrutiny which the State's classification fails to satisfy, I respectfully dissent.

California's disability insurance program was enacted to supplement the State's unemployment insurance and workmen's compensation programs by providing benefits to wage earners to cushion the economic effects of income loss and medical expenses resulting from sickness or injury.

To achieve the Act's broad humanitarian goals, the legislature fashioned a pooled-risk disability fund covering all employees at the same rate of contribution, regardless of individual risk. The only requirement that must be satisfied before an employee becomes eligible to receive disability benefits is that the employee must have contributed one percent of a minimum income of $300 during a one-year base period. The "basic benefits," varying from $25 to $119 per week, depending upon the employee's base-period earnings, begin on the eighth day of disability or on the first day of hospitalization. Benefits are payable for a maximum of 26 weeks, but may not exceed one-half of the employee's total base-period earnings. Finally, compensation is paid for virtually all disabling conditions without regard to cost, voluntariness, uniqueness, predictability, or "normalcy" of the disability. Thus, for example, workers are compensated for costly disabilities such as heart attacks, voluntary disabilities such as cosmetic surgery or sterilization, disabilities unique to sex or race such as prostatectomies or sickle-cell anemia, pre-existing conditions inevitably resulting in

disability such as degenerative arthritis or cataracts, and "normal" disabilities such as removal of irritating wisdom teeth or other orthodontia.

Despite the Code's broad goals and scope of coverage, compensation is denied for disabilities suffered in connection with a "normal" pregnancy—disabilities suffered only by women. Disabilities caused by pregnancy, however, like other physically disabling conditions covered by the Code, require medical care, often include hospitalization, anesthesia and surgical procedures, and may involve genuine risk to life. Moreover, the economic effects caused by pregnancy-related disabilities are functionally indistinguishable from the effects caused by any other disability: wages are lost due to a physical inability to work, and medical expenses are incurred for the delivery of the child and for postpartum care. In my view, by singling out for less favorable treatment a gender-linked disability peculiar to women, the State has created a double standard for disability compensation: a limitation is imposed upon the disabilities for which women workers may recover, while men receive full compensation for all disabilities suffered, including those that affect only or primarily their sex, such as prostatectomies, circumcision, hemophilia, and gout. In effect, one set of rules is applied to females and another to males. Such dissimilar treatment of men and women, on the basis of physical characteristics inextricably linked to one sex, inevitably constitutes sex discrimination.

In the past, when a legislative classification has turned on gender, the Court has justifiably applied a standard of judicial scrutiny more strict than that generally accorded economic or social welfare programs. Yet, by its decision today, the Court appears willing to abandon that higher standard of review without satisfactorily explaining what differentiates the gender-based classification employed in this case from those found unconstitutional in *Reed* and *Frontiero*.

I cannot join the Court's apparent retreat. I continue to adhere to my view that "classifications based upon sex, like classifications based upon race, alienage, or national origin, are inherently suspect, and must therefore be subjected to strict judicial scrutiny." *Frontiero v. Richardson*. When, as in this case, the State employs a legislative classification that distinguishes between beneficiaries solely by reference to gender-linked disability risks, "[t]he Court is not . . . free to sustain the statute on the ground that it rationally promotes legitimate governmental interests; rather, such suspect classifications can be sustained only when the State bears the burden of demonstrating that the challenged legislation serves overriding or compelling interests that cannot be achieved either by a more carefully tailored legislative

classification or by the use of feasible, less drastic means." *Kahn v. Shevin*.

The State has clearly failed to meet that burden in the present case. The essence of the State's justification for excluding disabilities caused by a normal pregnancy from its disability compensation scheme is that covering such disabilities would be too costly. To be sure, as presently funded, inclusion of normal pregnancies "would be substantially more costly than the present program." The present level of benefits for insured disabilities could not be maintained without increasing the employee contribution rate, raising or lifting the yearly contribution ceiling, or securing state subsidies. But whatever role such monetary considerations may play in traditional equal protection analysis, the State's interest in preserving the fiscal integrity of its disability insurance program simply cannot render the State's use of a suspect classification constitutional.

CRAIG v. BOREN

429 U.S. 190 (1976)

Opinion: Brennan, joined by White, Marshall, Powell, Stevens, and in all but Part II-D by Blackmun
Concurrence: Stewart
Concurrence: Blackmun
Concurrence: Powell
Concurrence: Stevens
Dissent: Rehnquist
Dissent: Burger

In the following case, the Court examines a distinction based on sex that disadvantages men. Consider the strategy employed by proponents of equal rights for women to find cases in which men, rather than women, were discri-

minated against. How might the fact that this case concerns discrimination against men have impacted the Court's jurisprudence? Specifically, pay special attention to the way that U.S. Supreme Court Justice William Brennan, now writing in the majority, draws from his earlier dissent in Geduldig v. Aiello. As you read the case, also pay attention to the Court's announcement of what has come to be called intermediate scrutiny. In what ways does it differ from both rational basis review and strict scrutiny? What difference, if any, would it have made in the prior cases that we have read if the Court had adopted this standard earlier? Moreover, do you think that the Court was mistaken in not adopting *a strict level of scrutiny as the ERA would have required? What effect, if any, should the rejection of the ERA have on the Court's determination as to what level of scrutiny is appropriate for gender discrimination?*

MR. JUSTICE BRENNAN *delivered the opinion of the Court.*

The interaction of two sections of an Oklahoma statute prohibits the sale of "nonintoxicating" 3.2% beer to males under the age of 21 and to females under the age of 18. The question to be decided is whether such a gender-based differential constitutes a denial to males 18–20 years of age of the equal protection of the laws in violation of the Fourteenth Amendment.

This action was brought in the District Court for the Western District of Oklahoma on December 20, 1972, by appellant Craig, a male then between 18 and 21 years of age, and by appellant Whitener, a licensed vendor of 3.2% beer. The complaint sought declaratory and injunctive relief against enforcement of the gender-based differential on the ground that it constituted invidious discrimination against males 18–20 years of age. . . .

II

A

Before 1972, Oklahoma defined the commencement of civil majority at age 18 for females and age 21 for males. In contrast, females were held criminally responsible as adults at age 18, and males at age 16. After the Court of Appeals for the Tenth Circuit held, in 1972, on the authority of *Reed v. Reed*, that the age distinction was unconstitutional for purposes of establishing criminal responsibility as adults, the Oklahoma Legislature fixed age 18 as applicable to both males and females. In 1972, 18 also was established as the age of

majority for males and females in civil matters, except that §§241 and 245 of the 3.2% beer statute were simultaneously codified to create an exception to the gender-free rule.

Analysis may appropriately begin with the reminder that *Reed* emphasized that statutory classifications that distinguish between males and females are "subject to scrutiny under the Equal Protection Clause." To withstand constitutional challenge, previous cases establish that classifications by gender must serve important governmental objectives and must be substantially related to achievement of those objectives. . . .

Reed v. Reed has also provided the underpinning for decisions that have invalidated statutes employing gender as an inaccurate proxy for other, more germane bases of classification. In light of the weak congruence between gender and the characteristic or trait that gender purported to represent, it was necessary that the legislatures choose either to realign their substantive laws in a gender-neutral fashion or to adopt procedures for identifying those instances where the sex-centered generalization actually comported with fact.

We turn then to the question whether, under *Reed*, the difference between males and females with respect to the purchase of 3.2% beer warrants the differential in age drawn by the Oklahoma statute. We conclude that it does not.

We accept for purposes of discussion the District Court's identification of the objective underlying §§241 and 245 as the enhancement of traffic safety.

The appellees introduced a variety of statistical surveys. First, an analysis of arrest statistics for 1973 demonstrated that 18–20-year-old male arrests for "driving under the influence" and "drunkenness" substantially exceeded female arrests for that same age period. Similarly, youths aged 17–21 were found to be overrepresented among those killed or injured in traffic accidents, with males again numerically exceeding females in this regard. Third, a random roadside survey in Oklahoma City revealed that young males were more inclined to drive and drink beer than were their female counterparts. Conceding that "the case is not free from doubt," the District Court nonetheless concluded that this statistical showing substantiated "a rational basis for the legislative judgment underlying the challenged classification."

Even were this statistical evidence accepted as accurate, it nevertheless offers only a weak answer to the equal protection question presented here.

. . . [T]he showing offered by the appellees does not satisfy us that sex represents a legitimate, accurate proxy for the regulation of drinking and driving. In fact, when it is further recognized that Oklahoma's statute prohibits only the selling of 3.2% beer to young males, and not their drinking the beverage once acquired (even after purchase by their 18-20-year-old female companions), the relationship between gender and traffic safety becomes far too tenuous to satisfy *Reed*'s requirement that the gender-based difference be substantially related to achievement of the statutory objective.

MR. JUSTICE STEVENS, *concurring.*

There is only one Equal Protection Clause. It requires every State to govern impartially. It does not direct the courts to apply one standard of review in some cases and a different standard in other cases. Whatever criticism may be leveled at a judicial opinion implying that there are at least three such standards applies with the same force to a double standard.

I am inclined to believe that what has become known as the two-tiered analysis of equal protection claims does not describe a completely logical method of deciding cases, but rather is a method the Court has employed to explain decisions that actually apply a single standard in a reasonably consistent fashion. I also suspect that a careful explanation of the reasons motivating particular decisions may contribute more to an identification of that standard than an attempt to articulate it in all-encompassing terms. It may therefore be appropriate for me to state the principal reasons which persuaded me to join the Court's opinion.

In this case, the classification is not as obnoxious as some the Court has condemned, nor as inoffensive as some the Court has accepted. It is objectionable because it is based on an accident of birth, because it is a mere remnant of the now almost universally rejected tradition of discriminating against males in this age bracket, and because, to the extent it reflects any physical difference between males and females, it is actually perverse. The question then is whether the traffic safety justification put forward by the State is sufficient to make an otherwise offensive classification acceptable.

The classification is not totally irrational. For the evidence does indicate that there are more males than females in this age bracket who drive, and also more who drink. Nevertheless, there are several reasons why I regard the justification as unacceptable. It is difficult to believe that the statute was actually intended to cope with the problem of traffic safety, since it has only a minimal effect on access to a not very intoxicating beverage, and does not prohibit its consumption. Moreover, the empirical data submitted by the State accentuate the unfairness of treating all 18–20-year-old males as inferior to their female counterparts. The legislation imposes a restraint on 100% of the males in the class allegedly because about 2% of them have probably violated one or more laws relating to the consumption of alcoholic beverages. It is unlikely that this law will have a significant deterrent effect either on that 2% or on the law-abiding 98%. But even assuming some such slight benefit, it does not seem to me that an insult to all of the young men of the State can be justified by visiting the sins of the 2% on the 98%.

MR. CHIEF JUSTICE BURGER,
dissenting.

On the merits, we have only recently recognized that our duty is not "to create substantive constitutional rights in the name of guaranteeing equal protection of the laws." *San Antonio School Dist. v. Rodriguez.* Thus, even interests of such importance in our society as public education and housing do not qualify as "fundamental rights"

for equal protection purposes, because they have no textually independent constitutional status. Though today's decision does not go so far as to make gender-based classifications "suspect," it makes gender a disfavored classification. Without an independent constitutional basis supporting the right asserted or disfavoring the classification adopted, I can justify no substantive constitutional protection other than the normal *McGowan v. Maryland* protection afforded by the Equal Protection Clause.

The means employed by the Oklahoma Legislature to achieve the objectives sought may not be agreeable to some judges, but since eight Members of the Court think the means not irrational, I see no basis for striking down the statute as violative of the Constitution simply because we find it unwise, unneeded, or possibly even a bit foolish.

CALIFANO v. WEBSTER
430 U.S. 313 (1977)

Opinion: Per Curiam

As with the issue of race, the Court was soon confronted with the constitutionality of laws giving preferential treatment to women. Such laws are often justified by a desire to rectify the effects of past discrimination. Consider how the Court answers the question in this case. Is the Court's answer similar to the one it has given with respect to race-based affirmative action? Should it be? Should the lesser level of scrutiny afforded to gender classifications affect the Court's assessment of the constitutionality of discrimination that benefits women?

PER CURIAM

Under §215 of the Social Security Act, old-age insurance benefits are computed

on the basis of the wage earner's "average monthly wage" earned during his "benefit computation years" which are the "elapsed years" (reduced by five) during which the wage earner's covered wages were highest. Until a 1972 amendment, "elapsed years" depended upon the sex of the wage earner. Section 215(b)(3) prescribed that the number of "elapsed years" for a male wage earner would be three higher than for an otherwise similarly situated female wage earner; for a male, the number of "elapsed years" equaled the number of years that elapsed after 1950 and before the year in which he attained age 65; for a female, the number of "elapsed years" equaled the number of years that elapsed after 1950 and before the year in which she attained age 62.

A single-judge District Court for the Eastern District of New York, on review under §205(g) of the Social Security Act of a denial, after hearing, of appellee's request that the more favorable formula be used to compute his benefits, held that, on two grounds, the statutory scheme violated the equal protection component of the Due Process Clause of the Fifth Amendment: (1) that to give women who reached age 62 before 1975 greater benefits than men of the same age and earnings record was irrational, and (2) that, in any event, the 1972 amendment was to be construed to apply retroactively, because construing the amendment to give men who reach age 62 in 1975 or later the benefit of the 1972 amendments but to deny older men the same benefit would render the amendment irrational, and therefore unconstitutional. We reverse.

To withstand scrutiny under the equal protection component of the Fifth Amendment's Due Process Clause, "classifications by gender must serve important governmental objectives, and must be substantially related to achievement of those objectives." *Craig v. Boren.* Reduction of the disparity in economic condition between men and women caused by the long history of discrimination against women has been recognized as such an important governmental objective.

The more favorable treatment of the female wage earner enacted here was not a result of "archaic and overbroad generalizations" about women, or of "the role-typing society has long imposed" upon women, such as casual assumptions that women are "the weaker sex" or are more likely to be childrearers or dependents.

The challenged statute operated directly to compensate women for past economic discrimination. Retirement benefits under the Act are based on past earnings.

Thus, allowing women, who as such have been unfairly hindered from earning as much as men, to eliminate additional low-earning years from the calculation of their retirement benefits works directly to remedy some part of the effect of past discrimination.

That Congress changed its mind in 1972 and equalized the treatment of men and women does not, as the District Court concluded, constitute an admission by Congress that its previous policy was invidiously discriminatory. Moreover, elimination of the more favorable benefit computation for women wage earners, even in the remedial context, is wholly consistent with those reforms, which require equal treatment of men and women in preference to the attitudes of "romantic paternalism" that have contributed to the "long and unfortunate history of sex discrimination."

ORR v. ORR

440 U.S. 268 (1979)

Opinion: Brennan, joined by Stewart, White, Marshall, Blackmun, Stevens
Concurrence: Blackmun
Concurrence: Stevens
Dissent: Rehnquist, joined by Burger
Dissent: Powell

This case concerns an Alabama law that imposed alimony obligations only on men. Like the statute at issue in Califano v. Webster, *this law categorically benefited women at the expense of men. However, the outcome is different in this case because the law was predicated on a stereotype. Is this a distinction without a difference? Is it correct to distinguish* Califano v. Webster *from this case?*

MR. JUSTICE BRENNAN *delivered the opinion of the Court.*

The question presented is the constitutionality of Alabama alimony statutes which provide that husbands, but not wives, may be required to pay alimony upon divorce.

On February 26, 1974, a final decree of divorce was entered, dissolving the marriage of William and Lillian Orr. That decree directed appellant, Mr. Orr, to pay appellee, Mrs. Orr, $1,240 per month in alimony. We now hold the challenged Alabama statutes unconstitutional, and reverse.

. . . "To withstand scrutiny" under the Equal Protection Clause, "classifications by gender must serve important governmental objectives, and must be substantially related to achievement of those objectives." *Califano v. Webster.* We shall, therefore, examine the three governmental objectives that might arguably be served by Alabama's statutory scheme.

Appellant views the Alabama alimony statutes as effectively announcing the State's preference for an allocation of family responsibilities under which the wife plays a dependent role, and as seeking for their objective the reinforcement of that model among the State's citizens. We agree, as he urges, that prior cases settle that this purpose cannot sustain the statutes. "No longer is the female destined solely for the home and the rearing of the family, and only the male for the marketplace and the world of ideas." If the statute is to survive constitutional attack, therefore, it must be validated on some other basis.

The opinion of the Alabama Court of Civil Appeals suggests other purposes that the statute may serve. Its opinion states that the Alabama statutes were "designed" for "the wife of a broken marriage who needs financial assistance." This may be read as asserting either of two legislative objectives. One is a legislative purpose to provide help for needy spouses, using sex as a proxy for need. The other is a goal of compensating women for past discrimination during marriage, which assertedly has left them unprepared to fend for themselves in the working world following divorce. We concede, of course, that assisting needy spouses is a legitimate and important governmental objective. We have also recognized "[r]eduction of the disparity in economic condition between men and women caused by the long history of discrimination against women . . . as . . . an important governmental objective," *Califano v. Webster.* It only remains, therefore, to determine whether the classification at issue here is "substantially related to achievement of those objectives."

Ordinarily, we would begin the analysis of the "needy spouse" objective by considering whether sex is a sufficiently "accurate proxy," for dependency to establish that the gender classification rests "upon some ground of difference having a fair and substantial relation to the object of the legislation." Similarly, we would initially approach the "compensation" rationale by asking whether women had, in fact, been significantly discriminated against in the sphere to which the statute applied a sex-based classification, leaving the sexes "not similarly situated with respect to opportunities" in that sphere.

But in this case, even if sex were a reliable proxy for need, and even if the institution of marriage did discriminate against women, these factors still would "not adequately justify the salient features of" Alabama's statutory scheme. Under the statute, individualized hearings at which the parties' relative financial circumstances are considered already occur. There is no reason, therefore, to use sex as a proxy for need. Needy males could be helped along with needy females with little if any additional burden on the State. In such circumstances, not even an administrative convenience rationale exists to justify operating by generalization or proxy.

Moreover, use of a gender classification actually produces perverse results in this case. As compared to a gender-neutral law placing alimony obligations on the spouse able to pay, the present Alabama statutes give an advantage only to the financially secure wife whose husband is in need. A gender-based classification which, as compared to a gender-neutral one, generates additional benefits only for those it has no reason to prefer cannot survive equal protection scrutiny.

Legislative classifications which distribute benefits and burdens on the basis of gender carry the inherent risk of reinforcing stereotypes about the "proper place" of women and their need for special protection. Thus, even statutes purportedly designed to compensate for and ameliorate the effects of past discrimination must be carefully tailored. Where, as here, the State's compensatory and ameliorative purposes are as well served by a gender-neutral classification as one that gender classifies, and therefore carries with it the baggage of sexual stereotypes, the State cannot be permitted to classify on the basis of sex. And this is doubly so where the choice made by the State appears to redound—if only indirectly—to the benefit of those without need for special solicitude.

MICHAEL M. v. SUPERIOR COURT OF SONOMA COUNTY

450 U.S. 464 (1981)

Opinion: Rehnquist, joined by Burger, Stewart, Powell
Concurrence: Stewart
Concurrence: Blackmun
Dissent: Brennan, joined by White, Marshall
Dissent: Stevens

We have already noted that one of the real differences between men and women concerns the ability to become pregnant. In this case, the Court considers whether that real difference justifies laws that make a distinction based on gender in matters of statutory rape. Given that women can be impregnated while men cannot, can an argument be made for laws that favor the protection of women in matters of statutory rape? Should the state be able to take this fact into account in passing criminal laws?

JUSTICE REHNQUIST *announced the judgment of the Court and delivered an opinion, in which* **THE CHIEF JUSTICE,** **JUSTICE STEWART,** *and* **JUSTICE POWELL** *joined.*

The question presented in this case is whether California's "statutory rape" law, §261.5 of the Cal. Penal Code Ann., violates the Equal Protection Clause of the Fourteenth Amendment. Section 261.5 defines unlawful sexual intercourse as "an act of sexual intercourse accomplished with a female not the wife of the perpetrator, where the female is under the age of 18 years." The statute thus makes men alone criminally liable for the act of sexual intercourse.

In July, 1978, a complaint was filed in the Municipal Court of Sonoma County, Cal., alleging that petitioner, then a

17½-year-old male, had had unlawful sexual intercourse with a female under the age of 18, in violation of §261.5. The evidence adduced at a preliminary hearing showed that, at approximately midnight on June 3, 1978, petitioner and two friends approached Sharon, a 16 1/2-year-old female, and her sister as they waited at a bus stop. Petitioner and Sharon, who had already been drinking, moved away from the others and began to kiss. After being struck in the face for rebuffing petitioner's initial advances, Sharon submitted to sexual intercourse with petitioner. Prior to trial, petitioner sought to set aside the information on both state and federal constitutional grounds, asserting that §261.5 unlawfully discriminated on the basis of gender. The trial court and the California Court of Appeal denied petitioner's request for relief, and petitioner sought review in the Supreme Court of California.

The Supreme Court held that "section 261.5 discriminates on the basis of sex, because only females may be victims and only males may violate the section." The court then subjected the classification to "strict scrutiny," stating that it must be justified by a compelling state interest. It found that the classification was "supported not by mere social convention, but by the immutable physiological fact that it is the female exclusively who can become pregnant." Canvassing "the tragic human costs of illegitimate teenage pregnancies," including the large number of teenage abortions, the increased medical risk associated with teenage pregnancies, and the social consequences of teenage childbearing, the court concluded that the State has a compelling interest in preventing such pregnancies. Because males alone can "physiologically cause the result which the law properly seeks to avoid," the court further held that the gender classification was readily justified as a means of identifying offender and victim.

For the reasons stated below, we affirm the judgment of the California Supreme Court.

As is evident from our opinions, the Court has had some difficulty in agreeing upon the proper approach and analysis in cases involving challenges to gender-based classifications. Unlike the California Supreme Court, we have not held that gender-based classifications are "inherently suspect," and thus we do not apply so-called "strict scrutiny" to those classifications. Our cases have held, however, that the traditional minimum rationality test takes on a somewhat "sharper focus" when gender-based classifications are challenged. *See Craig v. Boren*. In *Reed v. Reed*, for example, the Court stated that a gender-based classification will be upheld if it bears a "fair and substantial relationship" to legitimate state ends, while in *Craig v. Boren*, the Court restated the test to require the classification to bear a "substantial relationship" to "important governmental objectives."

Underlying these decisions is the principle that a legislature may not "make overbroad generalizations based on sex which are entirely unrelated to any differences between men and women or which demean the ability or social status of the affected class." But because the Equal Protection Clause does not "demand that a statute necessarily apply equally to all persons" or require "things which are different in fact ... to be treated in law as though they were the same," this Court has consistently upheld statutes where the gender classification is not invidious, but rather realistically reflects the fact that the sexes are not similarly situated in certain circumstances. As the Court has stated, a legislature may "provide for the special problems of women."

We are satisfied not only that the prevention of illegitimate pregnancy is at least one of the "purposes" of the statute, but also that the State has a strong interest in preventing such pregnancy. At the risk of stating the obvious, teenage pregnancies, which have increased dramatically over the last two decades, have significant social, medical, and economic consequences for both the mother and her child, and the State. Of particular concern to the State is that approximately half of all teenage pregnancies end in abortion. And of those children who are born, their illegitimacy makes them likely candidates to become wards of the State.

We need not be medical doctors to discern that young men and young women are not similarly situated with respect to the problems and the risks of sexual intercourse. Only women may become pregnant, and they suffer disproportionately the profound physical, emotional, and psychological consequences of sexual activity. The statute at issue here protects women from sexual intercourse at an age when those consequences are particularly severe.

The question thus boils down to whether a State may attack the problem of sexual intercourse and teenage pregnancy directly by prohibiting a male from having sexual intercourse with a minor female. We hold that such a statute is sufficiently related to the State's objectives to pass constitutional muster.

Because virtually all of the significant harmful and inescapably identifiable consequences of teenage pregnancy fall on the young female, a legislature acts well within its authority when it elects to punish only the participant who, by nature, suffers few of the consequences of his conduct. It is hardly unreasonable for a legislature acting to protect minor females to exclude them from punishment. Moreover, the risk of pregnancy itself constitutes a substantial deterrence to young females. No similar natural sanctions deter males. A criminal sanction imposed solely on males thus serves to roughly "equalize" the deterrents on the sexes.

There remains only petitioner's contention that the statute is unconstitutional as it is applied to him because he, like Sharon, was under 18 at the time of sexual intercourse. Petitioner argues that the statute is flawed because it presumes that, as between two persons under 18, the male is the culpable aggressor. We find petitioner's contentions unpersuasive. Contrary to his assertions, the statute does not rest on the assumption that males are generally the aggressors. It is, instead, an attempt by a legislature to prevent illegitimate teenage pregnancy by providing an additional deterrent for men. The age of the man is irrelevant, since young men are as capable as older men of inflicting the harm sought to be prevented.

In upholding the California statute, we also recognize that this is not a case where a statute is being challenged on the grounds that it "invidiously discriminates" against females. To the contrary, the statute places a burden on males which is not shared by females. But we find nothing to suggest that men, because of past discrimination or peculiar disadvantages, are in need of the special solicitude of the courts. Nor is this a case where the gender classification is made "solely for . . . administrative convenience," or rests on "the baggage of sexual stereotypes." As we have held, the statute instead reasonably reflects the fact that the consequences of sexual intercourse and pregnancy fall more heavily on the female than on the male.

Accordingly the judgment of the California Supreme Court is

Affirmed.

JUSTICE BRENNAN, *with whom* **JUSTICES WHITE** *and* **MARSHALL** *join, dissenting.*

It is disturbing to find the Court so splintered on a case that presents such a straightforward issue: whether the admittedly gender-based classification in Cal.

Penal Code Ann. §261.5 bears a sufficient relationship to the State's asserted goal of preventing teenage pregnancies to survive the "mid-level" constitutional scrutiny mandated by *Craig v. Boren.* Applying the analytical framework provided by our precedents, I am convinced that there is only one proper resolution of this issue: the classification must be declared unconstitutional. I fear that the plurality opinion and Justices Stewart and Blackmun reach the opposite result by placing too much emphasis on the desirability of achieving the State's asserted statutory goal— prevention of teenage pregnancy—and not enough emphasis on the fundamental question of whether the sex-based discrimination in the California statute is substantially related to the achievement of that goal.

However, a State's bare assertion that its gender-based statutory classification substantially furthers an important governmental interest is not enough to meet its burden of proof under *Craig v. Boren.* Rather, the State must produce evidence that will persuade the court that its assertion is true.

The State has not produced such evidence in this case. Moreover, there are at least two serious flaws in the State's assertion that law enforcement problems created by a gender-neutral statutory rape law would make such a statute less effective than a gender-based statute in deterring sexual activity.

First, the experience of other jurisdictions, and California itself, belies the plurality's conclusion that a gender-neutral statutory rape law "may well be incapable of enforcement." There are now at least 37 States that have enacted gender-neutral statutory rape laws. Although most of these laws protect young persons (of either sex) from the sexual exploitation of older individuals, the laws of Arizona, Florida, and Illinois permit prosecution of both minor females and minor males for engaging in mutual sexual conduct.

California has introduced no evidence that those States have been handicapped by the enforcement problems the plurality finds so persuasive. Surely, if those States could provide such evidence, we might expect that California would have introduced it.

In addition, the California Legislature in recent years has revised other sections of the Penal Code to make them gender-neutral. For example, Cal. Penal Code Ann. §§286(b)(1) and 288a(b)(1), prohibiting sodomy and oral copulation with a "person who is under 18 years of age," could cause two minor homosexuals to be subjected to criminal sanctions for engaging in mutually consensual conduct. Again, the State has introduced no evidence to explain why a gender-neutral statutory rape law would be any more difficult to enforce than those statutes.

The second flaw in the State's assertion is that, even assuming that a gender-neutral statute would be more difficult to enforce, the State has still not shown that those enforcement problems would make such a statute less effective than a gender-based statute in deterring minor females from engaging in sexual intercourse. Common sense, however, suggests that a gender-neutral statutory rape law is potentially a greater deterrent of sexual activity than a gender-based law, for the simple reason that a gender-neutral law subjects both men and women to criminal sanctions, and thus arguably has a deterrent effect on twice as many potential violators. Even if fewer persons were prosecuted under the gender-neutral law, as the State suggests, it would still be true that twice as many persons would be subject to arrest. The State's failure to prove that a gender-neutral law would be a less effective deterrent than a gender-based law, like the State's failure to prove that a gender-neutral law would be difficult to enforce, should have led this Court to invalidate §261.5.

ROSTKER v. GOLDBERG

453 U.S. 57 (1981)

Opinion: Rehnquist, joined by Burger,
  Stewart, Blackmun, Powell, Stevens
Dissent: White, joined by Brennan
Dissent: Marshall, joined by Brennan

JUSTICE REHNQUIST *delivered the
opinion of the Court.*

The question presented is whether the
Military Selective Service Act violates the
Fifth Amendment to the United States
Constitution in authorizing the President
to require the registration of males, and not
females.

Section 3 of the Act, as amended,
empowers the President, by proclamation,
to require the registration of "every male
citizen" and male resident aliens between
the ages of 18 and 26. The purpose of this
registration is to facilitate any eventual
conscription: pursuant to §4 (a) of the Act,
as amended, those persons required to register under §3 are liable for training and
service in the Armed Forces. The MSSA registration provision serves no other purpose
beyond providing a pool for subsequent
induction.

Registration for the draft under §3
was discontinued in 1975. In early 1980,
President Carter determined that it was
necessary to reactivate the draft registration process. The immediate impetus for
this decision was the Soviet armed invasion
of Afghanistan. He also recommended that
Congress take action to amend the MSSA
to permit the registration and conscription
of women as well as men.

Congress agreed that it was necessary
to reactivate the registration process, and
allocated funds for that purpose in a Joint
Resolution which passed the House on

April 22 and the Senate on June 12. The
Resolution did not allocate all the funds
originally requested by the President, but
only those necessary to register males.
Although Congress considered the question at great length, it declined to amend
the MSSA to permit the registration of
women.

These events of last year breathed new
life into a lawsuit which had been essentially dormant in the lower courts for
nearly a decade. It began in 1971, when
several men subject to registration for the
draft and subsequent induction into the
Armed Services filed a complaint in the
United States District Court for the Eastern
District of Pennsylvania challenging the
MSSA on several grounds. On July 1, 1980,
the court certified a plaintiff class of "all
male persons who are registered or subject
to registration under 50 U.S.C. App. §453
or are liable for training and service in the
armed forces of the United States under 50
U.S.C. App. §§454, 456 (h) and 467 (c)."

On Friday, July 18, 1980, three days before
registration was to commence, the District
Court issued an opinion finding that the
Act violated the Due Process Clause of
the Fifth Amendment and permanently
enjoined the Government from requiring
registration under the Act. . . . [T]he court
rejected plaintiffs' suggestions that the
equal protection claim should be tested
under "strict scrutiny," and also rejected
defendants' argument that the deference
due Congress in the area of military affairs
required application of the traditional "minimum scrutiny" test. Applying the "important government interest" test articulated
in *Craig v. Boren*, the court struck down the
MSSA. The court stressed that it was not
deciding whether or to what extent women

should serve in combat, but only the issue of registration. . . .

The Solicitor General argues, largely on the basis of the foregoing cases emphasizing the deference due Congress in the area of military affairs and national security, that this Court should scrutinize the MSSA only to determine if the distinction drawn between men and women bears a rational relation to some legitimate Government purpose, and should not examine the Act under the heightened scrutiny with which we have approached gender-based discrimination; *see Michael M. v. Superior Court of Sonoma County, Craig v. Boren, Reed v. Reed.* In this case, the courts are called upon to decide whether Congress, acting under an explicit constitutional grant of authority, has by that action transgressed an explicit guarantee of individual rights which limits the authority so conferred. Simply labeling the legislative decision "military" on the one hand, or "gender-based," on the other, does not automatically guide a court to the correct constitutional result.

No one could deny that, under the test of *Craig v. Boren*, the Government's interest in raising and supporting armies is an "important governmental interest." Congress and its Committees carefully considered and debated two alternative means of furthering that interest: the first was to register only males for potential conscription, and the other was to register both sexes. Congress chose the former alternative. When that decision is challenged on equal protection grounds, the question a court must decide is not which alternative it would have chosen, had it been the primary decisionmaker, but whether that chosen by Congress denies equal protection of the laws.

> . . . "We cannot say that, in exercising its broad constitutional power here, Congress has violated the Due Process Clause of the Fifth Amendment."

Or, as put a generation ago in a case not involving any claim of gender-based discrimination:

> [J]udges are not given the task of running the Army. The responsibility for setting up channels through which . . . grievances can be considered and fairly settled rests upon the Congress and upon the President of the United States and his subordinates. The military constitutes a specialized community governed by a separate discipline from that of the civilian. Orderly government requires that the judiciary be as scrupulous not to interfere with legitimate Army matters as the Army must be scrupulous not to intervene in judicial matters.

This case is quite different from several of the gender-based discrimination cases we have considered in that, despite appellees' assertions, Congress did not act "unthinkingly" or "reflexively and not for any considered reason."

The issue was considered at great length, and Congress clearly expressed its purpose and intent.

Congress determined that any future draft, which would be facilitated by the registration scheme, would be characterized by a need for combat troops. The purpose of registration, therefore, was to prepare for a draft *of combat troops.*

Women as a group, however, unlike men as a group, are not eligible for combat. The restrictions on the participation of women in combat in the Navy and Air Force are statutory. Under 10 U.S.C. §6015, "women may not be assigned to duty on vessels or in aircraft that are engaged in combat missions," and under 10 U.S.C. §8549 female members of the Air Force "may not be assigned to duty in aircraft engaged in combat missions." The Army and Marine Corps preclude the use of women in combat as a matter of established policy. Congress specifically recognized and endorsed the exclusion of women from combat in exempting women from registration. In the words of the Senate Report:

> The principle that women should not intentionally and routinely engage in combat is fundamental, and enjoys wide support among our people. It is universally supported by military leaders who have testified before the Committee.... Current law and policy exclude women from being assigned to combat in our military forces, and the Committee reaffirms this policy.

Since women are excluded from combat, Congress concluded that they would not be needed in the event of a draft, and therefore decided not to register them.

This is not a case of Congress arbitrarily choosing to burden one of two similarly situated groups, such as would be the case with an all-black or all-white, or an all-Catholic or all-Lutheran, or an all-Republican or all-Democratic registration. Men and women, because of the combat restrictions on women, are simply not similarly situated for purposes of a draft or registration for a draft.

The exemption of women from registration is not only sufficiently, but also closely, related to Congress' purpose in authorizing registration. The Constitution requires that Congress treat similarly situated persons similarly, not that it engage in gestures of superficial equality.

In light of the foregoing, we conclude that Congress acted well within its constitutional authority when it authorized the registration of men, and not women, under the Military Selective Service Act. The decision of the District Court holding otherwise is accordingly

Reversed.

JUSTICE WHITE, *with whom* **JUSTICE BRENNAN** *joins, dissenting.*

I assume what has not been challenged in this case—that excluding women from combat positions does not offend the Constitution. . . . I perceive little, if any, indication that Congress itself concluded that every position in the military, no matter how far removed from combat, must be filled with combat-ready men. Common sense and experience in recent wars, where women volunteers were employed in substantial numbers, belie this view of reality. . . .

I would also have little difficulty agreeing to a reversal if all the women who could serve in wartime without adversely affecting combat readiness could predictably be obtained through volunteers. In that event, the equal protection component of the Fifth Amendment would not require the United States to go through, and a large segment of the population to be burdened with, the expensive and essentially useless procedure of registering women. But again I cannot agree with the Court . . . that Congress concluded or that the legislative record indicates that each of the services could rely on women volunteers to fill all the positions for which they might be eligible in the event of mobilization. On the contrary, the record, as I understand it, supports the District Court's finding that the services would have to conscript at least 80,000 persons to fill positions for which combat-ready men would not be required. The consistent position of the Defense Department representatives was that their best estimate of the number of women draftees who could be used productively by the services in the event of a major mobilization would be approximately 80,000 over the first six months. *See* Hearings on S. 2294 before the Senate Committee on Armed Services, 96th Cong., 2d Sess., 1681, 1688 (1980); Hearings on H.R. 6569 before the Subcommittee on Military Personnel of the House Committee on Armed Services, 96th Cong., 2d Sess., 16 (1980). This number took into account the estimated number of women volunteers; *see* Deposition of Director of Selective Service Bernard Rostker 8; Deposition of Principal Deputy Assistant Secretary of Defense Richard Danzig, App. 276. Except for a single, unsupported, and ambiguous statement in the Senate Report to the effect that "women volunteers would fill the requirements for women," there is no indication that Congress rejected the Defense Department's figures or relied upon an alternative set of figures. . . .

As I understand the record, then, in order to secure the personnel it needs during mobilization, the Government cannot rely on volunteers, and must register and draft not only to fill combat positions and those noncombat positions that must be filled by combat-trained men, but also to secure the personnel needed for jobs that can be performed by persons ineligible for combat without diminishing military effectiveness. The claim is that, in providing for the latter category of positions, Congress is free to register and draft only men. I discern no adequate justification for this kind of discrimination between men and women. Accordingly, with all due respect, I dissent.

JUSTICE MARSHALL, *with whom* **JUSTICE BRENNAN** *joins, dissenting.*

The Court today places its imprimatur on one of the most potent remaining public expressions of "ancient canards about the proper role of women," *Phillips v. Martin Marietta Corp.* . . .

B

. . . By now it should be clear that statutes like the MSSA, which discriminate on the basis of gender, must be examined under the "heightened" scrutiny mandated by *Craig v. Boren*. Under this test, a gender-based classification cannot withstand constitutional challenge unless the classification is substantially related to the achievement of an important governmental objective . . .

C

. . . When, as here, a federal law that classifies on the basis of gender is challenged as violating this constitutional guarantee, it is ultimately for this Court, not Congress, to decide whether there exists the constitutionally required "close and substantial relationship" between the discriminatory means employed and the asserted governmental objective. . . .

II

A

The Government does not defend the exclusion of women from registration on the ground that preventing women from serving in the military is substantially related to the effectiveness of the Armed Forces. Indeed, the successful experience of women serving in all branches of the Armed Services would belie any such claim . . .

B

. . . The relevant inquiry under the *Craig v. Boren* test is not whether a *gender-neutral* classification would substantially advance important governmental interests. Rather, the question is whether the gender-based classification is itself substantially related to the achievement of the asserted governmental interest. Thus, the Government's task in this case is to demonstrate that excluding women from registration substantially furthers the goal of preparing for a draft of combat troops. Or to put it another way, the Government must show that registering women would substantially impede its efforts to prepare for such a draft. Under our precedents, the Government cannot meet this burden without showing that a gender-neutral statute would be a less effective means of attaining this end. . . .

VI

After reviewing the discussion and findings contained in the Senate Report, the most I am able to say of the Report is that it demonstrates that drafting *very large numbers* of women would frustrate the achievement of a number of important governmental objectives that relate to the ultimate goal of maintaining "an adequate armed strength . . . to insure the security of this Nation," 50 U.S.C. App. §451(b). Or to put it another way, the Senate Report establishes that

induction of a large number of men, but only a limited number of women, as determined by the military's personnel requirements, would be substantially related to important governmental interests. But the discussion and findings in the Senate Report do not enable the Government to carry its burden of demonstrating that *completely* excluding women from the draft by excluding them from registration substantially furthers important governmental objectives. . . .

In an attempt to avoid its constitutional obligation, the Court today "pushes back the limits of the Constitution" to accommodate an Act of Congress.

I would affirm the judgment of the District Court.

UNITED STATES v. VIRGINIA

518 U.S. 515 (1996)

Opinion: Ginsburg, joined by Stevens, O'Connor, Kennedy, Souter, Breyer
Concurrence: Rehnquist
Dissent: Scalia

The following case concerns a controversy over whether the Virginia Military Institute (VMI), a public school, should be allowed to exclude women from admission. Are there any real differences between men and women that justify the exclusion? For instance, how should the supposedly generalized difference in the physical strengths of the sexes factor into the distinction? Moreover, even if this single factor is a "real difference" between men and women, is it enough to justify VMI's admissions policy excluding women?

JUSTICE GINSBURG *delivered the opinion of the Court.*

Virginia's public institutions of higher learning include an incomparable military college, Virginia Military Institute (VMI). The United States maintains that the Constitution's equal protection guarantee precludes Virginia from reserving exclusively to men the unique educational opportunities VMI affords. We agree.

Founded in 1839, VMI is today the sole single-sex school among Virginia's 15 public institutions of higher learning. VMI's distinctive mission is to produce "citizen-soldiers," men prepared for leadership in civilian life and in military service. VMI constantly endeavors to instill physical and mental discipline in its cadets and impart to them a strong moral code.

Neither the goal of producing citizen-soldiers nor VMI's implementing methodology is inherently unsuitable to women. And the school's impressive record in producing leaders has made admission desirable to some women. Nevertheless, Virginia has elected to preserve exclusively for men the advantages and opportunities a VMI education affords.

VMI cadets live in spartan barracks where surveillance is constant and privacy nonexistent; they wear uniforms, eat together in the mess hall, and regularly participate in drills. Entering you are incessantly exposed to the rat line, "an extreme form of the adversative model," comparable in intensity to Marine Corps boot camp. Tormenting and punishing, the rat line bonds new cadets to their fellow sufferers and, when they have completed the 7-month experience, to their former tormentors.

VMI's "adversative model" is further characterized by a hierarchical "class system" of privileges and responsibilities, a "dyke system" for assigning a senior class mentor to each entering class "rat," and a stringently enforced "honor code," which prescribes that a cadet "does not lie, cheat, steal nor tolerate those who do."

In 1990, prompted by a complaint filed with the Attorney General by a female high-school student seeking admission to VMI, the United States sued the Commonwealth of Virginia and VMI, alleging that VMI's exclusively male admission policy violated the Equal Protection Clause of the Fourteenth Amendment.

In the two years preceding the lawsuit, the District Court noted, VMI had received inquiries from 347 women, but had responded to none of them. "[S]ome women, at least," the court said, "would want to attend the school if they had the opportunity." And it was also established that "some women are capable of all of the individual activities required of VMI cadets."

The District Court ruled in favor of VMI, however, and rejected the equal protection challenge pressed by the United States. That court correctly recognized that *Mississippi Univ. for Women v. Hogan* was the closest guide. There, this Court underscored that a party seeking to uphold government action based on sex must establish an "exceedingly persuasive justification" for the classification. To succeed, the defender of the challenged action must show "at least that the classification serves important governmental objectives and that the discriminatory means employed are substantially related to the achievement of those objectives."

The District Court reasoned that education in "a single-gender environment, be it male or female," yields substantial benefits. If single-gender education for males ranks as an important governmental objective, it becomes obvious, the District Court concluded, that the only means of achieving the objective "is to exclude women from the all-male institution—VMI."

The Court of Appeals for the Fourth Circuit disagreed and vacated the District Court's judgment.

The appeals court greeted with skepticism Virginia's assertion that it offers single-sex education at VMI as a facet of the State's overarching and undisputed policy to advance "autonomy and diversity." Furthermore, the appeals court observed, in urging "diversity" to justify an all-male VMI, the State had supplied "no explanation for the movement away from [single-sex education] in Virginia by public colleges and universities." In short, the court concluded, "[a] policy of diversity which aims to provide an array of educational opportunities, including single-gender institutions, must do more than favor one gender."

In response to the Fourth Circuit's ruling, Virginia proposed a parallel program for women: Virginia Women's Institute for Leadership (VWIL). The 4-year, state-sponsored undergraduate program would be located at Mary Baldwin College, a private liberal arts school for women, and would be open, initially, to about 25 to 30 students. Although VWIL would share VMI's mission—to produce "citizen-soldiers"—the VWIL program would differ, as does Mary Baldwin College, from VMI in academic offerings, methods of education, and financial resources.

The average combined SAT score of entrants at Mary Baldwin is about 100 points lower than the score for VMI freshmen. While VMI offers degrees in liberal arts, the sciences, and engineering, Mary Baldwin, at the time of trial, offered only bachelor of arts degrees.

The VMI Alumni Association has developed a network of employers interested in hiring VMI graduates. The Association has agreed to open its network to VWIL graduates, but those graduates will not have the advantage afforded by a VMI degree.

The cross-petitions in this case present two ultimate issues. First, does Virginia's exclusion of women from the educational opportunities provided by VMI—extraordinary opportunities for military training and civilian leadership development—deny to women "capable of all of the individual activities required of VMI cadets," the equal protection of the laws guaranteed by the Fourteenth Amendment? Second, if VMI's "unique" situation—as Virginia's sole single-sex public institution of higher education—offends the Constitution's equal protection principle, what is the remedial requirement?

Parties who seek to defend gender-based government action must demonstrate an "exceedingly persuasive justification" for that action.

Today's skeptical scrutiny of official action denying rights or opportunities based on sex responds to volumes of history. As a plurality of this Court acknowledged a generation ago, "our Nation has had a long and unfortunate history of sex discrimination." Through a century plus three decades and more of that history, women did not count among voters composing "We the People"; not until 1920 did women gain a constitutional right to the franchise. And for a half century thereafter, it remained the prevailing doctrine that government, both federal and state, could withhold from women opportunities accorded men so long as any "basis in reason" could be conceived for the discrimination.

In 1971, for the first time in our Nation's history, this Court ruled in favor of a woman who complained that her State had denied her the equal protection of its laws. *Reed v. Reed*. Since *Reed*, the Court has repeatedly recognized that neither federal nor state government acts compatibly with the equal protection principle when a law or official policy denies to women, simply because they are women, full citizenship stature—equal opportunity to aspire, achieve, participate in and contribute to society based on their individual talents and capacities.

Without equating gender classifications, for all purposes, to classifications based on race or national origin, the Court, in post-*Reed* decisions, has carefully inspected official action that closes a door or denies opportunity to women (or to men). To summarize the Court's current directions for cases of official classification based on gender: Focusing on the differential treatment or denial of opportunity for which relief is sought, the reviewing court must determine whether the proffered justification is "exceedingly persuasive." The burden of justification is demanding, and it rests entirely on the State. The justification must be genuine, not hypothesized or invented post hoc in response to litigation. And it must not rely on overbroad generalizations about the different talents, capacities, or preferences of males and females.

The heightened review standard our precedent establishes does not make sex a proscribed classification. Supposed "inherent differences" are no longer accepted as a ground for race or national origin classifications. See *Loving v. Virginia*. Physical differences between men and women, however, are enduring: "[T]he two sexes are not fungible; a community made up exclusively of one [sex] is different from a community composed of both."

"Inherent differences" between men and women, we have come to appreciate, remain cause for celebration, but not for denigration of the members of either sex or for artificial constraints on an individual's opportunity. Sex classifications may be used to compensate women "for particular economic disabilities [they have] suffered," *Califano v. Webster*, to "promot[e] equal employment opportunity," *California Fed. Sav. & Loan Assn. v. Guerra*, to advance full development of the talent and capacities of our Nation's people. But such classifications may not be used, as they once were, to create or perpetuate the legal, social, and economic inferiority of women.

Measuring the record in this case against the review standard just described, we conclude that Virginia has shown no "exceedingly persuasive justification" for excluding all women from the citizen-soldier training afforded by VMI. We therefore affirm the Fourth Circuit's initial judgment, which held that Virginia had violated the Fourteenth Amendment's Equal Protection Clause. Because the remedy proffered by Virginia—the Mary Baldwin VWIL program—does not cure the constitutional violation, i.e., it does not provide equal opportunity, we reverse the Fourth Circuit's final judgment in this case.

VMI . . . offers an educational opportunity no other Virginia institution provides, and the school's "prestige"—associated with its success in developing "citizen-soldiers"—is unequaled. Virginia has closed this facility to its daughters and, instead, has devised for them a "parallel program," with a faculty less impressively credentialed and less well paid, more limited course offerings, fewer opportunities for military training and for scientific specialization. VMI, beyond question, "possesses to a far greater degree" than the VWIL program "those qualities which are incapable of objective measurement but which make for greatness in a . . . school," including "position and influence of the alumni, standing in the community, traditions and prestige." Women seeking and fit for a VMI-quality education cannot be offered anything less, under the State's obligation to afford them genuinely equal protection.

A prime part of the history of our Constitution, historian Richard Morris recounted, is the story of the extension of constitutional rights and protections to people once ignored or excluded. VMI's story continued as our comprehension of "We the People" expanded. There is no reason to believe that the admission of women capable of all the activities required of VMI cadets would destroy the Institute rather than enhance its capacity to serve the "more perfect Union."

JUSTICE SCALIA, *dissenting.*

Much of the Court's opinion is devoted to deprecating the closed mindedness of our forebears with regard to women's education, and even with regard to the treatment of women in areas that have nothing to do with education. Closed minded they were— as every age is, including our own, with regard to matters it cannot guess, because it simply does not consider them debatable. The virtue of a democratic system with a First Amendment is that it readily enables the people, over time, to be persuaded that what they took for granted is not so, and to change their laws accordingly. That system is destroyed if the smug assurances of each age are removed from the democratic process and written into the Constitution. So to counterbalance the Court's criticism of our ancestors, let me say a word in their praise: they left us free to change. The same cannot be said of this most illiberal Court, which has embarked on a course of inscribing one after another of the current preferences of the society (and in some cases only the counter majoritarian preferences of the society's law-trained elite) into our Basic Law. Today it enshrines the notion that no substantial educational value is to be served by an all men's military academy—so that the decision by the people of Virginia to maintain such an institution denies equal protection to women who cannot attend that institution but can attend others. Since it is entirely clear that the Constitution of the United States—the old one—takes no sides in this educational debate, I dissent.

I shall devote most of my analysis to evaluating the Court's opinion on the basis of our current equal-protection jurisprudence, which regards this Court as free to evaluate everything under the sun by applying one of three tests: "rational basis" scrutiny, intermediate scrutiny, or strict scrutiny. These tests are no more scientific than their names suggest, and a further element of randomness is added by the fact that it is largely up to us which test will be applied in each case. Strict scrutiny, we have said, is reserved for state "classifications based on race or national origin and classifications affecting fundamental rights," *Clark v. Jeter*. It is my position that the term "fundamental rights" should be limited to "interest[s] traditionally protected by our society," *Michael H. v. Gerald D.*; but the Court has not accepted that view, so that strict scrutiny will be applied to the deprivation of whatever sort of right we consider "fundamental." We have no established

criterion for "intermediate scrutiny" either, but essentially apply it when it seems like a good idea to load the dice. So far it has been applied to content neutral restrictions that place an incidental burden on speech, to disabilities attendant to illegitimacy, and to discrimination on the basis of sex.

I have no problem with a system of abstract tests such as rational basis, intermediate, and strict scrutiny (though I think we can do better than applying strict scrutiny and intermediate scrutiny whenever we feel like it). Such formulas are essential to evaluating whether the new restrictions that a changing society constantly imposes upon private conduct comport with that "equal protection" our society has always accorded in the past. But in my view the function of this Court is to *preserve* our society's values regarding (among other things) equal protection, not to *revise* them.

It is beyond question that Virginia has an important state interest in providing effective college education for its citizens. That single-sex instruction is an approach substantially related to that interest should be evident enough from the long and continuing history in this country of men's and women's colleges. But beyond that, as the Court of Appeals here stated: "That single-gender education at the college level is beneficial to both sexes is a *fact established in this case.*"

The evidence establishing that fact was overwhelming—indeed, "virtually uncontradicted" in the words of the court that received the evidence. As an initial matter, Virginia demonstrated at trial that "[a] substantial body of contemporary scholarship and research supports the proposition that, although males and females have significant areas of developmental overlap, they also have differing developmental needs that are deep seated." While no one questioned that for many students a coeducational environment was nonetheless not inappropriate, that could not obscure the demonstrated benefits of single-sex colleges.

There are few extant single-sex public educational programs. The potential of today's decision for widespread disruption of existing institutions lies in its application to *private* single-sex education. Government support is immensely important to private educational institutions. Mary Baldwin College—which designed and runs VWIL—notes that private institutions of higher education in the 1990–1991 school year derived approximately 19 percent of their budgets from federal, state, and local government funds, *not including financial aid to students*. Charitable status under the tax laws is also highly significant for private educational institutions, and it is certainly not beyond the Court that rendered today's decision to hold that a donation to a single-sex college should be deemed contrary to public policy and therefore not deductible if the college discriminates on the basis of sex.

The Court adverts to private single-sex education only briefly, and only to make the assertion (mentioned above) that "[w]e address specifically and only an educational opportunity recognized by the District Court and the Court of Appeals as 'unique.'" As I have already remarked, that assurance assures nothing, unless it is to be taken as a promise that in the future the Court will disclaim the reasoning it has used today to destroy VMI. The Government, in its briefs to this Court, at least purports to address the consequences of its attack on VMI for public support of private single-sex education. It contends that private colleges which are the direct or indirect beneficiaries of government funding are not thereby necessarily

converted into state actors to which the Equal Protection Clause is then applicable. That is true. It is also virtually meaningless.

The issue will be not whether government assistance turns private colleges into state actors, but whether the government *itself* would be violating the Constitution by providing state support to single-sex colleges. For example, in *Norwood* v. *Harrison*, we saw no room to distinguish between state operation of racially segregated schools and state support of privately run segregated schools. "Racial discrimination in state operated schools is barred by the Constitution and '[i]t is also axiomatic that a state may not induce, encourage or promote private persons to accomplish what it is constitutionally forbidden to accomplish.'" When the Government was pressed at oral argument concerning the implications of these cases for private single-sex education if government provided single-sex education is unconstitutional, it stated that the implications will not be so disastrous, since States *can* provide funding to *racially* segregated private schools, "depend[ing] on the circumstances." I cannot imagine what those "circumstances" might be, and it would be as foolish for private-school administrators to think that that assurance from the Justice Department will outlive the day it was made, as it was for VMI to think that the Justice Department's "unequivoca[l]" support for an intermediate scrutiny standard in this case would survive the Government's loss in the courts below.

The only hope for state-assisted single-sex private schools is that the Court will not apply in the future the principles of law it has applied today. That is a substantial hope, I am happy and ashamed to say. After all, did not the Court today abandon the principles of law it has applied in our earlier sex-classification cases? And does not the Court positively invite private colleges to rely upon our ad-hocery by assuring them this case is "unique"? I would not advise the foundation of any new single-sex college (especially an all-male one) with the expectation of being allowed to receive any government support; but it is too soon to abandon in despair those single-sex colleges already in existence. It will certainly be possible for this Court to write a future opinion that ignores the broad principles of law set forth today, and that characterizes as utterly dispositive the opinion's perceptions that VMI was a uniquely prestigious all-male institution, conceived in chauvinism, etc., etc. I will not join that opinion.

SYNTHESIS QUESTIONS FOR FURTHER DISCUSSION: CHAPTER 9 SECTION A

1. Does intermediate scrutiny provide a way both to recognize that there are real differences between the sexes, yet also to eliminate arbitrary distinctions based on gender? One worry among critics of intermediate scrutiny as a level of review for sex discrimination is that it will allow the Court to conflate issues of sex and of gender. Is this a danger inherent in such a test? Consider, for instance, the test's ability to handle the arguments on behalf of the Virginia Military Institute that "real differences" between the sexes justified excluding women from the school.

2. The effect of the ERA, had it been adopted, would likely have been to subject distinctions based on sex or gender to the "strict scrutiny" test, doing away with the current "intermediate scrutiny" standard. Critics of the ERA, most notably Phyllis Schlafly, argue that the Amendment would make it impossible to acknowledge "real differences" between the sexes. In her article, Jane Mansbridge suggests that such worries are exaggerated. As we have seen, even a strict scrutiny test for distinctions based on race does not render all laws that employ such distinctions unconstitutional. Would this level of review have had any beneficial or problematic differences from an intermediate level of review? In thinking about the appropriateness of strict scrutiny for evaluating laws that distinguish based on sex or gender, you might think about whether such a test is compatible with all-female education. For instance, imagine a state-funded all-girls high school that is challenged on equal protection grounds by a male seeking admission to the school. Would it make a difference in such a case whether strict or intermediate scrutiny were applied?

B.   SEXUAL ORIENTATION

What level of scrutiny should discrimination on the basis of sexual orientation receive? How is it like gender or race? Are the rights of gay people liberty rights, equality rights, or both? Is the debate over same-sex marriage somehow distinct from other rights for gay people?

We saw in the last section that the Supreme Court has struck a balance in cases of discrimination based on sex between rational review and strict scrutiny. While strict scrutiny requires a strong presumption against the validity of the law, and rational review a strong presumption in favor of a law, intermediate scrutiny lies somewhere in between. As you will see, for much of its history, the Supreme Court did not regard discrimination against gay people as analogous to either sex-based discrimination or race-based discrimination. Indeed, as our first case makes clear, well into the twentieth century the Court regarded being gay as akin to a kind of pathology or illness. Thus the level of protection the Court afforded to sexual orientation was quite low.

Another assumption in the Court's earlier jurisprudence is that being gay is not a status, but a kind of chosen behavior. In our reading selection, John Finnis argues that the purpose of sex is procreation and that homosexuality therefore involves behaviors that should not be protected. In contrast, Andrew Koppelman argues that it is a mistake to see only the particular sex acts of gay citizens in isolation from their more general status. On his view, because discrimination against gays is a kind of status discrimination, it should be seen as similar to discrimination based on gender and should receive intermediate scrutiny.

Instead of heightening the level of scrutiny as it did with gender, the Court has recently protected the rights of gay citizens under the Equal Protection Clause without looking further than rational review. According to the Supreme Court's "animus" doctrine, laws based solely on hatred towards gay citizens cannot survive even rational-basis review. The increasing use of the animus doctrine has led some commentators to suggest that the Court is actually using a level of review that should be called rational basis with "a bite," or rational basis "plus." Another way to see this doctrine of animus, however, is to suggest that the presence of animus implies the absence of any rational reason for a law. Consider as you read these cases whether Finnis's arguments do or do not constitute a rational basis for the laws discussed in *Romer v. Evans* and *Lawrence v. Texas*.

While the Supreme Court could employ rational basis review in discussing the rights of gay citizens under the Equal Protection Clause, it has also avoided the discussion of whether gay people should enjoy a heightened level of scrutiny. However, in state courts, there is a lively debate about this issue. In particular, state courts have recently begun to recognize a right to same-sex marriage under heightened levels of scrutiny. The Iowa Supreme Court, for instance, invoked intermediate scrutiny in establishing a right to same-sex marriage. However, the Supreme Judicial Court of Massachusetts employed a rational review level in order to guarantee a right to marriage for its gay citizens. California employed a third approach, using a strict level of scrutiny in analyzing same-sex marriage. As you think about the appropriate level of scrutiny, you might use these different state opinions to consider what the

Supreme Court might say about this issue. Does the Supreme Court's jurisprudence and animus doctrine commit us to defending a right to same-sex marriage based in the Equal Protection Clause? To date, that issue has not been decided, but it might in the future come before the Court.

Andrew Koppelman

WHY DISCRIMINATION AGAINST LESBIANS AND GAY MEN IS SEX DISCRIMINATION

69 N.Y.U. L. Rev. 197 (1994)

As you will see in this section, unlike both race and gender, distinctions based on sexual orientation receive the lowest level of judicial scrutiny. In this excerpt, we consider an argument for why the harms involved in discrimination against gay people are analogous to those in gender discrimination. Is Andrew Koppelman's argument convincing? If so, should distinctions based on sexual orientation receive intermediate scrutiny?

The principal arguments for lesbian and gay rights are quite old. The privacy argument, that an individual has a right to do what she likes with her body so long as she doesn't harm others, and the oppressed class argument, that lesbians and gay men have suffered persecution and discrimination in much the same way blacks have, both have been made for centuries, and these are the arguments one most often encounters. But there is a third argument, one that was first developed at about the same time as the emergence of radical feminism in the 1970s, and which, though it is less familiar than the other two, may turn out to be the most insightful and persuasive of the three. This is the argument that in contemporary American society, discrimination against lesbians and gay men reinforces the hierarchy of males over females and thus is wrong because it oppresses women.

Both the privacy and oppressed class arguments face a common difficulty: neither takes account of any reason for the oppression of lesbians and gay men. Each of the arguments implicitly holds that there is no good reason for laws that discriminate against homosexuals. The privacy argument presupposes that there is no valid societal interest that justifies interference with (at least this kind of) sexual freedom—that homosexual sex acts are of legitimate concern only to the consenting adults who participate in them—and the oppressed class argument presupposes that discrimination on the basis of sexual orientation or behavior is as arbitrary and unfair as discrimination on the basis of race. In other words, each argument requires its proponent to carry the heavy burden of proving a negative: that no good reason exists for discriminating against lesbians and gay men. If an argument were available that shifted the burden of proof to the state to justify discrimination against lesbians and gays, this might be a more strategically promising alternative for gay rights advocates. The sex discrimination argument, I argue, has this strength.

. . . [T]he taboo against homosexuality is not entirely irrational, but serves a function, and . . . that function is similar to the function served by the taboo against miscegenation. Both taboos police the boundary that separates the dominant from the dominated in a social hierarchy that rests on a condition of birth. In the same way that the prohibition of miscegenation preserved the polarities of race on which white supremacy rested, the prohibition of homosexuality preserves the polarities of gender on which rests the subordination of women.

One might have attacked miscegenation laws by asserting the right to privacy, or by arguing that such laws impermissibly "legislate morality," or by claiming that "miscegenosexuals" are a special group, born into that class and unable to change their preferences, who therefore do not deserve the social and legal disadvantages that have traditionally been heaped upon them. Whatever varying degrees of validity these arguments have, they all miss a crucial dimension of miscegenation laws which the Supreme Court recognized in 1967: such laws are "measures designed to maintain White Supremacy.... [T]he notion that discrimination against gays involves only the rights of gays is similarly shallow. It fails to recognize that the stigmatization of gays in contemporary American society functions as part of a larger system of social control based on gender.

If this is so, then the question of whether homosexuality is genetically caused or immutable, which has been the object of excited debate and intense scientific investigation in recent years, is altogether irrelevant to the constitutional status of laws that discriminate against lesbians and gay men. To repeat, when we assess the constitutionality of laws that discriminate against interracial couples, we do not ask whether sexual desire for a person of a different race is biologically caused or whether it can be "cured." The very question is weird, racist, and insulting. Its answer, if there is one, clearly has no constitutional significance. The same should be true of laws that discriminate against lesbians and gay men. Even if some persons who are attracted to persons of

the same sex could choose heterosexual partners—and there are bisexuals, for whom the immutability argument is no help—the state has no legitimate interest in influencing that choice....

As a matter of definition, if the same conduct is prohibited or stigmatized when engaged in by a person of one sex, while it is tolerated when engaged in by a person of the other sex, then the party imposing the prohibition or stigma is discriminating on the basis of sex.... That is what happens whenever gays are discriminated against. If a business fires Ricky, or if the state prosecutes him, because of his sexual activities with Fred, while these actions would not be taken against Lucy if she did exactly the same things with Fred, then Ricky is being discriminated against because of his sex. If Lucy is permitted to marry Fred, but Ricky may not marry Fred, then (assuming that Fred would be a desirable spouse for either) Ricky is being discriminated against because of his sex.

... [T]he taboo against homosexuality reinforces the inequality of the sexes, and that is, at least in large part, why the taboo exists. From an antidiscrimination perspective, the problem with the prohibitions of both miscegenation and homosexuality is not that they interfere with individual liberty—the incest prohibition also interferes with sexual freedom—but the reasons for the interference.... The equal respect that the state owes its citizens, and that the citizens owe one another, is incompatible with the idea that sexual penetration is a nasty, degrading violation of the self, and that there are some people (black women, or women simpliciter) to whom, because of their inferior social status, it is acceptable to do it, and others (white women, or men) who, because of their superior social status, must be rescued (or, if necessary, forcibly prevented) from having it done to them.

What this conclusion requires of legal doctrine should be clear by analogy with the miscegenation cases. Just as inter-racial couples cannot be made to suffer any legal disadvantage that same-race couples are spared, gay couples cannot be made to suffer any legal disadvantage that heterosexual couples are spared. Lesbians and gay men must be permitted to marry. Nonmarital sex cannot be more heavily criminalized when it is homosexual than when it is heterosexual.

Societal disapproval is not a permissible ground for denying custody of a child to a gay parent. In short, any state action that discriminates against lesbians and gay men solely because they are gay is impermissible.

For far too long, heterosexuality has connoted the dominance of men over women. If our culture's devaluation of women is ever to be eliminated, then the homosexuality taboo, in which that devaluation is so deeply encoded, has got to go.

John Finnis

THE GOOD OF MARRIAGE AND THE MORALITY OF SEXUAL RELATIONS: SOME PHILOSOPHICAL AND HISTORICAL OBSERVATIONS

42 Am. J. Juris. 97 (1997)

In this excerpt, we read the arguments of a scholar who argues for the illegitimacy of homosexuality in a society that endorses the good of marriage. John Finnis's arguments are part of a "natural law" tradition, which according to Finnis dates back to the time of Thomas Aquinas. Even if you disagree with his conclusions, are his arguments for the immorality of homosexuality enough to show that legislation outlawing gay sodomy constitutes a legitimate interest and that laws banning it meet the Court's rational basis standard? Should the Constitution take account of the idea of a natural law in deciding whether laws have a rational basis? You should also consider how his arguments might figure into the current controversy over whether the Constitution protects a right of same-sex couples to marry.

Aquinas organized his account of the morality of sexual relations around the good of marriage. The good of marriage is one of the basic human goods to which human choice and action are directed by the first principles of practical reason. Sex acts are immoral when they are "against the good of marriage," and therefore unreasonable (and, inasmuch as unreasonable, unnatural). Considered precisely as kinds of morally bad sex— rather than as, say, unjust (as rapes and some other morally bad sex acts obviously also are)—wrongful sex acts are more seriously immoral the "more distant" they are from marital sexual intercourse. Aquinas' account of what it is to act sexually "against the good of marriage" leaves a good deal to be clarified. But he did deploy a line of thought that lawyers and philosophical theologians had articulated in the preceding century, and that brilliantly illuminates the ways in which sex acts, even when performed consensually between spouses, can be against the good of marriage and therefore unreasonable.

Germain Grisez's 1993 treatise on sex, marriage, and family life clarifies large tracts of sexual morality which Aquinas' account left more or less obscure. For it shows how various kinds of sex act, even when performed (e.g., as solitary masturbation, or homosexual sodomy) by unmarried people who have no intention of marrying, violate the good of marriage.

In 1994 I published an article which explored the reasons why "Plato and Socrates, Xenophon, Aristotle, Musonius Rufus, and Plutarch, right at the heart of their reflections on the homoerotic culture around them, make the very deliberate and careful judgment that homosexual conduct (and indeed all extramarital sexual gratification) is radically incapable of participating in, actualizing, the common good of friendship." The article then considered why homosexual conduct is "never a valid, humanly acceptable choice and form of life" and is (rightly) "repudiated as destructive of human character and relationships." The primary reason I summarized thus:

it treats human sexual capacities in a way which is deeply hostile to the self-understanding of those members of the community who are willing to commit themselves to real marriage in the understanding that its sexual joys are not mere instruments or accompaniments to, or mere compensations for, the accomplishment of marriage's responsibilities, but rather enable the spouses to actualize and experience their intelligent commitment to share in those responsibilities, in that genuine self-giving.

To emphasize the point, I added:

. . . the deliberate willingness to promote and engage in homosexual acts . . . treats human sexual capacities in a way which is deeply hostile to the self-understanding of those members of the community who are willing to commit

themselves to real marriage. . . . [It] is, in fact, a standing denial of the intrinsic aptness of sexual intercourse to actualize and in that sense give expression to the exclusiveness and open-ended commitment of marriage as something good in itself.

Thus, like Aquinas and Grisez, I argued that approval of homosexual and other nonmarital sex acts is not simply nonmarital, in the sense of being utterly incapable of consummating or actualizing the human good of marriage, but actually "contrary to" or "violative of" that good.

Andrew Koppelman now offers a critique of Aquinas, Grisez, and me which overlooks this central argument entirely. He constructs for Aquinas a sex ethics based on alleged principles—about respect for "the natural order of things" or "normality"—which are remote from those which Aquinas actually employs in his account of why some sex acts are morally unacceptable.

Aquinas' reasons for judging certain types of sex act wrongful neither depend upon nor even include the lines of argument which Koppelman . . . ascribe[s] to him. His reasons are concerned rather with the preconditions for instantiating, and the ways of disrespecting, the good of marriage, viz. the way of life made intelligible and choiceworthy by its twin orientation towards the procreation, support, and education of children and the mutual support and amicitia of spouses who, at all levels of their being, are sexually complementary. How, then, is this good violated by nonmarital sex acts, including even the sex acts of someone who perhaps could never marry?

. . . [M]arriage is rational and natural primarily because it is the institution which physically, biologically, emotionally, and in every other practical way is peculiarly apt to promote suitably the reproduction of the couple by the generation, nurture, and education of ultimately mature offspring. The version of "gay" ideology defended by Koppelman . . . and others who claim that sex acts between persons of the same sex can be truly marital, and that to perform such acts two such persons can indeed marry each other, suggests (without clearly affirming) that homosexual sex acts should be evaluated by focusing upon this sort of activity of this sort of couple.

The fact is that "gay" ideology . . . has no serious account whatever of why faithfulness— reservation of one's sex acts exclusively for one's spouse—is an intelligible, intelligent, and reasonable requirement. Only a small proportion of men who live as "gays" seriously attempt anything even resembling marriage as a permanent commitment. Only a tiny proportion seriously attempt marital fidelity, the commitment to exclusiveness; the proportion who find that the attempt seems to make sense, in view of the other aspects of their "gay identity," is even tinier. Thus, even at the level of behavior—i.e. even leaving aside its inherent sterility—gay "marriage," precisely because it excludes or makes no sense of a commitment utterly central to marriage, is a sham.

. . . [S]ame-sex partners cannot engage in acts of the reproductive kind, i.e., in marital sexual intercourse. For them the permanent, exclusive commitment of marriage—in which bodily union in such acts is the biological actuation of the multi-level (bodily, emotional, intellectual, and volitional) marital relationship—is inexplicable. Of course, two, three, four, five or any number of persons of the same sex can band together to raise a child or children. That may, in some circumstances, be a praiseworthy commitment. It has nothing to do with marriage.

Those who propound "gay" ideology or theories of same-sex marriage or "sexual activity" have no principled moral case to offer against (prudent and moderate) promiscuity, indeed the getting of orgasmic sexual pleasure in whatever friendly touch or welcoming orifice (human or otherwise) one may opportunely find it in. In debate with opponents of their ideology or theories, some of these proponents are fond of postulating an idealized (two-person, lifelong . . .) category of relationship, and of challenging their opponents to say how relationships of such a (not too carefully delimited) kind differ from marriage at least where husband and wife know themselves to be infertile. . . . [T]he principal difference is simple and fundamental: the artificially delimited category named "gay marriage" or "same-sex marriage" corresponds to no intrinsic reason or set of reasons at all. When we realize that—and why—the core of marriage is fides, the stringently exclusive commitment whose rationale and implications for sexual activity's integrity, purity, and reasonableness were well understood by Aquinas, we realize that—and why—the world of same-sex partnerships (in the real world outside the artifice of debate) offers no genuine instantiations, equivalents, or counterparts to marriage, and so very few whole-hearted imitations. Marriage is the coherent, stable category of relationships, activities, satisfactions, and responsibilities which can be intelligently and reasonably chosen by a man together with a woman, and adopted as their demanding mutual commitment and common good, because its components respond and correspond fully reasonably to that complex of interlocking, complementary good reasons.

Plato, Aristotle, and other great philosophers, like the mass of ordinary participants in the tradition of civilized life, understand that complex as constitutive of (the good of) marriage. And I have been arguing that true and valid sexual morality does no more, and no less, than unfold what is involved in understanding, promoting, and respecting (not violating) that basic human good, and what are the conditions for instantiating that common good of the two spouses in a real, non-illusory way, integrating all the levels of their human reality, in the marital act.

BOUTILIER v. INS

387 U.S. 118 (1967)

Opinion: Clark, joined by Warren, Black, Harlan, Stewart, White
Dissent ("for the reasons stated by Judge Moore of the Court of Appeals"): Brennan
Dissent: Douglas, joined by Fortas

This case stands as an example of the Court's early attitude towards the protection of gay citizens before it began to expand the Equal Protection Clause to offer protection in instances of discrimination against this group. As you read, consider how the Court's idea of homosexuality as a pathology informs its reluctance to extend protection to the petitioner before it. In what ways does the dissent excerpted here respond to the majority opinion? Is it convincing?

MR. JUSTICE CLARK *delivered the opinion of the Court.*

The petitioner, an alien, has been ordered deported to Canada as one who upon entry into this country was a homosexual and therefore "afflicted with psychopathic personality" and excludable under §212(a)(4) of the Immigration and Nationality Act of 1952.

In 1963, he applied for citizenship and submitted to the Naturalization Examiner an affidavit in which he admitted that he was arrested in New York in October 1959, on a charge of sodomy, which was later reduced to simple assault and thereafter dismissed on default of the complainant. In 1964, petitioner, at the request of the Government, submitted another affidavit which revealed the full history of his sexual deviate behavior. It stated that his first homosexual experience occurred when he was 14 years of age, some seven years before his entry into the United States.

The 1964 affidavit was submitted to the Public Health Service for its opinion as to whether petitioner was excludable for any reason at the time of his entry. The Public Health Service issued a certificate in 1964 stating that, in the opinion of the subscribing physicians, petitioner "was afflicted with a class A condition, namely, psychopathic personality, sexual deviate" at the time of his admission. Deportation proceedings were then instituted.

The legislative history of the Act indicates beyond a shadow of a doubt that the Congress intended the phrase "psychopathic personality" to include homosexuals such as petitioner.

Beginning in 1950, a subcommittee of the Senate Committee on the Judiciary conducted a comprehensive study of the immigration laws, and in its report found

> "that the purpose of the provision against 'persons with constitutional psychopathic inferiority' will be more adequately served by changing that term to 'persons afflicted with psychopathic personality,' and that the classes of mentally defectives should be enlarged to include homosexuals and other sex perverts."

We, therefore, conclude that the Congress used the phrase "psychopathic personality" not in the clinical sense, but to effectuate its purpose to exclude from entry all homosexuals and other sex perverts.

The section imposes neither regulation of nor sanction for conduct. In this situation, therefore no necessity exists for guidance so that one may avoid the applicability of the law. The petitioner is not being deported for conduct engaged in after his entry into the United States, but rather for characteristics he possessed at the time of his entry. Here, when petitioner first presented himself at our border for entrance, he was already afflicted with homosexuality. The pattern was cut, and under it he was not admissible.

It has long been held that the Congress has plenary power to make rules for the admission of aliens and to exclude those who possess those characteristics which Congress has forbidden.

Here, Congress commanded that homosexuals not be allowed to enter. The petitioner was found to have that characteristic, and was ordered deported. The basis of the deportation order was his affliction for a long period of time *prior to entry, i.e.,* six and one-half years before his entry. It may be, as some claim, that "psychopathic personality" is a medically ambiguous term, including several separate and distinct afflictions. But the test here is what the Congress intended, not what differing psychiatrists may think. It was not laying down a clinical test, but an exclusionary standard which it declared to be inclusive of those having homosexual and perverted characteristics.

MR. JUSTICE DOUGLAS, *with whom* **MR. JUSTICE FORTAS** *concurs, dissenting.*

The term "psychopathic personality" is a treacherous one like "communist" or, in an earlier day, "Bolshevik." A label of this kind, when freely used, may mean only an unpopular person. It is much too vague by constitutional standards for the imposition of penalties or punishment.

It is common knowledge that in this century homosexuals have risen high in our own public service—both in Congress and in the Executive Branch—and have served with distinction. It is therefore not credible that Congress wanted to deport everyone and anyone who was a sexual deviate, no matter how blameless his social conduct had been nor how creative his work nor how valuable his contribution to society.

If we are to hold, as the Court apparently does, that any acts of homosexuality suffice to deport the alien, whether or not they are part of a fabric of antisocial behavior, then we face a serious question of due process. By that construction, a person is judged by a standard that is almost incapable of definition.

Caprice of judgment is almost certain under this broad definition. Anyone can be caught who is unpopular, who is off-beat, who is nonconformist.

BOWERS v. HARDWICK

478 U.S. 186 (1986)

Opinion: White, joined by Burger, Powell, Rehnquist, O'Connor
Concurrence: Burger
Concurrence: Powell
Dissent: Blackmun, joined by Brennan, Marshall, Stevens
Dissent: Stevens, joined by Brennan, Marshall

Like Boutilier v. INS, Bowers v. Hardwick *is an example of the Court's jurisprudence before it began extending equal protection to gay persons. In what ways does the Court make the argument for the rational basis underlying laws that ban sodomy? Importantly, the law before the Court is one that banned both homosexual and heterosexual sodomy. Is this case thus not a good candidate for equal protection, or should the Court have employed equal protection analysis anyway?*

JUSTICE WHITE *delivered the opinion of the Court.*

In August, 1982, respondent Hardwick was charged with violating the Georgia statute criminalizing sodomy by committing that act with another adult male in the bedroom of respondent's home.

This case does not require a judgment on whether laws against sodomy between consenting adults in general, or between homosexuals in particular, are wise or desirable. It raises no question about the right or propriety of state legislative decisions to repeal their laws that criminalize homosexual sodomy, or of state court decisions invalidating those laws on state constitutional grounds. The issue presented is whether the Federal Constitution confers a fundamental right upon homosexuals to engage in sodomy, and hence invalidates the laws of the many States that still make such conduct illegal,

and have done so for a very long time. The case also calls for some judgment about the limits of the Court's role in carrying out its constitutional mandate.

Accepting the decisions in these cases and the above description of them, we think it evident that none of the rights announced in those cases bears any resemblance to the claimed constitutional right of homosexuals to engage in acts of sodomy that is asserted in this case. No connection between family, marriage, or procreation, on the one hand, and homosexual activity, on the other, has been demonstrated, either by the Court of Appeals or by respondent. Moreover, any claim that these cases nevertheless stand for the proposition that any kind of private sexual conduct between consenting adults is constitutionally insulated from state proscription is unsupportable. Indeed, the Court's opinion in *Carey* twice asserted that the privacy right, which the *Griswold* line of cases found to be one of the protections provided by the Due Process Clause, did not reach so far.

Precedent aside, however, respondent would have us announce, as the Court of Appeals did, a fundamental right to engage in homosexual sodomy. This we are quite unwilling to do. It is true that, despite the language of the Due Process Clauses of the Fifth and Fourteenth Amendments, which appears to focus only on the processes by which life, liberty, or property is taken, the cases are legion in which those Clauses have been interpreted to have substantive content, subsuming rights that to a great extent are immune from federal or state regulation or proscription. Among such cases are those recognizing rights that have little or no textual support in the constitutional language. *Meyer, Prince,* and *Pierce* fall in this category, as do the privacy cases from *Griswold* to *Carey.*

Striving to assure itself and the public that announcing rights not readily identifiable in the Constitution's text involves much more than the imposition of the Justices' own choice of values on the States and the Federal Government, the Court has sought to identify the nature of the rights qualifying for heightened judicial protection. In *Palko v. Connecticut*, it was said that this category includes those fundamental liberties that are "implicit in the concept of ordered liberty," such that "neither liberty nor justice would exist if [they] were sacrificed." A different description of fundamental liberties appeared in *Moore v. East Cleveland* (opinion of Powell, J.), where they are characterized as those liberties that are "deeply rooted in this Nation's history and tradition."

It is obvious to us that neither of these formulations would extend a fundamental right to homosexuals to engage in acts of consensual sodomy. Proscriptions against that conduct have ancient roots. Sodomy was a criminal offense at common law, and was forbidden by the laws of the original 13 States when they ratified the Bill of Rights. Against this background, to claim that a right to engage in such conduct is "deeply rooted in this Nation's history and tradition" or "implicit in the concept of ordered liberty" is, at best, facetious.

Even if the conduct at issue here is not a fundamental right, respondent asserts that there must be a rational basis for the law, and that there is none in this case other than the presumed belief of a majority of the electorate in Georgia that homosexual sodomy is immoral and unacceptable. This is said to be an inadequate rationale to support the law. The law, however, is constantly based on notions of morality, and if all laws representing essentially moral choices are to be invalidated under the Due Process Clause, the courts will be very busy indeed. Even respondent makes no such claim, but insists that majority sentiments about the morality of homosexuality should be declared inadequate. We do not agree, and are unpersuaded that the sodomy laws of some 25 States should be invalidated on this basis.

JUSTICE BLACKMUN, *with whom* **JUSTICE BRENNAN, JUSTICE MARSHALL,** *and* **JUSTICE STEVENS** *join, dissenting.*

I believe we must analyze respondent Hardwick's claim in the light of the values that underlie the constitutional right to privacy. If that right means anything, it means that, before Georgia can prosecute its citizens for making choices about the most intimate aspects of their lives, it must do more than assert that the choice they have made is an "abominable crime not fit to be named among Christians."

First, the Court's almost obsessive focus on homosexual activity is particularly hard to justify in light of the broad language Georgia has used. Unlike the Court, the Georgia Legislature has not proceeded on the assumption that homosexuals are so different from other citizens that their lives may be controlled in a way that would not be tolerated if it limited the choices of those other citizens. Rather, Georgia has provided that "[a] person commits the offense of sodomy when he performs or submits to any sexual act involving the sex organs of one person and the mouth or anus of another." The sex or status of the persons who engage in the act is irrelevant as a matter of state law. In fact, to the extent I can discern a legislative purpose for Georgia's 1968 enactment of §16-6-2, that purpose seems to have been to broaden the coverage of the law to reach heterosexual as well as homosexual activity. Michael Hardwick's standing may rest in significant part on Georgia's apparent willingness to enforce against homosexuals a law it seems not to have any desire to enforce against heterosexuals. But his claim that §16-6-2 involves an unconstitutional intrusion into his privacy and his right of intimate association does not depend in any way on his sexual orientation....

. . . The Court's failure to comprehend the magnitude of the liberty interests at stake in this case leads it to slight the question whether petitioner, on behalf of the State, has justified Georgia's infringement on these interests.

First, petitioner asserts that the acts made criminal by the statute may have serious adverse consequences for "the general public health and welfare," such as spreading communicable diseases or fostering other criminal activity. Inasmuch as this case was dismissed by the District Court on the pleadings, it is not surprising that the record before us is barren of any evidence to support petitioner's claim.

The core of petitioner's defense of §16-6-2, however, is that respondent and others who engage in the conduct prohibited by §16-6-2 interfere with Georgia's exercise of the "right of the Nation and of the States to maintain a decent society." Essentially, petitioner argues, and the Court agrees, that the fact that the acts described in §16-6-2 "for hundreds of years, if not thousands, have been uniformly condemned as immoral" is a sufficient reason to permit a State to ban them today.

The assertion that "traditional Judeo-Christian values proscribe" the conduct involved, cannot provide an adequate justification for §16-6-2. That certain, but by no means all, religious groups condemn the behavior at issue gives the State no license to impose their judgments on the entire citizenry. The legitimacy of secular legislation depends, instead, on whether the State can advance some justification for its law beyond its conformity to religious doctrine. Thus, far from buttressing his case, petitioner's invocation of Leviticus, Romans, St. Thomas Aquinas, and sodomy's heretical status during the Middle Ages undermines his suggestion that §16-6-2 represents a

legitimate use of secular coercive power. A State can no more punish private behavior because of religious intolerance than it can punish such behavior because of racial animus. "The Constitution cannot control such prejudices, but neither can it tolerate them. Private biases may be outside the reach of the law, but the law cannot, directly or indirectly, give them effect."

Nor can §16-6-2 be justified as a "morally neutral" exercise of Georgia's power to "protect the public environment." Certainly, some private behavior can affect the fabric of society as a whole. Reasonable people may differ about whether particular sexual acts are moral or immoral, but "we have ample evidence for believing that people will not abandon morality, will not think any better of murder, cruelty and dishonesty, merely because some private sexual practice which they abominate is not punished by the law." Petitioner and the Court fail to see the difference between laws that protect public sensibilities and those that enforce private morality. Statutes banning public sexual activity are entirely consistent with protecting the individual's liberty interest in decisions concerning sexual relations: the same recognition that those decisions are intensely private which justifies protecting them from governmental interference can justify protecting individuals from unwilling exposure to the sexual activities of others. But the mere fact that intimate behavior may be punished when it takes place in public cannot dictate how States can regulate intimate behavior that occurs in intimate places.

I can only hope that . . . the Court soon will reconsider its analysis and conclude that depriving individuals of the right to choose for themselves how to conduct their intimate relationships poses a far greater threat to the values most deeply rooted in our Nation's history than tolerance of nonconformity could ever do. Because I think the Court today betrays those values, I dissent.

ROMER v. EVANS

517 U.S. 620 (1996)

Opinion: Kennedy, joined by Stevens, O'Connor, Souter, Ginsburg, Breyer
Dissent: Scalia, joined by Rehnquist, Thomas

In Romer v. Evans, *the Court considered an amendment to the Constitution of Colorado that repealed several cities' non-discrimination ordinances and prohibited any part of the government of Colorado or its subdivisions from providing any protection to gays and lesbians. For the first time in history, the Supreme Court used the Equal Protection Clause to protect gay people from discrimination. Why did the Court decide that this legislation fails rational basis review? Moreover, should it make any difference that this law was passed by a directly democratic process? Does this heighten the counter-majoritarian difficulty in striking down this law?*

JUSTICE KENNEDY *delivered the opinion of the Court.*

The enactment challenged in this case is an amendment to the Constitution of the State of Colorado, adopted in a 1992 statewide referendum. The parties and the state courts refer to it as "Amendment 2," its designation when submitted to the voters. The impetus for the amendment and the contentious campaign that preceded its adoption came in large part from ordinances that had been passed in various Colorado municipalities. For example, the cities of Aspen and Boulder and the City and County of Denver each had enacted ordinances which banned discrimination in many transactions and activities, including housing, employment, education, public accommodations, and health and welfare services. What gave rise to the statewide controversy was the protection the ordinances afforded to persons discriminated against by reason of their sexual orientation. Amendment 2 repeals these ordinances to the extent they prohibit discrimination on the basis of "homosexual, lesbian or bisexual orientation, conduct, practices or relationships."

Yet Amendment 2, in explicit terms, does more than repeal or rescind these provisions. It prohibits all legislative, executive or judicial action at any level of state or local government designed to protect the named class, a class we shall refer to as homosexual persons or gays and lesbians. The amendment reads:

"No Protected Status Based on Homosexual, Lesbian, or Bisexual Orientation. Neither the State of Colorado, through any of its branches or departments, nor any of its agencies, political subdivisions, municipalities or school districts, shall enact, adopt or enforce any statute, regulation, ordinance or policy whereby homosexual, lesbian or bisexual orientation, conduct, practices or relationships shall constitute or otherwise be the basis of or entitle any person or class of persons to have or claim any minority status, quota preferences, protected status or claim of discrimination. This Section of the Constitution shall be in all respects self executing."

Among the plaintiffs (respondents here) were homosexual persons, some of them government employees. They alleged that enforcement of Amendment 2 would subject them to immediate and substantial risk of discrimination on the basis of their sexual orientation.

The State's principal argument in defense of Amendment 2 is that it puts gays and lesbians in the same position as all other persons. So, the State says, the measure does no more than deny homosexuals special rights. This reading of the amendment's language is implausible.

Sweeping and comprehensive is the change in legal status effected by this law. So much is evident from the ordinances that the Colorado Supreme Court declared would be void by operation of Amendment 2. Homosexuals, by state decree, are put in a solitary class with respect to transactions and relations in both the private and governmental spheres. The amendment withdraws from homosexuals, but no others, specific legal protection from the injuries caused by discrimination, and it forbids reinstatement of these laws and policies.

The change that Amendment 2 works in the legal status of gays and lesbians in the private sphere is far reaching, both on its own terms and when considered in light of the structure and operation of modern anti-discrimination laws.

Colorado's state and municipal laws typify [an] emerging tradition of statutory protection and follow a consistent pattern. The laws first enumerate the persons or entities subject to a duty not to discriminate. The list goes well beyond the entities covered by the common law. The Boulder ordinance, for example, has a comprehensive definition of entities deemed places of "public accommodation." They include "any place of business engaged in any sales to the general public and any place that offers services, facilities, privileges, or advantages to the general public or that receives financial support through solicitation of the general public or through governmental subsidy of any kind."

These statutes and ordinances also depart from the common law by enumerating the groups or persons within their ambit of protection. Enumeration is the essential device used to make the duty not to discriminate concrete and to provide

guidance for those who must comply. In following this approach, Colorado's state and local governments have not limited anti-discrimination laws to groups that have so far been given the protection of heightened equal protection scrutiny under our cases. Rather, they set forth an extensive catalogue of traits which cannot be the basis for discrimination, including age, military status, marital status, pregnancy, parenthood, custody of a minor child, political affiliation, physical or mental disability of an individual or of his or her associates—and, in recent times, sexual orientation.

Amendment 2 bars homosexuals from securing protection against the injuries that these public accommodations laws address. That in itself is a severe consequence, but there is more. Amendment 2, in addition, nullifies specific legal protections for this targeted class in all transactions in housing, sale of real estate, insurance, health and welfare services, private education, and employment.

Not confined to the private sphere, Amendment 2 also operates to repeal and forbid all laws or policies providing specific protection for gays or lesbians from discrimination by every level of Colorado government. The State Supreme Court cited two examples of protections in the governmental sphere that are now rescinded and may not be reintroduced. The repeal of these measures and the prohibition against their future reenactment demonstrates that Amendment 2 has the same force and effect in Colorado's governmental sector as it does elsewhere and that it applies to policies as well as ordinary legislation.

. . . [E]ven if, as we doubt, homosexuals could find some safe harbor in laws of general application, we cannot accept the view that Amendment 2's prohibition on specific legal protections does no more than deprive homosexuals of special rights. To the contrary, the amendment imposes a special disability upon those persons alone. Homosexuals are forbidden the safeguards that others enjoy or may seek without constraint. They can obtain specific protection against discrimination only by enlisting the citizenry of Colorado to amend the state constitution or perhaps, on the State's view, by trying to pass helpful laws of general applicability. These are protections taken for granted by most people either because they already have them or do not need them; these are protections against exclusion from an almost limitless number of transactions and endeavors that constitute ordinary civic life in a free society.

The Fourteenth Amendment's promise that no person shall be denied the equal protection of the laws must co-exist with the practical necessity that most legislation classifies for one purpose or another, with resulting disadvantage to various groups or persons. We have attempted to reconcile the principle with the reality by stating that, if a law neither burdens a fundamental right nor targets a suspect class, we will uphold the legislative classification so long as it bears a rational relation to some legitimate end.

Amendment 2 fails, indeed defies, even this conventional inquiry. First, the amendment has the peculiar property of imposing a broad and undifferentiated disability on a single named group, an exceptional and, as we shall explain, invalid form of legislation. Second, its sheer breadth is so discontinuous with the reasons offered for it that the amendment seems inexplicable by anything but animus toward the class that it affects; it lacks a rational relationship to legitimate state interests.

Amendment 2 confounds this normal process of judicial review. It is at once too narrow and too broad. It identifies persons by a single trait and then denies them protection across the board. The resulting disqualification of a class of persons from the

right to seek specific protection from the law is unprecedented in our jurisprudence. The absence of precedent for Amendment 2 is itself instructive; "[d]iscriminations of an unusual character especially suggest careful consideration to determine whether they are obnoxious to the constitutional provision."

It is not within our constitutional tradition to enact laws of this sort. Central both to the idea of the rule of law and to our own Constitution's guarantee of equal protection is the principle that government and each of its parts remain open on impartial terms to all who seek its assistance. Respect for this principle explains why laws singling out a certain class of citizens for disfavored legal status or general hardships are rare. A law declaring that in general it shall be more difficult for one group of citizens than for all others to seek aid from the government is itself a denial of equal protection of the laws in the most literal sense.

The primary rationale the State offers for Amendment 2 is respect for other citizens' freedom of association, and in particular the liberties of landlords or employers who have personal or religious objections to homosexuality. Colorado also cites its interest in conserving resources to fight discrimination against other groups. The breadth of the Amendment is so far removed from these particular justifications that we find it impossible to credit them. We cannot say that Amendment 2 is directed to any identifiable legitimate purpose or discrete objective. It is a status based enactment divorced from any factual context from which we could discern a relationship to legitimate state interests; it is a classification of persons undertaken for its own sake, something the Equal Protection Clause does not permit.

We must conclude that Amendment 2 classifies homosexuals not to further a proper legislative end but to make them unequal to everyone else. This Colorado cannot do. A State cannot so deem a class of persons a stranger to its laws. Amendment 2 violates the Equal Protection Clause, and the judgment of the Supreme Court of Colorado is affirmed.

JUSTICE SCALIA, *with whom* **THE CHIEF JUSTICE** *and* **JUSTICE THOMAS** *join, dissenting.*

The Court has mistaken a Kulturkampf for a fit of spite. The constitutional amendment before us here is not the manifestation of a "bare . . . desire to harm" homosexuals, but is rather a modest attempt by seemingly tolerant Coloradans to preserve traditional sexual mores against the efforts of a politically powerful minority to revise those mores through use of the laws. That objective, and the means chosen to achieve it, are not only unimpeachable under any constitutional doctrine hitherto pronounced (hence the opinion's heavy reliance upon principles of righteousness rather than judicial holdings); they have been specifically approved by the Congress of the United States and by this Court.

In holding that homosexuality cannot be singled out for disfavorable treatment, the Court contradicts a decision, unchallenged here, pronounced only 10 years ago, see *Bowers v. Hardwick*, and places the prestige of this institution behind the proposition that opposition to homosexuality is as reprehensible as racial or religious bias. Whether it is or not is precisely the cultural debate that gave rise to the Colorado constitutional amendment (and to the preferential laws against which the amendment was directed). Since the Constitution of the United States says nothing about this subject, it is left to be resolved by normal democratic means, including the democratic adoption of provisions in state constitutions. This Court has no business imposing upon all Americans the resolution favored

by the elite class from which the Members of this institution are selected, pronouncing that "animosity" toward homosexuality is evil. I vigorously dissent. . . .

II

I turn next to whether there was a legitimate rational basis for the substance of the constitutional amendment—for the prohibition of special protection for homosexuals. It is unsurprising that the Court avoids discussion of this question, since the answer is so obviously yes. The case most relevant to the issue before us today is not even mentioned in the Court's opinion: In *Bowers v. Hardwick*, we held that the Constitution does not prohibit what virtually all States had done from the founding of the Republic until very recent years—making homosexual conduct a crime. That holding is unassailable, except by those who think that the Constitution changes to suit current fashions. But in any event it is a given in the present case: Respondents' briefs did not urge overruling *Bowers*, and at oral argument respondents' counsel expressly disavowed any intent to seek such overruling. If it is constitutionally permissible for a State to make homosexual conduct criminal, surely it is constitutionally permissible for a State to enact other laws merely disfavoring homosexual conduct. And a fortiori it is constitutionally permissible for a State to adopt a provision not even disfavoring homosexual conduct, but merely prohibiting all levels of state government from bestowing special protections upon homosexual conduct. Respondents (who, unlike the Court, cannot afford the luxury of ignoring inconvenient precedent) counter *Bowers* with the argument that a greater-includes-the-lesser rationale cannot justify Amendment 2's application to individuals who do not engage in homosexual acts, but are merely of homosexual "orientation." Some courts of appeals have concluded that, with respect to laws of this sort at least, that is a distinction without a difference.

But assuming that, in Amendment 2, a person of homosexual "orientation" is someone who does not engage in homosexual conduct but merely has a tendency or desire to do so, *Bowers* still suffices to establish a rational basis for the provision. If it is rational to criminalize the conduct, surely it is rational to deny special favor and protection to those with a self-avowed tendency or desire to engage in the conduct. Indeed, where criminal sanctions are not involved, homosexual "orientation" is an acceptable stand-in for homosexual conduct. A State "does not violate the Equal Protection Clause merely because the classifications made by its laws are imperfect," *Dandridge v. Williams*. . . .

IV

. . . The Court today, announcing that Amendment 2 "defies . . . conventional [constitutional] inquiry," and "confounds [the] normal process of judicial review," employs a constitutional theory heretofore unknown to frustrate Colorado's reasonable effort to preserve traditional American moral values. . . .

To suggest, for example, that this constitutional amendment springs from nothing more than "a bare . . . desire to harm a politically unpopular group," is nothing short of insulting. (It is also nothing short of preposterous to call "politically unpopular" a group which enjoys enormous influence in American media and politics, and which, as the trial court here noted, though composing no more than 4% of the population had the support of 46% of the voters on Amendment 2.)

When the Court takes sides in the culture wars, it tends to be with the knights rather than the villains—and more specifically with the Templars, reflecting the views and values of the lawyer class from which the Court's Members are drawn. How that class feels about homosexuality will be evident to anyone who wishes to interview job applicants at virtually any of the Nation's law schools. The interviewer may refuse to offer a job because the applicant is a Republican; because he is an adulterer; because he went to the wrong prep school or belongs to the wrong country club; because he eats snails; because he is a womanizer; because she wears real-animal fur; or even because he hates the Chicago Cubs. But if the interviewer should wish not to be an associate or partner of an applicant because he disapproves of the applicant's homosexuality, then he will have violated the pledge which the Association of American Law Schools requires all its member-schools to exact from job interviewers: "assurance of the employer's willingness" to hire homosexuals. This law-school view of what "prejudices" must be stamped out may be contrasted with the more plebeian attitudes that apparently still prevail in the United States Congress, which has been unresponsive to repeated attempts to extend to homosexuals the protections of federal civil rights laws, and which took the pains to exclude them specifically from the Americans With Disabilities Act of 1990.

. . . Today's opinion has no foundation in American constitutional law, and barely pretends to. The people of Colorado have adopted an entirely reasonable provision which does not even disfavor homosexuals in any substantive sense, but merely denies them preferential treatment. Amendment 2 is designed to prevent piecemeal deterioration of the sexual morality favored by a majority of Coloradans, and is not only an appropriate means to that legitimate end, but a means that Americans have employed before. Striking it down is an act, not of judicial judgment, but of political will. I dissent.

LAWRENCE v. TEXAS

539 U.S. 558 (2003)

Opinion: Kennedy, joined by Stevens, Souter, Ginsburg, Breyer
Concurrence: O'Connor
Dissent: Scalia, joined by Rehnquist, Thomas
Dissent: Thomas

As we saw in Chapter 7, the Supreme Court reversed its decision in Bowers v. Hardwick *in* Lawrence v. Texas *and declared invalid all laws banning same-sex sodomy. Reread that excerpt from* Lawrence v. Texas *before turning to U.S. Supreme Court Justice Sandra Day O'Connor's concurrence excerpted here. Justice O'Connor provides an alternative rationale to that of substantive due process for striking down this law. Do you agree that equal protection would have been a better basis than substantive due process on which to decide this case? Notice how Justice O'Connor refuses to agree with the Court's majority that* Bowers v. Hardwick, *which she had previously joined, should be overturned. Do you think that it is possible to reconcile Justice O'Connor's opinion with the majority opinion in* Bowers v. Hardwick? *Is this opinion consistent with* Bowers v. Hardwick, *as she seems to think? Looking ahead to the same-sex marriage cases you will read next, do you agree with Justice O'Connor's statement that "preserving the traditional institution of marriage" is a legitimate state interest?*

JUSTICE O'CONNOR, *concurring in the judgment.*

The Court today overrules *Bowers v. Hardwick.* I joined *Bowers*, and do not join the Court in overruling it. Nevertheless, I agree with the Court that Texas' statute banning same-sex sodomy is unconstitutional. Rather than relying on the substantive component of the Fourteenth Amendment's Due Process Clause, as the Court does, I base my conclusion on the Fourteenth Amendment's Equal Protection Clause.

Under our rational basis standard of review, "legislation is presumed to be valid and will be sustained if the classification drawn by the statute is rationally related to a legitimate state interest."

Laws such as economic or tax legislation that are scrutinized under rational basis review normally pass constitutional muster, since "the Constitution presumes that even improvident decisions will eventually be rectified by the democratic processes." We have consistently held, however, that some objectives, such as "a bare ... desire to harm a politically unpopular group," are not legitimate state interests. When a law exhibits such a desire to harm a politically unpopular group, we have applied a more searching form of rational basis review to strike down such laws under the Equal Protection Clause.

We have been most likely to apply rational basis review to hold a law unconstitutional under the Equal Protection Clause where, as here, the challenged legislation inhibits personal relationships. In *Department of Agriculture v. Moreno*, for example, we held that a law preventing those households containing an individual unrelated to any other member of the household from receiving food stamps violated equal protection because the purpose of the law was to "discriminate against hippies." The asserted governmental interest in preventing food stamp fraud was not deemed sufficient to satisfy rational basis review. In *Eisenstadt v. Baird*, we refused to sanction a law that discriminated between married and unmarried persons by prohibiting the distribution of contraceptives to single persons. Likewise, in *Cleburne v. Cleburne Living Center*, we held that it was irrational for a State to require a home for the mentally disabled to obtain a special use permit when other residences—like fraternity houses and apartment buildings—did not have to obtain such a permit. And in *Romer v. Evans*, we disallowed a state statute that "impos[ed] a broad and undifferentiated disability on a single named group"—specifically, homosexuals.

The statute at issue here makes sodomy a crime only if a person "engages in deviate sexual intercourse with another individual of the same sex." Sodomy between opposite-sex partners, however, is not a crime in Texas. That is, Texas treats the same conduct differently based solely on the participants. Those harmed by this law are people who have a same-sex sexual orientation and thus are more likely to engage in behavior prohibited by §21.06.

The Texas statute makes homosexuals unequal in the eyes of the law by making particular conduct—and only that conduct—subject to criminal sanction.

And the effect of Texas' sodomy law is not just limited to the threat of prosecution or consequence of conviction. Texas' sodomy law brands all homosexuals as criminals, thereby making it more difficult for homosexuals to be treated in the same manner as everyone else. Indeed, Texas itself has previously acknowledged the collateral effects of the law, stipulating in a prior challenge to this action that the law "legally sanctions discrimination against [homosexuals] in a variety of ways unrelated to the criminal law," including in the areas of "employment, family issues, and housing."

Texas attempts to justify its law, and the effects of the law, by arguing that the statute satisfies rational basis review because it furthers the legitimate governmental interest of the promotion of morality. In *Bowers*, we held that a state law criminalizing sodomy as applied to homosexual couples did not violate substantive due process. We rejected the argument that no rational basis existed to justify the law, pointing to the government's interest in promoting morality. The only question in front of the Court in *Bowers* was whether the substantive component of the Due Process Clause protected a right to engage in homosexual sodomy. *Bowers* did not hold that moral disapproval of a group is a rational basis under the Equal Protection Clause to criminalize homosexual sodomy when heterosexual sodomy is not punished.

This case raises a different issue than *Bowers*: whether, under the Equal Protection Clause, moral disapproval is a legitimate state interest to justify by itself a statute that bans homosexual sodomy, but not heterosexual sodomy. It is not. Moral disapproval of this group, like a bare desire to harm the group, is an interest that is insufficient to satisfy rational basis review under the Equal Protection Clause. Indeed, we have never held that moral disapproval, without any other asserted state interest, is a sufficient rationale under the Equal Protection Clause to justify a law that discriminates among groups of persons.

And because Texas so rarely enforces its sodomy law as applied to private, consensual acts, the law serves more as a statement of dislike and disapproval against homosexuals than as a tool to stop criminal behavior. The Texas sodomy law "raise[s] the inevitable inference that the disadvantage imposed is born of animosity toward the class of persons affected."

Texas argues, however, that the sodomy law does not discriminate against homosexual persons. Instead, the State maintains that the law discriminates only against homosexual conduct. While it is true that the law applies only to conduct, the conduct targeted by this law is conduct that is closely correlated with being homosexual. Under such circumstances, Texas' sodomy law is targeted at more than conduct. It is instead directed toward gay persons as a class. When a State makes homosexual conduct criminal, and not "deviate sexual intercourse" committed by persons of different sexes, "that declaration in and of itself is an invitation to subject homosexual persons to discrimination both in the public and in the private spheres."

Indeed, Texas law confirms that the sodomy statute is directed toward homosexuals as a class. In Texas, calling a person a homosexual is slander *per se* because the word "homosexual" "impute[s] the commission of a crime." The State has admitted that because of the sodomy law, *being* homosexual carries the presumption of being a criminal. Texas' sodomy law therefore results in discrimination against homosexuals as a class in an array of areas outside the criminal law. In *Romer v. Evans,* we refused to sanction a law that singled out homosexuals "for disfavored legal status." The same is true here. The Equal Protection Clause "neither knows nor tolerates classes among citizens." *Id.*

That this law as applied to private, consensual conduct is unconstitutional under the Equal Protection Clause does not mean that other laws distinguishing between heterosexuals and homosexuals would similarly fail under rational basis review. Texas cannot assert any legitimate state interest here, such as national security or preserving the traditional institution of marriage. Unlike the moral disapproval of same-sex relations—the asserted state interest in this case—other reasons exist to promote the institution of marriage beyond mere moral disapproval of an excluded group.

A law branding one class of persons as criminal solely based on the State's moral disapproval of that class and the conduct associated with that class runs contrary to the values of the Constitution and the Equal Protection Clause, under any standard of review. I therefore concur in the Court's judgment that Texas' sodomy law banning "deviate sexual intercourse" between consenting adults of the same sex, but not between consenting adults of different sexes, is unconstitutional.

The Defense of Marriage Act (September 21, 1996)

In 1993, the Supreme Court of Hawaii ruled that restrictions on same-sex marriage must pass the strict scrutiny test. Although the voters of Hawaii later passed a constitutional amendment essentially nullifying that decision, Congress passed the following law to prevent the Hawaii Court ruling from influencing the nation as a whole.

An Act
To define and protect the institution of marriage.
Be it enacted by the Senate and House of Representatives of the
United States of America in Congress assembled,

SECTION 1.
This Act may be cited as the "Defense of Marriage Act."

SEC. 2. POWERS RESERVED TO THE STATES.

(a) In General.—Chapter 115 of title 28, United States Code, is amended by adding after section 1738B the following:

"§1738C. Certain acts, records, and proceedings and the effect thereof

"No State, territory, or possession of the United States, or Indian tribe, shall be required to give effect to any public act, record, or judicial proceeding of any other State, territory, possession, or tribe respecting a relationship between persons of the same sex that is treated as a marriage under the laws of such other State, territory, possession, or tribe, or a right or claim arising from such relationship."

SEC. 3. DEFINITION OF MARRIAGE.

(a) In General.—Chapter 1 of title 1, United States Code, is amended by adding at the end the following:

"§7. Definition of 'marriage' and 'spouse'

"In determining the meaning of any Act of Congress, or of any ruling, regulation, or interpretation of the various administrative bureaus and agencies of the United States, the word 'marriage' means only a legal union between one man and one woman as husband and wife, and the word 'spouse' refers only to a person of the opposite sex who is a husband or a wife."

GOODRIDGE v. DEP'T OF PUBLIC HEALTH

798 N.E.2d 941 (Mass. 2003)

Opinion: Marshall, joined by Greaney, Ireland, Cowin
Concurrence: Greaney
Dissent: Spina, joined by Sosman, Cordy
Dissent: Sosman, joined by Spina, Cordy
Dissent: Cordy, joined by Spina, Sosman

Throughout this book we have examined almost exclusively decisions of the U.S. Supreme Court, but, at times, Supreme Court decisions are presaged by state court decisions. We include here three state court decisions that address the question of same-sex marriage. As you will see, although they all recognize a right to same-sex marriage, *they differ in the level of scrutiny applied. As you read, consider which level of scrutiny you believe is appropriate, regardless of your opinion on the rulings. Could any of these decisions serve as the basis for a U.S. Supreme Court guarantee of same-sex marriage under the Equal Protection Clause of the U.S. Constitution?*

CHIEF JUSTICE MARGARET H. MARSHALL *for the majority.*

The question before us is whether, consistent with the Massachusetts Constitution, the Commonwealth may deny the protections, benefits, and obligations conferred by civil marriage to two individuals of the same sex who wish to marry. We conclude that it may not. The Massachusetts Constitution affirms the dignity and equality of all individuals. It forbids the creation of second class citizens. In reaching our conclusion we have given full deference to the arguments made by the Commonwealth. But it has failed to identify any constitutionally adequate reason for denying civil marriage to same-sex couples.

We are mindful that our decision marks a change in the history of our marriage law. Many people hold deep-seated religious, moral, and ethical convictions that marriage should be limited to the union of one man and one woman, and that homosexual conduct is immoral. Many hold equally strong religious, moral, and ethical convictions that same-sex couples are entitled to be married, and that homosexual persons should be treated no differently than their heterosexual neighbors. Neither view answers the question before us. Our concern is with the Massachusetts Constitution as a charter of governance for every person properly within its reach.

The plaintiffs are fourteen individuals from five Massachusetts counties. The plaintiffs Hillary Goodridge, forty-four years old, and Julie Goodridge, forty-three years old, had been in a committed relationship for thirteen years and lived with their five-year-old daughter.

In March and April, 2001, each of the plaintiff couples attempted to obtain a marriage license from a city or town clerk's office. In each case, the clerk either refused to accept the notice of intention to marry or denied a marriage license to the couple on the ground that Massachusetts does not recognize same-sex marriage.

The plaintiffs' claim that the marriage restriction violates the Massachusetts Constitution can be analyzed in two ways. Does it offend the Constitution's guarantees of equality before the law? Or do the liberty and due process provisions of the Massachusetts Constitution secure the plaintiffs' right to marry their chosen partner?

We begin by considering the nature of civil marriage itself. Simply put, the government creates civil marriage. In Massachusetts, civil marriage is, and since pre-Colonial days has been, precisely what its name implies: a wholly secular institution.

In a real sense, there are three partners to every civil marriage: two willing spouses and an approving State. While only the parties can mutually assent to marriage, the terms of the marriage—who may marry and what obligations, benefits, and liabilities attach to civil marriage—are set by the Commonwealth.

Civil marriage is created and regulated through exercise of the police power. "Police power" (now more commonly termed the State's regulatory authority) is an old fashioned term for the Commonwealth's lawmaking authority, as bounded by the liberty and equality guarantees of the Massachusetts Constitution and its express delegation of power from the people to their government. In broad terms, it is the Legislature's power to enact rules to regulate conduct, to the extent that such laws are "necessary to secure the health, safety, good order, comfort, or general welfare of the community."

Without question, civil marriage enhances the "welfare of the community." It is a "social institution of the highest importance." Civil marriage anchors an ordered society by encouraging stable relationships over transient ones. It is central to the way the Commonwealth identifies individuals, provides for the orderly distribution of property, ensures that children and adults are cared for and supported whenever possible from private rather than public funds, and tracks important epidemiological and demographic data.

Tangible as well as intangible benefits flow from marriage. The marriage license grants valuable property rights to those who meet the entry requirements, and who agree to what might otherwise be a burdensome degree of government regulation of their activities.

The benefits accessible only by way of a marriage license are enormous, touching nearly every aspect of life and death. The department states that "hundreds of statutes" are related to marriage and to marital benefits. With no attempt to be comprehensive, we note that some of the statutory benefits conferred by the Legislature on those who enter into civil marriage include, as to property: joint Massachusetts income tax filing; automatic rights to inherit the property of a deceased spouse who does not leave a will; entitlement to wages owed to a deceased employee; the right to share the medical policy of one's spouse; preferential options under the Commonwealth's pension; the equitable division of marital property on divorce; the right to separate support on separation of the parties that does not result in divorce; and the right to bring claims for wrongful death and loss of consortium, and for funeral and burial expenses and punitive damages resulting from tort actions.

It is undoubtedly for these concrete reasons, as well as for its intimately personal significance, that civil marriage has long been termed a "civil right."

The United States Supreme Court has described the right to marry as "of fundamental importance for all individuals" and as "part of the fundamental 'right of privacy' implicit in the Fourteenth Amendment's Due Process Clause." See *Loving v. Virginia*.

Whether and whom to marry, how to express sexual intimacy, and whether and how to establish a family—these are among the most basic of every individual's liberty and due process rights. And central to personal freedom and security is the assurance that the laws will apply equally to persons in similar situations. The liberty interest in choosing whether and whom to marry would be hollow if the Commonwealth could, without sufficient justification,

foreclose an individual from freely choosing the person with whom to share an exclusive commitment in the unique institution of civil marriage.

The Massachusetts Constitution requires, at a minimum, that the exercise of the State's regulatory authority not be "arbitrary or capricious." Under both the equality and liberty guarantees, regulatory authority must, at very least, serve "a legitimate purpose in a rational way"; a statute must "bear a reasonable relation to a permissible legislative objective."

The plaintiffs challenge the marriage statute on both equal protection and due process grounds. With respect to each such claim, we must first determine the appropriate standard of review. Where a statute implicates a fundamental right or uses a suspect classification, we employ "strict judicial scrutiny." For all other statutes, we employ the "'rational basis' test." For due process claims, rational basis analysis requires that statutes "bear[] a real and substantial relation to the public health, safety, morals, or some other phase of the general welfare." For equal protection challenges, the rational basis test requires that "an impartial lawmaker could logically believe that the classification would serve a legitimate public purpose that transcends the harm to the members of the disadvantaged class."

For the reasons we explain below, we conclude that the marriage ban does not meet the rational basis test for either due process or equal protection. Because the statute does not survive rational basis review, we do not consider the plaintiffs' arguments that this case merits strict judicial scrutiny.

The department posits three legislative rationales for prohibiting same-sex couples from marrying: (1) providing a "favorable setting for procreation"; (2) ensuring the optimal setting for child rearing, which the department defines as "a two-parent family with one parent of each sex"; and (3) preserving scarce State and private financial resources. We consider each in, turn.

Our laws of civil marriage do not privilege procreative heterosexual intercourse between married people above every other form of adult intimacy and every other means of creating a family. General Laws c.207 contains no requirement that the applicants for a marriage license attest to their ability or intention to conceive children by coitus. Fertility is not a condition of marriage, nor is it grounds for divorce. People who have never consummated their marriage, and never plan to, may be and stay married. . . .

The "marriage is procreation" argument singles out the one unbridgeable difference between same-sex and opposite-sex couples, and transforms that difference into the essence of legal marriage. Like "Amendment 2" to the Constitution of Colorado, which effectively denied homosexual persons equality under the law and full access to the political process, the marriage restriction impermissibly "identifies persons by a single trait and then denies them protection across the board." *Romer v. Evans.* In so doing, the State's action confers an official stamp of approval on the destructive stereotype that same-sex relationships are inherently unstable and inferior to opposite-sex relationships and are not worthy of respect.

The department's first stated rationale, equating marriage with unassisted heterosexual procreation, shades imperceptibly into its second: that confining marriage to opposite-sex couples ensures that children are raised in the "optimal" setting. Protecting the welfare of children is a paramount State policy. Restricting marriage to opposite-sex couples, however, cannot plausibly further this policy.

The department has offered no evidence that forbidding marriage to people of the same sex will increase the number of couples choosing to enter into opposite-sex marriages in order to have and raise children. There is thus no rational relationship between the marriage statute and the Commonwealth's proffered goal of protecting the "optimal" child rearing unit. Moreover, the department readily concedes that people in same-sex couples may be "excellent" parents. . . .

In this case, we are confronted with an entire, sizeable class of parents raising children who have absolutely no access to civil marriage and its protections because they are forbidden from procuring a marriage license. It cannot be rational under our laws, and indeed it is not permitted, to penalize children by depriving them of State benefits because the State disapproves of their parents' sexual orientation. . . .

The third rationale advanced by the department is that limiting marriage to opposite-sex couples furthers the Legislature's interest in conserving scarce State and private financial resources.

An absolute statutory ban on same-sex marriage bears no rational relationship to the goal of economy. First, the department's conclusory generalization—that same-sex couples are less financially dependent on each other than opposite-sex couples— ignores that many same-sex couples, such as many of the plaintiffs in this case, have children and other dependents (here, aged parents) in their care. The department does not contend, nor could it, that these dependents are less needy or deserving than the dependents of married couples. Second, Massachusetts marriage laws do not condition receipt of public and private financial benefits to married individuals on a demonstration of financial dependence on each other.

Here, the plaintiffs seek only to be married, not to undermine the institution of civil marriage. They do not want marriage abolished. They do not attack the binary nature of marriage, the consanguinity provisions, or any of the other gate-keeping provisions of the marriage licensing law. Recognizing the right of an individual to marry a person of the same sex will not diminish the validity or dignity of opposite-sex marriage, any more than recognizing the right of an individual to marry a person of a different race devalues the marriage of a person who marries someone of her own race.

The department has had more than ample opportunity to articulate a constitutionally adequate justification for limiting civil marriage to opposite-sex unions. It has failed to do so. The department has offered purported justifications for the civil marriage restriction that are starkly at odds with the comprehensive network of vigorous, gender-neutral laws promoting stable families and the best interests of children. It has failed to identify any relevant characteristic that would justify shutting the door to civil marriage to a person who wishes to marry someone of the same sex.

The marriage ban works a deep and scarring hardship on a very real segment of the community for no rational reason. The absence of any reasonable relationship between, on the one hand, an absolute disqualification of same-sex couples who wish to enter into civil marriage and, on the other, protection of public health, safety, or general welfare, suggests that the marriage restriction is rooted in persistent prejudices against persons who are (or who are believed to be) homosexual.

Limiting the protections, benefits, and obligations of civil marriage to opposite-sex couples violates the basic premises of individual liberty and equality under law protected by the Massachusetts Constitution.

SPINA, J. *(dissenting, with whom* **SOSMAN** *and* **CORDY, JJ.,** *join).*

What is at stake in this case is not the unequal treatment of individuals or whether individual rights have been impermissibly burdened, but the power of the Legislature to effectuate social change without interference from the courts. . . . The power to regulate marriage lies with the Legislature, not with the judiciary. See *Commonwealth v. Stowell.* Today, the court has transformed its role as protector of individual rights into the role of creator of rights, and I respectfully dissent.

SOSMAN, J. *(dissenting, with whom* **SPINA** *and* **CORDY, JJ.,** *join).*

In applying the rational basis test to any challenged statutory scheme, the issue is not whether the Legislature's rationale behind that scheme is persuasive to us, but only whether it satisfies a minimal threshold of rationality. Today, rather than apply that test, the court announces that, because it is persuaded that there are no differences between same-sex and opposite-sex couples, the Legislature has no rational basis for treating them differently with respect to the granting of marriage licenses. Reduced to its essence, the court's opinion concludes that, because same-sex couples are now raising children, and withholding the benefits of civil marriage from their union makes it harder for them to raise those children, the State must therefore provide the benefits of civil marriage to same-sex couples just as it does to opposite-sex couples. Of course, many people are raising children outside the confines of traditional marriage, and, by definition, those children are being deprived of the various benefits that would flow if they were being raised in a household with married parents. That does not mean that the Legislature must accord the full benefits of marital status on every household raising children. Rather, the Legislature need only have some rational basis for concluding that, at present, those alternate family structures have not yet been conclusively shown to be the equivalent of the marital family structure that has established itself as a successful one over a period of centuries. . . .

Based on our own philosophy of child rearing, and on our observations of the children being raised by same-sex couples to whom we are personally close, we may be of the view that what matters to children is not the gender, or sexual orientation, or even the number of the adults who raise them, but rather whether those adults provide the children with a nurturing, stable, safe, consistent, and supportive environment in which to mature. Same-sex couples can provide their children with the requisite nurturing, stable, safe, consistent, and supportive environment in which to mature, just as opposite-sex couples do. It is therefore understandable that the court might view the traditional definition of marriage as an unnecessary anachronism, rooted in historical prejudices that modern society has in large measure rejected and biological limitations that modern science has overcome.

It is not, however, our assessment that matters. Conspicuously absent from the court's opinion today is any acknowledgment that the attempts at scientific study of the ramifications of raising children in same-sex couple households are themselves in their infancy and have so far produced inconclusive and conflicting results. . . .

As a matter of social history, today's opinion may represent a great turning point that many will hail as a tremendous step toward a more just society. As a matter of constitutional jurisprudence, however, the case stands as an aberration. To reach the result it does, the court has tortured the rational basis test beyond recognition. I fully appreciate the strength of the temptation to find this particular law unconstitutional: there is much to be said for the argument that excluding gay and lesbian couples from the benefits of civil marriage is cruelly unfair and hopelessly outdated; the inability to marry has a profound impact on the personal lives of committed gay and lesbian couples (and their children) to whom we are personally close (our friends, neighbors, family members, classmates, and coworkers); and our resolution of this issue takes place under the intense glare of national and international publicity. Speaking metaphorically, these factors have combined to turn the case before us into a "perfect storm" of a constitutional question. In my view, however, such factors make it all the more imperative that we adhere precisely and scrupulously to the established guideposts of our constitutional jurisprudence, a jurisprudence that makes the rational basis test an extremely deferential one that focuses on the rationality, not the persuasiveness, of the potential justifications for the classifications in the legislative scheme. I trust that, once this particular "storm" clears, we will return to the rational basis test as it has always been understood and applied. Applying that deferential test in the manner it is customarily applied, the exclusion of gay and lesbian couples from the institution of civil marriage passes constitutional muster. I respectfully dissent.

CORDY, J. (*dissenting, with whom* **SPINA** *and* **SOSMAN, JJ.**, *join*).

D. Conclusion

While "[t]he Massachusetts Constitution protects matters of personal liberty against government incursion as zealously, and often more so, than does the

Federal Constitution," . . . this case is not about government intrusions into matters of personal liberty. It is not about the rights of same-sex couples to choose to live together, or to be intimate with each other, or to adopt and raise children together. It is about whether the State must endorse and support their choices by changing the institution of civil marriage to make its

benefits, obligations, and responsibilities applicable to them. While the courageous efforts of many have resulted in increased dignity, rights, and respect for gay and lesbian members of our community, the issue presented here is a profound one, deeply rooted in social policy, that must, for now, be the subject of legislative not judicial action.

IN RE MARRIAGE CASES

183 P.3d 384 (Cal. 2008)

Opinion: George, joined by Kennard, Werdegar, Moreno
Partial Concurrence, Partial Dissent: Corrigan
Concurrence: Kennard
Partial Concurrence, Partial Dissent: Baxter, joined by Chin

GEORGE, C.J.

. . . [T]he legal issue we must resolve is not whether it would be constitutionally permissible under the California Constitution for the state to limit marriage only to opposite-sex couples while denying same-sex couples any opportunity to enter into an official relationship with all or virtually all of the same substantive attributes, but rather whether our state Constitution prohibits the state from establishing a statutory scheme in which both opposite-sex and same-sex couples are granted the right to enter into an officially recognized family relationship that affords all of the significant legal rights and obligations traditionally associated under state law with the institution of marriage, but under which the union of an opposite-sex couple is officially designated a "marriage" whereas the union of a

same-sex couple is officially designated a "domestic partnership."

In defending the constitutionality of the current statutory scheme, the Attorney General of California maintains that even if the constitutional right to marry under the California Constitution applies to same-sex couples as well as to opposite-sex couples, this right should not be understood as requiring the Legislature to designate a couple's official family relationship by the term "marriage," as opposed to some other nomenclature. The Attorney General, observing that fundamental constitutional rights generally are defined by substance rather than by form, reasons that so long as the state affords a couple all of the constitutionally protected substantive incidents of marriage, the state does not violate the couple's constitutional right to marry simply by assigning their official relationship a name other than marriage. Because the Attorney General maintains that California's current domestic partnership legislation affords same-sex couples all of the core substantive rights that plausibly may be guaranteed to an individual or couple as elements of the fundamental state constitutional right to marry, the Attorney General concludes that the current California statutory scheme relating to marriage and domestic partnership does not violate the fundamental constitutional right to marry embodied in the California Constitution.

One of the core elements of the right to establish an officially recognized family that is embodied in the California constitutional right to marry is a couple's right to have their family relationship accorded dignity and respect equal to that accorded other officially recognized families, and assigning a different designation for the family relationship of same-sex couples while reserving the historic designation of "marriage" exclusively for opposite-sex couples poses at least a serious risk of denying the family relationship of same-sex couples such equal dignity and respect. We therefore conclude that although the provisions of the current domestic partnership legislation afford same-sex couples most of the substantive elements embodied in the constitutional right to marry, the current California statutes nonetheless must be viewed as potentially impinging upon a same-sex couple's constitutional right to marry under the California Constitution.

Furthermore, the circumstance that the current California statutes assign a different name for the official family relationship of same-sex couples as contrasted with the name for the official family relationship of opposite-sex couples raises constitutional concerns not only under the state constitutional right to marry, but also under the state constitutional equal protection clause. In analyzing the validity of this differential treatment under the latter clause, we first must determine which standard of review should be applied to the statutory classification here at issue. Although in most instances the deferential "rational basis" standard of review is applicable in determining whether different treatment accorded by a statutory provision violates the state equal protection clause, a more

exacting and rigorous standard of review — "strict scrutiny" — is applied when the distinction drawn by a statute rests upon a so-called "suspect classification" or impinges upon a fundamental right. . . . [A]lthough we do not agree with the claim advanced by the parties challenging the validity of the current statutory scheme that the applicable statutes properly should be viewed as an instance of discrimination on the basis of the suspect characteristic of sex or gender and should be subjected to strict scrutiny on that ground, we conclude that strict scrutiny nonetheless is applicable here because (1) the statutes in question properly must be understood as classifying or discriminating on the basis of sexual orientation, a characteristic that we conclude represents—like gender, race, and religion—a constitutionally suspect basis upon which to impose differential treatment, and (2) the differential treatment at issue impinges upon a same-sex couple's fundamental interest in having their family relationship accorded the same respect and dignity enjoyed by an opposite-sex couple.

Under the strict scrutiny standard, unlike the rational basis standard, in order to demonstrate the constitutional validity of a challenged statutory classification the state must establish (1) that the state interest intended to be served by the differential treatment not only is a constitutionally legitimate interest, but is a compelling state interest, and (2) that the differential treatment not only is reasonably related to but is necessary to serve that compelling state interest. Applying this standard to the statutory classification here at issue, we conclude that the purpose underlying differential treatment of opposite-sex and same-sex couples embodied in California's current marriage statutes — the interest in retaining the traditional and well-established definition of marriage — cannot properly be viewed as a compelling state interest for purposes of the equal protection clause, or as necessary to serve such an interest.

A number of factors lead us to this conclusion. First, the exclusion of same-sex couples from the designation of marriage clearly is not necessary in order to afford full protection to all of the rights and benefits that currently are enjoyed by married opposite-sex couples; permitting same-sex couples access to the designation of marriage will not deprive opposite-sex couples of any rights and will not alter the legal framework of the institution of marriage, because same-sex couples who choose to marry will be subject to the same obligations and duties that currently are imposed on married opposite-sex couples. Second, retaining the traditional definition of marriage and affording same-sex couples only a separate and differently named family relationship will, as a realistic matter, impose appreciable harm on same-sex couples and their children, because denying such couples access to the familiar and highly favored designation of marriage is likely to cast doubt on whether the official family relationship of same-sex couples enjoys dignity equal to that of opposite-sex couples. Third, because of the widespread disparagement that gay individuals historically have faced, it is all the more probable that excluding same-sex couples from the legal institution of marriage is likely to be viewed as reflecting an official view that their committed relationships are of lesser stature than the comparable relationships of opposite-sex couples. Finally, retaining the designation of marriage exclusively for opposite-sex couples and providing only a separate and distinct designation for same-sex couples may well have the effect of perpetuating a more general premise — now emphatically rejected by this state — that gay individuals and same-sex couples are in some respects "second-class citizens"

who may, under the law, be treated differently from, and less favorably than, heterosexual individuals or opposite-sex couples. Under these circumstances, we cannot find that retention of the traditional definition of marriage constitutes a compelling state interest. Accordingly, we conclude that to the extent the current California statutory provisions limit marriage to opposite-sex couples, these statutes are unconstitutional.

. . . [I]n light of the conclusions we reach concerning the constitutional questions brought to us for resolution, we determine that the language . . . limiting the designation of marriage to a union "between a man and a woman" is unconstitutional and must be stricken from the statute, and that the remaining statutory language must be understood as making the designation of marriage available both to opposite-sex and same-sex couples. In addition, because the limitation of marriage to opposite-sex couples imposed by section 308.5 can have no constitutionally permissible effect in light of the constitutional conclusions set forth in this opinion, that provision cannot stand.

BAXTER, J., *Concurring and dissenting.*

. . . Nothing in our Constitution, express or implicit, compels the majority's startling conclusion that the age-old understanding of marriage—an understanding recently confirmed by an initiative law—is no longer valid. California statutes already recognize same-sex unions and grant them all the substantive legal rights this state can bestow. If there is to be a further sea change in the social and legal understanding of marriage itself, that evolution should occur by similar democratic means. The majority forecloses this ordinary democratic process, and, in doing so, oversteps its authority. . . .

In doing so, the majority holds, in effect, that the Legislature has done indirectly what the Constitution prohibits it from doing directly. Under article II, section 10, subdivision (c), that body cannot unilaterally repeal an initiative statute, such as Family Code section 308.5, unless the initiative measure itself so provides. Section 308.5 contains no such provision. Yet the majority suggests that, by enacting other statutes which do provide substantial rights to gays and lesbians—including domestic partnership rights which, under section 308.5, the Legislature could not call "marriage"—the Legislature has given "explicit official recognition" (maj. opn. . . .) to a California right of equal treatment which, because it includes the right to marry, thereby invalidates section 308.5.

I cannot join this exercise in legal jujitsu, by which the Legislature's own weight is used against it to create a constitutional right from whole cloth, defeat the People's will, and invalidate a statute otherwise immune from legislative interference. Though the majority insists otherwise, its pronouncement seriously oversteps the judicial power. The majority purports to apply certain fundamental provisions of the state Constitution, but it runs afoul of another just as fundamental—article III, section 3, the separation of powers clause. This clause declares that "[t]he powers of state government are legislative, executive, and judicial," and that "[p]ersons charged with the exercise of one power may not exercise either of the others" except as the Constitution itself specifically provides.

CORRIGAN, J., *concurring and dissenting.*

In my view, Californians should allow our gay and lesbian neighbors to call their unions marriages. But I, and this court, must acknowledge that a majority of Californians hold a different view, and have explicitly said so by their vote. This court can overrule a vote of the people only if the Constitution compels us to do so. Here, the Constitution does not. Therefore, I must dissent.

It is important to be clear. Under California law, domestic partners have "virtually all of the benefits and responsibilities" available to traditional spouses. (Maj. opn. . . .) I believe the Constitution requires this as a matter of equal protection. However, the single question in this case is whether domestic partners have a constitutional right to the name of "marriage. . . ."

The majority refers to the race cases, from which our equal protection jurisprudence has evolved. The analogy does not hold. The civil rights cases banning racial discrimination were based on duly enacted amendments to the United States Constitution, proposed by Congress and ratified by the people through the states. To our nation's great shame, many individuals and governmental entities obdurately refused to follow these constitutional imperatives for nearly a century. By overturning Jim Crow and other segregation laws, the courts properly and courageously held the people accountable to their own constitutional mandates. Here the situation is quite different. In less than a decade, through the democratic process, same-sex couples have been given the equal legal rights to which they are entitled. . . .

Certainly initiative measures are not immune from constitutional review. However, we should hesitate to use our authority to take one side in an ongoing political debate. The accommodation of disparate views is democracy's essential challenge. Democracy is never more tested than when its citizens honestly disagree, based on deeply held beliefs. In such circumstances, the legislative process should be given leeway to work out the differences.

It is inappropriate for the judiciary to interrupt that process and impose the views of its individual members, while the opinions of the people are still evolving. . . .

We should allow the significant achievements embodied in the domestic partnership statutes to continue to take root. If there is to be a new understanding of the meaning of marriage in California, it should develop among the people of our state and find its expression at the ballot box.

AP / Marcio Jose Sanchet

Like abortion, same-sex marriage is a major, divisive issue in U.S. politics.

Box 9-3 **A Note on Proposition 8**

In November 2008, the California Marriage Protection Act, known popularly as Proposition 8, narrowly passed in the California state elections. It effectively overturned the decisions of the *In re Marriage Cases* by amending the California Constitution to define marriage as strictly between opposite-sex couples, thus barring a constitutional right to same-sex marriage. The amendment held heterosexual marriage as "fundamental" to American society, claiming that gay citizens had no right to redefine marriage. The decision was followed by rampant and vocal protests in many parts of California.

In 2010, U.S. District Court Judge Vaughn R. Walker overturned Proposition 8 on the grounds that it violated the Equal Protection and Due Process Clauses, and his ruling is currently stayed pending appeal.

VARNUM v. BRIEN

763 N.W.2D 862 (IOWA 2009)

Opinion: Cady, joined by Ternus, Streit, Wiggins, Hecht, Appel, Baker

Although the Supreme Judicial Court of Massachusetts was the first state supreme court to require same-sex marriage, it was not the last. Several other courts came to the same (and others to a different) conclusion. In 2009, the Iowa Supreme Court unanimously held that discrimination against gays and lesbians should be subject at least to intermediate scrutiny, and struck down that state's same-sex marriage ban. Because equal protection analysis under the Iowa Constitution is usually identical to that under the Federal Constitution, in reaching its conclusion the Supreme Court of Iowa relies almost exclusively on U.S. Supreme Court cases. How persuasive is its argumentation? Do you think the U.S. Supreme Court would come to a similar result? Should it?

CADY, *Justice. All justices concur.*

In this case, we must decide if our state statute limiting civil marriage to a union between a man and a woman violates the Iowa Constitution, as the district court ruled. On our review, we hold the Iowa marriage statute violates the equal protection clause of the Iowa Constitution. Therefore, we affirm the decision of the district court. . . .

Our responsibility . . . is to protect constitutional rights of individuals from legislative enactments that have denied those rights, even when the rights have not yet been broadly accepted, were at one time unimagined, or challenge a deeply ingrained practice or law viewed to be impervious to the passage of time. The framers of the Iowa Constitution knew, as did the drafters of the United States Constitution, that

"times can blind us to certain truths and later generations can see that laws once thought necessary and proper in fact serve only to oppress," and as our constitution "endures, persons in every generation can invoke its principles in their own search for greater freedom" and equality. *See Lawrence v. Texas.* . . .

IV. Equal Protection

A. Background Principles. The primary constitutional principle at the heart of this case is the doctrine of equal protection. The concept of equal protection is deeply rooted in our national and state history, but that history reveals this concept is often expressed far more easily than it is practiced. For sure, our nation has struggled to achieve a broad national consensus on equal protection of the laws when it has been forced to apply that principle to some of the institutions, traditions, and norms woven into the fabric of our society. This observation is important today because it reveals equal protection can only be defined by the standards of each generation.

The same-sex-marriage debate waged in this case is part of a strong national dialogue centered on a fundamental, deepseated, traditional institution that has excluded, by state action, a particular class of Iowans. This class of people asks a simple and direct question: How can a state premised on the constitutional principle of equal protection justify exclusion of a class of Iowans from civil marriage?

In most cases, we apply a very deferential standard known as the "rational basis test." Under the rational basis test, "[t]he plaintiff has the heavy burden of showing the statute unconstitutional and must negate every reasonable basis upon which the classification may be sustained." In deference to the legislature, a statute will satisfy the requirements of the equal protection clause

Although the rational basis test is "deferential to legislative judgment, 'it is not a toothless one' in Iowa." The rational basis test defers to the legislature's prerogative to make policy decisions by requiring only a plausible policy justification, mere rationality of the facts underlying the decision and, again, a merely rational relationship between the classification and the policy justification. Nonetheless, the deference built into the rational basis test is not dispositive because this court engages in a meaningful review of all legislation challenged on equal protection grounds by applying the rational basis test to the facts of each case. . . .

E. Classification Undertaken in Iowa Code Section 595.2. Plaintiffs believe Iowa Code section 595.2 classifies on the bases of gender and sexual orientation. The County argues the same-sex marriage ban does not discriminate on either basis. The district court held section 595.2 classifies according to gender. As we will explain, we believe the ban on civil marriages between two people of the same sex classifies on the basis of sexual orientation.

The County initially points out that section 595.2 does not explicitly refer to "sexual orientation" and does not inquire into whether either member of a proposed civil marriage is sexually attracted to the other. Consequently, it seizes on these observations to support its claim that the statute does not establish a classification on the basis of sexual orientation because the same-sex civil marriage ban does not grant or withhold the benefits flowing from the statute based on sexual preference. Instead, the County argues, section 595.2 only incidentally impacts disparately upon gay and lesbian people.

The County's position reveals the importance of accurately and precisely defining the classification in analyzing all equal protection challenges. The manner in which a classification is defined impacts the utility of an equal protection analysis as a means of revealing discrimination. Therefore, it is critical that a court reviewing the statute identify the true nature of the classification.

It is true the marriage statute does not expressly prohibit gay and lesbian persons from marrying; it does, however, require that if they marry, it must be to someone of the opposite sex. Viewed in the complete context of marriage, including intimacy, civil marriage with a person of the opposite sex is as unappealing to a gay or lesbian person as civil marriage with a person of the same sex is to a heterosexual. Thus, the right of a gay or lesbian person under the marriage statute to enter into a civil marriage only with a person of the opposite sex is no right at all. Under such a law, gay or lesbian individuals cannot simultaneously fulfill their deeply felt need for a committed personal relationship, as influenced by their sexual orientation, and gain the civil status and attendant benefits granted by the statute. Instead, a gay or lesbian person can only gain the same rights under the statute as a heterosexual person by negating the very trait that defines gay and lesbian people as a class—their sexual orientation. The benefit denied by the marriage statute—the status of civil marriage for same-sex couples—is so "closely correlated with being homosexual" as to make it apparent the law is targeted at gay and lesbian people as a class. *See Lawrence* (O'connor, J., concurring.) The Court's decision in *Romer v. Evans* supports this conclusion. *Romer* can be read to imply that sexual orientation is a trait that defines an individual and is not merely a means to associate a group with a type of behavior.

By purposefully placing civil marriage outside the realistic reach of gay and lesbian individuals, the ban on same-sex civil marriages differentiates implicitly on the basis of sexual orientation. Thus, we proceed to analyze the constitutionality of the statute based on sexual orientation discrimination. . . .

H. Application of Heightened Scrutiny. Plaintiffs argue sexual-orientation-based statutes should be subject to the most searching scrutiny. The County asserts Iowa's marriage statute, section 595.2, may be reviewed, at most, according to an intermediate level of scrutiny. Because we conclude Iowa's same-sex marriage statute cannot withstand intermediate scrutiny, we need not decide whether classifications based on sexual orientation are subject to a higher level of scrutiny. Thus, we turn to a discussion of the intermediate scrutiny standard.

1. *Intermediate scrutiny standard.* "To withstand intermediate scrutiny, a statutory classification must be substantially related to an important governmental objective." *Clark v. Jeter.* In applying an intermediate standard to review gender-based classifications, the Supreme Court has stated: "Focusing on the differential treatment or denial of opportunity for which relief is sought, the reviewing court must determine whether the proffered justification is 'exceedingly persuasive.'" *Virginia.* To this end, courts evaluate whether the proffered governmental objectives are important and whether the statutory classification is "substantially related to the achievement of those objectives."

2. *Statutory classification: exclusion of gay and lesbian people from civil marriage.* To identify the statutory classification, we focus on the "differential treatment or denial of opportunity for which relief is sought." Plaintiffs bring this lawsuit complaining of their exclusion from the institution of civil marriage. In response, the County offers support for the legislature's decision to statutorily establish *heterosexual* civil marriage. Because the relevant focal point is the opportunity sought by the plaintiffs, the issue presented by this lawsuit is whether the state has "exceedingly persuasive" reasons for denying civil marriage to same-sex couples, not whether state-sanctioned, heterosexual marriage is constitutional. Thus, the question we must answer is whether excluding gay and lesbian people from civil marriage is substantially related to any important governmental objective.

3. *Governmental objectives.* The County has proffered a number of objectives supporting the marriage statute. These objectives include support for the "traditional" institution of marriage, the optimal procreation and rearing of children, and financial considerations.

The first step in scrutinizing a statutory classification can be to determine whether the objectives purportedly advanced by the classification are important. "The burden of justification is demanding and it rests entirely on the State." Where we find, or can assume, the proffered governmental interests are sufficiently weighty to be called "important," the critical inquiry is whether these governmental objectives can fairly be said to be advanced by the legislative classification. In this analysis, we drill down to analyze the "link between classification and objective." *Romer.*

a. *Maintaining traditional marriage.* First, the County argues the same-sex marriage ban promotes the "integrity of traditional marriage" by "maintaining the historical and traditional marriage norm ([as] one between a man and a woman)." This argument is straightforward and has superficial appeal. A specific tradition sought to be maintained cannot be an important governmental objective for equal protection purposes, however, when the tradition is nothing more than the historical classification currently expressed in the statute being challenged. When a certain tradition is used as both the governmental objective and the classification to further that objective, the equal protection analysis is transformed into the circular question of whether the classification accomplishes the governmental objective, which objective is to maintain the classification. In other words, the equal protection clause is converted into a "barren form of words" when "'discrimination . . . is made an end in itself.'" *Truax v. Raich.*

This precise situation is presented by the County's claim that the statute in this case exists to preserve the traditional understanding of marriage. The governmental objective identified by the County—to maintain the traditional understanding of marriage—is simply another way of saying the governmental objective is to limit civil marriage to opposite-sex couples. Opposite-sex marriage, however, is the classification made under the statute, and this classification must comply with our principles of equal protection. Thus, the use of traditional marriage as both the governmental objective and the classification of the statute transforms the equal protection analysis into the question of whether restricting marriage to opposite-sex couples accomplishes the governmental objective of maintaining opposite-sex marriage.

This approach is, of course, an empty analysis. It permits a classification to be maintained "for its own sake." *Romer.* Moreover, it can allow discrimination to become acceptable as tradition and helps to explain how discrimination can exist for such a long time. If a simple showing that discrimination is traditional satisfies equal protection, previous successful equal protection challenges of invidious racial and gender classifications would have failed.

Consequently, equal protection demands that "the classification ([that is], the exclusion of gay [persons] from civil marriage) must advance a state interest that is separate from the classification itself."

The reasons underlying traditional marriage may include the other objectives asserted by the County, objectives we will separately address in this decision. However, some underlying reason other than the preservation of tradition must be identified. Because the County offers no particular *governmental* reason underlying the tradition of limiting civil marriage to heterosexual couples, we press forward to consider other plausible reasons for the legislative classification.

b. Promotion of optimal environment to raise children. Another governmental objective proffered by the County is the promotion of "child rearing by a father and a mother in a marital relationship which social scientists say with confidence is the optimal milieu for child rearing." This objective implicates the broader governmental interest to promote the best interests of children. The "best interests of children" is, undeniably, an important governmental objective. Yet, we first examine the underlying premise proffered by the County that the optimal environment for children is to be raised within a marriage of both a mother and a father.

Plaintiffs presented an abundance of evidence and research, confirmed by our independent research, supporting the proposition that the interests of children are served equally by same-sex parents and opposite-sex parents. On the other hand, we acknowledge the existence of reasoned opinions that dual-gender parenting is the optimal environment for children. These opinions, while thoughtful and sincere, were largely unsupported by reliable scientific studies.

Even assuming there may be a rational basis at this time to believe the legislative classification advances a legitimate government interest, this assumed fact would not be sufficient to survive the equal protection analysis applicable in this case. In order to ensure this classification based on sexual orientation is not borne of prejudice and stereotype, intermediate scrutiny demands a closer relationship between the legislative classification and the purpose of the classification than mere rationality. Under intermediate scrutiny, the relationship between the government's goal and the classification employed to further that goal must be "substantial." *Clark*. In order to evaluate that relationship, it is helpful to consider whether the legislation is over-inclusive or under-inclusive.

A statute is under-inclusive when the classification made in the statute "does not include all who are similarly situated with respect to the purpose of the law." An under-inclusive statute means all people included in the statutory classification have the trait that is relevant to the aim of the statute, but other people with the trait are not included in the classification. A statute is over-inclusive when the classification made in the statute includes more persons than those who are similarly situated with respect to the purpose of the law. An over-inclusive statute "imposes a burden upon a wider range of individuals than are included in the class of those" with the trait relevant to the aim of the law. As the degree to which a statutory classification is shown to be over-inclusive or under-inclusive increases, so does the difficulty in demonstrating the classification substantially furthers the legislative goal.

We begin with the County's argument that the goal of the same-sex marriage ban is to ensure children will be raised only in the optimal milieu. In pursuit of this objective, the statutory exclusion of gay and lesbian people is both under-inclusive and over-inclusive. The civil marriage statute is under-inclusive because it does not exclude from marriage other groups of parents—such as child abusers, sexual predators, parents neglecting to provide child support, and violent felons—that are undeniably less than optimal parents. Such under-inclusion tends to demonstrate that the sexual-orientation-based classification is grounded in prejudice or "overbroad generalizations about the different talents, capacities, or preferences" of gay and lesbian people, rather than having a substantial relationship to some important objective. *See Virginia*. If the marriage statute was truly focused on optimal parenting, many classifications of people would be excluded, not merely gay and lesbian people.

Of course, "[r]eform may take one step at a time, addressing itself to the phase of the problem which seems most acute to the legislative mind." Thus, "[t]he legislature may select one phase of one field and apply a remedy there, neglecting the others." *Williamson v. Lee Optical of Oklahoma*. While a statute does not automatically violate equal protection merely by being under-inclusive, the degree of under-inclusion nonetheless indicates the substantiality of the relationship between the legislative means and end. . . .

The ban on same-sex marriage is substantially over-inclusive because not all same-sex couples choose to raise children. Yet, the marriage statute denies civil marriage to all gay and lesbian people in order to discourage the limited number of same-sex couples who desire to raise children. In doing so, the legislature includes a consequential number of "individuals within the statute's purview who are not afflicted with the evil the statute seeks to remedy."

At the same time, the exclusion of gay and lesbian people from marriage is under-inclusive, even in relation to the narrower goal of improving child rearing by limiting same-sex parenting. Quite obviously, the statute does not prohibit same-sex couples from raising children. Same-sex couples currently raise children in Iowa, even while being excluded from civil marriage, and such couples will undoubtedly continue to do so. Recognition of this under-inclusion puts in perspective just how minimally the same-sex marriage ban actually advances the purported legislative goal. A law so simultaneously over-inclusive and under-inclusive is not substantially related to the government's objective. In the end, a careful analysis of the over- and under-inclusiveness of the statute reveals it is less about using marriage to achieve an optimal environment for children and more about merely precluding gay and lesbian people from civil marriage.

If the statute was truly about the best interest of children, some benefit to children derived from the ban on same-sex civil marriages would be observable. Yet, the germane analysis does not show how the best interests of children of gay and lesbian parents, who are denied an environment supported by the benefits of marriage under the statute, are served by the ban. Likewise, the exclusion of gays and lesbians from marriage does not benefit the interests of those children of heterosexual parents, who are able to enjoy the environment supported by marriage with or without the inclusion of same-sex couples.

The ban on same-sex civil marriage can only logically be justified as a means to ensure the asserted optimal environment for raising children if fewer children will be raised within same-sex relationships or more children will be raised in dual-gender marriages. Yet, the same-sex-marriage ban will accomplish these outcomes only when people in same-sex relationships choose not to raise children without the benefit of marriage or when children are adopted by dual-gender couples who would have

been adopted by same-sex couples but for the same-sex civil marriage ban. We discern no substantial support for this proposition. These outcomes, at best, are minimally advanced by the classification. Consequently, a classification that limits civil marriage to opposite-sex couples is simply not substantially related to the objective of promoting the optimal environment to raise children. This conclusion suggests stereotype and prejudice, or some other unarticulated reason, could be present to explain the real objectives of the statute....

4. *Conclusion.* Having examined each proffered governmental objective through the appropriate lens of intermediate scrutiny, we conclude the sexual-orientation-based classification under the marriage statute does not substantially further any of the objectives. While the objectives asserted may be important (and many undoubtedly are important), none are furthered in a substantial way by the exclusion of same-sex couples from civil marriage. Our equal protection clause requires more than has been offered to justify the continued existence of the same-sex marriage ban under the statute....

J. Constitutional Infirmity. We are firmly convinced the exclusion of gay and lesbian people from the institution of civil marriage does not substantially further any important governmental objective. The legislature has excluded a historically disfavored class of persons from a supremely important civil institution without a constitutionally sufficient justification. There is no material fact, genuinely in dispute, that can affect this determination....

V. Remedy

Because our civil marriage statute fails to provide equal protection of the law under the Iowa Constitution, we must decide how to best remedy the constitutional violation. The sole remedy requested by plaintiffs is admission into the institution of civil marriage. The County does not suggest an alternative remedy. The high courts of other jurisdictions have remedied constitutionally invalid bans on same-sex marriage in two ways. Some courts have ordered gay and lesbian people to be allowed to access the institution of civil marriage. Other courts have allowed their state legislatures to create parallel civil institutions for same-sex couples.

Iowa Code section 595.2 is unconstitutional because the County has been unable to identify a constitutionally adequate justification for excluding plaintiffs from the institution of civil marriage. A new distinction based on sexual orientation would be equally suspect and difficult to square with the fundamental principles of equal protection embodied in our constitution. This record, our independent research, and the appropriate equal protection analysis do not suggest the existence of a justification for such a legislative classification that substantially furthers any governmental objective. Consequently, the language in Iowa Code section 595.2 limiting civil marriage to a man and a woman must be stricken from the statute, and the remaining statutory language must be interpreted and applied in a manner allowing gay and lesbian people full access to the institution of civil marriage.

SYNTHESIS QUESTIONS FOR FURTHER DISCUSSION: CHAPTER 9 SECTION B

1. In *Romer v. Evans*, the Supreme Court applied rational review in considering a Colorado state constitutional amendment passed by plebiscite that denied gay citizens protection from discrimination based on sexual orientation. Although rational review is usually considered a weak standard, here it has "bite" because the Court struck down the law by finding that it was based in animus and therefore was not "rationally related" to a "legitimate" purpose. Even among those who agree with the outcome, however, the Court's level of review raises yet another question about tiered levels of scrutiny. Why should laws that discriminate against gay people receive a lower level of scrutiny than those that discriminate on the basis of race or sex? One very controversial claim for this lower level of review would suggest that being gay is a choice. While race and sex are immutable characteristics, sexual orientation, in this view, is not. Such an argument, however, is perhaps one of the most contested claims in current discussions about gay rights. In reading the cases in this section, does it seem as though the Court has taken a position on this controversial issue simply by invoking rational review? Is this a mistake?

2. In considering whether rational basis review is an appropriate standard by which to judge gay rights cases, pay close attention to the differing approaches taken by the California and Massachusetts supreme courts in the same-sex marriage cases in this section. While both state courts found a right to same-sex marriage in their respective state constitutions,

the courts applied different levels of scrutiny in reaching this analysis. While Massachusetts followed the U.S. Supreme Court in applying rational review, the California court applied strict scrutiny. In yet another case, *Kerrigan v. Commissioner of Public Health*, the Connecticut Supreme Court in 2008 used intermediate scrutiny in finding a right to same-sex marriage in that state's constitution. Which approach would be the best route for the Supreme Court in establishing a level of scrutiny for evaluating distinctions based on sexual orientation? Ask too, whether in light of the Supreme Court's ruling in *Loving v. Virginia*—which, as you saw in Chapter 8, demonstrated that equal protection guarantees the right to interracial marriage—similar reasoning should apply to a right to same-sex marriage.

3. In the context of equality, we have discussed discrimination based on race in the previous chapter and discrimination based on gender and sexual orientation in this chapter. However, many scholars often raise the point that discussions of equality should also include the issues of discrimination based on age, disability, and wealth. Indeed, in *San Antonio Independent School District v. Rodriguez*, the Court considered an equal protection claim based on financial status. The San Antonio Independent School District questioned the constitutionality of the State of Texas's use of local property taxes to fund public schools, on the grounds that it perpetuated educational disparities between rich students, whose parents generally paid high property taxes, and poor students, whose parents did not. The Court, deciding that the standard of strict scrutiny was not applicable in this case, ruled that Texas's funding scheme was constitutional. Reflect upon this case, as well as the ones we have seen in this chapter and Chapter 8, in considering why the Court has applied different standards of scrutiny to different equal protection claims. Has it been justified in doing so?

KEY TERMS

animus doctrine: The doctrine used to strike down discriminatory laws under the rational basis test. The doctrine suggests that a law based on a hostile sentiment is towards a particular group fails to meet even the lowest level of scrutiny for evaluating legitimate state interest.

discrete and insular: The Court's phrase in *United States v. Carolene Products* to describe racial minorities who deserve heightened review under the Equal Protection Clause, "*discrete*" meaning "noticeable," and *insular* meaning "isolated" or segregated from the rest of the population.

gender: Often distinguished from biological or "sex" differentiation between men and women, gender is thought to be a socially constructed difference.

intermediate scrutiny: Used by the Court in gender discrimination cases, this level of scrutiny requires an "important interest" by the state and a means that is "substantially related" to state goals. The standard is called intermediate because it lies between strict scrutiny and rational basis review.

invidious discrimination: Unequal treatment that is hateful or based in hostility to a minority and is therefore considered unacceptable by courts. Legislation that is based on invidious discrimination fails to meet even the rational review level of scrutiny.

natural law: The theory of John Finnis, which dates back at least to Thomas Aquinas, claiming there is a universal law that transcends both space and time. It is used by Finnis as a justification for opposing some constitutional protections for gay citizens.

GLOSSARY

animus   Term used by the Court to refer to rationales for legislation that fail the rational basis test because they exhibit an unconstitutional hostility to a particular group as the basis for law. Although these rationales might be stated as reasons, in the Court's current jurisprudence, they fail to meet a standard of "rationality."

animus doctrine   The doctrine used to strike down discriminatory laws under the rational basis test. The doctrine suggests that a law based on a hostile sentiment is towards a particular group fails to meet even the lowest level of scrutiny for evaluating legitimate state interest.

bicameralism   The principle that the legislative branch should be composed of two chambers.

bill of attainder   Legislation that declares an individual guilty of a crime without the benefit of a trial.

bipartisan gerrymander   A district drawn on a bipartisan basis in order to guarantee the reelection of incumbents of both parties.

Democratic-Republican Party   The party of Thomas Jefferson, the President of the United States when *Marbury v. Madison* was decided.

clear and present danger   A test in free speech jurisprudence that balanced free speech with the need for security.

colorblind   The view that the Constitution cannot take race into account in equal protection analysis, often used as a basis for opposing affirmative action and racial gerrymanders.

color-conscious   The view that we must take race into account to combat discrimination in matters of deep segregation and equal protection.

comprehensive doctrine   John Rawls's term for a religious or secular view that encompasses an understanding not just of justice, but of all moral questions. Comprehensive doctrines are contrasted with doctrines that are solely about politics.

1333

consequentialism   View in moral, political, and legal theory that good results justify a decision. Often contrasted with "deontological" views, which emphasize that decisions should be constrained for moral and other reasons even if they would lead to good consequences.

content neutrality   The First Amendment doctrine that suggests that the court should not discriminate based on the content of speech; broader than the idea of **viewpoint neutrality**. Exclusions include obscenity and threats.

de facto   A practical reality that is not established in law.

de jure   Established in or concerned with law.

departmentalism   The view that the various branches of government ought to have a say in constitutional interpretation.

discrete and insular   The Court's phrase in *United States v. Carolene Products* to describe racial minorities who deserve heightened review under the Equal Protection Clause, "*discrete*" meaning "noticeable," and *insular* meaning "isolated" or segregated from the rest of the population.

dual-sovereignty   The theory that suggests that both the states and the federal government are sovereign entities under the Constitution. On this theory, each retains certain exclusive powers. In particular, it holds that the Tenth Amendment and other provisions ensure a particular role for state power and limit federal power.

entanglement   The Court's term for programs or legislation that overly involve relations between government and religion, relevant in Establishment Clause jurisprudence.

enumerated powers   Those powers specifically granted to Congress by the Constitution, in contrast to the states' more general police powers to regulate the "welfare, health, safety, and morals" of its population.

euthanasia   In contrast to instances in which an individual is able to take his or her own life, euthanasia involves another person initiating such a course of action. It is distinguished into two categories, voluntary (the ending of life by another with consent) and involuntary (no consent). Sometimes it is colloquially referred to as mercy-killing. In the context of this book, euthanasia is discussed with reference to individuals who have an incurable, debilitating, or fatal disease.

executive privilege   Areas in which the president might be immune or exempt from certain powers of Congress, including the subpoena power.

exemption   When the Court grants an exception to otherwise generally valid laws to individuals or groups for religious reasons.

ex post facto law A law retroactively imposed on parties, in contrast to laws that govern future action.

facially invalid The idea that a law as written, as opposed to how it is applied to a specific instance, is invalid.

facially neutral As the Court explains in *Church of Lukumi Babalu Aye v. City of Hialeah*, a law that does not by its express terms discriminate against one religion or another, though it may have the incidental effect of doing so.

Federalist Party The party of President John Adams, Chief Justice John Marshall, and William Marbury.

fighting words doctrine The Court's doctrine for limiting threatening speech. Established in *Chaplinsky v. New Hampshire*. Relevant in some hate speech cases.

gender Often distinguished from biological or "sex" differentiation between men and women, gender is thought to be a socially constructed difference.

gerrymandering The attempt by a state legislature to draw districts in a way that will benefit or disadvantage a particular political party or racial group.

habeas corpus The right of all citizens held by the government against their will to be provided with the legal justification for their incarceration; includes the right to be released if a court determines they are held without cause.

implied powers Powers not explicitly stated in the Constitution, but thought granted by general phrases such as the Necessary and Proper Clause and the General Welfare Clause, often thought central to the decision in *McCulloch v. Maryland*.

incorporation doctrine The constitutional doctrine that holds that the Fourteenth Amendment's Due Process Clause creates a protection of the basic liberties of the Bill of Rights against the states in addition to Congress. At this point, most of the Bill of Rights has been subject to this doctrine, including the Free Speech and Religion Clauses. Provisions that have not been formally subject to the doctrine include but are not limited to the right to a jury trial in certain civil trials, guaranteed by the Seventh Amendment, as well as the right to an indictment by a grand jury in a criminal trial, guaranteed by the Fifth Amendment.

interpretivism As defined by John Hart Ely, the middle ground between strict textualism and open-ended non-textualism.

intermediate scrutiny Used by the Court in gender discrimination cases, this level of scrutiny requires an "important interest" by the state and a means that is "substantially related" to state goals. The standard is called intermediate because it lies between strict scrutiny and rational basis review.

invidious discrimination   Unequal treatment that is hateful or based in hostility to a minority and is therefore considered unacceptable by courts. Legislation that is based on invidious discrimination fails to meet even the rational review level of scrutiny.

Jim Crow   A name for the system of segregation at one time prevailing in the southern United States.

judicial review   The power to strike down legislative or executive acts on grounds that they are incompatible with a provision or provisions of the Constitution.

judicial supremacy   The view that the Court is the final and supreme interpreter of constitutional meaning.

justiciable   Adjective describing a controversy that can be adjudicated by the courts.

legal positivism   The view that there is a separation between legal validity and morality.

legislative veto   A statutory mechanism formerly used by Congress to permit overriding an executive agency's action or determination.

libertarianism   The political philosophy that holds that the primary purpose of government is the protection of private property. This theory also rejects the notion of government provision for welfare.

line item veto   A proposed presidential power to veto specific sections of a bill, rather than the whole bill.

majority-minority districts   Districts drawn in such a way as to make a traditionally disadvantaged population the majority. The result aims for the election of minority officials.

martial law   The declaration of military rule and the suspension of normal civil liberties in times of emergency.

***Miller* test**   The current test for recognizing obscenity. Chief Warren E. Justice Burger wrote, "The basic guidelines for the trier of fact must be   (a) whether 'the average person, applying contemporary community standards' would find that the work, taken as a whole, appeals to the prurient interest . . . (b) whether the work depicts or describes, in a patently offensive way, sexual conduct specifically defined by the applicable state law ; and (c) whether the work, taken as a whole, lacks serious literary, artistic, political, or scientific value."

Missouri Compromise   An agreement passed by Congress in 1820 to ban slavery in parts of the former Louisiana Territory; struck down in *Dred Scott v. Sandford*.

natural law   The theory of John Finnis, which dates back at least to Thomas Aquinas, claiming there is a universal law that transcends both space and time. It is used by Finnis as a justification for opposing some constitutional protections for gay citizens.

negative rights   Rights to be free from government coercion.

New Federalism   The philosophy usually associated with the Reagan revolution, which sought to retrench the role of the federal government in the economic sphere; this also might refer to the Court's jurisprudence in pulling back congressional power under the Commerce Clause.

non-textualism   The view, most clearly articulated by Justice Arthur Goldberg in *Griswold v. Connecticut*, that there are rights not explicitly mentioned in the constitutional text. In making his case, Justice Goldberg cites the Ninth Amendment.

original jurisdiction   The power of the Court to be the first court to hear a case. This is in contrast to appellate jurisdiction, where the Court reviews a lower court decision.

overbreadth doctrine   The idea in First Amendment jurisprudence that a particular law that aims at banning unprotected speech might also impact protected speech, and therefore should be struck down. This concept is related to the idea of vagueness, which suggests that if it is not clear which kind of speech is being regulated, a law can be invalid under the First Amendment.

penumbra   A concept used to defend the idea that the Constitution guarantees rights based on implicit meanings of the text. Most famously used in Justice William O. Douglas's concurrence in *Griswold v. Connecticut* to articulate a right to privacy in the shadow of various provisions of the Bill of Rights.

per curiam opinion   An unsigned opinion.

plenary powers   Exclusive powers explicitly granted to Congress, not shared with the states.

police powers   The state's entitlement to regulate the welfare, health, safety, and morals of its population.

political question doctrine   The idea that the Supreme Court should not intervene in matters concerning the other branches of government because the issue is fundamentally "political," not legal; the doctrine is sometimes applied to issues of foreign policy.

poll tax   A tax imposed on each citizen as a prerequisite to voting. Given the extreme poverty of many African Americans after the Civil War, the poll tax was often used as a strategy for disenfranchisement.

positive rights   Rights to be given certain material goods by the state.

prerogative   The discretionary power of the president not subject to control by legislation.

prior restraint   Attempts to censor speech before it occurs, for instance through an injunction, as opposed to attempts to punish speech, for instance through libel laws.

Progressive movement   A movement of the early twentieth century that sought increased roles for government in guaranteeing basic welfare for all and increased federal regulation of the economy and in stimulating economic growth.

public reason   Rawls's phrase for the appropriate kind of arguments that are appealed to in justifying coercion.

quickening   The moment during pregnancy in which a woman can feel her fetus, dismissed by the Court in *Roe v. Wade* as an inappropriate guideline for regulating abortion.

racial gerrymander   The shaping of legislative districts to account for race. In particular, in the modern context, this refers to an attempt to create by gerrymander majority-minority districts or some density of minority voters that falls short of a majority.

racial quota   A method of affirmative action whereby numerical floors are used to ensure the representation of racial minorities.

rational review   When the Court presumes that a law is valid so long as the state can demonstrate that the law is "rationally related" to pursuing a "legitimate interest."

seditious libel   Libel that calls into question one's fidelity to the government, usually a statement thought to incite hatred towards the government. It is usually considered unconstitutional to punish someone for seditious libel under the First Amendment protection of free speech, given that it is usually a statement of political viewpoint. Criminalized by Congress during President John Adams's administration in the "Alien and Sedition Acts," which were allowed to expire according to a sunset provision during the presidency of Thomas Jefferson.

standing doctrine   The doctrine the Court uses to determine whether an individual has suffered a constitutionally cognizable harm sufficient to permit his or her claim to be heard in federal court.

stare decisis   Literally, "let the decision stand." The idea that the Supreme Court should defer to legal precedents in the hope of treating "like cases like."

state action   The doctrine that suggests that free speech claims are only triggered when the government has acted.

state of nature   A rhetorical device used by political theorists such as John Locke to describe situations in which there is no state. It is often used to consider what fundamental rights exist independently of government. In turn, the state of nature is used by Locke and his followers to constrain the actions of government.

strict scrutiny   When the Court presumes that a law is invalid unless it is a "narrowly tailored" means of pursuing a "compelling interest."

substantive due process   The theory famously articulated in *Lochner v. New York* and in *Griswold v. Connecticut* suggesting that the Due Process Clause protects some fundamental rights, even if they are unrelated to due process of law.

textualism   The view articulated by originalists and other thinkers that we should read the text of the Constitution in as literal a way as possible, and that constitutional interpretation should not look beyond the explicit text of the document.

trimester framework   The framework announced in *Roe v. Wade* regulating abortion, dividing pregnancy into three sections, each lasting three months.

undue burden   The standard announced by the Court in *Planned Parenthood v. Casey* for determining whether infringements on the right to have an abortion, such as spousal or parental notification laws, can be sustained. It provides a test for balancing the interests of the individual woman seeking an abortion with the interests of the state.

unitary executive   The notion that the executive power must be held solely by one individual, not a committee. Its modern usage suggests that executive power should not be shared with the legislative branch or with independent agencies in matters such as the appointment and removal of officers. Also a theory associated with presidential control over federal agencies and with expanded presidential power during wartime.

viewpoint neutrality   The notion that the laws that discriminate based on the opinion expressed by a given act of speech are unconstitutional.

viability   The ability of the fetus to live outside the womb, cited as the key point at which the state could lawfully prohibit abortion in the trimester framework employed in *Roe v. Wade*.

vote dilution   The drawing of districts in such a way so as to weaken the voting power of a particular voting bloc.

wall of separation   The metaphor employed by some theorists of the First Amendment that suggests that the prohibition on the establishment of religion creates a sharp divide between religious and governmental institutions.

TABLE OF CASES

Principal cases are in italics.

INDEX